BaseBall

MW00332180

2002 Almanac

A Comprehensive Review of the 2001 Season, Featuring Statistics and Commentary

PUBLISHED BY
Baseball America Inc.

EDITOR
Allan Simpson

ASSISTANT EDITORS
John Royster, Geoff Wilson

CONTRIBUTING EDITORS
Josh Boyd, Mark Derewicz, Will Lingo,
Blair Lovern, John Manuel

CONTRIBUTING WRITERS
Jim Callis, John Perrotto, Alan Schwarz

PRODUCTION
Phillip Daquila, Matthew Eddy, Linwood Webb

STATISTICAL CONSULTANT
SportsTicker
Boston

BaseBall america

PRESIDENT/Catherine Silver
PUBLISHER/Lee Folger
EDITOR/Allan Simpson
MANAGING EDITOR/Will Lingo
DESIGN & PRODUCTION DIRECTOR/Phillip Daquila

COVER PHOTOS/Barry Bonds by Larry Goren; Dodger fans Sept. 17 by Larry Goren;
Josh Beckett by Ken Babbitt; Miami celebration by David Gonzalez

---

EDITOR'S NOTE

Major league statistics are based on final, unofficial 2001 averages. Minor league statistics are official.

The organization statistics, which begin on Page 55, include all players who participated in at least one game during the 2001 season. Pitchers' batting statistics are not included, nor are the pitching statistics of field players who pitched on rare occasions. For players who played with more than one team in the same league, the player's cumulative statistics appear on the line immediately after the player's last-team statistics.

Innings have been rounded off to the nearest full inning.

ALL THROUGH 2002...

BaseBall america

BEST TOOLS

Boston's Manny Ramirez swings his way onto our annual honor roll

Subscribing is easy and you'll save $32⁵⁵ off the cover price!

We know the Almanac has a valuable place on your bookshelf as the essential reference for baseball happenings in 2001.

But what about all the exciting action on and off the field that takes place in the new year? From spring training to winter leagues—including the most complete draft coverage anywhere, a front-row seat at the College World Series and statistics for every minor league team—Baseball America magazine is the best source for baseball information. Since 1981, BA has been finding the prospects and tracking them from the bushes to the big leagues. That means you get comprehensive reporting and commentary every step of the way.

When you subscribe to Baseball America, you also gain access to Baseball America Online premium content.

So join the team now to receive Baseball America every other week, and be the first to know about today's rising stars.

It's baseball news you can't get anywhere else.

you need Baseball America

baseballamerica.com

CONTENTS

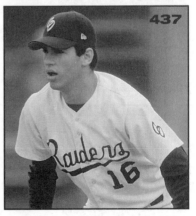

MAJOR LEAGUES

2001 IN REVIEW

Terrorist attacks overshadow eventful season

BY JOHN PERROTTO

When historians look back on 2001 in baseball, they are likely to say it was one of the greatest seasons in the game's history.

How could they not?

Consider what happened in 2001: Barry Bonds set a single-season home run record, breaking what was thought to be the unbreakable mark set by Mark McGwire just three years earlier; Cal Ripken and Tony Gwynn ended their distinguished careers in the same uniforms in which they began them; Rickey Henderson recorded his 3,000th hit; the Mariners tied the major league record for wins in a season and established an American League mark; and the Braves became the first major professional sports team to win 10 straight division titles as they captured yet another National League East crown.

That alone would have made for quite a season. Yet those events occurred in just the final weekend of the regular season and were a prelude for an exciting postseason, including one of the most drama-packed World Series in history. The Arizona Diamondbacks beat the three-time defending champion New York Yankees in seven games.

What made the season even more special was that the grand finale came as the United States was in the midst of recovering from a national tragedy of horrific proportions, and in the beginning of a war in Afghanistan.

To Every Thing There Is A Season

On Sept. 11, the worst terrorist attack ever left more than 5,000 people dead.

Four jetliners were hijacked in a plan masterminded by terrorist leader Osama bin Laden. Two of the planes crashed into the twin towers of the World Trade Center in New York, causing both 110-story structures to topple, while another slammed into a section of the Pentagon in suburban Washington. A fourth plane, believed to be headed toward the Washington area crashed in rural Shanksville, Pa.

American-led bombing of Afghanistan, which was harboring bin Laden, began Oct. 7, the final day of baseball's regular season.

The tragedies suspended major league play for six days, causing the addition of an extra week of makeup games to the regular season schedule and a one-week delay for the playoffs. Championship series were called off in 10 of the

Derek Jeter: Showing support for New York firefighters

STEVE MOORE

LARRY GOREN

Bud Selig

16 minor leagues, while the other six leagues had already concluded their playoffs before the attacks.

"You're hoping as a ballplayer you can bring some of that joy back from the tragedy we had," Henderson said. "It was a good year for baseball, with all the records and the great ballplayers retiring."

Commissioner Bud Selig said he hoped baseball could help heal the nation and provide a diversion from the continual news reports of the tragedy. Not long after the attacks on Sept. 11, Selig postponed that night's games, then called off the slate for the next two days a few hours later.

Selig had difficulty in determining when to resume play. He leaned toward starting again Sept. 15 but met with criticism from fans, some government leaders and the Players Association. Finally, Selig decided to call off games until Sept 18.

"We could do so much good, and I think the people in Washington and elsewhere understood that," Selig said. "At the same time, we needed to proceed with caution and sensitivity. It was a very, very difficult decision on when to come back, because we never had anything like this ever happen to our country. Who knew for sure how long we should not play?

"But I feel it was helpful for us to play again. Baseball is woven so deeply into the national fabric. It means so

PLAYER OF THE YEAR

In the end, no one knew how to react. When Barry Bonds' 71st home run disappeared into the San Francisco night on Oct. 5, the 41,730 fans on hand at Pacific Bell Park, the millions watching on television and even Bonds himself hadn't decided the significance of the feat they had just witnessed.

The United States was only tentatively dipping its toe back into sports as entertainment three weeks after the cataclysm of the World Trade Center attack. Baseball had feted Mark McGwire and his 70 home runs just three years before, and wasn't sure how special 71 was so soon. Bonds' own Giants were in the process of getting knocked out of the National League playoff race with their 11-10 loss to the Dodgers, and were in no celebratory mood. And finally neither was Bonds, who that morning had attended the funeral of a friend, and who maintained before, during and after his moment that individual accomplishments meant little without the World Series ring that remains beyond his grasp.

It was all that eluded Barry Bonds in 2001, though, as the Giants slugger put up a season so dominant that even comparisons to Babe Ruth seemed inadequate. His .328-73-137 numbers were merely the start. His .863 slugging percentage and 177 walks beat Ruth's all-time records. Bonds' .515 on-base percentage was the first to top .500 since Mickey Mantle and Ted Williams in 1957.

"If I knew how to do this, I would have done it a long time ago," said Bonds, 37. "Some things you just don't have an answer for."

Bonds' peers were lost for answers, too. "What he's done, it's absolutely phenomenal," McGwire said. "It's in the stratosphere. It's almost like he's playing tee-ball."

Added Sammy Sosa, "In '98, (the record) was only 61. And then Mark McGwire came and hit 70 and that was like 'Wow.' Now you see 73—that's unbelievable."

For all his accomplishments, Bonds was named Baseball America's 2001 Major League Player of the Year.

As Bonds neared the record, opposing pitchers rarely put the ball anywhere near the plate. In the last 18 games of the season, Bonds walked 27 times. During the season's final week, when Bonds had 69 home runs and played three games against the Astros, he came to the plate 14 times and was walked in eight of them. After Bonds reached 70, the Dodgers' Chan Ho Park decided to challenge Bonds and paid dearly. In the first inning, Bonds slammed a Park fastball 442 feet for the record. In his next at-bat, he went deep off Park again. He added his 73rd homer on the last day of the season off the Dodgers' Dennis Springer.

Bonds already has the greatest combination of power (567 career home runs) and speed (484 stolen bases) of anyone who has ever played the game. A free agent entering the offseason, he said he plans to play at least four more years; if he averages 50 home runs, he would break Hank Aaron's all-time record of 755.

"After I hit 73 home runs," he said, "anything's possible."

Apparently.

—ALAN SCHWARZ

Barry Bonds: Baseball's new home run king

LARRY GOREN

PREVIOUS **WINNERS**

1998—Mark McGwire, 1b, Cardinals
1999—Pedro Martinez, rhp, Red Sox
2000—Alex Rodriguez, ss, Mariners

---

much to so many people, though what happened Sept. 11 certainly trivializes it."

The minor leagues also debated calling off the playoffs before deciding it was the right thing to do. Six of the 10 leagues declared co-champions, while the other four gave the title to teams already ahead in the playoff series.

"We would have loved to have played, but with the tragedy we thought we should pay the proper respect to the victims and their families," Midwest League president George Spelius said.

Travel Trials

The postponements, and the grounding of all commercial flights for nearly two full days in the wake of the attacks, led to trying travel arrangements for clubs accustomed to speed and luxury.

The Rangers were in Oakland at the time of the attack, and they began an 1,800-mile trip back to Arlington that figured to take 30 hours. Not long after the bus trip began, Rangers traveling secretary Chris Lyngos made arrangements to charter an airplane in Bakersfield, Calif., to get home.

The White Sox were in New York to begin a series with the Yankees on the night of Sept. 11, staying at a Manhattan hotel just four miles from the World Trade Center. They then bused 15 hours back to Chicago and even played a small part to help in the relief effort. Their bus was stopped by a police blockade as it approached the George Washington Bridge to leave New York City. The police asked the White Sox to take some nurses to a New

Jersey hospital. The White Sox gladly took the small detour before heading west toward home.

"We normally have guys who, if a plane is 10 minutes late or a bus is 10 minutes late or if they don't get what drink they want, there is complaining like you wouldn't believe," White Sox first baseman Paul Konerko said. "I didn't hear one person complain on the trip, even though it took 15 hours."

With air traffic still scrambled after the shutdown, two teams went on buses when Selig decided Sept. 13 to call off the games of the weekend of Sept. 14-16. The Pirates were on their way to Chicago to open a three-game series with the Cubs. They had pulled over at a rest stop on the Ohio Turnpike near Sandusky when word came that the series was off. So, they turned around and rode three hours back to Pittsburgh.

"In a situation like this, nobody considered it an inconvenience," Pirates left fielder Brian Giles said. "Spending a day on a bus was nothing compared to what some people are going through in this country."

The Phillies had stayed in Atlanta after their series with the Braves was called off, and were headed to Cincinnati for a series with the Reds when they were told to go home. The Phillies continued on to Cincinnati, spent a night in a hotel there, then returned to Philadelphia.

The Red Sox were in St. Petersburg, Fla., to face the Devil Rays and weren't sure if they would be heading to Baltimore for a series with the Orioles. They took a bus to catch an Amtrak train near Orlando and headed to Baltimore. Once they got there and learned their series had been called off, they flew to Providence, R.I., then took buses to Boston.

While the delay made for baseball's version of "Planes, Trains and Automobiles," the mood was anything but comical. Clubs worked out and played intrasquad games to stay sharp, then returned to action Sept. 17 with emotions running high.

Everyone ♥ N.Y.

The New York Mets quickly became America's Team as they returned in Pittsburgh with a game against the Pirates. The Mets took the field at PNC Park wearing caps emblazoned with "NYPD" and "FDNY" to honor the police and fire departments of New York.

In St. Louis, longtime Cardinals broadcaster Jack Buck read a stirring poem that brought many in the Busch Stadium crowd to tears before a game with the Cubs. In Los Angeles, players and coaches from the Dodgers and Padres helped police and fire officers unfurl a giant American flag in the Dodger Stadium outfield. In Philadelphia, the fans chanted "U.S.A." as the Phillies rallied to beat Atlanta in a pivotal game.

The most moving ceremonies occurred Sept. 21 when the Mets returned home to Shea Stadium against Atlanta, in the first professional sporting event played in New York since the attacks. Days earlier, the Shea Stadium parking lot had been used as a staging area for rescue

TOP 10 MAJOR LEAGUE STORIES OF 2001

1 **The most gripping World Series ever?** The Diamondbacks became the youngest expansion franchise to win the Fall Classic, surviving three death-blows at Yankee Stadium and making an improbable Game Seven comeback against the previously unbeatable Mariano Rivera.

2 **Terrorist attacks postpone season.** As big as this story was, it was the resumption of play and the patriotism baseball showed in the weeks after Sept. 11 that touched hearts nationwide.

3 **Barry Bonds breaks the Mark.** No one—even Bonds himself—really thought he could do it, but the Giants outfielder launched 73 homers and also broke major league single-season records for walks and slugging percentage.

4 **Seattle celebrates Sweet 116.** Though they couldn't get past the Yankees in the playoffs, the Mariners—with the help of über-rookie Ichiro Suzuki—set a new AL standard for victories in a season.

5 **Cal Ripken and Tony Gwynn ride off into the sunset.** Both anomalies in this day and age, they broke in together in 1982 and spent every day of their careers with the same team.

6 **Rickey Henderson passes Ty and the Babe.** He set the stolen-base record 10 seasons ago, but breaking Cobb's career runs mark and Ruth's walks mark to go with his 3,000th hit made Rickey very happy.

7 **Sammy Sosa sets sights on 60 again.** The effusive Cubs slugger became the first player ever to hit the big six-oh three times.

8 **Braves' old world.** Atlanta did something no team in major professional sports has ever done by winning its 10th straight division title.

9 **Rocket leads the Yankees.** Though New York didn't win it all in 2001, it kept getting to the final act. The team's lead playwright was Roger Clemens, who became the first pitcher ever to go 20-1.

10 **Storm clouds on the horizon again.** Despite the damage done during the 1994-95 labor unrest, Major League Baseball's players and owners still had unresolved problems heading into the offseason. Another work stoppage could significantly alter the sport's landscape.

workers. The Mets players donated their day's salary, about $450,000, to the relief effort.

In solemn yet uplifting pregame ceremonies, Diana Ross sang "God Bless America," Mark Anthony sang the national anthem and bagpipers played "Amazing Grace." Liza Minelli drew a roar during the seventh-inning stretch when she led the crowd of 41,235 in the singing of "New York, New York."

Even New York mayor Rudolph Giuliani received a loud ovation when he took part in pregame ceremonies. A devout Yankees fan, Giuliani had always been roundly booed during his visits to Shea for World Series and inter-league games.

"This is the way that life gets back to normality," Giuliani said. "You can't just concentrate on the tragedy. It's so wonderful that these people have such confidence to turn out in such large numbers."

The most poignant scene might have been on the miniature New York skyline atop the right-field scoreboard. The World Trade Center's twin towers were still standing, covered by a red, white and blue ribbon.

"I'm glad they left it up," Mets pitcher Al Leiter said. "Those people will never be forgotten."

Chasing History

Once baseball resumed and the nation began to get back to what passed for normal, the most compelling drama was Bonds' chase of McGwire's home run record.

The Giants left fielder served notice early that he was ready to take aim at 70, the total McGwire amassed in 1998 when he broke Roger Maris' 37-year-old record of 61.

Bonds hit 11 homers in April, 17 in May and 11 in

BARRY BONDS SCOREBOARD

A home run-by-home run accounting of Barry Bonds' record-shattering 2001 season:

No.	Date	Opponent	H/A	Pitcher	Inn.	Outs	Count	ROB	Dist.	Score
1	April 2	San Diego	H	Woody Williams	5	1	0-0	0	420	Giants, 3-2
2	April 12	San Diego	A	Adam Eaton	4	1	1-0	0	417	Padres, 8-3
3	April 13	Milwaukee	A	Jamey Wright	1	1	0-1	1	440	Giants, 7-3
4	April 14	Milwaukee	A	Jimmy Haynes	5	0	2-0	2	410	Brewers, 11-6
5	April 15	Milwaukee	A	Dave Weathers	8	2	1-1	0	390	Brewers, 7-4
6	April 17	Los Angeles	H	Terry Adams	8	0	2-0	1	417	Giants, 3-2
7	April 18	Los Angeles	H	Chan Ho Park	7	2	0-0	0	420	Giants, 5-4
8	April 20	Milwaukee	H	Jimmy Haynes	4	1	0-0	1	410	Giants, 3-1
9	April 24	Cincinnati	H	Jim Brower	3	1	3-2	1	380	Reds, 9-5
10	April 26	Cincinnati	H	Scott Sullivan	8	2	3-2	1	430	Reds, 7-5
11	April 29	Chicago (N)	H	Manny Aybar	4	2	2-1	0	370	Cubs, 11-2
12	May 2	Pittsburgh	A	Todd Ritchie	5	2	3-2	1	420	Giants, 7-6
13	May 3	Pittsburgh	A	Jimmy Anderson	1	1	3-1	1	400	Pirates, 4-3
14	May 4	Philadelphia	A	Bruce Chen	6	1	1-1	1	360	Giants, 4-2
15	May 11	New York (N)	H	Steve Trachsel	4	0	3-2	0	410	Giants, 3-2 (10)
16	May 17	Florida	A	Chuck Smith	3	1	0-1	1	420	Marlins, 8-3
17	May 18	Atlanta	A	Mike Remlinger	8	1	0-1	0	391	Braves, 6-5
18	May 19	Atlanta	A	Odalis Perez	3	0	3-2	0	416	Giants, 6-3
19	May 19	Atlanta	A	Jose Cabrera	7	0	2-0	0	440	Giants, 6-3
20	May 19	Atlanta	A	Jason Marquis	8	2	3-0	0	410	Giants, 6-3
21	May 20	Atlanta	A	John Burkett	1	2	2-2	0	415	Braves, 11-6
22	May 20	Atlanta	A	Mike Remlinger	7	1	0-0	0	436	Braves, 11-6
23	May 21	Arizona	A	Curt Schilling	4	0	2-0	0	430	D'backs, 4-2
24	May 22	Arizona	A	Russ Springer	9	0	0-0	1	410	D'backs, 12-8
25	May 24	Colorado	H	John Thomson	3	2	2-2	0	400	Giants, 5-1
26	May 27	Colorado	H	Denny Neagle	1	1	3-1	1	390	Giants, 5-4
27	May 30	Arizona	H	Robert Ellis	2	0	0-0	0	420	D'backs, 4-3
28	May 30	Arizona	H	Robert Ellis	6	1	3-1	1	410	D'backs, 4-3
29	June 1	Colorado	A	Shawn Chacon	3	1	2-0	1	420	Giants, 11-7
30	June 4	San Diego	H	Bobby Jones	4	0	2-1	0	410	Giants, 3-1
31	June 5	San Diego	H	Wascar Serrano	3	1	1-1	1	410	Giants, 7-6
32	June 7	San Diego	H	Brian Lawrence	7	1	1-1	1	450	Padres, 10-7
33	June 12	Anaheim	H	Pat Rapp	1	2	0-0	0	320	Giants, 3-2
34	June 14	Anaheim	H	Lou Pote	6	1	2-1	0	430	Giants, 10-4
35	June 15	Oakland	H	Mark Mulder	1	2	3-1	0	380	Giants, 3-1
36	June 15	Oakland	H	Mark Mulder	6	0	1-1	0	375	Giants, 3-1
37	June 19	San Diego	A	Adam Eaton	5	1	2-1	0	375	Padres, 4-3 (15)
38	June 20	San Diego	A	Rodney Myers	8	0	2-1	1	347	Giants, 8-6
39	June 23	St. Louis	A	Darryl Kile	1	1	3-1	1	380	Cardinals, 6-5
40	July 12	Seattle	A	Paul Abbott	1	2	2-0	0	429	Mariners, 4-3 (11)
41	July 18	Colorado	H	Mike Hampton	4	0	2-1	0	320	Giants, 10-0
42	July 18	Colorado	H	Mike Hampton	5	1	0-1	1	360	Giants, 10-0
43	July 26	Arizona	A	Curt Schilling	4	0	0-0	0	375	Giants, 11-3
44	July 26	Arizona	A	Curt Schilling	5	1	0-0	3	370	Giants, 11-3
45	July 27	Arizona	A	Brian Anderson	4	0	1-1	0	440	Giants, 9-5
46	Aug. 1	Pittsburgh	H	Joe Beimel	1	2	1-0	0	400	Giants, 3-1
47	Aug. 4	Philadelphia	H	Nelson Figueroa	6	1	2-2	1	405	Phillies, 12-2
48	Aug. 7	Cincinnati	A	Danny Graves	11	0	1-1	0	430	Giants, 9-3 (11)
49	Aug. 9	Cincinnati	A	Scott Winchester	3	1	0-0	0	350	Giants, 6-4
50	Aug. 11	Chicago (N)	A	Joe Borowski	2	2	2-2	2	396	Giants, 9-4
51	Aug. 14	Florida	H	Ricky Bones	6	1	0-2	3	410	Giants, 13-7
52	Aug. 16	Florida	H	A.J. Burnett	4	0	1-0	0	380	Giants, 5-3
53	Aug. 16	Florida	H	Vic Darensbourg	8	0	1-2	2	430	Giants, 5-3
54	Aug. 18	Atlanta	H	Jason Marquis	8	1	2-2	0	415	Braves, 3-1
55	Aug. 23	Montreal	A	Graeme Lloyd	9	1	3-1	0	380	Giants, 10-5
56	Aug. 27	New York (N)	A	Kevin Appier	5	0	1-0	0	375	Giants, 6-5
57	Aug. 31	Colorado	H	John Thomson	8	1	0-2	1	400	Rockies, 5-2
58	Sept. 3	Colorado	H	Jason Jennings	4	0	1-0	0	435	Rockies, 4-1
59	Sept. 4	Arizona	H	Miguel Batista	7	2	0-0	0	420	Giants, 5-2
60	Sept. 6	Arizona	H	Albie Lopez	2	2	2-2	0	420	Giants, 9-5
61	Sept. 9	Colorado	A	Scott Elarton	1	1	1-1	0	488	Giants, 9-4 (11)
62	Sept. 9	Colorado	A	Scott Elarton	5	2	2-2	0	361	Giants, 9-4 (11)
63	Sept. 9	Colorado	A	Todd Belitz	11	1	0-1	2	394	Giants, 9-4 (11)
64	Sept. 20	Houston	H	Wade Miller	5	2	1-0	1	410	Astros, 5-4 (10)
65	Sept. 23	San Diego	A	Jason Middlebrook	2	2	2-1	0	411	Giants, 11-2
66	Sept. 23	San Diego	A	Jason Middlebrook	4	1	2-0	0	365	Giants, 11-2
67	Sept. 24	Los Angeles	A	James Baldwin	7	2	1-1	0	360	Giants, 2-1
68	Sept. 28	San Diego	H	Jason Middlebrook	2	2	3-0	0	440	Giants, 10-5
69	Sept. 29	San Diego	H	Chuck McElroy	6	0	2-1	0	435	Giants, 3-1
70	Oct. 4	Houston	A	Wilfredo Rodriguez	9	0	1-1	0	454	Giants, 10-2
71	Oct. 5	Los Angeles	H	Chan Ho Park	1	2	1-0	0	442	Dodgers, 11-10
72	Oct. 5	Los Angeles	H	Chan Ho Park	3	0	1-1	0	404	Dodgers, 11-10
73	Oct. 7	Los Angeles	H	Dennis Springer	1	2	3-2	0	385	Giants, 2-1

June. That gave him 39 after three months and put him on pace to surpass McGwire. He slumped in July as he connected just six times. But he heated up again down the stretch, going deep 12 times in August to raise his season total to 57, then blasting 12 homers in September to run his count to 69. He drew within one of the record Sept. 29 when he hit a long drive off Padres reliever Chuck McElroy in San Francisco.

With six games remaining in the regular season, Bonds looked like a lock to break the record. The Astros, though, were determined not to let Bonds make history in Houston's Enron Field.

In the first game of the series, Bonds was 1-for-2 while being walked twice and getting hit by a pitch. Astros manager Larry Dierker, his team locked in a tight NL Central race with St. Louis, also had his pitchers pitch around Bonds the next night, as he walked three times while going 1-for-2.

It was more of the same during the first eight innings of the series finale Oct. 4. Bonds walked three times in his first four trips to the plate. Finally, with San Francisco ahead 9-2 and the Houston crowd of 42,734 booing more loudly with each walk, Astros rookie Wilfredo Rodrgiuez challenged Bonds with three straight fastballs. Bonds responded by launching a 1-1 pitch into the right-center upper deck for No. 70.

"I was so happy to finally get a fastball," Bonds said. "I forgot what one looked like."

Barry Bonds: Home run No. 73 off the Dodgers' Dennis Springer

BILL NICHOLS

The Giants returned home to Pacific Bell Park the next night against the Dodgers, and Bonds wasted little time in breaking the record.

He stepped to the plate in the bottom of the first inning and drove a 1-0 fastball from the Dodgers' Chan Ho Park into the arcade seats in right-center for the history-making homer. In his next at-bat, in the third, Bonds homered again as he belted a 1-1 pitch over the wall in left-center, sending the 41,730 on hand into a frenzy.

"I didn't expect anything like this in my career, so this is all strange to me," the 37-year-old Bonds said.

"Barry didn't need this record to get into the Hall of Fame, but I think this pretty much solidifies it now," Giants shortstop Rich Aurilia said.

The most interesting part of the evening came in the 30-minute ceremonies at the pitcher's mound after the game. The festivities were emotional, to say the least, with Bonds, a San Francisco native, eligible to file for free agency after nine seasons with the Giants.

Accused of being aloof and arrogant throughout his career, Bonds broke into tears twice as he spoke. The first time came when he looked at his teammates standing behind him.

"I love you very much," Bonds said. "It's an honor to play with you guys behind me. I'll play for you any time, any day of the week, any hour, any year."

He choked up again when the fans began chanting "four more years." Bonds was willing to sign a four-year, $60 million contract extension in spring training, but Giants president Peter Magowan balked at the idea then.

"I love San Francisco and I love you fans," Bonds said. "My family knows and God knows I'm proud to put on this uniform."

Bonds also set the record with a heavy heart. Earlier in the day, he attended the funeral of his close friend Franklin Bradley. The 37-year-old Bradley had served as a bodyguard for both Bonds and NFL star Jerry Rice, and died during abdominal surgery a week earlier in a Bay Area hospital.

"It seems like it's been hard to enjoy what has happened," Bonds said. "There have been tragedies all the way along, with the attacks and Franklin dying. It has made things tough."

Bonds finished his season for the ages with a bang two days later when he hit

PROGRESSION OF THE RECORD

How major league baseball's home run record has evolved over the years:

Mark McGwire

Year	Player, Team	HRs	Record stood
1900	Herman Long, Red Sox	12	1 year
1901	Sam Crawford, Reds	16	10 years
1911	Frank Schulte, Cubs	21	4 years
1915	Gavvy Cravath, Phillies	24	4 years
1919	Babe Ruth, Red Sox	29	1 year
1920	Babe Ruth, Yankees	54	1 year
1921	Babe Ruth, Yankees	59	6 years
1927	Babe Ruth, Yankees	60	34 years
1961	Roger Maris, Yankees	61	37 years
1998	Mark McGwire, Cardinals	70	3 years
2001	Barry Bonds, Giants	73	?

2001 MAJOR LEAGUE ALL-STARS

Mike Piazza: Led all catchers with 36 homers

Jason Giambi: Produced 87 extra-base hits for the A's

Selected by Baseball America

FIRST TEAM

Pos.	Player, Team	B-T	Ht.	Wt.	Age	AVG	AB	R	H	2B	3B	HR	RBI	SB
C	Mike Piazza, Mets	R-R	6-3	223	32	.300	503	81	151	29	0	36	94	0
1B	Jason Giambi, Athletics	L-R	6-3	235	30	.342	520	109	178	47	2	38	120	2
2B	Bret Boone, Mariners	R-R	5-10	180	32	.331	623	118	206	37	3	37	141	5
3B	Albert Pujols, Cardinals	R-R	6-3	210	21	.329	590	112	194	47	4	37	130	1
SS	Alex Rodriguez, Rangers	R-R	6-3	195	25	318	632	133	201	34	1	52	135	18
OF	Barry Bonds, Giants	L-L	6-1	206	36	.328	476	129	156	32	2	73	137	13
OF	Sammy Sosa, Cubs	R-R	6-0	210	32	.328	577	146	189	34	5	64	160	0
OF	Ichiro Suzuki, Mariners	L-R	5-11	157	27	.350	692	127	242	34	8	8	69	56
DH	Luis Gonzalez, Diamondbacks	L-R	6-2	190	33	.325	609	128	198	36	7	57	142	1

						W	L	ERA	G	SV	IP	H	BB	SO
SP	Roger Clemens, Yankees	R-R	6-4	238	38	20	3	3.51	33	0	220	205	72	213
	Randy Johnson, Diamondbacks	R-L	6-10	230	37	21	6	2.49	35	0	250	181	71	372
	Matt Morris, Cardinals	R-R	6-5	210	26	22	8	3.16	34	0	216	218	54	185
	Curt Schilling, Diamondbacks	R-R	6-4	231	34	22	6	2.98	35	0	257	237	39	293
RP	Mariano Rivera, Yankees	R-R	6-2	195	31	4	6	2.34	71	50	81	61	12	83

SECOND TEAM

Pos.	Player, Team	B-T	Ht.	Wt.	Age	AVG	AB	R	H	2B	3B	HR	RBI	SB
C	Paul LoDuca, Dodgers	R-R	5-10	185	29	.320	460	71	147	28	0	25	90	2
1B	Todd Helton, Rockies	L-L	6-2	195	27	.336	587	132	197	54	2	49	146	7
2B	Roberto Alomar, Indians	B-R	6-0	185	33	.336	575	113	193	34	12	20	100	30
3B	Chipper Jones, Braves	B-R	6-4	210	29	.330	572	113	189	33	5	38	102	9
SS	Rich Aurilia, Giants	R-R	6-1	185	29	.324	636	114	206	37	5	37	97	1
OF	Lance Berkman, Astros	B-L	6-1	205	25	.331	577	110	191	55	5	34	126	7
OF	Juan Gonzalez, Indians	R-R	6-3	220	31	.325	532	97	173	34	1	35	140	1
OF	Larry Walker, Rockies	L-R	6-3	237	34	.350	497	107	174	35	3	38	123	14
DH	Jim Thome, Indians	L-R	6-4	240	30	.291	526	101	153	26	1	49	124	0

						W	L	ERA	G	SV	IP	H	BB	SO
SP	Freddy Garcia, Mariners	R-R	6-4	235	24	18	6	3.05	34	0	239	199	69	163
	Greg Maddux, Braves	R-R	6-0	185	35	17	11	3.05	34	0	233	220	27	173
	Jamie Moyer, Mariners	L-L	6-0	175	38	20	6	3.43	33	0	210	187	44	119
	Mark Mulder, Athletics	L-L	6-6	200	23	21	8	3.45	34	0	229	214	51	153
RP	Robb Nen, Giants	R-R	6-5	215	31	4	5	3.01	79	45	78	58	22	93

Ages as of July 1, 2001

Player of the Year: Barry Bonds, of, Giants. **Pitcher of the Year:** Curt Schilling, rhp, Diamondbacks. **Rookie of the Year:** Albert Pujols, 3b/of, Cardinals. **Manager of the Year:** Lou Piniella, Mariners. **Executive of the Year:** Pat Gillick, Mariners.

homer No. 73 in the season finale, going deep against Dodgers knuckleballer Dennis Springer.

"The chance of hitting a home run off a guy who throws slow is slim," Bonds said. "I just said, 'What else can you give me, God? Enough is enough.' "

Bonds finished the season hitting .328 with a career-high 137 RBIs. His most impressive statistic, other than the 73 homers, was his .863 slugging percentage, which also set a new major league record. The old mark of .847 was 81 years old, set in 1920 by Babe Ruth.

"The slugging percentage is the one that's not going to be broken," Bonds said. "I wouldn't be surprised if someone breaks 73. I don't know if that record will still exist next year, the way the game is now."

Bonds set his homer and slugging marks despite being continually pitched around. He also established still another big league season mark with 177 walks, eclipsing Ruth's record of 170 in 1923. Bonds' amazing .515 on-base percentage was the highest in the NL since John McGraw's .547 in 1899.

"If Barry had been pitched to on a consistent basis, he might have hit 100 home runs," Los Angeles manager Jim Tracy said.

Bonds homered every 6.52 at-bats during the season, which bettered the mark of a homer every 7.27 at-bats by McGwire in 1998. Bonds also hit his 500th career homer on April 17 in San Francisco off the Dodgers' Terry Adams. By season's end, Bonds' career total was at 567, ranking him seventh on the all-time list.

"You can't ask for anything better," Bonds said of his season. "I never thought I'd get to 500 home runs. I never thought I'd play long enough to reach a number like that. And now I've got a chance to reach 600 next year."

All the gaudy numbers led many to believe Bonds may have had the greatest offensive season in baseball history.

"It seems Babe Ruth ain't going to have many records, is he?" San Francisco manager Dusty Baker said. "It's the greatest year I've seen from a single player."

"To play left field like a center fielder in Gold Glove fashion, to be able to steal bases, along with Barry's production as a hitter, it hasn't been done in the history of baseball," Giants general manager Brian Sabean said.

The new home run standard of 73 also had many wondering exactly how high the record could go.

McGwire shattered Maris' long-standing mark by nine in '98, and Cubs outfielder Sammy Sosa hit 66 that same season. McGwire came back to homer 65 times in 1999, while Sosa hit 63. Sosa then hit 64 homers in 2001 to become the first player in history to hit 60 homers in three different seasons. Bonds

400-HOME RUN CLUB

No.	Player	Home Runs
1.	Hank Aaron	755
2.	Babe Ruth	714
3.	Willie Mays	660
4.	Frank Robinson	586
5.	**Mark McGwire**	**583**
6.	Harmon Killebrew	573
7.	**Barry Bonds**	**567**
8.	Reggie Jackson	563
9.	Mike Schmidt	548
10.	Mickey Mantle	536
11.	Jimmie Foxx	534
12.	Ted Williams	521
	Willie McCovey	521
14.	Eddie Mathews	512
	Ernie Banks	512
16.	Mel Ott	511
17.	Eddie Murray	504
18.	Lou Gehrig	493
19.	Stan Musial	475
	Willie Stargell	475
21.	Dave Winfield	465

No.	Player	Home Runs
22.	Jose Canseco	462
23.	Ken Griffey	460
24.	Carl Yastrzemski	452
25.	**Sammy Sosa**	**450**
26.	**Fred McGriff**	**448**
27.	**Rafael Palmeiro**	**447**
28.	Dave Kingman	442
29.	Andre Dawson	438
30.	Cal Ripken	431
31.	Billy Williams	426
32.	Darrell Evans	414
33.	Duke Snider	407

Bold indicates active player

Waiting in the Wings

No.	Player	Home Runs
36.	Juan Gonzalez	397
40.	Harold Baines	384
†47.	Andres Galarraga	377
53.	Matt Williams	362
61.	Jeff Bagwell	349
62.	Frank Thomas	348
64.	Greg Vaughn	344

and Sosa were two of four players to crack the 50 mark in 2001, along with the Diamondbacks' Luis Gonzalez (57) and Rangers' Alex Rodriguez, whose 52 homers set a major league record for shortstops.

"It's unbelievable what Barry has done," McGwire said. "He's totally blown away what I did.

"The game is not the same anymore, though. Before, 30 home runs and 100 RBIs were your goals. Now, if you hit 30 home runs and 100 RBIs, supposedly you have a bad year. So everything has shot up."

Into The Sunset

While Bonds is a surefire Hall of Famer, he will be going into the shrine after Ripken and Gwynn.

The two perennial all-stars retired at the end of the season to complete a perfect symmetry. The duo broke into the major leagues in 1982, spent their entire careers with one club in baseball's most transient era, retired in 2001 and are locks to be inducted in Cooperstown in 2007.

Ripken, the Orioles' shortstop turned third baseman, played his final game Oct. 6 against the Red Sox in Baltimore. Gwynn, the Padres' right fielder, wrapped up his career a day later against the Rockies in San Diego.

Ripken finished up by going 0-for-3 in a 5-1 loss, but that didn't deter the crowd of 48,807 at Camden Yards. Ripken was on deck with the crowd chanting "We want Cal, we want Cal" in the ninth inning when Brady Anderson struck out for the final out.

The Orioles honored Ripken before and after the game. In pregame ceremonies, they retired his No. 8 and unveiled a drawing of a Ripken bronze statue that will be

60-HOME RUN SEASONS

STEVE MOORE

Sammy Sosa

Year	Player, Team	Home Runs
2001	Barry Bonds, Giants	73
1998	Mark McGwire, Cardinals	70
1998	Sammy Sosa, Cubs	66
1999	Mark McGwire, Cardinals	65
2001	Sammy Sosa, Cubs	64
1999	Sammy Sosa, Cubs	63
1961	Roger Maris, Yankees	61
1927	Babe Ruth, Yankees	60

CAREERS FOR THE AGES

TONY GWYNN, of, Padres

JEFF GOLDEN

Proper Name: Anthony Keith Gwynn.
Born: May 9, 1960, in Los Angeles. **Resides:** Poway, Calif.
Ht.: 5-11. **Wt.:** 225. **Bats:** L. **Throws:** L.
School: San Diego State University.
Career Transactions: Selected by Padres in fourth round of June 1981 draft; signed June 16, 1981 . . . Granted free agency, Oct. 31, 2000; re-signed by Padres, Dec. 7, 2000.
Awards/Honors: 1981—Northwest League most valuable player . . . 1984-87, 1989, 1991-99, 2001—Selected to major league All-Star Game . . . 1986-87, 1989-91—National League Gold Glove (outfield).

CAREER RECORD

Yr	Club (League)	Class	AVG	G	AB	R	H	2B	3B	HR	RBI	BB	SO	SB
1981	Walla Walla (NWL)	A	.331	42	178	46	59	12	1	12	37	23	21	17
	Amarillo (TL)	AA	.462	23	91	22	42	8	2	4	19	5	7	5
1982	Hawaii (PCL)	AAA	.328	93	366	65	120	23	2	5	46	18	18	14
	San Diego (NL)	MAJ	.289	54	190	33	55	12	2	1	17	14	16	8
1983	Las Vegas (PCL)	AAA	.342	17	73	15	25	6	0	0	7	6	5	3
	San Diego (NL)	MAJ	.309	86	304	34	94	12	2	1	37	23	21	7
1984	San Diego (NL)	MAJ	.351	158	606	88	213	21	10	5	71	59	23	33
1985	San Diego (NL)	MAJ	.317	154	622	90	197	29	5	6	46	45	33	14
1986	San Diego (NL)	MAJ	.329	160	642	107	211	33	7	14	59	52	35	37
1987	San Diego (NL)	MAJ	.370	157	589	119	218	36	13	7	54	82	35	56
1988	San Diego (NL)	MAJ	.313	133	521	64	163	22	5	7	70	51	40	26
1989	San Diego (NL)	MAJ	.336	158	604	82	203	27	7	4	62	56	30	40
1990	San Diego (NL)	MAJ	.309	141	573	79	177	29	10	4	72	44	23	17
1991	San Diego (NL)	MAJ	.317	134	530	69	168	27	11	4	62	34	19	8
1992	San Diego (NL)	MAJ	.317	128	520	77	165	27	3	6	41	46	16	3
1993	San Diego (NL)	MAJ	.358	122	489	70	175	41	3	7	59	36	19	14
1994	San Diego (NL)	MAJ	.394	110	419	79	165	35	1	12	64	48	19	5
1995	San Diego (NL)	MAJ	.368	135	535	82	197	33	1	9	90	35	15	17
1996	San Diego (NL)	MAJ	.353	116	451	67	159	27	2	3	50	39	17	11
1997	San Diego (NL)	MAJ	.372	149	592	97	220	49	2	17	119	43	28	12
1998	San Diego (NL)	MAJ	.321	127	461	65	148	35	0	16	69	35	18	3
1999	San Diego (NL)	MAJ	.338	111	411	59	139	27	0	10	62	29	14	7
2000	San Diego (NL)	MAJ	.323	36	127	17	41	12	0	1	17	9	4	0
2001	San Diego (NL)	MAJ	.324	71	102	5	33	9	1	1	17	10	9	1
MAJOR LEAGUE TOTALS			**.338**	**2440**	**9288**	**1383**	**3141**	**543**	**85**	**135**	**1138**	**790**	**434**	**319**
MINOR LEAGUE TOTALS			**.347**	**175**	**708**	**148**	**246**	**49**	**5**	**21**	**109**	**52**	**51**	**39**

CAL RIPKEN, 3b, Orioles

LARRY GOREN

Proper Name: Calvin Edwin Ripken.
Born: Aug. 24, 1960, in Havre de Grace, Md. **Resides:** Reisterstown, Md.
Ht.: 6-4. **Wt.:** 220. **Bats:** R. **Throws:** R.
School: Aberdeen (Md.) HS.
Career Transactions: Selected by Orioles in second round of June 1978 draft; signed June 13, 1978.
Awards/Honors: 1979—Florida State League all-star ss . . . 1980—Southern League all-star 3B . . . 1981—International League all-star 3B . . . 1982—American League rookie of the year . . . 1983—American League most valuable player . . . 1983-2001—Selected to major league All-Star Game . . . 1991—American League most valuable player . . . 1991-92—American League Gold Glove (shortstop).

CAREER RECORD

Yr	Club (League)	Class	AVG	G	AB	R	H	2B	3B	HR	RBI	BB	SO	SB
1978	Bluefield (Appy)	R	.264	63	239	27	63	7	1	0	24	24	46	1
1979	Miami (FSL)	A	.303	105	393	51	119	28	1	5	54	31	64	4
	Charlotte (SL)	AA	.180	17	61	6	11	0	1	3	8	3	13	1
1980	Charlotte (SL)	AA	.276	144	522	91	144	28	5	25	78	77	81	4
1981	Rochester (IL)	AAA	.288	114	437	74	126	31	4	23	75	66	85	0
	Baltimore (AL)	MAJ	.128	23	39	1	5	0	0	0	0	1	8	0
1982	Baltimore (AL)	MAJ	.264	160	598	90	158	32	5	28	93	46	95	3
1983	Baltimore (AL)	MAJ	.318	162	663	121	211	47	2	27	102	58	97	0
1984	Baltimore (AL)	MAJ	.304	162	641	103	195	37	7	27	86	71	89	2
1985	Baltimore (AL)	MAJ	.282	161	642	116	181	32	5	26	110	67	68	2
1986	Baltimore (AL)	MAJ	.282	162	627	98	177	35	1	25	81	70	60	4
1987	Baltimore (AL)	MAJ	.252	162	624	97	157	28	3	27	98	81	77	3
1988	Baltimore (AL)	MAJ	.264	161	575	87	152	25	1	23	81	102	69	2
1989	Baltimore (AL)	MAJ	.257	162	646	80	166	30	0	21	93	57	72	3
1990	Baltimore (AL)	MAJ	.250	161	600	78	150	28	4	21	84	82	66	3
1991	Baltimore (AL)	MAJ	.323	162	650	99	210	46	5	34	114	53	46	6
1992	Baltimore (AL)	MAJ	.251	162	637	73	160	29	1	14	72	64	50	4
1993	Baltimore (AL)	MAJ	.257	162	641	87	165	26	3	24	90	65	58	1
1994	Baltimore (AL)	MAJ	.315	112	444	71	140	19	3	13	75	32	41	1
1995	Baltimore (AL)	MAJ	.262	144	550	71	144	33	2	17	88	52	59	0
1996	Baltimore (AL)	MAJ	.278	163	640	94	178	40	1	26	102	59	78	1
1997	Baltimore (AL)	MAJ	.270	162	615	79	166	30	0	17	84	56	73	1
1998	Baltimore (AL)	MAJ	.271	161	601	65	163	27	1	14	61	51	68	0
1999	Baltimore (AL)	MAJ	.340	86	332	51	113	27	0	18	57	13	31	0
2000	Baltimore (AL)	MAJ	.256	83	309	43	79	16	0	15	56	23	37	0
2001	Baltimore (AL)	MAJ	.239	128	477	43	114	16	0	14	68	26	63	0
MAJOR LEAGUE TOTALS			**.277**	**3001**	**11551**	**1647**	**3184**	**603**	**44**	**431**	**1695**	**1129**	**1305**	**36**
MINOR LEAGUE TOTALS			**.280**	**443**	**1652**	**249**	**463**	**94**	**12**	**56**	**239**	**201**	**289**	**10**

erected outside Camden Yards. He was driven around the field in a 1964 red convertible Corvette following the game. Then the stadium went dark, and Orioles Hall of Famers Eddie Murray, Jim Palmer, Frank Robinson and Earl Weaver escorted Ripken to the left side of the infield, where he gave a speech after taking several minutes to compose himself.

"Imagine playing for my hometown team my whole career," Ripken said. "I'm just thrilled that people cared so much about me. People asked me many times how I want to be remembered. Just being remembered at all was special."

Ripken finished his 20-year career batting .276 with 3,184 hits, 431 homers and 1,695 RBIs. He won two AL MVP awards and appeared in 19 All-Star Games, but will be best remembered for playing in a major league record 2,632 consecutive games, an iron man streak that seems as unbreakable as any baseball record.

Tony Gwynn: One final salute to San Diego fans

"I often heard players say they wished they had taken better care of themselves or taken the game more seriously," Ripken said. "Maybe that was my motivation, to maximize my talent and show up and play every day. I didn't want to be in a position at the end of my career to look back over it and regret not going about it in a certain way."

Ripken will stay in baseball, fulfilling a dream by working with amateur players. He returned home to Aberdeen, Md., where he continued work on changing a cow pasture into a baseball complex that will have a minor league stadium, six youth fields and dormitory space to take care of 400 young players a week. The Cal Ripken Jr. Youth Baseball Academy will sit on 50 acres and cost $38 million.

"I want to bring the experience of playing in a major league kind of setting to as many people as I can," Ripken said. "Most people's baseball lives will end pretty early. I want to bring the facility feeling to the grassroots level."

West Coast Party

Like Ripken, Gwynn went out quietly in his final game. Unable to play regularly since August because of a knee injury, Gwynn pinch-hit in the ninth inning of a 14-5 loss to Colorado and grounded out in his final at-bat.

"I was trying to hit the 5.5 hole," Gwynn said, referring to his favorite spot, between the third baseman and shortstop. "I probably could have done a little bit better. Bottom line is, is it going to matter? No. Wasn't going to win the game, wasn't going to lose the game.

"I'm at peace. It's been wonderful."

Gwynn was feted during a postgame ceremony, circling the field while shaking hands and waving to the fans. Gwynn's teammates presented him with a Harley-Davidson motorcycle, and the Padres announced their new downtown ballpark, scheduled to open in 2004, will have an address of No. 19 Tony Gwynn Drive.

In 20 seasons, Gwynn hit .338 with 3,141 hits. He also won eight NL batting titles.

"It's been unbelievable," Gwynn said. "Never in my wildest dreams did I imagine I'd be standing here after 20 years feeling good about a decision I made a year and a half ago. But I do. I feel I've done all I can do as a baseball player."

Like Ripken, Gwynn is headed to amateur baseball now that his playing career is over. He will serve as a volunteer assistant coach at San Diego State, his alma mater, in 2002, and then will take over for head coach Jim Dietz, who will retire. Gwynn's son Anthony is an outfielder for the Aztecs.

"Like my older brother—he's been a teacher for more than 20 years—now it's my turn to teach," Gwynn said.

"There wouldn't be a better recruiting tool in the country than to say, 'Come to San Diego State and be tutored by one of the best hitters to ever play the game,' " Padres

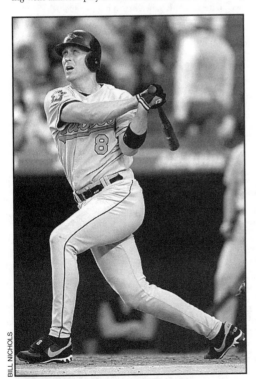

Cal Ripken: Historic career ended in 2001

BILL NICHOLS

LARRY GOREN

ORGANIZATIONOF THEYEAR

Given its middle-class payroll and conservative budget approach, Houston never would have reached the playoffs or captured a fourth National League Central title in five years without a strong scouting and player-development system.

Houston's farm system groomed players such as young pitchers Wade Miller, Roy Oswalt, Tim Redding and Carlos Hernandez. It drafted and developed an all-star outfielder in Lance Berkman, who contended all season for the National League batting title.

Those are just a few of the home-grown names to surface in the majors. They don't begin to reveal the minor league success, the depth of prospects and the wealth of quality, experienced instructors up and down the Houston system. That depth and its accompanying success made the Astros Baseball America's 2001 Organization of the Year.

The franchise worked toward reaching this point systematically. Its ascent includes a significant chronology of key front-office appointments:

Morris Fostoff

Gerry Hunsicker

■ Nov. 22, 1994: Tal Smith became president of baseball operations.

■ Nov. 10, 1995: Gerry Hunsicker was hired as general manager.

■ Sept. 26, 1996: Tim Purpura came on board as assistant GM.

■ Oct. 24, 1997: Purpura added farm director to his duties, overseeing the club's player development and six minor league affiliates.

Smith placed qualified and capable people in key positions of responsibility during his first two years. Over the past three years, Astros minor league affiliates have won a championship at each of the Triple-A, Double-A and Class A levels.

"Our goal four years ago was to become the best organization in major league baseball," Purpura says. "In order to do that, we had to be dogged in our pursuit of setting the goals higher every year. That's the standard we continue to set for ourselves."

Hunsicker and Purpura have strived to improve numerous aspects of the system over the past five years. They have upgraded minor league facilities and the caliber of competition, and they want to win consistently at all levels.

While Hunsicker and Purpura have received more notoriety, each works closely with and gives credit to scouting director David Lakey and his assistant, Pat Murphy. The unsung heroes of any major league operation, the scouts are critical.

"There's no way you can overestimate their importance," Purpura says.

Roy Oswalt: Won 14 games as an Astros rookie

LARRY GOREN

"They have to find the right guys. We've been very fortunate to have scouts who identify players that can help us at the major league level."

The Astros have allowed their minor league managers, coaches and instructors as much freedom as possible. Yet the front office is adamant about monitoring each player's progress and his adherence to high standards.

"You've got to let coaches coach and managers manage," Purpura says. "You can't run six farm clubs from the front office.

"My management style is to find good people and give them the support they need to do their jobs. But one thing we do is set some standards for our players, and then we expect them to live up to them."

In improving the farm system through the past five years, club executives have achieved their goal while staying focused on the basics, including a heavy accent on pitching. The emphasis on pitching has extended beyond drafting good prospects. The meat of the system has been its capable, talented and experienced pitching coaches up and down the system. Finding and keeping high-caliber pitching coaches is an underappreciated but vital part of the Astros' success.

Scouting has accounted for the selection of many key position prospects. Western scout Doug Deutsch saw enough Southern California games in recent years to like the futures for infielder Morgan Ensberg and outfielder Jason Lane, two former Trojan stars.

"The organization has done a great job, starting with scouts in identifying players who can help us at the major league level," Purpura says. "They have really gone the distance for us to be successful."

—TOM HALLIBURTON

PREVIOUS	WINNERS
1982—Oakland Athletics	
1983—New York Mets	
1984—New York Mets	
1985—Milwaukee Brewers	
1986—Milwaukee Brewers	
1987—Milwaukee Brewers	
1988—Montreal Expos	
1989—Texas Rangers	
1990—Montreal Expos	
1991—Atlanta Braves	
1992—Cleveland Indians	
1993—Toronto Blue Jays	
1994—Kansas City Royals	
1995—New York Mets	
1996—Atlanta Braves	
1997—Detroit Tigers	
1998—New York Yankees	
1999—Oakland Athletics	
2000—Chicago White Sox	

closer Trevor Hoffman said.

Like Ripken, Gwynn was most proud of spending his career with one franchise.

"Cal and I both played 20 years, we've both been consistent players and played the game in a professional manner," Gwynn said. "I think we've been good for baseball, and we're very proud of the fact we spent our whole careers in one place.

"Not too many people can say they spent their entire career with one team. I could have gone to different places, but I'm so glad I stayed. It was important to me and my family."

While Ripken and Gwynn were the most significant, they were just two of many players who retired in 2001.

Orioles outfielder Albert Belle decided to give up the game in spring training after a degenerative right hip condition worsened. Belle hit 381 homers and drove in 1,239 runs in his 12-year career, stamping him as a borderline Hall of Fame candidate.

Others who decided to hang it up in '01 included Yankees outfielder Paul O'Neill and infielder Luis Sojo, Giants outfielder Eric Davis, Angels first baseman Wally Joyner, Marlins righthander Alex Fernandez, Blue Jays infielder Tony Fernandez and Braves first baseman Rico Brogna.

The season also featured a couple of stirring comebacks. After sitting out five seasons and undergoing five elbow operations, righthander Jose Rijo returned to the mound for the Reds at age 36. Rijo, the MVP of the 1990 World Series when the Reds swept the Athletics, had a 2.12 ERA in 13 relief appearances.

Tim Raines, 42, made the Expos roster in spring training after sitting out the 2000 season because of lupus. He hit .303-1-9, his playing time limited by a shoulder injury.

Raines was traded to the Orioles during the final weekend of the season so he could play with his son Tim Raines Jr., a rookie outfielder. They joined Ken Griffey Sr. and Jr., who played together with the Mariners in 1990-91, as the only father-son teammates in major league history. But they added a twist because they played against each other in the minors before Tim Sr. was traded, believed to be the first time a father and son have played against each other in a regular season professional game.

Rickey Rocks

Henderson looked as if he might have to go into forced retirement in 2001. The outfielder, 42, received no interest as a free agent after hitting a combined .233 with 36 steals in 123 games with the Mets and Mariners in 2000.

3,000-HIT CLUB

Rickey Henderson

STEVE MOORE

No.	Player	Hits
1.	Pete Rose	4,256
2.	Ty Cobb	4,191
3.	Hank Aaron	3,771
4.	Stan Musial	3,630
5.	Tris Speaker	3,514
6.	Honus Wagner	3,430
7.	Carl Yastrzemski	3,419
8.	Paul Molitor	3,319
9.	Eddie Collins	3,313
10.	Willie Mays	3,283
11.	Eddie Murray	3,255
12.	Nap Lajoie	3,251
13.	Cal Ripken	3,184
14.	George Brett	3,154
15.	Paul Waner	3,152
16.	Robin Yount	3,142
17.	Tony Gwynn	3,141
18.	Dave Winfield	3,110
19.	Rod Carew	3,053
20.	Lou Brock	3,023
21.	Cap Anson	3,022
22.	Wade Boggs	3,010
23.	Al Kaline	3,007
24.	Roberto Clemente	3,000
	Rickey Henderson	**3,000**

Bold indicates active player

The Padres finally decided to give Henderson a chance in spring training, and he wound up making history.

On the final day of the season as Gwynn played his last game, Henderson collected his 3,000th career hit by doubling off the Rockies' John Thomson. Henderson needed 86 hits coming into his 23rd season, and had to go down to the final day to reach the milestone.

"I thought I would never get to 3,000 because I walk so much," said Henderson, widely regarded as the greatest leadoff hitter in history. "If you continue to play as long as I've been playing, you get the opportunity to do it."

The hit capped off a big final week for Henderson. Three days earlier, he homered off Los Angeles' Luke Prokopec in San Diego to break the all-time runs scored record, sliding into home to mark the 2,246th run, eclipsing the mark of Ty Cobb.

Henderson also is baseball's all-time leader in walks (2,141) and stolen bases (1,395). Henderson broke the old walk record of 2,063, held by Ruth, on April 25 in a game with Philadelphia. He set the steal standard in 1991.

"Of all the records, the runs record means the most to me," Henderson said. "As a leadoff hitter, my job is to get on base and find a way to score. Scoring runs is what it's all about. I think it's the most important statistic of all."

Henderson found it appropriate that he would break the runs record held by Cobb.

"Maybe I'm most like Ty Cobb," Henderson said. "We're just more controversial than anything else. It doesn't bother me. It doesn't get to me. I don't have any take on it. I don't understand it. I haven't done anything wrong. I've just always played the game hard. You know, I don't even know how I got to be controversial."

Gwynn could only marvel at seeing Henderson hold three of baseball's major career offensive records.

"To me, Rickey has done more in this game than just about anybody who has played it, with the exception of Hank Aaron and maybe Pete Rose to a certain degree," Gwynn said. "He's the all-time leader in three categories, and that just doesn't happen."

Henderson wasn't alone in reaching milestones, though.

Diamondbacks lefthander Randy Johnson became the first pitcher to strike out 300 or more batters in four consecutive seasons. Johnson finished the year with 372, coming up 11 short of the major league record of 383 set by Nolan Ryan in 1973. Johnson was scheduled to pitch on the final day of the regular season but skipped his start to rest for the playoffs, as the Diamondbacks had

ROOKIE OF THE YEAR

Tony La Russa was having dinner with members of his staff one evening late in the 2001 season, and talk turned to the superstar players he had managed over the years.

Names such as Harold Baines, Jose Canseco, Rickey Henderson and Mark McGwire were invoked, along with several others.

La Russa thought long and hard about that cream of the crop. Then the Cardinals manager contemplated the rookie season of Albert Pujols. And he uttered a statement that caught some of his dinner party by surprise.

"I said, 'I believe this is the best year by a position player that I've ever watched,' " La Russa says. "And I mean no disrespect to any of those other guys.

"I just think what this guy has done with batting average, clutch RBIs and good defense, I don't think I've ever had a better one."

Which tells you all you need to know about the impact Pujols made in his first season with the Cardinals. It added up to enough for the 21-year-old to edge out the Mariners' Ichiro Suzuki as Baseball America's choice for Major League Rookie of the Year.

As the season wound down to its final days and the Cardinals surged to the National League's wild-card playoff berth, the young Dominican had compiled a list of incredible offensive numbers to propel the charge. He led the Cardinals in average (.329), home runs (37), doubles (47), RBIs (130) and runs (112).

No St. Louis player had won the team's triple crown since Ted Simmons in 1973, much less a

Albert Pujols

rookie. But as remarkable as those numbers were, La Russa says there was much more to the story.

"This is a case where the numbers don't really paint enough of a picture of how important this guy has been," he says. "And that's saying a lot with his numbers."

Not bad for someone who wasn't even supposed to make the St. Louis roster in spring training. Not wanting to rush the young prospect who began the 2000 season at low Class A Peoria, the Cardinals had no intention of keeping Pujols when camp opened.

But with each passing day, Pujols played better and better. By the time the exhibition season was half over, the idea of keeping him started to sound not as crazy.

"His teammates were the ones who started yapping, 'Come on, this guy's got to be on the club,' " La Russa says.

The opening Pujols needed appeared at the end of camp when Bobby Bonilla went on the disabled list with a strained hamstring. With Mark McGwire limping on a surgically repaired knee that eventually landed him on the DL as well, the Cardinals decided to gamble and keep Pujols.

If Pujols was surprised by that decision, he never showed it.

"The whole time I was in spring training I thought I could make the team," he said. "I just went out

there with the attitude to make the team. Then it happened and I was very excited.

"I knew they were impressed with me and they would give me a chance. I went with the attitude to make the team and did the best that I can. I have been blessed this year."

Though Pujols was a baby in terms of professional baseball, he had prepared his entire life for this chance. The youngest of 11 children, he began playing at age 5 in the Dominican Republic.

When Pujols was 16, his father moved the family to Independence, Mo., which has a large community of Dominican immigrants. Pujols starred at Fort Osage High, leading the team to a state title as a junior. He was never drafted out of high school because he enrolled at Maple Woods Community College in Kansas City at the semester break.

TOP 20 ROOKIES

Selected by Baseball America

1.	Albert Pujols, 3b/1b/of, Cardinals
2.	Ichiro Suzuki, of, Mariners
3.	Roy Oswalt, rhp, Astros
4.	C.C. Sabathia, lhp, Indians
5.	Jimmy Rollins, ss, Phillies
6.	Alfonso Soriano, 2b, Yankees
7.	David Eckstein, ss, Angels
8.	Adam Dunn, of, Reds
9.	Bud Smith, lhp, Cardinals
10.	Ben Sheets, rhp, Brewers
11.	Joel Pineiro, rhp, Mariners
12.	Danys Baez, rhp, Indians
13.	Luis Rivas, 2b, Twins
14.	Brandon Duckworth, rhp, Phillies
15.	Brian Lawrence, rhp, Padres
16.	Bret Prinz, rhp, Diamondbacks
17.	Joe Kennedy, lhp, Devil Rays
18.	Shawn Chacon, rhp, Rockies
19.	Tsuyoshi Shinjo, of, Mets
20.	Juan Uribe, ss, Rockies

The next June, he wasn't selected until the 13th round of the draft and didn't sign until the end of the summer.

Having taken the bullet train to the big leagues, Pujols quickly showed he was a one-in-a-million performer. In fact, a strong case could be made that he had the finest offensive season of any rookie in major league history.

—TOM HAUDRICOURT

PREVIOUS WINNERS

1989—Gregg Olson, rhp, Orioles
1990—Sandy Alomar, c, Indians
1991—Jeff Bagwell, 1b, Astros
1992—Pat Listach, ss, Brewers
1993—Mike Piazza, c, Dodgers
1994—Raul Mondesi, of, Dodgers
1995—Hideo Nomo, rhp, Dodgers
1996—Derek Jeter, ss, Yankees
1997—Nomar Garciaparra, ss, Red Sox
1998—Kerry Wood, rhp, Cubs
1999—Carlos Beltran, of, Royals
2000—Rafael Furcal, ss/2b, Braves

clinched the NL West title.

Yankees righthander Roger Clemens set the AL record for career strikeouts with 3,717, while tying the league record for longest winning streak in a season with 16 in a row. He also became the first pitcher to start a season 20-1, though he lost his final two decisions, both to the lowly Devil Rays, to finish 20-3.

Three pitchers spun no-hitters. Red Sox righthander Hideo Nomo threw his second career no-hitter April 4 against the Orioles in Baltimore in his Boston debut. The Padres were no-hit twice at home, by Florida's A.J. Burnett on May 12 as he walked nine, and by Cardinals rookie lefthander Bud Smith on Sept. 3 in his 11th major league start.

Rockies first baseman Todd Helton became the first player with 100 extra-base hits in consecutive seasons. The Padres' Hoffman became the first pitcher to have four consecutive 40-save seasons, and the first with five career 40-save seasons.

Mariners Sail Along

Individual records weren't the only ones to fall in 2001, as Seattle had a season for the ages.

Led by right fielder Ichiro Suzuki, a rookie sensation as the first Japanese position player to reach the major leagues, the Mariners finished 116-46. That tied the major league wins record established by the 1906 Cubs and broke the AL mark of 114 set by the 1998 Yankees.

"When we left spring training, if you would have told me we'd win 116 ballgames and tie the record, I would have thought you'd have been smoking dope or something," Mariners manager Lou Piniella said.

What made the Mariners' season even more remarkable is that they weren't even the consensus favorite to win the AL West. The Athletics were considered the team to beat after edging the Mariners by a game in the division race the year before.

Seattle steamrolled its way to an incredible season, taking the division crown by 14 games over a 102-win Oakland team. The Mariners led the AL in hitting, pitching and defense with a .288 team average, a 3.54 staff ERA and a .986 fielding percentage.

"It was an amazing season, right from Opening Day," Mariners outfielder Al Martin said. "Every day, we just felt like we were going to win the game. There was never any doubt in our minds—never a day when guys seemed to be dragging. I've never seen anything like it. I don't know if anyone will ever experience this again."

Seattle made history despite losing three potential Hall of Famers in the previous three seasons. The Mariners traded Randy Johnson to the Astros during the 1998 season, dealt center fielder Ken Griffey to the Reds before the 2000 season and lost Rodriguez to the Rangers prior to the 2001 season as he signed a 10-year, $252 million contract, the largest in professional sports history.

Mariners GM Pat Gillick did an outstanding job of retooling the franchise as it moved from the hitter-friendly Kingdome to larger Safeco Field midway through the 1999 season.

"The ballpark necessitated a change of philosophy within the organization," Piniella said. "We had to prioritize pitching, defense and versatility. We used to be a home run-bashing team and had some great offensive teams, but pitching and defense wins. It's hard to

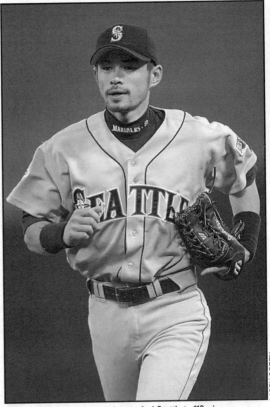

Ichiro Suzuki: Japanese sensation sparked Seattle to 116 wins

LARRY GOREN

outscore opponents consistently.

"We've added more depth in our bullpen, and some experience and a blend of youth to our starting rotation. It's been a winning mix."

Seattle had a chance to break the wins record on the final day of the season but wound up stuck on 116, as Texas pulled out a 4-3 win on Rafael Palmiero's go-ahead single off Jeff Nelson in the ninth inning.

"I'm sure everyone here knows this opportunity doesn't come around very often," Mariners DH Edgar Martinez said. "But it's still been a great year, and we're still in the record books."

Suzuki helped put the Mariners there with a phenomenal rookie season. The Mariners spent nearly $30 million to obtain Suzuki's rights and sign him. He left the Orix BlueWave after seven straight batting titles in Japan's Pacific League.

While skeptics said Suzuki would meet his match against major league pitching, he wore out the best the AL had to offer. The speedster won the AL batting title with a .350 average and set a major league record for rookies with 242 hits. He also topped the league with 56 stolen bases, a .445 average with runners in scoring position and 75 multi-hit games.

"To me, what I have won is not important," Suzuki said. "To me, what is important is how I prepare for the game every day. I get a lot of fulfillment in how I prepare."

Suzuki's manager and teammates were awed by his transition from Japan to the United States.

"I said when we signed him I thought he was going to

EXECUTIVEOF THEYEAR

Pat Gillick is enjoying a very nice retirement.

Since packing it in after the 1994 season after 18 years with the Blue Jays, planning to take up a hobby or two, Gillick has won a wild card and division in Baltimore. He chaired the committee that built the silver-medal-winning Team USA at the 1999 Pan American Games. And the past two seasons, his Mariners have reached the playoffs, winning an American League-record 116 games in 2001.

Gillick turned the Ken Griffey mess into Mike Cameron and built (from scratch) a dominant bullpen that scares opponents as much as the former Mariners bullpen scared Seattle. He has imported two straight rookies of the year from Japan. Almost every free-agent signing—Bret Boone, Mark McLemore, John Olerud, Aaron Sele, take your pick—has worked out positively. In short, more than half (13 of 25) of the players on the Mariners' 2001 postseason roster were procured in his two years, turning Seattle into one of the most formidable franchises in the game.

Yes, Gillick's retirement is humming along quite nicely.

"It's going well," he says, oddly serious. "I really have enjoyed it."

Seven years after walking away from his baseball career, Pat Gillick again stands at the top of his profession. No general manager in baseball has more shrewdly exploited so many avenues for talent, from trades to the farm system to free agency to overseas. No GM's moves worked so well for his team in 2001. And for that, Gillick was named Baseball America's 2001 Executive of the Year.

"Pat would be great at his job just judging people only on talent and character," Mariners chairman Howard Lincoln says. "But then he's very good at molding all of those constituent parts into one whole. And he's done it in every city he's operated in.

"Players see that. When they arrive in the morning at spring training, Pat's car is there. When they leave at night, Pat's car is there. They know their GM is working just as hard, if not harder, than they are."

"What I always said is that every general manager, if he's going to do his job, has to use every possible area to improve the club," Gillick says. "As new ones arise, then you have to take advantage of that."

Gillick will go down among

Pat Gillick

LARRY GOREN

Sandy Alderson and John Schuerholz as one of the most successful and innovative baseball men of his era. It's easy to forget that club executives have a spot in the Hall of Fame—Branch Rickey and George Weiss to name two—and it's hard to imagine Gillick not winding up there someday. Two World Series championships and getting three different teams into seven of the last eight postseasons is unmatched.

His record-breaking 2001 season with the Mariners will go down among Gillick's greatest accomplishments. Few teams have been built so quickly and with such unerring precision. All that is retired, it appears, is the notion that he can't do it at will.

—ALAN SCHWARZ

PREVIOUS WINNERS

| 1998—Doug Melvin, Rangers |
| 1999—Jim Bowden, Reds |
| 2000—Walt Jocketty, Cardinals |

MANAGEROF THEYEAR

Whether his team's 2001 season will be remembered as a triumph or a failure, Mariners manager Lou Piniella—Baseball America's Manager of the Year—figured out how to do the impossible. He made Seattle a better team even while losing his best players.

Faced with the departures of all-stars Randy Johnson, Ken Griffey and Alex Rodriguez over the past three seasons, Piniella molded a patchwork of free agents, veterans and rookies (at least to American baseball) to produce 116 wins for the Mariners, setting an American League record for victories.

Piniella juggled the personalities of his players, keeping everyone loose despite their torrid win pace,

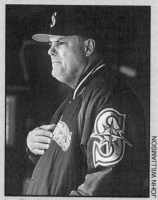
Lou Piniella

JOHN WILLIAMSON

and deftly handled a pitching staff that kept Seattle from losing a road

PREVIOUS WINNERS

| 1998—Larry Dierker, Astros |
| 1999—Jimy Williams, Red Sox |
| 2000—Dusty Baker, Giants |

series until the season's final month. Still, the team's regular season accomplishments failed to console him after the Yankees beat the Mariners for the second straight season in the AL Championship Series.

"The amazing thing about baseball is that no matter how many games you win, unless you win a World Series, you're going to feel disappointment," he said after Game Five of the ALCS.

—GEOFF WILSON

hit around .300, steal some bases and play an excellent right field," Piniella said. "He's exceeded everything I thought. It's rather amazing."

Rookie Sensations

Suzuki was the rookie who received the lion's share of hype in 2001, and understandably so. He was far from the only outstanding rookie in '01, though. In fact, it was one of the best crops of new players in years.

The Cardinals' Albert Pujols seemingly came from nowhere to turn in an incredible rookie year. While playing at third base, first base, left field and right field, Pujols set NL rookie records with 130 RBIs, 88 extra-base hits and 360 total bases. He also hit .329 with 37 homers.

Pujols went to spring training with little chance to make the club after spending almost all of 2000 in Class A. He forced his way onto the roster with a strong spring, then gave the Cardinals a lift at four different positions in leading them to a playoff berth.

"Albert was our one constant," Cardinals GM Walt Jocketty said. "Every single day he gave us something. If you look at the criteria for what an MVP is, I think he fits."

Pujols wasn't the only Cardinals rookie to make an impact, as lefthander Bud Smith threw a no-hitter. And they were just two of the rookies who made a major impact in the NL.

Astros righthander Roy Oswalt debuted with a dominating 14-3 record, his .824 winning percentage leading the league. Oswalt also had a 2.73 ERA and would have ranked second in the NL if he hadn't fallen 20 innings short of the 162-inning minimum to qualify.

Shortstop Jimmy Rollins played a big role in Philadelphia nearly going from worst to first in the East. He led the NL with 46 stolen bases and 12 triples while batting .274-14-54.

Brewers righthander Ben Sheets, who pitched the U.S. to an upset of Cuba in the gold-medal game of the 2000 Olympics, won 10 games in the first half and made the NL all-star team. Sheets was bothered by shoulder tendinitis in the second half and finished 11-10, 4.76, but he left little doubt he is ready to become a premier pitcher.

Reds outfielder Adam Dunn, after tearing up the minors at Double-A Chattanooga and Triple-A Louisville, got 244 at-bats with the Reds and made a huge impact, batting .262-19-43 in just 66 games.

Pirates catcher/first baseman/outfielder Craig Wilson tied the major league single-season record with seven pinch-hit

Jimmy Rollins

homers. Rockies righthander Jason Jennings became the first pitcher in modern times to throw a shutout and hit a home run in his major league debut, on Aug. 23 against the Mets.

Not to be outdone by the NL, Suzuki was one of many rookies to make an impact in the AL.

Indians lefthander C.C. Sabathia went 17-5 to finish sixth in the league in wins, and posted a 4.39 ERA in 33 starts. Alfonso Soriano's big spring prompted the Yankees to open up second base by moving veteran Chuck Knoblauch to left field. Soriano responded by hitting .268-18-73 with 43 steals. Angels shortstop David Eckstein hit .285-4-41 with 29 steals.

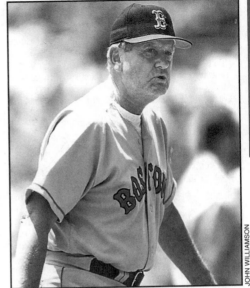

Jimy Williams: Fired by the Red Sox

Job Insecurity

While such high-profile players as Ripken and Gwynn retired in 2001, one of the game's more recognizable managers also called it quits at the end of the season.

Tom Kelly decided to retire, though the Twins were one of the biggest surprises in the game in 2001. Kelly replaced Ray Miller as manager late in the 1986 season and had the longest tenure of any coach or manager in professional sports.

While Kelly's lifetime record was 1,140-1,244, the Twins won World Series titles under his guidance in 1987 and 1991.

After eight straight losing seasons, primarily because of penny pinching by owner Carl Pohlad, the Twins went 85-77 in '01. They put themselves on the brink of becoming a contender for years with a strong rotation and a nucleus of good, young hitters.

Though just 51, Kelly said he no longer had the energy necessary to manage effectively.

"Whether it's the travel catching up to me or the stress of the job, there were days this year when I felt somewhat tired, a little worn out," Kelly said. "The time had come to leave, but it's just been a fantastic ride for me. Everybody's been wonderful to me. It's a good time for me to step aside and let somebody take over."

Kelly was one of eight managers who left their posts in 2001, along with Boston's Jimy Williams, Florida's John Boles and Tony Perez, Houston's Larry Dierker, Montreal's Felipe Alou, Tampa Bay's Larry Rothschild and Texas' Johnny Oates.

Williams got the ax Aug. 16, though he was a candidate for AL manager of the year with the Red Sox in playoff contention despite a slew of injuries to key players. Williams had long feuded with Red Sox GM Dan Duquette and finally lost the power struggle, as pitching coach Joe Kerrigan was promoted to manager.

The Marlins fired Boles on May 26, a day after pitcher Dan Miceli roundly criticized him and said the players had no faith in their manager because he had never

2001 MAJOR LEAGUE ALL-STAR GAME

Cal Ripken made his 19th and final All-Star Game his most memorable.

The Orioles third baseman, who retired at the end of the 2001 season, homered in his first at-bat to lead the American League to a 4-1 victory over the National League at Safeco Field in Seattle. Ripken was named the game's Most Valuable Player.

"It's been a great one," Ripken said. "To have things so great in the game, to hit a home run, it's been special. It's a greet feeling."

Leading off the bottom of the third inning of a scoreless game, Ripken homered off Dodgers righthander Chan Ho Park on the first pitch for his second career All-Star Game homer. At 40, Ripken became the oldest player to ever homer in the game. Ripken's other All-Star Game homer also netted him MVP honors in 1991 in Toronto.

LARRY GOREN

Kazuhiro Sasaki

The AL used two more homers to put the game away. Yankees shortstop Derek Jeter and White Sox outfielder Magglio Ordonez hit back-to-back shots leading off the sixth against the Cubs' Jon Lieber to extend the lead to 4-1.

Hometown pitchers from the Mariners got the win and the save. Freddy Garcia worked one perfect relief inning for the victory and Kazuhiro Sasaki retired the side in the ninth to record the save. Park was tagged with the loss.

TOP VOTE-GETTERS

NATIONAL LEAGUE

CATCHER: 1. Mike Piazza, Mets, 1,995,594; 2. Charles Johnson, Marlins, 522,144; 3. Jason Kendall, Pirates, 371,595.

FIRST BASE: 1. Todd Helton, Rockies, 1,166,838; 2. Mark McGwire, Cardinals, 919,636; 3. Jeff Bagwell, Astros, 632,114.

SECOND BASE: 1. Jeff Kent, Giants, 979,744; 2. Craig Biggio, Astros, 693,449; 3. Jay Bell, Diamondbacks, 480, 174.

THIRD BASE: 1. Chipper Jones, Braves, 1,162,434; 2. Robin Ventura, Mets, 494,306; 3. Phil Nevin, Padres 426,882.

SHORTSTOP: 1. Rich Aurilia, Giants, 1,036,528; 2. Barry Larkin, Reds, 599,322; 3. Rey Ordonez, Mets, 512,107.

OUTFIELD: 1. Barry Bonds, Giants, 2,140,315; 2. Sammy Sosa, Cubs, 1,640,322; 3. Luis Gonzalez, Diamondbacks, 1,194,254; 4. Larry Walker, Rockies, 871,036; 5. Ken Griffey, Reds, 863,559; 6. Jim Edmonds, Cardinals, 482,690; 7. Vladimir Guerrero, Expos, 479,590; 8. J.D. Drew, Cardinals, 454,595; 9. Andruw Jones, Braves, 430,875.

AMERICAN LEAGUE

CATCHER: 1. Ivan Rodriguez, Rangers, 2,043,613; 2. Dan Wilson, Mariners, 917,101; 3. Jorge Posada, Yankees, 632,503.

FIRST BASE: 1. John Olerud, Mariners, 1,565,445; 2. Jason Giambi, Athletics, 741,191; 3. Carlos Delgado, Blue Jays, 677,819.

SECOND BASE: 1. Bret Boone, Mariners, 2,262,819; 2. Roberto Alomar, Indians, 1,379,581; 3. Alfonso Soriano, Yankees, 348,085.

THIRD BASE: 1. Cal Ripken, Orioles, 1,108,383; 2. David Bell, Mariners, 1,063,772; 3. Troy Glaus, Angels, 1,039,155.

SHORTSTOP: 1. Alex Rodriguez, Rangers, 1,352,910; 2. Derek Jeter, Yankees, 1,088,985; 3. Carlos Guillen, Mariners, 745,077.

OUTFIELD: 1. Ichiro Suzuki, Mariners, 3,373,035; 2. Manny Ramirez, Red Sox, 1,834,981; 3. Juan Gonzalez, Indians, 1,354,583; 4. Mike Cameron, Mariners, 1,215,233; 5. Bernie Williams, Yankees, 817,517; 6. Kenny Lofton, Indians, 552,868; 7. Ellis Burks, Indians, 516,185; 8. Al Martin, Mariners, 460,248; 9. Paul O'Neill, Yankees, 405,769.

DESIGNATED HITTER: 1. Edgar Martinez, Mariners, 2,584,643; 2. David Justice, Yankees, 575,877; 3. Andres Galarraga, Rangers, 502,059.

ROSTERS

NATIONAL LEAGUE

MANAGER: Bobby Valentine, Mets.

PITCHERS: John Burkett, Braves; Mike Hampton, Rockies; **Randy Johnson, Diamondbacks**; Jon Lieber, Cubs; Matt Morris, Cardinals; Chan Ho Park, Dodgers; x-Rick Reed, Mets; Curt Schilling, Diamondbacks; Jeff Shaw, Dodgers; Ben Sheets, Brewers; Billy Wagner, Astros.

CATCHERS: Charles Johnson, Marlins; **Mike Piazza, Mets**.

INFIELDERS: **Rich Aurilia, Giants (ss)**; Sean Casey, Reds; **Todd Helton, Rockies (1b)**; **Chipper Jones, Braves (3b)**; **Jeff Kent, Giants (2b)**; Ryan Klesko, Padres; Phil Nevin, Padres; Albert Pujols, Cardinals; Jimmy Rollins, Phillies.

OUTFIELDERS: Moises Alou, Astros; Lance Berkman, Astros; **Barry Bonds, Giants (lf)**; Cliff Floyd, Marlins; Brian Giles, Pirates; **Luis Gonzalez, Diamondbacks (cf)**; Vladimir Guerrero, Expos; **Sammy Sosa, Cubs (rf)**.

AMERICAN LEAGUE

MANAGER: Joe Torre, Yankees.

PITCHERS: **Roger Clemens, Yankees**; Freddy Garcia, Mariners; Joe Mays, Twins; Eric Milton, Twins; Jeff Nelson, Mariners; Troy Percival, Angels; Andy Pettitte, Yankees; Paul Quantrill, Blue Jays; x-Mariano Rivera, Yankees; Kazuhiro Sasaki, Mariners; Mike Stanton, Yankees.

CATCHERS: Jorge Posada, Yankees; **Ivan Rodriguez, Rangers**.

INFIELDERS: Roberto Alomar, Indians; **Bret Boone, Mariners (2b)**; Tony Clark, Tigers; Jason Giambi, Athletics; Troy Glaus, Angels; Cristian Guzman, Twins; Derek Jeter, Yankees; **John Olerud, Mariners (1b)**; **Cal Ripken, Orioles (3b)**; **Alex Rodriguez, Rangers (ss)**; Mike Sweeney, Royals.

OUTFIELDERS: Mike Cameron, Mariners; **Juan Gonzalez, Indians (rf)**; Magglio Ordonez, White Sox; **Manny Ramirez, Indians (lf)**; **Ichiro Suzuki, Mariners (cf)**; x-Greg Vaughn, Devil Rays; Bernie Williams, Yankees.

Starters in **boldface**.
x-injured, did not play.

July 10 in Seattle
American League 4, National League 1

NATIONAL	ab	r	h	bi	AMERICAN	ab	r	h	bi
L. Gonzalez cf	2	0	1	0	Suzuki cf-rf	3	0	1	0
Berkman cf	2	0	1	0	Williams cf	1	0	0	0
Helton 1b	2	0	0	0	A. Rodriguez 3b-ss	2	0	0	0
Klesko ss	1	0	0	1	Jeter ss	1	1	1	1
Bonds lf	2	0	0	0	Guzman ph-ss	1	0	0	0
Guerrero ph-rf	1	0	0	0	Ramirez lf	1	0	0	0
Giles ph	1	0	0	0	Ordonez lf	3	1	2	1
Sosa rf	2	0	0	0	Boone 2b	2	0	0	0
Alou rf-lf	1	0	0	0	Alomar 2b	2	0	0	0
Casey ph	1	0	0	0	J. Gonzalez rf	1	0	0	0
Walker dh	2	0	0	0	Cameron cf-rf	3	0	1	0
Floyd dh	2	0	0	0	Olerud 1b	2	0	0	0
Piazza c	2	0	0	0	Giambi pr-1b	1	1	0	0
Pujols 3b-2b	0	0	0	0	Sweeney 1b	1	0	0	0
C. Jones 3b	2	0	0	0	E. Martinez dh	2	0	0	0
C. Johnson c	1	0	0	0	Clark dh	1	0	0	0
Kent 2b	2	1	1	0	Ripken ss-3b	2	1	1	1
Nevin ph-3b	1	0	0	0	Glaus 3b	1	0	0	0
Aurilia ss	2	0	0	0	I. Rodriguez c	2	0	1	0
Rollins ss	0	0	0	0	Posada c	1	0	1	0
Totals	**29**	**1**	**3**	**1**	**Totals**	**33**	**4**	**8**	**4**

National	000	001	000—1
American	001	012	00x—4

E—Kent. **LOB**—National 4, American 5. **2B**—Kent, Cameron, Posada. **HR**—Ripken, Jeter, Ordonez. **SF**—Klesko. **SB**—Rollins, Suzuki.

National	ip	h	r	er	bb	so	American	ip	h	r	er	bb	so
R Johnson	2	1	0	0	0	3	Clemens	2	0	0	0	0	1
Park L	1	1	1	1	0	1	Garcia W	1	0	0	0	0	0
Burkett	1	0	0	0	0	1	Pettitte	1	1	0	0	0	1
Hampton	1	1	1	0	0	0	Mays	1	0	0	0	0	0
Lieber	1	3	2	2	0	1	Quantrill	⅓	2	1	1	0	0
Morris	1	0	0	0	0	1	Stanton	⅔	0	0	0	0	0
Shaw	⅓	1	0	0	0	0	Nelson	1	0	0	1	1	0
Wagner	⅓	0	0	0	0	0	Percival	1	0	0	0	1	1
Sheets	⅓	0	0	0	0	0	Sasaki S	1	0	0	0	0	1

Umpires: HP—Dana DeMuth; **1B**—Dale Scott; **2B**—Jim Joyce; **3B**—Jerry Layne; **LF**—Ron Kulpa; **RF**—Tony Randazzo.

T—2:48. **A**—47,364.

played professionally. Perez, a special assistant to Florida GM Dave Dombrowski, took over the team and had it contending for a time before it slumped in the second half. At season's end he decided to return to the front office.

Dierker resigned a week after the Astros were swept by Atlanta in the NL Division Series. Though he guided the Astros to four NL Central titles in five seasons, he was under heavy fire in Houston for the team's playoff failures. The franchise still has never won a playoff series.

Alou had his 10-year tenure with the Expos end May 31 as he was fired with Montreal standing at 21-32. Former White Sox and Mets manager Jeff Torborg, who had been serving as a spring training catching instructor with the Expos, took over.

Felipe Alou (Expos) and Tom Kelly (Twins): Longtime managers stepped aside in 2001

Rothschild got canned quickly, the pink slip coming April 18 after the Devil Rays started 4-10. He was replaced by hitting coach Hal McRae.

Oates resigned under pressure May 5 after the Rangers, following on an offseason in which they gave Rodriguez his record-setting deal, got off to an 11-17 start. Third-base coach Jerry Narron was promoted to manager.

One of the game's most successful general managers, Cleveland's John Hart, decided to step down. Hart took over one of the sorriest franchises in baseball in 1991 and transformed the Indians into a team that won six AL Central titles from 1995-2001, though they never got over the hurdle of winning a World Series. Indians assistant GM Mark Shapiro took over on Nov. 1.

"It's been an incredible run, better than I ever could have imagined," said Hart, who immediately was named GM of the Rangers when his contract with Cleveland expired. "But I think it is time for the organization to have a change in the GM's chair. You run the risk of things getting stale."

Dodgers GM Kevin Malone had a bizarre exit April 19. The team fired him five days after he reportedly challenged a taunting Padres fan to a fight in the stands at Qualcomm Stadium in San Diego.

Special assistant Dave Wallace replaced Malone for the remainder of the season, with the assurance that he would not have to take the job full-time. The Dodgers hired former White Sox assistant GM Dan Evans in the middle of the season and then promoted him to GM in October.

Kevin Malone

Three other GMs were also fired, including Pittsburgh's Cam Bonifay, who got the ax June 11 with the Pirates on their way to a ninth straight losing season. Pittsburgh hired Florida assistant GM Dave Littlefield to try to right its struggling team.

Toronto's Gord Ash and Texas' Doug Melvin were jettisoned in the season's final days, while Montreal GM Jim Beattie resigned at season's end.

New Beginnings

PNC Park in Pittsburgh was one of two new stadiums to open in 2001, along with Miller Park in Milwaukee.

The Brewers unveiled their 42,500-seat park with a retractable roof on April 6, when they edged Cincinnati 5-4. The park, which cost $400 million, opened with plenty of pomp and circumstance, with President George W. Bush on hand to throw out the first pitch.

Miller Park was supposed to open at the start of the 2000 season, but a crane accident that killed three ironworkers on July 14, 1999, pushed the opening back a year.

The Brewers, though, were more than happy with the new ballpark, particularly after playing in County Stadium since the franchise moved from Seattle in 1970.

"I'll sit in my office, which overlooks the field, and just shake my head in disbelief," Brewers president Wendy Selig-Prieb said. "It's hard to believe that this is in Milwaukee. For all those years that our fans sat outside at County Stadium and shivered on Opening Day, then wondered if games were going to be played the rest of the year because of the weather . . . Well, they deserve this."

And the fans came out in record numbers, a total of 2,811,041 despite seeing the home team suffer through a 68-94 year.

The Pirates opened 37,898-seat PNC Park to rave reviews, its breathtaking views of the Pittsburgh skyline and Allegheny River a stark contrast to Three Rivers Stadium, the concrete bowl they had called home since 1970.

The Pirates opened the park on a sour note April 9, Stargell's death hanging heavily over an 8-2 loss to Cincinnati. Just as he did in Miller Park three days earlier, Reds first baseman Sean Casey delivered the first hit.

While the Pirates suffered through their first 100-loss season since 1985, they set a club attendance record at 2,402,890.

"The ballpark is absolutely awesome," Pirates catcher Jason Kendall said. "When I squat behind the plate, it becomes hard to concentrate sometimes. You look out at the city and it's an incredible sight. It's the best thing that could have ever happened to Pittsburgh."

Changing Calls

As seems to be the case with increasing regularity in recent years, the umpires again were one of the game's focal points in 2001.

Kirby Puckett and Dave Winfield: 2001 inductees

PAMELA SMITH

The Hall of Fame welcomed four new members during Aug. 5, 2001, induction ceremonies in Cooperstown, then overhauled its veterans committee the next day.

Outfielders Kirby Puckett and Dave Winfield went into the hall along with slick-fielding second baseman Bill Mazeroski and Negro League star pitcher Hilton Smith.

Mazeroski did not have the gaudy offensive credentials of Puckett and Winfield. He hit just .260-138-853 in 17 seasons with Pittsburgh from 1956-72. He got into the hall on the strength of eight Gold Gloves, and then stole the show with one of the shortest induction speeches in history.

Mazeroski waited 23 years to be inducted since first going on the Baseball Writers Association of America ballot in 1978. The emotions of all those years came out, as he had to cut his speech short after 2½ minutes when he couldn't hold back the tears. In addition to being passed over 15 times by the writers, Mazeroski lost out five times in veterans committee balloting.

"This is going to be hard," Mazeroski said before breaking down. "I thought having my Pirates number retired was the greatest thing that ever happened to me. I didn't think I would make it into the Hall of Fame."

With that, Mazeroski held up his 12-page speech to the crowd of 20,000-plus and said, "I don't think I'm going to make it." He then left the podium to a rousing ovation.

Puckett spent all 12 of his major league seasons with the Twins from 1984-95, his career cut short by glaucoma. He hit .318-207-1,085. Winfield logged 3,110 hits to go with 465 homers and 1,833 RBIs over 22 seasons (1973-88, 1990-95) with the Padres, Yankees, Angels, Blue Jays, Twins and Indians.

Stung by criticism of Mazeroski's election, the Hall of Fame decided to make sweeping changes with the veterans committee, which had been made up of 15 members—five former players, five former executives and five former writers—who met each March.

Under the new format, the committee will consist of  all living Hall of Fame players, writers and broadcasters. They will vote every two years, and candidates will have to be on 75 percent of the ballots to be elected.

"We just felt the time had come to make it tougher to get into the Hall of Fame," said Hall of Famer Joe Morgan, the vice chairman of the hall's board of directors.

Willie Stargell

Three Hall of Fame players died in 2001, including Pittsburgh icon Willie Stargell.

The slugging first baseman/outfielder died on April 9 in Wilmington, N.C., because of complications of kidney disease and diabetes. Stargell died on the day the Pirates opened their new ballpark, $262 million PNC Park.

Stargell spent his entire 21-year career with the Pirates from 1962-82, hitting .282 with 475 homers and 1,340 RBIs. He helped the Pirates to World Series titles in 1971 and 1979 and shared the NL MVP award in '79.

Another slugger, Eddie Mathews, died Feb. 18 in La Jolla, Calif., after being hospitalized for more than five months. He died at 69 due to complications from pneumonia.

Mathews was the only man to play for the Braves in Boston, Milwaukee and Atlanta. He also spent time with the Astros and Tigers late in his career and wound up hitting 512 homers and driving in 1,453 runs in 17 seasons from 1952-68, while compiling a .271 batting average.

Lou Boudreau, the youngest manager in baseball history, died Aug. 11 of heart failure at age 84 in Olympia Fields, Ill.

Boudreau took over as Cleveland's skipper at age 24 in 1942 and stayed with the Indians through 1950, leading them to their last World Series title in 1948. He also managed Boston from 1952-54, the Kansas City Athletics from 1955-57 and the Cubs in 1960. He then was a radio broadcaster for the Cubs for 28 years before retiring in 1988.

Sandy Alderson, Major League Baseball's executive vice president of baseball operations, decreed in the offseason that umpires would call a uniform strike zone in an effort to help the pitchers regain a bit of an edge in an offensive era.

In recent years, umpires called strikes from the knees to the waist. Alderson instructed them to follow the rule book, which says a strike is any pitch over home plate from the top of the knees to the midpoint between the top of the shoulders and the top of the uniform pants.

The umpires attended special camps over the winter to gain consistency with the strike zone, then spent time in spring training demonstrating to players and managers how balls and strikes would be called. While both sides had adjustment periods early in the season and some players claimed the umpires went back to calling the strike zone the way they had in the past, offense did decrease somewhat in 2001.

Scoring was down 7.1 percent, home runs were down 4.2 percent and the overall ERA dipped 7.4 percent. Runs a game dropped to 9.55 from 10.28, the overall batting average fell to .264 from .270 and overall ERA declined from 4.76 to 4.41.

What really gave the indication the strike zone got bigger was that strikeouts went up 3.3 percent, to 13.34 a game from 12.90 in 2000. Meanwhile, walks decreased 13.3 percent, to 6.51 a game from 7.50.

"I think we have made real progress," Alderson said. "I don't think we're there yet with consistency among all umpires and from game to game. I think the vast majority of umpires made the effort to make the adjustment, and I would expect next year you will see even greater conformity to the rule book definition."

MLB also installed $1 million of camera equipment in various ballparks to precisely identify balls and strikes.

Alderson rankled many of the umpires in early July by counting pitches in games. Alderson sent e-mails to certain umpires with high pitch counts, urging them to enlarge their strike zones in order to "find more strikes."

The umpires union quickly filed a grievance, which was dropped when Alderson agreed to abandon the pitch counting.

"I think I can speak for a lot of umpires and say I'm relieved," umpire Tim Tschida said. "I don't know if pitch count is really a very accurate tool for an umpire to gauge his performance."

The failed mass-resignation plan of former union head Richie Phillips in 1999 continued to have an effect two

Milwaukee's Miller Park opened in 2001

New PNC Park was the only bright spot for the Pirates in 2001

seasons later. MLB terminated 22 of those umpires who resigned, and nine were ordered rehired May 11 by arbitrator Alan Symonette, who concluded in his 100-page decision that former NL president Len Coleman "abused his discretion" in deciding to fire the umpires.

Thirteen umpires were left out in the ruling, including well-known personalities such as Richie Garcia and Eric Gregg.

The nine reinstated umpires did not go back onto the field, though. Both sides appealed Symonette's ruling, and the case had yet to be decided by season's end.

Labor Undercurrents

Speaking of labor issues, the uncertainly of whether the 2002 season would start on time simmered beneath the surface throughout 2001. The collective bargaining agreement in effect since 1996 expired at the conclusion of the World Series.

Whether Major League Baseball and the Players Association made any progress on a new contract during the 2001 season was unknown.

Commissioner Selig would not discuss negotiations during the year, and also threatened people on ownership's side with a $1 million fine if they commented publicly about the labor situation. Unon boss Don Fehr also stayed mum on the subject.

Owners did send the union a letter Sept. 4 stating they would seek to make changes in the Basic Agreement. The letter was a formality under the National Labor Relations Act.

There was also bad news on the labor front during the World Series, when Selig admitted many owners were favorable to the idea of folding two franchises. The Twins and Expos looked like the candidates to be contracted, though the union figured to fight that idea tooth and nail.

Baseball has had eight work stoppages since 1972, including a 232-day strike in 1994 and 1995 that caused the first cancellation of the World Series since 1904.

Following the terrorist actions of Sept. 11, neither side seemed to have the stomach for a labor fight under the prevailing national climate. There were many reports the sides would agree to extend the current agreement by either one or two years.

"You would hope we could come to some kind of agreement," said the Braves' Glavine, long an active member of the union. "I just don't think the time is right to have a very public battle over a labor contract. We need to find a way to resolve it and make sure we're playing baseball in 2002."

MAJOR LEAGUE DEBUTS, 2001

AMERICAN LEAGUE

Anaheim Angels

Larry Barnes, 1b	April 11
Jamie Burke, c-3b	May 9
David Eckstein, ss	April 3
Steve Green, rhp	April 7
Mark Lukasiewicz, lhp	May 11
Bart Miadich, rhp	Sept. 2
Scot Shields, rhp	May 26

Baltimore Orioles

Rick Bauer, rhp	Sept. 2
Larry Bigbie, of	June 23
Sean Douglass, rhp	July 18
Kris Foster, rhp	Aug. 3
Jay Gibbons, 1b	April 6
Geronimo Gil, c	Sept. 8
Willie Harris, of-2b	Sept. 2
Jorge Julio, rhp	April 26
Chad Paronto, rhp	April 18
Tim Raines Jr., of	Oct. 1
Brian Roberts, ss	June 14
Josh Towers, rhp	May 2

Boston Red Sox

Casey Fossum, lhp	July 28
Shea Hillenbrand, 3b	April 2
Sun-Woo Kim, rhp	June 15
James Lofton, ss	Sept. 19
Angel Santos, 2b	Sept. 8

Chicago White Sox

Josh Fogg, rhp	Sept. 2
Aaron Rowand, of	June 16
Ken Vining, lhp	May 23
Dan Wright, rhp	July 27

Cleveland Indians

Mike Bacsik, lhp	Aug. 5
Danys Baez, rhp	May 13
Ryan Drese, rhp	July 29
C.C. Sabathia, lhp	April 8
Roy Smith, rhp	May 26

Detroit Tigers

Jermaine Clark, 2b	April 3
Nate Cornejo, rhp	Aug. 8
Brandon Inge, c	April 3
Matt Miller, lhp	May 8
Jarrod Patterson, 3b	June 16
Adam Pettyjohn, lhp	July 16
Luis Pineda, rhp	Aug. 4
Mike Rivera, c	Sept. 18
Pedro Santana, 2b	July 16
Victor Santos, rhp	April 9
Chris Wakeland, of	Sept. 4

Kansas City Royals

Jeff Austin, rhp	June 26
Brandon Berger, of	Sept. 9
Angel Berroa, ss	Sept. 18
Endy Chavez, of	May 29
Tony Cogan, lhp	April 2
Chris George, lhp	July 26
Ken Harvey, 1b	Sept. 18
Mike MacDougal, rhp	Sept. 22
Brad Voyles, rhp	Sept. 8

Minnesota Twins

Grant Balfour, rhp	July 22
Michael Cuddyer, 3b	Sept. 23
Adam Johnson, rhp	July 16
Bobby Kielty, of	April 10
Kyle Lohse, rhp	June 22
Dustan Mohr, of	Aug. 29
Juan Rincon, rhp	June 7
Brad Thomas, lhp	May 26

New York Yankees

Erick Almonte, ss	Sept. 4
Adrian Hernandez, rhp	April 21
Brett Jodie, rhp	July 20
Nick Johnson, 1b	Aug. 21
Brandon Knight, rhp	June 5
Donzell McDonald, of	April 19

Christian Parker, rhp	April 6
Juan Rivera, of	Sept. 4
Scott Seabol, 3b	April 8

Oakland Athletics

Andy Abad, of	Sept. 10
Tom Wilson, c	May 19

Seattle Mariners

Brian Fuentes, lhp	June 2
Scott Podsednik, of	July 6
Ichiro Suzuki, of	April 2
Ramon Vazquez, ss	Sept. 7

Tampa Bay Devil Rays

Brent Abernathy, 2b	June 25
Jesus Colome, rhp	June 21
Paul Hoover, 3b	Sept. 8
Joe Kennedy, lhp	June 6
Travis Phelps, rhp	April 19
Jared Sandberg, 3b	Aug. 7
Bobby Seay, lhp	Aug. 14
Jason Standridge, rhp	July 29
Victor Zambrano, rhp	June 21

Texas Rangers

Joaquin Benoit, rhp	Aug. 8
Cliff Brumbaugh, of	May 30
R.A. Dickey, rhp	April 22
Justin Duchscherer, rhp	July 25
Chris Magruder, of	Sept. 4
Craig Monroe, of	July 28
Juan Moreno, lhp	May 17
Carlos Pena, 1b	Sept. 5

Toronto Blue Jays

Brian Bowles, rhp	June 27
Bob File, rhp	April 14
Ryan Freel, 2b-of	April 4
Cesar Izturis, ss	June 23
Felipe Lopez, ss	Aug. 3
Luis Lopez, 3b	April 29
Brandon Lyon, rhp	Aug. 4

NATIONAL LEAGUE

Arizona Diamondbacks

Nick Bierbrodt, lhp	June 7
Troy Brohawn, lhp	April 14
Alex Cintron, ss	July 24
Jack Cust, of-1b	Sept. 26
Ken Huckaby, c	Oct. 6
Eric Knott, lhp	Sept. 1
Mike Koplove, rhp	Sept. 6
Lyle Overbay, 1b	Sept. 19
Bret Prinz, rhp	April 22
Junior Spivey, 2b	June 2

Atlanta Braves

Cory Aldridge, of	Sept. 5
Wilson Betemit, ss	Sept. 18
Marcus Giles, 2b	April 17
Damian Moss, lhp	April 26
Joe Nelson, rhp	June 13
Scott Sobkowiak, rhp	Oct. 7
Tim Spooneybarger, rhp	Sept. 5
Steve Torrealba, c	Oct. 6

Chicago Cubs

Scott Chiasson, rhp	Sept. 19
Juan Cruz, rhp	Aug. 21
Courtney Duncan, rhp	April 2
Jason Smith, ss	June 17
Carlos Zambrano, rhp	Aug. 20

Cincinnati Reds

Jose Acevedo, of	June 19
Justin Atchley, lhp	April 7
Lance Davis, lhp	June 16
Adam Dunn, of	July 20
Jared Fernandez, rhp	Sept. 19
Brandon Larson, 3b	May 4
Scott MacRae, rhp	July 24
Corky Miller, c	Sept. 4
Chris Piersoll, rhp	Aug. 31
Brian Reith, rhp	May 16

Chris Reitsma, rhp	April 4

Colorado Rockies

Brent Butler, 2b	July 4
Shawn Chacon, rhp	April 29
Tim Christman, rhp	April 21
Mario Encarnacion, of	Aug. 26
Jason Jennings, rhp	Aug. 23
Juan Uribe, ss	April 8

Florida Marlins

Benito Baez, lhp	Aug. 25
Josh Beckett, rhp	Sept. 4
Gary Knotts, rhp	July 28
Blaine Neal, rhp	Sept. 3
Kevin Olsen, rhp	Sept. 7

Houston Astros

Adam Everett, ss	Aug. 30
Carlos Hernandez, lhp	Aug. 18
Roy Oswalt, rhp	May 6
Tim Redding, rhp	June 24
Wilfredo Rodriguez, lhp	Sept. 21
Ricky Stone, rhp	Sept. 21

Los Angeles Dodgers

Jose Nunez, lhp	April 3

Milwaukee Brewers

Mike Coolbaugh, ss	July 16
Gus Gandarillas, rhp	July 17
Nick Neugebauer, rhp	Aug. 19
Alex Sanchez, of	June 15
Ben Sheets, rhp	April 5

Montreal Expos

Henry Mateo, 2b	July 28
Troy Mattes, rhp	June 19
Scott Stewart, lhp	April 5
Brad Wilkerson, of	July 12

New York Mets

Mark Corey, rhp	Oct. 2
Alex Escobar, of	May 8
Dicky Gonzalez, rhp	May 1
Jason Phillips, c	Sept. 19
Tsuyoshi Shinjo, of	April 3

Philadelphia Phillies

Brandon Duckworth, rhp	Aug. 7
Johnny Estrada, c	May 15
Jason Michaels, of	April 6
Eddie Oropesa, lhp	April 2
Nick Punto, 2b-ss	Sept. 9
Eric Valent, of	June 8

Pittsburgh Pirates

Andy Barkett, 1b	May 28
Joe Beimel, lhp	April 8
Humberto Cota, c	Sept. 9
Luis Figueroa, ss	June 27
Rob Mackowiak, 2b	May 19
David Williams, lhp	June 6
Craig Wilson, c-1b	April 22
Jack Wilson, ss	April 3

St. Louis Cardinals

Stubby Clapp, 2b	June 18
Chad Hutchinson, rhp	April 4
Jason Karnuth, rhp	April 20
Bill Ortega, of	Sept. 7
Albert Pujols, 3b-of	April 2
Bud Smith, lhp	June 10

San Diego Padres

Cesar Crespo, of	May 29
Jeremy Fikac, rhp	Aug. 16
Junior Herndon, rhp	Aug. 2
Brian Lawrence, rhp	April 15
Donaldo Mendez, ss	April 5
Jason Middlebrook, rhp	Sept. 17
Jimmy Osting, lhp	May 2
Wascar Serrano, rhp	May 12

San Francisco Giants

Kurt Ainsworth, rhp	Sept. 5
Ryan Jensen, rhp	May 19
Jalal Leach, of	Sept. 5
Cody Ransom, ss	Sept. 5
Yorvit Torrealba, c	Sept. 5

WORLD SERIES

BY JOHN PERROTTO

It was the only way the 2001 World Series could possibly end.

The Diamondbacks entered the bottom of the ninth inning of the decisive Game Seven trailing the three-time defending champion Yankees 2-1 at Bank One Ballpark in Phoenix.

Furthermore, the Diamondbacks were facing Yankees closer Mariano Rivera, who hadn't blown a postseason save since 1996 and was a big reason why New York had won four World Series in five years. The same Rivera who walked to the mound having converted 23 straight postseason saves and owning a 0.70 postseason ERA, the best mark in baseball history.

Yet in keeping with the tenor of a classic World Series, the Diamondbacks found a way to overcome impossible odds. They scored two runs off Rivera in the ninth, the game-winner coming on Luis Gonzalez' broken-bat bloop single to center with one out.

It was a fitting end to a World Series in which the improbable became the probable time and again.

How improbable was the series? In both Game Four and Game Five at Yankee Stadium, the Yankees trailed by two runs with two outs in the bottom of the ninth inning. Each time, the Yankees hit a game-tying home run—Tino Martinez coming through in Game Four and Scott Brosius following suit in Game Five, both off Arizona closer Byung-Hyun Kim—then went on to win in extra innings to take a 3-2 lead in the series.

How improbable was the series? After two seemingly devastating losses, Arizona bounced back in Game Six and set a World Series record by pounding out 22 hits and winning 15-2. Randy Johnson pitched seven innings to get the win.

How improbable was the series? In an era when no one pitches effectively on three days' rest, Curt Schilling did it twice, in Game Four and Game Seven. He gave up three runs in 14⅓ innings in those two starts, though he didn't receive a decision in either.

How improbable was the series? After pitching so well in the Game Six rout, Johnson came out of the bullpen one night later in Game Seven to get the final out of the eighth inning and retire the side in order in the ninth. He wound up getting the win as Arizona staged its rally to win a title in just its fourth year of existence, the fastest an expansion team has ever walked off with the World Series trophy.

"This was a World Series that had it all," Arizona

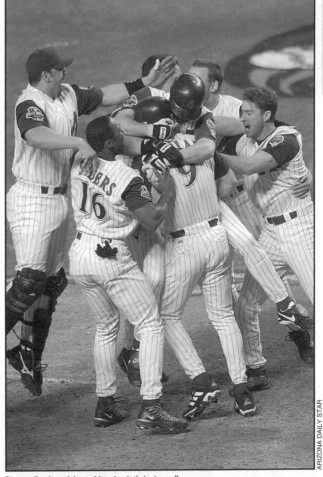

Diamondbacks celebrate historic ninth-inning rally

ARIZONA DAILY STAR

first baseman Mark Grace said. "So I don't think it surprised anybody that the seventh game of this World Series ended crazy. It didn't end normal because it couldn't end normal. I don't think anybody expected it to."

Classic Game Seven Matchup

Game Seven was not only unconventional but also a classic as Schilling and the Yankees' Roger Clemens, both 20-game winners in the regular season, took shutouts into the sixth inning.

Arizona broke through for a run in the sixth on Danny Bautista's RBI double. Schilling couldn't hold the 1-0 lead, though, as Martinez' run-scoring single in the seventh tied it and rookie second baseman Alfonso Soriano's leadoff home run in the eighth put the Yankees ahead 2-1.

Rivera relieved Clemens to start the eighth and struck

WORLD SERIES YEAR-BY-YEAR

Year	Winner	Manager	Loser	Manager	Result	MVP
1903	Boston (AL)	Jimmy Collins	Pittsburgh (NL)	Fred Clarke	5-3	None Selected
1904	NO SERIES					
1905	New York (NL)	John McGraw	Philadelphia (AL)	Connie Mack	4-1	None Selected
1906	Chicago (AL)	Fielder Jones	Chicago (NL)	Frank Chance	4-2	None Selected
1907	Chicago (NL)	Frank Chance	Detroit (AL)	Hugh Jennings	4-0	None Selected
1908	Chicago (NL)	Frank Chance	Detroit (AL)	Hugh Jennings	4-1	None Selected
1909	Pittsburgh (NL)	Fred Clarke	Detroit (AL)	Hugh Jennings	4-3	None Selected
1910	Philadelphia (AL)	Connie Mack	Chicago (NL)	Frank Chance	4-1	None Selected
1911	Philadelphia (AL)	Connie Mack	New York (NL)	John McGraw	4-2	None Selected
1912	Boston (AL)	Jake Stahl	New York (NL)	John McGraw	4-3-1	None Selected
1913	Philadelphia (AL)	Connie Mack	New York (NL)	John McGraw	4-1	None Selected
1914	Boston (NL)	George Stallings	Philadelphia (AL)	Connie Mack	4-0	None Selected
1915	Boston (AL)	Bill Carrigan	Philadelphia (NL)	Pat Moran	4-1	None Selected
1916	Boston (AL)	Bill Carrigan	Brooklyn (NL)	Wilbert Robinson	4-1	None Selected
1917	Chicago (AL)	Pants Rowland	New York (NL)	John McGraw	4-2	None Selected
1918	Boston (AL)	Ed Barrow	Chicago (NL)	Fred Mitchell	4-2	None Selected
1919	Cincinnati (NL)	Pat Moran	Chicago (AL)	Kid Gleason	5-3	None Selected
1920	Cleveland (AL)	Tris Speaker	Brooklyn (NL)	Wilbert Robinson	5-2	None Selected
1921	New York (NL)	John McGraw	New York (AL)	Miller Huggins	5-3	None Selected
1922	New York (NL)	John McGraw	New York (AL)	Miller Huggins	4-0	None Selected
1923	New York (AL)	Miller Huggins	New York (NL)	John McGraw	4-2	None Selected
1924	Washington (AL)	Bucky Harris	New York (NL)	John McGraw	4-3	None Selected
1925	Pittsburgh (NL)	Bill McKechnie	Washington (AL)	Bucky Harris	4-3	None Selected
1926	St. Louis (NL)	Rogers Hornsby	New York (AL)	Miller Huggins	4-3	None Selected
1927	New York (AL)	Miller Huggins	Pittsburgh (NL)	Donie Bush	4-0	None Selected
1928	New York (AL)	Miller Huggins	St. Louis (NL)	Bill McKechnie	4-0	None Selected
1929	Philadelphia (AL)	Connie Mack	Chicago (NL)	Joe McCarthy	4-1	None Selected
1930	Philadelphia (AL)	Connie Mack	St. Louis (NL)	Gabby Street	4-2	None Selected
1931	St. Louis (NL)	Gabby Street	Philadelphia (AL)	Connie Mack	4-3	None Selected
1932	New York (AL)	Joe McCarthy	Chicago (NL)	Charlie Grimm	4-0	None Selected
1933	New York (NL)	Bill Terry	Washington (AL)	Joe Cronin	4-1	None Selected
1934	St. Louis (NL)	Frankie Frisch	Detroit (AL)	Mickey Cochrane	4-3	None Selected
1935	Detroit (AL)	Mickey Cochrane	Chicago (NL)	Charlie Grimm	4-2	None Selected
1936	New York (AL)	Joe McCarthy	New York (NL)	Bill Terry	4-2	None Selected
1937	New York (AL)	Joe McCarthy	New York (NL)	Bill Terry	4-1	None Selected
1938	New York (AL)	Joe McCarthy	Chicago (NL)	Gabby Hartnett	4-0	None Selected
1939	New York (AL)	Joe McCarthy	Cincinnati (NL)	Bill McKechnie	4-0	None Selected
1940	Cincinnati (NL)	Bill McKechnie	Detroit (AL)	Del Baker	4-3	None Selected
1941	New York (AL)	Joe McCarthy	Brooklyn (NL)	Leo Durocher	4-1	None Selected
1942	St. Louis (NL)	Billy Southworth	New York (AL)	Joe McCarthy	4-1	None Selected
1943	New York (AL)	Joe McCarthy	St. Louis (NL)	Billy Southworth	4-1	None Selected
1944	St. Louis (NL)	Billy Southworth	St. Louis (AL)	Luke Sewell	4-2	None Selected
1945	Detroit (AL)	Steve O'Neill	Chicago (NL)	Charlie Grimm	4-3	None Selected
1946	St. Louis (NL)	Eddie Dyer	Boston (AL)	Joe Cronin	4-3	None Selected
1947	New York (AL)	Bucky Harris	Brooklyn (NL)	Burt Shotton	4-3	None Selected
1948	Cleveland (AL)	Lou Boudreau	Boston (NL)	Billy Southworth	4-2	None Selected
1949	New York (AL)	Casey Stengel	Brooklyn (NL)	Burt Shotton	4-1	None Selected
1950	New York (AL)	Casey Stengel	Philadelphia (NL)	Eddie Sawyer	4-0	None Selected
1951	New York (AL)	Casey Stengel	New York (NL)	Leo Durocher	4-2	None Selected
1952	New York (AL)	Casey Stengel	Brooklyn (NL)	Chuck Dressen	4-3	None Selected
1953	New York (AL)	Casey Stengel	Brooklyn (NL)	Chuck Dressen	4-2	None Selected
1954	New York (NL)	Leo Durocher	Cleveland (AL)	Al Lopez	4-0	None Selected
1955	Brooklyn (NL)	Walter Alston	New York (AL)	Casey Stengel	4-3	Johnny Podres, p, Brooklyn
1956	New York (AL)	Casey Stengel	Brooklyn (NL)	Walter Alston	4-3	Don Larsen, p, New York
1957	Milwaukee (NL)	Fred Haney	New York (AL)	Casey Stengel	4-3	Lew Burdette, p, Milwaukee
1958	New York (AL)	Casey Stengel	Milwaukee (NL)	Fred Haney	4-3	Bob Turley, p, New York
1959	Los Angeles (NL)	Walter Alston	Chicago (AL)	Al Lopez	4-2	Larry Sherry, p, Los Angeles
1960	Pittsburgh (NL)	Danny Murtaugh	New York (AL)	Casey Stengel	4-3	Bobby Richardson, 2b, New York
1961	New York (AL)	Ralph Houk	Cincinnati (NL)	Fred Hutchinson	4-1	Whitey Ford, p, New York
1962	New York (AL)	Ralph Houk	San Francisco (NL)	Alvin Dark	4-3	Ralph Terry, p, New York
1963	Los Angeles (NL)	Walter Alston	New York (AL)	Ralph Houk	4-0	Sandy Koufax, p, Los Angeles
1964	St. Louis (NL)	Johnny Keane	New York (AL)	Yogi Berra	4-3	Bob Gibson, p, St. Louis
1965	Los Angeles (NL)	Walter Alston	Minnesota (AL)	Sam Mele	4-3	Sandy Koufax, p, Los Angeles
1966	Baltimore (AL)	Hank Bauer	Los Angeles (NL)	Walter Alston	4-0	Frank Robinson, of, Baltimore
1967	St. Louis (NL)	Red Schoendienst	Boston (AL)	Dick Williams	4-3	Bob Gibson, p, St. Louis
1968	Detroit (AL)	Mayo Smith	St. Louis (NL)	Red Schoendienst	4-3	Mickey Lolich, p, Detroit
1969	New York (NL)	Gil Hodges	Baltimore (AL)	Earl Weaver	4-1	Donn Clendenon, 1b, New York
1970	Baltimore (AL)	Earl Weaver	Cincinnati (NL)	Sparky Anderson	4-1	Brooks Robinson, 3b, Baltimore
1971	Pittsburgh (NL)	Danny Murtaugh	Baltimore (AL)	Earl Weaver	4-3	Roberto Clemente, of, Pittsburgh
1972	Oakland (AL)	Dick Williams	Cincinnati (NL)	Sparky Anderson	4-3	Gene Tenace, c, Oakland
1973	Oakland (AL)	Dick Williams	New York (NL)	Yogi Berra	4-3	Reggie Jackson, of, Oakland
1974	Oakland (AL)	Alvin Dark	Los Angeles (NL)	Walter Alston	4-1	Rollie Fingers, p, Oakland
1975	Cincinnati (NL)	Sparky Anderson	Boston (AL)	Darrell Johnson	4-3	Pete Rose, 3b, Cincinnati
1976	Cincinnati (NL)	Sparky Anderson	New York (AL)	Billy Martin	4-0	Johnny Bench, c, Cincinnati
1977	New York (AL)	Billy Martin	Los Angeles (NL)	Tom Lasorda	4-2	Reggie Jackson, of, New York
1978	New York (AL)	Bob Lemon	Los Angeles (NL)	Tom Lasorda	4-2	Bucky Dent, ss, New York
1979	Pittsburgh (NL)	Chuck Tanner	Baltimore (AL)	Earl Weaver	4-3	Willie Stargell, 1b, Pittsburgh
1980	Philadelphia (NL)	Dallas Green	Kansas City (AL)	Jim Frey	4-2	Mike Schmidt, 3b, Philadelphia
1981	Los Angeles (NL)	Tom Lasorda	New York (AL)	Bob Lemon	4-2	Cey/Guerrero/Yeager, L.A.
1982	St. Louis (NL)	Whitey Herzog	Milwaukee (AL)	Harvey Kuenn	4-3	Darrell Porter, c, St. Louis
1983	Baltimore (AL)	Joe Altobelli	Philadelphia (NL)	Paul Owens	4-1	Rick Dempsey, c, Baltimore
1984	Detroit (AL)	Sparky Anderson	San Diego (NL)	Dick Williams	4-1	Alan Trammell, ss, Detroit
1985	Kansas City (AL)	Dick Howser	St. Louis (NL)	Whitey Herzog	4-3	Bret Saberhagen, p, Kansas City
1986	New York (NL)	Dave Johnson	Boston (AL)	John McNamara	4-3	Ray Knight, 3b, New York
1987	Minnesota (AL)	Tom Kelly	St. Louis (NL)	Whitey Herzog	4-3	Frank Viola, p, Minnesota
1988	Los Angeles (NL)	Tom Lasorda	Oakland (AL)	Tony La Russa	4-1	Orel Hershiser, p, Los Angeles
1989	Oakland (AL)	Tony La Russa	San Francisco (NL)	Roger Craig	4-0	Dave Stewart, p, Oakland
1990	Cincinnati (NL)	Lou Piniella	Oakland (AL)	Tony La Russa	4-0	Jose Rijo, p, Cincinnati
1991	Minnesota (AL)	Tom Kelly	Atlanta (NL)	Bobby Cox	4-3	Jack Morris, p, Minnesota
1992	Toronto (AL)	Cito Gaston	Atlanta (NL)	Bobby Cox	4-2	Pat Borders, c, Toronto
1993	Toronto (AL)	Cito Gaston	Philadelphia (NL)	Jim Fregosi	4-2	Paul Molitor, dh, Toronto
1994	NO SERIES					
1995	Atlanta (NL)	Bobby Cox	Cleveland (AL)	Mike Hargrove	4-2	Tom Glavine, p, Atlanta
1996	New York (AL)	Joe Torre	Atlanta (NL)	Bobby Cox	4-2	John Wetteland, p, New York
1997	Florida (NL)	Jim Leyland	Cleveland (AL)	Mike Hargrove	4-3	Livan Hernandez, p, Florida
1998	New York (AL)	Joe Torre	San Diego (NL)	Bruce Bochy	4-0	Scott Brosius, 3b, New York
1999	New York (AL)	Joe Torre	Atlanta (NL)	Bobby Cox	4-0	Mariano Rivera, p, New York
2000	New York (AL)	Joe Torre	New York (NL)	Bobby Valentine	4-1	Derek Jeter, ss, New York
2001	Arizona (NL)	Bob Brenly	New York (AL)	Joe Torre	4-3	Johnson, p/Schilling, p, Arizona

out the side. Rivera, who had converted 19 consecutive two-inning postseason save opportunities since 1996, seemed a lock to deliver the Yankees their fourth consecutive World Series title.

Diamondbacks first-year manager Bob Brenly said before the game that his fantasy of winning a World Series included getting to Rivera in the ninth inning. That is exactly what unfolded.

Grace led off the inning with a line single up the middle. David Dellucci pinch-ran, and Damian Miller followed by dropping down a bunt. Rivera pounced on the bunt but threw wildly to second base to put runners on first and second. Veteran Jay Bell pinch-hit for Johnson and also bunted. Rivera redeemed himself

Diamondbacks pitchers Randy Johnson and Curt Schilling
Won all four games for the Diamondbacks and World Series co-MVP honors

by fielding the ball and throwing to third base to get Dellucci.

Rivera couldn't work his way out of the jam, though. Speedy shortstop Tony Womack followed by a ripping a double into the right-field corner. Midre Cummings, pinch-running for Miller, raced home with the tying run and Bell advanced to third.

The rattled Rivera then hit Craig Counsell with a pitch to load the bases, and Gonzalez followed with his game-winning hit, a flare into center that scored Bell and sent the crowd of 49,589 at Bank One Ballpark into a frenzy.

Gonzalez hit 57 home runs during the regular season but struggled with a wrist injury throughout the postseason. In fact, he was hurting enough that he cut down his power stroke in favor of just making contact in his final at-bat.

"To be honest with you, that's the first time I choked up all year," Gonzalez said. "I was just looking in on everything and got jammed. I knew the infield was playing in and I didn't have to try to hit it hard, just loop something out there and get it in play.

"The series could not have finished in a more dramatic fashion. Womack coming up with a big hit, us being down by one run in the ninth inning . . . It could not have been scripted better for our ballclub. The way we have battled, fighting tooth and nail all year, up 2-0 in this series, going back down 3-2, then coming back. It was just a storybook ending."

Turning The Tables

That Arizona did it against the Yankees, the kings of late-inning comebacks during their run of titles, and Rivera, the greatest playoff closer in history, made it even sweeter.

It also made a bitter pill to swallow for the Yankees. After Gonzalez' hit, the Yankees slowly filed off the field. There were looks of disbelief all around as the tables had turned, an upstart franchise rallying against one that has won 26 World Series championships.

"We're obviously disappointed in the outcome, but our players should be very proud of what went on here," Yankees manager Joe Torre said. "I congratulate the Diamondbacks organization. They played hard and they certainly earned it, doing it off our best guy in Rivera.

"We realize how many times we snatched it away from people when they were close, so you really have to take

both sides of this thing, but I certainly am proud of the way my ballclub responded to the pressure. We were not hitting, but our guys seemed to get in a situation that put us with a lead, and we put Mo in the game and that's all we really wanted."

Rivera, though, couldn't save the day for a team that was on the cusp of winning the series despite being outscored 37-14 in the seven games.

"There's nobody in the history of baseball I'd rather have out there," Yankees reliever Mike Stanton said.

"I feel bad about what happened and I apologize to all my teammates," Rivera said. "I'm not perfect, though. I lost the game and that's baseball."

Schilling and Johnson were nearly perfect in pitching Arizona to the title. They wound up sharing the series MVP award. Schilling won Game One and kept his team in Game Four and Game Seven despite pitching on short rest. In all, he had a 2.21 ERA in 20⅓ innings.

"This is one of those things that's going to take a whole lot of time to absorb," Schilling said. "Euphoric would be the beginning of my description."

Johnson, another 20-game winner in the regular season, won his starts in Game Two and Game Six, then came back to get the victory in relief in Game Seven. He became the first pitcher to win three games in a World Series since Detroit's Mickey Lolich in 1968, and the first starter to win consecutive games since St. Louis' Harry Brecheen won Game Six as a starter and Game Seven in relief in 1946.

"Me and Curt fed off each other all year long," said Johnson, who had a 1.04 ERA in 17⅓ World Series innings. "And you know, I think we made ourselves better."

Two-Man Team

Combining the regular season and postseason, Schilling and Johnson went 52-13, 2.52 with 768 strikeouts in 596 innings. In the postseason, they were 9-1, 1.30.

"I don't think there's anybody that can rearrange a lineup as well as those two guys can," Torre said. "It really affects your thinking on the other side. Normally, I will just write our lineup down and don't care who is pitching against us. But these two guys make a difference."

Schilling and Johnson set the tone right away as the series started with two games in Phoenix.

LARRY GOREN

Luis Gonzalez: His base hit scored winning run for Diamondbacks

After throwing three straight complete games against St. Louis and Atlanta in the National League playoffs, Schilling worked seven strong innings as Arizona rolled to a 9-1 win in Game One. He allowed one run on three hits.

After New York took a 1-0 lead in the first, Arizona beat up on Yankees starter Mike Mussina, scoring five runs in three innings. Craig Counsell got Arizona started with a solo homer in the first inning, and Gonzalez' two-run shot in the third snapped the 1-1 tie and put the Diamondbacks ahead for good.

"Just getting a win in Game One was huge," said Brenly, who left the broadcast booth to become the first rookie manager to win a World Series since the Yankees' Ralph Houk in 1961.

Johnson gave the Diamondbacks a 2-0 lead by pitching a three-hit shutout and striking out 11 in Game Two. Bautista's RBI single in the second was all Johnson needed, though Matt Williams' three-run homer off loser Andy Pettitte in the seventh didn't hurt.

"I got to enjoy Game One, watching Curt pitch," Johnson said. "It gave me incentive to try to match him."

The series shifted to New York, and the trip was a somber one for the Diamondbacks. New York was still recovering after the Sept. 11 terrorist attacks leveled the twin towers of the World Trade Center and left more than 5,000 people dead. On the off day before Game Three, 20 of Arizona's players visited Ground Zero.

LARRY GOREN

Mark Grace: Led off ninth with single

"A lot of us weren't prepared to see what we did," Gonzalez said. "We are in Arizona and we see it on TV. We see all of the different stuff going on with the rescue workers and stuff. But to actually go out there and walk on the site, it's mind-boggling."

The city had used the Yankees' upset victories over Oakland and Seattle in the American League playoffs as a rallying point. In turn, the Yankees fed off the fans' energy once the series got to Yankee Stadium.

New York got back into the series by squeaking out a 2-1 victory in Game Three. Brosius' RBI single in the sixth off 42-year-old reliever Mike Morgan, pitching in his first World Series, snapped a 1-1 tie and gave the Yankees the win.

Clemens allowed only one run on three hits in seven innings for the win, while Jorge Posada homered for New York. Brian Anderson took the loss.

"I knew it was a game we had to have," Clemens said. "It was exciting to be part of everything. It was something I'll always have with me."

The Yankees then won two of the more dramatic games in World Series history, posting extra-inning wins in Game Four and Game Five to take a 3-2 series lead.

Arizona had a 3-1 lead with two outs in the ninth when Martinez clouted a two-run homer to dead center off Kim to force extra innings. Derek Jeter then homered down the right-field line off Kim to lead off the 10th and give New York the 4-3 victory.

Jeter became baseball's first Mr. November with the home run. The season was pushed back a week following the Sept. 11 attacks and Game Four stretched until 12:04 a.m., meaning Jeter's homer was hit Nov 1. It was the first major league game ever played in November.

Rivera got the win in relief, while Shane Spencer homered for the Yankees and Grace went deep for Arizona.

"We always feel as though we have a chance to win a game," Jeter said. "When you get to the postseason, you can throw everything out that you've done in the regular season."

The Yankees faced a near-identical situation in Game Five, down 2-0 with two outs in the bottom of the ninth. Incredibly, they got the same result as Brosius belted a two-run homer off Kim over the left-field fence to knot the score. The Yankees won it 3-2 in the 12th on Soriano's RBI single against loser Albie Lopez.

Sterling Hitchcock won in relief. Steve Finley, who had three hits, and Rod Barajas both homered for Arizona.

While seemingly everyone in the crowd of 56,018 was stunned by Brosius' heroics, Torre took it all in stride. "I can't be surprised," Torre said. "It just happened the day before."

Home-Field Advantage

The Yankees seemed to have all the momentum as the series shifted back to Phoenix. But the Diamondbacks turned the tide and the Yankees never got the elusive fourth win.

Arizona ripped Pettitte for six runs in just two-plus innings in posting the 15-2 win in Game Six. The Diamondbacks led 15-0 by the fourth inning and everyone got into the act as Reggie Sanders had four hits, Bautista had three hits and five RBIs and Womack and Williams had three hits each.

Johnson cruised to the win, giving up two runs on six hits in seven innings and conserving enough energy to win again the next night.

"These games, especially in the postseason, are an aberration, a freak thing," Brenly said. "As heartbreaking as those games were, all three losses in New York, they had no bearing on the last two games. You can stink up the joint one night and come back and win the next."

And that's exactly what Arizona did at the end, as it came away with the title in a most memorable World Series.

"I would have to say this has to be one of the very classic World Series," Diamondbacks owner Jerry Colangelo said. "The ebbs and the flows and the great games and plays. This World Series will be remembered for a long, long time."

WORLD SERIES
BOX SCORES

GAME ONE: October 27
Arizona 9, New York 1

New York	ab	r	h	bi	bb	so	Arizona	ab	r	h	bi	bb	so
Knoblauch, lf	4	0	0	0	0	0	Womack, ss	4	1	0	0	0	1
Stanton, p	0	0	0	0	0	0	Counsell, 2b	4	1	1	1	0	2
Jeter, ss	3	1	0	0	0	0	Gonzalez, lf	5	2	2	2	0	2
Justice, rf-lf	3	0	0	0	0	3	Sanders, rf	3	2	2	0	1	0
Spencer, ph	1	0	0	0	0	0	Finley, cf	4	2	1	1	0	1
B. Williams, cf	4	0	1	1	0	2	M. Williams, 3b	3	1	1	1	0	1
Martinez, 1b	3	0	0	0	1	0	Grace, 1b	3	0	1	2	1	0
Posada, c	3	0	1	0	1	1	Miller, c	4	0	2	1	0	1
Soriano, 2b	3	0	0	0	0	1	Schilling, p	3	0	0	0	0	2
Brosius, 3b	3	0	1	0	0	1	Bell, ph	1	0	0	0	0	1
Mussina, p	1	0	0	0	0	1	Morgan, p	0	0	0	0	0	0
Choate, p	0	0	0	0	0	0	Swindell, p	0	0	0	0	0	0
Wilson, p	0	0	0	0	0	0							
Hitchcock, p	0	0	0	0	0	0							
O'Neill, ph-rf	1	0	0	0	0	0							
Totals	30	1	3	1	2	9	Totals	34	9	10	8	2	11
New York							100	000	000—1				
Arizona							104	400	00x—9				

E—Justice (1), Brosius (1). LOB—New York 5, Arizona 6. 2B—B. Williams (1), Brosius (1), Miller (1), Gonzalez (1), Grace (1), Gonzalez (1). SH—Counsell. SF—M. Williams.

New York	ip	h	r	er	bb	so	Arizona	ip	h	r	er	bb	so
Mussina L	3	6	5	3	1	4	Schilling W	7	3	1	1	1	8
Choate	1	3	4	1	1	4	Morgan	1	0	0	0	0	0
Hitchcock	3	1	0	0	0	6	Swindell	1	0	0	0	1	1
Stanton	1	0	0	0	0	0							

IBB—Grace (by Mussina), Sanders (by Choate). HBP—Jeter (by Schilling), Womack (by Mussina).

Umpires: HP—Rippley; 1B—Hirschbeck; 2B—Scott; 3B—Rapuano; LF—Joyce; RF—DeMuth.

T—2:44. A—49,646.

GAME TWO: October 28
Arizona 4, New York 0

New York	ab	r	h	bi	bb	so	Arizona	ab	r	h	bi	bb	so
Knoblauch, lf	4	0	0	0	0	1	Womack, ss	4	0	0	0	0	1
Velarde, 1b	3	0	0	1	1	1	Counsell, 2b	4	0	0	0	0	2
Jeter, ss	4	0	0	0	0	1	Gonzalez, lf	2	0	0	0	2	0
B. Williams, cf	3	0	0	0	0	1	Sanders, rf	3	2	1	0	0	0
Posada, c	3	0	1	0	0	1	Bautista, lf	3	1	2	1	0	0
Spencer, rf	3	0	1	0	0	1	Finley, cf	0	0	0	0	0	0
Soriano, 2b	3	0	1	0	0	2	M. Williams, 3b	3	1	2	3	0	0
Brosius, 3b	3	0	0	0	0	2	Grace, 1b	3	0	0	0	1	0
Pettitte, p	2	0	0	0	0	0	Miller, c	3	0	0	0	0	1
Sojo, ph	1	0	0	0	0	0	Johnson, p	3	0	0	0	0	1
Stanton, p	0	0	0	0	0	0							
Totals	29	0	3	0	1	11	Totals	28	4	5	4	0	8
New York							000	000	000—0				
Arizona							010	000	30x—4				

DP—New York 1, Arizona 1. LOB—New York 3, Arizona 1. 2B—Bautista (1). HR—M. Williams (1).

New York	ip	h	r	er	bb	so	Arizona	ip	h	r	er	bb	so
Pettitte L	7	5	4	4	0	8	Johnson W	9	3	0	0	1	11
Stanton	1	0	0	0	0	0							

HBP—Gonzalez (by Pettitte).

Umpires: HP—Hirschbeck; 1B—Scott; 2B—Rapuano; 3B—Joyce; LF—DeMuth; RF—Rippley.

T—2:35. A—49,646.

GAME THREE: October 30
New York 2, Arizona 1

Arizona	ab	r	h	bi	bb	so	New York	ab	r	h	bi	bb	so
Counsell, 2b	4	0	0	0	0	1	Knoblauch, dh	4	0	0	0	0	0
Finley, cf	2	1	0	0	2	1	Jeter, ss	4	0	1	0	0	1
Gonzalez, lf	4	0	1	0	0	3	O'Neill, rf	4	0	2	0	0	0
Sanders, rf	3	0	0	0	0	2	Bellinger, pr-lf	0	0	0	0	0	0
Durazo, dh	3	0	2	0	1	1	B. Williams, cf	3	1	1	0	1	0
M. Williams, 3b	3	0	0	1	0	1	Martinez, 1b	4	0	0	0	0	0
Grace, 1b	3	0	0	0	0	0	Posada, c	3	1	1	1	1	0
Miller, c	3	0	0	0	0	2	Spencer, lf	1	0	0	0	1	0
Womack, ss	3	0	0	0	0	2	Justice, ph-lf-rf	2	0	0	0	0	2
							Brosius, 3b	3	0	1	1	0	0
							Soriano, 2b	3	0	1	0	0	0
Totals	28	1	3	1	3	13	Totals	31	2	7	2	3	3
Arizona							000	100	000—1				
New York							010	001	00x—2				

E—Womack (1), Miller (1), Grace (1), Soriano (1). DP—Arizona 1, New York 1. LOB—Arizona 5, New York 8. HR—Posada (1). SB—O'Neill (1). CS—Finley. SF—M. Williams.

Arizona	ip	h	r	er	bb	so	New York	ip	h	r	er	bb	so
Anderson L	5⅓	5	2	2	3	1	Clemens W	7	3	1	1	3	9
Morgan	1⅓	1	0	0	0	1	Rivera S	2	0	0	0	0	4
Swindell	1⅓	1	0	0	0	1							

WP—Anderson, Morgan, Swindell. HBP—Sanders (by Clemens).

Umpires: HP—Scott; 1B—Rapuano; 2B—Joyce; 3B—DeMuth; LF—Rippley; RF—Hirschbeck.

T—3:26. A—55,820.

GAME FOUR: October 31
New York 4, Arizona 3 (10)

Arizona	ab	r	h	bi	bb	so	New York	ab	r	h	bi	bb	so
Womack, ss	4	0	2	0	1	0	Jeter, ss	5	1	1	1	0	0
Counsell, 2b	2	0	0	0	0	0	O'Neill, rf	4	1	1	0	0	1
Gonzalez, lf	3	1	1	0	1	0	B. Williams, cf	4	0	1	0	0	2
Durazo, dh	3	0	1	1	1	1	Martinez, 1b	3	1	1	2	1	1
Cummings, pr	0	1	0	0	0	0	Posada, c	3	0	0	1	1	1
Bautista, lf	1	0	0	0	0	0	Justice, dh	4	0	1	0	0	3
M. Williams, 3b	4	0	1	0	1	0	Spencer, lf	4	1	1	1	0	2
Finley, cf	4	0	1	0	0	1	Brosius, 3b	4	0	1	0	0	2
Sanders, rf	4	0	0	0	0	1	Soriano, 2b	4	0	0	0	0	2
Grace, 1b	3	1	1	1	1	0							
Miller, c	3	0	0	0	0	2							
Totals	31	3	6	3	4	6	Totals	35	4	7	4	2	14
Arizona							000	100	020	0—3			
New York							001	000	002	1—4			

DP—Arizona 1, New York 3. LOB—Arizona 7, New York 4. 2B—Womack (1), Durazo (1), Brosius (2). HR—Grace (1), Spencer (1), Martinez (1), Jeter (1). SH—Counsell 3.

Arizona	ip	h	r	er	bb	so	New York	ip	h	r	er	bb	so
Schilling	7	3	1	1	1	9	Hernandez	6⅓	4	1	1	4	5
Kim L	2⅔	4	3	3	1	5	Stanton	1	2	2	2	0	0
							Mendoza	1⅔	0	0	0	0	1
							Rivera W	1	0	0	0	0	0

HBP—Gonzalez (by Hernandez), Miller (by Hernandez).

Umpires: HP—Rapuano; 1B—Joyce; 2B—DeMuth; 3B—Rippley; LF—Hirschbeck; RF—Scott.

T—3:31. A—55,863.

GAME FIVE: November 1
New York 3, Arizona 2 (12)

Arizona	ab	r	h	bi	bb	so	New York	ab	r	h	bi	bb	so
Womack, ss	6	0	1	0	0	1	Jeter, ss	5	0	1	0	0	2
Counsell, 2b	6	0	0	0	0	2	O'Neill, rf	3	0	0	2	0	0
Gonzalez, lf	4	0	0	0	0	1	B. Williams, cf	4	0	1	0	1	0
Bautista, lf	1	0	0	0	0	1	Martinez, 1b	5	0	1	0	0	0
Durazo, dh	4	0	1	0	1	1	Posada, c	5	1	1	0	0	2
M. Williams, 3b	4	0	0	0	0	0	Spencer, lf	4	0	1	0	1	1
Finley, cf	4	1	3	1	1	1	Justice, dh	2	0	0	0	1	1
Sanders, rf	5	0	0	0	0	3	Knoblauch, pr-dh	2	1	1	0	0	1
Grace, 1b	3	0	0	0	2	0	Brosius, 3b	4	1	1	2	0	0
Barajas, c	5	1	2	1	0	0	Soriano, 2b	5	0	2	1	0	0
Totals	42	2	8	2	4	10	Totals	39	3	9	3	5	7

Arizona	000 020 000 000—2
New York	000 000 002 001—3

E—Posada (1). DP—Arizona 2, New York 1. LOB—Arizona 9, New York 8. 2B—Posada (1). HR—Finley (1), Barajas (1), Brosius (1). SB—Womack (1). CS—Soriano. SH—M. Williams, Brosius.

Arizona	ip	h	r	er	bb	so	New York	ip	h	r	er	bb	so
Batista	7⅔	5	0	0	5	6	Mussina	8	5	2	2	3	10
Swindell	⅓	0	0	0	0	0	Mendoza	1	1	0	0	0	0
Kim	⅔	2	2	2	0	1	Rivera	2	2	0	0	1	0
Morgan	2⅓	0	0	0	1	0	Hitchcock W	1	0	0	0	0	0
Lopez L	⅓	2	1	1	0	0							

WP—Batista, Mussina. IBB—Grace (by Mussina), Durazo (by Mussina), Finley (by Rivera).

Umpires: HP—Joyce; 1B—DeMuth; 2B—Rippley; 3B—Hirschbeck; LF—Scott; RF—Rapuano.

T—4:15. A—56,018.

GAME SIX: November 3
Arizona 15, New York 2

New York	ab	r	h	bi	bb	so	Arizona	ab	r	h	bi	bb	so
Knoblauch, lf	3	0	0	0	1	0	Womack, ss	6	2	3	2	0	1
Stanton, p	0	0	0	0	0	0	Bautista, cf	4	0	3	5	0	0
Jeter, ss	2	0	0	0	0	1	Finley, cf	1	0	0	1	0	0
Wilson, ss	2	0	0	0	0	0	Gonzalez, lf	4	1	2	2	0	0
B. Williams, cf	2	1	1	0	2	0	Dellucci, pr-lf	2	0	1	0	0	0
Posada, c	2	0	0	0	0	0	Colbrunn, 1b	5	2	2	1	1	1
Greene, c	2	1	1	0	0	0	M. Williams, 3b	5	1	3	1	0	0
Spencer, rf	4	0	1	1	0	2	Sanders, rf	5	2	4	1	0	1
Martinez, 1b	2	0	1	0	0	0	Bell, 2b	5	2	1	1	0	1
Sojo, 1b	2	0	1	1	0	0	Miller, c	4	3	2	1	1	2
Soriano, 2b	4	0	1	0	0	1	Barajas, c	0	0	0	0	0	0
Brosius, 3b	4	0	0	0	0	1	Johnson, p	4	2	1	1	0	1
Pettitte, p	1	0	1	0	0	0	Durazo, ph	1	0	0	0	0	1
Witasick, p	0	0	0	0	0	0	Witt, p	0	0	0	0	0	0
Choate, p	1	0	0	0	0	1	Brohawn, p	0	0	0	0	0	0
Bellinger, ph-lf	2	0	0	0	0	2							
Totals	33	2	7	2	3	9	Totals	46	15	22	15	3	9

New York	000 002 000— 2
Arizona	138 300 00x—15

E—Soriano (2). DP—New York 1, Arizona 1. LOB—New York 10, Arizona 7. 2B—Greene (1), Womack (2), Sanders (1), M. Williams 2 (2), Gonzalez (2), Miller (1).

New York	ip	h	r	er	bb	so	Arizona	ip	h	r	er	bb	so
Pettitte L	2	7	6	6	2	1	Johnson W	7	6	2	2	2	7
Witasick	1⅓	10	9	8	0	4	Witt	1	0	0	0	1	1
Choate	2⅔	4	0	0	0	1	Brohawn	1	1	0	0	0	1
Stanton	2	1	0	0	1	3							

Pettitte pitched to 2 batters in the 3rd.
WP—Witasick. IBB—Miller (by Pettitte).

Umpires: HP—DeMuth; 1B—Rippley; 2B—Hirschbeck; 3B—Scott; LF—Rapuano; RF—Joyce.

T—3:33. A—49,707.

GAME SEVEN: November 4
Arizona 3, New York 2

New York	ab	r	h	bi	bb	so	Arizona	ab	r	h	bi	bb	so
Jeter, ss	4	1	1	0	0	1	Womack, ss	5	0	2	1	0	1
O'Neill, rf	3	0	2	0	0	1	Counsell, 2b	4	0	1	0	0	0
Knoblauch, ph-lf	1	0	0	0	0	0	Gonzalez, lf	5	1	1	0	2	0
B. Williams, cf	4	0	0	0	0	0	M. Williams, 3b	4	0	1	0	0	2
Martinez, 1b	4	0	1	1	0	1	Finley, cf	4	1	2	0	0	1
Posada, c	4	0	0	0	0	2	Bautista, rf	3	0	1	1	1	1
Spencer, lf-rf	3	0	0	0	0	0	Grace, 1b	4	0	3	0	0	0
Soriano, 2b	3	1	1	1	0	1	Dellucci, pr	0	0	0	0	0	0
Brosius, 3b	3	0	0	0	0	2	Miller, c	4	0	0	0	0	3
Clemens, p	2	0	0	0	0	0	Cummings, pr	0	1	0	0	0	0
Stanton, p	0	0	0	0	0	0	Schilling, p	3	0	0	0	0	3
Justice, ph	1	0	1	0	0	0	Batista, p	0	0	0	0	0	0
Rivera, p	0	0	0	0	0	0	Johnson, p	0	0	0	0	0	0
							Bell, ph	1	1	0	0	0	0
Totals	32	2	6	2	0	10	Totals	37	3	11	3	1	13

New York	000 000 110—2
Arizona	000 001 002—3

E—Clemens (1), Soriano (3), Rivera (1). LOB—New York 3, Arizona 11. 2B—O'Neill (1), Bautista (2), Womack (3). HR—Soriano (1). CS—Womack.

New York	ip	h	r	er	bb	so	Arizona	ip	h	r	er	bb	so
Clemens	6⅓	7	1	1	1	10	Schilling	7⅓	6	2	2	0	9
Stanton	⅔	0	0	0	0	0	Batista	⅓	0	0	0	0	0
Rivera L	1⅓	4	2	2	0	3	Johnson W	1⅓	0	0	0	0	1

HBP—Counsell (by Rivera).

Umpires: HP—Rippley; 1B—Hirschbeck; 2B—Scott; 3B—Rapuano; LF—Joyce; RF—DeMuth.

T—3:20. A—49,589.

COMPOSITE BOX

NEW YORK

Player, Pos.	AVG	G	AB	R	H	2B	3B	HR	RBI	BB	SO	SB
Todd Greene, c	.500	1	2	1	1	1	0	0	0	0	0	0
Paul O'Neill, ph-rf	.333	5	15	1	5	1	0	0	0	2	2	1
Andy Pettitte, p	.333	2	3	0	1	0	0	0	0	0	1	0
Luis Sojo, ph-1b	.333	2	3	0	1	0	0	0	1	0	0	0
Alfonso Soriano, 2b	.240	7	25	1	6	0	0	1	2	0	7	0
Bernie Williams, cf	.208	7	24	2	5	1	0	0	1	4	6	0
Shane Spencer, ph-lf-rf	.200	7	20	1	4	0	0	1	2	2	6	0
Tino Martinez, 1b	.190	6	21	1	4	0	0	1	3	2	2	0
Jorge Posada, c	.174	7	23	2	4	1	0	1	1	3	8	0
Scott Brosius, 3b	.167	7	24	1	4	2	0	1	3	0	8	0
Dave Justice, ph-dh-rf	.167	5	12	0	2	0	0	0	0	1	9	0
Derek Jeter, ss	.148	7	27	3	4	0	0	1	1	0	6	0
Chuck Knoblauch, ph-dh-lf	.056	6	18	1	1	0	0	0	0	1	2	0
Randy Velarde, 1b	.000	1	3	0	0	0	0	0	0	1	1	0
Enrique Wilson, ph-ss	.000	2	3	0	0	0	0	0	0	0	1	0
Clay Bellinger, ph-lf	.000	2	2	0	0	0	0	0	0	0	2	0
Roger Clemens, p	.000	1	2	0	0	0	0	0	0	0	1	0
Randy Choate, p	.000	2	1	0	0	0	0	0	0	0	1	0
Mike Mussina, p	.000	1	1	0	0	0	0	0	0	0	1	0
Totals	.183	7	229	14	42	6	0	6	14	16	63	1

Pitcher	W	L	ERA	G	GS	SV	IP	H	R	ER	BB	SO
Sterling Hitchcock	1	0	0.00	2	0	0	3	1	0	0	0	6
Ramiro Mendoza	0	0	0.00	2	0	0	3	1	0	0	0	1
Roger Clemens	1	0	1.35	2	2	0	13	10	2	2	4	19
Orlando Hernandez	0	0	1.42	1	1	0	6	4	1	1	4	5
Randy Choate	0	0	2.45	2	0	0	4	7	4	1	1	2
Mariano Rivera	1	1	2.84	4	0	1	6	6	2	2	1	7
Mike Stanton	0	0	3.18	5	0	0	6	3	2	2	1	3
Mike Mussina	0	1	4.09	2	2	0	11	11	7	5	4	14
Andy Pettitte	0	2	10.00	2	2	0	9	12	10	10	2	9
Jay Witasick	0	0	54.00	1	0	0	1	10	9	8	0	4
Totals	3	4	4.41	7	7	1	63	65	37	31	17	70

ARIZONA

Player, Pos.	AVG	G	AB	R	H	2B	3B	HR	RBI	BB	SO	SB
Danny Bautista, cf-dh-rf	.583	5	12	1	7	2	0	0	7	1	1	0
David Dellucci, pr-lf	.500	2	2	0	1	0	0	0	0	1	0	0
Rod Barajas, c	.400	2	5	1	2	0	0	1	1	0	0	0
Greg Colbrunn, 1b	.400	1	5	2	2	0	0	0	1	1	1	0
Steve Finley, cf	.368	7	19	5	7	0	0	1	2	4	5	0
Erubiel Durazo, ph-dh	.364	4	11	0	4	1	0	0	1	3	4	0
Reggie Sanders, rf	.304	6	23	6	7	1	0	0	1	1	7	1
Matt Williams, 3b	.269	7	26	3	7	2	0	1	7	0	6	0
Mark Grace, 1b	.263	6	19	1	5	1	0	1	3	4	1	0
Luis Gonzalez, lf	.259	7	27	4	7	2	0	1	5	1	11	0
Tony Womack, ss	.250	7	32	3	8	3	0	0	3	1	7	1
Damian Miller, c	.190	6	21	3	4	2	0	0	2	1	11	0
Jay Bell, ph-2b	.143	3	7	3	1	0	0	0	1	0	2	0
Randy Johnson, p	.143	3	7	2	1	0	0	0	1	0	2	0
Craig Counsell, 2b	.083	6	24	1	2	0	0	1	1	0	7	0
Curt Schilling, p	.000	2	6	0	0	0	0	0	0	0	5	0
Midre Cummings, pr	.000	2	0	2	0	0	0	0	0	0	0	0
Totals	.264	7	246	37	65	14	0	6	36	17	70	2

Pitcher	W	L	ERA	G	GS	SV	IP	H	R	ER	BB	SO
Miguel Batista	0	0	0.00	2	1	0	8	5	0	0	5	6
Mike Morgan	0	0	0.00	3	0	0	5	1	0	0	1	0
Greg Swindell	0	0	0.00	3	0	0	3	1	0	0	1	2
Troy Brohawn	0	0	0.00	1	0	0	1	1	0	0	0	1
Bobby Witt	0	0	0.00	1	0	0	1	0	0	0	1	1
Randy Johnson	3	0	1.04	3	2	0	17	9	2	2	3	19
Curt Schilling	1	0	1.69	3	3	0	21	12	4	4	2	26
Brian Anderson	0	1	3.38	1	1	0	5	5	2	2	3	1
Byung-Hyun Kim	0	1	13.50	2	0	0	3	6	5	5	1	6
Albie Lopez	0	1	27.00	1	0	0	2	1	1	0	0	0
Totals	4	3	1.94	7	7	0	65	42	14	14	16	63

SCORE BY INNINGS

New York	111 003 114 2—14
Arizona	24(12) 921 322 0—37

E—Justice, Brosius, Soriano 3, Posada, Clemens, Rivera, Womack, Miller, Grace. DP—New York 7, Arizona 6. LOB—New York 41, Arizona 46. CS—Soriano, Finley, Womack. SH—Brosius, Counsell 4, M. Williams. SF—M. Williams 2. HBP—Jeter (by Schilling), Womack (by Mussina), Gonzalez 2 (by Pettitte, by Hernandez), Sanders (by Clemens), Miller (by Hernandez), Counsell (by Rivera). IBB—Grace 2 (2 by Mussina), Sanders (by Choate), Durazo (by Mussina), Finley (by Rivera), Miller (by Pettitte). WP—Mussina, Witasick, Anderson, Morgan, Swindell, Batista.

BY BLAIR LOVERN

Yankees catcher Todd Greene coined a scary adjective for his team in the fall, calling it "Octoberized."

The Athletics, ahead of New York two games to none in the American League Division Series, know all about Octoberization. The Mariners, who won more regular season games in 2001 than any other AL team, do too. After the Yankees cleared those two clubs out of the way in the playoffs for their 38th pennant, they were 53-18 in post-season games since 1996.

"I don't think it's that we do anything different," outfielder Paul O'Neill said. "I think we're used to winning big games."

Oakland could have ended New York's season in Game Three of the Division Series. Barry Zito pitched a gem, allowing two hits in eight innings. But the Athletics scored no runs for him. New York won 1-0 and the rest of the series went down the drain for the Athletics.

Seattle topped New York's 1998 AL record of 114 wins in the regular season by two, tying for the major league record with the 1906 Cubs. The Mariners were the first team in 53 years to lead the league in batting average, fielding and ERA.

"You don't win 116 games because you luck into it," Seattle second baseman Bret Boone said. "You win 116 games because you've got something special going."

Call it special, but don't call it Octoberized. The Yankees beat them four games to one in the AL Championship Series.

"It's not the uniform," said Seattle manager Lou Piniella, who played in the World Series four times with the Yankees. "You can put purple and green on this bunch over there, and they are going to play well. Yeah, you've got the monuments, and you've got this and that and there's lots of things to lean on. But you've still got to play baseball when the umpire says, 'Play ball.' "

Seattle's batting average fell from a league-leading .288 in the season to .228 in the playoffs. The Indians took the Mariners to five games in the Division Series, so Piniella didn't have his optimal rotation for the Championship Series. One of his top pitchers, Jamie Moyer, had his best season at age 38 (20-6, 4.21). But he did not start in the Championship Series until Game Three. The Yankees' top starters, Andy Pettitte and Mike Mussina, were rested, winning the first two games in Seattle, and the Mariners never bounced back.

STEVE MOORE

Lou Piniella

The Yankees played with more emotion after terrorist attacks that brought down the World Trade Center towers. Following playoff games, manager Joe Torre often wore a hat that read, "It ain't over till it's over" on the front. The left side had the logo of the Port Authority police.

The Mariners did come to life in Game Three of the ALCS and won 14-3. The Yankees won the next game 3-1, and in Game Five they beat the daylights out of the Mariners, 12-3, for the pennant.

STEVE MOORE

Roger Clemens: Went 20-3 for Yankees

Western Heat

Because they won a record number of games, the Mariners earned a lot of attention during the year. But Oakland was about as good in the second half as the Mariners. The Athletics were 58-17 (.773) after the all-star break—the second-best record behind the 1954 Indians (.775).

The A's started miserably (8-18) but finished with the best record in the short history of the wild card (102-60). Oakland was the only team to sweep Seattle all season.

Aside from the Yankees, Seattle and Oakland dominated pitching in the league. Mariners ace Freddy Garcia won the ERA title (3.05). Moyer and Oakland's Mark Mulder joined the Yankees' Roger Clemens as the AL's only 20-game winners.

A decade earlier the A's had the promise of four pitching prospects nicknamed the Four Aces, but they never panned out. In 2001 the A's had a core of starters who did: Mulder (21-8, 3.45), Tim Hudson (18-9, 3.37), Zito (17-8, 3.49) and Cory Lidle (13-6, 3.59). In the bullpen Jason Isringhausen (34 saves) had his second straight solid year as a closer, after coming up as a starter in the Mets system. The A's 3.59 team ERA was a close second in the league to Seattle's 3.54.

Two three-team trades helped the A's in 2001. In the offseason they acquired outfielder Johnny Damon to improve defense and the leadoff spot. Halfway through the season they acquired outfielder Jermaine Dye, who hit .297-13-59 in 232 at-bats for the A's.

Jason Giambi went on a rampage on his way to becoming a free agent. The 30-year-old first baseman hit a career-best .342, with 38 home runs and 120 RBIs. He

AMERICAN LEAGUE CHAMPIONS, 1901-2001

	PENNANT	PCT	GA
1901	Chicago	.610	4
1902	Philadelphia	.610	5
1903	Boston	.659	14½
1904	Boston	.617	1½
1905	Philadelphia	.622	2
1906	Chicago	.616	3
1907	Detroit	.613	1½
1908	Detroit	.588	½
1909	Detroit	.645	3½
1910	Philadelphia	.680	14½
1911	Philadelphia	.669	13½
1912	Boston	.691	14
1913	Philadelphia	.627	6½
1914	Philadelphia	.651	8½
1915	Boston	.669	2½
1916	Boston	.591	2
1917	Chicago	.649	9
1918	Boston	.595	2½
1919	Chicago	.629	3½
1920	Cleveland	.636	2
1921	New York	.641	4½
1922	New York	.610	1
1923	New York	.645	16
1924	Washington	.597	2
1925	Washington	.636	8½
1926	New York	.591	3
1927	New York	.714	19
1928	New York	.656	2½
1929	Philadelphia	.693	18
1930	Philadelphia	.662	8

	PENNANT	PCT	GA	MVP
1931	Philadelphia	.704	13½	Lefty Grove, lhp, Philadelphia
1932	New York	.695	13	Jimmie Foxx, 1b, Philadelphia
1933	Washington	.651	7	Jimmie Foxx, 1b, Philadelphia
1934	Detroit	.656	7	Mickey Cochrane, c, Detroit
1935	Detroit	.616	3	Hank Greenberg, 1b, Detroit
1936	New York	.667	19½	Lou Gehrig, 1b, New York
1937	New York	.662	13	Charlie Gehringer, 2b, Detroit
1938	New York	.651	9½	Jimmie Foxx, 1b, Boston
1939	New York	.702	17	Joe DiMaggio, of, New York
1940	Detroit	.584	1	Hank Greenberg, 1b, Detroit
1941	New York	.656	17	Joe DiMaggio, of, New York
1942	New York	.669	9	Joe Gordon, 2b, New York
1943	New York	.636	13½	Spud Chandler, rhp, New York
1944	St. Louis	.578	1	Hal Newhouser, lhp, Detroit
1945	Detroit	.575	1½	Hal Newhouser, lhp, Detroit
1946	Boston	.675	12	Ted Williams, of, Boston
1947	New York	.630	12	Joe DiMaggio, of, New York
1948	Cleveland	.626	1	Lou Boudreau, ss, Cleveland
1949	New York	.630	1	Ted Williams, of, Boston
1950	New York	.636	3	Phil Rizzuto, ss, New York
1951	New York	.636	5	Yogi Berra, c, New York
1952	New York	.617	2	Bobby Shantz, lhp, Philadelphia
1953	New York	.656	8½	Al Rosen, 3b, Cleveland
1954	Cleveland	.721	8	Yogi Berra, c, New York
1955	New York	.623	3	Yogi Berra, c, New York
1956	New York	.630	9	Mickey Mantle, of, New York
1957	New York	.636	8	Mickey Mantle, of, New York
1958	New York	.597	10	Jackie Jensen, of, Boston
1959	Chicago	.610	5	Nellie Fox, 2b, Chicago
1960	New York	.630	8	Roger Maris, of, New York
1961	New York	.673	8	Roger Maris, of, New York
1962	New York	.593	5	Mickey Mantle, of, New York
1963	New York	.646	10½	Elston Howard, c, New York
1964	New York	.611	1	Brooks Robinson, 3b, Baltimore
1965	Minnesota	.630	7	Zoilo Versalles, ss, Minnesota
1966	Baltimore	.606	9	Frank Robinson, of, Baltimore
1967	Boston	.568	1	Carl Yastrzemski, of, Boston
1968	Detroit	.636	12	Denny McLain, rhp, Detroit

	EAST	PCT	GA	WEST	PCT	GA	PENNANT		MVP
1969	Baltimore	.673	19	Minnesota	.599	9	Baltimore	3-0	Harmon Killebrew, 1b-3b, Minnesota
1970	Baltimore	.667	15	Minnesota	.605	9	Baltimore	3-0	Boog Powell, 1b, Baltimore
1971	Baltimore	.639	12	Oakland	.627	16	Baltimore	3-0	Vida Blue, lhp, Oakland
1972	Detroit	.551	½	Oakland	.600	5½	Oakland	3-2	Dick Allen, 1b, Chicago
1973	Baltimore	.599	8	Oakland	.580	6	Oakland	3-2	Reggie Jackson, of, Oakland
1974	Baltimore	.562	2	Oakland	.556	5	Oakland	3-1	Jeff Burroughs, of, Texas
1975	Boston	.594	4½	Oakland	.605	7	Boston	3-0	Fred Lynn, of, Boston
1976	New York	.610	10½	Kansas City	.556	2½	New York	3-2	Thurman Munson, c, New York
1977	New York	.617	2½	Kansas City	.630	8	New York	3-2	Rod Carew, 1b, Minnesota
1978	New York	.613	1	Kansas City	.568	5	New York	3-1	Jim Rice, of, Boston
1979	Baltimore	.642	8	California	.543	3	Baltimore	3-0	Don Baylor, dh, California
1980	New York	.636	3	Kansas City	.599	14	Kansas City	3-0	George Brett, 3b, Kansas City
1981	New York*	.607	2	Oakland**	.587	—	New York	3-0	Rollie Fingers, rhp, Milwaukee
	Milwaukee	.585	1½	Kansas City	.566	1			
1982	Milwaukee	.586	1	California	.574	3	Milwaukee	3-2	Robin Yount, ss, Milwaukee
1983	Baltimore	.605	6	Chicago	.611	20	Baltimore	3-1	Cal Ripken, ss, Baltimore
1984	Detroit	.642	15	Kansas City	.519	3	Detroit	3-0	Willie Hernandez, lhp, Detroit
1985	Toronto	.615	2	Kansas City	.562	1	Kansas City	4-3	Don Mattingly, 1b, New York
1986	Boston	.590	5½	California	.568	5	Boston	4-3	Roger Clemens, rhp, Boston
1987	Detroit	.605	2	Minnesota	.525	2	Minnesota	4-1	George Bell, of, Toronto
1988	Boston	.549	1	Oakland	.642	13	Oakland	4-0	Jose Canseco, of, Oakland
1989	Toronto	.549	2	Oakland	.611	7	Oakland	4-1	Robin Yount, of, Milwaukee
1990	Boston	.543	2	Oakland	.636	9	Oakland	4-0	Rickey Henderson, of, Oakland
1991	Toronto	.562	7	Minnesota	.586	8	Minnesota	4-1	Cal Ripken, ss, Baltimore
1992	Toronto	.593	4	Oakland	.593	6	Toronto	4-2	Dennis Eckersley, rhp, Oakland
1993	Toronto	.586	7	Chicago	.580	8	Toronto	4-2	Frank Thomas, 1b, Chicago

* Won first half; defeated Milwaukee 3-2 in best-of-5 playoff.   ** Won first half; defeated Kansas City 3-0 in best-of-5 playoff.

	EAST	PCT	GA	CENTRAL	PCT	GA	WEST	PCT	GA	WILD CARD	PCT
1994	New York	.619	6½	Chicago	.593	1	Texas	.456	1	None	
	PENNANT: None (season incomplete)						MVP: Frank Thomas, 1b, Chicago				
1995	Boston	.597	7	Cleveland	.694	30	Seattle	.545	1	New York (East)	.549
	PENNANT: Cleveland def. Seattle 4-2						MVP: Mo Vaughn, 1b, Boston				
1996	New York	.568	4	Cleveland	.615	14½	Texas	.556	4	Baltimore (East)	.543
	PENNANT: New York def. Baltimore 4-1						MVP: Juan Gonzalez, of, Texas				
1997	Baltimore	.605	2	Cleveland	.534	6	Seattle	.556	6	New York (East)	.593
	PENNANT: Cleveland def. Baltimore 4-2						MVP: Ken Griffey, of, Seattle				
1998	New York	.704	22	Cleveland	.549	9	Texas	.543	3	Boston (East)	.568
	PENNANT: New York def. Cleveland 4-2						MVP: Juan Gonzalez, of, Texas				
1999	New York	.605	4	Cleveland	.599	21½	Texas	.586	8	Boston (East)	.580
	PENNANT: New York def. Boston 4-1						MVP: Ivan Rodriguez, c, Texas				
2000	New York	.540	2½	Chicago	.586	5	Oakland	.565	½	Seattle (West)	.562
	PENNANT: New York def. Seattle 4-2						MVP: Jason Giambi, 1b, Oakland				
2001	New York	.594	13½	Cleveland	.562	6	Seattle	.716	14	Oakland (West)	.630
	PENNANT: New York def. Seattle 4-1						MVP: Ichiro Suzuki, of, Seattle				

Page	EAST	W	L	PCT	GB	Manager(s)	General Manager	Attendance (Avg.)	Last Penn.
182	New York Yankees	95	65	.594	—	Joe Torre	Brian Cashman	3,264,777 (40,810)	2001
85	Boston Red Sox	82	79	.509	13½	J. Williams/J. Kerrigan	Dan Duquette	2,625,333 (32,412)	1986
259	Toronto Blue Jays	80	82	.494	16	Buck Martinez	Gord Ash	1,915,438 (23,647)	1993
78	Baltimore Orioles	63	98	.391	32½	Mike Hargrove	Syd Thrift	3,094,841 (38,686)	1983
246	Tampa Bay Devil Rays	62	100	.383	34	L. Rothschild/H. McRae	Chuck LaMar	1,298,365 (16,029)	None
Page	CENTRAL	W	L	PCT	GB	Manager	General Manager	Attendance (Avg.)	Last Penn.
113	Cleveland Indians	91	71	.562	—	Charlie Manuel	John Hart	3,175,523 (39,694)	1997
169	Minnesota Twins	85	77	.525	6	Tom Kelly	Terry Ryan	1,782,926 (22,287)	1991
92	Chicago White Sox	83	79	.512	8	Jerry Manuel	Ken Williams	1,766,142 (22,077)	1959
128	Detroit Tigers	66	96	.407	25	Phil Garner	Randy Smith	1,921,305 (24,016)	1984
148	Kansas City Royals	65	97	.401	26	Tony Muser	Allard Baird	1,536,371 (18,968)	1985
Page	WEST	W	L	PCT	GB	Manager(s)	General Manager	Attendance (Avg.)	Last Penn.
239	Seattle Mariners	116	46	.716	—	Lou Piniella	Pat Gillick	3,507,507 (43,303)	None
198	*Oakland Athletics	102	60	.630	14	Art Howe	Billy Beane	2,133,277 (26,337)	1990
57	Anaheim Angels	75	87	.463	41	Mike Scioscia	Bill Stoneman	2,000,919 (24,703)	None
252	Texas Rangers	73	89	.451	43	J. Oates/J. Narron	Doug Melvin	2,831,111 (34,952)	None

*Won wild-card playoff berth
NOTE: Teams' individual batting, pitching and fielding statistics can be found on page indicated in lefthand column.

led the league in on-base percentage (.477), slugging (.660), doubles (47) and walks (129).

Oakland went into the postseason with momentum, thanks to a 17-game winning streak at home. On the last day of the season, Zito won his ninth straight, Eric Chavez broke the franchise home run (32) and RBI marks (114) for a third baseman and the team won its sixth straight.

But after two Oakland wins in the ALDS, the Yankees summoned up whatever postseason witchery they've had since 1996. New York became the first team to win a best-of-five series after losing the first two at home.

Up the Pacific coast, the Mariners set the AL record for road wins in a season (59) and set a major league mark with 29 consecutive road series won or tied.

Bret Boone: AL RBI leader with 141

LARRY GOREN

The Mariners had the AL batting champion in Japanese rookie sensation Ichiro Suzuki (.350) and the RBI leader in Bret Boone (141).

Suzuki, who played nine years with the Orix Blue Wave in Japan's Pacific League, carried his success across the Pacific. The Mariners spent $13.1 million just to negotiate with Suzuki and then worked out a three-year, $14 million deal.

The 27-year-old right fielder led the AL with 242 hits and 56 stolen bases and showed off his superior arm: In one game, fear kept Mike Young of Texas from trying to score from third on a single.

Suzuki was second in the league with 127 runs. His hit total was the seventh-highest in history and the most since 1930. He also tied the major league mark with hits in 135 games.

Boone set a career high with 37 homers. His home run and RBI numbers were the most by any AL player who played at least 100 games at second base.

During the winter Rangers owner Tom Hicks spent $252 million on shortstop Alex Rodriguez, who didn't wilt under the pressure of signing the largest contract in sports history. Rodriguez had the best season of his career, hitting .318-52-135.

"I've seen a lot of great shortstops," Angels manager Mike Scioscia said. "Some guys can play tremendous defense and some are talented offensive players. I would say none are the complete package the way Alex is."

But as in 2000, when Texas finished last in the West, the team had no pitching. The Rangers (73-89) ended with almost the same record as in 2000 (71-91), and because of Seattle's surge they finished 43 games back.

Eastern Standard

Of the 25 players on the Yankees' postseason roster, 19 had played in the World Series before. One of the six who had not was Mussina. During the winter, the former Orioles ace sought a team close to his Pennsylvania home that would score more than 3.71 runs a game for him. The Yankees signed him to a six-year, $88.5 million contract and Mussina delivered, going 17-11, 3.15. His 214 strikeouts were the second-most of his 11-year career.

Clemens became the first pitcher in major league history to win 20 of his first 21 decisions. He bettered the record of Rube Marquard, who started 1912 for the New York Giants by going 19-1.

Yankees righthander Mariano Rivera was his usual self, becoming the sixth closer to earn 50 saves. New York continued with its usual mix of hitters, except that rookie second baseman Alfonso Soriano (.268-18-73) moved Chuck Knoblauch to left field.

The Red Sox were the only team in the East to give the Yankees a run for their money, but with the Red Sox being the Red Sox, they made sure things ended on a

AL YEAR-BY-YEAR BATTING LEADERS

Year	Batting Average	Home Runs	RBIs
1901	Nap Lajoie, Philadelphia .422	Nap Lajoie, Philadelphia 14	Nap Lajoie, Philadelphia 125
1902	Ed Delahanty, Washington .376	Socks Seybold, Philadelphia 16	Buck Freeman, Boston 121
1903	Nap Lajoie, Cleveland .355	Buck Freeman, Boston 13	Buck Freeman, Boston 104
1904	Nap Lajoie, Cleveland .381	Harry Davis, Philadelphia 10	Nap Lajoie, Cleveland 102
1905	Elmer Flick, Cleveland .306	Harry Davis, Philadelphia 8	Harry Davis, Philadelphia 83
1906	George Stone, St. Louis .358	Harry Davis, Philadelphia 12	Harry Davis, Philadelphia 96
1907	Ty Cobb, Detroit .350	Harry Davis, Philadelphia 8	Ty Cobb, Detroit 119
1908	Ty Cobb, Detroit .324	Sam Crawford, Detroit 7	Ty Cobb, Detroit 108
1909	Ty Cobb, Detroit .377	Ty Cobb, Detroit 9	Ty Cobb, Detroit 107
1910	Ty Cobb, Detroit .385	Jake Stahl, Boston 10	Sam Crawford, Detroit 120
1911	Ty Cobb, Detroit .420	Frank Baker, Philadelphia 11	Ty Cobb, Detroit 127
1912	Ty Cobb, Detroit .410	Two tied at 10	Frank Baker, Philadelphia 130
1913	Ty Cobb, Detroit .390	Frank Baker, Philadelphia 12	Frank Baker, Philadelphia 117
1914	Ty Cobb, Detroit .368	Frank Baker, Philadelphia 9	Sam Crawford, Detroit 104
1915	Ty Cobb, Detroit .370	Braggo Roth, Cleveland 7	Sam Crawford, Detroit 112
1916	Tris Speaker, Cleveland .386	Wally Pipp, New York 12	Wally Pipp, New York 93
1917	Ty Cobb, Detroit .383	Wally Pipp, New York 9	Bobby Veach, Detroit 103
1918	Ty Cobb, Detroit .382	Two tied at 11	Bobby Veach, Detroit 78
1919	Ty Cobb, Detroit .384	Babe Ruth, Boston 29	Babe Ruth, Boston 114
1920	George Sisler, St. Louis .407	Babe Ruth, New York 54	Babe Ruth, New York 137
1921	Harry Heilmann, Detroit .394	Babe Ruth, New York 59	Babe Ruth, New York 171
1922	George Sisler, St. Louis .420	Ken Williams, St. Louis 39	Ken Williams, St. Louis 155
1923	Harry Heilmann, Detroit .403	Babe Ruth, New York 41	Babe Ruth, New York 131
1924	Babe Ruth, New York .378	Babe Ruth, New York 46	Goose Goslin, Washington 129
1925	Harry Heilmann, Detroit .393	Bob Meusel, New York 33	Bob Meusel, New York 138
1926	Heinie Manush, Detroit .378	Babe Ruth, New York 47	Babe Ruth, New York 145
1927	Harry Heilmann, Detroit .398	Babe Ruth, New York 60	Lou Gehrig, New York 175
1928	Goose Goslin, Washington .379	Babe Ruth, New York 54	Two tied at 142
1929	Lew Fonseca, Cleveland .369	Babe Ruth, New York 46	Al Simmons, Philadelphia 157
1930	Al Simmons, Philadelphia .381	Babe Ruth, New York 49	Lou Gehrig, New York 174
1931	Al Simmons, Philadelphia .390	Two tied at 46	Lou Gehrig, New York 184
1932	Dale Alexander, Det.-Bos. .367	Jimmie Foxx, Philadelphia 58	Jimmie Foxx, Philadelphia 169
1933	Jimmie Foxx, Philadelphia .356	Jimmie Foxx, Philadelphia 48	Jimmie Foxx, Philadelphia 163
1934	Lou Gehrig, New York .363	Lou Gehrig, New York 49	Lou Gehrig, New York 165
1935	Buddy Myer, Washington .349	Two tied at 36	Hank Greenberg, Detroit 170
1936	Luke Appling, Chicago .388	Lou Gehrig, New York 49	Hal Trosky, Cleveland 162
1937	Charlie Gehringer, Detroit .371	Joe DiMaggio, New York 46	Hank Greenberg, Detroit 183
1938	Jimmie Foxx, Boston .349	Hank Greenberg, Detroit 58	Jimmie Foxx, Boston 175
1939	Joe DiMaggio, New York .381	Jimmie Foxx, Boston 35	Ted Williams, Boston 145
1940	Joe DiMaggio, New York .352	Hank Greenberg, Detroit 41	Hank Greenberg, Detroit 150
1941	Ted Williams, Boston .406	Ted Williams, Boston 37	Joe DiMaggio, New York 125
1942	Ted Williams, Boston .356	Ted Williams, Boston 36	Ted Williams, Boston 137
1943	Luke Appling, Chicago .328	Rudy York, Detroit 34	Rudy York, Detroit 118
1944	Lou Boudreau, Cleveland .327	Nick Etten, New York 22	Vern Stephens, St. Louis 109
1945	Snuffy Stirnweiss, New York .309	Vern Stephens, St. Louis 24	Nick Etten, New York 111
1946	Mickey Vernon, Wash. .353	Hank Greenberg, Detroit 44	Hank Greenberg, Detroit 127
1947	Ted Williams, Boston .343	Ted Williams, Boston 32	Ted Williams, Boston 114
1948	Ted Williams, Boston .369	Joe DiMaggio, New York 39	Joe DiMaggio, New York 155
1949	George Kell, Detroit .343	Ted Williams, Boston 43	Two tied at 159
1950	Billy Goodman, Boston .354	Al Rosen, Cleveland 37	Two tied at 144
1951	Ferris Fain, Philadelphia .344	Gus Zernial, Chi.-Phil. 33	Gus Zernial, Chi.-Phil. 129
1952	Ferris Fain, Philadelphia .327	Larry Doby, Cleveland 32	Al Rosen, Cleveland 105
1953	Mickey Vernon, Washington .337	Al Rosen, Cleveland 43	Al Rosen, Cleveland 145
1954	Bobby Avila, Cleveland .341	Larry Doby, Cleveland 32	Larry Doby, Cleveland 126
1955	Al Kaline, Detroit .340	Mickey Mantle, New York 37	Two tied at 116
1956	Mickey Mantle, New York .353	Mickey Mantle, New York 52	Mickey Mantle, New York 130
1957	Ted Williams, Boston .388	Roy Sievers, Washington 42	Roy Sievers, Washington 114
1958	Ted Williams, Boston .328	Mickey Mantle, New York 42	Jackie Jensen, Boston 122
1959	Harvey Kuenn, Detroit .353	Two tied at 42	Jackie Jensen, Boston 112
1960	Pete Runnels, Boston .320	Mickey Mantle, New York 40	Roger Maris, New York 112
1961	Norm Cash, Detroit .361	Roger Maris, New York 61	Roger Maris, New York 142
1962	Pete Runnels, Boston .326	Harmon Killebrew, Minnesota 48	Harmon Killebrew, Minnesota 126
1963	Carl Yastrzemski, Boston .321	Harmon Killebrew, Minnesota 45	Dick Stuart, Boston 118
1964	Tony Oliva, Minnesota .323	Harmon Killebrew, Minnesota 49	Brooks Robinson, Baltimore 118
1965	Tony Oliva, Minnesota .321	Tony Conigliaro, Boston 32	Rocky Colavito, Cleveland 108
1966	Frank Robinson, Baltimore .316	Frank Robinson, Baltimore 49	Frank Robinson, Baltimore 122
1967	Carl Yastrzemski, Boston .326	Carl Yastrzemski, Boston 44	Carl Yastrzemski, Boston 121
1968	Carl Yastrzemski, Boston .301	Frank Howard, Washington 44	Ken Harrelson, Boston 109
1969	Rod Carew, Minnesota .332	Harmon Killebrew, Minnesota 49	Harmon Killebrew, Minnesota 140
1970	Alex Johnson, California .329	Frank Howard, Washington 44	Frank Howard, Washington 126
1971	Tony Oliva, Minnesota .337	Bill Melton, Chicago 33	Harmon Killebrew, Minnesota 119
1972	Rod Carew, Minnesota .318	Dick Allen, Chicago 37	Dick Allen, Chicago 113
1973	Rod Carew, Minnesota .350	Reggie Jackson, Oakland 32	Reggie Jackson, Oakland 117
1974	Rod Carew, Minnesota .364	Dick Allen, Chicago 32	Jeff Burroughs, Texas 118
1975	Rod Carew, Minnesota .359	Two tied at 36	George Scott, Milwaukee 109
1976	George Brett, Kansas City .333	Graig Nettles, New York 32	Lee May, Baltimore 109
1977	Rod Carew, Minnesota .388	Jim Rice, Boston 39	Larry Hisle, Minnesota 119
1978	Rod Carew, Minnesota .333	Jim Rice, Boston 46	Jim Rice, Boston 139
1979	Fred Lynn, Boston .333	Gorman Thomas, Milwaukee 45	Don Baylor, California 139
1980	George Brett, Kansas City .390	Two tied at 41	Cecil Cooper, Milwaukee 122
1981	Carney Lansford, Boston .336	Four tied at 22	Eddie Murray, Baltimore 78
1982	Willie Wilson, Kansas City .332	Two tied at 39	Hal McRae, Kansas City 133
1983	Wade Boggs, Boston .361	Jim Rice, Boston 39	Two tied at 126
1984	Don Mattingly, New York .343	Tony Armas, Boston 43	Tony Armas, Boston 123
1985	Wade Boggs, Boston .368	Darrell Evans, Detroit 40	Don Mattingly, New York 145
1986	Wade Boggs, Boston .357	Jesse Barfield, Toronto 40	Joe Carter, Cleveland 121
1987	Wade Boggs, Boston .363	Mark McGwire, Oakland 49	George Bell, Toronto 134
1988	Wade Boggs, Boston .366	Jose Canseco, Oakland 42	Jose Canseco, Oakland 124
1989	Kirby Puckett, Minnesota .339	Fred McGriff, Toronto 36	Ruben Sierra, Texas 119
1990	George Brett, Kansas City .329	Cecil Fielder, Detroit 51	Cecil Fielder, Detroit 132
1991	Julio Franco, Texas .341	Two tied at 44	Cecil Fielder, Detroit 133
1992	Edgar Martinez, Seattle .343	Juan Gonzalez, Texas 43	Cecil Fielder, Detroit 124
1993	John Olerud, Toronto .363	Juan Gonzalez, Texas 46	Albert Belle, Cleveland 129
1994	Paul O'Neill, New York .359	Ken Griffey, Seattle 40	Kirby Puckett, Minnesota 112
1995	Edgar Martinez, Seattle .356	Albert Belle, Cleveland 50	Albert Belle, Cleveland 126
1996	Alex Rodriguez, Seattle .358	Mark McGwire Oakland 52	Albert Belle, Cleveland 148
1997	Frank Thomas, Chicago .347	Ken Griffey, Seattle 56	Ken Griffey, Seattle 147
1998	Bernie Williams, New York .339	Ken Griffey, Seattle 56	Juan Gonzalez, Texas 157
1999	Nomar Garciaparra, Boston .357	Ken Griffey, Seattle 48	Manny Ramirez, Cleveland 165
2000	Nomar Garciaparra, Boston .372	Troy Glaus, Anaheim 47	Edgar Martinez, Seattle 145
2001	Ichiro Suzuki, Seattle .350	Alex Rodriguez, Texas 52	Bret Boone, Seattle 141

sour note.

David Cone (9-7, 4.31) made a nice comeback after injuring his right shoulder in spring training. Hideo Nomo accomplished a rare double by leading the AL in walks (96) and strikeouts (220).

Outfielders Manny Ramirez (.306-41-125) and Trot Nixon (.280-27-88) had solid years, as did rookie Shea Hillenbrand (.263-12-49). But Boston was without its two mainstays for too long: Pedro Martinez on the mound and Nomar Garciaparra at short.

Martinez was limited to 18 starts because of rotator-cuff damage. He made three starts after June 26 and finally went home to the Dominican Republic in September to concentrate on 2002.

In spring training Garciaparra again injured a tendon in his right wrist (which was hit by a pitch in 1999) and required surgery. He missed the first half and played sporadically during the remainder of the year, getting just 83 at-bats.

Outfielder Carl Everett provided several interesting moments. In late March, the Red Sox suspended Everett for a game and fined him more than $97,000 for not riding the team bus to an exhibition game and missing practice the next day. He was fined an estimated $5,000 by Major League Baseball for grabbing his crotch while he crossed home plate Aug. 14 after hitting a home run. He got into several shouting matches during the year and was suspended for four games after arriving late for practice in September. With two weeks left in the season, he injured his right knee and Boston just let him go home.

Still, the Red Sox set themselves up in early August for a legitimate run at the Eastern Division title. Then to the surprise of many Boston fans, general manager Dan Duquette fired manager Jimy Williams. A few weeks after that, with the team in a tailspin, Boston fans were in for another miserable winter after a season that cost the team about $110 million.

In Baltimore, Cal Ripken retired, ending 21 seasons with the Orioles. At the time of his June announcement, Ripken was hitting .210. He went on a 15-game hitting streak and finished the All-Star Game as MVP. He later had a 16-game hitting streak before cooling off at the end of the year.

One of the surprises the Orioles gave Ripken in his final game in Baltimore came when he took his position at third base in the first inning. First baseman Jeff Conine threw a terrible warm-up grounder on purpose that skidded to the stands. After Ripken chased it and picked up the ball, he turned around and saw the starting lineup from his first major league game in place of the regulars. The spot at short was left empty in tribute to the late Mark Belanger.

Jason Giambi: 120 RBIs for the A's

LARRY GOREN

Ripken said his immediate plans will involve guiding his minor league and youth stadium projects in Aberdeen, Md., which are scheduled to be finished in 2002, a year behind schedule.

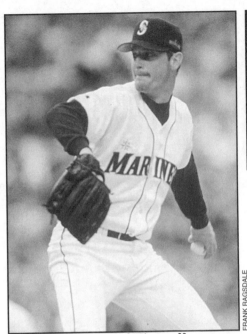

Jamie Moyer: Won 20 games for Seattle at age 38

FRANK RAGSDALE

"It's very exiting what we can accomplish there, and I'm looking forward to diving into that," Ripken said. "But it's even more exciting trying to take a lifetime of baseball and share that.

"I always thought I had the encyclopedia of baseball in dad. Every time I had a question, he could direct me and I could find the answer. And I thought about where do other kids, where do they go to learn about the game of baseball? They don't have a dad who's the encyclopedia of baseball. So dad shared his information and I intend to share it as widely as I can."

The Devil Rays lost 100 games and had the fewest wins in their four-year history. But they turned their dismal season around in the second half by bringing up young talent. Tampa Bay went 24-23 the final two months.

Fluke Central

The Twins had finished above .500 once since 1993 and were two years removed from a 63-win season. Few expected Minnesota to be on top of the Central at any point in 2001. But by midseason the Twins built a five-game lead over the Indians.

A solid rotation led by Brad Radke (15-11, 3.94), Joe Mays (17-13, 3.16) and Eric Milton (15-7, 4.32) helped in Minnesota's hot first half. A good group of young position players also came together: Cristian Guzman, Torii Hunter, Corey Koskie, Doug Mientkiewicz, A.J. Pierzynski and Luis Rivas.

After the all-star break, the dream year turned to dust. The once-reliable rotation went 4-10, 6.11 in August. All-star shortstop Guzman was out for a month, rehabilitating a shoulder. Team leader Matt Lawton was traded to the Mets for pitcher Rick Reed, who struggled. Young hitters stopped hitting and the bullpen faltered.

AL YEAR-BY-YEAR PITCHING LEADERS

Year	Wins	W	ERA	ERA	Strikeouts	SO
1901	Cy Young, Boston	33	Cy Young, Boston	1.63	Cy Young, Boston	158
1902	Cy Young, Boston	32	Ed Siever, Detroit	1.91	Rube Waddell, Philadelphia	210
1903	Cy Young, Boston	28	Earl Moore, Cleveland	1.77	Rube Waddell, Philadelphia	302
1904	Jack Chesbro, New York	41	Addie Joss, Cleveland	1.59	Rube Waddell, Philadelphia	349
1905	Rube Waddell, Philadelphia	26	Rube Waddell, Philadelphia	1.48	Rube Waddell, Philadelphia	287
1906	Al Orth, New York	27	Doc White, Chicago	1.52	Rube Waddell, Philadelphia	196
1907	Two tied at	27	Ed Walsh, Chicago	1.60	Rube Waddell, Philadelphia	232
1908	Ed Walsh, Chicago	40	Addie Joss, Cleveland	1.16	Ed Walsh, Philadelphia	269
1909	George Mullin, Detroit	29	Harry Krause, Philadelphia	1.39	Frank Smith, Chicago	177
1910	Jack Coombs, Philadelphia	31	Ed Walsh, Chicago	1.27	Walter Johnson, Washington	313
1911	Jack Coombs, Philadelphia	28	Vean Gregg, Cleveland	1.81	Ed Walsh, Chicago	255
1912	Joe Wood, Boston	34	Walter Johnson, Washington	1.39	Walter Johnson, Washington	303
1913	Walter Johnson, Washington	36	Walter Johnson, Washington	1.14	Walter Johnson, Washington	243
1914	Walter Johnson, Washington	28	Dutch Leonard, Boston	1.00	Walter Johnson, Washington	225
1915	Walter Johnson, Washington	27	Joe Wood, Boston	1.49	Walter Johnson, Washington	203
1916	Walter Johnson, Washington	25	Babe Ruth, Boston	1.75	Walter Johnson, Washington	228
1917	Ed Cicotte, Chicago	28	Ed Cicotte, Chicago	1.53	Walter Johnson, Washington	188
1918	Walter Johnson, Washington	23	Walter Johnson, Washington	1.27	Walter Johnson, Washington	162
1919	Ed Cicotte, Chicago	29	Walter Johnson, Washington	1.49	Walter Johnson, Washington	147
1920	Jim Bagby, Cleveland	31	Bob Shawkey, New York	2.45	Stan Coveleski, Cleveland	133
1921	Two tied at	27	Red Faber, Chicago	2.48	Walter Johnson, Washington	143
1922	Eddie Rommel, Phil.	27	Red Faber, Chicago	2.80	Urban Shocker, St. Louis	149
1923	George Uhle, Cleveland	26	Stan Coveleski, Cleveland	2.76	Walter Johnson, Washington	130
1924	Walter Johnson, Washington	23	Walter Johnson, Washington	2.72	Walter Johnson, Washington	158
1925	Two tied at	21	Stan Coveleski, Washington	2.84	Stan Coveleski, Washington	116
1926	George Uhle, Cleveland	27	Lefty Grove, Philadelphia	2.51	Lefty Grove, Philadelphia	194
1927	Two tied at	22	Wilcy Moore, New York	2.28	Lefty Grove, Philadelphia	174
1928	Two tied at	24	Garland Braxton, Washington	2.52	Lefty Grove, Philadelphia	183
1929	George Earnshaw, Philadelphia	24	Lefty Grove, Philadelphia	2.82	Lefty Grove, Philadelphia	170
1930	Lefty Grove, Philadelphia	28	Lefty Grove, Philadelphia	2.54	Lefty Grove, Philadelphia	209
1931	Lefty Grove, Philadelphia	31	Lefty Grove, Philadelphia	2.05	Lefty Grove, Philadelphia	175
1932	General Crowder, Washington	26	Lefty Grove, Philadelphia	2.84	Red Ruffing, New York	190
1933	Two tied at	24	Monte Pearson, Cleveland	2.33	Lefty Gomez, New York	163
1934	Lefty Gomez, New York	26	Lefty Gomez, New York	2.33	Lefty Gomez, New York	158
1935	Wes Ferrell, Boston	25	Lefty Grove, Boston	2.70	Tommy Bridges, Detroit	163
1936	Tommy Bridges, Detroit	23	Lefty Grove, Boston	2.81	Tommy Bridges, Detroit	175
1937	Lefty Gomez, New York	21	Lefty Gomez, New York	2.33	Lefty Gomez, New York	194
1938	Red Ruffing, New York	21	Lefty Grove, Philadelphia	3.07	Bob Feller, Cleveland	240
1939	Bob Feller, Cleveland	24	Lefty Grove, Philadelphia	2.54	Bob Feller, Cleveland	246
1940	Bob Feller, Cleveland	27	Bob Feller, Cleveland	2.62	Bob Feller, Cleveland	261
1941	Bob Feller, Cleveland	25	Thornton Lee, Chicago	2.37	Bob Feller, Cleveland	260
1942	Tex Hughson, Boston	22	Ted Lyons, Chicago	2.10	Two tied at	113
1943	Two tied at	20	Spud Chandler, New York	1.64	Allie Reynolds, Cleveland	151
1944	Hal Newhouser, Detroit	29	Dizzy Trout, Detroit	2.12	Hal Newhouser, Detroit	187
1945	Hal Newhouser, Detroit	25	Hal Newhouser, Detroit	1.81	Hal Newhouser, Detroit	212
1946	Two tied at	26	Hal Newhouser, Detroit	1.94	Bob Feller, Cleveland	348
1947	Bob Feller, Cleveland	20	Spud Chandler, New York	2.46	Bob Feller, Cleveland	196
1948	Hal Newhouser, Detroit	21	Gene Bearden, Cleveland	2.43	Bob Feller, Cleveland	164
1949	Mel Parnell, Boston	25	Mel Parnell, Boston	2.78	Virgil Trucks, Detroit	153
1950	Bob Lemon, Cleveland	23	Early Wynn, Cleveland	3.20	Bob Lemon, Cleveland	170
1951	Bob Feller, Cleveland	22	Saul Rogovin, Det.-Chi.	2.78	Vic Raschi, New York	164
1952	Bobby Shantz, Philadelphia	24	Allie Reynolds, New York	2.07	Allie Reynolds, New York	160
1953	Bob Porterfield, Washington	22	Eddie Lopat, New York	2.43	Billy Pierce, Chicago	186
1954	Three tied at	23	Mike Garcia, Cleveland	2.64	Bob Turley, Baltimore	185
1955	Three tied at	18	Billy Pierce, Chicago	1.97	Herb Score, Cleveland	245
1956	Frank Lary, Detroit	21	Whitey Ford, New York	2.47	Herb Score, Cleveland	263
1957	Two tied at	20	Bobby Shantz, New York	2.45	Early Wynn, Cleveland	184
1958	Bob Turley, New York	21	Whitey Ford, New York	2.01	Early Wynn, Chicago	179
1959	Early Wynn, Chicago	22	Hoyt Wilhelm, Baltimore	2.19	Jim Bunning, Detroit	201
1960	Two tied at	18	Frank Baumann, Detroit	2.68	Jim Bunning, Detroit	201
1961	Whitey Ford, New York	25	Dick Donovan, Washington	2.40	Camilo Pascual, Minnesota	221
1962	Ralph Terry, New York	23	Hank Aguirre, Detroit	2.21	Camilo Pascual, Minnesota	206
1963	Whitey Ford, New York	24	Gary Peters, Chicago	2.33	Camilo Pascual, Minnesota	202
1964	Two tied at	20	Dean Chance, L.A.	1.65	Al Downing, New York	217
1965	Mudcat Grant, Minnesota	21	Sam McDowell, Cleveland	2.18	Sam McDowell, Cleveland	325
1966	Jim Kaat, Minnesota	25	Gary Peters, Chicago	1.98	Sam McDowell, Cleveland	225
1967	Two tied at	22	Joel Horlen, Chicago	2.06	Jim Lonborg, Boston	246
1968	Denny McLain, Detroit	31	Luis Tiant, Cleveland	1.60	Sam McDowell, Cleveland	283
1969	Denny McLain, Detroit	24	Dick Bosman, Washington	2.19	Sam McDowell, Cleveland	279
1970	Three tied at	24	Diego Segui, Oakland	2.56	Sam McDowell, Cleveland	304
1971	Mickey Lolich, Detroit	25	Vida Blue, Oakland	1.82	Mickey Lolich, Detroit	308
1972	Two tied at	24	Luis Tiant, Boston	1.91	Nolan Ryan, California	329
1973	Wilbur Wood, Chicago	24	Jim Palmer, Baltimore	2.40	Nolan Ryan, California	383
1974	Two tied at	25	Catfish Hunter, Oakland	2.49	Nolan Ryan, California	367
1975	Jim Palmer, Baltimore	23	Jim Palmer, Baltimore	2.09	Frank Tanana, California	269
1976	Jim Palmer, Baltimore	22	Mark Fidrych, Detroit	2.34	Nolan Ryan, California	327
1977	Three tied at	20	Frank Tanana, California	2.54	Nolan Ryan, California	341
1978	Ron Guidry, New York	25	Ron Guidry, New York	1.74	Nolan Ryan, California	260
1979	Mike Flanagan, Baltimore	23	Ron Guidry, New York	2.78	Nolan Ryan, California	223
1980	Steve Stone, Baltimore	25	Rudy May, New York	2.47	Len Barker, Cleveland	187
1981	Steve McCatty, Oak.	14	Steve McCatty, Oak.	2.32	Len Barker, Cleveland	127
1982	LaMarr Hoyt, Chicago	19	Rick Sutcliffe, Cleveland	2.96	Floyd Bannister, Seattle	209
1983	LaMarr Hoyt, Chicago	24	Rick Honeycutt, Texas.	2.42	Jack Morris, Detroit	232
1984	Mike Boddicker, Baltimore	20	Mike Boddicker, Baltimore	2.79	Mark Langston, Seattle	204
1985	Ron Guidry, New York	22	Dave Stieb, Toronto	2.48	Bert Blyleven, Cleve.-Minn.	206
1986	Roger Clemens, Boston	24	Roger Clemens, Boston	2.48	Mark Langston, Seattle	245
1987	Two tied at	20	Jimmy Key, Toronto.	2.76	Mark Langston, Seattle	262
1988	Frank Viola, Minnesota	24	Allan Anderson, Minnesota	2.45	Roger Clemens, Boston	291
1989	Bret Saberhagen, Kansas City	23	Bret Saberhagen, Kansas City	2.16	Nolan Ryan, Texas	301
1990	Bob Welch, Oakland	27	Roger Clemens, Boston	1.93	Nolan Ryan, Texas	232
1991	Roger Clemens, Boston	21	Roger Clemens, Boston	2.62	Roger Clemens, Boston	241
1992	Two tied at	21	Roger Clemens, Boston	2.41	Randy Johnson, Seattle	241
1993	Jack McDowell, Chicago	22	Kevin Appier, Kansas City	2.56	Randy Johnson, Seattle	308
1994	Jimmy Key, New York	17	Steve Ontiveros, Oakland	2.65	Randy Johnson, Seattle	204
1995	Mike Mussina, Baltimore	19	Randy Johnson, Seattle	2.48	Randy Johnson, Seattle	294
1996	Andy Pettitte, New York	21	Juan Guzman, Toronto.	2.93	Roger Clemens, Boston	257
1997	Roger Clemens, Boston	21	Roger Clemens, Toronto.	2.05	Roger Clemens, Boston	292
1998	Three tied at	20	Roger Clemens, Toronto.	2.65	Roger Clemens, Toronto	271
1999	Pedro Martinez, Boston.	23	Pedro Martinez, Boston.	2.07	Pedro Martinez, Boston	313
2000	Two tied at	20	Pedro Martinez, Boston.	1.74	Pedro Martinez, Boston	284
2001	Mark Mulder, Oakland	21	Freddy Garcia, Seattle	3.05	Hideo Nomo, Boston	220

Reliever Eddie Guardado had been on the team the longest—his rookie year was 1993, the first of eight straight losing seasons. "Even when we weren't in contention, we didn't play this bad," he said as the team hit the skids.

Tom Kelly: Retired after 15 years

Cleveland passed the Twins and won the division. Minnesota played for pride and second place in its final series against the White Sox. The Twins won two of three and ended the year 85-77, two games ahead of Chicago.

"It was fun to have a chance to manage," Minnesota manager Tom Kelly said. "It has been a few years since I had that opportunity. Our greatest accomplishment this year is we got the fans in Minnesota interested in baseball again."

Kelly announced his retirement less than a week after the season. His 15 years with Minnesota had been the longest tenure of any active head coach in major professional sports, and under Kelly the Twins won two World Series titles. The Twins were in no hurry to name a replacement for Kelly, as they were one of the teams mentioned most prominently for contraction.

The Indians added power in the offseason after losing Manny Ramirez to free agency. They signed 32-year-old Juan Gonzalez for $10 million for one year after his disappointing 2000 for the Tigers. Gonzalez rebounded and hit .325-35-140. Jim Thome set career highs with 49 homers and 124 RBIs. Bartolo Colon (14-12) and rookie C.C. Sabathia (17-5) anchored the rotation.

Cleveland took Seattle to the limit in the Division Series before losing 3-1 in Game Five.

General manager John Hart announced in the middle of the year he would retire at season's end. Hart did leave the Indians, but not baseball. Shortly after the season, the Rangers hired him as GM to replace Doug Melvin. In Cleveland, Hart orchestrated six Central Division championships in seven years and two World Series appearances. New GM Mark Shapiro and owner Larry Dolan, who bought the team in 2000 for $323 million, spelled out plans for the next few years after the season ended: The era of big contracts was over.

"We will spend as much as we make," Dolan said, with the Indians' payroll expected to drop from $92 million to roughly $75 million for 2002.

John Hart

Around the AL

■ Joe Torre joined John McGraw (New York Giants 1921-24), Joe McCarthy (Yankees 1936-39) and Casey Stengel (Yankees 1949-53 and 1955-58) as the only managers to win four straight pennants.

■ Sure there was turmoil with the Red Sox in 2001. But Helen Robinson, 85, was one in the front office whom all the players adored. She was the switchboard operator for the team for 60 years until she died Oct. 3. Robinson knitted sweaters for the players and had helped the equipment manager sew American flags on the backs of uniforms. She worked the switchboard until the day before she died.

■ The Angels are bringing back the halo in 2002. After five seasons wearing a Disney-designed hat with an angel's wing, Anaheim will restore the halo that was on the hat from the team's start in 1961 until 1996.

■ Gord Ash of the Blue Jays and Melvin of the Rangers were AL general managers fired in 2001—both during the final week of the season. Ash was on the job for seven years, as Toronto went 465-489. Melvin also led the Rangers (491-463) for seven years.

■ Clemens struck out 213, which moved him to third on the all-time list (3,717) behind Steve Carlton (4,136) and Nolan Ryan (5,714).

AL: BEST TOOLS

A Baseball America survey of American League managers, conducted at midseason 2001, ranked AL players with the best tools:

BEST HITTER
1. Manny Ramírez, Red Sox
2. Ichiro Suzuki, Mariners
3. Edgar Martinez, Mariners

BEST POWER HITTER
1. Manny Ramírez, Red Sox
2. Juan Gonzalez, Indians
3. Carlos Delgado, Blue Jays

BEST BUNTER
1. Roberto Alomar, Indians
2. Omar Vizquel, Indians
3. Ichiro Suzuki, Mariners

BEST HIT-AND-RUN BATTER
1. Roberto Alomar, Indians
2. Derek Jeter, Yankees
3. Edgar Martinez, Seattle

BEST BASERUNNER
1. Ichiro Suzuki, Mariners
2. Roberto Alomar, Indians
3. Mark McLemore, Mariners

FASTEST BASERUNNER
1. Ichiro Suzuki, Mariners
2. Kenny Lofton, Indians
3. Cristian Guzman, Twins

BEST PITCHER
1. Pedro Martinez, Red Sox
2. Roger Clemens, Yankees
3. Joe Mays, Twins

BEST FASTBALL
1. Pedro Martinez, Red Sox
2. Troy Percival, Angels
3. Bartolo Colon, Indians

BEST CURVEBALL
1. Mike Mussina, Yankees
2. Aaron Sele, Mariners
3. Troy Percival, Angels

BEST SLIDER
1. Jeff Nelson, Mariners
2. Pedro Martinez, Red Sox
3. Tim Hudson, Athletics

BEST CHANGEUP
1. Pedro Martinez, Red Sox
2. Brad Radke, Twins
3. Jamie Moyer, Mariners

BEST CONTROL
1. Pedro Martinez, Red Sox
2. Brad Radke, Twins
3. Mike Mussina, Yankees

BEST PICKOFF MOVE
1. Andy Pettitte, Yankees
2. Chris Michalak, Rangers
3. Kenny Rogers, Rangers

BEST RELIEVER
1. Mariano Rivera, Yankees
2. Troy Percival, Angels
3. Kazuhiro Sasaki, Mariners

BEST DEFENSIVE C
1. Ivan Rodriguez, Rangers
2. Brandon Inge, Tigers
3. Dan Wilson, Mariners

BEST DEFENSIVE 1B
1. John Olerud, Mariners
2. Rafael Palmeiro, Rangers
3. Doug Mientkiewicz, Twins

BEST DEFENSIVE 2B
1. Roberto Alomar, Indians
2. Bret Boone, Mariners
3. Jerry Hairston, Orioles

BEST DEFENSIVE 3B
1. Scott Brosius, Yankees
2. Troy Glaus, Angels
3. Travis Fryman, Indians

BEST DEFENSIVE SS
1. Omar Vizquel, Indians
2. Alex Rodriguez, Mariners
3. Rey Sanchez, Royals

BEST INFIELD ARM
1. Alex Rodriguez, Mariners
2. Troy Glaus, Angels
3. Miguel Tejada, Athletics

BEST DEFENSIVE OF
1. Torii Hunter, Twins
2. Mike Cameron, Mariners
3. Ichiro Suzuki, Mariners

BEST OUTFIELD ARM
1. Ichiro Suzuki, Mariners
2. Raul Mondesi, Blue Jays
3. Jermaine Dye, Athletics

MOST EXCITING PLAYER
1. Ichiro Suzuki, Mariners
2. Alex Rodriguez, Rangers
3. Manny Ramirez, Red Sox

BEST MANAGER
1. Joe Torre, Yankees
2. Lou Piniella, Mariners
3. Tom Kelly, Twins

MAJOR LEAGUES

BATTING

GAMES
Carlos Delgado, Blue Jays	162
Terrence Long, Athletics	162
Alex Rodriguez, Rangers	162
Miguel Tejada, Athletics	162
Garret Anderson, Angels	161
Troy Glaus, Angels	161

AT-BATS
Ichiro Suzuki, Mariners	692
Garret Anderson, Angels	672
Johnny Damon, Athletics	644
Shannon Stewart, Blue Jays	640
Alex Gonzalez, Blue Jays	636

RUNS
Alex Rodriguez, Rangers	133
Ichiro Suzuki, Mariners	127
Bret Boone, Mariners	118
Roberto Alomar, Indians	113
Derek Jeter, Yankees	110

HITS
Ichiro Suzuki, Mariners	242
Bret Boone, Mariners	206
Shannon Stewart, Blue Jays	202
Alex Rodriguez, Rangers	201
Garret Anderson, Angels	194

TOTAL BASES
Alex Rodriguez, Rangers	393
Bret Boone, Mariners	360
Jason Giambi, Athletics	343
Rafael Palmeiro, Rangers	338
Jim Thome, Indians	328

EXTRA-BASE HITS
Jason Giambi, Athletics	87
Alex Rodriguez, Rangers	87
Troy Glaus, Angels	81
Rafael Palmeiro, Rangers	80
Bret Boone, Mariners	77

SINGLES
Ichiro Suzuki, Mariners	192
Shannon Stewart, Blue Jays	139
David Eckstein, Angels	134
Derek Jeter, Yankees	132
Bret Boone, Mariners	129

DOUBLES
Jason Giambi, Athletics	47
Mike Sweeney, Royals	46

Alex Rodriguez: 52 homers

Shannon Stewart, Blue Jays	44
Eric Chavez, Athletics	43
Ray Durham, White Sox	42

TRIPLES
Cristian Guzman, Twins	14
Roberto Alomar, Indians	12
Carlos Beltran, Royals	12
Roger Cedeno, Tigers	11
Ray Durham, White Sox	10

HOME RUNS
Alex Rodriguez, Rangers	52
Jim Thome, Indians	49
Rafael Palmeiro, Rangers	47
Troy Glaus, Angels	41
Manny Ramirez, Red Sox	41

HOME RUN RATIO
(At-Bats per Home Run)
Jim Thome, Indians	10.7
Alex Rodriguez, Rangers	12.2
Rafael Palmeiro, Rangers	12.8
Manny Ramirez, Red Sox	12.9
Jason Giambi, Athletics	13.7

RUNS BATTED IN
Bret Boone, Mariners	141
Juan Gonzalez, Indians	140
Alex Rodriguez, Rangers	135
Manny Ramirez, Red Sox	125
Jim Thome, Indians	124

SACRIFICE BUNTS
David Eckstein, Angels	16
Omar Vizquel, Indians	15
Chris Singleton, White Sox	14
Mark Johnson, White Sox	10
Six tied at	9

SACRIFICE FLIES
Juan Gonzalez, Indians	16
Bret Boone, Mariners	13
Mike Cameron, Mariners	13
Jermaine Dye, Royals/Athletics	11
Alex Gonzalez, Blue Jays	10

HIT BY PITCH
David Eckstein, Angels	21
Frank Menechino, Athletics	19
Carlos Delgado, Blue Jays	16
Einar Diaz, Indians	16
Alex Rodriguez, Rangers	16

WALKS
Jason Giambi, Athletics	129
Carlos Delgado, Blue Jays	111
Jim Thome, Indians	111
Troy Glaus, Angels	107
Rafael Palmeiro, Rangers	101

INTENTIONAL WALKS
Manny Ramirez, Red Sox	25
Jason Giambi, Athletics	24
Carlos Delgado, Blue Jays	22
John Olerud, Mariners	19
Mike Sweeney, Royals	13
Jim Thome, Indians	13

STRIKEOUTS
Jim Thome, Indians	185
Ben Grieve, Devil Rays	159
Troy Glaus, Angels	158
Mike Cameron, Mariners	155
Alex Gonzalez, Blue Jays	149

TOUGHEST TO STRIKE OUT
(Plate Appearances per SO)
Ichiro Suzuki, Mariners	13.9
David Eckstein, Angels	11.1
Johnny Damon, Athletics	10.3
Jose Macias, Tigers	9.9

Jim Thome: 49 home runs, 111 walks

RICK BATTLE

Mike Sweeney, Royals	9.9

STOLEN BASES
Ichiro Suzuki, Mariners	56
Roger Cedeno, Tigers	55
Alfonso Soriano, Yankees	43
Mark McLemore, Mariners	39
Chuck Knoblauch, Yankees	38

CAUGHT STEALING
Roger Cedeno, Tigers	15
Alfonso Soriano, Yankees	14
Ichiro Suzuki, Mariners	14
Johnny Damon, Athletics	12
Bob Higginson, Tigers	12

GIDP
John Olerud, Mariners	21
Paul O'Neill, Yankees	20
Darrin Fletcher, Blue Jays	18
Juan Gonzalez, Indians	18
Aubrey Huff, Devil Rays	18

HITTING STREAKS
Ichiro Suzuki, Mariners	23
Marty Cordova, Indians	22
Rey Sanchez, Royals	21
Ichiro Suzuki, Mariners	21
Jose Cruz, Blue Jays	19

MULTIPLE-HIT GAMES
Ichiro Suzuki, Mariners	75
Bret Boone, Mariners	65
Shannon Stewart, Blue Jays	60
Derek Jeter, Yankees	58
Garret Anderson, Angels	56

SLUGGING PERCENTAGE
Jason Giambi, Athletics	.660
Jim Thome, Indians	.624
Alex Rodriguez, Rangers	.622
Manny Ramirez, Red Sox	.609
Juan Gonzalez, Indians	.590

ON-BASE PERCENTAGE
Jason Giambi, Athletics	.477
Edgar Martinez, Mariners	.423
Jim Thome, Indians	.416
Roberto Alomar, Indians	.415
Carlos Delgado, Blue Jays	.408

PITCHING

WINS
Mark Mulder, Athletics	21
Roger Clemens, Yankees	20
Jamie Moyer, Mariners	20

LARRY GOREN

Freddy Garcia, Mariners 18
Tim Hudson, Athletics 18

LOSSES
Jose Mercedes, Orioles 17
Chad Durbin, Royals 16
Jeff Weaver, Tigers 16
Jeff Suppan, Royals 14
Joe Mays, Twins 13
Bryan Rekar, Devil Rays 13
Ismael Valdes, Angels 13

WINNING PERCENTAGE
Roger Clemens, Yankees .... .870
Paul Abbott, Mariners .... .810
C.C. Sabathia, Indians .... .773
Jamie Moyer, Mariners .... .769
Freddy Garcia, Mariners .... .750

GAMES
Paul Quantrill, Blue Jays 80
Mike Stanton, Yankees 76
Jason Grimsley, Royals 73
Keith Foulke, White Sox 72
Arthur Rhodes, Mariners 72

GAMES STARTED
Tim Hudson, Athletics 35
Barry Zito, Athletics 35
Nine tied at 34

COMPLETE GAMES
Steve Sparks, Tigers 8
Mark Mulder, Athletics 6
Brad Radke, Twins 6
Jeff Weaver, Tigers 5
Four tied at 4

SHUTOUTS
Mark Mulder, Athletics 4
Freddy Garcia, Mariners 3
Mike Mussina, Yankees 3
Six tied at 2

GAMES FINISHED
Keith Foulke, White Sox 69
Mariano Rivera, Yankees 66
Kazuhiro Sasaki, Mariners 63
Billy Koch, Blue Jays 56
Bob Wickman, Indians 56

SAVES
Mariano Rivera, Yankees 50
Kazuhiro Sasaki, Mariners 45
Keith Foulke, White Sox 42
Troy Percival, Angels 39
Billy Koch, Blue Jays 36

INNINGS
Freddy Garcia, Mariners 239
Tim Hudson, Athletics 235
Joe Mays, Twins 234
Steve Sparks, Tigers 232
Mark Mulder, Athletics 229
Jeff Weaver, Tigers 229
Mike Mussina, Yankees 229

HITS ALLOWED
Rick Helling, Rangers 256
Steve Sparks, Tigers 244
Esteban Loaiza, Blue Jays 239
Brad Radke, Twins 235
Jeff Weaver, Tigers 235

RUNS ALLOWED
Rick Helling, Rangers 134
Jose Mercedes, Orioles 125
Scott Schoeneweis, Angels 122
Jeff Suppan, Royals 120
Jeff Weaver, Tigers 116

HOME RUNS ALLOWED
Rick Helling, Rangers 38
Eric Milton, Twins 35
Ryan Rupe, Devil Rays 30
Chris Carpenter, Blue Jays 29
Jason Johnson, Orioles 28

WALKS
Hideo Nomo, Red Sox 96
C.C. Sabathia, Indians 95

Mark Mulder: Four shutouts

Bartolo Colon, Indians 90
Paul Abbott, Mariners 87
Barry Zito, Athletics 80

FEWEST WALKS PER 9 INNINGS
Brad Radke, Twins 1.04
Mike Mussina, Yankees 1.65
Andy Pettitte, Yankees 1.84
Esteban Loaiza, Blue Jays 1.89
Jamie Moyer, Mariners 1.89

HIT BATSMEN
Tim Wakefield, Red Sox 18
Chris Carpenter, Blue Jays 16
Scott Schoeneweis, Angels 14
Jeff Weaver, Tigers 14
Jason Johnson, Orioles 13
Paul Wilson, Devil Rays 13
Barry Zito, Athletics 13

STRIKEOUTS
Hideo Nomo, Red Sox 220
Mike Mussina, Yankees 214
Roger Clemens, Yankees 213
Barry Zito, Athletics 205
Bartolo Colon, Indians 201

STRIKEOUTS PER 9 INNINGS
Hideo Nomo, Red Sox 10.00
Roger Clemens, Yankees 8.70
Barry Zito, Athletics 8.61
C.C. Sabathia, Indians 8.53
Mike Mussina, Yankees 8.42

PICKOFFS
Doug Davis, Rangers 10
Chris Michalak, Blue Jays/Rangers 9
Jarrod Washburn, Angels 8
Ted Lilly, Yankees 6
Mark Mulder, Athletics 6

WILD PITCHES
Roger Clemens, Yankees 14
Kip Wells, White Sox 14
Dan Reichert, Royals 12
Paul Abbott, Mariners 11
Joe Mays, Twins 11
Tanyon Sturtze, Devil Rays 11

BALKS
Chris Michalak, Blue Jays/Rangers 6
Mark Buehrle, White Sox 5
Juan Moreno, Rangers 3
C.C. Sabathia, Indians 3
Steve Woodard, Indians 3

OPPONENTS BATTING AVERAGE
Kelvim Escobar, Blue Jays .... .204
Freddy Garcia, Mariners .... .225
C.C. Sabathia, Indians .... .228
Mark Buehrle, White Sox .... .230
Barry Zito, Athletics .... .230

FIELDING

PITCHER
PCT Andy Pettitte, Yankees 1.000
PO Freddy Garcia, Mariners 30
A Mark Buehrle, White Sox 49
E Ramon Ortiz, Angels 6
TC Freddy Garcia, Mariners 70
    Tim Hudson, Athletics 70
DP Chris Carpenter, Blue Jays 6

CATCHER
PCT Dan Wilson, Mariners .... .999
PO Jorge Posada, Yankees 997
A Einar Diaz, Indians 92
E Ramon Hernandez, Athletics 11
    Jorge Posada, Yankees 11
TC Einar Diaz, Indians 1059
    Jorge Posada, Yankees 1059
DP Ramon Hernandez, Athletics 15
PB Jorge Posada, Yankees 18

FIRST BASE
PCT Scott Spiezio, Angels .... .999
PO Carlos Delgado, Blue Jays 1517
A John Olerud, Mariners 120
E Mike Sweeney, Royals 12
TC Carlos Delgado, Blue Jays 1629
DP Carlos Delgado, Blue Jays 165

SECOND BASE
PCT Roberto Alomar, Indians .... .993
PO Jerry Hairston, Orioles 323
A Damion Easley, Tigers 496
E Jerry Hairston, Orioles 19
    Alfonso Soriano, Yankees 19
TC Jerry Hairston, Orioles 800
DP Damion Easley, Tigers 113

THIRD BASE
PCT Eric Chavez, Athletics .... .972
PO Joe Randa, Royals 111
A Eric Chavez, Athletics 321
E Scott Brosius, Yankees 22
TC Eric Chavez, Athletics 431
DP Joe Randa, Royals 30

SHORTSTOP
PCT Rey Sanchez, Royals .... .994
PO Alex Rodriguez, Rangers 280
A Alex Gonzalez, Blue Jays 510
E Cristian Guzman, Twins 21
TC Alex Gonzalez, Blue Jays 768
DP Alex Gonzalez, Blue Jays 120

OUTFIELD
PCT Chris Richard, Orioles 1.000
PO Torii Hunter, Twins 460
A Raul Mondesi, Blue Jays 17
E Roger Cedeno, Tigers 12
TC Torii Hunter, Twins 478
DP Carlos Beltran, Royals 6

Hideo Nomo: 220 strikeouts

2001 AMERICAN LEAGUE STATISTICS

CLUB BATTING

	AVG	G	AB	R	H	2B	3B	HR	BB	SO	SB
Seattle	.288	162	5680	927	1637	310	38	169	614	989	174
Cleveland	.278	162	5600	897	1559	294	37	212	577	1076	79
Texas	.275	162	5685	890	1566	326	23	246	548	1093	97
Minnesota	.272	162	5560	771	1514	328	38	164	495	1083	146
Chicago	.268	162	5464	798	1463	300	29	214	520	998	123
New York	.267	161	5577	804	1488	289	20	203	519	1035	161
Boston	.266	161	5605	772	1493	316	29	198	520	1131	46
Kansas City	.266	162	5643	729	1503	277	37	152	406	898	100
Oakland	.264	162	5573	884	1469	334	22	199	640	1021	68
Toronto	.263	162	5663	767	1489	287	36	195	470	1094	156
Anaheim	.261	162	5551	691	1447	275	26	158	494	1001	116
Detroit	.260	162	5537	724	1439	291	60	139	466	972	133
Tampa Bay	.258	162	5524	672	1426	311	21	121	456	1116	115
Baltimore	.248	162	5472	687	1359	262	24	136	514	989	133

CLUB PITCHING

	ERA	G	CG	SHO	SV	IP	H	R	ER	BB	SO
Seattle	3.54	162	8	14	56	1465.0	1293	627	576	465	1051
Oakland	3.58	162	13	9	44	1463.1	1384	645	583	440	1117
New York	4.02	161	7	9	57	1451.1	1429	713	649	465	1266
Boston	4.14	161	3	9	48	1448.0	1412	745	667	544	1259
Anaheim	4.20	162	6	1	43	1437.2	1452	730	671	525	947
Toronto	4.28	162	7	10	41	1462.2	1553	753	696	490	1041
Minnesota	4.51	162	12	8	45	1441.1	1494	766	722	445	965
Chicago	4.55	162	8	7	51	1433.1	1465	795	725	500	921
Cleveland	4.64	162	3	4	42	1446.2	1512	821	746	573	1218
Baltimore	4.67	162	10	6	31	1432.1	1504	829	744	528	938
Kansas City	4.87	162	5	1	30	1440.0	1537	858	779	576	911
Tampa Bay	4.94	162	1	6	30	1423.2	1513	887	781	569	1030
Detroit	5.00	162	16	2	34	1429.1	1624	876	795	553	859
Texas	5.71	162	4	3	37	1438.1	1670	968	913	596	951

CLUB FIELDING

	PCT	PO	A	E	DP		PCT	PO	A	E	DP
Seattle	.986	4395	1534	83	137	Boston	.981	4344	1558	113	129
Toronto	.985	4388	1831	97	184	Texas	.981	4315	1638	114	167
Anaheim	.983	4313	1690	103	142	Chicago	.981	4300	1731	118	149
Cleveland	.982	4340	1610	107	137	Oakland	.980	4390	1756	125	151
Minnesota	.982	4324	1542	108	118	Baltimore	.979	4297	1598	125	137
New York	.982	4354	1529	109	132	Detroit	.979	4288	1775	131	164
Kansas City	.981	4320	1801	117	204	Tampa Bay	.977	4271	1531	139	144

INDIVIDUAL BATTING LEADERS
(Minimum 502 Plate Appearances)

	AVG	G	AB	R	H	2B	3B	HR	RBI	BB	SO	SB
Suzuki, Ichiro, Seattle	.350	157	692	127	242	34	8	8	69	30	53	56
Giambi, Jason, Oakland	.342	154	520	109	178	47	2	38	120	129	83	2
Alomar, Roberto, Cleveland	.336	157	575	113	193	34	12	20	100	80	71	30
Boone, Bret, Seattle	.331	158	623	118	206	37	3	37	141	40	110	5
Catalanotto, Frank, Texas	.330	133	463	77	153	31	5	11	54	39	55	15
Gonzalez, Juan, Cleveland	.325	140	532	97	173	34	1	35	140	41	94	1
Rodriguez, Alex, Texas	.318	162	632	133	201	34	1	52	135	75	131	18
Stewart, Shannon, Toronto	.316	155	640	103	202	44	7	12	60	46	72	27
Conine, Jeff, Baltimore	.311	139	524	75	163	23	2	14	97	64	75	12
Jeter, Derek, New York	.311	150	614	110	191	35	3	21	74	56	99	27

INDIVIDUAL PITCHING LEADERS
(Minimum 162 Innings)

	W	L	ERA	G	GS	CG	SV	IP	H	R	ER	BB	SO
Garcia, Freddy, Seattle	18	6	3.05	34	34	4	0	239	199	88	81	69	163
Hudson, Tim, Oakland	18	9	3.37	35	35	3	0	235	216	100	88	71	181
Mays, Joe, Minnesota	17	13	3.16	34	34	4	0	234	205	87	82	64	123
Mulder, Mark, Oakland	21	8	3.45	34	34	6	0	229	214	92	88	51	153
Mussina, Mike, New York	17	11	3.15	34	34	4	0	229	202	87	80	42	214
Buehrle, Mark, Chicago	16	8	3.29	32	32	4	0	221	188	89	81	48	126
Clemens, Roger, New York	20	3	3.51	33	33	0	0	220	205	94	86	72	213
Zito, Barry, Oakland	17	8	3.49	35	35	3	0	214	184	92	83	80	205
Moyer, Jamie, Seattle	20	6	3.43	33	33	1	0	210	187	84	80	44	119
Lidle, Cory, Oakland	13	6	3.59	29	29	1	0	188	170	84	75	47	118

CLEVELAND

Player, Pos.	AVG	G	AB	R	H	2B	3B	HR	RBI	BB	SO	SB
Jolbert Cabrera, lf	1.000	2	1	1	1	0	0	0	1	0	0	0
Omar Vizquel, ss	.409	5	22	2	9	1	1	0	6	1	1	1
Juan Gonzalez, rf	.348	5	23	4	8	3	0	2	5	0	7	0
Russell Branyan, ph-lf	.333	2	3	1	1	0	0	0	0	0	0	0
Marty Cordova, lf	.333	3	9	0	3	0	0	0	1	0	3	0
Ellis Burks, dh	.316	5	19	4	6	1	0	1	1	1	3	0
Einar Diaz, c	.312	5	16	3	5	0	0	0	2	2	1	0
Roberto Alomar, 2b	.190	5	21	3	4	3	0	0	3	2	5	0
Travis Fryman, 3b	.176	5	17	4	3	1	0	0	2	2	7	0
Jim Thome, 1b	.158	5	19	2	3	0	0	1	1	8	8	0
Kenny Lofton, cf	.105	5	19	2	2	0	0	1	3	3	5	0
Wil Cordero, ph-lf	.000	2	4	0	0	0	0	0	0	0	2	0
Totals	.260	5	173	26	45	9	1	5	25	13	43	1

Pitcher	W	L	ERA	G	GS	SV	IP	H	R	ER	BB	SO
David Riske	0	0	0.00	3	0	0	4	2	0	0	1	5
Dave Burba	0	0	0.00	1	0	0	1	0	0	0	0	1
John Rocker	0	0	0.00	1	0	0	1	1	0	0	0	1
Bob Wickman	0	0	0.00	1	0	1	0	0	0	0	0	2
Bartolo Colon	1	1	1.84	2	2	0	15	12	3	3	6	13
Danys Baez	0	0	2.45	3	0	0	4	4	1	1	0	6
C.C. Sabathia	1	0	3.00	1	1	0	6	6	2	2	5	5
Paul Shuey	0	0	6.75	2	0	0	1	3	1	1	0	2
Chuck Finley	0	2	7.27	2	2	0	9	9	7	7	6	10
Ricardo Rincon	0	0	9.00	3	0	0	2	2	2	2	0	3
Totals	2	3	3.35	5	5	0	43	39	16	16	18	48

SCORE BY INNINGS

Cleveland	235 314 260—26
Seattle	520 010 512—16

E—Garcia, McLemore, Suzuki, Boone, Buhner, Vizquel, Diaz, Colon. **DP**—Cleveland 3, Seattle 4. **LOB**—Cleveland 30, Seattle 35. **CS**—Suzuki 2, Cameron. **SH**—Javier 2. **SF**—Lofton, Bell. **HBP**—Cabrera (by Paniagua), Cameron (by Finley). **IBB**—Martinez (by Sabathia). **WP**—Rhodes.

NEW YORK VS. OAKLAND
COMPOSITE BOX

NEW YORK

Player, Pos.	AVG	G	AB	R	H	2B	3B	HR	RBI	BB	SO	SB
Derek Jeter, ss	.444	5	18	2	8	1	0	0	1	1	0	0
Jorge Posada, c	.444	5	18	3	8	1	0	1	2	2	2	1
Chuck Knoblauch, lf	.273	5	22	1	6	1	0	0	1	0	0	1
Shane Spencer, rf-ph	.250	3	8	1	2	1	0	0	1	4	0	0
David Justice, dh-rf	.231	4	13	3	3	0	1	1	2	5	0	0
Alfonso Soriano, 2b	.222	5	18	2	4	0	0	3	3	1	5	2
Bernie Williams, cf	.222	5	18	4	4	3	0	0	5	3	3	0
Randy Velarde, dh	.200	2	5	0	1	0	0	0	0	0	1	0
Tino Martinez, 1b	.111	5	18	1	2	0	0	1	2	1	6	0
Paul O'Neill, rf-dh	.091	3	11	1	1	0	0	0	0	0	0	0
Scott Brosius, 3b	.059	5	17	0	1	0	0	0	1	0	3	0
Clay Bellinger, pr	.000	1	0	0	0	0	0	0	0	0	0	0
Totals	.241	5	166	18	40	8	1	3	16	11	29	4

Pitcher	W	L	ERA	G	GS	SV	IP	H	R	ER	BB	SO
Mike Mussina	1	0	0.00	1	1	0	7	4	0	0	1	4
Mariano Rivera	0	0	0.00	3	0	2	5	4	1	0	0	4
Mike Stanton	1	0	0.00	3	0	0	5	3	0	0	0	1
Ramiro Mendoza	0	0	0.00	3	0	0	4	2	0	0	1	5
Andy Pettitte	0	1	1.42	1	1	0	6	7	1	1	2	4
Orlando Hernandez	1	0	3.18	1	1	0	6	8	2	2	2	5
Roger Clemens	0	1	5.40	2	2	0	8	9	5	5	4	6
Sterling Hitchcock	0	0	6.00	1	0	0	3	5	2	2	0	2
Jay Witasick	0	0	13.50	1	0	0	1	1	1	1	1	0
Totals	3	2	2.20	5	5	2	45	43	12	11	11	31

OAKLAND

Player, Pos.	AVG	G	AB	R	H	2B	3B	HR	RBI	BB	SO	SB
Johnny Damon, cf	.409	5	22	3	9	2	1	0	0	1	1	2
Terrence Long, lf	.389	5	18	3	7	3	0	2	3	1	2	0
Jason Giambi, 1b	.353	5	17	2	6	0	0	1	4	4	2	0
F.P. Santangelo, 2b	.333	2	3	0	1	1	0	0	0	0	0	0
Jeremy Giambi, dh	.308	5	13	0	4	1	0	0	2	1	0	1
Miguel Tejada, ss	.286	5	21	1	6	3	0	1	0	3	3	0
Jermaine Dye, rf	.231	4	13	0	3	2	0	0	2	2	0	0
Ron Gant, dh	.182	4	11	1	2	0	0	1	1	0	3	0
Eric Chavez, 3b	.143	5	21	0	3	1	0	0	0	0	5	0
Greg Myers, ph-c	.143	3	7	0	1	0	0	0	0	0	3	0
Frank Menechino, 2b	.083	4	12	2	1	0	0	0	0	1	4	0
Ramon Hernandez, c	.000	5	10	0	0	0	0	0	0	1	4	0
Olmedo Saenz, ph	.000	3	4	0	0	0	0	0	0	1	0	0
Eric Byrnes, ph	.000	2	2	0	0	0	0	0	0	0	1	0
Totals	.247	5	174	12	43	13	1	4	11	11	31	3

Juan Gonzalez: Hit .325-35-140 for Indians

LARRY GOREN

AMERICAN LEAGUE
DIVISION SERIES
SEATTLE VS. CLEVELAND
COMPOSITE BOX

SEATTLE

Player, Pos.	AVG	G	AB	R	H	2B	3B	HR	RBI	BB	SO	SB
Ichiro Suzuki, rf	.600	5	20	4	12	1	0	0	2	1	0	1
David Bell, 3b	.313	5	16	2	5	1	0	1	2	1	6	0
Edgar Martinez, dh	.313	5	16	3	5	1	0	2	5	5	2	1
Stan Javier, lf	.250	4	8	2	2	1	0	0	0	2	1	0
Mike Cameron, cf	.222	5	18	2	4	3	0	1	3	2	7	0
Dan Wilson, c	.200	5	15	0	3	1	0	0	0	0	5	0
John Olerud, 1b	.176	5	17	1	3	0	0	0	1	3	5	0
Mark McLemore, ss	.167	5	18	0	3	0	0	0	3	1	8	0
Bret Boone, 2b	.095	5	21	1	2	0	0	0	0	1	11	1
Jay Buhner, lf	.000	2	3	0	0	0	0	0	0	2	1	0
Tom Lampkin, c	.000	2	2	0	0	0	0	0	0	0	2	0
Al Martin, ph	.000	3	2	1	0	0	0	0	0	0	0	0
Charles Gipson, ph	.000	1	1	0	0	0	0	0	0	0	0	0
Ed Sprague, ph	.000	1	1	0	0	0	0	0	0	0	0	0
Ramon Vazquez, ss	.000	1	0	0	0	0	0	0	0	0	0	0
Totals	.247	5	158	16	39	8	0	4	16	18	48	3

Pitcher	W	L	ERA	G	GS	SV	IP	H	R	ER	BB	SO
John Halama	0	0	0.00	2	0	0	3	3	0	0	0	3
Jeff Nelson	0	0	0.00	3	0	0	3	1	0	0	1	5
Kazuhiro Sasaki	0	0	0.00	3	0	1	3	1	0	0	0	5
Arthur Rhodes	0	0	0.00	3	0	0	3	1	0	0	0	1
Norm Charlton	0	0	0.00	1	0	0	2	0	0	0	0	2
Jamie Moyer	2	0	1.50	2	2	0	12	8	2	2	2	10
Freddy Garcia	1	1	3.86	2	2	0	12	13	6	5	3	13
Aaron Sele	0	1	9.00	1	1	0	2	5	4	2	0	0
Paul Abbott	0	0	24.00	1	0	0	3	9	8	8	5	3
Jose Paniagua	0	0	27.00	2	0	0	2	4	6	6	2	1
Totals	3	2	4.70	5	5	1	44	45	26	23	13	43

Pitcher	W	L	ERA	G	GS	SV	IP	H	R	ER	BB	SO
Chad Bradford	0	0	0.00	1	0	0	1	0	0	0	0	1
Mark Guthrie	0	0	0.00	2	0	0	3	0	0	0	0	1
Jason Isringhausen	0	0	0.00	2	0	2	2	1	0	0	1	3
Mike Magnante	0	0	0.00	1	0	0	1	3	0	0	1	1
Tim Hudson	1	0	0.93	2	1	0	10	8	1	1	1	5
Barry Zito	0	1	1.13	1	1	0	8	2	1	1	1	6
Mark Mulder	1	1	2.45	2	2	0	11	14	5	3	2	7
Jim Mecir	0	0	5.40	2	0	0	3	4	2	2	0	4
Cory Lidle	0	1	10.80	1	1	0	3	5	6	4	3	0
Jeff Tam	0	0	18.00	1	0	0	1	3	2	2	0	0
Erik Hiljus	0	0	27.00	1	0	0	0	0	1	1	2	0
Totals	2	3	2.86	5	5	2	44	40	18	14	11	29

SCORE BY INNINGS

New York	043 421 022—18
Oakland	212 210 121—12

E—Menechino, Tejada, Myers, Chavez, Ja. Giambi, Santangelo, Knoblauch, Brosius 3. **DP**—Oakland 4, New York 4. **LOB**—Oakland 43, New York 34. **CS**—Soriano, Jeter, Williams, Knoblauch, Velarde. **SH**—Brosius, Velarde. **SF**—Ja. Giambi, Tejada, Jeter. **HBP**—Martinez 2 (by Mulder, Zito), Brosius (by Mulder), Jeter (by Zito), R. Hernandez (by Clemens), Santangelo (by O. Hernandez), Tejada (by Clemens). **IBB**—Ja. Giambi (by Mendoza). **WP**—O. Hernandez, Clemens.

CHAMPIONSHIP SERIES

NEW YORK VS. SEATTLE

COMPOSITE BOX

NEW YORK

Player, Pos.	AVG	G	AB	R	H	2B	3B	HR	RBI	BB	SO	SB
Enrique Wilson, ph	1.000	1	1	0	1	0	0	0	0	0	0	0
Paul O'Neill, rf	.417	5	12	2	5	0	0	2	3	1	0	0
Alfonso Soriano, 2b	.400	5	15	5	6	0	0	1	2	3	3	2
Chuck Knoblauch, lf	.333	5	18	0	6	1	0	0	3	2	3	0
Shane Spencer, ph-rf ...	.286	5	7	1	2	1	0	0	0	1	1	1
David Justice, dh	.278	5	18	3	5	1	0	0	4	3	1	0
Tino Martinez, 1b	.250	5	20	3	5	1	0	1	3	0	4	0
Bernie Williams, cf	.235	5	17	4	4	0	0	3	5	5	4	0
Jorge Posada, c	.214	5	14	4	3	1	0	0	6	7	0	0
Scott Brosius, 3b	.187	5	16	3	3	2	0	0	2	0	6	0
Derek Jeter, ss	.118	5	17	0	2	0	0	0	2	2	2	0
Clay Bellinger, ph-2b ...	.000	1	1	0	0	0	0	0	0	0	0	0
Todd Greene, ph-c	.000	1	1	0	0	0	0	0	0	0	0	0
Luis Sojo, ph-1b	.000	1	1	0	0	0	0	0	0	0	0	0
Randy Velarde, ph-2b ...	.000	1	1	0	0	0	0	0	0	0	0	0
Totals	.264	5	159	25	42	7	0	7	24	23	31	3

Pitcher	W	L	ERA	G	GS	SV	IP	H	R	ER	BB	SO
Roger Clemens	0	0	0.00	1	1	0	5	1	0	0	4	7
Ramiro Mendoza	0	0	1.69	3	0	0	5	3	1	1	2	4
Mariano Rivera	1	0	1.93	4	0	2	5	2	1	1	1	3
Andy Pettitte	2	0	2.51	2	2	0	14	11	4	4	2	8
Mike Mussina	1	0	3.00	1	1	0	6	4	2	2	1	3
Orlando Hernandez	0	1	7.20	1	1	0	5	5	5	4	5	7
Jay Witasick	0	0	9.00	1	0	0	3	6	3	3	0	2
Mark Wohlers	0	0	13.50	1	0	0	1	3	3	1	1	1
Mike Stanton	0	0	27.00	2	0	0	1	1	3	3	2	0
Totals	4	1	3.80	5	5	2	45	36	22	19	18	35

SEATTLE

Player, Pos.	AVG	G	AB	R	H	2B	3B	HR	RBI	BB	SO	SB
Al Martin, ph-lf	.500	2	2	1	1	0	1	0	0	0	0	0
Jay Buhner, lf-rf	.333	3	6	2	2	0	1	1	1	1	3	0
Bret Boone, 2b	.316	5	19	2	6	0	0	2	6	2	2	0
Carlos Guillen, ss	.250	3	8	1	2	0	0	0	0	0	1	0
Tom Lampkin, c	.250	2	4	0	1	0	0	0	0	1	2	0
Ichiro Suzuki, rf-lf	.222	5	18	3	4	1	0	0	1	4	4	2
Stan Javier, lf-ph	.214	5	14	2	3	0	0	1	2	1	3	1
John Olerud, 1b	.211	5	19	2	4	0	0	1	3	2	4	0

Mariano Rivera: Saved 50 games for Yankees

LARRY GOREN

	AVG	G	AB	R	H	2B	3B	HR	RBI	BB	SO	SB
David Bell, 3b	.187	5	16	1	3	0	0	0	4	0	3	0
Mike Cameron, cf	.176	5	17	3	3	2	0	0	0	4	4	0
Dan Wilson, c	.154	4	13	2	2	0	0	0	0	0	1	0
Edgar Martinez, dh	.150	5	20	1	3	1	0	0	1	6	0	0
Mark McLemore, ss	.143	5	14	1	2	0	1	0	3	2	2	0
Charles Gipson, ph-rf-lf	.000	2	1	1	0	0	0	0	0	0	0	0
Totals	.211	5	171	22	36	4	2	5	20	18	35	3

Pitcher	W	L	ERA	G	GS	SV	IP	H	R	ER	BB	SO
Paul Abbott	0	0	0.00	1	1	0	5	0	0	0	8	2
Norm Charlton	0	0	0.00	2	0	0	2	1	0	0	2	2
Jeff Nelson	0	0	0.00	2	0	0	2	1	0	0	1	3
Jamie Moyer	1	0	2.57	1	1	0	7	4	2	2	1	5
Aaron Sele	0	2	3.60	2	2	0	10	11	8	4	4	5
Freddy Garcia	0	1	3.68	1	1	0	7	7	3	3	4	6
Joel Pineiro	0	0	4.50	1	0	0	2	4	1	1	2	5
Arthur Rhodes	0	0	4.50	2	0	0	2	2	1	1	0	2
Jose Paniagua	0	0	12.27	3	0	0	4	7	5	5	1	1
John Halama	0	0	13.50	2	0	0	2	3	3	3	0	0
Kazuhiro Sasaki	0	1	54.00	1	0	0	0	2	2	2	0	0
Totals	1	4	4.36	5	5	0	43	42	25	21	23	31

SCORE BY INNINGS

New York	244 304 053—25
Seattle	000 237 523—22

E—B. Williams, Soriano, Stanton, Wohlers, Bell. **DP**—New York 4, Seattle 5. **LOB**—New York 34, Seattle 34. **CS**—Knoblauch, T. Martinez, B. Williams. **SH**—Brosius 2, Jeter, Knoblauch, Bell. **SF**—Jeter. **HBP**—Cameron (by Mussina), Justice (by Moyer), Soriano (by Sele). **IBB**—Suzuki 2 (by Mendoza, Stanton), Posada (by Charlton). **WP**—Rivera 2, Clemens, Pineiro, Paniagua.

BY GEOFF WILSON

The postseason party in the National League had its usual cast of characters in 2001.

The perennial but aging Braves were there again, the up-and-coming young talent of the Astros again yearned to break through, and the Cardinals brought their classic blend of pitching and hitting. But in the end the story was much the same as it always is—pitching wins championships, and so does money. And in that sense, the Diamondbacks prevailed.

Behind the amazing arms of righthander Curt Schilling and lefthander Randy Johnson, Arizona made major league history by becoming the youngest expansion franchise to reach the World Series, defeating Atlanta 4-1 in the NL Championship Series. The Diamondbacks finished off their dream season by dethroning the three-time defending champion Yankees in the World Series.

In addition to the playoffs' familiar participants, there were familiar storylines.

Atlanta again beat Houston, as it has done all three times the teams have met in the playoffs since 1997, but it couldn't beat anyone else. St. Louis, despite having a solid pitching staff and a potent lineup sprinkled with veterans and exciting young players—as well as a seasoned playoff manager in Tony La Russa—couldn't get to the World Series in its third playoff run in the last six seasons.

No, in the end it was the best rotation money could buy that brought a championship to Phoenix. The Diamondbacks combined the right free-agent signings and players having career years, but the dominant pitching of Schilling and Johnson pushed them over the top.

An Affair To Remember

The only team that came close to solving the Schilling-Johnson riddle was St. Louis, which lost 1-0 to Schilling in Game One of the NL Division Series and beat Johnson in Game Two. The two teams split Games Three and Four in St. Louis, setting the stage for one of the best battles in recent playoff memory.

Cardinals righthander Matt Morris, who won 22 games during the regular season to tie Schilling for the NL lead and took the hard-luck loss in Game One, again faced Schilling in Game Five.

Outfielder Reggie Sanders, who rebounded from an atrocious 2000 with the Braves (.232 with 11 home runs) to hit 33 homers for the Diamondbacks, went deep off Morris in the fourth to give Arizona a 1-0 lead. Outfielder J.D. Drew answered for St. Louis in the eighth with a solo shot off Schilling to tie the game at 1-1. Then the drama really began.

Bob Brenly

Schilling, pitching his 18th inning in five days, gave up a leadoff single to Jim Edmonds in the ninth. Mark McGwire was due up next, but he had struggled so mightily that La Russa pinch-hit Kerry Robinson, who sacrificed Edmonds to second. But Schilling's adrenaline erased the Cardinals threat—he struck out Edgar Renteria

Curt Schilling: Came up big in NL playoffs

and catcher Mike Matheny while hitting 98 mph.

Matt Williams, roundly booed at Bank One Ballpark because of his 0-for-15 series at the plate to that point, greeted reliever Dave Veres with a double down the left-field line to start the bottom of the ninth. Damian Miller sacrificed pinch-runner Midre Cummings to third, and a series of moves between La Russa and first-year Diamondbacks manager Bob Brenly resulted in a walk to pinch-hitter Greg Colbrunn. That set up a first-and-third, one-out situation for Tony Womack against Cardinals reliever Steve Kline.

Brenly gambled and called for the squeeze, but Kline's slider eluded Womack's bat, and Matheny tagged Cummings out easily. Brenly inserted speedster Danny Bautista as a pinch-runner for Colbrunn after Colbrunn had advanced to second on the failed squeeze. Womack turned from goat to hero when he lofted a single to left that scored Bautista with the series-clinching run.

"You could just see it in his eyes," Brenly said of

NATIONAL LEAGUE CHAMPIONS, 1901-2001

	PENNANT	PCT	GA
1901	Pittsburgh	.647	1½
1902	Pittsburgh	.741	27½
1903	Pittsburgh	.650	6½
1904	New York	.693	13
1905	New York	.686	9
1906	Chicago	.763	20
1907	Chicago	.704	17
1908	Chicago	.643	1
1909	Pittsburgh	.724	6½
1910	Chicago	.675	13
1911	New York	.647	7½
1912	New York	.682	10
1913	New York	.664	12½
1914	Boston	.614	10½
1915	Philadelphia	.592	7
1916	Brooklyn	.610	2½
1917	New York	.636	10
1918	Chicago	.651	10½
1919	Cincinnati	.686	9
1920	Brooklyn	.604	7
1921	New York	.614	4
1922	New York	.604	7
1923	New York	.621	4½
1924	New York	.608	1½
1925	Pittsburgh	.621	8½
1926	St. Louis	.578	2
1927	Pittsburgh	.610	1½
1928	St. Louis	.617	2
1929	Chicago	.645	10½
1930	St. Louis	.597	2

	PENNANT	PCT	GA	MVP
1931	St. Louis	.656	13	Frankie Frisch, 2b, St. Louis
1932	Chicago	.584	4	Chuck Klein, of, Philadelphia
1933	New York	.599	5	Carl Hubbell, lhp, New York
1934	St. Louis	.621	2	Dizzy Dean, rhp, St. Louis
1935	Chicago	.649	4	Gabby Hartnett, c, Chicago
1936	New York	.597	5	Carl Hubbell, lhp, New York
1937	New York	.625	3	Joe Medwick, of, St. Louis
1938	Chicago	.586	2	Ernie Lombardi, c, Cincinnati
1939	Cincinnati	.630	4½	Bucky Walters, rhp, Cincinnati
1940	Cincinnati	.654	12	Frank McCormick, 1b, Cincinnati
1941	Brooklyn	.649	2½	Dolf Camilli, 1b, Brooklyn
1942	St. Louis	.688	2	Mort Cooper, rhp, St. Louis
1943	St. Louis	.682	18	Stan Musial, of, St. Louis
1944	St. Louis	.682	14½	Marty Marion, ss, St. Louis
1945	Chicago	.636	3	Phil Cavarretta, 1b, Chicago
1946	St. Louis	.628	2	Stan Musial, 1b, St. Louis
1947	Brooklyn	.610	5	Bob Elliott, 3b, Boston
1948	Boston	.595	6½	Stan Musial, of, St. Louis
1949	Brooklyn	.630	1	Jackie Robinson, 2b, Brooklyn
1950	Philadelphia	.591	2	Jim Konstanty, rhp, Philadelphia
1951	New York	.624	1	Roy Campanella, c, Brooklyn
1952	Brooklyn	.627	4½	Hank Sauer, of, Chicago
1953	Brooklyn	.682	13	Roy Campanella, c, Brooklyn
1954	New York	.630	5	Willie Mays, of, New York
1955	Brooklyn	.641	13½	Roy Campanella, c, Brooklyn
1956	Brooklyn	.604	1	Don Newcombe, rhp, Brooklyn
1957	Milwaukee	.617	8	Hank Aaron, of, Milwaukee
1958	Milwaukee	.597	8	Ernie Banks, ss, Chicago
1959	Los Angeles	.564	2	Ernie Banks, ss, Chicago
1960	Pittsburgh	.617	7	Dick Groat, ss, Pittsburgh
1961	Cincinnati	.604	4	Frank Robinson, of, Cincinnati
1962	San Francisco	.624	1	Maury Wills, ss, Los Angeles
1963	Los Angeles	.611	6	Sandy Koufax, lhp, Los Angeles
1964	St. Louis	.574	1	Ken Boyer, 3b, St. Louis
1965	Los Angeles	.599	2	Willie Mays, of, San Francisco
1966	Los Angeles	.586	1½	Roberto Clemente, of, Pittsburgh
1967	St. Louis	.627	10½	Orlando Cepeda, 1b, St. Louis
1968	St. Louis	.599	9	Bob Gibson, rhp, St. Louis

	EAST	PCT	GA	WEST	PCT	GA	PENNANT		MVP
1969	New York	.617	8	Atlanta	.574	3	New York	3-0	Willie McCovey, 1b, San Francisco
1970	Pittsburgh	.549	5	Cincinnati	.630	14½	Cincinnati	3-0	Johnny Bench, c, Cincinnati
1971	Pittsburgh	.599	7	San Francisco	.556	1	Pittsburgh	3-1	Joe Torre, 3b, St. Louis
1972	Pittsburgh	.619	11	Cincinnati	.617	10½	Cincinnati	3-2	Johnny Bench, c, Cincinnati
1973	New York	.509	1½	Cincinnati	.611	3½	New York	3-2	Pete Rose, of, Cincinnati
1974	Pittsburgh	.543	1½	Los Angeles	.630	4	Los Angeles	3-1	Steve Garvey, 1b, Los Angeles
1975	Pittsburgh	.571	6½	Cincinnati	.667	20	Cincinnati	3-0	Joe Morgan, 2b, Cincinnati
1976	Philadelphia	.623	9	Cincinnati	.630	10	Cincinnati	3-0	Joe Morgan, 2b, Cincinnati
1977	Philadelphia	.623	5	Los Angeles	.605	10	Los Angeles	3-1	George Foster, of, Cincinnati
1978	Philadelphia	.556	1½	Los Angeles	.586	2½	Los Angeles	3-1	Dave Parker, of, Pittsburgh
1979	Pittsburgh	.605	2	Cincinnati	.559	1½	Pittsburgh	3-0	Hernandez, St. Louis; Stargell, Pittsburgh
1980	Philadelphia	.562	1	Houston	.571	1	Philadelphia	3-2	Mike Schmidt, 3b, Philadelphia
1981	Montreal*	.566	½	Los Angeles**	.632	½	Los Angeles	3-2	Mike Schmidt, 3b, Philadelphia
	Philadelphia	.618	1½	Houston	.623	1			
1982	St. Louis	.568	3	Atlanta	.549	1	St. Louis	3-0	Dale Murphy, of, Atlanta
1983	Philadelphia	.556	6	Los Angeles	.562	3	Philadelphia	3-1	Dale Murphy, of, Atlanta
1984	Chicago	.596	6½	San Diego	.568	12	San Diego	3-2	Ryne Sandberg, 2b, Chicago
1985	St. Louis	.623	3	Los Angeles	.586	5½	St. Louis	4-2	Willie McGee, of, St. Louis
1986	New York	.667	21½	Houston	.593	10	New York	4-2	Mike Schmidt, 3b, Philadelphia
1987	St. Louis	.586	3	San Francisco	.556	6	St. Louis	4-3	Andre Dawson, of, Chicago
1988	New York	.625	15	Los Angeles	.584	7	Los Angeles	4-3	Kirk Gibson, of, Los Angeles
1989	Chicago	.571	6	San Francisco	.568	3	San Francisco	4-1	Kevin Mitchell, of, San Francisco
1990	Pittsburgh	.586	4	Cincinnati	.562	5	Cincinnati	4-2	Barry Bonds, of, Pittsburgh
1991	Pittsburgh	.605	14	Atlanta	.580	1	Atlanta	4-3	Terry Pendleton, 3b, Atlanta
1992	Pittsburgh	.593	9	Atlanta	.605	8	Atlanta	4-3	Barry Bonds, of, Pittsburgh
1993	Philadelphia	.599	3	Atlanta	.642	1	Philadelphia	4-2	Barry Bonds, of, San Francisco

* Won second half; defeated Philadelphia 3-2 in best-of-5 playoff.   ** Won first half; defeated Houston 3-2 in best-of-5 playoff.

	EAST	PCT	GA	CENTRAL	PCT	GA	WEST	PCT	GA	WILD CARD	PCT
1994	Montreal	.649	6	Cincinnati	.593	½	Los Angeles	.509	3½	None	
	PENNANT: None (season incomplete)						MVP: Jeff Bagwell, 1b, Houston				
1995	Atlanta	.625	21	Cincinnati	.590	9	Los Angeles	.542	1	Colorado (West)	.535
	PENNANT: Atlanta def. Cincinnati, 4-2						MVP: Barry Larkin, ss, Cincinnati				
1996	Atlanta	.593	8	St. Louis	.543	6	San Diego	.562	1	L.A. (West)	.556
	PENNANT: Atlanta def. St. Louis 4-3						MVP: Ken Caminiti, 3b, San Diego				
1997	Atlanta	.623	9	Houston	.519	5	San Francisco	.556	2	Florida (East)	.568
	PENNANT: Florida def. Atlanta 4-2						MVP: Larry Walker, of, Colorado				
1998	Atlanta	.654	18	Houston	.630	12½	San Diego	.605	9½	Chicago (Central)	.552
	PENNANT: San Diego def. Atlanta 4-2						MVP: Sammy Sosa, of, Chicago				
1999	Atlanta	.636	6½	Houston	.599	1½	Arizona	.617	14	New York (East)	.595
	PENNANT: Atlanta def. New York 4-2						MVP: Chipper Jones, 3b, Atlanta				
2000	Atlanta	.586	1	St. Louis	.586	10	San Francisco	.599	11	New York (East)	.580
	PENNANT: New York def. St. Louis 4-1						MVP: Jeff Kent, 2b, San Francisco				
2001	Atlanta	.543	2	Houston	.574	—	Arizona	.599	11	St. Louis (Central)	.574
	PENNANT: Arizona def. Atlanta 4-1						MVP: Barry Bonds, of, San Francisco				

Page	EAST	W	L	PCT	GB	Manager	General Manager	Attendance (Avg.)	Last Penn.
71	Atlanta Braves	88	74	.543	—	Bobby Cox	John Schuerholz	2,823,494 (34,858)	1999
204	Philadelphia Phillies	86	76	.531	2	Larry Bowa	Ed Wade	1,782,054 (22,847)	1993
190	New York Mets	82	80	.506	6	Bobby Valentine	Steve Phillips	2,658,279 (32,818)	2000
135	Florida Marlins	76	86	.469	12	J. Boles/T. Perez	Dave Dombrowski	1,261,220 (15,765)	1997
175	Montreal Expos	68	94	.420	20	F. Alou/J. Torborg	Jim Beattie	619,451 (7,648)	None
Page	CENTRAL	W	L	PCT	GB	Manager	General Manager	Attendance (Avg.)	Last Penn.
142	#Houston Astros	93	69	.574	—	Larry Dierker	Gerry Hunsicker	2,904,280 (35,855)	None
218	*St. Louis Cardinals	93	69	.574	—	Tony La Russa	Walt Jocketty	3,113,091 (38,433)	1987
99	Chicago Cubs	88	74	.543	5	Don Baylor	Andy MacPhail	2,779,464 (35,183)	1945
162	Milwaukee Brewers	68	94	.420	25	Davey Lopes	Dean Taylor	2,811,041 (34,704)	None
106	Cincinnati Reds	66	96	.407	27	Bob Boone	Jim Bowden	1,879,872 (23,796)	1990
211	Pittsburgh Pirates	62	100	.383	31	Lloyd McClendon	C. Bonifay/D. Littlefield	2,436,290 (30,839)	1979
Page	WEST	W	L	PCT	GB	Manager	General Manager	Attendance (Avg.)	Last Penn.
64	Arizona Diamondbacks	92	70	.568	—	Bob Brenly	Joe Garagiola Jr.	2,744,433 (33,882)	2001
232	San Francisco Giants	90	72	.556	2	Dusty Baker	Brian Sabean	3,307,686 (40,836)	1989
155	Los Angeles Dodgers	86	76	.531	6	Jim Tracy	K. Malone/D. Wallace	3,017,502 (37,253)	1988
225	San Diego Padres	79	83	.488	13	Bruce Bochy	Kevin Towers	2,378,116 (29,726)	1998
121	Colorado Rockies	73	89	.451	19	Buddy Bell	Dan O'Dowd	3,140,416 (38,771)	None

#Houston declared champion by virtue of head-to-head record vs. St. Louis   *Won wild-card playoff berth
NOTE: Teams' individual batting, pitching and fielding statistics can be found on page indicated in lefthand column.

Womack. "He was a very focused man today. I was confident he would do something to help bail me out."

"It's a hair-pulling, nail-biting, teeth-grinding experience," Schilling said. "We gave the fans everything they could want in this series. It was fitting that it would go down to the fifth game and the ninth inning."

Aside from the nail-biting Diamondbacks-Cardinals series, it was business as usual. The Astros couldn't get it together against the Braves, who swept their opening-round series, and Schilling and Johnson came up with two more dominating performances in the NLCS to put Atlanta out of its misery quickly. The NLCS win ended a seven-game playoff losing streak for the Big Unit.

Desert Heat

The Diamondbacks' success didn't come cheaply, as the season began in bizarre fashion for the eventual NL champions. Arizona owner Jerry Colangelo secured a $20 million loan from Major League Baseball to help cover his 2001 costs, and a number of players agreed to defer part of their salaries to keep the team competitive.

"I think the guys want to prove that the fluke was last year, not the year before," said lefthander Brian Anderson, referring to the Diamondbacks' 2000 meltdown after they won the NL West in 1999. "We know we don't have much time together. We're not stupid. You see what the core of this team is, and we're an older team. Let's face it—we realize time is running out."

Of the 10 players 34 or older on the Arizona Opening Day 25-man roster, two were named Johnson and Schilling. The former had signed with the club as a free agent in '99 and was instrumental in the D'backs winning the division title that year. The latter came over from the Phillies in a trade that was designed to help the team climb back into the race in 2000, though that climb never materialized.

From the start of the 2001 season, both pitched as men on a mission. Johnson was a workhorse the first six weeks of the season, going at least seven innings in seven of his first nine starts. And Schilling was even better, going at least seven in his first 15 starts. Johnson went 21-6, and led the National League with a 2.49 ERA and 372 strikeouts. Schilling went 22-6, 2.98 and had 293 strikeouts,

Randy Johnson: Led NL with 2.49 ERA, 372 strikeouts

LARRY GOREN

second to Johnson.

Offensively, outfielder Luis Gonzalez set a blistering home run pace to begin the season, going deep in 20 of his first 40 games. His .326 average was the second-best of his career behind his .336 mark in 1999, and he shattered his previous bests of 31 homers and 114 RBIs in 2000 with 57 bombs and 142 RBIs on the year.

To 500 And Beyond

The Diamondbacks' resurgence and Gonzalez' banner year never really had a chance to make front-page news, though. Barry Bonds was the story before the 2001 season

NL YEAR-BY-YEAR BATTING LEADERS

Year	Batting Average	AVG	Home Runs	HR	RBIs	RBI
1901	Jesse Burkett, St. Louis	.382	Sam Crawford, Cincinnati	16	Honus Wagner, Pittsburgh	126
1902	Ginger Beaumont, Pitt.	.357	Tom Leach, Pittsburgh	6	Honus Wagner, Pittsburgh	91
1903	Honus Wagner, Pittsburgh	.355	Jim Sheckard, Brooklyn	9	Sam Mertes, New York	104
1904	Honus Wagner, Pittsburgh	.349	Harry Lumley, Brooklyn	9	Bill Dahlen, New York	80
1905	Cy Seymour, Cincinnati	.377	Fred Odwell, Cincinnati	9	Cy Seymour, Cincinnati	121
1906	Honus Wagner, Pittsburgh	.339	Tim Jordan, Brooklyn	12	Two tied at	83
1907	Honus Wagner, Pittsburgh	.350	Dave Brain, Boston	10	Sherry Magee, Philadelphia	85
1908	Honus Wagner, Pittsburgh	.354	Tim Jordan, Brooklyn	12	Honus Wagner, Pittsburgh	109
1909	Honus Wagner, Pittsburgh	.339	Red Murray, New York	7	Honus Wagner, Pittsburgh	100
1910	Sherry Magee, Phil.	.331	Two tied at	10	Sherry Magee, Philadelphia	123
1911	Honus Wagner, Pittsburgh	.334	Wildfire Schulte, Chicago	21	Wildfire Schulte, Chicago	121
1912	Heinie Zimmerman, Chi.	.372	Heinie Zimmerman, Chicago	14	Heinie Zimmerman, Chicago	103
1913	Jake Daubert, Brooklyn	.350	Gavvy Cravath, Philadelphia	19	Gavvy Cravath, Philadelphia	128
1914	Jake Daubert, Brooklyn	.329	Gavvy Cravath, Philadelphia	19	Sherry Magee, Philadelphia	103
1915	Larry Doyle, New York	.320	Gavvy Cravath, Philadelphia	24	Gavvy Cravath, Philadelphia	115
1916	Hal Chase, Cincinnati	.339	Two tied at	12	Heinie Zimmerman, Chi.-N.Y.	83
1917	Edd Roush, Cincinnati	.341	Two tied at	12	Heinie Zimmerman, N.Y.	102
1918	Zack Wheat, Brooklyn	.335	Gavvy Cravath, Philadelphia	8	Sherry Magee, Cincinnati	76
1919	Edd Roush, Cincinnati	.321	Gavvy Cravath, Philadelphia	12	Hy Myers, Brooklyn	73
1920	Rogers Hornsby, St. Louis	.370	Cy Williams, Philadelphia	15	Rogers Hornsby, St. Louis	94
1921	Rogers Hornsby, St. Louis	.397	George Kelly, New York	23	Rogers Hornsby, St. Louis	126
1922	Rogers Hornsby, St. Louis	.401	Rogers Hornsby, St. Louis	42	Rogers Hornsby, St. Louis	152
1923	Rogers Hornsby, St. Louis	.384	Cy Williams, Philadelphia	41	Emil Meusel, New York	125
1924	Rogers Hornsby, St. Louis	.424	Jack Fournier, Brooklyn	27	George Kelly, New York	136
1925	Rogers Hornsby, St. Louis	.403	Rogers Hornsby, St. Louis	39	Rogers Hornsby, St. Louis	143
1926	Bubbles Hargrave, Cin.	.353	Hack Wilson, Chicago	21	Jim Bottomley, St. Louis	120
1927	Paul Waner, Pittsburgh	.380	Two tied at	30	Paul Waner, Pittsburgh	131
1928	Rogers Hornsby, Boston	.387	Two tied at	31	Jim Bottomley, St. Louis	136
1929	Lefty O'Doul, Philadelphia	.398	Chuck Klein, Philadelphia	43	Hack Wilson, Chicago	159
1930	Bill Terry, New York	.401	Hack Wilson, Chicago	56	Hack Wilson, Chicago	190
1931	Chick Hafey, St. Louis	.349	Chuck Klein, Philadelphia	31	Chuck Klein, Philadelphia	121
1932	Lefty O'Doul, Brooklyn	.368	Two tied at	38	Frank Hurst, Philadelphia	143
1933	Chuck Klein, Philadelphia	.368	Chuck Klein, Philadelphia	28	Chuck Klein, Philadelphia	120
1934	Paul Waner, Pittsburgh	.362	Two tied at	35	Mel Ott, New York	135
1935	Arky Vaughan, Pittsburgh	.385	Wally Berger, Boston	34	Wally Berger, Boston	130
1936	Paul Waner, Pittsburgh	.373	Mel Ott, New York	33	Joe Medwick, St. Louis	138
1937	Joe Medwick, St. Louis	.374	Two tied at	31	Joe Medwick, St. Louis	154
1938	Ernie Lombardi, Cincinnati	.342	Mel Ott, New York	36	Joe Medwick, St. Louis	122
1939	Johnny Mize, St. Louis	.349	Johnny Mize, St. Louis	28	Frank McCormick, Cincinnati	128
1940	Debs Garms, Pittsburgh	.355	Johnny Mize, St. Louis	43	Johnny Mize, St. Louis	137
1941	Pete Reiser, Brooklyn	.343	Dolff Camilli, Brooklyn	34	Dolff Camilli, Brooklyn	120
1942	Ernie Lombardi, Boston	.330	Mel Ott, New York	30	Johnny Mize, New York	110
1943	Stan Musial, St. Louis	.357	Bill Nicholson, Chicago	29	Bill Nicholson, Chicago	128
1944	Dixie Walker, Brooklyn	.357	Bill Nicholson, Chicago	33	Bill Nicholson, Chicago	122
1945	Phil Cavarretta, Chicago	.355	Tommy Holmes, Boston	28	Dixie Walker, Brooklyn	124
1946	Stan Musial, St. Louis	.365	Ralph Kiner, Pittsburgh	23	Enos Slaughter, St. Louis	130
1947	Harry Walker, St.L.-Phil.	.363	Two tied at	51	Johnny Mize, New York	138
1948	Stan Musial, St. Louis	.376	Two tied at	40	Stan Musial, St. Louis	131
1949	Jackie Robinson, Brooklyn	.342	Ralph Kiner, Pittsburgh	54	Ralph Kiner, Pittsburgh	127
1950	Stan Musial, St. Louis	.346	Ralph Kiner, Pittsburgh	47	Del Ennis, Philadelphia	126
1951	Stan Musial, St. Louis	.355	Ralph Kiner, Pittsburgh	42	Monte Irvin, New York	121
1952	Stan Musial, St. Louis	.336	Two tied at	37	Hank Sauer, Chicago	121
1953	Carl Furillo, Brooklyn	.344	Eddie Mathews, Milwaukee	47	Roy Campanella, Brooklyn	142
1954	Willie Mays, New York	.345	Ted Kluszewski, Cincinnati	49	Ted Kluszewski, Cincinnati	141
1955	Richie Ashburn, Phil.	.338	Willie Mays, New York	51	Duke Snider, Brooklyn	136
1956	Hank Aaron, Milwaukee	.328	Duke Snider, Brooklyn	43	Stan Musial, St. Louis	109
1957	Stan Musial, St. Louis	.351	Hank Aaron, Milwaukee	44	Hank Aaron, Milwaukee	132
1958	Richie Ashburn, Phil.	.350	Ernie Banks, Chicago	47	Ernie Banks, Chicago	129
1959	Hank Aaron, Milwaukee	.355	Eddie Mathews, Milwaukee	46	Ernie Banks, Chicago	143
1960	Dick Groat, Pittsburgh	.325	Ernie Banks, Chicago	41	Hank Aaron, Milwaukee	126
1961	Roberto Clemente, Pitt.	.351	Orlando Cepeda, S.F.	46	Orlando Cepeda, S.F.	142
1962	Tommy Davis, L.A.	.346	Willie Mays, San Francisco	49	Tommy Davis, Los Angeles	153
1963	Tommy Davis, L.A.	.326	Two tied at	44	Hank Aaron, Milwaukee	130
1964	Roberto Clemente, Pitt.	.339	Willie Mays, San Francisco	47	Ken Boyer, St. Louis	119
1965	Roberto Clemente, Pitt.	.329	Willie Mays, San Francisco	52	Deron Johnson, Cincinnati	130
1966	Matty Alou, Pittsburgh	.342	Hank Aaron, Atlanta	44	Hank Aaron, Atlanta	127
1967	Roberto Clemente, Pitt.	.357	Hank Aaron, Atlanta	39	Orlando Cepeda, S.F.	111
1968	Pete Rose, Cincinnati	.335	Willie McCovey, S.F.	36	Willie McCovey, S.F.	105
1969	Pete Rose, Cincinnati	.348	Willie McCovey, S.F.	45	Willie McCovey, S.F.	126
1970	Rico Carty, Atlanta	.366	Johnny Bench, Cincinnati	45	Johnny Bench, Cincinnati	148
1971	Joe Torre, St. Louis	.363	Willie Stargell, Pittsburgh	48	Joe Torre, St. Louis	137
1972	Billy Williams, Chicago	.333	Johnny Bench, Cincinnati	40	Johnny Bench, Cincinnati	125
1973	Pete Rose, Cincinnati	.338	Willie Stargell, Pittsburgh	44	Willie Stargell, Pittsburgh	119
1974	Ralph Garr, Atlanta	.353	Johnny Bench, Cincinnati	36	Johnny Bench, Cincinnati	129
1975	Bill Madlock, Chicago	.354	Mike Schmidt, Philadelphia	38	Greg Luzinski, Philadelphia	120
1976	Bill Madlock, Chicago	.339	Mike Schmidt, Philadelphia	38	George Foster, Cincinnati	121
1977	Dave Parker, Pittsburgh	.338	George Foster, Cincinnati	52	George Foster, Cincinnati	149
1978	Dave Parker, Pittsburgh	.334	George Foster, Cincinnati	40	George Foster, Cincinnati	120
1979	Keith Hernandez, St. Louis	.344	Dave Kingman, Chicago	48	Dave Winfield, San Diego	118
1980	Bill Buckner, Chicago	.324	Mike Schmidt, Philadelphia	48	Mike Schmidt, Philadelphia	121
1981	Bill Madlock, Pittsburgh	.341	Mike Schmidt, Philadelphia	31	Mike Schmidt, Philadelphia	91
1982	Al Oliver, Montreal	.331	Dave Kingman, New York	37	Dale Murphy, Atlanta	109
1983	Bill Madlock, Pittsburgh	.323	Mike Schmidt, Philadelphia	40	Dale Murphy, Atlanta	121
1984	Tony Gwynn, San Diego	.351	Two tied at	36	Two tied at	106
1985	Willie McGee, St. Louis	.353	Dale Murphy, Atlanta	37	Dave Parker, Cincinnati	125
1986	Tim Raines, Montreal	.334	Mike Schmidt, Philadelphia	37	Mike Schmidt, Philadelphia	119
1987	Tony Gwynn, San Diego	.370	Andre Dawson, Chicago	49	Andre Dawson, Chicago	137
1988	Tony Gwynn, San Diego	.313	Darryl Strawberry, New York	39	Will Clark, San Francisco	109
1989	Tony Gwynn, San Diego	.336	Kevin Mitchell, San Francisco	47	Kevin Mitchell, San Francisco	125
1990	Willie McGee, St. Louis	.335	Matt Williams, S.F.	40	Matt Williams, S.F.	122
1991	Terry Pendleton, Atlanta	.319	Howard Johnson, New York	38	Howard Johnson, New York	117
1992	Gary Sheffield, San Diego	.330	Fred McGriff, San Diego	35	Darren Daulton, Philadelphia	109
1993	Andres Galarraga, Colo.	.370	Barry Bonds, San Francisco	46	Barry Bonds, San Francisco	123
1994	Tony Gwynn, San Diego	.394	Matt Williams, San Francisco	43	Jeff Bagwell, Houston	116
1995	Tony Gwynn, San Diego	.368	Dante Bichette, Colorado	40	Dante Bichette, Colorado	128
1996	Tony Gwynn, San Diego	.353	Andres Galarraga, Colorado	47	Andres Galarraga, Colorado	150
1997	Tony Gwynn, San Diego	.372	Larry Walker, Colorado	49	Andres Galarraga, Colorado	140
1998	Larry Walker, Colorado	.363	Mark McGwire, St. Louis	70	Sammy Sosa, Chicago	158
1999	Larry Walker, Colorado	.379	Mark McGwire, St. Louis	65	Mark McGwire, St. Louis	147
2000	Todd Helton, Colorado	.372	Sammy Sosa, Chicago	50	Todd Helton, Colorado	147
2001	Larry Walker, Colorado	.350	Barry Bonds, San Francisco	73	Sammy Sosa, Chicago	160

even started, hiring agent Scott Boras before spring training in anticipation of his free agency after the season.

Though the left fielder is a Bay Area native and wanted to stay in San Francisco, Giants management balked at his requests for a four-year contract. After all, Bonds was 36 and was looking for at least $20 million a year.

Even as he passed the 500-homer plateau in April and began a pace that made people talk about the possibility of McGwire's single-season record falling, Bonds made it clear he was more interested in earning a World Series ring like Big Mac's than in surpassing his record. To that end, his offensive performance helped keep the Giants afloat in the NL West, as San Francisco, Los Angeles and Arizona waged a fierce three-team battle for the division crown.

Injuries to righthanders Kevin Brown and Darren Dreifort made the Dodgers' run a futile one, and offensive inconsistency from the Giants' outfielders (save Bonds, of course) and corner infielders kept San Francisco from making a better charge in September.

In fact, an interesting trend developed during the final month. On Sept. 9, the Diamondbacks led the division by two games over the Giants. From that point, everything San Francisco did in second place, Arizona did in first. If the Giants won, so did the Diamondbacks. If the Giants lost, so did the Diamondbacks. The margin remained at two games every day until the last Friday of the regular season, when Bonds hit home runs No. 71 and 72 to break McGwire's record of 70. But the Giants lost to the Dodgers, while Arizona won in Milwaukee to clinch its second division flag in three years.

It made for a scene in the post-midnight chill in San Francisco that might have been called "Pride of the Giants." Bonds, addressing an adoring crowd that was still stunned by the 11-10 loss that eliminated the Giants, could barely hold back tears as he spoke into the microphone.

"To my teammates, we worked real hard, and we're going to work real hard again," he said. "I love you all very much. It's an honor to play with a bunch of guys like this behind me. I'll play for you any time, any day of the week, any hour, any year."

Later, he told the San Francisco Chronicle he had finally overcome his often negative image, in spite of the rancor over his contract.

Luis Gonzalez: 57 homers

"I've seen a lot of changes out there this year," he said. "You guys (media) and the fans of San Francisco enjoyed me. It's very hard. Things start turning around, and you don't know where you're going to be. It's tough. Everybody worked hard here to mend some fences together."

New Beginnings

While fences were mended with the Giants, new ones were erected in Pittsburgh and Milwaukee.

Matt Morris: Went 22-8, 3.16 for Cardinals

At the Brewers' new Miller Park, where the opening was delayed a year because of a construction accident that killed three workers in 1999, the team looked to rewrite the record books. That it did—just not in the way it would've liked.

Milwaukee lost more games than it had in 17 years, thanks to a 9-31 slump in July and August that knocked the club from just above .500 to well below it. In addition, the Brewers made history as the first team to have more strikeouts (1,399) than hits (1,378). The strikeout mark broke the major league record by more than 130.

The Pirates fared even worse. Things started off tragically on Opening Day at PNC Park, when the franchise learned that one of its most beloved players, Willie Stargell, passed away the morning the gates were scheduled to open.

A shaken squad took the field and lost 8-2 to the Reds as Cincinnati's Sean Casey got the first hit at PNC—just as he had at Miller Park a few days earlier. It was the first of 100 losses on the season for the Pirates—the worst total in the Steel City in nearly 20 years. General manager Cam Bonifay didn't make it to July before he was fired.

On the bright side, both franchises set records at the gate, as the Brewers drew 2.8 million fans and the Pirates 2.4 million.

Central Issues

While both Pittsburgh and Milwaukee looked up from the bottom with Cincinnati, the NL Central provided a gripping pennant race. The Cubs, who took over the division lead in June and held it until mid-August, faltered down the stretch when ace righthander Kerry Wood went down for a month with a shoulder injury. Closer Tom Gordon followed with elbow problems after Wood finally came back.

MORRIS FOSTOFF

LEE SCHMID

NL YEAR-BY-YEAR PITCHING LEADERS

Year	Wins		ERA		Strikeouts	
1901	Bill Donovan, Brooklyn	25	Jesse Tannehill, Pittsburgh	2.18	Noodles Hahn, Cincinnati	233
1902	Jack Chesbro, Pittsburgh	28	Jack Taylor, Chicago	1.33	Vic Willis, Boston	226
1903	Joe McGinnity, New York	31	Sam Leever, Pittsburgh	2.06	Christy Mathewson, N.Y.	267
1904	Joe McGinnity, New York	35	Joe McGinnity, New York	1.61	Christy Mathewson, N.Y.	212
1905	Christy Mathewson, N.Y.	32	Christy Mathewson, N.Y.	1.27	Christy Mathewson, N.Y.	206
1906	Joe McGinnity, New York	27	Mordecai Brown, Chicago	1.04	Fred Beebe, Chi.-St.L.	171
1907	Christy Mathewson, New York	24	Jack Pfiester, Chicago	1.15	Christy Mathewson, N.Y.	178
1908	Christy Mathewson, N.Y.	37	Christy Mathewson, N.Y.	1.43	Christy Mathewson, N.Y.	259
1909	Mordecai Brown, Chicago	27	Christy Mathewson, N.Y.	1.14	Orval Overall, Chicago	205
1910	Christy Mathewson, N.Y.	27	George McQuillan, Phil.	1.60	Christy Mathewson, N.Y.	190
1911	Grover Alexander, Phil.	28	Christy Mathewson, N.Y.	1.99	Rube Marquard, New York	237
1912	Two tied at	26	Jeff Tesreau, New York	1.96	Grover Alexander, Phil.	195
1913	Tom Seaton, Philadelphia	27	Christy Mathewson, N.Y.	2.06	Tom Seaton, Philadelphia	168
1914	Two tied at	27	Bill Doak, St. Louis	1.72	Grover Alexander, Phil.	214
1915	Grover Alexander, Phil.	31	Grover Alexander, Phil.	1.22	Grover Alexander, Phil.	241
1916	Grover Alexander, Phil.	33	Grover Alexander, Phil.	1.55	Grover Alexander, Phil.	167
1917	Grover Alexander, Phil.	30	Grover Alexander, Phil.	1.85	Grover Alexander, Phil.	200
1918	Hippo Vaughn, Chicago	22	Hippo Vaughn, Chicago	1.74	Hippo Vaughn, Chicago	148
1919	Jesse Barnes, New York	25	Grover Alexander, Chicago	1.72	Hippo Vaughn, Chicago	141
1920	Grover Alexander, Chicago	27	Grover Alexander, Chicago	1.91	Grover Alexander, Chicago	173
1921	Two tied at	22	Bill Doak, St. Louis	2.58	Burleigh Grimes, Brooklyn	136
1922	Eppa Rixey, Cincinnati	25	Rosy Ryan, New York	3.00	Dazzy Vance, Brooklyn	134
1923	Dolf Luque, Cincinnati	27	Dolf Luque, Cincinnati	1.93	Dazzy Vance, Brooklyn	197
1924	Dazzy Vance, Brooklyn	28	Dazzy Vance, Brooklyn	2.16	Dazzy Vance, Brooklyn	262
1925	Dazzy Vance, Brooklyn	22	Dolf Luque, Cincinnati	2.63	Dazzy Vance, Brooklyn	221
1926	Four tied at	20	Ray Kremer, Pittsburgh	2.61	Dazzy Vance, Brooklyn	140
1927	Charlie Root, Chicago	26	Ray Kremer, Pittsburgh	2.47	Dazzy Vance, Brooklyn	184
1928	Two tied at	25	Bill Walker, New York	2.82	Dazzy Vance, Brooklyn	200
1929	Pat Malone, Chicago	22	Bill Walker, New York	3.08	Pat Malone, Chicago	166
1930	Two tied at	20	Dazzy Vance, Brooklyn	2.61	Bill Hallahan, St. Louis	177
1931	Three tied at	19	Bill Walker, New York	2.26	Bill Hallahan, St. Louis	159
1932	Lon Warneke, Chicago	22	Lon Warneke, Chicago	2.37	Dizzy Dean, St. Louis	191
1933	Carl Hubbell, New York	23	Carl Hubbell, New York	1.66	Dizzy Dean, St. Louis	199
1934	Dizzy Dean, St. Louis	30	Carl Hubbell, New York	2.30	Dizzy Dean, St. Louis	195
1935	Dizzy Dean, St. Louis	28	Cy Blanton, Pittsburgh	2.59	Dizzy Dean, St. Louis	182
1936	Carl Hubbell, New York	26	Carl Hubbell, New York	2.31	Van Lingle Mungo, Brooklyn	238
1937	Carl Hubbell, New York	22	Jim Turner, Boston	2.38	Carl Hubbell, New York	159
1938	Bill Lee, Chicago	22	Bill Lee, Chicago	2.66	Clay Bryant, Chicago	135
1939	Bucky Walters, Cincinnati	27	Bucky Walters, Cincinnati	2.29	Two tied at	137
1940	Bucky Walters, Cincinnati	22	Bucky Walters, Cincinnati	2.48	Kirby Higbe, Philadelphia	137
1941	Two tied at	22	Elmer Riddle, Cincinnati	2.24	Johnny Vander Meer, Cin.	202
1942	Mort Cooper, St. Louis	22	Mort Cooper, St. Louis	1.77	Johnny Vander Meer, Cin.	186
1943	Three tied at	21	Howie Pollet, St. Louis	1.75	Johnny Vander Meer, Cin.	174
1944	Bucky Walters, Cincinnati	23	Ed Heusser, Cincinnati	2.38	Bill Voiselle, New York	161
1945	Red Barrett, Bos.-St.L.	23	Hank Borowy, Chicago	2.14	Preacher Roe, Pittsburgh	148
1946	Howie Pollet, St. Louis	21	Howie Pollet, St. Louis	2.10	John Schmitz, Chicago	135
1947	Ewell Blackwell, Cincinnati	22	Warren Spahn, Boston	2.33	Ewell Blackwell, Cincinnati	193
1948	Johnny Sain, Boston	24	Harry Brecheen, St. Louis	2.24	Harry Brecheen, St. Louis	149
1949	Warren Spahn, Boston	21	Dave Koslo, New York	2.50	Warren Spahn, Boston	151
1950	Warren Spahn, Boston	21	Jim Hearn, St.L.-N.Y.	2.49	Warren Spahn, Boston	191
1951	Two tied at	23	Chet Nichols, Boston	2.88	Two tied at	164
1952	Robin Roberts, Philadelphia	28	Hoyt Wilhelm, New York	2.43	Warren Spahn, Boston	183
1953	Two tied at	23	Warren Spahn, Milwaukee	2.10	Robin Roberts, Philadelphia	198
1954	Robin Roberts, Philadelphia	23	John Antonelli, New York	2.29	Robin Roberts, Philadelphia	185
1955	Robin Roberts, Philadelphia	23	Bob Friend, Pittsburgh	2.84	Sam Jones, Chicago	198
1956	Two tied at	20	Lew Burdette, Milwaukee	2.71	Sam Jones, Chicago	176
1957	Warren Spahn, Milwaukee	21	Johnny Podres, Brooklyn	2.66	Jack Sanford, Philadelphia	188
1958	Two tied at	22	Stu Miller, San Francisco	2.47	Sam Jones, St. Louis	225
1959	Three tied at	21	Sam Jones, San Francisco	2.82	Don Drysdale, Los Angeles	242
1960	Two tied at	21	Mike McCormick, S.F.	2.70	Don Drysdale, Los Angeles	246
1961	Warren Spahn, Milwaukee	21	Warren Spahn, Milwaukee	3.01	Sandy Koufax, Los Angeles	269
1962	Don Drysdale, Los Angeles	25	Sandy Koufax, Los Angeles	2.54	Don Drysdale, Los Angeles	232
1963	Two tied at	25	Sandy Koufax, Los Angeles	1.88	Sandy Koufax, Los Angeles	306
1964	Larry Jackson, Chicago	24	Sandy Koufax, Los Angeles	1.74	Bob Veale, Pittsburgh	250
1965	Sandy Koufax, Los Angeles	26	Sandy Koufax, Los Angeles	2.04	Sandy Koufax, Los Angeles	382
1966	Sandy Koufax, Los Angeles	27	Sandy Koufax, Los Angeles	1.73	Sandy Koufax, Los Angeles	317
1967	Mike McCormick, S.F.	22	Phil Niekro, Atlanta	1.87	Jim Bunning, Philadelphia	253
1968	Juan Marichal, S.F.	26	Bob Gibson, St. Louis	1.12	Bob Gibson, St. Louis	268
1969	Tom Seaver, New York	25	Juan Marichal, S.F.	2.10	Ferguson Jenkins, Chicago	273
1970	Two tied at	23	Tom Seaver, New York	2.81	Tom Seaver, New York	283
1971	Ferguson Jenkins, Chicago	24	Tom Seaver, New York	1.76	Tom Seaver, New York	289
1972	Steve Carlton, Philadelphia	27	Steve Carlton, Philadelphia	1.98	Steve Carlton, Philadelphia	310
1973	Ron Bryant, San Francisco	24	Tom Seaver, New York	2.08	Tom Seaver, New York	251
1974	Two tied at	20	Buzz Capra, Atlanta	2.28	Steve Carlton, Philadelphia	240
1975	Tom Seaver, New York	22	Randy Jones, San Diego	2.24	Tom Seaver, New York	243
1976	Randy Jones, San Diego	22	John Denny, St. Louis	2.52	Tom Seaver, New York	235
1977	Steve Carlton, Philadelphia	23	John Candelaria, Pittsburgh	2.34	Phil Niekro, Atlanta	252
1978	Gaylord Perry, San Diego	21	Craig Swan, New York	2.43	J.R. Richard, Houston	303
1979	Two tied at	21	J.R. Richard, Houston	2.71	J.R. Richard, Houston	313
1980	Steve Carlton, Philadelphia	24	Don Sutton, Los Angeles	2.21	Steve Carlton, Philadelphia	286
1981	Tom Seaver, Cincinnati	14	Nolan Ryan, Houston	1.69	Fernando Valenzuela, L.A.	180
1982	Steve Carlton, Philadelphia	23	Steve Rogers, Montreal	2.40	Steve Carlton, Philadelphia	286
1983	John Denny, Philadelphia	19	Atlee Hammaker, S.F.	2.25	Steve Carlton, Philadelphia	275
1984	Joaquin Andujar, St. Louis	20	Alejandro Pena, Los Angeles	2.48	Dwight Gooden, New York	276
1985	Dwight Gooden, New York	24	Dwight Gooden, New York	1.53	Dwight Gooden, New York	268
1986	Fernando Valenzuela, L.A.	21	Mike Scott, Houston	2.22	Mike Scott, Houston	306
1987	Rick Sutcliffe, Chicago	18	Nolan Ryan, Houston	2.76	Nolan Ryan, Houston	270
1988	Two tied at	23	Joe Magrane, St. Louis	2.18	Nolan Ryan, Houston	228
1989	Mike Scott, Houston	20	Scott Garrelts, S.F.	2.28	Jose DeLeon, St. Louis	201
1990	Doug Drabek, Pittsburgh	22	Danny Darwin, Houston	2.21	David Cone, New York	233
1991	Two tied at	20	Dennis Martinez, Montreal	2.39	David Cone, New York	241
1992	Two tied at	20	Bill Swift, San Francisco	2.08	John Smoltz, Atlanta	215
1993	Two tied at	22	Greg Maddux, Atlanta	2.36	Jose Rijo, Cincinnati	227
1994	Greg Maddux, Atlanta	16	Greg Maddux, Atlanta	1.56	Andy Benes, San Diego	189
1995	Greg Maddux, Atlanta	19	Greg Maddux, Atlanta	1.63	Hideo Nomo, Los Angeles	236
1996	John Smoltz, Atlanta	24	Kevin Brown, Florida	1.89	John Smoltz, Atlanta	276
1997	Denny Neagle, Atlanta	20	Pedro Martinez, Montreal	1.90	Curt Schilling, Philadelphia	319
1998	Tom Glavine, Atlanta	20	Greg Maddux, Atlanta	2.22	Curt Schilling, Philadelphia	300
1999	Mike Hampton, Houston	22	Randy Johnson, Arizona	2.48	Randy Johnson, Arizona	364
2000	Tom Glavine, Atlanta	21	Kevin Brown, San Diego	2.58	Randy Johnson, Arizona	347
2001	Two tied at	22	Randy Johnson, Arizona	2.49	Randy Johnson, Arizona	372

STEVE MOORE

Greg Maddux: Went a steady 17-11, 3.05 for Atlanta

NL: BEST TOOLS

A Baseball America survey of National League managers, conducted at midseason 2001, ranked NL players with the best tools:

BEST HITTER
1. Todd Helton, Rockies
2. Luis Gonzalez, Diamondbacks
3. Moises Alou, Astros

BEST POWER HITTER
1. Barry Bonds, Giants
2. Sammy Sosa, Cubs
3. Mark McGwire, Cardinals

BEST BUNTER
1. Luis Castillo, Marlins
2. Juan Pierre, Rockies
3. Fernando Vina, Cardinals

BEST HIT-AND-RUN BATTER
1. Jay Bell, Diamondbacks
2. Rich Aurilia, Giants
3. Jeff Cirillo, Rockies

BEST BASERUNNER
1. Larry Walker, Rockies
2. Luis Castillo, Marlins
3. Jimmy Rollins, Phillies

FASTEST BASERUNNER
1. Luis Castillo, Marlins
2. Juan Pierre, Rockies
3. Tom Goodwin, Dodgers

BEST PITCHER
1. Curt Schilling, Diamondbacks
2. Randy Johnson, D'backs
3. Greg Maddux, Braves

BEST FASTBALL
1. Randy Johnson, D'backs
2. Kyle Farnsworth, Cubs
3. Robb Nen, Giants

BEST CURVEBALL
1. Darryl Kile, Cardinals
2. Kerry Wood, Cubs
3. Chan Ho Park, Dodgers

BEST SLIDER
1. Randy Johnson, D'backs
2. Robb Nen, Giants
3. Kevin Brown, Dodgers

BEST CHANGEUP
1. Greg Maddux, Braves
2. Trevor Hoffman, Padres
3. Tom Glavine, Braves

BEST CONTROL
1. Greg Maddux, Braves
2. Rick Reed, Mets
3. Kevin Brown, Dodgers

BEST PICKOFF MOVE
1. Brian Anderson, D'backs
2. Terry Mulholland, Dodgers
3. Armando Reynoso, D'backs

BEST RELIEVER
1. Robb Nen, Giants
2. Jeff Shaw, Dodgers
3. Trevor Hoffman, Padres

BEST DEFENSIVE C
1. Mike Matheny, Cardinals
2. Charles Johnson, Marlins
3. Henry Blanco, Brewers

BEST DEFENSIVE 1B
1. J.T. Snow, Giants
2. Todd Helton, Rockies
3. Mark Grace, Diamondbacks

BEST DEFENSIVE 2B
1. Pokey Reese, Reds
2. Luis Castillo, Marlins
3. Edgardo Alfonzo, Mets

BEST DEFENSIVE 3B
1. Scott Rolen, Phillies
2. Mike Lowell, Marlins
3. Robin Ventura, Mets

BEST DEFENSIVE SS
1. Neifi Perez, Rockies
2. Rey Ordonez, Mets
3. Jimmy Rollins, Phillies

BEST INFIELD ARM
1. Rafael Furcal, Braves
2. Scott Rolen, Phillies
3. Jimmy Rollins, Phillies

BEST DEFENSIVE OF
1. Andruw Jones, Braves
2. Larry Walker, Rockies
3. Jim Edmonds, Cardinals

BEST OUTFIELD ARM
1. Vladimir Guerrero, Expos
2. Andruw Jones, Braves
3. Larry Walker, Rockies

MOST EXCITING PLAYER
1. Vladimir Guerrero, Expos
2. Barry Bonds, Giants
3. Todd Helton, Rockies

BEST MANAGER
1. Bobby Cox, Braves
2. Dusty Baker, Giants
3. Larry Bowa, Phillies

One of the primary reasons the Cubs' pitching couldn't measure up was that the starting staffs in Houston and St. Louis were two of the league's best. The Astros did it with youth, as hard-throwing rookie righthander Roy Oswalt went 14-3 and led the NL in winning percentage, and righthander Wade Miller won 16 to lead the staff. Add in set-up man/spot starter Octavio Dotel and resurgent closer Billy Wagner, and Houston's pitching was solid enough to take the division crown despite its relative inexperience.

"There's too much attention paid to their ages and not enough to their abilities," Astros manager Larry Dierker said. "These guys are still learning how to get big league hitters out, but I don't think there's any doubt they belong at this level."

Oswalt injured his groin in mid-September and was unavailable for the playoffs, and Houston's fourth playoff meltdown in five years helped bring about Dierker's resignation before the World Series started.

The Cardinals' solid pitching and timely hitting helped them tie the Astros for the division crown. St. Louis could have won the title outright and faced Atlanta in the first round if it had beaten Houston on the final day of the season. Morris' comeback from Tommy John surgery was complete when the righthander posted his 22 wins. Darryl Kile (16-11, 3.09) was solid all year, rookie lefthander Bud Smith pitched well and threw a no-hitter against the Padres in his 11th big league start and Woody Williams—acquired from the Padres for disgruntled outfielder Ray Lankford—went 7-1 down the stretch and pitched well in the playoffs.

But the biggest story under the Arch was versatile rookie Albert Pujols, who forced his way onto the Opening Day roster and never slowed down. He won Baseball America Rookie-of-the-Year honors by setting National League rookie records for RBIs (130) and total bases (360).

"Everybody is amazed at what he has done," said Cardinals first base coach Jose Oquendo, who took Pujols under his wing in the early days of spring training. "The accomplishments he has made this year, you don't see a rookie doing. We all knew he was a good hitter and has a lot of ability, but you don't expect this."

Another Year, Another Title

In the NL East, it was business as usual for the Braves, who won their 10th consecutive division title. Atlanta held off a charge by the Phillies, who led the division the first half of the season, and a belated rally by the Mets, who occupied the cellar early on but rallied just as their city did in the wake of the terrorist attacks.

Because they overcame significant injuries to both the pitching staff and everyday lineup, this division title may have been the sweetest for the Braves. The team lost sparkplug shortstop Rafael Furcal to a season-ending injury and had a yearlong open tryout for a first baseman, with the job eventually going to 40-year-old Julio Franco, who was plucked out of the Mexican League.

NATIONAL LEAGUE
DEPARTMENT LEADERS

BATTING

GAMES
Bob Abreu, Phillies 162
Orlando Cabrera, Expos 162
Luis Gonzalez, Diamondbacks 162
Jeff Bagwell, Astros 161
Shawn Green, Dodgers 161
Andruw Jones, Braves 161
Albert Pujols, Cardinals 161

AT-BATS
Jimmy Rollins, Phillies 656
Rich Aurilia, Giants 636
Doug Glanville, Phillies 634
Fernando Vina, Cardinals 631
Orlando Cabrera, Expos 626

RUNS
Sammy Sosa, Cubs 146
Todd Helton, Rockies 132
Barry Bonds, Giants 129
Luis Gonzalez, Diamondbacks 128
Jeff Bagwell, Astros 126

HITS
Rich Aurilia, Giants 206
Juan Pierre, Rockies 202
Luis Gonzalez, Diamondbacks 198
Todd Helton, Rockies 197
Albert Pujols, Cardinals 194

TOTAL BASES
Sammy Sosa, Cubs 425
Luis Gonzalez, Diamondbacks 419
Barry Bonds, Giants 411
Todd Helton, Rockies 402
Shawn Green, Dodgers 370

EXTRA-BASE HITS
Barry Bonds, Giants 107
Todd Helton, Rockies 105
Sammy Sosa, Cubs 103
Luis Gonzalez, Diamondbacks 100
Lance Berkman, Astros 94

SINGLES
Juan Pierre, Rockies 163
Fernando Vina, Cardinals 144
Placido Polanco, Cardinals 140
Rich Aurilia, Giants 127
Jason Kendall, Pirates 127

DOUBLES
Lance Berkman, Astros 55

Sammy Sosa: 146 runs, 425 total bases

Todd Helton, Rockies 54
Jeff Kent, Giants 49
Bob Abreu, Phillies 48
Albert Pujols, Cardinals 47

TRIPLES
Jimmy Rollins, Phillies 12
Juan Pierre, Rockies 11
Juan Uribe, Rockies 11
Luis Castillo, Marlins 10
Neifi Perez, Rockies 8
Fernando Vina, Cardinals 8

HOME RUNS
Barry Bonds, Giants 73
Sammy Sosa, Cubs 64
Luis Gonzalez, Diamondbacks 57
Shawn Green, Dodgers 49
Todd Helton, Rockies 49

HOME RUN RATIO
(At-Bats per Home Run)
Barry Bonds, Giants 6.5
Sammy Sosa, Cubs 9.0
Luis Gonzalez, Diamondbacks 10.7
Todd Helton, Rockies 12.0
Shawn Green, Dodgers 12.6

RUNS BATTED IN
Sammy Sosa, Cubs 160
Todd Helton, Rockies 146
Luis Gonzalez, Diamondbacks 142
Barry Bonds, Giants 137
Jeff Bagwell, Astros 130
Albert Pujols, Cardinals 130

SACRIFICE BUNTS
Tom Glavine, Braves 17
Ricky Gutierrez, Cubs 17
Jack Wilson, Pirates 17
Ryan Dempster, Marlins 16
Javier Vazquez, Expos 16

SACRIFICE FLIES
Jeff Kent, Giants 13
Scott Rolen, Phillies 12
Sammy Sosa, Cubs 12
Ricky Gutierrez, Cubs 11
Richard Hidalgo, Astros 11

HIT BY PITCH
Craig Biggio, Astros 28
Fernando Vina, Cardinals 22
Jason Kendall, Pirates 20
Richard Hidalgo, Astros 16
Luis Gonzalez, Diamondbacks 14
Larry Walker, Rockies 14

WALKS
Barry Bonds, Giants 177
Sammy Sosa, Cubs 116
Bob Abreu, Phillies 106
Jeff Bagwell, Astros 106
Luis Gonzalez, Diamondbacks 100

INTENTIONAL WALKS
Sammy Sosa, Cubs 37
Barry Bonds, Giants 35
Luis Gonzalez, Diamondbacks 24
Vladimir Guerrero, Expos 24
Chipper Jones, Braves 20

STRIKEOUTS
Jose Hernandez, Brewers 185
Richie Sexson, Brewers 178
Pat Burrell, Phillies 162
Lee Stevens, Expos 157
Sammy Sosa, Cubs 150

TOUGHEST TO STRIKE OUT
(Plate Appearances per SO)
Juan Pierre, Rockies 23.6
Fernando Vina, Cardinals 19.7

Jimmy Rollins: 12 triples, 46 steals

Paul LoDuca, Dodgers 17.3
Mark Grace, Diamondbacks 15.4
Eric Young, Cubs 14.9

STOLEN BASES
Juan Pierre, Rockies 46
Jimmy Rollins, Phillies 46
Vladimir Guerrero, Expos 37
Bob Abreu, Phillies 36
Luis Castillo, Marlins 33

CAUGHT STEALING
Juan Pierre, Rockies 17
Luis Castillo, Marlins 16
Vladimir Guerrero, Expos 16
Bob Abreu, Phillies 14
Jason Kendall, Pirates 14
Eric Young, Cubs 14

GIDP
Vladimir Guerrero, Expos 24
Ron Coomer, Cubs 23
Placido Polanco, Cardinals 22
Dmitri Young, Reds 22
Albert Pujols, Cardinals 21

HITTING STREAKS
Moises Alou, Astros 23
Lance Berkman, Astros 21
Placido Polanco, Cardinals 20
Peter Bergeron, Expos 19
Mark Grace, Diamondbacks 18
Craig Biggio, Astros 18
Cliff Floyd, Marlins 18

MULTIPLE-HIT GAMES
Luis Gonzalez, Diamondbacks 64
Juan Pierre, Rockies 62
Rich Aurilia, Giants 61
Albert Pujols, Cardinals 60
Todd Helton, Rockies 59

SLUGGING PERCENTAGE
Barry Bonds, Giants .... .863
Sammy Sosa, Cubs .... .737
Luis Gonzalez, Diamondbacks .... .688
Todd Helton, Rockies .... .685
Larry Walker, Rockies .... .662

ON-BASE PERCENTAGE
Barry Bonds, Giants .... .515
Larry Walker, Rockies .... .449
Sammy Sosa, Cubs .... .437
Todd Helton, Rockies .... .432
Lance Berkman, Astros .... .430

PITCHING

WINS
Matt Morris, Cardinals 22
Curt Schilling, Diamondbacks 22
Randy Johnson, Diamondbacks 21
Jon Lieber, Cubs 20
Greg Maddux, Braves 17
Russ Ortiz, Giants 17

LOSSES
Bobby Jones, Padres 19
Jimmy Anderson, Pirates 17
Jimmy Haynes, Brewers 17
Livan Hernandez, Giants 15
Chris Reitsma, Reds 15
Todd Ritchie, Pirates 15

WINNING PERCENTAGE
Roy Oswalt, Astros .... .824
Curt Schilling, Diamondbacks .... .786
Randy Johnson, Diamondbacks .... .778
Jon Lieber, Cubs .... .769
Matt Morris, Cardinals .... .733

GAMES
Steve Kline, Cardinals 89
Graeme Lloyd, Expos 84
Jeff Fassero, Cubs 82
Ray King, Brewers 82
Felix Rodriguez, Giants 80

GAMES STARTED
Tom Glavine, Braves 35
Chan Ho Park, Dodgers 35
Curt Schilling, Diamondbacks 35
13 tied at 34

COMPLETE GAMES
Curt Schilling, Diamondbacks 6
Jon Lieber, Cubs 5
Javier Vazquez, Expos 5
Pedro Astacio, Rockies/Astros 4
Todd Ritchie, Pirates 4
Randy Wolf, Phillies 4

SHUTOUTS
Greg Maddux, Braves 3
Javier Vazquez, Expos 3
Randy Johnson, Diamondbacks 2
Albie Lopez, Diamondbacks 2
Todd Ritchie, Pirates 2
Randy Wolf, Phillies 2

GAMES FINISHED
Robb Nen, Giants 71
Jeff Shaw, Dodgers 66
Armando Benitez, Mets 64
Jose Mesa, Phillies 59
Curtis Leskanic, Brewers 58
Billy Wagner, Astros 58

SAVES
Robb Nen, Giants 45
Armando Benitez, Mets 43
Trevor Hoffman, Padres 43
Jeff Shaw, Dodgers 43
Jose Mesa, Phillies 42

INNINGS
Curt Schilling, Diamondbacks 257
Randy Johnson, Diamondbacks 250
Chan Ho Park, Dodgers 234
Greg Maddux, Braves 233
Jon Lieber, Cubs 232

HITS ALLOWED
Livan Hernandez, Giants 266
Bobby Jones, Padres 250
Curt Schilling, Diamondbacks 237
Mike Hampton, Rockies 236
Jimmy Anderson, Pirates 232

RUNS ALLOWED
Livan Hernandez, Giants 143
Mike Hampton, Rockies 138
Bobby Jones, Padres 137
Jimmy Anderson, Pirates 123
Ryan Dempster, Marlins 123

HOME RUNS ALLOWED
Kevin Jarvis, Padres 37

Bobby Jones, Padres 37
Curt Schilling, Diamondbacks 37
Dustin Hermanson, Cardinals 34
Robert Person, Phillies 34

WALKS
Ryan Dempster, Marlins 112
Jamey Wright, Brewers 98
Tom Glavine, Braves 97
Kerry Wood, Cubs 92
Tony Armas, Expos 91
Russ Ortiz, Giants 91
Chan Ho Park, Dodgers 91

FEWEST WALKS PER 9 INNINGS
Greg Maddux, Braves 1.04
Curt Schilling, Diamondbacks 1.37
Jon Lieber, Cubs 1.59
Bobby Jones, Padres 1.75
Shane Reynolds, Astros 1.77
Javier Vazquez, Expos 1.77

HIT BATSMEN
Chan Ho Park, Dodgers 20
Jamey Wright, Brewers 20
Randy Johnson, Diamondbacks 18
Eric Gagne, Dodgers 16
Kevin Appier, Mets 15
Matt Clement, Marlins 15

STRIKEOUTS
Randy Johnson, Diamondbacks 372
Curt Schilling, Diamondbacks 293
Chan Ho Park, Dodgers 218
Kerry Wood, Cubs 217
Javier Vazquez, Expos 208

STRIKEOUTS PER 9 INNINGS
Randy Johnson, Diamondbacks 13.41
Kerry Wood, Cubs 11.20
Curt Schilling, Diamondbacks 10.27
Randy Wolf, Phillies 8.39
Jason Bere, Cubs 8.38

PICKOFFS
Brian Anderson, Diamondbacks 7
Kerry Wood, Cubs 7
Joe Beimel, Pirates 6
Bruce Chen, Phillies/Mets 6
Lance Davis, Reds 6

WILD PITCHES
Matt Clement, Marlins 15
Kevin Appier, Mets 12
Darren Dreifort, Dodgers 10
Shawn Estes, Giants 10
Robert Person, Phillies 10
Mac Suzuki, Rockies/Brewers 10

BALKS
Omar Daal, Phillies 3
Chan Ho Park, Dodgers 3
Odalis Perez, Braves 3
Eight tied at 2

OPPONENTS BATTING AVERAGE
Kerry Wood, Cubs .... .202

Robb Nen: 45 saves

Brad Ausmus: .997 fielding average

Randy Johnson, Diamondbacks .... .203
Chan Ho Park, Dodgers .... .216
John Burkett, Braves .... .230
A.J. Burnett, Marlins .... .231

FIELDING

PITCHER
PCT	Kirk Rueter, Giants	1.000
PO	Javier Vazquez, Expos	23
A	Greg Maddux, Braves	53
E	Three tied at	4
TC	Greg Maddux, Braves	73
DP	Kirk Rueter, Giants	11

CATCHER
PCT	Brad Ausmus, Astros	.997
PO	Damian Miller, D'backs	966
A	Damian Miller, D'backs	78
E	Jason Kendall, Pirates	12
	Kelly Stinnett, Reds	12
TC	Damian Miller, D'backs	1051
DP	Ben Davis, Padres	15
	Charles Johnson, Marlins	15
PB	Jason LaRue, Reds	15

FIRST BASE
PCT	Todd Helton, Rockies	.999
PO	Richie Sexson, Brewers	1354
A	Jeff Bagwell, Astros	141
E	Lee Stevens, Expos	19
TC	Richie Sexson, Brewers	1490
DP	Derrek Lee, Marlins	142

SECOND BASE
PCT	Three tied at	.987
PO	Fernando Vina, Cardinals	312
A	Jeff Kent, Giants	391
E	Luis Castillo, Marlins	13
TC	Fernando Vina, Cardinals	703
DP	Luis Castillo, Marlins	100
	Fernando Vina, Cardinals	100

THIRD BASE
PCT	Placido Polanco, Cardinals	.985
PO	Mike Lowell, Marlins	107
A	Aramis Ramirez, Pirates	335
E	Phil Nevin, Padres	27
TC	Aramis Ramirez, Pirates	453
DP	Mike Lowell, Marlins	35

SHORTSTOP
PCT	Orlando Cabrera, Expos	.986
PO	Orlando Cabrera, Expos	246
A	Orlando Cabrera, Expos	517
E	Alex Gonzalez, Marlins	26
TC	Orlando Cabrera, Expos	774
DP	Rich Aurilia, Giants	108

OUTFIELD
PCT	Luis Gonzalez, D'backs	1.000
PO	Andruw Jones, Braves	456
A	Pat Burrell, Phillies	18
E	Vladimir Guerrero, Expos	12
TC	Andruw Jones, Braves	472
DP	Andruw Jones, Braves	6

2001 NATIONAL LEAGUE STATISTICS

CLUB BATTING

	AVG	G	AB	R	H	2B	3B	HR	BB	SO	SB
Colorado	.292	162	5690	923	1663	324	61	213	511	1027	132
Houston	.271	162	5528	847	1500	313	29	208	581	1119	64
St. Louis	.270	162	5450	814	1469	274	32	199	529	1089	91
Arizona	.267	162	5595	818	1494	284	35	208	587	1052	71
San Francisco	.266	162	5612	799	1493	304	40	235	625	1090	57
Florida	.264	162	5542	742	1461	325	30	166	470	1145	89
Cincinnati	.262	162	5583	735	1464	304	22	176	468	1172	103
Chicago	.261	162	5406	777	1409	268	32	194	577	1077	67
Atlanta	.260	162	5498	729	1432	263	24	174	493	1039	85
Philadelphia	.260	162	5497	746	1431	295	29	164	551	1125	153
Los Angeles	.255	162	5493	758	1399	264	27	206	519	1062	89
Montreal	.253	162	5379	670	1361	320	28	131	478	1071	101
San Diego	.252	162	5482	789	1379	273	26	161	678	1273	129
Milwaukee	.251	162	5488	740	1378	273	30	209	488	1399	66
New York	.249	162	5459	642	1361	273	18	147	545	1062	66
Pittsburgh	.247	162	5398	657	1333	256	25	161	467	1106	93

CLUB PITCHING

	ERA	G	CG	SHO	SV	IP	H	R	ER	BB	SO
Atlanta	3.59	162	5	13	41	1447	1363	643	578	499	1133
Arizona	3.87	162	12	13	34	1460	1352	677	627	461	1297
St. Louis	3.93	162	8	11	38	1435	1389	684	627	526	1083
Chicago	4.03	162	8	6	41	1437	1357	701	643	550	1344
New York	4.07	162	6	14	48	1446	1418	713	654	438	1191
Philadelphia	4.15	162	8	7	47	1445	1417	719	667	527	1086
San Francisco	4.18	162	3	8	47	1463	1437	748	680	579	1080
Los Angeles	4.25	162	3	5	46	1451	1387	744	685	524	1212
Florida	4.32	162	5	11	32	1438	1397	744	691	617	1119
Houston	4.37	162	7	6	48	1455	1453	769	707	486	1228
San Diego	4.52	162	5	6	46	1441	1519	812	724	476	1088
Milwaukee	4.64	162	3	8	28	1436	1452	806	740	667	1057
Montreal	4.68	162	5	11	28	1431	1509	812	745	525	1103
Cincinnati	4.77	162	2	2	35	1443	1572	850	765	515	943
Pittsburgh	5.04	162	8	9	36	1416	1493	858	794	549	908
Colorado	5.29	162	8	8	26	1430	1522	906	841	598	1058

CLUB FIELDING

	PCT	PO	A	E	DP		PCT	PO	A	E	DP
Arizona	.986	4379	1559	84	148	Montreal	.982	4294	1621	108	139
Philadelphia	.985	4318	1603	91	145	St. Louis	.982	4306	1664	110	156
Colorado	.984	4290	1693	96	167	Chicago	.982	4311	1493	109	113
Milwaukee	.983	4309	1727	103	156	Los Angeles	.981	4352	1586	116	138
New York	.983	4337	1576	101	132	San Francisco	.981	4390	1649	118	170
Florida	.983	4314	1666	103	174	Pittsburgh	.978	4249	1799	133	168
Atlanta	.983	4342	1636	103	133	Cincinnati	.978	4328	1733	138	136
Houston	.982	4364	1662	110	138	San Diego	.976	4322	1607	145	127

INDIVIDUAL BATTING LEADERS
(Minimum 502 Plate Appearances)

	AVG	G	AB	R	H	2B	3B	HR	RBI	BB	SO	SB
Walker, Larry, Colorado	.350	142	497	107	174	35	3	38	123	82	103	14
Helton, Todd, Colorado	.336	159	587	132	197	54	2	49	146	98	104	7
Alou, Moises, Houston	.331	136	513	79	170	31	1	27	108	57	57	5
Berkman, Lance, Houston	.331	157	577	110	191	55	5	34	126	92	121	7
Jones, Chipper, Atlanta	.330	159	572	113	189	33	5	38	102	98	82	9
Pujols, Albert, St. Louis	.329	161	590	112	194	47	4	37	130	69	93	1
Bonds, Barry, San Francisco	.328	153	476	129	156	32	2	73	137	177	93	13
Sosa, Sammy, Chicago	.328	160	577	146	189	34	5	64	160	116	153	0
Pierre, Juan, Colorado	.327	156	617	108	202	26	11	2	55	41	29	46
Gonzalez, Luis, Arizona	.325	162	609	128	198	36	7	57	142	100	83	1

INDIVIDUAL PITCHING LEADERS
(Minimum 162 Innings)

	W	L	ERA	G	GS	CG	SV	IP	H	R	ER	BB	SO
Johnson, Randy, Arizona	21	6	2.49	35	34	3	0	250	181	74	69	71	372
Schilling, Curt, Arizona	22	6	2.98	35	35	6	0	257	237	86	85	39	293
Burkett, John, Atlanta	12	12	3.04	34	34	1	0	219	187	83	74	70	187
Maddux, Greg, Atlanta	17	11	3.05	34	34	3	0	233	220	86	79	27	173
Kile, Darryl, St. Louis	16	11	3.09	34	34	2	0	227	228	83	78	65	179
Morris, Matt, St. Louis	22	8	3.16	34	34	2	0	216	218	86	76	54	185
Ortiz, Russ, San Francisco	17	9	3.29	33	33	1	0	219	187	90	80	91	169
Leiter, Al, New York	11	11	3.31	29	29	0	0	187	178	81	69	46	142
Wood, Kerry, Chicago	12	6	3.36	28	28	1	0	174	127	70	65	92	217
Miller, Wade, Houston	16	8	3.40	32	32	1	0	212	183	91	80	76	183

AWARD WINNERS

Selected by Baseball Writers Association of America

MVP

Player, Team	1st	2nd	3rd	Total
Barry Bonds, S.F.	30	2	0	438
Sammy Sosa, Chicago	2	17	8	278
Luis Gonzalez, Ariz.	0	8	21	261
Albert Pujols, St.L.	0	5	3	222
Lance Berkman, Hou.	0	0	0	125
Shawn Green, L.A.	0	0	0	112
Jeff Bagwell, Hou.	0	0	0	109
Chipper Jones, Atl.	0	0	0	100
Todd Helton, Colo.	0	0	0	90
Curt Schilling, Ariz.	0	0	0	24
Randy Johnson, Ariz.	0	0	0	23
Rich Aurilia, S.F.	0	0	0	20
Mike Piazza, N.Y.	0	0	0	14
Moises Alou, Hou.	0	0	0	13
Matt Morris, St. Louis	0	0	0	13
Bob Abreu, Phil.	0	0	0	9
Jimmy Rollins, Phil.	0	0	0	8
Brian Jordan, Atl.	0	0	0	7
Paul LoDuca, L.A.	0	0	0	6
Felix Rodriguez, S.F.	0	0	0	4
Phil Nevin, S.D.	0	0	0	3
Cliff Floyd, Fla.	0	0	0	2
Roy Oswalt, Hou.	0	0	0	2
Brian Giles, Pitt.	0	0	0	1
Vladimir Guerrero, Mon.	0	0	0	1
Steve Kline, St.L.	0	0	0	1
Scott Rolen, Phil.	0	0	0	1
Larry Walker, Colo.	0	0	0	1

CY YOUNG AWARD

Player, Team	1st	2nd	3rd	Total
Randy Johnson, Ariz.	30	2	0	156
Curt Schilling, Ariz.	2	29	1	98
Matt Morris, St. Louis	0	1	28	31
Jon Lieber, Chicago	0	0	2	2
Roy Oswalt, Hou.	0	0	1	1

ROOKIE OF THE YEAR

Player, Team	1st	2nd	3rd	Total
Albert Pujols, St. Louis	32	0	0	160
Roy Oswalt, Hou.	0	25	7	82
Jimmy Rollins, Phil.	0	7	23	44
Bud Smith, St. Louis	0	1	1	1
Adam Dunn, Cin.	0	0	1	1

MANAGER OF THE YEAR

Manager, Team	1st	2nd	3rd	Total
Larry Bowa, Phil.	18	6	5	113
Jim Tracy, L.A.	4	8	4	48
Tony La Russa, St.L.	4	5	3	38
Bob Brenly, Ariz.	3	4	6	33
Larry Dierker, Hou.	1	4	4	21
Don Baylor, Chicago	0	3	4	13
Bobby Cox, Atlanta	2	0	2	12
Dusty Baker, S.F.	0	2	4	10

NOTE: MVP balloting based on 14 points for first place vote, nine for second, eight for third, etc.; Cy Young Award, Rookie of the Year and Manager of the Year balloting based on five points for first-place vote, three for second and one for third.

GOLD GLOVE AWARDS

Selected by NL managers

C—Brad Ausmus, Houston. 1B—Todd Helton, Colorado. 2B—Fernando Vina, St. Louis. 3B—Scott Rolen, Philadelphia. SS—Orlando Cabrera, Montreal. OF—Jim Edmonds, St. Louis; Andruw Jones, Atlanta; Larry Walker, Colorado. P—Greg Maddux, Atlanta.

Righthander Kevin Millwood had another disappointing year, but Tom Glavine (16-7, 3.57) and Greg Maddux (17-11, 3.05) were reliable as ever as the Braves led the NL in ERA for the fifth straight season. John Smoltz also overcame his elbow injury to become a big success as a closer.

Still, it was a rather ho-hum year in terms of individual accomplishments in Atlanta. Third baseman Chipper Jones (.330-38-102) had a solid year, but the only significant record set was by Maddux, who raised the NL mark for consecutive innings without a walk to 72⅓. True to Maddux' nature, he didn't even fret when the streak ended on an intentional walk to Arizona's Steve Finley.

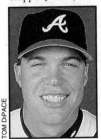

TOM DiPACE

Chipper Jones

"If you pitch better, you don't have to walk anybody," Maddux said. "If I was the manager, I would have walked him, too . . . It never meant that much to me. Walks are a big part of pitching. You've got good walks and you've got bad walks. That's why the streak doesn't matter."

Perhaps it's that consistency and lack of excitement, combined with a flair for the postseason fizzle, that led to more than 15,000 empty seats at Turner Field for two weekend games during the NLCS.

The End

The NL saw record after record fall in a magic final weekend, as Bonds made his way to the summit of baseball history on the backs of his teammates.

Bonds' three-homer weekend series against the Dodgers gave him 73 for the season, breaking the record McGwire had worked so tirelessly to shatter just three years earlier.

As the Padres were drubbed by the Rockies on the final Sunday in San Diego, Tony Gwynn said goodbye to the only team he'd ever played for in his 20 seasons as a major leaguer, grounding out as a pinch-hitter in the ninth. And Rickey Henderson, playing only because Gwynn simply wouldn't let him sit out, capped a remarkable record-setting season, collecting his 3,000th hit after earlier in the year breaking Babe Ruth's record for career walks and Ty Cobb's mark for career runs.

LARRY GOREN

Tony Gwynn

However, the records weren't what made the end of the 2001 season special. It was the "FDNY" and "NYPD" hats the Mets wore as they took the field over the final two weeks. It was the unfurling of the American flag and the heart-wrenching renditions of the new seventh-inning-stretch standard, "God Bless America." It was baseball rediscovering why it came to be known as the national pastime.

From no-hitters to McCovey Cove splashdowns, from Randy Johnson and Curt Schilling to Sammy Sosa and Luis Gonzalez, from a fractious and bickering Mets clubhouse in May to a united and anonymous Mets volunteer effort at Ground Zero in September, the 2001 season was one that won't soon be forgotten.

NATIONAL LEAGUE
DIVISION SERIES

ST. LOUIS VS. ARIZONA
COMPOSITE BOX

ST. LOUIS

Player, Pos.	AVG	G	AB	R	H	2B	3B	HR	RBI	BB	SO	SB
Kerry Robinson, ph-pr	.500	4	2	0	1	0	0	0	1	0	0	0
Woody Williams, p	.333	1	3	1	1	1	0	0	0	0	1	0
Fernando Vina, 2b	.316	5	19	2	6	0	0	1	2	0	1	1
Placido Polanco, 3b	.267	5	15	1	4	0	0	1	1	1	1	1
Jim Edmonds, cf	.235	5	17	3	4	1	0	2	3	3	6	0
Edgar Renteria, ss	.235	5	17	2	4	1	0	1	1	2	4	0
Miguel Cairo, ph-lf	.200	3	5	0	1	0	0	0	0	0	1	1
Mike Matheny, c	.200	4	10	0	2	0	0	0	0	0	3	0
J.D. Drew, rf	.154	5	13	1	2	0	0	1	2	3	1	0
Craig Paquette, 1b	.143	2	7	0	1	0	0	0	0	0	5	0
Albert Pujols, 1b-lf	.111	5	18	1	2	0	0	1	2	2	2	0
Mark McGwire, 1b	.091	4	11	0	1	0	0	0	0	0	6	0
Eli Marrero, c	.000	3	7	0	0	0	0	0	0	0	2	0
Matt Morris, p	.000	2	4	0	0	0	0	0	0	0	3	0
Darryl Kile, p	.000	1	2	0	0	0	0	0	0	0	2	0
Bud Smith, p	.000	1	1	1	0	0	0	0	0	1	1	0
Dustin Hermanson, p	.000	1	1	0	0	0	0	0	0	0	1	0
Totals	.191	5	152	12	29	3	0	6	12	12	38	3

Pitcher	W	L	ERA	G	GS	SV	IP	H	R	ER	BB	SO
Dustin Hermanson	0	0	0.00	1	0	0	3	0	0	0	0	0
Gene Stechschulte	0	0	0.00	2	0	0	3	0	0	0	0	0
Mike Timlin	0	0	0.00	1	0	0	1	0	0	0	0	0
Dave Veres	0	0	0.00	2	0	0	1	1	0	0	1	1
Matt Morris	0	1	1.20	2	2	0	15	13	2	2	5	12
Woody Williams	1	0	1.29	1	1	0	7	4	1	1	1	9
Bud Smith	1	0	1.80	1	1	0	5	4	1	1	4	2
Steve Kline	0	1	2.08	4	0	2	4	4	1	1	2	0
Darryl Kile	0	0	3.00	1	1	0	6	3	2	2	5	5
Mike Matthews	0	1	40.50	1	0	0	1	4	3	3	0	0
Totals	2	3	2.06	5	5	2	44	37	10	10	18	29

ARIZONA

Player, Pos.	AVG	G	AB	R	H	2B	3B	HR	RBI	BB	SO	SB
Steve Finley, cf	.421	5	19	1	8	1	0	0	2	0	2	0
Reggie Sanders, rf	.357	5	14	2	5	1	0	1	1	3	3	1
Greg Colbrunn, ph-1b	.333	4	6	0	2	0	0	0	1	1	0	0
Tony Womack, ss	.294	5	17	1	5	1	0	0	1	3	2	0
Damian Miller, c	.267	5	15	1	4	0	0	0	0	1	3	0
Luis Gonzalez, lf	.263	5	19	1	5	0	0	1	1	2	4	0
Jay Bell, ss	.250	2	4	0	1	0	0	0	0	0	1	0
Mark Grace, 1b	.214	4	14	0	3	1	0	0	0	2	3	0
Craig Counsell, 2b	.187	5	16	2	3	0	0	1	3	2	2	0
Matt Williams, 3b	.062	5	16	0	1	1	0	0	0	4	4	0
Danny Bautista, cf	.000	3	6	1	0	0	0	0	1	0	1	0
Curt Schilling, p	.000	2	5	0	0	0	0	0	0	0	2	0
Randy Johnson, p	.000	1	2	0	0	0	0	0	0	0	0	0
Erubiel Durazo, ph	.000	1	1	0	0	0	0	0	0	0	0	0
Miguel Batista, p	.000	1	1	0	0	0	0	0	0	0	0	0
Albie Lopez, p	.000	1	1	0	0	0	0	0	0	0	0	0
Rod Barajas, c	.000	1	0	0	0	0	0	0	0	0	0	0
Midre Cummings, pr	.000	2	0	1	0	0	0	0	0	0	0	0
Dave Dellucci, ph	.000	2	0	0	0	0	0	0	0	0	0	0
Totals	.237	5	156	10	37	5	0	3	10	18	29	1

Pitcher	W	L	ERA	G	GS	SV	IP	H	R	ER	BB	SO
Byung-Hyun Kim	0	0	0.00	1	0	1	1	1	0	0	2	1
Greg Swindell	0	0	0.00	2	0	0	2	1	0	0	0	2
Curt Schilling	2	0	0.50	2	2	0	18	9	1	1	2	18
Brian Anderson	0	0	2.25	2	0	0	4	3	1	1	0	3
Miguel Batista	1	0	2.70	2	1	0	7	3	2	2	1	4
Randy Johnson	0	1	3.38	1	1	0	8	6	3	3	2	9
Mike Morgan	0	0	6.75	3	0	0	1	2	1	1	2	1
Albie Lopez	0	1	12.00	1	1	0	3	4	4	4	3	0
Totals	3	2	2.45	5	5	1	44	29	12	12	12	38

SCORE BY INNINGS

St. Louis	313 200 111—12
Arizona	100 111 411—10

E—Womack 2, Pujols, Polanco, Renteria, M. Williams, Batista. **DP**—St. Louis 4, Arizona 4. **LOB**—St. Louis 30, Arizona 40. **CS**—Womack, Cummings. **SH**—Morris, Vina, Kline, Drew, Polanco 3, Robinson, Schilling 2, Womack 2, Batista, Miller. **SF**—Polanco. **HBP**—Miller (by Morris), Vina (by Anderson). **IBB**—Miller (by Veres), Colbrunn (by Kline). **WP**—Kim.

MAJOR LEAGUES

ATLANTA VS. HOUSTON
COMPOSITE BOX

ATLANTA

Player, Pos.	AVG	G	AB	R	H	2B	3B	HR	RBI	BB	SO	SB
Mark DeRosa, ss	1.000	1	1	0	1	0	0	0	0	0	0	0
Steve Torrealba, c	1.000	1	1	0	1	1	0	0	0	0	0	0
Andruw Jones, cf	.500	3	12	2	6	0	0	1	1	0	3	0
Keith Lockhart, ph-2b	.500	1	2	1	1	1	0	0	0	0	0	0
Chipper Jones, 3b	.444	3	9	2	4	0	0	2	5	3	1	0
Tom Glavine, p	.333	1	3	0	1	0	0	0	0	0	0	0
Julio Franco, 1b	.308	3	13	3	4	0	0	1	1	0	1	0
Paul Bako, c	.286	3	7	1	2	1	0	1	3	1	0	0
B.J. Surhoff, lf	.273	3	11	1	3	1	0	0	0	0	0	1
Marcus Giles, 2b	.250	3	12	2	3	1	0	0	1	0	3	0
Rey Sanchez, ss	.222	3	9	1	2	1	0	0	0	0	2	0
Brian Jordan, rf	.182	3	11	1	2	0	0	1	2	0	5	0
Greg Maddux, p	.000	1	2	0	0	0	0	0	0	0	1	0
John Burkett, p	.000	1	2	0	0	0	0	0	0	0	1	0
Ken Caminiti, ph	.000	2	2	0	0	0	0	0	0	0	1	0
John Smoltz, p	.000	3	1	0	0	0	0	0	0	0	0	0
Dave Martinez, ph	.000	1	1	0	0	0	0	0	0	0	0	0
Totals	.303	3	99	14	30	6	0	6	13	4	18	1

Pitcher	W	L	ERA	G	GS	SV	IP	H	R	ER	BB	SO
Tom Glavine	1	0	0.00	1	1	0	8	6	0	0	2	3
Steve Karsay	0	0	0.00	1	0	0	1	0	0	0	0	3
Steve Reed	0	0	0.00	1	0	0	0	0	0	0	0	0
Mike Remlinger	0	0	0.00	1	0	0	0	0	0	0	0	0
Rudy Seanez	1	0	0.00	1	0	0	1	0	0	0	1	0
John Smoltz	0	0	2.25	3	0	2	4	3	1	1	0	3
John Burkett	1	0	2.84	1	1	0	6	6	2	2	2	4
Greg Maddux	0	0	3.00	1	1	0	6	4	3	2	3	5
Totals	3	0	1.67	3	3	2	27	19	6	5	8	16

HOUSTON

Player, Pos.	AVG	G	AB	R	H	2B	3B	HR	RBI	BB	SO	SB
Tony Eusebio, c	.667	1	3	1	2	1	0	0	0	0	0	0
Daryle Ward, ph	.500	2	2	1	1	0	0	1	2	0	0	0
Jeff Bagwell, 1b	.429	3	7	0	3	0	0	0	0	5	1	0
Vinny Castilla, 3b	.273	3	11	1	3	0	0	1	1	0	3	0
Brad Ausmus, c	.250	3	8	1	2	0	0	1	2	0	0	0
Moises Alou, rf	.167	3	12	0	2	1	0	0	1	0	1	0
Lance Berkman, lf	.167	3	12	0	2	0	0	0	0	0	4	0
Craig Biggio, 2b	.167	3	12	0	2	0	0	0	0	0	1	0
Jose Vizcaino, ph-ss	.167	3	6	0	1	0	0	0	0	0	1	0
Richard Hidalgo, cf	.125	3	8	1	1	0	0	0	0	3	2	0
Julio Lugo, ss	.000	3	8	1	0	0	0	0	0	0	2	0
Wade Miller, p	.000	1	2	0	0	0	0	0	0	0	0	0
Dave Mlicki, p	.000	1	1	0	0	0	0	0	0	0	0	0
Shane Reynolds, p	.000	1	1	0	0	0	0	0	0	0	1	0
Orlando Merced, ph	.000	1	1	0	0	0	0	0	0	0	0	0
Chris Truby, ph	.000	1	1	0	0	0	0	0	0	0	1	0
Totals	.200	3	95	6	19	2	0	3	6	8	16	0

Pitcher	W	L	ERA	G	GS	SV	IP	H	R	ER	BB	SO
Nelson Cruz	0	0	0.00	2	0	0	3	1	0	0	1	1
Dave Mlicki	0	1	0.00	1	1	0	5	4	1	0	2	0
Ron Villone	0	0	0.00	1	0	0	1	0	0	0	0	0
Wade Miller	0	0	2.57	1	1	0	7	7	2	2	0	6
Octavio Dotel	0	0	5.40	2	0	0	3	5	2	2	0	5
Billy Wagner	0	0	5.40	2	0	0	2	1	0	0	0	3
Shane Reynolds	0	1	9.00	1	1	0	4	6	4	4	1	1
Mike Williams	0	0	9.00	2	0	0	1	3	1	1	0	1
Mike Jackson	0	1	27.00	2	0	0	1	3	3	2	0	1
Totals	0	3	4.15	3	3	0	26	30	14	12	4	18

SCORE BY INNINGS

Atlanta	131 200 061—14
Houston	000 021 201—6

E—Sanchez, Lugo 3. DP—Atlanta 5, Houston 7. LOB—Atlanta 14, Houston 16. CS—C. Jones, Franco, Jordan, Bagwell. SH—Bako. SF—Jordan. HBP—Surhoff (by Wagner). IBB—C. Jones (by Cruz). WP—Wagner.

CHAMPIONSHIP SERIES
ATLANTA VS. ARIZONA
COMPOSITE BOX

ATLANTA

Player, Pos.	AVG	G	AB	R	H	2B	3B	HR	RBI	BB	SO	SB
Greg Maddux, p	.333	2	3	0	1	1	0	0	0	0	2	0
Rey Sanchez, ss	.294	5	17	1	5	1	0	0	1	0	4	0
Chipper Jones, 3b	.263	5	19	1	5	1	0	0	2	6	0	0
Julio Franco, 1b	.261	5	23	2	6	0	0	1	2	0	2	0
B.J. Surhoff, lf	.231	4	13	1	3	0	0	1	2	0	1	0
Marcus Giles, 2b	.200	5	20	4	4	1	0	1	3	4	0	
Bernard Gilkey, ph-lf	.200	3	5	0	1	0	0	0	0	2	1	0
Dave Martinez, ph-lf	.200	4	5	0	1	0	0	0	0	0	1	0
Brian Jordan, rf	.190	5	21	1	4	2	0	0	3	0	6	0
Andruw Jones, cf	.176	5	17	4	3	0	0	1	1	1	5	0
Javy Lopez, c	.143	5	14	1	2	0	0	1	2	1	4	0
Mark DeRosa, ph-ss	.000	4	4	0	0	0	0	0	0	1	0	0
Paul Bako, c	.000	3	3	0	0	0	0	0	0	0	1	0
Tom Glavine, p	.000	2	3	0	0	0	0	0	0	0	2	0
Keith Lockhart, ph	.000	2	1	0	0	0	0	0	0	0	1	0
John Burkett, p	.000	1	1	0	0	0	0	0	0	0	0	0
Totals	.207	5	169	15	35	6	0	5	14	11	39	0

Pitcher	W	L	ERA	G	GS	SV	IP	H	R	ER	BB	SO
Kerry Ligtenberg	0	0	0.00	2	0	0	3	0	0	0	1	2
John Smoltz	0	0	0.00	2	0	0	3	0	0	0	0	1
Jason Marquis	0	0	0.00	2	0	0	2	2	4	0	2	3
Mike Remlinger	0	0	0.00	3	0	0	2	3	0	0	2	2
Rudy Seanez	0	0	0.00	2	0	0	2	1	0	0	3	3
Kevin Millwood	0	0	0.00	1	0	0	1	0	0	0	0	1
Steve Reed	0	0	0.00	1	0	0	0	0	0	0	0	0
Tom Glavine	1	1	1.50	2	2	0	12	10	4	2	5	5
Steve Karsay	0	0	2.08	4	0	0	4	3	1	1	1	6
Greg Maddux	0	2	5.40	2	2	0	10	14	8	6	2	7
John Burkett	0	1	8.31	1	1	0	4	7	5	4	2	2
Totals	1	4	2.66	5	5	0	44	40	22	13	18	32

ARIZONA

Player, Pos.	AVG	G	AB	R	H	2B	3B	HR	RBI	BB	SO	SB
Dave Dellucci, ph	.500	2	2	1	1	0	0	0	0	0	0	0
Craig Counsell, 2b	.381	5	21	5	8	3	0	0	4	0	3	1
Mark Grace, 1b	.375	5	16	1	6	0	0	0	1	2	1	0
Erubiel Durazo, ph-1b	.333	2	3	1	1	0	0	1	2	0	1	0
Steve Finley, cf	.286	5	14	1	4	1	0	0	4	3	1	1
Matt Williams, 3b	.278	5	18	1	5	1	0	0	2	2	3	0
Danny Bautista, cf	.250	2	4	1	1	0	0	0	1	1	1	0
Curt Schilling, p	.250	2	4	1	1	0	0	0	0	0	2	0
Luis Gonzalez, lf	.211	5	19	4	4	0	0	1	4	3	3	0
Tony Womack, ss	.200	4	20	4	4	1	0	0	0	2	0	
Damian Miller, c	.176	5	17	0	3	0	0	0	0	2	5	0
Reggie Sanders, rf	.118	5	17	2	2	0	0	0	1	5	5	1
Randy Johnson, p	.000	2	6	0	0	0	0	0	0	0	2	0
Jay Bell, 2b	.000	1	4	0	0	0	0	0	0	0	0	0
Miguel Batista, p	.000	2	2	0	0	0	0	0	0	0	1	0
Greg Colbrunn, ph	.000	1	1	0	0	0	0	0	0	0	0	0
Midre Cummings, ph	.000	1	1	0	0	0	0	0	0	0	1	0
Brian Anderson, p	.000	1	1	0	0	0	0	0	0	0	1	0
Byung-Hyun Kim, p	.000	3	1	0	0	0	0	0	0	0	0	0
Albie Lopez, p	.000	1	1	0	0	0	0	0	0	0	1	0
Totals	.233	5	172	22	40	6	0	2	19	18	32	3

Pitcher	W	L	ERA	G	GS	SV	IP	H	R	ER	BB	SO
Byung-Hyun Kim	0	0	0.00	3	0	2	5	0	0	0	1	3
Curt Schilling	1	0	1.00	1	1	0	9	4	1	1	2	13
Randy Johnson	2	0	1.13	2	2	0	16	10	2	2	3	19
Brian Anderson	1	0	2.70	1	0	0	3	4	1	1	1	0
Miguel Batista	0	1	5.14	2	1	0	7	5	4	4	2	3
Albie Lopez	0	0	6.00	1	1	0	3	5	2	2	1	1
Mike Morgan	0	0	27.00	2	0	0	1	3	3	3	1	1
Greg Swindell	0	0	27.00	2	0	0	1	1	1	1	0	0
Bobby Witt	0	0	27.00	1	0	0	3	1	1	1	0	0
Totals	4	1	3.00	5	5	2	45	35	15	15	11	39

SCORE BY INNINGS

Atlanta	210 200 460—15
Arizona	106 361 014—22

E—Giles 2, J. Lopez, C. Jones, Sanchez 2, Maddux, Williams 3. DP—Atlanta 5, Arizona 3. LOB—Atlanta 30, Arizona 39. CS—Surhoff, Womack. SH—Counsell 2. HBP—Gonzalez (by Maddux). IBB—Finley 2 (by Maddux, Seanez), Gonzalez 2 (by Burkett, Karsay), Grace (by Seanez). WP—Karsay, Glavine. PB—Bako.

ORGANIZATION STATS

ANAHEIM ANGELS

BY BILL SHAIKIN

David Eckstein singled home the tying run off Mariano Rivera in the ninth inning, Garret Anderson doubled home the winning run in the 10th, and the Angels were feeling pretty good about themselves on that August night. They had defeated the mighty Yankees, again, and were six games out in the wild-card race.

To say the Angels did not win another game the rest of the season would be incorrect, but not by much: They lost 25 of 31. Anaheim finished 41 games out of first. Troy Percival, the Angels' all-star closer, asked to be traded. Mo Vaughn, rarely seen or heard in Anaheim during his season-long rehab from arm surgery, popped up on a Boston radio station in October and asked the Red Sox to trade for him.

Disney kept its corporate fingers crossed that, if major league officials actually implemented contraction, the company could sell its money-losing baseball team to the owner of one of the teams going out of business.

The Angels would like to believe that a team that hit well and pitched poorly in 2000 and pitched well and hit poorly in 2001 can hit well and pitch well in 2002. The hitting, presumably, cannot get any worse.

"We've been bad," manager Mike Scioscia said. "I don't know how else you can say it. It's not like we've been middle of the pack. We're at the bottom. There will be years that people struggle, but it should never get as bad as this."

The Angels scored fewer runs than all but two other American League teams, hitting 78 fewer home runs and scoring 173 fewer runs than in the previous year.

Vaughn did not play, one year after hitting 36 homers and driving in 117. Darin Erstad dropped from .355-25-100 in 2000 to .258-9-63 in 2001, amid knee and back injuries. Tim Salmon, rewarded for his consistent excellence with a four-year, $40-million contract extension, dropped from .290-34-97 to .227-17-49 after shoulder and foot surgery.

Garret Anderson · Jose Fernandez

PLAYERS OF THE YEAR

MAJOR LEAGUE: Garret Anderson, of
About the only Angel who produced consistently with men on base in 2001, Anderson drove in 123 runs—a left-handed hitters' record for Anaheim—and had a personal high 194 hits.

MINOR LEAGUE: Jose Fernandez, 3b
He hit .338-30-114 in 122 games for Triple-A Salt Lake, shattering all previous career highs in an eight-year career. The Angels put him on waivers at the end of the season and he was claimed by the Cubs.

With comebacks from those three, and with the reliable Anderson (.289-28-123) and Troy Glaus emerging as a feared slugger (.250-41-108), the Angels could have the makings of a formidable offense. Rookie Eckstein, plucked off waivers in 2000, emerged as a suitably pesky leadoff hitter (.355 on-base percentage, 29 stolen bases) and could play second base or shortstop in 2002.

For the first time in four years, the Angels produced three 10-game winners in Ramon Ortiz (13-11, 4.36), Jarrod Washburn (11-10, 3.77) and Scott Schoeneweis (10-11, 5.08). Ortiz and Schoeneweis topped 200 innings, and Washburn threw 193, so the Angels appear to have developed stability and consistency in their rotation. Ortiz and Washburn could advance to top-of-the-rotation status, but Schoeneweis needs to develop his changeup (and as a sinkerball specialist get better infield defense).

Matt Wise (9-9, 5.04 at Triple-A Salt Lake City) will get first shot at winning a rotation spot in spring training. Salt Lake teammates Brian Cooper, Bart Miadich, Elvin Nina and Scot Shields figure to compete for spots in the bullpen.

By the end of the 2002 season, the Angels hope John Lackey (12-11, 4.48 in Triple-A and Double-A Arkansas) and Chris Bootcheck (11-7, 4.38 at Arkansas and Class A Rancho Cucamonga) can contend for rotation spots. Salt Lake third baseman Jose Fernandez, signed as a six-year free agent, hit .338-30-114.

The Angels had barely finished celebrating a strong draft when their top three picks—first baseman Casey Kotchman, catcher Jeff Mathis and third baseman Dallas McPherson—all were lost to season-ending injuries. Arkansas, in its first year as an Angel affiliate, was named Texas League champion. Provo won its division in the Pioneer League.

ORGANIZATION LEADERS

BATTING

*AVG	Jose Fernandez, Salt Lake	.338
R	Jose Fernandez, Salt Lake	99
H	Jose Fernandez, Salt Lake	153
TB	Jose Fernandez, Salt Lake	282
2B	Scott Morgan, Salt Lake	39
3B	Alfredo Amezaga, Salt Lake/Arkansas	9
HR	Jose Fernandez, Salt Lake	30
RBI	Jose Fernandez, Salt Lake	114
BB	Johnny Raburn, Cedar Rapids	63
	Scott Bikowski, Rancho Cucamonga	63
SO	Tommy Murphy, Rancho Cucamonga/Cedar Rapids	163
SB	Johnny Raburn, Cedar Rapids	37

PITCHING

W	Brian Cooper, Salt Lake	12
	John Lackey, Salt Lake/Arkansas	12
L	Dusty Bergman, Arkansas	13
#ERA	Pedro Liriano, Provo	2.78
G	Brendan Donnelly, Salt Lake/Arkansas	56
CG	Scot Shields, Salt Lake	4
	John Lackey, Salt Lake/Arkansas	4
SV	Bart Miadich, Salt Lake	27
IP	John Lackey, Salt Lake/Arkansas	185
BB	Elvin Nina, Salt Lake	79
SO	Francisco Rodriguez, Rancho Cucamonga	147

*Minimum 250 At-Bats #Minimum 75 Innings

ANAHEIM ANGELS

Manager: Mike Scioscia

2001 Record: 75-87, .463 (3rd, AL West)

BATTING	AVG	G	AB	R	H	2B	3B	HR	RBI	BB	SO	SB	CS	SLG	OBP	B	T	HT	WT	DOB	1st Yr	Resides
Anderson, Garret	.289	161	672	83	194	39	2	28	123	27	100	13	6	.478	.314	L	L	6-3	220	6-30-72	1990	Sand Canyon, Calif.
Barnes, Larry	.100	16	40	2	4	0	0	1	2	1	9	0	0	.175	.122	L	L	6-1	195	7-23-74	1995	Bakersfield, Calif.
Burke, Jamie	.200	9	5	1	1	0	0	0	0	0	2	0	0	.200	.200	R	R	6-0	195	9-24-71	1993	Roseburg, Ore.
DaVanon, Jeff	.193	40	88	7	17	2	1	5	9	11	29	1	3	.409	.280	B	R	6-0	185	12-8-73	1995	Del Mar, Calif.
Eckstein, David	.285	153	582	82	166	26	2	4	41	43	60	29	4	.357	.355	R	R	5-8	168	1-20-75	1997	Sanford, Fla.
Erstad, Darin	.258	157	631	89	163	35	1	9	63	62	113	24	10	.360	.331	L	L	6-2	212	6-4-74	1995	Fargo, N.D.
Fabregas, Jorge	.223	53	148	9	33	4	2	2	16	3	15	0	0	.318	.235	L	R	6-3	215	3-13-70	1991	Miami Beach, Fla.
Fernandez, Jose	.080	13	25	1	2	1	0	0	0	2	10	0	1	.120	.148	R	R	6-3	220	11-2-74	1993	Santiago, D.R.
Gil, Benji	.296	104	260	33	77	15	4	8	39	14	57	3	4	.477	.330	R	R	6-2	190	10-6-72	1991	San Diego, Calif.
Glaus, Troy	.250	161	588	100	147	38	2	41	108	107	158	10	3	.531	.367	R	R	6-5	229	8-3-76	1997	Anaheim Hills, Calif.
Hill, Glenallen	.136	16	66	4	9	0	0	1	2	0	20	0	0	.182	.136	R	R	6-3	230	3-22-65	1983	Santa Cruz, Calif.
Joyner, Wally	.243	53	148	14	36	5	1	3	14	13	18	1	1	.351	.304	L	L	6-2	200	6-16-62	1983	Rancho Santa Fe, Calif.
Kennedy, Adam	.270	137	478	48	129	25	3	6	40	27	71	12	7	.372	.318	L	R	6-1	180	1-10-76	1997	Riverside, Calif.
Molina, Bengie	.262	96	325	31	85	11	0	6	40	16	51	0	1	.351	.309	R	R	5-11	207	7-20-74	1993	San Luis, Ariz.
Molina, Jose	.270	15	37	8	10	3	0	2	4	3	8	0	0	.514	.325	R	R	6-1	195	6-3-75	1993	Vega Alta, P.R.
Nieves, Jose	.245	29	53	5	13	3	1	2	3	2	20	0	1	.453	.298	R	R	6-0	180	6-16-75	1992	Carabobo, Venez.
Palmeiro, Orlando	.243	104	230	29	56	10	1	2	23	25	24	6	6	.322	.319	L	R	5-11	175	1-19-69	1991	Miami, Fla.
Salmon, Tim	.227	137	475	63	108	21	1	17	49	96	121	9	3	.383	.365	R	R	6-3	231	8-24-68	1989	Scottsdale, Ariz.
Spiezio, Scott	.271	139	457	57	124	29	4	13	54	34	65	5	2	.438	.326	B	R	6-2	222	9-21-72	1993	Morris, Ill.
Wooten, Shawn	.312	79	221	24	69	8	1	8	32	5	42	2	0	.466	.332	R	R	5-10	205	7-24-72	1993	La Verne, Calif.

PITCHING	W	L	ERA	G	GS	CG	SV	IP	H	R	ER	BB	SO	AVG	B	T	HT	WT	DOB	1st Yr	Resides
Borland, Toby	0	1	10.80	2	0	0	0	3	8	5	4	1	0	.470	R	R	6-6	204	5-29-69	1989	Quitman, La.
Cooper, Brian	0	0	2.63	7	1	0	0	14	10	5	4	4	7	.200	R	R	6-1	185	8-19-74	1995	Glendora, Calif.
Green, Steve	0	0	3.00	1	1	0	0	6	4	2	2	6	4	.190	R	R	6-2	180	1-26-78	1997	Longueuil, Quebec
Hasegawa, Shigetoshi	5	6	4.04	46	0	0	0	56	52	28	25	20	41	.247	R	R	5-11	178	8-1-68	1997	Newport Beach, Calif.
Holtz, Mike	1	2	4.86	63	0	0	0	37	40	24	20	15	38	.273	L	L	5-9	188	10-12-72	1994	Hollidaysburg, Pa.
Levine, Alan	8	10	2.38	64	1	0	2	76	71	25	20	28	40	.257	L	R	6-3	198	5-22-68	1991	Gilbert, Ariz.
Lukasiewicz, Mark	0	2	6.04	24	0	0	0	22	21	17	15	9	25	.247	L	L	6-5	230	3-8-73	1994	Secaucus, N.J.
Miadich, Bart	0	0	4.50	11	0	0	0	10	6	5	5	8	11	.181	R	R	6-4	205	2-3-76	1997	Lake Oswego, Ore.
Ortiz, Ramon	13	11	4.36	32	32	2	0	209	223	114	101	76	135	.274	R	R	6-0	175	3-23-76	1995	Cotui, D.R.
Percival, Troy	4	2	2.65	57	0	0	39	58	39	19	17	18	71	.186	R	R	6-3	236	8-9-69	1990	Riverside, Calif.
Pote, Lou	2	0	4.15	44	1	0	2	87	88	41	40	32	66	.258	R	R	6-3	208	8-27-71	1991	Chicago, Ill.
Rapp, Pat	5	12	4.76	31	28	1	0	170	169	96	90	71	82	.260	R	R	6-3	215	7-13-67	1989	Sulphur, La.
Schoeneweis, Scott	10	11	5.08	32	32	1	0	205	227	122	116	77	104	.280	L	L	6-0	186	10-2-73	1996	Scottsdale, Ariz.
Shields, Scot	0	0	0.00	8	0	0	0	11	8	1	0	7	7	.200	R	R	6-1	175	7-22-75	1997	Fort Lauderdale, Fla.
Valdes, Ismael	9	13	4.45	27	27	1	0	164	177	82	81	50	100	.277	R	R	6-3	215	8-21-73	1991	Victoria, Mexico
Washburn, Jarrod	11	10	3.77	30	30	1	0	193	196	89	81	54	126	.263	L	L	6-1	198	8-13-74	1995	Danbury, Wis.
Weber, Ben	6	2	3.42	56	0	0	0	68	66	28	26	31	40	.250	R	R	6-4	180	11-17-69	1991	Groves, Texas
Wise, Matt	1	4	4.38	11	9	0	0	49	47	27	24	18	50	.250	R	R	6-4	190	11-18-75	1997	La Verne, Calif.

FIELDING

Catcher	PCT	G	PO	A	E	DP	PB
Burke	1.000	8	10	1	0	0	0
Fabregas	.990	53	267	23	3	3	2
B. Molina	.991	94	527	36	5	4	4
J. Molina	1.000	15	78	6	0	1	2
Wooten	1.000	25	97	11	0	0	8

First Base	PCT	G	PO	A	E	DP
Barnes	1.000	16	86	7	0	5
Burke	1.000	1	2	0	0	0
Erstad	1.000	12	64	7	0	8
Fernandez	.000	2	0	0	1	0
Gil	1.000	18	69	8	0	7
Joyner	.997	39	270	18	1	27
Nieves	1.000	1	2	0	0	0
Spiezio	.999	105	819	74	1	64
Wooten	.986	21	134	11	2	19

Second Base	PCT	G	PO	A	E	DP
Eckstein	.948	14	21	34	3	9
Gil	.965	21	30	53	3	14
Kennedy	.984	131	236	376	10	64
Nieves	1.000	11	21	31	0	10

Third Base	PCT	G	PO	A	E	DP
Fernandez	.000	2	0	0	0	0
Glaus	.953	159	103	286	19	21
Nieves	1.000	2	0	3	0	1
Spiezio	.917	10	2	9	1	1
Wooten	.000	1	0	0	0	0

Shortstop	PCT	G	PO	A	E	DP
Eckstein	.971	126	178	332	15	66
Gil	.945	44	78	110	11	24
Glaus	1.000	2	0	1	0	0
Nieves	.957	10	10	12	1	2

Outfield	PCT	G	PO	A	E	DP
Anderson	.994	149	313	9	2	2
Barnes	.000	1	0	0	0	0
DaVanon	.980	29	45	3	1	1
Erstad	.998	146	398	10	1	3
Gil	.000	1	0	0	0	0
Palmeiro	.989	59	87	2	1	1
Salmon	.989	125	254	13	3	5
Spiezio	1.000	18	19	0	0	0

Troy Percival

Director, Player Development: Darrell Miller

Class	Farm Team	League	W	L	Pct.	Finish*	Manager	First Yr.
AAA	Salt Lake (Utah) Stingers	Pacific Coast	79	64	.552	4th (16)	Garry Templeton	2001
AA	Arkansas Travelers	Texas	66	70	.485	+6th (8)	Mike Brumley	2001
A#	Rancho Cucamonga (Calif.) Quakes	California	63	77	.450	7th (10)	Tim Wallach	2001
A	Cedar Rapids (Iowa) Kernels	Midwest	60	77	.438	10th (14)	Tyrone Boykin	1993
Rookie#	Provo (Utah) Angels	Pioneer	53	23	.697	1st (8)	Tom Kotchman	2001
Rookie	Mesa (Ariz.) Angels	Arizona	22	34	.393	7th (7)	Brian Harper	2001

*Finish in overall standings (No. of teams in league) #Advanced level +League champion

SALT LAKE   Class AAA

PACIFIC COAST LEAGUE

BATTING	AVG	G	AB	R	H	2B	3B	HR	RBI	BB	SO	SB	CS	SLG	OBP	B	T	HT	WT	DOB	1st Yr	Resides
Abbott, Chuck	.000	4	9	1	0	0	0	0	0	2	4	0	0	.000	.182	R	R	6-1	180	1-26-75	1996	Schaumburg, Ill.
Amezaga, Alfredo	.250	49	200	28	50	5	4	1	16	14	45	9	6	.330	.307	B	R	5-10	165	1-16-78	1999	Obregon, Mexico
Barnes, Larry	.290	100	404	78	117	21	8	18	73	29	90	6	1	.515	.337	L	L	6-1	195	7-23-77	1996	Bakersfield, Calif.
Bartee, Kimera	.275	40	167	23	46	13	2	3	27	19	26	5	1	.431	.348	R	R	6-0	200	7-21-72	1993	Peoria, Ariz.
Baughman, Justin	.302	77	288	52	87	15	5	3	32	20	54	21	6	.420	.356	R	R	5-11	180	8-1-74	1995	Portland, Ore.
Burke, Jamie	.219	61	215	25	47	10	3	0	27	19	28	1	0	.293	.292	R	R	6-0	195	9-24-71	1993	Roseburg, Ore.
Caceres, Wilmy	.249	87	325	38	81	5	4	0	21	12	45	12	6	.289	.281	R	R	6-0	165	10-2-78	1997	Moca, D.R.
DaVanon, Jeff	.313	69	256	46	80	19	8	10	48	32	57	8	3	.566	.390	B	R	6-0	185	12-8-73	1995	Del Mar, Calif.
Diaz, Angel	.231	7	26	5	6	2	0	0	4	0	7	0	0	.308	.259	R	R	6-0	198	7-27-76	1998	Lakeland, Fla.
Durrington, Trent	.328	39	122	20	40	11	4	3	21	11	24	7	4	.557	.387	R	R	5-10	188	8-27-75	1994	Queensland, Australia
2-team (22 Las Vegas)	.294	61	177	30	52	15	5	4	23	19	43	10	5	.503	.368							
Encarnacion, Bien	.304	6	23	6	7	0	0	3	2	6	0	0	0	.304	.360	R	R	5-11	180	2-24-78	1995	Bani, D.R.
Fernandez, Jose	.338	122	452	99	153	37	1	30	114	55	91	9	7	.624	.421	R	R	6-3	220	11-2-74	1993	Santiago, D.R.
Guiel, Jeff	.321	61	224	37	72	14	1	10	35	17	39	2	0	.527	.370	L	R	5-11	195	1-12-74	1997	Langley, B.C.
Hill, Jason	.370	8	27	3	10	1	1	0	3	2	4	0	0	.481	.414	R	R	6-3	210	3-17-77	1998	Danville, Calif.
Lidle, Kevin	.295	30	88	10	26	7	0	1	10	9	27	2	1	.409	.376	B	R	5-11	170	3-22-72	1992	West Covina, Calif.
Lopez, Norberto	.000	2	5	0	0	0	0	0	0	0	1	0	0	.000	.000	R	R	5-8	190	12-9-76	1999	Hialeah, Fla.
Molina, Bengie	.278	5	18	2	5	1	0	0	3	2	3	0	0	.333	.350	R	R	5-11	207	7-20-74	1993	San Luis, Ariz.
Molina, Jose	.300	61	213	29	64	11	1	5	31	14	49	1	2	.432	.349	R	R	6-1	195	6-3-75	1993	Vega Alta, P.R.
Moreta, Ramon	.286	2	7	0	2	0	0	0	1	0	0	0	1	.286	.286	R	R	5-11	185	9-5-75	1994	La Romana, D.R.
2-team (23 Tacoma)	.224	25	76	8	17	3	1	1	14	6	31	3	4	.329	.287							
Morgan, Scott	.265	128	501	93	133	39	3	28	83	41	117	2	0	.523	.326	R	R	6-7	230	7-19-73	1995	Lompoc, Calif.
Murphy, Nate	.249	53	177	28	44	8	1	5	21	16	53	1	3	.390	.318	L	L	6-0	195	4-15-75	1996	Montague, Mass.
Nieves, Jose	.329	61	258	50	85	15	4	11	37	8	36	8	7	.547	.354	R	R	6-0	180	6-16-75	1992	Carabobo, Venez.
Pritchett, Chris	.303	125	476	66	144	36	3	17	75	45	102	3	2	.498	.362	L	R	6-4	212	1-31-70	1991	Modesto, Calif.
t'Hoen, E.J.	.219	18	64	8	14	5	0	2	7	1	18	0	1	.391	.254	R	R	6-2	185	11-8-75	1996	Alphen Aan Denryn, Netherlands
Tolentino, Juan	.277	114	452	70	125	35	3	11	66	25	87	17	4	.440	.320	R	R	6-0	165	3-12-76	1995	San Pedro de Marcois, D.R.
Zamora, Junior	.300	6	20	3	6	1	1	2	4	2	3	0	0	.750	.364	R	R	6-2	193	5-3-76	1994	San Pedro de Macoris, D.R.

PITCHING	W	L	ERA	G	GS	CG	SV	IP	H	R	ER	BB	SO	AVG	B	T	HT	WT	DOB	1st Yr	Resides
Alvarez, Juan	2	2	4.95	48	1	0	0	67	68	42	37	27	44	.264	L	L	6-0	175	8-9-73	1995	Miami, Fla.
Beverlin, Jason	6	2	4.23	19	12	1	0	83	82	41	39	29	74	.260	L	R	6-5	220	11-27-73	1994	Royal Oak, Mich.
Borland, Toby	2	3	2.30	45	1	0	3	74	53	25	19	29	92	.197	R	R	6-6	204	5-29-69	1989	Quitman, La.
Brunson, Will	2	2	4.39	39	1	0	0	70	73	37	34	20	52	.271	L	L	6-5	185	3-20-70	1992	Bulverde, Texas
Bruske, Jim	3	1	4.89	27	5	0	1	57	70	35	31	10	58	.295	R	R	6-1	185	10-7-64	1986	Phoenix, Ariz.
Cooper, Brian	12	8	4.63	28	28	1	0	173	181	98	89	58	109	.272	R	R	6-1	185	8-19-74	1995	Glendora, Calif.
Donnelly, Brendan	5	1	2.40	29	0	0	1	41	38	11	11	8	50	.245	R	R	6-3	205	7-4-71	1992	Albuquerque, N.M.
Espina, Rendy	0	0	3.86	2	0	0	0	2	1	1	1	0	1	.142	L	L	6-0	180	5-11-78	1995	Cabimas, Venez.
Green, Steve	3	3	3.66	10	10	1	0	59	59	30	24	13	40	.256	R	R	6-2	180	12-26-78	1997	Longueuil, Quebec
Janzen, Marty	0	0	12.27	2	0	0	0	4	5	5	5	3	3	.333	R	R	6-3	197	5-31-73	1991	Gainesville, Fla.
Lackey, John	3	4	6.71	10	10	1	0	58	75	44	43	16	42	.321	R	R	6-6	200	10-23-78	1999	Abilene, Texas
Lukasiewicz, Mark	0	1	1.48	20	0	0	2	30	12	5	5	2	41	.116	L	L	6-5	230	3-8-73	1994	Secaucus, N.J.
Miadich, Bart	4	4	2.44	55	0	0	27	59	40	20	16	29	73	.189	R	R	6-4	205	2-3-76	1997	Lake Oswego, Ore.
Mintz, Steve	1	2	5.79	13	3	0	0	37	50	28	24	11	21	.318	L	R	5-11	190	11-24-68	1990	Vero Beach, Fla.
Nina, Elvin	10	11	5.47	29	28	1	0	158	195	112	96	79	101	.306	R	R	6-0	185	11-25-75	1997	East Orange, N.J.
Shields, Scot	6	11	4.97	21	21	4	0	138	141	84	76	31	104	.266	R	R	6-1	175	7-22-75	1997	Fort Lauderdale, Fla.
Small, Aaron	0	1	1.69	3	0	0	0	5	8	1	1	1	5	.363	R	R	6-5	225	11-23-71	1989	Loudon, Tenn.
Washburn, Jarrod	0	1	5.87	1	1	0	0	8	9	5	5	1	5	.300	L	L	6-1	198	8-13-74	1995	Danbury, Wis.
Williams, Shad	0	0	8.78	8	1	0	0	13	26	13	13	7	9	.426	R	R	6-0	198	3-10-71	1991	Fresno, Calif.
Wise, Matt	9	9	5.04	21	21	0	0	123	134	79	69	17	111	.271	R	R	6-4	190	11-18-75	1997	La Verne, Calif.

FIELDING

Catcher	PCT	G	PO	A	E	DP	PB
Burke	.987	36	284	20	4	1	3
Diaz	1.000	7	59	4	0	0	0
Hill	.951	8	55	3	3	0	1
Lidle	.979	29	162	25	4	1	2
Lopez	1.000	2	8	0	0	0	0
B. Molina	1.000	4	27	2	0	0	0
J. Molina	.996	61	451	43	2	4	5

First Base	PCT	G	PO	A	E	DP
Barnes	.990	83	676	53	7	76
Burke	.980	6	44	5	1	6
Fernandez	1.000	1	6	0	0	6

	PCT	G	PO	A	E	DP
Morgan	1.000	1	9	0	0	2
Pritchett	.990	55	472	30	5	46

Second Base	PCT	G	PO	A	E	DP
Abbott	1.000	3	3	3	0	1
Baughman	.980	63	121	166	6	34
Caceres	.960	17	30	42	3	12
Durrington	.974	17	30	44	2	15
Nieves	.959	45	92	121	9	28
t'Hoen	1.000	5	4	14	0	4

Third Base	PCT	G	PO	A	E	DP
Abbott	.800	1	0	4	1	0

	PCT	G	PO	A	E	DP
Burke	1.000	13	12	28	0	0
Durrington	.800	5	2	6	2	0
Encarnacion	.889	2	1	7	1	0
Fernandez	.953	114	71	234	15	22
Guiel	1.000	2	0	1	0	0
Nieves	.889	5	3	5	1	0
Pritchett	1.000	1	0	4	0	0
t'Hoen	.941	5	3	13	1	2
Zamora	.875	3	0	7	1	1

Shortstop	PCT	G	PO	A	E	DP
Amezaga	.954	49	91	137	11	34
Baughman	1.000	1	3	4	0	2

Caceres	.963	70	128	206	13	47
Durrington	1.000	1	1	2	0	0
Encarnacion	1.000	4	8	16	0	2
Nieves	.945	14	17	35	3	6
t'Hoen	.929	7	5	21	2	4

Outfield	PCT	G	PO	A	E	DP
Barnes	1.000	3	4	0	0	0

Bartee	.989	39	88	4	1	1
Baughman	.920	13	22	1	2	0
Burke	1.000	2	4	0	0	0
DaVanon	.992	66	123	5	1	1
Durrington	1.000	11	12	0	0	0
Fernandez	.000	1	0	0	0	0
Guiel	.977	44	84	2	2	0

Moreta	1.000	2	5	0	0	0
Morgan	.972	118	207	4	6	1
Murphy	1.000	38	55	2	0	1
Tolentino	.961	109	214	5	9	0

ARKANSAS Class AA

TEXAS LEAGUE

BATTING	AVG	G	AB	R	H	2B	3B	HR	RBI	BB	SO	SB	CS	SLG	OBP	B	T	HT	WT	DOB	1st Yr	Resides
Amezaga, Alfredo	.312	70	285	50	89	10	5	4	21	22	55	24	15	.425	.370	B	R	5-10	165	1-16-78	1999	Obregon, Mexico
Christensen, Mike	.235	86	298	32	70	23	2	6	33	19	76	4	2	.386	.281	R	R	6-2	190	5-24-76	1998	Fort Myers, Fla.
Diaz, Angel	.265	35	117	17	31	9	0	4	15	8	23	0	1	.444	.328	R	R	6-0	198	7-27-76	1998	Lakeland, Fla.
Durrington, Trent	.291	51	182	37	53	12	0	10	35	26	47	22	2	.522	.398	R	R	5-10	188	8-27-75	1994	Queensland, Australia
Figgins, Chone	.268	39	138	21	37	12	2	0	12	14	26	7	2	.384	.329	B	R	5-8	155	1-22-78	1997	Brandon, Fla.
Gregorio, Tom	.191	45	157	15	30	10	0	1	23	7	37	0	0	.274	.243	R	R	6-2	200	5-5-77	1999	Staten Island, N.Y.
Guiel, Jeff	.313	55	176	33	55	12	2	13	36	21	52	3	2	.625	.390	L	R	5-11	195	1-12-74	1997	Langley, B.C.
Guzman, Elpidio	.244	117	459	58	112	21	8	7	46	17	89	18	14	.370	.272	L	L	6-2	165	2-24-79	1996	Santo Domingo, D.R.
Haynes, Nathan	.310	79	316	49	98	11	5	5	23	32	65	33	15	.424	.379	L	L	5-9	170	9-7-79	1997	Hercules, Calif.
Hill, Jason	.258	85	298	42	77	18	0	11	45	18	58	1	1	.430	.306	R	R	6-3	210	3-17-77	1998	Danville, Calif.
Hood, Jay	.291	17	55	8	16	2	0	1	9	3	15	0	1	.382	.328	R	R	6-0	185	3-8-77	1998	Germantown, Tenn.
Huisman, Jason	.278	109	371	55	103	22	0	10	51	39	63	4	9	.418	.349	R	R	6-3	195	4-16-76	1998	Thornton, Ill.
Johnson, Gary	.245	128	466	63	114	24	2	11	72	60	93	8	7	.376	.336	L	L	6-3	210	10-29-75	1999	Atherton, Calif.
Leday, A.J.	.125	4	16	1	2	0	0	2	2	8	0	0	0	.125	.211	R	R	6-3	225	2-17-73	1995	Rancho Cucamonga, Calif.
Lopez, Norberto	.167	2	6	0	1	0	0	0	1	3	0	0	0	.333	.286	R	R	5-8	190	12-9-76	1999	Hialeah, Fla.
Mott, Bill	.319	25	94	9	30	5	4	0	9	9	21	10	4	.457	.379	L	R	6-2	180	1-2-76	1998	San Luis Obispo, Calif.
Quinlan, Robb	.295	129	492	82	145	33	7	14	79	53	84	0	4	.476	.366	R	R	6-1	195	3-17-77	1999	Maplewood, Minn.
Socarras, Tony	.167	3	6	0	1	0	0	0	1	0	1	0	0	.167	.167	L	R	6-0	200	11-8-78	2000	Miami, Fla.
Specht, Brian	.265	45	155	14	41	9	2	2	15	13	32	2	2	.387	.325	B	R	5-11	175	10-19-80	1999	Colorado Springs, Colo.
t'Hoen, E.J.	.172	30	93	11	16	5	1	2	7	12	31	5	3	.312	.278	R	R	6-2	185	11-8-75	1996	Alphen Aan Denryn, Netherlands
Urquhart, Derick	.264	81	250	42	66	11	2	5	45	33	37	4	1	.384	.344	L	L	5-8	175	12-20-75	1998	Florence, S.C.
Zamora, Junior	.208	42	144	15	30	5	1	4	18	9	32	1	1	.340	.256	R	R	6-2	193	5-3-76	1994	San Pedro de Macoris, D.R.

PITCHING	W	L	ERA	G	GS	CG	SV	IP	H	R	ER	BB	SO	AVG	B	T	HT	WT	DOB	1st Yr	Resides
Bergman, Dusty	7	13	5.11	27	25	1	0	153	196	100	87	53	83	.313	L	L	6-4	200	2-1-78	1999	Carson City, Nev.
Beverlin, Jason	4	2	2.75	6	0	0	0	39	36	15	12	11	30	.241	L	R	6-5	220	11-27-73	1994	Royal Oak, Mich.
Bootcheck, Chris	3	3	5.45	6	6	1	0	36	39	25	22	11	22	.265	R	R	6-5	205	10-24-78	2001	La Porte, Ind.
Brummett, Sean	2	4	5.62	25	5	2	0	66	65	46	41	28	45	.253	L	L	6-0	200	1-10-78	1999	Brookston, Ind.
Callier, Jeremy	2	0	7.13	16	0	0	1	24	31	19	19	10	6	.316	R	R	6-0	195	11-18-75	1998	Ballwin, Mo.
Clark, Chris	3	3	6.78	28	6	0	0	66	74	53	50	35	34	.289	R	R	6-1	180	10-29-74	1994	Tucson, Ariz.
Cummings, Ryan	6	3	3.56	42	0	0	6	66	61	34	26	21	42	.239	R	R	6-0	210	6-3-76	1997	Marietta, Ga.
Demouy, Chris	2	0	6.11	24	0	0	0	35	42	25	24	22	16	.302	R	L	6-1	205	11-3-75	1998	Baton Rouge, La.
Donnelly, Brendan	4	1	2.48	27	0	0	12	29	21	8	8	13	37	.200	R	R	6-3	205	7-4-71	1992	Albuquerque, N.M.
Dykhoff, Radhames	2	3	4.57	27	14	0	0	81	85	46	41	35	37	.273	L	L	6-0	200	9-27-74	1993	Oranjestad, Aruba
Harriger, Mark	2	3	4.65	10	9	0	0	50	52	33	26	23	31	.266	R	R	6-2	196	4-29-75	1996	Lakewood, Calif.
Hundley, Jeff	2	6	6.17	10	9	0	0	54	63	48	37	25	31	.290	L	L	6-2	205	2-19-77	1998	Warren, Ohio
Jenks, Bobby	1	0	3.60	2	2	0	0	10	8	5	4	5	10	.200	R	R	6-3	225	3-14-81	2000	Spirit Lake, Idaho
Kelley, Rich	1	1	3.72	5	3	0	0	19	19	13	8	8	14	.250	L	L	6-3	210	5-27-70	1991	Scituate, Mass.
Kirkreit, Daron	2	1	6.92	17	0	0	0	26	38	23	20	9	9	.339	R	R	6-6	225	8-7-72	1993	Corona, Calif.
Lackey, John	9	7	3.46	18	18	3	0	127	106	55	49	29	94	.227	R	R	6-6	200	10-23-78	1999	Abilene, Texas
Milo, Tony	1	2	5.34	19	2	0	1	30	29	18	18	17	35	.250	L	L	6-5	225	5-5-78	2000	Tucson, Ariz.
Peralta, Joel	0	1	6.30	9	0	0	2	10	15	10	7	5	14	.333	R	R	5-11	155	3-23-80	1996	Bonao, D.R.
Pine, Chris	1	0	4.15	4	0	0	1	4	6	3	2	6	4	.333	R	R	6-2	205	9-25-76	1998	Tigard, Ore.
Stephens, Jason	6	7	3.92	19	19	2	0	119	117	64	52	26	75	.253	R	R	6-0	180	9-10-75	1996	Springhill, La.
Suarez, Felipe	2	5	4.46	34	1	0	3	67	77	37	33	18	46	.289	R	R	6-2	185	3-12-76	1998	Sunrise, Fla.
Turnbow, Derrick	0	0	2.57	3	3	0	0	14	12	4	4	5	11	.240	R	R	6-3	180	1-25-78	1997	Franklin, Tenn.
Williams, Shad	3	4	5.86	11	6	0	1	35	42	26	23	13	26	.283	R	R	6-0	198	3-10-71	1991	Fresno, Calif.
Wilson, Phil	1	1	11.37	2	2	0	0	6	10	12	8	6	5	.333	R	R	6-8	210	4-1-81	1999	Ramona, Calif.

FIELDING

Catcher	PCT	G	PO	A	E	DP	PB
Diaz	1.000	18	94	8	0	0	4
Gregorio	.989	43	245	33	3	3	4
Hill	.989	76	415	36	5	3	10
Lopez	1.000	2	10	2	0	0	0
Socarras	1.000	3	8	2	0	0	1

First Base	PCT	G	PO	A	E	DP
Christensen	1.000	1	10	0	0	1
Diaz	1.000	1	10	0	0	1
Guiel	1.000	7	67	1	0	6
Hill	1.000	2	21	1	0	1
Huisman	1.000	5	29	3	0	3
Quinlan	.993	113	963	97	8	86
Zamora	1.000	9	84	12	0	6

Second Base	PCT	G	PO	A	E	DP
Durrington	.966	38	68	75	5	17
Figgins	.950	34	72	80	8	23

Hood	.833	1	1	4	1	1
Huisman	.975	57	105	131	6	27
t'Hoen	.983	13	23	36	1	10
Zamora	1.000	4	5	7	0	2

Third Base	PCT	G	PO	A	E	DP
Christensen	.925	81	51	158	17	16
Durrington	.917	4	3	8	1	1
Figgins	.750	1	0	3	1	0
Guiel	.839	10	6	20	5	1
Hill	1.000	1	0	2	0	1
Hood	.957	12	4	18	1	1
Huisman	.750	9	7	14	7	1
t'Hoen	1.000	6	3	6	0	0
Zamora	.930	25	20	46	5	4

Shortstop	PCT	G	PO	A	E	DP
Amezaga	.964	70	132	214	13	43
Durrington	.892	8	12	21	4	2

Figgins	.947	3	6	12	1	1
Hood	1.000	3	6	7	0	2
Huisman	1.000	2	2	8	0	0
Specht	.906	44	73	140	22	24
t'Hoen	.909	10	13	27	4	5

Outfield	PCT	G	PO	A	E	DP
Diaz	1.000	1	2	1	0	1
Durrington	1.000	1	1	0	0	0
Guiel	1.000	16	28	1	0	0
Guzman	.984	110	231	10	4	1
Haynes	.985	71	190	3	3	0
Hill	1.000	3	1	0	0	0
Huisman	1.000	26	35	3	0	0
Johnson	.989	105	178	8	2	2
Leday	.000	1	0	0	0	0
Mott	.971	15	32	2	1	0
Quinlan	1.000	8	17	0	0	0
Urquhart	.992	63	126	5	1	0

CALIFORNIA LEAGUE

BATTING	AVG	G	AB	R	H	2B	3B	HR	RBI	BB	SO	SB	CS	SLG	OBP	B	T	HT	WT	DOB	1st Yr	Resides
Abruzzo, Jared	.208	28	101	13	21	1	0	2	13	9	30	1	0	.277	.270	B	R	6-3	225	11-15-81	2000	La Mesa, Calif.
Barski, Chris	.213	30	89	9	19	3	2	1	10	9	23	0	1	.326	.293	L	R	6-2	210	1-14-78	1999	Langley, B.C.
Bartee, Kimera	.267	7	30	3	8	2	0	0	1	1	11	3	0	.333	.290	B	R	6-0	200	7-21-72	1993	Peoria, Ariz.
Bikowski, Scott	.297	128	482	81	143	28	5	10	53	63	94	24	9	.438	.382	L	L	6-0	185	2-12-77	1999	Suffield, Conn.
Contreras, Sergio	.271	104	351	47	95	15	5	3	37	29	68	15	9	.368	.333	L	L	5-11	180	4-30-80	1999	Esperanza, Mexico
Diaz, Angel	.167	26	84	9	14	4	1	0	5	7	27	1	0	.238	.247	R	R	6-0	198	7-27-76	1998	Lakeland, Fla.
Encarnacion, Bien	.202	35	104	13	21	4	1	0	4	8	31	0	1	.260	.272	R	R	5-11	180	2-24-78	1995	Bani, D.R.
Gastelum, Carlos	.204	118	363	39	74	11	6	0	28	15	57	20	6	.267	.242	R	R	5-9	165	10-29-81	1999	Huatabampo, Mexico
Hill, Glenallen	.167	3	12	1	2	1	0	1	3	0	5	0	0	.500	.167	R	R	6-3	230	3-22-65	1983	Santa Cruz, Calif.
Kennedy, Adam	.375	3	8	3	3	2	0	1	2	1	3	0	0	.625	.545	L	R	6-1	180	1-10-76	1997	Riverside, Calif.
Lehr, Ryan	.269	54	197	28	53	14	3	4	25	13	40	1	1	.431	.324	R	R	5-11	205	2-15-79	1997	La Mesa, Calif.
Lopez, Norberto	.150	9	20	0	3	0	0	0	0	0	8	0	0	.150	.150	R	R	5-8	190	12-9-76	1999	Hialeah, Fla.
Molina, Bengie	.545	3	11	1	6	1	0	0	2	0	1	0	0	.636	.545	R	R	5-11	207	7-20-74	1993	San Luis, Ariz.
Moreta, Ramon	.321	34	137	23	44	13	1	1	13	9	32	19	7	.453	.367	R	R	5-11	185	9-5-75	1994	La Romana, D.R.
Mott, Bill	.304	17	69	14	21	5	1	3	16	8	11	5	1	.536	.367	L	R	6-2	180	1-2-76	1998	San Luis Obispo, Calif.
Mounts, J.R.	.220	106	378	45	83	15	4	9	38	15	145	13	6	.352	.252	R	R	6-0	190	11-13-78	1997	Key West, Fla.
Murphy, Tommy	.190	50	200	16	38	8	0	0	11	5	69	7	3	.230	.214	R	R	6-0	180	8-27-79	2000	Port Charlotte, Fla.
Napoli, Mike	.200	7	20	3	4	0	0	1	4	8	11	0	0	.350	.429	R	R	6-1	205	10-31-81	2000	Cooper City, Fla.
O'Keefe, Mike	.330	115	409	75	135	25	5	15	91	42	81	20	1	.526	.389	L	L	5-10	205	6-28-78	1999	Hamden, Conn.
Pichardo, Maximo	.300	3	10	1	3	0	1	0	0	0	2	0	1	.500	.300	R	R	6-0	150	6-27-79	1999	Santo Domingo, D.R.
Raymundo, G.J.	.293	109	389	49	114	30	2	9	58	25	75	4	4	.450	.362	R	R	6-1	188	3-3-77	1999	Clovis, Calif.
Rogers, Brandon	.211	24	76	4	16	4	0	1	11	6	20	0	1	.303	.274	R	R	6-0	200	3-1-78	2000	El Cajon, Calif.
Salmon, Tim	.143	2	7	1	1	0	0	0	1	4	0	0	.143	.250	R	R	6-3	231	8-24-68	1989	Scottsdale, Ariz.
Shaffer, Josh	.280	58	193	17	54	7	2	2	20	11	34	2	4	.368	.322	L	R	6-1	175	6-26-80	1999	Las Vegas, Nev.
Socarras, Tony	.131	56	176	10	23	4	0	5	9	14	68	1	1	.239	.195	L	R	6-0	200	11-8-78	2000	Miami, Fla.
Specht, Brian	.242	65	264	45	64	13	6	7	31	24	78	17	3	.417	.312	B	R	5-11	175	10-19-80	1999	Colorado Springs, Colo.
Urquhart, Derick	.244	25	41	8	10	3	0	1	2	6	6	4	0	.390	.354	L	L	5-8	175	12-20-75	1998	Florence, S.C.
Wagner, Jeff	.291	113	402	51	117	37	1	8	56	38	82	4	3	.448	.364	R	R	6-3	230	1-5-77	1999	Louisville, Ky.
Zamora, Junior	.288	12	52	9	15	2	1	3	8	1	14	3	0	.538	.302	R	R	6-2	193	5-3-76	1994	San Pedro de Macoris, D.R.
Zeber, Ryan	.239	31	92	11	22	4	0	2	12	10	29	0	0	.348	.317	R	R	6-2	190	5-24-78	1996	Santa Ana, Calif.

GAMES BY POSITION: C—Abruzzo 22, Barski 8, Diaz 18, Lopez 9, Molina 3, Napoli 7, Rogers 23, Socarras 53, Zeber 13. **1B**—Barski 9, Contreras 52, Lehr 4, O'Keefe 1, Wagner 90, Zamora 4. **2B**—Encarnacion 19, Gastelum 108, Kennedy 3, Pichardo 3, Raymundo 1, Shaffer 20. **3B**—Encarnacio 7, Gastelum 5, Lehr 36, Raymundo 77, Shaffer 16, Zamora 8. **SS**—Encarnacion 6, Gastelum 4, Murphy 49, Shaffer 22, Specht 63. **OF**—Bartee 7, Bikowski 125, Contreras 51, Encarnacion 1, Lehr 6, Moreta 34, Mott 17, Mounts 104, O'Keefe 92, Salmon 2, Urquhart 21.

PITCHING	W	L	ERA	G	GS	CG	SV	IP	H	R	ER	BB	SO	AVG	B	T	HT	WT	DOB	1st Yr	Resides
Bootcheck, Chris	8	4	3.93	15	14	1	0	87	84	45	38	23	86	.250	R	R	6-5	205	10-24-78	2001	La Porte, Ind.
Brummett, Sean	2	4	4.93	7	6	1	0	38	46	24	21	10	28	.298	L	L	6-0	200	1-10-78	1999	Brookston, Ind.
Callier, Jeremy	0	0	0.00	2	1	0	0	4	1	0	0	0	3	.076	R	R	6-0	195	11-18-75	1998	Ballwin, Mo.
Crawford, Wesley	6	7	5.21	21	13	0	0	93	109	60	54	28	56	.286	B	L	6-3	200	12-12-76	1999	Panama City Beach, Fla.
Demouy, Chris	0	1	2.70	2	0	0	0	10	7	3	3	3	4	.194	R	L	6-1	205	11-3-75	1998	Baton Rouge, La.
Espina, Rendy	0	0	21.60	2	1	0	0	2	4	4	4	0	2	.500	L	L	6-0	180	5-11-78	1995	Cabimas, Venez.
Grezlovski, Ben	2	4	4.20	48	0	0	8	64	60	37	30	29	74	.246	R	R	5-11	180	11-22-76	1999	Miami, Fla.
Harris, Julian	0	1	3.28	25	0	0	0	36	36	22	13	17	31	.257	L	L	6-3	175	9-26-77	1998	San Jose, Calif.
Hasegawa, Shigetoshi	0	0	0.00	2	2	0	0	2	3	1	0	0	1	.375	R	R	5-11	178	8-1-68	1997	Newport Beach, Calif.
Haworth, Brent	0	0	13.50	5	0	0	0	8	15	13	12	2	4	.405	R	R	6-6	205	2-26-77	1999	Orlando, Fla.
Hensley, Matt	2	7	5.93	14	12	0	0	68	85	57	45	24	58	.305	R	R	6-2	215	8-18-78	2000	San Diego, Calif.
Holtz, Mike	0	0	9.00	2	2	0	0	2	3	2	2	1	3	.375	L	L	5-9	188	10-10-72	1994	Hollidaysburg, Pa.
Hundley, Jeff	2	1	4.19	13	7	0	0	54	48	25	25	17	38	.243	L	L	6-2	205	2-19-77	1998	Warren, Ohio
Jacobs, Greg	2	4	7.57	31	0	0	0	44	59	47	37	22	49	.318	L	L	5-10	180	10-9-76	1998	Anaheim Hills, Calif.
Jones, Greg	1	3	3.23	6	6	0	0	28	25	15	13	11	27	.238	R	R	6-2	190	11-15-76	1997	Seminole, Fla.
Martinez, Renan	4	3	4.33	43	1	0	0	54	65	34	26	28	49	.294	L	L	5-10	164	4-22-82	1999	Obregon, Mexico
McClain, Kevin	2	0	4.25	23	0	0	0	36	33	17	17	12	40	.246	R	R	6-4	180	2-22-78	1998	Palm Bay, Fla.
Mendoza, Mario	2	4	5.44	8	0	0	0	43	56	37	26	12	22	.307	R	R	6-3	200	1-19-79	1999	Navojoa, Mexico
Milo, Tony	3	1	0.97	24	0	0	2	37	24	5	4	17	45	.187	L	L	6-5	225	5-5-78	2000	Tucson, Ariz.
O'Neal, Brandon	0	3	5.63	10	6	0	0	32	37	24	20	25	20	.298	B	R	6-1	195	10-17-78	2000	Olathe, Kan.
Pace, Adam	1	1	4.15	3	3	1	0	22	30	11	10	6	13	.326	L	L	6-1	192	9-20-79	2000	Brooklyn, N.Y.
Rodriguez, Francisco	5	7	5.38	20	20	1	0	114	127	72	68	55	147	.275	R	R	6-0	180	1-7-82	1999	Caracas, Venez.
Schneider, Scott	4	6	4.23	53	0	0	3	79	81	37	37	42	79	.264	R	R	6-4	210	5-4-78	2000	Virginia Beach, Va.
Stephens, Jason	3	2	2.20	8	5	0	0	33	35	11	8	4	19	.275	R	R	6-0	180	9-10-75	1996	Springhill, La.
Stokley, Billy	2	2	4.18	27	0	0	10	28	27	15	13	18	24	.252	L	R	6-4	200	5-13-77	2000	Pasadena, Texas
Thames, Charlie	4	2	1.52	29	0	0	13	30	21	9	5	9	26	.194	R	R	6-1	190	5-23-79	2000	Humble, Texas
Wilson, Phil	8	10	5.23	26	26	1	0	160	173	102	93	55	134	.276	R	R	6-8	210	4-1-81	1999	Ramona, Calif.
Wolensky, Dave	2	0	3.34	8	7	0	0	32	24	13	12	14	26	.212	R	R	6-0	190	1-15-80	2000	Atlanta, Ga.

MIDWEST LEAGUE

BATTING	AVG	G	AB	R	H	2B	3B	HR	RBI	BB	SO	SB	CS	SLG	OBP	B	T	HT	WT	DOB	1st Yr	Resides
Abruzzo, Jared	.241	87	323	41	78	20	0	10	53	44	104	1	1	.396	.340	B	R	6-3	225	11-15-81	2000	La Mesa, Calif.
Adames, Epidaro	.238	53	202	16	48	11	1	0	17	9	46	2	3	.302	.292	R	R	6-1	170	3-29-80	1996	Santo Domingo, D.R.
Cahill, Jon	.273	44	172	21	47	7	0	1	13	8	28	2	2	.331	.306	R	R	6-0	185	2-21-78	2001	Peabody, Mass.
Campo, Mike	.313	100	358	69	112	20	3	7	46	43	65	21	11	.444	.419	L	R	5-10	185	11-14-76	2000	Absecon, N.J.
Coulie, Jason	.242	117	434	49	105	22	3	9	50	23	105	9	7	.369	.294	R	R	6-2	200	4-13-78	2000	Manchester, N.H.
Doudt, Anthony	.186	39	129	13	24	7	0	3	15	2	32	1	1	.310	.216	R	R	6-4	204	5-22-77	1999	Muncie, Ind.
Duran, Frank	.171	50	170	26	29	4	0	2	16	30	40	12	3	.229	.313	R	R	5-11	160	6-8-79	1996	La Vega, D.R.
Eylward, Tom	.233	23	90	12	21	6	1	2	12	5	21	0	0	.389	.286	R	R	6-2	210	9-28-79	2001	Clearwater, Fla.
Knight, Marcus	.250	27	92	13	23	4	0	5	17	5	14	0	1	.457	.287	B	R	6-0	190	9-10-78	1996	Pembroke Pines, Fla.
Lehr, Ryan	.259	22	81	12	21	8	0	3	16	7	7	0	0	.469	.319	R	R	5-11	205	2-15-79	1997	La Mesa, Calif.

BATTING	AVG	G	AB	R	H	2B	3B	HR	RBI	BB	SO	SB	CS	SLG	OBP	B	T	HT	WT	DOB	1st Yr	Resides
Lindsey, Del	.250	65	248	31	62	14	1	7	32	14	46	4	4	.399	.292	R	R	6-1	190	3-8-78	1999	Houston, Texas
Murphy, Tommy	.204	74	280	32	57	15	3	4	31	16	94	7	10	.321	.259	R	R	6-0	180	8-27-79	2000	Port Charlotte, Fla.
Napoli, Mike	.232	43	155	23	36	10	1	5	18	24	54	3	2	.406	.341	R	R	6-1	205	10-31-81	2000	Cooper City, Fla.
Pichardo, Maximo	.208	44	178	21	37	4	1	1	12	9	30	11	7	.258	.254	R	R	6-0	150	6-27-79	1999	Santo Domingo, D.R.
Raburn, Johnny	.315	68	235	56	74	2	1	0	12	63	43	37	7	.332	.467	B	R	6-1	165	2-16-79	2000	Plant City, Fla.
Rogers, Brandon	.343	19	70	13	24	7	0	0	10	8	16	0	1	.443	.432	R	R	6-0	200	3-1-78	2000	El Cajon, Calif.
Roper, Zach	.310	124	471	64	146	27	2	15	87	29	82	8	3	.471	.364	R	R	6-2	200	9-26-77	2000	Pompano Beach, Fla.
Seever, Brian	.223	45	166	25	37	6	1	1	14	31	34	14	7	.289	.348	R	R	6-0	196	8-18-76	1999	Fairfield, Calif.
Socarras, Tony	.216	16	51	10	11	1	0	2	11	7	20	0	0	.353	.339	L	R	6-0	200	11-8-78	2000	Miami, Fla.
Stockton, Jeff	.120	7	25	3	3	1	0	0	0	0	7	0	0	.160	.120	R	R	6-1	185	6-6-78	2000	St. Petersburg, Fla.
Stockton, Rick	.273	8	22	2	6	2	0	0	3	2	5	1	0	.364	.346	L	L	6-1	185	11-5-79	2001	Calabasas, Calif.
Tolli, Barry	.141	23	71	5	10	1	0	1	2	2	23	3	4	.197	.164	R	R	6-2	195	8-17-79	1998	Newbury Park, Calif.
Tolzien, Ed	.183	20	71	9	13	2	0	0	8	6	20	0	0	.211	.275	L	L	6-4	207	7-11-79	2001	Arlington Heights, Ill.
Valdez, Angel	.246	31	114	19	28	8	0	3	11	4	29	3	1	.395	.283	R	R	6-2	178	5-22-78	1996	Santo Domingo, D.R.
Warner, J.R.	.189	14	53	9	10	2	1	0	4	4	11	1	0	.264	.259	L	L	6-2	195	6-21-79	2000	Chesterfield, Mo.
Webb, Ryan	.310	44	145	14	45	5	1	0	14	7	28	7	4	.359	.346	R	R	6-3	190	5-30-78	2001	Upland, Calif.
Withey, Ryan	.248	62	202	31	50	11	0	6	28	20	53	20	5	.391	.335	R	R	6-2	195	7-4-77	2000	Boynton Beach, Fla.

GAMES BY POSITION: C—Abruzzo 66, Doudt 16, Napoli 35, Rogers 13, Socarras 12. **1B**—Doudt 21, Eylward 20, Lindsey 33, Napoli 5, Roper 28, Tolzien 20, Warner 14. **2B**—Cahill 2, Duran 36, Pichardo 43, Raburn 52, J. Stockton 5. **3B**—Adames 53, Duran 3, Eylward 1, Lehr 14, Lindsey 30, Roper 38, J. Stockton 1. **SS**—Cahill 42, Duran 11, Murphy 71, Raburn 13. **OF**—Campo 87, Coulie 114, Knight 15, Roper 5, Seever 43, R. Stockton 7, Tolli 21, Valdez 28, Webb 41, Withey 57.

PITCHING	W	L	ERA	G	GS	CG	SV	IP	H	R	ER	BB	SO	AVG	B	T	HT	WT	DOB	1st Yr	Resides
Andrade, Steve	2	1	6.52	20	0	0	0	29	33	24	21	8	31	.284	R	R	6-1	200	2-6-78	2001	Woodland, Calif.
Andujar, Jesse	0	0	5.40	5	0	0	0	5	6	4	3	2	6	.285	R	R	6-4	230	7-23-79	1996	San Pedro de Macoris, D.R.
Arthur, Tony	3	1	2.57	5	5	0	0	28	33	11	8	9	28	.294	L	L	6-4	205	12-16-78	2001	Rolla, Mo.
Bukowski, Stan	2	4	6.61	8	8	1	0	48	53	39	35	25	29	.291	R	R	6-5	220	9-16-81	1999	Clearwater, Fla.
Fischer, Rich	9	7	4.20	20	20	2	0	131	131	73	61	33	97	.261	R	R	6-3	170	10-21-80	2000	Riverside, Calif.
Flading, Cameron	0	0	5.29	15	0	0	1	17	12	13	10	16	29	.190	R	R	6-2	190	8-25-78	1999	Anaheim, Calif.
Gruban, Jarret	0	2	5.29	13	2	0	0	34	44	30	20	14	22	.307	R	R	6-4	185	10-14-78	2000	Surrey, B.C.
Harris, Julian	2	2	5.61	18	3	0	0	26	28	18	16	14	20	.274	L	L	6-3	175	9-26-77	1998	San Jose, Calif.
Hensley, Matt	5	3	3.64	11	11	1	0	72	80	42	29	19	63	.270	R	R	6-2	215	8-18-78	2000	San Diego, Calif.
Jackson, Dan	1	1	2.40	8	5	0	0	30	24	9	8	14	24	.218	R	R	6-2	210	7-12-78	2000	Lyons, Ill.
Jenks, Bobby	3	7	5.27	21	21	0	0	99	90	74	58	64	98	.244	R	R	6-3	225	3-14-81	2000	Spirit Lake, Idaho
LaCorte, Vince	3	10	4.37	36	10	0	2	105	119	61	51	19	87	.276	R	R	6-3	203	9-10-78	1999	Gilroy, Calif.
Landestoy, Gilbert	3	2	4.15	36	0	0	2	65	51	40	30	33	54	.212	R	R	6-4	200	3-31-77	2000	Friendswood, Texas
McClain, Kevin	2	1	2.27	24	0	0	0	32	22	9	8	9	36	.191	R	R	6-4	180	2-22-78	1998	Palm Bay, Fla.
Morris, Will	6	6	4.44	40	0	0	2	81	99	51	40	23	88	.294	R	R	6-0	180	3-26-78	2000	Rancho Cucamonga, Calif.
O'Neal, Brandon	2	8	5.88	16	15	0	0	83	95	67	54	40	51	.287	B	R	6-1	195	10-17-78	2000	Olathe, Kan.
Pace, Adam	5	6	3.92	17	12	1	0	87	84	52	38	24	68	.246	L	L	6-1	192	9-20-79	2000	Brooklyn, N.Y.
Peralta, Joel	0	0	2.13	41	0	0	23	42	27	13	10	5	53	.175	R	R	5-11	153	3-23-80	1996	Bonao, D.R.
Pine, Chris	1	1	1.76	12	0	0	2	15	6	3	3	7	24	.117	R	R	6-2	205	9-25-76	1998	Tigard, Ore.
Stokley, Billy	5	3	1.98	22	0	0	1	41	31	14	9	18	45	.203	L	R	6-4	200	5-13-77	2000	Pasadena, Calif.
Thomas, Adam	4	7	5.14	19	16	2	0	96	109	63	55	23	61	.288	R	R	6-4	195	5-22-79	2000	Clearwater, Fla.
Torres, Joe	0	3	5.82	4	4	0	0	17	16	12	11	14	14	.258	L	L	6-2	175	9-3-82	2000	Kissimmee, Fla.
Wawrzyniak, Alan	2	2	3.57	5	5	0	0	23	25	16	9	22	21	.280	R	R	6-3	205	9-14-77	1999	Blandon, Pa.

PROVO · Rookie

PIONEER LEAGUE

BATTING	AVG	G	AB	R	H	2B	3B	HR	RBI	BB	SO	SB	CS	SLG	OBP	B	T	HT	WT	DOB	1st Yr	Resides
Adames, Epidaro	.000	1	4	0	0	0	0	0	0	0	1	0	0	.000	.000	R	R	6-1	170	3-29-80	1996	Santo Domingo, D.R.
Batista, Christian	.296	17	54	10	16	1	1	2	8	10	13	0	1	.463	.415	R	R	6-1	195	6-5-82	2000	Santo Domingo, D.R.
Cahill, Jon	.419	8	31	7	13	3	0	0	5	2	4	1	0	.516	.471	R	R	6-0	185	2-21-78	2001	Peabody, Mass.
Corbeil, Al	.359	60	217	48	78	18	0	6	49	40	41	0	1	.525	.463	L	L	6-0	190	12-16-78	2001	Margate, Fla.
Del Chiaro, Brent	.158	52	57	2	9	1	0	0	5	7	20	1	0	.175	.242	R	R	6-3	217	6-26-79	2001	Oakley, Calif.
Eylward, Tom	.300	7	20	7	6	3	0	0	5	2	5	0	0	.450	.440	R	R	6-2	210	9-28-79	2001	Clearwater, Fla.
Gates, David	.294	48	170	31	50	13	0	3	33	29	43	4	3	.424	.415	R	R	6-1	205	9-23-80	2001	Huntsville, Ala.
Gorneault, Nick	.315	54	168	38	53	12	4	6	30	11	65	5	2	.542	.373	R	R	6-3	200	4-19-79	2001	Springfield, Mass.
Gray, Josh	.240	57	200	32	48	6	0	6	31	22	58	2	1	.360	.328	R	R	6-3	210	2-22-81	2000	Durant, Okla.
Guzman, Junior	.343	11	35	11	12	0	0	5	13	4	5	0	0	.771	.400	R	R	5-11	185	8-10-82	2000	Bonao, D.R.
Johnson, Dale	.277	27	83	12	23	3	0	0	12	4	17	0	1	.313	.330	R	R	5-9	175	5-24-79	2001	MacClenny, Fla.
Kotchman, Casey	.500	7	22	6	11	3	0	0	7	2	0	0	0	.636	.542	L	L	6-3	210	2-22-83	2001	Seminole, Fla.
Lagana, Shawn	.266	38	143	27	38	6	1	1	17	10	22	5	2	.343	.321	R	R	6-2	175	4-28-81	1999	Cypress, Calif.
Mathis, Jeff	.299	22	77	14	23	6	3	0	18	11	13	1	0	.455	.387	R	R	6-0	190	3-31-83	2001	Marianna, Fla.
McPherson, Dallas	.395	31	124	30	49	11	0	5	29	12	22	1	0	.605	.449	L	R	6-4	210	7-23-80	2001	Randleman, N.C.
Nevins, Ryan	.286	4	7	0	2	1	0	0	3	0	1	0	0	.429	.250	L	R	5-11	175	12-29-78	2001	Flushing, N.Y.
Pichardo, Maximo	.364	22	88	16	32	7	1	2	16	6	8	12	5	.534	.430	R	R	6-0	150	6-27-79	1999	Santo Domingo, D.R.
Porter, Greg	.331	39	127	34	42	3	1	10	34	18	21	3	1	.606	.412	R	R	6-4	225	8-15-80	2001	Keller, Texas
Smith, Casey	.321	62	249	60	80	11	1	1	34	37	40	6	4	.386	.411	R	R	6-2	200	3-18-79	2001	Ashford, Ala.
Swenson, Sam	.351	63	225	61	79	16	4	13	55	24	64	7	1	.631	.438	L	L	6-0	190	2-28-78	2001	South Jordan, Utah
Tolzien, Ed	.265	39	132	27	35	9	1	2	23	18	22	4	1	.394	.370	L	L	6-4	207	7-11-79	2001	Arlington Heights, Ill.
Turner, Justin	.216	52	176	36	38	3	0	6	27	28	65	9	4	.335	.327	L	R	6-1	195	12-19-79	2001	Cape Coral, Fla.
Webb, Ryan	.500	7	6	1	3	0	1	0	1	2	0	0	0	.833	.667	R	R	6-3	190	5-30-78	2001	Upland, Calif.
Welch, Ed	.282	59	216	47	61	9	5	1	26	16	59	18	4	.384	.328	L	R	6-0	190	2-22-80	1998	Richmond, B.C.

GAMES BY POSITION: C—Corbeil 33, Del Chiaro 22, Guzman 10, Mathis 20. **1B**—Corbeil 21, Eylward 6, Kotchman 7, McPherson 6, Tolzien 38, Turner 6, Welch 1. **2B**—Batista 3, Johnson 22, Lagana 32, Nevins 4, Pichardo 22, Turner 1. **3B**—Adames 1, Batista 14, Johnson 2, McPherson 21, Turner 46. **SS**—Cahill 8, Johnson 3, Lagana 5, Smith 62. **OF**—Gates 43, Gorneault 48, Porter 35, Swenson 59, Tolzien 1, Webb 3, Welch 57.

PITCHING	W	L	ERA	G	GS	CG	SV	IP	H	R	ER	BB	SO	AVG	B	T	HT	WT	DOB	1st Yr	Resides
Allen, Blake	7	3	2.13	28	0	0	8	51	35	13	12	8	55	.191	L	L	6-4	190	7-12-79	2001	Alexander City, Ala.
Andrade, Steve	0	0	0.00	1	0	0	0	2	3	0	0	0	5	.333	R	R	6-1	200	2-6-78	2001	Woodland, Calif.
Arthur, Tony	7	1	3.76	10	10	1	0	55	48	32	23	11	49	.233	L	L	6-4	205	12-16-78	2001	Rolla, Mo.

PITCHING	W	L	ERA	G	GS	CG	SV	IP	H	R	ER	BB	SO	AVG	B	T	HT	WT	DOB	1st Yr	Resides
Bailey, Ryan	4	1	3.96	15	6	0	1	52	62	29	23	16	48	.281	R	R	6-2	215	5-10-80	2001	Chula Vista, Calif.
Bowles, Larry	4	1	5.60	19	1	0	0	27	32	18	17	6	25	.296	L	L	5-11	195	3-18-79	2000	Boones Mill, Va.
Bukowski, Stan	0	0	1.29	5	0	0	0	7	9	3	1	2	2	.321	R	R	6-5	220	9-16-81	1999	Clearwater, Fla.
D'Amico, Leonardo	1	0	9.00	1	0	0	0	2	4	2	2	1	4	.400	R	R	6-2	180	12-14-81	1999	Mariara, Venez.
Dennis, Jason	5	0	2.05	14	13	0	0	75	53	20	17	21	79	.193	L	L	6-0	195	8-12-78	2001	Concord, Calif.
Gruban, Jarret	0	0	0.00	1	0	0	0	1	2	1	0	0	0	.400	R	R	6-4	185	10-14-78	2000	Surrey, B.C.
Jackson, Dan	0	0	6.00	7	0	0	3	9	11	6	6	5	13	.297	R	R	6-2	210	7-12-78	2000	Lyons, Ill.
Liriano, Pedro	11	2	2.78	15	14	0	0	78	80	39	24	31	76	.264	R	R	6-2	150	10-23-80	1999	Fantino, D.R.
Luther, Heath	0	0	0.00	3	0	0	0	3	4	0	0	1	2	.285	L	L	5-11	185	1-7-79	2001	Fort Wayne, Ind.
O'Sullivan, Mark	1	2	3.97	22	0	0	2	34	35	23	15	16	36	.263	R	R	6-2	200	10-24-78	2001	Andover, Mass.
Pinkerton, Brad	0	2	5.60	17	1	0	0	35	37	24	22	13	35	.262	L	L	6-2	192	6-15-80	2001	Charlotte, N.C.
Santana, Johan	2	1	7.71	4	4	0	0	19	19	17	16	12	22	.246	R	R	6-2	150	11-28-83	2001	San Cristobal, D.R.
Shell, Steven	0	3	7.17	14	4	0	1	38	52	31	30	15	33	.331	R	R	6-5	195	3-10-83	2001	Cleburne, Texas
Smith, Cliff	2	1	3.34	21	0	0	1	35	29	20	13	15	47	.219	R	R	6-6	205	10-13-79	2001	Haverhill, Mass.
Steward, Jaime	1	0	5.40	1	0	0	0	7	7	4	4	1	9	.259	L	L	6-0	185	1-26-79	2001	Blackwood, N.J.
Sutton, Kris	2	1	3.96	23	0	0	4	25	43	20	11	8	20	.361	R	R	6-2	205	10-3-78	2001	Apopka, Fla.
Torres, Joe	2	2	4.02	9	8	0	0	31	32	20	14	15	39	.260	L	L	6-2	175	9-3-82	2000	Kissimmee, Fla.
Woods, Jake	4	3	5.29	15	14	1	0	65	70	41	38	29	84	.274	R	R	6-1	195	9-3-81	2001	Kingsburg, Calif.
Wright, Shayne	0	0	3.00	1	1	0	0	6	3	2	2	0	5	.142	R	R	6-5	195	8-21-80	2000	Auburn, Calif.

MESA — Rookie

ARIZONA LEAGUE

BATTING	AVG	G	AB	R	H	2B	3B	HR	RBI	BB	SO	SB	CS	SLG	OBP	B	T	HT	WT	DOB	1st Yr	Resides
Abad, Noel	.293	19	58	9	17	1	1	1	7	3	14	6	1	.397	.344	R	R	6-1	165	9-9-82	2000	Santo Domingo, D.R.
Batista, Christian	.268	35	127	26	34	7	0	2	17	18	33	4	5	.370	.367	R	R	6-1	195	6-5-82	2000	Santo Domingo, D.R.
Batista, Juan	.125	36	72	8	9	2	2	0	7	9	36	4	0	.208	.229	B	R	6-0	165	7-14-84	2001	Santo Domingo, D.R.
Brown, Matt	.163	46	141	14	23	7	1	1	21	18	30	1	3	.248	.275	R	R	6-0	180	8-8-82	2001	Hayden, Idaho
Collins, Mike	.179	20	39	2	7	0	0	0	1	3	11	1	0	.179	.256	R	R	6-2	175	7-18-84	2001	Sydney, Australia
Cosby, Quantwan	.243	41	148	21	36	4	1	0	8	9	40	8	7	.284	.289	B	R	5-10	185	12-23-82	2001	Mart, Texas
Del Chiaro, Brent	.259	20	58	15	15	1	1	1	4	7	18	0	0	.362	.368	R	R	6-3	217	6-26-79	2001	Oakley, Calif.
DeLeon, Carlos	.172	27	58	9	10	5	1	0	3	3	28	3	1	.293	.250	R	R	6-2	185	10-9-82	2000	Santo Domingo, D.R.
Felix, Kelvin	.217	23	46	4	10	2	1	0	5	3	18	2	0	.304	.265	R	R	5-11	160	8-30-83	2001	San Pedro de Macoris, D.R.
Gregorio, Tom	.273	4	11	1	3	0	0	0	1	3	2	0	0	.273	.429	R	R	6-2	200	5-5-77	1999	Staten Island, N.Y.
Guzman, Junior	.307	28	101	12	31	4	1	0	13	5	10	2	2	.366	.360	R	R	5-11	185	8-10-82	2000	Bonao, D.R.
Jenkins, Kevin	.174	42	115	15	20	3	1	1	11	12	39	5	5	.243	.280	L	L	6-0	200	4-6-82	2000	Miami, Fla.
Kimpton, Nick	.269	49	186	30	50	4	2	0	23	21	39	9	5	.312	.354	L	L	6-1	170	10-27-83	2001	Sydney, Australia
Kotchman, Casey	.600	4	15	5	9	1	0	1	5	3	2	0	0	.867	.632	L	L	6-3	210	2-22-83	2001	Seminole, Fla.
Mathis, Jeff	.304	7	23	1	7	1	0	0	3	2	4	0	0	.348	.346	R	R	6-0	180	3-31-83	2001	Marianna, Fla.
Melgarejo, Ransel	.283	45	138	25	39	7	2	1	20	19	19	12	5	.384	.390	R	R	6-0	180	8-28-81	2001	Miami, Fla.
Mott, Bill	.083	5	12	2	1	0	1	0	2	4	0	0	0	.250	.333	L	R	6-2	180	1-2-76	1998	San Luis Obispo, Calif.
Nevins, Ryan	.329	25	82	12	27	4	4	0	17	5	15	1	2	.476	.371	L	R	5-11	175	12-29-78	2001	Flushing, N.Y.
Seever, Brian	.412	5	17	5	7	0	1	0	1	0	2	1	1	.529	.412	R	R	6-0	196	8-18-76	1999	Fairfield, Calif.
Selmo, Wilson	.301	48	183	23	55	5	2	0	21	1	24	10	0	.350	.314	B	R	5-11	160	9-27-82	2000	Santo Domingo, D.R.
Stockton, Rick	.263	36	118	17	31	2	2	1	11	7	20	8	2	.339	.318	L	L	6-1	185	11-5-79	2001	Calabasas, Calif.
Vega, Jesus	.333	25	54	3	18	3	0	1	9	7	14	1	1	.444	.431	R	R	6-0	213	4-10-82	1999	Navojoa, Mexico
Wallace, Kellen	.119	27	67	5	8	0	1	1	5	6	19	1	0	.194	.192	L	R	6-4	200	11-20-80	1999	Baltimore, Md.

GAMES BY POSITION: C—Collins 15, Del Chiaro 15, Gregorio 3, Guzman 17, Mathis 3, Vega 23. **1B**—C. Batista 5, DeLeon 17, Guzman 1, Jenkins 24, Kimpton 1, Kotchman 4, Stockton 17, Wallace 2. **2B**—C. Batista 1, J. Batista 1, Brown 31, DeLeon 1, Felix 18, Nevins 4, Selmo 4. **3B**—C. Batista 30, J. Batista 1, Brown 17, DeLeon 1, Nevins 15. **SS**—C. Batista 3, J. Batista 19, Selmo 45, Stockton 12, Wallace 11. **OF**—Abad 14, Cosby 37, Felix 1, Guzman 4, Jenkins 18, Kimpton 45, Mathis 1, Melgarejo 42, Mott 3, Seever 4, Stockton 12, Wallace 11.

PITCHING	W	L	ERA	G	GS	CG	SV	IP	H	R	ER	BB	SO	AVG	B	T	HT	WT	DOB	1st Yr	Resides
Andujar, Jesse	0	0	5.06	3	0	0	0	5	6	3	3	4	6	.300	R	R	6-4	230	7-23-79	1996	San Pedro de Macoris, D.R.
Arias, Daniel	1	2	3.02	16	3	0	1	48	64	25	16	9	42	.329	R	R	6-1	185	6-19-82	2000	Bani, D.R.
Astacio, Hector	3	2	3.07	22	4	0	1	44	46	21	15	6	36	.267	R	R	6-0	165	8-10-83	2000	Hato Mayor, D.R.
Balser, Jeffrey	2	3	8.87	20	0	0	3	22	50	29	22	5	12	.423	R	R	6-1	205	12-31-80	2001	Venice, Fla.
Bukowski, Stan	0	1	4.09	4	4	0	0	11	11	6	5	5	8	.239	R	R	6-5	220	9-16-81	1999	Clearwater, Fla.
Cimorelli, Brett	2	2	7.08	11	2	0	0	20	25	22	16	13	14	.280	R	R	6-4	215	2-22-82	2000	Zephyrhills, Fla.
D'Amico, Leonardo	0	6	5.17	14	5	0	0	38	44	32	22	13	33	.283	R	R	6-2	180	12-14-81	1999	Mariara, Venez.
Jones, Greg	0	0	0.00	2	2	0	0	2	3	0	0	2	2	.375	R	R	6-2	190	11-15-76	1997	Seminole, Fla.
Luther, Heath	1	3	4.66	13	6	0	0	39	52	26	20	15	34	.320	L	L	5-11	185	1-7-79	2001	Fort Wayne, Ind.
Mendoza, Mario	0	0	2.25	3	0	0	0	4	2	1	1	0	2	.142	R	R	6-3	200	1-19-79	1999	Navojoa, Mexico
Morban, Carlos	0	1	13.14	11	1	0	0	12	17	22	18	12	10	.314	R	R	6-6	185	1-29-83	2001	Nigua, D.R.
Pine, Chris	0	1	4.50	3	0	0	0	4	5	3	2	0	2	.277	R	R	6-2	205	9-25-76	1998	Tigard, Ore.
Reynoso, Roberto	1	4	5.40	14	6	0	0	52	70	46	31	9	34	.305	R	R	6-2	195	12-16-81	2000	Santo Domingo, D.R.
Rouwenhorst, Jon	1	0	0.00	7	0	0	0	9	2	1	0	5	14	.068	L	L	6-1	175	9-25-79	2001	Anaheim, Calif.
Santana, Johan	3	2	3.22	10	9	1	0	59	40	27	21	35	69	.184	R	R	6-2	150	11-28-83	2001	San Cristobal, D.R.
Shell, Steven	1	0	0.00	3	0	0	0	4	1	0	0	2	3	.076	R	R	6-5	195	3-10-83	2001	Cleburne, Texas
Shull, Johnathan	2	3	4.89	17	8	0	0	53	61	42	29	24	40	.281	R	R	6-3	200	6-23-82	2001	Butler, Ind.
Steward, Jaime	5	3	2.02	19	4	1	1	49	47	19	11	11	40	.247	L	L	6-0	185	1-26-79	2001	Blackwood, N.J.
Wright, Shayne	0	1	2.84	9	2	0	2	13	20	9	4	1	11	.344	R	R	6-5	195	8-21-80	2000	Auburn, Calif.

ARIZONA DIAMONDBACKS

BY JACK MAGRUDER

Call it a season of hiss-tory. Powered by the best 1-2 pitching punch in major league annals—Randy Johnson and Curt Schilling—and home run-hitter Luis Gonzalez, the Diamondbacks became the first four-year-old franchise to win the World Series with a thrilling seven-game victory over the Yankees.

No expansion team had done it as quickly, the Marlins taking five years to win in 1997. The Marlins were disbanded after that run, but Diamondbacks owner Jerry Colangelo—who got a dozen players to defer money at simple interest in the offseason to help the bottom line—emphatically denied that will happen here.

Johnson and Schilling had their best seasons, combining for 43 victories and 665 strikeouts during the 2001 regular season while turning the year of the high strike into the year of the often strike. Johnson and Schilling claimed nine of the 'Backs' 11 postseason victories, Johnson setting a playoff record with five. Johnson won Game Six of the World Series as a starter and Game Seven as a reliever, the third pitcher in history to do that and the first to do it without a day off in between. Johnson had 372 strikeouts in the regular season and 47 more in six playoff appearances, enabling him to break Sandy Koufax' 1965 record for strikeouts (412) in a season.

Gonzalez was a fitting hero in Game Seven, blooping a single over a drawn-in infield for a 3-2 victory in the last of the ninth inning, the sixth walkoff Game Seven in Series history. He was the main power source during the season, hitting 60 homers—57 in the regular season, including a major league record-tying 13 in April.

Manager Bob Brenly, in his first season on the job after broadcasting the team's games for three years as a TV analyst, became the fourth manager in history to win a World Series in his first season, and the first since the Yankees' Ralph Houk in 1961.

Brenly replaced Buck Showalter to create a lighter clubhouse mood. While some of his moves seemed unorthodox, he got the most out of his talent at the most critical

Luis Gonzalez

Lyle Overbay

JOHN SPEAR

PLAYERS OF THE YEAR

MAJOR LEAGUE: Luis Gonzalez, of

In his 12th season Gonzalez had his best year ever, hitting .325-57-142. He became the 15th player in major league history to have at least 100 extra-base hits.

MINOR LEAGUE: Lyle Overbay, 1b

He hit .352-13-100 at Double-A El Paso—missing by .002 having the highest full-season batting average in the minors in 2001. He also had 49 doubles and earned a promotion to the majors.

times—such as the Series-record 22-hit, 15-2 victory over the Yankees in Game Six. That followed consecutive blown saves in New York by closer Byung-Hyun Kim, who yielded two-out, two-run homers in the last of the ninth inning of Games Four and Five.

"I feel like I came here and this yacht was sitting at the dock and I just happened to get behind the wheel," Brenly said. "It could have been any one of a number of people. This is a ballclub that was primed and focused and knew what (it) had to do to get to this position."

The Diamondbacks mixed and matched well. Craig Counsell, who entered spring training on the bubble, emerged as the everyday second baseman. Mark Grace and Reggie Sanders, signed as free agents in the offseason, combined for 48 homers and 168 RBIs. And when injuries kept Todd Stottlemyre, Matt Mantei and Armando Reynoso from contributing to the pitching staff, Kim developed into a steady closer, and heretofore journeyman Miguel Batista won a career-high 11 games.

The minor league system does not have a good reputation, but seemed to take a step forward in 2001. Double-A El Paso first baseman Lyle Overbay led the Texas League in hitting (.352), hits (187), doubles (49) and on-base percentage (.423). He led the minor leagues in hits and doubles. Another minor league hitting hero was first baseman Jesus Cota, who won a triple crown in the Rookie-level Pioneer League. He hit .368-16-71 for Missoula.

El Paso closer Jose Valverde struck out 72 batters in 41 innings with a fastball in the high 90s. His season was cut short because of a strained elbow, but he is the top pitching prospect in a system that also includes U.S. World Cup team members Jeremy Ward and Chris Capuano and righthander Beltran Perez, who went 12-4, 2.81 at Class A South Bend.

ORGANIZATION LEADERS

BATTING

*AVG	Jesus Cota, Missoula	.368
R	Billy Martin, El Paso/Lancaster	101
H	Lyle Overbay, El Paso	187
TB	Lyle Overbay, El Paso	281
2B	Lyle Overbay, El Paso	49
3B	Victor Hall, South Bend	12
HR	Jack Cust, Tucson	27
RBI	Billy Martin, El Paso/Lancaster	107
BB	Jack Cust, Tucson	102
SO	Jack Cust, Tucson	160
SB	Victor Hall, South Bend	60

PITCHING

W	Beltran Perez, South Bend	12
L	Enrique Gonzalez, South Bend	12
#ERA	Ryan Holsten, Missoula	2.53
G	Jason Martines, Tucson/El Paso	63
CG	Three tied at	2
SV	Greg Belson, South Bend	16
IP	Kennie Steenstra, Tucson	170
BB	Chris Capuano, El Paso	75
SO	Chris Capuano, El Paso	167

*Minimum 250 At-Bats #Minimum 75 Innings

ARIZONA DIAMONDBACKS

Manager: Bob Brenly

2001 Record: 92-70, .568 (1st, NL West)

BATTING	AVG	G	AB	R	H	2B	3B	HR	RBI	BB	SO	SB	CS	SLG	OBP	B	T	HT	WT	DOB	1st Yr	Resides
Barajas, Rod	.160	51	106	9	17	3	0	3	9	4	26	0	0	.274	.191	R	R	6-2	220	9-5-75	1996	Norwalk, Calif.
Bautista, Danny	.302	100	222	26	67	11	2	5	26	14	31	3	2	.437	.346	R	R	5-11	170	5-24-72	1989	Santo Domingo, D.R.
Bell, Jay	.248	129	428	59	106	24	1	13	46	65	79	0	1	.400	.349	R	R	6-0	182	12-11-65	1984	Valrico, Fla.
Christenson, Ryan	.250	19	4	3	1	0	0	0	1	1	1	0	0	.500	.400	R	R	6-0	191	3-28-74	1995	Apple Valley, Calif.
Cintron, Alex	.286	8	7	0	2	0	1	0	0	0	0	0	0	.571	.286	B	R	6-2	180	12-17-78	1997	Yabucoa, P.R.
Colbrunn, Greg	.289	59	97	12	28	8	0	4	18	9	14	0	0	.495	.373	R	R	6-0	200	7-26-69	1988	Weston, Fla.
Conti, Jason	.250	5	4	1	1	0	0	0	0	1	2	0	0	.250	.400	L	R	5-11	180	1-27-75	1996	Cranberry Township, Pa.
Counsell, Craig	.275	141	458	76	126	22	3	4	38	61	76	6	8	.362	.359	L	R	6-0	175	8-21-70	1992	Fort Lauderdale, Fla.
Cummings, Midre	.300	20	20	1	6	1	0	0	1	0	4	0	0	.350	.286	L	R	6-0	195	10-14-71	1990	Tarpon Springs, Fla.
Cust, Jack	.500	3	2	0	1	0	0	0	0	1	0	0	0	.500	.667	L	R	6-1	205	1-16-79	1997	Flemington, N.J.
Dellucci, David	.276	115	217	28	60	10	2	10	40	22	52	2	1	.479	.349	L	L	5-10	180	10-31-73	1995	Baton Rouge, La.
Difelice, Mike	.048	12	21	1	1	0	0	0	1	0	10	0	0	.048	.091	R	R	6-2	205	5-28-69	1991	Safety Harbor, Fla.
Durazo, Erubiel	.269	92	175	34	47	11	0	12	38	28	49	0	0	.537	.372	L	L	6-3	225	1-23-74	1997	Hermosillo, Mexico
Finley, Steve	.275	140	495	66	136	27	4	14	73	47	67	11	7	.430	.337	L	L	6-2	180	3-12-65	1987	Del Mar, Calif.
Gonzalez, Luis	.325	162	609	128	198	36	7	57	142	100	83	1	1	.688	.429	L	R	6-2	190	9-2-67	1988	Sugar Land, Texas
Grace, Mark	.298	145	476	66	142	31	2	15	78	67	36	1	0	.466	.386	L	L	6-2	200	6-28-64	1986	Chicago, Ill.
Huckaby, Ken	.000	1	1	0	0	0	0	0	0	0	1	0	0	.000	.000	R	R	6-1	205	1-27-71	1991	Philadelphia, Pa.
Miller, Damian	.271	123	380	45	103	19	0	13	47	35	80	0	1	.424	.337	R	R	6-2	190	10-13-69	1990	La Crosse, Wis.
Moeller, Chad	.232	25	56	8	13	0	1	1	2	6	12	0	0	.321	.306	R	R	6-3	210	2-18-75	1996	Manhattan Beach, Fla.
Overbay, Lyle	.500	2	2	0	1	0	0	0	0	0	1	0	0	.500	.500	L	L	6-2	215	1-28-77	1999	Centralia, Wash.
Ryan, Rob	.000	1	1	0	0	0	0	0	0	0	1	0	0	.000	.000	L	L	5-11	190	6-24-73	1996	Spokane, Wash.
Sanders, Reggie	.263	126	441	84	116	21	3	33	90	46	126	14	10	.549	.337	R	R	6-1	185	12-1-67	1988	Tampa, Fla.
Sosa, Juan	.000	2	0	0	0	0	0	0	0	0	1	0	0	.000	.000	R	R	6-1	175	8-19-75	1993	San Francisco de Macoris, D.R.
Spivey, Junior	.258	72	163	33	42	6	3	5	21	23	47	3	0	.423	.354	R	R	6-0	185	1-28-75	1996	Oklahoma City, Okla.
Williams, Matt	.275	106	408	58	112	30	0	16	65	22	70	1	0	.466	.314	R	R	6-2	210	11-28-65	1986	Scottsdale, Ariz.
Womack, Tony	.266	125	481	66	128	19	5	3	30	23	54	28	7	.345	.307	L	R	5-9	155	9-25-69	1991	Greensboro, N.C.

PITCHING	W	L	ERA	G	GS	CG	SV	IP	H	R	ER	BB	SO	AVG	B	T	HT	WT	DOB	1st Yr	Resides
Anderson, Brian	4	9	5.20	29	22	1	0	133	156	93	77	30	55	.294	B	L	6-1	190	4-26-72	1993	North Olmstead, Ohio
Batista, Miguel	11	8	3.36	48	18	0	0	139	113	57	52	60	90	.226	R	R	6-0	190	2-19-71	1988	San Pedro de Macoris, D.R.
Bierbrodt, Nick	2	2	8.22	5	5	0	0	23	29	21	21	12	17	.305	L	L	6-5	190	5-16-78	1996	Long Beach, Calif.
Brohawn, Troy	2	3	4.93	59	0	0	1	49	55	27	27	23	30	.289	L	L	6-1	190	1-14-73	1994	Woolford, Md.
Ellis, Robert	6	5	5.77	19	17	0	0	92	106	61	59	34	41	.292	R	R	6-5	220	12-15-70	1991	Carthage, Texas
Guzman, Geraldo	0	0	2.89	4	0	0	0	9	7	4	3	3	4	.205	R	R	6-1	160	11-28-72	1990	Arroyo Seco, D.R.
Johnson, Randy	21	6	2.49	35	34	3	0	250	181	74	69	71	372	.203	R	L	6-10	230	9-10-63	1985	Glendale, Ariz.
Kim, Byung-Hyun	5	6	2.94	78	0	0	19	98	58	32	32	44	113	.173	R	R	5-11	176	1-21-79	1999	Kwangsan, Korea
Knott, Eric	0	1	1.93	3	1	0	0	5	8	9	1	0	4	.347	L	L	6-0	188	9-23-74	1997	Sebring, Fla.
Koplove, Mike	0	1	3.60	9	0	0	0	10	8	7	4	9	14	.210	R	R	6-0	160	8-30-76	1998	Philadelphia, Pa.
Lopez, Albie	4	7	4.00	13	13	0	0	81	74	36	36	24	69	.246	R	R	6-2	240	8-18-71	1991	Gilbert, Ariz.
Mantei, Matt	0	0	2.57	8	0	0	2	7	6	2	2	4	12	.222	R	R	6-1	190	7-7-73	1991	Pembroke Pines, Fla.
Mohler, Mike	0	0	7.24	13	0	0	0	14	14	11	11	9	7	.285	R	L	6-2	208	7-26-68	1990	Gonzales, La.
Morgan, Mike	1	0	4.26	31	1	0	0	38	45	20	18	17	24	.306	R	R	6-2	220	10-8-59	1978	Park City, Utah
Prinz, Bret	4	1	2.63	46	0	0	9	41	33	13	12	19	27	.220	R	R	6-3	200	6-15-77	1998	Peoria, Ariz.
Reynoso, Armando	1	6	5.98	9	9	0	0	47	58	32	31	13	15	.311	R	R	6-0	196	5-1-66	1989	Jalisco, Mexico
Sabel, Erik	3	2	4.38	42	0	0	0	51	57	26	25	12	25	.282	R	R	6-3	193	10-14-74	1996	West Lafayette, Ind.
Schilling, Curt	22	6	2.98	35	35	6	0	257	237	86	85	39	293	.244	R	R	6-4	231	11-14-66	1986	Philadelphia, Pa.
Springer, Russ	0	0	7.13	18	0	0	1	18	20	16	14	4	12	.273	R	R	6-4	205	11-7-68	1989	Pollack, La.
Swindell, Greg	2	6	4.53	64	0	0	2	54	51	27	27	8	42	.250	R	L	6-3	230	1-2-65	1986	Paradise Valley, Ariz.
Witt, Bobby	4	1	4.78	14	7	0	0	43	36	23	23	25	31	.222	R	R	6-2	205	5-11-64	1985	Colleyville, Texas

FIELDING

Catcher	PCT	G	PO	A	E	DP	PB
Barajas	.995	50	179	11	1	3	0
Difelice	.982	12	53	3	1	1	1
Huckaby	1.000	1	5	0	0	0	0
Miller	.993	121	966	81	7	6	10
Moeller	1.000	25	111	7	0	0	1

First Base	PCT	G	PO	A	E	DP
Colbrunn	.987	14	67	9	1	7
Counsell	1.000	2	1	0	0	0
Durazo	.993	38	248	17	2	22
Grace	.995	135	997	62	5	99

Second Base	PCT	G	PO	A	E	DP
Bell	.994	80	153	168	2	43
Counsell	.996	55	96	133	1	34
Spivey	.985	66	46	104	3	27

Third Base	PCT	G	PO	A	E	DP
Bell	.940	40	22	56	5	3
Colbrunn	.875	10	6	8	2	1
Counsell	.977	38	27	58	2	4
Sosa	1.000	1	0	1	0	0

	PCT	G	PO	A	E	DP
Williams	.963	102	57	177	9	17

Shortstop	PCT	G	PO	A	E	DP
Cintron	1.000	7	2	6	0	0
Counsell	.975	58	70	124	5	31
Spivey	.000	1	0	0	0	0
Williams	1.000	2	3	5	0	1
Womack	.955	118	151	312	22	74

Outfield	PCT	G	PO	A	E	DP
Bautista	1.000	61	102	4	0	2
Christenson	1.000	5	1	0	0	0
Conti	.000	1	0	0	0	0
Cummings	1.000	4	4	0	0	0
Cust	.000	1	0	0	0	0
Dellucci	.989	58	90	0	1	0
Durazo	1.000	2	4	1	0	0
Finley	.993	131	299	6	2	3
Gonzalez	1.000	161	280	8	0	1
Sanders	.996	119	232	5	1	3
Womack	.000	1	0	0	0	0

Randy Johnson

LARRY GOREN

FARM SYSTEM

Director, Minor League Operations: Tommy Jones

Class	Farm Team	League	W	L	Pct.	Finish*	Manager	First Yr.
AAA	Tucson (Ariz.) Sidewinders	Pacific Coast	65	77	.458	12th (16)	Tom Spencer	1998
AA	El Paso (Texas) Diablos	Texas	57	83	.407	7th (8)	Al Pedrique	1999
A#	Lancaster (Calif.) JetHawks	California	61	79	.436	t-8th (10)	Scott Coolbaugh	2001
A	South Bend (Ind.) Silver Hawks	Midwest	70	66	.515	6th (14)	Steve Scarsone	1997
A	Yakima (Wash.) Bears	Northwest	33	42	.440	6th (8)	Greg Lonigro	2001
Rookie#	Missoula (Mont.) Osprey	Pioneer	52	24	.684	2nd (8)	Chip Hale	1999

*Finish in overall standings (No. of teams in league)   #Advanced level

TUCSON   Class AAA

ORGANIZATION STATISTICS

PACIFIC COAST LEAGUE

BATTING	AVG	G	AB	R	H	2B	3B	HR	RBI	BB	SO	SB	CS	SLG	OBP	B	T	HT	WT	DOB	1st Yr	Resides
Barajas, Rod	.321	45	162	23	52	13	0	9	32	9	23	3	1	.568	.366	R	R	6-2	220	9-5-75	1996	Norwalk, Calif.
Christenson, Ryan	.288	57	215	32	62	17	0	6	27	23	43	5	2	.451	.353	R	R	6-0	191	3-28-74	1995	Apple Valley, Calif.
2-team (19 Sacra.)	.260	76	285	39	74	21	0	7	30	27	56	7	2	.407	.321							
Cintron, Alex	.292	107	425	53	124	24	3	3	35	15	48	9	6	.384	.315	B	R	6-2	180	12-17-78	1997	Yabucoa, P.R.
Colbrunn, Greg	.385	5	13	1	5	1	0	0	4	2	0	0	0	.462	.467	R	R	6-0	200	7-26-69	1988	Weston, Fla.
Conti, Jason	.331	92	362	68	120	23	6	9	52	33	54	2	5	.503	.402	L	R	5-11	180	1-27-75	1996	Cranberry Township, Pa.
Cummings, Midre	.331	77	263	38	87	23	9	5	38	24	49	2	3	.544	.383	L	R	6-0	195	10-14-71	1990	Tarpon Springs, Fla.
Cust, Jack	.278	135	442	81	123	24	2	27	79	102	160	6	3	.525	.415	L	R	6-1	205	1-16-79	1997	Flemington, N.J.
Difelice, Mike	.346	7	26	6	9	0	0	1	2	3	6	0	0	.462	.414	R	R	6-2	205	5-28-69	1991	Safety Harbor, Fla.
Durazo, Erubiel	.273	3	11	3	3	0	0	1	1	1	3	0	0	.545	.333	L	L	6-3	225	1-23-74	1997	Hermosillo, Mexico
Epke, Brian	.000	2	3	1	0	0	0	0	0	1	2	0	0	.000	.400	R	R	6-0	195	5-2-79	2001	Waco, Neb.
Gann, Jamie	.267	7	15	2	4	1	0	1	4	0	0	0	0	.533	.267	R	R	6-1	197	5-1-75	1996	Norman, Okla.
Gibson, Derrick	.247	32	97	8	24	8	1	2	15	5	19	5	0	.412	.311	R	R	6-2	244	2-5-75	1993	Winter Haven, Fla.
Huckaby, Ken	.290	78	262	31	76	15	1	2	34	7	62	1	3	.378	.313	R	R	6-1	205	1-27-71	1991	Philadelphia, Pa.
Klassen, Danny	.222	7	18	5	4	0	0	1	3	2	3	0	0	.389	.333	R	R	6-0	175	9-22-75	1993	Stuart, Fla.
Lemonis, Chris	.217	9	23	3	5	2	0	0	1	3	0	0	0	.304	.250	L	R	5-11	185	8-21-73	1995	New York, N.Y.
2-team (9 Calgary)	.188	18	48	6	9	2	0	0	1	3	10	0	0	.229	.250							
McNally, Sean	.241	74	249	24	60	5	2	6	28	24	77	4	1	.349	.314	R	R	6-4	210	12-14-72	1994	Rye, N.Y.
Moeller, Chad	.274	78	274	41	75	20	0	8	36	25	54	1	4	.434	.337	R	R	6-3	210	2-18-75	1996	Manhattan Beach, Calif.
Nelson, Bryant	.301	85	326	37	98	15	0	6	41	16	20	9	5	.402	.332	B	R	5-10	205	1-27-74	1994	Crossett, Ark.
Petersen, Chris	.211	43	123	16	26	2	0	2	8	8	18	2	0	.276	.274	R	R	5-11	175	11-6-70	1992	Southington, Conn.
2-team (21 Nashville)	.264	64	178	25	47	7	0	4	26	11	33	2	2	.371	.325							
Romero, Willie	.231	9	26	2	6	1	0	0	1	2	7	0	1	.269	.286	R	R	5-9	192	8-5-74	1991	Maracay, Venez.
Rosario, Mel	.243	19	37	1	9	3	0	0	3	1	8	0	0	.324	.263	B	R	6-0	200	5-25-73	1992	Miami, Fla.
2-team (41 Omaha)	.250	60	188	19	47	13	2	6	28	8	50	1	1	.436	.283							
Rose, Mike	.182	20	55	9	10	1	2	0	8	12	16	0	0	.273	.324	B	R	6-1	185	8-25-76	1995	Sacramento, Calif.
Ryan, Rob	.329	63	216	45	71	17	5	12	50	29	34	1	3	.620	.417	L	L	5-11	190	6-24-73	1996	Spokane, Wash.
Sanders, Reggie	.333	2	6	0	2	1	0	0	1	2	0	1	0	.500	.500	R	R	6-1	185	12-1-67	1988	Tampa, Fla.
Sell, Chip	.262	94	248	34	65	10	2	6	28	12	49	3	2	.391	.299	L	R	6-2	205	6-19-71	1994	Otis, Ore.
Sosa, Juan	.192	64	182	17	35	6	1	0	12	9	22	5	1	.236	.232	R	R	6-1	175	8-19-75	1993	San Francisco de Macoris, D.R.
2-team (14 Colo. Spr.)	.198	78	222	19	44	7	1	0	14	14	29	6	2	.239	.246							
Spivey, Junior	.232	54	194	25	45	6	0	6	27	27	32	9	6	.356	.326	R	R	6-0	185	1-28-75	1996	Oklahoma City, Okla.
Steenstra, Kennie	.163	29	43	4	7	2	0	0	1	1	21	0	0	.209	.182	R	R	6-5	215	10-13-70	1992	Liberty, Mo.
White, Walt	.215	35	79	11	17	4	1	0	8	8	23	1	0	.291	.287	R	R	6-0	195	12-12-71	1994	Trenton, Fla.
Williams, Matt	.353	5	17	4	6	2	0	2	5	2	2	1	0	.824	.421	R	R	6-2	210	11-28-65	1986	Scottsdale, Ariz.
Wilson, Desi	.328	83	320	45	105	20	1	3	38	14	48	4	2	.425	.359	L	L	6-7	230	5-9-69	1991	Glen Cove, N.Y.
Womack, Tony	.385	4	13	1	5	0	1	0	2	0	1	0	1	.538	.385	L	R	5-9	155	9-25-69	1991	Greensboro, N.C.

PITCHING	W	L	ERA	G	GS	CG	SV	IP	H	R	ER	BB	SO	AVG	B	T	HT	WT	DOB	1st Yr	Resides
Anderson, Brian	1	0	1.50	2	2	0	0	12	7	2	2	2	8	.166	B	L	6-1	190	4-26-72	1993	North Olmstead, Ohio
Belflower, Jay	0	0	0.00	1	0	0	0	2	2	0	0	1	2	.285	R	R	6-4	215	11-12-79	2001	Sebring, Fla.
Bierbrodt, Nick	4	1	2.18	7	6	0	0	45	48	15	11	9	56	.280	L	L	6-5	190	5-16-78	1996	Long Beach, Calif.
Boskie, Shawn	4	6	6.93	12	11	1	0	62	95	55	48	17	31	.347	R	R	6-3	225	3-28-67	1986	Reno, Nev.
Brohawn, Troy	0	0	0.00	2	0	0	0	3	1	0	0	1	4	.083	L	L	6-1	190	1-14-73	1994	Woolford, Md.
Chavez, Anthony	7	6	4.57	51	8	1	1	87	109	59	44	37	76	.307	R	R	5-11	180	10-22-70	1992	Merced, Calif.
Crawford, Joe	2	4	5.23	8	7	1	0	41	58	30	24	12	32	.329	L	L	6-3	225	5-2-70	1991	Hillsboro, Ohio
Dace, Derek	0	3	5.40	17	0	0	0	22	29	19	13	7	14	.311	L	L	6-7	200	4-11-75	1994	Rolla, Mo.
Ellis, Robert	1	1	3.08	5	5	0	0	26	25	12	9	5	13	.250	R	R	6-5	220	12-15-70	1991	Carthage, Texas
Eppolito, Vince	0	0	4.50	2	0	0	0	2	1	1	1	3	2	.142	R	R	6-5	225	7-29-77	2000	Lansdale, Pa.
Guzman, Geraldo	3	6	4.85	20	14	0	0	95	92	56	51	30	85	.254	R	R	6-1	160	11-28-72	1990	Arroyo Seco, D.R.
Jacome, Jason	1	8	5.33	35	16	0	0	120	149	78	71	37	72	.308	L	L	6-0	180	11-24-70	1991	Tucson, Ariz.
Johnson, Jonathan	4	4	5.25	15	12	0	0	74	63	48	43	42	51	.232	R	R	6-0	180	7-16-74	1995	Irmo, S.C.
Knott, Eric	6	2	3.80	25	8	0	1	73	82	34	31	8	43	.284	L	L	6-0	188	9-23-74	1997	Sebring, Fla.
Koplove, Mike	4	1	2.82	17	0	0	9	22	17	7	7	10	22	.207	R	R	6-0	160	8-30-76	1998	Philadelphia, Pa.
Lawrence, Sean	1	3	3.57	18	0	0	0	23	20	15	9	9	22	.230	L	L	6-4	215	9-2-70	1992	Hillside, Ill.
2-team (25 Portland)	1	6	3.55	43	0	0	0	58	52	31	23	22	76	.230							
Lee, Jon	0	0	3.38	2	0	0	0	3	3	1	1	1	1	.300	R	R	6-5	215	7-24-78	2000	Houston, Texas
Martines, Jason	3	0	9.00	12	0	0	1	18	31	19	18	7	15	.378	L	R	6-2	190	1-21-76	1997	Hanover, Mich.
Mohler, Mike	5	0	3.18	40	0	0	3	45	52	28	16	14	48	.279	R	L	6-2	208	7-26-68	1990	Gonzales, La.
Morgan, Mike	0	0	3.00	2	2	0	0	3	5	1	1	0	4	.357	R	R	6-2	220	10-8-59	1978	Park City, Utah
Patterson, John	2	7	5.85	13	12	0	0	68	82	50	44	31	40	.301	R	R	6-4	195	1-30-78	1996	Orange, Texas
Prinz, Bret	0	0	0.00	5	0	0	3	6	1	0	0	6	6	.055	R	R	6-3	200	6-15-77	1998	Peoria, Ariz.
Randolph, Steve	2	0	6.33	18	0	0	0	21	24	15	15	19	16	.282	L	L	6-3	185	5-1-74	1995	Austin, Texas
Revenig, Todd	4	5	5.07	46	0	0	0	66	82	39	37	12	42	.301	R	R	6-1	185	6-28-69	1990	Baxter, Minn.

PITCHING

PITCHING	W	L	ERA	G	GS	CG	SV	IP	H	R	ER	BB	SO	AVG	B	T	HT	WT	DOB	1st Yr	Resides
Reyes, Carlos	0	1	8.68	8	0	0	0	9	13	10	9	5	7	.333	B	R	6-0	190	4-4-69	1991	Tampa, Fla.
2-team (17 Sacramento)	2	1	6.81	25	0	0	0	40	44	31	30	19	33	.282							
Reynoso, Armando	0	0	0.00	1	1	0	0	4	3	0	0	2	5	.214	R	R	6-0	196	5-1-66	1989	Jalisco, Mexico
Sabel, Erik	2	2	2.95	18	2	0	2	40	35	14	13	7	32	.239	R	R	6-3	193	10-14-74	1996	West Lafayette, Ind.
Sikaras, Pete	0	1	12.00	4	0	0	0	6	11	10	8	4	4	.392	R	R	6-2	204	5-5-79	2000	Niles, Ill.
Springer, Russ	0	0	4.91	7	3	0	0	7	7	4	4	3	6	.250	R	R	6-4	205	11-7-68	1989	Pollack, La.
Steenstra, Kennie	9	6	4.18	28	28	1	0	170	187	101	79	42	114	.277	R	R	6-5	215	10-13-70	1992	Liberty, Mo.
Ward, Jeremy	3	4	3.52	40	0	0	13	46	53	23	18	17	35	.286	R	R	6-3	220	2-24-78	1999	Rocky Mount, N.C.
Witt, Bobby	0	3	3.63	5	5	0	0	22	18	11	9	8	18	.222	R	R	6-2	205	5-11-64	1985	Colleyville, Texas

FIELDING

Catcher	PCT	G	PO	A	E	DP	PB
Barajas	.992	19	112	7	1	0	0
Difelice	.952	5	40	0	2	0	0
Epke	1.000	1	1	0	0	0	0
Huckaby	.970	36	237	24	8	3	3
Moeller	.989	70	442	20	5	1	6
Rosario	1.000	7	34	6	0	0	1
Rose	1.000	15	101	13	0	1	2

First Base	PCT	G	PO	A	E	DP
Barajas	.989	21	163	14	2	16
Colbrunn	1.000	5	24	3	0	4
Cummings	1.000	5	39	1	0	1
Difelice	.875	1	7	0	1	1
Durazo	1.000	3	18	2	0	1
Huckaby	.990	28	188	11	2	11
McNally	1.000	7	29	1	0	4
Nelson	1.000	1	7	1	0	0
Rosario	1.000	1	3	0	0	0
Sell	.985	34	240	23	4	25
Wilson	.989	58	470	48	6	38

Second Base	PCT	G	PO	A	E	DP
Cintron	.970	19	26	38	2	5

Huckaby	.000	1	0	0	0	0
Klassen	1.000	1	3	3	0	0
Lemonis	.962	5	7	18	1	2
Nelson	.974	16	33	43	2	12
Petersen	1.000	16	25	33	0	8
Sosa	.959	36	61	78	6	19
Spivey	.990	50	131	152	3	25
White	.932	24	35	61	7	10

Third Base	PCT	G	PO	A	E	DP
Barajas	.000	1	0	0	0	0
Huckaby	.879	11	7	22	4	1
Klassen	.909	5	2	8	1	1
McNally	.954	68	37	109	7	10
Nelson	.918	62	45	111	14	11
Sosa	.889	8	0	8	1	0
White	1.000	2	1	0	0	0
Williams	.833	4	1	4	1	1

Shortstop	PCT	G	PO	A	E	DP
Cintron	.931	93	139	267	30	36
Klassen	1.000	1	1	3	0	0
McNally	1.000	6	2	16	0	2
Petersen	.991	31	40	66	1	13

Sosa	.981	16	18	35	1	4
Spivey	1.000	3	4	11	0	3
White	1.000	6	14	13	0	6
Womack	.846	4	3	8	2	2

Outfield	PCT	G	PO	A	E	DP
Christenson	.950	57	130	2	7	0
Conti	.991	89	205	5	2	1
Cummings	.978	46	84	5	2	1
Cust	.948	117	195	6	11	1
Gann	1.000	6	2	1	0	0
Gibson	.962	28	49	2	2	0
Nelson	1.000	5	7	0	0	0
Romero	.933	6	12	2	1	0
Ryan	.988	51	77	2	1	0
Sanders	1.000	2	2	0	0	0
Sell	.987	48	74	1	1	0
Sosa	.900	5	9	0	1	0
Wilson	.913	15	18	3	2	0

EL PASO

TEXAS LEAGUE

BATTING

BATTING	AVG	G	AB	R	H	2B	3B	HR	RBI	BB	SO	SB	CS	SLG	OBP	B	T	HT	WT	DOB	1st Yr	Resides
Camilli, Jason	.333	13	39	7	13	0	0	3	2	8	0	2	.359	.357	R	R	6-0	190	10-18-75	1994	Phoenix, Ariz.
Cresse, Brad	.289	118	429	55	124	39	1	14	81	44	116	0	1	.483	.373	R	R	6-4	215	7-31-78	2000	Rancho Mirage, Calif.
Dallimore, Brian	.327	127	517	74	169	38	6	8	67	30	56	11	13	.470	.378	R	R	6-1	185	11-15-73	1996	Las Vegas, Nev.
Devore, Doug	.294	128	476	67	140	32	11	15	74	46	118	11	3	.502	.358	L	L	6-4	200	12-14-77	1999	Dublin, Ohio
Gann, Jamie	.216	55	190	20	41	5	0	2	18	7	44	5	3	.274	.259	R	R	6-1	197	5-1-75	1996	Norman, Okla.
Gibson, Derrick	.347	18	72	13	25	4	0	2	16	6	18	3	1	.486	.407	R	R	6-2	244	2-5-75	1993	Winter Haven, Fla.
Glassey, Josh	.167	8	18	1	3	0	0	0	3	5	0	0	0	.167	.286	L	R	6-1	190	5-6-77	1996	Longview, Texas
Glendenning, Mike	.236	40	140	17	33	9	0	3	18	18	46	1	0	.364	.329	R	R	6-0	225	8-26-76	1996	West Hills, Calif.
2-team (60 Shreveport)	.205	100	347	37	71	12	0	10	36	39	117	1	0	.326	.291							
Gonzalez, Manny	.192	9	26	3	5	1	0	0	1	1	4	0	0	.231	.222	B	R	6-2	195	5-5-76	1994	Santo Domingo, D.R.
Hammock, Rob	.162	26	74	6	12	5	0	0	4	7	18	2	2	.230	.235	R	R	5-11	190	5-13-77	1998	Marietta, Ga.
Harris, Cedrick	.204	16	49	4	10	1	0	1	4	2	15	1	0	.286	.231	R	R	6-2	190	11-14-77	2000	Ashdown, Ark.
Hernandez, John	.143	8	21	1	3	1	0	0	0	0	6	0	0	.190	.143	R	R	6-2	205	9-1-79	1997	La Puente, Calif.
Huckaby, Ken	.346	30	104	16	36	4	0	2	14	3	16	0	0	.442	.368	R	R	6-1	205	1-27-71	1991	Philadelphia, Pa.
Kata, Matt	.438	4	16	4	7	2	0	0	4	2	2	0	1	.563	.500	B	R	6-1	185	3-14-78	1999	Willoughby Hills, Ohio
Lemonis, Chris	.309	87	333	45	103	19	2	6	52	23	51	8	3	.396	.357	L	R	5-11	185	8-21-73	1995	New York, N.Y.
Martin, Billy	.176	4	17	3	3	0	1	0	1	1	4	0	0	.294	.222	R	R	6-2	205	6-10-76	1998	Abilene, Texas
Melton, John	.500	2	4	0	2	1	0	0	2	1	2	0	0	.750	.600	R	R	6-2	200	9-17-78	2000	Ashland City, Tenn.
Montas, Ricardo	.250	28	96	5	24	5	0	1	9	10	17	0	1	.333	.321	R	R	6-1	170	3-9-77	1994	Marietta, Ga.
Murphy, Nate	.262	38	122	22	32	8	3	4	18	19	29	6	1	.475	.359	L	L	6-0	195	4-15-75	1996	Montague, Mass.
Neal, Steve	.172	7	29	0	5	3	0	0	1	1	10	0	0	.276	.200	L	L	6-2	200	2-14-77	1998	Pine Bluff, Ark.
Olson, Tim	.317	46	167	29	53	13	0	2	24	11	36	4	4	.431	.378	R	R	6-2	200	8-1-78	2000	Bismarck, N.D.
Overbay, Lyle	.352	138	532	82	187	49	3	13	100	67	92	5	4	.528	.423	L	L	6-2	215	1-28-77	1999	Centralia, Wash.
Owens, Ryan	.232	16	56	4	13	2	0	0	1	5	18	0	1	.268	.295	R	R	6-2	200	3-18-78	1999	Anaheim Hills, Calif.
Rose, Mike	.259	62	205	28	53	13	1	3	23	37	40	4	4	.376	.370	B	R	6-1	185	8-25-76	1995	Sacramento, Calif.
Santora, Jack	.234	86	265	35	62	14	0	0	13	35	48	4	5	.287	.327	B	R	5-7	145	10-6-76	1999	Monterey, Calif.
Sell, Chip	.194	17	62	12	12	5	0	0	11	2	15	0	0	.274	.215	L	R	6-2	205	6-19-71	1994	Otis, Ore.
Sosa, Juan	.257	29	113	14	29	5	1	0	8	7	20	5	2	.319	.298	R	R	6-1	175	8-19-75	1993	San Francisco de Macoris, D.R.
Sykes, Jamie	.250	66	216	22	54	7	0	3	16	13	75	9	2	.324	.300	R	R	5-11	198	1-14-75	1997	Kankakee, Ill.
Terrero, Luis	.299	34	147	29	44	13	3	3	8	4	45	9	2	.490	.331	R	R	6-2	185	5-18-80	1997	Barahona, D.R.
Urquiola, Carlos	.281	41	153	26	43	7	1	0	9	10	16	7	3	.340	.325	L	R	5-8	150	4-22-80	1997	Caracas, Venez.
White, Walt	.151	27	86	7	13	2	0	0	3	7	25	0	1	.174	.215	R	R	6-0	195	12-21-74	1994	Torrance, Calif.

PITCHING

PITCHING	W	L	ERA	G	GS	CG	SV	IP	H	R	ER	BB	SO	AVG	B	T	HT	WT	DOB	1st Yr	Resides
Bevis, P.J.	0	0	2.16	14	0	0	6	17	11	4	4	6	19	.183	R	R	6-3	175	7-28-80	1998	Capalaba, Australia
Bierbrodt, Nick	2	1	1.37	4	4	0	0	20	13	3	3	6	18	.185	L	L	6-5	190	5-16-78	1996	Long Beach, Calif.
Capuano, Chris	10	11	5.31	28	28	2	0	159	184	109	94	75	167	.289	L	L	6-3	215	8-19-78	1999	West Springfield, Mass.
Carlson, Dan	4	2	3.68	32	0	0	5	51	53	22	21	12	55	.258	R	R	6-1	185	1-26-70	1990	Portland, Ore.
Cervantes, Chris	3	7	5.44	45	7	0	1	96	110	68	58	36	87	.284	L	L	6-1	165	2-4-79	1998	Tucson, Ariz.
Crawford, Joe	0	4	5.31	7	7	0	0	41	49	30	24	12	30	.306	L	L	6-3	225	5-2-70	1991	Hillsboro, Ohio
Fuller, Jody	1	2	5.52	12	0	0	0	19	23	13	12	12	12	.288	R	R	6-3	225	9-12-76	1998	Huntingdon, Tenn.
Good, Andrew	2	3	5.88	10	9	0	0	57	79	44	37	20	46	.323	R	R	6-2	195	9-19-79	1998	Rochester Hills, Mich.
Gray, Mike	3	1	1.72	29	0	0	4	31	32	11	6	8	13	.264	L	L	6-1	170	12-6-76	1999	Paso Robles, Calif.
Hartmann, Pete	0	4	7.76	19	3	0	0	31	46	32	27	31	27	.328	L	L	6-2	200	5-13-71	1993	Scottsdale, Ariz.

PITCHING	W	L	ERA	G	GS	CG	SV	IP	H	R	ER	BB	SO	AVG	B	T	HT	WT	DOB	1st Yr	Resides
Knott, Eric	4	1	3.12	17	0	0	0	26	29	13	9	8	20	.276	L	L	6-0	188	9-23-74	1997	Sebring, Fla.
Koplove, Mike	3	2	2.66	34	0	0	4	44	44	18	13	19	43	.263	R	R	6-0	160	8-30-76	1998	Philadelphia, Pa.
Lee, Jon	0	0	6.75	3	0	0	0	3	3	3	2	6	1	.375	R	R	6-5	215	7-24-78	2000	Houston, Texas
Lopez, Javier	1	0	7.43	22	1	0	0	40	64	39	33	14	21	.369	L	L	6-4	220	7-11-77	1998	Fairfax, Va.
Martines, Jason	4	3	3.00	51	0	0	1	69	62	32	23	20	49	.245	L	R	6-2	190	1-21-76	1997	Hanover, Mich.
Matzenbacher, Brian	1	0	1.80	1	0	0	0	5	5	1	1	2	4	.263	R	R	6-3	205	3-23-77	1999	Marissa, Ill.
Mendoza, Hatuey	1	5	6.28	8	5	0	0	29	29	25	20	17	20	.256	R	R	6-1	175	3-16-80	1997	Santo Domingo, D.R.
Newman, Eric	1	0	8.84	13	0	0	1	18	26	19	18	13	20	.346	R	R	6-4	205	8-27-72	1995	Phoenix, Ariz.
Norris, Ben	1	6	7.25	16	10	0	0	58	104	61	47	30	25	.403	L	L	6-3	185	12-6-77	1996	Austin, Texas
Patterson, John	1	2	4.26	5	5	0	0	25	30	15	12	9	19	.297	R	R	6-6	197	1-30-78	1996	Orange, Texas
Ramirez, Joslin	1	0	1.42	4	0	0	0	6	5	2	1	2	9	.208	R	R	5-11	182	11-19-80	1998	Santo Domingo, D.R.
Randolph, Steve	5	6	5.16	18	14	1	0	75	69	50	43	53	66	.243	L	L	6-3	185	5-1-74	1995	Austin, Texas
Sanchez, Duaner	3	7	6.78	13	13	0	0	70	92	56	53	25	41	.323	R	R	6-0	160	10-14-79	1996	Cotui, D.R.
Valverde, Jose	2	2	3.92	39	0	0	13	41	36	19	18	27	72	.225	R	R	6-4	220	7-24-79	1997	El Seibo, D.R.
Villarreal, Oscar	6	9	4.41	27	27	0	0	141	154	96	69	63	108	.274	L	R	6-1	190	11-22-81	1999	San Nicolas de la Garza, Mexico
Ward, Jeremy	0	0	1.13	6	0	0	0	8	2	2	1	1	6	.080	R	R	6-3	220	2-24-78	1999	Rocky Mount, N.C.
White, Bill	0	4	4.54	7	7	0	0	38	38	23	19	20	26	.275	L	L	6-3	210	11-20-78	2000	Alexander City, Ala.

FIELDING

Catcher	PCT	G	PO	A	E	DP	PB
Cresse	.991	96	665	83	7	3	17
Glassey	.955	4	20	1	1	0	0
Hammock	.929	2	11	2	1	0	1
Hernandez	1.000	7	40	2	0	0	0
Huckaby	.978	12	77	11	2	0	0
Melton	1.000	1	1	0	0	0	0
Rose	.987	27	209	23	3	0	3

First Base	PCT	G	PO	A	E	DP
Hammock	.960	7	38	10	2	4
Huckaby	.986	16	129	12	2	13
Lemonis	1.000	1	6	0	0	0
Martin	1.000	2	14	2	0	2
Montas	1.000	3	15	2	0	2
Neal	1.000	7	61	5	0	8
Overbay	.990	106	874	75	10	83
Sell	1.000	1	7	0	0	0

Second Base	PCT	G	PO	A	E	DP
Camilli	.933	4	4	10	1	1

		PCT	G	PO	A	E	DP
Dallimore		.945	19	44	42	5	14
Kata		1.000	4	8	9	0	2
Lemonis		.972	80	168	184	10	59
Montas		.983	13	24	33	1	2
Santora		.990	24	45	53	1	10
W. White		1.000	1	16	24	0	2

Third Base	PCT	G	PO	A	E	DP
Camilli	.800	3	3	5	2	1
Dallimore	.938	106	85	216	20	17
Hammock	.900	7	5	13	2	1
Montas	.842	9	3	13	3	2
Owens	.839	16	8	18	5	3
Rose	.000	1	0	0	1	0
Santora	1.000	5	2	13	0	1
Sell	.000	1	0	0	0	0
W. White	1.000	1	1	2	0	0

Shortstop	PCT	G	PO	A	E	DP
Camilli	.867	4	4	9	2	0
Montas	.923	4	1	11	1	2

		PCT	G	PO	A	E	DP
Olson		.914	46	74	138	20	26
Santora		.930	52	75	151	17	27
Sosa		.947	29	48	78	7	17
W. White		.935	16	18	40	4	12

Outfield	PCT	G	PO	A	E	DP
Devore	.953	120	231	11	12	3
Gann	.992	53	124	6	1	1
Gibson	.960	18	47	1	2	0
Glendenning	1.000	25	33	0	0	0
Gonzalez	1.000	3	4	0	0	0
Hammock	1.000	7	13	0	0	0
Harris	1.000	14	29	1	0	0
Murphy	.967	34	55	3	2	0
Overbay	.897	25	25	1	3	0
Rose	1.000	11	6	1	0	0
Sell	1.000	14	16	1	0	0
Sykes	.977	54	83	2	2	0
Terrero	.943	34	78	4	5	0
Urquiola	.972	26	35	0	1	0

LANCASTER
Class A

CALIFORNIA LEAGUE

BATTING	AVG	G	AB	R	H	2B	3B	HR	RBI	BB	SO	SB	CS	SLG	OBP	B	T	HT	WT	DOB	1st Yr	Resides
Burns, Kevan	.361	74	255	48	92	21	7	11	45	23	42	11	4	.627	.414	L	L	6-0	185	11-10-76	1999	Beloit, Wis.
Closser, J.D.	.291	128	468	85	136	26	6	21	87	65	106	6	7	.506	.377	B	R	5-10	195	1-15-80	1998	Alexandria, Ind.
Edge, Dwight	.194	20	62	5	12	1	0	0	6	6	23	3	3	.210	.261	R	R	6-6	235	7-7-78	2001	St. Cloud, Fla.
Gann, Jamie	.200	31	90	14	18	2	0	1	10	5	21	1	2	.256	.253	R	R	6-1	197	5-1-75	1996	Norman, Okla.
Glassey, Josh	.150	8	20	6	3	0	0	0	1	8	2	1	1	.150	.414	L	R	6-1	190	5-6-77	1996	Longview, Texas
Glendenning, Mike	.242	9	33	2	8	4	0	2	6	4	13	0	0	.545	.324	R	R	6-0	225	8-26-76	1996	West Hills, Calif.
Goldfield, Josh	.176	5	17	2	3	0	0	0	1	1	2	0	0	.176	.222	L	R	6-1	195	7-11-79	1999	Thousand Oaks, Calif.
Gordon, Brian	.304	103	392	74	119	21	10	16	70	26	100	13	7	.531	.345	L	R	6-0	180	8-16-78	1997	Taylor, Texas
Hammock, Rob	.311	45	190	33	59	11	3	4	36	16	42	3	2	.463	.378	R	R	5-11	190	5-13-77	1998	Marietta, Ga.
Harris, Cedrick	.276	84	319	63	88	13	1	6	34	26	77	21	8	.379	.333	R	R	6-2	190	11-14-77	2000	Ashdown, Ark.
Jones, Ryan	.271	125	446	74	121	25	3	22	77	44	100	2	3	.489	.343	R	R	6-2	225	11-5-74	1993	Irvine, Calif.
Kata, Matt	.296	119	494	80	146	19	6	10	54	41	79	30	8	.419	.355	B	R	6-1	185	3-14-78	1999	Willoughby Hills, Ohio
Martin, Billy	.299	130	472	98	141	33	4	26	106	95	130	6	5	.551	.420	R	R	6-2	205	6-30-78	1999	Abilene, Texas
Melton, John	.200	31	85	10	17	3	1	1	8	13	36	0	1	.294	.320	R	R	6-1	170	3-9-77	1994	Marietta, Ga.
Montas, Ricardo	.293	70	205	28	60	8	0	1	16	24	46	3	4	.346	.371	R	R	6-1	170	3-9-77	1994	Marietta, Ga.
Myers, Corey	.284	53	183	20	52	13	1	5	33	15	49	0	0	.448	.338	R	R	6-2	220	6-5-80	1999	Phoenix, Ariz.
Olson, Tim	.289	61	239	36	69	12	4	6	32	14	49	13	9	.448	.336	R	R	6-2	200	8-1-78	2000	Bismarck, N.D.
Santos, Luis	.189	14	37	4	7	0	0	1	1	2	0	0	0	.189	.211	R	R	5-11	190	5-21-79	1999	Huntington Beach, Calif.
Sykes, Jamie	.245	43	155	21	38	11	0	4	19	10	42	4	5	.394	.295	R	R	5-11	198	1-14-75	1997	Kankakee, Ill.
Terrero, Luis	.451	19	71	16	32	9	1	4	11	1	14	5	0	.775	.466	R	R	6-2	193	5-18-80	1997	Barahona, D.R.
Urquiola, Carlos	.328	14	61	9	20	5	0	0	12	6	3	5	2	.410	.397	L	R	5-8	150	4-22-80	1997	Caracas, Venez.
Waldron, Jeff	.291	54	151	13	44	12	1	2	35	13	22	0	0	.424	.351	L	R	6-1	205	10-4-76	1999	Lynn, Mass.
Williams, Jason	.210	95	295	38	62	14	2	3	29	35	78	6	5	.302	.295	R	R	5-11	170	12-6-78	2000	Fairfield, Calif.
Woodward, Steve	.201	47	144	19	29	6	1	0	6	17	40	5	5	.257	.290	B	L	5-11	200	12-28-77	2000	Clovis, Calif.
Yakopich, Joe	.190	14	42	3	8	0	0	2	2	9	0	0	0	.190	.244	L	R	6-0	175	6-19-81	1999	Amherstburg, Ontario

GAMES BY POSITION: C—Closser 95, Glassey 8, Goldfield 4, Hammock 14, Melton 6, Sykes 1, Waldron 27. **1B**—Hammock 3, Jones 90, Martin 58, Montas 1, Myers 4, Waldron 1. **2B**—Hammock 1, Kata 113, Montas 18, Williams 14, Yakopich 7. **3B**—Hammock 4, Martin 47, Montas 25, Myers 50, Olson 28, Santos 10, Yakopich 3. **SS**—Kata 6, Montas 32, Olson 33, Williams 77. **OF**—Burns 50, Closser 1, Edge 20, Gann 21, Glendenning 8, Gordon 95, Hammock 31, Harris 81, Jones 28, Olson 1, Santos 4, Sykes 39, Terrero 18, Urquiola 12, Williams 1, Woodward 44.

PITCHING	W	L	ERA	G	GS	CG	SV	IP	H	R	ER	BB	SO	AVG	B	T	HT	WT	DOB	1st Yr	Resides
Barber, Scott	7	7	7.20	29	12	0	2	85	121	76	68	27	83	.325	R	R	6-3	205	12-17-78	2000	Belton, S.C.
Belflower, Jay	2	2	0.62	27	0	0	11	29	15	5	2	6	24	.145	R	R	6-4	215	11-12-79	2001	Sebring, Fla.
Castillo, Dan	1	3	5.30	23	7	0	4	53	56	33	31	21	64	.267	R	R	6-0	155	8-20-76	1994	Santiago, D.R.
Eriksen, Tanner	3	6	6.46	19	13	0	0	71	95	66	51	49	52	.326	R	R	6-6	240	4-13-79	2001	Henderson, Nev.
Fuller, Jody	2	3	4.50	23	1	0	0	36	43	23	18	19	27	.291	R	R	6-3	225	9-12-76	1998	Huntingdon, Tenn.
Gann, Jamie	0	1	6.10	9	0	0	0	10	5	7	7	7	10	.000	R	R	6-1	197	5-1-75	1996	Norman, Okla.
Garber, Mike	0	2	6.38	25	0	0	0	24	41	22	17	14	21	.379	L	L	6-2	190	1-9-81	2001	Palos Heights, Ill.
Good, Andrew	8	6	4.80	19	18	0	0	101	108	63	54	27	104	.267	R	R	6-2	195	9-19-79	1998	Rochester Hills, Mich.

PITCHING	W	L	ERA	G	GS	CG	SV	IP	H	R	ER	BB	SO	AVG	B	T	HT	WT	DOB	1st Yr	Resides
Jacobs, Greg	1	1	5.23	20	0	0	0	21	20	12	12	8	22	.253	L	L	5-10	180	10-9-76	1998	Anaheim Hills, Calif.
2-team (31 Rancho Cuca.)	3	5	6.82	51	0	0	0	65	79	59	49	30	71	.299							
Lee, Jonathan	0	1	11.37	5	0	0	0	6	14	12	8	1	4	.451	R	R	6-5	215	7-24-78	2000	Houston, Texas
Lopez, Javier	1	3	2.63	17	0	0	1	24	30	9	7	5	18	.312	L	L	6-4	220	7-11-77	1998	Fairfax, Va.
Matzenbacher, Brian	5	4	3.55	48	0	0	3	79	85	39	31	23	85	.279	R	R	6-3	205	3-23-77	1999	Marissa, Ill.
McCutcheon, Mike	1	2	10.38	10	0	0	1	9	9	10	10	7	8	.281	L	L	5-11	170	7-5-77	1996	Mauna Loa, Hawaii
Medders, Brandon	1	2	1.32	31	0	0	3	41	26	8	6	15	53	.181	R	R	6-2	185	1-26-80	2001	Duncanville, Ala.
Mendoza, Hatuey	8	5	4.70	24	16	1	0	105	114	69	55	43	72	.284	R	R	6-1	175	3-16-80	1997	Santo Domingo, D.R.
Montoya, Saul	0	1	5.65	9	0	0	0	14	20	11	9	7	8	.338	R	R	6-2	220	12-17-80	1998	Los Mochis, Mexico
Norris, Ben	1	0	5.68	2	2	0	0	13	16	9	8	2	18	.307	L	L	6-3	185	12-6-77	1996	Austin, Texas
Patterson, John	0	0	5.79	2	2	0	0	9	9	6	6	3	9	.243	R	R	6-6	197	1-30-78	1996	Orange, Texas
Sanchez, Duaner	2	4	4.58	10	10	1	0	59	65	44	30	18	49	.274	R	R	6-0	160	10-14-79	1996	Cotui, D.R.
Shabansky, Rob	0	2	7.42	29	0	0	0	30	41	31	25	17	35	.320	L	L	6-0	185	2-27-77	2000	Las Vegas, Nev.
Sikaras, Pete	1	1	6.20	18	0	0	1	25	25	22	17	18	20	.271	R	R	6-2	204	5-5-79	2000	Niles, Ill.
Slaten, Doug	9	8	4.79	28	27	1	0	158	207	105	84	45	110	.312	L	L	6-5	190	2-4-80	2000	Venice, Calif.
Stockman, Phil	0	0	5.09	8	0	0	0	18	11	11	10	9	18	.200	R	R	6-8	220	1-25-80	1997	Brisbane, Australia
Trejo, Francisco	0	0	4.00	5	0	0	0	9	14	4	4	4	7	.368	L	L	6-0	154	3-6-80	1997	Santo Domingo, D.R.
Valera, Greg	2	5	8.14	25	4	0	0	42	59	40	38	24	39	.331	R	R	6-0	150	4-11-79	1996	Palenque, D.R.
Webb, Brandon	6	10	3.99	29	28	0	0	162	174	90	72	44	158	.275	R	R	6-2	200	5-9-79	2000	Ashland, Ky.

SOUTH BEND — Class A

MIDWEST LEAGUE

BATTING	AVG	G	AB	R	H	2B	3B	HR	RBI	BB	SO	SB	CS	SLG	OBP	B	T	HT	WT	DOB	1st Yr	Resides
Ansman, Craig	.330	97	345	73	114	30	4	21	82	29	85	4	1	.623	.402	R	R	6-4	225	3-10-78	2000	West Islip, N.Y.
Brand, Kevin	.243	14	37	3	9	1	1	0	3	2	5	2	0	.324	.300	B	R	5-10	175	1-24-80	2001	Mesa, Ariz.
Brooks, Jeff	.169	18	65	2	11	2	1	0	8	3	24	0	0	.231	.229	R	R	6-5	235	9-4-79	1997	Nottingham, Pa.
Delgado, Jorge	.302	101	348	53	105	26	2	4	50	46	43	0	2	.422	.400	R	R	6-0	220	7-8-80	1997	Acarigua, Venez.
Edge, Dwight	.232	46	164	15	38	5	1	2	18	16	42	5	2	.311	.306	R	R	6-6	235	7-7-78	2001	St. Cloud, Fla.
Epke, Brian	.250	18	56	5	14	1	0	0	5	3	11	1	0	.268	.311	R	R	6-0	195	5-2-79	2001	Waco, Neb.
Foreman, Julius	.311	61	212	47	66	6	5	0	16	42	25	23	7	.387	.425	L	R	5-7	155	2-8-79	2000	Girard, Ga.
Gil, Jerry	.215	105	363	40	78	14	5	2	31	8	103	19	7	.298	.240	R	R	6-3	183	10-14-82	1999	Santo Domingo, D.R.
Green, Andy	.300	128	477	76	143	18	6	5	59	59	50	51	15	.394	.379	R	R	5-9	170	7-7-77	2000	Lexington, Ky.
Hall, Victor	.275	113	415	82	114	13	12	0	39	52	71	60	15	.364	.362	L	L	6-0	170	9-16-80	1998	Arleta, Calif.
Hammock, Rob	.248	34	125	16	31	3	2	2	14	14	21	5	6	.352	.324	R	R	5-11	190	5-13-77	1998	Marietta, Ga.
Jacobo, Kervin	.267	9	30	5	8	2	1	1	6	4	10	4	0	.500	.353	B	R	6-2	160	9-26-82	1999	Haina, D.R.
Kroeger, Josh	.274	79	292	36	80	15	1	3	37	18	49	4	4	.363	.324	L	L	6-2	190	8-31-82	2000	San Diego, Calif.
Lagana, Shawn	.239	43	134	13	32	7	0	1	16	2	25	5	2	.313	.246	R	R	6-2	175	4-28-81	1999	Cypress, Calif.
Loeb, Bryan	.208	16	48	7	10	3	0	0	4	5	8	0	0	.271	.291	R	R	6-2	190	4-8-78	2000	Sugar Land, Texas
Myers, Corey	.327	59	211	28	69	17	2	3	36	12	33	2	0	.469	.360	R	R	6-2	220	6-5-80	1999	Phoenix, Ariz.
Neal, Steve	.256	121	453	71	116	23	3	20	92	39	137	7	1	.453	.324	L	L	6-0	260	2-14-77	1998	Pine Bluff, Ark.
Nunez, Argelis	.215	82	284	36	61	13	2	3	25	16	108	11	5	.306	.273	R	R	6-1	170	10-25-81	1998	San Cristobal, D.R.
Sandoval, Jhensy	.200	9	35	6	7	1	0	2	5	4	13	0	0	.400	.275	R	R	6-2	195	9-11-78	1996	Santo Domingo, D.R.
Terrero, Luis	.157	24	89	4	14	2	0	1	8	0	29	3	0	.213	.176	R	R	6-2	193	5-18-80	1997	Barahona, D.R.
Tracy, Chad	.340	54	215	43	73	11	0	4	36	19	19	3	0	.447	.393	L	R	6-2	190	5-22-80	2001	Charlotte, N.C.
Vizcaino, Maximo	.236	52	165	18	39	8	1	0	16	6	35	2	5	.297	.262	R	R	6-2	183	11-28-80	1997	Palenque, D.R.

GAMES BY POSITION: C—Ansman 67, Delgado 34, Epke 16, Hammock 19, Loeb 6. **1B**—Ansman 5, Brooks 9, Loeb 1, Myers 5, Neal 119, Tracy 1. **2B**—Brand 4, Green 125, Lagana 1, Vizcaino 14. **3B**—Brand 2, Lagana 22, Myers 53, Tracy 52, Vizcaino 14. **SS**—Brand 4, Gil 103, Jacobo 9, Lagana 3, Vizcaino 21. **OF**—Edge 46, Foreman 60, Hall 111, Kroeger 71, Lagana 8, Loeb 8, Nunez 76, Sandoval 5, Terrero 24.

PITCHING	W	L	ERA	G	GS	CG	SV	IP	H	R	ER	BB	SO	AVG	B	T	HT	WT	DOB	1st Yr	Resides
Belson, Greg	6	4	2.50	46	0	0	16	58	54	24	16	17	50	.246	R	R	5-10	170	8-16-78	2000	Staten Island, N.Y.
Bruney, Brian	1	4	4.13	26	0	0	8	33	24	19	15	19	40	.205	R	R	6-3	220	2-17-82	2000	Warrenton, Ore.
Castellanos, Jon	1	3	4.86	8	0	0	0	37	47	24	20	15	34	.311	R	R	6-0	191	9-17-81	2000	Nuevo Leon, Mexico
Cramblitt, Joey	5	7	3.36	35	8	0	2	104	104	54	39	19	91	.262	R	R	6-3	225	7-27-78	2000	Meridian, Miss.
Daigle, Casey	10	10	4.12	28	27	2	0	164	180	100	75	55	85	.278	R	R	6-7	215	4-4-81	1999	Vinton, La.
Eppolito, Vince	2	1	5.40	25	0	0	1	37	34	24	22	28	31	.244	R	R	6-5	225	7-29-77	2000	Lansdale, Pa.
Gonzalez, Cesar	4	12	4.01	26	26	1	0	146	142	81	65	53	92	.256	R	R	5-10	155	8-6-82	1999	Bolivar, Venez.
Heiberger, Heath	1	1	3.86	12	0	0	1	19	15	10	8	7	21	.217	L	L	6-4	200	6-20-80	2001	Hennepin, Ill.
LeClair, Aric	3	1	3.42	37	2	0	1	53	48	28	20	34	53	.235	L	L	6-0	195	4-12-78	2000	Swanzey, N.H.
Montoya, Saul	0	0	3.95	7	1	0	0	14	17	6	6	5	11	.326	R	R	6-2	220	12-17-80	1998	Los Mochis, Mexico
Perez, Beltran	12	4	2.81	27	27	2	0	160	142	59	50	35	157	.235	R	R	6-2	157	10-24-81	1999	San Francisco de Macoris, D.R.
Ramirez, Joslin	6	5	3.28	18	18	0	0	104	109	48	38	28	73	.271	R	R	5-11	182	11-19-80	1998	Santo Domingo, D.R.
Ricciardi, Joe	5	4	6.27	20	0	0	0	33	43	25	23	19	28	.318	R	R	6-2	230	8-2-79	2000	Tampa, Fla.
Sundberg, Cody	0	1	3.77	11	0	0	0	14	8	6	6	10	16	.165	R	R	6-1	205	2-22-78	1999	Plano, Texas
Wells, Carl	4	4	2.89	40	0	0	2	72	74	31	23	13	52	.264	L	L	6-2	210	3-25-80	2000	Tampa, Fla.
White, Bill	9	3	3.80	19	19	0	0	111	90	53	47	53	103	.223	L	L	6-3	210	11-20-78	2000	Alexander City, Ala.
Wilkinson, Matthew	1	2	7.23	14	0	0	0	19	27	17	15	10	23	.341	L	R	6-3	195	10-25-77	2001	Edwardsville, Ill.

YAKIMA — Short-Season Class A

NORTHWEST LEAGUE

BATTING	AVG	G	AB	R	H	2B	3B	HR	RBI	BB	SO	SB	CS	SLG	OBP	B	T	HT	WT	DOB	1st Yr	Resides
Barrera, Reinaldo	.207	45	140	12	29	4	0	0	5	10	22	1	2	.236	.260	B	R	6-2	170	12-27-82	1999	Caracas, Venez.
Barrett, Rich	.225	73	227	29	51	8	0	2	19	12	68	14	3	.286	.288	R	R	6-6	205	8-20-79	2001	Hartsville, Pa.
Boll, Javier	.323	17	62	10	20	7	0	2	8	4	13	2	1	.532	.358	R	R	6-2	175	3-18-82	1999	Caracas, Venez.
Brooks, Jeff	.243	72	268	30	65	14	2	5	35	13	83	2	1	.366	.289	R	R	6-5	235	9-4-79	1997	Nottingham, Pa.
DiRosa, Michael	.307	45	127	20	39	9	0	4	25	23	35	0	0	.472	.429	R	R	5-11	195	1-17-80	2001	Miami, Fla.
Edge, Dwight	.115	8	26	0	3	0	0	2	2	14	1	0	0	.115	.179	R	R	6-6	235	7-7-78	2001	St. Cloud, Fla.
Epke, Brian	.083	5	12	2	1	0	0	0	4	1	3	0	0	.083	.143	R	R	6-0	195	5-2-79	2001	Waco, Neb.
Hilinski, Scott	.250	6	12	1	3	2	0	0	5	3	4	0	0	.417	.400	R	R	6-0	170	12-12-79	2001	Lake Mary, Fla.
Loeb, Bryan	.243	40	115	12	28	8	1	1	12	8	29	1	0	.357	.315	R	R	6-2	190	4-8-78	2000	Sugar Land, Texas

BATTING	AVG	G	AB	R	H	2B	3B	HR	RBI	BB	SO	SB	CS	SLG	OBP	B	T	HT	WT	DOB	1st Yr	Resides
Mace, Clark	.218	53	165	22	36	9	2	1	9	11	45	0	4	.315	.287	L	L	6-2	190	4-21-79	2001	London, Ohio
Macha, Erick	.245	52	196	24	48	3	2	1	16	12	40	1	4	.296	.289	R	R	6-1	180	12-13-79	2001	Victoria, Texas
Nichols, Kyle	.278	75	284	41	79	24	0	12	51	29	69	1	0	.489	.347	R	R	6-2	215	3-29-78	2001	Southport, Fla.
Santos, Sneideer	.173	31	81	11	14	2	2	2	10	7	32	1	1	.321	.239	L	R	6-2	192	9-29-79	1997	Santo Domingo, D.R.
Simpson, Bodie	.236	56	195	25	46	11	0	1	19	16	39	4	2	.308	.301	R	R	6-2	185	12-13-77	2001	Lubbock, Texas
Terrero, Luis	.317	11	41	7	13	2	1	0	0	2	8	0	3	.415	.349	R	R	6-2	193	5-18-80	1997	Barahona, D.R.
Thiessen, Mike	.308	27	104	14	32	4	0	0	11	6	17	6	2	.346	.353	R	R	5-11	185	11-10-78	2001	Modesto, Calif.
Tiesing, Tyler	.186	30	86	6	16	6	0	0	5	7	30	0	1	.256	.263	R	R	6-3	205	8-15-79	2001	Pratt, Kan.
Tracy, Chad	.278	10	36	2	10	1	0	0	5	3	5	1	0	.306	.350	L	R	6-2	190	5-22-80	2001	Charlotte, N.C.
Uggla, Dan	.277	72	278	39	77	21	0	5	40	20	52	8	4	.406	.341	R	R	5-11	190	3-11-80	2001	Columbia, Tenn.
Yakopich, Joe	.228	45	101	16	23	3	0	0	6	21	23	2	2	.257	.363	L	R	6-0	175	6-19-81	1999	Amherstburg, Ontario

GAMES BY POSITION: C—DiRosa 40, Epke 5, Loeb 26, Tiesing 17. **1B**—Barrera 1, Brooks 16, Nichols 60, Thiessen 2. **2B**—Barrera 4, Macha 2, Uggla 71, Yakopich 1. **3B**—Barrera 14, Brooks 54, Yakopich 11. **SS**—Barrera 26, Hilinski 4, Macha 51. **OF**—Barrett 72, Boll 16, Edge 8, Loeb 5, Mace 50, Santos 16, Simpson 54, Terrero 11, Thiessen 19, Tiesing 4, Yakopich 1.

PITCHING	W	L	ERA	G	GS	CG	SV	IP	H	R	ER	BB	SO	AVG	B	T	HT	WT	DOB	1st Yr	Resides
Barber, Scott	2	0	2.25	2	2	0	0	12	11	3	3	3	11	.250	R	R	6-3	205	12-12-78	2000	Belton, S.C.
Bevis, P.J.	1	1	0.64	12	0	0	8	14	9	1	1	7	22	.180	R	R	6-3	175	7-28-80	1998	Capalaba, Australia
Bruney, Brian	1	2	5.14	15	0	0	2	21	19	14	12	11	28	.226	R	R	6-3	220	2-17-82	2000	Warrenton, Ore.
Castellanos, Jon	2	3	4.08	15	15	0	0	86	100	43	39	26	73	.294	R	R	6-0	191	9-17-81	2000	Nuevo Leon, Mexico
Clark, Josh	1	4	5.80	17	7	0	0	50	58	38	32	17	42	.292	R	R	6-5	235	3-9-79	2001	Olalla, Wash.
Eriksen, Tanner	1	1	3.45	3	3	0	0	16	17	9	6	4	14	.269	R	R	6-6	240	4-13-79	2001	Henderson, Nev.
Garber, Mike	0	0	3.38	3	0	0	0	3	3	2	1	0	2	.300	L	L	6-2	190	1-9-81	2001	Palos Heights, Ill.
Gonzalez, Carlos	0	1	3.38	13	0	0	3	24	19	12	9	15	21	.215	R	R	6-0	163	11-4-79	1996	San Cristobal, D.R.
Lee, Jonathan	2	3	4.40	18	0	0	1	31	32	17	15	10	23	.266	R	R	6-5	215	7-24-78	2000	Houston, Texas
McMachen, Cliff	2	3	2.86	20	6	0	0	57	54	24	18	28	62	.247	L	L	6-1	185	1-14-81	2001	North Las Vegas, Nev.
Montoya, Saul	1	2	4.58	4	4	0	0	18	22	13	9	8	12	.293	R	R	6-2	220	12-17-80	1998	Los Mochis, Mexico
Ovalles, Juan	2	5	3.95	16	6	0	0	43	48	21	19	19	28	.277	R	R	6-1	165	5-15-82	1999	Caracas, Venez.
Ricciardi, Joe	1	3	4.95	19	2	0	3	36	34	21	20	9	48	.239	R	R	6-2	230	8-2-79	2000	Tampa, Fla.
Shabansky, Rob	4	1	5.12	19	2	0	0	39	45	24	22	18	32	.294	L	L	6-0	185	2-27-77	2000	Las Vegas, Nev.
Sikaras, Pete	2	5	3.56	16	0	0	3	30	31	16	12	15	24	.254	R	R	6-2	204	5-5-79	2000	Niles, Ill.
Stockman, Phil	3	4	4.26	15	14	0	0	76	81	39	36	22	48	.271	R	R	6-8	220	1-25-80	1997	Brisbane, Australia
Sundbeck, Cody	0	0	3.00	4	0	0	0	6	7	2	2	4	3	.291	R	R	6-1	205	2-22-78	1999	Plano, Texas
Trejo, Francisco	2	2	5.90	13	6	0	1	40	61	38	26	17	23	.352	L	L	6-0	154	3-6-80	1997	Santo Domingo, D.R.
Valera, Greg	4	2	3.30	8	8	0	0	46	39	18	17	14	39	.229	R	R	6-0	150	4-11-79	1996	Palenque, D.R.
Wilkinson, Matthew	2	0	1.72	9	0	0	1	16	14	8	3	8	23	.241	L	R	6-3	195	10-25-77	2001	Edwardsville, Ill.

MISSOULA — Rookie

PIONEER LEAGUE

BATTING	AVG	G	AB	R	H	2B	3B	HR	RBI	BB	SO	SB	CS	SLG	OBP	B	T	HT	WT	DOB	1st Yr	Resides
Ball, Jarred	.246	19	57	13	14	2	1	0	3	7	14	1	1	.316	.348	B	R	6-0	175	4-18-83	2001	Tomball, Texas
Boll, Javier	.269	35	119	17	32	7	1	3	21	11	19	2	2	.420	.353	R	R	6-2	175	3-18-82	1999	Caracas, Venez.
Brand, Kevin	.220	18	59	6	13	0	0	0	2	3	8	1	1	.220	.270	B	R	5-10	175	1-24-80	2001	Mesa, Ariz.
Chilsom, Marques	.194	21	36	6	7	1	0	0	2	7	14	0	1	.222	.326	R	R	5-11	190	3-6-82	2000	Brandon, Fla.
Corporan, Roberto	.000	3	5	1	0	0	0	0	0	2	3	0	0	.000	.286	B	R	6-2	170	8-12-82	1999	San Pedro de Macoris, D.R.
Cota, Jesus	.368	75	272	74	100	22	0	16	71	56	52	2	0	.625	.476	L	R	6-3	200	11-7-81	2001	Tucson, Ariz.
Diredo, Curtis	.246	19	61	8	15	2	0	0	5	4	15	3	2	.279	.303	R	R	5-10	215	7-7-78	2001	Fresno, Calif.
Fisher, Tim	.071	16	28	5	2	0	0	0	0	2	12	0	0	.071	.235	R	R	6-1	210	3-9-80	2001	Beatrice, Neb.
Garcia, Lino	.243	46	140	34	34	6	2	4	22	14	32	8	2	.400	.333	R	R	6-3	180	10-12-83	2001	Biruaca, Venez.
Hairston, Scott	.347	74	291	81	101	16	6	14	65	38	50	2	2	.588	.432	R	R	6-0	190	5-25-80	2001	Oro Valley, Ariz.
Hilinski, Scott	.246	42	138	34	34	5	2	2	18	25	45	4	1	.355	.361	R	R	6-0	170	12-12-79	2001	Lake Mary, Fla.
Jacobo, Kervin	.269	59	219	36	59	10	3	5	36	22	72	4	3	.411	.336	B	R	6-2	160	9-26-82	1999	Haina, D.R.
Janz, Jeramy	.293	67	259	40	76	14	8	5	62	16	46	2	2	.467	.336	L	R	6-3	190	8-5-79	2001	Fresno, Calif.
Lopez, Mike	.313	73	284	70	89	21	4	8	37	36	52	6	2	.500	.418	R	R	5-10	190	9-19-77	2001	Glendale, Ariz.
Melton, John	.281	13	32	5	9	1	0	2	6	7	11	1	0	.500	.410	R	R	6-2	200	9-17-78	2000	Ashland City, Tenn.
Montilla, Samuel	.264	46	159	21	42	8	2	0	20	2	20	2	1	.340	.276	R	R	5-11	208	2-7-82	1998	Santo Domingo, D.R.
Nevels, Craig	.230	48	135	21	31	8	0	1	20	10	32	1	0	.311	.325	R	R	6-2	215	10-31-78	2001	Millington, Mich.
Robinson, Carlos	.246	43	122	12	30	8	1	3	28	6	25	0	2	.402	.290	R	R	6-2	200	8-28-81	1999	Providencia Isla, Colombia
Sherlock, Jon	.226	25	53	11	12	1	0	0	3	11	16	1	1	.245	.414	R	R	6-3	225	1-15-82	2000	Minnetonka, Minn.
Vugteveen, Dustin	.293	60	232	40	68	14	1	6	51	11	58	7	3	.440	.333	R	R	6-1	205	8-26-79	2001	Grandville, Mich.

GAMES BY POSITION: C—Fisher 13, Melton 13, Montilla 46, Sherlock 23. **1B**—Cota 66, Nevels 1, Robinson 17. **2B**—Brand 5, Hairston 62, Jacobo 9, Lopez 2. **3B**—Brand 1, Hilinski 1, Jacobo 7, Lopez 65, Nevels 12. **SS**—Brand 9, Corporan 3, Hilinski 40, Jacobo 34. **OF**—Ball 17, Boll 34, Chilsom 18, Diredo 14, Garcia 43, Jacobo 1, Janz 63, Robinson 10, Vugteveen 57.

PITCHING	W	L	ERA	G	GS	CG	SV	IP	H	R	ER	BB	SO	AVG	B	T	HT	WT	DOB	1st Yr	Resides
Davis, Mikael	4	1	3.86	15	4	0	0	40	44	25	17	12	33	.275	R	R	6-4	195	7-6-80	1999	Eddyville, Ky.
DeJesus, Henky	0	1	11.57	3	0	0	0	5	7	7	6	3	0	.333	L	R	6-1	185	6-17-81	1997	Villa Mella, D.R.
Gonzalez, Carlos	0	2	5.27	10	0	0	0	14	19	13	8	6	15	.316	R	R	6-0	163	11-4-79	1996	San Cristobal, D.R.
Heiberger, Heath	0	0	1.69	7	0	0	0	11	5	4	2	3	13	.131	L	L	6-4	200	6-20-80	2001	Hennepin, Ill.
Holsten, Ryan	9	3	2.53	17	12	0	0	89	84	33	25	12	60	.242	R	R	6-4	220	5-5-79	2001	Wilmington, Del.
Lizarraga, Sergio	6	2	5.09	15	15	0	0	81	104	57	46	23	57	.307	R	R	6-4	170	7-23-81	2001	Mazatlan, Mexico
Marquez, Jose	1	0	6.52	15	0	0	0	19	22	23	14	19	10	.271	R	R	6-4	205	3-19-81	1998	San Cristobal, D.R.
Medina, Franklin	8	2	3.39	15	14	1	0	88	89	42	33	28	55	.258	R	R	6-2	160	3-25-82	1998	San Cristobal, D.R.
Medina, Roberto	3	2	3.67	21	0	0	0	34	32	18	14	17	29	.248	L	L	6-0	168	8-6-80	2001	Hermosillo, Mexico
Medlin, Corbey	2	1	2.38	21	0	0	6	42	27	12	11	16	46	.184	R	R	6-3	185	8-4-81	2001	Katy, Texas
Mercedes, Gabriel	8	3	3.71	15	14	0	0	80	81	47	33	30	66	.254	R	R	6-2	166	11-30-82	1999	Villa Mella, D.R.
Perkin, Greg	1	2	4.96	12	5	0	0	33	43	29	18	9	34	.307	R	R	6-3	195	4-15-81	1999	Kingwood, Texas
Silva, Jesus	3	0	2.35	26	2	0	14	38	33	12	10	8	43	.217	R	R	5-11	170	12-24-82	1999	Maracay, Venez.
Taulli, Sam	1	1	6.27	15	0	0	0	19	26	16	13	12	18	.329	L	L	6-1	180	9-19-79	2001	Lafayette, La.
Waroff, Shane	4	1	2.48	26	0	0	1	40	38	16	11	9	24	.245	R	R	6-5	220	8-19-80	2001	Walnut, Calif.
Wechsler, Justin	2	3	2.89	10	10	0	0	37	35	21	12	15	29	.243	R	R	6-2	230	4-6-80	2001	Pendleton, Ind.

ATLANTA BRAVES

BY BILL BALLEW

The Braves extended their major league record to a 10th consecutive division title and reached the National League Championship Series for the ninth time during that span, yet they may have overachieved in 2001 more than at any point since 1991.

Manager Bobby Cox was forced to juggle a patchwork lineup into a team that managed to hold off the upstart Phillies and win the National League East by two games with an 88-74 record.

The Atlanta roster experienced constant change, including the release of one Opening Day starter (second baseman Quilvio Veras), the retirement of a second (first baseman Rico Brogna) and the loss of a third (shortstop Rafael Furcal, with a season-ending shoulder injury in early July). Two projected members of the rotation, John Smoltz and Kevin Millwood, spent significant time on the disabled list, with Smoltz returning as the eventual replacement for closer John Rocker, who was traded to the Indians in June. Making matters even more difficult were significant drops in production at the plate from starting catcher Javy Lopez and outfielders B.J. Surhoff and Andruw Jones.

Such unexpected bumps in the road forced general manager John Schuerholz to spend most of his time working the phones. In addition to acquiring relievers Steve Karsay and Steve Reed from the Indians in the Rocker deal, Schuerholz tried to fill the void at first base with Ken Caminiti before signing the 40-something Julio Franco out of the Mexican League. The Braves also obtained veteran shortstop Rey Sanchez from the Royals at the trading deadline, after giving the inexperienced Mark DeRosa a look for most of July.

While the Braves surprised many observers by sweeping Houston in the Division Series before losing to Arizona 4-1 in the NLCS, signs that the team's reign may be coming to an end were obvious. Atlanta became the first team to reach the playoffs with a losing record at home (40-41).

Chipper Jones

Wilson Betemit

PLAYERS OF THE YEAR

MAJOR LEAGUE: Chipper Jones, 3b

Jones hit .330-38-102 to become the first third baseman in major league history to drive in at least 100 runs in six consecutive seasons.

MINOR LEAGUE: Wilson Betemit, ss

He started the 2001 season in Class A, but advanced all the way to the big leagues after the chain reaction following Rafael Furcal's injury. Betemt, 19, shone at Double-A Greenville, hitting .355-5-19 in 183 at-bats.

The Braves tied for eighth in the league with a .260 batting average and scored 81 fewer runs than in 2000. The club's saving grace again was pitching, with Greg Maddux and Tom Glavine carrying the load. The team led the NL in ERA for the fifth straight season and the sixth time in seven years.

The farm system continued its steady production by providing a starter for the second time in as many seasons. Second baseman Marcus Giles took over the starting duties after Veras was released in July.

Another new infielder also showed he is on the verge of contributing in Atlanta. Shortstop Wilson Betemit turned up the juice after a July promotion from Class A Myrtle Beach to Double-A Greenville. Ranked as the top prospect in the Carolina League and the third-best in the Southern League, Betemit hit .355-5-19 with the G-Braves after batting .277-7-43 as a Pelican.

Overall, Atlanta's seven minor league clubs posted a record of 370-387 (.489). Class A Jamestown of the short-season New York-Penn League was the only team to reach the postseason.

From an individual standpoint, righthander Trey Hodges was named the co-pitcher of the year in the Carolina League after leading the league with 15 wins and 173 innings. He ranked third with a 2.76 ERA. Shortstop Kelly Johnson was recognized as the top prospect in the South Atlantic League after hitting 23 home runs and having a .404 on-base percentage. Catcher Brayan Pena won the Appalachian League batting crown (.370) and led the league with 87 hits.

Injuries also played a role in the minors. Righthander Matt Belisle missed the entire season after undergoing back surgery at the end of spring training. Third baseman Scott Thorman, Atlanta's second first-round draft pick in 2000, did not play because of shoulder surgery.

ORGANIZATION LEADERS

BATTING

*AVG	Marcus Giles, Richmond	.333
R	Alph Coleman, Macon	84
H	Wilson Betemit, Greenville/Myrtle Beach	153
TB	Wilson Betemit, Greenville/Myrtle Beach	225
2B	Wilson Betemit, Greenville/Myrtle Beach	34
3B	Alph Coleman, Macon	7
	Ramon Castro, Richmond/Greenville	7
HR	Michael Hessman, Greenville	26
RBI	Michael Hessman, Greenville	80
BB	Mike Forbes, Macon	72
SO	Cory Aldridge, Greenville	139
SB	Alph Coleman, Macon	38

PITCHING

W	Trey Hodges, Myrtle Beach	15
L	Marc Valdes, Richmond	11
#ERA	Brett Evert, Myrtle Beach/Macon	1.74
G	Ray Beasley, Richmond	65
CG	Chris Waters, Macon	3
SV	Billy Sylvester, Richmond/Greenville	23
IP	Trey Hodges, Myrtle Beach	173
BB	Kenny Nelson, Macon	57
	Matt McClendon, Richmond/Greenville	57
SO	Adam Wainwright, Macon	184

*Minimum 250 At-Bats #Minimum 75 Innings

ATLANTA BRAVES

Manager: Bobby Cox

2001 Record: 88-74, .543 (1st, NL East)

BATTING	AVG	G	AB	R	H	2B	3B	HR	RBI	BB	SO	SB	CS	SLG	OBP	B	T	HT	WT	DOB	1st Yr	Resides
Abbott, Kurt	.222	6	9	0	2	0	0	0	0	0	3	1	0	.222	.222	R	R	6-0	200	6-2-69	1989	Davie, Fla.
Aldridge, Cory	.000	8	5	1	0	0	0	0	0	0	4	0	0	.000	.000	L	R	6-0	210	6-13-79	1997	Abilene, Texas
Bako, Paul	.212	61	137	19	29	10	1	2	15	20	34	1	0	.343	.312	L	R	6-2	205	6-20-72	1993	Lafayette, La.
Betemit, Wilson	.000	8	3	1	0	0	0	0	2	3	1	0	0	.000	.400	B	R	6-2	155	11-2-81	1996	Santo Domingo, D.R.
Brogna, Rico	.248	72	206	15	51	9	0	3	21	14	46	3	1	.335	.297	L	L	6-2	203	4-18-70	1988	Watertown, Conn.
Caminiti, Ken	.222	64	171	12	38	9	0	6	16	21	44	0	1	.380	.306	B	R	6-0	200	4-21-63	1985	Richmond, Texas
DeRosa, Mark	.287	66	164	27	47	8	0	3	20	12	19	2	1	.390	.350	R	R	6-1	195	2-2-75	1996	Carlstadt, N.J.
Franco, Julio	.300	25	90	13	27	4	0	3	11	10	20	0	0	.444	.376	R	R	6-1	188	8-23-61	1978	San Pedro de Macoris, D.R.
Furcal, Rafael	.275	79	324	39	89	19	0	4	30	24	56	22	6	.370	.321	B	R	5-10	150	8-24-80	1997	Loma de Cabrera, D.R.
Garcia, Jesse	.200	22	5	3	1	0	0	0	0	0	1	6	2	.200	.200	R	R	5-10	171	9-24-73	1993	Robstown, Texas
Giles, Marcus	.262	68	244	36	64	10	2	9	31	28	37	2	5	.430	.338	R	R	5-8	180	5-18-78	1997	El Cajon, Calif.
Gilkey, Bernard	.274	69	106	8	29	6	0	2	14	11	31	0	1	.387	.339	R	R	6-0	200	9-24-66	1985	St. Louis, Mo.
Helms, Wes	.222	100	216	28	48	10	3	10	36	21	56	1	1	.435	.293	R	R	6-4	230	5-12-76	1994	Gastonia, N.C.
Jones, Andruw	.251	161	625	104	157	25	2	34	104	56	142	11	4	.461	.312	R	R	6-1	185	4-23-77	1994	Willemstad, Curacao
Jones, Chipper	.330	159	572	113	189	33	5	38	102	98	82	9	10	.605	.427	B	R	6-4	210	4-24-72	1990	Alpharetta, Ga.
Jordan, Brian	.295	148	560	82	165	32	3	25	97	31	88	3	2	.496	.334	R	R	6-1	205	3-29-67	1988	Alpharetta, Ga.
Lockhart, Keith	.219	104	178	17	39	6	0	3	12	16	22	1	2	.303	.289	L	R	5-10	170	11-10-64	1986	Overland Park, Kan.
Lopez, Javy	.267	128	438	45	117	16	1	17	66	28	82	1	0	.425	.322	R	R	6-3	200	11-5-70	1988	Ponce, P.R.
Maddux, Greg	.188	35	64	3	12	0	0	0	3	2	19	0	0	.188	.235	R	R	6-0	185	4-14-66	1984	Las Vegas, Nev.
Martinez, Dave	.287	120	237	33	68	11	3	2	20	21	44	3	3	.384	.347	L	L	5-10	190	9-26-64	1983	Safety Harbor, Fla.
Perez, Eddie	.300	5	10	0	3	0	0	0	0	0	2	0	0	.300	.300	R	R	6-1	185	5-4-68	1987	Duluth, Ga.
Sanchez, Rey	.227	49	154	10	35	4	1	0	9	4	15	2	0	.266	.245	R	R	5-9	175	10-5-67	1986	San Juan, P.R.
Surhoff, B.J.	.271	141	484	68	131	33	1	10	58	38	48	9	3	.405	.321	L	R	6-0	175	8-4-64	1985	Cockeysville, Md.
Torrealba, Steve	.500	2	2	0	1	0	0	0	0	0	0	0	0	.500	.500	R	R	6-0	175	2-24-78	1995	Barquisimeto, Venez.
Veras, Quilvio	.252	71	258	39	65	14	2	3	25	24	52	7	4	.357	.330	B	R	5-8	168	4-3-71	1990	Santo Domingo, D.R.

PITCHING	W	L	ERA	G	GS	CG	SV	IP	H	R	ER	BB	SO	AVG	B	T	HT	WT	DOB	1st Yr	Resides
Burkett, John	12	12	3.04	34	34	1	0	219	187	83	74	70	187	.230	R	R	6-3	215	11-28-64	1983	Southlake, Texas
Cabrera, Jose	7	4	2.88	55	0	0	2	59	52	24	19	25	43	.238	R	R	6-0	180	3-24-72	1991	Santiago, D.R.
Glavine, Tom	16	7	3.57	35	35	1	0	219	213	92	87	97	116	.260	L	L	6-0	185	3-25-66	1984	Alpharetta, Ga.
Karsay, Steve	3	4	3.43	43	0	0	7	45	44	21	17	17	39	.265	R	R	6-3	207	3-24-72	1990	Westlake, Ohio
Ligtenberg, Kerry	3	3	3.02	53	0	0	1	60	50	22	20	30	56	.226	R	R	6-2	215	5-11-71	1994	Cottage Grove, Minn.
Maddux, Greg	17	11	3.05	34	34	3	0	233	220	86	79	27	173	.252	R	R	6-0	185	4-14-66	1984	Las Vegas, Nev.
Marquis, Jason	5	6	3.48	38	16	0	0	129	113	62	50	59	98	.234	L	R	6-1	185	8-21-78	1996	Coral Springs, Fla.
Millwood, Kevin	7	7	4.31	21	21	0	0	121	121	66	58	40	84	.260	R	R	6-4	220	12-24-74	1993	Bessemer City, N.C.
Moore, Trey	0	0	11.25	2	0	0	0	4	7	5	5	2	1	.368	L	L	6-0	190	10-2-72	1994	Southlake, Texas
Moss, Damian	0	0	3.00	5	1	0	0	9	3	3	3	9	4	.096	R	L	6-0	187	11-24-76	1996	Sadler, Australia
Nelson, Joe	0	0	36.00	2	0	0	0	2	7	9	8	2	0	.583	R	R	6-2	185	10-25-74	1996	Alameda, Calif.
Perez, Odalis	7	8	4.91	24	16	0	0	95	108	55	52	39	71	.290	L	L	6-0	150	6-7-78	1994	Las Matas de Farfan, D.R.
Reed, Steve	2	2	3.48	39	0	0	1	31	30	14	12	13	25	.258	R	R	6-2	212	3-11-66	1988	Arvada, Colo.
Remlinger, Mike	3	3	2.76	74	0	0	1	75	67	25	23	23	93	.234	L	L	6-1	210	3-23-66	1987	Scottsdale, Ariz.
Rocker, John	2	2	3.09	30	0	0	19	32	25	13	11	16	36	.215	R	L	6-4	225	10-17-74	1994	Macon, Ga.
Seanez, Rudy	0	0	3.00	12	0	0	0	12	8	4	4	4	17	.181	R	R	5-11	205	10-20-68	1986	El Centro, Calif.
2-team (26 San Diego)	0	0	2.75	38	0	0	1	36	23	12	11	19	41	.178							
Seelbach, Chris	0	0	7.88	5	0	0	0	8	9	7	7	5	8	.272	R	R	6-4	180	12-18-72	1991	Lufkin, Texas
Slusarski, Joe	0	0	9.00	4	0	0	0	6	9	6	6	1	5	.346	R	R	6-4	195	12-19-66	1989	Springfield, Ill.
Smoltz, John	3	3	3.36	36	5	0	10	59	53	24	22	10	57	.237	R	R	6-3	220	5-15-67	1986	Duluth, Ga.
Sobkowiak, Scott	0	0	9.00	1	0	0	0	1	2	1	1	0	0	.400	R	R	6-3	180	10-26-77	1998	Loveland, Ohio
Spoonybarger, Tim	0	1	2.25	4	0	0	0	4	5	1	1	2	3	.312	R	R	6-3	180	10-21-79	1999	Pensacola, Fla.
Valdes, Marc	1	0	7.71	9	0	0	0	7	7	6	6	1	3	.259	R	R	6-0	180	12-20-71	1993	Tampa, Fla.
Whiteside, Matt	0	1	7.16	13	0	0	0	16	23	14	13	7	10	.319	R	R	6-0	200	8-8-67	1990	Arlington, Texas

FIELDING

Catcher	PCT	G	PO	A	E	DP	PB
Bako	.991	60	319	29	3	1	4
Lopez	.989	127	826	50	10	7	5
E. Perez	1.000	5	10	1	0	0	0
Torrealba	1.000	2	2	0	0	0	0

First Base	PCT	G	PO	A	E	DP
Brogna	.994	67	431	42	3	30
Caminiti	.977	33	240	14	6	19
Franco	.995	23	181	16	1	20
Helms	.991	77	433	31	4	41
Martinez	1.000	10	51	6	0	6

Second Base	PCT	G	PO	A	E	DP
Abbott	1.000	1	1	6	0	0
DeRosa	1.000	5	7	20	0	3

	PCT	G	PO	A	E	DP
Garcia	1.000	4	3	2	0	1
Giles	.978	62	104	166	6	31
Lockhart	1.000	47	66	84	0	20
Veras	.991	67	132	181	3	37

Third Base	PCT	G	PO	A	E	DP
Caminiti	.933	13	9	19	2	3
DeRosa	.000	1	0	0	0	0
Helms	1.000	17	4	10	0	1
C. Jones	.945	149	75	233	18	12
Lockhart	1.000	4	1	0	0	0

Shortstop	PCT	G	PO	A	E	DP
Abbott	1.000	1	1	2	0	0
Betemit	.000	1	0	0	0	0
DeRosa	.960	48	51	118	7	21

	PCT	G	PO	A	E	DP
Furcal	.970	79	126	224	11	49
Garcia	1.000	2	0	1	0	0
Sanchez	.986	48	62	146	3	31

Outfield	PCT	G	PO	A	E	DP
Aldridge	1.000	4	2	0	0	0
DeRosa	.000	1	0	0	0	0
Gilkey	1.000	36	40	0	0	0
Helms	1.000	1	2	0	0	0
A. Jones	.987	161	461	10	6	6
C. Jones	1.000	8	16	0	0	0
Jordan	.991	144	321	11	3	2
Martinez	1.000	52	69	2	0	1
Surhoff	.986	129	200	8	3	0

Director, Player Development: Dick Balderson

Class	Farm Team	League	W	L	Pct.	Finish*	Manager	First Yr.
AAA	Richmond (Va.) Braves	International	68	76	.472	t-7th (14)	Carlos Tosca	1966
AA	Greenville (S.C.) Braves	Southern	60	79	.432	8th (10)	Paul Runge	1984
A#	Myrtle Beach (S.C.) Pelicans	Carolina	71	67	.514	3rd (8)	Brian Snitker	1999
A	Macon (Ga.) Braves	South Atlantic	72	61	.541	5th (16)	Randy Ingle	1991
A	Jamestown (N.Y.) Jammers	New York-Penn	39	36	.520	5th (14)	Jim Saul	1999
Rookie#	Danville (Va.) Braves	Appalachian	30	38	.441	9th (10)	Ralph Henriquez	1993
Rookie	Kissimmee (Fla.) Braves	Gulf Coast	30	30	.500	8th (13)	Rick Albert	1998

*Finish in overall standings (No. of teams in league)   #Advanced level

RICHMOND   Class AAA

INTERNATIONAL LEAGUE

BATTING	AVG	G	AB	R	H	2B	3B	HR	RBI	BB	SO	SB	CS	SLG	OBP	B	T	HT	WT	DOB	1st Yr	Resides
Abbott, Kurt	.214	4	14	0	3	1	0	0	0	0	7	1	0	.286	.313	R	R	6-0	200	6-2-69	1989	Davie, Fla.
Battle, Howard	.275	131	491	53	135	21	0	10	76	25	77	2	5	.379	.308	R	R	6-0	197	3-25-72	1990	Ocean Springs, Miss.
Carter, Michael	.294	104	388	55	114	16	3	2	20	10	45	10	10	.366	.316	R	R	5-9	170	5-5-69	1990	Vicksburg, Miss.
Castro, Ramon	.222	36	135	14	30	8	2	1	15	7	30	1	2	.333	.266	R	R	6-0	195	10-23-79	1996	Valencia, Venez.
DeRosa, Mark	.296	49	186	31	55	18	0	2	17	17	22	7	3	.425	.351	R	R	6-1	195	2-2-75	1996	Carlstadt, N.J.
Garcia, Jesse	.267	105	375	50	100	22	3	2	22	22	54	18	6	.357	.313	R	R	5-10	171	9-24-73	1993	Robstown, Texas
Giles, Marcus	.333	67	252	48	84	19	1	6	44	22	48	13	5	.488	.387	R	R	5-8	180	5-18-78	1997	El Cajon, Calif.
Gilkey, Bernard	.271	13	48	5	13	3	0	0	2	4	8	0	1	.333	.315	R	R	6-0	200	9-24-66	1985	St. Louis, Mo.
Glavine, Mike	.136	23	44	1	6	2	0	0	4	6	11	0	0	.182	.235	L	L	6-3	210	1-24-73	1995	Billerica, Mass.
Green, Nick	.200	2	5	0	1	0	0	0	1	0	3	0	0	.200	.200	R	R	6-0	178	9-10-78	1999	Duluth, Ga.
Greene, Charlie	.167	23	66	4	11	1	0	0	4	3	17	0	0	.182	.203	R	R	6-2	170	1-23-71	1991	Miami, Fla.
Hollins, Damon	.263	43	160	27	42	10	2	5	24	14	34	2	2	.444	.318	R	L	5-11	180	6-12-74	1992	Fairfield, Calif.
Jones, Chris	.246	32	65	7	16	4	0	0	4	10	26	0	3	.308	.351	R	R	6-2	210	11-16-65	1984	Utica, N.Y.
Levis, Jesse	.297	67	192	18	57	6	0	1	27	24	15	2	0	.344	.381	L	R	5-9	200	4-14-68	1989	Elkins Park, Pa.
Lombard, George	.318	13	44	7	14	2	1	4	8	6	14	3	2	.682	.423	L	R	6-0	212	9-14-75	1994	Atlanta, Ga.
Martinez, Lou	.042	9	24	1	1	0	0	0	2	0	3	0	1	.042	.040	R	R	6-0	175	11-1-76	1999	Tampa, Fla.
Norris, Dax	.281	95	317	26	89	25	0	3	38	16	44	2	2	.388	.323	R	R	5-10	190	1-14-73	1996	La Grange, Ga.
Perry, Chan	.274	98	350	38	96	15	3	8	39	19	60	1	6	.403	.316	R	R	6-2	200	9-13-72	1994	Mayo, Fla.
Robertson, Mike	.272	127	434	42	118	19	5	6	40	30	56	4	12	.380	.321	L	L	6-0	190	10-9-70	1991	Las Vegas, Nev.
Ross, Jason	.208	49	125	15	26	5	1	5	7	7	45	3	2	.384	.265	R	R	6-4	215	6-10-74	1996	Augusta, Ga.
Swann, Pedro	.291	139	488	68	142	33	5	8	72	52	95	12	6	.428	.362	L	R	6-0	195	10-27-70	1991	Townsend, Del.
Tebbs, Nate	.096	28	83	2	8	0	0	0	2	5	24	1	0	.096	.148	B	R	5-10	170	12-14-72	1993	Riverton, Utah
2-team (46 Pawtucket)	.183	74	219	17	40	7	0	0	8	14	59	6	2	.215	.232							
Villegas, Ismael	.083	36	12	0	1	0	0	0	0	1	4	0	0	.083	.154	R	R	6-0	188	8-12-76	1995	Caguas, P.R.
Wilson, Travis	.243	103	383	34	93	22	3	3	38	7	81	4	2	.339	.263	R	R	6-2	185	7-10-77	1996	Christchurch, New Zealand
Woods, Kenny	.271	23	70	8	19	4	0	0	3	2	7	1	1	.329	.301	R	R	5-10	175	8-2-70	1992	Los Angeles, Calif.

PITCHING	W	L	ERA	G	GS	CG	SV	IP	H	R	ER	BB	SO	AVG	B	T	HT	WT	DOB	1st Yr	Resides
Beasley, Ray	1	3	3.76	65	0	0	0	55	58	26	23	22	37	.272	R	L	5-11	168	10-26-76	1996	Lake City, Fla.
Cumberland, Chris	2	3	4.86	13	1	0	1	17	23	11	9	7	10	.338	R	L	6-1	189	1-15-73	1993	Mandeville, La.
Dawley, Joey	1	0	2.84	3	0	0	0	6	3	2	2	1	5	.142	R	R	6-4	205	9-19-71	1993	Moreno Valley, Calif.
Hammond, Chris	3	1	2.35	21	0	0	1	31	32	9	8	4	29	.280	L	L	6-1	195	1-21-66	1986	Hallandale, Fla.
2-team (28 Buffalo)	10	4	2.95	49	4	0	1	82	85	31	27	24	83	.268							
Lewis, Derrick	4	4	4.45	12	12	0	0	61	50	34	30	37	50	.231	R	R	6-5	215	5-7-76	1997	Montgomery, Ala.
Ligtenberg, Kerry	0	0	0.00	1	0	0	0	1	0	0	0	1	2	.000	R	R	6-2	215	5-11-71	1994	Cottage Grove, Minn.
McClendon, Matt	0	6	8.16	10	10	0	0	46	50	45	42	31	31	.277	R	R	6-6	220	10-13-77	1999	Orlando, Fla.
Moore, Trey	9	8	3.31	26	25	2	0	163	140	64	60	41	122	.232	L	L	6-0	190	10-2-72	1994	Southlake, Texas
Moss, Damian	5	4	3.15	17	16	0	0	89	75	34	31	38	94	.231	R	L	6-0	187	11-24-76	1994	Sadler, Australia
Nelson, Joe	1	2	1.13	29	0	0	8	40	23	5	5	14	40	.171	R	R	6-2	185	10-25-74	1996	Alameda, Calif.
Pacheco, Delvis	1	4	5.28	22	9	1	0	58	78	36	34	24	51	.318	R	R	6-2	180	6-25-78	1995	Maracay, Venez.
Perez, Odalis	1	0	2.74	5	5	0	0	23	23	7	7	2	22	.255	L	L	6-0	150	6-7-78	1994	Las Matas de Farfan, D.R.
Robbins, Jake	5	3	5.51	57	0	0	1	78	73	51	48	51	53	.251	R	R	6-5	190	5-23-76	1994	Charlotte, N.C.
Seelbach, Chris	7	7	5.09	22	14	0	1	88	85	50	50	36	82	.256	R	R	6-4	180	12-18-72	1991	Lufkin, Texas
Slusarski, Joe	0	0	2.25	6	0	0	0	8	9	2	2	2	5	.290	R	R	6-4	195	12-19-66	1989	Springfield, Ill.
Small, Aaron	10	7	3.83	41	11	0	0	96	97	50	41	31	61	.256	R	R	6-5	225	11-23-71	1989	Loudon, Tenn.
Spooneybarger, Tim	3	0	0.71	42	0	0	5	51	33	5	4	21	58	.185	R	R	6-3	190	10-21-79	1999	Pensacola, Fla.
Stevens, Dave	2	1	6.90	39	0	0	1	59	67	49	45	31	47	.295	R	R	6-3	215	3-4-70	1990	Yorba Linda, Calif.
Sylvester, Billy	0	4	5.11	36	0	0	11	37	28	21	21	27	41	.208	R	R	6-5	218	10-1-76	1997	Florence, S.C.
Valdes, Marc	9	11	4.51	29	21	0	2	124	133	67	62	41	97	.278	R	R	6-0	180	12-20-71	1993	Tampa, Fla.
Villegas, Ismael	4	7	4.15	34	20	0	1	134	128	65	62	39	100	.252	R	R	6-0	188	8-12-76	1995	Caguas, P.R.
Whiteside, Matt	0	0	0.00	9	0	0	4	10	4	0	0	1	9	.114	R	R	6-0	200	8-8-67	1990	Arlington, Texas

FIELDING

Catcher	PCT	G	PO	A	E	DP	PB
Greene	.987	22	136	11	2	1	1
Levis	.995	61	398	43	2	2	6
Norris	.993	74	531	38	4	4	2

First Base	PCT	G	PO	A	E	DP
Battle	1.000	4	28	5	0	3
Glavine	.950	3	17	2	1	2
Norris	1.000	4	26	1	0	5
Perry	.991	68	536	41	5	47
Robertson	.995	71	562	29	3	45

	PCT	G	PO	A	E	DP
Wilson	1.000	8	38	4	0	2

Second Base	PCT	G	PO	A	E	DP
Abbott	1.000	1	3	1	0	0
Castro	1.000	6	14	10	0	3
DeRosa	1.000	7	16	17	0	3
Garcia	.953	16	24	37	3	11
Giles	.974	63	130	166	8	32
Green	.833	1	4	1	1	0
Martinez	1.000	8	14	28	0	5
Tebbs	.975	17	14	37	2	9

	PCT	G	PO	A	E	DP
Wilson	.952	38	72	86	8	19

Third Base	PCT	G	PO	A	E	DP
Battle	.972	114	69	208	8	22
Castro	.000	1	0	0	0	0
DeRosa	.977	18	15	28	1	5
Garcia	1.000	4	3	6	0	1
Giles	1.000	1	1	0	0	0
Martinez	1.000	1	0	2	0	0
Perry	.889	5	2	6	1	1
Tebbs	1.000	1	1	2	0	1

	PCT	G	PO	A	E	DP
Wilson	.880	11	6	16	3	2
Shortstop	PCT	G	PO	A	E	DP
Abbott	1.000	1	1	2	0	0
Battle	1.000	1	4	3	0	0
Castro	.967	29	33	83	4	17
DeRosa	.971	25	31	71	3	11
Garcia	.954	84	120	233	17	39
Giles	1.000	2	4	2	0	0

	PCT	G	PO	A	E	DP
Tebbs	1.000	8	9	15	0	3
Outfield	PCT	G	PO	A	E	DP
Carter	.981	96	201	6	4	0
Giles	1.000	1	3	0	0	0
Gilkey	1.000	13	18	1	0	0
Hollins	.981	43	100	1	2	0
Jones	1.000	23	42	3	0	1
Lombard	1.000	12	19	1	0	0

	PCT	G	PO	A	E	DP
Perry	1.000	14	17	0	0	0
Robertson	1.000	21	28	1	0	0
Ross	.957	47	84	4	4	0
Swann	.985	124	245	10	4	1
Villegas	.000	1	0	0	0	0
Wilson	.972	55	68	1	2	0
Woods	1.000	17	28	0	0	0

GREENVILLE   Class AA

ORGANIZATION STATISTICS

SOUTHERN LEAGUE

BATTING	AVG	G	AB	R	H	2B	3B	HR	RBI	BB	SO	SB	CS	SLG	OBP	B	T	HT	WT	DOB	1st Yr	Resides
Abbott, Kurt	.000	2	6	0	0	0	0	0	0	1	1	0	0	.000	.143	R	R	6-0	200	6-2-69	1989	Davie, Fla.
Aldridge, Cory	.246	131	452	57	111	19	2	19	56	48	139	12	6	.423	.323	L	R	6-0	210	6-13-79	1997	Abilene, Texas
Betemit, Wilson	.355	47	183	22	65	14	0	5	19	12	36	6	2	.514	.394	B	R	6-2	155	11-2-81	1996	Santo Domingo, D.R.
Brignac, Junior	.202	62	203	21	41	9	1	1	12	22	70	4	2	.271	.293	R	R	6-3	175	2-15-78	1996	Sun Valley, Calif.
Castro, Ramon	.307	76	261	35	80	19	5	6	31	25	56	5	8	.487	.383	R	R	6-0	195	10-23-79	1996	Valencia, Venez.
DeRenne, Keoni	.238	130	453	42	108	15	2	3	42	44	57	4	2	.300	.311	R	R	5-7	162	4-30-79	2000	Honolulu, Hawaii
Fiore, Curt	.154	13	39	2	6	2	0	0	0	0	13	0	0	.205	.195	R	R	6-2	195	7-28-77	1999	San Juan Capistrano, Calif.
Hessman, Michael	.230	129	478	66	110	23	2	26	80	39	124	2	4	.450	.298	R	R	6-5	215	3-5-78	1996	Westminster, Calif.
Horn, Jeff	.257	72	187	18	48	10	0	2	16	26	42	1	0	.342	.347	R	R	6-1	213	8-23-70	1992	Las Vegas, Nev.
Martinez, Lou	.182	46	99	11	18	3	0	0	2	4	14	1	0	.212	.229	R	R	6-0	175	11-1-76	1999	Tampa, Fla.
Moore, Mike	.159	27	63	8	10	2	0	2	6	4	33	0	0	.286	.232	R	R	6-4	225	3-7-71	1992	San Pedro, Calif.
Mortimer, Mark	.253	33	87	9	22	2	1	3	8	6	13	0	0	.402	.316	R	R	6-1	215	9-15-75	1997	Forest Park, Ga.
Otanez, Willis	.266	93	308	39	82	14	2	12	43	42	60	2	2	.442	.357	R	R	6-1	215	4-19-73	1990	Cotui, D.R.
Perez, Eddie	.342	10	38	7	13	2	0	4	5	0	9	0	0	.711	.359	R	R	6-1	185	5-4-68	1987	Duluth, Ga.
Rivera, Roberto	.237	121	392	49	93	19	1	6	27	30	78	9	4	.337	.300	B	R	6-2	180	11-25-76	1994	La Romana, D.R.
Ross, Jason	.257	63	187	27	48	7	1	11	30	33	55	15	6	.481	.387	R	R	6-4	215	6-10-74	1996	Augusta, Ga.
Smothers, Stewart	.233	39	120	10	28	7	0	0	5	14	34	1	2	.292	.313	R	R	5-10	180	4-29-76	1997	Los Angeles, Calif.
Torrealba, Steve	.271	90	295	37	80	21	0	8	34	33	54	0	0	.424	.347	R	R	6-0	175	2-24-78	1995	Barquisimeto, Venez.
Urquiola, Carlos	.303	40	132	18	40	5	0	0	10	15	15	6	4	.341	.373	L	R	5-8	150	4-22-80	1997	Caracas, Venez.
Wilson, Travis	.325	31	123	13	40	8	1	2	21	3	24	2	5	.455	.344	R	R	6-2	185	7-10-77	1996	Christchurch, New Zealand
Zapp, A.J.	.233	75	292	36	68	17	0	8	34	21	87	5	1	.373	.296	L	R	6-3	190	4-24-78	1996	Greenwood, Ind.

PITCHING	W	L	ERA	G	GS	CG	SV	IP	H	R	ER	BB	SO	AVG	B	T	HT	WT	DOB	1st Yr	Resides
Abreu, Winston	3	5	4.64	34	7	0	0	74	56	40	38	45	93	.213	R	R	6-2	155	4-5-77	1994	Cotui, D.R.
Brooks, Antone	0	1	6.62	11	0	0	0	18	18	13	13	9	10	.285	L	L	6-0	170	12-20-73	1995	Florence, S.C.
Cortes, David	0	3	8.15	14	0	0	0	18	19	18	16	11	10	.263	R	R	5-11	195	10-15-73	1996	El Centro, Calif.
Cumberland, Chris	3	7	3.46	20	20	2	0	125	126	51	48	40	85	.266	R	L	6-1	189	1-15-73	1993	Mandeville, La.
Dawley, Joey	7	5	3.04	22	21	1	0	127	95	50	43	46	130	.207	R	R	6-4	205	9-19-71	1993	Moreno Valley, Calif.
Foster, John	8	7	3.01	50	0	0	7	69	71	30	23	33	63	.279	L	L	6-0	200	5-17-78	1999	Stockton, Calif.
Gray, Mike	3	1	3.79	25	0	0	0	40	41	23	17	13	22	.259	L	L	6-1	170	12-6-76	1999	Paso Robles, Calif.
Kent, Nathan	8	10	4.07	26	26	0	0	155	186	89	70	38	111	.295	R	R	6-6	210	8-16-78	1999	Frankfort, Ky.
Lee, Garrett	4	9	4.60	32	9	1	0	92	103	55	47	17	63	.283	R	R	6-3	210	8-17-76	1996	Montrose, Calif.
Lontayo, Alex	3	5	5.19	9	9	0	0	50	59	34	29	26	43	.292	L	L	6-1	195	12-12-75	1999	Chula Vista, Calif.
McClendon, Matt	0	1	5.91	2	2	0	0	11	10	7	7	7	9	.256	R	R	6-6	220	10-13-77	1999	Orlando, Fla.
Millwood, Kevin	0	1	4.50	2	2	0	0	10	9	6	5	3	10	.243	R	R	6-4	220	12-24-74	1993	Bessemer City, N.C.
Moss, Damian	0	1	3.00	2	2	0	0	9	7	3	3	0	10	.209	R	L	6-0	187	11-24-76	1994	Sadler, Australia
Parra, Christian	3	8	5.44	18	18	0	0	89	87	58	54	56	82	.257	R	R	6-1	255	2-28-78	1999	Yuma, Ariz.
Ramirez, Horacio	1	1	4.91	3	3	0	0	15	17	8	8	17	.309		L	L	6-1	170	11-24-79	1997	Inglewood, Calif.
Saipe, Mike	4	2	2.39	7	7	0	0	49	43	13	13	13	36	.242	R	R	6-3	220	5-15-67	1986	Duluth, Ga.
Smoltz, John	0	0	0.00	3	1	0	0	6	3	0	0	0	6	.150	R	R	6-3	220	5-15-67	1986	Duluth, Ga.
Sobkowiak, Scott	2	5	5.54	12	12	0	0	65	71	45	40	40	48	.279	R	R	6-5	230	10-26-77	1998	Loveland, Ohio
Spooneybarger, Tim	1	1	5.14	15	0	0	0	21	20	12	12	4	24	.246	R	R	6-3	190	10-21-79	1999	Pensacola, Fla.
Stevens, Dave	1	0	3.09	9	0	0	2	12	4	5	4	6	8	.111	R	R	6-3	215	3-4-70	1990	Yorba Linda, Calif.
Sylvester, Billy	1	0	2.37	26	0	0	12	30	18	8	8	24	41	.176	R	R	6-4	190	1-25-75	2001	Shiga, Japan
Takeoka, Kazuhiro	5	3	2.68	45	0	0	3	74	76	31	22	21	46	.267	R	R	6-1	190	8-18-76	1999	West Sacramento, Calif.
Veronie, Shanin	0	0	0.00	2	0	0	0	3	4	0	0	4	4	.307	R	R	6-1	195	12-30-76	1998	Green Bay, Wis.
Voyles, Brad	0	0	1.08	15	0	0	6	17	11	3	2	10	25	.192	R	R	6-1	195	12-30-76	1998	Green Bay, Wis.
Winkelsas, Joe	4	2	3.27	20	0	0	3	33	24	12	12	14	14	.205	R	R	6-3	188	9-14-73	1996	Buffalo, N.Y.

FIELDING

Catcher	PCT	G	PO	A	E	DP	PB
Horn	.986	48	325	24	5	1	1
Mortimer	.965	11	74	8	3	0	1
Perez	1.000	6	35	4	0	0	0
Torrealba	.979	85	596	64	14	3	10

First Base	PCT	G	PO	A	E	DP
Fiore	1.000	1	9	0	0	0
Hessman	1.000	5	25	1	0	0
Horn	.984	7	55	6	1	10
Mortimer	1.000	2	12	1	0	2
Otanez	.994	53	450	30	3	34
Perez	.955	5	21	0	1	1
Wilson	1.000	1	10	0	0	0
Zapp	.992	74	592	66	5	59

Second Base	PCT	G	PO	A	E	DP
Abbott	1.000	1	6	7	0	3

	PCT	G	PO	A	E	DP
Castro	.957	9	18	27	2	4
DeRenne	.986	94	183	232	6	48
Martinez	.955	24	31	54	4	11
Wilson	.973	24	48	59	3	15
Third Base	PCT	G	PO	A	E	DP
Castro	1.000	5	2	7	0	1
Fiore	.840	9	9	12	4	1
Hessman	.918	113	74	217	26	20
Horn	.000	2	0	0	0	0
Martinez	1.000	6	1	9	0	1
Mortimer	1.000	1	1	0	0	0
Otanez	.900	19	9	27	4	2
Shortstop	PCT	G	PO	A	E	DP
Betemit	.954	47	56	132	9	24
Castro	.972	62	80	164	7	27
DeRenne	.970	31	39	89	4	22

	PCT	G	PO	A	E	DP
Martinez	.857	6	5	13	3	3
Outfield	PCT	G	PO	A	E	DP
Aldridge	.964	117	208	7	8	0
Brignac	.970	61	123	7	4	0
Hessman	.964	18	24	3	1	0
Moore	.929	13	11	2	1	0
Mortimer	.833	4	5	0	1	0
Otanez	1.000	8	9	0	0	0
Rivera	.965	99	158	6	6	0
Ross	.991	58	108	4	1	1
Smothers	.977	38	82	4	2	0
Urquiola	.980	28	48	0	1	0
Wilson	1.000	7	9	0	0	0

CAROLINA LEAGUE

BATTING	AVG	G	AB	R	H	2B	3B	HR	RBI	BB	SO	SB	CS	SLG	OBP	B	T	HT	WT	DOB	1st Yr	Resides
Betemit, Wilson	.277	84	318	38	88	20	1	7	43	23	71	8	5	.412	.324	B	R	6-2	155	11-2-81	1996	Santo Domingo, D.R.
Boscan, Jean	.167	18	54	3	9	2	0	0	6	3	25	0	1	.204	.220	R	R	6-2	160	12-26-79	1996	Maracaibo, Venez.
Brignac, Junior	.193	66	233	28	45	8	0	6	19	24	68	6	9	.305	.273	R	R	6-3	175	2-15-78	1996	Sun Valley, Calif.
Cameron, Troy	.251	65	223	27	56	13	1	7	38	23	62	2	6	.413	.335	B	R	6-2	180	8-31-78	1997	Plantation, Fla.
Coates, Brad	.113	18	53	4	6	1	0	0	3	5	20	0	0	.132	.200	R	R	6-2	180	4-7-79	2001	Benson, N.C.
Crocker, Nick	.215	81	246	27	53	10	1	6	27	20	91	6	5	.337	.285	L	L	6-3	215	8-8-77	1999	Carlyle, Ill.
Fiore, Curtis	.283	100	329	56	93	20	2	6	42	47	69	5	1	.410	.398	R	R	6-2	195	7-28-77	1999	San Juan Capistrano, Calif.
Green, Nick	.266	80	297	49	79	18	1	10	42	32	70	9	2	.434	.348	R	R	6-0	178	9-10-78	1999	Duluth, Ga.
Jones, Damien	.265	129	460	57	122	20	3	1	41	38	114	9	12	.328	.323	L	L	6-2	200	7-10-79	1998	Mobile, Ala.
Langerhans, Ryan	.287	125	450	66	129	30	3	7	48	55	104	22	13	.413	.374	L	L	6-3	195	2-20-80	1998	Round Rock, Texas
LaRoche, Adam	.251	126	471	49	118	31	0	7	47	30	108	10	8	.361	.305	L	L	6-3	180	11-6-79	2000	Fort Scott, Kan.
Leal, Jaeme	.214	63	215	32	46	7	1	15	39	20	88	0	0	.465	.317	R	R	6-0	235	8-23-78	1999	Riverside, Calif.
Manning, Pat	.223	62	220	23	49	12	0	10	30	28	41	2	3	.414	.322	R	R	6-1	185	2-27-80	1999	Anaheim Hills, Calif.
Martinez, Lou	.143	2	7	0	1	0	0	0	0	0	0	0	0	.143	.143	R	R	6-0	175	11-1-76	1999	Tampa, Fla.
Mortimer, Mark	.193	50	181	18	35	4	0	2	17	17	31	0	0	.249	.277	R	R	6-1	215	9-15-75	1997	Forest Park, Ga.
Orr, Pete	.233	92	317	38	74	10	1	4	23	19	70	17	6	.309	.299	L	R	6-1	175	6-8-79	1999	Newmarket, Ontario
Rodriguez, Jeff	.206	76	248	22	51	10	0	4	27	24	57	0	1	.294	.288	R	R	5-11	195	12-20-76	1999	Miami, Fla.
Terveen, Bryce	.180	20	61	7	11	3	0	2	7	4	17	0	0	.328	.261	L	R	6-1	205	3-1-78	1999	Modesto, Calif.
Thomas, Charles	.159	12	44	4	7	1	0	0	6	3	8	1	0	.182	.208	L	L	6-0	190	12-26-78	2000	Asheville, N.C.
Um, Jong	.153	24	72	5	11	1	0	1	7	7	33	0	0	.208	.247	R	R	6-0	200	7-9-73	2001	Seoul, Korea

GAMES BY POSITION: C—Boscan 18, Mortimer 22, Rodriguez 64, Terveen 17, Um 24. **1B**—Fiore 1, LaRoche 120, Leal 15, Mortimer 5, Rodriguez 1, Terveen 2. **2B**—Coates 1, Fiore 7, Green 74, Manning 46, Orr 21. **3B**—Cameron 62, Fiore 60, Manning 8, Martinez 2, Orr 4. **SS**—Betemit 83, Coates 18, Green 3, Orr 39. **OF**—Brignac 66, Crocker 59, Fiore 26, Jones 110, Langerhans 121, LaRoche 3, Orr 25, Thomas 11.

PITCHING	W	L	ERA	G	GS	CG	SV	IP	H	R	ER	BB	SO	AVG	B	T	HT	WT	DOB	1st Yr	Resides
Bent, Andy	1	5	3.38	29	0	0	1	56	44	29	21	25	53	.217	R	R	6-2	190	12-19-78	2000	Beatrice, Neb.
Bong, Jung	13	9	3.00	28	0	0	168	151	67	56	47	145	.244	L	L	6-3	175	7-15-80	1997	Norcross, Ga.
Butler, Matt	7	8	5.89	22	22	1	0	115	127	81	75	48	78	.284	R	R	6-3	190	9-24-79	1998	Hattiesburg, Miss.
Clontz, Brad	0	1	1.59	9	0	0	0	11	8	4	2	5	12	.186	R	R	6-1	195	4-25-71	1992	Alpharetta, Ga.
Cortes, David	0	2	5.91	9	0	0	2	11	11	7	7	5	9	.245	R	R	5-11	195	10-15-73	1996	El Centro, Calif.
Curtiss, Tom	0	1	4.26	12	0	0	0	13	11	7	6	8	10	.229	R	L	6-4	215	12-19-76	1999	Ardmore, Pa.
Dawley, Joey	1	0	1.80	5	0	0	0	10	4	2	2	0	16	.117	R	R	6-4	205	9-19-71	1993	Moreno Valley, Calif.
Ennis, John	6	8	3.58	25	25	1	0	138	111	63	55	45	144	.224	R	R	6-5	220	10-17-79	1998	North Hills, Calif.
Evert, Brett	7	2	2.24	13	13	1	0	72	63	25	18	15	75	.225	L	R	6-6	200	10-23-80	1999	Salem, Ore.
Gawer, Matt	2	0	2.51	42	0	0	14	43	41	18	12	16	46	.239	L	L	6-4	235	4-15-78	1999	Sullivan, Mo.
Hernandez, Buddy	1	1	1.17	34	0	0	6	54	28	7	7	18	77	.146	R	R	5-9	170	3-3-79	2000	Birdsboro, Pa.
Herndon, Eric	2	2	2.42	24	0	0	2	45	39	13	12	11	38	.242	L	R	6-1	190	10-4-76	1998	Upper Marlboro, Md.
Hodges, Trey	15	8	2.76	26	26	1	0	173	156	64	53	18	139	.237	R	R	6-3	187	6-29-78	2000	Spring, Texas
Kelly, Dan	2	1	2.03	18	1	0	1	40	31	10	9	7	22	.215	B	L	6-1	175	10-5-77	2000	Niceville, Fla.
Kozlowski, Ben	0	2	3.77	2	2	0	0	14	15	7	6	3	13	.283	L	L	6-6	220	8-16-80	1999	Seminole, Fla.
Lontayo, Alex	5	2	4.29	20	4	0	0	50	56	26	24	27	42	.282	L	L	6-1	195	12-7-75	1999	Chula Vista, Calif.
McClendon, Matt	1	2	8.68	8	0	0	0	9	7	10	9	9	10	.212	R	R	6-6	220	10-13-77	1999	Orlando, Fla.
Pacheco, Delvis	1	0	0.00	2	0	0	0	10	4	0	0	2	7	.117	R	R	6-2	180	6-25-78	1999	Maracay, Venez.
Smalley, Mike	0	6	6.67	9	5	0	0	30	42	25	22	10	25	.338	R	L	6-1	200	6-22-79	2000	Maitland, Fla.
Truitt, Derrick	2	2	8.39	16	0	0	0	25	37	24	23	10	25	.345	R	R	6-1	170	2-2-78	1998	Columbia, Tenn.
Veronie, Shanin	1	2	2.48	35	0	0	9	54	47	17	15	10	57	.224	R	R	6-1	190	8-18-76	1999	West Sacramento, Calif.
Voyles, Brad	0	0	0.00	2	0	0	1	2	0	0	0	1	3	.000	R	R	6-1	195	12-30-76	1998	Green Bay, Wis.
Winkelsas, Joe	1	0	0.00	4	0	0	3	6	2	0	0	1	5	.105	R	R	6-3	188	9-14-73	1996	Buffalo, N.Y.
Yankosky, L.J.	2	3	2.60	9	8	0	0	55	50	20	16	4	50	.238	R	R	6-2	208	2-1-75	1998	Springfield, Va.

SOUTH ATLANTIC LEAGUE

BATTING	AVG	G	AB	R	H	2B	3B	HR	RBI	BB	SO	SB	CS	SLG	OBP	B	T	HT	WT	DOB	1st Yr	Resides
Bernard, Miguel	.189	47	159	19	30	1	0	3	17	8	41	5	2	.252	.233	R	R	5-11	170	1-1-81	1997	San Pedro de Macoris, D.R.
Boscan, Jean	.282	35	124	16	35	7	0	4	22	14	27	2	0	.435	.357	R	R	6-2	160	12-26-79	1996	Maracaibo, Venez.
Burrows, Angelo	.256	117	426	52	109	15	2	4	36	28	61	31	15	.329	.303	L	R	5-11	170	7-2-80	1999	Freeport, Bahamas
Coleman, Alph	.300	120	476	84	143	18	7	7	57	24	73	38	13	.412	.342	R	R	6-3	187	4-8-79	2000	Houston, Texas
Donato, Greg	.250	3	12	1	3	0	0	1	2	1	0	0	0	.250	.357	R	R	6-0	185	11-10-80	1998	Clovis, Calif.
Forbes, Mike	.257	117	378	53	97	23	0	10	64	72	106	10	8	.397	.377	L	R	6-1	175	5-27-80	1999	West Lakes, Australia
Green, Kevin	.147	17	34	5	5	2	0	1	3	3	18	0	0	.294	.250	R	R	6-0	180	9-10-78	1999	Duluth, Ga.
Jeffcoat, Bryon	.222	26	90	11	20	5	1	2	7	10	28	3	2	.367	.311	R	R	6-1	190	5-14-79	2001	West Columbia, S.C.
Johnson, Kelly	.289	124	415	75	120	22	1	23	66	71	111	25	6	.513	.404	L	R	6-1	180	2-22-82	2000	Austin, Texas
Lopez, Raul	.207	45	150	14	31	9	1	4	25	8	26	0	1	.360	.245	L	R	6-3	182	11-9-78	1996	Obregon, Mexico
Machado, Alejandro	.271	82	306	43	83	6	3	1	24	34	56	20	13	.320	.368	R	R	6-0	160	4-26-82	1998	Caracas, Venez.
Manning, Pat	.284	62	211	40	60	13	1	13	29	37	46	6	2	.540	.399	R	R	6-1	185	2-27-80	1999	Anaheim Hills, Calif.
Morales, Michael	.188	26	69	8	13	2	0	1	6	6	15	1	0	.261	.282	R	R	6-1	185	4-4-79	2001	West Palm Beach, Fla.
Oropeza, Asdrubal	.207	109	362	37	75	18	0	8	40	38	105	4	5	.323	.289	R	R	6-2	170	7-3-80	1996	Barquisimeto, Venez.
Rodriguez, Ricardo	.188	5	16	2	3	0	0	0	2	1	5	1	0	.188	.316	R	R	6-0	140	4-28-81	1998	Caracas, Venez.
Salas, Jose	.158	12	38	1	6	2	0	0	3	4	11	1	0	.211	.175	B	R	6-3	210	2-16-82	1998	Caracas, Venez.
Serrano, Ray	.200	63	215	20	43	10	0	4	27	11	37	2	0	.302	.238	R	R	5-9	180	1-19-81	1999	Ponce, P.R.
Terveen, Bryce	.226	61	190	25	43	5	0	4	26	32	42	1	3	.316	.362	L	R	6-1	205	3-1-78	1999	Modesto, Calif.
Thomas, Charles	.250	108	408	59	102	19	5	11	59	32	87	17	7	.402	.307	L	L	6-0	190	12-26-78	2000	Asheville, N.C.
Thompson, Alva	.157	17	51	7	8	1	0	0	1	2	11	0	0	.176	.170	R	R	6-1	180	9-15-81	1999	Atlanta, Ga.
Zumwalt, Alec	.209	101	349	43	73	20	2	6	38	34	101	8	1	.330	.286	R	R	6-2	190	1-20-81	1999	Kernersville, N.C.

GAMES BY POSITION: C—Bernard 42, Boscan 31, Salas 9, Serrano 46, Terveen 20, Thompson 2. **1B**—Forbes 76, Jeffcoat 4, Lopez 42, Morales 1, Terveen 19, Thompson 3. **2B**—Green 8, Jeffcoat 16, Machado 68, Manning 35, Morales 20, Rodriguez 1. **3B**—Forbes 12, Green 1, Jeffcoat 5, Manning 21, Oropeza 108. **SS**—Jeffcoat 116, Machado 14, Manning 1, Morales 5, Rodriguez 3. **OF**—Burrows 107, Coleman 105, Donato 1, Forbes 12, Rodriguez 1, Thomas 98, Zumwalt 91.

PITCHING	W	L	ERA	G	GS	CG	SV	IP	H	R	ER	BB	SO	AVG	B	T	HT	WT	DOB	1st Yr	Resides
Baker, Ryan	2	3	2.09	40	0	0	18	47	40	13	11	15	56	.228	R	R	6-0	200	3-20-78	2000	Linthicum, Md.
Collazo, Willie	3	2	2.70	12	0	0	1	23	13	9	7	4	23	.171	L	L	5-9	170	11-7-79	2001	Miami, Fla.
Colon, Roman	7	7	3.59	23	21	0	0	128	136	69	51	26	91	.270	R	R	6-3	170	8-13-79	1996	El Centro, Calif.
Cortes, David	1	0	7.11	10	0	0	0	13	14	11	10	5	8	.259	R	R	5-11	195	10-15-73	1996	El Centro, Calif.
Davies, Kyle	1	0	0.00	1	1	0	0	6	2	0	0	1	7	.105	R	R	6-2	190	9-9-83	2001	McDonough, Ga.
Digby, Bryan	1	0	1.13	3	1	0	0	8	3	1	1		7	.120	R	R	6-2	190	12-31-81	2000	Peachtree City, Ga.
Evert, Brett	1	0	0.74	6	6	0	0	36	25	5	3	3	34	.182	L	R	6-6	200	10-23-80	1999	Salem, Ore.
Hernandez, Buddy	0	0	3.21	7	0	0	0	14	13	8	5	1	29	.232	R	R	5-9	170	3-3-79	2000	Birdsboro, Pa.
Herndon, Eric	0	2	1.93	10	0	0	2	19	13	5	4	6	15	.203	L	R	6-1	190	10-4-76	1998	Upper Marlboro, Md.
Jones, Quentin	1	2	5.59	35	0	0	9	37	32	26	23	33	51	.244	R	R	6-4	217	4-14-79	2000	Danville, Va.
Kozlowski, Ben	10	7	2.48	26	23	1	0	145	134	60	40	27	147	.247	L	L	6-6	220	8-16-80	1999	Seminole, Fla.
Mathiesen, Ryan	0	0	9.00	1	0	0	0	2	5	2	2	2	1	.500	R	R	6-1	200	2-13-81	2001	Corvallis, Ore.
Mendez, Dave	5	4	4.08	35	1	0	2	68	55	34	31	29	55	.216	L	L	6-2	190	10-1-79	1996	Pueblo Nuevo, Panama
Mikels, Jason	1	4	5.00	23	1	0	0	36	43	28	20	16	27	.288	R	R	6-4	185	7-27-79	1999	Rio Linda, Calif.
Millwood, Kevin	0	0	0.00	1	1	0	0	3	0	0	0	0	5	.000	R	R	6-4	220	12-24-74	1993	Bessemer City, N.C.
Nelson, Kenny	12	8	3.93	25	24	2	0	151	144	76	66	57	154	.251	R	R	6-2	200	8-26-81	2000	Fort Washington, Md.
Perez, Elvis	5	5	2.98	27	0	0	0	51	35	22	17	19	48	.186	R	R	6-3	160	7-4-79	1996	Santo Domingo, D.R.
Pierce, Tony	0	0	13.50	2	0	0	0	4	7	6	6	3	4	.368	R	R	6-0	170	6-21-76	1999	Midland, Ga.
Sclafani, Anthony	1	0	1.93	5	0	0	1	14	11	4	3	4	12	.215	R	R	6-1	175	7-28-81	1999	Staten Island, N.Y.
Smalley, Mike	0	0	12.46	5	0	0	0	4	12	10	6	2	3	.500	R	L	6-1	190	6-22-79	2000	Maitland, Fla.
Smoltz, John	0	0	1.80	1	1	0	0	5	4	1	1	0	5	.235	R	R	6-3	220	5-15-67	1986	Duluth, Ga.
Wainwright, Adam	10	10	3.77	28	28	1	0	165	144	89	69	48	184	.230	R	R	6-6	190	8-30-81	2000	St. Simons Island, Ga.
Waters, Chris	8	6	3.35	25	24	3	0	148	131	71	55	52	78	.238	L	L	6-0	190	8-17-80	2000	Lakeland, Fla.
Watkins, Dave	3	1	2.76	24	0	0	2	49	33	17	15	27	59	.194	R	R	6-1	190	8-18-81	1999	Leitchfield, Ky.
Yankosky, L.J.	0	0	0.00	1	1	0	0	4	2	1	0	0		.133	R	R	6-2	208	2-1-75	1998	Springfield, Va.

JAMESTOWN — Short-Season Class A

NEW YORK-PENN LEAGUE

BATTING	AVG	G	AB	R	H	2B	3B	HR	RBI	BB	SO	SB	CS	SLG	OBP	B	T	HT	WT	DOB	1st Yr	Resides
Anderson, Travis	.246	37	130	16	32	11	0	1	17	11	19	1	0	.354	.338	R	R	6-0	195	8-29-79	2001	Burney, Calif.
Brown, Kevin	.158	49	158	17	25	8	0	6	20	33	70	0	1	.323	.322	R	R	6-4	230	4-11-79	2001	North Fort Myers, Fla.
Cummings, Frank	.000	3	1	0	0	0	0	0	0	0	1	0	0	.000	.000	R	R	6-2	200	2-10-77	2000	Ripley, W.Va.
Green, Kevin	.091	11	33	2	3	0	0	1	2	2	20	0	0	.182	.189	R	R	6-3	180	9-10-78	1999	Duluth, Ga.
Guzman, Carlos	.000	6	6	2	0	0	0	0	0	3	0	0	0	.000	.000	R	R	6-3	180	7-5-83	1999	La Vega, D.R.
Hambrick, Marcus	.144	36	97	8	14	7	1	0	1	8	32	1	3	.237	.217	L	L	5-11	170	6-19-79	1999	Montgomery, Ala.
Jeffcoat, Bryon	.238	36	122	15	29	3	3	2	16	12	24	1	1	.361	.324	R	R	6-1	190	5-14-79	2001	West Columbia, S.C.
Kent, Mailon	.310	50	187	26	58	9	3	2	27	21	20	5	3	.422	.383	R	R	6-0	183	9-2-78	2001	Birmingham, Ala.
Lewis, Richard	.242	71	285	37	69	7	1	4	27	20	54	10	4	.316	.298	R	R	6-1	190	6-29-80	2001	Marietta, Ga.
McCarthy, Bill	.295	74	285	38	84	17	2	2	39	20	47	7	4	.389	.351	R	R	6-2	200	12-2-79	2001	Sewell, N.J.
Miller, Greg	.279	61	240	24	67	10	2	0	17	20	28	9	5	.338	.343	R	R	6-1	180	1-9-79	2001	Sterling, Va.
Parrott, Tom	.256	42	117	17	30	5	1	1	8	15	39	3	1	.342	.343	R	R	6-1	205	9-22-80	2000	Titusville, Fla.
Pena, Tony	.246	72	264	26	65	12	2	0	18	10	48	8	6	.307	.278	R	R	6-1	160	3-23-81	1999	Santiago, D.R.
Pimentel, Hector	.271	53	181	22	49	8	3	5	24	7	39	6	2	.431	.306	R	R	5-10	185	5-14-80	2001	Coweta, Okla.
Roat, Kyle	.215	33	107	10	23	5	0	4	10	10	22	2	0	.262	.288	R	R	6-4	185	1-1-80	2001	Yuma, Ariz.
Ruiz, Daniel	.250	9	28	3	7	1	0	0	1	1	5	0	0	.286	.276	B	R	6-2	175	6-11-84	2001	Maracay, Venez.
Salas, Michael	.217	37	129	8	28	8	0	2	17	9	21	0	1	.326	.285	B	R	5-11	185	2-12-80	2001	London, Ontario
Stern, Adam	.307	21	75	20	23	4	2	0	11	15	11	9	4	.413	.413	L	R	5-11	185	2-12-80	2001	London, Ontario

GAMES BY POSITION: C—Anderson 31, Green 1, Roat 32, Salas 13. 1B—K. Brown 49, Green 1, Jeffcoat 1, Parrott 28. 2B—Jeffcoat 6, Lewis 69. 3B—Cummings 2, Jeffcoat 21, Parrott 6, Pimentel 49. SS—Jeffcoat 4, Pena 71. OF—Guzman 3, Hambrick 24, Kent 50, McCarthy 73, G. Miller 59, Stern 21.

PITCHING	W	L	ERA	G	GS	CG	SV	IP	H	R	ER	BB	SO	AVG	B	T	HT	WT	DOB	1st Yr	Resides
Abrams, Grant	3	3	3.03	22	0	0	0	36	40	14	12	17	31	.273	R	R	6-0	180	11-20-79	2000	Dunedin, Fla.
Aguilar, Ray	1	1	1.50	2	2	0	0	12	7	4	2	3	16	.162	B	L	5-11	200	1-18-80	1999	South El Monte, Calif.
Arteaga, Francisco	0	0	2.45	3	0	0	1	4	3	1	1	2	5	.250	R	R	6-1	170	10-4-81	2001	Los Angeles, Calif.
Barry, Kevin	1	0	0.86	29	0	0	12	31	14	5	3	18	54	.130	R	R	6-2	215	8-18-78	2001	Princeton Junction, N.J.
Brown, Andrew	3	4	3.92	14	12	0	0	64	50	29	28	31	59	.000	R	R	6-6	230	2-17-81	1999	Deltona, Fla.
Cetani, Bryan	0	0	16.20	3	0	0	0	2	1	5	3	4	0	.200	L	L	6-4	200	10-9-81	1999	Ukiah, Calif.
Collazo, Willie	3	1	0.60	9	0	0	1	15	9	2	1	0	13	.169	L	L	5-9	170	11-7-79	2001	Miami, Fla.
Colton, Kyle	1	4	7.11	8	0	0	0	38	45	32	30	23	26	.292	R	R	6-2	175	11-16-80	1999	Longwood, Fla.
Furnald, Donnie	4	1	6.64	11	5	0	0	39	37	30	29	34	34	.256	R	R	6-3	210	12-2-79	2001	Alta Loma, Calif.
Hopper, Kevin	1	0	5.00	7	0	0	2	9	15	6	5	0	8	.375	R	R	6-2	190	6-4-78	2000	Boston, Ga.
Mikels, Jason	1	1	3.48	7	3	0	0	21	18	8	8	5	13	.236	R	R	6-4	185	7-27-79	1999	Rio Linda, Calif.
Miller, Matt	2	4	3.15	28	0	0	1	40	40	14	14	12	36	.258	L	L	6-2	205	6-6-78	2000	Devon, Pa.
Miner, Zach	3	4	1.89	15	15	0	0	91	76	26	19	16	68	.226	R	R	6-3	190	3-12-82	2001	Jupiter, Fla.
Rodriguez, Jose	5	5	3.52	12	12	1	0	64	55	27	25	20	30	.234	R	R	6-0	175	1-15-82	1998	Carora, Venez.
Sclafani, Anthony	1	2	3.00	8	0	0	1	21	17	7	7	7	15	.226	R	R	6-1	175	7-28-81	1999	Staten Island, N.Y.
Smith, Toebius	4	0	3.90	14	0	0	0	28	27	13	12	14	24	.254	R	R	6-8	180	10-27-79	1998	Clarkton, N.C.
Staveland, Toby	3	2	4.14	15	11	0	0	54	62	33	25	21	42	.289	R	R	6-3	225	3-27-80	2000	Juneau, Alaska
Tillery, Josh	2	0	2.33	21	1	0	2	39	43	14	10	12	39	.290	R	R	6-6	250	8-2-78	2000	La Verne, Okla.
Trevino, Chris	1	4	3.77	15	6	0	0	43	44	27	18	11	43	.257	L	L	6-3	195	11-14-80	1999	Andrews, Texas

DANVILLE — Rookie

APPALACHIAN LEAGUE

BATTING	AVG	G	AB	R	H	2B	3B	HR	RBI	BB	SO	SB	CS	SLG	OBP	B	T	HT	WT	DOB	1st Yr	Resides
Bernard, Miguel	.242	39	128	13	31	8	1	1	16	8	29	1	1	.344	.297	R	R	5-11	170	1-1-81	1997	San Pedro de Macoris, D.R.
Bessa, Laumin	.243	55	173	24	42	10	3	3	17	11	49	3	2	.480	.296	R	R	6-3	175	1-23-83	1999	Caracas, Venez.
Castellanos, Jose	.310	42	129	14	40	10	1	3	21	10	21	0	0	.473	.364	R	R	6-1	180	8-23-80	1999	Santo Domingo, D.R.
Copeland, Nate	.272	43	81	13	22	3	0	0	8	13	24	2	1	.309	.375	L	L	6-6	205	7-30-78	2001	Elizabethton, Tenn.
Cust, Kevin	.129	24	62	2	8	0	0	1	4	1	32	0	1	.177	.167	R	R	6-1	200	9-9-81	2000	Flemington, N.J.
Farmer, John	.250	12	16	1	4	1	0	0	1	1	4	0	0	.313	.368	R	R	6-0	175	3-30-79	2001	Eugene, Ore.

ORGANIZATION STATISTICS

BATTING

BATTING	AVG	G	AB	R	H	2B	3B	HR	RBI	BB	SO	SB	CS	SLG	OBP	B	T	HT	WT	DOB	1st Yr	Resides
Guilliams, Earl	.167	18	48	3	8	0	0	0	2	1	12	0	0	.167	.200	R	R	6-0	190	6-22-81	1999	Danville, Va.
Herr, Aaron	.243	64	239	31	58	12	1	2	21	24	64	6	4	.326	.326	R	R	5-11	183	3-7-81	2000	Lancaster, Pa.
Jansen, Ardley	.223	64	211	25	47	3	0	6	23	15	64	9	7	.322	.287	R	R	6-2	160	2-16-83	1999	Willemstad, Curacao
Jones, Garrett	.289	40	149	13	43	11	0	3	23	9	58	0	1	.423	.333	L	L	6-4	205	6-21-81	1999	Tinley Park, Ill.
Marte, Andy	.200	37	125	12	25	6	0	1	12	20	45	3	0	.272	.306	R	R	6-1	185	10-21-83	2001	Villa Tapia, D.R.
Melo, Hanlet	.225	55	178	22	40	7	3	1	12	9	47	7	3	.315	.265	R	R	6-2	175	3-3-82	1999	Bani, D.R.
O'Kelly, Mike	.200	52	165	14	33	12	1	3	22	9	60	0	0	.339	.249	R	R	6-3	210	12-3-78	2001	Midlothian, Va.
Pena, Brayan	.370	64	235	39	87	16	2	1	33	31	30	3	1	.468	.440	B	R	5-11	210	1-7-82	2001	San Jose, Costa Rica
Rodriguez , Ricardo	.190	58	231	30	44	5	2	2	14	17	62	12	5	.255	.267	R	R	6-0	140	4-28-81	1998	Caracas, Venez.
Ruiz, Daniel	.244	23	78	9	19	7	0	0	6	4	15	2	0	.333	.298	R	R	6-4	185	1-1-80	2001	Yuma, Ariz.

GAMES BY POSITION: C—Bernard 28, Guilliams 18, Pena 31. **1B**—Cust 11, Jones 39, O'Kelly 22. **2B**—Farmer 5, Herr 64, Marte 1, Rodriguez 3. **3B**—Bessa 4, Farmer 1, Marte 37, O'Kelly 28. **SS**—Farmer 2, Rodriguez 53, Ruiz 16. **OF**—Bessa 50, Castellanos 32, Copeland 32, Cust 1, Jansen 64, Melo 53.

PITCHING

PITCHING	W	L	ERA	G	GS	CG	SV	IP	H	R	ER	BB	SO	AVG	B	T	HT	WT	DOB	1st Yr	Resides
Albertus, Roberto	3	2	2.39	16	5	0	2	60	46	20	16	13	56	.204	L	L	6-4	190	11-14-81	1998	San Nicholaas, Aruba
Belicic, Adam	0	2	4.78	21	0	0	1	26	31	18	14	16	22	.279	R	L	6-1	195	11-17-78	2000	Harrisburg, Pa.
Boyer, Blaine	4	5	4.32	13	12	0	0	50	48	35	24	19	57	.250	R	R	6-3	195	7-11-81	2000	Marietta, Ga.
Capellan, Jose	0	0	1.72	3	3	0	0	15	12	7	3	4	25	.000	R	R	6-3	175	1-13-81	1998	Cotui, D.R.
Cetani, Bryan	1	1	6.11	15	0	0	2	18	29	20	12	17	13	.358	L	L	6-4	200	10-9-81	1999	Ukiah, Calif.
Digby, Bryan	3	5	3.38	12	12	1	0	61	52	33	23	32	49	.222	R	R	6-2	190	12-31-81	2000	Peachtree City, Ga.
Ewin, Ryan	2	2	4.54	10	9	0	0	38	36	20	19	13	39	.251	R	R	6-7	180	11-15-81	1999	Spring Valley, Calif.
Fries, Tim	2	3	4.91	24	0	0	5	37	39	22	20	20	54	.267	R	R	6-2	195	4-2-80	2001	Evans, Ga.
Mabry, Barry	3	3	3.20	20	2	0	0	56	60	26	20	18	55	.269	R	R	6-5	185	11-2-81	2000	Spartanburg, S.C.
Merricks, Matt	4	5	2.79	12	11	0	0	58	42	19	18	18	78	.208	L	L	5-11	180	8-6-82	2000	Oxnard, Calif.
Roberts, Ralph	0	1	1.80	17	0	0	6	20	18	6	4	4	31	.243	R	R	6-2	208	3-28-80	2001	Cherryville, N.C.
Rogers, Jon	0	1	2.16	6	0	0	1	8	5	7	2	2	11	.156	R	R	6-1	180	7-2-81	2000	Midland, Texas
Sokoll, Adam	2	3	6.21	22	0	0	0	29	21	28	20	19	19	.196	R	R	6-4	195	7-26-79	2001	Clarkston, Mich.
Wray, Fred	3	0	6.00	17	0	0	0	33	30	26	22	17	25	.243	R	R	6-6	215	8-13-79	2001	Durham, N.C.
Wright, Matt	3	5	3.72	14	14	1	0	73	60	40	30	26	89	.221	R	R	6-4	220	3-13-82	2000	Lorena, Texas

KISSIMMEE

Rookie

GULF COAST LEAGUE

BATTING

BATTING	AVG	G	AB	R	H	2B	3B	HR	RBI	BB	SO	SB	CS	SLG	OBP	B	T	HT	WT	DOB	1st Yr	Resides
Albert, Luke	.211	38	114	5	24	3	0	1	12	10	30	0	1	.263	.280	B	R	6-2	205	4-25-79	2001	Hollywood, Fla.
Aristigueta, Darwin	.162	37	117	11	19	4	0	1	8	8	31	3	0	.222	.233	B	R	6-0	180	9-26-82	1999	Guatire, Venez.
Barthel, Cole	.217	45	152	14	33	1	0	0	12	14	27	8	3	.224	.302	R	R	6-2	208	8-11-82	2001	Decatur, Ala.
Boscan, Jean	.333	8	30	5	10	4	0	0	6	0	3	0	1	.467	.323	R	R	6-2	160	12-26-79	1996	Maracaibo, Venez.
Burrus, Josh	.193	52	197	24	38	8	2	3	19	14	40	10	2	.299	.271	R	R	5-11	185	8-20-83	2001	Marietta, Ga.
Cust, Kevin	.269	17	52	6	14	2	0	2	5	6	14	1	0	.423	.356	R	R	6-1	200	9-9-81	2000	Flemington, N.J.
Duran, Carlos	.304	54	204	35	62	10	3	2	17	12	30	16	4	.412	.349	L	L	6-1	165	12-27-82	1999	Barquisimeto, Venez.
Farmer, John	.000	2	6	0	0	0	0	0	0	0	2	0	0	.000	.000	R	R	6-0	175	3-30-79	2001	Eugene, Ore.
Guzman, Carlos	.266	40	139	20	37	7	0	3	23	15	44	3	2	.381	.352	B	R	5-9	155	3-16-82	1999	Santo Domingo, D.R.
Infante, Franklin	.242	43	128	10	31	7	2	0	16	1	38	3	0	.328	.256	R	R	6-0	175	2-11-83	2000	Santiago, D.R.
Morales, Michael	.163	16	49	8	8	2	0	0	4	4	4	0	1	.204	.333	R	R	6-1	185	4-4-79	2001	West Palm Beach, Fla.
Partridge, Dominique	.205	26	83	13	17	2	0	2	9	6	26	3	1	.301	.272	R	R	6-2	215	7-28-83	2001	Palmetto, Ga.
Polo, Roberto	.203	38	118	13	24	3	0	3	13	10	33	5	2	.305	.266	R	R	6-2	160	7-24-82	1999	San Pedro de Macoris, D.R.
Ruelas, Alonzo	.276	47	134	16	37	10	0	2	12	12	16	6	0	.396	.347	R	R	6-1	195	4-2-81	2001	El Paso, Texas
Salas, Jose	.250	3	4	0	1	0	0	0	0	0	0	0	0	.250	.250	B	R	6-3	210	2-16-82	1998	Caracas, Venez.
Santana, Roberto	.225	48	138	15	31	4	0	1	14	11	21	1	0	.275	.288	L	R	5-11	180	3-2-83	2001	Las Piedras, P.R.
Strong, Brian	.283	37	106	11	30	3	1	3	16	6	24	1	5	.415	.333	L	R	6-3	205	7-14-79	2001	Glade Hill, Va.
Tejero, Armando	.098	20	51	2	5	2	0	0	0	11	19	1	0	.137	.258	L	L	6-3	180	7-11-82	2000	Santa Isabel, P.R.
White, Dean	.143	2	7	1	1	0	0	0	0	1	2	1	0	.143	.250	R	R	6-2	180	2-12-83	2001	Perth, Australia
Woods, Ahmad	.173	38	110	18	19	4	1	1	8	6	42	12	5	.255	.233	R	R	6-2	185	11-27-82	2001	Stone Mountain, Ga.

GAMES BY POSITION: C—Albert 22, Boscan 7, Cust 1, Ruelas 39, Salas 2, Strong 8. **1B**—Cust 8, Santana 44, Tejero 18. **2B**—Aristigueta 13, Farmer 2, Infante 30, Morales 16, Santana 1, Strong 5. **3B**—Aristigueta 119, Barthel 43, Infante 1, Santana 1, Strong 1. **SS**—Burrus 48, Infante 12, White 2. **OF**—Duran 53, Guzman 40, Partridge 25, Polo 35, Santana 2, Woods 38.

PITCHING

PITCHING	W	L	ERA	G	GS	CG	SV	IP	H	R	ER	BB	SO	AVG	B	T	HT	WT	DOB	1st Yr	Resides
Aguilar, Ray	3	1	1.50	7	5	0	0	30	18	5	5	6	42	.166	B	L	5-11	200	1-18-80	1999	South El Monte, Calif.
Almeida, Brian	0	1	2.25	2	0	0	0	4	2	1	1	2	3	.153	L	R	6-5	210	7-26-81	2000	Englewood, Fla.
Alvarez, Juan	3	1	1.73	11	6	0	0	42	36	15	8	13	39	.223	L	L	6-0	170	5-6-82	1999	Coahuila, Mexico
Arteaga, Francisco	0	1	2.41	18	0	0	5	34	20	13	9	13	30	.182	R	R	5-11	170	10-4-81	2001	Los Angeles, Calif.
Cooper, Dexter	2	1	4.66	12	1	0	0	19	19	19	10	18	21	.236	R	R	6-2	210	7-14-82	2001	Acworth, Ga.
Davies, Kyle	4	2	2.25	12	9	1	0	56	47	17	14	8	53	.223	R	R	6-2	190	9-9-83	2001	McDonough, Ga.
Douglas, Rod	0	2	7.71	4	0	0	0	7	8	6	6	7	9	.285	R	R	6-0	185	12-24-81	2000	Colmesneil, Texas
Ewin, Ryan	0	0	9.00	1	0	0	0	2	2	2	2	1	4	.400	R	R	6-7	180	10-5-81	1999	Spring Valley, Calif.
Furnald, Donnie	0	0	1.13	4	0	0	3	8	3	1	1	1	7	.125	R	R	6-3	210	12-2-79	2001	Alta Loma, Calif.
Lerew, Anthony	1	2	2.92	12	7	0	0	49	43	25	16	14	40	.237	L	R	6-3	215	10-28-82	2001	Wellsville, Pa.
Lopez, Gonzalo	5	4	2.45	12	11	0	0	59	44	19	16	10	69	.207	R	R	6-2	175	10-6-83	2000	Managua, Nicaragua
Machen, Mike	2	2	4.85	13	0	0	0	26	25	17	14	10	30	.242	R	R	6-4	190	10-5-81	2000	Mobile, Ala.
Mason, Robert	3	2	3.41	14	0	0	1	34	28	16	9	10	34	.223	L	L	5-11	190	9-5-83	2001	Walnut, Calif.
Mathiesen, Ryan	0	2	3.00	22	0	0	10	27	25	9	9	5	38	.238	R	R	6-1	200	2-13-81	2001	Corvallis, Ore.
McBride, Macay	4	4	3.76	13	11	0	0	55	51	30	23	23	67	.247	L	L	5-11	180	10-24-82	2001	Sylvania, Ga.
McClendon, Matt	0	0	1.35	3	0	0	0	7	3	2	1	10	15	.130	R	R	6-6	220	10-13-77	1999	Orlando, Fla.
McGlinchy, Kevin	0	0	0.00	2	2	0	0	2	1	0	0	0	2	.166	R	R	6-5	220	6-28-77	1996	Ocala, Fla.
Paz, Jackson	2	1	3.58	12	0	0	0	33	40	19	13	7	31	.291	R	L	6-1	160	7-10-82	1999	Maracaibo, Venez.
Sexton, Joey	0	0	0.00	2	0	0	0	2	0	0	0	2	5	.000	R	R	6-2	210	4-13-82	2001	Savannah, Ga.
Sobkowiak, Scott	0	0	1.29	2	2	0	0	7	4	2	1	1	11	.153	R	R	6-5	230	10-26-77	1998	Loveland, Ohio
Yankosky, L.J.	1	1	1.93	4	3	0	0	14	10	3	3	1	11	.204	R	R	6-2	208	2-1-75	1998	Springfield, Va.

BALTIMORE ORIOLES

BY ROCH KUBATKO

An emphasis on youth was supposed to send the Orioles in a new direction in 2001. So how did they wind up in the same old place?

They finished fourth in the American League East for the fourth consecutive season. The team's 63-98 record was 10 games worse than 2000 and the worst since a 54-107 in 1988. Not exactly the kind of sendoff they intended for Cal Ripken, who retired after 21 years with the team.

There was lots of blame to spread around.

September's expanded roster did nothing to counter a series of injuries that punched holes in manager Mike Hargrove's rotation, lineup and bench. The most damaging was the loss of No. 1 starter Pat Hengten, a free agent who went 2-3, 3.47 and didn't pitch after May 16. He underwent ligament-transplant surgery on his right elbow and might not pitch again for the Orioles after signing a two-year contract.

Shortstop Mike Bordick, another veteran who was supposed to ease the club's growing pains, also missed most of the season. First baseman David Segui went on the disabled list twice and appeared in one game after Aug. 23. Righthander Sidney Ponson, still with undelivered potential, succumbed to a sore arm after going 5-10, 4.94.

The Orioles also endured a season-ending hand injury to Rule 5 pick Jay Gibbons, another reason for an offensive brownout that contributed to their 23-51 second half. Their .248 batting average was the league's worst.

The problems began at the top, with their leadoff hitters batting .192. Brady Anderson struggled all season to reach .200. Hargrove eventually lowered him in the order and brought in unproven players like Jerry Hairston, Luis Matos and Tim Raines Jr. He didn't have a true No. 3 or 4 hitter, though veteran Jeff Conine filled in admirably in both slots (.311-14-97) and was named the team's MVP.

Hargrove used four closers. Rookie righthander Ryan Kohlmeier was optioned to Triple-A Rochester before June. Another rookie, righthander Willis Roberts, audi-

Jeff Conine — MORRIS FOSTOFF

John Stephens — RODGER WOOD

ORGANIZATION STATISTICS

PLAYERS OF THE YEAR

MAJOR LEAGUE: Jeff Conine, of
After the career-ending injury to slugger Albert Belle, Conine was the rock in the Baltimore lineup in 2001. He hit .311-14-97 and led the Orioles in runs, RBIs, hits, average and walks.

MINOR LEAGUE: John Stephens, rhp
The 21-year-old Australian was one of the few bright spots in the Orioles system in 2001. He went 11-4, 1.84 at Bowie and led the Double-A Eastern League in ERA.

tioned over the final month but the Orioles rarely had a late-inning lead. Lefthander Buddy Groom emerged as the saves leader (11).

Ripken provided a nice distraction from all the losses. He went on an offensive tear after announcing his retirement on June 19, homering in six cities and becoming the oldest player to be named MVP in the All-Star Game. A 2-for-48 slump left him at .239-14-68 as the season—and an era—drew to a close.

Another sentimental touch was provided when the Orioles traded for Tim Raines Sr. during the final week, creating the second father-son teammates in baseball history.

With little to play for over the second half, the Orioles used the remaining months to evaluate their young pitching talent. The back end of the bullpen had the power arms of Jorge Julio and Kris Foster. Rick Bauer and Sean Douglass made cases for their inclusion in the 2002 rotation. Jason Johnson should be a lock after leading the staff with 10 wins. The biggest disappointment may have been Jose Mercedes, who led the club with 14 victories in 2000 but went 8-17, 5.82.

The search for victories didn't prove more fruitful at the highest levels of the farm system. Rochester finished 60-84 and 32 games behind Buffalo in the Northern Division of the International League. The Red Wings, who sent 15 players to the Orioles, again led the International League in errors with 197.

Double-A Bowie was 59-82 in the Eastern League and manager Dave Machemer was dismissed after the season. Class A Frederick qualified for the playoffs as the wild card in the Carolina League's Northern Division, but was swept in the first round. Bluefield was crowned champion of the Rookie-level Appalachian League, despite finishing the regular season with a .500 record, fourth-best in the 10-team league.

ORGANIZATION LEADERS

BATTING
*AVG	Willie Harris, Bowie	.305
R	B.J. Littleton, Delmarva	84
H	Franky Figueroa, Bowie	160
TB	Jose Leon, Rochester/Bowie	237
2B	Doug Gredvig, Frederick	40
3B	B.J. Littleton, Delmarva	18
HR	Calvin Pickering, Rochester	21
RBI	Calvin Pickering, Rochester	98
BB	Calvin Pickering, Rochester	64
SO	Calvin Pickering, Rochester	149
SB	Willie Harris., Bowie	54
	Tim Raines Jr., Rochester/Bowie	54

PITCHING
W	John Stephens, Rochester/Bowie	13
L	Mike Paradis, Bowie	13
#ERA	Erik Bedard, Frederick/GCL Orioles	2.20
G	Lesli Brea, Rochester	63
CG	Matt Schwager, Delmarva	4
SV	Jayme Sperring, Delmarva	26
IP	John Stephens, Rochester/Bowie	190
BB	Mike Paradis, Bowie	62
SO	John Stephens, Rochester/Bowie	191

*Minimum 250 At-Bats #Minimum 75 Innings

BALTIMORE ORIOLES

Manager: Mike Hargrove

2001 Record: 63-98, .391 (4th, AL East)

BATTING	AVG	G	AB	R	H	2B	3B	HR	RBI	BB	SO	SB	CS	SLG	OBP	B	T	HT	WT	DOB	1st Yr	Resides
Anderson, Brady	.202	131	430	50	87	12	3	8	45	60	77	12	4	.300	.311	L	L	6-1	202	1-18-64	1985	Lake Tahoe, Nev.
Batista, Tony	.266	84	308	41	82	16	5	12	42	19	47	5	1	.468	.305	R	R	6-0	205	12-9-73	1992	Valverde, D.R.
2-team (72 Toronto)	.238	156	579	70	138	27	6	25	87	32	113	5	2	.435	.280							
Bigbie, Larry	.229	47	131	15	30	6	0	2	11	17	42	4	1	.321	.318	L	L	6-4	190	11-4-77	1999	Hobart, Ind.
Blake, Casey	.133	6	15	2	2	0	0	1	2	1	4	2	0	.333	.188	R	R	6-2	205	8-23-73	1996	Indianola, Iowa
2-team (13 Minnesota)	.243	19	37	3	9	1	0	1	4	4	12	3	0	.351	.317							
Bordick, Mike	.249	58	229	32	57	13	0	7	30	17	36	9	3	.397	.314	R	R	5-11	175	7-21-65	1986	Ruxton, Md.
Conine, Jeff	.311	139	524	75	163	23	2	14	97	64	75	12	8	.443	.386	R	R	6-1	220	6-27-66	1988	Weston, Fla.
DeShields, Delino	.197	58	188	29	37	8	2	3	21	31	42	11	1	.309	.312	L	R	6-1	175	1-15-69	1987	Fairburn, Ga.
Fordyce, Brook	.209	95	292	30	61	18	0	5	19	21	56	1	2	.322	.268	R	R	6-0	190	5-7-70	1989	Jensen Beach, Fla.
Gibbons, Jay	.236	73	225	27	53	10	0	15	36	17	39	0	1	.480	.301	L	L	6-0	200	3-2-77	1998	Lakewood, Calif.
Gil, Geronimo	.293	17	58	3	17	2	0	0	6	5	7	0	0	.328	.369	R	R	6-2	195	8-7-75	1996	Oaxaca, Mexico
Hairston, Jerry	.233	159	532	63	124	25	5	8	47	44	73	29	11	.344	.305	R	R	5-10	172	5-29-76	1997	Tucson, Ariz.
Harris, Willie	.125	9	24	3	3	1	0	0	0	0	7	0	0	.167	.125	L	R	5-9	175	6-22-78	1999	Cairo, Ga.
Kingsale, Eugene	.000	3	4	0	0	0	0	0	0	0	2	1	1	.000	.000	B	R	6-3	190	8-20-76	1994	Oranjestad, Aruba
Kinkade, Mike	.275	61	160	19	44	5	0	4	16	14	31	2	1	.381	.345	R	R	6-1	210	5-6-73	1995	Pullman, Wash.
Lunar, Fernando	.246	64	167	8	41	7	0	0	16	7	32	0	0	.287	.287	R	R	6-1	190	5-25-77	1994	Anaco Aneoa, Venez.
Matos, Luis	.214	31	98	16	21	7	0	4	12	11	30	7	0	.408	.300	R	R	6-0	179	10-30-78	1996	Bayamon, P.R.
Mora, Melvin	.250	128	436	49	109	28	0	7	48	41	91	11	4	.362	.329	R	R	5-10	180	2-2-72	1991	Naquanqua, Venez.
Myers, Greg	.270	25	74	11	20	2	0	4	18	8	17	0	0	.459	.341	L	R	6-2	225	4-14-66	1984	Riverside, Calif.
Raines, Tim Sr.	.273	4	11	1	3	0	0	1	5	0	3	0	0	.545	.250	B	R	5-8	195	9-16-59	1977	Heathrow, Fla.
Raines, Tim Jr.	.174	7	23	6	4	2	0	0	3	8	3	0	0	.261	.269	B	R	5-10	183	8-31-79	1998	Heathrow, Fla.
Richard, Chris	.265	136	483	74	128	31	3	15	61	45	100	11	9	.435	.335	L	L	6-2	185	6-7-74	1995	San Diego, Calif.
Ripken, Cal	.239	128	477	43	114	16	0	14	68	26	63	0	2	.361	.276	R	R	6-4	220	8-24-60	1978	Reisterstown, Md.
Roberts, Brian	.253	75	273	42	69	12	3	2	17	13	36	12	3	.341	.284	B	R	5-9	170	10-9-77	1999	Chapel Hill, N.C.
Segui, David	.301	82	292	48	88	18	1	10	46	49	61	1	1	.473	.406	B	L	6-1	202	7-19-66	1988	Kansas City, Kan.

PITCHING	W	L	ERA	G	GS	CG	SV	IP	H	R	ER	BB	SO	AVG	B	T	HT	WT	DOB	1st Yr	Resides
Bale, John	1	0	3.04	14	0	0	0	27	18	14	9	17	21	.193	L	L	6-4	205	5-22-74	1996	Crestview, Fla.
Bauer, Rick	0	5	4.64	6	6	0	0	33	35	22	17	9	16	.265	R	R	6-6	212	1-10-77	1997	Eagle, Idaho
Brea, Lesli	0	0	18.00	2	0	0	0	2	6	4	4	3	0	.545	R	R	5-11	170	10-12-78	1996	Phoenix, Ariz.
Douglass, Sean	2	1	5.31	4	4	0	0	20	21	12	12	11	17	.259	R	R	6-6	200	4-28-79	1997	Lancaster, Calif.
Foster, Kris	0	0	2.70	7	0	0	0	10	9	4	3	8	8	.230	R	R	6-1	200	8-30-74	1992	Lehigh Acres, Fla.
Groom, Buddy	1	4	3.55	70	0	0	11	66	64	28	26	9	54	.251	L	L	6-2	208	7-10-65	1987	Red Oak, Texas
Hentgen, Pat	2	3	3.47	9	9	1	0	62	51	25	24	19	33	.220	R	R	6-2	195	11-13-68	1986	Palm Harbor, Fla.
Johnson, Jason	10	12	4.09	32	32	2	0	196	194	109	89	77	114	.257	R	R	6-6	235	10-27-73	1992	Henderson, Nev.
Julio, Jorge	1	1	3.80	18	0	0	0	21	25	13	9	9	22	.287	R	R	6-1	190	3-3-79	1996	Caracas, Venez.
Kohlmeier, Ryan	1	2	7.30	34	1	0	6	41	48	33	33	19	29	.290	R	R	6-2	195	6-25-77	1996	Cottonwood Falls, Kan.
Maduro, Calvin	5	6	4.23	22	12	0	0	94	83	44	44	36	51	.239	R	R	6-0	180	9-5-74	1992	Santa Cruz, Aruba
McElroy, Chuck	1	2	5.36	18	5	0	0	45	49	29	27	28	22	.269	L	L	6-0	205	10-1-67	1986	Lindale, Texas
Mercedes, Jose	8	17	5.82	33	31	2	0	184	219	125	119	63	123	.293	R	R	6-1	180	3-5-71	1992	La Romana, D.R.
Mills, Alan	1	1	9.64	15	0	0	0	14	20	15	15	11	9	.333	R	R	6-1	195	10-18-66	1986	Lakeland, Fla.
Paronto, Chad	1	3	5.00	24	0	0	0	27	33	24	15	15	16	.289	R	R	6-5	255	7-28-75	1996	North Haverhill, N.H.
Parrish, John	1	2	6.14	16	1	0	0	22	22	17	15	17	20	.255	L	L	5-11	181	11-26-77	1996	Lancaster, Pa.
Ponson, Sidney	5	10	4.94	23	23	3	0	138	161	83	76	37	84	.289	R	R	6-1	220	11-2-76	1994	Noord, Aruba
Roberts, Willis	9	10	4.91	46	18	1	6	132	142	75	72	55	95	.274	R	R	6-3	175	6-19-75	1992	San Cristobal, D.R.
Ryan, B.J.	2	4	4.25	61	0	0	2	53	47	31	25	30	54	.232	L	L	6-6	230	12-28-75	1998	Benton, La.
Towers, Josh	8	10	4.49	24	20	1	0	140	165	74	70	16	58	.296	R	R	6-1	165	2-26-77	1996	Port Hueneme, Calif.
Trombley, Mike	3	4	3.46	50	0	0	6	55	38	23	21	27	45	.200	R	R	6-2	204	4-14-67	1989	Fort Myers, Fla.
Wasdin, John	1	1	4.17	26	0	0	0	50	54	25	23	16	47	.276	R	R	6-2	195	8-5-72	1993	Jacksonville, Fla.

FIELDING

Catcher	PCT	G	PO	A	E	DP	PB
Fordyce	.983	95	541	30	10	7	8
Gil	.985	17	121	10	2	1	5
Kinkade	1.000	2	11	1	0	0	0
Lunar	.987	64	267	32	4	3	2
Myers	1.000	8	41	4	0	0	0

First Base	PCT	G	PO	A	E	DP
Blake	.967	5	29	0	1	3
Conine	.994	80	646	45	4	61
Gibbons	1.000	7	36	1	0	3
Kinkade	1.000	3	3	0	0	0
Richard	1.000	18	127	9	0	10
Segui	.983	65	487	33	9	49

Second Base	PCT	G	PO	A	E	DP
Hairston	.976	156	326	458	19	93

	PCT	G	PO	A	E	DP
Mora	.500	1	0	1	1	0
B. Roberts	.950	12	13	25	2	6

Third Base	PCT	G	PO	A	E	DP
Batista	.934	29	18	53	5	5
Blake	.800	5	1	3	1	0
Conine	1.000	17	15	24	0	0
Kinkade	1.000	10	8	11	0	0
Ripken	.956	111	97	209	14	23

Shortstop	PCT	G	PO	A	E	DP
Batista	.990	20	33	63	1	11
Bordick	.977	58	107	146	6	28
Mora	.965	43	69	125	7	21
B. Roberts	.939	51	84	131	14	25

Outfield	PCT	G	PO	A	E	DP
Anderson	.988	120	239	8	3	4
Bigbie	1.000	40	71	2	0	1
Conine	1.000	36	85	2	0	0
DeShields	.967	47	87	2	3	0
Gibbons	1.000	28	62	3	0	0
Harris	1.000	8	16	1	0	1
Kingsale	1.000	1	1	0	0	0
Kinkade	.962	32	50	1	2	0
Matos	.985	31	65	2	1	2
Mora	.987	88	218	4	3	1
Raines Sr.	1.000	3	7	0	0	0
Raines Jr.	1.000	7	12	0	0	0
Richard	1.000	96	228	6	0	2

Director, Minor League Operations: Don Buford

Class	Farm Team	League	W	L	Pct.	Finish*	Manager	First Yr.
AAA	Rochester (N.Y.) Red Wings	International	60	84	.417	14th (14)	Andy Etchebarren	1961
AA	Bowie (Md.) Baysox	Eastern	59	82	.418	11th (12)	Dave Machemer	1993
A#	Frederick (Md.) Keys	Carolina	70	69	.504	5th (8)	Dave Cash	1989
A	Delmarva (Md.) Shorebirds	South Atlantic	61	79	.436	13th (16)	Joe Ferguson	1997
Rookie#	Bluefield (W.Va.) Orioles	Appalachian	33	33	.500	+4th (10)	Joe Almaraz	1958
Rookie	Sarasota (Fla.) Orioles	Gulf Coast	22	34	.393	t-11th (14)	Jesus Alfaro	1991

*Finish in overall standings (No. of teams in league)   #Advanced level   +League champion

ROCHESTER   Class AAA

INTERNATIONAL LEAGUE

BATTING	AVG	G	AB	R	H	2B	3B	HR	RBI	BB	SO	SB	CS	SLG	OBP	B	T	HT	WT	DOB	1st Yr	Resides
Almonte, Wady	.215	87	316	25	68	8	4	3	31	16	54	7	3	.294	.260	R	R	6-0	200	4-20-75	1993	Higuey, D.R.
Bigbie, Larry	.310	10	42	5	13	4	0	1	2	3	8	1	1	.476	.356	L	L	6-4	190	11-4-77	1999	Hobart, Ind.
Brinkley, Darryl	.306	9	36	4	11	3	0	2	7	0	3	1	1	.556	.308	R	R	5-11	210	12-23-68	1995	Stamford, Conn.
Buford, Damon	.255	39	149	20	38	10	0	4	12	22	26	3	1	.403	.358	R	R	5-10	180	6-12-70	1990	Dallas, Texas
Casimiro, Carlos	.235	48	166	21	39	9	1	4	14	7	41	5	1	.373	.274	R	R	5-11	179	11-8-76	1994	San Pedro de Macoris, D.R.
Charles, Frank	.242	68	240	15	58	12	0	1	24	11	56	1	1	.304	.279	R	R	6-4	210	2-23-69	1991	Van Nuys, Calif.
Coffie, Ivanon	.267	56	206	33	55	10	1	8	35	15	47	3	0	.442	.317	L	R	6-1	192	5-16-77	1995	Curacao, Netherlands Antilles
Garabito, Eddy	.267	127	517	65	138	29	6	3	34	31	76	24	11	.364	.311	B	R	5-8	172	12-7-78	1996	Manrreza, D.R.
Garcia, Guillermo	.053	5	19	1	1	0	0	0	2	5	0	0	0	.053	.143	R	R	6-3	215	4-4-72	1990	Santiago, D.R.
Gil, Geronimo	.268	23	82	7	22	6	1	2	14	0	23	0	0	.439	.271	R	R	6-2	195	8-7-75	1996	Oaxaca, Mexico
Hughes, Bobby	.000	1	3	0	0	0	0	0	0	0	0	0	0	.000	.000	R	R	6-4	229	3-10-71	1992	North Hollywood, Calif.
Kingsale, Eugene	.201	64	244	31	49	12	2	0	15	26	44	16	2	.266	.283	B	R	6-3	190	8-20-76	1994	Oranjestad, Aruba
Leon, Jose	.279	109	416	54	116	20	4	12	53	25	96	7	3	.433	.322	R	R	6-0	175	12-8-76	1994	Cayey, P.R.
Lopez-Cao, Mike	.000	2	1	0	0	0	0	0	0	0	0	0	0	.000	.500	L	R	5-9	187	8-14-75	1997	Miami, Fla.
Martinez, Eddy	.271	90	314	42	85	14	1	7	33	21	66	7	0	.389	.324	R	R	6-2	173	10-23-77	1995	San Pedro de Macoris, D.R.
McDonald, Darnell	.238	104	391	37	93	19	2	2	35	29	75	13	9	.312	.291	R	R	5-11	201	11-17-78	1997	Glendale, Colo.
Morales, Willie	.232	52	164	18	38	7	0	1	11	5	32	2	1	.293	.256	R	R	5-11	180	9-7-72	1993	Tucson, Ariz.
Mulligan, Sean	.333	7	27	5	9	2	0	1	4	1	5	0	1	.519	.357	R	R	6-2	205	4-25-70	1991	Diamond Bar, Calif.
Pickering, Calvin	.282	131	461	62	130	25	0	21	98	64	149	0	1	.473	.379	L	L	6-5	290	9-29-76	1995	Temple Terrace, Fla.
Raines, Tim Jr.	.256	40	133	19	34	5	1	2	12	11	30	11	3	.353	.313	B	R	5-10	183	8-31-79	1998	Heathrow, Fla.
Reed, Keith	.311	20	74	11	23	7	1	2	11	5	14	1	1	.514	.354	R	R	6-4	215	10-8-78	1999	Yarmouth Port, Mass.
Roberts, Brian	.267	44	161	16	43	4	1	1	12	28	22	23	3	.323	.376	B	R	5-9	170	10-9-77	1999	Chapel Hill, N.C.
Rust, Brian	.204	55	186	24	38	12	0	9	29	22	50	4	0	.414	.302	R	R	6-2	205	8-1-74	1995	Portland, Ore.
Sisco, Steve	.237	92	338	38	80	17	0	6	29	28	66	6	5	.340	.302	R	R	5-10	190	12-2-69	1992	Thousand Oaks, Calif.
Vinas, Julio	.218	38	142	17	31	5	1	3	21	13	23	0	0	.331	.283	R	R	6-1	205	2-14-73	1991	Hialeah, Fla.
Woods, Kenny	.240	26	75	6	18	3	1	0	8	13	7	4	2	.307	.352	R	R	5-10	175	8-2-70	1992	Los Angeles, Calif.

PITCHING	W	L	ERA	G	GS	CG	SV	IP	H	R	ER	BB	SO	AVG	B	T	HT	WT	DOB	1st Yr	Resides
Bale, John	1	1	2.05	9	7	0	0	31	31	8	7	5	41	.262	L	L	6-4	205	5-22-74	1996	Crestview, Fla.
Bauer, Rick	10	4	3.89	19	18	1	0	113	119	63	49	28	89	.263	R	R	6-6	212	1-10-77	1997	Eagle, Idaho
Bechler, Steve	1	1	15.95	2	2	0	0	7	14	14	13	5	6	.358	R	R	6-2	207	11-18-79	1998	Medford, Ore.
Brea, Lesli	2	6	3.83	63	0	0	1	82	80	44	35	35	98	.248	R	R	5-11	170	10-12-78	1996	Phoenix, Ariz.
Brown, Derek	2	1	8.68	9	0	0	0	19	25	18	18	6	14	.316	R	R	6-1	184	7-23-76	1994	Clear Spring, Md.
Douglass, Sean	8	9	3.49	27	27	0	0	162	160	79	63	61	156	.251	R	R	6-5	200	4-28-79	1997	Lancaster, Calif.
Felix, Miguel	0	1	11.57	1	1	0	0	5	5	6	6	3	3	.263	R	R	6-3	180	12-30-76	1994	La Romana, D.R.
Foster, Kris	0	1	5.40	9	0	0	6	10	11	8	6	6	11	.289	R	R	6-1	200	8-30-74	1992	Lehigh Acres, Fla.
Hamilton, Jimmy	0	3	4.53	36	1	0	1	56	58	29	28	27	49	.274	L	L	6-5	205	8-1-75	1996	Weyers Cave, Va.
Huisman, Rick	0	1	6.35	15	0	0	1	17	24	13	12	9	13	.328	R	R	6-3	210	5-17-69	1990	Holland, Mich.
Julio, Jorge	1	2	3.74	34	0	0	12	43	39	27	18	19	48	.232	R	R	6-1	190	3-3-79	1996	Caracas, Venez.
Kohlmeier, Ryan	1	4	2.36	14	7	0	4	42	36	15	11	8	28	.226	R	R	6-1	200	6-25-77	1996	Cottonwood Falls, Kan.
Lakman, Jason	1	0	3.42	19	0	0	1	26	32	13	10	9	12	.304	R	R	6-4	220	10-17-76	1995	Seattle, Wash.
Maduro, Calvin	2	7	4.03	12	11	1	0	67	61	37	30	22	48	.238	R	R	6-0	180	9-5-74	1992	Santa Cruz, Aruba
Paronto, Chad	3	3	4.57	33	0	0	1	43	44	28	22	24	39	.263	R	R	6-5	225	7-28-75	1996	North Haverhill, N.H.
Parrish, John	7	7	3.52	26	19	1	0	133	115	68	52	51	126	.231	L	L	5-11	181	11-26-77	1996	Lancaster, Pa.
Pina, Rafael	1	2	2.48	13	6	1	0	40	45	17	11	12	30	.284	R	R	6-1	170	8-16-71	1991	Alta Loma, Calif.
Shumaker, Anthony	8	7	3.96	53	0	0	4	73	70	35	32	31	53	.255	L	L	6-5	219	5-14-73	1995	Kokomo, Ind.
Snyder, Matt	0	0	4.91	9	0	0	0	11	13	8	6	10	9	.302	R	R	5-11	201	7-7-74	1995	Newtown, Pa.
Spurgeon, Jay	3	5	4.55	15	15	1	0	87	85	48	44	27	61	.253	R	R	6-6	211	7-5-76	1997	Coarsegold, Calif.
Stephens, John	2	5	4.03	9	9	0	0	58	52	31	26	19	61	.236	R	R	6-1	200	11-15-79	1996	Berala, Australia
Towers, Josh	3	1	3.51	6	6	1	0	41	40	18	16	8	27	.254	R	R	6-1	165	2-26-77	1996	Port Hueneme, Calif.
Wasdin, John	2	1	3.98	5	3	0	0	20	27	9	9	5	20	.321	R	R	6-2	195	8-5-72	1993	Jacksonville, Fla.
Wilson, Jeff	2	11	6.05	28	12	1	0	100	118	73	67	42	56	.289	R	L	6-2	180	5-30-76	1997	Greensboro, N.C.

FIELDING

Catcher	PCT	G	PO	A	E	DP	PB
Charles	.971	68	508	37	16	4	6
Gil	.986	23	185	22	3	2	6
Hughes	1.000	1	1	0	0	0	0
Lopez-Cao	1.000	2	8	0	0	0	0
Morales	.990	52	359	25	4	2	6
Mulligan	.942	7	48	1	3	1	1

First Base	PCT	G	PO	A	E	DP
Charles	1.000	1	6	1	0	0
Coffie	.934	12	91	8	7	11

	PCT	G	PO	A	E	DP
Garcia	1.000	2	18	1	0	0
Pickering	.986	69	516	31	8	52
Rust	.986	22	130	11	2	10
Sisco	.995	27	180	16	1	11
Vinas	.988	23	158	9	2	15

Second Base	PCT	G	PO	A	E	DP
Casimiro	1.000	1	2	1	0	1
Garabito	.956	106	209	247	21	58
Martinez	.917	5	10	12	2	6
Rust	1.000	2	2	2	0	0

	PCT	G	PO	A	E	DP
Sisco	.977	39	79	92	4	20

Third Base	PCT	G	PO	A	E	DP
Coffie	.932	16	15	26	3	5
Leon	.933	108	74	219	21	18
Rust	.933	3	11	1	1	1
Sisco	.922	17	14	45	5	5

Shortstop	PCT	G	PO	A	E	DP
Garabito	.927	24	29	60	7	15
Martinez	.926	83	119	155	22	33

	PCT	G	PO	A	E	DP
Roberts	.927	44	62	104	13	16

Outfield	PCT	G	PO	A	E	DP
Almonte	.984	80	169	11	3	0
Bigbie	1.000	10	20	2	0	0
Brinkley	1.000	7	11	0	0	0
Buford	1.000	32	86	0	0	0
Casimiro	.955	42	84	1	4	0
Kingsale	.965	57	134	2	5	1
McDonald	.957	101	264	5	12	1
Raines	.986	37	70	1	1	0
Reed	.933	19	28	0	2	0
Rust	1.000	22	37	0	0	0
Sisco	1.000	12	11	0	0	0
Woods	.968	22	53	7	2	1

BOWIE

Class AA

EASTERN LEAGUE

BATTING	AVG	G	AB	R	H	2B	3B	HR	RBI	BB	SO	SB	CS	SLG	OBP	B	T	HT	WT	DOB	1st Yr	Resides
Alley, Charles	.216	19	51	5	11	0	1	0	4	7	3	2	0	.255	.317	B	R	6-2	205	12-20-76	1995	Salisbury, Md.
Amezcua, Adan	.215	38	135	19	29	7	2	4	21	9	25	0	0	.385	.282	R	R	6-1	195	3-9-74	1993	Mazatlan, Mexico
Bigbie, Larry	.294	71	262	41	77	13	3	8	33	40	54	10	7	.458	.386	L	L	6-4	190	11-4-77	1999	Hobart, Ind.
Bordick, Mike	.250	1	4	0	1	0	0	0	0	0	1	0	0	.250	.250	R	R	5-11	175	7-21-65	1986	Ruxton, Md.
Briggs, Stoney	.244	55	164	25	40	5	1	8	22	24	40	2	2	.433	.349	R	R	6-3	215	12-26-71	1991	Seaford, Del.
Casimiro, Carlos	.222	80	302	22	67	15	1	4	24	18	81	2	5	.318	.268	R	R	5-11	179	11-8-76	1994	San Pedro de Macoris, D.R.
Del Rosario, Manny	.357	7	14	0	5	0	0	0	1	0	2	0	0	.357	.357	B	R	5-11	149	7-8-81	1997	Hato Mayor, D.R.
Figueroa, Franky	.300	137	534	61	160	32	0	14	72	21	138	0	4	.438	.326	R	R	6-6	239	2-9-77	1996	Hialeah, Fla.
Gibbs, Mark	.228	32	79	7	18	2	0	0	6	4	23	0	1	.253	.262	R	R	6-0	185	8-16-77	2000	Davidsonville, Md.
Goodell, Steve	.244	41	135	27	33	6	1	6	26	24	36	1	3	.437	.373	R	R	6-3	196	4-23-75	1995	Danville, Calif.
Hackett, Richard	.125	3	8	0	1	0	0	0	0	1	5	0	1	.125	.222	R	R	6-1	200	4-30-79	2001	Stockton, Calif.
Hammond, Joey	.278	102	342	49	95	13	2	1	26	42	59	2	3	.336	.365	R	R	6-1	184	10-27-77	1998	Frederick, Md.
Harris, Willie	.305	133	525	83	160	27	4	9	49	46	71	54	16	.423	.364	L	R	5-9	175	6-22-78	1999	Cairo, Ga.
Keylor, Cory	.143	3	7	0	1	1	0	0	1	0	2	0	0	.286	.125	L	R	6-3	200	8-25-79	2001	Westerville, Ohio
Leon, Jose	.358	26	95	18	34	9	1	4	20	8	21	1	1	.600	.413	R	R	6-0	175	12-8-76	1994	Cayey, P.R.
Lopez-Cao, Mike	.201	61	174	18	35	11	0	4	20	17	34	0	2	.333	.289	L	R	5-9	187	8-14-75	1997	Miami, Fla.
Martinez, Eddy	.287	32	122	21	35	1	0	1	10	14	31	5	3	.320	.360	R	R	6-2	173	10-23-77	1995	San Pedro de Macoris, D.R.
Matos, Luis	.304	13	46	6	14	5	0	1	8	5	7	0	1	.478	.385	R	R	6-0	179	10-30-78	1996	Bayamon, P.R.
McDonald, Darnell	.282	30	117	16	33	7	1	3	21	9	28	3	3	.436	.336	R	R	5-11	201	11-17-78	1997	Glendale, Colo.
McGee, Tom	.160	48	156	15	25	6	0	2	14	12	32	0	1	.237	.234	R	R	5-11	193	1-29-75	1997	Rialto, Calif.
Mulligan, Sean	.217	6	23	2	5	0	0	2	7	0	6	0	0	.478	.217	R	R	6-2	205	4-25-70	1991	Diamond Bar, Calif.
Ndungidi, Ntema	.212	104	339	34	72	17	1	3	35	37	90	3	5	.295	.296	L	R	6-2	199	3-15-79	1997	Montreal, Quebec
Phoenix, Wynter	.225	81	267	32	60	17	4	4	20	26	62	11	5	.363	.297	L	L	6-2	208	12-7-74	1996	El Cajon, Calif.
2-team (24 Portland)	.229	105	327	41	75	19	4	6	26	29	77	11	6	.367	.295							
Raines, Tim Jr.	.291	65	254	46	74	14	1	4	30	34	60	29	10	.402	.380	B	R	5-10	183	8-31-79	1998	Heathrow, Fla.
Reed, Keith	.254	18	67	7	17	3	0	1	8	6	10	2	2	.343	.315	R	R	6-4	215	10-8-78	1999	Yarmouth Port, Mass.
Roberts, Brian	.296	22	81	12	24	7	0	1	7	9	12	10	0	.420	.366	B	R	5-9	170	10-9-77	1999	Chapel Hill, N.C.
Rogers, Ed	.199	53	191	11	38	10	1	0	13	6	40	10	2	.262	.231	R	R	6-1	150	8-10-81	1997	San Pedro de Macoris, D.R.
Rust, Brian	.302	38	129	16	39	6	0	5	19	6	33	1	5	.465	.338	R	R	6-2	205	8-1-74	1995	Portland, Ore.
Ullery, Dave	.283	14	53	3	15	3	0	2	12	1	15	0	0	.453	.304	L	R	6-3	225	12-16-74	1997	Brazil, Ind.

PITCHING	W	L	ERA	G	GS	CG	SV	IP	H	R	ER	BB	SO	AVG	B	T	HT	WT	DOB	1st Yr	Resides
Babula, Shaun	2	4	3.26	28	0	0	2	39	37	18	14	12	27	.258	B	L	6-0	190	5-21-77	1999	Burlington, N.J.
Bauer, Rick	2	6	3.54	9	9	2	0	61	52	27	24	10	34	.227	R	R	6-6	212	1-10-77	1997	Eagle, Idaho
Bechler, Steve	3	5	3.08	12	12	2	0	79	63	31	27	15	58	.217	R	R	6-2	207	11-18-79	1998	Medford, Ore.
Brown, Derek	4	4	3.76	34	3	1	1	67	69	31	28	19	44	.263	R	R	6-1	184	7-23-76	1994	Clear Spring, Md.
Corcoran, Tim	1	0	0.77	7	0	0	0	12	4	1	1	3	13	.105	R	R	6-2	195	4-15-78	1997	Slaughter, La.
Eibey, Scott	0	3	6.13	38	0	0	0	69	84	53	47	22	48	.294	L	L	6-4	208	1-19-74	1995	Waterloo, Iowa
Falteisek, Steve	1	6	7.87	11	5	0	0	42	59	45	37	15	25	.333	R	R	6-2	200	1-28-72	1992	Floral Park, N.Y.
Felix, Miguel	5	5	4.39	15	14	1	0	80	73	44	39	32	58	.246	R	R	6-3	180	12-30-76	1994	La Romana, D.R.
Figueroa, Juan	3	10	4.89	18	17	1	0	99	126	63	54	26	52	.313	R	R	6-3	150	6-24-79	1996	Santo Domingo, D.R.
Fleming, Travis	0	0	9.00	3	0	0	0	4	15	11	4	0	2	.535	R	R	6-4	190	9-26-76	1999	McKinleyville, Calif.
Garcia, Sonny	1	3	5.72	5	5	1	0	28	33	22	18	9	21	.272	R	R	6-3	215	9-10-76	1998	Houston, Texas
Hale, Beau	1	5	5.11	12	12	0	0	62	74	39	35	15	40	.305	R	R	6-2	220	12-1-78	2000	Mauriceville, Texas
Hamilton, Jimmy	3	1	3.34	13	0	0	1	30	30	11	11	8	22	.275	L	L	6-3	205	8-1-75	1996	Weyers Cave, Va.
Julio, Jorge	0	0	0.73	12	0	0	7	12	5	1	1	2	14	.125	R	R	6-1	190	3-3-79	1996	Caracas, Venez.
Lakman, Jason	0	2	8.13	18	1	0	0	34	48	34	31	12	26	.335	R	R	6-4	220	10-17-76	1995	Seattle, Wash.
Mills, Alan	0	0	2.25	7	0	0	0	8	5	2	2	3	10	.178	R	R	6-1	195	10-18-66	1986	Lakeland, Fla.
Ormond, Rodney	0	0	21.60	1	0	0	0	2	4	4	4	1	0	.500	R	R	6-4	210	6-17-77	1999	Princeton, N.C.
Paradis, Mike	8	13	4.71	27	26	1	0	138	157	98	72	62	108	.279	R	R	6-3	190	5-3-78	1999	Clemson, S.C.
Pina, Rafael	0	1	2.08	4	0	0	0	9	6	3	2	1	5	.171	R	R	6-1	170	8-16-71	1991	Alta Loma, Calif.
Ponson, Sidney	0	0	0.00	1	1	0	0	4	3	0	0	1	2	.230	R	R	6-1	220	11-2-76	1994	Noord, Aruba
Rakers, Aaron	4	4	2.39	51	0	0	14	60	53	21	16	20	74	.227	R	R	6-3	205	1-22-77	1999	Trenton, Ill.
Rodriguez, Eddy	1	1	2.08	5	0	0	2	9	7	2	2	6	10	.241	R	R	6-1	170	8-8-81	1999	San Pedro de Macoris, D.R.
Sims, Ken	8	4	4.10	24	14	1	1	112	123	54	51	26	51	.283	R	R	6-4	215	7-24-75	1996	Union, S.C.
Stephens, John	11	4	1.84	18	17	3	0	132	95	32	27	21	130	.201	R	R	6-1	200	11-15-79	1996	Berala, Australia
Wilson, Jeff	1	1	3.97	5	5	0	0	34	32	19	15	9	31	.240	R	L	6-2	180	5-30-76	1997	Greensboro, N.C.

FIELDING

Catcher	PCT	G	PO	A	E	DP	PB
Alley	.967	16	109	9	4	1	1
Amezcua	.982	27	192	22	4	3	6
Lopez-Cao	.990	46	263	34	3	5	3
McGee	.994	46	284	46	2	2	5
Mulligan	1.000	6	34	3	0	0	1
Ullery	.979	6	40	7	1	1	2

First Base	PCT	G	PO	A	E	DP
F. Figueroa	.992	120	969	84	8	71
Gibbs	.000	1	0	0	0	0
Goodell	1.000	11	101	6	0	7
Hammond	1.000	1	1	0	0	0
Rust	1.000	9	69	8	0	6
Ullery	.978	5	40	4	1	3

Second Base	PCT	G	PO	A	E	DP
Del Rosario	.789	7	6	9	4	2
Gibbs	.963	20	32	46	3	11
Goodell	.714	2	1	4	2	0
Hammond	1.000	2	3	2	0	1
Harris	.979	90	212	212	9	56
Lopez-Cao	1.000	1	0	2	0	0
Martinez	.976	8	16	25	1	3
Roberts	.966	21	30	54	3	9

Third Base	PCT	G	PO	A	E	DP
Brown	1.000	1	2	2	0	0
Casimiro	.931	65	46	130	13	11
F. Figueroa	.857	5	1	5	1	0
Gibbs	.826	8	8	11	4	1
Hammond	.951	16	8	31	2	3
Leon	.879	24	18	33	7	3
Lopez-Cao	.600	3	1	2	2	0
Martinez	.927	16	9	29	3	3
McGee	1.000	2	1	0	0	0
Rust	.880	10	5	17	3	1
Ullery	1.000	4	2	4	0	0

Shortstop	PCT	G	PO	A	E	DP
Casimiro	.857	2	2	4	1	1
Gibbs	.857	3	3	3	1	1
Hammond	.957	78	106	204	14	36
Martinez	.880	9	5	17	3	3
Roberts	1.000	1	1	5	0	1
Rogers	.960	53	90	147	10	20

Outfield	PCT	G	PO	A	E	DP
Bigbie	.972	70	136	4	4	1
Briggs	1.000	30	50	0	0	0
Casimiro	.941	15	16	0	1	0
Goodell	1.000	3	1	0	0	0
Hackett	1.000	3	9	0	0	0

	PCT	G	PO	A	E	DP
Hammond	.000	1	0	0	0	0
Harris	.956	41	101	8	5	0
Keylor	1.000	3	2	0	0	0
Matos	.955	9	20	1	1	1
McDonald	.968	30	59	1	2	0
Ndungidi	.933	64	110	1	8	1

	PCT	G	PO	A	E	DP
Phoenix	.948	76	156	8	9	0
Raines	.976	65	159	6	4	4
Reed	1.000	18	40	3	0	0
Rust	1.000	8	9	0	0	0

FREDERICK — Class A

CAROLINA LEAGUE

BATTING	AVG	G	AB	R	H	2B	3B	HR	RBI	BB	SO	SB	CS	SLG	OBP	B	T	HT	WT	DOB	1st Yr	Resides
Alley, Charles	.183	43	126	13	23	5	0	1	10	27	25	2	1	.246	.340	R	R	6-2	205	12-20-76	1995	Salisbury, Md.
Ascencion, Quincy	.182	18	55	7	10	2	0	2	9	3	13	1	0	.327	.250	R	R	6-0	205	11-1-82	1999	Willemstad, Curacao
Cabrera, Ray	.274	123	460	62	126	21	4	14	65	23	73	16	7	.428	.325	R	R	6-3	211	11-10-78	1996	Upata, Venez.
Calzado, Napolean	.287	121	464	50	133	20	2	5	41	16	52	34	14	.371	.316	R	R	6-3	160	2-9-80	1996	Santo Domingo, D.R.
Cates, Gary	.242	28	91	8	22	4	0	0	4	4	16	0	1	.286	.274	R	R	5-7	160	7-3-81	1999	Brandon, Fla.
Diaz, Maikell	.248	95	310	34	77	14	1	2	18	11	75	9	9	.319	.282	R	R	6-0	185	8-16-77	2000	Davidsonville, Md.
Gibbs, Mark	.207	42	121	12	25	4	0	3	12	8	42	2	1	.314	.273	L	L	6-4	211	3-3-80	1998	Seattle, Wash.
Gordon, Alex	.275	27	80	4	22	3	1	1	15	4	31	2	0	.375	.322	R	R	6-3	225	8-25-79	2000	Sacramento, Calif.
Gredvig, Doug	.254	129	484	71	123	35	2	20	62	37	125	2	3	.459	.313	R	R	6-4	184	10-27-77	1998	Frederick, Md.
Hammond, Joey	.319	25	94	12	30	5	1	0	8	16	18	1	3	.394	.414	R	R	6-0	185	3-14-80	1996	Puerto Ordaz, Venez.
Leon, Alfredo	.188	10	32	2	6	1	0	0	0	2	7	0	1	.219	.257	R	R	6-0	185	3-19-80	1996	Miami, Fla.
Lopez-Cao, Mike	.372	15	43	4	16	1	0	3	8	4	10	0	1	.605	.438	L	R	5-9	187	8-14-75	1997	Orlando, Fla.
Mack, Tony	.199	110	332	33	66	12	0	5	33	18	102	9	8	.280	.243	R	R	5-11	185	3-19-79	1998	Bakersfield, Calif.
Martinez, Octavio	.217	98	336	23	73	14	0	1	29	10	47	3	2	.268	.263	R	R	6-0	195	7-30-79	1999	Bakersfield, Calif.
Matos, Luis	.429	2	7	3	3	0	0	1	2	1	3	0	0	.857	.500	R	R	6-0	179	10-30-78	1996	Bayamon, P.R.
Moreno, Christopher	.063	19	32	7	2	2	0	0	2	4	15	0	0	.125	.167	R	R	5-9	180	5-9-78	2001	Stockton, Calif.
Rachels, Wes	.261	108	357	43	93	12	0	0	26	58	52	4	5	.294	.371	R	R	5-9	180	1-19-76	1998	Las Vegas, Nev.
Raines, Tim Jr.	.250	23	84	15	21	3	1	3	13	13	23	14	4	.417	.351	B	R	5-10	183	8-31-79	1998	Heathrow, Fla.
Reed, Keith	.270	72	267	28	72	14	0	7	29	13	57	8	6	.401	.305	R	R	6-4	215	10-8-78	1999	Yarmouth Port, Mass.
Rogers, Ed	.260	73	292	39	76	20	3	8	41	14	47	18	6	.432	.310	R	R	6-1	150	8-10-81	1997	San Pedro de Macoris, D.R.
Shier, Peter	.200	13	40	5	8	1	0	0	3	2	7	1	1	.225	.238	R	R	6-2	170	3-16-81	1999	Columbus, Ohio
Sosa, Jovanny	.179	64	207	27	37	4	0	7	25	34	72	1	1	.300	.296	R	R	6-2	207	4-10-80	1997	Santo Domingo, D.R.
Tucker, Mamon	.285	69	256	33	73	9	1	1	23	25	46	7	5	.340	.344	R	R	5-9	215	2-7-78	2001	New Caney, Texas
Webster, Robert	.438	5	16	3	7	2	0	0	2	1	2	0	0	.563	.500	R	R	6-3	188	10-18-79	1998	Austin, Texas
White, Kenneth	.182	3	11	0	2	0	0	0	0	4	4	0	0	.273	.182	R	R	6-1	175	11-27-78	2001	Webster, Fla.

GAMES BY POSITION: C—Alley 39, Leon 4, Lopez-Cao 3, Martinez 91, Webster 5. **1B**—Gredvig 125, Rachels 14. **2B**—Cates 25, Diaz 47, Gibbs 31, Hammond 15, Moreno 3, Rachels 27, White 2. **3B**—Calzado 118, Diaz 3, Hammond 13, Leon 2, Moreno 9. **SS**—Calzado 2, Cates 4, Diaz 45, Gibbs 8, Rogers 73, Shier 13. **OF**—Ascencion 15, Cabrera 116, Gordon 17, Mack 98, Rachels 19, Raines 19, Reed 67, Sosa 22, Tucker 67.

PITCHING	W	L	ERA	G	GS	CG	SV	IP	H	R	ER	BB	SO	AVG	B	T	HT	WT	DOB	1st Yr	Resides
Andrade, Jancy	5	5	4.44	20	13	0	0	75	80	47	37	28	57	.283	R	R	6-2	223	6-29-78	1995	Cumana, Venez.
Bechler, Steve	5	2	2.27	13	13	1	0	83	73	24	21	22	71	.244	R	R	6-2	207	11-18-79	1998	Medford, Ore.
Bedard, Erik	9	2	2.15	17	17	0	0	96	68	27	23	26	130	.198	L	L	6-1	180	3-6-79	1999	Naum, Ontario
Corcoran, Tim	6	5	2.68	33	0	0	6	50	37	16	15	19	42	.207	R	R	6-3	150	4-15-78	1997	Slaughter, La.
Figueroa, Juan	5	0	1.59	7	7	0	0	40	37	8	7	3	26	.241	R	R	6-4	190	9-26-79	1999	McKinleyville, Calif.
Fleming, Travis	1	3	2.51	44	0	0	23	57	53	18	16	20	59	.240	L	L	6-0	200	11-8-76	2000	Santa Rosa, Calif.
Ford, Tom	1	1	3.21	33	0	0	5	48	45	18	17	16	68	.268	L	L	6-1	175	10-30-78	2000	Palos Park, Ill.
Forystek, Brian	1	2	2.88	41	1	0	0	59	61	27	19	30	68	.268	L	L	6-1	195	10-18-76	1998	Houston, Texas
Garcia, Sonny	8	9	3.27	25	20	2	1	143	132	67	52	33	139	.244	R	R	6-3	215	9-10-76	1998	Houston, Texas
Hale, Beau	1	2	1.32	5	5	1	0	34	30	8	5	4	30	.236	R	R	6-4	220	12-1-78	2000	Mauriceville, Texas
Jones, Sean	5	4	3.24	39	0	0	1	83	86	35	30	21	57	.266	R	R	6-7	184	4-12-78	1997	Hamilton, Ontario
Lakman, Jason	1	0	1.69	3	0	0	0	5	4	1	1	0	8	.190	R	R	6-4	220	10-17-76	1995	Seattle, Wash.
Lewis, Richard	0	1	9.00	1	0	0	0	4	8	7	4	1	2	.400	R	R	6-1	190	6-29-80	2001	Marietta, Ga.
Mills, Alan	0	0	1.80	5	0	0	1	5	3	4	1	0	10	.157	R	R	6-1	195	10-18-66	1986	Lakeland, Fla.
Morris, Cory	3	5	3.38	13	12	0	0	69	50	30	26	24	81	.201	R	R	6-2	185	6-2-79	2001	Beckville, Texas
Perez, Randy	8	7	3.96	20	20	3	0	123	145	56	54	23	101	.300	L	L	6-1	169	4-13-80	1998	Sarasota, Fla.
Plank, Terry	2	8	5.32	38	4	0	1	71	71	51	42	43	58	.261	L	R	6-5	195	4-19-78	1999	Hampton, Va.
Ramirez, Enrique	2	1	1.54	7	0	0	1	12	5	2	2	4	9	.131	R	R	6-2	195	8-15-79	1996	El Seibo, D.R.
Schwager, Matt	0	1	3.62	7	3	0	1	27	28	13	11	3	30	.261	R	R	6-6	229	10-10-77	1998	Orchard, Neb.
Sequea, Jacobo	6	9	3.97	18	18	0	0	102	85	54	45	37	80	.224	R	R	6-1	198	8-31-81	1997	Anaco, Venez.
Stahl, Rich	1	1	1.95	6	6	1	0	32	26	13	7	15	24	.232	R	L	6-7	185	4-11-81	1999	Covington, Ga.

DELMARVA — Class A

SOUTH ATLANTIC LEAGUE

BATTING	AVG	G	AB	R	H	2B	3B	HR	RBI	BB	SO	SB	CS	SLG	OBP	B	T	HT	WT	DOB	1st Yr	Resides
Ascencion, Quincy	.211	48	152	11	32	3	2	1	13	12	38	5	1	.276	.284	R	R	6-0	205	11-1-82	1999	Willemstad, Curacao
Bordick, Mike	.000	3	8	0	0	0	0	0	1	2	1	0	0	.000	.200	R	R	5-11	175	7-21-65	1986	Ruxton, Md.
Cates, Gary	.292	101	342	44	100	14	3	2	33	17	30	16	8	.368	.341	R	R	5-7	160	7-3-81	1999	Brandon, Fla.
Del Rosario, Manny	.224	106	313	44	70	9	2	1	24	35	38	16	1	.275	.314	R	R	5-11	149	7-8-81	1997	Hato Mayor, D.R.
Elder, Rick	.251	112	382	66	96	20	5	16	64	63	130	7	1	.455	.359	L	L	6-6	221	2-24-80	1998	Marietta, Ga.
Francisco, Ruben	.214	39	103	14	22	4	4	0	13	6	17	1	3	.330	.257	L	L	6-0	160	5-13-81	1997	San Pedro de Macoris, D.R.
Garcia, Nick	.262	130	442	42	116	14	1	2	42	20	59	2	3	.312	.305	R	R	5-11	165	5-2-80	1999	Sonora, Mexico
Kessick, Jon	.278	34	115	14	32	9	0	5	21	15	40	0	2	.487	.366	L	R	6-3	200	8-25-79	2001	Westerville, Ohio
Keylor, Cory	.230	56	191	28	44	13	0	5	19	19	64	4	2	.377	.316	L	R	6-0	185	3-14-80	1996	Puerto Ordaz, Venez.
Leon, Alfredo	.239	90	318	26	76	12	0	4	41	14	48	3	0	.277	.288	R	R	6-0	185	3-14-80	1996	Puerto Ordaz, Venez.
Littleton, B.J.	.252	133	508	84	128	11	18	3	45	61	108	17	9	.362	.341	B	L	5-10	175	10-3-79	2000	Arlington, Texas
Manley, Adam	.152	23	66	1	10	3	1	1	9	7	26	1	1	.273	.243	L	L	6-3	205	7-18-79	1997	Lakewood, Wash.
Ridley, Shayne	.235	53	153	13	36	6	0	18	17	48	0	0	.275	.310	R	R	6-2	190	11-21-77	2000	Milton, Ontario
Riordan, Matt	.224	59	210	29	47	8	0	2	21	15	38	5	0	.290	.276	R	R	6-2	195	6-24-78	1999	Thousand Oaks, Calif.
Rodriguez, Mike	.193	26	57	3	11	0	0	0	2	6	16	3	0	.193	.277	L	R	5-9	165	5-30-79	2001	San Antonio, Texas
Russell, Michael	.267	17	45	4	12	2	0	1	7	3	16	0	0	.378	.313	R	R	6-0	180	8-14-81	2000	Bothell, Wash.

BATTING	AVG	G	AB	R	H	2B	3B	HR	RBI	BB	SO	SB	CS	SLG	OBP	B	T	HT	WT	DOB	1st Yr	Resides
Saucke, Casey	.200	20	45	4	9	2	0	0	5	7	20	0	1	.244	.308	R	R	6-0	200	3-21-78	2000	Rochester, N.Y.
Seestedt, Mike	.221	90	231	28	51	9	0	1	18	39	37	0	0	.273	.354	R	R	6-0	195	11-10-77	1999	Mount Pleasant, Mich.
Sosa, Jovanny	.274	36	117	17	32	5	0	5	18	16	37	1	0	.444	.365	R	R	6-2	207	4-10-80	1997	Santo Domingo, D.R.
Tucker, Mamon	.246	59	224	37	55	7	1	2	24	28	44	10	3	.313	.329	R	R	6-3	188	10-18-79	1998	Austin, Texas
Whiteside, Eli	.250	61	212	30	53	11	0	7	28	9	45	1	1	.401	.300	R	R	6-2	215	10-22-79	2001	New Albany, Miss.
Wilken, Kris	.211	93	304	26	64	13	2	3	30	43	81	0	1	.296	.313	B	R	5-11	190	4-11-79	2000	Albuquerque, N.M.

GAMES BY POSITION: C—Kessick 23, Russell 17, Seestedt 63, Whiteside 54. **1B**—Elder 49, Leon 12, Manley 2, Ridley 22, Saucke 1, Seestedt 11, Wilken 59. **2B**—Cates 72, Del Rosario 68, Ridley 2, M. Rodriguez 21, Saucke 7, Wilken 2. **3B**—Cates 7, Del Rosario 31, Leon 74, Ridley 17, Saucke 2, Seestedt 1, Wilken 29. **SS**—Cates 20, Del Rosario 6, Garcia 129. **OF**—Ascencion 34, Cates 14, Del Rosario 1, Elder 43, Francisco 23, Keylor 55, Littleton 128, Manley 21, Riordan 53, Saucke 6, Sosa 19, Tucker 54, Wilken 1.

PITCHING	W	L	ERA	G	GS	CG	SV	IP	H	R	ER	BB	SO	AVG	B	T	HT	WT	DOB	1st Yr	Resides
Advincola, Jose	0	0	9.26	11	0	0	0	12	20	14	12	5	7	.350	L	L	6-0	160	5-20-80	1996	San Cristobal, D.R.
Andrade, Jancy	2	4	3.72	8	8	0	0	48	46	22	20	16	43	.250	R	R	6-2	223	6-29-78	1995	Cumana, Venez.
Anez, Omar	0	0	8.04	12	0	0	0	16	23	16	14	18	17	.348	R	R	6-4	226	2-1-81	1997	Valencia, Venez.
Bartlett, Richard	5	9	4.53	19	18	0	0	95	109	54	48	30	60	.293	R	R	6-3	200	10-6-81	2000	Kennewick, Wash.
Deza, Fredy	0	2	3.00	3	2	0	0	15	10	6	5	0	12	.178	R	R	6-2	130	12-11-82	1999	La Romana, D.R.
Farren, Dave	4	7	3.93	32	19	0	0	121	113	66	53	30	84	.241	R	R	6-1	175	3-20-81	1999	Texarkana, Texas
Ford, Tom	2	0	4.50	13	0	0	0	14	13	8	7	8	23	.245	L	L	6-0	200	11-8-76	2000	Santa Rosa, Calif.
Gutierrez, Fernando	1	1	3.45	22	0	0	0	29	18	16	11	21	28	.176	R	R	6-2	210	9-25-80	1997	Portuguesa, Venez.
Jones, D.J.	1	4	3.98	17	6	0	0	41	52	23	18	7	30	.320	L	L	6-1	205	6-3-78	2001	Forney, Texas
Marchetti, Dan	1	1	2.45	10	0	0	1	18	10	5	5	8	17	—	R	R	6-1	185	7-20-78	2000	Gaithersburg, Md.
Montilla, Elvis	7	6	4.19	26	18	0	0	107	104	53	50	28	53	.257	R	R	6-3	165	8-26-81	1997	Ramon Santana, D.R.
Ormond, Rodney	4	4	4.18	24	8	0	0	56	59	37	26	14	59	.257	R	R	6-4	210	6-17-77	1999	Princeton, N.C.
Pruitt, Jason	0	0	5.29	12	0	0	1	17	14	10	10	9	13	.218	L	L	6-3	197	8-6-80	1998	Marana. Ariz.
Ramirez, Enrique	6	4	5.18	45	0	0	1	66	76	47	38	33	66	.286	R	R	6-1	165	8-15-79	1996	El Seibo, D.R.
Rleal, Sendy	3	6	3.57	20	20	1	0	103	79	50	41	27	83	.207	R	R	6-1	165	6-21-80	1999	San Pedro de Macoris, D.R.
Rodriguez, Eddy	5	3	3.39	41	0	0	1	61	58	27	23	23	64	.246	R	R	6-1	170	8-8-81	1999	San Pedro de Macoris, D.R.
Rogers, Brad	3	7	4.58	34	14	0	1	92	106	63	47	36	79	.290	R	R	6-4	195	12-6-81	1999	Nanaimo, B.C.
Schwager, Matt	10	8	2.26	27	14	4	1	103	85	41	26	14	80	.220	R	R	6-6	229	10-10-77	1998	Orchard, Neb.
Seestedt, Mike	0	0	9.00	4	0	0	0	6	9	6	6	2	5	.000	R	R	6-0	195	11-10-77	1999	Mount Pleasant, Mich.
Sperring, Jayme	2	4	2.97	53	0	0	26	64	50	25	21	30	75	.215	R	R	6-4	220	11-16-78	2000	Cypress, Texas
Stahl, Rich	2	3	2.67	6	6	0	0	34	24	15	10	15	31	.205	R	L	6-7	185	4-11-81	1999	Covington, Ga.
Tate, Matt	2	3	6.14	13	3	0	0	37	33	29	25	21	25	.239	R	R	6-2	180	9-21-80	1999	Bonifay, Fla.
Tomaszewski, Eliot	1	3	4.43	18	4	0	2	41	59	25	20	7	32	.337	R	R	6-4	190	1-13-80	1998	Albuquerque, N.M.

BLUEFIELD   Rookie

APPALACHIAN LEAGUE

BATTING	AVG	G	AB	R	H	2B	3B	HR	RBI	BB	SO	SB	CS	SLG	OBP	B	T	HT	WT	DOB	1st Yr	Resides
Arko, Tommy	.194	36	124	16	24	4	1	5	16	13	47	0	1	.363	.271	R	R	6-1	195	7-28-82	2000	Abilene, Texas
Bass, Bryan	.324	19	71	17	23	6	1	5	20	10	17	0	0	.648	.407	B	R	6-1	180	4-12-82	2001	Seminole, Fla.
Cliffords, Woody	.278	62	198	36	55	13	2	6	29	32	40	8	1	.455	.381	L	R	6-2	185	12-2-80	2001	West Hills, Calif.
Francisco, Ruben	.327	57	199	35	65	16	0	3	21	17	32	18	5	.452	.399	L	L	6-0	160	5-13-81	1997	San Pedro de Macoris, D.R.
Hackett, Richard	.247	39	97	19	24	4	0	5	20	18	32	1	4	.443	.380	R	R	6-1	200	4-30-79	2001	Stockton, Calif.
Johnson, Tripper	.261	43	157	24	41	6	1	2	26	11	37	4	0	.350	.312	R	R	6-1	195	4-28-82	2000	Bellevue, Wash.
Keylor, Cory	.538	3	13	5	7	1	1	1	4	2	4	0	0	1.000	.600	L	R	6-3	200	8-25-79	2001	Westerville, Ohio
Manley, Adam	.190	27	84	13	16	3	1	3	17	4	30	1	0	.357	.253	L	L	6-3	205	7-18-78	2001	Lakewood, Wash.
Martin, Kyle	.308	44	130	16	40	11	0	1	13	13	39	1	2	.415	.368	R	R	5-11	215	6-12-80	1999	Yakima, Wash.
Perez, Felipe	.212	55	189	27	40	9	2	7	32	9	66	9	3	.392	.260	R	R	6-3	190	9-2-79	1996	La Romana, D.R.
Pickering, Kelvin	.091	14	22	3	2	0	0	0	1	2	13	0	0	.091	.160	R	R	6-1	215	9-7-79	1999	Tampa, Fla.
Rivas, Arturo	.147	11	34	4	5	0	0	0	2	5	13	4	0	.147	.286	R	R	6-0	150	2-2-84	2001	San Francisco, Venez.
Rodriguez, Jose	.147	22	34	5	5	0	1	0	4	5	15	2	1	.206	.256	B	R	5-10	175	11-23-79	2000	Cayey, P.R.
Rogers, Omar	.323	63	226	41	73	12	1	2	32	29	41	22	10	.412	.419	R	R	6-0	160	8-12-82	1999	San Pedro de Macoris, D.R.
Russell, Michael	.281	10	32	7	9	2	0	2	6	2	7	1	0	.531	.343	R	R	6-0	180	8-14-81	2000	Bothell, Wash.
Shier, Peter	.238	65	202	30	48	10	2	1	19	36	51	17	4	.322	.360	R	R	6-2	170	3-16-81	1999	Columbus, Ohio
Soriano, Jairo	.206	41	102	14	21	4	3	0	15	12	30	4	4	.304	.319	R	R	6-1	160	12-13-80	1999	Villa Mella, D.R.
Thomas, Adam	.295	62	227	45	67	8	3	4	26	36	39	16	5	.410	.405	L	L	6-0	170	12-7-79	2001	Pottsboro, Texas
Webster, Robert	.238	10	21	2	5	0	0	0	1	5	4	1	0	.238	.407	R	R	5-9	215	2-7-78	2001	New Caney, Texas

GAMES BY POSITION: C—Arko 35, Martin 21, Pickering 8, Russell 8, Webster 6. **1B**—Cliffords 15, Manley 17, Martin 1, Perez 43. **2B**—Rodriguez 15, Rogers 57, Soriano 5. **3B**—Johnson 14, Rodriguez 1, Rogers 10, Shier 24, Soriano 28. **SS**—Bass 19, Shier 42, Soriano 8. **OF**—Cliffords 48, Francisco 55, Hackett 34, Keylor 2, Manley 9, Perez 4, Rivas 11, Thomas 58.

PITCHING	W	L	ERA	G	GS	CG	SV	IP	H	R	ER	BB	SO	AVG	B	T	HT	WT	DOB	1st Yr	Resides
Advincola, Jose	1	2	5.26	22	0	0	0	39	37	28	23	22	50	.253	L	L	6-0	160	5-20-80	1996	San Cristobal, D.R.
Anez, Omar	2	7	7.62	15	6	0	0	41	51	46	35	17	46	.291	R	R	6-4	226	2-1-81	1997	Valencia, Venez.
Berube, Martin	2	6	6.11	11	11	0	0	53	78	42	36	10	49	.340	L	L	6-1	195	9-12-81	2000	Montreal, Quebec
Birkins, Kurt	4	1	2.92	6	6	0	0	37	28	14	12	5	42	.205	L	L	6-2	175	8-11-80	2001	Canoga Park, Calif.
Crouthers, Dave	2	3	4.43	10	10	1	0	45	41	28	22	18	45	.242	R	R	6-3	190	12-18-79	2001	Edwardsville, Ill.
Crump, Joel	0	0	2.25	10	0	0	1	12	10	4	3	6	15	.222	L	L	6-2	190	8-20-81	2000	Yuma, Ariz.
Edwards, Brad	0	1	5.60	16	1	0	0	35	25	23	22	28	37	.200	L	L	6-3	184	4-10-80	2001	Dumfries, Va.
Forbes, Derek	1	1	6.48	6	0	0	0	8	12	7	6	6	11	.324	R	R	6-2	185	9-11-78	1999	Scottsdale, Ariz.
Jones, D.J.	1	0	0.75	4	1	0	0	12	8	2	1	2	8	.195	L	L	6-1	205	6-3-78	2001	Forney, Texas
Keefer, Ryan	1	0	0.59	29	0	0	15	31	21	4	2	8	46	.178	L	R	6-3	190	8-10-81	2000	Catawissa, Pa.
Mincey, T.W.	1	1	6.75	15	1	0	1	31	38	31	23	21	29	.299	L	L	6-3	195	5-17-80	2001	Winston, Ga.
Montani, Jeff	0	0	2.25	7	0	0	0	8	5	2	2	4	9	.166	R	R	5-11	175	11-22-80	2001	Liverpool, N.Y.
Montilla, Elvis	2	2	4.68	5	4	1	0	25	28	13	13	8	18	.285	R	R	6-3	165	8-26-81	1997	Ramon Santana, D.R.
Morris, Cory	1	0	0.00	1	0	0	0	3	1	0	0	2	4	.100	R	R	6-2	185	6-2-79	2001	Beckville, Texas
Phillips, James	3	5	5.13	25	2	0	0	40	52	32	23	18	37	.311	R	R	6-2	180	10-24-80	1999	Zanesville, Ohio
Pruitt, Jason	0	0	5.40	1	0	0	0	2	2	1	1	1	2	.285	L	L	6-3	197	8-6-80	1998	Marana. Ariz.
Rice, Scott	4	3	4.12	12	12	0	0	63	58	44	29	28	53	.239	L	L	6-6	210	9-21-81	1999	Simi Valley, Calif.
Salazar, Richard	1	0	3.86	2	0	0	0	5	5	2	2	0	7	.263	L	L	5-11	185	1-6-81	2001	Miami, Fla.
Tate, Matt	5	5	4.94	12	12	0	0	62	80	37	34	18	64	.314	R	R	6-2	180	9-21-80	1999	Bonifay, Fla.

GULF COAST LEAGUE

BATTING	AVG	G	AB	R	H	2B	3B	HR	RBI	BB	SO	SB	CS	SLG	OBP	B	T	HT	WT	DOB	1st Yr	Resides
Baez, Federico	.259	28	81	9	21	3	0	0	6	14	29	2	3	.296	.368	R	R	6-2	185	8-4-81	2001	Dorado, P.R.
Banks, Almonzo	.150	38	100	8	15	4	1	1	8	12	39	3	0	.240	.252	R	R	6-1	190	5-28-81	1999	Washington, D.C.
Bass, Bryan	.297	21	74	12	22	3	6	0	7	5	25	4	0	.500	.333	B	R	6-1	180	4-12-82	2001	Seminole, Fla.
Coffie, Ivanon	.278	6	18	2	5	1	0	1	2	2	5	0	0	.500	.350	L	R	6-1	192	5-16-77	1995	Willemstad, Curacao
Gordon, Alex	.333	9	24	7	8	2	0	3	10	4	14	1	0	.792	.448	L	L	6-4	211	3-3-80	1998	Seattle, Wash.
Hackett, Richard	.238	7	21	2	5	1	0	0	1	2	4	0	1	.286	.304	R	R	6-1	200	4-30-79	2001	Stockton, Calif.
Hadad, Jorge	.234	15	47	4	11	4	0	0	5	3	11	0	0	.319	.294	R	R	6-2	170	5-4-82	2001	Mexico City, Mexico
Horsman, Stephen	.071	5	14	0	1	0	0	0	1	3	5	0	1	.071	.235	L	R	6-6	220	5-24-78	2001	Abington, Mass.
Jordan, Ed	.276	50	156	32	43	9	1	6	22	17	35	16	2	.462	.360	R	R	6-1	190	11-18-78	2001	Falls Church, Va.
Joyce, Tom	.217	49	152	18	33	8	1	0	12	20	45	2	4	.283	.305	L	L	5-11	170	3-1-82	2000	Macon, Ga.
Manley, Adam	.176	9	34	3	6	1	1	1	5	0	9	0	0	.353	.200	L	L	6-3	205	7-18-78	2001	Lakewood, Wash.
Martinez, Raul	.248	35	101	13	25	4	1	1	17	15	23	2	0	.337	.342	L	R	6-0	190	10-7-79	2001	San Lorenzo, P.R.
Matos, Luis	.286	3	14	1	4	2	0	0	2	0	3	0	0	.429	.286	R	R	6-0	179	10-30-78	1996	Bayamon, P.R.
McMahon, James	.261	18	46	1	12	0	0	0	3	7	19	0	1	.261	.352	R	R	5-10	189	8-27-82	2001	Lake Orion, Mich.
Mitchell, Andy	.300	19	20	1	6	1	0	0	1	1	6	0	0	.350	.333	R	R	6-3	210	9-10-78	2001	Conyers, Ga.
Moreno, Chris	.250	6	20	1	5	0	0	0	0	0	5	1	0	.250	.250	R	R	6-0	180	5-9-78	2001	Stockton, Calif.
Recio, Bolivar	.308	29	91	14	28	8	2	2	7	4	18	1	0	.505	.357	R	R	6-2	180	1-14-81	1999	San Francisco de Macoris, D.R.
2-team (6 Pirates)	.274	35	113	18	31	9	2	2	9	6	25	1	1	.442	.325							
Rijo, Carlos	.279	53	201	18	56	10	4	1	23	6	32	8	3	.383	.305	R	R	6-0	170	9-11-82	1999	La Romana, D.R.
Rivas, Arturo	.308	8	26	6	8	1	0	0	2	4	5	2	1	.346	.412	R	R	6-0	150	2-2-84	2001	San Francisco, Venez.
Rodriguez, Jose	.176	5	17	0	3	1	0	0	0	2	4	0	0	.235	.263	B	R	5-10	175	11-23-79	2000	Cayey, P.R.
Severino, Wanell	.304	34	125	21	38	5	0	0	16	6	17	8	5	.344	.338	R	R	6-2	155	7-20-82	1999	La Romana, D.R.
Webster, Kevin	.231	17	52	4	12	2	0	1	9	0	12	0	1	.327	.255	R	R	5-9	215	2-7-78	2001	New Caney, Texas
White, Ken	.294	49	160	22	47	11	1	1	12	12	42	5	2	.394	.354	B	R	6-1	175	11-27-81	2001	Webster, Fla.
Yount, Dustin	.228	44	145	15	33	11	1	3	18	22	38	0	2	.379	.333	L	R	6-1	210	10-27-82	2001	Scottsdale, Ariz.

GAMES BY POSITION: C—Hadad 5, Martinez 28, McMahon 16, Webster 15. **1B**—Joyce 3, Manley 5, Martinez 4, Recio 4, Rijo 1, Yount 40. **2B**—Baez 10, Moren o 1, Recio 7, Severino 31, White 14. **3B**—Baez 4, Moreno 1, Recio 3, Rijo 49, Yount 1. **SS**—Baez 16, Bass 18, Jordan 1, Moreno 3, Recio 7, Rijo 1, Rodriguez 5, White 13. **OF**—Banks 36, Gordon 8, Hackett 6, Horsman 3, Jordan 48, Joyce 45, Manley 4, Recio 5, Severino 1, White 21.

PITCHING	W	L	ERA	G	GS	CG	SV	IP	H	R	ER	BB	SO	AVG	B	T	HT	WT	DOB	1st Yr	Resides
Bale, John	0	0	2.25	2	2	0	0	4	1	1	1	2	7	.090	L	L	6-4	205	5-22-74	1996	Crestview, Fla.
Bartsch, John	2	1	4.00	10	0	0	0	18	19	8	8	1	10	.271	R	R	6-2	180	7-6-79	2001	Naum, Ontario
Bedard, Erik	0	1	3.00	2	2	0	0	6	4	2	2	3	7	.200	L	L	6-1	180	3-6-79	1999	Seminole, Fla.
Birkins, Kurt	2	1	2.05	5	4	0	0	22	13	5	5	3	24	.166	L	L	6-2	175	8-11-80	2001	Canoga Park, Calif.
Britton, Chris	2	3	2.76	12	3	0	0	33	35	20	10	12	20	.265	R	R	6-3	215	12-16-82	2001	Plantation, Fla.
Cabrera, Daniel	2	3	5.53	12	7	0	0	41	31	29	25	39	36	.215	R	R	6-7	195	5-28-81	1999	San Pedro de Macoris, D.R.
Coppinger, Joe	2	4	5.85	11	8	0	0	40	53	37	26	17	28	.296	R	R	6-3	205	7-23-82	2001	El Paso, Texas
Crump, Joel	1	0	2.35	7	0	0	0	15	15	5	4	12	11	.000	R	R	6-2	190	8-20-81	2000	La Romana, D.R.
Deza, Fredy	1	4	3.14	9	7	1	0	49	49	26	17	15	42	.262	R	R	6-5	210	6-27-83	2001	Endicott, N.Y.
Johnson, James	0	1	3.86	7	4	0	0	19	17	10	8	7	19	.239	R	R	6-6	200	9-2-82	2001	Bellevue, Wash.
Lewis, Rommie	1	1	2.14	10	7	0	0	34	37	16	8	6	27	.276	L	L	6-2	175	11-23-79	2000	Conyers, Ga.
Mitchell, Andy	4	2	2.55	12	0	0	2	24	18	10	7	10	21	.000	R	R	6-1	150	5-20-82	2001	San Pedro de Macoris, D.R.
Perez, Carlos	1	1	5.46	14	0	0	0	29	29	22	18	17	29	.000	R	R	6-0	160	2-2-81	1998	Hato Mayor, D.R.
Sala, Marino	1	5	4.82	15	0	0	6	19	21	12	10	13	10	.287	R	R	6-2	155	6-1-81	2001	Miami, Fla.
Salazar, Richard	0	0	0.00	1	0	0	0	2	2	0	0	1	2	.285	L	L	5-11	185	1-6-81	2001	Miami, Fla.
Smith, Chris	0	0	0.00	2	0	0	0	2	2	2	0	1	0	.222	L	L	5-11	190	12-10-79	2001	Wantagh, N.Y.
Spillers, Larry	3	3	4.01	10	10	0	0	52	53	25	23	19	13	.270	R	L	6-3	195	3-12-82	2001	Roberta, Ga.
Stahl, Rich	0	0	0.00	1	1	0	0	2	1	0	0	1	1	.166	R	L	6-7	185	4-11-81	1999	Covington, Ga.
Tiller, James	0	3	3.68	16	1	0	0	37	30	18	15	15	44	.218	R	R	6-5	185	4-13-83	2001	Waskom, Texas
White, Ken	0	1	1.50	4	0	0	0	6	9	3	1	2	2	.000	B	R	6-1	175	11-27-78	2001	Webster, Fla.

BOSTON RED SOX

BY JOHN TOMASE

Dan Duquette fired Jimy Williams on Aug. 16, hoping for a spark. He got one. But he couldn't douse the resulting inferno.

The 2001 season dissolved like a sugar cube after general manager Duquette promoted pitching coach Joe Kerrigan to manager for the stretch run.

Two games out in the wild-card race at the time, the Red Sox went 17-26 under Kerrigan and finished 82-79—13½ games behind the Yankees in the American League East. A 6-23 stretch effectively ended the season in early September, and then things got ugly.

Recalcitrant outfielder Carl Everett cursed out Kerrigan at a practice and was exiled to Florida. Ace Pedro Martinez, out most of the season with a rotator-cuff injury, left with three weeks remaining for his native Dominican Republic. Fans booed Duquette lustily on Cal Ripken Night at Fenway Park.

A season that started with the acquisition of power-hitting outfielder Manny Ramirez and expectations of World Series contention ended in disarray.

The first bad news came at the start of spring training, when two-time defending AL batting champ Nomar Garciaparra revealed a sore right wrist had left him unable to swing or throw. The saga lasted all spring, with player and team hoping to avoid surgery.

They couldn't. After an Opening Day loss in Baltimore, Garciaparra had surgery and missed the team's first 104 games.

Fortune changed two nights later against the Orioles when free-agent signee Hideo Nomo, in his Red Sox debut, pitched the team's first no-hitter since Dave Morehead's in 1965.

The Red Sox stayed in contention for the first two months behind Ramirez, who was hitting .400-16-56 on May 26. His production then lagged, and he finished at

Manny Ramirez   Seung Song

PLAYERS OF THE YEAR

MAJOR LEAGUE: Manny Ramirez, of
One year into an eight-year, $160 million contract, Ramirez bore much of the offensive load without the injured Nomar Garciaparra in the lineup. Ramirez hit .306-41-125.

MINOR LEAGUE: Seung Song, rhp
Too good for low Class A Augusta (3-2, 2.04), Song moved to high Class A Sarasota after appearing in the Futures Game and was again too good for that league (5-2, 1.68).

.306-41-125.

Injuries mounted. Catcher Jason Varitek, emerging as a team leader and potential all-star, broke his elbow diving for a foul ball June 7, ending his season.

Martinez went down June 26 against the Devil Rays with an inflamed rotator cuff. He made three starts thereafter and the team ERA rose from 3.57 in the first half to 4.90 in the second.

Everett had his worst season in five years, limited to 102 games because of knee injuries.

Outfielder Trot Nixon set career highs in average (.288), homers (27) and RBIs (88), and emerged as a team leader.

Bret Saberhagen made a stirring comeback on July 27, beating the White Sox in his first game since 1999. He made two more starts before a tattered shoulder forced him to call it a career.

Garciaparra returned to electrify Fenway Park with a home run and game-winning single on July 29 against Chicago. But he played just 21 more games before the pain became too great. His departure coincided with a nine-game losing streak.

As it was, Garciaparra, Ramirez and Everett—the team's dream 3-4-5 hitters—never played a game together.

In the minors, only Augusta of the Class A South Atlantic League and the Rookie-level Red Sox of the Gulf Coast League reached the postseason. Every other affiliate compiled a losing record.

Bright spots included Korean righthander Seung Song, who excelled at Augusta and Class A Sarasota; Double-A Trenton lefty Casey Fossum, who earned a promotion to the big leagues; and shortstop Freddy Sanchez, who led the organization with a .334 average.

Izzy Alcantara tied Triple-A Pawtucket's franchise record with 36 homers, but also literally kicked off a brawl with a cleat to the facemask of Scranton/Wilkes-Barre catcher Jeremy Salazar.

ORGANIZATION LEADERS

BATTING
*AVG	Freddy Sanchez, Trenton/Sarasota	.334
R	Israel Alcantara, Pawtucket	80
	Rontrez Johnson, Pawtucket/Trenton	80
H	Freddy Sanchez, Trenton/Sarasota	153
TB	Israel Alcantara, Pawtucket	270
2B	Freddy Sanchez, Trenton/Sarasota	39
3B	Three tied at	6
HR	Israel Alcantara, Pawtucket	36
RBI	Israel Alcantara, Pawtucket	90
BB	Kevin Youkilis, Augusta/Lowell	73
SO	Mark Fischer, Trenton	148
SB	Antron Seiber, Augusta	36

PITCHING
W	Greg Montalbano, Trenton/Sarasota	12
L	Anastacio Martinez, Sarasota	12
	Derrin Ebert, Pawtucket/Trenton	12
#ERA	Seung Song, Sarasota/Augusta	1.90
G	Corey Spencer, Trenton	55
C	Carlos Castillo, Pawtucket	5
SV	Rodney Dickinson, Sarasota/Augusta	22
IP	Carlos Castillo, Pawtucket	164
BB	Brad Baker, Sarasota	64
SO	Seung Song, Sarasota/Augusta	135

*Minimum 250 At-Bats #Minimum 75 Innings

Managers: Jimy Williams, Joe Kerrigan

2001 Record: 82-79, .509 (2nd, AL East)

BATTING	AVG	G	AB	R	H	2B	3B	HR	RBI	BB	SO	SB	CS	SLG	OBP	B	T	HT	WT	DOB	1st Yr	Resides
Alcantara, Israel	.263	14	38	3	10	1	0	0	3	3	13	1	0	.289	.317	R	R	6-2	180	5-6-73	1991	Santo Domingo, D.R.
Bichette, Dante	.286	107	391	45	112	30	1	12	49	20	76	2	2	.460	.325	R	R	6-2	235	11-18-63	1984	Longwood, Fla.
Burkhart, Morgan	.182	11	33	3	6	1	0	1	4	1	11	0	0	.303	.206	B	L	5-11	225	1-29-72	1995	St. Louis, Mo.
Daubach, Brian	.263	122	407	54	107	28	3	22	71	53	108	1	0	.509	.350	L	R	6-1	201	2-11-72	1990	Belleville, Ill.
Everett, Carl	.257	102	409	61	105	24	4	14	58	27	104	9	2	.438	.323	B	R	6-0	190	6-3-71	1990	Tampa, Fla.
Garciaparra, Nomar	.289	21	83	13	24	3	0	4	8	7	9	0	1	.470	.352	R	R	6-0	180	7-23-73	1994	Boston, Mass.
Grebeck, Craig	.049	23	41	1	2	1	0	0	2	2	9	0	0	.073	.093	R	R	5-7	155	12-29-64	1987	Laguna Niguel, Calif.
Hatteberg, Scott	.245	94	278	34	68	19	0	3	25	33	26	1	1	.345	.332	L	R	6-1	205	12-14-69	1991	Tacoma, Wash.
Hillenbrand, Shea	.263	139	468	52	123	20	2	12	49	13	61	3	4	.391	.291	R	R	6-1	200	7-27-75	1996	Mesa, Ariz.
Jensen, Marcus	.250	1	4	0	1	0	0	0	0	1	0	0	0	.250	.250	B	R	6-4	204	12-14-72	1990	Scottsdale, Ariz.
Lansing, Mike	.250	106	352	45	88	23	0	8	34	22	50	3	3	.384	.294	R	R	6-0	195	4-3-68	1990	Palm Beach Gardens, Fla.
Lewis, Darren	.280	82	164	18	46	9	1	1	12	8	25	5	5	.366	.326	R	R	6-0	189	8-28-67	1988	Hillsborough, Calif.
Lofton, James	.192	8	26	1	5	1	0	0	1	1	4	2	1	.231	.214	B	R	5-9	170	3-6-74	1993	Los Angeles, Calif.
Merloni, Lou	.267	52	146	21	39	10	0	3	13	6	31	2	1	.397	.306	R	R	5-10	194	4-6-71	1993	Framingham, Mass.
Mirabelli, Doug	.270	54	141	16	38	8	0	9	26	17	36	0	0	.518	.360	R	R	6-1	218	10-18-70	1992	Wichita, Kan.
2-team (23 Texas)	.226	77	190	20	43	10	0	11	29	27	57	0	0	.453	.332							
Nixon, Trot	.280	148	535	100	150	31	4	27	88	79	113	7	4	.505	.376	L	L	6-2	200	4-11-74	1993	Wilmington, N.C.
O'Leary, Troy	.240	104	341	50	82	16	6	13	50	25	73	1	3	.437	.298	L	L	6-0	200	8-4-69	1987	Phoenix, Ariz.
Offerman, Jose	.267	128	524	76	140	23	3	9	49	61	97	5	2	.374	.342	B	R	6-0	190	11-11-68	1988	Toluca Lake, Calif.
Oliver, Joe	.250	5	12	1	3	1	0	0	1	1	3	0	0	.333	.308	R	R	6-3	220	7-24-65	1983	Orlando, Fla.
2-team (12 New York)	.250	17	48	4	12	2	0	1	3	2	15	0	0	.354	.275							
Pickering, Calvin	.280	17	50	4	14	1	0	3	7	8	13	0	0	.480	.379	L	L	6-5	290	9-29-76	1995	Temple Terrace, Fla.
Ramirez, Manny	.306	142	529	93	162	33	2	41	125	81	147	0	1	.609	.405	R	R	6-0	205	5-30-72	1991	New York, N.Y.
Santos, Angel	.125	9	16	2	2	1	0	0	1	2	7	0	0	.188	.211	B	R	5-11	178	8-14-79	1997	Cayey, P.R.
Stynes, Chris	.280	96	361	52	101	19	2	8	33	20	56	4	5	.410	.332	R	R	5-10	185	1-19-73	1991	Deerfield Beach, Fla.
Valentin, John	.200	20	60	8	12	2	0	1	5	9	8	0	0	.283	.314	B	R	6-0	185	2-18-67	1988	Homdel, N.J.
Varitek, Jason	.293	51	174	19	51	11	1	7	25	21	35	0	0	.489	.371	B	R	6-2	220	4-11-72	1995	Suwanee, Ga.

PITCHING	W	L	ERA	G	GS	CG	SV	IP	H	R	ER	BB	SO	AVG	B	T	HT	WT	DOB	1st Yr	Resides
Arrojo, Rolando	5	4	3.48	41	9	0	5	103	88	44	40	35	78	.229	R	R	6-4	220	7-18-68	1997	St. Petersburg, Fla.
Banks, Willie	0	0	0.84	5	0	0	0	11	5	4	1	4	10	.131	R	R	6-1	200	2-27-69	1987	Miami, Fla.
Beck, Rod	6	4	3.90	68	0	0	6	81	77	42	35	28	63	.251	R	R	6-2	250	4-21-75	1994	Miami, Fla.
Castillo, Carlos	0	0	6.00	2	0	0	0	3	3	2	2	0	0	.272	R	R	6-1	200	4-1-69	1987	Cave Creek, Ariz.
Castillo, Frank	10	9	4.21	26	26	0	0	137	138	72	64	35	89	.250	R	R	6-1	200	1-2-63	1981	Greenwich, Conn.
Cone, David	9	7	4.31	25	25	0	0	136	148	74	65	57	115	.274	L	R	6-1	200	8-4-77	1995	Morrilton, Ark.
Crawford, Paxton	3	0	4.75	8	7	0	0	36	40	19	19	13	25	.275	R	R	6-3	205	8-4-77	1995	Meadville, Pa.
Erdos, Todd	0	0	4.96	10	0	0	0	16	15	9	9	8	7	.263	R	R	6-1	204	11-21-73	1992	Meadville, Pa.
Florie, Bryce	0	1	11.42	7	0	0	0	9	12	11	11	7	7	.315	R	R	5-11	192	5-21-70	1988	Goose Creek, S.C.
Fossum, Casey	3	2	4.87	13	7	0	0	44	44	26	24	20	26	.258	B	L	6-1	160	1-9-78	1999	Nashville, Tenn.
Garces, Rich	6	1	3.90	62	0	0	1	67	55	32	29	25	51	.219	R	R	6-0	215	5-18-71	1988	Maracay, Venez.
Kim, Sun-Woo	0	2	5.83	20	2	0	0	42	54	27	27	21	27	.312	R	R	6-2	180	9-4-77	1997	Seoul, Korea
Lowe, Derek	5	10	3.53	67	3	0	24	92	103	39	36	29	82	.282	R	R	6-6	200	6-1-73	1991	Fort Myers, Fla.
Martinez, Pedro	7	3	2.39	18	18	1	0	117	84	33	31	25	163	.198	R	R	5-11	170	10-25-71	1988	Santo Domingo, D.R.
McDill, Allen	0	0	5.52	15	0	0	0	15	13	9	9	7	16	.236	L	L	6-1	170	8-23-71	1992	Arkadelphia, Ark.
Nomo, Hideo	13	10	4.50	33	33	2	0	198	171	105	99	96	220	.231	R	R	6-2	210	8-31-68	1995	Kobe, Japan
Ohka, Tomo	2	5	6.19	12	11	0	0	52	69	40	36	19	37	.316	R	R	6-1	179	3-18-76	1999	Kyoto, Japan
Pichardo, Hipolito	2	1	4.93	30	0	0	0	35	42	23	19	10	17	.300	R	R	6-1	195	8-22-69	1988	Esperanza, D.R.
Pulsipher, Bill	0	0	5.32	23	0	0	0	22	25	15	13	14	16	.294	L	L	6-3	200	10-9-73	1992	Port St. Lucie, Fla.
Saberhagen, Bret	1	2	6.00	3	3	0	0	15	19	11	10	0	10	.301	R	R	6-1	200	4-11-64	1983	Babylon, N.Y.
Schourek, Pete	1	5	4.45	33	0	0	0	30	35	19	15	15	20	.291	L	L	6-5	220	5-10-69	1987	Clifton, Va.
Urbina, Ugueth	0	1	2.25	19	0	0	9	20	16	5	5	3	32	.219	R	R	6-0	205	2-15-74	1991	Ocumare del Tuy, Venez.
Wakefield, Tim	9	12	3.90	45	17	0	3	169	156	84	73	73	148	.248	R	R	6-2	210	8-2-66	1988	Melbourne, Fla.

FIELDING

Catcher	PCT	G	PO	A	E	DP	PB
Hatteberg	.992	72	491	29	4	3	13
Jensen	1.000	1	12	1	0	0	0
Mirabelli	.995	52	329	33	2	8	6
Oliver	.971	5	33	1	1	0	1
Varitek	.996	50	425	32	2	2	3

First Base	PCT	G	PO	A	E	DP
Alcantara	.950	4	17	2	1	1
Burkhart	1.000	5	29	2	0	4
Daubach	.988	106	839	75	11	71
Hillenbrand	1.000	6	50	3	0	4
Offerman	.991	43	297	39	3	26
Pickering	1.000	12	90	6	0	8

Second Base	PCT	G	PO	A	E	DP
Lansing	.970	31	53	75	4	15

	PCT	G	PO	A	E	DP
Merloni	.947	5	10	8	1	3
Offerman	.974	91	161	249	11	44
Santos	.905	6	7	12	2	0
Stynes	.995	43	73	116	1	18

Third Base	PCT	G	PO	A	E	DP
Hillenbrand	.941	129	88	200	18	16
Merloni	.000	1	0	0	0	0
Stynes	.949	46	31	63	5	5
Valentin	1.000	3	1	1	0	0

Shortstop	PCT	G	PO	A	E	DP
Garciaparra	.968	21	34	56	3	13
Grebeck	1.000	23	16	32	0	4
Lansing	.966	76	108	172	10	37
Lofton	.920	7	9	14	2	3
Merloni	.987	45	54	100	2	19

	PCT	G	PO	A	E	DP
Valentin	.970	18	22	42	2	9

Outfield	PCT	G	PO	A	E	DP
Alcantara	.900	8	8	1	1	0
Bichette	.955	53	80	4	4	1
Daubach	1.000	14	22	0	0	0
Everett	.974	93	185	4	5	1
Lewis	1.000	69	102	4	0	2
Nixon	.973	145	280	7	8	4
O'Leary	.994	89	163	3	1	0
Ramirez	1.000	55	98	1	0	0
Stynes	1.000	3	5	0	0	0

FARM SYSTEM

Director, Player Development: Kent Qualls

Class	Farm Team	League	W	L	Pct.	Finish*	Manager	First Yr.
AAA	Pawtucket (R.I.) Red Sox	International	60	82	.423	13th (14)	Gary Jones	1973
AA	Trenton (N.J.) Thunder	Eastern	67	75	.472	8th (12)	Billy Gardner	1995
A#	Sarasota (Fla.) Red Sox	Florida State	54	83	.394	14th (14)	Ron Johnson	1994
A	Augusta (Ga.) GreenJackets	South Atlantic	74	65	.532	7th (16)	Mike Boulanger	1999
A	Lowell (Mass.) Spinners	New York-Penn	33	43	.434	10th (14)	Arnie Beyeler	1996
Rookie	Fort Myers (Fla.) Red Sox	Gulf Coast	37	22	.627	2nd (14)	John Sanders	1993

*Finish in overall standings (No. of teams in league)   #Advanced level

ORGANIZATION STATISTICS

PAWTUCKET   Class AAA

INTERNATIONAL LEAGUE

BATTING	AVG	G	AB	R	H	2B	3B	HR	RBI	BB	SO	SB	CS	SLG	OBP	B	T	HT	WT	DOB	1st Yr	Resides
Alcantara, Israel	.297	119	451	80	134	26	1	36	90	57	107	9	2	.599	.380	R	R	6-2	180	5-6-73	1991	Santo Domingo, D.R.
Burkhart, Morgan	.269	120	412	64	111	19	1	25	62	68	113	1	0	.502	.382	B	L	5-11	225	1-29-72	1995	St. Louis, Mo.
Chamblee, Jim	.241	103	378	40	91	22	0	10	32	31	104	8	5	.378	.308	R	R	6-4	175	5-6-75	1995	Denton, Texas
Chevalier, Virgil	.259	7	27	2	7	2	0	0	4	0	3	0	0	.333	.259	R	R	6-2	240	10-31-73	1995	Scotia, N.Y.
Clemente, Edgard	.247	86	300	32	74	14	0	12	35	25	84	2	0	.413	.312	R	R	6-0	170	12-15-75	1993	Guaynabo, P.R.
Daubach, Brian	.250	1	4	0	1	0	0	0	0	0	2	0	0	.250	.250	L	R	6-1	201	2-11-72	1990	Belleville, Ill.
DeLeon, Jorge	.167	9	30	3	5	2	0	0	3	3	8	0	0	.233	.235	R	R	6-2	164	9-26-74	1997	Guayama, P.R.
Diaz, Juan	.269	74	279	45	75	17	1	20	51	17	85	0	0	.552	.323	R	R	6-2	228	2-19-76	1996	Santo Domingo, D.R.
Encarnacion, Angelo	.265	47	155	16	41	5	1	1	11	8	17	1	0	.329	.305	R	R	5-9	190	4-18-73	1990	Santo Domingo, D.R.
Garciaparra, Nomar	.438	4	16	3	7	0	1	4	1	2	0	0	0	.750	.500	R	R	6-0	180	7-23-73	1994	Boston, Mass.
Jensen, Marcus	.235	27	102	11	24	7	2	4	12	6	27	0	0	.461	.278	B	R	6-4	204	12-14-72	1990	Scottsdale, Ariz.
Johnson, Rontrez	.299	44	187	32	56	16	3	4	22	10	35	8	4	.481	.358	R	R	5-10	165	12-8-76	1995	Marshall, Texas
Lofton, James	.318	42	151	19	48	8	0	6	13	10	29	3	3	.490	.360	R	R	5-9	170	3-6-74	1993	Los Angeles, Calif.
Lomasney, Steve	.286	17	63	10	18	4	0	2	9	4	21	2	0	.444	.338	R	R	6-0	195	8-29-77	1995	Peabody, Mass.
Maddox, Garry	.111	8	27	1	3	0	0	1	0	8	0	0	0	.111	.111	L	R	6-3	180	10-24-74	1996	Philadelphia, Pa.
Merloni, Lou	.262	52	195	30	51	12	0	4	20	15	37	2	0	.385	.330	R	R	5-10	194	4-6-71	1993	Framingham, Mass.
Neill, Mike	.245	67	208	27	51	10	2	5	22	31	70	2	1	.385	.342	L	L	6-2	200	4-27-70	1991	Seaford, Del.
Oliver, Joe	.244	13	41	3	10	1	0	2	6	0	9	1	0	.415	.244	R	R	6-3	220	7-24-65	1983	Orlando, Fla.
Ramos, Kelly	.231	5	13	0	3	0	0	0	0	0	3	0	0	.231	.231	B	R	6-0	168	10-15-76	1994	San Pedro de Macoris, D.R.
Rodriguez, Luis	.263	33	99	17	26	4	0	3	5	6	27	1	0	.394	.305	R	R	5-11	185	1-3-74	1971	Tampa, Fla.
Samuels, Scott	.256	38	125	14	32	9	1	4	14	14	21	5	2	.440	.331	L	R	5-11	190	5-19-71	1992	San Jose, Calif.
Santos, Angel	.200	4	15	1	3	1	0	0	2	1	4	1	0	.267	.235	B	R	5-11	178	8-14-79	1997	Cayey, P.R.
Shave, Jon	.256	84	308	35	79	10	0	6	27	22	49	3	3	.347	.322	R	R	6-0	185	11-4-67	1990	Fernandina Beach, Fla.
Stenson, Dernell	.237	122	464	53	110	18	1	16	69	43	116	0	0	.384	.302	L	L	6-3	230	6-17-78	1996	La Grange, Ga.
Stynes, Chris	.333	4	15	1	5	1	0	0	1	1	2	0	0	.400	.412	R	R	5-10	185	1-19-73	1991	Deerfield Beach, Fla.
Tebbs, Nate	.235	46	136	15	32	7	0	0	6	9	35	5	2	.287	.283	B	R	5-10	170	12-14-72	1993	Riverton, Utah
Valentin, John	.250	10	36	7	9	1	0	2	4	8	4	0	0	.444	.380	R	R	6-0	185	2-18-67	1988	Homdel, N.J.
Veras, Quilvio	.300	3	10	1	3	1	0	0	0	0	3	0	0	.400	.300	B	R	5-8	168	4-3-71	1990	Santo Domingo, D.R.
Veras, Wilton	.230	136	521	44	120	16	2	8	52	14	63	5	6	.315	.259	R	R	6-2	198	1-19-78	1995	Santo Domingo, D.R.
Williams, George	.130	17	46	6	6	2	0	0	1	4	13	0	0	.174	.250	B	R	5-10	215	4-22-69	1991	West Salem, Wis.

PITCHING	W	L	ERA	G	GS	CG	SV	IP	H	R	ER	BB	SO	AVG	B	T	HT	WT	DOB	1st Yr	Resides
Ambrose, John	0	0	10.80	2	0	0	0	3	7	6	4	3	0	.388	R	R	6-5	180	11-1-74	1994	Evansville, Ind.
Banks, Willie	2	0	1.42	2	2	0	0	13	8	3	2	3	12	.173	R	R	6-1	200	2-27-69	1987	Miami, Fla.
2-team (24 Syracuse)	10	5	3.11	26	25	0	0	159	150	66	55	56	133	.258							
Castillo, Carlos	9	11	3.41	28	21	5	0	164	179	78	62	24	114	.277	R	R	6-2	250	4-21-75	1994	Miami, Fla.
Castillo, Frank	0	0	0.00	2	2	0	0	8	7	1	0	0	3	.250	R	R	6-1	200	4-1-69	1987	Cave Creek, Ariz.
Cho, Jin Ho	3	10	4.51	37	16	0	10	118	133	62	59	17	77	.287	R	R	6-3	220	8-16-75	1998	Yeok, Korea
Crawford, Paxton	1	3	5.52	6	6	1	0	29	43	19	18	7	15	.349	R	R	6-3	205	8-4-77	1995	Morrilton, Ark.
Ebert, Derrin	2	3	4.53	10	7	1	0	44	50	29	22	10	34	.279	R	L	6-3	200	8-21-76	1994	Hesperia, Calif.
Erdos, Todd	5	1	3.06	49	0	0	7	68	59	25	23	24	54	.236	R	R	6-1	204	11-21-73	1992	Meadville, Pa.
Farrell, Jim	0	0	0.00	1	0	0	0	1	1	0	0	0	0	.250	R	R	6-1	174	11-1-73	1995	Hartville, Ohio
Gandarillas, Gus	2	1	4.30	12	0	0	1	15	19	9	7	10	7	.327	R	R	6-0	190	7-19-71	1992	Miami, Fla.
Hazlett, Andy	2	0	1.59	9	1	0	1	23	14	4	4	3	18	.171	L	L	6-3	187	8-27-75	1997	The Dalles, Ore.
Heiserman, Rick	0	0	6.23	3	0	0	0	4	4	3	3	4	2	.250	R	R	6-7	225	2-22-73	1994	Omaha, Neb.
Hill, Ken	2	1	6.54	8	8	0	0	32	42	27	23	11	17	.311	R	R	6-2	215	12-14-65	1985	Southlake, Texas
2-team (6 Louisville)	4	2	5.57	14	14	0	0	63	75	46	39	23	33	.291							
Kim, Sun-Woo	6	7	5.36	19	14	0	0	89	93	55	53	27	79	.271	R	R	6-2	180	9-4-77	1997	Seoul, Korea
Kusiewicz, Mike	2	2	4.66	8	7	0	0	37	42	23	19	12	31	.285	R	L	6-2	190	11-1-76	1995	Nepean, Ontario
Lee, Sang	3	5	5.43	43	0	0	4	53	52	33	32	16	44	.252	L	L	6-1	190	3-11-71	2000	Seoul, Korea
McDill, Allen	3	3	3.42	47	0	0	2	71	62	27	27	19	72	.235	L	L	6-1	170	8-23-71	1992	Arkadelphia, Ark.
McLeary, Marty	1	2	3.00	18	0	0	0	30	28	13	10	15	20	.259	R	R	6-5	220	10-26-74	1997	Mansfield, Ohio
Miller, Trever	3	11	5.20	33	15	0	0	116	142	79	67	34	93	.306	R	L	6-4	195	5-29-73	1991	Mount Washington, Ky.
Mix, Greg	0	0	8.53	8	1	0	0	13	15	12	12	7	15	.294	R	R	6-4	225	8-21-71	1993	Albuquerque, N.M.
Ohka, Tomo	2	5	5.57	8	8	1	0	42	55	35	26	9	33	.321	R	R	6-1	179	3-18-76	1999	Kyoto, Japan
Pena, Jesus	3	5	6.59	26	8	0	0	72	92	59	53	38	42	.313	L	L	6-0	170	3-8-75	1993	Santo Domingo, D.R.
Pichardo, Hipolito	0	0	5.40	3	3	0	0	5	3	3	3	4	2	.176	R	R	6-1	195	8-22-69	1988	Esperanza, D.R.
Pulsipher, Bill	1	1	2.87	24	0	0	10	31	27	12	10	10	23	.228	L	L	6-3	200	10-9-73	1992	Port St. Lucie, Fla.
Roque, Rafael	8	5	4.20	20	19	0	0	99	101	52	46	35	68	.261	L	L	6-4	180	1-1-72	1991	Santo Domingo, D.R.
Saberhagen, Bret	0	0	3.00	1	1	0	0	6	3	2	2	1	4	.150	R	R	6-1	200	4-11-64	1983	Babylon, N.Y.
Sekany, Jason	0	3	8.62	7	2	0	0	16	22	16	15	7	8	.328	R	R	6-4	214	7-20-75	1996	Pleasanton, Calif.
Ward, Bryan	0	3	4.28	19	1	0	0	34	47	23	16	6	18	.324	L	L	6-2	205	1-25-72	1993	Mount Holly, N.J.
Williams, Brian	0	0	0.00	3	0	0	0	4	2	0	0	1	3	.153	R	R	6-2	195	2-15-69	1990	Cayce, S.C.

Tony Blanco: Hit .265-17-69 for Class A Augusta

Casey Fossum: Impressive year despite 3-7 record

BILL SETLIFF

FIELDING

Catcher	PCT	G	PO	A	E	DP	PB
Encarnacion	.994	45	316	39	2	4	5
Jensen	.994	25	146	11	1	3	2
Lomasney	.969	17	121	2	4	0	2
Neill	.000	2	0	0	0	0	0
Oliver	.986	12	66	5	1	1	0
Ramos	.955	5	19	2	1	0	2
Rodriguez	.985	30	178	21	3	2	3
G. Williams	.990	16	94	5	1	0	1

First Base	PCT	G	PO	A	E	DP
Alcantara	.978	6	43	1	1	3
Burkhart	.992	98	789	58	7	78
Chevalier	1.000	2	16	3	0	2
Diaz	.970	36	307	11	10	30
Merloni	1.000	1	1	0	0	0
Oliver	.000	1	0	0	0	0
Shave	.944	3	17	0	1	1

Second Base	PCT	G	PO	A	E	DP
Chamblee	.979	87	161	220	8	61
Merloni	.964	18	31	50	3	6
Neill	1.000	1	1	3	0	1
Rodriguez	1.000	1	1	0	0	0
Santos	1.000	4	8	7	0	3
Shave	.962	30	55	71	5	19
Stynes	1.000	1	2	3	0	1
Tebbs	.947	4	7	11	1	2
Q. Veras	1.000	3	2	5	0	0

Third Base	PCT	G	PO	A	E	DP
Merloni	1.000	3	2	2	0	0
Stynes	1.000	1	1	0	0	0
Valentin	.850	8	5	12	3	4
W. Veras	.933	131	128	234	26	31

Shortstop	PCT	G	PO	A	E	DP
DeLeon	.911	9	17	24	4	9
Garciaparra	.941	3	4	12	1	1
Lofton	.946	42	49	125	10	14
Merloni	.945	31	46	75	7	11
Shave	.946	49	77	133	12	30
Tebbs	.931	19	26	41	5	8

Outfield	PCT	G	PO	A	E	DP
Alcantara	.975	61	145	8	4	2
Burkhart	1.000	3	1	0	0	0
Chamblee	1.000	13	23	0	0	1
Chevalier	1.000	3	9	0	0	0
Clemente	.986	83	200	13	3	4
Johnson	.989	43	91	1	1	0
Maddox	1.000	4	12	0	0	0
Neill	.992	54	110	7	1	2
Samuels	.980	35	98	0	2	0
Stenson	.964	120	204	9	8	2
Tebbs	1.000	20	25	1	0	1

TRENTON · Class AA

EASTERN LEAGUE

BATTING	AVG	G	AB	R	H	2B	3B	HR	RBI	BB	SO	SB	CS	SLG	OBP	B	T	HT	WT	DOB	1st Yr	Resides
Ahumada, Alex	.267	4	15	3	4	0	0	0	1	0	4	0	0	.267	.313	R	R	6-1	171	1-20-79	1996	Culiacan, Mexico
Brown, Tonayne	.290	111	396	41	115	21	1	4	31	16	76	4	12	.379	.330	B	R	6-2	189	5-31-79	1997	Tallahassee, Fla.
Capista, Aaron	.213	117	404	48	86	25	4	2	40	20	48	2	1	.309	.252	R	R	6-2	240	10-31-73	1995	Scotia, N.Y.
Chevalier, Virgil	.261	121	456	59	119	25	1	16	67	43	58	3	3	.425	.324	R	R	6-2	170	12-15-75	1993	Guaynabo, P.R.
Clemente, Edgard	.356	11	45	7	16	3	1	3	7	2	6	0	1	.667	.383	R	R	6-2	164	9-26-74	1997	Guayama, P.R.
DeLeon, Jorge	.252	29	111	14	28	6	2	1	10	12	12	2	1	.369	.325	L	R	6-2	215	4-24-75	1996	Jensen Beach, Fla.
DiPace, Danny	.129	12	31	1	4	1	0	0	1	1	14	0	0	.161	.182	R	R	6-1	205	4-15-76	1997	Marietta, Ga.
Fischer, Mark	.222	127	463	48	103	22	2	11	55	25	148	3	1	.350	.260	R	R	6-4	184	11-5-78	1997	Guadalajara, Mexico
Garcia, Luis	.310	63	229	35	71	20	1	14	45	28	68	0	1	.590	.384	R	R	6-0	180	10-12-75	1997	Maracaibo, Venez.
Graham, Jess	.274	49	124	9	34	7	0	4	18	15	36	0	1	.427	.350	L	L	6-0	180	1-4-76	1997	Fairmont, W.Va.
Haas, Danny	.175	29	80	10	14	3	0	0	5	8	20	1	0	.213	.258	L	R	5-11	180	10-27-75	1997	Paducah, Ky.
Johnson, Rontrez	.282	73	255	48	72	15	1	10	31	22	40	17	7	.467	.356	R	R	5-10	165	12-8-76	1995	Marshall, Texas
Leon, Carlos	.222	11	27	4	6	0	2	0	2	1	4	2	2	.370	.276	B	R	5-10	169	8-31-79	1997	Cabimas, Venez.
Lofton, James	.315	29	111	22	35	7	0	5	11	10	23	3	1	.514	.377	R	R	5-9	170	3-6-74	1993	Los Angeles, Calif.
Lomasney, Steve	.249	58	209	24	52	14	2	10	29	23	76	0	1	.478	.332	R	R	6-0	195	8-29-77	1995	Peabody, Mass.
Maddox, Garry	.300	84	287	47	86	25	5	11	48	40	76	4	5	.537	.386	L	R	6-3	180	10-24-74	1996	Philadelphia, Pa.
Nadeau, Rick	.167	6	18	1	3	1	0	0	1	0	5	0	0	.222	.167	R	R	6-0	195	11-20-75	1999	Granada Hills, Calif.
Ramos, Kelly	.209	56	182	14	38	6	1	7	27	6	49	0	0	.368	.236	B	R	6-0	168	10-15-76	1994	San Pedro de Macoris, D.R.
Rodriguez, Luis	.209	51	163	21	34	7	2	6	22	6	36	2	1	.387	.237	R	R	5-11	185	1-3-74	1991	Tampa, Fla.
Rose, Mike	.167	9	24	3	4	0	0	1	2	6	10	0	1	.292	.333	B	R	6-1	185	8-25-76	1995	Sacramento, Calif.
Salzano, Jerry	.283	125	453	65	128	31	1	7	54	50	90	15	6	.402	.368	R	R	6-0	175	10-27-74	1992	Trenton, N.J.
Sanchez, Freddy	.326	44	178	25	58	20	0	2	19	9	21	3	1	.472	.363	R	R	5-11	185	12-21-77	2000	Burbank, Calif.
Santos, Angel	.271	129	510	75	138	32	0	14	52	54	106	26	9	.416	.343	B	R	5-11	178	8-14-79	1997	Cayey, P.R.
Valentin, John	.154	3	13	1	2	1	0	0	1	3	0	0	0	.231	.214	R	R	6-0	185	2-18-67	1988	Homdel, N.J.

PITCHING	W	L	ERA	G	GS	CG	SV	IP	H	R	ER	BB	SO	AVG	B	T	HT	WT	DOB	1st Yr	Resides
Ambrose, John	0	0	14.21	5	0	0	0	6	12	10	10	5	7	.413	R	R	6-5	180	11-1-74	1994	Evansville, Ind.
Arroyo, Luis	0	1	9.22	7	0	0	0	14	28	17	14	10	10	.405	L	L	6-0	174	9-29-73	1992	Bajadero, P.R.
Betancourt, Rafael	0	1	5.63	16	0	0	4	24	28	16	15	3	27	.294	R	R	6-2	176	4-29-75	1994	Cumana, Venez.
Cisar, Mark	1	1	4.31	21	0	0	3	31	30	15	15	7	21	.263	R	R	5-11	176	5-22-75	1998	New Martinsville, W.Va.

ORGANIZATION STATISTICS

PITCHING	W	L	ERA	G	GS	CG	SV	IP	H	R	ER	BB	SO	AVG	B	T	HT	WT	DOB	1st Yr	Resides
De la Rosa, Jorge	1	3	5.84	29	0	0	0	37	56	35	24	20	27	.347	L	L	6-1	192	4-5-81	1998	San Nicolas, Mexico
Duchscherer, Justin	6	3	2.44	12	12	1	0	74	49	25	20	14	69	.178	R	R	6-3	164	11-19-77	1996	Lubbock, Texas
Ebert, Derrin	7	9	4.64	20	20	0	0	116	134	67	60	23	89	.290	R	L	6-3	203	8-21-76	1994	Hesperia, Calif.
Elmore, Chris	5	3	2.29	14	13	0	0	79	76	34	20	19	56	.255	L	L	6-1	195	4-28-77	2000	Virginia Beach, Va.
Farrell, Jim	0	0	0.00	1	0	0	0	2	1	0	0	1	2	.142	R	R	6-1	174	11-1-73	1995	Hartville, Ohio
Florie, Bryce	0	1	1.64	6	1	0	2	11	5	4	2	6	17	.135	R	R	5-11	192	5-21-70	1988	Goose Creek, S.C.
Fossum, Casey	3	7	2.83	20	20	0	0	118	102	47	37	28	130	.230	B	L	6-1	160	1-9-78	1999	Nashville, Tenn.
Garrett, Josh	3	6	5.64	46	4	0	0	81	84	61	51	44	68	.266	R	R	6-4	205	1-12-78	1997	Richland, Ind.
Hancock, Josh	8	6	3.65	24	24	0	0	131	138	60	53	37	119	.272	R	R	6-3	217	4-11-78	1998	Tupelo, Miss.
Hazlett, Andy	6	1	3.81	14	7	0	1	52	51	24	22	13	39	.261	L	L	6-3	187	8-27-75	1997	The Dalles, Ore.
Hill, Terry	1	3	3.79	22	0	0	0	38	38	25	16	10	42	.251	L	L	5-10	179	10-17-75	1998	Thibodaux, La.
Kusiewicz, Mike	4	5	3.44	18	17	0	0	89	83	39	34	19	92	.250	R	L	6-2	190	11-1-76	1995	Nepean, Ontario
Leach, B.J.	2	2	4.50	23	0	0	1	40	42	21	20	11	40	.265	R	R	5-11	175	8-3-77	1999	Seminole, Fla.
McLeary, Marty	9	6	3.46	35	0	0	2	55	58	30	21	30	42	.273	R	R	6-5	220	10-26-74	1997	Mansfield, Ohio
Montalbano, Greg	3	3	4.50	10	10	0	0	48	50	25	24	14	45	.273	L	L	6-2	185	8-24-77	2000	Westboro, Mass.
Norton, Jason	0	2	12.12	6	4	0	0	16	24	25	22	8	17	.347	R	R	6-3	205	4-9-76	1998	Mobile, Ala.
Pena, Jesus	2	4	5.06	14	2	0	1	32	46	20	18	7	35	.330	L	L	6-0	170	3-8-75	1993	Santo Domingo, D.R.
Saberhagen, Bret	0	0	2.45	1	1	0	0	4	5	1	1	1	4	.384	R	R	6-1	200	4-11-64	1983	Babylon, N.Y.
Sekany, Jason	1	5	6.07	15	7	0	0	56	71	40	38	19	41	.319	R	R	6-4	214	7-20-75	1996	Pleasanton, Calif.
Spencer, Corey	3	5	4.52	55	0	0	20	78	85	41	39	31	82	.276	L	L	6-1	220	9-4-76	1999	Andover, Mass.

FIELDING

Catcher	PCT	G	PO	A	E	DP	PB
Chevalier	1.000	1	6	0	0	0	1
Lomasney	.987	53	399	48	6	4	9
Ramos	.994	55	442	52	3	8	8
Rodriguez	.982	36	239	29	5	1	5
Rose	1.000	9	51	8	0	0	1

First Base	PCT	G	PO	A	E	DP
Chevalier	.989	79	582	55	7	52
DiPace	.800	3	12	0	3	1
Garcia	.990	57	446	32	5	49
Rodriguez	1.000	3	22	2	0	3
Salzano	.857	3	18	0	3	1

Second Base	PCT	G	PO	A	E	DP
Ahumada	.846	2	5	6	2	0
Capista	.962	6	14	11	1	6

	PCT	G	PO	A	E	DP	PB
DeLeon	1.000	2	2	3	0	1	
Leon	.833	1	3	2	1	1	
Lofton	.960	7	12	12	1	3	
Santos	.966	127	274	273	19	81	

Third Base	PCT	G	PO	A	E	DP
Ahumada	1.000	2	3	11	0	2
Capista	.894	39	20	81	12	5
DeLeon	.987	26	19	55	1	3
Lofton	.913	10	5	16	2	2
Rodriguez	.875	7	2	12	2	3
Salzano	.905	68	46	135	19	16

Shortstop	PCT	G	PO	A	E	DP
Capista	.954	78	113	199	15	37
DeLeon	1.000	2	2	8	0	0
Leon	.935	11	10	19	2	5

	PCT	G	PO	A	E	DP
Lofton	.964	12	22	31	2	9
Sanchez	.948	44	55	110	9	26
Valentin	.917	3	3	8	1	0

Outfield	PCT	G	PO	A	E	DP
Brown	.985	109	191	10	3	1
Chevalier	.982	26	50	5	1	1
Clemente	1.000	11	29	1	0	0
Fischer	.987	120	215	7	3	2
Graham	.965	42	52	3	2	0
Haas	1.000	12	15	2	0	0
Johnson	.964	72	156	3	6	0
Maddox	.963	47	72	6	3	0
Nadeau	1.000	3	8	0	0	0
Rodriguez	1.000	6	8	0	0	0

SARASOTA — Class A

FLORIDA STATE LEAGUE

BATTING	AVG	G	AB	R	H	2B	3B	HR	RBI	BB	SO	SB	CS	SLG	OBP	B	T	HT	WT	DOB	1st Yr	Resides
Ahumada, Alex	.243	112	379	48	92	23	0	6	42	34	73	22	9	.351	.320	R	R	6-1	171	1-20-79	1996	Culiacan, Mexico
Anderson, Jon	.000	4	7	0	0	0	0	0	1	1	1	0	1	.000	.125	B	R	5-9	150	10-17-76	1999	South Barrington, Ill.
Everett, Carl	.429	2	7	0	3	0	0	0	2	0	0	0	0	.429	.556	B	R	6-0	190	6-3-71	1990	Tampa, Fla.
Garcia, Luis	.303	65	267	38	81	14	1	12	44	18	61	2	2	.498	.348	R	R	6-4	184	11-5-78	1997	Guadalajara, Mexico
Graham, Jess	.255	17	47	6	12	2	0	1	2	6	11	0	1	.362	.340	L	L	6-0	180	10-12-75	1997	Fairmont, W.Va.
Headley, Justin	.254	114	409	54	104	28	1	6	53	54	60	13	6	.372	.343	L	L	6-2	200	4-27-76	2000	Memphis, Tenn.
Kerrigan, Joe	.248	103	367	43	91	14	2	5	31	49	51	5	3	.338	.342	L	R	5-10	180	11-1-77	1999	Ardmore, Pa.
Larned, Drew	.182	69	192	23	35	10	0	1	18	32	53	3	5	.250	.301	R	R	6-0	195	11-13-75	1998	Concord, Ohio
Minus, Steve	.227	112	387	41	88	10	4	8	40	59	102	6	2	.336	.331	R	R	6-2	210	12-30-76	1999	San Antonio, Texas
Nadeau, Rick	.261	96	348	32	91	17	2	5	45	33	55	6	5	.365	.328	R	R	6-0	195	11-20-75	1999	Granada Hills, Calif.
Pena, Rodolfo	.237	64	198	13	47	4	0	2	11	8	40	0	2	.288	.286	R	R	6-0	197	3-7-79	1997	Montecristi, D.R.
Ramos, Kelly	.167	17	66	4	11	2	0	0	3	1	15	0	0	.197	.191	B	R	6-0	168	10-15-76	1994	San Pedro de Macoris, D.R.
Riepe, Andy	.182	5	11	2	2	0	0	0	1	1	2	0	0	.182	.250	R	R	6-1	200	3-26-77	1999	Danbury, Conn.
Rodriguez, Carlos	.213	128	502	56	107	21	2	12	54	27	144	15	15	.335	.262	R	R	6-2	210	12-6-77	1998	Louisville, Ky.
Sanchez, Freddy	.339	69	280	40	95	19	4	1	24	22	30	5	3	.446	.388	R	R	5-11	185	12-21-77	2000	Burbank, Calif.
Santoro, Pat	.206	106	335	44	69	10	1	10	35	30	112	3	4	.331	.278	R	R	6-0	175	11-9-78	1998	River Forest, Ill.
Sherrod, Justin	.305	37	141	20	43	8	3	7	23	11	37	5	1	.553	.357	R	R	6-2	210	1-11-78	2000	Boynton Beach, Fla.
Warren, Chris	.264	106	382	49	101	20	3	10	51	32	112	11	5	.411	.342	R	R	6-3	205	9-30-76	1998	Fayetteville, N.C.
Williams, Brady	.195	79	251	37	49	20	3	5	21	43	80	5	3	.359	.318	R	R	6-1	180	10-18-79	1999	Dunedin, Fla.

GAMES BY POSITION: C—Larned 66, R. Pena 63, Ramos 17, Riepe 4. **1B**—Ahumada 1, Garcia 54, Minus 59, Williams 25. **2B**—Kerrigan 48, Santoro 74, Williams 16. **3B**—Ahumada 51, Garcia 1, Minus 36, Sherrod 36, Williams 18. **SS**—Ahumada 54, Sanchez 69, Williams 17. **OF**—Anderson 3, Garcia 10, Graham 15, Headley 102, Nadeau 81, Rodriguez 127, Warren 83, Williams 1.

PITCHING	W	L	ERA	G	GS	CG	SV	IP	H	R	ER	BB	SO	AVG	B	T	HT	WT	DOB	1st Yr	Resides
Ambrose, John	0	1	2.87	10	1	0	1	16	13	8	5	5	18	.224	R	R	6-5	180	11-1-74	1994	Evansville, Ind.
An, Byeong	2	8	3.62	23	21	1	0	119	122	68	48	42	84	.263	L	L	6-2	190	7-1-80	2001	Kyong Ki-Do, Korea
Arrojo, Rolando	0	1	6.00	2	2	0	0	3	4	2	2	1	5	.307	R	R	6-4	220	7-18-68	1997	St. Petersburg, Fla.
Baker, Brad	7	9	4.73	24	23	0	0	120	132	77	63	64	103	.272	R	R	6-2	180	11-6-80	1999	Leyden, Mass.
Cisar, Mark	1	1	4.50	27	0	0	6	38	41	21	19	15	39	.278	R	R	5-11	176	5-22-75	1998	New Martinsville, W.Va.
Cone, David	0	0	0.00	1	1	0	0	4	2	0	0	0	6	.142	L	R	6-1	200	1-2-63	1981	Greenwich, Conn.
De La Rosa, Jorge	0	1	1.21	12	0	0	2	30	13	7	4	12	27	.127	L	L	6-1	192	4-5-81	1998	San Nicolas de la Garza, Mexico
Dickinson, Rodney	3	5	6.75	29	0	0	11	46	46	29	22	13	27	.254	R	R	5-10	175	1-9-75	1998	Bethlehem, Ga.
Elmore, Chris	6	2	2.41	17	5	0	1	60	58	25	16	12	40	.254	L	L	6-1	195	4-28-77	2000	Virginia Beach, Va.
Florie, Bryce	0	0	0.00	2	0	0	0	5	3	0	0	5	7	.187	R	R	5-11	192	5-21-70	1988	Goose Creek, S.C.
Fontana, Frank	2	3	3.51	9	7	0	0	49	57	25	19	8	32	.293	R	R	6-3	175	5-21-79	2000	Parma Heights, Ohio
Gamble, Jerome	0	0	7.88	3	2	0	1	8	11	8	7	4	7	.333	R	R	6-2	202	4-5-80	1998	Alexander City, Ala.
Glaser, Eric	4	3	2.54	37	5	0	1	89	74	28	25	27	82	.225	R	R	6-6	239	1-23-78	1997	Fort Thomas, Ky.
Graham, Frank	2	10	5.82	39	1	0	0	82	119	68	53	27	52	.340	R	R	6-2	180	8-7-78	1998	Johnstown, Ohio
Jacob, Russell	0	0	6.75	3	0	0	0	4	4	3	2	0	.266	R	R	6-6	240	1-2-75	1994	Winter Haven, Fla.
Lara, Nelson	1	3	10.50	27	0	0	1	30	40	40	35	28	29	.327	R	R	6-4	185	7-15-78	1995	Santo Domingo, D.R.

PITCHING	W	L	ERA	G	GS	CG	SV	IP	H	R	ER	BB	SO	AVG	B	T	HT	WT	DOB	1st Yr	Resides
Martinez, Anastacio	9	12	3.35	25	24	1	0	145	130	69	54	39	123	.235	R	R	6-2	180	11-3-80	1998	Santo Domingo, D.R.
Miller, Trever	0	0	2.25	3	2	0	0	8	3	2	2	1	6	.115	R	L	6-4	195	5-29-73	1991	Mount Washington, Ky.
Montalbano, Greg	9	3	2.96	17	15	0	0	91	66	36	30	25	77	.200	L	L	6-2	185	8-24-77	2000	Westboro, Mass.
Pena, Juan	0	3	5.19	8	8	0	0	26	29	15	15	11	31	.273	R	R	6-5	215	6-27-77	1995	Carol City, Fla.
Pichardo, Hipolito	0	0	4.50	3	3	0	0	6	8	3	3	2	8	.296	R	R	6-1	195	8-22-69	1988	Esperanza, D.R.
Riccobono, Rick	1	3	5.81	35	6	0	0	79	100	62	51	38	50	.302	R	R	6-2	225	1-3-80	1998	Commack, N.Y.
Saberhagen, Bret	0	0	6.75	1	1	0	0	4	5	3	3	0	3	.294	R	R	6-1	200	4-11-64	1983	Babylon, N.Y.
Sams, Aaron	0	0	0.00	2	0	0	1	3	1	2	0	2		.090	L	L	6-1	205	4-30-76	1998	Bedford, Pa.
Solano, Alex	2	9	4.78	39	2	0	1	90	113	71	48	32	61	.303	R	R	6-1	150	4-22-80	1997	La Romana, D.R.
Song, Seung	5	2	1.68	8	8	0	0	48	28	11	9	18	56	.163	R	R	6-1	192	6-29-80	1999	Pusan, Korea
Viera, Rolando	0	2	6.00	6	0	0	0	12	12	8	8	6	12	.250	L	L	5-10	182	8-1-73	2001	Tampa, Fla.
Ward, Bryan	0	1	33.75	1	0	0	0	1	7	7	5	1	1	.583	L	L	6-2	205	1-25-72	1993	Mount Holly, N.J.

AUGUSTA — Class A

SOUTH ATLANTIC LEAGUE

BATTING	AVG	G	AB	R	H	2B	3B	HR	RBI	BB	SO	SB	CS	SLG	OBP	B	T	HT	WT	DOB	1st Yr	Resides
Anderson, Jon	.211	47	128	12	27	2	0	0	6	8	30	5	4	.227	.261	B	R	5-9	150	10-17-76	1999	South Barrington, Ill.
Asadoorian, Rick	.212	116	406	50	86	13	6	6	40	47	139	13	4	.318	.299	R	R	6-2	185	7-23-80	1999	Whitinsville, Mass.
Barnowski, Bryan	.189	42	143	17	27	6	0	3	15	13	50	0	1	.294	.282	R	R	6-2	205	9-3-80	1999	Granville, Mass.
Blanco, Tony	.265	96	370	44	98	23	2	17	69	17	78	1	0	.476	.308	R	R	6-1	176	11-10-81	1998	Haina, D.R.
Brisson, Dustin	.295	90	319	49	94	13	1	10	53	40	76	3	0	.436	.376	L	R	6-3	210	3-18-78	2000	Orlando, Fla.
Cooper, Matt	.177	37	124	9	22	4	0	3	12	14	46	1	1	.282	.293	R	R	6-3	200	10-10-80	2000	Stillwater, Okla.
Dorta, Melvin	.267	36	135	19	36	4	1	0	18	8	16	6	5	.311	.320	R	R	5-11	160	1-15-82	1999	Guscara, Venez.
Esposito, Brian	.190	90	311	21	59	13	0	3	30	13	81	0	0	.260	.224	R	R	6-1	195	2-24-79	2000	Tolland, Conn.
Gambino, Mike	.077	7	26	2	2	1	0	0	0	2	4	0	1	.115	.143	R	R	5-9	175	7-9-77	2000	Garrison, N.Y.
Guerrero, Julio	.197	94	314	27	62	9	1	1	25	21	56	14	6	.242	.249	R	R	6-3	182	10-18-80	1998	Don Gregorio, D.R.
Hattig, John	.285	50	179	25	51	9	1	1	23	22	42	4	1	.363	.371	R	R	6-2	215	2-27-80	1999	Piti, Guam
Money, Freddie	.189	21	74	9	14	2	1	1	7	10	21	5	5	.284	.282	R	R	6-0	165	1-11-79	2000	Webb, Ala.
Mooney, Dan	.239	27	88	11	21	8	0	3	14	2	23	1	0	.432	.299	R	R	6-0	195	2-14-77	2000	Forked River, N.J.
Nieves, Raul	.246	114	390	49	96	13	0	1	37	26	75	12	2	.287	.300	B	R	6-2	185	1-1-79	2000	Barranquitas, P.R.
Perez, Kenny	.248	120	407	44	101	21	2	6	37	48	62	11	6	.354	.330	B	R	6-2	190	9-28-81	2000	Miami, Fla.
Riepe, Andy	.234	33	107	11	25	2	0	0	17	13	23	0	0	.252	.320	R	R	6-1	200	3-26-77	1999	Danbury, Conn.
Seiber, Antron	.223	120	462	59	103	16	3	5	27	50	113	36	12	.303	.308	R	R	6-1	185	5-19-80	1999	Independence, La.
Sherrod, Justin	.290	87	307	53	89	24	3	11	43	34	102	16	7	.495	.396	R	R	6-2	210	1-11-78	2000	Boynton Beach, Fla.
Smith, Will	.285	72	228	45	65	13	0	0	13	37	44	19	9	.342	.393	R	R	5-11	180	5-7-77	2000	Prattville, Ala.
Youkilis, Kevin	.167	5	12	0	2	0	0	0	3	3	0	0	0	.167	.375	R	R	6-1	220	3-15-79	2001	Cincinnati, Ohio

GAMES BY POSITION: C—Barnowski 23, Esposito 89, Mooney 21, Riepe 13. **1B**—Brisson 82, Cooper 31, Hattig 27, Riepe 1. **2B**—Anderson 33, Dorta 36, Gambino 7, Hattig 2, Nieves 68. **3B**—Anderson 8, Blanco 51, Hattig 11, Mooney 5, Nieves 23, Riepe 1, Sherrod 49, Youkilis 1. **SS**—Anderson 4, Nieves 21, Perez 118, Sherrod 1. **OF**—Anderson 1, Asadoorian 96, Guerrero 84, Hattig 1, Money 19, Nieves 5, Riepe 9, Seiber 117, Sherrod 34, Smith 58.

PITCHING	W	L	ERA	G	GS	CG	SV	IP	H	R	ER	BB	SO	AVG	B	T	HT	WT	DOB	1st Yr	Resides
Adams, Brian	9	8	3.52	34	2	0	1	79	81	45	31	36	60	.275	L	L	6-3	190	10-2-77	2000	Bishopville, S.C.
Dickinson, Rodney	2	0	1.86	23	0	0	11	29	28	7	6	0	30	.250	R	R	5-10	175	1-9-75	1998	Bethlehem, Ga.
Fontana, Tony	2	2	1.94	24	4	0	6	70	66	21	15	9	62	.236	R	R	6-3	175	5-21-79	2000	Parma Heights, Ohio
Francisco, Franklin	4	3	2.91	37	0	0	2	68	40	25	22	30	90	.168	R	R	6-2	179	6-11-80	1997	Santo Domingo, D.R.
Giese, Dan	6	4	2.19	46	0	0	9	74	65	27	18	8	95	.225	R	R	6-3	200	5-19-77	1999	San Clemente, Calif.
Lara, Mauricio	7	6	3.02	20	19	1	0	107	114	45	36	24	96	.279	B	L	5-11	185	4-2-79	1999	Hermosillo, Mexico
Miniel, Rene	8	4	2.73	27	23	0	0	122	93	49	37	38	114	.210	R	R	6-2	175	4-26-81	1998	Santo Domingo, D.R.
Peres, Luis	8	8	3.58	26	25	0	0	126	118	69	50	42	113	.231	R	L	6-0	150	2-10-81	1999	Villa Riva, D.R.
Prendes, Alex	1	0	2.57	8	0	0	0	21	22	7	6	5	14	.275	L	L	6-0	185	12-30-78	2001	Miami, Fla.
Rundles, Rich	7	6	2.43	19	19	0	0	115	109	46	31	10	94	.247	L	L	6-5	180	6-3-81	1999	New Market, Tenn.
Sams, Aaron	1	1	2.83	17	0	0	1	29	25	10	9	18	31	.231	L	L	6-1	205	4-30-76	1998	Bedford, Pa.
Sclafani, Anthony	1	3	5.63	8	0	0	0	16	20	10	10	6	10	.307	R	R	6-1	175	7-28-81	1999	Staten Island, N.Y.
2-team (5 Macon)	2	3	3.90	13	0	0	1	30	31	14	13	10	22	.267							
Song, Seung	3	2	2.04	14	14	0	0	75	56	24	17	18	79	.208	R	R	6-1	192	6-29-80	1999	Pusan, Korea
Thompson, Matt	9	10	3.22	25	24	0	0	134	115	58	48	19	97	.228	R	R	6-2	205	8-28-81	1999	Boise, Idaho
Troilo, Joe	4	3	3.55	30	2	0	1	58	49	33	23	21	40	.221	R	R	6-0	190	9-27-77	2000	Avondale, Pa.
Villegas, Felix	2	5	3.59	34	7	0	6	90	100	63	36	30	65	.273	R	R	6-2	195	8-8-78	2000	San Juan, P.R.

LOWELL — Short-Season Class A

NEW YORK-PENN LEAGUE

BATTING	AVG	G	AB	R	H	2B	3B	HR	RBI	BB	SO	SB	CS	SLG	OBP	B	T	HT	WT	DOB	1st Yr	Resides
Bailie, Stefan	.233	23	90	9	21	4	0	2	15	6	21	0	0	.344	.303	R	R	6-0	215	5-16-80	2001	Mesa, Wash.
Barnowski, Bryan	.157	14	51	7	8	5	0	1	2	6	22	0	0	.314	.271	R	R	6-2	205	9-3-80	1999	Granville, Mass.
Brackley, Carlos	.360	6	25	6	9	3	1	1	6	1	8	0	1	.680	.407	R	R	6-2	225	10-19-79	2001	Hamilton, N.J.
Brunner, Ryan	.241	69	261	35	63	16	1	1	34	41	57	1	0	.322	.350	L	L	6-0	220	1-20-79	2001	Charles City, Iowa
Campos, Mario	.231	60	225	22	52	16	0	5	31	11	80	2	3	.369	.270	R	R	6-6	235	11-24-78	2001	Miami, Fla.
Coffey, Kris	.274	69	274	27	75	5	0	0	13	28	50	22	9	.292	.342	R	R	5-9	175	4-27-79	2001	Newark, Calif.
Daubach, Brian	.000	1	2	0	0	0	0	0	0	1	1	0	0	.000	.333	L	R	6-1	201	2-11-72	1990	Belleville, Ill.
Gambino, Mike	.243	46	169	20	41	10	2	0	25	18	25	0	1	.325	.314	R	R	5-9	175	7-9-77	2000	Garrison, N.Y.
Gonzalez, Carlos	.222	3	9	1	2	0	0	0	1	3	0	0	0	.222	.300	R	L	6-1	220	10-1-81	1999	Santo Domingo, D.R.
Hattig, John	.111	11	45	4	5	0	1	1	5	3	7	1	0	.222	.184	B	R	6-2	215	2-27-80	1999	Piti, Guam
Johnson, Patrick	.143	6	21	1	3	0	0	0	2	4	6	0	1	.143	.280	L	L	6-1	225	2-6-79	2000	Magee, Miss.
Kent, Bryan	.231	40	117	16	27	6	0	0	13	15	26	7	2	.282	.343	R	R	6-0	190	6-27-78	2001	Waco, Texas
Lewis, Russell	.292	47	168	26	49	14	3	2	27	22	34	0	1	.446	.378	L	R	5-8	175	3-3-78	2000	Blue Ridge, Texas
Martinez, Edgar	.320	49	175	21	56	12	3	2	25	10	23	1	0	.463	.370	R	R	6-0	160	10-23-81	1998	Guigue, Venez.
Money, Freddie	.249	57	221	40	55	13	1	2	21	29	46	27	5	.344	.339	R	R	6-0	165	1-11-79	2000	Webb, Ala.
Nathans, John	.160	31	75	16	12	2	0	0	3	18	30	2	0	.187	.323	R	R	6-1	215	6-10-79	2001	Warwick, N.Y.
Noboa, Joel	.181	46	155	16	28	2	0	5	19	1	60	4	2	.290	.196	R	R	6-1	184	11-27-79	1997	Santo Domingo, D.R.
Peterson, Brian	.259	8	27	5	7	2	0	0	6	6	3	5	0	.333	.429	R	R	6-2	205	10-22-78	1999	Greencastle, Pa.
Porzel, Alec	.256	44	172	16	44	10	2	1	19	13	19	2	1	.355	.310	R	R	5-11	190	1-14-79	2001	Lisle, Ill.

BATTING	AVG	G	AB	R	H	2B	3B	HR	RBI	BB	SO	SB	CS	SLG	OBP	B	T	HT	WT	DOB	1st Yr	Resides
Reed, Robert	.267	4	15	2	4	1	0	0	0	0	5	0	0	.333	.267	R	R	6-1	210	9-17-77	2000	Conshohocken, Pa.
Rodriguez, Ivan	.307	25	88	11	27	3	0	1	10	8	20	6	4	.375	.365	R	R	5-11	170	4-4-81	1998	Esperanza, D.R.
Salazar, Juan	.269	7	26	1	7	0	0	0	4	3	4	2	2	.269	.375	B	R	5-11	156	10-17-81	1999	Barquisimeto, Venez.
Youkilis, Kevin	.317	59	183	52	58	14	2	3	28	70	28	4	3	.464	.512	R	R	6-1	220	3-15-79	2001	Cincinnati, Ohio

GAMES BY POSITION: C—Barnowski 10, Gonzalez 3, Martinez 38, Nathans 12, Reed 4, Rodriguez 18. **1B**—Bailie 21, Brunner 42, Daubach 1, Hattig 4, Nathans 7, Noboa 5. **2B**—Gambino 27, Kent 2, Lewis 37, Noboa 6, Peterson 2, Salazar 6. **3B**—Hattig 1, Kent 5, Lewis 6, Nathans 2, Peterson 8, Youkilis 59. **SS**—Gambino 3, Kent 31, Porzel 44, Salazar 2. **OF**—Brackley 47, Brunner 20, Campos 56, Coffey 62, Johnson 6, Money 56, Noboa 29.

PITCHING	W	L	ERA	G	GS	CG	SV	IP	H	R	ER	BB	SO	AVG	B	T	HT	WT	DOB	1st Yr	Resides
Benitez, Fabricio	0	3	4.20	9	9	0	0	49	47	25	23	11	23	.258	R	R	6-3	175	5-10-81	1997	Santo Domingo, D.R.
Dumatrait, Phil	1	1	3.48	2	2	0	0	10	9	4	4	4	15	.225	R	L	6-2	170	7-12-81	2000	Bakersfield, Calif.
Friske, Parker	3	2	5.23	19	3	0	1	53	70	38	31	23	38	.313	L	L	6-4	210	5-1-79	2001	Virginia Beach, Va.
Garces, Rich	0	0	0.00	2	2	0	0	2	1	0	0	0	1	.142	R	R	6-0	215	5-18-71	1988	Maracay, Venez.
Generelli, Daniel	1	8	4.71	16	14	0	0	71	69	49	37	38	51	.257	R	R	6-2	200	8-25-80	1999	Hubbardston, Mass.
Grant, Michael	0	2	6.10	5	1	0	1	10	14	7	7	6	7	.318	R	R	6-1	190	11-12-79	2000	Beech Grove, Ind.
Hall, Shane	0	3	4.67	14	0	0	2	27	36	19	14	9	21	.318	R	R	6-5	225	6-14-80	2000	Herford, Ariz.
Howell, Jason	4	2	5.64	20	0	0	2	53	55	38	33	16	38	.263	L	L	6-2	195	5-25-79	2001	Millers Creek, N.C.
Huang, Jun-chung	5	2	2.25	10	8	0	0	48	41	16	12	12	55	.234	R	R	6-0	172	4-25-82	2001	Chau Chou, Taiwan
Kennedy, Jodie	0	1	3.06	9	0	0	1	18	17	6	6	6	6	.253	R	L	6-0	180	7-16-79	2001	Shubuta, Miss.
Lane, Brian	1	2	5.33	6	6	0	0	27	29	19	16	12	22	.261	R	R	6-3	220	12-5-80	2001	Crofton, Md.
Prendes, Alex	1	2	1.37	15	0	0	2	20	13	7	3	15	20	.188	L	L	6-0	185	12-30-78	2001	Miami, Fla.
Rhodes, Shane	4	4	2.89	15	14	1	0	72	62	28	23	25	58	.233	L	L	6-2	200	1-19-80	2001	Monkton, Md.
Rogers, Jed	2	2	3.83	23	0	0	4	40	43	21	17	26	35	.279	R	R	6-2	205	12-15-78	2001	Westerly, R.I.
Rudrude, Brett	5	3	2.95	17	7	0	1	73	65	30	24	21	44	.239	R	R	6-3	195	1-23-79	2001	Alta Loma, Calif.
Sams, Aaron	2	1	5.91	4	0	0	0	11	14	7	7	6	7	.325	L	L	6-1	205	4-30-76	1998	Bedford, Pa.
Sander, Richard	1	0	2.79	4	0	0	1	10	9	3	3	3	20	.236	R	R	6-2	225	10-27-80	2001	Colton, Calif.
Weatherby, Charlie	2	3	3.02	13	10	0	0	51	45	21	17	15	41	.239	R	R	6-0	200	12-23-78	2001	Beaufort, N.C.
Zervas, Paul	0	3	4.60	17	0	0	1	29	27	18	15	11	16	.238	R	R	6-0	175	11-2-79	2001	Boca Raton, Fla.

FORT MYERS — Rookie

GULF COAST LEAGUE

BATTING	AVG	G	AB	R	H	2B	3B	HR	RBI	BB	SO	SB	CS	SLG	OBP	B	T	HT	WT	DOB	1st Yr	Resides
Bonvechio, Brett	.217	19	69	4	15	5	1	1	5	9	12	0	2	.362	.304	L	R	6-1	190	11-13-82	2001	Santa Clara, Calif.
Brackley, Carlos	.329	49	152	24	50	8	1	6	21	9	27	3	3	.513	.376	R	R	6-2	225	10-10-79	2001	Hamilton, N.J.
Brown, Dustin	.254	36	126	15	32	5	4	0	14	7	24	1	2	.357	.289	R	R	6-0	187	6-19-82	2001	Prescott Valley, Ariz.
Caraballo, Carlos	.212	47	137	16	29	3	3	1	14	8	39	8	3	.299	.270	R	R	6-0	160	5-26-80	2000	Salinas, P.R.
Cooper, Matt	.267	56	187	33	50	14	1	7	34	32	57	2	0	.465	.397	R	R	6-3	200	10-10-80	2000	Stillwater, Okla.
Cruz, Luis	.259	53	197	18	51	9	3	1	8	7	17	1	4	.350	.285	R	R	6-1	185	2-10-84	2001	Sonora, Mexico
DeLeon, Jorge	.208	10	24	6	5	2	0	0	0	4	4	1	0	.292	.345	R	R	6-2	164	9-26-74	1997	Guayama, P.R.
Devries, Jonathan	.316	21	57	8	18	5	0	0	6	6	19	0	0	.404	.418	R	R	6-3	205	8-22-82	2001	Irvine, Calif.
Dorta, Melvin	.408	21	76	19	31	6	0	2	8	11	5	7	3	.566	.489	R	R	5-11	160	1-15-82	1999	Guscara, Venez.
Encarnacion, Angelo	.200	3	5	1	1	1	0	0	0	2	0	1	0	.400	.429	R	R	5-9	190	4-18-73	1990	Santo Domingo, D.R.
Everett, Carl	.200	3	10	2	2	0	0	2	2	1	3	0	0	.800	.333	B	R	6-0	190	6-3-71	1990	Tampa, Fla.
Figueroa, Daniel	.256	27	86	16	22	4	1	6	24	21	28	3	0	.535	.389	L	L	6-2	170	1-7-82	1998	Santo Domingo, D.R.
Gonzalez, Carlos	.214	8	14	0	3	0	0	0	1	2	3	0	0	.214	.313	R	R	6-1	220	10-1-81	1999	Santo Domingo, D.R.
Haas, Danny	.107	11	28	6	3	1	0	0	1	9	1	0	0	.143	.161	L	R	5-11	180	1-4-76	1997	Paducah, Ky.
Nathans, John	.200	5	5	1	1	1	0	0	0	1	2	0	0	.400	.333	R	R	6-1	215	6-10-79	2001	Warwick, N.Y.
Oh, Chul	.192	42	130	16	25	4	0	1	9	17	41	1	0	.246	.287	L	R	6-3	196	5-17-81	1999	Kwangju City, Korea
Oliver, Joe	1.000	5	2	5	2	2	0	0	1	1	0	0	0	1.600	1.000	R	R	6-3	220	7-24-65	1983	Orlando, Fla.
Petersen, Ryan	.280	49	143	26	40	11	0	1	17	10	32	11	3	.378	.344	R	R	5-9	175	10-21-77	2001	Plantsville, Conn.
Rodriguez, Ivan	.356	19	59	11	21	3	2	3	7	8	12	8	0	.627	.441	R	R	5-11	170	4-4-81	1998	Esperanza, D.R.
Rodriguez, Ronny	.000	1	0	0	0	0	0	0	0	0	0	0	0	.000	.000	R	R	6-0	168	1-7-81	1998	Maracaibo, Venez.
Salazar, Juan	.248	46	161	23	40	2	0	0	12	15	12	16	7	.261	.322	B	R	5-11	156	10-17-81	1999	Barquisimeto, Venez.
Tarbett, Brent	.225	47	138	20	31	8	0	5	20	19	40	2	3	.391	.355	R	R	6-2	225	11-30-81	2001	Las Vegas, Nev.
West, Jose	.256	25	82	11	21	5	1	4	11	9	12	0	1	.488	.344	R	R	5-11	170	3-24-83	2001	Nashville, Tenn.

GAMES BY POSITION: C—Brown 29, Devries 16, Encarnacion 3, C. Gonzalez 5, Nathans 4, Oliver 2, I. Rodriguez 16. **1B**—Cooper 56, Figueroa 1, Oh 5. **2B**—DeLeon 1, Dorta 17, Petersen 10, Salazar 36. **3B**—Bonvechio 18, Brown 2, Cruz 15, DeLeon 10, Petersen 24, Salazar 1. **SS**—Cruz 38, Dorta 2, Salazar 6, West 18. **OF**—Brackley 47, Caraballo 46, Everett 3, Figueroa 13, Haas 10, Oh 25, Petersen 12, Tarbett 41.

PITCHING	W	L	ERA	G	GS	CG	SV	IP	H	R	ER	BB	SO	AVG	B	T	HT	WT	DOB	1st Yr	Resides
Delcarmen, Manny	4	2	2.54	14	14	0	1	46	35	16	13	19	62	.210	R	R	6-2	190	2-16-82	2000	Pompano Beach, Fla.
Dumatrait, Phil	3	0	2.76	8	8	0	0	33	27	10	10	9	33	.228	R	L	6-2	170	7-12-81	2000	Bakersfield, Calif.
Farley, Chris	0	1	16.62	3	2	0	0	4	8	8	8	8	3	.421	R	R	6-2	175	2-24-83	2001	Orange, Mass.
Gabbard, Kason	0	1	5.65	6	6	0	0	14	11	11	9	9	17	.207	L	L	6-4	210	4-8-82	2001	Royal Palm Beach, Fla.
Gonzalez, Jose	0	0	0.00	1	0	0	0	2	0	0	0	2	0	.000	R	R	6-2	170	6-10-80	1997	Santo Domingo, D.R.
Hall, Shane	1	2	2.89	4	0	0	1	9	6	3	3	3	10	.181	R	R	6-5	225	6-14-80	2000	Herford, Ariz.
Hill, Terry	2	0	1.23	3	0	0	0	7	2	1	1	0	11	.083	L	L	5-10	170	10-17-75	1998	Thibodaux, La.
Hollis, Barton	2	0	8.38	7	0	0	2	10	17	10	9	8	5	.395	R	R	6-7	220	5-21-81	2000	Moulton, Ala.
Huang, Jun-chung	0	2	3.65	10	0	0	3	12	14	5	5	10	15	.291	R	R	6-0	172	4-25-82	2001	Chau Chou, Taiwan
Jacob, Russell	1	1	4.85	5	0	0	0	13	14	7	7	4	7	.285	R	R	6-6	240	1-2-75	1994	Winter Haven, Fla.
Kennedy, Jodie	0	0	1.80	3	0	0	2	5	3	2	1	0	6	.176	R	L	6-0	180	7-16-79	2001	Shubuta, Miss.
Leach, B.J.	2	0	8.38	6	0	0	2	8	6	2	2	1	10	.200	R	R	5-11	175	8-3-77	1999	Seminole, Fla.
Lundgren, Wayne	4	4	5.31	13	1	0	2	42	48	26	25	15	20	.290	R	R	6-2	170	8-4-81	2000	Baulkham Hills, Australia
Mateo, Aneudis	0	1	0.00	3	2	0	0	8	4	0	0	6	6	.200	R	R	6-4	185	10-3-82	2000	San Pedro de Macoris, D.R.
Mims, Brandon	2	4	4.09	11	6	0	1	56	56	25	23	14	34	.287	L	L	6-2	180	12-2-81	2000	Prattville, Ala.
Rodriguez, Miguel	3	2	2.59	11	7	0	0	56	52	18	16	12	53	.244	R	R	6-3	182	3-9-82	2000	Santo Domingo, D.R.
Royal, Shannon	0	1	3.38	10	0	0	0	11	7	4	4	3	5	.194	L	L	6-2	205	4-6-78	2001	Fort Myers, Fla.
Saberhagen, Bret	1	1	1.59	2	2	0	0	6	3	1	1	0	2	.150	R	R	6-1	200	4-11-64	1983	Babylon, N.Y.
Sanchez, Rafael	5	1	1.78	10	8	0	0	51	36	12	10	7	45	.200	R	R	6-2	195	5-24-82	1999	Higuey, D.R.
Simon, Billy	0	0	1.00	3	0	0	0	9	6	2	1	1	7	.206	R	R	6-6	220	11-8-82	2001	Wellington, Fla.
Suarez, Pedro	0	5	5.65	8	0	0	1	14	17	9	9	13	14	.293	R	R	6-3	195	10-22-83	2001	Spring Valley, Calif.
Thigpen, Joshua	4	2	2.52	10	6	0	1	39	20	15	11	14	44	.152	R	R	6-4	185	6-27-82	2001	Killen, Ala.
Valdez, Henry	5	2	4.35	16	0	0	3	39	42	22	19	17	29	.269	L	L	6-4	185	5-24-81	1998	Azua, D.R.
Ward, Bryan	0	0	18.00	1	0	0	0	2	4	4	4	0	2	.400	L	L	6-2	205	1-25-72	1993	Mount Holly, N.J.

BY PHIL ROGERS

Ambition is an admirable quality, but it can sure make you look foolish. That turned out to be the case for the White Sox in 2001.

Following a 95-win season in 2000, rookie general manager Ken Williams not only traded for David Wells but said he did it because he wanted to know who would start Game One of the World Series. The organization followed that lead, building its marketing campaign about the phrase, "It's time."

But by the middle of May the word around Chicago was, "It's over."

If it could go wrong it did for Williams, manager Jerry Manuel and many of the team's players. The White Sox broke from the gate more like Mr. Ed than Secretariat, stumbling to a 14-29 start.

This was a shocking development for Williams, who was sure he had addressed his team's one clear weakness—fielding—by trading for shortstop Royce Clayton and moving Jose Valentin to center field. But Valentin never got comfortable in the outfield and Frank Thomas, Harold Baines and Clayton hit a combined .166 in April.

Thomas, runner-up for American League MVP honors a year before, was lost for the season with a torn biceps tendon in his right arm on April 27. Eight pitchers sustained season-ending injuries, including starters Jim Parque (partially torn rotator cuff), Cal Eldred (stress fracture, elbow) and Wells (herniated disc).

"For whatever reason," Williams said, "this is just our time."

It was a tribute to Manuel's leadership and a deep talent base of young pitching that the White Sox did not implode after their awful start. Rather than grow disinterested, they actually made up nine games of their huge hole in the American League Central by going 58-37 from May 24 to Sept. 5. They climbed as high as eight games

Magglio Ordonez | Corwin Malone

PLAYERS OF THE YEAR

MAJOR LEAGUE: Magglio Ordonez, of
Chicago's offensive leader with slugger Frank Thomas missing from the lineup for much of the 2001 season, Ordonez led the team in average (.305), RBIs (113) and stolen bases (25).

MINOR LEAGUE: Corwin Malone, lhp
He intimidated hitters with the low Class A Kannapolis Intimidators, going 11-4, 2.00. That earned him a promotion to high Class A Winston-Salem (0-1, 1.72) and Double-A Birmingham (2-0, 2.33).

over .500 before finishing the year 83-79 and in third place, eight games behind Cleveland.

Those who formed the foundation for 2001 were second-year lefty Mark Buehrle, closer Keith Foulke, three-time all-star outfielder Magglio Ordonez and first baseman Paul Konerko. Buehrle, who had made little previous impression, was 16-8, 3.29. He would have been the AL's best rookie pitcher but missed the eligibility requirement by 1⅓ innings.

Clayton, who was hitting .099 as late as May 29, hit .313 the rest of the season to finish at .263. He filled a defensive void at shortstop but the Sox had enough holes elsewhere to finish 10th in the league in fielding, their sixth straight year near the bottom. Valentin never really settled in anywhere, playing through leg injuries to start at least 18 games in center, at shortstop and at third base.

While the Sox offset their poor fielding by scoring a majors-best 6.0 runs per game in 2000, this time they were sixth in the league with an average of 4.9 runs. They tried 11 starting pitchers. Only Buehrle (32), Rocky Biddle (21) and Kip Wells (20) made more than 16 starts.

Beneath the surface, it was another strong developmental year for pitching. While 6-foot-11 righthander Jon Rauch, Baseball America's Minor League Player of the Year in 2000, was forced to undergo shoulder surgery after six starts, the Sox were excited by the progress of lefthander Corwin Malone and righthanders Matt Guerrier and Edwin Almonte.

Malone, 21, started the season in the South Atlantic League and ended it pitching a shutout in the Southern League playoffs. He was 14-5, 2.07 between three levels. Guerrier, 23, led the minor leagues with 18 wins in a season he split between Double-A Birmingham and Triple-A Charlotte. Almonte, 25, set a Southern League record with 36 saves for Birmingham.

ORGANIZATION LEADERS

BATTING
*AVG	Aaron Rowand, Charlotte	.295
	Joe Borchard, Birmingham	.295
R	Joe Borchard, Birmingham	95
H	Tim Hummel, Birmingham	152
TB	Joe Borchard, Birmingham	262
2B	Three tied at	34
3B	Three tied at	7
HR	Joe Borchard, Birmingham	27
RBI	Joe Borchard, Birmingham	98
BB	Eric Battersby, Birmingham	94
SO	Darron Ingram, Birmingham	188
SB	Chad Durham, Winston-Salem	50

PITCHING
W	Matt Guerrier, Charlotte/Birmingham	18
L	Eric Fischer, Winston-Salem	13
	Dario Ferrand, Kannapolis	13
#ERA	Joe Valentine, Winston-Salem/Kannapolis	1.79
G	Arnaldo Munoz, Kannapolis	60
CG	Dennis Ulacia, Charlotte/Birmingham/Win.-Salem/Kann.	5
SV	Ed Almonte, Birmingham	36
IP	Dennis Ulacia, Charlotte/Birmingham/Win.-Salem/Kann.	180
BB	Eduardo Lantigua, Birmingham/Winston-Salem	76
SO	Corwin Malone, Birmingham/Winston-Salem/Kannapolis	177

*Minimum 250 At-Bats #Minimum 75 Innings

CHICAGO
WHITE SOX

Manager: Jerry Manuel

2001 Record: 83-79, .512 (3rd, AL Central)

BATTING	AVG	G	AB	R	H	2B	3B	HR	RBI	BB	SO	SB	CS	SLG	OBP	B	T	HT	WT	DOB	1st Yr	Resides
Alomar, Sandy	.245	70	220	17	54	8	1	4	21	12	17	1	2	.345	.288	R	R	6-5	215	6-18-66	1984	Westlake, Ohio
Baines, Harold	.131	32	84	3	11	1	0	0	6	8	16	0	0	.143	.202	L	L	6-2	195	3-15-59	1977	St. Michaels, Md.
Canseco, Jose	.258	76	256	46	66	8	0	16	49	45	75	2	1	.477	.366	R	R	6-4	240	7-2-64	1982	Westin, Fla.
Christensen, McKay	.250	7	4	0	1	0	0	0	0	0	2	0	0	.250	.400	L	L	5-11	180	8-14-75	1995	Alpine, Utah
Clayton, Royce	.263	135	433	62	114	21	4	9	60	33	72	10	7	.393	.315	R	R	6-0	183	1-2-70	1988	Scottsdale, Ariz.
Crede, Joe	.220	17	50	1	11	1	1	0	7	3	11	1	0	.280	.273	R	R	6-3	195	4-26-78	1996	Westphalia, Mo.
Dalesandro, Mark	.000	1	0	0	0	0	0	0	0	0	0	0	0	.000	.000	R	R	6-0	195	5-14-68	1990	Chicago, Ill.
Durham, Ray	.267	152	611	104	163	42	10	20	65	64	110	23	10	.466	.337	B	R	5-8	170	11-30-71	1990	Charlotte, N.C.
Graffanino, Tony	.303	74	145	23	44	9	0	2	15	16	29	4	1	.407	.370	R	R	6-1	195	6-6-72	1990	Marietta, Ga.
Johnson, Mark	.249	61	173	21	43	6	1	5	18	23	31	2	1	.382	.338	L	R	6-0	185	9-12-75	1994	Warner Robins, Ga.
Konerko, Paul	.282	156	582	92	164	35	0	32	99	54	89	1	0	.507	.349	R	R	6-3	211	3-5-76	1994	Scottsdale, Ariz.
Lee, Carlos	.269	150	558	55	150	33	3	24	84	38	85	17	7	.468	.321	R	R	6-2	220	6-20-76	1994	Aguadulce, Panama
Liefer, Jeff	.256	83	254	36	65	13	0	18	39	20	69	0	1	.520	.313	L	R	6-3	195	8-17-74	1996	Upland, Calif.
Ordonez, Magglio	.305	160	593	97	181	40	1	31	113	70	70	25	7	.533	.382	R	R	6-0	200	1-28-74	1991	Coro Falcon, Venez.
Paul, Josh	.266	57	139	20	37	11	0	3	18	13	25	6	2	.410	.327	R	R	6-1	185	5-19-75	1996	Buffalo Grove, Ill.
Perry, Herbert	.256	92	285	38	73	21	1	7	32	23	55	2	2	.411	.326	R	R	6-2	220	9-15-69	1991	Mayo, Fla.
Ramirez, Julio	.081	22	37	2	3	0	0	0	1	2	15	2	0	.081	.128	R	R	5-11	170	8-10-77	1994	Santo Domingo, D.R.
Rowand, Aaron	.293	63	123	21	36	5	0	4	20	15	28	5	1	.431	.385	R	R	6-1	200	8-29-77	1998	Glendora, Calif.
Singleton, Chris	.298	140	392	57	117	21	5	7	45	20	61	12	11	.431	.331	L	L	6-2	195	8-15-72	1993	Mesa, Ariz.
Thomas, Frank	.221	20	68	8	15	3	0	4	10	10	12	0	0	.441	.316	R	R	6-5	270	5-27-68	1989	Oak Brook, Ill.
Valentin, Jose	.258	124	438	74	113	22	2	28	68	50	114	9	6	.509	.336	L	R	5-10	175	10-12-69	1987	Manati, P.R.

PITCHING	W	L	ERA	G	GS	CG	SV	IP	H	R	ER	BB	SO	AVG	B	T	HT	WT	DOB	1st Yr	Resides
Baldwin, James	7	5	4.61	17	16	2	0	96	109	56	49	38	42	.286	R	R	6-3	210	7-15-71	1990	Southern Pines, N.C.
Barcelo, Lorenzo	1	0	4.71	17	0	0	0	21	24	13	11	8	15	.282	R	R	6-2	220	8-10-77	1994	San Pedro de Macoris, D.R.
Biddle, Rocky	7	8	5.39	30	21	0	0	129	137	87	77	52	85	.271	R	R	6-3	230	5-21-76	1997	Arcadia, Calif.
Buehrle, Mark	16	8	3.29	32	32	4	0	221	188	89	81	48	126	.230	L	L	6-2	200	3-23-79	1999	St. Charles, Mo.
Eldred, Cal	0	1	13.50	2	2	0	0	6	12	9	9	3	6	.428	R	R	6-4	235	11-24-67	1989	Chandler, Ariz.
Embree, Alan	1	2	5.03	39	0	0	0	34	31	21	19	7	34	.242	L	L	6-2	190	1-23-70	1990	Vancouver, Wash.
Fogg, Josh	0	0	2.03	11	0	0	0	13	10	3	3	3	17	.208	R	R	6-2	205	12-13-76	1998	Margate, Fla.
Foulke, Keith	4	9	2.33	72	0	0	42	81	57	21	21	22	75	.198	R	R	6-0	200	10-19-72	1994	Huffman, Texas
Garland, Jon	6	7	3.69	35	16	0	1	117	123	59	48	55	61	.277	R	R	6-6	205	9-27-79	1997	Granada Hills, Calif.
Ginter, Matt	1	0	5.22	20	0	0	0	40	34	23	23	14	24	.237	R	R	6-1	215	12-24-77	1999	Jacksonville, Fla.
Glover, Gary	5	5	4.93	46	11	0	0	100	98	61	55	32	63	.251	R	R	6-5	205	12-3-76	1994	DeLand, Fla.
Howry, Bobby	4	5	4.69	69	0	0	5	79	85	41	41	30	64	.278	L	R	6-5	215	8-4-73	1994	Glendale, Ariz.
Lowe, Sean	9	4	3.61	45	11	0	3	127	123	55	51	32	71	.256	R	R	6-2	205	3-29-71	1992	Mesquite, Texas
Osuna, Antonio	0	0	20.77	4	0	0	0	4	8	10	10	2	6	.421	R	R	5-11	206	4-12-73	1991	Sinaloa, Mexico
Parque, Jim	0	3	8.04	5	5	1	0	28	36	26	25	10	15	.307	L	L	5-11	165	2-8-75	1997	La Crescenta, Calif.
Pulsipher, Bill	0	0	7.88	14	0	0	0	8	11	8	7	7	4	.314	L	L	6-3	200	10-9-73	1992	Port St. Lucie, Fla.
2-team (23 Boston)	0	0	6.00	37	0	0	0	30	36	23	20	21	20	.300							
Vining, Ken	0	0	17.55	8	0	0	0	7	15	14	13	7	3	.441	L	L	6-0	180	12-5-74	1996	Hopkins, S.C.
Wells, David	5	7	4.47	16	16	1	0	101	120	55	50	21	59	.297	L	L	6-4	235	5-20-63	1982	Clearwater, Fla.
Wells, Kip	10	11	4.79	40	20	0	0	133	145	80	71	61	99	.281	R	R	6-3	196	4-21-77	1999	Missouri City, Texas
Wright, Danny	5	3	5.70	13	12	0	0	66	78	45	42	39	36	.300	R	R	6-5	225	12-14-77	1999	Batesville, Ark.
Wunsch, Kelly	2	1	7.66	33	0	0	0	22	21	19	19	9	16	.247	L	L	6-5	192	7-12-72	1993	Houston, Texas

FIELDING

Catcher	PCT	G	PO	A	E	DP	PB
Alomar	.990	69	367	19	4	5	5
Dalesandro	.000	1	0	0	0	0	0
Johnson	.992	61	326	31	3	2	4
Paul	.980	56	267	24	6	3	4

First Base	PCT	G	PO	A	E	DP
Graffanino	1.000	1	3	0	0	1
Konerko	.994	144	1276	90	8	120
Liefer	.973	15	100	9	3	12
Perry	1.000	12	60	3	0	8
Thomas	.955	3	20	1	1	2

Second Base	PCT	G	PO	A	E	DP
Durham	.986	150	280	446	10	88
Graffanino	.988	20	32	51	1	13

Third Base	PCT	G	PO	A	E	DP
Crede	1.000	15	17	18	0	3
Graffanino	.923	38	16	44	5	1
Liefer	.867	15	7	19	4	2

	PCT	G	PO	A	E	DP
Perry	.940	68	45	112	10	5
Valentin	.926	66	49	113	13	9

Shortstop	PCT	G	PO	A	E	DP
Clayton	.988	133	196	367	7	74
Graffanino	.857	5	2	4	1	2
Valentin	.953	43	64	118	9	34

Outfield	PCT	G	PO	A	E	DP
Canseco	1.000	2	1	0	0	0
Christensen	1.000	6	2	0	0	0
Graffanino	1.000	3	3	0	0	0
Lee	.969	130	241	9	8	0
Liefer	1.000	38	52	2	0	0
Ordonez	.983	155	286	11	5	0
Ramirez	.978	21	43	2	1	1
Rowand	.991	61	102	3	1	0
Singleton	.991	133	310	8	3	2
Valentin	1.000	24	46	3	0	1

LARRY GOREN

Mark Buehrle

FARM SYSTEM

Vice President, Player Development: Bob Fontaine

Class	Farm Team	League	W	L	Pct.	Finish*	Manager	First Yr.
AAA	Charlotte (N.C.) Knights	International	67	77	.465	10th (14)	Nick Leyva	1999
AA	Birmingham (Ala.) Barons	Southern	80	60	.571	t-2nd (10)	Nick Capra	1986
A#	Winston-Salem (N.C.) Warthogs	Carolina	54	86	.386	8th (8)	Wally Backman	1997
A	Kannapolis (N.C.) Intimidators	South Atlantic	76	63	.547	4th (16)	Razor Shines	1999
Rookie#	Bristol (Va.) Sox	Appalachian	38	26	.594	2nd (10)	John Orton	1995
Rookie	Phoenix (Ariz.) White Sox	Arizona	23	33	.411	6th (7)	Jerry Hairston	1998

*Finish in overall standings (No. of teams in league)   #Advanced level

JOHN WILLIAMSON

Paul Konerko: Led the White Sox with 32 homers

DAVID SEELIG

Keith Foulke: Had 46 saves and 2.33 ERA

CHARLOTTE   Class AAA

INTERNATIONAL LEAGUE

BATTING	AVG	G	AB	R	H	2B	3B	HR	RBI	BB	SO	SB	CS	SLG	OBP	B	T	HT	WT	DOB	1st Yr	Resides
Ashby, Chris	.228	62	197	21	45	8	1	2	12	16	39	2	2	.310	.286	R	R	6-3	196	12-15-74	1993	Boca Raton, Fla.
Baines, Harold	.000	2	8	0	0	0	0	0	0	1	0	0	0	.000	.000	L	L	6-2	195	3-15-59	1977	St. Michaels, Md.
Barry, Jeff	.122	13	41	6	5	1	0	0	2	5	7	0	0	.146	.224	B	R	6-1	210	9-22-68	1990	Medford, Ore.
Bravo, Danny	.190	39	126	11	24	2	0	3	13	7	16	1	1	.278	.233	B	R	5-11	175	5-27-77	1996	Maracaibo, Venez.
Christensen, McKay	.275	69	273	53	75	15	6	7	25	30	52	17	3	.451	.347	L	L	5-11	180	8-14-75	1995	Alpine, Utah
Crede, Joe	.276	124	463	67	128	34	1	17	65	46	88	2	1	.464	.349	R	R	6-3	195	4-26-78	1996	Westphalia, Mo.
Dalesandro, Mark	.260	75	262	16	68	18	0	4	23	6	24	0	1	.374	.281	R	R	6-0	195	5-14-68	1990	Chicago, Ill.
Dellaero, Jason	.178	115	377	32	67	10	0	11	28	17	113	4	4	.292	.217	B	R	6-2	195	12-17-76	1997	Brewster, N.Y.
Garcia, Amaury	.237	34	118	9	28	4	1	0	7	7	26	4	0	.288	.286	R	R	5-10	160	5-20-75	1993	Santo Domingo, D.R.
Gubanich, Creighton	.246	32	114	19	28	3	0	7	19	13	32	0	0	.456	.318	R	R	6-3	200	3-27-72	1991	Phoenixville, Pa.
2-team (30 Ind.)	.218	62	197	25	43	8	0	9	23	17	51	0	0	.396	.281							
Hardtke, Jason	.260	57	208	33	54	14	0	10	25	18	27	2	1	.471	.330	B	R	5-10	175	9-15-71	1990	Port Washington, N.Y.
2-team (39 Buffalo)	.259	96	336	52	87	21	3	10	39	34	43	2	2	.429	.336							
Heintz, Chris	.100	5	10	1	1	1	0	0	1	0	3	0	0	.200	.091	R	R	6-1	200	8-6-74	1996	Clearwater, Fla.
Inglin, Jeff	.272	128	481	66	131	25	6	24	75	43	103	3	4	.499	.338	R	R	5-11	185	10-8-75	1996	Petaluma, Calif.
Johnson, Adam	.444	7	18	1	8	2	0	0	4	0	0	0	1	.556	.474	L	L	6-0	185	7-18-75	1996	Naples, Fla.
Johnson, Mark	.270	55	196	24	53	5	2	4	24	29	34	2	1	.378	.363	L	R	6-0	185	9-12-75	1994	Warner Robins, Ga.
Liefer, Jeff	.286	32	119	23	34	7	0	6	21	15	41	3	1	.496	.381	L	R	6-3	195	8-17-74	1996	Upland, Calif.
Paul, Josh	.280	22	75	11	21	4	0	4	14	7	18	0	0	.493	.337	R	R	6-1	185	5-19-75	1996	Buffalo Grove, Ill.
Prieto, Rick	.231	11	26	4	6	0	0	0	1	6	6	0	0	.231	.375	B	R	5-10	175	8-24-72	1993	Carmel, Calif.
Ramirez, Julio	.216	88	319	36	69	11	1	8	25	20	80	15	6	.332	.266	R	R	5-11	170	8-10-77	1994	Santo Domingo, D.R.
Rodriguez, Liu	.291	118	444	53	129	25	0	0	37	41	60	7	4	.347	.352	B	R	5-9	170	11-5-76	1995	Caracas, Venez.
Rowand, Aaron	.295	82	329	54	97	28	0	16	48	21	47	8	2	.526	.353	R	R	6-1	200	8-29-77	1998	Glendora, Calif.
Rumfield, Toby	.272	121	463	49	126	28	0	20	69	28	64	0	0	.462	.319	R	R	6-3	190	9-4-72	1991	Belton, Texas
Saunders, Chris	.205	12	39	3	8	1	0	2	3	5	7	0	0	.385	.311	R	R	6-1	203	7-19-70	1992	Clovis, Calif.
Valenzuela, Mario	.261	49	176	19	46	7	1	10	26	8	34	2	0	.483	.291	R	R	6-2	190	3-10-77	1996	Isla San Marcos, Mexico

PITCHING	W	L	ERA	G	GS	CG	SV	IP	H	R	ER	BB	SO	AVG	B	T	HT	WT	DOB	1st Yr	Resides
Baldwin, James	1	0	5.25	2	0	0	0	12	12	7	7	2	11	.272	R	R	6-3	210	7-15-71	1990	Southern Pines, N.C.
Baptist, Travis	2	5	5.14	33	9	0	3	61	74	38	35	19	43	.289	L	L	6-0	202	12-30-71	1990	Aloha, Ore.
Barcelo, Lorenzo	1	0	5.40	2	0	0	0	5	6	3	3	1	5	.300	R	R	6-4	220	8-10-77	1994	San Pedro de Macoris, D.R.
Bullinger, Kirk	0	3	3.58	36	1	0	5	50	44	23	20	21	34	.247	R	R	6-2	170	10-28-69	1992	Gretna, La.
Corbin, Archie	6	7	3.14	58	0	0	4	77	58	29	27	54	64	.214	R	R	6-4	230	12-30-67	1986	Beaumont, Texas
Curreri, Joe	1	0	0.00	1	0	0	0	3	4	0	0	0	3	.333	R	R	6-1	190	6-29-77	1999	Valley Cottage, N.Y.
Fogg, Josh	4	7	4.79	40	16	0	4	115	129	68	61	30	89	.282	R	R	6-2	205	12-13-76	1998	Margate, Fla.
Garland, Jon	0	3	2.73	5	5	1	0	33	31	10	10	11	26	.260	R	R	6-6	205	9-27-79	1997	Granada Hills, Calif.
Ginter, Matt	2	3	2.59	22	10	0	0	76	62	26	22	24	67	.219	R	R	6-1	215	12-24-77	1999	Jacksonville, Fla.
Glover, Gary	2	1	1.88	6	6	1	0	38	21	8	8	5	29	.157	R	R	6-5	205	12-3-76	1994	DeLand, Fla.
Guerrier, Matt	7	1	3.54	12	12	3	0	81	75	33	32	18	43	.250	R	R	6-3	190	8-2-78	1999	Shaker Heights, Ohio
Hasselhoff, Derek	6	1	2.03	34	0	0	6	44	29	14	10	12	41	.183	R	R	6-2	185	10-10-73	1995	Pasadena, Md.
Juden, Jeff	5	5	3.32	12	11	1	0	65	44	34	24	46	63	.188	R	R	6-8	271	1-19-71	1991	Salem, Mass.
Kane, Kyle	0	0	6.00	1	1	0	0	3	4	2	2	1	0	.333	L	R	6-3	215	2-4-76	1997	Reno, Nev.
Lowe, Sean	1	1	4.50	2	2	0	0	10	9	6	5	2	8	.230	R	R	6-2	205	3-29-71	1992	Mesquite, Texas
Masaoka, Onan	0	1	4.30	14	0	0	5	15	11	8	7	5	22	.211	R	L	6-0	188	10-27-77	1995	Hilo, Hawaii
Mendoza, Geronimo	5	8	4.95	17	15	0	0	96	103	57	53	31	68	.279	L	R	6-4	180	1-23-78	1995	Santo Domingo, D.R.
Porzio, Mike	6	6	4.35	31	23	0	0	134	138	76	65	55	107	.266	L	L	6-3	190	8-20-72	1993	Norwalk, Conn.
Rauch, Jon	1	3	5.79	6	6	0	0	28	28	20	18	7	27	.247	R	R	6-10	230	9-27-78	1999	Westport, Ky.
Schrenk, Steve	5	3	3.00	30	0	0	2	39	38	13	13	13	43	.255	R	R	6-3	215	11-20-68	1987	Parrish, Fla.
Secoda, Jason	3	9	5.18	34	20	1	1	139	168	90	80	56	105	.302	R	R	6-1	195	9-2-74	1995	Fullerton, Calif.
Sinclair, Steve	4	6	4.69	53	0	0	1	63	66	35	33	23	57	.270	L	L	6-2	190	8-21-71	1991	Victoria, B.C.
Ulacia, Dennis	1	0	2.57	1	1	1	0	7	6	2	2	1	3	.230	L	L	6-1	185	4-2-81	1999	Hialeah, Fla.
Vining, Ken	2	3	1.96	41	0	0	4	46	35	10	10	19	47	.212	L	L	6-0	180	12-5-74	1996	Hopkins, S.C.
Wells, Kip	2	1	3.55	4	4	0	0	25	26	11	10	8	24	.260	R	R	6-3	196	4-21-77	1999	Missouri City, Texas

FIELDING

Catcher	PCT	G	PO	A	E	DP	PB
Dalesandro	.998	65	429	37	1	2	5
Gubanich	.981	13	92	10	2	3	3
Heintz	1.000	5	21	1	0	0	0
M. Johnson	.990	47	385	24	4	3	3
Paul	1.000	18	125	7	0	0	1

First Base	PCT	G	PO	A	E	DP
Barry	1.000	1	10	1	0	0
Dalesandro	1.000	4	24	2	0	1
Gubanich	.941	2	15	1	1	1
Hardtke	1.000	1	2	0	0	0
M. Johnson	1.000	3	28	0	0	5
Liefer	.996	28	250	21	1	17
Rumfield	.992	108	901	62	8	79
Saunders	1.000	3	19	1	0	3

Second Base	PCT	G	PO	A	E	DP
Bravo	1.000	12	21	37	0	12
Dalesandro	.750	1	2	1	1	1
Garcia	.974	27	39	72	3	9
Hardtke	.986	14	28	40	1	5
Prieto	.889	3	7	1	1	2
Rodriguez	.979	94	179	245	9	54

Third Base	PCT	G	PO	A	E	DP
Bravo	1.000	5	2	0	0	0
Crede	.946	123	93	258	20	25
Hardtke	1.000	7	8	0	0	0
Liefer	.800	2	2	6	2	1
Saunders	.935	9	9	20	2	5

Shortstop	PCT	G	PO	A	E	DP
Bravo	.957	18	25	42	3	8

	PCT	G	PO	A	E	DP
Dellaero	.968	114	157	299	15	57
Garcia	1.000	1	2	4	0	2
Rodriguez	.942	19	30	51	5	11

Outfield	PCT	G	PO	A	E	DP
Ashby	.990	58	93	2	1	1
Barry	1.000	8	9	1	0	1
Christensen	.981	68	147	4	3	1
Hardtke	1.000	24	36	2	0	0
Inglin	.955	63	79	6	4	0
A. Johnson	1.000	5	8	0	0	0
Prieto	1.000	6	10	0	0	0
Ramirez	.962	88	191	9	8	0
Rowand	.966	79	170	1	6	0
Valenzuela	.957	48	84	5	4	0

BIRMINGHAM   Class AA

SOUTHERN LEAGUE

BATTING	AVG	G	AB	R	H	2B	3B	HR	RBI	BB	SO	SB	CS	SLG	OBP	B	T	HT	WT	DOB	1st Yr	Resides
Acevas, Jon	.222	12	36	5	8	1	0	2	6	2	13	0	0	.417	.275	R	R	6-2	187	3-7-78	1997	Sonora, Mexico
Battersby, Eric	.253	133	438	69	111	19	1	14	67	80	87	6	4	.397	.366	R	L	6-1	205	2-28-76	1998	San Antonio, Texas
Borchard, Joe	.295	133	515	95	152	27	1	27	98	67	158	5	4	.509	.384	B	R	6-5	220	11-25-78	2000	Camarillo, Calif.
Bravo, Danny	.292	42	168	22	49	12	2	2	22	17	17	3	2	.423	.360	B	R	5-11	175	5-27-77	1996	Maracaibo, Venez.
Caradonna, Brett	.000	1	1	0	0	0	0	0	0	0	0	0	0	.000	.000	L	R	6-1	185	12-3-78	1997	San Diego, Calif.
Garcia, Tony	.143	2	7	1	1	0	0	1	1	0	3	0	0	.571	.143	R	R	6-1	213	3-12-78	1998	Miami, Fla.
Heintz, Chris	.235	37	119	14	28	8	0	2	8	10	23	0	2	.353	.303	R	R	6-1	200	8-6-74	1996	Clearwater, Fla.
Hummel, Tim	.290	134	524	83	152	33	6	7	63	62	69	14	3	.416	.364	R	R	6-2	195	11-18-78	2000	Montgomery, N.Y.
Ingram, Darron	.263	136	514	77	135	34	4	22	91	52	188	6	6	.473	.330	R	R	6-3	226	6-7-76	1994	Lexington, Ky.
Johnson, Adam	.257	43	148	13	38	9	0	2	11	9	28	0	0	.358	.304	L	L	6-0	185	7-18-75	1996	Naples, Fla.
Miles, Aaron	.259	84	343	53	89	16	3	8	42	26	35	3	5	.394	.313	L	B	5-8	170	12-15-76	1995	Antioch, Calif.
Mitchell, Derek	.211	82	237	37	50	8	2	1	21	34	68	5	4	.278	.313	R	R	6-2	170	3-9-75	1995	Gurnee, Ill.
Olivo, Miguel	.259	93	316	45	82	23	1	14	55	37	62	6	3	.472	.347	R	R	6-1	215	7-15-78	1996	Villa Vazquez, D.R.
Prieto, Rick	.240	92	313	51	75	12	4	4	34	52	47	9	6	.342	.352	B	R	5-10	175	8-24-72	1993	Carmel, Calif.
Quintero, Humberto	.211	5	19	0	4	0	0	0	2	0	2	0	0	.211	.250	R	R	5-10	190	8-2-79	1997	Maracaibo, Venez.
Sandoval, Danny	.281	58	203	24	57	7	1	0	29	17	26	17	4	.325	.335	R	R	5-11	180	4-7-79	1997	Lara, Venez.
Saunders, Chris	.294	118	442	74	130	33	0	10	68	60	85	4	1	.437	.383	R	R	6-1	203	7-19-70	1992	Clovis, Calif.
Suarez, Luis	.118	6	17	4	2	2	0	0	2	1	6	0	0	.235	.211	R	R	6-1	175	9-5-78	1998	Hialeah, Fla.
Valenzuela, Mario	.290	88	341	50	99	17	3	12	53	21	61	4	5	.463	.330	R	R	6-2	190	3-10-77	1996	Isla San Marcos, Mexico

PITCHING	W	L	ERA	G	GS	CG	SV	IP	H	R	ER	BB	SO	AVG	B	T	HT	WT	DOB	1st Yr	Resides
Almonte, Ed	1	4	1.49	54	0	0	36	66	58	16	11	16	62	.228	R	R	6-3	200	12-17-76	1998	New York, N.Y.
Bajenaru, Jeff	0	0	0.00	2	0	0	0	4	4	0	0	3	5	.222	R	R	6-1	190	3-21-78	2000	Rancho Cucamonga, Calif.
Baptist, Travis	1	4	1.93	10	3	0	2	37	37	16	8	9	42	.266	L	L	6-0	202	12-30-71	1990	Aloha, Ore.
Beaumont, Matt	1	0	18.00	4	0	0	0	4	8	8	8	2	3	.421	L	L	6-3	210	4-22-73	1994	Rittman, Ohio
Bohannan, Brad	3	5	5.65	29	0	0	0	51	61	36	32	21	25	.303	R	R	6-3	170	9-2-77	2000	Springdale, Ark.
Freeman, Kai	5	3	5.08	28	10	0	0	83	100	53	47	33	38	.304	R	R	6-2	182	3-11-77	1998	Shorewood, Ill.
Guerrier, Matt	11	3	3.10	15	15	1	0	99	85	42	34	32	75	.236	R	R	6-3	190	8-2-78	1999	Shaker Heights, Ohio
Kane, Kyle	2	1	1.85	26	0	0	3	34	20	9	7	13	43	.172	L	R	6-3	215	2-4-76	1997	Reno, Nev.
Lantigua, Eduardo	4	0	3.71	7	7	2	0	44	40	19	18	18	34	.248	R	R	6-0	176	1-5-80	1998	La Vega, D.R.
Malone, Corwin	2	0	2.33	4	4	0	0	19	8	5	5	12	20	.126	R	L	6-3	200	7-3-80	1999	Thomasville, Ala.
McDaniel, Denny	1	2	7.71	18	0	0	0	21	30	18	18	9	13	.340	L	L	6-3	215	8-12-76	1996	Austin, Texas
Mendoza, Geronimo	5	4	5.06	12	12	0	0	69	84	51	39	28	38	.303	L	R	6-4	180	1-23-78	1995	Santo Domingo, D.R.
Parrish, Wade	4	0	1.38	16	1	0	0	26	19	4	4	5	15	.213	L	L	6-1	205	11-13-77	1999	Othello, Wash.
2-team (4 Jacksonville)	5	1	2.18	20	1	0	0	33	26	8	8	10	20	.224							
Porzio, Mike	1	0	1.38	2	2	0	0	13	3	2	2	5	10	.069	L	L	6-3	190	8-20-72	1993	Norwalk, Conn.

PITCHING	W	L	ERA	G	GS	CG	SV	IP	H	R	ER	BB	SO	AVG	B	T	HT	WT	DOB	1st Yr	Resides
Purvis, Rob	5	9	5.27	24	23	0	0	140	165	96	82	70	53	.301	R	R	6-2	200	8-11-77	1999	Tipton, Ind.
Sanders, Dave	3	0	2.65	36	0	0	0	34	27	12	10	25	25	.226	L	L	6-0	200	8-29-79	1999	Derby, Kan.
Stewart, Josh	3	4	6.67	16	16	0	0	82	110	68	61	42	47	.330	L	L	6-3	205	12-5-78	1999	Ledbetter, Ky.
Tokarse, Brian	2	6	3.97	39	0	0	0	66	56	33	29	39	81	.229	R	R	6-3	200	2-28-75	1997	Whittier, Calif.
Ulacia, Dennis	1	1	2.25	3	3	0	0	20	11	7	5	5	18	.154	L	L	6-1	185	4-2-81	1999	Hialeah, Fla.
Weaver, Eric	3	3	3.45	24	0	0	2	31	25	14	12	16	31	.217	R	R	6-5	230	8-4-73	1991	Springfield, Ill.
Weymouth, Marty	0	0	7.45	10	0	0	0	10	13	9	8	5	5	.317	R	R	6-2	180	8-6-77	1995	Romeo, Mich.
Wright, Danny	7	7	2.82	20	20	0	0	134	112	54	42	41	128	.228	R	R	6-5	225	12-14-77	1999	Batesville, Ark.
Wylie, Mitch	15	4	4.21	24	24	0	0	141	138	70	66	46	123	.252	R	R	6-3	190	1-14-77	1998	Princeton, Iowa

FIELDING

Catcher	PCT	G	PO	A	E	DP	PB
Acevas	.967	12	76	13	3	0	3
Garcia	1.000	2	10	1	0	0	1
Heintz	.991	36	191	26	2	0	7
Olivo	.988	90	633	78	9	4	19
Quintero	.971	5	26	7	1	2	0

First Base	PCT	G	PO	A	E	DP
Battersby	.995	133	1183	93	7	119
Johnson	.984	7	58	3	1	6
Saunders	.978	5	42	2	1	6

Second Base	PCT	G	PO	A	E	DP
Bravo	.967	16	25	62	3	13
Hummel	.973	93	178	254	12	70
Miles	.970	16	24	41	2	5
Mitchell	.941	6	7	9	1	3
Prieto	.982	10	21	35	1	7
Suarez	1.000	4	7	11	0	3

Third Base	PCT	G	PO	A	E	DP
Bravo	1.000	1	0	1	0	0
Heintz	.500	1	0	2	2	0
Hummel	.857	5	3	3	1	1
Miles	.917	23	16	28	4	1
Mitchell	.875	4	3	4	1	0
Prieto	.750	2	2	1	1	0
Sandoval	.925	16	9	28	3	3
Saunders	.941	88	50	173	14	13
Suarez	.800	2	0	4	1	0

Shortstop	PCT	G	PO	A	E	DP
Bravo	.973	15	31	42	2	12
Hummel	.926	36	62	100	13	21
Mitchell	.958	72	113	231	15	55
Sandoval	.960	21	33	62	4	16

Outfield	PCT	G	PO	A	E	DP
Borchard	.964	133	316	10	12	3
Bravo	.944	12	17	0	1	0
Ingram	.985	77	128	3	2	0
Johnson	.939	19	30	1	2	0
Prieto	.959	80	111	7	5	0
Sandoval	.941	21	30	2	2	2
Saunders	1.000	2	3	0	0	0
Valenzuela	.963	88	169	11	7	0

WINSTON-SALEM — Class A

CAROLINA LEAGUE

BATTING	AVG	G	AB	R	H	2B	3B	HR	RBI	BB	SO	SB	CS	SLG	OBP	B	T	HT	WT	DOB	1st Yr	Resides
Acevas, Jon	.214	70	220	33	47	8	2	6	27	24	65	2	0	.350	.302	R	R	6-2	187	3-7-78	1997	Sonora, Mexico
Aspito, Jason	.254	127	402	46	102	30	3	6	35	21	113	7	10	.388	.306	L	R	6-0	185	1-3-79	2000	Itasca, Ill.
Berger, Matt	.259	70	239	20	62	18	1	5	24	20	74	0	3	.406	.326	R	R	6-1	195	10-2-74	1997	Fort Mitchell, Ky.
Calahan, Larry	.250	13	44	5	11	2	0	1	11	4	8	0	2	.364	.320	L	R	5-9	195	5-24-78	2001	Crossville, Tenn.
Caradonna, Brett	.235	104	345	34	81	14	1	2	25	29	66	7	7	.299	.300	L	R	6-1	185	12-3-78	1997	San Diego, Calif.
Durham, Chad	.254	133	528	56	134	16	4	2	38	43	92	50	22	.311	.310	R	R	5-8	175	6-23-78	1997	Charlotte, N.C.
Fennell, Jason	.189	63	175	17	33	5	0	0	14	18	33	1	1	.217	.276	B	R	6-3	210	11-15-77	1996	Pittsburgh, Pa.
Flores, Ralphs	.200	25	80	5	16	0	0	0	6	4	14	1	1	.200	.238	R	R	5-11	160	2-13-80	1997	Caracas, Venez.
Garcia, Tony	.223	63	206	12	46	6	3	1	18	7	45	4	4	.296	.270	R	R	6-1	213	3-12-78	1998	Miami, Fla.
Hankins, Ryan	.267	108	389	54	104	26	0	15	58	57	76	4	5	.450	.370	R	R	5-11	200	6-30-76	1997	Simi Valley, Calif.
Merriman, Terrell	.104	17	48	4	5	0	0	0	1	9	17	4	0	.104	.246	L	L	6-0	180	7-30-77	1998	Cheraw, S.C.
Muro, Robert	.246	96	354	39	87	25	0	12	54	47	71	4	4	.418	.348	R	R	5-9	180	1-16-76	1998	Riverside, Calif.
Nicholson, Tommy	.245	138	477	46	117	22	1	2	40	42	97	10	14	.308	.311	L	R	5-9	165	8-23-79	2000	Anaheim, Calif.
Oborn, Spencer	.274	120	402	54	110	25	2	3	37	20	64	13	3	.368	.309	R	R	6-3	190	8-22-77	1999	Diamond Bar, Calif.
Pena, Amaury	.181	62	127	9	23	5	1	1	12	11	45	4	6	.260	.266	R	R	6-0	188	10-9-79	1996	Santiago, D.R.
Quintero, Humberto	.240	43	154	15	37	6	0	0	12	5	19	9	3	.279	.268	R	R	5-10	190	8-2-79	1997	Maracaibo, Venez.
Reyes, Guillermo	.208	59	216	24	45	4	1	0	24	14	33	16	4	.236	.271	B	R	5-9	160	12-29-81	1999	Villa Vazquez, D.R.
Sandoval, Danny	.273	48	176	25	48	11	0	3	14	11	31	11	2	.386	.323	R	R	5-11	180	4-7-79	1997	Lara, Venez.
Santamarina, Juan	.200	17	60	9	12	2	0	2	8	3	16	0	0	.333	.238	L	R	6-1	180	10-3-79	1998	Miami, Fla.
Suarez, Luis	.133	6	15	0	2	1	0	0	1	0	7	0	0	.200	.133	R	R	6-1	175	9-5-78	1998	Hialeah, Fla.

GAMES BY POSITION: C—Acevas 48, Fennell 4, Garcia 52, Quintero 43. **1B**—Acevas 13, Berger 67, Fennell 38, Garcia 3, Hankins 22, Oborn 1, Pena 1, Santamarina 7. **2B**—Calahan 5, Flores 1, Nicholson 131, Pena 14, Suarez 2. **3B**—Calahan 9, Hankins 45, Muro 59, Pena 26, Santamarina 11, Suarez 1. **SS**—Flores 25, Nicholson 4, Pena 15, Reyes 59, Sandoval 48. **OF**—Aspito 121, Caradonna 58, Durham 132, Fennell 5, Hankins 1, Merriman 15, Oborn 114, Pena 1.

PITCHING	W	L	ERA	G	GS	CG	SV	IP	H	R	ER	BB	SO	AVG	B	T	HT	WT	DOB	1st Yr	Resides
Bajenaru, Jeff	2	4	3.35	35	0	0	10	40	32	16	15	21	51	.216	R	R	6-1	190	3-21-78	2000	Rancho Cucamonga, Calif.
Bohannon, Brad	2	1	1.73	23	0	0	5	36	33	10	7	10	33	.240	R	R	5-11	180	5-13-75	1997	Lindale, Ga.
Curreri, Joe	3	3	4.81	33	0	0	1	49	46	27	26	19	44	.254	R	R	6-1	190	6-29-77	1999	Valley Cottage, N.Y.
Fischer, Eric	3	13	5.31	25	22	0	0	124	144	87	73	47	84	.293	B	L	6-7	205	2-19-80	1998	Cincinnati, Ohio
Hollifield, Alec	0	8	4.97	9	9	0	0	42	53	29	23	21	28	.311	R	R	6-3	170	7-18-80	1999	Fort Lauderdale, Fla.
Hughes, Rocky	1	0	1.93	16	0	0	1	28	20	8	6	16	19	.198	L	L	6-0	155	4-29-79	1999	Owasso, Okla.
Kane, Kyle	1	0	2.08	14	0	0	1	22	10	5	5	8	32	.142	L	R	6-3	215	2-4-76	1997	Reno, Nev.
Lantigua, Eduardo	8	6	3.06	22	19	1	0	121	92	46	41	58	113	.215	R	R	6-0	176	1-5-80	1998	La Vega, D.R.
Lopez, Juan	0	1	3.93	26	0	0	0	37	34	23	16	21	37	.248	L	L	6-2	195	3-19-80	1997	Caracas, Venez.
Majewski, Gary	4	2	2.93	9	6	1	0	43	42	15	14	10	31	.265	R	R	6-2	200	2-26-80	1999	Houston, Texas
Malone, Corwin	0	1	1.72	5	5	0	0	37	25	10	7	10	38	.192	R	L	6-3	200	7-3-80	1999	Thomasville, Ala.
McDaniel, Denny	1	3	2.93	32	0	0	0	46	43	18	15	21	25	.248	L	L	6-3	215	8-12-76	1996	Austin, Texas
McWhirter, Kris	2	3	5.34	13	10	0	0	57	60	39	34	25	49	.275	L	R	6-4	175	5-11-79	1999	Goodlettsville, Tenn.
Mozingo, Dan	0	3	11.91	3	3	0	0	11	21	19	15	6	17	.381	L	L	6-2	210	6-3-80	1998	Ashtabula, Ohio
Murray, Brad	3	2	1.98	32	0	0	0	50	42	13	11	30	30	.229	L	L	5-11	175	8-20-78	2000	La Belle, Fla.
Olivo, Rigal	0	0	4.73	8	0	0	1	13	16	9	7	3	9	.296	R	R	6-0	175	10-28-81	2001	Montecristi, D.R.
Ortega, Carlos	0	3	4.73	10	6	0	0	40	43	23	21	10	33	.282	L	L	6-1	170	9-20-78	1995	Falcon, Venez.
Patten, Scott	0	1	27.00	2	1	0	0	1	2	3	3	3	0	.500	R	R	6-3	210	11-26-80	1999	Tecumseh, Okla.
Pena, Ed	1	6	4.18	31	5	0	0	47	52	30	22	24	35	.282	L	L	5-10	170	8-12-79	2001	Caguas, P.R.
Rupp, Mike	2	3	3.38	27	3	0	0	53	56	29	20	17	45	.274	R	R	6-3	203	2-21-78	1997	La Mesa, Calif.
Stewart, Josh	4	6	3.82	12	12	1	0	64	64	41	27	28	38	.258	L	L	6-3	205	12-5-78	1999	Ledbetter, Ky.
Ulacia, Dennis	5	3	3.64	10	10	4	0	64	57	27	26	26	47	.247	L	L	6-1	185	4-2-81	1999	Hialeah, Fla.
Valentine, Joe	5	1	1.01	27	0	0	8	45	18	7	5	27	50	.121	R	R	6-2	195	12-24-79	1999	Pensacola, Fla.
West, Brian	7	12	3.46	28	28	3	0	169	179	75	65	70	130	.280	R	R	6-4	230	8-4-80	1999	West Monroe, La.
Wylie, Mitch	0	1	3.60	1	1	0	0	5	7	2	2	1	4	.318	R	R	6-3	190	1-14-77	1998	Princeton, Iowa

SOUTH ATLANTIC LEAGUE

BATTING	AVG	G	AB	R	H	2B	3B	HR	RBI	BB	SO	SB	CS	SLG	OBP	B	T	HT	WT	DOB	1st Yr	Resides
Amador, Chris	.196	102	322	42	63	8	6	3	28	15	127	29	12	.286	.248	R	R	5-10	160	12-14-82	2000	Camuy, P.R.
Calahan, Larry	.154	6	13	1	2	0	0	0	2	1	2	0	0	.154	.214	L	R	5-9	195	5-24-78	2001	Crossville, Tenn.
Ciraco, Darren	.253	111	388	43	98	15	7	5	52	25	92	14	11	.366	.299	R	R	6-2	205	4-6-81	2000	New Rochelle, N.Y.
Daniel, Stevie	.194	57	180	25	35	5	3	1	13	23	39	4	3	.272	.301	R	R	5-11	175	1-16-80	2001	Jacks Creek, Tenn.
Fennell, Jason	.136	10	22	1	3	0	0	0	3	2	0	0	0	.136	.240	B	R	6-3	210	11-15-77	1996	Pittsburgh, Pa.
Flores, Ralphs	.285	61	186	18	53	7	0	1	19	13	39	3	3	.339	.337	R	R	5-11	160	2-13-80	1997	Caracas, Venez.
Gillikin, Joe	.240	77	221	27	53	11	2	8	35	18	74	3	7	.416	.309	R	R	5-10	200	3-17-77	2000	Yukon, Okla.
Hickman, Brian	.263	7	19	1	5	0	0	0	2	4	4	0	0	.263	.417	R	R	6-2	205	2-7-78	2001	Yuba City, Calif.
Ison, Jeremy	.154	21	52	7	8	1	0	1	2	6	21	0	0	.231	.241	R	R	6-0	195	9-5-78	2001	Hudson, Ohio
Lackaff, John	.246	127	451	68	111	21	3	11	65	33	75	24	11	.379	.313	R	R	5-11	195	5-3-79	2000	Downers Grove, Ill.
Lebron, Francisco	.286	35	112	13	32	8	0	5	14	16	31	0	1	.491	.369	R	R	6-6	230	5-10-75	1999	Bayamon, P.R.
Martel, Normand	.281	71	135	15	38	2	2	1	7	18	29	7	3	.348	.374	L	R	6-0	185	8-4-78	2001	Newport News, Va.
Quintero, Humberto	.269	60	197	32	53	7	1	1	20	8	20	7	3	.330	.321	R	R	5-10	190	8-2-79	1997	Maracaibo, Venez.
Reyes, Guillermo	.279	71	280	49	78	8	5	0	26	27	30	29	8	.343	.344	B	R	5-9	160	12-29-81	1999	Villa Vazquez, D.R.
Rogowski, Casey	.287	130	439	66	126	18	3	14	69	62	95	16	8	.437	.382	L	L	6-3	230	5-1-81	1999	Livonia, Mich.
Rosa, Wally	.226	98	305	27	69	14	0	4	23	13	88	6	6	.311	.277	R	R	6-1	175	11-28-81	2000	Miami, Fla.
Santamarina, Juan	.259	13	27	5	7	2	0	3	6	0	9	0	0	.667	.259	L	R	6-1	180	10-3-79	1998	Miami, Fla.
Spidale, Mike	.232	126	431	51	100	8	0	0	32	52	65	35	15	.251	.331	R	R	5-9	180	3-12-82	2000	Broadview, Ill.
Tapia, Roman	.100	18	30	2	3	2	0	0	0	2	17	0	0	.167	.156	R	R	6-3	190	12-7-79	1999	Santiago, D.R.
Teilon, Nilson	.190	67	163	20	31	6	1	3	8	11	47	2	2	.294	.244	R	R	6-0	168	5-10-81	1998	San Pedro de Macoris, D.R.
Wigginton, Derek	.263	114	373	42	98	16	4	8	50	23	95	2	6	.391	.310	L	L	6-1	215	4-20-79	2000	Antioch, Tenn.

GAMES BY POSITION: C—Fennell 5, Gillikin 13, Hickman 6, Quintero 57, Rosa 72. 1B—Fennell 1, Gillikin 2, Lebron 10, Rogowski 128, Tapia 4. 2B—Amador 101, Calahan 1, Daniel 2, Flores 23, Ison 18, Lackaff 1. 3B—Calahan 4, Flores 10, Lackaff 123, Santamarina 6, Tapia 5. SS—Amador 1, Daniel 54, Flores 17, Ison 2, Reyes 70. OF—Ciraco 102, Gillikin 30, Martel 58, Spidale 120, Teilon 56, Wigginton 97.

PITCHING	W	L	ERA	G	GS	CG	SV	IP	H	R	ER	BB	SO	AVG	B	T	HT	WT	DOB	1st Yr	Resides
Allen, Wyatt	4	5	3.16	12	11	2	0	63	60	29	22	16	45	.253	R	R	6-4	205	4-12-80	2001	Brentwood, Tenn.
Bittner, Tim	0	3	4.43	4	4	0	0	20	21	18	10	9	15	.269	L	L	6-2	210	6-9-80	2001	Wilmington, Del.
Bullard, Jim	3	2	2.98	8	8	1	0	45	45	18	15	6	26	.264	L	L	6-7	210	12-29-79	2001	West Covina, Calif.
Castro, Julio	3	1	2.67	40	0	0	4	54	46	22	16	21	68	.223	R	R	6-1	160	1-19-81	1998	San Pedro de Macoris, D.R.
Ferrand, Dario	9	13	3.06	27	27	3	0	162	156	67	55	36	111	.252	R	R	6-1	160	1-19-81	1998	Santo Domingo, D.R.
Garza, Rolando	1	0	9.64	9	0	0	0	9	12	10	10	9	10	.315	R	R	6-3	180	12-14-79	1997	Coachella, Calif.
Hollifield, Alec	0	2	10.97	5	3	0	0	11	22	20	13	7	6	.400	R	R	6-5	179	7-18-80	1999	Fort Lauderdale, Fla.
Hughes, Rocky	0	1	5.08	19	0	0	1	28	30	16	16	19	21	.280	L	L	6-5	195	4-29-79	1999	Owasso, Okla.
Madril, Steve	2	2	2.89	42	2	0	2	65	68	28	21	21	59	.268	L	L	5-11	185	6-20-78	2000	Riverside, Calif.
Malone, Corwin	11	4	2.00	18	18	2	0	112	83	30	25	44	119	.207	R	L	6-3	200	7-3-80	1999	Thomasville, Ala.
McWhirter, Kris	7	6	3.09	14	14	2	0	90	79	37	31	23	91	.238	L	R	6-4	175	5-11-79	1999	Goodlettsville, Tenn.
Mozingo, Dan	8	4	2.39	37	9	1	1	94	59	30	25	43	114	.182	L	L	6-2	210	6-3-80	1998	Ashtabula, Ohio
Munoz, Arnaldo	6	3	2.49	60	0	0	12	80	41	24	22	42	115	.160	L	L	5-9	170	6-21-82	1999	Mao, D.R.
Murray, Brad	0	0	6.59	9	0	0	0	14	16	12	10	7	12	.290	L	L	5-11	175	8-20-78	2000	La Belle, Fla.
Phillips, Mike	2	7	3.64	14	12	1	0	72	74	36	29	18	54	.276	L	L	6-3	185	3-24-82	2001	Evansville, Ind.
Rohling, Stuart	0	0	9.64	5	0	0	0	5	6	5	5	6	5	.333	R	R	6-4	185	6-29-78	1998	Leoma, Tenn.
Smith, Matthew	2	3	5.00	20	0	0	1	27	26	15	15	26	14	.262	R	R	6-5	234	8-14-78	1999	Godfrey, Ill.
Sweeney, James	8	4	2.65	21	16	0	0	102	83	35	30	37	110	.232	R	L	6-2	200	7-12-79	2000	Norwood, Mass.
Ulacia, Dennis	8	1	2.43	15	15	0	0	89	68	25	24	36	93	.215	L	L	6-1	185	4-2-81	1999	Hialeah, Fla.
Valentine, Joe	2	2	2.93	30	0	0	14	31	21	10	10	10	33	.194	R	R	6-2	195	12-24-79	1999	Pensacola, Fla.
Young, Curtis	0	0	2.70	6	0	0	0	7	9	12	2	4	7	.290	L	R	6-1	185	1-30-80	2000	Grand Junction, Colo.

APPALACHIAN LEAGUE

BATTING	AVG	G	AB	R	H	2B	3B	HR	RBI	BB	SO	SB	CS	SLG	OBP	B	T	HT	WT	DOB	1st Yr	Resides
Callahan, Stephen	.255	18	51	10	13	2	2	1	7	11	9	1	1	.431	.391	L	L	6-1	190	1-7-67	1989	Lewiston, Idaho
Cavin, Jonathan	.317	54	183	24	58	7	1	3	21	17	45	3	1	.415	.383	L	R	6-3	220	3-19-80	2000	Stilwell, Okla.
Cochrane, Mark	.294	6	17	3	5	2	0	0	2	1	3	0	0	.412	.333	R	R	6-0	185	5-31-80	1999	Coral Springs, Fla.
Encarnacion, Julio	.211	26	76	11	16	3	0	2	12	0	31	2	0	.329	.221	R	R	6-0	175	10-16-81	2000	La Romana, D.R.
Hilario, Enderson	.292	26	89	9	26	11	0	0	11	2	14	0	0	.416	.323	R	R	5-10	175	9-17-81	1999	Santiago, D.R.
Huson, Tim	.183	50	153	23	28	5	0	2	9	24	68	2	4	.255	.306	L	R	6-3	190	4-8-80	2001	Cottonwood, Ariz.
Ison, Jeremy	.260	29	96	12	25	9	0	2	12	9	32	0	1	.417	.330	R	R	6-0	195	9-5-78	2001	Hudson, Ohio
Ivy, Bo	.199	56	156	30	31	4	2	0	11	25	47	18	3	.250	.321	R	R	5-10	175	9-20-81	2000	Shannon, Miss.
Lisk, Charles	.289	13	38	8	11	1	0	0	6	7	14	3	0	.316	.404	R	R	6-3	200	1-3-83	2001	Fort Mill, S.C.
Luna, Leonardo	.196	17	46	6	9	0	0	1	0	15	3	2	.196	.208	R	R	6-0	180	2-14-82	1999	Santiago, D.R.
Molina, Gustavo	.283	46	166	18	47	9	0	2	24	9	26	3	1	.373	.333	R	R	6-0	219	2-24-82	2000	Catia la Mar, Venez.
Monegan, Anthony	.286	55	192	37	55	6	2	1	19	22	59	22	8	.354	.358	L	R	6-1	175	5-11-79	2000	Flossmoor, Ill.
Morse, Michael	.227	57	181	23	41	7	3	4	27	17	57	6	2	.365	.324	B	R	6-3	185	3-22-82	2000	Plantation, Fla.
Reyes, Julio	.251	57	199	19	50	11	0	8	38	6	47	1	2	.427	.284	L	R	6-2	185	6-30-80	1999	San Luis, Mexico
Salvesen, Matthew	.000	2	8	0	0	0	0	0	0	0	4	0	0	.000	.000	L	R	6-3	225	11-18-79	2000	Aniwa, Wis.
Salvo, Andrew	.297	63	212	37	63	12	0	3	35	27	23	14	6	.396	.387	L	R	5-10	175	8-27-79	2001	East Islip, N.Y.
Santamarina, Juan	.259	10	27	4	7	1	1	1	3	7	8	0	1	.481	.412	L	R	6-1	180	10-3-79	1998	Miami, Fla.
Santana, Mayobanex	.269	42	145	27	39	3	1	16	8	36	2	3	.379	.310	R	R	6-1	180	8-23-81	1999	Santo Domingo, D.R.

GAMES BY POSITION: C—Cochrane 5, Hilario 11, Ison 1, Lisk 11, Molina 40. 1B—Huson 23, Molina 4, Salvesen 2, Santana 40. 2B—Callahan 4, Ison 1, Luna 5, Salvo 60. 3B—Callahan 11, Huson 28, Ison 19, Luna 8, Reyes 1, Santamarina 6. SS—Ison 9, Luna 5, Morse 53. OF—Cavin 42, Encarnacion 23, Ivy 51, Molina 1, Moneghan 54, Reyes 27, Santana 1.

PITCHING	W	L	ERA	G	GS	CG	SV	IP	H	R	ER	BB	SO	AVG	B	T	HT	WT	DOB	1st Yr	Resides
Asencio, Dalmiro	0	1	4.91	6	3	0	0	18	24	10	10	4	6	.342	R	R	6-3	165	1-26-84	2001	Mao, D.R.
Bittner, Tim	6	1	1.10	8	8	1	0	49	34	14	6	12	53	.189	L	L	6-2	210	6-9-80	2001	Wilmington, Del.
Bullard, Jim	1	2	3.05	4	4	1	0	21	20	12	7	1	31	.243	L	L	6-7	210	12-29-79	2001	West Covina, Calif.
Dobyns, Heath	0	3	3.63	13	0	0	1	17	21	9	7	3	15	.291	R	R	6-4	205	1-16-79	2001	Fountain, Colo.
Fields, Josh	3	1	3.67	18	0	0	2	34	34	22	14	8	37	.257	R	R	6-1	195	1-20-80	2001	Hungry Horse, Mont.
Fryson, Andrew	2	0	2.50	3	3	0	0	18	17	6	5	3	11	.250	R	R	6-7	215	10-14-80	2001	Tallahassee, Fla.

PITCHING	W	L	ERA	G	GS	CG	SV	IP	H	R	ER	BB	SO	AVG	B	T	HT	WT	DOB	1st Yr	Resides
Garza, Rolando	0	1	7.04	5	0	0	0	8	9	6	6	10	4	.300	R	R	6-3	180	12-14-79	1997	Coachella, Calif.
Hollifield, Alec	2	1	4.73	4	2	0	0	13	19	7	7	4	15	.333	R	R	6-3	170	7-18-80	1999	Fort Lauderdale, Fla.
Honel, Kris...........................	2	3	3.13	8	8	0	0	46	41	19	16	9	45	.239	R	R	6-5	180	11-7-82	2001	Bourbonnais, Ill.
Hooker, Jon	2	2	5.46	17	0	0	2	30	27	24	18	14	35	.236	R	R	6-3	205	12-18-78	2001	London, Ky.
Lubisich, Nik	5	2	2.83	11	11	2	0	70	65	26	22	12	49	.254	L	L	6-2	195	4-19-79	2001	Portland, Ore.
Martinez, Dan	3	1	1.38	18	0	0	6	26	21	8	4	11	24	.230	L	L	6-6	235	12-31-78	1999	National City, Calif.
Olivo, Rigal	1	4	3.95	11	6	0	0	41	41	22	18	11	40	.248	R	R	6-0	175	10-28-81	2001	Montecristi, D.R.
Patten, Scott	3	4	5.46	12	12	1	0	61	67	42	37	21	43	.282	R	R	6-3	210	11-26-80	1999	Tecumseh, Okla.
Smith, Matthew...................	1	0	4.50	4	0	0	2	8	4	4	4	5	6	.142	R	R	6-5	234	8-14-78	1999	Godfrey, Ill.
Szado, Craig	2	3	3.05	15	8	0	1	56	52	23	19	12	56	.245	L	L	6-1	180	3-19-79	2001	Monson, Mass.
Wing, Ryan	1	0	9.00	1	0	0	0	1	1	1	1	0	2	.200	L	L	6-2	170	2-1-82	2001	Murrieta, Calif.
Young, Curtis	3	0	6.75	10	0	0	1	13	17	12	10	9	14	.320	L	R	6-1	185	1-30-80	2000	Grand Junction, Colo.

PHOENIX — Rookie

ARIZONA LEAGUE

BATTING	AVG	G	AB	R	H	2B	3B	HR	RBI	BB	SO	SB	CS	SLG	OBP	B	T	HT	WT	DOB	1st Yr	Resides
Aybar, Francisco..............	.265	46	162	23	43	11	2	0	17	12	41	7	2	.358	.320	R	R	6-1	160	12-16-81	1999	San Pedro de Macoris, D.R.
Bounds, Brandon	.239	37	113	13	27	4	2	1	4	10	33	2	1	.336	.301	L	R	6-6	205	8-10-81	2001	Mansfield, Texas
Cochrane, Mark..............	.275	21	51	6	14	2	0	0	7	11	11	0	1	.314	.403	R	R	6-0	185	5-31-80	1999	Coral Springs, Fla.
Davis, Tyrel.....................	.243	43	140	11	34	4	1	0	11	10	37	1	3	.286	.301	R	R	5-10	185	4-1-81	2001	Kennewick, Wash.
Gomez, Raul....................	.229	39	131	8	30	7	2	0	16	19	42	1	2	.313	.325	B	R	6-1	200	7-18-79	2001	Miami, Fla.
Gonzalez, Andy...............	.323	48	189	33	61	18	1	5	30	15	36	13	2	.508	.382	R	R	6-2	175	12-15-81	2001	Rio Piedras, P.R.
Hickman, Brian................	.127	23	55	8	7	2	0	0	2	8	17	0	0	.164	.294	R	R	6-2	205	2-7-78	2001	Yuba City, Calif.
Hilario, Enderson.............	.167	3	12	1	2	1	0	0	0	1	1	0	0	.250	.231	R	R	5-10	175	9-17-81	1999	Santiago, D.R.
Koslowski, Kasey	.238	43	147	17	35	4	0	0	9	13	22	3	2	.265	.304	R	R	5-11	195	5-29-79	2001	Ozone Park, N.Y.
Lebron, Freddie	.233	39	120	22	28	8	0	0	13	11	29	7	1	.300	.316	B	R	5-9	170	1-23-82	2001	Humacao, P.R.
Lee, Carlos	.278	23	90	14	25	3	0	2	18	3	4	2	0	.378	.323	R	R	6-1	217	9-29-81	2000	Provincia, Panama
Lopez, Pedro	.312	50	199	26	62	11	3	1	19	16	24	12	6	.412	.359	R	R	6-1	160	4-28-84	2001	Moca, D.R.
Luna, Leonardo	.243	28	103	12	25	4	2	0	14	5	14	1	4	.320	.278	R	R	6-0	165	2-14-82	1999	Santiago, D.R.
Moreno, Alberto	.138	17	29	2	4	1	0	0	2	1	16	1	0	.172	.167	R	R	6-2	200	12-5-81	1999	Monte Plata, D.R.
Terrero, Wandy................	.400	13	30	3	12	1	0	0	3	3	3	0	1	.433	.455	R	R	5-11	160	9-24-81	1999	La Romana, D.R.
Webster, Anthony...........	.307	55	225	38	69	9	7	0	30	9	33	18	7	.409	.332	L	R	6-0	190	4-10-83	2001	Parsons, Tenn.
Young, Eddie	.200	43	145	22	29	5	0	0	13	11	42	8	3	.234	.284	R	R	6-2	195	2-6-82	2000	Macon, Ga.

GAMES BY POSITION: C—Cochrane 13, Hickman 22, Hilario 2, Koslowski 24, Terrero 7. **1B**—Bounds 25, Davis 1, Gomez 23, Gonzalez 1, Koslowski 14. **2B**—Aybar 1, Lebron 25, Lopez 20, Luna 11. **3B**—Gomez 9, Koslowski 6, Lebron 1, Lee 21, Lopez 9, Luna 12, Webster 1. **SS**—Gomez 1, Gonzalez 38, Lopez 18, Luna 1. **OF**—Aybar 44, Bounds 3, Davis 32, Luna 1, Moreno 9, Webster 54, Young 38.

PITCHING	W	L	ERA	G	GS	CG	SV	IP	H	R	ER	BB	SO	AVG	B	T	HT	WT	DOB	1st Yr	Resides
Asencio, Domingo...............	2	1	2.44	7	7	0	0	48	45	23	13	8	29	.245	R	L	6-3	160	8-20-81	1998	Bani, D.R.
Cruz, Ramon	1	2	1.11	6	5	0	0	24	15	6	3	3	21	.174	R	R	6-3	185	5-30-81	1999	Santo Domingo, D.R.
Dowdy, Justin	5	3	3.74	18	1	0	1	43	46	26	18	8	46	.262	L	L	6-1	165	8-13-83	2001	San Diego, Calif.
Fryson, Andrew	0	3	3.09	8	6	0	0	23	29	14	8	3	23	.302	R	R	6-7	215	10-14-80	2001	Tallahassee, Fla.
Haeger, Charles	3	3	6.39	13	4	0	0	31	44	29	22	17	17	.335	R	R	6-1	205	9-19-83	2001	Plymouth, Mich.
Honel, Kris.........................	2	0	1.80	3	1	0	0	10	9	3	2	3	8	.257	R	R	6-5	180	11-7-82	2001	Bourbonnais, Ill.
Jones, Alvin	0	3	12.63	11	2	0	0	21	25	34	29	26	19	.287	R	R	6-2	225	5-21-82	2000	Seguin, Texas
Kirkland, Aaron	0	2	0.40	29	0	0	13	45	25	5	2	4	62	.158	R	R	6-5	195	3-1-70	2001	Chatom, Ala.
Morales, Ruddy	3	2	2.48	6	5	0	0	29	31	15	8	6	26	.262	R	R	6-5	183	1-20-82	1999	La Romana, D.R.
Ortega, Carlos	2	0	2.45	4	0	0	0	11	10	3	3	0	13	.232	L	L	6-1	170	9-20-78	1995	Falcon, Venez.
Perez, Armando.................	3	3	2.98	15	5	1	0	63	56	27	21	23	44	.235	L	L	6-2	185	12-26-80	2000	San Ysidro, Calif.
Reed, Rylan	4	4	3.10	13	13	0	0	58	56	46	20	34	53	.247	R	R	6-7	245	11-18-81	2000	Crossett, Ark.
Reynoso, Paulino	0	2	3.66	15	3	0	1	39	41	27	16	13	31	.262	L	L	6-3	190	8-10-80	1999	Santiago, D.R.
Stumm, Jason...................	0	2	2.25	4	4	0	0	12	6	4	3	5	12	.153	R	R	6-2	215	4-13-81	1999	Centralia, Wash.
Zorrilla, Reinaldo................	1	3	4.18	25	0	0	1	32	35	20	15	9	25	.277	R	R	6-0	170	5-31-82	1999	El Seibo, D.R.

CHICAGO CUBS

BY JEFF VORVA

Though the Cubs went 88-74 and improved 23 games in the standings from 2000, history is clearly not on Chicago's side.

Since 1972—the end of a six-year span in which the Cubs had winning records—the team has not put together back-to-back winning seasons.

But manager Don Baylor called the 2001 season a success, especially after last-place finishes in 1999 and 2000.

"Absolutely," Baylor said. "I know we fell short in our goal of making the playoffs. But this club was expected to finish fifth. We made it a run all the way into the last week of the season. We'll be looking to improve on what has happened. And if we do that, and win maybe 95 games, we'll be in the playoffs."

The Cubs spent most of May, June and July in first place. But in mid-August, Houston caught them and passed them and in early September, St. Louis caught them and passed them and they had to settle for a third-place finish in the National League Central.

"We won 88 games and we should have won some more," said Cubs right fielder Sammy Sosa, who hit an astounding .328-64-160. "What can you do? When we left spring training, no one was thinking we would do the great job we did. But we feel we belong at the top and we want that again next year."

Baylor pointed out two obstacles the Cubs couldn't overcome. First was Kerry Wood's shoulder injury, which kept him out of action from Aug. 4-Sept. 6. Then, when Wood returned, closer Tom Gordon, who had 27 saves, felt pain in his elbow and did not pitch again. Baylor said the fact that the Cubs had the lead in nine of their final 12 losses demonstrates how much the team missed Gordon.

For the most part, the pitching staff was strong in 2001. Righthander Jon Lieber (20-6) became the first

Sammy Sosa   Nic Jackson

JOHN SPEAR

PLAYERS OF THE YEAR

MAJOR LEAGUE: Sammy Sosa, of
Another year, another second-fiddle, 60-plus homer season. But Sosa's 425 total bases in 2001 edged Hack Wilson's mark for the top single-season total in Cubs history.

MINOR LEAGUE: Nic Jackson, of
He was much improved after 2000, his first year in pro ball when he was coming off a wrist injury. In 2001, Jackson hit .296-19-85 with 30 doubles at Class A Daytona. He also stole 24 bases.

Cubs pitcher since 1992 to win 20, while Wood (11-2, 2.71 in his final 20 starts) also picked up double-digit victories.

Rookie Juan Cruz, 20, made eight starts and was 3-1, 3.22. He impressed the Cubs to the point where he should have a spot in the starting rotation reserved for him in 2002. The only concern with Cruz is that he averaged fewer than six innings per start.

Cubs pitchers set a major league record with 1,344 strikeouts, passing Atlanta's mark of 1,245 set in 1996. They also racked up a 4.03 ERA, a huge improvement over 2000's 5.25.

But at the end of the season, pitching coach Oscar Acosta resigned after he found out Baylor was going to fire him for "personality conflicts." Cubs pitchers were puzzled and outspoken about the move, and Baylor said he thought the issue will be all but forgotten by spring training.

Some of the Cubs' heralded prospects received major league experience, with varying results.

Chicago twice called up top prospect Corey Patterson, an outfielder who hit .221-4-14 with four stolen bases in 131 at-bats—including a four-hit game against Cincinnati Oct. 3. Pitchers Scott Chiasson and Carlos Zambrano picked up some late-season major league experience after enjoying success in the minors.

Triple-A Iowa finished 83-60 and lost in the Pacific Coast League playoffs to New Orleans.

Double-A West Tenn could not keep the momentum going from its 2000 Southern League title and finished 59-80, though Cruz and Chiasson honed their skills there en route to the big leagues.

Also, talent-laden Boise won the Northwest League Eastern Division title as outfielder Syketo Anderson spent most of the summer flirting with .400. He won the batting title with a .376 average.

ORGANIZATION LEADERS

BATTING
*AVG	Roosevelt Brown, Iowa	.346
R	Chad Meyers, Iowa	92
H	Blair Barbier, Lansing	153
TB	Jason Dubois, Lansing	249
2B	Blair Barbier, Lansing	38
	Ryan Gripp, West Tenn/Daytona	38
3B	Adam Morrissey, Lansing	11
HR	Chris Haas, West Tenn	25
RBI	Ryan Gripp, West Tenn/Daytona	94
BB	Adam Morrissey, Lansing	80
SO	Chris Haas, West Tenn	151
SB	Syketo Anderson, Lansing/Boise	29

PITCHING
W	Nate Teut, Iowa	13
	Todd Wellemeyer, Lansing	13
L	Matt Achilles, West Tenn/Daytona	12
#ERA	Tim Lavery, Lansing	2.43
G	Scott Chiasson, Iowa/West Tenn	63
CG	Steve Smyth, West Tenn	3
SV	Scott Chiasson, Iowa/West Tenn	34
IP	Nate Teut, Iowa	167
BB	Todd Wellemeyer, Lansing	74
SO	Aaron Krawiec, Lansing	170

*Minimum 250 At-Bats #Minimum 75 Innings

CHICAGO CUBS

Manager: Don Baylor

2001 Record: 88-74, .543 (3rd, NL Central)

BATTING

BATTING	AVG	G	AB	R	H	2B	3B	HR	RBI	BB	SO	SB	CS	SLG	OBP	B	T	HT	WT	DOB	1st Yr	Resides
Brown, Roosevelt	.265	39	83	13	22	6	1	4	22	7	12	0	0	.506	.326	L	R	5-10	200	8-3-75	1993	Midland, Ga.
Buford, Damon	.176	35	85	11	15	2	0	3	8	4	23	0	0	.306	.213	R	R	5-10	180	6-12-70	1990	Dallas, Texas
Cairo, Miguel	.285	66	123	20	35	3	1	2	9	16	21	2	1	.374	.364	R	R	6-1	200	5-4-74	1991	St. Petersburg, Fla.
Coomer, Ron	.261	94	349	25	91	19	1	8	53	29	70	0	0	.390	.316	R	R	6-00	215	11-18-66	1987	Minneapolis, Minn.
DeShields, Delino	.276	68	163	26	45	9	3	2	16	28	35	12	1	.405	.380	L	R	6-1	175	1-15-69	1987	Fairburn, Ga.
Dunwoody, Todd	.213	33	61	6	13	4	0	1	3	3	14	0	1	.328	.250	L	L	6-1	210	4-11-75	1993	West Lafayette, Ind.
Girardi, Joe	.253	78	229	22	58	10	1	3	25	21	50	0	1	.345	.315	R	R	5-11	200	10-14-64	1986	Chicago, Ill.
Gutierrez, Ricky	.290	147	528	76	153	23	3	10	66	40	56	4	3	.402	.345	R	R	6-1	190	5-23-70	1988	Pembroke Pines, Fla.
Hundley, Todd	.187	79	246	23	46	10	0	12	31	25	89	0	0	.374	.268	B	R	5-11	199	5-27-69	1987	Port St. Lucie, Fla.
Machado, Rob	.222	52	135	13	30	10	0	2	13	7	26	0	0	.341	.266	R	R	6-1	205	6-3-73	1994	Caracas, Venez.
Matthews, Gary	.217	106	258	41	56	9	1	9	30	38	55	5	3	.364	.320	B	R	6-3	210	8-25-74	1994	Canoga Park, Calif.
McGriff, Fred	.282	49	170	27	48	7	2	12	41	26	37	0	1	.559	.383	L	L	6-3	215	10-31-63	1981	Tampa, Fla.
Meyers, Chad	.118	18	17	1	2	0	0	0	0	2	5	0	1	.118	.348	R	R	5-11	190	8-8-75	1996	Omaha, Neb.
Mueller, Bill	.295	70	210	38	62	12	1	6	23	37	19	1	1	.448	.403	B	R	5-10	180	3-17-71	1993	Maryland Heights, Mo.
Ojeda, Augie	.201	78	144	16	29	5	1	1	12	12	20	1	0	.271	.269	B	R	5-8	165	12-20-74	1996	South Gate, Calif.
Patterson, Corey	.221	59	131	26	29	3	0	4	14	6	33	4	0	.336	.266	L	R	5-9	180	8-13-79	1999	Kennesaw, Ga.
Smith, Jason	.000	2	1	0	0	0	0	0	0	0	1	0	0	.000	.000	L	R	6-3	195	7-24-77	1997	Coatopa, Ala.
Sosa, Sammy	.328	160	577	146	189	34	5	64	160	116	153	0	2	.737	.437	R	R	6-0	225	11-12-68	1986	San Pedro de Macoris, D.R.
Stairs, Matt	.250	128	340	48	85	21	0	17	61	52	76	2	3	.462	.358	L	R	5-9	215	2-27-69	1989	Bangor, Maine
Tucker, Michael	.263	63	205	31	54	9	7	5	31	23	47	4	3	.449	.339	L	R	6-2	185	6-25-71	1992	Chase City, Va.
2-team (86 Cincinnati)	.252	149	436	62	110	19	8	12	61	46	102	16	8	.415	.322							
White, Rondell	.307	95	323	43	99	19	1	17	50	26	56	1	0	.529	.371	R	R	6-1	215	2-23-72	1990	Gray, Ga.
Young, Eric	.279	149	603	98	168	43	4	6	42	42	45	31	14	.393	.333	R	R	5-9	180	5-18-67	1989	Chattanooga, Tenn.
Zuleta, Julio	.217	49	106	11	23	3	0	6	24	8	32	0	1	.415	.288	R	R	6-5	235	3-28-75	1993	Chandler, Ariz.

PITCHING

PITCHING	W	L	ERA	G	GS	CG	SV	IP	H	R	ER	BB	SO	AVG	B	T	HT	WT	DOB	1st Yr	Resides
Aybar, Manny	2	1	6.35	17	1	0	0	23	28	19	16	17	16	.304	R	R	6-1	177	10-5-74	1991	Bani, D.R.
Bere, Jason	11	11	4.31	32	32	2	0	188	171	99	90	77	175	.240	R	R	6-3	225	5-26-71	1990	North Andover, Mass.
Borowski, Joe	0	1	32.40	1	1	0	0	2	6	6	6	3	1	.666	R	R	6-2	225	5-4-71	1989	Bayonne, N.J.
Chiasson, Scott	1	1	2.70	6	0	0	0	7	5	2	2	2	6	.200	R	R	6-3	200	8-4-77	1998	Norwich, Conn.
Cruz, Juan	3	1	3.22	8	8	0	0	45	40	16	16	17	39	.243	R	R	6-2	155	10-15-80	1997	Bonao, D.R.
Duncan, Courtney	3	3	5.06	36	0	0	0	43	42	24	24	25	49	.259	L	R	6-0	185	10-9-74	1996	Huntsville, Ala.
Farnsworth, Kyle	4	6	2.74	76	0	0	2	82	65	26	25	29	107	.213	R	R	6-4	220	4-14-76	1995	Roswell, Ga.
Fassero, Jeff	4	4	3.42	82	0	0	12	74	66	31	28	23	79	.234	L	L	6-1	200	1-5-63	1984	Scottsdale, Ariz.
Fyhrie, Mike	0	2	4.20	15	0	0	0	15	16	7	7	7	6	.280	R	R	6-2	203	12-9-69	1991	Huntington Beach, Calif.
Gordon, Tom	1	2	3.38	47	0	27	0	32	18	17	16	16	67	.188	R	R	5-10	195	11-18-67	1986	Avon Park, Fla.
Heredia, Felix	2	2	6.17	48	0	0	0	35	45	27	24	16	28	.314	L	L	6-0	180	6-18-76	1993	Miami, Fla.
Lieber, Jon	20	6	3.80	34	34	5	0	232	226	104	98	41	148	.254	L	R	6-2	230	4-2-70	1992	Mobile, Ala.
Mahay, Ron	0	0	2.61	17	0	0	0	21	14	6	6	15	24	.197	L	L	6-2	195	6-28-71	1991	Crestwood, Ill.
Ohman, Will	0	1	7.71	11	0	0	0	12	14	10	10	6	12	.291	L	L	6-2	195	8-13-77	1998	Phoenix, Ariz.
Tapani, Kevin	9	14	4.49	29	29	0	0	168	186	93	84	40	149	.278	R	R	6-0	190	2-18-64	1986	Chicago, Ill.
Tavarez, Julian	10	9	4.52	34	28	0	0	161	172	98	81	69	107	.277	L	R	6-2	190	5-22-73	1990	Broadview, Ohio
Van Poppel, Todd	4	1	2.52	59	0	0	0	75	63	22	21	38	90	.223	R	R	6-5	235	12-9-71	1990	Southlake, Texas
Weathers, David	1	1	3.18	28	0	0	0	28	28	10	10	9	20	.250	R	R	6-3	230	9-25-69	1988	Loretto, Tenn.
2-team (52 Milwaukee)	4	5	2.41	80	0	0	4	86	65	24	23	34	66	.215							
Wood, Kerry	12	6	3.36	28	28	1	0	174	127	70	65	92	217	.201	R	R	6-5	230	6-16-77	1995	Irving, Texas
Zambrano, Carlos	1	2	15.26	6	1	0	0	8	11	13	13	8	4	.354	L	R	6-4	220	6-1-81	1997	Puerto Cabello, Venez.

FIELDING

Catcher	PCT	G	PO	A	E	DP	PB
Girardi	1.000	71	504	33	0	2	6
Hundley	.993	70	547	25	4	3	6
Machado	.997	47	317	20	1	3	1
DeShields	.667	5	0	4	2	0	
Meyers	.000	1	0	0	0	0	
Mueller	.942	64	33	96	8	6	
Ojeda	.913	35	8	34	4	4	

First Base	PCT	G	PO	A	E	DP
Coomer	1.000	36	136	13	0	19
DeShields	1.000	1	1	0	0	0
McGriff	.990	49	366	23	4	29
Stairs	.993	89	516	51	4	38
Tucker	.909	4	14	6	2	2
Zuleta	.991	35	213	7	2	11

Second Base	PCT	G	PO	A	E	DP
Cairo	.938	11	11	19	2	2
DeShields	1.000	16	28	21	0	1
Meyers	1.000	4	3	10	0	1
Mueller	1.000	1	0	1	0	0
Ojeda	1.000	10	8	13	0	3
Stairs	.000	1	0	0	0	0
Young	.981	147	263	366	12	67

Third Base	PCT	G	PO	A	E	DP
Cairo	.900	40	13	32	5	6
Coomer	.954	76	43	101	7	11

Shortstop	PCT	G	PO	A	E	DP
Cairo	1.000	1	1	1	0	0
Gutierrez	.971	144	173	360	16	67
Ojeda	.978	31	34	56	2	10
Smith	1.000	1	2	0	0	0

Outfield	PCT	G	PO	A	E	DP
Brown	.952	22	20	0	1	0
Buford	1.000	34	53	0	0	0
DeShields	.976	33	40	1	1	0
Dunwoody	.973	26	35	1	1	0
Matthews	.976	100	159	3	4	0
Meyers	1.000	4	3	0	0	0
Patterson	.976	54	82	0	2	0
Sosa	.982	160	326	8	6	1
Stairs	1.000	22	31	1	0	0
Tucker	.991	57	111	2	1	0
White	.979	90	133	4	3	0

LARRY GOREN

Kerry Wood

Eric Young: Cubs second baseman stole 31 bases

JOHN WILLIAMSON

Jon Lieber: Led the Cubs with 20 wins

JOHN WILLIAMSON

FARM SYSTEM

Director, Player Development: Jim Hendry

Class	Farm Team	League	W	L	Pct.	Finish*	Manager	First Yr.
AAA	Iowa Cubs	Pacific Coast	83	60	.580	3rd (16)	Bruce Kimm	1981
AA	West Tenn Diamond Jaxx	Southern	59	80	.424	9th (10)	Dave Bialas	1998
A#	Daytona (Fla.) Cubs	Florida State	68	68	.500	6th (12)	Dave Trembley	1993
A	Lansing (Mich.) Lugnuts	Midwest	65	75	.464	9th (14)	Julio Garcia	1999
A	Boise (Idaho) Hawks	Northwest	52	23	.693	1st (8)	Steve McFarland	2001
Rookie	Mesa (Ariz.) Cubs	Arizona	26	30	.464	5th (7)	Carmelo Martinez	1997

*Finish in overall standings (No. of teams in league)   #Advanced level

IOWA
Class AAA

PACIFIC COAST LEAGUE

BATTING	AVG	G	AB	R	H	2B	3B	HR	RBI	BB	SO	SB	CS	SLG	OBP	B	T	HT	WT	DOB	1st Yr	Resides
Abreu, Dennis	.500	4	12	3	6	1	0	0	1	0	2	0	0	.583	.500	R	R	6-0	180	4-22-78	1995	Tumero, Venez.
Banks, Brian	.179	17	39	2	7	2	0	1	4	4	11	0	0	.308	.256	B	R	6-3	210	9-28-70	1993	Mesa, Ariz.
Bass, Jayson	.327	70	226	34	74	17	1	8	42	26	65	7	6	.518	.402	L	L	6-3	225	6-22-74	1993	Seattle, Wash.
Brown, Roosevelt	.346	88	364	68	126	34	1	22	77	14	67	3	5	.626	.381	L	R	5-10	200	8-3-75	1993	Midland, Ga.
Cairo, Miguel	.301	34	123	22	37	7	1	3	14	8	11	3	4	.447	.348	R	R	6-1	200	5-4-74	1991	St. Petersburg, Fla.
Choi, Hee Seop	.229	77	266	38	61	11	0	13	45	34	67	5	1	.417	.313	L	L	6-5	235	3-16-79	1999	Mesa, Ariz.
Coomer, Ron	.333	4	12	0	4	0	0	0	0	1	3	0	0	.333	.385	R	R	6-00	215	11-18-66	1987	Minneapolis, Minn.
Dunwoody, Todd	.283	75	251	31	71	18	3	8	32	17	75	6	4	.474	.331	L	L	6-1	210	4-11-75	1993	West Lafayette, Ind.
Gload, Ross	.297	133	475	70	141	32	10	15	93	35	88	9	7	.501	.344	L	L	6-0	185	4-5-76	1997	East Hampton, N.Y.
Hubbard, Trenidad	.316	49	171	38	54	11	3	6	31	37	27	17	5	.520	.439	R	R	5-9	203	5-11-66	1986	Houston, Texas
2-team (49 Omaha)	.301	98	346	73	104	20	4	16	59	67	61	25	10	.520	.416							
Hundley, Todd	.196	15	51	7	10	1	0	3	8	4	23	0	0	.392	.263	B	R	5-11	199	5-27-69	1987	Port St. Lucie, Fla.
Kopitzke, Casey	.200	4	5	1	1	0	0	0	2	0	1	0	0	.200	.200	R	R	6-2	210	5-31-78	1999	Greenleaf, Wis.
Lopez, Pee Wee	.167	24	54	6	9	3	0	0	2	3	12	0	0	.222	.211	R	R	6-0	200	10-22-76	1996	Miami, Fla.
Machado, Rob	.283	53	180	20	51	11	0	8	30	11	36	0	0	.478	.332	R	R	6-1	205	6-3-73	1989	Caracas, Venez.
Mahoney, Mike	.225	95	289	22	65	14	1	3	27	22	63	1	3	.311	.287	R	R	6-1	200	12-5-72	1995	Johnston, Iowa
Meyers, Chad	.300	132	446	92	134	31	5	9	54	58	72	27	9	.453	.407	R	R	5-11	190	8-8-75	1996	Omaha, Neb.
Mueller, Bill	.423	8	26	3	11	3	0	0	4	1	2	0	0	.538	.444	B	R	5-10	180	3-17-71	1993	Maryland Heights, Mo.
Patterson, Corey	.253	89	367	63	93	22	3	7	32	29	65	19	8	.387	.308	L	R	5-9	180	8-13-79	1999	Kennesaw, Ga.
Roskos, John	.256	34	90	10	23	5	0	2	14	12	20	0	0	.378	.346	R	R	5-11	195	11-19-74	1993	Rio Rancho, N.M.
2-team (46 Portland)	.246	80	224	25	55	14	1	5	34	23	51	0	0	.384	.313							
Short, Rick	.275	105	313	38	86	19	1	5	34	22	42	2	1	.390	.327	R	R	6-0	200	12-6-72	1994	South Elgin, Ill.
Smith, Jason	.233	70	240	31	56	8	6	4	15	12	71	6	3	.367	.271	L	R	6-3	195	7-24-77	1997	Coatopa, Ala.
Snopek, Chris	.277	130	470	65	130	33	0	14	57	32	67	6	5	.436	.322	R	R	6-1	190	9-20-70	1992	Cynthiana, Ky.
Woods, Ken	.250	11	36	3	9	1	0	0	2	0	9	0	0	.278	.270	R	R	5-10	175	8-2-70	1992	Los Angeles, Calif.
Zuleta, Julio	.308	37	146	18	45	13	0	7	29	7	33	3	1	.541	.348	R	R	6-5	235	3-28-75	1993	Chandler, Ariz.

PITCHING

PITCHING	W	L	ERA	G	GS	CG	SV	IP	H	R	ER	BB	SO	AVG	B	T	HT	WT	DOB	1st Yr	Resides
Aybar, Manny	1	2	5.02	8	7	1	0	43	42	26	24	16	32	.251	R	R	6-1	177	10-5-74	1991	Bani, D.R.
Borowski, Joe	8	7	2.62	39	12	1	1	110	87	35	32	26	131	.215	R	R	6-2	225	5-4-71	1989	Bayonne, N.J.
Chiasson, Scott	0	0	2.25	11	0	0	10	12	11	3	3	0	14	.234	R	R	6-3	200	8-14-77	1998	Norwich, Conn.
Daneker, Pat	3	1	9.14	16	0	0	0	22	41	26	22	9	9	.414	R	R	6-3	195	1-14-76	1997	Williamsport, Pa.
Duncan, Courtney	1	0	3.24	7	0	0	0	8	7	3	3	5	15	.225	L	R	6-0	185	10-9-74	1996	Huntsville, Ala.
Ford, Ben	2	3	5.79	5	5	0	0	23	31	15	15	9	16	.326	R	R	6-7	225	8-15-75	1994	Tampa, Fla.
Fyhrie, Mike	1	0	4.80	13	0	0	2	15	14	8	8	8	15	.233	R	R	6-2	203	12-9-69	1991	Huntington Beach, Calif.
Gordon, Tom	0	0	0.00	2	0	0	0	2	1	0	0	1	2	.166	R	R	5-10	195	11-18-67	1986	Avon Park, Fla.
Kamieniecki, Scott	1	4	3.65	8	4	0	0	37	34	16	15	10	38	.255	R	R	6-0	200	4-19-64	1987	Goodrich, Mich.
Mahay, Ron	3	1	2.31	36	0	0	14	47	29	12	12	10	52	.182	L	L	6-2	190	6-28-71	1991	Crestwood, Ill.
2-team (14 Portland)	4	3	2.70	50	0	0	14	63	42	21	19	15	70	.190							
Meyers, Mike	7	4	3.23	25	25	0	0	148	129	58	53	64	124	.232	R	R	6-2	210	10-18-77	1997	Tillsonburg, Ontario
Nation, Joey	3	2	3.02	14	9	0	0	45	39	16	15	13	48	.233	L	L	6-2	205	9-28-78	1997	Oklahoma City, Okla.
Norton, Phil	6	3	2.69	46	3	0	2	74	65	27	22	41	75	.250	R	L	6-0	190	2-1-76	1996	Texarkana, Texas
Ohman, Will	5	2	4.06	40	1	0	4	51	51	24	23	18	66	.258	L	L	6-2	195	8-13-77	1998	Phoenix, Ariz.
Quevedo, Ruben	9	5	2.99	22	22	1	0	142	124	54	47	48	150	.237	R	R	6-1	245	1-5-79	1996	Valencia, Venez.
Rain, Steve	0	0	11.74	9	0	0	1	8	10	12	10	6	9	.322	R	R	6-6	260	6-2-75	1993	Walnut, Calif.
Snyder, Matt	0	0	9.00	1	0	0	0	1	1	1	1	1	3	.250	R	R	5-11	201	7-7-74	1995	Newtown, Pa.
Sollecito, Gabe	0	0	4.82	7	0	0	0	9	9	5	5	1	9	.257	R	R	6-1	190	3-3-72	1993	Monterey, Calif.
Stanifer, Rob	7	8	4.24	54	0	0	6	74	85	38	35	28	79	.296	R	R	6-2	220	3-10-72	1994	Largo, Fla.
Teut, Nate	13	8	5.12	29	29	0	0	167	184	109	95	69	125	.275	R	L	6-7	220	3-11-76	1997	Des Moines, Iowa
Wainhouse, Dave	3	5	4.16	49	1	0	6	76	86	38	35	24	61	.292	R	R	6-2	200	11-7-67	1989	Kent, Wash.
Zambrano, Carlos	10	5	3.88	26	25	1	0	151	124	73	65	68	155	.225	L	R	6-4	220	6-1-81	1997	Puerto Cabello, Venez.

FIELDING

Catcher	PCT	G	PO	A	E	DP	PB
Hundley	1.000	9	51	5	0	0	0
Kopitzke	1.000	1	3	0	0	0	0
Lopez	.993	19	140	10	1	2	2
Machado	.988	45	396	27	5	3	3
Mahoney	.996	85	680	42	3	10	6

First Base	PCT	G	PO	A	E	DP
Banks	1.000	2	6	1	0	2
Choi	.995	72	518	39	3	49
Coomer	1.000	2	9	0	0	2
Gload	.997	50	345	35	1	30
Mahoney	1.000	1	1	0	0	0
Roskos	.978	8	38	7	1	2
Short	1.000	4	10	0	0	0
Zuleta	.982	20	151	9	3	15

Second Base	PCT	G	PO	A	E	DP
Cairo	.991	27	51	54	1	11

	PCT	G	PO	A	E	DP
Meyers	.965	106	188	227	15	52
Short	1.000	6	10	12	0	4
Snopek	.951	14	24	34	3	9

Third Base	PCT	G	PO	A	E	DP
Abreu	1.000	2	2	4	0	2
Cairo	.750	1	0	3	1	0
Coomer	1.000	2	1	4	0	0
Hubbard	1.000	7	3	8	0	1
Mahoney	.000	1	0	0	0	0
Meyers	1.000	4	1	6	0	0
Mueller	1.000	6	1	6	0	1
Short	.959	90	67	121	8	15
Snopek	.966	45	31	54	3	4
Zuleta	.826	12	9	10	4	0

Shortstop	PCT	G	PO	A	E	DP
Abreu	1.000	1	0	1	0	0
Cairo	.960	7	7	17	1	1

	PCT	G	PO	A	E	DP
Smith	.942	67	108	199	19	47
Snopek	.970	71	82	178	8	28

Outfield	PCT	G	PO	A	E	DP
Banks	1.000	10	12	0	0	0
Bass	.967	58	111	5	4	2
Brown	.971	79	127	7	4	1
Dunwoody	.974	63	107	7	3	2
Gload	.983	72	112	6	2	0
Hubbard	.987	43	76	1	1	1
Meyers	.972	22	35	0	1	0
Patterson	.968	87	180	3	6	0
Roskos	1.000	14	14	2	0	0
Short	.000	1	0	0	0	0
Woods	1.000	10	13	0	0	0
Zuleta	1.000	3	5	0	0	0

WEST TENN

Class AA

SOUTHERN LEAGUE

BATTING	AVG	G	AB	R	H	2B	3B	HR	RBI	BB	SO	SB	CS	SLG	OBP	B	T	HT	WT	DOB	1st Yr	Resides
Abreu, Dennis	.254	102	331	35	84	7	1	4	30	19	74	14	4	.317	.299	R	R	6-0	180	4-22-78	1995	Turmero, Venez.
Amrhein, Mike	.241	96	311	30	75	14	0	4	33	23	45	0	1	.325	.310	R	R	6-2	215	6-14-75	1997	Oak Park, Ill.
Bass, Jayson	.309	48	162	17	50	5	1	6	24	14	42	6	3	.463	.371	L	L	6-3	225	6-22-74	1993	Seattle, Wash.
Curry, Chris	.213	42	108	9	23	3	0	1	11	12	34	0	0	.269	.289	R	R	6-1	205	11-17-77	1999	Conway, Ark.
Frese, Nate	.180	72	233	25	42	5	1	4	19	38	62	0	1	.262	.306	R	R	6-3	200	7-10-77	1998	Norway, Iowa
Goldbach, Jeff	.204	32	98	11	20	4	1	3	6	9	17	1	0	.357	.278	R	R	6-0	190	12-20-79	1998	Princeton, Ind.
Grice, Daniel	.143	7	14	1	2	1	0	0	1	1	3	0	0	.214	.235	R	R	5-11	180	10-5-75	2001	Creswell, Ore.
Gripp, Ryan	.227	68	255	31	58	19	0	8	45	25	60	2	0	.396	.313	R	R	6-1	210	4-20-78	1999	Indianola, Iowa
Haas, Chris	.245	126	417	64	102	16	4	25	72	65	151	2	2	.482	.348	L	R	6-2	210	10-15-76	1995	Paducah, Ky.
Hill, Bobby	.301	57	209	30	63	8	1	3	21	32	39	20	8	.392	.396	B	R	5-10	180	4-3-78	2000	San Jose, Calif.
Hundley, Todd	.333	4	12	1	4	2	0	0	1	1	3	0	0	.500	.385	B	R	5-11	199	5-27-69	1987	Port St. Lucie, Fla.
Johnson, Gary	.261	135	463	87	121	28	5	8	64	58	105	15	5	.395	.357	R	R	6-4	210	9-6-76	1997	Rancho Cucamonga, Calif.
Jorgensen, Ryan	.119	32	109	8	13	4	0	2	7	11	38	0	0	.211	.195	R	R	6-2	195	5-4-79	2000	Kingwood, Texas
Kelton, Dave	.313	58	224	33	70	9	4	12	45	24	55	1	3	.549	.378	R	R	6-3	205	12-17-79	1998	West Point, Ga.
Lopez, Pee Wee	.333	22	69	8	23	4	1	1	12	5	9	0	0	.464	.378	R	R	6-0	180	10-22-76	1996	Miami, Fla.
Meadows, Randy	.257	64	140	16	36	7	1	0	15	6	35	1	3	.321	.300	R	R	6-0	185	8-15-76	1998	Nesbit, Miss.
Meadows, Tydus	.269	67	197	42	53	10	3	10	29	40	57	0	2	.503	.412	L	L	6-2	215	9-5-77	1998	Evans, Ga.
Piedra, Jorge	.245	124	441	55	108	26	6	8	54	37	80	12	5	.385	.310	L	L	6-0	175	4-17-79	1997	Van Nuys, Calif.
Ramsey, Brad	.250	9	20	5	5	0	0	2	4	3	6	0	0	.600	.375	B	R	6-4	225	11-7-76	1997	West Monroe, La.
Randolph, Jaisen	.230	102	365	43	84	11	1	0	17	50	61	23	15	.266	.327	B	R	6-0	180	1-19-79	1997	Tampa, Fla.
Rodriguez, Tony	.282	33	131	13	37	5	0	1	15	4	23	3	3	.344	.324	R	R	5-11	165	8-15-70	1991	Cidra, P.R.
Schrager, Tony	.244	26	78	9	19	4	0	1	10	7	16	0	0	.333	.314	R	R	6-1	185	6-14-77	1998	Omaha, Neb.
Short, Rick	.263	8	19	5	5	0	0	0	5	1	0	1	0	.263	.440	R	R	6-0	200	12-6-72	1994	South Elgin, Ill.
White, Rondell	.143	9	28	2	4	1	0	2	4	1	7	0	0	.393	.226	R	R	6-1	215	2-23-72	1990	Gray, Ga.

PITCHING	W	L	ERA	G	GS	CG	SV	IP	H	R	ER	BB	SO	AVG	B	T	HT	WT	DOB	1st Yr	Resides
Achilles, Matt	3	4	4.10	9	9	0	0	53	56	26	24	22	39	.285	R	R	6-3	180	8-18-76	1996	East Moline, Ill.
Booker, Chris	2	6	4.33	45	0	0	1	52	39	29	25	36	76	.205	R	R	6-3	230	12-9-76	1995	Monroeville, Ala.
Bruback, Matt	2	5	9.00	9	9	0	0	38	58	44	38	20	43	.345	R	R	6-7	215	1-12-79	1998	Sarasota, Fla.
Chiasson, Scott	3	4	1.76	52	0	0	24	61	43	15	12	20	62	.197	R	R	6-3	200	8-14-77	1998	Norwich, Conn.
Christensen, Ben	2	1	6.48	3	3	0	0	17	20	12	12	9	9	.312	R	R	6-4	205	2-7-78	1999	Wichita, Kan.
Cook, Derrick	0	2	8.10	4	0	0	0	7	9	6	6	5	3	.346	R	R	6-2	195	8-6-75	1996	Staunton, Va.
Cruz, Juan	9	6	4.01	23	23	0	0	121	107	56	54	60	137	.237	R	R	6-2	155	10-15-80	1997	Bonao, D.R.
Cueto, Jose	0	1	8.68	2	2	0	0	9	10	9	9	6	10	.285	R	R	6-2	175	9-13-78	1996	San Pedro de Macoris, D.R.
Daneker, Pat	0	0	13.50	2	0	0	0	1	3	2	2	1	2	.429	R	R	6-3	195	1-14-76	1997	Williamsport, Pa.
Gagliano, Steve	1	2	4.25	35	1	0	0	49	49	24	23	23	44	.260	R	R	6-4	200	8-4-77	1997	Rolling Meadows, Ill.
Gissell, Chris	5	11	4.51	28	27	0	0	160	159	91	80	63	136	.260	R	R	6-5	210	1-4-78	1996	Vancouver, Wash.

PITCHING

PITCHING	W	L	ERA	G	GS	CG	SV	IP	H	R	ER	BB	SO	AVG	B	T	HT	WT	DOB	1st Yr	Resides
Gonzalez, Lariel	1	0	4.63	11	0	0	0	12	15	11	6	7	8	.300	R	R	6-4	228	5-25-76	1994	San Cristobal, D.R.
Kramer, Aaron	0	0	20.25	2	0	0	0	1	3	3	3	0	2	.428	B	R	6-1	210	6-25-75	1998	Glendale, Ariz.
2-team (23 Mobile)	2	7	5.65	25	4	0	0	51	56	35	32	12	43	.274							
Krug, Dustin	0	0	9.90	7	0	0	0	10	16	12	11	5	9	.363	R	R	6-5	225	6-4-77	1998	Kodiak, Alaska
Mallard, Randi	0	0	9.90	8	0	0	0	10	13	12	11	9	7	.325	R	R	6-1	180	8-11-75	1998	Tampa, Fla.
Meadows, Randy	0	0	7.71	2	0	0	0	2	3	2	2	1	0	.000	R	R	6-0	185	8-15-76	1998	Nesbit, Miss.
Moraga, David	4	5	4.10	23	12	1	0	83	82	44	38	21	58	.255	L	L	6-0	184	7-8-75	1994	Suisun, Calif.
Noyce, Dave	3	8	4.03	50	8	0	1	96	98	53	43	48	87	.263	L	L	6-5	195	3-2-77	1998	West Melbourne, Fla.
Palma, Rick	4	9	3.06	57	0	0	7	71	61	29	24	25	70	.235	L	L	6-1	160	9-26-79	1996	Maracay, Venez.
Robinson, Dustin	1	1	4.35	17	0	0	1	21	24	10	10	9	18	.296	R	R	6-6	225	9-13-75	1997	Stroud, Okla.
Smyth, Steve	9	3	2.54	18	18	3	0	120	110	38	34	40	93	.246	L	L	6-1	220	6-3-78	1999	Temecula, Calif.
Snyder, Matt	2	1	8.90	25	0	0	1	31	36	33	31	17	31	.288	R	R	5-11	201	7-7-74	1995	Newtown, Pa.
Waligora, Tom	4	1	3.48	22	0	0	0	31	22	13	12	13	36	.192	R	R	6-8	240	8-7-76	1997	Richmond, Va.
Wuertz, Mike	4	9	3.99	27	27	1	0	160	160	80	71	58	135	.260	R	R	6-3	190	12-15-78	1997	Austin, Minn.

FIELDING

Catcher	PCT	G	PO	A	E	DP	PB
Amrhein	.985	45	351	35	6	5	6
Curry	.992	34	219	18	2	2	5
Goldbach	.992	27	224	13	2	1	6
Hundley	1.000	2	7	1	0	0	0
Jorgensen	.981	32	240	23	5	0	0
Lopez	1.000	16	98	12	0	1	2

First Base	PCT	G	PO	A	E	DP
Abreu	.000	1	0	0	0	0
Amrhein	1.000	40	274	14	0	31
Haas	.991	100	708	39	7	51
Ramsey	1.000	4	22	2	0	3
Schrager	1.000	1	2	0	0	0
Short	1.000	2	18	2	0	3

Second Base	PCT	G	PO	A	E	DP
Abreu	.979	49	81	102	4	19
Grice	1.000	1	3	4	0	0

Haas	1.000	1	1	2	0	1
Hill	.973	54	98	118	6	28
R. Meadows	.990	32	50	48	1	10
Rodriguez	1.000	2	3	6	0	2
Schrager	.968	22	45	46	3	13
Short	1.000	1	0	1	0	

Third Base	PCT	G	PO	A	E	DP
Abreu	.882	7	4	11	2	1
Gripp	.892	62	50	99	18	16
Haas	.892	13	12	21	4	2
Kelton	.883	54	26	87	15	5
R. Meadows	1.000	7	3	15	0	1
Short	.000	2	0	0	0	0

Shortstop	PCT	G	PO	A	E	DP
Abreu	.956	37	44	87	6	20
Frese	.996	70	97	178	1	35
Grice	1.000	5	5	5	0	2

Hill	1.000	1	3	0	0	0
R. Meadows	.786	4	2	9	3	3
Rodriguez	.964	31	37	71	4	9

Outfield	PCT	G	PO	A	E	DP
Abreu	1.000	2	1	1	0	0
Amrhein	1.000	2	1	0	0	0
Bass	.971	35	63	3	2	0
Haas	1.000	2	4	0	0	0
Johnson	.980	127	286	11	6	2
Lopez	.000	1	0	0	0	0
R. Meadows	1.000	2	1	0	0	0
T. Meadows	.971	54	93	7	3	3
Piedra	.980	118	231	9	5	1
Randolph	1.000	96	181	9	0	3
Short	1.000	2	4	0	0	0
White	1.000	3	2	0	0	0

DAYTONA — Class A

FLORIDA STATE LEAGUE

BATTING

BATTING	AVG	G	AB	R	H	2B	3B	HR	RBI	BB	SO	SB	CS	SLG	OBP	B	T	HT	WT	DOB	1st Yr	Resides
Bass, Kevin	.188	87	276	32	52	11	0	7	20	28	106	4	2	.304	.263	B	R	6-2	205	6-22-79	1998	Fayette, Ala.
Blasi, Blake	.243	46	144	17	35	1	1	0	14	25	14	3	4	.264	.355	B	R	5-8	165	3-23-79	2000	Wichita, Kan.
Chapman, Scott	.061	18	66	3	4	0	0	0	2	5	15	0	0	.061	.127	R	R	6-2	200	1-30-78	1995	Davenport, Ohio
Cooper, Sam	.108	13	37	6	4	1	0	0	0	4	8	1	0	.135	.250	B	R	5-10	175	11-9-77	2000	Mesa, Ariz.
Curry, Chris	.263	12	38	2	10	4	0	0	5	4	12	0	0	.368	.333	R	R	6-1	205	11-17-77	1999	Conway, Ark.
Deschaine, James	.289	134	485	68	140	26	2	21	82	62	103	6	10	.480	.372	R	R	6-0	200	9-18-77	1999	Bristol, Conn.
Dzurilla, Mike	.288	123	434	60	125	21	2	8	45	38	77	9	6	.401	.349	R	R	6-0	190	5-4-78	1999	Bayside, N.Y.
German, Franklin	.184	71	196	29	36	6	2	0	12	25	63	13	7	.235	.286	R	R	5-10	175	2-28-80	1997	Santo Domingo, D.R.
Goldbach, Jeff	.193	46	145	14	28	5	1	4	17	15	28	0	0	.324	.276	R	R	6-0	190	12-20-79	1998	Princeton, Ind.
Grice, Daniel	.128	28	94	7	12	2	0	0	7	6	16	2	0	.149	.193	R	R	5-11	180	10-5-75	2001	Creswell, Ore.
Gripp, Ryan	.295	67	241	35	71	19	0	5	49	27	57	6	5	.436	.375	R	R	6-1	210	4-20-78	1999	Indianola, Iowa
Jackson, Nic	.296	131	503	87	149	30	6	19	85	39	96	24	10	.493	.355	L	R	6-3	205	9-25-79	2000	Richmond, Va.
Johnstone, Ben	.266	82	308	39	82	6	0	1	30	10	32	20	13	.295	.294	R	R	6-0	195	2-5-78	1999	Atlanta, Ga.
Jones, Jack	.238	9	21	3	5	1	0	0	2	0	4	0	0	.286	.273	R	R	5-10	175	11-7-74	1996	Modesto, Calif.
Jorgensen, Ryan	.282	54	188	24	53	12	1	8	29	23	39	1	3	.484	.366	R	R	6-2	195	5-4-79	2000	Kingwood, Texas
Kopitzke, Casey	.240	38	96	15	23	1	0	0	8	11	17	0	2	.250	.351	R	R	6-2	210	5-31-78	1999	Greenleaf, Wis.
Martinez, Dionnar	.267	26	60	10	16	3	0	0	7	11	11	0	0	.317	.353	B	R	6-5	185	1-15-81	1998	Barcelona, Venez.
Meadows, Randy	.100	5	20	0	2	0	0	0	0	1	6	1	0	.100	.143	R	R	6-0	185	8-15-76	1998	Nesbit, Miss.
2-team (5 Jupiter)	.088	10	34	1	3	0	0	0	0	1	11	1	0	.088	.114							
Meadows, Tydus	.350	5	20	5	7	1	0	1	4	3	4	0	0	.550	.480	R	R	6-2	215	9-5-77	1998	Evans, Ga.
Navarro, Mandy	.333	3	6	2	2	0	0	0	2	3	0	0	0	.333	.500	R	R	6-0	175	4-24-81	2001	Miami, Fla.
Ramsey, Brad	.226	96	332	28	75	16	0	7	41	23	75	2	3	.337	.288	R	R	6-4	225	11-7-76	1997	West Monroe, La.
Schrager, Tony	.314	89	299	55	94	22	2	14	56	54	49	10	6	.542	.423	R	R	6-1	185	6-14-77	1998	Omaha, Neb.
Sledd, Joseph	.118	7	17	1	2	0	0	0	1	3	6	0	0	.118	.238	L	L	5-11	200	12-27-75	1998	Germantown, Tenn.
Theriot, Ryan	.204	30	103	20	21	5	0	0	9	21	17	2	4	.252	.341	R	R	5-10	175	12-7-79	2001	Baton Rouge, La.
Zoccolillo, Peter	.264	96	326	42	86	18	4	2	35	35	57	7	5	.362	.332	L	R	6-2	205	2-6-77	1999	White Plains, N.Y.

GAMES BY POSITION: C—Curry 4, Goldbach 33, Jorgensen 40, Kopitzke 36, Ramsey 5. **1B**—Curry 1, Dzurilla 107, Gripp 1, Ramsey 23, Zoccolillo 13. **2B**—Blasi 40, Cooper 6, Dzurilla 12, German 10, Jones 4, Martinez 5, R. Meadows 4, Schrager 70. **3B**—Blasi 4, Deschaine 48, Dzurilla 4, German 2, Grice 9, Gripp 61, Jones 1, Martinez 11, Schrager 5. **SS**—Cooper 6, Deschaine 57, German 37, Grice 19, Jones 3, Martinez 9, R. Meadows 3, Navarro 3, Schrager 12, Theriot 30. **OF**—Bass 53, Chapman 11, Deschaine 18, German 57, Jackson 129, Johnstone 79, Kopitzke 1, T. Meadows 5, Sledd 6, Zoccolillo 76.

PITCHING

PITCHING	W	L	ERA	G	GS	CG	SV	IP	H	R	ER	BB	SO	AVG	B	T	HT	WT	DOB	1st Yr	Resides
Achilles, Matt	4	8	2.59	16	15	1	0	94	84	37	27	22	60	.243	R	R	6-3	180	8-18-76	1996	East Moline, Ill.
Bailey, Dave	0	2	4.99	34	0	0	8	40	45	25	22	15	39	.288	R	R	6-1	200	2-2-77	1998	Chesapeake, Va.
Beltran, Frank	6	9	5.00	21	18	0	0	95	93	62	53	40	72	.251	R	R	6-5	220	7-25-80	1997	Santo Domingo, D.R.
Blanton, Jason	3	0	0.44	4	0	0	0	21	10	3	1	15	21	.149	R	R	6-3	200	9-10-79	2001	Titusville, Fla.
Bruback, Matt	6	3	3.00	14	14	0	0	84	70	33	28	21	87	.222	R	R	6-7	215	1-12-79	1998	Sarasota, Fla.
Chavez, Wilton	3	4	4.12	17	16	0	0	90	96	46	41	30	59	.268	R	R	6-2	175	4-30-81	1998	Montecristi, D.R.
Corbin, John	2	0	3.74	10	0	0	2	22	26	9	9	4	12	.292	R	R	6-2	205	6-18-77	2000	Hollywood, Fla.
Cueto, Jose	1	2	3.03	6	6	0	0	39	31	19	13	13	41	.210	R	R	6-2	175	9-13-78	1996	San Pedro de Macoris, D.R.
Eppender, James	4	2	3.48	42	0	0	5	67	54	37	26	34	56	.210	L	L	6-3	215	11-17-78	1999	Antioch, Calif.
Fisher, Marc	0	0	2.25	2	1	0	0	4	5	1	1	1	4	.312	R	R	6-4	195	5-17-79	2001	Conshohocken, Pa.
Frachiseur, Zach	1	3	5.10	22	0	0	4	30	34	19	17	10	34	.290	R	R	6-1	190	9-30-76	1998	Conyers, Ga.
Freed, Mark	6	8	3.12	23	22	1	0	130	120	54	45	51	90	.249	L	L	6-5	215	8-10-78	2000	Pennsville, N.J.
Gagliano, Steve	1	2	4.22	17	0	0	7	21	23	11	10	14	16	.277	R	R	6-4	200	8-4-77	1997	Rolling Meadows, Ill.

PITCHING	W	L	ERA	G	GS	CG	SV	IP	H	R	ER	BB	SO	AVG	B	T	HT	WT	DOB	1st Yr	Resides
Gomer, Jeramy	3	1	6.24	24	2	0	1	49	51	36	34	29	44	.274	L	L	6-2	195	6-12-79	1998	Plant City, Fla.
Gordon, Tom	0	0	0.00	2	0	0	0	2	0	0	0	0	3	.000	R	R	5-10	195	11-18-67	1986	Avon Park, Fla.
Hammons, Matt	1	1	3.70	7	6	0	0	24	25	16	10	13	27	.257	R	R	6-3	205	4-9-77	1995	San Diego, Calif.
Krug, Dustin	3	2	5.23	20	0	0	1	31	46	21	18	12	22	.340	R	R	6-5	225	3-6-77	1998	Kodiak, Alaska
Montero, Oscar	2	0	3.38	11	1	0	0	16	7	6	6	14	13	.129	R	R	6-4	215	5-9-78	1997	Caracas, Venez.
Murphy, Matt	4	6	3.96	53	0	0	0	75	82	44	33	25	77	.278	L	L	6-2	190	10-31-78	1998	Delano, Tenn.
Negrette, Richard	0	1	33.00	4	0	0	0	3	11	12	11	7	1	.523	R	R	6-2	210	3-6-76	1994	Maracaibo, Venez.
Orr, Ben	0	1	5.40	5	0	0	1	5	6	4	3	6	6	.352	L	L	6-1	190	2-24-78	2001	La Mirada, Calif.
Robinson, Dustin	0	0	2.08	2	0	0	0	4	2	1	1	1	7	.133	R	R	6-6	225	9-13-75	1997	Stroud, Okla.
Shaffar, Ben	6	4	3.12	19	19	2	0	107	83	42	37	45	118	.210	B	R	6-3	195	9-28-77	1999	Leitchfield, Ky.
Tranchina, Scott	11	3	3.59	42	8	0	1	93	91	50	37	42	89	.257	R	R	6-0	190	6-3-77	2000	Harvey, La.
Webb, John	1	1	5.40	5	4	0	0	20	23	13	12	7	20	.280	R	R	6-3	190	5-23-79	1999	Pensacola, Fla.

LANSING — Class A

MIDWEST LEAGUE

BATTING	AVG	G	AB	R	H	2B	3B	HR	RBI	BB	SO	SB	CS	SLG	OBP	B	T	HT	WT	DOB	1st Yr	Resides
Anderson, Syketo	.161	18	62	4	10	1	0	0	3	2	9	5	3	.177	.188	L	R	5-11	180	2-12-79	1999	Prattville, Ala.
Barbier, Blair	.314	131	488	77	153	38	1	16	77	52	63	3	6	.494	.392	R	R	5-10	190	2-13-78	2000	Harvey, La.
Blasi, Blake	.272	61	228	34	62	7	0	1	19	33	29	7	4	.316	.364	B	R	5-8	165	3-23-79	2000	Wichita, Kan.
Cameron, Antoine	.265	94	343	47	91	20	2	9	47	37	87	2	2	.414	.339	L	L	6-1	215	3-17-80	2000	Chino Hills, Calif.
Cedeno, Ronny	.196	17	56	9	11	4	1	1	2	2	18	0	2	.357	.237	R	R	6-0	170	2-2-83	1999	Carabobo, Venez.
Cooper, Sam	.273	3	11	0	3	0	0	0	1	0	1	0	0	.273	.273	R	R	5-10	175	11-9-77	2000	Mesa, Ariz.
Curry, Chris	.116	29	95	7	11	4	0	0	8	9	21	0	0	.158	.202	R	R	6-1	205	11-17-77	1999	Conway, Ark.
Dubois, Jason	.296	118	443	76	131	28	9	24	92	46	120	1	2	.562	.377	R	R	6-05	225	3-26-79	2000	Virginia Beach, Va.
Harris, Brendan	.274	32	113	25	31	5	1	4	22	17	26	5	1	.442	.370	R	R	6-0	180	8-26-80	2001	Queensbury, N.Y.
Harris, Josh	.303	22	76	10	23	5	1	0	9	2	6	0	1	.395	.337	R	R	5-9	170	11-27-78	2001	West Hills, Calif.
Kweon, Yoon-Min	.270	68	326	33	88	15	1	6	51	15	44	0	0	.377	.304	R	R	6-2	210	1-22-79	1999	Inchon, Korea
Mallory, Mike	.228	127	434	51	99	17	3	12	47	28	132	17	3	.364	.291	R	R	6-4	210	12-8-80	1999	Dinwiddie, Va.
Martinez, Dionnar	.321	17	56	8	18	2	1	0	6	3	8	0	1	.393	.367	B	R	6-5	185	1-15-81	1998	Barcelona, Venez.
Mejia, Andy	.135	12	37	3	5	2	0	0	3	1	9	0	0	.189	.158	R	R	6-2	170	6-15-82	1999	Hato Mayor, D.R.
Montanez, Luis	.255	124	499	70	127	33	6	5	54	34	121	20	7	.375	.316	R	R	6-2	175	12-15-81	2000	Miami, Fla.
Morrissey, Adam	.309	122	418	88	129	26	11	14	62	80	82	10	9	.524	.427	R	R	5-11	170	6-8-81	1999	Ourimbah, Australia
Sadler, Ray	.341	94	378	74	129	27	3	10	50	22	58	18	7	.508	.378	R	R	6-1	195	9-19-80	2000	Clifton, Texas
Silver, Travis	.158	22	57	7	9	0	0	0	4	6	23	0	1	.158	.269	R	R	6-3	215	6-11-78	2001	Weaverville, N.C.
Sing, Brandon	.245	121	417	54	102	27	2	16	50	46	109	3	5	.434	.328	R	R	6-3	200	3-13-81	1999	Joliet, Ill.
Sprowl, Jon-Mark	.219	54	155	12	34	9	0	3	28	18	24	0	3	.335	.311	R	R	6-1	200	8-1-80	1999	Panama City, Fla.

GAMES BY POSITION: C—Barbier 1, Curry 23, Kweon 83, Mejia 11, Silver 20, Sprowl 17. **1B**—Barbier 71, Dubois 13, Sing 52, Sprowl 7. **2B**—Blasi 61, B. Harris 11, J. Harris 20, Martinez 2, Morrissey 46. **3B**—Barbier 48, Cedeno 5, B. Harris 9, Martinez 3, Morrissey 27, Sing 52, Sprowl 1. **SS**—Cedeno 6, Cooper 2, B. Harris 8, J. Harris 2, Martinez 11, Montanez 112, Morrissey 2. **OF**—Anderson 17, Barbier 6, Cameron 73, Curry 2, Dubois 87, Mallory 123, Morrissey 32, Sadler 90.

PITCHING	W	L	ERA	G	GS	CG	SV	IP	H	R	ER	BB	SO	AVG	B	T	HT	WT	DOB	1st Yr	Resides
Albright, Eric	1	5	6.20	34	0	0	8	41	49	31	28	11	50	.288	R	R	6-2	180	10-4-77	2000	Long Beach, Calif.
Alvarez, Larry	1	2	2.25	30	0	0	2	44	38	13	11	14	54	.231	R	R	6-3	225	9-24-79	1998	Rowland Heights, Calif.
Blanton, Jason	0	0	4.09	7	0	0	0	11	14	6	5	3	7	.311	R	R	6-3	220	9-10-79	2001	Titusville, Fla.
Brown, Eric	3	1	2.61	16	0	0	1	21	18	6	6	5	23	.230	R	R	6-3	205	12-5-78	2001	Basking Ridge, N.J.
Chavez, Wilton	2	6	4.02	8	8	2	0	47	38	24	21	27	60	.219	R	R	6-1	175	4-30-81	1998	Montecristi, D.R.
Corbin, Jason	3	1	3.60	14	0	0	1	25	37	16	10	4	23	.333	R	R	6-3	205	6-18-77	2000	Hollywood, Fla.
Cordero, Frangil	2	0	7.24	9	0	0	0	14	18	16	11	15	11	.300	L	L	5-10	175	12-8-80	1997	Bani, D.R.
Cueto, Jose	4	4	3.79	22	14	2	0	95	71	50	40	44	105	.288	R	R	6-2	175	9-13-78	1996	San Pedro de Macoris, D.R.
Diaz, Eddy	0	2	6.99	20	6	0	0	57	71	55	44	34	41	.303	R	R	6-3	215	2-5-81	1998	Azua, D.R.
Fries, Scott	6	5	3.27	43	0	0	5	72	65	35	26	11	64	.236	L	L	6-1	190	12-3-77	2000	Dannebrog, Neb.
Gomer, Jeramy	0	0	2.45	10	1	0	0	22	22	8	6	12	22	.268	L	L	6-2	195	6-12-79	1998	Plant City, Fla.
Jongejan, Ferenc	2	5	1.99	48	0	0	16	59	64	21	13	31	52	.290	L	L	6-2	165	10-20-78	2001	Houten, Netherlands
Krawiec, Aaron	7	11	4.58	27	26	1	0	153	183	108	78	51	170	.296	L	L	6-6	210	3-17-79	2000	Hamburg, N.Y.
Lavery, Tim	2	1	2.43	30	1	0	2	85	74	25	23	13	55	.232	L	L	6-3	210	11-16-78	1999	Naperville, Ill.
Leicester, Jon	9	10	5.29	28	27	1	0	153	182	117	90	58	109	.296	R	R	6-2	210	2-7-79	2000	Sherman Oaks, Calif.
Martin, Nick	0	1	18.00	1	1	0	0	2	6	5	4	3	0	.500	L	L	6-3	195	3-5-80	2001	Houston, Texas
Miniel, Roberto	2	1	4.78	8	5	0	0	32	26	18	17	11	23	.222	R	R	6-4	160	5-12-80	1996	Santo Domingo, D.R.
2-team (25 Beloit)	6	6	4.25	33	21	1	0	136	130	75	64	38	140	.248							
Pinto, Renyel	4	8	5.22	20	20	1	0	88	94	64	51	44	69	.278	L	L	6-4	195	7-8-82	1999	Cupira, Venez.
Szuminski, Jason	4	3	6.44	14	4	0	0	36	56	27	26	17	22	.358	R	R	6-4	215	12-11-78	2000	San Antonio, Texas
Wellemeyer, Todd	13	9	4.16	27	27	1	0	147	165	85	68	74	167	.287	R	R	6-3	195	8-30-78	2000	Louisville, Ky.

BOISE — Short-Season Class A

NORTHWEST LEAGUE

BATTING	AVG	G	AB	R	H	2B	3B	HR	RBI	BB	SO	SB	CS	SLG	OBP	B	T	HT	WT	DOB	1st Yr	Resides
Anderson, Syketo	.376	70	290	70	109	13	6	6	41	12	34	24	7	.524	.404	L	R	5-11	180	2-12-79	1999	Prattville, Ala.
Arteaga, Joshua	.318	40	157	31	50	13	0	3	27	10	28	3	4	.459	.359	R	R	5-9	170	3-14-80	2001	Homestead, Fla.
Bacon, Dwaine	.193	57	150	22	29	5	0	0	3	17	51	8	5	.227	.288	B	R	5-11	190	4-11-79	2001	Fort Washington, Md.
Banks, Gary	.250	2	4	0	1	0	0	0	1	0	1	0	0	.250	.250	R	R	6-1	190	11-4-81	2000	Gilbertown, Ala.
Bouras, Brad	.349	62	238	44	83	25	0	6	60	27	39	1	1	.529	.419	R	R	6-3	220	8-10-79	2001	Lilburn, Ga.
Cash, Condor	.347	66	245	33	85	18	4	10	49	26	37	6	3	.576	.404	R	R	6-2	190	9-22-79	1999	Toccoa, Ga.
Ceminaro, Michael	.237	41	131	23	31	4	1	0	7	5	23	2	1	.282	.263	R	R	6-0	175	4-1-79	2001	Howell, N.J.
Hairr, Kevin	.284	28	109	29	31	7	0	4	13	8	24	5	4	.459	.350	L	R	5-11	185	2-15-79	2001	Fayetteville, N.C.
Hanna, Warren	.233	39	133	13	31	3	0	0	11	13	28	4	3	.256	.313	R	R	6-2	190	9-12-79	2001	Pensacola, Fla.
Johnson, J.J.	.317	70	287	55	91	15	7	7	61	20	50	18	4	.477	.362	R	R	6-2	195	11-3-81	2000	Appling, Ga.
Lawler, Daniel	.269	40	104	17	28	8	0	2	11	16	23	1	3	.404	.374	L	R	6-3	210	6-12-79	2001	Rochester, Minn.
McKnight, Lukas	.290	27	69	8	20	3	1	3	14	6	18	0	0	.493	.347	L	R	6-0	195	2-19-80	2000	Libertyville, Ill.
Mejia, Andy	.200	24	80	9	16	4	1	2	14	6	21	0	0	.350	.256	R	R	6-2	170	6-15-82	1999	Hato Mayor, D.R.
Navarro, Mandy	.229	30	96	10	22	5	0	2	11	10	17	1	1	.344	.303	B	R	6-0	175	4-24-81	2001	Miami, Fla.
Servais, Eric	.245	36	106	9	26	5	2	2	12	11	29	0	1	.387	.319	L	R	6-1	185	11-15-79	2001	La Crosse, Wis.

BATTING	AVG	G	AB	R	H	2B	3B	HR	RBI	BB	SO	SB	CS	SLG	OBP	B	T	HT	WT	DOB	1st Yr	Resides
Silver, Travis	.167	3	6	1	1	0	0	1	2	0	2	0	0	.667	.167	R	R	6-3	215	6-11-78	2001	Weaverville, N.C.
Slavik, Corey	.286	63	227	43	65	15	1	10	31	39	47	5	3	.493	.388	L	R	6-0	190	3-24-80	2001	Winston-Salem, N.C.
Thornton-Murray, Jandin	.239	56	205	24	49	14	5	4	26	12	45	4	1	.415	.283	B	R	6-0	190	6-24-81	1999	Ewa Beach, Hawaii

GAMES BY POSITION: C—Hanna 39, McKnight 19, Mejia 24, Silver 30. **1B**—Bouras 49, Lawler 36. **2B**—Ceminaro 39, Navarro 21, Servais 3, Thornton-Murray 18. **3B**—Navarro 1, Servais 16, Slavik 62, Thornton-Murray 3. **SS**—Arteaga 40, Ceminaro 1, Navarro 9, Thornton-Murray 30. **OF**—Anderson 31, Bacon 55, Banks 2, Cash 62, Hairr 27, Johnson 65.

PITCHING	W	L	ERA	G	GS	CG	SV	IP	H	R	ER	BB	SO	AVG	B	T	HT	WT	DOB	1st Yr	Resides
Benik, B.J.	6	2	3.82	20	0	0	2	33	34	30	14	9	29	.250	R	R	6-1	189	9-13-78	2001	Delray Beach, Fla.
Blanton, Jason	0	3	4.11	8	0	0	0	15	16	9	7	8	9	.266	R	R	6-3	220	9-10-79	2001	Titusville, Fla.
Carlsen, Jeff	1	0	1.50	16	0	0	3	36	23	7	6	5	41	.175	R	R	6-6	230	3-6-79	2001	Poulsbo, Wash.
Carter, Mark	2	1	4.62	16	0	0	1	25	30	15	13	17	31	.288	L	L	6-2	185	8-27-80	2001	Birmingham, Ala.
Earley, Andrew	1	1	3.56	14	3	0	0	30	32	16	12	20	15	.275	R	R	6-4	165	8-19-79	2001	Norcross, Ga.
Ellis, Steve	2	1	2.45	20	0	0	6	26	18	8	7	11	31	.200	R	R	6-2	205	2-4-79	2001	Elsah, Ill.
Ferreras, Yorkin	1	0	3.16	18	0	0	6	26	27	12	9	13	23	.278	L	L	6-1	180	1-28-81	1998	Santo Domingo, D.R.
Guzman, Angel	9	1	2.23	14	14	0	0	77	68	27	19	6	63	.232	R	R	6-2	180	12-14-81	1999	Caracas, Venez.
Mitre, Sergio	8	4	3.07	15	15	1	0	91	85	37	31	18	71	.242	R	R	6-3	220	2-16-81	2001	San Ysidro, Calif.
Orr, Ben	0	3	9.99	12	1	0	4	24	37	27	27	11	21	.339	L	L	6-1	190	2-24-78	2001	La Mirada, Calif.
Pignatiello, Carmen	7	3	3.00	16	12	0	1	78	70	37	26	22	83	.230	R	L	6-0	175	9-12-82	2001	Frankfort, Ill.
Reyes, Junior	1	0	3.33	13	0	0	1	24	22	10	9	15	17	.241	L	L	6-3	160	7-16-81	1997	Santo Domingo, D.R.
Sanchez, Felix	2	0	1.56	3	3	0	0	17	11	4	3	10	16	.180	L	L	6-3	165	8-3-82	1999	Puerto Plata, D.R.
Willis, Dontrelle	8	2	2.98	15	15	0	0	94	76	36	31	19	77	.216	L	L	6-4	200	1-12-82	2000	Alameda, Calif.
Wynegar, Adam	4	2	2.92	14	12	0	0	71	77	34	23	19	63	.275	L	L	6-1	185	9-11-80	2001	Centreville, Va.

MESA — Rookie

ARIZONA LEAGUE

BATTING	AVG	G	AB	R	H	2B	3B	HR	RBI	BB	SO	SB	CS	SLG	OBP	B	T	HT	WT	DOB	1st Yr	Resides
Banks, Gary	.170	53	200	30	34	3	1	1	14	20	80	11	3	.210	.280	R	R	6-1	190	11-4-81	2000	Gilbertown, Ala.
Cedeno, Ronny	.350	52	206	36	72	13	4	1	17	13	32	17	10	.466	.398	R	R	6-0	170	2-2-83	1999	Carabobo, Venez.
Chirinos, Robinson	.234	47	154	15	36	12	0	2	15	10	42	4	3	.351	.292	R	R	6-1	175	6-5-84	2000	Punto Fijo, Venez.
Coats, Buck	.260	33	123	11	32	3	3	1	18	4	19	3	4	.358	.292	L	R	6-3	195	6-6-82	2000	Valdosta, Ga.
Collins, Kevin	.280	39	132	25	37	6	6	3	16	22	55	2	2	.485	.385	L	L	6-2	205	5-6-81	2000	Land O' Lakes, Fla.
Devinney, Rick	.333	6	18	1	6	1	0	0	1	2	3	0	0	.389	.400	R	R	6-2	195	11-21-83	2001	Fullerton, Calif.
Esterlin, Ivan	.221	24	77	11	17	4	2	1	10	7	19	4	0	.364	.287	L	L	6-1	180	11-24-80	1997	San Pedro de Macoris, D.R.
Golden, Bryan	.140	22	57	11	8	1	0	2	4	11	15	0	3	.263	.290	R	R	6-0	200	7-24-80	2000	Dillsburg, Pa.
Harris, Josh	.250	2	8	3	2	0	0	0	2	0	2	1	0	.250	.250	R	R	5-9	170	11-27-78	2001	West Hills, Calif.
Hill, Bobby	.222	3	9	1	2	0	0	0	1	2	3	1	0	.222	.364	B	R	5-10	180	4-3-78	2000	San Jose, Calif.
Marmol, Carlos	.295	40	129	15	38	11	0	0	12	9	30	4	3	.380	.355	R	R	6-2	190	10-14-82	1999	Bonao, D.R.
Meadows, Tydus	.000	1	2	0	0	0	0	0	0	0	1	0	0	.000	.000	R	R	6-2	215	9-5-77	1998	Evans, Ga.
Mejia, Andy	.250	4	12	1	3	0	0	0	1	1	2	0	0	.250	.308	R	R	6-2	170	6-15-82	1999	Hato Mayor, D.R.
Miliano, Hector	.260	52	196	22	51	10	3	3	25	7	52	6	6	.388	.298	R	R	6-2	170	3-26-82	1998	Santo Domingo, D.R.
Navarro, Mandy	.318	8	22	3	7	0	2	0	1	1	4	1	0	.500	.348	B	R	6-0	175	4-24-81	2001	Miami, Fla.
Paulino, Robert	.327	47	153	20	50	10	4	2	28	9	26	4	1	.484	.376	R	R	5-11	160	3-29-82	1998	San Cristobal, D.R.
Queroz, Pedro	.287	49	164	24	47	9	1	2	21	13	18	8	3	.390	.346	R	R	5-11	180	9-26-81	1999	Puerto Cabello, Venez.
Salas, Francisco	.353	15	51	10	18	2	0	1	4	2	8	3	1	.451	.411	R	R	5-10	175	7-25-82	2001	San Diego, Calif.
Soto, Geovany	.260	41	150	18	39	16	0	1	20	15	33	1	0	.387	.339	R	R	6-1	195	1-20-83	2001	San Juan, P.R.
Vazquez, Rafael	.467	6	15	2	7	1	0	0	3	0	2	0	0	.533	.438	R	R	6-3	185	4-2-81	1999	Lara, Venez.
Williamson, Chad	.174	11	23	1	4	0	0	0	2	2	10	0	1	.174	.240	R	R	5-11	180	12-15-80	2001	Richmond, Va.

GAMES BY POSITION: C—Devinney 4, Golden 10, Marmol 11, Mejia 3, Queroz 20, Soto 18. **1B**—Coats 1, Collins 25, Esterlin 8, Golden 6, Mejia 1, Queroz 9, Soto 12. **2B**—Cedeno 1, Chirinos 14, Hill 2, Miliano 1, Paulino 34, Salas 11. **3B**—Chirinos 33, Esterlin 1, Navarro 1, Paulino 2, Queroz 21, Soto 2, Vazquez 4. **SS**—Banks 1, Cedeno 50, Chirinos 3, Harris 2, Navarro 1, Paulino 2, Salas 1, Vazquez 1. **OF**—Banks 52, Cedeno 1, Chirinos 1, Coats 26, Esterlin 9, Golden 1, Marmol 20, Miliano 51, Navarro 4, Salas 3, Soto 2, Williamson 4.

PITCHING	W	L	ERA	G	GS	CG	SV	IP	H	R	ER	BB	SO	AVG	B	T	HT	WT	DOB	1st Yr	Resides
Brown, Eric	0	1	1.04	11	0	0	4	17	15	4	2	4	14	.217	R	R	6-3	205	12-5-78	2001	Basking Ridge, N.J.
Burnau, Ryan	3	6	4.89	14	9	0	0	50	58	43	27	20	46	.285	R	R	6-4	190	12-10-81	2000	Markle, Ind.
Caminero, Concepcion	1	1	5.01	15	0	0	0	23	27	19	13	14	18	.300	R	R	6-2	200	11-4-81	1999	Sabana Grande, D.R.
Fisher, Marc	0	1	1.20	15	1	0	7	30	19	5	4	3	35	.182	R	R	6-4	195	5-17-79	2001	Conshohocken, Pa.
Foli, Daniel	2	5	4.82	11	10	0	0	47	40	29	25	15	40	.232	R	R	6-2	180	3-30-81	2001	Kodak, Tenn.
Ford, Ben	0	1	2.00	3	3	0	0	9	10	4	2	2	9	.270	R	R	6-7	225	8-15-75	1994	Tampa, Fla.
Fyhrie, Mike	0	0	0.00	2	2	0	0	2	1	0	0	0	4	.142	R	R	6-2	203	12-9-69	1991	Huntington Beach, Calif.
Glascock, John-Paul	0	1	9.61	16	1	0	0	20	22	23	21	24	15	.278	R	R	6-2	190	1-25-80	2000	Downey, Calif.
Lebron, Obispo	1	1	5.11	12	0	0	3	12	16	7	7	5	14	.271	R	R	6-1	190	4-24-82	1998	Las Matas de Farfan, D.R.
Martin, Nick	3	0	3.32	10	0	0	0	22	26	9	8	5	18	.309	L	L	6-3	195	3-5-80	2001	Houston, Texas
Nolasco, Ricky	1	0	1.50	5	4	0	0	18	11	3	3	5	23	.174	R	R	6-2	205	12-13-82	2001	Rialto, Calif.
O'Brien, Weston	3	3	3.27	13	3	0	0	41	49	18	15	8	34	.308	R	R	6-6	220	10-4-82	2001	Chino Hills, Calif.
Olivero, Pedro	2	0	6.60	17	0	0	3	30	38	24	22	10	27	.308	R	R	6-3	175	3-26-82	1999	Santo Domingo, D.R.
Reyes, Luis	4	1	6.23	15	0	0	0	26	38	21	18	15	12	.355	R	R	6-2	200	6-26-81	2001	Toa Baja, P.R.
Ryu, Jae-kuk	1	0	0.61	4	3	0	0	15	11	2	1	5	20	.196	R	R	6-3	175	5-30-83	2001	Seoul, Korea
Sanchez, Felix	2	5	4.01	12	9	0	0	61	57	38	27	22	55	.250	L	L	6-3	165	8-3-82	1999	Puerto Plata, D.R.
Sanchez, Jesus	1	0	3.86	3	0	0	0	5	7	3	2	3	5	.333	R	R	6-5	180	4-25-79	1996	Carabobo, Venez.
Sisco, Andy	1	0	5.24	10	7	0	0	34	36	28	20	10	31	.266	L	L	6-8	260	1-13-83	2001	Sammamish, Wash.
Valdez, Richard	1	4	8.23	12	4	0	0	35	50	39	32	15	25	.333	R	R	6-3	165	7-11-81	2001	Bani, D.R.

CINCINNATI REDS

BY CHRIS HAFT

The Cincinnati Reds began 2001 sensing they had enough talent to contend in the National League Central, while knowing they had little margin for error.

Their 66-96 record demonstrated just how much went wrong.

Injuries plagued the team from start to finish. Center fielder Ken Griffey was hampered by a spring training hamstring injury and appeared in just 111 games, hitting .286-22-65.

The Opening Day infield of first baseman Sean Casey, second baseman Pokey Reese, shortstop Barry Larkin and third baseman Aaron Boone missed 222 games.

The disappearance of Larkin, the team's acknowledged leader on and off the field, bore the most impact since he was the leadoff hitter. The 37-year-old hit more than .350 and maintained a league-leading on-base percentage as the Reds wrestled with the Chicago Cubs for first place through early May. After a groin injury and hernia sidelined Larkin, the Reds sagged.

That wasn't all. Poor pitching truly hastened the Reds' collapse. Injuries and ineffectiveness derailed the bulk of the season-opening rotation—Pete Harnisch, Osvaldo Fernandez and Rob Bell—forcing the Reds to start five rookies at one time or another, the most since 1945. The starters' overall ERA of 5.47 and average of 5⅓ innings per outing were the league's worst.

"We had to live through some badness," Reds manager Bob Boone said.

While matching the franchise's fifth-highest loss total, Cincinnati generated sources of hope. Outfielder Adam Dunn, Baseball America's No. 1 prospect in the Southern and International leagues, stormed through those two levels, hitting .334-32-84 combined, before breaking in with Cincinnati on July 20. He hit .262-19-43 in 66 games, prompting dreams of a Griffey-Dunn tandem that could rival any power combination in baseball.

Sean Casey | Adam Dunn

PLAYERS OF THE YEAR

MAJOR LEAGUE: Sean Casey, 1b

A steady producer as always in 2001, Casey had to do it without Barry Larkin and Ken Griffey in the lineup consistently. He led the team in average (.310), runs (69) and RBIs (89).

MINOR LEAGUE: Adam Dunn, of

Dunn is 6-foot-6, 235 pounds of pure monster hitting. He went .343-12-31 in Double-A, .329-20-53 in Triple-A and .262-19-43 in his first trip to the majors.

Rookie starters Jose Acevedo (5-7, 5.44), Lance Davis (8-4, 4.74) and Chris Reitsma (7-15, 5.29) also showed promise. Scott Sullivan, the righthanded setup specialist, became the first reliever to lead the majors in relief innings four years in a row. Danny Graves posted 32 saves, becoming the first Red since John Franco to exceed 25 in three consecutive seasons.

But the Reds' small-market payroll didn't allow them to find any quick fixes. Instead, they were expected to conduct open auditions for the starting rotation in the spring of 2002, featuring veterans such as Harnisch, Joey Hamilton and the resurgent Jose Rijo, assuming they agreed to incentive-laden contracts.

The lineup almost surely will change, perhaps drastically. "We're going to have to look at all different avenues," said general manager Jim Bowden, referring to the possibility of a significant trade.

Two-time Gold Glove winner Reese expressed his desire to be traded. Outfielder Dmitri Young, who's perpetually on the trading block, also could go. Even Casey, the hugely popular two-time all-star, could be moved.

The scene was brighter in the minors, where five of Cincinnati's six affiliates reached the postseason in 2001. Louisville captured the Triple-A International League championship, while Billings took the Rookie-level Pioneer League title.

Double-A Chattanooga's Austin Kearns, the organization's reigning No. 1 prospect, tore the ulnar collateral ligament in his right thumb and hit just .268-6-36. But Kearns finished strong and kept hitting proficiently in the Arizona Fall League, suggesting he had righted himself.

Outfielder Wily Mo Pena, named the No. 3 prospect in the Midwest League, hit .264-26-113 with 26 stolen bases for Class A Dayton while inviting comparisons to Sammy Sosa.

ORGANIZATION LEADERS

BATTING

*AVG	Gary Varner, Billings	.351
R	Ben Broussard, Chattanooga/Mudville	95
H	Raul Gonzalez, Louisville	161
TB	Ben Broussard, Chattanooga/Mudville	254
2B	Steve Smitherman, Dayton	45
3B	Elvin Andujar, Dayton/GCL Reds	9
HR	Adam Dunn, Louisville/Chattanooga	32
RBI	Wily Mo Pena, Dayton	113
BB	Mark Burnett, Mudville	84
SO	Wily Mo Pena, Dayton	177
SB	Ranier Olmedo, Mudville	38

PITCHING

W	Ryan Mottl, Dayton	15
L	Three tied at	10
#ERA	Ty Howington, Chattanooga/Mudville/Dayton	2.30
G	Michael Neu, Mudville	53
CG	Jared Fernandez, Louisville	4
SV	Frank Bludau, Dayton	21
	Michael Neu, Mudville	21
IP	Jared Fernandez, Louisville	196
BB	Scott Dunn, Chattanooga/Mudville	102
SO	Scott Dunn, Chattanooga/Mudville	160

*Minimum 250 At-Bats #Minimum 75 Innings

CINCINNATI REDS

Manager: Bob Boone

2001 Record: 66-96, .407 (5th, NL Central)

BATTING	AVG	G	AB	R	H	2B	3B	HR	RBI	BB	SO	SB	CS	SLG	OBP	B	T	HT	WT	DOB	1st Yr	Resides
Boone, Aaron	.294	103	381	54	112	26	2	14	62	29	71	6	3	.483	.351	R	R	6-2	200	3-9-73	1994	Villa Park, Calif.
Casey, Sean	.310	145	533	69	165	40	0	13	89	43	63	3	1	.458	.369	L	R	6-2	225	7-2-74	1995	Pittsburgh, Pa.
Castro, Juan	.223	96	242	25	54	10	0	3	13	13	50	0	0	.302	.261	R	R	5-10	187	6-20-72	1991	Glendale, Ariz.
Clark, Brady	.264	89	129	22	34	3	0	6	18	22	16	4	1	.426	.373	R	R	6-2	195	4-18-73	1996	Beaverton, Ore.
Cromer, D.T.	.281	50	57	7	16	3	0	5	12	3	19	0	0	.596	.302	L	L	6-2	220	3-19-71	1992	Columbia, S.C.
Dessens, Elmer	.193	35	57	3	11	1	0	0	2	3	12	0	0	.211	.233	R	R	6-0	187	1-13-72	1993	Hermosillo, Mexico
Dunn, Adam	.262	66	244	54	64	18	1	19	43	38	74	4	2	.578	.371	L	R	6-6	235	11-9-79	1998	Porter, Texas
Gonzalez, Raul	.214	11	14	0	3	0	0	0	1	3	0	0	0	.214	.267	R	R	5-9	190	12-27-73	1991	Villa Carolina, P.R.
Griffey, Ken	.286	111	364	57	104	20	2	22	65	44	72	2	0	.533	.365	L	L	6-3	205	11-21-69	1987	Orlando, Fla.
Guerrero, Wilton	.338	60	142	16	48	5	1	1	8	3	17	5	2	.408	.352	B	R	6-0	175	10-24-74	1992	Bani, D.R.
Jennings, Robin	.286	27	77	10	22	5	2	3	14	5	11	0	0	.519	.329	L	L	6-2	210	4-11-72	1992	Park City, Utah
2-team (1 Colorado)	.275	28	80	10	22	5	2	3	14	5	12	0	0	.500	.318							
Larkin, Barry	.256	45	156	29	40	12	0	2	17	27	25	3	2	.372	.373	R	R	6-0	185	4-28-64	1985	Orlando, Fla.
Larson, Brandon	.121	14	33	2	4	2	0	0	1	2	10	0	0	.182	.171	R	R	6-0	210	5-24-76	1997	San Antonio, Texas
LaRue, Jason	.236	121	364	39	86	21	2	12	43	27	106	3	3	.404	.303	R	R	5-11	200	3-19-74	1995	San Antonio, Texas
Miller, Corky	.184	17	49	5	9	2	0	3	7	4	16	1	0	.408	.263	R	R	6-1	215	3-18-76	1998	Calimesa, Calif.
Ochoa, Alex	.289	90	349	48	101	20	4	7	35	24	53	12	9	.430	.337	R	R	6-0	195	3-29-72	1991	Pembroke Pines, Fla.
Pickering, Calvin	.250	4	4	0	1	0	0	0	1	0	2	0	0	.250	.250	L	L	6-5	290	9-29-76	1995	Temple Terrace, Fla.
Reese, Pokey	.224	133	428	50	96	20	2	9	40	34	82	25	4	.343	.284	R	R	5-11	180	6-10-73	1991	Columbia, S.C.
Rivera, Ruben	.255	117	263	37	67	13	1	10	34	21	83	6	3	.426	.321	R	R	6-3	208	11-14-73	1992	La Chorrera, Panama
Sadler, Donnie	.202	39	84	9	17	3	0	1	3	9	20	3	3	.274	.280	R	R	5-6	175	6-17-75	1994	Valley Mills, Texas
Sanders, Deion	.173	32	75	6	13	2	0	1	4	4	10	3	4	.240	.235	L	L	6-1	195	8-9-67	1988	Alpharetta, Ga.
Selby, Bill	.228	36	92	7	21	7	1	2	12	5	13	0	0	.391	.273	L	R	5-9	190	6-11-70	1992	Walls, Miss.
Stinnett, Kelly	.257	63	187	27	48	11	0	9	25	17	61	2	2	.460	.333	R	R	5-11	195	2-4-70	1990	Lawton, Okla.
Tucker, Michael	.242	86	231	31	56	10	1	7	30	23	55	12	5	.385	.308	L	R	6-2	185	6-25-71	1992	Chase City, Va.
Walker, Todd	.295	66	261	41	77	17	0	5	32	26	42	0	5	.418	.361	L	R	6-0	181	5-25-73	1994	Bossier City, La.
2-team (85 Colorado)	.296	151	551	93	163	35	2	17	75	51	82	1	8	.459	.355							
Young, Dmitri	.302	142	540	68	163	28	3	21	69	37	77	8	5	.481	.350	B	R	6-2	235	10-11-73	1991	Erlanger, Ky.

PITCHING	W	L	ERA	G	GS	CG	SV	IP	H	R	ER	BB	SO	AVG	B	T	HT	WT	DOB	1st Yr	Resides
Acevedo, Jose	5	7	5.44	18	18	0	0	96	101	61	58	34	68	.272	R	R	6-0	185	12-18-77	1997	Santiago, D.R.
Atchley, Justin	0	0	6.10	15	0	0	0	10	12	7	7	5	8	.285	L	L	6-3	215	9-5-73	1995	Mount Vernon, Wash.
Bell, Rob	0	5	5.48	9	9	0	0	44	46	28	27	17	33	.275	R	R	6-5	225	1-17-77	1995	Marlboro, N.Y.
Brower, Jim	7	10	3.97	46	10	0	1	129	119	65	57	60	94	.246	R	R	6-2	205	12-29-72	1994	Minnetonka, Minn.
Davis, Lance	8	4	4.74	20	20	1	0	106	124	60	56	34	53	.293	R	L	6-0	160	9-1-76	1995	Polk City, Fla.
Dessens, Elmer	10	14	4.48	34	34	1	0	205	221	103	102	56	128	.279	R	R	6-0	187	1-13-72	1993	Hermosillo, Mexico
Fernandez, Jared	0	1	4.38	5	2	0	0	12	13	9	6	6	5	.265	R	R	6-2	223	2-2-72	1994	West Valley, Utah
Fernandez, Osvaldo	5	6	6.92	20	14	0	0	79	103	62	61	33	35	.315	R	R	6-2	190	11-4-68	1996	Miami, Fla.
Graves, Danny	6	5	4.15	66	0	0	32	80	83	41	37	18	49	.267	R	R	5-11	185	8-7-73	1995	Lake Mary, Fla.
Hamilton, Joey	1	2	6.23	4	4	0	0	17	23	12	12	6	10	.328	R	R	6-4	240	9-9-70	1991	McDonough, Ga.
Harnisch, Pete	1	3	6.37	7	7	0	0	35	48	29	25	17	17	.317	R	R	6-0	228	9-23-66	1987	Lake Mary, Fla.
MacRae, Scott	0	1	4.02	24	0	0	0	31	33	15	14	8	18	.266	R	R	6-3	205	8-13-74	1995	Marietta, Ga.
Mercado, Hector	3	2	4.08	56	0	0	0	53	55	27	24	30	59	.265	L	L	6-3	205	4-29-74	1992	Dorado, P.R.
Nichting, Chris	0	3	4.46	36	0	0	1	36	46	24	18	8	33	.306	R	R	6-1	205	5-13-66	1988	Cincinnati, Ohio
Piersoll, Chris	0	0	2.38	11	0	0	0	11	12	4	3	6	7	.266	R	R	6-4	195	9-25-77	1997	Carlsbad, Calif.
Reith, Brian	0	7	7.81	9	8	0	0	40	56	37	35	16	22	.333	R	R	6-5	190	2-28-78	1996	Fort Wayne, Ind.
Reitsma, Chris	7	15	5.29	36	29	0	0	182	209	121	107	49	96	.288	R	R	6-5	214	12-31-77	1996	Lutz, Fla.
Reyes, Dennys	2	6	4.92	35	6	0	0	53	51	35	29	35	52	.247	R	L	6-3	246	4-19-77	1994	Higuera de Zaragoza, Mexico
Riedling, John	1	1	2.41	29	0	0	1	34	22	9	9	14	23	.186	R	R	5-11	190	8-29-75	1994	Pompano Beach, Fla.
Rijo, Jose	0	0	2.12	13	0	0	0	17	19	6	4	9	12	.271	R	R	6-3	200	5-13-65	1981	Parkland, Fla.
Rodriguez, Frank	0	0	11.42	7	0	0	0	9	16	12	11	5	9	.400	R	R	6-0	210	12-11-72	1991	New York, N.Y.
Sullivan, Scott	7	1	3.31	79	0	0	0	103	94	44	38	36	82	.242	R	R	6-3	210	3-13-71	1993	Livingston, Ala.
Williamson, Scott	0	0	0.00	2	0	0	0	1	1	0	0	2	0	.333	R	R	6-0	185	2-17-76	1997	Friendswood, Texas
Winchester, Scott	0	2	4.50	12	1	0	0	24	29	19	12	4	9	.315	R	R	6-2	210	4-20-73	1995	Midland, Mich.
Wohlers, Mark	3	1	3.94	30	0	0	0	32	36	20	14	7	21	.285	R	R	6-4	207	1-23-70	1988	Alpharetta, Ga.

FIELDING

Catcher	PCT	G	PO	A	E	DP	PB
LaRue	.991	107	569	75	6	8	15
Miller	.991	17	104	12	1	2	2
Stinnett	.966	59	322	21	12	3	4

First Base	PCT	G	PO	A	E	DP
Casey	.994	136	1145	63	7	89
Castro	1.000	1	10	3	0	0
Cromer	.973	8	32	4	1	3
Jennings	1.000	8	51	6	0	9
LaRue	1.000	1	5	0	0	0
Selby	1.000	2	5	0	0	0
Young	1.000	38	219	19	0	16

Second Base	PCT	G	PO	A	E	DP
Castro	1.000	37	45	59	0	10
Guerrero	1.000	11	21	23	0	4

	PCT	G	PO	A	E	DP
Reese	.980	51	101	141	5	28
Sadler	.947	15	15	21	2	5
Selby	1.000	21	34	49	0	13
Walker	.987	65	138	168	4	33

Third Base	PCT	G	PO	A	E	DP
Boone	.936	103	72	207	19	17
Castro	.958	19	3	20	1	3
Guerrero	.889	4	3	5	1	0
Larson	.939	9	10	21	2	2
LaRue	.909	3	4	6	1	0
Selby	.882	8	7	8	2	2
Young	.890	36	16	57	9	9

Shortstop	PCT	G	PO	A	E	DP
Castro	.944	46	38	81	7	14
Guerrero	.927	16	20	31	4	9

	PCT	G	PO	A	E	DP
Larkin	.951	44	65	108	9	23
Reese	.972	78	117	224	10	34
Sadler	1.000	12	10	31	0	4
Walker	1.000	1	0	1	0	0

Outfield	PCT	G	PO	A	E	DP
Clark	.981	43	52	0	1	0
Dunn	.986	63	136	3	2	1
Gonzalez	1.000	2	4	0	0	0
Griffey	.985	90	195	1	3	0
Guerrero	1.000	6	6	0	0	0
Jennings	.893	15	23	2	3	1
LaRue	1.000	2	1	0	0	0

Pokey Reese: Split time between short and second

Ken Griffey.: Hit 22 homers in 364 at-bats

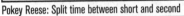

FARM SYSTEM

Director, Player Development: Bill Doran

Class	Farm Team	League	W	L	Pct.	Finish*	Manager	First Yr.
AAA	Louisville (Ky.) RiverBats	International	84	60	.583	+3rd (14)	Dave Miley	2000
AA	Chattanooga (Tenn.) Lookouts	Southern	72	67	.518	5th (10)	Phillip Wellman	1988
A#	Mudville (Stockton, Calif.) Nine	California	74	66	.529	4th (10)	Dave Oliver	2001
A	Dayton (Ohio) Dragons	Midwest	82	57	.590	4th (14)	Donnie Scott	2000
Rookie#	Billings (Mont.) Mustangs	Pioneer	46	29	.613	+3rd (8)	Rick Burleson	1974
Rookie	Sarasota (Fla.) Reds	Gulf Coast	36	22	.621	3rd (14)	Edgar Caceres	1999

*Finish in overall standings (No. of teams in league)   #Advanced level   +League champion

LOUISVILLE   Class AAA

INTERNATIONAL LEAGUE

BATTING	AVG	G	AB	R	H	2B	3B	HR	RBI	BB	SO	SB	CS	SLG	OBP	B	T	HT	WT	DOB	1st Yr	Resides
Anderson, Bryan	.333	6	21	3	7	0	0	0	0	1	6	1	0	.333	.364	R	R	6-2	170	7-10-78	2000	San Antonio, Texas
Beattie, Andy	.222	7	9	0	2	0	0	0	0	0	5	0	0	.222	.222	B	R	5-10	170	2-28-78	1998	Clearwater, Fla.
Boone, Aaron	.250	1	4	0	1	0	0	0	0	0	0	0	0	.250	.250	R	R	6-2	200	3-9-73	1994	Villa Park, Calif.
Buford, Damon	.370	13	54	14	20	5	1	3	14	10	17	0	1	.667	.462	R	R	5-10	180	6-12-70	1990	Dallas, Texas
2-team (39 Roch.)	.286	52	203	34	58	15	1	7	26	32	43	3	2	.473	.386							
Clark, Brady	.263	49	167	24	44	5	1	2	18	18	17	6	2	.341	.354	R	R	6-2	195	4-18-73	1996	Beaverton, Ore.
Cromer, D.T.	.285	62	242	35	69	12	2	11	49	15	48	4	2	.488	.330	L	L	6-2	220	3-19-71	1992	Columbia, S.C.
Davis, Tommy	.270	112	396	48	107	25	2	6	47	27	97	1	1	.389	.318	R	R	6-1	210	5-21-73	1994	Semmes, Ala.
Dunn, Adam	.329	55	210	44	69	13	0	20	53	38	51	5	1	.676	.441	L	R	6-6	235	11-9-79	1998	Porter, Texas
Gonzalez, Raul	.299	142	539	90	161	39	1	11	66	64	70	6	8	.436	.371	R	R	5-9	190	12-27-73	1991	Villa Carolina, P.R.
Guerrero, Wilton	.304	54	227	23	69	14	2	0	28	12	30	12	5	.383	.342	B	R	6-0	175	10-24-74	1992	Bani, D.R.
Hall, Noah	.000	1	2	0	0	0	0	0	0	0	0	0	0	.000	.000	R	R	5-11	200	6-9-77	1996	Aptos, Calif.
Jennings, Robin	.301	28	113	18	34	6	0	8	15	9	22	2	2	.566	.352	L	L	6-2	210	4-11-72	1992	Park City, Utah
Larson, Brandon	.255	115	424	61	108	22	2	14	55	24	123	5	6	.415	.312	R	R	6-0	210	5-24-76	1997	San Antonio, Texas
Malloy, Marty	.303	126	468	69	142	36	4	6	49	27	51	8	7	.436	.340	L	R	5-10	165	7-6-72	1992	Trenton, Fla.
Mateo, Ruben	.251	65	251	35	63	16	4	2	25	13	45	2	0	.371	.307	R	R	6-0	185	2-10-78	1995	San Cristobal, D.R.
Metcalfe, Mike	.150	6	20	1	3	0	0	0	0	4	5	2	1	.150	.292	B	R	5-10	175	1-2-73	1994	Orlando, Fla.
Miller, Corky	.347	44	144	30	50	11	0	7	28	10	19	2	0	.569	.431	R	R	6-1	215	3-18-76	1998	Calimesa, Calif.
Nevers, Tom	.105	5	19	0	2	1	0	0	3	1	5	0	0	.158	.143	R	R	6-1	190	9-13-71	1990	Edina, Minn.
Pickering, Calvin	.250	1	4	1	1	0	0	1	1	1	2	0	0	1.000	.400	L	L	6-5	290	9-29-76	1995	Temple Terrace, Fla.
2-team (131 Roch.)	.282	132	465	63	131	25	0	22	99	65	151	0	1	.477	.379							
Sanders, Deion	.459	19	74	12	34	4	5	1	9	2	4	6	3	.689	.494	L	L	6-1	195	8-9-67	1988	Alpharetta, Ga.
Selby, Bill	.258	88	330	47	85	19	1	14	56	25	47	1	0	.448	.310	L	R	5-9	190	6-11-70	1992	Walls, Miss.
Sexton, Chris	.279	105	409	59	114	25	3	2	47	40	57	5	5	.369	.338	R	R	5-11	180	8-3-71	1993	Cincinnati, Ohio
Sheff, Chris	.276	94	312	54	86	19	1	9	51	40	73	4	3	.429	.369	R	R	6-3	215	2-4-71	1992	Laguna Hills, Calif.
Spehr, Tim	.163	68	184	22	30	7	0	5	25	18	73	2	1	.283	.261	R	R	6-2	200	7-2-66	1988	Dallas, Texas

BATTING

BATTING	AVG	G	AB	R	H	2B	3B	HR	RBI	BB	SO	SB	CS	SLG	OBP	B	T	HT	WT	DOB	1st Yr	Resides
Tyler, Brad	.278	13	36	7	10	5	0	1	2	2	16	0	1	.500	.316	L	R	6-2	180	3-3-69	1990	Aurora, Ind.
Walbeck, Matt	.228	67	197	20	45	7	0	3	25	23	26	1	0	.310	.309	B	R	5-11	188	10-2-69	1987	Sacramento, Calif.

PITCHING

PITCHING	W	L	ERA	G	GS	CG	SV	IP	H	R	ER	BB	SO	AVG	B	T	HT	WT	DOB	1st Yr	Resides
Andrews, Clayton	2	2	4.81	8	8	0	0	43	57	28	23	13	19	.316	R	L	6-0	175	5-15-78	1996	Largo, Fla.
Atchley, Justin	1	0	0.64	15	0	0	2	14	14	1	1	3	15	.264	L	L	6-3	215	9-5-73	1995	Mount Vernon, Wash.
Bell, Rob	2	2	3.33	5	4	0	0	27	32	10	10	4	26	.288	R	R	6-5	225	1-17-77	1995	Marlboro, N.Y.
Brower, Jim	1	0	4.09	2	2	0	0	11	12	5	5	2	11	.272	R	R	6-2	205	12-29-72	1994	Minnetonka, Minn.
Darnell, Paul	2	0	2.57	21	0	0	0	21	15	6	6	11	32	.194	R	L	6-5	190	6-4-76	1999	Hubbard, Texas
Davis, Lance	7	2	3.05	13	13	1	0	80	81	31	27	15	47	.262	R	L	6-0	160	9-1-76	1995	Polk City, Fla.
2-team (8 Norfolk)	3	1	4.50	42	6	0	1	89	90	43	40	35	47	.293							
Estrella, Leo	1	1	4.88	34	5	0	1	63	67	36	34	27	37	.276	R	R	6-1	185	2-20-75	1994	Port St. Lucie, Fla.
Fernandez, Jared	10	9	4.13	33	28	4	0	196	218	105	90	54	118	.280	R	R	6-2	223	2-2-72	1994	West Valley, Utah
Fernandez, Ozvaldo	3	2	3.86	9	9	0	0	54	54	26	23	12	31	.263	R	R	6-2	190	11-4-68	1996	Miami, Fla.
Forster, Scott	1	0	1.74	9	0	0	0	10	7	3	2	9	9	.194	R	L	6-1	185	10-27-71	1994	Flourtown, Pa.
Glauber, Keith	3	3	5.65	23	0	0	0	37	45	30	23	10	24	.302	R	R	6-2	195	11-12-76	1994	Doylestown, Pa.
Gooch, Arnie	7	10	5.63	28	26	1	1	149	175	101	93	43	95	.293	R	R	6-2	195	11-12-76	1994	Doylestown, Pa.
Hamilton, Joey	1	0	5.40	1	1	0	0	5	4	3	3	1	1	.222	R	R	6-4	240	9-9-70	1991	McDonough, Ga.
Harnisch, Pete	0	1	54.00	1	1	0	0	3	3	3	2	0	0	.750	R	R	6-0	228	9-23-66	1987	Lake Mary, Fla.
Hill, Ken	2	1	4.60	6	6	0	0	31	33	19	16	12	16	.270	R	R	6-2	215	12-14-65	1985	Southlake, Texas
Luebbers, Larry	7	6	3.57	21	18	2	0	121	129	54	48	24	60	.282	R	R	6-6	190	10-11-69	1990	Florence, Ky.
MacRae, Scott	2	2	1.23	11	0	0	2	22	14	5	3	6	15	.186	R	R	6-3	205	8-13-74	1995	Marietta, Ga.
Maurer, Dave	0	1	4.15	18	0	0	1	22	18	11	10	7	23	.225	R	L	6-2	205	2-23-75	1997	Burnsville, Minn.
McNichol, Brian	4	1	1.59	26	0	0	0	28	23	8	5	5	22	.223	L	L	6-5	220	5-20-74	1995	Woodbridge, Va.
Mercado, Hector	1	0	1.35	12	0	0	1	13	12	2	2	6	13	.250	L	L	6-3	205	4-29-74	1992	Dorado, P.R.
Nichting, Chris	2	1	2.97	27	0	0	17	33	24	11	11	10	45	.200	R	R	6-1	205	5-13-66	1988	Cincinnati, Ohio
Peters, Chris	3	1	6.89	8	6	0	0	31	46	26	24	18	16	.343	L	L	6-1	170	1-28-72	1993	Bethel Park, Pa.
Reith, Brian	0	0	3.60	1	1	0	0	5	7	2	2	1	6	.368	R	R	6-5	190	2-28-78	1996	Fort Wayne, Ind.
Reyes, Dennys	4	2	3.67	7	6	0	0	34	34	15	14	16	34	.259	R	L	6-3	246	4-19-77	1994	Higuera de Zaragoza, Mexico
Riedling, John	0	0	0.00	1	0	0	1	0	0	0	0	1	1	.000	R	R	5-11	190	8-29-75	1994	Pompano Beach, Fla.
Rijo, Jose	0	0	5.14	6	4	0	0	14	16	9	8	5	7	.301	R	R	6-3	200	5-13-65	1981	Parkland, Fla.
Rodriguez, Frank	8	6	2.46	43	0	0	5	80	67	25	22	24	56	.227	R	R	6-0	210	12-11-72	1991	New York, N.Y.
Ruffin, Johnny	0	0	0.00	9	0	0	5	8	6	1	0	3	11	.206	R	R	6-3	170	7-29-71	1988	Tampa, Fla.
Service, Scott	2	0	4.74	20	0	0	5	25	22	13	13	10	27	.241	R	R	6-6	240	2-26-67	1986	Cincinnati, Ohio
Skrmetta, Matt	2	4	2.48	46	0	0	6	54	41	17	15	20	58	.210	R	R	6-3	220	11-6-72	1993	Satellite Beach, Fla.
Winchester, Scott	6	3	3.54	23	6	0	0	53	50	26	21	10	37	.245	R	R	6-2	210	4-20-73	1995	Midland, Mich.

FIELDING

Catcher	PCT	G	PO	A	E	DP	PB
T. Davis	1.000	12	55	8	0	0	0
Miller	.994	41	294	35	2	6	8
Spehr	.982	48	303	33	6	3	8
Walbeck	1.000	56	300	34	0	5	8

First Base	PCT	G	PO	A	E	DP
Cromer	.989	42	398	34	5	33
T. Davis	.997	73	704	51	2	63
Larson	.923	3	11	1	1	0
Pickering	1.000	1	4	0	0	1
Selby	.984	24	171	11	3	17
Sheff	1.000	2	18	1	0	3
Spehr	1.000	6	40	4	0	5
Tyler	.968	4	29	1	1	4

Second Base	PCT	G	PO	A	E	DP
Anderson	1.000	5	10	13	0	5
Beattie	1.000	1	2	1	0	0

	PCT	G	PO	A	E	DP
Guerrero	.963	35	71	85	6	21
Malloy	.961	69	128	169	12	41
Metcalfe	1.000	6	9	13	0	2
Selby	.977	36	60	113	4	24
Sexton	1.000	4	10	9	0	2

Third Base	PCT	G	PO	A	E	DP
Boone	1.000	1	1	2	0	1
T. Davis	.896	17	11	32	5	3
Larson	.948	109	67	279	19	30
Malloy	1.000	2	1	1	0	0
Selby	.903	18	8	20	3	0
Sexton	.944	7	3	14	1	0
Tyler	.000	1	0	0	0	0

Shortstop	PCT	G	PO	A	E	DP
Beattie	1.000	2	3	0	0	0
Guerrero	.956	12	17	26	2	5
Larson	1.000	6	7	7	0	2

	PCT	G	PO	A	E	DP
Malloy	.938	38	50	100	10	22
Nevers	.850	5	5	12	3	2
Sexton	.970	93	132	284	13	50

Outfield	PCT	G	PO	A	E	DP
Anderson	1.000	1	2	0	0	0
Buford	.958	13	22	1	1	0
Clark	.981	46	105	1	2	0
T. Davis	1.000	6	7	0	0	0
Dunn	.954	54	93	10	5	3
Gonzalez	.973	137	313	7	9	2
Guerrero	1.000	4	10	0	0	0
Hall	1.000	1	1	0	0	0
Jennings	.952	27	36	4	2	2
Mateo	.954	62	100	3	5	2
Sanders	.973	19	36	0	1	0
Selby	1.000	8	11	0	0	0
Sheff	.980	63	91	6	2	1
Tyler	.944	7	15	2	1	1

CHATTANOOGA

Class AA

SOUTHERN LEAGUE

BATTING	AVG	G	AB	R	H	2B	3B	HR	RBI	BB	SO	SB	CS	SLG	OBP	B	T	HT	WT	DOB	1st Yr	Resides
Alvarez, Gabe	.253	99	336	59	85	23	1	16	50	61	82	4	4	.470	.377	R	R	6-1	205	3-6-74	1995	El Monte, Calif.
Beattie, Andy	.266	51	169	32	45	12	0	3	24	21	30	4	2	.391	.349	B	R	5-10	170	2-28-78	1998	Clearwater, Fla.
Broussard, Ben	.320	100	353	81	113	27	0	23	69	61	69	10	3	.592	.428	L	L	6-2	220	9-24-76	1999	Southlake, Texas
Dawkins, Travis	.226	104	394	59	89	16	3	8	40	32	88	14	4	.343	.285	R	R	6-1	180	5-12-79	1997	Chappells, S.C.
Diaz, Alejandro	.299	25	87	13	26	2	0	3	10	2	12	0	1	.425	.319	R	R	5-9	190	7-9-78	1999	Constanza, D.R.
Dunn, Adam	.343	39	140	30	48	9	0	12	31	24	31	6	3	.664	.449	L	R	6-6	235	11-9-79	1998	Porter, Texas
Gibralter, Steve	.275	82	306	51	84	21	1	16	53	25	66	10	2	.507	.337	R	R	6-0	195	10-9-72	1990	Duncanville, Texas
Gomez, Heber	.189	10	37	2	7	2	0	0	1	1	7	1	0	.243	.250	R	R	5-10	190	11-3-77	2001	Veracruz, Mexico
Kearns, Austin	.268	59	205	30	55	11	2	6	36	26	43	7	5	.429	.364	R	R	6-3	220	5-20-80	1998	Lexington, Ky.
Melian, Jackson	.237	120	426	64	101	20	2	16	52	36	95	10	7	.401	.311	R	R	6-2	190	1-7-80	1996	Barcelona, Venez.
Metcalfe, Mike	.289	123	474	68	137	25	4	3	47	38	59	32	10	.378	.344	B	R	5-10	175	1-2-73	1994	Orlando, Fla.
Miller, Corky	.276	59	170	25	47	12	0	9	42	25	32	1	2	.506	.425	R	R	6-1	215	3-18-76	1998	Calimesa, Calif.
Morris, Bobby	.281	85	224	35	63	18	1	9	44	41	41	4	4	.491	.393	L	R	6-0	175	11-22-72	1993	Munster, Ind.
Nevers, Tom	.251	120	402	63	101	33	1	17	67	43	101	4	5	.465	.327	R	R	6-1	190	9-13-71	1990	Edina, Minn.
Rose, Pete	.264	35	91	8	24	6	0	1	14	7	16	0	0	.363	.313	L	R	6-1	225	11-16-69	1989	Cincinnati, Ohio
Sollmann, Scott	.314	47	121	28	38	3	1	0	8	19	17	12	6	.355	.407	L	L	5-10	167	5-2-75	1996	Cincinnati, Ohio
Thompson, Travis	.170	31	47	5	8	4	0	1	1	2	13	0	1	.319	.204	R	R	6-5	215	7-3-77	1999	Matthews, N.C.
Thurston, Jerry	.160	28	81	11	13	2	0	2	3	4	29	0	0	.259	.209	R	R	6-4	200	4-17-72	1990	Longwood, Fla.
Tyler, Brad	.255	14	47	7	12	4	1	1	11	5	13	1	1	.447	.327	L	R	6-2	180	3-3-69	1990	Aurora, Ind.
Valencia, Vic	.230	76	230	24	53	8	2	6	33	27	59	2	0	.361	.316	R	R	6-2	185	5-13-77	1994	Maracay, Venez.
Van Rossum, Chris	.222	18	27	5	6	2	0	0	3	1	12	0	0	.296	.250	L	L	6-1	175	2-15-74	1996	Turlock, Calif.
Welsh, Eric	.203	25	69	5	14	2	0	3	11	3	24	0	2	.362	.230	L	L	6-3	200	9-17-76	1997	Tinley Park, Ill.

PITCHING	W	L	ERA	G	GS	CG	SV	IP	H	R	ER	BB	SO	AVG	B	T	HT	WT	DOB	1st Yr	Resides
Acevedo, Jose	4	4	3.69	16	11	0	0	78	68	34	32	25	82	.238	R	R	6-0	185	12-18-77	1997	Santiago, D.R.
Andrews, Clayton	1	3	6.00	6	6	0	0	36	41	27	24	16	19	.286	R	L	6-0	175	5-15-78	1996	Largo, Fla.
Aramboles, Ricardo	0	2	8.00	2	1	0	0	9	12	8	8	0	5	.324	R	R	6-2	170	12-4-81	1996	Santo Domingo, D.R.
Booker, Chris	2	0	3.94	16	0	0	1	16	13	7	7	11	25	.286	R	R	6-3	230	12-9-76	1995	Monroeville, Ala.
2-team (45 West Tenn)	4	6	4.24	61	0	0	2	68	52	36	32	47	101	.208							
Darnell, Paul	3	1	2.58	21	4	0	0	38	39	13	11	13	43	.261	R	L	6-5	190	6-4-76	1999	Hubbard, Texas
De la Rosa, Maximo	2	6	5.21	38	0	0	2	47	57	31	27	13	52	.295	R	R	5-11	170	7-12-71	1998	Villa Mella, D.R.
Dunn, Scott	7	2	4.12	17	17	0	0	98	96	51	45	71	87	.261	R	R	6-3	180	5-23-78	1999	San Antonio, Texas
Estrella, Leo	0	1	3.68	3	3	0	0	15	13	6	6	4	14	.240	R	R	6-1	185	2-20-75	1994	Port St. Lucie, Fla.
Gil, David	6	1	3.10	11	10	0	1	61	65	23	21	30	55	.277	R	R	6-4	215	10-1-78	2000	Miami, Fla.
Glauber, Keith	2	1	4.26	22	4	0	0	44	53	21	21	8	30	.304	R	R	6-2	190	1-18-72	1994	Morganville, N.J.
Grace, Mike	3	2	5.67	21	1	0	0	33	44	26	21	15	27	.314	R	R	6-4	210	6-20-70	1991	Clearwater, Fla.
Howington, Ty	1	3	3.27	7	7	0	0	41	36	18	15	24	38	.240	B	L	6-4	225	11-4-80	1999	Vancouver, Wash.
Koronka, John	1	5	5.73	9	9	0	0	55	62	37	35	28	44	.285	L	L	6-1	180	6-3-80	1998	Orlando, Fla.
Lowe, Benny	3	2	4.19	26	1	0	0	39	29	21	18	24	35	.210	L	L	5-10	185	6-13-74	1994	Key West, Fla.
Luebbers, Larry	2	3	2.98	8	8	1	0	54	48	23	18	12	48	.233	R	R	6-6	190	10-11-69	1990	Florence, Ky.
MacRae, Scott	5	2	3.68	19	8	1	0	59	60	29	24	14	42	.260	R	R	6-3	205	8-13-74	1995	Marietta, Ga.
Manias, Jim	1	1	3.12	24	0	0	0	26	13	9	9	6	23	.151	L	L	6-4	190	10-21-74	1996	Florham Park, N.J.
Martinez, Javier	0	0	135.00	1	0	0	0	0	2	6	5	3	0	.666	R	R	6-2	235	2-5-77	1994	Toa Alta, P.R.
McNichol, Brian	4	0	1.04	21	1	0	0	26	19	4	3	9	32	.206	L	L	6-5	220	5-20-74	1995	Woodbridge, Va.
Piersoll, Chris	1	4	3.38	50	0	0	19	56	48	24	21	30	78	.225	R	R	6-4	195	9-25-77	1997	Carlsbad, Calif.
Reith, Brian	6	4	3.97	18	18	1	0	104	103	63	46	42	89	.258	R	R	6-5	190	2-28-78	1996	Fort Wayne, Ind.
Rijo, Jose	0	0	0.00	1	1	0	0	3	1	0	0	1	3	.100	R	R	6-3	200	5-13-65	1981	Parkland, Fla.
Smith, Cam	1	5	5.03	29	1	0	0	54	49	32	30	36	49	.293	R	R	6-3	190	9-20-73	1993	Selkirk, N.Y.
Taglienti, Jeff	5	5	4.72	51	0	0	7	55	64	30	29	14	45	.296	R	R	6-0	210	11-13-75	1997	Walpole, Mass.
Thompson, Travis	12	10	3.88	28	28	3	0	167	170	82	72	46	118	.264	R	R	6-5	215	7-3-77	1999	Matthews, N.C.

FIELDING

Catcher	PCT	G	PO	A	E	DP	PB
Miller	.985	54	432	39	7	8	1
Thurston	.988	21	163	7	2	2	2
Valencia	.984	66	522	43	9	2	3

First Base	PCT	G	PO	A	E	DP
Alvarez	.984	17	121	5	2	12
Broussard	.990	93	737	55	8	58
Morris	.986	9	65	4	1	4
Nevers	1.000	2	26	1	0	3
Rose	1.000	2	23	0	0	0
Thurston	1.000	1	6	0	0	2
Valencia	1.000	3	4	0	0	0
Welsh	.980	20	142	8	3	16

Second Base	PCT	G	PO	A	E	DP
Beattie	.978	29	53	79	3	8

	PCT	G	PO	A	E	DP
Gomez	.909	2	6	4	1	1
Metcalfe	.982	84	149	223	7	45
Morris	.978	21	38	50	2	15
Nevers	.967	7	8	21	1	4

Third Base	PCT	G	PO	A	E	DP
Alvarez	.838	67	31	109	27	6
Beattie	.944	6	10	7	1	1
Gomez	1.000	5	3	7	0	0
Nevers	.946	62	33	89	7	11
Rose	.818	4	1	8	2	1
Valencia	.000	1	0	0	0	0

Shortstop	PCT	G	PO	A	E	DP
Beattie	.968	6	8	22	1	4
Dawkins	.964	98	166	261	16	47
Gomez	.929	2	5	8	1	2

	PCT	G	PO	A	E	DP
Nevers	.952	36	56	104	8	22

Outfield	PCT	G	PO	A	E	DP
Alvarez	.958	16	22	1	1	0
Beattie	1.000	2	1	0	0	0
Broussard	1.000	3	3	0	0	0
Diaz	.964	25	51	3	2	0
A. Dunn	.961	39	65	8	3	1
Gibralter	.970	81	155	6	5	1
Kearns	.979	55	92	2	2	0
Melian	.948	114	184	15	11	1
Metcalfe	.962	32	75	0	3	0
Morris	.960	20	22	2	1	0
Sollmann	1.000	32	70	1	0	0
Tyler	.968	11	29	1	1	1
Van Rossum	1.000	6	11	1	0	0

MUDVILLE — Class A

CALIFORNIA LEAGUE

BATTING	AVG	G	AB	R	H	2B	3B	HR	RBI	BB	SO	SB	CS	SLG	OBP	B	T	HT	WT	DOB	1st Yr	Resides
Amado, Jose	.241	52	174	17	42	7	0	2	17	19	15	2	0	.316	.328	R	R	6-1	180	2-7-75	1994	San Cristobal, Venez.
Beattie, Andy	.313	60	227	37	71	17	0	7	31	28	50	11	2	.480	.394	B	R	5-10	170	2-28-78	1998	Clearwater, Fla.
Broussard, Ben	.245	30	102	14	25	5	0	5	21	16	31	0	0	.441	.360	L	L	6-2	220	9-24-76	1999	Southlake, Texas
Burnett, Mark	.224	123	434	67	97	16	5	5	43	84	88	11	4	.318	.346	L	R	5-11	175	2-16-77	1999	Benton, Ark.
Burress, Andy	.270	33	122	13	33	6	1	3	16	10	40	8	2	.410	.324	R	R	6-0	200	7-18-77	1995	McRae, Ga.
Calitri, Mike	.176	22	74	8	13	2	0	2	10	11	28	0	0	.284	.291	R	R	6-3	215	3-14-78	2000	Canton, Mass.
Campana, Wandel	.228	43	167	14	38	9	0	1	15	7	34	2	2	.299	.271	R	R	6-2	215	5-18-78	2000	Miami, Fla.
Huguet, J.C.	.400	3	5	2	2	0	0	1	1	0	2	0	0	1.000	.400	R	R	6-0	187	10-24-78	1996	Caracas, Venez.
Hurtado, Omar	.104	17	48	8	5	2	0	0	1	10	16	1	3	.146	.254	R	R	6-0	172	4-10-74	1996	Santa Clara, Calif.
Kiil, Skip	.300	5	20	1	6	0	0	1	3	0	4	1	1	.450	.364	R	R	5-10	155	5-11-77	1999	Bradenton, Fla.
Kison, Robbie	.250	67	204	31	51	11	0	2	23	24	38	4	4	.333	.330	R	R	6-1	200	11-26-76	1999	Oklahoma City, Okla.
Lundquist, Ryan	.273	122	436	66	119	31	0	14	72	54	117	9	2	.440	.357	R	R	5-11	155	5-31-81	1999	Maracay, Venez.
Olmedo, Ranier	.244	129	536	57	131	23	4	0	28	24	121	38	17	.302	.285	R	R	6-0	180	10-12-78	1997	Sinaloa, Mexico
Rios, Fernando	.277	114	426	57	118	16	4	4	49	34	45	6	5	.362	.334	R	R	6-0	180	10-12-78	1997	Tlacotalpan, Mexico
Rodriguez, Serafin	.240	58	200	22	48	9	1	2	25	8	27	0	0	.325	.274	R	R	5-11	205	4-8-79	2001	Kahuku, Hawaii
Sardinha, Dane	.235	109	422	45	99	24	2	9	55	12	97	0	1	.365	.259	L	R	6-3	225	5-27-79	1997	St. Paul, Minn.
Senjem, Guye	.355	42	141	25	50	9	1	10	32	22	31	0	1	.645	.442	L	L	5-11	200	12-27-75	1998	Germantown, Tenn.
Sledd, Aaron	.000	1	3	0	0	0	0	0	0	0	0	0	0	.000	.000	L	L	5-10	167	5-2-75	1996	Cincinnati, Ohio
Sollmann, Scott	.333	4	18	2	6	2	1	0	1	0	5	1	0	.556	.333	R	R	6-2	230	9-30-78	1999	Mesquite, Texas
Spoerl, Josh	.257	116	420	56	108	23	6	12	60	47	124	1	2	.426	.340	R	R	6-4	200	4-17-72	1990	Longwood, Fla.
Thurston, Jerrey	.190	7	21	2	4	0	0	0	3	7	0	1	0	.190	.292							
2-team (14 Lake Els.)	.167	21	66	5	11	0	0	0	2	5	27	0	0	.167	.236							
Van Rossum, Chris	.167	47	156	14	26	2	0	0	5	5	37	5	3	.199	.198	L	L	6-1	175	2-15-74	1996	Turlock, Calif.
Welsh, Eric	.258	105	399	65	103	24	0	20	64	38	107	0	0	.469	.333	L	L	6-3	200	9-17-76	1997	Tinley Park, Ill.

GAMES BY POSITION: C—Huguet 2, Sardinha 109, Senjem 26, Thurston 7. **1B**—Amado 1, Broussard 30, Calitri 2, Spoerl 12, Welsh 100. **2B**—Beattie 11, Burnett 67, Campana 44, Kison 21. **3B**—Amado 29, Beattie 5, Calitri 21, Kison 34, Lundquist 62. **SS**—Beattie 6, Kison 13, Olmedo 129. **OF**—Amado 17, Beattie 39, Burnett 52, Burress 32, Hurtado 17, Kiil 5, Lundquist 61, Rios 113. Rodriguez 55, Sollmann 4, Van Rossum 47, Welsh 2.

PITCHING	W	L	ERA	G	GS	CG	SV	IP	H	R	ER	BB	SO	AVG	B	T	HT	WT	DOB	1st Yr	Resides
Ammons, Cary	1	4	2.94	14	9	0	0	64	53	28	21	31	81	.219	L	L	5-11	165	10-14-76	1998	Durant, Okla.
Birdsong, Tim	3	4	5.02	23	0	0	5	29	39	21	16	15	31	.314	R	R	6-5	210	5-4-77	1998	Bokchito, Okla.
Bradley, Dave	1	1	6.32	15	1	0	1	31	36	25	22	24	31	.297	R	R	6-3	210	8-28-77	1999	Walker, Wyo.
Carter, Justin	3	5	4.35	10	10	1	0	50	42	32	24	38	43	.233	R	L	6-2	185	3-8-77	1998	Birmingham, Ala.
Cordova, Jorge	9	8	3.72	30	25	0	0	155	157	81	64	67	132	.267	R	R	6-0	190	1-13-78	1998	La Asuncion, Venez.
Culp, Brandon	1	0	4.07	9	3	0	0	24	24	15	11	14	25	.260	R	R	6-6	240	8-27-77	2000	Jemison, Ala.

PITCHING	W	L	ERA	G	GS	CG	SV	IP	H	R	ER	BB	SO	AVG	B	T	HT	WT	DOB	1st Yr	Resides
Darnell, Paul	2	1	3.38	5	5	0	0	32	27	13	12	8	33	.223	R	L	6-5	190	6-4-76	1999	Hubbard, Texas
DeHart, Casey	4	3	2.23	49	0	0	4	69	54	20	17	36	64	.219	L	L	6-1	180	11-1-77	1998	Burleson, Texas
Dent, Doug	6	3	3.92	24	3	0	2	64	69	34	28	24	63	.276	R	R	6-8	210	3-23-77	1998	Bellevue, Wash.
Dunn, Scott	5	3	2.11	10	10	1	0	60	45	17	14	31	73	.208	R	R	6-3	180	5-23-78	1999	San Antonio, Texas
Gray, Brett	10	4	2.42	29	18	0	0	141	133	48	38	37	110	.246	R	R	6-0	185	8-19-76	1998	Wyoming, Ontario
Howington, Ty	3	2	2.43	7	7	0	0	37	33	18	10	20	44	.234	B	L	6-4	225	11-4-80	1999	Vancouver, Wash.
Kison, Robbie	0	0	0.00	2	0	0	0	2	1	0	0	3	1	1.000	R	R	5-10	155	5-11-77	1999	Bradenton, Fla.
Koronka, John	5	2	4.94	12	12	0	0	71	78	44	39	39	66	.280	L	L	6-1	180	6-3-80	1998	Orlando, Fla.
Lara, Nelson	0	0	16.88	2	0	0	0	3	4	5	5	7	0	.333	R	R	6-4	185	7-15-78	1995	Santo Domingo, D.R.
Lowe, Benny	1	1	4.05	4	0	0	0	7	4	3	3	7		.181	L	L	5-10	185	6-13-74	1994	Key West, Fla.
Manias, Jim	3	2	2.78	24	0	0	2	45	38	16	14	12	45	.222	L	L	6-4	190	10-21-74	1996	Florham Park, N.J.
Martinez, Javier	3	0	2.16	16	0	0	0	17	14	4	4	6	21	.229	R	R	6-2	235	2-5-77	1994	Toa Alta, P.R.
Neu, Michael	3	2	2.37	53	0	0	21	66	50	21	17	30	102	.209	B	R	5-10	190	3-9-78	1999	Napa, Calif.
Pugmire, Rob	0	2	7.79	4	4	0	0	17	25	16	15	10	19	.337	R	R	6-3	205	9-5-78	1997	Snohomish, Wash.
Robinson, Dustin	2	4	3.98	30	0	0	3	54	53	28	24	19	43	.254	R	R	6-6	225	9-13-75	1997	Stroud, Okla.
Salmon, Brad	5	8	4.06	33	18	1	0	135	132	75	61	51	110	.252	R	R	6-4	210	1-3-80	1999	Pensacola, Fla.
Shaffar, Ben	3	2	3.52	6	6	0	0	31	29	15	12	12	24	.254	B	R	6-3	195	9-28-77	1998	Leitchfield, Ky.
Therneau, Dave	1	5	6.07	10	9	0	0	46	64	39	31	11	41	.320	R	R	6-5	195	12-23-75	1998	Denton, Texas

DAYTON — Class A

MIDWEST LEAGUE

BATTING	AVG	G	AB	R	H	2B	3B	HR	RBI	BB	SO	SB	CS	SLG	OBP	B	T	HT	WT	DOB	1st Yr	Resides
Anderson, Bryan	.226	80	270	33	61	14	4	1	26	13	66	9	2	.319	.268	R	R	6-2	170	7-10-78	2000	San Antonio, Texas
Andujar, Elvin	.188	5	16	2	3	0	0	0	1	1	6	1	0	.188	.235	R	R	6-3	195	1-19-81	1999	San Cristobal, D.R.
Calitri, Mike	.249	97	317	57	79	18	0	16	44	57	98	1	3	.457	.367	R	R	6-3	215	3-14-78	2000	Canton, Mass.
Campana, Wandel	.264	79	295	46	78	19	3	0	23	10	41	8	5	.349	.296	R	R	6-0	175	6-13-80	1998	Santo Domingo, D.R.
Encarnacion, Edwin	.162	9	37	2	6	2	0	1	6	1	5	0	1	.297	.184	R	R	6-1	175	1-7-83	2000	Caguas, P.R.
Espinosa, David	.262	122	493	88	129	29	8	7	37	55	120	15	10	.396	.340	B	R	6-1	200	12-16-81	2001	Miami, Fla.
Garabito, Vianney	.087	10	23	4	2	1	0	1	2	1	4	0	0	.261	.160	R	R	6-2	195	12-12-79	1996	San Cristobal, D.R.
Hargreaves, Brad	.222	7	18	4	4	1	0	0	2	3	4	0	0	.278	.318	R	R	6-0	175	10-30-77	1997	Cincinnati, Ohio
Hawes, B.J.	.188	25	69	8	13	2	2	0	6	4	14	1	2	.275	.253	R	R	6-0	170	6-2-79	1999	Appling, Ga.
Huguet, J.C.	.224	38	107	10	24	2	0	1	5	23	31	2	3	.271	.368	R	R	6-2	215	5-18-78	2000	Miami, Fla.
Hurtado, Omar	.234	63	205	23	48	7	2	5	20	19	59	3	3	.361	.304	R	R	6-0	187	10-24-78	1996	Caracas, Venez.
Jones, Brian	.230	63	191	17	44	10	0	5	19	11	47	4	1	.361	.273	L	R	6-4	220	7-19-77	1999	Myrtle Beach, S.C.
Patchett, Gary	.243	85	259	42	63	8	1	0	17	27	52	6	3	.282	.350	R	R	6-2	180	9-25-78	2000	Gardena, Calif.
Pena, Wily Mo	.264	135	511	85	135	25	5	26	113	33	177	26	10	.485	.327	R	R	6-3	215	1-23-82	1998	Laguna Salada, D.R.
Peters, Samone	.206	120	452	61	93	20	0	28	78	29	158	2	2	.436	.265	R	R	6-7	235	7-30-78	1998	Santa Rosa, Calif.
Peterson, Brian	.248	35	113	14	28	5	0	2	18	14	33	0	0	.345	.331	R	R	6-2	205	10-22-78	1999	Greencastle, Pa.
Ruiz, Randy	.268	123	466	82	125	34	3	20	92	48	116	21	9	.483	.352	R	R	6-3	225	10-19-77	1999	Bronx, N.Y.
Sledd, Aaron	.243	13	37	6	9	3	0	0	3	7	14	0	0	.324	.356	L	L	5-11	180	12-27-75	1998	Germantown, Tenn.
Smitherman, Steve	.280	134	497	89	139	45	2	20	73	43	113	16	7	.499	.348	R	R	6-4	230	9-1-78	2000	Hartshorne, Okla.
Suarez, Marc	.253	47	150	18	38	9	6	2	13	4	44	4	0	.433	.325	R	R	6-0	175	1-18-76	1997	Miami, Fla.
Williamson, Chris	.211	37	114	16	24	5	1	5	18	22	39	0	2	.404	.345	L	L	6-5	229	8-21-78	2000	Houston, Texas

GAMES BY POSITION: C—Hargreaves 7, Huguet 32, Jones 30, Peterson 35, Suarez 46. **1B**—Peters 71, Ruiz 67, Williamson 4. **2B**—Anderson 1, Campana 76, Garabito 5, Patchett 66. **3B**—Anderson 27, Calitri 96, Encarnacion 9, Garabito 1, Hurtado 3, Patchett 7. **SS**—Anderson 10, Espinosa 121, Patchett 11. **OF**—Anderson 38, Andujar 4, Calitri 1, Hawes 25, Huguet 2, Hurtado 59, Pena 127, Sledd 12, Smitherman 133, Williamson 33.

PITCHING	W	L	ERA	G	GS	CG	SV	IP	H	R	ER	BB	SO	AVG	B	T	HT	WT	DOB	1st Yr	Resides
Arambles, Ricardo	1	2	3.66	4	4	0	0	20	23	8	8	4	9	.298	R	R	6-2	170	12-4-81	1996	Santo Domingo, D.R.
Bladau, Frank	6	3	2.52	42	0	0	21	54	42	16	15	10	39	.205	R	R	6-0	195	11-19-76	2000	Hallettsville, Texas
Boutwell, Andy	4	4	4.92	32	2	0	2	68	57	41	37	34	83	.224	L	R	6-1	180	7-24-79	2000	Valdosta, Ga.
Bradley, Dave	0	2	3.72	16	0	0	0	29	30	15	12	9	33	.270	R	R	6-1	175	8-28-77	1999	Walker, Wyo.
Brannon, Nick	0	0	12.46	2	0	0	0	4	8	6	6	2	4	.400	L	L	6-4	190	4-23-78	2001	Sevierville, Tenn.
Collins, Clint	2	1	4.63	6	1	0	0	12	20	7	6	3	7	.377	R	R	5-11	200	3-6-79	2000	Bamberg, S.C.
Cotton, Nathan	0	1	3.24	12	0	0	2	25	36	15	9	3	17	.339	L	R	6-2	195	7-19-79	2000	Southside, Ala.
Edwards, Bryan	6	7	4.68	29	14	1	0	108	127	75	56	40	58	.293	B	R	5-11	185	8-21-79	2000	Pflugerville, Texas
George, Brad	2	1	5.97	8	0	0	0	35	44	26	23	13	33	.333	R	R	6-5	200	5-31-82	2000	New Braunfels, Texas
Gil, David	1	0	0.77	2	2	0	0	12	11	1	1	3	15	.255	R	R	6-4	215	10-1-78	2000	Miami, Fla.
Hall, Josh	11	5	2.65	22	22	2	0	132	117	52	39	39	122	.231	R	R	6-2	170	12-16-80	1998	Lynchburg, Va.
Howington, Ty	4	0	1.15	6	1	0	0	39	15	7	5	9	47	.116	B	L	6-4	225	11-4-80	1999	Vancouver, Wash.
Koronka, John	3	1	0.75	5	5	0	0	24	23	12	2	8	25	.255	L	L	6-1	180	6-3-80	1998	Orlando, Fla.
Koziara, Matt	0	0	4.34	14	0	0	2	19	27	10	9	4	14	.333	R	R	6-2	205	11-8-76	1999	Franklin, Pa.
Laesch, Michael	2	3	3.91	29	0	0	3	51	41	25	22	25	62	.218	R	R	6-4	190	4-27-78	2000	Ames, Iowa
Markray, Thad	2	3	3.60	32	0	0	3	65	70	32	26	30	54	.277	R	R	6-4	220	9-20-79	1997	Springhill, La.
Martinez, Javier	1	0	3.38	8	0	0	4	8	6	4	3	4	13	.206	R	R	6-3	170	12-8-82	2000	Merida, Mexico
Moseley, Dustin	10	8	4.20	25	25	0	0	148	158	83	69	42	108	.271	R	R	6-3	190	12-26-81	2001	Texarkana, Ark.
Mottl, Ryan	15	6	3.60	26	26	2	0	153	155	74	61	42	119	.261	B	R	6-3	190	12-9-77	2000	Florissant, Mo.
Pape, Stace	0	0	8.18	7	0	0	0	11	20	13	10	2	13	.363	R	R	6-1	180	8-3-77	2000	San Antonio, Texas
Patchett, Gary	0	0	7.71	3	0	0	0	4	3	4	4	2	3	.000	R	R	6-2	180	9-25-78	2000	Gardena, Calif.
Pike, Matt	0	1	5.40	2	1	0	0	7	7	4	4	3	8	.269	R	R	6-1	185	9-5-78	2000	White Lake, Mich.
Rijo, Jose	0	0	3.00	1	1	0	0	3	3	1	1	0	1	.272	R	R	6-3	200	5-13-65	1981	Parkland, Fla.
Service, Scott	0	0	0.00	4	0	0	2	6	2	0	0	0	6	.095	R	R	6-6	240	2-26-67	1986	Cincinnati, Ohio
Sheefel, Adam	3	4	4.04	40	2	0	1	69	80	37	31	25	59	.288	L	L	6-0	190	12-20-77	2000	Fort Wayne, Ind.
Snare, Ryan	9	5	3.05	21	20	0	0	115	101	45	39	37	118	.238	L	L	6-0	190	2-8-79	2000	Palm Harbor, Fla.

BILLINGS — Rookie

PIONEER LEAGUE

BATTING	AVG	G	AB	R	H	2B	3B	HR	RBI	BB	SO	SB	CS	SLG	OBP	B	T	HT	WT	DOB	1st Yr	Resides
Bannon, Jeff	.260	60	235	37	61	11	3	1	31	16	33	5	2	.345	.311	R	R	6-2	190	8-21-78	2001	Camarillo, Calif.
Bautista, Augusto	.083	6	12	1	1	0	0	0	0	1	5	1	0	.083	.214	R	R	6-1	165	10-25-81	1999	San Pedro de Macoris, D.R.
Bergolla, William	.323	57	232	47	75	5	3	4	24	24	21	22	7	.422	.387	R	R	6-0	150	2-4-83	1999	Valencia, Venez.
Chourio, Jorjanis	.233	45	133	24	31	6	3	1	12	10	37	5	5	.346	.297	R	R	6-1	175	12-18-80	1997	Burere, Venez.
Davis, Justin	.295	25	88	16	26	7	1	0	18	13	11	3	0	.398	.392	L	L	6-3	195	7-17-78	2001	Chino, Calif.

BATTING	AVG	G	AB	R	H	2B	3B	HR	RBI	BB	SO	SB	CS	SLG	OBP	B	T	HT	WT	DOB	1st Yr	Resides
Encarnacion, Edwin	.261	52	211	27	55	8	2	5	26	15	29	8	1	.389	.307	R	R	6-1	175	1-7-83	2000	Caguas, P.R.
Fry, Ryan	.222	3	9	1	2	0	0	0	2	0	4	0	0	.222	.222	R	R	6-1	195	5-11-80	2001	Stockertown, Pa.
Garabito, Vianney	.179	10	39	9	7	4	0	0	4	3	5	0	0	.282	.233	R	R	6-2	195	12-12-79	1996	San Cristobal, D.R.
Gutierrez, Jesse	.294	72	269	45	79	21	0	16	61	29	43	1	0	.550	.369	R	R	6-2	190	6-16-78	2001	McAllen, Texas
Hawes, B.J.	.269	47	182	30	49	5	0	0	19	11	26	5	4	.297	.320	R	R	6-0	170	6-2-79	1999	Appling, Ga.
Lewis, Domonique	.257	41	148	33	38	3	1	2	15	18	27	15	1	.331	.349	R	R	5-9	175	8-6-79	2001	Channelview, Texas
Mateo, Daniel	.556	4	9	1	5	0	0	0	2	0	3	0	1	.556	.556	R	R	6-0	150	10-27-82	1999	San Cristobal, D.R.
Mercado, Onix	.279	29	86	15	24	6	1	1	13	7	26	0	1	.407	.354	R	R	5-11	195	6-15-80	1999	Isabela, P.R.
Molidor, David	.246	53	191	28	47	10	0	3	30	31	55	5	1	.346	.368	R	R	6-5	220	8-9-78	2001	Santa Rosa, Calif.
Nelson, Chris	.233	8	30	4	7	1	0	0	2	1	7	0	0	.267	.258	R	R	5-10	185	10-5-79	2001	Alta Loma, Calif.
Paula, Manuel	.271	49	170	24	46	7	0	3	23	12	53	5	3	.412	.333	R	R	6-2	190	1-25-81	1999	Bonao, D.R.
Peterson, Brian	.325	10	40	5	13	2	1	1	7	5	9	0	0	.500	.413	R	R	6-2	205	10-22-78	1999	Greencastle, Pa.
Prince, Bryan	.255	51	157	26	40	12	1	3	25	17	36	2	1	.401	.335	R	R	6-2	200	11-4-78	2001	Fort Oglethorpe, Ga.
Ruiz, Junior	.000	5	9	1	0	0	0	0	0	4	0	0	0	.000	.400	L	R	5-10	180	6-7-80	2001	San Jose, Calif.
Varner, Gary	.351	72	291	55	102	20	5	8	55	29	64	7	4	.536	.411	L	L	6-5	229	12-7-80	2000	Cynthiana, Ky.
Williamson, Chris	.271	29	96	21	26	3	0	6	18	20	39	0	0	.490	.398	L	L	6-2	198	8-21-78	2000	Houston, Texas

GAMES BY POSITION: C—Mercado 25, Peterson 9, Prince 50. **1B**—Fry 2, Garabito 5, Gutierrez 52, Mercado 2, Molidor 18. **2B**—Bautista 4, Bergolla 42, Lewis 31, Ruiz 3. **3B**—Bautista 1, Encarnacion 51, Fry 1, Garabito 1, Molidor 8, Varner 14. **SS**—Bannon 58, Bergolla 15, Lewis 1, Mateo 3. **OF**—Bautista 1, Chourio 43, Davis 19, Hawes 38, Lewis 7, Mercado 1, Nelson 8, Paula 47, Ruiz 2, Varner 48, Williamson 28.

PITCHING	W	L	ERA	G	GS	CG	SV	IP	H	R	ER	BB	SO	AVG	B	T	HT	WT	DOB	1st Yr	Resides
Adams, Jay	1	1	3.93	28	0	0	0	37	41	20	16	5	28	.262	R	R	6-1	190	3-14-79	2001	Del Mar, Calif.
Basham, Bobby	1	2	4.85	6	6	0	0	30	36	23	16	17	37	.300	R	R	6-3	205	3-7-80	2001	Hardy, Va.
Childress, Daylan	6	1	3.55	14	8	0	1	63	59	32	25	17	54	.245	R	R	6-2	200	7-31-78	2001	Floresville, Texas
Coffey, Todd	2	2	3.51	14	2	0	1	33	34	21	13	15	33	.257	R	R	6-5	242	9-9-80	1998	Caroleen, N.C.
Collins, Clint	5	2	2.75	10	10	0	0	56	46	19	17	14	45	.228	R	R	5-11	200	3-6-79	2000	Southside, Ala.
Cotton, Nathan	4	1	2.79	28	0	0	13	29	30	10	9	3	37	.252	L	R	6-2	195	7-19-79	2000	New Braunfels, Texas
George, Brad	0	2	9.26	5	5	0	0	23	29	31	24	8	16	.292	R	R	6-5	200	5-31-82	2000	Panama City, Fla.
Gillman, Justin	1	0	0.00	1	1	0	0	6	0	1	0	5	2	.000	R	R	6-3	185	6-27-83	2001	San Antonio, Texas
Howton, Jared	1	1	4.71	18	1	0	0	36	39	25	19	7	35	.263	L	L	6-3	190	2-8-78	2001	Hamilton, Ohio
Kelly, Steve	4	2	2.30	12	7	0	0	55	50	16	14	11	54	.235	R	R	6-3	210	4-27-79	2001	Lawrenceburg, Ky.
McWilliams, Matt	2	2	3.32	14	0	0	0	22	17	10	8	12	26	.215	L	L	6-0	185	11-19-78	2001	Hamilton, Ohio
Moak, Curtus	3	1	3.72	20	0	0	0	36	34	18	15	11	24	.250	L	L	6-0	185	9-5-78	2000	White Lake, Mich.
Pike, Matthew	3	4	5.20	13	8	0	0	55	60	39	32	15	57	.272	R	R	6-1	185	9-5-78	2000	Cincinnati, Ohio
Powers, Joe	3	1	2.70	27	0	0	0	30	25	17	9	13	30	.215	R	R	6-3	220	8-5-78	2001	
Severino, Cleris	3	3	4.30	15	13	1	0	67	66	37	32	30	54	.258	L	L	5-11	160	12-23-81	1999	Santo Domingo, D.R.
Tisdale, Marlyn	7	4	3.05	14	14	1	0	83	88	31	28	13	76	.281	L	R	6-2	215	11-1-77	2000	Jacksonville, Fla.

SARASOTA
Rookie

GULF COAST LEAGUE

BATTING	AVG	G	AB	R	H	2B	3B	HR	RBI	BB	SO	SB	CS	SLG	OBP	B	T	HT	WT	DOB	1st Yr	Resides
Acevedo, Juan	.140	37	100	10	14	6	0	0	3	8	50	2	1	.200	.211	B	R	6-2	180	8-4-81	1999	San Cristobal, D.R.
Andujar, Elvin	.294	58	197	32	58	9	9	3	34	16	43	21	4	.477	.359	R	R	6-3	195	1-19-81	1999	San Cristobal, D.R.
Bautista, Augusto	.190	20	42	7	8	0	0	1	7	1	16	0	3	.262	.239	R	R	6-1	165	10-25-81	1999	San Pedro de Macoris, D.R.
Espino, Damaso	.250	39	104	8	26	2	0	1	11	5	26	6	2	.298	.292	R	R	6-0	165	5-8-83	1999	Panama City, Panama
Fry, Ryan	.276	56	181	30	50	9	3	4	22	25	61	9	2	.425	.376	R	R	6-1	195	5-11-80	2001	Spring, Texas
Ghutzman, Phillip	.206	27	68	6	14	6	0	0	7	10	11	0	0	.294	.304	R	R	6-0	200	10-1-78	1998	Lexington, Ky.
Kearns, Austin	.176	6	17	2	3	2	0	0	4	2	7	0	0	.294	.227	B	R	6-0	150	10-27-82	1999	San Cristobal, D.R.
Mateo, Daniel	.244	53	180	29	44	6	0	1	14	15	48	27	6	.294	.323	L	L	6-1	175	9-30-81	1999	Nigua, D.R.
Morban, Dany	.143	27	63	4	9	1	0	0	3	1	22	3	1	.159	.169	R	R	6-0	170	8-18-82	2000	Sao Paulo, Brazil
Motooka, Rafael	.250	26	80	5	20	2	0	1	10	6	8	1	0	.313	.302	R	R	6-2	185	10-8-82	2001	Longview, Texas
Moye, Alan	.287	48	171	24	49	9	2	2	18	8	34	12	3	.398	.330	R	R	6-2	200	12-4-80	1999	Jefferson City, Mo.
Oetting, Todd	.238	23	63	7	15	2	0	0	8	4	11	1	0	.270	.310	B	R	6-1	175	8-20-79	2000	San Jose, Calif.
Ramirez, Jordy	.000	2	3	0	0	0	0	0	0	0	2	0	0	.000	.000	B	R	6-1	175	8-20-79	2000	San Jose, Calif.
Ruiz, Junior	.289	45	149	31	43	4	3	0	12	33	17	13	3	.356	.424	L	R	5-10	180	6-7-80	2001	San Jose, Calif.
Smith, Brenton	.261	47	138	16	36	7	0	0	10	22	35	11	6	.312	.391	L	R	6-2	210	2-2-79	2001	Rohnert Park, Calif.
Vavao, Jason	.217	53	175	30	38	9	2	1	19	10	38	2	2	.309	.282	R	R	6-4	220	5-5-81	2001	Carson, Calif.

GAMES BY POSITION: C—Ghutzman 21, Motooka 25, Oetting 15. **1B**—Fry 2, Ghutzman 1, Motooka 1, Smith 4, Vavao 53. **2B**—Bautista 11, Espino 1, Mateo 8, Ruiz 41. **3B**—Espino 25, Fry 39. **SS**—Bautista 4, Espino 12, Mateo 45. **OF**—Acevedo 23, Andujar 58, Fry 12, Kearns 4, Morban 24, Moye 46, Ruiz 1, Smith 19.

PITCHING	W	L	ERA	G	GS	CG	SV	IP	H	R	ER	BB	SO	AVG	B	T	HT	WT	DOB	1st Yr	Resides
Bartel, Richard	0	0	0.00	1	0	0	0	1	0	0	0	0	0	.000	R	R	6-5	198	2-3-83	2001	Grapevine, Texas
Batista, Gorky	5	3	2.77	10	8	2	1	52	55	18	16	10	53	.265	R	R	6-0	184	3-20-81	2000	Barahona, D.R.
Brannon, Nick	1	2	0.42	17	0	0	10	21	13	4	1	9	25	.166	L	L	6-4	190	4-23-78	2001	Swannanoa, N.C.
Burnette, Weston	2	1	8.49	10	0	0	0	12	13	13	11	5	17	.270	L	R	6-4	190	10-21-81	2001	Birmingham, Ala.
Carter, Justin	1	0	0.61	4	4	1	0	15	9	3	1	6	20	.163	R	L	6-2	185	3-8-77	1998	Caroleen, N.C.
Coffey, Todd	1	0	4.26	3	2	0	0	13	11	11	6	5	15	.234	R	R	6-5	242	9-9-80	1998	Jemison, Ala.
Culp, Brandon	1	1	1.59	6	4	0	0	28	23	6	5	13	33	.225	R	R	6-6	240	8-27-77	2000	New Braunfels, Texas
George, Brad	6	1	1.29	7	7	0	0	42	33	7	6	14	33	.212	R	R	6-5	200	5-31-82	2000	Miami, Fla.
Gil, David	0	2	7.36	4	4	0	0	11	19	15	9	6	14	.372	R	R	6-2	185	10-1-78	2000	Panama City, Fla.
Gillman, Justin	4	2	1.75	9	7	0	0	36	19	10	7	11	38	.155	R	R	6-3	185	11-27-81	1999	Chihuahua, Mexico
Gomez, Jose	0	1	1.42	14	0	0	1	32	24	7	5	6	27	.208	R	R	6-2	185	7-15-78	1995	Santo Domingo, D.R.
Lara, Nelson	0	0	2.16	4	1	0	0	8	2	2	2	4	9	.074	R	R	6-1	185	2-22-80	2001	Danville, Va.
Light, Scott	1	1	3.41	8	7	0	0	29	23	12	11	15	30	.214	R	R	6-2	215	10-4-81	1999	Collinsville, Ill.
Lutz, Kenny	1	1	4.96	6	3	0	0	16	20	10	9	13	10	.303	R	R	6-3	178	6-19-79	2001	Clifton Park, N.Y.
Meyer, Scott	5	2	1.78	14	0	0	3	30	24	7	6	13	34	.214	L	L	6-2	195	6-19-79	2001	Maracaibo, Venez.
Nunez, Renny	0	0	4.67	4	0	0	0	17	18	11	9	6	12	.253	R	R	6-3	178	12-10-81	1999	Maracaibo, Venez.
Rodriguez, Enoc	0	0	2.25	4	0	0	0	4	5	2	1	2		.312	L	L	6-3	175	1-13-81	1998	Tamaulipas, Mexico
Ross, Brian	0	0	60.75	2	2	0	0	1	10	9	9	1	2	.769	L	L	6-0	175	12-8-77	2000	Portland, Maine
Therneau, Dave	2	2	2.40	5	5	0	0	30	26	12	8	0	35	.232	R	R	6-5	195	12-23-75	1999	Denton, Texas
Torres, Carlos	1	2	2.97	11	4	0	0	39	27	13	13	18	29	.197	R	R	6-2	176	7-11-80	1999	La Romana, D.R.
Valera, Luis	5	1	2.40	10	0	0	3	15	7	4	4	6	16	.000	R	R	5-11	177	1-30-82	1999	Maracaibo, Venez.
Wagnon, Dwayne	1	1	3.05	10	0	0	0	21	14	9	7	14	23	.189	R	R	6-4	215	12-27-81	2001	Corpus Christi, Texas

CLEVELAND INDIANS

BY JIM INGRAHAM

The Indians in 2001 returned to the postseason—but not for long.

After taking a 2-1 lead over Seattle in the American League Division Series, and leading the Mariners 1-0 as late as the seventh inning of Game Four, the Indians stopped hitting. They lost 6-2 in Game Four and 3-1 in the deciding Game Five, trudging into the winter having failed again to win the World Series.

Cleveland won the Central Division title for the sixth time in the past seven years. But the club's World Series drought goes back to 1948, though it came close a couple of times in the 1990s. The Indians haven't won a postseason series since 1998.

John Hart, chief architect of the Indians' rebirth into a contender in the mid-1990s, stepped down after a 10-year run as general manager. The new GM is Mark Shapiro, 34, Hart's assistant the past three years.

During the regular season the Indians were as advertised. Using the usual Hart formula of great hitting and passable pitching, the Indians rallied in the second half to catch and pass the surprising Twins in the Central Division race.

Cleveland trailed Minnesota by five games at the all-star break. A second-half Minnesota slump allowed the Indians to finish six games ahead of the second-place Twins.

The Indians' return to the top of the division in 2001 was in large part because of their improved record against division opponents—21-30 in 2000 compared to 47-29 in 2001.

As usual, the Indians rode a potent lineup into the postseason. Three MVP candidates filled the middle of their lineup: Roberto Alomar, Juan Gonzalez and Jim Thome.

Alomar finished third in the league in hitting (.336), Gonzalez was second in RBIs (140) and Thome was second in home runs (49).

Thome surpassed Albert Belle as the franchise's all-time leader in home runs when he hit No. 243 in May. By the

Juan Gonzalez   Victor Martinez

PLAYERS OF THE YEAR

MAJOR LEAGUE: Juan Gonzalez, of
He took over in right field for the Indians in 2001 after Manny Ramirez left for the Red Sox. He let everyone know Detroit was an aberration in 2000 by driving in 140 runs.

MINOR LEAGUE: Victor Martinez, c
He won the Class A Carolina League batting title (.329) and was named the league's MVP. League managers also raved about his defensive skills and arm strength.

end of the season he had extended his record to 282.

On Sept. 4, Thome broke Tris Speaker's club record for career walks, drawing the 858th free pass of his career.

Improbably enough, rookie lefthander C.C. Sabathia anchored the Indians' pitching staff. The 20-year-old pitched his way into the Opening Day rotation then proved he belonged by going 17-5. He was the first Indians rookie lefthander in 53 years to win that many games. Sabathia held opposing batters to a .228 average, the second-lowest mark among AL starters.

The rest of the rotation was inconsistent. Bartolo Colon lost nearly as many as he won (14-12). Dave Burba (10-10, 6.21) was pulled from the rotation two different times in the second half. Chuck Finley (8-7, 5.54) was hampered by ribcage and neck injuries.

The bullpen was again very consistent, surviving an ill-advised midseason trade with Atlanta that brought controversial John Rocker to Cleveland in exchange for Steve Karsay and Steve Reed.

Rocker was a disaster, going 3-7, 5.45 in 38 appearances that also included three hit batters, 25 walks in 34 innings, six wild pitches and two balks.

Fortunately for the Indians, Bob Wickman, who was briefly deposed as closer following the Rocker trade, eventually returned to that role and had a career year, going 5-0, 2.39 with 32 saves.

The trade of Karsay also led to the emergence of Cuban defector Danys Baez into a quality setup man. In 43 appearances Baez held opposing batters to a .191 average.

The Indians' minor league system received a much-needed infusion of talent through what could potentially be one of the club's best June drafts ever. The Indians signed three of four first-round picks, including high school righthander J.D. Martin. Martin had a sensational debut at Rookie-level Burlington, going 5-1, 1.38.

ORGANIZATION LEADERS

BATTING
*AVG	Victor Martinez, Kinston	.329
R	Ryan Church, Kinston/Columbus	80
H	Nate Grindell, Akron/Kinston	140
TB	Karim Garcia, Buffalo	239
2B	Simon Pond, Akron/Kinston	37
3B	J.J. Sherrill, Columbus	11
HR	Karim Garcia, Buffalo	31
RBI	Ryan Church, Kinston/Columbus	91
BB	Ryan Church, Kinston/Columbus	72
SO	Corey Smith, Columbus	149
SB	Alex Requena, Kinston/Columbus	47

PITCHING
W	Jason Davis, Columbus	14
L	Jason Stanford, Buffalo/Akron	11
#ERA	Ryan Larson, Kinston/Columbus	0.88
G	Martin Vargas, Buffalo/Akron	54
CG	Mike Bacsik, Buffalo/Akron	3
SV	Brian Jackson, Kinston	25
IP	Brian Tallet, Kinston	160
	Jason Davis, Columbus	160
BB	Matt White, Akron	60
SO	Brian Tallet, Kinston	164

*Minimum 250 At-Bats #Minimum 75 Innings

CLEVELAND INDIANS

Manager: Charlie Manuel

2001 Record: 91-71, .562 (1st, AL Central)

BATTING	AVG	G	AB	R	H	2B	3B	HR	RBI	BB	SO	SB	CS	SLG	OBP	B	T	HT	WT	DOB	1st Yr	Resides
Alomar, Roberto	.336	157	575	113	193	34	12	20	100	80	71	30	6	.541	.415	B	R	6-0	185	2-5-68	1985	Bradenton, Fla.
Bradley, Milton	.222	10	18	3	4	1	0	0	2	3	1	1		.278	.300	B	R	6-0	190	4-15-78	1996	Long Beach, Calif.
Branyan, Russell	.232	113	315	48	73	16	2	20	54	38	132	1	1	.486	.316	L	R	6-3	195	12-19-75	1994	Warner Robins, Ga.
Burks, Ellis	.280	124	439	83	123	29	1	28	74	62	85	5	1	.542	.369	R	R	6-2	205	9-11-64	1983	Denver, Colo.
Cabrera, Jolbert	.261	141	287	50	75	16	3	1	38	16	41	10	4	.348	.312	R	R	6-0	177	12-8-72	1991	Cartagena, Colombia
Cordero, Wil	.250	89	268	30	67	11	1	4	21	22	50	0	0	.343	.313	R	R	6-2	200	10-3-71	1988	Mayaguez, P.R.
Cordova, Marty	.301	122	409	61	123	20	2	20	69	23	81	0	3	.506	.348	R	R	6-0	206	7-10-69	1989	Las Vegas, Nev.
Cruz, Jacob	.221	28	68	12	15	4	0	3	11	5	23	0	2	.412	.303	L	L	6-0	179	1-28-73	1994	Tempe, Ariz.
Diaz, Einar	.277	134	437	54	121	34	1	4	56	17	44	1	2	.387	.328	R	R	5-10	165	12-28-72	1991	Chesnee, S.C.
Fryman, Travis	.263	94	334	34	88	15	0	3	38	30	63	1	2	.335	.327	R	R	6-1	195	3-25-69	1987	Pensacola, Fla.
Garcia, Karim	.311	20	45	8	14	3	0	5	9	3	13	0	0	.711	.360	L	L	6-0	172	10-29-75	1992	Ciudad Obregon, Mexico
Gonzalez, Juan	.325	140	532	97	173	34	1	35	140	41	94	1	0	.590	.370	R	R	6-3	220	10-16-69	1986	Levittown, P.R.
Hollins, Dave	.200	2	5	0	1	0	0	0	0	1	2	0	0	.200	.333	B	R	6-1	232	5-25-66	1987	Orchard Park, N.Y.
Laker, Tim	.182	16	33	5	6	0	0	1	5	6	8	0	0	.273	.308	R	R	6-3	225	11-27-69	1988	Simi Valley, Calif.
Lewis, Mark	.077	6	13	1	1	0	0	0	0	0	4	0	0	.077	.077	R	R	6-1	195	11-30-69	1988	Hamilton, Ohio
Lofton, Kenny	.261	133	517	91	135	21	4	14	66	47	69	16	8	.398	.322	L	L	6-0	180	5-31-67	1988	Tucson, Ariz.
McDonald, John	.091	17	22	1	2	1	0	0	2	1	7	0	0	.136	.167	R	R	5-11	175	9-24-74	1996	East Lyme, Conn.
Roberts, Dave	.333	15	12	3	4	1	0	0	2	1	2	0	1	.417	.385	L	L	5-10	175	5-31-72	1994	Oceanside, Calif.
Taubensee, Eddie	.250	52	116	16	29	2	1	3	11	10	19	0	0	.362	.315	L	R	6-3	220	10-31-68	1989	Windermere, Fla.
Thome, Jim	.291	156	526	101	153	26	1	49	124	111	185	0	1	.624	.416	L	R	6-4	220	8-27-70	1989	Aurora, Ohio
Vizquel, Omar	.255	155	611	84	156	26	8	2	50	61	72	13	9	.334	.323	B	R	5-9	175	4-24-67	1984	Issaquah, Wash.

PITCHING	W	L	ERA	G	GS	CG	SV	IP	H	R	ER	BB	SO	AVG	B	T	HT	WT	DOB	1st Yr	Resides
Bacsik, Mike	0	0	9.00	3	0	0	0	9	13	9	9	3	4	.325	L	L	6-3	190	11-17-77	1996	Duncanville, Texas
Baez, Danny	5	3	2.50	43	0	0	0	50	34	22	14	20	52	.191	R	R	6-4	225	9-10-77	2000	Miami, Fla.
Burba, Dave	10	10	6.21	32	27	1	0	151	188	112	104	54	118	.305	R	R	6-4	240	7-7-66	1987	Gilbert, Ariz.
Colon, Bartolo	14	12	4.09	34	34	1	0	222	220	106	101	90	201	.260	R	R	6-0	225	5-24-75	1994	Westlake, Ohio
Drese, Ryan	1	2	3.44	9	4	0	0	37	32	15	14	15	24	.242	R	R	6-3	220	4-5-76	1998	Oakland, Calif.
Drew, Tim	0	2	7.97	8	6	0	0	35	51	39	31	16	15	.340	R	R	6-3	188	8-31-78	1997	Hahira, Ga.
Finley, Chuck	8	7	5.54	22	22	1	0	114	131	78	70	35	96	.290	L	L	6-6	226	11-26-62	1985	Newport Beach, Calif.
Karsay, Steve	0	1	1.25	31	0	0	1	43	29	6	6	8	44	.188	R	R	6-3	207	3-24-72	1990	Westlake, Ohio
Nagy, Charles	5	6	6.40	15	13	0	0	70	102	53	50	20	29	.342	L	R	6-3	200	5-5-67	1989	Westlake, Ohio
Radinsky, Scott	0	0	27.00	2	0	0	0	2	4	6	6	3	3	.400	L	L	6-3	215	3-3-68	1986	Simi Valley, Calif.
Reed, Steve	1	1	3.62	31	0	0	0	27	22	11	11	10	21	.211	R	R	6-2	212	3-11-66	1988	Arvada, Colo.
Rincon, Ricardo	2	1	2.83	67	0	0	2	54	44	18	17	21	50	.223	L	L	5-10	187	4-13-70	1997	Veracruz, Mexico
Riske, David	2	0	1.98	26	0	0	1	27	20	7	6	18	29	.206	R	R	6-2	175	10-23-76	1997	Kent, Wash.
Rocker, John	3	7	5.45	38	0	0	0	35	33	23	21	25	43	.250	R	L	6-4	225	10-17-74	1994	Macon, Ga.
Rodriguez, Rich	2	2	4.15	53	0	0	0	39	41	24	18	17	31	.269	L	L	6-0	200	3-1-63	1984	Duluth, Ga.
Sabathia, C.C.	17	5	4.39	33	33	0	0	180	149	93	88	95	171	.228	L	L	6-7	235	7-21-80	1998	Vallejo, Calif.
Shuey, Paul	5	3	2.82	47	0	0	0	54	53	25	17	26	70	.251	R	R	6-3	215	9-16-70	1992	Wake Forest, N.C.
Smith, Roy	0	0	6.06	9	0	0	0	16	16	14	11	13	17	.246	R	R	6-6	235	5-18-76	1994	Pinellas Park, Fla.
Speier, Justin	2	0	6.97	12	0	0	0	21	24	16	16	8	15	.292	R	R	6-4	205	11-6-73	1995	Paradise Valley, Ariz.
Westbrook, Jake	4	4	5.85	23	6	0	0	65	79	43	42	22	48	.306	R	R	6-3	185	9-29-77	1996	Danielsville, Ga.
Wickman, Bob	5	0	2.39	70	0	0	32	68	61	18	18	14	66	.240	R	R	6-1	234	2-6-69	1990	Wausaukee, Wis.
Woodard, Steve	3	3	5.20	29	10	0	0	97	129	59	56	17	52	.324	L	R	6-4	217	5-15-75	1994	Hartselle, Ala.
Wright, Jaret	2	2	6.52	7	7	0	0	29	36	23	21	22	18	.313	R	R	6-2	230	12-29-75	1994	Newport Beach, Calif.

FIELDING

Catcher	PCT	G	PO	A	E	DP	PB
Diaz	.992	134	959	93	8	11	7
Laker	.988	14	76	6	1	2	0
Taubensee	.986	38	212	3	3	0	5

First Base	PCT	G	PO	A	E	DP
Cordero	.994	22	161	10	1	17
Garcia	1.000	2	3	0	0	1
Thome	.992	148	1177	78	10	105

Second Base	PCT	G	PO	A	E	DP
Alomar	.993	157	268	423	5	88
Cabrera	.983	28	20	37	1	5
Diaz	1.000	1	0	1	0	0
Lewis	1.000	3	2	1	0	0
McDonald	1.000	3	2	2	0	1
Taubensee	.000	1	0	0	0	0

Third Base	PCT	G	PO	A	E	DP
Branyan	.930	72	39	108	11	8
Cabrera	.970	27	9	23	1	2
Fryman	.944	96	65	137	12	14

Lewis	.889	4	2	6	1	1
McDonald	1.000	3	0	2	0	0

Shortstop	PCT	G	PO	A	E	DP
Cabrera	.951	14	11	28	2	4
Fryman	1.000	1	1	2	0	1
McDonald	.955	9	8	13	1	2
Vizquel	.989	154	219	414	7	88

Outfield	PCT	G	PO	A	E	DP
Bradley	.929	9	12	1	1	0
Branyan	.933	32	39	3	3	0
Burks	1.000	20	25	2	0	0
Cabrera	.978	83	90	1	2	1
Cordero	.985	51	64	1	1	0
Cordova	.990	106	200	8	2	1
Cruz	.976	22	40	0	1	0
Garcia	.905	18	15	4	2	0
Gonzalez	.987	119	214	10	3	0
Lofton	.981	130	310	3	6	0
Roberts	1.000	13	8	0	0	0

Roberto Alomar

Jim Thome: Drilled 49 homers for Cleveland

STEVE MOORE

C.C. Sabathia: Rookie lefthander won 17 games for Cleveland

TYLER BOLDEN

FARM SYSTEM

Director, Player Development: Neal Huntington

Class	Farm Team	League	W	L	Pct.	Finish*	Manager	First Yr.
AAA	Buffalo (N.Y.) Bisons	International	91	51	.641	1st (14)	Eric Wedge	1995
AA	Akron (Ohio) Aeros	Eastern	68	74	.479	7th (12)	Chris Bando	1997
A#	Kinston (N.C.) Indians	Carolina	89	51	.636	1st (8)	Brad Komminsk	1987
A	Columbus (Ga.) RedStixx	South Atlantic	77	59	.566	3rd (16)	Ted Kubiak	1991
A	Mahoning Valley (Ohio) Scrappers	New York-Penn	26	49	.347	14th (14)	Dave Turgeon	1999
Rookie#	Burlington (N.C.) Indians	Appalachian	31	37	.456	t-7th (10)	Rouglas Odor	1986

*Finish in overall standings (No. of teams in league)   #Advanced level

BUFFALO   Class AAA

INTERNATIONAL LEAGUE

BATTING	AVG	G	AB	R	H	2B	3B	HR	RBI	BB	SO	SB	CS	SLG	OBP	B	T	HT	WT	DOB	1st Yr	Resides
Andreopoulos, Alex	.216	37	102	14	22	5	0	3	9	13	16	1	0	.353	.310	L	R	5-10	190	8-19-72	1995	Toronto, Ontario
Bard, Josh	.000	1	4	0	0	0	0	0	0	0	1	0	0	.000	.000	B	R	6-3	205	3-30-78	1999	Englewood, Colo.
Bradley, Milton	.254	30	114	18	29	3	0	5	15	19	31	9	2	.412	.361	B	R	6-0	190	4-15-78	1996	Long Beach, Calif.
2-team (35 Ottawa)	.264	65	250	39	66	10	2	7	28	42	61	23	3	.404	.373							
Budzinski, Mark	.256	122	438	69	112	26	4	2	39	28	125	13	4	.347	.308	L	L	6-2	175	8-26-73	1995	Severna Park, Md.
Coquillette, Trace	.208	55	178	27	37	5	3	6	22	19	38	1	2	.371	.299	R	R	5-11	185	6-4-74	1993	Orangevale, Calif.
Coste, Chris	.288	75	271	31	78	16	2	7	50	15	50	0	1	.439	.330	R	R	6-1	205	2-4-73	1995	Fargo, N.D.
Edwards, Mike	.222	3	9	1	2	0	0	0	1	1	3	0	0	.222	.300	R	R	6-1	185	11-24-76	1995	Mechanicsburg, Pa.
Erickson, Corey	.000	3	6	1	0	0	0	0	0	0	3	0	0	.000	.000	R	R	5-11	190	1-10-77	1995	Springfield, Ill.
Fryman, Travis	.481	8	27	9	13	1	0	2	8	5	6	1	0	.741	.545	R	R	6-1	195	3-25-69	1987	Pensacola, Fla.
Garcia, Karim	.264	125	462	73	122	16	4	31	85	44	106	4	4	.517	.326	L	L	6-0	172	10-29-75	1992	Ciudad Obregon, Mexico
Goelz, Jim	.250	4	4	0	1	0	0	0	0	0	2	0	0	.250	.250	R	R	5-10	170	2-13-76	1998	St. James, N.Y.
Hamilton, Jon	.000	2	4	0	0	0	0	0	0	1	1	0	0	.000	.200	L	L	6-1	195	10-23-77	1997	San Ramon, Calif.
Hardtke, Jason	.258	39	128	19	33	7	3	0	14	16	16	0	1	.359	.345	B	R	5-10	175	9-15-71	1990	Port Washington, N.Y.
Hollins, Dave	.272	89	316	50	86	25	2	16	67	45	79	0	0	.516	.373	B	R	6-1	232	5-25-66	1987	Orchard Park, N.Y.
Laker, Tim	.247	86	320	45	79	13	0	20	57	28	53	2	1	.475	.314	R	R	6-3	225	11-27-69	1988	Simi Valley, Calif.
LaRocca, Greg	.310	61	216	39	67	12	1	12	37	12	35	2	1	.542	.362	R	R	5-11	185	11-10-72	1994	Bedford, N.H.
Lewis, Mark	.299	48	184	22	55	10	1	4	29	18	26	0	1	.429	.372	R	R	6-1	195	11-30-69	1988	Hamilton, Ohio
McDonald, John	.244	116	410	52	100	17	1	2	33	33	72	17	10	.305	.305	R	R	5-11	175	9-24-74	1996	East Lyme, Conn.
McNally, Sean	.225	51	178	24	40	10	1	8	29	24	71	0	1	.427	.320	R	R	6-4	210	12-14-72	1994	Rye, N.Y.
Medrano, Tony	.290	121	466	68	135	28	1	7	52	54	40	21	7	.399	.367	R	R	5-10	175	12-8-74	1993	Long Beach, Calif.
Milliard, Ralph	.267	5	15	2	4	1	0	0	1	2	2	0	0	.333	.353	R	R	5-11	175	12-30-73	1993	Amsterdam, Netherlands
Peoples, Danny	.222	106	370	62	82	20	1	17	48	56	133	0	3	.419	.324	R	R	6-1	225	1-20-75	1996	Austin, Texas
Roberts, Dave	.303	62	241	34	73	12	4	0	22	18	44	17	6	.386	.352	L	L	5-10	175	5-31-72	1994	Oceanside, Calif.
Sefcik, Kevin	.197	70	233	30	46	10	2	5	24	18	20	4	3	.322	.260	R	R	5-10	182	2-10-71	1993	Orland Park, Ill.

BATTING	AVG	G	AB	R	H	2B	3B	HR	RBI	BB	SO	SB	CS	SLG	OBP	B	T	HT	WT	DOB	1st Yr	Resides
Snusz, Chris	.000	1	1	0	0	0	0	0	0	0	0	0	0	.000	.000	R	R	6-0	190	11-8-72	1995	Buffalo, N.Y.
Sorensen, Zach	.286	2	7	2	2	0	0	0	1	0	0	0	0	.286	.286	B	R	6-0	190	1-3-77	1998	Mesquite, Nev.
Taubensee, Eddie	.269	7	26	5	7	1	0	2	7	2	6	0	0	.538	.321	L	R	6-3	220	10-31-68	1986	Windermere, Fla.

PITCHING	W	L	ERA	G	GS	CG	SV	IP	H	R	ER	BB	SO	AVG	B	T	HT	WT	DOB	1st Yr	Resides
Bacsik, Mike	12	5	3.26	21	20	2	0	121	115	47	44	25	81	.244	L	L	6-3	190	11-11-77	1996	Duncanville, Texas
Baez, Danny	2	0	3.20	16	0	0	3	25	18	9	9	9	30	.200	R	R	6-4	225	9-10-77	2000	Miami, Fla.
Blair, Willie	4	3	2.75	11	10	1	0	72	72	30	22	7	50	.251	R	R	6-1	185	12-18-65	1986	Lexington, Ky.
Byrdak, Tim	2	0	4.67	4	3	0	0	17	18	10	9	5	17	.264	L	L	5-11	180	10-31-73	1994	Oak Forest, Ill.
Darwin, Dave	0	1	3.06	4	3	0	0	18	20	12	6	8	13	.289	L	L	6-0	185	12-19-73	1996	Macon, Ga.
Day, Zach	1	0	1.50	1	1	0	0	6	3	1	1	1	4	.142	R	R	6-4	185	6-15-78	1996	West Harrison, Ind.
DePaula, Sean	1	0	1.04	6	0	0	1	9	2	1	1	4	6	.074	R	R	6-4	215	11-7-73	1996	Derry, N.H.
Deschenes, Marc	2	2	6.37	22	0	0	0	30	38	23	21	23	29	.311	R	R	6-0	175	1-6-73	1995	Dracut, Mass.
Drese, Ryan	5	1	4.01	11	10	0	0	61	60	28	27	17	52	.262	R	R	6-3	220	4-5-76	1998	Oakland, Calif.
Drew, Tim	8	6	3.92	18	18	1	0	108	115	54	47	27	75	.268	R	R	6-1	195	8-31-78	1997	Hahira, Ga.
Gunderson, Eric	0	0	0.00	2	0	0	0	2	2	1	0	0	3	.222	R	L	6-0	190	3-29-66	1987	Portland, Ore.
Hammond, Chris	7	3	3.31	28	4	0	0	52	53	22	19	20	54	.261	L	L	6-1	195	1-21-66	1986	Hallandale, Fla.
Hooten, Dave	1	0	1.80	1	1	0	0	5	5	1	1	1	2	.263	R	R	6-0	176	5-8-75	1996	Shreveport, La.
Lewis, Richie	2	0	2.10	7	5	0	1	30	19	8	7	13	11	.182	R	R	5-10	175	1-25-66	1987	Muncie, Ind.
Nagy, Charles	5	1	2.56	6	6	0	0	39	40	12	11	9	18	.266	L	R	6-3	200	5-5-67	1989	Westlake, Ohio
Phillips, Jason	2	2	3.34	8	6	1	0	35	27	15	13	8	25	.212	R	R	6-6	225	3-22-74	1992	Hughesville, Pa.
Radinsky, Scott	0	1	4.11	16	0	0	0	15	13	7	7	1	7	.250	L	L	6-3	215	3-3-68	1986	Simi Valley, Calif.
Reinike, Chris	0	0	9.00	1	0	0	0	1	0	1	1	3	1	.000	R	R	6-0	195	11-16-76	1998	Gulfport, Miss.
Riske, David	1	2	2.36	38	0	0	15	53	45	16	14	17	72	.231	R	R	6-2	175	10-23-76	1997	Kent, Wash.
Rodriguez, Nerio	2	3	5.35	11	5	0	1	39	41	24	23	15	21	.277	R	R	6-1	205	3-22-73	1991	San Pedro de Macoris, D.R.
2-team (1 Norfolk)	2	3	5.82	12	5	0	1	39	43	26	25	15	21	.286							
Smith, Dan	6	4	4.50	21	16	1	0	106	110	58	53	44	68	.273	R	R	6-3	210	9-15-75	1993	Girard, Kan.
Smith, Roy	0	5	2.19	48	0	0	18	74	59	25	18	29	86	.224	R	R	6-6	235	5-18-76	1994	Pinellas Park, Fla.
Spoljaric, Paul	0	1	17.36	4	0	0	0	5	11	11	9	4	3	.458	L	L	6-3	210	9-24-70	1990	Kelowna, B.C.
Stanford, Jason	1	0	0.00	1	1	1	0	9	3	0	0		10	.103	L	L	6-2	200	1-23-77	1999	Lawrence, Kan.
Vargas, Martin	0	3	2.93	22	0	0	4	28	20	11	9	17	22	.202	R	R	6-0	155	2-22-78	1996	San Pedro de Macoris, D.R.
Veras, Dario	5	1	4.57	48	0	0	6	67	69	35	34	21	69	.265	R	R	6-1	155	3-13-73	1991	Villa Vazquez, D.R.
Walker, Jamie	7	2	3.87	38	8	0	2	93	104	44	40	27	51	.281	L	L	6-2	190	7-1-71	1992	Overland Park, Kan.
Watson, Mark	0	1	13.50	1	0	0	0	4	9	7	6	3	3	.409	R	L	6-4	215	1-23-74	1996	Dunwoody, Ga.
Westbrook, Jake	8	1	3.20	12	12	0	0	65	60	27	23	23	45	.248	R	R	6-3	185	9-29-77	1996	Danielsville, Ga.
Woodard, Steve	4	2	2.39	6	6	1	0	38	36	11	10	1	32	.248	L	R	6-4	217	5-15-75	1994	Hartselle, Ala.
Wright, Jaret	3	1	4.71	7	7	0	0	29	25	18	15	13	28	.233	R	R	6-2	230	12-29-75	1994	Newport Beach, Calif.

FIELDING

Catcher	PCT	G	PO	A	E	DP	PB
Andreopoulos	.990	34	191	11	2	1	1
Coste	.989	32	257	17	3	2	1
Laker	.990	80	549	41	6	6	4
Snusz	1.000	1	3	0	0	0	0
Taubensee	.960	5	23	1	1	0	0

First Base	PCT	G	PO	A	E	DP
Coste	.994	19	162	14	1	20
Edwards	1.000	3	28	4	0	3
Garcia	.941	6	32	0	2	4
Hollins	.979	16	134	9	3	15
Laker	1.000	3	32	1	0	2
McNally	.988	10	75	10	1	9
Peoples	.988	87	713	50	9	82

Second Base	PCT	G	PO	A	E	DP
Coquillette	.952	11	16	24	2	6
Erickson	1.000	1	4	3	0	0
Goelz	.714	2	2	3	2	0
Hardtke	.967	27	46	73	4	15
LaRocca	1.000	1	1	2	0	1
M. Lewis	.939	9	15	16	2	4
McDonald	.933	2	6	8	1	2
Medrano	.984	48	105	135	4	41
Milliard	.913	5	7	14	2	3
Sefcik	.981	45	79	130	4	33
Sorensen	1.000	2	3	4	0	1

Third Base	PCT	G	PO	A	E	DP
Coste	1.000	1	1	0	1	0
Erickson	1.000	2	0	2	0	0
Fryman	1.000	7	7	11	0	1
Hardtke	1.000	8	8	18	0	1
Hollins	1.000	1	1	3	0	0
LaRocca	.955	49	24	103	6	8
M. Lewis	.878	33	28	44	10	2
McDonald	1.000	2	1	0	0	0
McNally	.955	33	24	61	4	6
Medrano	1.000	17	7	34	0	1

Shortstop	PCT	G	PO	A	E	DP
Sefcik	.875	2	2	5	1	0
Goelz	.000	1	0	0	0	0
LaRocca	1.000	8	16	28	0	7
McDonald	.958	111	170	328	22	81
Medrano	.981	26	40	65	2	19

Outfield	PCT	G	PO	A	E	DP
Bradley	1.000	29	57	3	0	1
Budzinski	1.000	121	253	11	0	3
Coquillette	.987	42	72	4	1	1
Coste	1.000	12	26	1	0	0
Garcia	.978	112	208	11	5	1
Hamilton	1.000	1	3	0	0	0
Hollins	1.000	2	1	0	0	0
Medrano	.986	37	72	1	1	0
Peoples	1.000	10	14	1	0	0
Roberts	.978	56	132	1	3	0
Sefcik	1.000	16	27	0	0	0

AKRON — Class AA

EASTERN LEAGUE

BATTING	AVG	G	AB	R	H	2B	3B	HR	RBI	BB	SO	SB	CS	SLG	OBP	B	T	HT	WT	DOB	1st Yr	Resides
Abbott, Chuck	.195	17	41	6	8	1	1	3	8	2	17	1	1	.488	.233	R	R	6-1	180	1-26-75	1996	Schaumburg, Ill.
Bard, Josh	.278	51	194	26	54	11	0	4	25	16	27	0	0	.397	.338	B	R	6-3	205	3-30-78	1999	Englewood, Colo.
Benefield, Brian	.204	63	157	16	32	7	0	2	9	10	28	5	4	.287	.249	R	R	6-0	181	8-12-76	1997	Carrollton, Texas
Bost, Tom	.176	29	91	7	16	2	0	0	7	5	34	6	0	.198	.227	L	R	6-2	220	10-5-75	1998	Columbia, Tenn.
Coste, Chris	.125	6	24	1	3	0	0	0	1	3	0	1	0	.125	.160	R	R	6-1	205	2-4-73	1995	Fargo, N.D.
DePippo, Jeff	.263	82	240	32	63	10	2	6	28	14	51	5	8	.396	.335	R	R	5-7	170	4-29-76	1998	Garden Grove, Calif.
Edwards, Mike	.333	29	111	21	37	3	2	4	24	13	26	0	0	.613	.403	R	R	6-1	185	11-24-76	1995	Mechanicsburg, Pa.
Erickson, Corey	.228	133	483	67	110	28	2	22	65	33	132	7	4	.431	.285	R	R	5-11	190	1-10-77	1995	Springfield, Ill.
Fitzgerald, Jason	.272	61	239	23	65	12	1	4	19	10	38	10	2	.381	.300	L	L	6-1	190	9-16-75	1997	Belle Chasse, La.
Fryman, Travis	.360	6	25	3	9	2	0	1	3	2	5	0	0	.560	.407	R	R	6-1	195	3-25-69	1987	Pensacola, Fla.
Goelz, Jim	.261	101	283	30	74	20	2	1	28	13	43	6	3	.357	.292	R	R	5-10	170	2-13-76	1998	St. James, N.Y.
Gonzalez, Luis	.302	52	199	41	60	12	2	5	17	7	26	2	3	.457	.329	R	R	5-11	170	6-26-79	1997	El Tigre, Venez.
Green, Chad	.260	37	127	23	33	8	2	3	16	11	28	8	2	.425	.317	R	R	5-10	180	6-28-75	1996	Cincinnati, Ohio
Grindell, Nate	.284	63	229	34	65	17	1	10	45	10	45	6	4	.498	.317	R	R	6-0	185	4-9-77	1998	Carrollton, Texas
Hamilton, Jon	.280	134	471	60	132	24	4	17	65	42	118	9	12	.456	.341	L	L	6-1	195	10-23-77	1997	San Ramon, Calif.
Hernandez, Jesus	.357	4	14	1	5	1	0	0	0	3	5	1	1	.429	.471	L	R	6-2	170	6-6-77	1995	Laguna Salada, D.R.
Jenkins, Jesus	.217	6	23	4	5	4	0	0	3	0	5	0	0	.391	.240	R	R	5-11	215	10-11-78	1997	Port St. Joe, Fla.
Krause, Scott	.254	87	303	47	77	16	1	15	52	26	84	0	3	.462	.317	R	R	6-1	187	8-16-73	1994	Willowick, Ohio
Lackey, Steve	.222	13	27	4	6	1	0	0	0	4	7	2	0	.259	.323	R	R	5-11	159	9-25-74	1992	Riverside, Calif.
LaRocca, Greg	.317	31	104	16	33	9	0	3	19	18	11	0	2	.490	.421	R	R	5-11	185	11-10-72	1994	Bedford, N.H.

BATTING	AVG	G	AB	R	H	2B	3B	HR	RBI	BB	SO	SB	CS	SLG	OBP	B	T	HT	WT	DOB	1st Yr	Resides
Malave, Dennis	.000	4	7	0	0	0	0	0	0	0	2	0	0	.000	.000	L	L	5-9	165	1-6-80	1997	Caracas, Venez.
Munoz, Billy	.184	34	114	5	21	4	0	4	12	12	21	0	0	.325	.260	L	L	6-2	220	6-30-75	1998	Mesa, Ariz.
Pond, Simon	.268	114	388	46	104	29	3	11	46	30	70	2	3	.443	.320	L	R	6-1	190	10-27-76	1994	North Vancouver, B.C.
Pratt, Scott	.280	68	264	33	74	13	4	4	24	26	48	16	11	.405	.349	L	R	5-10	185	2-4-77	1998	Tooele, Utah
Rickon, Jim	.154	12	26	0	4	1	0	0	0	1	9	1	0	.192	.185	R	R	6-4	225	6-1-76	1999	Maple Heights, Ohio
Roberts, Dave	.203	17	64	9	13	5	0	0	2	9	8	4	0	.281	.307	L	L	5-10	175	5-31-72	1994	Oceanside, Calif.
Santana, Osmany	.125	11	40	1	5	0	0	0	1	2	10	1	0	.125	.167	L	L	5-11	185	8-9-76	1998	Hialeah, Fla.
Smith, Casey	.176	30	91	8	16	1	0	3	5	6	27	3	0	.286	.235	R	R	6-3	200	5-7-77	1997	Carrollton, Texas
Snusz, Chris	.143	2	7	0	1	0	0	0	0	0	0	0	0	.143	.143	R	R	6-0	190	11-8-72	1995	Buffalo, N.Y.
Sorensen, Zach	.232	46	194	24	45	6	1	5	16	11	30	10	8	.351	.273	B	R	6-0	190	1-3-77	1998	Mesquite, Nev.
Taubensee, Eddie	.143	2	7	1	1	0	0	0	1	1	1	0	0	.143	.250	L	R	6-3	220	10-31-68	1986	Windermere, Fla.
Tillman, Kevin	.286	2	7	1	2	0	0	0	1	0	2	1	0	.286	.286	L	R	5-10	190	1-24-78	2001	San Jose, Calif.
Whitaker, Chad	.239	51	155	16	37	9	1	6	18	13	34	2	1	.426	.295	L	R	6-2	190	9-16-76	1995	Fort Lauderdale, Fla.

PITCHING	W	L	ERA	G	GS	CG	SV	IP	H	R	ER	BB	SO	AVG	B	T	HT	WT	DOB	1st Yr	Resides
Bacsik, Mike	1	1	1.98	4	4	1	0	27	21	7	6	3	19	.207	L	L	6-3	190	11-11-77	1996	Duncanville, Texas
Baez, Danny	0	0	0.00	1	0	0	0	2	1	0	0	0	2	.142	R	R	6-4	225	9-10-77	2000	Miami, Fla.
Brown, Jamie	1	1	5.03	4	4	0	0	20	22	11	11	7	12	.278	R	R	6-2	205	3-31-77	1997	Collinsville, Miss.
Bullinger, Kirk	0	1	4.91	3	0	0	1	4	5	2	2	1	4	.357	R	R	6-2	170	10-28-69	1992	Gretna, La.
Cooper, Chris	0	0	4.50	2	0	0	0	2	2	1	1	0	3	.250	L	L	5-11	190	10-31-78	2001	Sewickley, Pa.
Darwin, Dave	3	2	4.15	19	7	0	0	56	62	34	26	18	43	.281	L	L	6-0	185	12-19-73	1996	Macon, Ga.
Day, Zach	9	10	3.10	22	22	2	0	137	123	57	47	45	94	.236	R	R	6-4	185	6-15-78	1996	West Harrison, Ind.
Delgado, Ernie	0	1	3.24	1	0	0	0	8	5	3	3	1	9	.178	R	R	6-2	190	7-21-75	1993	Tucson, Ariz.
Deschenes, Marc	2	2	1.72	22	0	0	0	31	25	9	6	18	30	.225	R	R	6-0	175	1-6-73	1995	Dracut, Mass.
Drese, Ryan	5	7	3.35	14	13	1	0	86	64	34	32	29	73	.215	R	R	6-3	220	4-5-76	1998	Oakland, Calif.
Field, Luke	0	1	10.80	1	1	0	0	5	8	6	6	2	1	.363	R	R	5-11	178	1-27-79	2000	Tempe, Ariz.
Finley, Chuck	1	1	0.82	2	2	0	0	11	7	3	1	2	11	.189	L	L	6-6	226	11-26-62	1985	Newport Beach, Calif.
Fitch, Steve	0	0	7.71	1	1	0	0	2	4	4	2	1	2	.307	R	R	6-1	180	2-15-78	2000	West Chester, Pa.
Garrett, Hal	1	4	5.61	11	2	0	0	26	21	17	16	14	19	.221	R	R	6-2	175	4-27-75	1993	Mount Juliet, Tenn.
Gronkiewicz, Lee	0	0	0.00	2	0	0	0	2	4	0	0	0	1	.400	R	R	5-11	183	8-21-78	2001	Lancaster, S.C.
Herrera, Alex	3	0	2.83	15	0	0	2	29	24	9	9	9	22	.228	L	L	5-11	175	11-5-79	1997	Maracaibo, Venez.
Hooten, Dave	4	0	1.37	17	6	0	4	46	43	7	7	12	31	.259	R	R	6-0	176	5-8-75	1996	Shreveport, La.
Johnson, James	4	0	2.91	31	0	0	0	46	35	15	15	19	55	.205	B	L	6-1	175	8-7-76	1998	San Diego, Calif.
Lantz, Doug	0	0	0.00	1	1	0	0	6	1	0	0	0	3	.055	R	R	6-1	185	8-26-79	2001	Southlake, Texas
Perkins, Dan	0	0	15.00	1	1	0	0	3	7	5	5	0	4	.437	R	R	6-2	193	3-15-75	1993	South Miami, Fla.
Phillips, Jason	2	1	4.13	10	3	0	0	24	18	11	11	15	20	.214	R	R	6-6	225	3-22-74	1992	Hughesville, Pa.
2-team (6 Altoona)	2	2	5.73	16	4	0	0	33	36	22	21	19	24	.283							
Pinales, Aquiles	0	0	9.00	5	0	0	0	8	13	9	8	4	6	.361	R	R	5-11	190	9-26-74	1996	La Romana, D.R.
Radinsky, Scott	2	2	3.47	23	0	0	3	23	30	10	9	3	19	.319	L	L	6-3	215	3-3-68	1986	Simi Valley, Calif.
Reinike, Chris	1	3	5.33	27	0	0	5	52	55	34	31	18	40	.266	R	R	6-0	195	11-16-76	1998	Gulfport, Miss.
Rodriguez, Nerio	6	2	3.91	11	11	2	0	71	64	34	31	17	49	.243	R	R	6-1	205	3-22-73	1991	San Pedro de Macoris, D.R.
Rodriguez, Rich	0	0	0.00	4	0	0	1	5	2	0	0	0	4	.117	L	L	6-0	200	3-1-63	1984	Duluth, Ga.
Sadler, Carl	2	3	6.50	11	0	0	0	18	23	16	13	9	14	.302	L	L	6-2	180	10-11-76	1996	Perry, Fla.
Sanders, Frankie	0	0	189.00	1	0	0	0	0	3	7	7	3	0	.750	R	R	5-11	165	8-27-75	1995	Sarasota, Fla.
Sexton, Jeff	0	0	2.04	11	0	0	1	18	22	7	4	5	14	.301	R	R	6-2	190	10-4-71	1993	Kingston, Okla.
Shuey, Paul	0	0	0.00	1	1	0	0	1	0	0	0	1	2	.000	R	R	6-3	215	9-16-70	1992	Wake Forest, N.C.
Sido, Wilson	1	0	2.30	3	2	0	0	16	15	4	4	9	13	.263	R	R	6-2	178	6-18-76	1998	Barahona, D.R.
Spiegel, Mike	0	0	9.53	1	1	0	0	6	10	6	6	3	0	.333	L	L	6-5	200	11-24-75	1996	Carmichael, Calif.
Spoljaric, Paul	0	0	0.00	3	0	0	0	3	4	0	0	0	3	.333	L	L	6-3	210	9-24-70	1990	Kelowna, B.C.
Stanford, Jason	6	11	4.07	24	24	1	0	142	152	71	64	32	108	.276	L	L	6-2	200	1-23-77	1999	Lawrence, Kan.
Tucker, Julien	0	0	9.72	5	1	0	0	8	10	9	9	5	6	.303	L	R	6-7	200	4-19-73	1993	Chateauguay, Quebec
2-team (23 Erie)	1	6	5.67	28	1	0	0	54	62	39	34	35	27	.293							
Turnbow, Mark	0	0	3.00	1	0	0	0	3	1	1	1	2	1	.125	R	R	6-3	205	11-26-78	1997	Saltillo, Tenn.
Vargas, Martin	1	5	5.63	32	0	0	9	40	52	29	25	23	35	.325	R	R	6-0	155	2-22-78	1996	San Pedro de Macoris, D.R.
Watson, Mark	3	1	4.12	30	0	0	4	39	34	19	18	13	34	.226	R	R	6-4	215	1-23-74	1996	Dunwoody, Ga.
White, Matt	8	10	4.81	25	25	0	0	144	151	84	77	60	72	.276	R	L	6-1	180	8-19-77	1998	Windsor, Mass.
Wolff, Bryan	2	3	4.05	8	8	1	0	53	52	24	24	15	47	.258	R	R	6-2	189	3-16-72	1993	Herrin, Ill.
Woodard, Steve	0	0	3.00	1	1	0	0	3	3	1	1	1	2	.272	L	R	6-4	217	5-15-75	1994	Hartselle, Ala.
Wright, Jaret	0	0	1.29	1	1	0	0	7	2	1	1	0	4	.086	R	R	6-2	230	12-29-75	1994	Newport Beach, Calif.

FIELDING

Catcher	PCT	G	PO	A	E	DP	PB
Bard	.986	43	255	36	4	2	2
Coste	.977	5	35	7	1	2	2
DePippo	.989	64	395	46	5	3	15
Rickon	1.000	9	44	3	0	0	3
Smith	.991	28	197	30	2	3	1
Snusz	1.000	1	10	0	0	0	0
Taubensee	1.000	2	9	0	0	0	0

First Base	PCT	G	PO	A	E	DP
Abbott	1.000	1	11	1	0	0
Edwards	.994	19	147	8	1	17
Erickson	1.000	10	60	8	0	3
Goelz	1.000	1	1	0	0	0
Grindell	1.000	15	128	9	0	0
Munoz	.997	32	278	22	1	16
Pond	.996	75	641	29	3	60
Smith	1.000	1	2	1	0	0

Second Base	PCT	G	PO	A	E	DP
Abbott	.958	12	14	32	2	9
Benefield	.957	10	23	21	2	5
Erickson	.975	12	21	18	1	4
Goelz	.911	17	24	27	5	10
Gonzalez	.987	48	106	117	3	32
LaRocca	.900	2	5	4	1	1
Pratt	.964	55	96	145	9	21
Tillman	1.000	2	3	0	0	1

Third Base	PCT	G	PO	A	E	DP
Abbott	1.000	1	2	0	0	0
Benefield	1.000	11	2	15	0	1
Edwards	.885	9	7	16	3	1
Erickson	.950	116	79	223	16	28
Goelz	.909	7	3	7	1	0
Gonzalez	1.000	1	0	2	0	0
Grindell	1.000	4	3	7	0	2
LaRocca	.950	6	6	13	1	0
Pond	1.000	1	3	0	0	

Shortstop	PCT	G	PO	A	E	DP
Abbott	1.000	3	3	3	0	0
Benefield	1.000	8	11	18	0	2
Goelz	.961	58	97	150	10	31
Gonzalez	1.000	2	3	4	0	0
Lackey	.925	10	17	32	4	5

	PCT	G	PO	A	E	DP
LaRocca	.944	25	32	69	6	10
Pratt	.889	3	3	5	1	1
Sorensen	.956	45	77	140	10	28

Outfield	PCT	G	PO	A	E	DP
Benefield	.958	16	21	2	1	1
Bost	.982	28	54	2	1	0
DePippo	.846	6	11	0	2	0
Fitzgerald	.991	55	112	0	1	0
Goelz	1.000	13	27	1	0	0
Green	.975	36	71	6	2	2
Grindell	.962	40	70	5	3	2
Hamilton	.978	133	209	17	5	5
Hernandez	1.000	1	2	0	0	0
Jenkins	1.000	6	6	0	0	0
Krause	.974	42	70	5	2	0
Malave	1.000	4	7	1	0	0
Pond	.818	8	9	0	2	0
Pratt	1.000	8	16	0	0	0
Roberts	.969	12	31	0	1	0
Santana	.960	11	23	1	1	0
Whitaker	1.000	35	48	3	0	0

CAROLINA LEAGUE

BATTING	AVG	G	AB	R	H	2B	3B	HR	RBI	BB	SO	SB	CS	SLG	OBP	B	T	HT	WT	DOB	1st Yr	Resides
Becker, Jeff	.246	24	69	7	17	5	0	1	11	9	16	0	0	.362	.358	R	R	6-2	200	12-20-76	2000	Thiells, N.Y.
Benefield, Brian	.333	17	57	14	19	5	1	1	8	8	9	5	0	.509	.451	R	R	6-0	181	8-12-76	1997	Carrollton, Texas
Bost, Tom	.254	50	130	18	33	7	1	6	21	16	31	3	1	.462	.355	L	R	6-2	220	10-5-75	1998	Columbia, Tenn.
Cameron, Troy	.250	61	224	39	56	14	1	8	38	36	53	0	0	.429	.361	B	R	5-11	180	8-31-78	1997	Plantation, Fla.
2-team (65 M.B.)	.251	126	447	66	112	27	2	15	76	59	115	2	6	.421	.348							
Church, Ryan	.241	24	83	16	20	7	0	5	15	18	23	1	0	.506	.379	L	L	6-1	190	10-14-78	2000	Lompoc, Calif.
Cruz, Edgar	.128	15	47	5	6	1	0	0	3	3	10	0	0	.149	.180	R	R	6-3	195	8-12-78	1997	Juncos, P.R.
Ewing, Byron	.243	90	301	41	73	14	1	7	38	35	67	7	7	.365	.337	R	R	6-3	215	10-22-76	1999	Jacksonville, Fla.
Gonzalez, Luis	.322	52	183	31	59	14	0	5	19	14	36	3	5	.481	.391	R	R	5-11	170	6-26-79	1997	El Tigre, Venez.
Grindell, Nate	.276	69	272	41	75	17	1	6	41	16	42	1	3	.412	.318	R	R	6-1	180	4-9-77	1998	Carrollton, Texas
Haase, Jeff	.200	19	60	4	12	2	1	2	9	4	20	0	0	.367	.273	R	R	6-2	205	5-15-78	2000	Eastlake, Ohio
Hernandez, Jesus	.159	23	82	15	13	3	2	3	7	10	20	1	1	.354	.263	L	L	6-2	170	6-6-77	1995	Laguna Salada, D.R.
Izturis, Maicer	.240	114	433	47	104	16	6	1	39	31	81	32	9	.312	.300	B	R	5-8	155	9-12-80	1998	Barquisimeto, Venez.
Janowicz, Nate	.253	46	154	21	39	7	1	0	23	18	30	4	1	.312	.333	L	L	5-10	183	5-16-78	2000	Atascadero, Calif.
Jenkins, Brian	.349	23	83	10	29	5	2	1	14	7	13	2	3	.494	.402	R	R	5-11	215	10-11-78	1997	Port St. Joe, Fla.
Johnson, Eric	.230	127	482	77	111	17	5	7	45	57	124	22	14	.330	.322	R	R	6-1	210	8-14-77	1999	Shallotte, N.C.
Katz, Damon	.161	13	31	0	5	1	0	0	3	3	9	0	0	.194	.297	R	R	5-11	180	11-23-77	2000	Danville, Calif.
Martinez, Victor	.329	114	420	59	138	33	2	10	57	39	60	3	3	.488	.394	B	R	6-2	160	12-23-78	1997	Ciudad Bolivar, Venez.
Minges, Tyler	.252	66	250	30	63	12	2	5	35	12	48	3	2	.376	.294	R	R	6-0	185	11-15-79	1998	Hamilton, Ohio
Moraga, Omar	.233	13	43	4	10	1	0	1	2	1	6	0	1	.326	.250	L	R	5-9	180	5-23-77	1998	Tucson, Ariz.
Moreno, Jorge	.204	101	368	31	75	7	1	5	35	26	94	7	8	.269	.261	R	R	6-0	175	10-26-80	1998	Ciudad Ojeda, Venez.
Peralta, John	.240	125	441	57	106	24	2	7	47	58	148	4	8	.351	.328	R	R	6-1	185	5-28-82	1999	Santiago, D.R.
Pichardo, Henry	.289	14	45	6	13	3	0	1	7	4	11	0	1	.422	.360	R	R	5-10	145	1-15-79	1996	Tamboril, D.R.
Pond, Simon	.340	25	97	13	33	8	1	4	24	10	12	1	1	.567	.400	L	R	6-0	190	10-27-76	1994	North Vancouver, B.C.
Requena, Alex	.212	62	259	30	55	7	4	2	13	19	80	32	10	.293	.277	B	R	5-11	155	8-13-80	1998	Maracay, Venez.
Rickon, Jim	.225	29	80	13	18	3	0	4	13	11	20	1	0	.413	.295	R	R	6-4	225	6-1-76	1999	Maple Heights, Ohio

GAMES BY POSITION: C—Cruz 14, Haase 10, Martinez 106, Rickon 17. **1B**—Becker 10, Ewing 85, Grindell 17, Haase 5, Pichardo 1, Pond 22, Rickon 8. **2B**—Becker 6, Benefield 7, Gonzalez 13, Izturis 102, Katz 8, Moraga 7, Pichardo 2. **3B**—Becker 6, Benefield 7, Cameron 60, Gonzalez 22, Grindell 47, Katz 1, Pichardo 1. **SS**—Becker 2, Gonzalez 8, Katz 5, Peralta 125, Pichardo 4. **OF**—Becker 1, Bost 26, Church 21, Haase 1, Hernandez 20, Janowicz 30, Jenkins 21, E. Johnson 117, Minges 47, Moreno 86, Pichardo 4, Requena 55.

PITCHING	W	L	ERA	G	GS	CG	SV	IP	H	R	ER	BB	SO	AVG	B	T	HT	WT	DOB	1st Yr	Resides
Baker, Jason	4	1	3.44	13	8	1	0	50	44	21	19	22	44	.234	R	R	6-4	195	11-21-74	1993	Midland, Texas
Cowie, Stephen	0	0	1.50	2	0	0	0	6	5	1	1	4		.263	R	R	6-2	190	11-9-76	1999	Belmont, N.C.
Denney, Kyle	5	3	2.05	11	10	0	0	57	32	14	13	13	80	.159	R	R	6-2	195	7-27-77	1999	Prague, Okla.
Evans, Kyle	2	1	2.70	7	0	0	0	30	35	9	9	9	16	.312	R	R	6-3	190	10-10-78	2000	Albuquerque, N.M.
Fitch, Steve	4	4	4.15	13	11	0	0	65	77	36	30	22	45	.293	R	R	6-1	180	2-15-78	2000	West Chester, Pa.
Garza, Alberto	5	3	3.17	41	0	0	2	77	60	29	27	48	123	.215	R	R	6-3	195	5-25-77	1996	Wapato, Wash.
Guillory, Dan	2	1	1.24	23	0	0	7	29	19	5	4	6	36	.180	L	L	5-11	175	11-5-79	1997	Maracaibo, Venez.
Herrera, Alex	4	0	0.60	28	0	0	3	60	36	6	4	18	83	.170	L	L	6-4	190	8-12-77	1998	Tiburon, Calif.
Jackson, Damon	2	6	2.65	53	0	0	25	68	66	25	20	28	53	.259	R	R	6-4	190	8-12-77	1998	Tiburon, Calif.
Johnson, James	0	0	0.73	4	1	0	0	12	8	2	1	2	13	.190	B	L	6-1	175	8-7-76	1998	San Diego, Calif.
Larson, Ryan	3	1	1.55	12	0	0	2	29	20	7	5	6	30	.186	R	R	5-10	195	5-13-79	2000	Rocklin, Calif.
Matsko, Rick	0	0	5.63	10	0	0	0	16	14	15	10	9	19	.241	R	R	6-2	210	4-26-77	1998	Johnstown, Pa.
Neil, Dan	3	0	0.82	16	0	0	0	33	26	6	3	3	27	.213	L	L	6-0	185	8-8-78	1999	Bardonia, N.Y.
Pinales, Aquiles	5	4	4.47	36	0	0	3	58	65	34	29	25	55	.277	R	R	5-11	190	9-26-74	1996	La Romana, D.R.
Sadler, Carl	6	0	1.88	27	2	0	2	62	51	19	13	18	78	.216	L	L	6-2	180	10-11-76	1996	Perry, Fla.
Sido, Wilson	9	2	2.33	17	17	1	0	93	69	29	24	20	96	.204	R	R	6-2	178	6-18-76	1998	Barahona, D.R.
Spiegel, Mike	7	7	2.82	21	17	0	0	109	83	37	34	38	90	.212	L	L	6-5	200	11-24-75	1996	Carmichael, Calif.
Tallet, Brian	9	7	3.04	27	27	2	0	160	134	62	54	38	164	.224	L	L	6-7	208	9-21-77	2000	Bethany, Okla.
Thoms, Hank	7	2	2.26	14	14	1	0	80	70	26	20	20	74	.236	R	R	6-4	210	6-7-76	1999	Newton, Miss.
Vargas, Jose	0	1	1.35	8	0	0	1	13	6	2	2	7	22	.136	R	R	6-0	175	3-25-77	1998	Barahona, D.R.
Wallace, Shane	10	2	1.61	13	13	1	0	84	65	22	15	16	60	.212	L	L	6-2	200	12-29-80	1999	Carrollton, Texas
Young, Simon	3	5	6.75	15	13	0	0	60	85	54	45	21	48	.323	L	L	6-4	240	9-14-77	1999	Flowery Branch, Ga.

SOUTH ATLANTIC LEAGUE

BATTING	AVG	G	AB	R	H	2B	3B	HR	RBI	BB	SO	SB	CS	SLG	OBP	B	T	HT	WT	DOB	1st Yr	Resides
Baker, Casey	.083	4	12	1	1	0	0	0	0	0	2	2	1	.083	.214	R	R	5-9	165	8-7-80	1999	Wysox, Pa.
2-team (8 Greens.)	.077	12	26	2	2	0	0	0	1	2	8	3	2	.077	.200							
Becker, Jeff	.257	65	206	33	53	10	1	1	19	34	38	2	2	.330	.398	R	R	6-2	200	12-20-76	2000	Thiells, N.Y.
Choy Foo, Rodney	.250	12	40	2	10	0	0	0	5	4	9	1	0	.250	.311	B	R	6-1	185	12-12-81	2000	Waimanalo, Hawaii
Church, Ryan	.287	101	363	64	104	23	3	17	76	54	79	4	6	.507	.385	L	L	6-1	190	10-14-78	2000	Lompoc, Calif.
Colmenter, Jesus	.279	39	136	12	38	1	1	0	8	4	26	1	2	.301	.306	B	R	5-10	155	12-1-81	1998	Cabudare, Venez.
Crozier, Eric	.235	67	221	41	52	9	2	4	19	37	84	5	3	.348	.346	L	L	6-4	200	8-11-78	2000	Columbus, Ohio
Cruz, Edgar	.205	33	112	11	23	6	0	4	10	10	28	2	2	.366	.288	R	R	6-3	195	8-12-78	1997	Juncos, P.R.
Garcia, Oscar	.106	16	47	3	5	1	0	0	0	5	15	0	2	.128	.222	R	R	5-9	160	11-3-80	1998	Colon, Panama
Haase, Jeff	.237	41	135	15	32	9	0	1	12	13	26	2	5	.326	.327	R	R	6-2	205	5-15-78	2000	Eastlake, Ohio
Inglett, Joe	.300	52	190	30	57	11	9	2	33	24	22	5	3	.505	.380	L	R	5-10	175	6-29-78	2000	Citrus Heights, Calif.
Janowicz, Nate	.294	51	201	29	59	10	5	2	26	9	38	4	1	.423	.324	L	L	5-10	183	5-16-78	2000	Atascadero, Calif.
Katz, Damon	.119	14	42	3	5	0	0	1	3	1	9	1	0	.190	.196	R	R	5-11	180	11-23-77	2000	Danville, Calif.
Luna, Hector	.266	66	241	36	64	8	3	3	23	23	48	15	4	.361	.333	R	R	6-1	170	2-1-82	1999	Montecristi, D.R.
Minges, Tyler	.373	15	59	9	22	5	0	1	7	3	12	2	0	.508	.431	R	R	6-0	185	11-15-79	1998	Hamilton, Ohio
Moreno, Jorge	.204	24	93	13	19	5	2	3	6	4	28	4	0	.398	.237	R	R	6-0	175	10-26-80	1998	Ciudad Ojeda, Venez.
Ochoa, Javier	.225	51	173	21	39	7	0	0	15	15	24	2	1	.266	.295	R	R	5-10	170	1-8-79	1996	Maracay, Venez.
Pichardo, Henry	.241	84	299	49	72	12	1	16	44	36	67	11	6	.448	.333	R	R	5-10	145	1-15-79	1996	Tamboril, D.R.
Requena, Alex	.255	33	137	22	35	6	0	2	13	9	40	15	7	.343	.306	B	R	5-11	155	8-13-80	1998	Maracay, Venez.
Sherrill, J.J.	.251	111	407	62	102	19	11	4	50	32	123	29	9	.383	.361	B	R	5-7	170	4-6-78	1999	Seaside, Calif.
Smith, Corey	.260	130	500	59	130	26	5	18	85	37	149	10	9	.440	.312	R	R	6-1	205	4-15-82	2000	Piscataway, N.J.
Swedlow, Sean	.200	106	401	30	80	18	2	4	35	28	146	1	2	.284	.259	L	R	6-3	220	5-25-82	2000	Glendora, Calif.

BATTING	AVG	G	AB	R	H	2B	3B	HR	RBI	BB	SO	SB	CS	SLG	OBP	B	T	HT	WT	DOB	1st Yr	Resides
Taveras, Willy	.271	97	395	55	107	15	7	3	32	22	73	29	9	.367	.317	R	R	6-0	160	12-25-81	1999	Tenares, D.R.
Wilson, Heath	.175	39	114	14	20	5	0	3	16	26	41	2	1	.298	.371	R	R	6-2	190	8-9-78	1996	Torquay, Australia

GAMES BY POSITION: C—Cruz 32, Haase 25, Ochoa 45, Wilson 39. **1B**—Becker 14, Crozier 20, Haase 10, Swedlow 96. **2B**—Baker 1, Becker 17, Choy Foo 12, Garcia 9, Haase 1, Inglett 57, Pichardo 48. **3B**—Becker 16, Garcia 3, Pichardo 4, Smith 114. **SS**—Baker 3, Becker 7, Colmenter 39, Katz 13, Luna 63, Pichardo 19. **OF**—Church 96, Crozier 34, Janowicz 43, Minges 15, Moreno 23, Pichardo 9, Requena 25, Sherrill 81, Taveras 91.

PITCHING	W	L	ERA	G	GS	CG	SV	IP	H	R	ER	BB	SO	AVG	B	T	HT	WT	DOB	1st Yr	Resides
Altman, Heath	1	0	15.75	3	0	0	0	4	6	7	7	5	6	.333	R	R	6-5	200	6-2-71	1993	Hamlet, N.C.
Alvarez, Oscar	5	9	4.17	17	17	0	0	95	94	54	44	37	69	.261	L	L	6-0	165	9-17-80	1997	Anzoategui, Venez.
Barr, Adam	0	0	12.91	6	0	0	0	8	9	14	11	11	6	.290	L	L	6-0	175	4-30-81	1999	South Williamsport, Pa.
Blethen, Matt	0	0	13.50	1	0	0	0	2	7	5	3	3	1	.538	L	L	6-3	210	2-23-80	2001	Havre de Grace, Md.
Cabrera, Fernando	5	6	3.61	20	20	0	0	95	89	49	38	37	96	.241	R	R	6-4	175	11-16-81	1999	Toa Baja, P.R.
Canale, Tom	3	1	3.14	8	0	0	0	14	18	9	5	2	7	.310	R	R	6-3	185	7-21-79	2000	Peoria, Ariz.
Christ, John	0	0	5.00	4	0	0	0	9	14	7	5	3	8	.350	L	R	6-2	215	9-10-77	1999	East Amherst, N.Y.
Colon, Jose	2	3	1.92	44	0	0	22	52	38	19	11	6	47	.191	R	R	6-0	175	7-24-77	1993	Puerto Plata, D.R.
Davis, Jason	14	6	2.70	27	27	1	0	160	147	72	48	51	115	.242	R	R	6-6	195	5-8-80	2000	Cleveland, Tenn.
De la Cruz, Carlos	2	1	4.30	6	0	0	0	29	29	17	14	13	31	.268	R	R	6-1	167	1-14-82	1999	Santo Domingo, D.R.
Donaghey, Steve	2	3	4.17	23	0	0	4	50	58	28	23	7	23	.290	R	R	6-6	235	7-17-78	1999	Woburn, Mass.
Fitch, Steve	0	1	1.00	4	4	0	0	27	23	7	3	3	16	.232	R	R	6-1	180	2-15-78	2000	West Chester, Pa.
Garza, Alberto	1	0	0.00	1	0	0	0	2	2	0	0	1	2	.250	R	R	6-3	195	5-25-77	1996	Wapato, Wash.
Kleine, Victor	0	0	3.86	1	1	0	0	7	5	5	3	0	9	.178	L	L	6-4	185	9-12-79	2000	Florence, Ky.
Larson, Ryan	5	1	0.51	31	0	0	4	53	30	5	3	7	60	.163	R	R	5-10	195	5-13-79	2000	Rocklin, Calif.
Matheny, Brandon	7	8	2.97	24	22	1	0	115	90	45	38	45	97	.214	L	L	6-3	205	10-22-78	2000	Damascus, Va.
Matsko, Rick	3	2	3.74	24	0	0	4	46	53	25	19	10	41	.288	R	R	6-2	210	4-26-77	1998	Johnstown, Pa.
Montano, Ignacio	1	1	3.06	11	0	0	1	18	16	8	6	6	17	.242	L	L	5-8	155	3-8-80	2001	Veracruz, Mexico
Neil, Dan	3	4	1.69	24	0	0	2	48	33	14	9	8	35	.189	L	L	6-0	185	8-8-78	1999	Bardonia, N.Y.
Percell, Brody	1	2	3.81	26	0	0	2	54	55	34	23	22	41	.269	L	L	6-2	200	8-29-75	1998	Portland, Ore.
Prahm, Ryan	7	2	2.41	11	11	0	0	60	53	18	16	12	47	.236	R	R	6-5	210	5-17-79	2000	Cedar Rapids, Iowa
Rogers, Devin	2	3	5.14	7	7	0	0	28	32	20	16	21	22	.285	R	R	6-6	215	8-4-78	1999	Harvey, La.
Skyles, Matt	0	0	2.90	11	1	0	2	31	30	13	10	8	23	.241	R	L	6-1	185	6-12-78	2000	Mansfield, Mo.
Suttles, Donnie	4	0	3.50	21	0	0	4	44	36	19	17	15	29	.230	R	R	6-2	185	1-8-77	1998	Marion, N.C.
Tetz, Kris	0	0	0.00	1	0	0	0	2	0	0	0	1	3	.000	R	R	6-5	245	9-3-78	1997	Lodi, Calif.
Thompson, Derek	0	2	9.75	2	2	0	0	12	16	13	13	3	5	.320	L	L	6-2	180	1-8-81	2000	Land O' Lakes, Fla.
Thoms, Hank	1	3	2.98	19	1	0	1	45	40	20	15	15	51	.231	R	R	6-4	210	6-7-76	1999	Newton, Miss.
Wade, Matt	4	2	3.36	10	10	0	0	59	61	23	22	16	33	.269	R	R	6-2	195	1-14-80	1998	Lilburn, Ga.
Young, Simon	0	0	3.89	8	7	0	0	39	48	18	17	13	35	.320	L	L	6-4	240	9-14-77	1999	Flowery Branch, Ga.

NEW YORK-PENN LEAGUE

BATTING	AVG	G	AB	R	H	2B	3B	HR	RBI	BB	SO	SB	CS	SLG	OBP	B	T	HT	WT	DOB	1st Yr	Resides
Alayon, Jean	.125	3	8	1	1	0	0	0	0	0	3	0	0	.125	.125	B	R	6-0	165	1-25-84	2000	Caracas, Venez.
Bard, Josh	.273	13	44	7	12	4	0	2	8	6	2	0	1	.500	.373	B	R	6-3	205	3-30-78	1999	Englewood, Colo.
Bastardo, Angel	.262	36	130	12	34	8	0	3	13	6	19	1	1	.392	.304	R	R	6-0	170	4-2-79	1997	Miraflores, Venez.
Colmenter, Jesus	.185	17	65	6	12	0	2	0	6	3	15	2	0	.246	.229	B	R	5-10	155	12-1-81	1998	Cabudare, Venez.
Edwards, Mike	.366	20	71	19	26	5	0	6	24	12	7	0	1	.690	.464	R	R	6-1	185	11-24-76	1995	Mechanicsburg, Pa.
Finnerty, Francis	.163	45	153	7	25	3	0	1	10	6	26	2	0	.203	.200	L	R	6-3	200	3-19-81	1999	West Palm Beach, Fla.
Gay, Curt	.141	29	92	8	13	3	0	1	5	11	31	0	3	.207	.233	L	L	6-6	225	9-12-77	1999	Enid, Okla.
Guglielmelli, Brad	.141	20	64	4	9	3	0	2	5	3	22	0	1	.281	.225	R	R	6-0	190	10-31-79	2001	San Luis Obispo, Calif.
Kirby, Brian	.202	37	124	12	25	11	1	2	14	19	45	1	1	.355	.308	L	R	6-2	190	8-3-79	2001	North Little Rock, Ark.
Lillash, Keith	.255	33	94	17	24	5	2	1	2	14	19	2	1	.383	.369	R	R	5-11	200	4-8-79	2001	Mentor, Ohio
Made, Maximo	.204	50	157	14	32	8	0	1	7	11	31	6	2	.274	.277	R	R	5-11	150	5-12-82	1999	San Cristobal, D.R.
Malave, Dennis	.195	40	128	19	25	3	1	0	8	21	23	4	8	.234	.316	L	L	5-9	165	1-6-80	1997	Caracas, Venez.
Morton, Rickie	.282	69	238	34	67	15	3	12	40	37	55	3	3	.521	.378	R	R	6-0	200	9-15-78	2001	Citrus Heights, Calif.
Munoz, Billy	.302	12	43	3	13	3	1	0	8	3	6	0	0	.419	.348	L	L	6-2	220	6-30-75	1998	Mesa, Ariz.
Myers, Kenton	.215	24	79	9	17	0	0	6	7	19	0	2	.215	.287	R	R	6-1	200	4-14-80	2001	Albuquerque, N.M.
Peshke, Chad	.250	52	168	23	42	10	1	2	14	19	21	2	5	.357	.337	R	R	5-9	185	9-10-79	2001	Redondo Beach, Calif.
Quintana, Miguel	.222	69	279	29	62	17	4	5	33	13	65	6	3	.366	.266	L	R	6-1	195	6-29-79	2001	Miami, Fla.
Santini, Travis	.214	34	117	9	25	9	0	3	13	1	30	0	1	.368	.220	R	R	5-11	175	11-23-80	1999	Naples, Fla.
Scott, Charles	.133	6	15	0	2	0	0	0	1	1	3	0	0	.133	.176	R	R	5-11	198	11-28-77	2000	Lynchburg, Va.
Small, Chris	.500	2	2	0	1	0	0	0	0	1	1	0	0	.500	.667	R	R	6-0	210	1-27-78	2000	Alpharetta, Ga.
Sorensen, Zach	.245	14	53	10	13	0	1	1	11	2	8	2	0	.340	.263	B	R	6-0	190	1-3-77	1998	Mesquite, Nev.
Thompson, Eric	.212	26	66	5	14	0	0	3	8	3	28	2	2	.212	.246	L	L	6-0	170	5-1-79	1997	Fayetteville, N.C.
Uegawachi, Bryce	.204	55	162	14	33	0	1	0	5	28	32	4	5	.216	.325	B	R	5-6	150	4-28-79	2001	Honolulu, Hawaii
Van Every, Jon	.252	41	135	30	34	4	2	6	17	28	50	1	2	.444	.406	L	L	6-3	205	11-27-79	2001	Brandon, Miss.

GAMES BY POSITION: C—Bard 3, Bastardo 33, Guglielmelli 18, Kirby 1, Myers 22, Scott 4, Small 2. **1B**—Finnerty 5, Gay 21, Morton 47, Munoz 7. **2B**—Colmenter 6, Lillash 32, Made 46, Peshke 8. **3B**—Edwards 11, Finnerty 34, Lillash 1, Peshke 34, Scott 1. **SS**—Alayon 3, Colmenter 11, Lillash 3, Made 2, Peshke 1, Sorensen 8, Uegawachi 55. **OF**—Kirby 36, Malave 40, Peshke 4, Quintana 69, Santini 32, Thompson 25, Van Every 38.

PITCHING	W	L	ERA	G	GS	CG	SV	IP	H	R	ER	BB	SO	AVG	B	T	HT	WT	DOB	1st Yr	Resides
Colvard, Ron	0	1	8.31	17	0	0	0	22	26	25	20	17	16	.288	R	R	6-4	205	11-27-77	2000	Lincolnton, N.C.
Cooper, Chris	0	5	2.38	25	0	0	11	34	34	24	9	10	40	.248	L	L	5-11	190	10-31-78	2001	Sewickley, Pa.
Culp, Todd	2	2	3.63	22	0	0	2	45	36	21	18	21	60	.219	R	R	6-4	215	8-7-78	2001	Sacramento, Calif.
Curtin, Brian	1	3	3.82	21	0	0	2	31	36	14	13	16	26	.302	R	R	6-6	235	1-9-78	2000	Lansing, Iowa
Farman, Brian	0	2	2.81	10	0	0	1	16	16	5	5	2	12	.258	R	R	6-3	210	10-9-78	2001	Bremerton, Wash.
Fernley, Nate	0	2	4.42	13	0	0	0	18	30	18	9	8	21	.352	R	R	6-3	160	1-13-77	2001	Orem, Utah
Field, Luke	4	5	3.89	14	14	0	0	69	80	48	30	25	53	.289	R	R	5-11	178	1-27-79	2000	Tempe, Ariz.
Gomez, Mariano	1	0	5.40	1	1	0	0	5	5	3	3	2	6	.263	L	L	6-6	170	9-12-82	1998	San Pedro Sula, Honduras
Kleine, Victor	1	8	5.25	14	14	0	0	70	88	42	41	25	50	.307	L	L	6-4	185	9-12-79	2000	Florence, Ky.
Lantz, Doug	4	6	3.44	11	11	0	0	55	65	28	21	11	33	.302	R	R	6-3	185	8-26-79	2001	Southlake, Texas
Mackintosh, Jason	1	1	7.43	6	1	0	0	13	20	13	11	2	14	.333	R	L	6-0	205	7-2-80	2001	South Weber, Utah
Martin, Kevin	0	2	5.35	19	1	0	1	39	39	27	23	18	25	.253	R	R	6-2	185	1-3-79	2001	Las Vegas, Nev.
Martinez, Paul	0	0	4.50	2	0	0	0	4	5	2	2	4	6	.312	L	L	5-10	155	9-28-81	1999	Navarrete, D.R.
Mendoza, Marcos	4	3	3.51	11	11	0	0	49	40	23	19	28	39	.231	L	L	5-10	180	10-31-80	2001	Santee, Calif.

PITCHING	W	L	ERA	G	GS	CG	SV	IP	H	R	ER	BB	SO	AVG	B	T	HT	WT	DOB	1st Yr	Resides
Moran, Nick	5	2	3.40	15	15	0	0	79	82	36	30	13	66	.260	R	R	6-5	195	1-3-80	2001	Elk Grove, Calif.
Pennington, Todd	0	2	3.52	13	0	0	0	31	27	12	12	18	32	.238	R	R	6-2	214	4-6-80	2001	McClure, Ill.
Rogers, Devin	0	1	5.91	3	3	0	0	11	10	8	7	10	7	.263	R	R	6-6	215	8-4-78	1999	Harvey, La.
Sturkie, Scott	2	1	6.00	18	4	0	1	39	53	27	26	12	28	.327	R	R	6-3	210	6-12-79	2001	West Columbia, S.C.
Turnbow, Mark	1	3	3.77	21	0	0	0	31	30	15	13	8	34	.245	R	R	6-3	205	11-26-78	1997	Saltillo, Tenn.

BURLINGTON · Rookie

APPALACHIAN LEAGUE

BATTING	AVG	G	AB	R	H	2B	3B	HR	RBI	BB	SO	SB	CS	SLG	OBP	B	T	HT	WT	DOB	1st Yr	Resides
Baxter, Andy	.244	63	209	41	51	16	4	11	46	35	60	3	1	.517	.370	L	R	6-4	210	4-8-79	2001	Erwin, Tenn.
Camacaro, Armando	.205	40	122	11	25	3	0	1	8	12	27	3	4	.254	.312	R	R	5-11	170	10-5-80	1998	Guarenas, Venez.
Choy Foo, Rodney	.333	7	24	2	8	2	0	1	3	1	5	0	2	.542	.360	B	R	6-1	185	12-12-81	2000	Waimanalo, Hawaii
Conroy, Mike	.244	43	156	19	38	7	1	2	23	13	49	5	5	.340	.302	L	L	6-3	190	10-3-82	2001	Scituate, Mass.
Eldridge, Rashad	.258	61	229	39	59	8	6	5	27	27	65	3	2	.410	.341	B	R	6-1	185	10-16-81	2000	Macon, Ga.
Esprit, Jermaine	.241	35	112	13	27	1	0	0	2	4	29	8	4	.250	.280	B	R	6-0	165	11-10-79	1998	Willemstad, Curacao
Folsom, Mark	.210	29	100	15	21	7	1	2	23	17	41	0	1	.360	.325	R	R	6-5	215	6-7-81	2000	Winter Garden, Fla.
Garcia, Rafaelito	.256	51	195	28	50	6	1	1	12	20	37	12	5	.313	.329	B	R	6-2	165	1-7-82	2000	Santo Domingo, D.R.
Kirby, Brian	.190	25	84	14	16	3	1	4	14	15	31	1	1	.393	.340	L	R	6-2	190	8-3-79	2001	North Little Rock, Ark.
Knox, Matt	.207	62	222	26	46	11	1	2	33	20	46	1	1	.293	.276	R	R	6-4	215	12-29-79	2001	Lebanon, Pa.
Nixon, Jason	.154	9	26	2	4	1	0	1	3	2	13	0	0	.308	.241	R	R	6-2	225	11-24-81	2000	Coeburn, Va.
Noviskey, Josh	.140	38	114	16	16	2	0	0	4	23	50	1	1	.158	.290	B	R	6-4	215	3-15-83	2001	Newton, N.J.
Ochoa, Ivan	.216	51	176	30	38	2	0	0	14	24	57	14	5	.227	.346	R	R	5-10	140	12-16-82	2000	Guacara, Venez.
Santana, Hector	.194	29	103	7	20	3	2	2	8	7	45	0	1	.320	.245	R	R	6-0	165	7-13-82	2000	San Pedro de Macoris, D.R.
Scott, Charles	.212	11	33	5	7	0	0	3	6	4	12	0	1	.485	.297	R	R	5-11	198	11-28-77	2000	Lynchburg, Va.
Tavarez, Ydel	.194	13	36	5	7	1	0	0	2	2	20	1	0	.222	.237	R	R	6-1	185	4-9-81	2001	New York, N.Y.
Threinen, Scott	.200	37	110	19	22	2	1	1	12	25	34	6	3	.264	.360	L	R	6-0	195	8-23-81	2001	Mantorville, Minn.
Tillman, Kevin	.238	40	126	22	30	6	0	6	23	17	39	3	0	.429	.333	L	R	5-10	190	1-24-78	2001	San Jose, Calif.

GAMES BY POSITION: C—Camacaro 39, Kirby 1, Santana 29, Scott 2. **1B**—Baxter 62, Knox 5, Noviskey 1, Scott 3. **2B**—Choy Foo 4, Garcia 18, Ochoa 13, Tavarez 1, Threinen 9, Tillman 30. **3B**—Baxter 1, Knox 57, Tavarez 1, Threinen 11. **SS**—Garcia 32, Knox 1, Ochoa 38. **OF**—Conroy 40, Eldridge 58, Esprit 31, Folsom 27, Kirby 14, Nixon 9, Noviskey 26, Ochoa 1, Tavarez 1, Threinen 8.

PITCHING	W	L	ERA	G	GS	CG	SV	IP	H	R	ER	BB	SO	AVG	B	T	HT	WT	DOB	1st Yr	Resides
Alvarado, Luis	1	0	4.60	16	0	0	0	31	34	18	16	12	31	.272	L	L	5-11	165	9-11-82	2001	Bayamon, P.R.
Aquino, Danny	1	0	8.22	6	0	0	0	8	8	7	7	4	3	.250	R	R	6-2	165	1-20-82	1999	San Juan, D.R.
Barr, Adam	2	0	3.91	8	3	0	0	23	17	15	10	25	29	.204	L	L	6-6	170	4-30-81	1999	South Williamsport, Pa.
Blethen, Matt	4	1	2.76	18	0	0	1	49	42	17	15	15	42	.229	L	L	6-3	210	2-23-80	2001	Havre de Grace, Md.
Chourio, Jorge	0	1	23.63	3	0	0	0	3	8	7	7	1	1	.533	R	R	6-0	150	10-30-82	2000	Maracaibo, Venez.
Cislak, Chad	0	1	27.00	1	0	0	0	0	4	1	4	0	.000	R	R	6-2	197	3-29-79	2000	Tucson, Ariz.
D'Frank, Carlos	0	0	3.86	5	0	0	0	7	5	3	3	1	6	.200	R	R	6-1	175	1-2-83	1999	Santo Domingo, D.R.
De la Cruz, Carlos	1	1	2.83	6	4	0	0	29	17	11	9	12	33	.166	R	R	6-2	195	12-24-82	2001	Santo Domingo, D.R.
Denham, Dan	0	4	4.40	8	8	0	0	31	30	21	15	26	31	.256	R	R	6-2	195	12-24-82	2001	Stateline, Nev.
Dittler, Jake	1	2	3.68	6	5	0	0	22	25	14	9	12	20	.287	R	R	6-4	220	11-24-82	2001	Henderson, Nev.
Foley, Travis	2	3	2.80	10	10	0	0	45	26	16	14	15	59	.171	R	R	6-1	180	3-11-83	2001	Louisville, Ky.
Gomez, Mariano	2	8	6.07	13	12	0	0	59	69	47	40	21	57	.288	L	L	6-6	170	9-12-82	1999	San Pedro Sula, Honduras
Gronkiewicz, Lee	3	3	2.56	25	0	0	10	32	18	11	9	8	47	.160	R	R	5-11	183	8-21-78	2001	Lancaster, S.C.
Martin, J.D.	5	1	1.38	10	10	0	0	46	26	9	7	11	72	.163	R	R	6-4	170	1-2-83	2001	Las Vegas, Nev.
Martinez, Paul	2	2	6.43	19	0	0	0	35	39	29	25	26	40	.280	L	L	5-10	155	9-28-81	1999	Navarrete, D.R.
Prahm, Ryan	0	0	10.38	1	1	0	0	4	8	5	5	1	4	.380	R	R	6-5	210	5-17-79	2000	Cedar Rapids, Iowa
Romero, Luis	2	3	3.82	16	0	0	3	33	37	25	14	16	24	.291	R	R	6-0	165	5-18-81	1999	Mariara, Venez.
Skyles, Matt	0	2	4.00	6	3	0	0	27	35	17	12	4	15	.315	R	L	6-1	185	6-12-78	2000	Mansfield, Mo.
Spaulding, Richard	0	0	7.02	14	0	0	0	17	19	16	13	15	9	.287	L	L	6-3	160	10-27-80	2001	Lexington, Ky.
Thomas, Scott	0	0	6.52	9	0	0	0	10	7	8	7	12	10	.189	R	R	6-5	195	3-5-80	2001	Benton Harbor, Mich.
Valdez, Fernando	1	0	1.80	7	0	0	1	15	12	6	3	2	20	.200	R	R	6-2	175	12-26-79	1996	Santo Domingo, D.R.
Warden, Jim Ed	4	5	4.27	12	12	0	0	53	56	32	25	13	52	.265	R	R	6-7	195	5-7-79	2001	Murfreesboro, Tenn.

BY BARNEY HUTCHINSON

The Rockies opened the 2001 season with great optimism. But it ended in bitter disappointment, considering how they opened their checkbooks in the offseason to make the most significant additions to the pitching staff in their history.

Colorado landed Mike Hampton and Denny Neagle for the top of their rotation, and baseball observers envisioned the National League West as a four-team race.

Hopes soared in spring training, and Hampton delivered on Opening Day with eight shutout innings as the Rockies blanked the Cardinals.

But Colorado had a disturbingly thin team. When Todd Hollandsworth went down with a season-ending shin injury in mid-May and Mark Little landed on the disabled list twice, it uncovered a lack of depth in the outfield. Righthander Pedro Astacio had a good April but threw inconsistently after that, and lefthander Ron Villone was not the answer as the No. 5 starter.

The Rockies were a decent 36-32 on June 17—5½ games out—when the season fell apart.

For the next 45 games, Colorado went 10-35 and sank to the bottom of the division. Hampton and Neagle made 18 starts between them in that stretch, and the Rockies went 4-14 in those games.

"It's been a really disappointing, frustrating season," Neagle said. "I have 17 decisions and 14 or 15 no-decisions (actually 13), and in those 14 or 15 no-decisions, I think I was leading in about nine or 10 of them. That's baseball and you have to deal with that sometimes. It's been tough, but it's been a good learning experience for me.

"I've always been one that says you're always learning in this game, always trying to figure out ways to improve yourself. As soon as you think you've got this game made, the old humble bee will come up and sting you on your butt pretty hard."

Consider the Rockies and general manager Dan

Todd Helton

Ryan Kibler

PLAYERS OF THE YEAR

MAJOR LEAGUE: Todd Helton, 1b

He became the first player in history with at least 100 extra-base hits in consecutive seasons. He hit .336 with 54 doubles and 49 home runs, along with 132 runs and 146 RBIs.

MINOR LEAGUE: Ryan Kibler, rhp

He started 2001 at low Class A Asheville, going 3-5, 2.93, and got better as he advanced to high Class A Salem (7-0, 1.55) and Double-A Carolina (4-1, 2.11).

O'Dowd stung. O'Dowd undertook his third roster makeover in a 22-month period in July and August, dissatisfied with the club's progress and willing to wheel and deal. He traded Villone and Astacio, catcher Brent Mayne, second baseman Todd Walker, shortstop Neifi Perez and outfielder Ron Gant in major deals that affected half the starting lineup and pitching staff.

In return, the Rockies found themselves with defensively sound Alex Ochoa plugging the Hollandsworth void in the outfield, rookie Juan Uribe at shortstop, Oakland prospect Jose Ortiz at second, Jay Powell in the bullpen and Scott Elarton on the mend before he got on the mound.

After the dust cleared on the trade front, the Rockies settled in and played marginally better, finishing at 73-89. It was the team's third losing season in four years.

The minor league system started out slowly as well, but steadily improved. Three of the organization's four lowest-level farm teams made the playoffs, the most in Rockies history.

Class A Salem produced the lone champion of the three, winning the Carolina League title. Rookie-level Casper was eliminated in the Pioneer League playoffs and Asheville was declared the runner-up when the Class A South Atlantic League playoffs were halted in mid-September by the terrorist attack.

Asheville's Rene Reyes won the Sally League batting title (.322) and was named MVP. The Rockies selected righthander Ryan Kibler and first baseman Garrett Atkins as their minor league pitcher and player of the year. Kibler went a combined 11-1 at Double-A Carolina and Salem. Atkins hit .325-5-67 in 465 at-bats at Salem.

"The bottom line is, you want all the players to continue to get better on a daily basis," minor league director Michael Hill said. "At the beginning things were not clicking like we wanted, but in the second half guys understood the process better and played better."

ORGANIZATION LEADERS

BATTING

*AVG	Brent Butler, Colorado Springs	.335
R	Brad Hawpe, Asheville	78
H	Rene Reyes, Asheville	156
TB	Butch Huskey, Colorado Springs	236
2B	Garrett Atkins, Salem	43
3B	Three tied at	7
HR	Brad Hawpe, Asheville	22
RBI	Butch Huskey, Colorado Springs	87
BB	Garrett Atkins, Salem	74
SO	Justin Lincoln, Salem/Asheville	160
SB	Rene Reyes, Asheville	53

PITCHING

W	Ryan Kibler, Carolina/Salem/Asheville	14
L	Robert Averette, Colorado Springs	14
#ERA	Ryan Kibler, Carolina/Salem/Asheville	2.15
G	Justin Huisman, Asheville	55
CG	Jason Jennings, Colorado Springs/Carolina	4
SV	Justin Huisman, Asheville	30
IP	Ryan Kibler, Carolina/Salem/Asheville	184
BB	Ryan Price, Salem	85
SO	Ryan Kibler, Carolina/Salem/Asheville	161

*Minimum 250 At-Bats #Minimum 75 Innings

COLORADO ROCKIES

Manager: Buddy Bell

2001 Record: 73-89, .451 (5th, NL West)

BATTING	AVG	G	AB	R	H	2B	3B	HR	RBI	BB	SO	SB	CS	SLG	OBP	B	T	HT	WT	DOB	1st Yr	Resides
Bartee, Kimera	.000	12	15	0	0	0	0	0	1	2	5	0	0	.000	.158	B	R	6-0	200	7-21-72	1993	Peoria, Ariz.
Bennett, Gary	.273	19	55	7	15	3	0	1	4	3	5	0	0	.382	.317	R	R	6-0	208	4-17-72	1990	Waukegan, Ill.
3-team (26 Phil./1 N.Y.)	.244	46	131	15	32	6	1	2	10	12	24	0	0	.351	.308							
Brumbaugh, Cliff	.278	14	36	5	10	2	0	1	4	2	9	0	1	.417	.316	R	R	6-2	205	4-21-74	1995	New Castle, Del.
Butler, Brent	.244	53	119	17	29	7	1	1	14	7	7	1	1	.345	.287	R	R	6-0	180	2-11-78	1996	Laurinburg, N.C.
Cirillo, Jeff	.313	138	528	72	165	26	4	17	83	43	63	12	2	.473	.364	R	R	6-1	195	9-23-69	1991	Redmond, Wash.
Cruz, Jacob	.211	44	76	7	16	1	0	1	7	10	27	0	2	.263	.303	L	L	6-0	179	1-28-73	1994	Tempe, Ariz.
Encarnacion, Mario	.226	20	62	3	14	1	0	0	3	5	14	2	1	.242	.284	R	R	6-2	210	9-24-77	1994	Bani, D.R.
Fasano, Sal	.254	25	63	10	16	5	0	3	9	4	19	0	0	.476	.329	R	R	6-2	230	8-10-71	1993	Overland Park, Kan.
Gant, Ron	.257	59	171	31	44	8	2	8	22	24	56	3	1	.468	.345	R	R	6-0	196	3-2-65	1983	Alpharetta, Ga.
Hampton, Mike	.291	43	79	20	23	2	0	7	16	2	21	0	1	.582	.309	R	L	5-10	180	9-9-72	1990	Houston, Texas
Helton, Todd	.336	159	587	132	197	54	2	49	146	98	104	7	5	.685	.432	L	L	6-2	206	8-20-73	1995	Knoxville, Tenn.
Hollandsworth, Todd	.368	33	117	21	43	15	1	6	19	8	20	5	0	.667	.408	L	L	6-2	215	4-20-73	1991	Pleasanton, Calif.
Jennings, Robin	.000	1	3	0	0	0	0	0	0	0	1	0	0	.000	.000	L	L	6-2	210	4-11-72	1992	Park City, Utah
Kieschnick, Brooks	.238	35	42	5	10	2	1	3	9	3	13	0	0	.548	.289	L	R	6-4	228	6-6-72	1993	Caldwell, Texas
Little, Mark	.341	51	85	18	29	6	0	3	13	1	20	5	2	.518	.378	R	R	6-0	195	7-11-72	1994	Edwardsville, Ill.
Mayne, Brent	.331	49	160	15	53	7	0	0	20	16	24	0	0	.375	.385	L	R	6-1	192	4-19-68	1989	Corona Del Mar, Calif.
Melhuse, Adam	.183	40	71	5	13	2	0	1	8	6	18	1	0	.254	.241	B	R	6-2	185	3-27-72	1993	Stockton, Calif.
Norton, Greg	.267	117	225	30	60	13	2	13	40	19	65	1	0	.516	.321	B	R	6-1	205	7-6-72	1993	Norman, Okla.
Ochoa, Alex	.251	58	187	25	47	10	3	1	17	21	23	5	4	.353	.330	R	R	6-0	180	3-29-72	1991	Pembroke Pines, Fla.
2-team (90 Cinc.)	.276	148	536	73	148	30	7	8	52	45	76	17	13	.403	.334							
Ortiz, Jose	.255	53	204	38	52	8	1	13	35	14	36	3	1	.495	.314	R	R	5-10	182	6-13-77	1995	Santo Domingo, D.R.
Perez, Neifi	.298	87	382	65	114	19	8	7	47	16	49	6	2	.445	.326	B	R	6-0	175	6-2-75	1993	Villa Mella, D.R.
Petrick, Ben	.238	85	244	41	58	15	3	11	39	31	67	3	3	.459	.327	R	R	6-0	205	4-7-77	1996	Hillsboro, Ore.
Pierre, Juan	.327	156	617	108	202	26	11	2	55	41	29	46	17	.415	.378	L	L	6-0	170	8-14-77	1998	Alexandria, La.
Sefcik, Kevin	.000	1	1	0	0	0	0	0	0	0	0	0	0	.000	.000	R	R	5-10	182	2-10-71	1993	Orland Park, Ill.
Shumpert, Terry	.289	114	242	37	70	14	5	4	24	15	44	14	3	.438	.337	R	R	6-0	200	8-16-66	1987	Lees Summit, Mo.
Uribe, Juan	.300	72	273	32	82	15	11	8	53	8	55	3	0	.524	.325	R	R	5-11	173	7-22-79	1997	San Cristobal, D.R.
Walker, Larry	.350	142	497	107	174	35	3	38	123	82	103	14	5	.662	.449	L	R	6-3	237	12-1-66	1985	Evergreen, Colo.
Walker, Todd	.297	85	290	52	86	18	2	12	43	25	40	1	3	.497	.349	L	R	6-0	181	5-25-73	1994	Bossier City, La.

PITCHING	W	L	ERA	G	GS	CG	SV	IP	H	R	ER	BB	SO	AVG	B	T	HT	WT	DOB	1st Yr	Resides
Acevedo, Juan	0	2	5.63	39	0	0	0	32	37	24	20	19	26	.284	R	R	6-2	228	5-5-70	1992	Algonquin, Ill.
Astacio, Pedro	6	13	5.49	22	22	4	0	141	151	91	86	50	125	.275	R	R	6-2	210	11-28-69	1988	Hato Mayor, D.R.
Belitz, Todd	1	1	7.71	8	0	0	0	9	9	8	8	3	5	.250	L	L	6-3	200	10-23-75	1997	Spokane, Wash.
Bohanon, Brian	5	8	7.14	20	19	0	0	97	127	79	77	47	47	.323	L	L	6-2	240	8-1-68	1987	Houston, Texas
Chacon, Shawn	6	10	5.06	27	27	0	0	160	157	96	90	87	134	.259	R	R	6-3	212	12-23-77	1996	Greeley, Colo.
Chouinard, Bobby	0	0	8.22	8	0	0	0	8	10	7	7	1	5	.303	R	R	6-1	188	5-1-72	1990	Forest Grove, Ore.
Christman, Tim	0	0	4.50	1	0	0	0	2	1	1	1	0	2	.142	L	L	6-0	195	3-31-75	1996	Oneonta, N.Y.
Davenport, Joe	0	0	3.48	7	0	0	0	10	8	7	4	7	8	.222	R	R	6-5	225	3-24-76	1994	Santee, Calif.
Davis, Kane	2	4	4.35	57	0	0	0	68	66	36	33	32	47	.251	R	R	6-3	194	6-25-75	1993	Reedy, W.Va.
Dingman, Craig	0	0	13.50	7	0	0	1	7	11	11	11	3	2	.354	R	R	6-4	215	3-12-74	1994	Wichita, Kan.
Elarton, Scott	0	2	6.65	4	4	0	0	23	20	17	17	10	11	.232	R	R	6-7	240	2-23-76	1994	Lamar, Colo.
2-team (20 Houston)	4	10	7.06	24	24	0	0	133	146	105	104	59	87	.280							
Estrada, Horacio	1	1	14.54	4	0	0	0	4	8	7	7	1	4	.400	L	L	6-0	160	10-19-75	1992	San Joaquin, Venez.
Hampton, Mike	14	13	5.41	32	32	2	0	203	236	138	122	85	122	.296	R	L	5-10	180	9-9-72	1990	Houston, Texas
Jennings, Jason	4	1	4.58	7	7	1	0	39	42	21	20	19	26	.276	L	R	6-2	230	7-17-78	1999	Mesquite, Texas
Jimenez, Jose	6	1	4.09	56	0	0	17	55	56	27	25	22	37	.264	R	R	6-3	190	7-7-73	1992	Boca Chica, D.R.
Miceli, Danny	2	0	2.21	22	0	0	1	20	18	8	5	5	17	.230	R	R	6-0	216	9-9-70	1990	Winter Springs, Fla.
2-team (29 Florida)	2	5	4.80	51	0	0	1	45	47	29	24	16	48	.262							
Myers, Mike	2	3	3.60	73	0	0	0	40	32	17	16	24	36	.225	L	L	6-4	214	6-26-69	1990	Port St. Lucie, Fla.
Neagle, Denny	9	8	5.38	30	30	0	0	171	192	107	102	60	139	.284	L	L	6-3	225	9-13-68	1989	Morrison, Colo.
Nichting, Chris	0	0	4.50	7	0	0	0	6	9	3	3	0	7	.346	R	R	6-1	205	5-13-66	1988	Cincinnati, Ohio
2-team (36 Cincinnati)	0	3	3.46	43	0	0	1	42	55	27	21	8	40	.312							
Powell, Jay	3	1	2.79	39	0	0	7	39	34	18	12	12	26	.244	R	R	6-4	225	1-9-72	1993	Madison, Miss.
2-team (35 Houston)	5	3	3.24	74	0	0	7	75	75	36	27	31	54	.260							
Speier, Justin	4	3	3.70	42	0	0	0	56	47	24	23	12	47	.229	R	R	6-4	205	11-6-73	1995	Paradise Valley, Ariz.
Suzuki, Mac	0	2	15.63	3	1	0	0	6	9	12	11	11	5	.333	R	R	6-3	205	5-31-75	1992	Kobe, Japan
Thomson, John	4	5	4.04	14	14	1	0	94	84	46	42	25	68	.239	R	R	6-3	187	10-1-73	1993	Sulphur, La.
Villone, Ron	1	3	6.36	22	6	0	0	47	56	35	33	29	48	.294	L	L	6-3	237	1-16-70	1992	River Vale, N.J.
Wasdin, John	2	1	7.03	18	0	0	0	24	32	19	19	8	17	.320	R	R	6-2	195	8-5-72	1993	Jacksonville, Fla.
White, Gabe	1	7	6.25	69	0	0	0	68	70	47	47	26	47	.270	L	L	6-2	200	11-20-71	1990	Sebring, Fla.

FIELDING

Catcher	PCT	G	PO	A	E	DP	PB
Bennett	1.000	19	96	4	0	1	0
Fasano	.982	25	153	14	3	5	0
Mayne	.997	44	317	19	1	4	1
Melhuse	.991	23	104	4	1	0	2
Petrick	.984	77	456	29	8	8	11

First Base	PCT	G	PO	A	E	DP
Helton	.999	157	1303	119	2	139

	PCT	G	PO	A	E	DP
Kieschnick	1.000	1	1	0	0	0
Mayne	.000	1	0	0	0	0
Melhuse	1.000	1	1	0	0	0
Norton	1.000	13	66	4	0	6
Petrick	1.000	2	3	0	0	1

Second Base	PCT	G	PO	A	E	DP
Butler	.959	23	44	49	4	14
Ortiz	.965	51	86	137	8	30

	PCT	G	PO	A	E	DP
Shumpert	.968	41	51	71	4	20
T. Walker	.981	77	155	198	7	49

Third Base	PCT	G	PO	A	E	DP
Butler	1.000	9	4	6	0	1
Cirillo	.982	137	78	308	7	25
Norton	.895	24	8	26	4	2
Shumpert	.870	12	2	18	3	1

Mike Hampton: Won 14 games and batted .291-7-16

Jason Jennings: Pitched four complete games in Triple-A

Shortstop	PCT	G	PO	A	E	DP
Butler	.947	10	5	13	1	3
Perez	.976	87	145	264	10	64
Shumpert	1.000	4	5	1	0	1
Uribe	.983	69	108	184	5	45

Outfield	PCT	G	PO	A	E	DP
Bartee	.889	10	8	0	1	0

Brumbaugh	1.000	11	15	0	0	0
Cruz	.931	24	26	1	2	0
Encarnacion	1.000	20	35	1	0	2
Gant	.965	51	81	2	3	0
Hollandsworth	.981	31	51	2	1	0
R. Jennings	.000	1	0	0	1	0
Kieschnick	.818	12	9	0	2	0

Little	1.000	29	36	3	0	3
Norton	1.000	25	16	1	0	0
Ochoa	.990	52	90	6	1	3
Pierre	.979	154	362	3	8	1
Shumpert	.976	24	38	2	1	0
L. Walker	.984	129	243	8	4	4

FARM SYSTEM

Director, Player Development: Michael Hill

Class	Farm Team	League	W	L	Pct.	Finish*	Manager	First Yr.
AAA	Colo. Springs (Colo.) Sky Sox	Pacific Coast	62	79	.440	14th (16)	Chris Cron	1993
AA	Carolina (Zebulon, N.C.) Mudcats	Southern	62	76	.449	7th (10)	Ron Gideon	1999
A#	Salem (Va.) Avalanche	Carolina	70	68	.507	+4th (8)	Dave Collins	1995
A	Asheville (N.C.) Tourists	South Atlantic	68	71	.489	9th (16)	Joe Mikulik	1994
A	Tri-City (Wash.) Dust Devils	Northwest	39	36	.520	3rd (8)	Stu Cole	2001
Rookie#	Casper (Wyo.) Rockies	Pioneer	37	39	.487	t-4th (10)	P.J. Carey	2001

*Finish in overall standings (No. of teams in league)   #Advanced level   +League champion

COLORADO SPRINGS   Class AAA

PACIFIC COAST LEAGUE

BATTING	AVG	G	AB	R	H	2B	3B	HR	RBI	BB	SO	SB	CS	SLG	OBP	B	T	HT	WT	DOB	1st Yr	Resides
Alviso, Jerome	.241	111	266	30	64	12	0	1	18	14	43	3	1	.297	.286	B	R	6-1	180	9-4-75	1997	Livermore, Calif.
Bartee, Kimera	.192	24	78	14	15	2	0	5	15	6	31	3	4	.410	.256	B	R	6-0	200	7-21-72	1993	Peoria, Ariz.
2-team (40 Salt Lake)	.249	64	245	37	61	15	2	8	42	25	57	8	1	.424	.319							
Bell, Mike	.281	84	320	43	90	21	1	13	53	16	80	0	4	.475	.322	R	R	6-2	195	12-7-74	1993	Cincinnati, Ohio
Brumbaugh, Cliff	.332	53	208	31	69	18	1	3	39	34	52	5	3	.471	.419	R	R	6-2	205	4-21-74	1995	New Castle, Del.
2-team (54 Okla.)	.320	107	410	69	131	29	4	11	81	67	93	8	6	.490	.412							
Bullett, Scott	.256	21	78	7	20	4	1	2	11	0	17	1	0	.410	.253	L	L	6-2	225	12-25-68	1988	Welland, Ontario
Butler, Brent	.335	65	272	51	91	20	3	7	38	15	26	4	2	.507	.375	R	R	6-0	180	2-11-78	1996	Laurinburg, N.C.
Carpenter, Bubba	.264	49	125	22	33	14	0	2	10	18	23	3	2	.424	.370	L	L	6-1	185	7-23-68	1991	Springdale, Ark.
Cirillo, Jeff	.750	1	4	2	3	1	0	0	3	1	0	0	0	1.000	.800	R	R	6-1	195	9-23-69	1991	Redmond, Wash.
Cox, Darron	.278	76	209	33	58	10	1	3	25	24	42	3	1	.378	.364	R	R	6-1	205	11-21-67	1989	Mustang, Okla.
Cruz, Jacob	.326	20	86	18	28	5	2	6	25	1	23	1	0	.640	.337	L	L	6-0	179	1-28-73	1994	Tempe, Ariz.
Encarnacion, Mario	.378	16	45	8	17	5	0	2	10	4	8	0	1	.622	.440	R	R	6-2	210	9-24-77	1994	Bani, D.R.
2-team (51 Sacra.)	.303	67	231	37	70	13	2	14	43	21	69	4	4	.558	.372							
Espada, Joe	.259	7	27	8	7	2	0	1	2	5	6	3	2	.444	.375	R	R	5-10	175	8-30-75	1996	Carolina, P.R.
2-team (79 Calgary)	.297	86	317	69	94	22	2	4	32	44	55	16	9	.416	.386							
Fasano, Sal	.305	26	82	16	25	4	0	7	23	9	26	0	0	.610	.396	R	R	6-2	230	8-10-71	1993	Overland Park, Kan.
2-team (13 Omaha)	.281	39	128	22	36	5	0	9	30	13	37	0	0	.531	.384							
Flores, Jose	.294	100	316	61	93	21	5	2	36	48	57	8	2	.411	.391	R	R	5-11	180	6-28-73	1994	Corpus Christi, Texas
Hamilton, Darryl	.154	4	13	0	2	0	0	0	0	2	2	0	0	.154	.267	L	R	6-1	180	12-3-64	1986	Houston, Texas

BATTING	AVG	G	AB	R	H	2B	3B	HR	RBI	BB	SO	SB	CS	SLG	OBP	B	T	HT	WT	DOB	1st Yr	Resides
Huskey, Butch	.323	122	458	76	148	29	1	19	87	42	95	2	2	.515	.372	R	R	6-3	244	11-10-71	1989	Lawton, Okla.
Jennings, Robin	.282	11	39	8	11	1	0	2	5	1	10	1	0	.462	.317	L	L	6-2	210	4-11-72	1992	Park City, Utah
2-team (38 Sacra.)	.301	49	183	34	55	12	3	7	31	10	36	6	2	.514	.345							
Johnson, Lance	.341	35	135	26	46	8	2	2	16	4	14	9	4	.474	.355	L	L	5-11	165	7-6-63	1984	Mobile, Ala.
Kelly, Roberto	.288	63	212	32	61	10	0	12	48	18	48	1	2	.505	.347	R	R	6-2	202	10-1-64	1982	Panama City, Panama
Kieschnick, Brooks	.294	71	252	44	74	9	3	13	45	24	72	3	2	.508	.360	L	R	6-4	228	6-6-72	1993	Caldwell, Texas
Lamb, David	.222	5	9	1	2	0	0	0	0	0	4	0	0	.222	.222	B	R	6-2	165	6-6-75	1993	Newbury Park, Calif.
Little, Mark	.375	9	40	6	15	2	0	0	4	3	9	0	2	.425	.432	R	R	6-0	195	7-11-72	1994	Edwardsville, Ill.
McKeel, Walt	.241	28	79	13	19	4	1	1	4	6	22	0	0	.354	.294	R	R	6-2	200	1-17-72	1990	Stantonsburg, N.C.
Melhuse, Adam	.266	54	184	26	49	10	1	7	32	31	42	0	1	.446	.378	B	R	6-2	185	3-27-72	1993	Stockton, Calif.
Morales, Willie	.157	17	51	4	8	1	0	1	2	1	8	2	0	.235	.170	R	R	5-11	180	9-7-72	1993	Tucson, Ariz.
Nicholson, Kevin	.385	23	78	14	30	5	0	1	11	5	7	1	1	.487	.422	B	R	6-0	195	3-29-76	1997	Surrey, B.C.
2-team (11 Portland)	.330	34	109	15	36	6	0	1	12	9	10	1	2	.413	.381							
Nieves, Melvin	.233	13	43	7	10	5	1	1	4	8	20	1	0	.465	.365	B	R	6-2	220	12-18-71	1988	Pinehurst, N.C.
Peeples, Mike	.300	115	424	71	127	23	4	19	69	27	63	9	9	.507	.346	R	R	6-3	175	9-3-76	1994	Green Cove Springs, Fla.
Petrick, Ben	.250	18	64	11	16	2	0	1	9	13	21	1	0	.328	.367	R	R	6-0	205	4-7-77	1996	Hillsboro, Ore.
Powers, Jeff	.125	7	16	1	2	0	0	1	3	1	3	0	0	.313	.176	L	R	6-0	175	3-20-76	1998	Scottsdale, Ariz.
Sefcik, Kevin	.312	49	199	37	62	14	0	2	22	24	26	5	6	.412	.387	R	R	5-10	182	2-10-71	1993	Orland Park, Ill.
Sosa, Juan	.225	14	40	2	9	1	0	0	2	5	7	1	1	.250	.304	R	R	6-1	175	8-19-75	1993	San Francisco de Macoris, D.R.
Uribe, Juan	.310	74	281	40	87	27	7	7	48	12	43	11	8	.530	.340	R	R	5-11	173	7-22-79	1997	San Cristobal, D.R.
Ventura, Juan	.167	2	6	1	1	0	0	0	1	0	2	0	1	.167	.286	R	R	6-1	170	12-10-80	1997	Puerto Plata, D.R.

PITCHING	W	L	ERA	G	GS	CG	SV	IP	H	R	ER	BB	SO	AVG	B	T	HT	WT	DOB	1st Yr	Resides
Acevedo, Juan	0	0	1.29	6	0	0	1	7	3	2	1	4	7	.130	R	R	6-2	228	5-5-70	1992	Algonquin, Ill.
Averette, Robert	6	14	6.11	27	27	0	0	166	204	131	113	48	125	.299	R	R	6-2	195	9-30-76	1997	Sylacauga, Ala.
Belitz, Todd	0	2	9.82	14	0	0	2	11	19	15	12	3	8	.358	L	L	6-3	200	10-23-75	1997	Spokane, Wash.
2-team (38 Sacramento)	4	4	5.94	52	0	0	2	64	71	53	42	19	62	.279							
Bergman, Sean	2	1	2.04	3	2	0	0	18	15	7	4	4	12	.227	R	R	6-4	225	4-11-70	1991	Joliet, Ill.
Bohanon, Brian	0	0	1.80	1	1	0	0	5	8	1	1	1	2	.363	L	L	6-2	240	8-1-68	1987	Houston, Texas
Bost, Heath	2	2	4.32	45	2	0	0	75	82	37	36	23	64	.275	R	R	6-3	195	10-13-74	1995	Taylorsville, N.C.
Chacon, Shawn	2	0	2.25	4	4	0	0	24	18	6	6	7	28	.206	R	R	6-3	212	12-23-77	1996	Greeley, Colo.
Chouinard, Bobby	3	1	3.66	39	0	0	1	39	44	19	16	13	47	.276	R	R	6-1	188	5-1-72	1990	Forest Grove, Ore.
Christman, Tim	2	5	6.30	38	0	0	2	40	52	31	28	21	42	.307	L	L	6-0	195	3-31-75	1996	Oneonta, N.Y.
Clontz, Brad	2	1	9.00	21	0	0	0	23	37	26	23	10	23	.362	R	R	6-1	195	4-25-71	1992	Alpharetta, Ga.
Davenport, Joe	2	2	8.47	31	0	0	0	34	62	38	32	15	23	.389	R	R	6-5	225	3-24-76	1994	Santee, Calif.
Davis, Kane	0	0	3.60	4	0	0	0	5	5	2	2	3	7	.263	R	R	6-3	194	6-25-75	1993	Reedy, W.Va.
Difelice, Mark	3	2	5.28	8	8	0	0	46	56	29	27	8	43	.297	R	R	6-2	190	8-23-76	1998	Havertown, Pa.
Dingman, Craig	3	5	3.75	46	0	0	7	48	57	28	20	9	55	.293	R	R	6-4	215	3-12-74	1994	Wichita, Kan.
Estrada, Horacio	8	4	4.73	16	16	0	0	91	102	51	48	20	77	.283	L	L	6-0	160	10-19-75	1992	San Joaquin, Venez.
Gross, Kip	1	7	6.04	18	12	1	0	82	112	65	55	12	48	.327	R	R	6-2	190	8-24-64	1987	Moreno Valley, Calif.
2-team (10 Las Vegas)	4	8	5.87	28	12	1	0	100	138	76	65	16	56	.330							
House, Craig	2	2	4.45	54	0	0	6	59	50	32	29	31	62	.231	R	R	6-2	210	7-8-77	1999	Bartlett, Tenn.
Jennings, Jason	7	8	4.72	22	22	4	0	132	145	80	69	41	110	.281	L	R	6-2	230	7-17-78	1999	Mesquite, Texas
Larkin, Andy	4	8	5.40	26	18	0	0	120	134	78	72	41	99	.282	R	R	6-4	210	6-27-74	1992	Sunrise, Fla.
Miceli, Danny	0	2	6.00	4	0	0	0	3	2	2	2	1	4	.200	R	R	6-0	216	9-9-70	1990	Winter Springs, Fla.
Moraga, David	0	1	10.95	3	3	0	0	12	21	16	15	8	9	.368	L	L	6-0	184	7-8-75	1994	Suisun, Calif.
Pauls, Matthew	0	1	7.04	2	2	0	0	8	14	6	6	0	8	.378	R	R	6-1	190	7-26-74	1994	Monahans, Texas
Randall, Scott	6	5	5.48	19	12	0	0	71	74	48	43	34	47	.263	R	R	6-3	178	10-29-75	1995	Goleta, Calif.
Speier, Justin	1	0	1.46	11	0	0	2	12	10	2	2	7	16	.227	R	R	6-4	205	11-6-73	1995	Paradise Valley, Ariz.
Tessmer, Jay	1	0	6.59	10	0	0	0	14	23	14	10	6	10	.377	R	R	6-3	190	12-26-71	1995	Port St. Lucie, Fla.
Thompson, Travis	0	2	17.65	9	0	0	0	9	20	19	17	6	9	.476	R	R	6-3	189	1-10-75	1996	Greenfield, Wis.
Thomson, John	5	3	3.31	12	12	0	0	68	74	29	25	13	52	.274	R	R	6-3	187	10-1-73	1993	Sulphur, La.
Watkins, Scott	0	1	10.57	10	0	0	0	8	13	10	9	10	4	.351	L	L	6-2	195	5-15-70	1992	Sand Springs, Okla.

FIELDING

Catcher	PCT	G	PO	A	E	DP	PB
Bell	1.000	1	3	0	0	0	0
Cox	.998	56	380	32	1	3	2
Fasano	.984	25	167	15	3	2	3
McKeel	1.000	13	76	2	0	0	1
Melhuse	.986	38	264	21	4	3	5
Morales	1.000	15	119	8	0	1	0
Petrick	.982	8	51	5	1	0	0

First Base	PCT	G	PO	A	E	DP
Alviso	1.000	20	77	3	0	13
Bell	.971	11	29	4	1	3
Brumbaugh	1.000	6	32	4	0	7
Flores	.939	4	27	4	2	1
Huskey	.985	107	915	66	15	91
R. Jennings	.944	2	17	0	1	1
Kieschnick	.961	7	49	0	2	3
McKeel	1.000	6	31	2	0	4
Melhuse	.985	7	59	7	1	7
Petrick	.947	2	17	1	1	1

Second Base	PCT	G	PO	A	E	DP
Alviso	.974	46	67	84	4	24
Bell	.966	24	38	46	3	5
Brumbaugh	.000	1	0	0	0	0
Butler	.979	54	103	134	5	33
Flores	.975	23	44	73	3	16
Lamb	1.000	1	2	0	0	0
Nicholson	1.000	6	4	15	0	2
Powers	.964	4	14	13	1	3
Sefcik	.903	7	15	13	3	4

Third Base	PCT	G	PO	A	E	DP
Alviso	.727	9	3	5	3	1
Bell	.938	65	84	124	11	14
Brumbaugh	.878	26	11	32	6	0
Butler	1.000	5	3	11	0	1
Cirillo	1.000	1	1	2	0	1
Flores	.947	26	7	47	3	8
Morales	1.000	1	0	1	0	0
Nicholson	1.000	12	8	21	0	2
Peeples	.929	10	7	19	2	1
Sefcik	.909	6	2	18	2	1
Sosa	.909	8	2	18	2	3

Shortstop	PCT	G	PO	A	E	DP
Alviso	.963	18	32	47	3	9
Butler	1.000	7	6	15	0	3
Espada	1.000	7	11	22	0	3
Flores	.930	35	53	79	10	14
Lamb	.857	3	3	3	1	2
Nicholson	1.000	4	2	6	0	1
Sosa	.864	5	5	14	3	3
Uribe	.960	73	156	230	16	58

Outfield	PCT	G	PO	A	E	DP
Alviso	.944	14	17	0	1	0
Bartee	1.000	23	43	2	0	1
Brumbaugh	.940	34	45	2	3	1
Bullett	.964	20	25	2	1	1
Carpenter	.955	42	63	1	3	0
Cruz	1.000	19	39	5	0	2
Encarnacion	1.000	14	22	1	0	0
Flores	1.000	7	6	0	0	0
Hamilton	1.000	3	7	1	0	0
Huskey	1.000	5	10	0	0	0
R. Jennings	1.000	10	14	2	0	0
Johnson	.980	30	49	1	1	0
Kelly	1.000	39	44	5	0	1
Kieschnick	1.000	44	56	3	0	0
Little	1.000	9	20	2	0	0
Melhuse	1.000	3	3	0	0	0
Nieves	1.000	13	22	0	0	0
Peeples	.990	84	99	2	1	0
Petrick	.882	12	13	2	2	1
Sefcik	.972	40	69	0	2	0
Ventura	1.000	2	2	1	0	0

CAROLINA — Class AA

SOUTHERN LEAGUE

BATTING	AVG	G	AB	R	H	2B	3B	HR	RBI	BB	SO	SB	CS	SLG	OBP	B	T	HT	WT	DOB	1st Yr	Resides
Bair, Rod	.253	72	273	25	69	13	0	7	31	10	49	5	6	.377	.290	R	R	5-11	195	10-29-74	1996	Tempe, Ariz.

BATTING

BATTING	AVG	G	AB	R	H	2B	3B	HR	RBI	BB	SO	SB	CS	SLG	OBP	B	T	HT	WT	DOB	1st Yr	Resides
Bard, Josh	.258	35	124	14	32	13	0	1	24	19	23	0	1	.387	.359	B	R	6-3	205	3-30-78	1999	Englewood, Colo.
Burford, Kevin	.289	101	363	51	105	21	4	6	35	45	79	4	1	.419	.377	L	L	6-0	190	11-7-77	1997	Westminster, Calif.
Carpenter, Bubba	.230	32	100	12	23	7	0	1	12	16	17	3	1	.330	.342	L	L	6-1	185	7-23-68	1991	Springdale, Ark.
Colina, Javier	.042	7	24	0	1	0	0	0	2	0	10	0	1	.042	.042	R	R	6-1	180	2-15-79	1997	Cocorote, Venez.
Dewey, Jason	.239	71	243	24	58	21	0	5	27	23	78	1	0	.387	.307	R	R	6-0	200	4-18-77	1997	Tampa, Fla.
Figgins, Chone	.220	86	332	41	73	14	5	2	25	40	73	27	8	.310	.306	B	R	5-8	155	1-22-78	1997	Brandon, Fla.
Keck, Brian	.263	100	327	35	86	15	1	4	41	22	46	12	5	.352	.307	R	R	6-3	185	1-15-74	1996	Dodge City, Kan.
Kuilan, Hector	.186	12	43	3	8	2	0	1	3	3	6	0	0	.302	.239	R	R	5-11	190	4-3-76	1994	Vega Alta, P.R.
Lamb, Dave	.272	82	287	32	78	16	0	5	32	37	39	2	3	.380	.361	L	L	6-2	165	6-6-75	1993	Newbury Park, Calif.
Landaeta, Luis	.282	66	241	27	68	11	4	1	23	16	27	8	6	.373	.321	L	L	6-0	180	3-4-77	1996	Valencia, Venez.
Martinez, Belvani	.260	115	430	46	112	21	7	5	37	37	59	29	13	.377	.287	R	R	5-11	172	12-14-78	1996	Palenque, D.R.
Mashore, Justin	.250	57	172	21	43	12	0	4	23	11	42	4	3	.390	.296	R	R	5-9	190	2-14-72	1991	Concord, Calif.
McKeel, Walt	.221	24	68	11	15	2	0	3	9	14	14	0	0	.382	.384	R	R	6-2	200	1-17-72	1990	Stantonsburg, N.C.
Murphy, Mike	.263	114	410	57	108	19	1	7	43	62	114	21	5	.366	.368	R	R	6-2	185	1-23-72	1990	Martinez, Calif.
Owens, Ryan	.268	111	392	66	105	20	2	8	47	63	107	12	4	.390	.378	R	R	6-2	200	3-18-78	1999	Anaheim Hills, Calif.
Phillips, J.R.	.294	31	119	18	35	8	0	8	23	12	33	0	1	.563	.364	L	L	6-1	185	4-29-70	1988	Moreno Valley, Calif.
Powers, Jeff	.190	30	84	5	16	2	1	0	5	6	12	0	1	.238	.253	L	R	6-0	175	3-20-76	1998	Scottsdale, Ariz.
Seal, Scott	.204	70	186	24	38	7	1	4	26	33	34	2	2	.317	.332	L	L	6-1	205	8-16-75	1997	Irvine, Calif.
Stoner, Mike	.265	45	155	25	41	7	3	2	27	14	19	0	0	.387	.343	R	R	6-0	210	5-23-73	1996	Shelbyville, Ky.
Uribe, Juan	.231	3	13	1	3	1	0	0	1	0	4	1	0	.308	.231	R	R	5-11	173	7-22-79	1997	San Cristobal, D.R.

PITCHING

PITCHING	W	L	ERA	G	GS	CG	SV	IP	H	R	ER	BB	SO	AVG	B	T	HT	WT	DOB	1st Yr	Resides
Brantley, Brian	0	2	7.36	14	0	0	0	22	31	19	18	16	23	.352	R	R	6-4	185	4-23-76	1998	Chesapeake, Va.
Cameron, Ryan	7	6	5.22	18	13	0	0	90	112	64	52	45	81	.301	R	R	6-1	180	9-13-77	1998	Williamstown, Mass.
Crowder, Chuck	6	6	5.35	32	14	0	1	101	126	64	60	63	71	.309	L	L	6-2	190	9-30-76	1999	Mantua, Ohio
DeWitt, Scott	2	6	3.57	43	1	0	1	63	66	36	25	28	52	.271	R	L	6-4	200	10-6-74	1995	Springfield, Ore.
Difelice, Mark	6	4	3.15	19	18	2	0	123	108	47	43	23	98	.232	R	R	6-2	190	8-23-76	1998	Havertown, Pa.
Dorame, Randey	0	4	4.82	5	5	0	0	28	33	17	15	6	17	.297	L	L	6-2	205	1-23-79	1997	Huatabampo, Mexico
Emiliano, Jamie	3	6	3.34	50	0	0	2	65	56	29	24	30	38	.233	R	R	5-10	210	8-2-74	1995	Andrews, Texas
Esslinger, Cam	1	1	4.93	40	0	0	16	42	32	26	23	31	51	.209	R	R	6-0	170	12-28-76	1999	Hewitt, N.J.
Hudson, Luke	7	12	4.20	29	28	1	0	165	159	90	77	68	145	.249	R	R	6-3	195	5-2-77	1998	Fountain Valley, Calif.
Jennings, Jason	2	0	2.88	4	4	0	0	25	25	9	8	8	24	.257	L	R	6-2	230	7-17-78	1999	Mesquite, Texas
Kalinowski, Josh	7	8	4.06	25	25	0	0	137	151	76	62	65	116	.283	L	L	6-2	190	12-12-76	1997	Casper, Wyo.
Kibler, Ryan	4	1	2.11	8	8	1	0	47	38	17	11	19	41	.215	R	R	6-2	185	9-17-80	1999	Tampa, Fla.
Osting, Jimmy	1	0	1.80	1	1	0	0	5	3	1	1	3	3	.157	R	L	6-5	190	4-7-77	1997	Louisville, Ky.
Randall, Scott	0	0	0.00	1	1	0	0	6	5	0	0	3	2	.238	R	R	6-3	185	10-29-75	1995	Goleta, Calif.
Seifert, Ryan	4	6	3.14	33	12	1	1	103	103	42	36	28	88	.261	R	R	6-5	215	8-14-75	1997	Chaska, Minn.
Thompson, Doug	2	5	3.76	26	0	0	1	38	33	16	16	19	33	.242	R	R	6-1	195	7-22-76	1998	Biloxi, Miss.
Thompson, Mark	3	2	5.06	8	8	1	0	48	43	29	27	15	38	.236	R	R	6-2	212	4-7-71	1992	Russellville, Ky.
Thompson, Travis	1	1	4.58	28	0	0	5	37	39	20	19	13	28	.270	R	R	6-3	189	1-10-75	1996	Greenfield, Wis.
Wrigley, Jase	6	6	6.30	47	0	0	2	64	93	53	45	28	33	.341	R	R	6-4	220	11-6-75	1998	Atlanta, Ga.

FIELDING

Catcher	PCT	G	PO	A	E	DP	PB
Bard	.993	35	258	26	2	1	4
Dewey	.987	69	504	42	7	2	8
Kuilan	.990	12	90	9	1	0	5
McKeel	.971	23	148	20	5	4	2

First Base	PCT	G	PO	A	E	DP
Burford	.971	77	621	70	21	55
Keck	.992	16	122	7	1	13
McKeel	1.000	1	5	1	0	4
Murphy	1.000	4	44	0	0	4
Phillips	.993	29	245	26	2	18
Seal	1.000	2	10	0	0	1
Stoner	.976	15	116	6	3	11

Second Base	PCT	G	PO	A	E	DP
Colina	1.000	1	0	2	0	0

	PCT	G	PO	A	E	DP
Figgins	.974	77	155	221	10	45
Keck	1.000	2	1	5	0	1
Lamb	.946	8	14	21	2	5
Martinez	.969	35	66	92	5	19
Powers	.968	23	35	55	3	14

Third Base	PCT	G	PO	A	E	DP
Bair	1.000	7	7	9	0	1
Colina	.929	7	3	10	1	1
Keck	.952	25	20	39	3	5
Lamb	1.000	6	2	4	0	1
Owens	.922	103	65	171	20	21

Shortstop	PCT	G	PO	A	E	DP
Figgins	.872	10	15	26	6	5
Keck	.972	54	73	137	6	24
Lamb	.967	70	106	212	11	40

	PCT	G	PO	A	E	DP
Owens	.953	7	19	22	2	4
Powers	1.000	2	2	6	0	0
Uribe	.833	3	4	6	2	1

Outfield	PCT	G	PO	A	E	DP
Bair	.978	51	89	2	2	1
Carpenter	1.000	26	60	0	0	0
Landaeta	.947	54	84	5	5	1
Martinez	.951	76	123	12	7	2
Mashore	.942	43	61	4	4	0
Murphy	.992	102	235	3	2	0
Phillips	1.000	1	1	0	0	0
Seal	.991	53	100	5	1	0
Stoner	1.000	21	34	1	0	0

SALEM — Class A

CAROLINA LEAGUE

BATTING

BATTING	AVG	G	AB	R	H	2B	3B	HR	RBI	BB	SO	SB	CS	SLG	OBP	B	T	HT	WT	DOB	1st Yr	Resides
Atkins, Garrett	.325	135	465	70	151	43	5	5	67	74	98	6	4	.471	.421	R	R	6-3	210	12-12-79	2000	Irvine, Calif.
Barmes, Clint	.248	38	121	17	30	3	3	0	9	15	20	4	1	.322	.350	R	R	6-1	190	3-6-79	2000	Vincennes, Ind.
Bell, Mike	.385	4	13	1	5	1	0	0	9	5	1	1	0	.462	.556	R	R	6-2	195	12-7-74	1993	Cincinnati, Ohio
Catalanotte, Greg	.217	119	401	45	87	20	4	11	40	44	125	8	5	.359	.301	B	R	6-3	210	6-18-77	1999	Glendale, Ariz.
Colina, Javier	.285	113	439	67	125	33	7	9	58	22	61	9	4	.453	.324	R	R	6-1	180	2-15-79	1997	Cocorote, Venez.
Freeman, Choo	.240	132	517	63	124	16	5	8	42	31	108	19	7	.337	.292	R	R	6-2	200	10-20-79	1998	Dallas, Texas
Holliday, Matt	.275	72	255	36	70	16	1	11	52	33	42	11	3	.475	.358	R	R	6-4	215	1-10-80	1998	Stillwater, Okla.
Lincoln, Justin	.167	50	156	15	26	6	0	3	10	9	63	1	0	.263	.229	R	R	6-2	200	4-4-79	1999	Sarasota, Fla.
Lindsey, John	.280	51	168	19	47	13	0	7	32	13	51	1	1	.482	.349	R	R	6-3	220	1-30-77	1995	Hattiesburg, Miss.
McQueen, Eric	.000	2	5	0	0	0	0	0	0	1	5	0	0	.000	.167	R	R	6-0	200	1-10-77	1999	Winder, Ga.
Moore, Chris	.159	19	44	3	7	2	0	0	1	9	11	0	0	.205	.296	L	R	5-11	180	11-16-76	1999	Wilmington, N.C.
Phillips, Dan	.262	132	493	65	129	35	0	16	68	27	106	11	12	.430	.315	R	R	6-3	190	8-23-78	1999	Northridge, Calif.
Powers, Jeff	.186	44	118	9	22	4	1	0	6	7	15	0	2	.237	.238	L	R	6-0	175	3-20-76	1998	Scottsdale, Calif.
Sanchez, Tino	.233	91	283	32	66	9	0	3	26	32	30	4	4	.297	.316	B	R	6-0	154	2-2-79	1997	Yauco, P.R.
Seal, Scott	.181	34	94	9	17	4	0	2	9	8	20	1	1	.287	.260	L	L	6-1	205	8-16-75	1997	Irvine, Calif.
Taylor, Seth	.263	131	480	52	126	26	1	8	45	26	66	6	8	.371	.305	R	R	6-1	180	8-23-77	1999	Cantonment, Fla.
Viloria, Miguel	.356	12	45	6	16	2	0	0	0	0	9	1	0	.400	.356	R	R	5-10	152	7-22-79	1997	Santo Domingo, D.R.
Warren, Chris	.197	74	132	20	26	7	1	6	18	26	51	3	4	.402	.344	R	R	6-0	175	11-24-76	1999	Athens, Ga.
Winchester, Jeff	.161	95	304	29	49	13	0	7	26	23	75	2	2	.273	.237	R	R	6-0	205	1-21-80	1998	Metairie, La.

GAMES BY POSITION: C—McQueen 2, Sanchez 51, Winchester 95. **1B**—Atkins 130, Bell 2, Moore 9, Powers 1, Sanchez 1, Seal 3, Warren 2. **2B**—Colina 113, Powers 5, Taylor 5, Vilorio 12, Warren 15. **3B**—Atkins 6, Bell 3, Lincoln 49, Powers 16, Sanchez 23, Taylor 40, Warren 17. **SS**—Barmes 38, Powers 21,

Taylor 76, Warren 12. **OF**—Catalanotte 103, Freeman 123, Holliday 30, Phillips 122, Sanchez 17, Seal 25, Warren 20.

PITCHING	W	L	ERA	G	GS	CG	SV	IP	H	R	ER	BB	SO	AVG	B	T	HT	WT	DOB	1st Yr	Resides
Ayala, Luis	0	1	4.05	13	0	0	7	13	19	10	6	5	10	.358	R	R	6-2	175	1-12-78	1999	Los Mochis, Mexico
Brantley, Brian	5	3	2.78	28	1	0	2	58	43	23	18	21	55	.200	R	R	6-4	185	4-23-76	1998	Chesapeake, Va.
Brueggemann, Dean	2	0	4.78	48	0	0	2	64	66	40	34	37	36	.276	L	L	6-1	186	3-11-76	1996	Smithton, Ill.
Cameron, Ryan	0	1	2.25	2	2	0	0	8	5	4	2	5	12	.166	R	R	6-1	180	9-13-77	1998	Williamstown, Mass.
Cercy, Rick	4	1	3.16	39	0	0	5	57	47	22	20	24	51	.227	R	R	6-1	195	10-10-76	1999	Ormond Beach, Fla.
Cook, Aaron	11	11	3.08	27	27	0	0	155	157	73	53	38	122	.263	R	R	6-3	175	2-8-79	1997	Loveland, Ohio
Cowie, Stephen	0	1	10.80	1	1	0	0	3	6	4	4	2	1	.400	R	R	6-2	190	11-9-76	1999	Belmont, N.C.
2-team (2 Kinston)	0	1	4.82	3	1	0	0	9	11	5	5	3	5	.323							
Dorame, Randey	2	5	5.26	17	14	0	0	79	95	50	46	28	57	.302	L	L	6-2	205	1-23-79	1997	Huatabampo, Mexico
Kibler, Ryan	7	0	1.55	11	11	0	0	76	53	19	13	16	61	.194	R	R	6-2	185	9-17-80	1999	Tampa, Fla.
Martin, Chandler	3	5	4.74	9	9	0	0	57	68	35	30	14	32	.294	R	R	6-1	180	10-23-73	1995	Salem, Ore.
Matcuk, Steve	4	1	2.98	24	0	0	3	42	47	19	14	13	33	.286	R	R	6-2	185	4-8-76	1996	Pasadena, Md.
Pacheco, Enemencio	4	2	4.68	27	3	0	1	42	55	27	22	18	29	.312	R	R	6-0	160	3-30-79	1997	Santo Domingo, D.R.
Price, Ryan	4	11	7.34	28	21	0	0	103	101	93	84	85	79	.255	R	R	6-3	190	1-31-78	1997	Roswell, N.M.
Randall, Scott	0	0	4.50	2	0	0	0	6	9	3	3	1	7	.346	R	R	6-3	178	10-29-75	1995	Goleta, Calif.
Stepka, Tom	2	2	3.72	32	2	0	2	68	72	36	28	25	42	.269	R	R	6-2	185	11-29-75	1996	Williamsville, N.Y.
Thompson, Doug	2	2	4.02	17	0	0	1	31	30	15	14	16	35	.256	R	R	6-1	195	7-22-76	1998	Biloxi, Miss.
Tsao, Chin-hui	0	4	4.67	4	4	0	0	17	23	11	9	5	18	.333	R	R	6-2	178	6-2-81	1999	Hualien, Taiwan
Vance, Cory	10	8	3.10	26	26	1	0	154	129	65	53	65	142	.232	L	L	6-1	195	6-20-79	2000	Vandalia, Ohio
Warren, Chris	0	0	0.00	2	0	0	0	2	1	0	0	0	0	.000	B	R	6-0	175	11-24-76	1999	Athens, Ga.
Young, Colin	4	3	1.42	47	0	0	21	57	35	11	9	12	72	.172	L	L	6-0	185	8-1-77	1999	West Newbury, Mass.
Young, Jason	6	7	3.44	17	17	2	0	105	104	47	40	28	91	.259	B	R	6-5	205	9-28-79	2001	Henderson, Nev.

ASHEVILLE — Class A

SOUTH ATLANTIC LEAGUE

BATTING	AVG	G	AB	R	H	2B	3B	HR	RBI	BB	SO	SB	CS	SLG	OBP	B	T	HT	WT	DOB	1st Yr	Resides
Auterson, Jeff	.206	28	97	9	20	4	1	2	9	7	32	4	1	.330	.274	R	R	6-2	190	2-22-78	1996	Riverside, Calif.
Barmes, Clint	.260	74	285	40	74	14	1	5	24	17	37	21	7	.368	.314	R	R	6-1	190	3-6-79	2000	Vincennes, Ind.
Bernard, Dagoberto	.275	38	109	9	30	7	0	0	11	1	24	3	7	.339	.288	R	R	6-0	159	2-23-80	1997	San Pedro de Macoris, D.R.
Conway, Ben	.227	86	273	31	62	12	1	5	27	38	82	2	1	.333	.327	R	R	6-2	195	10-13-79	2000	Delmar, N.Y.
Figueroa, Carlos	.250	12	40	6	10	2	0	0	5	4	8	4	1	.300	.318	L	R	5-10	160	5-25-81	1999	Carolina, P.R.
Gretz, Nick	.556	3	9	1	5	0	0	0	0	0	0	0	0	.556	.556	L	R	5-11	205	1-26-78	2001	Apple Valley, Minn.
Hawpe, Brad	.267	111	393	78	105	22	3	22	72	59	113	7	4	.506	.363	L	L	6-2	200	6-22-79	2000	Fort Worth, Texas
Lincoln, Justin	.274	62	226	37	62	12	4	10	41	17	84	2	2	.496	.325	R	R	6-2	200	4-4-79	1999	Sarasota, Fla.
Moore, Chris	.154	7	26	1	4	0	0	0	3	1	9	0	0	.154	.179	L	R	5-11	180	11-16-76	1999	Wilmington, N.C.
Muth, Edmund	.261	117	398	53	104	21	3	18	70	44	105	13	3	.465	.346	L	L	6-0	195	12-1-77	2000	Long Beach, Calif.
Peck, Bryan	.271	72	214	48	58	13	0	5	26	47	51	7	2	.402	.410	R	R	5-11	195	8-9-77	2000	Athens, Tenn.
Powers, Jeff	.236	19	72	11	17	3	0	2	6	2	11	0	0	.361	.257	L	R	6-0	175	3-20-76	1998	Scottsdale, Ariz.
Reyes, Rene	.322	128	484	71	156	27	2	11	61	28	80	53	12	.455	.371	B	R	5-11	202	2-21-78	1996	Margarita, Venez.
Rock, Jamie	.198	30	106	8	21	6	0	1	17	3	25	1	1	.283	.223	R	R	6-0	195	12-23-77	2000	Nettleton, Miss.
Rosario, Melvin	.228	102	276	44	63	4	0	0	18	44	89	23	13	.243	.345	L	L	6-2	175	9-22-78	1998	Carolina, P.R.
Smith, Sam	.152	30	105	5	16	4	0	0	7	8	37	1	1	.190	.239	R	R	6-1	180	3-21-79	1997	Jasper, Texas
Storey, Eric	.250	87	300	45	75	10	3	10	53	50	116	6	4	.403	.355	R	R	6-0	175	10-12-77	2000	Indianapolis, Ind.
Sullivan, Cory	.275	67	258	36	71	12	1	5	22	25	56	13	9	.388	.344	L	L	6-0	180	8-20-79	2001	Evanston, Wyo.
Tejada, Mike	.204	107	363	35	74	17	0	15	49	22	102	3	0	.375	.249	R	R	6-1	215	3-8-79	2000	Provo, Utah
Tena, Hector	.146	32	103	5	15	1	0	2	19	5	32	0	0	.214	.175	R	R	6-0	155	6-20-82	1999	San Cristobal, D.R.
Vilorio, Miguel	.254	143	453	55	115	15	7	3	32	22	58	20	15	.338	.302	R	R	6-0	152	7-22-79	1997	Santo Domingo, D.R.

GAMES BY POSITION: C—Conway 84, Peck 4, Tejada 60. **1B**—Bernard 3, Hawpe 52, Moore 2, Reyes 60, Rock 10, Storey 15. **2B**—Bernard 10, Figueroa 11, Peck 2, Storey 6, Vilorio 113. **3B**—Bernard 3, Lincoln 62, Peck 16, Smith 19, Storey 43. **SS**—Barmes 74, Bernard 13, Powers 19, Storey 6, Tena 32. **OF**—Auterson 18, Hawpe 54, Muth 96, Peck 32, Reyes 63, Rock 17, Rosario 97, Sullivan 65.

PITCHING	W	L	ERA	G	GS	CG	SV	IP	H	R	ER	BB	SO	AVG	B	T	HT	WT	DOB	1st Yr	Resides
Abell, Joe	2	2	2.51	16	6	1	0	43	40	14	12	12	38	.246	R	R	6-2	190	3-7-78	2000	Boulder, Colo.
Berney, Scott	2	2	5.04	33	1	0	0	50	59	37	28	21	28	.301	R	R	6-3	200	10-25-77	2000	Wallingford, Conn.
Buglovsky, Chris	8	10	4.08	26	26	0	0	143	158	83	65	32	119	.273	L	R	6-1	170	11-22-79	2000	Iselin, N.J.
DePaula, Julio	1	1	3.78	3	3	0	0	17	19	13	7	2	26	.267	R	R	6-1	160	7-27-79	1997	Santo Domingo, D.R.
Dohmann, Scott	11	13	4.32	28	28	3	0	173	165	88	83	33	154	.250	R	R	6-1	190	2-13-78	2000	Morgan City, La.
Gomez, Diogenes	12	4	2.25	50	1	0	3	84	82	34	21	21	55	.259	R	R	5-11	165	3-27-79	1997	Chorrera, Panama
Green, Sean	3	4	5.90	43	0	0	0	58	66	43	38	37	28	.282	R	R	6-6	230	4-20-79	2000	Louisville, Ky.
Huisman, Justin	0	3	1.70	55	0	0	30	58	35	20	11	14	53	.166	R	R	6-1	195	4-16-79	2000	Thornton, Ill.
Kibler, Ryan	3	5	2.93	10	10	1	0	61	50	26	20	27	59	.226	R	R	6-2	185	9-17-80	1999	Tampa, Fla.
LaRoche, Jeff	1	2	4.82	26	0	0	0	37	45	37	20	24	21	.298	L	L	6-3	185	3-17-78	1998	Fort Scott, Kan.
Lorenzo, Javier	0	0	5.17	38	0	0	1	47	42	35	27	35	55	.234	R	R	6-0	180	12-26-78	1999	Hialeah, Fla.
Martin, Chandler	2	0	1.32	2	2	0	0	14	10	2	2	5	8	.217	R	R	6-1	180	10-23-73	1995	Salem, Ore.
Matos, Jesus	1	1	5.06	21	0	0	0	32	36	19	18	8	25	.281	R	R	6-0	165	7-21-79	1997	San Pedro de Macoris, D.R.
Pacheco, Enemencio	1	2	4.21	7	7	0	0	36	38	23	17	9	34	.263	R	R	6-0	160	3-30-79	1997	Santo Domingo, D.R.
Roney, Matt	8	10	4.98	23	23	1	0	121	131	74	67	43	115	.274	R	R	6-4	225	1-10-80	1998	Edmond, Okla.
Serrano, Alex	0	0	.66	14	0	0	0	14	13	4	1	5	13	.240	R	R	6-1	200	2-18-81	1998	Barcelona, Venez.
Stepka, Tom	0	0	3.18	2	0	0	0	6	5	4	2	1	4	.217	R	R	6-2	185	11-29-75	1996	Williamsville, N.Y.
Vazquez, Will	4	7	5.67	16	14	0	0	86	92	62	54	35	64	.272	R	R	6-0	140	12-26-79	2000	Guayama, P.R.
Webb, Nicholas	9	5	3.33	19	18	1	1	116	111	52	43	27	92	.253	L	L	6-3	200	7-8-79	2000	Houston, Texas

TRI-CITY — Short-Season Class A

NORTHWEST LEAGUE

BATTING	AVG	G	AB	R	H	2B	3B	HR	RBI	BB	SO	SB	CS	SLG	OBP	B	T	HT	WT	DOB	1st Yr	Resides
Bird, T.J.	.244	52	164	20	40	10	1	4	22	13	37	0	0	.390	.308	L	L	5-11	195	6-20-79	2000	Cloverdale, Calif.
Burkholder, David	.268	13	41	5	11	3	0	2	9	3	10	1	0	.488	.326	L	L	6-1	225	11-30-77	2001	Menahga, Minn.
Colina, Alvin	.213	47	164	12	35	10	0	5	17	12	50	0	2	.366	.283	R	R	6-3	193	12-26-81	1999	Puerto Cabello, Venez.
Figueroa, Carlos	.156	42	128	10	20	0	0	0	11	13	23	1	3	.164	.236	L	R	5-10	160	5-25-81	1999	Carolina, P.R.
Freeman, Ashley	.203	66	236	39	48	13	3	1	28	18	52	6	1	.297	.292	R	R	6-1	195	1-27-79	2001	Town Creek, Ala.
Frome, Jason	.224	58	219	28	49	12	4	1	21	23	64	6	3	.329	.304	L	L	6-0	190	7-3-79	2001	Appleton, Wis.

BATTING	AVG	G	AB	R	H	2B	3B	HR	RBI	BB	SO	SB	CS	SLG	OBP	B	T	HT	WT	DOB	1st Yr	Resides
Gearlds, Aaron	.239	58	197	30	47	9	5	0	19	17	61	21	1	.335	.324	R	R	6-1	190	12-13-79	1999	Jackson, Miss.
Gretz, Nick	.348	29	92	5	32	6	2	0	21	11	18	0	1	.457	.419	L	R	5-11	205	1-26-78	2001	Apple Valley, Minn.
Guance, Walkill	.197	59	218	31	43	7	2	3	17	15	57	15	6	.289	.261	R	R	5-9	160	3-6-82	1999	Palenque, D.R.
Lambert, Casey	.227	55	172	20	39	5	1	1	16	28	31	3	4	.285	.348	R	R	5-9	165	8-31-79	2001	St. Amant, La.
Montero, Esteban	.194	57	165	23	32	10	4	2	16	12	63	1	1	.339	.266	R	R	5-11	170	4-16-83	2000	Santo Domingo, D.R.
Morency, Vernand	.230	54	183	30	42	12	2	4	27	20	59	16	3	.383	.333	R	R	5-11	220	2-4-80	1998	Miami, Fla.
Ortega, Sixto	.159	18	63	8	10	1	0	0	3	0	14	1	0	.175	.172	R	R	5-10	195	12-24-79	1997	Santo Domingo, D.R.
Pride, Joshua	.260	42	127	12	33	10	0	3	22	15	40	1	1	.409	.338	R	R	6-0	200	9-16-77	2000	Brentwood, Tenn.
Testa, Chris	.269	54	182	23	49	12	3	2	22	21	49	5	4	.401	.359	L	L	6-2	175	5-23-81	1999	Palmdale, Calif.
Ventura, Juan	.204	47	162	26	33	5	3	0	8	15	38	7	4	.272	.291	R	R	6-1	170	12-10-80	1997	Puerto Plata, D.R.

GAMES BY POSITION: C—Colina 46, Ortega 15, Pride 16. **1B**—Bird 25, Burkholder 11, Freeman 26, Gretz 22, Ventura 1. **2B**—Figueroa 25, Guance 54, Lambert 3, Ventura 1. **3B**—Figueroa 5, Freeman 47, Guance 1, Lambert 31. **SS**—Figueroa 1, Guance 6, Lambert 25, Montero 57. **OF**—Bird 11, Frome 55, Gearlds 46, Morency 47, Testa 42, Ventura 37.

PITCHING	W	L	ERA	G	GS	CG	SV	IP	H	R	ER	BB	SO	AVG	B	T	HT	WT	DOB	1st Yr	Resides
Almond, Casey	0	0	2.57	4	0	0	0	7	5	3	2	8	5	.250	R	R	6-2	185	11-2-78	2001	Moss Point, Miss.
Bouknight, Kip	3	5	2.78	15	15	0	0	81	69	29	25	19	86	.229	R	R	6-0	190	11-16-78	2001	Gaston, S.C.
Cruz, Jeffrey	0	1	8.49	12	0	0	0	12	21	15	11	8	6	.355	L	L	6-0	190	3-14-79	2001	Fullerton, Calif.
Dannemiller, Beau	3	2	2.15	23	1	0	6	46	33	13	11	17	53	.196	R	R	6-0	210	12-26-79	2001	Munroe Falls, Ohio
Frary, Levi	1	1	5.40	22	0	0	9	22	27	17	13	5	11	.317	R	R	6-2	215	3-27-79	2001	Lewiston, Idaho
Gallagher, Shawn	0	3	4.58	17	0	0	1	18	22	12	9	8	19	.314	L	L	5-11	175	1-3-79	2001	Billings, Mont.
Haase, Frank	2	1	1.45	19	0	0	0	31	22	11	5	19	25	.200	R	L	6-3	175	7-21-79	1999	Atwater, Calif.
Hampson, Justin	4	6	4.52	15	15	0	0	82	84	55	41	23	63	.265	L	L	6-1	180	5-24-80	2000	Worden, Ill.
Labitzke, Jesse	0	0	3.22	17	0	0	0	22	16	12	8	15	15	.186	L	L	6-5	220	11-23-77	1996	Laramie, Wyo.
Lynch, Pat	1	0	2.00	4	0	0	1	9	4	2	2	0	10	.129	R	R	6-3	195	6-27-78	1996	Milton, Ontario
Martin, Chandler	1	0	3.00	4	4	0	0	18	14	6	6	1	11	.205	R	R	6-1	180	10-23-73	1995	Salem, Ore.
Matos, Jesus	2	1	2.79	4	0	0	0	10	8	3	3	3	11	.216	R	R	6-0	165	7-21-79	1997	San Pedro de Macoris, D.R.
Merricks, Charles	3	2	5.69	13	13	0	0	55	71	48	35	24	35	.322	L	L	6-0	200	12-6-78	2000	Oxnard, Calif.
Moore, Greg	4	2	4.29	22	3	0	0	50	65	27	24	11	50	.303	R	R	6-6	215	5-23-79	1999	San Ramon, Calif.
Nicholson, Scott	4	3	2.93	14	14	1	0	77	69	29	25	12	50	.242	L	L	6-0	175	8-24-79	2001	Longview, Wash.
Simpson, Gerrit	2	1	1.11	8	3	1	1	24	14	5	3	3	40	.157	R	R	6-3	200	12-18-79	2001	Austin, Texas
Songster, Judd	1	1	1.99	17	0	0	1	23	15	6	5	5	32	.182	R	R	6-3	195	12-26-79	2001	North Platte, Neb.
Thompson, Mark	1	1	1.29	4	2	0	0	14	9	3	2	5	7	.180	R	R	6-2	212	4-7-71	1992	Russellville, Ky.
Tricoglou, Jamie	1	1	2.83	24	0	0	2	29	19	11	9	20	29	.188	L	R	6-2	195	6-28-80	2001	Hixson, Tenn.
Van Buren, Jermaine	1	0	7.20	1	1	0	0	5	7	4	4	3	2	.304	R	R	6-2	212	7-2-80	1998	Hattiesburg, Miss.
Vazquez, Will	0	5	7.89	8	4	0	0	22	30	25	19	17	15	.312	R	R	6-0	140	12-26-79	2000	Guayama, P.R.
Villacis, Eduardo	4	1	4.26	11	0	0	0	19	14	9	9	8	20	.200	R	R	6-2	178	8-29-79	2001	Miranda, Venez.

CASPER   Rookie

PIONEER LEAGUE

BATTING	AVG	G	AB	R	H	2B	3B	HR	RBI	BB	SO	SB	CS	SLG	OBP	B	T	HT	WT	DOB	1st Yr	Resides
Bello, Vladimir	.304	49	161	27	49	5	1	27	7	36	16	3		.416	.339	R	R	5-11	165	6-2-82	2000	Santo Domingo, D.R.
Chavez, Endy	.342	64	228	49	78	9	1	0	22	38	31	24	7	.390	.438	L	L	5-11	155	3-9-81	1999	Valencia, Venez.
Diaz, Eduardo	.279	71	269	44	75	17	6	7	51	31	63	13	10	.465	.349	R	R	5-11	160	5-20-81	1998	Santo Domingo, D.R.
Essery, Frederick	.150	24	60	4	9	0	0	0	9	1	12	0	0	.150	.161	R	R	6-1	180	9-26-77	2000	Havertown, Pa.
Ingram, Bryan	.237	22	19	7	18	3	2	1	10	6	25	0	2	.368	.322	R	R	6-1	200	4-17-79	2001	Everett, Wash.
Materano, Oscar	.251	69	271	34	68	11	0	6	38	9	59	5	5	.358	.291	R	R	6-1	170	11-18-81	1998	Valera, Venez.
Miller, Tony	.306	70	268	68	82	17	3	10	34	41	63	28	10	.504	.399	R	R	5-9	180	8-18-80	2001	Lorain, Ohio
Morel, Robinson	.250	36	108	19	27	3	1	5	16	9	32	5	3	.435	.325	R	R	5-10	160	2-5-82	1999	Esperanza, D.R.
Mulqueen, Dave	.280	73	286	49	80	19	0	12	49	36	89	8	2	.472	.366	B	R	6-3	225	10-16-80	1999	Milwaukee, Wis.
Nix, Jayson	.294	42	153	28	45	10	1	5	24	21	43	1	5	.471	.385	R	R	5-11	180	8-26-82	2001	Midland, Texas
Ortega, Sixto	.324	10	37	4	12	1	0	1	5	2	7	0	1	.432	.375	R	R	5-10	195	12-24-79	1997	Santo Domingo, D.R.
Perez, Jay	.354	35	127	22	45	7	1	6	27	16	28	3	0	.567	.432	B	R	6-2	210	2-24-80	1999	Seymour, Conn.
Pilkington, Ross	.225	41	129	19	29	9	0	1	9	19	34	0	5	.318	.331	R	R	6-0	185	7-21-81	2000	Loveland, Colo.
Sweeney, James	.278	26	90	19	25	4	1	3	12	8	32	1	1	.444	.359	R	R	6-1	197	6-13-83	2001	Austin, Texas
Tena, Hector	.236	35	123	15	29	6	1	3	16	6	36	3	7	.350	.291	R	R	6-0	155	6-20-82	1999	San Cristobal, D.R.
Vasquez, Jose	.232	64	228	40	53	6	3	14	39	27	96	1	6	.469	.332	L	L	6-3	220	12-28-82	2000	Sarasota, Fla.

GAMES BY POSITION: C—Essery 23, Ingram 14, Ortega 10, Perez 21, Sweeney 19. **1B**—Materano 6, Mulqueen 71. **2B**—Diaz 69, Morel 10. **3B**—Essery 1, Materano 58, Morel 22. **SS**—Morel 2, Nix 40, Tena 35. **OF**—Bello 47, Chavez 63, Materano 2, Miller 70, Pilkington 36, Vasquez 30.

PITCHING	W	L	ERA	G	GS	CG	SV	IP	H	R	ER	BB	SO	AVG	B	T	HT	WT	DOB	1st Yr	Resides
Almond, Casey	2	2	7.39	11	0	0	0	32	37	30	26	15	20	.296	R	R	6-2	185	11-2-78	2001	Moss Point, Miss.
Beckstead, Jentry	1	0	2.89	23	0	0	12	28	23	13	9	12	28	.225	R	R	6-1	175	6-9-80	2001	Sandy, Utah
Buret, Jorge	4	6	5.24	16	15	1	0	81	110	66	47	23	54	.316	R	R	6-0	160	10-17-81	1999	Santo Domingo, D.R.
Clarke, Darren	3	6	6.02	14	14	0	0	55	76	47	37	33	42	.336	R	R	6-8	235	3-19-81	2001	Tampa, Fla.
Collado, Jerry	0	2	5.59	21	0	0	1	29	36	24	18	15	18	.297	R	R	6-7	252	5-12-80	1997	Santiago, D.R.
Davies, Michael	2	2	4.50	10	7	0	0	36	40	23	18	10	37	.279	L	L	6-3	195	3-29-81	2000	Beaverton, Ore.
Dotel, Melido	0	0	162.00	2	0	0	0	0	3	6	6	5	0	.750	R	R	6-3	216	4-20-77	1993	San Cristobal, D.R.
Ferrand, Julian	0	6	6.59	17	0	0	0	29	40	27	21	11	26	.322	R	R	6-2	165	11-22-79	2001	Santo Domingo, D.R.
Gonzalez, Miguel	2	2	3.35	24	0	0	0	40	40	21	15	12	41	.254	R	R	6-3	200	11-7-79	1999	Guasave, Mexico
Granados, Daniel	0	0	6.84	21	0	0	0	25	33	24	19	13	23	.308	R	R	6-5	185	6-6-79	1999	San Jose, Costa Rica
Greenbush, Peter	4	2	5.10	14	6	0	1	42	55	32	24	15	26	.316	R	R	6-1	195	10-5-78	2001	North Adams, Mass.
Martinez, Angel	4	3	4.37	18	8	0	0	58	56	34	28	18	44	.253	R	R	6-2	172	1-27-82	1999	Santo Domingo, D.R.
Mitchell, Jay	5	4	6.34	14	14	0	0	55	54	47	39	38	35	.251	R	R	6-7	205	1-5-83	2001	La Grange, Ga.
Parker, Zach	1	2	7.52	8	8	0	0	26	42	26	22	12	19	.388	R	L	6-2	215	8-19-81	2001	Austin, Texas
Serrano, Alex	2	0	0.00	12	0	0	6	18	10	0	0	1	23	.161	R	R	6-1	200	2-18-81	1998	Barcelona, Venez.
Simpson, Joe	0	1	8.24	19	0	0	0	20	30	19	18	14	13	.344	R	R	6-2	190	10-10-78	1999	Fairfield, Ohio
Speier, Ryan	1	2	3.16	17	0	0	1	26	19	12	9	9	24	.195	R	R	6-7	200	7-24-79	2001	Springfield, Va.
Van Buren, Jermaine	3	0	5.32	6	3	1	0	24	25	15	14	10	25	.274	R	R	6-2	212	7-2-80	1998	Hattiesburg, Miss.
Vargas, Reynardo	3	4	6.11	21	0	0	0	28	43	25	19	14	21	.364	R	R	6-1	160	11-13-82	1999	Santo Domingo, D.R.
Villacis, Eduardo	1	0	0.00	1	1	0	0	6	5	1	0	2	3	.217	R	R	6-2	178	8-29-79	1998	Miranda, Venez.

DETROIT TIGERS

BY PAT CAPUTO

Every time the Tigers seem to take even a small step forward, they immediately take a huge step back. The 2001 season was the latest example of the team's maddeningly inconsistent play.

Detroit won 79 games a year earlier and got to the fringe of the wild-card race in the American League before faltering. In 2001, the Tigers were awful in every way, winning 66 games.

If players weren't bickering with manager Phil Garner, they were feuding with each other.

Owner Mike Ilitch cut the major league payroll to below $50 million after topping $60 million in 2000. He also reduced spending in player development. This all happened despite opening a new stadium in 2000, Comerica Park, which has defied the conventional wisdom presented in "Field of Dreams." They built it all right, but they did not come. Home attendance fell from 2,533,753 in 2000 to 1,921,305—a drop of more than 600,000.

By the end of May, team president John McHale Jr. departed after seven years.

Two key players who had big seasons in 2000 slid in 2001.

After signing a four-year, $35.5 million contract extension, outfielder Bobby Higginson hit .277-17-71. He hit .300-30-102 the season before.

Closer Todd Jones, who led the American League in saves in 2000, quibbled with Denise Ilitch, the daughter of the owner, during spring training. She was upset that he referred to the owner's children as "kids" and called Garner to protest. Jones then turned down a contract extension and was eventually traded to Minnesota.

Starting pitcher Brian Moehler, who led the team with 12 wins in 2000, made one start in 2001 and then missed the remainder of the season with a shoulder injury that required surgery. Third baseman Dean Palmer, who hit .256-29-102 in 2000, was limited to DH duty because of a shoulder injury that also eventually required surgery.

Steve Sparks   Nate Cornejo

PLAYERS OF THE YEAR

MAJOR LEAGUE: Steve Sparks, rhp

He isn't a strikeout king, but the 36-year-old righthander was the most dependable pitcher on the Tigers staff in 2001, going 14-9, 3.65 in 236 innings. His eight complete games led the American League.

MINOR LEAGUE: Nate Cornejo, rhp

He made the Tigers' rotation after starting the season with Double-A Erie (12-3, 2.68) and moving to Triple-A Toledo (4-0, 2.12). He struggled in his first trip to the majors, going 4-4, 7.38 in 42 innings.

One of the few bright spots in 2001 was 1997 first overall draft choice Matt Anderson. He had 22 saves after replacing Jones as the closer.

Knuckleballer Steve Sparks was Detroit's best starting pitcher. He went 14-9, 3.65 and led the major leagues in complete games—the first Detroit pitcher to do so since Frank Lary in 1961.

Center fielder Roger Cedeno had been Detroit's best player for much of the season, but Garner benched him in September. The two had a heated exchange during an intrasquad game the team held when Major League Baseball shut down for a week because of the terrorist attacks on Sept. 11.

First baseman Tony Clark got off to a good start and was the Tigers' representative at the All-Star Game. However, he developed wrist and shoulder injuries, in addition to combating a chronic back problem. He hit three home runs after the break.

When the Tigers' season was over, Garner called it his most disappointing as a manager. Considering he hasn't had a winning season since managing the Brewers in 1992, that summed up the situation perfectly.

All was not lost, however. The farm system had a number of bright developments in 2001.

The Tigers' new Double-A affiliate at Erie went 84-58. Righthander Nate Cornejo went 12-3, 2.68 and won four more games at both Triple-A Toledo and Detroit to finish with 20 on the year. Catcher Mike Rivera had a breakout year, hitting 33 homers, while first baseman Eric Munson led the organization with 102 RBIs.

Detroit's Rookie-level club in Lakeland also had a rewarding season, producing the top two prospects in the Gulf Coast League, lefthander Chad Petty and shortstop Anderson Hernandez.

ORGANIZATION LEADERS

BATTING
*AVG	Brian Rios, Toledo	.325
R	Eric Munson, Erie	88
H	Omar Infante, Erie	163
TB	Chris Wakeland, Toledo	263
2B	Eric Munson, Erie	35
3B	Anderson Hernandez, Lakeland/GCL Tigers	12
HR	Mike Rivera, Erie	33
RBI	Eric Munson, Erie	102
BB	Eric Munson, Erie	84
SO	Eric Munson, Erie	141
SB	Nook Logan, West Michigan	67

PITCHING
W	Nate Cornejo, Toledo/Erie	16
L	Mark Woodyard, West Michigan	12
#ERA	Michael Howell, West Michigan/Oneonta	1.79
G	Terry Pearson, Erie	59
CG	Tim Kalita, Erie	5
SV	Terry Pearson, Erie	23
	Mike Steele, Lakeland/West Michigan	23
IP	Tim Kalita, Erie	200
BB	Calvin Chipperfield, Lakeland	81
SO	Lee Rodney, West Michigan	149

*Minimum 250 At-Bats #Minimum 75 Innings

DETROIT TIGERS

Manager: Phil Garner

2001 Record: 66-96, .407 (4th, AL Central)

BATTING	AVG	G	AB	R	H	2B	3B	HR	RBI	BB	SO	SB	CS	SLG	OBP	B	T	HT	WT	DOB	1st Yr	Resides
Cardona, Javier	.260	46	96	10	25	8	0	1	10	2	12	0	1	.375	.280	R	R	6-1	185	9-15-75	1994	Dorado, P.R.
Cedeno, Roger	.293	131	523	79	153	14	11	6	48	36	83	55	15	.396	.337	B	R	6-1	205	8-16-74	1992	Valencia, Venez.
Clark, Jermaine	.000	3	0	1	0	0	0	0	0	0	0	0	0	.000	.000	L	R	5-10	175	9-29-76	1997	Vacaville, Calif.
Clark, Tony	.287	126	428	67	123	29	3	16	75	62	108	0	1	.481	.374	B	R	6-7	245	6-15-72	1990	Glendale, Ariz.
Cruz, Deivi	.256	110	414	39	106	28	1	7	52	17	46	4	1	.379	.291	R	R	6-0	184	11-6-75	1993	Bani, D.R.
Easley, Damion	.250	154	585	77	146	27	7	11	65	52	90	10	5	.376	.323	R	R	5-11	185	11-11-69	1988	Glendale, Ariz.
Encarnacion, Juan	.242	120	417	52	101	19	7	12	52	25	93	9	5	.408	.292	R	R	6-3	187	3-8-76	1992	Las Matas de Farfan, D.R.
Fick, Robert	.272	124	401	62	109	21	2	19	61	39	62	0	3	.476	.339	L	R	6-1	189	3-15-74	1996	Thousand Oaks, Calif.
Halter, Shane	.284	136	450	53	128	32	7	12	65	37	100	3	3	.467	.344	R	R	6-0	180	11-8-69	1991	Overland Park, Kan.
Higginson, Bobby	.277	147	541	84	150	28	6	17	71	80	65	20	12	.445	.367	L	R	5-11	195	8-18-70	1992	Bloomfield Hills, Mich.
Inge, Brandon	.180	79	189	13	34	11	0	0	15	9	41	1	4	.238	.215	R	R	5-11	185	5-19-77	1998	Evington, Va.
Jackson, Ryan	.212	79	118	19	25	4	2	2	11	5	26	3	1	.331	.250	L	L	6-2	205	11-15-71	1994	Sarasota, Fla.
Macias, Jose	.268	137	488	62	131	24	6	8	51	32	54	21	6	.391	.316	B	R	5-10	173	1-25-74	1992	Panama City, Panama
Magee, Wendell	.213	90	207	26	44	11	4	5	17	23	44	3	0	.377	.293	R	R	6-0	220	8-3-72	1994	Birmingham, Ala.
McMillon, Billy	.088	20	34	1	3	1	0	1	4	2	12	0	0	.206	.162	L	L	5-11	179	11-17-71	1993	Indianapolis, Ind.
Munson, Eric	.152	17	66	4	10	3	1	1	6	3	21	0	1	.273	.188	L	R	6-3	220	10-3-77	1999	San Diego, Calif.
Palmer, Dean	.222	57	216	34	48	11	0	11	40	27	59	4	1	.426	.317	R	R	6-1	210	12-27-68	1986	Tallahassee, Fla.
Patterson, Jarrod	.268	13	41	6	11	1	1	2	4	0	4	0	1	.488	.302	L	R	6-1	195	9-7-73	1993	Clanton, Ala.
Rivera, Mike	.333	4	12	2	4	2	0	0	1	0	2	0	0	.500	.333	R	R	6-0	190	9-8-76	1997	Bayamon, P.R.
Santana, Pedro	.000	1	0	0	0	0	0	0	0	0	0	0	0	.000	.000	R	R	5-11	160	9-21-76	1994	San Pedro de Macoris, D.R.
Simon, Randall	.305	81	256	28	78	14	2	6	37	15	28	0	1	.445	.341	L	L	6-0	180	5-26-75	1993	Willemstad, Curacao
Wakeland, Chris	.250	10	36	5	9	2	0	2	6	0	13	0	0	.472	.250	L	L	6-0	185	6-15-74	1996	St. Helens, Ore.

PITCHING	W	L	ERA	G	GS	CG	SV	IP	H	R	ER	BB	SO	AVG	B	T	HT	WT	DOB	1st Yr	Resides
Anderson, Matt	3	1	4.82	62	0	0	22	56	56	33	30	18	52	.256	R	R	6-4	200	8-17-76	1997	Louisville, Ky.
Bernero, Adam	0	0	7.30	5	0	0	0	12	13	13	10	4	8	.260	R	R	6-5	205	11-28-76	1999	Elk Grove, Calif.
Blair, Willie	1	4	10.50	9	4	0	0	24	38	30	28	11	15	.368	R	R	6-1	185	12-18-65	1986	Lexington, Ky.
Borkowski, Dave	0	2	6.37	15	0	0	0	30	30	21	21	15	30	.260	R	R	6-0	200	2-7-77	1995	Monroe, Mich.
Cornejo, Nate	4	4	7.38	10	10	0	0	43	63	38	35	28	22	.342	R	R	6-5	200	9-24-79	1998	Wellington, Kan.
Holt, Chris	7	9	5.77	30	22	1	0	151	197	102	97	57	80	.319	R	R	6-4	205	9-18-71	1992	Dallas, Texas
Jones, Todd	4	5	4.62	45	0	0	11	49	60	31	25	22	39	.303	R	R	6-3	230	4-24-68	1989	Pell City, Ala.
Lima, Jose	5	10	4.71	18	18	2	0	113	120	66	59	22	43	.273	R	R	6-2	205	9-30-72	1989	Houston, Texas
Miller, Matt	0	0	7.45	13	0	0	0	10	16	8	8	4	6	.372	L	L	6-3	175	8-2-74	1996	Lubbock, Texas
Mlicki, Dave	4	8	7.33	15	15	0	0	81	118	69	66	41	48	.348	R	R	6-4	205	6-8-68	1989	Columbus, Ohio
Moehler, Brian	0	0	3.38	1	1	0	0	8	6	3	3	1	2	.206	R	R	6-3	235	12-31-71	1993	Marietta, Ga.
Murray, Heath	1	7	6.54	40	4	0	0	63	82	48	46	40	42	.321	L	L	6-4	210	4-19-73	1994	Troy, Ohio
Nitkowski, C.J.	0	3	5.56	56	0	0	0	45	51	30	28	31	38	.283	L	L	6-3	205	3-9-73	1994	Houston, Texas
Patterson, Danny	5	4	3.06	60	0	0	1	65	64	24	22	12	27	.273	R	R	6-0	185	2-17-71	1989	Colleyville, Texas
Perisho, Matt	2	3	5.72	30	4	0	0	39	54	29	25	14	19	.327	L	L	6-0	205	6-8-75	1993	Chandler, Ariz.
Pettyjohn, Adam	1	6	5.82	16	9	0	0	65	81	48	42	21	40	.309	R	L	6-3	190	6-11-77	1998	Exeter, Calif.
Pineda, Luis	0	1	4.91	16	0	0	0	18	16	10	10	14	13	.238	R	R	6-1	160	6-10-78	1995	San Cristobal, D.R.
Redman, Mark	2	6	2.00	2	2	0	0	9	11	6	6	4	4	.305	L	L	6-5	220	1-5-74	1995	Catoosa, Okla.
2-team (9 Minnesota)	2	6	4.50	11	11	0	0	58	68	32	29	23	33	.289							
Santos, Victor	2	2	3.30	33	7	0	0	76	62	33	28	49	52	.222	R	R	6-3	175	10-2-76	1995	Garfield, N.J.
Sparks, Steve	14	9	3.65	35	33	8	0	232	244	110	94	64	116	.271	R	R	6-0	180	7-2-65	1987	Sugar Land, Texas
Tolar, Kevin	0	0	6.75	9	0	0	0	11	7	8	8	13	11	.189	R	L	6-3	225	1-28-71	1989	Venice, Fla.
Weaver, Jeff	13	16	4.08	33	33	5	0	229	235	116	104	68	152	.265	R	R	6-5	200	8-22-76	1998	Simi Valley, Calif.

FIELDING

Catcher	PCT	G	PO	A	E	DP	PB
Cardona	.980	44	132	15	3	1	8
Fick	.986	78	412	26	6	3	12
Inge	.989	79	330	40	4	3	10
Rivera	.929	4	24	2	2	0	0

First Base	PCT	G	PO	A	E	DP
T. Clark	.996	78	647	48	3	69
Fick	.995	26	169	12	1	10
Halter	1.000	8	69	7	0	10
Jackson	1.000	35	126	12	0	14
Munson	.994	17	142	14	1	14
Simon	.992	43	353	26	3	39

Second Base	PCT	G	PO	A	E	DP
Easley	.982	153	279	496	14	113
Macias	1.000	18	25	31	0	3
Santana	1.000	1	1	0	0	0

Third Base	PCT	G	PO	A	E	DP
Cruz	1.000	7	5	7	0	0

	PCT	G	PO	A	E	DP
Halter	.924	74	57	150	17	12
Macias	.955	89	68	187	12	23
J. Patterson	.923	13	9	15	2	0

Shortstop	PCT	G	PO	A	E	DP
Cruz	.964	109	157	292	17	69
Halter	.967	62	97	169	9	46

Outfield	PCT	G	PO	A	E	DP
Cedeno	.953	120	236	5	12	1
Encarnacion	.977	116	247	5	6	0
Fick	1.000	8	15	1	0	0
Higginson	.976	142	321	10	8	1
Jackson	.943	34	33	0	2	0
Macias	1.000	29	72	1	0	0
Magee	.992	74	123	7	1	0
McMillon	1.000	7	10	0	0	0
Wakeland	.941	10	32	0	2	0

LARRY GOREN

Bobby Higginson

Tony Clark: Led the Tigers with 75 RBIs

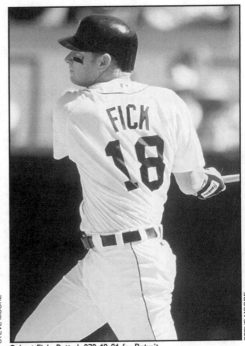

Robert Fick: Batted .272-19-61 for Detroit

FARM SYSTEM

Director, Player Development: Greg Smith

Class	Farm Team	League	W	L	Pct.	Finish*	Manager(s)	First Yr.
AAA	Toledo (Ohio) Mud Hens	International	65	79	.451	12th (14)	Bruce Fields	1987
AA	Erie (Pa.) SeaWolves	Eastern	84	58	.592	2nd (12)	Luis Pujols	2001
A#	Lakeland (Fla.) Tigers	Florida State	67	69	.493	9th (12)	Kevin Bradshaw	1960
A	West Michigan Whitecaps	Midwest	65	72	.474	8th (14)	Brent Gates	1997
A	Oneonta (N.Y.) Tigers	New York-Penn	37	37	.500	7th (14)	Gary Green	1999
Rookie	Lakeland (Fla.) Tigers	Gulf Coast	34	26	.567	5th (14)	Howard Bushong	1995

*Finish in overall standings (No. of teams in league)   #Advanced level

TOLEDO — Class AAA

INTERNATIONAL LEAGUE

BATTING	AVG	G	AB	R	H	2B	3B	HR	RBI	BB	SO	SB	CS	SLG	OBP	B	T	HT	WT	DOB	1st Yr	Resides
Airoso, Kurt	.200	10	30	2	6	0	2	1	1	4	7	0	1	.433	.294	R	R	6-2	190	2-12-75	1996	Tulare, Calif.
Allen, Dusty	.218	29	87	18	19	1	0	4	11	19	31	0	0	.368	.352	R	R	6-4	235	8-9-73	1995	Las Vegas, Nev.
Allensworth, Jermaine	.272	133	485	57	132	22	7	10	52	49	74	13	9	.408	.347	R	R	6-0	190	1-11-72	1993	Anderson, Ind.
Becker, Rich	.244	67	234	37	57	8	3	5	17	48	63	7	3	.368	.377	L	L	5-10	193	2-1-72	1990	Cape Coral, Fla.
Bierek, Kurt	.272	105	394	64	107	27	1	16	53	32	76	2	2	.467	.326	L	R	6-4	220	9-13-72	1993	Hillsboro, Ore.
Cardona, Javier	.235	26	98	7	23	2	0	1	10	8	18	1	0	.286	.292	R	R	6-1	185	9-15-75	1994	Dorado, P.R.
Coquillette, Trace	.200	28	85	13	17	6	1	3	10	13	29	0	0	.400	.310	R	R	5-11	185	6-4-74	1993	Orangevale, Calif.
2-team (55 Buffalo)	.205	83	263	40	54	11	4	9	32	32	67	1	2	.380	.303							
Evans, Tom	.266	50	169	26	45	12	2	5	19	26	33	1	3	.450	.377	R	R	6-1	200	7-9-74	1992	Issaquah, Wash.
Gazarek, Marty	.214	17	56	10	12	4	0	1	3	5	5	2	0	.339	.279	R	R	6-2	205	6-1-73	1994	Findlay, Ohio
Guevara, Giomar	.235	109	400	50	94	15	3	6	36	33	97	8	2	.333	.294	R	R	5-8	150	10-23-72	1990	Kirkland, Wash.
Inge, Brandon	.289	27	90	11	26	11	1	2	15	7	24	1	0	.500	.337	R	R	5-11	185	5-19-77	1998	Evington, Va.
Jackson, Ryan	.286	9	35	2	10	1	0	1	9	5	6	0	0	.400	.375	L	L	6-2	205	11-15-71	1994	Sarasota, Fla.
Lindstrom, David	.256	61	203	21	52	16	1	1	22	10	24	1	1	.360	.300	R	R	5-10	185	8-6-74	1996	Brooklyn Park, Minn.
Magee, Wendell	.444	2	9	0	4	0	0	0	1	0	0	0	0	.444	.444	R	R	6-0	220	8-3-72	1994	Birmingham, Ala.
Mendez, Carlos	.246	102	398	45	98	27	1	18	76	9	53	0	0	.455	.268	R	R	6-0	210	6-18-74	1991	Caracas, Venez.
Meran, Jorge	.190	7	21	0	4	0	0	0	2	2	7	1	0	.190	.250	R	R	6-4	230	5-13-69	1991	Tarpon Springs, Fla.
Mouton, Lyle	.317	67	262	59	83	18	2	18	49	29	66	4	1	.607	.394	R	R	6-4	230	12-27-68	1986	Tallahassee, Fla.
Palmer, Dean	.500	1	2	0	1	0	0	0	0	0	2	0	0	.500	.750	R	R	6-1	210	12-27-68	1986	Tallahassee, Fla.
Patterson, Jarrod	.296	69	213	41	63	15	2	7	25	30	47	2	1	.484	.381	L	R	6-1	195	9-7-73	1993	Clanton, Ala.
Perez, Jhonny	.250	32	120	19	30	7	2	1	14	9	24	7	2	.367	.305	R	R	5-10	180	10-23-76	1994	Santo Domingo, D.R.
Rios, Brian	.325	104	372	47	121	29	5	14	62	22	66	2	4	.543	.368	R	R	6-3	190	7-25-74	1996	Corona, Calif.
Santana, Pedro	.227	115	432	45	98	10	3	5	30	27	97	36	8	.299	.274	R	R	5-11	160	9-21-76	1994	San Pedro de Macoris, D.R.
Simon, Randall	.338	59	222	27	75	13	0	10	31	21	21	0	3	.532	.400	L	L	6-0	180	5-26-75	1993	Willemstad, Curacao
Wakeland, Chris	.283	140	547	85	155	33	3	23	84	39	126	7	8	.481	.338	L	L	6-0	185	6-15-74	1996	St. Helens, Ore.

PITCHING

PITCHING	W	L	ERA	G	GS	CG	SV	IP	H	R	ER	BB	SO	AVG	B	T	HT	WT	DOB	1st Yr	Resides
Arias, Pablo	0	0	8.31	1	1	0	0	4	4	5	4	2	1	.250	R	R	6-2	160	1-9-79	1996	Bani, D.R.
Bernero, Adam	6	11	5.13	26	25	1	0	140	172	90	80	54	99	.303	R	R	6-4	205	11-28-76	1999	Elk Grove, Calif.
Borkowski, Dave	1	2	3.54	18	0	0	1	28	22	14	11	9	22	.213	R	R	6-1	200	2-7-77	1995	Monroe, Mich.
Buller, Sean	1	0	1.69	5	0	0	0	11	8	2	2	5	9	.245	L	L	6-5	235	11-28-75	1998	Signal Hill, Calif.
Cornejo, Nate	4	0	2.12	4	4	0	0	30	24	8	7	7	22	.228	R	R	6-5	200	9-24-79	1998	Wellington, Kan.
DeLucia, Rich	1	1	2.54	28	0	0	5	39	27	11	11	15	45	.192	R	R	6-0	190	10-7-65	1986	Shillington, Pa.
Florie, Bryce	2	1	6.17	10	0	0	0	12	14	8	8	13	10	.304	R	R	5-11	192	5-21-70	1988	Goose Creek, S.C.
Hannah, Shawn	0	0	7.50	1	1	0	0	6	5	5	5	1	1	.260	R	R	6-3	205	3-22-77	2000	Clovis, Calif.
Heams, Shane	1	2	9.00	14	0	0	0	18	20	19	18	27	21	.281	R	R	6-1	175	9-29-75	1994	Lambertville, Mich.
Johnson, Mark	7	11	4.79	24	24	2	0	141	170	83	75	24	79	.297	R	R	6-3	226	5-2-75	1997	Leesburg, Fla.
Keller, Kris	5	2	4.48	52	0	0	4	68	64	42	34	38	60	.249	R	R	6-2	225	3-1-78	1996	Atlantic Beach, Fla.
Leek, Randy	0	0	3.86	1	1	0	0	7	7	3	3	0	3	.259	L	L	6-0	175	4-18-77	1999	Levittown, N.Y.
Loux, Shane	10	11	5.78	28	27	2	0	151	203	111	97	73	72	.304	R	R	6-2	205	8-13-79	1997	Gilbert, Ariz.
Maroth, Mike	7	10	4.65	24	23	0	0	132	158	80	68	50	63	.302	L	L	6-0	180	8-17-77	1998	Orlando, Fla.
Miller, Matt	1	2	2.87	50	0	0	4	63	60	26	20	18	49	.258	L	L	6-3	175	8-2-74	1996	Lubbock, Texas
Moehler, Brian	0	2	4.35	2	2	0	0	10	12	6	5	2	6	.293	R	R	6-3	235	12-31-71	1993	Marietta, Ga.
Murray, Heath	1	1	2.00	11	3	0	1	36	22	9	8	2	44	.170	L	L	6-4	210	4-19-73	1994	Troy, Ohio
Nitkowski, C.J.	0	0	0.00	1	0	0	0	1	1	0	0	0	1	.250	L	L	6-3	205	3-9-73	1994	Houston, Texas
Perisho, Matt	2	3	1.71	25	2	0	9	42	42	10	8	11	28	.260	L	L	6-0	205	6-8-75	1993	Chandler, Ariz.
Persails, Mark	2	3	5.77	12	5	0	0	48	53	37	31	21	24	.278	R	R	6-3	190	10-25-75	1995	Millington, Mich.
Pettyjohn, Adam	5	8	3.44	17	17	0	0	107	107	51	41	26	78	.260	R	L	6-3	190	6-11-77	1998	Exeter, Calif.
Phelps, Tommy	3	2	3.62	29	0	0	1	60	74	30	24	19	53	.288	L	L	6-3	192	3-4-74	1993	Tampa, Fla.
Pineda, Luis	1	0	0.00	2	0	0	0	8	3	0	0	0	6	.111	R	R	6-1	160	6-10-78	1995	San Cristobal, D.R.
Redman, Mark	0	1	5.27	3	3	0	0	14	14	10	8	1	12	.259	L	L	6-5	220	1-5-74	1995	Catoosa, Okla.
Runyan, Sean	0	1	8.44	11	0	0	0	11	15	17	10	11	6	.333	L	L	6-3	210	6-21-74	1992	Haines City, Fla.
Santos, Victor	2	1	6.37	6	6	0	0	35	50	27	25	12	22	.340	R	R	6-3	175	10-2-76	1995	Garfield, N.J.
Tolar, Kevin	3	4	2.73	44	0	0	7	56	49	18	17	21	73	.236	R	L	6-3	225	1-28-71	1989	Venice, Fla.

FIELDING

Catcher	PCT	G	PO	A	E	DP	PB
Cardona	.989	26	156	22	2	2	3
Inge	.989	27	160	20	2	1	6
Lindstrom	.981	54	349	22	7	4	4
Mendez	.989	41	240	21	3	6	1
Meran	1.000	7	32	5	0	0	1

First Base	PCT	G	PO	A	E	DP
Allen	.962	3	22	3	1	2
Bierek	.991	35	302	30	3	42
Jackson	1.000	1	12	0	0	2
Mendez	.994	55	479	28	3	49
Patterson	.979	6	45	1	1	0
Simon	.986	55	462	23	7	45

Second Base	PCT	G	PO	A	E	DP
Coquillette	.964	12	24	29	2	11

	PCT	G	PO	A	E	DP
Lindstrom	.944	6	8	9	1	5
Patterson	1.000	2	2	4	0	1
Perez	.913	6	10	11	2	3
Rios	.918	9	23	33	5	6
Santana	.948	112	234	328	31	87

Third Base	PCT	G	PO	A	E	DP
Bierek	1.000	1	1	2	0	0
Coquillette	.900	4	3	6	1	3
Evans	.936	49	33	99	9	12
Patterson	.946	41	16	89	6	4
Rios	.921	59	36	127	14	16

Shortstop	PCT	G	PO	A	E	DP
Evans	1.000	1	2	1	0	0
Guevara	.954	108	163	354	25	73
Perez	.958	27	44	93	6	18

	PCT	G	PO	A	E	DP
Rios	.927	15	14	37	4	9

Outfield	PCT	G	PO	A	E	DP
Airoso	1.000	7	18	1	0	0
Allen	.000	1	0	0	1	0
Allensworth	.985	133	318	8	5	0
Becker	.974	46	72	3	2	0
Bierek	.992	61	110	9	1	1
Coquillette	1.000	4	5	0	0	0
Gazarek	.964	16	26	1	1	0
Jackson	.900	7	9	0	1	0
Lindstrom	.875	3	7	0	1	0
Magee	1.000	2	2	0	0	0
Mouton	.983	53	113	6	2	2
Patterson	1.000	1	1	0	0	0
Wakeland	.966	113	213	13	8	2

ERIE

Class AA

EASTERN LEAGUE

BATTING	AVG	G	AB	R	H	2B	3B	HR	RBI	BB	SO	SB	CS	SLG	OBP	B	T	HT	WT	DOB	1st Yr	Resides
Airoso, Kurt	.236	82	276	45	65	16	1	14	44	32	62	1	0	.453	.313	R	R	6-2	190	2-12-75	1996	Tulare, Calif.
Baker, Derek	.278	6	18	2	5	0	0	0	3	3	4	0	0	.278	.409	L	R	6-2	220	10-5-75	1996	Tustin, Calif.
Camilo, Juan	.282	33	110	14	31	3	1	5	17	7	27	1	1	.464	.322	L	R	6-0	205	6-24-78	1996	Santo Domingo, D.R.
Cruz, Deivi	.417	4	12	2	5	1	0	1	3	0	1	0	0	.750	.417	R	R	6-0	184	11-6-75	1993	Bani, D.R.
Freire, Alejandro	.295	133	501	73	148	33	0	17	82	46	113	2	3	.463	.365	R	R	6-2	185	8-23-74	1992	Caracas, Venez.
Gazarek, Marty	.267	31	101	13	27	4	0	0	6	8	16	1	1	.307	.342	R	R	6-2	205	6-1-73	1999	Findlay, Ohio
Gomez, Rich	.269	93	346	60	93	21	2	14	44	25	75	2	1	.462	.344	R	R	5-11	190	8-19-77	1996	San Francisco de Macoris, D.R.
Infante, Omar	.302	132	540	86	163	21	4	2	62	46	87	27	12	.367	.355	R	R	6-0	150	12-26-81	1999	Guanta, Venez.
Kropf, Andy	.333	5	15	1	5	2	0	0	1	1	4	0	0	.467	.375	R	R	6-1	195	7-19-78	2000	Roswell, Ga.
Lindsey, Rodney	.252	111	385	51	97	14	1	2	34	23	77	29	12	.309	.311	R	R	5-8	175	1-28-76	1994	Opelika, Ala.
McClure, Brian	.251	75	255	29	64	14	2	1	22	23	45	0	0	.333	.317	L	R	6-0	170	1-15-74	1996	Chatham, Ill.
Meran, Jorge	.265	35	117	11	31	4	0	3	17	4	39	0	0	.376	.310	L	L	6-1	168	5-4-77	1993	Santo Domingo, D.R.
Merrill, Ronnie	.293	37	147	22	43	14	0	4	18	12	27	0	1	.469	.342	B	R	6-1	185	11-13-78	2000	Seffner, Fla.
Munson, Eric	.260	142	519	88	135	35	1	26	102	84	141	0	3	.482	.371	L	R	6-3	220	10-3-77	1999	San Diego, Calif.
Nicholson, Derek	.330	30	94	19	31	8	3	2	13	13	13	0	0	.543	.422	R	R	6-0	205	10-27-78	1998	Redondo Beach, Calif.
Patterson, Jarrod	.400	20	70	17	28	5	1	7	18	11	11	0	0	.800	.476	L	R	5-11	195	9-7-73	1993	Clanton, Ala.
Perez, Jhonny	.266	83	293	42	78	13	3	5	30	20	46	10	4	.382	.314	R	R	5-10	180	10-23-76	1994	Santo Domingo, D.R.
Rivera, Mike	.289	112	415	76	120	19	1	33	101	44	96	2	2	.578	.368	R	R	6-0	190	9-8-76	1997	Bayamon, P.R.
Torres, Andres	.294	64	252	54	74	16	3	1	23	36	50	19	11	.393	.391	B	R	5-10	175	1-26-78	1998	Aguada, P.R.
Ust, Brant	.238	87	323	36	77	16	1	6	31	15	81	1	1	.350	.282	R	R	6-2	200	7-17-78	1999	Redmond, Wash.

PITCHING	W	L	ERA	G	GS	CG	SV	IP	H	R	ER	BB	SO	AVG	B	T	HT	WT	DOB	1st Yr	Resides
Baugh, Kenny	1	3	2.97	5	5	1	0	30	23	16	10	6	30	.207	R	R	6-4	185	2-5-79	2001	Houston, Texas
Bess, Stephen	0	2	2.89	10	1	0	0	19	15	6	6	4	8	.227	R	R	6-4	225	9-1-76	1999	Nashville, Tenn.
Buller, Sean	2	1	5.82	16	0	0	2	22	27	15	14	4	11	.296	L	L	6-5	235	11-28-75	1998	Signal Hill, Calif.
Camp, Jared	1	1	4.82	11	0	0	1	19	16	11	10	16	18	.238	R	R	6-2	195	5-4-75	1995	Huntington, W.Va.
Cornejo, Nate	12	3	2.68	19	19	3	0	124	107	37	37	41	105	.228	R	R	6-5	200	9-24-79	1998	Wellington, Kan.
Eckenstahler, Eric	4	2	3.90	46	0	0	4	65	65	32	28	31	73	.256	L	L	6-7	210	12-17-76	2000	Lake Villa, Ill.
Farmer, Tom	0	0	2.53	2	2	0	0	11	12	3	3	4	8	.300	R	R	6-3	185	7-27-79	2001	Crestwood, Ill.
Heams, Shane	3	2	3.15	36	0	0	6	54	22	15	13	37	57	.122	R	R	6-1	175	9-29-75	1994	Lambertville, Mich.
Kalita, Tim	15	9	3.83	30	29	5	0	200	190	98	85	49	147	.251	R	L	6-2	220	11-21-78	1999	Oak Park, Ill.
Kirsten, Rick	14	8	4.62	28	27	1	0	162	161	93	83	53	143	.256	R	R	6-0	165	7-23-78	1996	Rolling Meadows, Ill.
Leek, Randy	11	7	3.86	29	27	4	1	179	190	87	77	27	123	.272	L	L	6-0	175	4-18-77	1999	Levittown, N.Y.
Pearson, Terry	4	4	2.93	59	0	0	23	61	65	26	20	16	62	.261	R	R	6-0	200	11-10-71	1995	Carrollton, Ala.

PITCHING

PITCHING	W	L	ERA	G	GS	CG	SV	IP	H	R	ER	BB	SO	AVG	B	T	HT	WT	DOB	1st Yr	Resides
Persails, Mark	1	4	7.28	9	7	0	0	38	62	37	31	18	15	.380	R	R	6-3	190	10-25-75	1995	Millington, Mich.
Phelps, Tommy	1	1	3.58	15	2	0	2	33	33	14	13	8	31	.268	L	L	6-3	192	3-4-74	1993	Tampa, Fla.
Pineda, Luis	6	2	3.05	16	12	0	0	86	68	33	29	28	92	.225	R	R	6-1	160	6-10-78	1995	San Cristobal, D.R.
Rivera, Homero	1	2	4.75	16	2	0	2	30	35	16	16	11	19	.299	L	L	5-10	165	8-13-78	1995	Nizao, D.R.
Rodney, Fernando	0	0	4.26	4	0	0	1	6	7	3	3	3	8	.291	R	R	5-11	170	3-17-81	1997	Santo Domingo, D.R.
Tekavec, Nate	0	1	6.75	1	1	0	0	1	3	1	1	0	2	.428	R	R	6-5	200	5-2-79	2000	Concord, Ohio
Tucker, Julien	1	5	4.93	23	0	0	0	46	52	30	25	30	21	.292	L	R	6-7	200	4-19-73	1993	Chateauguay, Quebec
Van Hekken, Andy	5	0	4.69	8	8	0	0	48	63	29	25	8	29	.319	R	L	6-3	175	7-31-79	1998	Holland, Mich.

FIELDING

Catcher	PCT	G	PO	A	E	DP	PB
Kropf	1.000	5	28	2	0	1	0
Meran	.967	33	209	23	8	2	5
M. Rivera	.989	109	793	83	10	8	7

First Base	PCT	G	PO	A	E	DP
Baker	.964	3	25	2	1	0
Freire	.980	10	92	6	2	6
Munson	.985	129	1031	93	17	94
Nicholson	1.000	1	4	0	0	1

Second Base	PCT	G	PO	A	E	DP
McClure	.978	29	56	80	3	19

Merrill	.958	32	61	75	6	20
Perez	.972	83	156	219	11	48

Third Base	PCT	G	PO	A	E	DP
Cruz	1.000	2	1	6	0	0
McClure	.952	35	19	60	4	4
Nicholson	.667	3	0	2	1	0
Patterson	.920	20	14	32	4	3
Ust	.949	87	47	158	11	15

Shortstop	PCT	G	PO	A	E	DP
Cruz	.857	3	3	3	1	0
Infante	.955	132	206	370	27	71

McClure	1.000	6	7	14	0	3
Merrill	1.000	6	10	19	0	4

Outfield	PCT	G	PO	A	E	DP
Airoso	.981	80	145	6	3	1
Camilo	.955	32	62	1	3	0
Freire	.971	18	33	0	1	0
Gazarek	.938	28	45	0	3	0
Gomez	.966	92	163	6	6	0
Lindsey	.982	111	258	11	5	4
McClure	1.000	2	1	0	0	0
Nicholson	.941	20	31	1	2	0
Torres	.993	55	136	3	1	1

LAKELAND — Class A

FLORIDA STATE LEAGUE

BATTING	AVG	G	AB	R	H	2B	3B	HR	RBI	BB	SO	SB	CS	SLG	OBP	B	T	HT	WT	DOB	1st Yr	Resides
Baker, Derek	.268	77	213	31	57	16	0	0	34	60	43	1	2	.343	.432	L	R	6-2	220	10-5-75	1996	Tustin, Calif.
Bautista, Rayner	.260	101	354	43	92	18	4	8	43	20	89	8	4	.401	.298	R	R	5-11	155	8-17-79	1995	Nizao, D.R.
Boone, Matt	.256	104	375	47	96	16	5	4	33	29	95	8	3	.357	.309	R	R	6-2	175	7-18-79	1997	Villa Park, Calif.
Camilo, Juan	.301	55	193	34	58	10	5	8	37	26	52	7	2	.528	.393	L	R	6-0	205	6-24-78	1996	Santo Domingo, D.R.
Daigle, Leo	.252	95	313	42	79	19	1	11	58	24	77	4	1	.425	.311	R	R	6-3	225	9-18-79	1997	Spring Valley, Calif.
Downing, Brad	.255	34	94	15	24	7	0	5	27	16	19	0	0	.489	.357	L	R	6-0	200	5-10-76	1998	Celina, Texas
Garland, Ross	.250	1	4	0	1	0	0	0	0	0	2	0	0	.250	.250	R	R	6-0	190	2-27-80	2000	Johnson City, Tenn.
Hernandez, Anderson	.190	7	21	2	4	0	1	0	1	0	8	0	0	.286	.190	B	R	5-9	150	10-30-82	2001	Santo Domingo, D.R.
Jenkins, Neil	.302	23	86	14	26	8	1	1	6	2	25	0	1	.453	.315	R	R	6-5	205	7-17-80	1999	Jupiter, Fla.
Jimenez, Carlos	.193	54	135	17	26	7	1	0	11	17	47	6	2	.259	.288	R	R	5-11	165	5-26-80	1996	San Pedro de Macoris, D.R.
Kropf, Andy	.231	48	169	16	39	8	0	5	15	16	27	1	0	.331	.296	B	R	6-1	195	7-19-78	2000	Roswell, Ga.
Lara, David	.238	16	42	4	10	5	1	0	4	2	11	2	0	.405	.289	R	R	6-3	180	6-19-78	1995	Santo Domingo, D.R.
Leer, David	.209	50	129	17	27	6	3	0	5	3	36	8	1	.302	.255	R	R	6-1	175	2-2-77	1997	San Nicolas, Aruba
Nicholson, Derek	.267	39	116	12	31	4	1	0	18	16	16	2	0	.319	.358	L	R	6-0	205	6-17-76	1998	Redondo Beach, Calif.
Richardson, Corey	.263	131	498	76	131	23	3	2	38	71	93	31	11	.333	.363	R	L	5-11	180	12-23-80	1999	Carlsbad, N.M.
Ross, Cody	.276	127	482	84	133	34	5	15	80	44	96	28	5	.461	.337	R	R	5-9	180	12-23-80	1998	Las Matas de Farfan, D.R.
Santiago, Ramon	.268	120	429	64	115	15	3	2	46	54	60	34	8	.331	.361	B	R	6-3	186	3-14-78	1997	Bayamon, P.R.
Santos, Juan	.161	23	62	7	10	2	1	1	4	3	18	0	0	.274	.197	B	R	5-10	165	10-1-80	1998	Anaco, Venez.
Sequea, Jorge	.247	104	328	39	81	16	1	6	54	32	47	9	7	.357	.318	R	R	5-11	180	10-20-80	1998	Montreal, Quebec
St. Pierre, Maxim	.248	99	330	42	82	15	0	4	43	43	50	2	5	.330	.338	R	R	6-0	175	4-17-80	1997	Montreal, Quebec
Tousa, Scott	.216	39	111	18	24	4	0	0	8	18	21	3	1	.252	.341	L	R	5-11	180	8-3-79	2001	St. George, Utah
Vargas, Inakel	.182	7	22	1	4	0	0	0	2	3	3	0	0	.182	.308	R	R	6-0	185	3-1-78	1995	Santo Domingo, D.R.

GAMES BY POSITION: C—Garland 1, Kropf 23, Santos 20, St. Pierre 98, Vargas 7. **1B**—Baker 60, Daigle 84, Downing 1, Nicholson 12. **2B**—Bautista 1, Jimenez 45, Sequea 63, Tousa 38. **3B**—Boone 104, Daigle 4, Jimenez 2, Kropf 25, Nicholson 6, Sequea 2. **SS**—Bautista 99, Boone 1, Hernandez 7, Jimenez 1, Sequea 33. **OF**—Baker 1, Camilo 52, Downing 34, Jenkins 21, Lara 15, Leer 43, Nicholson 17, Richardson 130, Ross 126.

PITCHING	W	L	ERA	G	GS	CG	SV	IP	H	R	ER	BB	SO	AVG	B	T	HT	WT	DOB	1st Yr	Resides
Arias, Pablo	3	1	4.89	8	7	0	0	42	48	26	23	16	28	.282	R	R	6-2	160	1-9-79	1996	Bani, D.R.
Bess, Stephen	2	3	2.65	33	0	0	19	37	25	12	11	12	39	.189	R	R	6-4	225	9-1-76	1999	Nashville, Tenn.
Chipperfield, Calvin	7	8	4.79	24	24	1	0	124	132	73	66	81	109	.276	R	R	6-1	170	3-7-78	1998	Adelaide, Australia
Corrado, Matt	3	7	5.68	16	12	1	0	63	62	45	40	31	48	.259	L	R	6-6	205	8-4-78	2001	Sevierville, Tenn.
Dunn, Gerald	1	1	4.50	2	1	0	0	6	11	3	3	1	2	.407	R	R	6-4	210	6-30-81	2001	Charlotte, N.C.
Eckenstahler, Eric	1	0	1.50	4	0	0	1	6	3	1	1	2	7	.157	L	L	6-7	210	12-17-76	2000	Lake Villa, Ill.
Graves, Robert	0	1	2.73	15	0	0	0	26	21	12	8	14	14	.221	L	L	5-10	175	1-20-80	2001	Las Vegas, Nev.
Hannah, Shawn	7	5	3.35	34	17	0	0	129	128	63	48	54	55	.264	R	R	6-3	205	3-22-77	2000	Clovis, Calif.
Herauf, Jeremy	0	0	10.80	6	0	0	0	7	13	8	8	5	3	.406	R	R	6-4	195	7-7-78	2001	Regina, Saskatchewan
Johnson, Jeremy	1	1	5.25	4	2	0	0	12	15	8	7	6	6	.319	R	R	6-3	170	7-19-82	2000	Mooresville, N.C.
Marx, Tommy	8	11	4.91	28	27	1	0	150	160	92	82	78	97	.277	R	L	6-7	200	9-5-79	1998	West Bloomfield, Mich.
Matthews, Barry	2	2	4.04	22	7	1	0	62	70	31	28	23	42	.280	L	L	6-0	185	4-6-78	2001	Northridge, Calif.
Persails, Mark	0	0	2.84	3	0	0	1	6	6	2	2	1	6	.250	R	R	6-3	190	10-25-75	1995	Millington, Mich.
Rivas, Gabriel	0	0	0.00	1	0	0	0	2	0	0	0	1	2	.000	R	R	6-5	170	5-24-82	1999	Ciudad Bolivar, Venez.
Rivera, Homero	3	4	2.19	35	0	0	3	49	30	13	12	18	31	.177	L	R	5-10	165	8-13-78	1995	Nizao, D.R.
Rodney, Fernando	4	2	3.42	16	9	0	0	55	53	26	21	19	44	.248	R	R	6-1	160	3-17-81	1997	Santo Domingo, D.R.
Serrano, Willy	3	8	3.17	50	6	0	4	82	91	41	29	28	56	.279	R	R	6-4	185	9-4-76	1998	Claremore, Okla.
Smith, Clint	0	2	4.60	20	0	0	0	29	25	18	15	24	37	.221	R	R	6-3	190	8-30-77	1995	Albanvale, Australia
Spear, Russ	1	1	5.11	8	0	0	0	12	5	8	7	13	18	.128	R	R	6-2	205	8-22-78	2000	Midland, Mich.
Steele, Mike	0	1	3.86	15	0	0	0	14	17	12	8	7	10	.246	R	R	6-5	200	5-2-79	2000	Concord, Ohio
Tekavec, Nate	1	1	2.84	18	11	0	0	79	77	27	25	17	56	.258	R	R	6-5	200	5-2-79	2000	Concord, Ohio
Van Hekken, Andy	10	4	3.17	19	19	2	0	111	105	43	39	33	82	.251	R	L	6-3	175	7-31-79	1998	Holland, Mich.
Watson, Greg	3	6	3.14	57	0	0	9	66	55	35	23	35	53	.226	R	R	6-2	165	1-8-77	1999	Tampa, Fla.

WEST MICHIGAN — Class A

MIDWEST LEAGUE

BATTING	AVG	G	AB	R	H	2B	3B	HR	RBI	BB	SO	SB	CS	SLG	OBP	B	T	HT	WT	DOB	1st Yr	Resides
Amador, Jerry	.221	81	289	24	64	7	1	4	31	15	47	4	3	.294	.271	R	R	6-0	185	1-13-80	1999	Camuy, P.R.
Cleveland, Russ	.244	61	205	18	50	9	0	2	13	13	51	0	3	.317	.299	R	R	6-3	205	12-26-79	1998	Las Vegas, Nev.

BATTING	AVG	G	AB	R	H	2B	3B	HR	RBI	BB	SO	SB	CS	SLG	OBP	B	T	HT	WT	DOB	1st Yr	Resides
Downing, Brad	.266	49	154	19	41	4	2	5	23	15	18	0	3	.416	.335	L	R	6-0	200	5-10-76	1998	Celina, Texas
Durham, Miles	.218	68	257	29	56	6	3	0	20	25	74	33	7	.265	.289	L	R	6-3	195	8-19-78	2000	Dallas, Texas
Hannahan, Jack	.318	46	170	24	54	11	0	1	27	26	39	4	2	.400	.409	L	R	6-2	205	3-4-80	2001	St. Paul, Minn.
Inge, Brandon	.188	4	16	3	3	1	0	0	2	2	5	0	0	.250	.316	R	R	5-11	185	5-19-77	1998	Evington, Va.
Johnson, Forrest	.260	114	420	64	109	19	1	15	61	36	89	3	0	.417	.327	R	R	6-2	190	3-21-79	2000	Rialto, Calif.
Logan, Nook	.262	128	522	82	137	19	8	1	27	53	129	67	19	.335	.330	B	R	6-2	180	11-28-79	2000	Nashville, Tenn.
Luuloa, Miles	.184	84	250	30	46	9	2	2	17	35	76	5	4	.260	.283	R	R	5-9	180	9-23-80	2000	Kaunakakai, Hawaii
Merrill, Ronnie	.317	83	309	53	98	11	3	8	53	36	47	15	7	.450	.394	B	R	6-1	185	11-13-78	2000	Seffner, Fla.
Neill, Ryan	.239	130	419	68	100	13	6	7	61	71	122	35	8	.372	.372	R	R	6-2	205	10-23-77	2000	Broken Arrow, Okla.
Parker, Chris	.253	74	237	25	60	13	0	1	22	23	46	2	1	.321	.337	R	R	6-2	185	8-16-79	1997	Thousand Oaks, Calif.
Peguero, Miguel	.226	109	368	31	83	15	1	1	30	22	73	5	6	.280	.270	R	R	6-0	180	9-29-80	1997	Santo Domingo, D.R.
Quattlebaum, Hugh	.239	121	415	63	99	26	4	3	55	68	68	8	4	.342	.355	R	R	6-4	205	6-26-78	2000	Andover, Mass.
Walker, Matt	.260	112	415	53	108	23	2	10	65	34	80	11	4	.398	.322	R	R	6-2	205	12-3-77	2000	Gibsonia, Pa.
Woods, Michael	.270	44	163	30	44	8	4	0	17	32	44	13	7	.368	.401	R	R	6-1	180	9-11-80	2001	Baton Rouge, La.

GAMES BY POSITION: C—Cleveland 57, Inge 2, F. Johnson 19, Parker 67. **1B**—F. Johnson 32, Neill 70, Quattlebaum 42. **2B**—Luuloa 66, Peguero 33, Woods 44. **3B**—Hannahan 45, Luuloa 2, Peguero 22, Quattlebaum 74. **SS**—Luuloa 11, Merrill 82, Peguero 53. **OF**—Amador 66, Cleveland 1, Downing 11, Durham 65, Logan 126, Neill 57, Walker 101.

PITCHING	W	L	ERA	G	GS	CG	SV	IP	H	R	ER	BB	SO	AVG	B	T	HT	WT	DOB	1st Yr	Resides
Arias, Pablo	9	4	3.17	20	17	0	0	108	100	44	38	33	81	.243	R	R	6-2	160	1-9-79	1996	Bani, D.R.
Baugh, Kenny	2	1	1.59	6	6	0	0	34	31	14	6	10	39	.238	R	R	6-4	185	2-5-79	2001	Houston, Texas
Campbell, Dayle	1	7	7.04	21	13	0	1	69	83	67	54	57	47	.301	R	R	6-7	200	9-30-78	1999	Carson, Calif.
Cuello, Manolin	2	3	5.40	23	3	0	0	55	47	44	33	47	61	.223	R	R	6-3	185	5-5-81	2000	Santo Domingo, D.R.
Detillion, Jamie	2	3	2.10	48	0	0	4	77	66	21	18	27	66	.228	L	L	6-2	210	6-22-78	2000	Tiffin, Ohio
Farmer, Tom	3	2	2.37	6	6	0	0	38	30	10	10	8	28	.220	R	R	6-3	185	7-27-79	2001	Crestwood, Ill.
Fuell, Jerrod	0	1	2.91	14	0	0	1	22	13	8	7	12	13	.175	R	R	6-4	210	10-3-80	1999	Tucson, Ariz.
Hernandez, Fausto	1	1	5.40	9	0	0	0	17	21	11	10	6	16	.304	R	R	6-3	175	11-20-79	1997	Santo Domingo, D.R.
Howell, Michael	3	0	1.76	8	8	0	0	51	41	12	10	7	42	.219	R	R	6-4	200	11-9-79	2001	Binghamton, N.Y.
Johnson, Jeremy	1	1	4.67	3	3	0	0	17	18	10	9	6	7	.264	R	R	6-3	170	7-19-82	2000	Mooresville, N.C.
Johnston, Rikki	2	8	4.38	13	13	0	0	74	72	43	36	28	59	.255	L	L	6-4	185	4-2-81	1998	Victoria, Australia
Leu, Trevor	1	3	5.57	13	0	0	0	21	23	18	13	16	28	.264	L	L	6-2	220	12-29-78	2001	Bartlesville, Okla.
Leuenberger, Jeff	3	2	3.10	30	0	0	0	49	46	19	17	19	40	.255	R	R	5-11	185	10-15-78	2000	Orange, Calif.
Lewis, Jeremy	3	4	2.90	9	9	1	0	50	41	20	16	21	35	.227	R	L	6-4	180	9-12-80	1999	Concord, N.C.
Perez, Franklin	7	2	2.65	36	1	0	2	78	63	27	23	29	81	.223	R	R	5-11	185	5-11-80	1998	San Francisco de Macoris, D.R.
Pitney, Jim	1	0	3.42	15	0	0	1	26	23	12	10	12	27	.232	R	R	6-2	190	6-3-78	2000	Eastport, N.Y.
Rodney, Lee	8	8	3.87	27	27	0	0	158	149	85	68	70	149	.248	R	R	6-2	187	11-6-77	2000	Dacula, Ga.
Sierra, Auvin	2	2	5.09	17	1	0	0	23	24	15	13	16	20	.282	L	L	5-10	170	1-4-78	2000	La Puente, Calif.
Steele, Mike	4	3	1.16	38	0	0	19	47	23	13	6	26	78	.141	R	R	6-2	205	8-22-78	2000	Midland, Mich.
Stockman, Landon	2	2	2.42	18	0	0	6	26	21	7	7	13	23	.221	R	R	6-2	190	8-28-79	2000	Dickson, Tenn.
Swindell, Jeremy	0	0	16.20	4	0	0	0	2	1	3	3	6	1	.166	L	L	6-2	220	8-4-77	2000	Houston, Texas
Warren, Andy	1	1	3.45	3	3	0	0	16	17	7	6	3	12	.265	R	R	6-4	190	6-11-78	2000	Conroe, Texas
Wheatland, Matt	0	2	10.93	3	3	0	0	14	21	18	17	4	17	.333	R	R	6-5	215	10-18-81	2000	Poway, Calif.
Woodyard, Mark	7	12	4.51	25	25	2	0	144	147	81	72	69	84	.266	R	R	6-2	185	12-19-78	2000	Grand Bay, Ala.

ONEONTA
Short-Season Class A

NEW YORK-PENN LEAGUE

BATTING	AVG	G	AB	R	H	2B	3B	HR	RBI	BB	SO	SB	CS	SLG	OBP	B	T	HT	WT	DOB	1st Yr	Resides
Brostrom, Jeremy	.333	2	3	2	1	1	0	0	0	4	0	0	0	.667	.714	L	L	6-3	190	1-19-78	2001	Peachtree City, Ga.
Dean, Herman	.208	7	24	3	5	1	1	0	0	1	10	1	0	.333	.240	R	R	6-3	190	11-25-80	2001	Monrovia, Calif.
Francia, Juan	.340	47	191	30	65	5	2	0	8	11	32	17	14	.387	.380	B	R	5-9	145	1-4-82	1998	San Antonio de los Altos, Venez.
Garland, Ross	.151	32	106	8	16	3	1	1	10	5	31	0	1	.226	.211	R	R	6-0	190	2-27-80	2000	Johnson City, Tenn.
Gomersall, Richard	.167	43	120	18	20	2	0	1	8	11	45	3	2	.208	.246	R	R	6-1	180	2-12-79	2001	West Palm Beach, Fla.
Gonzalez, Juan	.344	10	32	5	11	2	1	0	8	3	5	2	2	.469	.405	R	R	6-0	165	2-23-82	1999	Valencia, Venez.
Hannahan, Jack	.291	14	55	11	16	4	1	0	8	5	7	2	1	.400	.333	L	R	6-2	205	3-4-80	2001	St. Paul, Minn.
Heath, Demetrius	.313	6	16	0	5	0	0	0	1	1	2	0	1	.313	.353	R	R	5-10	170	1-23-81	2001	Bethel, N.C.
Kelly, Donald	.286	67	262	41	75	8	3	0	25	25	16	8	5	.340	.345	L	R	6-4	185	2-15-80	2001	Pittsburgh, Pa.
Knoedler, Jason	.226	59	208	30	47	3	4	4	20	28	61	11	4	.337	.319	R	R	6-0	200	7-17-80	2001	Springfield, Ill.
Kolodzey, Chris	.249	65	237	29	59	13	5	2	25	20	37	4	5	.371	.314	R	R	6-0	200	7-15-79	2001	Cherry Hill, N.J.
Mattle, David	.204	40	142	14	29	8	1	1	22	17	33	2	0	.296	.293	L	R	6-0	200	12-21-79	2000	Barberton, Ohio
Rabelo, Mike	.325	53	194	27	63	4	2	0	32	23	45	1	2	.366	.405	L	R	6-1	195	1-17-80	2001	New Port Richey, Fla.
Raburn, Ryan	.363	44	171	25	62	17	8	8	42	17	42	1	3	.696	.418	R	R	6-0	185	4-17-81	2001	Plant City, Fla.
Rueffert, Mark	.221	24	68	6	15	1	0	0	3	13	26	1	1	.235	.346	R	R	6-1	185	12-2-78	2001	Herndon, Va.
Ryan, Billy	.182	11	33	2	6	0	0	0	4	1	7	1	0	.182	.289	R	R	6-3	200	7-21-81	2001	Brooklyn, N.Y.
Scott, Mike	.000	2	3	0	0	0	0	0	1	0	2	0	0	.000	.000	L	L	5-10	175	11-17-78	2001	Darien, Conn.
Stringham, Jed	.187	44	134	10	25	5	0	1	11	8	38	1	1	.246	.238	R	R	6-3	215	12-28-77	2001	Provo, Utah
Tousa, Scott	.167	8	24	6	4	0	0	0	1	2	5	2	0	.167	.259	L	R	5-11	180	8-3-79	2001	St. George, Utah
Trezza, Alex	.224	53	183	23	41	11	2	1	19	13	65	0	1	.322	.281	L	R	6-3	215	9-1-80	2001	Middletown, N.Y.
Woods, Michael	.270	9	37	6	10	2	0	0	3	4	5	5	1	.324	.357	R	R	6-1	180	9-11-80	2001	Baton Rouge, La.
Yount, Andy	.271	63	207	31	56	8	4	6	31	32	83	11	4	.435	.381	R	R	6-2	185	2-14-77	1995	Kingwood, Texas

GAMES BY POSITION: C—Garland 32, Rabelo 42, Rueffert 4. **1B**—Gomersall 7, Gonzalez 7, Rueffert 13, Stringham 32, Trezza 26. **2B**—Francia 40, Gomersall 19, Gonzalez 1, Heath 5, Raburn 1, Woods 7. **3B**—Francia 1, Gomersall 8, Gonzalez 2, Hannahan 12, Raburn 42, Ryan 11. **SS**—Gomersall 9, Gonzalez 1, Kelly 67. **OF**—Brostrom 1, Dean 7, Knoedler 58, Kolodzey 54, Mattle 38, Scott 2, Stringham 8, Yount 61.

PITCHING	W	L	ERA	G	GS	CG	SV	IP	H	R	ER	BB	SO	AVG	B	T	HT	WT	DOB	1st Yr	Resides
Birtwell, John	1	2	3.76	23	0	0	7	26	25	12	11	6	43	.242	R	R	6-2	225	9-4-79	2001	Walpole, Mass.
Coenen, Matt	3	2	3.04	10	9	1	1	47	44	26	16	16	37	.236	L	L	6-6	230	3-13-80	2001	St. Michaels, Md.
Connolly, Jon	0	1	18.00	1	1	0	0	3	8	6	6	1	1	.533	R	L	6-0	205	8-24-83	2001	Oneonta, N.Y.
Farmer, Tom	1	1	2.86	4	4	0	0	22	24	13	7	4	11	.266	R	R	6-3	185	7-27-79	2001	Crestwood, Ill.
Gerk, Jordan	0	2	0.25	4	0	0	0	8	10	3	2	2	10	.285	L	L	6-1	180	7-6-79	2000	Kelowna, B.C.
Gonzales, Jim	3	3	2.55	16	0	0	2	25	24	10	7	8	20	.252	R	R	6-0	185	8-4-79	2001	Las Vegas, Nev.
Herauf, Jeremy	0	1	2.31	5	0	0	0	12	10	5	3	3	13	.227	R	R	6-4	195	7-7-78	2001	Regina, Saskatchewan
Howell, Michael	0	1	1.82	6	6	0	0	35	27	12	7	6	26	.212	R	R	6-4	200	11-9-79	2001	Binghamton, N.Y.
Johnson, Jeremy	7	1	3.42	12	12	1	0	76	76	39	29	13	48	.264	R	R	6-3	170	7-19-82	2000	Mooresville, N.C.
Kobow, Mike	1	0	6.55	7	0	0	0	11	16	8	8	1	13	.340	R	R	6-4	190	4-9-79	2001	Hutchinson, Minn.

PITCHING	W	L	ERA	G	GS	CG	SV	IP	H	R	ER	BB	SO	AVG	B	T	HT	WT	DOB	1st Yr	Resides
Koenig, Ross	4	2	3.67	16	8	0	0	54	43	31	22	30	58	.211	R	R	6-3	175	5-4-80	2001	Festus, Mo.
Larrison, Preston	1	3	2.47	10	8	0	0	47	37	22	13	21	50	.207	R	R	6-4	215	11-19-80	2001	Aurora, Ill.
Leu, Trevor	3	0	1.02	8	0	0	0	18	13	5	2	7	18	.213	L	L	6-2	200	12-29-78	2001	Bartlesville, Okla.
Lewis, Jeremy	2	5	7.95	15	7	1	1	49	83	56	43	19	29	.373	L	L	6-4	180	9-12-80	1999	Concord, N.C.
McDowell, Kevin	2	4	2.74	14	7	0	0	46	40	25	14	27	35	.236	L	L	6-2	200	11-20-78	2001	Cheswick, Pa.
Moates, Jason	0	0	0.00	1	0	0	0	2	1	0	0	0	4	.142	R	R	6-3	230	8-22-78	2001	Columbia, Tenn.
Ostlund, Ian	2	5	3.15	14	10	0	0	66	63	29	23	20	44	.250	L	L	6-1	200	10-17-78	2001	Singers Glen, Va.
Petty, Chad	0	1	2.84	1	1	0	0	6	6	5	2	2	0	.250	L	L	6-4	200	2-17-82	2000	West Farmington, Ohio
Sierra, Auvin	1	2	2.12	18	0	0	1	30	30	10	7	8	31	.267	L	L	5-10	170	1-4-78	2000	La Puente, Calif.
Smith, Dan	1	2	4.00	20	0	0	0	36	27	24	16	22	27	.204	R	R	6-4	215	11-29-78	2001	Bonne Terre, Mo.
Stockman, Landon	0	1	2.53	11	0	0	6	11	9	4	3	1	7	.214	R	R	6-2	190	8-28-79	2001	Dickson, Tenn.
Vargas, Javier	0	1	13.50	2	1	0	0	5	14	12	8	6	4	.482	R	R	6-3	170	7-17-81	1999	Salcedo, D.R.

LAKELAND

Rookie

GULF COAST LEAGUE

BATTING	AVG	G	AB	R	H	2B	3B	HR	RBI	BB	SO	SB	CS	SLG	OBP	B	T	HT	WT	DOB	1st Yr	Resides
Anderson, Samuel	.268	33	82	9	22	1	0	0	5	10	16	0	1	.280	.362	R	R	5-11	188	3-23-79	2001	Mesquite, Texas
Birkett, Matt	.189	35	90	14	17	1	1	0	3	6	16	2	3	.222	.247	R	R	5-11	160	1-13-82	2001	Torrance, Calif.
Blue, Vincent	.248	42	113	16	28	2	2	0	4	24	24	8	4	.301	.380	L	R	6-2	180	2-8-83	2001	Houston, Texas
Davis, Daniel	.161	9	31	2	5	1	0	0	1	1	15	1	0	.194	.188	L	L	6-2	195	6-11-81	1999	Kissimmee, Fla.
DeLeon, Virgilio	.243	9	37	2	9	2	0	1	5	1	5	1	1	.378	.282	R	R	6-3	190	11-25-80	2001	San Pedro de Macoris, D.R.
Dean, Herman	.256	28	82	18	21	4	0	3	10	4	24	13	0	.415	.315	B	R	6-0	165	2-23-82	1999	Valencia, Venez.
Gonzalez, Juan	.333	54	192	30	64	6	0	3	33	19	30	19	6	.411	.396	R	R	5-10	170	1-23-81	2001	Bethel, N.C.
Heath, Demetrius	.303	50	175	34	53	5	6	0	19	18	16	21	4	.400	.364	B	R	5-9	150	10-30-82	2001	Santo Domingo, D.R.
Hernandez, Anderson	.264	55	216	37	57	5	11	0	18	13	38	34	8	.389	.303	R	R	5-11	185	5-19-77	1998	Evington, Va.
Inge, Brandon	.100	3	10	1	1	0	0	1	2	2	2	0	0	.400	.250	R	R	6-3	215	12-28-81	2000	Clovis, Calif.
Lambert, Shawn	.131	16	107	5	14	3	0	1	5	9	49	0	1	.187	.202	R	R	6-2	195	5-19-78	1998	Peak Hurst, Australia
Lehmann, Thomas	.178	34	90	8	16	3	0	0	12	9	21	1	0	.211	.250	L	L	5-10	145	7-3-83	2001	Plant City, Fla.
Raburn, Ryan	.155	19	58	4	9	2	0	1	5	9	19	2	1	.241	.300	R	R	6-0	185	4-17-81	2001	Lancaster, Calif.
Rosado, Francisco	.184	34	98	9	18	4	0	2	4	13	26	2	0	.286	.298	R	R	5-10	230	11-27-81	2001	Lancaster, Calif.
Ryan, Billy	.246	20	57	7	14	1	0	0	5	10	10	0	0	.263	.389	R	R	6-3	200	7-21-81	2001	Brooklyn, N.Y.
Sanchez, Danilo	.185	38	108	15	20	2	0	4	17	17	27	2	0	.315	.326	R	R	5-11	155	10-25-80	1997	Santo Domingo, D.R.
Santana, Isidro	.357	7	28	6	10	2	0	0	1	2	6	1	0	.429	.400	B	R	5-10	155	5-15-81	1997	San Pedro de Macoris, D.R.
Tejeda, Juan	.295	50	173	17	51	8	1	4	37	8	32	0	0	.422	.344	R	R	6-2	195	1-26-82	1999	Santiago, D.R.
Ust, Brant	.308	7	26	4	8	1	0	0	5	2	4	1	0	.346	.357	R	R	6-2	200	7-17-78	1999	Redmond, Wash.
Williams, Matt	.164	28	73	13	12	1	0	0	6	5	14	2	3	.178	.228	B	R	6-2	173	11-18-83	2001	Fontana, Calif.
Wise, Bradley	.200	11	25	2	5	0	0	0	3	3	10	0	0	.200	.300	L	R	6-2	175	1-18-84	2000	Parkwood, Australia

GAMES BY POSITION: C—Anderson 30, Inge 3, Sanchez 37. **1B**—Gonzalez 2, Lambert 26, Tejeda 40. **2B**—Gonzalez 9, Heath 49, Santana 5. **3B**—Gonzalez 33, Hernandez 1, Raburn 13, Ryan 15, Ust 3, Wise 1. **SS**—Gonzalez 10, Hernandez 54. **OF**—Birkett 31, Blue 34, Davis 9, DeLeon 9, Dean 24, Gonzalez 2, Lehmann 28, Rosado 31, Williams 24.

PITCHING	W	L	ERA	G	GS	CG	SV	IP	H	R	ER	BB	SO	AVG	B	T	HT	WT	DOB	1st Yr	Resides
Barrios, Rafael	3	3	2.14	23	0	0	6	34	24	12	8	17	29	.200	R	R	6-3	175	7-10-81	1998	Zaraza, Venez.
Brandon, Keith	2	0	5.67	19	0	0	0	33	44	28	21	20	35	.312	R	R	6-1	185	9-27-79	2001	Brandon, Fla.
Connolly, Jon	1	1	3.82	8	6	0	0	35	30	16	15	10	23	.227	R	R	6-0	205	8-24-83	2001	Oneonta, N.Y.
Cuello, Manolin	0	0	0.00	1	0	0	0	1	1	0	0	0	1	.500	R	R	6-3	185	5-5-81	2000	Santo Domingo, D.R.
Diaz, Luis	2	4	4.39	13	10	0	0	55	53	30	27	27	71	.256	B	R	6-4	210	6-30-81	2001	Charlotte, N.C.
Dunn, Gerald	2	4	3.50	12	8	1	2	54	47	26	21	20	46	.228	R	R	6-0	180	10-8-81	2001	Carolina, P.R.
Figueroa, Juan	1	4	4.66	17	4	0	0	39	33	28	20	30	41	.226	L	L	5-10	175	1-20-80	2001	Las Vegas, Nev.
Graves, Robert	2	0	0.83	9	1	0	0	22	13	5	2	6	31	.178	R	R	6-4	185	2-8-80	1997	La Victoria, D.R.
Herrera, Junior	0	2	7.53	18	3	0	7	29	44	30	24	13	19	.335	R	R	6-2	195	3-22-83	2001	Downers Grove, Ill.
Lyons, Thomas	1	0	6.43	5	3	0	0	14	17	11	10	5	22	.278	R	R	6-4	200	2-17-82	2000	West Farmington, Ohio
Petty, Chad	6	0	1.11	12	10	2	0	57	35	17	7	13	52	.170	L	L	6-4	200	2-17-82	2000	West Farmington, Ohio
Rivas, Gabriel	5	3	5.94	18	4	0	0	36	46	25	24	21	33	.321	R	R	6-1	170	5-24-82	1999	Ciudad Bolivar, Venez.
Rodney, Fernando	0	0	0.00	1	1	0	0	1	0	0	0	1	1	.000	R	R	5-11	170	3-17-77	1997	Santo Domingo, D.R.
Valentin, Emmanuel	7	1	4.11	21	0	0	0	35	32	16	16	21	34	.238	R	R	6-2	175	10-11-82	2000	Guayama, P.R.
Vargas, Javier	2	4	3.55	9	7	1	0	38	31	19	15	11	25	.215	R	R	6-3	170	7-17-81	1999	Salcedo, D.R.
Wheatland, Matt	0	0	0.00	3	3	0	0	9	3	0	0	3	5	.100	R	R	6-5	215	10-18-81	2000	Poway, Calif.

BY MIKE BERARDINO

What began as a season of great promise for the Marlins wound up as the most disappointing in their nine-year history. In the end even the very existence of the franchise was in doubt.

 Instead of posting their third straight improvement of 10 or more wins, something that hadn't been done in more than 90 years, they went backward. Plagued by inconsistent pitching and streaky hitting, they finished 76-86 and fell to fourth place, 12 games behind the suddenly vulnerable Atlanta Braves.

Manager John Boles, who guaranteed a winning season, was fired May 28 with the club floundering at 22-26. Boles, who never played professionally, was dismissed after journeyman reliever Dan Miceli ripped him publicly, saying the team had lost confidence in his ability to lead. Marlins president and general manager Dave Dombrowski concurred and fired his longtime friend.

Hall of Famer Tony Perez took over and spurred the young roster to a 19-9 turnaround. But a five-game series sweep by the Phillies before the all-star break stripped the Marlins of confidence and momentum. Perez voluntarily returned to his front-office post at season's end.

Righthander A.J. Burnett became the third pitcher in franchise history to throw a no-hitter, but his was easily the wildest. Burnett, 24, walked nine on May 12 at San Diego, his second start of the season after missing the first five weeks with a broken foot.

Righthander Ryan Dempster won a career-best 15 games and tied Pat Rapp's franchise mark with his 37th career win in a Marlins uniform. But Dempster failed to win any of his final five starts.

Florida lost center fielder Preston Wilson for nearly six weeks after he suffered a sprained thumb in July, then endured a family tragedy with the death of his newborn son.

Catcher Charles Johnson, the linchpin of the 1997 World Series champions, returned to his hometown in

Cliff Floyd   Josh Beckett

PLAYERS OF THE YEAR

MAJOR LEAGUE: Cliff Floyd, of
Floyd, one of baseball's best prospects in the early '90s, had his best year ever in 2001, hitting .317 with 31 homers and 103 RBIs—all career highs.

MINOR LEAGUE: Josh Beckett, rhp
Beckett, 21, started the 2001 season at Class A Brevard County (6-0, 1.23), was promoted to Double-A Portland (8-1, 1.82) at midseason and finished in the big leagues.

the offseason with a five-year, $35 million free-agent deal. Johnson enjoyed a big first half, making his second All-Star Game team, but hit one home run after July 15.

Left fielder Cliff Floyd set career highs in the triple-crown categories, but he slumped in the final two months when he was bothered by wrist and heel injuries.

A late-spring trade with the Padres backfired. Righthander Matt Clement went 9-10, 5.05 and right fielder Eric Owens lost his job after a poor first half. Former first-round pick Mark Kotsay, meanwhile, had his best year after going to San Diego in the deal.

Positives included the emergence of Kevin Millar (.314-20-85) as the starting right fielder and the September callup of Josh Beckett (2-2, 1.50), Baseball America's Minor League Player of the Year. Beckett was expected to open the 2002 season in the rotation.

Off the field, a deal for a publicly-financed, baseball-only stadium in downtown Miami fell apart in May when the state legislature refused to vote on the issue. The setback proved a devastating blow to Marlins owner John Henry, who projected losses of up to $20 million on a $35 million payroll that ranked among the game's lowest.

Without the promise of a new ballpark, particularly in the wake of the Sept. 11 terrorist attacks, Henry was considering another steep cut in payroll in order to stem the tide of red ink.

Attendance rose 3 percent to 15,663 per game, the first increase since the 1997 World Series season, but it still represented the second-worst figure in the majors. By the final week of the season, home crowds barely topped 1,500 at Pro Player Stadium.

Two Marlins Class A affiliates came away with shares of their league titles after the attacks forced suspension of all uncompleted minor league playoffs. Kane County was declared Midwest League champion, while Brevard County split the Florida State League title with the Tampa Yankees.

ORGANIZATION LEADERS

BATTING

*AVG	Ramon Castro, Calgary	336
R	Jesus Medrano, Brevard County	93
H	Kevin Hooper, Portland/Kane County	163
TB	Mike Gulan, Calgary	271
2B	Mike Gulan, Calgary	44
3B	Abraham Nunez, Portland	9
HR	Ramon Castro, Calgary	27
RBI	Adrian Gonzalez, Kane County	103
BB	Abraham Nunez, Portland	83
SO	Abraham Nunez, Portland	155
SB	Jesus Medrano, Brevard County	61

PITCHING

W	Hansel Izquierdo, Portland/Brevard/K.C.	16
L	Mike Drumright, Calgary/Portland	13
#ERA	Josh Beckett, Portland/Brevard	1.54
G	Tim McClaskey, Portland/Brevard	63
CG	Three tied at	2
SV	Johnny Ruffin, Calgary	22
IP	Joe Roa, Calgary/Portland	160
BB	Claudio Vargas, Portland	67
SO	Josh Beckett, Portland/Brevard	203

*Minimum 250 At-Bats #Minimum 75 Innings

FLORIDA MARLINS

Managers: John Boles, Tony Perez

2001 Record: 76-86, .469 (4th, NL East)

BATTING	AVG	G	AB	R	H	2B	3B	HR	RBI	BB	SO	SB	CS	SLG	OBP	B	T	HT	WT	DOB	1st Yr	Resides
Abbott, Jeff	.262	28	42	5	11	3	0	0	5	3	7	0	0	.333	.326	R	L	6-2	200	8-17-72	1994	Dunwoody, Ga.
Berg, Dave	.242	82	215	26	52	12	1	4	16	14	39	0	1	.363	.292	R	R	5-11	185	9-3-70	1993	Roseville, Calif.
Castillo, Luis	.263	134	537	76	141	16	10	2	45	67	90	33	16	.341	.344	B	R	5-11	175	9-12-75	1993	Roseville, Calif.
Castro, Ramon	.182	7	11	0	2	0	0	0	1	1	1	0	0	.182	.250	R	R	6-3	225	3-1-76	1994	Vega Baja, P.R.
Floyd, Cliff	.317	149	555	123	176	44	4	31	103	59	101	18	3	.578	.390	L	R	6-4	235	12-5-72	1991	Weston, Ill.
Fox, Andy	.185	54	81	8	15	0	1	3	7	15	17	1	0	.321	.327	L	R	6-4	185	1-12-71	1989	Sacramento, Calif.
Gonzalez, Alex	.250	145	515	57	129	36	1	9	48	30	107	2	2	.377	.303	R	R	6-0	170	2-15-77	1994	Turmero, Venez.
Gulan, Mike	.000	6	6	1	0	0	0	0	0	2	2	0	0	.000	.250	R	R	6-1	190	12-18-70	1992	Steubenville, Ohio
Johnson, Charles	.259	128	451	51	117	32	0	18	75	38	133	0	0	.450	.321	R	R	6-2	220	7-20-71	1992	Pembroke Pines, Fla.
Lee, Derrek	.282	158	561	83	158	37	4	21	75	50	126	4	2	.474	.346	R	R	6-5	225	9-6-75	1993	Folsom, Calif.
Lowell, Mike	.283	146	551	65	156	37	0	18	100	43	79	1	2	.448	.340	R	R	6-4	205	2-24-74	1995	Coral Gables, Fla.
Mabry, John	.218	82	147	14	32	7	0	6	20	13	44	1	0	.388	.299	L	R	6-4	210	10-17-70	1991	Chesapeake, Md.
2-team (5 St. Louis)	.208	87	154	14	32	7	0	6	20	13	46	1	0	.370	.287							
McGuire, Ryan	.185	48	54	8	10	2	0	1	8	7	15	1	0	.278	.270	L	L	6-0	215	11-23-71	1993	Woodland Hills, Calif.
Millar, Kevin	.314	144	449	62	141	39	5	20	85	39	70	0	0	.557	.374	R	R	6-0	210	9-24-71	1993	Encino, Calif.
Mottola, Chad	.000	5	7	1	0	0	0	0	1	2	2	0	0	.000	.200	R	R	6-3	220	10-15-71	1992	Casselberry, Fla.
Mouton, Lyle	.059	21	17	1	1	0	0	0	1	0	7	0	0	.059	.059	R	R	6-4	230	5-13-69	1991	Tarpon Springs, Fla.
Owens, Eric	.253	119	400	51	101	16	1	5	28	29	59	8	6	.335	.302	R	R	6-1	184	2-3-71	1992	Rocky Mount, Va.
Redmond, Mike	.312	48	141	19	44	4	0	4	14	13	13	0	0	.426	.376	R	R	6-1	185	5-5-71	1993	Spokane, Wash.
Thompson, Ryan	.290	18	31	6	9	5	0	0	2	1	8	0	0	.452	.313	R	R	6-3	215	11-4-67	1987	Edesville, Md.
Wilson, Preston	.274	123	468	70	128	30	2	23	71	36	107	20	8	.494	.331	R	R	6-2	193	7-19-74	1993	Eastover, S.C.

PITCHING	W	L	ERA	G	GS	CG	SV	IP	H	R	ER	BB	SO	AVG	B	T	HT	WT	DOB	1st Yr	Resides
Acevedo, Juan	2	3	2.54	20	0	0	0	28	31	11	8	16	21	.284	R	R	6-2	228	5-5-70	1992	Algonquin, Ill.
2-team (39 Colorado)	2	5	4.18	59	0	0	0	60	68	35	28	35	47	.284							
Alfonseca, Antonio	4	4	3.06	58	0	0	28	62	68	24	21	15	40	.280	R	R	6-5	235	4-16-72	1990	La Romana, D.R.
Almanza, Armando	2	2	4.83	52	0	0	0	41	34	24	22	26	45	.229	L	L	6-3	205	10-26-72	1993	El Paso, Texas
Baez, Benito	0	0	13.50	8	0	0	0	9	22	14	14	6	14	.448	L	L	6-0	160	5-6-77	1994	Bonao, D.R.
Beckett, Josh	2	2	1.50	4	4	0	0	24	14	9	4	11	24	.160	R	R	6-4	190	5-15-80	2000	Spring, Texas
Bones, Ricky	4	4	5.06	61	0	0	0	64	71	39	36	33	41	.286	R	R	6-0	202	4-7-69	1986	Guayama, P.R.
Burnett, A.J.	11	12	4.05	27	27	2	0	173	145	82	78	83	128	.230	R	R	6-3	190	8-12-74	1994	Butler, Pa.
Clement, Matt	9	10	5.05	31	31	0	0	169	172	102	95	85	134	.267	R	R	6-4	185	11-13-70	1992	Las Vegas, Nev.
Darensbourg, Vic	1	2	4.25	58	0	0	1	49	52	24	23	10	33	.276	L	L	5-10	165	11-13-70	1992	Las Vegas, Nev.
Dempster, Ryan	15	12	4.94	34	34	2	0	211	218	123	116	112	171	.269	R	R	6-1	201	5-3-77	1995	Gibsons, B.C.
Grilli, Jason	2	2	6.08	6	5	0	0	27	30	18	18	11	17	.297	R	R	6-4	185	11-11-76	1997	Orlando, Fla.
Knotts, Gary	0	1	6.00	2	1	0	0	6	7	4	4	1	9	.280	R	R	6-4	200	2-12-77	1996	Decatur, Ala.
Looper, Braden	3	3	3.55	71	0	0	3	71	63	28	28	30	52	.242	R	R	6-5	225	10-28-74	1996	Palm Beach Gardens, Fla.
Miceli, Danny	0	5	6.93	29	0	0	0	25	29	21	19	11	31	.287	R	R	6-0	216	9-9-70	1990	Winter Springs, Fla.
Neal, Blaine	0	0	6.75	4	0	0	0	5	7	4	4	5	3	.304	L	R	6-5	205	4-6-78	1996	Haddon Heights, N.J.
Nunez, Vladimir	4	5	2.74	52	3	0	0	92	79	33	28	30	64	.233	R	R	6-4	229	3-15-75	1996	Miramar, Fla.
Olsen, Kevin	0	0	1.20	4	2	0	0	15	11	2	2	2	13	.203	R	R	6-2	200	7-26-76	1998	Norco, Calif.
Penny, Brad	10	10	3.69	31	31	1	0	205	183	92	84	54	154	.240	R	R	6-4	200	5-24-78	1996	Broken Arrow, Okla.
Ruffin, Johnny	0	0	4.91	3	0	0	0	4	5	4	2	4	4	.312	L	L	5-10	155	10-11-74	1992	Bani, D.R.
Sanchez, Jesus	2	4	4.74	16	9	0	0	63	61	33	33	31	46	.256	L	L	5-10	155	10-21-69	1991	Hillside, Ill.
Smith, Chuck	5	5	4.70	15	15	0	0	88	89	47	46	35	71	.264	R	R	6-1	185	10-21-69	1991	Hillside, Ill.
Strong, Joe	0	0	1.35	5	0	0	0	7	3	1	1	3	4	.136	B	R	6-0	200	9-9-62	1984	Seattle, Wash.

FIELDING

Catcher	PCT	G	PO	A	E	DP	PB
Castro	1.000	4	10	1	0	0	0
Gonzalez	.000	1	0	0	0	0	0
Johnson	.996	125	846	62	4	15	8
Redmond	.994	47	291	23	2	5	2

First Base	PCT	G	PO	A	E	DP
Lee	.994	156	1271	114	8	142
Mabry	1.000	1	7	1	0	0
McGuire	1.000	4	7	0	0	0
Millar	1.000	15	117	6	0	10

Second Base	PCT	G	PO	A	E	DP
Berg	.965	34	54	85	5	21
Castillo	.980	133	260	387	13	99
Fox	1.000	2	4	4	0	0

Third Base	PCT	G	PO	A	E	DP
Berg	.895	16	1	16	2	2
Fox	1.000	9	6	6	0	1
Gulan	1.000	1	2	2	0	0

Lowell	.976	144	108	261	9	35
Millar	1.000	10	5	11	0	1

Shortstop	PCT	G	PO	A	E	DP
Berg	.976	19	11	29	1	3
Fox	.938	12	14	31	3	9
Gonzalez	.959	142	219	396	26	101

Outfield	PCT	G	PO	A	E	DP
Abbott	.963	17	26	0	1	0
Floyd	.972	142	268	8	8	2
Fox	1.000	2	1	0	0	0
Mabry	.958	39	44	2	2	0
McGuire	1.000	9	16	0	0	0
Millar	.987	86	145	2	2	0
Mottola	1.000	5	8	1	0	0
Mouton	1.000	1	4	0	0	0
Owens	.984	106	180	6	3	1
Thompson	.923	16	11	1	1	0
Wilson	.993	121	287	12	2	4

Kevin Millar

MORRIS FOSTOFF

Cliff Floyd: Batted .317-31-103 for Florida

LARRY GOREN

Ryan Dempster: Led Marlins with 15 wins

FARM SYSTEM

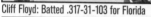

Director, Player Development: Rick Williams.

Class	Farm Team	League	W	L	Pct.	Finish*	Manager	First Yr.
AAA	Calgary (Alberta) Cannons	Pacific Coast	72	71	.503	7th (16)	Chris Chambliss	1999
AA	Portland (Maine) Sea Dogs	Eastern	77	65	.542	t-4th (12)	Rick Renteria	1994
A#	Brevard County (Fla.) Manatees	Florida State	80	55	.593	+1st (14)	Dave Huppert	1994
A	Kane County (Ill.) Cougars	Midwest	88	50	.638	+1st (14)	Russ Morman	1993
A	Utica (N.Y.) Blue Sox	New York-Penn	27	47	.365	13th (14)	Kevin Boles	1996
Rookie	Melbourne (Fla.) Marlins	Gulf Coast	29	31	.483	9th (14)	Jon Deeble	1992

*Finish in overall standings (No. of teams in league)   #Advanced level   +League champion

CALGARY   Class AAA

PACIFIC COAST LEAGUE

BATTING	AVG	G	AB	R	H	2B	3B	HR	RBI	BB	SO	SB	CS	SLG	OBP	B	T	HT	WT	DOB	1st Yr	Resides
Abbott, Jeff	.320	47	175	25	56	9	0	9	24	6	33	1	2	.526	.337	R	L	6-2	200	8-17-72	1994	Dunwoody, Ga.
Banks, Brian	.291	101	357	70	104	27	4	23	63	32	97	5	4	.583	.352	B	R	6-3	210	9-28-70	1993	Mesa, Ariz.
2-team (17 Iowa)	.280	118	396	72	111	29	4	24	67	36	108	5	4	.556	.342							
Becker, Rich	.264	50	163	35	43	9	0	8	28	28	40	3	1	.466	.368	L	L	5-10	193	2-1-72	1990	Cape Coral, Fla.
Brown, Jason	.308	12	39	7	12	3	0	1	7	1	11	0	0	.462	.341	R	R	6-2	208	5-22-74	1997	Rolling Hills Estates, Calif.
Candelaria, Ben	.319	61	163	23	52	17	1	5	29	7	19	0	0	.528	.343	L	R	5-11	167	1-29-75	1992	Hatillo, P.R.
Castro, Ramon	.336	108	390	81	131	33	0	27	90	38	74	1	1	.628	.393	R	R	6-3	225	3-1-76	1994	Vega Baja, P.R.
Clapinski, Chris	.251	58	199	31	50	10	1	7	20	17	43	1	2	.417	.317	B	R	6-0	175	8-20-71	1992	Cape Canaveral, Fla.
Easterday, Matt	.196	15	46	6	9	1	1	0	3	2	10	0	1	.261	.245	R	R	6-1	188	5-3-79	2000	Covington, Ga.
Erickson, Matt	.310	115	413	66	128	21	1	2	29	39	69	11	4	.380	.386	L	R	5-11	190	7-30-75	1997	Appleton, Wis.
Espada, Joe	.300	79	290	61	87	20	2	3	30	39	49	13	7	.414	.387	R	R	5-10	175	8-30-75	1996	Carolina, P.R.
Fox, Andy	.429	11	42	10	18	2	1	2	8	3	2	1	1	.667	.478	L	R	6-4	185	1-12-71	1989	Sacramento, Calif.
Grijak, Kevin	.246	45	142	17	35	7	0	5	27	12	13	1	0	.401	.317	L	R	6-2	215	8-6-70	1991	Sterling Heights, Mich.
Gulan, Mike	.324	124	485	78	157	44	2	22	92	35	145	2	6	.559	.375	R	R	6-1	190	12-18-70	1992	Steubenville, Ohio
Lamb, David	.299	23	67	15	20	6	0	1	6	11	11	0	0	.433	.413	B	R	6-2	165	6-6-75	1993	Newbury Park, Calif.
2-team (5 Colo. Spr.)	.289	28	76	16	22	6	0	1	6	11	15	0	0	.408	.393							
Lemonis, Chris	.160	9	25	3	4	0	0	0	1	2	7	0	0	.160	.250	L	R	5-11	185	8-21-73	1995	New York, N.Y.
Martin, Paco	.306	93	333	45	102	20	4	5	38	14	41	8	3	.435	.334	R	R	5-10	164	12-10-66	1984	Hato Rey, P.R.
McGuire, Ryan	.301	62	239	45	72	14	2	8	42	26	49	0	1	.477	.369	L	L	6-0	215	11-23-71	1993	Woodland Hills, Calif.
Morales, Steve	.500	2	2	0	1	0	0	0	0	0	1	0	0	.500	.500	B	R	5-10	195	5-4-78	1996	Mayaguez, P.R.
Mottola, Chad	.295	119	457	66	135	23	2	15	66	30	85	11	5	.453	.343	R	R	6-3	220	10-15-71	1992	Casselberry, Fla.
Owens, Eric	.267	3	15	2	4	2	0	0	2	0	2	1	0	.400	.267	R	R	6-1	184	2-3-71	1992	Rocky Mount, Va.
Rolison, Nate	.167	3	12	1	2	0	0	0	1	1	3	0	0	.167	.231	L	R	6-6	240	3-27-77	1995	Petal, Miss.
Romero, Mandy	.000	3	6	0	0	0	0	0	0	3	3	0	0	.000	.333	B	R	5-11	196	10-19-67	1988	Miami, Fla.
Saylor, Jamie	.111	15	27	5	3	0	0	1	3	3	11	0	0	.222	.200	L	R	5-11	185	9-11-74	1994	Garland, Texas
Thompson, Ryan	.310	78	300	53	93	26	0	19	69	14	65	4	3	.587	.342	R	R	6-3	215	11-4-67	1987	Edesville, Md.
Waszgis, B.J.	.251	96	311	50	78	18	0	23	65	31	90	0	1	.531	.332	R	R	6-2	215	8-24-70	1991	Camilla, Ga.
Wilson, Preston	.500	4	10	3	5	2	0	0	1	5	1	2	0	.700	.667	R	R	6-2	193	7-19-74	1993	Eastover, S.C.

ORGANIZATION STATISTICS

PITCHING

PITCHING	W	L	ERA	G	GS	CG	SV	IP	H	R	ER	BB	SO	AVG	B	T	HT	WT	DOB	1st Yr	Resides
Ahearne, Pat	6	10	6.28	28	26	0	0	145	212	112	101	35	80	.346	R	R	6-3	195	12-10-69	1992	Atascadero, Calif.
Almonte, Hector	0	0	8.39	18	0	0	0	25	36	29	23	15	21	.339	R	R	6-2	190	10-17-75	1993	Santo Domingo, D.R.
Baez, Benito	7	1	3.03	49	0	0	1	59	53	22	20	7	56	.239	L	L	6-0	160	5-6-77	1994	Bonao, D.R.
DeSilva, John	1	2	6.75	26	3	0	1	39	59	33	29	9	29	.337	R	R	6-0	193	9-30-67	1989	Fort Bragg, Calif.
Drumright, Mike	0	5	3.73	19	0	0	1	31	30	15	13	24	39	.267	L	R	6-4	210	4-19-74	1995	Valley Center, Kan.
Edmondson, Brian	2	5	8.49	23	0	0	0	30	43	33	28	15	20	.335	R	R	6-2	175	1-29-73	1991	Riverside, Calif.
Grilli, Jason	1	2	4.02	8	8	0	0	47	46	26	21	20	35	.255	R	R	6-4	185	11-11-76	1997	Orlando, Fla.
Knotts, Gary	6	7	5.46	21	21	0	0	119	136	77	72	43	104	.285	R	R	6-4	200	2-12-77	1996	Decatur, Ala.
Leese, Brandon	3	3	6.95	9	9	0	0	44	68	36	34	7	30	.356	R	R	6-4	205	10-8-75	1996	Lincolnshire, Ill.
Lorraine, Andrew	9	5	5.40	30	25	1	0	150	209	100	90	36	101	.330	L	L	6-3	205	8-11-72	1993	Scottsdale, Ariz.
Mairena, Oswaldo	3	2	7.55	31	0	0	0	39	52	33	33	13	44	.320	L	L	5-11	165	7-30-75	1996	Chinandega, Nicaragua
Molina, Gabe	5	9	5.89	40	16	0	0	107	126	75	70	39	105	.288	R	R	6-1	220	5-3-75	1996	Denver, Colo.
Roa, Joe	6	6	3.92	19	19	1	0	124	134	58	54	12	81	.275	R	R	6-1	194	10-11-71	1989	Hazel Park, Mich.
Roberts, Mark	6	3	4.50	33	0	0	8	36	47	21	18	15	35	.313	R	R	6-2	205	9-29-75	1996	Zephyrhills, Fla.
Rodgers, Bobby	1	3	6.03	18	2	0	0	37	35	25	25	20	28	.253	R	R	6-3	225	7-22-74	1996	St. Charles, Mo.
Ruffin, Johnny	2	3	4.36	37	0	0	22	33	37	17	16	10	47	.278	R	R	6-3	170	7-29-71	1988	Tampa, Fla.
Sanchez, Jesus	6	1	3.21	16	11	0	0	76	61	32	27	33	58	.215	L	L	5-10	155	10-11-74	1992	Bani, D.R.
Smith, Chuck	2	0	2.84	2	2	0	0	13	12	4	4	2	9	.255	R	R	6-1	185	10-21-69	1991	Hillside, Ill.
Strong, Joe	6	3	6.25	46	0	0	1	59	80	45	41	18	48	.326	B	R	6-0	200	9-9-62	1984	Seattle, Wash.
Wojciechowski, Steve	0	1	6.97	8	1	0	0	10	16	8	8	3	7	.347	L	L	6-2	185	7-29-70	1991	Calgary, Alberta

FIELDING

Catcher	PCT	G	PO	A	E	DP	PB
Banks	.981	9	48	5	1	0	0
Brown	1.000	6	41	2	0	0	0
Castro	.989	86	589	45	7	3	8
Romero	1.000	3	18	1	0	0	0
Saylor	1.000	1	2	0	0	0	0
Waszgis	.988	47	299	28	4	2	6

First Base	PCT	G	PO	A	E	DP
Banks	.992	79	603	58	5	62
Fox	1.000	1	7	0	0	1
Grijak	.977	23	165	7	4	14
McGuire	.992	29	228	28	2	22
Rolison	1.000	3	19	2	0	1
Waszgis	.969	22	178	10	6	15

Second Base	PCT	G	PO	A	E	DP
Clapinski	.985	15	26	39	1	12
Easterday	.952	8	6	14	1	1
Erickson	.978	56	107	159	6	35
Espada	1.000	5	11	7	0	2

	PCT	G	PO	A	E	DP
Fox	1.000	3	9	7	0	1
Lamb	.968	14	27	34	2	10
Lemonis	.909	7	17	23	4	4
Martin	.995	39	73	121	1	21
Saylor	1.000	3	0	3	0	0

Third Base	PCT	G	PO	A	E	DP
Clapinski	.963	12	8	18	1	2
Erickson	1.000	1	0	4	0	0
Espada	.933	3	4	10	1	0
Fox	1.000	1	1	0	0	0
Gulan	.935	118	62	196	18	17
Lamb	.000	1	0	0	0	0
Martin	1.000	10	5	19	0	2

Shortstop	PCT	G	PO	A	E	DP
Clapinski	.970	7	12	20	1	4
Erickson	.965	56	73	146	8	34
Espada	.973	68	101	188	8	38
Fox	.900	3	1	8	1	1
Lamb	.963	6	13	13	1	5

Martin	.930	10	20	33	4	8

Outfield	PCT	G	PO	A	E	DP
Abbott	.974	44	72	2	2	0
Banks	.846	10	10	1	2	0
Becker	.956	45	61	4	3	1
Brown	1.000	3	5	0	0	0
Candelaria	.986	44	68	2	1	0
Clapinski	.969	17	30	1	1	0
Easterday	.889	6	7	1	1	0
Fox	1.000	2	1	0	0	0
Grijak	1.000	18	35	1	0	0
Martin	1.000	25	53	2	0	0
McGuire	.985	34	61	3	1	0
Mottola	.968	119	235	9	8	2
Owens	.667	3	2	1	0	0
Saylor	.667	3	2	0	1	0
Thompson	.948	77	159	6	9	2
Wilson	1.000	4	9	0	0	0

PORTLAND
Class AA

EASTERN LEAGUE

BATTING	AVG	G	AB	R	H	2B	3B	HR	RBI	BB	SO	SB	CS	SLG	OBP	B	T	HT	WT	DOB	1st Yr	Resides
Abbott, Jeff	.462	7	26	4	12	1	0	2	6	2	0	0	1	.731	.500	R	L	6-2	200	8-17-72	1994	Dunwoody, Ga.
Aguila, Chris	.257	64	241	25	62	16	1	4	29	18	50	5	7	.382	.312	R	R	5-11	182	2-23-79	1997	Reno, Nev.
Bailey, Jeff	.241	129	432	56	104	28	2	13	66	64	136	7	2	.405	.347	R	R	6-2	205	11-19-78	1997	Kelso, Wash.
Brown, Jason	.333	17	51	6	17	3	0	1	10	5	12	0	0	.451	.393	R	R	6-2	208	5-22-74	1997	Rolling Hills Estates, Calif.
Candelaria, Ben	.305	29	95	11	29	6	1	2	15	16	13	0	1	.453	.407	L	R	5-11	167	1-29-75	1992	Hatillo, P.R.
Clapinski, Chris	.222	5	18	4	4	0	0	1	2	4	2	1	0	.389	.364	L	R	6-0	175	8-20-71	1992	Cape Canaveral, Fla.
Foster, Quincy	.215	68	200	34	43	2	3	2	14	25	31	23	9	.285	.308	L	R	5-10	200	6-6-75	1996	Long Beach, Calif.
Gillespie, Eric	.225	82	240	28	54	16	2	4	35	45	3	1	.358	.309	L	R	6-4	200	4-29-76	1997	Houston, Texas
Harper, Brandon	.239	76	247	21	59	13	0	3	24	27	52	0	0	.328	.323	R	R	6-4	210	7-30-76	1998	Alpharetta, Ga.
Honeycutt, Heath	.242	132	475	56	115	24	2	9	59	41	129	10	8	.358	.316	R	R	5-10	160	12-7-76	1999	Lawrence, Kan.
Hooper, Kevin	.308	117	468	70	144	19	6	2	39	59	78	24	12	.387	.392	L	L	6-3	190	8-2-76	1995	Poway, Calif.
Jones, Jaime	.202	31	94	9	19	4	0	1	10	12	29	2	1	.277	.299	L	L	6-1	185	2-16-76	1998	Pensacola, Fla.
Kelly, Heath	.162	17	37	3	6	2	1	1	1	13	0	1	.351	.184	R	R	6-1	175	3-17-77	1998	Irmo, S.C.
Niles, Drew	.237	71	194	22	46	7	2	4	18	17	55	2	7	.356	.306	B	R	6-2	186	2-5-80	1996	Haina, D.R.
Nunez, Abraham	.240	136	467	75	112	14	9	17	53	83	155	26	19	.418	.357	L	L	6-2	205	12-7-74	1996	El Cajon, Calif.
Phoenix, Wynter	.250	24	60	9	15	2	0	2	6	3	15	0	1	.383	.308	L	R	6-6	240	3-27-77	1995	Petal, Miss.
Rolison, Nate	.211	5	19	1	4	1	0	0	2	1	7	0	0	.263	.250	L	R	6-5	245	2-5-77	1994	Cairns, Australia
Roneberg, Brett	.262	49	164	17	43	11	0	5	19	17	25	1	0	.421	.335	L	L	6-2	205	2-5-79	1996	Cairns, Australia
Smith, Bubba	.180	31	122	11	22	4	0	6	22	6	29	0	0	.361	.223	R	R	6-2	225	12-18-69	1991	Winston-Salem, N.C.
Treanor, Matt	.157	35	89	7	14	2	0	2	8	13	18	1	1	.247	.324	R	R	6-2	205	3-3-76	1994	Anaheim, Calif.
Wathan, Derek	.252	127	469	65	118	12	8	4	35	45	83	25	16	.337	.317	B	R	6-3	190	12-13-76	1998	Blue Springs, Mo.
Wathan, Dusty	.269	55	134	24	36	10	0	2	21	13	28	0	1	.388	.402	R	R	6-4	215	8-22-73	1994	Blue Springs, Mo.
Wilcox, Luke	.241	69	220	25	53	14	0	9	41	21	43	1	1	.427	.310	L	R	6-4	190	11-15-73	1995	St. Johns, Mich.

PITCHING	W	L	ERA	G	GS	CG	SV	IP	H	R	ER	BB	SO	AVG	B	T	HT	WT	DOB	1st Yr	Resides
Beckett, Josh	8	1	1.82	13	13	0	0	74	50	16	15	19	102	.190	R	R	6-4	190	5-15-80	2000	Spring, Texas
Bowe, Brandon	0	2	1.56	9	0	0	0	17	13	4	3	6	10	.209	R	R	6-3	215	3-13-76	1998	Stockton, Calif.
Bump, Nate	4	5	5.27	11	8	0	0	55	55	41	32	10	41	.259	R	R	6-2	185	7-24-76	1998	Monroeton, Pa.
Clark, Chris	1	0	3.18	4	0	0	0	6	3	2	2	5	6	.150	R	R	6-4	210	4-19-74	1995	Valley Center, Kan.
Drumright, Mike	5	8	4.06	18	16	1	0	102	100	54	46	27	85	.258	L	R	6-4	210	1-29-74	1991	Riverside, Calif.
Edmondson, Brian	2	3	1.73	14	0	0	1	26	16	7	5	5	16	.183	R	R	6-2	175	1-29-73	1991	Lutz, Fla.
Goetz, Geoff	2	2	1.53	25	0	0	0	29	22	10	5	12	24	.205	L	L	5-11	163	4-3-79	1997	Orlando, Fla.
Grilli, Jason	0	1	2.25	1	1	0	0	4	3	1	1	0	3	.200	R	R	6-4	185	11-11-76	1997	Orlando, Fla.
Henderson, Scott	5	7	4.76	39	0	0	4	57	52	31	30	23	55	.250	R	R	6-3	195	2-27-75	1997	Villa Park, Calif.
Izquierdo, Hansel	7	2	3.81	10	9	1	0	57	47	24	24	10	45	.224	R	R	6-2	205	1-2-77	1995	Miami, Fla.
Levan, Matt	0	0	4.15	4	0	0	0	9	8	5	4	7	8	.235	L	L	6-3	200	6-24-75	1996	Coatesville, Pa.
Mairena, Oswaldo	4	2	1.57	22	0	0	3	34	27	12	6	8	27	.223	L	L	5-11	165	7-30-75	1996	Chinandega, Nicaragua

PITCHING	W	L	ERA	G	GS	CG	SV	IP	H	R	ER	BB	SO	AVG	B	T	HT	WT	DOB	1st Yr	Resides
McClaskey, Tim	2	2	2.86	37	0	0	2	50	38	17	16	10	52	.207	R	R	5-10	170	1-11-76	1996	Wilton, Iowa
McCurtain, Paul	0	0	5.02	10	0	0	0	14	17	9	8	13	14	.293	R	R	6-1	190	2-5-76	1998	Mesa, Ariz.
Moskau, Ryan	3	2	3.48	39	10	0	2	103	103	45	40	29	78	.268	R	L	6-3	210	8-22-77	1998	Tucson, Ariz.
Neal, Blaine	2	3	2.36	54	0	0	21	53	43	17	14	21	45	.218	L	R	6-5	205	4-6-78	1996	Haddon Heights, N.J.
Olsen, Kevin	10	3	2.68	26	26	0	0	155	123	56	46	21	144	.213	R	R	6-2	200	7-26-76	1998	Norco, Calif.
Roa, Joe	0	2	3.00	7	7	0	0	36	36	15	12	3	26	.266	R	R	6-1	194	10-11-71	1989	Hazel Park, Mich.
Rodgers, Bobby	3	2	2.03	26	0	0	4	40	30	9	9	11	39	.202	R	R	6-3	225	7-22-74	1996	St. Charles, Mo.
Scheffer, Aaron	2	1	1.02	24	0	0	1	35	16	4	4	9	39	.141	L	R	6-2	175	10-15-75	1994	Westland, Mich.
Tejera, Michael	9	8	3.57	25	25	0	0	141	143	61	56	41	131	.265	L	L	5-9	175	10-18-76	1995	Miami, Fla.
Vargas, Claudio	8	9	4.19	27	27	0	0	159	122	77	74	67	151	.211	R	R	6-3	210	5-19-79	1996	Santiago, D.R.

FIELDING

Catcher	PCT	G	PO	A	E	DP	PB
Bailey	1.000	7	7	0	0	0	0
Brown	.983	16	111	3	2	0	0
Harper	.997	69	556	47	2	6	4
Treanor	.996	32	235	12	1	1	2
Du. Wathan	.990	45	278	22	3	1	0

First Base	PCT	G	PO	A	E	DP
Bailey	.989	96	737	48	9	46
Gillespie	.993	21	125	13	1	19
Kelly	.000	1	0	0	0	0
Rolison	1.000	4	28	2	0	4
Roneberg	1.000	1	10	1	0	1
Smith	.991	27	218	15	2	20
Treanor	.000	1	0	0	0	0
Du. Wathan	1.000	6	22	2	0	1

Second Base	PCT	G	PO	A	E	DP
Clapinski	1.000	1	2	2	0	0
Hooper	.986	117	231	257	7	63
Kelly	.947	10	8	10	1	2
Niles	.972	21	44	62	3	12

Third Base	PCT	G	PO	A	E	DP
Clapinski	1.000	2	1	5	0	0
Gillespie	.944	18	6	28	2	0
Honeycutt	.945	125	77	217	17	20
Kelly	1.000	3	0	2	0	0
Niles	.889	7	6	10	2	2
Smith	.000	1	0	0	0	0
Du. Wathan	1.000	1	1	0	0	0

Shortstop	PCT	G	PO	A	E	DP
Clapinski	1.000	1	4	2	0	0
Kelly	1.000	1	1	1	0	0
Niles	.981	26	37	64	2	15
De. Wathan	.973	125	176	297	13	48

Outfield	PCT	G	PO	A	E	DP
Abbott	1.000	7	9	0	0	0
Aguila	.969	64	93	2	3	2
Bailey	.944	15	16	1	1	0
Candelaria	.958	26	41	5	2	0
Foster	.975	60	76	3	2	1
Gillespie	.952	25	36	4	2	1
Jones	.959	23	45	2	2	0
Kelly	.000	1	0	0	0	0
Niles	.000	1	0	0	0	0
Nunez	.976	134	315	13	8	1
Phoenix	.920	14	22	1	2	0
Roneberg	1.000	46	51	2	0	1
Wilcox	.963	42	74	3	3	1

BREVARD COUNTY · Class A

FLORIDA STATE LEAGUE

BATTING	AVG	G	AB	R	H	2B	3B	HR	RBI	BB	SO	SB	CS	SLG	OBP	B	T	HT	WT	DOB	1st Yr	Resides
Abbott, Jeff	.250	3	8	2	2	0	0	0	2	1	1	0	0	.250	.300	R	L	6-2	200	8-17-72	1994	Dunwoody, Ga.
Aguila, Chris	.276	73	272	44	75	15	3	10	34	21	54	8	4	.463	.328	R	R	5-11	180	2-23-79	1997	Reno, Nev.
Arroyo, William	.231	6	13	3	3	0	0	0	2	2	0	0	0	.231	.333	B	R	5-10	170	11-8-81	1999	Cabudare, Venez.
Brown, Jason	.276	34	127	14	35	6	1	2	20	10	29	0	0	.386	.361	R	R	6-2	208	5-22-74	1997	Rolling Hills Estates, Calif.
Callahan, Dave	.254	123	476	68	121	14	2	9	68	54	89	10	7	.349	.332	L	L	5-11	200	12-7-69	1998	Palm Bay, Fla.
Clapinski, Chris	.345	10	29	10	10	0	0	1	6	14	5	0	0	.448	.568	B	R	6-0	175	8-20-71	1992	Cape Canaveral, Fla.
Ferrand, Francisco	.195	31	113	14	22	0	1	3	13	4	28	0	0	.292	.222	L	L	5-10	170	5-20-80	1997	Santo Domingo, D.R.
Foster, Quincy	.299	41	154	29	46	6	1	0	12	19	25	16	5	.351	.381	L	R	6-2	175	10-30-74	1996	Hendersonville, N.C.
Frick, Matt	.226	42	133	19	30	12	0	2	12	10	30	1	0	.361	.297	R	R	6-2	220	1-2-76	1998	Scottsdale, Calif.
Goodman, Scott	.242	34	99	12	24	12	0	1	13	12	23	0	0	.394	.330	L	L	6-1	210	8-15-77	1999	San Luis Obispo, Calif.
Harper, Brandon	.238	29	101	14	24	6	0	2	16	12	14	0	1	.356	.330	R	R	6-4	200	4-29-76	1997	Houston, Texas
Hicks, Scott	.286	2	7	0	2	0	0	0	0	0	0	0	0	.286	.286	L	R	6-4	210	6-6-80	2000	Altamonte Springs, Fla.
Hill, Willy	.297	10	37	6	11	0	0	0	2	2	7	1	2	.297	.350	L	L	5-9	160	9-21-76	1998	Sapulpa, Okla.
Lush, Zach	.150	10	20	2	3	1	0	0	0	2	7	0	0	.200	.261	R	R	6-3	190	1-18-77	2001	North Andover, Mass.
Mabry, John	.154	4	13	0	2	0	0	0	4	2	1	0	0	.154	.250	L	R	6-4	210	10-17-70	1991	Chesapeake, Md.
Magness, Pat	.274	35	117	11	32	7	0	1	16	16	28	0	0	.359	.363	L	R	6-3	230	1-19-78	2000	Overland Park, Kan.
Medrano, Jesus	.251	124	454	49	114	15	2	1	32	51	81	61	8	.300	.331	R	R	6-0	185	9-11-78	1997	La Puente, Calif.
Morales, Steve	.248	48	157	19	39	7	0	4	15	10	15	0	0	.369	.312	B	R	5-10	195	5-4-78	1996	Mayaguez, P.R.
Padgett, Matt	.293	125	440	68	129	37	2	8	81	64	101	10	1	.441	.390	L	L	6-2	215	7-22-77	1998	Lexington, S.C.
Perkins, Kevin	.236	56	195	25	46	3	1	6	18	15	45	0	4	.354	.317	R	R	6-2	185	8-27-79	1999	Whittier, Calif.
Rigsby, Randy	.272	95	320	41	87	15	3	3	38	22	62	14	5	.366	.329	L	L	6-0	190	8-7-76	1998	Goldsboro, N.C.
Rolison, Nate	.378	14	45	7	17	3	0	1	6	10	7	0	0	.511	.491	L	R	6-6	240	3-27-77	1995	Petal, Miss.
Roneberg, Brett	.299	88	331	49	99	20	4	11	63	50	54	5	3	.483	.388	L	L	6-2	205	2-5-79	1996	Cairns, Australia
Santos, Jose	.265	121	411	73	109	22	0	18	81	78	93	10	5	.450	.391	R	R	5-10	195	3-1-78	1995	Santiago, D.R.
Soto, Jose	.200	2	5	1	1	0	0	0	0	0	2	0	0	.200	.333	B	R	6-0	160	6-20-80	1996	San Cristobal, D.R.
Ugueto, Luis	.263	121	392	53	103	12	5	3	43	38	96	22	7	.342	.330	R	R	5-11	170	2-15-79	1996	Macaracuay, Venez.

GAMES BY POSITION: C—Brown 19, Frick 41, Harper 29, Lush 8, Morales 45. **1B**—Brown 2, Callahan 106, Lush 1, Magness 6, Rolison 12, Roneberg 12. **2B**—Arroyo 4, Clapinski 4, Medrano 99, Perkins 24, Ugueto 16. **3B**—Clapinski 3, Medrano 1, Perkins 19, Santos 115. **SS**—Arroyo 1, Clapinski 3, Medrano 21, Perkins 9, Ugueto 107. **OF**—Abbott 3, Aguila 73, Callahan 9, Ferrand 27, Foster 40, Goodman 27, Hicks 2, Hill 8, Mabry 4, Medrano 1, Padgett 68, Perkins 7, Rigsby 90, Roneberg 66, Soto 2.

PITCHING	W	L	ERA	G	GS	CG	SV	IP	H	R	ER	BB	SO	AVG	B	T	HT	WT	DOB	1st Yr	Resides
Anderson, Wes	1	6	5.63	8	8	0	0	32	48	26	20	21	17	.352	R	R	6-4	175	9-10-79	1997	Pine Bluff, Ark.
Beckett, Josh	6	0	1.23	13	12	0	0	66	32	13	9	15	101	.145	R	R	6-4	190	5-15-80	2000	Spring, Texas
Bowe, Brandon	6	4	1.55	42	0	0	11	58	52	21	10	11	45	.242	R	R	6-3	215	3-13-76	1999	Stockton, Calif.
Burnett, A.J.	0	0	1.93	2	2	0	0	9	4	2	2	4	10	.129	R	R	6-5	205	1-3-77	1995	North Little Rock, Ark.
Byron, Terence	0	0	10.29	4	0	0	0	7	7	9	8	5	7	.250	R	R	6-0	200	3-28-79	1999	St. Croix, Virgin Islands
Clark, Chris	0	1	5.68	4	0	0	1	6	6	5	4	9	7	.250	R	R	6-1	180	10-29-74	1994	Tucson, Ariz.
Edmondson, Brian	5	2	1.73	16	0	0	3	26	23	8	5	4	21	.242	R	R	6-2	175	1-29-73	1991	Riverside, Calif.
Farizo, Brad	4	2	2.15	9	7	0	0	46	39	13	11	5	31	.238	R	R	6-4	190	11-3-78	1996	Marrero, La.
Grilli, Jason	2	0	1.98	3	3	0	0	14	12	4	3	5	14	.230	R	R	6-4	185	11-11-76	1997	Orlando, Fla.
Hamulack, Tim	2	4	3.15	40	0	0	1	71	83	42	25	21	39	.287	L	L	6-4	215	11-14-76	1996	Edgewood, Md.
Harber, Ryan	6	4	3.49	29	5	0	1	90	94	44	35	30	48	.252	L	L	6-2	190	9-25-76	1998	Fort Wayne, Ind.
Henriquez, Hector	0	1	6.18	25	0	0	0	39	36	28	27	33	28	.248	L	L	6-3	190	8-27-78	1994	Santo Domingo, D.R.
Izquierdo, Hansel	2	0	2.70	4	4	0	0	27	15	8	8	6	22	.159	R	R	6-2	205	1-2-77	1995	Miami, Fla.
Levan, Matt	1	0	3.48	15	0	0	1	21	21	10	8	10	18	.253	L	L	6-3	200	4-25-76	1996	Coatesville, Pa.
Lopez, Gustavo	3	3	3.21	6	6	2	0	34	32	18	12	6	19	.244	R	R	5-9	180	12-31-78	1996	Santiago, D.R.
McClaskey, Tim	3	1	0.88	26	0	0	14	31	21	3	3	8	41	.187	R	R	5-10	170	1-11-76	1996	Wilton, Iowa
McCurtain, Paul	0	1	6.97	7	0	0	1	10	11	10	8	6	10	.268	R	R	6-1	190	2-5-76	1998	Mesa, Ariz.

PITCHING	W	L	ERA	G	GS	CG	SV	IP	H	R	ER	BB	SO	AVG	B	T	HT	WT	DOB	1st Yr	Resides
Messenger, Randy	7	4	4.08	18	18	0	0	93	99	55	42	35	42	.277	R	R	6-0	220	8-13-81	1999	Sparks, Nev.
Morse, Bryan	3	2	4.06	37	0	0	3	62	57	32	28	36	33	.253	L	L	5-11	165	9-12-77	1999	California, Md.
Moser, Todd	0	0	1.69	2	2	0	0	5	3	3	1	1	2	.166	L	L	6-5	180	10-28-76	1999	Davie, Fla.
Ortiz, Omar	4	10	5.38	28	21	0	0	112	120	78	67	65	78	.279	B	R	6-1	210	9-11-77	1999	Brownsville, Texas
Padilla, Roy	0	0	5.68	6	0	0	0	6	6	4	4	12	3	.285	L	L	6-5	227	8-4-75	1993	Panama City, Panama
Reyes, Eddy	2	0	3.60	13	0	0	2	15	13	13	6	10	9	.228	R	R	6-4	204	4-24-76	1997	Miami, Fla.
Robertson, Nathan	11	4	2.88	19	19	2	0	106	95	44	34	43	67	.244	R	L	6-2	215	9-3-77	1999	Valley Center, Kan.
Scheffer, Aaron	0	0	0.00	3	0	0	0	5	1	0	0	1	4	.062	L	R	6-2	175	10-15-75	1994	Westland, Mich.
Sergent, Joe	12	6	3.33	27	25	0	0	143	154	70	53	32	89	.272	L	L	6-0	185	8-29-78	1999	Manteca, Calif.
Smith, Chuck	0	0	3.38	2	2	0	0	8	7	3	3	1	6	.233	R	R	6-1	185	10-21-69	1991	Hillside, Ill.
Tejada, Frailyn	0	2	6.35	2	1	0	0	6	13	8	4	1	4	.481	L	L	6-2	175	7-25-82	1999	Santiago, D.R.
Woodards, Orlando	0	0	1.88	9	0	0	0	14	15	5	3	2	13	.263	R	R	6-2	200	1-2-78	1997	Sacramento, Calif.
2-team (17 Dunedin)	2	1	4.39	26	0	0	0	41	52	26	20	17	28	.305							

MIDWEST LEAGUE

BATTING	AVG	G	AB	R	H	2B	3B	HR	RBI	BB	SO	SB	CS	SLG	OBP	B	T	HT	WT	DOB	1st Yr	Resides
Ambres, Chip	.265	96	377	80	100	26	8	5	41	53	81	19	15	.416	.369	R	R	6-1	190	12-19-79	1998	Beaumont, Texas
Anderson, Dennis	.236	78	242	43	57	14	2	6	35	37	45	2	3	.384	.365	B	R	6-0	200	2-1-78	1999	Tucson, Ariz.
Cabrera, Miguel	.268	110	422	61	113	19	4	7	66	37	76	3	0	.382	.328	R	R	6-3	185	4-18-83	1999	Maracay, Venez.
DeMarco, Matt	.252	77	222	25	56	6	2	0	22	20	31	9	2	.297	.317	L	R	5-10	160	1-24-80	1999	Clayton, N.J.
Easterday, Matt	.262	72	195	42	51	7	2	2	16	33	37	10	3	.349	.374	L	L	6-1	188	5-3-79	2000	Covington, Ga.
Ferrand, Francisco	.290	85	297	43	86	20	2	6	45	17	49	3	1	.431	.331	L	L	5-10	170	5-20-80	1997	Santo Domingo, D.R.
Gonzalez, Adrian	.312	127	516	86	161	37	1	17	103	57	83	5	5	.486	.382	L	L	6-2	190	5-8-82	2000	Bonita, Calif.
Hicks, Scott	.667	1	3	1	2	1	0	0	0	0	0	1	0	1.000	.667	L	R	6-4	210	6-6-80	2000	Altamonte Springs, Fla.
Hill, Willy	.333	6	21	3	7	1	0	0	1	0	2	0	1	.381	.333	L	L	5-9	160	9-21-76	1998	Sapulpa, Okla.
Hooper, Kevin	.292	17	65	11	19	2	0	0	4	11	13	3	1	.323	.390	R	R	5-10	160	12-7-76	1999	Lawrence, Kan.
Kavourias, Jim	.261	120	460	77	120	30	4	23	88	48	126	11	3	.493	.340	L	R	6-4	230	10-4-79	2000	Strongsville, Ohio
Kelly, Heath	.176	11	34	1	6	0	0	0	3	1	10	0	1	.176	.200	R	R	6-1	185	2-16-76	1998	Pensacola, Fla.
Magness, Pat	.256	68	227	25	58	14	0	6	39	53	41	2	1	.396	.400	L	R	6-3	230	1-19-78	2000	Overland Park, Kan.
Postell, Matt	.284	34	95	16	27	6	0	3	6	11	36	2	2	.442	.364	L	R	6-4	187	1-10-77	1999	Gastonia, N.C.
Smith, Will	.280	125	535	92	150	26	2	16	91	32	74	4	5	.426	.324	L	R	6-1	185	10-23-81	2000	Tucson, Ariz.
Treanor, Matt	1.000	1	1	2	1	0	0	0	0	3	0	0	0	1.000	1.000	R	R	6-2	225	3-3-76	1994	Anaheim, Calif.
Willingham, Josh	.259	97	320	57	83	20	2	7	36	53	85	24	2	.400	.382	R	R	6-1	200	2-17-79	2000	Florence, Ala.
Wilson, Josh	.285	123	506	65	144	28	5	4	61	28	60	17	11	.383	.325	R	R	6-1	165	3-26-81	1999	Pittsburgh, Pa.
Woody, Dominic	.238	66	227	38	54	11	3	6	33	21	47	6	2	.392	.319	R	R	6-3	210	8-17-78	1999	Richland, Wash.
Wyant, Hunter	.000	7	13	0	0	0	0	0	0	0	3	0	0	.000	.000	R	R	6-2	195	10-4-78	2001	Whitehall, Va.
Zapey, Winton	.000	1	1	0	0	0	0	0	0	0	1	0	0	.000	.000	R	R	5-11	170	3-21-80	1997	Santo Domingo, D.R.

GAMES BY POSITION: C—Anderson 78, Postell 18, Treanor 1, Woody 51. **1B**—DeMarco 4, Gonzalez 116, Magness 14, Postell 7, Woody 1. **2B**—DeMarco 27, Easterday 33, Hooper 17, Kelly 5, Willingham 2, Wilson 67, Wyant 3. **3B**—Cabrera 8, DeMarco 37, Easterday 1, Kelly 4, Postell 2, Willingham 87, Wilson 11, Wyant 3. **SS**—Cabrera 98, DeMarco 2, Kelly 1, Wilson 52. **OF**—Ambres 91, DeMarco 2, Easterday 32, Ferrand 75, Hicks 1, Hill 4, Kavourias 106, Magness 2, Smith 118, Willingham 4.

PITCHING	W	L	ERA	G	GS	CG	SV	IP	H	R	ER	BB	SO	AVG	B	T	HT	WT	DOB	1st Yr	Resides
Bautista, Denny	3	1	4.35	8	7	0	0	39	43	21	19	14	20	.281	R	R	6-5	170	10-23-82	2000	Santo Domingo, D.R.
Byron, Terence	1	2	7.90	4	2	0	0	14	12	13	12	7	11	.230	R	R	6-0	200	3-28-79	1999	St. Croix, Virgin Islands
Castillo, Ramon	11	2	3.80	28	28	0	0	159	178	79	67	31	108	.277	R	R	6-0	165	5-30-80	1997	Cartagena, Colombia
Esquivia, Manuel	8	7	5.13	24	18	0	1	105	92	66	60	51	82	.232	R	R	6-1	195	9-20-79	2000	Collings Lakes, N.J.
Flannery, Michael	3	4	4.79	53	0	0	16	56	58	35	30	31	47	.262	R	R	6-2	195	9-18-79	2000	Canovanas, P.R.
Geigel, Rolando	3	3	4.06	30	1	0	0	44	39	22	20	28	19	.246	R	R	6-1	190	10-23-77	2001	Costa Mesa, Calif.
Halamicek, Kevin	0	3	4.70	20	0	0	0	31	31	17	16	13	17	.267	R	R	6-5	187	9-29-81	1999	Glasgow, Ky.
Haynes, Brad	7	3	3.81	17	17	0	0	90	86	50	38	39	73	.250	R	R	6-2	210	8-3-78	2001	La Mesa, Calif.
Henkel, Rob	0	0	4.50	1	1	0	0	4	6	3	2	1	2	.315	R	L	6-2	205	1-2-77	1995	Miami, Fla.
Izquierdo, Hansel	7	1	1.32	24	2	0	2	48	27	8	7	13	42	.164	R	R	6-2	190	10-30-77	2000	Reno, Nev.
Key, Chris	7	0	2.35	54	1	0	3	92	89	30	24	10	71	.255	R	L	6-3	210	10-30-77	2000	Santo Domingo, D.R.
Lajara, Gustavo	5	2	4.44	36	0	0	0	49	44	29	24	21	48	.247	L	L	5-10	160	8-20-79	1996	Santiago, D.R.
Lopez, Gustavo	6	4	3.58	17	17	0	0	93	89	42	37	27	63	.247	R	R	5-9	180	12-31-78	1996	Cincinnati, Ohio
McNutt, Mike	9	5	3.94	28	25	1	1	146	152	72	64	20	107	.267	R	R	6-0	220	8-13-81	1999	Sparks, Nev.
Messenger, Randy	2	1	3.93	14	0	0	0	18	22	13	8	5	14	.301	R	R	6-4	229	3-15-75	1996	Miramar, Fla.
Nunez, Vladimir	0	0	9.00	1	1	0	0	1	3	1	1	0	0	.600	R	R	6-2	190	6-30-80	1999	Gloucester City, N.J.
Sauer, Marc	2	2	4.20	9	5	0	0	30	30	15	14	1	13	.256	R	R	6-1	195	7-31-78	2000	Hammond, La.
Sawyer, Steve	10	2	4.20	55	0	0	7	71	78	39	33	27	37	.280	R	R	6-1	185	6-15-77	2001	Dublin, Calif.
Skinner, John	1	4	3.00	25	0	0	0	36	36	16	12	8	26	.257	R	R	6-1	185	12-25-78	2000	Wichita, Kan.
Sloan, Brandon	3	4	3.36	41	13	0	9	107	108	48	40	26	65	.274	B	R	6-2	190	10-26-77	2000	Wichita, Kan.

NEW YORK-PENN LEAGUE

BATTING	AVG	G	AB	R	H	2B	3B	HR	RBI	BB	SO	SB	CS	SLG	OBP	B	T	HT	WT	DOB	1st Yr	Resides
Alvarez, Aaron	.208	20	48	7	10	1	0	1	2	6	13	0	0	.292	.291	R	R	6-3	210	11-5-79	1999	Duluth, Ga.
Asahina, Ken	.217	30	60	5	13	1	0	0	4	6	14	0	0	.233	.292	B	R	6-1	190	12-31-80	2001	Fresno, Calif.
Blackburn, Franco	.224	37	107	14	24	4	0	2	11	21	37	0	0	.318	.352	R	R	6-1	185	2-18-79	2001	Huntsville, Ala.
Clute, Kris	.191	29	94	11	18	2	1	0	12	13	25	1	1	.234	.296	R	R	5-9	175	4-20-79	2001	Miami, Fla.
Frazier, Charles	.243	67	243	35	59	15	3	2	18	27	72	11	4	.354	.322	R	R	6-3	185	7-6-80	1999	Toms River, N.J.
Hartig, Philip	.259	46	170	12	44	4	4	3	17	8	37	0	3	.382	.292	B	R	6-3	210	12-17-77	2001	Asheville, N.C.
Helps, Jason	.138	24	65	6	9	3	0	0	4	12	17	0	1	.185	.317	B	R	6-3	185	12-20-78	2001	Wyoming, Ontario
Hicks, Scott	.308	56	211	25	65	15	1	4	36	24	52	7	2	.445	.379	L	R	6-4	210	6-6-80	2000	Altamonte Springs, Fla.
Kelly, Heath	.222	7	18	5	4	1	0	1	3	0	2	0	0	.444	.222	R	R	6-1	185	2-16-76	1998	Pensacola, Fla.
Laidlaw, Jake	.229	65	223	27	51	12	2	5	25	29	59	2	1	.368	.326	R	R	6-3	210	10-5-81	1999	North Las Vegas, Nev.
Louwsma, Chris	.229	44	140	20	32	6	2	2	17	10	34	0	0	.343	.276	R	R	6-0	200	1-11-79	2001	Gainesville, Fla.
Lovelady, Greg	.154	20	65	4	10	1	0	0	5	3	21	0	1	.169	.191	R	R	5-11	195	10-27-80	2001	Williamstown, N.J.
Lynam, Guy	.351	22	57	10	20	5	0	1	10	4	10	1	0	.491	.406	R	R	6-3	200	11-4-82	2001	Naples, Fla.
Resop, Chris	.333	2	3	0	1	0	0	0	0	0	2	0	0	.333	.333	R	R	6-3	210	11-4-82	2001	Naples, Fla.
Rittenhouse, Marc	.234	40	128	21	30	6	0	3	12	16	43	0	1	.352	.333	R	R	5-10	180	6-9-79	2001	Bellevue, Wash.

BATTING	AVG	G	AB	R	H	2B	3B	HR	RBI	BB	SO	SB	CS	SLG	OBP	B	T	HT	WT	DOB	1st Yr	Resides
Rundgren, Rex	.251	55	195	15	49	5	1	3	25	5	33	3	5	.333	.275	R	R	6-1	170	11-20-80	2001	Princeville, Hawaii
Soto, Jose	.229	48	192	22	44	7	3	2	17	13	52	15	3	.328	.277	R	R	6-0	160	6-20-80	1996	San Cristobal, D.R.
Stokes, Jason	.231	35	130	12	30	2	1	6	19	11	48	0	0	.400	.299	R	R	6-4	225	1-23-82	2000	Coppell, Texas
Tucker, Michael	.214	49	159	29	34	4	0	2	9	23	40	0	2	.277	.317	R	R	6-3	200	11-7-79	2001	Lakeland, Fla.
Wyant, Hunter	.277	30	94	11	26	6	0	0	6	6	14	1	2	.340	.340	R	R	6-2	195	10-4-78	2001	Whitehall, Mont.
Zapey, Winton	.195	32	77	6	15	3	1	1	8	7	24	0	0	.299	.279	R	R	5-11	170	3-21-80	1997	Santo Domingo, D.R.

GAMES BY POSITION: C—Alvarez 20, Lovelady 20, Lynam 20, Zapey 32. 1B—Hartig 40, Hicks 26, Louwsma 14. 2B—Clute 28, Helps 3, Kelly 6, Rittenhouse 33, Wyant 12. 3B—Kelly 1, Louwsma 21, Tucker 47, Wyant 11. SS—Helps 21, Rundgren 55, Wyant 5. OF—Blackburn 25, Frazier 67, Hicks 29, Laidlaw 56, Resop 2, Rittenhouse 3, Soto 46, Stokes 5.

PITCHING	W	L	ERA	G	GS	CG	SV	IP	H	R	ER	BB	SO	AVG	B	T	HT	WT	DOB	1st Yr	Resides
Akens, Phil	2	5	3.24	9	9	0	0	50	40	24	18	22	34	.222	R	R	6-6	200	8-9-82	2000	Bel Air, Md.
Asahina, Jon	4	6	2.58	15	13	0	0	69	56	27	20	19	55	.236	B	R	6-1	190	12-31-80	2000	Fresno, Calif.
Bautista, Denny	3	1	2.08	7	7	0	0	39	25	16	9	6	31	.173	R	R	6-5	170	10-23-82	2000	Santo Domingo, D.R.
Baxter, Allen	0	0	3.60	1	1	0	0	5	3	2	2	3	5	.176	R	R	6-4	215	7-6-83	2001	Sandston, Va.
Bell, Tom	1	0	7.99	18	0	0	0	24	29	22	21	13	21	.305	R	R	6-0	185	1-5-81	1999	Vienna, Va.
Cautaulin, Heath	0	3	7.41	25	0	0	4	38	44	37	31	19	32	.295	R	R	6-1	205	12-8-79	2001	Norfolk, Va.
Cave, Kevin	1	2	3.26	14	5	0	1	39	38	16	14	14	23	.260	R	R	6-3	215	5-25-80	2001	Levittown, Pa.
David, Toby	0	3	5.19	20	0	0	0	35	41	25	20	11	18	.294	L	L	6-4	225	6-1-78	2001	Kissimmee, Fla.
Fulchino, Jeff	3	8	3.56	14	13	0	0	61	48	34	24	31	33	.211	R	R	6-5	240	11-26-79	2001	Hollis, N.H.
Goodwin, Ron	3	3	3.60	20	0	0	3	45	51	22	18	10	25	.291	R	R	6-1	175	8-30-79	2001	Sherwood, Ark.
Halamicek, Kevin	4	0	3.52	7	0	0	0	15	12	12	6	10	12	.203	R	R	6-1	190	10-23-77	2001	Costa Mesa, Calif.
Henkel, Rob	0	0	4.32	3	3	0	0	8	7	4	4	6	11	.212	R	L	6-2	210	8-3-78	2001	La Mesa, Calif.
Khoury, Josh	2	4	4.78	29	0	0	1	38	34	28	20	26	33	.241	R	R	6-1	205	5-20-78	2001	Indianapolis, Ind.
Kupper, Dustin	0	1	5.27	8	3	0	0	14	10	13	8	7	14	.197	R	R	6-6	190	2-22-81	2001	Tucson, Ariz.
McCrotty, Wes	1	7	4.12	17	9	0	0	63	50	34	29	24	39	.210	L	L	6-1	190	6-22-79	2001	Russellville, Ark.
Skinner, John	0	0	3.86	4	0	0	2	5	5	3	2	1	6	.238	R	R	6-1	185	6-15-77	2001	Dublin, Calif.
Thomas, Stephen	1	2	3.98	24	0	0	3	41	48	23	18	9	26	.303	R	R	6-1	205	5-3-78	2001	Plantation, Fla.
Ungs, Nick	3	1	1.62	12	11	0	0	61	57	14	11	0	40	.245	R	R	6-1	220	9-3-79	2001	Dyersville, Iowa

MELBOURNE — Rookie

GULF COAST LEAGUE

BATTING	AVG	G	AB	R	H	2B	3B	HR	RBI	BB	SO	SB	CS	SLG	OBP	B	T	HT	WT	DOB	1st Yr	Resides
Arroyo, William	.257	42	144	15	37	1	1	0	14	12	28	5	1	.278	.321	B	R	5-10	170	11-8-81	1999	Cabudare, Venez.
Bastardo, Frederick	.238	44	147	18	35	12	0	2	14	9	32	7	4	.361	.294	R	R	5-11	160	8-2-81	1998	Maracay, Venez.
Brewer, Anthony	.251	58	211	35	53	7	3	0	16	28	55	27	10	.313	.359	R	R	6-0	165	8-2-82	2000	Chicago, Ill.
Brown, Jason	.333	1	3	0	1	0	0	0	1	0	2	0	0	.333	.333	R	R	6-2	208	5-22-74	1997	Rolling Hills Estates, Calif.
Carofiles, Vladimir	.259	43	147	13	38	9	1	1	20	4	20	13	4	.354	.295	R	R	5-11	165	8-11-81	1999	Panama City, Panama
Coffey, Josh	.033	9	30	1	1	0	0	0	0	0	10	1	0	.033	.033	R	R	6-2	180	8-4-83	2001	Mechanicsville, Va.
Estilow, Chris	.125	18	40	3	5	0	0	0	3	7	20	0	0	.125	.255	R	R	6-2	220	3-14-81	2001	Cherry Hill, N.J.
Garcia, Juan Carlos	.185	40	108	8	20	4	0	1	10	14	44	2	3	.250	.276	B	R	6-1	185	3-10-82	1998	Santiago, D.R.
Gerlits, Gooby	.163	16	43	1	7	1	0	0	2	1	12	0	0	.186	.200	R	R	6-0	200	11-17-82	2001	Parkland, Fla.
Graham, Tyson	.172	35	93	12	16	1	1	1	6	8	32	1	0	.237	.252	R	R	6-3	215	1-12-83	2001	Gastonia, N.C.
Guerrero, Jorge	.293	46	140	18	41	9	1	2	13	18	27	11	6	.414	.379	R	R	6-0	152	8-13-80	1997	Palenque, D.R.
Guzman, Wander	.226	51	199	16	45	7	0	0	13	3	34	14	2	.261	.252	B	R	5-11	165	12-3-82	1999	Santo Domingo, D.R.
Lindberg, Russell	.127	20	55	2	7	2	0	0	5	3	8	0	3	.164	.200	R	R	6-4	225	7-3-79	2001	Cleveland Heights, Ohio
Lush, Zach	.115	7	26	4	3	0	0	0	1	5	5	5	0	.115	.303	R	R	6-3	190	1-18-77	2001	North Andover, Mass.
Molina, Angel	.255	36	110	9	28	7	0	1	13	10	26	0	2	.345	.317	R	R	6-2	200	11-4-82	2000	Santa Isabel, P.R.
Rengifo, Amado	.308	3	13	4	4	0	0	0	0	1	2	2	2	.308	.357	R	R	5-10	160	12-7-81	1998	Yaracuy, Venez.
Resop, Chris	.116	26	86	5	10	2	0	0	5	7	34	0	3	.140	.189	R	R	6-3	200	11-4-82	2001	Naples, Fla.
Rolison, Nate	.500	2	4	1	2	0	0	0	1	3	1	0	0	.500	.714	L	R	6-6	240	3-27-77	1995	Petal, Miss.
Rudecindo, Carlos	.000	3	9	0	0	0	0	0	1	1	7	0	0	.000	.100	R	R	6-1	170	11-4-82	1999	La Victoria, D.R.
Searage, Ray	.088	12	34	4	3	0	0	0	1	3	10	0	1	.088	.162	R	R	6-0	175	10-16-80	2001	St. Petersburg, Fla.
Taveras, Frank	.213	28	89	12	19	2	0	0	4	12	29	6	2	.236	.317	R	R	6-2	182	8-14-81	1997	Moca, D.R.
Timaure, Jesus	.224	44	156	18	35	12	0	1	21	10	45	3	0	.321	.301	R	R	6-0	170	2-25-80	1997	Cabudare, Venez.
Treanor, Matt	.412	11	34	10	14	4	0	1	4	7	7	3	0	.618	.512	R	R	6-2	225	3-3-76	1994	Anaheim, Calif.

GAMES BY POSITION: C—Brown 1, Coffey 1, Estilow 17, Gerlits 12, Lush 3, Molina 34, Treanor 6. 1B—Bastardo 7, Carofiles 9, Coffey 1, Garcia 17, Gerlits 2, Guerrero 5, Lindberg 17, Lush 2, Rolison 2, Taveras 1, Timaure 4. 2B—Arroyo 5, Bastardo 21, Guerrero 12, Guzman 8, Rudecindo 2. 3B—Bastardo 12, Garcia 19, Guerrero 17, Taveras 18. SS—Arroyo 36, Garcia 1, Guzman 23. OF—Bastardo 2, Brewer 58, Carofiles 32, Graham 30, Rengifo 3, Resop 23, Searage 12, Timaure 3.

PITCHING	W	L	ERA	G	GS	CG	SV	IP	H	R	ER	BB	SO	AVG	B	T	HT	WT	DOB	1st Yr	Resides
Akens, Phil	2	0	1.60	6	3	0	0	33	19	11	6	9	24	.158	R	R	6-6	200	8-9-82	2000	Bel Air, Md.
Anderson, Wes	0	1	27.00	1	1	0	0	1	3	2	1	1	0	.600	R	R	6-4	175	9-10-79	1997	Pine Bluff, Ark.
Banks, Tyler	0	2	2.30	10	2	0	1	31	24	9	8	6	26	.206	R	R	6-2	200	2-9-81	2001	Palm Harbor, Fla.
Baxter, Allen	2	3	2.38	9	7	0	0	34	25	13	9	8	40	.206	R	R	6-4	215	7-6-83	2001	Sandston, Va.
Belizario, Ronald	4	6	2.34	13	10	1	0	73	62	29	19	20	54	.228	R	R	6-2	148	12-31-82	1999	Aragua, Venez.
Birk, Ben	0	0	0.00	3	0	0	0	6	3	0	0	1	4	.142	L	L	6-5	215	11-6-77	2001	St. Paul, Minn.
Bostick, Adam	1	1	4.26	7	1	0	0	13	16	8	6	3	13	.301	L	L	6-2	220	3-17-83	2001	Greensburg, Pa.
Davis, Lance	2	1	3.19	14	3	0	1	31	33	15	11	4	26	.282	R	R	6-3	195	1-18-83	2001	Lucedale, Miss.
DeJesus, Elvis	0	4	5.18	13	7	0	2	42	49	35	24	12	33	.284	R	R	6-3	150	5-9-81	1999	Moca, D.R.
Espaillat, Ezequiel	0	0	5.06	15	0	0	3	32	34	22	18	10	23	.276	R	R	6-5	180	3-31-81	1998	Santiago, D.R.
Evans, Louis	3	3	2.16	14	0	0	0	25	18	10	6	12	26	.204	L	L	6-5	213	10-5-80	2001	San Jose, Calif.
Frawley, Patrick	0	1	4.05	6	0	0	0	7	5	4	3	2	6	.192	R	R	6-0	195	3-25-77	2001	Fort Lauderdale, Fla.
Grilli, Jason	0	0	0.00	2	2	0	0	4	2	0	0	0	6	.142	R	R	6-4	185	11-11-76	1997	Orlando, Fla.
Henkel, Rob	1	3	1.52	9	8	0	0	30	17	9	5	11	38	.155	R	L	6-2	210	8-3-78	2001	La Mesa, Calif.
Hickman, Ben	0	0	1.42	5	0	0	0	6	6	1	1	1	6	.285	R	R	6-0	170	11-10-76	1999	Bryant, Ark.
Holdzkom, Lincoln	1	3	2.49	12	7	0	2	43	26	18	12	27	43	.175	R	R	6-4	240	3-23-82	2001	Lacey, Wash.
Mau, Ryan	1	0	0.90	4	0	0	0	10	6	1	1	3	6	.176	R	R	6-5	210	11-27-78	2001	Mount Pleasant, S.C.
Moser, Todd	0	0	9.00	1	1	0	0	2	2	2	2	0	3	.250	L	L	6-5	180	10-28-76	1999	Davie, Fla.
Padilla, Roy	0	0	0.00	4	0	0	0	1	6	1	1	0	1	.055	L	L	6-5	227	4-4-75	1993	Panama City, Panama
Selmo, Steven	5	2	2.97	17	0	0	4	36	28	16	12	7	22	.207	R	R	6-4	185	11-21-82	1999	Santo Domingo, D.R.
Sterrett, Adam	0	0	9.00	3	0	0	0	1	1	1	1	3	0	.333	B	R	6-4	185	8-11-82	2000	Staunton, Va.
Tejada, Frailyn	6	1	2.58	10	8	0	0	52	47	19	15	7	54	.237	L	L	6-2	175	7-25-82	1999	Santiago, D.R.

HOUSTON ASTROS

BY TOM HALLIBURTON

The good news is that 2001 saw Houston's fourth National League Central title in the past five years.

The bad news is the Astros extended their playoff futility, failing to win even a game. In their 40-year history, the Astros have lost all seven playoff series they've appeared in.

The latest setback cost manager Larry Dierker his job. Though the Astros improved to 93-69 from 72-90 in 2000, delivering their largest single-season turnaround ever and capturing a club-record 49 road victories, Dierker resigned under pressure after the season. He stepped down after six years on the job.

Houston went three-and-out against Atlanta in the NL Division Series, despite owning the home-field advantage for every possible playoff round. Its overall postseason record fell to 8-22. To add insult to injury, the Braves are 9-1 against the Astros in postseason games.

With several key players having outstanding years in the regular season, some familiar faces continued to struggle in the playoffs. Jeff Bagwell now has a .174 batting average with no extra-base hits in 46 career postseason at-bats. Craig Biggio stands at .130 with one extra-base hit in 54 career postseason at-bats. Moises Alou has hit .179 with no extra-base hits in 28 playoff at-bats with the Astros.

Through the course of the 2001 season, general manager Gerry Hunsicker tapped into his organization's rich minor league system for pitching reinforcements. Dierker used a club-record 25 pitchers, including 14 different starters, as he managed to keep his team in first place most of the season.

Righthander Roy Oswalt began the season in Triple-A and became the Astros' best pitcher at one point, winning 14 games. But he was unavailable down the stretch as he was sidelined by a leg injury.

Second-year righthander Wade Miller led the team with 16 wins, while veteran Shane Reynolds won 13. Closer Billy Wagner bounced back from an injury-plagued 2000

Lance Berkman

Jason Lane

TYLER BOLDEN

RODGER WOOD

PLAYERS OF THE YEAR

MAJOR LEAGUE: Lance Berkman, of
Berkman hit .331-34-126 and became the first switch-hitter with 30 home runs and 50 doubles in a season. He also had the most doubles in a season, 55, by a switch-hitter.

MINOR LEAGUE: Jason Lane, of
Lane led Astros minor leaguers in RBIs for the second year in a row in 2001, finishing with 124 while hitting .316 with 38 home runs. He was also named the Texas League player of the year.

season to tie a franchise record with 39 saves. Octavio Dotel emerged as one of baseball's premier setup men, leading major league relievers in strikeouts (128).

Outfielders Lance Berkman and Alou stayed among the National League batting leaders all season, and tied for the team lead at .331. In his first full big league season, Berkman became the first switch-hitter in major league history to have 50 doubles (55) and 30 home runs (34) in a season.

Despite their postseason failings, Bagwell and Biggio continued distinguished Houston careers. Bagwell led the team in home runs (39), RBIs (130), runs (126) and walks (106), and became the only player in major league history with 30 homers, 100 RBIs, 100 runs and 100 walks in six consecutive seasons.

Rebounding from major knee surgery, Biggio became the franchise leader in games played (1,955). He also led the majors in being hit by pitches (28).

Houston was faced with some serious thinking during the winter, because the team was unlikely to stick with a $62 million payroll. The team had 13 free agents.

At the minor league level, the Astros had a banner 2001 season. The organization posted the best cumulative won-lost record in the minors and Baseball America chose the Astros as its Organization of the Year. Double-A Round Rock's Jackie Moore was named Minor League Manager of the Year by BA.

Triple-A New Orleans and Class A Lexington won championships in the Pacific Coast and South Atlantic leagues. Round Rock and Class A Michigan also reached the playoffs.

Round Rock fashioned a Texas League-best 86-54 record while Moore, MVP Jason Lane and top pitcher Tim Redding combined for the sixth postseason awards sweep in league history.

ORGANIZATION LEADERS

BATTING
*AVG	Jason Maule, Michigan	.347
R	Jason Lane, Round Rock	103
H	Jason Lane, Round Rock	166
TB	Jason Lane, Round Rock	320
2B	Felix Escalona, Lexington	42
3B	Henri Stanley, Michigan	12
HR	Jason Lane, Round Rock	38
RBI	Jason Lane, Round Rock	124
BB	Jon Topolski, Lexington	75
SO	Keith Ginter, New Orleans	147
SB	Jason Maule, Michigan	56

PITCHING
W	Three tied at	15
L	Darwin Peguero, Lexington	10
#ERA	D.J. Houlton, Martinsville	2.69
G	Travis Wade, Round Rock	60
CG	Mike Nannini, Lexington	4
SV	Jim Mann, New Orleans	27
IP	Mike Nannini, Lexington	190
BB	Anthony Pluta, Lexington	86
SO	Carlos Hernandez, Round Rock	167

*Minimum 250 At-Bats #Minimum 75 Innings

HOUSTON ASTROS

Manager: Larry Dierker

2001 Record: 93-69, .574 (t-1st, NL Central)

BATTING	AVG	G	AB	R	H	2B	3B	HR	RBI	BB	SO	SB	CS	SLG	OBP	B	T	HT	WT	DOB	1st Yr	Resides
Alou, Moises	.331	136	513	79	170	31	1	27	108	57	57	5	1	.554	.396	R	R	6-3	195	7-3-66	1986	Santo Domingo, D.R.
Ausmus, Brad	.232	128	422	45	98	23	4	5	34	30	64	4	1	.341	.284	R	R	5-11	195	4-14-69	1987	San Diego, Calif.
Bagwell, Jeff	.288	161	600	126	173	43	4	39	130	106	135	11	3	.568	.397	R	R	6-0	195	5-27-68	1989	Houston, Texas
Barker, Glen	.083	70	24	12	2	0	0	0	1	3	6	4	6	.083	.233	B	R	5-10	180	5-10-71	1993	Albany, N.Y.
Berkman, Lance	.331	156	577	110	191	55	5	34	126	92	121	7	4	.620	.430	B	L	6-1	205	2-10-76	1997	Houston, Texas
Biggio, Craig	.292	155	617	118	180	35	3	20	70	66	100	7	4	.455	.382	R	R	5-11	180	12-14-65	1987	Houston, Texas
Castilla, Vinny	.270	122	445	62	120	28	1	23	82	32	86	1	4	.492	.320	R	R	6-1	205	7-4-67	1990	Littleton, Colo.
Eusebio, Tony	.253	59	154	16	39	8	0	5	14	17	34	0	0	.403	.339	R	R	6-2	210	4-27-67	1985	Kissimmee, Fla.
Everett, Adam	.000	9	3	1	0	0	0	0	0	0	1	1	0	.000	.000	R	R	6-0	156	2-6-77	1998	Kennesaw, Ga.
Ginter, Keith	.000	1	1	0	0	0	0	0	0	0	0	0	0	.000	.000	R	R	5-9	190	5-5-76	1998	Fullerton, Calif.
Hayes, Charlie	.200	31	50	4	10	2	0	0	4	7	16	0	0	.240	.293	R	R	6-0	215	5-29-65	1983	Tomball, Texas
Hidalgo, Richard	.275	146	512	70	141	29	3	19	80	54	107	3	5	.455	.356	R	R	6-3	190	7-2-75	1991	Guarenas, Venez.
Lopez, Mendy	.267	10	15	3	4	0	0	1	3	2	4	0	0	.467	.389	R	R	6-2	190	10-15-74	1992	Santo Domingo, D.R.
Lugo, Julio	.263	140	513	93	135	20	3	10	37	46	116	12	11	.372	.326	R	R	6-2	165	11-16-75	1995	Brooklyn, N.Y.
Merced, Orlando	.263	94	137	19	36	6	1	6	29	14	32	5	1	.453	.333	L	R	6-1	195	11-2-66	1985	Orlando, Fla.
Servais, Scott	.375	11	16	1	6	0	0	0	0	2	3	0	0	.375	.444	R	R	6-2	210	6-4-67	1989	Castle Rock, Colo.
Spiers, Bill	.333	4	3	0	1	0	0	0	0	1	0	0	0	.333	.500	L	R	6-2	190	6-5-66	1987	Cameron, S.C.
Truby, Chris	.206	48	136	11	28	6	1	8	23	13	38	1	2	.441	.276	R	R	6-2	190	12-9-73	1993	Mukilteo, Wash.
Vizcaino, Jose	.277	107	256	38	71	8	3	1	14	15	33	3	2	.344	.322	B	R	6-1	180	3-26-68	1986	Jamul, Calif.
Ward, Daryle	.263	95	213	21	56	15	0	9	39	19	48	0	0	.460	.323	L	L	6-2	230	6-27-75	1994	Riverside, Calif.

PITCHING	W	L	ERA	G	GS	CG	SV	IP	H	R	ER	BB	SO	AVG	B	T	HT	WT	DOB	1st Yr	Resides
Astacio, Pedro	2	1	3.14	4	4	0	0	29	30	10	10	4	19	.280	R	R	6-2	210	11-28-69	1988	Hato Mayor, D.R.
2-team (22 Colorado)	8	14	5.09	26	26	4	0	170	181	101	96	54	144	.276							
Bottenfield, Kent	2	5	6.40	13	9	0	1	52	61	44	37	16	39	.287	R	R	6-3	240	11-14-68	1986	Brownsburg, Ind.
Cruz, Nelson	3	3	4.15	66	0	0	2	82	72	41	38	24	75	.236	R	R	6-1	185	9-13-72	1989	Washington, D.C.
Dotel, Octavio	7	5	2.66	61	4	0	2	105	79	35	31	47	145	.205	R	R	6-0	175	11-25-75	1993	Santo Domingo, D.R.
Elarton, Scott	4	8	7.14	20	20	0	0	110	126	88	87	49	76	.289	R	R	6-7	240	2-23-76	1994	Lamar, Colo.
Franklin, Wayne	0	0	6.75	11	0	0	0	12	17	9	9	9	9	.333	L	L	6-2	195	3-9-74	1996	North East, Md.
Hernandez, Carlos	1	0	1.02	3	3	0	0	18	11	2	2	7	17	.177	L	L	5-10	145	4-22-80	1997	Yagua, Venez.
Jackson, Mike	5	3	4.70	67	0	0	4	69	68	36	36	22	46	.259	R	R	6-2	225	12-22-64	1984	Spring, Texas
Lima, Jose	1	2	7.30	14	9	0	0	53	77	48	43	16	41	.350	R	R	6-2	205	9-30-72	1989	Houston, Texas
Linebrink, Scott	0	0	2.61	5	0	0	0	6	4	3	6	9	.176	R	R	6-3	185	8-4-76	1997	Austin, Texas
Mann, Jim	0	0	3.38	4	0	0	0	5	3	2	2	4	5	.176	R	R	6-3	225	11-17-74	1994	Holbrook, Mass.
McKnight, Tony	1	0	4.00	3	3	0	0	18	21	8	8	3	10	.287	L	R	6-5	205	6-29-77	1995	Texarkana, Ark.
Miller, Wade	16	8	3.40	32	32	1	0	212	183	91	80	76	183	.234	R	R	6-2	185	9-13-76	1996	Reading, Pa.
Mlicki, Dave	7	3	5.09	19	14	0	0	87	85	53	49	33	49	.259	R	R	6-4	205	6-8-68	1989	Columbus, Ohio
Oswalt, Roy	14	3	2.73	28	20	3	0	142	126	48	43	24	144	.234	R	R	6-0	170	8-29-77	1997	Weir, Miss.
Powell, Brian	0	1	18.00	1	1	0	0	3	5	6	6	3	3	.357	R	R	6-2	205	10-10-73	1995	Bainbridge, Ga.
Powell, Jay	2	2	3.72	35	0	0	0	36	41	18	15	19	28	.275	R	R	6-4	225	1-9-72	1993	Madison, Miss.
Redding, Tim	3	1	5.50	13	9	0	0	56	62	38	34	24	55	.283	R	R	6-0	180	2-12-78	1998	Churchville, N.Y.
Reynolds, Shane	14	11	4.34	28	28	3	0	183	208	95	88	36	102	.290	R	R	6-3	210	3-26-68	1989	Houston, Texas
Rodriguez, Wilfredo	0	0	15.00	2	0	0	0	3	6	5	5	1	3	.428	L	L	6-3	180	3-20-79	1996	San Felix, Venez.
Slusarski, Joe	0	1	9.00	8	0	0	0	10	16	10	10	3	6	.363	R	R	6-4	195	12-19-66	1989	Springfield, Ill.
2-team (4 Atlanta)	0	1	9.00	12	0	0	0	16	25	16	16	4	11	.357							
Stone, Ricky	0	0	2.35	6	0	0	0	8	8	3	2	2	4	.258	R	R	6-1	168	2-28-75	1994	Hamilton, Ohio
Villone, Ron	5	7	5.56	31	6	0	0	68	77	46	42	24	65	.282	L	L	6-3	237	1-16-70	1992	River Vale, N.J.
2-team (22 Colorado)	6	10	5.89	53	12	0	0	115	133	81	75	53	113	.287							
Wagner, Billy	2	5	2.73	64	0	0	39	63	44	19	19	20	79	.198	L	L	5-11	180	7-25-71	1993	Pearland, Texas
Williams, Mike	4	0	4.03	25	0	0	0	22	21	10	10	14	16	.244	R	R	6-2	204	7-29-68	1990	Newport, Va.
2-team (40 Pittsburgh)	6	4	3.80	65	0	0	22	60	60	28	27	35	59	.243							

FIELDING

Catcher	PCT	G	PO	A	E	DP	PB
Ausmus	.997	127	948	62	3	9	1
Eusebio	.991	48	300	22	3	4	2
Servais	1.000	9	38	1	0	0	1

First Base	PCT	G	PO	A	E	DP
Bagwell	.992	160	1291	143	12	123
Hayes	1.000	2	7	0	0	0
Merced	1.000	1	1	0	0	0
Truby	1.000	1	1	0	0	0
Ward	1.000	9	19	0	0	0

Second Base	PCT	G	PO	A	E	DP
Biggio	.984	154	280	389	11	86
Lopez	1.000	3	5	2	0	0
Lugo	.000	2	0	0	0	0
Vizcaino	.980	18	22	26	1	6

Third Base	PCT	G	PO	A	E	DP
Castilla	.963	121	82	230	12	18
Hayes	1.000	11	7	12	0	2

	PCT	G	PO	A	E	DP
Lopez	1.000	2	0	1	0	1
Merced	.000	2	0	0	0	0
Truby	.923	35	17	55	6	4
Vizcaino	.500	7	0	2	2	0

Shortstop	PCT	G	PO	A	E	DP
Castilla	1.000	3	1	1	0	0
Everett	.667	6	2	2	2	1
Lugo	.964	133	211	373	22	74
Vizcaino	.937	53	50	114	11	21

Outfield	PCT	G	PO	A	E	DP
Alou	.991	130	205	10	2	3
Barker	1.000	60	36	0	0	0
Berkman	.981	155	306	6	6	1
Hidalgo	.991	144	332	11	3	4
Lugo	1.000	8	2	0	0	0
Merced	.975	31	38	1	1	0
Ward	.985	42	62	2	1	1

Roy Oswalt

LARRY GOREN

Director, Player Development: Tim Purpura

Class	Farm Team	League	W	L	Pct.	Finish*	Manager	First Yr.
AAA	New Orleans (La.) Zephyrs	Pacific Coast	82	57	.590	+2nd (16)	Tony Pena	1997
AA	Round Rock (Texas) Express	Texas	86	54	.614	1st (8)	Jackie Moore	2000
A	Michigan Battle Cats	Midwest	82	55	.599	3rd (14)	John Massarelli	1999
A	Lexington (Ky.) Legends	South Atlantic	92	48	.657	+1st (16)	J.J. Cannon	2001
A	Pittsfield (Mass.) Astros	New York-Penn	45	30	.600	4th (14)	Ivan DeJesus	2001
Rookie#	Martinsville (Va.) Astros	Appalachian	31	37	.456	t-7th (10)	Jorge Orta	1999

*Finish in overall standings (No. of teams in league)   #Advanced level   +League champion

NEW ORLEANS   Class AAA

PACIFIC COAST LEAGUE

BATTING	AVG	G	AB	R	H	2B	3B	HR	RBI	BB	SO	SB	CS	SLG	OBP	B	T	HT	WT	DOB	1st Yr	Resides
Barker, Glen	.280	46	168	28	47	2	4	2	20	12	45	7	3	.375	.333	B	R	5-10	180	5-10-71	1993	Albany, N.Y.
Berroa, Cristian	.133	8	15	1	2	0	0	0	1	3	4	0	1	.133	.278	B	R	5-11	150	4-27-79	1996	Haina, D.R.
Bruntlett, Eric	.125	5	16	3	2	0	0	0	1	2	1	0	0	.125	.222	R	R	6-0	200	3-29-78	2000	Lafayette, Ind.
Burns, Kevin	.263	34	99	19	26	5	3	1	11	15	18	0	1	.404	.376	L	L	6-5	220	9-9-75	1995	El Dorado, Ark.
Chamblee, Jim	.257	11	35	3	9	2	0	1	4	4	13	0	0	.400	.350	R	R	6-4	175	5-6-75	1995	Denton, Texas
Charles, Frank	.333	3	3	0	1	0	0	0	0	0	0	0	0	.333	.500	R	R	6-4	210	2-23-69	1991	Van Nuys, Calif.
Chavez, Raul	.302	85	278	38	84	17	0	8	40	19	34	1	1	.450	.361	R	R	5-11	210	3-18-74	1990	Valencia, Venez.
Cole, Eric	.264	121	397	47	105	25	2	3	41	38	94	1	4	.360	.339	R	R	6-0	185	11-15-75	1995	Boulder City, Nev.
Ensberg, Morgan	.310	87	316	65	98	20	0	23	61	45	60	6	3	.592	.397	R	R	6-2	210	8-26-75	1998	Hermosa Beach, Calif.
Everett, Adam	.249	114	441	69	110	20	8	5	40	39	74	24	5	.365	.330	R	R	6-0	156	2-6-77	1998	Kennesaw, Ga.
Ginter, Keith	.269	132	457	76	123	31	5	16	70	61	147	8	6	.464	.380	R	R	5-10	190	5-5-76	1998	Fullerton, Calif.
Lopez, Mendy	.279	63	208	37	58	11	1	14	36	18	49	2	2	.543	.343	R	R	6-2	190	10-15-74	1992	Santo Domingo, D.R.
Luuloa, Keith	.204	36	93	14	19	7	0	2	11	13	17	0	0	.344	.312	R	R	6-0	185	12-24-74	1994	Canyon Lake, Calif.
2-team (64 Portland)	.252	100	310	45	78	20	2	6	27	26	41	1	1	.387	.321							
Lydy, Scott	.265	95	283	37	75	20	1	7	43	47	62	8	5	.417	.371	R	R	6-5	195	10-28-68	1989	Chandler, Ariz.
Matranga, Dave	.313	4	16	3	5	1	0	1	3	0	5	1	0	.563	.333	R	R	6-0	196	1-8-77	1998	Aliso Viejo, Calif.
Mouton, Lyle	.333	2	9	1	3	1	0	1	1	0	3	0	0	.778	.333	R	R	6-4	230	5-13-69	1991	Tarpon Springs, Fla.
Porter, Colin	.237	101	312	48	74	14	1	7	33	34	105	11	6	.356	.314	L	L	6-2	200	11-23-75	1998	Tucson, Ariz.
Pose, Scott	.271	17	59	5	16	2	0	0	3	4	6	6	2	.305	.317	L	R	5-11	190	2-11-67	1989	Raleigh, N.C.
Ramirez, Omar	.251	118	363	40	91	20	0	2	39	29	42	9	4	.322	.307	R	R	5-9	170	11-2-70	1990	Anaheim Hills, Calif.
Servais, Scott	.222	11	9	2	2	0	0	0	1	1	3	0	0	.222	.300	R	R	6-1	195	11-11-74	1987	Castle Rock, Colo.
Schifano, Tony	.338	44	148	22	50	10	1	6	31	12	21	0	0	.541	.392	R	R	6-0	215	10-17-69	1992	New Waverly, Texas
Tremie, Chris	.118	8	17	0	2	1	0	0	2	4	2	0	0	.176	.273	R	R	6-2	200	12-9-73	1993	Mukilteo, Wash.
Truby, Chris	.312	81	321	53	100	25	6	12	71	24	66	10	5	.539	.365	R	R	6-2	190	12-9-73	1993	Mukilteo, Wash.
Zinter, Alan	.265	104	332	58	88	16	0	19	65	33	85	1	1	.485	.334	B	R	6-2	200	5-19-68	1989	Tucson, Ariz.

PITCHING	W	L	ERA	G	GS	CG	SV	IP	H	R	ER	BB	SO	AVG	B	T	HT	WT	DOB	1st Yr	Resides
Arteaga, J.D.	8	6	3.07	32	21	1	1	138	143	60	47	27	90	.266	L	L	6-3	227	8-2-74	1997	Miami, Fla.
Brocail, Doug	0	0	0.00	2	0	0	0	2	2	0	0	1	2	.222	L	R	6-5	235	5-16-67	1986	Missouri City, Texas
Driskill, Travis	11	5	3.78	28	28	1	0	179	175	83	75	33	145	.255	R	R	6-0	185	8-1-71	1993	Austin, Texas
Evans, Dave	2	1	6.38	25	7	1	1	42	50	37	30	27	40	.294	R	R	6-3	205	1-1-68	1990	Houston, Texas
Franklin, Wayne	2	1	3.81	41	0	0	0	50	47	28	21	18	51	.243	L	L	6-2	195	3-9-74	1996	North East, Md.
Guerra, Mark	7	8	3.90	28	15	1	0	108	129	56	47	21	56	.293	R	R	6-2	200	11-4-71	1994	Pensacola Beach, Fla.
Kessel, Kyle	1	3	7.90	15	6	0	0	41	64	40	36	24	24	.365	R	L	6-0	160	6-2-76	1994	Mundelein, Ill.
Linebrink, Scott	7	6	3.50	50	0	0	8	72	52	28	28	24	72	.203	R	R	6-3	185	8-4-76	1997	Austin, Texas
Mann, Jim	6	3	2.51	53	0	0	27	68	52	21	19	17	81	.211	R	R	6-3	225	11-17-74	1994	Holbrook, Mass.
McKnight, Tony	9	5	4.76	18	18	1	0	93	104	56	49	24	61	.286	L	R	6-5	205	6-29-77	1995	Texarkana, Ark.
Oswalt, Roy	2	3	4.35	5	5	0	0	31	32	16	15	6	34	.266	R	R	6-0	170	8-29-77	1997	Weir, Miss.
Powell, Brian	9	8	3.17	24	23	3	0	145	142	65	51	39	96	.259	R	R	6-2	205	10-10-73	1995	Bainbridge, Ga.
Redding, Tim	4	1	4.54	6	6	0	0	38	22	21	19	19	42	.171	R	R	6-3	210	3-26-68	1989	Houston, Texas
Reynolds, Shane	1	0	0.00	1	1	0	0	7	8	0	0	0	7	.275	R	R	6-3	210	3-26-68	1989	Houston, Texas
Shouse, Brian	2	2	2.89	56	1	0	1	53	51	21	17	15	56	.248	L	L	5-11	180	9-26-68	1990	Peoria, Ill.
Slusarski, Joe	5	2	2.48	31	0	0	1	40	37	17	11	8	24	.243	R	R	6-4	195	12-19-66	1988	Springfield, Ill.
Smith, Travis	0	0	0.00	1	0	0	0	2	3	0	0	1	0	.333	R	R	5-10	170	11-7-72	1995	Bend, Ore.
Stone, Ricky	6	3	3.59	51	8	0	2	95	98	42	38	27	78	.269	R	R	6-1	168	2-28-75	1994	Hamilton, Ohio

FIELDING

Catcher	PCT	G	PO	A	E	DP	PB
Charles	1.000	1	4	0	0	0	0
Chavez	.992	82	533	62	5	10	3
Servais	.997	42	288	34	1	8	1
Tremie	1.000	5	43	3	0	1	0
Zinter	.992	21	117	5	1	0	4

First Base	PCT	G	PO	A	E	DP
Burns	.972	28	224	18	7	23
Chamblee	1.000	3	19	4	0	3
Chavez	.000	1	0	0	0	0
Lopez	.981	5	48	3	1	3
Luuloa	.959	9	44	3	2	5
Lydy	.991	25	195	19	2	15
Truby	.992	30	231	11	2	26
Zinter	.993	57	398	22	3	32

Second Base	PCT	G	PO	A	E	DP
Berroa	1.000	3	1	11	0	2
Chamblee	.958	4	14	9	1	2

Ginter	.971	93	163	236	12	52
Lopez	.995	33	75	109	1	28
Luuloa	.980	10	21	29	1	6
Matranga	1.000	2	4	4	0	2
Schifano	.857	2	3	3	1	0

Third Base	PCT	G	PO	A	E	DP
Chamblee	1.000	3	0	3	0	0
Chavez	1.000	1	0	3	0	0
Ensberg	.929	81	50	172	17	22
Ginter	1.000	3	3	6	0	1
Lopez	1.000	1	1	0	0	0
Luuloa	1.000	2	3	5	0	0
Lydy	.000	2	0	0	0	0
Truby	.946	57	48	109	9	6

Shortstop	PCT	G	PO	A	E	DP
Berroa	1.000	1	1	5	0	1
Bruntlett	1.000	4	5	11	0	2
Chamblee	1.000	1	1	0	0	0

Ensberg	.000	1	0	0	0	0
Everett	.956	113	189	329	24	70
Lopez	.983	16	22	36	1	9
Luuloa	.786	5	7	15	6	0
Matranga	1.000	2	1	7	0	0
Schifano	.000	2	0	0	0	0

Outfield	PCT	G	PO	A	E	DP
Barker	.980	42	91	6	2	2
Chamblee	1.000	1	1	0	0	0
Cole	.979	112	175	9	4	1
Ginter	1.000	36	49	3	0	1
Lopez	1.000	3	3	0	0	0
Lydy	.988	49	81	3	1	0
Mouton	1.000	2	2	0	0	0
Porter	1.000	89	174	3	0	1
Pose	.968	16	30	0	1	0
Ramirez	.989	104	170	13	2	4
Zinter	.000	1	0	0	0	0

TEXAS LEAGUE

BATTING	AVG	G	AB	R	H	2B	3B	HR	RBI	BB	SO	SB	CS	SLG	OBP	B	T	HT	WT	DOB	1st Yr	Resides
Alfaro, Jason	.243	87	284	26	69	16	2	2	29	7	40	2	1	.335	.264	R	R	5-10	189	11-29-77	1997	Fort Worth, Texas
Berroa, Cristian	.204	38	113	12	23	3	1	0	2	7	15	6	4	.248	.246	B	R	5-11	150	4-27-79	1996	Haina, D.R.
Bruntlett, Eric	.266	123	503	84	134	23	3	3	40	50	76	23	7	.342	.340	R	R	6-0	200	3-29-78	2000	Lafayette, Ind.
Burns, Kevin	.272	89	305	57	83	20	2	20	56	45	79	2	0	.548	.374	L	L	6-5	220	9-9-75	1995	El Dorado, Ark.
Carter, Charley	.263	133	525	65	138	26	1	25	97	35	106	1	1	.459	.309	R	R	6-2	205	12-11-75	1998	Mount Pleasant, Texas
Chapman, Scott	.300	3	10	2	3	1	0	0	1	0	3	0	0	.400	.300	R	R	6-2	200	1-30-78	1995	Davenport, Ohio
Fatheree, Danny	.130	8	23	3	3	0	0	1	2	2	2	0	0	.261	.200	R	R	5-11	232	8-25-78	1997	Grand Prairie, Texas
Hodges, Kerry	.000	1	3	0	0	0	0	0	0	0	3	0	0	.000	.000	R	R	6-4	220	11-7-79	2001	Glendale, Ariz.
Huffman, Royce	.309	137	511	75	158	35	1	4	49	51	90	13	8	.405	.382	R	R	6-0	195	1-11-77	1999	Missouri City, Texas
Lane, Jason	.316	137	526	103	166	36	2	38	124	61	98	14	2	.608	.407	R	L	6-2	220	12-22-76	1999	Sebastopol, Calif.
Logan, Kyle	.314	73	258	36	81	22	3	6	32	19	44	12	3	.492	.369	L	R	6-0	196	7-11-75	1997	Hattiesburg, Miss.
Maldonado, Carlos	.286	76	262	29	75	14	0	4	33	27	55	1	2	.385	.356	R	R	6-2	185	1-3-79	1996	Maracaibo, Venez.
Matranga, Dave	.302	103	387	78	117	34	2	10	60	45	91	17	7	.439	.391	R	R	6-0	196	1-8-77	1998	Aliso Viejo, Calif.
Morillo, Cesar	.183	33	93	11	17	1	2	1	8	6	12	2	0	.269	.232	B	R	5-11	180	7-21-73	1990	Eugene, Ore.
Porter, Colin	.320	25	100	14	32	5	5	2	12	5	25	1	3	.530	.358	L	L	6-2	200	11-23-75	1998	Tucson, Ariz.
Rosamond, Mike	.290	31	107	14	31	5	2	1	12	12	27	3	5	.402	.358	R	R	6-5	220	4-18-78	1999	Madison, Miss.
Tremie, Chris	.227	66	220	28	50	7	0	5	28	22	33	0	4	.327	.302	R	R	6-0	215	10-17-69	1992	New Waverly, Texas
Wesson, Barry	.252	133	472	67	119	23	7	16	54	41	135	20	10	.432	.317	R	R	6-2	195	4-6-77	1995	Glen Allan, Miss.
Whiteman, Tommy	.250	4	16	1	4	0	0	1	1	0	5	0	0	.438	.294	R	R	6-3	175	7-14-79	2000	Edmond, Okla.

PITCHING	W	L	ERA	G	GS	CG	SV	IP	H	R	ER	BB	SO	AVG	B	T	HT	WT	DOB	1st Yr	Resides
Bottenfield, Kent	0	1	20.25	1	1	0	0	3	4	6	6	3	3	.400	R	R	6-3	240	11-14-68	1986	Brownsburg, Ind.
Brocail, Doug	0	0	0.00	1	1	0	0	1	0	0	0	0	1	.000	L	R	6-5	235	5-16-67	1986	Missouri City, Texas
Evans, Chris	0	0	9.64	1	1	0	0	5	6	5	5	0	4	.300	R	R	6-3	205	1-1-68	1990	Houston, Texas
Guerra, Mark	2	0	1.75	9	4	1	0	36	21	8	7	5	27	.169	R	R	6-2	200	11-4-71	1994	Pensacola Beach, Fla.
Hernandez, Carlos	12	3	3.69	24	23	0	0	139	115	60	57	69	167	.228	L	L	5-10	145	4-22-80	1997	Yagua, Venez.
Jamison, Ryan	5	2	3.50	10	9	0	0	46	49	25	18	23	32	.267	R	R	6-3	185	1-5-78	1999	El Cajon, Calif.
Kessel, Kyle	3	6	5.97	13	10	0	0	57	75	43	38	26	39	.317	R	L	6-0	160	6-21-76	1994	Mundelein, Ill.
Lidge, Brad	2	0	1.73	5	5	0	0	26	21	5	5	7	42	.218	R	R	6-5	200	12-23-76	1998	Englewood, Colo.
Lira, Jon	0	1	3.00	27	0	0	2	39	32	16	13	10	27	.225	R	R	6-1	160	5-19-78	1998	Bishop, Texas
Miller, Greg	5	3	3.25	14	14	0	0	55	38	22	20	35	37	.196	L	L	6-5	215	9-30-79	1997	Aurora, Ill.
Persails, Mark	0	0	13.50	1	0	0	0	1	2	2	2	0	1	.333	R	R	6-3	190	10-25-75	1995	Millington, Mich.
Puffer, Brandon	6	1	2.07	56	0	0	8	83	52	19	19	35	91	.181	R	R	6-3	190	10-5-75	1994	Mission Viejo, Calif.
Redding, Tim	10	2	2.18	14	14	1	0	91	64	26	22	25	113	.192	R	R	6-0	180	2-12-78	1998	Churchville, N.Y.
Reynolds, Shane	1	0	1.29	1	1	0	0	7	5	1	1	2	5	.200	R	R	6-3	210	3-26-68	1989	Houston, Texas
Roberts, Nick	2	4	5.16	8	7	0	0	45	52	27	26	10	26	.295	R	R	6-2	185	11-6-76	1999	Annabella, Utah
Robertson, Jeriome	5	1	3.91	57	0	0	3	74	89	33	32	21	72	.295	L	L	6-1	190	3-30-77	1996	Exeter, Calif.
Rodriguez, Wilfredo	5	9	4.78	42	10	0	0	92	94	61	49	56	94	.267	L	L	6-3	180	3-20-79	1996	San Felix, Venez.
Sessions, Doug	6	4	4.37	41	9	0	1	103	98	53	50	33	78	.252	R	R	6-1	192	9-28-76	1998	Orange Park, Fla.
Shearn, Tom	5	6	3.85	43	8	0	1	110	94	54	47	51	136	.233	R	R	6-4	200	8-28-77	1994	Columbus, Ohio
Smith, Travis	15	8	3.09	29	22	1	1	160	154	66	55	26	85	.251	R	R	5-10	170	11-7-72	1995	Bend, Ore.
Wade, Travis	2	3	3.15	60	0	0	23	66	67	33	23	22	56	.262	R	R	6-3	220	7-8-75	1997	Climax, Mich.
Wagner, Billy	0	0	0.00	1	1	0	0	1	0	0	0	0	2	.000	L	L	5-11	180	7-25-71	1993	Pearland, Texas

FIELDING

Catcher	PCT	G	PO	A	E	DP	PB
Chapman	.966	2	25	3	1	0	1
Fatheree	.964	7	50	3	2	0	1
Maldonado	.992	74	590	50	5	2	8
Tremie	.992	63	472	47	4	1	1

First Base	PCT	G	PO	A	E	DP
Burns	.984	42	340	25	6	30
Carter	.993	100	790	40	6	81
Huffman	.000	1	0	0	0	0
Tremie	1.000	4	21	0	0	0

Second Base	PCT	G	PO	A	E	DP
Alfaro	.976	28	56	68	3	19

	PCT	G	PO	A	E	DP
Berroa	.950	15	26	31	3	10
Matranga	.987	100	178	268	6	57
Morillo	.941	3	8	8	1	0
Third Base	PCT	G	PO	A	E	DP
Alfaro	.900	14	4	23	3	3
Huffman	.918	134	72	229	27	14
Morillo	.800	2	2	2	1	0
Shortstop	PCT	G	PO	A	E	DP
Alfaro	.948	16	19	36	3	8
Berroa	.938	13	16	29	3	7
Bruntlett	.956	111	174	329	23	67
Whiteman	1.000	4	4	10	0	2

Outfield	PCT	G	PO	A	E	DP
Alfaro	1.000	19	28	1	0	0
Carter	1.000	20	20	0	0	0
Chapman	1.000	1	1	0	0	0
Hodges	1.000	1	1	0	0	0
Lane	.992	134	226	8	2	1
Logan	.964	68	104	4	4	0
Porter	.983	25	58	1	1	0
Rosamond	.989	31	83	3	1	1
Wesson	.990	133	288	10	3	2

MIDWEST LEAGUE

BATTING	AVG	G	AB	R	H	2B	3B	HR	RBI	BB	SO	SB	CS	SLG	OBP	B	T	HT	WT	DOB	1st Yr	Resides
Acevedo, Anthony	.259	120	429	74	111	35	4	12	70	69	130	21	5	.443	.368	L	L	6-5	200	5-5-78	2000	Bakersfield, Calif.
Andrianoff, Jon	.184	14	38	5	7	1	0	0	1	8	12	3	1	.211	.340	R	R	6-2	165	2-25-81	1999	Olean, N.Y.
Angel, Tony	.260	65	219	35	57	16	0	5	26	8	30	3	3	.402	.301	R	R	6-0	190	7-2-78	2000	Los Angeles, Calif.
Berroa, Cristian	.325	36	123	19	40	4	0	2	23	7	13	5	7	.407	.382	B	R	5-11	150	4-27-79	1996	Haina, D.R.
Buckley, Brandon	.203	67	197	17	40	7	0	1	14	19	31	0	1	.254	.275	R	R	6-2	205	1-25-77	1998	Danville, Calif.
Burke, Chris	.300	56	233	47	70	11	6	3	17	26	31	21	8	.438	.376	R	R	5-11	180	3-11-80	2001	Knoxville, Tenn.
Fatheree, Danny	.296	9	27	5	8	4	1	0	3	3	6	0	0	.519	.355	R	R	5-11	232	8-25-78	1997	Grand Prairie, Texas
Gentry, Garett	.299	98	358	62	107	18	3	24	103	39	45	5	0	.567	.376	L	R	5-10	210	6-27-81	1999	Victorville, Calif.
Hamilton, Mark	.251	107	371	59	93	23	4	13	50	37	98	15	7	.439	.327	L	L	6-2	200	4-23-78	2000	Hurst, Texas
Helquist, Jon	.241	112	415	55	100	17	5	14	47	37	107	10	3	.407	.315	R	R	6-0	175	8-17-80	1999	Jacksonville, Fla.
Lee, Eric	.262	69	210	27	55	8	2	1	26	21	58	6	5	.333	.336	R	R	5-10	180	2-14-78	2000	Houston, Texas
Lydic, Joe	.245	94	330	38	81	22	1	5	38	8	95	2	4	.364	.270	R	R	6-4	190	2-20-79	2000	Bethel Park, Pa.
Maule, Jason	.347	124	412	101	143	23	5	1	63	74	62	56	6	.434	.448	L	R	6-0	170	7-1-77	1999	East Berlin, Conn.
O'Connor, Brian	.071	24	42	2	3	0	0	0	5	20	0	1	.071	.188	R	R	6-2	225	6-21-77	1999	Arlington Heights, Ill.
Obradovich, Mark	.214	8	28	1	6	2	0	0	3	0	7	0	0	.286	.241	B	R	6-2	190	10-26-80	2001	Tuscaloosa, Ala.
Soto, T.J.	.287	110	404	73	116	27	5	22	62	35	128	19	5	.542	.347	R	R	5-11	200	8-31-77	2000	Ruston, La.
Stanley, Henri	.300	114	400	75	120	24	12	14	76	73	84	30	5	.525	.408	L	L	5-10	190	12-15-77	2000	Columbia, S.C.
Wright, Gavin	.273	100	392	68	107	17	6	8	52	28	76	26	6	.408	.326	R	R	6-2	175	5-6-79	1999	Lufkin, Texas

ORGANIZATION STATISTICS

GAMES BY POSITION: C—Buckley 63, Fatheree 2, Gentry 71, O'Connor 16, Obradovich 8. **1B**—Acevedo 1, Angel 25, Hamilton 3, Lydic 15, Maule 3, Soto 99. **2B**—Angel 19, Berroa 10, Helquist 64, Maule 48. **3B**—Andrianoff 7, Angel 8, Lydic 74, Maule 49, Soto 7. **SS**—Andrianoff 8, Berroa 26, Burke 55, Helquist 42, Maule 10, Soto 1. **OF**—Acevedo 106, Angel 1, Hamilton 97, Helquist 2, Lee 61, Soto 1, Stanley 72, Wright 94.

PITCHING	W	L	ERA	G	GS	CG	SV	IP	H	R	ER	BB	SO	AVG	B	T	HT	WT	DOB	1st Yr	Resides
Aguilar, Edwin	2	1	4.08	14	0	0	3	29	25	15	13	15	30	.240	R	R	6-2	165	3-18-80	1996	Sarare, Venez.
Anderson, Travis	6	8	5.72	31	22	1	1	140	165	102	89	52	99	.293	R	R	6-4	235	3-18-78	1999	Bellevue, Wash.
Barrett, Jimmy	10	5	4.48	27	25	1	0	131	122	76	65	62	98	.242	R	R	6-2	190	6-7-81	1999	Cumberland, Md.
Burns, Mike	7	7	3.95	29	21	1	1	132	131	67	58	27	108	.260	R	R	6-1	190	7-14-78	2000	Diamond Bar, Calif.
Campos, Juan	5	4	4.60	13	13	2	0	78	90	50	40	10	69	.281	R	R	6-1	200	6-17-78	2000	Dunbar, Pa.
Coughenour, Jory	11	5	3.78	35	14	0	2	126	152	66	53	22	65	.291	L	L	6-0	170	3-18-78	1999	Long Beach, Calif.
Gallo, Mike	9	2	3.84	44	0	0	4	84	83	38	36	19	67	.251	L	L	6-2	200	4-23-78	2000	Hurst, Texas
Hamilton, Mark	0	0	4.22	10	0	0	0	10	16	7	5	3	13	.000	R	R	6-4	220	8-12-79	2001	Yorba Linda, Calif.
Houlton, Dennis	0	1	5.40	1	1	0	0	5	7	5	3	1	4	.304	R	R	6-1	160	5-19-78	1998	Bishop, Texas
Lira, Jim	2	1	1.72	25	0	0	12	31	17	7	6	12	33	.161	R	R	6-4	215	3-22-81	2000	Hesperia, Calif.
Mansfield, Monte	5	4	5.60	40	3	0	2	72	72	52	45	42	81	.254	R	R	6-5	205	8-17-78	2000	Reno, Nev.
Qualls, Chad	15	6	3.72	26	26	3	0	162	149	77	67	31	125	.239	R	R	6-2	195	6-21-75	1995	Sarasota, Fla.
Ribaudo, Mike	2	2	3.59	30	0	0	0	48	50	26	19	30	37	.270	R	R	6-4	195	1-18-78	1998	Kansas City, Mo.
Ryan, Jeremy	0	3	5.86	15	7	0	0	43	47	33	28	13	39	.271	R	R	5-11	165	5-22-78	1996	San Pedro de Macoris, D.R.
Saladin, Miguel	7	3	2.93	46	0	0	11	74	72	27	24	24	66	.252	R	R	6-2	190	9-6-78	1998	Temple, Texas
Stanford, Derek	1	2	2.74	5	5	0	0	23	24	11	7	11	14	.279							

LEXINGTON

Class A

SOUTH ATLANTIC LEAGUE

BATTING	AVG	G	AB	R	H	2B	3B	HR	RBI	BB	SO	SB	CS	SLG	OBP	B	T	HT	WT	DOB	1st Yr	Resides
Buck, John	.275	122	443	72	122	24	1	22	73	37	84	4	9	.483	.345	R	R	6-2	200	7-7-80	1998	Salt Lake City, Utah
Escalona, Felix	.289	130	536	92	155	42	2	16	64	30	85	46	12	.465	.342	R	R	6-0	185	3-12-79	1996	Puerto Cabello, Venez.
Fatheree, Danny	.230	21	61	8	14	3	0	1	9	7	13	0	0	.328	.319	R	R	5-11	160	1-15-80	1997	Santo Domingo, D.R.
German, Ramon	.265	129	461	72	122	37	3	13	65	48	102	27	9	.443	.352	R	R	6-4	210	9-30-76	1999	Lawton, Okla.
Hill, Mike	.305	119	465	83	142	31	6	12	65	48	107	21	9	.475	.381	R	R	5-10	185	5-12-76	1998	Highland, Calif.
Joyce, Jesse	.113	18	53	12	6	1	0	2	4	15	16	3	1	.245	.329	R	R	6-0	185	8-12-77	2001	Santa Rosa, Calif.
Lentini, Fehlandt	.295	29	122	27	36	11	2	1	21	10	16	10	4	.443	.351	R	R	6-0	185	2-2-78	2000	Bellingham, Wash.
Lockhart, Paul	.247	99	320	48	79	17	4	6	40	29	73	3	2	.381	.317	B	L	6-0	195	4-12-78	2000	Fullerton, Calif.
Lucas, Matt	.269	29	67	9	18	6	0	3	8	0	18	0	1	.522	.279	R	R	6-1	185	11-21-78	2000	Houston, Texas
McKee, Mickey	.269	73	238	35	64	16	4	5	35	21	61	4	3	.433	.333	R	R	6-1	200	2-8-77	2000	Cypress, Texas
Nelson, Nate	.234	19	64	3	15	1	0	0	6	1	10	2	3	.250	.242	R	R	6-5	220	4-18-78	1999	Madison, Miss.
Rosamond, Mike	.266	101	394	62	105	19	3	16	55	37	112	32	13	.452	.336	R	R	6-0	170	2-4-80	1996	Falcon, Venez.
Ruiz, Reinaldo	.200	3	5	0	1	0	0	0	1	0	0	0	0	.200	.200	R	R	6-2	200	5-16-79	1999	Jayton, Texas
Schmitt, Brian	.242	99	376	51	91	22	3	9	50	31	100	5	8	.388	.314	L	L	6-2	200	5-16-79	1999	Jayton, Texas
Topolski, Jon	.287	136	550	98	158	27	7	24	96	75	128	28	11	.493	.375	L	R	5-10	185	12-28-76	1999	Houston, Texas
Toven, John	.257	56	167	34	43	5	0	2	16	8	32	12	5	.323	.304	R	R	5-8	165	11-10-74	1998	Los Angeles, Calif.
Truitt, Steve	.295	28	88	18	26	7	0	3	13	9	26	7	1	.477	.364	R	R	5-9	185	12-2-77	1999	Missouri City, Texas
Whiteman, Tom	.319	114	389	58	124	26	8	18	57	34	106	17	13	.566	.380	R	R	6-3	175	7-14-79	2000	Edmond, Okla.

GAMES BY POSITION: C—Buck 120, Fatheree 13, Lucas 25, Ruiz 3. **1B**—McKee 36, Nelson 12, Schmitt 98. **2B**—Escalona 109, McKee 1, Toven 34. **3B**—German 126, McKee 13, Nelson 7. **SS**—Escalona 20, Toven 10, Whiteman 110. **OF**—Hill 112, Joyce 1, Lentini 29, Lockhart 51, McKee 3, Rosamond 101, Topolski 106, Truitt 27.

PITCHING	W	L	ERA	G	GS	CG	SV	IP	H	R	ER	BB	SO	AVG	B	T	HT	WT	DOB	1st Yr	Resides
Dorn, Grant	0	0	2.05	10	0	0	1	22	23	6	5	2	17	.273	R	R	6-4	210	2-26-78	1999	New Alexandria, Pa.
George, Chris	5	1	3.88	40	0	0	2	51	43	26	22	30	65	.216	R	R	6-3	190	8-6-77	1999	St. Louis, Mo.
Jamison, Ryan	4	2	2.28	9	8	0	0	55	40	17	14	9	63	.203	R	R	6-3	185	1-5-78	1999	El Cajon, Calif.
Krysa, Jon	1	3	3.68	16	0	0	1	29	24	13	12	8	25	.226	R	R	6-0	175	8-27-78	2000	Lees Summit, Mo.
Middleton, Jim	1	1	5.30	11	1	0	0	19	18	13	11	11	19	.250	R	R	6-2	200	11-30-78	2001	Woodbury, N.J.
Nannini, Mike	15	5	2.70	28	27	4	0	190	176	70	57	36	151	.246	B	L	6-0	165	12-5-78	1996	Hato Mayor, D.R.
Peguero, Darwin	8	10	4.05	34	15	0	2	124	112	67	56	37	134	.244	R	R	6-0	165	10-28-82	2000	Las Vegas, Nev.
Pluta, Anthony	12	4	3.20	26	26	0	0	132	107	52	47	86	138	.231	R	R	6-3	205	7-27-80	1999	Las Vegas, Nev.
Ramirez, Santiago	8	2	3.63	45	0	0	4	79	69	35	32	28	85	.237	R	R	5-11	160	11-6-76	1999	Annabella, Utah
Roberts, Nick	10	1	2.95	20	20	3	0	137	118	49	45	21	128	.232	R	R	6-2	185	11-6-76	1999	Annabella, Utah
Rosario, Rodrigo	13	4	2.14	30	21	1	2	147	105	46	35	36	131	.198	R	R	6-0	185	12-14-79	1996	La Romana, D.R.
Saarloos, Kirk	1	1	1.17	22	0	0	11	31	18	5	4	7	40	.165	R	R	6-0	165	5-23-79	2001	Long Beach, Calif.
Santillan, Manny	6	5	3.54	38	7	0	1	97	83	43	38	43	90	.237	R	R	6-0	165	8-20-79	1996	La Romana, D.R.
Stanford, Derek	2	0	6.94	3	3	0	0	12	9	9	9	7	5	.230	R	R	6-3	205	12-9-80	2000	Torrance, Calif.
Stiehl, Robert	2	3	1.98	14	12	0	0	50	28	17	11	34	59	.163	R	R	6-2	190	9-6-78	1998	Temple, Texas
Tremblay, Max	6	4	4.14	48	0	0	4	67	74	37	31	29	84	.275	L	L	6-0	190	6-18-76	1998	San Dimas, Calif.

PITTSFIELD

Short-Season Class A

NEW YORK-PENN LEAGUE

BATTING	AVG	G	AB	R	H	2B	3B	HR	RBI	BB	SO	SB	CS	SLG	OBP	B	T	HT	WT	DOB	1st Yr	Resides
Alvarado, Oscar	.155	26	71	9	11	2	0	1	4	8	28	0	0	.225	.250	R	R	6-1	185	5-19-80	1998	Guigue, Venez.
Andrianoff, Jon	.145	23	55	5	8	3	0	0	6	6	19	4	1	.200	.254	R	R	6-2	165	2-25-81	1999	Olean, N.Y.
Ayala, Abraham	.238	8	21	2	5	1	0	0	2	4	0	0	0	.286	.360	R	R	6-3	230	6-11-79	2001	Hurley, N.Y.
Checksfield, Steve	.190	60	200	32	38	7	4	7	23	18	49	5	3	.370	.263	B	R	6-3	210	1-16-80	2001	Spring Valley, Calif.
Conrad, Brooks	.280	65	232	41	65	16	5	4	39	26	52	14	2	.444	.375	B	R	5-11	150	2-14-79	1996	La Romana, D.R.
De Aza, Modesto	.280	58	168	30	47	6	1	0	20	14	50	27	11	.345	.356	R	R	6-0	150	11-23-80	1998	Azua, D.R.
Franco, Esterlin	.246	42	134	20	33	5	1	0	10	15	22	5	1	.299	.318	R	R	5-11	155	10-9-80	1997	Farriar, Venez.
Garcia, Kevys	.182	20	44	3	8	0	1	0	9	6	13	1	0	.295	.269	R	R	6-3	205	3-26-79	2001	Moraga, Calif.
Hoover, Clint	.286	27	84	7	24	8	0	0	16	8	29	1	0	.381	.381	R	R	6-3	205	9-22-79	2001	Hayward, Calif.
Jimerson, Charlton	.234	51	197	35	46	12	1	9	31	18	79	15	4	.442	.304	R	R	6-3	210	12-14-80	2001	Broken Arrow, Okla.
Jones, Kendall	.177	36	113	11	20	6	0	1	14	19	20	1	0	.257	.295	R	R	6-2	195	6-13-79	2001	Batavia, Ill.
Kochen, Ryan	.412	4	17	4	7	4	0	0	5	0	3	0	0	.647	.412	R	R	6-0	185	8-12-77	2001	Santa Rosa, Calif.
Lentini, Fehlandt	.346	15	52	10	18	0	1	0	8	4	6	8	1	.442	.393	R	R	5-10	170	2-2-78	2001	Port St. Joe, Fla.
Likely, Cameron	.291	40	79	20	23	1	1	1	11	8	10	6	3	.367	.371	R	R	6-1	200	2-8-77	2000	Cypress, Texas
Nelson, Nate	.231	38	134	9	31	8	0	1	14	7	22	7	5	.313	.280	R	R	6-5	220	4-18-78	1999	Tuscaloosa, Ala.
Obradovich, Mark	.248	42	141	21	35	10	1	2	23	21	36	7	5	.376	.343	B	R	6-2	190	10-26-80	2001	Tuscaloosa, Ala.

BATTING	AVG	G	AB	R	H	2B	3B	HR	RBI	BB	SO	SB	CS	SLG	OBP	B	T	HT	WT	DOB	1st Yr	Resides
Rodriguez, Michael	.318	47	157	38	50	14	4	0	14	33	30	13	5	.459	.443	L	L	5-10	165	10-15-80	2001	Cooper City, Fla.
Sandoval, Jlallil	.190	23	58	9	11	2	0	0	2	9	19	3	2	.224	.309	B	R	5-9	160	12-17-79	2001	Montebello, Calif.
Self, Todd	.303	73	261	52	79	13	4	3	49	46	61	10	6	.418	.403	L	R	6-5	210	11-9-78	2000	Stonewall, La.
Stegall, Ryan	.230	67	235	29	54	17	0	3	26	20	47	5	4	.340	.300	R	R	6-0	187	11-13-79	2001	Liberty, Mo.
Truitt, Steve	.308	11	39	8	12	1	1	1	6	0	5	1	2	.462	.308	R	R	5-9	185	12-2-77	1999	Missouri City, Texas

GAMES BY POSITION: C—Alvarado 25, Ayala 8, Jones 34, Obradovich 19. **1B**—Checksfield 34, Franco 1, Hoover 26, Nelson 11, Obradovich 13, Stegall 1. **2B**—Conrad 62, Garcia 2, Sandoval 21. **3B**—Andrianoff 14, Conrad 2, Franco 34, Kochen 4, Nelson 26, Stegall 4. **SS**—Andrianoff 9, Garcia 18, Hoover 1, Stegall 59. **OF**—Checksfield 19, De Aza 50, Jimerson 33, Lentini 14, Likely 29, Rodriguez 39, Self 55, Truitt 10.

PITCHING	W	L	ERA	G	GS	CG	SV	IP	H	R	ER	BB	SO	AVG	B	T	HT	WT	DOB	1st Yr	Resides
Aguilar, Edwin	2	0	0.00	3	0	0	0	8	1	0	0	2	12	.040	R	R	6-2	165	3-18-80	1996	Sarare, Venez.
Barzilla, Philip	4	5	4.71	16	14	0	0	78	87	52	41	34	56	.277	L	L	6-0	180	1-25-79	2001	Sugar Land, Texas
Bayrer, Thomas	0	0	2.25	5	0	0	1	8	5	2	2	11	5	.200	R	R	6-4	205	1-2-80	2001	Roanoke, Va.
Bobbitt, Seth	0	0	1.61	8	5	0	0	28	27	8	5	10	23	.247	R	R	6-1	180	3-24-79	2001	Alabaster, Ala.
Calvo, Jose	0	0	0.00	1	0	0	0	2	1	0	0	1	3	.166	R	R	6-3	180	1-14-80	1996	Chame, Panama
Clifton, Derek	2	0	5.56	9	0	0	0	11	11	9	7	6	6	.261	R	R	6-3	185	11-7-80	1999	League City, Texas
Durham, Chad	1	2	2.30	8	0	0	0	16	13	4	4	2	23	.228	R	R	6-2	185	12-27-78	2001	Austin, Texas
Hamilton, Ryan	1	0	4.80	9	1	0	0	15	15	13	8	14	9	.267	R	R	5-9	195	1-5-78	2000	San Rafael, Calif.
Perry, Andrew	1	6	5.79	23	1	0	0	42	50	37	27	23	39	.285	R	R	6-5	220	12-31-78	2001	Upland, Calif.
Powell, Greg	1	1	0.48	8	1	0	0	19	13	7	1	2	9	.191	R	R	6-4	200	8-26-78	2001	Holland, Pa.
Roberson, Brandon	5	4	3.72	14	14	0	0	87	81	41	36	12	70	.241	R	R	6-3	190	4-26-78	2001	Aledo, Texas
Rodaway, Brian	7	3	2.34	17	13	1	1	88	76	28	23	11	56	.228	L	L	6-4	190	9-11-78	2001	Lincoln, Neb.
Rohlicek, Russ	4	1	2.74	12	9	0	1	43	32	28	13	37	33	.207	R	L	6-6	220	12-26-79	2001	Pleasant Hill, Calif.
Ryan, Jeremy	1	0	3.60	2	2	0	0	10	8	4	4	6	12	.222	R	R	6-4	195	1-18-78	1998	Kansas City, Mo.
Santos, Bernaldo	2	2	3.50	24	0	0	5	36	39	25	14	15	19	.284	R	R	6-3	190	3-27-79	1997	Constanza, D.R.
Sinclair, Ernnie	5	4	4.15	16	15	0	0	80	86	46	37	29	70	.274	R	R	6-0	165	4-2-80	1998	Bluefields, Nicaragua
Smith, Jared	1	0	1.50	8	0	0	1	12	4	2	2	12	22	.105	L	R	6-2	200	12-1-78	2001	Vestavia Hills, Ala.
Valles, Rolando	2	2	5.50	22	0	0	0	34	48	29	21	20	35	.335	L	L	6-4	190	7-27-79	1997	Coro, Venez.
Wood, Brandon	6	0	2.28	29	0	0	9	51	44	13	13	12	61	.227	R	R	6-0	200	2-20-79	1999	Nacogdoches, Texas

MARTINSVILLE

Rookie

APPALACHIAN LEAGUE

BATTING	AVG	G	AB	R	H	2B	3B	HR	RBI	BB	SO	SB	CS	SLG	OBP	B	T	HT	WT	DOB	1st Yr	Resides
Acevedo, Freddy	.173	56	173	16	30	3	2	2	10	4	66	7	1	.249	.227	R	R	6-2	170	8-23-81	1999	La Romana, D.R.
Alvarado, Oscar	.190	5	21	1	4	2	0	0	2	1	5	0	0	.286	.227	R	R	6-1	185	5-19-80	1998	Guigue, Venez.
Avila, Esteban	.206	44	155	12	32	4	1	2	14	4	29	1	1	.284	.236	L	R	6-1	165	10-14-81	1998	Maracaibo, Venez.
Ayala, Abraham	.135	33	111	5	15	2	0	1	8	6	13	1	2	.180	.197	R	R	6-1	190	10-5-80	2000	Bayamon, P.R.
Cuevas, Aneudi	.283	57	173	23	49	9	1	1	16	12	57	8	7	.364	.351	R	R	6-1	160	10-6-81	1999	Nizao, D.R.
Fagan, John	.209	59	201	20	42	12	0	5	22	19	50	1	0	.343	.294	R	R	6-5	207	8-8-79	2001	San Jose, Calif.
Hodges, Kerry	.246	49	179	19	44	15	0	1	16	8	43	5	5	.346	.305	R	R	6-4	220	11-7-79	2001	Glendale, Ariz.
Humphries, Justin	.225	19	40	3	9	2	0	0	5	3	20	0	0	.275	.279	R	R	6-4	225	2-24-83	2001	Richmond, Texas
Jacobson, Billy	.458	26	24	6	11	1	0	0	2	1	6	0	0	.500	.519	R	R	6-2	190	12-16-78	2001	Spring, Texas
Kochen, Ryan	.300	56	180	29	54	12	3	5	23	10	37	5	1	.483	.337	R	R	6-2	195	6-13-79	2001	Batavia, Ill.
Lentini, Fehlandt	.283	12	46	8	13	1	1	1	4	5	5	11	1	.413	.346	R	R	6-0	185	8-12-77	2001	Santa Rosa, Calif.
Macchi, Brandon	.106	42	113	12	12	4	0	0	5	9	30	5	2	.142	.171	B	L	6-0	185	9-23-79	2001	Santa Clara, Calif.
Mote, Trevor	.250	47	168	18	42	8	1	1	13	14	36	9	3	.327	.308	B	R	6-1	190	7-22-79	2001	Kingman, Ariz.
Rojas, Randy	.251	62	223	23	56	10	2	2	19	12	36	17	7	.341	.308	R	R	6-0	170	3-12-80	2001	Brooklyn, N.Y.
Ruiz, Reinaldo	.262	46	168	15	44	5	0	4	18	8	27	0	1	.363	.304	R	R	6-0	170	2-4-80	1996	Falcon, Venez.
Whitesides, Jake	.230	53	178	20	41	6	4	1	8	10	55	5	1	.326	.281	L	R	5-11	190	6-23-81	2000	Columbia, Mo.

GAMES BY POSITION: C—Alvarado 5, Ayala 20, Humphries 2, Ruiz 44. **1B**—Ayala 8, Fagan 55, Humphries 4, Mote 4. **2B**—Hodges 2, Mote 16, Rojas 52. **3B**—Avila 39, Kochen 26, Mote 6, Rojas 3. **SS**—Cuevas 57, Kochen 13, Rojas 2. **OF**—Acevedo 56, Hodges 44, Kochen 1, Lentini 11, Macchi 34, Mote 14, Whitesides 48.

PITCHING	W	L	ERA	G	GS	CG	SV	IP	H	R	ER	BB	SO	AVG	B	T	HT	WT	DOB	1st Yr	Resides
Aguilar, Edwin	0	0	0.00	1	0	0	0	1	0	0	0	1	0	.000	R	R	6-2	165	3-18-80	1996	Sarare, Venez.
Barrios, Angel	3	5	3.15	11	10	0	0	46	45	17	16	16	54	.261	R	R	6-2	160	8-6-81	1998	Ciudad Bolivar, Venez.
Bayrer, Thomas	0	3	5.19	16	0	0	1	26	27	19	15	22	33	.275	R	R	6-4	205	1-2-80	2001	Roanoke, Va.
Cabreja, Eny	4	3	1.58	12	12	1	0	74	54	19	13	20	67	.207	B	L	5-11	160	8-18-81	1999	Santiago Rodriguez, D.R.
Camacho, Jose	1	0	1.46	8	0	0	0	12	8	2	2	0	14	.173	R	R	6-4	175	12-8-80	1999	Guabina, Venez.
DeLeon, Joey	1	2	2.32	13	7	0	0	43	27	12	11	11	44	.181	R	R	5-11	180	10-21-82	2001	Nixon, Texas
Doyne, Cory	4	3	3.54	13	13	0	0	61	57	31	24	30	56	.251	R	R	6-2	185	8-13-81	2001	Lutz, Fla.
Hamilton, Ryan	0	0	0.00	2	1	0	0	3	0	0	0	3	3	.000	R	R	5-9	195	1-5-78	2000	San Rafael, Calif.
Houlton, Dennis	5	4	2.50	13	13	1	0	72	67	24	20	7	71	.240	R	R	6-4	220	8-12-79	2001	Yorba Linda, Calif.
Jacobson, Billy	0	1	1.06	18	0	0	3	34	20	7	4	8	25	.000	R	R	6-2	190	12-16-78	2001	Spring, Texas
Little, Chris	2	6	5.45	20	0	0	0	38	51	31	23	16	43	.316	R	R	6-3	185	11-18-81	2001	University City, Mo.
McNair, James	1	2	5.08	18	0	0	0	34	35	20	19	11	26	.282	R	R	6-4	205	5-15-79	2001	Arlington, Va.
Middleton, Brian	1	3	3.10	10	0	0	0	20	13	9	7	16	22	.180	R	R	6-2	200	11-30-78	2001	Woodbury, N.J.
Nieve, Fernando	4	2	3.79	12	8	1	0	38	27	20	16	21	49	.197	R	R	6-0	170	7-15-82	1999	San Felipe, Venez.
Santana, Leonardo	3	0	1.80	19	0	0	10	35	23	9	7	14	44	.191	L	L	6-2	180	5-6-82	1999	Hato Mayor, D.R.
Williams, Ruddy	2	3	4.50	15	4	0	0	36	40	23	18	16	24	.281	R	R	5-11	160	10-29-80	1998	Villa Isabela, D.R.

BY ALAN ESKEW

The Royals entered 2001 with expectations of being in the playoff hunt in September—or, at the very least, finishing above .500 for the first time since 1994.

Instead, the Royals lost nine of their first 11 and eventually dropped 97 altogether. That number matched the club record for defeats and the Royals finished last in the American League Central for the third time in six years.

With outfielders Johnny Damon and Jermaine Dye gone in separate trades to Oakland, and shortstop Rey Sanchez traded to Atlanta at the July 31 trading deadline after hitting .303 in 100 games, the offense sagged. The Royals had set team records with 856 runs and a .288 average in 2000, but those numbers dropped to 729 and .266 in 2001. The Royals were last in the American League in on-base percentage (.318) and walks (406).

First baseman Mike Sweeney, who hit a commendable .304-29-99, lost production after an August brawl. He charged the mound to get at Detroit pitcher Jeff Weaver and injured his wrist during a dugout-clearing fight. The normally mild-mannered Sweeney received a 10-game suspension and had just three home runs and 17 RBIs after he returned. Third baseman Joe Randa's average fell from .304 in 2000 to .259.

One offensive plus was outfielder Carlos Beltran, who led the team with a .306 average, 101 RBIs, 106 runs and 31 stolen bases.

Kansas City's pitching staff never measured up to expectations, either. The rotation had an 80 percent turnover from April to September. Jeff Suppan, who led the team with 10 victories, was the only starter to remain in the rotation all season. Other April starters were righthanders Dan Reichert, Brian Meadows, Mac Suzuki and Blake Stein.

Meadows was sent to Triple-A Omaha after going 1-6, 6.97 in 10 starts. Reichert was shipped to Omaha in late July; when he returned, he was used in relief. Suzuki was traded in June to Colorado for catcher Brent Mayne. Stein

Mike Sweeney

LARRY GOREN

Angel Berroa

RODGER WOOD

ORGANIZATION STATISTICS

PLAYERS OF THE YEAR

MAJOR LEAGUE: Mike Sweeney, 1b

It took Sweeney a couple of months to crack the .300 mark, but after he reached it he stayed there, hitting .304-29-99 on a team with few bright spots. His 46 doubles missed leading the American League by one.

MINOR LEAGUE: Angel Berroa, ss

Acquired from Oakland in the offseason in a three-way trade also involving the Devil Rays, Berroa began the 2001 season in Class A and finished it in the big leagues. He hit .302 with the Royals.

vacillated between the bullpen and rotation.

Rookie Kris Wilson, who at 6-5 was the only pitcher to finish above .500, ended the season with a tender elbow. Another rookie, Mike MacDougal, sustained a fractured skull in the final home game when he was struck by a bat that flew out of Beltran's hands and into the dugout.

Lefthander Jose Rosado, once one of the team's most dependable starters, had a second shoulder operation and missed the entire season.

The bullpen improved with the additions of Cory Bailey, Jason Grimsley and Roberto Hernandez (28 saves in 34 opportunities). But the bullpen blew 20 saves in 50 chances, and had 22 losses and a 4.61 ERA.

As the losses piled up, attendance at Kauffman Stadium waned. It dropped 141,544 from the previous year to 1,536,371. Only Montreal and both Florida franchises drew fewer fans.

Several top minor league prospects made their major league debuts in 2001, including shortstop Angel Berroa, first baseman Ken Harvey and pitchers Jeff Austin, Brad Voyles, Chris George and MacDougal. Also debuting was outfielder Brandon Berger, who had a breakout season in his sixth year in the minors, hitting .308 with 40 home runs at Double-A Wichita.

The Royals minor league system produced two playoff teams: Wichita in the Texas League and Wilmington in the Class A Carolina League. Two highly touted lefthanders, Jeremy Affeldt (10-6, 3.90 with Wichita) and Jimmy Gobble (10-6, 2.55 with Wilmington), had strong seasons and could make their big league debuts as early as 2002.

With their first pick in the draft, the Royals selected Marshall (Texas) righthander Colt Griffin, whose fastball was clocked at 100 mph—the fastest ever recorded by a high school pitcher.

ORGANIZATION LEADERS

BATTING

*AVG	Ken Harvey, Wichita/Wilmington	.350
R	Angel Berroa, Wichita/Wilmington	106
H	Ken Harvey, Wichita/Wilmington	158
TB	Brandon Berger, Wichita	294
2B	Angel Berroa, Wichita/Wilmington	38
3B	Jonathan Guzman, Burlington	12
HR	Brandon Berger, Wichita	40
RBI	Brandon Berger, Wichita	118
BB	Marco Cunningham, Wilmington	95
SO	Donovan Ross, Wilmington	159
SB	Jonathan Guzman, Burlington	34

PITCHING

W	Kiko Calero, Wichita	14
L	Shawn Sedlacek, Omaha/Wichita	15
#ERA	Micah Mangrum, Wilmington/Burlington	2.63
G	Nathan Field, Wichita	52
	Micah Mangrum, Wilmington/Burlington	52
CG	Ryan Baerlocher, Wichita	2
SV	Nathan Field, Wichita	19
IP	Ryan Baerlocher, Wichita	181
BB	Mike MacDougal, Omaha	76
SO	Jimmy Gobble, Wilmington	154

*Minimum 250 At-Bats #Minimum 75 Innings

KANSAS CITY
ROYALS

Manager: Tony Muser

BATTING	AVG	G	AB	R	H	2B	3B	HR	RBI	BB	SO	SB	CS	SLG	OBP	B	T	HT	WT	DOB	1st Yr	Resides
Alicea, Luis	.274	113	387	44	106	16	4	4	32	23	56	8	6	.367	.320	B	R	5-9	176	7-29-65	1988	Loxahatchie, Fla.
Beltran, Carlos	.306	155	617	106	189	32	12	24	101	52	120	31	1	.514	.362	B	R	6-1	190	4-24-77	1995	Manati, P.R.
Berger, Brandon	.313	6	16	4	5	1	1	2	2	2	2	0	0	.875	.389	R	R	5-11	200	2-21-75	1996	Fort Mitchell, Ky.
Berroa, Angel	.302	15	53	8	16	2	0	0	4	3	10	2	0	.340	.339	R	R	6-0	175	1-27-80	1997	Santo Domingo, D.R.
Brown, Dee	.245	106	380	39	93	19	0	7	40	22	81	5	3	.350	.286	L	R	6-0	215	3-27-78	1996	Orlando, Fla.
Chavez, Endy	.208	29	77	4	16	2	0	0	5	3	8	0	2	.234	.238	L	L	6-0	148	2-7-78	1996	Valencia, Venez.
Delgado, Wilson	.120	14	25	1	3	0	0	0	1	3	10	0	0	.120	.214	B	R	5-11	165	7-15-75	1993	San Cristobal, D.R.
Dye, Jermaine	.272	97	367	50	100	14	0	13	47	30	68	7	1	.417	.333	R	R	6-5	220	1-28-74	1993	Overland Park, Kan.
Fasano, Sal	.000	3	1	0	0	0	0	0	0	0	0	0	0	.000	.000	R	R	6-2	230	8-10-71	1993	Overland Park, Kan.
2-team (11 Oakland)	.045	14	22	2	1	0	0	0	1	1	12	0	0	.045	.125							
Febles, Carlos	.236	79	292	45	69	9	2	8	25	22	58	5	2	.363	.291	R	R	5-11	185	5-24-76	1994	La Romana, D.R.
Harvey, Ken	.250	4	12	1	3	1	0	0	2	0	4	0	1	.333	.250	R	R	6-2	240	3-1-78	1999	Cerritos, Calif.
Hinch, A.J.	.157	45	121	10	19	3	0	6	15	8	26	1	1	.331	.226	R	R	6-1	205	5-15-74	1996	Scottsdale, Ariz.
Hubbard, Trenidad	.250	5	12	2	3	0	1	0	0	0	2	0	0	.417	.250	R	R	5-9	203	5-11-66	1986	Houston, Texas
Ibanez, Raul	.280	104	279	44	78	11	5	13	54	32	51	0	2	.495	.353	L	R	6-2	200	6-2-72	1992	Miami, Fla.
Mayne, Brent	.241	51	166	13	40	4	1	2	20	10	17	1	2	.313	.283	L	R	6-1	192	4-19-68	1989	Corona Del Mar, Calif.
McCarty, Dave	.250	98	200	26	50	10	0	7	26	24	45	0	0	.405	.328	R	L	6-5	215	11-23-69	1991	Menlo Park, Calif.
Ordaz, Luis	.250	28	56	8	14	3	0	0	4	3	8	0	0	.304	.295	R	R	5-11	170	8-12-75	1993	Maracaibo, Venez.
Ortiz, Hector	.247	56	154	12	38	6	1	0	11	9	24	1	3	.299	.293	R	R	6-0	205	10-14-69	1988	Canovanas, P.R.
Perez, Neifi	.241	49	199	18	48	7	1	1	12	10	19	3	4	.302	.277	B	R	6-0	175	6-2-75	1993	Villa Mella, D.R.
Quinn, Mark	.269	118	453	57	122	31	2	17	60	12	69	9	5	.459	.298	R	R	6-1	195	5-21-74	1995	West Covina, Calif.
Randa, Joe	.253	151	581	59	147	34	2	13	83	42	80	3	2	.386	.307	R	R	5-11	190	12-18-69	1991	Overland Park, Kan.
Sadler, Donnie	.129	54	101	19	13	3	0	0	2	9	17	4	1	.158	.212	R	R	5-6	175	6-17-75	1994	Valley Mills, Texas
Sanchez, Rey	.303	100	390	46	118	14	5	0	28	11	34	9	1	.364	.322	R	R	5-9	175	10-5-67	1986	San Juan, P.R.
Sweeney, Mike	.304	147	559	97	170	46	0	29	99	64	64	10	3	.542	.374	R	R	6-3	225	7-22-73	1991	Overland Park, Kan.
Zaun, Greg	.320	39	125	15	40	9	0	6	18	12	16	1	2	.536	.377	B	R	5-10	190	4-14-71	1989	Weston, Fla.

PITCHING	W	L	ERA	G	GS	CG	SV	IP	H	R	ER	BB	SO	AVG	B	T	HT	WT	DOB	1st Yr	Resides
Austin, Jeff	0	0	5.54	21	0	0	0	26	27	17	16	14	27	.272	R	R	6-0	185	10-19-76	1999	Kingwood, Texas
Bailey, Cory	1	1	3.48	53	0	0	0	67	57	28	26	33	61	.233	R	R	6-1	210	1-24-71	1991	El Cajon, Calif.
Byrd, Paul	6	6	4.05	16	15	1	0	93	110	45	42	22	49	.297	R	R	6-1	184	12-3-70	1991	Louisville, Ky.
Cogan, Tony	0	4	5.84	39	0	0	0	25	32	17	16	13	17	.320	L	L	6-2	195	12-21-76	1999	Highland Park, Ill.
Durbin, Chad	9	16	4.93	29	29	2	0	179	201	109	98	58	95	.287	R	R	6-2	200	12-3-77	1996	Baton Rouge, La.
George, Chris	4	8	5.59	13	13	1	0	74	83	48	46	18	32	.288	L	L	6-1	165	9-16-79	1998	Spring, Texas
Grimsley, Jason	1	5	3.02	73	0	0	0	80	71	32	27	28	61	.241	R	R	6-3	205	8-7-67	1985	Lafayette, La.
Henry, Doug	2	2	6.07	53	0	0	0	76	75	53	51	45	52	.263	R	R	6-4	205	12-10-63	1986	Chandler, Ariz.
Hernandez, Roberto	5	6	4.12	63	0	0	28	68	69	34	31	26	46	.266	R	R	6-4	250	11-11-64	1986	Largo, Fla.
MacDougal, Mike	1	1	4.70	3	3	0	0	15	18	10	8	4	7	.290	B	R	6-4	195	3-5-77	1999	Marco Island, Fla.
Meadows, Brian	1	6	6.97	10	10	0	0	50	73	41	39	12	21	.350	R	R	6-4	220	11-21-75	1994	Troy, Ala.
Mullen, Scott	0	0	4.50	17	0	0	0	10	13	6	5	9	3	.309	R	L	6-2	190	1-17-75	1996	Beaufort, S.C.
Reichert, Dan	8	8	5.63	27	19	0	0	123	131	83	77	67	77	.277	R	R	6-3	175	7-12-76	1997	Turlock, Calif.
Santiago, Jose	2	2	6.75	20	0	0	0	29	40	22	22	9	15	.333	R	R	6-3	215	11-5-74	1994	Loiza, P.R.
Stein, Blake	7	8	4.74	36	15	0	1	131	112	73	69	79	113	.232	R	R	6-7	240	8-3-73	1994	Folsom, La.
Suppan, Jeff	10	14	4.37	34	34	1	0	218	227	120	106	74	120	.267	R	R	6-2	210	1-2-75	1993	West Hills, Calif.
Suzuki, Mac	2	5	5.30	15	9	0	0	56	61	38	33	25	37	.277	R	R	6-3	205	5-31-75	1992	Kobe, Japan
Voyles, Brad	0	0	3.86	7	0	0	0	9	5	4	4	8	6	.161	R	R	6-1	195	12-30-76	1998	Green Bay, Wis.
Wilson, Kris	6	5	5.19	29	15	0	1	109	132	78	63	32	67	.297	R	R	6-4	225	8-6-76	1997	Palm Harbor, Fla.

FIELDING

Catcher	PCT	G	PO	A	E	DP	PB
Fasano	1.000	3	2	0	0	0	1
Hinch	.987	43	220	14	3	2	4
Mayne	.993	49	269	19	2	2	4
Ortiz	.990	55	280	28	3	1	1
Zaun	.975	35	181	11	5	4	0

First Base	PCT	G	PO	A	E	DP
Harvey	1.000	3	11	1	0	1
Ibanez	.971	10	58	8	2	11
McCarty	.988	68	441	45	6	56
Sweeney	.989	108	945	88	12	124

Second Base	PCT	G	PO	A	E	DP
Alicea	.958	67	105	194	13	47
Delgado	1.000	2	2	4	0	0
Febles	.981	78	128	224	7	62
Ordaz	.987	19	21	53	1	16
Perez	1.000	4	9	13	0	1
Randa	1.000	1	3	1	0	1
Sadler	1.000	13	28	38	0	12

Third Base	PCT	G	PO	A	E	DP
Alicea	.973	18	12	24	1	3
Delgado	1.000	3	0	7	0	0

	PCT	G	PO	A	E	DP
Ibanez	.000	1	0	0	1	0
Ordaz	.000	1	0	0	0	0
Randa	.966	137	111	255	13	31
Sadler	1.000	15	9	27	0	5

Shortstop	PCT	G	PO	A	E	DP
Berroa	.953	14	21	40	3	9
Delgado	1.000	6	2	10	0	2
Ordaz	.905	8	6	13	2	1
Perez	.978	46	96	131	5	38
Sadler	.923	6	7	17	2	3
Sanchez	.994	100	155	333	3	99

Outfield	PCT	G	PO	A	E	DP
Beltran	.988	152	404	14	5	6
Berger	1.000	5	7	0	0	0
Brown	.988	83	159	3	2	1
Chavez	1.000	28	40	2	0	0
Dye	.984	93	178	5	3	0
Hubbard	1.000	3	2	0	0	0
Ibanez	.967	42	56	3	2	0
McCarty	.750	9	6	0	2	0
Quinn	.976	99	197	8	5	1
Sadler	1.000	16	27	2	0	0

Carlos Beltran

JOHN WILLIAMSON

Joe Randa: Batted .253-13-83 in 581 at-bats for Royals

Neifi Perez: Batted .241 after coming over from Colorado

JOHN WILLIAMSON

FARM SYSTEM

Director, Minor League Operations: Bob Hegman

Class	Farm Team	League	W	L	Pct.	Finish*	Manager	First Yr.
AAA	Omaha (Neb.) Royals	Pacific Coast	70	74	.486	10th (16)	John Mizerock	1969
AA	Wichita (Kan.) Wranglers	Texas	79	58	.577	2nd (8)	Keith Bodie	1995
A#	Wilmington (Del.) Blue Rocks	Carolina	78	62	.557	2nd (8)	Jeff Garber	1993
A	Burlington (Iowa) Bees	Midwest	55	79	.410	14th (16)	Joe Szekely	2001
A	Spokane (Wash.) Indians	Northwest	22	54	.289	8th (8)	Tom Poquette	1995
Rookie	Baseball City (Fla.) Royals	Gulf Coast	20	40	.333	t-13th (14)	Lino Diaz	1993

*Finish in overall standings (No. of teams in league)   #Advanced level

OMAHA   Class AAA

PACIFIC COAST LEAGUE

BATTING	AVG	G	AB	R	H	2B	3B	HR	RBI	BB	SO	SB	CS	SLG	OBP	B	T	HT	WT	DOB	1st Yr	Resides
Alou, Felipe	.219	11	32	1	7	1	0	0	2	1	15	1	0	.250	.257	R	R	5-11	165	11-29-78	1998	Santo Domingo, D.R.
Berblinger, Jeff	.215	73	270	36	58	12	3	5	23	22	54	8	5	.337	.276	R	R	6-0	190	11-19-70	1993	Goddard, Kan.
Brown, Dee	.297	10	37	5	11	0	0	2	6	3	5	0	0	.459	.357	L	R	6-0	215	3-27-78	1996	Orlando, Fla.
Chavez, Endy	.337	23	104	18	35	6	0	0	4	0	13	4	3	.394	.333	L	L	6-0	148	2-7-78	1996	Valencia, Venez.
Delgado, Wilson	.247	76	255	24	63	11	2	4	30	16	43	8	3	.353	.293	B	R	5-11	165	7-15-75	1993	San Cristobal, D.R.
Fasano, Sal	.239	13	46	6	11	1	0	2	7	4	11	0	0	.391	.364	R	R	6-2	230	8-10-71	1993	Overland Park, Kan.
Febles, Carlos	.337	25	98	23	33	7	1	2	9	9	14	6	2	.490	.414	R	R	5-11	185	5-24-76	1994	La Romana, D.R.
Felix, Hersy	.250	1	4	1	1	1	0	0	1	0	0	0	0	.500	.250	R	R	6-3	180	4-11-78	1996	Puerto Plata, D.R.
Guiel, Aaron	.267	121	442	78	118	27	3	21	73	51	92	6	4	.484	.355	L	R	5-10	190	10-5-72	1993	Langley, B.C.
Hallmark, Pat	.247	32	93	10	23	5	0	0	10	7	17	3	0	.301	.330	R	R	6-0	170	12-31-73	1995	Houston, Texas
Hansen, Jed	.253	80	288	37	73	14	1	10	22	34	86	10	6	.413	.335	R	R	6-1	195	8-19-72	1994	Olympia, Wash.
Hinch, A.J.	.321	45	168	28	54	14	0	10	33	11	33	1	0	.583	.365	R	R	6-1	205	5-15-74	1996	Scottsdale, Ariz.
Hubbard, Trenidad	.286	49	175	35	50	9	1	10	28	30	34	8	5	.520	.392	R	R	5-9	203	5-11-66	1986	Houston, Texas
Ibanez, Raul	.148	8	27	3	4	1	0	2	5	1	10	0	0	.407	.179	L	R	6-2	200	6-2-72	1992	Miami, Fla.
King, Cesar	.286	19	56	5	16	6	0	2	12	1	5	1	0	.500	.288	R	R	6-0	215	2-28-78	1995	La Romana, D.R.
Nunnally, Jon	.209	97	316	50	66	9	0	18	53	54	109	11	3	.408	.329	L	R	5-10	190	11-9-71	1992	Keeling, Va.
Ordaz, Luis	.308	14	52	5	16	1	0	1	4	2	10	3	0	.385	.368	R	R	6-0	205	10-14-69	1988	Canovanas, P.R.
Ortiz, Hector	.260	42	150	19	39	7	0	2	15	15	26	0	3	.347	.320	R	R	6-0	160	7-9-73	1991	Cidra, P.R.
Ortiz, Nick	.250	99	316	39	79	20	1	6	40	33	65	2	6	.377	.323	R	R	6-1	205	8-28-73	1996	Olathe, Kan.
Pellow, Kit	.291	129	484	81	141	15	0	20	81	37	101	4	3	.446	.353	R	R	5-11	175	6-19-76	1993	Caracas, Venez.
Prieto, Alejandro	.282	105	376	45	106	21	3	8	44	36	59	9	2	.418	.344	R	R	5-11	185	5-21-74	1995	West Covina, Calif.
Quinn, Mark	.186	11	43	4	8	1	0	2	3	0	9	0	0	.349	.186	R	R	6-0	200	5-25-73	1992	Miami, Fla.
Rosario, Mel	.252	41	151	18	38	10	2	6	25	7	42	1	1	.464	.288	B	R	6-0	200	5-25-73	1992	Miami, Fla.
Ullery, Dave	.157	17	51	4	8	1	1	0	1	5	20	1	0	.216	.246	L	R	6-3	225	12-16-74	1997	Brazil, Ind.
Watkins, Pat	.253	67	245	29	62	12	1	7	29	13	41	2	7	.396	.298	R	R	6-2	195	9-2-72	1993	Garner, N.C.

BATTING	AVG	G	AB	R	H	2B	3B	HR	RBI	BB	SO	SB	CS	SLG	OBP	B	T	HT	WT	DOB	1st Yr	Resides
Wilson, Craig	.296	125	473	78	140	27	3	11	69	45	58	6	4	.436	.356	R	R	6-0	185	9-3-70	1992	Phoenix, Ariz.
Zaun, Greg	.279	11	43	5	12	6	1	2	5	5	4	0	0	.442	.333	B	R	5-10	190	4-14-71	1989	Weston, Fla.

PITCHING	W	L	ERA	G	GS	CG	SV	IP	H	R	ER	BB	SO	AVG	B	T	HT	WT	DOB	1st Yr	Resides
Austin, Jeff	3	7	6.88	28	8	0	2	71	89	56	54	27	55	.314	R	R	6-0	185	10-19-76	1999	Kingwood, Texas
Bailey, Cory	1	0	0.00	5	0	0	1	10	2	0	0	5	7	.064	R	R	6-1	210	1-24-71	1991	El Cajon, Calif.
Cogan, Tony	1	1	2.79	9	0	0	2	10	14	3	3	3	8	.341	L	L	6-2	195	12-21-76	1999	Highland Park, Ill.
D'Amico, Jeff	5	7	3.54	32	20	0	0	140	151	65	55	40	92	.280	R	R	6-3	200	11-9-74	1993	Seattle, Wash.
Durbin, Chad	2	2	3.33	5	5	0	0	27	22	11	10	6	35	.215	R	R	6-2	200	12-3-77	1996	Baton Rouge, La.
Fussell, Chris	2	6	9.61	9	9	0	0	39	58	47	42	24	35	.341	R	R	6-2	200	5-19-76	1994	Oregon, Ohio
George, Chris	11	3	3.53	20	20	0	0	117	103	54	46	51	84	.237	L	L	6-1	165	9-16-79	1998	Spring, Texas
Laxton, Brett	3	7	4.02	45	5	0	2	96	92	49	43	35	75	.252	L	R	6-2	210	10-5-73	1996	Audubon, N.J.
MacDougal, Mike	8	8	4.68	28	27	1	0	144	144	90	75	76	110	.258	B	R	6-4	195	3-5-77	1999	Marco Island, Fla.
Meadows, Brian	6	5	6.17	18	18	0	0	105	143	73	72	20	74	.331	R	R	6-4	220	11-21-75	1994	Troy, Ala.
Moreno, Orber	1	1	4.71	17	0	0	3	21	19	11	11	8	25	.231	R	R	6-3	200	4-27-77	1994	Los Altos, Venez.
Mullen, Scott	5	4	6.62	48	0	0	5	53	66	39	39	22	38	.315	R	L	6-2	190	1-17-75	1996	Beaufort, S.C.
Murray, Dan	3	3	3.95	48	1	0	8	98	105	49	43	30	70	.276	R	R	6-1	193	11-21-73	1995	Garden Grove, Calif.
Rakers, Jason	6	4	4.45	44	5	0	5	97	100	50	48	16	99	.264	R	R	6-2	200	6-29-73	1995	Pittsburgh, Pa.
Reichert, Dan	1	5	8.27	10	5	1	0	33	45	30	30	16	30	.333	R	R	6-3	175	7-12-76	1997	Turlock, Calif.
Sedlacek, Shawn	5	4	5.00	14	13	0	0	81	98	49	45	22	44	.309	R	R	6-4	200	6-29-77	1998	Cedar Rapids, Iowa
Sonnier, Shawn	5	5	4.82	47	2	0	6	71	69	41	38	33	63	.249	R	R	6-5	210	7-5-76	1998	Carencro, La.
Thurman, Corey	0	0	5.40	1	1	0	0	5	6	4	3	2	4	.272	R	R	6-1	215	11-5-78	1996	Wake Village, Texas
Wilson, Kris	2	2	2.79	6	5	0	0	29	31	9	9	6	18	.279	R	R	6-4	225	8-6-76	1997	Palm Harbor, Fla.

FIELDING

Catcher	PCT	G	PO	A	E	DP	PB
Fasano	.972	12	62	8	2	0	1
Felix	1.000	1	7	0	0	0	0
Hinch	.995	24	188	6	1	0	0
King	.983	19	107	12	2	1	5
H. Ortiz	.991	29	198	11	2	0	0
Rosario	.961	40	279	20	12	3	8
Ullery	.964	17	98	9	4	0	3
Zaun	.985	8	63	3	1	0	1

First Base	PCT	G	PO	A	E	DP
Berblinger	1.000	2	16	2	0	4
Fasano	.933	1	10	4	1	0
Pellow	.993	121	1030	88	8	130
C. Wilson	.994	21	153	13	1	13

Second Base	PCT	G	PO	A	E	DP
Berblinger	.976	36	58	104	4	27
Delgado	.960	42	87	106	8	34

Febles	1.000	23	45	66	0	19
Hansen	.889	4	2	6	1	1
Ordaz	1.000	3	4	8	0	1
Prieto	1.000	39	68	116	0	33
C. Wilson	1.000	6	11	22	0	3

Third Base	PCT	G	PO	A	E	DP
Berblinger	.903	8	14	14	3	1
Delgado	.949	18	13	24	2	3
Hansen	.800	2	1	3	1	0
Ordaz	.800	2	1	3	1	0
Prieto	.972	44	26	79	3	7
C. Wilson	.974	73	53	136	5	14

Shortstop	PCT	G	PO	A	E	DP
Delgado	.982	15	18	38	1	8
Ibanez	1.000	1	1	0	0	0
Ordaz	.952	5	8	12	1	6
N. Ortiz	.975	98	167	292	12	68

Prieto	.953	21	26	55	4	14
C. Wilson	1.000	12	26	38	0	15

Outfield	PCT	G	PO	A	E	DP
Alou	.889	11	16	0	2	0
Brown	.950	8	16	3	1	2
Chavez	1.000	23	38	2	0	0
Guiel	.973	113	202	13	6	3
Hallmark	.976	24	38	3	1	0
Hansen	.978	69	131	5	3	0
Hinch	.000	1	0	0	0	0
Hubbard	1.000	45	99	4	0	1
Ibanez	.833	5	5	0	1	0
Nunnally	.975	84	154	3	4	1
Prieto	1.000	3	2	0	0	0
Quinn	1.000	6	12	1	0	0
Watkins	.981	56	97	7	2	0

WICHITA   Class AA

TEXAS LEAGUE

BATTING	AVG	G	AB	R	H	2B	3B	HR	RBI	BB	SO	SB	CS	SLG	OBP	B	T	HT	WT	DOB	1st Yr	Resides
Benefield, Brian	.150	9	20	2	3	0	1	2	4	2	6	0	0	.550	.261	R	R	6-0	181	8-12-76	1997	Carrollton, Texas
Berger, Brandon	.308	120	454	98	140	28	3	40	118	43	91	14	6	.648	.383	R	R	5-11	200	2-21-75	1996	Fort Mitchell, Ky.
Berroa, Angel	.296	80	304	63	90	20	4	8	42	17	55	15	6	.467	.373	R	R	6-0	175	1-27-80	1997	Santo Domingo, D.R.
Brito, Juan	.267	70	236	22	63	10	0	4	28	17	29	3	3	.360	.315	R	R	5-11	185	11-7-79	1996	Santiago Rodriguez, D.R.
Calderon, Henry	.263	97	327	50	86	21	5	5	49	18	51	4	8	.404	.318	R	R	6-1	170	8-3-77	1996	Santo Domingo, D.R.
Caruso, Joe	.264	120	424	75	112	26	1	8	59	50	65	12	6	.387	.369	R	R	5-9	190	12-30-74	1997	Lock Haven, Pa.
Chavez, Endy	.298	43	168	27	50	6	1	1	13	16	13	11	6	.363	.353	L	L	6-0	148	2-7-78	1996	Valencia, Venez.
Dillon, Joe	.287	101	369	62	106	19	3	15	59	36	60	4	3	.477	.361	R	R	6-2	205	8-2-75	1997	Santa Rosa, Calif.
Dodson, Jeremy	.204	35	113	13	23	1	1	1	7	11	31	3	0	.257	.286	L	R	6-2	200	5-3-77	1998	Sherman, Texas
Felix, Hersy	.222	3	9	1	2	0	0	1	1	0	5	0	0	.556	.222	R	R	6-3	180	4-11-78	1996	Puerto Plata, D.R.
Gallagher, Shawn	.264	96	345	44	91	19	4	12	48	25	62	5	7	.446	.315	R	R	6-0	205	11-8-76	1995	Lakeland, Fla.
Gomez, Alexis	.281	83	342	55	96	15	6	4	34	27	70	16	10	.395	.337	L	L	6-2	160	8-6-80	1997	Loma de Cabrera, D.R.
Hansen, Jed	.368	17	57	17	21	8	0	3	6	9	11	4	1	.667	.463	R	R	6-1	195	8-19-72	1994	Olympia, Wash.
Hart, Corey	.220	17	41	8	9	2	0	0	1	10	5	0	1	.268	.373	B	R	6-0	180	9-5-75	1998	Oklahoma City, Okla.
Harvey, Ken	.338	79	314	54	106	20	3	9	63	18	60	3	0	.506	.372	R	R	6-2	240	3-1-78	1999	Cerritos, Calif.
Medrano, Steve	.243	46	140	16	34	5	0	0	15	14	22	3	2	.279	.312	R	R	6-0	180	10-8-77	1996	La Puente, Calif.
Metzler, Rod	.283	110	381	62	108	20	3	4	62	46	81	13	11	.383	.366	B	R	5-11	185	11-19-74	1997	Zionsville, Ind.
Shackelford, Brian	.260	110	366	62	95	18	3	20	72	33	79	4	4	.489	.326	L	L	6-1	190	8-30-76	1998	McAlester, Okla.
Tonis, Mike	.270	63	226	36	61	11	1	9	43	22	41	1	1	.447	.344	R	R	6-3	215	2-9-79	2000	Elk Grove, Calif.
Ullery, Dave	.286	12	42	8	12	3	0	0	9	6	6	0	0	.357	.375	L	R	6-3	225	12-16-74	1997	Brazil, Ind.

PITCHING	W	L	ERA	G	GS	CG	SV	IP	H	R	ER	BB	SO	AVG	B	T	HT	WT	DOB	1st Yr	Resides
Affeldt, Jeremy	10	6	3.90	25	25	0	0	145	153	74	63	46	128	.276	L	L	6-4	185	6-6-79	1997	Medical Lake, Wash.
Baerlocher, Ryan	13	8	3.99	28	28	2	0	181	180	94	80	55	124	.256	R	R	6-5	220	8-6-77	1998	Lewiston, Idaho
Bochtler, Doug	0	0	2.90	15	2	0	4	31	26	10	10	9	38	.234	R	R	6-3	200	7-5-70	1989	West Palm Beach, Fla.
Bukvich, Ryan	0	0	3.75	7	0	0	0	12	9	6	5	2	14	.200	R	R	6-3	237	5-13-78	2000	Brandon, Miss.
Calero, Kiko	14	5	3.33	27	19	0	0	124	110	57	46	51	94	.237	R	R	6-1	170	1-9-75	1996	Rio Piedras, P.R.
Camp, Jared	1	2	5.05	33	0	0	2	46	44	28	26	35	44	.248	R	R	6-2	195	5-4-75	1995	Huntington, W.Va.
Cogan, Tony	1	1	2.08	8	0	0	1	17	13	6	4	4	12	.213	L	L	6-2	195	12-21-76	1999	Highland Park, Ill.
DeHart, Rick	2	2	6.56	13	0	0	0	23	30	20	17	7	16	.303	L	L	6-1	180	3-21-70	1992	Topeka, Kan.
Field, Jason	4	2	1.48	52	0	0	19	73	61	16	12	18	67	.221	R	R	6-2	185	12-11-75	1998	Littleton, Colo.
Gilfillan, Jason	0	0	6.23	11	0	0	0	17	23	13	12	13	13	.319	R	R	6-6	215	8-31-76	1997	Blacksburg, S.C.
Guerrero, Junior	1	2	8.62	15	0	0	1	16	30	18	15	14	11	.394	R	R	6-2	175	8-21-79	1996	Santo Domingo, D.R.
Lamber, Justin	0	2	5.50	19	0	0	1	36	42	22	22	24	21	.297	R	L	6-0	210	5-22-76	1997	Hackensack, N.J.
McMullen, Mike	0	0	11.42	6	1	0	0	9	13	11	11	12	5	.342	R	R	6-6	230	11-3-73	1993	St. Louis, Mo.
Moreno, Orber	0	0	0.00	7	0	0	0	9	3	0	0	2	10	.107	R	R	6-3	200	4-27-77	1994	Los Altos, Venez.
Sanches, Brian	7	9	5.98	29	21	0	0	134	152	96	89	61	95	.288	R	R	6-1	195	8-8-78	1999	Nederland, Texas

PITCHING	W	L	ERA	G	GS	CG	SV	IP	H	R	ER	BB	SO	AVG	B	T	HT	WT	DOB	1st Yr	Resides
Sedlacek, Shawn	6	7	3.63	14	14	1	0	87	85	37	35	14	66	.253	R	R	6-4	200	6-29-77	1998	Cedar Rapids, Iowa
Thurman, Corey	13	5	3.37	25	25	0	0	155	117	66	58	65	148	.206	R	R	6-1	215	11-5-78	1996	Wake Village, Texas
Villano, Mike	6	7	4.50	37	2	0	4	68	79	43	34	29	40	.292	R	R	6-0	195	8-10-71	1994	Bay City, Mich.
Voyles, Brad	1	0	0.00	11	0	0	4	15	8	0	0	10	19	.163	R	R	6-1	195	12-30-76	1998	Green Bay, Wis.

FIELDING

Catcher	PCT	G	PO	A	E	DP	PB
Brito	.996	66	451	47	2	2	7
Caruso	.000	1	0	0	0	0	0
Felix	1.000	3	25	2	0	0	1
Hansen	1.000	1	3	1	0	0	0
Tonis	.985	59	412	43	7	1	2
Ullery	1.000	12	82	8	0	0	2

First Base	PCT	G	PO	A	E	DP
Caruso	1.000	1	2	0	0	0
Dillon	.987	54	410	46	6	32
Gallagher	.987	36	297	10	4	18
Harvey	.990	55	442	34	5	28
Shackelford	1.000	1	9	2	0	0

Second Base	PCT	G	PO	A	E	DP
Benefield	.947	4	10	8	1	2
Caruso	.968	20	23	37	2	5

	PCT	G	PO	A	E	DP
Dillon	.965	11	30	25	2	2
Hansen	1.000	1	0	6	0	1
Medrano	.975	14	18	21	1	6
Metzler	.971	102	197	231	13	44

Third Base	PCT	G	PO	A	E	DP
Calderon	.949	94	57	185	13	11
Caruso	.950	16	11	27	2	0
Dillon	.938	31	21	69	6	2
Hansen	1.000	2	2	4	0	0

Shortstop	PCT	G	PO	A	E	DP
Benefield	1.000	1	0	2	0	0
Berroa	.965	78	148	213	13	44
Caruso	.933	16	29	27	4	6
Dillon	.714	1	1	4	2	0
Hansen	1.000	3	0	3	0	0
Hart	.923	16	12	36	4	9

	PCT	G	PO	A	E	DP
Medrano	.975	33	49	70	3	9

Outfield	PCT	G	PO	A	E	DP
Benefield	1.000	2	2	0	0	0
Berger	.971	88	131	4	4	0
Brito	1.000	1	1	0	0	0
Calderon	.000	1	0	0	0	0
Caruso	.992	68	119	3	1	1
Chavez	.990	42	95	4	1	1
Dodson	1.000	34	55	4	0	0
Gallagher		9	12	1	0	0
Gomez	.971	83	203	1	6	0
Hansen	1.000	8	7	0	0	0
Harvey	.000	1	0	0	0	0
Metzler	.909	10	9	1	1	0
Shackelford	.959	95	155	7	7	2

WILMINGTON — Class A

CAROLINA LEAGUE

BATTING	AVG	G	AB	R	H	2B	3B	HR	RBI	BB	SO	SB	CS	SLG	OBP	B	T	HT	WT	DOB	1st Yr	Resides
Berroa, Angel	.317	51	199	43	63	18	4	6	25	9	41	10	6	.538	.382	R	R	6-0	175	1-27-80	1997	Santo Domingo, D.R.
Cunningham, Marco	.284	138	497	82	141	22	4	4	61	95	119	17	8	.368	.417	R	R	5-10	185	8-3-77	2000	Silt, Colo.
Dodson, Jeremy	.214	70	215	27	46	8	2	5	30	32	78	7	0	.340	.333	L	R	6-2	200	5-3-77	1998	Sherman, Texas
Felix, Hersy	.071	4	14	1	1	0	0	0	1	1	1	0	0	.071	.125	R	R	6-3	180	4-11-78	1996	Puerto Plata, D.R.
Gettis, Byron	.251	82	303	34	76	21	2	6	51	20	70	4	5	.393	.321	R	R	6-2	220	3-13-80	1998	Centreville, Ill.
Gomez, Alexis	.302	48	169	29	51	8	2	1	9	11	43	7	3	.391	.348	L	L	6-2	160	8-6-80	1997	Loma de Cabrera, D.R.
Hansen, Jed	.328	17	64	8	21	3	1	5	20	10	18	2	2	.641	.413	R	R	6-1	195	8-19-72	1994	Olympia, Wash.
Hart, Corey	.287	75	282	53	81	14	0	4	26	55	62	1	6	.379	.408	B	R	6-2	240	3-1-78	1999	Oklahoma City, Okla.
Harvey, Ken	.380	35	137	22	52	9	1	6	27	13	21	3	1	.591	.455	R	R	6-2	240	3-1-78	1999	Cerritos, Calif.
Hattenburg, Ray	.209	83	244	28	51	9	0	0	25	39	67	4	4	.246	.332	B	R	6-1	190	10-6-76	2000	Mead, Wash.
Hopper, Norris	.247	110	389	38	96	6	2	1	38	32	60	16	4	.280	.312	R	R	5-10	170	3-24-79	1998	Shelby, N.C.
McAuley, Jimbo	.209	54	163	17	34	5	0	0	15	19	46	1	0	.239	.297	R	R	6-0	185	12-17-79	1999	Dunwoody, Ga.
Medrano, Steve	.205	42	146	22	30	3	0	0	7	14	37	2	2	.226	.293	R	R	6-2	185	10-5-78	1996	La Puente, Calif.
Mercado, Wilkins	.145	60	165	10	24	7	0	1	13	11	43	0	0	.206	.203	R	R	6-2	185	10-5-78	1996	Esperanza, D.R.
Nelson, Eric	.271	113	421	44	114	27	6	2	41	30	99	6	6	.378	.328	B	R	5-11	180	5-2-77	1999	Missouri City, Texas
Neubart, Adam	.182	26	55	13	10	3	0	0	5	6	13	0	2	.236	.303	R	R	5-11	165	7-23-77	1998	Livingston, N.J.
Ross, Donovan	.209	134	459	60	96	18	1	13	59	62	159	1	0	.338	.321	L	R	6-1	215	8-1-77	1999	Mount Juliet, Tenn.
Ruiz, Willy	.240	105	337	45	81	6	0	0	30	29	44	26	13	.258	.298	R	R	5-11	150	10-15-78	1996	Nagua, D.R.
Tonis, Mike	.252	33	123	15	31	8	0	3	18	15	34	0	0	.390	.343	R	R	6-3	215	2-9-79	2000	Elk Grove, Calif.
Walter, Scott	.249	60	201	19	50	9	0	7	33	18	36	1	0	.398	.336	R	R	6-2	200	12-28-78	2000	Manhattan Beach, Calif.

GAMES BY POSITION: C—Felix 2, McAuley 54, Tonis 33, Walter 60. **1B**—Harvey 20, Hattenburg 6, Mercado 7, Nelson 2, Ross 114. **2B**—Hattenburg 1, Hopper 1, Nelson 103, Ruiz 40. **3B**—Hansen 17, Hart 21, Hattenburg 7, Mercado 50, Nelson 1, Ruiz 60. **SS**—Berroa 51, Hart 47, Medrano 40, Ruiz 7. **OF**—Cunningham 109, Dodson 66, Gettis 78, Gomez 10, Hattenburg 10, Hopper 108, Medrano 19, Ross 2.

PITCHING	W	L	ERA	G	GS	CG	SV	IP	H	R	ER	BB	SO	AVG	B	T	HT	WT	DOB	1st Yr	Resides
Ammons, Cary	2	6	3.88	12	12	1	0	58	50	26	25	21	64	.241	L	L	5-11	165	10-14-76	1998	Durant, Okla.
Bukvich, Ryan	0	1	1.72	37	0	0	13	58	41	16	11	31	80	.194	R	R	6-3	237	5-13-78	2000	Brandon, Miss.
Burch, Matt	11	10	3.70	28	22	0	0	148	145	73	61	50	92	.262	R	R	6-4	195	12-21-76	1998	Horseheads, N.Y.
DeHart, Rick	0	1	1.59	0	0	0	0	6	5	2	1	3	2	.250	L	L	6-1	180	3-21-70	1992	Topeka, Kan.
Douglass, Ryan	1	0	0.00	1	1	0	0	5	1	0	0	3	7	.066	R	R	6-3	200	12-3-78	1997	Pittsburgh, Pa.
Ferguson, Ian	10	3	3.83	18	18	0	0	96	85	47	41	27	72	.234	R	R	6-4	220	8-23-79	2000	Bellingham, Wash.
Fuller, Jody	1	1	4.08	15	0	0	1	18	20	8	8	10	11	.298	R	R	6-3	225	9-12-76	1998	Huntingdon, Tenn.
Gehrke, Jay	5	7	5.65	42	0	0	3	72	82	51	45	32	65	.291	R	R	6-2	195	11-1-77	1999	Scottsdale, Ariz.
Gilfillan, Jason	4	1	0.98	33	0	0	9	55	35	8	6	17	68	.179	R	R	6-6	215	8-31-76	1997	Blacksburg, S.C.
Gobble, Jimmy	10	6	2.55	27	27	0	0	162	134	58	46	33	154	.225	L	L	6-3	175	7-19-81	1999	Bristol, Va.
Guerrero, Junior	5	4	3.66	16	14	0	0	84	78	35	34	24	59	.256	R	R	6-2	175	8-21-79	1996	Santo Domingo, D.R.
Hill, Jeremy	4	0	0.73	9	0	0	2	12	10	2	1	8	13	.232	R	R	5-10	185	8-8-77	1996	Dallas, Texas
King, Jay	4	3	2.92	11	9	1	0	52	41	20	17	11	46	.219	B	L	5-11	195	7-21-77	1999	Pensacola, Fla.
Lamber, Justin	4	4	1.71	20	1	0	2	47	32	11	9	13	34	.184	R	L	6-2	210	5-22-76	1997	Hackensack, N.J.
Mangrum, Micah	4	2	3.07	29	0	0	3	59	52	27	20	11	55	.232	R	R	6-2	175	9-11-77	2000	Sandy, Utah
Moreno, Orber	1	1	2.53	8	1	0	0	11	12	5	3	1	16	.260	R	R	6-3	200	4-27-77	1994	Los Altos, Venez.
Natale, Mike	9	8	3.28	28	27	0	0	159	152	75	58	33	134	.250	R	R	6-2	195	9-2-79	2000	Whittier, Calif.
Newell, Mark	2	0	5.96	18	0	0	0	26	34	22	17	15	7	.326	R	R	6-1	170	3-3-77	2000	Salem, Ore.
Obermueller, Wes	0	2	3.08	20	6	0	0	38	38	15	13	16	28	.265	R	R	6-2	195	12-22-76	1999	Vinton, Iowa
Pichardo, Carlos	1	2	4.52	31	2	0	2	66	67	36	33	19	38	.262	R	R	5-10	145	3-5-78	1999	Esperanza, D.R.
Stiles, Brad	0	0	0.00	1	0	0	0	1	1	0	0	1	2	.333	L	L	6-6	215	2-9-81	1999	Lamar, Colo.

BURLINGTON — Class A

MIDWEST LEAGUE

BATTING	AVG	G	AB	R	H	2B	3B	HR	RBI	BB	SO	SB	CS	SLG	OBP	B	T	HT	WT	DOB	1st Yr	Resides
Alvarez, Henrry	.205	45	161	21	33	7	1	4	23	3	44	1	0	.335	.241	R	R	6-0	193	10-20-79	1997	Las Matas de Farfan, D.R.
Arnerich, Tony	.162	11	37	0	6	2	0	0	3	3	9	0	0	.216	.220	R	R	6-0	190	12-14-79	2001	Santa Rosa, Calif.
Ayala, Odannis	.211	53	180	16	38	6	5	2	16	17	25	2	1	.333	.298	R	R	5-11	175	7-2-80	2000	Carolina, P.R.
Cordova, Ben	.294	108	384	58	113	30	6	6	44	38	55	7	2	.419	.359	L	L	6-0	205	12-3-79	1998	Chula Vista, Calif.
Cotto, Luis	.147	46	143	14	21	0	0	0	9	17	41	2	2	.147	.261	R	R	6-0	175	7-9-81	2000	Trujillo Alto, P.R.
Cowan, Justin	.219	88	319	34	70	20	1	7	38	23	63	0	1	.354	.281	R	R	5-10	195	11-24-77	2000	Tumwater, Wash.

BATTING	AVG	G	AB	R	H	2B	3B	HR	RBI	BB	SO	SB	CS	SLG	OBP	B	T	HT	WT	DOB	1st Yr	Resides
Felix, Hersy	.211	35	114	9	24	4	0	1	8	12	23	0	0	.272	.286	R	R	6-3	180	4-11-78	1996	Puerto Plata, D.R.
Fenster, Darren	.287	97	356	47	102	19	0	2	45	33	63	1	3	.357	.353	R	R	5-9	175	9-11-78	2000	Middletown, N.J.
Gemoll, Byron	.272	128	482	78	131	27	3	10	70	50	90	5	1	.402	.353	R	R	6-2	205	11-19-77	2000	San Jose, Calif.
Gettis, Byron	.314	37	140	26	44	9	2	5	26	14	25	4	3	.514	.385	R	R	6-2	220	3-13-80	1998	Centreville, Ill.
Guzman, Jonathan	.236	121	411	58	97	12	12	13	46	36	155	34	11	.418	.302	R	R	6-1	170	8-8-80	1998	Santiago, D.R.
Guzman, Juan	.240	54	171	20	41	9	1	1	13	13	64	4	4	.322	.297	B	R	5-10	170	5-27-80	1997	Santiago, D.R.
Keppinger, Billy	.244	76	279	42	68	13	1	2	26	43	45	9	3	.319	.349	L	L	6-0	180	12-15-78	2000	Auburn, Ga.
Llamas, Juan	.237	42	152	17	36	7	0	4	25	15	37	0	0	.362	.320	R	R	6-1	165	6-24-80	1997	Cartagena, Colombia
Lora, Thomas	.249	112	442	80	110	11	7	2	28	45	84	27	15	.319	.325	B	R	5-10	165	10-14-78	1997	Montecristi, D.R.
Machado, Alejandro	.239	28	109	17	26	5	0	0	11	10	16	5	2	.284	.311	R	R	6-0	160	4-26-82	1998	Caracas, Venez.
Ridley, Shayne	.050	7	20	0	1	0	0	0	1	4	8	0	1	.050	.200	B	R	6-2	190	11-21-77	2000	Milton, Ontario
Rodgers, Mackeel	.200	4	10	1	2	0	0	0	1	1	1	0	0	.200	.273	B	R	6-1	180	4-30-81	1999	Miami, Fla.
Santos, Chad	.252	121	444	58	112	32	0	16	83	52	101	0	1	.432	.337	L	L	6-1	215	4-28-81	1999	Kaneohe, Hawaii
Walter, Scott	.274	33	124	24	34	12	1	6	22	6	16	0	0	.532	.324	R	R	6-2	200	12-28-78	2000	Manhattan Beach, Calif.

GAMES BY POSITION: C—Alvarez 42, Arnerich 11, Cowan 20, Felix 35, Walter 33. **1B**—Cowan 7, Keppinger 10, Llamas 1, Santos 121. **2B**—Fenster 33, Ju. Guzman 1, Lora 105. **3B**—Fenster 7, Gemoll 83, Ju. Guzman 10, Llamas 27, Ridley 7. **SS**—Cotto 46, Fenster 20, Jo. Guzman 1, Ju. Guzman 41, Machado 28. **OF**—Ayala 52, Cordova 108, Cowan 29, Gemoll 3, Gettis 37, Jo. Guzman 120, Ju. Guzman 1, Keppinger 59, Lora 2, Rodgers 3.

PITCHING	W	L	ERA	G	GS	CG	SV	IP	H	R	ER	BB	SO	AVG	B	T	HT	WT	DOB	1st Yr	Resides
Baker, Joey	7	10	5.34	27	23	0	0	140	155	97	83	45	71	.281	R	R	6-5	200	8-30-78	2000	Monterey, Calif.
Bass, Brian	3	10	4.65	26	26	1	0	139	138	82	72	53	75	.256	R	R	6-2	185	1-6-82	2000	Montgomery, Ala.
Coa, Jesus	2	3	6.68	36	0	0	1	63	82	52	47	28	38	.312	R	R	6-0	170	1-25-80	1997	Bolivar, Venez.
Douglass, Ryan	1	2	5.87	7	1	0	0	15	18	10	10	5	7	.285	R	R	6-3	200	12-3-78	1997	Pittsburgh, Pa.
Ferguson, Ian	3	2	5.28	10	10	0	0	58	62	39	34	10	30	.281	R	R	6-4	220	8-23-79	2000	Bellingham, Wash.
Fingers, Jason	1	6	3.71	33	0	0	4	44	46	21	18	10	37	.270	R	R	6-6	185	8-17-78	2000	Las Vegas, Nev.
Hernandez, Runelvys	7	5	3.40	17	17	0	0	101	94	46	38	29	100	.241	R	R	6-5	185	9-27-80	1998	Santo Domingo, D.R.
Hill, Jeremy	0	2	1.51	40	0	0	12	48	22	11	8	25	66	.137	R	R	5-10	185	8-8-77	1996	Dallas, Texas
Mangrum, Micah	7	2	1.95	23	0	0	2	37	33	10	8	6	34	.239	R	R	6-2	175	9-11-77	2000	Sandy, Utah
McClellan, Zach	5	10	4.54	24	22	0	0	127	142	79	64	36	87	.280	R	R	6-6	200	11-25-78	2000	Toledo, Ohio
McGill, Trae	0	2	4.62	5	5	1	0	25	29	17	13	5	27	.290	R	R	6-0	200	8-7-77	2001	Mobile, Ala.
Stiles, Brad	5	5	5.04	30	6	0	0	61	81	45	34	33	49	.326	L	L	6-6	215	2-9-81	1999	Lamar, Colo.
Stodolka, Mike	3	8	4.67	20	20	0	0	94	105	67	49	30	49	.281	L	L	6-2	210	9-24-81	2000	Corona, Calif.
Wilkerson, Wes	1	4	4.84	43	0	0	8	61	67	39	33	26	46	.281	R	R	6-4	205	9-11-76	2000	Nashville, Tenn.
Wrightsman, Dusty	5	6	4.29	34	4	0	0	80	90	43	38	22	54	.285	R	R	6-4	225	12-7-79	2000	Terre Haute, Ind.
Zurita, Thomas	5	2	4.76	35	0	0	2	57	71	34	30	22	39	.302	R	R	5-11	165	6-28-80	1999	Anzoategui, Venez.

SPOKANE — Short-Season Class A

NORTHWEST LEAGUE

BATTING	AVG	G	AB	R	H	2B	3B	HR	RBI	BB	SO	SB	CS	SLG	OBP	B	T	HT	WT	DOB	1st Yr	Resides
Alleva, J.D.	.283	67	247	25	70	23	1	2	38	18	26	0	1	.409	.336	L	R	5-11	195	11-2-78	2001	Durham, N.C.
Chandler, Marcus	.244	41	119	15	29	4	2	0	10	8	29	4	2	.311	.287	B	R	6-0	180	7-25-79	2001	Houston, Texas
Cleveland, Matt	.239	37	134	12	32	5	2	1	17	11	33	1	5	.328	.305	R	R	5-10	188	6-18-79	2001	FtortLauderdale, Fla.
Cotto, Luis	.216	72	236	28	51	5	0	2	20	31	60	7	5	.263	.311	R	R	6-0	175	7-9-81	2000	Trujillo Alto, P.R.
Draper, John	.261	58	222	34	58	7	0	6	31	22	37	7	2	.374	.353	R	R	6-2	190	8-11-80	2001	Whittier, Calif.
Durand, Jose	.130	16	46	4	6	2	1	0	0	3	19	0	0	.217	.216	R	R	6-0	160	11-17-80	1997	Valencia, Venez.
Fallon, Chris	.253	64	198	28	50	8	0	2	26	32	57	2	0	.323	.350	L	R	6-2	185	3-9-79	2001	Bayonne, N.J.
Fox, Matt	.274	58	226	25	62	6	2	1	29	6	39	5	2	.332	.304	R	R	6-0	175	12-25-78	2001	Houston, Texas
Gunny, Peter	.182	29	77	7	14	1	0	1	7	4	26	3	1	.234	.229	R	R	6-0	175	5-24-80	2001	Woodland Hills, Calif.
Laureano, Wilfredo	.158	6	19	1	3	0	0	0	1	0	7	0	0	.158	.158	R	R	6-0	175	11-4-80	1997	Hato Mayor, D.R.
Lindsey, Cordell	.095	6	21	2	2	0	0	1	4	1	4	1	0	.238	.136	R	R	6-1	190	3-8-78	1999	Houston, Texas
Llamas, Juan	.260	57	204	31	53	13	1	5	25	15	46	2	2	.407	.318	R	R	6-1	165	6-24-80	1997	Cartagena, Colombia
Pieper, William	.142	37	106	8	15	1	1	1	8	14	43	0	1	.198	.254	R	R	6-2	225	5-31-78	2001	Kailua, Hawaii
Rosario, Victor	.243	69	247	36	60	5	5	3	24	28	63	18	3	.340	.319	L	R	5-8	170	12-26-80	2001	Poinciana, Fla.
Shanks, James	.295	67	251	39	74	7	3	0	13	21	50	24	5	.347	.361	R	R	6-0	180	1-26-79	1998	Appling, Ga.
Smiley, Jermaine	.225	61	182	22	41	5	2	0	17	25	56	4	4	.275	.329	L	L	6-2	208	3-5-80	1999	Seattle, Wash.
Stocker, Mel	.233	28	73	10	17	2	2	0	7	14	20	4	2	.315	.356	B	R	5-10	160	8-15-80	2001	Tucson, Ariz.

GAMES BY POSITION: C—Alleva 37, Draper 31, Durand 16. **1B**—Fallon 48, Lindsey 3, Llamas 14, Pieper 24. **2B**—Cleveland 33, Fox 27, Stocker 24. **3B**—Cleveland 1, Fox 32, Lindsey 2, Llamas 42, Pieper 11. **SS**—Cleveland 3, Cotto 71, Fox 6. **OF**—Chandler 33, Draper 20, Gunny 21, Rosario 63, Shanks 67, Smiley 50.

PITCHING	W	L	ERA	G	GS	CG	SV	IP	H	R	ER	BB	SO	AVG	B	T	HT	WT	DOB	1st Yr	Resides
Adinolfi, Tim	2	3	4.72	18	4	0	0	48	48	29	25	19	39	.252	L	L	6-4	220	12-5-77	2001	San Jose, Calif.
Arias, Miguel	0	0	10.57	5	0	0	0	8	12	13	9	10	6	.363	R	R	6-0	165	1-11-80	1996	Puerto Plata, D.R.
Armitage, Barry	1	7	6.10	15	14	0	0	72	79	57	49	26	70	.276	R	R	6-1	230	5-11-79	2000	Durban, South Africa
Barnett, John	0	3	4.50	20	0	0	1	34	40	20	17	10	29	.291	R	R	6-5	205	6-26-82	2001	Moreno Valley, Calif.
Doble, Eric	3	3	4.46	18	0	0	3	34	41	22	17	11	31	.288	R	R	6-2	190	11-3-78	2001	Casa Grande, Ariz.
Dossett, William	1	2	5.91	12	0	0	0	21	34	20	14	7	13	.365	R	R	6-2	175	4-11-80	2001	Athens, Texas
Freeman, Eric	1	3	4.82	21	0	0	1	37	40	23	20	18	24	.270	L	L	6-0	210	9-23-79	2001	Pembroke, N.C.
Garcia, Rafael	2	5	7.13	10	10	0	0	42	54	41	33	17	33	.310	R	R	6-1	190	6-11-78	1996	Caracas, Venez.
Gonzalez, Giovanni	0	3	14.29	4	3	0	0	11	21	18	18	3	8	.388	R	R	6-5	235	6-18-80	1998	North Miami Beach, Fla.
Griffin, Colt	0	1	27.00	3	2	0	0	2	4	7	7	7	0	.368	R	R	6-4	198	9-29-82	2001	Marshall, Texas
Kaanoi, Jason	0	1	9.00	2	2	0	0	6	7	7	6	4	4	.346	L	R	5-11	175	8-19-82	2001	Kaneohe, Hawaii
Lord, Justin	0	0	3.00	2	2	0	0	3	5	3	1	0	4	.357	R	R	6-4	215	11-15-79	2001	Marianna, Fla.
Melnyk, Brian	0	0	0.00	4	1	0	1	9	4	1	0	2	11	.185	L	L	6-2	205	8-2-80	2001	Colliers, N.J.
Middleton, Kyle	3	6	4.65	16	14	0	0	79	92	48	41	23	68	.299	R	R	6-6	230	6-13-80	2000	Pensacola, Fla.
Ortega, Jesus	2	2	2.83	21	0	0	1	35	25	11	11	20	33	.196	L	L	5-11	145	8-2-78	1996	San Francisco de Macoris, D.R.
Reyes, Hipolito	3	5	5.19	19	0	0	0	43	31	26	25	27	49	.200	R	R	6-2	190	6-17-81	1998	Hato Mayor, D.R.
Tamayo, Danny	3	3	4.54	14	14	1	0	67	60	39	34	16	64	.234	R	R	6-1	230	6-3-79	2001	Miami, Fla.
Thomas, Jeb	2	0	2.97	15	2	0	3	39	36	18	13	15	33	.235	R	R	6-4	205	10-3-80	2000	Boone, N.C.
Vasquez, Jorge	1	6	5.01	10	8	0	0	50	50	33	28	13	67	.259	R	R	6-1	165	7-16-81	1999	Nagua, D.R.
Zary, Richard	1	1	4.18	15	0	0	0	28	30	18	13	11	12	.260	R	R	6-3	200	6-18-78	2001	Mount Holly Springs, Pa.

GULF COAST LEAGUE

BATTING	AVG	G	AB	R	H	2B	3B	HR	RBI	BB	SO	SB	CS	SLG	OBP	B	T	HT	WT	DOB	1st Yr	Resides
Alexander, Alexis	.185	36	108	11	20	5	0	0	5	8	29	9	3	.231	.268	R	R	5-11	200	11-18-82	2001	Spokane, Wash.
Alou, Felipe	.250	18	76	8	19	3	0	0	9	1	14	1	1	.289	.260	R	R	5-11	165	11-29-78	1998	Santo Domingo, D.R.
Batista, Jose	.263	49	167	18	44	7	0	1	22	11	22	4	3	.323	.326	R	R	5-10	160	11-18-81	1999	Montecristi, D.R.
Escobar, Luis	.277	34	94	8	26	3	0	2	10	12	18	0	0	.372	.378	L	R	6-0	185	9-5-82	2000	Manati, P.R.
Figuereo, Anibal	.227	51	176	18	40	7	2	2	18	18	47	8	2	.324	.310	R	R	6-1	175	1-21-82	1999	Barahona, D.R.
Gotay, Ruben	.315	52	184	29	58	15	1	3	19	26	22	5	6	.457	.398	B	R	5-11	170	12-25-82	2001	Fajardo, P.R.
Guzman, Jacob	.184	29	76	4	14	2	0	0	4	10	19	0	1	.211	.287	R	R	6-0	195	8-2-82	2001	Santee, Calif.
Legendre, Curtis	.321	48	168	23	54	15	2	0	29	16	25	7	1	.435	.383	R	R	6-0	185	9-1-81	2001	Port Neches, Texas
McDonald, Chamar	.208	40	125	13	26	7	1	1	11	9	43	5	1	.304	.272	R	R	6-4	200	6-18-83	2001	Madison, Miss.
Pereyra, Joel	.182	21	66	6	12	3	0	0	3	21	0	0	.227	.229	R	R	5-11	165	6-20-83	1999	Nagua, D.R.
Roberts, Mike	.000	1	3	0	0	0	0	0	0	1	1	0	0	.000	.250	R	R	6-4	220	8-28-75	1997	Wilbraham, Mass.
Rodgers, Mackeel	.217	21	69	4	15	5	0	1	6	4	18	1	0	.333	.270	B	R	6-1	180	4-30-81	1999	Miami, Fla.
Rodriguez, Alexander	.235	50	166	24	39	4	0	0	13	19	43	8	2	.259	.319	B	R	5-11	155	9-2-82	1999	La Romana, D.R.
Sanchez, Angel	.242	30	95	10	23	4	0	0	6	6	28	3	1	.284	.287	R	R	6-1	170	9-20-83	2001	Las Piedras, P.R.
Suarez, Victor	.192	28	78	6	15	4	1	0	4	4	16	2	1	.269	.232	B	R	6-2	160	3-15-82	1999	Santo Domingo, D.R.
Watkins, Cedric	.140	35	93	9	13	0	0	0	5	9	38	0	1	.140	.273	R	R	5-11	210	5-25-83	2001	Bassett, Va.
Williams, Mervin	.186	39	113	15	21	1	0	0	9	14	35	10	4	.195	.281	L	R	5-10	180	9-1-83	2001	Garyville, La.
Zaun, Greg	.056	6	18	3	1	0	0	0	1	7	5	0	0	.056	.320	B	R	5-10	190	4-14-71	1989	Weston, Fla.

GAMES BY POSITION: C—Escobar 32, Guzman 12, Legendre 8, Pereyra 16, Zaun 3. **1B**—Figuereo 51, Guzman 8, McDonald 5. **2B**—Batista 11, Gotay 47, Rodriguez 2, A. Sanchez 1. **3B**—Batista 13, Gotay 2, Legendre 19, A. Sanchez 13, Suarez 15. **SS**—Rodriguez 48, A. Sanchez 16. **OF**—Alexander 35, Alou 18, Batista 8, McDonald 36, Roberts 1, Rodgers 21, Suarez 4, Watkins 33, Williams 37.

PITCHING	W	L	ERA	G	GS	CG	SV	IP	H	R	ER	BB	SO	AVG	B	T	HT	WT	DOB	1st Yr	Resides
Baker, Bo	0	0	0.00	1	0	0	0	2	2	0	0	0	1	.333	R	R	6-4	190	10-12-80	2001	Snowflake, Ariz.
Brown, Ira	2	5	4.99	11	10	0	0	40	40	27	22	25	42	.254	R	R	6-4	215	8-3-82	2001	Conroe, Texas
Carter, Ramsey	2	0	1.69	9	0	0	2	16	13	5	3	5	15	.232	R	R	6-2	190	11-26-80	2001	El Paso, Texas
Dossett, William	2	2	2.20	8	0	0	0	16	11	5	4	0	11	.192	R	R	6-3	200	12-3-78	1997	Pittsburgh, Pa.
Douglass, Ryan	0	0	0.00	2	1	0	0	2	0	0	0	0	2	.000	R	R	6-6	180	7-4-83	2001	Columbus, Ga.
Frost, Clint	0	1	3.18	4	2	0	0	17	14	6	6	3	15	.218	R	R	5-11	190	7-29-74	1997	Cambridge, Ontario
Gooding, Jason	0	1	18.00	1	1	0	0	1	3	2	2	0	0	.500	R	L	5-11	190	7-29-74	1997	Cambridge, Ontario
Kaanoi, Jason	2	5	5.87	14	3	0	1	38	40	29	25	8	24	.263	L	R	5-11	175	8-19-82	2000	Kaneohe, Hawaii
Lopez, Samuel	0	0	5.40	3	0	0	0	5	6	4	3	5	5	.272	R	R	6-4	160	6-15-82	1999	Montecristi, D.R.
Lowery, Devon	2	3	4.17	11	6	0	1	41	38	25	19	12	19	.237	L	R	6-1	190	3-24-83	2001	Belmont, N.C.
Metzger, Jon	0	0	4.00	6	5	0	0	9	9	5	4	4	11	.243	L	L	6-3	205	10-27-78	2000	Fairfax Station, Va.
Morrison, Robbie	0	0	0.00	2	2	0	0	2	1	0	0	0	2	.142	R	R	6-0	215	12-7-76	1998	Loxahatchee, Fla.
Nelson, Justin	1	6	4.35	12	10	0	0	39	49	33	19	21	31	.291	R	R	6-4	185	12-15-82	2001	Kersey, Colo.
Newell, Mark	0	1	12.27	5	0	0	0	7	12	18	10	13	4	.363	R	R	6-1	170	3-3-77	2000	Salem, Ore.
Nunez, Kelvin	3	1	4.50	19	0	0	2	48	49	33	24	24	25	.259	R	R	6-6	187	3-18-83	1999	La Romana, D.R.
Pena, Geronimo	1	3	3.93	17	0	0	0	37	42	22	16	8	29	.295	L	R	6-4	165	11-10-82	1999	Puerto Plata, D.R.
Rosado, Hector	3	5	1.73	14	6	1	2	52	44	19	10	15	48	.215	L	L	5-11	175	3-13-81	2000	Dorado, P.R.
Sanchez, Elby	2	3	3.24	18	0	0	0	42	39	26	15	17	25	.242	R	R	6-2	157	2-6-83	1999	Dajabon, D.R.
Sanchez, Roberto	0	1	4.50	12	9	0	1	30	30	18	15	12	18	.258	B	R	6-2	160	12-12-82	1999	Puerto Plata, D.R.
Suarez, Victor	0	0	2.25	7	0	0	1	8	7	2	2	5	4	.000	B	R	6-2	160	3-15-82	1999	Santo Domingo, D.R.
Tierney, Chris	0	2	6.65	8	3	0	0	22	31	19	16	8	21	.326	L	L	6-6	205	9-1-83	2001	Lockport, Ill.
Vasquez, Jorge	0	1	1.13	4	2	0	0	16	10	2	2	1	19	.166	R	R	6-1	165	7-16-81	1999	Nagua, D.R.

ORGANIZATION STATISTICS

BY MATT McHALE

Though the Dodgers were in the National League West race until the final week, their 2001 season will be remembered more for what happened off the field.

It began in spring training when left fielder Gary Sheffield repeatedly blasted the organization for not tearing up the final four years of his contract and giving him a new one. His ploy was unsuccessful.

It continued with the firing of embattled general manager Kevin Malone in May as the result of an alleged confrontation with a fan in San Diego. The fallout from that led to the outright release of Malone's shakiest player acquisition, lefthander Carlos Perez, and farm director Jerry Weinstein.

Then came the loss of righthanders Kevin Brown, Andy Ashby and Darren Dreifort to season-ending elbow operations. Chan Ho Park, one of the top pitchers on the free-agent market after the season, did his best to hold the team's starting staff together. But he fell apart when stories started leaking in August that he was seeking a $20 million-a-year contract.

It all added up to another unfulfilling year for a team with a $110 million payroll, with $80 million in contracts already guaranteed for 2002.

"There was a lot of stuff going on," said Dodgers manager Jim Tracy, who finished his first season at 86-76. "But not everything was bad."

The emergence of career minor leaguer Paul LoDuca (.320-25-90), who became the regular catcher and a bright light in the traditionally dreary Dodgers clubhouse, was one of the brighter developments.

Brown and Ashby were expected to return by spring training. Dreifort may not be back until the middle of 2002.

The task of leading the Dodgers to their first postseason victory since 1988 was given to former White Sox assistant general manager Dan Evans, who came aboard as a consultant to Dave Wallace after Malone was let go.

Wallace, a highly respected pitching coach in the orga-

Shawn Green   Ricardo Rodriguez

PLAYERS OF THE YEAR

MAJOR LEAGUE: Shawn Green, of
Proving that his 2000 season with the Dodgers was simply an off year, Green bounced back in 2001 by hitting .297-49-125. He set the Dodgers' team record for home runs in a year.

MINOR LEAGUE: Ricardo Rodriguez, rhp
Rodriguez led the farm system in wins and was named the Class A Florida State League's most valuable pitcher. He went 14-6, 3.21 with 154 strikeouts and 60 walks in 154 innings.

nization for years, took over as GM on an interim basis after Malone was fired, but always said his focus was on rebuilding the Dodgers farm system. Wallace assumed that role from the hub of minor league operations in Vero Beach, Fla., after the season. Evans was installed on a permanent basis as the GM.

In the farm system, Double-A Jacksonville, Class A Vero Beach and the Rookie-level Gulf Coast League team advanced to postseason play. Outfielder Chin-Feng Chen, the organization's player of the year in 1999, rebounded from an off year in 2000 to put up big numbers in the second half at Jacksonville. The Suns won both halves in the Southern League and shared the league title.

Righthander Ricardo Rodriguez was selected the Dodgers' top pitcher in 2001 after going 14-6, 3.21 at Vero Beach. Righthander Ben Diggins, the club's first-round draft pick in 2000, impressed scouts with his 95-mph fastball and went 4-0 in his final month at Class A Wilmington.

The Dodgers landed one of the year's top international talents, Irvin Joel Guzman, a 16-year-old shortstop who signed for a Dominican record $2.5 million. He drew raves in instructional league for his skill and poise.

Not everything went as hoped in the minors. The Dodgers got little help from Triple-A Las Vegas, which was composed mostly of six-year minor league free agents. Veteran infielder Phil Hiatt tied the club's minor league record by hitting 44 homers.

Righthander Carlos Garcia and infielder Joe Thurston, the top players in the system in 2000, struggled. Garcia needed shoulder surgery and missed the entire season. Thurston was moved from short to second in Double-A. He stole 20 bases but was caught 18 times.

Righthander Brian Pilkington, the team's first draft pick (second round) and the nephew of ex-big leaguer Bert Blyleven, required surgery shortly after signing. He was expected to be ready for spring training.

ORGANIZATION LEADERS

BATTING

*AVG	Phil Hiatt, Las Vegas	.330
R	Phil Hiatt, Las Vegas	107
H	Koyie Hill, Wilmington	150
TB	Phil Hiatt, Las Vegas	315
2B	Luke Allen, Las Vegas/Jacksonville	33
3B	Shane Victorino, Vero Beach/Wilmington	9
HR	Phil Hiatt, Las Vegas	44
RBI	Phil Hiatt, Las Vegas	99
BB	Lamont Matthews, Jacksonville/Vero Beach	107
SO	Reggie Abercrombie, Wilmington	154
SB	Candido Martinez, Wilmington	54

PITCHING

W	Ricardo Rodriguez, Vero Beach	14
L	Ben Simon, Las Vegas/Jacksonville	12
#ERA	Shane Nance, Jacksonville/Vero Beach	2.12
G	Pedro Feliciano, Las Vegas/Jacksonville	60
CG	Three tied at	3
SV	Kris Foster, Las Vegas/Jacksonville	25
IP	Eric Junge, Jacksonville	164
BB	Steve Colyer, Vero Beach	77
SO	Mark Kiefer, Las Vegas	174

*Minimum 250 At-Bats #Minimum 75 Innings

LOS ANGELES DODGERS

Manager: Jim Tracy

2001 Record: 86-76, .531 (3rd, NL West)

BATTING	AVG	G	AB	R	H	2B	3B	HR	RBI	BB	SO	SB	CS	SLG	OBP	B	T	HT	WT	DOB	1st Yr	Resides
Aven, Bruce	.333	21	24	3	8	2	0	1	2	0	5	0	0	.542	.385	R	R	5-9	180	3-4-72	1994	Orange, Texas
Beltre, Adrian	.265	126	475	59	126	22	4	13	60	28	82	13	4	.411	.310	R	R	5-11	170	4-7-79	1994	Santo Domingo, D.R.
Bocachica, Hiram	.233	75	133	15	31	11	1	2	9	9	33	4	1	.376	.287	R	R	5-11	165	3-4-76	1994	Toa Alta, P.R.
Bogar, Tim	.333	12	15	4	5	2	0	2	2	2	1	0	0	.867	.412	R	R	6-2	198	10-28-66	1987	Normal, Ill.
Branson, Jeff	.286	13	21	3	6	0	0	0	0	0	4	0	0	.286	.286	L	R	6-0	180	1-26-67	1989	Union, Ky.
Christensen, McKay	.327	28	49	7	16	2	0	1	7	3	10	3	2	.429	.400	L	L	5-11	180	8-14-75	1995	Alpine, Utah
Cora, Alex	.217	134	405	38	88	18	3	4	29	31	58	0	2	.306	.285	L	R	6-0	180	10-18-75	1996	Caguas, P.R.
Donnels, Chris	.170	66	88	8	15	2	0	3	8	12	25	0	0	.295	.277	L	R	6-0	185	4-21-66	1987	Aliso Viejo, Calif.
Goodwin, Tom	.231	105	286	51	66	8	5	4	22	23	58	22	8	.336	.286	L	R	6-1	175	7-27-68	1989	Fresno, Calif.
Green, Shawn	.297	161	619	121	184	31	4	49	125	72	107	20	4	.598	.372	L	L	6-4	200	11-10-72	1991	Newport Beach, Calif.
Grissom, Marquis	.221	135	448	56	99	17	1	21	60	16	107	7	5	.404	.250	R	R	5-11	188	4-17-67	1988	Fairburn, Ga.
Grudzielanek, Mark	.271	133	539	83	146	21	3	13	55	28	83	4	3	.393	.317	R	R	6-1	185	6-30-70	1991	West Palm Beach, Fla.
Hansen, Dave	.236	92	140	13	33	10	0	2	20	32	29	0	1	.350	.371	L	R	6-0	195	11-24-68	1986	San Juan Capistrano, Calif.
Hiatt, Phil	.240	30	50	6	12	3	0	2	6	3	19	0	0	.420	.283	R	R	6-3	200	5-1-69	1990	Pensacola, Fla.
Johnson, Brian	.250	3	4	0	1	0	0	0	1	0	1	0	0	.250	.250	R	R	6-2	210	1-8-68	1989	Chicago, Ill.
Karros, Eric	.235	121	438	42	103	22	0	15	63	41	101	3	1	.388	.303	R	R	6-4	226	11-4-67	1988	Manhattan Beach, Calif.
Kreuter, Chad	.215	73	191	21	41	11	1	6	17	41	52	0	0	.377	.355	B	R	6-2	200	8-26-64	1985	La Quinta, Calif.
LoDuca, Paul	.320	125	460	71	147	28	4	25	90	39	30	2	4	.543	.374	R	R	5-10	185	4-12-72	1993	Peoria, Ariz.
Pena, Angel	.204	22	54	3	11	1	0	1	2	1	17	0	0	.278	.214	R	R	5-10	228	2-16-75	1992	San Pedro de Macoris, D.R.
Reboulet, Jeff	.266	94	214	35	57	15	2	3	22	33	48	0	1	.397	.367	R	R	6-0	175	4-30-64	1986	Kettering, Ohio
Sheffield, Gary	.311	143	515	98	160	28	2	36	100	94	67	10	4	.583	.417	R	R	5-11	205	11-18-68	1986	St. Petersburg, Fla.

PITCHING	W	L	ERA	G	GS	CG	SV	IP	H	R	ER	BB	SO	AVG	B	T	HT	WT	DOB	1st Yr	Resides
Adams, Terry	12	8	4.33	43	22	0	0	166	172	84	80	54	141	.266	R	R	6-3	215	3-6-73	1991	Semmes, Ala.
Ashby, Andy	2	0	3.86	2	2	0	0	12	14	5	5	1	7	.291	R	R	6-1	202	7-11-67	1986	Pittston, Pa.
Baldwin, James	3	6	4.20	12	12	0	0	79	82	39	37	25	53	.274	R	R	6-3	210	7-15-71	1990	Southern Pines, N.C.
Brown, Kevin	10	4	2.65	20	19	1	0	116	94	41	34	38	104	.223	R	R	6-4	200	3-14-65	1986	Macon, Ga.
Carrara, Giovanni	6	1	3.16	47	3	0	0	85	73	30	30	24	70	.231	R	R	6-2	210	3-4-68	1990	Anzoategui, Venez.
Dreifort, Darren	4	7	5.13	16	16	0	0	95	89	62	54	47	91	.250	R	R	6-2	211	5-3-72	1993	Wichita, Kan.
Fetters, Mike	2	1	6.07	34	0	0	1	30	33	23	20	13	26	.272	R	R	6-4	226	12-19-64	1986	Gilbert, Ariz.
Gagne, Eric	6	7	4.75	33	24	0	0	152	144	90	80	46	130	.251	R	R	6-2	195	1-7-76	1995	Montreal, Quebec
Herges, Matt	9	8	3.44	75	0	0	1	99	97	39	38	46	76	.259	L	R	6-0	200	4-1-70	1992	Champaign, Ill.
Mulholland, Terry	1	1	5.83	19	3	0	0	29	40	20	19	7	25	.314	R	L	6-3	220	3-9-63	1984	Scottsdale, Ariz.
2-team (22 Pittsburgh)	1	1	4.66	41	4	0	0	66	78	35	34	17	42	.295							
Nunez, Jose	0	1	13.50	6	0	0	0	7	14	15	11	5	11	.388	L	L	6-2	173	3-14-79	1996	Montecristi, D.R.
Olson, Gregg	0	1	8.03	28	0	0	0	25	26	24	22	20	24	.268	R	R	6-4	210	10-11-66	1988	Reisterstown, Md.
Orosco, Jesse	0	1	3.94	35	0	0	0	16	17	7	7	7	21	.278	R	L	6-2	205	4-21-57	1978	San Diego, Calif.
Park, Chan Ho	15	11	3.50	36	35	2	0	234	183	98	91	91	218	.216	R	R	6-2	204	6-30-73	1994	Beverly Hills, Calif.
Prokopec, Luke	8	7	4.88	29	22	0	0	138	146	80	75	40	91	.267	L	R	5-11	166	2-23-78	1994	Renmark, Australia
Reyes, Al	2	1	3.86	19	0	0	1	26	28	13	11	13	23	.269	R	R	6-0	165	4-10-71	1988	Santo Domingo, D.R.
Shaw, Jeff	3	5	3.62	77	0	0	43	75	63	32	30	18	58	.226	R	R	6-2	200	7-7-66	1986	Washington Court House, Ohio
Springer, Dennis	1	1	3.32	4	3	0	0	19	19	7	7	2	7	.275	R	R	5-10	185	2-12-65	1987	Fresno, Calif.
Trombley, Mike	0	4	6.56	19	0	0	0	23	27	17	17	10	27	.290	R	R	6-2	204	4-14-67	1989	Fort Myers, Fla.
Williams, Jeff	2	1	6.29	15	1	0	0	24	26	18	17	17	9	.295	R	L	6-0	185	6-6-72	1996	Page, Australia

FIELDING

Catcher	PCT	G	PO	A	E	DP	PB
Johnson	1.000	2	3	0	0	0	0
Kreuter	1.000	70	486	29	0	4	5
LoDuca	.991	99	643	53	6	8	4
Pena	1.000	15	125	11	0	0	0

First Base	PCT	G	PO	A	E	DP
Bogar	1.000	3	9	0	0	1
Donnels	1.000	7	40	2	0	4
Green	1.000	1	5	0	0	1
Hansen	.984	25	169	12	3	11
Hiatt	.952	6	20	0	1	3
Karros	.996	119	964	71	4	82
LoDuca	.990	33	185	17	2	17

Second Base	PCT	G	PO	A	E	DP
Bocachica	.941	19	23	41	4	8
Branson	1.000	6	7	10	0	2
Cora	1.000	1	1	1	0	0
Grudzielanek	.984	133	245	359	10	75
Reboulet	.984	22	25	35	1	8

Third Base	PCT	G	PO	A	E	DP
Beltre	.952	124	99	215	16	18
Bocachica	.778	8	1	6	2	0
Bogar	.000	1	0	0	0	0

	PCT	G	PO	A	E	DP
Branson	.000	1	0	0	0	0
Donnels	.897	14	6	20	3	2
Hansen	.927	21	4	34	3	5
Hiatt	1.000	17	9	8	0	1
Reboulet	.714	7	1	4	2	0

Shortstop	PCT	G	PO	A	E	DP
Beltre	1.000	2	4	3	0	0
Bogar	1.000	2	1	2	0	0
Branson	.000	2	0	0	1	0
Cora	.962	132	178	328	20	63
Hansen	.000	1	0	0	0	0
Reboulet	.961	56	77	96	7	33

Outfield	PCT	G	PO	A	E	DP
Aven	1.000	9	5	0	0	0
Bocachica	.889	13	8	0	1	0
Christensen	.917	14	22	0	2	0
Goodwin	.994	78	153	1	1	0
Green	.982	159	312	8	6	0
Grissom	1.000	123	227	6	0	2
LoDuca	.900	5	9	0	1	0
Reboulet	.000	2	0	0	0	0
Sheffield	.972	141	195	17	6	0

Paul LoDuca

LARRY GOREN

Director, Player Development: Jerry Weinstein, Dave Wallace

Class	Farm Team	League	W	L	Pct.	Finish*	Manager(s)	First Yr.
AAA	Las Vegas (Nev.) 51s	Pacific Coast	68	76	.472	11th (16)	Rick Sofield	2001
AA	Jacksonville (Fla.) Suns	Southern	83	56	.597	+1st (10)	John Shoemaker	2001
A#	Vero Beach (Fla.) Dodgers	Florida State	67	66	.504	t-4th (12)	Bob Mariano	1980
A	Wilmington (N.C.) Waves	South Atlantic	73	63	.537	6th (16)	Dino Ebel	2001
Rookie#	Great Falls (Mont.) Dodgers	Pioneer	37	39	.487	t-4th (8)	Dave Silvestri	1984
Rookie	Vero Beach (Fla.) Dodgers	Gulf Coast	41	19	.683	1st (14)	Juan Bustabad	2001

*Finish in overall standings (No. of teams in league)   #Advanced level   +League champion

LAS VEGAS   Class AAA

PACIFIC COAST LEAGUE

BATTING	AVG	G	AB	R	H	2B	3B	HR	RBI	BB	SO	SB	CS	SLG	OBP	B	T	HT	WT	DOB	1st Yr	Resides
Allen, Luke	.222	2	9	1	2	1	0	0	0	0	0	0	0	.333	.222	L	R	6-2	208	8-4-78	1996	Covington, Ga.
Aven, Bruce	.260	86	292	43	76	17	0	8	32	24	59	5	1	.401	.325	R	R	5-9	180	3-4-72	1994	Orange, Texas
Barry, Jeff	.290	89	314	49	91	20	2	12	42	33	66	11	5	.481	.360	B	R	6-1	210	9-22-68	1990	Medford, Ore.
Beltre, Adrian	.600	2	5	2	3	1	0	1	2	2	0	0	1	.400	.714	R	R	5-11	170	4-7-79	1994	Santo Domingo, D.R.
Bogar, Tim	.250	16	52	8	13	5	0	0	4	3	11	0	1	.346	.291	R	R	6-2	198	10-28-66	1987	Normal, Ill.
Branson, Jeff	.273	96	289	28	79	18	0	4	20	26	71	3	2	.377	.334	L	R	6-0	180	1-26-67	1989	Union, Ky.
Christensen, McKay	.246	16	57	8	14	2	1	1	3	5	11	3	1	.368	.317	L	L	5-11	180	8-14-75	1995	Alpine, Utah
Cookson, Brent	.284	59	190	30	54	13	2	12	48	22	34	1	1	.563	.370	R	R	5-11	200	9-7-69	1991	Santa Paula, Calif.
Cotton, John	.205	42	127	15	26	2	0	8	17	11	44	1	1	.409	.279	L	R	6-0	190	10-30-70	1989	Houston, Texas
2-team (30 Nashville)	.203	72	207	22	42	6	0	9	26	16	66	1	3	.362	.267							
Crosby, Bubba	.214	13	42	5	9	2	1	0	5	1	8	1	1	.310	.233	L	L	5-11	185	8-11-76	1998	Bellaire, Texas
Donnels, Chris	.234	39	137	17	32	5	0	7	25	21	24	0	1	.423	.333	L	R	6-0	185	4-21-66	1987	Aliso Viejo, Calif.
Durrington, Trent	.218	22	55	10	12	4	1	2	8	19	3	1	.382	.328	R	R	5-10	188	8-27-75	1994	Broadbeach Waters, Australia
Gil, Geronimo	.295	82	281	40	83	15	0	9	40	16	56	0	1	.445	.334	R	R	6-2	195	8-7-75	1996	Oaxaca, Mexico
Gilbert, Shawn	.330	59	224	25	74	14	2	8	36	20	43	11	4	.518	.383	R	R	5-9	185	3-12-65	1987	Glendale, Ariz.
Hernandez, John	.067	5	15	1	1	0	0	0	1	0	3	1	0	.133	.067	R	R	6-2	205	9-1-79	1997	La Puente, Calif.
Hiatt, Phil	.330	113	436	107	144	29	5	44	99	52	109	6	4	.722	.406	R	R	6-3	200	5-1-69	1990	Pensacola, Fla.
Johnson, Brian	.301	48	166	21	50	12	0	6	31	11	39	0	0	.482	.346	L	R	6-2	210	1-8-68	1989	Chicago, Ill.
Johnson, Keith	.251	125	435	55	109	32	4	12	50	17	87	4	5	.425	.289	R	R	5-11	200	4-17-71	1992	Stockton, Calif.
Lipowicz, Nathan	.125	2	8	0	1	0	0	0	0	0	3	0	0	.250	.125	R	R	5-10	175	2-9-78	2000	Buckner, Mo.
LoDuca, Paul	.333	3	9	3	3	2	0	0	3	1	0	0	0	.556	.400	R	R	5-10	185	4-12-72	1993	Peoria, Ariz.
Mota, Tony	.296	120	442	62	131	29	8	8	57	40	79	16	7	.452	.355	R	R	6-1	170	10-31-77	1995	Miami, Fla.
Pachot, John	.318	6	22	3	7	1	0	1	1	0	3	1	0	.500	.318	R	R	6-2	168	11-11-74	1993	Ponce, P.R.
Pena, Angel	.313	53	198	39	62	8	2	16	41	18	52	1	0	.616	.370	R	R	5-10	228	2-16-75	1992	San Pedro de Macoris, D.R.
Post, Dave	.294	67	180	24	53	14	1	2	31	26	21	2	3	.417	.385	R	R	5-11	170	9-3-73	1992	Kingston, N.Y.
Prieto, Chris	.291	118	446	98	130	27	6	19	58	67	79	25	7	.507	.398	L	L	5-11	180	8-24-72	1993	Carmel, Calif.
Rosario, Mel	.260	24	77	11	20	2	1	4	15	2	19	1	5	.468	.298	B	R	6-0	200	5-25-73	1992	Miami, Fla.
Stankiewicz, Andy	.262	66	202	18	53	7	0	0	13	25	29	5	2	.297	.351	R	R	5-9	165	8-10-64	1986	Gilbert, Ariz.
Stocker, Kevin	.000	1	0	1	0	0	0	0	0	0	0	0	0	.000	.000	B	R	6-1	180	2-13-70	1991	Liberty Lake, Wash.
Theodorou, Nick	.000	1	1	0	0	0	0	0	0	0	1	0	0	.000	.000	B	R	5-11	182	6-7-75	1998	Rialto, Calif.

PITCHING	W	L	ERA	G	GS	CG	SV	IP	H	R	ER	BB	SO	AVG	B	T	HT	WT	DOB	1st Yr	Resides
Alvarez, Victor	7	4	4.27	20	20	0	0	118	115	63	56	41	94	.256	L	L	5-10	150	11-8-76	1997	Culiacan, Mexico
Bevel, Bobby	0	1	4.58	25	1	0	0	35	36	19	18	16	29	.254	L	L	5-10	180	10-10-73	1995	West Plains, Mo.
Bruske, Jim	2	2	5.47	10	8	0	0	49	59	31	30	15	49	.297	R	R	6-1	185	10-7-64	1986	Phoenix, Ariz.
2-team (27 Salt Lake)	5	3	5.16	37	13	0	1	106	129	66	61	25	107	.296							
Carrara, Giovanni	1	2	3.10	6	6	0	0	29	27	10	10	9	35	.247	R	R	6-2	210	3-4-68	1990	Anzoategui, Venez.
Devey, Phil	0	2	11.05	3	3	0	0	15	25	18	18	9	7	.396	L	L	6-0	170	5-31-77	1999	Lachute, Quebec
DeSilva, John	1	1	2.16	14	0	0	0	25	23	7	6	6	27	.252	R	R	6-0	193	9-30-67	1989	Fort Bragg, Calif.
Dougherty, Jim	4	5	4.22	59	0	0	14	81	82	39	38	34	85	.267	R	R	6-1	225	3-8-68	1991	Kitty Hawk, N.C.
Feliciano, Pedro	0	1	7.27	6	0	0	0	9	16	11	7	5	5	.390	L	L	5-11	165	8-25-76	1995	Dorado, P.R.
Foster, Kris	0	1	3.86	21	0	0	12	21	25	13	9	4	17	.294	R	R	6-1	200	8-30-74	1992	Lehigh Acres, Fla.
Gagne, Eric	3	0	1.52	4	4	0	0	24	15	4	4	8	31	.194	R	R	6-2	195	1-7-76	1995	Montreal, Quebec
Gross, Kip	3	1	5.09	10	0	0	0	18	26	11	10	4	8	.346	R	R	6-2	195	8-24-64	1987	Moreno Valley, Calif.
Husted, Brent	0	0	3.66	14	0	0	0	20	25	9	8	7	11	.312	R	R	6-3	198	3-30-76	1997	Reno, Nev.
Kiefer, Mark	11	7	4.20	32	17	2	1	146	126	75	68	46	174	.225	R	R	6-4	184	11-13-68	1988	Kingsland, Texas
Masaoka, Onan	8	4	5.55	31	5	0	1	73	87	49	45	28	61	.298	R	L	6-0	175	10-27-77	1995	Hilo, Hawaii
Montgomery, Matt	0	0	0.00	1	0	0	0	2	1	0	0	2	3	.125	R	R	6-4	210	5-13-76	1997	Anaheim, Calif.
Mota, Danny	1	2	7.71	12	0	0	1	12	16	10	10	9	7	.355	R	R	6-0	180	10-9-75	1994	La Romana, D.R.
2-team (34 Edmonton)	4	5	6.25	46	0	0	3	59	68	41	41	31	50	.300							
Orosco, Jesse	1	0	0.00	10	0	0	0	7	4	0	0	2	11	.160	L	L	6-2	205	4-21-57	1978	San Diego, Calif.
Perez, Carlos	2	1	6.53	6	6	0	0	30	42	24	22	11	20	.320	L	L	6-3	210	4-14-71	1988	Santo Domingo, D.R.
Priest, Eddie	4	8	6.17	23	15	0	0	93	132	75	64	31	67	.341	R	L	6-0	200	4-8-74	1994	Altoona, Ala.
Prokopec, Luke	1	0	3.00	1	1	0	0	6	3	2	2	2	8	.142	L	R	5-11	166	2-23-78	1994	Renmark, Australia
Reyes, Al	0	1	3.38	19	0	0	0	29	24	11	11	10	37	.218	R	R	6-0	165	4-10-71	1988	Santo Domingo, D.R.
Ricketts, Chad	1	3	2.91	48	0	0	3	59	49	24	19	25	70	.225	R	R	6-5	225	2-12-75	1995	Thorold, Ontario
Rizzo, Todd	1	0	3.63	13	0	0	0	17	17	9	7	14	19	.257	L	L	6-2	220	5-24-71	1992	Philadelphia, Pa.
Ryan, Jason	0	3	13.83	5	5	0	0	14	28	25	21	7	6	.424	B	R	6-3	195	1-23-76	1994	Charlotte, N.C.
2-team (9 Nashville)	3	8	6.42	14	14	1	0	67	80	59	48	26	31	.295							
Simon, Ben	2	6	7.35	12	9	0	0	53	64	48	43	23	43	.300	R	R	6-1	185	11-12-74	1996	Berlin Heights, Ohio
Smith, Cam	0	1	8.74	8	0	0	0	11	12	14	11	19	9	.260	R	R	6-3	190	9-20-73	1993	Selkirk, N.Y.
Springer, Dennis	7	7	5.27	19	18	2	0	114	142	74	67	28	51	.309	R	R	5-10	185	2-12-65	1987	Fresno, Calif.
Whisenant, Matt	1	7	7.31	24	10	0	1	60	83	49	49	36	42	.342	L	L	6-3	215	6-8-71	1990	La Canada, Calif.
Williams, Jeff	7	5	3.97	16	16	1	0	91	102	49	40	24	61	.287	L	L	6-0	185	6-6-72	1996	Page, Australia

FIELDING

Catcher	PCT	G	PO	A	E	DP	PB
Gil	.996	64	492	36	2	2	7
Hernandez	.974	4	34	3	1	0	1
B. Johnson	.995	27	207	13	1	1	6
LoDuca	1.000	2	15	1	0	0	0
Pachot	1.000	6	37	4	0	1	1
Pena	.992	31	227	16	2	1	0
Rosario	.978	14	125	11	3	1	1

First Base	PCT	G	PO	A	E	DP
Barry	.985	20	125	10	2	19
Cotton	1.000	21	148	5	0	17
Donnels	.995	26	200	11	1	24
Gil	.991	16	92	14	1	14
Gilbert	.000	1	0	0	0	0
Hiatt	.984	19	116	8	2	16
B. Johnson	.986	21	139	6	2	19
K. Johnson	1.000	8	44	1	0	2
LoDuca	.750	1	2	1	1	0
Pena	.967	15	113	3	4	9
Post	.994	24	161	11	1	12

Second Base	PCT	G	PO	A	E	DP
Branson	.973	43	78	103	5	33
Cotton	1.000	14	22	23	0	7
Durrington	.973	16	32	41	2	9
Gilbert	.984	25	51	73	2	19
K. Johnson	1.000	4	4	12	0	2
Post	.917	8	6	16	2	4
Stankiewicz	.969	61	89	129	7	37

Third Base	PCT	G	PO	A	E	DP
Beltre	.833	2	2	3	1	0
Bogar	.800	3	2	2	1	0
Branson	1.000	17	6	22	0	2
Cotton	1.000	2	0	4	0	0
Donnels	.929	4	4	9	1	3
Gilbert	1.000	2	0	1	0	0
Hiatt	.932	91	56	164	16	18
K. Johnson	.919	32	27	41	6	2
Post	.969	12	13	18	1	2

Shortstop	PCT	G	PO	A	E	DP
Bogar	.968	13	26	35	2	11

	PCT	G	PO	A	E	DP
Branson	.975	42	61	93	4	27
Gil	.000	1	0	0	0	0
Gilbert	.974	23	21	55	2	14
K. Johnson	.954	89	133	221	17	59

Outfield	PCT	G	PO	A	E	DP
Allen	.667	2	1	1	1	0
Aven	.983	70	108	5	2	3
Barry	.984	69	122	2	2	1
Christensen	.943	15	32	1	2	0
Cookson	.940	44	59	4	4	1
Cotton	1.000	2	1	0	0	0
Crosby	1.000	12	38	0	0	0
Gilbert	.933	13	26	2	2	1
Lipowicz	1.000	2	7	0	0	0
T. Mota	.966	110	161	10	6	1
Post	.957	14	22	0	1	0
Prieto	.989	115	244	14	3	2
Rosario	1.000	2	1	0	0	0

JACKSONVILLE — Class AA

SOUTHERN LEAGUE

BATTING

	AVG	G	AB	R	H	2B	3B	HR	RBI	BB	SO	SB	CS	SLG	OBP	B	T	HT	WT	DOB	1st Yr	Resides
Allen, Luke	.290	125	486	74	141	32	6	16	73	42	111	13	3	.479	.345	L	R	6-2	208	8-4-78	1996	Covington, Ga.
Bell, Ricky	.255	63	188	21	48	9	0	3	22	13	29	1	1	.351	.304	R	R	6-2	180	4-5-79	1997	Cincinnati, Ohio
Chen, Chin-Feng	.313	66	224	47	70	16	2	17	50	41	65	5	4	.629	.422	R	R	6-1	189	10-28-77	1997	Tainan City, Taiwan
Collins, Mike	.128	17	39	1	5	0	0	0	3	5	9	2	1	.128	.217	R	R	5-10	172	1-29-77	1998	Phoenix, Ariz.
Crosby, Bubba	.302	107	384	68	116	22	5	6	47	37	60	22	6	.432	.369	L	L	5-11	185	8-11-76	1998	Bellaire, Texas
Davis, Glenn	.243	134	478	62	116	29	8	20	89	67	142	14	5	.462	.335	B	L	6-1	200	11-25-75	1997	Aston, Pa.
Dent, Darrell	.279	117	376	50	105	15	2	4	32	42	91	31	12	.362	.359	L	L	6-2	175	5-26-77	1995	Van Nuys, Calif.
Duplissea, Bill	.150	17	40	1	6	2	0	0	4	5	14	0	0	.200	.292	R	R	6-0	200	9-27-77	1999	San Carlos, Calif.
Kellner, Ryan	.297	25	91	5	27	4	0	1	9	3	20	0	0	.374	.319	R	R	6-2	205	12-9-77	1997	Morganton, N.C.
Matthews, Lamont	.145	18	55	4	8	4	0	0	7	12	25	0	1	.218	.294	L	L	6-2	210	6-15-78	1999	Petersburg, Va.
Nunez, Jorge	.260	123	473	63	123	15	2	4	28	33	88	44	11	.326	.310	R	R	5-10	158	3-3-78	1995	Villa Mella, D.R.
Pachot, John	.243	46	152	12	37	15	1	4	22	4	20	0	2	.434	.259	R	R	6-2	168	11-11-74	1993	Ponce, P.R.
Paciorek, Pete	.213	65	150	17	32	8	1	4	20	15	42	3	1	.360	.289	L	L	6-3	205	5-19-76	1995	San Gabriel, Calif.
Post, Dave	.286	5	14	3	4	1	0		3	1	3	0	0	.500	.333	R	R	5-11	195	9-3-73	1992	Kingston, N.Y.
Riggs, Eric	.256	118	394	52	101	28	1	6	36	42	49	7	4	.378	.333	R	R	6-2	190	8-19-76	1998	Miami, Fla.
Ross, David	.264	74	246	35	65	13	1	11	45	34	72	1	1	.459	.372	R	R	6-2	205	3-19-77	1998	Tallahassee, Fla.
Soto, Saul	.333	3	3	1	1	0	0	0	0	0	0	0	0	.333	.333	R	R	6-3	225	8-11-78	1997	Los Mochis, Mexico
Theodorou, Nick	.294	55	102	15	30	5	0	0	11	25	15	2	1	.343	.438	B	R	5-11	182	6-7-75	1998	Rialto, Calif.
Thurston, Joe	.267	134	544	80	145	25	7	4	46	48	65	20	18	.377	.338	L	R	5-11	175	9-29-79	1999	Vallejo, Calif.
Wright, Nate	.000	1	1	0	0	0	0	0	0	0	1	0	0	.000	.000	R	R	5-10	170	1-22-78	2000	Saugus, Calif.

PITCHING

	W	L	ERA	G	GS	CG	SV	IP	H	R	ER	BB	SO	AVG	B	T	HT	WT	DOB	1st Yr	Resides
Alvarez, Victor	2	0	1.20	8	8	0	0	45	27	6	6	7	40	.176	L	L	5-10	150	11-8-76	1997	Culiacan, Mexico
Bauer, Greg	0	1	6.28	6	0	0	0	14	17	13	10	10	8	.293	R	R	6-1	195	11-30-77	2000	Tulsa, Okla.
Berry, Jon	0	1	3.00	3	1	0	0	9	6	3	3	4	5	.200	R	R	6-1	185	11-17-77	1999	Branchville, S.C.
Bevel, Bobby	2	2	1.96	31	0	0	6	46	42	14	10	11	33	.244	L	L	5-10	180	10-10-73	1995	West Plains, Mo.
Burnside, Adrian	4	3	2.66	13	12	0	0	68	44	21	20	30	67	.181	R	L	6-3	168	3-15-77	1996	Alice Springs, Australia
Caraccioli, Lance	8	4	4.64	28	18	0	1	130	139	76	67	45	87	.280	L	L	6-4	190	12-14-77	1998	Walker, La.
Devey, Phil	8	2	3.77	24	17	0	1	112	121	56	47	21	76	.271	L	L	6-0	170	5-31-77	1999	Lachute, Quebec
Feliciano, Pedro	5	4	1.94	54	0	0	17	60	41	14	13	11	55	.194	L	L	5-11	165	8-25-76	1995	Dorado, P.R.
Fischer, Mike	1	0	5.14	12	4	0	0	28	30	18	16	8	28	.272	R	R	6-4	200	12-10-76	1998	Crestline, Ohio
Foster, Kris	3	0	1.00	17	0	0	7	18	6	2	2	2	29	.098	R	R	6-1	200	8-30-74	1992	Lehigh Acres, Fla.
Gomes, Tony	1	1	2.86	17	0	0	2	28	30	13	9	15	31	.267	R	R	6-0	190	9-10-77	1998	Galt, Calif.
Gulin, Lindsay	7	5	2.64	26	21	1	0	126	128	46	37	46	111	.266	L	L	6-3	175	11-22-76	1995	Issaquah, Wash.
Harrell, Tim	5	4	3.00	47	1	0	5	81	70	32	27	29	71	.231	R	R	6-4	215	10-31-75	1998	Weaverville, N.C.
Husted, Brent	3	3	5.50	23	0	0	1	38	52	25	23	13	21	.339	R	R	6-3	198	3-30-76	1997	Reno, Nev.
Junge, Eric	10	11	3.46	27	27	1	0	164	143	72	63	56	116	.237	R	R	6-5	215	1-5-77	1999	Rye, N.Y.
Langone, Steve	0	0	1.50	1	1	0	0	6	2	1	1	0	8	.105	R	R	6-2	195	1-12-78	2000	Reading, Mass.
McBride, Chris	2	1	4.74	4	0	0	0	19	24	12	10	3	19	.307	L	R	6-5	210	10-13-73	1994	Leland, N.C.
Montgomery, Matt	0	1	3.20	14	0	0	0	25	20	9	9	8	17	.219	R	R	6-4	210	5-13-76	1997	Anaheim, Calif.
Nance, Shane	7	0	1.59	28	0	0	1	45	31	11	8	17	44	.194	L	L	5-8	180	9-7-77	2000	Houston, Texas
Parrish, Wade	1	1	5.14	4	0	0	0	7	7	4	4	5	5	.259	L	L	6-1	205	11-13-77	1999	Othello, Wash.
Proctor, Scott	4	3	4.17	10	9	0	0	50	39	26	23	31	48	.220	R	R	6-1	198	1-2-77	1998	Jensen Beach, Fla.
Regalado, Maximo	2	3	6.35	18	0	0	1	23	20	18	16	22	33	.232	R	R	6-2	165	11-18-76	1994	Montecristi, D.R.
Simon, Ben	7	6	3.32	15	15	0	0	81	64	34	30	21	76	.218	R	R	6-1	185	11-12-74	1996	Berlin Heights, Ohio
Stephenson, Brian	1	0	1.13	7	1	0	0	8	6	4	1	2	3	.200	R	R	6-3	210	7-17-73	1994	Fullerton, Calif.

FIELDING

Catcher	PCT	G	PO	A	E	DP	PB
Duplissea	.990	13	88	14	1	1	1
Kellner	.989	25	168	18	2	1	1
Pachot	1.000	39	264	31	0	1	6
Ross	.985	70	530	51	9	1	6
Theodorou	1.000	2	11	1	0	0	0

First Base	PCT	G	PO	A	E	DP
Davis	.991	132	1064	96	10	91
Paciorek	1.000	6	48	6	0	6
Theodorou	1.000	1	3	0	0	1

Second Base	PCT	G	PO	A	E	DP
Collins	1.000	3	6	11	0	3
Nunez	.926	9	11	14	2	3
Riggs	1.000	5	8	15	0	3
Theodorou	.905	3	12	7	2	4
Thurston	.976	121	287	275	14	64

Third Base	PCT	G	PO	A	E	DP
Bell	.942	52	27	102	8	8
Collins	.944	8	3	14	1	1
Post	1.000	2	1	4	0	1

	PCT	G	PO	A	E	DP
Riggs	.941	85	51	157	13	17
Theodorou	1.000	5	3	5	0	3
Wright	1.000	1	0	1	0	0

Shortstop	PCT	G	PO	A	E	DP
Collins	1.000	2	4	5	0	1
Nunez	.940	111	148	287	28	48
Riggs	.952	19	21	39	3	9
Thurston	.943	12	20	30	3	7

Outfield	PCT	G	PO	A	E	DP
Allen	.972	120	225	15	7	3

Chen	.966	50	80	5	3	1	Matthews	.970	15	28	4	1	0	Riggs	1.000	1	0	1	0	0
Crosby	.985	100	197	5	3	0	Paciorek	1.000	12	20	0	0	0	Theodorou	1.000	24	51	0	0	0
Dent	1.000	105	235	6	0	1	Post	1.000	2	4	0	0	0							

VERO BEACH — Class A

FLORIDA STATE LEAGUE

BATTING	AVG	G	AB	R	H	2B	3B	HR	RBI	BB	SO	SB	CS	SLG	OBP	B	T	HT	WT	DOB	1st Yr	Resides
Alvarez, Nick	.286	118	420	63	120	15	2	21	71	29	80	14	7	.481	.353	R	R	6-3	205	2-8-77	2000	Miami, Fla.
Aracena, Sandy	.333	2	6	0	2	0	0	0	0	1	0	0	0	.333	.429	R	R	6-0	180	3-3-81	1998	La Vega, D.R.
Aybar, Willy	.286	2	7	0	2	0	0	0	0	1	2	0	0	.286	.375	B	R	6-0	175	3-9-83	2000	Bani, D.R.
Bell, Ricky	.250	6	24	3	6	0	0	0	0	0	3	0	1	.250	.280	R	R	6-2	180	4-5-79	1997	Cincinnati, Ohio
Beltre, Adrian	.444	3	9	0	4	1	0	0	1	2	1	0	0	.556	.583	R	R	5-11	170	4-7-79	1994	Santo Domingo, D.R.
Bledsoe, Hunter	.323	65	232	28	75	8	0	4	25	24	27	5	2	.409	.390	R	R	6-4	215	1-24-76	1999	Nashville, Tenn.
Chen, Chin-Feng	.268	62	235	38	63	15	3	5	41	28	56	2	0	.421	.359	R	R	6-1	189	10-28-77	1999	Tainan City, Taiwan
Collins, Mike	.276	74	268	29	74	11	0	2	24	37	26	5	3	.340	.366	R	R	5-10	172	1-29-77	1998	Phoenix, Ariz.
Duplissea, Bill	.187	39	107	8	20	4	2	0	6	11	37	1	0	.262	.304	R	R	6-0	200	9-27-77	1999	San Carlos, Calif.
Feliciano, Jesus	.262	116	401	48	105	11	3	3	29	31	35	22	10	.327	.320	L	L	5-11	170	6-6-79	1997	Bayamon, P.R.
Gallo, Ismael	.253	64	237	26	60	9	3	2	22	24	15	2	1	.342	.318	L	R	5-11	165	1-14-77	1996	Ontario, Calif.
Guerrero, Hector	.257	39	148	16	38	11	1	0	10	4	35	2	3	.345	.281	L	L	6-0	170	12-22-81	1998	San Pedro de Macoris, D.R.
Hansen, Dave	.000	3	9	1	0	0	0	0	0	1	2	0	0	.000	.100	L	R	6-0	195	11-24-68	1986	San Juan Capistrano, Calif.
Hernandez, John	.202	38	114	8	23	9	0	0	22	5	19	1	1	.281	.248	R	R	6-2	205	9-1-79	1997	La Puente, Calif.
Jaramillo, Milko	.183	50	153	15	28	2	2	1	5	4	25	1	0	.242	.209	R	R	5-11	165	1-21-80	1996	Caracas, Venez.
Kellner, Ryan	.208	66	236	15	49	8	1	4	21	17	52	0	2	.301	.277	R	R	6-2	205	12-9-77	1997	Morganton, N.C.
King, Brennan	.243	73	255	24	62	10	0	1	28	13	48	0	0	.294	.286	R	R	6-3	190	1-20-81	1999	Murfreesboro, Tenn.
Langs, Ronte	.273	5	11	3	3	0	0	0	1	2	1	1	1	.273	.385	R	R	5-10	200	1-29-79	2000	Memphis, Tenn.
Lipowicz, Nathan	.238	33	101	8	24	4	0	0	9	7	12	0	0	.277	.297	R	R	5-10	175	2-9-78	2000	Buckner, Mo.
Matthews, Lamont	.307	107	349	61	107	26	3	10	57	95	106	1	3	.484	.458	L	L	6-2	210	6-15-78	1999	Petersburg, Va.
Nelson, Reggie	.227	102	348	51	79	12	0	0	23	46	54	22	13	.261	.333	R	R	5-10	165	3-30-79	1998	San Diego, Calif.
Nunez, Manuel	.136	16	44	5	6	1	0	1	5	3	21	0	1	.227	.191	R	R	6-1	153	3-9-80	1997	Santiago, D.R.
Paciorek, Pete	.196	46	143	13	28	5	1	4	17	13	33	0	0	.329	.261	L	L	6-3	205	5-19-76	1995	San Gabriel, Calif.
Schifano, Tony	.281	62	199	23	56	12	0	4	23	15	39	6	1	.402	.341	R	R	6-3	225	8-11-78	1997	Los Mochis, Mexico
Soto, Saul	.000	1	2	0	0	0	0	0	0	2	0	0	0	.000	.500	R	R	6-3	225	8-11-78	1997	Los Mochis, Mexico
Theodorou, Nick	.000	8	17	3	0	0	0	0	1	8	4	0	0	.000	.308	B	R	5-11	182	6-7-75	1998	Rialto, Calif.
Thomas, Charles	.261	66	253	28	66	18	0	1	20	23	58	9	6	.344	.321	R	R	6-2	180	11-4-78	2000	Fresno, Calif.
Victorino, Shane	.167	2	6	2	1	0	0	0	3	1	0	0	0	.167	.444	R	R	5-9	160	11-30-80	1999	Wailuku, Hawaii
Wright, Nate	.000	2	2	0	0	0	0	0	1	1	0	0	0	.000	.333	R	R	5-10	170	1-22-78	2000	Saugus, Calif.

GAMES BY POSITION: C—Aracena 1, Duplissea 37, Hernandez 37, Kellner 66, Nelson 1, Soto 1. **1B**—Alvarez 59, Bledsoe 47, Hernandez 1, Paciorek 32, Schifano 1. **2B**—Collins 15, Gallo 60, Jaramillo 1, Nelson 51, Nunez 1, Schifano 4. **3B**—Aybar 2, Bell 6, Beltre 2, Bledsoe 1, Collins 2, Hansen 3, Jaramillo 3, King 72, Nelson 16, Schifano 36, Theodorou 3. **SS**—Collins 57, Jaramillo 44, Nelson 24, Nunez 14. **OF**—Alvarez 47, Chen 11, Feliciano 111, Guerrero 26, Jaramillo 1, Langs 4, Lipowicz 30, Matthews 107, Nelson 5, Paciorek 1, Schifano 2, Theodorou 4, Thomas 60, Victorino 2.

PITCHING	W	L	ERA	G	GS	CG	SV	IP	H	R	ER	BB	SO	AVG	B	T	HT	WT	DOB	1st Yr	Resides
Bauer, Greg	2	3	3.91	12	0	0	1	23	28	13	10	13	15	.294	R	R	6-1	195	11-30-77	2000	Tulsa, Okla.
Berry, Jon	2	4	3.78	33	5	0	8	69	58	34	29	37	71	.225	R	R	6-1	185	11-17-77	1999	Branchville, S.C.
Caraccioli, Lance	2	1	1.82	5	5	0	0	30	23	6	6	7	22	.219	L	L	6-4	190	12-14-77	1998	Walker, La.
Colyer, Steve	4	8	3.96	24	24	0	0	120	101	62	53	77	118	.233	L	L	6-4	205	2-22-79	1998	St. Peters, Mo.
Cordero, Jesus	0	1	4.32	4	1	0	0	8	7	5	4	3	10	.225	R	R	6-2	195	5-5-79	1998	San Pedro de Macoris, D.R.
Devey, Phil	0	0	2.57	3	0	0	1	7	8	2	2	0	6	.275	L	L	6-0	170	5-31-77	1999	Lachute, Quebec
Fischer, Mike	1	0	1.59	26	0	0	2	45	31	8	8	18	44	.190	R	R	6-4	200	12-10-76	1998	Crestline, Ohio
Gomes, Tony	1	1	2.31	11	0	0	4	23	13	6	6	11	26	.166	R	R	6-0	190	9-10-77	1998	Galt, Calif.
Hadden, Randy	4	4	5.10	34	1	0	2	67	75	44	38	29	58	.283	R	R	6-2	191	11-1-77	1999	Jacksonville, Fla.
Harrell, Tim	0	0	0.00	2	0	0	0	4	1	0	0	1	3	.076	R	R	6-4	215	10-31-75	1998	Weaverville, N.C.
Langone, Steve	9	3	2.46	23	13	1	0	99	94	32	27	18	89	.250	R	R	6-2	195	1-12-78	2000	Reading, Mass.
Majewski, Gary	4	5	6.24	23	13	0	1	75	103	57	52	36	41	.339	R	R	6-2	200	2-26-80	1999	Houston, Texas
McCrotty, Will	0	2	4.37	20	0	0	5	23	22	11	11	14	17	.252	R	R	6-2	195	6-22-79	1997	Russellville, Ark.
Meyer, Dave	1	1	6.28	12	0	0	3	14	20	11	10	6	13	.350	R	R	6-0	185	8-6-75	1999	Austin, Minn.
Montero, Agustin	1	0	3.45	16	0	0	1	31	29	14	12	13	23	.250	R	R	6-2	207	8-26-77	1995	San Pedro de Macoris, D.R.
Nance, Dave	6	3	2.63	21	0	0	4	48	28	15	14	21	63	.163	L	L	5-8	180	9-7-77	2000	Houston, Texas
Parrish, Wade	4	1	1.85	23	0	0	6	39	34	9	8	7	42	.234	L	L	6-1	205	11-13-77	1999	Othello, Wash.
Proctor, Scott	6	4	2.48	15	15	0	0	91	73	30	25	30	79	.226	R	R	6-1	198	1-2-77	1998	Jensen Beach, Fla.
Rijo, Fernando	0	1	5.73	2	2	0	0	11	7	7	7	10	11	.189	R	R	5-11	155	11-14-77	1995	La Romana, D.R.
Roberts, Rick	4	5	2.72	29	14	0	4	86	70	42	26	47	92	.218	L	L	6-1	200	5-20-79	1997	Summer Hill, Pa.
Rodriguez, Ricardo	14	6	3.21	26	26	2	0	154	133	67	55	60	154	.232	R	R	6-3	195	5-21-79	1996	Guayubin, D.R.
Rojas, Jose	0	0	6.00	1	0	0	0	3	3	2	2	1	3	.250	R	R	5-10	160	3-20-82	1998	San Pedro de Macoris, D.R.
Simpson, Andre	1	3	8.69	5	5	0	0	20	23	24	19	20	17	.302	R	R	6-3	170	7-1-80	1998	Lemon Grove, Calif.
Totten, Heath	0	8	7.07	9	9	2	0	50	64	40	39	10	25	.315	R	R	6-3	210	9-30-78	2000	Groves, Texas
Williams, Adam	0	1	6.43	10	0	0	0	14	16	13	10	12	13	.285	R	L	6-3	215	11-29-78	1997	Montgomery, Ala.

WILMINGTON — Class A

SOUTH ATLANTIC LEAGUE

BATTING	AVG	G	AB	R	H	2B	3B	HR	RBI	BB	SO	SB	CS	SLG	OBP	B	T	HT	WT	DOB	1st Yr	Resides
Abercrombie, Reggie	.226	125	486	63	110	17	3	10	41	19	154	44	11	.335	.272	R	R	6-3	210	7-15-81	2000	Damascus, Ga.
Aybar, Willy	.237	120	431	45	102	25	2	4	48	43	64	7	9	.332	.307	B	R	6-0	175	3-9-83	2000	Bani, D.R.
Canales, Josh	.227	52	163	14	37	2	1	1	12	14	28	10	5	.270	.294	R	R	5-11	175	1-15-79	2001	Carson, Calif.
Dacey, Ryan	.253	66	198	22	50	8	0	1	24	32	45	10	7	.308	.367	R	R	6-3	200	5-31-78	2000	Edgewater, Md.
Detienne, Dave	.264	83	280	36	74	10	3	1	13	14	63	25	4	.332	.309	R	R	6-3	190	8-16-79	1997	Dartmouth, Nova Scotia
Diaz, Jose	.175	23	80	7	14	4	0	2	5	4	31	1	0	.300	.214	R	R	6-0	205	4-13-80	1996	San Pedro de Macoris, D.R.
Escalera, Jose	.147	8	34	4	5	0	0	0	5	0	7	0	0	.147	.143	R	R	6-3	230	10-21-80	1998	Loiza, P.R.
Gatti, William	.217	6	23	3	5	1	0	1	3	1	10	1	0	.391	.269	R	R	6-2	220	7-20-77	2001	Louisville, Ky.
Goodwin, Tom	.400	2	5	2	2	0	1	0	1	1	0	0	0	.800	.429	L	R	6-1	175	7-27-68	1989	Fresno, Calif.
Hill, Koyie	.301	134	498	65	150	20	2	8	79	49	82	21	12	.398	.368	B	R	6-0	190	3-9-79	2000	Lawton, Okla.
Langs, Ronte	.269	105	376	49	101	14	8	1	29	43	88	18	7	.356	.353	R	R	5-10	200	1-29-79	2000	Memphis, Tenn.
Martinez, Candido	.260	120	443	69	115	27	4	7	66	29	138	54	18	.386	.310	R	R	6-2	170	10-26-80	1996	Sabana Perdida, D.R.

ORGANIZATION STATISTICS

BATTING	AVG	G	AB	R	H	2B	3B	HR	RBI	BB	SO	SB	CS	SLG	OBP	B	T	HT	WT	DOB	1st Yr	Resides
Michaelis, Derek	.197	33	117	10	23	4	1	0	17	6	36	6	0	.248	.248	L	L	6-7	230	12-2-78	2000	Waco, Texas
Pierce, Sean	.250	3	12	0	3	0	0	0	0	0	2	1	1	.250	.250	R	R	5-9	190	11-26-78	2001	Covina, Calif.
Repko, Jason	.220	88	337	36	74	17	4	4	32	15	68	17	8	.329	.257	R	R	5-11	175	12-27-80	1999	West Richland, Wash.
Soto, Saul	.262	75	252	32	66	17	0	6	34	33	34	4	4	.401	.366	R	R	6-3	225	8-11-78	1997	Los Mochis, Mexico
Story-Harden, Thomari	.191	22	68	4	13	2	1	1	5	4	29	0	1	.294	.233	R	R	6-6	235	4-6-80	1998	Richmond, Calif.
Van Buizen, Rodney	.221	90	285	29	63	16	0	5	34	23	54	12	7	.330	.296	R	R	6-0	190	9-25-80	1998	Sydney, Australia
Victorino, Shane	.283	112	435	71	123	21	9	4	32	36	61	47	13	.400	.344	R	R	5-9	160	11-30-80	1999	Wailuku, Hawaii

GAMES BY POSITION: C—Diaz 22, Hill 91, Michaelis 1, Soto 24. **1B**—Dacey 29, Detienne 8, Michaelis 31, Soto 49, Story-Harden 15, Van Buizen 12. **2B**—Canales 11, Dacey 16, Detienne 46, Van Buizen 67. **3B**—Aybar 118, Dacey 6, Detienne 10, Van Buizen 6. **SS**—Canales 39, Dacey 4, Detienne 18, Repko 77. **OF**—Abercrombie 122, Escalera 4, Gatti 5, Goodwin 2, Langs 92, Martinez 77, Pierce 1, Van Buizen 3, Victorino 109.

PITCHING	W	L	ERA	G	GS	CG	SV	IP	H	R	ER	BB	SO	AVG	B	T	HT	WT	DOB	1st Yr	Resides
Aguilera, Adrian	0	1	6.75	5	0	0	1	5	8	5	4	2	4	.347	L	L	5-09	198	7-10-79	1997	Obregon, Mexico
Andrews, Aron	4	3	2.05	15	1	0	2	44	40	14	10	7	26	.246	R	R	6-0	175	8-24-77	2000	Tuscaloosa, Ala.
Bauer, Greg	1	1	1.78	25	0	0	17	30	22	6	6	8	32	.209	R	R	6-1	195	11-30-77	2000	Tulsa, Okla.
Bridenbaugh, Christian	3	6	3.68	21	20	1	0	127	131	58	52	30	76	.269	L	L	6-1	185	9-26-79	1998	Martinsburg, Pa.
Cordero, Jesus	8	4	2.47	33	1	0	9	69	49	20	19	25	56	.205	R	R	6-2	195	5-5-79	1998	San Pedro de Macoris, D.R.
Diggins, Ben	7	6	3.58	21	21	0	0	106	88	49	42	48	79	.223	R	R	6-7	230	6-13-79	2000	Tucson, Ariz.
Gonzalez, Alfredo	1	0	3.00	2	1	0	0	9	10	4	3	3	12	.270	R	R	6-2	181	9-17-79	1997	Nagua, D.R.
Hanrahan, Joel	9	11	3.38	27	26	0	0	144	136	71	54	55	116	.250	R	R	6-3	215	10-6-81	2000	Norwalk, Iowa
Hughes, Nial	1	4	4.24	25	1	0	2	40	25	27	19	45	57	.182	R	L	6-3	210	11-5-77	1997	Charlottetown, P.E.I.
Keirstead, Michael	0	1	4.82	7	1	0	0	9	9	7	5	5	12	.243	R	R	6-3	210	1-26-81	2000	Musquash, New Brunswick
Lizarraga, Edgar	0	0	0.00	3	0	0	0	6	2	0	0	1	10	.105	R	R	6-0	180	1-27-81	2000	Culiacan, Mexico
Lugo, Ruddy	0	2	3.77	16	0	0	2	31	29	14	13	13	23	.258	R	R	6-0	190	5-22-80	1999	Brooklyn, N.Y.
McCrotty, Will	2	1	1.96	21	0	0	4	37	24	9	8	10	46	.183	R	R	6-2	195	6-22-79	1997	Russellville, Ark.
Montero, Agustin	2	1	3.29	18	0	0	1	27	13	11	10	19	30	.147	R	R	6-2	207	8-26-77	1995	San Pedro de Macoris, D.R.
Olson, Jason	2	4	3.68	15	0	0	1	29	23	12	12	15	28	.216	R	R	6-2	180	6-12-78	2000	Chino Valley, Ariz.
Rijo, Fernando	11	7	2.98	26	26	0	0	139	107	64	46	54	128	.217	R	R	5-11	155	11-14-77	1995	La Romana, D.R.
Roberts, Rick	3	1	2.75	7	2	0	0	20	12	7	6	7	26	.173	L	L	6-1	200	5-20-79	1997	Summer Hill, Pa.
Rojas, Jose	10	3	2.12	24	23	1	0	136	107	42	32	42	116	.221	R	R	5-10	160	3-20-82	1999	San Pedro de Macoris, D.R.
Simpson, Andre	9	3	2.30	24	9	0	1	98	75	27	25	20	96	.210	R	R	6-3	170	7-1-80	1998	Lemon Grove, Calif.
Steffek, Brian	0	1	1.93	9	1	0	2	23	12	5	5	8	22	.157	R	R	6-2	195	3-2-78	2000	Stafford, Texas
Urdaneta, Lino	1	2	7.61	10	4	0	0	24	31	23	20	11	16	.329	R	R	6-1	168	11-20-79	1996	Guarenas, Venez.
Williams, Adam	1	1	2.65	25	1	0	2	54	41	21	16	21	47	.203	R	L	6-3	215	11-29-78	1997	Montgomery, Ala.

GREAT FALLS — Rookie

PIONEER LEAGUE

BATTING	AVG	G	AB	R	H	2B	3B	HR	RBI	BB	SO	SB	CS	SLG	OBP	B	T	HT	WT	DOB	1st Yr	Resides
Aracena, Sandy	.256	44	164	26	42	9	1	4	25	12	20	2	0	.396	.313	R	R	6-0	180	3-3-81	1998	La Vega, D.R.
Canales, Josh	.500	9	30	4	15	2	0	0	6	2	3	0	0	.567	.559	R	R	5-11	175	1-15-79	2001	Carson, Calif.
Cordova, Ricardo	.198	34	116	17	23	3	1	0	11	12	22	0	1	.241	.267	B	R	5-11	160	7-5-81	1998	Aragua, Venez.
De los Santos, Omar	.186	37	102	13	19	1	0	1	7	5	32	2	1	.225	.229	R	R	6-0	162	8-13-81	1998	San Pedro de Macoris, D.R.
Diaz, Jose	.189	48	159	18	30	8	0	3	17	15	38	2	1	.296	.284	R	R	6-0	205	4-13-80	1996	San Pedro de Macoris, D.R.
Escalera, Jose	.167	9	42	4	7	0	0	0	2	3	5	0	0	.167	.217	R	R	6-3	230	10-21-80	1999	Loiza, P.R.
Garcia, Jose	.291	74	306	46	89	23	4	8	50	13	49	15	9	.471	.330	R	R	6-1	198	8-22-80	1996	Santo Domingo, D.R.
Gillitzer, Scott	.261	66	253	34	66	11	0	1	41	21	23	10	1	.316	.324	R	R	6-1	185	6-11-79	2001	Prairie du Chien, Wis.
Guerrero, Hector	.210	31	124	18	26	5	2	3	12	6	15	6	2	.355	.258	L	L	6-0	170	12-22-81	1998	San Pedro de Macoris, D.R.
Johnson, Michael	.247	45	154	32	38	3	3	0	13	31	32	14	4	.305	.380	L	L	6-3	180	8-28-78	2001	Sherwood, Ark.
Lanoix, Gilbert	.250	1	4	0	1	0	0	0	0	0	0	0	0	.250	.250	L	R	5-11	172	7-15-78	2001	New Orleans, La.
Malone, Billy	.210	55	176	23	37	5	1	0	18	25	49	15	6	.250	.321	R	R	5-10	185	5-8-78	2001	La Grange Park, Ill.
Michaelis, Derek	.276	37	134	21	37	9	1	4	28	17	31	2	1	.448	.362	L	L	6-7	230	12-2-78	2000	Waco, Texas
Nickerson, Brian	.158	9	38	3	6	0	0	0	3	0	5	0	0	.158	.179	R	R	5-10	195	2-20-78	2001	Arcadia, Calif.
Nunez, Manuel	.250	69	244	46	61	8	0	6	29	38	60	32	8	.357	.350	R	R	6-1	153	3-9-80	1997	Santiago, D.R.
O'Connell, Bradley	.310	23	84	12	26	3	2	2	11	3	16	3	3	.464	.370	R	R	5-10	185	2-1-78	2001	Elk Mound, Wis.
Pierce, Sean	.311	72	273	59	85	11	7	6	43	43	54	29	6	.469	.414	R	R	5-9	190	11-26-78	2001	Covina, Calif.
Story-Harden, Thomari	.263	24	80	11	21	4	0	3	14	12	25	2	2	.425	.394	R	R	6-6	235	4-6-80	1998	Richmond, Calif.
Virgen, Constancio	.262	31	107	13	28	4	0	1	16	15	17	3	2	.327	.347	R	R	6-3	172	5-5-82	2000	Nayarit, Mexico

GAMES BY POSITION: C—Aracena 26, Diaz 43, Virgen 9. **1B**—Aracena 5, de los Santos 5, Diaz 2, Gillitzer 11, Michaelis 34, Story-Harden 18, Virgen 8. **2B**—Canales 2, Cordova 5, de los Santos 7, Gillitzer 53, Malone 11, O'Connell 3. **3B**—Aracena 3, Canales 1, Cordova 12, de los Santos 23, Diaz 1, Malone 23, Nickerson 9, O'Connell 11. **SS**—Canales 2, Cordova 6, de los Santos 1, Nunez 68. **OF**—Canales 4, de los Santos 1, Escalera 9, Garcia 74, Guerrero 29, Johnson 29, Malone 12, O'Connell 6, Pierce 72, Virgen 2.

PITCHING	W	L	ERA	G	GS	CG	SV	IP	H	R	ER	BB	SO	AVG	B	T	HT	WT	DOB	1st Yr	Resides
Astacio, Andres	2	6	5.01	17	12	0	0	74	87	52	41	13	62	.282	R	R	6-2	155	8-5-80	1999	La Romana, D.R.
Gonzalez, Alfredo	3	4	3.56	11	8	0	0	48	43	26	19	12	56	.233	R	R	6-2	181	9-17-79	1997	Nagua, D.R.
Hickman, Jason	1	2	4.91	17	2	0	2	40	45	29	22	29	31	.283	L	L	6-2	205	7-11-78	2000	Terre Haute, Ind.
Hosford, Clinton	6	3	2.50	15	12	0	0	79	72	28	22	16	69	.240	R	R	6-2	185	8-8-80	1998	North Vancouver, B.C.
Kauffman, Matt	0	0	8.59	10	0	0	0	15	21	20	14	14	13	.318	L	L	6-3	190	10-8-78	2001	San Francisco, Calif.
Keirstead, Michael	1	1	2.34	25	3	0	5	35	35	14	9	12	52	.250	R	R	6-3	210	1-26-81	2000	Musquash, New Brunswick
Lizarraga, Edgar	4	2	3.54	14	4	0	2	48	43	25	19	11	56	.232	R	R	6-0	180	1-27-81	2000	Culiacan, Mexico
Lorenzen, Jonathan	0	0	10.80	5	0	0	0	10	15	14	12	8	11	.326	R	R	6-2	170	5-13-82	2000	Anaheim, Calif.
McCracken, Vance	4	5	3.84	14	9	0	1	63	63	31	27	11	46	.262	R	R	6-7	220	4-16-79	2001	St. Albans, W.Va.
Nall, T.J.	2	2	5.01	7	2	0	0	23	26	18	13	6	25	.268	R	R	6-1	185	11-4-80	1999	Schaumburg, Ill.
Olson, Jason	2	0	1.17	5	0	0	1	8	2	1	1	1	13	.071	R	R	6-2	180	6-12-78	2000	Chino Valley, Ariz.
Ott, Thom	2	1	4.84	14	0	0	2	22	29	19	12	7	24	.295	R	R	6-3	195	3-28-80	2001	Lincoln, Neb.
Pilkington, Brian	0	1	5.63	5	2	0	0	16	19	11	10	2	17	.296	R	R	6-5	210	9-17-82	2001	Garden Grove, Calif.
Rodriguez, Orlando	3	3	4.15	15	10	0	1	61	58	41	28	26	79	.239	L	L	5-10	155	11-28-80	2000	Santiago, D.R.
Stefani, Jason	3	1	5.03	19	2	0	1	39	48	30	22	19	35	.296	L	L	6-1	194	4-11-79	2001	Sacramento, Calif.
Steffek, Brian	0	2	7.71	8	3	0	1	21	28	18	18	11	19	.325	R	R	6-2	195	3-2-78	2000	Stafford, Texas
Strayhorn, Kole	0	0	15.43	2	0	0	0	2	4	4	4	1	1	.363	R	R	6-0	185	10-1-82	2001	Shawnee, Okla.
Tibbs, Jeff	2	5	10.02	15	7	0	0	41	62	57	46	30	25	.346	R	R	6-2	180	12-11-81	2000	Farmington, Utah
Turuda, Miyoki	2	1	3.14	17	0	0	2	29	25	16	10	18	32	.221	R	R	6-1	165	1-8-79	1997	Nuevo Leon, Mexico

ORGANIZATION STATISTICS

GULF COAST LEAGUE

BATTING	AVG	G	AB	R	H	2B	3B	HR	RBI	BB	SO	SB	CS	SLG	OBP	B	T	HT	WT	DOB	1st Yr	Resides
Bellorin, Edwin	.175	28	80	11	14	1	0	0	6	8	6	1	0	.188	.283	R	R	5-11	170	2-21-82	1998	Bolivar, Venez.
Bledsoe, Hunter	.385	4	13	2	5	1	0	0	1	1	1	1	0	.462	.429	R	R	6-4	215	1-24-76	1999	Nashville, Tenn.
Cardona, David	.232	47	168	20	39	5	1	0	21	10	42	2	1	.274	.283	R	R	6-2	175	11-7-82	2001	San Juan, P.R.
Carter, Ryan	.272	30	92	16	25	3	1	1	10	10	29	4	0	.359	.393	R	R	6-2	175	1-4-83	2001	Fort Myers, Fla.
De los Santos, Omar	.303	9	33	7	10	4	0	0	3	3	4	1	1	.424	.351	R	R	6-0	162	8-13-81	1998	San Pedro de Macoris, D.R.
Diaz, Victor	.354	53	195	36	69	22	2	3	31	16	23	6	3	.533	.414	R	R	6-0	200	12-10-81	2001	Chicago, Ill.
Ezi, Travis	.231	58	238	33	55	10	4	2	24	17	90	15	1	.332	.293	R	L	6-0	175	9-5-81	2000	Baltimore, Md.
Fahey, Patrick	.176	8	17	3	3	0	0	0	2	3	4	0	0	.176	.333	R	R	5-9	180	8-23-79	2001	Chicago, Ill.
Gallo, Ismael	.167	4	6	2	1	0	0	0	0	1	1	1	0	.167	.375	L	R	5-11	165	1-14-77	1996	Ontario, Calif.
Gatti, William	.161	11	31	5	5	0	0	0	1	3	8	0	0	.161	.278	R	R	6-2	220	7-20-77	2001	Louisville, Ky.
Gonzalez, Juan	.269	26	67	9	18	0	0	0	7	3	8	3	0	.269	.292	R	R	5-9	165	8-21-82	2001	Carolina, P.R.
Gutierrez, Franklin	.269	56	234	38	63	16	0	4	30	16	39	9	3	.389	.324	R	R	6-2	175	2-21-83	2001	Caracas, Venez.
Herrera, Christian	.320	46	153	24	49	3	0	0	20	12	23	9	2	.340	.378	R	R	5-11	169	4-9-82	2001	Aguascalientes, Mexico
Jackson, Edwin	.308	20	26	5	8	0	0	1	2	3	6	0	0	.423	.379	R	R	6-3	190	9-9-83	2001	Columbus, Ga.
Jaramillo, Milko	.250	3	8	2	2	0	1	0	1	1	0	0	0	.500	.400	B	R	5-11	165	1-21-80	1996	Caracas, Venez.
Johnson, Brian	.444	5	18	4	8	0	0	2	3	2	0	0	0	.778	.500	R	R	6-2	210	1-8-68	1989	Chicago, Ill.
King, Brennan	.556	3	9	3	5	2	0	1	4	0	0	0	0	1.111	.545	R	R	6-3	190	1-20-81	1999	Murfreesboro, Tenn.
Lanoix, Gilbert	.250	2	8	1	2	1	0	0	0	0	1	0	0	.375	.250	L	R	5-11	172	7-15-78	2001	New Orleans, La.
Mendoza, Adrian	.302	52	172	34	52	7	1	4	37	29	55	9	4	.424	.421	L	L	6-2	190	8-30-78	2000	Simi Valley, Calif.
Nickerson, Brian	.252	36	103	9	26	4	0	0	14	5	14	4	1	.291	.317	R	R	5-10	195	2-20-78	2001	Arcadia, Calif.
Pachot, John	.200	1	5	1	1	0	0	1	1	0	1	0	0	.800	.200	R	R	6-2	168	11-11-74	1993	Ponce, P.R.
Perozo, Hector	.223	55	184	32	41	4	3	1	26	27	63	2	2	.293	.368	R	R	6-2	190	9-20-83	2000	Caracas, Venez.
Post, Dave	.000	1	2	0	0	0	0	0	0	0	1	0	0	.000	.000	R	R	5-11	170	9-3-73	1992	Kingston, N.Y.
Price, Jared	.096	33	94	10	9	1	0	0	5	14	41	0	2	.106	.252	R	R	6-1	190	3-18-82	2001	Rupert, Idaho
Thomas, Chuck	.250	7	16	5	4	0	0	0	2	3	0	3	0	.250	.368	R	R	6-1	200	6-10-80	1998	Fresno, Calif.
Wright, Nate	.200	4	10	3	2	0	0	0	1	1	1	0	0	.200	.273	R	R	6-0	170	1-22-78	2000	Saugus, Calif.

GAMES BY POSITION: C—Bellorin 27, Fahey 8, Johnson 4, Pachot 1, Price 32. **1B**—Bellorin 1, Bledsoe 4, Mendoza 42, Nickerson 20, Price 1. **2B**—de los Santos 7, Diaz 50, Gallo 4, J. Gonzalez 7, Nickerson 1. **3B**—de los Santos 2, Diaz 3, J. Gonzalez 1, King 3, Nickerson 7, Perozo 51, Post 1. **SS**—J. Gonzalez 15, Herrera 46, Jaramillo 3. **OF**—Cardona 47, Carter 11, Ezi 57, Gatti 10, Gutierrez 55, Thomas 6, Wright 4.

PITCHING	W	L	ERA	G	GS	CG	SV	IP	H	R	ER	BB	SO	AVG	B	T	HT	WT	DOB	1st Yr	Resides
Aguilera, Adrian	0	0	7.71	4	0	0	0	5	2	4	4	3	6	.117	L	L	5-9	198	7-10-79	1997	Obregon, Mexico
Andrews, Aron	0	0	0.00	6	0	0	3	7	2	0	0	1	9	.083	R	R	6-0	175	8-24-77	2000	Tuscaloosa, Ala.
Blaney, Matthew	1	3	9.56	11	0	0	1	16	21	17	17	5	8	.338	B	R	5-11	185	5-7-79	2001	Oxnard, Calif.
Cuen, David	4	1	1.42	13	6	0	0	51	32	14	8	17	49	.178	L	L	6-4	170	8-4-83	2001	Somerton, Ariz.
Escobedo, Edgar	4	1	1.66	17	4	0	0	43	42	9	8	9	24	.257	R	R	6-4	155	2-6-83	2001	Tijuana, Mexico
Gonzalez, Luis	4	2	3.55	13	2	0	0	25	25	15	10	14	25	.247	L	L	6-3	190	2-27-83	2001	Carolina, P.R.
Hughes, Nial	1	0	1.80	2	2	0	0	10	5	2	2	4	10	.151	R	L	6-3	210	11-5-77	1997	Charlottetown, P.E.I.
Jackson, Edwin	2	1	2.45	12	2	0	0	22	14	12	6	19	23	.000	R	R	6-3	190	9-9-83	2001	Columbus, Ga.
Johansen, Ryan	2	2	2.43	21	0	0	2	37	26	10	10	6	39	.203	R	R	6-0	180	6-19-80	2001	Jensen Beach, Fla.
Kuo, Hong-Chih	0	0	2.33	7	6	0	0	19	13	5	5	4	21	.185	L	L	6-0	200	7-23-81	1999	Tainan City, Taiwan
Lopez, Javier	5	1	2.04	14	7	0	1	62	46	20	14	12	45	.212	L	L	5-10	165	2-22-83	2001	Sinaloa, Mexico
Lorenzen, Jonathan	2	1	1.77	7	1	0	0	20	18	5	4	5	19	.240	R	R	6-2	170	5-13-82	2000	Anaheim, Calif.
Nall, T.J.	0	0	4.50	4	4	0	0	12	14	6	6	5	10	.297	R	R	6-1	185	11-4-80	1999	Schaumburg, Ill.
Nelson, Stephen	1	2	2.17	10	6	0	0	29	19	9	7	4	26	.180	L	R	6-3	200	11-10-82	2001	Dartmouth, Nova Scotia
Neuage, Leigh	0	0	1.59	3	2	0	0	6	2	1	1	3	3	.111	R	R	6-4	210	7-6-83	2001	South Australia, Australia
Reina, Dimas	3	1	1.30	25	0	0	8	42	34	6	6	6	35	.220	R	R	6-0	170	2-23-82	1998	Caracas, Venez.
Stewart, James	1	1	3.09	11	1	0	0	23	19	9	8	4	14	.215	R	R	6-2	190	5-9-82	2001	Vail, Ariz.
Strayhorn, Kole	5	3	2.19	12	6	0	0	53	41	15	13	17	47	.215	R	R	6-5	185	10-1-82	2001	Shawnee, Okla.
Taylor, David	0	1	3.00	3	3	0	0	6	5	3	2	0	6	.227	B	R	6-5	190	12-4-82	2001	Clermont, Fla.
Totten, Heath	1	0	0.82	2	2	0	0	11	5	1	1	0	8	.135	R	R	6-3	210	9-30-78	2000	Groves, Texas
Withelder, Greg	1	0	4.15	6	6	0	0	17	15	8	8	11	15	.250	R	L	6-3	200	5-11-79	2000	Wallingford, Pa.

MILWAUKEE BREWERS

BY TOM HAUDRICOURT

The last thing any new regime wants to do is take a step backward in its second year on the job.

Unfortunately for Brewers general manager Dean Taylor and his staff, that's exactly what happened in

2001. Expecting to contend in the National League Central, the Brewers instead collapsed like a house of cards and finished with 94 losses—five more than the previous year and the most since 1984.

The good news was that a club-record 2.8 million fans went through the turnstiles at new Miller Park. The bad news was that more people than ever before witnessed a very bad product on the field.

"We're all judged by results," Taylor said. "Certainly, we realize that. We're all disappointed by the results.

"We had much higher expectations for this team, as did a number of people throughout the game. I think it's safe to say many people had higher expectations. And I don't think those expectations were necessarily unrealistic."

Those expectations seemed realistic indeed when the Brewers were 38-34 in late June and in the thick of the division race. But they quickly bottomed out, losing 31 of the next 40 games, and never recovered.

Injuries played a role in that collapse as the Brewers placed 19 players on the disabled list, including a club-record 12 at one time. Center fielder Jeffrey Hammonds, Taylor's key acquisition during the previous winter, went down early with a shoulder injury and played in just 49 games.

But the casualty list did not tell the full story. The offense degenerated into an all-or-nothing mode too reliant on home runs to win. The Brewers obliterated the major league record for strikeouts (1,268) by whiffing 1,399 times, becoming the first team ever to finish with more strikeouts than hits (1,378).

Richie Sexson   Jim Rushford

MEL BAILEY

PLAYERS OF THE YEAR

MAJOR LEAGUE: Richie Sexson, 1b
He hit his 45th homer on the last day of the 2001 season, tying him for the club record set by Gorman Thomas in 1979. Sexson also led the Brewers in RBIs (125).

MINOR LEAGUE: Jim Rushford, of
A 27-year-old with no prior experience in the affiliated minor leagues, Rushford led minor league baseball with a .354 average while advancing to Double-A.

Shortstop Jose Hernandez played his position well and showed good pop (25 homers, 78 RBIs) but struck out 185 times, four shy of the major league record. First baseman Richie Sexson tied the club record with 45 home runs and was one shy of the club mark with 125 RBIs, but finished second in the NL to Hernandez with 178 strikeouts.

Right fielder Jeromy Burnitz socked 34 homers and drove in 100 runs but combined with Hernandez and Sexson to give the Brewers the first trio of players ever with 150 Ks apiece. The situation got so bad that hitting coach Rod Carew, one of the greatest contact hitters in the history of the game, resigned during the final week of the season.

The pitching also had its share of problems. At one time or another, every member of the starting rotation spent time on the disabled list. The Brewers led the major leagues with 667 walks, contributing to the dismissal of pitching coach Bob Apodaca at season's end.

Jeff D'Amico, expected to be the No. 1 starter after a comeback from a two-year absence in 2000, was bitten by the injury bug again and pitched in just 10 games.

Even the sparkling debut of top pitching prospect Ben Sheets was tarnished. Sheets won 10 games in the first half and became the first Brewers rookie to be named to the All-Star Game, but later experienced shoulder problems and won one game after the break.

While the cupboard remained mostly bare at the top levels of the farm system, the overall situation improved as Double-A Huntsville, Class A Beloit and Rookie-level Ogden made the playoffs. Righthander Nick Neugebauer was named the organization's minor league pitcher of the year, and Class A High Desert shortstop Bill Hall earned player of the year honors.

Center fielder David Krynzel, 19, a first-round draft pick in 2000, got off to a good start at Beloit and was promoted to High Desert, where he was the youngest player in the California League.

ORGANIZATION LEADERS

BATTING

*AVG	Jim Rushford, Huntsville/High Desert	.354
R	Jim Rushford, Huntsville/High Desert	103
H	Jim Rushford, Huntsville/High Desert	158
TB	Jim Rushford, Huntsville/High Desert	265
2B	Bill Scott, High Desert	42
3B	Bobby Darula, Huntsville/High Desert	7
	Bill Hall, Huntsville/High Desert	7
HR	Lance Burkhart, Huntsville/High Desert	32
RBI	Bill Scott, High Desert	102
BB	Steve Scarborough, High Desert	65
	Lance Burkhart, Huntsville/High Desert	65
SO	Dave Krynzel, High Desert/Beloit	150
SB	Dave Krynzel, High Desert/Beloit	45
	Ryan Knox, Huntsville/High Desert	45

PITCHING

W	Matt Parker, High Desert	13
L	Matt Childers, Huntsville/High Desert	11
#ERA	Rocky Coppinger, Indianapolis/Huntsville	1.97
G	Brian Mallette, Indianapolis/Huntsville	56
CG	Six tied at	1
SV	Brian Mallette, Indianapolis/Huntsville	19
IP	Tim Harikkala, Indianapolis	172
BB	Carlos Chantres, Indianapolis	93
SO	Nick Neugebauer, Indianapolis/Huntsville	175

*Minimum 250 At-Bats #Minimum 75 Innings

ORGANIZATION STATISTICS

MILWAUKEE BREWERS

Manager: Davey Lopes

2001 Record: 68-94, .420 (4th, NL Central)

BATTING	AVG	G	AB	R	H	2B	3B	HR	RBI	BB	SO	SB	CS	SLG	OBP	B	T	HT	WT	DOB	1st Yr	Resides
Belliard, Ronnie	.264	101	364	69	96	30	3	11	36	35	65	5	2	.453	.335	R	R	5-8	180	4-7-75	1994	Miami, Fla.
Blanco, Henry	.210	104	314	33	66	18	3	6	31	34	72	3	1	.344	.290	R	R	5-11	190	8-29-71	1990	Guarenas, Venez.
Brown, Kevin	.209	17	43	7	9	0	1	4	12	2	18	0	0	.535	.261	R	R	6-2	215	4-21-73	1994	Mount Vernon, Ind.
Burnitz, Jeromy	.251	154	562	104	141	32	4	34	100	80	150	0	4	.504	.347	L	R	6-0	205	4-14-69	1990	Tavernier, Fla.
Casanova, Raul	.260	71	192	21	50	10	0	11	33	12	29	0	0	.484	.303	B	R	6-0	195	8-23-72	1990	Ponce, P.R.
Collier, Lou	.252	50	127	19	32	8	1	2	14	17	30	5	1	.378	.340	R	R	5-10	182	8-21-73	1993	Chicago, Ill.
Coolbaugh, Mike	.200	39	70	10	14	6	0	2	7	5	16	0	0	.371	.273	R	R	6-1	185	6-5-72	1990	San Antonio, Texas
Echevarria, Angel	.256	75	133	12	34	11	0	5	13	8	29	0	1	.451	.310	R	R	6-3	226	5-25-71	1992	Aurora, Colo.
Fernandez, Tony	.281	28	64	6	18	0	0	1	3	7	9	1	2	.328	.352	B	R	6-2	195	6-30-62	1980	Boca Raton, Fla.
Hammonds, Jeffrey	.247	49	174	20	43	11	1	6	21	14	42	5	3	.425	.314	R	R	6-0	200	3-5-71	1992	Scotch Plains, N.J.
Hernandez, Jose	.249	152	542	67	135	26	2	25	78	39	185	5	4	.443	.300	R	R	6-1	180	7-14-69	1987	Dorado, P.R.
Houston, Tyler	.289	75	235	36	68	7	0	12	38	18	62	0	0	.472	.343	L	R	6-1	210	1-17-71	1989	Las Vegas, Nev.
Jenkins, Geoff	.264	105	397	60	105	21	1	20	63	36	120	4	2	.474	.334	L	R	6-1	204	7-21-74	1996	Scottsdale, Ariz.
Levis, Jesse	.242	12	33	6	8	2	0	0	3	3	7	0	0	.303	.306	L	R	5-9	200	4-14-68	1989	Elkins Park, Pa.
Lopez, Luis	.270	92	222	22	60	8	3	4	18	14	44	0	1	.387	.326	B	R	5-11	166	9-4-70	1988	Cidra, P.R.
Loretta, Mark	.289	102	384	40	111	14	2	2	29	28	46	1	2	.352	.346	R	R	6-0	190	8-14-71	1993	Scottsdale, Ariz.
Mouton, James	.246	75	138	20	34	8	0	2	10	11	40	7	3	.348	.329	R	R	5-9	175	12-29-68	1991	Missouri City, Texas
Pena, Elvis	.225	15	40	5	9	2	0	0	6	6	6	2	0	.275	.333	B	R	5-11	155	9-15-76	1994	Santo Domingo, D.R.
Perez, Robert	.000	2	5	0	0	0	0	0	0	0	0	0	0	.000	.000	R	R	6-3	230	6-4-69	1990	Bolivar, Venez.
Sanchez, Alex	.206	30	68	7	14	3	2	0	4	5	13	6	2	.309	.260	L	L	5-10	180	8-26-76	1996	Miami, Fla.
Sexson, Richie	.271	158	598	94	162	24	3	45	125	60	178	2	4	.547	.342	R	R	6-7	205	12-29-74	1993	Brush Prairie, Wash.
Sweeney, Mark	.258	48	89	9	23	3	1	3	11	12	23	2	1	.416	.347	L	L	6-1	195	10-26-69	1991	Scottsdale, Ariz.
White, Devon	.277	126	390	52	108	25	2	14	47	28	95	18	3	.459	.343	B	R	6-2	190	12-29-62	1981	Paradise Valley, Ariz.

PITCHING	W	L	ERA	G	GS	CG	SV	IP	H	R	ER	BB	SO	AVG	B	T	HT	WT	DOB	1st Yr	Resides
Buddie, Mike	0	1	3.89	31	0	0	2	42	34	20	18	17	22	.225	R	R	6-3	215	12-12-70	1992	Advance, N.C.
Coppinger, Rocky	1	0	6.75	8	3	0	0	23	24	17	17	15	15	.282	R	R	6-5	240	3-19-74	1994	El Paso, Texas
Cunnane, Will	0	3	5.40	31	1	0	0	52	66	34	31	22	37	.320	R	R	6-2	200	4-24-74	1993	Congers, N.Y.
D'Amico, Jeff	2	4	6.08	10	10	0	0	47	60	42	32	16	32	.306	R	R	6-7	250	12-27-75	1993	Pinellas Park, Fla.
DeJean, Mike	4	2	2.77	75	0	0	2	84	75	31	26	39	68	.235	R	R	6-2	212	9-28-70	1992	Castle Rock, Colo.
De los Santos, Valerio	0	0	9.00	1	0	0	0	1	1	1	1	1	1	.250	L	L	6-2	180	10-6-75	1993	Santo Domingo, D.R.
Fox, Chad	5	2	1.89	65	0	0	2	67	44	16	14	36	80	.181	R	R	6-1	190	9-3-70	1992	Houston, Texas
Gandarillas, Gus	0	0	5.49	16	0	0	0	20	25	13	12	10	7	.320	R	R	6-0	190	7-19-71	1992	Miami, Fla.
Haynes, Jimmy	8	17	4.85	31	29	0	0	173	182	98	93	78	112	.278	R	R	6-3	180	9-5-72	1991	La Grange, Ga.
King, Ray	0	4	3.60	82	0	0	1	55	49	22	22	25	49	.241	L	L	6-1	230	1-15-74	1995	Chicago, Ill.
Kolb, Brandon	0	0	13.03	10	0	0	0	10	16	16	14	8	8	.372	R	R	6-1	190	11-20-73	1995	Lubbock, Texas
Leiter, Mark	2	1	3.75	20	3	0	0	36	32	16	15	8	26	.231	R	R	6-3	220	4-13-63	1983	Lanoka Harbor, N.J.
Leskanic, Curt	2	6	3.63	70	0	0	17	69	63	30	28	31	64	.241	R	R	6-0	186	4-2-68	1990	Highlands Ranch, Colo.
Levrault, Allen	6	10	6.06	32	20	1	0	131	146	93	88	59	80	.280	R	R	6-3	230	8-15-77	1996	Westport, Mass.
Neugebauer, Nick	1	1	7.50	2	2	0	0	6	6	5	5	6	11	.250	R	R	6-3	225	7-15-80	1999	Riverside, Calif.
Painter, Lance	1	0	4.22	13	0	0	0	11	11	5	5	7	6	.268	L	L	6-1	200	7-21-67	1990	Highlands Ranch, Colo.
Peterson, Kyle	1	2	5.52	3	2	0	0	15	19	10	9	4	12	.301	R	R	6-3	215	4-9-76	1997	Elkhorn, Neb.
Quevedo, Ruben	4	5	4.61	10	10	0	0	57	56	30	29	30	60	.256	R	R	6-1	245	1-5-79	1996	Valencia, Venez.
Rigdon, Paul	3	5	5.79	15	15	0	0	79	86	52	51	46	49	.286	R	R	6-5	210	11-2-75	1996	Jacksonville, Fla.
Sheets, Ben	11	10	4.76	25	25	1	0	151	166	89	80	48	94	.282	R	R	6-1	195	7-18-78	1999	Baton Rouge, La.
Suzuki, Mac	3	5	5.30	15	9	0	0	56	52	37	33	37	47	.251	R	R	6-3	205	5-31-75	1992	Kobe, Japan
2-team (3 Colorado)	3	7	6.35	18	10	0	0	62	61	49	44	48	52	.260							
Weathers, David	3	4	2.03	52	0	0	4	58	37	14	13	25	46	.187	R	R	6-3	230	9-25-69	1988	Loretto, Tenn.
Wright, Jamey	11	12	4.90	33	33	1	0	195	201	115	106	98	129	.272	R	R	6-5	201	12-24-74	1993	Oklahoma City, Okla.

FIELDING

Catcher	PCT	G	PO	A	E	DP	PB
Blanco	.992	102	645	68	6	9	6
Brown	1.000	16	68	6	0	0	2
Casanova	.991	56	305	25	3	6	2
Levis	.984	11	59	3	1	1	1

First Base	PCT	G	PO	A	E	DP
Echevarria	1.000	10	47	2	0	5
Houston	1.000	3	12	0	0	1
Sexson	.995	158	1356	129	8	126
Sweeney	1.000	2	3	0	0	2

Second Base	PCT	G	PO	A	E	DP
Belliard	.990	96	213	290	5	66
Lopez	1.000	15	24	34	0	7
Loretta	.992	52	115	144	2	31
Pena	.980	11	14	36	1	7

Third Base	PCT	G	PO	A	E	DP
Collier	.914	16	8	24	3	2
Coolbaugh	.971	27	11	23	1	5
Fernandez	.966	13	3	25	1	4

	PCT	G	PO	A	E	DP
Houston	.928	62	30	99	10	11
Lopez	.922	46	30	53	7	9
Loretta	.933	39	16	54	5	0

Shortstop	PCT	G	PO	A	E	DP
Coolbaugh	1.000	3	2	5	0	1
Hernandez	.972	150	204	427	18	90
Lopez	.978	17	16	29	1	5
Loretta	.969	9	11	20	1	4

Outfield	PCT	G	PO	A	E	DP
Burnitz	.981	153	295	13	6	4
Collier	.976	23	40	1	1	0
Echevarria	.931	23	27	0	2	0
Hammonds	.982	46	106	2	2	0
Hernandez	1.000	2	2	0	0	0
Jenkins	.986	104	210	8	3	2
Mouton	.965	53	81	2	3	1
Perez	1.000	1	3	0	0	0
Sanchez	.963	19	24	2	1	0
Sweeney	.968	20	30	0	1	0
White	1.000	100	190	3	0	1

LARRY GOREN

Ben Sheets

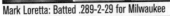
Mark Loretta: Batted .289-2-29 for Milwaukee | Jeromy Burnitz: Batted .251-34-100, but had 150 strikeouts

STEVE MOORE

JOHN WILLIAMSON

FARM SYSTEM

Director, Player Development: Greg Riddoch

Class	Farm Team	League	W	L	Pct.	Finish*	Manager	First Yr.
AAA	Indianapolis (Ind.) Indians	International	66	78	.458	11th (14)	Wendell Kim	2000
AA	Huntsville (Ala.) Stars	Southern	75	63	.543	+4th (10)	Ed Romero	1999
A#	High Desert (Calif.) Mavericks	California	71	69	.507	5th (10)	Frank Kremblas	2001
A	Beloit (Wis.) Snappers	Midwest	67	71	.486	7th (14)	Don Money	1982
Rookie#	Ogden (Utah) Raptors	Pioneer	36	38	.486	6th (8)	Ed Sedar	1996
Rookie	Maryvale (Ariz.) Brewers	Arizona	27	29	.482	4th (7)	Carlos Lezcano	2001

*Finish in overall standings (No. of teams in league)   #Advanced level   +League champion

INDIANAPOLIS

Class AAA

INTERNATIONAL LEAGUE

BATTING	AVG	G	AB	R	H	2B	3B	HR	RBI	BB	SO	SB	CS	SLG	OBP	B	T	HT	WT	DOB	1st Yr	Resides
Barker, Kevin	.189	51	159	12	30	5	0	4	20	20	40	0	0	.296	.282	L	L	6-3	205	7-26-75	1996	Mendota, Va.
Brown, Brant	.201	50	154	22	31	8	1	5	13	12	47	1	2	.364	.272	L	L	6-3	220	6-22-71	1992	Fresno, Calif.
Brown, Kevin	.231	82	290	19	67	16	1	9	34	18	110	0	1	.386	.284	R	R	6-2	215	4-21-73	1994	Mount Vernon, Ind.
Cancel, Robinson	.215	51	172	16	37	5	0	1	18	9	38	0	0	.262	.254	R	R	6-0	195	5-4-76	1994	Lajas, P.R.
Cesar, Dionys	.310	35	129	12	40	11	1	1	17	10	23	1	0	.434	.368	B	R	5-10	155	9-27-76	1994	Santo Domingo, D.R.
Collier, Lou	.288	86	312	48	90	17	2	14	36	24	64	9	3	.490	.350	R	R	5-10	182	8-21-73	1993	Chicago, Ill.
Coolbaugh, Mike	.268	94	347	49	93	24	3	10	50	39	92	3	2	.441	.347	R	R	6-1	185	6-5-72	1990	San Antonio, Texas
Franklin, Micah	.230	110	331	54	76	12	4	23	63	47	73	1	3	.498	.344	B	R	6-0	205	4-25-72	1990	San Francisco, Calif.
Gibralter, Dave	.327	27	98	10	32	9	0	3	17	6	10	0	1	.510	.361	R	R	6-3	224	6-19-75	1993	Duncanville, Texas
Gubanich, Creighton	.181	30	83	6	15	5	0	2	4	4	19	0	0	.313	.227	R	R	6-3	200	3-27-72	1991	Phoenixville, Pa.
Jacobsen, Bucky	.247	86	300	42	74	18	1	12	53	26	78	0	0	.433	.312	R	R	6-4	220	8-30-75	1997	Hermiston, Ore.
Jones, Chris	.283	31	113	20	32	2	1	7	21	9	25	0	0	.504	.339	R	R	6-2	210	11-16-65	1984	Utica, N.Y.
3-team (37 Syr./32 Rich.)	.248	100	315	44	78	8	3	10	40	32	86	7	5	.387	.318							
Klimek, Josh	.260	30	104	13	27	6	0	1	4	10	26	0	0	.346	.330	L	R	6-1	175	2-2-74	1996	St. Louis, Mo.
Lesher, Brian	.283	93	346	51	98	17	4	7	63	40	78	1	1	.416	.356	R	L	6-5	216	3-5-71	1992	Scottsdale, Ariz.
Levis, Jesse	.150	12	40	4	6	1	0	2	7	2	6	0	0	.325	.209	L	R	5-9	200	4-14-68	1989	Elkins Park, Pa.
2-team (67 Rich.)	.272	79	232	22	63	7	0	3	34	26	21	2	0	.341	.352							
Loretta, Mark	.097	8	31	4	3	0	0	0	1	2	4	0	0	.097	.152	R	R	6-0	190	8-14-71	1993	Scottsdale, Ariz.
Mouton, James	.444	2	9	0	4	2	0	0	2	0	2	0	0	.667	.444	R	R	5-9	175	12-29-68	1991	Santo Domingo, D.R.
Pena, Elvis	.240	127	437	56	105	15	3	1	28	30	76	12	5	.295	.300	B	R	5-11	155	9-15-76	1994	Santo Domingo, D.R.
Perez, Robert	.333	20	84	13	28	9	0	3	16	4	11	0	1	.548	.378	R	R	6-3	230	6-4-69	1990	Bolivar, Venez.
2-team (36 Col.)	.326	56	230	33	75	16	3	10	43	8	34	6	6	.552	.361							
Sanchez, Alex	.313	83	335	52	105	14	5	1	26	22	44	27	8	.394	.359	L	L	5-10	180	8-26-76	1996	Miami, Fla.
Scutaro, Marcos	.295	132	495	87	146	29	4	11	50	62	83	11	11	.432	.382	R	R	5-10	170	10-30-75	1995	San Felipe, Venez.
Sell, Chip	.321	17	56	4	18	4	1	0	5	4	14	3	0	.429	.365	L	R	6-2	205	6-19-71	1994	Otis, Ore.
Sweeney, Mark	.287	109	404	65	116	34	1	6	69	56	71	3	1	.421	.373	L	L	6-1	195	10-26-69	1991	Scottsdale, Ariz.

PITCHING	W	L	ERA	G	GS	CG	SV	IP	H	R	ER	BB	SO	AVG	B	T	HT	WT	DOB	1st Yr	Resides
Buddie, Mike	4	1	2.31	27	0	0	3	47	36	13	12	25	31	.215	R	R	6-3	215	12-12-70	1992	Advance, N.C.
Chantres, Carlos	7	11	4.41	28	28	0	0	167	176	93	82	93	87	.273	R	R	6-3	175	4-1-76	1994	Miami, Fla.
Coppinger, Rocky	6	1	1.88	15	5	0	0	48	25	10	10	20	42	.158	R	R	6-5	240	3-19-74	1994	El Paso, Texas
Cunnane, Will	0	1	3.86	7	3	0	1	23	25	10	10	6	25	.277	R	R	6-2	200	4-24-74	1993	Congers, N.Y.
Fordham, Tom	1	2	2.58	18	5	1	0	38	25	15	11	13	35	.182	L	L	6-2	205	2-20-74	1993	El Cajon, Calif.
Fox, Chad	3	0	1.50	4	0	0	0	6	4	1	1	3	8	.190	R	R	6-3	190	9-3-70	1992	Houston, Texas
Gandarillas, Gus	2	2	2.70	28	5	0	1	67	62	30	20	13	52	.248	R	R	6-0	190	7-19-71	1992	Miami, Fla.
2-team (12 Pawtucket)	4	3	2.99	40	5	0	2	81	81	39	27	23	59	.262							
Harikkala, Tim	11	10	4.76	31	27	1	0	172	210	104	91	42	96	.304	R	R	6-2	185	7-15-71	1992	Lake Worth, Fla.
Henry, Butch	3	0	6.00	5	5	1	0	36	39	25	24	9	27	.276	L	L	6-1	205	10-7-68	1987	El Paso, Texas
Kolb, Brandon	3	5	4.28	40	0	0	14	55	49	28	26	22	57	.231	R	R	6-1	190	11-20-73	1995	Lubbock, Texas
Levrault, Allen	2	1	2.64	5	5	0	0	31	22	9	9	8	30	.200	R	R	6-3	230	8-15-77	1996	Westport, Mass.
Mallette, Brian	0	1	1.06	12	0	0	2	17	10	4	2	8	23	.169	R	R	6-0	185	1-19-75	1997	Glenwood, Ga.
Mieses, Jose	0	3	6.08	3	3	0	0	13	23	12	9	7	13	.359	R	R	6-1	180	10-14-79	1997	Santo Domingo, D.R.
Neugebauer, Nick	2	1	1.50	4	4	0	0	24	10	5	4	9	26	.128	R	R	6-3	225	7-15-80	1999	Riverside, Calif.
Painter, Lance	0	0	5.00	8	0	0	0	9	10	5	5	6	7	.294	L	L	6-1	200	7-21-67	1990	Highlands Ranch, Colo.
Penney, Mike	4	3	5.37	22	5	0	1	57	70	38	34	23	35	.309	R	R	6-3	215	3-29-77	1998	Laguna Niguel, Calif.
Peterson, Kyle	2	10	5.71	21	20	0	0	115	143	81	73	26	73	.306	R	R	6-3	215	4-9-76	1997	Elkhorn, Neb.
Rain, Steve	2	2	7.39	25	0	0	1	35	35	34	29	34	34	.251	R	R	6-6	260	6-2-75	1993	Walnut, Calif.
Roberts, Chris	0	0	6.48	5	0	0	0	8	12	6	6	5	5	.363	R	L	6-0	190	6-25-71	1992	Middleburg, Fla.
Serafini, Dan	2	2	5.96	9	4	0	0	23	30	17	15	2	18	.309	B	L	6-1	195	1-25-74	1992	San Bruno, Calif.
2-team (31 Norfolk)	7	4	4.14	40	6	0	1	72	78	35	33	18	56	.274							
Sheets, Ben	1	1	3.38	2	2	0	0	11	14	5	4	3	6	.318	R	R	6-1	195	7-18-78	1999	Baton Rouge, La.
Snyder, John	3	11	5.56	32	23	0	0	147	202	115	91	37	84	.322	R	R	6-3	200	8-16-74	1992	Thousand Oaks, Calif.
Tessmer, Jay	7	5	2.79	35	0	0	4	58	56	23	18	9	39	.250	R	R	6-3	188	12-26-71	1995	Port St. Lucie, Fla.
Williams, Matt	2	2	3.88	51	0	0	0	72	65	33	31	42	45	.241	B	L	6-0	175	4-12-71	1992	Atlanta, Ga.

FIELDING

Catcher	PCT	G	PO	A	E	DP	PB
K. Brown	.992	76	439	45	4	7	3
Cancel	.993	45	262	43	2	6	4
Gubanich	.993	22	135	12	1	3	2
Levis	1.000	11	81	8	0	3	0

First Base	PCT	G	PO	A	E	DP
Barker	1.000	16	150	12	0	13
B. Brown	.997	39	338	18	1	29
Franklin	1.000	3	18	0	0	1
Gibralter	1.000	1	8	2	0	0
Jacobsen	.986	81	661	45	10	56
Lesher	.971	6	32	2	1	8
Sweeney	.985	7	59	7	1	10

Second Base	PCT	G	PO	A	E	DP
Cesar	1.000	2	3	2	0	0
Collier	.986	14	31	37	1	9
Loretta	.714	1	1	4	2	2

	PCT	G	PO	A	E	DP	
Pena	.929	14	25	27	4	6	
Scutaro	.973	122	244	300	15	69	

Third Base	PCT	G	PO	A	E	DP
Cancel	.857	2	0	6	1	0
Cesar	.870	9	6	14	3	2
Collier	.917	6	7	15	2	1
Coolbaugh	.953	79	74	191	13	15
Franklin	.863	30	21	42	10	1
Klimek	.939	18	10	21	2	4
Loretta	1.000	1	0	2	0	0
Pena	.750	3	6	3	3	0
Scutaro	.857	5	3	9	2	1

Shortstop	PCT	G	PO	A	E	DP
Cesar	.974	25	26	48	2	10
Coolbaugh	.987	15	25	50	1	13
Loretta	.909	3	2	8	1	2
Pena	.949	107	161	283	24	54

	PCT	G	PO	A	E	DP
Scutaro	.889	4	4	12	2	2

Outfield	PCT	G	PO	A	E	DP
Barker	1.000	30	64	3	0	0
B. Brown	1.000	7	15	1	0	1
Cesar	.000	1	0	0	1	0
Collier	.981	63	146	8	3	2
Franklin	.988	43	76	3	1	1
Gibralter	1.000	24	49	3	0	1
Jones	.957	30	62	4	3	1
Klimek	.950	11	18	1	1	0
Lesher	.979	78	137	4	3	0
Mouton	1.000	2	4	0	0	0
Perez	.959	20	47	0	2	0
Sanchez	.968	79	178	2	6	0
Sell	.909	16	38	2	4	1
Snyder	.000	1	0	0	0	0
Sweeney	1.000	49	105	0	0	0

HUNTSVILLE

Class AA

SOUTHERN LEAGUE

BATTING	AVG	G	AB	R	H	2B	3B	HR	RBI	BB	SO	SB	CS	SLG	OBP	B	T	HT	WT	DOB	1st Yr	Resides
Barker, Kevin	.323	66	232	42	75	16	1	8	38	35	51	0	2	.504	.410	L	L	6-3	205	7-26-75	1996	Mendota, Va.
Burkhart, Lance	.235	52	170	34	40	10	0	12	38	21	54	0	1	.506	.327	R	R	5-9	220	12-16-74	1997	Florissant, Mo.
Cancel, Robinson	.174	29	86	8	15	2	0	0	5	6	17	0	5	.198	.234	R	R	6-0	195	5-4-76	1994	Lajas, P.R.
Cesar, Dionys	.282	60	227	38	64	12	1	8	31	25	50	4	3	.449	.350	B	R	5-10	155	9-27-76	1994	Santo Domingo, D.R.
Cridland, Mark	.231	70	234	25	54	8	1	7	31	12	56	3	4	.363	.271	L	R	6-3	205	5-15-75	1998	Galveston, Texas
Darula, Bobby	.277	22	65	6	18	2	1	2	7	4	7	1	1	.431	.329	L	R	5-10	175	10-29-74	1996	New York, N.Y.
Deardorff, Jeff	.279	58	201	30	56	11	1	14	43	13	66	1	1	.552	.327	R	R	6-3	226	8-14-78	1997	Clermont, Fla.
DeRosso, Tony	.234	65	218	21	51	17	0	6	25	19	36	0	1	.394	.296	R	R	6-3	226	11-7-75	1994	Moultrie, Ga.
Ernster, Mark	.148	28	81	6	12	4	0	1	4	4	23	0	1	.235	.216	R	R	6-0	190	12-10-77	1999	Glendale, Ariz.
Fox, Jason	.246	90	289	32	71	10	2	3	28	18	74	19	7	.325	.290	B	R	5-8	185	3-30-77	1998	York, Pa.
Gibralter, Dave	.271	95	354	54	96	19	0	13	48	36	48	1	2	.435	.352	R	R	6-3	224	6-19-75	1993	Duncanville, Texas
Hall, Bill	.256	41	160	14	41	8	1	3	14	5	46	5	3	.375	.279	R	R	6-0	175	12-28-79	1998	Nettleton, Miss.
Jacobsen, Bucky	.441	27	93	21	41	9	0	8	28	15	14	1	2	.860	.518	R	R	6-4	220	8-30-75	1997	Hermiston, Ore.
Kirby, Scott	.228	68	184	27	42	13	0	6	23	22	63	3	0	.397	.322	R	R	6-2	190	7-18-77	1996	Lakeland, Fla.
Klimek, Josh	.284	96	310	48	88	12	2	18	51	45	65	2	1	.510	.372	R	R	6-1	175	2-2-74	1996	St. Louis, Mo.
Knox, Ryan	.188	28	96	11	18	2	0	0	4	5	15	8	2	.208	.235	R	R	6-5	185	6-28-77	1999	Peoria, Ill.
Mathis, Jared	.245	87	204	15	50	11	1	2	17	6	25	1	1	.338	.284	R	R	5-10	180	8-8-75	1997	Port Orange, Fla.
Moon, Brian	.157	97	287	17	45	11	2	0	16	20	50	0	2	.209	.216	B	R	6-0	190	7-15-77	1997	Mansfield, Ga.
Pickler, Jeff	.287	134	523	74	150	17	2	0	32	60	51	34	14	.327	.360	L	R	5-10	180	1-6-76	1998	Santa Ana, Calif.
Rushford, Jim	.342	57	187	35	64	16	1	7	30	23	22	3	2	.551	.422	L	L	6-1	225	3-24-74	1996	San Diego, Calif.
Sanchez, Wellington	.226	89	212	28	48	10	0	1	14	22	56	4	3	.288	.299	R	R	6-0	162	5-27-77	1995	Nigua, D.R.

PITCHING	W	L	ERA	G	GS	CG	SV	IP	H	R	ER	BB	SO	AVG	B	T	HT	WT	DOB	1st Yr	Resides
Brownson, Mark	10	5	4.47	24	23	0	0	131	143	67	65	35	115	.273	L	R	6-2	185	6-17-75	1994	Wellington, Fla.
Childers, Jason	7	6	2.87	40	2	0	2	88	76	32	28	30	85	.231	R	R	6-0	165	1-13-75	1997	Douglas, Ga.
Childers, Matt	2	2	3.43	7	7	0	0	39	41	19	15	12	21	.267	R	R	6-5	215	12-3-78	1997	Augusta, Ga.
Coppinger, Rocky	2	0	2.12	16	0	0	4	30	28	9	7	11	24	.254	R	R	6-5	240	3-19-74	1994	El Paso, Texas
D'Amico, Jeff	0	2	0.57	1	1	0	0	7	3	2	2	2	5	.130	R	R	6-7	250	12-27-75	1993	Pinellas Park, Fla.
Davis, Tim	1	2	2.87	28	0	0	2	38	36	15	12	18	32	.255	R	R	6-0	180	1-16-78	1997	Pearson, Ga.
Forster, Scott	1	1	6.23	6	1	0	0	9	18	8	6	7	6	.303	R	L	6-1	185	10-27-71	1994	Flourtown, Pa.
Garcia, Jose	6	5	3.73	21	21	1	0	111	99	52	46	49	84	.239	R	R	6-3	195	4-29-78	1996	Las Vegas, Nev.
High, Andy	2	1	2.12	6	5	0	0	30	22	9	7	6	28	.207	L	L	6-4	220	5-22-74	1996	Fayetteville, N.C.
Jacobs, Ryan	0	1	2.77	10	0	0	0	13	10	6	4	5	15	.196	R	L	6-2	215	2-3-74	1992	Lexington, N.C.
Kimball, Andy	8	6	3.03	48	0	0	2	71	73	32	24	28	39	.266	R	R	6-0	190	8-23-75	1997	Oshkosh, Wis.

PITCHING

PITCHING	W	L	ERA	G	GS	CG	SV	IP	H	R	ER	BB	SO	AVG	B	T	HT	WT	DOB	1st Yr	Resides
Krawczyk, Jack	6	2	3.43	47	0	0	1	81	67	33	31	16	66	.224	R	R	6-4	210	8-12-75	1998	Scottsdale, Ariz.
Lee, Derek	7	11	3.38	28	28	0	0	162	173	76	61	39	109	.269	L	L	6-4	185	8-20-74	1997	Fort Worth, Texas
Mallette, Brian	7	2	1.96	44	0	0	17	55	43	13	12	23	71	.213	R	R	6-0	185	1-19-75	1997	Glenwood, Ga.
Martinez, Luis	0	0	6.75	7	0	0	0	9	13	7	7	9	13	.333	L	L	6-7	225	1-20-80	1997	Boca Chica, D.R.
Mieses, Jose	0	0	2.22	5	4	0	0	24	21	7	6	3	35	.230	R	R	6-1	180	10-14-79	1997	Santo Domingo, D.R.
Myers, Aaron	3	4	3.60	34	7	0	2	70	53	31	28	40	68	.205	R	R	6-2	205	5-14-76	1994	Santa Maria, Calif.
Neugebauer, Nick	5	6	3.46	21	21	1	0	107	94	46	41	52	149	.240	R	R	6-3	225	7-15-80	1999	Riverside, Calif.
Penney, Mike	4	3	3.31	21	5	0	7	49	50	24	18	22	30	.259	R	R	6-1	190	3-29-77	1998	Laguna Niguel, Calif.
Poe, Ryan	1	2	3.86	7	7	0	0	35	30	15	15	7	40	.232	R	R	6-2	220	9-3-77	1998	Mission Viejo, Calif.
Shumate, Jacob	0	1	15.43	8	0	0	0	9	18	17	16	6	10	.428	R	R	6-2	190	1-22-76	1994	Hartsville, S.C.
Sismondo, Bobby	2	1	2.18	8	2	0	1	21	24	9	5	4	16	.292	L	L	6-1	180	11-14-76	1998	Mingo Junction, Ohio
Stull, Everett	1	1	3.86	6	4	0	1	26	21	11	11	5	23	.221	R	R	6-3	200	8-24-71	1992	Stone Mountain, Ga.

FIELDING

Catcher	PCT	G	PO	A	E	DP	PB
Burkhart	.995	30	217	4	1	0	5
Cancel	.991	22	193	25	2	1	2
Mathis	1.000	8	42	3	0	0	0
Moon	.985	94	651	74	11	9	11
First Base	**PCT**	**G**	**PO**	**A**	**E**	**DP**	
Barker	.992	57	471	33	4	35	
Burkhart	1.000	2	13	0	0	3	
Deardorff	.968	7	55	5	2	5	
DeRosso	1.000	2	2	0	0	0	
Gibralter	.998	51	381	30	1	22	
Jacobsen	.984	23	174	11	3	8	
Klimek	1.000	4	20	2	0	3	
Second Base	**PCT**	**G**	**PO**	**A**	**E**	**DP**	
Cesar	1.000	4	8	9	0	1	

	PCT	G	PO	A	E	DP
Mathis	1.000	8	9	9	0	0
Pickler	.979	132	269	326	13	56
Sanchez	1.000	1	2	3	0	1
Third Base	**PCT**	**G**	**PO**	**A**	**E**	**DP**
Burkhart	.750	5	1	5	2	0
Cesar	1.000	1	0	1	0	0
Deardorff	1.000	3	1	1	0	0
DeRosso	.898	61	29	120	17	8
Klimek	.924	51	35	74	9	7
Mathis	.973	15	7	29	1	1
Sanchez	.918	16	8	37	4	5
Shortstop	**PCT**	**G**	**PO**	**A**	**E**	**DP**
Cesar	.947	55	63	151	12	18
Ernster	.903	26	35	49	9	9
Hall	.925	41	60	125	15	18

	PCT	G	PO	A	E	DP
Mathis	1.000	3	1	3	0	1
Sanchez	.931	27	31	50	6	9
Outfield	**PCT**	**G**	**PO**	**A**	**E**	**DP**
Barker	1.000	7	11	1	0	0
Cridland	.982	65	101	9	2	2
Darula	.952	10	20	0	1	0
Deardorff	.973	42	70	1	2	0
Fox	.982	86	165	3	3	0
Gibralter	.987	40	70	4	1	0
Kirby	.971	62	97	2	3	1
Klimek	.889	29	39	1	5	1
Knox	.981	28	51	1	1	0
Mathis	1.000	37	54	2	0	0
Rushford	.989	46	83	3	1	0
Sanchez	.943	21	32	1	2	0

HIGH DESERT — Class A

CALIFORNIA LEAGUE

BATTING	AVG	G	AB	R	H	2B	3B	HR	RBI	BB	SO	SB	CS	SLG	OBP	B	T	HT	WT	DOB	1st Yr	Resides
Alvarado, Joel	.141	22	64	9	9	1	0	1	5	8	12	2	2	.203	.240	R	R	6-2	190	6-30-80	2001	Cayey, P.R.
Burkhart, Lance	.313	65	233	57	73	23	1	20	55	44	58	4	2	.678	.434	R	R	5-9	220	12-16-74	1997	Florissant, Mo.
Ceriani, Matt	.190	25	84	5	16	3	0	1	8	4	22	0	1	.262	.227	R	R	6-2	220	10-9-76	1998	Vacaville, Calif.
Cridland, Mark	.326	12	46	13	15	5	1	3	6	15	4	1	1	.674	.404	L	R	6-3	205	5-15-75	1998	Galveston, Texas
Darula, Bobby	.303	74	254	42	77	10	6	2	39	42	26	15	4	.413	.417	L	L	5-10	175	10-29-74	1996	New York, N.Y.
De la Cruz, Erickson	.304	9	23	4	7	0	0	0	1	0	4	1	1	.304	.333	R	R	5-10	175	12-6-78	1997	Santo Domingo, D.R.
Deardorff, Jeff	.304	69	260	40	79	18	1	15	57	22	70	5	4	.554	.360	R	R	6-3	220	8-14-78	1997	Clermont, Fla.
Foster, Brian	.250	9	28	6	7	3	1	2	5	5	14	1	0	.643	.364	R	R	6-2	205	8-21-81	1999	Burlington, N.C.
Guerrero, Cristian	.312	85	327	50	102	18	2	7	41	18	79	22	11	.443	.349	R	R	6-5	200	4-12-80	1997	Bani, D.R.
Hall, Bill	.303	89	346	61	105	21	6	15	51	22	78	8	9	.529	.348	R	R	6-0	175	12-28-79	1998	Nettleton, Miss.
Johnson, Kade	.254	101	370	57	94	21	1	21	67	35	118	9	2	.486	.336	R	R	6-1	205	9-28-78	1999	Baytown, Texas
Kenney, Jeff	.290	49	169	32	49	12	1	3	21	25	46	8	2	.426	.398	R	R	6-0	185	6-28-77	1998	Peoria, Ill.
Knox, Ryan	.319	75	304	65	97	15	4	29	45	57	37	13	4	.447	.417	R	R	6-1	180	11-7-81	2000	Henderson, Nev.
Krynzel, Dave	.277	89	383	65	106	19	5	5	33	27	122	34	17	.392	.329	L	L	6-1	215	12-8-78	1997	Tempe, Ariz.
Patten, Chris	.226	103	345	42	78	5	1	2	34	35	123	11	5	.264	.317	R	R	6-1	195	3-18-79	1997	Mount Vernon, N.Y.
Rowan, Chris	.222	90	320	45	71	15	5	13	44	12	124	7	3	.422	.268	R	R	6-1	225	3-24-74	1996	San Diego, Calif.
Rushford, Jim	.363	65	259	68	94	22	2	14	61	38	35	3	3	.625	.449	L	L	6-1	225	3-24-74	1996	Duncanville, Texas
Scarborough, Steve	.255	138	546	101	139	36	4	14	91	65	126	21	6	.412	.335	R	R	6-1	210	4-8-79	2001	Granada Hills, Calif.
Scott, Bill	.283	132	513	73	145	42	1	16	102	50	135	9	11	.462	.350	L	L	6-0	175	12-30-81	2000	Jackson, Miss.
Thompson, Zachary	.077	5	13	2	1	0	0	0	1	3	3	0	0	.077	.250	L	L	6-0	175	12-30-81	2000	Jackson, Miss.

GAMES BY POSITION: C—Alvarado 22, Burkhart 49, Ceriani 19, Foster 8, Johnson 52. **1B**—Burkhart 11, Ceriani 3, Darula 5, Deardorff 30, Foster 1, Kenney 4, Patten 11, Rushford 26, Scott 53. **2B**—Kenney 13, Patten 41, Scarborough 90. **3B**—Burkhart 3, Kenney 20, Patten 38, Rowan 85. **SS**—Hall 89, Kenney 3, Scarborough 51. **OF**—Cridland 61, Darula 24, de la Cruz 9, Deardorff 37, Guerrero 84, Johnson 16, Kenney 9, Knox 75, Krynzel 89, Patten 10, Rowan 1, Rushford 38, Scott 32, Thompson 4.

PITCHING	W	L	ERA	G	GS	CG	SV	IP	H	R	ER	BB	SO	AVG	B	T	HT	WT	DOB	1st Yr	Resides
Allen, Rod	4	6	4.37	43	0	0	1	78	72	44	38	28	95	.248	R	R	6-2	205	6-29-74	1996	Lewisburg, W.Va.
Altman, Gene	2	2	7.85	38	0	0	12	39	46	36	34	39	46	.283	R	R	6-7	235	9-1-78	1996	Lynchburg, S.C.
Childers, Matt	6	11	6.44	20	20	0	0	117	155	95	84	29	76	.320	R	R	6-2	215	12-3-78	1997	Augusta, Ga.
Corey, Mike	3	3	4.14	47	0	0	2	76	83	45	35	35	70	.282	R	R	6-2	215	9-29-74	1998	Pendleton, Ore.
Giron, Roberto	3	2	3.27	45	0	0	12	63	64	33	23	20	86	.253	R	R	6-2	190	3-24-76	1994	Miami, Fla.
Huggins, Dave	2	1	6.92	14	9	0	0	53	68	51	41	24	35	.298	R	R	6-0	210	12-12-75	1998	Evansville, Ind.
Lynch, Jim	2	5	6.64	37	8	0	0	85	98	71	63	40	114	.276	R	R	6-7	225	1-20-80	1997	Boca Chica, D.R.
Martinez, Luis	8	9	5.19	22	22	0	0	113	112	67	65	64	121	.262	L	L	6-7	225	12-22-75	1998	South Bend, Ind.
Mathews, Dan	4	3	6.14	36	0	0	1	51	61	38	35	25	59	.293	R	R	6-3	225	12-13-78	1999	Hartsfield, Ga.
Parker, Matt	13	6	4.30	28	28	1	0	161	167	88	77	67	134	.269	R	R	6-3	225	5-24-78	1999	Knoxville, Tenn.
Pember, Dave	9	6	4.82	20	20	0	0	121	135	73	65	35	96	.280	R	R	6-3	195	3-10-78	1994	Puerto Cabello, Venez.
Polanco, Elvis	3	3	4.50	42	0	0	2	84	98	47	42	19	77	.286	R	R	6-4	215	6-2-77	1999	Lake Charles, La.
Robinson, Jeff	2	1	5.56	5	5	0	0	23	20	16	14	15	24	.235	R	R	6-5	215	1-31-76	1995	Mount Vernon, Wash.
Seabury, Jaron	0	1	19.89	3	0	0	0	6	18	17	14	6	5	.461	B	L	6-3	180	6-24-75	1998	Columbus, Ohio
Stafford, Mike	1	1	4.35	24	0	0	0	21	20	10	10	6	17	.243	R	R	6-5	240	10-21-78	1996	Raleigh, N.C.
Stewart, Paul	9	8	5.16	28	27	0	0	152	169	106	87	64	127	.280	R	R	6-3	200	8-24-71	1992	Stone Mountain, Ga.
Stull, Everett	0	1	16.88	1	1	0	0	3	6	5	5	1	1	.428	R	R	6-3	200	8-24-71	1992	Stone Mountain, Ga.

BELOIT — Class A

MIDWEST LEAGUE

BATTING	AVG	G	AB	R	H	2B	3B	HR	RBI	BB	SO	SB	CS	SLG	OBP	B	T	HT	WT	DOB	1st Yr	Resides
Alfonzo, Eliezer	.277	106	397	52	110	28	2	14	48	13	65	0	1	.463	.311	R	R	6-0	170	2-7-79	1996	Puerto la Cruz, Venez.

BATTING	AVG	G	AB	R	H	2B	3B	HR	RBI	BB	SO	SB	CS	SLG	OBP	B	T	HT	WT	DOB	1st Yr	Resides
Ayala, Elio	.265	101	400	65	106	19	2	0	25	34	61	11	2	.323	.331	R	R	5-9	160	11-7-78	1998	Bronx, N.Y.
Belcher, Jason	.326	38	144	23	47	6	0	2	23	15	16	0	1	.410	.394	L	R	6-1	190	1-13-82	2000	Walnut Ridge, Ark.
Brito, Obispo	.224	21	76	5	17	5	0	0	5	1	16	1	0	.289	.250	R	R	6-1	170	3-17-78	1996	Monte Plata, D.R.
Candelaria, Scott	.250	69	256	35	64	11	0	2	27	12	50	3	4	.316	.287	R	R	6-2	190	11-2-78	2000	Albuquerque, N.M.
Ceriani, Matt	.266	22	79	8	21	3	0	1	6	8	16	2	0	.342	.337	R	R	6-2	220	10-9-76	1998	Vacaville, Calif.
Clark, Daryl	.283	133	501	76	142	24	2	21	92	61	135	4	5	.465	.364	L	R	6-2	205	9-25-79	2000	Boalsburg, Pa.
De la Cruz, Erickson	.201	67	224	20	45	8	0	1	14	4	41	3	1	.250	.220	R	R	5-10	175	12-6-78	1997	Santo Domingo, D.R.
De los Santos, Nelson	.196	28	107	9	21	3	0	1	10	2	22	0	2	.252	.209	B	R	5-10	180	10-19-78	1997	San Juan de la Maguana, D.R.
Foster, Brian	.146	36	123	14	18	8	0	4	9	10	55	0	0	.309	.216	R	R	6-2	205	8-21-81	1999	Burlington, N.C.
Garcia, Hector	.265	109	404	43	107	14	2	6	37	9	71	20	6	.354	.283	R	R	6-3	165	12-19-79	1997	Haina, D.R.
Hake, Travis	.200	6	15	2	3	3	0	0	0	3	3	0	0	.400	.333	R	R	6-0	165	8-11-76	2000	Brogue, Pa.
Hammond, Derry	.269	96	360	57	97	23	0	19	73	32	109	2	1	.492	.330	R	R	6-2	205	10-19-79	1998	West Point, Miss.
Houston, Tyler	.000	1	3	0	0	0	0	0	0	0	1	0	0	.000	.000	L	R	6-1	210	1-17-71	1989	Las Vegas, Nev.
Jenkins, Geoff	.333	1	3	1	1	1	0	0	1	1	1	0	0	.667	.500	L	R	6-1	204	7-21-74	1996	Scottsdale, Ariz.
Kenney, Jeff	.212	41	151	21	32	6	0	3	19	26	33	6	3	.311	.355	R	R	5-11	185	9-14-77	1999	Pitman, N.J.
Krynzel, Dave	.305	35	141	22	43	1	1	1	19	9	28	11	5	.348	.364	L	L	6-1	180	11-7-81	2000	Henderson, Nev.
Martinez, Hipolito	.200	7	25	3	5	1	1	1	2	0	13	0	0	.440	.200	R	R	6-1	170	1-30-77	1994	Bani, D.R.
Pregnalato, Bob	.247	81	259	43	64	30	1	0	19	24	57	11	1	.371	.317	R	R	6-0	173	7-5-77	1999	Burlington, Ontario
Serafini, Matt	.105	4	19	2	2	0	0	0	0	0	3	0	0	.105	.105	R	R	6-1	230	3-4-80	2001	Lockport, Ill.
Voltz, Jude	.236	126	462	68	109	18	1	18	69	55	135	3	2	.396	.320	L	L	6-6	215	5-5-78	2000	Metairie, La.
West, Todd	.235	132	408	62	96	14	0	0	40	60	62	16	4	.270	.341	R	R	5-11	165	3-2-79	2000	Highlands Ranch, Colo.
Zoccolillo, Peter	.333	31	123	16	41	8	0	6	23	10	19	0	2	.545	.385	L	R	6-2	205	2-6-77	1999	White Plains, N.Y.

GAMES BY POSITION: C—Alfonzo 55, Belcher 17, Brito 18, Ceriani 21, Foster 29, Pregnalato 2, Serafini 3. **1B**—Garcia 14, Kenney 4, Voltz 124. **2B**—Ayala 80, Candelaria 21, Hake 6, Kenney 34. **3B**—Ayala 10, Candelaria 7, Clark 123, Houston 1. **SS**—Candelaria 6, Kenney 1, West 132. **OF**—Candelaria 16, Clark 1, de la Cruz 65, de los Santos 15, Foster 5, Garcia 97, Hammond 95, Jenkins 1, Krynzel 35, Martinez 4, Pregnalato 75, Zoccolillo 29.

PITCHING	W	L	ERA	G	GS	CG	SV	IP	H	R	ER	BB	SO	AVG	B	T	HT	WT	DOB	1st Yr	Resides
Artieta, Corey	2	1	4.55	26	4	0	0	63	62	40	32	38	36	.261	L	L	6-6	180	10-8-76	1999	Monroe, La.
Cordero, Victor	7	5	4.56	46	0	0	5	81	61	45	41	45	98	.205	R	R	6-1	175	9-7-79	1997	Santo Domingo, D.R.
D'Amico, Jeff	0	0	5.40	2	2	0	0	8	11	6	5	1	6	.305	R	R	6-7	250	12-27-75	1993	Pinellas Park, Fla.
Gordon, Justin	3	4	4.42	27	24	0	0	124	112	83	61	84	103	.244	L	L	6-5	215	5-26-79	1999	Taunton, Mass.
Gray, Rusty	1	0	6.75	7	0	0	0	17	26	13	13	4	7	.376	R	R	6-1	190	9-2-77	2000	Salt Lake City, Utah
Hall, Dan	4	3	4.10	38	0	0	13	53	47	30	24	27	53	.231	R	R	6-3	220	6-18-79	2000	Plymouth, N.C.
Hendrickson, Ben	8	9	2.84	25	25	1	0	133	122	58	42	72	133	.245	R	R	6-3	185	2-4-81	1999	Eden Prairie, Minn.
Lansford, Dustin	1	1	2.16	3	1	0	0	8	3	2	2	10	12	.130	R	R	6-0	165	4-8-80	2000	Baytown, Texas
Leiter, Mark	0	1	2.45	1	0	0	0	4	4	1	1	0	4	.285	R	R	6-3	220	4-13-63	1983	Lanoka Harbor, N.J.
Lugo, Ruddy	1	0	0.60	10	0	0	5	15	10	1	1	6	20	.192	R	R	6-0	190	5-22-80	1999	Brooklyn, N.Y.
Maysonet, Roberto	5	10	4.22	28	17	0	0	111	99	64	52	61	109	.238	R	R	6-0	204	1-16-80	1998	Vega Baja, P.R.
McGee, Chris	4	2	4.19	37	2	0	1	69	69	40	32	34	51	.264	R	R	6-3	215	7-28-77	1999	Laceyville, Pa.
McMurray, Heath	3	0	4.70	9	0	0	0	15	13	9	8	8	20	.228	R	R	6-3	200	5-22-79	2000	Splendora, Texas
Miller, Ryan	10	6	5.30	22	22	0	0	105	100	70	62	47	112	.251	R	R	6-1	200	2-12-78	2000	Newburgh, Ind.
Miniel, Roberto	4	6	4.08	25	16	1	0	104	104	57	47	27	117	.255	R	R	6-4	160	5-12-80	1996	Santo Domingo, D.R.
Pember, Dave	3	4	3.27	8	8	0	0	44	49	20	16	10	39	.284	R	R	6-5	225	5-24-78	1999	Knoxville, Tenn.
Ramos, Luis	0	0	4.50	2	0	0	1	4	4	2	2	2	8	.250	R	R	6-2	210	8-3-77	1999	Tampa, Fla.
Schaub, Greg	0	2	3.70	25	0	0	1	41	37	24	17	24	47	.234	R	R	6-1	185	3-30-77	1995	Oxford, Pa.
Shrout, Kevin	1	1	8.31	6	0	0	0	13	22	13	12	4	11	.379	R	R	6-1	205	12-24-77	2000	Murrysville, Pa.
Shwam, Mike	9	3	2.60	47	0	0	9	93	75	36	27	31	97	.219	R	R	6-2	200	12-22-77	2000	Huntington Beach, Calif.
Smart, Pete	0	8	3.07	11	11	0	0	70	64	30	24	24	47	.246	R	L	6-7	200	11-22-77	2001	Lawrence, Kan.
Wagner, Frank	0	1	21.60	8	0	0	0	8	18	20	20	13	8	.428	L	L	6-2	230	9-25-77	1999	Colstrip, Mont.
Wallace, Ben	1	4	9.55	8	6	0	0	27	44	32	29	14	15	.376	L	L	6-3	200	2-18-81	1999	Hubbardston, Mass.

OGDEN — Rookie

PIONEER LEAGUE

BATTING	AVG	G	AB	R	H	2B	3B	HR	RBI	BB	SO	SB	CS	SLG	OBP	B	T	HT	WT	DOB	1st Yr	Resides
Alvarado, Joel	.192	18	52	5	10	0	0	0	3	3	5	0	1	.192	.250	R	R	6-2	190	6-30-80	2001	Cayey, P.R.
Barnwell, Chris	.307	69	261	49	80	19	5	0	37	7	28	17	2	.418	.337	R	R	5-10	180	3-1-79	2001	Jacksonville, Fla.
Boyd, Dan	.357	5	14	1	5	1	0	0	1	1	1	0	0	.429	.400	R	R	5-11	190	9-28-78	2001	Dade City, Fla.
Carrow, Tom	.331	45	157	37	52	7	0	5	20	33	34	7	3	.471	.454	R	R	6-2	185	7-31-80	2001	Lutz, Fla.
Esparragoza, Pedro	.000	1	1	0	0	0	0	0	0	0	1	0	0	.000	.000	R	R	5-11	165	3-16-82	1999	Caracas, Venez.
Eure, Jeff	.215	50	144	16	31	7	0	3	24	7	41	6	2	.326	.278	R	R	6-1	200	8-17-80	2001	Pillow, Pa.
Gemoll, Brandon	.308	6	13	1	4	0	0	0	0	1	2	0	1	.308	.357	L	L	6-3	210	9-15-80	2001	San Jose, Calif.
Haggard, Chris	.193	34	83	14	16	0	0	2	12	19	28	1	0	.265	.373	R	R	6-1	190	11-10-78	2001	Tulsa, Okla.
Hardy, J.J.	.248	35	125	20	31	5	0	2	15	15	12	1	2	.336	.326	R	R	6-1	170	8-19-82	2001	Tucson, Ariz.
Hart, Jon	.340	69	262	53	89	18	1	11	62	26	47	14	1	.542	.395	R	R	6-6	190	3-24-82	2000	Bowling Green, Ky.
Hicks, Brian	.233	28	103	17	24	10	2	1	12	9	24	1	1	.398	.295	L	R	6-3	195	6-28-82	2000	Natchitoches, La.
Hinton, Travis	.277	69	235	44	65	17	0	8	41	29	58	3	4	.451	.349	L	L	6-1	215	11-21-80	2001	Phoenix, Ariz.
January, Javerro	.263	11	19	6	5	1	1	0	3	2	6	0	0	.421	.364	R	R	6-1	185	10-31-80	1999	Jackson, Miss.
Mayo, Terry	.235	8	17	3	4	2	0	0	1	3	8	0	1	.353	.333	R	R	6-4	210	7-1-81	1999	Greensboro, N.C.
McClanahan, Jonah	.296	26	98	17	29	5	3	0	8	2	13	2	0	.408	.317	R	R	6-2	195	3-25-81	2000	Monterey, Calif.
Nelson, Brad	.262	13	42	5	11	4	0	0	10	3	9	0	0	.357	.298	L	R	6-2	220	12-23-82	2001	Algona, Iowa
Parrott, Corry	.197	31	71	9	14	1	1	0	3	3	17	1	1	.239	.230	R	R	6-1	190	7-4-79	2001	Burbank, Calif.
Santana, Ralph	.337	68	261	57	88	6	1	1	26	37	37	30	12	.379	.425	L	R	6-1	170	9-30-80	2001	Orlando, Fla.
Serafini, Matt	.161	20	62	6	10	1	0	2	4	4	8	1	0	.274	.212	R	R	6-1	230	3-4-80	2001	Lockport, Ill.
Soriano, Carlos	.308	60	224	39	69	15	2	7	43	20	77	18	6	.487	.364	R	R	5-11	170	9-19-79	1997	San Cristobal, D.R.
Torres, Erik	.172	20	58	9	10	3	0	0	4	4	16	0	2	.224	.226	R	R	6-0	180	11-6-78	2001	Tucson, Ariz.
Villanueva, Florian	.308	68	273	52	84	21	2	6	53	18	27	5	3	.465	.358	R	R	6-2	155	10-5-80	1997	Santo Domingo, D.R.

GAMES BY POSITION: C—Alvarado 16, Esparragoza 1, Eure 9, Haggard 34, Serafini 16, Soriano 1, Villanueva 17. **1B**—Gemoll 2, Hart 65, Hinton 10, Nelson 2. **2B**—Barnwell 2, Santana 60, Torres 16, Villanueva 1. **3B**—Barnwell 32, Eure 14, Torres 3, Villanueva 30. **SS**—Barnwell 35, Hardy 35, Santana 6. **OF**—Boyd 4, Carrow 35, Eure 16, Hart 3, Hicks 28, Hinton 37, January 11, Mayo 7, McClanahan 25, Parrott 25, Soriano 42, Villanueva 15.

PITCHING	W	L	ERA	G	GS	CG	SV	IP	H	R	ER	BB	SO	AVG	B	T	HT	WT	DOB	1st Yr	Resides
Adams, Jon	2	2	2.81	23	0	0	12	32	26	10	10	6	44	.220	R	R	6-5	185	7-29-78	2001	Sinton, Texas
Artman, Dane	0	3	15.88	6	3	0	0	11	21	22	20	8	10	.396	L	L	6-3	215	6-3-82	2000	Key West, Fla.
Castillo, Geraldo	6	4	4.35	15	10	0	0	68	77	42	33	11	49	.275	R	R	6-3	175	4-5-82	1999	Boca Chica, D.R.

PITCHING	W	L	ERA	G	GS	CG	SV	IP	H	R	ER	BB	SO	AVG	B	T	HT	WT	DOB	1st Yr	Resides
DeSalme, Gene	0	0	5.02	8	0	0	0	14	15	11	8	14	16	.263	L	L	6-5	215	9-14-79	2001	Rolla, Mo.
Gold, J.M.	1	1	2.17	7	7	0	0	29	20	12	7	9	42	.192	R	R	6-5	220	4-18-80	1998	Toms River, N.J.
Horne, Travis	0	0	6.75	4	0	0	0	11	11	9	8	8	11	.282	L	L	6-4	240	4-16-81	1999	Jacksonville, Fla.
Huggins, Rusty	0	0	3.55	10	0	0	0	13	18	6	5	2	6	.346	L	L	6-2	205	6-17-80	2001	Pooler, Ga.
Jones, Mike	4	1	3.74	9	7	0	0	34	29	17	14	10	32	.235	R	R	6-4	200	4-23-83	2001	Phoenix, Ariz.
Kolb, Dan	4	0	7.12	16	2	0	0	43	53	35	34	13	33	.000	R	R	6-1	190	6-5-80	2001	Palmetto, Fla.
McMurray, Heath	2	3	3.28	10	0	0	1	25	24	14	9	7	24	.263	R	R	6-3	200	5-22-79	2000	Splendora, Texas
Mieses, Jose	0	1	27.00	1	1	0	0	1	3	3	3	1	2	.500	R	R	6-1	180	10-14-79	1997	Santo Domingo, D.R.
Nolasco, Dave	3	3	4.43	20	2	0	2	43	38	27	21	14	35	.231	R	R	6-2	200	4-3-79	2001	Rialto, Calif.
Nunez, Severino	0	0	2.00	7	0	0	0	9	3	2	2	3	12	.107	L	L	6-2	160	11-8-80	1997	Santo Domingo, D.R.
Ramos, Luis	2	3	8.87	15	0	0	0	23	31	26	23	7	25	.306	R	R	6-2	210	8-3-77	1999	Tampa, Fla.
Richardson, Judd	0	1	5.00	5	0	0	0	18	23	12	10	2	18	.328	L	R	6-4	200	2-13-80	2001	Caledon, Ontario
Saenz, Chris	3	1	4.24	21	4	0	0	47	43	25	22	14	48	.251	R	R	6-3	205	8-14-81	2001	Tucson, Ariz.
Sarfate, Dennis	1	2	4.63	9	4	0	1	23	20	13	12	10	32	.229	R	R	6-4	210	4-9-81	2000	Chandler, Ariz.
Shorey, Jeremy	3	2	5.53	22	1	0	1	41	47	32	25	16	30	.291	R	R	6-4	210	12-7-80	2001	Lisbon, Maine
Smart, Pete	1	0	3.78	4	2	0	0	17	18	9	7	2	11	.268	R	L	6-7	200	11-22-77	2001	Lawrence, Kan.
Steitz, Jon	2	4	6.68	11	10	0	0	34	44	32	25	25	28	.314	R	R	6-3	205	9-5-80	2001	Stoney Creek, Conn.
Wallace, Ben	0	3	7.29	13	8	0	0	46	64	43	37	23	33	.329	L	L	6-3	200	2-18-81	1999	Hubbardston, Mass.
Yeatman, Matt	2	4	4.95	13	8	0	1	60	72	40	33	27	61	.301	R	R	6-4	200	8-2-82	2000	Tomball, Texas

MARYVALE · Rookie

ARIZONA LEAGUE

BATTING	AVG	G	AB	R	H	2B	3B	HR	RBI	BB	SO	SB	CS	SLG	OBP	B	T	HT	WT	DOB	1st Yr	Resides
Bell, Paul	.292	18	65	13	19	2	0	0	9	3	12	1	0	.323	.352	R	R	5-10	170	6-24-80	2000	Capetown, South Africa
Chavez, Ozzie	.305	52	210	38	64	12	6	0	27	13	36	9	8	.419	.346	B	R	6-1	155	7-31-83	1999	Villa Mella, D.R.
De los Santos, Nelson	.253	26	95	15	24	8	3	1	15	11	15	1	0	.411	.327	B	R	5-10	185	8-16-82	1999	San Juan de la Maguana, D.R.
Esparragoza, Pedro	.242	48	153	25	37	5	1	2	22	16	39	4	1	.327	.339	R	R	5-11	165	3-16-82	1999	Caracas, Venez.
Franke, Michael	.151	26	86	8	13	4	0	0	5	5	34	4	0	.198	.213	R	R	6-2	185	9-22-81	2001	Straussberg, Germany
Gelotti, Matt	.167	4	18	0	3	0	1	0	4	1	4	0	0	.278	.211	R	R	5-10	185	10-19-76	2000	Houston, Texas
Gemoll, Brandon	.323	8	31	8	10	2	1	0	9	3	7	0	0	.452	.361	L	L	6-3	210	9-15-80	2001	San Jose, Calif.
Hammonds, Jeffrey	.333	1	3	0	1	0	0	0	0	0	0	0	0	.333	.333	R	R	6-0	200	3-5-71	1992	Scotch Plains, N.J.
Hardy, J.J.	.250	5	20	6	5	2	1	0	1	1	2	0	0	.450	.286	R	R	6-1	170	8-19-82	2001	Tucson, Ariz.
Hicks, Brian	.222	15	54	5	12	3	0	0	6	1	18	0	0	.278	.311	L	R	6-3	195	6-28-82	2000	Natchitoches, La.
January, Javerro	.284	38	134	27	38	6	1	0	10	13	42	5	5	.343	.370	R	R	5-11	195	1-6-79	2001	Temple, Texas
Martin, Craig	.224	21	76	6	17	3	0	0	7	9	21	0	0	.289	.314	R	R	6-4	210	7-1-81	1999	Greensboro, N.C.
Mayo, Terry	.213	18	61	4	13	1	2	1	6	3	31	0	1	.344	.275	R	R	6-2	190	10-20-82	2001	Palm Harbor, Fla.
McCormack, Taylor	.198	36	131	15	26	4	1	0	18	13	48	1	0	.244	.279	R	R	6-2	220	12-23-82	2001	Algona, Iowa
Nelson, Brad	.302	17	63	10	19	6	1	0	13	8	18	0	0	.429	.392	L	R	6-2	160	1-11-82	1999	San Cristobal, D.R.
Nova, Willian	.213	25	80	7	17	2	1	1	8	7	22	2	0	.300	.270	B	R	6-1	190	7-4-79	2001	Burbank, Calif.
Parrott, Corry	.250	4	12	1	3	0	0	0	0	3	3	0	0	.250	.400	R	R	6-2	155	6-19-84	2000	Baranita, Venez.
Plasencia, Francisco	.270	49	200	38	54	7	1	0	19	31	46	10	4	.315	.368	L	L	6-0	165	7-7-82	2000	Portuguesa, Venez.
Ramirez, Manuel	.303	46	175	27	53	17	4	5	30	12	20	0	2	.531	.356	R	R	6-1	230	3-4-80	2001	Lockport, Ill.
Serafini, Matt	.351	20	74	16	26	6	0	7	24	6	19	0	0	.716	.390	L	L	6-0	175	12-30-81	2000	Jackson, Miss.
Thompson, Zachary	.194	22	67	7	13	1	0	0	3	10	32	1	1	.209	.341	L	L	6-0	180	11-6-78	2001	Tucson, Ariz.
Torres, Erik	.000	1	3	0	0	0	0	0	0	0	0	0	0	.000	.250	R	R	6-0	176	11-6-78	2001	Tucson, Ariz.
Viera, Orlando	.265	27	83	8	22	2	1	0	4	6	27	1	1	.313	.319	L	L	6-0	175	14-83	2001	Gurabo, P.R.

GAMES BY POSITION: C—Bell 1, Esparragoza 40, M. Ramirez 18, Serafini 4. **1B**—de los Santos 13, Esparragoza 2, Franke 3, Gemoll 6, Nelson 17, M. Ramirez 1. **2B**—Bell 3, Chavez 4, de los Santos 3, Martin 21, Nova 23, Torres 1. **3B**—Bell 4, Franke 19, McCormack 33, M. Ramirez 1. **SS**—Bell 4, Chavez 48, Hardy 5, Nova 1. **OF**—de los Santos 12, Esparragoza 1, Franke 1, Gelotti 4, Gemoll 1, Hammonds 1, Hicks 10, January 37, Mayo 18, Nova 2, Parrott 2, Plasencia 49, Thompson 16, Viera 25.

PITCHING	W	L	ERA	G	GS	CG	SV	IP	H	R	ER	BB	SO	AVG	B	T	HT	WT	DOB	1st Yr	Resides
Artman, Dane	0	1	5.84	5	5	0	0	12	15	8	8	5	14	.300	L	L	6-3	215	6-3-82	2000	Key West, Fla.
Batista, Cristian	0	1	5.06	13	0	0	0	21	26	24	12	10	16	.282	R	R	6-7	190	4-27-81	1998	San Cristobal, D.R.
Carpenter, Calvin	3	3	4.06	11	10	0	0	38	39	24	17	22	29	.274	R	R	6-2	195	9-23-82	2001	Natchitoches, La.
Chirinos, Jesus	5	3	4.08	11	7	0	0	53	56	31	24	11	36	.265	R	R	6-0	175	1-14-82	1998	Bachaquero, Venez.
Correa, Alexander	1	0	5.85	12	3	0	0	32	42	23	21	13	29	.328	L	L	6-4	170	7-17-82	1999	Chaguarama, Venez.
De la Rosa, Felix	0	1	5.17	6	0	0	0	16	20	10	9	7	5	.338	R	R	6-3	185	8-2-81	2001	Lake Forest, Calif.
Gelatka, Todd	0	0	6.75	1	0	0	0	1	2	1	1	0	1	.333	L	R	6-3	190	11-2-82	2001	Louisville, Ky.
Gittings, Chris	1	1	7.71	6	3	0	0	12	15	10	10	1	12	.319	R	R	6-5	220	4-18-80	1998	Toms River, N.J.
Gold, J.M.	0	1	7.56	4	4	0	0	8	17	7	7	2	7	.447	R	R	6-2	185	5-21-81	2000	Crawford, Australia
Michaels, Carl	2	1	3.57	9	0	0	0	18	23	7	7	3	10	.333	R	R	6-1	180	10-14-79	1997	Santo Domingo, D.R.
Mieses, Jose	1	1	0.00	2	2	0	0	4	3	1	0	1	5	.166	R	R	6-5	210	5-29-83	2001	Apopka, Fla.
Moreira, Greg	1	1	4.91	4	0	0	0	15	17	10	8	1	11	.227	R	R	6-2	195	9-8-81	2000	Sanford, Fla.
Nielsen, Brian	1	1	3.70	7	6	0	0	24	21	12	10	5	21	.223	L	L	6-4	158	4-3-83	2000	Oviedo, Fla.
Nova, Wander	4	1	5.64	16	0	0	0	22	32	15	14	9	10	.355	L	L	6-2	160	11-8-80	1997	Santo Domingo, D.R.
Nunez, Severino	0	0	4.70	9	0	0	0	15	11	8	8	4	19	.180	L	L	6-2	160	11-8-80	1997	Santo Domingo, D.R.
Oakes, Gerry	2	4	2.85	12	7	0	0	54	50	24	17	25	44	.251	L	R	6-4	175	4-29-82	2000	Upper Darby, Pa.
Pena, Luismar	3	4	4.63	11	2	0	0	35	42	23	18	13	20	.300	R	R	6-4	230	4-14-79	2001	Monroe, N.C.
Price, Jon	0	0	12.00	2	0	0	0	3	4	4	4	1	0	.307	R	R	6-3	165	8-12-84	2001	Azua, D.R.
Ramirez, Carlos	2	2	4.66	11	2	0	0	37	43	22	19	9	25	.296	L	L	6-3	165	7-28-81	1998	Barinas, Venez.
Rodriguez, Ken	0	1	1.15	8	0	0	1	16	16	3	2	8	12	.275	R	R	6-2	160	8-14-81	2001	Marietta, Ga.
Sheffield, Aaron	1	1	7.82	8	0	0	0	13	14	12	11	7	11	.311	R	R	6-3	215	8-14-81	2001	Eugene, Ore.
Stavros, Tony	0	1	0.61	5	0	0	0	15	13	2	1	3	11	.250	R	R	6-3	200	8-7-80	2001	Stone Mountain, Ga.
Stull, Everett	0	0	0.00	2	1	0	0	4	2	0	0	0	4	.125	R	R	6-3	200	8-24-71	1992	Stone Mountain, Ga.
Trytten, Ryan	2	0	3.96	18	0	0	6	25	23	12	11	11	21	.234	R	R	6-3	204	5-10-81	2001	Agency, Iowa

BY JOHN MILLEA

For the first time since 1992, the Twins experienced the lofty air of first place in the American League Central for a significant portion of the season. They eventually ended up in second at 85-77, despite again having the lowest payroll in the league.

That showing provides reason for optimism for 2002, but for the first time since 1986, Tom Kelly won't be the manager.

Five days after the Twins' finest season in nearly a decade came to an end, Kelly announced he was stepping down. He had the longest tenure of any head coach in Major League Baseball, the NBA, NFL or NHL.

Kelly was on a one-year contract and was expected to continue to play a role in the organization in an undefined capacity. Regardless, the future of the Twins appeared solid.

They were 55-32 at the all-star break and enjoyed a five-game lead over Cleveland. A second-half fade took some of the luster off the season—the Twins went only 29-45 after the break and finished seven games behind the Indians—but positive signs abounded.

Starting pitchers Joe Mays, Eric Milton and Brad Radke all won at least 15 games. The Twins hadn't had three starters accomplish that since 1991, when they won the World Series. Third baseman Corey Koskie also had a strong season and became the first Twins player to drive in 100 runs since 1996.

The experience gained by a young team in a pennant race might have been the biggest story of the 2001 season. The Twins were 18-6 in April and 16-11 in May, lending a Cinderella air to the Metrodome for a few short weeks. The Twins won just five of 19 games with Cleveland but were still 47-29 in the division.

Still, questions remain about the future. The Twins need to shore up their bullpen and find some power-hitting outfielders.

Closer LaTroy Hawkins finished the year with 28 saves, but he struggled badly during the second half, ending

Corey Koskie | Michael Cuddyer

RODGER WOOD

PLAYERS OF THE YEAR

MAJOR LEAGUE: Corey Koskie, 3b

Koskie put everything together for the Twins in 2001, hitting 26 home runs, stealing 27 bases and driving in 103 runs. He became the first American League third baseman with 20 homers, 100 RBIs and 20 stolen bases in a season.

MINOR LEAGUE: Michael Cuddyer, 3b

Cuddyer saw action at three positions in 2001 and set across-the-board career highs on offense. He hit .301-30-87 in 509 at-bats at Double-A New Britain.

with a 5.72 ERA. Injuries also played a role in the Twins' fade. Shortstop Cristian Guzman, a first-time all-star, was sidelined because of a shoulder problem and David Ortiz sustained a broken wrist.

General manager Terry Ryan made two trades before the July 31 deadline, picking up starter Rick Reed and reliever Todd Jones. Neither of them contributed much. The bigger downside of the trades was that the Twins gave up Matt Lawton to the Mets but never replaced his bat in right field.

That was expected to be one of Ryan's main tasks during the offseason. If owner Carl Pohlad continues to loosen the pursestrings, Ryan is hopeful of finding the right guy.

The nucleus—first baseman Doug Mientkiewicz, second baseman Luis Rivas, shortstop Guzman, third baseman Koskie, center fielder Torii Hunter and catcher A.J. Pierzynski—will be back, as will Radke, Milton and Mays. Jones and reliever Hector Carrasco were the team's only free agents, and both could end up elsewhere in 2002.

In the minors, the New Britain Rock Cats were the flagship franchise in the Twins system in 2001. The Rock Cats had the Double-A Eastern League's best record and shared the EL title with Reading after the terrorist attacks of Sept. 11 forced cancellation of the championship series.

Rookie-level Elizabethton had the best record in the Rookie-level Appalachian League, but lost to Bluefield 2-1 in the best-of-three playoffs. The team featured catcher Joe Mauer, the No. 1 pick in the 2001 draft and a product of St. Paul's Cretin-Derham Hall. Mauer signed for $5.15 million and played with his older brother Jake, drafted by Minnesota in the 23rd round. The younger Mauer hit .400-0-14 and was voted the Appalachian League's No. 1 prospect.

ORGANIZATION LEADERS

BATTING

*AVG	Quinton McCracken, Edmonton	.338
R	Michael Cuddyer, New Britain	95
H	Dustan Mohr, New Britain	174
TB	Dustan Mohr, New Britain	293
2B	Dustan Mohr, New Britain	41
3B	Nestor Smith, New Britain	8
HR	Michael Cuddyer, New Britain	30
RBI	Justin Morneau, New Britain/Fort Myers/Quad City	97
BB	Luis Rodriguez, Fort Myers	82
SO	Mike Restovich, New Britain	125
SB	Rafael Boitel, Quad City	36

PITCHING

W	Juan Rincon, New Britain	14
L	Brent Schoening, New Britain/Fort Myers	15
#ERA	Kevin Frederick, New Britain/Fort Myers	1.52
G	Juan Padilla, Fort Myers	56
CG	Six tied at	2
SV	Henry Bonilla, Quad City	25
IP	Matt Kinney, Edmonton	162
BB	Matt Kinney, Edmonton	74
SO	Matt Kinney, Edmonton	146

*Minimum 250 At-Bats #Minimum 75 Innings

MINNESOTA TWINS

Manager: Tom Kelly

2001 Record: 85-77, .525 (2nd, AL Central)

BATTING	AVG	G	AB	R	H	2B	3B	HR	RBI	BB	SO	SB	CS	SLG	OBP	B	T	HT	WT	DOB	1st Yr	Resides
Allen, Chad	.263	57	175	20	46	13	2	4	20	19	37	1	2	.429	.333	R	R	6-1	195	2-6-75	1996	Dallas, Texas
Barnes, John	.048	9	21	1	1	0	0	0	0	1	3	0	0	.048	.130	R	R	6-2	205	4-24-76	1996	El Cajon, Calif.
Blake, Casey	.318	13	22	1	7	1	0	0	2	3	8	1	0	.364	.400	R	R	6-2	205	8-23-73	1996	Indianola, Iowa
Buchanan, Brian	.274	69	197	28	54	12	0	10	32	19	58	1	1	.487	.342	R	R	6-4	230	7-21-73	1994	Fort Myers, Fla.
Cuddyer, Michael	.222	8	18	1	4	2	0	0	1	2	6	1	0	.333	.300	R	R	6-2	202	3-27-79	1997	Chesapeake, Va.
Guzman, Cristian	.302	118	493	80	149	28	14	10	51	21	78	25	8	.477	.337	B	R	6-0	195	3-21-78	1995	Santo Domingo, D.R.
Hocking, Denny	.251	112	327	34	82	16	2	3	25	29	67	6	1	.339	.315	B	R	5-10	183	4-2-70	1989	Tustin, Calif.
Hunter, Torii	.261	148	564	82	147	32	5	27	92	29	125	9	6	.479	.306	R	R	6-2	205	7-18-75	1993	Pine Bluff, Ark.
Jones, Jacque	.276	149	475	57	131	25	0	14	49	39	92	12	9	.417	.335	L	L	5-10	176	4-25-75	1996	San Diego, Calif.
Kielty, Bobby	.250	37	104	8	26	8	0	2	14	8	25	3	0	.385	.297	B	R	6-1	215	8-5-76	1999	Fort Myers, Fla.
Koskie, Corey	.276	153	562	100	155	37	2	26	103	68	118	27	6	.488	.362	L	R	6-3	217	6-28-73	1994	White Rock, B.C.
Lawton, Matt	.293	103	376	71	110	25	0	10	51	63	46	19	6	.439	.396	L	R	5-10	186	11-3-71	1991	Saucier, Miss.
LeCroy, Matthew	.425	15	40	6	17	5	0	3	12	0	8	0	1	.775	.429	R	R	6-2	225	12-13-75	1997	Belton, S.C.
Maxwell, Jason	.191	39	68	4	13	4	0	1	10	9	23	2	0	.294	.286	R	R	6-1	180	3-26-72	1993	Lewisburg, Tenn.
McCracken, Quinton	.219	24	64	7	14	2	2	0	3	5	13	0	1	.313	.275	B	R	5-7	173	3-16-70	1992	Scottsdale, Ariz.
Mientkiewicz, Doug	.306	151	543	77	166	39	1	15	74	67	92	2	6	.464	.387	L	R	6-2	200	6-19-74	1995	Miami, Fla.
Mohr, Dustan	.235	20	51	6	12	2	0	0	4	5	17	1	1	.275	.298	R	R	6-2	210	6-19-76	1997	Hattiesburg, Miss.
Ortiz, David	.234	89	303	46	71	17	1	18	48	40	68	1	0	.475	.324	L	L	6-4	230	11-18-75	1993	Haina, D.R.
Pierzynski, A.J.	.289	114	381	51	110	33	2	7	55	16	57	1	7	.441	.322	L	R	6-3	220	12-30-76	1994	Jacksonville, Fla.
Prince, Tom	.219	64	196	19	43	4	1	7	23	12	39	3	1	.357	.284	R	R	5-11	206	8-13-64	1984	Bradenton, Fla.
Rivas, Luis	.266	153	563	70	150	21	6	7	47	40	99	31	11	.362	.319	R	R	5-11	175	8-30-79	1995	La Guaira, Venez.

PITCHING	W	L	ERA	G	GS	CG	SV	IP	H	R	ER	BB	SO	AVG	B	T	HT	WT	DOB	1st Yr	Resides
Balfour, Grant	0	0	13.50	2	0	0	0	3	3	4	4	3	2	.333	R	R	6-2	170	12-30-77	1997	Sydney, Australia
Carrasco, Hector	4	3	4.64	56	0	0	1	74	77	40	38	30	70	.276	R	R	6-2	220	10-22-69	1988	San Pedro de Macoris, D.R.
Cressend, Jack	3	2	3.67	44	0	0	0	56	50	24	23	16	40	.236	R	R	6-1	185	5-13-75	1996	Covington, La.
Duvall, Mike	0	0	7.71	8	0	0	0	5	7	4	4	2	4	.368	R	L	6-0	200	10-11-74	1995	Windham, Maine
Fiore, Tony	0	1	5.68	4	0	0	0	6	5	4	4	2	5	.208	R	R	6-1	210	10-12-71	1992	Chicago, Ill.
2-team (3 Tampa Bay)	0	1	5.59	7	0	0	0	10	9	6	6	3	8	.243							
Guardado, Eddie	7	1	3.51	67	0	0	12	67	47	27	26	23	67	.197	R	L	6-0	194	10-2-70	1990	Stockton, Calif.
Hawkins, LaTroy	1	5	5.96	62	0	0	28	51	59	34	34	39	36	.290	R	R	6-5	204	12-21-72	1991	Frisco, Texas
Johnson, Adam	1	2	8.28	7	4	0	0	25	32	25	23	13	17	.323	R	R	6-2	210	7-12-79	2000	Fort Myers, Fla.
Jones, Todd	1	0	3.26	24	0	0	2	19	27	8	7	7	15	.333	R	R	6-3	230	4-24-68	1989	Pell City, Ala.
2-team (45 Detroit)	5	5	4.24	69	0	0	13	68	87	39	32	29	54	.311							
Lohse, Kyle	4	7	5.68	19	16	0	0	90	102	60	57	29	64	.284	R	R	6-2	190	10-4-78	1997	Glenn, Calif.
Mays, Joe	17	13	3.16	34	34	4	0	234	205	87	82	64	123	.235	B	R	6-1	185	12-10-75	1995	Sarasota, Fla.
Miller, Travis	1	4	4.81	45	0	0	0	49	54	30	26	20	30	.282	R	L	6-3	215	11-2-72	1994	Eaton, Ohio
Milton, Eric	15	7	4.32	35	34	2	0	221	222	109	106	61	157	.256	L	L	6-3	220	8-4-75	1996	Fort Myers, Fla.
Radke, Brad	15	11	3.94	33	33	6	0	226	235	105	99	26	137	.271	R	R	6-2	188	10-27-72	1991	Largo, Fla.
Redman, Mark	2	4	4.22	9	9	0	0	49	57	26	23	19	29	.286	L	L	6-5	220	1-5-74	1995	Catoosa, Okla.
Reed, Rick	4	6	5.19	12	12	0	0	68	92	45	39	14	43	.325	R	R	6-1	195	8-16-65	1986	Proctorville, Ohio
Rincon, Juan	0	0	6.35	4	0	0	0	6	7	5	4	5	4	.318	R	R	5-11	190	1-23-79	1996	Maracaibo, Venez.
Romero, J.C.	1	4	6.23	14	11	0	0	65	71	48	45	24	39	.277	B	L	5-11	195	6-4-76	1997	San Juan, P.R.
Santana, Johan	1	0	4.74	15	4	0	0	44	50	25	23	16	28	.292	L	L	6-0	195	3-13-79	1996	Tovar, Venez.
Thomas, Brad	0	2	9.37	5	5	0	0	16	20	17	17	14	6	.303	L	L	6-4	220	10-27-77	1995	Sydney, Australia
Wells, Bob	8	5	5.11	65	0	0	2	69	72	39	39	18	49	.272	R	R	6-0	200	11-1-66	1989	Cowiche, Wash.

FIELDING

Catcher	PCT	G	PO	A	E	DP	PB
LeCroy	1.000	3	6	1	0	0	0
Pierzynski	.985	110	611	44	10	7	4
Prince	1.000	64	380	41	0	3	0

First Base	PCT	G	PO	A	E	DP
Blake	1.000	3	15	2	0	1
Cuddyer	.975	5	37	2	1	4
Hocking	1.000	11	47	6	0	3
LeCroy	1.000	2	4	0	0	0
Mientkiewicz	.997	148	1263	69	4	95
Ortiz	1.000	8	60	2	0	2

Second Base	PCT	G	PO	A	E	DP
Hocking	.979	17	23	24	1	6
Maxwell	1.000	9	4	17	0	0
Rivas	.974	150	230	335	15	65

Third Base	PCT	G	PO	A	E	DP
Cuddyer	.000	2	0	0	0	0
Hocking	.900	6	1	8	1	0

Koskie	.964	150	95	306	15	19
Maxwell	1.000	11	8	17	0	1

Shortstop	PCT	G	PO	A	E	DP
Guzman	.959	118	165	327	21	58
Hocking	.983	47	65	111	3	26
Maxwell	.893	12	8	17	3	3

Outfield	PCT	G	PO	A	E	DP
Allen	.968	27	57	3	2	0
Barnes	.895	9	16	1	2	0
Buchanan	.973	46	70	1	2	0
Hocking	1.000	16	27	1	0	1
Hunter	.992	147	460	14	4	3
J. Jones	.983	140	278	8	5	0
Kielty	.956	34	63	2	3	1
Lawton	.980	94	193	2	4	2
McCracken	1.000	10	13	0	0	0
Mohr	1.000	19	45	0	0	0

Doug Mientkiewicz

Director, Minor Leagues: Jim Rantz

Class	Farm Team	League	W	L	Pct.	Finish*	Manager	First Yr.
AAA	Edmonton (Alberta) Trappers	Pacific Coast	60	83	.420	16th (16)	John Russell	2001
AA	New Britain (Conn.) Rock Cats	Eastern	87	55	.613	+1st (12)	Stan Cliburn	1995
A#	Fort Myers (Fla.) Miracle	Florida State	68	69	.496	t-7th (12)	Jose Marzan	1993
A	Quad City (Iowa) River Bandits	Midwest	80	57	.584	5th (14)	Jeff Carter	1999
Rookie#	Elizabethton (Tenn.) Twins	Appalachian	41	22	.651	1st (10)	Rudy Hernandez	1974
Rookie	Fort Myers (Fla.) Twins	Gulf Coast	32	26	.552	6th (14)	Al Newman	1989

*Finish in overall standings (No. of teams in league) #Advanced level +League champion

EDMONTON
Class AAA

PACIFIC COAST LEAGUE

BATTING

	AVG	G	AB	R	H	2B	3B	HR	RBI	BB	SO	SB	CS	SLG	OBP	B	T	HT	WT	DOB	1st Yr	Resides
Allen, Chad	.364	6	22	4	8	2	0	1	4	1	2	0	.591	.481	R	R	6-1	195	2-6-75	1996	Dallas, Texas
Ardoin, Danny	.255	88	302	37	77	18	1	5	37	22	81	2	6	.371	.304	R	R	6-0	220	7-8-74	1995	Ville Platte, La.
Barnes, John	.293	81	311	42	91	21	2	8	42	27	28	3	2	.450	.368	R	R	6-2	205	4-24-76	1996	El Cajon, Calif.
Blake, Casey	.309	94	375	64	116	24	6	10	49	34	66	14	3	.485	.376	R	R	6-2	205	8-23-73	1996	Indianola, Iowa
Diaz, Edwin	.273	113	381	59	104	26	3	11	56	25	65	3	6	.444	.324	R	R	5-11	170	1-15-75	1993	Vega Alta, P.R.
Frias, Hanley	.183	49	142	15	26	6	0	0	7	10	28	2	3	.225	.237	B	R	6-0	165	12-5-73	1991	Villa Altagracia, D.R.
Hollins, Damon	.276	69	232	29	64	8	2	6	30	22	44	3	3	.405	.342	R	L	5-11	180	6-12-74	1992	Fairfield, Calif.
Huff, Larry	.313	27	67	10	21	2	2	1	11	7	13	2	1	.448	.368	R	R	6-0	175	1-24-72	1994	Palm Harbor, Fla.
Kielty, Bobby	.287	94	341	58	98	25	2	12	50	53	76	5	0	.478	.391	B	R	6-1	215	8-5-76	1999	Fort Myers, Fla.
LeCroy, Matthew	.328	101	396	53	130	17	0	20	80	36	95	0	2	.523	.390	R	R	6-2	225	12-13-75	1997	Belton, S.C.
McCracken, Quinton	.338	81	361	53	122	27	4	4	45	21	54	8	10	.468	.374	B	R	5-7	173	3-16-70	1992	Scottsdale, Ariz.
Moriarty, Mike	.243	131	404	66	98	17	2	13	50	50	94	5	4	.391	.354	R	R	6-0	195	3-8-74	1995	Mount Laurel, N.J.
Ryan, Mike	.288	135	527	89	152	36	7	18	73	52	121	1	6	.486	.353	L	R	5-10	182	7-6-77	1996	Indiana, Pa.
Sagmoen, Marc	.081	9	37	2	3	1	0	0	1	2	8	0	0	.108	.128	L	L	5-11	185	4-16-71	1993	Seattle, Wash.
Sears, Todd	.311	118	408	61	127	25	2	13	50	41	71	2	1	.478	.376	R	R	6-5	215	10-23-75	1997	Ankeny, Iowa
Sutton, Larry	.252	45	147	23	37	7	3	3	24	23	32	0	1	.401	.351	L	L	6-0	185	5-14-70	1992	Temecula, Calif.
2-team (29 Memphis)	.256	74	246	35	63	12	3	5	37	44	48	1	2	.390	.367							
Valentin, Javier	.281	121	431	53	121	29	2	17	71	47	108	0	1	.476	.352	B	R	5-10	200	9-19-75	1993	Manati, P.R.

PITCHING

	W	L	ERA	G	GS	CG	SV	IP	H	R	ER	BB	SO	AVG	B	T	HT	WT	DOB	1st Yr	Resides
Balfour, Grant	2	2	5.51	11	0	0	0	16	18	11	10	10	17	.305	R	R	6-2	170	12-30-77	1997	Sydney, Australia
Bochtler, Doug	2	5	2.76	34	1	0	3	46	41	16	14	19	65	.238	R	R	6-3	200	7-5-70	1989	West Palm Beach, Fla.
Brewington, Jamie	2	8	5.91	35	4	0	0	67	87	48	44	31	53	.317	R	R	6-4	175	9-28-71	1992	Phoenix, Ariz.
Cressend, Jack	2	2	3.50	12	0	0	1	18	19	12	7	7	9	.283	R	R	6-1	185	5-13-75	1996	Covington, La.
Duvall, Mike	2	2	4.45	55	0	0	3	63	73	32	31	21	63	.290	R	L	6-0	200	10-11-74	1995	Windham, Maine
Fiore, Tony	5	0	3.68	32	6	0	1	81	85	35	33	25	58	.272	R	R	6-4	210	10-12-71	1992	Chicago, Ill.
Hooten, Dave	1	1	9.00	7	0	0	0	10	17	10	10	4	4	.386	R	R	6-0	176	5-8-75	1996	Shreveport, La.
Johnson, Adam	1	1	5.70	4	4	0	0	24	19	15	15	10	25	.226	R	R	6-2	210	7-12-79	2000	Fort Myers, Fla.
Kinney, Matt	6	11	5.07	29	29	2	0	162	178	101	91	74	146	.278	R	R	6-5	220	12-16-76	1995	Bangor, Maine
Lohse, Kyle	4	2	3.12	8	8	1	0	49	50	21	17	13	48	.261	R	R	6-2	190	10-4-78	1997	Glenn, Calif.
Marshall, Lee	4	2	2.35	39	0	0	11	54	50	18	14	20	37	.243	R	R	6-5	217	9-25-76	1995	Ariton, Ala.
Martinez, Willie	7	8	5.61	21	20	0	0	112	147	80	70	39	86	.317	R	R	6-2	210	1-4-78	1995	Barquisimeto, Venez.
McMullen, Mike	0	0	3.38	14	0	0	0	16	12	10	6	15	11	.222	R	R	6-6	230	10-13-73	1993	St. Louis, Mo.
Mix, Greg	1	1	2.45	7	0	0	1	11	12	6	3	0	5	.285	R	R	6-4	225	8-21-71	1993	Albuquerque, N.M.
Mota, Danny	3	3	5.89	34	0	0	2	47	52	31	31	23	43	.287	R	R	6-0	180	10-9-75	1994	La Romana, D.R.
Oquist, Mike	5	8	4.15	21	20	2	0	111	132	62	51	29	76	.294	R	R	6-2	190	5-30-68	1989	Swink, Colo.
Pumphrey, Ken	1	6	7.22	7	7	0	0	39	55	39	31	18	17	.337	L	L	6-5	220	1-5-74	1995	Glen Burnie, Md.
Redman, Mark	0	0	13.50	1	1	0	0	1	3	2	2	1	0	.375	L	L	6-5	220	1-5-74	1995	Catoosa, Okla.
Romero, J.C.	3	3	3.68	12	10	0	0	64	67	33	26	24	55	.275	B	L	5-11	195	6-4-76	1997	San Juan, P.R.
Simontacchi, Jason	7	13	5.34	32	18	2	0	143	192	97	85	23	83	.326	R	R	6-2	185	11-13-73	1996	Santa Clara, Calif.
Stentz, Brent	0	0	5.65	17	0	0	7	14	19	9	9	5	12	.311	R	R	6-5	235	7-24-75	1995	Brooksville, Fla.
Sturdy, Tim	0	1	16.71	2	2	0	0	7	15	14	13	6	3	.454	R	R	6-2	179	10-8-78	1997	Albuquerque, N.M.
Wolff, Bryan	2	4	6.08	15	13	0	0	74	96	51	50	22	52	.321	R	R	6-2	189	3-16-72	1993	Herrin, Ill.

FIELDING

Catcher	PCT	G	PO	A	E	DP	PB
Ardoin	.989	81	501	54	6	4	6
LeCroy	.986	21	135	11	2	3	2
Valentin	.987	49	343	32	5	3	6

First Base	PCT	G	PO	A	E	DP
Blake	.969	5	26	5	1	2
LeCroy	.969	10	92	3	3	11
Sagmoen	1.000	1	3	0	0	0
Sears	.993	107	842	69	6	107
Sutton	.985	9	62	5	1	4
Valentin	.994	20	137	19	1	11

Second Base	PCT	G	PO	A	E	DP
Blake	1.000	4	6	13	0	3
Diaz	.991	75	115	203	3	54

	PCT	G	PO	A	E	DP
Frias	1.000	28	34	55	0	15
Huff	.983	12	22	35	1	4
Moriarty	.000	1	0	0	0	0
Ryan	.945	39	66	89	9	28

Third Base	PCT	G	PO	A	E	DP
Blake	.955	86	59	155	10	14
Diaz	.928	33	28	49	6	8
Frias	.000	1	0	0	0	0
Huff	1.000	5	0	7	0	1
Moriarty	1.000	3	3	3	0	0
Sears	.000	1	0	0	0	0
Valentin	.887	25	19	44	8	6

Shortstop	PCT	G	PO	A	E	DP
Blake	1.000	3	2	2	0	1

	PCT	G	PO	A	E	DP
Diaz	.947	5	6	12	1	3
Frias	.958	17	29	40	3	11
Moriarty	.965	125	198	359	20	89

Outfield	PCT	G	PO	A	E	DP
Allen	1.000	6	10	1	0	0
Ardoin	1.000	1	3	0	0	0
Barnes	1.000	78	132	8	0	1
Blake	.000	1	0	0	0	0
Hollins	.954	47	98	6	5	2
Huff	1.000	11	9	0	0	0
Kielty	.991	94	221	11	2	1
McCracken	.971	72	164	3	5	1
Ryan	.988	94	152	7	2	3
Sagmoen	1.000	9	16	1	0	0
Sutton	.982	33	54	1	1	0

NEW BRITAIN
Class AA

EASTERN LEAGUE

BATTING

	AVG	G	AB	R	H	2B	3B	HR	RBI	BB	SO	SB	CS	SLG	OBP	B	T	HT	WT	DOB	1st Yr	Resides
Bolivar, Papo	.268	43	142	15	38	7	0	2	20	9	25	1	1	.359	.327	R	R	5-9	195	10-18-78	1995	La Guaira, Venez.

BATTING	AVG	G	AB	R	H	2B	3B	HR	RBI	BB	SO	SB	CS	SLG	OBP	B	T	HT	WT	DOB	1st Yr	Resides
Borrego, Ramon	.184	60	136	17	25	6	2	1	3	14	30	5	0	.279	.265	B	R	5-6	170	6-7-78	1995	Gamacho Marcar, Venez.
Cuddyer, Michael	.301	141	509	95	153	36	3	30	87	75	106	5	9	.560	.395	R	R	6-2	202	3-27-79	1997	Chesapeake, Va.
Ford, Lew	.218	62	252	30	55	9	3	7	25	20	35	5	5	.361	.289	R	R	6-0	190	8-12-76	1999	Grand Prairie, Texas
Hodge, Kevin	.173	44	139	16	24	4	1	1	6	14	39	1	2	.237	.258	R	R	5-11	182	10-28-76	1998	Bryan, Texas
Lorenzo, Juan	.235	101	319	32	75	9	3	3	24	5	32	2	2	.310	.255	B	R	5-11	172	6-10-78	1995	Cambito Garabitos, D.R.
Marcinczyk, T.R.	.125	7	16	0	2	0	0	0	1	3	5	0	0	.125	.263	R	R	6-2	210	10-11-73	1996	Farmington, Conn.
Marsters, Brandon	.221	100	349	35	77	16	1	9	36	29	75	2	1	.350	.285	R	R	5-11	190	3-14-75	1996	Sarasota, Fla.
Mohr, Dustan	.336	135	518	90	174	41	3	24	91	49	111	9	9	.566	.395	R	R	6-2	210	6-19-76	1997	Hattiesburg, Miss.
Morneau, Justin	.158	10	38	3	6	1	0	0	4	3	8	0	0	.184	.214	L	R	6-4	205	5-15-81	1999	Fort Myers, Fla.
Ortiz, David	.243	9	37	3	9	4	0	0	3	9	9	0	0	.351	.293	L	L	6-4	230	11-18-75	1993	Haina, D.R.
Peterman, Tommy	.238	88	302	35	72	16	1	3	34	21	40	1	1	.328	.291	L	L	6-0	228	5-21-75	1996	Marietta, Ga.
Restovich, Mike	.269	140	501	69	135	33	4	23	84	54	125	15	7	.489	.345	R	R	6-4	233	1-3-79	1997	Rochester, Minn.
Salazar, Ruben	.298	131	530	70	158	29	2	10	66	37	77	6	1	.417	.348	R	R	5-10	186	1-16-78	1997	San Felix, Venez.
Shrum, Allen	.000	7	12	0	0	0	0	0	0	0	4	0	0	.000	.000	R	R	6-3	215	5-13-76	1998	Heritage, Tenn.
Smith, Jeff	.285	102	351	38	100	15	1	7	42	15	57	0	0	.393	.320	L	R	6-3	216	6-17-74	1995	Naples, Fla.
Smith, Nestor	.248	95	294	29	73	5	8	3	17	8	74	5	6	.350	.271	B	R	5-11	188	1-21-78	1995	Maturin, Venez.
Stevens, Tony	.171	72	245	19	42	7	1	1	21	10	29	3	3	.220	.210	R	R	5-10	160	9-18-78	1997	Jacksonville, Fla.
Torres, Gabby	.308	41	133	24	41	12	1	2	13	10	11	0	2	.459	.378	R	R	5-10	200	3-22-78	1995	Acarigua, Venez.

PITCHING	W	L	ERA	G	GS	CG	SV	IP	H	R	ER	BB	SO	AVG	B	T	HT	WT	DOB	1st Yr	Resides
Balfour, Grant	2	1	1.08	35	0	0	13	56	26	6	22	72	.149	R	R	6-2	170	12-30-77	1997	Sydney, Australia
Carnes, Matt	4	5	3.76	28	7	0	2	65	64	31	27	20	63	.254	R	R	6-3	208	8-18-75	1997	Miami, Okla.
Cento, Tony	0	1	9.00	9	0	0	0	10	19	10	10	3	8	.404	L	L	5-11	170	8-16-77	1999	Edgewood, Ky.
Fisher, Pete	5	2	1.89	8	8	0	0	52	52	20	11	11	39	.256	R	R	6-3	215	7-7-77	1998	Stoneham, Mass.
Flohr, Adam	3	5	4.86	18	12	0	0	74	94	43	40	15	49	.313	L	L	6-2	185	3-29-77	1998	Benton City, Wash.
Frederick, Kevin	6	2	1.63	44	0	0	7	83	56	17	15	28	109	.195	L	R	6-4	208	11-4-76	1998	Lincolnshire, Ill.
Hoard, Brent	1	0	0.00	1	1	0	0	6	2	1	0	1	2	.105	R	L	6-4	210	11-3-76	1998	Los Gatos, Calif.
Howard, Tom	0	0	9.00	4	0	0	0	4	6	4	4	4	2	.375	R	L	6-5	211	7-29-75	1993	Cocoa Beach, Fla.
Johnson, Adam	5	6	3.82	18	18	0	0	113	105	53	48	39	110	.247	R	R	6-2	210	7-12-79	2000	Fort Myers, Fla.
Lohse, Kyle	3	1	2.37	6	6	0	0	38	32	10	10	4	32	.230	R	R	6-2	190	10-4-78	1997	Glenn, Calif.
Marshall, Lee	1	3	1.93	11	0	0	2	19	20	6	4	4	15	.253	R	R	6-5	217	9-25-76	1995	Ariton, Ala.
McDonald, Jon	8	3	3.44	17	17	0	0	97	88	47	37	34	68	.241	R	R	6-3	195	10-16-77	2000	Orlando, Fla.
Mills, Ryan	2	5	6.42	8	8	0	0	41	45	31	29	14	29	.279	L	L	6-5	205	7-21-77	1998	Scottsdale, Ariz.
Nakamura, Mike	5	1	1.77	48	1	0	5	86	75	20	17	24	109	.229	R	R	6-0	215	4-14-76	1995	Oakland, Ore.
Palki, Jeromy	3	1	2.83	31	2	0	1	60	50	19	19	22	52	.234	R	R	6-6	208	9-10-76	1994	Glen Burnie, Md.
Pumphrey, Ken	8	2	2.88	22	14	2	1	103	89	38	33	26	52	.234	L	L	5-11	190	1-23-79	1996	Maracaibo, Venez.
Rincon, Juan	14	6	2.88	29	23	2	0	153	130	60	49	57	133	.226	R	R	5-11	155	12-7-77	1998	San Juan, P.R.
Rivera, Saul	5	2	3.16	33	0	0	13	43	35	16	15	18	55	.220	R	R	6-1	195	4-7-78	1999	Columbus, Ga.
Schoening, Brent	2	6	4.73	12	6	0	0	46	48	25	24	16	37	.272	L	L	6-4	220	10-27-77	1995	Sydney, Australia
Thomas, Brad	10	3	1.96	19	19	1	0	119	91	37	26	26	97	.206	L	L	6-4	220	10-22-77	1998	Winter Park, Fla.
Weis, Brad	0	0	5.14	4	0	0	0	7	9	5	4	1	8	.321	L	L	5-11	185	11-29-77	1999	Winter Park, Fla.

FIELDING

Catcher	PCT	G	PO	A	E	DP	PB
Marsters	.994	75	594	58	4	4	4
Shrum	1.000	2	4	0	0	0	0
J. Smith	.992	60	472	57	4	3	3
Torres	.976	9	76	5	2	1	1

First Base	PCT	G	PO	A	E	DP
Cuddyer	.984	57	467	32	8	46
Marcinczyk	1.000	3	23	0	0	3
Morneau	1.000	7	63	4	0	2
Ortiz	1.000	9	78	4	0	9
Peterman	.993	76	608	63	5	44
Restovich	1.000	2	1	1	0	1

Second Base	PCT	G	PO	A	E	DP
Borrego	.988	26	44	38	1	10
Hodge	1.000	14	16	21	0	5
Lorenzo	.919	6	11	23	3	4
Salazar	.962	115	183	299	19	60

Third Base	PCT	G	PO	A	E	DP
Borrego	.842	10	8	8	3	0
Cuddyer	.922	81	46	166	18	14
Hodge	.889	17	9	31	5	0
Lorenzo	.938	46	17	103	8	10
Salazar	.867	6	4	9	2	0

Shortstop	PCT	G	PO	A	E	DP
Borrego	.920	23	27	42	6	12
Hodge	.887	15	20	43	8	6
Lorenzo	.948	53	64	117	10	18
Stevens	.952	72	94	203	15	35

Outfield	PCT	G	PO	A	E	DP
Bolivar	1.000	20	23	0	0	0
Cuddyer	.920	19	22	1	2	0
Ford	.974	60	108	5	3	0
Mohr	.978	133	261	9	6	1
Restovich	.989	140	257	8	3	1
J. Smith	1.000	2	1	0	0	0
N. Smith	.991	72	102	4	1	0

FORT MYERS · Class A

FLORIDA STATE LEAGUE

BATTING	AVG	G	AB	R	H	2B	3B	HR	RBI	BB	SO	SB	CS	SLG	OBP	B	T	HT	WT	DOB	1st Yr	Resides
Baron, Brian	.306	69	265	38	81	10	3	1	37	18	40	0	0	.377	.348	L	R	5-11	195	9-12-78	2001	Santa Clarita, Calif.
Bolivar, Papo	.291	57	227	42	66	6	2	3	25	22	33	15	3	.374	.356	R	R	5-9	195	10-18-78	1995	La Guaira, Venez.
Edwards, John	.209	87	278	24	58	14	2	4	33	22	77	4	2	.317	.275	R	R	6-1	180	6-27-78	1998	Melton, Australia
Ford, Lew	.298	67	265	42	79	15	2	2	24	21	30	19	9	.392	.373	R	R	6-0	190	8-12-76	1999	Grand Prairie, Texas
Garbe, B.J.	.242	127	463	55	112	14	4	6	61	51	86	13	7	.328	.331	R	R	6-2	195	2-3-81	1999	Moses Lake, Wash.
Gomon, Dusty	.278	6	18	2	5	0	0	1	3	0	6	0	0	.444	.278	R	R	6-3	220	9-3-82	2001	Jacksonville, Fla.
Gulledge, Kelley	.268	61	213	33	57	16	0	10	45	20	60	1	1	.484	.349	R	R	6-1	200	1-25-79	2000	Arlington, Texas
Hawthorne, Kyle	.218	47	165	16	36	5	0	4	21	7	29	3	2	.321	.265	R	R	6-1	195	3-13-78	1998	Baton Rouge, La.
Hodge, Kevin	.235	61	221	35	52	13	0	7	27	36	51	3	1	.389	.351	R	R	5-11	182	10-28-76	1998	Bryan, Texas
Maxwell, Jason	.444	2	9	1	4	1	0	0	2	0	0	0	0	.556	.444	R	R	6-1	180	3-26-72	1993	Lewisburg, Tenn.
McMillin, Brian	.180	93	250	31	45	10	0	2	15	29	76	15	3	.244	.267	R	R	5-10	190	5-24-77	1998	Fort Myers, Fla.
Morneau, Justin	.294	53	197	25	58	10	3	4	40	24	41	0	0	.437	.385	L	R	6-4	230	11-18-75	1993	Haina, D.R.
Ortiz, David	.000	3	0	0	0	0	0	0	0	0	0	0	0	.000	.250	L	L	6-4	220	2-1-78	1996	Sanford, N.C.
Osborne, Mark	.219	47	137	14	30	4	0	3	8	21	36	1	1	.314	.325	R	R	5-9	180	12-28-78	2001	Sarasota, Fla.
Renick, Josh	.268	49	142	17	38	7	0	0	17	25	17	3	1	.317	.371	L	L	5-11	155	8-8-79	1996	Santo Domingo, D.R.
Reyes, Deurys	.240	95	263	47	63	10	1	0	20	33	82	18	5	.285	.340	L	L	5-9	170	6-27-80	1997	Cojedes, Venez.
Rodriguez, Luis	.274	125	463	71	127	21	3	4	64	82	42	11	8	.359	.387	B	R	6-1	215	8-15-79	1998	Spokane, Wash.
Sandberg, Eric	.234	81	274	37	64	11	1	2	33	35	50	0	1	.303	.331	L	R	5-11	205	6-19-78	1999	Richfield, Minn.
Scanlon, Matt	.253	107	348	39	88	12	2	3	35	45	67	2	1	.320	.340	L	R	5-10	160	9-18-78	1997	Jacksonville, Fla.
Stevens, Tony	.178	65	197	23	35	5	1	0	12	17	35	7	5	.213	.253	R	R	5-10	200	3-22-78	1995	Acarigua, Venez.
Torres, Gabby	.261	49	157	17	41	8	0	1	18	7	28	2	0	.331	.308	R	R	5-10	200	3-22-78	1995	Acarigua, Venez.
Ward, Brian	.255	15	47	5	12	1	0	0	6	7	6	0	1	.277	.345	R	R	5-8	188	7-7-77	1999	Orlando, Fla.

ORGANIZATION STATISTICS

GAMES BY POSITION: C—Edwards 60, Gulledge 53, Osborne 12, Torres 26. **1B**—Gomon 5, Hawthorne 4, Morneau 48, Ortiz 1, Osborne 6, Renick 7, Sandberg 70, Scanlon 4. **2B**—Hawthorne 9, Hodge 38, Maxwell 1, Renick 41, Rodriguez 58, Scanlon 1, Ward 6. **3B**—Hawthorne 25, Hodge 28, Maxwell 1, Rodriguez 2, Scanlon 97, Ward 6. **SS**—Hawthorne 9, Hodge 3, Rodriguez 68, Stevens 65. **OF**—Baron 49, Bolivar 14, Edwards 21, Ford 66, Garbe 127, Hawthorne 1, Hodge 5, McMillin 80, Reyes 87.

PITCHING	W	L	ERA	G	GS	CG	SV	IP	H	R	ER	BB	SO	AVG	B	T	HT	WT	DOB	1st Yr	Resides
Cento, Tony	3	2	3.43	39	1	0	0	58	49	27	22	21	47	.234	L	L	5-11	170	8-16-77	1999	Edgewood, Ky.
Contreras, J.C.	0	0	3.38	6	0	0	1	8	6	3	3	6	4	.222	L	L	6-0	140	4-24-82	1998	Caracas, Venez.
Corona, Ronnie	3	1	2.19	16	7	0	0	49	45	15	12	16	47	.241	R	R	6-0	180	1-27-79	2000	Apple Valley, Calif.
Eyre, Willie	2	5	2.52	32	0	0	1	64	54	27	18	33	51	.231	R	R	6-1	200	7-21-78	1999	Magna, Utah
Fisher, Pete	4	5	3.34	31	9	0	2	92	91	48	34	32	77	.254	R	R	6-3	215	7-7-77	1998	Stoneham, Mass.
Flohr, Adam	1	2	5.09	21	2	0	1	41	47	31	23	9	40	.291	L	L	6-2	185	3-29-77	1998	Benton City, Wash.
Foote, Joe	2	8	3.87	17	14	0	0	86	101	45	37	25	57	.300	R	R	6-4	196	8-30-79	1997	Bradenton, Fla.
Frederick, Kevin	2	0	1.00	9	0	0	1	18	9	2	2	3	19	.145	L	R	6-1	208	11-4-76	1998	Lincolnshire, Ill.
Hoard, Brent	7	4	3.36	17	15	0	0	80	78	31	30	28	70	.262	R	L	6-4	210	11-3-76	1998	Los Gatos, Calif.
Hodge, Kevin	0	0	0.00	2	0	0	1	1	0	0	0	0	2	.000	R	R	5-11	182	10-28-76	1998	Bryan, Texas
Howard, Tom	6	3	6.02	33	1	0	0	58	58	45	39	64	57	.272	R	L	6-5	211	7-29-75	1993	Cocoa Beach, Fla.
McDonald, Jon	4	2	1.98	9	9	0	0	50	44	15	11	15	44	.231	R	R	6-3	195	10-16-77	2000	Orlando, Fla.
Padilla, Juan	6	4	2.99	56	0	0	23	69	72	35	23	25	77	.260	R	R	6-0	188	2-17-77	1998	Levittown, P.R.
Palki, Jeromy	1	1	1.80	12	0	0	1	20	13	5	4	10	24	.183	R	R	6-0	215	4-14-76	1995	Oakland, Ore.
Persby, Andy	1	3	6.92	18	0	0	0	26	25	22	20	23	14	.252	R	R	6-3	247	5-2-78	2000	North St. Paul, Minn.
Pridie, Jon	1	3	4.58	14	9	0	0	57	54	31	29	37	42	.251	R	R	6-4	205	12-7-79	1998	Prescott, Ariz.
Richardson, Jason	1	0	2.19	8	1	0	0	12	10	5	3	7	6	.238	R	R	6-3	210	6-11-80	1999	Lakeland, Fla.
Sampson, Benj	2	3	3.20	15	15	0	0	70	61	30	25	31	36	.239	R	L	6-2	210	4-27-75	1993	Bondurant, Iowa
Schoening, Brent	5	9	4.88	17	16	0	0	87	97	54	47	32	69	.291	R	R	6-1	195	4-7-78	1999	Columbus, Ga.
Sneed, John	8	3	3.24	25	19	0	0	114	95	51	41	49	88	.223	L	R	6-6	250	6-30-76	1997	Houston, Texas
Sturdy, Tim	8	10	3.82	28	19	1	0	130	122	74	55	53	54	.256	R	R	6-2	179	10-8-78	1997	Albuquerque, N.M.
Weis, Brad	1	1	2.61	17	0	0	0	21	20	9	6	10	26	.259	L	L	5-11	185	11-29-77	1999	Winter Park, Fla.

QUAD CITY
Class A

MIDWEST LEAGUE

BATTING	AVG	G	AB	R	H	2B	3B	HR	RBI	BB	SO	SB	CS	SLG	OBP	B	T	HT	WT	DOB	1st Yr	Resides
Boitel, Rafael	.238	116	462	65	110	15	5	1	32	43	87	36	15	.299	.305	B	L	6-1	169	1-21-81	1998	Lehigh Acres, Fla.
Bowen, Rob	.255	106	385	47	98	18	2	18	70	37	112	4	0	.452	.321	B	R	6-2	206	2-24-81	1999	Fort Myers, Fla.
De los Santos, Hector	.226	99	336	35	76	4	4	0	29	14	58	25	11	.262	.269	R	R	6-2	155	1-19-80	1997	San Pedro de Macoris, D.R.
DeCola, Dan	.218	34	101	6	22	4	0	1	13	6	23	0	0	.287	.310	R	R	6-1	202	7-24-79	2000	Chicora, Pa.
Gonzalez, Reggie	.225	51	173	23	39	11	1	6	23	5	30	2	0	.405	.247	R	R	5-10	162	10-14-79	1998	Santurce, P.R.
Gulledge, Kelley	.275	39	131	15	36	9	0	3	16	8	37	0	2	.412	.324	L	R	6-1	200	1-25-79	2000	Arlington, Texas
Guzman, Robert	.234	21	77	12	18	1	1	0	5	4	14	4	0	.273	.298	L	L	5-11	200	1-22-80	2001	Hanford, Calif.
Kennedy, Bryan	.200	14	40	8	8	3	0	0	5	9	13	0	0	.275	.385	L	R	6-2	200	10-4-78	2001	Riverside, Calif.
Maza, Luis	.280	116	429	74	120	24	1	9	46	30	66	12	4	.403	.357	R	R	5-9	145	6-22-80	1997	Cumana, Venez.
Morneau, Justin	.356	64	236	50	84	17	2	12	53	36	38	0	0	.597	.420	L	R	6-4	205	5-15-81	1999	Fort Myers, Fla.
Rabe, Josh	.282	119	397	58	112	25	3	6	44	32	64	9	7	.406	.345	R	R	6-2	214	10-15-78	2000	Mendon, Ill.
Sandberg, Eric	.319	42	166	28	53	8	2	4	23	16	25	1	1	.464	.390	L	L	6-1	215	8-15-79	1998	Spokane, Wash.
Sandoval, Michael	.222	47	153	18	34	6	0	1	22	11	32	2	0	.281	.278	R	R	5-9	160	7-8-81	1997	Puerto Cabello, Venez.
Southward, Deshawn	.143	10	21	3	3	2	0	0	1	2	4	1	0	.238	.217	R	R	5-11	187	5-16-78	1997	Dade City, Fla.
Tamburrino, Brett	.262	42	141	23	37	3	5	0	16	15	32	4	2	.355	.350	B	R	5-11	184	11-10-81	1998	Sunbury, Australia
Tiffee, Terry	.309	128	495	65	153	32	1	11	86	32	48	3	1	.444	.347	B	R	6-3	225	4-21-79	1999	North Little Rock, Ark.
Torres, Digno	.193	88	264	31	51	15	2	3	27	33	72	1	2	.299	.296	L	L	6-4	190	8-27-79	1999	Morouis, P.R.
Watkins, Tommy	.230	73	191	31	44	9	0	2	16	28	36	4	2	.309	.333	R	R	5-7	185	6-18-80	1999	Fort Myers, Fla.
West, Kevin	.271	126	443	74	120	23	5	20	75	38	124	4	4	.413	.390	R	R	6-2	195	1-1-80	1999	Redwood Valley, Calif.

GAMES BY POSITION: C—Bowen 98, DeCola 15, Gulledge 16, Kennedy 14. **1B**—Morneau 61, Sandberg 40, Tiffee 27, Torres 22. **2B**—Gonzalez 30, Maza 1, Sandoval 1, Tamburrino 16, Watkins 7. **3B**—de los Santos 4, Rabe 1, Sandoval 32, Tamburrino 4, Tiffee 98, Watkins 13. **SS**—de los Santos 3, Maza 107, Watkins 36. **OF**—Boitel 113, Guzman 17, Rabe 113, Southward 8, Tamburrino 12, Torres 42, Watkins 12, West 121.

PITCHING	W	L	ERA	G	GS	CG	SV	IP	H	R	ER	BB	SO	AVG	B	T	HT	WT	DOB	1st Yr	Resides
Blackwell, Scott	1	2	5.12	13	0	0	0	19	17	11	9	19	19	.229	R	R	6-2	206	11-26-79	2000	Havana, Ill.
Bonilla, Henry	5	6	3.22	53	0	0	25	59	61	22	21	23	55	.264	R	R	6-0	189	8-16-78	2000	Reno, Nev.
Contreras, J.C.	2	0	2.67	26	0	0	2	34	28	14	10	11	38	.227	L	L	6-0	140	4-24-82	1998	Caracas, Venez.
Eyre, Willie	3	0	2.42	17	0	0	4	22	19	6	6	2	21	.234	R	R	6-1	200	7-21-78	1999	Magna, Utah
Foote, Joe	3	2	5.17	13	8	0	0	56	64	37	32	10	46	.285	R	R	6-4	196	8-30-79	1997	Bradenton, Fla.
Gates, Brian	2	1	2.17	15	0	0	0	29	25	10	7	8	24	.225	R	R	6-0	195	9-25-79	2001	Granite Bay, Calif.
Holubec, Ken	4	8	3.22	27	22	1	1	134	107	57	48	63	129	.218	L	L	6-0	218	9-1-78	2000	Houma, La.
Kemp, Beau	0	1	2.51	31	0	0	4	43	29	17	12	15	46	.190	R	R	6-0	182	10-31-80	2000	Tulsa, Okla.
Lincoln, Jeff	7	4	3.63	31	12	0	1	97	83	47	39	67	101	.229	R	R	6-2	185	4-30-78	2000	Citrus Heights, Calif.
Martin, Lucas	8	6	3.99	33	19	1	1	138	146	74	61	32	117	.270	L	L	5-10	206	3-9-78	1999	Fort Myers, Fla.
Moseley, Marcus	3	5	6.28	20	8	0	0	57	52	44	40	46	35	.246	R	R	6-2	210	8-12-80	1998	Hohenwald, Tenn.
Persby, Andy	3	0	1.00	20	0	0	1	27	18	6	3	13	17	.194	R	R	6-3	247	5-2-78	2000	North St. Paul, Minn.
Pridie, Jon	6	3	3.40	12	11	1	0	56	40	26	21	24	48	.203	R	R	6-4	205	12-7-79	1998	Prescott, Ariz.
Randazzo, Jeff	9	3	4.62	20	18	0	0	103	116	58	53	31	69	.294	R	L	6-7	195	8-12-81	1999	Brooman, Pa.
Romero, Josmir	7	7	4.44	30	14	2	1	122	134	72	60	40	61	.283	R	R	6-2	193	11-18-80	1997	Guarenas, Venez.
Tejada, Sandy	0	1	4.50	4	2	0	0	10	7	8	5	9	13	.194	R	R	6-2	188	4-16-82	1998	Puerto Plata, D.R.
Weis, Brad	4	0	0.69	22	0	0	2	39	38	15	3	19	43	.240	L	L	5-11	185	11-29-77	1999	Winter Park, Fla.
Wolfe, Brian	13	8	2.81	28	23	2	0	160	128	64	50	32	128	.214	R	R	6-2	200	11-29-80	1999	Fulton, Calif.

ELIZABETHTON
Rookie

APPALACHIAN LEAGUE

BATTING	AVG	G	AB	R	H	2B	3B	HR	RBI	BB	SO	SB	CS	SLG	OBP	B	T	HT	WT	DOB	1st Yr	Resides
Abram, Matt	.242	55	190	26	46	11	0	5	24	16	38	3	3	.379	.311	R	R	6-0	190	6-13-80	2001	Scottsdale, Ariz.
Agar, Cory	.275	57	193	26	53	15	1	8	33	17	62	0	0	.487	.344	R	R	5-11	204	4-9-81	2000	Palm Harbor, Fla.
Guante, Domingo	.131	40	84	16	11	1	0	0	5	16	27	4	1	.143	.277	R	R	6-2	188	11-28-80	1999	San Pedro de Macoris, D.R.
Guzman, Robert	.333	25	78	10	26	4	2	1	8	5	17	1	1	.474	.395	L	L	5-11	200	1-22-80	2001	Hanford, Calif.
Huff, Ken	.262	43	126	11	33	6	1	0	14	9	33	0	1	.325	.309	L	L	6-0	200	9-17-79	2001	Phoenix, Ariz.
Kennedy, Bryan	.250	10	28	2	7	1	0	0	1	4	6	0	0	.286	.344	L	R	6-2	200	10-4-78	2001	Riverside, Calif.

BATTING	AVG	G	AB	R	H	2B	3B	HR	RBI	BB	SO	SB	CS	SLG	OBP	B	T	HT	WT	DOB	1st Yr	Resides
Kuhaulua, Kaulana	.246	20	69	8	17	4	1	0	6	1	19	4	1	.333	.268	R	R	6-0	170	1-30-80	2001	Waianae, Hawaii
Lebron, Edgardo	.209	38	115	15	24	3	0	2	10	8	42	1	2	.287	.272	B	R	6-3	179	8-16-82	2000	Las Piedras, P.R.
Manning, Ricky	.253	22	75	15	19	4	0	4	9	15	4	3		.333	.364	L	L	5-11	177	11-18-80	1999	Fresno, Calif.
Martinez, Peter	.224	35	98	11	22	11	0	0	12	13	26	5	2	.337	.342	R	R	5-11	173	11-20-81	1999	Santo Domingo, D.R.
Matos, Bernie	.227	14	44	5	10	3	0	0	4	1	9	0	1	.295	.244	R	R	6-0	175	7-30-81	1999	Barahona, D.R.
Mauer, Jake	.155	27	58	8	9	1	0	0	6	8	5	3	1	.172	.310	R	R	6-2	170	12-20-78	2001	St. Paul, Minn.
Mauer, Joe	.400	32	110	14	44	6	2	0	14	19	10	4	0	.491	.492	L	R	6-4	215	4-19-83	2001	St. Paul, Minn.
Merchan, Jesus	.271	47	133	19	36	10	1	1	14	6	18	4	0	.383	.306	R	R	5-11	160	3-26-81	1999	Maracay, Venez.
Nunez, Alexis	.298	21	57	10	17	3	0	0	11	11	9	3	2	.351	.406	L	R	5-11	170	4-30-81	1999	Valencia, Venez.
Oeltjen, Trent	.233	9	30	4	7	1	0	0	4	0	6	2	0	.267	.226	L	L	6-0	180	2-28-83	2001	Sydney, Australia
Quickstad, Barry	.274	42	117	20	32	4	0	9	23	14	45	5	0	.538	.356	R	R	6-0	191	7-20-80	1999	Waseca, Minn.
Tomlin, James	.300	63	237	38	71	14	4	1	23	21	33	15	7	.405	.373	R	R	6-1	170	1-28-82	1999	Los Angeles, Calif.
Tope, Stephen	.215	40	130	13	28	7	1	1	9	6	30	1	1	.308	.252	R	R	5-11	176	1-12-82	1999	Perth, Australia

GAMES BY POSITION: C—Agar 23, Guante 1, Kennedy 10, Matos 13, Jo. Mauer 19. **1B**—Huff 22, Kuhaulua 5, Lebron 6, Tope 38. **2B**—Abram 5, Martinez 31, Ja. Mauer 9, Merchan 6, Nunez 21. **3B**—Abram 39, Lebron 13, Ja. Mauer 16, Merchan 5, Quickstad 1. **SS**—Kuhaulua 13, Lebron 21, Merchan 33. **OF**—Abram 7, Guante 34, Guzman 23, Huff 21, Manning 21, Martinez 4, Merchan 1, Oeltjen 9, Quickstad 26, Tomlin 63.

PITCHING	W	L	ERA	G	GS	CG	SV	IP	H	R	ER	BB	SO	AVG	B	T	HT	WT	DOB	1st Yr	Resides
Bowyer, Travis	2	5	6.10	9	8	0	0	38	38	30	26	20	34	.265	R	R	6-4	200	8-3-81	1999	Big Island, Va.
Brown, Jeremy	0	0	3.27	3	2	0	0	11	10	4	4	3	9	.232	R	R	6-3	210	1-3-79	2001	London, Ky.
Cameron, Kevin	1	1	1.57	22	0	0	13	23	16	4	4	5	30	.186	R	R	6-1	175	12-15-79	2001	Joliet, Ill.
Daws, Josh	1	1	1.39	20	1	0	2	45	34	8	7	5	56	.213	R	R	6-0	180	12-8-78	2001	Palm Beach, Fla.
Durbin, J.D.	3	2	1.87	8	7	0	0	34	23	13	7	17	39	.190	R	R	6-0	177	2-24-82	2000	Scottsdale, Ariz.
Hemus, Jared	6	1	1.48	16	6	0	3	49	33	9	8	16	49	.195	L	L	6-0	175	1-1-81	2001	Spring Valley, Calif.
Lawson, Brett	1	0	9.49	10	1	0	0	12	14	19	13	16	14	.259	R	R	6-8	250	2-21-79	2001	Mississauga, Ontario
Lohse, Eric	1	1	4.15	3	2	0	0	9	12	7	4	1	5	.315	R	R	6-2	195	6-6-80	2001	Glen, Calif.
Miller, Colby	5	1	2.44	15	6	0	0	48	39	15	13	12	61	.216	R	R	6-2	185	3-19-82	2000	Weatherford, Okla.
Miller, Jason	4	3	4.05	12	11	0	0	53	46	26	24	19	64	.228	L	L	6-0	192	7-20-82	2000	Sarasota, Fla.
Serafini, Vince	3	3	3.81	14	9	0	0	52	54	24	22	8	40	.272	R	L	6-3	215	3-4-80	2001	Lockport, Ill.
Smart, Richard	3	0	3.31	17	0	0	0	33	32	22	12	25	31	.246	R	R	6-4	192	10-15-79	2000	Panama City, Fla.
Tarkington, Shawn	0	0	11.25	6	0	0	0	8	17	10	10	3	7	.447	L	L	6-4	230	8-21-79	2001	Middletown, N.Y.
Tejada, Sandy	5	3	3.20	11	10	0	0	56	43	26	20	20	87	.208	R	R	6-2	188	4-16-82	1998	Puerto Plata, D.R.
Vorwald, Matt	6	1	1.16	23	0	0	4	47	31	12	6	22	60	.180	R	R	6-3	180	11-29-79	2001	Freeport, Ill.

FORT MYERS — Rookie

GULF COAST LEAGUE

BATTING	AVG	G	AB	R	H	2B	3B	HR	RBI	BB	SO	SB	CS	SLG	OBP	B	T	HT	WT	DOB	1st Yr	Resides
Fermin, Angelo	.279	13	43	5	12	0	0	0	5	6	10	2	2	.279	.365	B	R	5-9	150	11-6-83	2000	Santo Domingo, D.R.
Gomon, Dusty	.324	19	74	13	24	6	0	2	10	5	15	1	0	.486	.367	B	R	6-3	220	9-3-82	2001	Jacksonville, Fla.
Guzman, Cristian	.250	5	16	4	4	0	1	0	0	2	4	0	1	.375	.368	B	R	6-0	195	3-21-78	1995	Santo Domingo, D.R.
Guzman, Garrett	.355	39	138	22	49	14	5	2	22	9	16	4	2	.572	.401	L	L	5-10	170	2-7-83	2001	Henderson, Nev.
Hiraldo, Inocencio	.282	49	163	26	46	12	4	2	18	13	31	12	3	.442	.339	R	R	5-11	157	1-25-82	1999	Santiago, D.R.
Johnson, Joshua	.141	24	64	5	9	1	1	0	2	7	14	1	0	.188	.243	R	R	6-0	185	11-3-82	2001	Ridgway, Pa.
Kubel, Jason	.331	37	124	14	41	10	4	1	30	19	14	3	2	.500	.422	L	R	6-0	180	5-25-82	2000	Palmdale, Calif.
Marin, Daniel	.274	31	95	16	26	5	0	1	11	10	10	5	1	.326	.349	L	R	5-11	170	3-2-83	1999	Anzoategui, Venez.
Masino, Adam	.220	39	123	10	27	7	0	1	10	10	41	3	0	.301	.284	R	R	6-3	247	1-2-82	2000	Cape Coral, Fla.
Maxwell, Jason	.500	3	10	2	5	2	0	0	1	2	0	0	0	.700	.545	R	R	6-1	180	3-26-72	1993	Lewisburg, Tenn.
Molina, Felix	.286	51	189	27	54	12	3	2	21	16	25	8	6	.413	.340	B	R	5-8	168	5-5-83	2001	Mayaguez, P.R.
Morales, Jose	.248	35	117	13	29	6	2	0	18	6	26	4	1	.333	.296	R	R	5-11	180	4-30-81	2001	Valencia, Venez.
Nunez, Alexis	.182	4	11	1	2	0	0	0	0	0	1	0	0	.182	.182	L	R	5-11	175	2-20-83	2001	Rio Piedras, P.R.
Oeltjen, Trent	.321	45	134	21	43	7	3	0	18	14	16	10	3	.418	.387	L	L	6-0	180	2-28-83	2001	Sydney, Australia
Ortiz, David	.400	4	10	3	4	0	0	0	1	3	1	1	0	.400	.538	L	L	6-4	230	11-18-75	1993	Haina, D.R.
Pospishil, Jason	.175	19	57	5	10	4	0	0	2	6	19	1	1	.246	.266	B	R	5-8	155	1-28-83	2001	Sydney, Australia
Smith, Ryan	.198	44	121	14	24	4	0	2	7	25	32	6	2	.281	.355	L	R	5-11	185	1-9-82	2001	West Covina, Calif.
Spataro, Ryan	.208	16	48	4	10	0	0	2	3	16	1	1		.326	.370	B	R	6-2	210	10-21-80	2001	Barrie, Ontario
Taylor, Sam	.261	59	92	14	24	1	1	1	8	13	10	8	2	.326	.370	R	R	5-8	165	11-6-82	2001	San Leandro, Calif.
Thomman, John	.203	36	79	7	16	5	0	1	10	6	30	0	2	.304	.292	R	R	6-4	212	7-8-81	2000	Levelland, Texas
Whitrock, Scott	.171	36	105	11	18	4	0	0	6	7	40	7	2	.210	.230	R	R	6-2	195	12-18-80	2001	Wisconsin Rapids, Wis.

GAMES BY POSITION: C—Johnson 22, Marin 30, Smith 14. **1B**—Gomon 24, Marin 1, Masino 24, Smith 26. **2B**—Fermin 9, Molina 8, Morales 23, Nunez 2, Pospishil 6, Taylor 18. **3B**—Fermin 2, Gomon 3, Hiraldo 13, Marin 2, Maxwell 1, Molina 37, Morales 5, Nunez 1, Pospishil 1. **SS**—Fermin 2, C. Guzman 2, Hiraldo 34, Maxwell 2, Morales 9, Taylor 16. **OF**—G. Guzman 33, Kubel 34, Molina 9, Oeltjen 43, Spataro 14, Thomman 32, Whitrock 30.

PITCHING	W	L	ERA	G	GS	CG	SV	IP	H	R	ER	BB	SO	AVG	B	T	HT	WT	DOB	1st Yr	Resides
Abbott, Jim	0	0	5.40	2	0	0	0	2	1	1	1	2	1	.166	R	R	6-3	185	10-12-79	2001	Caledonia, Mich.
Blake, Peter	0	1	3.52	6	0	0	0	8	5	3	3	1	7	.208	R	L	6-2	228	1-15-79	1997	Indianola, Iowa
Brewington, Jamie	0	0	0.00	4	0	0	0	7	4	0	0	1	8	.166	R	R	6-4	175	9-28-71	1992	Phoenix, Ariz.
Carrasco, Edelyn	3	4	3.51	14	9	1	0	51	49	26	20	15	45	.248	R	R	6-3	168	11-23-82	1999	Browns Plaines, Australia
Crawford, Tristan	0	0	2.20	13	0	0	3	16	15	5	4	6	19	.227	R	R	6-3	172	7-22-82	2000	La Luisa Blanca, D.R.
Ferreira, Emilo	8	1	1.20	12	10	0	0	60	52	16	8	10	47	.235	R	R	6-6	200	10-28-83	2001	Dorado, P.R.
Garcia, Angel	0	3	5.60	9	6	0	0	18	20	15	11	12	22	.285	R	R	5-11	193	5-3-82	2001	Maracaibo, Venez.
Gutierrez, Jannio	0	0	0.31	23	0	0	16	29	11	2	1	13	48	.115	R	R	6-2	194	3-27-83	2001	Sydney, Australia
Hill, Joshua	2	2	3.63	12	0	0	0	17	15	8	7	8	17	.000	R	R	6-2	195	6-6-80	2000	Glen, Calif.
Lohse, Eric	4	3	2.55	10	10	1	0	49	42	16	14	4	34	.237	R	R	6-5	230	1-18-83	2001	Chermside, Australia
Mutch, Paul	1	0	8.39	17	1	0	0	25	35	28	23	15	14	.330	R	L	6-3	180	11-3-80	2001	St. Louis, Mo.
Niedbalski, Nick	2	2	4.24	14	8	0	0	47	44	25	22	16	41	.247	R	R	6-2	215	10-4-80	2001	Vancleave, Miss.
Pylate, Chad	1	1	3.44	10	3	0	0	18	18	9	7	14	12	.173	R	R	6-3	210	6-11-80	1999	Lakeland, Fla.
Richardson, Jason	0	1	1.35	4	1	0	0	7	4	1	1	5	7	.166	R	R	5-11	155	12-7-77	1996	San Juan, P.R.
Rivera, Saul	0	0	0.00	3	0	0	0	3	2	0	0	1	5	.166	R	R	6-1	200	2-9-78	1998	Puerto Plata, D.R.
Simon, Janewrys	2	5	4.74	13	7	0	0	44	51	29	23	22	33	.300	R	R	6-5	235	7-24-75	1995	Brooksville, Fla.
Stentz, Brent	2	1	1.93	8	0	0	0	9	7	3	2	7	6	.205	R	R	6-4	230	8-21-79	2001	Middletown, N.Y.
Tarkington, Shawn	1	0	3.00	13	0	0	1	21	25	8	7	1	25	.294	R	R	6-2	188	4-16-82	1998	Paris, Ill.
Tingley, Pat	4	1	8.86	15	0	0	1	21	35	22	21	8	18	.330	L	L	6-6	215	7-5-80	2001	Downingtown, Pa.
Tyler, Scott	0	1	6.75	5	3	0	0	11	11	9	8	2	14	.255	R	R	6-3	205	2-12-84	2001	Perth, Australia
Wheldon, Rhys	2	0	1.17	13	0	0	0	15	11	5	2	13	12	.200	R	R	6-3	205			Perth, Australia

MONTREAL EXPOS

BY MICHAEL LEVESQUE

After another disappointing year, when whatever could go wrong on and off the field did, the Expos went into the offseason not knowing what the future holds for the franchise.

The team roared out of the gate to a 6-1 start in 2001, and then it was all downhill. Montreal endured its fourth straight season with at least 94 losses, despite seeing its payroll quadruple since 1998.

Manager Felipe Alou, one of the most popular figures in team history, was fired May 31 when the team was 21-32. Owner Jeffrey Loria replaced Alou with broadcaster Jeff Torborg, and he didn't fare much better as Montreal finished dead last in the National League East at 68-94, 20 games behind division-winning Atlanta.

General manager Jim Beattie, who had been with the club since 1995, resigned during the team's final homestand, effective Oct. 31. His assistant Larry Beinfest was appointed interim general manager. The fallout prompted the departure of director of professional scouting Michael Berger.

The team never fared well at the gate, either. The Expos drew 619,451 fans, the lowest figure in the major leagues—an average of 7,648 a game.

Montreal's big offseason acquisition proved disappointing, as third baseman Fernando Tatis, acquired from St. Louis, was placed on the disabled list. Surgery on his left knee in August ended his season. The team also parted ways with Hideki Irabu, who was released after he was hospitalized for excessive consumption of alcohol in August. Josh Girdley, the team's first-round pick in 1999, missed the majority of the year after a dirt-bike accident.

There were bright spots, however: most notably, the talented young core of the team led by outfielder Vladimir Guerrero, second baseman Jose Vidro, shortstop

RICK BATTLE

Vladimir Guerrero   Brandon Phillips

PLAYERS OF THE YEAR

MAJOR LEAGUE: Vladimir Guerrero, of

Guerrero was one of the few bright lights in an otherwise dismal 2001 showing by the Expos—both on and off the field. He hit .307-34-108. At age 25, he has 170 career home runs.

MINOR LEAGUE: Brandon Phillips, ss

Phillips started well at Class A Jupiter in 2001 and did even better after a promotion to Double-A Harrisburg. He hit .292-11-59 between the two stops and also stole 30 bases.

Orlando Cabrera and righthanders Javier Vazquez and Tony Armas.

Guerrero became the first Expos player in history to become a member of the 30-30 club. The 25-year-old outfielder hit .307-34-108, adding 45 doubles and 37 stolen bases.

On defense, Cabrera led all National League shortstops with the most total chances and a .986 fielding percentage. He hit .276-14-96 and stole 19 bases, while also hitting 41 doubles. Vazquez led the pitching staff by going 16-11, 3.42 with 208 strikeouts in 223 innings. A beaning on Sept. 17 broke bones in his right eye socket, ending his season.

Only Class A Jupiter had a winning record among Expos farm teams. Low Class A Clinton, short-season Vermont and the Rookie-level Gulf Coast Expos all finished last in their respective leagues.

Shortstop Brandon Phillips, who turned 20 in June, emerged as the organization's top prospect after hitting a combined .292-11-59 with 31 doubles and 30 stolen bases between Jupiter and Double-A Harrisburg.

Outfielder Grady Sizemore, a coveted quarterback recruit who turned down a University of Washington football scholarship in 2000 to sign for $2 million, improved in his first full season. The 19-year-old hit .218 through June, then finished with a .327 surge to finish the year at .268-2-61 for Clinton.

But the obvious strength of the system remained pitching. No matter the fate of the franchise, the team has stockpiled an impressive group of righthanders, including Donnie Bridges, Ron Chiavacci, Zach Day, Shawn Hill, Josh Karp, Don Levinski, Juan Lima, Ignacio Puello, T.J. Tucker and Justin Wayne; and lefthanders Anthony Ferrari, Girdley, Eric Good, Cliff Lee, Luke Lockwood, Rich Rundles and Phil Seibel.

ORGANIZATION LEADERS

BATTING

*AVG	Matt Watson, Jupiter	330
R	Val Pascucci, Harrisburg	79
	Jason Bay, Jupiter/Clinton	79
H	Brandon Watson, Clinton	160
TB	Ron Calloway, Ottawa/Harrisburg	254
2B	Ron Calloway, Ottawa/Harrisburg	34
3B	Henry Mateo, Ottawa	12
HR	Val Pascucci, Harrisburg	21
RBI	Ron Calloway, Ottawa/Harrisburg	82
BB	Grady Sizemore, Clinton	81
SO	Tootie Myers, Harrisburg	118
	Rich Lane, Jupiter	118
SB	Henry Mateo, Ottawa	47

PITCHING

W	Justin Wayne, Harrisburg/Jupiter	16
L	Pat Collins, Jupiter	12
	Ben Washburn, Clinton	12
#ERA	Luke Lockwood, Clinton	2.70
G	Jim Serrano, Ottawa/Harrisburg	56
CG	Luke Lockwood, Clinton	3
SV	Bob Scanlan, Ottawa	23
IP	T.J. Tucker, Ottawa/Harrisburg	166
BB	Ron Chiavacci, Harrisburg	81
SO	Ron Chiavacci, Harrisburg	161

*Minimum 250 At-Bats #Minimum 75 Innings

MONTREAL EXPOS

Managers: Felipe Alou, Jeff Torborg

2001 Record: 68-94, .420 (5th, NL East)

BATTING	AVG	G	AB	R	H	2B	3B	HR	RBI	BB	SO	SB	CS	SLG	OBP	B	T	HT	WT	DOB	1st Yr	Resides
Barrett, Michael	.250	132	472	42	118	33	2	6	38	25	54	2	1	.367	.289	R	R	6-2	200	10-22-76	1995	West Palm Beach, Fla.
Bergeron, Peter	.211	102	375	53	79	11	4	3	16	28	87	10	7	.285	.275	L	R	6-0	190	11-9-77	1996	St. Petersburg, Fla.
Blum, Geoff	.236	148	453	57	107	25	0	9	50	43	94	9	5	.351	.313	B	R	6-3	200	4-26-73	1994	Los Angeles, Calif.
Bradley, Milton	.223	67	220	19	49	16	3	1	19	19	62	7	4	.336	.288	B	R	6-0	190	4-15-78	1996	Long Beach, Calif.
Cabrera, Orlando	.276	162	626	64	173	41	6	14	96	43	54	19	7	.428	.324	R	R	5-10	185	11-2-74	1994	Cartagena, Colombia
De la Rosa, Tomas	.000	1	1	0	0	0	0	0	0	0	0	0	0	.000	.000	R	R	5-10	170	1-28-78	1996	La Victoria, D.R.
Ducey, Rob	.239	27	46	6	11	2	0	2	8	10	14	0	1	.413	.379	L	R	6-2	183	5-24-65	1984	Palm Harbor, Fla.
2-team (30 Phil.)	.233	57	73	10	17	3	0	3	12	16	25	0	1	.397	.374							
Guerrero, Vladimir	.307	159	599	107	184	45	4	34	108	60	88	37	16	.566	.377	R	R	6-3	210	2-9-76	1993	Bani, D.R.
Jones, Terry	.260	30	77	8	20	5	0	0	2	2	11	3	0	.325	.278	B	R	5-10	170	2-15-71	1993	Birmingham, Ala.
Knorr, Randy	.220	34	91	13	20	2	0	3	10	8	22	0	0	.341	.287	R	R	6-2	215	11-12-68	1986	Tampa, Fla.
Martinez, Sandy	.000	1	0	0	0	0	0	0	0	0	0	0	0	.000	.000	L	R	6-2	215	10-3-72	1990	Santo Domingo, D.R.
Mateo, Henry	.333	5	9	1	3	1	0	0	0	1	0	1	0	.444	.333	B	R	5-11	180	10-14-76	1995	Santurce, P.R.
Minor, Ryan	.158	55	95	10	15	2	0	2	13	9	31	0	1	.242	.234	R	R	6-7	245	1-5-74	1996	Edmond, Okla.
Mordecai, Mike	.280	96	254	28	71	17	2	3	32	19	53	2	2	.398	.330	R	R	5-10	185	12-13-67	1989	Kennesaw, Ga.
Pride, Curtis	.250	36	76	8	19	3	1	1	9	9	22	3	2	.355	.345	L	R	6-0	210	12-17-68	1986	West Palm Beach, Fla.
Raines, Tim Sr.	.308	47	78	13	24	8	1	0	4	18	6	1	0	.436	.433	B	R	5-8	195	9-16-59	1977	Heathrow, Fla.
Schneider, Brian	.317	27	41	4	13	3	0	1	6	6	3	0	0	.463	.396	L	R	6-1	200	11-26-76	1995	Chadds Ford, Pa.
Seguignol, Fernando	.140	46	50	0	7	2	0	0	5	2	17	0	0	.180	.185	B	R	6-5	230	1-19-75	1993	Panama City, Panama
Smith, Mark	.242	80	194	28	47	13	1	6	18	23	38	0	2	.412	.326	R	R	6-3	225	5-7-70	1991	Arcadia, Calif.
Stevens, Lee	.245	152	542	77	133	35	1	25	95	74	157	2	1	.452	.338	L	L	6-4	235	10-3-67	1986	Grapevine, Texas
Tatis, Fernando	.255	41	145	20	37	9	0	2	11	16	43	0	0	.359	.330	R	R	5-10	180	1-1-75	1993	San Pedro de Macoris, D.R.
Tracy, Andy	.109	38	55	4	6	1	0	2	8	6	26	0	0	.236	.190	L	R	6-3	225	12-11-73	1996	Bowling Green, Ohio
Vidro, Jose	.319	124	486	82	155	34	1	15	59	31	49	4	1	.486	.371	B	R	5-11	195	8-27-74	1992	Sabana Grande, P.R.
Wilkerson, Brad	.205	47	117	11	24	7	2	1	5	17	41	2	1	.325	.304	L	L	6-0	200	6-1-77	1999	Owensboro, Ky.

PITCHING	W	L	ERA	G	GS	CG	SV	IP	H	R	ER	BB	SO	AVG	B	T	HT	WT	DOB	1st Yr	Resides
Armas, Tony	9	14	4.03	34	34	0	0	197	180	101	88	91	176	.246	R	R	6-4	215	4-29-78	1994	Puerto Piritu, Venez.
Blank, Matt	2	2	5.16	5	4	0	0	23	23	14	13	13	11	.267	L	L	6-2	195	4-5-79	1997	Arlington, Texas
Cubillan, Darwin	0	0	4.10	29	0	0	0	26	31	13	12	12	19	.295	R	R	6-2	170	11-15-74	1994	Bobure, Venez.
Eischen, Joey	0	1	4.85	24	0	0	0	30	29	17	16	16	19	.256	L	L	6-6	216	5-25-70	1989	Rotonda West, Fla.
Irabu, Hideki	0	2	4.86	3	3	0	0	17	22	9	9	3	18	.314	R	R	6-4	250	5-5-69	1997	Chiba, Japan
Johnson, Mike	0	4	4.76	10	0	0	0	11	13	6	6	4	10	.295	L	R	6-2	180	10-3-75	1993	Jupiter, Fla.
Lira, Felipe	0	0	12.60	4	0	0	0	5	11	7	7	2	3	.440	R	R	6-1	215	4-26-72	1990	Miranda, Venez.
Lloyd, Graeme	9	5	4.35	84	0	0	1	70	74	38	34	21	44	.272	L	L	6-7	225	4-9-67	1988	Gnarwarre, Australia
Mattes, Troy	3	3	6.00	8	8	0	0	45	51	33	30	21	26	.284	R	R	6-7	230	8-26-75	1994	Sarasota, Fla.
Mota, Guillermo	1	3	5.26	53	0	0	0	50	51	30	29	18	31	.271	R	R	6-4	205	7-25-73	1991	San Pedro de Macoris, D.R.
Munoz, Bobby	0	4	5.14	15	7	0	0	42	53	25	24	21	21	.321	R	R	6-7	210	3-3-68	1989	Irving, Texas
Ohka, Tomo	1	4	4.77	10	10	0	0	55	65	30	29	10	31	.302	R	R	6-5	230	3-18-76	1999	Kyoto, Japan
Pavano, Carl	1	6	6.33	8	8	0	0	43	59	33	30	16	36	.331	R	R	6-5	230	1-8-76	1994	Palm Beach Gardens, Fla.
Peters, Chris	2	4	7.55	13	6	0	0	31	47	26	26	15	14	.367	L	L	6-1	170	1-28-72	1993	Bethel Park, Pa.
Reames, Britt	4	8	5.59	41	13	0	0	95	101	68	59	48	86	.272	R	R	5-11	175	8-19-73	1995	Seneca, S.C.
Scanlan, Bob	0	0	7.86	18	0	0	0	26	37	23	23	14	5	.339	R	R	6-7	215	8-9-66	1984	Beverly Hills, Calif.
Stewart, Scott	3	1	3.78	62	0	0	3	48	43	20	20	13	39	.242	R	L	6-2	225	8-14-75	1994	Stanley, N.C.
Strickland, Scott	2	6	3.21	77	0	0	9	81	67	36	29	41	85	.221	R	R	5-11	180	4-26-76	1997	Spring, Texas
Telford, Anthony	0	1	10.29	8	0	0	0	7	14	12	8	5	5	.411	R	R	6-0	195	3-6-66	1987	Pinellas Park, Fla.
Thurman, Mike	9	11	5.33	28	26	0	0	147	172	90	87	50	96	.294	R	R	6-5	210	7-22-73	1994	West Palm Beach, Fla.
Urbina, Ugueth	2	1	4.24	45	0	0	15	47	42	24	22	21	57	.235	R	R	6-0	205	2-15-74	1991	Ocumare del Tuy, Venez.
Vazquez, Javier	16	11	3.42	32	32	5	0	224	197	92	85	44	208	.234	R	R	6-2	195	7-25-76	1994	Ponce, P.R.
Yoshii, Masato	4	7	4.78	42	11	0	0	113	127	65	60	26	63	.279	R	R	6-2	210	4-20-65	1998	Tokyo, Japan

FIELDING

Catcher	PCT	G	PO	A	E	DP	PB
Barrett	.993	131	880	50	7	6	8
Knorr	.989	27	168	5	2	0	2
Martinez	1.000	1	2	0	0	0	0
Mordecai	1.000	1	1	0	0	0	0
Schneider	1.000	14	77	7	0	1	2

First Base	PCT	G	PO	A	E	DP
Blum	.988	14	74	9	1	9
Minor	.750	1	3	0	1	0
Mordecai	1.000	1	1	0	0	0
Seguignol	.920	7	20	3	2	3
Smith	1.000	1	0	0	0	0
Stevens	.986	152	1287	92	19	113
Tracy	1.000	3	11	0	0	1

Second Base	PCT	G	PO	A	E	DP
Blum	.989	25	39	47	1	5
Mateo	.818	2	3	6	2	0
Mordecai	.990	32	46	58	1	13
Vidro	.983	121	204	315	9	63

Third Base	PCT	G	PO	A	E	DP
Blum	.966	72	49	120	6	12
Minor	.970	24	12	20	1	0
Mordecai	.974	42	21	53	2	2
Tatis	.889	41	18	54	9	2
Tracy	1.000	11	5	12	0	0

Shortstop	PCT	G	PO	A	E	DP
Blum	1.000	4	2	3	0	1
Cabrera	.986	162	246	514	11	106

Outfield	PCT	G	PO	A	E	DP
Mordecai	1.000	4	3	6	0	2
Bergeron	.996	101	220	6	1	1
Blum	1.000	35	51	1	0	0
Bradley	.988	65	155	5	2	1
Ducey	1.000	14	23	1	0	0
Guerrero	.965	158	320	14	12	5
Jones	.977	22	41	2	1	1
Minor	.000	2	0	0	0	0
Mordecai	1.000	1	2	0	0	0
Pride	1.000	23	32	1	0	0
Raines	1.000	20	23	0	0	0
Seguignol	1.000	13	8	1	0	0
Smith	1.000	60	99	2	0	1
Wilkerson	.970	38	62	2	2	0

Javier Vazquez: Expos righthander went 16-11 with 208 strikeouts

STEVE MOORE

Tony Armas: Nine wins and 176 strikeouts in 2001

MORRIS FOSTOFF

FARM SYSTEM

Director, Player Development: Tony LaCava

Class	Farm Team	League	W	L	Pct.	Finish*	Manager(s)	First Yr.
AAA	Ottawa (Ontario) Lynx	International	68	76	.472	t-7th (14)	Stan Hough	1993
AA	Harrisburg (Pa.) Senators	Eastern	66	76	.465	9th (12)	Luis Dorante	1991
A#	Jupiter (Fla.) Hammerheads	Florida State	70	69	.504	t-4th (12)	Tim Leiper	1998
A	Clinton (Iowa) Lumber Kings	Midwest	51	85	.375	14th (14)	Steve Phillips	2001
A	Vermont Expos	New York-Penn	28	47	.373	12th (14)	Steve Balboni	1994
Rookie	Jupiter (Fla.) Expos	Gulf Coast	20	40	.333	t-14th (14)	Dave Dangler	1998

*Finish in overall standings (No. of teams in league)   #Advanced level

OTTAWA
Class AAA

INTERNATIONAL LEAGUE

BATTING	AVG	G	AB	R	H	2B	3B	HR	RBI	BB	SO	SB	CS	SLG	OBP	B	T	HT	WT	DOB	1st Yr	Resides
Bergeron, Peter	.238	52	206	29	49	5	3	0	8	20	42	15	7	.291	.307	L	R	6-0	190	11-9-77	1996	St. Petersburg, Fla.
Berroa, Geronimo	.286	16	56	8	16	3	0	2	2	9	8	0	0	.446	.394	R	R	6-0	210	3-18-65	1984	New York, N.Y.
Bradley, Milton	.272	35	136	21	37	7	2	2	13	23	30	14	1	.397	.383	B	R	6-0	190	4-15-78	1996	Long Beach, Calif.
Bruce, Mo	.133	6	15	1	2	0	0	0	0	2	7	0	0	.133	.235	R	R	5-10	190	5-1-75	1996	Kansas City, Mo.
Calloway, Ron	.264	61	239	27	63	12	0	10	35	16	64	11	1	.439	.323	L	L	6-0	190	9-4-76	1997	Los Banos, Calif.
Carroll, Jamey	.240	83	267	26	64	8	2	0	16	18	41	5	5	.285	.292	R	R	5-10	175	2-18-74	1996	St. Petersburg, Fla.
Cotton, John	.280	24	93	11	26	8	1	5	15	6	25	2	1	.548	.330	R	R	6-0	190	10-30-70	1989	Houston, Texas
De la Rosa, Tomas	.238	121	420	56	100	24	0	7	30	40	63	12	9	.345	.309	R	R	5-10	170	1-28-78	1996	La Victoria, D.R.
Gonzalez, Jimmy	.177	58	215	18	38	8	1	6	19	8	49	0	0	.307	.212	R	R	6-3	235	3-8-73	1991	Hartford, Conn.
Johannes, Todd	.000	4	10	0	0	0	0	0	0	0	5	0	0	.000	.000	R	R	6-3	185	10-25-76	1999	Sunnyvale, Calif.
Jones, Terry	.294	17	68	6	20	2	0	0	5	3	13	2	3	.324	.319	B	R	5-10	170	2-15-71	1993	Birmingham, Ala.
Mateo, Henry	.268	118	500	71	134	14	12	5	43	33	89	47	14	.374	.322	B	R	5-11	180	10-14-76	1995	Santurce, P.R.
McKinley, Dan	.281	105	360	31	101	18	6	5	39	20	85	12	6	.406	.325	L	R	6-0	185	5-15-76	1997	Chandler, Ariz.
Minor, Ryan	.245	42	143	20	35	6	2	5	19	16	41	0	0	.420	.343	R	R	6-7	245	1-5-74	1996	Edmond, Okla.
Nunnari, Talmadge	.219	110	343	35	75	15	1	4	35	38	81	13	2	.303	.301	L	L	6-1	200	4-9-75	1997	Pensacola, Fla.
Ortiz, Luis	.281	16	57	4	16	5	1	0	8	3	6	0	0	.404	.311	R	R	6-0	195	5-25-70	1991	Santo Domingo, D.R.
Pride, Curtis	.333	22	81	14	27	4	1	5	15	12	26	6	1	.593	.432	L	R	6-0	210	12-17-68	1986	West Palm Beach, Fla.
Raines, Tim Sr.	.143	2	7	1	1	1	0	0	0	1	1	0	0	.286	.250	B	R	5-8	195	9-16-59	1977	Heathrow, Fla.
Reding, Josh	.111	6	18	0	2	1	0	0	2	1	6	0	0	.167	.227	R	R	6-3	175	3-7-77	1997	Anaheim, Calif.
Sasser, Rob	.232	52	181	20	42	9	3	3	25	22	41	7	1	.365	.317	R	R	6-3	205	3-9-75	1993	Oakland, Calif.
Schneider, Brian	.275	97	338	33	93	27	1	6	43	27	55	2	0	.414	.336	L	R	6-1	200	11-26-76	1995	Chadds Ford, Pa.
Seguignol, Fernando	.310	60	242	36	75	12	0	14	45	15	49	0	1	.533	.363	B	R	6-5	230	1-19-75	1993	Panama City, Panama
Smith, Mark	.207	40	145	20	30	8	0	6	17	15	38	4	2	.386	.290	R	R	6-3	225	5-7-70	1991	Arcadia, Calif.
Thompson, Ryan	.165	21	85	6	14	4	0	2	9	3	22	0	2	.282	.202	R	R	6-3	215	11-4-67	1987	Edesville, Md.
Tracy, Andy	.205	53	190	17	39	11	1	4	19	24	72	4	2	.337	.300	L	R	6-3	225	12-11-73	1996	Bowling Green, Ohio

BATTING	AVG	G	AB	R	H	2B	3B	HR	RBI	BB	SO	SB	CS	SLG	OBP	B	T	HT	WT	DOB	1st Yr	Resides
Ware, Jeremy	.265	53	147	13	39	13	0	2	13	6	24	2	0	.395	.294	R	R	6-0	205	10-23-75	1995	Guelph, Ontario
Wilkerson, Brad	.270	69	233	43	63	10	0	12	48	60	68	12	5	.468	.423	L	L	6-0	200	6-1-77	1999	Owensboro, Ky.
Zech, Scott	.167	13	36	2	6	2	0	0	2	5	8	1	1	.222	.286	R	R	5-10	175	6-6-74	1997	Wellington, Fla.

PITCHING	W	L	ERA	G	GS	CG	SV	IP	H	R	ER	BB	SO	AVG	B	T	HT	WT	DOB	1st Yr	Resides
Agamennone, Brandon	1	0	2.38	8	0	0	0	11	6	5	3	3	7	.146	R	R	6-2	190	11-6-75	1998	Crofton, Md.
Billingsley, Brent	0	0	15.00	1	1	0	0	3	6	5	5	2	2	.461	L	L	6-2	200	4-19-75	1996	Chino Hills, Calif.
Blank, Matt	6	7	5.18	14	14	1	0	82	89	52	47	30	58	.277	L	L	6-2	195	4-5-76	1997	Arlington, Texas
Bridges, Donnie	3	5	7.48	13	13	0	0	55	60	50	46	43	49	.281	R	R	6-4	220	12-10-78	1997	Hattiesburg, Miss.
Burrows, Terry	0	1	3.24	6	0	0	0	8	7	7	3	5	6	.225	L	L	6-1	190	11-28-68	1990	Lake Charles, La.
Cubillan, Darwin	2	2	5.28	17	4	0	2	31	31	22	18	15	29	.267	R	R	6-2	170	11-15-74	1994	Bobure, Venezuela
Day, Zach	2	2	7.43	6	5	0	0	27	38	23	22	8	15	.348	R	R	6-4	185	6-15-78	1996	West Harrison, Ind.
2-team (1 Buffalo)	3	2	6.34	7	6	0	0	33	41	24	23	9	19	.315							
Eischen, Joey	2	3	3.24	34	1	0	1	52	42	16	13	11	54	.219	L	L	6-6	216	5-25-70	1989	Rotonda West, Fla.
Evans, Keith	7	3	3.98	45	2	0	1	84	94	40	37	13	72	.279	R	R	6-5	220	11-2-75	1996	San Pedro, Calif.
Flury, Pat	0	1	4.63	10	0	0	0	12	8	6	6	8	9	.205	R	R	6-2	215	3-14-73	1993	Sparks, Nev.
Irabu, Hideki	1	2	4.43	4	4	0	0	22	22	12	11	6	21	.261	R	R	6-4	250	5-5-69	1997	Chiba, Japan
Johnson, Mike	2	0	4.50	2	2	0	0	10	7	5	5	3	8	.205	L	R	6-2	180	10-3-75	1993	Jupiter, Fla.
Lira, Felipe	5	4	2.08	42	0	0	6	61	56	17	14	10	47	.247	R	R	6-1	215	4-26-72	1990	Miranda, Venez.
Manon, Julio	1	4	3.11	15	14	0	0	84	71	31	29	34	67	.234	R	R	6-0	200	4-21-73	1995	Houston, Texas
Marquez, Robert	6	2	2.97	34	0	0	6	61	57	23	20	12	27	.252	R	R	6-7	230	8-26-75	1994	Sarasota, Fla.
Mattes, Troy	5	5	3.61	15	15	0	0	82	75	38	33	33	70	.242	R	R	6-0	185	3-19-73	1995	Sicklerville, N.J.
Mitchell, Scott	0	1	4.12	6	2	0	0	20	17	10	9	10	10	.239	R	R	6-2	205	7-25-73	1991	San Pedro de Macoris, D.R.
Mota, Guillermo	0	0	2.25	4	0	0	0	4	1	1	1	0	4	.076	R	R	6-7	210	3-3-68	1989	Irving, Texas
Munoz, Bobby	4	6	3.44	19	18	1	0	110	98	47	42	39	66	.245	R	R	6-5	230	1-8-76	1994	Palm Beach Gardens, Fla.
Pavano, Carl	2	1	3.58	4	4	0	0	28	27	13	11	5	19	.247	R	R	5-11	215	8-19-73	1995	Seneca, S.C.
Reames, Britt	4	3	3.50	8	8	1	0	54	47	24	21	13	38	.242	R	R	6-1	185	8-23-73	1996	St. Clairsville, Ohio
Rose, Ted	7	9	4.03	37	15	1	0	121	125	59	54	35	98	.270	R	R	6-7	215	8-9-66	1984	Beverly Hills, Calif.
Scanlan, Bob	0	5	3.90	32	0	0	23	32	41	20	14	10	21	.297	R	R	5-10	170	5-9-76	1998	Grand Junction, Colo.
Serrano, Jim	0	1	4.50	9	0	0	0	8	11	5	4	6	11	.314	R	R	5-11	185	5-29-75	1996	Port Orchard, Wash.
Spencer, Sean	2	1	2.94	52	0	0	0	64	53	23	21	27	59	.224	L	L	5-11	185	5-29-75	1996	Port Orchard, Wash.
Stewart, Scott	0	0	1.80	4	0	0	0	5	5	1	1	1	4	.277	R	L	6-2	225	8-14-75	1994	Stanley, N.C.
Telford, Anthony	3	5	4.50	28	8	0	1	76	79	42	38	17	62	.275	R	R	6-0	195	3-6-66	1987	Pinellas Park, Fla.
Tucker, T.J.	3	5	3.11	14	14	1	0	84	68	42	29	33	63	.220	R	R	6-3	245	8-20-78	1997	New Port Richey, Fla.

FIELDING

Catcher	PCT	G	PO	A	E	DP	PB
Gonzalez	.990	57	368	27	4	4	3
Johannes	.950	3	18	1	1	1	0
Schneider	.994	89	629	79	4	4	2

First Base	PCT	G	PO	A	E	DP
Berroa	1.000	3	26	0	0	4
Minor	1.000	9	68	3	0	3
Nunnari	.995	62	527	39	3	56
Ortiz	.992	13	119	6	1	10
Seguignol	.992	54	452	37	4	47
Thompson	.964	3	26	1	1	1
Tracy	1.000	8	73	4	0	6

Second Base	PCT	G	PO	A	E	DP
Carroll	.984	28	57	67	2	15
Cotton	1.000	1	2	5	0	0

	PCT	G	PO	A	E	DP
Mateo	.963	116	251	328	22	76

Third Base	PCT	G	PO	A	E	DP
Bruce	.875	5	2	12	2	2
Carroll	.956	22	16	49	3	5
Cotton	.827	19	9	34	9	3
Minor	1.000	12	5	21	0	1
Ortiz	1.000	1	1	1	0	0
Reding	.905	6	7	12	2	1
Sasser	.860	41	29	75	17	4
Tracy	.932	37	25	85	8	15
Zech	.958	11	3	20	1	2

Shortstop	PCT	G	PO	A	E	DP
Carroll	.968	23	46	74	4	16
De La Rosa	.965	121	190	368	20	75

Outfield	PCT	G	PO	A	E	DP
Bergeron	.983	50	110	3	2	1
Berroa	1.000	4	6	0	0	0
Bradley	.966	34	80	4	3	1
Calloway	.959	56	113	3	5	0
Jones	1.000	13	20	5	0	1
McKinley	1.000	91	161	0	0	0
Minor	1.000	17	29	0	0	0
Nunnari	1.000	14	28	2	0	1
Pride	.963	19	26	0	1	0
Seguignol	1.000	3	5	0	0	0
Smith	.974	38	72	4	2	0
Thompson	1.000	15	30	2	0	0
Ware	.986	33	64	4	1	1
Wilkerson	.973	55	101	6	3	1

HARRISBURG

Class AA

EASTERN LEAGUE

BATTING	AVG	G	AB	R	H	2B	3B	HR	RBI	BB	SO	SB	CS	SLG	OBP	B	T	HT	WT	DOB	1st Yr	Resides
Bruce, Mo.	.228	45	136	19	31	6	0	3	15	8	36	14	2	.338	.274	R	R	5-10	190	5-1-75	1996	Kansas City, Mo.
Calloway, Ron	.330	74	279	48	92	22	4	9	47	24	46	25	7	.534	.385	L	L	6-0	190	9-4-76	1997	Los Banos, Calif.
Carreno, Jose	.158	40	120	3	19	1	0	0	8	12	24	0	2	.167	.237	R	R	5-11	190	4-23-78	1996	El Tigre, Venez.
Cepicky, Matt	.264	122	459	59	121	23	8	19	77	21	97	5	12	.473	.294	L	R	6-2	215	11-10-77	1999	Sun City Center, Fla.
Cotton, John	.294	5	17	5	5	0	0	3	8	1	5	0	0	.824	.333	R	R	6-0	190	10-30-70	1989	Houston, Texas
Fuentes, Javier	.280	22	50	7	14	3	1	0	6	7	4	0	0	.380	.379	R	R	6-1	182	9-27-74	1996	Austin, Texas
Gingrich, Troy	.000	13	34	0	0	0	0	0	3	10	0	0	0	.000	.081	L	L	5-10	175	1-17-77	2000	Apache Junction, Ariz.
Hodges, Scott	.275	85	305	30	84	11	2	5	32	25	56	3	2	.374	.328	L	R	6-0	190	12-26-78	1997	Lexington, Ky.
James, Kenny	.189	41	95	17	18	3	1	0	3	6	13	9	3	.242	.290	B	R	6-0	198	10-9-76	1995	Ocala, Fla.
Machado, Albenis	.261	99	341	57	89	13	3	3	33	44	56	10	7	.343	.352	B	R	5-9	175	3-20-79	1996	Caracas, Venez.
Melucci, Lou	.200	6	15	1	3	0	0	0	2	0	7	1	0	.200	.188	R	R	5-9	175	9-20-77	1999	Clarks Summit, Pa.
Myers, Tootie	.263	123	396	49	104	15	8	10	49	34	118	17	7	.417	.329	R	L	5-11	178	9-8-78	1997	Petal, Miss.
Nunnari, Talmadge	.156	9	32	4	5	2	0	1	4	1	6	0	0	.313	.200	L	L	6-1	204	4-9-75	1997	Pensacola, Fla.
Pascucci, Val	.244	138	476	79	116	17	1	21	67	65	114	8	8	.416	.344	R	R	6-6	235	11-17-78	1999	Cerritos, Calif.
Phillips, Brandon	.298	67	265	35	79	19	0	7	36	12	42	13	6	.449	.337	R	R	5-11	185	6-28-81	1999	Stone Mountain, Ga.
Reding, Josh	.202	117	372	25	75	9	4	3	34	18	94	10	5	.272	.239	R	R	6-0	170	11-18-79	1996	Anaheim, Calif.
Ruan, Wilken	.248	30	117	14	29	7	0	0	6	3	18	6	0	.308	.279	R	R	6-0	170	3-6-76	1998	Guaymate, D.R.
Sandusky, Scott	.248	114	387	36	96	20	1	2	33	35	76	7	2	.320	.321	R	R	6-0	200	3-6-76	1998	Arvada, Colo.
Sledge, Terrmel	.277	129	448	66	124	22	6	9	48	51	72	30	8	.413	.359	L	L	6-0	205	10-23-76	1999	Granada Hills, Calif.
Ware, Jeremy	.287	27	87	12	25	6	0	3	16	7	14	1	1	.460	.340	R	R	6-0	205	10-23-75	1995	Guelph, Ontario
Zech, Scott	.259	34	85	3	14	3	4	2	12	9	21	1	0	.294	.360	R	R	5-10	175	6-6-74	1997	Wellington, Fla.

PITCHING	W	L	ERA	G	GS	CG	SV	IP	H	R	ER	BB	SO	AVG	B	T	HT	WT	DOB	1st Yr	Resides
Agamennone, Brandon	4	0	4.13	45	0	0	3	61	59	31	28	23	51	.255	R	R	6-2	190	11-6-75	1998	Crofton, Md.
Albin, Scott	0	0	4.91	4	0	0	0	4	4	2	2	2	4	.266	R	R	6-0	185	9-27-75	1999	Carson City, Nev.
Andrews, Jeff	1	0	5.56	9	0	0	0	11	15	7	7	4	13	.312	R	R	6-3	190	9-1-74	1997	Beverly, Mass.
Arthurs, Shane	0	0	1.69	5	0	0	0	5	7	3	1	2	5	.318	L	L	6-5	185	8-30-79	1997	Oklahoma City, Okla.
Billingsley, Brent	7	9	5.37	19	19	1	0	112	128	77	67	34	97	.285	L	L	6-2	200	4-19-75	1996	Chino Hills, Calif.

PITCHING	W	L	ERA	G	GS	CG	SV	IP	H	R	ER	BB	SO	AVG	B	T	HT	WT	DOB	1st Yr	Resides
Bridges, Donnie	1	2	3.24	3	3	0	0	17	14	10	6	13	14	.233	R	R	6-4	220	12-10-78	1997	Hattiesburg, Miss.
Chapman, Jake	7	3	2.39	53	0	0	2	68	55	26	18	27	69	.218	R	L	6-1	190	1-11-74	1996	Rensselaer, Ind.
Chiavacci, Ron	3	11	3.97	25	25	2	0	147	137	77	65	76	161	.247	R	R	6-2	220	9-5-77	1998	Scranton, Pa.
Crumpton, Chuck	2	6	4.32	52	0	0	4	67	73	39	32	25	44	.286	R	R	6-4	210	12-30-76	1999	Mesquite, Texas
Darrell, Tommy	0	2	7.79	24	1	0	0	35	45	37	30	19	15	.302	R	R	6-6	220	7-21-76	1995	Dunbar, Pa.
Davis, Allen	2	2	2.89	8	8	1	0	53	48	20	17	9	36	.240	L	L	6-4	195	10-1-75	1998	Ovilla, Texas
Hebson, Bryan	2	8	4.44	26	8	2	0	75	78	40	37	19	54	.271	R	R	6-5	210	3-12-76	1997	Phenix City, Ala.
Mangum, Mark	7	8	4.62	26	26	2	0	140	161	88	72	36	59	.291	R	R	6-2	180	8-24-78	1997	Kingwood, Texas
Manon, Julio	4	3	3.12	10	7	0	1	52	50	20	18	16	44	.264	L	R	6-0	200	6-10-73	1992	St. Petersburg, Fla.
Matz, Brian	1	8	5.49	37	13	0	0	97	116	68	59	28	62	.294	L	L	6-1	205	9-23-74	1996	Towson, Md.
Mitchell, Scott	1	2	4.15	9	4	0	0	22	24	11	10	6	14	.282	R	R	6-0	185	3-19-73	1995	Sicklerville, N.J.
Salyers, Jeremy	4	2	5.56	16	1	0	0	23	24	15	14	6	13	.272	R	R	6-3	200	1-31-76	1996	Pound, Va.
Serrano, Jim	6	3	2.18	47	0	0	20	54	30	20	13	24	73	.160	R	R	5-10	170	5-9-76	1998	Grand Junction, Colo.
Tucker, T.J.	5	5	3.73	13	13	0	0	82	77	38	34	37	57	.254	R	R	6-3	245	8-20-78	1997	New Port Richey, Fla.
Wamback, Trevor	0	0	10.57	3	0	0	0	8	12	9	9	0	3	.375	R	R	6-3	205	12-22-76	1998	Halifax, Nova Scotia
Wayne, Justin	9	2	2.62	14	14	0	0	93	87	28	27	34	70	.247	R	R	6-3	200	4-16-79	2000	Honolulu, Hawaii

FIELDING

Catcher	PCT	G	PO	A	E	DP	PB
Carreno	.989	37	252	22	3	2	7
Sandusky	.985	108	739	72	12	9	9

First Base	PCT	G	PO	A	E	DP
Cotton	.857	3	10	2	2	0
Fuentes	1.000	1	1	0	0	0
Nunnari	1.000	3	24	2	0	3
Pascucci	.992	19	110	8	1	5
Sandusky	1.000	7	37	4	0	3
Sledge	.985	120	887	74	15	90

Second Base	PCT	G	PO	A	E	DP
Bruce	.978	30	56	79	3	24
Fuentes	.714	1	2	3	2	1
Machado	.966	81	150	162	11	48
Melucci	1.000	2	0	1	0	0
Myers	.938	32	40	65	7	14

	PCT	G	PO	A	E	DP
Phillips	1.000	1	2	2	0	0
Reding	1.000	10	14	11	0	2
Zech	.947	11	20	16	2	3

Third Base	PCT	G	PO	A	E	DP
Bruce	1.000	15	11	9	0	1
Cotton	1.000	2	0	3	0	0
Fuentes	.840	11	10	11	4	0
Hodges	.918	76	54	137	17	11
Machado	1.000	4	0	8	0	0
Melucci	1.000	4	3	6	0	0
Phillips	1.000	1	0	1	0	0
Reding	.940	35	28	51	5	9
Zech	.956	17	12	31	2	3

Shortstop	PCT	G	PO	A	E	DP
Bruce	1.000	1	2	1	0	1
Machado	.931	16	19	35	4	8

	PCT	G	PO	A	E	DP
Phillips	.957	66	105	165	12	31
Reding	.961	71	123	173	12	37
Zech	1.000	3	2	5	0	1

Outfield	PCT	G	PO	A	E	DP
Calloway	.969	63	121	6	4	0
Cepicky	.986	104	199	8	3	0
Cotton	.000	1	0	0	0	0
Gingrich	.875	6	7	0	1	0
James	1.000	20	35	1	0	0
Myers	.983	77	168	8	3	2
Nunnari	.900	3	8	1	1	0
Pascucci	.978	119	220	7	5	2
Reding	1.000	5	4	3	0	0
Ruan	.976	28	81	2	2	0
Sledge	1.000	3	5	0	0	0
Ware	1.000	22	45	3	0	2

FLORIDA STATE LEAGUE

BATTING	AVG	G	AB	R	H	2B	3B	HR	RBI	BB	SO	SB	CS	SLG	OBP	B	T	HT	WT	DOB	1st Yr	Resides
Ackerman, Scott	.250	90	324	31	81	12	1	3	44	25	52	1	4	.321	.301	R	R	6-1	215	4-23-79	1997	Oregon City, Ore.
Bay, Jason	.195	38	123	12	24	4	1	1	10	18	26	10	3	.268	.306	R	R	6-2	200	9-20-78	2000	Trail, B.C.
Blum, Greg	.194	64	201	22	39	13	0	3	22	21	53	2	2	.303	.315	R	R	6-1	205	8-7-78	2000	Chino, Calif.
Downing, Phil	.238	67	227	48	54	15	3	3	30	29	69	6	4	.370	.324	L	L	6-1	190	8-22-78	2000	Sandy, Utah
Gingrich, Troy	.241	70	199	30	48	9	3	0	15	37	37	6	7	.317	.380	L	L	5-10	175	1-17-77	2000	Apache Junction, Ariz.
James, Kenny	.273	74	282	49	77	8	5	2	19	17	40	22	8	.358	.326	B	R	6-0	198	10-9-76	1995	Ocala, Fla.
Johannes, Todd	.086	22	58	5	5	0	0	1	2	7	23	0	0	.138	.197	R	R	6-3	185	10-25-76	1999	Sunnyvale, Calif.
Jones, Terry	.160	7	25	4	4	1	0	0	1	1	3	0	0	.200	.192	B	R	5-10	170	2-15-71	1993	Birmingham, Ala.
Kerner, Craig	.200	8	15	2	3	0	0	0	3	6	0	0		.200	.400	L	R	6-1	195	11-13-78	2000	Whitesboro, N.Y.
Lane, Rich	.235	125	447	41	105	20	3	4	49	33	118	2	5	.320	.295	L	L	6-2	200	1-4-80	1999	Tustin, Calif.
Lugo, Felix	.245	77	269	31	66	12	6	5	36	14	89	7	3	.390	.294	B	R	6-2	200	8-1-80	1996	Bani, D.R.
McKinley, Josh	.252	128	464	63	117	19	2	2	54	70	83	28	10	.315	.351	B	R	6-2	205	9-14-79	1998	Windermere, Fla.
Meadows, Randy	.071	5	14	1	1	0	0	0	0	0	5	0	0	.071	.071	R	R	6-3	185	8-15-76	1998	Nesbit, Miss.
Melucci, Lou	.219	65	201	20	44	6	1	1	16	25	61	3	4	.274	.308	R	R	5-9	175	9-20-77	1999	Clarks Summit, Pa.
Miller, Eric	.270	19	63	4	17	3	1	0	7	3	8	2	1	.349	.309	R	R	6-2	175	12-9-77	2000	Tempe, Ariz.
Phillips, Brandon	.284	55	194	36	55	12	2	4	23	38	45	17	3	.428	.414	R	R	5-11	185	6-28-81	1999	Stone Mountain, Ga.
Pittman, Tom	.214	78	281	31	60	7	3	4	37	23	83	2	2	.302	.287	R	R	6-4	270	11-2-79	1997	Garyville, La.
Pride, Curtis	.190	6	21	3	4	1	0	0	0	3	3	0	1	.238	.292	L	R	6-0	210	12-17-68	1986	West Palm Beach, Fla.
Raines, Tim Sr.	.348	8	23	7	8	1	1	1	5	5	4	1	0	.609	.448	B	R	5-8	195	9-16-59	1977	Heathrow, Fla.
Ruan, Wilken	.283	72	293	41	83	8	2	2	26	10	35	25	14	.345	.313	R	R	6-0	170	11-18-79	1996	Guaymate, D.R.
Valdez, Wilson	.249	64	233	34	58	13	2	2	19	10	33	7	3	.348	.286	R	R	5-11	160	5-20-80	1997	Bani, D.R.
Wallis, Jacob	.143	2	7	0	1	0	0	0	0	0	3	0	0	.143	.143	R	R	6-3	200	2-1-80	1998	Joshua, Texas
Watson, Matt	.330	124	446	70	147	33	4	5	74	63	45	17	9	.455	.417	L	R	5-11	190	9-5-78	1999	Lancaster, Pa.
Wilkerson, Brad	.231	6	26	3	6	3	0	0	1	3	10	0	0	.346	.310	L	L	6-0	200	6-1-77	1999	Owensboro, Ky.
Zech, Scott	.222	32	99	10	22	1	0	0	7	14	17	2	0	.232	.325	R	R	5-10	175	6-6-74	1997	Wellington, Fla.

GAMES BY POSITION: C—Ackerman 68, Blum 56, Johannes 16, Wallis 2. **1B**—Lane 120, Miller 2, Pittman 23. **2B**—Bay 1, McKinley 128, Melucci 14. **3B**—Lugo 76, Meadows 4, Melucci 28, Miller 11, Zech 26. **SS**—Melucci 13, Miller 7, Phillips 55, Valdez 64, Zech 6. **OF**—Bay 1, Downing 65, Gingrich 63, James 74, Jones 4, Kerner 4, Meadows 1, Melucci 2, Pride 5, Raines 3, Ruan 72, Watson 107.

PITCHING	W	L	ERA	G	GS	CG	SV	IP	H	R	ER	BB	SO	AVG	B	T	HT	WT	DOB	1st Yr	Resides
Arthurs, Shane	2	0	3.54	28	3	0	1	56	69	29	22	19	33	.297	R	R	6-5	185	8-30-79	1997	Oklahoma City, Okla.
Bridges, Donnie	0	1	6.75	1	1	0	0	4	7	6	3	3	2	.368	R	R	6-4	220	12-10-78	1997	Hattiesburg, Miss.
Bye, Chris	1	0	3.04	19	0	0	0	24	24	8	8	9	15	.263	R	R	5-11	190	9-10-77	2000	Englewood, Colo.
Charron, Eric	0	1	6.00	2	0	0	0	3	4	3	2	1	1	.333	R	R	5-11	170	4-3-79	1999	Montreal, Quebec
Collins, Pat	9	12	4.31	33	12	0	1	111	101	71	53	71	90	.239	R	R	6-5	235	3-3-78	1999	Union, N.J.
Corcoran, Roy	0	0	0.00	1	0	0	0	2	0	0	0	2	0	.000	R	R	5-10	170	5-11-80	2001	Slaughter, La.
Crumpton, Chuck	0	1	1.50	3	0	0	0	6	4	2	1	3	3	.200	R	R	6-4	210	12-30-76	1999	Mesquite, Texas
Darrell, Tommy	1	1	2.57	11	0	0	0	21	14	6	6	16	18	.189	R	R	6-6	220	7-21-76	1995	Dunbar, Pa.
Ferrari, Anthony	2	3	0.79	51	0	0	21	57	36	11	5	17	45	.180	L	L	5-9	165	6-22-78	2000	Greenbrae, Calif.
George, Todd	1	0	0.00	1	0	0	0	3	4	0	0	0	2	.307	R	R	6-3	215	10-24-77	2001	Oklahoma City, Okla.
Good, Eric	5	5	2.82	21	20	1	0	108	104	42	34	26	70	.248	R	L	6-3	185	4-10-80	1998	Port Charlotte, Fla.
Irabu, Hideki	0	0	3.00	3	3	0	0	9	9	3	3	4	9	.151	R	R	6-4	250	5-5-69	1997	Chiba, Japan
Klepacki, Ed	9	9	3.50	26	26	1	0	136	135	69	53	49	74	.263	R	R	6-5	185	4-26-78	1998	Midwest City, Okla.
Lee, Cliff	6	7	2.79	21	20	0	0	110	78	43	34	46	129	.199	L	L	6-3	190	8-30-78	2000	Benton, Ark.

PITCHING	W	L	ERA	G	GS	CG	SV	IP	H	R	ER	BB	SO	AVG	B	T	HT	WT	DOB	1st Yr	Resides
Lewis, Craig	2	1	1.05	17	0	0	0	26	20	10	3	5	9	.202	R	R	6-5	210	12-30-76	1997	Sydney, Australia
Lima, Juan	0	0	0.00	1	0	0	0	2	0	0	0	0	1	.000	R	R	6-0	160	4-10-82	1999	San Pedro de Macoris, D.R.
Marrero, Darwin	5	8	3.67	21	17	1	0	103	103	47	42	25	62	.260	R	R	6-1	190	2-9-81	1997	Valencia, Venez.
Maust, David	0	1	15.00	1	1	0	0	3	7	5	5	1	0	.500	L	L	6-2	205	11-6-78	2001	Morgantown, W.Va.
McAvoy, Jeff	2	2	2.70	46	1	0	3	77	70	31	23	20	52	.240	R	R	6-3	215	3-15-77	2000	Palmer, Mass.
McCasland, Ralph	0	1	4.50	17	0	0	0	28	32	15	14	6	10	.285	L	L	6-4	190	2-2-79	2000	Jefferson City, Mo.
Pavano, Carl	1	1	2.19	3	3	0	0	12	10	7	3	2	11	.212	R	R	6-5	230	1-8-76	1994	Palm Beach Gardens, Fla.
Perez, Julio	6	3	3.61	34	0	0	4	47	58	26	19	16	46	.298	R	R	6-2	175	8-6-78	1997	Miami, Fla.
Reames, Jay	0	0	1.46	12	0	0	0	12	11	5	2	8	4	.244	R	R	6-1	205	10-31-74	1996	Seneca, S.C.
Rodriguez, Cristobal	1	0	3.29	14	0	0	7	14	11	5	5	7	19	.220	R	R	6-1	210	1-27-79	1996	Chichiriviche, Venez.
Russo, Scott	0	0	0.00	5	0	0	0	6	3	0	0	1	8	.142	L	L	6-2	180	3-1-78	2000	Turnersville, N.J.
Salyers, Jeremy	3	1	3.57	9	1	0	0	23	22	10	9	6	10	.255	R	R	6-3	200	1-31-76	1996	Pound, Va.
Schroder, Chris	1	0	2.30	10	0	0	0	16	12	5	4	4	20	.200	R	R	6-3	210	8-20-78	2001	Okarche, Okla.
Seibel, Phil	10	7	3.95	29	21	0	0	134	144	70	59	28	88	.273	L	L	6-1	195	1-28-79	2000	Cypress, Calif.
Telford, Anthony	0	1	7.20	4	2	0	0	5	9	5	4	1	5	.375	R	R	6-0	195	3-6-66	1987	Pinellas Park, Fla.
Tetz, Kris	0	0	3.00	2	0	0	0	3	1	1	1	1	3	.100	R	R	6-5	245	9-3-78	1997	Lodi, Calif.
Thurman, Mike	1	0	0.00	1	1	1	0	5	2	0	0	0	3	.133	R	R	6-3	200	7-22-73	1994	West Palm Beach, Fla.
Wayne, Justin	2	3	3.02	8	7	0	0	42	31	16	14	9	35	.203	R	R	6-3	200	4-16-79	2000	Honolulu, Hawaii

CLINTON — Class A

MIDWEST LEAGUE

BATTING	AVG	G	AB	R	H	2B	3B	HR	RBI	BB	SO	SB	CS	SLG	OBP	B	T	HT	WT	DOB	1st Yr	Resides
Ambrosini, Anthony	.250	3	8	1	2	0	0	0	1	0	2	0	0	.250	.333	R	R	5-9	185	9-22-78	2001	Ronkonkoma, N.Y.
Ambrosini, Dom	.194	67	252	19	49	8	1	0	21	17	58	3	4	.234	.246	L	L	5-10	185	2-21-81	1999	Ronkonkoma, N.Y.
Bay, Jason	.362	87	318	67	115	20	4	13	61	48	62	15	2	.572	.449	R	R	6-2	200	9-20-78	2000	Trail, B.C.
Boyer, Bret	.250	107	420	58	105	21	1	3	23	22	90	29	5	.326	.291	B	R	6-0	180	8-8-80	1999	Indian Rocks Beach, Fla.
Dempsey, Nick	.304	34	115	16	35	6	0	1	18	8	29	0	0	.383	.365	B	R	6-5	215	12-15-78	1997	Durban, South Africa
Docen, Jose	.246	87	301	28	74	12	0	0	32	25	54	11	14	.286	.304	L	L	5-9	160	1-10-80	1998	La Romana, D.R.
Downing, Phil	.252	37	123	18	31	4	6	4	20	22	35	2	0	.480	.363	L	L	6-1	190	8-22-78	2000	Sandy, Utah
Kerner, Craig	.189	53	190	21	36	7	0	3	17	21	49	10	4	.274	.276	L	R	6-1	195	11-13-78	2000	Whitesboro, N.Y.
Langill, Eric	.201	47	134	14	27	8	0	1	9	16	31	1	2	.284	.301	R	R	5-9	190	4-4-79	2000	Kirkland, Quebec
Lutz, David	.240	7	25	4	6	1	0	0	2	2	2	1	0	.280	.296	L	R	6-3	195	9-25-81	1999	Spring Valley, Calif.
McMillan, Andrew	.197	94	320	25	63	12	0	6	30	12	67	1	0	.291	.259	R	R	6-3	205	10-25-80	1999	Yorba Linda, Calif.
Miller, Eric	.286	69	276	28	79	11	3	2	35	16	42	8	1	.370	.324	R	R	6-2	175	12-9-77	2000	Tempe, Ariz.
Rivas, Norberto	.148	7	27	2	4	0	0	1	2	0	9	0	1	.259	.148	R	R	5-10	170	11-26-81	2000	Caracas, Venez.
Rombley, Danny	.191	35	136	14	26	5	1	1	9	7	35	9	1	.265	.236	R	R	6-1	185	11-26-79	1999	Amersfoort, Netherlands
Rooi, Vince	.254	120	422	53	107	22	0	9	60	61	94	5	4	.370	.349	R	R	6-1	195	12-13-81	1999	Amsterdam, Netherlands
Schnabel, Nick	.256	16	39	4	10	2	0	0	2	4	7	0	0	.308	.341	R	R	5-9	170	3-16-76	2000	Greenville, N.C.
Sizemore, Grady	.268	123	451	64	121	16	4	2	61	81	92	32	11	.335	.381	L	L	6-2	200	8-2-82	2000	Mill Creek, Wash.
Valdez, Wilson	.252	59	214	31	54	8	1	0	11	9	22	6	7	.299	.286	R	R	5-11	160	5-20-80	1997	Bani, D.R.
Wallis, Jacob	.213	26	80	5	17	1	0	1	7	4	18	2	0	.263	.259	R	R	6-3	200	2-1-80	1998	Joshua, Texas
Watson, Brandon	.327	117	489	74	160	16	9	2	38	29	65	33	20	.409	.364	L	R	6-1	170	9-30-81	1999	Inglewood, Calif.
Williams, Clyde	.251	88	347	45	87	12	3	10	52	11	92	7	2	.389	.275	L	L	6-2	190	7-7-79	1998	Sanford, Fla.

GAMES BY POSITION: C—A. Ambrosini 3, Docen 1, Langill 41, Lutz 5, McMillan 84, Wallis 19. **1B**—D. Ambrosini 51, Dempsey 20, Miller 5, Williams 65. **2B**—Boyer 56, Docen 69, Miller 1, Schnabel 14. **3B**—Boyer 16, Miller 6, Rooi 117. **SS**—Boyer 24, Docen 11, Miller 47, Valdez 58. **OF**—D. Ambrosini 6, Bay 78, Downing 23, Kerner 40, Miller 7, Rivas 6, Rombley 34, Sizemore 114, Watson 108.

PITCHING	W	L	ERA	G	GS	CG	SV	IP	H	R	ER	BB	SO	AVG	B	T	HT	WT	DOB	1st Yr	Resides
Bye, Chris	1	1	0.91	21	0	0	3	30	18	7	3	13	34	.178	R	R	5-11	190	9-10-77	2000	Englewood, Colo.
Caputo, Rob	0	2	5.00	4	0	0	0	5	4	4	5	8	.190	R	R	6-6	200	11-7-79	2001	New Fairfield, Conn.
Casadiego, Gerardo	5	3	5.98	42	1	0	6	72	67	37	32	28	43	.250	R	R	6-0	181	12-19-80	1998	Barquisimeto, Venez.
Charron, Eric	1	0	1.77	14	0	0	0	20	19	11	4	5	21	.226	R	R	5-11	170	4-3-79	1999	Montreal, Quebec
Chisnall, Wes	2	3	4.76	24	1	0	0	51	67	31	27	7	18	.325	R	R	6-4	190	7-18-80	1998	Alta Loma, Calif.
Crowther, Jackson	0	0	6.39	8	0	0	0	13	19	10	9	1	9	.351	R	R	6-4	195	9-14-76	1999	Riverside, Calif.
Dequin, Benji	6	11	5.30	26	24	0	0	129	125	81	76	70	129	.255	R	L	5-10	170	6-20-80	2000	Gilroy, Calif.
Dorn, Grant	4	1	5.59	31	0	0	4	48	56	33	30	21	33	.294	R	R	6-4	210	2-26-78	1998	New Alexandria, Pa.
Garris, Antonio	0	3	5.29	15	0	0	1	17	16	14	10	18	11	.253	L	R	6-0	190	3-23-78	1999	Wadesboro, N.C.
George, Todd	0	2	7.36	2	2	0	0	11	12	9	9	4	8	.272	R	R	6-3	215	12-20-78	2001	Oklahoma City, Okla.
Girdley, Josh	0	2	3.68	6	6	0	0	29	28	15	12	18	21	.247	L	L	6-3	185	8-29-80	1998	Jasper, Texas
Humrich, Chris	2	3	3.64	33	0	0	0	47	44	22	19	33	45	.247	R	R	5-11	188	12-28-77	1999	Bethune, Calif.
Lockwood, Luke	5	10	2.70	26	26	3	0	163	152	78	49	49	114	.248	L	L	6-3	170	7-21-81	1999	Victorville, Calif.
McCasland, Ralph	1	2	3.07	26	0	0	4	41	31	15	14	13	22	.208	L	L	6-4	190	2-2-79	2000	Jefferson City, Mo.
Mitchell, Thomas	0	4	6.45	5	5	0	0	22	29	20	16	9	5	.305	R	R	6-3	185	11-20-80	2000	Bladenboro, N.C.
Miyamoto, Eiji	2	4	4.08	20	0	0	1	29	22	21	13	19	23	.211	R	R	6-3	185	10-26-79	2000	Fukushima, Japan
Norderum, Jason	4	7	4.88	28	28	2	0	155	176	96	84	60	101	.284	L	L	6-3	220	11-21-81	2000	Redding, Calif.
Puello, Ignacio	3	3	5.57	7	7	0	0	32	29	21	20	26	21	.243	R	R	6-1	170	10-16-80	1998	San Pedro de Macoris, D.R.
Rundles, Rich	1	1	2.33	4	4	0	0	27	26	10	7	3	20	.247	L	L	6-5	180	6-3-81	1999	New Market, Tenn.
Russo, Scott	1	1	1.80	15	0	0	1	20	13	9	4	12	21	.175	L	L	6-2	180	3-1-78	2000	Turnersville, N.J.
Torres, Luis	6	8	5.18	18	18	0	0	104	116	76	60	42	56	.285	R	R	6-4	200	3-12-81	1999	Caracas, Venez.
Washburn, Ben	4	12	4.79	30	15	1	0	130	141	84	69	30	89	.274	R	R	6-2	200	5-17-79	2000	Redlands, Calif.

VERMONT — Short-Season Class A

NEW YORK-PENN LEAGUE

BATTING	AVG	G	AB	R	H	2B	3B	HR	RBI	BB	SO	SB	CS	SLG	OBP	B	T	HT	WT	DOB	1st Yr	Resides
Ambrosini, Dom	.226	44	159	19	36	7	1	2	19	14	37	1	3	.321	.289	L	L	5-10	185	2-21-81	1999	Ronkonkoma, N.Y.
Brown, Matt	.218	53	197	22	43	14	1	4	22	15	61	4	3	.360	.277	B	R	6-1	195	9-23-80	1999	Randleman, N.C.
Caracciolo, Tony	.211	52	171	18	36	5	0	1	8	19	38	13	1	.257	.304	R	R	6-1	180	7-12-79	1997	Henderson, Nev.
Dempsey, Nick	.300	15	60	4	18	3	0	2	10	3	10	0	0	.450	.333	B	R	6-5	215	12-15-78	1997	Durban, South Africa
Ellis, Ryan	.234	42	137	15	32	3	3	1	13	24	24	4	2	.321	.307	R	R	6-0	185	7-19-78	2000	Munhall, Pa.
Emmerick, Josh	.181	43	144	11	26	5	0	0	10	11	32	0	0	.215	.248	R	R	6-4	195	2-22-81	1999	Oceanside, Calif.
Fitzpatrick, Reggie	.125	4	16	2	2	0	0	0	1	0	2	1	1	.125	.125	L	L	5-10	180	2-28-83	2001	Atlanta, Ga.
Freeman, Miguel	.172	54	180	21	31	3	2	6	26	19	73	3	0	.311	.254	R	R	6-2	195	5-20-80	1997	San Pedro de Macoris, D.R.

BATTING	AVG	G	AB	R	H	2B	3B	HR	RBI	BB	SO	SB	CS	SLG	OBP	B	T	HT	WT	DOB	1st Yr	Resides
Griffin, Daniel	.195	38	118	12	23	4	2	1	6	9	60	2	1	.288	.258	R	R	6-3	190	2-21-81	1997	San Pedro de Macoris, D.R.
Johnson, Seth	.178	57	208	15	37	7	0	1	19	13	37	2	2	.226	.229	R	R	6-2	190	6-3-82	2000	Longview, Wash.
Labandeira, Josh	.333	1	3	2	1	0	0	0	0	0	0	0	0	.333	.333	R	R	5-7	180	2-25-79	2001	Porterville, Calif.
Lutz, David	.228	46	167	19	38	7	1	0	16	16	30	2	1	.281	.292	L	R	6-3	195	9-25-81	1999	Spring Valley, Calif.
Norris, Shawn	.218	57	197	18	43	4	0	2	21	38	57	0	4	.269	.347	L	R	6-2	190	8-1-80	2001	Draper, Utah
Padilla, Juan	.159	28	88	6	14	4	1	0	7	6	43	0	2	.227	.237	R	R	6-1	185	9-13-80	1997	Valencia, Venez.
Rombley, Danny	.210	70	267	42	56	4	2	0	12	19	70	19	12	.240	.276	R	R	6-1	185	11-26-79	1999	Amersfoort, Netherlands
Schnabel, Nick	.205	27	83	11	17	2	0	0	6	17	13	6	2	.229	.359	R	R	5-9	170	3-16-78	2000	Greenville, N.C.
Thissen, Greg	.235	59	221	27	52	13	0	1	19	20	43	9	4	.308	.306	R	R	6-4	185	6-1-81	2001	Davenport, Iowa
Wallis, Jacob	.063	6	16	0	1	0	0	0	0	0	8	0	0	.063	.118	R	R	6-3	200	2-1-80	1998	Joshua, Texas

GAMES BY POSITION: C—Ellis 1, Emmerick 43, Lutz 28, Wallis 6. **1B**—Ambrosini 10, Brown 21, Dempsey 8, Ellis 1, Johnson 35, Lutz 1, Norris 1, Thissen 1. **2B**—Ellis 24, Schnabel 27, Thissen 28. **3B**—Brown 5, Ellis 11, Johnson 5, Norris 2, Thissen 2. **SS**—Caracciolo 48, Ellis 1, Labandeira 1, Norris 1, Thissen 26. **OF**—Ambrosini 29, Brown 12, Ellis 3, Fitzpatrick 4, Freeman 52, Griffin 37, Padilla 27, Rombley 67.

PITCHING	W	L	ERA	G	GS	CG	SV	IP	H	R	ER	BB	SO	AVG	B	T	HT	WT	DOB	1st Yr	Resides
Bentz, Chad	1	3	4.91	8	8	0	0	37	39	23	20	11	38	.263	R	L	6-2	215	5-5-80	2001	Juneau, Alaska
Caputo, Rob	0	2	4.75	20	1	0	3	30	32	20	16	16	28	.264	R	R	6-6	200	11-7-79	2001	New Fairfield, Conn.
Charron, Eric	0	0	3.72	7	0	0	0	10	9	4	4	2	12	.243	R	R	5-11	170	4-3-79	1999	Montreal, Quebec
Chisnall, Wes	2	2	2.65	18	2	0	0	37	37	16	11	7	30	.251	R	R	6-4	190	7-18-80	1998	Alta Loma, Calif.
Clelland, James	3	1	4.73	18	0	0	0	32	40	22	17	6	24	.291	R	R	6-4	180	9-28-79	2001	Pasadena, Calif.
Garris, Antonio	0	0	1.62	15	0	0	5	17	12	7	3	9	20	.193	R	R	6-0	190	3-23-78	1999	Wadesboro, N.C.
George, Todd	0	0	4.24	5	2	0	0	17	20	8	8	4	15	.307	R	R	6-3	215	12-20-78	2001	Oklahoma City, Okla.
Guerrero, Thomas	0	0	4.91	2	0	0	0	4	4	2	2	2	3	.286	R	R	6-0	160	1-6-82	1999	Bani, D.R.
Hashimoto, Kei	0	1	6.46	10	0	0	0	15	17	15	11	9	10	.269	R	R	6-3	200	9-5-79	2001	Osaka, Japan
Hill, Shawn	2	2	2.27	7	7	0	0	36	22	12	9	8	23	.171	R	R	6-2	185	4-28-81	2000	Georgetown, Ontario
Lewis, Craig	1	1	1.80	6	0	0	0	15	17	5	3	0	5	.283	R	R	6-5	210	12-30-76	1997	Sydney, Australia
Lima, Juan	2	6	4.68	12	9	0	0	50	55	34	26	17	34	.283	R	R	6-0	160	4-10-82	1999	San Pedro de Macoris, D.R.
Marceau, Pierre-Luc	1	7	5.59	15	15	0	0	74	86	54	46	30	64	.298	L	L	6-2	190	4-11-81	1999	Fleurimont, Quebec
Marrero, Darwin	1	0	3.00	1	1	0	0	6	7	4	2	3	5	.291	R	R	6-1	190	2-9-81	1997	Valencia, Venez.
Mata, Gustavo	0	3	6.86	4	4	0	0	20	22	16	15	5	14	.271	R	R	6-1	190	5-20-83	2001	Carupano, Venez.
Maust, David	4	2	0.72	18	3	1	1	50	30	10	4	6	45	.173	L	L	6-2	205	11-6-78	2001	Morgantown, W.Va.
Milner, Robbie	0	1	5.40	19	0	0	0	33	42	23	20	14	37	.306	R	R	6-1	210	10-19-78	2001	Phoenix, Ariz.
Mitchell, Thomas	2	7	6.93	14	14	0	0	61	84	55	47	39	33	.336	R	R	6-2	185	11-20-80	2000	Bladenboro, N.C.
Miyamoto, Eiji	0	0	0.00	1	0	0	0	1	0	0	0	0	1	.000	R	R	6-3	185	10-26-79	2000	Fukushima, Japan
Schroder, Chris	0	0	1.50	11	0	0	0	12	8	2	2	5	18	.186	R	R	6-3	210	8-20-78	2001	Okarche, Okla.
Stevenson, Jason	6	3	5.83	25	1	0	0	42	49	31	27	17	33	.302	L	L	6-1	175	8-8-81	2001	Redding, Calif.
Walker, Jason	3	6	4.96	18	8	0	1	53	48	31	29	26	35	.236	L	L	6-0	180	1-15-80	2001	Ontario, Calif.

JUPITER
Rookie

GULF COAST LEAGUE

BATTING	AVG	G	AB	R	H	2B	3B	HR	RBI	BB	SO	SB	CS	SLG	OBP	B	T	HT	WT	DOB	1st Yr	Resides
Ambrosini, Anthony	.224	25	85	5	19	1	0	0	5	5	24	1	1	.235	.290	R	R	5-9	185	9-22-78	2001	Ronkonkoma, N.Y.
Blanco, Luis	.199	45	151	11	30	6	0	2	13	6	54	1	0	.278	.245	R	R	6-3	200	7-6-81	1999	Caracas, Venez.
Diaz, Frank	.219	38	128	10	28	5	1	0	8	12	27	10	3	.273	.297	R	R	6-2	180	10-6-83	2000	Guacara, Venez.
Encarnacion, Henry	.205	50	146	23	34	4	1	0	10	26	38	10	0	.241	.314	B	R	6-0	175	5-20-82	1999	Santo Domingo, D.R.
Fitzpatrick, Reggie	.280	31	118	17	33	1	0	0	7	9	28	5	4	.288	.331	L	L	5-10	180	2-28-83	2001	Atlanta, Ga.
Greene, Jason	.279	31	104	14	29	7	3	0	13	18	30	2	2	.404	.390	L	R	5-11	180	9-9-82	2001	Minford, Ohio
Honeycutt, Shedrick	.198	38	131	9	26	3	0	0	8	5	38	4	3	.221	.230	L	L	6-2	190	1-21-81	2001	Tallahassee, Fla.
Kahr, Danny	.169	16	59	5	10	2	1	1	6	4	24	0	0	.288	.234	B	R	6-3	180	9-25-82	2001	Las Vegas, Nev.
Lababera, Michael	.231	34	104	9	24	2	0	0	4	3	11	3	2	.250	.266	R	R	5-10	165	11-25-79	2001	Nesconset, N.Y.
Louisa, Lorvin	.173	46	156	9	27	1	1	2	16	11	54	1	3	.231	.241	R	R	6-4	200	2-7-83	1999	Willemstad, Curacao
Mancebo, Deni	.193	46	166	21	32	2	1	0	7	17	44	6	3	.217	.295	B	R	5-10	160	11-17-83	2001	Santo Domingo, D.R.
Manriquez, Salomon	.217	34	120	8	26	9	0	0	8	7	30	0	0	.292	.277	R	R	6-0	175	9-15-82	1999	Guacara, Venez.
Medina, Ricardo	.217	38	129	12	28	5	1	3	14	8	37	0	3	.341	.268	R	R	6-3	205	5-22-82	2001	Santo Domingo, D.R.
Mujica, Jean	.258	41	128	16	33	4	1	1	12	11	34	1	0	.328	.326	R	R	6-1	185	8-15-82	2000	Carabobo, Venez.
Rivas, Norberto	.188	19	48	6	9	1	0	1	6	8	17	3	2	.271	.310	R	R	5-10	170	11-26-81	2000	Caracas, Venez.
Thede, Matt	.208	34	120	9	25	4	1	0	8	9	31	3	3	.258	.276	R	R	6-1	180	6-21-78	2001	Reinbeck, Iowa

GAMES BY POSITION: C—Ambrosini 15, Encarnacion 1, Kahr 8, Manriquez 29, Thede 11. **1B**—Blanco 43, Honeycutt 9, Thede 12. **2B**—Encarnacion 15, Greene 22, Lababera 25, Mancebo 1. **3B**—Encarnacion 18, Lababera 5, Mujica 41. **SS**—Encarnacion 18, Lababera 1, Mancebo 43. **OF**—F. Diaz 34, Fitzpatrick 31, Honeycutt 29, Lababera 1, Louisa 45, Medina 31, Rivas 19.

PITCHING	W	L	ERA	G	GS	CG	SV	IP	H	R	ER	BB	SO	AVG	B	T	HT	WT	DOB	1st Yr	Resides
Acuna, Jose	2	4	1.93	14	5	0	0	51	44	13	11	11	45	.226	R	R	6-2	180	8-15-81	1999	Cartagena, Colombia
Bridges, Donnie	1	0	8.44	2	2	0	0	5	2	6	5	5	9	.105	R	R	6-4	220	12-10-78	1997	Hattiesburg, Miss.
Corcoran, Roy	2	0	1.56	13	0	0	2	17	12	4	3	2	21	.184	R	R	5-10	170	5-11-80	2001	Slaughter, La.
Diaz, Eddie	1	7	10.34	13	6	0	0	31	33	42	36	27	30	.268	R	R	6-0	170	1-25-83	2001	Orlando, Fla.
Figueroa, Williams	1	4	4.67	12	0	0	0	17	9	10	9	19	13	.155	R	R	6-1	190	1-5-84	2000	Caracas, Venez.
Galarraga, Armando	1	3	3.12	14	1	0	2	35	37	21	12	15	24	.274	R	R	6-3	170	1-15-82	1999	Caracas, Venez.
George, Todd	0	0	2.70	8	0	0	1	10	8	3	3	3	13	.210	R	R	6-3	215	12-20-78	2001	Oklahoma City, Okla.
Gomez, Warmar	0	1	7.89	18	0	0	0	22	32	22	19	5	14	.333	R	R	6-2	210	5-8-83	2001	Rio Grande, P.R.
Griswold, Jordan	1	0	2.48	16	0	0	0	29	31	13	8	16	22	.287	L	L	6-3	195	4-25-82	2000	Lilburn, Ga.
Guerrero, Thomas	3	2	5.46	19	0	0	3	28	31	21	17	7	37	.267	R	R	6-0	160	1-6-82	1999	Bani, D.R.
Hinckley, Mike	3	2	5.24	8	5	0	0	34	46	23	20	12	28	.328	R	L	6-3	170	10-5-82	2001	Moore, Okla.
Imotichey, Tory	1	5	3.12	10	8	0	0	40	39	23	14	16	32	.250	L	L	6-3	180	8-20-82	2001	Purcell, Okla.
Kirkman, Tyler	0	0	11.57	2	0	0	0	2	5	3	3	1	1	.500	L	L	6-3	180	12-21-82	2001	Mount Carmel, Ill.
Levinski, Don	0	0	3.46	3	3	0	0	13	15	5	5	7	15	.300	R	R	6-4	205	10-20-82	2001	Weimar, Texas
Long, Nick	1	1	3.32	4	3	0	0	19	24	8	7	4	13	.300	R	R	6-3	180	11-24-82	2001	Columbus, Ga.
Mata, Gustavo	3	4	2.05	10	9	0	0	48	44	27	11	13	38	.229	R	R	6-1	190	5-20-83	2001	Carupano, Venez.
Puello, Ignacio	1	3	2.06	8	8	0	0	35	28	11	8	10	37	.213	R	R	6-1	170	10-16-80	1998	San Pedro de Macoris, D.R.
Reames, Jay	0	0	4.91	3	0	0	0	4	4	2	2	2	7	.266	R	R	6-1	205	10-31-74	1996	Seneca, S.C.
Rengifo, Nohemar	0	2	5.87	14	0	0	0	31	38	30	20	13	28	.296	R	R	5-11	185	10-12-82	2001	Tucupido, Venez.
Rose, Michael	0	0	2.35	3	1	0	0	8	9	3	2	1	5	.300	R	R	6-3	215	5-16-77	2000	Owasso, Okla.
Stevens, Kris	1	0	0.00	4	4	0	0	11	7	0	0	5	7	.175	R	L	6-2	190	9-19-77	1996	Fontana, Calif.
Vaughn, Josh	0	3	8.22	11	2	0	0	23	38	27	21	6	17	.365	L	L	6-3	165	1-15-80	2001	Ardmore, Okla.

BY GEORGE KING

The pain of losing Game Seven of the 2001 World Series in the ninth inning was severe. For a team that won three straight World Series and four of the previous five, being dethroned cut deep.

However, to manager Joe Torre, Luis Gonzalez' broken-bat single against Mariano Rivera wasn't as bad as 1997, when the Indians eliminated the Yankees in the American League Division Series.

"The feeling was different because the quality of the World Series is one thing," Torre said. "Plus the fact that when the last game is played, everybody goes home. You don't have to turn the TV on and watch somebody else playing baseball. We were there at the end, and that makes it a lot different than '97."

Of course, there were similarities. Rivera gave up a big home run to Sandy Alomar in Game Four of the 1997 division series, and the Diamondbacks victimized the best reliever in baseball, too.

Yet it took three broken-bat hits and Rivera's throwing error to kill the Yankees' fourpeat effort.

"It absolutely didn't surprise me that was the kind of hit that beat him," Torre said of Gonzalez' bloop single over a drawn-in infield. "That's what he makes you do."

What the Yankees didn't do most of the year was hit well enough. Injuries took their toll on Derek Jeter, who batted .311, his lowest average since a .291 in 1997. Bernie Williams had an off year, batting .307-26-94. David Justice never fully recovered from offseason hernia surgery. Chuck Knoblauch had a great April and was miserable for the next five months.

After the team hit .183 in the World Series, hitting coach Gary Denbo, who replaced Chris Chambliss after the Yankees won three straight World Series titles, was fired.

Paul O'Neill and Luis Sojo retired. Scott Brosius, Tino Martinez and Knoblauch were likely to leave via free

Roger Clemens   Brandon Claussen

STEVE MOORE

PLAYERS OF THE YEAR

MAJOR LEAGUE: Roger Clemens, rhp

Clemens became the first pitcher since 1900 to start the season 20-1. He also fanned 213 in 2001 and now has 3,717 career K's—advancing from eighth to third on the all-time list.

MINOR LEAGUE: Brandon Claussen, lhp

Claussen was the strikeout king in the minors in 2001, recording 220. He earned a promotion to Double-A Norwich (9-2, 2.13) after starting the year at Class A Tampa (5-2, 2.73).

agency. But a strong core of Jorge Posada, Jeter, Williams, Mike Mussina, Roger Clemens, Andy Pettitte, Mike Stanton, Ramiro Mendoza and Rivera remained intact. And the Yankees found they have a very special talent in Alfonso Soriano.

While seasoned veterans came unglued in the postseason, Soriano didn't flinch. He won Game Four of the AL Championship Series with a ninth-inning homer against Seattle. His 12th-inning RBI single won Game Five of the World Series.

"The kid handled it like Jeter handled it," Torre said. "That's the only one I can compare him to, because they both . . . not only to perform in the postseason or the World Series, but to understand that wearing the Yankee pinstripes is not easy to do."

As for the farm system, it was used as trade bait again. Wily Mo Pena, a power-hitting outfield prospect, was dealt to the Reds in March for Drew Henson, the third baseman of the future.

Switch-hitting infielder D'Angelo Jimenez was traded to the Padres for reliever Jay Witasick. Righthander Ricardo Aramboles fetched Mark Wohlers from the Reds. Righthander Bret Jodie and outfielder Darren Blakely were used to get Sterling Hitchcock from the Padres.

Yet, a new wave of prospects emerged. Lefties Brandon Claussen and Alex Graman established themselves in and out of the organization as pitchers with big league futures after solid seasons at Double-A Norwich. Despite being rushed to Triple-A, Henson is considered a can't-miss deal.

First baseman Nick Johnson received his first taste of the big leagues. Along with Henson, Johnson represents the Yankees' future. However, they never get into a rebuilding mode.

"We are still in a win-now mentality," Torre said. "We have to figure out if they are not ready. We have to be ready, that's the important thing."

ORGANIZATION LEADERS

BATTING

*AVG	Juan Rivera, Columbus/Norwich	.322
R	Marcus Thames, Norwich	114
H	Marcus Thames, Norwich	167
TB	Marcus Thames, Norwich	311
2B	Marcus Thames, Norwich	43
3B	Mike Vento, Tampa	10
HR	Marcus Thames, Norwich	31
RBI	Juan Rivera, Columbus/Norwich	98
BB	Nick Johnson, Columbus	81
	Mitch Jones, Tampa	81
SO	Mitch Jones, Tampa	135
SB	Bernabel Castro, Greensboro/Staten Island	37

PITCHING

W	Julio DePaula, Tampa/Greensboro	16
L	Jason Anderson, Greensboro/Staten Island	10
#ERA	Dave Martinez, Tampa/Greensboro	2.10
G	Kevin Lovingier, Columbus/Norwich	62
	Jason Faigin, Greensboro	62
CG	Sam Marsonek, Tampa	5
SV	Alex Pacheco, Norwich	26
IP	Brandon Claussen, Norwich/Tampa	187
BB	Julio DePaula, Tampa/Greensboro	76
SO	Brandon Claussen, Norwich/Tampa	220

*Minimum 250 At-Bats #Minimum 75 Innings

NEW YORK YANKEES

Manager: Joe Torre

2001 Record: 95-65, .594 (1st, AL East)

BATTING	AVG	G	AB	R	H	2B	3B	HR	RBI	BB	SO	SB	CS	SLG	OBP	B	T	HT	WT	DOB	1st Yr	Resides
Almonte, Erick	.500	8	4	0	2	1	0	0	0	0	1	2	0	.750	.500	R	R	6-2	180	2-1-78	1996	Santo Domingo, D.R.
Bellinger, Clay	.160	51	81	12	13	1	1	5	12	4	23	1	2	.383	.207	R	R	6-3	215	11-18-68	1989	Oneonta, N.Y.
Bragg, Darren	.250	5	4	1	1	0	0	0	0	1	0	0	0	.500	.250	L	R	5-9	180	9-7-69	1991	Roswell, Ga.
Brosius, Scott	.287	120	428	57	123	25	2	13	49	34	83	3	1	.446	.343	R	R	6-1	202	8-15-66	1987	McMinnville, Ore.
Coleman, Michael	.211	12	38	5	8	0	0	1	7	0	15	0	1	.289	.205	R	R	5-11	215	8-16-75	1994	Nashville, Tenn.
Estalella, Bobby	.000	3	4	1	0	0	0	0	0	1	2	0	0	.000	.333	R	R	6-1	205	8-23-74	1993	Pembroke Pines, Fla.
Greene, Todd	.208	35	96	9	20	4	0	1	11	3	21	0	0	.281	.240	R	R	5-10	208	5-8-71	1993	Evans, Ga.
Jeter, Derek	.311	150	614	110	191	35	3	21	74	56	99	27	3	.480	.377	R	R	6-3	195	6-26-74	1992	Tampa, Fla.
Johnson, Nick	.194	23	67	6	13	2	0	2	8	7	15	0	0	.313	.308	L	L	6-3	224	9-19-78	1996	Sacramento, Calif.
Justice, David	.241	111	381	58	92	16	1	18	51	54	83	1	2	.430	.333	L	L	6-3	200	4-14-66	1985	Cincinnati, Ohio
Knoblauch, Chuck	.250	137	521	66	130	20	3	9	44	58	73	38	9	.351	.339	R	R	5-9	175	7-7-68	1989	Houston, Texas
Martinez, Tino	.280	154	589	89	165	24	2	34	113	42	89	1	2	.501	.329	L	R	6-2	210	12-7-67	1989	Tampa, Fla.
McDonald, Donzell	.333	5	3	0	1	0	0	0	0	0	2	0	0	.333	.333	B	R	5-11	180	2-20-75	1995	Glendale, Colo.
O'Neill, Paul	.267	137	510	77	136	33	1	21	70	48	59	22	3	.459	.330	L	L	6-4	215	2-25-63	1981	Cincinnati, Ohio
Oliver, Joe	.250	12	36	3	9	1	0	1	2	1	12	0	0	.361	.263	R	R	6-3	220	7-24-65	1983	Orlando, Fla.
Perez, Robert	.267	6	15	1	4	1	0	0	1	1	7	0	1	.333	.313	R	R	6-3	230	6-4-69	1990	Bolivar, Venez.
Posada, Jorge	.277	138	484	59	134	28	1	22	95	62	132	2	6	.475	.363	B	R	6-2	205	8-17-71	1991	Rio Piedras, P.R.
Rivera, Juan	.000	3	4	0	0	0	0	0	0	0	1	0	0	.000	.000	R	R	6-2	170	7-3-78	1996	Guarenas, Venez.
Rodriguez, Henry	.000	5	8	0	0	0	0	0	0	0	6	0	0	.000	.000	L	L	6-2	220	11-8-67	1986	Santo Domingo, D.R.
Seabol, Scott	.000	1	2	0	0	0	0	0	0	0	0	0	0	.000	.000	R	R	6-4	200	5-17-75	1996	McKeesport, Pa.
Sojo, Luis	.165	39	79	5	13	2	0	0	9	4	12	1	0	.190	.214	R	R	5-11	175	1-3-66	1987	Barquisimeto, Venez.
Soriano, Alfonso	.268	158	574	77	154	34	3	18	73	29	125	43	14	.432	.304	R	R	6-1	180	1-7-78	1999	Los Angeles, Calif.
Spencer, Shane	.258	80	283	40	73	14	2	10	46	21	58	4	1	.428	.315	R	R	5-11	225	2-20-72	1990	El Cajon, Calif.
Velarde, Randy	.152	15	46	4	7	3	0	0	1	5	13	2	0	.217	.278	R	R	6-0	200	11-24-62	1985	Midland, Texas
2-team (78 Texas)	.278	93	342	50	95	19	2	9	32	34	86	6	2	.424	.356							
Williams, Bernie	.307	146	540	102	166	38	0	26	94	78	67	11	5	.522	.395	B	R	6-2	205	9-13-68	1986	Armonk, N.Y.
Williams, Gerald	.170	38	47	12	8	1	0	0	2	5	13	3	1	.191	.264	R	R	6-2	187	8-10-66	1987	Tampa, Fla.
2-team (62 T.B.)	.201	100	279	42	56	18	0	4	19	18	55	13	5	.308	.262							
Wilson, Enrique	.242	48	99	10	24	5	1	1	12	6	14	0	2	.343	.283	B	R	5-11	160	7-27-75	1992	Santo Domingo, D.R.

PITCHING	W	L	ERA	G	GS	CG	SV	IP	H	R	ER	BB	SO	AVG	B	T	HT	WT	DOB	1st Yr	Resides
Almanzar, Carlos	0	1	3.38	10	0	0	0	11	14	4	4	2	6	.333	R	R	6-2	200	11-6-73	1991	Santo Domingo, D.R.
Boehringer, Brian	0	1	3.12	22	0	0	1	35	35	15	12	12	33	.255	B	R	6-2	190	1-8-70	1989	Fenton, Mo.
Choate, Randy	3	1	3.35	37	0	0	0	48	34	21	18	27	35	.202	L	L	6-3	180	9-5-75	1997	Tallahassee, Fla.
Clemens, Roger	20	3	3.51	33	33	0	0	220	205	94	86	72	213	.246	R	R	6-4	238	8-4-62	1983	Houston, Texas
Hernandez, Adrian	3	4	3.68	6	3	0	0	22	15	10	9	10	10	.189	R	R	6-2	185	8-30-79	2000	Tampa, Fla.
Hernandez, Orlando	4	7	4.85	17	16	0	0	95	90	51	51	42	77	.247	R	R	6-2	220	10-11-69	1998	Miami, Fla.
Hitchcock, Sterling	4	4	6.49	10	9	1	0	51	67	37	37	18	28	.314	L	L	6-0	205	4-29-71	1989	Tampa, Fla.
Jodie, Brett	0	1	27.00	1	1	0	0	2	7	6	6	1	0	.583	R	R	6-4	208	3-25-77	1998	Lexington, S.C.
Keisler, Randy	1	2	6.22	10	10	0	0	51	52	36	35	34	36	.258	L	L	6-3	190	2-24-76	1998	Richardson, Texas
Knight, Brandon	0	0	10.13	4	0	0	0	11	18	12	12	3	7	.367	L	R	6-0	170	10-1-75	1995	Ventura, Calif.
Lilly, Ted	5	6	5.37	26	21	0	0	121	126	81	72	51	112	.266	L	L	6-0	185	1-4-76	1996	Oakhurst, Calif.
Mendoza, Ramiro	8	4	3.75	56	2	0	6	101	89	44	42	23	70	.241	R	R	6-2	195	6-15-72	1992	Los Santos, Panama
Mussina, Mike	17	11	3.15	34	34	4	0	229	202	87	80	42	214	.237	B	R	6-2	185	12-8-68	1990	Montoursville, Pa.
Parker, Christian	0	1	21.00	1	1	0	0	3	8	7	7	1	1	.470	R	R	6-2	190	7-3-75	1996	Albuquerque, N.M.
Pettitte, Andy	15	10	3.99	31	31	2	0	201	224	103	89	41	164	.281	L	L	6-5	225	6-15-72	1991	Deer Park, Texas
Rivera, Mariano	4	6	2.34	71	0	0	50	81	61	24	21	12	83	.208	R	R	6-2	195	11-29-69	1990	La Chorrera, Panama
Stanton, Mike	9	4	2.58	76	0	0	0	80	80	25	23	29	78	.263	L	L	6-1	215	6-2-67	1987	Houston, Texas
Williams, Todd	1	0	4.70	15	0	0	0	15	22	9	8	9	13	.323	R	R	6-3	210	2-13-71	1991	Syracuse, N.Y.
Witasick, Jay	3	0	4.69	32	0	0	0	40	47	27	21	18	53	.283	R	R	6-4	235	8-28-72	1993	Bel Air, Md.
Wohlers, Mark	1	0	4.54	10	0	0	0	36	33	20	18	18	33	.240	R	R	6-4	207	1-23-70	1988	Alpharetta, Ga.

FIELDING

Catcher	PCT	G	PO	A	E	DP	PB
Estalella	1.000	3	14	1	0	0	0
Greene	1.000	34	187	14	0	2	1
Oliver	.999	12	102	3	1	1	2
Posada	.990	131	996	52	11	11	18

First Base	PCT	G	PO	A	E	DP
Bellinger	1.000	6	8	1	0	3
Johnson	1.000	15	90	5	0	4
Martinez	.996	149	1144	99	5	105
Posada	1.000	2	7	0	0	1
Sojo	1.000	8	32	3	0	2
Velarde	1.000	1	9	2	0	0

Second Base	PCT	G	PO	A	E	DP
Sojo	1.000	7	5	8	0	0

	PCT	G	PO	A	E	DP
Soriano	.973	156	318	366	19	93
Wilson	1.000	7	9	17	0	3

Third Base	PCT	G	PO	A	E	DP
Bellinger	.939	17	16	30	3	5
Brosius	.935	120	81	238	22	21
Sojo	.933	17	7	21	2	2
Velarde	.952	7	4	16	1	1
Wilson	1.000	19	7	29	0	2

Shortstop	PCT	G	PO	A	E	DP
Almonte	.875	4	4	3	1	1
Bellinger	1.000	2	0	3	0	0
Jeter	.974	150	212	343	15	68
Sojo	1.000	5	7	10	0	2
Wilson	.952	20	13	27	2	4

Outfield	PCT	G	PO	A	E	DP
Bellinger	1.000	25	21	0	0	0
Bragg	1.000	3	2	0	0	0
Brosius	1.000	2	1	0	0	0
Coleman	1.000	9	8	0	0	0
Justice	.981	25	49	4	1	1
Knoblauch	.989	108	171	8	2	4
McDonald	1.000	3	2	0	0	0
O'Neill	.981	130	210	1	4	0
Perez	1.000	5	7	0	0	0
J. Rivera	1.000	3	1	0	0	0
Spencer	.993	68	139	7	1	0
Velarde	1.000	3	5	0	0	0
B. Williams	.994	144	348	3	2	1
G. Williams	.967	26	29	0	1	0

Tino Martinez: Led the Yankees with 34 homers

Mike Mussina: Led the Yankees in strikeouts, innings and ERA

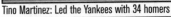

FARM SYSTEM

Vice President, Player Development: Mark Newman

Class	Farm Team	League	W	L	Pct.	Finish*	Manager	First Yr.
AAA	Columbus (Ohio) Clippers	International	67	76	.469	9th (14)	Trey Hillman	1979
AA	Norwich (Conn.) Navigators	Eastern	83	59	.585	3rd (12)	Stump Merrill	1995
A#	Tampa (Fla.) Yankees	Florida State	77	62	.554	+2nd (12)	Brian Butterfield	1994
A	Greensboro (N.C.) Bats	South Atlantic	70	70	.500	8th (16)	Mitch Seoane	1990
A	Staten Island (N.Y.) Yankees	New York-Penn	48	28	.632	3rd (14)	Dave Jorn	1999
Rookie	Tampa (Fla.) Yankees	Gulf Coast	35	25	.583	+4th (14)	Derek Shelton	1980

*Finish in overall standings (No. of teams in league)   #Advanced level   +League champion

COLUMBUS   Class AAA

INTERNATIONAL LEAGUE

BATTING	AVG	G	AB	R	H	2B	3B	HR	RBI	BB	SO	SB	CS	SLG	OBP	B	T	HT	WT	DOB	1st Yr	Resides
Almonte, Erick	.287	97	345	55	99	19	3	12	55	44	90	4	5	.464	.369	R	R	6-2	180	2-1-78	1996	Santo Domingo, D.R.
Bellinger, Clay	.214	26	98	13	21	10	0	1	9	5	22	3	0	.347	.260	R	R	6-3	215	11-18-68	1989	Oneonta, N.Y.
Bragg, Darren	.291	53	199	30	58	11	2	7	21	27	51	3	2	.472	.379	L	R	5-9	180	9-7-69	1991	Roswell, Ga.
2-team (32 Norfolk)	.305	85	298	52	91	15	2	11	28	50	73	8	4	.480	.410							
Brazoban, Yhency	.200	1	5	2	1	1	0	0	0	0	2	0	0	.400	.200	R	R	6-1	170	6-11-80	1997	Santo Domingo, D.R.
Bridges, Kary	.297	109	408	59	121	17	1	5	39	36	29	5	8	.380	.352	L	R	5-10	170	10-27-72	1993	Hattiesburg, Miss.
Coleman, Michael	.238	29	101	16	24	3	3	4	17	13	35	3	3	.446	.336	R	R	5-11	215	8-16-75	1994	Nashville, Tenn.
Estalella, Bobby	.257	48	171	26	44	10	1	10	38	21	45	0	2	.503	.340	R	R	6-0	205	8-23-74	1993	Pembroke Pines, Fla.
Figga, Mike	.000	1	5	0	0	0	0	0	0	0	2	0	0	.000	.000	R	R	6-0	200	7-31-70	1990	Tampa, Fla.
Flanagan, Kevin	.000	3	5	1	0	0	0	0	0	2	2	0	0	.000	.286	R	R	6-0	195	12-23-76	2000	Virginia Beach, Va.
Fonville, Chad	.224	16	58	9	13	3	1	0	7	4	13	1	1	.310	.286	B	R	5-7	155	3-5-71	1992	Midway Park, N.C.
Frank, Mike	.253	106	356	45	90	20	2	10	53	41	52	11	3	.404	.333	L	L	6-2	195	1-14-75	1997	Upland, Calif.
Garcia, Carlos	.251	61	215	22	54	12	0	3	19	14	39	8	1	.349	.303	R	R	6-1	193	10-15-67	1987	Lancaster, N.Y.
Greene, Todd	.252	34	131	16	33	8	0	6	17	4	19	3	2	.450	.279	R	R	5-10	208	5-8-71	1993	Evans, Ga.
Henson, Drew	.222	71	270	29	60	6	0	11	38	10	85	2	1	.367	.249	R	R	6-5	222	2-13-80	1998	Brighton, Mich.
Jimenez, D'Angelo	.262	56	214	33	56	11	1	5	19	24	31	5	6	.393	.333	B	R	6-0	194	12-21-77	1995	Santo Domingo, D.R.
Johnson, Nick	.256	110	359	68	92	20	0	18	49	81	105	9	2	.462	.407	L	L	6-3	224	9-19-78	1996	Sacramento, Calif.
Lennon, Patrick	.136	14	44	6	6	1	1	1	2	9	14	0	0	.273	.296	R	R	6-2	200	4-27-68	1986	Whiteville, N.C.
Leon, Donny	.163	12	43	4	7	1	0	0	3	3	14	1	0	.186	.213	B	R	6-2	185	5-7-76	1995	Ponce, P.R.
Matos, Pascual	.219	77	256	23	56	12	1	4	26	12	60	1	3	.320	.258	R	R	6-2	180	12-23-74	1992	Barahona, D.R.
McDonald, Donzell	.257	105	374	59	96	11	9	8	36	42	79	20	4	.398	.342	B	R	5-11	180	2-20-75	1995	Glendale, Colo.
Mosquera, Julio	.244	16	41	6	10	2	0	0	2	1	10	0	0	.293	.311	R	R	6-0	190	1-29-72	1991	Dunedin, Fla.
Nettles, Jeff	.185	12	27	1	5	0	0	1	5	9	2	1	.185	.313		R	R	6-2	200	8-20-78	1998	Encinitas, Calif.
Ottavinia, Paul	.272	42	147	20	40	11	4	2	14	14	16	3	4	.442	.345	L	L	6-1	190	4-22-73	1994	Drakestown, N.J.
Perez, Robert	.322	36	146	20	47	7	3	7	27	4	23	6	5	.555	.351	R	R	6-3	230	6-4-69	1990	Bolivar, Venez.

BATTING	AVG	G	AB	R	H	2B	3B	HR	RBI	BB	SO	SB	CS	SLG	OBP	B	T	HT	WT	DOB	1st Yr	Resides
Rivera, Juan	.327	55	199	39	65	11	1	14	40	15	31	4	5	.603	.372	R	R	6-2	170	7-3-78	1996	Guarenas, Venez.
Rodriguez, Henry	.238	18	63	9	15	2	0	5	13	7	21	0	0	.508	.319	L	L	6-2	220	11-8-67	1986	Santo Domingo, D.R.
Seabol, Scott	.266	78	282	32	75	19	1	10	42	14	56	3	4	.447	.308	R	R	6-4	200	5-17-75	1996	McKeesport, Pa.
Spencer, Shane	.231	49	173	17	40	10	1	3	14	23	21	4	1	.353	.323	R	R	5-11	225	2-20-72	1990	El Cajon, Calif.
Wilcox, Luke	.150	11	40	3	6	1	0	2	6	3	6	0	1	.325	.205	L	R	6-4	190	11-15-73	1995	St. Johns, Mich.

PITCHING	W	L	ERA	G	GS	CG	SV	IP	H	R	ER	BB	SO	AVG	B	T	HT	WT	DOB	1st Yr	Resides
Adkins, Tim	0	0	0.00	1	0	0	0	2	0	0	0	1		.666	L	L	6-0	205	5-12-74	1992	Lavalette, W.Va.
Almanzar, Carlos	2	1	2.43	35	0	0	18	33	36	10	9	6	26	.279	R	R	6-2	200	11-6-73	1991	Santo Domingo, D.R.
Aramboles, Ricardo	1	3	3.04	4	4	0	0	24	26	11	8	4	14	.282	R	R	6-2	170	12-4-81	1996	Santo Domingo, D.R.
Bertotti, Mike	1	2	3.70	19	4	0	0	41	37	21	17	28	43	.238	L	L	6-1	185	1-18-70	1991	Highland Mills, N.Y.
Choate, Randy	1	1	2.08	4	0	0	0	4	7	1	1	3	4	.388	L	L	6-3	180	9-5-75	1997	Tallahassee, Fla.
Fernandez, Sid	0	0	13.50	1	1	0	0	2	3	3	3	2	3	.375	L	L	6-1	220	10-12-62	1981	Honolulu, Hawaii
Flores, Randy	0	1	4.76	3	0	0	0	6	5	4	3	2	4	.238	L	L	6-0	180	7-31-75	1997	Pico Rivera, Calif.
Flury, Pat	3	2	2.47	34	0	0	3	47	31	13	13	19	66	.184	R	R	6-2	215	3-14-73	1993	Sparks, Nev.
2-team (10 Ottawa)	3	3	2.90	44	0	0	3	59	39	19	19	27	75	.188	R	R					
Gunderson, Eric	2	4	3.05	56	0	0	6	74	70	32	25	24	60	.255	R	L	6-0	190	3-29-66	1987	Portland, Ore.
2-team (2 Buffalo)	2	4	2.97	58	0	0	7	76	72	33	25	24	63	.254							
Henry, Butch	0	1	27.00	1	1	0	0	2	10	7	6	0	1	.625	L	L	6-1	205	10-7-68	1987	El Paso, Texas
3-team (12 Syr./5 Ind.)	8	8	5.03	18	18	2	0	116	140	70	65	18	77	.301							
Hernandez, Adrian	8	7	5.51	21	21	0	0	118	116	75	72	60	97	.265	R	R	6-2	185	8-30-79	2000	Tampa, Fla.
Jean, Domingo	2	4	3.92	35	0	0	3	41	51	23	18	22	45	.291	R	R	6-2	175	1-9-69	1990	Coventry, Conn.
Jodie, Brett	10	4	3.01	19	19	2	0	120	123	46	40	25	59	.265	R	R	6-4	208	3-25-77	1998	Lexington, S.C.
Johnson, Barry	4	2	4.12	38	1	0	1	63	64	32	29	19	37	.265	R	R	6-4	200	8-21-69	1991	Joliet, Ill.
Keisler, Randy	5	7	5.18	18	18	3	0	97	111	67	56	39	88	.280	L	L	6-3	190	2-24-76	1998	Richardson, Texas
Knight, Brandon	12	7	3.66	25	25	3	0	162	174	77	66	45	173	.276	L	R	6-0	170	10-1-75	1995	Ventura, Calif.
Lail, Denny	6	6	4.61	33	20	0	0	137	144	84	70	46	105	.273	R	R	6-1	172	9-10-74	1995	Taylorsville, N.C.
Lilly, Ted	0	0	2.84	5	5	0	0	25	16	10	8	8	30	.175	L	L	6-0	185	1-4-76	1996	Oakhurst, Calif.
Lovingier, Kevin	2	4	2.50	7	0	0	0	10	13	9	5	7	9	.302	L	L	6-1	190	8-29-71	1994	Wichita, Kan.
Ogea, Chad	0	4	7.81	6	6	0	0	28	34	24	24	15	21	.306	R	R	6-2	220	11-9-70	1991	Baton Rouge, La.
Peters, Chris	2	4	4.27	9	8	0	0	53	56	36	25	25	29	.264	L	L	6-1	170	1-28-72	1993	Bethel Park, Pa.
2-team (8 Louisville)	5	5	5.25	17	14	0	0	84	102	62	49	43	45	.294							
Reed, Brandon	1	2	3.48	24	0	0	1	34	27	18	13	8	30	.212	R	R	6-4	195	12-18-74	1993	Flint, Mich.
Scott, Tim	2	3	5.01	14	0	0	0	23	24	14	13	6	28	.258	R	R	6-2	185	11-16-66	1984	Hanford, Calif.
Stoops, Jim	0	0	2.25	5	0	0	0	12	8	4	3	5	10	.177	R	R	6-2	195	6-30-72	1995	Somerset, N.J.
Walling, Dave	0	1	6.00	1	1	0	0	6	5	5	4	0	7	.227	R	R	6-6	200	11-12-78	1999	Las Vegas, Nev.
Williams, Brian	0	1	5.43	16	9	0	0	58	72	43	35	26	33	.307	R	R	6-2	195	2-15-69	1990	Cayce, S.C.
2-team (3 Pawtucket)	5	6	5.08	19	9	0	0	62	74	43	35	27	36	.299							
Williams, Todd	0	1	7.11	17	0	0	2	19	31	19	15	9	14	.352	R	R	6-3	210	2-13-71	1991	Syracuse, N.Y.

FIELDING

Catcher	PCT	G	PO	A	E	DP	PB
Estalella	.993	36	259	18	2	1	0
Figga	1.000	1	7	0	0	0	0
Greene	.982	27	201	15	4	3	2
Matos	.991	74	512	44	5	3	11
Mosquera	.989	16	87	5	1	1	0

First Base	PCT	G	PO	A	E	DP
Bellinger	1.000	1	5	0	0	1
Estalella	1.000	2	8	1	0	0
Garcia	.968	8	57	3	2	8
N. Johnson	.989	109	856	63	10	87
Matos	.963	5	26	0	1	4
Nettles	1.000	3	15	1	0	0
Ottavinia	1.000	11	78	9	0	7
Seabol	1.000	9	61	5	0	9

Second Base	PCT	G	PO	A	E	DP
Bellinger	.000	1	0	0	0	0
Bridges	.987	95	170	207	5	48
Fonville	.964	13	25	29	2	4
Garcia	1.000	10	19	19	0	3
Jimenez	.956	30	66	63	6	24
Nettles	1.000	1	1	0	0	0

Third Base	PCT	G	PO	A	E	DP
Bellinger	1.000	4	2	12	0	0
Bridges	.857	2	1	5	1	1
Garcia	.958	18	14	32	2	2
Henson	.912	68	45	121	16	13
Jimenez	.833	3	2	3	1	0
Leon	.769	11	7	13	6	1
Nettles	1.000	3	1	1	0	0
Seabol	.885	40	25	75	13	5

Shortstop	PCT	G	PO	A	E	DP
Almonte	.936	96	134	258	27	53
Bellinger	.952	9	12	28	2	6
Bridges	.900	2	2	7	1	0
Garcia	.923	16	23	49	6	12
Jimenez	1.000	15	16	43	0	8
Nettles	.900	2	6	3	1	1
Seabol	1.000	7	11	16	0	5

Outfield	PCT	G	PO	A	E	DP
Bellinger	.933	13	14	0	1	0
Bragg	1.000	27	52	4	0	1
Brazoban	1.000	1	3	0	0	0
Coleman	.926	25	48	2	4	0
Fonville	1.000	3	4	0	0	0
Frank	.988	91	165	6	2	2
Greene	1.000	2	3	0	0	0
Knight	.000	1	0	0	0	0
Lennon	1.000	2	5	0	0	0
McDonald	.979	101	232	4	5	1
Nettles	1.000	2	4	0	0	0
Ottavinia	.982	28	51	3	1	1
Perez	1.000	32	68	2	0	1
Rivera	.970	55	124	5	4	0
Rodriguez	1.000	3	3	0	0	0
Seabol	1.000	12	28	2	0	0
Spencer	.985	32	64	2	1	0

NORWICH — Class AA

EASTERN LEAGUE

BATTING	AVG	G	AB	R	H	2B	3B	HR	RBI	BB	SO	SB	CS	SLG	OBP	B	T	HT	WT	DOB	1st Yr	Resides
Almonte, Erick	.250	3	12	2	3	0	0	0	0	1	6	1	0	.250	.308	R	R	6-2	180	2-1-78	1996	Santo Domingo, D.R.
Blakely, Darren	.300	10	20	2	6	0	0	0	2	2	4	3	2	.300	.417	B	R	6-0	190	3-14-77	1998	Pensacola, Fla.
Brown, Rich	.349	11	43	7	15	2	0	3	7	5	9	1	1	.605	.408	L	L	6-1	196	4-28-77	1996	Plantation, Fla.
Cervenak, Mike	.274	128	463	63	127	37	1	11	60	44	75	2	4	.430	.347	R	R	5-11	185	8-17-76	1999	New Boston, Mich.
Emmons, Scott	.133	10	15	2	2	1	0	0	0	1	4	1	0	.200	.188	R	R	6-4	205	12-25-73	1995	Norco, Calif.
Henson, Drew	.368	5	19	2	7	1	0	0	2	1	4	0	1	.421	.429	R	R	6-5	222	2-13-80	1998	Brighton, Mich.
Hernandez, Michel	.227	51	128	10	29	6	0	2	10	10	20	1	0	.320	.291	R	R	6-0	211	8-12-78	1998	Caracas, Venez.
Jackson, Brandon	.316	11	38	5	12	1	0	1	5	2	7	0	2	.421	.350	R	R	6-1	180	10-28-75	1998	House Springs, Mo.
Justice, David	.000	2	8	0	0	0	0	0	0	5	0	0	0	.000	.000	L	L	6-3	200	4-14-66	1985	Cincinnati, Ohio
Kiil, Skip	.188	10	16	5	3	2	0	1	5	8	1	0	0	.500	.391	R	R	6-0	172	4-10-74	1996	Santa Clara, Calif.
Leach, Nick	.210	55	167	17	35	13	0	3	22	28	39	2	2	.341	.320	L	R	6-1	190	12-7-77	1996	Madera, Calif.
Leon, Donny	.255	116	436	45	111	26	2	15	74	19	115	0	2	.427	.290	B	R	6-2	185	5-7-76	1995	Ponce, P.R.
Loggins, Josh	.267	52	176	24	47	12	0	2	27	16	52	2	2	.369	.332	R	R	6-1	190	6-21-76	1998	West Lafayette, Ind.
Morales, Andy	.231	48	160	15	37	3	1	1	14	10	25	1	1	.281	.287	R	R	6-1	200	12-3-74	2001	Lima, Peru
Mosquera, Julio	.269	88	268	31	72	18	0	9	33	14	64	2	1	.437	.317	R	R	6-0	190	1-29-72	1991	Dunedin, Fla.
Nettles, Jeff	.118	6	17	1	2	0	0	0	1	3	6	0	0	.118	.167	R	R	6-2	200	8-20-78	1998	Encinitas, Calif.
Olivares, Teuris	.212	128	439	55	93	15	3	4	30	22	93	5	4	.287	.253	R	R	6-0	164	12-15-78	1996	San Pedro de Macoris, D.R.
Ottavinia, Paul	.258	76	302	52	78	19	2	6	34	30	45	11	1	.394	.335	L	L	6-1	190	4-22-73	1994	Drakestown, N.J.

BATTING	AVG	G	AB	R	H	2B	3B	HR	RBI	BB	SO	SB	CS	SLG	OBP	B	T	HT	WT	DOB	1st Yr	Resides
Phillips, Andy	.268	51	183	23	49	9	2	6	25	21	54	1	0	.437	.340	R	R	6-0	205	4-6-77	1999	Demopolis, Ala.
Pierce, Kirk	.286	12	28	5	8	2	0	1	4	4	8	0	0	.464	.459	R	R	6-3	200	5-26-73	1995	Murrieta, Calif.
Rivera, Juan	.320	77	316	50	101	18	3	14	58	15	50	5	7	.528	.353	R	R	6-2	170	7-3-78	1996	Guarenas, Venez.
Rodriguez, John	.285	103	393	64	112	31	1	22	66	26	117	2	3	.537	.345	L	L	6-0	185	1-20-78	1997	New York, N.Y.
Rodriguez, Victor	.294	57	218	33	64	9	1	3	17	15	18	2	3	.385	.342	R	R	6-0	205	10-25-76	1994	Aguirre, P.R.
Seabol, Scott	.250	31	128	16	32	7	0	4	19	5	30	1	1	.398	.290	R	R	6-4	200	5-17-75	1996	McKeesport, Pa.
Snusz, Chris	.336	42	125	17	42	4	2	2	21	9	23	1	0	.448	.384	R	R	6-0	190	11-8-72	1995	Buffalo, N.Y.
2-team (2 Akron)	.326	44	132	17	43	4	2	2	22	9	24	1	0	.432	.372							
Thames, Marcus	.321	139	520	114	167	43	4	31	97	73	101	10	4	.598	.410	R	R	6-2	205	3-6-77	1997	Louisville, Miss.
Tyson, Torre	.246	71	224	43	55	8	0	0	14	34	49	9	3	.281	.354	B	R	5-10	185	12-31-75	1998	Columbia, Mo.

PITCHING	W	L	ERA	G	GS	CG	SV	IP	H	R	ER	BB	SO	AVG	B	T	HT	WT	DOB	1st Yr	Resides
Adkins, Tim	3	1	3.38	40	5	0	0	80	70	36	30	30	83	.228	L	L	6-0	205	5-12-74	1992	Lavalette, W.Va.
Aldred, Scott	4	3	3.65	11	7	0	0	37	36	19	15	7	43	.250	L	L	6-4	220	6-12-68	1987	Fenton, Mich.
Bean, Colter	0	1	9.00	1	0	0	0	1	1	1	1	1	0	.250	R	R	6-6	255	1-16-77	2000	Anniston, Ala.
Blevins, Jeremy	1	6	2.98	50	0	0	6	63	46	30	21	26	63	.198	R	R	6-3	190	10-5-77	1995	Bristol, Tenn.
Bradley, Ryan	4	5	6.63	16	12	0	0	58	47	51	43	48	53	.221	R	R	6-4	226	10-26-75	1997	Chino Hills, Calif.
Claussen, Brandon	9	2	2.13	21	21	1	0	131	101	42	31	55	151	.209	L	L	6-2	175	5-1-79	1999	Roswell, N.M.
Flores, Randy	14	6	2.78	25	25	3	0	159	156	64	49	63	115	.257	L	L	6-0	180	7-31-75	1997	Pico Rivera, Calif.
Flury, Pat	1	0	1.59	4	0	0	0	6	2	1	1	2	9	.105	R	R	6-2	215	3-14-73	1993	Sparks, Nev.
Garcia, Rosman	1	0	0.00	1	1	0	0	6	5	4	0	2	6	.200	R	R	6-2	165	1-3-79	1996	San Joaquin, Venez.
Graman, Alex	12	9	3.52	28	28	1	0	166	174	83	65	60	138	.267	L	L	6-4	200	11-17-77	1999	Huntingburg, Ind.
Jean, Domingo	3	2	1.21	21	0	0	6	30	20	5	4	4	43	.192	R	R	6-2	175	1-9-69	1990	Coventry, Conn.
Jensen, Justin	0	0	3.68	4	0	0	0	7	7	3	3	4	6	.250	L	L	6-3	210	12-19-73	1994	Santa Cruz, Calif.
Jerzembeck, Mike	1	2	5.14	10	4	0	0	28	30	20	16	8	31	.277	R	R	6-1	185	5-18-72	1993	Sanford, N.C.
Jodie, Brett	2	0	0.64	2	2	0	0	14	10	1	1	2	14	.208	R	R	6-4	208	3-25-77	1998	Lexington, S.C.
Johnson, Barry	1	1	4.63	8	0	0	0	12	12	7	6	5	16	.260	R	R	6-4	200	8-21-69	1991	Joliet, Ill.
Looney, Brian	0	0	8.44	11	0	0	0	16	23	18	15	10	16	.328	L	L	5-10	180	6-26-69	1991	Cheshire, Conn.
Lovingier, Kevin	3	5	1.91	53	0	0	0	90	56	22	19	31	94	.180	L	L	6-1	190	8-29-71	1994	Wichita, Kan.
Marte, Damaso	3	1	3.50	23	0	0	1	36	29	16	14	7	36	.214	L	L	6-0	170	2-14-75	1993	San Carlos, D.R.
Pacheco, Alexander	5	4	1.26	43	0	0	26	50	25	9	7	16	65	.142	R	R	6-3	170	7-19-73	1990	Caracas, Venez.
Padua, Geraldo	1	0	2.89	5	0	0	0	9	5	3	3	3	11	.156	R	R	6-2	165	2-9-77	1995	Santo Domingo, D.R.
2-team (10 Altoona)	1	1	6.85	15	0	0	0	22	22	17	17	9	21	.265							
Reynoso, Edison	1	0	3.93	5	3	0	0	18	19	12	8	5	17	.260	R	R	6-1	170	11-10-75	1993	Montecristi, D.R.
Rogers, Brian	10	9	3.96	29	29	1	0	177	187	97	78	63	150	.270	R	R	6-6	200	2-13-77	1998	Carthage, N.C.
Roller, Adam	0	0	0.00	2	0	0	0	3	3	0	0	0	2	.300	R	R	6-3	208	6-27-78	1997	Lakeland, Fla.
Stoops, Jim	0	0	6.00	6	0	0	0	9	14	10	6	6	9	.333	R	R	6-2	195	6-30-72	1995	Somerset, N.J.
Walling, David	3	2	5.40	5	5	1	0	32	44	23	19	4	24	.328	R	R	6-6	200	11-12-78	1999	Las Vegas, Nev.
Whiteley, Shad	0	0	4.50	1	0	0	0	2	2	1	1	0	2	.250	R	R	6-6	220	3-19-75	1998	Fort Worth, Texas
Wiggins, Scott	0	0	0.00	4	0	0	0	4	0	0	0	1	5	.000	L	L	6-3	205	3-24-76	1997	Newport, Ky.
Williams, Todd	1	0	0.00	6	0	0	1	8	4	0	0	0	5	.148	R	R	6-3	210	2-13-71	1991	Syracuse, N.Y.

FIELDING

Catcher	PCT	G	PO	A	E	DP	PB
Emmons	1.000	7	23	2	0	0	1
Hernandez	.981	47	338	31	7	4	6
Loggins	.875	2	7	0	1	0	2
Mosquera	.991	82	629	46	6	6	10
Pierce	.962	11	69	6	3	1	1
Snusz	.983	25	163	11	3	2	6

First Base	PCT	G	PO	A	E	DP
Cervenak	.980	33	223	19	5	16
Emmons	1.000	3	6	1	0	0
Leach	.988	53	377	18	5	35
Leon	.965	12	50	5	2	3
Mosquera	1.000	1	0	0	0	1
Ottavinia	.993	48	364	39	3	33
Seabol	.893	4	23	2	3	1
Snusz	.947	5	34	2	2	3

Second Base	PCT	G	PO	A	E	DP
Cervenak	.951	27	62	35	5	12
Jackson	.957	11	23	22	2	7
Phillips	.915	47	92	91	17	20
Rodriguez	.981	57	79	130	4	23
Tyson	.960	14	21	27	2	9

Third Base	PCT	G	PO	A	E	DP
Cervenak	.942	40	21	77	6	2
Henson	.842	5	8	8	3	0
Leon	.867	63	47	103	23	10
Morales	.960	25	20	28	2	3
Nettles	.833	4	0	5	1	0
Seabol	.875	25	10	39	7	2

Shortstop	PCT	G	PO	A	E	DP
Almonte	.900	3	4	5	1	1
Cervenak	.955	18	18	24	2	5

	PCT	G	PO	A	E	DP
Nettles	1.000	1	0	1	0	0
Olivares	.932	128	184	324	37	61
Tyson	.815	7	6	16	5	2

Outfield	PCT	G	PO	A	E	DP
Blakely	1.000	6	12	0	0	0
Kiil	1.000	6	8	0	0	0
Leon	1.000	1	1	0	0	0
Loggins	.963	40	77	2	3	0
Nettles	1.000	2	3	0	0	0
Ottavinia	1.000	30	48	1	0	1
Rivera	.963	76	141	16	6	4
Rodriguez	.976	101	153	9	4	0
Seabol	.750	4	3	0	1	0
Thames	.973	137	277	7	8	0
Tyson	.968	42	86	4	3	0

FLORIDA STATE LEAGUE

BATTING	AVG	G	AB	R	H	2B	3B	HR	RBI	BB	SO	SB	CS	SLG	OBP	B	T	HT	WT	DOB	1st Yr	Resides
Blakely, Darren	.256	86	313	47	80	14	5	12	39	41	94	24	11	.447	.363	B	R	6-0	190	3-14-77	1998	Pensacola, Fla.
Bozanich, Sam	.182	14	44	6	8	0	0	0	8	10	1	3	.182	.321	R	R	5-9	190	11-10-78	2000	Bakersfield, Calif.
Brown, Andy	.193	93	306	45	59	13	3	11	45	52	129	7	5	.363	.315	L	L	6-6	190	4-14-80	1998	Richmond, Ind.
Brown, Richard	.600	1	5	0	3	1	0	0	2	0	0	0	0	.800	.600	L	L	6-1	196	4-28-77	1996	Plantation, Fla.
Calabrese, Tony	.233	20	60	8	14	2	0	0	3	8	9	3	1	.267	.343	R	R	6-4	195	11-5-78	2000	Riverside, Conn.
Coleman, Andy	.059	7	17	3	1	1	0	0	1	3	7	0	0	.118	.273	R	R	5-11	210	11-11-77	2001	Pasadena, Calif.
Elwood, Brad	.212	45	118	11	25	6	0	0	10	8	21	1	1	.263	.273	R	R	6-1	195	10-22-75	1998	Clear Spring, Md.
Fuentes, Omar	.833	2	6	4	5	1	0	1	3	2	0	0	0	1.500	.875	R	R	6-1	175	4-6-80	1996	Maracay, Venez.
Grove, Jason	.400	1	5	1	2	2	0	0	2	0	2	0	0	.800	.400	L	L	6-2	200	8-15-78	2000	Walla Walla, Wash.
Henson, Drew	.143	5	14	2	2	0	0	1	3	2	7	1	0	.357	.316	R	R	6-5	222	2-13-80	1998	Brighton, Mich.
Hooper, Clay	.216	93	268	43	58	10	2	1	20	35	44	3	9	.280	.317	R	R	6-1	190	4-9-77	2000	Greensboro, N.C.
Jackson, Brandon	.231	69	225	23	52	8	3	6	26	25	45	3	7	.307	.311	R	R	6-1	180	10-28-75	1998	House Springs, Mo.
Jones, Mitch	.224	137	487	85	109	36	3	21	71	81	135	9	2	.439	.340	R	R	6-2	215	10-15-77	2000	Orem, Utah
Leach, Nick	.269	59	201	24	54	6	2	8	33	19	42	0	6	.438	.338	L	R	6-1	190	12-7-77	1996	Madera, Calif.
Leaumont, Jeff	.241	76	249	28	60	11	3	6	22	21	50	1	1	.382	.302	L	L	6-4	200	3-22-77	1999	Baton Rouge, La.
Myrow, Brian	.255	48	149	30	38	11	1	3	28	32	29	5	1	.403	.399	L	R	5-11	190	9-4-76	1999	Fort Worth, Texas
Nettles, Jeff	.202	77	253	28	51	14	0	4	31	24	53	0	2	.304	.270	R	R	6-2	200	8-20-78	1998	Encinitas, Calif.
Nettles, Tim	.056	10	18	2	1	0	0	0	1	1	5	1	0	.056	.105	R	R	6-1	195	6-23-77	2000	Encinitas, Calif.
Olivares, Teuris	.267	4	15	2	4	2	0	0	2	3	1	0	0	.400	.353	R	R	6-0	164	12-15-78	1996	San Pedro de Macoris, D.R.
Osborne, Steve	.200	6	15	2	3	1	0	0	1	0	5	0	0	.267	.250	R	R	6-1	195	12-21-78	2001	Millinocket, Maine

BATTING

BATTING	AVG	G	AB	R	H	2B	3B	HR	RBI	BB	SO	SB	CS	SLG	OBP	B	T	HT	WT	DOB	1st Yr	Resides
Parrish, David	.253	115	367	43	93	25	0	6	49	54	88	2	1	.371	.355	R	R	6-3	220	6-13-79	2000	Yorba Linda, Calif.
Phillips, Andy	.302	75	288	43	87	17	4	11	50	25	55	3	3	.503	.353	R	R	6-0	205	4-6-77	1999	Demopolis, Ala.
Reyes, Ivan	.500	3	4	2	2	0	0	1	1	3	1	0	0	1.250	.714	R	R	6-2	185	6-6-81	1999	Toa Baja, P.R.
Rodriguez, Victor	.272	41	151	22	41	10	2	1	15	21	15	5	3	.384	.374	R	R	6-0	205	10-25-76	1994	Aguirre, P.R.
Rojas, Tom	.000	1	0	0	0	0	0	0	0	0	0	0	0	.000	.000	R	R	6-2	185	3-31-82	2001	Henderson, Nev.
Santana, Pedro	.241	17	54	4	13	3	0	1	6	2	17	1	1	.352	.305	R	R	6-1	190	5-19-79	1996	Santo Domingo, D.R.
Tyson, Torre	.254	31	114	28	29	6	2	0	10	24	19	6	4	.342	.390	B	R	5-10	185	12-31-75	1998	Columbia, Mo.
Valdez, Angel	.236	46	148	22	35	9	2	1	7	7	43	5	1	.345	.277	R	R	6-2	178	5-22-78	1996	Santo Domingo, D.R.
Vento, Mike	.300	130	457	71	137	20	10	20	87	45	88	13	10	.519	.372	R	R	6-0	195	5-25-78	1998	Corrales, N.M.
Washington, Dion	.190	29	84	5	16	4	1	0	8	10	22	0	1	.262	.284	R	R	6-4	235	12-21-76	1997	Las Vegas, Nev.

GAMES BY POSITION: C—Coleman 6, Elwood 40, Fuentes 2, Parrish 104. **1B**—Leach 57, Leaumont 68, Washington 22. **2B**—Bozanich 13, Calabrese 1, Hooper 7, Jackson 4, Phillips 73, Reyes 2, Rodriguez 40. **3B**—Calabrese 14, Henson 5, Hooper 1, Jackson 10, Jones 20, Myrow 32, J. Nettles 68. **SS**—Calabrese 5, Hooper 79, Jones 53, J. Nettles 5, Olivares 4. **OF**—Blakely 86, Elwood 1, Grove 1, Hooper 3, Jones 115, Leaumont 2, J. Nettles 3, T. Nettles 8, Osborne 6, Santana 17, Tyson 31, Valdez 39, Vento 122.

PITCHING

PITCHING	W	L	ERA	G	GS	CG	SV	IP	H	R	ER	BB	SO	AVG	B	T	HT	WT	DOB	1st Yr	Resides
Acosta, Manuel	0	1	7.71	2	2	0	0	7	7	7	6	6	8	.280	R	R	6-4	170	5-1-81	1998	Colon, Panama
Aramboles, Ricardo	7	2	4.06	12	11	0	0	69	72	37	31	19	59	.270	R	R	6-2	170	12-4-81	1996	Santo Domingo, D.R.
Artiles, Carlos	0	1	5.00	5	0	0	0	9	7	5	5	5	9	.218	L	L	5-11	165	1-21-81	1997	Santo Domingo, D.R.
Beal, Andy	5	5	3.00	17	17	0	0	99	101	57	33	30	72	.256	L	L	6-2	185	10-31-78	2000	Paducah, Ky.
Bean, Colter	7	1	1.46	32	0	0	2	49	27	9	8	18	77	.155	R	R	6-6	255	1-16-77	2000	Anniston, Ala.
Borrell, Danny	7	9	3.97	22	20	0	0	111	109	58	49	38	84	.258	L	L	6-3	190	1-24-79	2000	Sanford, N.C.
Bradley, Ryan	3	1	3.08	7	7	0	0	38	27	15	13	22	32	.194	R	R	6-4	226	10-26-75	1997	Chino Hills, Calif.
Claussen, Brandon	5	2	2.73	8	8	0	0	56	47	21	17	13	69	.223	L	L	6-2	175	5-1-79	1999	Roswell, N.M.
DePaula, Julio	9	5	3.58	16	13	0	0	83	65	43	33	53	77	.212	R	R	6-1	160	7-27-79	1997	Santo Domingo, D.R.
Garcia, Rosman	2	6	3.47	26	7	0	1	60	56	30	23	22	42	.243	R	R	6-2	165	1-3-79	1996	San Joaquin, Venez.
Grace, Bryan	0	0	13.50	3	0	0	0	2	5	4	3	1	5	.454	R	R	6-1	190	4-1-76	1999	Baton Rouge, La.
Hernandez, Orlando	0	0	0.00	2	2	0	0	7	6	2	0	1	8	.214	R	R	6-2	220	10-11-69	1998	Miami, Fla.
Jensen, Justin	3	3	2.32	37	2	0	0	62	52	22	16	36	67	.225	L	L	6-3	210	12-19-73	1994	Santa Cruz, Calif.
Knowles, Mike	0	0	10.13	8	0	0	2	8	15	10	9	8	9	.428	R	R	6-5	215	7-15-79	1997	Daytona Beach, Fla.
Kremer, John	0	0	6.00	6	0	0	0	9	15	7	6	3	8	.357	R	R	6-1	220	11-19-76	1999	Indianapolis, Ind.
Marsonek, Sam	8	8	3.51	24	23	5	0	138	128	67	54	39	120	.244	R	R	6-6	225	7-10-78	1997	Tampa, Fla.
Martinez, Dave	0	3	6.05	4	3	1	0	19	20	15	13	9	19	.266	L	L	6-1	165	6-7-80	1997	Ciudad, Venez.
Martinez, Oscar	2	3	3.07	29	0	0	14	29	26	12	10	10	40	.226	R	R	6-2	185	10-7-78	1996	Araure, Venez.
Mosley, Eric	0	1	4.50	1	1	0	0	6	5	3	3	3	0	.272	R	R	6-3	185	5-27-81	2000	Tulsa, Okla.
Ogea, Chad	0	0	3.00	2	2	0	0	9	10	3	3	3	6	.285	R	R	6-2	220	11-9-70	1991	Baton Rouge, La.
Padua, Geraldo	0	0	0.00	1	0	0	0	1	0	0	0	1	1	.000	R	R	6-2	165	2-9-77	1995	Santo Domingo, D.R.
Reynoso, Edison	0	0	0.00	1	1	0	0	4	1	0	0	0	5	.083	R	R	6-1	170	11-10-75	1993	Montecristi, D.R.
Roller, Adam	2	3	1.20	51	0	0	23	68	42	14	9	15	76	.173	R	R	6-3	208	6-27-78	1997	Lakeland, Fla.
Smith, Jason	1	0	0.00	1	0	0	0	3	1	0	0	2	1	.100	B	R	6-5	205	3-7-82	2000	Kennewick, Wash.
Smith, Matt	6	2	2.24	11	11	0	0	68	54	21	17	22	71	.215	L	L	6-5	225	6-15-79	2000	Henderson, Nev.
Stafford, Mike	0	1	7.71	4	0	0	0	2	8	2	2	1	4	.000	B	L	6-3	180	6-24-75	1998	Columbus, Ohio
Stanton, Tim	1	0	1.89	26	0	0	1	48	46	15	10	13	39	.258	L	L	6-1	190	12-31-76	1999	Sandwich, Mass.
Walling, David	1	1	5.19	4	4	0	0	17	23	12	10	2	9	.302	R	R	6-6	200	11-12-78	1999	Las Vegas, Nev.
Whiteley, Shad	1	0	2.79	9	0	0	0	10	9	4	3	6	9	.243	R	R	6-6	220	3-19-75	1998	Fort Worth, Texas
Wiggins, Scott	4	3	3.03	36	5	0	1	68	72	29	23	23	77	.270	L	L	6-3	205	3-24-76	1997	Newport, Ky.
Witte, Lou	3	1	2.67	29	0	0	0	34	39	13	10	5	29	.307	R	R	6-0	180	10-30-76	1999	Richmond, Ind.

GREENSBORO

Class A

SOUTH ATLANTIC LEAGUE

BATTING

BATTING	AVG	G	AB	R	H	2B	3B	HR	RBI	BB	SO	SB	CS	SLG	OBP	B	T	HT	WT	DOB	1st Yr	Resides
Baker, Casey	.071	8	14	1	1	0	0	0	1	2	6	1	1	.071	.188	R	R	5-9	165	8-7-80	1999	Wysox, Pa.
Bozanich, Sam	.270	65	204	30	55	12	2	3	17	18	51	5	5	.392	.327	R	R	5-9	190	11-10-78	2000	Bakersfield, Calif.
Brazoban, Yhency	.273	124	469	51	128	23	3	6	52	19	98	6	3	.373	.311	R	R	6-1	170	6-11-80	1997	Santo Domingo, D.R.
Calabrese, Tony	.291	43	134	25	39	8	1	5	20	22	29	1	1	.478	.386	R	R	6-4	195	11-5-78	2000	Riverside, Conn.
Castro, Bernabel	.260	101	389	71	101	15	7	1	36	54	67	20	20	.342	.350	B	R	5-10	165	7-14-81	1997	Santo Domingo, D.R.
Coleman, Andy	.125	3	8	0	1	0	0	0	0	0	4	0	0	.125	.125	R	R	5-11	210	11-11-77	2001	Pasadena, Calif.
Corporan, Elvis	.225	135	484	65	109	25	6	15	53	35	124	15	8	.395	.279	B	R	6-3	200	6-9-80	1999	Catano, P.R.
Cronin, Shane	.251	58	191	23	48	6	0	4	25	7	32	1	0	.346	.282	R	R	6-1	210	2-26-76	1996	Renton, Wash.
Fowler, David	.199	110	291	30	58	15	3	5	26	27	125	8	12	.323	.277	R	R	6-3	190	10-17-79	1998	St. Louis, Mo.
Fuentes, Omar	.266	100	342	59	91	24	1	8	62	45	57	0	2	.412	.360	R	R	6-1	175	4-6-80	1996	Maracay, Venez.
Grove, Jason	.296	115	446	68	132	21	8	15	68	36	108	0	2	.480	.353	L	L	6-2	200	8-15-78	2000	Walla Walla, Wash.
Jackson, Brandon	.250	5	20	3	5	0	0	0	2	2	5	2	0	.250	.304	R	R	6-1	180	10-28-75	1998	House Springs, Mo.
Kinchen, Jason	.309	134	489	81	151	24	1	30	82	50	102	2	0	.546	.380	L	R	6-0	210	7-30-75	1997	Baton Rouge, La.
Leaumont, Jeff	.245	27	94	9	23	5	0	5	8	8	25	0	1	.298	.298	L	L	6-4	200	3-22-77	1999	Baton Rouge, La.
Mendez, Deivi	.215	49	172	25	37	6	0	2	15	14	35	5	2	.285	.279	R	R	6-1	165	6-24-83	1999	Santo Domingo, D.R.
Nettles, Tim	.364	3	11	0	4	0	0	0	1	0	3	0	0	.364	.364	R	R	6-1	195	6-23-77	2000	Encinitas, Calif.
Ramistella, John	.286	2	7	0	2	0	0	0	0	0	5	0	0	.286	.286	R	R	6-2	220	8-29-81	2001	Monterey, Calif.
Reyes, Ivan	.247	51	170	17	42	9	1	7	23	20	58	3	2	.435	.326	R	R	6-2	185	6-6-81	1999	Toa Baja, P.R.
Rojas, Tom	.333	1	3	0	1	0	0	0	0	0	2	0	0	.333	.333	R	R	6-2	185	3-31-82	2001	Henderson, Nev.
Santa, Alex	.000	3	9	0	0	0	0	0	0	1	0	0	0	.000	.000	L	L	6-0	175	12-27-82	1999	Santo Domingo, D.R.
Santana, Pedro	.105	6	19	2	2	1	0	0	0	2	0	0	0	.158	.190	R	R	6-1	190	5-19-79	1996	Santo Domingo, D.R.
Segar, Jeff	.167	27	84	5	14	2	2	0	8	19	0	0	.238	.234	R	R	6-3	210	11-1-78	2000	Syracuse, N.Y.
Sutter, Tony	.163	16	43	7	7	0	0	1	6	8	9	0	1	.233	.302	B	R	6-0	185	2-26-78	2000	Staten Island, N.Y.
Svihlik, D.J.	.143	4	7	1	1	0	1	0	0	0	1	0	0	.429	.143	L	R	5-10	180	10-29-77	2000	Garfield Heights, Ohio
Turner, Jason	.261	88	303	43	79	15	2	8	47	45	63	5	2	.403	.352	L	L	6-3	205	7-30-77	2000	Versailles, Ohio
Winrow, Tommy	.167	63	222	17	37	5	0	7	24	15	56	2	1	.284	.228	L	L	6-2	187	7-12-80	1999	Fort Myers, Fla.

GAMES BY POSITION: C—Coleman 3, Cronin 48, Fuentes 95, Rojas 1. **1B**—Calabrese 3, Cronin 8, Kinchen 44, Leaumont 22, Sutter 7, Turner 68. **2B**—Baker 4, Bozanich 42, Castro 96, Reyes 1, Svihlik 3. **3B**—Bozanich 1, Calabrese 7, Corporan 135, Sutter 4. **SS**—Calabrese 32, Jackson 5, Mendez 49, Reyes 49, Sutter 5. **OF**—Brazoban 122, Fowler 109, Grove 104, Leaumont 4, Nettles 3, Ramistella 2, Santa 3, Santana 3, Segar 27, Turner 15, Winrow 60.

PITCHING

PITCHING	W	L	ERA	G	GS	CG	SV	IP	H	R	ER	BB	SO	AVG	B	T	HT	WT	DOB	1st Yr	Resides
Acosta, Manuel	5	2	1.51	9	9	0	0	66	37	14	11	37	67	.165	R	R	6-4	170	5-1-81	1998	Colon, Panama
Anderson, Jason	7	9	3.76	23	19	1	1	124	127	68	52	40	101	.267	L	R	6-0	170	6-9-79	2000	Danville, Ill.

PITCHING	W	L	ERA	G	GS	CG	SV	IP	H	R	ER	BB	SO	AVG	B	T	HT	WT	DOB	1st Yr	Resides
Beal, Andy	1	0	0.00	2	2	0	0	10	10	1	0	3	6	.270	L	L	6-2	185	10-31-78	2000	Paducah, Ky.
Blankenship, John	5	5	2.38	27	9	0	0	76	53	21	20	28	85	.197	L	L	5-10	180	11-6-78	2000	Tuscaloosa, Ala.
Buchanan, Brian	4	2	4.08	37	4	0	0	79	82	42	36	34	82	.272	L	L	6-3	190	4-23-77	1995	Oviedo, Fla.
Correa, Dominic	2	2	4.42	16	0	0	3	18	12	9	9	9	17	.187	R	R	5-11	185	6-12-77	1999	Los Angeles, Calif.
Currier, Rik	0	4	4.55	6	6	0	0	32	32	22	16	17	25	.264	R	R	5-10	180	5-26-78	2001	Aliso Viejo, Calif.
DePaula, Julio	6	1	2.75	8	8	0	0	56	35	19	17	21	67	.179	R	R	6-1	160	7-27-79	1997	Santo Domingo, D.R.
2-team (3 Asheville)	7	2	2.99	11	11	0	0	72	54	32	24	23	93	.203							
Faigin, Jason	4	8	3.41	60	1	0	8	66	63	32	25	26	67	.241	R	R	6-2	195	9-20-78	1999	Marlboro, N.J.
Gomez, Ricardo	2	2	8.80	9	2	0	1	15	20	19	15	12	10	.322	R	R	6-2	165	6-14-78	1995	Puerto Plata, D.R.
Gonzales, Jose	2	6	5.14	35	0	0	0	49	52	30	28	19	36	.282	R	R	6-0	185	11-17-77	1996	Chiriqui, Panama
Goodrum, Kevin	2	4	4.19	7	7	0	0	39	45	21	18	12	25	.296	L	L	6-3	225	6-17-79	2001	Ashtabula, Ohio
King, Jeremy	0	1	12.60	1	1	0	0	5	8	7	7	3	5	.380	R	R	6-2	210	11-12-81	2000	Nocatee, Fla.
Knowles, Mike	3	4	3.22	38	7	0	21	64	63	26	23	35	62	.257	R	R	6-5	215	7-15-79	1997	Daytona Beach, Fla.
Kremer, John	4	1	2.49	40	0	0	1	51	40	26	14	26	39	.210	R	R	6-1	220	11-19-76	1999	Indianapolis, Ind.
Laplante, Reggie	0	2	8.10	7	0	0	2	7	9	7	6	4	5	.333	L	R	6-2	190	12-2-79	1999	Beauport, Quebec
Marietta, Ron	1	0	18.00	4	1	0	0	3	4	6	6	4	1	.307	L	L	6-0	190	8-12-77	1998	Brooklyn, N.Y.
Martin, Larry	1	0	4.02	13	0	0	0	16	15	11	7	19	20	.258	L	L	6-3	180	5-9-77	2001	Andrews, Texas
Martinez, Dave	6	0	1.13	11	11	3	0	79	54	17	10	28	67	.192	L	L	6-1	165	6-7-80	1997	Ciudad, Venez.
Mosley, Eric	1	4	4.93	11	10	0	0	46	48	31	25	22	32	.266	R	R	6-3	185	5-27-81	2000	Tulsa, Okla.
Padua, Geraldo	1	1	3.86	3	3	0	0	19	20	8	8	3	14	.285	R	R	6-2	165	2-9-77	1995	Santo Domingo, D.R.
Peeples, Jim	0	0	0.00	1	0	0	0	1	0	0	0	0	0	.000	L	L	6-0	195	7-5-80	1999	Jacksonville, Fla.
Reynolds, Eric	0	0	0.00	1	0	0	0	1	1	0	0	1	1	.333	L	L	6-3	215	4-20-80	2000	Saltillo, Miss.
Schmitt, Eric	2	1	3.38	7	7	0	0	37	32	15	14	9	35	.230	R	R	6-4	210	7-23-78	2000	Fairfax, Va.
Smith, Jason	1	2	5.73	5	4	0	0	22	34	19	14	7	13	.369	B	R	6-5	205	3-7-82	2000	Kennewick, Wash.
Smith, Joe	3	6	5.23	11	10	1	0	52	68	35	30	12	25	.313	R	R	6-0	185	4-1-78	2000	San Luis Obispo, Calif.
2-team (24 Hagerstown)	10	8	3.70	35	12	1	0	122	132	56	50	33	70	.276							
Smith, Matt	5	3	2.59	16	16	1	0	97	69	37	28	32	116	.197	L	L	6-5	225	6-15-79	2000	Henderson, Nev.
Stevens, Josh	1	0	2.95	19	2	0	0	37	29	12	12	9	42	.216	R	R	6-4	200	6-6-79	1998	Riverside, Calif.
Wombacher, Mike	1	2	3.62	38	0	0	0	50	54	26	20	13	41	.275	L	L	6-5	235	10-13-77	2000	Clarkdale, Ariz.

STATEN ISLAND — Short-Season Class A

NEW YORK-PENN LEAGUE

BATTING	AVG	G	AB	R	H	2B	3B	HR	RBI	BB	SO	SB	CS	SLG	OBP	B	T	HT	WT	DOB	1st Yr	Resides
Baker, Casey	.071	6	14	0	1	0	0	0	0	1	3	0	0	.071	.133	R	R	5-9	165	8-7-80	1999	Wysox, Pa.
Camacho, Juan	.277	72	274	42	76	14	3	10	51	20	36	0	1	.460	.338	B	R	6-2	175	1-13-81	1997	San Carlos, Venez.
Cannizaro, Andy	.283	67	254	38	72	9	2	0	20	22	21	5	3	.335	.351	R	R	5-10	170	12-19-78	2001	Mandeville, La.
Cano, Robinson	.250	2	8	0	2	0	0	0	2	0	2	0	0	.250	.250	L	R	6-0	172	10-22-82	2001	San Pedro de Macoris, D.R.
Castro, Bernabel	.351	15	57	6	20	1	0	0	7	11	12	8	3	.368	.464	B	R	5-10	165	7-14-81	1997	Santo Domingo, D.R.
Christensen, Jeff	.224	19	58	13	13	4	2	2	9	5	14	7	1	.466	.338	L	L	6-1	205	10-12-78	2001	Knoxville, Tenn.
DeGroote, Casey	.182	14	22	0	4	3	0	0	4	4	10	0	0	.318	.308	L	L	6-4	185	7-13-79	1998	Harte, Ind.
Duncan, Shelley	.245	70	273	43	67	17	2	8	39	21	62	5	3	.410	.311	R	R	6-5	215	9-29-79	2001	Tucson, Ariz.
Evans, Mitch	.122	26	49	1	6	2	0	0	3	8	16	0	0	.163	.259	R	R	6-1	180	4-11-81	1999	Sydney, Australia
Faulkner, Todd	.218	24	55	4	12	1	1	0	3	4	13	1	0	.273	.279	R	R	6-4	210	12-12-77	2001	Powder Springs, Ga.
Fernandez, Alejandro	.190	29	84	7	16	2	0	1	5	8	26	0	0	.250	.284	R	R	6-2	175	12-19-80	1997	Maracaibo, Venez.
Griffin, John-Ford	.311	66	238	46	74	17	1	5	43	40	41	10	4	.454	.413	L	L	6-2	215	11-19-79	2001	Sarasota, Fla.
Martin, Chris	.200	27	75	8	15	2	0	1	5	4	18	0	0	.267	.250	R	R	5-9	190	1-31-79	2001	Quincy, Ill.
Mendez, Deivi	.231	53	186	23	43	10	2	1	21	9	31	2	4	.323	.272	R	R	6-1	165	6-24-83	1999	Santo Domingo, D.R.
Pitney, Jared	.000	3	7	0	0	0	0	0	0	1	6	1	0	.000	.125	L	L	6-0	185	3-26-79	2001	Agoura, Calif.
Rifkin, Aaron	.318	69	245	41	78	19	5	10	49	31	47	3	2	.559	.392	L	L	6-3	220	3-12-79	2001	Upland, Calif.
Santos, Omir	.274	44	117	11	32	5	1	0	8	6	25	0	1	.333	.310	R	R	6-0	200	4-29-81	2001	Toa Baja, P.R.
Segar, Jeff	.267	34	116	16	31	14	0	1	21	9	18	4	1	.414	.318	R	R	6-3	210	11-1-78	2000	Syracuse, N.Y.
Summerville, Kaazim	.186	35	59	14	11	0	0	0	4	7	18	13	1	.186	.314	R	R	5-10	185	9-18-78	2001	Hayward, Calif.
Thompson, Kevin	.262	68	260	46	68	11	4	6	33	36	48	11	5	.404	.360	R	R	6-3	185	9-18-79	2000	Fort Worth, Texas
Turner, Jason	.336	33	110	24	37	7	2	1	19	18	31	1	1	.464	.430	L	L	6-3	205	7-30-77	2000	Versailles, Ohio

GAMES BY POSITION: C—Evans 25, Fernandez 29, Santos 44, Summerville 1. **1B**—Christensen 4, DeGroote 2, Faulkner 9, Pitney 2, Rifkin 67. **2B**—Baker 6, Cannizaro 44, Castro 15, Martin 20. **3B**—Camacho 70, Cano 1, DeGroote 4, Faulkner 1, Martin 7. **SS**—Camacho 2, Cannizaro 24, Cano 1, Martin 1, Mendez 53. **OF**—Christensen 15, DeGroote 1, Evans 1, Faulkner 7, Griffin 66, Segar 33, Summerville 22, Thompson 67, Turner 33.

PITCHING	W	L	ERA	G	GS	CG	SV	IP	H	R	ER	BB	SO	AVG	B	T	HT	WT	DOB	1st Yr	Resides
Anderson, Jason	5	1	1.70	7	7	0	0	48	32	9	9	12	56	.190	L	R	6-0	170	6-9-79	2000	Danville, Ill.
Arnold, Jason	7	2	1.50	10	10	2	0	66	35	13	11	15	74	.157	R	R	6-3	210	5-2-79	2001	Palm Bay, Fla.
Artiles, Carlos	0	0	0.00	1	1	0	0	5	1	0	0	3	4	.066	L	L	5-11	165	1-21-81	1997	Santo Domingo, D.R.
Blankenship, John	4	0	3.09	5	5	0	0	35	29	16	12	8	22	.218	L	L	5-10	180	11-6-78	2000	Tuscaloosa, Ala.
Carlson, Steve	1	0	0.00	3	0	0	0	3	1	0	0	1	2	.111	R	L	6-1	205	1-9-79	2001	Newark, Ill.
Clark, Ryan	2	0	1.15	29	0	0	7	31	14	5	4	7	37	.131	L	L	6-3	210	8-3-79	2001	North Baltimore, Ohio
Cooksey, Wes	1	0	4.71	20	0	0	1	29	27	16	15	11	13	.245	L	R	6-3	215	5-22-78	2001	Port Arthur, Texas
Currier, Rik	2	2	3.77	7	7	0	0	31	37	20	13	13	27	.280	R	R	5-10	180	5-26-78	2001	Aliso Viejo, Calif.
Garcia, Anderson	0	1	5.79	1	1	0	0	5	7	3	3	1	1	.368	R	R	6-2	178	12-23-83	2001	Santo Domingo, D.R.
Gill, Ryan	2	2	5.63	19	0	0	0	24	23	20	15	16	25	.247	R	R	6-3	200	2-1-77	2000	Baton Rouge, La.
Gomez, Ricardo	1	1	1.47	8	0	0	0	18	13	7	3	10	11	.203	R	R	6-2	165	6-14-78	1995	Puerto Plata, D.R.
Goodrum, Kevin	1	1	3.78	7	3	0	0	17	18	9	7	6	14	.264	L	L	6-3	225	6-17-79	2001	Ashtabula, Ohio
Henn, Sean	3	1	3.00	9	8	0	1	42	26	15	14	15	49	.178	R	L	6-5	205	4-23-81	2001	Fort Worth, Texas
Hernandez, Orlando	1	0	0.00	1	1	0	0	6	2	0	0	1	11	.100	R	R	6-2	220	10-11-69	1998	Miami, Fla.
Landaeta, Argenis	0	1	6.00	1	1	0	0	6	8	4	4	2	6	.333	R	R	6-2	175	11-8-81	1998	Valencia, Venez.
Laplante, Reggie	0	1	5.26	19	0	0	0	26	28	15	15	17	32	.266	L	R	6-2	190	12-2-79	1999	Beauport, Quebec
Manning, Charlie	8	4	3.49	14	14	0	0	80	73	33	31	21	87	.244	L	L	6-2	180	3-31-79	2001	Winter Haven, Fla.
Nunez, Mike	0	0	1.50	4	0	0	0	6	6	2	1	3	5	.260	R	R	6-0	190	3-28-79	2001	San Jose, Calif.
Ortiz, Javier	1	1	1.98	3	3	0	0	14	11	4	3	4	12	.215	R	R	6-0	155	11-28-79	1996	Cartagena, Colombia
Peeples, Jim	1	0	9.20	11	0	0	0	15	18	15	15	19	14	.305	L	L	6-0	195	7-5-80	1999	Jacksonville, Fla.
Reynolds, Eric	0	0	6.75	2	0	0	0	3	3	2	2	2	3	.272	L	L	6-3	215	4-20-80	2000	Saltillo, Miss.
Reynoso, Edison	1	0	0.00	1	1	0	0	5	3	1	0	2	9	.157	R	R	6-1	170	11-10-75	1993	Montecristi, D.R.
Russ, Chris	1	2	1.88	20	0	0	12	24	15	7	5	4	21	.174	R	R	5-11	175	3-27-79	2001	Comfort, Texas
Skaggs, Jon	0	0	1.93	1	1	0	0	5	4	1	1	1	4	.222	R	R	6-5	225	3-27-78	2001	Houston, Texas

PITCHING	W	L	ERA	G	GS	CG	SV	IP	H	R	ER	BB	SO	AVG	B	T	HT	WT	DOB	1st Yr	Resides
Smith, Jason	0	1	4.50	1	1	0	0	6	8	4	3	0	6	.333	B	R	6-5	205	3-7-82	2000	Kennewick, Wash.
Strelitz, Brian	3	3	3.35	24	0	0	1	38	37	23	14	14	21	.255	R	R	6-2	200	1-8-80	2001	Temple City, Calif.
Tacker, Trevor	0	0	6.30	3	0	0	0	10	8	7	7	4	8	.205	R	R	6-3	190	3-19-81	2001	Southlake, Texas
Wood, Bobby	3	4	4.02	12	12	2	0	69	69	33	31	28	59	.257	R	R	6-4	205	11-27-79	2001	Englewood, Colo.

TAMPA — Rookie

GULF COAST LEAGUE

BATTING	AVG	G	AB	R	H	2B	3B	HR	RBI	BB	SO	SB	CS	SLG	OBP	B	T	HT	WT	DOB	1st Yr	Resides
Brown, Richard	.167	2	6	1	1	1	0	0	2	2	4	0	0	.333	.375	L	L	6-1	196	4-28-77	1996	Plantation, Fla.
Cano, Robinson	.230	57	200	37	46	14	2	3	34	28	27	11	2	.365	.330	L	R	6-0	172	10-22-82	2001	San Pedro de Macoris, D.R.
Chauncey, Clinton	.111	10	18	1	2	0	0	0	0	1	8	0	0	.111	.200	R	R	6-1	180	1-1-81	2000	Jacksonville, Fla.
Crosby, Kelly	.290	22	62	9	18	3	0	0	5	4	8	1	1	.339	.353	R	R	6-2	205	8-22-78	2001	Wheaton, Ill.
Faulkner, Todd	.105	7	19	2	2	1	0	0	0	2	6	0	0	.158	.190	R	R	6-4	210	12-12-77	2000	Powder Springs, Ga.
Feliz, Henry	.203	25	64	7	13	2	1	1	9	2	22	0	1	.313	.235	L	R	6-0	187	4-11-81	1999	Santo Domingo, D.R.
Garcia, Sandy	.250	35	112	18	28	8	2	3	18	10	37	3	1	.438	.317	R	R	6-2	165	6-8-80	1997	Santo Domingo, D.R.
Hernandez, Michel	.000	2	5	0	0	0	0	0	0	1	0	0	0	.000	.167	R	R	6-0	211	8-12-78	1998	Caracas, Venez.
Jimenez, Luis	.200	10	30	2	6	1	0	0	2	1	10	0	0	.233	.250	B	R	6-2	175	7-1-83	2000	Caracas, Venez.
Martin, Chris	.000	2	5	1	0	0	0	0	1	1	1	0	0	.000	.167	R	R	5-9	190	1-31-79	2001	Quincy, Ill.
Navarro, Dioner	.280	43	143	27	40	10	1	2	22	17	23	6	0	.406	.345	B	R	5-10	185	2-9-84	2000	Caracas, Venez.
Nunez, Andres	.228	55	180	21	41	2	1	1	15	21	28	5	1	.267	.316	R	R	6-2	150	7-20-82	1999	Valencia, Venez.
Osborne, Steve	.000	1	2	0	0	0	0	0	0	0	0	0	0	.000	.000	R	R	6-1	195	12-21-78	2001	Millinocket, Maine
Pitney, Jared	.272	44	147	21	40	8	0	2	24	10	36	3	0	.367	.321	L	L	6-0	185	3-26-79	2001	Agoura, Calif.
Ramistella, John	.272	53	180	30	49	11	1	5	33	21	48	5	2	.428	.367	R	R	6-2	200	8-29-81	2001	Monterey, Calif.
Rodriguez, John	.833	2	6	2	5	0	0	0	2	0	0	0	0	.833	.833	L	L	6-0	185	1-20-78	1997	New York, N.Y.
Rojas, Tom	.348	25	66	12	23	6	0	0	8	7	10	2	1	.439	.419	R	R	6-3	185	3-31-82	2001	Henderson, Nev.
Santa, Alex	.263	52	179	32	47	1	4	2	16	23	52	10	5	.346	.356	L	L	6-0	175	12-27-82	1999	Santo Domingo, D.R.
Santana, Pedro	.396	15	48	6	19	3	1	1	10	1	7	3	1	.563	.408	R	R	6-1	190	5-19-79	1996	Santo Domingo, D.R.
Sardinha, Bronson	.303	55	188	42	57	14	3	4	27	28	51	11	2	.473	.398	L	R	6-1	195	4-6-83	2001	Kahuku, Hawaii
Singer, Matt	.181	41	105	11	19	1	1	1	13	9	22	4	4	.238	.252	L	L	6-2	200	11-16-78	2001	Cincinnati, Ohio
Vasquez, Wuillians	.221	41	136	19	30	3	1	2	16	21	33	5	1	.286	.321	R	R	6-0	152	7-26-83	1999	Puerto Piritu, Venez.

GAMES BY POSITION: C—Chauncey 6, Hernandez 2, Navarro 40, Rojas 22. **1B**—Faulkner 3, Feliz 20, Garcia 2, Nunez 1, Pitney 41. **2B**—Cano 33, Nunez 3, Vasquez 29. **3B**—Cano 10, Garcia 2, Martin 2, Nunez 51. **SS**—Cano 19, Sardinha 46, Vasquez 1. **OF**—Chauncey 2, Crosby 20, Garcia 25, Jimenez 4, Nunez 1, Ramistella 48, Santa 52, Santana 12, Singer 35.

PITCHING	W	L	ERA	G	GS	CG	SV	IP	H	R	ER	BB	SO	AVG	B	T	HT	WT	DOB	1st Yr	Resides
Artiles, Carlos	1	3	3.72	10	5	0	1	36	41	15	15	12	37	.288	L	L	5-11	165	1-21-81	1997	Santo Domingo, D.R.
Carlson, Steve	2	2	1.15	21	0	0	3	31	19	7	4	12	41	.175	R	L	6-1	205	1-9-79	2001	Newark, Ill.
Dominguez, Raul	1	0	5.59	12	0	0	0	19	21	13	12	13	20	.280	L	L	6-1	180	7-25-81	2001	Panama City, Panama
Kennard, Jeff	0	0	1.52	19	0	0	9	24	17	4	4	10	30	.197	R	R	6-2	195	7-26-81	2001	Centerville, Ohio
King, Jeremy	5	2	4.44	11	9	0	0	49	50	26	24	26	40	.273	R	R	6-2	210	11-12-81	2000	Nocatee, Fla.
Landaeta, Argenis	6	1	2.40	10	7	0	0	45	35	17	12	15	42	.210	R	R	6-2	175	11-8-81	1998	Valencia, Venez.
Marietta, Ron	0	0	2.70	2	0	0	0	3	1	1	1	1	5	.100	L	L	6-0	190	8-12-77	1998	Brooklyn, N.Y.
Mendoza, Cristian	0	0	5.06	3	0	0	0	5	5	3	3	2	8	.238	R	R	6-3	160	5-1-82	1998	Cartagena, Colombia
Mosley, Eric	4	1	1.62	6	6	0	0	33	28	8	6	9	21	.225	R	R	6-3	185	5-27-81	2000	Tulsa, Okla.
Nettles, Tim	0	0	5.40	3	0	0	0	3	6	3	2	2	2	.333	R	R	6-1	195	6-23-77	2000	Encinitas, Calif.
Newton, Stan	2	2	3.24	19	0	0	1	33	38	14	12	13	34	.277	R	R	6-2	220	5-16-79	2001	Russellville, Ark.
Ortiz, Javier	0	0	0.00	2	0	0	0	4	1	0	0	1	2	.083	R	R	6-0	155	11-28-79	1996	Cartagena, Colombia
Rada, Gerald	1	0	8.27	8	1	0	0	16	20	16	15	5	21	.303	R	R	6-1	160	8-20-81	1998	Miranda, Venez.
Reynolds, Eric	1	3	6.91	11	2	0	2	27	35	23	21	13	21	.318	L	L	6-3	215	4-20-80	2000	Saltillo, Miss.
Santana, Eddy	2	0	3.44	7	2	0	0	18	11	7	7	11	12	.177	R	R	6-2	165	10-12-80	1997	Santo Domingo, D.R.
Smith, Jason	5	2	1.93	11	11	2	0	61	52	25	13	11	44	.226	B	R	6-5	205	3-7-82	2000	Kennewick, Wash.
Tacker, Trevor	1	3	4.75	9	4	1	0	30	35	19	16	11	16	.286	R	R	6-3	190	3-19-81	2001	Southlake, Texas
Wheeler, Adam	3	2	3.90	10	5	0	0	30	24	16	13	15	28	.218	R	R	6-6	190	4-26-83	2001	Smyrna, Ga.
Williams, Todd	0	0	0.00	1	1	0	0	2	1	0	0	0	5	.142	R	R	6-3	210	2-13-71	1991	Syracuse, N.Y.
Wright, Chase	2	3	7.92	10	7	0	0	25	33	28	22	21	33	.317	L	L	6-2	190	2-8-83	2001	Iowa Park, Texas

BY MARTY NOBLE

The Mets scored one run against the Pirates in their 158th game, giving up 10. The starting pitching and defense could have been better. Their lack of speed was evident.

How appropriate it was that a loss that took hope from their final week also took the shape of so many of the defeats that led to their elimination from the division race that night.

New York finished third in the National League East in 2001, going 82-80, because they scored neither early nor often, didn't hit with runners in scoring position, didn't exercise enough power and didn't have enough speed to offset their shortcomings in the other areas.

They unquestionably would have produced a better record if second baseman Edgardo Alfonzo had been healthy and not a shell of his former self most of the summer, if the rotation had been more resilient during Al Leiter's April absence, if Steve Trachsel hadn't needed a Triple-A refresher, if Glendon Rusch had performed at the level envisioned in March, if the bullpen hadn't endured the inevitable spells of inadequacy, if Robin Ventura hadn't begun to act his 2006 age and if Amando Benitez hadn't dissolved at the least opportune moments.

But each of those shortcomings, and some combinations thereof, could have been overcome if only the offense hadn't performed so inadequately for so long. The bottom line was that the offense was the bottom line. A year after playing in the World Series, the Mets finished last in runs in the National League.

Earned runs can be produced only via power hitting, timely hitting, so-called small ball and speed. The Mets were lacking in each area. No team hit so few home runs (147) or stole so few bases (66). And no team produced so low a batting average (.239) with runners in scoring position.

The Mets' pitching was better than most. Their 4.07 ERA ranked fifth in the league. But they scored 642 runs

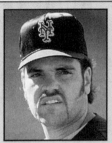

Mike Piazza   Jose Reyes

DAVID SCHOFIELD

PLAYERS OF THE YEAR

MAJOR LEAGUE: Mike Piazza, c
Offensively, Piazza continued to be the most productive catcher in the majors in 2001. He led the Mets in average (.300), home runs (36), RBIs (94) and runs (81).

MINOR LEAGUE: Jose Reyes, ss
Compared to Mets shortstop wizard Rey Ordonez because of his defensive skills, Reyes, 18, made the fewest errors in the Class A South Atlantic League (18). He also hit .307-5-48 with 15 triples.

in a season when other league teams averaged 770.

Consequently, upgrading the offense was the primary objective of general manager Steve Phillips once the off-season began.

The Mets made a remarkable and late run at the division championship, fueled by their rotation and the awakened offense. But Phillips knew better than to dismiss the first 122 games as an aberration and base his judgments on what followed.

As well as they performed in the 25-victories-in-31-games surge that preceded their final 4-A collapse (almost annual and always in Atlanta), they never deceived him.

Phillips faced a daunting assignment, fraught with uncertainty and potential restrictions. What effect would the team's disappointing performance have on its appeal to prospective free agents, advertisers and season-ticket buyers? And how would those factors and the changing economic landscape—within and outside the game—affect what they could afford to pay for talent?

If the club had planned to use the possibility of a new stadium as a selling point to free agents and advertisers, how could it with the costs of construction and improving access to a new stadium subordinate to other, more urgent issues facing New York City?

The roster Phillips intended to upgrade included two older players whose lack of production was critical to the offensive shortfall—Ventura, 34, and Todd Zeile, 36—and whose 2002 salaries ($8.25 million and $6 million) made them a payroll drain and less than appealing to other clubs.

In the minors, the short-season Brooklyn Cyclones celebrated the opening of Keyspan Park by sharing the New York-Penn League championship with Williamsport. Triple-A Norfolk had the second-best record in the International League, but lost to eventual champion Louisville in the playoffs.

ORGANIZATION LEADERS

BATTING

*AVG	Angel Pagan, Capital City/Brooklyn	.312
R	Chris Basak, Binghamton/St. Lucie	82
H	Ronald Acuna, St. Lucie/Capital City	136
TB	Rob Stratton, Norfolk/Binghamton	243
2B	Earl Snyder, Norfolk/Binghamton	38
3B	Jose Reyes, Capital City	15
HR	Rob Stratton, Norfolk/Binghamton	30
RBI	Rob Stratton, Norfolk/Binghamton	86
BB	Marvin Seale, St. Lucie	61
	Earl Snyder, Norfolk/Binghamton	61
SO	Rob Stratton, Norfolk/Binghamton	203
SB	Jeff Duncan, Capital City	41

PITCHING

W	Pete Walker, Norfolk	13
L	Jason Saenz, Binghamton	15
#ERA	Jaime Cerda, Norfolk/Binghamton/St. Lucie	1.67
G	Corey Brittan, Norfolk	58
CG	Jeremy Griffiths, Binghamton/St. Lucie	3
SV	Mark Corey, Norfolk/Binghamton	27
IP	Pete Walker, Norfolk	168
BB	Jason Saenz, Binghamton	80
SO	Neal Musser, St. Lucie/Capital City	138

*Minimum 250 At-Bats #Minimum 75 Innings

NEW YORK METS

Manager: Bobby Valentine

2001 Record: 82-80, .506 (3rd, NL East)

BATTING	AVG	G	AB	R	H	2B	3B	HR	RBI	BB	SO	SB	CS	SLG	OBP	B	T	HT	WT	DOB	1st Yr	Resides
Agbayani, Benny	.277	91	296	28	82	14	2	6	27	36	73	4	5	.399	.364	R	R	6-0	225	12-28-71	1993	Aiea, Hawaii
Alfonzo, Edgardo	.243	124	457	64	111	22	0	17	49	51	62	5	0	.403	.322	R	R	5-11	187	11-8-73	1991	Santa Teresa, Venez.
Bennett, Gary	1.000	1	1	0	1	0	0	0	0	0	0	0	0	1.000	1.000	R	R	6-0	208	4-17-72	1990	Waukegan, Ill.
Bragg, Darren	.263	18	57	4	15	6	0	0	5	4	23	3	2	.368	.323	L	R	5-9	180	9-7-69	1991	Roswell, Ga.
Escobar, Alex	.200	18	50	3	10	1	0	3	8	3	19	1	0	.400	.245	R	R	6-1	180	9-6-78	1996	Valencia, Venez.
Figueroa, Luis	.000	4	2	0	0	0	0	0	0	0	0	0	0	.000	.000	B	R	5-9	144	2-16-74	1997	Vega Alta, P.R.
Hamilton, Darryl	.214	52	126	15	27	7	1	1	5	19	20	3	1	.310	.322	L	R	6-1	180	12-3-64	1986	Houston, Texas
Harris, Lenny	.222	110	135	12	30	5	1	0	9	8	9	3	2	.274	.266	L	R	5-10	210	10-28-64	1983	Miami, Fla.
Johnson, Mark	.254	71	118	17	30	6	1	6	23	16	31	0	2	.475	.338	L	L	6-4	230	10-17-67	1990	Pittsburgh, Pa.
Lawton, Matt	.246	48	183	24	45	11	1	3	13	22	34	10	2	.366	.352	L	R	5-10	186	11-3-71	1991	Saucier, Miss.
McEwing, Joe	.283	116	283	40	80	17	3	8	30	17	57	8	5	.449	.342	R	R	5-10	170	10-19-72	1992	Bristol, Pa.
Ordonez, Rey	.247	149	461	31	114	24	4	3	44	34	43	3	2	.336	.299	R	R	5-9	159	11-11-72	1993	Parkland, Fla.
Payton, Jay	.255	104	361	44	92	16	1	8	34	18	52	4	3	.371	.298	R	R	5-10	185	11-22-72	1994	Zanesville, Ohio
Perez, Timo	.247	85	239	26	59	9	1	5	22	12	25	1	6	.356	.287	L	L	5-9	167	4-8-77	2000	San Cristobal, D.R.
Phillips, Jason	.143	6	7	2	1	1	0	0	0	0	1	0	0	.286	.143	R	R	6-1	177	9-27-76	1997	El Cajon, Calif.
Piazza, Mike	.300	141	503	81	151	29	0	36	94	67	87	0	2	.573	.384	R	R	6-3	215	9-4-68	1989	Boynton Beach, Fla.
Pratt, Todd	.163	45	80	6	13	5	0	2	4	15	36	1	0	.300	.306	R	R	6-3	230	2-9-67	1985	Deerfield Beach, Fla.
Relaford, Desi	.302	120	301	43	91	27	0	8	36	27	65	13	5	.472	.364	B	R	5-9	174	9-16-73	1991	Jacksonville, Fla.
Shinjo, Tsuyoshi	.268	123	400	46	107	23	1	10	56	25	70	4	5	.405	.320	R	R	6-1	185	1-28-72	2001	Kobe, Japan
Toca, Jorge	.176	13	17	3	3	0	0	0	1	0	8	0	0	.176	.176	R	R	6-3	220	1-7-75	1999	Miami, Fla.
Velandia, Jorge	.000	9	9	1	0	0	0	0	0	2	1	0	0	.000	.182	R	R	5-9	185	1-12-75	1992	Caracas, Venez.
Ventura, Robin	.237	142	456	70	108	20	0	21	61	88	101	2	5	.419	.359	L	R	6-1	198	7-14-67	1989	Santa Maria, Calif.
Wilson, Vance	.298	32	57	3	17	3	0	0	6	2	16	0	1	.351	.339	R	R	5-11	190	3-17-73	1994	Mesa, Ariz.
Zeile, Todd	.266	151	531	66	141	25	1	10	62	73	102	1	0	.373	.359	R	R	6-1	200	9-9-65	1986	Westlake Village, Calif.

PITCHING	W	L	ERA	G	GS	CG	SV	IP	H	R	ER	BB	SO	AVG	B	T	HT	WT	DOB	1st Yr	Resides
Appier, Kevin	11	10	3.57	33	33	1	0	207	181	89	82	64	172	.236	R	R	6-2	200	12-6-67	1987	Paola, Kan.
Benitez, Armando	6	4	3.77	73	0	0	43	76	59	32	32	40	93	.213	R	R	6-4	229	11-3-72	1990	San Pedro de Macoris, D.R.
Chen, Bruce	3	2	4.68	11	11	0	0	60	56	37	31	28	47	.254	B	L	6-1	180	6-19-77	1994	Panama City, Panama
2-team (16 Philadelphia)	7	7	4.87	27	27	0	0	146	146	90	79	59	126	.259							
Cook, Dennis	1	1	4.25	43	0	0	0	36	28	18	17	10	34	.207	L	L	6-3	190	10-4-62	1985	Austin, Texas
Corey, Mark	0	0	16.20	2	0	0	0	2	5	3	3	3	3	.500	R	R	6-3	210	11-16-74	1995	Austin, Pa.
Franco, John	6	2	4.05	58	0	0	2	53	55	25	24	19	50	.264	L	L	5-10	185	9-17-60	1981	Staten Island, N.Y.
Gonzalez, Dicky	3	2	4.88	16	7	0	0	59	72	33	32	17	31	.300	R	R	5-11	170	12-21-78	1996	Bayamon, P.R.
Hinchliffe, Brett	0	1	36.00	1	1	0	0	2	9	8	8	1	2	.642	R	R	6-5	190	7-21-74	1992	Detroit, Mich.
Leiter, Al	11	11	3.31	29	29	0	0	187	178	81	69	46	142	.251	L	L	6-3	220	10-23-65	1984	Plantation, Fla.
Martin, Tom	1	0	10.06	14	0	0	0	17	23	22	19	10	12	.319	L	L	6-1	200	5-21-70	1989	Panama City, Fla.
Nitkowski, C.J.	1	0	0.00	5	0	0	0	6	3	0	0	3	4	.166	L	L	6-3	205	3-9-73	1994	Houston, Texas
Reed, Rick	8	6	3.48	20	20	3	0	135	119	53	52	17	99	.236	R	R	6-1	195	8-16-65	1986	Proctorville, Ohio
Riggan, Jerrod	3	3	3.40	35	0	0	0	48	42	19	18	24	41	.242	R	R	6-4	205	11-4-74	1996	Brewster, Wash.
Roberts, Grant	1	0	3.81	16	0	0	0	26	24	11	11	8	29	.240	R	R	6-3	205	9-13-77	1995	El Cajon, Calif.
Rose, Brian	0	1	4.15	3	0	0	0	9	10	4	4	2	4	.285	R	R	6-3	215	2-13-76	1995	Dartmouth, Mass.
Rusch, Glendon	8	12	4.63	33	33	1	0	179	216	101	92	43	156	.300	L	L	6-1	200	11-7-74	1993	Seattle, Wash.
Trachsel, Steve	11	13	4.46	28	28	1	0	174	168	90	86	47	144	.254	R	R	6-4	205	10-31-70	1991	Mesa, Ariz.
Walker, Pete	0	0	2.70	2	0	0	0	7	6	2	2	0	4	.240	R	R	6-2	195	4-8-69	1990	East Lyme, Conn.
Wall, Donne	0	4	4.85	32	0	0	0	43	51	24	23	17	31	.300	R	R	6-1	205	7-11-67	1989	Houston, Texas
Wendell, Turk	4	3	3.51	49	0	0	1	51	42	23	20	22	41	.223	L	R	6-2	180	5-19-67	1988	Castle Rock, Colo.
White, Rick	4	5	3.88	55	0	0	2	70	71	38	30	17	51	.257	R	R	6-4	230	12-23-68	1990	Springfield, Ohio

FIELDING

Catcher	PCT	G	PO	A	E	DP	PB
Phillips	1.000	5	15	0	0	0	0
Piazza	.991	131	919	58	9	5	7
Pratt	.994	31	152	4	1	0	2
Wilson	.993	27	130	9	1	1	2

First Base	PCT	G	PO	A	E	DP
Harris	.949	7	33	4	2	1
Johnson	.991	21	101	7	1	10
McEwing	.750	3	2	1	1	1
Toca	1.000	3	14	1	0	1
Zeile	.992	149	1184	112	11	105

Second Base	PCT	G	PO	A	E	DP
Alfonzo	.987	122	211	301	7	61
Figueroa	1.000	3	1	4	0	1
Harris	1.000	1	1	0	0	0
McEwing	1.000	5	5	6	0	2
Relaford	.969	54	85	105	6	24

Third Base	PCT	G	PO	A	E	DP
Harris	.875	11	3	4	1	0
McEwing	.977	25	15	28	1	5
Relaford	.939	20	10	21	2	0

	PCT	G	PO	A	E	DP
Velandia	.000	1	0	0	0	0
Ventura	.957	139	91	264	16	24

Shortstop	PCT	G	PO	A	E	DP
McEwing	.966	12	7	21	1	1
Ordonez	.980	148	213	383	12	79
Relaford	.958	25	50	48	3	7
Velandia	1.000	8	2	8	0	2

Outfield	PCT	G	PO	A	E	DP
Agbayani	.954	84	123	1	6	0
Bragg	1.000	16	21	1	0	0
Escobar	.935	15	26	3	2	1
Hamilton	1.000	37	66	2	0	0
Harris	1.000	8	5	0	0	0
Johnson	1.000	19	10	0	0	0
Lawton	1.000	48	96	1	0	0
McEwing	1.000	62	72	2	0	1
Payton	.984	103	237	6	4	1
Perez	1.000	73	128	5	0	1
Shinjo	.989	119	256	12	3	3
Toca	1.000	2	2	0	0	0

Kevin Appier

STEVE MOORE

Al Leiter: Mets lefthander went 11-11, 3.31 in 2001

Billy Traber: '00 first-rounder went 6-5, 2.00 at St. Lucie

FARM SYSTEM

Director, Player Development: Jim Duquette

Class	Farm Team	League	W	L	Pct.	Finish*	Manager	First Yr.
AAA	Norfolk (Va.) Tides	International	85	57	.599	2nd (14)	John Gibbons	1969
AA	Binghamton (N.Y.) Mets	Eastern	73	68	.518	6th (12)	Howie Freiling	1992
A#	St. Lucie (Fla.) Mets	Florida State	63	76	.453	13th (14)	Tony Tijerina	1988
A	Capital City (S.C.) Bombers	South Atlantic	62	73	.459	11th (16)	Ken Oberkfell	1983
A	Brooklyn (N.Y.) Cyclones	New York-Penn	52	24	.684	+1st (14)	Edgar Alfonzo	2001
Rookie#	Kingsport (Tenn.) Mets	Appalachian	31	35	.470	t-5th (10)	Joey Cora	1980

*Finish in overall standings (No. of teams in league)　　#Advanced level　　+League champion

NORFOLK　　　　　　　　　　　　　　　　　　　　　　　　　　　　　　Class AAA

INTERNATIONAL LEAGUE

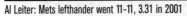

BATTING	AVG	G	AB	R	H	2B	3B	HR	RBI	BB	SO	SB	CS	SLG	OBP	B	T	HT	WT	DOB	1st Yr	Resides
Agbayani, Benny	.313	4	16	3	5	1	0	1	3	1	0	0	0	.563	.353	R	R	6-0	225	12-28-71	1993	Aiea, Hawaii
Alfonzo, Edgardo	.000	2	8	0	0	0	0	0	0	0	0	0	0	.000	.000	R	R	5-11	187	11-8-73	1991	Santa Teresa, Venez.
Baez, Kevin	.219	100	311	35	68	16	0	4	28	33	62	0	3	.309	.302	R	R	5-11	175	1-10-67	1988	Brooklyn, N.Y.
Bennett, Gary	.299	20	67	7	20	5	0	2	14	4	12	0	0	.463	.342	R	R	6-0	208	4-17-72	1990	Waukegan, Ill.
Bennett, Ryan	.143	12	21	2	3	0	0	0	1	4	7	0	0	.143	.280	R	R	6-0	201	7-26-74	1996	Waukegan, Ill.
Bragg, Darren	.333	32	99	22	33	4	0	4	7	23	22	5	2	.495	.468	L	R	5-9	180	9-7-69	1991	Roswell, Ga.
Carpenter, Bubba	.244	28	82	12	20	3	1	1	13	13	19	2	3	.341	.354	L	L	6-1	185	7-23-68	1991	Springdale, Ark.
Curry, Mike	.121	12	33	3	4	0	0	1	1	10	17	2	1	.212	.326	L	R	5-10	190	2-15-77	1998	Jacksonville, Fla.
Dina, Allen	.000	7	12	0	0	0	0	0	2	0	2	0	0	.000	.000	R	R	5-10	190	9-28-73	1998	Stratford, Conn.
Escobar, Alex	.267	111	397	55	106	21	4	12	52	35	146	18	3	.431	.327	R	R	6-1	180	9-6-78	1996	Valencia, Venez.
Figga, Mike	.191	36	110	13	21	4	0	5	16	4	26	0	1	.364	.224	R	R	6-0	200	7-31-70	1990	Tampa, Fla.
2-team (1 Columbus)	.183	37	115	13	21	4	0	5	16	4	28	0	1	.348	.215							
Figueroa, Luis	.259	17	58	7	15	3	1	1	5	5	6	0	0	.397	.317	B	R	5-9	144	2-16-74	1997	Vega Alta, P.R.
Franco, Matt	.245	124	433	49	106	25	1	8	47	52	72	5	2	.363	.325	L	R	6-1	210	8-19-69	1987	Thousand Oaks, Calif.
Hernandez, Carlos	.227	56	194	22	44	5	0	0	10	15	31	4	1	.253	.303	R	R	5-9	175	12-12-75	1993	Caracas, Venez.
Howard, Dave	.125	4	8	0	1	1	0	0	0	0	4	0	0	.250	.125	B	R	6-0	175	2-26-67	1987	Sarasota, Fla.
Hunter, Scott	.280	65	239	23	67	12	4	2	31	8	40	6	3	.389	.306	R	R	6-1	210	12-17-75	1994	Philadelphia, Pa.
Johnson, Mark	.316	42	152	27	48	15	0	8	25	22	20	2	1	.572	.407	L	L	6-4	230	10-17-67	1990	Pittsburgh, Pa.
Martinez, Gabby	.262	48	149	23	39	6	1	0	6	12	19	9	5	.315	.321	R	R	6-2	170	1-7-74	1992	Santurce, P.R.
Miller, Ryan	.179	22	56	5	10	3	0	0	3	3	14	0	0	.232	.246	R	R	6-0	175	10-22-72	1994	Tulare, Calif.
Montgomery, Ray	.320	57	194	37	62	7	1	7	33	27	36	4	2	.474	.400	R	R	6-3	215	8-8-70	1990	Pearland, Texas
Perez, Timo	.359	48	192	37	69	10	2	6	19	12	18	15	2	.526	.399	L	L	5-9	167	4-8-77	2000	San Cristobal, D.R.
Phillips, Jason	.303	19	66	8	20	2	0	2	14	7	8	0	0	.424	.365	R	R	6-1	177	9-27-76	1997	El Cajon, Calif.
Probst, Alan	.150	23	60	4	9	2	0	1	5	4	19	0	0	.233	.197	R	R	6-4	215	10-24-70	1992	Avis, Pa.
Snyder, Earl	.474	6	19	5	9	3	0	0	3	3	1	0	1	.632	.565	R	R	6-0	207	5-6-76	1998	Plainville, Conn.

BATTING	AVG	G	AB	R	H	2B	3B	HR	RBI	BB	SO	SB	CS	SLG	OBP	B	T	HT	WT	DOB	1st Yr	Resides
Stratton, Rob	.143	2	7	1	1	0	0	1	3	0	2	0	0	.571	.125	R	R	6-2	251	10-7-77	1996	Santa Barbara, Calif.
Tamargo, John	.288	40	111	11	32	3	0	1	11	12	16	0	0	.342	.357	B	R	5-9	165	5-3-75	1996	Tampa, Fla.
Tarasco, Tony	.292	105	366	53	107	31	4	7	57	48	43	14	8	.456	.371	L	R	6-0	205	12-9-70	1988	Santa Monica, Calif.
Toca, Jorge	.268	111	407	53	109	13	1	11	51	25	63	12	2	.386	.314	R	R	6-3	220	1-7-75	1999	Miami, Fla.
Velandia, Jorge	.250	67	260	25	65	21	0	5	37	16	47	9	4	.388	.303	R	R	5-9	185	1-12-75	1992	Caracas, Venez.
Wigginton, Ty	.250	78	260	29	65	12	0	7	24	27	66	3	3	.377	.323	R	R	6-0	200	10-11-77	1998	Chula Vista, Calif.
Wilson, Vance	.246	65	228	24	56	14	0	6	31	12	34	0	1	.386	.306	R	R	5-11	190	3-17-73	1994	Mesa, Ariz.

PITCHING	W	L	ERA	G	GS	CG	SV	IP	H	R	ER	BB	SO	AVG	B	T	HT	WT	DOB	1st Yr	Resides
Brittan, Corey	4	2	1.98	58	0	0	4	82	86	22	18	26	45	.272	R	R	6-6	209	2-23-75	1996	Scott City, Kan.
Brunette, Justin	2	2	9.69	24	0	0	0	26	42	32	28	15	23	.368	L	L	6-1	200	10-7-77	1997	Huntington Beach, Calif.
Cerda, Jaime	0	0	3.86	3	0	0	0	5	2	2	2	2	4	.125	L	L	6-0	175	10-26-78	1999	Fresno, Calif.
Cerros, Juan	1	3	3.95	38	1	0	1	57	65	33	25	22	32	.291	R	R	6-1	203	9-25-76	1996	Nuevo Leon, Mexico
Corey, Mark	8	2	1.47	28	0	0	10	37	24	7	6	22	42	.196	R	R	6-3	210	11-16-74	1995	Austin, Pa.
Croushore, Rich	0	0	3.38	10	1	0	0	13	8	5	5	5	10	.181	R	R	6-4	210	8-7-70	1993	Benton, Ark.
Eshelman, Vaughn	2	0	3.18	7	1	0	0	11	13	6	4	7	4	.302	L	L	6-3	205	5-22-69	1991	Houston, Texas
Estrella, Leo	2	0	3.12	8	1	0	0	17	23	7	6	8	10	.353	R	R	6-1	185	2-20-75	1994	Port St. Lucie, Fla.
Gonzalez, Dicky	6	5	3.09	17	16	2	0	96	96	35	33	20	70	.268	R	R	5-11	170	12-21-78	1996	Bayamon, P.R.
Henriquez, Oscar	4	2	2.82	39	0	0	19	38	30	13	12	19	44	.222	R	R	6-6	220	1-28-74	1991	La Guaira, Venez.
Hinchliffe, Brett	3	2	3.02	11	10	0	0	60	67	30	20	17	46	.279	R	R	6-5	190	7-21-74	1992	Detroit, Mich.
Jones, Bobby	0	0	0.00	1	1	0	0	2	0	0	0	0	4	—	R	L	6-0	175	4-11-72	1992	Rutherford, N.J.
Lewis, Richie	7	4	4.03	17	16	0	0	92	83	46	41	47	66	.241	R	R	5-10	175	1-25-66	1987	Muncie, Ind.
2-team (7 Buffalo)	9	4	3.55	24	21	0	1	122	102	54	48	60	77	.227							
Linton, Doug	7	3	3.21	12	12	0	0	76	74	28	27	10	67	.261	R	R	6-1	190	9-2-65	1987	Overland Park, Kan.
Lohrman, Dave	0	0	6.00	2	0	0	0	3	4	2	2	0	3	.333	R	R	6-6	200	9-16-75	1997	East Amherst, N.Y.
Martin, Tom	2	1	6.26	23	0	0	1	23	31	17	16	10	24	.329	L	L	6-1	200	5-21-70	1989	Panama City, Fla.
Montane, Ivan	1	4	4.14	15	2	0	0	37	40	23	17	23	26	.277	R	R	6-2	195	6-3-73	1992	Miami, Fla.
Ochoa, Pablo	3	4	3.67	19	13	0	0	74	71	38	30	27	49	.251	R	R	6-1	185	10-21-75	1996	Nuevo Leon, Mexico
Ontiveros, Steve	2	2	2.83	7	7	1	0	41	32	13	13	9	28	.210	R	R	6-0	180	3-5-61	1982	Stafford, Texas
Riggan, Jerrod	2	0	1.95	28	0	0	13	32	26	7	7	4	37	.222	R	R	6-3	197	5-16-74	1996	Brewster, Wash.
Roach, Jason	1	2	7.16	4	4	0	0	16	21	13	13	7	7	.318	R	R	6-4	199	4-20-76	1997	Kinston, N.C.
Roberts, Grant	3	5	4.52	30	6	0	2	68	80	38	34	19	54	.297	R	R	6-3	205	9-13-77	1995	El Cajon, Calif.
Rodriguez, Nerio	0	0	0.00	1	0	0	0	2	2	2	0	0	1	0	1.000	R	R	6-1	205	3-22-73	1991	San Pedro de Macoris, D.R.
Seo, Jae	2	2	3.42	9	9	0	0	47	53	18	18	6	25	.296	R	R	6-1	215	5-24-77	1997	Naebang, Korea
Serafini, Dan	5	2	3.31	31	2	0	1	49	48	18	18	16	38	.256	B	L	6-1	195	1-25-74	1992	San Bruno, Calif.
Strange, Pat	1	0	0.00	1	1	0	0	6	4	0	0	1	6	.181	R	R	6-5	243	8-23-80	1998	Springfield, Mass.
Traber, Billy	0	1	1.29	1	1	0	0	7	5	3	1	0	0	.192	L	L	6-5	205	9-18-79	2001	El Segundo, Calif.
Trachsel, Steve	2	0	2.79	3	3	1	0	19	13	6	6	6	12	.188	R	R	6-4	205	10-31-70	1991	Mesa, Ariz.
Wagner, Paul	1	1	8.10	2	1	0	0	7	12	6	6	2	2	.387	R	R	6-1	210	11-14-67	1989	Slinger, Wis.
Walker, Pete	13	4	2.99	26	26	0	0	168	145	64	56	46	106	.233	R	R	6-2	195	4-8-69	1990	East Lyme, Conn.
Walker, Tyler	3	2	4.02	8	8	0	0	40	34	19	18	8	35	.229	R	R	6-3	225	5-15-76	1997	Ross, Calif.
Wall, Donne	0	0	10.38	4	0	0	1	4	8	6	5	1	4	.400	R	R	6-1	205	7-11-67	1989	Houston, Texas

FIELDING

Catcher	PCT	G	PO	A	E	DP	PB
G. Bennett	1.000	15	94	5	0	1	2
R. Bennett	1.000	10	46	2	0	0	0
Figga	.995	29	186	27	1	6	3
Phillips	1.000	18	103	5	0	2	0
Probst	.974	18	103	8	3	0	1
Wigginton	.000	1	0	0	0	0	0
Wilson	.984	64	436	47	8	4	6

First Base	PCT	G	PO	A	E	DP
Franco	.997	40	282	26	1	37
Johnson	.998	40	379	32	1	36
Montgomery	.962	4	23	2	1	1
Snyder	.981	5	52	1	1	3
Toca	.987	59	499	47	7	53
Wigginton	1.000	5	27	1	0	3

Second Base	PCT	G	PO	A	E	DP
Alfonzo	1.000	2	6	8	0	5
Baez	.980	28	39	57	2	8
Figueroa	1.000	2	6	11	0	1
Hernandez	.964	44	71	118	7	30

	PCT	G	PO	A	E	DP
Howard	1.000	2	2	3	0	0
Martinez	.980	27	37	62	2	17
Miller	.974	9	17	21	1	7
Tamargo	.983	30	49	66	2	22
Velandia	1.000	3	6	10	0	2
Wigginton	.979	24	42	53	2	16

Third Base	PCT	G	PO	A	E	DP
Baez	.958	18	22	24	2	3
G. Bennett	.000	1	0	0	0	0
Franco	.940	85	38	166	13	16
Hernandez	.950	6	6	13	1	0
Miller	1.000	3	1	0	0	0
Tamargo	1.000	8	0	12	0	0
Wigginton	.845	44	17	65	15	5

Shortstop	PCT	G	PO	A	E	DP
Baez	.980	54	86	160	5	46
Figueroa	.968	16	20	41	2	7
Hernandez	.976	7	13	27	1	7
Martinez	1.000	2	3	3	0	1
Miller	.923	11	14	22	3	6

	PCT	G	PO	A	E	DP
Velandia	.977	63	91	205	7	41

Outfield	PCT	G	PO	A	E	DP
Agbayani	1.000	4	5	0	0	0
Bragg	1.000	23	41	2	0	0
Carpenter	.889	17	23	1	3	0
Curry	1.000	9	14	2	0	0
Dina	1.000	5	4	0	0	0
Escobar	.980	108	242	8	5	2
Franco	1.000	1	2	0	0	0
Hernandez	.000	1	0	0	0	0
Hunter	1.000	50	98	4	0	1
Johnson	1.000	1	1	0	0	0
Martinez	.895	14	15	2	2	0
Montgomery	.932	35	55	0	4	0
Perez	.951	46	90	8	5	2
Stratton	1.000	2	2	0	0	0
Tarasco	.991	98	204	13	2	4
Toca	.963	41	75	2	3	1
Wigginton	1.000	1	3	0	0	0

EASTERN LEAGUE

BATTING	AVG	G	AB	R	H	2B	3B	HR	RBI	BB	SO	SB	CS	SLG	OBP	B	T	HT	WT	DOB	1st Yr	Resides
Basak, Chris	.372	13	43	11	16	6	1	1	7	3	10	2	0	.628	.429	R	R	6-2	185	12-6-78	2000	Joliet, Ill.
Bennett, Ryan	.167	2	6	0	1	0	0	0	0	3	0	0	0	.167	.167	R	R	6-0	201	7-26-74	1996	Waukegan, Ill.
Curry, Mike	.290	107	400	65	116	16	4	5	28	40	100	24	16	.388	.360	L	R	5-10	190	2-15-77	1998	Jacksonville, Fla.
Dina, Allen	.275	85	269	33	74	17	1	3	35	17	53	9	6	.379	.320	R	R	5-10	190	9-28-73	1998	Stratford, Conn.
Figga, Mike	.323	8	31	2	10	2	0	1	7	0	8	0	0	.484	.313	R	R	6-0	200	7-31-70	1990	Tampa, Fla.
Hernandez, Carlos	.316	70	266	49	84	18	1	5	32	22	42	20	9	.447	.380	R	R	5-9	175	12-12-75	1993	Caracas, Venez.
Hietpas, Joe	.000	2	3	0	0	0	0	0	0	0	1	0	0	.000	.000	R	R	6-3	220	5-1-79	2001	Appleton, Wis.
Huff, B.J.	.050	7	20	0	1	0	0	0	0	0	13	0	1	.050	.050	R	R	6-1	195	8-1-75	1996	Chandler, Ind.
Hunter, Scott	.269	65	253	44	68	9	0	15	41	7	47	13	6	.482	.294	R	R	6-1	210	12-17-75	1994	Philadelphia, Pa.
LeBron, Juan	.245	113	363	43	89	16	4	18	52	39	121	2	4	.460	.332	R	R	6-4	195	6-7-77	1995	Arroyo, P.R.
Malave, Jaime	.105	7	19	2	2	1	0	0	1	1	4	0	0	.158	.190	R	R	6-0	215	3-22-75	1995	Yakima, Wash.
Martinez, Gabby	.264	25	87	6	23	6	2	1	10	3	14	8	2	.414	.304	R	R	6-2	170	1-7-74	1992	Santurce, P.R.
McNeal, Aaron	.201	70	264	26	53	7	0	11	25	12	77	1	3	.352	.236	R	R	6-3	230	4-28-76	1996	Castro Valley, Calif.

BATTING	AVG	G	AB	R	H	2B	3B	HR	RBI	BB	SO	SB	CS	SLG	OBP	B	T	HT	WT	DOB	1st Yr	Resides
Miller, Ryan	.167	22	60	5	10	2	0	2	3	0	17	1	0	.300	.180	R	R	6-0	175	10-22-72	1994	Tulare, Calif.
Nye, Rodney	.270	109	366	45	99	23	0	7	45	49	82	5	5	.391	.358	R	R	6-4	215	12-2-76	1999	Cameron, Okla.
Phillips, Jason	.293	93	317	42	93	21	0	11	55	31	25	0	1	.464	.362	R	R	6-1	177	9-27-76	1997	El Cajon, Calif.
Randolph, Jaisen	.179	11	39	7	7	1	0	0	0	6	5	0	4	.205	.289	R	R	6-0	180	1-19-79	1997	Tampa, Fla.
Rodriguez, Sammy	.245	53	159	20	39	12	0	5	13	18	39	1	0	.415	.326	R	R	5-9	196	8-20-75	1995	New York, N.Y.
Saylor, Jamie	.224	56	156	18	35	6	1	4	21	16	42	2	4	.353	.301	L	R	5-11	185	9-11-74	1994	Garland, Texas
Snyder, Earl	.281	114	405	69	114	35	2	20	75	58	111	4	2	.526	.374	R	R	6-0	207	5-6-76	1998	Plainville, Conn.
Stratton, Rob	.248	133	483	70	120	30	1	29	83	53	201	9	5	.495	.332	R	R	6-2	251	10-7-77	1996	Santa Barbara, Calif.
Tamargo, John	.252	49	151	13	38	8	1	1	10	13	19	3	3	.338	.311	B	R	5-9	165	5-3-75	1996	Tampa, Fla.
Terhune, Mike	.133	5	15	3	2	1	0	0	3	0	1	0	0	.200	.235	R	R	6-1	185	10-14-75	1996	Pocono Manor, Pa.
Velazquez, Gil	.207	106	358	33	74	11	2	3	19	26	84	1	1	.274	.266	R	R	6-2	170	10-17-79	1998	Paramount, Calif.
Wigginton, Ty	.286	8	28	5	8	3	0	0	0	5	5	1	0	.393	.394	R	R	6-0	200	10-11-77	1998	Chula Vista, Calif.

PITCHING	W	L	ERA	G	GS	CG	SV	IP	H	R	ER	BB	SO	AVG	B	T	HT	WT	DOB	1st Yr	Resides
Barrios, Manny	0	0	9.00	4	0	0	0	6	6	6	6	5	3	.272	R	R	6-0	185	9-21-74	1993	Rock Island, Ill.
Bell, Heath	3	1	6.02	43	0	0	4	61	82	44	41	19	55	.320	R	R	6-2	237	9-29-77	1998	Tustin, Calif.
Braswell, Bryan	1	1	4.42	5	3	0	0	18	26	9	9	7	14	.342	L	L	6-1	200	6-30-75	1996	Concord Township, Ohio
Brunette, Justin	3	1	5.46	23	0	0	4	30	43	20	18	7	33	.346	L	L	6-1	200	10-7-75	1997	Huntington Beach, Calif.
Cerda, Jaime	1	0	3.10	12	0	0	3	20	17	7	7	6	22	.232	L	L	6-0	175	10-26-78	1999	Fresno, Calif.
Cerros, Juan	1	2	4.91	13	0	0	0	18	24	10	10	7	14	.303	R	R	6-1	203	9-25-76	1996	Nuevo Leon, Mexico
Cook, Andy	2	2	4.75	22	2	1	1	47	51	28	25	16	33	.275	R	R	6-5	195	2-26-77	1998	Danville, Va.
Corey, Mark	1	2	1.80	25	0	0	17	35	23	10	7	12	50	.188	R	R	6-3	210	11-16-74	1995	Austin, Pa.
Della Ratta, Pete	4	2	6.30	22	0	0	0	30	36	25	21	8	30	.288	R	R	6-4	223	2-14-74	1996	Gulf Breeze, Fla.
Griffiths, Jeremy	2	0	0.69	2	2	1	0	13	8	3	1	4	12	.173	R	R	6-3	230	3-22-78	1999	Avon Lakes, Ohio
Jones, Bobby	0	0	0.00	2	1	0	0	5	0	0	0	0	6	.000	R	L	6-0	175	4-11-72	1992	Rutherford, N.J.
Kessel, Kyle	0	1	8.00	3	2	0	0	9	12	10	8	2	7	.307	R	L	6-0	160	6-2-76	1994	Mundelein, Ill.
Lohrman, Dave	2	1	2.10	13	0	0	6	26	20	9	6	12	26	.212	R	R	6-6	200	9-16-75	1997	East Amherst, N.Y.
Maness, Nick	6	12	4.97	28	26	1	0	143	168	94	79	65	107	.294	R	R	6-4	210	10-17-78	1997	Robbins, N.C.
Martinez, Jesus	2	0	5.10	17	0	0	0	30	33	17	17	16	24	.279	L	L	6-2	190	3-13-74	1991	Santo Domingo, D.R.
Medina, Carlos	0	1	3.55	24	0	0	1	33	36	15	13	13	17	.272	L	L	6-2	160	5-16-77	1994	La Vega, D.R.
Montane, Ivan	2	2	2.97	21	0	0	2	33	31	13	11	11	32	.244	R	R	6-2	195	6-3-73	1992	Miami, Fla.
Moreno, Julio	3	2	4.87	12	0	0	0	20	21	13	11	9	17	.265	R	R	6-1	180	10-23-75	1994	Los Llanos, D.R.
Roach, Jason	8	7	3.26	22	21	0	0	116	129	54	42	28	70	.281	R	R	6-4	199	4-20-76	1997	Kinston, N.C.
Saenz, Jason	8	15	5.66	28	23	0	0	143	167	97	90	80	95	.295	L	L	6-2	190	2-13-77	1998	Santa Ana, Calif.
Seo, Jae	5	1	1.94	12	10	0	0	60	44	14	13	11	47	.205	R	R	6-1	215	5-24-77	1997	Naebang, Korea
Strange, Pat	11	6	4.87	26	24	1	0	153	171	94	83	52	106	.287	R	R	6-5	243	8-23-80	1998	Springfield, Mass.
Traber, Billy	4	3	4.43	8	8	0	0	43	50	25	21	13	45	.295	L	L	6-5	205	9-18-79	2001	El Segundo, Calif.
Vega, Rene	3	6	3.64	41	10	0	2	106	117	48	43	32	69	.287	L	L	5-10	175	8-4-76	1998	Bronx, N.Y.
Walker, Adam	0	0	0.00	2	0	0	0	4	3	0	0	2	7	.200	L	L	6-7	205	5-28-76	1997	Albuquerque, N.M.
2-team (15 Reading)	7	4	1.80	17	17	3	0	95	53	22	19	30	88	.160							
Walker, Tyler	1	0	0.40	4	3	0	0	22	9	2	1	13	13	.126	R	R	6-3	225	5-15-76	1997	Ross, Calif.
Wall, Donne	0	0	0.00	4	4	0	0	5	1	0	0	1	5	.066	R	R	6-1	205	7-11-67	1989	Houston, Texas

FIELDING

Catcher	PCT	G	PO	A	E	DP	PB
Bennett	1.000	2	11	0	0	0	0
Figga	1.000	8	51	5	0	0	1
Hietpas	1.000	1	3	0	0	0	0
Malave	.966	7	26	2	1	0	0
Phillips	.995	83	561	54	3	6	4
Rodriguez	.989	49	316	35	4	3	6

First Base	PCT	G	PO	A	E	DP
Huff	1.000	1	1	0	0	0
G. Martinez	1.000	1	2	0	0	0
McNeal	.987	59	484	47	7	60
Nye	1.000	5	24	2	0	4
Snyder	.989	83	733	52	9	67

Second Base	PCT	G	PO	A	E	DP
Hernandez	.978	65	128	184	7	57
G. Martinez	.982	12	21	33	1	6

	PCT	G	PO	A	E	DP
Miller	1.000	4	4	10	0	1
Saylor	.990	23	42	61	1	19
Tamargo	.984	28	55	67	2	13
Terhune	1.000	4	5	6	0	1
Velazquez	1.000	11	23	37	0	9
Wigginton	.813	5	5	8	3	1

Third Base	PCT	G	PO	A	E	DP
G. Martinez	1.000	3	3	10	0	2
Miller	.846	4	3	8	2	2
Nye	.927	107	61	230	23	26
Saylor	.880	11	4	18	3	0
Snyder	1.000	18	8	27	0	5
Tamargo	1.000	9	4	7	0	0
Wigginton	1.000	3	2	5	0	0

Shortstop	PCT	G	PO	A	E	DP
Basak	1.000	12	12	40	0	9

	PCT	G	PO	A	E	DP
Hernandez	.778	2	3	4	2	1
G. Martinez	.900	9	16	29	5	5
Miller	.939	8	9	22	2	7
Saylor	.923	11	8	28	3	2
Tamargo	.960	10	16	32	2	4
Velazquez	.942	94	150	273	26	65

Outfield	PCT	G	PO	A	E	DP
Curry	.991	98	221	4	2	2
Dina	.970	68	123	7	4	1
Huff	1.000	4	3	0	0	0
Hunter	.933	53	81	3	6	1
LeBron	.962	95	173	5	7	1
Randolph	1.000	8	15	0	0	0
Saylor	.000	2	0	0	0	0
Snyder	1.000	8	8	0	0	0
Stratton	.975	110	184	14	5	3

ST. LUCIE — Class A

FLORIDA STATE LEAGUE

BATTING	AVG	G	AB	R	H	2B	3B	HR	RBI	BB	SO	SB	CS	SLG	OBP	B	T	HT	WT	DOB	1st Yr	Resides
Abreu, David	.250	20	40	6	10	0	0	1	2	4	5	2	4	.325	.318	B	R	6-0	160	6-28-79	1996	San Pedro de Macoris, D.R.
Acuna, Ronald	.244	33	119	13	29	9	0	2	13	6	22	7	1	.370	.283	R	R	5-11	200	6-30-79	1998	Guatire, Venez.
Arias, Leandro	.200	5	15	1	3	1	0	0	1	0	5	1	0	.267	.200	R	R	5-10	160	5-4-81	1998	Santiago, D.R.
Basak, Chris	.233	126	472	71	110	19	4	4	46	47	125	30	9	.316	.305	R	R	6-2	185	12-6-78	2000	Joliet, Ill.
Bates, Fletcher	.247	82	300	45	74	18	2	11	46	27	48	13	5	.430	.307	B	R	6-1	193	3-24-74	1994	Rocky Point, N.C.
Bennett, Ryan	.293	26	82	12	24	2	0	1	5	12	13	1	0	.354	.392	R	R	6-0	201	7-26-74	1996	Waukegan, Ill.
Burns, Pat	.238	131	466	54	111	22	1	8	66	48	131	1	4	.341	.311	B	L	6-1	212	9-16-77	1996	Denton, Texas
Deschenes, Pat	.258	65	213	26	55	8	1	1	24	27	32	1	1	.319	.344	L	R	6-0	205	4-26-78	1999	Quebec City, Quebec
Dina, Allen	.361	16	61	13	22	6	1	3	12	2	10	4	0	.639	.381	R	R	5-10	190	9-28-73	1998	Stratford, Conn.
Figga, Mike	.278	25	90	10	25	3	1	4	11	4	22	0	1	.467	.305	R	R	6-2	201	7-31-70	1990	Tampa, Fla.
Guyton, Eric	.182	5	11	0	2	1	0	0	0	2	6	0	0	.273	.308	R	R	6-3	190	11-1-77	1999	Hagerstown, Md.
Hill, Bobby	.249	63	173	22	43	6	2	2	18	15	34	6	9	.341	.311	L	R	5-9	165	6-25-79	1997	Waldo, Fla.
Huber, Justin	.000	2	6	0	0	0	0	0	0	0	2	0	0	.000	.000	R	R	6-2	190	7-1-82	2000	Emerald, Australia
Huff, B.J.	.226	31	106	12	24	7	0	1	13	7	35	5	4	.321	.278	R	R	6-1	195	8-1-75	1996	Chandler, Ind.
Jenkins, Brian	.270	35	126	15	34	5	1	4	15	5	26	4	3	.421	.314	R	R	5-11	215	10-11-78	1997	Port St. Joe, Fla.
Malave, Jaime	.444	2	9	2	4	0	0	0	0	0	5	0	1	.444	.444	R	R	6-0	215	3-22-75	1995	Yakima, Wash.
McAffee, Josh	.067	5	15	0	1	0	0	0	0	0	6	0	0	.067	.176	R	R	6-1	209	11-4-77	1996	Rock Springs, Wyo.

ORGANIZATION STATISTICS

BATTING

BATTING	AVG	G	AB	R	H	2B	3B	HR	RBI	BB	SO	SB	CS	SLG	OBP	B	T	HT	WT	DOB	1st Yr	Resides
Payton, Jay	.375	4	16	7	6	3	0	0	4	1	0	0	0	.563	.500	R	R	5-10	185	11-22-72	1994	Zanesville, Ohio
Piercy, Mike	.286	7	14	4	4	1	0	0	2	1	1	2	0	.357	.375	L	L	6-0	210	6-24-76	1999	Hillside, N.J.
Probst, Alan	.152	37	112	6	17	6	0	1	9	12	38	0	1	.232	.252	R	R	6-4	215	10-24-70	1992	Avis, Pa.
Redman, Prentice	.261	132	495	70	129	18	1	9	65	42	91	29	8	.356	.322	R	R	6-3	185	8-23-79	1999	Duncanville, Ala.
Rodriguez, Sammy	.159	21	63	2	10	4	0	1	6	5	14	0	0	.270	.217	R	R	5-9	196	8-20-75	1995	New York, N.Y.
Seale, Marvin	.238	129	479	72	114	24	4	10	38	61	127	37	18	.367	.335	B	R	6-0	190	6-16-79	1998	Durango, Colo.
Shipp, Brian	.277	114	372	47	103	21	6	8	48	25	107	25	6	.430	.337	R	R	6-2	195	8-15-78	1999	Zachary, La.
Smith, Ryan	.286	31	70	9	20	3	0	0	5	11	18	2	1	.329	.407	R	R	5-10	195	6-20-79	1998	Mifflinburg, Pa.
Tarasco, Tony	.231	3	13	1	3	2	0	0	2	0	4	0	0	.385	.231	L	R	6-0	205	12-9-70	1988	Santa Monica, Calif.
Terhune, Mike	.260	80	262	26	68	15	2	3	31	28	30	6	5	.366	.330	B	R	6-1	185	10-14-75	1996	Pocono Manor, Pa.
Tucci, Pete	.258	77	264	43	68	17	2	9	49	42	56	15	9	.439	.358	R	R	6-2	210	10-8-75	1996	Norwalk, Conn.
Wigginton, Ty	.333	3	9	1	3	1	0	0	1	4	2	0	0	.444	.571	R	R	6-0	200	10-11-77	1998	Chula Vista, Calif.

GAMES BY POSITION: C—R. Bennett 26, Figga 25, Probst 37, Rodriguez 21, Smith 31. **1B**—Bates 4, Burns 127, Deschenes 8, Guyton 1, Huff 5, Terhune 1. **2B**—Abreu 11, Arias 4, Hill 9, Shipp 104, Terhune 15, Wigginton 3. **3B**—Deschenes 55, Guyton 1, Hill 29, Shipp 2, Terhune 6. **SS**—Basak 119, Hill 19, Shipp 2, Terhune 2. **OF**—Acuna 27, Bates 57, Burns 3, Dina 13, Hill 1, Huff 18, Jenkins 23, Payton 2, Piercy 5, Redman 118, Seale 2, Tarasco 2, Tucci 57.

PITCHING

PITCHING	W	L	ERA	G	GS	CG	SV	IP	H	R	ER	BB	SO	AVG	B	T	HT	WT	DOB	1st Yr	Resides
Bennett, Steve	0	1	7.86	7	6	0	0	26	31	26	23	12	20	.289	R	R	6-4	250	10-1-76	2000	Helena, Mont.
Bohannon, Gary	1	0	3.64	15	0	0	1	30	35	15	12	10	11	.315	R	R	6-4	179	2-19-76	1998	Harrison, Tenn.
Braswell, Bryan	1	1	3.63	4	2	0	0	17	15	8	7	5	12	.230	L	L	6-1	200	6-30-75	1996	Concord Township, Ohio
Cerda, Jaime	2	1	0.97	28	0	0	6	56	40	8	6	12	56	.204	L	L	6-0	175	10-26-78	1999	Fresno, Calif.
Chenard, Ken	0	2	37.80	2	2	0	0	2	3	7	7	4	2	.428	R	R	6-3	185	8-30-78	1999	Victorville, Calif.
Cole, Joey	1	0	6.00	1	1	0	0	6	3	4	4	6	2	.150	L	R	6-7	240	9-15-77	1998	Nacogdoches, Texas
Cook, Andy	5	2	2.29	16	6	0	0	51	39	16	13	22	50	.207	R	R	6-5	195	2-26-77	1998	Danville, Va.
Croushore, Rich	0	0	0.00	2	2	0	0	3	1	0	0	6	5	.100	R	R	6-4	210	8-7-70	1993	Benton, Ark.
Dunning, Justin	5	4	3.43	39	0	0	1	66	46	31	25	62	64	.200	R	R	6-3	210	2-16-77	1998	Tustin, Calif.
German, Yon	1	0	3.86	2	0	0	0	5	5	2	2	4	0	.312	L	L	5-11	170	2-28-78	1995	Bani, D.R.
Gonzalez, Gilberto	0	1	5.25	7	0	0	0	12	11	9	7	7	6	.224	L	L	5-11	200	11-24-76	2000	Veracruz, Mexico
Griffiths, Jeremy	7	8	3.75	23	20	2	0	132	126	63	55	35	95	.252	R	R	6-3	220	3-22-78	1999	Avon Lakes, Ohio
Halvorson, Greg	5	6	4.32	22	13	2	2	100	109	55	48	24	47	.275	R	R	6-5	235	1-17-77	1998	Scottsdale, Ariz.
Hee, Aaron	0	0	6.00	2	0	0	1	3	4	2	2	3	3	.307	L	L	6-0	193	3-4-79	1998	Las Vegas, Nev.
Heilman, Aaron	1	2	2.35	7	7	0	0	38	26	11	10	13	39	.189	R	R	6-5	220	11-12-78	2001	Logansport, Ind.
Jones, Bobby	0	1	0.93	4	4	0	0	10	6	2	1	4	9	.171	R	L	6-0	175	4-11-72	1992	Rutherford, N.J.
Joseph, Jake	4	12	5.34	25	24	0	0	128	162	93	76	52	69	.315	R	R	6-1	210	1-24-78	1999	Citrus Heights, Calif.
LaVigne, Tim	1	0	0.00	4	0	0	0	5	4	2	0	2	2	.210	R	R	5-11	180	7-4-78	2000	Virginia Beach, Va.
Lohrman, Dave	3	1	1.67	20	0	0	2	38	18	8	7	20	53	.145	R	R	6-6	200	9-16-75	1997	East Amherst, N.Y.
Maberry, Mark	1	0	0.00	3	0	0	0	6	2	0	0	2	2	.111	R	R	6-5	205	7-31-74	1997	Cookeville, Tenn.
Moreno, Julio	5	4	3.09	20	5	1	2	55	52	22	19	9	43	.240	R	R	6-1	180	10-23-75	1994	Los Llanos, D.R.
Musser, Neal	3	4	3.55	9	9	0	0	46	45	24	18	19	40	.257	L	L	6-2	185	8-25-80	1999	Otterbein, Ind.
Polk, Scott	1	0	7.04	6	0	0	0	8	9	6	6	10	4	.333	R	R	6-2	218	8-25-76	1999	Ridgeland, Miss.
Queen, Mike	4	3	3.47	31	0	0	1	62	60	32	24	23	39	.255	L	L	6-4	232	12-5-77	1996	Gravette, Ark.
Reynolds, Josh	3	6	4.95	17	11	0	0	60	83	39	33	20	48	.333	R	R	6-2	195	9-27-79	2000	Holts Summit, Mo.
Seo, Jae	2	3	3.55	6	5	0	0	25	21	11	10	6	19	.221	R	R	6-1	215	5-24-77	1997	Naebang, Korea
Traber, Billy	6	5	2.66	18	18	0	0	102	85	36	30	23	79	.222	L	L	6-5	205	9-18-79	2001	El Segundo, Calif.
Viole, Paul	1	5	3.47	46	0	0	11	60	47	32	23	50	55	.214	R	R	5-10	170	11-12-77	1999	Demarest, N.J.
Walker, Tyler	0	2	8.04	4	4	0	0	16	19	14	14	3	11	.287	R	R	6-3	225	5-15-76	1997	Ross, Calif.
Weslowski, Rob	1	3	5.94	9	0	0	0	17	25	16	11	6	10	.324	R	R	6-2	180	9-23-78	1997	Marcellus, N.Y.

CAPITAL CITY
Class A

SOUTH ATLANTIC LEAGUE

BATTING

BATTING	AVG	G	AB	R	H	2B	3B	HR	RBI	BB	SO	SB	CS	SLG	OBP	B	T	HT	WT	DOB	1st Yr	Resides
Abreu, David	.169	16	59	10	10	3	0	1	4	9	15	5	1	.271	.290	B	R	6-0	160	6-28-79	1996	San Pedro de Macoris, D.R.
Acuna, Ronald	.285	96	376	63	107	17	3	6	62	19	67	23	8	.394	.332	R	R	5-11	200	6-30-79	1996	Guatire, Venez.
Arias, Leandro	.177	15	62	7	11	3	0	0	2	1	16	3	2	.226	.190	R	R	5-10	160	5-4-81	1998	Santiago, D.R.
Brazell, Craig	.308	83	331	51	102	25	5	19	72	15	74	0	3	.586	.343	L	R	6-3	195	5-10-80	1998	Montgomery, Ala.
Castaneda, Jose	.164	38	116	8	19	2	0	1	8	14	39	0	0	.207	.269	R	R	5-11	195	10-16-77	2000	Del Rio, Texas
Castillo, Carlos	.242	83	310	42	75	8	6	2	30	21	63	9	4	.326	.290	B	R	5-10	165	10-22-80	1999	Valencia, Venez.
Cruz, Enrique	.251	124	438	60	110	20	2	9	59	59	106	33	7	.368	.346	R	R	6-1	175	11-21-81	1998	Santo Domingo, D.R.
Deschenes, Pat	.272	53	195	26	53	10	1	0	36	24	33	2	2	.333	.348	L	R	6-0	175	4-26-78	1999	Quebec City, Quebec
Devarez, Noel	.156	9	32	4	5	2	0	1	3	3	12	0	0	.313	.250	R	R	6-0	175	12-24-81	1998	San Francisco de Macoris, D.R.
Duncan, Jeff	.217	88	318	49	69	16	8	3	23	46	97	41	3	.346	.320	L	L	6-2	180	12-9-78	2000	Frankfort, Ill.
Flannigan, Tim	.208	15	53	3	11	1	0	0	3	3	10	2	1	.226	.276	R	R	6-0	180	7-29-78	2000	Crestwood, Ill.
Garcia, Daniel	.301	30	103	25	31	12	1	2	16	15	18	7	3	.495	.409	R	R	6-0	180	4-12-80	2001	Anaheim, Calif.
Harper, Brett	.182	10	33	1	6	1	0	0	4	3	14	0	0	.212	.250	L	R	6-4	185	7-31-81	2001	Scottsdale, Ariz.
Harris, Cory	.258	102	357	50	92	23	1	8	49	43	57	13	9	.395	.356	R	R	5-10	180	12-7-79	1999	Davenport, Iowa
Hensler, Brad	.194	23	72	11	14	3	0	1	3	4	24	1	0	.278	.275	R	R	6-0	195	3-4-78	2001	Bridgeville, Pa.
Hernandez, Vladimir	.143	5	21	2	3	1	0	0	1	1	2	1	0	.190	.182	R	R	5-11	180	2-27-81	2001	McAllen, Texas
Jacobs, Mike	.278	46	180	18	50	13	0	2	26	13	46	0	1	.383	.328	L	R	6-4	200	10-30-80	1999	Chula Vista, Calif.
Lawson, Forrest	.157	23	70	4	11	1	0	0	6	6	25	2	1	.171	.234	R	R	6-3	195	11-9-80	1999	Federal Way, Wash.
Pagan, Angel	.298	15	57	4	17	1	1	0	5	6	5	3	2	.351	.365	B	R	6-1	175	7-2-81	2000	Rio Piedras, P.R.
Perich, Josh	.242	89	297	32	72	11	3	7	38	23	78	6	2	.370	.301	R	R	6-4	215	11-15-79	1998	Allentown, Pa.
Raffo, John	.167	17	60	6	10	1	0	1	4	8	17	1	1	.233	.261	L	L	6-2	205	11-4-77	2000	Orange Park, Fla.
Reyes, Jose	.307	108	407	71	125	22	15	5	48	18	71	30	10	.472	.337	B	R	6-0	160	6-11-83	1999	Santiago, D.R.
Royer, Lissandro	.265	35	102	15	27	3	0	0	7	10	15	4	4	.294	.336	R	R	6-5	185	2-11-82	1997	Alexandria, La.
Smith, Ryan	.094	20	53	5	5	0	0	0	1	6	20	0	1	.094	.210	R	R	5-10	195	6-20-79	1998	Mifflinburg, Pa.
Todd, Jeremy	.164	19	61	5	10	5	1	2	0	1	7	7	35	0	0	.239	.237	L	R	6-2	210	1-30-78	2000	Maylene, Ala.
Wilson, John	.250	88	304	41	76	10	1	3	32	47	41	7	6	.319	.364	R	R	6-1	205	9-29-78	2000	Newbury Park, Calif.

GAMES BY POSITION: C—Castaneda 34, Cruz 1, Hensler 2, Jacobs 37, Smith 12, Wilson 55. **1B**—Brazell 58, Deschenes 42, Harper 9, Hensler 5, Perich 3, Raffo 9, Royer 1, Todd 14. **2B**—Abreu 16, Arias 15, Castillo 63, Garcia 30, Hernandez 5, Royer 9. **3B**—Castillo 5, Cruz 102, Deschenes 1, Flannigan 15, Hensler 1, Royer 13. **SS**—Castaneda 1, Castillo 8, Cruz 22, Reyes 108. **OF**—Acuna 95, Devarez 9, Duncan 87, Garcia 1, Harris 101, Hensler 6, Lawson 23, Pagan 15, Perich 70, Royer 8.

PITCHING	W	L	ERA	G	GS	CG	SV	IP	H	R	ER	BB	SO	AVG	B	T	HT	WT	DOB	1st Yr	Resides
Bennett, Steve	0	4	2.94	12	11	0	0	52	37	26	17	25	77	.189	R	R	6-4	250	10-1-76	2000	Helena, Mont.
Chenard, Ken	0	1	4.50	4	4	0	0	16	14	8	8	8	12	.241	R	R	6-3	185	8-30-78	1999	Victorville, Calif.
Cole, Joey	7	6	3.87	25	25	0	0	137	125	69	59	67	123	.247	L	R	6-7	240	9-15-77	1999	Nacogdoches, Texas
Cox, Mike	2	3	4.45	15	0	0	1	32	27	18	16	19	40	.225	L	L	5-11	195	11-3-78	2000	Pasadena, Texas
Deaton, Kevin	0	0	4.50	1	1	0	0	4	4	2	2	3	6	.250	R	R	6-4	265	8-7-81	2000	Merritt Island, Fla.
Elliott, Chad	4	4	3.32	35	3	0	5	84	78	44	31	26	91	.240	R	L	6-1	192	1-28-78	2000	Yorba Linda, Calif.
Gahan, Matt	0	3	5.79	5	4	0	0	14	20	14	9	4	11	.317	R	R	6-0	185	11-26-75	2001	Goonellabah, Australia
Gonzalez, Gilberto	1	2	2.37	5	4	0	0	19	15	6	5	5	24	.208	L	L	5-11	200	11-24-76	2000	Veracruz, Mexico
Hee, Aaron	6	4	2.55	35	0	0	2	78	62	28	22	43	95	.219	L	L	6-0	193	3-4-79	1998	Las Vegas, Nev.
Herbison, Brett	1	0	4.00	5	0	0	0	9	11	4	4	4	4	.333	R	R	6-5	208	6-13-77	1995	Elgin, Ill.
Keppel, Bob	6	7	3.11	26	20	1	0	124	118	58	43	25	87	.249	R	R	6-5	185	6-11-82	2000	Chesterfield, Mo.
LaVigne, Tim	5	3	2.29	33	0	0	12	63	51	24	16	21	44	.216	R	R	5-11	180	7-4-78	2000	Virginia Beach, Va.
Lopez, Rafael	6	7	4.13	25	24	0	0	122	127	66	56	36	87	.271	R	R	6-4	205	10-24-80	1997	Hato Mayor, D.R.
Mattioni, Nick	4	8	2.95	37	0	0	6	79	77	35	26	23	98	.246	R	R	6-3	195	3-14-79	2000	Deerfield Beach, Fla.
Musser, Neal	7	4	2.84	17	17	1	0	95	86	38	30	18	98	.240	L	L	6-2	185	8-25-80	1999	Otterbein, Ind.
Olson, Ryan	0	0	2.45	1	0	0	0	4	5	1	1	1	4	.357	B	L	6-5	190	1-16-80	2001	Oakhurst, Calif.
Patterson, Quenten	3	4	6.11	33	1	0	6	63	62	46	43	29	43	.259	R	R	6-5	215	12-29-77	2000	Killeen, Texas
Peterson, Matt	2	6	4.99	18	14	0	0	79	87	46	44	29	72	.275	R	R	6-5	185	2-11-82	2000	Alexandria, La.
Portobanco, Luz	0	1	4.50	1	1	0	0	6	7	3	3	1	5	.291	R	R	6-2	205	9-15-79	2000	Miami, Fla.
Roman, Orlando	1	2	5.74	4	1	0	0	16	17	11	10	8	20	.269	R	R	6-2	195	11-28-78	1999	Vega Baja, P.R.
Sherman, Chris	0	0	2.08	2	0	0	0	9	10	2	2	2	5	.294	R	R	6-2	195	7-2-79	2001	Aptos, Calif.
Templet, Eric	0	2	9.00	2	0	0	0	8	7	6	1	1	9	.333	R	R	6-2	201	4-20-79	2001	Gonzales, La.
Weslowski, Rob	3	6	4.28	23	5	0	1	61	68	32	29	16	59	.289	R	R	6-2	180	9-23-78	1997	Marcellus, N.Y.

BROOKLYN — Short-Season Class A

NEW YORK-PENN LEAGUE

BATTING	AVG	G	AB	R	H	2B	3B	HR	RBI	BB	SO	SB	CS	SLG	OBP	B	T	HT	WT	DOB	1st Yr	Resides
Abreu, David	.182	4	11	1	2	0	0	1	2	0	2	0	0	.455	.182	B	R	6-0	160	6-28-79	1996	San Pedro de Macoris, D.R.
Arias, Leandro	.241	36	112	12	27	7	1	3	11	10	31	2	2	.402	.303	R	R	5-10	160	5-4-81	1998	Santiago, D.R.
Bacani, Dave	.295	23	95	13	28	6	0	0	9	5	12	5	4	.358	.340	R	R	5-7	170	7-30-79	2001	Long Beach, Calif.
Beuerlein, Tyler	.253	21	75	10	19	5	0	0	6	8	20	1	0	.320	.341	B	R	6-2	205	5-29-79	2001	Cave Creek, Ariz.
Caligiuri, Jay	.328	66	238	38	78	14	3	5	34	26	31	4	2	.475	.403	R	R	6-0	190	3-29-80	2001	Camarillo, Calif.
Corr, Frank	.302	61	212	38	64	21	1	13	46	14	32	6	6	.594	.365	R	R	5-9	205	9-19-78	2001	Deltona, Fla.
Coyne, Anthony	.000	1	2	0	0	0	0	0	0	1	0	0	0	.000	.000	R	R	5-10	190	2-22-79	2000	Huntingtown, Md.
Devarez, Noel	.250	54	188	30	47	10	0	10	33	10	63	3	3	.463	.296	R	R	6-0	175	12-24-81	1998	San Francisco de Macoris, D.R.
Garcia, Danny	.321	15	56	10	18	2	0	1	6	4	10	3	2	.411	.387	R	R	6-0	180	4-12-80	2001	Anaheim, Calif.
Hernandez, Vladimir	.245	15	49	2	12	1	1	0	4	2	7	2	2	.306	.269	R	R	5-11	180	2-2-77	2001	McAllen, Texas
Huber, Justin	.000	3	9	0	0	0	0	0	0	4	0	0	0	.000	.000	R	R	6-2	190	7-1-82	2000	Emerald, Australia
Jacobs, Mike	.288	19	66	12	19	5	0	1	15	6	11	1	1	.409	.364	L	R	6-4	200	10-30-80	1999	Chula Vista, Calif.
Jiannetti, Joe	.348	41	158	24	55	13	0	3	29	18	29	8	5	.487	.420	R	R	6-1	190	9-25-81	2001	St. Petersburg, Fla.
Kay, Brett	.311	49	180	28	56	13	0	5	18	16	28	2	1	.467	.380	R	R	6-1	195	10-31-79	2001	Orange, Calif.
Lawson, Forrest	.280	49	164	18	46	6	2	1	15	6	23	7	4	.360	.314	R	R	6-3	195	11-9-80	1999	Federal Way, Wash.
Lydon, Wayne	.246	21	57	12	14	1	1	0	1	7	18	10	1	.298	.348	B	R	6-2	190	4-17-81	1999	Jessup, Pa.
McIntyre, Robert	.197	67	233	35	46	10	1	8	35	18	67	7	5	.352	.263	B	R	5-10	170	12-8-80	1999	Tampa, Fla.
Pagan, Angel	.315	62	238	46	75	10	2	0	15	22	30	30	18	.374	.388	B	R	6-1	175	7-2-81	2000	Rio Piedras, P.R.
Piercy, Mike	.000	3	1	0	0	0	0	0	1	1	0	1	0	.000	.000	L	L	6-0	210	6-24-76	1999	Hillside, N.J.
Pittman, Sean	.333	5	12	0	4	0	0	0	1	0	5	0	0	.333	.385	B	R	5-10	180	4-24-78	2001	Lawrenceville, Ga.
Rodriguez, Elbi	.239	27	92	8	22	5	0	5	13	4	23	0	0	.457	.287	R	R	6-3	180	3-21-84	2001	Santo Domingo, D.R.
Shinjo, Tsuyoshi	.286	2	7	0	2	0	0	0	1	1	2	0	0	.286	.375	R	R	6-1	185	1-28-72	2001	Kobe, Japan
Sosa, Francisco	.389	24	72	12	28	3	1	1	8	2	7	2	4	.500	.421	R	R	5-11	180	2-12-81	1998	Esperanza, D.R.
Todd, Jeremy	.182	17	44	4	8	1	0	0	3	7	13	0	1	.205	.291	L	R	6-2	210	1-30-78	2000	Maylene, Ala.
Toner, John	.258	38	124	10	32	8	1	1	16	8	33	3	4	.363	.326	R	R	6-3	215	9-22-79	2001	St. Joseph, Mich.
Zaragoza, Joel	.170	28	53	5	9	2	0	0	1	3	16	1	1	.208	.228	R	R	5-10	180	8-26-78	2001	Bayamon, P.R.

GAMES BY POSITION: C—Beuerlein 8, Huber 3, Jacobs 14, Kay 34, Sosa 23. **1B**—Beuerlein 7, Caligiuri 55, Todd 17, Zaragoza 9. **2B**—Abreu 2, Arias 27, Bacani 23, Garcia 15, Hernandez 10, Zaragoza 1. **3B**—Arias 8, Caligiuri 10, Hernandez 1, Jiannetti 34, Rodriguez 24, Zaragoza 13. **SS**—Hernandez 5, McIntyre 67, Pittman 4, Zaragoza 7. **OF**—Corr 44, Devarez 49, Lawson 48, Lydon 17, Pagan 54, Shinjo 2, Toner 28.

PITCHING	W	L	ERA	G	GS	CG	SV	IP	H	R	ER	BB	SO	AVG	B	T	HT	WT	DOB	1st Yr	Resides
Bowen, Chad	1	2	4.82	3	2	0	0	9	14	5	5	3	11	.358	R	R	6-4	205	4-28-82	2000	Hendersonville, Tenn.
Braswell, Bryan	1	0	2.08	5	2	0	0	13	12	3	3	2	13	.235	L	L	6-0	200	6-30-75	1996	Concord Township, Ohio
Byard, David	3	1	1.46	22	0	0	9	37	21	7	6	11	32	.164	R	R	6-3	235	6-1-78	2000	Mount Vernon, Ohio
Cabrera, Yunior	0	0	3.00	1	0	0	0	3	4	1	1	2	4	.307	L	L	6-0	166	7-25-80	1996	San Pedro de Macoris, D.R.
Cox, Mike	6	1	2.91	13	7	0	0	53	40	25	17	41	73	.212	L	L	5-11	195	11-3-78	2000	Pasadena, Texas
DiNardo, Len	1	2	2.00	9	5	0	0	36	26	10	8	17	40	.200	L	L	6-4	190	9-19-79	2001	High Springs, Fla.
Eckert, Harold	9	1	3.34	13	11	0	0	70	51	31	26	21	75	.200	R	R	6-3	208	7-18-77	1999	Edison, N.J.
Gahan, Matt	4	1	1.99	10	3	0	4	41	29	16	9	7	42	.187	R	R	6-0	185	11-26-75	2001	Goonellabah, Australia
Herbison, Brett	0	2	6.75	6	5	0	0	12	15	11	9	6	9	.294	R	R	6-5	208	6-13-77	1995	Elgin, Ill.
Martin, Tom	0	0	0.00	1	1	0	0	1	2	0	0	0	0	.500	L	L	6-1	200	5-21-70	1989	Panama City, Fla.
Mattox, David	1	0	0.90	2	2	0	0	10	5	2	1	3	12	.147	R	R	6-2	180	5-24-80	2001	Spartanburg, S.C.
McGinley, Blake	5	0	1.94	18	0	0	4	46	30	12	10	11	50	.189	L	L	6-1	170	8-2-78	2001	Bakersfield, Calif.
Ogle, Rylie	0	1	1.26	6	0	0	0	14	15	3	2	5	14	.277	B	L	6-5	190	1-16-80	2001	Oakhurst, Calif.
Olson, Ryan	0	1	2.16	7	1	0	0	25	15	6	6	9	22	.168	R	R	6-2	205	11-27-78	2000	Townsville, Australia
Ough, Mike	0	1	6.48	7	3	0	0	17	11	12	12	17	19	.180	R	R	6-4	190	2-20-80	2001	Cordele, Ga.
Peeples, Ross	9	3	1.34	16	15	1	0	80	63	19	12	29	67	.214	R	R	6-4	196	2-20-80	2001	Cordele, Ga.
Peterson, Matt	2	2	1.62	6	6	0	0	33	26	7	6	14	59	.209	R	R	6-5	185	2-11-82	2000	Alexandria, La.
Portobanco, Luz	5	3	2.04	13	12	0	0	71	51	20	16	29	52	.200	R	R	6-2	205	9-15-79	2000	Miami, Fla.
Roman, Orlando	1	1	5.03	9	0	0	2	20	14	13	11	8	18	.191	R	R	6-2	195	11-28-78	1999	Vega Baja, P.R.
Scobie, Jason	3	0	0.89	18	0	0	7	40	22	4	4	8	32	.160	R	R	6-1	195	9-1-78	2001	Austin, Texas
Sherman, Chris	0	0	3.72	3	0	0	1	10	10	4	4	3	6	.285	R	R	6-2	195	7-2-79	2001	Aptos, Calif.
Walker, Brian	1	2	2.57	13	1	0	2	28	26	11	8	12	24	.236	L	L	6-3	210	2-20-80	2001	Miami, Fla.

APPALACHIAN LEAGUE

BATTING

BATTING	AVG	G	AB	R	H	2B	3B	HR	RBI	BB	SO	SB	CS	SLG	OBP	B	T	HT	WT	DOB	1st Yr	Resides
Bacani, Dave	.352	19	71	19	25	8	1	2	13	13	12	5	2	.577	.459	R	R	5-7	170	7-30-79	2001	Long Beach, Calif.
Furbush, Mark	.271	40	144	18	39	12	1	3	19	10	35	8	4	.431	.318	R	R	6-4	225	3-2-78	2001	Framingham, Mass.
Garcia, Kenji	.021	17	48	1	1	1	0	0	1	6	25	0	1	.042	.145	R	R	6-4	234	7-29-80	1998	Caracas, Venez.
Harper, Brett	.336	38	146	24	49	9	1	0	19	8	30	3	2	.411	.386	L	R	6-4	185	7-31-81	2001	Scottsdale, Ariz.
Hensler, Brad	.333	4	9	4	3	1	0	1	2	2	1	0	0	.778	.571	R	R	6-0	195	3-4-78	2001	Bridgeville, Pa.
Hietpas, Joe	.185	11	27	3	5	1	0	0	1	6	11	0	0	.222	.353	R	R	6-3	220	5-1-79	2001	Appleton, Wis.
Housel, David	.182	23	66	6	12	1	0	0	5	5	21	2	3	.197	.247	B	R	6-2	165	9-6-81	2001	DeBary, Fla.
Huber, Justin	.314	47	159	24	50	11	1	7	31	17	42	4	2	.528	.415	R	R	6-2	190	7-1-82	2000	Emerald, Australia
Jiannetti, Joe	.271	23	85	13	23	5	2	2	17	9	11	4	2	.447	.330	R	R	6-1	190	9-25-81	2001	St. Petersburg, Fla.
Lydon, Wayne	.184	26	98	14	18	7	0	0	8	11	35	15	1	.255	.266	B	R	6-2	190	4-17-81	1999	Jessup, Pa.
Martinez, Luis	.122	29	82	14	10	3	0	1	4	7	26	2	1	.195	.209	R	R	6-0	170	10-11-80	1998	Santiago, D.R.
Paulk, Barry	.250	31	88	24	22	3	3	1	4	17	17	11	2	.386	.393	L	R	5-10	185	3-20-79	2001	Miami, Fla.
Perez, Juan	.293	42	140	18	41	4	4	3	15	8	35	14	7	.443	.344	R	R	6-2	165	12-10-80	1998	San Francisco de Macoris, D.R.
Pittman, Sean	.320	47	181	24	58	11	3	1	26	21	36	17	7	.431	.385	B	R	5-10	180	4-24-78	2001	Lawrenceville, Ga.
Ragsdale, Corey	.141	23	71	9	10	3	2	1	5	10	38	4	5	.282	.256	R	R	6-4	175	11-10-82	2001	Cordova, Tenn.
Reynoso, Danilo	.167	12	30	0	5	1	0	0	0	0	13	0	0	.200	.167	R	R	5-10	160	4-5-81	1997	San Cristobal, D.R.
Rodriguez, Andres	.322	27	90	10	29	8	0	2	10	5	23	2	1	.478	.354	R	R	6-4	180	4-14-81	1998	San Cristobal, D.R.
Sassanella, Justin	.172	20	64	7	11	2	0	0	5	8	29	4	3	.203	.260	L	R	6-3	190	6-6-83	2001	Austin, Ind.
Sosa, Francisco	.000	1	4	0	0	0	0	0	1	0	1	0	0	.000	.000	R	R	5-11	180	2-12-81	1998	Esperanza, D.R.
Turay, Alhaji	.245	43	163	21	40	8	3	2	20	9	46	8	3	.368	.286	R	R	6-0	205	9-22-82	2001	Auburn, Wash.
Watts, Derran	.245	17	53	10	13	0	0	0	3	9	21	5	0	.245	.365	R	R	6-2	180	6-28-80	2001	Brampton, Ontario
Wendt, Justin	.275	30	91	16	25	3	0	1	17	16	21	0	6	.341	.402	L	R	6-3	225	12-24-81	2000	Waterloo, Ontario
Wilson, Brandon	.215	30	93	9	20	2	0	3	12	14	43	3	0	.333	.315	R	R	6-4	195	9-1-82	2000	Baton Rouge, La.
Wright, David	.300	36	120	27	36	7	0	4	17	16	30	9	1	.458	.391	R	R	6-0	195	12-20-82	2001	Chesapeake, Va.

GAMES BY POSITION: C—Hensler 2, Hietpas 10, Huber 47, Reynoso 11, Sosa 1. **1B**—Garcia 13, Harper 26, Martinez 1, Rodriguez 23, Wendt 9. **2B**—Bacani 19, Garcia 1, Housel 21, Martinez 8, Pittman 20. **3B**—Harper 12, Hensler 1, Jiannetti 20, Martinez 1, Wendt 1, Wright 35. **SS**—Martinez 18, Pittman 26, Ragsdale 22. **OF**—Furbush 39, Lydon 25, Paulk 27, Perez 40, Pittman 1, Rodriguez 1, Sassanella 19, Turay 41, Watts 15.

PITCHING

PITCHING	W	L	ERA	G	GS	CG	SV	IP	H	R	ER	BB	SO	AVG	B	T	HT	WT	DOB	1st Yr	Resides
Acosta, Domingo	0	5	5.54	17	5	0	0	39	49	31	24	11	39	.302	R	R	6-1	188	10-5-80	2001	New York, N.Y.
Cabrera, Yunior	3	3	3.89	11	10	0	0	44	38	22	19	19	49	.231	L	L	6-0	166	7-25-80	1996	San Pedro de Macoris, D.R.
Danly, Kevin	1	2	4.62	15	1	0	3	25	33	13	13	7	31	.308	L	L	6-7	190	6-23-81	2001	Cedar Rapids, Iowa
Deaton, Kevin	5	2	2.09	17	4	0	1	47	40	17	11	10	43	.227	R	R	6-4	265	8-7-81	2000	Merritt Island, Fla.
Eckert, Harold	1	0	2.25	2	2	0	0	12	8	3	3	1	17	.186	R	R	6-3	208	7-18-77	1999	Edison, N.J.
Farrell, Sean	1	0	6.43	19	0	0	0	28	31	25	20	17	28	.274	L	L	6-4	220	10-24-81	2001	Huntington Station, N.Y.
Gomez, Jose	0	1	1.00	3	2	0	0	9	3	2	1	4	14	.096	R	R	6-3	220	5-16-81	1998	Brooksville, Fla.
Kentner, Brandon	1	0	4.30	21	0	0	1	29	26	18	14	36	37	.230	R	R	6-3	210	8-7-81	2000	Benton, Ark.
Maberry, Mark	0	0	0.00	2	0	0	1	3	1	0	0	0	1	.100	R	R	6-3	205	7-31-74	1997	Cookeville, Tenn.
Mattox, David	5	1	2.40	14	8	1	0	56	48	22	15	19	58	.225	R	R	6-2	180	5-24-80	2001	Spartanburg, S.C.
Morban, Domingo	1	4	7.77	16	0	0	1	22	29	20	19	16	26	.315	L	L	6-2	150	8-22-81	1998	San Cristobal, D.R.
Ogle, Rylie	2	2	3.42	6	5	0	0	24	31	15	9	7	18	.306	L	L	6-4	180	12-29-77	2001	Seal Beach, Calif.
Olson, Ryan	0	0	2.45	2	1	0	0	7	9	4	2	1	6	.300	B	L	6-5	190	1-16-80	2001	Oakhurst, Calif.
Osberg, Tanner	2	2	4.28	13	13	0	0	67	72	34	32	22	36	.283	L	R	6-4	189	9-10-82	2000	Red Deer, Alberta
Pinango, Miguel	3	8	4.42	14	13	0	0	59	63	35	29	13	49	.271	R	R	6-1	160	1-20-83	1999	Santa Teresa, Venez.
Roman, Orlando	1	0	1.00	4	1	0	1	9	4	2	1	2	13	.129	R	R	6-2	205	11-28-78	1999	Vega Baja, P.R.
Sherman, Chris	3	3	3.28	14	0	0	2	25	25	15	9	9	19	.247	R	R	6-2	195	7-2-79	2001	Aptos, Calif.
Templet, Eric	1	2	5.23	12	2	0	0	21	30	14	12	4	27	.326	R	R	6-2	201	4-20-79	2001	Gonzales, La.
Weintraub, Jason	1	2	5.70	11	0	0	1	24	27	15	15	11	25	.290	R	R	6-3	165	8-13-82	2001	Tampa, Fla.
Weir, Jayson	0	0	6.43	9	0	0	0	14	21	13	10	6	16	.344	L	L	5-10	180	4-3-83	2001	Orlando, Fla.

OAKLAND ATHLETICS

BY CASEY TEFERTILLER

The 2001 season seemed over almost before it began for the Athletics. The team picked by many to win the American League West staggered to an 8-18 beginning, and seemed virtually out of the race by the end of May.

But baseball is the sort of game where what seems incomprehensible in April can become reality in September. With a late-season drive that reached epic proportion, Oakland ran away to capture the wild card, then finish the season in a memorable five-game playoff loss to the New York Yankees.

This was to be the year of the big opportunity for the A's. Before the season, the team acquired leadoff man Johnny Damon from Kansas City to add balance to an offense that had relied on slow-footed sluggers.

After the miserable start, the A's began a slow uphill climb, reaching 44-43 at the all-star break, then winning six of their next seven by dominating interleague play.

The threesome of young starters—Mark Mulder, Tim Hudson and Barry Zito—matured during the second half, leading the team on a 58-17 surge that would push Oakland to 102-60. After trailing Boston by six games for the wild card at the all-star break, the A's pulled ahead on Aug. 10 and ran away.

The big move came July 25 when the A's acquired right fielder Jermaine Dye from Kansas City in a three-team trade. Dye did not come cheaply, as Oakland dealt three of its top 15 prospects, Jose Ortiz, Mario Encarnacion and Todd Belitz.

It was a coming-of-age season for the young Athletics. The 24-year-old Mulder was 21-8, 3.45. Zito, 23, won 12 of his final 13 decisions. Third baseman Eric Chavez, 23, showed the offensive form that had long been predicted, hitting 32 homers and driving in 114 runs.

Chavez and shortstop Miguel Tejada became the first third-short combination to top 30 homers each in baseball history. And Giambi continued to prove himself one

Jason Giambi   Mario Ramos

PLAYERS OF THE YEAR

MAJOR LEAGUE: Jason Giambi, 1b
Giambi was again the heart of the Athletics' order in 2001. In the year before free agency you can just smell the piles of cash behind these statistics: .342-38-120.

MINOR LEAGUE: Mario Ramos, lhp
With a fastball in the mid-80s he doesn't overpower hitters, but he keeps getting them out. He was 8-3, 3.14 with Triple-A Sacramento and 8-1, 3.07 with Double-A Midland.

of the finest hitters in the game, mixing a career-high .342 average with 38 homers and 120 RBIs.

It was as the hottest team in baseball that Oakland went to New York for an emotional Division Series, in a Yankee Stadium strewn with firefighters and police officers still mourning their departed brethren.

Before the first game, Giambi, Damon and some of their teammates visited the smoldering site of what was once the World Trade Center, then visited police stations and firehouses. From this tense atmosphere, the A's emerged to win the first two ALDS games at Yankee Stadium. But they returned to Oakland to be shut down by Mike Mussina and Mariano Rivera, and stopped by an otherworldly defensive play by shortstop Derek Jeter, as Zito lost 1-0. The Yankees followed by winning Game Four in Oakland as Dye broke his left leg, fouling a ball off his fully-extended leg.

Back in New York, the Yankees claimed a 5-3 win to become the first team ever to win a divisional series after losing the first two at home. It was an emotional end for one of the most remarkable seasons in Oakland baseball history.

Oakland began the year with only one first-round pick in the farm system—pitcher Chris Enochs, the club's top choice in 1997. Nearly all the other top prospects had either reached the majors or been traded in the effort to build a contender.

Though Triple-A Sacramento and Double-A Midland finished above .500, it was not a great year for the system, with the only championship coming in the Rookie-level Arizina League.

The six farm teams finished a combined 344-362 after the promotions and trades that depleted talent. Lefthander Mario Ramos emerged as the organization's top pitching prospect, with a combined 16-4, 3.10 record between Midland and Sacramento.

ORGANIZATION LEADERS

BATTING

*AVG	Eddy Furniss, Midland/Visalia	.317
R	Esteban German, Sacramento/Midland	119
H	Esteban German, Sacramento/Midland	151
TB	Jacques Landry, Midland	252
2B	Marshall McDougall, Visalia	43
3B	Austin Nagle, AZL Athletics	9
HR	Jacques Landry, Midland	36
RBI	Ryan Ludwick, Sacramento/Midland	103
BB	Esteban German, Sacramento/Midland	81
SO	Jacques Landry, Midland	184
SB	Carlos Rosario, Visalia	54

PITCHING

W	Mario Ramos, Sacramento/Midland	16
L	Mark Gwyn, Modesto	13
#ERA	Mike Wood, Modesto/Vancouver	2.59
G	Tyler Yates, Sacramento/Midland	60
CG	Erik Hiljus, Sacramento	3
SV	Franklyn German, Visalia	19
IP	Mario Ramos, Sacramento/Midland	174
BB	Justin Miller, Sacramento	64
SO	Wayne Nix, Midland/Visalia	179

*Minimum 250 At-Bats #Minimum 75 Innings

OAKLAND ATHLETICS

Manager: Art Howe

2001 Record: 102-60, .630 (2nd, AL West)

BATTING	AVG	G	AB	R	H	2B	3B	HR	RBI	BB	SO	SB	CS	SLG	OBP	B	T	HT	WT	DOB	1st Yr	Resides
Abad, Andy	.000	1	0	0	0	0	0	0	0	0	0	0	0	.000	.000	L	L	6-1	184	8-25-72	1993	Jupiter, Fla.
Bellhorn, Mark	.135	38	74	11	10	1	2	1	4	7	37	0	0	.243	.210	B	R	6-0	209	8-23-74	1995	Oviedo, Fla.
Byrnes, Eric	.237	19	38	9	9	1	0	3	5	4	6	1	0	.500	.326	R	R	6-2	210	2-16-76	1998	Woodside, Calif.
Chavez, Eric	.288	151	552	91	159	43	0	32	114	41	99	8	2	.540	.338	L	R	6-1	206	12-7-77	1996	Poway, Calif.
Christenson, Ryan	.000	7	4	1	0	0	0	0	0	1	0	0	0	.000	.000	R	R	6-0	191	3-28-74	1995	Apple Valley, Calif.
Damon, Johnny	.256	155	644	108	165	34	4	9	49	61	70	27	12	.363	.324	L	L	6-2	190	11-5-73	1992	Overland Park, Kan.
Dye, Jermaine	.297	61	232	41	69	17	1	13	59	27	44	2	0	.547	.366	R	R	6-5	220	1-28-74	1993	Overland Park, Kan.
2-team (97 K.C.)	.282	158	599	91	169	31	1	26	106	57	112	9	1	.467	.346							
Fasano, Sal	.048	11	21	2	1	0	0	0	0	1	12	0	0	.048	.130	R	R	6-2	230	8-10-71	1993	Overland Park, Kan.
Gant, Ron	.259	34	81	15	21	5	1	2	13	11	24	2	0	.420	.344	R	R	6-0	196	3-2-65	1983	Alpharetta, Ga.
Giambi, Jason	.342	154	520	109	178	47	2	38	120	129	83	2	0	.660	.477	L	R	6-3	235	1-8-71	1992	Palm Desert, Calif.
Giambi, Jeremy	.283	124	371	64	105	26	0	12	57	63	83	0	1	.450	.391	L	L	5-11	218	9-30-74	1996	Covina, Calif.
Hernandez, Ramon	.254	136	453	55	115	25	0	15	60	37	68	1	1	.408	.316	R	R	6-0	210	5-20-76	1994	Aragua, Venez.
Jaha, John	.089	12	45	2	4	3	0	0	8	6	15	0	0	.156	.192	R	R	6-1	240	5-27-66	1985	Camas, Wash.
Jennings, Robin	.250	20	52	4	13	3	0	0	4	2	6	0	0	.308	.273	L	L	6-2	210	4-11-72	1992	Park City, Utah
Long, Terrance	.283	162	629	90	178	37	4	12	85	52	103	9	3	.412	.335	L	L	6-1	197	2-29-76	1994	Millbrook, Ala.
McMillon, Billy	.293	20	58	6	17	7	1	0	10	5	13	1	0	.448	.354	L	L	5-11	179	11-17-71	1993	Indianapolis, Ind.
2-team (20 Detroit)	.217	40	92	7	20	8	1	1	14	7	25	1	0	.359	.284							
Menechino, Frank	.242	139	471	82	114	22	2	12	60	79	97	2	3	.374	.369	R	R	5-8	199	1-7-71	1993	Staten Island, N.Y.
Myers, Greg	.184	33	87	13	16	1	0	7	13	13	21	0	0	.437	.290	L	R	6-2	225	4-14-66	1984	Riverside, Calif.
2-team (25 Baltimore)	.224	58	161	24	36	3	0	11	31	21	38	0	0	.447	.313							
Ortiz, Jose	.167	11	42	4	7	0	0	3	3	5	1	0	0	.167	.217	R	R	5-10	182	6-13-77	1995	Santo Domingo, D.R.
Piatt, Adam	.211	36	95	9	20	5	1	0	6	13	26	0	0	.284	.300	R	R	6-2	218	2-8-76	1997	Missouri City, Texas
Ryan, Rob	.000	7	7	0	0	0	0	0	0	0	5	0	0	.000	.000	L	L	5-11	190	6-24-73	1996	Spokane, Wash.
Saenz, Olmedo	.220	106	305	33	67	21	1	9	32	19	64	0	1	.384	.291	R	R	5-11	200	10-8-70	1990	Chitre, Panama
Santangelo, F.P.	.197	32	71	16	14	4	0	0	8	11	17	1	1	.254	.341	B	R	5-10	185	10-24-67	1989	El Dorado Hills, Calif.
Tejada, Miguel	.267	162	622	107	166	31	3	31	113	43	89	11	5	.476	.326	R	R	5-9	196	5-25-76	1994	Santo Domingo, D.R.
Valdez, Mario	.278	32	54	7	15	1	0	1	8	12	18	0	0	.352	.418	L	R	6-1	210	11-19-74	1994	Obregon, Mexico
Wilson, Tom	.190	9	21	4	4	0	0	2	4	1	5	0	0	.476	.250	R	R	6-3	220	12-19-70	1991	Lake Havasu City, Ariz.

PITCHING	W	L	ERA	G	GS	CG	SV	IP	H	R	ER	BB	SO	AVG	B	T	HT	WT	DOB	1st Yr	Resides
Bradford, Chad	2	1	2.70	35	0	0	1	37	41	12	11	6	34	.280	R	R	6-5	205	9-14-74	1996	Jackson, Miss.
Fyhrie, Mike	0	0	0.00	3	0	0	0	5	2	0	0	1	5	.125	R	R	6-2	203	12-9-69	1991	Huntington Beach, Calif.
Guthrie, Mark	6	2	4.47	54	0	0	1	52	49	29	26	20	52	.248	R	L	6-4	215	9-22-65	1987	Bradenton, Fla.
Harville, Chad	0	0	0.00	3	0	0	0	3	2	0	0	0	2	.181	R	R	5-9	186	9-16-76	1997	Savannah, Tenn.
Heredia, Gil	7	8	5.58	24	18	0	0	110	144	75	68	29	48	.316	R	R	6-1	220	10-26-65	1987	Tucson, Ariz.
Hiljus, Erik	5	0	3.41	16	11	0	0	66	70	29	25	21	67	.263	R	R	6-5	230	12-25-72	1991	Northridge, Calif.
Hudson, Tim	18	9	3.37	35	35	3	0	235	216	100	88	71	181	.244	R	R	6-1	165	7-14-75	1997	Auburn, Ala.
Isringhausen, Jason	4	3	2.65	65	0	0	34	71	54	24	21	23	74	.203	R	R	6-3	230	9-7-72	1992	Godfrey, Ill.
Lidle, Cory	13	6	3.59	29	29	1	0	188	170	84	75	47	118	.242	R	R	5-11	180	3-22-72	1991	Las Vegas, Nev.
Magnante, Mike	3	1	2.77	65	0	0	0	55	50	23	17	13	23	.243	L	L	6-2	220	6-17-65	1988	Burbank, Calif.
Mathews, T.J.	0	1	5.09	20	0	0	1	23	28	14	13	11	19	.294	R	R	6-1	225	1-19-70	1992	Columbia, Ill.
Mecir, Jim	2	8	3.43	54	0	0	3	63	54	25	24	26	61	.230	B	R	6-1	210	5-16-70	1991	Gulfport, Fla.
Mulder, Mark	21	8	3.45	34	34	6	0	229	214	92	88	51	153	.248	L	L	6-6	210	8-5-77	1999	Scottsdale, Ariz.
Tam, Jeff	2	4	3.01	70	0	0	3	75	68	27	25	29	44	.250	R	R	6-1	214	8-19-70	1993	Melbourne, Fla.
Vizcaino, Luis	2	1	4.66	36	0	0	1	37	38	19	19	12	31	.265	R	R	5-11	193	6-1-77	1995	Bani, D.R.
Zito, Barry	17	8	3.49	35	35	3	0	214	184	92	83	80	205	.230	L	L	6-4	210	5-13-78	1999	Las Vegas, Nev.

FIELDING

Catcher	PCT	G	PO	A	E	DP	PB
Fasano	.952	9	37	3	2	0	0
Hernandez	.989	135	907	70	11	15	4
Myers	1.000	28	153	14	0	2	0
Wilson	.974	9	35	3	1	0	0

First Base	PCT	G	PO	A	E	DP
Abad	1.000	1	2	0	0	1
Chavez	.000	1	0	0	0	0
Damon	.000	1	0	0	0	0
Giambi	.992	136	1224	76	11	107
Giambi	.974	10	74	2	2	6
Hernandez	.800	2	4	0	1	0
Jennings	1.000	6	35	3	0	2
Saenz	.986	28	196	16	3	13
Valdez	1.000	6	15	0	0	2

Second Base	PCT	G	PO	A	E	DP
Bellhorn	.953	12	15	26	2	4
Menechino	.978	136	253	406	15	90
Ortiz	.951	10	16	23	2	7
Santangelo	1.000	20	33	40	0	7

Third Base	PCT	G	PO	A	E	DP
Bellhorn	.900	9	3	15	2	0
Chavez	.972	149	100	321	12	27

	PCT	G	PO	A	E	DP
Menechino	.000	1	0	0	0	0
Saenz	.923	14	5	19	2	3
Santangelo	.000	3	0	0	0	0

Shortstop	PCT	G	PO	A	E	DP
Bellhorn	.900	5	3	6	1	0
Chavez	.000	1	0	0	0	0
Menechino	.500	3	0	1	1	0
Tejada	.973	162	256	473	20	93

Outfield	PCT	G	PO	A	E	DP
Bellhorn	.000	1	0	0	0	0
Byrnes	.933	12	14	0	1	0
Chavez	.000	1	0	0	0	0
Christenson	1.000	4	1	0	0	0
Damon	.991	154	345	4	3	1
Dye	.972	61	96	7	3	1
Gant	1.000	11	4	0	0	0
Giambi	.943	47	49	1	3	0
Jennings	1.000	13	13	1	0	0
Long	.980	162	332	5	7	3
McMillon	.950	16	18	1	1	0
Piatt	.962	32	48	3	2	0
Ryan	1.000	5	2	0	0	0
Santangelo	1.000	6	10	0	0	0
Valdez	1.000	7	10	1	0	1

Mark Mulder

Director, Player Development: Keith Lieppman

Class	Farm Team	League	W	L	Pct.	Finish*	Manager	First Yr.
AAA	Sacramento (Calif.) RiverCats	Pacific Coast	75	69	.521	5th (16)	Bob Geren	2000
AA	Midland (Texas) RockHounds	Texas	71	69	.507	4th (8)	Tony DeFrancesco	1999
A#	Modesto (Calif.) A's	California	55	85	.393	10th (10)	Greg Sparks	1975
A#	Visalia (Calif.) Oaks	California	61	79	.436	8th (10)	Juan Navarrete	1997
A	Vancouver (B.C.) Canadians	Northwest	37	39	.487	4th (8)	Webster Garrison	2000
Rookie	Phoenix (Ariz.) Athletics	Arizona	35	21	.625	+1st (7)	Ricky Nelson	1988

*Finish in overall standings (No. of teams in league)   #Advanced level   +League champion

SACRAMENTO
Class AAA

PACIFIC COAST LEAGUE

BATTING	AVG	G	AB	R	H	2B	3B	HR	RBI	BB	SO	SB	CS	SLG	OBP	B	T	HT	WT	DOB	1st Yr	Resides
Abad, Andy	.301	124	462	72	139	19	2	19	82	58	67	4	2	.474	.379	L	L	6-1	184	8-25-72	1993	Jupiter, Fla.
Bellhorn, Mark	.269	43	156	30	42	6	0	12	36	22	60	3	0	.538	.370	B	R	6-0	209	8-23-74	1995	Oviedo, Fla.
Byrnes, Eric	.289	100	415	81	120	23	2	20	51	33	66	25	3	.499	.343	R	R	6-2	210	2-16-76	1998	Woodside, Calif.
Castillo, Carlos	.000	1	1	0	0	0	0	0	0	0	1	0	0	.000	.000	R	R	6-0	175	5-6-81	1998	Santo Domingo, D.R.
Christenson, Ryan	.171	19	70	7	12	4	0	1	3	4	13	2	0	.271	.216	R	R	6-0	191	3-28-74	1995	Apple Valley, Calif.
De la Cruz, Jose	.000	2	1	0	0	0	0	0	0	0	1	0	0	.000	.000	R	R	6-0	165	1-27-78	1995	Santo Domingo, D.R.
Ellis, Mark	.273	132	472	71	129	38	0	10	53	54	78	21	7	.417	.351	R	R	5-11	180	6-6-77	1999	Rapid City, S.D.
Encarnacion, Mario	.285	51	186	29	53	8	2	12	33	17	61	4	3	.543	.356	R	R	6-2	210	9-24-77	1994	Bani, D.R.
German, Esteban	.373	38	150	40	56	8	0	4	14	18	20	17	2	.507	.457	R	R	5-10	180	12-26-78	1996	Santo Domingo, D.R.
Giambi, Jeremy	.333	9	27	1	9	1	0	1	1	6	0	0	0	.370	.357	L	L	5-11	218	9-30-74	1996	Covina, Calif.
Hart, Jason	.247	134	494	71	122	26	1	19	75	57	102	3	3	.419	.325	R	R	6-4	237	9-5-77	1998	Springfield, Mo.
Hinske, Eric	.282	121	436	71	123	27	1	25	79	54	113	20	7	.521	.373	L	R	6-2	225	8-5-77	1998	Menasha, Wis.
Jaha, John	.190	23	84	9	16	5	0	4	11	11	32	0	0	.393	.284	R	R	6-1	240	5-27-66	1985	Camas, Wash.
Jennings, Robin	.306	38	144	26	44	11	3	5	26	9	26	5	2	.528	.353	L	L	6-2	210	4-11-72	1992	Park City, Utah
Lane, Ryan	.210	56	186	17	39	8	0	4	14	21	39	6	1	.317	.292	R	R	6-1	185	7-6-74	1993	Bellefontaine, Ohio
Ludwick, Ryan	.228	17	57	10	13	3	0	1	7	2	16	2	0	.333	.246	R	L	6-3	203	7-13-78	1999	Las Vegas, Nev.
McKay, Cody	.263	99	350	36	92	19	0	6	41	27	64	1	0	.369	.324	L	R	6-0	212	1-11-74	1996	Scottsdale, Ariz.
Myers, Greg	.000	2	5	0	0	0	0	0	1	3	2	0	0	.000	.000	L	R	6-2	225	4-14-66	1984	Riverside, Calif.
Ortiz, Jose	.273	65	256	41	70	16	4	7	39	25	50	7	4	.449	.345	R	R	5-10	182	6-13-77	1995	Santo Domingo, D.R.
Piatt, Adam	.257	35	109	14	28	9	0	1	15	11	27	2	0	.367	.339	R	R	6-2	218	2-8-76	1997	Missouri City, Texas
Pujols, Rafael	.233	9	30	4	7	1	0	1	3	3	5	0	0	.367	.303	R	R	6-0	165	1-20-78	1995	Bani, D.R.
Romero, Mandy	.183	19	60	4	11	4	0	1	5	5	13	0	0	.300	.246	B	R	5-11	196	10-19-67	1988	Miami, Fla.
2-team (3 Calgary)	.167	22	66	4	11	4	0	1	5	8	16	0	0	.273	.257							
Rosario, Omar	.237	21	59	6	14	3	0	1	8	7	18	1	2	.339	.328	L	L	6-1	170	1-14-78	1996	Santo Domingo, D.R.
Ryan, Rob	.225	62	218	35	49	8	3	7	32	39	51	1	3	.385	.346	L	L	5-11	190	6-24-73	1996	Spokane, Wash.
2-team (63 Tucson)	.276	125	434	80	120	25	8	19	82	68	85	2	6	.502	.381							
Salazar, Oscar	.063	5	16	0	1	0	0	0	1	1	5	0	0	.063	.118	R	R	5-11	178	6-27-78	1994	Maracay, Venez.
Santangelo, F.P.	.202	71	188	32	38	7	1	5	17	30	49	5	4	.330	.333	B	R	5-10	165	10-24-67	1989	El Dorado Hills, Calif.
Wilson, Tom	.282	77	259	43	73	15	1	8	48	49	62	0	1	.440	.394	R	R	6-3	220	12-19-70	1991	Lake Havasu City, Ariz.

PITCHING	W	L	ERA	G	GS	CG	SV	IP	H	R	ER	BB	SO	AVG	B	T	HT	WT	DOB	1st Yr	Resides
Adkins, Jon	1	0	4.26	3	2	0	0	13	17	9	6	8	7	.333	L	R	6-0	200	8-30-77	1998	Wayne, W.Va.
Belitz, Todd	4	2	5.13	38	0	0	0	53	52	38	30	16	54	.258	L	L	6-3	200	10-23-75	1997	Spokane, Wash.
Bowie, Micah	6	8	5.04	38	10	1	3	116	123	68	65	44	102	.271	L	L	6-4	210	11-10-74	1993	New Braunfels, Texas
Bradford, Chad	0	0	0.38	12	0	0	2	24	15	2	1	2	24	.180	R	R	6-5	205	9-14-74	1996	Jackson, Miss.
Brink, Jim	0	0	3.00	1	0	0	0	3	2	1	1	0	5	.181	R	R	6-0	185	9-11-76	1998	Stockton, Calif.
Cotton, Joe	0	2	8.53	6	0	0	0	6	7	6	6	5	7	.291	R	R	6-2	185	3-25-75	1996	Uniontown, Ohio
Galva, Claudio	1	0	3.60	4	0	0	0	5	7	2	2	5	6	.368	L	L	6-2	205	11-28-79	1996	Santo Domingo, D.R.
Harville, Chad	5	2	3.98	33	0	0	8	41	35	20	18	12	55	.230	R	R	5-9	186	9-16-76	1997	Savannah, Tenn.
Henderson, Rod	4	1	7.85	8	8	0	0	37	50	33	32	18	30	.326	R	R	6-4	195	3-11-71	1992	Glasgow, Ky.
Hiljus, Erik	8	5	3.63	15	15	3	0	102	79	46	41	26	108	.212	R	R	6-5	230	12-25-72	1991	Northridge, Calif.
Ireland, Eric	8	11	5.24	29	28	0	0	168	215	120	98	56	102	.308	R	R	6-1	170	3-11-77	1996	Long Beach, Calif.
Jones, Marcus	2	3	4.54	27	9	1	1	73	81	39	37	20	51	.281	R	R	6-3	235	3-29-75	1997	Yorba Linda, Calif.
Lankford, Frank	5	5	4.80	40	0	0	2	69	87	44	37	23	37	.311	R	R	6-2	196	3-26-71	1993	Atlanta, Ga.
Lidle, Cory	1	0	3.00	1	1	0	0	6	6	2	2	3	2	.260	R	R	5-11	180	3-22-72	1991	Las Vegas, Nev.
Maurer, Dave	0	0	5.54	11	0	0	0	13	14	9	8	8	21	.269	R	L	6-2	205	2-23-75	1997	Burnsville, Minn.
2-team (17 Portland)	0	0	4.83	28	0	0	1	32	25	18	17	17	42	.215							
Mecir, Jim	0	0	0.00	1	1	0	0	1	1	0	0	0	0	.250	B	R	6-1	210	5-16-70	1991	Gulfport, Fla.
Miller, Justin	7	10	4.75	29	28	1	0	165	174	94	87	64	134	.276	R	R	6-2	209	8-27-77	1997	Torrance, Calif.
Ontiveros, Steve	7	6	4.55	16	15	0	0	85	94	50	43	28	64	.280	R	R	6-0	180	3-5-61	1982	Stafford, Texas
Ramos, Mario	8	3	3.14	13	13	1	0	80	74	32	28	27	82	.241	L	L	5-11	165	10-19-77	1999	Pflugerville, Texas
Ratliff, Jon	1	7	7.86	18	14	0	0	63	84	58	55	38	41	.319	R	R	6-5	208	12-22-71	1993	Pittsford, N.Y.
Reyes, Carlos	2	0	6.23	17	0	0	0	30	31	21	21	14	26	.264	B	R	6-0	190	4-4-69	1991	Tampa, Fla.
Schrenk, Steve	2	1	2.49	16	0	0	3	22	21	9	6	6	22	.253	R	R	6-3	215	11-20-68	1987	Parrish, Fla.
Vasquez, Leo	0	1	5.28	36	0	0	0	44	52	28	26	31	36	.292	L	L	6-4	193	7-1-73	1996	La Romana, D.R.
Vizcaino, Luis	2	2	2.14	27	0	0	7	42	35	10	10	10	56	.220	R	R	5-11	193	6-1-77	1995	Bani, D.R.
Yates, Tyler	1	0	0.00	4	0	0	1	5	4	0	0	1	3	.166	R	R	6-4	220	8-7-77	1998	Koloa, Hawaii

FIELDING

Catcher	PCT	G	PO	A	E	DP	PB
Castillo	1.000	1	3	0	0	0	0
De la Cruz	1.000	2	1	0	0	0	0
McKay	.991	78	600	49	6	4	8
Myers	1.000	1	5	0	0	0	0
Pujols	.889	1	8	0	1	0	0

	PCT	G	PO	A	E	DP
Romero	.987	18	145	8	2	1	3
Wilson	.989	50	348	27	4	1	4
First Base	PCT	G	PO	A	E	DP
Abad	.987	12	72	6	1	8
Hart	.988	132	1130	62	15	122
Jennings	.833	1	4	1	1	0

	PCT	G	PO	A	E	DP
Wilson	1.000	2	11	0	0	1
Second Base	PCT	G	PO	A	E	DP
Bellhorn	1.000	16	35	51	0	16
German	.962	35	78	97	7	27
Hinske	.500	1	1	0	1	0
Lane	.970	16	25	39	2	11

	PCT	G	PO	A	E	DP
Ortiz	.961	60	112	134	10	42
Salazar	1.000	5	7	6	0	2
Santangelo	.991	26	46	61	1	14
Third Base	**PCT**	**G**	**PO**	**A**	**E**	**DP**
Bellhorn	.875	2	2	5	1	2
Hinske	.944	120	72	197	16	14
Lane	.974	13	9	28	1	6
McKay	1.000	8	4	15	0	2
Salazar	1.000	1	0	2	0	1
Santangelo	1.000	1	0	4	0	0
Wilson	.923	6	3	9	1	1

Shortstop	**PCT**	**G**	**PO**	**A**	**E**	**DP**
Bellhorn	.929	4	3	10	1	3
Ellis	.968	131	199	382	19	87
Lane	1.000	10	12	17	0	5
Ortiz	1.000	4	4	15	0	1
Santangelo	1.000	1	1	3	0	0
Outfield	**PCT**	**G**	**PO**	**A**	**E**	**DP**
Abad	.966	88	141	2	5	0
Bellhorn	1.000	17	24	2	0	0
Byrnes	.973	93	175	6	5	5
Christenson	1.000	16	30	1	0	1

	PCT	G	PO	A	E	DP
Encarnacion	.947	41	66	5	4	2
Giambi	1.000	6	7	0	0	0
Jennings	.955	28	41	1	2	0
Lane	.967	21	28	1	1	0
Ludwick	.981	17	51	1	1	1
McKay	1.000	1	2	0	0	0
Piatt	.933	32	40	2	3	0
Rosario	.962	17	24	1	1	0
Ryan	.980	52	98	2	2	1
Santangelo	1.000	42	78	2	0	1
Wilson	1.000	3	5	0	0	0

MIDLAND — Class AA

TEXAS LEAGUE

BATTING

	AVG	G	AB	R	H	2B	3B	HR	RBI	BB	SO	SB	CS	SLG	OBP	B	T	HT	WT	DOB	1st Yr	Resides
Asche, Kirk	.214	16	56	9	12	2	0	3	5	9	16	0	0	.411	.333	R	R	6-2	195	7-10-77	1999	Brandon, Fla.
Cosme, Caonabo	.192	34	99	9	19	2	2	0	4	4	32	1	2	.253	.223	R	R	6-2	160	3-18-79	1996	La Vega, D.R.
Furniss, Eddy	.250	38	132	11	33	10	2	1	13	19	43	0	0	.379	.349	L	L	6-2	225	9-18-75	1998	Nacogdoches, Texas
German, Esteban	.284	92	335	79	95	20	3	6	30	63	66	31	11	.415	.415	R	R	5-10	180	12-26-78	1996	Santo Domingo, D.R.
Hochgesang, Josh	.231	83	303	48	70	18	3	6	33	30	84	8	3	.370	.320	R	R	6-3	210	4-16-77	1999	Fullerton, Calif.
Keith, Rusty	.261	89	291	39	76	20	1	3	31	46	43	1	4	.368	.360	R	R	6-0	209	9-18-77	1998	Brookings, Ore.
Landry, Jacques	.241	134	506	102	122	14	4	36	95	64	184	37	7	.498	.341	R	R	6-3	205	8-15-73	1996	LaMarque, Texas
Lockwood, Mike	.260	131	493	71	128	36	3	6	69	49	80	9	4	.381	.333	L	L	6-0	190	12-27-76	1999	Powell, Ohio
Luderer, Brian	.257	86	307	30	79	20	1	5	34	23	49	1	1	.378	.314	R	R	5-11	160	8-19-78	1996	Tarzana, Calif.
Ludwick, Ryan	.269	119	443	82	119	23	3	25	96	56	113	9	10	.503	.356	R	L	6-3	203	7-13-78	1999	Las Vegas, Nev.
Madonna, Chris	.236	40	106	21	25	2	1	4	16	17	31	0	1	.387	.344	L	R	5-11	193	3-13-73	1995	Smithtown, N.Y.
Mensik, Todd	.283	132	502	69	142	35	1	21	79	60	104	0	1	.482	.361	L	L	6-2	195	2-27-75	1996	Orland Park, Ill.
Nieckula, Aaron	.385	12	39	8	15	5	0	1	10	2	7	0	0	.590	.432	R	R	5-11	200	9-7-76	1998	Stickney, Ill.
Pecci, Jay	.260	125	469	72	122	31	7	3	49	42	56	16	7	.375	.353	B	R	5-11	185	9-26-76	1998	Novato, Calif.
Pujols, Rafael	.220	19	59	5	13	3	1	0	6	4	13	0	0	.305	.277	R	R	6-0	165	1-20-78	1995	Bani, D.R.
Romero, Mandy	.311	29	103	12	32	8	0	1	12	11	10	0	0	.417	.379	B	R	5-11	196	10-19-67	1988	Miami, Fla.
Salazar, Oscar	.267	130	521	75	139	31	4	18	95	49	100	10	3	.445	.329	R	R	5-11	178	6-27-78	1994	Maracay, Venez.

PITCHING

	W	L	ERA	G	GS	CG	SV	IP	H	R	ER	BB	SO	AVG	B	T	HT	WT	DOB	1st Yr	Resides
Adkins, Jon	8	8	4.46	24	24	1	0	137	147	71	68	36	74	.273	R	R	6-0	200	8-30-77	1998	Wayne, W.Va.
Bazzell, Shane	0	2	19.64	2	2	0	0	7	20	17	16	2	4	.476	L	R	6-2	180	3-22-79	1998	Columbus, Miss.
Brink, Jim	0	1	4.02	20	0	0	2	31	34	15	14	20	24	.290	R	R	6-0	185	9-11-76	1998	Stockton, Calif.
Cotton, Joe	6	1	2.77	47	0	0	7	65	50	21	20	28	63	.210	R	R	6-2	185	3-25-75	1996	Uniontown, Ohio
Enochs, Chris	5	4	4.33	39	10	0	1	100	102	57	48	39	67	.260	R	R	6-3	225	10-11-75	1997	Newell, W.Va.
Galva, Claudio	1	2	2.82	55	0	0	11	61	56	24	19	27	44	.240	L	L	6-2	205	11-28-79	1996	Santo Domingo, D.R.
Gregg, Kevin	5	5	4.54	44	1	0	1	81	88	48	41	40	72	.274	R	R	6-6	200	6-20-78	1996	Corvallis, Ore.
Harang, Aaron	10	8	4.14	27	27	0	0	150	173	81	69	37	112	.284	R	R	6-7	240	5-9-78	1999	San Diego, Calif.
Lehr, Justin	11	12	5.45	29	27	0	0	155	206	107	94	43	103	.318	R	R	6-1	200	8-3-77	1999	West Covina, Calif.
Mazur, Bryan	0	0	1.93	6	0	0	0	5	10	1	1	1	2	.454	L	L	6-0	175	7-26-77	1998	Elizabethtown, N.C.
Nix, Wayne	0	2	8.71	2	2	0	0	10	24	15	10	1	12	.461	R	R	6-5	210	9-16-76	1995	North Hills, Calif.
Noriega, Ray	0	1	9.41	17	0	0	0	22	34	24	23	16	20	.346	R	L	5-10	170	3-28-74	1996	Tucson, Ariz.
Pena, Juan	11	9	4.07	27	27	0	0	148	164	88	67	46	106	.278	L	L	6-3	189	6-4-79	1998	Santo Domingo, D.R.
Ramos, Mario	8	1	3.07	15	15	0	0	94	71	37	32	28	68	.204	L	L	5-11	165	10-19-77	1999	Pflugerville, Texas
Snyder, Bill	1	3	5.53	31	0	0	0	42	59	32	26	21	24	.329	R	R	6-0	190	1-29-75	1997	Martville, N.Y.
Thompson, Eric	1	4	4.31	35	5	0	2	65	74	32	31	21	69	.285	R	R	6-2	195	9-7-77	1998	Fairborn, Ohio
Yates, Tyler	4	6	4.31	56	0	0	17	63	66	39	30	27	61	.260	R	R	6-4	220	8-7-77	1998	Koloa, Hawaii

FIELDING

Catcher	PCT	G	PO	A	E	DP	PB
Luderer	.978	73	470	56	12	4	6
Madonna	.979	24	131	10	3	0	6
Nieckula	.970	12	82	15	3	0	1
Pujols	1.000	12	75	8	0	1	3
Romero	.991	27	199	12	2	2	2

First Base	PCT	G	PO	A	E	DP
Furniss	1.000	5	35	3	0	0
Landry	.880	3	21	1	3	2
Madonna	.982	8	50	5	1	4
Mensik	.985	130	1178	87	19	100
Pujols	1.000	2	2	0	0	0

Second Base	PCT	G	PO	A	E	DP
German	.963	78	170	242	16	48
Pecci	.976	52	92	154	6	22
Salazar	.962	12	32	44	3	14

Third Base	PCT	G	PO	A	E	DP
Cosme	.944	14	8	26	2	1
Hochgesang	.907	74	44	170	22	13
Landry	1.000	10	3	12	0	1
Pecci	.962	12	3	22	1	3
Salazar	.880	34	16	79	13	6

Shortstop	PCT	G	PO	A	E	DP
Cosme	.943	17	30	52	5	13

	PCT	G	PO	A	E	DP
Landry	.800	1	2	2	1	0
Pecci	.958	47	67	136	9	29
Salazar	.947	77	125	253	21	36
Outfield	**PCT**	**G**	**PO**	**A**	**E**	**DP**
Asche	1.000	15	26	2	0	1
Keith	.991	61	103	3	1	0
Landry	.965	107	159	7	6	1
Lockwood	.992	127	252	9	2	0
Ludwick	.977	116	250	4	6	1
Mensik	.000	3	0	0	0	0
Salazar	1.000	1	3	0	0	0

MODESTO — Class A

CALIFORNIA LEAGUE

BATTING

	AVG	G	AB	R	H	2B	3B	HR	RBI	BB	SO	SB	CS	SLG	OBP	B	T	HT	WT	DOB	1st Yr	Resides
Allegra, Matt	.209	51	153	19	32	3	2	2	17	21	61	3	1	.294	.315	R	R	6-3	195	7-10-81	2000	Lake Mary, Fla.
Basabe, Jesus	.258	119	426	74	110	21	7	21	93	47	130	12	5	.488	.365	R	R	6-2	175	5-14-77	1995	Aragua, Venez.
Bynum, Freddie	.261	120	440	59	115	19	7	2	46	41	95	28	11	.350	.325	L	R	6-1	180	3-15-80	2000	Stantonsburg, N.C.
Castillo, Carlos	.143	3	7	1	1	0	0	0	0	2	3	0	0	.143	.333	R	R	6-0	175	5-6-81	1998	Santo Domingo, D.R.
Cosme, Caonabo	.292	58	236	43	69	16	1	1	21	20	54	22	6	.381	.350	R	R	6-2	160	3-18-79	1996	La Vega, D.R.
Crosby, Bobby	.395	11	38	7	15	5	0	1	3	3	8	0	0	.605	.439	R	R	6-3	195	1-12-80	2001	Cypress, Calif.
Garcia, Isaac	.250	53	168	11	42	7	1	2	16	8	40	5	1	.339	.283	R	R	6-1	165	6-29-81	1998	Las Matas de Farfan, D.R.
Hall, Justin	.253	32	87	10	22	3	0	1	9	9	20	2	2	.322	.343	R	R	5-10	175	9-23-76	1998	Mesa, Ariz.
Hoffpauir, Josh	.237	71	228	27	54	3	2	0	21	19	66	12	2	.320	.299	L	R	5-10	175	9-21-77	2000	Vidalia, La.
Holt, Daylan	.179	101	341	31	61	15	1	2	39	40	90	5	2	.246	.266	R	R	6-1	200	10-4-78	2000	Mesquite, Texas
Howe, Matt	.254	134	507	81	129	28	4	22	73	67	123	13	3	.456	.347	R	R	6-0	190	9-16-76	1998	Houston, Texas
Laird, Gerald	.255	119	443	71	113	13	5	5	46	48	101	10	9	.341	.337	R	R	6-2	195	11-13-79	1999	Garden Grove, Calif.
Nieckula, Aaron	.289	26	83	12	24	1	1	3	11	8	19	0	1	.434	.385	R	R	5-11	200	9-7-76	1998	Stickney, Ill.
Piatt, Adam	.467	4	15	4	7	2	0	1	2	1	5	0	0	.800	.529	R	R	6-2	218	2-8-76	1997	Missouri City, Texas

BATTING	AVG	G	AB	R	H	2B	3B	HR	RBI	BB	SO	SB	CS	SLG	OBP	B	T	HT	WT	DOB	1st Yr	Resides
Pujols, Rafael	.269	64	223	33	60	13	1	1	23	45	34	4	1	.350	.393	R	R	6-0	165	1-20-78	1995	Bani, D.R.
Reyes, Christian	.198	31	91	13	18	4	0	1	4	15	32	1	1	.275	.318	B	R	6-2	160	6-22-78	1995	Santiago, D.R.
Rosario, Omar	.186	60	188	24	35	9	1	1	17	40	61	9	1	.261	.346	L	L	6-1	170	1-14-78	1996	Santo Domingo, D.R.
2-team (30 Visalia)	.219	90	301	41	66	13	1	3	29	66	88	19	4	.299	.375							
Sosa, Nick	.277	125	462	54	128	31	0	13	63	65	157	1	2	.429	.368	R	R	6-2	205	7-18-77	1996	Longwood, Fla.
Soto, Jorge	.200	19	55	5	11	2	1	3	12	12	31	0	0	.436	.343	R	R	6-0	210	4-14-78	1999	Patillas, P.R.
Valdez, Mario	.421	6	19	3	8	1	0	2	5	2	1	0	1	.789	.500	L	L	6-1	210	11-19-74	1994	Obregon, Mexico
Vaz, Roberto	.294	48	180	24	53	13	0	1	25	23	35	19	2	.383	.377	L	L	5-9	195	3-15-75	1997	Tuscaloosa, Ala.
Wenner, Michael	.276	114	427	57	118	14	3	5	48	18	73	33	10	.338	.313	R	R	6-1	200			Allentown, Pa.

GAMES BY POSITION: C—Castillo 3, Laird 85, Nieckula 23, Pujols 40. **1B**—Howe 26, Laird 7, Nieckula 1, Pujols 28, Rosario 3, Sosa 85, Soto 14. **2B**—Bynum 53, Garcia 28, Hall 24, Hoffpauir 56, Howe 4, Laird 1. **3B**—Bynum 7, Cosme 10, Hoffpauir 9, Howe 105, Laird 1, Reyes 26, Sosa 1. **SS**—Bynum 68, Cosme 49, Crosby 10, Garcia 25, Hall 1, Hoffpauir 1, Laird 1, Reyes 4. **OF**—Allegra 51, Basabe 114, Holt 99, Laird 9, Piatt 4, Pujols 4, Rosario 58, Valdez 4, Wenner 112.

PITCHING	W	L	ERA	G	GS	CG	SV	IP	H	R	ER	BB	SO	AVG	B	T	HT	WT	DOB	1st Yr	Resides
Bazzell, Shane	10	4	2.73	28	20	0	0	135	116	51	41	38	129	.230	L	R	6-2	180	3-22-79	1998	Columbus, Miss.
Brink, Jim	0	3	3.03	24	0	0	4	33	33	17	11	10	26	.272	R	R	6-0	185	9-11-76	1998	Stockton, Calif.
Crowell, Kyle	3	10	5.37	37	10	0	2	112	135	70	67	33	97	.302	R	R	6-0	190	6-16-79	2000	Webster, Texas
Cullen, Ryan	2	4	4.23	40	3	0	1	83	112	58	39	24	53	.321	L	L	6-2	170	1-20-80	1999	Satellite Beach, Fla.
Flores, Ronald	5	2	2.86	47	0	0	6	66	53	24	21	29	71	.217	L	L	5-11	190	8-9-79	2000	Pico Rivera, Calif.
Gwyn, Mark	3	13	4.63	28	25	0	0	140	137	85	72	59	101	.254	R	R	6-3	230	11-4-77	2000	The Woodlands, Texas
Harville, Chad	0	0	3.00	2	1	0	0	3	2	2	1	0	3	.181	R	R	5-9	186	9-16-76	1997	Savannah, Tenn.
Leyva, Julian	0	0	7.71	5	0	0	0	14	21	16	12	2	7	.328	L	R	6-0	200	2-11-78	1998	Riverside, Calif.
McCall, Derell	1	6	4.15	39	4	0	3	87	105	50	40	20	55	.300	R	R	6-3	205	9-22-81	2000	Cantonment, Fla.
McGerry, Kevin	1	7	8.49	15	9	0	0	35	39	45	33	45	30	.274	R	R	6-3	215	8-24-79	2000	Philadelphia, Pa.
Miller, Corey	5	4	3.45	43	0	0	2	70	70	29	27	25	65	.262	R	R	5-11	175	7-31-76	1999	Oakhurst, Calif.
Noriega, Ray	3	1	1.69	13	0	0	2	21	13	4	4	7	19	.180	R	L	5-10	170	3-28-79	1996	Tucson, Ariz.
Ratliff, Jon	0	0	1.29	4	0	0	0	7	4	1	1	3	6	.160	R	R	6-5	208	12-22-71	1993	Pittsford, N.Y.
Rheinecker, John	0	1	6.30	2	2	0	0	10	10	7	7	5	5	.256	L	L	6-2	215	5-29-79	2001	Waterloo, Ill.
Sanchez, Cade	3	6	3.93	39	0	0	3	55	57	30	24	34	54	.274	L	R	6-0	205	3-7-77	1999	Salina, Kan.
Surkont, Keith	8	9	5.31	24	24	0	0	124	152	90	73	42	93	.297	R	R	5-11	180	12-28-77	2000	West Hills, Calif.
Trosper, Tanner	0	0	18.00	2	0	0	0	2	5	6	4	1	3	.454	R	R	6-0	205	11-8-76	1999	Castlewood, Va.
Wagner, Denny	7	9	3.99	30	30	1	0	169	181	101	75	59	127	.273	R	R	6-0	190	9-8-73	1992	Kent, Wash.
Wolcott, Bob	0	3	7.20	3	0	0	0	15	22	13	12	1	10	.333	R	R	6-3	175	4-26-80	2001	West Palm Beach, Fla.
Wood, Mike	4	3	3.09	10	9	0	0	58	46	22	20	10	52	.211							

VISALIA Class A

CALIFORNIA LEAGUE

BATTING	AVG	G	AB	R	H	2B	3B	HR	RBI	BB	SO	SB	CS	SLG	OBP	B	T	HT	WT	DOB	1st Yr	Resides
Asche, Kirk	.267	105	405	64	108	24	2	21	89	33	111	10	6	.491	.335	R	R	6-2	195	7-10-77	1999	Brandon, Fla.
Bowser, Matt	.273	131	479	92	131	32	7	21	83	70	92	10	5	.501	.371	L	L	6-3	205	3-8-79	2000	Palm Harbor, Fla.
Chirinos, Germain	.267	94	251	47	67	11	0	5	27	38	78	12	7	.371	.370	B	R	5-10	170	2-12-79	2000	Santee, Calif.
Craig, Beau	.195	96	344	34	67	16	1	1	32	23	77	1	1	.256	.248	R	R	6-0	170	1-27-78	1995	Santo Domingo, D.R.
De la Cruz, Jose	.177	45	130	10	23	7	0	1	23	15	32	4	1	.254	.254	R	R	6-2	225	9-18-75	1998	Nacogdoches, Texas
Furniss, Eddy	.347	80	294	54	102	20	2	16	49	72	74	4	0	.592	.440	L	L	6-2	225	9-18-75	1998	Nacogdoches, Texas
Gomez, Francis	.234	120	384	43	90	15	2	5	45	28	100	9	7	.323	.291	R	R	6-1	165	9-2-81	1999	La Romana, D.R.
Gregg, Mitch	.247	121	401	66	99	22	1	17	68	58	110	14	2	.434	.343	L	R	6-5	235	12-13-77	2000	Yakima, Wash.
Jackson, Steve	.253	121	435	72	110	27	3	16	64	46	123	5	5	.439	.332	R	R	5-10	170	6-4-77	1999	Bakersfield, Calif.
Keller, G.W.	.094	11	32	3	3	0	0	0	3	2	9	0	0	.094	.194	R	R	6-1	200	12-19-78	2000	Valrico, Fla.
McDougall, Marshall	.257	134	534	79	137	43	7	12	84	46	110	14	2	.431	.321	R	R	5-11	200	9-7-76	1998	Stickney, Ill.
Nieckula, Aaron	.295	43	129	26	38	6	0	4	15	11	34	2	1	.434	.386							
2-team (26 Modesto)	.292	69	212	38	62	7	1	7	26	19	53	2	2	.434	.386							
Rosario, Carlos	.261	116	441	91	115	15	3	6	42	73	98	54	24	.349	.366	B	R	5-8	160	2-22-80	1997	Bani, D.R.
Rosario, Omar	.274	30	113	17	31	4	0	2	12	26	27	10	3	.363	.423	L	L	6-1	170	1-14-78	1996	Santo Domingo, D.R.
Schmidt, J.P.	.270	18	63	5	17	3	0	0	3	4	13	4	3	.317	.313	L	R	6-1	160	1-4-80	1998	Palmdale, Calif.
Schneidmiller, Gary	.278	113	390	60	104	17	4	3	34	53	83	12	8	.369	.375	R	R	6-1	185	1-26-80	1998	Chino, Calif.

GAMES BY POSITION: C—Craig 84, de la Cruz 34, Nieckula 31. **1B**—de la Cruz 2, Furniss 2, Gregg 22, Jackson 117, McDougall 2, Nieckula 6. **2B**—Keller 2, McDougall 38, C. Rosario 104, Schmidt 14. **3B**—de la Cruz 3, McDougall 83, Nieckula 1, Schneidmiller 75. **SS**—Gomez 117, Keller 1, McDougall 27, C. Rosario 13. **OF**—Asche 104, Bowser 126, Chirinos 86, Craig 1, Gregg 71, Keller 4, Nieckula 2, C. Rosario 2, O. Rosario 30, Schmidt 3, Schneidmiller 34.

PITCHING	W	L	ERA	G	GS	CG	SV	IP	H	R	ER	BB	SO	AVG	B	T	HT	WT	DOB	1st Yr	Resides
Brooks, Conor	5	5	4.48	45	4	0	0	84	98	55	42	22	64	.289	L	R	6-1	195	6-11-78	2000	Plymouth, Mass.
Coleman, Jeff	0	4	6.45	16	0	0	0	38	57	32	27	16	38	.345	R	R	5-11	190	10-6-80	2001	San Dimas, Calif.
Cotts, Neal	3	2	2.32	7	7	0	0	31	27	14	8	15	34	.245	L	L	6-2	200	3-25-80	2001	Lebanon, Ill.
DePaula, Freddy	2	1	5.63	15	5	0	0	32	31	20	20	19	30	.258	L	L	6-3	160	6-2-81	1997	Santo Domingo, D.R.
Diaz, Alex	3	1	5.55	32	0	0	0	49	62	39	30	12	33	.311	R	R	6-2	160	7-15-79	1996	Benicia, Calif.
Fischer, Steve	7	7	4.61	34	20	0	1	121	140	77	62	41	88	.261	R	R	6-4	170	1-20-80	1996	San Cristobal, D.R.
German, Franklyn	3	4	3.98	53	0	0	19	63	67	34	28	31	93	.261	R	R	5-9	186	9-16-77	1997	Savannah, Tenn.
Harville, Chad	0	0	0.00	1	1	0	0	3	3	0	0	0	3	.250							
2-team (2 Modesto)	0	0	1.50	3	2	0	0	6	5	2	1	0	6	.217							
Mazur, Bryan	0	3	5.95	48	0	0	5	62	67	48	41	27	45	.324	L	L	6-0	175	7-26-77	1999	Elizabethtown, N.C.
Minaya, Edwin	0	3	5.34	13	3	0	2	29	41	33	17	16	22	.330	R	R	6-1	160	6-20-80	1997	Montecristi, D.R.
Moore, Darin	4	8	8.74	38	3	0	0	59	66	69	57	51	76	.276	R	R	6-1	185	12-19-76	1999	Acampo, Calif.
Navarro, Scott	0	1	5.06	14	0	0	1	21	20	12	12	7	22	.246	L	L	6-1	185	11-13-74	1997	Chico, Calif.
Nix, Wayne	9	7	4.01	26	25	1	0	148	149	81	66	36	167	.256	R	R	6-5	210	9-16-76	1995	North Hills, Calif.
O'Brien, Matt	9	9	4.70	27	24	0	0	146	161	86	76	39	148	.275	L	L	6-0	190	2-22-77	2000	Seattle, Wash.
Rodarmel, Richie	0	0	11.57	2	0	0	1	9	7	3	3	3	3	.300	R	R	5-10	180	2-12-77	2000	Williamsport, Pa.
Schultz, Jeff	3	6	3.45	56	0	0	2	73	75	34	28	33	60	.264	R	R	6-1	200	5-22-76	1998	Long Beach, Calif.
Withers, Darvin	4	7	5.00	28	17	0	0	117	128	75	65	43	85	.279	R	R	6-2	190	5-31-80	2000	Aiken, S.C.
Ziegler, Mike	9	11	4.32	29	27	0	0	152	181	87	73	39	142	.297	R	R	6-3	225	7-25-79	2000	Glen Burnie, Md.

NORTHWEST LEAGUE

BATTING	AVG	G	AB	R	H	2B	3B	HR	RBI	BB	SO	SB	CS	SLG	OBP	B	T	HT	WT	DOB	1st Yr	Resides
Allegra, Matt	.220	71	273	36	60	16	2	11	39	30	104	5	6	.414	.307	R	R	6-3	195	7-10-81	2000	Lake Mary, Fla.
Basil, Jason	.260	50	177	23	46	8	1	5	30	23	42	1	0	.401	.351	R	R	6-3	225	8-5-78	2001	Cincinnati, Ohio
Brack, Josh	.221	42	136	16	30	7	1	0	12	25	41	2	1	.287	.346	R	R	6-1	185	6-5-77	2000	Falls Church, Va.
Christy, Jeff	.000	3	0	1	0	0	0	0	0	0	0	0	1	.000	.000	L	R	5-9	180	10-3-79	2001	Tampa, Fla.
Cirone, Joe	.226	37	133	13	30	5	0	0	10	7	43	3	2	.263	.262	R	R	6-3	215	11-20-77	2000	San Jose, Calif.
Ellis, Alvyn	.213	31	89	8	19	4	2	1	11	11	38	0	1	.337	.320	R	R	6-3	200	6-14-80	1999	Beaverton, Ore.
Hoffpauir, Josh	.312	28	93	18	29	3	0	0	5	11	7	15	4	.344	.387	L	R	5-10	175	9-21-77	2000	Vidalia, La.
Johnson, Dan	.283	69	247	36	70	15	2	11	41	27	63	0	0	.494	.354	L	R	6-2	220	8-10-79	2001	Coon Rapids, Minn.
Madera, Sandy	.234	35	77	8	18	3	1	1	12	15	24	0	1	.338	.375	R	R	6-2	175	1-11-81	1998	Santo Domingo, D.R.
Myers, Casey	.278	59	198	24	55	15	0	7	35	22	34	0	0	.460	.372	R	R	5-11	210	10-23-78	2001	Phoenix, Ariz.
Neufeld, Andy	.178	55	157	15	28	5	1	1	13	19	41	8	3	.242	.272	L	R	5-11	180	2-21-79	2001	Winter Springs, Fla.
Pierce, Justin	.186	36	97	11	18	5	0	0	5	5	36	0	3	.237	.233	R	R	6-3	210	10-4-79	2001	Wichita Falls, Texas
Reyes, Christian	.221	59	195	30	43	12	1	0	20	26	55	3	0	.292	.309	B	R	6-2	160	6-22-78	1995	Santiago, D.R.
Rooke, Brian	.148	47	108	12	16	5	1	0	8	16	43	9	4	.213	.277	R	R	6-2	197	8-8-79	2001	Pacific Palisades, Calif.
Schmidt, J.P.	.295	32	122	18	36	9	2	0	10	9	24	7	4	.402	.344	L	R	6-1	160	1-4-80	1998	Palmdale, Calif.
Soto, Jason	.206	44	165	16	34	12	1	7	21	8	84	0	0	.418	.264	R	R	6-0	210	4-14-78	1999	Patillas, P.R.
Stotts, J.T.	.270	62	241	35	65	5	2	0	17	26	34	19	4	.307	.348	R	R	5-11	185	1-21-80	2001	Weatherford, Texas

GAMES BY POSITION: C—Basil 4, Madera 16, Myers 42, Soto 24. **1B**—Brack 1, Ellis 23, Johnson 59, Soto 1. **2B**—Brack 19, Hoffpauir 23, Neufeld 36, Schmidt 5. **3B**—Brack 18, Neufeld 8, Reyes 58. **SS**—Neufeld 10, Schmidt 7, Stotts 62. **OF**—Allegra 70, Basil 40, Cirone 34, Madera 3, Pierce 32, Rooke 41, Schmidt 20.

PITCHING	W	L	ERA	G	GS	CG	SV	IP	H	R	ER	BB	SO	AVG	B	T	HT	WT	DOB	1st Yr	Resides
Cotts, Neal	1	0	3.09	9	7	0	0	35	28	14	12	13	44	.215	L	L	6-2	200	3-25-80	2001	Lebanon, Ill.
Crider, George	1	3	3.27	22	0	0	3	33	20	15	12	26	29	.175	R	R	6-1	195	12-7-79	2001	Phoenix, Ariz.
DePaula, Freddy	2	4	3.52	7	7	0	0	31	27	16	12	20	37	.232	L	L	6-3	160	6-2-81	1997	Santo Domingo, D.R.
Diaz, Alex	0	2	2.55	10	0	0	1	18	20	6	5	5	12	.270	R	R	6-2	160	7-15-79	1996	Santo Domingo, D.R.
Frick, Mike	7	2	2.70	21	1	0	3	40	38	15	12	15	54	.243	R	R	6-3	230	3-18-80	2001	Ventura, Calif.
Gage, Matt	1	1	4.11	17	3	0	0	35	46	25	16	7	18	.306	R	R	6-5	205	3-23-78	1999	Westmont, Ill.
Gilpatrick, Tyler	2	2	3.83	19	1	0	1	42	42	23	18	14	34	.265	R	R	6-3	205	5-3-79	2000	Cody, Wyo.
Gonzalez, Christian	2	7	2.67	16	16	0	0	88	90	36	26	15	59	.261	R	R	5-11	170	6-17-79	1996	San Cristobal, D.R.
Harden, James	2	4	3.39	18	14	0	0	74	47	29	28	30	100	.190	L	R	6-1	180	11-30-81	2001	Victoria, B.C.
Mabeus, Chris	2	5	4.50	20	8	0	2	62	75	34	31	18	28	.300	R	R	6-3	210	2-11-79	2001	Soldotna, Alaska
McGerry, Kevin	0	1	19.50	8	0	0	0	6	4	15	13	17	7	.190	R	R	6-3	215	8-24-79	2000	Philadelphia, Pa.
Minaya, Edwin	1	0	1.74	13	0	0	5	21	13	7	4	7	19	.173	R	R	6-1	160	6-20-80	1997	Montecristi, D.R.
Price, Brett	7	2	2.34	20	4	0	0	50	32	18	13	31	59	.184	L	L	5-10	165	12-7-79	2001	Leesville, S.C.
Rheineheimer, John	0	1	1.59	6	5	0	0	23	13	5	4	4	17	.160	L	L	6-2	215	5-29-79	2001	Waterloo, Ill.
Scarcella, Chris	1	1	8.55	8	4	0	0	20	29	25	19	11	11	.309	R	R	6-2	200	12-9-79	2000	League City, Texas
Sobscuk, Justin	2	2	6.91	17	2	0	0	27	35	25	21	15	30	.309	L	R	6-2	195	11-19-80	1999	Bellingham, Wash.
Trosper, Tanner	4	2	3.05	18	2	0	2	44	26	16	15	18	47	.160	R	R	5-11	180	12-28-77	2000	West Hills, Calif.
Wood, Mike	2	0	1.25	5	2	0	0	22	17	4	3	4	24	.209	R	R	6-3	175	4-26-80	2001	West Palm Beach, Fla.

ARIZONA LEAGUE

BATTING	AVG	G	AB	R	H	2B	3B	HR	RBI	BB	SO	SB	CS	SLG	OBP	B	T	HT	WT	DOB	1st Yr	Resides
Castillo, Carlos	.190	7	21	4	0	0	0	3	3	4	0	0	0	.190	.320	R	R	6-0	175	5-6-81	1998	Santo Domingo, D.R.
Castillo, Oscar	.183	35	120	8	22	5	0	1	19	11	31	4	0	.250	.248	R	R	6-0	185	8-6-81	1997	San Pedro de Macoris, D.R.
Cruz, Nelson	.250	23	88	11	22	3	1	3	16	4	29	6	3	.409	.283	R	R	6-3	175	7-1-81	1998	Montecristi, D.R.
Francois, Francisco	.168	46	155	22	26	5	2	0	7	15	37	10	8	.226	.275	R	R	6-1	155	11-30-82	2000	La Romana, D.R.
Groff, Matt	.333	24	72	14	24	4	2	0	9	12	9	6	6	.444	.449	R	R	6-2	185	3-28-78	2001	Fort Myers, Fla.
Jimenez, Luis	.214	24	70	8	15	1	1	0	12	8	23	2	0	.257	.280	L	L	6-2	185	5-7-82	1999	Bobare, Venez.
Kelly, Otis	.311	45	164	34	51	13	2	5	26	32	36	5	2	.506	.433	R	R	6-2	221	5-27-79	2001	Florence, S.C.
Lachapel, Juan	.256	10	43	7	11	1	1	0	3	1	11	3	0	.326	.304	R	R	6-2	160	5-1-81	1997	Santo Domingo, D.R.
Nagle, Austin	.250	50	188	36	47	7	9	0	22	26	53	7	5	.383	.346	R	R	6-1	190	10-20-82	2001	Lake Charles, La.
Perez, Radhame	.198	25	86	9	17	1	2	0	8	10	29	1	1	.256	.290	R	R	6-3	165	3-23-80	1996	Santo Domingo, D.R.
Reyes, Jose	.272	42	158	25	43	4	2	0	9	15	40	13	9	.323	.359	B	R	5-11	160	6-23-80	1997	Anzoategui, Venez.
Suomi, Richard	.257	52	175	31	45	14	2	4	43	27	36	7	2	.429	.374	L	R	5-11	180	10-5-80	2000	Toronto, Ontario
Todd, Kelvin	.235	5	17	2	4	1	0	0	4	1	5	0	0	.294	.278	R	R	6-3	185	3-11-81	1997	San Pedro de Macoris, D.R.
Trinidad, Edgar	.294	44	163	29	48	6	4	0	17	32	28	9	10	.380	.414	R	R	6-0	160	8-16-82	1999	Santo Domingo, D.R.
Tritle, Chris	.336	52	214	47	72	6	8	9	42	22	55	26	1	.565	.402	R	R	6-3	195	6-22-82	2000	Center Point, Iowa
Wayment, Kory	.229	51	192	24	44	9	2	0	16	16	53	7	4	.297	.289	R	R	6-1	175	2-18-81	2001	Ogden, Utah

GAMES BY POSITION: C—C. Castillo 1, O. Castillo 23, Suomi 35. **1B**—C. Castillo 3, Jimenez 5, Kelly 42, Perez 1, Reyes 1, Suomi 2, Tritle 1, Wayment 3. **2B**—Francois 11, Reyes 9, Trinidad 39, Wayment 1. **3B**—C. Castillo 2, Francois 1, Groff 5, Reyes 31, Trinidad 4, Wayment 21. **SS**—Francois 32, Wayment 26. **OF**—Cruz 21, Francois 1, Groff 13, Jimenez 3, Lachapel 10, Neagle 47, Perez 15, Reyes 2, Suomi 6, Todd 3, Trinidad 1, Tritle 51, Wayment 4.

PITCHING	W	L	ERA	G	GS	CG	SV	IP	H	R	ER	BB	SO	AVG	B	T	HT	WT	DOB	1st Yr	Resides
Amancio, Jose	7	3	3.71	14	8	0	0	53	51	23	22	16	33	.257	R	R	6-3	175	8-16-81	1999	Azua, D.R.
Atencio, Donald	0	2	4.50	15	2	0	0	28	33	19	14	13	29	.292	R	R	6-4	195	8-1-81	2000	Kirtland, N.M.
Baez, Hebel	1	2	3.57	12	4	0	0	35	41	24	14	7	22	.269	R	R	6-3	170	6-2-81	1997	San Cristobal, D.R.
Beck, David	0	0	1.00	18	0	0	9	18	13	3	2	7	32	.200	L	L	6-5	230	2-23-78	2001	North Olmstead, Ohio
Coleman, Jeff	0	0	1.54	8	0	0	6	12	7	2	2	3	8	.189	R	R	5-11	190	10-6-80	2001	San Dimas, Calif.
Garcia, Jairo	4	2	2.85	12	7	0	0	47	37	19	15	6	50	.213	R	R	6-0	164	3-7-83	2000	Palenque, D.R.
Gill, Chris	3	1	6.00	13	1	0	0	24	23	20	16	9	21	.247	R	R	6-0	188	2-17-81	2001	Phoenix, Ariz.
Johnson, Thad	2	1	3.72	13	8	0	0	46	45	25	19	10	44	.252	R	R	6-4	205	4-22-79	2001	Santa Rosa, Calif.
Landeros, Leonard	2	1	2.82	11	4	0	1	38	35	16	12	13	31	.238	L	L	6-3	170	12-12-80	2001	Hanford, Calif.
Leon, Brigmer	4	3	3.28	14	7	0	0	47	46	26	17	7	40	.252	R	R	6-3	165	4-7-81	1997	Cumana, Venez.
Martinez, Pedro	1	1	4.09	16	3	0	0	22	24	13	10	6	22	.275	L	L	6-2	165	9-8-82	1999	Santo Domingo, D.R.
Muessig, Jeff	5	0	2.41	14	0	0	0	19	14	5	5	7	18	.212	R	R	6-1	185	2-27-82	2001	Mount Sinai, N.Y.
Rodriguez, Manuel	2	2	4.12	17	0	0	0	20	25	14	9	9	21	.304	R	R	6-2	165	5-2-81	1999	Jusepin, Venez.
Sierra, Eduardo	2	1	3.02	12	0	0	1	45	45	19	15	9	41	.261	R	R	6-3	165	4-15-82	1999	San Cristobal, D.R.
Simmering, Bryan	2	2	2.40	13	0	0	0	49	41	16	13	5	57	.231	R	R	6-0	160	11-11-80	2001	North East, Md.

PHILADELPHIA PHILLIES

BY PAUL HAGEN

The Phillies even exceeded the expectations of new manager Larry Bowa in 2001. And Bowa expected a lot.

The day before the regular season opened, he wrote down his predicted number of wins, sealed it in an envelope and handed it to pitching coach Vern Ruhle for safekeeping.

On the last day of the season, it was revealed that he anticipated 81 victories. The Phillies actually won five more, a 21-game improvement from the previous season, and weren't eliminated from the National League East race until the final weekend.

One of the reasons Bowa underestimated how well his team would do was concern about the pitching coming out of spring training. That turned out to be one of the Phillies' strengths.

A bullpen that was baseball's worst (5.66 ERA) was rebuilt with the free-agent additions of Jose Mesa, Rheal Cormier and Ricky Bottalico. Mesa, considered by many to be washed up, responded with 42 saves, one short of the franchise record set by Mitch Williams in 1993.

The season also featured the emergence of three rookie pitchers—David Coggin, Nelson Figueroa and Brandon Duckworth—who at one point in July and August were in the rotation at the same time. Duckworth showed why he was considered one of the organization's top prospects by going 3-2, 3.52 in 11 starts.

The Phillies went into spring training unsure of what to expect from rookie shortstop Jimmy Rollins. He established himself as a fixture, batting .274, leading the league with 12 triples and tying for the top spot in stolen bases with 46.

Right fielder Bobby Abreu became the first 30-30 player in franchise history. He ended the year with 31 homers. No Phillies player has hit more since Hall of Famer Mike Schmidt in 1987.

The year wasn't an unqualified success, however.

Opening Day starter Omar Daal got off to a 10-2 start,

Bob Abreu

Marlon Byrd

PLAYERS OF THE YEAR

MAJOR LEAGUE: Bob Abreu, of

At .289, Abreu dipped below his previous career batting average of .313, but he had career highs in RBIs (110), doubles (48), stolen bases (36) and home runs (31).

MINOR LEAGUE: Marlon Byrd, of

Byrd's package of speed, power and defense spells trouble for other teams. He hit .316-28-89 and stole 32 bases for Double-A Reading in 2001, leading the organization in homers and RBIs.

but then had a 6.02 ERA in 16 outings from June 15 to Sept. 9. When he had his final start of the season pushed back in the final week so that Randy Wolf, Robert Person and Duckworth could face the Braves in a crucial series, he complained that he wasn't being given the respect he deserved.

The Phillies roared out to a 35-18 start and had an eight-game lead on June 1. From that point until the end of the season, they were 51-58 and ended the year two games behind the Atlanta Braves.

There were reports at midseason that many players were put off by Bowa's intensity and about controversies involving third baseman Scott Rolen, who rebuffed attempts to sign him to a long-term contract extension during spring training.

Public criticism of Rolen by senior advisor Dallas Green and Bowa was muted by the fact that Rolen got hot and ended up batting .289-25-107. But the lingering effect was more difficult to gauge, since the potential franchise player finished the season just a year away from free agency.

All-star catcher Mike Lieberthal was lost for most of the season after he tore the anterior cruciate ligament in his right knee May 12.

Bowa didn't waste any time raising the expectations, though.

"The big thing is that I don't want this to be a one-year thing," he said. "I would be very disappointed if we didn't do much better (in 2002). I want to get into the 90s (in wins), and I think we're capable of that."

The farm system had a successful 2001 season, particularly Double-A Reading, which shared the Eastern League championship. Outfielder Marlon Byrd earned EL top-player honors by leading the organization in total bases, homers and RBIs. Reading righthander Carlos Silva led the organization with 15 wins.

ORGANIZATION LEADERS

BATTING

*AVG	Gary Burnham, Reading	.318
R	Marlon Byrd, Reading	108
H	Marlon Byrd, Reading	161
TB	Marlon Byrd, Reading	283
2B	Scott Youngbauer, Lakewood	35
3B	Reggie Taylor, Scranton	9
HR	Marlon Byrd, Reading	28
RBI	Marlon Byrd, Reading	89
BB	Nate Espy, Clearwater	88
SO	Juan Richardson, Lakewood	147
SB	Nick Punto, Scranton	33

PITCHING

W	Carlos Silva, Reading	15
L	Taylor Buchholz, Lakewood	14
#ERA	Adam Walker, Reading	1.88
G	Jason Boyd, Scranton	52
CG	Taylor Buchholz, Lakewood	5
SV	Trevor Bullock, Lakewood	16
	Brad Pautz, Reading/Clearwater	16
IP	Carlos Silva, Reading	180
BB	Miguel Ascencio, Clearwater	70
	Ryan Carter, Clearwater/Lakewood	70
SO	Robinson Tejeda, Lakewood	152

*Minimum 250 At-Bats #Minimum 75 Innings

PHILADELPHIA
PHILLIES

Manager: Larry Bowa

2001 Record: 86-76, .531 (2nd, NL East)

BATTING	AVG	G	AB	R	H	2B	3B	HR	RBI	BB	SO	SB	CS	SLG	OBP	B	T	HT	WT	DOB	1st Yr	Resides
Abreu, Bob	.289	162	588	118	170	48	4	31	110	106	137	36	14	.543	.393	L	R	6-0	197	3-11-74	1991	Turmero, Venez.
Anderson, Marlon	.293	147	522	69	153	30	2	11	61	35	74	8	5	.421	.337	L	R	5-11	198	1-6-74	1995	Prattville, Ala.
Bennett, Gary	.213	26	75	8	16	3	1	1	6	9	19	0	0	.320	.294	R	R	6-0	208	4-17-72	1990	Waukegan, Ill.
Burrell, Pat	.258	155	539	70	139	29	2	27	89	70	162	2	1	.469	.346	R	R	6-4	225	10-10-76	1998	Boulder Creek, Calif.
Crespo, Felipe	.171	33	41	1	7	3	1	0	5	4	8	0	0	.293	.234	B	R	5-11	200	3-5-73	1991	Caguas, P.R.
2-team (40 S.F.)	.187	73	107	9	20	4	1	4	15	11	34	1	1	.355	.266							
Ducey, Rob	.222	30	27	4	6	1	0	1	4	6	11	0	0	.370	.364	L	R	6-2	183	5-24-65	1984	Palm Harbor, Fla.
Estrada, Johnny	.228	89	298	26	68	15	0	8	37	16	32	0	0	.359	.273	B	R	5-11	209	6-27-76	1997	Fresno, Calif.
Forbes, P.J.	.286	3	7	1	2	0	0	0	1	0	2	0	0	.286	.286	R	R	5-10	160	9-22-67	1990	Pittsburg, Kan.
Glanville, Doug	.262	153	634	74	166	24	3	14	55	19	91	28	6	.375	.285	R	R	6-2	172	8-25-70	1991	Teaneck, N.J.
Hunter, Brian	.276	83	145	22	40	6	0	2	16	16	25	14	3	.359	.344	R	L	6-0	195	3-4-68	1987	Anaheim, Calif.
Jordan, Kevin	.239	68	113	9	27	5	0	1	13	14	21	0	0	.310	.323	R	R	6-1	201	10-9-69	1990	Birkdale, Australia
Lee, Travis	.258	157	555	75	143	34	2	20	90	71	109	3	4	.434	.341	L	L	6-3	210	5-26-75	1997	Olympia, Wash.
Lieberthal, Mike	.231	34	121	21	28	8	0	2	11	12	21	0	0	.347	.316	R	R	6-0	190	1-18-72	1990	Westlake Village, Calif.
Michaels, Jason	.167	6	6	0	1	0	0	0	1	0	2	0	0	.167	.167	R	R	6-0	204	5-4-76	1998	Tampa, Fla.
Newhan, David	.333	7	6	2	2	1	0	0	1	1	0	0	0	.500	.375	L	R	5-10	180	9-7-73	1995	Yorba Linda, Calif.
Perez, Tomas	.304	62	135	11	41	7	1	3	19	7	22	0	1	.437	.347	B	R	5-11	177	12-29-73	1991	Barquisimeto, Venez.
Pratt, Todd	.204	35	93	12	19	3	0	2	7	19	25	0	0	.301	.345	R	R	6-3	230	2-9-67	1985	Deerfield, Fla.
2-team (45 N.Y.)	.185	80	173	18	32	8	0	4	11	34	61	1	0	.301	.327							
Punto, Nick	.400	4	5	0	2	0	0	0	0	0	0	0	0	.400	.400	B	R	5-9	170	11-8-77	1998	Mission Viejo, Calif.
Rolen, Scott	.289	151	554	96	160	39	1	25	107	74	127	16	5	.498	.378	R	R	6-4	226	4-4-75	1993	Holmes Beach, Fla.
Rollins, Jimmy	.274	158	656	97	180	29	12	14	54	48	108	46	8	.419	.323	B	R	5-8	160	11-27-78	1996	Alameda, Calif.
Taylor, Reggie	.000	5	7	1	0	0	0	0	0	1	1	0	0	.000	.125	L	R	6-1	178	1-12-77	1995	Newberry, S.C.
Valent, Eric	.098	22	41	3	4	2	0	0	1	4	11	0	0	.146	.196	L	L	6-0	191	4-4-77	1998	Anaheim, Calif.
Walbeck, Matt	1.000	1	1	0	1	0	0	0	0	0	0	0	0	1.000	1.000	B	R	5-11	188	10-2-69	1987	Sacramento, Calif.
Ward, Turner	.267	17	15	1	4	1	0	0	2	1	6	0	0	.333	.353	B	R	6-2	204	4-11-65	1986	Saraland, Ala.

PITCHING	W	L	ERA	G	GS	CG	SV	IP	H	R	ER	BB	SO	AVG	B	T	HT	WT	DOB	1st Yr	Resides
Bottalico, Ricky	3	4	3.90	66	0	0	3	67	58	31	29	25	57	.240	L	R	6-1	217	8-26-69	1991	Rocky Hill, Conn.
Brock, Chris	3	0	4.13	24	0	0	0	33	35	16	15	15	26	.275	R	R	6-0	185	2-5-71	1992	Altamonte Springs, Fla.
Byrd, Paul	0	1	8.10	3	1	0	0	10	10	9	9	4	3	.277	R	R	6-1	184	12-3-70	1991	Louisville, Ky.
Chen, Bruce	4	5	5.00	16	16	0	0	86	90	53	48	31	79	.262	B	L	6-1	180	6-19-77	1994	Panama City, Panama
Coggin, Dave	6	7	4.17	17	17	0	0	95	99	46	44	39	62	.271	R	R	6-4	205	10-30-76	1995	Upland, Calif.
Cook, Dennis	0	0	5.59	19	0	0	0	10	15	6	6	4	4	.384	L	L	6-3	190	10-4-62	1985	Austin, Texas
2-team (43 New York)	1	1	4.53	62	0	0	0	46	43	24	23	14	38	.247							
Cormier, Rheal	5	6	4.21	60	0	0	1	51	49	26	24	17	37	.247	L	L	5-10	185	4-23-67	1989	West Palm Beach, Fla.
Daal, Omar	13	7	4.46	32	32	0	0	186	199	100	92	56	107	.273	L	L	6-3	185	3-1-72	1990	Maracaibo, Venez.
Duckworth, Brandon	3	2	3.52	11	11	0	0	69	57	29	27	29	40	.233	B	R	6-2	185	1-23-76	1997	Kearns, Utah
Figueroa, Nelson	4	5	3.94	19	13	0	0	89	95	40	39	37	61	.275	B	R	6-1	155	5-18-74	1995	Brooklyn, N.Y.
Gomes, Wayne	4	3	4.31	42	0	0	1	48	51	23	23	22	35	.275	R	R	6-2	227	1-15-73	1993	Cherry Hill, N.J.
Mesa, Jose	3	3	2.34	71	0	0	42	69	65	26	18	20	59	.246	R	R	6-3	225	5-22-66	1982	Westlake, Ohio
Nickle, Doug	0	0	0.00	2	0	0	0	2	1	0	0	0	1	.142	R	R	6-4	210	10-2-74	1997	Sonoma, Calif.
Oropesa, Eddie	1	0	4.74	30	0	0	0	19	16	10	10	17	15	.231	L	L	6-3	215	11-23-71	1993	Conoga Park, Calif.
Padilla, Vicente	3	1	4.24	23	0	0	0	34	36	18	16	12	29	.272	R	R	6-2	200	9-27-77	1998	Managua, Nicaragua
Person, Robert	15	7	4.19	33	33	3	0	208	179	103	97	80	183	.233	R	R	6-0	194	1-8-69	1989	St. Louis, Mo.
Politte, Cliff	2	3	2.42	23	0	0	0	26	24	8	7	8	23	.250	R	R	5-11	185	2-27-74	1995	St. Louis, Mo.
Santiago, Jose	2	4	3.61	53	0	0	0	62	66	25	25	13	28	.271	R	R	6-3	215	11-5-74	1994	Loiza, P.R.
Telemaco, Amaury	5	5	5.54	24	14	1	0	89	93	59	55	32	59	.273	R	R	6-3	222	1-19-74	1991	La Romana, D.R.
Vosberg, Ed	0	0	2.84	18	0	0	0	13	8	4	4	3	11	.186	L	L	6-1	210	9-28-61	1983	Tucson, Ariz.
Wendell, Turk	0	2	7.47	21	0	0	0	16	21	13	13	12	15	.323	L	R	6-2	180	5-19-67	1988	Castle Rock, Colo.
2-team (49 New York)	4	5	4.43	70	0	0	1	67	63	36	33	34	56	.249							
Wolf, Randy	10	11	3.70	28	25	4	0	163	150	74	67	51	152	.247	L	L	6-0	194	8-22-76	1997	West Hills, Calif.

FIELDING

Catcher	PCT	G	PO	A	E	DP	PB
Bennett	.987	24	151	5	2	2	3
Estrada	.993	89	543	30	4	4	3
Lieberthal	.992	33	243	9	2	3	0
Pratt	.985	34	190	7	3	1	3

First Base	PCT	G	PO	A	E	DP
Crespo	1.000	2	21	0	0	3
Jordan	.948	10	53	2	3	4
Lee	.996	156	1332	75	6	121
Pratt	1.000	1	6	1	0	0

Second Base	PCT	G	PO	A	E	DP
Anderson	.982	140	270	387	12	86
Crespo	1.000	1	2	0	0	0
Forbes	1.000	1	2	2	0	0
Jordan	.953	10	13	28	2	4
Newhan	1.000	1	2	0	0	0
Perez	1.000	29	36	49	0	11

Third Base	PCT	G	PO	A	E	DP
Jordan	1.000	10	4	7	0	0

	PCT	G	PO	A	E	DP
Perez	.969	9	13	18	1	2
Rolen	.973	151	104	325	12	22

Shortstop	PCT	G	PO	A	E	DP
Perez	1.000	8	8	20	0	4
Punto	1.000	1	1	2	0	0
Rollins	.979	157	216	426	14	99

Outfield	PCT	G	PO	A	E	DP
Abreu	.976	162	308	11	8	4
Burrell	.972	146	226	18	7	2
Crespo	1.000	4	6	1	0	0
Ducey	1.000	3	5	0	0	0
Glanville	.991	150	413	8	4	3
Hunter	1.000	41	69	3	0	2
Michaels	.000	1	0	0	0	0
Perez	.000	1	0	0	0	0
Taylor	1.000	2	4	0	0	0
Valent	1.000	8	20	2	0	0

STEVE MOORE

Jimmy Rollins

Pat Burrell: Second on the team with 27 homers

Robert Person: Led the Phillies with 15 wins

STEVE MOORE

LARRY GOREN

FARM SYSTEM

Director, Minor Leagues: Mike Arbuckle

Class	Farm Team	League	W	L	Pct.	Finish*	Manager(s)	First Yr.
AAA	Scranton/W-B (Pa.) Red Barons	International	78	65	.545	4th (14)	Marc Bombard/Jerry Martin	1989
AA	Reading (Pa.) Phillies	Eastern	77	65	.542	+4th (12)	Gary Varsho	1967
A#	Clearwater (Fla.) Phillies	Florida State	68	69	.496	t-7th (12)	Ramon Aviles	1985
A	Lakewood (N.J.) Blue Claws	South Atlantic	60	79	.432	14th (16)	Greg Legg	2001
A	Batavia (N.Y.) Muckdogs	New York-Penn	37	39	.487	8th (14)	Frank Klebe	1988
Rookie	Clearwater (Fla.) Phillies	Gulf Coast	31	29	.517	7th (14)	Roly de Armas	1999

*Finish in overall standings (No. of teams in league)   #Advanced level   +League champion

SCRANTON/WILKES-BARRE   Class AAA

INTERNATIONAL LEAGUE

BATTING	AVG	G	AB	R	H	2B	3B	HR	RBI	BB	SO	SB	CS	SLG	OBP	B	T	HT	WT	DOB	1st Yr	Resides
Bates, Fletcher	.000	3	5	0	0	0	0	0	0	0	1	0	0	.000	.000	B	R	6-1	193	3-24-74	1994	Rocky Point, N.C.
Dominique, Andy	.170	40	135	16	23	6	0	3	18	12	34	0	0	.281	.243	R	R	6-0	224	10-30-75	1997	Granada Hills, Calif.
Ducey, Rob	.300	4	20	3	6	1	0	1	5	2	6	0	0	.500	.364	L	R	6-2	183	5-24-65	1984	Palm Harbor, Fla.
Estrada, Johnny	.290	32	131	13	38	13	0	0	16	5	6	0	0	.389	.319	B	R	5-11	209	6-27-76	1997	Fresno, Calif.
Forbes, P.J.	.305	133	514	79	157	29	2	5	61	48	72	5	0	.399	.367	R	R	5-10	160	9-22-67	1990	Pittsburg, Kan.
Francia, Dave	.228	110	347	34	79	13	2	3	37	25	58	19	7	.303	.290	L	L	6-0	167	4-16-75	1996	Mobile, Ala.
Hunter, Brian	.111	2	9	1	1	0	0	0	0	1	3	0	0	.111	.200	R	R	6-3	210	3-25-71	1989	Vancouver, Wash.
Knupfer, Jason	.239	90	276	41	66	12	2	1	25	30	59	10	5	.308	.326	R	R	6-0	185	9-21-74	1996	Redwood City, Calif.
McNamara, Rusty	.143	5	14	2	2	0	0	1	2	1	1	0	0	.357	.278	R	R	5-9	190	1-23-75	1997	Riverside, Calif.
Michaels, Jason	.261	109	418	58	109	19	3	17	69	37	126	11	3	.443	.332	R	R	6-0	204	5-4-76	1998	Tampa, Fla.
Newhan, David	.109	13	55	4	6	1	0	0	2	4	11	0	0	.127	.183	L	R	5-10	180	9-7-73	1995	Yorba Linda, Calif.
Orie, Kevin	.293	134	509	77	149	34	2	13	45	77	63	11	6	.444	.394	R	R	6-4	215	9-1-72	1993	Pittsburgh, Pa.
Punto, Nick	.229	123	463	57	106	19	5	1	39	68	114	33	9	.298	.327	B	R	5-9	170	11-8-77	1998	Mission Viejo, Calif.
Reed, Jeff	.235	31	98	12	23	1	0	4	8	14	24	0	0	.367	.327	L	R	6-2	200	11-12-62	1980	Elizabethton, Tenn.
Roberge, J.P.	.271	26	96	10	26	8	0	0	10	9	18	0	1	.354	.336	R	R	6-0	177	9-12-72	1994	Arcadia, Calif.
Royster, Aaron	.316	8	19	3	6	1	0	0	1	0	5	0	0	.368	.316	R	R	6-1	215	11-30-72	1994	Chicago, Ill.
Salazar, Jeremy	.231	47	160	16	37	13	0	1	16	10	35	0	0	.331	.275	R	R	6-0	190	3-18-76	1998	Breaux Bridge, La.
Schall, Gene	.281	73	263	40	74	20	1	14	54	31	57	0	0	.525	.370	R	R	6-3	200	6-5-70	1991	Willow Grove, Pa.
Sisco, Steve	.231	3	13	0	3	0	0	0	0	0	4	1	0	.231	.231	R	R	5-10	190	12-2-69	1992	Thousand Oaks, Calif.
2-team (92 Roch.)	.236	95	351	38	83	17	0	6	29	28	70	7	5	.336	.300							
Taylor, Reggie	.263	111	464	56	122	20	9	7	50	24	94	31	15	.390	.301	L	R	6-1	178	1-12-77	1995	Newberry, S.C.
Valdez, Jerry	.308	5	13	1	4	0	0	1	2	0	3	0	0	.538	.357	R	R	5-11	185	6-6-74	1997	El Paso, Texas
Valent, Eric	.272	117	448	65	122	30	2	21	78	49	105	0	1	.489	.362	L	L	6-0	191	4-4-77	1998	Anaheim, Calif.
Walbeck, Matt	.298	40	141	18	42	11	0	2	21	11	20	0	2	.418	.355	B	R	5-11	188	10-2-69	1987	Sacramento, Calif.
2-team (67 Louisville)	.257	107	338	38	87	18	0	5	46	34	46	1	2	.355	.328							
Ward, Turner	.275	70	222	28	61	22	4	4	27	30	31	9	0	.464	.362	B	R	6-2	204	4-11-65	1986	Saraland, Ala.
Woods, Kenny	.000	1	4	2	0	0	0	0	0	1	0	1	0	.000	.200	R	R	5-10	175	8-2-70	1992	Los Angeles, Calif.
3-team (26 Roch./23 Rich.)	.248	50	149	16	37	7	1	0	11	16	14	6	3	.309	.325							

PITCHING	W	L	ERA	G	GS	CG	SV	IP	H	R	ER	BB	SO	AVG	B	T	HT	WT	DOB	1st Yr	Resides
Bailie, Matt	0	0	0.00	1	0	0	0	1	0	0	0	0	0	.000	R	R	5-10	195	10-1-75	1998	Aloha, Ore.
Beltran, Rigo	2	5	2.96	37	11	0	2	116	87	40	38	41	113	.210	L	L	5-11	200	11-13-69	1991	Delray Beach, Fla.
Boyd, Jason	2	7	1.97	52	0	0	12	59	44	17	13	22	66	.204	R	R	6-3	173	2-23-73	1994	Edwardsville, Ill.
Brock, Chris	6	2	3.55	13	13	2	0	79	75	31	31	16	56	.254	R	R	6-0	185	2-5-71	1992	Altamonte Springs, Fla.
Byrd, Paul	1	3	3.65	5	5	0	0	37	34	18	15	7	35	.239	R	R	6-1	184	12-3-70	1991	Louisville, Ky.
Cedeno, Blas	3	4	4.45	35	0	0	1	59	56	29	29	23	52	.252	R	R	6-0	165	11-15-72	1991	Campo Carabobo, Venez.
Chen, Bruce	1	0	3.86	3	3	0	0	19	14	8	8	5	14	.212	B	L	6-1	180	6-19-77	1994	Panama City, Panama
Coggin, Dave	5	5	3.05	15	15	0	0	97	93	36	33	31	53	.253	R	R	6-4	205	10-30-76	1995	Upland, Calif.
Cook, Dennis	0	0	9.00	1	1	0	0	1	1	1	1	2	1	.200	L	L	6-3	190	10-4-62	1985	Austin, Texas
Duckworth, Brandon	13	2	2.63	22	20	2	0	147	122	46	43	36	150	.228	B	R	6-2	185	1-23-76	1997	Kearns, Utah
Figueroa, Nelson	4	2	2.47	13	12	3	0	87	74	33	24	18	74	.223	R	R	6-1	155	5-18-74	1995	Brooklyn, N.Y.
Geary, Geoff	0	3	6.95	7	3	0	0	22	35	17	17	6	21	.376	R	R	6-0	175	8-26-76	1998	El Cajon, Calif.
Jacquez, Tom	10	6	3.13	33	9	1	0	109	100	43	38	29	86	.246	L	L	6-2	195	12-29-75	1997	Stockton, Calif.
Kershner, Jason	1	1	3.60	6	1	0	0	15	12	8	6	3	7	.206	L	L	6-2	165	12-19-76	1995	Scottsdale, Ariz.
Lira, Felipe	0	1	5.19	2	2	0	0	9	17	5	5	0	6	.414	R	R	6-1	215	4-26-72	1990	Miranda, Venez.
2-team (42 Ottawa)	5	5	2.47	44	2	0	6	69	73	22	19	10	53	.273							
Nickle, Doug	9	3	1.68	47	1	0	7	86	62	19	16	37	60	.205	R	R	6-4	210	10-2-74	1997	Sonoma, Calif.
Oropesa, Eddie	1	1	2.35	14	1	0	0	15	14	5	4	4	11	.245	L	L	6-3	215	11-23-71	1993	Conoga Park, Calif.
Padilla, Vicente	7	0	2.42	16	16	0	0	82	64	24	22	11	75	.216	R	R	6-2	200	9-27-77	1998	Managua, Nicaragua
Sodowsky, Clint	0	0	3.86	7	0	0	3	7	8	4	3	3	8	.285	L	R	6-4	200	7-13-72	1991	Lamont, Okla.
Telemaco, Amaury	1	2	4.01	4	4	0	0	25	31	11	11	6	25	.306	R	R	6-3	222	1-19-74	1991	La Romana, D.R.
Thomas, Evan	3	13	5.28	19	18	0	0	104	123	68	61	36	74	.292	R	R	5-10	171	6-14-74	1996	Pembroke Pines, Fla.
Vosberg, Ed	1	0	3.00	27	0	0	5	27	24	9	9	13	22	.244	L	L	6-1	210	9-28-61	1983	Tucson, Ariz.
Wolf, Randy	0	1	5.00	2	2	0	0	9	10	6	5	5	7	.285	L	L	6-0	194	8-22-76	1997	West Hills, Calif.
Zamora, Pete	8	4	2.93	45	6	0	3	89	64	29	29	41	79	.201	L	L	6-3	185	8-13-75	1997	Mission Viejo, Calif.

FIELDING

Catcher	PCT	G	PO	A	E	DP	PB
Dominique	1.000	1	8	1	0	0	0
Estrada	1.000	30	246	19	0	2	2
Reed	.995	29	187	15	1	2	2
Salazar	.987	47	360	19	5	2	4
Valdez	1.000	5	21	3	0	0	0
Walbeck	1.000	39	288	19	0	3	5

First Base	PCT	G	PO	A	E	DP
Dominique	.985	37	318	17	5	22
Knupfer	.987	18	147	7	2	18
Roberge	1.000	16	128	13	0	18
Schall	.994	54	484	38	3	37
Valent	.996	27	209	15	1	18
Walbeck	1.000	1	10	1	0	1
Ward	1.000	1	1	0	0	0

Second Base	PCT	G	PO	A	E	DP
Forbes	.989	92	186	266	5	50
Knupfer	.955	51	99	112	10	19
Newhan	.969	6	15	16	1	6
Roberge	1.000	2	2	5	0	0
Sisco	1.000	3	7	7	0	1

Third Base	PCT	G	PO	A	E	DP
Dominique	.000	1	0	0	0	0
Forbes	.000	1	0	0	0	0
Knupfer	.964	14	1	26	1	0
Orie	.965	133	91	267	13	14

Shortstop	PCT	G	PO	A	E	DP
Forbes	.973	22	31	76	3	14
Knupfer	1.000	3	1	5	0	0

Punto		.964	123	158	398	21	80

Outfield	PCT	G	PO	A	E	DP
Bates	1.000	3	3	0	0	0
Ducey	1.000	2	4	0	0	0
Forbes	1.000	21	33	1	0	0
Francia	.977	82	164	5	4	2
Hunter	.833	2	5	0	1	0
Michaels	1.000	104	168	4	0	1
Roberge	1.000	4	6	0	0	0
Royster	1.000	3	5	1	0	0
Taylor	.980	108	243	6	5	0
Valent	.988	95	155	12	2	3
Ward	.946	23	34	1	2	0
Woods	1.000	1	2	0	0	0

READING

Class AA

EASTERN LEAGUE

BATTING	AVG	G	AB	R	H	2B	3B	HR	RBI	BB	SO	SB	CS	SLG	OBP	B	T	HT	WT	DOB	1st Yr	Resides
Bates, Fletcher	.135	15	37	5	5	2	0	1	4	7	5	0	2	.270	.273	B	R	6-1	193	3-24-74	1994	Rocky Point, N.C.
Batson, Tom	.083	7	24	1	2	0	0	0	2	4	0	0	0	.083	.154	R	R	5-11	180	2-9-77	1999	Alvin, Texas
Burnham, Gary	.318	109	371	59	118	25	2	15	77	35	43	1	2	.518	.385	L	L	5-11	200	10-13-74	1997	Windsor, Conn.
Byrd, Marlon	.316	137	510	108	161	22	8	28	89	52	93	32	5	.555	.386	R	R	6-0	225	8-30-77	1999	Marietta, Ga.
Casillas, Uriel	.240	113	384	46	92	17	2	5	40	27	47	4	5	.333	.304	R	R	5-11	185	8-22-75	1997	Downey, Calif.
Chapman, Travis	.182	7	22	3	4	0	0	1	3	0	5	0	0	.318	.250	R	R	6-2	206	9-6-80	2001	Fort Walton Beach, Fla.
Dominique, Andy	.280	76	261	43	73	16	0	12	49	37	45	3	1	.479	.369	R	R	6-0	224	10-30-75	1997	Granada Hills, Calif.
Gomez, Ramon	.190	38	105	7	20	7	3	0	10	5	42	2	2	.314	.246	B	R	6-2	175	10-6-75	1994	San Pedro de Macoris, D.R.
Gonzalez, Manny	.294	64	238	32	70	19	0	3	24	13	37	2	3	.412	.336	B	R	6-2	195	5-5-76	1994	Santo Domingo, D.R.
Harris, Brian	.245	135	511	71	125	27	5	13	58	45	62	20	9	.393	.313	B	R	5-10	171	4-28-75	1997	Carmel, Ind.
Hitchcox, Brian	.120	9	25	1	3	0	0	0	1	0	5	1	0	.120	.120	L	R	5-11	175	7-21-78	1999	Dayton, Tenn.
Johnson, Jason	.264	65	197	26	52	10	0	0	9	41	9	4	.315	.310	R	R	6-1	170	8-21-77	1996	Collinsville, Va.
Lopez, Mickey	.272	107	382	71	104	18	6	11	47	63	58	21	6	.437	.383	B	R	5-10	165	11-17-73	1995	Miami, Fla.
Machado, Anderson	.149	31	101	13	15	2	0	1	8	12	25	5	2	.198	.237	B	R	5-11	165	1-25-81	1999	Caracas, Venez.
McNamara, Rusty	.280	33	118	18	33	10	0	1	16	6	10	0	1	.390	.312	R	R	5-9	190	1-23-75	1997	Riverside, Calif.
Perez, Josue	.168	50	167	12	28	4	0	1	6	14	38	3	3	.210	.236	L	L	6-0	180	8-12-77	1998	Santo Domingo, D.R.
Roberge, J.P.	.321	87	343	61	110	13	1	19	71	25	40	12	4	.531	.371	R	R	6-0	177	9-12-72	1994	Arcadia, Calif.
Rose, Pete	.500	9	30	4	15	3	0	0	1	3	0	0	0	.600	.516	L	R	6-1	225	11-16-69	1989	Cincinnati, Ohio
Royster, Aaron	.260	42	146	19	38	3	3	7	19	11	37	6	0	.466	.321	R	R	6-1	215	11-30-72	1994	Chicago, Ill.
Valdez, Jerry	.248	74	242	32	60	14	2	9	39	11	47	1	2	.434	.291	R	R	5-11	185	6-6-74	1997	El Paso, Texas
Van Iten, Bob	.228	113	404	46	92	23	1	7	52	36	120	1	1	.342	.302	L	R	6-1	186	7-1-77	1996	Independence, Mo.

PITCHING	W	L	ERA	G	GS	CG	SV	IP	H	R	ER	BB	SO	AVG	B	T	HT	WT	DOB	1st Yr	Resides
Bailie, Matt	1	6	6.85	35	6	0	2	67	76	52	51	30	72	.291	R	R	5-10	195	10-1-75	1998	Aloha, Ore.
Baisley, Brad	5	4	6.50	12	10	0	0	62	82	50	45	14	37	.314	R	R	6-9	205	8-24-79	1998	Tampa, Fla.
Bottalico, Ricky	0	1	1.80	3	3	0	0	5	3	2	1	1	5	.166	L	R	6-1	217	8-26-69	1991	Rocky Hill, Conn.
Cedeno, Blas	1	0	2.25	7	0	0	1	12	12	4	3	3	10	.255	R	R	6-0	165	11-15-72	1991	Campo Carabobo, Venez.
Chen, Bruce	1	0	0.00	1	1	0	0	6	3	0	0	0	7	.136	B	L	6-1	180	6-19-77	1994	Panama City, Panama
Cormier, Rheal	0	0	0.00	1	1	0	0	2	0	0	0	1	2	.000	L	L	5-10	185	4-23-67	1989	West Palm Beach, Fla.
Geary, Geoff	9	7	3.61	29	13	0	2	112	101	48	45	21	88	.244	R	R	6-0	175	8-26-76	1998	El Cajon, Calif.
Hiles, Cary	2	3	2.42	51	0	0	11	82	60	24	22	21	62	.205	R	R	5-10	173	11-29-75	1998	Memphis, Tenn.
Kershner, Jason	5	9	4.80	26	19	0	0	124	147	75	66	26	70	.302	L	L	6-2	165	12-19-76	1995	Scottsdale, Ariz.
Kubes, Greg	0	0	3.67	6	5	0	0	27	32	12	11	7	12	.316	R	L	6-6	205	11-10-76	1998	East Bernard, Texas
Myers, Brett	13	4	3.87	26	23	1	0	156	156	71	67	43	130	.258	R	R	6-4	215	8-17-80	1999	Jacksonville, Fla.
Nunez, Franklin	8	7	4.42	39	14	0	3	110	107	68	54	51	112	.252	R	R	6-0	185	1-18-77	1995	Nagua, D.R.
Outlaw, Mark	4	6	5.01	49	3	0	7	65	74	38	36	28	59	.289	L	L	5-11	180	2-7-77	1999	Waco, Texas
Pautz, Brad	0	0	1.93	5	0	0	0	5	3	2	1	4	4	.187	R	R	6-3	190	1-3-77	1999	Reedsville, Wis.

PITCHING	W	L	ERA	G	GS	CG	SV	IP	H	R	ER	BB	SO	AVG	B	T	HT	WT	DOB	1st Yr	Resides
Serrano, Elio	1	1	2.89	30	0	0	2	37	22	12	12	9	30	.166	R	R	6-3	215	12-4-78	1996	Valencia, Venez.
Silva, Carlos	15	8	3.90	28	28	4	0	180	197	85	78	27	100	.283	R	R	6-4	225	4-23-79	1996	Bolivar, Venez.
Sismondo, Bobby	0	1	4.24	26	0	0	2	34	32	20	16	19	27	.248	L	L	6-1	180	11-14-76	1998	Mingo Junction, Ohio
Walker, Adam	7	4	1.88	15	15	3	0	91	50	22	19	28	81	.158	L	L	6-7	205	5-28-76	1997	Albuquerque, N.M.
Wedel, Jeremy	5	3	3.71	45	0	0	5	63	67	33	26	16	43	.264	R	R	6-0	195	11-27-76	1998	Wasco, Calif.
Wolf, Randy	0	0	4.50	1	1	0	0	6	5	3	3	2	7	.208	L	L	6-0	194	8-22-76	1997	West Hills, Calif.

FIELDING

Catcher	PCT	G	PO	A	E	DP	PB
Dominique	.990	51	358	44	4	0	2
Valdez	.993	58	391	47	3	3	10
Van Iten	.993	41	249	22	2	1	7

First Base	PCT	G	PO	A	E	DP
Burnham	.999	79	671	45	1	64
Casillas	1.000	1	12	1	0	0
Dominique	.972	10	97	6	3	7
McNamara	.000	1	0	0	0	0
Roberge	.994	21	157	10	1	9
Rose	1.000	1	2	0	0	0
Van Iten	.991	40	304	25	3	25

Second Base	PCT	G	PO	A	E	DP
Casillas	.944	9	10	24	2	3
Harris	.984	75	147	230	6	40

	PCT	G	PO	A	E	DP
Hitchcox	1.000	2	3	4	0	2
Lopez	.991	48	93	133	2	22
Roberge	.948	16	21	34	3	8

Third Base	PCT	G	PO	A	E	DP
Batson	1.000	6	2	8	0	2
Casillas	.922	81	55	157	18	13
Chapman	1.000	5	1	9	0	1
Dominique	.944	4	3	14	1	2
Harris	1.000	5	4	14	0	0
Roberge	.888	40	25	62	11	1
Rose	.714	7	6	9	6	1
Van Iten	.875	4	0	7	1	0

Shortstop	PCT	G	PO	A	E	DP
Casillas	.943	18	37	46	5	15
Harris	.952	55	95	161	13	29

	PCT	G	PO	A	E	DP
Hitchcox	1.000	7	10	15	0	4
Lopez	.918	36	56	78	12	12
Machado	.941	30	49	95	9	16

Outfield	PCT	G	PO	A	E	DP
Bates	.923	14	10	2	1	0
Byrd	.994	134	304	6	2	1
Gomez	.966	29	55	1	2	0
Gonzalez	.973	61	99	8	3	0
Hiles	.000	1	0	0	0	0
Johnson	.972	63	98	8	3	1
Lopez	.962	20	24	1	1	1
Perez	.972	48	99	5	3	1
Roberge	.939	19	30	1	2	1
Royster	.984	35	59	4	1	0
Van Iten	.923	32	36	0	3	0

CLEARWATER — Class A

FLORIDA STATE LEAGUE

BATTING	AVG	G	AB	R	H	2B	3B	HR	RBI	BB	SO	SB	CS	SLG	OBP	B	T	HT	WT	DOB	1st Yr	Resides
Batson, Tom	.216	9	37	3	8	0	0	0	1	2	6	3	0	.216	.256	R	R	5-11	180	2-9-77	1999	Alvin, Texas
Bush, Brian	.100	4	10	0	1	0	0	0	2	1	2	1	0	.100	.167	R	R	6-1	180	1-3-77	1999	Warren, Ohio
Bush, Darren	.175	46	137	15	24	5	1	2	18	18	33	1	1	.270	.286	L	R	6-0	200	1-18-74	1996	Dunedin, Fla.
Campos, Julio	.208	9	24	1	5	1	0	0	1	0	4	1	0	.250	.208	R	R	5-11	180	6-6-78	2000	Birmingham, Ala.
Carroll, Wes	.200	7	15	2	3	0	0	0	1	3	2	0	0	.200	.368	R	R	5-11	185	1-5-79	2001	Evansville, Ind.
Chapman, Travis	.307	96	329	39	101	22	0	4	50	44	39	3	1	.410	.400	R	R	6-2	185	6-5-78	2000	Jacksonville, Fla.
Deitrick, Jeremy	.205	55	195	12	40	11	2	5	28	8	62	3	3	.359	.248	R	R	6-0	210	9-14-76	1998	Williamsport, Pa.
Duarte, Justin	.236	48	157	17	37	10	0	1	22	8	42	0	0	.318	.287	R	R	6-2	210	9-14-76	1998	Azusa, Calif.
Duran, Deudis	.190	5	21	1	4	1	0	0	2	0	7	0	0	.238	.190	B	R	5-9	170	7-5-81	1999	Maracaibo, Venez.
Espy, Nate	.285	133	470	75	134	31	2	11	68	88	90	6	2	.430	.399	R	R	6-3	215	4-24-78	1998	Pensacola, Fla.
Giron, Alejandro	.261	113	418	59	109	26	3	6	41	19	84	9	9	.380	.298	R	R	6-2	180	4-26-79	1996	Santo Domingo, D.R.
Gomez, Ramon	.338	21	77	16	26	3	2	1	8	13	21	13	3	.468	.433	R	R	6-2	175	10-6-75	1994	San Pedro de Macoris, D.R.
Hannahan, Buzz	.261	82	268	43	70	10	1	1	27	39	44	17	7	.317	.364	R	R	6-2	180	6-29-76	1998	St. Paul, Minn.
Hensley, Anthony	.158	12	38	4	6	3	1	0	3	6	8	2	0	.289	.209	B	R	5-10	185	12-10-77	2000	College Station, Texas
Hitchcox, Brian	.195	32	87	9	17	2	1	1	6	8	6	2	3	.276	.268	L	R	5-11	175	7-21-78	1999	Dayton, Tenn.
Jacobson, Russ	.208	102	351	35	73	21	2	4	40	27	99	1	0	.313	.280	R	R	6-3	210	10-14-77	1999	Scottsdale, Ariz.
Johnson, Jason	.289	46	187	26	54	12	0	2	32	12	32	22	3	.385	.328	R	R	6-1	170	8-21-77	1996	Collinsville, Va.
Machado, Anderson	.261	82	272	49	71	5	8	5	36	31	66	23	9	.393	.342	B	R	5-11	165	1-25-81	1998	Caracas, Venez.
McNamara, Rusty	.429	9	28	5	12	6	0	0	11	6	2	0	0	.643	.556	R	R	5-9	190	1-23-75	1997	Riverside, Calif.
Padilla, Jorge	.260	100	358	62	93	13	2	16	66	40	73	23	6	.441	.343	R	R	6-2	200	8-11-79	1998	Carolina, P.R.
Reyes, Ambiorix	.305	27	95	17	29	2	0	0	7	5	12	7	1	.326	.347	R	R	5-11	166	2-6-79	1996	Rancho Viejo, D.R.
Sitzman, Jay	.247	118	465	63	115	21	6	6	34	35	100	31	17	.357	.300	L	L	6-3	195	3-13-78	1999	Scottsdale, Ariz.
Utley, Chase	.257	122	467	65	120	25	2	16	59	37	88	19	8	.422	.324	L	R	6-1	185	12-17-78	2000	Wilmington, Calif.

GAMES BY POSITION: C—Deitrick 27, Duarte 28, Jacobson 85. **1B**—Duarte 14, Espy 125. **2B**—Carroll 5, Duran 1, Hannahan 14, Hitchcox 6, Reyes 1, Utley 114. **3B**—Batson 6, Campos 1, Carroll 1, Chapman 89, Duran 4, Hannahan 31, Hitchcox 9. **SS**—Campos 4, Carroll 2, Hannahan 27, Hitchcox 1, Machado 82, Reyes 26. **OF**—B. Bush 4, D. Bush 19, Deitrick 7, Giron 108, Gomez 17, Hensley 4, Hitchcox 1, Johnson 46, Padilla 93, Sitzman 117.

PITCHING	W	L	ERA	G	GS	CG	SV	IP	H	R	ER	BB	SO	AVG	B	T	HT	WT	DOB	1st Yr	Resides
Alston, Travis	1	2	5.40	12	1	0	0	18	19	13	11	16	7	.260	R	R	6-2	195	7-24-76	1999	Birmingham, Ala.
Asencio, Miguel	12	5	2.84	28	21	2	0	155	124	62	49	70	123	.218	R	R	6-2	160	9-29-80	1998	La Victoria, D.R.
Baisley, Brad	2	4	3.78	11	9	0	0	64	59	31	27	18	43	.245	R	R	6-9	205	8-24-79	1998	Tampa, Fla.
Brooks, Frank	5	10	4.71	37	15	0	1	113	113	70	59	58	92	.262	L	L	6-1	195	9-6-78	1999	Brooklyn, N.Y.
Byrd, Paul	0	3	3.42	4	4	0	0	24	24	10	9	5	17	.266	R	R	6-1	184	12-3-70	1991	Louisville, Ky.
Carter, Tony	3	4	5.55	11	11	1	0	58	67	39	36	36	56	.293	L	L	6-7	245	8-1-79	2000	Modesto, Calif.
Franco, Martire	11	8	4.13	26	24	4	0	161	178	84	74	41	97	.280	R	R	6-0	170	5-20-81	1998	Bani, D.R.
Fry, Justin	2	2	4.67	30	0	0	1	54	54	34	28	34	43	.262	R	R	6-3	195	8-20-76	1999	Munhall, Pa.
Keelin, Chris	2	4	2.00	46	0	0	14	72	44	22	16	40	87	.180	R	R	6-2	190	3-3-77	1999	Sussex, N.J.
Kubes, Greg	10	6	3.79	20	19	0	0	112	124	59	47	50	89	.283	R	L	6-6	205	11-10-76	1998	East Bernard, Texas
Madson, Ryan	9	9	3.90	22	21	1	0	118	137	68	51	49	101	.290	L	R	6-6	180	8-28-80	1998	Moreno Valley, Calif.
Meldahl, Todd	0	0	1.59	7	0	0	0	11	8	2	2	5	10	.200	L	L	6-1	190	12-17-77	2000	Butte, Mont.
Oropesa, Eddie	0	0	0.00	2	0	0	0	2	1	0	0	1	3	.250	L	L	6-3	215	11-23-71	1993	Canoga Park, Calif.
Pautz, Brad	3	2	3.38	44	0	0	16	64	62	29	24	24	51	.258	R	R	6-3	190	1-3-77	1999	Reedsville, Wis.
Perez, Franklin	4	2	3.52	31	0	0	3	64	58	29	25	26	45	.244	R	R	6-2	175	6-10-81	1998	Bani, D.R.
Politte, Cliff	0	1	2.45	7	7	0	0	11	8	4	3	3	15	.200	R	R	5-11	185	2-27-74	1995	St. Louis, Mo.
Rodriguez, George	0	2	10.22	8	0	0	0	12	14	14	14	13	7	.297	R	R	6-0	170	12-1-79	1997	Loma de Cabrera, D.R.
Serrano, Elio	0	2	3.31	17	1	0	1	35	34	14	13	7	22	.265	R	R	6-3	215	12-4-78	1996	Valencia, Venez.
Sismondo, Bobby	2	2	3.00	6	4	1	0	30	26	13	10	15	22	.232	L	L	6-1	180	11-14-76	1998	Mingo Junction, Ohio
Squires, Matt	0	1	6.75	4	0	0	0	5	5	4	4	7	8	.238	L	L	5-10	200	1-24-79	2001	Lewiston, Idaho

LAKEWOOD — Class A

SOUTH ATLANTIC LEAGUE

BATTING	AVG	G	AB	R	H	2B	3B	HR	RBI	BB	SO	SB	CS	SLG	OBP	B	T	HT	WT	DOB	1st Yr	Resides
Acevedo, Carlos	.252	109	409	33	103	18	3	2	47	28	74	10	10	.325	.302	R	R	6-0	167	1-31-81	1997	Santo Domingo, D.R.
Anderson, Melvin	.103	21	39	8	4	1	0	0	1	4	17	1	1	.128	.217	R	R	6-0	205	8-18-79	2000	Baton Rouge, La.

ORGANIZATION STATISTICS

BATTING

BATTING	AVG	G	AB	R	H	2B	3B	HR	RBI	BB	SO	SB	CS	SLG	OBP	B	T	HT	WT	DOB	1st Yr	Resides
Avila, Rob	.272	91	305	31	83	21	1	0	32	24	50	1	3	.348	.340	R	R	5-11	200	9-4-78	1999	Fresno, Calif.
Barnette, Jason	.236	126	449	54	106	18	5	0	25	24	130	30	10	.298	.284	L	L	6-2	180	10-19-76	1999	Hoover, Ala.
Bush, Brian	.181	20	83	10	15	2	1	1	3	3	15	2	2	.265	.218	R	R	6-1	180	1-3-77	1999	Warren, Ohio
Carroll, Wes	.346	36	130	17	45	8	0	1	11	10	24	3	3	.431	.399	R	R	5-11	185	1-5-79	2001	Evansville, Ind.
Ciofrone, Paul	.000	7	12	0	0	0	0	0	0	2	5	0	0	.000	.143	L	R	6-3	220	6-19-78	2000	Smithtown, N.Y.
Collazo, Julio	.203	44	128	12	26	4	0	0	5	10	33	2	3	.234	.270	R	R	5-10	155	12-24-80	1999	Ponce, P.R.
Dancy, Cliff	.111	7	18	0	2	0	0	0	0	1	7	0	0	.111	.158	R	R	6-1	185	2-7-80	2001	Casselberry, Fla.
Delgado, Dario	.192	84	281	19	54	11	1	3	27	11	53	0	0	.270	.243	R	R	6-1	186	3-30-80	1997	Santo Domingo, D.R.
Delgado, Mario	.268	60	224	27	60	11	2	9	36	12	58	3	2	.455	.310	L	L	6-0	220	8-5-79	2001	San Diego, Calif.
Foster, Gregg	.224	87	281	37	63	11	2	6	23	21	74	17	5	.342	.297	R	R	6-0	205	10-3-78	2000	Commack, N.Y.
Griggs, Reggie	.245	13	49	3	12	3	0	1	4	1	22	0	0	.367	.269	L	L	6-6	245	2-22-78	2000	West Palm Beach, Fla.
Hensley, Anthony	.220	64	214	38	47	10	4	2	13	46	57	19	12	.332	.361	B	R	5-10	185	12-10-77	2000	College Station, Texas
Johnston, Ryan	.167	4	6	1	1	1	0	0	0	1	2	0	0	.333	.286	R	R	6-3	220	10-2-78	2001	McKinleyville, Calif.
Lankford, Derrick	.257	49	171	14	44	14	0	4	21	34	49	2	1	.409	.389	L	R	6-2	228	9-21-74	1997	Knoxville, Tenn.
McArthur, Kennon	.141	22	71	3	10	2	0	0	5	3	29	0	0	.169	.187	B	R	6-3	196	10-23-79	1998	Sylacauga, Ala.
McNamara, Rusty	.176	5	17	4	3	1	0	0	1	4	3	1	0	.235	.333	R	R	5-9	190	1-23-75	1997	Riverside, Calif.
Reyes, Ambiorix	.285	72	267	30	76	7	1	0	16	13	33	13	8	.318	.319	R	R	5-11	166	2-6-79	1996	Rancho Viejo, D.R.
Richardson, Juan	.240	137	505	68	121	31	2	22	83	51	147	7	9	.440	.325	R	R	6-1	175	1-10-81	1998	Bani, D.R.
Ruiz, Carlos	.261	73	249	21	65	14	3	4	32	10	27	5	4	.390	.290	R	R	5-10	185	1-22-80	1999	Chiriqui, Panama
Tosca, Daniel	.158	56	183	16	29	9	0	1	12	22	66	1	1	.224	.246	L	R	6-0	180	11-1-80	1999	Seffner, Fla.
Voshell, Key	.270	36	111	8	30	8	0	0	12	6	27	2	3	.342	.317	R	R	5-11	190	8-25-76	1999	Milford, Ohio
Youngbauer, Scott	.218	125	467	40	102	35	1	5	40	30	97	4	6	.330	.265	B	R	6-1	175	1-14-79	2000	Powder Springs, Ga.

GAMES BY POSITION: C—Avila 42, Johnston 3, McArthur 20, Ruiz 41, Tosca 49. **1B**—Anderson 3, Avila 2, D. Delgado 68, M. Delgado 50, Griggs 7, Lankford 24. **2B**—Carroll 33, Collazo 42, Reyes 46, Voshell 25, Youngbauer 1. **3B**—Anderson 2, Avila 1, Carroll 4, Dancy 2, Johnston 1, Reyes 3, Richardson 132. **SS**—Carroll 1, Reyes 23, Youngbauer 119. **OF**—Acevedo 109, Anderson 12, Avila 14, Barnette 121, Bush 19, Ciofrone 5, Dancy 5, Foster 71, Hensley 63, Lankford 16, Ruiz 2.

PITCHING

PITCHING	W	L	ERA	G	GS	CG	SV	IP	H	R	ER	BB	SO	AVG	B	T	HT	WT	DOB	1st Yr	Resides
Adams, Daniel	4	6	2.10	50	0	0	3	69	67	25	16	12	55	.250	R	R	6-0	200	2-21-78	2000	Burlington, Wash.
Brito, Eude	4	3	2.73	44	0	0	6	69	53	28	21	14	58	.210	L	L	6-0	160	8-19-81	1998	Sabana de la Mar, D.R.
Buchholz, Taylor	9	14	3.36	28	26	5	0	177	165	83	66	57	136	.249	R	R	6-4	225	10-13-81	2000	Springfield, Pa.
Bucktrot, Keith	6	11	5.28	24	24	3	0	135	139	93	79	58	97	.269	L	R	6-3	190	11-27-80	2000	Claremore, Okla.
Bullock, Trevor	5	3	1.13	48	0	0	16	72	53	14	9	17	62	.208	L	L	6-2	190	1-4-77	2000	Lincoln, Neb.
Carter, Ryan	3	7	3.92	14	13	0	0	80	73	39	35	34	76	.244	L	L	6-7	245	8-1-79	2000	Modesto, Calif.
Elskamp, Andy	0	1	2.27	23	0	0	1	40	28	15	10	19	41	.194	R	R	5-11	190	8-11-78	2000	Potosi, Wis.
Gomes, Wayne	0	0	3.00	2	2	0	0	3	2	1	1	3	3	.200	R	R	6-2	227	1-15-73	1993	Cherry Hill, N.J.
Hernandez, Yoel	6	9	3.47	25	25	1	0	161	153	94	62	42	111	.243	R	R	6-2	170	4-15-82	1999	Ciudad Bolivar, Venez.
Lawson, Jarrod	2	5	4.35	23	11	0	0	72	76	42	35	22	62	.269	R	R	6-4	195	4-2-79	1998	Potosi, Mo.
Meldahl, Todd	1	2	2.66	11	0	0	0	20	16	12	6	11	14	.207	L	L	6-1	190	12-17-77	2000	Butte, Mont.
Riethmaier, Matt	4	4	5.68	19	11	2	0	78	90	53	49	38	48	.293	R	R	6-5	215	6-16-79	2000	Arkadelphia, Ark.
Rodriguez, George	4	3	0.80	31	2	0	3	56	39	12	5	16	45	.201	R	R	6-0	170	12-1-79	1997	Loma de Cabrera, D.R.
Sadowski, Chad	4	2	2.14	35	1	0	2	59	48	17	14	11	41	.222	R	R	6-3	220	12-8-77	2000	Cudahy, Wis.
Tejeda, Robinson	8	9	3.40	26	24	1	0	151	128	74	57	58	152	.227	R	R	6-3	188	3-24-82	1999	Bani, D.R.

BATAVIA Short-Season Class A

NEW YORK-PENN LEAGUE

BATTING	AVG	G	AB	R	H	2B	3B	HR	RBI	BB	SO	SB	CS	SLG	OBP	B	T	HT	WT	DOB	1st Yr	Resides
Bennett, Kris	.242	44	157	13	38	4	1	0	14	14	22	5	5	.280	.324	R	R	5-10	170	10-3-79	2001	Huntingdon, Tenn.
Carroll, Wes	.286	12	42	7	12	2	0	0	3	4	2	2	1	.333	.348	R	R	5-11	185	1-5-79	2001	Evansville, Ind.
Ciofrone, Paul	.111	3	9	0	1	0	0	0	0	1	5	0	0	.222	.200	L	R	6-3	220	6-19-78	2000	Smithtown, N.Y.
Dancy, Cliff	.191	47	141	13	27	6	0	1	10	17	61	8	3	.255	.283	R	R	6-1	185	2-7-80	2001	Casselberry, Fla.
Foster, Gregg	.176	8	17	5	3	2	0	0	1	2	6	1	0	.294	.250	R	R	6-0	205	10-3-78	2000	Commack, N.Y.
Gonzalez, Daniel	.238	73	281	33	67	9	4	0	20	18	52	1	3	.299	.289	R	R	6-0	185	11-20-81	2000	Trujillo Alto, P.R.
Howard, Ryan	.272	48	169	26	46	7	6	8	35	30	55	0	0	.456	.384	L	L	6-4	220	11-19-79	2001	Wildwood, Mo.
Johnston, Ryan	.200	13	40	3	8	1	0	0	1	3	10	0	0	.225	.289	R	R	6-3	220	10-2-78	2001	McKinleyville, Calif.
Margalski, Ben	.223	40	130	16	29	6	3	1	18	12	41	0	0	.338	.287	L	R	6-2	210	9-2-79	2001	High Ridge, Mo.
McArthur, Kennon	.000	1	3	0	0	0	0	0	0	0	1	0	0	.000	.000	B	R	6-3	196	10-23-79	1998	Sylacauga, Ala.
McRoberts, Mark	.350	7	20	2	7	2	0	0	3	0	3	0	0	.450	.409	R	R	6-2	195	1-15-82	2000	El Cajon, Calif.
Perry, Rod	.248	70	278	35	69	13	2	1	28	26	47	8	8	.320	.327	R	R	5-11	185	2-1-79	2001	San Diego, Calif.
Phelps, Jeff	.226	40	133	18	30	7	1	2	16	10	35	2	0	.338	.278	R	R	6-0	195	11-20-79	2001	Tempe, Ariz.
Pohle, Richard	.241	50	187	24	45	12	0	5	30	17	22	0	1	.385	.300	L	R	5-10	190	5-30-79	2001	Buena Park, Calif.
Rivera, Erick	.257	68	261	28	67	11	2	1	30	14	54	4	7	.326	.289	R	R	6-2	200	5-22-81	1999	Utuado, P.R.
Sato, G.G.	.261	37	138	22	36	10	3	4	21	6	33	2	1	.464	.297	R	R	6-2	220	8-9-78	2001	Chiba, Japan
Silvera, Andres	.281	58	195	24	43	10	2	4	20	18	63	13	4	.354	.289	R	R	6-0	170	7-23-81	1999	Caracas, Venez.
Vukovich, Vince	.201	46	149	19	30	6	0	1	14	14	25	4	2	.262	.274	L	R	6-0	175	5-6-80	2001	Voorhees, N.J.
Walsh, Sean	.274	63	215	35	59	20	2	2	24	27	44	8	6	.414	.379	R	R	6-4	220	11-15-79	2001	Aiken, S.C.

GAMES BY POSITION: C—Johnston 11, Margalski 33, McRoberts 7, Sato 31. **1B**—Howard 44, Phelps 21, Walsh 18. **2B**—K. Bennett 24, Carroll 1, Silvera 56. **3B**—K. Bennett 16, Carroll 8, Phelps 13, Pohle 9, Walsh 36. **SS**—K. Bennett 6, Gonzalez 73. **OF**—Ciofrone 3, Dancy 45, Foster 6, Perry 68, Rivera 68, Vukovich 46.

PITCHING

PITCHING	W	L	ERA	G	GS	CG	SV	IP	H	R	ER	BB	SO	AVG	B	T	HT	WT	DOB	1st Yr	Resides
Ally, Ben	3	2	1.05	21	0	0	1	43	42	15	5	14	26	.257	R	R	6-2	205	2-9-79	2001	Lakeland, Fla.
Bennett, Jamie	1	1	3.60	18	0	0	1	30	26	14	12	11	31	.226	R	L	5-10	164	1-15-78	2000	Gallatin, Tenn.
Bernard, Jason	2	6	3.90	13	12	0	0	65	79	43	28	24	30	.300	R	R	6-5	220	8-14-78	2001	Panama City, Fla.
Cable, Taft	1	3	3.34	14	12	1	0	67	65	33	25	19	64	.247	R	R	6-2	210	7-25-80	2001	Greensboro, N.C.
Davis, Tim	2	0	3.51	16	0	0	0	33	25	16	13	13	26	.215	L	L	6-4	230	4-8-79	2001	Lucedale, Miss.
Glaser, Nick	3	4	2.51	24	0	0	6	29	27	13	8	7	21	.232	R	R	6-1	195	7-12-78	2001	Aberdeen, Wash.
Hutchison, Ryan	3	1	0.55	26	0	0	9	33	21	3	2	10	31	.181	R	R	6-0	205	8-9-78	2001	Vincennes, Ind.
Kim, In	6	4	3.08	13	13	2	0	76	72	28	26	9	48	.245	R	R	6-3	225	2-15-80	2001	Taegu, Korea
Lee, Seung	0	3	7.65	4	4	0	0	20	31	24	17	4	14	.340	R	R	6-4	225	6-2-79	2001	Pusan, Korea
Mayfield, James	5	5	4.24	15	14	0	0	85	88	47	40	27	42	.271	R	R	6-7	220	10-17-78	2000	Birmingham, Ala.
Meldahl, Todd	0	0	2.25	2	0	0	0	4	3	1	1	1	3	.214	L	L	6-1	190	12-17-77	2000	Butte, Mont.
Miller, Josh	2	1	2.59	17	0	0	0	31	36	11	9	4	21	.283	R	R	6-1	200	2-7-79	2001	Melbourne, Fla.

PITCHING	W	L	ERA	G	GS	CG	SV	IP	H	R	ER	BB	SO	AVG	B	T	HT	WT	DOB	1st Yr	Resides
Nall, Mike	1	1	8.67	16	0	0	0	27	34	27	26	20	26	.306	R	R	6-1	190	5-1-79	2001	Schaumburg, III.
Scott, Josh	1	2	3.27	14	0	0	0	22	17	10	8	11	12	.212	L	L	6-3	190	10-24-79	2001	Downey, Calif.
Silverio, Carlos	3	2	4.54	9	7	0	0	34	31	19	17	12	25	.242	R	R	6-2	180	4-1-79	1997	Puerto Plata, D.R.
Wilson, Mike	4	4	2.58	14	14	1	0	80	89	37	23	23	51	.277	R	R	6-6	220	6-12-80	1998	Las Vegas, Nev.

CLEARWATER Rookie

GULF COAST LEAGUE

BATTING	AVG	G	AB	R	H	2B	3B	HR	RBI	BB	SO	SB	CS	SLG	OBP	B	T	HT	WT	DOB	1st Yr	Resides
Abreu, Nielsen	.275	35	131	14	36	3	0	1	10	6	19	3	5	.321	.304	R	R	5-11	160	4-1-81	1999	Aragua, Venez.
Alexander, Lawrence	.276	39	127	21	35	3	0	0	10	16	26	3	4	.299	.366	R	R	6-1	170	12-16-80	2000	Chandler, Okla.
Brito, Anyelo..................	.186	27	86	9	16	5	0	1	15	7	27	2	0	.279	.253	R	R	6-1	170	8-15-83	1999	Bonao, D.R.
Campos, Julio	.150	13	40	2	6	2	0	0	1	1	9	0	1	.200	.186	R	R	5-11	180	6-6-78	2000	Birmingham, Ala.
Cancio, Tony..................	.292	49	171	22	50	13	0	2	29	16	51	0	0	.404	.363	R	R	6-2	220	12-20-81	2000	Tampa, Fla.
Ciofrone, Paul..................	.269	42	134	23	36	7	1	4	21	33	42	2	0	.425	.414	L	R	6-3	220	6-19-78	2000	Smithtown, N.Y.
Cisneros, Josh	.288	24	73	8	21	3	0	0	7	6	9	1	0	.329	.381	R	R	5-10	190	11-9-79	2001	Wilmington, Calif.
Delgado, Mario................	.500	2	8	1	4	0	0	1	4	0	1	0	0	.875	.500	L	L	6-0	220	8-5-79	2001	San Diego, Calif.
De los Santos, Esteban ...	.195	38	123	18	24	6	4	2	13	8	27	3	5	.358	.254	B	R	6-1	160	12-26-82	1999	Santo Domingo, D.R.
Duran, Deudis	.256	35	117	17	30	8	2	2	14	8	21	0	0	.410	.315	B	R	5-9	170	7-5-81	1999	Maracaibo, Venez.
Hansen, Bryan	.243	30	111	9	27	2	0	1	11	10	21	1	0	.288	.303	L	L	6-2	170	5-8-83	2001	Coram, N.Y.
Jones, Terry	.194	9	36	3	7	0	0	0	4	2	5	0	0	.194	.237	R	R	6-2	195	3-20-83	2001	Upland, Calif.
Marshall, Andre...............	.287	36	115	22	33	9	0	1	13	11	32	5	1	.391	.364	B	R	6-5	205	10-2-80	2001	Oak Harbor, Wash.
McNamara, Rusty	.000	1	4	0	0	0	0	0	0	0	3	0	0	.000	.000	R	R	5-9	190	1-23-75	1997	Riverside, Calif.
McRoberts, Mark	.200	27	80	14	16	3	1	4	6	10	25	0	0	.413	.289	R	R	6-2	195	1-15-82	2000	El Cajon, Calif.
Ortega, Felix	.250	20	56	10	14	4	1	1	9	12	15	0	0	.411	.394	R	R	5-7	175	12-16-81	2000	Trujillo Alto, P.R.
Perez, Josue..................	.308	10	39	9	12	3	1	0	3	5	4	3	1	.436	.386	R	R	6-0	180	8-12-77	1998	Santo Domingo, D.R.
Rivera, Carlos	.141	24	71	3	10	2	0	0	5	2	30	0	0	.169	.164	R	R	5-11	180	1-29-82	2000	Toa Baja, P.R.
Rivero, Luis	.250	38	128	17	32	7	1	1	11	9	27	4	1	.344	.309	R	R	6-1	178	10-10-80	1998	Manicuare, Venez.
Roberson, Chris	.248	38	133	17	33	8	1	0	13	16	30	6	2	.323	.336	R	R	6-2	175	8-23-79	2001	San Pablo, Calif.
Rodriguez, Carlos............	.297	35	128	22	38	10	1	3	23	11	25	6	4	.461	.368	R	R	6-0	170	10-4-83	2001	Santo Domingo, D.R.

GAMES BY POSITION: C—Cisneros 24, McRoberts 22, Ortega 20. **1B**—Cancio 31, Delgado 1, Hansen 19, Rivera 11, Rivero 1. **2B**—Abreu 34, Campos 2, Duran 30. **3B**—Campos 10, de los Santos 38, Duran 7, Jones 9. **SS**—Brito 27, Rodriguez 34. **OF**—Abreu 2, Alexander 35, Ciofrone 30, Marshall 36, Perez 10, Rivera 1, Rivero 36, Roberson 38.

PITCHING	W	L	ERA	G	GS	CG	SV	IP	H	R	ER	BB	SO	AVG	B	T	HT	WT	DOB	1st Yr	Resides
Arteaga, Erick	4	1	3.63	10	9	0	0	52	58	28	21	7	28	.277	R	R	6-7	170	4-2-81	1999	Yaracuy, Venez.
Astacio, Ezequiel	4	2	2.30	9	9	0	0	47	48	16	12	10	42	.268	R	R	6-3	156	11-4-80	1998	Hato Mayor, D.R.
Butto, Francisco	2	3	2.42	15	0	0	2	26	22	10	7	12	20	.231	R	R	6-1	170	5-11-82	1999	Monagas, Venez.
Cabrera, Carlos	2	2	2.91	10	8	0	0	43	35	23	14	23	40	.220	R	R	6-4	174	2-19-83	1999	Santiago, D.R.
Dawson, Carl	3	3	2.08	10	8	0	1	48	42	20	11	5	51	.221	R	R	6-2	180	9-13-79	2001	Somerville, Tenn.
DeChristofaro, Vinny	1	2	2.17	9	9	0	0	37	32	12	9	14	33	.226	L	L	6-2	168	4-2-82	2001	Richmond Hill, Ga.
Lammers, Kris................	0	1	3.63	12	1	0	0	22	23	12	9	8	25	.270	L	L	6-2	195	12-7-78	2001	Manchester, Tenn.
Lee, Seung	1	0	3.00	3	3	0	0	9	12	7	3	0	4	.307	R	R	6-4	225	6-2-79	2001	Pusan, Korea
McCall, Dan..................	5	3	2.43	16	0	0	2	33	23	13	9	11	34	.188	L	L	6-0	175	6-5-79	2001	Boalsburg, Pa.
Moreno, Victor	4	2	1.69	15	0	0	0	27	21	9	5	6	25	.205	R	R	6-1	193	6-10-80	1997	Puerto Cabello, Venez.
Reyes, Maximo	1	2	2.42	17	0	0	2	26	16	9	7	7	33	.166	R	R	5-9	170	9-24-81	2001	San Luis, Mexico
Rollandini, David	0	4	3.43	9	8	0	0	39	37	23	15	14	38	.245	R	R	6-5	220	2-6-79	2001	Montclair, Va.
Schriner, Brian...............	2	0	5.40	16	0	0	2	25	36	21	15	10	14	.346	R	R	6-3	215	9-4-78	2001	Great Bend, Kan.
Squires, Matt	0	2	1.21	17	0	0	0	30	16	5	4	11	33	.164	L	L	5-10	200	1-24-79	2001	Lewiston, Idaho
Sweeney, Matt...............	2	2	3.38	9	5	0	0	29	28	12	11	16	16	.266	R	R	6-2	185	2-25-83	2001	Yardville, N.J.

PITTSBURGH PIRATES

BY JOHN PERROTTO

In 1997 the Pirates set forth on a five-year plan that was supposed to culminate with a contending team moving into a new ballpark in 2001.

Well, the only thing that went according to plan in 2001 was the ballpark. PNC Park opened to rave reviews and the Pirates set the franchise single-season attendance record by drawing 2,436,139.

On the field, the Pirates had one of the most miserable seasons of their 115-year history. They finished 62-100, good for last place in the National League Central, 31 games behind division co-champions Houston and St. Louis.

Pittsburgh got off to a 19-41 start and it cost general manager Cam Bonifay his job.

In reality, the Pirates' season was over before it ever began. Righthanders Kris Benson and Francisco Cordova hurt their elbows in spring training and wound up missing the season after undergoing reconstructive surgery. In all, the Pirates had 17 players go on the disabled list.

The epitome of the Pirates' injury woes came Sept. 9 when rookie righthander Ryan Vogelsong, acquired from the Giants in a July 30 trade, blew out his elbow and had to have reconstructive surgery.

Adrian Brown began the season as the starting center fielder and leadoff hitter, but played in eight games before succumbing to season-ending shoulder surgery. Righthander Jose Silva, who might have been groomed as the closer, was knocked out for the season with a broken shinbone June 3.

Injuries weren't the only reason the Pirates had an awful year. There were plenty of poor performances, particularly from free agents signed by Bonifay.

Right fielder Derek Bell hit .173-5-13 in 46 games while missing most of the season with knee and hamstring injuries. Lefthander Terry Mulholland was injured twice

Brian Giles   Sean Burnett

PLAYERS OF THE YEAR

MAJOR LEAGUE: Brian Giles, of
Giles was one of the few bright spots in an otherwise dismal 2001 season for the Pirates. He hit .309-37-95 and led the team in average, home runs and runs (116).

MINOR LEAGUE: Sean Burnett, lhp
One of several promising young arms in the system, Burnett went 11-8, 2.62 with 134 strikeouts and 33 walks in 161 innings for Class A Hickory.

and pitched in 22 games before being traded to Los Angeles on July 31.

Two other high-priced players had poor years: second baseman Pat Meares (.211-4-25) and first baseman Kevin Young (.232-14-65). They have a combined $19.5 million and two years left on their contracts.

The Pirates also got disappointing seasons from catcher Jason Kendall and lefthander Jimmy Anderson. Kendall, who signed a six-year, $60 million contract extension, hit a career-low .266-10-52. His left thumb eventually needed reconstructive surgery. Anderson finished strong just to go 9-17, 5.10.

While it was mostly doom and gloom, not everything was bad for the Pirates. They watched the emergence of a potential superstar, third baseman Aramis Ramirez (.300-34-112). Steady left fielder Brian Giles (.309-37-95) continued to quietly be one of the premier players in the league.

Righthander Todd Ritchie overcame a 0-8 start, worst in club history, to go 11-15, 4.47. Rookie lefthander Dave Williams, who joined the Pirates in early June, showed promise by going 3-7, 3.71.

Rookie Craig Wilson tied the major league record for pinch-hit homers in a season (seven) and finished at .310-13-32.

While the Pirates are counting on the improvement of young players, getting things turned around will be a tough task as there is little talent in the pipeline. The Pirates' farm system also had a weak year as it mirrored the major league club with injuries and ineffectiveness. Only one of the six minor league affiliates had a winning season.

Double-A Altoona catcher J.R. House, rated as the organization's best prospect by Baseball America in the spring, hit .258-11-56 while flirting with the idea of playing quarterback at West Virginia. Top pitching prospect Bobby Bradley made nine starts at Class A Lynchburg before having elbow surgery.

ORGANIZATION LEADERS

BATTING

*AVG	Tony Alvarez, Altoona/Lynchburg	.326
R	Chad Hermansen, Nashville	75
H	Shaun Skrehot, Nashville/Altoona	138
TB	Jeremy Cotten, Hickory	211
2B	Shaun Skrehot, Nashville/Altoona	33
	James Langston, Altoona/Lynchburg	33
3B	Tike Redman, Nashville	10
HR	Jeremy Cotten, Hickory	25
RBI	Jeremy Cotten, Hickory	78
	Yurendell DeCaster, Lynchburg/Hickory	78
BB	Chris Combs, Lynchburg	66
SO	Chad Hermansen, Nashville	154
SB	Manny Ravelo, Lynchburg/Hickory	70

PITCHING

W	Three tied at	11
L	Ryan Ledden, Lynchburg	13
#ERA	Ian Oquendo, Williamsport/GCL Pirates	1.18
G	Clint Chrysler, Nashville/Altoona	58
CG	Ryan Ledden, Lynchburg	3
	Brady Borner, Hickory/Williamsport	3
SV	Tony Pavlovich, Altoona/Lynchburg	25
IP	Jeff Bennett, Altoona/Lynchburg	173
BB	Steve Sparks, Nashville/Altoona	89
SO	Sean Burnett, Hickory	134

*Minimum 250 At-Bats #Minimum 75 Innings

PITTSBURGH PIRATES

Manager: Lloyd McClendon

2001 Record: 62-100, .383 (6th, NL Central)

BATTING	AVG	G	AB	R	H	2B	3B	HR	RBI	BB	SO	SB	CS	SLG	OBP	B	T	HT	WT	DOB	1st Yr	Resides
Barkett, Andy	.304	17	46	5	14	2	0	1	3	4	7	1	0	.413	.373	L	L	6-1	205	9-5-74	1995	Raleigh, N.C.
Bell, Derek	.173	46	156	14	27	3	0	5	13	25	38	0	2	.288	.287	R	R	6-2	215	12-11-68	1987	Tampa, Fla.
Brown, Adrian	.194	8	31	3	6	0	0	1	2	3	3	2	1	.290	.265	B	R	6-0	185	2-7-74	1992	Summit, Miss.
Brown, Emil	.203	61	123	18	25	4	1	3	13	15	42	10	4	.325	.300	R	R	6-2	193	12-29-74	1994	Chicago, Ill.
Cota, Humberto	.222	7	9	0	2	0	0	0	1	0	5	0	0	.222	.222	R	R	6-0	175	2-7-79	1995	San Luis Rio Colorado, Mex.
Figueroa, Luis	.000	4	0	0	0	0	0	0	0	0	0	0	0	.000	.000	B	R	5-9	144	2-16-74	1997	Vega Alta, P.R.
Giles, Brian	.309	160	576	116	178	37	7	37	95	90	67	13	6	.590	.404	L	L	5-10	200	1-20-71	1989	Pittsburgh, Pa.
Hermansen, Chad	.164	22	55	5	9	1	0	2	5	1	18	0	1	.291	.179	R	R	6-2	185	9-10-77	1995	Provo, Utah
Hernandez, Alex	.091	7	11	0	1	0	0	0	0	0	2	0	0	.091	.091	L	L	6-4	186	5-28-77	1995	Levittown, P.R.
Hyzdu, Adam	.208	51	72	7	15	1	0	5	9	4	18	0	1	.431	.260	R	R	6-2	220	12-6-71	1990	Mesa, Ariz.
Kendall, Jason	.266	157	606	84	161	22	2	10	53	44	48	13	14	.358	.335	R	R	6-0	195	6-26-74	1992	Manhattan Beach, Calif.
Lopez, Mendy	.233	22	43	5	10	3	1	0	4	4	16	0	0	.349	.292	R	R	6-2	190	10-15-74	1992	Santo Domingo, D.R.
2-team (10 Houston)	.241	32	58	8	14	3	1	1	7	6	20	0	0	.379	.318							
Mackowiak, Rob	.266	83	214	30	57	15	2	4	21	15	52	4	3	.411	.319	L	R	5-10	166	6-20-76	1996	Schererville, Ind.
Matthews, Gary	.245	46	147	22	36	6	1	5	14	22	45	3	2	.401	.341	B	R	6-3	210	8-25-74	1994	Canoga Park, Calif.
2-team (106 Chicago)	.227	152	405	63	92	15	2	14	46	60	100	8	5	.378	.328							
Meares, Pat	.211	87	270	27	57	11	1	4	25	10	45	0	2	.304	.244	R	R	6-0	187	9-6-68	1990	Wichita, Kan.
Morris, Warren	.204	48	103	6	21	6	0	2	11	3	9	2	3	.320	.239	L	R	5-11	179	1-11-74	1996	Alexandria, La.
Nunez, Abraham	.262	115	301	30	79	11	4	1	21	28	53	8	2	.336	.326	B	R	5-11	185	3-16-76	1994	Santo Domingo, D.R.
Osik, Keith	.208	56	120	9	25	4	0	2	13	13	24	1	0	.292	.299	R	R	6-0	192	10-22-68	1990	Shoreham, N.Y.
Ramirez, Aramis	.300	158	603	83	181	40	0	34	112	40	100	5	4	.536	.350	R	R	6-1	219	6-25-78	1994	Santo Domingo, D.R.
Redman, Tike	.224	37	125	8	28	4	1	1	4	4	25	3	5	.296	.246	L	L	5-11	166	3-10-77	1996	Duncanville, Ala.
Rios, Armando	.333	2	3	0	1	0	0	0	1	2	1	0	0	.333	.500	L	L	5-9	185	9-13-71	1994	Supply, N.C.
2-team (93 S.F.)	.260	95	319	38	83	17	3	14	50	36	74	3	2	.464	.332							
Vander Wal, John	.278	97	313	39	87	22	3	11	50	42	84	7	4	.473	.361	L	L	6-1	180	4-29-66	1987	Hudsonville, Mich.
Wehner, John	.196	43	51	3	10	1	0	0	2	10	12	2	1	.216	.328	R	R	6-3	205	6-29-67	1988	Cranberry Township, Pa.
Wilson, Craig	.310	88	158	27	49	3	1	13	32	15	53	3	1	.589	.390	R	R	6-2	217	11-30-76	1995	Huntington Beach, Calif.
Wilson, Enrique	.186	46	129	7	24	3	0	1	8	3	23	0	3	.233	.203	B	R	5-11	160	7-27-75	1992	Santo Domingo, D.R.
Wilson, Jack	.223	108	390	44	87	17	1	3	25	16	70	1	3	.295	.255	R	R	6-0	170	12-29-77	1998	Thousand Oaks, Calif.
Young, Kevin	.232	142	449	53	104	33	0	14	65	42	119	15	11	.399	.310	R	R	6-3	222	6-16-69	1990	Phoenix, Ariz.

PITCHING	W	L	ERA	G	GS	CG	SV	IP	H	R	ER	BB	SO	AVG	B	T	HT	WT	DOB	1st Yr	Resides
Anderson, Jimmy	9	17	5.10	34	34	1	0	206	232	123	117	83	89	.287	L	L	6-1	207	1-22-76	1994	Chesapeake, Va.
Arroyo, Bronson	5	7	5.09	24	13	1	0	88	99	54	50	34	39	.289	R	R	6-5	180	2-24-77	1995	Brooksville, Fla.
Beimel, Joe	7	11	5.23	42	15	0	0	115	131	72	67	49	58	.289	L	L	6-2	201	4-19-77	1998	Kersey, Pa.
Fetters, Mike	1	1	4.58	20	0	0	8	18	16	9	9	13	11	.235	R	R	6-4	226	12-19-64	1986	Gilbert, Ariz.
2-team (34 Los Angeles)	3	2	5.51	54	0	0	9	47	49	32	29	26	37	.259							
Lincoln, Mike	2	1	2.68	31	0	0	0	40	34	16	12	11	24	.225	R	R	6-2	210	4-10-75	1996	Citrus Heights, Calif.
Loiselle, Rich	0	1	11.50	18	0	0	1	18	28	24	23	17	9	.358	R	R	6-5	253	1-12-72	1991	Phoenix, Ariz.
Manzanillo, Josias	3	2	3.39	71	0	0	2	80	60	32	30	26	80	.210	R	R	6-0	190	10-16-67	1983	Hyde Park, Mass.
Marte, Damaso	0	1	4.71	23	0	0	0	36	34	21	19	12	39	.250	L	L	6-0	170	2-14-75	1993	San Carlos, D.R.
Martinez, Ramon	2	8	8.62	4	4	0	0	16	16	15	15	16	9	.275	B	R	6-4	184	3-22-68	1985	Montecristi, D.R.
McKnight, Tony	2	6	5.19	12	12	0	0	69	88	44	40	21	36	.306	L	R	6-5	205	6-29-77	1995	Texarkana, Ark.
2-team (3 Houston)	3	6	4.95	15	15	0	0	87	109	52	48	24	46	.302							
Mulholland, Terry	0	0	3.72	22	1	0	0	36	38	15	15	10	17	.277	R	L	6-3	220	3-9-63	1984	Scottsdale, Ariz.
Olivares, Omar	6	9	6.55	45	12	1	1	110	123	87	80	42	69	.282	R	R	6-1	210	7-6-67	1987	San German, P.R.
Ritchie, Todd	11	15	4.47	33	33	4	0	207	211	118	103	52	124	.259	R	R	6-3	222	11-7-71	1990	Kerens, Texas
Sauerbeck, Scott	2	2	5.60	70	0	0	2	63	61	41	39	40	79	.257	R	L	6-3	197	11-9-71	1994	Cincinnati, Ohio
Schmidt, Jason	6	6	4.61	14	14	1	0	84	81	46	43	28	77	.255	R	R	6-5	213	1-29-73	1991	Longview, Wash.
Silva, Jose	3	3	6.75	26	0	0	0	32	35	24	24	9	23	.271	R	R	6-5	235	12-19-73	1991	San Diego, Calif.
Taylor, Bill	0	0	4.50	1	0	0	0	2	2	1	1	0	3	.250	R	R	6-8	230	10-16-61	1980	Thomasville, Ga.
Vogelsong, Ryan	0	2	12.00	2	2	0	0	6	10	10	8	6	7	.357	R	R	6-3	195	7-22-77	1998	North Grafton, Mass.
2-team (13 S.F.)	0	5	6.75	15	2	0	0	35	39	31	26	20	24	.276							
Wengert, Don	0	2	12.38	4	4	0	0	16	33	22	22	6	4	.428	R	R	6-3	205	11-6-69	1992	Des Moines, Iowa
Wilkins, Marc	0	1	6.75	14	0	0	0	17	22	13	13	8	11	.318	R	R	5-11	212	10-21-70	1992	Palmetto, Fla.
Williams, Dave	3	7	3.71	22	18	0	0	114	100	53	47	45	57	.244	L	L	6-2	203	3-12-79	1998	Camden, Del.
Williams, Mike	2	4	3.67	40	0	0	22	42	39	18	17	21	43	.243	R	R	6-2	204	7-29-68	1990	Newport, Va.

FIELDING

Catcher	PCT	G	PO	A	E	DP	PB
Cota	1.000	3	11	0	0	0	0
Kendall	.985	133	739	52	12	7	7
Osik	.995	39	188	12	1	1	1
Wehner	1.000	1	1	0	0	0	1
C. Wilson	.960	10	22	2	1	0	1

First Base	PCT	G	PO	A	E	DP
Barkett	1.000	4	36	3	0	2
Hernandez	1.000	2	4	0	0	1
Hyzdu	1.000	4	15	2	0	0
Mackowiak	.000	1	0	0	0	0
Osik	1.000	5	21	0	0	0
Vander Wal	.991	13	111	4	1	13
Wehner	1.000	11	51	1	0	2

	PCT	G	PO	A	E	DP
C. Wilson	.994	26	166	12	1	16
Young	.994	137	1154	70	7	118
Second Base	**PCT**	**G**	**PO**	**A**	**E**	**DP**
Lopez	.970	9	14	18	1	4
Mackowiak	.947	21	34	55	5	8
Meares	.973	85	149	213	10	53
Morris	.965	29	41	69	4	15
Nunez	.990	48	93	103	2	27
Osik	1.000	2	1	2	0	0
Wehner	1.000	1	3	1	0	1
E. Wilson	.972	10	16	19	1	9
Third Base	**PCT**	**G**	**PO**	**A**	**E**	**DP**
Lopez	1.000	4	2	5	0	0
Mackowiak	1.000	2	0	2	0	1

	PCT	G	PO	A	E	DP
Morris	1.000	1	0	1	0	0
Nunez	.000	1	0	0	0	0
Osik	1.000	3	1	3	0	0
Ramirez	.945	157	92	335	25	33
Wehner	.857	6	0	6	1	2
E. Wilson	1.000	2	0	1	0	1
Shortstop	**PCT**	**G**	**PO**	**A**	**E**	**DP**
Lopez	1.000	6	6	12	0	4
Nunez	.989	48	51	131	2	24
E. Wilson	.974	28	40	72	3	15
J. Wilson	.968	107	136	342	16	67
Outfield	**PCT**	**G**	**PO**	**A**	**E**	**DP**
Barkett	1.000	10	14	1	0	0
Bell	.988	46	78	3	1	1

A. Brown	1.000	7	18	0	0	0	Kendall	.906	27	47	1	5	0	Rios	.000	2	0	0	0	0
E. Brown	.988	54	79	4	1	1	Mackowiak	.986	46	70	3	1	1	Vander Wal	.973	73	106	2	3	0
Giles	.969	159	307	7	10	2	Matthews	.971	44	100	1	3	0	Wehner	1.000	8	7	0	0	0
Hermansen	1.000	20	30	1	0	1	Nunez	.000	1	0	0	0	0	C. Wilson	.947	14	17	1	1	0
Hernandez	1.000	4	3	1	0	0	Osik	1.000	1	2	0	0	0							
Hyzdu	1.000	27	27	0	0	0	Redman	.980	35	92	5	2	2							

FARM SYSTEM

Director, Player Development: Paul Tinnell

Class	Farm Team	League	W	L	Pct.	Finish*	Manager	First Yr.
AAA	Nashville (Tenn.) Sounds	Pacific Coast	64	77	.454	13th (16)	Marty Brown	1998
AA	Altoona (Pa.) Curve	Eastern	63	79	.444	10th (12)	Dale Sveum	1999
A#	Lynchburg (Va.) Hillcats	Carolina	58	79	.423	7th (8)	Curtis Wilkerson	1995
A	Hickory (N.C.) Crawdads	South Atlantic	67	73	.479	10th (16)	Pete Mackanin	1999
A	Williamsport (Pa.) Crosscutters	New York-Penn	48	26	.649	2nd (14)	Tony Beasley	1999
Rookie	Bradenton (Fla.) Pirates	Gulf Coast	22	34	.393	t-11th (14)	Woody Huyke	1967

*Finish in overall standings (No. of teams in league)   #Advanced level

NASHVILLE   Class AAA

PACIFIC COAST LEAGUE

BATTING	AVG	G	AB	R	H	2B	3B	HR	RBI	BB	SO	SB	CS	SLG	OBP	B	T	HT	WT	DOB	1st Yr	Resides
Barkett, Andy	.242	91	273	37	66	17	0	6	42	37	46	2	2	.370	.335	L	L	6-1	205	9-5-74	1995	Raleigh, N.C.
Bell, Derek	.162	22	68	12	11	3	0	1	9	9	19	0	0	.250	.266	R	R	6-2	215	12-11-68	1987	Tampa, Fla.
Berblinger, Jeff	.333	6	18	3	6	1	0	1	1	4	1	0	.556	.368	R	R	6-0	190	11-19-70	1993	Goddard, Kan.
2-team (73 Omaha)	.222	79	288	39	64	13	3	6	24	23	58	9	5	.351	.282							
Cota, Humberto	.297	111	377	61	112	22	2	14	72	25	74	7	2	.477	.351	R	R	6-0	175	2-7-79	1995	San Luis Rio Colorado, Mex.
Cotton, John	.200	30	80	7	16	4	0	1	9	5	22	0	2	.288	.247	L	R	6-0	190	10-30-70	1989	Houston, Texas
Figueroa, Luis	.300	92	347	45	104	11	1	4	29	31	26	8	5	.372	.357	B	R	5-9	144	2-16-74	1997	Vega Alta, P.R.
Green, Scarborough	.155	33	58	8	9	2	1	0	4	8	16	2	1	.224	.254	B	R	5-10	185	6-9-74	1993	St. Louis, Mo.
Haad, Yamid	.257	51	144	14	37	5	0	2	10	7	27	0	3	.333	.291	R	R	6-2	204	9-2-77	1994	Cartagena, Colombia
Haverbusch, Kevin	.333	50	147	24	49	7	2	7	30	4	34	3	1	.551	.373	R	R	6-3	199	6-16-76	1997	Massapequa, N.Y.
Hermansen, Chad	.246	123	447	75	110	22	6	17	63	41	154	22	5	.436	.315	R	R	6-2	185	9-10-77	1995	Provo, Utah
Hernandez, Alex	.295	88	342	45	101	16	1	8	36	13	65	3	4	.418	.325	L	L	6-4	186	5-28-77	1995	Levittown, P.R.
Howard, Thomas	.200	13	30	2	6	2	0	0	1	2	7	0	0	.267	.273	B	R	6-2	205	12-11-64	1986	Elk Grove, Calif.
Hyzdu, Adam	.291	69	261	38	76	17	2	11	39	17	68	1	3	.498	.332	R	R	6-2	220	12-6-71	1990	Mesa, Ariz.
Mackowiak, Rob	.263	32	118	14	31	5	0	4	14	7	39	1	1	.407	.302	L	R	5-10	166	6-20-76	1996	Schererville, Ind.
Monahan, Shane	.220	16	41	3	9	0	0	1	3	2	9	0	0	.293	.250	L	L	6-0	195	8-12-74	1995	Marietta, Ga.
Morris, Warren	.305	57	223	26	68	16	2	5	40	12	21	3	4	.462	.342	L	R	5-11	179	1-11-74	1996	Alexandria, La.
Nelson, Bry	.314	49	185	23	58	7	0	5	15	10	16	1	3	.432	.348	B	R	5-10	205	1-27-74	1994	Crossett, Ark.
2-team (85 Tucson)	.305	134	511	60	156	22	0	11	56	26	36	12	8	.413	.338							
Petersen, Chris	.382	21	55	9	21	5	0	2	18	3	15	0	2	.582	.435	R	R	5-11	175	11-6-70	1992	Southington, Conn.
Radmanovic, Ryan	.287	31	94	17	27	8	0	5	14	11	26	1	0	.532	.358	L	R	6-2	200	8-9-71	1993	Calgary, Alberta
2-team (92 Portland)	.269	123	390	61	105	25	1	19	66	70	108	3	4	.485	.376							
Redman, Tike	.304	95	398	53	121	18	10	3	42	24	37	21	7	.422	.347	L	L	5-11	166	3-10-77	1996	Duncanville, Ala.
Secrist, Reed	.305	104	338	61	103	21	1	22	61	48	81	4	0	.565	.398	L	R	6-1	205	5-7-70	1992	Farmington, Utah
Skrehot, Shaun	.224	18	58	8	13	3	0	1	7	8	12	1	2	.328	.328	R	R	5-9	172	5-2-75	1998	Spring, Texas
Wilson, Craig	.289	11	45	4	13	2	1	3	2	14	0	0	.444	.333	R	R	6-2	217	11-30-76	1995	Huntington Beach, Calif.
Wilson, Jack	.369	27	103	20	38	6	1	1	6	9	13	2	2	.476	.430	R	R	6-0	170	12-29-77	1998	Thousand Oaks, Calif.
Wood, Jason	.243	113	379	46	92	19	1	8	38	27	73	0	0	.361	.303	R	R	6-1	200	12-16-69	1991	Fresno, Calif.

PITCHING	W	L	ERA	G	GS	CG	SV	IP	H	R	ER	BB	SO	AVG	B	T	HT	WT	DOB	1st Yr	Resides
Ah Yat, Paul	1	4	9.30	8	4	0	0	20	37	22	21	9	15	.406	R	L	6-1	192	10-13-74	1996	Honolulu, Hawaii
Arroyo, Bronson	6	2	3.93	9	9	2	0	66	63	32	29	15	49	.247	R	R	6-5	180	2-24-77	1995	Brooksville, Fla.
Ayers, Mike	0	0	9.00	5	0	0	0	4	5	4	4	5	3	.384	L	L	5-10	206	3-23-73	1996	Cincinnati, Ohio
Camp, Shawn	0	0	2.12	11	0	0	0	17	11	4	4	8	15	.189	R	R	6-1	200	11-18-75	1997	Fairfax, Va.
2-team (4 Portland)	1	0	1.50	15	1	0	0	24	13	4	4	9	21	.164							
Chrysler, Clint	0	0	2.70	7	0	0	0	10	14	4	3	4	6	.325	L	L	6-0	190	11-4-75	1997	St. Petersburg, Fla.
Cordova, Francisco	0	0	18.00	1	1	0	0	1	2	2	2	0	1	.400	R	R	6-1	197	4-26-72	1996	Veracruz, Mexico
Dewey, Mark	1	1	1.74	11	0	0	0	10	9	3	2	3	3	.230	R	R	6-0	216	1-3-65	1987	Jenison, Mich.
Donaldson, Bo	1	1	0.64	11	0	0	0	14	9	4	1	9	17	.187	R	R	6-2	200	10-10-74	1997	Philadelphia, Pa.
Guy, Brad	2	2	4.24	22	2	0	0	47	47	26	22	16	35	.267	R	R	6-2	192	10-25-75	1997	Eureka, Calif.
Karl, Scott	4	3	3.83	14	14	0	0	85	79	40	36	29	54	.246	L	L	6-2	209	8-9-71	1992	Solana Beach, Calif.
Lincoln, Mike	5	4	3.44	18	13	1	0	92	90	39	35	25	71	.251	R	R	6-2	210	4-10-75	1996	Citrus Heights, Calif.
Loiselle, Rich	0	2	6.15	26	1	0	0	34	33	24	23	23	18	.264	R	R	6-5	253	1-12-72	1991	Phoenix, Ariz.
Marte, Damaso	0	0	3.38	4	0	0	0	5	3	2	2	0	4	.166	L	L	6-0	170	2-14-75	1993	San Carlos, D.R.
McConnell, Sam	7	10	6.03	26	23	1	0	134	159	103	90	41	98	.291	L	L	6-1	213	12-31-75	1997	Fairfield, Ohio
McDade, Neal	1	1	3.00	8	0	0	0	15	14	5	5	7	8	.254	R	R	6-3	170	6-16-76	1995	Orange Park, Fla.
Moody, Eric	5	6	3.45	42	8	1	0	112	112	47	43	14	50	.259	R	R	6-6	215	1-6-71	1993	Williamston, S.C.
O'Connor, Brian	6	9	6.21	37	16	0	1	112	124	87	77	58	74	.279	L	L	6-2	190	1-4-77	1995	Cincinnati, Ohio
Pavlas, Dave	1	4	2.61	41	1	0	6	41	34	17	12	8	40	.217	R	R	6-2	205	8-12-62	1985	Shiner, Texas
Ryan, Jason	3	5	4.53	9	9	1	0	54	52	34	27	19	25	.253	B	R	6-3	195	1-23-76	1994	Charlotte, N.C.
Schmidt, Jason	1	0	0.00	1	1	0	0	7	4	0	0	0	6	.160	R	R	6-5	213	1-29-73	1991	Longview, Wash.
Smith, Brian	1	2	3.69	36	0	0	11	39	37	22	16	7	34	.238	R	R	6-0	190	7-19-72	1994	Toney, Ala.
Sparks, Steve	3	5	5.06	31	10	1	3	75	77	50	42	64	63	.269	R	R	6-4	210	3-28-75	1998	Mobile, Ala.
Taylor, Bill	0	3	7.20	20	0	0	8	20	29	17	16	3	16	.337	R	R	6-8	230	10-16-61	1980	Thomasville, Ga.
Vogelsong, Ryan	2	3	3.98	6	6	0	0	32	26	15	14	15	33	.230	R	R	6-3	195	7-22-77	1998	North Grafton, Mass.
2-team (10 Fresno)	5	6	3.21	16	16	0	0	90	61	33	32	33	86	.191							
Wengert, Don	7	7	4.10	18	18	0	0	112	135	60	51	20	67	.301	R	R	6-3	205	11-6-69	1992	Des Moines, Iowa
Wilkins, Marc	4	1	4.75	32	0	0	1	36	38	21	19	13	24	.279	R	R	5-11	212	10-21-70	1992	Palmetto, Fla.

PITCHING

PITCHING	W	L	ERA	G	GS	CG	SV	IP	H	R	ER	BB	SO	AVG	B	T	HT	WT	DOB	1st Yr	Resides
Williams, Dave	1	1	3.38	2	2	0	0	11	9	5	4	5	6	.230	L	L	6-2	203	3-12-79	1998	Camden, Del.
Wimberly, Larry	2	1	5.27	4	3	0	0	14	16	8	4	3		.301	L	L	6-0	190	8-22-75	1994	Zellwood, Fla.

FIELDING

Catcher	PCT	G	PO	A	E	DP	PB
Cota	.986	91	523	27	8	0	5
Haad	.988	37	222	22	3	4	6
Secrist	.955	21	101	6	5	1	1
C. Wilson	1.000	4	27	3	0	0	0

	PCT	G	PO	A	E	DP
Mackowiak	.981	10	27	25	1	9
Morris	.967	47	103	131	8	32
Nelson	.978	41	98	127	5	25
Petersen	1.000	14	30	41	0	10
Wood	1.000	2	6	7	0	4

	PCT	G	PO	A	E	DP
Skrehot	.898	18	24	55	9	17
J. Wilson	.974	27	30	81	3	19
Wood	.924	33	41	93	11	19

First Base	PCT	G	PO	A	E	DP
Barkett	.990	70	560	43	6	58
Cotton	.975	4	37	2	1	3
Haad	1.000	2	10	1	0	0
Hernandez	.984	48	415	18	7	42
Hyzdu	1.000	4	36	0	0	4
Secrist	.994	19	150	11	1	24
C. Wilson	.963	6	50	2	2	3
Wood	1.000	1	10	0	0	0

Third Base	PCT	G	PO	A	E	DP
Berblinger	1.000	1	0	10	0	0
Cotton	.850	8	5	12	3	2
Figueroa	1.000	1	0	3	0	1
Hyzdu	1.000	1	1	1	0	0
Mackowiak	.889	8	7	25	4	3
Morris	.955	8	3	18	1	0
Nelson	.333	2	0	1	2	0
Secrist	.946	45	21	101	7	9
Wood	.944	78	52	151	12	12

Outfield	PCT	G	PO	A	E	DP
Barkett	.857	12	11	1	2	0
Bell	.938	12	15	0	1	0
Cotton	1.000	2	2	0	0	0
Green	.970	20	29	3	1	2
Haverbusch	.966	24	27	1	1	0
Hermansen	.984	117	237	8	4	3
Hernandez	.969	36	59	4	2	1
Howard	.800	3	3	1	1	0
Hyzdu	.993	58	132	3	1	0
Mackowiak	.926	14	23	2	2	0
Monahan	1.000	11	18	0	0	0
Radmanovich	.976	27	41	0	1	0
Redman	.970	94	216	12	7	3
Secrist	.966	23	27	1	1	0

Second Base	PCT	G	PO	A	E	DP
Berblinger	1.000	1	2	3	0	1
Figueroa	.965	25	44	65	4	13
Haverbusch	.813	7	12	14	6	2

Shortstop	PCT	G	PO	A	E	DP
Figueroa	.959	67	113	235	15	47
Petersen	.889	2	3	5	1	0

ALTOONA — Class AA

EASTERN LEAGUE

BATTING

BATTING	AVG	G	AB	R	H	2B	3B	HR	RBI	BB	SO	SB	CS	SLG	OBP	B	T	HT	WT	DOB	1st Yr	Resides
Alvarez, Tony	.319	67	254	34	81	16	1	6	25	9	30	17	11	.461	.359	R	R	6-1	202	5-10-79	1995	Los Teques, Venez.
Barns, B.J.	.220	30	109	12	24	6	2	6	15	7	37	3	1	.477	.286	L	L	6-4	195	7-21-77	1997	Loysville, Pa.
Bass, Jayson	.235	67	170	18	40	14	3	1	13	10	47	9	5	.371	.284	B	R	6-0	180	6-2-76	1994	Fayette, Ala.
Brown, Adrian	.333	7	30	7	10	1	1	0	1	1	7	1	2	.433	.344	B	R	6-0	185	2-7-74	1992	Summit, Miss.
Bruce, Mo.	.118	10	34	4	4	1	0	0	2	4	11	0	2	.147	.211	R	R	5-10	190	5-1-75	1996	Kansas City, Mo.
2-team (45 Harrisburg)	.206	55	170	23	35	7	0	3	17	12	47	14	4	.300	.261							
Burton, Darren	.288	85	299	36	86	15	2	7	32	23	62	5	1	.421	.348	B	R	6-1	185	9-16-72	1990	Somerset, Ky.
Davis, J.J.	.250	67	228	21	57	13	3	4	26	21	79	2	5	.386	.317	R	R	6-4	250	10-25-78	1997	Pomona, Calif.
Doumit, Ryan	.250	2	4	0	1	0	0	0	2	1	1	0	0	.250	.400	B	R	6-0	180	4-3-81	1999	Moses Lake, Wash.
Evans, Lee	.248	118	428	53	106	21	8	11	48	37	116	12	5	.411	.314	B	R	6-1	185	7-20-77	1996	Northport, Ala.
Green, Scarborough	.253	27	91	10	23	1	0	0	6	6	19	10	0	.264	.303	B	R	5-10	185	6-9-74	1993	St. Louis, Mo.
Haad, Yamid	.000	1	3	0	0	0	0	0	0	0	0	0	0	.000	.000	R	R	6-2	204	9-2-77	1994	Cartagena, Colombia
Haverbusch, Kevin	.261	43	153	17	40	10	2	2	19	5	23	1	2	.392	.287	R	R	6-3	199	6-16-76	1997	Massapequa, N.Y.
House, J.R.	.258	112	426	51	110	25	1	11	56	37	103	1	1	.399	.323	B	R	6-1	202	11-11-79	1999	Ormond Beach, Fla.
Langston, James	.282	28	103	9	29	3	1	0	7	2	22	0	1	.330	.295	B	R	6-3	198	3-23-78	1999	Lawrenceville, Ga.
Lankford, Derrick	.158	16	19	2	3	1	1	0	2	1	6	0	0	.316	.200	L	R	6-2	228	9-21-74	1997	Knoxville, Tenn.
Mann, Derek	.000	1	3	0	0	0	0	0	0	1	0	0	0	.000	.000	L	R	6-0	166	3-8-78	1996	Columbus, Ga.
Martin, Justin	.329	63	161	20	53	7	0	0	13	14	21	16	6	.373	.388	B	R	5-8	160	2-19-76	1999	Reno, Nev.
Meier, Dan	.256	97	312	43	80	14	4	13	38	45	80	1	1	.452	.355	L	L	6-0	200	8-13-77	1998	Aurora, Colo.
Monahan, Shane	.296	21	71	9	21	6	1	2	10	4	12	1	2	.493	.333	L	R	6-0	195	8-12-74	1995	Marietta, Ga.
Paz, Richard	.238	85	248	30	59	15	1	4	30	52	55	7	6	.355	.374	R	R	5-8	172	7-30-77	1994	Los Teques, Venez.
Petersen, Chris	.210	38	100	7	21	6	0	0	11	17	20	1	2	.270	.333	R	R	5-11	175	11-6-70	1992	Southington, Conn.
Rivera, Carlos	.234	111	389	44	91	30	0	10	50	13	71	0	2	.388	.258	L	L	5-11	230	6-10-78	1996	Rio Grande, P.R.
Secrist, Reed	.071	4	14	0	1	0	0	0	1	1	6	0	0	.071	.133	L	R	6-1	205	5-7-70	1992	Farmington, Utah
Skrehot, Shaun	.267	117	468	61	125	30	6	6	45	30	63	24	15	.395	.315	R	R	5-9	172	12-5-75	1998	Spring, Texas
Stoner, Mike	.252	42	135	15	34	7	3	3	21	2	21	0	3	.385	.282	R	R	6-0	210	5-23-73	1996	Shelbyville, Ky.
Washington, Rico	.302	75	291	31	88	17	0	4	29	21	49	5	5	.402	.360	L	R	5-10	182	5-30-78	1997	Gray, Ga.
Wehner, John	.228	25	92	10	21	3	0	0	8	3	11	4	0	.261	.258	R	R	6-3	205	6-29-67	1988	Cranberry Township, Pa.

PITCHING

PITCHING	W	L	ERA	G	GS	CG	SV	IP	H	R	ER	BB	SO	AVG	B	T	HT	WT	DOB	1st Yr	Resides
Alvarado, Carlos	5	7	3.36	26	10	0	0	83	74	46	31	29	73	.233	R	R	6-3	213	1-24-78	1995	Arecibo, P.R.
Ayers, Mike	1	1	2.25	7	0	0	0	8	8	2	2	3	6	.275	L	L	5-10	206	12-23-73	1996	Cincinnati, Ohio
Bennett, Jeff	0	1	3.86	1	1	0	0	7	9	3	3	2	6	.275	R	R	6-1	201	6-10-80	1998	Brush Creek, Tenn.
Burnside, Adrian	0	2	3.62	6	6	0	0	32	28	15	13	14	32	.235	R	L	6-3	168	3-15-77	1996	Alice Springs, Australia
Camp, Shawn	4	0	4.24	8	3	0	0	23	25	14	11	8	19	.277	R	R	6-1	200	11-18-75	1997	Fairfax, Va.
Carrasco, Dan	2	2	4.14	27	1	0	1	37	34	22	17	25	35	.239	R	R	6-3	191	4-12-77	1997	Safford, Ariz.
Chaney, Mike	0	0	6.75	4	0	0	0	9	18	7	7	2	2	.418	B	L	6-3	200	10-3-74	1996	Westchester, Ohio
Chrysler, Clint	4	3	3.28	51	0	0	3	49	52	24	18	12	31	.262	L	L	6-0	190	11-4-75	1997	St. Petersburg, Fla.
Cordova, Francisco	0	0	4.15	1	1	0	0	4	6	2	2	1	4	.333	R	R	6-1	197	4-26-72	1996	Veracruz, Mexico
Diorio, Mike	1	4	7.91	18	0	0	0	33	40	34	29	19	14	.303	R	R	6-2	215	3-1-73	1993	Kenner, La.
Donaldson, Bo	3	1	3.10	17	0	0	5	20	12	7	7	7	22	.169	R	R	6-0	200	10-10-74	1997	Philadelphia, Pa.
France, Aaron	1	2	5.68	7	5	0	0	25	36	19	16	10	17	.352	L	R	6-3	188	4-17-74	1994	Anaheim, Calif.
Galvez, Randy	5	6	3.45	15	15	0	0	86	93	40	33	22	45	.280	R	R	6-2	167	7-26-78	1995	Guasave, Mexico
Garcia, Mike	2	0	0.45	18	0	0	4	20	15	1	1	4	15	.211	R	R	6-2	220	5-11-68	1989	Moreno Valley, Calif.
Gonzalez, Mike	5	4	3.71	14	14	1	0	87	81	38	36	36	66	.250	R	L	6-2	217	5-23-78	1997	Pasadena, Texas
Grabow, John	2	5	3.38	10	10	0	0	51	30	23	19	39	42	.175	L	L	6-2	189	11-4-78	1997	San Gabriel, Calif.
Guy, Brad	3	4	4.03	28	4	0	4	51	59	32	23	17	30	.292	R	R	6-2	192	10-25-75	1997	Eureka, Calif.
Lopez, Jose	1	2	4.83	6	5	0	0	32	38	20	17	11	23	.290	R	R	5-11	195	1-28-76	1999	Corpus Christi, Texas
Manzueta, Roberto	1	1	5.40	12	0	0	0	20	19	13	12	11	14	.256	L	R	6-1	197	12-28-78	1995	Cotui, D.R.
McDade, Neal	5	4	5.05	19	9	0	0	73	85	38	33	24	55	.289	R	R	6-3	216	6-16-76	1993	Orange Park, Fla.
Mulholland, Terry	0	2	3.86	2	2	0	0	2	5	3	1	1	3	.416	R	L	6-3	220	3-9-63	1984	Scottsdale, Ariz.
Padua, Geraldo	0	1	9.69	10	0	0	0	13	17	14	14	6	10	.333	R	R	6-2	165	2-9-77	1995	Santo Domingo, D.R.
Pavlovich, Tony	0	3	2.98	31	0	0	12	42	38	15	14	13	26	.245	R	R	5-10	190	8-23-74	1994	Pavo, Ga.
Phillips, Jason	1	0	10.00	6	1	0	0	9	13	10	10	4	4	.418	R	R	6-6	225	3-22-74	1992	Hughesville, Pa.
Reid, Justin	5	5	2.54	17	16	1	0	110	104	38	31	14	70	.244	R	R	6-6	200	6-30-77	1999	Folsom, Calif.
Rodriguez, Frank	0	0	4.82	7	0	0	0	9	9	6	5	8	5	.243	R	R	5-9	160	1-6-73	1992	Rowland Heights, Calif.
Schmidt, Jason	0	1	0.96	3	3	0	0	9	7	1	1	1	17	.200	R	R	6-5	213	1-29-73	1991	Longview, Wash.

ORGANIZATION STATISTICS

PITCHING

	W	L	ERA	G	GS	CG	SV	IP	H	R	ER	BB	SO	AVG	B	T	HT	WT	DOB	1st Yr	Resides
Silva, Jose	0	0	0.00	2	0	0	0	1	2	0	0	1	2	.333	R	R	6-5	235	12-19-73	1991	San Diego, Calif.
Smith, Brian	0	0	0.00	2	0	0	0	4	3	0	0	0	3	.187	R	R	6-0	190	7-19-72	1994	Toney, Ala.
Sparks, Steve	1	4	3.76	7	6	1	0	38	31	19	16	25	32	.224	R	R	6-4	210	3-28-75	1998	Mobile, Ala.
Spurling, Chris	5	7	3.11	34	15	0	1	122	133	48	42	28	63	.279	R	R	6-6	240	6-28-77	1998	Englewood, Ohio
Williams, Dave	5	2	2.61	9	8	1	0	59	45	17	17	12	39	.211	L	L	6-2	203	3-12-79	1998	Camden, Del.
Wimberly, Larry	3	2	4.17	24	7	0	0	69	75	36	32	18	43	.279	L	L	6-0	190	8-22-75	1994	Zellwood, Fla.

FIELDING

Catcher	PCT	G	PO	A	E	DP	PB
Doumit	1.000	1	3	1	0	0	0
Evans	.988	49	276	48	4	4	4
Haad	1.000	1	8	1	0	0	0
House	.991	88	590	61	6	1	14
Secrist	1.000	2	6	1	0	0	0
Washington	1.000	2	13	0	0	0	0
Martin	.978	30	59	73	3	9	
Paz	.973	48	96	124	6	29	
Petersen	.976	20	59	61	3	17	
Washington	.936	23	54	48	7	13	
Wehner	1.000	1	5	5	0	2	
Wehner	.962	18	26	50	3	8	

First Base	PCT	G	PO	A	E	DP
Evans	.979	7	45	2	1	6
Haverbusch	.966	6	28	0	1	5
House	.990	12	100	3	1	8
Meier	.992	35	231	17	2	18
Rivera	.989	100	863	48	10	80
Stoner	1.000	3	17	2	0	1

Second Base	PCT	G	PO	A	E	DP
Alvarez	1.000	1	1	0	0	0
Bruce	.981	8	23	29	1	7
Haverbusch	.958	25	51	63	5	13
Mann	.800	1	3	1	1	0

Third Base	PCT	G	PO	A	E	DP
Bruce	.667	2	1	1	1	0
Evans	.868	30	22	37	9	3
Langston	.942	28	22	43	4	3
Martin	.800	1	2	2	1	0
Paz	.893	30	20	47	8	4
Petersen	.955	8	9	12	1	1
Washington	.953	49	39	102	7	6
Wehner	1.000	1	1	0	0	0

Shortstop	PCT	G	PO	A	E	DP
Paz	1.000	6	8	12	0	2
Petersen	.906	10	11	18	3	3
Skrehot	.951	113	190	350	28	73
Washington	.000	1	0	0	0	0

Outfield	PCT	G	PO	A	E	DP
Alvarado	.000	1	0	0	0	0
Alvarez	.968	65	112	8	4	0
Barns	.948	30	71	2	4	1
Bass	.962	49	74	2	3	0
Burton	.980	74	142	5	3	0
Davis	1.000	62	110	1	0	0
Evans	1.000	26	32	4	0	0
Green	.983	25	56	3	1	0
Haverbusch	1.000	4	5	1	0	0
Lankford	1.000	4	3	1	0	1
Martin	.976	29	40	1	1	0
Meier	.976	52	78	4	2	0
Monahan	.967	19	28	1	1	0
Rivera	.000	1	0	0	0	0
Secrist	1.000	1	3	0	0	0
Skrehot	1.000	6	11	1	0	0
Stoner	1.000	21	29	0	0	0
Wehner	1.000	4	8	0	0	0

LYNCHBURG — Class A

CAROLINA LEAGUE

BATTING

	AVG	G	AB	R	H	2B	3B	HR	RBI	BB	SO	SB	CS	SLG	OBP	B	T	HT	WT	DOB	1st Yr	Resides
Alvarez, Tony	.344	25	93	10	32	4	0	2	11	7	11	7	3	.452	.390	R	R	6-1	202	5-10-79	1995	Los Teques, Venez.
Barns, B.J.	.246	103	386	60	95	18	4	6	57	31	87	5	2	.360	.321	L	L	6-4	195	7-21-77	1999	Loysville, Pa.
Bass, Chris	.150	7	20	4	3	0	0	3	5	8	1	1	.200	.320	R	R	6-2	185	10-18-81	2000	Madison, Ind.
Bonifay, Josh	.297	85	323	42	96	14	1	13	41	26	87	5	4	.467	.355	R	R	6-0	190	7-30-78	1999	Gibsonia, Pa.
Brown, Adrian	.333	4	18	2	6	0	0	0	1	1	3	2	0	.333	.400	B	R	6-0	185	2-7-74	1992	Summit, Miss.
Castillo, Jose	.245	125	485	57	119	20	7	7	49	21	94	23	10	.359	.288	R	R	5-11	185	3-19-81	1997	Las Mercedes, Venez.
Cleto, Ambioris	.166	71	193	22	32	12	0	1	14	9	53	7	1	.244	.214	R	R	5-10	158	1-5-80	1996	Santo Domingo, D.R.
Combs, Chris	.227	133	463	68	105	18	4	12	53	66	153	2	1	.361	.328	L	R	6-7	234	5-19-75	1997	Raleigh, N.C.
DeCaster, Yurendell	.104	13	48	1	5	2	0	0	4	3	16	0	0	.146	.157	R	R	6-1	202	9-26-79	1996	Curacao, Netherlands Antilles
Espinoza, Efren	.145	19	62	4	9	2	0	0	4	2	19	1	1	.177	.185	R	R	6-0	174	9-13-80	1998	Obregon, Mexico
Garrett, Shawn	.294	52	194	28	57	13	0	9	28	17	64	6	4	.500	.360	B	R	6-3	190	11-2-78	1998	Kinmundy, Ill.
Haad, Yamid	.182	3	11	0	2	1	0	0	1	0	3	1	0	.273	.182	R	R	6-2	204	9-2-77	1994	Cartagena, Colombia
Harts, Jeremy	.210	125	410	50	86	17	1	3	34	46	151	10	11	.278	.297	B	L	6-1	186	6-6-80	1998	Decatur, Ga.
Hernandez, Jose	.163	24	80	7	13	3	0	0	6	4	13	1	0	.200	.221	R	R	6-1	194	11-3-80	1998	Valencia, Venez.
Langston, James	.265	101	381	29	101	30	0	2	45	15	83	0	4	.360	.294	B	R	6-3	198	3-23-78	1999	Lawrenceville, Ga.
Mann, Derek	.275	38	102	14	28	3	2	0	11	9	25	4	2	.343	.333	L	R	6-0	186	3-8-78	1996	Columbus, Ga.
Martin, Justin	.287	50	181	25	52	8	1	0	7	17	34	4	9	.343	.353	R	R	5-8	160	2-19-76	1998	Reno, Nev.
Meier, Dan	.288	20	73	11	21	7	0	3	12	10	21	1	1	.507	.369	L	L	6-0	202	8-13-77	1998	Aurora, Colo.
Paulino, Ron	.290	103	352	30	102	16	1	6	51	36	76	4	1	.392	.353	R	R	6-1	194	4-21-81	1997	Santo Domingo, D.R.
Prieto, Jonathan	.210	115	395	41	83	12	2	1	32	37	76	21	7	.258	.285	R	R	5-9	179	6-24-80	1997	San Bernardino, Venez.
Ravelo, Manny	.250	20	80	17	20	0	2	0	2	9	15	16	3	.300	.355	R	R	5-10	158	8-8-81	1997	Santo Domingo, D.R.
Reyes, Milver	.103	19	29	2	3	0	0	0	1	2	7	0	0	.103	.188	R	R	5-11	170	9-3-82	1999	San Felipe, Venez.
Sickles, Jeremy	.239	29	92	4	22	6	0	2	6	6	23	1	2	.370	.300	R	R	6-4	194	1-16-78	1999	Long Beach, Calif.
Weichard, Paul	.243	19	70	10	17	1	0	0	5	3	22	1	0	.257	.270	B	L	5-10	195	11-7-79	1997	Ringwood, Australia

GAMES BY POSITION: C—Haad 3, Hernandez 22, Paulino 87, Reyes 9, Sickles 20. **1B**—Bonifay 6, Combs 111, Langston 11, Meier 5, Sickles 6. **2B**—Bonifay 12, Cleto 18, Mann 15, Martin 14, Prieto 83. **3B**—Bonifay 5, Cleto 34, DeCaster 9, Espinoza 15, Langston 87. **SS**—Castillo 121, Cleto 19, Espinoza 2, Mann 7. **OF**—Alvarez 21, Barns 101, Bass 4, Bonifay 51, Cleto 2, Espinoza 3, Garrett 42, Harts 124, Langston 1, Martin 33, Meier 7, Ravelo 20, Weichard 13.

PITCHING

	W	L	ERA	G	GS	CG	SV	IP	H	R	ER	BB	SO	AVG	B	T	HT	WT	DOB	1st Yr	Resides
Alcala, Jason	0	2	2.36	18	0	0	7	27	21	7	7	5	27	.216	R	R	6-2	183	9-18-80	1997	Cumana, Venez.
Alvarado, Carlos	0	0	3.27	4	1	0	0	11	8	5	4	7	8	.228	R	R	6-3	213	1-24-78	1995	Arecibo, P.R.
Bennett, Jeff	11	10	3.42	25	25	2	0	166	171	78	63	30	98	.267	R	R	6-1	201	6-10-80	1998	Brush Creek, Tenn.
Bradley, Bobby	1	2	3.12	9	9	0	0	49	44	23	17	20	46	.237	R	R	6-1	185	6-14-81	1998	Wellington, Fla.
Bumatay, Mike	1	7	7.27	23	1	0	2	43	55	39	35	26	40	.302	L	L	5-11	176	10-9-79	1998	Clovis, Calif.
Carrasco, Dan	4	0	1.50	22	0	0	7	36	18	7	6	14	40	.145	R	R	6-2	191	4-12-77	1997	Safford, Ariz.
Chaney, Mike	3	3	3.71	28	3	0	2	68	69	31	28	22	44	.263	B	L	6-3	200	10-3-74	1996	Westchester, Ohio
Dukeman, Greg	6	6	4.01	27	12	0	0	108	108	66	48	36	70	.262	R	R	6-7	203	12-6-78	1997	Costa Mesa, Calif.
Gonzalez, Mike	2	2	2.93	14	2	0	0	31	28	14	10	7	32	.241	R	L	6-2	217	5-23-78	1997	Pasadena, Texas
Grabow, John	3	6	6.38	7	7	0	0	37	42	30	26	26	35	.293	L	L	6-2	189	11-4-78	1997	San Gabriel, Calif.
Hurley, Derek	0	3	3.52	17	1	0	1	38	39	23	15	19	20	.284	L	L	6-2	185	7-25-77	1999	Staten Island, N.Y.
Jacobsen, Landon	5	7	3.34	17	17	1	0	105	101	50	39	38	83	.255	R	R	6-0	210	5-4-79	1999	Canova, S.D.
Johnston, Clint	1	1	5.29	11	0	0	0	17	15	11	10	14	20	.300	L	L	6-2	210	7-2-77	1998	Nashville, Tenn.
Johnston, Mike	4	4	3.34	11	10	1	0	62	66	27	23	24	44	.271	L	L	6-3	198	3-30-79	1998	Colwyn, Pa.
Ledden, Ryan	9	13	5.42	27	25	3	0	153	184	112	92	53	73	.298	R	R	6-4	195	10-19-77	1997	Lilburn, Ga.
Lopez, Jose	5	4	2.37	13	13	0	0	76	63	28	20	23	70	.232	R	R	5-11	195	1-28-76	1999	Corpus Christi, Texas
Manzueta, Roberto	0	3	2.66	15	0	0	1	24	18	11	7	12	30	.204	L	R	6-1	197	12-28-78	1995	Cotui, D.R.
Montilla, Felix	0	1	9.00	7	0	0	1	7	11	7	7	2	3	.354	R	R	6-1	191	3-7-80	1997	Santo Domingo, D.R.
Pavlovich, Tony	1	0	0.39	20	0	0	13	23	13	1	1	5	27	.181	R	R	5-10	193	8-23-74	1994	Pavo, Ga.
Pena, Alex	2	4	6.11	25	3	0	3	53	61	39	36	35	31	.293	R	R	6-2	205	9-9-77	1994	Santo Domingo, D.R.
Reid, Justin	2	4	2.25	8	8	1	0	56	50	15	14	6	48	.235	R	R	6-6	200	6-30-77	1999	Folsom, Calif.
Torres, Luis	0	0	13.50	4	0	0	0	3	6	7	5	3	4	.375	R	R	5-10	177	6-6-80	1998	Falcon, Venez.

SOUTH ATLANTIC LEAGUE

BATTING	AVG	G	AB	R	H	2B	3B	HR	RBI	BB	SO	SB	CS	SLG	OBP	B	T	HT	WT	DOB	1st Yr	Resides
Aliendo, Humberto	.130	19	69	3	9	1	0	0	5	2	21	1	0	.145	.176	R	R	6-1	170	10-31-80	1998	Miranda, Venez.
Bass, Chris	.247	106	352	34	87	18	1	3	34	22	80	6	3	.330	.299	R	R	6-2	185	10-18-81	2000	Madison, Ind.
Bonifay, Josh	.323	17	65	10	21	4	0	2	10	5	15	2	3	.477	.380	R	R	6-0	190	7-30-78	1999	Gibsonia, Pa.
Buttler, Vic	.244	92	299	38	73	10	2	2	23	15	49	11	3	.311	.287	L	L	5-11	180	8-12-80	2000	Hawthorne, Calif.
Castro, Vince	.215	55	172	16	37	6	2	1	20	7	47	6	2	.291	.254	R	R	6-0	180	5-19-80	1997	San Pedro de Macoris, D.R.
Chaves, Brandon	.199	110	356	29	71	12	4	2	32	28	89	8	4	.272	.273	R	R	6-3	175	8-5-79	2000	Hilo, Hawaii
Ciarrachi, Kevin	.000	2	7	1	0	0	0	0	0	1	3	0	0	.000	.125	R	R	6-1	195	3-27-78	1999	Lombard, Ill.
Cotten, Jeremy	.253	125	443	58	112	20	2	25	78	42	132	12	5	.476	.337	R	R	6-3	229	9-24-80	1998	Fuquay-Varina, N.C.
Cuello, Domingo	.220	18	59	6	13	0	1	0	2	2	11	6	1	.254	.242	R	R	5-11	160	4-12-83	1999	Santo Domingo, D.R.
DeCaster, Yurendell	.290	97	341	56	99	17	4	19	74	35	83	4	4	.531	.365	R	R	6-1	202	9-26-79	1996	Curacao, Netherlands Antilles
De la Cruz, Miguel	.222	12	36	3	8	1	0	0	1	4	12	0	1	.250	.349	R	R	6-2	180	10-18-79	1997	Santo Domingo, D.R.
Doumit, Ryan	.270	39	148	14	40	6	0	2	14	10	32	2	1	.351	.333	B	R	6-0	180	4-3-81	1999	Moses Lake, Wash.
Espinoza, Efren	.222	50	162	18	36	9	0	5	21	5	49	2	0	.370	.266	R	R	6-0	174	9-13-80	1998	Obregon, Mexico
Hernandez, Jose	.161	53	161	19	26	4	0	1	13	12	35	3	0	.205	.239	R	R	6-1	194	11-3-80	1998	Valencia, Venez.
McLouth, Nathan	.285	96	351	59	100	17	5	12	54	43	54	21	5	.464	.371	L	R	5-11	170	10-28-81	2000	Whitehall, Mich.
Mejia, Manuel	.216	46	125	6	27	2	0	2	13	18	37	0	0	.280	.327	R	R	6-3	190	11-5-79	1996	Santo Domingo, D.R.
Navarrete, Ray	.268	92	354	53	95	23	2	10	49	21	70	9	4	.429	.320	R	R	6-0	185	5-28-80	2000	Cotts Neck, N.J.
Nicolas, Jose	.206	31	102	13	21	7	1	3	10	9	41	3	0	.382	.281	R	R	6-3	217	1-1-79	1997	Miami, Fla.
Ravelo, Manny	.299	93	365	57	109	12	7	1	20	28	64	54	17	.378	.358	R	R	5-10	158	8-8-81	1997	Santo Domingo, D.R.
Riera, Zack	.143	34	98	11	14	4	0	0	6	9	21	0	1	.184	.288	B	R	6-0	195	4-16-79	2000	Tallahassee, Fla.
Weston, Aron	.122	20	74	8	9	2	1	0	2	3	25	5	1	.176	.195	L	L	6-6	172	11-5-80	1999	Solon, Ohio
Yan, Edwin	.283	128	446	58	126	8	4	2	24	42	62	56	21	.332	.347	B	R	6-0	165	2-18-82	1999	Santo Domingo, D.R.

GAMES BY POSITION: C—Ciarrachi 2, Doumit 23, Hernandez 50, Mejia 39, Riera 33, Yan 1. **1B**—Bass 35, Cotton 110, Espinoza 1, Mejia 4. **2B**—Bass 1, Bonifay 8, Cuello 17, Espinoza 33, Hernandez 1, McLouth 1, Navarrete 19, Yan 68. **3B**—Bass 28, Chaves 18, DeCaster 62, Doumit 10, Espinoza 9, Navarrete 20. **SS**—Chaves 90, Espinoza 1, Yan 53. **OF**—Aliendo 19, Bonifay 8, Buttler 87, Castro 52, Espinoza 3, McLouth 93, Navarrete 43, Nicolas 30, Ravelo 90, Weston 16.

PITCHING	W	L	ERA	G	GS	CG	SV	IP	H	R	ER	BB	SO	AVG	B	T	HT	WT	DOB	1st Yr	Resides
Alcala, Jason	3	1	1.76	34	0	0	7	41	35	12	8	13	56	.222	R	R	6-2	183	9-18-80	1997	Cumana, Venez.
Almonte, Henry	2	2	6.58	20	1	0	0	26	39	25	19	17	17	.351	R	R	6-2	160	5-31-81	1998	Hato Mayor, D.R.
Borner, Brady	5	1	2.43	9	8	3	0	59	43	18	16	12	58	.201	L	L	5-10	175	4-12-79	2001	Chaska, Minn.
Bumatay, Mike	1	0	2.73	15	1	0	0	26	20	10	8	8	31	.208	L	L	5-11	176	10-9-79	1998	Clovis, Calif.
Burnett, Sean	11	8	2.62	26	26	1	0	161	164	63	47	33	134	.264	L	L	6-1	172	9-17-82	2000	Wellington, Fla.
Cabell, Shannon	1	9	3.45	42	0	0	2	63	73	35	24	26	58	.296	L	L	6-0	185	4-7-79	2000	Ona, W.Va.
Connolly, Mike	11	7	3.94	33	15	2	0	121	116	59	53	41	107	.255	L	L	5-11	175	6-2-82	2000	Oneonta, N.Y.
De los Santos, Carlos	2	5	6.69	13	7	0	0	38	44	33	28	28	31	.305	R	R	6-0	175	4-11-81	1998	Santo Domingo, D.R.
Friedberg, Drew	0	1	6.20	17	0	0	1	20	26	16	14	9	15	.320	L	L	6-2	205	3-3-79	2001	Middleton, Wis.
Guerrero, Julio	1	4	4.45	11	9	0	0	55	65	37	27	17	24	.290	R	R	6-4	185	1-4-81	1999	San Pedro de Macoris, D.R.
Hawk, David	2	1	4.01	17	3	0	0	25	25	15	11	17	18	.257	L	L	6-5	179	6-20-79	1998	Bakersfield, Calif.
Henderson, Kenny	0	3	5.29	27	0	0	1	34	29	22	20	16	35	.224	R	L	6-4	205	11-9-77	2000	Port Washington, N.Y.
Higgins, Josh	2	2	2.07	55	0	0	23	61	40	15	14	11	71	.182	R	R	6-6	180	6-16-79	2000	Santee, Calif.
Hurley, Derek	4	7	4.37	17	14	0	0	82	97	59	40	32	42	.296	L	L	6-2	185	7-25-77	1999	Staten Island, N.Y.
Jacobsen, Landon	1	4	3.38	9	9	0	0	53	45	24	20	9	50	.227	R	R	6-0	210	5-4-79	1999	Canova, S.D.
Johnston, Mike	4	5	3.38	16	16	0	0	93	88	47	35	42	80	.249	L	L	6-3	198	3-30-79	1998	Colwyn, Pa.
Levesque, Ben	1	2	9.33	16	0	0	0	18	23	20	19	15	8	.333	R	R	6-3	187	10-9-79	1998	Longwood, Fla.
Messer, Ben	1	0	5.84	17	0	0	0	25	27	19	16	9	13	.281	R	R	6-4	208	4-6-77	1999	Shawnee, Kan.
O'Brien, Patrick	6	5	3.16	11	11	0	0	74	73	30	26	14	67	.257	R	R	6-5	195	11-20-80	1999	Bath, Ohio
Pearson, Brent	2	0	0.00	3	0	0	0	5	3	0	0	2	4	.200	R	R	6-0	170	8-6-79	2001	Tallahassee, Fla.
Sabens, Mike	0	1	10.95	10	0	0	0	12	22	16	15	10	10	.379	R	R	6-1	200	1-21-77	1999	Hiram, Ga.
Shafer, Kurt	0	0	1.42	1	1	0	0	6	5	1	1	3	5	.227	R	R	6-4	190	12-4-81	2000	Land O' Lakes, Fla.
Sharber, Jeff	2	2	1.99	7	7	0	0	45	34	13	10	19	57	.207	R	R	6-3	215	2-24-82	2000	Murfreesboro, Tenn.
Young, Chris	5	3	4.12	12	12	2	0	74	79	39	34	20	72	.268	R	R	6-10	255	5-25-79	2001	Dallas, Texas

NEW YORK-PENN LEAGUE

BATTING	AVG	G	AB	R	H	2B	3B	HR	RBI	BB	SO	SB	CS	SLG	OBP	B	T	HT	WT	DOB	1st Yr	Resides
Aliendo, Humberto	.211	45	152	17	32	9	1	2	15	11	45	1	0	.322	.268	R	R	6-1	170	10-31-80	1998	Miranda, Venez.
Asprilla, Avelino	.257	56	183	28	47	9	2	1	20	7	36	9	3	.344	.285	R	R	5-11	155	1-1-82	1998	Panama City, Panama
Bautista, Jose	.286	62	220	43	63	10	3	5	30	21	41	8	1	.427	.364	R	R	6-0	190	10-19-80	2001	Santo Domingo, D.R.
Brown, Adrian	.333	4	18	4	6	0	1	0	4	1	2	2	0	.444	.368	B	R	6-0	185	2-7-74	1992	Summit, Miss.
Cabrera, Yoelmis	.181	42	127	12	23	5	1	1	12	7	27	5	5	.260	.228	R	R	5-11	155	10-4-81	1997	Santo Domingo, D.R.
Chapman, Travis	.291	17	55	6	16	3	1	0	4	1	9	0	1	.382	.322	R	R	6-2	206	9-6-80	2001	Fort Walton Beach, Fla.
Cortes, Jorge	.254	51	189	23	48	17	1	2	31	20	25	2	2	.386	.329	L	L	5-8	185	10-17-80	1997	Barranquilla, Colombia
Cruz, Alex	.181	26	83	9	15	1	1	0	11	4	14	1	0	.217	.213	R	R	6-0	170	4-9-81	2000	Ridge Manor, Fla.
Cuello, Domingo	.278	62	230	35	64	9	2	6	30	16	40	28	6	.413	.328	R	R	5-11	160	4-12-83	1999	Santo Domingo, D.R.
Davis, Rajai	.083	6	12	1	1	0	0	0	2	4	0	1	0	.083	.214	B	R	5-11	170	10-19-80	2001	New London, Conn.
De la Cruz, Miguel	.206	42	131	19	27	9	2	0	15	18	33	1	2	.305	.303	R	R	6-2	180	10-18-79	1997	Santo Domingo, D.R.
Duffy, Chris	.317	64	221	50	70	12	4	1	24	33	33	30	5	.421	.440	B	L	5-10	185	4-20-80	2001	Glendale, Ariz.
Hudnall, Josh	.282	40	124	17	35	4	3	0	16	7	31	17	2	.363	.338	R	R	6-3	171	2-22-80	1999	Monroe, La.
Meath, Matt	.324	32	102	22	33	5	2	1	8	21	24	13	3	.441	.446	R	R	6-0	175	10-6-79	2001	Boca Raton, Fla.
Myler, Jonathan	.189	23	74	6	14	5	0	1	8	10	20	0	0	.297	.286	R	R	6-0	175	8-5-79	2001	Warren, Pa.
Riera, Zack	.500	2	4	3	2	0	0	0	0	4	0	1	1	.500	.750	B	R	6-0	195	4-16-79	2000	Tallahassee, Fla.
Shelton, Chris	.305	50	174	22	53	11	0	2	33	33	31	4	1	.402	.415	R	R	6-0	205	6-26-80	2001	Salt Lake City, Utah
VanBenschoten, John	.227	32	75	9	17	5	0	0	8	7	23	3	2	.293	.302	R	R	6-4	215	4-14-80	2001	Milford, Ohio
Veleber, Troy	.154	14	26	8	4	1	0	1	2	1	8	6	0	.308	.185	B	R	5-10	165	6-7-79	2000	Jacksonville, Fla.
Young, Walter	.289	66	232	40	67	10	1	13	47	19	43	1	1	.509	.353	L	R	6-5	309	2-18-80	1999	Purvis, Miss.

GAMES BY POSITION: C—Chapman 12, Myler 23, Riera 2, Shelton 40. **1B**—Aliendo 1, de la Cruz 24, Shelton 9, Young 48. **2B**—Aliendo 1, Asprilla 2, Cruz 12, Cuello 62, Davis 2, Hudnall 3. **3B**—Bautista 59, Cruz 2, de la Cruz 15, Hudnall 2. **SS**—Asprilla 54, Cruz 13, Cuello 1, Hudnall 13. **OF**—Aliendo 17, Bautista 3, Cabrera 39, Cortes 49, Davis 3, Duffy 60, Hudnall 22, Meath 32, Veleber 9.

PITCHING	W	L	ERA	G	GS	CG	SV	IP	H	R	ER	BB	SO	AVG	B	T	HT	WT	DOB	1st Yr	Resides
Biddlestone, Jason	3	1	1.44	16	1	0	1	31	28	11	5	17	25	.245	R	R	6-4	202	8-12-78	1999	Westerville, Ohio
Borner, Brady	1	0	0.71	3	1	0	0	13	4	1	1	1	13	.100	L	L	5-10	175	4-12-79	2001	Chaska, Minn.
Burruezo, Joe	1	2	3.60	14	2	0	1	20	22	16	8	10	17	.271	R	R	5-11	174	9-10-80	1999	Tampa, Fla.
Clark, Claudell	1	4	3.86	18	0	0	1	30	17	19	13	24	26	.171	R	L	5-11	185	11-20-79	2001	Chesapeake, Va.
D'Amato, Dan	4	1	2.17	20	0	0	2	29	21	10	7	13	32	.203	L	L	6-1	190	11-8-79	2001	Coatesville, Pa.
De los Santos, Carlos	5	3	2.98	14	13	0	0	82	73	34	27	29	80	.244	R	R	6-0	175	4-11-81	1998	Santo Domingo, D.R.
Dutremble, Jeff	1	0	6.85	17	0	0	0	24	29	20	18	27	25	.311	L	L	6-2	200	10-8-78	2001	Biddeford, Maine
Fortin, Michael	1	0	6.00	4	0	0	0	6	5	4	4	6	5	.250	R	R	6-5	205	7-31-77	2000	Holyoke, Mass.
Friedberg, Drew	0	0	0.00	4	0	0	3	4	2	0	0	0	6	.153	L	L	6-2	205	3-3-79	2001	Middleton, Wis.
Gilchrist, Ron	4	0	3.18	16	0	0	0	23	21	8	8	8	27	.247	L	L	6-0	200	1-17-78	2001	Plaquemine, La.
Guerrero, Julio	2	4	4.50	7	0	0	0	16	18	14	8	4	13	.285	R	R	6-4	185	1-4-81	1999	San Pedro de Macoris, D.R.
Hawk, David	0	0	4.50	2	0	0	0	4	2	2	2	2	4	.166	L	L	6-5	179	6-20-79	1998	Bakersfield, Calif.
Lissir, Alexander	0	0	1.80	2	0	0	0	5	4	1	1	2	6	.235	R	R	6-0	170	12-29-82	1999	Tucacas, Venez.
Miller, Jeff	0	0	1.13	21	0	0	15	24	17	3	3	5	28	.197	R	R	6-4	225	2-1-80	2001	Springfield, N.J.
Novoa, Roberto	5	5	3.39	14	13	1	0	80	76	40	30	20	55	.255	R	R	6-5	200	8-16-81	1999	Santo Domingo, D.R.
Oquendo, Ian	7	0	1.39	10	9	1	0	65	55	16	10	10	56	.204	R	R	5-11	160	10-30-81	2000	Bradenton, Fla.
Rodriguez, Juan	8	2	1.89	13	13	0	0	81	61	23	17	15	58	.207	R	R	6-1	190	6-10-81	1999	Montecristi, D.R.
Searles, Jon	5	4	3.82	14	11	0	0	73	63	38	31	23	65	.229	R	R	6-3	200	1-18-81	1999	Huntington, N.Y.
Silva, Jose	0	0	0.00	2	2	0	0	2	2	0	0	2	2	.250	R	R	6-5	235	12-19-73	1991	San Diego, Calif.
Story, Aaron	0	0	9.00	3	0	0	0	4	7	4	4	3	5	.411	L	L	6-0	179	10-2-80	1999	Lawrenceburg, Tenn.
VanBenschoten, John	0	2	3.51	9	9	0	0	25	23	11	10	10	19	.000	R	R	6-4	215	4-14-80	2001	Milford, Ohio

BRADENTON — Rookie

GULF COAST LEAGUE

BATTING	AVG	G	AB	R	H	2B	3B	HR	RBI	BB	SO	SB	CS	SLG	OBP	B	T	HT	WT	DOB	1st Yr	Resides
Acosta, Johe	.212	20	66	7	14	2	2	0	10	8	17	2	0	.303	.333	R	R	6-5	190	12-19-81	2000	Santo Domingo, D.R.
Brown, Tim	.211	46	142	11	30	4	1	2	18	29	32	1	0	.296	.356	L	L	6-3	225	2-21-83	2001	Eugene, Ore.
Cockrell, Mike	.280	48	168	32	47	7	1	0	11	19	17	31	5	.333	.354	R	R	5-10	160	7-25-81	2001	Wilmington, Calif.
Collum, Michael	.289	35	114	17	33	9	2	5	21	15	40	2	1	.535	.383	R	R	6-3	185	7-16-81	2001	Wellington, Fla.
Cruz, Alex	.292	19	65	12	19	3	2	1	7	13	8	3	0	.446	.410	R	R	6-0	170	4-9-81	2000	Ridge Manor, Fla.
Davis, J.J.	.471	4	17	3	8	1	0	2	6	1	2	0	0	.882	.500	R	R	6-4	250	10-25-78	1997	Pomona, Calif.
Davis, Rajai	.262	26	84	19	22	1	0	0	4	13	26	11	3	.274	.364	B	R	5-11	170	10-19-80	2001	New London, Conn.
Doumit, Ryan	.235	7	17	2	4	2	0	0	3	2	0	0	0	.353	.316	B	R	6-0	180	4-3-81	1999	Moses Lake, Wash.
Johnson, Tristan	.143	25	77	5	11	1	0	0	4	6	32	1	0	.156	.202	R	L	6-3	230	3-1-82	2000	Woonsocket, R.I.
Mariot, Lino	.165	31	85	6	14	0	0	0	2	4	22	4	1	.165	.220	R	R	6-2	170	10-21-82	2001	Woodbridge, N.J.
McCuistion, Mike	.220	27	82	4	18	3	0	0	3	9	8	0	0	.256	.304	L	R	6-2	195	5-14-82	2001	Yucaipa, Calif.
Meath, Matt	.147	14	34	7	5	2	0	0	1	12	6	5	1	.206	.396	B	R	6-0	175	10-6-79	2001	Boca Raton, Fla.
Milauskas, Adam	.217	31	92	8	20	0	0	0	3	10	18	0	0	.217	.305	R	R	6-1	185	3-18-83	2001	St. Charles, Ill.
Navarrete, Ray	.222	3	9	1	2	1	0	0	1	2	3	0	1	.333	.364	R	R	6-0	185	5-20-78	2000	Cotts Neck, N.J.
Ramos, Victor	.200	29	80	5	16	2	0	0	4	6	10	0	1	.225	.261	L	R	6-3	192	10-4-81	2000	Cayey, P.R.
Recio, Bolivar	.136	6	22	4	3	1	0	0	2	2	7	0	1	.182	.200	R	R	6-2	180	1-14-81	1999	San Francisco de Macoris, D.R.
Rethwisch, Justin	.193	39	135	11	26	8	0	0	11	5	41	4	1	.252	.225	L	L	6-1	187	4-5-81	2001	Lancaster, Calif.
Reyes, Milver	.054	13	37	3	2	1	0	0	1	2	5	0	0	.081	.122	R	R	5-11	170	9-3-82	1999	San Felipe, Venez.
Rush, Travis	.244	33	82	4	20	5	1	1	5	12	16	5	2	.366	.361	R	R	6-0	180	12-7-81	2000	Americus, Ga.
Smith, Sean	.203	46	148	14	30	7	1	3	14	20	56	12	1	.324	.306	R	R	5-10	175	8-24-82	2000	Joliet, Ill.
Taylor, Mark	.215	38	130	9	28	5	1	0	10	0	32	0	3	.269	.226	R	R	6-6	205	7-14-79	2001	St. Augustine, Fla.

GAMES BY POSITION: C—Doumit 4, McCuistion 18, Ramos 29, Reyes 12, Rush 1. **1B**—Brown 36, Johnson 22. **2B**—Cockrell 45, Collum 1, Cruz 13, Meath 1. **3B**—Collum 7, Navarrete 2, Recio 5, Rush 9, Taylor 38. **SS**—Collum 22, Cruz 8, Mariot 31. **OF**—Acosta 19, J. Davis 1, R. Davis 26, Meath 13, Milauskas 31, Navarrete 1, Rethwisch 37, Rush 8, Smith 41.

PITCHING	W	L	ERA	G	GS	CG	SV	IP	H	R	ER	BB	SO	AVG	B	T	HT	WT	DOB	1st Yr	Resides
Albaladejo, Jonathan	0	3	4.74	10	2	0	1	19	22	13	10	2	24	.285	R	R	6-5	215	10-30-82	2001	Vega Alta, P.R.
Almonte, Henry	1	0	2.70	2	1	0	0	10	11	4	3	1	10	.282	R	R	6-2	160	5-31-81	1998	Hato Mayor, D.R.
Alvarez, Melvin	1	4	4.00	7	3	0	0	27	34	16	12	7	16	.323	L	L	6-4	165	11-24-81	1998	Puerto Plata, D.R.
Andara, Miguel	0	4	3.62	8	3	0	0	32	28	18	13	20	20	.239	R	R	6-2	175	11-14-81	1998	Caracas, Venez.
Beigh, David	0	5	6.46	10	7	0	0	31	30	28	22	28	24	.258	R	R	6-5	230	2-2-81	2000	Battle Ground, Ind.
Burzynski, Cole	1	2	6.46	7	5	0	0	24	26	19	17	23	28	.279	R	R	6-4	200	9-3-81	2000	Navasota, Texas
Grabow, John	0	1	3.75	6	6	0	0	12	11	6	5	4	9	.244	L	L	6-2	189	11-4-78	1997	San Gabriel, Calif.
Guerrero, Julio	0	2	2.84	3	2	0	0	6	5	2	2	1	6	.227	R	R	6-4	185	1-4-81	1999	San Pedro de Macoris, D.R.
Johnston, Clint	0	0	0.00	2	0	0	0	3	1	0	0	1	4	.111	L	L	6-2	210	7-2-77	1998	Nashville, Tenn.
Kiley, Jason	1	2	9.18	8	1	0	0	17	29	20	17	10	9	.408	R	R	6-4	220	10-15-82	2001	St. Charles, Ill.
Lee, Kevin	2	2	2.08	9	0	0	0	22	16	6	5	7	23	.200	R	R	6-4	200	11-18-81	2000	Wheaton, Ill.
Lissir, Alexander	2	0	0.66	6	0	0	1	14	13	5	1	6	18	.228	R	R	6-0	170	12-29-82	1999	Tucacas, Venez.
Morel, Jhosandy	0	0	1.93	6	0	0	0	9	7	2	2	5	12	.200	L	L	6-1	160	1-9-82	2001	Union City, N.J.
Nunez, Leo	2	2	4.39	10	7	1	0	53	62	28	26	9	34	.284	R	R	6-1	150	8-14-83	2000	Moca, D.R.
Oquendo, Ian	3	0	0.47	3	3	0	0	19	12	2	1	5	13	.184	R	R	5-11	160	10-30-81	2000	Bradenton, Fla.
Owens, Henry	1	0	1.29	6	0	0	1	7	5	1	1	2	8	.192	R	R	6-3	230	4-23-79	2001	Miami, Fla.
Pearson, Brent	0	2	1.35	11	0	0	7	13	8	4	2	8	15	.160	R	R	6-0	170	8-6-79	2001	Tallahassee, Fla.
Purcell, Brian	2	0	4.41	9	0	0	1	16	17	10	8	6	15	.257	L	L	6-4	190	1-4-81	2000	Gadsden, Ala.
Shafer, Kurt	3	4	3.50	12	6	1	1	54	54	24	21	9	41	.270	R	R	6-4	190	12-4-81	2000	Land O' Lakes, Fla.
Sharber, Jeff	1	0	0.50	3	3	0	0	18	5	1	1	4	19	.090	R	R	6-3	215	2-24-82	2000	Murfreesboro, Tenn.
Shortslef, Josh	2	3	3.63	10	4	1	0	35	39	23	14	9	14	.293	R	L	6-4	205	2-1-82	2000	Hannibal, N.Y.
Shroyer, Dustin	0	0	17.36	5	0	0	0	5	3	11	9	11	4	.187	R	L	6-3	205	12-20-79	2001	Nashport, Ohio
Torres, Luis	0	0	3.00	3	1	0	0	3	3	3	1	1	2	.230	R	R	5-10	177	6-6-80	1998	Falcon, Venez.

ORGANIZATION STATISTICS

ST. LOUIS CARDINALS

BY MIKE EISENBATH

The Cardinals went into the 2001 season with lofty expectations. Not only were they almost universally picked to repeat their championship in the National League Central but, thanks to a strong offense and deep pitching staff, they were considered a favorite to win their 16th NL pennant.

At season's end, though, the Cardinals were still stuck on 15.

They didn't win the Central title outright because the Astros beat them in a head-to-head matchup on the final day of the season. The two teams ended with the same record (93-69), but Houston won the tiebreaker, forcing St. Louis to become the wild-card team in the playoffs. Without home-field advantage, they lost a five-game series to the Diamondbacks.

Scoring runs often was a problem for the Cardinals, especially in the first half. Outfielder Jim Edmonds battled through a right shoulder injury, while outfielder J.D. Drew missed more than a month with a broken hand. Shortstop Edgar Renteria struggled to bust out of a miserable slump, and outfielder Ray Lankford struck out in record numbers before he was sent to San Diego in a trade for righthander Woody Williams. And Mark McGwire, who probably tried to come back too soon after offseason knee surgery, hit eight homers before the all-star break.

Cardinals pitchers had their problems, too. Lefthander Rick Ankiel failed to find his control in the big leagues and was dispatched to Rookie ball in June. Righthander Andy Benes pitched his way out of the starting rotation, while closer Dave Veres missed time with a circulatory problem in his hand.

If not for pitching, though, the Cardinals would have been out of the race by July. Righthander Matt Morris, who didn't pitch in 1999 because of elbow surgery, went 22-8. Righthanders Darryl Kile and Dustin Hermanson combined to win 30 games, while rookie lefthander Bud

Albert Pujols

Jim Journell

STEVE MOORE

JOHN SPEAR

PLAYERS OF THE YEAR

MAJOR LEAGUE: Albert Pujols, 3b/1b
Pujols joined Ted Williams as the only rookies with a .300 batting average, .400 on-base percentage and .600 slugging percentage in the same season.

MINOR LEAGUE: Jim Journell, rhp
Almost two years removed from Tommy John surgery, Journell dominated the Class A Carolina League, going 14-6, 2.50 with 156 strikeouts and 42 walks in 151 innings.

Smith won six of his 14 starts, including a no-hitter against the Padres. Williams, who had an 8-8 record when the Cardinals traded for him in early August, went 7-1 the rest of the way.

Lefthander Steve Kline anchored a strong, if unpredictable, bullpen by posting a 1.80 ERA in 89 appearances. He had the closer's job by the end of the season.

It's not that the lineup was completely disappointing. Albert Pujols (.329-37-130), who had significant playing time at first and third base and in left and right field, proved to be the team's most valuable player.

Second baseman Fernando Vina and third baseman Placido Polanco, the top two batters in the order, each finished with batting averages above .300 and played excellent defense.

The rest of the offense finally came around. Edmonds finished with a .300-plus average, 30 homers and 100 RBIs for the first time in his career. Drew hit .323-27-73 in 375 at-bats. Even McGwire, with a .187 average and pondering retirement, contributed 29 homers and 64 RBIs.

The Cardinals went 50-24 after July 13, when they were tied for third place and nine games out in the Central. They sat in first place alone on the next-to-last day of the season, but losing to the Astros on the final day cost them the division title.

None of the farm system's six clubs had a winning record. The overall record was 296-408, the worst showing in the organization since 1991 and the worst in the game. It was the third-lowest winning percentage (.420) for Cardinals farm clubs since Branch Rickey perfected the chain system in the 1920s.

The Cardinals' minor league player and pitcher of the year came from Class A Potomac: outfielder Covelli Crisp (.306-11-47) and righthander Jim Journell (14-6, 2.50). Journell threw a no-hitter in his lone Double-A start and overall struck out 162 and walked 45 in 158 innings.

ORGANIZATION LEADERS

BATTING
*AVG	John Gall, Potomac/Peoria	.311
R	Chris Morris, Peoria	89
H	John Gall, Potomac/Peoria	163
TB	John Gall, Potomac/Peoria	235
2B	John Gall, Potomac/Peoria	48
3B	Chris Morris, Peoria	9
HR	Andy Bevins, Memphis/New Haven	20
RBI	John Gall, Potomac/Peoria	77
BB	Chris Morris, Peoria	83
SO	Tim Lemon, Peoria	165
SB	Chris Morris, Peoria	111

PITCHING
W	Jim Journell, New Haven/Potomac	15
L	Frank Tejada, Potomac	14
	Dave Zancanaro, Memphis/New Haven	14
#ERA	Rick Ankiel, Memphis/Johnson City	2.25
G	Mike Crudale, New Haven	62
CG	Three tied at	2
SV	Scotty Layfield, Potomac	31
IP	Josh Pearce, Memphis/New Haven	185
BB	Chad Hutchinson, Memphis	104
SO	Rick Ankiel, Memphis/Johnson City	162
	Jim Journell, New Haven/Potomac	162

*Minimum 250 At-Bats #Minimum 75 Innings

ST. LOUIS CARDINALS

Manager: Tony La Russa

2001 Record: 93-69, .574 (t-1st, NL Central)

Jim Edmonds

ORGANIZATION STATISTICS

BATTING	AVG	G	AB	R	H	2B	3B	HR	RBI	BB	SO	SB	CS	SLG	OBP	B	T	HT	WT	DOB	1st Yr	Resides
Bonilla, Bobby	.213	93	174	17	37	7	0	5	21	23	53	1	1	.339	.308	B	R	6-4	240	2-23-63	1981	Greenwich, Conn.
Cairo, Miguel	.333	27	33	5	11	5	0	1	7	2	2	0	0	.576	.371	R	R	6-1	200	5-4-74	1991	St. Petersburg, Fla.
2-team (66 Chicago)	.295	93	156	25	46	8	1	3	16	18	23	2	1	.417	.366							
Clapp, Stubby	.200	23	25	0	5	2	0	0	1	1	7	0	0	.280	.231	L	R	5-8	175	2-24-73	1996	Windsor, Ontario
Drew, J.D.	.323	109	375	80	121	18	5	27	73	57	75	13	3	.613	.414	L	R	6-1	195	11-20-75	1997	Hahira, Ga.
Edmonds, Jim	.304	150	500	95	152	38	1	30	110	93	136	5	5	.564	.410	L	L	6-1	212	6-27-70	1988	Orange, Calif.
Lankford, Ray	.235	91	264	38	62	18	3	15	39	44	105	4	2	.496	.345	L	L	5-11	200	6-5-67	1987	St. Louis, Mo.
Mabry, John	.000	5	7	0	0	0	0	0	0	0	2	0	0	.000	.000	L	R	6-4	210	10-17-70	1991	Chesapeake, Md.
Marrero, Eli	.266	86	203	37	54	11	3	6	23	15	36	6	3	.438	.312	R	R	6-1	180	11-17-73	1993	Miami, Fla.
Matheny, Mike	.218	121	381	40	83	12	0	7	42	28	76	0	1	.304	.276	R	R	6-3	205	9-22-70	1991	Weldon Springs, Mo.
McDonald, Keith	.000	2	2	0	0	0	0	0	0	0	1	0	0	.000	.000	R	R	6-2	215	2-8-73	1994	Anaheim Hills, Calif.
McGwire, Mark	.187	97	299	48	56	4	0	29	64	56	118	0	0	.492	.316	R	R	6-5	250	10-1-63	1984	Long Beach, Calif.
Ortega, Bill	.200	5	5	0	1	0	0	0	0	0	1	0	0	.200	.200	R	R	6-4	205	7-24-75	1997	Hialeah, Fla.
Paquette, Craig	.282	123	340	47	96	17	0	15	64	18	67	3	1	.465	.326	R	R	6-0	190	3-28-69	1989	Tempe, Ariz.
Polanco, Placido	.307	144	564	87	173	26	4	3	38	25	43	12	3	.383	.342	R	R	5-10	168	10-10-75	1994	Miami, Fla.
Pujols, Albert	.329	161	590	112	194	47	4	37	130	69	93	1	3	.610	.403	R	R	6-3	210	1-16-80	1999	Roeland Park, Kan.
Renteria, Edgar	.260	141	493	54	128	19	3	10	57	39	73	17	4	.371	.314	R	R	6-1	180	8-7-75	1992	Barranquilla, Colombia
Robinson, Kerry	.285	114	186	34	53	6	1	1	15	12	20	11	2	.344	.330	L	L	6-0	175	10-3-73	1994	Spanish Lake, Mo.
Saturria, Luis	.200	13	5	0	1	0	0	1	0	1	1	1	0	.400	.200	R	R	6-2	165	7-21-76	1994	Boca Chica, D.R.
Sutton, Larry	.119	33	42	3	5	1	0	1	3	1	10	0	0	.214	.140	L	L	6-0	185	5-14-70	1992	Temecula, Calif.
Vina, Fernando	.303	154	631	95	191	30	8	9	56	32	35	17	7	.418	.357	L	R	5-9	174	4-16-69	1991	Stateline, Nev.

PITCHING	W	L	ERA	G	GS	CG	SV	IP	H	R	ER	BB	SO	AVG	B	T	HT	WT	DOB	1st Yr	Resides
Ankiel, Rick	1	2	7.13	6	6	0	0	24	25	21	19	25	27	.274	L	L	6-1	210	7-19-79	1997	Fort Pierce, Fla.
Benes, Alan	2	0	7.36	9	1	0	0	15	14	12	12	12	10	.250	R	R	6-5	235	1-21-72	1993	Cedar Hill, Mo.
Benes, Andy	7	7	7.38	27	19	0	0	107	122	92	88	61	78	.286	R	R	6-6	245	8-20-67	1989	Phoenix, Ariz.
Christiansen, Jason	1	1	4.66	30	0	0	3	19	15	10	10	10	19	.211	R	L	6-5	241	9-21-69	1991	Omaha, Neb.
Hackman, Luther	2	4	4.29	35	0	0	1	36	28	18	17	14	24	.212	R	R	6-4	195	10-10-74	1994	Memphis, Tenn.
Hermanson, Dustin	14	13	4.45	33	33	0	0	192	195	106	95	73	123	.263	R	R	6-2	200	12-21-72	1994	Springfield, Ohio
Hutchinson, Chad	0	0	24.75	3	0	0	0	4	9	11	11	6	2	.450	R	R	6-5	230	2-21-77	1998	Henderson, Nev.
James, Mike	1	2	5.21	40	0	0	0	38	43	24	22	17	26	.292	R	R	6-3	205	8-15-67	1988	Mary Esther, Fla.
Karnuth, Jason	0	0	1.80	4	0	0	0	5	6	1	1	4	1	.315	R	R	6-2	190	5-15-76	1997	Glen Ellyn, Ill.
Kile, Darryl	16	11	3.09	34	34	2	0	227	228	83	78	65	179	.264	R	R	6-5	212	12-2-68	1988	Englewood, Colo.
Kline, Steve	3	3	1.80	89	0	0	9	75	53	16	15	29	54	.203	B	L	6-1	215	8-22-72	1993	Winfield, Pa.
Mathews, T.J.	1	0	3.07	10	0	0	0	15	11	6	5	1	10	.203	R	R	6-1	225	1-19-70	1992	Columbia, Ill.
Matthews, Mike	3	4	3.24	51	10	0	1	89	74	32	32	33	72	.226	L	L	6-2	175	10-24-73	1992	Woodbridge, Va.
Morris, Matt	22	8	3.16	34	34	2	0	216	218	86	76	54	185	.264	R	R	6-5	210	8-9-74	1995	Middletown, N.Y.
Smith, Bud	6	3	3.83	16	14	1	0	85	79	40	36	24	59	.250	L	L	6-0	170	10-23-79	1998	Lakewood, Calif.
Stechschulte, Gene	1	5	3.86	67	0	0	6	70	71	35	30	30	51	.273	R	R	6-5	210	8-12-73	1996	Kalida, Ohio
Tabaka, Jeff	0	0	7.36	8	0	0	0	4	6	3	3	1	3	.375	R	L	6-2	201	1-17-64	1986	Clinton, Ohio
Timlin, Mike	4	5	4.09	67	0	0	3	73	78	35	33	19	47	.276	R	R	6-4	210	3-10-66	1987	Oldsmar, Fla.
Veres, Dave	3	2	3.70	71	0	0	15	66	57	29	27	28	61	.231	R	R	6-2	220	10-19-66	1986	Sugar Land, Texas
Williams, Woody	7	1	2.28	11	11	3	0	75	54	22	19	19	52	.205	R	R	6-0	195	8-19-66	1988	Fresno, Texas
2-team (23 San Diego)	15	9	4.05	34	34	3	0	220	224	110	99	56	154	.267							

FIELDING

Catcher	PCT	G	PO	A	E	DP	PB
Marrero	.984	65	352	21	6	2	1
Matheny	.995	121	772	69	4	9	6
McDonald	1.000	2	1	1	0	0	0

First Base	PCT	G	PO	A	E	DP
Bonilla	.992	33	228	10	2	27
Cairo	.000	1	0	0	0	0
Edmonds	1.000	2	14	2	0	2
Mabry	1.000	2	3	0	0	1
Marrero	1.000	6	19	1	0	4
Matheny	1.000	2	7	0	0	2
McGwire	.994	90	686	33	4	60
Paquette	.978	23	125	10	3	17
Pujols	.984	42	283	19	5	27
Renteria	1.000	1	2	0	0	1
Sutton	1.000	11	38	5	0	3

Second Base	PCT	G	PO	A	E	DP
Cairo	1.000	5	2	4	0	2
Clapp	1.000	4	1	6	0	0
Paquette	1.000	4	3	5	0	0
Polanco	1.000	15	22	36	0	10
Vina	.987	151	313	383	9	100

Third Base	PCT	G	PO	A	E	DP
Cairo	.000	3	0	0	1	0
Paquette	.965	33	20	35	2	5
Polanco	.985	103	60	199	4	16
Pujols	.938	55	40	111	10	17

Shortstop	PCT	G	PO	A	E	DP
Cairo	.000	1	0	0	0	0
Polanco	1.000	42	51	109	0	16
Renteria	.961	137	207	390	24	85

Outfield	PCT	G	PO	A	E	DP
Bonilla	1.000	10	11	1	0	0
Cairo	1.000	6	7	0	0	0
Clapp	1.000	4	3	0	0	0
Drew	.973	107	209	7	6	1
Edmonds	.982	147	311	12	6	1
Lankford	.966	85	135	5	5	1
Mabry	.000	2	0	0	0	0
Marrero	.923	15	11	1	1	0
Paquette	1.000	56	70	2	0	1
Pujols	.964	78	128	6	5	0
Robinson	.981	74	101	2	2	0
Saturria	1.000	9	2	0	0	0
Sutton	1.000	3	1	0	0	0

LARRY GOREN

Matt Morris: Led the Cardinals with 22 wins

LARRY GOREN

Albert Pujols: Led the Cardinals with 37 homers

FARM SYSTEM

Director, Player Development: Mike Jorgensen

Class	Farm Team	League	W	L	Pct.	Finish*	Manager	First Yr.
AAA	Memphis (Tenn.) Redbirds	Pacific Coast	62	81	.434	15th (16)	Gaylen Pitts	1998
AA	New Haven (Conn.) Ravens	Eastern	47	95	.331	12th (12)	Danny Sheaffer	2001
A#	Potomac (Va.) Cannons	Carolina	66	74	.471	6th (8)	Joe Cunningham	1997
A	Peoria (Ill.) Chiefs	Midwest	57	81	.413	11th (14)	Joe Hall	1995
A	New Jersey Cardinals	New York-Penn	35	41	.461	9th (14)	Brian Rupp	1994
Rookie#	Johnson City (Tenn.) Cardinals	Appalachian	31	35	.470	t-5th (10)	Chris Maloney	1975

*Finish in overall standings (No. of teams in league)   #Advanced level

MEMPHIS   Class AAA

PACIFIC COAST LEAGUE

BATTING	AVG	G	AB	R	H	2B	3B	HR	RBI	BB	SO	SB	CS	SLG	OBP	B	T	HT	WT	DOB	1st Yr	Resides
Andrews, Shane	.218	62	193	30	42	9	1	9	31	33	63	2	0	.415	.339	R	R	6-1	220	8-28-71	1990	Carlsbad, N.M.
Balfe, Ryan	.319	67	232	35	74	20	2	8	37	23	59	1	1	.526	.384	B	R	6-1	180	11-11-75	1997	Cornwall, N.Y.
Bevins, Andy	.253	43	146	24	37	8	0	7	20	12	47	0	2	.452	.325	R	R	6-3	215	10-10-75	1997	Port Coquitlam, B.C.
Bieser, Steve	.000	7	8	1	0	0	0	0	0	1	5	0	0	.000	.200	L	R	5-10	180	8-4-67	1989	St. Genevieve, Mo.
Brown, Brant	.277	52	188	30	52	4	1	4	19	21	60	2	1	.372	.349	L	L	6-3	220	6-22-71	1992	Fresno, Calif.
Clapp, Stubby	.304	86	299	48	91	14	7	5	33	43	46	8	4	.448	.392	L	R	5-8	175	2-24-73	1996	Windsor, Ontario
Frias, Hanley	.242	58	240	27	58	8	2	2	19	16	44	6	4	.317	.293	B	R	6-0	165	12-5-73	1991	Villa Altagracia, D.R.
2-team (49 Edm.)	.220	107	382	42	84	14	2	2	26	26	72	8	7	.283	.273							
Garcia, Luis	.256	118	422	42	108	20	1	7	44	8	71	2	1	.358	.275	R	R	6-0	175	5-20-75	1993	San Francisco de Macoris, D.R.
Hernandez, Carlos	.500	2	4	1	2	0	0	1	1	0	0	0	0	1.250	.500	R	R	5-11	215	5-24-67	1985	Caracas, Venez.
Lidle, Kevin	.057	13	35	1	2	1	0	0	2	2	14	0	0	.086	.108	B	R	5-11	170	3-22-72	1992	West Covina, Calif.
2-team (30 Salt Lake)	.228	43	123	11	28	8	0	1	12	11	41	2	1	.317	.304							
Lucca, Lou	.265	135	479	58	127	32	1	9	64	27	67	2	3	.392	.317	R	R	5-11	210	10-13-70	1992	South San Francisco, Calif.
Maier, T.J.	.235	6	17	4	4	0	0	0	1	2	3	0	0	.235	.300	R	R	6-0	180	2-24-75	1997	Santa Clara, Calif.
Mashore, Damon	.298	79	289	35	86	17	1	7	37	18	62	3	4	.436	.347	R	R	5-11	195	10-31-69	1991	Concord, Calif.
McDonald, Keith	.261	94	333	42	87	22	1	11	42	24	60	1	0	.432	.312	R	R	6-2	215	2-8-73	1994	Anaheim Hills, Calif.
McNaughton, Troy	.130	6	23	5	3	2	0	1	1	2	5	0	0	.348	.200	L	L	6-0	195	1-27-75	1998	Tacoma, Wash.
Ortega, Bill	.287	134	495	55	142	26	4	6	62	40	74	6	6	.392	.344	L	L	6-4	205	7-24-75	1997	Hialeah, Fla.
Polcovich, Kevin	.295	72	183	35	54	10	2	3	20	12	39	4	0	.421	.363	R	R	5-9	185	6-28-70	1992	Auburn, N.Y.
Robinson, Kerry	.325	10	40	4	13	1	0	0	3	4	10	4	1	.350	.386	L	L	6-0	175	10-3-73	1994	Spanish Lake, Mo.
Sagmoen, Marc	.250	12	52	7	13	4	0	0	9	4	15	1	0	.327	.304	L	L	5-11	185	4-16-71	1993	Seattle, Wash.
Saturria, Luis	.225	119	413	63	93	16	5	13	49	31	115	6	8	.383	.286	R	R	6-2	165	7-21-76	1994	Boca Chica, D.R.
Stefanski, Mike	.262	61	164	25	43	8	1	6	26	13	31	1	2	.433	.322	R	R	6-2	190	9-12-69	1991	Redford, Mich.
Sutton, Larry	.263	29	99	12	26	5	0	2	13	21	16	1	1	.374	.392	L	L	6-0	185	5-14-70	1992	Temecula, Calif.
Whitmore, Darrell	.277	112	328	47	91	22	0	11	52	22	61	2	3	.445	.326	L	R	6-1	220	11-18-68	1990	Miramar, Fla.
Woolf, Jason	.188	5	16	3	3	0	0	1	4	2	2	2	0	.375	.263	B	R	6-1	170	6-6-77	1995	Miami, Fla.

PITCHING	W	L	ERA	G	GS	CG	SV	IP	H	R	ER	BB	SO	AVG	B	T	HT	WT	DOB	1st Yr	Resides
Ankiel, Rick	0	2	20.77	3	3	0	0	4	3	10	10	17	4	.200	L	L	6-1	210	7-19-79	1997	Fort Pierce, Fla.
Benes, Alan	7	6	3.55	25	25	1	0	142	164	71	56	51	96	.287	R	R	6-5	235	1-21-72	1993	Cedar Hill, Mo.
Bullinger, Jim	1	8	6.96	10	10	0	0	53	68	47	41	30	36	.316	R	R	6-2	190	8-21-65	1986	Sarasota, Fla.
Carlson, Dan	1	0	4.71	7	3	0	0	21	25	13	11	8	21	.294	R	R	6-1	185	1-26-70	1990	Portland, Ore.
Cather, Mike	1	1	5.82	15	0	0	0	22	27	14	14	9	21	.296	R	R	6-2	205	12-17-70	1993	Folsom, Calif.
Christiansen, Jason	0	0	2.25	7	1	0	0	8	9	2	2	0	9	.281	R	L	6-5	241	9-21-69	1991	Omaha, Neb.
Cole, Victor	0	1	6.75	3	0	0	0	5	7	6	4	4	4	.280	L	R	5-10	180	1-23-68	1988	Cordova, Tenn.
Crafton, Kevin	1	1	8.05	13	0	0	0	19	34	20	17	6	13	.373	R	R	6-5	185	5-10-74	1996	Russellville, Ark.
Hackman, Luther	0	2	2.78	16	0	0	0	23	21	7	7	1	12	.253	R	R	6-4	195	10-10-74	1994	Memphis, Tenn.
Heiserman, Rick	1	1	4.59	24	4	0	0	49	61	26	25	11	33	.309	R	R	6-7	225	2-22-73	1994	Omaha, Neb.
Huisman, Rick	0	1	7.20	8	0	0	0	15	18	17	12	9	16	.295	R	R	6-3	210	5-17-69	1990	Holland, Mich.
Hutchinson, Chad	4	9	7.92	27	20	0	0	98	99	91	86	104	111	.267	R	R	6-5	230	2-21-77	1998	Henderson, Nev.
James, Mike	0	2	4.00	10	0	0	0	9	10	6	4	4	9	.303	R	R	6-3	205	8-15-67	1988	Mary Esther, Fla.
Joseph, Kevin	0	2	6.75	12	0	0	0	12	8	9	9	11	6	.190	R	R	6-4	200	8-1-76	1997	Dallas, Texas
2-team (5 Fresno)	0	3	7.08	17	0	0	0	20	17	16	16	15	8	.236							
Karnuth, Jason	4	4	4.28	55	0	0	3	74	82	37	35	24	42	.283	R	R	6-2	190	5-15-76	1997	Glen Ellyn, Ill.
Krivda, Rick	4	6	4.35	14	13	0	0	81	87	50	39	20	46	.278	R	L	6-1	185	1-19-70	1991	Cockeysville, Md.
Lambert, Jeremy	5	1	3.23	28	0	0	3	31	23	14	11	8	39	.211	R	R	6-1	195	1-10-79	1997	Kearns, Utah
Mathews, T.J.	1	1	1.80	15	0	0	4	15	16	4	3	1	14	.266	R	R	6-1	225	1-19-70	1992	Columbia, Ill.
Medina, Rafael	3	1	3.72	27	0	0	0	39	30	17	16	16	36	.208	R	R	6-3	203	2-15-75	1993	Panama City, Panama
Pearce, Josh	4	4	4.26	10	10	0	0	70	72	43	33	12	36	.265	R	R	6-3	215	8-20-77	1999	Yakima, Wash.
Rath, Fred	4	5	6.69	27	10	0	0	78	103	60	58	33	57	.314	R	R	6-3	220	1-5-73	1995	Tampa, Fla.
Rodriguez, Jose	2	1	3.56	54	0	0	1	61	52	25	24	31	54	.231	L	L	6-0	205	12-18-74	1997	Cayey, P.R.
Smith, Bud	8	5	2.75	17	17	0	0	108	114	38	33	28	78	.272	L	L	6-0	170	10-23-79	1998	Lakewood, Calif.
Spradlin, Jerry	4	1	2.20	29	0	0	14	33	17	8	8	7	28	.157	R	R	6-7	246	6-14-67	1988	Anaheim, Calif.
Stephenson, Garrett	0	0	0.00	1	1	0	0	2	2	0	0	0	2	.250	R	R	6-5	208	1-2-72	1992	Kimberly, Idaho
Tabaka, Jeff	0	2	2.60	32	0	0	2	28	24	10	8	10	23	.240	R	L	6-2	201	1-17-64	1986	Clinton, Ohio
Weibl, Clint	1	0	2.25	2	2	0	0	12	10	3	3	2	9	.232	R	R	6-3	180	3-17-75	1996	Dawson, Pa.
Zancanaro, Dave	6	14	5.99	27	24	1	1	143	171	103	95	48	107	.298	L	L	6-1	190	1-8-69	1990	Carmichael, Calif.

FIELDING

Catcher	PCT	G	PO	A	E	DP	PB
Hernandez	1.000	2	5	0	0	0	0
Lidle	.953	11	52	9	3	1	2
McDonald	.998	91	600	53	1	4	3
Stefanski	.994	52	323	29	2	2	3

First Base	PCT	G	PO	A	E	DP
Andrews	.986	46	331	29	5	32
Balfe	1.000	12	83	8	0	4
Bevins	.974	17	112	2	3	7
Brown	.998	48	384	33	1	35
Sagmoen	1.000	1	10	0	0	3
Stefanski	1.000	2	17	3	0	0
Sutton	.995	27	202	14	1	23

Second Base	PCT	G	PO	A	E	DP
Clapp	.977	82	184	236	10	53
Frias	.988	19	42	42	1	8

Garcia	1.000	1	1	1	0	0
Lucca	.931	18	33	48	6	8
Maier	1.000	6	11	10	0	3
Polcovich	.962	26	42	58	4	12

Third Base	PCT	G	PO	A	E	DP
Andrews	.935	16	5	24	2	3
Balfe	.925	17	11	26	3	3
Garcia	.879	15	4	25	4	2
Lucca	.947	108	47	205	14	11
Polcovich	1.000	7	5	9	0	1

Shortstop	PCT	G	PO	A	E	DP
Frias	.927	41	63	90	12	25
Garcia	.955	87	153	208	17	49
Lucca	1.000	5	3	11	0	2
Polcovich	.947	21	24	47	4	7
Woolf	1.000	1	2	1	0	0

Outfield	PCT	G	PO	A	E	DP
Balfe	.972	34	68	1	2	0
Bevins	1.000	19	28	2	0	0
Bieser	1.000	1	2	0	0	0
Brown	1.000	1	1	0	0	0
Clapp	1.000	2	2	1	0	0
Garcia	.000	1	0	0	0	0
Mashore	1.000	72	151	7	0	4
McNaughton	.889	5	8	0	1	0
Ortega	.970	124	219	8	7	0
Robinson	1.000	10	15	0	0	0
Sagmoen	1.000	11	34	1	0	1
Saturria	.972	115	344	7	10	1
Whitmore	.958	45	67	1	3	0
Woolf	1.000	3	4	0	0	0

NEW HAVEN — Class AA

EASTERN LEAGUE

BATTING	AVG	G	AB	R	H	2B	3B	HR	RBI	BB	SO	SB	CS	SLG	OBP	B	T	HT	WT	DOB	1st Yr	Resides
Ametller, Jesus	.000	3	3	0	0	0	0	0	0	0	1	0	0	.000	.000	L	R	5-8	175	7-25-74	1997	Hialeah, Fla.
Bailey, Travis	.273	27	88	9	24	3	1	4	10	4	35	2	2	.466	.316	R	R	6-2	198	1-26-77	1999	Loxahatchee, Fla.
Benham, David	.242	46	132	8	32	5	0	1	15	4	31	2	0	.303	.273	R	R	6-2	187	10-12-75	1998	Fort Myers, Fla.
Bevins, Andy	.198	99	348	43	69	14	1	13	40	36	65	5	7	.356	.290	R	R	6-3	215	10-10-75	1997	Port Coquitlam, B.C.
Bowers, Jason	.239	137	460	35	110	19	4	3	33	25	111	10	10	.317	.280	R	R	5-11	170	1-27-78	1998	Uniontown, Pa.
Diaz, Miguel	.274	58	117	7	32	4	1	0	6	4	20	2	5	.325	.309	R	R	5-11	160	9-29-77	1995	San Pedro de Macoris, D.R.
Dishington, Nate	.194	39	129	12	25	5	0	7	22	7	61	1	0	.395	.252	L	R	6-3	290	1-8-75	1993	Glendale, Calif.
Eckelman, Alex	.212	130	411	33	87	17	0	5	38	20	68	14	5	.290	.257	R	R	5-11	190	7-16-74	1997	St. Louis, Mo.
Farnsworth, Troy	.232	115	422	47	98	21	1	18	70	28	104	4	7	.415	.301	R	R	6-2	215	2-4-76	1998	West Valley City, Utah
Garcia, Guillermo	.167	7	18	2	3	0	0	1	1	0	5	0	0	.333	.167	R	R	6-3	215	4-4-72	1990	Santiago, D.R.
Garrick, Matt	.220	40	127	10	28	6	0	2	10	9	25	1	0	.315	.270	R	R	6-0	185	8-19-75	1997	Duncanville, Texas
Green, Scarborough	.250	47	160	14	40	7	1	0	10	21	38	12	4	.306	.327	B	R	5-10	185	6-9-74	1993	St. Louis, Mo.
2-team (27 Altoona)	.251	74	251	24	63	8	1	0	16	27	57	22	4	.291	.325							
Maier, T.J.	.282	74	255	46	72	20	2	4	35	38	58	9	4	.424	.385	R	R	6-0	180	2-24-75	1997	Santa Clara, Calif.
Martine, Chris	.211	62	180	21	38	6	0	0	5	12	46	2	2	.244	.267	R	R	6-2	190	7-10-75	1997	Cherry Hill, N.J.
McNaughton, Troy	.235	115	387	57	91	29	3	8	39	37	108	6	10	.388	.307	L	L	6-0	195	1-27-75	1998	Tacoma, Wash.
Munoz, Juan	.276	126	456	39	126	19	2	9	56	24	48	9	7	.386	.311	L	L	5-9	170	3-27-74	1995	Miami, Fla.
Nunez, Jose	.159	39	82	7	13	2	0	0	1	5	20	5	1	.183	.216	R	R	5-10	175	12-8-78	1997	Cotui, D.R.
Ortiz, Matt	.167	4	12	0	2	2	0	0	2	2	5	0	0	.333	.286	R	R	5-11	195	4-18-78	2000	San Diego, Calif.
Pogue, Jamie	.200	5	15	3	3	0	1	0	0	2	1	0	0	.333	.294	R	R	6-4	235	8-17-77	1999	Guelph, Ontario
Saturria, Luis	.276	8	29	5	8	3	0	0	4	3	7	0	0	.379	.333	R	R	6-1	175	7-21-76	1994	Boca Chica, D.R.
Schumacher, Shawn	.221	41	122	8	27	5	0	2	11	3	10	3	1	.311	.246	L	R	6-1	200	8-18-76	1999	Carthage, Texas
Snead, Esix	.233	133	520	71	121	21	6	1	33	44	115	64	23	.302	.307	B	R	5-10	175	6-7-76	1998	Williston, Fla.
Thames, Damon	.200	34	65	9	13	0	1	2	4	3	21	0	1	.323	.257	R	R	6-0	170	11-15-76	1999	Humble, Texas

PITCHING	W	L	ERA	G	GS	CG	SV	IP	H	R	ER	BB	SO	AVG	B	T	HT	WT	DOB	1st Yr	Resides
Coogan, Patrick	8	8	5.09	33	23	1	0	149	168	91	84	43	115	.285	R	R	6-3	195	9-12-75	1997	Baton Rouge, La.
Cook, B.R.	5	8	3.94	20	20	0	0	122	115	68	54	34	84	.247	R	R	6-4	200	3-2-78	1999	Salem, Ore.
Crudale, Mike	4	9	3.25	62	0	0	9	80	76	42	29	22	85	.243	R	R	6-2	190	1-3-77	1999	Danville, Calif.
Daniels, David	1	1	2.86	13	0	0	0	22	19	7	7	8	17	.237	R	R	6-2	182	7-25-73	1996	Nashville, Tenn.
Franks, Lance	2	8	4.08	28	11	0	0	90	86	60	41	48	72	.248	R	R	5-11	180	8-20-75	1997	Russellville, Ark.
Hackman, Luther	0	0	2.25	3	1	0	0	4	2	2	1	1	5	.153	R	R	6-4	195	10-10-74	1994	Memphis, Tenn.

PITCHING	W	L	ERA	G	GS	CG	SV	IP	H	R	ER	BB	SO	AVG	B	T	HT	WT	DOB	1st Yr	Resides
Heiserman, Rick	0	0	3.52	5	0	0	0	8	7	4	3	3	5	.241	R	R	6-7	225	2-22-73	1994	Omaha, Neb.
Janke, Cheyenne	1	4	5.52	17	5	0	0	44	65	31	27	14	20	.351	R	R	6-5	235	2-16-77	1999	Elk Mound, Wis.
Journell, Jimmy	1	0	0.00	1	1	1	0	7	0	0	0	3	6	.000	R	R	6-4	205	12-29-77	1999	Springfield, Ohio
Lambert, Jeremy	2	2	2.97	31	0	0	14	33	32	17	11	17	48	.256	R	R	6-1	195	1-10-79	1997	Kearns, Utah
Marr, Jason	3	4	4.96	51	0	0	0	62	68	36	34	25	27	.279	R	R	6-1	195	9-9-75	1998	Downey, Calif.
Navarro, Jason	1	2	5.25	52	0	0	0	62	64	47	36	37	48	.266	L	L	6-4	225	7-5-75	1997	Lilburn, Ga.
Pearce, Josh	6	8	3.75	18	18	0	0	115	111	55	48	34	96	.253	R	R	6-3	215	8-20-77	1999	Yakima, Wash.
Perkins, Mike	0	1	12.00	1	1	0	0	3	6	4	4	2	2	.461	R	R	6-1	195	5-29-79	1999	Sarasota, Fla.
Prather, Scott	1	3	3.70	23	4	0	0	49	52	20	20	17	38	.270	L	L	6-2	185	10-8-76	1998	Atlanta, Ga.
Rath, Fred	0	0	16.20	1	0	0	0	2	3	3	3	3	0	.375	R	R	6-3	220	1-5-73	1995	Tampa, Fla.
Sansom, Trevor	0	0	4.50	1	0	0	0	2	1	1	1	1	1	.142	R	R	6-4	190	5-6-76	1999	Winfield, W.Va.
Sheredy, Kevin	0	7	2.95	48	0	0	1	64	46	29	21	34	58	.205	R	R	6-4	211	1-3-75	1996	Antioch, Calif.
Sprague, Kevin	1	0	3.00	1	1	0	0	6	4	3	2	2	4	.173	L	L	6-4	215	3-10-77	1999	Kansas City, Kan.
Stemle, Steve	7	10	4.77	26	25	0	0	134	159	76	71	43	75	.292	R	R	6-4	200	5-20-77	1998	New Albany, Ind.
Stocks, Nick	2	12	5.16	16	15	1	0	82	89	52	47	33	63	.276	R	R	6-2	185	8-27-78	1999	Tampa, Fla.
Walrond, Les	2	8	3.87	16	16	1	0	81	68	41	35	46	67	.226	L	L	6-0	195	11-7-76	1998	Tulsa, Okla.
Zancanaro, Dave	0	0	1.80	1	1	0	0	5	4	1	1	4	5	.222	L	L	6-1	190	1-8-69	1990	Carmichael, Calif.

FIELDING

Catcher	PCT	G	PO	A	E	DP	PB
Benham	.984	27	172	15	3	1	5
Garcia	1.000	3	16	1	0	0	2
Garrick	.976	34	263	19	7	1	2
Martine	.981	54	323	30	7	4	6
Pogue	1.000	5	36	7	0	0	6
Schumacher	.994	29	160	18	1	0	6

First Base	PCT	G	PO	A	E	DP
Bailey	1.000	2	12	0	0	0
Farnsworth	.990	27	184	10	2	22
Garcia	1.000	1	8	0	0	1
Munoz	.988	123	1001	58	13	92

Second Base	PCT	G	PO	A	E	DP
Bowers	.000	1	0	0	0	0

	PCT	G	PO	A	E	DP
Eckelman	.965	58	106	139	9	34
Maier	.986	72	139	213	5	52
McNaughton	.000	1	0	0	0	0
Nunez	1.000	2	1	2	0	1
Thames	.966	21	29	28	2	8

Third Base	PCT	G	PO	A	E	DP
Bailey	.898	22	10	43	6	2
Eckelman	.975	34	18	60	2	9
Farnsworth	.937	93	68	185	17	13
Nunez	.875	10	1	6	1	1
Thames	1.000	2	0	1	0	0

Shortstop	PCT	G	PO	A	E	DP
Bowers	.930	130	191	366	42	79
Eckelman	1.000	13	10	24	0	7

	PCT	G	PO	A	E	DP
Nunez	.900	7	8	10	2	4
Thames	.917	5	3	8	1	2

Outfield	PCT	G	PO	A	E	DP
Bailey	1.000	3	3	0	0	0
Bevins	.978	82	132	4	3	1
Diaz	.942	31	47	2	3	0
Dishington	.978	28	44	1	1	0
Eckelman	1.000	20	24	1	0	0
Green	1.000	46	104	5	0	0
McNaughton	.988	99	161	8	2	1
Munoz	.000	1	0	0	0	0
Saturria	.846	6	11	0	2	0
Snead	.983	132	347	10	6	4

POTOMAC

Class A

CAROLINA LEAGUE

BATTING	AVG	G	AB	R	H	2B	3B	HR	RBI	BB	SO	SB	CS	SLG	OBP	B	T	HT	WT	DOB	1st Yr	Resides
Bailey, Travis	.216	73	227	25	49	13	4	6	24	15	75	3	6	.388	.274	R	R	6-2	198	1-26-77	1999	Loxahatchee, Fla.
Brandes, Landon	.220	27	82	6	18	4	0	3	13	3	23	1	2	.378	.244	R	R	5-11	190	3-15-79	2000	Knob Noster, Mo.
Carvajal, Ramon	.217	125	456	59	99	16	4	8	39	22	115	17	4	.322	.260	B	R	5-10	155	3-4-81	1997	Bani, D.R.
Clark, Greg	.200	8	15	0	3	2	0	0	2	0	4	0	1	.333	.200	R	R	6-2	175	1-5-77	1998	Phoenix, Ariz.
Crisp, Covelli	.306	139	530	80	162	23	3	11	47	52	64	39	21	.423	.368	B	R	6-0	185	11-1-79	1999	Desert Hot Springs, Calif.
Duncan, Chris	.179	49	168	12	30	6	0	3	16	10	47	4	4	.268	.229	L	R	6-5	210	5-5-81	1999	Tucson, Ariz.
Escobar, Gustavo	.375	4	8	0	3	0	0	0	0	1	0	0	0	.375	.444	R	R	5-10	170	1-30-80	1997	Barcelona, Venez.
Fatur, Brian	.235	60	226	20	53	13	0	2	20	6	38	3	1	.319	.271	R	R	6-0	180	6-5-79	2000	Calabasas Hills, Calif.
Friar, Roddy	.220	18	41	4	9	2	0	0	2	6	20	1	1	.268	.333	R	R	6-0	190	5-10-76	2000	Pueblo, Colo.
Galante, Matt	.167	4	6	0	1	0	0	0	0	0	2	0	0	.167	.286	R	R	5-8	165	10-10-78	2000	Staten Island, N.Y.
Gall, John	.317	84	319	44	101	25	0	4	33	24	40	5	6	.433	.369	R	R	6-0	195	4-2-78	2000	Portola Valley, Calif.
Green, Steve	.200	2	5	0	1	0	0	0	0	0	3	0	0	.000	.167	L	R	6-1	180	7-22-78	2001	Monticello, Ark.
Hart, Bo	.305	81	279	48	85	23	3	5	34	17	69	16	7	.462	.375	R	R	5-11	175	9-27-76	1999	Laselva Beach, Calif.
Haynes, Dee	.290	114	417	45	121	24	3	13	72	14	82	5	1	.456	.329	R	R	6-0	205	2-22-78	2000	Columbus, Miss.
Hernandez, Johnny	.231	131	464	42	107	20	4	1	28	32	108	7	12	.297	.281	B	L	6-1	185	9-11-79	1999	Brooklyn, N.Y.
Johnson, Gabe	.189	86	281	24	53	14	0	4	22	21	113	2	3	.281	.250	R	R	6-1	195	9-21-79	1999	Delray Beach, Fla.
Pogue, Jamie	.240	108	354	48	85	15	0	8	42	55	61	11	7	.350	.353	R	R	6-4	235	8-17-77	1999	Guelph, Ontario
Pollaro, Dallas	.253	50	162	15	41	7	0	0	15	10	26	4	0	.296	.297	R	R	6-0	170	6-27-80	2000	Henderson, Nev.
Rodgers, Albert	.271	36	129	19	35	9	0	2	10	6	39	0	2	.388	.319	R	R	6-2	190	6-8-79	2000	Long Beach, Calif.
Schumacher, Shawn	.285	68	249	15	71	8	1	2	38	13	20	2	1	.349	.331	L	R	6-1	200	8-18-76	1999	Carthage, Texas
Thames, Damon	.190	44	116	16	22	4	0	1	6	3	28	6	1	.250	.228	R	R	6-1	170	11-15-76	1999	Humble, Texas
Williams, Charles	.141	42	85	10	12	1	0	1	6	16	25	1	4	.188	.284	B	L	6-0	185	2-9-78	1999	Humble, Texas

GAMES BY POSITION: C—Clark 7, Friar 18, Pogue 86, Schumacher 43. **1B**—Bailey 18, Duncan 47, Gall 47, Johnson 1, Rodgers 34. **2B**—Bailey 1, Escobar 2, Fatur 10, Galante 4, Hart 72, Pollaro 43, Thames 20. **3B**—Bailey 9, Brandes 1, Fatur 14, Gall 32, Hart 6, Johnson 83, Rodgers 2, Thames 1. **SS**—Carvajal 125, Escobar 2, Fatur 2, Johnson 1, Thames 17. **OF**—Bailey 20, Brandes 3, Crisp 137, Fatur 40, Green 2, Hart 1, Haynes 77, Hernandez 131, Pollaro 1, C. Williams 41.

PITCHING	W	L	ERA	G	GS	CG	SV	IP	H	R	ER	BB	SO	AVG	B	T	HT	WT	DOB	1st Yr	Resides
Axelson, Josh	2	5	5.56	10	10	1	0	57	61	41	35	19	38	.274	R	R	6-1	201	12-4-78	2000	Brooklyn, Mich.
Cali, Carmen	1	0	2.19	12	0	0	0	12	12	4	3	6	9	.279	L	L	5-11	190	11-4-78	2000	Naples, Fla.
Cook, B.R.	4	2	2.86	8	8	0	0	50	35	20	16	12	36	.194	R	R	6-4	200	3-2-78	1999	Salem, Ore.
Cummings, Jeremy	0	3	8.53	4	4	0	0	19	25	18	18	2	15	.324	R	R	6-2	215	11-7-76	1999	Hurricane, W.Va.
Grassing, Bryan	5	1	4.91	48	0	0	1	62	80	51	34	22	25	.317	R	R	6-0	220	1-12-78	2000	Longwood, Fla.
Grippo, Mike	0	0	18.00	6	0	0	0	4	9	8	8	5	2	.409	L	L	5-11	185	5-6-76	1999	Staten Island, N.Y.
Janke, Cheyenne	0	0	2.48	15	5	0	0	36	44	16	10	9	17	.299	R	R	6-5	235	2-16-77	1999	Elk Mound, Wis.
Journell, Jimmy	14	2	2.50	26	26	0	0	151	121	54	42	42	156	.220	R	R	6-4	205	12-29-77	1999	Springfield, Ohio
Kohl, Doug	3	5	2.08	51	0	0	6	56	40	21	13	21	44	.191	R	R	6-4	210	7-9-79	1997	Henderson, Nev.
Langen, Brian	2	2	2.77	43	0	0	0	49	48	28	15	27	32	.255	L	L	6-7	210	2-13-78	1998	Farmersville, Ill.
Layfield, Scotty	1	2	1.84	47	0	0	31	54	36	13	11	18	66	.187	R	R	6-2	205	9-13-76	1999	Montezuma, Ga.
Medlock, Chet	1	1	0.55	12	0	0	0	16	17	5	1	5	14	.274	R	R	6-1	175	10-23-78	2000	Brusly, La.
Narveson, Chris	4	3	2.57	11	11	1	0	67	52	22	19	13	53	.212	L	L	6-3	180	12-20-81	2000	Arden, N.C.
Perkins, Mike	1	3	3.94	11	5	0	0	30	32	15	13	13	25	.278	R	R	6-1	195	5-29-79	1999	Sarasota, Fla.
Ponce de Leon, Damon	1	4	2.85	23	3	0	0	41	30	19	13	12	30	.196	R	R	5-11	185	11-2-77	2000	Demarest, N.J.
Prather, Scott	2	1	3.60	20	0	0	0	25	24	15	10	7	27	.235	L	L	6-2	185	10-8-76	1998	Atlanta, Ga.
Sansom, Trevor	6	4	2.71	50	0	0	0	70	72	33	21	22	45	.263	R	R	6-4	190	5-6-76	1999	Winfield, W.Va.

PITCHING	W	L	ERA	G	GS	CG	SV	IP	H	R	ER	BB	SO	AVG	B	T	HT	WT	DOB	1st Yr	Resides
Sprague, Kevin	9	8	3.40	26	26	2	0	164	155	64	62	43	113	.252	L	L	6-4	215	3-10-77	1999	Kansas City, Kan.
Tejeda, Franklin	6	14	4.43	25	25	2	0	136	152	76	67	19	70	.280	R	R	6-3	225	4-7-80	1998	Bani, D.R.
Williams, Blake	4	10	2.43	17	17	2	0	107	82	43	29	30	92	.210	R	R	6-5	210	2-22-79	2000	San Marcos, Texas

PEORIA — Class A

MIDWEST LEAGUE

BATTING	AVG	G	AB	R	H	2B	3B	HR	RBI	BB	SO	SB	CS	SLG	OBP	B	T	HT	WT	DOB	1st Yr	Resides
Boyd, Shaun	.282	81	277	42	78	12	2	5	27	33	42	20	3	.394	.357	R	R	5-10	175	8-15-81	2000	Pala, Calif.
Brandes, Landon	.205	47	161	20	33	10	1	3	12	11	38	2	3	.335	.254	R	R	5-11	190	3-15-79	2000	Knob Noster, Mo.
Diaz, Aneuris	.239	120	418	43	100	22	5	3	43	16	122	10	8	.337	.269	R	R	6-2	165	1-20-81	1998	Azua, D.R.
Dogero, Matt	.235	17	34	3	8	1	0	1	3	3	6	2	1	.353	.297	R	R	6-0	210	7-3-80	2000	San Bernardino, Calif.
Drew, J.D.	.545	3	11	3	6	2	0	0	1	0	0	0	0	.727	.583	L	R	195	11-20-75	1997	Hahira, Ga.
Duncan, Chris	.306	80	297	44	91	23	2	13	59	36	55	13	3	.529	.386	L	R	6-5	210	5-5-81	1999	Tucson, Ariz.
Fatur, Brian	.207	56	193	27	40	7	0	5	24	25	35	9	10	.321	.305	R	R	6-0	180	6-5-79	2000	Calabasas Hills, Calif.
Fera, Aaron	.169	16	59	5	10	4	0	2	9	4	32	1	1	.339	.222	R	R	6-2	225	11-13-77	1999	Sault Ste. Marie, Ontario
Firlit, Dan	.210	41	105	12	22	6	0	1	7	9	33	2	1	.295	.288	R	R	6-1	180	11-22-78	2000	Orland Park, Ill.
Floyd, Mike	.215	83	246	26	53	9	0	2	23	17	62	18	9	.276	.267	R	R	6-1	210	9-1-77	1999	Brandon, Fla.
Friar, Roddy	.165	36	85	10	14	5	0	0	5	18	38	0	1	.224	.324	R	R	6-0	190	5-10-76	2000	Pueblo, Colo.
Gall, John	.302	57	205	27	62	23	0	4	44	16	18	0	3	.473	.353	R	R	6-0	195	4-2-78	2000	Portola Valley, Calif.
Hamill, Ryan	.264	110	371	44	98	23	0	10	45	33	62	2	2	.407	.328	R	R	6-0	200	10-3-78	2000	Woodland Hills, Calif.
Johnson, Gabe	.224	36	134	17	30	10	4	2	17	16	49	1	1	.403	.312	R	R	6-1	195	9-21-79	1998	Delray Beach, Fla.
Lemon, Tim	.222	130	482	60	107	32	3	15	61	27	165	31	7	.394	.270	R	R	6-1	180	9-23-80	1998	La Mirada, Calif.
Morris, Chris	.294	134	480	89	141	11	9	2	39	83	101	111	24	.367	.398	B	R	5-8	180	7-1-79	2000	Andrews, S.C.
Ortiz, Matt	.245	65	216	23	53	13	1	0	23	19	31	4	3	.315	.308	R	R	5-11	195	4-18-78	2000	San Diego, Calif.
Rodgers, Albert	.215	77	261	31	56	14	1	9	33	18	83	8	5	.379	.280	R	R	6-2	190	6-8-79	2000	Long Beach, Calif.
Santana, Sandy	.203	65	197	19	40	7	1	1	17	7	36	5	5	.264	.249	R	R	5-10	150	7-11-80	1997	San Pedro de Macoris, D.R.
Vasquez, Geraldo	.000	4	9	1	0	0	0	0	2	4	1	0	.000	.182	R	R	5-11	145	11-5-79	1997	San Pedro de Macoris, D.R.
Voshell, Chase	.258	90	325	53	84	19	3	5	23	33	80	9	5	.382	.333	R	R	6-2	185	3-29-79	2000	Milford, Ohio

GAMES BY POSITION: C—Dogero 15, Friar 34, Hamill 100, Ortiz 16, Voshell 1. **1B**—Brandes 2, Diaz 3, Duncan 79, Gall 45, Rodgers 17. **2B**—Boyd 80, Diaz 1, Fatur 13, Firlit 4, Santana 48. **3B**—Brandes 25, Diaz 74, Fatur 2, G. Johnson 35, Rodgers 15, Santana 3. **SS**—Brandes 1, Diaz 4, Fatur 20, Firlit 34, Ortiz 1, Santana 1, Vasquez 3, Voshell 87. **OF**—Diaz 21, Drew 3, Fatur 23, Fera 7, Floyd 66, Lemon 130, Morris 132, Ortiz 8, Rodgers 45, Santana 1.

PITCHING	W	L	ERA	G	GS	CG	SV	IP	H	R	ER	BB	SO	AVG	B	T	HT	WT	DOB	1st Yr	Resides
Axelson, Josh	5	7	4.61	18	18	1	0	109	112	62	56	28	77	.264	R	R	6-1	201	12-4-78	2000	Brooklyn, Mich.
Cali, Carmen	7	3	6.00	39	0	0	1	48	53	40	32	29	47	.274	L	L	5-11	190	11-4-78	2000	Naples, Fla.
Cook, Jeremy	3	7	3.71	52	0	0	14	68	78	37	28	20	61	.276	R	R	6-6	235	5-11-78	2000	Yuba City, Calif.
Cummings, Jeremy	4	6	3.22	18	18	0	0	95	93	45	34	10	75	.250	R	R	6-2	215	11-7-76	1999	Hurricane, W.Va.
Graves, Donovan	2	6	5.02	34	15	0	0	104	99	67	58	53	71	.247	R	R	6-4	205	1-3-81	1999	Boonville, Mo.
Johnson, Kelly	1	0	5.03	13	0	0	0	20	20	13	11	5	11	.270	R	R	6-1	205	5-9-80	2000	Tucson, Ariz.
Johnson, Tyler	0	1	3.95	3	3	0	0	14	14	9	6	10	15	.254	B	L	6-2	180	6-7-81	2001	Newbury Park, Calif.
Kinney, Josh	1	4	4.39	27	0	0	0	41	47	24	20	15	35	.286	R	R	6-1	195	3-31-79	2001	Port Allegheny, Pa.
Martinez, Miguel	5	8	4.44	18	18	1	0	97	114	72	48	27	52	.284	R	R	6-1	168	9-29-81	1999	Montecristi, D.R.
Medlock, Chet	2	2	3.71	30	0	0	0	44	45	23	18	15	27	.272	R	R	6-1	175	10-23-78	2000	Brusly, La.
Meyer, Mike	2	3	0.00	17	0	0	1	24	29	19	8	5	17	.281	R	R	6-2	185	12-18-77	2000	Tucson, Ariz.
Narveson, Chris	3	3	1.98	8	8	0	0	50	32	14	11	11	53	.184	L	L	6-3	180	12-20-81	2000	Arden, N.C.
Novinsky, John	9	11	5.52	25	25	1	0	139	165	95	85	43	115	.296	R	R	6-3	190	4-25-79	2001	Hauppauge, N.Y.
Perkins, Mike	0	0	0.79	7	0	0	0	11	3	2	1	2	8	.075	R	R	1-95	5-29-79	1999	Sarasota, Fla.
Polo, Bienvenido	1	0	4.50	18	1	0	0	28	25	22	14	19	19	.235	R	R	6-2	165	1-4-79	1997	El Seibo, D.R.
Ponce de Leon, Damon	1	1	4.57	19	0	0	2	22	17	13	11	8	15	.209	R	R	5-11	185	11-2-77	2000	Demarest, N.J.
Russelburg, Aaron	4	3	4.56	10	10	0	0	51	53	31	26	27	31	.271	R	R	6-4	215	10-17-79	2001	Hawesville, Ky.
Samora, Santo	1	7	4.21	52	0	0	12	62	62	50	29	27	38	.241	R	R	6-1	152	12-10-79	1997	San Pedro de Macoris, D.R.
Shouse, Dan	1	0	5.14	11	0	0	0	14	17	9	8	4	11	.298	L	L	6-3	200	9-21-78	2001	Wildwood, Mo.
Stokes, Shaun	2	7	7.14	13	13	0	0	58	87	57	46	22	42	.349	R	R	6-2	210	8-23-78	2000	Oak Ridge, N.J.
Vincent, Matt	0	1	3.24	14	0	0	0	17	18	7	6	4	10	.276	L	L	6-1	190	5-10-77	1999	Floyds Knobs, Ind.
Vriesenga, Matt	4	1	4.01	35	9	0	0	92	103	50	41	11	48	.276	R	R	6-5	190	8-28-77	2000	Grand Rapids, Mich.

NEW JERSEY — Short-Season Class A

NEW YORK-PENN LEAGUE

BATTING	AVG	G	AB	R	H	2B	3B	HR	RBI	BB	SO	SB	CS	SLG	OBP	B	T	HT	WT	DOB	1st Yr	Resides
Davidson, Seth	.276	63	217	18	60	7	1	0	15	23	13	5	13	.318	.352	B	R	6-0	170	2-26-79	2001	San Diego, Calif.
De los Santos, Rene	.226	66	252	34	57	9	1	0	17	29	57	18	4	.270	.309	R	R	6-1	160	12-29-80	1998	Santo Domingo, D.R.
Dogero, Matt	.000	4	5	0	0	0	0	0	0	0	1	0	0	.000	.000	R	R	6-0	210	7-3-80	2000	San Bernardino, Calif.
Espino, Jose	.283	20	53	10	15	5	1	1	11	5	13	0	2	.472	.339	R	R	6-0	165	11-6-79	1997	Cotui, D.R.
Fox, Matt	.222	37	90	13	20	7	0	2	5	13	29	1	1	.367	.324	R	R	6-1	195	8-13-79	2001	Coral Springs, Fla.
Jones, Jeff	.289	37	90	20	26	6	1	1	12	8	17	11	1	.411	.398	R	R	5-8	180	3-12-79	2001	Elk Grove, Calif.
Moylan, Dan	.292	59	192	23	56	9	1	1	22	45	31	6	7	.365	.424	L	R	6-0	190	4-24-79	2000	Keene, N.H.
Nelson, Bruce	.250	16	40	6	10	1	1	0	3	2	6	2	1	.325	.286	R	R	6-0	180	8-27-78	2001	Gladstone, Mo.
Nelson, John	.238	66	252	43	60	16	3	8	26	35	76	14	3	.421	.332	R	R	6-1	190	3-3-79	2000	Denton, Texas
Netwall, Chris	.272	28	81	13	22	4	1	0	7	8	14	0	0	.346	.348	R	R	6-1	205	11-17-79	2001	Allentown, Pa.
Pearl, Matt	.278	22	54	6	15	3	0	0	6	6	4	1	.333	.371	R	R	6-0	190	9-8-78	2001	Bakersfield, Calif.
Robison, Jordan	.255	66	243	27	62	17	3	7	34	15	79	7	6	.436	.303	R	R	6-3	190	5-26-79	2001	Iona, Idaho
Roman, Jesse	.271	71	255	39	69	16	3	3	39	51	39	5	5	.392	.395	L	L	6-0	190	4-21-79	2000	Houston, Texas
Santor, John	.227	54	185	17	42	12	2	2	26	22	64	3	2	.346	.308	B	R	6-1	215	11-16-81	2001	Palmdale, Calif.
Schmitt, Billy	.244	62	238	14	58	9	3	2	37	9	59	1	2	.332	.270	R	R	6-1	200	8-16-82	2001	Henderson, Nev.
Schumaker, Skip	.253	49	162	22	41	10	1	0	14	29	33	11	2	.327	.368	L	R	5-10	175	2-3-80	2001	Laguna Niguel, Calif.
Williams, Matt	.294	41	136	25	40	7	2	3	17	25	43	1	2	.449	.416	R	R	6-0	180	3-24-79	2001	Signal Hill, Calif.

GAMES BY POSITION: C—Dogero 1, Moylan 48, B. Nelson 8, Netwall 28. **1B**—Roman 49, Santor 22, Schmitt 8. **2B**—Davidson 30, de los Santos 26, Fox 23, Williams 1. **3B**—Fox 2, Santor 21, Schmitt 23, Williams 34. **SS**—Davidson 34, de los Santos 40, J. Nelson 6. **OF**—Espino 12, Jones 23, J. Nelson 59, Pearl 17, Robison 65, Roman 18, Santor 3, Schmitt 1, Schumaker 46.

PITCHING	W	L	ERA	G	GS	CG	SV	IP	H	R	ER	BB	SO	AVG	B	T	HT	WT	DOB	1st Yr	Resides
Blasdell, Jared	0	1	1.26	26	0	0	11	29	18	6	4	7	36	.176	R	R	6-3	185	5-14-79	2001	Las Vegas, Nev.

PITCHING	W	L	ERA	G	GS	CG	SV	IP	H	R	ER	BB	SO	AVG	B	T	HT	WT	DOB	1st Yr	Resides
Burgess, Richie	3	3	4.02	16	6	0	1	63	66	31	28	28	44	.269	R	R	6-4	210	10-9-79	2000	Redlands, Calif.
Correa, Cristobal	1	3	5.40	15	1	0	3	40	48	34	24	17	32	.294	R	R	6-1	175	12-27-79	1998	Guarico, Venez.
Greco, Sam	1	4	4.50	21	0	0	0	30	30	19	15	11	29	.263	B	R	6-2	200	1-22-79	2001	East Greenbush, N.Y.
Hall, Chris	0	0	3.68	18	0	0	0	22	26	11	9	11	13	.298	L	L	6-3	195	3-14-79	2001	Little Rock, Ark.
Haren, Dan	3	3	3.10	12	8	0	1	52	47	22	18	8	57	.238	R	R	6-5	220	9-17-80	2001	West Covina, Calif.
Johnson, Kelly	0	0	2.35	13	0	0	0	15	15	8	4	6	17	.250	R	R	6-1	205	5-9-80	2000	Tucson, Ariz.
Julianel, Ben	6	6	3.48	15	15	0	0	85	88	38	33	26	86	.269	B	L	6-2	180	9-4-79	2001	Belmont, Calif.
Kinney, Josh	2	0	0.00	3	0	0	0	6	2	0	0	0	5	.111	R	R	6-1	195	3-31-79	2001	Port Allegheny, Pa.
Mattison, Corey	5	7	3.86	15	15	0	0	79	70	44	34	26	59	.234	R	R	6-6	220	12-1-77	2001	Graham, N.C.
Merrigan, Josh	4	2	2.14	29	0	0	4	34	33	13	8	8	30	.264	L	L	6-4	225	6-30-78	2001	Yankton, S.D.
Meyer, Mike	1	2	4.50	10	0	0	5	12	16	8	6	4	12	.313	R	R	6-2	185	12-18-77	2000	Tucson, Ariz.
Parrott, Rhett	1	3	4.93	11	11	0	0	46	45	27	25	28	58	.261	R	R	6-2	190	11-12-79	2001	Dalton, Ga.
Pope, Justin	2	4	2.60	15	15	0	0	69	64	32	20	14	66	.240	B	R	6-2	185	1-19-80	2001	Lake Worth, Fla.
Rawson, Anthony	0	0	3.00	3	0	0	0	3	3	1	1	2	3	.250	L	L	5-11	180	7-31-80	2001	Kosciusko, Miss.
Russelburg, Aaron	3	0	1.40	5	5	0	0	26	19	6	4	10	17	.215	R	R	6-4	215	10-17-79	2001	Hawesville, Ky.
Teekel, Josh	1	0	1.75	15	0	0	3	36	23	7	7	15	31	.186	R	R	6-5	200	9-18-80	1999	Greenwell Springs, La.
Wodnicki, Mike	2	3	2.43	22	0	0	0	30	17	10	8	13	26	.170	R	R	6-3	210	1-17-80	2001	Southington, Conn.

JOHNSON CITY
Rookie

APPALACHIAN LEAGUE

BATTING	AVG	G	AB	R	H	2B	3B	HR	RBI	BB	SO	SB	CS	SLG	OBP	B	T	HT	WT	DOB	1st Yr	Resides
Amaya, Pilar	.213	54	169	24	36	11	0	3	16	22	40	2	2	.331	.316	B	R	6-3	190	3-29-80	2001	San Diego, Calif.
Ankiel, Rick	.286	41	105	21	30	7	0	10	35	11	26	0	0	.638	.364	L	L	6-1	210	7-19-79	1997	Fort Pierce, Fla.
Davie, Andrew	.221	39	113	8	25	6	0	2	22	20	43	2	1	.327	.348	L	R	6-5	230	1-5-80	2001	Little Rock, Ark.
Gomez, Jose	.143	16	35	4	5	1	1	0	0	6	13	1	0	.229	.268	R	R	6-2	170	1-8-81	1998	Caracas, Venez.
Green, Steve	.296	44	125	21	37	4	2	2	9	10	28	4	1	.408	.380	L	R	6-1	180	7-22-78	2001	Monticello, Ark.
Gunn, Cody	.197	25	71	4	14	5	0	0	5	6	30	1	1	.268	.288	L	R	6-0	185	3-9-82	2001	Brewster, Wash.
Hileman, Jutt	.255	61	220	36	56	8	2	9	35	25	81	4	4	.432	.332	R	R	6-1	180	7-13-81	2000	Palmyra, Mo.
Kantrovitz, Dan	.333	1	3	0	1	0	0	0	0	0	0	0	0	.333	.333	R	R	5-8	180	9-8-78	2001	St. Louis, Mo.
Levy, Mike	.256	19	43	7	11	1	2	8	6	18	0	0	.465	.347	R	R	5-11	205	3-11-79	2001	Atlanta, Ga.
Mather, Joe	.248	45	165	25	41	3	0	5	21	7	60	2	2	.358	.288	R	R	6-4	195	7-23-82	2001	Phoenix, Ariz.
Mojica, Robinson	.220	36	118	7	26	5	1	0	8	3	25	0	3	.280	.242	R	R	6-2	170	5-31-82	2000	Bani, D.R.
Molina, Yadier	.259	44	158	18	41	6	0	4	18	12	23	1	1	.405	.320	R	R	5-11	187	7-13-82	2000	Vega Alta, P.R.
Moore, Bryan	.229	54	179	20	41	7	0	3	26	21	37	4	1	.318	.336	L	L	6-2	225	3-20-80	2001	Fort Lauderdale, Fla.
Nolasco, Jose	.204	55	191	25	39	7	0	3	22	22	48	8	3	.288	.290	B	R	6-2	162	6-20-81	1999	Santo Domingo, D.R.
Reyes, Eduardo	.190	19	42	5	8	2	0	1	4	2	15	0	1	.310	.234	R	R	5-11	155	1-14-82	2001	San Pedro de Macoris, D.R.
Simoneaux, Neil	.203	49	153	29	31	6	3	2	5	20	42	5	1	.320	.301	R	R	6-1	180	3-16-80	2001	Lake Charles, La.
Woodrow, Justin	.313	60	211	32	66	11	3	2	21	38	27	4	4	.422	.418	L	R	6-1	185	3-26-82	2000	Sarver, Pa.

GAMES BY POSITION: C—Gunn 24, Levy 6, Molina 42. **1B**—Amaya 1, Davie 10, Moore 53, Nolasco 4. **2B**—Amaya 2, Hileman 6, Nolasco 10, Reyes 13, Simoneaux 40. **3B**—Amaya 2, Mather 41, Nolasco 24. **SS**—Hileman 52, Mather 4, Nolasco 4, Simoneaux 7. **OF**—Amaya 49, Davie 3, J. Gomez 15, Green 41, Mojica 35, Nolasco 13, Woodrow 59.

PITCHING	W	L	ERA	G	GS	CG	SV	IP	H	R	ER	BB	SO	AVG	B	T	HT	WT	DOB	1st Yr	Resides
Ankiel, Rick	5	3	1.33	14	14	1	0	87	42	20	13	18	158	.000	L	L	6-1	210	7-19-79	1997	Fort Pierce, Fla.
Batista, Roberto	2	3	3.38	20	3	0	0	43	54	23	16	9	30	.308	R	R	6-1	165	3-10-82	1999	Guaymate, D.R.
Bravo, Edgar	0	3	5.06	18	0	0	1	21	17	15	12	16	15	.232	R	R	6-4	180	5-5-82	2000	Carabobo, Venez.
Frey, Jason	1	0	4.15	3	3	0	0	13	11	6	6	4	13	.250	R	R	6-6	210	5-24-78	2001	Highland, Ill.
Gomez, Deibis	0	1	3.00	4	0	0	1	3	6	2	1	2	2	.000	R	R	6-2	165	3-16-80	1998	Maracaibo, Venez.
Johnson, Tyler	1	1	2.66	9	9	0	0	41	26	17	12	21	58	.180	B	L	6-2	180	6-7-81	2001	Newbury Park, Calif.
Killalea, John	0	3	6.39	7	7	0	0	25	32	19	18	16	29	.320	L	L	6-1	200	2-23-83	2001	Seminole, Fla.
Ledbetter, Aaron	1	7	6.13	11	11	0	0	47	72	40	32	12	54	.346	R	R	6-5	210	6-28-81	2001	Fort Smith, Ark.
Martinez, Wilmer	6	3	2.10	23	0	0	0	34	32	18	8	11	25	.244	R	R	6-3	155	4-3-81	1998	Miranda, Venez.
Morales, Juan	0	0	5.40	4	3	0	0	13	17	12	8	2	10	.320	R	R	6-4	170	12-1-82	2000	Bonao, D.R.
Palmer, Travis	1	2	4.19	10	7	0	0	39	45	22	18	14	29	.294	R	R	6-3	190	10-5-79	2001	Sandy, Utah
Plancich, Nick	2	2	1.18	9	9	0	0	38	32	12	5	10	19	.225	R	R	6-2	190	9-12-78	2001	Redondo Beach, Calif.
Rawson, Anthony	3	1	0.60	23	0	0	10	30	19	3	2	7	45	.184	L	L	5-11	180	7-31-80	2001	Kosciusko, Miss.
Rogers, Joe	1	1	3.21	15	0	0	1	28	22	15	10	8	46	.211	L	L	6-2	175	7-19-81	2001	Fullerton, Calif.
Rojas, Yorlan	2	0	3.96	19	0	0	0	25	23	15	11	12	25	.247	R	R	6-1	170	5-15-80	1997	San Joaquin, Venez.
Shouse, Dan	2	2	4.96	12	0	0	0	16	23	15	9	5	12	.328	L	L	6-3	200	9-21-78	2001	Wildwood, Mo.
Thomas, Matt	4	2	4.68	20	0	0	0	25	23	17	13	7	22	.237	R	R	6-2	205	2-19-79	2001	Palo Pinto, Texas
Turner, Brad	0	1	2.81	15	0	0	0	26	18	14	8	15	37	.193	R	R	6-0	200	12-9-77	2001	Clarksville, Ind.

SAN DIEGO PADRES

BY JOHN MAFFEI

The veterans—lefthander Sterling Hitchcock and righthander Woody Williams—were traded. The kids—righthanders Brian Lawrence, Jason Middlebrook and Junior Herndon—were given a chance.

And while the deals probably cost the Padres some games in the National League West and a realistic shot at finishing .500, the experience the young starters gained in 2001 could pay huge dividends in 2002 and beyond.

"We needed to trim payroll, but we also needed to provide some of our young starters the chance to pitch in the big leagues," said Padres general manager Kevin Towers, whose team finished 79-83, in fourth place.

The Padres saved about $8 million by trading Hitchcock to the Yankees and Williams to the Cardinals. Those deals allowed Lawrence 14 starts, Herndon eight and Middlebrook three. Even Brett Jodie, who was acquired in the Hitchcock deal, started twice.

Righthander Adam Eaton (8-5, 5.32) was scheduled to miss the 2002 season because of Tommy John surgery; the same goes for lefthander Kevin Walker. Jeremy Fikac, called up from Double-A Mobile, took some of the sting out of losing Walker by going 2-0, 1.37 in 23 appearances.

Padres executives will have to decide where to play third baseman Phil Nevin (.306-41-125), first baseman Ryan Klesko (.286-30-113) and outfielder Bubba Trammell (.261-25-91) in 2002, to accommodate third baseman Sean Burroughs, the organization's top prospect. At Triple-A Portland, Burroughs hit .322-9-55.

The middle infield is shaky but appears set for 2002. D'Angelo Jimenez, acquired from the Yankees during the 2001 season, hit .276-2-32 but in the field his concentration often was lacking. He committed 21 errors.

The catching position is in solid hands with Ben Davis and Wiki Gonzalez, and Mark Kotsay is locked into center field. Kotsay (.291-10-58), acquired before the season from Florida, could assume the leadoff role.

Phil Nevin   Sean Burroughs

PLAYERS OF THE YEAR

MAJOR LEAGUE: Phil Nevin, 3b
Though he faces a stiff challenge from Padres prospects for the third base job in San Diego, Nevin solidified his case by leading the team in the three triple-crown categories—average (.306), homers (41) and RBIs (126).

MINOR LEAGUE: Sean Burroughs, 3b
Burroughs remains on course to knock Nevin off third base in San Diego. He had another big year in 2001 at Triple-A Portland, hitting .322-9-55.

If Trammell, Kotsay and Klesko are the outfielders, it leaves youngster Mike Darr (.278-2-34) and $7 million man Ray Lankford (.252-19-58) as reserves.

Still at least two years away from moving into their new downtown ballpark, the Padres will probably have a player budget of between $30 million and $40 million. So Towers has to be creative in filling in the gaps.

There appears to be little immediate help in the minor leagues. The organization's six farm teams finished 334-374 (.471), with 91 of those wins coming at Class A Lake Elsinore, co-champion of the California League and Baseball America's Minor League Team of the Year.

The signing of expensive six-year free agents proved to be a bust at Portland (71-73), San Diego's new Triple-A club. Farm director Tye Waller said the Padres will not go that route again in 2002.

The strength of the organization is clearly its young arms. In lefthanders Mike Bynum, bothered by a knee injury in 2001, Eric Cyr, Oliver Perez and Mark Phillips; righthanders Ben Howard, Jake Peavy, Dennis Tankersley and Chris Rojas; and closers J.J. Trujillo and Andy Shibilo, the Padres have a number of pitchers on the horizon with big league stuff.

The majority will probably be at Double-A Mobile in 2002, united again with manager Craig Colbert and pitching coach Darren Balsley, who have gone a combined 163-114 at Class A Fort Wayne and Lake Elsinore in the last two years.

Outside of Burroughs, position help appears to be a year or two away. Speedy outfielder Jeremy Owens had a disappointing season at Mobile and was demoted to Lake Elsinore, where outfielders Todd Donovan, Vince Faison and Ben Johnson had breakthrough seasons. First baseman Xavier Nady was the anchor of that club, leading Padres minor leaguers with 26 homers and 100 RBIs.

ORGANIZATION LEADERS

BATTING
*AVG	Abner Arroyo, Fort Wayne	.338
R	Xavier Nady, Lake Elsinore	96
H	Xavier Nady, Lake Elsinore	158
TB	Xavier Nady, Lake Elsinore	276
2B	Xavier Nady, Lake Elsinore	38
3B	Shawn Garrett, Lake Elsinore	8
HR	Kevin Witt, Portland	27
RBI	Xavier Nady, Lake Elsinore	100
BB	Graham Koonce, Portland/Mobile	94
SO	Jeremy Owens, Mobile/Lake Elsinore	188
SB	Jeremy Owens, Mobile/Lake Elsinore	37

PITCHING
W	Jimmy Osting, Portland/Mobile	11
L	Rick Guttormson, Portland/Mobile	17
#ERA	Eric Cyr, Lake Elsinore	1.61
G	Clay Condrey, Portland/Mobile	66
	J.J. Trujillo, Portland/Mobile	66
CG	Justin Germano, Fort Wayne/Eugene	2
SV	J.J. Trujillo, Portland/Mobile	19
IP	Chris Rojas, Lake Elsinore	160
BB	Chris Rojas, Lake Elsinore	71
SO	Jake Peavy, Mobile/Lake Elsinore	188

*Minimum 250 At-Bats #Minimum 75 Innings

SAN DIEGO PADRES

Manager: Bruce Bochy

2001 Record: 79-83, .488 (4th, NL West)

ORGANIZATION STATISTICS

BATTING	AVG	G	AB	R	H	2B	3B	HR	RBI	BB	SO	SB	CS	SLG	OBP	B	T	HT	WT	DOB	1st Yr	Resides
Arias, Alex	.226	70	137	19	31	9	0	2	12	17	22	1	0	.336	.312	R	R	6-3	202	11-20-67	1987	Hollywood, Fla.
Brown, Emil	.071	13	14	3	1	0	0	0	0	1	7	2	0	.071	.133	R	R	6-2	193	12-29-74	1994	Chicago, Ill.
2-team (61 Pitt.)	.190	74	137	21	26	4	1	3	13	16	49	12	4	.299	.284							
Colangelo, Mike	.242	50	91	10	22	3	3	2	8	8	30	0	0	.407	.310	R	R	6-1	185	10-22-76	1997	Dumfries, Va.
Crespo, Cesar	.209	55	153	27	32	6	0	4	12	25	50	6	2	.327	.320	B	R	5-11	170	5-23-79	1997	Caguas, P.R.
Darr, Mike	.277	105	289	36	80	13	1	2	34	39	72	6	2	.349	.363	L	R	6-3	205	3-21-76	1994	Corona, Calif.
Davis, Ben	.239	138	448	56	107	20	0	11	57	66	112	4	4	.357	.337	B	R	6-4	215	3-10-77	1995	West Chester, Pa.
Gomez, Chris	.188	40	112	6	21	3	0	0	7	9	14	1	0	.214	.244	R	R	6-1	195	6-16-71	1992	Carlsbad, Calif.
Gonzalez, Wiki	.275	64	160	16	44	6	0	8	27	11	28	2	0	.463	.335	R	R	5-11	203	5-17-74	1992	Palo Negro, Venez.
Gwynn, Tony	.324	71	102	5	33	9	1	1	17	10	9	1	0	.461	.384	L	L	5-11	225	5-9-60	1981	Poway, Calif.
Henderson, Rickey	.227	123	379	70	86	17	3	8	42	81	84	25	7	.351	.366	L	L	5-10	190	12-25-58	1976	Hillsborough, Calif.
Jackson, Damian	.241	122	440	67	106	21	6	4	38	44	128	23	6	.343	.316	R	R	5-11	185	8-16-73	1992	Concord, Calif.
Jimenez, D'Angelo	.276	86	308	45	85	19	0	3	33	39	68	2	3	.367	.355	B	R	6-0	194	12-21-77	1995	Santo Domingo, D.R.
Klesko, Ryan	.286	146	538	105	154	34	6	30	113	88	89	23	4	.539	.384	L	L	6-3	220	6-12-71	1989	Covington, Ga.
Kotsay, Mark	.291	119	406	67	118	29	1	10	58	48	58	13	5	.441	.366	L	L	6-0	190	12-2-75	1996	Pembroke Pines, Fla.
Lankford, Ray	.288	40	125	20	36	10	1	4	19	18	40	6	0	.480	.386	L	L	5-11	200	6-5-67	1987	St. Louis, Mo.
2-team (91 St. Louis)	.252	131	389	58	98	28	4	19	58	62	145	10	2	.491	.358							
Magadan, Dave	.250	91	128	12	32	7	0	1	12	12	20	0	0	.328	.317	L	R	6-4	215	9-30-62	1983	Tampa, Fla.
Mendez, Donaldo	.153	46	118	11	18	2	1	1	5	5	37	1	2	.212	.206	R	R	6-1	155	6-7-78	1996	Barquisimeto, Venez.
Nevin, Phil	.306	149	546	97	167	31	0	41	126	71	147	4	4	.588	.388	R	R	6-2	231	1-19-71	1992	San Diego, Calif.
Perez, Santiago	.198	43	81	13	16	1	0	0	4	15	29	5	1	.210	.320	B	R	6-2	150	12-30-75	1993	Santo Domingo, D.R.
Riggs, Adam	.194	12	36	2	7	1	0	0	1	2	8	1	1	.222	.237	R	R	6-0	190	10-4-72	1994	Andover, N.J.
Trammell, Bubba	.261	142	490	66	128	20	3	25	92	48	78	2	2	.467	.330	R	R	6-2	220	11-6-71	1994	Clearwater, Fla.
Wilkins, Rick	.182	12	22	3	4	1	0	1	8	2	8	0	0	.364	.250	L	R	6-2	215	6-4-67	1987	Jacksonville, Fla.
Witt, Kevin	.185	14	27	5	5	0	0	2	5	2	7	0	0	.407	.233	L	R	6-4	210	1-5-76	1994	Jacksonville, Fla.

PITCHING	W	L	ERA	G	GS	CG	SV	IP	H	R	ER	BB	SO	AVG	B	T	HT	WT	DOB	1st Yr	Resides
Davey, Tom	2	4	4.50	39	0	0	0	38	41	22	19	17	37	.271	R	R	6-7	230	9-11-73	1994	Canton, Mich.
Eaton, Adam	8	5	4.32	17	17	2	0	117	108	61	56	40	109	.240	R	R	6-2	190	11-23-77	1996	Snohomish, Wash.
Fikac, Jeremy	2	0	1.37	23	0	0	0	26	15	6	4	5	19	.164	R	R	6-2	195	4-8-75	1998	Shiner, Texas
Herndon, Junior	2	6	6.33	12	8	0	0	43	55	34	30	25	14	.321	R	R	6-1	190	9-11-78	1997	Craig, Colo.
Hitchcock, Sterling	2	1	3.32	3	3	0	0	19	22	9	7	3	15	.275	L	L	6-0	205	4-29-71	1989	Tampa, Fla.
Hoffman, Trevor	3	4	3.43	62	0	0	43	60	48	25	23	21	63	.216	R	R	6-0	215	10-13-67	1989	Del Mar, Calif.
Jarvis, Kevin	12	11	4.79	32	32	1	0	193	189	107	103	49	133	.254	B	R	6-2	200	8-1-69	1991	Lexington, Ky.
Jodie, Brett	0	1	4.63	7	2	0	0	23	19	12	12	12	13	.228	R	R	6-4	208	3-25-77	1998	Lexington, S.C.
Jones, Bobby	8	19	5.12	33	33	1	0	195	250	137	111	38	113	.304	R	R	6-4	225	2-10-70	1991	Fresno, Calif.
Lawrence, Brian	5	5	3.45	27	15	1	0	115	107	53	44	34	84	.244	R	R	6-0	195	5-14-76	1998	Linden, Texas
Lee, David	1	0	3.70	41	0	0	0	49	52	20	20	27	42	.278	R	R	6-1	202	3-12-73	1995	Pittsburgh, Pa.
Loewer, Carlton	0	2	24.92	2	2	0	0	4	13	12	12	3	1	.520	R	R	6-6	211	9-24-73	1995	Eunice, La.
Lundquist, David	0	1	5.95	17	0	0	0	20	20	13	13	7	19	.259	R	R	6-2	200	6-4-73	1993	Carson City, Nev.
Maurer, Dave	0	0	10.80	3	0	0	0	5	8	6	6	4	4	.347	R	L	6-2	205	2-23-75	1997	Burnsville, Minn.
McElroy, Chuck	1	1	5.16	31	0	0	0	30	38	24	17	18	25	.306	L	L	6-0	205	10-1-67	1986	Lindale, Texas
Middlebrook, Jason	2	1	5.12	4	3	0	0	19	18	11	11	10	10	.246	R	R	6-3	215	6-26-75	1996	Grass Lake, Mich.
Myers, Rodney	1	2	5.32	37	0	0	1	47	53	31	28	20	29	.291	R	R	6-1	205	6-26-69	1990	Chandler, Ariz.
Nunez, Jose	4	1	3.31	56	0	0	0	52	48	20	19	20	49	.244	L	L	6-2	173	3-14-79	1996	Montecristi, D.R.
2-team (6 Los Angeles)	4	2	4.58	62	0	0	0	59	62	35	30	25	60	.267							
Osting, Jimmy	0	0	0.00	3	0	0	0	2	1	0	0	2	3	.142	R	L	6-5	190	4-7-77	1995	Louisville, Ky.
Seanez, Rudy	0	2	2.63	26	0	0	1	24	15	8	7	15	24	.176	R	R	5-11	205	10-20-68	1986	El Centro, Calif.
Serrano, Wascar	3	3	6.56	20	5	0	0	47	60	37	34	21	39	.312	R	R	6-2	178	6-2-78	1995	Bani, D.R.
Tollberg, Brian	10	4	4.30	19	19	0	0	117	133	58	56	25	71	.286	R	R	6-3	195	9-16-72	1994	Bradenton, Fla.
Walker, Kevin	0	0	3.00	16	0	0	0	12	5	4	4	8	17	.121	L	L	6-4	190	9-20-76	1995	Glen Rose, Texas
Williams, Woody	8	8	4.97	23	23	0	0	145	170	88	80	37	102	.296	R	R	6-0	195	8-19-66	1988	Fresno, Texas
Witasick, Jay	5	2	1.86	31	0	0	1	39	31	14	8	15	53	.218	R	R	6-4	235	8-28-72	1993	Bel Air, Md.

FIELDING

Catcher	PCT	G	PO	A	E	DP	PB
Davis	.990	135	845	60	9	14	8
Gonzalez	.989	47	246	21	3	3	6
Wilkins	1.000	7	38	0	0	0	1

First Base	PCT	G	PO	A	E	DP
Arias	.980	17	91	9	2	6
Davis	1.000	2	9	1	0	0
Klesko	.991	145	1135	84	11	92
Magadan	.963	9	24	2	1	2
Wilkins	1.000	1	1	0	0	0
Witt	1.000	9	69	3	0	4

Second Base	PCT	G	PO	A	E	DP
Arias	.974	13	19	19	1	3
Crespo	.970	34	62	67	4	12
Gomez	1.000	8	9	11	0	5
Jackson	.986	118	241	323	8	68

	PCT	G	PO	A	E	DP
Magadan	.000	1	0	0	0	0
Perez	1.000	2	4	2	0	0
Riggs	1.000	11	12	20	0	5

Third Base	PCT	G	PO	A	E	DP
Arias	.957	18	5	17	1	1
Crespo	1.000	2	1	0	0	0
Magadan	.950	22	15	23	2	2
Nevin	.930	145	96	265	27	26
Riggs	1.000	1	1	4	0	0

Shortstop	PCT	G	PO	A	E	DP
Arias	.971	13	17	16	1	3
Crespo	1.000	1	1	1	0	0
Gomez	.937	36	31	58	6	14
Jackson	1.000	3	2	6	0	0
Jimenez	.948	85	130	255	21	47
Magadan	.000	1	0	0	0	0

	PCT	G	PO	A	E	DP
Mendez	.920	46	47	91	12	15
Perez	.900	8	8	10	2	1

Outfield	PCT	G	PO	A	E	DP
Brown	1.000	11	9	0	0	0
Colangelo	.979	40	45	1	1	0
Crespo	1.000	18	29	1	0	0
Darr	.990	93	183	6	2	2
Gwynn	1.000	17	17	2	0	0
Henderson	.982	104	158	5	3	2
Jackson	1.000	2	2	0	0	0
Kotsay	.986	111	277	4	4	1
Lankford	.985	38	63	1	1	0
Perez	.947	26	35	1	2	0
Trammell	.985	132	261	5	4	0

Vice President, Minor Leagues/Scouting: Tye Waller

Class	Farm Team	League	W	L	Pct.	Finish*	Manager	First Yr.
AAA	Portland (Ore.) Beavers	Pacific Coast	71	73	.493	8th (16)	Rick Sweet	2001
AA	Mobile (Ala.) BayBears	Southern	65	73	.471	6th (10)	Tracy Woodson	1997
A#	Lake Elsinore (Calif.) Storm	California	91	49	.650	+1st (10)	Craig Colbert	2001
A	Fort Wayne (Ind.) Wizards	Midwest	54	83	.394	13th (14)	Tom Lawless	1999
A	Eugene (Ore.) Emeralds	Northwest	32	44	.421	7th (8)	Jeff Gardner	2001
Rookie#	Idaho Falls (Idaho) Braves	Pioneer	21	54	.280	7th (8)	Jake Molina	1995

*Finish in overall standings (No. of teams in league) #Advanced level +League champion

PORTLAND   Class AAA

PACIFIC COAST LEAGUE

BATTING	AVG	G	AB	R	H	2B	3B	HR	RBI	BB	SO	SB	CS	SLG	OBP	B	T	HT	WT	DOB	1st Yr	Resides
Brown, Emil	.321	22	78	10	25	8	2	3	8	6	17	3	1	.590	.384	R	R	6-2	193	12-29-74	1994	Chicago, Ill.
Burroughs, Sean	.322	104	394	60	127	28	1	9	55	37	54	9	2	.467	.386	L	R	6-2	200	9-12-80	1999	Long Beach, Calif.
Colangelo, Mike	.261	61	180	27	47	11	1	3	22	31	44	5	3	.383	.385	R	R	6-1	185	10-22-76	1997	Dumfries, Va.
Crespo, Cesar	.260	78	273	46	71	18	3	8	29	39	66	23	3	.436	.354	B	R	5-11	170	5-23-79	1997	Caguas, P.R.
DeCinces, Tim	.056	7	18	1	1	0	0	0	1	8	0	0	0	.056	.105	L	R	6-2	195	4-26-74	1996	Newport Beach, Calif.
DeHaan, Kory	.253	87	304	35	77	9	5	7	28	20	71	12	9	.385	.303	L	R	6-2	187	7-16-76	1997	Pella, Iowa
Eberwein, Kevin	.266	27	94	16	25	8	1	3	11	10	22	0	2	.468	.349	R	R	6-4	200	3-30-77	1998	Las Vegas, Nev.
Gautreau, Jake	.286	2	7	2	2	0	0	1	2	2	2	0	0	.714	.444	L	R	6-0	185	11-14-79	2001	South Padre Island, Texas
Gomez, Chris	.300	11	40	5	12	3	0	1	5	2	4	1	0	.450	.333	R	R	6-1	195	6-16-71	1992	Carlsbad, Calif.
Green, Chad	.224	21	67	12	15	4	1	2	2	9	28	4	1	.403	.316	B	R	5-10	180	6-28-75	1996	Cincinnati, Ohio
Greene, Charlie	.137	67	211	11	29	2	0	1	10	9	47	0	0	.161	.173	R	R	6-2	170	1-23-71	1991	Miami, Fla.
Hellman, Matthew	.000	1	3	0	0	0	0	0	0	0	1	0	0	.000	.000	R	R	5-11	185	11-18-78	2001	Burbank, Calif.
Henderson, Rickey	.275	9	40	5	11	3	0	0	2	1	9	1	0	.350	.392	R	L	5-10	190	12-25-58	1976	Hillsborough, Calif.
Jackson, Damian	.300	3	10	4	3	3	0	0	3	1	0	1	0	.600	.462	R	R	5-11	185	8-16-73	1992	Concord, Calif.
Koonce, Graham	.214	6	14	5	3	1	0	1	2	5	6	0	0	.500	.421	L	L	6-4	225	5-15-75	1994	Julian, Calif.
Leyritz, Jim	.261	16	46	8	12	1	0	5	10	5	13	1	0	.609	.340	R	R	6-0	220	12-27-63	1986	Cooper City, Fla.
Lorenzana, Luis	.000	2	4	0	0	0	0	0	0	0	1	0	0	.000	.000	R	R	6-2	193	11-9-78	1996	San Diego, Calif.
Loyd, Brian	.239	25	88	7	21	3	0	3	10	4	11	0	0	.375	.280	R	R	6-2	205	12-3-73	1996	Yorba Linda, Calif.
Luuloa, Keith	.272	64	217	31	59	13	2	4	16	13	24	1	1	.406	.323	R	R	6-0	190	5-23-74	1994	Canyon Lake, Calif.
Matos, Julius	.279	106	383	40	107	12	2	7	34	15	48	6	8	.376	.314	R	R	5-11	175	12-12-74	1994	Racine, Wis.
Nicholson, Kevin	.194	11	31	1	6	1	0	0	1	4	3	0	1	.226	.286	B	R	5-10	190	3-29-76	1997	Surrey, B.C.
Perez, Santiago	.272	46	184	31	50	12	0	5	10	15	59	18	3	.418	.333	B	R	6-2	150	12-30-75	1993	Santo Domingo, D.R.
Radmanovich, Ryan	.264	92	296	44	78	17	1	14	52	59	82	2	4	.470	.382	L	R	6-2	200	8-9-71	1993	Calgary, Alberta
Riggins, Auntwan	.000	1	1	0	0	0	0	0	0	1	0	0	0	.000	.000	B	R	6-1	170	6-17-76	1998	Houston, Texas
Riggs, Adam	.261	110	394	42	103	18	2	21	65	12	78	8	3	.477	.282	R	R	6-0	190	10-4-72	1994	Andover, N.J.
Roskos, John	.239	46	134	15	32	9	1	3	20	11	31	0	0	.388	.291	R	R	5-11	195	11-19-74	1993	Rio Rancho, N.M.
Thrower, Jake	.204	15	54	3	11	1	0	0	1	2	8	1	0	.222	.232	B	R	5-11	180	11-19-75	1997	Yuma, Ariz.
Wilkins, Rick	.212	68	222	18	47	15	2	6	33	15	77	0	1	.378	.257	L	R	6-2	215	6-4-67	1987	Jacksonville, Fla.
Witt, Kevin	.289	129	456	66	132	28	5	27	87	22	127	1	1	.550	.322	L	R	6-4	210	1-5-76	1994	Jacksonville, Fla.
Young, Ernie	.274	116	409	66	112	21	2	20	67	38	115	0	3	.482	.355	R	R	6-1	234	7-8-69	1990	Mesa, Ariz.

PITCHING	W	L	ERA	G	GS	CG	SV	IP	H	R	ER	BB	SO	AVG	B	T	HT	WT	DOB	1st Yr	Resides
Camp, Shawn	1	0	0.00	4	1	0	0	7	2	0	0	1	6	.095	R	R	6-0	200	11-18-75	1997	Fairfax, Va.
Condrey, Clay	1	3	4.75	39	0	0	2	53	63	37	28	13	45	.304	R	R	6-3	195	11-19-75	1998	Navasota, Texas
Corey, Bryan	8	7	4.67	47	12	0	6	106	124	55	55	31	66	.300	R	R	6-0	170	10-21-73	1993	Phoenix, Ariz.
Crowell, Jim	0	0	5.49	11	2	0	0	20	22	15	12	15	7	.293	R	L	6-4	230	5-14-74	1995	Valparaiso, Ind.
Donaldson, Bo	2	0	0.46	8	2	0	0	20	6	2	1	2	18	.092	R	R	6-2	200	10-10-74	1997	Philadelphia, Pa.
2-team (11 Nashville)	3	1	0.53	19	2	0	0	34	15	6	2	11	35	.132							
Fikac, Jeremy	0	0	3.00	1	0	0	0	3	3	1	1	0	3	.250	R	R	6-2	195	4-8-75	1998	Shiner, Texas
Giron, Isabel	4	1	4.87	44	0	0	0	65	74	36	35	27	69	.284	R	R	6-2	170	11-17-77	1995	Villa Mella, D.R.
Gonzalez, Gabe	0	1	12.46	3	0	0	0	4	9	6	6	3	1	.450	L	L	6-1	170	5-24-72	1995	Long Beach, Calif.
Guttormson, Rick	0	1	10.80	1	0	0	0	5	9	6	6	1	1	.409	R	R	6-2	185	1-11-77	1997	Anacortes, Wash.
Guzman, Domingo	1	2	6.75	11	0	0	1	17	20	13	13	5	16	.294	R	R	6-0	210	4-5-75	1994	San Cristobal, D.R.
Herbert, John	0	0	0.00	1	0	0	0	1	0	0	0	1	0	.000	R	R	6-8	230	10-23-77	2000	San Francisco, Calif.
Herndon, Junior	9	5	4.58	21	21	0	0	116	132	72	59	39	47	.286	R	R	6-1	190	9-11-78	1997	Craig, Colo.
Hitchcock, Sterling	2	0	3.71	3	3	0	0	17	20	7	7	2	11	.307	L	L	6-0	205	4-29-71	1989	Tampa, Fla.
Jodie, Brett	2	1	4.75	5	5	0	0	30	33	16	16	8	19	.277	R	R	6-4	208	3-25-77	1998	Lexington, S.C.
Lawrence, Brian	1	3	3.80	9	8	0	1	45	42	22	19	17	42	.238	R	R	6-0	195	5-14-76	1998	Linden, Texas
Lawrence, Sean	0	3	3.53	25	0	0	0	36	32	16	14	13	44	.233	L	L	6-4	215	9-2-70	1992	Hillside, Ill.
Lee, David	1	0	0.75	9	0	1	0	12	5	1	1	5	14	.131	R	R	6-2	202	3-12-73	1995	Pittsburgh, Pa.
Loewer, Carlton	5	4	3.87	14	12	0	0	81	97	42	35	15	64	.304	B	R	6-6	211	9-24-73	1995	Eunice, La.
Lopez, Rodrigo	2	2	3.44	11	8	0	0	52	45	22	20	15	37	.229	R	R	6-1	180	12-14-75	1995	Mexico City, Mexico
Lundquist, David	4	7	3.11	50	0	0	7	64	59	25	22	20	67	.245	R	R	6-2	200	6-4-73	1993	Carson City, Nev.
Mahay, Ron	1	2	3.78	14	0	0	0	17	13	9	7	5	18	.209	L	L	6-2	190	6-28-71	1991	Crestwood, Ill.
Maurer, Dave	0	0	4.34	17	0	0	1	19	11	9	9	9	21	.171	R	L	6-2	205	2-23-75	1997	Burnsville, Minn.
Middlebrook, Jason	7	4	3.29	15	15	0	0	90	86	34	33	23	66	.252	R	R	6-3	215	6-26-75	1996	Grass Lake, Mich.
Miller, Matt	1	7	3.63	44	0	0	17	45	44	22	18	14	43	.254	R	R	6-3	215	11-23-71	1997	Greenville, Miss.
Myers, Rodney	1	1	3.00	8	1	0	0	15	12	5	5	5	14	.245	R	R	6-1	205	6-26-69	1990	Chandler, Ariz.
Osting, Jimmy	1	4	9.59	5	5	0	0	25	41	27	27	10	15	.362	R	L	6-5	190	4-7-77	1995	Louisville, Ky.
Powell, Jeremy	4	2	1.59	11	11	0	0	74	43	14	13	14	63	.169	R	R	6-5	230	6-18-76	1994	Sacramento, Calif.
Serrano, Wascar	6	5	4.53	27	13	0	0	93	98	50	47	35	73	.277	R	R	6-2	178	6-2-78	1995	Bani, D.R.
Spencer, Stan	5	6	5.09	20	18	0	0	99	110	62	56	30	81	.282	R	R	6-4	223	8-7-69	1991	Battle Ground, Wash.
Tankersley, Dennis	1	2	6.91	3	3	0	0	14	16	13	11	8	16	.285	R	R	6-2	185	2-24-79	1999	St. Charles, Mo.
Tollberg, Brian	1	0	4.50	4	4	0	0	20	24	11	10	4	10	.292	R	R	6-3	195	9-16-72	1994	Bradenton, Fla.

FIELDING

Catcher	PCT	G	PO	A	E	DP	PB
DeCinces	1.000	6	32	2	0	0	1
Greene	.987	64	435	33	6	6	5
Loyd	.990	23	177	14	2	1	0
Roskos	1.000	1	3	0	0	0	0
Wilkins	.989	57	401	29	5	1	8

First Base	PCT	G	PO	A	E	DP
Eberwein	.976	14	113	7	3	10
Koonce	1.000	5	37	0	0	4
Leyritz	.980	11	88	9	2	0
Luuloa	1.000	17	123	9	0	8
Roskos	.995	27	180	13	1	11
Wilkins	1.000	6	40	3	0	2
Witt	.987	79	651	41	9	56

Second Base	PCT	G	PO	A	E	DP
Crespo	.982	34	66	94	3	15
Gomez	1.000	1	3	1	0	0
Luuloa	.988	18	32	47	1	14
Matos	1.000	10	20	22	0	3

	PCT	G	PO	A	E	DP
Perez	.941	7	13	19	2	5
Riggs	.964	82	150	221	14	41
Thrower	1.000	6	10	16	0	3

Third Base	PCT	G	PO	A	E	DP
Burroughs	.964	96	79	192	10	18
Crespo	.968	11	5	25	1	1
Eberwein	1.000	13	8	19	0	1
Gautreau	1.000	2	0	5	0	0
Luuloa	.950	10	5	14	1	1
Riggs	.923	12	7	17	2	3
Thrower	.833	7	3	7	2	1
Witt	1.000	1	0	1	0	0

Shortstop	PCT	G	PO	A	E	DP
Crespo	1.000	14	15	37	0	6
Gomez	.956	10	10	33	2	5
Jackson	1.000	3	3	11	0	2
Lorenzana	1.000	2	1	3	0	0
Luuloa	.957	16	14	30	2	3
Matos	.967	96	145	266	14	46

	PCT	G	PO	A	E	DP
Nicholson	.950	9	18	20	2	4
Perez	1.000	3	2	6	0	1
Thrower	1.000	2	2	3	0	0

Outfield	PCT	G	PO	A	E	DP
Brown	1.000	21	39	2	0	0
Colangelo	.991	56	99	6	1	0
Crespo	1.000	23	43	2	0	1
DeHaan	.990	80	198	9	2	2
Green	.950	17	38	0	2	0
Greene	.000	1	0	0	0	0
Hellman	1.000	1	1	1	0	0
Henderson	.933	9	14	0	1	0
Leyritz	.000	1	0	0	0	0
Luuloa	1.000	4	7	0	0	0
Perez	.987	36	73	4	1	0
Radmanovich	1.000	84	140	5	0	0
Riggs	1.000	1	1	0	0	0
Witt	.947	38	51	3	3	0
Young	.974	89	140	11	4	2

MOBILE Class AA

SOUTHERN LEAGUE

BATTING	AVG	G	AB	R	H	2B	3B	HR	RBI	BB	SO	SB	CS	SLG	OBP	B	T	HT	WT	DOB	1st Yr	Resides
Benjamin, Al	.273	110	374	50	102	23	2	12	50	18	73	8	3	.441	.305	R	R	6-1	200	9-9-77	1996	Houston, Texas
Blakely, Darren	.217	28	115	19	25	4	2	6	15	11	41	4	4	.443	.300	B	R	6-0	190	3-14-77	1998	Pensacola, Fla.
Colangelo, Mike	.265	9	34	5	9	0	1	1	4	4	8	0	0	.412	.342	R	R	6-1	185	10-22-76	1997	Dumfries, Va.
Cosentino, Tony	.000	5	10	0	0	0	0	0	0	2	2	0	0	.000	.167	R	R	6-0	195	12-7-78	1997	Torrance, Calif.
Darr, Mike	.200	2	5	1	1	0	0	0	0	2	4	0	0	.200	.429	L	R	6-3	205	3-21-76	1994	Corona, Calif.
Davidson, Cleatus	.218	125	467	39	102	18	4	2	34	23	101	13	8	.287	.254	B	R	5-10	180	11-1-76	1994	Haines City, Fla.
DeRosso, Tony	.234	28	94	8	22	5	0	3	18	9	20	0	0	.383	.318	R	R	6-3	226	11-7-75	1994	Moultrie, Ga.
2-team (65 Huntsville)	.234	93	312	29	73	22	0	9	43	28	56	0	1	.391	.303							
DeCinces, Tim	.206	56	180	11	37	4	1	4	25	19	29	0	0	.306	.277	L	R	6-2	195	4-26-74	1996	Newport Beach, Calif.
DeHaan, Kory	.296	42	159	29	47	8	2	4	23	22	27	12	4	.447	.382	L	R	6-2	187	7-16-76	1997	Pella, Iowa
Green, Chad	.226	42	137	14	31	8	3	1	15	11	42	3	2	.350	.282	B	R	5-10	180	6-28-75	1996	Cincinnati, Ohio
Hopper, Shane	.257	69	191	27	49	10	0	2	23	16	52	5	4	.340	.325	R	R	6-1	205	9-22-75	1999	Winder, Ga.
Koonce, Graham	.266	109	320	52	85	18	0	13	48	89	83	0	0	.444	.429	L	L	6-4	225	5-15-75	1994	Julian, Calif.
Loggins, Josh	.191	34	89	10	17	3	0	2	6	6	27	0	0	.292	.247	R	R	6-1	190	11-29-76	1998	West Lafayette, Ind.
Lorenzana, Luis	.182	5	11	1	2	0	0	0	0	1	5	0	0	.182	.250	R	R	6-2	193	11-9-78	1996	San Diego, Calif.
Matos, Julius	.328	19	67	13	22	6	0	0	2	1	5	1	2	.418	.343	R	R	5-11	175	12-12-74	1994	Racine, Wis.
McNeal, Aaron	.291	59	220	27	64	13	1	6	29	16	53	0	1	.441	.343	R	R	6-3	230	4-28-76	1996	Castro Valley, Calif.
Nieves, Wil	.300	95	330	28	99	24	0	3	41	18	40	1	0	.400	.336	R	R	5-11	190	9-25-77	1996	Santurce, P.R.
Owens, Jeremy	.215	107	395	46	85	20	6	7	26	55	149	33	12	.349	.311	R	R	6-1	200	12-9-76	1998	Johnson City, Tenn.
Pelaez, Alex	.281	114	416	44	117	22	1	10	53	32	52	2	0	.411	.332	R	R	5-9	190	4-6-76	1998	Chula Vista, Calif.
Powers, John	.276	96	315	41	87	15	6	4	35	37	58	7	5	.400	.352	L	R	5-9	165	6-2-74	1996	Scottsdale, Ariz.
Riggins, Auntwan	.147	14	34	0	5	0	0	1	2	8	1	1	1	.147	.216	B	R	6-1	170	6-17-76	1998	Houston, Texas
Scheschuk, John	.181	21	83	8	15	4	0	1	9	5	14	1	0	.265	.244	L	L	6-2	208	2-2-77	1999	Houston, Texas
Thrower, Jake	.272	103	386	46	105	25	1	4	31	45	66	3	3	.373	.355	R	R	5-11	180	11-19-75	1997	Yuma, Ariz.
Tucci, Pete	.185	18	65	3	12	0	0	0	7	3	22	1	1	.185	.217	R	R	6-2	210	10-8-75	1996	Norwalk, Conn.

PITCHING	W	L	ERA	G	GS	CG	SV	IP	H	R	ER	BB	SO	AVG	B	T	HT	WT	DOB	1st Yr	Resides
Bartosh, Cliff	1	2	3.97	20	0	0	2	23	20	12	10	13	20	.232	L	L	6-2	175	9-5-79	1998	Duncanville, Texas
Bausher, Andy	0	1	12.00	4	0	0	0	6	9	8	8	9	4	.000	R	L	6-2	200	8-17-76	1997	Bechtelsville, Pa.
Bynum, Mike	2	7	5.02	16	15	0	0	84	90	53	47	35	69	.278	L	L	6-4	200	3-20-78	1999	Middleburg, Fla.
Camp, Shawn	6	2	4.44	35	1	0	0	49	46	24	24	15	55	.261	R	R	6-1	200	11-18-75	1997	Fairfax, Va.
Condrey, Clay	2	4	4.54	27	0	0	12	34	33	23	17	15	21	.268	R	R	6-3	195	11-19-75	1998	Navasota, Texas
Crowell, Jim	1	0	2.08	5	0	0	0	4	2	1	1	4	0	.000	R	L	6-4	230	5-14-74	1995	Valparaiso, Ind.
Dent, Doug	0	1	10.13	3	1	0	0	5	10	6	6	5	2	.400	R	R	6-8	210	3-23-77	1998	Bellevue, Wash.
Fikac, Jeremy	0	0	1.97	53	0	0	18	69	54	16	15	20	75	.218	R	R	6-2	195	4-8-75	1998	Shiner, Texas
Giron, Isabel	0	0	1.96	14	0	0	0	18	15	5	4	4	20	.220	R	R	6-2	170	11-17-77	1995	Villa Mella, D.R.
Gonzalez, Gabe	1	0	1.32	8	0	0	0	14	18	6	2	1	8	.333	L	L	6-1	170	5-24-72	1995	Long Beach, Calif.
Guttormson, Rick	5	16	4.71	27	24	0	0	143	146	84	75	51	68	.264	R	R	6-2	185	1-11-77	1997	Anacortes, Wash.
Howard, Ben	2	0	2.40	7	5	0	0	30	17	9	8	15	29	.166	R	R	6-2	190	1-15-79	1997	Jackson, Tenn.
Hunter, Johnny	3	6	4.85	19	16	1	0	98	105	57	53	37	61	.277	R	R	6-1	190	6-14-75	1997	Mansfield, Texas
Kramer, Aaron	2	7	5.26	23	4	0	0	50	53	32	29	12	41	.269	B	R	6-1	210	6-25-75	1998	Glendale, Ariz.
Lee, David	0	0	0.00	2	0	0	0	2	2	0	0	0	3	.285	R	R	6-2	202	3-12-73	1995	Pittsburgh, Pa.
Middlebrook, Jason	3	0	1.20	10	9	0	0	53	36	10	7	9	51	.191	R	R	6-3	215	6-26-75	1996	Grass Lake, Mich.
Osting, Jimmy	9	4	3.59	18	18	0	0	98	85	41	39	42	69	.236	R	L	6-5	190	4-7-77	1998	Louisville, Ky.
2-team (1 Carolina)	10	4	3.51	19	19	0	0	103	88	42	40	45	72	.232							
Pearson, Jason	5	5	4.17	54	5	0	1	86	88	40	40	30	67	.268	L	L	6-0	195	12-29-75	1998	Cambridge, Mass.
Peavy, Jake	2	1	2.57	5	5	0	0	28	19	8	8	12	44	.191	R	R	6-1	180	5-31-81	1999	Semmes, Ala.
Pelaez, Alex	1	1	3.48	8	0	0	0	10	13	4	4	3	1	.000	R	R	5-9	190	4-6-76	1998	Chula Vista, Calif.
Shiell, Jason	2	3	4.44	45	2	0	0	81	91	46	40	32	60	.295	R	R	6-0	180	10-19-76	1996	Savannah, Ga.
Stevenson, Jason	1	2	3.57	10	1	0	0	18	20	8	7	10	9	.289	R	R	6-3	180	8-11-74	1994	Phenix City, Ala.
Tankersley, Dennis	4	1	2.07	13	13	0	0	70	44	23	16	24	89	.173	R	R	6-2	185	2-24-79	1999	St. Charles, Mo.
Trujillo, J.J.	3	3	2.65	43	0	0	6	51	44	20	15	20	44	.236	R	R	6-0	180	10-9-75	1999	Grand Prairie, Texas
Watkins, Steve	4	8	5.73	23	19	0	0	97	108	74	62	53	55	.283	R	R	6-4	190	7-19-78	1998	Lubbock, Texas

FIELDING

Catcher	PCT	G	PO	A	E	DP	PB
Cosentino	1.000	4	21	0	0	0	1
DeCinces	.997	49	308	18	1	3	2
Nieves	.996	91	696	63	3	9	12

First Base	PCT	G	PO	A	E	DP
Derosso	1.000	1	10	0	0	0
DeCinces	1.000	1	3	0	0	0
Hopper	1.000	1	1	0	0	0

	PCT	G	PO	A	E	DP
Koonce	.998	56	409	27	1	32
McNeal	.978	49	400	46	10	35
Pelaez	1.000	17	153	7	0	13
Scheschuk	.995	21	179	9	1	20

Second Base	PCT	G	PO	A	E	DP
Davidson	1.000	7	12	15	0	7
Lorenzana	.889	4	6	10	2	1
Matos	1.000	7	12	18	0	5
Pelaez	1.000	4	6	3	0	1
Powers	.966	43	79	119	7	21
Thrower	.981	85	152	208	7	38
Third Base	**PCT**	**G**	**PO**	**A**	**E**	**DP**
Bausher	.000	1	0	0	0	0
Crowell	1.000	1	1	0	0	0
Derosso	1.000	17	11	27	0	1

Hopper	.813	7	4	9	3	2
Pelaez	.964	89	57	156	8	23
Powers	.938	37	16	60	5	3
Thrower	.667	3	3	1	2	0
Shortstop	**PCT**	**G**	**PO**	**A**	**E**	**DP**
Davidson	.947	117	178	343	29	54
Matos	.909	13	18	32	5	8
Thrower	.967	16	24	35	2	5
Outfield	**PCT**	**G**	**PO**	**A**	**E**	**DP**
Benjamin	.966	98	162	6	6	1
Blakely	.988	28	82	0	1	0

Colangelo	.909	9	7	3	1	1
Darr	1.000	2	2	0	0	0
DeHaan	.988	42	80	3	1	0
Green	.971	39	68	0	2	0
Hopper	.984	38	60	0	1	0
Hunter	.000	1	0	0	0	0
Koonce	.941	27	31	1	2	0
Loggins	.979	27	44	3	1	0
Owens	.985	106	251	15	4	5
Riggins	1.000	10	17	0	0	0
Tucci	1.000	17	34	5	0	1

LAKE ELSINORE Class A

CALIFORNIA LEAGUE

BATTING	AVG	G	AB	R	H	2B	3B	HR	RBI	BB	SO	SB	CS	SLG	OBP	B	T	HT	WT	DOB	1st Yr	Resides
Benjamin, Al	.215	16	65	6	14	3	1	0	5	1	15	1	1	.292	.224	R	R	6-1	200	9-9-77	1996	Houston, Texas
Bitter, Jarrod	.218	35	119	13	26	9	0	2	16	5	37	0	0	.345	.254	R	R	6-1	227	10-16-78	2000	Tyler, Texas
Cosentino, Tony	.213	53	174	21	37	9	1	4	21	20	32	1	1	.345	.293	R	R	6-0	195	12-7-78	1997	Torrance, Calif.
Donovan, Todd	.304	41	168	37	51	7	0	1	12	19	25	23	2	.363	.378	R	R	6-1	175	8-12-78	1999	East Lyme, Conn.
Eberwein, Kevin	.333	9	30	6	10	4	0	2	4	6	6	0	0	.667	.459	R	R	6-4	200	3-30-77	1998	Las Vegas, Nev.
Faison, Vince	.233	73	275	27	64	11	3	7	36	24	94	12	7	.371	.297	L	R	6-0	180	1-22-81	1999	Lyons, Ga.
Garrett, Shawn	.313	77	275	41	86	16	8	1	44	24	57	16	7	.505	.373	B	R	6-3	190	11-2-78	1998	Kinmundy, Ill.
Gomez, Andre	.229	21	70	7	16	3	0	1	11	3	24	0	0	.314	.257	R	R	6-2	185	9-6-78	2000	Playa del Rey, Calif.
Gonzalez, Wiki	.154	4	13	1	2	0	0	0	1	2	4	0	0	.154	.250	R	R	5-11	203	5-17-74	1992	Palo Negro, Venez.
Hopper, Shane	.270	31	126	24	34	7	1	4	21	11	33	5	3	.437	.326	R	R	6-1	200	9-22-75	1999	Winder, Ga.
Johnson, Ben	.276	136	503	79	139	35	6	12	63	54	141	22	7	.441	.358	R	R	6-1	200	6-18-81	1999	Memphis, Tenn.
Lorenzana, Luis	.269	70	234	32	63	7	1	0	17	24	48	5	1	.308	.357	R	R	6-2	193	11-9-78	1996	San Diego, Calif.
Loyd, Brian	.304	14	46	8	14	3	0	0	10	3	6	0	0	.370	.353	R	R	6-2	205	12-3-73	1996	Yorba Linda, Calif.
Moore, Jason	.253	132	509	79	129	30	2	13	67	61	110	1	3	.397	.333	R	R	6-0	180	1-4-78	1999	Miami, Fla.
Nady, Xavier	.302	137	524	96	158	38	1	26	100	62	109	6	0	.527	.381	R	R	6-1	185	11-14-78	2001	Salinas, Calif.
O'Donnell, Ryan	.255	15	51	7	13	2	0	0	1	5	10	0	1	.294	.333	L	R	6-0	185	8-21-78	2000	Tempe, Ariz.
Owens, Jeremy	.198	24	91	8	18	1	1	3	9	7	39	4	2	.330	.260	R	R	6-1	200	12-9-76	1998	Johnson City, Tenn.
Riggins, Auntwan	.227	17	66	7	15	0	0	0	5	4	22	2	2	.227	.282	B	R	6-1	170	6-17-76	1998	Houston, Texas
Risinger, Ben	.251	105	351	32	88	16	0	1	46	32	86	2	5	.305	.333	R	R	6-1	170	11-25-77	1999	Perth, Australia
Scales, Bobby	.271	98	362	46	98	24	4	5	42	44	78	20	7	.401	.365	B	R	6-0	175	10-4-77	1999	Roswell, Ga.
Schader, Troy	.242	94	363	55	88	17	4	14	55	28	111	1	4	.427	.307	R	R	6-1	205	3-5-77	1999	La Center, Wash.
Scheschuk, John	.283	96	346	48	98	28	2	7	46	55	60	3	3	.436	.381	L	L	6-2	208	2-2-77	1999	Houston, Texas
Thurston, Jeremy	.156	14	45	3	7	0	0	2	2	0	20	0	0	.156	.208	R	R	6-0	200	4-17-72	1990	Longwood, Fla.

GAMES BY POSITION: C—Bitter 31, Cosentino 47, Gomez 9, Gonzalez 4, Loyd 12, Risinger 39, Thurston 14. **1B**—Nady 110, Risinger 3, Scheschuk 28. **2B**—Lorenzana 4, Moore 56, Risinger 26, Scales 59. **3B**—Eberwein 6, Moore 15, Risinger 41, Schader 87. **SS**—Lorenzana 65, Moore 65, Riggins 15. **OF**—Benjamin 15, Donovan 37, Faison 71, Garrett 72, Gomez 13, Hopper 30, Johnson 133, O'Donnell 15, Owens 13, Riggins 2, Scales 22, Schader 8.

PITCHING	W	L	ERA	G	GS	CG	SV	IP	H	R	ER	BB	SO	AVG	B	T	HT	WT	DOB	1st Yr	Resides
Bartosh, Cliff	6	2	1.58	38	0	0	10	46	42	17	8	12	66	.237	L	L	6-2	175	9-5-79	1998	Duncanville, Texas
Bausher, Andy	2	2	2.76	37	2	0	1	65	55	28	20	16	53	.220	R	L	6-2	200	8-17-76	1997	Bechtelsville, Pa.
Bumstead, Mike	1	2	6.68	19	0	0	0	32	35	25	24	18	33	.273	R	R	6-3	210	7-8-77	2001	Big Bear Lake, Calif.
Cyr, Eric	7	4	1.61	21	16	0	0	101	68	28	18	24	131	.184	R	L	6-4	200	2-11-79	1999	Ada, Okla.
Gaal, Bryan	3	3	3.64	35	0	0	3	47	37	23	19	17	50	.216	R	R	6-4	203	12-17-76	1999	Syracuse, N.Y.
Hitchcock, Sterling	0	2	4.10	6	6	0	0	26	33	18	12	1	31	.292	L	L	6-0	205	4-29-71	1989	Tampa, Fla.
Howard, Jason	8	2	2.83	18	18	0	0	102	86	37	32	32	107	.228	R	R	6-2	190	1-15-79	1997	Jackson, Tenn.
Hunter, Johnny	3	0	3.82	7	5	0	0	33	27	19	14	11	29	.221	R	R	6-1	190	6-14-75	1997	Mansfield, Texas
Loewer, Carlton	0	1	1.59	4	4	0	0	11	6	7	2	4	14	.142	B	R	6-6	211	9-24-73	1995	Eunice, La.
Lopez, Rodrigo	0	1	6.09	9	0	0	0	13	15	7	1	4	9	.277	R	R	6-1	180	12-14-75	1995	Mexico City, Mexico
Luque, Roger	0	0	27.00	1	0	0	0	1	3	3	3	1	1	.500	L	L	6-1	170	1-8-80	1997	Charallave, Venez.
Montgomery, Steve	0	0	21.60	2	1	0	0	2	4	4	4	0	2	.500	R	R	6-4	200	12-25-70	1992	Corona Del Mar, Calif.
Nicolas, Mike	0	1	5.25	8	0	0	0	12	11	7	7	5	15	.250	R	R	6-3	207	11-5-81	2000	Santo Domingo, D.R.
Oxspring, Chris	0	0	0.64	7	0	0	0	14	10	2	1	6	17	.200	L	R	6-0	183	5-13-77	2001	Queensland, Australia
Peavy, Jake	7	5	3.08	19	19	0	0	105	76	41	36	33	144	.200	R	R	6-1	180	5-31-81	1999	Semmes, Ala.
Perez, Oliver	2	4	2.72	9	9	0	0	53	45	22	16	25	62	.225	L	L	6-3	160	8-15-81	1999	Culiacan, Mexico
Phillips, Mark	2	1	2.57	5	5	0	0	28	19	8	8	14	34	.190	L	L	6-3	205	12-30-81	2000	Hanover, Pa.
Rojas, Chris	10	5	3.43	28	28	0	0	160	135	72	61	71	149	.227	R	R	6-2	189	3-30-77	1998	Glendale, N.Y.
Seanez, Rudy	2	0	2.08	7	0	0	0	9	7	3	2	2	8	.218	R	R	5-11	205	10-20-68	1986	El Centro, Calif.
Shibilo, Andy	10	2	1.96	60	0	0	15	83	66	24	18	27	105	.215	R	R	6-7	220	9-16-76	1998	Massapequa, N.Y.
Shiyuk, Todd	6	3	3.98	50	0	0	2	72	66	35	32	28	75	.245	L	L	6-0	190	1-31-77	1999	Delta, B.C.
Stevenson, Jason	1	1	5.65	11	0	0	0	14	25	12	9	4	14	.384	R	R	6-3	180	8-11-74	1994	Phenix City, Ala.
Tankersley, Dennis	5	1	0.52	9	8	0	0	52	29	5	3	12	68	.158	R	R	6-2	185	2-24-79	1999	St. Charles, Mo.
Thompson, Mike	5	4	5.35	19	12	0	0	74	82	46	44	25	39	.289	R	R	6-4	185	11-6-80	1999	Lamar, Colo.
Tollberg, Brian	0	2	6.30	2	2	0	0	10	18	11	7	1	9	.391	R	R	6-3	195	9-16-72	1994	Bradenton, Fla.
Trujillo, J.J.	4	1	1.86	23	0	0	13	29	20	7	6	13	31	.192	R	R	6-0	180	10-9-75	1999	Grand Prairie, Texas
Watkins, Steve	2	0	1.84	5	5	1	0	29	23	6	6	7	23	.207	R	R	6-4	190	7-19-78	1998	Lubbock, Texas
Young, Doug	4	0	3.03	20	0	0	0	30	26	17	10	12	23	.213	R	R	6-2	190	1-23-76	1997	Roseville, Calif.

FORT WAYNE Class A

MIDWEST LEAGUE

BATTING	AVG	G	AB	R	H	2B	3B	HR	RBI	BB	SO	SB	CS	SLG	OBP	B	T	HT	WT	DOB	1st Yr	Resides
Arroyo, Abner	.338	68	266	41	90	19	0	8	38	28	62	1	4	.500	.402	L	L	6-0	181	12-16-79	2000	Maunabo, P.R.
Bitter, Jarrod	.205	26	83	6	17	3	0	2	8	8	26	1	0	.313	.333	R	R	6-1	227	10-16-78	2000	Tyler, Texas
Castro, Renato	.158	14	38	1	6	2	0	0	2	2	8	1	0	.211	.220	R	R	6-2	180	12-30-79	1996	Haina, D.R.
Davis, Michael	.272	80	294	40	80	16	2	4	45	28	57	10	4	.381	.353	R	R	5-8	190	10-10-76	2001	Chicago, Ill.
Day, Nick	.000	5	12	0	0	0	0	0	0	0	3	0	0	.000	.000	R	R	6-2	205	1-16-78	2000	Las Vegas, Nev.
Edwards, Dytarious	.214	69	220	35	47	4	0	6	24	50	23	5	.232	.290	L	R	6-0	165	8-5-76	1999	Detroit, Mich.
Faison, Vince	.200	41	140	14	28	5	0	1	8	18	35	10	3	.257	.302	L	R	6-0	180	1-22-81	1999	Lyons, Ga.

BATTING

BATTING	AVG	G	AB	R	H	2B	3B	HR	RBI	BB	SO	SB	CS	SLG	OBP	B	T	HT	WT	DOB	1st Yr	Resides
Fears, Chris	.251	86	263	30	66	5	1	1	19	30	53	20	7	.289	.337	B	R	5-9	170	8-12-77	2000	Ozark, Mo.
Furmaniak, J.J.	.220	123	436	57	96	24	3	5	35	55	117	11	6	.323	.309	R	R	6-0	190	7-31-79	2000	Bolingbrook, Ill.
McCool, Lee	.237	102	392	35	93	17	3	1	36	20	77	8	5	.304	.279	R	R	5-11	180	3-5-79	2000	Palatka, Fla.
O'Donnell, Ryan	.269	29	108	16	29	4	0	0	7	9	20	4	0	.306	.322	L	R	6-0	185	8-21-78	2000	Tempe, Ariz.
Pagan, Andres	.223	90	319	24	71	13	0	1	25	6	85	4	1	.273	.235	R	R	6-4	185	3-18-81	1999	Yauco, P.R.
Puccinelli, John	.190	64	179	14	34	8	0	2	13	25	49	1	2	.268	.289	R	R	6-4	180	3-5-81	1999	North Hollywood, Calif.
Reese, Kevin	.329	125	459	84	151	30	6	13	73	54	62	30	10	.505	.402	L	L	5-11	195	3-11-78	2000	San Diego, Calif.
Riggins, Auntwan	.239	32	117	15	28	4	0	0	5	16	29	12	3	.274	.336	B	R	6-1	170	6-17-76	1998	Houston, Texas
Saba, Cesar	.223	84	291	29	65	10	1	6	31	21	61	2	6	.326	.282	R	R	6-0	160	8-2-81	1998	San Cristobal, D.R.
Segura, Rolando	.196	12	46	3	9	0	0	1	2	2	9	0	0	.196	.240	R	R	6-2	209	12-21-78	1995	San Pedro de Macoris, D.R.
Stone, Jon	.231	53	169	15	39	10	0	1	20	18	48	3	0	.308	.318	B	R	5-11	185	12-23-78	1999	Lodi, Calif.
Thompson, Craig	.261	87	310	53	81	27	2	10	59	41	35	8	1	.458	.344	B	R	6-0	190	9-27-77	2000	Dallas, Texas
Woodward, J.P.	.196	116	414	48	81	23	1	15	64	49	114	7	4	.365	.289	L	R	6-3	220	11-10-76	2000	Spring, Texas

GAMES BY POSITION: C—Bitter 5, Pagan 90, Puccinelli 1, Stone 44. **1B**—Bitter 3, Puccinelli 9, Segura 3, Thompson 14, Woodward 110. **2B**—Davis 12, Day 1, Edwards 22, Fears 1, Furmaniak 3, McCool 95, Saba 7. **3B**—Davis 27, Edwards 10, McCool 1, Puccinelli 54, Saba 60, Stone 1. **SS**—Edwards 5, Furmaniak 117, Riggins 2, Saba 16. **OF**—Arroyo 46, Castro 11, Davis 3, Day 4, Edwards 31, Faison 41, Fears 73, O'Donnell 28, Reese 121, Riggins 30, Thompson 45.

PITCHING

PITCHING	W	L	ERA	G	GS	CG	SV	IP	H	R	ER	BB	SO	AVG	B	T	HT	WT	DOB	1st Yr	Resides
Belanger, Brandon	1	3	6.42	33	0	0	2	48	57	36	34	18	39	.308	R	R	6-0	180	5-13-78	2000	Houma, La.
Bumstead, Mike	4	2	2.27	36	0	0	17	40	26	12	10	15	52	.181	R	R	6-3	210	7-8-77	2001	Big Bear Lake, Calif.
Burns, Casey	5	8	5.08	20	16	0	0	89	87	60	50	43	59	.251	R	R	6-1	185	7-24-77	1999	Pennington, N.J.
Cassel, Jack	4	14	5.54	25	23	0	0	128	163	104	79	35	89	.304	R	R	6-2	190	8-8-80	2000	Northridge, Calif.
Devine, Travis	3	3	5.26	29	1	0	1	50	66	41	29	14	42	.312	R	R	6-5	190	12-3-79	1998	Lawrenceville, Ga.
Earey, Ryan	4	4	4.82	24	7	0	0	65	70	38	35	17	59	.275	R	R	6-4	225	3-5-79	2000	Greensboro, N.C.
Fox, Ben	1	1	7.48	11	5	0	0	28	43	25	23	13	22	.361	B	L	5-11	185	6-22-81	2001	Las Vegas, Nev.
Gaal, Bryan	1	1	1.95	23	0	0	2	32	20	7	7	4	42	.178	R	R	6-4	203	12-17-76	1999	Syracuse, N.Y.
Germano, Justin	2	6	4.98	13	13	0	0	65	80	47	36	16	55	.301	R	R	6-2	190	8-6-82	2000	Claremont, Calif.
Gutierrez, Laz	1	1	4.91	16	0	0	0	18	18	10	10	10	16	.253	L	L	6-2	195	2-7-76	1998	Hialeah, Fla.
Harvey, Ian	0	0	2.84	8	0	0	3	13	6	4	4	5	15	.139	R	R	6-1	190	10-11-76	1999	Oakville, Ontario
Herbert, John	1	0	7.20	2	0	0	0	5	6	5	4	4	2	.250	R	R	6-8	230	10-23-77	2000	San Francisco, Calif.
Luque, Roger	5	2	2.40	42	0	0	0	60	47	24	16	17	61	.211	L	L	6-1	170	1-8-80	1997	Charallave, Venez.
McAdoo, Duncan	6	16	3.54	28	28	0	0	158	173	87	62	36	121	.275	R	R	6-1	200	4-15-79	2000	Winnsboro, Texas
Mejia, Juan	0	2	5.14	9	0	0	0	14	18	8	8	7	6	.321	R	R	6-2	165	12-11-79	1996	Azua, D.R.
Nicolas, Mike	1	5	3.45	54	0	0	7	63	44	30	24	34	70	.205	R	R	6-3	207	11-5-81	2000	Santo Domingo, D.R.
Oxspring, Chris	4	1	4.15	41	2	0	0	56	66	29	26	25	54	.297	L	R	6-0	183	5-13-77	2001	Queensland, Australia
Percosky, Mark	2	2	5.65	8	6	0	0	29	33	20	18	12	30	.284	R	R	6-3	225	3-15-78	2000	Kent, Wash.
Perez, Oliver	8	5	3.46	19	19	0	0	101	84	46	39	43	98	.229	L	L	6-3	160	8-15-81	1999	Culiacan, Mexico
Phillips, Mark	4	1	2.64	5	5	0	0	31	19	11	9	14	27	.174	L	L	6-3	205	12-30-81	2000	Hanover, Pa.
Prater, Andy	0	0	54.00	1	0	0	0	1	3	4	4	1	0	.600	R	R	6-3	178	9-27-77	1996	Florissant, Mo.
Thompson, Mike	0	1	6.00	1	1	0	0	6	8	4	4	2	1	.307	R	R	6-4	185	11-6-80	1999	Lamar, Colo.
Webster, Jeremy	0	1	2.96	16	0	0	0	27	19	15	9	22	31	.208	L	L	6-0	195	3-20-79	1999	Sandy, Utah
Wiedmeyer, Jason	1	1	1.85	6	6	1	0	34	38	14	7	13	29	.273	L	L	6-3	200	10-15-78	2001	West Bend, Wis.
Yoshida, Nobuaki	1	2	3.86	5	5	1	0	23	23	13	10	13	12	.270	L	L	6-1	170	8-10-81	2000	Sendai, Japan

EUGENE — Short-Season Class A

NORTHWEST LEAGUE

BATTING	AVG	G	AB	R	H	2B	3B	HR	RBI	BB	SO	SB	CS	SLG	OBP	B	T	HT	WT	DOB	1st Yr	Resides
Bartlett, Jason	.300	68	267	49	80	12	4	3	37	28	47	12	4	.408	.371	R	R	6-0	175	10-30-79	2001	Lodi, Calif.
Benick, Jon	.262	64	237	31	62	12	1	10	45	19	53	2	2	.447	.315	B	R	6-1	215	9-26-79	2001	Glen Lyon, Pa.
Brooks, Doc	.236	39	127	21	30	5	2	7	22	13	57	4	2	.472	.338	R	R	5-10	190	1-21-80	2001	Phenix City, Ala.
Brown, Trevor	.280	31	75	11	21	5	0	2	17	15	17	0	0	.427	.423	R	R	6-2	220	4-17-79	2001	Eugene, Ore.
Carter, Josh	.186	23	86	6	16	3	1	1	9	3	14	2	0	.279	.220	R	R	6-2	210	11-5-80	2001	Fallbrook, Calif.
Castillo, David	.195	36	82	8	16	0	1	1	5	14	26	4	1	.256	.323	B	L	5-11	185	5-19-81	1998	Bani, D.R.
Castro, Renato	.194	9	31	2	6	1	0	0	3	1	9	0	0	.226	.212	R	R	6-2	180	12-30-79	1996	Haina, D.R.
DiBetta, John	.229	67	231	27	53	10	0	3	27	33	52	4	3	.312	.332	R	R	6-1	190	10-19-80	2001	Las Vegas, Nev.
Encarnacion, Santos	.186	33	102	11	19	3	1	0	3	5	35	4	0	.235	.231	R	R	6-4	176	8-21-79	1996	Haina, D.R.
Gautreau, Jake	.309	48	178	28	55	19	0	6	36	22	47	1	1	.517	.389	L	R	6-0	185	11-14-79	2001	South Padre Island, Texas
Gomez, Andre	.143	6	14	1	2	0	0	1	3	0	4	1	0	.357	.200	R	R	6-2	185	9-6-78	2000	Playa del Rey, Calif.
Hellman, Matthew	.220	57	200	28	44	6	1	3	15	24	41	2	2	.305	.303	R	R	5-11	185	11-9-78	2000	Burbank, Calif.
Nettles, Marcus	.300	55	213	37	64	3	0	0	10	27	54	35	17	.315	.385	L	L	5-11	185	5-15-80	2001	Chicago, Ill.
Puccinelli, John	.185	9	27	1	5	1	0	0	5	2	8	0	0	.222	.241	R	R	6-4	180	3-5-81	1999	North Hollywood, Calif.
Roenicke, Jarett	.160	9	25	2	4	0	0	0	2	1	10	0	0	.160	.192	L	L	6-2	195	1-15-80	2000	Nevada City, Calif.
Romero, Nick	.218	55	179	24	39	8	3	1	19	18	75	8	2	.313	.289	R	R	5-10	150	1-12-80	1997	Haina, D.R.
Sain, Greg	.293	67	256	48	75	19	1	16	40	21	68	1	2	.563	.356	R	R	6-2	205	12-26-79	2001	Torrance, Calif.
Serrano, Eddie	.294	7	17	2	5	1	0	1	1	2	5	0	0	.529	.400	R	R	6-2	180	12-30-79	1996	Haina, D.R.
Sobet, Renato	.194	9	31	2	6	1	0	0	3	1	9	0	0	.226	.212	R	R	6-2	180	12-30-79	1996	Haina, D.R.
Trzesniak, Nick	.233	57	193	24	45	8	1	2	21	22	59	0	1	.316	.324	R	R	6-0	215	11-19-80	1999	Tinley Park, Ill.

GAMES BY POSITION: C—Brown 22, Gomez 5, Sain 7, Trzesniak 49. **1B**—Benick 39, Brown 1, Encarnacion 11, Puccinelli 1, Roenicke 1, Romero 1, Sain 29, Trzesniak 1. **2B**—DiBetta 67, Encarnacion 1, Romero 10, Serrano 2. **3B**—Encarnacion 8, Gautreau 44, Puccinelli 8, Romero 2, Sain 14, Serrano 5. **SS**—Bartlett 67, Encarnacion 2, Romero 11. **OF**—Brooks 18, Carter 22, Castillo 35, Encarnacion 13, Hellman 57, Nettles 55, Roenicke 3, Romero 32, Sobet 8, Trzesniak 2.

PITCHING	W	L	ERA	G	GS	CG	SV	IP	H	R	ER	BB	SO	AVG	B	T	HT	WT	DOB	1st Yr	Resides
Anderegg, Jason	3	7	4.81	14	13	0	0	64	64	46	34	27	62	.258	R	R	6-1	215	11-22-78	2001	Mason City, Iowa
Brandt, Jon	3	2	3.20	13	6	0	0	45	45	25	16	13	44	.255	R	R	6-2	185	3-31-79	2000	Palo Alto, Calif.
Dulkowski, Marc	1	1	4.26	7	0	0	1	6	6	3	3	2	8	.250	R	R	6-0	190	5-28-82	2000	Tinley Park, Ill.
Germano, Justin	6	5	3.49	13	13	2	0	80	77	35	31	11	74	.246	R	R	6-2	190	8-6-82	2000	Claremont, Calif.
Herbert, John	3	1	2.75	28	0	0	4	36	25	13	11	11	39	.193	R	R	6-8	230	10-23-77	2000	San Francisco, Calif.
Hoyt, Michael	1	1	3.57	28	0	0	0	40	39	19	16	23	38	.265	R	R	6-2	180	12-9-77	2000	Corona, Calif.
Jones, Geoff	3	7	5.01	15	15	1	0	83	90	57	46	27	73	.271	L	L	6-6	230	8-10-79	1999	Dolores, Colo.
Kelly, Scott	2	4	5.06	14	14	0	0	64	73	42	36	26	66	.289	L	L	6-3	200	6-8-78	2001	Maple Valley, Wash.
King, Seth	0	0	0.00	1	0	0	0	1	1	0	0	1	1	.333	R	R	6-2	190	9-3-77	2001	Provo, Utah
Mejia, Juan	0	1	2.74	22	0	0	6	23	9	7	7	12	11	.112	R	R	6-2	165	12-11-79	1996	Azua, D.R.

ORGANIZATION STATISTICS

PITCHING	W	L	ERA	G	GS	CG	SV	IP	H	R	ER	BB	SO	AVG	B	T	HT	WT	DOB	1st Yr	Resides
Modica, Greg	2	4	6.20	17	1	0	0	25	37	21	17	8	15	.359	R	R	6-0	145	5-12-80	2001	Glendale, N.Y.
Phillips, Mark	3	1	3.74	4	4	0	0	22	16	10	9	9	19	.207	L	L	6-3	205	12-30-81	2000	Hanover, Pa.
Rodriguez, Jose	0	1	8.64	9	0	0	0	8	11	9	8	13	9	.314	R	R	6-2	180	2-9-81	1998	Santo Domingo, D.R.
Soto, Darwin	4	5	3.80	30	1	0	0	43	35	23	18	15	39	.218	R	R	6-2	180	1-15-82	1998	Bani, D.R.
Velazquez, Ernesto	0	0	0.00	1	0	0	0	1	1	0	0	2	0	.333	R	R	6-4	200	7-31-81	1999	Culiacan, Mexico
Vitek, Josh	0	0	2.45	11	0	0	3	11	7	4	3	4	11	.175	R	R	6-3	200	6-18-80	1999	Fayetteville, Texas
Webster, Jeremy	0	0	1.08	6	0	0	0	8	2	1	1	2	9	.076	L	L	6-0	195	3-20-79	1999	Sandy, Utah
Wiedmeyer, Jason	1	3	3.18	8	6	0	0	34	28	14	12	10	30	.229	L	L	6-3	200	10-15-78	2001	West Bend, Wis.
Wykoff, Zach	0	1	9.68	25	0	0	0	31	48	37	33	19	24	.363	R	R	6-1	195	8-6-79	2001	Oxford, Ga.
Yoshida, Nobuaki	0	0	1.19	8	3	0	0	23	23	7	3	4	17	.270	L	L	6-1	170	8-10-81	2000	Sendai, Japan

IDAHO FALLS — Rookie

PIONEER LEAGUE

BATTING	AVG	G	AB	R	H	2B	3B	HR	RBI	BB	SO	SB	CS	SLG	OBP	B	T	HT	WT	DOB	1st Yr	Resides
Aquino, Jack	.250	56	196	30	49	5	5	2	23	23	35	6	5	.357	.324	B	R	5-8	150	2-26-83	2000	Santo Domingo, D.R.
Baez, Carlos	.228	55	180	18	41	5	2	1	21	8	50	1	2	.294	.272	R	R	6-1	160	2-20-83	1999	Palenque, D.R.
Barfield, Josh	.310	66	277	51	86	15	4	4	53	16	54	12	4	.437	.350	R	R	6-0	185	12-17-82	2001	Spring, Texas
De los Santos, Pedro	.348	12	46	11	16	4	1	0	5	2	10	5	0	.478	.388	B	R	5-10	165	8-8-83	2000	Santo Domingo, D.R.
Falcon, Omar	.187	37	107	24	20	5	0	5	9	33	50	0	1	.374	.396	R	R	6-1	190	9-1-82	2000	Miami, Fla.
Giorgis, David	.289	65	242	28	70	16	0	7	41	24	69	2	4	.442	.359	B	R	6-2	190	8-14-81	2000	San Diego, Calif.
Hastings, Joseph	.339	34	124	24	42	16	0	5	34	15	32	1	1	.589	.407	L	R	6-3	205	6-25-78	2001	Connelly Springs, N.C.
Jung, Young-jin	.158	23	57	9	9	2	0	0	3	7	23	0	0	.193	.273	R	R	6-2	220	2-7-78	2000	Inchon, Korea
Klatt, Joel	.208	45	125	13	26	7	0	2	10	14	47	3	0	.312	.293	R	R	6-2	205	2-4-82	2000	Arvada, Colo.
Kulbe, Eric	.125	15	16	4	2	1	0	0	0	4	5	0	0	.188	.333	L	R	6-0	194	6-28-78	2001	Lakewood, Colo.
Martinez, Thomas	.274	36	117	15	32	7	0	2	16	1	26	0	0	.385	.292	R	R	5-11	180	2-27-83	2000	Villa Altagracia, D.R.
Millan, Carlos	.190	14	42	7	8	0	0	1	6	5	15	0	1	.262	.277	R	R	5-11	170	9-25-81	1999	Ocumare del Tuy, Venez.
Moore, Mewelde	.236	24	89	19	21	1	0	1	5	6	29	4	2	.281	.313	R	R	6-0	195	7-24-82	2001	Baton Rouge, La.
Mora, Ruben	.201	54	184	33	37	6	4	0	17	18	55	12	3	.277	.280	B	R	6-0	170	1-11-82	2000	Colon, Panama
Nulton, Kevin	.289	53	187	28	54	7	2	0	21	21	33	5	3	.348	.358	R	R	6-0	175	8-16-82	2000	Lakeside, Calif.
Olson, David	.245	48	98	21	24	1	0	0	9	10	45	4	5	.255	.330	R	R	5-9	155	1-19-82	2000	Caracas, Venez.
Pickens, Jordan	.235	52	183	29	43	13	1	8	26	19	57	0	0	.448	.335	R	R	6-2	195	6-10-81	2001	Atascadero, Calif.
Roenicke, Jarett	.286	24	84	10	24	2	0	0	6	5	25	0	0	.310	.326	L	L	6-2	195	1-15-80	2001	Nevada City, Calif.
Selmo, Francisco	.274	53	197	22	54	15	1	3	26	14	42	4	0	.406	.321	R	R	5-10	160	11-23-81	2000	Santo Domingo, D.R.
Serrano, Eddie	.324	20	68	9	22	2	0	2	10	2	20	1	0	.441	.351	R	R	6-0	170	10-26-81	2000	Chiriqui, Panama

GAMES BY POSITION: C—Falcon 34, T. Martinez 15, Selmo 34. **1B**—Hastings 29, Jung 11, Klatt 30, T. Martinez 11, Roenicke 7. **2B**—Aquino 2, Baez 1, Barfield 44, de los Santos 9, Nulton 21, Serrano 10. **3B**—Baez 47, Klatt 6, Nulton 28, Serrano 5. **SS**—Aquino 53, Baez 6, Barfield 23, Klatt 1. **OF**—Falcon 1, Giorgis 57, Kulbe 8, Millan 14, Moore 24, Mora 53, Olson 43, Pickens 45, Roenicke 11.

PITCHING	W	L	ERA	G	GS	CG	SV	IP	H	R	ER	BB	SO	AVG	B	T	HT	WT	DOB	1st Yr	Resides
Arellano, Salvador	0	1	3.65	3	3	0	0	12	17	13	5	5	8	.298	R	R	6-1	185	8-9-82	2000	Campeche, Mexico
Barbarossa, Josh	2	1	3.90	7	3	0	0	28	33	22	12	17	25	.284	L	L	6-3	215	1-4-80	1999	Valparaiso, Ind.
Dulkowski, Marc	0	1	5.33	22	0	0	2	25	25	17	15	16	25	.260	B	R	6-0	190	5-28-82	2000	Tinley Park, Ill.
Fox, Ben	1	1	9.00	13	0	0	0	5	16	22	16	16	8	17	.323	B	L	5-11	185	6-22-81	2001	Las Vegas, Nev.
Huber, Jon	5	9	6.04	15	15	0	0	73	77	61	49	48	75	.274	R	R	6-2	170	7-7-81	2000	North Fort Myers, Fla.
Lawton, Charles	1	4	8.51	23	7	0	0	61	99	69	58	32	34	.361	R	R	6-1	187	9-25-81	2000	Palatka, Fla.
Linderbaum, Mason	1	0	7.80	23	0	0	0	30	45	28	26	20	27	.333	L	L	6-8	225	1-9-79	2001	West Des Moines, Iowa
Martinez, Hancer	1	0	4.15	11	1	0	0	22	25	11	10	10	21	.294	R	R	6-0	170	6-23-83	2000	La Victoria, D.R.
Martinez, Javier	1	4	6.43	10	8	0	0	42	42	35	30	26	38	.260	B	R	6-3	170	12-9-82	2000	Merida, Mexico
Mordan, Pedro	1	7	8.22	21	8	0	0	58	86	63	53	37	43	.348	R	R	6-3	190	6-29-80	1998	Bani, D.R.
Morel, Eudy	0	2	4.95	14	0	0	0	20	24	15	11	6	25	.289	R	R	5-10	160	1-24-83	2000	Montecristi, D.R.
Pauley, David	4	9	6.03	15	15	0	0	69	88	57	46	24	53	.307	R	R	6-2	170	6-17-83	2001	Longmont, Colo.
Perez, Henry	4	8	6.28	15	15	0	0	72	79	60	50	39	82	.282	R	R	6-3	210	10-27-82	1999	Santo Domingo, D.R.
Richards, John	0	0	4.30	13	0	0	0	15	15	9	7	13	13	.267	L	L	6-4	205	11-12-78	2001	Coos Bay, Ore.
Rodriguez, Jose	0	1	7.29	18	0	0	0	21	27	23	17	21	28	.303	R	R	6-2	180	2-9-81	1998	Santo Domingo, D.R.
Scott, John	0	1	15.12	20	0	0	0	17	29	38	28	36	10	.386	R	R	6-1	170	2-7-82	2000	Ramona, Calif.
Tucker, Rusty	0	2	7.13	30	0	0	0	35	41	41	28	50	43	.297	R	L	6-1	190	7-15-80	2001	Gloucester, Mass.
Villatoro, Wilmer	0	3	5.26	30	0	0	3	38	39	24	22	21	35	.267	R	R	6-0	145	6-27-83	2000	San Salvador, El Salvador

SAN FRANCISCO GIANTS

Barry Bonds   Boof Bonser

BY JOE RODERICK

Some teams coming off a 90-win season might sit back and take a deep breath before immersing themselves in matters pertaining to the 2002 season.

And others, such as the Giants, work the phones, meet

behind closed doors and burn the candle at both ends preparing for the challenges that lie ahead. The Giants, led by general manager Brian Sabean, aren't about to freshen up while there's work to be done. The 2001-02 offseason will be unlike any Sabean and his staff have encountered.

"This year will probably be as big a challenge in turning the club around as we've faced since '97," Sabean said. "We've got a track record of doing it and we're confident we can do it."

The Giants completed their fifth straight winning season during the Sabean regime, but were eliminated by Arizona in their 160th game.

"We just came up short," Sabean said. "We had 90 wins. That will have us fourth in the league. I think everybody in this room believes this was a playoff team. On the other hand, we've won one playoff game in five years, so there's a lot of work to be done to figure out how we can get to the next level within our limitations."

Barry Bonds became a free agent after completing one of the greatest seasons ever. He not only established the single-season home run record with 73, he walked more times (177) than anyone in history and had the highest slugging percentage (.863) in major league history.

It was not merely Bonds who led the Giants to the brink of the National League West title. The team's pitching staff finished with a 4.18 ERA, ranking in the upper half of the league.

"As much as Barry did this year, our pitching staff really allowed us to be competitive, and that's an area we'll always try to be out in front on and try to take care of first," Sabean said.

PLAYERS OF THE YEAR

MAJOR LEAGUE: Barry Bonds, of

Bonds had a magical 2001 season, setting all-time major league records for home runs (73), slugging percentage (.863), walks (177) and homers per 100 at-bats (15.34).

MINOR LEAGUE: Boof Bonser, rhp

Bonser's got a great name and great stuff. He was the most valuable pitcher in the Class A South Atlantic League, going 16-4, 2.49 with 178 strikeouts and 61 walks in 134 innings.

Russ Ortiz (17-9, 3.39) led the staff in wins, with Kirk Rueter (14-12, 4.42) not far behind. Shawn Estes and Livan Hernandez, the top pitchers the season before, had what could be considered disappointing seasons. Estes was bothered by a left ankle injury and went 9-8, 4.02, while Hernandez was 13-15, 5.24.

Closer Robb Nen finished with a league-high 45 saves, though he blew seven. He was backed by Felix Rodriguez (9-1, 1.68), who has become one of the best set-up men in baseball.

Shortstop Rich Aurilia became the third San Francisco Giant to record 200 hits, joining Willie Mays (1958) and Bobby Bonds (1970). Aurilia put up remarkable numbers for a shortstop, hitting .324-27-97. The last National League shortstop with that many homers was Ernie Banks in 1960 (41).

Three of the team's six farm clubs reached the playoffs. The new Class A Hagerstown affiliate went 45-25 in the second half, but was swept in the South Atlantic League Northern Division playoffs. Hagerstown righthander Boof Bonser, the Giants' No. 1 draft choice in 2000, had the best season among the organization's top prospects, going 16-4, 2.49.

Short-season Salem-Keizer finished 49-25 and won the Northwest League playoffs behind the pitching of second-round pick Jesse Foppert (8-1, 1.93).

Class A San Jose went 40-30 in the second half in the California League to finish first in the Northern Division. San Jose received considerable contributions from righthander Vance Cozier (15-7, 3.61) and first baseman Tim Flaherty (.255-26-83).

Kurt Ainsworth, the Giants' 1999 No. 1 draft choice, struggled at times in the hitter-friendly Pacific Coast League and finished 10-9, 5.07 at Triple-A Fresno. Nonetheless, he was called up by the Giants in September and made his major league debut.

ORGANIZATION LEADERS

BATTING

*AVG	Tony Torcato, Fresno/Shreveport/San Jose	.323
R	Jason Ellison, Hagerstown	95
H	Tony Torcato, Fresno/Shreveport/San Jose	179
TB	Sean McGowan, Fresno/Shreveport	241
2B	Jason Ellison, Hagerstown	38
	Tony Torcato, Fresno/Shreveport/San Jose	38
3B	Arturo McDowell, San Jose	11
HR	Three tied at	26
RBI	Tim Flaherty, San Jose	83
BB	Jason Ellison, Hagerstown	71
SO	Tim Flaherty, San Jose	162
SB	Nelson Castro, Fresno/Shreveport	38

PITCHING

W	Boof Bonser, Hagerstown	16
L	Jeff Andra, Fresno/Shreveport	12
#ERA	Jon Cannon, Shreveport/San Jose	3.22
G	Robbie Crabtree, Fresno	63
CG	Jerome Williams, Shreveport	2
	Mike Riley, Fresno/Shreveport	2
SV	Jackson Markert, Fresno/Shreveport	39
IP	Vance Cozier, San Jose	170
BB	Joe Nathan, Fresno/Shreveport	70
SO	Boof Bonser, Hagerstown	178

*Minimum 250 At-Bats #Minimum 75 Innings

SAN FRANCISCO
GIANTS

Manager: Dusty Baker

2001 Record: 90-72, .556 (2nd, NL West)

BATTING	AVG	G	AB	R	H	2B	3B	HR	RBI	BB	SO	SB	CS	SLG	OBP	B	T	HT	WT	DOB	1st Yr	Resides
Aurilia, Rich	.324	156	636	114	206	37	5	37	97	47	83	1	3	.572	.369	R	R	6-1	185	9-2-71	1992	Hazlet, N.J.
Benard, Marvin	.265	129	392	70	104	19	2	15	44	29	66	10	5	.439	.320	L	L	5-09	185	1-20-70	1992	Scottsdale, Ariz.
Bonds, Barry	.328	153	476	129	156	32	2	73	137	177	93	13	3	.863	.515	L	L	6-2	210	7-24-64	1985	Redwood Shores, Calif.
Crespo, Felipe	.197	40	66	8	13	1	0	4	10	7	26	1	1	.394	.286	B	R	5-11	200	3-5-73	1991	Caguas, P.R.
Davis, Eric	.205	74	156	17	32	7	3	4	22	13	38	1	1	.365	.269	R	R	6-3	185	5-29-62	1980	Woodland Hills, Calif.
Davis, Russ	.257	53	167	16	43	13	1	7	17	17	49	1	0	.473	.326	R	R	6-0	195	9-13-69	1988	Birmingham, Ala.
Dunston, Shawon	.280	88	186	26	52	10	3	9	25	2	32	3	1	.511	.293	R	R	6-1	175	3-21-63	1982	Corona, N.Y.
Estalella, Bobby	.204	29	93	11	19	5	1	3	10	11	28	0	0	.376	.295	R	R	6-1	205	8-23-74	1993	Pembroke Pines, Fla.
Feliz, Pedro	.227	94	220	23	50	9	1	7	22	10	50	2	1	.373	.264	R	R	6-1	195	4-27-77	1994	Azua, D.R.
Galarraga, Andres	.288	49	156	17	45	12	1	7	35	13	49	0	3	.513	.351	R	R	6-3	235	6-18-61	1979	West Palm Beach, Fla.
Guzman, Edwards	.243	61	115	8	28	6	0	3	7	5	16	0	0	.374	.273	L	R	5-10	205	9-11-76	1996	Naranjito, P.R.
Kent, Jeff	.298	159	607	84	181	49	6	22	106	65	96	7	6	.507	.369	R	R	6-1	205	3-7-68	1989	Spicewood, Texas
Leach, Jalal	.100	8	10	0	1	0	0	0	1	2	3	0	0	.100	.250	L	L	6-2	200	3-14-69	1990	Novato, Calif.
Martinez, Ramon	.253	128	391	48	99	18	3	5	37	38	52	1	2	.353	.323	R	R	6-1	187	10-10-72	1993	Toa Alta, P.R.
Minor, Damon	.156	19	45	3	7	1	0	3	3	3	8	0	0	.178	.208	L	L	6-7	230	1-5-74	1996	Edmond, Okla.
Murray, Calvin	.245	106	326	54	80	14	2	6	25	32	57	8	8	.356	.319	R	R	5-11	190	7-30-71	1993	Houston, Texas
Powell, Dante	.333	13	6	5	2	0	0	0	0	0	0	0	0	.333	.333	R	R	6-2	185	8-25-73	1994	Long Beach, Calif.
Ransom, Cody	.000	9	7	1	0	0	0	0	0	0	5	0	0	.000	.000	R	R	6-2	190	2-17-76	1998	Chandler, Ariz.
Rios, Armando	.259	93	316	38	82	17	3	14	49	34	73	3	2	.465	.330	L	L	5-9	185	9-13-71	1994	Supply, N.C.
Santiago, Benito	.262	133	477	39	125	25	4	6	45	23	78	5	4	.369	.295	R	R	6-1	195	3-9-65	1983	Lighthouse Point, Fla.
Snow, J.T.	.246	101	285	43	70	12	1	8	34	55	81	0	0	.379	.371	L	L	6-2	205	2-26-68	1989	Corona Del Mar, Calif.
Torrealba, Yorvit	.500	3	4	0	2	0	1	0	2	0	0	0	0	1.000	.500	R	R	5-11	190	7-19-78	1995	Guarenas, Venez.
Vander Wal, John	.252	49	139	19	35	6	1	3	20	26	38	1	2	.374	.370	L	L	6-1	180	4-29-66	1987	Hudsonville, Mich.
2-team (97 Pitt.)	.270	146	452	58	122	28	4	14	70	68	122	8	6	.442	.364							

PITCHING	W	L	ERA	G	GS	CG	SV	IP	H	R	ER	BB	SO	AVG	B	T	HT	WT	DOB	1st Yr	Resides
Ainsworth, Kurt	0	0	13.50	2	0	0	0	2	3	3	3	2	3	.333	R	R	6-3	185	9-9-78	1999	Kingwood, Texas
Boehringer, Brian	3	3	4.19	29	0	0	1	34	32	20	16	17	27	.238	B	R	6-2	190	1-8-70	1991	Fenton, Mo.
Christiansen, Jason	1	0	1.59	25	0	0	0	17	14	3	3	5	12	.241	R	L	6-5	241	9-21-69	1991	Omaha, Neb.
2-team (30 St. Louis)	2	1	3.22	55	0	0	3	36	29	13	13	15	31	.224							
Embree, Alan	0	2	11.25	22	0	0	0	20	34	26	25	10	25	.373	L	L	6-2	190	1-23-70	1990	Vancouver, Wash.
Estes, Shawn	9	8	4.02	27	27	0	0	159	151	78	71	77	109	.252	R	L	6-2	195	2-18-73	1991	San Francisco, Calif.
Fultz, Aaron	3	1	4.56	66	0	0	1	71	70	40	36	21	67	.258	L	L	6-0	196	9-4-73	1992	Northport, Ala.
Gardner, Mark	5	5	5.40	23	15	0	0	92	93	57	55	34	53	.263	R	R	6-1	220	3-1-62	1985	Fresno, Calif.
Gomes, Wayne	2	0	8.40	13	0	0	0	15	21	14	14	7	17	.350	R	R	6-2	227	1-15-73	1993	Cherry Hill, N.J.
2-team (42 Philadelphia)	6	3	5.29	55	0	0	1	63	72	37	37	29	52	.293							
Hernandez, Livan	13	15	5.24	34	34	2	0	227	266	143	132	85	138	.296	R	R	6-2	222	2-20-75	1996	Miami Beach, Fla.
Jensen, Ryan	1	2	4.25	10	7	0	0	42	44	21	20	25	26	.268	R	R	6-0	205	9-17-75	1996	Murray, Utah
Nen, Robb	4	5	3.01	79	0	0	45	78	58	28	26	22	93	.202	R	R	6-5	215	11-28-69	1987	Dove Canyon, Calif.
Ortiz, Russ	17	9	3.29	33	33	1	0	219	187	90	80	91	169	.232	R	R	6-1	210	6-5-74	1995	Norman, Okla.
Rodriguez, Felix	9	1	1.68	80	0	0	0	80	53	16	15	27	91	.187	R	R	6-1	190	12-5-72	1990	Montecristi, D.R.
Rueter, Kirk	14	12	4.42	34	34	0	0	195	213	105	96	66	83	.282	L	L	6-2	205	12-1-70	1991	Nashville, Ill.
Schmidt, Jason	7	1	3.39	11	11	0	0	66	57	29	25	33	65	.229	R	R	6-5	213	1-29-73	1991	Longview, Wash.
2-team (14 Pittsburgh)	13	7	4.07	25	25	1	0	150	138	75	68	61	142	.244							
Vogelsong, Ryan	0	3	5.65	13	0	0	0	29	29	21	18	14	17	.256	R	R	6-3	195	7-22-77	1998	North Grafton, Mass.
Worrell, Tim	2	5	3.45	73	0	0	0	78	71	33	30	33	63	.239	R	R	6-4	215	7-5-67	1990	Glendale, Ariz.
Zerbe, Chad	3	0	3.92	27	1	0	0	39	41	21	17	10	22	.280	L	L	6-0	190	4-27-72	1991	Tampa, Fla.

FIELDING

Catcher	PCT	G	PO	A	E	DP	PB
Estalella	1.000	28	185	14	0	5	0
Guzman	.990	26	86	10	1	1	0
Santiago	.994	130	830	62	5	12	8
Torrealba	1.000	3	8	0	0	0	0

First Base	PCT	G	PO	A	E	DP
Crespo	.972	16	101	3	3	10
Dunston	.000	1	0	0	0	0
Galarraga	.984	41	288	13	5	38
Guzman	.973	7	34	2	1	2
Kent	.990	30	193	14	2	19
Minor	.984	11	86	4	1	4
Santiago	1.000	2	7	0	0	0
Snow	.999	92	659	46	1	76
Vander Wal	1.000	1	2	0	0	0

Second Base	PCT	G	PO	A	E	DP
Crespo	.833	2	2	3	1	1
Guzman	.750	3	3	0	1	0
Kent	.987	140	269	390	9	91
Martinez	.993	42	54	98	1	21

Third Base	PCT	G	PO	A	E	DP
R. Davis	.890	46	20	61	10	9

	PCT	G	PO	A	E	DP
Feliz	.908	86	40	79	12	6
Guzman	1.000	7	4	7	0	1
Martinez	.974	70	44	105	4	7

Shortstop	PCT	G	PO	A	E	DP
Aurilia	.975	149	246	423	17	108
Martinez	.965	24	25	58	3	16
Ransom	1.000	6	0	4	0	0

Outfield	PCT	G	PO	A	E	DP
Benard	.965	109	213	5	8	2
Bonds	.977	143	246	8	6	1
Crespo	1.000	1	2	0	0	0
E. Davis	.962	48	74	1	3	0
Dunston	.966	60	80	4	3	2
Guzman	.000	2	0	0	0	0
Leach	1.000	3	1	0	0	0
Murray	.979	104	232	4	5	1
Powell	1.000	9	8	0	0	0
Rios	.971	87	196	7	6	2
Vander Wal	1.000	41	82	1	0	0

Dusty Baker

JOHN WILLIAMSON

Rich Aurilia: Hit .327-37-97, batting in front of Barry Bonds

Jeff Kent: Hit .298-22-106, batting behind Bonds

FARM SYSTEM

Vice President, Player Personnel: Dick Tidrow

Class	Farm Team	League	W	L	Pct.	Finish*	Manager	First Yr.
AAA	Fresno (Calif.) Grizzlies	Pacific Coast	68	71	.489	9th (16)	Shane Turner	1998
AA	Shreveport (La.) Swamp Dragons	Texas	54	81	.400	8th (8)	Bill Russell	1979
A#	San Jose (Calif.) Giants	California	77	63	.550	+2nd (10)	Lenn Sakata	1988
A	Hagerstown (Md.) Suns	South Atlantic	83	57	.593	2nd (16)	Bill Hayes	2001
A	Salem-Keizer (Ore.) Volcanoes	Northwest	51	25	.671	+2nd (8)	Fred Stanley	1997
Rookie	Scottsdale (Ariz.) Giants	Arizona	29	27	.518	3rd (7)	Keith Comstock	2000

*Finish in overall standings (No. of teams in league)   #Advanced level   +League champion

FRESNO — Class AAA

PACIFIC COAST LEAGUE

BATTING	AVG	G	AB	R	H	2B	3B	HR	RBI	BB	SO	SB	CS	SLG	OBP	B	T	HT	WT	DOB	1st Yr	Resides
Byas, Mike	.190	17	21	4	4	1	0	0	1	7	5	0	0	.238	.393	B	R	6-0	170	4-21-76	1997	Chesterfield, Mo.
Campusano, Carlos	.136	13	22	1	3	1	0	0	3	0	5	0	0	.182	.136	R	R	5-11	160	9-2-75	1994	Palave, D.R.
Castro, Nelson	.130	6	23	3	3	1	0	0	1	1	5	0	0	.174	.167	R	R	5-10	190	6-4-76	1994	Villa Vazquez, D.R.
Chiaramonte, Giuseppe	.210	37	100	11	21	6	0	2	12	4	19	0	1	.330	.266	R	R	6-0	200	2-19-76	1997	Santa Cruz, Calif.
Crespo, Felipe	.375	3	8	2	3	1	0	1	1	0	3	0	0	.875	.375	B	R	5-11	200	3-5-73	1991	Caguas, P.R.
Estalella, Bobby	.318	6	22	3	7	1	0	1	4	1	9	0	0	.500	.348	R	R	6-1	205	8-23-74	1993	Pembroke Pines, Fla.
Fajardo, Alex	.281	27	32	5	9	1	0	0	3	4	14	0	0	.313	.361	R	R	6-0	180	2-6-76	1995	Moca, D.R.
Guzman, Edwards	.361	18	72	13	26	3	2	0	11	4	3	0	1	.458	.395	L	R	5-10	205	9-11-76	1996	Naranjito, P.R.
Hall, Justin	.500	1	4	1	2	0	0	0	1	0	0	0	0	.500	.500	R	R	5-10	175	9-23-76	1998	Mesa, Ariz.
Leach, Jalal	.285	130	467	68	133	30	3	16	70	31	94	13	6	.465	.329	L	L	6-2	200	3-14-69	1990	Novato, Calif.
Magruder, Chris	.280	54	214	37	60	7	1	10	30	18	45	3	1	.463	.354	B	R	5-11	200	4-26-77	1998	Yakima, Wash.
McGowan, Sean	.286	104	391	59	112	30	2	14	65	23	95	1	0	.481	.328	R	R	6-6	240	5-15-77	1999	Burlington, Mass.
Melo, Juan	.312	100	375	46	117	22	4	9	55	19	64	9	9	.464	.349	B	R	6-1	180	5-11-76	1994	Bani, D.R.
Minor, Damon	.308	112	406	74	125	22	3	24	71	44	83	1	1	.554	.380	L	L	6-7	230	1-5-74	1996	Edmond, Okla.
Murray, Calvin	.261	35	138	17	36	6	1	4	12	12	33	3	3	.406	.322	R	R	5-11	190	7-30-71	1993	Houston, Texas
Pernalete, Marco	.307	32	101	9	31	7	2	2	11	10	22	1	0	.475	.366	B	R	6-0	155	10-12-78	1996	Barquisimeto, Venez.
Powell, Dante	.282	114	426	74	120	23	3	22	62	34	122	25	5	.505	.339	R	R	6-2	185	8-25-73	1994	Long Beach, Calif.
Ransom, Cody	.241	134	469	77	113	21	6	23	78	44	137	17	2	.458	.303	R	R	6-2	190	2-17-76	1998	Chandler, Ariz.
Snow, J.T.	.000	4	12	1	0	0	0	0	0	2	7	0	0	.000	.143	L	L	6-2	205	2-26-68	1989	Corona Del Mar, Calif.
Torcato, Tony	.320	35	150	20	48	8	1	2	8	2	20	0	1	.427	.329	L	R	6-1	195	10-25-79	1998	Woodland, Calif.
Torrealba, Yorvit	.274	115	394	56	108	23	3	8	36	19	65	2	3	.409	.313	R	R	5-11	190	7-19-78	1995	Guarenas, Venez.
Tyler, Josh	.287	77	230	21	66	15	1	3	26	16	40	5	3	.400	.344	R	R	6-1	185	9-6-73	1994	Green Lane, Pa.
Wright, Mike	.375	2	8	2	3	0	0	1	3	0	2	0	0	.750	.375	R	R	6-2	210	3-13-76	1999	San Jose, Calif.
Young, Travis	.000	4	3	0	0	0	0	0	0	0	2	0	0	.000	.000	R	R	6-1	185	9-8-74	1997	Albuquerque, N.M.
Zuniga, Tony	.271	123	413	77	112	16	1	26	74	55	83	6	1	.504	.363	R	R	6-0	185	1-13-75	1996	Santa Ana, Calif.

PITCHING	W	L	ERA	G	GS	CG	SV	IP	H	R	ER	BB	SO	AVG	B	T	HT	WT	DOB	1st Yr	Resides
Ainsworth, Kurt	10	9	5.07	27	26	0	0	149	139	91	84	54	157	.246	R	R	6-3	185	9-9-78	1999	Kingwood, Texas
Andra, Jeff	1	3	6.38	9	6	0	0	37	50	32	26	14	22	.335	L	L	6-5	210	9-9-75	1997	Lenexa, Kan.
Arnold, Jeff	1	4	5.92	44	3	0	9	76	96	58	36	56	.310	R	R	6-2	188	3-24-74	1992	Salado, Texas
Brown, Elliot	2	2	7.86	8	7	0	0	34	61	32	30	18	21	.401	B	R	6-2	191	6-7-75	1996	Metairie, La.
Connelly, Steve	2	3	3.68	33	0	0	4	59	47	26	24	23	40	.223	R	R	6-4	210	4-27-74	1995	Long Beach, Calif.
Crabtree, Robbie	8	10	3.69	63	0	0	6	115	115	56	47	34	99	.268	R	R	6-1	175	11-25-72	1996	Anaheim, Calif.
Embree, Alan	1	0	1.13	7	0	0	1	8	5	3	1	1	6	.178	L	L	6-2	190	1-23-70	1990	Vancouver, Wash.
Estrella, Luis	8	3	4.51	30	17	0	0	116	123	60	58	52	73	.277	R	R	6-1	220	10-7-74	1996	Santa Ana, Calif.
Gardner, Mark	0	1	6.00	3	3	0	0	6	10	4	4	1	7	.370	R	R	6-1	220	3-1-62	1985	Fresno, Calif.
Hasselhoff, Derek	2	0	3.86	25	0	0	8	28	24	19	12	14	24	.230	R	R	6-2	185	10-10-73	1995	Pasadena, Md.
Horgan, Joe	0	0	5.87	3	1	0	0	7	11	5	5	3	5	.000	L	L	6-1	200	6-7-77	1996	Rancho Cordova, Calif.
Jensen, Ryan	11	2	3.48	20	17	1	0	106	97	43	41	34	95	.241	R	R	6-0	205	9-17-75	1996	Murray, Utah
Joseph, Kevin	0	1	7.56	5	0	0	0	8	9	7	7	4	2	.300	R	R	6-2	200	8-1-76	1997	Dallas, Texas
Knoll, Brian	0	3	7.18	22	9	0	0	63	88	52	50	29	47	.335	R	R	6-3	200	8-4-73	1995	Corona, Calif.
Nathan, Joe	0	5	7.77	10	10	0	0	46	63	47	40	33	21	.333	R	R	6-4	195	11-22-74	1995	Tempe, Ariz.
Riley, Mike	2	4	6.08	28	5	0	0	53	59	41	36	33	52	.271	L	L	6-1	162	1-2-75	1996	Seaford, Del.
Rizzo, Todd	3	4	4.50	36	0	0	6	46	49	26	23	22	39	.276	R	L	6-2	220	5-24-71	1992	Philadelphia, Pa.
2-team (13 Las Vegas)	4	4	4.26	49	0	0	6	63	66	35	30	36	58	.271							
Santana, Julio	8	8	5.83	25	25	0	0	133	160	94	86	50	125	.298	R	R	6-0	185	1-20-73	1992	Santo Domingo, D.R.
Serafini, Dan	1	1	10.32	7	0	0	0	11	17	14	13	9	9	.369	B	L	6-1	195	1-25-74	1992	San Bruno, Calif.
Verplancke, Jeff	2	1	2.92	8	0	0	1	12	9	4	4	6	13	.214	R	R	6-3	200	11-18-77	1999	Ontario, Calif.
Vogelsong, Ryan	3	3	2.79	10	10	0	0	58	35	18	18	18	53	.169	R	R	6-3	195	7-22-77	1998	North Grafton, Mass.
Zerbe, Chad	3	4	3.55	17	0	0	5	25	28	13	10	9	17	.271	L	L	6-0	190	4-27-72	1991	Tampa, Fla.

FIELDING

Catcher	PCT	G	PO	A	E	DP	PB
Chiaramonte	1.000	15	75	4	0	0	2
Estalella	1.000	1	8	0	0	0	0
Guzman	1.000	11	84	7	0	0	3
Torrealba	.989	114	779	62	9	5	6
Tyler	.983	10	54	5	1	0	3
Wright	1.000	2	10	0	0	0	0

First Base	PCT	G	PO	A	E	DP
Crespo	1.000	1	2	0	0	1
Estalella	1.000	1	9	1	0	1
Guzman	.000	1	0	0	0	0
McGowan	.983	34	274	21	5	26
Minor	.988	108	801	68	11	95
Snow	1.000	4	26	0	0	1
Tyler	.000	1	0	0	0	0
Zuniga	1.000	2	4	1	0	0

Second Base	PCT	G	PO	A	E	DP
Castro	1.000	4	7	9	0	1

	PCT				
Crespo	1.000	1	2	4	0	1
Fajardo	1.000	3	2	2	0	0
Guzman	1.000	1	1	1	0	0
Hall	1.000	1	5	3	0	3
Melo	.980	94	200	235	9	71
Pernalete	.963	24	43	62	4	13
Tyler	.934	17	23	48	5	9
Young	1.000	2	4	1	0	1

Third Base	PCT	G	PO	A	E	DP
Guzman	1.000	8	4	23	0	1
Melo	1.000	4	4	7	0	0
Tyler	.953	16	11	30	2	3
Zuniga	.946	117	79	219	17	24

Shortstop	PCT	G	PO	A	E	DP
Campusano	1.000	5	3	6	0	1
Castro	.938	2	3	12	1	4
Melo	1.000	2	2	2	0	0
Ransom	.980	133	202	374	12	82

Outfield	PCT	G	PO	A	E	DP
Byas	1.000	9	7	1	0	0
Crespo	1.000	1	2	0	0	0
Estrella	1.000	1	4	0	0	0
Fajardo	1.000	6	2	0	0	0
Horgan	.000	1	0	0	0	0
Leach	.966	111	197	4	7	0
Magruder	.992	53	118	2	1	0
McGowan	.925	53	73	1	6	0
Minor	1.000	1	3	1	0	1
Murray	.978	34	88	2	2	1
Powell	.966	106	189	7	7	0
Torcato	.985	34	64	3	1	0
Tyler	1.000	29	35	1	0	0

SHREVEPORT — Class AA

TEXAS LEAGUE

BATTING	AVG	G	AB	R	H	2B	3B	HR	RBI	BB	SO	SB	CS	SLG	OBP	B	T	HT	WT	DOB	1st Yr	Resides
Allen, Jeff	.217	20	60	5	13	2	0	0	8	10	16	0	1	.250	.324	R	R	6-1	190	6-8-76	1998	Walnut Creek, Calif.
Byas, Mike	.266	83	316	55	84	13	2	0	25	49	57	21	10	.320	.367	B	R	6-0	170	4-21-76	1997	Chesterfield, Mo.
Campusano, Carlos	.143	27	63	6	9	3	0	0	1	5	18	0	1	.190	.217	R	R	5-11	160	9-2-75	1994	Palave, D.R.
Casper, Brett	.077	10	26	1	2	0	0	0	1	5	15	0	0	.077	.242	R	R	6-3	215	11-24-75	1997	Omaha, Neb.
Castro, Nelson	.296	122	479	76	142	27	6	11	60	42	122	38	11	.447	.359	R	R	5-10	190	6-4-76	1994	Villa Vazquez, D.R.
Chiaramonte, Giuseppe	.205	13	44	3	9	2	0	0	3	4	6	0	1	.250	.265	R	R	6-0	200	2-19-76	1997	Santa Cruz, Calif.
Clark, Doug	.275	123	414	53	114	16	4	6	51	45	83	20	5	.377	.348	L	R	6-2	205	3-5-76	1998	Springfield, Mass.
Cordido, Julio	.217	121	433	45	94	14	2	1	47	31	68	11	3	.266	.272	R	R	6-1	192	7-30-80	1997	Caracas, Venez.
Glendenning, Mike	.184	60	207	20	38	3	0	7	18	21	71	0	0	.300	.264	R	R	6-0	225	8-26-76	1996	West Hills, Calif.
Jester, Joe	.320	40	150	26	48	14	2	6	27	12	33	4	1	.560	.380	R	R	5-10	180	7-17-78	1999	Ashdown, Ark.
Luster, Jeremy	.273	130	506	54	138	33	2	4	76	33	94	6	3	.370	.323	B	R	6-4	210	6-10-77	1999	Kennesaw, Ga.
Luther, Ryan	.280	127	453	54	127	26	2	4	42	32	78	6	8	.373	.347	R	R	6-5	185	1-21-77	1999	North Bend, Wash.
Magruder, Chris	.255	40	149	22	38	6	3	2	11	15	27	5	3	.376	.335	B	R	5-11	200	4-26-77	1998	Yakima, Wash.
McGowan, Sean	.304	31	125	11	38	6	0	3	17	5	19	0	1	.424	.326	R	R	6-6	240	5-15-77	1999	Burlington, Mass.
Moreta, Ramon	.284	30	109	14	31	4	0	2	14	6	15	9	6	.376	.331	R	R	5-11	185	9-5-75	1994	La Romana, D.R.
Pernalete, Marco	.280	29	93	9	26	5	1	2	12	9	17	0	1	.419	.339	R	R	6-0	155	10-12-78	1996	Barquisimeto, Venez.
Rodriguez, Guillermo	.204	65	216	21	44	7	0	5	25	8	40	3	0	.306	.249	R	R	5-11	195	5-15-78	1996	Barquisimeto, Venez.
Shabala, Adam	.343	12	35	9	12	0	0	1	4	7	10	2	0	.429	.452	L	R	6-1	190	2-6-78	2000	Streator, Ill.
Strankman, Elliott	.077	9	13	1	1	0	0	0	0	1	9	0	0	.077	.200	R	R	6-1	185	1-13-77	2000	Richland, Wash.
Torcato, Tony	.293	36	147	13	43	9	1	1	23	9	15	0	1	.388	.344	L	R	6-1	195	10-25-79	1998	Woodland, Calif.
Tyler, Josh	.273	17	44	3	12	3	0	0	3	4	8	3	2	.341	.333	R	R	6-1	185	9-6-73	1994	Green Lane, Pa.
Valderrama, Carlos	.308	41	159	29	49	12	2	1	8	18	29	11	5	.428	.379	R	R	5-11	175	11-30-77	1995	Maracaibo, Venez.
Walker, Mark	.233	43	90	14	21	6	1	3	9	8	36	2	1	.422	.293	R	R	6-1	195	8-17-78	2000	Miami, Fla.
Wright, Mike	.242	62	182	13	44	9	3	3	19	12	62	0	2	.346	.289	R	R	6-2	210	3-13-76	1999	San Jose, Calif.
Young, Travis	.357	6	14	2	5	1	0	0	1	0	3	0	0	.429	.357	R	R	6-1	185	9-8-74	1997	Albuquerque, N.M.

PITCHING	W	L	ERA	G	GS	CG	SV	IP	H	R	ER	BB	SO	AVG	B	T	HT	WT	DOB	1st Yr	Resides
Alfano, Jeff	0	0	0.00	1	0	0	0	1	0	0	0	1	0	.000	R	R	6-3	195	8-16-76	1996	Visalia, Calif.
Andra, Jeff	3	9	4.68	18	18	0	0	98	116	59	51	32	57	.292	L	L	6-5	210	9-9-75	1997	Lenexa, Kan.
Bermudez, Manny	2	3	3.71	12	0	0	0	27	25	11	11	7	13	.257	R	R	6-1	195	12-15-76	1995	Antioch, Calif.
Brown, Elliot	0	8	4.50	14	10	0	0	62	77	50	31	17	28	.303	B	R	6-2	191	6-7-75	1996	Metairie, La.
Cannon, Jon	2	0	3.19	17	2	0	1	37	23	15	13	19	39	.176	R	L	6-3	200	1-1-75	1996	Los Altos, Calif.
Cox, Ryan	8	8	3.69	24	24	1	0	137	145	70	56	24	61	.270	R	R	6-3	210	12-25-76	1999	Stewardson, Ill.
Estrella, Luis	1	0	3.12	7	0	0	0	9	10	6	3	5	8	.285	R	R	6-1	220	10-7-74	1996	Santa Ana, Calif.
Goodrich, Randy	1	1	7.56	19	0	0	0	33	46	28	28	12	19	.326	R	R	6-4	210	11-8-76	1998	Fresno, Calif.
Guzman, Leiby	2	1	3.14	11	0	0	0	14	17	9	5	2	14	.274	R	R	6-5	160	9-27-76	1994	Nato del Media Abajo, D.R.
2-team (25 Tulsa)	4	1	4.88	36	0	0	1	63	65	39	34	17	45	.260							

PITCHING	W	L	ERA	G	GS	CG	SV	IP	H	R	ER	BB	SO	AVG	B	T	HT	WT	DOB	1st Yr	Resides
Horgan, Joe	3	5	3.65	31	14	0	1	104	97	51	42	27	61	.246	L	L	6-1	200	6-7-77	1996	Rancho Cordova, Calif.
Joseph, Kevin	2	1	2.43	24	0	0	1	33	31	9	9	13	27	.242	R	R	6-4	200	8-1-76	1997	Dallas, Texas
Knoll, Brian	0	0	2.25	2	1	0	0	4	5	1	1	3	2	.294	R	R	6-3	200	8-4-73	1995	Corona, Calif.
Messman, Joe	1	1	4.10	12	1	0	0	26	24	15	12	14	13	.250	R	R	6-2	175	7-29-75	1997	Parkdale, Ore.
Miller, Benji	1	6	4.23	37	0	0	2	66	63	33	31	35	39	.249	R	R	6-2	180	5-2-76	1998	Lynchburg, Va.
Nathan, Joe	3	6	6.93	21	7	0	0	62	73	49	48	37	33	.299	R	R	6-4	195	11-22-74	1995	Tempe, Ariz.
Ozias, Todd	3	3	2.73	30	0	0	0	56	47	21	17	22	32	.224	R	R	6-1	185	8-19-76	1998	Coral Springs, Fla.
Ramirez, Erasmo	2	0	2.16	22	1	0	1	33	25	10	8	5	39	.204	L	L	6-0	180	4-29-76	1998	Santa Ana, Calif.
Riley, Mike	3	2	4.81	7	7	2	0	43	55	26	23	12	34	.327	L	L	6-1	162	1-2-75	1996	Seaford, Del.
Urban, Jeff	7	11	3.91	27	27	0	0	157	178	85	68	32	117	.288	R	R	6-8	215	1-25-77	1998	Alexandria, Ind.
Verplancke, Jeff	1	8	4.44	43	0	0	22	49	50	27	24	20	46	.270	R	R	6-3	200	11-18-77	1999	Ontario, Calif.
Villano, Mike	0	0	1.04	7	0	0	5	9	6	1	1	1	7	.206	R	R	6-0	195	8-10-71	1994	Bay City, Mich.
2-team (37 Wichita)	6	7	4.11	44	2	0	9	77	85	44	35	30	47	.284							
Williams, Jerome	9	7	3.95	23	23	2	0	130	116	69	57	34	84	.234	R	R	6-3	190	12-4-81	1999	Las Vegas, Nev.

FIELDING

Catcher	PCT	G	PO	A	E	DP	PB
Luther	.975	31	138	18	4	1	3
Rodriguez	.983	61	362	35	7	3	7
Wright	.989	59	306	40	4	6	6

First Base	PCT	G	PO	A	E	DP
Glendenning	1.000	1	2	0	0	1
Luster	.990	119	1046	78	11	78
McGowan	.992	13	112	6	1	7
Pernalete	1.000	4	30	0	0	2
Rodriguez	.941	3	15	1	1	1

Second Base	PCT	G	PO	A	E	DP
Campusano	1.000	2	5	6	0	0
Cordido	1.000	2	3	2	0	0
Jester	.970	40	82	115	6	17
Luther	.951	93	181	210	20	50
Pernalete	1.000	1	0	1	0	0
Strankman	.867	5	6	7	2	1

	PCT	G	PO	A	E	DP
Young	1.000	2	0	3	0	0

Third Base	PCT	G	PO	A	E	DP
Campusano	.500	1	0	1	1	0
Cordido	.940	118	86	245	21	10
Pernalete	.905	16	10	28	4	3
Strankman	1.000	1	0	2	0	1
Tyler	1.000	2	3	5	0	1
Young	1.000	2	0	7	0	1

Shortstop	PCT	G	PO	A	E	DP
Campusano	1.000	3	5	6	0	1
Castro	.948	122	207	373	32	61
Jester	.000	1	0	0	0	0
Pernalete	1.000	1	0	1	0	0
Strankman	.667	2	0	2	1	0
Tyler	.911	10	15	36	5	4
Young	1.000	2	4	5	0	2

Outfield	PCT	G	PO	A	E	DP
Allen	.963	16	26	0	1	0
Byas	.987	83	216	7	3	1
Casper	1.000	8	13	0	0	0
Clark	.982	110	219	5	4	1
Glendenning	.917	14	19	3	2	0
Luster	1.000	2	5	0	0	0
Luther	1.000	1	1	0	0	0
Magruder	.979	39	93	0	2	0
McGowan	1.000	2	3	0	0	0
Moreta	.965	30	52	3	2	0
Shabala	1.000	12	26	2	0	1
Torcato	.975	36	76	3	2	0
Tyler	1.000	2	2	0	0	0
Valderrama	1.000	41	85	3	0	1
Walker	.943	37	48	2	3	0

SAN JOSE — Class A

CALIFORNIA LEAGUE

BATTING	AVG	G	AB	R	H	2B	3B	HR	RBI	BB	SO	SB	CS	SLG	OBP	B	T	HT	WT	DOB	1st Yr	Resides
Alfano, Jeff	.213	56	164	15	35	7	0	6	22	10	57	0	3	.366	.278	R	R	6-3	195	8-16-76	1996	Visalia, Calif.
Allen, Jeff	.305	99	371	60	113	19	4	14	61	43	103	12	5	.491	.393	R	R	6-1	190	6-8-76	1998	Walnut Creek, Calif.
Campusano, Carlos	.200	11	40	2	8	3	0	1	7	0	9	0	1	.350	.200	R	R	5-11	160	9-2-75	1994	Palave, Venez.
Carvajal, Jhonny	.261	113	448	57	117	20	1	4	50	31	76	14	7	.337	.308	R	R	5-10	180	7-24-74	1993	Barcelona, Venez.
Cerda, Jose	.218	30	87	10	19	4	2	0	3	4	25	0	0	.310	.277	R	R	6-2	215	5-14-77	2000	Selma, Calif.
Chavez, Angel	.244	84	316	37	77	22	2	3	28	16	60	10	4	.354	.280	R	R	6-0	175	7-22-81	1999	Panama City, Panama
Cook, Josh	.421	8	19	2	8	3	0	0	5	2	0	2	0	.579	.476	R	R	6-2	195	6-1-78	1999	Yuba City, Calif.
Daeley, Scott	.226	114	411	77	93	14	1	3	29	64	76	30	5	.287	.337	R	R	5-10	178	2-25-77	1999	Orange, Calif.
Fajardo, Alex	.243	40	136	22	33	9	2	1	12	16	30	9	4	.360	.322	R	R	6-0	180	2-6-76	1995	Moca, D.R.
Flaherty, Tim	.255	135	466	69	119	26	5	26	83	66	162	2	5	.500	.355	R	R	6-4	220	7-11-76	1997	Williamstown, Mass.
Hall, Justin	.265	42	151	22	40	11	1	2	13	24	39	1	0	.391	.369	R	R	5-10	175	9-23-76	1998	Mesa, Ariz.
2-team (32 Modesto)	.261	74	238	32	62	14	1	3	22	33	59	3	2	.366	.360							
Jester, Joe	.254	81	295	51	75	17	2	7	41	35	77	20	5	.397	.356	R	R	5-10	180	7-17-78	1999	Ashdown, Ark.
Maldonado, Edwin	.325	44	160	23	52	9	1	7	24	3	34	0	2	.525	.343	R	R	6-0	175	1-3-79	2000	Manati, P.R.
McDowell, Arturo	.242	118	425	57	103	12	11	1	31	46	132	25	14	.329	.321	L	L	6-1	175	9-7-79	1998	Jackson, Miss.
Messner, Jake	.244	83	279	36	68	14	1	2	39	34	83	1	2	.323	.329	L	L	6-1	205	5-18-77	1995	Sacramento, Calif.
Moreta, Ramon	.200	11	40	5	8	0	0	0	2	3	9	3	3	.200	.256	R	R	5-11	185	9-5-75	1994	La Romana, D.R.
2-team (34 R.C.)	.294	45	177	28	52	13	1	1	15	12	41	22	10	.395	.342							
Niekro, Lance	.288	42	163	18	47	11	0	3	34	14	44	4	2	.411	.298	R	R	6-3	210	1-29-79	2000	Lakeland, Fla.
Pernalete, Marco	.351	48	171	25	60	11	1	2	22	17	45	3	1	.462	.411	B	R	6-0	155	10-12-78	1996	Barquisimeto, Venez.
Rodriguez, Guillermo	.270	35	126	18	34	10	0	2	21	9	26	2	2	.397	.354	R	R	5-11	175	5-15-78	1996	Barquisimeto, Venez.
Santana, Henry	.333	7	24	1	8	1	1		5	0	7	1	0	.583	.333	B	R	5-11	170	3-12-83	1999	Los Mameyes, D.R.
Serrano, Sammy	.209	39	139	14	29	12	1	1	12	7	38	0	0	.331	.248	R	R	6-2	205	12-3-76	1998	Woodbridge, Va.
Shabala, Adam	.143	3	7	1	1	0	0	0	0	2	4	0	0	.143	.333	L	R	6-1	190	2-26-78	2000	Streator, Ill.
Torcato, Tony	.341	67	258	38	88	21	2	2	47	17	40	9	3	.461	.381	L	R	6-1	195	10-25-79	1998	Woodland, Calif.
Wilfong, Nick	.208	17	48	7	10	2	0	1	7	9	23	1	1	.313	.328	R	R	6-1	190	11-6-78	2000	Wappapello, Mo.

GAMES BY POSITION: C—Alfano 49, Cerda 30, Rodriguez 32, Serrano 39. 1B—Flaherty 130, Messner 11, Pernalete 7, Rodriguez 4. 2B—Campusano 1, Hall 26, Jester 74, Maldonado 33, Pernalete 15. 3B—Campusano 6, Chavez 82, Cook 4, Flaherty 1, Hall 5, Jester 3, Niekro 32, Pernalete 15. SS—Campusano 6, Carvajal 112, Chavez 2, Pernalete 15, Santana 7. OF—Allen 91, Cook 2, Daeley 112, Fajardo 30, Flaherty 6, McDowell 114, Messner 37, Moreta 10, Shabala 2, Torcato 15, Wilfong 17.

PITCHING	W	L	ERA	G	GS	CG	SV	IP	H	R	ER	BB	SO	AVG	B	T	HT	WT	DOB	1st Yr	Resides
Ah Yat, Paul	2	1	4.50	5	4	0	0	18	14	13	9	7	17	.200	R	L	6-1	192	10-13-74	1996	Honolulu, Hawaii
Alfano, Jeff	0	0	5.63	8	0	0	0	8	8	8	5	5	5	.000	R	R	6-3	195	8-16-76	1996	Visalia, Calif.
Anderson, Luke	2	2	2.59	59	0	0	30	66	56	22	19	13	76	.220	R	R	6-5	210	4-9-78	2000	Las Vegas, Nev.
Bermudez, Manny	8	2	3.56	43	0	0	1	81	87	36	32	23	40	.282	R	R	6-1	195	12-15-76	1995	Antioch, Calif.
Brous, Dave	2	4	6.19	11	9	0	0	32	28	25	22	36	18	.239	L	L	6-2	195	3-9-80	1999	Crescent City, Calif.
Brown, Elliot	4	0	0.93	5	5	0	0	29	15	3	3	7	26	.150	B	R	6-2	191	6-7-75	1996	Metairie, La.
Cannon, Jon	3	1	3.24	22	0	0	2	42	36	17	15	18	48	.238	R	L	6-3	200	1-1-75	1996	Los Altos, Calif.
Cash, David	4	0	2.08	20	0	0	1	39	23	9	9	17	46	.170	R	R	6-1	180	7-25-79	2001	Modesto, Calif.
Cozier, Vance	15	7	3.61	30	29	1	0	170	158	71	68	45	98	.247	R	R	6-6	245	9-26-77	1999	Ajax, Ontario
Esteves, Jake	0	3	7.36	9	9	0	0	15	13	12	12	9	19	.236	R	R	6-1	200	7-31-75	1998	Auburn, Calif.
Farley, Joe	1	0	7.09	18	0	0	0	27	28	22	21	20	15	.271	B	L	6-8	230	4-23-79	1997	Olympia, Wash.
Farmer, Jason	6	1	4.62	14	13	0	0	62	77	37	32	20	52	.303	R	R	6-2	200	5-6-79	2000	Indio, Calif.
Frias, Juan	0	0	10.50	4	0	0	0	6	9	8	7	9	5	.346	R	R	6-0	179	6-27-79	1996	San Pedro de Macoris, D.R.

PITCHING	W	L	ERA	G	GS	CG	SV	IP	H	R	ER	BB	SO	AVG	B	T	HT	WT	DOB	1st Yr	Resides
Goodrich, Randy	0	9	8.63	15	13	0	0	56	89	58	54	23	34	.357	R	R	6-4	210	11-8-76	1998	Fresno, Calif.
Joseph, Kevin	0	0	3.38	9	0	0	3	13	12	6	5	1	15	.255	R	R	6-4	200	8-1-76	1997	Dallas, Texas
Messman, Joe	3	1	3.86	23	0	0	2	42	47	28	18	15	24	.284	R	R	6-2	175	7-29-75	1997	Parkdale, Ore.
Miller, Benji	0	0	0.00	1	0	0	0	1	0	0	0	0	2	.000	R	R	6-2	180	5-2-76	1998	Lynchburg, Va.
Pavon, Julio	1	0	8.74	6	0	0	0	11	14	12	11	2	14	.311	R	R	6-2	165	6-14-76	1999	Granada, Nicaragua
Ramirez, Erasmo	3	2	3.41	17	0	0	1	32	23	14	12	5	33	.193	L	L	6-0	180	4-29-76	1998	Santa Ana, Calif.
Taschner, Jack	4	4	4.11	14	14	0	0	66	62	33	30	29	72	.244	L	L	6-3	190	4-21-78	1999	Racine, Wis.
Threets, Erick	0	10	4.25	14	14	0	0	59	49	34	28	40	60	.223	L	L	6-5	220	11-4-81	2000	Livermore, Calif.
Uzzell, Todd	1	1	4.36	15	0	0	0	33	30	18	16	18	25	.243	R	R	6-3	205	6-22-78	2000	El Paso, Texas
Vent, Kevin	5	6	4.69	41	10	0	0	104	105	70	54	34	74	.256	R	R	6-0	185	6-1-77	1999	Maumelle, Ark.
Walk, Mitch	9	6	3.54	27	19	0	0	117	115	57	46	39	59	.259	L	L	6-1	185	4-7-78	2000	Mattoon, Ill.
Yacco, Anthony	1	0	3.38	7	0	0	0	13	10	7	5	12	15	.212	R	R	6-3	220	12-2-80	1999	Mahopac, N.Y.
Zirelli, Mike	3	3	5.75	38	1	0	0	83	119	62	53	13	62	.338	R	R	6-4	210	1-21-77	1999	San Carlos, Calif.

HAGERSTOWN — Class A

SOUTH ATLANTIC LEAGUE

BATTING	AVG	G	AB	R	H	2B	3B	HR	RBI	BB	SO	SB	CS	SLG	OBP	B	T	HT	WT	DOB	1st Yr	Resides
Alexander, Kevin	.229	83	266	25	61	14	1	2	30	25	58	5	1	.312	.299	R	R	5-10	162	9-15-80	2000	Eugene, Ore.
Athas, Jamie	.274	65	234	44	64	10	3	2	28	31	55	17	5	.368	.370	L	R	6-2	190	10-14-79	2001	Winston-Salem, N.C.
Bell, Derek	.252	111	381	50	96	30	2	2	49	62	76	1	3	.357	.355	B	R	6-1	195	9-22-76	2000	Rohnert Park, Calif.
Cabrera, Leonel	.300	10	30	8	9	1	0	0	1	1	7	3	3	.333	.323	R	R	5-11	165	1-10-81	1998	Santo Domingo, D.R.
Carter, Bryan	.183	56	197	18	36	7	2	2	14	15	63	11	3	.269	.251	L	L	6-0	194	2-25-78	2000	Frostproof, Fla.
Cerda, Jose	.242	13	33	4	8	0	0	0	2	6	7	0	0	.242	.381	R	R	6-2	215	5-14-77	2000	Selma, Calif.
Chavez, Angel	.189	13	37	5	7	2	0	2	3	1	12	1	0	.405	.231	R	R	6-0	175	7-22-81	1999	Panama City, Panama
Ellison, Jason	.291	130	494	95	144	38	3	8	55	71	68	19	15	.429	.388	R	R	5-10	180	4-4-78	2000	Lewiston, Idaho
Fajardo, Alex	.162	12	37	4	6	0	0	0	3	10	14	3	0	.162	.354	R	R	6-0	180	2-6-76	1995	Moca, D.R.
Gann, Bryan	.237	111	397	49	94	16	0	0	26	28	50	2	3	.277	.295	R	R	5-10	175	4-7-78	2000	Lexington, Okla.
Garrido, Tomas	.218	45	142	13	31	3	0	0	7	2	34	2	1	.239	.234	R	R	6-2	155	8-17-81	1999	Valencia, Venez.
Lunsford, Trey	.237	114	396	53	94	19	0	5	50	45	89	10	5	.333	.320	R	R	6-1	195	5-25-79	2000	San Angelo, Texas
Mapes, Jake	.000	2	6	0	0	0	0	0	0	0	2	0	0	.000	.000	R	R	6-4	210	3-1-79	1999	Hemet, Calif.
Santos, Deivis	.290	131	520	64	151	27	3	12	80	25	91	16	10	.423	.325	L	L	6-1	182	2-9-80	1997	Santo Domingo, D.R.
Shabala, Adam	.313	70	256	37	80	16	2	1	29	37	37	11	4	.402	.411	L	R	6-1	190	2-6-78	2000	Streator, Ill.
Shrum, Allen	.217	29	106	12	23	7	0	2	12	6	30	1	0	.340	.265	R	R	6-3	215	5-13-76	1998	Heritage, Tenn.
Strankman, Elliott	.259	39	116	16	30	12	0	0	10	5	29	3	4	.362	.312	R	R	6-1	185	1-13-77	2000	Richland, Wash.
Trumble, Dan	.236	119	399	70	94	18	1	26	75	63	157	10	5	.481	.346	R	R	6-2	205	9-29-79	2000	Nampa, Idaho
Walker, Mark	.160	58	169	19	27	4	2	4	12	32	74	8	2	.278	.291	R	R	6-1	190	8-17-78	2000	Miami, Fla.
Wilfong, Nick	.238	109	370	44	88	15	2	15	58	39	138	15	2	.411	.313	L	R	6-1	190	11-6-78	2000	Wappapello, Mo.

GAMES BY POSITION: C—Certa 13, Lunsford 109, Mapes 1, Shrum 21. **1B**—Bell 11, Lunsford 1, Santos 125, Trumble 9. **2B**—Alexander 28, Cabrera 9, Gann 108. **3B**—Alexander 38, Bell 95, Chavez 8, Strankman 8. **SS**—Alexander 5, Athas 64, Chavez 5, Gann 1, Garrido 45, Strankman 30. **OF**—Carter 52, Ellison 129, Fajardo 10, Santos 1, Shabala 70, Trumble 19, Walker 52, Wilfong 100.

PITCHING	W	L	ERA	G	GS	CG	SV	IP	H	R	ER	BB	SO	AVG	B	T	HT	WT	DOB	1st Yr	Resides
Bonser, Boof	16	4	2.49	27	27	0	0	134	91	40	37	61	178	.192	R	R	6-4	230	10-14-81	2000	Pinellas Park, Fla.
Brous, Dave	0	1	3.58	20	0	0	3	33	30	18	13	29	21	.254	L	L	6-2	195	3-9-80	1999	Crescent City, Calif.
Clark, Jeff	14	9	3.65	27	27	0	0	148	152	72	60	15	131	.265	R	R	6-6	240	5-6-80	2000	Ledyard, Conn.
Cunningham, Jeremy	1	1	5.89	10	0	0	0	18	23	16	12	7	17	.306	R	R	6-5	190	8-4-78	1999	Cupertino, Calif.
Diaz, Felix	1	4	3.66	15	12	0	0	52	49	27	21	16	56	.245	R	R	6-1	165	7-27-81	1998	Las Matas de Farfan, D.R.
Faust, Wesley	7	5	2.48	46	0	0	4	91	79	28	25	18	66	.237	R	R	6-7	190	12-3-77	2000	Glendora, Calif.
Frias, Juan	3	1	3.19	24	0	0	1	31	36	17	11	10	27	.305	R	R	6-0	179	6-27-79	1996	San Pedro de Macoris, D.R.
Graham, Elgin	3	4	5.91	32	9	0	1	67	75	56	44	43	37	.289	R	R	6-2	185	2-15-78	2000	Pensacola, Fla.
Gross, Kyle	2	6	6.45	22	12	0	0	53	43	45	38	51	46	.228	R	R	6-4	212	12-11-78	2000	Danville, Calif.
Hills, Matt	0	3	9.47	10	1	0	0	19	34	26	20	6	16	.382	L	L	6-01	200	8-12-78	1999	Salem, Ore.
Jones, Chris	6	3	4.52	39	4	0	1	74	77	42	37	40	60	.282	L	L	6-03	195	8-29-79	1998	Charlotte, N.C.
Malerich, Will	0	0	11.57	5	0	0	0	7	13	9	9	4	7	.406	L	L	6-0	180	10-25-75	1997	Alexandria, Va.
Markert, Jackson	3	3	2.82	58	0	0	39	61	57	26	19	18	45	.243	R	R	6-6	215	2-9-79	2000	Tulsa, Okla.
Munter, Scott	1	0	3.38	1	1	0	0	5	5	3	2	1	2	.277	R	R	6-6	235	3-7-80	2001	Wichita, Kan.
Padgett, Dan	0	1	6.66	19	0	0	0	24	24	18	18	18	16	.272	L	L	6-0	170	1-7-78	2000	Littleton, Colo.
Pavon, Julio	6	4	3.12	29	15	1	2	113	109	45	39	21	107	.254	R	R	6-2	165	6-14-76	1999	Granada, Nicaragua
Rigueiro, Rafael	5	3	3.19	26	14	0	0	96	77	37	34	35	104	.217	R	R	6-6	200	5-20-77	2000	Riverside, Calif.
Smith, Joe	7	2	2.57	24	2	0	0	70	64	21	20	21	45	.246	R	R	6-0	185	4-1-78	2000	San Luis Obispo, Calif.
Thomas, John	3	3	4.16	15	15	0	0	71	70	40	33	22	65	.259	L	L	6-0	190	7-24-81	1999	Orcutt, Calif.
Threets, Erick	2	0	0.75	12	0	0	1	24	13	3	2	9	32	.154	L	L	6-5	220	11-4-81	2000	Livermore, Calif.
Uzzell, Todd	0	0	3.60	1	1	0	0	5	5	2	2	3	3	.312	R	R	6-3	205	6-22-78	2000	El Paso, Texas
Yacco, Anthony	3	0	2.61	24	0	0	0	38	27	15	11	23	37	.198	R	R	6-3	220	12-2-80	1999	Mahopac, N.Y.

SALEM-KEIZER — Short-Season Class A

NORTHWEST LEAGUE

BATTING	AVG	G	AB	R	H	2B	3B	HR	RBI	BB	SO	SB	CS	SLG	OBP	B	T	HT	WT	DOB	1st Yr	Resides
Anderson, Keith	.206	57	155	18	32	9	0	4	21	18	34	1	0	.342	.299	R	R	6-1	205	1-6-79	2001	Escondido, Calif.
Benavidez, Julian	.319	50	188	36	60	12	1	9	39	24	54	2	1	.537	.395	R	R	6-2	215	4-14-82	2001	Oakland, Calif.
Carter, Bryan	.223	67	238	36	53	12	1	6	31	22	46	13	5	.357	.303	L	L	6-0	194	2-25-78	2000	Frostproof, Fla.
Florence, Branden	.274	32	124	20	34	6	1	1	15	12	18	2	0	.363	.352	R	R	6-0	200	4-3-78	2001	Boise, Idaho
Holm, Steve	.208	33	72	8	15	3	1	0	2	10	16	1	0	.278	.310	R	R	6-0	195	10-31-79	2001	Tulsa, Okla.
Holst, Micah	.272	60	217	41	59	15	1	4	36	18	38	10	4	.406	.346	R	R	6-2	205	3-5-77	1999	Independence, Mo.
Huntington, Matt	.227	62	220	35	50	5	5	3	37	13	37	8	3	.336	.301	L	L	6-1	175	3-5-79	2001	West Vancouver, B.C.
Keating, Matt	.224	26	49	7	11	3	0	1	2	4	9	0	0	.347	.283	L	R	6-2	190	8-14-77	2000	Arlington, Mass.
Maestrales, Peter	.258	19	66	6	17	5	1	1	11	3	19	0	0	.409	.300	B	R	5-11	180	7-4-79	2001	Delray Beach, Fla.
Maldonado, Edwin	.500	1	2	1	1	0	0	1	1	0	0	0	2	.000	.500	R	R	6-0	175	1-3-79	2000	Manati, P.R.
McAuliff, Jimbo	.242	20	66	10	16	2	0	1	4	10	18	3	1	.318	.359	R	R	5-9	180	5-21-79	2001	Stillwater, Okla.
McMains, Derin	.271	69	258	40	70	18	2	4	40	32	26	6	1	.403	.350	B	R	6-0	180	11-3-79	2001	Little Rock, Ark.
Meyer, Robbie	.292	70	274	47	80	19	1	5	35	25	53	0	0	.423	.359	R	R	6-2	195	12-15-78	2001	Berkeley, Calif.
Miranda, Miguel	.278	59	194	21	54	7	0	0	28	20	43	4	3	.314	.338	B	R	6-0	175	6-10-79	2001	Little Rock, Ark.

ORGANIZATION STATISTICS

BATTING	AVG	G	AB	R	H	2B	3B	HR	RBI	BB	SO	SB	CS	SLG	OBP	B	T	HT	WT	DOB	1st Yr	Resides
Pinon, Alex	.231	51	121	20	28	5	0	0	16	31	20	8	1	.273	.391	R	R	5-8	170	10-10-78	2001	Miami, Fla.
Turco, Anthony	.244	42	86	15	21	1	1	2	11	12	20	0	0	.349	.337	L	R	5-9	173	10-8-79	2000	Sarasota, Fla.
Von Schell, Tyler	.273	75	293	50	80	18	2	10	45	26	63	1	2	.451	.337	R	R	6-3	215	7-7-79	2001	Goleta, Calif.
Williams, Jon	.615	6	13	5	8	1	0	2	4	1	2	0	0	1.154	.643	L	R	5-10	190	5-18-79	2001	Columbia, Mo.

GAMES BY POSITION: C—Anderson 57, Holm 10, Turco 42, Williams 2. **1B**—Holm 2, Keating 6, Von Schell 74. **2B**—Maldonado 1, McMains 69, Pinon 11. **3B**—Benavidez 47, Holm 15, Maestrales 17, Pinon 2. **SS**—Meyer 1, Miranda 58, Pinon 25, Williams 1. **OF**—Carter 60, Florence 2, Holst 40, Huntingford 58, Keating 2, McAuliff 17, Meyer 64.

PITCHING	W	L	ERA	G	GS	CG	SV	IP	H	R	ER	BB	SO	AVG	B	T	HT	WT	DOB	1st Yr	Resides
Ashlock, Chad	4	3	4.44	11	10	0	0	47	46	26	23	15	39	.264	R	R	6-2	200	7-17-78	2000	Edmond, Okla.
Benjamin, Petersen	3	1	3.23	15	5	0	1	56	51	24	20	7	50	.240	R	R	6-4	210	10-2-78	2001	Boca Raton, Fla.
Burres, Brian	3	1	3.10	14	6	0	1	41	43	20	14	11	38	.273	L	L	6-1	175	4-8-81	2001	Clackamas, Ore.
Cram, Josh	5	2	3.03	19	0	0	0	36	41	16	12	10	34	.284	R	R	6-2	200	8-22-80	2001	Edmonds, Wash.
Foppert, Jesse	8	1	1.93	14	14	0	0	70	35	18	15	23	88	.150	R	R	6-6	210	7-10-80	2001	San Rafael, Calif.
Frias, Juan	0	0	9.00	4	0	0	0	5	7	5	5	3	2	.333	R	R	6-0	179	6-27-79	1996	San Pedro de Macoris, D.R.
Hannaman, Ryan	1	1	2.08	3	3	0	0	13	8	5	3	8	19	.170	L	L	6-3	190	8-28-81	2000	Mobile, Ala.
Hennessey, Brad	1	0	2.38	9	9	0	0	34	28	9	9	11	22	.224	R	R	6-2	185	2-7-80	2001	Toledo, Ohio
Hills, Mark	0	0	9.22	10	0	0	0	14	20	17	14	12	11	.333	L	L	6-01	180	8-12-78	1999	Salem, Ore.
Hixson, David	3	1	2.27	22	0	0	0	48	46	14	12	16	49	.255	R	R	6-1	195	9-13-78	2001	Spokane, Wash.
Hutchison, Wes	6	2	1.64	25	0	0	10	33	21	8	6	14	45	.185	R	R	6-1	195	5-31-79	2001	Lewiston, Idaho
Knoedler, Justin	1	1	1.26	13	0	0	1	29	22	4	4	9	38	.211	R	R	6-2	210	7-15-80	2001	Springfield, Ill.
Liriano, Francisco	0	0	5.00	2	2	0	0	9	7	5	5	1	12	.205	L	L	6-2	185	10-26-83	2001	San Cristobal, D.R.
Lowry, Noah	1	1	3.60	8	7	0	0	25	26	15	10	8	28	.265	L	L	6-2	190	10-10-80	2001	Ojai, Calif.
Meaux, Ryan	2	2	5.59	17	3	0	0	29	39	20	18	11	27	.325	R	L	5-11	175	10-5-78	2001	Lamar, Colo.
Montes, Albert	2	1	3.57	17	0	0	7	23	21	10	9	6	19	.241	R	R	6-2	210	12-11-79	2001	El Paso, Texas
Munter, Scott	1	2	5.91	15	0	0	0	35	42	26	23	12	28	.295	R	R	6-6	235	3-7-80	2001	Wichita, Kan.
Padgett, Dan	0	0	21.60	4	0	0	0	3	11	8	8	2	1	.578	L	L	6-0	170	1-7-78	2000	Littleton, Colo.
Pannone, Anthony	7	1	4.11	14	14	0	0	77	82	41	35	13	61	.271	R	R	6-3	220	7-7-81	2001	Olympia, Wash.
Ransom, Troy	0	2	6.41	17	0	0	0	20	31	15	14	11	13	.369	R	R	6-2	180	7-9-78	1999	Chandler, Ariz.
Uzzell, Todd	2	2	8.16	6	2	0	0	14	19	13	13	9	6	.327	R	R	6-3	205	6-22-78	2000	El Paso, Texas
Waddell, Jason	1	1	5.46	15	1	0	0	28	30	19	17	11	30	.270	R	L	6-2	182	6-11-81	2001	Riverside, Calif.

SCOTTSDALE — Rookie

ARIZONA LEAGUE

BATTING	AVG	G	AB	R	H	2B	3B	HR	RBI	BB	SO	SB	CS	SLG	OBP	B	T	HT	WT	DOB	1st Yr	Resides
Cabrera, Andres	.143	7	7	0	1	0	0	0	1	0	4	0	0	.143	.143	R	R	6-0	180	4-10-84	2001	San Pedro de Macoris, D.R.
Cabrera, Leonel	.322	46	205	45	66	14	2	1	31	6	22	12	1	.424	.344	R	R	6-1	165	1-10-81	1998	Santo Domingo, D.R.
Ciesluk, Chris	.253	51	170	22	43	3	3	0	17	17	31	4	1	.306	.328	R	R	6-1	185	2-6-83	2001	Taunton, Mass.
Cleto, Carlos	.262	54	214	38	56	10	4	1	35	14	55	6	1	.360	.322	L	L	6-1	175	5-19-83	2001	Santo Domingo, D.R.
D'Jesus, Francisco	.250	45	160	16	40	4	1	3	20	4	32	0	2	.344	.278	R	R	6-0	194	4-12-81	2000	Santo Domingo, D.R.
Davis, Jon	.285	54	193	23	55	11	2	0	20	19	34	6	2	.363	.356	L	L	6-2	190	11-2-78	2000	Fairfield, Calif.
Diaz, Randor	.286	16	21	3	6	1	0	0	2	3	6	1	0	.333	.375	R	R	6-0	180	10-13-82	2000	Santo Domingo, D.R.
Garrido, Tomas	.252	40	131	17	33	3	0	0	8	2	19	3	0	.275	.290	R	R	6-2	155	8-17-81	1998	Valencia, Venez.
Gonzalez, Jose	.200	6	15	1	3	0	0	0	2	2	7	0	0	.200	.278	R	R	5-11	155	7-5-81	1998	Santo Domingo, D.R.
Gustafson, Troy	.279	56	222	28	62	10	3	0	22	8	28	10	6	.351	.316	L	R	6-3	190	6-13-80	2000	Blaine, Minn.
Keating, Matt	.270	16	63	9	17	1	2	1	16	6	9	0	2	.397	.329	L	R	6-2	200	8-14-77	2000	Arlington, Mass.
Maestrales, Peter	.255	26	94	12	24	5	2	0	6	8	17	5	2	.351	.317	B	R	5-11	180	7-4-79	2001	Delray Beach, Fla.
McAuliff, Jimbo	.337	43	172	41	58	14	3	1	18	23	35	6	3	.471	.421	R	R	5-9	180	5-21-79	2001	Stillwater, Okla.
Montero, Roberto	.308	11	13	2	4	2	0	0	0	0	6	0	0	.462	.308	R	R	6-2	175	3-3-82	2000	Santo Domingo, D.R.
Morillo, Roberto	.250	4	4	1	1	0	0	0	0	0	2	0	0	.250	.400	B	R	6-0	155	7-24-84	2001	Maracaibo, Venez.
Pinango, Ever	.161	22	56	5	9	0	0	0	3	3	11	1	3	.161	.200	R	R	6-0	150	12-22-81	1999	Guiria, Venez.
Ramirez, Alexander	.243	33	111	14	27	2	4	0	10	10	39	1	1	.333	.323	R	R	6-1	160	3-15-82	1999	San Pedro de Macoris, D.R.
Williams, Jon	.324	39	136	24	44	7	3	3	26	16	14	1	1	.485	.406	L	R	5-10	190	5-18-79	2001	Columbia, Mo.

GAMES BY POSITION: C—D'Jesus 32, Gonzalez 6, Montero 2, Morillo 1, Williams 23. **1B**—D'Jesus 1, Davis 38, Diaz 8, Keating 16. **2B**—L. Cabrera 34, Cleto 1, D'Jesus 1, Maestrales 8, Montero 1, Pinango 3, A. Ramirez 13. **3B**—Ciesluk 42, Diaz 2, Garrido 5, Maestrales 5, Pinango 7. **SS**—L. Cabrera 10, Ciesluk 1, Garrido 32, Morillo 1, A. Ramirez 20. **OF**—A. Cabrera 4, Ciesluk 1, Cleto 50, Davis 8, Gustafson 56, Maestrales 8, McAuliff 43, Montero 1, Pinango 11.

PITCHING	W	L	ERA	G	GS	CG	SV	IP	H	R	ER	BB	SO	AVG	B	T	HT	WT	DOB	1st Yr	Resides
Abreu, Jonathan	2	2	4.93	23	0	0	1	35	39	20	19	10	31	.286	L	L	6-0	160	11-12-82	2000	Santo Domingo, D.R.
Bastardo, Jose	1	3	5.19	18	0	0	0	17	16	14	10	20	24	.235	L	L	6-2	192	6-25-81	1997	San Pedro de Macoris, D.R.
Featherstone, Deron	2	1	9.85	15	4	0	0	28	30	32	31	21	36	.283	R	R	6-2	175	6-20-77	1999	Hendersonville, N.C.
Garcia, Ruddy	0	0	3.18	5	0	0	0	6	7	3	2	5	3	.304	R	R	6-2	170	8-1-83	2001	Lake Worth, Fla.
Hannaman, Ryan	4	1	2.00	11	11	0	0	54	34	14	12	31	67	.181	L	L	6-3	190	8-28-81	2000	Mobile, Ala.
Hannaway, Patrick	1	1	2.70	12	0	0	0	13	13	5	4	9	7	.270	R	R	6-4	200	3-14-79	2001	Staten Island, N.Y.
King, Robert	2	0	5.29	12	1	0	0	17	21	11	10	7	19	.304	R	R	6-2	210	2-25-81	2001	Turlock, Calif.
Liriano, Francisco	5	4	3.63	13	12	0	0	62	51	26	25	24	67	.231	L	L	6-2	185	10-26-83	2001	San Cristobal, D.R.
Matos, Raymond	4	3	2.34	14	12	0	0	62	64	35	16	29	66	.260	L	L	6-1	150	2-23-83	1999	Santo Domingo, D.R.
Nacar, Leslie	0	3	2.54	22	0	0	5	28	27	9	8	9	35	.247	R	R	6-1	150	7-20-83	1999	Libertad de Baminas, Venez.
Nacar, Yimmy	1	0	5.14	17	5	0	0	42	40	25	24	22	38	.256	R	R	6-4	175	5-5-83	1999	Libertad de Baminas, Venez.
Ramirez, Hector	3	2	2.82	25	0	0	0	38	31	12	12	14	20	.226	R	R	6-1	175	6-5-80	1998	San Cristobal, D.R.
Ramirez, Rafael	1	0	3.55	9	9	0	0	38	35	17	15	15	32	.251	R	R	6-2	170	1-4-83	2000	San Pedro de Macoris, D.R.
Rojas, Ramon	3	5	3.40	27	0	0	0	45	43	21	17	14	27	.251	R	R	6-3	170	1-12-81	1998	Puerto Plata, D.R.
Waddell, Jason	0	1	3.00	1	1	0	0	6	8	3	2	0	3	.320	R	L	6-2	182	6-11-81	2001	Riverside, Calif.
Wells, Matt	0	1	18.00	1	0	0	0	1	3	2	2	1	1	.600	R	R	6-3	215	5-25-75	1996	Rocklin, Calif.
Worrell, Tim	0	0	0.00	1	1	0	0	3	1	0	0	1	2	.125	R	R	6-4	215	7-5-67	1990	Glendale, Ariz.

ORGANIZATION STATISTICS

SEATTLE MARINERS

BY SUSAN WADE

The Mariners raced to a 20-5 start by the end of April, putting them nine games ahead in the American League West. And the baseball world wondered when the other shoe was going to fall.

Seattle went on to win 116 games in 2001, setting a league record and tying the 1906 Cubs for the most victories in a major league season. The shoe never fell—until the New York Yankees dropped it with a decisive thud in Game Five of the AL Championship Series.

Historians might lament that the milestone became a millstone for Seattle.

"Nothing" is what those 116 victories meant ultimately, said Seattle's ALCS Game Five starter and loser Aaron Sele, who won 15 regular season games and was 0-3 in the playoffs. "It doesn't matter if you won 85 to get in the playoffs or 185 . . . It's how you finish."

Still, for the Mariners and their fans, nothing can taint the accomplishment.

"We won 116 games as a team," 20-game winner Jamie Moyer said. "We lived it. We breathed it. We ate it. We enjoyed it. Our fans enjoyed it. I think the baseball world enjoyed it. You know, it's something that can never be taken away from us."

Terrorist attacks on America subdued the Mariners' celebration as they won their third AL West championship in manager Lou Piniella's seven seasons. But that was the true tragedy that tinged their 2001 triumphs.

In the season-long swirl that saw Seattle host the All-Star Game, the Mariners treated the club-record 3,507,507 Safeco Field fans to some sparkling individual performances.

Players and fans alike marveled at the energy and ability of right fielder Ichiro Suzuki, the first Japanese position player to play in the major leagues. The 28-year-old megastar from Kobe, Japan, quickly earned first-name-only status as he hit .350 and stole 56 bases. He became

Ichiro Suzuki   Denny Stark

PLAYERS OF THE YEAR

MAJOR LEAGUE: Ichiro Suzuki, of

Suzuki, a seven-time batting champion in Japan's Pacific League, surpassed Shoeless Joe Jackson's major league rookie record for hits, getting 242 in his first season in the United States.

MINOR LEAGUE: Denny Stark, rhp

In his first season in Triple-A, Stark went 14-2, 2.37 with 130 strikeouts and 41 walks in 151 innings. He was named the Pacific Coast League's 2001 pitcher of the year.

the first player to win a batting crown and stolen base title since Jackie Robinson in 1949, and he set the major league rookie mark and club record with 242 hits.

Second baseman Bret Boone made a tortuous, but triumphant return to Seattle—and a case for MVP consideration. He set the AL record for home runs (36) and RBIs (141) by a second baseman. He was the first AL second baseman in history to bat .300 or better with more than 30 homers.

Edgar Martinez, the 38-year-old DH affectionately known as Papa, finished the season with a .306 average, marking the 10th time in his career he has batted .300 or better. He became Seattle's all-time hit leader with a single April 3 against Oakland. He has 1,882 career hits.

And Moyer, a 38-year-old testament to perseverance, became the oldest pitcher to win 20 games for the first time.

The Mariners set a major league record for most consecutive road series without losing a series (29). Among the club marks to fall were ones for consecutive victories (15), home victories (57), road wins (59), shutouts (14), saves (56), series swept (16), batting average (.287), stolen bases (174), fewest opponent runs (627), fewest walks allowed (465), highest fielding percentage (.986) and fewest errors (83).

Seattle will watch carefully how young pitchers Gil Meche and Ryan Anderson return from injuries that cost them the entire 2001 season. Lefthander Matt Thornton, the team's 1998 first-round draft pick, blossomed with a 14-7, 2.52 season at Class A San Bernardino and had an organization-best 192 strikeouts. Outfielder Chris Snelling, 19, won the California League batting title while outfielder Jamal Strong excelled at both Class A levels.

Each Mariner affiliate except short-season Everett finished with a record above .500. Tacoma shared the Pacific Coast League championship with New Orleans.

ORGANIZATION LEADERS

BATTING

*AVG	Chris Snelling, San Bernardino	.336
R	Jamal Strong, San Bernardino/Wisconsin	115
H	Jamal Strong, San Bernardino/Wisconsin	168
TB	Juan Thomas, Tacoma	263
2B	Chad Alexander, Tacoma	45
3B	Jaime Bubela, Wisconsin	12
HR	Juan Thomas, Tacoma	23
RBI	Juan Thomas, Tacoma	95
BB	Jamal Strong, San Bernardino/Wisconsin	91
SO	Justin Leone, San Bernardino	158
SB	Jamal Strong, San Bernardino/Wisconsin	82

PITCHING

W	Denny Stark, Tacoma/San Antonio	15
L	Rob Ramsay, Tacoma	11
	Aaron Looper, Tacoma	11
#ERA	Jared Hoerman, San Bernardino/Wisconsin	1.89
G	Kevin Gryboski, Tacoma	58
CG	Greg Wooten, Tacoma	5
SV	Julio Mateo, San Bernardino	26
IP	Craig Anderson, San Bernardino	179
BB	Rett Johnson, San Bernardino/Wisconsin	63
SO	Matt Thornton, San Bernardino	192

*Minimum 250 At-Bats #Minimum 75 Innings

SEATTLE MARINERS

Manager: Lou Piniella

2001 Record: 116-46, .716 (1st, AL West)

BATTING	AVG	G	AB	R	H	2B	3B	HR	RBI	BB	SO	SB	CS	SLG	OBP	B	T	HT	WT	DOB	1st Yr	Resides
Bell, David	.260	135	470	62	122	28	0	15	64	28	59	2	1	.415	.303	R	R	5-10	195	9-14-72	1990	Seattle, Wash.
Boone, Bret	.331	158	623	118	206	37	3	37	141	40	110	5	5	.578	.372	R	R	5-10	190	4-6-69	1990	Orlando, Fla.
Borders, Pat	.500	5	6	1	3	0	0	0	0	1	0	0	0	.500	.500	R	R	6-2	200	5-14-63	1982	Lake Wales, Fla.
Buhner, Jay	.222	19	45	4	10	2	0	2	5	8	9	0	0	.400	.340	R	R	6-3	210	8-13-64	1984	Issaquah, Wash.
Cameron, Mike	.267	150	540	99	144	30	5	25	110	69	155	34	5	.480	.353	R	R	6-2	195	1-8-73	1991	La Grange, Ga.
Gipson, Charles	.219	94	64	16	14	2	2	0	5	4	20	1	1	.313	.282	R	R	6-1	190	12-16-72	1992	Orange, Calif.
Guillen, Carlos	.259	140	456	72	118	21	4	5	53	53	89	4	1	.355	.333	B	R	6-1	180	9-30-75	1993	Maracay, Venez.
Javier, Stan	.292	89	281	44	82	14	1	4	33	36	47	11	1	.391	.375	B	R	6-0	200	1-9-64	1981	Santo Domingo, D.R.
Kingsale, Eugene	.333	10	15	4	5	0	0	0	1	2	2	2	0	.333	.444	B	R	6-3	190	8-20-76	1994	Oranjestad, Aruba
2-team (3 Baltimore)	.263	13	19	4	5	0	0	1	2	4	3	1	1	.263	.364							
Lampkin, Tom	.225	79	204	28	46	10	0	5	22	18	41	1	0	.348	.309	L	R	5-11	198	3-4-64	1986	Vancouver, Wash.
Martin, Al	.240	100	283	41	68	15	2	7	42	37	59	9	3	.382	.330	L	L	6-2	214	11-24-67	1985	Scottsdale, Ariz.
Martinez, Edgar	.306	132	470	80	144	40	1	23	116	93	90	4	1	.543	.423	R	R	5-11	210	1-2-63	1983	Kirkland, Wash.
McLemore, Mark	.286	125	409	78	117	16	9	5	57	69	84	39	7	.406	.384	B	R	5-11	207	10-4-64	1982	Southlake, Texas
Olerud, John	.302	159	572	91	173	32	1	21	95	94	70	3	1	.472	.401	L	L	6-5	220	8-5-68	1989	Fall City, Wash.
Podsednik, Scott	.167	5	6	1	1	0	1	0	3	0	1	0	0	.500	.167	L	L	6-0	170	3-18-76	1994	West, Texas
Sanders, Anthony	.176	9	17	1	3	2	0	0	2	2	3	0	0	.294	.263	R	R	6-2	200	3-2-74	1993	Tucson, Ariz.
Sprague, Ed	.298	45	94	9	28	7	0	2	16	11	18	0	0	.436	.374	R	R	6-2	205	7-25-67	1989	Stockton, Calif.
Suzuki, Ichiro	.350	157	692	127	242	34	8	8	69	30	53	56	14	.457	.381	L	R	5-9	160	10-22-73	2001	Kobe, Japan
Vazquez, Ramon	.229	17	35	5	8	0	0	0	4	0	3	0	0	.229	.222	L	R	5-11	170	8-21-76	1995	Cayey, P.R.
Wilson, Dan	.265	123	377	44	100	20	1	10	42	20	69	3	2	.403	.305	R	R	6-3	214	3-25-69	1990	Seattle, Wash.

PITCHING	W	L	ERA	G	GS	CG	SV	IP	H	R	ER	BB	SO	AVG	B	T	HT	WT	DOB	1st Yr	Resides
Abbott, Paul	17	4	4.25	28	27	1	0	163	145	79	77	87	118	.238	R	R	6-3	204	9-15-67	1985	Fullerton, Calif.
Charlton, Norm	4	2	3.02	44	0	0	1	48	36	19	16	11	48	.211	B	L	6-3	205	1-6-63	1984	Tilden, Texas
Franklin, Ryan	5	1	3.56	38	0	0	0	78	76	32	31	24	60	.250	R	R	6-3	165	3-5-73	1993	Spiro, Okla.
Fuentes, Brian	1	1	4.63	10	0	0	0	12	6	6	6	8	10	.171	L	L	6-4	220	8-9-75	1996	Merced, Calif.
Garcia, Freddy	18	6	3.05	34	34	4	0	239	199	88	81	69	163	.225	R	R	6-4	235	10-6-76	1994	Baruta, Venez.
Halama, John	10	7	4.73	31	17	0	0	110	132	69	58	26	50	.295	L	L	6-5	210	2-22-72	1994	Brooklyn, N.Y.
Moyer, Jamie	20	6	3.43	33	33	1	0	210	187	84	80	44	119	.239	L	L	6-0	175	11-18-62	1984	Seattle, Wash.
Nelson, Jeff	4	3	2.76	69	0	0	4	65	30	21	20	44	88	.135	R	R	6-8	235	11-17-66	1984	Issaquah, Wash.
Paniagua, Jose	4	3	4.36	60	0	0	3	66	59	35	32	38	46	.233	R	R	6-2	195	8-20-73	1991	Santo Domingo, D.R.
Pineiro, Joel	6	2	2.03	17	11	0	0	75	50	24	17	21	56	.190	R	R	6-1	180	9-25-78	1997	Rio Piedras, P.R.
Rhodes, Arthur	8	0	1.72	71	0	0	3	68	46	14	13	12	83	.188	L	L	6-2	205	10-24-69	1988	Baltimore, Md.
Sasaki, Kazuhiro	0	4	3.24	69	0	0	45	67	48	24	24	11	62	.195	R	R	6-4	220	2-22-68	2001	Yokohama, Japan
Sele, Aaron	15	5	3.60	34	33	2	0	215	216	93	86	51	114	.261	R	R	6-5	220	6-25-70	1991	Bellevue, Wash.
Stark, Denny	1	1	9.20	4	3	0	0	15	21	15	15	4	12	.333	R	R	6-2	210	10-27-74	1996	Edgerton, Ohio
Tomko, Brett	3	1	5.19	11	4	0	0	35	42	24	20	15	22	.287	R	R	6-4	215	4-7-73	1995	San Diego, Calif.

FIELDING

Catcher	PCT	G	PO	A	E	DP	PB
Borders	.923	5	10	2	1	0	0
Lampkin	.995	71	375	23	2	2	3
Sprague	1.000	1	1	0	0	0	0
Wilson	.999	122	711	32	1	1	3

First Base	PCT	G	PO	A	E	DP
Bell	1.000	2	6	0	0	1
Javier	1.000	6	26	3	0	4
Martinez	1.000	1	8	0	0	0
Olerud	.993	158	1211	121	9	116
Sprague	.981	12	52	1	1	4
Wilson	1.000	2	3	0	0	0

Second Base	PCT	G	PO	A	E	DP
Boone	.986	156	286	410	10	90
Gipson	.000	1	0	0	0	0
McLemore	.946	9	14	17	2	8
Vazquez	1.000	6	3	7	0	0

Third Base	PCT	G	PO	A	E	DP
Bell	.961	134	92	257	14	21
Gipson	.889	9	2	6	1	0
McLemore	.913	36	25	48	7	3

Sprague	.941	8	5	11	1	0
Vazquez	.500	2	0	1	1	0

Shortstop	PCT	G	PO	A	E	DP
Gipson	.952	6	9	11	1	1
Guillen	.980	137	187	313	10	75
McLemore	.984	35	41	79	2	20
Vazquez	1.000	10	11	9	0	3

Outfield	PCT	G	PO	A	E	DP
Buhner	1.000	12	15	0	0	0
Cameron	.986	149	410	8	6	2
Gipson	1.000	65	40	1	0	0
Javier	.993	76	139	1	1	1
Kingsale	1.000	9	12	0	0	0
Lampkin	.000	1	0	0	0	0
Martin	.971	73	132	3	4	2
McLemore	.988	68	81	3	1	2
Podsednik	1.000	5	3	0	0	0
Sanders	1.000	9	13	0	0	0
Sprague	1.000	9	11	0	0	0
Suzuki	.997	152	335	8	1	2

Bret Boone

LARRY GOREN

FRANK RAGSDALE

Freddy Garcia: Had an American League-best 3.05 ERA

Jamie Moyer: 20-game winner at age 38

FARM SYSTEM

Director, Player Development: Benny Looper

Class	Farm Team	League	W	L	Pct.	Finish*	Manager	First Yr.
AAA	Tacoma (Wash.) Rainiers	Pacific Coast	85	59	.590	+1st (16)	Dan Rohn	1995
AA	San Antonio (Texas) Missions	Texas	70	67	.511	3rd (8)	Dave Brundage	2001
A#	San Bernardino (Calif.) Stampede	California	76	64	.543	3rd (10)	Daren Brown	2001
A	Wisconsin Timber Rattlers	Midwest	84	52	.618	2nd (14)	Gary Thurman	1993
A	Everett (Wash.) Aquasox	Northwest	36	39	.480	5th (8)	Terry Pollreisz	1995
Rookie	Peoria (Ariz.) Mariners	Arizona	34	22	.607	2nd (7)	Omer Munoz	1988

*Finish in overall standings (No. of teams in league)   #Advanced level   +League champion

TACOMA
Class AAA

PACIFIC COAST LEAGUE

BATTING	AVG	G	AB	R	H	2B	3B	HR	RBI	BB	SO	SB	CS	SLG	OBP	B	T	HT	WT	DOB	1st Yr	Resides
Akers, Chad	.297	86	316	44	94	16	3	3	32	13	36	6	5	.396	.330	R	R	5-8	170	5-30-72	1993	Lake, W.Va.
Alexander, Chad	.290	137	527	76	153	45	0	14	77	53	92	1	1	.455	.355	R	R	6-1	195	5-22-74	1995	Norfolk, Va.
Alexander, Manny	.282	97	344	46	97	26	2	8	51	14	55	5	9	.439	.311	R	R	5-10	180	3-20-71	1988	San Pedro de Macoris, D.R.
Barthol, Blake	.277	79	278	37	77	15	1	9	37	24	67	5	0	.435	.340	R	R	6-0	200	4-7-73	1995	Schnecksville, Pa.
Betts, Todd	.308	135	506	87	156	40	5	14	65	51	55	3	4	.490	.372	L	R	6-0	185	6-24-73	1993	Scarborough, Ontario
Betzsold, James	.159	48	157	20	25	4	2	8	25	21	71	0	0	.363	.271	R	R	6-3	210	8-7-72	1994	Orange, Calif.
Borders, Pat	.273	3	11	2	3	0	0	1	2	1	1	0	0	.545	.385	R	R	6-2	200	5-14-63	1982	Lake Wales, Fla.
Buhner, Jay	.235	11	34	5	8	0	0	3	9	5	13	0	0	.500	.350	R	R	6-3	210	8-13-64	1984	Issaquah, Wash.
Clark, Jermaine	.250	74	216	35	54	7	3	1	26	27	39	13	2	.324	.340	L	R	5-10	175	9-29-76	1997	Vacaville, Calif.
Figueroa, Luis	.342	24	76	9	26	4	0	0	9	3	8	0	1	.395	.363	R	R	6-0	175	3-2-77	1995	Carolina, P.R.
Freeman, Corey	.214	7	14	3	3	0	0	0	1	0	5	0	0	.214	.214	R	R	5-11	165	10-13-79	1998	Tampa, Fla.
Grabowski, Jason	.297	114	394	60	117	32	3	9	58	61	94	7	4	.462	.390	L	R	6-3	200	5-24-76	1997	Clinton, Conn.
Horner, Jim	.284	65	236	45	67	16	0	6	29	10	41	1	0	.428	.342	R	R	6-0	210	11-11-73	1996	Twin Falls, Idaho
Kingsale, Eugene	.293	51	215	30	63	14	4	3	24	8	25	12	4	.437	.327	B	R	6-3	190	8-20-76	1994	Oranjestad, Aruba
Moreta, Ramon	.217	23	69	8	15	3	1	1	13	6	31	3	3	.333	.288	R	R	5-11	185	9-5-75	1994	La Romana, D.R.
Myers, Adrian	.254	71	260	30	66	10	8	0	33	18	59	4	4	.354	.304	R	R	5-10	175	5-10-75	1996	Bassfield, Miss.
Podsednik, Scott	.290	66	269	46	78	15	4	3	30	13	46	12	5	.409	.327	L	L	6-0	170	3-18-76	1994	West, Texas
Sprague, Ed	.316	5	19	6	6	2	0	2	4	1	5	0	0	.737	.391	R	R	6-2	205	7-25-67	1989	Stockton, Calif.
Thomas, Juan	.300	129	503	75	151	39	2	23	95	40	141	2	2	.523	.351	R	R	6-4	265	4-17-72	1991	Montgomery, Ala.
Vazquez, Ramon	.300	127	466	85	140	28	1	10	79	76	84	9	7	.429	.397	L	R	5-11	170	8-21-76	1995	Cayey, P.R.

PITCHING	W	L	ERA	G	GS	CG	SV	IP	H	R	ER	BB	SO	AVG	B	T	HT	WT	DOB	1st Yr	Resides
Abbott, Paul	0	0	0.00	1	1	0	0	4	1	0	0	4		4	.076	R	R	6-3	204	9-15-67	1985	Fullerton, Calif.
Charlton, Norm	0	1	3.00	4	2	0	0	6	4	2	2	2	9	.173	B	L	6-3	205	1-6-63	1984	Tilden, Texas
Falkenborg, Brian	2	4	4.47	8	8	0	0	48	50	25	24	18	27	.273	R	R	6-6	195	1-18-78	1996	Redmond, Wash.
Fitzgerald, Brian	2	1	3.89	20	1	0	0	35	40	19	15	11	26	.281	L	L	5-11	175	12-26-74	1996	Woodbridge, Va.

PITCHING	W	L	ERA	G	GS	CG	SV	IP	H	R	ER	BB	SO	AVG	B	T	HT	WT	DOB	1st Yr	Resides
Franklin, Ryan	0	0	0.00	1	0	0	0	4	2	0	0	0	3	.166	R	R	6-3	165	3-5-73	1993	Spiro, Okla.
Fuentes, Brian	3	2	2.94	35	0	0	6	52	35	19	17	25	70	.205	L	L	6-4	220	8-9-75	1996	Merced, Calif.
Gryboski, Kevin	2	5	3.90	58	0	0	22	60	64	29	26	19	50	.277	R	R	6-5	220	11-15-73	1995	Plains, Pa.
Halama, John	2	0	0.47	3	3	1	0	19	9	2	1	0	22	.138	L	L	6-5	210	2-22-72	1994	Brooklyn, N.Y.
Head, Daniel	1	0	0.00	2	0	0	0	2	1	0	0	1	1	.166	R	R	6-2	215	10-7-78	2000	Satsuma, Ala.
Hodges, Kevin	5	5	4.15	14	14	2	0	87	97	50	40	25	55	.284	R	R	6-4	200	6-24-73	1991	Spring, Texas
Jarvis, Matt	2	0	1.56	12	0	0	0	17	12	3	3	7	9	.196	R	L	6-4	185	2-22-72	1991	Albuquerque, N.M.
Kaye, Justin	3	2	2.92	56	0	0	4	77	51	27	25	46	107	.186	R	R	6-4	185	6-9-76	1995	Fort Lauderdale, Fla.
Martinez, Gustavo	1	0	1.50	1	1	0	0	6	2	1	1	4	7	.105	R	R	6-0	175	11-9-80	1998	Santo Domingo, D.R.
Meyer, Jake	0	0	6.32	9	1	0	0	16	15	11	11	7	18	.245	R	R	6-1	195	1-7-75	1997	San Diego, Calif.
Myers, Randy	0	0	0.00	1	0	0	0	0	3	4	4	1	0	1.000	L	L	6-1	210	9-19-62	1982	Brush Prairie, Wash.
Pineiro, Joel	6	3	3.62	18	10	0	0	77	68	31	31	33	64	.241	R	R	6-1	180	9-25-78	1997	Rio Piedras, P.R.
Ramsay, Rob	10	11	4.82	26	26	0	0	149	160	98	80	60	113	.270	L	L	6-5	215	12-3-73	1996	Issaquah, Wash.
Stark, Denny	14	2	2.37	24	24	0	0	152	124	52	40	41	130	.224	R	R	6-2	210	10-27-74	1996	Edgerton, Ohio
Tomko, Brett	10	6	4.04	19	18	3	0	127	124	64	57	25	117	.254	R	R	6-4	215	4-7-73	1995	San Diego, Calif.
Turman, Jason	7	5	2.26	29	5	0	1	76	54	26	19	26	85	.199	R	R	6-10	210	11-10-75	1996	Gordo, Ala.
Watson, Mark	0	1	2.25	3	0	0	1	4	4	2	1	2	1	.222	R	L	6-4	215	1-23-74	1996	Dunwoody, Ga.
Wooten, Greg	11	8	3.99	27	26	5	0	169	201	91	75	32	116	.298	R	R	6-7	210	3-30-74	1996	Vancouver, Wash.
Zimmerman, Jordan	4	3	6.94	41	4	0	4	58	83	52	45	23	45	.342	R	L	6-0	200	4-28-75	1995	Brenham, Texas

FIELDING

Catcher	PCT	G	PO	A	E	DP	PB
Barthol	.997	77	596	28	2	4	6
Borders	1.000	3	20	4	0	0	0
Horner	.991	65	493	42	5	5	4

First Base	PCT	G	PO	A	E	DP
Betts	.992	105	817	56	7	70
Grabowski	1.000	20	148	9	0	16
Thomas	.995	27	191	16	1	13

Second Base	PCT	G	PO	A	E	DP
Akers	1.000	25	49	53	0	13
M. Alexander	.974	60	87	136	6	31
Clark	.980	71	118	173	6	37
Freeman	1.000	5	10	8	0	1

Third Base	PCT	G	PO	A	E	DP
Akers	.893	30	23	44	8	5
M. Alexander	.969	18	10	21	1	1
Betts	.966	25	16	40	2	3
Figueroa	.979	24	11	35	1	2
Grabowski	.903	58	38	111	16	8
Sprague	.000	1	0	0	0	0

Shortstop	PCT	G	PO	A	E	DP
Akers	1.000	1	0	1	0	0
M. Alexander	.917	20	30	36	6	8
Grabowski	.600	1	1	2	2	1
Vazquez	.979	127	190	381	12	69

Outfield	PCT	G	PO	A	E	DP
Akers	.979	35	42	4	1	0
C. Alexander	.975	130	224	7	6	1
M. Alexander	.000	2	0	0	0	0
Betzsold	.966	42	52	5	2	2
Buhner	1.000	6	10	0	0	0
Grabowski	.912	23	28	3	3	2
Kingsale	.976	51	115	5	3	0
Moreta	1.000	23	48	3	0	0
A. Myers	.981	71	153	4	3	1
Podsednik	.967	65	147	0	5	0
Sprague	1.000	4	6	0	0	0

SAN ANTONIO — Class AA

TEXAS LEAGUE

BATTING	AVG	G	AB	R	H	2B	3B	HR	RBI	BB	SO	SB	CS	SLG	OBP	B	T	HT	WT	DOB	1st Yr	Resides
Beamon, Trey	.256	64	238	33	61	14	2	1	19	18	32	7	3	.345	.313	L	R	6-3	192	2-11-74	1992	Garland, Texas
Bloomquist, Willie	.255	123	491	59	125	23	2	0	28	28	55	34	9	.310	.294	R	R	5-11	185	11-27-77	1999	Port Orchard, Wash.
Castillo, Ruben	.198	40	126	12	25	4	0	0	7	7	27	1	0	.230	.244	R	R	6-2	155	8-16-80	1996	San Pedro de Macoris, D.R.
Connors, Greg	.240	121	455	68	109	14	6	11	69	32	94	5	5	.369	.294	R	R	6-2	185	8-22-74	1996	Smithtown, N.Y.
Curl, John	.259	52	174	23	45	7	0	6	20	23	47	3	1	.402	.350	L	R	6-3	205	11-10-72	1995	Logansport, Ind.
Figueroa, Luis	.141	18	64	5	9	2	0	0	4	1	6	1	0	.172	.167	R	R	6-0	175	3-2-77	1995	Carolina, P.R.
Foley, Steve	.230	30	87	9	20	5	1	0	10	6	14	4	1	.310	.292	R	R	5-9	200	4-6-75	2000	Toronto, Ontario
Freeman, Corey	.176	26	74	6	13	3	0	1	3	5	18	1	0	.257	.228	R	R	5-11	165	10-13-79	1998	Tampa, Fla.
Kelly, Kenny	.262	121	419	72	125	20	5	11	46	45	111	18	12	.393	.326	R	R	6-3	180	1-26-79	1997	Plant City, Fla.
King, Brad	.313	80	262	34	82	16	0	10	56	33	33	4	4	.489	.397	B	R	6-2	205	12-3-74	1996	Boca Raton, Fla.
Kuzmic, Craig	.282	131	479	79	135	31	5	15	91	67	133	7	4	.461	.373	R	R	6-2	215	8-28-77	1995	Laguna Niguel, Calif.
Maynard, Scott	.183	70	229	17	42	11	0	0	19	21	59	3	0	.231	.255	R	R	5-10	175	5-10-75	1996	Bassfield, Miss.
Myers, Adrian	.233	33	129	14	30	4	2	0	15	17	30	6	4	.295	.320	R	R	5-11	175	7-26-81	1998	Bani, D.R.
Perez, Antonio	.143	5	21	3	3	0	0	0	0	0	7	0	0	.143	.143	R	R	5-11	175	8-21-75	1998	Charlotte, N.C.
Robinson, Bo	.293	133	474	75	139	23	1	13	74	81	56	3	0	.428	.395	R	R	6-2	195	8-21-75	1998	San Pedro de Macoris, D.R.
Silvestre, Juan	.228	101	372	29	85	13	0	8	39	21	113	0	2	.328	.270	R	R	5-11	180	1-10-78	1994	San Pedro de Macoris, D.R.
Weber, Jake	.293	126	451	66	132	28	4	4	58	40	53	11	6	.399	.358	L	R	5-11	188	4-22-76	1998	Wappingers Falls, N.Y.
Williams, Peanut	.200	38	125	11	25	9	0	1	9	14	37	1	1	.296	.284	R	R	6-3	235	10-3-77	1996	Nacogdoches, Texas

PITCHING	W	L	ERA	G	GS	CG	SV	IP	H	R	ER	BB	SO	AVG	B	T	HT	WT	DOB	1st Yr	Resides
Atchison, Scott	9	10	4.24	24	24	1	0	136	171	84	64	28	83	.314	R	R	6-2	180	3-29-76	1999	Fort Worth, Texas
Ayala, Julio	0	0	6.35	3	0	0	0	6	7	4	4	2	4	.269	L	L	6-2	203	4-20-75	1996	Buffalo, Texas
Ellison, Jason	2	8	3.74	46	1	0	9	65	76	30	27	28	57	.296	R	R	6-4	188	7-24-75	1996	Redmond, Wash.
Falkenborg, Brian	5	6	5.45	12	12	2	0	66	80	47	40	24	56	.305	R	R	6-6	195	1-18-78	1996	Pensacola, Fla.
Farnsworth, Jeff	11	10	4.35	27	27	0	0	155	182	92	75	47	113	.290	R	R	6-2	190	10-6-75	1996	Woodbridge, Va.
Fitzgerald, Brian	4	1	1.96	30	0	0	1	41	33	10	9	16	26	.217	L	L	5-11	175	12-26-74	1996	Moses Lake, Wash.
Heaverlo, Jeff	11	6	3.12	27	27	4	0	179	164	75	62	40	173	.239	R	R	6-1	185	1-13-78	1999	Albuquerque, N.M.
Jarvis, Matt	1	1	5.09	23	0	0	0	23	23	14	13	11	18	.261	R	L	6-3	165	7-30-80	1997	Villa Altagracia, D.R.
Lopez, Aquilino	4	3	3.02	42	0	0	2	63	48	24	21	25	79	.208	R	R	6-0	175	11-9-80	1998	Santo Domingo, D.R.
Martinez, Gustavo	0	0	1.93	3	0	0	0	5	2	2	2	6		.161	R	R	6-1	195	1-7-75	1997	San Diego, Calif.
Meyer, Jake	1	4	5.94	25	1	0	1	36	43	26	24	17	35	.292	R	R	6-2	200	9-26-74	1998	Kelso, Wash.
Morrison, Cody	0	0	13.50	8	0	0	1	10	15	14	14	4	8	.357	R	R	6-5	220	2-22-77	1999	Trenton, Mich.
Putz, J.J.	7	9	3.83	27	26	0	0	148	145	80	63	59	135	.259	R	R	6-4	210	11-22-74	1997	Purvis, Miss.
Rayborn, Kenny	1	0	6.86	14	0	0	0	20	26	15	15	8	11	.329	R	R	6-4	185	8-26-77	1997	Las Vegas, Nev.
Simpson, Allan	2	1	1.86	22	0	0	9	39	25	8	5	14	37	.183	R	R	6-1	175	12-19-79	1996	San Jose, D.R.
Soriano, Rafael	2	2	3.35	8	8	0	0	48	34	18	18	14	53	.192	R	R	6-2	210	10-27-74	1996	Edgerton, Ohio
Stark, Denny	1	0	0.00	1	1	0	0	6	2	0	0	3	7	.095	R	R	6-2	185	6-13-74	1996	Yonkers, N.Y.
Sweeney, Brian	7	4	3.80	37	9	0	1	104	117	47	44	23	96	.282	R	R	6-2	170	11-26-78	1997	New York, N.Y.
Ulloa, Enmanuel	2	2	3.04	45	1	0	4	80	81	32	27	21	64	.257	R	R					

FIELDING

Catcher	PCT	G	PO	A	E	DP	PB
Connors	1.000	5	34	3	0	0	0
King	.991	72	508	61	5	6	14
Maynard	.993	70	526	73	4	8	5

First Base	PCT	G	PO	A	E	DP
Beamon	1.000	1	2	1	0	0
Connors	.992	85	738	42	6	57
Curl	.981	18	145	12	3	8
King	1.000	1	9	1	0	0

	PCT	G	PO	A	E	DP
Robinson	.985	20	129	4	2	12
Williams	.975	26	212	26	6	17

Second Base	PCT	G	PO	A	E	DP
Bloomquist	.979	57	82	146	5	33

	PCT	G	PO	A	E	DP
Connors	1.000	1	0	1	0	0
Figueroa	1.000	7	11	11	0	2
Kuzmic	.969	89	151	221	12	35
Weber	.000	1	0	0	0	0

Third Base	PCT	G	PO	A	E	DP
Connors	.500	2	1	2	3	0
Curl	.000	1	0	0	1	0
Figueroa	1.000	4	2	4	0	0
Kuzmic	.926	46	20	68	7	6
Robinson	.931	99	60	155	16	13

Shortstop	PCT	G	PO	A	E	DP
Bloomquist	.945	76	103	226	19	32
Castillo	.949	40	73	115	10	24
Figueroa	1.000	5	5	7	0	2
Freeman	.958	25	35	57	4	11
Kuzmic	.000	1	0	0	0	0
Perez	.818	5	9	18	6	4

Outfield	PCT	G	PO	A	E	DP
Beamon	.958	44	67	1	3	0
Connors	.917	9	9	2	1	1

	PCT	G	PO	A	E	DP
Curl	.962	13	25	0	1	0
Foley	.979	29	45	2	1	1
Kelly	.981	121	252	6	5	3
Kuzmic	1.000	9	6	0	0	0
Myers	1.000	27	46	0	0	0
Silvestre	.981	65	98	4	2	0
Weber	.962	122	220	6	9	1

SAN BERNARDINO — Class A

CALIFORNIA LEAGUE

BATTING	AVG	G	AB	R	H	2B	3B	HR	RBI	BB	SO	SB	CS	SLG	OBP	B	T	HT	WT	DOB	1st Yr	Resides
Alcala, Juan	.254	72	232	23	59	9	1	0	24	9	55	1	1	.302	.296	R	R	6-2	160	4-15-78	1995	San Pedro de Macoris, D.R.
Alvarado, Damien	.000	3	9	0	0	0	0	0	0	0	2	0	0	.000	.000	L	R	6-0	190	3-14-78	2000	Sacramento, Calif.
Castillo, Ruben	.222	76	270	31	60	7	2	1	26	5	53	10	2	.274	.243	R	R	6-2	155	8-16-80	1996	San Pedro de Macoris, D.R.
Christianson, Ryan	.248	134	528	65	131	42	5	12	85	53	112	3	2	.415	.320	R	R	6-2	210	4-21-81	1999	Riverside, Calif.
Crespo, Manny	.500	2	6	0	3	0	0	0	0	0	0	0	0	.500	.500	R	R	5-10	185	1-4-79	2000	Miami, Fla.
Cruz, Israel	.179	31	67	6	12	2	0	0	3	2	12	3	0	.209	.214	R	R	6-0	170	9-2-79	1998	Blue Springs, Mo.
Dobbs, Greg	.385	3	13	2	5	1	0	1	3	0	4	0	0	.692	.357	L	R	6-2	215	7-2-78	2001	Moreno Valley, Calif.
Durango, Ariel	.184	27	87	8	16	1	0	0	6	10	18	7	4	.195	.276	B	R	5-10	150	4-5-79	1996	Panama City, Panama
Fernandez, Alex	.286	111	416	51	119	21	6	8	52	35	67	17	6	.423	.344	L	L	6-1	205	5-15-81	1998	Cotui, D.R.
Figueroa, Luis	.323	32	124	24	40	10	1	0	16	17	15	2	0	.419	.410	R	R	6-0	175	3-2-77	1995	Carolina, P.R.
Foley, Steve	.252	34	127	20	32	4	1	1	9	10	25	2	0	.331	.333	R	R	5-9	200	4-6-75	2000	Toronto, Ontario
Fulse, Sheldon	.164	34	122	14	20	2	1	2	11	14	43	7	6	.246	.264	B	R	6-3	175	11-10-81	1999	Bartow, Fla.
Gandolfo, Rob	.205	94	312	33	64	6	3	0	26	23	47	4	6	.244	.265	L	R	5-9	175	8-24-77	1999	Dumont, N.J.
Hernandez, Orlando	.167	18	48	4	8	0	0	0	3	3	15	0	0	.167	.216	R	R	6-2	170	3-26-79	1996	Charallave, Venez.
Leone, Justin	.233	130	485	70	113	27	4	22	69	57	158	1	4	.441	.318	R	R	6-1	190	3-9-77	1999	Las Vegas, Nev.
Lopez, Chuck	.294	24	102	14	30	1	3	4	24	6	23	2	1	.480	.336	L	L	6-1	195	11-29-76	2000	Huntington Beach, Calif.
Martinez, Guillermo	.253	44	166	26	42	8	1	1	16	13	43	1	2	.331	.313	B	R	6-0	158	6-24-80	1997	Maracay, Venez.
McCallum, Geoff	.245	32	98	13	24	6	0	0	12	18	34	2	1	.306	.362	R	R	6-0	190	11-22-77	2000	London, Ontario
McCorkle, Shawn	.275	136	520	81	143	36	4	13	81	69	151	2	2	.435	.360	L	R	6-5	230	7-14-77	1998	Newton, N.J.
Pines, Greg	.200	18	35	1	7	0	0	0	4	2	8	0	0	.200	.243	R	R	6-0	180	8-3-78	1999	Garden Grove, Calif.
Quintana, Wilfredo	.223	48	175	21	39	7	1	3	27	10	50	1	1	.326	.281	R	R	5-11	181	6-22-78	1998	Loiza, P.R.
Rainey, Jason	.214	15	42	2	9	3	0	0	5	0	17	0	1	.286	.261	L	L	6-0	185	6-11-79	2001	Klondike, Texas
Snelling, Chris	.336	114	450	90	151	29	10	7	73	45	63	12	5	.491	.418	L	L	5-10	165	12-3-81	1999	Gorokan, Australia
Strong, Jamal	.311	81	331	74	103	11	2	0	32	51	60	47	8	.356	.411	R	R	5-10	180	8-5-78	2000	Altadena, Calif.
Williams, P.J.	.231	30	108	13	25	2	0	0	8	11	20	7	4	.250	.301	R	R	6-2	165	5-7-77	1997	Rockdale, Texas
Woods, Blake	.091	10	22	3	2	0	0	1	4	4	7	3	0	.227	.259	R	R	6-2	190	1-5-79	2001	Chandler, Ariz.

GAMES BY POSITION: C—Alcala 32, Alvarado 2, Christianson 109, Pines 1. **1B**—Alcala 3, McCorkle 136, Pines 2. **2B**—Cruz 18, Durango 26, Figueroa 12, Gandolfo 78, McCallum 17, Woods 7. **3B**—Cruz 3, Figueroa 11, Leone 127, Martinez 1, McCallum 2. **SS**—Castillo 76, Cruz 8, Gandolfo 16, Martinez 44, McCallum 8. **OF**—Cruz 1, Dobbs 3, Fernandez 64, Foley 34, Fulse 34, Hernandez 16, Leone 5, Lopez 12, Quintana 47, Rainey 7, Snelling 106, Strong 81, Williams 30.

PITCHING	W	L	ERA	G	GS	CG	SV	IP	H	R	ER	BB	SO	AVG	B	T	HT	WT	DOB	1st Yr	Resides
Anderson, Craig	11	4	2.26	28	28	0	0	179	142	65	45	39	178	.214	L	L	6-3	182	10-30-80	1999	Ourimbah, Australia
Baek, Cha	1	0	3.43	5	4	0	0	21	17	10	8	2	16	.223	R	R	6-4	190	5-29-80	1999	Pusan, Korea
Balbuena, Caleb	0	5	6.86	36	5	0	0	63	78	57	48	44	56	.298	R	R	6-7	240	3-23-77	1998	Tuolumne, Calif.
Delgado, Danny	4	7	5.40	36	10	0	1	103	130	68	62	24	90	.306	R	R	6-2	180	2-10-78	1997	Miami Lakes, Fla.
Hoerman, Jared	0	0	3.86	11	0	0	0	19	16	11	8	7	18	.222	R	R	6-4	215	4-25-77	1999	Ardmore, Okla.
Johnson, Rett	6	2	4.09	12	12	0	0	66	56	36	30	33	70	.230	L	R	6-2	211	7-6-79	2000	Aynor, S.C.
Kent, Steve	0	3	2.20	51	0	0	5	65	50	21	16	34	73	.204	B	L	5-11	170	10-3-78	1999	Killeen, Texas
Looper, Aaron	6	11	2.79	56	0	0	5	59	34	22	22	77	77	.168	R	R	6-2	185	9-7-76	1998	Ada, Okla.
Mateo, Julio	5	4	2.86	56	0	0	26	66	58	28	21	16	79	.230	R	R	6-0	177	8-22-79	1996	Bani, D.R.
Mears, Chris	7	6	4.46	38	12	0	0	107	104	59	53	49	74	.260	L	R	6-4	190	1-20-78	1996	Victoria, B.C.
Parker, Brandon	4	0	4.30	15	0	0	0	23	18	13	11	18	28	.219	R	R	6-1	200	12-9-75	1997	Long Beach, Miss.
Ramos, Juan	4	3	2.63	39	0	0	2	65	45	23	19	30	57	.190	R	R	6-0	160	2-1-76	1995	Santo Domingo, D.R.
Simpson, Allan	1	0	1.80	16	0	0	1	30	19	7	6	12	40	.177	R	R	6-4	185	8-26-77	1997	Las Vegas, Nev.
Soriano, Rafael	6	3	2.53	15	15	2	0	89	49	28	25	39	98	.163	R	R	6-1	175	12-19-79	1996	San Jose, D.R.
Thornton, Matt	14	7	2.52	27	27	0	0	157	126	56	44	60	192	.220	L	L	6-6	220	9-15-76	1998	Allendale, Mich.
Torres, Melqui	7	7	4.15	26	26	0	0	154	159	79	71	56	113	.277	R	R	6-1	165	5-27-77	1996	San Pedro de Macoris, D.R.
Van Dusen, Derrick	0	1	5.40	1	1	0	0	3	3	2	2	1	3	.230	L	L	6-2	175	6-6-81	2000	Fontana, Calif.

WISCONSIN — Class A

MIDWEST LEAGUE

BATTING	AVG	G	AB	R	H	2B	3B	HR	RBI	BB	SO	SB	CS	SLG	OBP	B	T	HT	WT	DOB	1st Yr	Resides
Bone, Blake	.218	78	257	40	56	19	1	7	36	37	50	8	3	.381	.318	L	R	6-1	190	1-12-79	2000	Southside, Ala.
Bubela, Jaime	.304	132	530	96	161	27	12	6	68	44	116	34	13	.434	.357	L	R	6-1	200	6-6-78	2000	Houston, Texas
Carroll, Mark	.230	84	257	34	59	10	0	1	27	45	63	2	4	.280	.362	R	R	6-0	185	10-19-78	1996	Athens, N.Y.
Castellano, John	.334	99	377	59	126	34	0	14	81	35	35	13	5	.536	.370	R	R	5-11	185	9-8-77	1997	North Babylon, N.Y.
Choo, Shin-Soo	.462	3	13	1	6	0	0	0	3	1	3	2	0	.462	.533	L	L	5-11	175	7-30-82	2000	Pusan, Korea
Daubert, Jake	.256	97	351	43	90	19	0	4	52	33	74	4	3	.345	.327	L	R	6-2	205	5-19-79	2000	Toms River, N.J.
Durango, Ariel	.287	87	307	48	88	10	4	4	31	25	71	32	11	.384	.348	B	R	5-10	150	4-5-79	1996	Panama City, Panama
Dusan, Joe	.233	119	378	49	88	19	1	7	52	41	100	4	3	.344	.305	L	L	6-1	190	7-30-77	1998	Bend, Ore.
Figueroa, Eduardo	.204	15	49	6	10	1	1	0	5	5	11	2	1	.265	.304	R	R	6-2	164	6-4-82	1999	Santo Domingo, D.R.
Floyd, Dan	.260	90	338	47	88	19	1	5	38	20	61	6	6	.367	.316	R	R	5-9	175	1-17-83	2000	South Gilford, Australia
Freeman, Corey	.151	37	106	14	16	4	0	1	10	8	24	3	6	.217	.240	R	R	5-11	165	10-13-79	1998	Tampa, Fla.
Fulse, Sheldon	.220	80	255	38	56	16	5	2	17	31	73	21	3	.345	.319	B	R	6-3	175	11-10-81	1999	Bartow, Fla.
Gutierrez, Derrick	.265	10	34	5	9	2	0	1	6	4	8	1	1	.412	.375	R	R	5-11	180	10-6-78	1998	Jacksonville, Fla.
Hudson, Ben	.349	14	43	4	15	1	0	0	6	3	12	0	0	.372	.396	R	R	6-4	210	11-4-79	2001	Decatur, Ga.
Liriano, Pedro	.326	113	442	76	144	28	3	4	47	30	50	65	20	.430	.373	R	R	5-11	165	2-20-82	1999	Pimentel, D.R.
Lopez, Chuck	.299	49	194	28	58	7	7	4	29	10	19	9	5	.469	.340	L	L	6-1	195	11-29-76	2000	Huntington Beach, Calif.

BATTING	AVG	G	AB	R	H	2B	3B	HR	RBI	BB	SO	SB	CS	SLG	OBP	B	T	HT	WT	DOB	1st Yr	Resides
Martinez, Guillermo	.239	58	184	24	44	6	2	1	23	4	47	2	2	.310	.258	B	R	6-0	158	6-24-80	1997	Maracay, Venez.
Merritt, Tim	.308	3	13	1	4	0	0	0	1	0	2	0	1	.308	.286	R	R	6-0	180	2-7-80	2001	Cantonment, Fla.
Quintana, Wilfredo	.229	35	131	21	30	6	2	8	29	8	43	1	1	.489	.280	R	R	5-11	181	6-22-78	1998	Loiza, P.R.
Richardson, Miguel	.321	9	28	7	9	1	0	2	5	9	10	1	1	.571	.486	R	R	6-5	180	8-5-80	1997	San Pedro de Macoris, D.R.
Rodriguez, Joe	.229	39	109	9	25	6	0	3	22	11	33	2	2	.367	.328	R	R	5-9	183	2-11-78	2001	Caguas, P.R.
Strong, Jamal	.353	51	184	41	65	12	1	0	19	40	27	35	4	.429	.478	R	R	5-10	180	8-5-78	2000	Altadena, Calif.
Villilo, Miguel	.167	14	42	1	7	1	0	0	3	3	14	0	4	.190	.239	B	R	6-1	180	10-10-81	1999	Santo Domingo, D.R.

GAMES BY POSITION: C—Carroll 74, Castellano 49, Hudson 10, Rodriguez 15. 1B—Bone 9, Carroll 1, Castellano 21, Daubert 5, Dusan 114. 2B—Bone 3, Durango 12, Floyd 13, Gutierrez 1, Liriano 106, Martinez 9, Merritt. 3B—Bone 35, Daubert 57, Durango 2, Floyd 35, Freeman 4, Martinez 8, Villilo 9. SS—Durango 68, Freeman 28, Gutierrez 8, Martinez 40, Villilo 1. OF—Bone 3, Bubela 131, Choo 3, Daubert 1, Dusan 1, Figueroa 14, Floyd 48, Freeman 4, Fulse 80, Lopez 47, Quintana 35, Richardson 9, Strong 48.

PITCHING	W	L	ERA	G	GS	CG	SV	IP	H	R	ER	BB	SO	AVG	B	T	HT	WT	DOB	1st Yr	Resides
Ayala, Julio	0	0	4.50	1	0	0	0	2	1	1	1	0	0	.142	L	L	6-2	203	4-20-75	1996	Guaynabo, P.R.
Barnes, Pat	1	0	0.82	10	0	0	0	11	4	2	1	4	10	.117	R	L	6-2	180	9-25-79	1998	Jacksonville, Fla.
Burton, O.J.	4	3	3.19	39	0	0	1	59	54	31	21	21	39	.238	R	R	6-3	225	12-16-76	1999	Stuart, Fla.
Butler, John	5	3	2.01	40	0	0	1	67	68	27	15	16	62	.257	R	R	6-3	210	8-23-77	2000	Villa Rica, Ga.
Grunwald, Erik	8	6	3.38	29	21	1	0	157	138	66	59	48	128	.235	R	R	6-4	220	4-25-77	1999	Upland, Calif.
Head, Daniel	3	1	3.03	16	1	0	1	33	24	15	11	11	27	.196	R	R	6-2	215	10-7-78	2000	Satsuma, Ala.
Herrera, Jose	1	0	3.07	4	1	0	0	15	10	7	5	3	20	.178	R	R	6-6	170	11-11-79	1996	Santo Domingo, D.R.
Hoerman, Jared	9	2	1.49	21	13	0	0	91	60	32	15	29	101	.184	R	R	6-4	215	4-25-77	1999	Ardmore, Okla.
Johnson, Rett	5	5	5.27	16	16	2	0	99	92	33	25	30	96	.247	L	R	6-2	211	7-6-79	2000	Aynor, S.C.
Morgan, Russ	2	1	2.25	17	0	0	1	28	22	10	7	18	38	.211	R	L	6-1	205	11-20-77	2000	New Hartford, N.Y.
Nageotte, Clint	11	8	3.13	28	26	0	0	152	141	65	53	50	187	.245	R	R	6-4	190	10-25-80	1999	New Port Richey, Fla.
Olore, Kevin	4	3	3.32	27	27	0	0	155	134	70	57	40	158	.231	L	R	6-2	200	9-21-78	1999	Southington, Conn.
Sosa, Jorge	0	0	9.00	2	0	0	0	2	3	2	2	0	4	.333	B	R	6-2	177	4-28-78	1995	San Jose, D.R.
Taylor, Aaron	3	1	2.45	28	0	0	9	29	19	9	8	11	50	.184	R	R	6-7	230	8-20-77	1996	Hahira, Ga.
Van Dusen, Derrick	5	4	3.19	18	18	1	0	96	82	40	34	24	103	.224	L	L	6-2	175	6-6-81	2000	Fontana, Calif.
Walton, Sam	0	1	4.76	3	2	0	0	6	7	3	3	6	8	.304	L	L	6-4	200	12-1-78	1997	Dallas, Texas
Wayne, Hawkeye	4	2	4.58	30	5	0	1	59	55	38	30	45	48	.250	R	R	6-1	205	11-24-77	1999	Honolulu, Hawaii
Wells, Roy	7	6	3.23	39	6	0	3	92	82	37	33	27	97	.230	R	R	6-3	195	11-17-78	1999	Hyden, Ky.
Wiles, Chad	3	4	2.18	39	0	0	17	45	49	19	11	8	45	.270	R	R	6-1	205	5-15-78	2000	Alda, Neb.

EVERETT

NORTHWEST LEAGUE

BATTING	AVG	G	AB	R	H	2B	3B	HR	RBI	BB	SO	SB	CS	SLG	OBP	B	T	HT	WT	DOB	1st Yr	Resides
Buhner, Jay	.600	3	10	3	6	1	0	2	3	1	2	0	0	1.300	.636	R	R	6-3	210	8-13-64	1984	Issaquah, Wash.
Cadena, Alejandro	.100	3	10	0	1	0	0	0	1	0	4	0	0	.200	.100	R	R	5-11	205	3-13-80	2000	Laredo, Texas
Cole, John	.291	13	55	8	16	4	0	0	6	3	14	2	1	.364	.328	R	R	5-11	185	1-11-80	2001	Ottawa, Ontario
Collins, Chris	.083	4	12	0	1	0	0	0	2	1	8	0	0	.083	.154	R	R	5-11	195	8-14-81	2001	Phoenix, Ariz.
Dobbs, Greg	.321	65	249	37	80	17	2	6	41	30	39	5	3	.478	.396	L	R	6-2	215	7-2-78	2001	Moreno Valley, Calif.
Figueroa, Eduardo	.310	49	187	35	58	10	2	3	24	17	45	7	5	.433	.380	R	R	6-2	164	6-4-82	1999	Santo Domingo, D.R.
Gutierrez, Derrick	.259	10	27	5	7	0	0	1	3	2	10	3	0	.370	.310	R	R	6-2	170	3-26-79	1996	Charallave, Venez.
Hernandez, Orlando	.304	32	115	16	35	5	1	1	17	10	21	3	4	.391	.364	R	R	6-2	170	11-24-83	2000	Anzoategui, Venez.
Lopez, Jose	.256	70	289	42	74	15	0	2	20	13	44	13	6	.329	.309	R	R	6-0	195	2-7-81	2001	Mesa, Ariz.
Menchaca, Eriberto	.000	3	5	1	0	0	0	0	0	1	1	1	0	.000	.286	R	R	6-0	180	2-7-80	2001	Cantonment, Fla.
Merritt, Tim	.306	51	196	33	60	13	3	5	30	9	35	11	3	.480	.332	R	R	6-1	180	6-18-83	2000	Guarenas, Venez.
Oliveros, Luis	.240	26	100	7	24	3	0	4	17	1	15	0	0	.390	.262	R	R	5-10	185	3-8-79	2001	New Lenox, Ill.
Olszta, Eddie	.162	27	74	5	12	2	0	0	4	3	34	3	1	.189	.205	L	L	6-0	185	6-11-79	2001	Klondike, Texas
Rainey, Jason	.226	33	106	17	24	4	1	1	9	9	31	7	2	.311	.311	L	L	6-0	190	7-31-83	2001	Bayamon, P.R.
Richardson, Miguel	.276	23	76	8	21	4	1	2	11	5	25	2	0	.434	.329	R	R	6-5	190	8-5-80	1997	San Pedro de Macoris, D.R.
Rivera, Rene	.089	15	45	3	4	1	0	2	3	1	19	0	0	.244	.106	R	R	5-9	180	2-2-78	1997	New York, N.Y.
Rosario, Vicente	.250	33	136	22	34	7	1	0	6	12	29	17	6	.316	.350	R	R	6-0	185	8-4-80	1998	Vega Alta, P.R.
Santana, Emmanuel	.268	68	250	35	67	13	3	6	49	24	47	0	2	.416	.343	L	R	6-0	185	8-4-80	1998	Henderson, Nev.
VanMeetren, Jason	.230	45	152	18	35	8	1	5	22	20	47	0	2	.395	.324	R	R	6-2	200	10-4-79	2001	Santo Domingo, D.R.
Villilo, Miguel	.246	50	195	33	48	10	0	5	22	22	69	7	2	.374	.329	B	R	6-1	180	10-10-81	1999	Santo Domingo, D.R.
Widger, Chris	.077	5	13	2	1	0	0	0	6	1	0	0	0	.077	.368	R	R	6-2	215	5-21-71	1992	Pennsville, N.J.
Williamson, John	.277	53	188	26	52	16	2	5	34	22	52	2	1	.463	.368	B	R	6-1	190	8-23-78	2001	Wilmington, N.C.
Woods, Blake	.260	43	146	20	38	7	1	5	19	18	36	4	3	.425	.349	R	R	6-2	190	1-5-79	2001	Chandler, Ariz.

GAMES BY POSITION: C—Oliveros 26, Olszta 25, Rivera 12, Santana 21. 1B—Cadena 3, Dobbs 50, Santana 26, Widger 2. 2B—Cole 13, Gutierrez 8, Lopez 7, Menchaca 3, Merritt 33, Woods 20. 3B—Collins 4, Dobbs 3, Merritt 3, Villilo 45, Woods 24. SS—Lopez 62, Merritt 15, Villilo 1. OF—Buhner 3, Dobbs 6, Figueroa 43, Hernandez 29, Rainey 24, Richardson 12, Rosario 33, Van Meetren 33, Williamson 52, Woods 2.

PITCHING	W	L	ERA	G	GS	CG	SV	IP	H	R	ER	BB	SO	AVG	B	T	HT	WT	DOB	1st Yr	Resides
Allen, Travis	0	0	4.76	4	0	0	0	6	7	4	3	2	6	.280	L	R	6-1	195	5-14-81	2001	Quartz Hill, Calif.
Bausher, Tim	0	3	8.62	11	0	0	1	16	25	15	15	8	18	.352	R	R	6-4	205	4-23-79	2001	Bechtelsville, Pa.
Blackley, Travis	6	1	3.32	14	14	0	0	79	60	34	29	29	90	.210	L	L	6-3	190	11-4-82	2001	Cheltenham, Australia
Blood, Justin	1	1	10.03	10	0	0	0	12	15	15	13	9	14	.319	L	L	6-3	215	11-20-79	2001	Swanzey, N.H.
Bott, Glenn	2	3	2.30	19	0	0	4	43	32	17	11	23	57	.196	L	L	6-0	178	9-17-81	2001	Houston, Texas
Cullen, Phil	1	4	5.08	14	14	0	0	57	52	36	32	49	64	.250	R	R	6-1	190	12-2-79	2000	Chelan, Wash.
Done, J.J.	0	0	8.35	8	1	0	0	18	24	21	17	14	13	.315	R	R	6-2	215	10-7-78	2000	Satsuma, Ala.
Head, Daniel	4	4	1.95	21	2	0	2	51	40	14	11	14	44	.209	R	R	6-2	215	10-7-78	2000	Stockton, Calif.
Hintz, Beau	3	4	6.39	15	11	0	1	56	63	50	40	15	43	.273	L	L	6-4	210	5-12-80	2001	San Pedro de Macoris, D.R.
Javier, Tony	1	0	12.15	5	0	0	0	7	8	9	9	4	9	.307	R	R	6-3	160	2-5-80	1997	Bellflower, Calif.
Kesten, Michael	0	2	10.80	5	0	0	0	7	8	8	8	8	5	.360	L	L	6-2	185	9-22-81	1999	Lantana, Fla.
Ketchner, Ryan	3	3	2.92	20	5	0	2	52	38	19	17	18	58	.198	L	L	6-1	190	4-19-82	2000	Santo Domingo, D.R.
Martinez, Gustavo	5	3	2.67	15	15	0	0	84	62	30	25	34	100	.207	R	R	6-0	175	11-9-80	1998	New Hartford, N.Y.
Morgan, Russ	2	5	5.23	22	2	0	1	52	60	34	30	17	56	.292	R	L	6-1	205	11-20-77	2000	Boise, Idaho
Royce, Ramon	2	0	5.87	20	3	0	0	38	42	27	25	19	29	.280	R	R	6-2	215	9-22-79	2001	San Jose, D.R.
Sosa, Jorge	3	1	1.69	21	7	0	7	59	45	22	11	19	57	.203	B	R	6-2	177	4-28-78	1995	San Jose, D.R.
Swanson, Erick	1	0	4.66	14	0	0	1	19	21	10	10	9	15	.269	L	L	6-6	215	10-30-78	2000	Berkley, Mich.
Watson, Tanner	0	0	0.00	1	0	0	0	2	1	0	0	1	2	.142	R	R	6-3	195	4-14-82	2000	Arnprior, Ontario
Wiley, Skip	1	0	6.30	4	0	0	1	10	19	7	7	3	11	.404	R	R	6-1	185	10-19-81	2000	Pembroke Pines, Fla.

ARIZONA LEAGUE

BATTING	AVG	G	AB	R	H	2B	3B	HR	RBI	BB	SO	SB	CS	SLG	OBP	B	T	HT	WT	DOB	1st Yr	Resides
Abreu, Lazaro	.375	4	8	3	3	0	0	0	2	2	3	0	0	.375	.500	R	R	6-2	195	12-2-81	2001	Miami, Fla.
Brown, Larry	.279	34	111	23	31	3	1	3	13	13	19	3	0	.405	.357	L	L	6-4	225	3-22-81	2000	San Fernando, Calif.
Cadena, Alejandro	.333	56	222	41	74	23	1	8	60	14	23	0	1	.554	.390	R	R	5-11	205	3-13-80	2000	Laredo, Texas
Choo, Shin-Soo	.302	51	199	51	60	10	10	4	35	34	49	12	4	.513	.420	L	L	5-11	175	7-30-82	2000	Pusan, Korea
Collins, Chris	.342	42	161	25	55	14	0	2	29	20	26	0	1	.466	.415	R	R	5-11	195	8-14-81	2001	Phoenix, Ariz.
Cordova, Roman	.343	42	140	25	48	6	3	0	14	9	23	4	4	.429	.414	B	R	6-1	180	9-2-84	2001	Aragua, Venez.
Ellison, Josh	.214	33	84	21	18	3	1	0	10	15	24	2	1	.274	.347	R	R	5-10	208	7-24-83	2001	West Palm Beach, Fla.
Hodges, Jarrod	.273	45	143	30	39	8	2	5	26	16	26	2	3	.462	.371	L	L	5-10	167	12-8-82	2000	Ringwood, Australia
Hrynio, Mike	.161	20	56	4	9	2	0	0	5	2	21	0	1	.196	.203	R	R	6-2	190	11-18-82	2001	Mine Hill, N.J.
Hudson, Ben	.167	5	18	3	3	1	0	0	1	1	1	0	0	.222	.286	R	R	6-4	210	11-4-79	2001	Decatur, Ga.
Imperiali, Francesco	.284	40	116	17	33	7	0	0	12	13	26	2	3	.345	.366	R	R	5-11	180	11-10-83	2000	Rome, Italy
Jones, Jared	.242	9	33	1	8	1	0	0	3	3	8	0	0	.273	.306	R	R	6-5	245	6-25-80	2000	College Place, Wash.
Menchaca, Eriberto	.271	49	170	30	46	7	2	0	18	8	29	1	0	.335	.306	R	R	6-0	195	2-7-81	2001	Mesa, Ariz.
Mujica, Andres	.283	45	159	27	45	6	3	0	24	15	36	5	3	.358	.352	R	R	6-1	174	7-7-82	1999	San Antonio Altos, Venez.
Oliveros, Luis	.374	25	91	21	34	6	1	1	15	5	10	2	2	.495	.424	R	R	6-1	180	6-18-83	2000	Guarenas, Venez.
Parnell, Sean	.370	8	27	2	10	2	1	0	4	1	7	0	0	.519	.424	R	R	6-3	225	11-8-77	1999	Deer Park, Wis.
Peless, Sean	.314	45	159	21	50	6	1	1	18	14	47	1	1	.384	.371	L	L	6-5	230	12-24-80	2001	Kirkland, Wash.
Rivera, Rene	.338	21	71	13	24	4	0	2	12	2	11	0	0	.479	.360	R	R	5-10	190	7-31-83	2001	Bayamon, P.R.
Varitek, Justin	.333	4	6	2	2	1	0	0	0	1	2	0	0	.500	.429	R	R	6-3	230	6-5-78	2001	Longwood, Fla.

GAMES BY POSITION: C—Cadena 11, Cordova 1, Hudson 5, Oliveros 21, Rivera 20, Varitek 4. **1B**—Cadena 18, Collins 1, Imperiali 1, Peless 44. **2B**—Cordova 34, Hodges 1, Imperiali 33, Mujica 1. **3B**—Collins 40, Hrynio 15, Imperiali 10, Oliveros 1. **SS**—Cordova 10, Menchaca 49. **OF**—Brown 27, Choo 51, Ellison 24, Hodges 39, Jones 4, Mujica 43.

PITCHING	W	L	ERA	G	GS	CG	SV	IP	H	R	ER	BB	SO	AVG	B	T	HT	WT	DOB	1st Yr	Resides
Allen, Travis	2	2	4.24	17	0	0	4	23	25	12	11	4	26	.284	L	R	6-1	195	5-14-81	2001	Quartz Hill, Calif.
Bott, Glenn	0	0	6.00	2	0	0	1	3	5	2	2	0	4	.357	L	L	6-0	178	9-17-81	2001	Houston, Texas
Cortez, Rene	2	0	4.42	11	9	0	0	53	60	34	26	10	52	.277	R	R	6-4	178	12-9-82	2000	Valencia, Venez.
Done, J.J.	0	0	1.00	5	0	0	2	9	5	3	1	6	12	.147	R	R	6-1	190	10-2-80	1999	Miami, Fla.
Fruto, Emiliano	5	3	5.84	12	12	0	0	62	73	45	40	22	51	.290	R	R	6-3	170	6-6-84	2000	Bolivar, Colombia
Hays, Sam	1	2	6.83	7	7	0	0	29	36	25	22	14	22	.313	L	L	6-4	210	10-7-81	2000	Waco, Texas
Heflin, Theo	2	1	6.56	18	0	0	1	23	34	21	17	13	21	.343	L	L	6-2	175	5-28-81	2000	Topeka, Kan.
Javier, Tony	3	1	2.28	12	2	0	2	28	27	10	7	11	23	.278	R	R	6-3	160	2-5-80	1997	San Pedro de Macoris, D.R.
Jobe, John	1	1	4.25	16	0	0	0	30	38	26	14	12	26	.299	R	L	6-4	217	8-14-78	2001	Hercules, Calif.
Korneev, Oleg	0	0	0.00	1	0	0	0	1	0	0	0	0	1	.000	L	R	6-7	210	5-10-82	2001	Moscow, Russia
Mendoza, Edgardo	3	3	4.29	13	4	0	0	42	38	25	20	21	34	.236	B	L	6-1	155	12-9-80	1998	Barranquilla, Colombia
Ockerman, Justin	1	4	4.91	10	10	0	0	40	49	30	22	16	27	.296	L	R	6-10	250	1-8-83	2001	Garden City, Mich.
Parker, Brandon	2	0	4.09	9	0	0	0	11	15	5	5	5	13	.326	R	R	6-1	200	12-9-75	1997	Long Beach, Miss.
Rivera, Jimmy	3	1	4.10	16	0	0	2	37	44	21	17	17	18	.301	R	R	6-2	180	1-27-80	2000	South Gate, Calif.
Rowland-Smith, Ryan	1	1	2.97	17	0	0	5	33	25	11	11	9	39	.215	L	L	6-3	205	1-26-83	2001	Newcastle, Australia
Sabourin, Brian	0	1	18.00	1	1	0	0	2	5	4	4	1	1	.625	R	R	6-3	195	8-26-83	2001	Winnipeg, Manitoba
Watson, Tanner	8	2	4.40	11	11	1	0	59	70	40	29	15	57	.291	R	R	6-3	195	6-14-82	2000	Arnprior, Ontario

ORGANIZATION STATISTICS

TAMPA BAY DEVIL RAYS

BY MARC TOPKIN

The Devil Rays took their biggest step back in 2001, losing 100 games for the first time in their four-year history.

But they also think they took their biggest step forward, committing to playing their young prospects and reaping the benefits of their inspired performance with a 35-39 second half that raises their hopes that the future actually is bright.

"It's as disappointing a season as we've had from a won-loss standpoint," general manager Chuck LaMar said. "But there were more positives, and more positive steps toward the future, than in any season we've had. You can't talk about the negatives without talking about the positives."

Most important, the Rays think they have assembled the nucleus of a good young pitching staff.

Twentysomething rookie lefthanders Joe Kennedy, an eighth-round pick in the '98 draft who hadn't pitched above Class A until the 2001 season, and Nick Bierbrodt looked as if they could be in the rotation for years to come. Bierbrodt, a former first-round pick, came over in a trade with the Diamondbacks.

Three relievers had the talent and, at times, the temperament to pitch at the end of games: Victor Zambrano, Travis Phelps (an 89th-round pick in the 1996 draft who is the lowest drafted player to ever reach the majors) and Jesus Colome.

With seven rookies, the Tampa Bay staff reduced its ERA from 5.63 in the first half to 4.12, an improvement that is second-best among American League teams in the past 10 years.

The Rays also got to see some of their top position players on an everyday basis. Catcher Toby Hall, second baseman Brent Abernathy and outfielder Jason Tyner all impressed and should be big parts of the team in 2002 and beyond. Third basemen Jared Sandberg and Aubrey Huff also got extended opportunities.

Overall the Rays used 16 rookies in 2001, including nine who made their major league debuts.

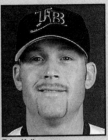

MORRIS FOSTOFF

Fred McGriff | Toby Hall

PLAYERS OF THE YEAR

MAJOR LEAGUE: Fred McGriff, 1b

He spent the last third of the year in a Cubs uniform, but even if McGriff had stayed with his hometown team all of the 2001 season he probably would have put up similar numbers (.306-31-102).

MINOR LEAGUE: Toby Hall, c

Hall was hitting .335-19-72 at the time of a midseason callup from Triple-A Durham. He led the Bulls in nine offensive categories and was the MVP of the Futures Game.

The decision to go with young players was accelerated as a direct result of the failures of some of their high-priced veterans. The Rays released third baseman Vinny Castilla and outfielder Gerald Williams; traded first baseman Fred McGriff, righthander Albie Lopez and catcher Mike Difelice; and benched catcher John Flaherty. Plus, for the second straight season, they got nothing out of injured pitchers Wilson Alvarez and Juan Guzman.

LaMar had envisioned the team making the transition to youth at the end of the 2001 season, but had no choice but to accelerate it. The turnover on the field was accompanied by turmoil off the field.

There was the mid-April decision to fire manager Larry Rothschild, after a 4-10 start, and replace him with bench coach Hal McRae.

There were reports of squabbling between the investors who own the team, which prompted managing general partner Vince Naimoli to step up to the position of team chairman. There was a restructuring of the front office to accommodate the hiring of John McHale Jr. as chief operating officer. And there were persistent rumors about the very existence of the franchise itself.

After the season, pitching coach Bill Fischer and third-base coach Terry Collins were fired.

The team's top prospect, outfielder Josh Hamilton, had a miserable season, playing just 27 games because of a combination of leg and back injuries. Righthander Matt White, who signed a record $10.2 million contract in 1996, struggled miserably in spring training and underwent season-ending shoulder surgery in May. Outfielder Kenny Kelly, once considered a future major league star, was traded to the Seattle organization.

Hall, who was named MVP of the International League, and Kennedy were named the organization's top minor leaguers.

ORGANIZATION LEADERS

BATTING

*AVG	Toby Hall, Durham	.335
R	Matt Diaz, Bakersfield	79
H	Matt Diaz, Bakersfield	172
TB	Matt Diaz, Bakersfield	267
2B	Matt Diaz, Bakersfield	40
3B	Dan DeMent, Bakersfield/Charleston	11
HR	Justin Schuda, Charleston	25
RBI	Matt Diaz, Bakersfield	81
BB	Justin Schuda, Charleston	65
SO	Justin Schuda, Charleston	166
SB	Irwin Centeno, Charleston	48

PITCHING

W	Travis Harper, Durham	12
L	Mark Malaska, Bakersfield/Charleston	13
#ERA	Chad Coward, Bakersfield/Charleston	1.86
G	Talley Haines, Durham/Orlando	59
CG	Three tied at	2
SV	Hans Smith, Bakersfield	17
IP	Jim Magrane, Orlando	182
BB	Brian Stokes, Bakersfield	64
SO	Seth McClung, Charleston	165

*Minimum 250 At-Bats #Minimum 75 Innings

TAMPA BAY
DEVIL RAYS

Managers: Larry Rothschild, Hal McRae

2001 Record: 62-100, .383 (5th, AL East)

BATTING	AVG	G	AB	R	H	2B	3B	HR	RBI	BB	SO	SB	CS	SLG	OBP	B	T	HT	WT	DOB	1st Yr	Resides
Abernathy, Brent	.270	79	304	43	82	17	1	5	33	27	35	8	3	.382	.328	R	R	6-0	185	9-23-77	1996	Marietta, Ga.
Castilla, Vinny	.215	24	93	7	20	6	0	2	9	3	22	0	0	.344	.247	R	R	6-1	205	7-4-67	1990	Littleton, Colo.
Cox, Steve	.257	108	342	37	88	22	0	12	51	24	75	2	2	.427	.323	L	L	6-4	222	10-31-74	1992	Strathmore, Calif.
Difelice, Mike	.208	48	149	13	31	5	1	2	9	8	39	1	1	.295	.259	R	R	6-2	205	5-28-69	1991	Safety Harbor, Fla.
Flaherty, John	.238	78	248	20	59	17	1	4	29	10	33	1	0	.363	.269	R	R	6-1	200	10-21-67	1988	Lutz, Fla.
Gomez, Chris	.302	58	189	31	57	16	0	8	36	8	24	3	0	.513	.332	R	R	6-1	195	6-16-71	1992	Carlsbad, Calif.
Grieve, Ben	.264	154	542	72	143	30	2	11	72	87	159	7	1	.387	.372	L	R	6-4	230	5-4-76	1994	Flower Mound, Texas
Guillen, Jose	.274	41	135	14	37	5	0	3	11	6	26	2	3	.378	.317	R	R	5-11	195	5-17-76	1993	San Cristobal, D.R.
Hall, Toby	.298	49	188	28	56	16	0	4	30	4	16	2	2	.447	.321	R	R	6-3	205	10-21-75	1997	Placerville, Calif.
Hoover, Paul	.250	3	4	1	1	0	0	0	0	1	0	0	0	.250	.250	R	R	6-1	210	4-14-76	1997	Steubenville, Ohio
Huff, Aubrey	.248	111	411	42	102	25	1	8	45	23	72	1	3	.372	.288	L	R	6-4	221	12-20-76	1998	Gulfport, Fla.
Johnson, Russ	.294	85	248	32	73	19	2	4	33	34	57	2	2	.435	.380	R	R	5-10	180	2-22-73	1994	Denham Springs, La.
Martinez, Felix	.247	77	219	24	54	13	1	1	14	10	46	6	5	.329	.294	B	R	6-0	180	5-18-74	1993	Nagua, D.R.
McGriff, Fred	.318	97	343	40	109	18	0	19	61	40	69	1	1	.536	.387	L	L	6-3	215	10-31-63	1981	Tampa, Fla.
Rolls, Damian	.262	81	237	33	62	11	1	2	12	10	47	12	4	.342	.291	R	R	6-2	205	9-15-77	1996	Kansas City, Kan.
Sandberg, Jared	.206	39	136	13	28	7	0	1	15	10	45	1	0	.279	.265	R	R	6-3	185	3-2-78	1996	Olympia, Wash.
Sheets, Andy	.196	49	153	10	30	8	0	1	14	12	35	2	0	.268	.251	R	R	6-2	180	11-19-71	1992	Lafayette, La.
Smith, Bobby	.105	6	19	1	2	0	0	0	1	3	10	0	0	.105	.227	R	R	6-3	190	4-10-74	1992	Oakland, Calif.
Tyner, Jason	.280	105	396	51	111	8	5	0	21	15	42	31	6	.326	.311	L	L	6-1	170	4-23-77	1998	Bedford, Texas
Vaughn, Greg	.233	136	485	74	113	25	0	24	82	71	130	11	5	.433	.333	R	R	6-0	202	7-3-65	1986	Elk Grove, Calif.
Williams, Gerald	.207	62	232	30	48	17	0	4	17	13	42	10	4	.332	.261	R	R	6-2	187	8-10-66	1987	Tampa, Fla.
Winn, Randy	.273	128	429	54	117	25	6	6	50	38	81	12	10	.401	.339	B	R	6-2	193	6-9-74	1995	Danville, Calif.

PITCHING	W	L	ERA	G	GS	CG	SV	IP	H	R	ER	BB	SO	AVG	B	T	HT	WT	DOB	1st Yr	Resides
Bierbrodt, Nick	3	4	4.55	11	11	0	0	61	71	38	31	27	56	.285	L	L	6-5	190	5-16-78	1996	Long Beach, Calif.
Callaway, Mickey	0	0	7.20	2	0	0	0	5	3	4	4	2	2	.166	R	R	6-2	209	5-13-75	1996	Memphis, Tenn.
Colome, Jesus	2	3	3.33	30	0	0	0	49	37	22	18	25	31	.207	R	R	6-2	170	6-2-80	1996	San Pedro de Macoris, D.R.
Creek, Doug	2	5	4.31	66	0	0	0	63	51	34	30	49	66	.229	L	L	6-0	200	3-1-69	1991	Dallas, Texas
Fiore, Tony	0	0	5.40	3	0	0	0	3	4	2	2	1	3	.307	R	R	6-4	210	10-12-71	1992	Chicago, Ill.
Harper, Travis	0	2	7.71	2	2	0	0	7	15	11	6	3	2	.454	L	R	6-4	193	5-21-76	1997	Riverton, W.Va.
Hill, Ken	0	1	12.27	5	0	0	0	7	10	11	10	5	2	.333	R	R	6-2	215	12-14-65	1985	Southlake, Texas
Judd, Mike	1	0	4.05	8	2	0	0	20	19	14	9	10	11	.250	R	R	6-1	217	6-30-75	1995	La Mesa, Calif.
Kennedy, Joe	7	8	4.44	20	20	0	0	118	122	63	58	34	78	.268	R	L	6-4	225	5-24-79	1998	El Cajon, Calif.
Lopez, Albie	5	12	5.34	20	20	1	0	125	152	87	74	51	67	.301	R	R	6-2	240	8-18-71	1991	Gilbert, Ariz.
Meacham, Rusty	1	3	5.60	24	0	0	0	35	39	24	22	10	13	.276	R	R	6-2	175	1-27-68	1988	Palm City, Fla.
Phelps, Travis	2	2	3.48	49	0	0	5	62	53	30	24	24	54	.225	R	R	6-2	165	7-25-77	1997	Rocky Comfort, Mo.
Prieto, Ariel	0	0	2.45	3	0	0	0	4	6	1	1	2	2	.375	R	R	6-2	245	10-22-66	1995	Miami, Fla.
Rekar, Bryan	3	13	5.89	25	25	0	0	141	167	104	92	45	87	.294	R	R	6-3	220	6-3-72	1993	Lutz, Fla.
Rose, Brian	0	2	8.85	7	3	0	0	20	31	20	20	12	11	.356	R	R	6-3	215	2-13-76	1995	Dartmouth, Mass.
Rupe, Ryan	5	12	6.59	28	26	0	0	143	161	111	105	48	123	.283	R	R	6-5	230	3-31-75	1998	Houston, Texas
Seay, Bobby	1	1	6.23	12	0	0	0	13	13	11	9	5	12	.260	L	L	6-2	221	6-20-78	1996	West Gulfport, Fla.
Standridge, Jason	0	0	4.66	9	1	0	0	19	19	10	10	14	9	.260	R	R	6-4	217	11-9-78	1997	Pinson, Ala.
Sturtze, Tanyon	11	12	4.42	39	27	0	1	195	200	98	96	79	110	.271	R	R	6-5	205	10-12-70	1990	St. Petersburg, Fla.
Wallace, Jeff	0	3	3.40	29	1	0	0	50	43	26	19	37	38	.232	L	L	6-2	240	4-12-76	1995	Louisville, Ohio
Wheeler, Dan	1	0	8.66	13	0	0	0	18	30	17	17	5	12	.375	R	R	6-3	222	12-10-77	1997	Warwick, R.I.
Wilson, Paul	8	9	4.88	37	24	0	0	151	165	94	82	52	119	.277	R	R	6-5	235	3-28-73	1994	Palm City, Fla.
Yan, Esteban	4	6	3.90	54	0	0	22	62	64	34	27	11	64	.262	R	R	6-4	230	6-22-74	1991	San Pedro de Macoris, D.R.
Zambrano, Victor	6	2	3.16	36	0	0	2	51	38	21	18	18	58	.201	R	R	6-0	190	8-6-74	1994	Valencia, Venez.

FIELDING

Catcher	PCT	G	PO	A	E	DP	PB
Difelice	.982	48	293	29	6	4	2
Flaherty	.986	78	458	28	7	4	4
Hall	.986	46	328	20	5	2	2
Hoover	1.000	2	2	1	0	0	0

First Base	PCT	G	PO	A	E	DP
Cox	.998	78	569	48	1	64
Huff	.966	19	129	15	5	13
McGriff	.986	74	558	59	9	53
Sandberg	.000	1	0	0	0	0

Second Base	PCT	G	PO	A	E	DP
Abernathy	.981	79	150	209	7	56
Johnson	1.000	33	60	83	0	21
Martinez	1.000	10	15	20	0	3
Rolls	.968	42	69	113	6	21
Smith	.958	6	12	11	1	3

Third Base	PCT	G	PO	A	E	DP
Castilla	.934	24	26	45	5	5

Huff	.918	73	41	126	15	13
Johnson	.922	36	21	50	6	6
Rolls	1.000	1	3	3	0	0
Sandberg	.944	38	33	68	6	7

Shortstop	PCT	G	PO	A	E	DP
Gomez	.968	58	80	131	7	29
Johnson	.857	6	3	3	1	0
Martinez	.944	67	103	148	15	38
Sheets	.990	49	80	121	2	29

Outfield	PCT	G	PO	A	E	DP
Cox	1.000	8	11	1	0	0
Grieve	.984	120	240	4	4	0
Guillen	.969	36	86	7	3	3
Rolls	1.000	25	38	2	0	0
Tyner	.978	100	219	8	5	1
Vaughn	.978	57	127	4	3	2
Williams	.989	59	179	5	2	1
Winn	.981	117	245	12	5	0

Hal McRae

LARRY GOREN

Director, Minor League Operations: Tom Foley

Class	Farm Team	League	W	L	Pct.	Finish*	Manager	First Yr.
AAA	Durham (N.C.) Bulls	International	74	70	.514	5th (14)	Bill Evers	1998
AA	Orlando (Fla.) Rays	Southern	59	81	.421	10th (10)	Mike Ramsey	1999
A#	Bakersfield (Calif.) Blaze	California	71	69	.507	t-5th (10)	Charlie Montoyo	2001
A	Charleston (S.C.) RiverDogs	South Atlantic	64	76	.457	12th (16)	Buddy Biancalana	1997
A	Hudson Valley (N.Y.) Renegades	New York-Penn	39	37	.513	6th (14)	David Howard	1996
Rookie#	Princeton (W.Va.) Devil Rays	Appalachian	28	39	.418	10th (10)	Edwin Rodriguez	1997

*Finish in overall standings (No. of teams in league)   #Advanced level

DURHAM   Class AAA

INTERNATIONAL LEAGUE

BATTING	AVG	G	AB	R	H	2B	3B	HR	RBI	BB	SO	SB	CS	SLG	OBP	B	T	HT	WT	DOB	1st Yr	Resides
Abernathy, Brent	.302	61	252	45	76	20	0	4	23	16	23	11	4	.429	.346	R	R	6-0	185	9-23-77	1996	Marietta, Ga.
Borders, Pat	.236	87	313	26	74	15	1	2	28	16	61	3	2	.310	.278	R	R	6-2	200	5-14-63	1982	Lake Wales, Fla.
Carr, Dustin	.242	73	227	25	55	6	1	4	26	25	47	5	2	.330	.329	R	R	5-11	189	6-7-75	1997	Mount Vernon, Texas
Caruso, Mike	.292	110	387	62	113	10	9	0	35	22	22	11	9	.364	.340	L	R	6-1	172	5-27-77	1996	Coral Springs, Fla.
Conti, Jason	.306	38	157	24	48	12	0	5	18	9	31	3	1	.478	.347	L	R	5-11	180	1-27-75	1996	Cranberry Township, Pa.
Gomez, Chris	.301	23	93	16	28	5	1	4	17	11	5	1	1	.505	.375	R	R	6-1	195	6-16-71	1992	Carlsbad, Calif.
Guillen, Jose	.294	33	119	18	35	9	0	7	29	3	28	0	0	.546	.306	R	R	5-11	195	10-21-75	1997	Placerville, Calif.
Hall, Toby	.335	94	373	59	125	28	1	19	72	29	22	1	3	.568	.385	R	R	6-3	205	10-21-75	1997	Council Bluffs, Iowa
Hatcher, Chris	.267	69	251	31	67	12	0	11	38	19	63	4	2	.446	.321	R	R	6-3	235	1-7-69	1990	Council Bluffs, Iowa
Hoover, Paul	.215	89	293	37	63	18	4	3	21	11	66	5	3	.334	.260	R	R	6-1	210	4-14-76	1997	Steubenville, Ohio
Huff, Aubrey	.288	17	66	14	19	6	0	3	10	5	7	0	0	.515	.338	L	R	6-4	221	12-20-76	1998	Gulfport, Fla.
Hutchins, Norm	.230	78	261	32	60	10	1	7	28	9	64	15	2	.356	.267	B	L	5-11	198	11-20-75	1994	Greenburgh, N.Y.
Lowery, Terrell	.261	71	253	28	66	14	3	1	18	28	69	6	3	.352	.335	R	R	6-3	195	10-25-70	1991	Vallejo, Calif.
Marconi, Alex	.000	1	4	0	0	0	0	0	0	0	1	0	0	.000	.000	R	R	6-0	181	3-25-78	2000	Cuyahoga Falls, Ohio
Martinez, Greg	.293	62	242	36	71	6	2	1	21	29	46	14	7	.347	.377	B	R	5-10	168	1-27-72	1993	Las Vegas, Nev.
Sandberg, Jared	.239	93	322	39	77	16	0	16	50	38	81	0	1	.438	.331	R	R	6-2	180	11-19-71	1992	Olympia, Wash.
Sheets, Andy	.280	66	225	28	63	14	2	4	22	25	45	8	3	.413	.356	R	R	6-2	180	4-10-74	1992	Lafayette, La.
Smith, Bobby	.301	107	396	67	119	25	2	22	70	45	91	10	2	.540	.379	R	R	6-3	190	4-10-74	1992	Oakland, Calif.
Smith, Jason	.194	8	31	2	6	1	0	0	3	0	11	0	0	.226	.194	L	R	6-3	195	7-24-77	1997	Coatopa, Ala.
Tyner, Jason	.312	39	157	25	49	2	1	0	12	15	10	11	5	.338	.371	L	L	6-1	170	4-23-77	1998	Bedford, Texas
Wright, Ron	.262	121	439	63	115	27	0	20	75	51	103	2	2	.460	.340	R	R	6-1	230	1-21-76	1994	St. George, Utah

PITCHING	W	L	ERA	G	GS	CG	SV	IP	H	R	ER	BB	SO	AVG	B	T	HT	WT	DOB	1st Yr	Resides
Agosto, Stevenson	0	0	10.13	3	0	0	0	5	5	6	6	5	5	.227	L	L	5-11	170	9-2-76	1994	Rio Grande, P.R.
Alvarez, Wilson	1	1	3.00	4	4	0	0	18	20	8	6	6	16	.281	L	L	6-1	245	3-24-70	1987	Sarasota, Fla.
Aybar, Manny	1	3	5.68	11	3	0	0	32	40	25	20	9	29	.320	R	R	6-1	177	10-5-74	1991	Bani, D.R.
Bowers, Cedrick	6	5	3.06	42	11	0	0	94	83	38	32	56	67	.240	R	L	6-2	223	2-10-78	1996	Chiefland, Fla.
Callaway, Mickey	11	7	3.07	29	21	2	0	129	131	50	44	24	81	.264	R	R	6-2	209	5-13-75	1996	Memphis, Tenn.
Colome, Jesus	0	3	6.23	13	0	0	0	17	22	13	12	6	18	.318	R	R	6-2	170	6-2-80	1996	San Pedro de Macoris, D.R.
Cornett, Brad	4	2	2.05	33	2	0	2	61	56	22	14	12	55	.236	R	R	6-3	190	2-4-69	1992	Odessa, Texas
2-team (6 Syracuse)	5	2	2.72	39	2	0	2	73	73	30	22	17	61	.257							
Davison, Scott	0	0	18.90	2	0	0	0	3	9	7	7	2	3	.500	R	R	6-0	190	10-16-70	1988	Redondo Beach, Calif.
Enders, Trevor	2	5	4.98	32	1	0	0	47	51	26	26	14	26	.291	R	L	6-4	214	12-22-74	1996	Houston, Texas
Fiore, Tony	1	0	0.00	15	0	0	3	20	7	0	0	8	11	.104	R	R	6-0	219	10-12-71	1992	Chicago, Ill.
Gardner, Lee	5	2	2.72	56	0	0	2	76	76	27	23	23	55	.258	R	R	6-0	219	1-16-75	1998	Hartland, Mich.
Guzman, Juan	4	2	4.77	10	10	0	0	60	50	35	32	30	42	.232	R	R	5-11	195	10-28-66	1985	Miami, Fla.
Haines, Talley	0	0	0.00	1	0	0	0	2	0	0	0	0	1	.000	R	R	6-5	203	11-16-76	1998	Cape Girardeau, Mo.
Harper, Travis	12	6	3.70	25	25	1	0	156	140	70	64	38	115	.241	L	R	6-4	193	5-21-76	1997	Riverton, W.Va.
James, Delvin	3	7	4.80	31	9	1	0	84	99	51	45	27	51	.295	R	R	6-4	222	1-3-78	1996	Nacogdoches, Texas
Jimenez, Jason	0	1	4.70	15	0	0	1	23	23	12	12	14	25	.261	R	L	6-2	205	1-10-76	1997	Elk Grove, Calif.
Kennedy, Joe	2	0	2.42	4	4	0	0	26	22	8	7	9	23	.226	R	L	6-4	225	5-24-79	1998	El Cajon, Calif.
Meacham, Rusty	2	1	0.87	27	0	0	15	31	17	4	3	5	30	.160	R	R	6-2	175	1-27-68	1988	Palm City, Fla.
Phelps, Travis	2	0	0.00	9	0	0	0	16	11	0	0	1	12	.203	R	R	6-2	165	7-25-77	1997	Rocky Comfort, Mo.
Prieto, Ariel	0	0	1.35	3	0	0	0	7	3	2	1	2	10	.130	R	R	6-2	245	10-22-66	1995	Miami, Fla.
Pujals, Denis	0	0	5.40	2	0	0	0	5	5	5	3	2	2	.277	R	R	6-3	228	2-5-73	1996	Miami, Fla.
Rose, Brian	9	2	3.10	19	15	0	1	99	88	35	34	19	88	.241	R	R	6-3	215	2-13-76	1995	Dartmouth, Mass.
Rupe, Ryan	0	1	0.82	2	1	0	0	11	3	1	1	1	17	.088	R	R	6-5	230	3-31-75	1998	Pinson, Ala.
Standridge, Jason	5	10	5.28	20	20	0	0	102	130	73	60	50	48	.314	R	R	6-4	217	11-9-78	1997	Louisville, Ohio
Wallace, Jeff	0	0	3.86	7	0	0	0	9	6	4	4	7	11	.181	L	L	6-2	240	4-12-76	1993	Louisville, Ohio
Wheeler, Dan	3	5	5.23	18	10	0	0	65	72	51	38	11	39	.270	R	R	6-3	222	12-10-77	1997	Warwick, R.I.
White, Matt	0	5	7.80	7	7	0	0	30	33	28	26	25	16	.300	R	R	6-5	230	8-13-78	1996	Largo, Fla.
Zambrano, Victor	1	2	2.08	29	0	0	12	30	26	10	7	12	29	.232	R	R	6-0	190	8-6-74	1994	Valencia, Venez.

FIELDING

Catcher	PCT	G	PO	A	E	DP	PB
Borders	.989	40	253	27	3	3	3
Hall	.987	64	408	43	6	3	2
Hoover	.993	43	263	19	2	3	7
Marconi	.909	1	10	1	0	1	0

First Base	PCT	G	PO	A	E	DP
Borders	.987	9	72	4	1	9
Carr	.984	8	55	5	1	5
Hoover	.992	13	117	11	1	8
Sheets	1.000	1	4	0	0	0
B. Smith	1.000	2	22	1	0	2
Wright	.992	118	980	66	8	102

Second Base	PCT	G	PO	A	E	DP
Abernathy	.969	61	107	179	9	41
Carr	.920	5	10	13	2	4
Caruso	.975	59	102	173	7	36
Hoover	1.000	1	1	1	0	0
Sheets	1.000	1	3	5	0	1
B. Smith	.975	24	51	68	3	13

Third Base	PCT	G	PO	A	E	DP
Carr	.887	20	13	34	6	3
Hoover	.952	15	11	29	2	5
Huff	.929	16	18	34	4	5
Sandberg	.948	92	56	181	13	17

	PCT	G	PO	A	E	DP
Sheets	1.000	4	4	3	0	0
B. Smith	1.000	2	2	2	0	0
Shortstop	PCT	G	PO	A	E	DP
Caruso	.956	52	82	133	10	29
Gomez	.978	23	23	65	2	11
Hoover	.000	2	0	0	0	0
Sheets	.958	61	103	145	11	38
B. Smith	.895	5	6	11	2	1
J. Smith	.917	8	9	24	3	6
Outfield	PCT	G	PO	A	E	DP
Carr	1.000	20	32	0	0	0
Conti	.987	38	71	7	1	0

ORGANIZATION STATISTICS

	PCT	G	PO	A	E	DP		PCT	G	PO	A	E	DP		PCT	G	PO	A	E	DP
Guillen	.982	28	49	5	1	1	Hutchins	.975	77	193	5	5	0	Sheets	.000	2	0	0	0	0
Hatcher	.978	27	44	1	1	0	Lowery	.976	69	159	7	4	0	B. Smith	.986	76	128	10	2	1
Hoover	.950	14	18	1	1	0	Martinez	1.000	58	132	0	0	0	Tyner	1.000	39	88	2	0	2

ORLANDO — Class AA

SOUTHERN LEAGUE

BATTING	AVG	G	AB	R	H	2B	3B	HR	RBI	BB	SO	SB	CS	SLG	OBP	B	T	HT	WT	DOB	1st Yr	Resides
Badeaux, Brooks	.249	127	470	48	117	11	6	1	27	33	50	14	7	.304	.304	B	R	5-10	175	10-20-76	1998	Scott, La.
Becker, Brian	.226	115	411	38	93	22	0	7	42	43	96	0	0	.331	.305	R	R	6-7	232	5-26-75	1996	Tempe, Ariz.
Beinbrink, Andrew	.273	126	443	51	121	22	6	5	49	55	69	4	2	.384	.356	R	R	6-3	207	9-24-76	1999	San Diego, Calif.
Brown, Jason	.364	3	11	2	4	2	0	0	1	0	2	0	0	.545	.364	R	R	6-2	208	5-22-74	1997	Rolling Hills Estates, Calif.
Cantu, Jorge	.256	130	512	58	131	26	3	4	45	17	93	4	9	.342	.287	R	R	6-1	178	1-30-82	1998	Reynosa, Mexico
Cox, Steve	.214	4	14	2	3	1	0	1	3	2	1	0	0	.500	.313	L	L	6-4	222	10-31-74	1992	Strathmore, Calif.
Crawford, Carl	.274	132	537	64	147	24	3	4	51	36	90	36	20	.352	.323	L	L	6-2	203	8-5-81	1999	Houston, Texas
De los Santos, Eddy	.258	114	415	33	107	13	1	2	38	22	60	14	11	.308	.302	R	R	6-2	170	2-24-78	1996	Santo Domingo, D.R.
Grummitt, Dan	.238	71	244	37	58	11	1	11	41	23	74	2	2	.426	.331	R	R	6-5	247	6-16-76	1998	Twinsburg, Ohio
Hamilton, Josh	.180	23	89	5	16	5	0	0	4	5	22	2	0	.236	.221	L	L	6-4	209	5-21-81	1999	Raleigh, N.C.
Hutchins, Norm	.219	30	105	14	23	1	1	2	9	6	30	4	2	.305	.281	B	L	5-11	198	11-20-75	1994	Greenburgh, N.Y.
Isenia, Chairon	.163	15	43	2	7	1	0	0	4	3	7	0	0	.186	.217	R	R	5-11	216	1-23-79	1996	Curacao, Netherlands Antilles
Johnson, Russ	.667	1	3	0	2	0	0	0	0	1	0	0	0	.667	.750	R	R	5-10	180	2-22-73	1994	Denham Springs, La.
LaForest, Pete	.095	7	21	3	2	0	0	1	1	5	9	0	0	.238	.269	L	R	6-2	208	1-27-78	1995	Hull, Quebec
Martinez, Felix	.100	3	10	1	1	1	0	0	0	0	2	1	0	.200	.100	B	R	6-0	180	5-18-74	1993	Nagua, D.R.
Neuberger, Scott	.265	120	419	49	111	25	1	4	43	36	83	5	3	.358	.328	R	R	6-3	213	8-14-77	1997	Tallahassee, Fla.
Pigott, Anthony	.240	82	250	29	60	10	1	2	28	7	39	8	3	.312	.264	R	R	6-1	194	6-13-76	1997	Wilmington, N.C.
Pressley, Josh	.279	30	111	10	31	2	1	1	12	6	22	0	0	.342	.316	L	R	6-6	223	4-2-80	1998	Fort Lauderdale, Fla.
Quatraro, Matt	.325	81	271	38	88	24	2	6	35	17	60	4	1	.494	.375	R	R	6-2	208	11-14-73	1996	East Selkirk, N.Y.
Sandberg, Jared	.286	8	28	4	8	2	0	1	4	4	10	0	0	.464	.412	R	R	6-3	185	3-2-78	1996	Olympia, Wash.
Valera, Yohanny	.256	75	250	26	64	20	3	6	32	13	67	0	2	.432	.323	R	R	6-1	205	8-17-76	1993	San Cristobal, D.R.

PITCHING	W	L	ERA	G	GS	CG	SV	IP	H	R	ER	BB	SO	AVG	B	T	HT	WT	DOB	1st Yr	Resides
Agosto, Stevenson	8	10	3.90	30	18	2	0	129	114	62	56	57	113	.242	L	L	5-11	170	9-2-76	1994	Rio Grande, P.R.
Alvarez, Wilson	1	3	4.43	5	5	0	0	20	24	10	10	6	18	.285	L	L	6-1	245	3-24-70	1987	Sarasota, Fla.
Backe, Brandon	1	0	5.73	14	0	0	0	22	20	14	14	11	20	.253	R	R	6-0	182	4-5-78	1998	Texas City, Texas
Enders, Trevor	3	3	4.94	13	8	0	0	47	51	26	26	5	38	.272	R	L	6-0	214	12-22-74	1996	Houston, Texas
Gardner, Lee	0	0	0.00	1	0	0	0	2	0	0	0	0	0	.000	R	R	6-0	219	1-16-75	1998	Hartland, Mich.
Garibaldi, Cecilio	5	6	4.49	35	12	0	1	104	111	57	52	37	66	.276	R	R	6-2	214	1-5-78	1998	Guasave, Mexico
Guzman, Juan	2	0	0.75	2	2	0	0	12	8	1	1	4	9	.195	R	R	5-11	195	10-28-66	1985	Miami, Fla.
Haines, Talley	6	6	3.64	58	0	0	8	72	73	32	29	29	73	.264	R	R	6-5	203	11-16-76	1998	Cape Girardeau, Mo.
James, Delvin	2	0	1.65	7	7	0	0	44	25	8	8	9	31	.167	R	R	6-4	222	1-3-78	1996	Nacogdoches, Texas
Jimenez, Jason	3	3	3.18	35	4	0	10	51	46	20	18	24	46	.244	R	L	6-2	205	1-10-76	1997	Elk Grove, Calif.
Kennedy, Joe	4	0	0.19	7	7	0	0	47	29	3	1	3	52	.177	L	L	6-4	225	5-24-79	1998	El Cajon, Calif.
Kofler, Ed	2	7	7.84	13	13	0	0	60	81	57	52	26	39	.318	R	R	6-2	175	12-23-77	1996	Palm Harbor, Fla.
Magrane, Jim	8	12	2.97	29	28	1	0	182	166	87	60	56	126	.243	R	R	6-2	208	7-23-78	1999	Ottumwa, Iowa
Powalski, Rick	0	0	5.40	3	0	0	0	3	6	2	2	3	5	.400	L	L	6-11	190	5-9-78	1997	Clearwater, Fla.
Pruett, Jason	2	5	5.12	38	0	0	1	51	59	38	29	19	29	.285	L	L	6-3	186	1-21-79	1999	Princeton, Texas
Pujals, Denis	0	0	7.36	7	0	0	0	11	19	9	9	4	3	.373	R	R	6-3	228	2-5-73	1996	Miami, Fla.
Rekar, Bryan	1	0	2.25	3	3	0	0	12	8	3	3	1	11	.177	R	R	6-3	220	6-3-72	1993	Lutz, Fla.
Reyes, Eddy	2	3	5.44	31	0	0	1	43	45	30	26	27	28	.269	R	R	6-4	204	4-24-76	1997	Miami, Fla.
Rosario, Juan	1	3	3.56	44	0	0	3	68	69	36	27	27	55	.266	R	R	6-4	219	11-17-75	1993	Perth Amboy, N.J.
Ruhl, Nathan	3	3	3.88	31	2	0	6	51	54	25	22	23	54	.272	R	R	6-4	236	7-16-76	1996	Lees Summit, Mo.
Seay, Bobby	2	5	5.98	15	13	0	0	65	81	48	43	26	49	.310	L	L	6-2	221	6-20-78	1996	West Gulfport, Fla.
Severino, Ronni	3	8	5.00	38	11	0	0	90	116	58	50	47	63	.318	L	L	6-1	199	8-6-75	1996	San Pedro de Macoris, D.R.
Shelby, Anthony	0	0	4.15	4	0	0	0	4	6	2	2	2	2	.333	L	L	6-3	230	12-11-73	1993	Bradenton, Fla.
Standridge, Jason	0	2	5.59	2	2	0	0	10	12	6	6	4	7	.300	R	R	6-4	217	11-9-78	1997	Pinson, Ala.
Wallace, Jeff	0	0	0.00	1	0	0	0	1	1	0	0	1	3	.250	L	L	6-2	240	4-12-76	1995	Louisville, Mich.
Wheeler, Dan	0	2	2.81	3	3	0	0	16	15	5	5	6	12	.241	R	R	6-3	222	12-10-77	1997	Warwick, R.I.
Yan, Esteban	0	0	3.00	2	2	0	0	3	3	1	1	0	4	.250	R	R	6-4	230	6-22-74	1991	San Pedro de Macoris, D.R.

FIELDING

Catcher	PCT	G	PO	A	E	DP	PB
Brown	1.000	3	9	1	0	0	0
Isenia	.981	15	99	7	2	0	2
LaForest	.968	7	55	5	2	0	6
Quatraro	.991	48	296	27	3	2	10
Valera	.995	75	509	62	3	5	17

First Base	PCT	G	PO	A	E	DP
Becker	.996	51	449	28	2	42
Beinbrink	1.000	1	1	0	0	0
Cox	.962	4	24	1	1	4
Grummitt	.993	51	409	31	3	40
Pressley	.981	18	140	13	3	11

	PCT	G	PO	A	E	DP
Quatraro	.995	22	165	17	1	17
Sandberg	1.000	1	4	0	0	1
Second Base	PCT	G	PO	A	E	DP
Badeaux	.956	53	123	138	12	37
De los Santos	.953	91	193	232	21	63
Johnson	.818	1	3	6	2	2
Third Base	PCT	G	PO	A	E	DP
Badeaux	.972	31	20	85	3	11
Beinbrink	.948	103	68	221	16	23
Sandberg	1.000	8	6	20	0	3
Shortstop	PCT	G	PO	A	E	DP
Cantu	.948	121	177	296	26	59

	PCT	G	PO	A	E	DP
De los Santos	.931	19	26	55	6	15
Martinez	.800	3	0	4	1	1
Outfield	PCT	G	PO	A	E	DP
Badeaux	.979	47	87	6	2	0
Crawford	.981	130	309	5	6	0
Hamilton	.957	23	40	5	2	2
Hutchins	.920	28	44	2	4	0
Neuberger	.990	120	202	5	2	1
Pigott	.969	74	117	7	4	0
Quatraro	1.000	11	13	2	0	0

BAKERSFIELD — Class A

CALIFORNIA LEAGUE

BATTING	AVG	G	AB	R	H	2B	3B	HR	RBI	BB	SO	SB	CS	SLG	OBP	B	T	HT	WT	DOB	1st Yr	Resides
Beinbrink, Andrew	.250	7	24	4	6	2	0	0	3	0	4	0	0	.333	.250	R	R	6-3	207	9-24-76	1999	San Diego, Calif.
Castillo, Alberto	.274	94	347	45	95	12	2	11	54	28	120	1	3	.415	.329	L	L	6-3	215	7-5-75	1994	New Port Richey, Fla.
DeMent, Dan	.059	5	17	0	1	0	0	0	1	3	0	0	0	.059	.111	R	R	5-10	179	6-17-78	2000	Frankfort, Ill.
Diaz, Matt	.328	131	524	79	172	40	2	17	81	24	73	11	5	.510	.370	R	R	6-1	206	3-3-78	1999	Lakeland, Fla.
Eddlemon, Kelly	.229	104	367	46	84	25	4	7	49	36	85	7	4	.376	.299	R	R	6-2	181	8-26-78	2000	Missouri City, Texas

ORGANIZATION STATISTICS

BATTING	AVG	G	AB	R	H	2B	3B	HR	RBI	BB	SO	SB	CS	SLG	OBP	B	T	HT	WT	DOB	1st Yr	Resides
Grummitt, Dan	.321	46	165	31	53	22	0	9	28	18	50	3	2	.618	.417	R	R	6-5	247	6-16-76	1998	Twinsburg, Ohio
Isenia, Chairon	.290	76	290	42	84	16	0	8	50	16	41	2	3	.428	.334	R	R	5-11	216	1-23-79	1996	Curacao, Netherlands Antilles
Kaup, Nate	.323	113	427	65	138	34	3	13	68	35	81	3	2	.508	.376	R	R	6-3	215	1-11-78	2000	Henderson, Nev.
Marconi, Alex	.239	34	109	11	26	3	0	1	11	6	27	0	0	.294	.278	R	R	6-0	187	3-25-78	2000	Cuyahoga Falls, Ohio
Massiatte, Danny	.212	96	330	37	70	20	2	4	29	26	84	1	2	.321	.279	R	R	5-11	181	7-25-78	2000	Houston, Texas
Moore, Frank	.307	129	505	75	155	29	6	7	60	25	106	9	3	.430	.346	L	R	6-2	217	7-2-78	1998	Douglas, Ga.
Murch, Jeremy	.235	72	221	27	52	12	4	9	32	18	63	1	1	.448	.295	L	L	6-1	185	9-22-78	1998	Sarasota, Fla.
Perez, Nestor	.241	118	407	44	98	16	3	0	37	27	57	11	4	.295	.289	R	R	5-10	172	11-24-76	1997	Tenerife, Canary Islands
Ryan, Kelvin	.264	103	363	46	96	26	1	6	36	9	83	4	2	.391	.311	R	R	6-1	202	8-10-78	1997	La Romana, D.R.
Schrock, Chris	.244	94	320	38	78	16	0	0	24	18	51	3	3	.294	.289	R	R	6-0	178	5-30-76	2000	Sarasota, Fla.
Soler, Ramon	.263	103	418	72	110	14	4	2	27	46	75	25	5	.330	.338	B	R	6-0	174	7-6-81	1997	Elias Pina, D.R.
Wilder, Paul	.265	30	98	15	26	5	0	2	13	15	45	1	0	.378	.379	L	R	6-4	250	1-9-78	1996	Clearwater, Fla.

GAMES BY POSITION: C—Isenia 39, Kaup 1, Marconi 18, Massiatte 93. **1B**—Castillo 82, Grummitt 39, Isenia 3, Kaup 18, Marconi 7, Moore 1, Schrock 3. **2B**—Eddlemon 45, Moore 26, Schrock 13, Soler 75. **3B**—Beinbrink 7, DeMent 5, Eddlemon 72, Kaup 19, Marconi 2, Schrock 55. **SS**—Moore 8, Perez 118, Schrock 24. **OF**—Castillo 4, Diaz 130, Kaup 56, Moore 97, Murch 59, Ryan 98, Schrock 9.

PITCHING	W	L	ERA	G	GS	CG	SV	IP	H	R	ER	BB	SO	AVG	B	T	HT	WT	DOB	1st Yr	Resides
Andersen, Derek	2	1	3.38	18	0	0	0	24	19	9	9	6	26	.223	L	L	6-3	190	10-6-77	1999	Lynnwood, Wash.
Backe, Brandon	1	0	1.09	17	0	0	3	25	13	7	3	8	33	.149	R	R	6-0	182	4-5-78	1998	Texas City, Texas
Carvajal, Alex	2	1	7.11	24	0	0	0	32	43	26	25	11	34	.316	L	L	6-2	194	11-6-77	2000	Rosemead, Calif.
Cornejo, Jesse	0	1	4.05	9	0	0	0	13	17	12	6	8	16	.288	R	L	6-3	196	10-26-76	1998	Wellington, Kan.
Coward, Chad	2	2	2.00	32	4	0	3	67	59	20	15	22	65	.233	R	R	6-3	176	9-10-78	2000	Siler City, N.C.
Frendling, Neal	6	8	4.58	20	20	0	0	112	105	62	57	38	107	.244	R	R	6-3	194	10-7-79	1999	Dyer, Ind.
Kofler, Ed	5	6	4.23	15	14	0	0	79	88	43	37	25	74	.278	R	R	6-2	175	12-23-77	1996	Palm Harbor, Fla.
Malaska, Mark	2	1	4.08	3	3	0	0	18	14	8	8	5	13	.218	L	L	6-3	191	1-17-78	2000	Youngstown, Ohio
Minix, Travis	5	1	3.34	44	0	0	10	67	67	27	25	19	70	.252	R	R	6-1	195	8-8-77	1999	Hamlet, Ind.
Montgomery, Matt	2	3	4.76	14	0	0	1	23	20	13	12	7	29	.238	R	R	6-4	210	5-13-76	1997	Anaheim, Calif.
Ortiz, Jose	3	3	3.79	35	0	0	0	71	77	34	30	29	57	.277	R	R	6-5	204	12-12-77	1995	Guayubin, D.R.
Renteria, Juan	0	0	0.00	1	0	0	0	1	0	0	0	0	1	.000	B	R	5-10	165	1-1-80	2000	Driskoll, Texas
Robinson, Jeremy	0	1	11.05	5	0	0	0	7	12	11	9	12	3	.400	L	L	6-2	209	10-19-77	1998	St. Amant, La.
Ruhl, Nathan	1	2	4.94	12	4	0	1	31	37	17	17	21	31	.300	R	R	6-4	236	7-16-76	1996	Lees Summit, Mo.
Santos, Alex	11	9	4.15	24	24	0	0	134	149	75	62	49	150	.275	R	R	6-1	201	8-9-77	1999	Lake Worth, Fla.
Smith, Hans	1	0	1.45	31	0	0	17	37	36	10	6	15	42	.244	L	L	6-9	265	8-3-78	2000	Central Point, Ore.
Stokes, Brian	8	6	3.92	32	20	1	1	129	118	65	56	64	92	.243	R	R	6-1	203	9-7-79	1999	Chino, Calif.
Veras, Enger	9	8	4.53	27	27	0	0	153	163	104	77	55	138	.274	R	R	6-5	230	7-9-81	1998	Santo Domingo, D.R.
Villalon, Julio	4	9	4.87	25	24	0	0	133	148	83	72	45	146	.282	R	R	6-2	189	5-11-78	2000	San Jose, Costa Rica
Wright, Chris	7	7	3.49	49	0	0	5	88	83	42	34	32	79	.253	R	R	6-2	195	6-6-77	1997	Dale, Okla.

CHARLESTON, S.C. — Class A

SOUTH ATLANTIC LEAGUE

BATTING	AVG	G	AB	R	H	2B	3B	HR	RBI	BB	SO	SB	CS	SLG	OBP	B	T	HT	WT	DOB	1st Yr	Resides
Baldelli, Rocco	.249	113	406	58	101	23	6	8	55	23	89	25	9	.394	.303	R	R	6-4	183	9-25-81	2000	Cumberland, R.I.
Bonner, Adam	.217	116	364	48	79	27	1	3	29	63	115	21	6	.321	.348	L	R	6-5	206	3-11-81	2000	Hueytown, Ala.
Brewer, Jace	.217	108	414	50	90	12	4	3	35	18	74	6	6	.287	.252	R	R	6-0	170	6-6-79	2000	Norman, Okla.
Centeno, Irwin	.231	102	372	61	86	8	3	1	22	41	91	48	12	.277	.326	R	R	6-2	176	6-1-81	1997	Maracay, Venez.
Cordell, Brent	.143	2	7	2	1	0	0	0	1	2	2	0	0	.143	.333	B	R	6-3	215	5-22-80	2001	Incline Village, Nev.
DeMent, Dan	.269	108	394	52	106	24	11	8	54	31	108	6	14	.447	.326	R	R	5-10	179	6-17-78	2000	Frankfort, Ill.
Franco, Iker	.200	87	265	15	53	10	2	3	21	19	81	1	2	.287	.253	R	R	6-1	212	5-5-81	1998	Ensenada, Mexico
Hamilton, Josh	.364	4	11	3	4	1	0	1	2	2	3	0	0	.727	.462	L	L	6-4	209	5-21-81	1999	Raleigh, N.C.
Jacobs, John	.187	79	198	18	37	5	2	1	11	15	69	6	2	.247	.255	R	R	6-1	179	11-7-79	1998	Rohnert Park, Calif.
Kaup, Nate	.267	4	15	0	4	2	0	0	2	0	3	0	0	.400	.250	R	R	6-3	215	1-11-78	2000	Henderson, Nev.
Marsh, Jason	.245	66	216	24	53	9	0	4	24	4	41	3	2	.343	.271	R	R	6-2	189	3-4-78	2000	Greensboro, N.C.
Martin, Brian	.232	131	456	42	106	22	3	8	44	35	150	7	15	.346	.300	R	R	6-2	217	6-14-80	1998	El Centro, Calif.
Merritt, Graig	.000	5	9	0	0	0	0	0	1	2	3	1	0	.000	.182	R	R	6-1	195	7-2-78	2001	Maple Ridge, B.C.
Monroy, Sam	.158	19	38	6	6	0	0	0	0	6	7	3	1	.158	.273	L	R	6-0	175	11-24-78	2001	Oxnard, Calif.
Nunez, Felix	.186	103	361	28	67	12	1	7	32	7	141	2	7	.283	.204	R	R	6-4	230	8-17-82	1999	San Cristobal, D.R.
Salas, Juan	.228	135	500	53	114	25	3	7	62	17	93	9	15	.332	.255	R	R	6-2	194	12-6-81	1998	Santo Domingo, D.R.
Schuda, Justin	.240	127	430	56	103	15	0	25	71	65	166	2	2	.449	.352	L	R	6-3	208	2-24-81	1999	San Juan Capistrano, Calif.
Scott, Ed	.000	3	2	1	0	0	0	0	0	0	1	0	0	.000	.000	R	R	5-11	175	9-18-79	2001	Compton, Calif.
Volquez, Bolivar	.167	38	126	13	21	3	0	0	7	14	39	4	1	.190	.259	R	R	6-3	186	7-3-81	1998	Santo Domingo, D.R.

GAMES BY POSITION: C—Cordell 2, Fanco 87, Marsh 60, Merritt 5. **1B**—Kaup 1, Marsh 3, Martin 1, Monroy 1, Nunez 61, Schuda 78, Volquez 1. **2B**—Centeno 96, DeMent 41, Jacobs 2, Monroy 6. **3B**—Bonner 1, DeMent 20, Jacobs 1, Salas 126. **SS**—Brewer 101, DeMent 7, Volquez 36. **OF**—Baldelli 112, Bonner 110, DeMent 28, Hamilton 1, Jacobs 67, Kaup 1, Martin 122, Salas 1, Schuda 1, Scott 2.

PITCHING	W	L	ERA	G	GS	CG	SV	IP	H	R	ER	BB	SO	AVG	B	T	HT	WT	DOB	1st Yr	Resides
Andersen, Derek	2	0	2.27	29	0	0	3	40	27	10	10	3	49	.188	L	L	6-3	190	10-6-77	1999	Lynnwood, Wash.
Backe, Brandon	2	1	2.92	16	0	0	7	25	17	8	8	7	20	.200	R	R	6-0	182	4-5-78	1998	Texas City, Texas
Benedetti, John	2	4	3.28	44	0	0	4	69	74	35	25	21	63	.272	R	R	6-0	188	6-27-78	2000	Palatine, Ill.
Campbell, Jarrett	3	6	3.95	39	5	0	0	84	90	51	37	18	71	.266	R	R	6-2	195	9-8-79	1998	Corpus Christi, Texas
Carney, Jake	1	0	0.64	10	0	0	0	28	20	5	2	8	24	.190	R	R	6-2	185	12-25-79	2001	Tyler, Texas
Coose, Austin	0	1	4.61	10	0	0	2	14	13	8	7	7	21	.250	R	R	6-2	230	1-27-79	2001	Norman, Okla.
Coward, Chad	0	0	0.90	5	0	0	0	10	11	3	1	4	13	.282	R	R	6-3	176	9-10-78	2000	Siler City, N.C.
Dorman, Rich	1	5	6.51	17	9	0	0	57	61	47	41	41	41	.282	R	R	6-2	202	9-30-78	2000	Salem, Ore.
Gomez, Benito	1	1	3.86	39	0	0	0	58	59	32	25	19	46	.253	R	L	6-3	197	4-25-79	2000	Mission, Texas
Malaska, Mark	7	12	2.92	25	25	1	0	157	153	71	51	35	152	.248	L	L	6-3	191	1-17-78	2000	Youngstown, Ohio
McClung, Seth	10	11	2.79	28	28	2	0	164	142	72	51	53	165	.231	R	R	6-6	235	2-7-81	1999	Lewisburg, W.Va.
McCormick, Terry	3	0	1.40	14	0	0	2	19	14	3	3	8	22	.215	L	L	6-1	175	10-14-78	1997	Tampa, Fla.
Parker, Josh	2	1	2.70	3	0	0	0	7	7	3	2	4	4	.269	R	R	6-5	220	1-12-81	2001	Calera, Ala.
Renteria, Juan	4	4	2.26	39	4	0	1	76	60	28	19	24	90	.218	B	R	5-10	165	1-1-80	2000	Driskoll, Texas
Ridgway, Jeff	7	8	4.07	22	22	0	0	104	110	55	47	42	71	.272	R	L	6-3	186	8-17-80	1999	Port Angeles, Wash.
Rust, Evan	7	6	3.06	35	11	0	12	97	88	47	33	27	88	.238	R	R	6-1	208	5-4-78	2000	Ben Lomond, Calif.
Shields, Jamie	4	5	2.65	10	10	2	0	71	63	24	21	10	60	.235	R	R	6-3	195	12-20-81	2000	Valencia, Calif.
Waechter, Doug	8	11	4.34	26	26	1	0	153	179	97	74	38	107	.285	R	R	6-4	209	1-28-81	1999	St. Petersburg, Fla.

NEW YORK-PENN LEAGUE

BATTING	AVG	G	AB	R	H	2B	3B	HR	RBI	BB	SO	SB	CS	SLG	OBP	B	T	HT	WT	DOB	1st Yr	Resides
Candelario, Luis	.258	56	225	26	58	16	0	6	28	7	62	9	1	.409	.287	R	R	6-2	192	8-9-81	1999	San Pedro de Macoris, D.R.
Clark, Aaron	.201	66	254	31	51	16	2	6	35	22	66	4	2	.350	.269	L	L	6-1	195	2-17-79	2001	Ennis, Texas
Cortez, Fernando	.278	55	234	36	65	14	3	1	25	15	26	6	3	.376	.327	L	R	6-1	170	8-10-81	2001	San Diego, Calif.
DePaula, Luis	.234	70	303	42	71	12	6	7	26	19	54	6	3	.383	.282	R	R	5-11	160	8-23-82	1999	Santo Domingo, D.R.
Dion, Nate	.221	52	172	18	38	5	3	1	9	9	54	0	2	.302	.272	R	R	6-3	175	11-13-81	2000	Yukon, Okla.
Gonzalez, Edgar	.332	73	277	49	92	19	4	9	34	37	56	6	3	.527	.411	R	R	6-0	174	6-14-78	2000	Bonita, Calif.
Harrison, Vince	.305	57	197	21	60	10	1	1	30	16	34	4	4	.381	.361	R	R	5-11	200	11-29-79	2001	Cincinnati, Ohio
Maduro, Jorge	.183	32	120	19	22	6	0	1	13	6	31	0	0	.258	.228	R	R	6-2	200	3-11-81	1999	Miami, Fla.
Merritt, Graig	.259	35	116	13	30	4	0	1	12	9	14	1	1	.319	.305	R	R	6-1	195	7-2-78	2001	Maple Ridge, B.C.
Monroy, Sam	.200	13	50	3	10	0	0	0	2	4	9	2	0	.200	.259	L	R	6-0	175	11-24-78	2001	Oxnard, Calif.
O'Brien, Kevin	.276	55	203	24	56	10	1	0	17	13	44	1	2	.335	.317	L	L	6-3	203	6-18-81	2000	Clearwater, Fla.
Reece, Eric	.273	68	271	35	74	20	1	3	48	29	56	6	1	.387	.345	L	R	6-3	210	6-16-78	2001	El Dorado Hills, Calif.
Rico, Matt	.221	46	154	21	34	5	0	1	16	12	34	1	1	.273	.284	R	R	6-3	200	10-8-81	2001	Clovis, Calif.
Wolotka, Brian	.266	39	124	14	33	6	3	4	20	12	39	1	0	.460	.345	L	L	6-5	195	7-7-80	2001	Munster, Ind.

GAMES BY POSITION: C—Maduro 31, Merritt 33, Reece 15. 1B—Clark 1, Merritt 1, O'Brien 46, Reece 29. 2B—Gonzalez 11, Harrison 56, Monroy 12. 3B—Cortez 54, Gonzalez 25. SS—DePaula 70, Gonzalez 6. OF—Candelario 56, Clark 64, Dion 49, Gonzalez 9, Rico 34, Wolotka 25.

PITCHING	W	L	ERA	G	GS	CG	SV	IP	H	R	ER	BB	SO	AVG	B	T	HT	WT	DOB	1st Yr	Resides
Aiello, Nick	6	1	2.48	22	0	0	0	40	36	17	11	8	24	.243	L	L	6-2	210	7-31-79	2001	Las Vegas, Nev.
Anderson, Julius	0	0	4.02	10	0	0	0	16	17	9	7	6	4	.274	R	R	6-5	185	7-16-79	2000	Grand Bay, Ala.
Bustillos, Oscar	4	3	2.70	26	0	0	13	33	25	21	10	16	44	.195	R	R	5-11	185	12-10-79	1999	Culiacan, Mexico
Carney, Jake	1	0	0.64	9	0	0	1	14	8	2	1	6	16	.160	R	R	6-2	185	12-25-79	2001	Tyler, Texas
Crawford, Chris	1	1	2.95	24	0	0	2	40	26	14	13	23	46	.189	L	L	6-3	215	10-14-77	1999	Marietta, Ga.
Cromer, Nathan	4	3	3.99	15	15	0	0	79	94	38	35	24	39	.298	L	L	6-4	208	12-11-80	1999	Des Moines, Iowa
Dischiavo, John	3	8	6.50	15	15	1	0	73	91	58	53	31	51	.306	R	R	6-4	155	1-1-82	2000	Las Vegas, Nev.
Dorman, Rich	3	0	2.58	17	3	0	0	45	37	14	13	20	34	.225	R	R	6-2	202	9-30-78	2000	Salem, Ore.
Flinn, Chris	3	4	2.36	15	10	0	2	69	54	33	18	21	72	.209	R	R	6-2	185	8-18-80	2001	Levittown, N.Y.
Fortunato, Bartolome	2	5	5.13	16	9	0	0	60	70	35	34	29	53	.299	R	R	6-1	178	7-27-80	1996	Santo Domingo, D.R.
Lockwood, Brian	4	5	3.24	12	10	0	0	58	50	28	21	20	48	.236	R	R	6-4	170	2-20-81	2001	Torrance, Calif.
Peguero, Radhame	2	0	4.76	17	1	0	0	40	30	29	21	40	22	.209	R	R	6-0	184	4-15-78	1996	San Pedro de Macoris, D.R.
Shields, Jamie	2	1	2.30	5	5	0	0	27	27	8	7	5	25	.254	R	R	6-3	195	12-20-81	2001	Valencia, Calif.
Switzer, Jon	2	0	0.63	5	0	0	0	14	9	3	1	2	20	.173	L	L	6-3	190	8-13-79	2001	Houston, Texas
Thompson, Tyson	0	1	6.75	12	0	0	1	20	21	18	15	21	15	.253	R	R	6-3	210	3-19-80	2001	Kenmore, Wash.
Vandermeer, Scott	2	5	6.02	12	8	1	1	55	74	44	37	23	31	.325	R	R	6-4	181	2-16-81	1999	New Orleans, La.

APPALACHIAN LEAGUE

BATTING	AVG	G	AB	R	H	2B	3B	HR	RBI	BB	SO	SB	CS	SLG	OBP	B	T	HT	WT	DOB	1st Yr	Resides
Blount, Pierre	.260	41	127	33	33	2	3	8	18	29	58	8	1	.512	.416	R	R	6-3	200	3-11-81	2001	Redlands, Calif.
Cordell, Brent	.307	48	163	23	50	13	0	7	26	12	32	0	3	.515	.366	B	R	6-3	215	5-22-80	2001	Incline Village, Nev.
Davis, J.P.	.223	49	166	20	37	10	0	4	13	11	37	0	2	.355	.301	R	R	6-4	220	12-20-78	2001	Russellville, Ark.
Dorner, Dwight	.202	27	84	13	17	2	0	1	4	8	18	0	0	.262	.272	L	R	6-0	175	5-23-78	2000	Houston, Texas
German, Amado	.283	52	184	25	52	10	5	5	31	19	50	16	4	.473	.348	B	R	6-2	175	6-26-81	1997	San Pedro de Macoris, D.R.
Gomes, Jonny	.291	62	206	58	60	11	2	16	44	33	73	15	4	.597	.442	R	R	6-1	205	11-22-80	2001	Petaluma, Calif.
Habel, Jason	.252	37	127	11	32	3	0	1	14	8	36	3	3	.299	.304	R	R	6-3	200	8-16-80	2001	Las Vegas, Nev.
Krga, Mike	.208	38	130	11	27	1	1	0	8	11	33	0	0	.231	.273	R	R	6-2	170	9-19-82	2000	Chicago, Ill.
Maddox, Jeremy	.271	53	188	20	51	11	0	5	27	12	47	1	1	.410	.327	R	R	6-3	235	4-5-79	2001	Lynn Haven, Fla.
Mercedes, Ramon	.252	48	163	22	41	5	0	1	19	11	26	5	3	.301	.303	R	R	5-11	160	7-9-81	1999	Nizao, D.R.
Nash, Toe	.240	47	171	23	41	10	1	8	29	19	69	0	1	.450	.318	B	R	6-5	220	2-16-82	2001	Sorrento, La.
Nichols, Tommy	.205	43	151	14	31	4	1	1	18	6	51	1	0	.265	.245	R	R	6-4	190	8-27-83	2001	Fairfield, Calif.
Riggans, Shawn	.345	15	58	15	20	4	0	8	17	9	18	1	0	.828	.433	R	R	6-2	195	7-25-80	2001	Fort Lauderdale, Fla.
Riley, Ryan	.257	46	140	25	36	6	3	1	16	11	23	3	5	.364	.325	R	R	5-10	185	11-10-78	2001	Seattle, Wash.
St. Clair, Jason	.241	32	116	16	28	6	1	0	8	2	25	1	4	.310	.266	R	R	5-10	175	9-27-82	2001	Phoenix, Ariz.

GAMES BY POSITION: C—Cordell 36, Dorner 23, Riggans 12. 1B—Davis 38, Nichols 31. 2B—Krga 38, Riley 12, St. Clair 24. 3B—Davis 2, Dorner 2, Maddox 49, Mercedes 1, Riley 23, St. Clair 1. SS—Mercedes 47, Riley 14, St. Clair 11. OF—Blount 35, Dorner 2, German 44, Gomes 61, Habel 32, Nash 35.

PITCHING	W	L	ERA	G	GS	CG	SV	IP	H	R	ER	BB	SO	AVG	B	T	HT	WT	DOB	1st Yr	Resides
Ayala, Roberto	0	0	12.00	5	0	0	0	3	5	5	4	5	1	.384	L	L	6-1	155	5-29-81	1998	Maracay, Venez.
Basilio, Manuel	2	4	5.59	11	9	0	0	48	49	32	30	23	57	.262	R	R	6-2	165	10-20-80	1998	San Pedro de Macoris, D.R.
Coose, Austin	0	0	0.00	8	0	0	2	9	4	2	0	2	16	.121	R	R	6-2	230	1-27-79	2001	Norman, Okla.
Cromer, Jason	2	0	1.59	5	2	0	0	23	14	5	4	8	18	.184	R	L	6-4	221	12-11-80	1999	Des Moines, Iowa
Febles, Hector	3	3	6.80	12	10	2	0	46	55	40	35	25	39	.292	R	R	6-2	175	11-8-82	1999	San Pedro de Macoris, D.R.
Gonzalez, Kiwi	3	2	4.44	14	8	0	0	51	52	31	25	18	38	.258	R	R	6-3	190	8-16-82	1999	Sucre, Venez.
Hines, Carlos	2	3	4.44	13	7	0	0	49	51	33	24	17	56	.260	R	R	6-4	190	9-26-80	1999	Smithfield, N.C.
King, Tim	1	3	4.54	11	7	0	0	36	40	20	18	15	26	.279	L	L	6-3	205	8-22-83	2001	Deer Park, Texas
Made, Luis	0	0	8.10	8	0	0	0	17	18	16	15	13	14	.276	L	L	6-1	180	10-17-82	2000	Bani, D.R.
Madere, Ronnie	1	2	10.71	19	0	0	0	21	32	35	25	14	22	.336	R	R	5-11	190	8-20-78	2001	La Place, La.
Miller, Eric	4	2	5.05	16	1	0	0	36	32	23	20	18	40	.230	R	R	6-2	195	7-31-82	2001	Naples, Fla.
Parker, Josh	2	1	2.35	22	0	0	5	31	29	12	8	6	34	.250	R	R	6-5	220	1-12-81	2001	Calera, Ala.
Sanchez, Juan	2	6	7.74	12	12	0	0	45	50	43	39	23	47	.287	R	R	6-3	215	9-25-82	2001	Imperial Beach, Calif.
Seddon, Chris	1	2	5.11	4	2	0	0	12	15	7	7	6	18	.300	L	L	6-3	170	10-13-83	2001	Santa Clarita, Calif.
Shaw, Elliott	0	0	5.93	6	0	0	0	14	15	10	9	11	17	.294	R	R	6-3	218	12-31-79	2000	Suisun, Calif.
Thompson, Tyson	0	1	3.18	3	1	0	0	6	9	7	2	2	6	.333	R	R	6-3	210	3-19-80	2001	Kenmore, Wash.
Victorino, Pedro	2	3	6.18	13	8	0	0	44	49	35	30	23	39	.284	R	R	6-1	170	2-25-82	1999	Santo Domingo, D.R.
Vigue, John	1	5	3.24	20	0	0	4	33	34	13	12	6	33	.263	R	R	6-0	175	8-18-78	2001	Seminole, Fla.
Volquez, Bolivar	2	2	2.43	19	0	0	0	30	28	9	8	7	37	.250	R	R	6-3	186	7-3-81	1998	Santo Domingo, D.R.

TEXAS RANGERS

BY EVAN GRANT

It started as the most anticipated season in Rangers history. By the time it ended, the Rangers were a team deep into transition.

The 2001 season actually started in December of 2000 with a bevy of free-agent signings at the Winter Meetings in Dallas. The shopping spree was headlined by the record-breaking 10-year, $252 million contract given to shortstop Alex Rodriguez.

Despite an inauspicious start that included tripping over his own feet on Opening Day in San Juan, Puerto Rico, Rodriguez delivered as promised. He hit 52 home runs, establishing both a new franchise record and a new single-season record for shortstops. It was, however, the extent of the good news for the Rangers, who finished 73-89 and in last place in the American League West for the second consecutive season.

The Rangers and their overmatched pitching staff were quickly left behind in the Seattle Mariners' wake. The changes came quickly. Manager Johnny Oates resigned on May 4, perhaps only days before he was to be fired. Farm director Reid Nichols soon relinquished his spot—on a permanent basis—to join the major league coaching staff. On the season's final day, owner Tom Hicks decided to make it a clean sweep and fired general manager Doug Melvin. All three had been in place since 1995, overseeing the only three playoff berths in Rangers history.

From the time Oates left until the end of the season, the Rangers committed to rebuilding. That meant long looks for lots of young players. Under new manager Jerry Narron, who infused the team with an energy it had lacked for several years, the Rangers did see improvement.

Rookie second baseman Michael Young, called up in May, established himself as a solid major leaguer. Lefthander Doug Davis continued the progress he made in the second half of 2000. There were glimpses that

Alex Rodriguez

Hank Blalock

PLAYERS OF THE YEAR

MAJOR LEAGUE: Alex Rodriguez, ss

Huge contract, huge numbers. Rodriguez set a major league record for home runs at his position (52) in 2001. At age 26, he has 241 career homers. He also hit .318 and drove in 135 runs in his first year as a Ranger.

MINOR LEAGUE: Hank Blalock, 3b

Blalock hit for the cycle in June at Double-A Tulsa, and then did it again two nights later. He hit well at Tulsa (.327-11-61), after a mid-season promotion from Class A Charlotte (.380-7-47).

rookie righthander Aaron Myette could be the power pitcher the Rangers have seen very rarely in recent years. And, in the final month of the season, the much-anticipated debut of first baseman Carlos Pena, the team's top prospect, went very well at the plate.

Only one minor league affiliate, Class A Charlotte, made the postseason, but there were individual cases of improvement. The most impressive were made by position players, particularly third baseman Hank Blalock. In an astonishing season, Blalock, 20, had the second-highest average in all of the minors. He batted .352-18-108 while splitting the season between Charlotte and Double-A Tulsa. In his first week at Tulsa, he hit for the cycle twice in a three-game span—a feat never previously accomplished in professional baseball.

Blalock wasn't the only third base prospect to earn some buzz in the organization. The Rangers' top pick in the June draft was third baseman Mark Teixeira from Georgia Tech. Despite acrimonious negotiations with agent Scott Boras that lasted deep into August, Teixeira signed a major league contract guaranteeing him $9.5 million.

The Rangers have had a history of developing good position players. Their challenge in 2002 and beyond is to develop solid pitchers. In that regard, it was a mixed season. While the Rangers got no-hitters from Andy Pratt and Nick Regilio, who threw a perfect game for Charlotte, prized righthander Jovanny Cedeno was slowed by a shoulder injury.

The season's breakthrough pitcher was righthander Ryan Dittfurth, who went 9-6, 3.48 at Charlotte. Dittfurth, 20, was the Rangers' minor league pitcher of the year.

The Rangers hope pitchers like Dittfurth offer a glimpse into the team's future. Then maybe the transition would be complete.

ORGANIZATION LEADERS

BATTING

*AVG	Hank Blalock, Tulsa/Charlotte	.352
R	Hank Blalock, Tulsa/Charlotte	96
H	Hank Blalock, Tulsa/Charlotte	179
TB	Hank Blalock, Tulsa/Charlotte	280
2B	Carlos Pena, Oklahoma	38
3B	Jose Morban, Savannah	11
HR	Kevin Mench, Tulsa	26
RBI	Hank Blalock, Tulsa/Charlotte	108
BB	Carlos Pena, Oklahoma	80
SO	Carlos Pena, Oklahoma	127
SB	Jose Morban, Savannah	46

PITCHING

W	R.A. Dickey, Oklahoma	11
	Colby Lewis, Tulsa/Charlotte	11
L	Corey Lee, Oklahoma/Tulsa	12
#ERA	Keith Stamler, Charlotte/Savannah	2.43
	Hayden Gardner, Charlotte/Pulaski	2.43
G	Greg Runser, Charlotte	50
CG	Three tied at	3
SV	Greg Runser, Charlotte	30
IP	Andy Pratt, Tulsa	168
BB	Dave Elder, Oklahoma/Tulsa	86
SO	Colby Lewis, Tulsa/Charlotte	170

*Minimum 250 At-Bats #Minimum 75 Innings

TEXAS RANGERS

Managers: Johnny Oates, Jerry Narron

2001 Record: 73-89, .451 (4th, AL West)

BATTING	AVG	G	AB	R	H	2B	3B	HR	RBI	BB	SO	SB	CS	SLG	OBP	B	T	HT	WT	DOB	1st Yr	Resides
Brumbaugh, Cliff	.000	7	10	1	0	0	0	0	0	1	5	0	0	.000	.091	R	R	6-2	205	4-21-74	1995	New Castle, Del.
Caminiti, Ken	.232	54	185	24	43	8	1	9	25	22	41	0	0	.432	.318	B	R	6-0	200	4-21-63	1985	Richmond, Texas
Catalanotto, Frank	.330	133	463	77	153	31	5	11	54	39	55	15	5	.490	.391	L	R	5-11	195	4-27-74	1992	Smithtown, N.Y.
Curtis, Chad	.252	38	115	24	29	3	0	3	10	14	21	7	1	.357	.338	R	R	5-10	185	11-6-68	1989	Ada, Mich.
Dransfeldt, Kelly	.000	4	3	0	0	0	0	0	0	0	0	0	0	.000	.000	R	R	6-2	195	4-16-75	1996	Morris, Ill.
Galarraga, Andres	.235	72	243	33	57	16	0	10	34	18	68	1	0	.424	.310	R	R	6-3	235	6-18-61	1979	West Palm Beach, Fla.
Greer, Rusty	.273	62	245	38	67	23	0	7	29	27	32	1	2	.453	.342	L	L	6-0	195	1-21-69	1990	Colleyville, Texas
Haselman, Bill	.285	47	130	12	37	6	0	3	25	8	27	0	1	.400	.331	R	R	6-3	225	5-25-66	1987	New Castle, Wash.
Hubbard, Mike	.273	5	11	3	3	1	0	1	1	0	4	0	0	.636	.273	R	R	6-1	205	2-16-71	1992	Madison Heights, Va.
Jensen, Marcus	.160	11	25	0	4	1	0	0	2	0	9	0	0	.200	.160	B	R	6-4	204	12-14-72	1990	Scottsdale, Ariz.
2-team (1 Boston)	.172	12	29	0	5	1	0	0	2	0	10	0	0	.207	.172							
Kapler, Gabe	.267	134	483	77	129	29	1	17	72	61	70	23	6	.437	.348	R	R	6-2	208	8-31-75	1995	Sherman Oaks, Calif.
Lamb, Mike	.306	76	284	42	87	18	0	4	35	14	27	2	1	.412	.348	L	R	6-1	195	8-9-75	1997	Valinda, Calif.
Ledee, Ricky	.231	78	242	33	56	21	1	2	36	23	58	3	3	.351	.303	L	L	6-1	190	11-22-73	1990	Salinas, P.R.
Magruder, Chris	.172	17	29	3	5	0	0	1	1	5	0	0	0	.172	.226	B	R	5-11	200	4-26-77	1998	Yakima, Wash.
Mateo, Ruben	.248	40	129	18	32	5	2	1	13	9	28	1	0	.341	.322	R	R	6-0	185	2-10-78	1995	San Cristobal, D.R.
Mirabelli, Doug	.102	23	49	4	5	2	0	2	3	6	10	0	0	.265	.254	R	R	6-1	218	10-18-70	1992	Wichita, Kan.
Monroe, Craig	.212	27	52	8	11	1	0	2	5	6	18	2	0	.346	.293	R	R	6-1	195	2-27-77	1995	Texarkana, Texas
Palmeiro, Rafael	.273	160	600	98	164	33	0	47	123	101	90	1	1	.563	.381	L	L	6-0	190	9-24-64	1985	Colleyville, Texas
Pena, Carlos	.258	22	62	6	16	4	1	3	12	10	17	0	0	.500	.361	L	L	6-2	210	5-17-78	1998	Haverhill, Mass.
Porter, Bo	.230	48	87	18	20	4	2	1	6	9	34	3	2	.356	.296	R	R	6-2	195	7-5-72	1994	Fresno, Texas
Rodriguez, Alex	.318	162	632	133	201	34	1	52	135	75	131	18	3	.622	.399	R	R	6-3	210	7-27-75	1994	Miami, Fla.
Rodriguez, Ivan	.308	111	442	70	136	24	2	25	65	23	73	10	3	.541	.347	R	R	5-9	205	11-30-71	1989	Rio Piedras, P.R.
Sheldon, Scott	.200	61	120	11	24	5	0	3	11	3	35	1	1	.317	.216	R	R	6-3	215	11-20-68	1991	Pearland, Texas
Sierra, Darren	.291	94	344	55	100	22	1	23	67	19	52	2	0	.561	.322	B	R	6-1	215	10-6-65	1983	Miami, Fla.
Velarde, Randy	.297	78	296	46	88	16	2	9	31	29	73	4	2	.456	.369	R	R	6-0	200	11-24-62	1985	Midland, Texas
Young, Mike	.249	106	386	57	96	18	4	11	49	26	91	3	1	.402	.298	R	R	6-1	190	10-19-76	1997	Los Angeles, Calif.

PITCHING	W	L	ERA	G	GS	CG	SV	IP	H	R	ER	BB	SO	AVG	B	T	HT	WT	DOB	1st Yr	Resides
Bell, Rob	5	5	7.18	18	18	0	0	105	130	87	84	47	64	.309	R	R	6-5	225	1-17-77	1995	Marlboro, N.Y.
Benoit, Joaquin	0	0	10.80	1	1	0	0	5	8	6	6	3	4	.363	R	R	6-3	205	7-26-79	1996	Santiago, D.R.
Brantley, Jeff	0	1	5.14	18	0	0	0	21	26	12	12	9	11	.309	R	R	5-10	197	9-5-63	1985	Clinton, Miss.
Cordero, Francisco	0	1	3.86	3	0	0	0	2	3	1	1	2	1	.300	R	R	6-2	200	8-11-77	1994	Santo Domingo, D.R.
Crabtree, Tim	0	5	6.56	21	0	0	4	23	37	18	17	14	16	.385	R	R	6-4	225	10-13-69	1992	Colleyville, Texas
Davis, Doug	11	10	4.45	30	30	1	0	186	220	103	92	69	115	.294	R	L	6-4	190	9-21-75	1996	Arlington, Texas
Dickey, R.A.	0	1	6.75	4	0	0	0	12	13	9	9	7	4	.282	R	R	6-3	205	10-29-74	1997	Nashville, Tenn.
Duchscherer, Justin	1	1	12.27	5	2	0	0	15	24	20	20	4	11	.352	R	R	6-3	164	11-19-77	1996	Lubbock, Texas
Foster, Kevin	0	1	6.62	9	0	0	0	18	21	14	13	10	16	.308	R	R	6-1	175	1-13-69	1988	Evanston, Ill.
Glynn, Ryan	1	5	7.04	12	9	0	0	46	59	38	36	26	15	.308	R	R	6-3	200	11-1-74	1995	Grand Prairie, Texas
Helling, Rick	12	11	5.17	34	34	2	0	216	256	134	124	63	154	.297	R	R	6-3	220	12-15-70	1992	Southlake, Texas
Johnson, Jonathan	0	0	9.58	5	0	0	0	10	13	11	11	7	11	.317	R	R	6-0	180	7-16-74	1995	Irmo, S.C.
Judd, Mike	0	1	8.00	4	1	0	0	9	15	10	8	5	5	.357	R	R	6-1	217	6-30-75	1995	La Mesa, Calif.
2-team (8 Tampa Bay)	1	1	5.28	12	3	0	0	29	34	24	17	15	16	.288							
Kolb, Dan	0	0	4.70	17	0	0	0	15	15	8	8	10	15	.258	R	R	6-3	215	3-29-75	1995	Walnut, Ill.
Mahomes, Pat	7	6	5.70	56	4	0	0	107	115	71	68	55	61	.279	R	R	6-4	212	8-9-70	1988	Lindale, Texas
Michalak, Chris	2	2	3.32	11	0	0	1	22	24	8	8	6	10	.279	L	L	6-2	195	1-4-71	1993	Lemont, Ill.
2-team (24 Toronto)	8	9	4.41	35	18	0	1	137	157	74	67	55	67	.293							
Moreno, Juan	3	3	3.92	45	0	0	0	41	22	21	18	28	36	.152	L	L	6-1	205	2-28-75	1994	Cagua, Venez.
Myette, Aaron	4	5	7.14	19	15	0	0	81	94	65	64	37	67	.292	R	R	6-4	195	9-26-77	1997	Gig Harbor, Wash.
Oliver, Darren	11	11	6.02	28	28	1	0	154	189	109	103	65	104	.305	R	L	6-2	220	10-6-70	1988	Southlake, Texas
Petkovsek, Mark	1	2	6.69	55	0	0	0	77	103	61	57	28	42	.322	R	R	6-0	198	11-18-65	1987	Beaumont, Texas
Rogers, Kenny	5	7	6.19	20	20	0	0	121	150	88	83	49	74	.307	L	L	6-1	217	11-10-64	1982	Southlake, Texas
Smart, J.D.	1	2	6.46	15	0	0	0	15	19	11	11	4	10	.306	L	R	6-2	185	11-12-73	1995	Austin, Texas
Venafro, Mike	5	5	4.80	70	0	0	4	60	54	35	32	28	29	.240	L	L	5-10	180	8-2-73	1995	Fort Myers, Fla.
Villafuerte, Brandon	0	0	14.29	6	0	0	0	6	12	9	9	3	4	.413	R	R	5-11	165	12-17-75	1995	Morgan Hill, Calif.
Zimmerman, Jeff	4	4	2.40	66	0	0	28	71	48	19	19	16	72	.192	R	R	6-1	200	8-9-72	1997	Vancouver, B.C.

FIELDING

Catcher	PCT	G	PO	A	E	DP	PB
Haselman	1.000	47	234	13	0	2	0
Hubbard	1.000	5	15	2	0	0	0
Jensen	1.000	11	35	3	0	0	0
Mirabelli	.990	23	84	16	1	4	0
I. Rodriguez	.990	106	631	52	7	11	2
Sheldon	1.000	1	4	0	0	0	0

First Base	PCT	G	PO	A	E	DP
Catalanotto	1.000	5	6	2	0	0
Galarraga	.995	25	195	16	1	26
Palmeiro	.992	113	906	83	8	112
Pena	.987	16	138	15	2	13
Velarde	1.000	9	70	2	0	5

Second Base	PCT	G	PO	A	E	DP
Catalanotto	.953	13	18	23	2	8

Velarde	.988	52	111	135	3	38
Young	.984	104	212	284	8	79

Third Base	PCT	G	PO	A	E	DP
Caminiti	.940	53	42	99	9	10
Catalanotto	.958	11	6	17	1	0
Dransfeldt	.000	1	0	0	0	0
Lamb	.914	74	52	139	18	14
Pena	.000	1	0	0	0	0
Sheldon	.951	38	37	61	5	1
Velarde	.929	7	4	9	1	2

Shortstop	PCT	G	PO	A	E	DP
Dransfeldt	1.000	3	0	4	0	0
A. Rodriguez	.976	161	279	452	18	118
Sheldon	.960	16	8	16	1	3

Outfield	PCT	G	PO	A	E	DP
Brumbaugh	1.000	6	6	0	0	0
Catalanotto	.995	92	187	2	1	0
Curtis	.988	33	80	2	1	1
Greer	.962	60	124	2	5	0
Kapler	.997	133	344	8	1	3
Ledee	.979	72	136	1	3	0
Magruder	1.000	12	21	1	0	0
Mateo	.986	39	70	0	1	0
Monroe	1.000	24	42	3	0	1
Porter	.969	40	61	1	2	0
Sheldon	1.000	3	2	0	0	0
Sierra	.938	36	60	0	4	0
Velarde	1.000	2	2	0	0	0

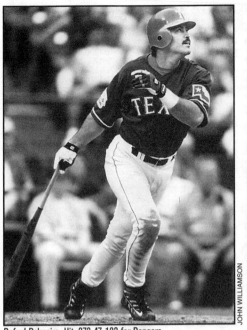

Rafael Palmeiro: Hit .273-47-123 for Rangers

Ivan Rodriguez: Gold Glove catcher hit .308-25-65

FARM SYSTEM

Director, Player Development: Reid Nichols, John Lombardo

Class	Farm Team	League	W	L	Pct.	Finish*	Manager(s)	First Yr.
AAA	Oklahoma RedHawks	Pacific Coast	74	69	.517	6th (16)	DeMarlo Hale	1983
AA	Tulsa (Okla.) Drillers	Texas	69	70	.496	5th (8)	Paul Carey	1977
A#	Charlotte (Fla.) Rangers	Florida State	67	70	.489	10th (12)	Darryl Kennedy	1987
A	Savannah (Ga.) Sand Gnats	South Atlantic	54	80	.403	14th (16)	Bill Slack/Pedro Lopez	1998
Rookie#	Pulaski (Va.) Rangers	Appalachian	38	30	.559	3rd (10)	Bruce Crabbe	1997
Rookie	Port Charlotte (Fla.) Rangers	Gulf Coast	24	35	.407	10th (14)	Carlos Subero	1973

*Finish in overall standings (No. of teams in league) #Advanced level

OKLAHOMA Class AAA

PACIFIC COAST LEAGUE

BATTING	AVG	G	AB	R	H	2B	3B	HR	RBI	BB	SO	SB	CS	SLG	OBP	B	T	HT	WT	DOB	1st Yr	Resides
Ashby, Chris	.231	33	121	11	28	7	0	2	16	12	24	0	2	.339	.301	R	R	6-3	196	12-15-74	1993	Boca Raton, Fla.
Berrios, Harry	.255	61	231	33	59	8	4	7	33	14	47	3	0	.416	.304	R	R	5-11	205	12-2-71	1993	Grand Rapids, Mich.
Brumbaugh, Cliff	.307	54	202	38	62	11	3	8	42	33	41	3	3	.510	.404	R	R	6-2	205	4-21-74	1995	New Castle, Del.
Cadiente, Brett	.400	2	5	0	2	0	0	0	0	0	2	0	0	.400	.400	L	L	5-11	180	6-17-77	1999	Mesa, Ariz.
Curtis, Chad	.286	4	14	3	4	0	0	0	1	2	2	0	0	.286	.375	R	R	5-10	185	11-6-68	1989	Ada, Mich.
Demetral, Chris	.236	92	322	33	76	11	1	2	27	34	32	1	1	.295	.307	L	R	5-11	175	12-8-69	1991	Sterling Heights, Mich.
Dransfeldt, Kelly	.250	143	551	76	138	29	5	9	63	50	116	12	9	.370	.313	R	R	6-2	195	4-16-75	1996	Morris, Ill.
Garcia, Osmani	.237	47	173	15	41	11	0	1	21	3	19	1	2	.318	.250	R	R	6-0	210	9-6-74	2000	Santiago, D.R.
Goodwin, Curtis	.229	73	236	24	54	3	1	2	19	10	45	3	3	.275	.258	L	L	5-11	180	9-30-72	1991	San Leandro, Calif.
Haselman, Bill	.143	8	28	2	4	0	0	0	1	1	10	0	0	.143	.194	R	R	6-3	225	5-25-66	1987	New Castle, Wash.
Hubbard, Mike	.310	35	129	22	40	8	1	6	23	11	20	0	1	.527	.373	R	R	6-1	205	2-16-71	1992	Madison Heights, Va.
Jensen, Marcus	.298	53	188	42	56	10	1	8	25	46	46	0	0	.489	.438	B	R	6-4	204	12-14-72	1990	Scottsdale, Ariz.
Lamb, Mike	.297	69	273	35	81	19	3	8	40	13	31	0	2	.476	.331	L	R	6-1	195	8-9-75	1997	Valinda, Calif.
Ledee, Ricky	.500	4	16	4	8	1	0	1	3	1	1	0	0	.750	.529	L	L	6-1	190	11-22-73	1990	Salinas, P.R.
Magruder, Chris	.362	33	127	28	46	14	4	5	21	21	19	1	2	.654	.464	B	R	5-11	200	4-26-77	1998	Yakima, Wash.
2-team (54 Fresno)	.311	87	341	65	106	21	5	15	51	39	64	4	3	.534	.397							
Mateo, Ruben	.216	14	51	3	11	3	0	1	8	2	8	1	2	.333	.241	R	R	6-0	185	2-10-78	1995	San Cristobal, D.R.
Meliah, Dave	.254	20	63	9	16	5	0	1	7	9	13	2	2	.381	.347	L	R	6-3	185	3-11-77	1998	Walla Walla, Wash.
Monroe, Craig	.280	114	410	60	115	25	5	20	75	46	85	10	8	.512	.358	R	R	6-1	195	2-27-77	1995	Texarkana, Texas
Pena, Carlos	.288	119	431	71	124	38	3	23	74	80	127	11	3	.550	.408	L	L	6-2	210	5-17-78	1998	Haverhill, Mass.
Porter, Bo	.246	58	224	40	55	9	2	13	40	26	60	10	4	.478	.329	R	R	6-2	195	7-5-72	1994	Fresno, Texas
Romano, Jason	.315	41	149	32	47	6	1	4	13	20	28	3	4	.450	.394	R	R	6-0	185	6-24-79	1997	Tampa, Fla.
Sagmoen, Marc	.238	59	235	22	56	10	1	4	16	8	53	3	2	.340	.261	L	L	5-11	185	4-16-71	1993	Seattle, Wash.
3-team (9 Edm./12 Mem.)	.222	80	324	31	72	15	1	4	26	14	76	4	2	.312	.253							
Sierra, Ruben	.266	24	94	14	25	2	1	3	12	10	14	2	0	.404	.337	B	R	6-1	215	10-6-65	1983	Miami, Fla.
Simons, Mitch	.240	34	121	14	29	7	0	0	7	11	23	0	2	.298	.308	R	R	5-9	172	12-13-68	1991	Midwest City, Okla.
Steed, Dave	.233	67	227	28	53	10	0	7	29	25	61	0	1	.370	.315	R	R	6-1	205	2-25-73	1993	Starkville, Miss.

BATTING

BATTING	AVG	G	AB	R	H	2B	3B	HR	RBI	BB	SO	SB	CS	SLG	OBP	B	T	HT	WT	DOB	1st Yr	Resides
Taveras, Luis	.182	12	33	3	6	0	0	0	3	3	12	0	1	.182	.250	R	R	5-10	185	8-1-77	1995	Santiago, D.R.
Young, Mike	.291	47	189	28	55	8	0	8	28	20	34	3	3	.460	.358	R	R	6-1	190	10-19-76	1997	Los Angeles, Calif.

PITCHING

PITCHING	W	L	ERA	G	GS	CG	SV	IP	H	R	ER	BB	SO	AVG	B	T	HT	WT	DOB	1st Yr	Resides
Beech, Matt	1	6	5.88	10	10	0	0	60	83	49	39	24	44	.328	L	L	6-2	195	1-20-72	1994	Clearwater, Fla.
Benoit, Joaquin	9	5	4.19	24	24	1	0	131	113	63	61	73	142	.233	R	R	6-3	205	7-26-79	1996	Santiago, D.R.
Cordero, Francisco	1	1	0.59	12	0	0	6	15	8	2	1	3	20	.148	R	R	6-2	200	8-11-77	1994	Santo Domingo, D.R.
Cubillan, Darwin	1	1	10.38	9	0	0	2	13	20	16	15	12	8	.350	R	R	6-2	170	11-15-74	1994	Bobure, Venez.
Davis, Doug	2	0	2.87	2	2	0	0	16	10	5	5	4	14	.188	R	L	6-4	190	9-21-75	1996	Arlington, Texas
Dickey, R.A.	11	7	3.75	24	24	3	0	163	164	77	68	45	120	.262	R	R	6-3	205	10-29-74	1997	Nashville, Tenn.
Duchscherer, Justin	3	3	2.84	7	7	1	0	51	48	20	16	10	52	.255	R	R	6-3	164	11-19-77	1996	Lubbock, Texas
Durocher, Jayson	4	1	4.99	31	0	0	6	40	34	25	22	23	52	.231	R	R	6-3	195	8-18-74	1993	Scottsdale, Ariz.
Elder, Dave	5	4	4.99	15	8	0	0	58	54	36	32	43	56	.248	R	R	6-0	180	9-23-75	1997	Conyers, Ga.
Foster, Kevin	3	1	2.80	16	3	0	0	55	33	18	17	22	65	.174	R	R	6-1	175	1-13-69	1988	Evanston, Ill.
Glynn, Ryan	2	6	6.49	13	13	1	0	79	87	62	57	41	52	.282	R	R	6-3	200	11-1-74	1995	Grand Prairie, Texas
Johnson, Mike	3	5	4.58	23	8	1	2	88	101	48	45	22	67	.286	L	R	6-2	180	10-3-75	1993	Jupiter, Fla.
Judd, Mike	0	1	10.13	2	0	0	0	3	6	3	3	2	3	.461	R	R	6-1	217	6-30-75	1995	La Mesa, Calif.
Kolb, Dan	0	1	1.42	12	0	0	3	19	13	3	3	4	21	.188	R	R	6-4	215	3-29-75	1995	Walnut, Ill.
Lee, Corey	0	0	18.00	2	0	0	0	3	5	7	6	4	1	.333	B	L	6-2	185	12-26-74	1996	Raleigh, N.C.
Lopez, Johan	0	0	3.52	3	0	0	0	8	8	4	3	2	4	.266	R	R	6-2	210	4-4-75	1992	Yaracuy, Venez.
Lundberg, Spike	3	5	6.71	13	8	0	0	55	72	51	41	15	31	.307	R	R	6-1	185	5-4-77	1997	San Diego, Calif.
Martinez, Jose	0	0	0.00	1	1	0	0	7	1	0	0	1	3	.047	R	R	6-0	165	2-4-75	1995	Santiago, D.R.
Mitchell, Dean	0	0	7.11	4	0	0	0	6	9	6	5	1	2	.360	R	R	5-11	175	3-19-74	1996	Waco, Texas
Moreno, Jason	0	1	1.86	7	0	0	0	10	4	2	2	2	13	.125	L	L	6-1	205	2-28-75	1994	Cagua, Venez.
Munro, Peter	8	6	4.67	33	8	0	0	89	89	50	46	43	73	.264	R	R	6-3	210	6-14-75	1994	Windham, N.H.
Myette, Aaron	4	3	3.73	12	12	2	0	70	64	32	29	30	76	.240	R	R	6-4	195	9-26-77	1997	Gig Harbor, Wash.
Oliver, Darren	0	0	0.00	1	1	0	0	3	3	0	0	0	3	.250	R	L	6-2	220	10-6-70	1988	Southlake, Texas
Schmack, Brian	2	2	4.08	40	0	0	1	53	56	31	24	14	34	.261	R	R	6-2	195	12-7-73	1996	Barrington, Ill.
Sikorski, Brian	6	4	3.61	14	14	1	0	87	89	37	35	23	73	.275	R	R	6-1	200	7-27-74	1995	Roseville, Mich.
Smart, J.D.	2	2	2.74	16	0	0	3	23	22	9	7	6	13	.255	L	R	6-2	185	11-12-73	1995	Austin, Texas
Villafuerte, Brandon	5	5	2.83	38	0	0	10	64	63	21	20	26	65	.266	R	R	5-11	165	12-17-75	1995	Morgan Hill, Calif.

FIELDING

Catcher	PCT	G	PO	A	E	DP	PB
Haselman	.957	3	22	0	1	0	0
Hubbard	.987	34	278	16	4	2	3
Jensen	1.000	47	375	18	0	3	4
Steed	.984	52	384	35	7	8	8
Taveras	.989	12	84	7	1	0	1

First Base	PCT	G	PO	A	E	DP
Brumbaugh	1.000	5	39	4	0	4
Demetral	1.000	1	3	0	0	0
Hubbard	1.000	1	1	0	0	0
Pena	.989	117	925	89	11	108
Sagmoen	.976	9	75	6	2	8
Steed	.992	13	116	10	1	12

Second Base	PCT	G	PO	A	E	DP
Demetral	.970	50	83	141	7	36

Romano	.975	18	26	52	2	13
Simons	.988	33	67	104	2	25
Young	.972	46	60	114	5	26

Third Base	PCT	G	PO	A	E	DP
Demetral	1.000	15	8	17	0	0
Garcia	.963	44	25	79	4	3
Lamb	.908	69	39	109	15	9
Meliah	.905	16	9	29	4	3
Steed	1.000	1	0	3	0	0

Shortstop	PCT	G	PO	A	E	DP
Demetral	.000	1	0	0	0	0
Dransfeldt	.965	142	268	400	24	105
Young	.909	2	2	8	1	2

Outfield	PCT	G	PO	A	E	DP
Ashby	.977	27	43	0	1	0

Berrios	.972	31	34	1	1	0
Brumbaugh	.976	50	115	5	3	3
Demetral	1.000	4	1	0	0	0
Goodwin	.969	71	120	7	4	4
Ledee	1.000	3	3	0	0	0
Magruder	.986	31	69	2	1	0
Mateo	.957	14	22	0	1	0
Meliah	.000	1	0	0	0	0
Monroe	.975	97	185	9	5	3
Porter	1.000	54	110	3	0	2
Romano	1.000	13	26	0	0	0
Sagmoen	.989	44	90	4	1	1
Sierra	1.000	1	2	0	0	0

TULSA — Class AA

TEXAS LEAGUE

BATTING	AVG	G	AB	R	H	2B	3B	HR	RBI	BB	SO	SB	CS	SLG	OBP	B	T	HT	WT	DOB	1st Yr	Resides
Berrios, Harry	.262	37	149	20	39	10	0	7	23	10	33	4	1	.470	.308	R	R	5-11	205	12-2-71	1993	Grand Rapids, Mich.
Blalock, Hank	.327	68	272	50	89	18	4	11	61	39	38	3	3	.544	.413	L	R	6-1	192	11-21-80	1999	San Diego, Calif.
Cadiente, Brett	.279	67	262	32	73	16	5	3	24	15	66	8	5	.412	.318	L	L	5-11	180	6-17-77	1999	Mesa, Ariz.
Camilli, Jason	.241	55	174	21	42	8	1	3	24	32	36	4	1	.351	.370	R	R	6-0	190	10-18-75	1994	Phoenix, Ariz.
2-team (13 El Paso)	.258	68	213	28	55	9	1	3	27	34	44	4	3	.352	.368							
Curtis, Chad	.182	6	22	3	4	0	0	1	2	5	6	1	0	.318	.379	R	R	5-10	185	11-6-68	1989	Ada, Mich.
Flores, Javier	.241	32	116	8	28	4	1	0	11	9	10	2	2	.293	.305	R	R	6-0	185	12-20-75	1997	Broken Arrow, Okla.
Garcia, Osmani	.258	71	260	29	67	14	4	6	35	10	27	0	2	.412	.284	R	R	6-0	210	9-6-74	2000	Santiago, D.R.
Greer, Rusty	.000	1	3	1	0	0	0	0	0	1	1	0	0	.000	.250	L	L	6-0	195	1-21-69	1990	Colleyville, Texas
Hafner, Travis	.282	88	323	59	91	25	0	20	74	59	82	3	1	.545	.396	L	R	6-3	240	6-3-77	1997	Sykeston, N.D.
Halloran, Matt	.214	27	70	7	15	5	0	1	4	4	15	1	0	.329	.276	R	R	6-1	180	3-3-78	1996	Niceville, Fla.
Jones, Jason	.215	30	107	8	23	6	0	2	8	3	17	0	0	.327	.243	R	R	6-3	210	10-17-76	1999	Marietta, Ga.
Jones, Jeremy	.232	93	311	34	72	13	0	4	29	30	61	1	3	.312	.305	R	R	6-3	195	8-12-77	1998	Raymore, Mo.
Kapler, Gabe	.333	5	15	2	5	1	0	0	0	6	1	0	1	.400	.524	R	R	6-2	208	8-31-75	1995	Sherman Oaks, Calif.
Meliah, Dave	.290	90	307	40	89	17	4	12	47	24	47	4	4	.489	.342	L	R	6-3	185	3-11-77	1998	Walla Walla, Wash.
Mench, Kevin	.265	120	475	78	126	34	2	26	83	34	76	4	6	.509	.319	R	R	6-0	215	1-7-78	1999	Newark, Del.
Oliver, Brian	.225	12	40	5	9	1	1	0	5	6	8	0	0	.300	.327	R	R	5-10	170	11-7-76	1998	Antioch, Calif.
Piniella, Juan	.260	110	373	51	97	24	2	3	34	38	98	13	3	.359	.333	R	R	5-10	160	3-13-78	1996	Stafford, Va.
Romano, Jason	.242	46	186	19	45	9	1	1	19	16	31	8	3	.317	.304	R	R	5-11	185	6-24-79	1997	Tampa, Fla.
Solano, Danny	.246	120	423	58	104	16	5	6	45	46	77	3	4	.350	.326	R	R	5-9	155	12-3-78	1997	Santo Domingo, D.R.
Taveras, Luis	.206	55	180	31	37	4	2	5	22	18	35	5	0	.333	.279	R	R	5-10	185	8-1-77	1995	Santiago, D.R.
Velarde, Randy	.381	6	21	5	8	2	0	0	5	1	5	0	0	.476	.375	R	R	6-0	200	11-24-62	1985	Midland, Texas
Warriax, Brandon	.135	23	74	4	10	5	0	0	3	3	31	0	0	.203	.169	R	R	6-0	165	6-23-79	1997	Maxton, N.C.
Wright, Corey	.254	117	418	62	106	19	3	0	26	58	103	23	15	.313	.360	L	L	5-11	165	11-26-79	1997	La Puente, Calif.
Zywica, Mike	.239	47	163	23	39	9	0	5	22	6	60	0	1	.387	.286	R	R	6-4	190	9-14-74	1996	Richton Park, Ill.

PITCHING	W	L	ERA	G	GS	CG	SV	IP	H	R	ER	BB	SO	AVG	B	T	HT	WT	DOB	1st Yr	Resides
Beech, Matt	3	1	3.13	7	7	1	0	46	41	17	16	10	39	.241	L	L	6-2	195	1-20-72	1994	Clearwater, Fla.
Benoit, Joaquin	1	0	3.32	4	4	0	0	22	23	8	8	6	23	.264	R	R	6-3	205	7-26-79	1996	Santiago, D.R.
Cook, Derrick	0	1	9.00	7	0	0	1	10	15	12	10	6	4	.357	R	R	6-2	195	8-6-75	1996	Staunton, Va.
Crabtree, Tim	0	0	3.00	2	2	0	0	3	3	1	1	1	0	.250	R	R	6-4	225	10-13-69	1992	Colleyville, Texas
Duchscherer, Justin	4	0	2.08	6	6	1	0	43	39	14	10	10	55	.242	R	R	6-3	164	11-19-77	1996	Lubbock, Texas

PITCHING	W	L	ERA	G	GS	CG	SV	IP	H	R	ER	BB	SO	AVG	B	T	HT	WT	DOB	1st Yr	Resides
Durocher, Jayson	0	0	0.00	3	0	0	0	4	0	0	0	3	4	.000	R	R	6-3	195	8-18-74	1993	Scottsdale, Ariz.
Elder, Dave	4	6	3.00	13	13	0	0	72	64	28	24	43	78	.246	R	R	6-0	180	9-23-75	1997	Conyers, Ga.
Figueroa, Carlos	0	1	2.08	3	0	0	0	4	3	1	1	3	2	.200	L	L	6-1	190	10-5-79	1997	Carolina, P.R.
Garza, Chris	0	1	3.09	16	0	0	0	23	15	11	8	16	23	.182	L	L	5-11	180	7-23-75	1996	Los Angeles, Calif.
Guzman, Leiby	2	0	5.40	25	0	0	1	48	48	30	29	15	31	.255	R	R	6-5	160	9-27-76	1994	Nato del Media Abajo, D.R.
Hughes, Travis	5	7	4.64	47	5	0	8	87	91	52	45	45	86	.270	R	R	6-5	215	5-25-78	1998	Elwood, Neb.
Kolb, Dan	1	0	0.00	1	0	0	0	2	0	0	0	1	0	.000	R	R	6-4	215	3-29-75	1995	Walnut, Ill.
Lee, Corey	5	12	5.31	25	17	1	0	125	117	78	74	51	103	.250	B	L	6-2	185	12-26-74	1996	Raleigh, N.C.
Lewis, Colby	10	10	4.50	25	25	1	0	156	150	85	78	62	162	.252	R	R	6-4	215	8-2-79	1999	Bakersfield, Calif.
Lundberg, Spike	5	3	3.48	18	8	1	6	67	75	27	26	9	41	.286	R	R	6-1	185	5-4-77	1997	San Diego, Calif.
Martinez, Jose	6	6	4.73	24	13	0	0	93	98	61	49	39	58	.265	R	R	6-0	165	2-4-75	1995	Santiago, D.R.
Mobley, Kevin	3	0	3.96	36	1	0	0	75	71	40	33	32	58	.256	R	R	6-7	245	1-26-75	1997	Vidalia, Ga.
Moreno, Juan	1	1	0.00	6	0	0	1	9	6	1	0	3	10	.222	L	L	6-1	205	2-28-77	1994	Cagua, Venez.
Myette, Aaron	1	0	0.00	1	1	0	0	6	3	0	0	1	2	.142	R	R	6-4	195	9-26-77	1997	Gig Harbor, Wash.
Oliver, Darren	0	1	5.40	1	1	0	0	5	4	3	3	2	5	.235	R	L	6-2	220	10-6-70	1988	Southlake, Texas
Ozias, Todd	0	0	7.30	9	0	0	0	12	15	10	10	8	10	.312	R	R	6-1	185	8-19-76	1998	Coral Springs, Fla.
2-team (30 Shreveport)	3	3	3.56	39	0	0	0	68	62	31	27	30	42	.241	R	R					
Pearsall, J.J.	6	4	3.26	43	0	0	10	58	54	27	21	18	58	.243	L	L	6-2	202	9-9-73	1995	Burnt Hills, N.Y.
Pratt, Andy	8	10	4.61	27	26	3	0	168	175	99	86	57	132	.267	L	L	5-11	160	8-27-79	1998	Chino Valley, Ariz.
Ramirez, Erasmo	2	1	4.41	12	0	0	0	16	17	8	8	5	18	.269	L	L	6-0	180	4-29-76	1998	Santa Ana, Calif.
2-team (22 Shreveport)	4	1	2.90	34	1	0	1	50	42	18	16	10	57	.227							
Regilio, Nick	1	3	5.54	10	10	0	0	52	62	34	32	20	40	.296	R	R	6-2	185	9-4-78	1999	Deltona, Fla.
Silva, Doug	0	1	3.32	14	0	0	1	19	19	10	7	5	15	.253	R	R	6-3	190	7-8-79	1997	Miranda, Venez.
Snyder, Matt	1	0	8.10	4	0	0	0	10	14	9	9	3	6	.325	R	R	5-11	201	7-7-74	1995	Newtown, Pa.

FIELDING

Catcher	PCT	G	PO	A	E	DP	PB
Flores	.990	14	86	15	1	2	2
Je. Jones	.989	77	594	56	7	0	9
Taveras	.988	55	390	37	5	1	9

First Base	PCT	G	PO	A	E	DP
Berrios	1.000	1	9	2	0	0
Flores	.956	5	42	1	2	3
Garcia	1.000	4	37	3	0	0
Hafner	.993	78	672	40	5	54
Halloran	1.000	3	26	1	0	3
Ja. Jones	.988	29	235	10	3	14
Je. Jones	.974	9	70	4	2	12
Meliah	1.000	13	83	6	0	9

Second Base	PCT	G	PO	A	E	DP
Camilli	.974	48	103	120	6	21

	PCT	G	PO	A	E	DP
Garcia	1.000	1	1	2	0	0
Halloran	.969	15	28	35	2	7
Meliah	.970	30	58	73	4	20
B. Oliver	.921	9	15	20	3	3
Romano	.962	45	105	97	8	17
Velarde	1.000	3	4	9	0	0

Third Base	PCT	G	PO	A	E	DP
Blalock	.953	67	37	125	8	9
Camilli	1.000	2	0	2	0	0
Garcia	.934	62	42	114	11	7
Meliah	.750	5	1	5	2	2
Solano	.909	7	2	8	1	0
Velarde	1.000	2	1	3	0	0

Shortstop	PCT	G	PO	A	E	DP
Garcia	.000	1	0	0	0	0

		PCT	G	PO	A	E	DP
Meliah		.773	5	4	13	5	1
Solano		.971	113	181	358	16	65
Warriax		.959	23	28	65	4	6

Outfield	PCT	G	PO	A	E	DP
Berrios	.950	23	38	0	2	0
Cadiente	.976	56	78	5	2	0
Curtis	.917	5	11	0	1	0
Kapler	1.000	3	2	0	0	0
Meliah	1.000	10	16	2	0	1
Mench	.983	117	228	10	4	3
Piniella	.977	98	167	4	4	0
Wright	.984	110	240	4	4	1
Zywica	.923	20	22	2	2	0

CHARLOTTE   Class A

FLORIDA STATE LEAGUE

BATTING	AVG	G	AB	R	H	2B	3B	HR	RBI	BB	SO	SB	CS	SLG	OBP	B	T	HT	WT	DOB	1st Yr	Resides
Agramonte, Marcos	.324	10	37	2	12	3	3	0	3	0	7	1	2	.568	.324	B	R	5-11	153	12-29-80	1997	Santiago, D.R.
Angell, Rick	.217	46	161	12	35	5	0	0	10	10	30	4	5	.248	.274	R	R	5-9	175	11-24-76	1999	Rhinelander, Wis.
Barningham, Steve	.279	70	219	50	61	15	4	1	24	42	38	17	8	.397	.401	L	R	5-9	175	1-8-74	1998	Meridian, Idaho
Blalock, Hank	.380	63	237	46	90	19	1	7	47	26	31	7	4	.557	.437	L	R	6-1	192	11-21-80	1999	San Diego, Calif.
Botts, Jason	.167	4	12	1	2	1	0	0	4	4	0	0	0	.250	.375	B	R	6-6	245	7-26-80	2000	Paso Robles, Calif.
Cadiente, Brett	.279	68	272	39	76	14	5	1	21	26	44	10	8	.379	.343	L	L	5-11	180	6-17-77	1999	Mesa, Ariz.
Flores, Javier	.173	19	52	3	9	3	0	0	2	7	3	0	0	.231	.295	R	R	6-0	185	12-20-75	1997	Broken Arrow, Okla.
Gajewski, Matt	.139	26	79	4	11	4	1	1	4	12	26	0	0	.253	.253	R	R	6-2	205	10-8-77	1999	Ashley, Ill.
Garcia, Douglas	.243	127	473	40	115	17	7	4	51	27	78	11	4	.334	.289	L	L	6-1	165	4-25-79	1997	Barquisimeto, Venez.
Halloran, Matt	.227	26	88	12	20	9	0	1	8	3	20	1	1	.364	.269	R	R	6-2	185	3-3-78	1996	Niceville, Fla.
Jaile, Chris	.219	42	151	17	33	5	0	2	10	12	31	0	0	.291	.277	R	R	6-3	195	2-20-81	1999	Miami, Fla.
Jones, Jason	.283	102	375	50	106	26	2	15	81	56	48	1	3	.483	.364	B	R	6-3	210	10-17-76	1999	Marietta, Ga.
Koone, Chuck	.333	7	18	1	6	0	0	0	1	4	0		2	.333	.368	R	R	6-0	175	9-19-75	1998	Marion, N.C.
Martin, Tyler	.218	47	147	24	32	6	2	4	15	20	30	0	1	.367	.306	B	R	6-2	185	8-31-77	2000	West Melbourne, Fla.
Martinez, Ramon	.241	128	515	69	124	20	1	2	32	28	65	28	18	.295	.286	B	R	5-10	170	2-22-80	1998	San Cristobal, D.R.
Nina, Amuarys	.232	99	323	27	75	9	3		18	25	99	8	3	.307	.295	R	R	5-11	155	8-10-77	1995	Santo Domingo, D.R.
Nix, Laynce	.297	9	37	4	11	3	1	0	2	1	13	0	0	.432	.316	L	L	6-0	190	10-30-80	2000	Midland, Texas
Nowlin, Cody	.250	53	188	16	47	10	3	2	25	17	48	0	0	.367	.316	L	R	6-3	190	11-7-76	1998	Fresno, Calif.
Oliver, Brian	.238	8	21	2	5	0	0	0	1	0	0	0	0	.238	.238	R	R	5-10	170	11-7-76	1998	Antioch, Calif.
Rapp, Travis	.154	5	13	0	2	0	0	0	0	1	7	0	0	.154	.214	R	R	6-2	205	1-24-75	1997	Sebring, Fla.
Romano, Jason	.400	3	10	3	4	2	0	0	1	4	1	1	0	.600	.571	R	R	6-0	185	6-24-79	1997	Tampa, Fla.
Roper, Chad	.210	42	143	13	30	9	0	2	14	14	31	0	0	.315	.280	R	R	6-1	223	3-29-74	1992	Belton, S.C.
Swenson, Leland	.175	47	120	16	21	3	0	0	12	21	30	0	2	.200	.301	R	R	6-1	170	6-13-77	2000	Saginaw, Minn.
Torres, Freddy	.248	111	407	37	101	18	1	9	52	20	103	1	0	.364	.287	R	R	6-0	165	3-16-80	1997	Santiago, D.R.
Villegas, Ernest	.270	34	126	7	34	5	0	2	15	2	35	3	0	.357	.311	R	R	6-1	200	11-29-78	1999	Irving, Texas
Warriax, Brandon	.191	97	320	34	61	13	4	6	30	22	84	4	6	.313	.249	R	R	6-0	165	6-23-79	1997	Maxton, N.C.

GAMES BY POSITION: C—Flores 19, Gajewski 2, Jaile 30, Torres 87. **1B**—Gajewski 11, Jones 98, Rapp 1, Roper 1, Swenson 1, Villegas 29. **2B**—Agramonte 10, Halloran 22, Martin 2, Martinez 94, Swenson 13. **3B**—Blalock 62, Gajewski 5, Halloran 5, Martin 36, Roper 24, Swenson 9. **SS**—Martinez 34, Swenson 10, Warriax 97. **OF**—Angell 45, Barningham 67, Botts 3, Cadiente 67, Garcia 125, Jones 1, Koone 6, Nina 93, Nix 9, Romano 3, Swenson 6, Villegas 1.

PITCHING	W	L	ERA	G	GS	CG	SV	IP	H	R	ER	BB	SO	AVG	B	T	HT	WT	DOB	1st Yr	Resides
Backsmeyer, Justin	1	2	3.75	33	0	0	0	60	56	32	25	42	47	.251	R	R	6-4	205	1-24-80	1998	Ballwin, Mo.
Beech, Matt	0	0	0.00	1	1	0	0	5	3	1	0	2	7	.187	L	L	6-2	195	1-20-72	1994	Clearwater, Fla.
Cedeno, Jovanny	0	0	1.86	3	3	0	0	10	3	2	2	5	12	.093	R	R	6-0	170	10-25-79		La Romana, D.R.
Cook, Derrick	0	0	0.00	2	2	0	0	8	7	2	0	1	5	.225	R	R	6-2	195	8-6-75	1996	Staunton, Va.
Dittfurth, Ryan	9	6	3.48	27	24	2	0	147	123	66	57	66	134	.227	R	R	6-6	180	10-18-79	1998	Plano, Texas
Dominguez, Jose	1	0	3.60	2	0	0	0	5	4	2	2	1	5	.235	R	R	6-2	180	8-7-82	2000	Valverde, D.R.

PITCHING	W	L	ERA	G	GS	CG	SV	IP	H	R	ER	BB	SO	AVG	B	T	HT	WT	DOB	1st Yr	Resides
Figueroa, Carlos	2	4	2.48	44	0	0	3	69	50	27	19	39	51	.211	L	L	6-1	190	10-5-79	1997	Carolina, P.R.
Garcia, Reynaldo	5	10	3.56	35	16	0	4	116	107	62	46	45	111	.247	R	R	6-3	170	4-15-78	1997	Santo Domingo, D.R.
Gardner, Hayden	1	0	1.59	1	1	0	0	6	5	1	1	2	3	.250	R	R	6-2	200	10-7-80	2000	Stafford, Va.
Graham, Tom	2	2	2.66	9	0	0	1	24	13	7	7	9	20	.168	R	R	6-7	250	1-26-78	2000	Modesto, Calif.
Haring, Brett	1	1	2.36	17	2	0	1	46	41	17	12	13	22	.241	R	L	5-11	180	2-7-75	1997	Coleman, Mich.
Hawkins, Chad	2	1	3.71	4	4	0	0	17	18	7	7	3	8	.281	R	R	6-7	205	7-24-78	2000	Euless, Texas
Huffaker, Mike	4	3	1.88	43	0	0	1	77	60	25	16	39	67	.222	R	R	6-2	215	8-10-75	1997	Florence, Ala.
Jones, Kiki	0	1	18.69	3	0	0	0	4	9	9	9	4	2	.428	R	R	5-11	175	6-8-70	1989	Tampa, Fla.
Kolb, Dan	1	2	3.86	7	3	0	0	19	21	8	8	2	16	.276	R	R	6-4	215	3-29-75	1995	Walnut, Ill.
Kosderka, Matt		1	6.75	7	0	0	0	12	16	11	9	6	10	.320	R	R	6-2	215	4-13-76	1998	Roseburg, Ore.
Lewis, Colby	1	0	0.00	1	0	0	0	4	0	0	0	0	8	.000	R	R	6-4	215	8-2-79	1999	Bakersfield, Calif.
Montero, Jose	0	4	10.57	6	0	0	0	8	9	10	9	7	5	.300	R	R	6-2	190	9-14-78	1996	Lara, Venez.
Moreno, Edwin	8	9	4.03	28	28	1	0	152	142	83	68	51	92	.246	R	R	6-1	170	7-30-80	1998	El Mojan, Venez.
Ramirez, Victor	0	3	11.00	3	3	0	0	9	11	16	11	13	11	.297	R	R	6-1	175	10-25-80	1997	La Romana, D.R.
Regilio, Nick	6	2	1.55	11	11	1	0	64	47	16	11	16	60	.200	R	R	6-2	185	9-4-78	1999	Deltona, Fla.
Rodriguez, Luis		3	7.58	5	5	0	0	19	20	17	16	20	15	.285	R	R	6-2	185	7-24-81	1998	Caracas, Venez.
Runner, Greg	3	4	2.93	50	0	0	30	68	66	26	22	28	66	.260	R	R	6-2	200	4-5-79	2000	The Woodlands, Texas
Russ, Chris	5	2	3.47	13	12	0	0	70	67	36	27	19	56	.250	L	L	6-3	185	10-26-79	2000	Laurel, Md.
Silva, Doug	3	1	2.29	23	1	0	1	55	45	16	14	10	50	.228	R	R	6-3	190	7-8-79	1997	Miranda, Venez.
Snyder, Matt	0	1	32.40	1	1	0	0	2	7	6	6	1	2	.636	R	R	5-11	201	7-7-74	1995	Newtown, Pa.
Stamler, Keith	8	4	2.48	23	11	1	0	87	64	35	24	28	61	.205	R	R	6-2	177	8-20-79	2000	Stockholm, N.J.
Valdez, Domingo	3	4	4.89	9	9	0	0	42	36	26	23	19	40	.225	R	R	6-3	220	6-27-80	1998	Corpus Christi, Texas

SAVANNAH — Class A

SOUTH ATLANTIC LEAGUE

BATTING	AVG	G	AB	R	H	2B	3B	HR	RBI	BB	SO	SB	CS	SLG	OBP	B	T	HT	WT	DOB	1st Yr	Resides
Acevedo, Inocencio	.232	109	392	52	91	14	6	2	26	23	79	34	11	.314	.284	R	R	5-10	155	6-15-79	1997	Santo Domingo, D.R.
Agramonte, Marcos	.183	72	252	20	46	8	2	3	19	3	62	8	8	.266	.194	R	R	5-11	153	12-29-80	1997	Santiago, D.R.
Botts, Jason	.309	114	392	63	121	24	2	9	50	53	88	13	7	.449	.416	B	R	6-6	245	7-26-80	2000	Paso Robles, Calif.
Bryan, Jason	.125	26	72	5	9	1	0	0	8	13	28	1	1	.139	.264	R	R	6-2	195	11-18-81	1999	Brooklyn, N.Y.
Cruz, Orlando	.184	34	114	3	21	0	0	1	6	3	31	1	4	.211	.217	R	R	6-0	170	10-5-81	1999	Juncos, P.R.
Dees, Charlie	.250	41	140	16	35	6	2	5	19	13	52	1	3	.429	.310	R	R	6-2	220	7-19-77	1999	Montgomery, Ala.
Dill, Jason	.121	43	132	8	16	4	0	1	7	22	35	1	0	.174	.247	L	L	6-1	200	9-22-78	2001	Punta Gorda, Fla.
Encarnacion, Edwin	.306	45	170	23	52	9	2	4	25	12	34	3	3	.453	.355	R	R	6-1	175	1-7-83	2000	Caguas, P.R.
Esquivel, Lale	.237	51	177	13	42	10	0	5	20	11	43	0	1	.379	.285	R	R	6-3	215	11-4-77	2001	Arlington, Texas
Evans, Austin	.197	51	147	18	29	5	0	0	5	12	27	5	2	.231	.263	L	L	5-8	155	3-28-78	2000	Buda, Texas
Gajewski, Matt	.238	30	84	7	20	2	0	2	8	10	30	0	2	.333	.323	R	R	6-2	205	10-8-77	1999	Ashley, Ill.
Heard, Scott	.228	77	268	25	61	13	1	5	36	30	71	1	2	.340	.308	L	R	6-2	190	9-2-81	2000	San Diego, Calif.
Hewes, Robert	.283	27	92	14	26	4	2	0	8	10	18	0	2	.370	.380	R	R	5-10	180	6-27-75	1997	Mesa, Ariz.
Koone, Chuck	.215	71	247	31	53	5	1	2	11	23	66	8	4	.267	.279	B	R	6-2	185	9-19-75	1998	Marion, N.C.
Martin, Tyler	.150	35	107	7	16	1	1	0	4	13	28	1	2	.178	.254	R	R	6-2	185	8-31-77	2000	West Melbourne, Fla.
Matos, Angel	.200	26	65	6	13	2	0	0	4	4	27	0	0	.231	.257	R	R	5-10	160	1-2-80	1997	Santiago, D.R.
Mongeluzzo, Anthony	.248	72	258	32	64	14	3	7	35	21	67	9	1	.407	.319	R	R	6-1	210	11-23-78	2000	Huntington, N.Y.
Morban, Jose	.251	122	474	71	119	20	11	8	47	42	119	46	18	.390	.313	R	R	6-1	170	12-2-79	1997	Santiago, D.R.
Nix, Laynce	.278	104	407	50	113	26	8	8	59	37	94	9	6	.440	.337	L	L	6-0	190	10-30-80	2000	Midland, Texas
Pack, Brandon	.220	99	327	37	72	17	1	5	34	33	111	4	6	.324	.293	B	R	6-3	215	1-22-79	2000	Salt Lake City, Utah
Stockton, Brad	.176	6	17	1	3	0	0	1	4	4	1	0	0	.353	.333	L	R	6-0	180	7-28-79	2001	Marietta, Ga.
Sulbaran, Orlando	.333	2	6	0	2	1	0	0	2	1	0	0	0	.500	.429	R	R	6-2	160	11-16-81	1998	Maracaibo, Venez.
Villegas, Ernest	.223	39	130	22	29	4	0	8	21	6	35	4	1	.438	.308	R	R	6-1	200	11-29-78	1999	Irving, Texas

GAMES BY POSITION: C—Gajewski 14, Heard 68, Matos 10, Pack 54, Sulbaran 2. **1B**—Botts 62, Dill 20, Esquivel 29, Gajewski 6, Hewes 1, Pack 18, Villegas 10. **2B**—Acevedo 66, Agramonte 63, Encarnacion 1, Martin 10. **3B**—Acevedo 14, Agramonte 4, Encarnacion 44, Gajewski 1, Hewes 25, Martin 10, Mongeluzzo 41, Pack 3. **SS**—Acevedo 22, Martin 1, Mongeluzzo 1, Morban 120. **OF**—Botts 45, Bryan 24, Cruz 34, Dees 35, Dill 26, Evans 46, Koone 64, Mongeluzzo 26, Nix 103, Stockton 4, Villegas 15.

PITCHING	W	L	ERA	G	GS	CG	SV	IP	H	R	ER	BB	SO	AVG	B	T	HT	WT	DOB	1st Yr	Resides
Bowers, Rob	0	0	6.27	11	0	0	0	19	26	13	13	5	8	.333	R	R	6-4	210	10-25-77	2000	Crawfordsville, Ind.
Burke, Erick	2	6	3.99	34	4	0	1	77	81	47	34	22	69	.269	L	L	6-4	230	8-14-77	1999	Houston, Texas
Cavazos, Andy	6	10	5.53	29	19	1	0	122	149	87	75	63	96	.303	R	R	6-3	185	1-5-81	1999	Clute, Texas
Echols, Justin	5	9	3.80	36	13	1	3	123	88	58	52	63	156	.200	R	R	6-3	185	10-6-80	1999	Roby, Mo.
Feliciano, Ruben	0	1	7.98	6	0	0	0	15	16	14	13	7	6	.266	R	R	6-2	175	11-1-79	2001	Brooklyn, N.Y.
Gilbert, Rich	6	11	4.23	21	20	3	0	134	120	75	63	44	155	.237	L	L	6-2	180	11-14-79	2000	Clyde Park, Mont.
Graham, Tom	1	4	2.50	40	0	0	17	54	46	19	15	10	71	.233	R	R	6-7	250	1-26-78	2000	Modesto, Calif.
Hawkins, Chad	1	0	0.32	4	4	0	0	28	13	2	1	5	25	.134	R	R	6-7	205	7-24-78	2000	Euless, Texas
Luna, Brandon	2	1	0.00	11	0	0	2	14	8	3	0	8	16	.170	R	R	6-5	215	6-13-79	2001	Lompoc, Calif.
Mead, David		10	5.51	19	19	0	0	96	91	63	59	64	79	.255	R	R	6-5	180	3-21-81	1999	Sale Creek, Tenn.
Meisenheimer, Matt	0	1	13.50	3	3	0	0	7	11	11	10	7	4	.379	R	R	6-1	180	10-1-81	2000	Greenville, Texas
Ramirez, Victor	5	8	5.08	19	16	0	0	89	93	60	50	57	94	.274	R	R	6-1	175	10-25-80	1997	La Romana, D.R.
Rivard, Reggie	5	4	3.26	44	1	0	1	77	84	35	28	21	52	.273	L	R	6-2	198	3-13-78	2000	Bonnyville, Alberta
Rodriguez, Luis	5	5	3.71	16	16	1	0	78	60	38	32	30	88	.211	R	R	6-2	185	7-24-81	1998	Caracas, Venez.
Scuglik, Mike	0	1	8.48	27	0	0	0	40	54	45	38	27	29	.325	L	L	6-1	190	5-24-77	1999	Kenosha, Wis.
Stamler, Keith	2	1	2.16	7	1	0	0	17	13	7	4	3	16	.203	R	R	6-2	177	8-20-79	2000	Stockholm, N.J.
Valdez, Domingo	6	4	3.24	15	15	1	0	86	50	33	31	38	107	.168	R	R	6-3	220	6-27-80	1998	Corpus Christi, Texas
Vigeland, Ole	5	4	2.48	39	0	0	2	73	55	27	20	34	67	.209	R	R	6-1	185	10-26-76	1998	Redmond, Wash.
Wilson, C.J.	1	2	3.18	5	5	2	0	34	30	13	12	9	26	.252	L	L	6-2	195	11-18-81	2001	Huntington Beach, Calif.

PULASKI — Rookie

APPALACHIAN LEAGUE

BATTING	AVG	G	AB	R	H	2B	3B	HR	RBI	BB	SO	SB	CS	SLG	OBP	B	T	HT	WT	DOB	1st Yr	Resides
Bourgeois, Jason	.311	62	251	60	78	12	2	7	34	26	47	21	7	.458	.387	R	R	5-9	170	1-4-82	2000	Houston, Texas
Bryan, Jason	.199	55	176	26	35	7	0	8	23	25	75	3	1	.375	.314	R	R	6-2	195	11-18-81	1999	Brooklyn, N.Y.
Caperton, Freddy	.234	17	47	5	11	1	0	0	5	7	15	0	0	.255	.345	R	R	6-0	190	10-25-79	2000	Culpeper, Va.
Cruz, Orlando	.247	47	178	25	44	9	3	1	18	12	59	9	2	.348	.295	R	R	6-0	170	10-5-81	1999	Juncos, P.R.

BATTING	AVG	G	AB	R	H	2B	3B	HR	RBI	BB	SO	SB	CS	SLG	OBP	B	T	HT	WT	DOB	1st Yr	Resides
Dorsey, Ryan	.132	16	38	1	5	2	1	0	2	5	20	2	0	.237	.250	R	R	6-1	164	8-29-81	1999	Wheaton, Md.
Esquivel, Lale	.259	7	27	2	7	2	0	2	8	2	5	0	0	.556	.310	R	R	6-3	215	11-4-77	2001	Arlington, Texas
Heard, Scott	.298	32	114	24	34	6	1	5	20	12	31	3	1	.500	.359	L	R	6-2	190	9-2-81	2000	San Diego, Calif.
Jaile, Chris	.250	29	100	15	25	5	0	0	12	13	20	0	0	.300	.339	R	R	6-3	195	2-20-81	1999	Miami, Fla.
Patty, Jason	.271	53	177	26	48	4	3	5	32	10	47	6	3	.412	.345	L	R	5-11	165	7-12-79	2001	El Dorado, Kan.
Perea, Jean	.305	68	256	40	78	15	0	3	39	24	53	13	1	.398	.370	R	R	6-3	175	1-28-79	1996	Zulia, Venez.
Rollins, Antwon	.254	65	240	43	61	15	2	12	37	16	80	18	1	.483	.314	R	R	6-1	195	3-18-80	1998	Alameda, Calif.
Shelley, Randall	.249	67	233	47	58	18	1	9	43	35	81	8	2	.451	.363	R	R	6-4	200	1-12-80	2001	Trabuco Canyon, Calif.
Stockton, Brad	.259	64	232	43	60	18	4	7	41	40	67	3	3	.461	.367	L	R	6-0	180	7-28-79	2001	Marietta, Ga.
Volquez, Julio	.219	48	178	25	39	10	2	0	15	4	37	11	6	.298	.249	B	R	5-11	150	7-24-80	1998	San Cristobal, D.R.

GAMES BY POSITION: C—Caperton 16, Heard 28, Jaile 28, Perea 1. **1B**—Esquivel 1, Perea 67, Shelley 1. **2B**—Bourgeois 61, Dorsey 6, Patty 2. **3B**—Dorsey 1, Patty 2, Shelley 67. **SS**—Dorsey 5, Patty 18, Volquez 48. **OF**—Bryan 35, Cruz 45, Patty 17, Rollins 62, Stockton 48.

PITCHING	W	L	ERA	G	GS	CG	SV	IP	H	R	ER	BB	SO	AVG	B	T	HT	WT	DOB	1st Yr	Resides
Abraham, Paul	3	2	4.94	15	0	0	2	31	26	22	17	16	28	.222	R	R	6-1		1-10-80	2001	Centreville, Va.
Beltre, Omar	6	3	3.38	13	12	0	0	69	56	28	26	23	83	.222	R	R	6-3	192	8-24-82	2000	Santo Domingo, D.R.
Berry, Casey	4	2	3.92	14	1	0	2	41	40	20	18	15	38	.243	R	R	6-1	180	10-30-80	2000	Granite, Okla.
Bowers, Rob	1	1	4.00	4	0	0	0	9	13	7	4	4	7	.317	R	R	6-4	210	10-25-77	2000	Crawfordsville, Ind.
Bradshaw, Chris	2	2	3.97	14	3	0	1	48	42	28	21	14	52	.227	R	R	6-4	210	2-16-79	2001	Fort Worth, Texas
Bright, Nathan	1	3	5.66	12	0	0	0	21	31	18	13	10	16	.336	R	R	6-3	180	10-6-79	2001	Byers, Colo.
Feliciano, Ruben	0	0	0.00	4	0	0	1	8	1	0	0	4	6	.045	R	R	6-2	175	11-4-79	2000	Brooklyn, N.Y.
Gardner, Hayden	4	4	2.48	13	13	2	0	83	71	32	23	15	70	.224	R	R	6-2	200	10-7-80	2000	Stafford, Va.
Jimenez, Kelvin	0	3	6.28	4	4	0	0	14	24	14	10	4	10	.352	R	R	6-2	153	10-27-82	2000	Santo Domingo, D.R.
Keiter, Ben	4	2	4.33	10	10	0	0	44	30	23	21	20	42	.188	R	R	6-3	210	4-23-80	2001	Arvada, Colo.
Marcano, Luis	3	2	3.71	11	0	0	5	27	27	15	11	8	27	.264	R	R	6-0	176	1-12-81	1998	Cumana, Venez.
Moravek, Rob	4	2	3.57	13	11	0	0	63	70	34	25	17	54	.283	R	R	6-4	205	2-20-80	2001	Alpharetta, Ga.
Paustian, Mike	2	1	3.38	14	2	0	5	29	25	16	11	16	27	.229	R	R	6-4	215	3-20-81	2001	Clovis, Calif.
Ramos, Eddy	2	1	4.83	17	0	0	3	32	39	20	17	8	30	.300	B	R	6-1	170	9-28-78	1996	Santiago, D.R.
Truselo, Randy	1	2	8.00	4	4	0	0	18	27	24	16	7	16	.325	R	R	6-3	190	1-11-81	2000	New Castle, Del.
Wilson, C.J.	1	0	0.96	8	8	0	0	38	24	6	4	9	49	.177	L	L	6-2	195	11-18-80	2001	Huntington Beach, Calif.

PORT CHARLOTTE — Rookie

GULF COAST LEAGUE

BATTING	AVG	G	AB	R	H	2B	3B	HR	RBI	BB	SO	SB	CS	SLG	OBP	B	T	HT	WT	DOB	1st Yr	Resides
Angell, Rick	.364	3	11	1	4	0	1	0	0	0	2	0	0	.545	.364	R	R	5-9	175	11-24-76	1999	Rhinelander, Wis.
Bunch, J.C.	.333	35	102	16	34	7	3	2	19	13	12	7	2	.520	.414	R	R	6-1	205	10-19-78	2001	Austin, Texas
Buscher, Greg	.240	40	121	14	29	9	2	1	10	11	35	1	0	.372	.313	R	R	6-0	200	10-26-82	2001	Jacksonville, Fla.
Cabrera, Ulises	.286	42	126	26	36	9	1	0	8	23	32	15	2	.373	.438	R	R	5-10	180	3-26-78	2001	Hawthorne, Calif.
Carroll, Rich	.259	48	158	22	41	15	1	1	18	13	37	2	0	.386	.316	R	R	6-3	225	12-24-79	2001	Nokomis, Fla.
Charles, Julin	.241	52	187	23	45	15	4	1	22	12	41	17	2	.380	.287	R	R	6-0	175	10-31-82	2000	Guaymate, D.R.
Gonzalez, Jose	.239	52	180	23	43	4	2	0	14	22	40	21	7	.283	.335	B	R	5-10	140	2-11-81	1998	Cumana, Venez.
Guy, Jason	.207	47	140	17	29	7	4	0	15	11	45	5	3	.314	.268	L	L	5-10	175	4-30-82	2001	Fort Myers, Fla.
Khairy, Masjid	.255	40	141	15	36	2	3	0	16	9	34	26	3	.312	.310	B	R	5-9	163	2-13-81	2001	Compton, Calif.
Mateo, Alejandro	.153	32	72	6	11	1	1	0	7	16	30	6	3	.194	.315	R	R	6-1	170	1-14-82	1999	Azua, D.R.
Nowlin, Cody	.273	6	22	2	6	3	0	1	7	1	3	0	0	.545	.333	L	R	6-3	190	11-27-79	1998	Fresno, Calif.
Olivari, Reinaldo	.232	54	203	24	47	14	4	2	27	12	45	8	5	.369	.284	R	R	6-0	140	10-10-80	1997	Maracaibo, Venez.
Quintin, Luis	.042	10	24	0	1	0	0	2	3	11	2	1		.083	.179	R	R	6-0	193	2-1-83	2000	Bani, D.R.
Romano, Jason	.143	5	21	2	3	0	0	0	0	1	8	1	0	.143	.182	R	R	6-0	185	6-24-79	1997	Tampa, Fla.
Sandoval, Abigail	.207	36	111	14	23	3	2	1	9	3	20	3	2	.297	.233	R	R	5-11	165	1-23-82	2001	Bolivar, Venez.
Smith, Dustin	.223	34	103	16	23	2	0	1	16	13	14	2	2	.272	.333	R	R	6-2	210	5-8-81	2001	Girard, Kan.
Sulbaran, Orlando	.262	36	122	18	32	7	1	2	12	9	25	8	2	.385	.316	R	R	6-2	160	11-16-81	1998	Maracaibo, Venez.

GAMES BY POSITION: C—Bunch 6, Smith 31, Sulbaran 25. **1B**—Bunch 11, Carroll 41, Olivari 9, Sulbaran 1. **2B**—Gonzalez 44, Olivari 15, Romano 3. **3B**—Bunch 5, Buscher 30, Olivari 30. **SS**—Cabrera 38, Gonzalez 8, Sandoval 14. **OF**—Angell 3, Bunch 8, Carroll 2, Charles 49, Gonzalez 1, Guy 46, Khairy 38, Mateo 31, Olivari 1, Quintin 7, Romano 2, Smith 1, Sulbaran 7.

PITCHING	W	L	ERA	G	GS	CG	SV	IP	H	R	ER	BB	SO	AVG	B	T	HT	WT	DOB	1st Yr	Resides
Campbell, Andrew	2	2	4.56	14	0	0	5	24	25	15	12	9	11	.271	L	L	6-0	175	8-22-81	2001	Lebanon, Ore.
Cristobal, Luis	0	1	4.24	11	4	0	0	34	34	20	16	20	35	.267	R	R	6-1	170	11-1-79	1998	La Romana, D.R.
Devenney, Nick	0	1	9.30	17	0	0	1	20	35	28	21	20	14	.384	R	R	6-3	245	7-31-80	2001	Denham Springs, La.
Dominguez, Jose	4	2	4.01	11	9	1	0	58	56	29	26	12	55	.250	R	R	6-2	180	8-7-82	2001	Valverde, D.R.
Engels, Jackson	2	2	2.22	10	0	0	0	28	21	8	7	15	11	.234	L	L	6-2	175	10-19-82	2001	Sheridan, Wyo.
Hampton, Royce	2	2	4.19	12	4	0	1	43	38	23	20	15	29	.234	R	R	6-2	153	10-27-82	2000	Lehi, Utah
Jimenez, Kelvin	3	3	2.56	9	6	1	1	46	36	19	13	9	51	.214	R	R	6-1	170	1-12-81	1998	Santo Domingo, D.R.
Marcano, Luis	0	1	9.00	3	2	0	0	10	16	10	10	5	10	.390	R	R	6-0	176	1-12-81	1998	Cumana, Venez.
Masset, Nick	0	6	4.35	15	14	0	0	31	34	21	15	7	32	.280	R	R	6-4	190	5-17-82	2001	Largo, Fla.
Meisenheimer, Matt	3	3	5.56	15	0	0	1	34	49	22	21	18	30	.355	R	R	6-3	180	10-1-81	2000	Greenville, Texas
Mendoza, Jorge	5	5	4.50	11	6	1	0	52	51	29	26	17	51	.254	R	R	6-2	180	2-22-82	1999	Quibor, Venez.
Montero, Jose	0	0	1.29	5	1	0	0	7	4	1	1	1	6	.153	R	R	6-2	190	9-14-78	1996	Lara, Venez.
Murray, A.J.	3	3	1.86	12	8	0	0	53	48	15	11	10	45	.247	B	L	6-3	200	3-17-82	2001	Vernal, Utah
Rahrer, Josh	0	1	3.00	5	0	0	0	6	9	4	2	1	8	.346	R	R	6-3	195	12-11-80	1999	Emmett, Idaho
Smiley, Gerald	0	0	1.59	3	0	0	0	6	4	1	1	4	2	.200	R	R	6-0	200	10-1-82	2001	Seattle, Wash.
Truselo, Randy	0	3	0.53	7	5	0	0	34	30	10	2	15	24	.240	R	R	6-3	190	1-11-81	2000	New Castle, Del.

BY LARRY MILLSON

A cloud of uncertainty hung over the Blue Jays in 2001 as they completed their first losing season since 1997.

First-year owner Rogers Communications had expected more with an increased payroll to about $75 million and a new manager, Buck Martinez.

A few days before another third-place finish in the American League East, general manager Gord Ash was fired with two years remaining on his contract. Only a year earlier, chief executive officer Paul Godfrey had praised Ash for the job he had done under the previously uncertain ownership.

Hitting coach Cito Gaston, who led the Blue Jays to World Series championships as manager in 1992 and 1993, and third base coach Terry Bevington were also let go. Gaston was offered another job in the organization.

Attendance improved, but not by much. The average for 2001 was 23,694, compared with 22,468 in 2000. But it still represents a far cry from the glory days of the Blue Jays, when they routinely sold out SkyDome.

Despite an uplifting 17-9 start, the Blue Jays entered the all-star break at 42-46, 11 games out of first. They were 31-24 after Aug. 1 with a greatly revamped starting rotation.

Rookie righthander Brandon Lyon, who pitched in the New York-Penn League in 2000, made an immediate impact when added to the rotation. So did the return of Kelvim Escobar after he had spent all season in the bullpen. Roy Halladay was superb after his return to Toronto in early July from the minors, where he rebuilt his pitching game.

Opening Day starter Esteban Loaiza found himself shuttled between the bullpen and rotation late in the season. Other members of the early-season rotation departed for various reasons. Steve Parris was put on the

| Carlos Delgado | Josh Phelps |

PLAYERS OF THE YEAR

MAJOR LEAGUE: Carlos Delgado, 1b

Though his offensive numbers slipped from 2000, when he hit .344-41-137, Delgado still was the dominant offensive player in the Blue Jays lineup in 2001.

MINOR LEAGUE: Josh Phelps, c

His defense is a step behind his offense, but Phelps had a huge season with the bat in 2001. He led Double-A Tennessee in total bases, doubles, homers and RBIs.

disabled list and required shoulder surgery. Righthander Joey Hamilton was released. Lefthander Chris Michalak, a minor league veteran who had been the club's feel-good story early in the season, was moved to the bullpen and eventually was claimed on waivers by the Rangers.

Also lost to waivers was third baseman Tony Batista, who hit 41 homers in 2000. After struggling for the Blue Jays in the first two months, he was claimed by the Orioles in June.

There were some solid individual accomplishments on offense, though players such as Carlos Delgado had lower production than in 2000.

Shannon Stewart became the fourth Blue Jay to have a 200-hit season, finishing with 202. Jose Cruz Jr. became the club's second 30-30 man with 34 homers and 32 stolen bases. In his fourth stint with Toronto, Tony Fernandez had a club-record 16 pinch-hits. Second baseman Jeff Frye hit for the cycle against the Rangers on Aug. 17.

Lyon was one of several top prospects to make their major league debuts in 2001. Felipe Lopez stepped in at third base in the latter part of the season, while Cesar Izturis moved in at second base. Righthander Bob File became an important part of the bullpen.

In the minors just two clubs, Double-A Tennessee and Class A Dunedin, had winning seasons. Both failed to qualify for the playoffs.

There were some individual success stories, particularly at Tennessee. Catcher Josh Phelps was named the Southern League MVP after hitting .292-31-97. Orlando Hudson (.307-4-52) was the SL's all-star second baseman despite being called up to Triple-A in July. Righthander Chris Baker was named the league's pitcher of the year.

ORGANIZATION LEADERS

BATTING

*AVG	Aaron McEachran, Medicine Hat	.336
R	Reed Johnson, Tennessee	104
H	Reed Johnson, Tennessee	174
TB	Josh Phelps, Tennessee	273
2B	Josh Phelps, Tennessee	36
	Orlando Hudson, Syracuse/Tennessee	36
3B	Orlando Hudson, Syracuse/Tennessee	11
HR	Josh Phelps, Tennessee	31
RBI	Josh Phelps, Tennessee	97
BB	Shawn Fagan, Dunedin	86
SO	Justin Singleton, Tennessee/Charleston	164
SB	Rich Thompson, Syracuse/Dunedin	44

PITCHING

W	Chris Baker, Tennessee	15
L	Tracy Thorpe, Charleston	13
#ERA	Mike Smith, Tennessee/Charleston	2.26
G	Brian Bowles, Syracuse	66
CG	Chris Baker, Tennessee	4
	Scott Cassidy, Syracuse/Tennessee	4
SV	Matt DeWitt, Syracuse	27
	Jarrod Kingrey, Tennessee	27
IP	Mike Smith, Tennessee/Charleston	187
BB	Charles Kegley, Dunedin	76
SO	Mike Smith, Tennessee/Charleston	129

*Minimum 250 At-Bats #Minimum 75 Innings

TORONTO BLUE JAYS

Manager: Buck Martinez

2001 Record: 80-82, .494 (3rd, AL East)

BATTING	AVG	G	AB	R	H	2B	3B	HR	RBI	BB	SO	SB	CS	SLG	OBP	B	T	HT	WT	DOB	1st Yr	Resides
Batista, Tony	.207	72	271	29	56	11	1	13	45	13	66	0	1	.399	.251	R	R	6-0	205	12-9-73	1992	Valverde, D.R.
Bush, Homer	.306	78	271	32	83	11	1	3	27	8	50	13	4	.387	.336	R	R	5-10	180	11-12-72	1991	Keller, Texas
Castillo, Alberto	.198	66	131	9	26	4	0	1	4	7	30	1	1	.252	.255	R	R	6-0	200	2-10-70	1987	Port St. Lucie, Fla.
Cruz, Jose	.274	146	577	92	158	38	4	34	88	45	138	32	5	.530	.326	B	R	6-0	200	4-19-74	1995	Houston, Texas
Delgado, Carlos	.279	162	574	102	160	31	1	39	102	111	136	3	0	.540	.408	L	R	6-3	230	6-25-72	1989	Aguadilla, P.R.
Fernandez, Tony	.305	48	59	5	18	4	0	1	12	1	8	0	1	.424	.323	B	R	6-2	195	6-30-62	1980	Boca Raton, Fla.
Fletcher, Darrin	.226	134	416	36	94	20	0	11	56	24	43	0	1	.353	.274	L	R	6-2	205	10-3-66	1987	Oakwood, Ill.
Freel, Ryan	.273	9	22	1	6	1	0	0	3	1	4	2	1	.318	.333	R	R	5-10	185	3-8-76	1995	Jacksonville, Fla.
Frye, Jeff	.246	74	175	24	43	6	1	2	15	12	18	2	1	.326	.305	R	R	5-9	170	8-31-66	1988	Mansfield, Texas
Fullmer, Brad	.274	146	522	71	143	31	2	18	83	38	88	5	2	.444	.326	L	R	6-0	215	1-17-75	1994	Chatsworth, Calif.
Gonzalez, Alex	.253	154	636	79	161	25	5	17	76	43	149	18	11	.388	.303	R	R	6-0	195	4-8-73	1991	Coral Gables, Fla.
Izturis, Cesar	.269	46	134	19	36	6	2	2	9	2	15	8	1	.388	.279	B	R	5-9	175	2-10-80	1996	Barquisimeto, Venez.
Latham, Chris	.274	43	73	12	20	3	1	2	10	10	28	4	1	.425	.369	B	R	6-0	198	5-26-73	1991	Las Vegas, Nev.
Lopez, Felipe	.260	49	177	21	46	5	4	5	23	12	39	4	3	.418	.304	R	R	6-0	175	5-12-80	1998	Apopka, Fla.
Lopez, Luis	.244	41	119	10	29	4	0	3	10	8	16	0	0	.353	.291	R	R	6-0	185	10-5-73	1996	Corpus Christi, Texas
Mondesi, Raul	.252	149	572	88	144	26	4	27	84	73	128	30	11	.453	.342	R	R	5-11	230	3-12-71	1988	San Cristobal, D.R.
Phelps, Josh	.000	8	12	3	0	0	0	0	1	2	5	1	0	.000	.143	R	R	6-3	215	5-12-78	1996	Rathdrum, Idaho
Simmons, Brian	.178	60	107	8	19	5	0	2	8	8	26	1	0	.280	.239	B	R	6-2	190	9-4-73	1995	McMurray, Pa.
Stewart, Shannon	.316	154	640	103	202	44	7	12	60	46	72	27	10	.463	.371	R	R	6-1	205	2-25-74	1992	Miami, Fla.
Wells, Vernon	.313	30	96	14	30	8	0	1	6	5	15	5	0	.427	.350	R	R	6-1	210	12-8-78	1997	Arlington, Texas
Woodward, Chris	.190	37	63	9	12	3	2	2	5	1	14	0	1	.397	.203	R	R	6-0	173	6-27-76	1995	Chino, Calif.

PITCHING	W	L	ERA	G	GS	CG	SV	IP	H	R	ER	BB	SO	AVG	B	T	HT	WT	DOB	1st Yr	Resides
Beirne, Kevin	0	0	12.86	5	0	0	0	7	13	10	10	6	5	.393	L	R	6-4	210	1-1-74	1995	The Woodlands, Texas
Borbon, Pedro	2	4	3.71	71	0	0	0	53	48	24	22	12	45	.243	L	L	6-1	224	11-15-67	1988	Houston, Texas
Bowles, Brian	0	0	0.00	2	0	0	0	4	4	0	0	1	4	.285	R	R	6-5	220	8-18-76	1995	Manhattan Beach, Calif.
Carpenter, Chris	11	11	4.09	34	34	3	0	216	229	112	98	75	157	.274	R	R	6-6	225	4-27-75	1994	Bedford, N.H.
Coco, Pasqual	1	0	4.40	7	1	0	0	14	12	8	7	6	9	.226	R	R	6-1	180	9-8-77	1995	Santo Domingo, D.R.
DeWitt, Matt	0	2	3.79	16	0	0	0	19	22	8	8	10	13	.293	R	R	6-3	210	9-4-77	1995	Las Vegas, Nev.
Escobar, Kelvim	6	8	3.50	59	11	1	0	126	93	51	49	52	121	.204	R	R	6-1	210	4-11-76	1992	Caracas, Venez.
Eyre, Scott	1	2	3.45	17	0	0	0	2	16	15	6	6	7	16	.263	L	L	6-1	200	5-30-72	1991	West Valley, Utah
File, Bob	5	3	3.27	60	0	0	0	74	57	28	27	29	38	.220	R	R	6-4	215	1-28-77	1998	Philadelphia, Pa.
Frascatore, John	1	0	2.20	12	0	0	0	16	16	4	4	4	9	.246	R	R	6-1	223	2-4-70	1991	New Port Richey, Fla.
Halladay, Roy	5	3	3.16	17	16	1	0	105	97	41	37	25	96	.241	R	R	6-6	230	5-14-77	1995	Arvada, Colo.
Hamilton, Joey	5	8	5.89	22	22	0	0	122	170	88	80	38	82	.339	R	R	6-4	240	9-9-70	1991	McDonough, Ga.
Koch, Billy	2	5	4.80	69	0	0	36	69	69	39	37	33	55	.265	R	R	6-3	215	12-14-74	1996	Largo, Fla.
Loaiza, Esteban	11	11	5.02	36	30	1	0	190	239	113	106	40	110	.307	R	R	6-3	215	12-31-71	1991	Gibsonia, Pa.
Lyon, Brandon	5	4	4.29	11	11	0	0	63	63	31	30	15	35	.265	R	R	6-1	175	8-10-79	2000	Salt Lake City, Utah
Michalak, Chris	6	7	4.62	24	18	0	0	115	133	66	59	49	57	.296	L	L	6-2	195	1-4-71	1993	Lemont, Ill.
Painter, Lance	0	1	7.85	10	0	0	0	18	27	17	16	11	14	.341	L	L	6-1	200	7-21-67	1990	Highlands Ranch, Colo.
Parris, Steve	4	6	4.60	19	19	1	0	106	126	60	54	41	49	.296	R	R	6-0	195	12-17-67	1988	Plainfield, Ill.
Plesac, Dan	4	5	3.57	62	0	0	1	45	34	18	18	24	68	.207	L	L	6-5	217	2-4-62	1983	Valparaiso, Ind.
Quantrill, Paul	11	2	3.04	80	0	0	2	83	86	29	28	12	58	.273	L	R	6-1	195	11-3-68	1989	Tarpon Springs, Fla.

FIELDING

Catcher	PCT	G	PO	A	E	DP	PB
Castillo	.989	66	324	25	4	0	2
Fletcher	.995	129	720	41	4	8	8
Phelps	1.000	7	28	2	0	0	0

First Base	PCT	G	PO	A	E	DP
Delgado	.994	161	1519	103	9	166
Fullmer	1.000	1	12	1	0	1
L. Lopez	1.000	5	10	1	0	0
Woodward	1.000	2	3	0	0	0

Second Base	PCT	G	PO	A	E	DP
Bush	.990	78	153	254	4	68
Freel	.969	7	11	20	1	4
Frye	.995	47	83	122	1	30
Izturis	.988	41	57	110	2	23
Woodward	.959	17	22	49	3	10

Third Base	PCT	G	PO	A	E	DP
Batista	.953	72	56	145	10	21
Frye	1.000	27	7	22	0	2

	PCT	G	PO	A	E	DP
F. Lopez	.940	47	26	100	8	6
L. Lopez	.936	28	17	56	5	4
Woodward	.839	10	6	20	5	5

Shortstop	PCT	G	PO	A	E	DP
Frye	1.000	2	0	2	0	0
Gonzalez	.987	154	249	509	10	120
Izturis	.964	6	16	11	1	5
F. Lopez	.917	3	6	5	1	1
Woodward	1.000	4	3	8	0	2

Outfield	PCT	G	PO	A	E	DP
Cruz	.990	143	286	5	3	1
Freel	.000	1	0	0	0	0
Frye	.000	1	0	0	0	0
Latham	1.000	31	47	2	0	1
Mondesi	.972	149	263	18	8	2
Simmons	1.000	37	59	1	0	0
Stewart	.981	142	257	7	5	0
Wells	.969	30	61	2	2	0

Raul Mondesi

LARRY GOREN

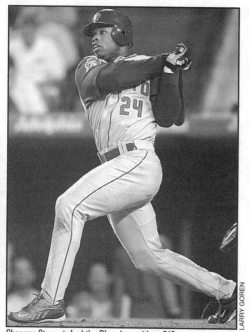

Shannon Stewart: Led the Blue Jays with a .316 average

Billy Koch: Notched 36 saves

FARM SYSTEM

Director, Player Development: Jim Hoff.

Class	Farm Team	League	W	L	Pct.	Finish*	Manager(s)	First Yr.
AAA	Syracuse (N.Y.) SkyChiefs	International	71	73	.493	6th (14)	Omar Malave	1978
AA	Tennessee Smokies	Southern	80	60	.571	2nd (10)	Rocket Wheeler	1980
A#	Dunedin (Fla.) Blue Jays	Florida State	71	64	.526	3rd (14)	Marty Pevey	1987
A	Charleston (W.Va.) Alley Cats	South Atlantic	51	87	.370	16th (16)	Rolando Pino	2001
A	Auburn (N.Y.) Doubledays	New York-Penn	32	42	.432	11th (14)	Paul Elliott	2001
Rookie#	Medicine Hat (Alberta) Blue Jays	Pioneer	20	56	.263	8th (8)	Tom Bradley	1978

*Finish in overall standings (No. of teams in league) #Advanced level

SYRACUSE
Class AAA

INTERNATIONAL LEAGUE

BATTING	AVG	G	AB	R	H	2B	3B	HR	RBI	BB	SO	SB	CS	SLG	OBP	B	T	HT	WT	DOB	1st Yr	Resides
Balfe, Ryan	.253	51	190	22	48	10	1	5	24	18	55	1	2	.395	.319	B	R	6-1	180	11-11-75	1994	Cornwall, N.Y.
Bush, Homer	.250	9	32	11	8	2	0	0	3	3	6	0	0	.313	.342	R	R	5-10	180	11-12-72	1991	Keller, Texas
Carter, Shannon	.111	4	9	1	1	1	0	0	1	1	2	0	0	.222	.273	L	L	6-0	180	3-23-79	1997	El Reno, Okla.
Freel, Ryan	.260	85	319	60	83	21	3	5	33	42	42	22	9	.392	.357	R	R	5-10	185	3-8-76	1995	Jacksonville, Fla.
Haltiwanger, Garrick	.233	23	73	8	17	1	1	2	12	11	21	2	2	.356	.345	R	L	6-0	195	3-3-75	1996	Irmo, S.C.
Holbert, Aaron	.245	55	212	25	52	10	2	2	19	8	33	9	0	.340	.276	R	R	6-0	160	1-9-73	1990	St. Petersburg, Fla.
Hudson, Orlando	.304	55	194	31	59	14	3	4	27	23	34	11	3	.469	.378	B	R	6-0	175	12-12-77	1998	Darlington, S.C.
Hunter, Brian	.238	30	105	21	25	5	0	3	16	15	21	1	0	.371	.350	R	L	6-0	195	3-4-68	1987	Anaheim, Calif.
Izturis, Cesar	.292	87	342	32	100	16	3	2	35	10	22	24	9	.374	.310	B	R	5-9	175	2-10-80	1996	Barquisimeto, Venez.
Jones, Chris	.219	37	137	17	30	2	2	3	15	13	35	7	2	.328	.286	R	R	6-2	210	11-16-65	1984	Utica, N.Y.
Kremblas, Mike	.222	4	9	3	2	0	0	0	0	1	4	0	0	.222	.364	R	R	6-0	180	10-1-75	1998	Carroll, Ohio
Langaigne, Selwyn	.239	62	201	31	48	7	1	3	23	17	53	4	2	.328	.299	L	L	6-0	190	3-22-76	1994	Las Acaias, Venez.
Latham, Chris	.278	79	288	57	80	20	9	13	54	51	90	14	11	.545	.382	B	R	6-0	198	5-26-73	1991	Las Vegas, Nev.
Lawrence, Joe	.220	93	318	27	70	11	4	1	26	36	62	6	9	.289	.310	R	R	6-2	190	2-13-77	1996	Lake Charles, La.
Liniak, Cole	.241	103	344	40	83	21	1	10	49	32	55	1	2	.395	.307	R	R	6-1	190	8-23-76	1995	Encinitas, Calif.
Lopez, Felipe	.279	89	358	65	100	19	7	16	44	30	94	13	5	.506	.337	B	R	6-0	175	5-12-80	1998	Apopka, Fla.
Lopez, Luis	.324	87	339	57	110	26	2	10	73	39	31	1	1	.501	.391	R	R	6-0	205	10-5-73	1996	Corpus Christi, Texas
Martinez, Casey	.600	5	5	1	3	0	0	0	1	0	1	0	0	.600	.600	R	R	5-11	200	8-31-77	2000	Holmdel, N.J.
Molina, Izzy	.305	73	256	34	78	20	1	16	38	18	52	1	0	.578	.353	R	R	6-1	200	6-3-71	1990	Miami, Fla.
Perez, Jersen	.125	5	16	1	2	1	0	0	0	1	7	0	0	.188	.176	R	R	5-10	185	1-20-76	1996	Lynn, Mass.
Sanders, Deion	.252	25	107	15	27	7	1	1	6	7	12	5	4	.364	.304	L	L	6-1	195	8-9-67	1988	Alpharetta, Ga.
2-team (19 Louisville)	.337	44	181	27	61	11	6	2	15	9	16	11	7	.497	.381							
Simmons, Brian	.264	52	201	24	53	10	1	2	20	19	36	4	5	.353	.332	B	R	6-2	190	9-4-73	1995	McMurray, Pa.
Thompson, Andy	.230	48	178	15	41	5	1	7	28	14	42	2	4	.388	.294	R	R	6-3	220	8-28-75	1995	Cottage Grove, Wis.
Thompson, Rich	.245	17	53	5	13	0	1	0	3	4	12	5	1	.283	.293	L	R	6-3	180	4-23-79	2000	Montrose, Pa.
Wells, Vernon	.281	107	413	57	116	27	4	12	52	29	68	15	11	.453	.333	R	R	6-1	210	12-8-78	1997	Arlington, Texas

BATTING

BATTING	AVG	G	AB	R	H	2B	3B	HR	RBI	BB	SO	SB	CS	SLG	OBP	B	T	HT	WT	DOB	1st Yr	Resides
Wise, Dewayne	.231	3	13	1	3	0	0	0	0	8	0	1	.231	.231	L	L	6-1	180	2-24-78	1997	Chapin, S.C.
Woodward, Chris	.306	51	193	29	59	14	3	11	31	16	40	0	0	.580	.360	R	R	6-0	173	6-27-76	1995	Chino, Calif.

PITCHING

PITCHING	W	L	ERA	G	GS	CG	SV	IP	H	R	ER	BB	SO	AVG	B	T	HT	WT	DOB	1st Yr	Resides
Banks, Willie	8	5	3.25	24	23	0	0	147	151	63	53	53	121	.265	R	R	6-1	200	2-27-69	1987	Miami, Fla.
Beirne, Kevin	1	1	1.57	18	0	0	0	29	24	6	5	3	17	.222	R	R	6-4	210	1-1-74	1995	The Woodlands, Texas
Bell, Jason	0	1	10.38	8	0	0	0	9	10	10	10	7	7	.277	R	R	6-3	210	9-30-74	1995	Orlando, Fla.
Bleazard, Dave	0	2	9.88	5	2	0	0	14	15	15	15	11	7	.277	R	R	6-0	175	3-7-74	1996	Tooele, Utah
Bowles, Brian	3	5	2.91	66	0	0	6	77	56	30	25	44	81	.199	R	R	6-5	220	8-18-76	1995	Manhattan Beach, Calif.
Cassidy, Scott	3	3	2.71	11	11	0	0	63	60	24	19	26	48	.246	R	R	6-2	175	10-3-75	1998	Clay, N.Y.
Chulk, Vinny	1	0	1.50	5	0	0	0	6	5	1	1	4	3	.238	R	R	6-2	185	12-19-78	2000	Miami, Fla.
Coco, Pasqual	8	6	4.66	22	22	0	0	122	128	67	63	50	82	.276	R	R	6-1	180	9-8-77	1995	Santo Domingo, D.R.
Comolli, Mark	0	0	0.00	1	1	0	0	4	4	1	0	1	1	.285	R	R	6-0	190	3-11-79	2001	Millville, Del.
Cornett, Brad	1	0	6.35	6	0	0	0	11	17	8	8	5	6	.361	R	R	6-3	190	2-4-69	1992	Odessa, Texas
Daneker, Pat	2	5	8.94	10	10	1	0	50	75	53	50	17	14	.353	R	R	6-3	195	1-4-76	1997	Williamsport, Pa.
DeWitt, Matt	3	2	2.78	53	0	0	27	58	45	20	18	17	44	.206	R	R	6-3	210	9-4-77	1995	Las Vegas, Nev.
Dickson, Jason	4	7	7.18	11	11	0	0	58	75	52	46	19	40	.320	L	R	6-0	195	3-30-73	1994	Chatham, New Brunswick
Dillinger, John	11	7	3.99	26	26	1	0	156	150	79	69	58	108	.255	R	R	6-5	240	8-28-73	1992	Dawson, Pa.
Espina, Rendy	6	1	3.64	36	0	0	0	47	41	26	19	17	33	.234	L	L	6-0	180	5-11-78	1995	Cabimas, Venez.
Eyre, Scott	4	6	3.18	62	2	0	0	79	67	30	28	26	96	.224	L	L	6-1	200	5-30-72	1991	West Valley, Utah
File, Bob	0	0	0.00	2	0	0	0	4	1	0	0	0	3	.083	R	R	6-4	215	1-28-77	1998	Philadelphia, Pa.
Flores, Neomar	0	0	3.86	2	1	0	0	7	4	3	3	2	2	.160	R	R	6-2	180	3-12-82	1998	Guarenas, Venez.
Frascatore, John	1	4	4.14	37	0	0	2	37	47	20	17	9	18	.307	R	R	6-1	223	2-4-70	1991	New Port Richey, Fla.
Halladay, Roy	1	0	3.21	2	2	0	0	14	12	5	5	0	13	.222	R	R	6-6	230	5-14-77	1995	Arvada, Colo.
Hendrickson, Mark	2	9	4.66	38	6	0	0	73	80	43	38	18	33	.273	L	L	6-9	230	6-23-74	1998	Mount Vernon, Wash.
Henry, Butch	6	4	4.02	12	12	1	0	78	91	38	35	9	49	.296	L	L	6-1	205	10-7-68	1987	El Paso, Texas
Lyon, Brandon	5	3	3.69	11	11	2	0	68	68	33	28	10	53	.256	R	R	6-1	175	8-10-79	2000	Salt Lake City, Utah
McClellan, Matt	3	3	3.27	29	1	0	2	52	49	21	19	20	44	.242	R	R	6-7	220	8-13-76	1997	Toledo, Ohio
Parris, Steve	0	0	4.70	2	2	0	0	8	6	4	4	2	8	.206	R	R	6-0	195	12-17-67	1989	Plainfield, Ill.
Renwick, Tyler	0	0	3.18	2	0	0	0	6	7	2	2	4	2	.333	R	R	6-4	206	8-12-78	1998	Langley, B.C.
Valdez, Santo	0	0	1.80	1	1	0	0	5	5	1	1	1	2	.312	R	R	6-1	170	3-30-82	1999	Bani, D.R.

FIELDING

Catcher	PCT	G	PO	A	E	DP	PB
Kremblas	.938	2	14	1	1	1	0
Lawrence	.994	75	502	37	3	1	15
Martinez	1.000	2	1	0	0	0	0
Molina	.987	70	451	19	6	6	1

First Base	PCT	G	PO	A	E	DP
Balfe	.983	12	113	5	2	13
Hunter	.990	23	199	8	2	19
Jones	1.000	5	58	3	0	2
Langaigne	.989	22	157	17	2	18
Lawrence	1.000	1	1	0	0	0
Lopez	1.000	80	728	45	0	78
Woodward	.971	4	33	1	1	3

Second Base	PCT	G	PO	A	E	DP
Bush	1.000	9	13	23	0	3
Freel	.953	10	18	23	2	2
Holbert	.982	29	67	93	3	27
Hudson	.989	53	106	163	3	34
Izturis	.992	26	50	77	1	18

	PCT	G	PO	A	E	DP
Liniak	.864	5	9	10	3	3
Lopez	.980	18	36	61	2	17
Woodward	1.000	4	7	13	0	2

Third Base	PCT	G	PO	A	E	DP
Balfe	.900	6	5	13	2	1
Freel	.885	8	8	15	3	2
Holbert	.857	13	6	24	5	0
Hudson	.909	5	4	6	1	0
Lawrence	.931	12	4	23	2	1
Liniak	.968	82	51	163	7	14
Lopez	.833	2	2	3	1	1
Lopez	1.000	6	3	11	0	2
Woodward	.957	21	20	47	3	7

Shortstop	PCT	G	PO	A	E	DP
Freel	.974	8	16	22	1	7
Holbert	1.000	2	2	3	0	1
Izturis	.949	57	104	174	15	45
Lawrence	.000	1	0	0	0	0
Lopez	.942	61	84	174	16	40

Perez	.950	5	5	14	1	2
Woodward	.907	12	12	37	5	8

Outfield	PCT	G	PO	A	E	DP
Balfe	1.000	10	18	1	0	0
Carter	1.000	4	10	0	0	0
Freel	.974	58	103	8	3	0
Haltiwanger	.981	21	51	0	1	0
Holbert	1.000	1	0	0	0	0
Hunter	1.000	3	8	0	0	0
Jones	.909	26	47	3	5	0
Kremblas	1.000	2	0	0	0	0
Langaigne	1.000	38	62	4	0	1
Latham	.965	77	159	7	6	0
Sanders	1.000	13	17	1	0	0
Simmons	.970	48	91	5	3	2
A. Thompson	.983	29	58	1	1	1
R. Thompson	1.000	17	43	1	0	0
Wells	.978	103	216	7	5	5
Wise	1.000	1	5	0	0	0

TENNESSEE

Class AA

SOUTHERN LEAGUE

BATTING	AVG	G	AB	R	H	2B	3B	HR	RBI	BB	SO	SB	CS	SLG	OBP	B	T	HT	WT	DOB	1st Yr	Resides
Alvarez, Jimmy	.227	8	22	4	5	0	1	0	1	4	6	1	0	.318	.346	B	R	5-10	168	10-4-79	1996	Santo Domingo, D.R.
Chiaffredo, Paul	.250	42	132	11	33	7	1	1	16	22	33	2	2	.341	.363	R	R	6-2	206	5-30-76	1997	San Jose, Calif.
Fleming, Ryan	.278	106	349	57	97	19	4	10	35	38	49	6	4	.441	.348	L	L	5-11	180	2-11-76	1998	Grove City, Ohio
Goudie, Jaime	.253	45	154	19	39	7	2	1	15	7	22	3	1	.344	.282	R	R	5-10	180	3-8-79	1998	Columbus, Ga.
Gross, Gabe	.244	11	41	8	10	1	0	3	11	6	12	0	1	.488	.373	L	R	6-3	205	10-21-79	2001	Dothan, Ala.
Haltiwanger, Garrick	.263	46	133	23	35	9	1	3	15	18	33	8	4	.414	.353	B	R	6-0	175	12-12-77	1998	Darlington, S.C.
Hudson, Orlando	.307	84	306	51	94	22	8	4	52	37	42	8	3	.471	.383	B	R	5-10	180	12-8-76	1998	Temecula, Calif.
Johnson, Reed	.314	136	554	104	174	29	4	13	74	45	79	42	12	.451	.383	R	R	5-10	180	12-8-76	1999	Las Acaias, Venez.
Langaigne, Selwyn	.274	19	62	6	17	4	0	0	7	3	11	1	2	.339	.318	L	L	6-0	190	3-22-76	1994	Las Acaias, Venez.
Logan, Matt	.206	96	277	32	57	12	1	9	34	28	82	3	1	.354	.288	L	R	6-3	210	7-22-79	1997	Brampton, Ontario
Lopez, Felipe	.222	19	72	12	16	2	1	2	4	9	23	4	0	.361	.309	B	R	6-0	175	5-12-80	1998	Apopka, Fla.
Loyd, Brian	.220	15	50	4	11	3	0	0	2	2	11	2	0	.280	.278	R	R	6-2	205	12-3-73	1996	Yorba Linda, Calif.
Peralta, Juan	.500	3	2	1	1	0	0	0	0	2	0	0	0	.500	.500	B	R	5-11	155	6-24-83	2000	Santiago Rodriguez, D.R.
Perez, Jersen	.282	116	422	60	119	23	4	4	49	30	96	14	3	.384	.334	R	R	6-0	210	10-28-74	1995	Mesa, Ariz.
Peters, Tony	.246	91	256	46	63	9	1	11	33	25	83	8	1	.418	.322	R	R	6-3	215	5-12-78	1996	Rathdrum, Idaho
Phelps, Josh	.292	136	486	95	142	36	1	31	97	80	127	3	3	.562	.406	R	R	5-11	185	4-1-75	1996	Stephenville, Texas
Rodriguez, Mike	.300	12	40	5	12	6	0	2	13	3	3	1	0	.600	.341	L	R	6-1	190	4-10-79	2001	Sparks, Md.
Singleton, Justin	.278	15	36	5	10	0	0	3	4	13	1	1	0	.278	.341	L	R	6-1	190	4-10-79	2001	Sparks, Md.
Weekly, Chris	.260	45	131	16	34	4	1	4	23	14	35	0	2	.397	.349	L	R	6-2	195	12-4-76	1999	Mesa, Ariz.
Werth, Jayson	.285	104	369	51	105	23	1	18	69	63	93	12	3	.499	.387	R	R	6-5	215	5-20-79	1997	Chatham, Ill.
Williams, Glenn	.255	130	487	63	124	28	0	11	65	45	120	1	5	.380	.321	B	R	6-2	195	7-18-77	1994	Chipping North, Australia
Wise, Dewayne	.239	87	351	44	84	13	6	8	44	21	58	13	5	.379	.283	L	L	6-1	180	2-24-78	1997	Chapin, S.C.

PITCHING	W	L	ERA	G	GS	CG	SV	IP	H	R	ER	BB	SO	AVG	B	T	HT	WT	DOB	1st Yr	Resides
Baker, Chris	15	6	3.37	28	26	4	1	179	162	73	67	42	121	.243	R	R	6-1	194	8-24-77	1999	Valencia, Calif.
Bauer, Peter	6	8	5.11	21	21	0	0	129	147	84	73	37	71	.283	L	R	6-7	250	11-6-78	2000	Hagerstown, Md.
Bleazard, Dave	0	0	1.35	3	3	0	0	20	15	3	3	5	11	.214	R	R	6-0	175	3-7-74	1996	Tooele, Utah

PITCHING

PITCHING	W	L	ERA	G	GS	CG	SV	IP	H	R	ER	BB	SO	AVG	B	T	HT	WT	DOB	1st Yr	Resides
Caraballo, Angel	3	3	5.47	26	5	1	1	53	51	36	32	21	36	.252	R	R	6-0	180	1-20-80	1997	Guanta, Venez.
Casey, Joe	4	3	4.72	42	0	0	1	61	74	36	32	16	42	.300	R	R	6-0	192	1-25-79	1997	Honeybrook, Pa.
Cassidy, Scott	6	6	3.44	16	15	4	0	97	78	45	37	27	81	.218	R	R	6-2	175	10-3-75	1998	Clay, N.Y.
Castellanos, Hugo	5	2	2.51	43	0	0	2	65	53	24	18	33	47	.224	R	R	6-4	204	6-30-80	1996	Nuevo Laredo, Mexico
Chacin, Gustavo	11	8	3.98	25	23	1	0	140	138	66	62	39	86	.256	L	L	5-11	185	12-4-80	1998	Maracaibo, Venez.
Chulk, Vinny	2	5	3.14	24	1	0	2	43	34	15	15	8	43	.226	R	R	6-2	185	12-19-78	2000	Miami, Fla.
Coco, Pasqual	0	1	3.94	3	3	0	0	16	13	7	7	5	13	.216	R	R	6-1	180	9-8-77	1995	Santo Domingo, D.R.
Dickson, Jason	2	1	3.31	5	5	0	0	33	30	12	12	11	21	.241	L	R	6-0	195	3-30-73	1994	Chatham, New Brunswick
Dimma, Doug	0	2	5.40	19	0	0	1	13	16	8	8	9	5	.333	R	L	5-11	175	7-3-78	1999	Richmond Hill, Ontario
File, Bob	0	0	3.00	3	0	0	1	3	3	1	1	0	2	.300	R	R	6-4	215	1-28-77	1998	Philadelphia, Pa.
Halladay, Roy	2	1	2.12	5	5	3	0	34	25	9	8	6	29	.201	R	R	6-6	230	5-14-77	1995	Arvada, Colo.
Hubbel, Travis	1	0	3.38	6	5	0	0	27	20	11	10	18	12	.219	R	R	6-0	190	6-27-79	1997	Edmonton, Alberta
Kingrey, Jarrod	5	3	2.47	51	0	0	27	55	41	17	15	32	52	.211	R	R	6-1	200	8-23-76	1998	Forston, Ga.
Lyon, Brandon	5	0	3.68	9	9	0	0	59	57	25	24	9	45	.252	R	R	6-1	175	8-10-79	2000	Salt Lake City, Utah
McClellan, Matt	2	2	2.41	19	0	0	1	19	17	10	5	8	20	.232	R	R	6-7	220	8-13-76	1997	Toledo, Ohio
Ozuna, Francisco	1	0	1.50	12	0	0	0	12	11	3	2	4	7	.250	L	L	6-2	180	5-17-81	1997	Santo Domingo, D.R.
Parris, Steve	0	0	0.00	1	1	0	0	3	2	0	0	1	2	.181	R	R	6-0	195	12-17-67	1989	Plainfield, Ill.
Payne, Jerrod	2	3	6.14	22	0	0	1	29	37	22	20	9	18	.303	R	R	5-10	198	8-27-77	2000	Jacksonville, Fla.
Reimers, Cameron	1	2	6.60	5	4	0	0	30	32	22	22	5	19	.273	R	R	6-5	205	9-15-78	1999	Missoula, Mont.
Smith, Mike	6	2	2.42	14	14	1	0	93	80	32	25	26	77	.225	R	R	5-11	195	11-9-77	2000	Westwood, Mass.
Woodards, Orlando	1	2	7.00	15	0	0	0	18	19	15	14	15	14	.267	R	R	6-2	200	1-2-78	1997	Sacramento, Calif.

FIELDING

Catcher	PCT	G	PO	A	E	DP	PB
Chiaffredo	.984	19	113	13	2	1	0
Loyd	.982	11	51	4	1	0	0
Peters	1.000	3	10	0	0	0	0
Phelps	.996	69	447	29	2	4	5
Rodriguez	1.000	1	1	0	0	0	0
Werth	.985	46	294	36	5	8	3

First Base	PCT	G	PO	A	E	DP
Chiaffredo	1.000	2	15	0	0	1
Langaigne	1.000	9	64	6	0	5
Logan	.987	93	716	50	10	59
Peters	.978	19	81	7	2	8
Rodriguez	.963	7	51	1	2	5
Weekly	.988	8	75	4	1	6
Werth	.992	28	227	14	2	22

Second Base	PCT	G	PO	A	E	DP
Williams	.982	8	50	4	1	8
Goudie	.960	45	101	141	10	28
Hudson	.979	72	131	203	7	46
Lopez	.923	6	16	20	3	6
Peralta	1.000	2	1	1	0	1
Perez	.964	7	16	11	1	5
Williams	.964	22	32	48	3	11

Third Base	PCT	G	PO	A	E	DP
Hudson	.971	13	7	27	1	4
Peters	.818	7	2	7	2	1
Rodriguez	.857	4	1	5	1	1
Weekly	.958	33	25	67	4	5
Williams	.934	98	62	223	20	27

Shortstop	PCT	G	PO	A	E	DP
Alvarez	.971	8	12	22	1	7
Lopez	.886	12	10	29	5	9
Perez	.939	108	159	304	30	54
Williams	.932	15	22	33	4	6

Outfield	PCT	G	PO	A	E	DP
Fleming	.981	97	153	6	3	0
Gross	1.000	9	25	3	0	1
Haltiwanger	.917	31	51	4	5	1
Johnson	.983	133	222	12	4	2
Langaigne	1.000	12	19	0	0	0
Peters	.984	66	118	8	2	2
Singleton	1.000	12	19	0	0	0
Wise	.976	86	198	9	5	5

DUNEDIN — Class A

FLORIDA STATE LEAGUE

BATTING

BATTING	AVG	G	AB	R	H	2B	3B	HR	RBI	BB	SO	SB	CS	SLG	OBP	B	T	HT	WT	DOB	1st Yr	Resides
Alvarez, Jimmy	.283	123	467	88	132	16	8	5	56	49	87	29	7	.392	.351	B	R	5-10	168	10-4-79	1996	Santo Domingo, D.R.
Bernhardt, Jossephang	.255	120	420	50	107	25	1	7	52	28	100	2	3	.369	.305	R	R	6-1	185	9-22-80	1996	San Pedro de Macoris, D.R.
Berry, Sean	.190	12	42	9	8	2	0	2	7	8	10	0	0	.381	.340	R	R	5-11	200	3-22-66	1986	Paso Robles, Calif.
Bush, Homer	.353	4	17	4	6	0	0	0	2	3	1	0	0	.353	.421	R	R	5-10	180	11-12-72	1991	Keller, Texas
Carter, Shannon	.273	48	161	25	44	7	1	0	17	5	44	6	6	.329	.306	L	L	6-0	185	3-23-79	1997	El Reno, Okla.
Cash, Kevin	.283	105	371	55	105	27	0	12	66	43	80	4	3	.453	.369	R	R	6-0	185	12-6-77	1999	Lutz, Fla.
Chiaffredo, Paul	.213	28	75	20	16	6	1	3	20	5	26	0	0	.394	.283	R	R	6-2	206	5-30-76	1997	San Jose, Calif.
Fagan, Shawn	.301	132	475	68	143	18	5	10	71	86	114	7	2	.423	.407	R	R	5-11	200	3-2-78	2000	Levittown, N.Y.
Frye, Jeff	.500	4	12	4	6	0	0	1	2	1	1	0	0	.500	.571	R	R	5-9	170	8-31-66	1988	Mansfield, Texas
Goudie, Jaime	.270	47	174	23	47	9	1	2	23	7	30	3	2	.368	.304	R	R	6-1	185	3-8-79	1997	Columbus, Ga.
Gross, Gabe	.302	35	126	23	38	9	2	4	15	26	29	4	2	.500	.426	L	R	6-3	205	10-21-79	2001	Dothan, Ala.
Keene, Kurt	.182	53	132	16	24	4	0	0	8	9	23	0	2	.212	.247	R	R	6-0	190	8-22-77	2000	Chattanooga, Tenn.
Kremblas, Mike	.191	49	141	17	27	6	1	0	15	18	34	0	3	.248	.305	R	R	6-0	180	10-1-75	1998	Carroll, Ohio
Martinez, Casey	.176	7	17	1	3	1	0	0	3	0	2	0	0	.235	.176	R	R	5-11	200	8-31-77	2000	Holmdel, N.J.
Mayorson, Manuel	.189	18	37	6	7	0	0	0	2	2	6	3	0	.189	.231	R	R	5-10	167	3-10-83	1999	La Romana, D.R.
McKinney, Antonio	.267	128	450	68	120	25	5	3	48	48	106	23	6	.364	.343	R	R	5-10	175	1-2-78	1996	Portland, Ore.
Morrow, Alvin	.213	52	174	20	37	8	1	2	30	23	65	1	1	.305	.307	R	R	6-4	240	4-28-78	1997	St. Louis, Mo.
Pearson, Shawn	.183	30	60	13	11	1	0	0	1	10	14	3	1	.200	.300	R	R	6-1	175	9-14-77	1999	Guelph, Ontario
Rodriguez, Mike	.184	13	38	4	7	0	0	0	6	0	5	0	0	.184	.179	R	R	5-11	185	4-1-75	1996	Stephenville, Texas
Rouse, Michael	.272	48	180	27	49	17	2	5	24	13	45	3	1	.472	.327	R	R	5-11	185	4-25-80	2001	San Jose, Calif.
Sisk, Aaron	.114	15	35	2	4	1	1	1	4	2	14	1	1	.286	.184	R	R	6-1	180	9-17-78	2000	Fort Worth, Texas
Thompson, Andy	.529	9	34	5	18	6	0	1	6	5	7	0	0	.794	.610	R	R	6-3	220	8-28-75	1995	Cottage Grove, Wis.
Thompson, Rich	.311	112	454	90	141	14	6	1	60	44	72	39	11	.374	.380	L	R	6-3	180	4-23-79	2000	Montrose, Pa.
Weekly, Chris	.254	67	240	33	61	12	1	4	47	26	66	2	2	.363	.333	L	R	5-9	195	12-4-76	1999	Mesa, Ariz.
Werth, Jayson	.200	21	70	9	14	3	0	2	14	17	19	1	3	.329	.356	R	R	6-5	215	5-20-79	1997	Chatham, Ill.
Wise, Dewayne	.223	25	103	9	23	3	1	2	16	5	13	5	0	.330	.252	L	L	6-1	180	2-24-78	1997	Chapin, S.C.
Yepez, Jose	.000	4	3	0	0	0	0	0	0	0	1	0	0	.000	.250	R	R	6-0	175	6-19-81	1997	Lara, Venez.
Zieour, Neesan	.256	29	86	19	22	9	0	2	11	11	16	1	0	.430	.363	R	R	5-11	185	11-2-80	2001	Rocklin, Calif.

GAMES BY POSITION: C—Cash 80, Chiaffredo 20, Fagan 5, Kremblas 25, Martinez 3, Rodriguez 2, Werth 9, Yepez 2. **1B**—Bernhardt 81, Chiaffredo 1, Keene 12, Kremblas 2, Martinez 2, Morrow 1, Rodriguez 1, Weekly 57, Zieour 3. **2B**—Alvarez 16, Bernhardt 30, Bush 4, Frye 4, Goudie 43, Keene 24, Mayorson 2, Rouse 29, Sisk 1. **3B**—Bernhardt 11, Berry 4, Fagan 115, Keene 8, Mayorson 10, Rouse 23. **OF**—Carter 46, Gross 35, Keene 1, Kremblas 15, McKinney 123, Morrow 26, Pearson 21, Rodriguez 4, Sisk 7, A. Thompson 2, R. Thompson 108, Weekly 1, Wise 25, Zieour 28. **SS**—Alvarez 106, Keene 8, Mayorson 10,

PITCHING

PITCHING	W	L	ERA	G	GS	CG	SV	IP	H	R	ER	BB	SO	AVG	B	T	HT	WT	DOB	1st Yr	Resides
Abbott, David	5	4	5.96	10	10	0	0	51	61	35	34	20	35	.303	R	R	6-4	230	10-19-77	2000	Tucson, Ariz.
Caraballo, Angel	3	1	4.80	12	2	0	0	30	30	19	16	18	21	.265	R	R	6-0	180	1-20-80	1997	Guanta, Venez.
Chulk, Vinny	1	2	3.12	16	1	0	1	35	38	16	12	13	50	.271	R	R	6-2	185	12-19-78	2000	Miami, Fla.
Colson, Jason	0	0	0.00	1	1	0	0	1	0	1	0	3	1	.000	L	R	6-2	220	11-19-78	2001	Weirton, W.Va.
Dean, Aaron	11	12	5.46	27	27	2	0	160	172	113	97	75	121	.276	R	R	6-4	190	4-9-79	1999	Pleasanton, Calif.
Dickson, Jason	1	1	1.50	4	4	0	0	18	14	3	3	1	20	.197	L	R	6-0	195	3-30-73	1994	Chatham, New Brunswick

PITCHING	W	L	ERA	G	GS	CG	SV	IP	H	R	ER	BB	SO	AVG	B	T	HT	WT	DOB	1st Yr	Resides
Dimma, Doug	1	2	4.88	24	2	0	0	48	58	31	26	30	27	.297	R	L	5-11	175	7-3-78	1999	Richmond Hill, Ontario
Ford, Matt	2	7	5.85	13	12	0	0	60	67	41	39	37	48	.293	B	L	6-1	175	4-8-81	1999	Tamarac, Fla.
Gracesqui, Franklyn	1	0	0.00	4	0	0	0	6	2	0	0	8	6	.125	B	L	6-5	210	8-20-79	1998	New York, N.Y.
Halladay, Roy	0	1	3.97	13	0	0	2	23	28	12	10	3	15	.304	R	R	6-6	230	5-14-77	1995	Arvada, Colo.
Hamann, Robert	4	0	4.41	39	0	0	5	65	69	40	32	17	44	.271	R	R	6-7	215	12-15-76	1999	Franklin Park, Ill.
Houston, Ryan	7	5	4.19	26	23	0	1	133	147	77	62	46	85	.285	R	R	6-4	192	9-22-79	1999	Pensacola, Fla.
Hubbel, Travis	1	3	6.14	12	4	0	0	29	26	31	20	25	20	.230	R	R	6-0	190	6-27-79	1997	Edmonton, Alberta
Kegley, Charlie	6	9	6.03	26	20	0	0	112	120	94	75	76	76	.275	R	R	6-3	205	12-17-79	1999	Orange Park, Fla.
Markwell, Diegomar	3	1	3.21	5	5	0	0	34	27	12	12	13	26	.225	L	L	6-2	197	8-8-80	1996	Curacao, Netherlands Antilles
Orloski, Joe	4	2	2.84	46	0	0	10	67	55	28	21	29	52	.221	R	R	6-3	180	5-17-79	1999	Las Vegas, Nev.
Painter, Lance	1	1	0.96	5	1	0	0	9	10	1	1	1	10	.294	L	L	6-1	200	7-21-67	1990	Highlands Ranch, Colo.
Payne, Jerrod	2	2	2.30	21	0	0	8	27	25	13	7	8	22	.229	R	R	6-4	220	3-20-79	1997	San Pedro de Macoris, D.R.
Perez, George	4	3	3.12	41	0	0	8	87	81	39	30	42	48	.250	R	R	6-1	195	3-18-77	1999	Doctors Inlet, Fla.
Porter, Scott	0	1	21.00	1	0	0	0	3	8	7	7	2	2	.533	R	R	6-2	185	12-29-80	1997	Carabobo, Venez.
Reimers, Cameron	10	6	4.40	22	22	3	0	141	150	81	69	24	88	.272	R	R	6-1	185	12-29-80	1999	Missoula, Mont.
Sandoval, Marcos	1	0	11.57	5	1	0	0	7	6	10	9	12	2	.222	R	R	6-3	215	12-13-79	2001	Richmond, Texas
Sheffield, Chris	1	0	22.85	6	0	0	0	4	9	11	11	11	2	.450	R	R	6-3	185	12-29-80	1997	Richmond, Texas
Woodards, Orlando	2	1	5.74	17	0	0	0	27	37	21	17	15	15	.327	R	R	6-2	200	1-2-78	1997	Sacramento, Calif.

SOUTH ATLANTIC LEAGUE

BATTING	AVG	G	AB	R	H	2B	3B	HR	RBI	BB	SO	SB	CS	SLG	OBP	B	T	HT	WT	DOB	1st Yr	Resides
Cosby, Rob	.228	120	412	48	94	22	1	5	43	32	60	6	4	.323	.286	R	R	6-2	205	4-2-81	1999	Rio Piedras, P.R.
Crespo, Manny	.220	61	186	21	41	9	0	3	12	27	45	0	2	.317	.327	R	R	5-10	185	1-4-79	2000	Miami, Fla.
Davenport, Ron	.289	79	298	37	86	18	2	4	54	20	53	11	5	.403	.328	L	R	6-2	190	10-16-81	2000	Raleigh, N.C.
Delfino, Lee	.267	41	146	16	39	10	2	0	13	12	29	2	1	.363	.340	R	R	5-10	196	5-21-80	2001	Pickering, Ontario
Gutierrez, Said	.071	11	28	0	2	0	0	0	0	2	5	0	0	.071	.133	R	R	5-10	196	3-26-80	1998	Merida, Mexico
Jimenez, Rich	.184	26	76	14	14	1	0	0	4	8	18	11	2	.197	.267	R	R	6-1	175	7-3-81	1997	Santo Domingo, D.R.
Jova, Maikel	.173	46	162	12	28	6	0	3	14	1	33	1	1	.265	.177	R	R	6-0	190	8-22-77	2000	San Jose, Costa Rica
Keene, Kurt	.172	16	58	7	10	2	0	1	4	0	10	0	0	.259	.172	R	R	6-0	190	8-22-77	2000	Chattanooga, Tenn.
Malpica, Martin	.183	15	60	4	11	1	0	0	6	1	14	0	0	.200	.197	R	R	6-2	208	9-21-79	1997	Lara, Venez.
Martinez, Casey	.145	27	83	7	12	2	0	1	4	2	23	1	0	.205	.174	R	R	5-10	167	3-10-83	1999	La Romana, D.R.
Mayorson, Manuel	.000	1	2	0	0	0	0	0	0	0	1	0	0	.000	.000	R	R	6-4	240	4-28-78	1997	St. Louis, Mo.
Morrow, Alvin	.250	54	172	22	43	8	1	6	23	36	73	0	4	.413	.383	L	L	6-2	170	8-22-82	2000	Caguas, P.R.
Negron, Miguel	.192	25	99	11	19	1	0	0	2	6	21	5	3	.202	.238	L	L	6-1	202	11-29-81	1999	Maracaibo, Venez.
Quiroz, Guillermo	.199	82	261	25	52	12	0	7	25	29	67	0	1	.326	.294	R	R	6-1	190	8-22-79	2000	Herndon, Pa.
Rich, Dominic	.278	91	327	67	91	16	1	4	32	47	54	20	8	.370	.382	L	R	5-10	185	2-18-81	1999	Guaynabo, P.R.
Rios, Alexis	.263	130	480	40	126	20	9	2	58	25	59	22	14	.354	.296	R	R	6-5	185	2-18-81	1999	Guaynabo, P.R.
Singleton, Justin	.232	100	345	51	80	15	5	2	25	33	138	24	7	.322	.299	L	R	6-1	190	4-10-79	2001	Sparks, Md.
Sisk, Aaron	.179	68	223	21	40	9	3	4	28	15	78	5	6	.300	.231	L	R	6-0	185	9-17-78	2000	Fort Worth, Texas
Snyder, Mike	.220	119	414	47	91	18	2	8	45	40	101	12	5	.331	.290	L	R	6-5	230	2-11-81	1999	Chino Hills, Calif.
Tablado, Raul	.253	122	388	49	98	23	2	9	44	45	127	5	10	.392	.336	R	R	6-2	175	3-3-82	2000	Miami, Fla.
Umbria, Jose	.234	45	128	12	30	3	0	1	19	15	27	1	2	.281	.317	R	R	6-2	215	1-20-78	1996	Barquisimeto, Venez.
Zieour, Neesan	.280	22	75	8	21	3	0	0	6	9	16	0	2	.320	.365	R	R	5-11	185	11-2-80	2001	Rocklin, Calif.

GAMES BY POSITION: C—Gutierrez 5, Martinez 21, Quiroz 82, Umbria 38. 1B—Gutierrez 6, Keene 3, Malpica 7, Sisk 7, Snyder 118, Umbria 2. 2B—Crespo 15, Delfino 12, Jimenez 13, Keene 6, Rich 78, Sisk 16. 3B—Cosby 116, Crespo 11, Jimenez 1, Malpica 2, Sisk 13. SS—Delfino 16, Jimenez 7, Keene 5, Sisk 2, Tablado 107. OF—Crespo 3, Davenport 64, Jova 40, Keene 2, Morrow 19, Negron 25, Rios 127, Singleton 97, Sisk 30, Zieour 19.

PITCHING	W	L	ERA	G	GS	CG	SV	IP	H	R	ER	BB	SO	AVG	B	T	HT	WT	DOB	1st Yr	Resides
Abbott, David	2	3	1.10	8	8	0	0	49	39	10	6	8	35	.214	R	R	6-4	230	10-19-77	2000	Tucson, Ariz.
Bauer, Peter	1	2	2.39	6	6	0	0	38	26	15	10	10	47	.192	L	R	6-7	250	11-6-78	2000	Hagerstown, Md.
Cardwell, Brian	3	10	5.18	19	19	2	0	92	101	70	53	33	60	.279	R	R	6-10	215	12-30-80	1999	Kiefer, Okla.
Comolli, Mark	1	2	3.90	8	5	0	0	32	28	16	14	6	27	.233	R	R	6-0	190	3-11-79	2001	Millville, Del.
Ford, Matt	4	4	2.42	11	11	1	0	71	62	28	19	22	62	.236	B	L	6-2	190	12-14-78	2001	Hortonville, Wis.
Gassner, Dave	4	4	3.03	13	11	0	0	74	72	30	25	11	51	.246	L	L	6-1	185	10-30-78	2000	Plainfield, Ind.
Glen, William	2	1	3.40	23	0	0	1	45	46	27	17	26	50	.259	R	R	6-5	210	8-20-79	1998	New York, N.Y.
Gracesqui, Franklyn	2	8	3.17	35	2	0	1	65	60	40	23	34	66	.244	B	L	6-5	210	8-20-79	1998	New York, N.Y.
Guzman, Alexis	2	7	3.58	52	0	0	2	78	82	38	31	10	45	.276	B	R	6-0	175	4-23-80	1997	Barcelona, Venez.
Markwell, Diegomar	5	7	3.87	22	21	3	0	123	121	58	53	32	99	.260	L	L	6-2	197	8-8-80	1996	Curacao, Netherlands Antilles
McCulloch, Andy	5	2	2.17	55	0	0	17	62	53	15	15	12	54	.225	R	R	6-1	205	2-26-78	2000	Las Vegas, Nev.
McMillan, Josh	1	1	5.40	9	1	0	0	18	21	11	13	18	18	.308	L	L	6-0	175	7-8-78	2000	Moreno Valley, Calif.
Mowday, Chris	0	1	5.64	13	1	0	0	22	22	16	14	9	22	.282	R	R	6-4	185	8-24-81	1997	Strathpine, Australia
Nunley, Derrek	1	2	3.93	14	0	0	0	18	22	12	8	8	23	.282	R	R	6-1	185	9-13-80	1999	Jacksonville, Fla.
Ozuna, Francisco	2	1	2.57	18	0	0	2	35	25	13	10	4	16	.200	L	L	6-2	180	5-17-81	1997	Santo Domingo, D.R.
Quick, Ben	3	1	3.71	17	5	0	0	51	51	23	21	9	39	.257	R	R	6-2	185	3-8-79	2001	San Jacinto, Calif.
Renwick, Tyler	1	2	11.57	7	0	0	0	12	17	16	15	13	8	.369	R	R	6-1	185	12-29-80	1997	Carabobo, Venez.
Sandoval, Marcos	1	6	6.83	21	8	1	0	55	47	44	42	33	28	.235	R	R	6-3	215	12-13-79	2001	Richmond, Texas
Sheffield, Chris	1	3	10.32	6	3	0	0	11	7	13	13	20	12	.184	R	R	6-3	185	12-29-80	1997	Richmond, Texas
Smith, Mike	5	5	2.10	14	14	2	0	94	78	32	22	21	85	.224	R	R	5-11	195	9-19-77	2000	Westwood, Mass.
Spillman, Jeromie	1	2	7.57	20	0	0	0	27	49	29	23	6	22	.388	L	L	5-11	180	9-24-78	2000	Phoenix, Ariz.
Thorpe, Tracy	4	13	5.08	24	23	0	0	103	108	77	58	51	81	.270	R	R	6-4	254	12-15-80	2000	Melbourne, Fla.

NEW YORK-PENN LEAGUE

BATTING	AVG	G	AB	R	H	2B	3B	HR	RBI	BB	SO	SB	CS	SLG	OBP	B	T	HT	WT	DOB	1st Yr	Resides
Arrieche, Gabriel	.264	41	121	11	32	4	3	0	12	11	15	8	4	.347	.327	R	R	6-0	170	3-8-79	1997	Lara, Venez.
Brosseau, Rick	.195	51	174	12	34	7	2	2	20	20	24	4	2	.293	.276	L	R	5-11	180	9-22-78	2000	North Oaks, Minn.
Davis, Morrin	.143	65	217	17	31	8	2	4	20	14	88	2	2	.253	.197	R	R	6-2	190	12-11-82	2000	Tampa, Fla.
Delfino, Lee	.220	13	50	5	11	2	0	0	5	7	5	3	0	.260	.350	R	R	6-0	185	5-21-80	2001	Pickering, Ontario
Durazo, Ernie	.273	64	238	26	65	22	0	1	36	21	54	1	1	.378	.332	L	R	6-0	200	7-10-79	2001	Council, N.C.
Godwin, Tyrell	.368	33	117	26	43	8	2	2	15	19	27	9	5	.521	.464	L	R	5-10	196	3-26-80	1998	Merida, Mexico
Gutierrez, Said	.214	41	131	10	28	6	0	3	13	7	28	1	1	.328	.273	R	R	5-10	196	3-26-80	1998	Merida, Mexico
Jimenez, Rich	.281	35	114	12	32	3	1	0	6	7	25	14	2	.325	.336	B	R	6-1	175	7-3-81	1997	Santo Domingo, D.R.

BATTING	AVG	G	AB	R	H	2B	3B	HR	RBI	BB	SO	SB	CS	SLG	OBP	B	T	HT	WT	DOB	1st Yr	Resides
Jova, Maikel	.268	67	261	44	70	12	0	9	39	7	37	6	2	.418	.299	R	R	6-0	195	3-5-81	1999	San Jose, Costa Rica
Malpica, Martin	.235	40	136	17	32	3	0	1	7	9	24	3	0	.279	.289	R	R	6-2	208	9-21-79	1997	Lara, Venez.
Mayorson, Manuel	.263	62	247	28	65	5	0	0	18	21	19	25	13	.283	.325	R	R	5-10	167	3-10-83	1999	La Romana, D.R.
Medina, Rodney	.179	11	39	4	7	1	0	0	3	4	5	1	0	.205	.256	B	R	6-1	180	10-17-81	1999	Maracaibo, Venez.
Negron, Miguel	.253	50	186	27	47	6	1	1	13	15	22	7	4	.312	.314	L	L	6-2	170	8-22-82	2000	Caguas, P.R.
Siriveaw, Nom	.167	66	239	32	40	8	3	6	25	23	88	8	1	.301	.245	B	R	6-3	195	12-9-80	2000	Vancouver, B.C.
Whittaker, Tim	.299	42	127	23	38	7	2	2	16	13	20	1	3	.433	.379	R	R	6-0	205	1-4-79	2001	Conway, S.C.
Wood, Stephen	.209	33	129	9	27	5	1	2	11	7	25	0	0	.310	.248	R	R	6-0	205	12-10-77	2000	West Covina, Calif.
Zieour, Neesan	.381	5	21	3	8	0	2	0	2	1	1	1	0	.571	.435	R	R	5-11	185	11-2-80	2001	Rocklin, Calif.

GAMES BY POSITION: C—Gutierrez 40, Malpica 1, Whittaker 42. **1B**—Durazo 47, Gutierrez 2, Jimenez 1, Malpica 18, Wood 12. **2B**—Arrieche 25, Brosseau 33, Jimenez 7, Mayorson 10, Medina 2. **3B**—Arrieche 3, Malpica 9, Siriveaw 63. **SS**—Brosseau 12, Delfino 12, Mayorson 51. **OF**—Arrieche 7, Davis 64, Godwin 20, Jimenez 23, Jova 65, Malpica 2, Medina 2, Negron 50, Zieour 2.

PITCHING	W	L	ERA	G	GS	CG	SV	IP	H	R	ER	BB	SO	AVG	B	T	HT	WT	DOB	1st Yr	Resides
Beirne, Kevin	0	0	5.40	2	2	0	0	3	6	2	2	1	2	.400	L	R	6-4	210	1-1-74	1995	The Woodlands, Texas
Colson, Jason	1	2	2.72	8	0	0	0	36	28	14	11	13	31	.207	L	R	6-2	220	11-19-78	2001	Weirton, W.Va.
Comolli, Mark	2	1	4.74	10	0	0	1	19	21	11	10	6	21	.287	R	R	6-0	190	3-11-79	2001	Millville, Del.
Esarey, Brad	2	0	3.86	17	0	0	0	35	33	18	15	12	34	.244	L	L	6-3	178	9-20-78	2001	Concord, N.C.
Flores, Neomar	3	1	4.80	12	4	0	0	54	45	33	29	19	51	.219	R	R	6-2	180	3-12-82	1998	Guarenas, Venez.
Harper, Jesse	3	4	4.79	14	14	0	0	68	79	40	36	20	58	.289	R	R	6-4	205	11-11-80	2000	Clute, Texas
Hecker, Steven	1	5	3.06	17	1	0	0	35	34	18	12	19	37	.253	R	R	6-3	200	11-22-78	2001	Buffalo Grove, Ill.
McGowan, Dustin	3	6	3.76	15	14	0	0	67	57	33	28	49	80	.233	R	R	6-3	190	3-24-82	2000	Palm Harbor, Fla.
Mora, Ramon	2	2	1.98	16	1	0	0	59	40	19	13	19	61	.189	R	R	6-2	175	3-18-81	1998	Monagas, Venez.
Mowday, Chris	4	3	3.89	17	2	0	0	37	28	17	16	21	50	.218	R	R	6-4	210	8-24-81	1997	Strathpine, Australia
Patten, Lanny	0	1	27.00	3	0	0	0	3	7	9	8	5	2	.437	R	R	6-3	205	5-30-79	2000	Drayton Valley, Alberta
Perkins, Vince	1	4	3.27	14	14	0	0	52	41	23	19	37	67	.220	L	R	6-5	220	9-27-81	2001	Victoria, B.C.
Renwick, Tyler	1	0	4.94	13	0	0	0	31	35	18	17	10	24	.277	R	R	6-4	206	8-12-78	1998	Langley, B.C.
Romero, Felix	2	0	4.85	26	0	0	12	26	27	14	14	9	35	.259	R	R	6-2	165	6-18-80	1997	San Pedro de Macoris, D.R.
Stephenson, Eric	3	6	4.04	15	14	0	0	78	80	45	35	44	62	.272	R	L	6-4	180	9-3-82	2000	Benson, N.C.
Taylor, John	1	2	4.25	12	0	0	0	30	32	16	14	9	23	.275	R	R	6-4	220	3-15-78	2000	Ridgeland, S.C.
Valdez, Santo	3	3	3.92	14	0	0	1	41	38	19	18	13	47	.243	R	R	6-1	170	3-30-82	1999	Bani, D.R.

MEDICINE HAT — Rookie

PIONEER LEAGUE

BATTING	AVG	G	AB	R	H	2B	3B	HR	RBI	BB	SO	SB	CS	SLG	OBP	B	T	HT	WT	DOB	1st Yr	Resides
Blackburn, John	.252	42	139	19	35	6	0	2	14	15	41	1	1	.338	.329	R	R	6-1	200	12-30-82	2000	London, Ontario
Corrente, David	.192	35	99	7	19	5	0	1	6	8	32	1	0	.273	.298	R	R	6-3	195	10-13-83	2001	Chatham, Ontario
Guerrero, Armando	.243	72	263	35	64	10	1	8	36	10	61	10	10	.380	.274	R	R	6-2	190	1-18-81	1998	Bani, D.R.
Hetherington, Luke	.207	51	174	22	36	3	4	2	14	18	54	6	1	.305	.299	R	R	6-1	190	4-13-83	2001	Covington, Wash.
Hyde, Nathan	.232	57	190	27	44	7	3	3	18	12	47	5	0	.347	.290	R	R	6-6	210	3-1-79	2001	Anderson, S.C.
Iorg, Isaac	.250	24	80	8	20	3	0	2	10	1	16	0	1	.363	.268	R	R	6-1	190	6-7-79	2001	Knoxville, Tenn.
Kimberley, Glynn	.232	52	190	21	44	8	1	9	26	18	64	0	4	.426	.312	R	R	6-4	220	7-30-81	2000	Bayswater, Australia
Martin, Cesar	.220	67	254	34	56	16	0	8	43	27	54	4	3	.378	.325	R	R	6-0	165	6-21-81	1998	San Pedro de Macoris, D.R.
McEachran, Aaron	.336	69	256	34	86	12	1	5	41	32	55	3	1	.449	.426	L	R	6-0	200	1-28-79	2001	St. Louis Park, Minn.
Medina, Rodney	.308	50	195	37	60	7	0	7	21	19	29	6	3	.451	.375	B	R	6-1	180	10-17-81	1999	Maracaibo, Venez.
Peralta, Juan	.231	71	299	45	69	8	3	0	13	26	47	18	8	.278	.291	R	R	6-2	190	6-24-83	2000	Santiago Rodriguez, D.R.
Rivera, William	.208	48	173	18	36	4	0	0	11	9	38	3	0	.231	.250	L	R	6-0	155	12-28-81	2000	Caguas, P.R.
Tempesta, Nick	.335	72	263	49	88	16	1	8	46	24	51	3	1	.494	.407	L	L	5-10	185	11-20-78	2001	Brockton, Mass.
Wood, Stephen	.333	2	6	2	2	1	0	0	2	0	1	0	0	.500	.429	R	R	6-4	215	12-10-77	2000	West Covina, Calif.
Yepez, Jose	.276	18	58	5	16	5	0	0	3	4	4	3	0	.362	.354	R	R	6-0	175	6-19-81	1997	Lara, Venez.

GAMES BY POSITION: C—Blackburn 40, Corrente 35, Tempesta 9, Yepez 9. **1B**—Guerrero 1, Martin 2, McEachran 55, Medina 17, Wood 2, Yepez 4. **2B**—Iorg 5, Medina 2, Rivera 45, Tempesta 31. **3B**—Iorg 1, Martin 65, Tempesta 12. **SS**—Iorg 4, Peralta 66, Tempesta 9. **OF**—Blackburn 1, Guerrero 70, Hetherington 43, Hyde 49, Kimberley 49, Martin 1, Medina 24, Rivera 1, Yepez 1.

PITCHING	W	L	ERA	G	GS	CG	SV	IP	H	R	ER	BB	SO	AVG	B	T	HT	WT	DOB	1st Yr	Resides
Chadwick, John	1	1	4.43	23	0	0	2	61	65	38	30	19	42	.262	L	R	6-4	225	5-3-78	2000	Brampton, Ontario
Costello, Ryan	1	5	3.83	14	8	0	1	52	38	33	22	21	56	.200	L	L	6-6	215	7-13-79	2001	Marlton, N.J.
Fuller, Brendan	0	1	6.75	18	0	0	0	25	21	20	19	16	38	.238	R	R	6-1	205	9-13-80	2001	Clearwater, Fla.
Grimes, Sean	1	4	4.97	12	7	0	0	38	48	26	21	20	21	.307	R	L	6-2	180	5-31-83	2001	London, Ontario
Heal, Darren	0	1	19.29	7	0	0	0	9	21	29	20	13	7	.411	B	R	6-2	198	9-5-79	2001	Staten Island, N.Y.
League, Brandon	2	2	4.66	9	9	0	0	39	36	23	20	11	38	.244	R	R	6-2	180	3-16-83	2001	Honolulu, Hawaii
McMillan, Josh	0	2	10.52	15	0	0	1	26	41	35	30	27	15	.327	L	L	6-0	175	7-8-78	2000	Moreno Valley, Calif.
Medina, Frewing	3	5	7.51	19	0	0	0	44	67	51	37	16	26	.345	R	R	6-2	170	10-8-80	1997	Lara, Venez.
Neylan, Chris	0	2	6.62	10	5	0	0	34	49	29	25	10	22	.342	R	L	6-6	192	9-27-82	2001	Hamilton, N.J.
Ogiltree, John	2	4	3.38	28	0	0	6	32	33	17	12	10	25	.277	R	R	6-6	225	6-3-78	2001	Mississauga, Ontario
Patten, Lanny	1	4	5.40	25	0	0	1	38	30	30	23	22	31	.215	R	R	6-3	205	5-30-79	2001	Drayton Valley, Alberta
Ramirez, Ismael	5	6	5.35	14	14	0	0	74	77	48	44	21	35	.267	R	R	6-2	175	3-3-81	1998	Anzoategui, Venez.
Rosario, Francisco	3	7	5.59	16	15	0	0	76	79	61	47	38	55	.271	R	R	6-0	160	9-28-80	1999	Del Yuma, D.R.
Spillman, Jeromie	0	3	4.12	28	0	0	1	39	41	23	18	18	42	.251	L	L	5-11	180	9-24-78	2000	Phoenix, Ariz.
Talanoa, Charles	1	8	5.73	15	15	0	0	55	65	53	35	33	30	.287	R	R	6-5	230	12-29-80	2001	El Segundo, Calif.
Taylor, John	0	0	4.76	6	0	0	0	11	15	11	6	4	8	.300	R	R	6-4	220	3-15-78	2000	Ridgeland, S.C.
Wassong, Michael	0	1	8.31	11	0	0	0	9	14	10	8	6	13	.350	L	L	5-9	180	11-19-79	2001	Jersey City, N.J.

MINORLEAGUES

Terrorist attacks cast pall over end of minor league season

BY WILL LINGO

As did most everything else, minor league baseball stopped on Sept. 11. And when we look back on the 2001 season, it will be hard not to think about the terrorist attacks instead of what happened on the field.

The regular season had already ended, and Minor League Baseball postponed league playoff games for several days after the attacks before finally deciding to cancel the remaining games altogether.

The only decision left to leagues that had not completed their seasons was how to determine their champions. Some went with teams that were leading championship series, while others went with co-champions. Though the decisions didn't satisfy everyone, in September 2001 it was clear that getting the playoffs completed was not an important consideration.

While weather has affected minor league playoffs in past years, this was the first wholesale disruption of a minor league season since World War II, when many leagues suspended play due to manpower shortages and wartime restrictions. The cancellations also marked the first time any minor league playoff series had been canceled or truncated for any reason other than poor weather.

Mike Weinberg

The attacks also tended to obscure the great performances of players like Marlins righthander Josh Beckett and Reds outfielder Adam Dunn. That's all right, because fans will have many more years to talk about their exploits.

The minor leaguer who was brought into sharpest focus was Mike Weinberg, a former outfielder in the Tigers organization who went on to become a New York firefighter and was killed in the World Trade Center collapse.

Weinberg, 34, was off duty on Sept. 11 and about to tee off at a golf course in Queens when he heard about the first plane hitting one of the towers. Concerned for his sister's safety, Weinberg, a member of one of the oldest firefighting companies in New York City—Manhattan Company, Engine 1—went to help her and others. He rushed to the scene with chaplain Mychal Judge and Capt. Daniel Brethel. None of the three was in either of the towers when they collapsed; all three were killed in the street by falling debris.

Weinberg's family thinks he was the person to whom Judge was administering last rites when he was killed. Weinberg's sister Patricia Gambino was working on the 72nd floor of Two World Trade Center, but escaped.

Weinberg batted .238 for Niagara Falls (New York-Penn) in 1990 and .217 for Fayetteville (South Atlantic) in 1991. He joined the fire department after the Tigers released him in the middle of the '91 season. He is remembered more for his play at St. John's, where he hit home runs in both the semifinal and final games of the 1988 Big East Conference tournament, which the Red Storm won.

Now, unfortunately, he'll be remembered as one of the victims. Like just about every corner of American life, minor league baseball was touched by the tragedy. The loss of a few playoff games was meaningless. The loss of life is still hard to fathom.

Determining Champions

The 2001 minor league season came to its official end Sept. 14, when the 10 leagues that had yet to complete their postseason schedules canceled the rest of their playoffs.

The New York-Penn League became the first to call it quits, making an announcement Sept. 12. Four other leagues nixed their playoffs that day, while five decided to resume on Sept. 14. But President George W. Bush marked that date as a national day of prayer and remembrance, and Minor League Baseball later decided to cancel all remaining games.

The New York-Penn League nixed the final two games of its championship series between Brooklyn and Williamsport, which were scheduled for KeySpan Park in Brooklyn, less than 15 miles from the World Trade Center.

"Due to the emergency situations in the New York metropolitan area, and out of respect to the friends and families of those who lost their lives or were injured in yesterday's tragic events, we are canceling the remainder of the championship series," league president Ben Hayes said.

ORGANIZATION STANDINGS

Cumulative farm club standings for the 30 major league farm systems:

	2001			2000	1999	1998
	W	L	Pct.	Pct.	Pct.	Pct.
Houston (6)	418	281	.598	.526	.499	.506
Cincinnati (6)	394	301	.567	.486	.521	.454
Seattle (6)	385	303	.560	.577	.483	.520
Cleveland (6)	382	321	.543	.517	.500	.513
New York-AL (6)	380	320	.543	.517	.558	.516
Minnesota (6)	368	312	.541	.537	.496	.548
Florida (6)	373	319	.539	.496	.477	.459
Los Angeles (6)	371	319	.538	.527	.457	.439
San Francisco (6)	362	324	.528	.444	.502	.490
New York-NL (6)	366	333	.524	.509	.516	.535
Chicago-NL (6)	353	336	.512	.513	.480	.515
Detroit (6)	352	341	.508	.478	.480	.501
Philadelphia (6)	351	346	.504	.568	.523	.503
Anaheim (6)	343	345	.499	.426	.486	.457
Milwaukee (6)	342	348	.496	.495	.442	.469
Chicago-AL (6)	338	345	.495	.483	.520	.493
Atlanta (7)	370	387	.489	.493	.496	.439
Oakland (6)	334	362	.480	.551	.573	.524
Colorado (6)	338	369	.478	.502	.472	.463
Texas (6)	326	356	.478	.530	.541	.526
Arizona (6)	338	371	.477	.466	.483	.446
Tampa Bay (6)	335	372	.474	.478	.508	.533
San Diego (6)	334	376	.470	.485	.505	.533
Kansas City (6)	324	367	.469	.457	.545	.558
Boston (6)	325	370	.468	.522	.526	.521
Pittsburgh (6)	322	368	.467	.491	.487	.449
Toronto (6)	325	382	.460	.529	.534	.558
Baltimore (6)	305	381	.445	.481	.453	.499
Montreal (6)	303	393	.435	.453	.493	.528
St. Louis (6)	298	407	.423	.472	.442	.506

Number of farm teams in parentheses

MINOR LEAGUES

The California League, the only league that had not reached its championship round, also decided to cancel the rest of its playoffs. "I feel with all the delays and this situation, it serves no particular purpose to go any further," president Joe Gagliardi said. "We are done."

The Texas League was the last to cancel, and the last to make news. League president Tom Kayser awarded the title to Arkansas, which held a 2-0 lead in its best-of-seven series against Round Rock. But Round Rock, which had 86 regular season wins to Arkansas' 66, wanted a share of the title despite its deficit in the series.

The Express called Travelers general manager Bill Valentine, asking to share the title. Valentine declined. In accordance with league bylaws, the Express filed an appeal, requesting to be named co-champion.

"The main reason we did it was I really felt we owed it to our players and fans for all the effort and support they had put in this season," Express president Reid Ryan said. "It wasn't us thinking the president's decision wasn't the right one."

The Express, Travelers and league officials all made cases in a conference call, and no one would second Round Rock's motion to share the crown.

"In the end there was precedent in the league, and precedent in other leagues, for this action," Kayser said, pointing out that Austin and Midland earned league titles in series shortened by inclement weather in 1966 and 1975.

In all, four leagues declared champions, six split titles and another six had finished their finals before the attacks. According to individual league records, it marked the first co-champions for every league except the Pacific Coast and Eastern, which have had a shared title before.

"It's certainly less than a desirable situation, but as evidenced by the fact of what was done in all the leagues but one, you're not going to ignore those games," said International League president Randy Mobley, who gave Louisville the title based on its 1-0 lead against Scranton/Wilkes-Barre. "The title's not the same as it is other years, but that's no fault of anyone involved."

Randy Mobley

No league president said the decision to cancel the playoffs was an easy one, especially given the history of postseason play. But most agreed it was the correct decision, even if the players were itching to get back on the field.

"Both clubs would have loved to have played, but with the tragedy we thought we should pay the proper respect to the victims and their families," Midwest League president George Spelius said.

"In difficult times you're going to make difficult decisions," Mobley said. "Sometimes they're not popular

ones. Any club which works hard all season long to get to that point, there's bound to be some disappointment."

In the absence of games, minor league teams came up with various ideas to raise money to help victims of the attacks. One of the most creative came from Carolina Mudcats radio broadcaster Patrick Kinas, who held a bowl-a-thon to raise money. He ended up setting a world record by bowling continuously for 33 hours and 24 minutes.

"Minor league baseball is predicated on a lot of interesting promotions," Kinas said. "This was a unique way to help out, and it meant a lot to everybody who was able to participate."

Successful Centennial

Though tragedy marked the end of the season, the minor leagues celebrated their 100th year in grand fashion with another season of record attendance.

The 2001 season was the 100th anniversary of the formation of the National Association of Professional Baseball Leagues, an organization created to help smaller leagues survive in the struggle between the American and National leagues.

Now the organization is known as Minor League Baseball, and survival is no longer an issue. The minor leagues have weathered wars and economic trouble and periods of flagging attendance, but now they enjoy a period of unprecedented success.

PLAYER OF THE YEAR

The Marlins were slogging through the final innings of another loss late in the 2001 season when Al Avila's cell phone rang. Avila, the Marlins' assistant general manager and former scouting director, answered and immediately recognized the voice on the other end.

"It's your first-ever draft pick," Josh Beckett said in his slight Texas drawl.

The two chatted for a few minutes, Beckett sharing details from that night's Double-A Portland Sea Dogs victory, Avila lamenting the stunning slide of the Marlins. At no point did Beckett inquire about his chances for a September promotion, which was announced the next day.

A week later, Beckett went out and held the Cubs to one single over six innings in his major league debut, coming after just two summers and 199 innings of minor league seasoning.

After a couple of shoulder injury scares in 2000, Beckett went 14-1, 1.54 in 2001, splitting his time between Class A Brevard County and Portland. He opened the year with 39 consecutive scoreless innings at Brevard, then pitched the first seven innings of a combined no-hitter in mid-August for Portland. His beginning-to-end dominance made him Baseball America's Minor League Player of the Year.

Beckett's top-shelf repertoire makes him formidable. Few pitchers in the majors can match Beckett's

KEN BABBITT
Josh Beckett's fastball produced a 14-1, 1.54 record

combination of a 97-mph fastball, knee-buckling curve and solid changeup. But if you really want to know why Beckett inspires such confidence, even awe, among those who have followed his progress, the phone call to Avila might be the best place to start.

How many 21-year-old employees would feel comfortable calling one of the highest-ranking members of the company just to shoot the breeze?

"I don't think it took a lot of courage for him to call me up," Avila says. "I think we've had a good relationship all along. I've always let him know he can call me and ask me for whatever, whenever. I genuinely like him."

Plenty of high school kids have come along throwing mid-90s heat, but Beckett was different coming out of Spring, Texas. He didn't just have a gift. He understood it.

"You would approach him, and he would explain to you exactly how he attacked a hitter and the reasons behind it," Avila says. "He could tell you how he gripped the ball, how it would react when you do this or do that. You don't hear that from many high school kids, let me tell you."

Beckett signed with the Marlins in 1999 just before he was to enroll at Blinn (Texas) Junior College. All it cost

them was a four-year, $7 million major league contract, making Beckett the third high school player ever given a big league deal. Todd Van Poppel and Alex Rodriguez were the others.

It was Beckett who, on a conference call the day he was drafted, said he could pitch in the 2001 All-Star Game. He took much grief from that moment of public hubris and has since learned to tone down his comments, but ask him if he's ready to pitch in the majors for good and he'll look you dead in the eye.

"I think I am," he says. "I'm sure I could go down there and I could learn some more in the minor leagues. But the things that I'm going to learn down there are so small. The deal is with a young guy, you don't want him to come up here and learn in the big leagues. It crushes most people.

"I don't think if I get hit around, it will bother me. It's still little lessons that I need to learn and I think I'll be on my way."

—MIKE BERARDINO

PREVIOUS WINNERS

1981—Mike Marshall, 1b, Albuquerque (Dodgers)	
1982—Ron Kittle, of, Edmonton (White Sox)	
1983—Dwight Gooden, rhp, Lynchburg (Mets)	
1984—Mike Bielecki, rhp, Hawaii (Pirates)	
1985—Jose Canseco, of, Huntsville/Tacoma (Athletics)	
1986—Gregg Jefferies, ss, Columbia/Lynch./Jackson (Mets)	
1987—Gregg Jefferies, ss, Jackson/Tidewater (Mets)	
1988—Tom Gordon, rhp, Apple./Memphis/Omaha (Royals)	
1989—Sandy Alomar, c, Las Vegas (Padres)	
1990—Frank Thomas, 1b, Birmingham (White Sox)	
1991—Derek Bell, of, Syracuse (Blue Jays)	
1992—Tim Salmon, of, Edmonton (Angels)	
1993—Manny Ramirez, of, Canton/Charlotte (Indians)	
1994—Derek Jeter, ss, Tampa/Albany/Columbus (Yankees)	
1995—Andruw Jones, of, Macon (Braves)	
1996—Andruw Jones, of, Durham/Green./Rich. (Braves)	
1997—Paul Konerko, 1b, Albuquerque (Dodgers)	
1998—Eric Chavez, 3b, Huntsville/Edmonton (Athletics)	
1999—Rick Ankiel, lhp, Arkansas/Memphis (Cardinals)	
2000—Jon Rauch, rhp, Winston-Salem/Birmingham (White Sox)	

Mike Moore, the president of Minor League Baseball, says nothing has been more important in 100 years than the creation of the National Association itself in a hotel in Chicago in 1901.

"The formation of the National Association was probably the most significant event in Minor League Baseball history," he said. "This action allowed the leagues to continue operation and eventually flourish, where prior to the agreement the future was very much in doubt. The phrase 'united we stand and divided we fall' was never more significant in our organizational history than at that moment."

Miles Wolff, the former president of Baseball America and a longtime minor league executive who is now the commissioner of the independent Northern League, says the mere existence of minor league baseball seems to defy logic.

"The amazing thing is that minor league baseball has survived 100 years at all," he said. "Because it's not something a town needs. You look at things like vaudeville from that time, they're all gone. Minor league baseball is one of the few things that has really survived."

The minor leagues have survived, and they thrived in the centennial season, which ended up being the second-most attended in history.

For the 176 teams in the 15 leagues that keep track of numbers, attendance was 38,808,339—up 3.1 percent over the 37.6 million in 2000. The raw-number increase was just more than 1.1 million.

The high-water mark Moore and his administration shoot for continues to be the 1949 season, when 39.8 million fans came through the turnstiles. That mark came from 448 teams playing in 59 leagues.

Four of the 15 leagues—Pacific Coast, International, South Atlantic and New York-Penn—set new season records. Four others—Eastern, Carolina, Appalachian and Pioneer—saw increases over 2000, and the Florida State and Southern leagues showed increases in average attendance even though overall attendance declined.

Six teams surpassed previous league attendance records: Sacramento (901,214) and Memphis (887,976) in the PCL, Round Rock (668,792) in the Texas League, Lakewood (482,206) and Lexington (451,076) in the SAL, and Brooklyn (289,381) in the NY-P.

The new Portland franchise aver-

TEAM OF THE YEAR

It's not uncommon to find so many top prospects on one Class A team. It's uncommon for them all to produce so well.

But that's what happened to the Lake Elsinore Storm, which raced to a 50-20 first-half record and was named California League co-champion when the championship series was canceled due to the tragedies of Sept. 11. The team's sustained success and prospect-heavy roster were more than enough to make Lake Elsinore Baseball America's choice for 2001 Minor League Team of the Year.

With 11 of the Padres' top 30 prospects, the Storm was scary on paper. But in losing three of its first four games to Rancho Cucamonga, Lake Elsinore didn't seem much more than that. From there the Storm ran off seven straight wins, beginning with a victory by righthander Ben Howard, who began the season as the fifth starter.

During the streak, the team allowed more than three runs in a game just twice as the pitching staff began to round into form. The staff carried the team to four winning streaks of five games or more in the first half, while never losing three in a row after the opening series.

"Every kid we had went out and threw extremely well this season," manager Craig Colbert said. "By the middle of May you could see everybody coming together. Everybody who played for us this season really wanted to win."

With Dennis Tankersley and Jake Peavy at the top of the rotation, and the development of Howard and Chris Rojas, the Storm's ERA stayed below 3.00 for most of the first half and ended up at 3.03.

With position prospects Xavier Nady and Ben Johnson aided by

veterans Al Benjamin, Kevin Eberwein, Shane Hopper and Ben Risinger, Tankersley and Co. received plenty of support.

Once Tankersley, Howard and Peavy were all promoted, others stepped up in their place. Lefthander Eric Cyr used a dominant fastball to limit opponents to 18 earned runs in 101 innings. He just missed out on qualifying for the Cal League ERA title.

"It was one of those teams where we just had great chemistry," Colbert said. "The nucleus for our lineup stayed the same all year, and the pitchers who joined the team understood what we were doing. So they went out and did what the rest of the guys were doing."

It all added up to victories for the Storm, 91 of them, the most in minor league baseball.

—PATRICK LAVERTY

MINOR LEAGUE ALL-STARS

Ken Harvey   Josh Beckett   Marlon Byrd   Jimmy Journell

FIRST TEAM

Pos., Player, Team (League)	AVG	AB	R	H	2B	3B	HR	RBI	BB	SO	SB
C Toby Hall, Durham (International)	.335	373	59	125	28	1	19	72	29	22	1
1B Lyle Overbay, El Paso (Texas)	.352	532	82	187	49	3	13	100	67	92	4
2B Orlando Hudson, Tennessee (SL)/Syracuse (IL)	.306	500	82	153	36	11	8	79	60	76	19
3B Hank Blalock, Charlotte (FSL)/Tulsa (TL)	.352	509	96	179	37	5	18	108	65	69	10
SS Angel Berroa, Wilmington (CL)/Wichita (TL)	.304	503	106	153	38	8	14	67	26	96	25
OF Marlon Byrd, Reading (Eastern)	.316	510	108	161	22	8	28	89	52	93	32
OF Adam Dunn, Chattanooga (SL)/Louisville (IL)	.334	350	74	117	22	0	32	84	62	82	11
OF Jason Lane, Round Rock (Texas)	.316	526	103	166	36	2	38	124	61	98	14
DH Jose Fernandez, Salt Lake (Pacific Coast)	.338	452	99	153	37	1	30	114	55	91	9

	W	L	ERA	G	GS	CG	SV	IP	H	BB	SO
P Josh Beckett, Brevard County (FSL)/Portland (EL)	14	1	1.54	26	25	0	0	140	82	34	203
P Boof Bonser, Hagerstown (South Atlantic)	16	4	2.49	27	27	0	0	134	91	61	178
P Brandon Claussen, Tampa (FSL)/Norwich (EL)	14	4	2.31	29	29	1	0	187	148	68	220
P Nate Cornejo, Erie (EL)/Toledo (IL)	16	3	2.57	23	23	3	0	154	131	48	127
P Brandon Duckworth, Scranton/W-B (International)	13	2	2.63	22	20	2	0	147	122	36	150

SECOND TEAM

Pos., Player, Team (League)	AVG	AB	R	H	2B	3B	HR	RBI	BB	SO	SB
C Josh Phelps, Tennessee (Southern)	.292	486	95	142	36	1	31	97	80	127	3
1B Ken Harvey, Wilmington (CL)/Wichita (TL)	.350	451	76	158	29	4	15	90	31	81	6
2B Chad Meyers, Iowa (Pacific Coast)	.300	446	92	134	31	5	9	54	58	72	27
3B Michael Cuddyer, New Britain (EL)	.301	509	95	153	36	3	30	87	75	106	5
SS Wilson Betemit, Myrtle Beach (CL)/Greenville (SL)	.305	501	60	153	34	1	12	62	35	107	14
OF Juan Rivera, Norwich (EL)/Columbus (IL)	.322	515	89	166	29	4	28	98	30	81	9
OF Jamal Strong, Wisconsin (MWL)/San Bern. (CAL)	.326	515	115	168	23	3	0	51	91	87	82
OF Marcus Thames, Norwich (Eastern)	.321	520	114	167	43	4	31	97	73	101	10
DH Jim Rushford, High Desert (CAL)/Huntsville (SL)	.354	446	103	158	38	3	21	91	61	57	6

	W	L	ERA	G	GS	CG	SV	IP	H	BB	SO
P Matt Guerrier, Birmingham (SL)/Charlotte (IL)	18	4	3.30	27	27	4	0	180	160	50	118
P Jimmy Journell, Potomac (CL)/New Haven (EL)	15	6	2.39	27	27	1	0	158	121	45	162
P Corwin Malone, Kannapolis (SAL)/Win.-Salem (CL)/Birm. (SL)	13	5	1.98	27	25	2	0	168	116	66	177
P Mario Ramos, Midland (TL)/Sacramento (PCL)	16	4	3.10	28	28	1	0	174	145	55	150
P Tim Redding, Round Rock (TL)/New Orleans (PCL)	14	3	2.88	20	20	1	0	128	86	44	155

Player of the Year: Josh Beckett, rhp, Brevard County/Portland. **Manager of the Year:** Jackie Moore, Round Rock (Texas).

money coming in, we didn't have the means to make payroll. And there's nothing for these people to do right now."

Quad City was only one team on its way out of town. Also in 2003, the Pacific Coast League's Calgary Cannons plan to move to Albuquerque, where voters approved more than $10 million in renovation to Albuquerque Sports Stadium, giving the Land of Enchantment a PCL team again after a two-year absence.

"There are mixed feelings, but nothing has changed since we made the difficult decision to sell," Cannons owner Russ Parker said.

Parker brought minor league baseball to the southern Alberta city when he purchased a Rookie-level Pioneer League franchise in 1977. In 1984, he bought the PCL's Salt Lake City franchise and moved it north. With the Vancouver Canadians moving to Sacramento at the end of the 1999 season, the demise of the Cannons will leave the Edmonton Trappers as the only Canadian team in the PCL.

Minor league franchises continue to find untapped markets to spur better and better attendance. In the South Atlantic League, new teams in Lexington and Lakewood broke league records for attendance as the Sally League expanded and the Florida State League contracted.

In an effort to provide major league teams 30 high Class

aged more than 5,000 a game in the PCL, while teams in new locations in short-season leagues (Brooklyn; Casper, Wyo.; Pasco, Wash.; and Provo, Utah) provided boosts as well.

Washed Out Of Quad City

It turned out the rising water of the Mississippi River was the least of the Quad City River Bandits' worries.

As the river crested at the end of April and left the field at John O'Donnell Stadium under five feet of water, employees of the team found out they had been laid off.

The next day, the Quad-City Times broke the story that a deal to sell the team to a group from Ohio was all but done. The official announcement came later, and the River Bandits will move to Eastlake, Ohio, for the 2003 season. Eastlake is a Cleveland suburb, and the team will become an Indians affiliate after 2002 as well.

"I'm not sure things can get any worse, really," said Tim Bawmann, the former general manager of the River Bandits who was fired along with almost everyone else who worked for the team.

"It's a pretty screwy situation down there," said the GM from another Midwest League team.

The trouble started with the flooding of the Mississippi River in Davenport, Iowa. As the story was reported across the nation, one of the most frequent pictures was O'Donnell Stadium—first surrounded by water, and eventually inundated with it.

The River Bandits had to abandon the ballpark in mid-April, and played its home dates in the ballparks of Midwest League neighbors or at Black Hawk Junior College, just across the river in Moline, Ill., before returning home in July. It was the third time the team has been forced out of its ballpark in the last nine seasons, with similar situations in 1993 and '97.

Team president Kevin Krause said he had no choice but to lay people off because the franchise wasn't bringing in any money, and he couldn't be sure when the team would be able to return to the ballpark.

"It's the hardest thing I've had to do—ever," he said. "These are people we're talking about. But without any

MANAGER**OF THE**YEAR

"Jackie Moore is a winner," Nolan Ryan flatly states.

The Round Rock Express namesake and principal owner was instrumental in bringing Moore to manage his team in 2000 and 2001, and there are few decisions in life he's been happier with.

"He's baseball through and through, but he's also a great human being," Ryan said. "To have someone who can be so successful and do so with such class and dignity is the best thing that's happened to this franchise."

Moore, who led Round Rock to a Texas League championship in its first year in 2000, had the team in the championship series again in 2001 when play was stopped by the terrorist attacks in New York and Washington. The Express improved

on its 2000 championship record, recording an 86-54 season, a three-win upgrade over 2000's 83-57. It made Moore a clear choice as Baseball America's 2001 Minor League Manager of the Year.

Round Rock opened the year playing the best baseball in the minors, using power pitching and opportunistic hitting to race to a 50-20 record.

"I knew we couldn't continue to play at that level, especially with players getting called up, but it was a special stretch and I enjoyed it while I could," Moore said. The stretch included 11 shutouts in the first 42 games, as Tim Redding, Brad Lidge, Travis Smith and Carlos Hernandez were dominant on the mound.

League player of the year Jason Lane led the offense, leading all minor leaguers in RBIs with 124. His success was a moderate surprise to some, but not to Round Rock broadcaster Mike Capps.

"It's certainly no coincidence that everyone seems to have a career year when Jackie Moore is their manager," Capps said. "He knows how to motivate these guys, and I can tell you they love playing for him."

Moore, with 44 years in pro ball, is a baseball lifer. His playing career, spanning 11 seasons with the Tigers and

TAYLOR JONES

Jackie Moore

Red Sox organizations, included only a single season in the big leagues. But that's where he spent many subsequent years in the game.

His major league coaching experience included work in six organizations. He also managed the Athletics during the 1985 season and parts of the 1984 and 1986 seasons. When Moore signed on to manage the Express, it had been a quarter-century since he was in the minors.

"I honestly didn't know exactly what I was getting into, but I trusted the Ryan family and the Astros organization," he said. "They said they were going to make Round Rock a first-class baseball situation, and that's exactly what they did."

—MICHAEL POINT

PREVIOUS **WINNERS**

1981—Ed Nottle, Tacoma (Athletics)
1982—Eddie Haas, Richmond (Braves)
1983—Bill Dancy, Reading (Phillies)
1984—Sam Perlozzo, Jackson (Mets)
1985—Jim Lefebvre, Phoenix (Giants)
1986—Brad Fischer, Huntsville (Athletics)
1987—Dave Trembley, Harrisburg (Pirates)
1988—Joe Sparks, Indianapolis (Expos)
1989—Buck Showalter, Albany (Yankees)
1990—Kevin Kennedy, Albuquerque (Dodgers)
1991—Butch Hobson, Pawtucket (Red Sox)
1992—Grady Little, Greenville (Braves)
1993—Terry Francona, Birmingham (White Sox)
1994—Tim Ireland, El Paso (Brewers)
1995—Marc Bombard, Indianapolis (Reds)
1996—Carlos Tosca, Portland (Marlins)
1997—Gary Jones, Edmonton (Athletics)
1998—Terry Kennedy, Iowa (Cubs)
1999—John Mizerock, Wichita (Royals)
2000—Joel Skinner, Buffalo (Indians)

MINOR LEAGUES

A affiliates and 30 low-A affiliates, the FSL lost two teams (Kissimmee and St. Petersburg) and the SAL gained two (Lexington and Wilmington, N.C.). But with the Athletics keeping two Cal League affiliates and the Astros keeping two low-A affiliates, the balance didn't quite work out.

Ankiel Highlights Appy Season

While Beckett and Dunn put on a great competition for Baseball America's 2001 Minor League Player of the Year award, the 1999 winner found himself back in the minors after losing the strike zone.

While Cardinals lefthander Rick Ankiel still had not proven he could get hitters out in the big leagues again, he impressed people with his performance both on and off the field as he fell all the way down to the Appalachian League.

Ankiel started the season in St. Louis but was terribly wild, and an assignment to Triple-A didn't work out much better. In his first start for Memphis, he went three-plus innings against Oklahoma, allowing two scratch hits and two runs and striking out three. He walked six and sent eight pitches to the backstop.

Things only got worse in subsequent outings, so Ankiel found himself all the way down at Rookie-level Johnson City for the first time in his career. He ended up with dominant performances as a pitcher (5-3, 1.33 with 158 strikeouts and 18 walks in 88 innings) and good work as a DH as well (.286-10-35 in 105 at-bats).

While he still had to prove himself at higher levels, at least Ankiel appeared to enjoy baseball again. And by all accounts he was a great teammate, carrying equipment bags and being one of the guys, away from the limelight.

Rick Ankiel

"He seemed like he was having fun," Bristol shortstop Mike Morse said. "He was running around smiling. I know we wanted to turn a double play when he was up so we could get on 'SportsCenter.'

"I'd love to hit against him. If you strike out, so what? He's a major league pitcher."

Ankiel avoided all questions about his control problems and when he might get back to the big leagues. But he did seem comfortable that Johnson City was the right place for this moment in his career.

"It's a great city," Ankiel said. "I mean as far as our location, we're staying downtown near the mall, and as far as I can see, there's more restaurants and stuff to do than many of the other cities I've played in."

It was the biggest happening in a dream season for the Appalachian League.

"There's been a lot of excitement with people coming from all over to watch baseball," Johnson City GM Vance Spinks said. "It's been fun, and hopefully it's something we can build on."

Spinks saw attendance nearly double to a league-best 42,816 at Howard Johnson Field thanks to Ankiel.

The league's other big attraction was Joe Mauer, the No. 1 pick in the 2001 draft. He lived up to his lofty

ALL-STAR FUTURES GAME

Reds outfield prospect Adam Dunn led a home run barrage for the U.S. team in its 5-1 victory over the World team in the third annual Futures Game. The game was featured as part of the 2001 All-Star Weekend at Seattle's Safeco Field.

Toby Hall

Devil Rays catcher Toby Hall also homered en route to claiming the game's MVP award, but Dunn's mammoth home run off Safeco's Hit It Here Cafe beyond the right-field bleachers had the stadium buzzing. Little did anyone know that the 21-year-old slugger would finish the season with 51 home runs, including 19 for Cincinnati during a two-month stint in the majors. Dunn added two home runs three days after the Futures Game in the Triple-A All-Star Game.

The U.S. pitching staff shut down the World behind the performances of starter Chris George (Royals) and Brett Myers (Phillies), who each pitched two scoreless innings. Carlos Hernandez (Astros) was the loser in his second consecutive Futures Game appearance.

UNITED STATES ROSTER
Pitchers: Scott Chiasson (Cubs), Nate Cornejo (Tigers), Chris George (Royals), Brett Myers (Phillies), Nick Neugebauer (Brewers), Josh Pearce (Cardinals), Richard Stahl (Orioles), Billy Sylvester (Braves), Dennis Tankersley (Padres), Jerome Williams (Giants), Jason Young (Rockies).
Catchers: Toby Hall (Devil Rays), J.R. House (Pirates).
Infielders: Hank Blalock (Rangers), Sean Burroughs (Padres), Adrian Gonzalez (Marlins), Nick Johnson (Yankees), Cody Ransom (Giants), Chase Utley (Phillies).
Outfielders: Joe Borchard (White Sox), Adam Dunn (Reds), Jason Lane (Astros), Ryan Ludwick (Athletics), Jamal Strong (Mariners).

WORLD TEAM ROSTER
Pitchers: Grant Balfour (Twins), Erik Bedard (Orioles), Juan Cruz (Cubs), Carlos Hernandez (Astros), Alex Herrera (Indians), Juan Pena (Athletics), Ricardo Rodriguez (Dodgers), Jae Seo (Mets), Seung Song (Red Sox), Jose Valverde (Diamondbacks).
Catchers: Humberto Cota (Pirates), Mike Rivera (Tigers).
Infielders: Alfredo Amezaga (Angels), Angel Berroa (Royals), Wilson Betemit (Braves), Miguel Cabrera (Marlins), Luis Garcia (Red Sox), Felipe Lopez (Blue Jays), Carlos Pena (Rangers).
Outfielders: Bill Ortega (Cardinals), Wily Mo Pena (Reds), Juan Rivera (Yankees), Wilken Ruan (Expos).

United States 5, World 1

WORLD	ab	r	h	bi	U.S.	ab	r	h	bi
Amezaga ss	2	0	0	0	Ransom ss	3	0	0	0
Berroa ss	2	0	0	0	Burroughs 3b	2	0	0	0
Betemit 3b	3	1	2	1	Blalock 3b	1	0	0	0
Ortega lf	3	0	1	0	Lane rf	2	0	0	0
JRivera rf	2	0	0	0	Dunn lf	2	1	1	1
WPena rf	1	0	0	0	NJohnson 1b	1	1	1	0
MRivera c	2	0	1	0	AGonzalez 1b	1	0	0	0
Cota c	1	0	0	0	Borchard dh	2	0	1	0
CPena 1b	2	0	0	0	House dh	1	0	0	0
Garcia 1b	1	0	0	0	Ludwick cf	2	0	0	0
Lopez 2b	3	0	1	0	Strong cf	1	0	0	0
Cabrera dh	2	0	0	0	Hall c	3	2	2	1
Ruan cf	3	0	2	0	Utley 2b	3	1	2	2
Totals	**27**	**1**	**7**	**1**	**Totals**	**24**	**5**	**7**	**4**

World	000	001	0—1
U.S.	021	200	x—5

E—Garcia. DP—World 1. LOB—World 6, U.S. 4. 2B—Ortega, Lopez. HR—Betemit, Dunn, Hall, Utley. SB—Hall, Utley.

World	ip	h	r	er	bb	so	U.S.	ip	h	r	er	bb	so
Seo	1	0	0	0	1	2	George W	2	2	0	0	0	2
Hernandez L	1	3	2	2	0	3	Myers	2	1	0	0	0	1
RRodriguez	⅓	0	0	0	0	0	Tankersley	1	1	0	0	0	2
JPena	⅓	2	1	1	0	0	Williams	1	2	1	1	0	2
Cruz	⅔	2	2	1	0	0	Pearce	⅓	0	0	0	0	1
Valverde	⅓	0	0	0	0	0	Chiasson	⅓	1	0	0	1	0
Song	1	0	0	0	1	1	Sylvester	⅓	0	0	0	0	0
Herrera	⅓	0	0	0	0	0							
Balfour	⅔	0	0	0	0	1							

WP—JPena, Tankersley. A—40,850.

CLASSIFICATION ALL-STARS

Selected by Baseball America

TRIPLE-A — International League, Pacific Coast League

Pos., Player, Team (League)	AVG	AB	R	H	2B	3B	HR	RBI	BB	SO	SB
C Toby Hall, Durham (International)	.335	373	59	125	28	1	19	72	29	22	1
1B Carlos Pena, Oklahoma (Pacific Coast)	.288	431	71	124	38	3	23	74	80	127	11
2B Chad Meyers, Iowa (Pacific Coast)	.300	446	92	134	31	5	9	54	58	72	27
3B Jose Fernandez, Salt Lake (Pacific Coast)	.338	452	99	153	37	1	30	114	55	91	9
SS Ramon Vazquez, Tacoma (Pacific Coast)	.300	466	85	140	28	1	10	79	76	84	9
OF Roosevelt Brown, Iowa (Pacific Coast)	.346	364	68	126	34	1	22	77	14	67	3
Ross Gload, Iowa (Pacific Coast)	.297	475	70	141	32	10	15	93	35	88	9
Chris Wakeland, Toledo (International)	.283	547	85	155	33	3	23	84	39	126	7
DH Phil Hiatt, Las Vegas (Pacific Coast)	.330	436	107	144	29	5	44	99	52	109	6

	W	L	ERA	G	GS	CG	SV	IP	H	BB	SO
SP Brandon Duckworth, Scranton/W-B (International)	13	2	2.63	22	20	2	0	147	122	36	150
Brandon Knight, Columbus (International)	12	7	3.66	25	25	3	0	162	174	45	173
Ruben Quevedo, Iowa (Pacific Coast)	9	5	2.99	22	22	1	0	142	124	48	150
Denny Stark, Tacoma (Pacific Coast)	14	2	2.37	24	24	0	0	152	124	41	130
RP Jim Mann, New Orleans (Pacific Coast)	6	3	2.51	53	0	0	27	68	52	17	81

Player of the Year: Brandon Duckworth, rhp, Scranton/Wilkes-Barre (International). **Manager of the Year:** Eric Wedge, Buffalo (International).

DOUBLE-A ALL-STARS — Eastern League, Southern League, Texas League

Pos., Player, Team (League)	AVG	AB	R	H	2B	3B	HR	RBI	BB	SO	SB
C Josh Phelps, Tennessee (Southern)	.292	486	95	142	36	1	31	97	80	127	3
1B Lyle Overbay, El Paso (Texas)	.352	532	82	187	49	3	13	100	67	92	4
2B Tim Hummel, Birmingham (Southern)	.290	524	83	152	33	6	7	63	62	69	14
3B Michael Cuddyer, New Britain (Eastern)	.301	509	95	153	36	3	30	87	75	106	5
SS Omar Infante, Erie (Eastern)	.302	540	86	163	21	4	2	62	46	87	27
OF Marlon Byrd, Reading (Eastern)	.316	510	108	161	22	8	28	89	52	93	32
Jason Lane, Round Rock (Texas)	.316	526	103	166	36	2	38	124	61	98	14
Marcus Thames, Norwich (Eastern)	.321	520	114	167	43	4	31	97	73	101	10
DH Brandon Berger, Wichita (Texas)	.308	454	98	140	28	3	40	118	43	91	14

	W	L	ERA	G	GS	CG	SV	IP	H	BB	SO
SP Chris Baker, Tennessee (Southern)	15	6	3.37	28	26	4	1	179	162	42	121
Brandon Claussen, Norwich (Eastern)	9	2	2.13	21	21	1	0	131	101	55	151
Tim Redding, Round Rock (Texas)	10	2	2.18	14	14	1	0	91	64	25	113
John Stephens, Bowie (Eastern)	11	4	1.84	18	17	3	0	132	95	21	130
RP Scott Chiasson, West Tenn (Southern)	3	4	1.76	52	0	0	24	61	43	20	62

Player of the Year: Marlon Byrd, of, Reading (Eastern). **Manager of the Year:** Jackie Moore, Round Rock (Texas).

HIGH CLASS A ALL-STARS — California League, Carolina League, Florida State League

Pos., Player, Team (League)	AVG	AB	R	H	2B	3B	HR	RBI	BB	SO	SB
C Victor Martinez, Kinston (Carolina)	.329	420	59	138	33	2	10	57	39	60	3
1B Xavier Nady, Lake Elsinore (California)	.302	524	96	158	38	1	26	100	62	109	6
2B Matt Kata, Lancaster (California)	.296	494	80	146	19	6	10	54	41	79	30
3B Hank Blalock, Charlotte (Florida State)	.380	237	46	90	19	1	7	47	26	31	7
SS Jim Deschaine, Daytona (Florida State)	.289	485	68	140	26	2	21	82	62	103	6
OF Nic Jackson, Daytona (Florida State)	.296	503	87	149	30	6	19	85	39	96	24
Chris Snelling, San Bernardino (California)	.336	450	90	151	29	10	7	73	45	63	12
Mike Vento, Tampa (Florida State)	.300	457	71	137	20	10	20	87	45	88	13
DH Billy Martin, Lancaster (California)	.299	472	98	141	33	4	26	106	95	130	0

	W	L	ERA	G	GS	CG	SV	IP	H	BB	SO
SP Craig Anderson, San Bernardino (California)	11	4	2.26	28	28	0	0	179	142	39	178
Jimmy Journell, Potomac (Carolina)	14	6	2.50	26	26	0	0	151	121	42	156
Ricardo Rodriguez, Vero Beach (Florida State)	14	6	3.21	26	26	2	0	154	133	60	154
Matt Thornton, San Bernardino (California)	14	7	2.52	27	27	0	0	157	126	60	192
RP Scotty Layfield, Potomac (Carolina)	1	2	1.84	47	0	0	31	54	36	18	66

Player of the Year: Jimmy Journell, Potomac (Carolina). **Manager of the Year:** Brad Komminsk, Kinston (Carolina).

MINOR LEAGUES

billing in Elizabethton, where attendance rose 33 percent over the 2000 season.

Triple-A World Series Withers

After three editions that failed to generate significant interest from fans in ballparks or on television, the Triple-A World Series went out with a whimper.

The event, which had been played in Las Vegas in September 1998-2000, was tentatively scheduled to return to Cashman Field with a reduced format. But failing attendance (none of the three series averaged more than 4,000 fans) and trouble negotiating a television contract meant the Las Vegas ownership group didn't have much interest in remaining as host.

At the joint Triple-A meeting at the 2000 Winter Meetings, Pacific Coast League owners rejected the possibility of playing a 2001 Triple-A World Series at Cooperstown, which had provided the only full-fledged offer to keep the series alive.

The International League never voted on the Hall of Fame site, but was known to be in favor of it. Without PCL approval, which was lacking in part because of concerns about the facilities at Doubleday Field, the series died. Both leagues were hoping to take proposals for renewing the championship in 2002. At past league meetings, the PCL favored a home-and-home format, while the IL sought neutral, rotating sites.

"After the close vote by the PCL to elect not to go to Cooperstown, I think it's done for now," IL president Mobley said.

CLASSIFICATION ALL-STARS

LOW CLASS A ALL-STARS — Midwest League, South Atlantic League

Pos., Player, Team (League)	AVG	AB	R	H	2B	3B	HR	RBI	BB	SO	SB
C Garett Gentry, Michigan (Midwest)	.299	358	62	107	18	3	24	103	39	45	5
1B Adrian Gonzalez, Kane County (Midwest)	.312	516	86	161	37	1	17	103	57	83	5
2B Felix Escalona, Lexington (South Atlantic)	.289	536	92	155	42	2	16	64	30	85	46
3B Blair Barbier, Lansing (Midwest)	.314	488	77	153	38	1	16	77	52	63	3
SS Jose Reyes, Capital City (South Atlantic)	.307	407	71	125	22	15	5	48	18	71	30
OF Wily Mo Pena, Dayton (Midwest)	.264	511	87	135	24	5	26	113	33	177	26
Will Smith, Kane County (Midwest)	.280	535	92	150	26	2	16	91	32	74	4
Jon Topolski, Lexington (South Atlantic)	.287	550	98	158	27	7	24	96	75	128	28
DH Kelly Johnson, Macon (South Atlantic)	.289	415	75	120	22	1	23	66	71	111	25

	W	L	ERA	G	GS	CG	SV	IP	H	BB	SO
SP Boof Bonser, Hagerstown (South Atlantic)	16	4	2.49	27	27	0	0	134	91	61	178
Corwin Malone, Kannapolis (South Atlantic)	11	4	2.00	18	18	2	0	112	83	44	119
Clint Nageotte, Wisconsin (Midwest)	11	8	3.13	28	26	0	0	152	141	50	187
Mike Nannini, Lexington (South Atlantic)	15	5	2.70	28	27	4	0	190	176	36	151
RP Mike Steele, West Michigan (Midwest)	4	3	1.16	38	0	0	19	47	23	26	78

Player of the Year: Boof Bonser, rhp, Hagerstown (South Atlantic). **Manager of the Year:** Gary Thurman, Wisconsin (Midwest).

SHORT-SEASON ALL-STARS — New York-Penn League, Northwest League

Pos., Player, Team (League)	AVG	AB	R	H	2B	3B	HR	RBI	BB	SO	SB
C Casey Myers, Vancouver (Northwest)	.278	198	24	55	15	0	7	35	22	34	0
1B Aaron Rifkin, Staten Island (New York-Penn)	.322	242	41	78	19	5	10	49	29	46	3
2B Tim Merritt, Everett (Northwest)	.306	196	33	60	13	3	5	30	9	35	11
3B Ryan Raburn, Oneonta (New York-Penn)	.368	163	24	60	16	8	8	41	15	41	1
SS Jason Bartlett, Eugene (Northwest)	.307	261	49	80	12	4	3	37	28	43	12
OF Syketo Anderson, Boise (Northwest)	.375	285	67	107	12	6	6	41	12	34	24
Condor Cash, Boise (Northwest)	.350	240	32	84	18	4	10	47	26	37	6
J.J. Johnson, Boise (Northwest)	.317	284	54	90	15	5	7	59	20	50	18
DH Greg Sain, Eugene (Northwest)	.294	248	46	73	19	1	16	40	20	63	1

	W	L	ERA	G	GS	CG	SV	IP	H	BB	SO
SP Jason Arnold, Staten Island (New York-Penn)	7	2	1.50	10	10	2	0	66	35	15	74
Jesse Foppert, Salem-Keizer (Northwest)	8	1	1.93	14	14	0	0	70	35	23	88
Angel Guzman, Boise (Northwest)	9	1	2.23	14	14	0	0	77	68	19	63
Ross Peeples, Brooklyn (New York-Penn)	9	3	1.34	16	15	1	0	80	63	29	67
RP Kevin Barry, Jamestown (New York-Penn)	1	0	0.86	29	0	0	12	31	14	18	54

Player of the Year: J.J. Johnson, Boise (Northwest). **Manager of the Year:** Edgar Alfonzo, Brooklyn (New York-Penn).

ROOKIE ALL-STARS — Appalachian League, Arizona League, Gulf Coast League, Pioneer League

Pos., Player, Team (League)	AVG	AB	R	H	2B	3B	HR	RBI	BB	SO	SB
C Brayan Pena, Danville (Appalachian)	.370	235	39	87	16	2	1	33	31	30	3
1B Jesus Cota, Missoula (Pioneer)	.368	272	74	100	22	0	16	71	56	52	2
2B Scott Hairston, Missoula (Pioneer)	.347	291	81	101	16	6	14	65	38	50	2
3B Florian Villanueva, Ogden (Pioneer)	.308	273	52	84	21	2	6	53	18	27	5
SS Casey Smith, Provo (Pioneer)	.321	249	60	80	11	1	1	34	37	40	6
OF Jonny Gomes, Princeton (Appalachian)	.291	206	58	60	11	2	16	44	33	73	15
Sam Swenson, Provo (Pioneer)	.351	225	61	79	16	4	13	55	24	64	7
Chris Tritle, Athletics (Arizona)	.336	214	47	72	6	8	9	42	22	55	26
DH Jesse Gutierrez, Billings (Pioneer)	.294	269	45	79	21	0	16	61	29	43	1

	W	L	ERA	G	GS	CG	SV	IP	H	BB	SO
SP Rick Ankiel, Johnson City (Appalachian)	5	3	1.33	14	14	1	0	88	42	18	158
Pedro Liriano, Provo (Pioneer)	11	2	2.78	15	14	0	0	78	80	31	76
J.D. Martin, Burlington (Appalachian)	5	1	1.38	10	10	0	0	46	26	11	72
Chad Petty, Tigers (Gulf Coast)	6	0	1.11	12	10	2	0	57	35	13	52
RP Ryan Keefer, Bluefield (Appalachian)	1	0	0.59	29	0	0	15	31	20	8	46

Player of the Year: Rick Ankiel, lhp/dh, Johnson City (Appalachian). **Manager of the Year:** Chip Hale, Missoula (Pioneer).

MINOR LEAGUES

It was the IL that voted out of the Triple-A Alliance with the American Association in 1990. The IL and AA clubs had played each other in the regular season and met in a championship that didn't include the PCL winner.

The American Association dissolved after the 1997 season, leaving the Triple-A classification with two leagues. One benefit of that realignment was the feasibility of a true Triple-A championship series. Even if the series is now a thing of the past, the leagues have no concrete plans to go back to three leagues with less travel.

Mobley and PCL president Branch Rickey clearly were disappointed a fourth Triple-A World Series might not get off the ground.

"If you believe in the potential of the event—and I do—then it is tough," Mobley said. "I think we should be forever grateful to the Las Vegas Convention and Visitors Authority for giving it a chance, but after three years out there we also came to the conclusion that they weren't the spot."

Rickey added: "We're disappointed not to be going forward with the event, but as one of the International League officials said today, when one door closes, somewhere a window opens . . . There were a variety of factors that we felt would be better resolved in advance. It's a little bit of a disruption on one front, but we'll go forward on to the next one and see what we can work out for the future."

The 1998 New Orleans Zephyrs (Astros), 1999 Vancouver Canadians (Athletics) and 2000 Indianapolis Indians (Brewers) were the three champions. Major leaguers who played in the event include Lance Berkman, Russell Branyan, Jon Garland, John Halama, Terrence

Long, Julio Lugo, Adam Piatt and Barry Zito.

And in Double-A, getting all the leagues together for an all-star game has become too much trouble.

At the Double-A association meetings in Round Rock, Texas, in July 2001, the three leagues voted to suspend the classification-wide game after it's played at Norwich in 2002.

The loss of a live television contract with ESPN, the lack of teams interested in staging the event and the creation of the Futures Game two years earlier were major factors in the decision. The Southern and Texas leagues already have their own all-star games, and the Eastern League will add one.

"It was something that's been talked about for a long time," Kayser said. "While these games have been successful, I think it was time to review its status.

"The general feeling among the Double-A executives is that it's time to step back for a while."

When It Raines . . .

When Tim Raines Jr. was young and his father played for the Expos, they were regulars in Montreal's annual father-son games.

But in 2001, Raines Jr. and Raines Sr. played father-and-son games that really counted. With Tim Jr. playing for Rochester and Tim Sr. on an injury rehabilitation assignment with Ottawa in the International League, the Red Wings and Lynx split a doubleheader Aug. 21 at Ottawa's JetForm Park. It is believed to be the first time a father and son played against each other in a regular season professional game at any level.

"It was a great day for the Raines family," Tim Sr. said. "Our main goal is to do it in the big leagues."

They did just that at the end of the season, as the Orioles acquired Tim Sr. and started father and son in the outfield in one September game. Ken Griffey Jr. and Sr. had been the only father and son to play in the big leagues at the same time.

"We set goals three or four years ago to do that," Raines Sr. said. "We wanted to be the second father-son to play in the big leagues."

Senior and Junior had played against each other in a spring training game in March in Jupiter, Fla. They each had a run-scoring single as the Orioles beat Montreal 7-6.

Before the game in Ottawa, father and son exchanged lineup cards at home plate. Each had a hit in his first at-bat: Raines Sr. hit a double and scored, while Raines Jr. reached on an infield single and stole second base.

"It was a great day," Raines Jr. said. "It was another learning experience. Every time he got up there, I was watching every little thing he was doing."

Too Much Tragedy

Even before the events of Sept. 11, it seemed the minors had experienced too much bad news in 2001, with the deaths of several active players.

■ Brian Cole, one of the brightest prospects in the Mets organization, died at the end of spring training from injuries suffered when he was thrown from his sport-utility vehicle.

According to a highway patrol report, Cole's vehicle flipped 1¾ times on a Florida interstate near the Georgia border.

Cole was 22, a rare combination of power and speed and an outstanding person.

"Off what I saw, he was a can't-miss kid who could

TRIPLE-A ALL-STAR GAME

After starring in the 2001 Futures Game, Adam Dunn hung around Seattle to watch the major league home run derby and wasn't able to compete in the Triple-A derby at Indianapolis' Victory Field. That was OK, though, because he decided to stage a Home Run Derby of his own during the actual Triple-A all-star game.

The Pacific Coast League beat the International League 9-5, but the player of the game and the recipient of the most electricity from the crowd was clearly the IL's Dunn. The former Texas quarterback entered the game with 30 home runs on the season, including 18 for the Louisville RiverBats after a strong start at Double-A Chattanooga. He slammed two long blasts in the Triple-A all-star game.

The two—and one in the Futures Game—didn't officially count as Nos. 31, 32 and 33 but displayed the long-bomb talents Dunn showed for more than three months of the minor league season before he was promoted to Cincinnati.

The Reds' lefthanded-hitting outfield prospect launched a 450-foot homer in the first inning that left the confines of the stadium. He hit one nearly that far just to the right of dead center field in the fourth.

"I kind of regret not coming to (the home run derby), but I missed a couple of flights," said Dunn, who homered in his first two at-bats. "I guess I made up for that tonight."

Dunn tied the Triple-A all-star game home run record, which was set by Richmond's Ryan Klesko in Albuquerque in 1993. Dunn's shots were the IL's only hits in the first eight innings. Hometown Indianapolis Indian Mike Coolbaugh hit a two-run homer in the ninth, but enough damage had already been done. DH Juan Thomas of the Tacoma Rainiers gave the PCL a 3-2 lead with a two-run homer in the fourth, and the IL could never get the lead back.

TRIPLE-A ALL-STAR GAME
July 11 at Indianapolis
Pacific Coast League 9, International League 5

PCL	ab	r	h	bi	IL	ab	r	h	bi
Redman cf	3	1	2	1	Forbes 2b	2	0	0	0
Prieto cf	2	1	1	1	Mateo 2b	1	1	0	0
Ginter 2b	2	0	0	0	NJohnson 1b	2	0	0	0
Figueroa 2b	3	0	1	1	Coolbaugh 1b	2	1	1	2
Betts 1b	3	1	1	1	Hall c	2	1	0	0
Pellow 1b	2	0	0	0	Norris c	2	0	0	0
Cust rf	2	1	2	1	Dunn lf	4	2	2	3
Mota rf	1	0	0	0	Lesher rf	2	0	0	0
Thomas dh	3	1	1	2	Sheff rf	2	0	1	0
Fernandez dh	1	0	0	0	Pickering dh	2	0	0	0
Gulan 3b	3	1	1	0	Wright dh	2	0	0	0
Burroughs 3b	1	0	0	0	Latham cf	2	0	0	0
Byrnes lf	3	0	0	0	Gonzalez cf	1	0	0	0
Monroe lf	1	1	1	0	Orie 3b	2	0	0	0
Castro c	3	1	0	0	Crede 3b	1	0	0	0
Valentin c	1	0	0	0	Almonte ss	2	0	0	0
Vazquez ss	2	1	0	0	Medrano ss	1	0	0	0
Ransom ss	0	0	0	0					
Uribe ss	1	0	0	0					
Totals	37	9	10	7	Totals	32	5	4	5

Pacific Coast League	100	231	002—9
International League	200	100	002—5

E—Gulan, Coolbaugh, Hall. DP—IL 1. LOB—PCL 3, IL 1. 2B—Prieto, Cust, Gulan. HR—Dunn 2, Thomas, Coolbaugh. SB—Redman 2, Monroe.

PCL	ip	h	r	er	bb	so	IL	ip	h	r	er	bb	so
B. Smith	2	1	2	0	0	3	Duckworth	2	1	1	0	1	5
Quevedo W	3	1	1	1	0	2	Roque	1	0	0	0	0	0
Wengert	1	0	0	0	0	1	M. Johnson	1	2	2	2	0	0
Ruffin	2	0	0	0	0	0	Jodie L	2	4	4	2	1	0
Mann	1	2	2	2	1	1	R. Smith	1	0	0	0	0	1
							Henriquez	1	0	0	0	0	1
							DeWitt	1	3	2	2	0	2

T—2:35. A—15,868.

have had a 15-year career as an impact player in the big leagues," Mets coach John Stearns said. "And he wanted it. He had a high ceiling and higher aspirations.

"This is the worst experience I've had in my professional career."

Cole was Baseball America's Junior College Player of the Year in 1998 at Navarro (Texas). He was a BA high Class A all-star in 2000 after he stole 69 bases and hit 19 homers between Class A St. Lucie and Double-A Binghamton.

RICH ABEL

Brian Cole

"He was the one you loved to dream about," Mets farm director Jim Duquette said. "What could he become? He did everything the right way."

■ Independent league righthander John LeRoy died June 25 due to complications during shoulder surgery at Mercy Medical Center in Sioux City, Iowa. He was 26.

LeRoy complained of numbness after his first two Northern League appearances for the Sioux City Explorers and decided to see a circulatory specialist. Doctors found a severe blockage in a main artery leading from LeRoy's heart to his shoulder.

LeRoy had surgery on June 20, but the next day another blockage was discovered in his forearm. On June 22, complications arose during a procedure to correct the second blockage.

"Our hearts go out to John's family and especially to his wife Aleata and their children," Explorers general manager George Stavrenos said. "The team is going through a lot of suffering; they're hurting. John was a veteran, a team leader even though he didn't have a lot of innings. Guys knew he had pitched in the major leagues. He was just a fun guy to be around."

LeRoy, the Braves' 15th-round draft pick in 1993 out of Sammamish (Wash.) High, moved quickly through the Braves system. In 1996, he went 7-4, 3.50 in 111 innings at Class A Durham and 1-1, 2.98 in 45 innings at Double-A Greenville. He was called up to Atlanta in 1997, earning a win in his only major league appearance.

■ Gerik Baxter, one of the top pitching prospects in the Padres system, and Mark Hilde, a 2001 draft pick of the Athletics, were killed July 29 in a car crash near Indio, Calif. Baxter was 21, and Hilde was 18.

Baxter, a righthander drafted in the first round in 1999, had been rated San Diego's fifth-best prospect by Baseball America entering the 2001 season. Hilde, a third baseman, was taken in the 32nd round in June but hadn't signed with Oakland.

"This is a shocker, something that stops you dead in your tracks," Padres farm director Tye Waller said. "It's very unfortunate, very sad."

Baxter, who had been injured all season, had gone to Phoenix to watch Hilde, his former teammate at Edmonds-Woodway (Wash.) High, play in a tournament. They were driving back to Southern California when the accident occurred.

According to police reports, Baxter's 2001 Ford F-350 blew a right rear tire while traveling on Interstate 10. The

DOUBLE-A ALL-STAR GAME

The Huntsville Stars' David Gibralter got to see old friends, make a few new ones and grab an extra $315 for his three-run homer in the 2001 Double-A all-star game at Dell Diamond in Round Rock, Texas. Gibralter led the National League affiliates to an 8-3 victory over their American League counterparts.

"Not bad at all, huh?" said Gibralter, a native Texan, as fireworks exploded behind him during the postgame celebration. "This is definitely one of the highlights of my career . . . so far."

Gibralter, 26, provided the first fireworks of the night. After the AL took a 1-0 lead on a homer by New Britain's Dustan Mohr in the top of the second, the starting NL third baseman smacked a three-run homer to left field in the bottom of the frame off Erie's Nate Cornejo to highlight a five-run outburst.

The blast was enough to make Gibralter the MVP of the game from the Southern League. And in a Round Rock Express tradition, a batting helmet was passed through the stands after the home team's homer, netting the Duncanville High graduate the cool $315.

"The main thing is to have fun," Gibralter said. "There's no question you want to do well, but you've got to have a good time with all these guys. There's a great pool of talent."

Later in the same inning, leadoff hitter Ramon Castro of Greenville hit a two-run homer to make it 5-1.

The 2002 Double-A all-star game is scheduled for Norwich (Eastern), but the three Double-A leagues voted to dissolve the game from that point on.

DOUBLE-A ALL-STAR GAME
July 11 at Round Rock, Texas
National League 8, American League 3

AMERICAN	ab	r	h	bi	NATIONAL	ab	r	h	bi
Amezaga 2b	4	1	2	0	RCastro ss	3	2	2	2
Infante ss	2	0	0	0	NCastro ss	1	1	1	0
Salazar ss	1	0	0	0	Matranga 2b	2	0	0	0
Cuddyer 3b	3	0	2	0	Luther 2b	2	0	0	0
Robinson 3b	1	0	1	0	Lane rf	3	0	1	2
Landry lf	3	0	0	0	Overbay 1b	3	1	2	0
Berger rf	1	0	0	1	Byrd cf	2	1	0	0
Borchard rf	2	1	1	1	Crosby cf	1	0	0	0
Rivera c	3	0	1	0	Snyder dh	4	1	1	1
Phelps c	1	0	0	0	Gibralter 3b	1	1	1	3
Quinlan 1b	2	0	1	0	Owens 3b	2	0	0	0
Kuzmic 1b	2	0	0	0	Cepicky lf	4	0	0	0
Mohr cf	2	1	1	1	House c	1	0	0	0
Crawford cf	2	0	0	0	Tremie c	1	0	0	0
Thames dh	3	0	0	0					
Totals	**32**	**3**	**9**	**3**	**Totals**	**30**	**8**	**8**	**8**

American League	011	001	000—3
National League	050	010	11x—8

DP—American 1, National 3. **LOB**—American 5, National 6. **2B**—Amezaga, Cuddyer, R. Castro, N. Castro, Overbay. **HR**—Borchard, Mohr, R. Castro, Snyder, Gibralter. **SF**—Berger, Lane. **SB**—Amezaga, Cuddyer, Landry, N. Castro.

American	ip	h	r	er	bb	so	National	ip	h	r	er	bb	so
Cornejo L	2	3	5	5	2	4	Silva W	2	3	1	1	1	3
White	1	1	0	0	0	0	Olsen	1	2	1	1	1	1
Stephens	1	0	0	0	1	2	Devey	1	1	0	0	0	0
Pratt	⅓	1	1	1	2	0	Smith	1	1	0	0	0	2
Yates	⅔	0	0	0	0	1	DiFelice	1	1	1	1	0	1
Thomas	1	0	0	0	0	1	Neugebauer	1	0	0	0	2	0
McLeary	1	2	1	1	0	1	Fikac	1	1	0	0	0	1
Almonte	⅓	1	1	1	0	1	Serrano	⅔	0	0	0	0	2
Pacheco	⅔	0	0	0	2	1	Puffer	⅓	0	0	0	0	0

T—2:54. **A**—12,046.

truck was traveling at 75-85 mph when the tire blew, causing it to veer to the right and sideswipe a Chevy Tahoe.

Baxter lost control of his truck, which left the road and rolled several times. Both Baxter and Hilde were ejected from the Ford. Neither was wearing his seatbelt.

MINOR LEAGUE
DEPARTMENT LEADERS
*Full-season teams only

TEAM

WINS
Lexington (South Atlantic) 92
Buffalo (International) 91
Lake Elsinore (California) 91
Kinston (Carolina) 89
Kane County (Midwest) 88

LONGEST WINNING STREAK
Missoula (Pioneer) 13
San Antonio (Texas) 13
Brooklyn (New York-Penn) 12
Myrtle Beach (Carolina) 11
Lexington (South Atlantic) 10
Norwich (Eastern) 10
Pittsfield (New York-Penn) 10
Round Rock (Texas) 10
Wichita (Texas) 10
Wisconsin (Midwest) 10

LOSSES
New Haven (Eastern) 95
Charleston, W. Va. (South Atlantic) 87
Winston-Salem (Carolina) 86
Clinton (Midwest) 85
Modesto (California) 85

LONGEST LOSING STREAK
Vermont (New York-Penn) 14
Lancaster (California) 13
Capital City (South Atlantic) 13
Charleston, W. Va. (South Atlantic) 10
Lancaster (California) 10
Trenton (Eastern) 10

BATTING AVERAGE*
Calgary (Pacific Coast) .... .292
Colorado Springs (Pacific Coast) .... .290
Salt Lake (Pacific Coast) .... .288
Edmonton (Pacific Coast) .... .285
Tacoma (Pacific Coast) .... .285

RUNS
High Desert (California) 837
Salt Lake (Pacific Coast) 820
Calgary (Pacific Coast) 810
Lancaster (California) 801
Lexington (South Atlantic) 781

HOME RUNS
Calgary (Pacific Coast) 187
Las Vegas (Pacific Coast) 184
Sacramento (Pacific Coast) 173
Pawtucket (International) 171
Fresno (Pacific Coast) 170

Lyle Overbay: .352 average

ROBERT GURGANUS

Hank Blalock: .352 average

MICHAEL WALBY

STOLEN BASES
Wilmington (South Atlantic) 275
Peoria (Midwest) 249
Wisconsin (Midwest) 245
Michigan (Midwest) 222
Lexington (South Atlantic) 221

EARNED RUN AVERAGE*
Kinston (Carolina) 2.73
Augusta (South Atlantic) 2.93
Wisconsin (Midwest) 2.96
New Britain (Eastern) 3.02
Lake Elsinore (California) 3.03

STRIKEOUTS
Lake Elsinore (California) 1,343
San Bernardino (California) 1,262
Kinston (Carolina) 1,260
Lexington (South Atlantic) 1,235
Iowa (Pacific Coast) 1,228

FIELDING AVERAGE*
Scranton/Wilkes-Barre (International) .... .982
Richmond (International) .... .980
Portland (Pacific Coast) .... .980
Portland (Eastern) .... .980
Seven tied at .... .978

INDIVIDUAL BATTING

BATTING AVERAGE
(Minimum 383 Plate Appearances)
Jim Rushford, High Desert/Huntsville ... .354
Hank Blalock, Charlotte (FSL)/Tulsa .... .352
Lyle Overbay, El Paso .... .352
Ken Harvey, Wilmington (CL)/Wichita ...... .350
Jason Maule, Michigan .... .347
Roosevelt Brown, Iowa .... .346
Ray Sadler, Lansing .... .341
Jose Fernandez, Salt Lake .... .338
Quinton McCracken, Edmonton .... .338
Dustan Mohr, New Britain .... .336

RUNS
Esteban German, Midland/Sacramento 119
Jamal Strong, Wisconsin/San Bernardino .. 115
Marcus Thames, Norwich 114
Marlon Byrd, Reading 108
Phil Hiatt, Las Vegas 107

HITS
Lyle Overbay, El Paso 187
Hank Blalock, Charlotte (FSL)/Tulsa 179
Tony Torcato, San Jose/Shreveport/Fresno .. 179
Dustan Mohr, New Britain 174
Reed Johnson, Tennessee 174

TOP HITTING STREAKS
Adam Hyzdu, Nashville 26
Chris Snelling, San Bernardino 25
Andy Phillips, Tampa 24
Kevin Sefcik, Colorado Springs 23

MOST HITS, ONE GAME
Syketo Anderson, Boise 6
Kevin Barker, Huntsville 6
Jesus Feliciano, Sarasota 6
Justin Martin, Lynchburg 6

TOTAL BASES
Jason Lane, Round Rock 320
Phil Hiatt, Las Vegas 315
Marcus Thames, Norwich 311
Brandon Berger, Wichita 294
Dustan Mohr, New Britain 293

EXTRA-BASE HITS
Phil Hiatt, Las Vegas 78
Marcus Thames, Norwich 78
Jason Lane, Round Rock 76
Brandon Berger, Wichita 71
Scott Morgan, Salt Lake 70

DOUBLES
Lyle Overbay, El Paso 49
John Gall, Peoria/Potomac 48
Steve Smitherman, Dayton 45
Chad Alexander, Tacoma 45
Mike Gulan, Calgary 44

TRIPLES
B.J. Littleton, Delmarva 18
Jose Reyes, Capital City 15
Jaime Bubela, Wisconsin 12
Henri Stanley, Michigan 12
Henry Mateo, Ottawa 12
Jonathan Guzman, Burlington (MWL) 12
Victor Hall, South Bend 12

HOME RUNS
Phil Hiatt, Las Vegas 44
Brandon Berger, Wichita 40
Jason Lane, Round Rock 38
Jacques Landry, Midland 36
Izzy Alcantara, Pawtucket 36

RUNS BATTED IN
Jason Lane, Round Rock 124
Brandon Berger, Wichita 118
Jose Fernandez, Salt Lake 114
Wily Mo Pena, Dayton 113
Hank Blalock, Charlotte (FSL)/Tulsa 108

MOST RBIs, ONE GAME
Mike Edwards, Mahoning Valley 10
Kirk Asche, Visalia 8
Jason Lane, Round Rock 8
Ryan Ludwick, Midland 8
Eric Welsh, Mudville 8

STOLEN BASES
Chris Morris, Peoria 111
Jamal Strong, Wisconsin/San Bernardino .. 82
Manny Ravelo, Hickory/Lynchburg 70
Nook Logan, West Michigan 67
Bernabel Castro, Greensboro 67

CAUGHT STEALING
Carlos Rosario, Visalia 24
Chris Morris, Peoria 24
Esix Snead, New Haven 23
Chad Durham, Winston-Salem 22
Dave Krynzel, Beloit/High Desert 22

HIT BY PITCHES
Angel Berroa, Wilmington (CL)/Wichita 36
Corky Miller, Chattanooga/Louisville 31
Kevin West, Quad City 28
J.J. Sherrill, Columbus (SAL) 27
Jesus Basabe, Modesto 27

MINOR LEAGUES

WALKS

Lamont Matthews, Vero Beach/Jacksonville .. 107
Jack Cust, Tucson 102
Billy Martin, Lancaster/El Paso 96
Marco Cunningham, Wilmington (CL) 95
Gray Koonce, Mobile/Portland (PCL) 94

STRIKEOUTS

Rob Stratton, Binghamton/Norfolk 203
Darron Ingram, Birmingham 188
Jeremy Owens, Lake Elsinore/Mobile 188
Jacques Landry, Midland 184
Wily Mo Pena, Dayton 177

SACRIFICE FLIES

Alexis Rios, Charleston, W. Va. 14
Andy Phillips, Tampa/Norwich 12
Butch Huskey, Colorado Springs 12
Javier Colina, Salem/Carolina 12
Nate Grindell, Kinston/Akron 11

SACRIFICE BUNTS

Todd West, Beloit 26
Tony Stevens, Fort Myers/New Britain 26
Carlos Gastelum, Rancho Cucamonga 23
Jesse Garcia, Richmond 21
Jermaine Allensworth, Toledo 21

SLUGGING PERCENTAGE

Phil Hiatt, Las Vegas .... .722
Adam Dunn, Chattanooga/Louisville .... .671
Brandon Berger, Wichita .... .648
Ramon Castro, Calgary .... .628
Roosevelt Brown, Iowa .... .626

ON-BASE PERCENTAGE

Jason Maule, Michigan .... .448
Adam Dunn, Chattanooga/Louisville .... .444
Jim Rushford, High Desert/Huntsville .... .438
Jamal Strong, Wisconsin/San Bernardino .. .436
Lamont Matthews, Vero Beach/Jacksonville .. .436

BATTING AVERAGE*
By Position
(Minimum 383 Plate Appearances)
Catchers
Ramon Castro, Calgary .... .336
Toby Hall, Durham .... .335
John Castellano, Wisconsin .... .334
Craig Ansman, South Bend .... .330
Victor Martinez, Kinston .... .329

First Basemen
Lyle Overbay, El Paso .... .352
Ken Harvey, Wilmington (CL)/Wichita .... .350
Garrett Atkins, Salem .... .325
Luis Lopez, Syracuse .... .324
Butch Huskey, Colorado Springs .... .323

Second Basemen
Pedro Liriano, Wisconsin .... .326
Luis Gonzalez, Kinston/Akron .... .312
Juan Melo, Fresno .... .312
Esteban German, Midland/Sacramento ...... .311
Matt Erickson, Calgary .... .310

Jackson Markert: 39 saves

Third Basemen

Hank Blalock, Charlotte (FSL)/Tulsa .... .352
Jason Maule, Michigan .... .347
Jose Fernandez, Salt Lake .... .338
Phil Hiatt, Las Vegas .... .330
Brian Dallimore, El Paso .... .327

Shortstops

Freddy Sanchez, Sarasota/Trenton .... .334
Tommy Whiteman, Lexington/Round Rock .. .316
Jose Reyes, Capital City .... .307
Wilson Betemit, Myrtle Beach/Greenville ... .305
Angel Berroa, Wilmington (CL)/Wichita .. .304

Outfielders

Jim Rushford, High Desert/Huntsville ...... .354
Roosevelt Brown, Iowa .... .346
Ray Sadler, Lansing .... .341
Quinton McCracken, Edmonton .... .338
Dustan Mohr, New Britain .... .336
Chris Snelling, San Bernardino .... .336

EARNED RUN AVERAGE
(Minimum 112 Innings)
Josh Beckett, Brevard County/Portland (EL) .. 1.54
Seung Song, Augusta/Sarasota 1.90
Brad Thomas, New Britain 1.96
Dennis Tankersley, Lake Elsinore/Mobile/LV .. 1.98
Corwin Malone, Kannapolis/W-S/Birm. 1.98
Rodrigo Rosario, Lexington 2.14
Ryan Kibler, Asheville/Salem/Carolina 2.15
Jose Rojas, Wilmington (SAL)/Vero Beach .. 2.21
Craig Anderson, San Bernardino 2.26
Mike Smith, Charleston, W. Va./Tennessee .. 2.26

WINS

Matt Guerrier, Birmingham/Charlotte (IL) .. 18
Nate Cornejo, Erie/Toledo 16
Mario Ramos, Midland/Sacramento 16
Boof Bonser, Hagerstown 16
Julio DePaula, Asheville/Greensboro/Tampa .. 16
Hansel Izquierdo, Kane Cty./Brevard/Port. (EL) .. 16

LOSSES

Rick Guttormson, Mobile/Portland (PCL) ... 17
Duncan McAdoo, Fort Wayne 16
Brent Schoening, Fort Myers/New Britian ... 15
Jason Saenz, Binghamton 15
Dave Zancanaro, New Haven/Memphis 14
Robert Averette, Colorado Springs 14
Taylor Buchholz, Lakewood 14
Franklin Tejeda, Potomac 14
Jack Cassel, Fort Wayne 14

GAMES

Brian Bowles, Syracuse 66
Clay Condrey, Mobile/Portland (PCL) 66
J.J. Trujillo, Lake Elsinore/Mobile 66
Ray Beasley, Richmond 65
Scott Chiasson, West Tenn/Iowa 63
Lesli Brea, Rochester 63
Robbie Crabtree, Fresno 63
Tim McClaskey, Brevard/Portland (EL) 63
Jason Martines, El Paso/Tucson 63

COMPLETE GAMES

Carlos Castillo, Pawtucket 5
Dennis Ulacia, Kann./W-S/Birm./Char. (IL) .. 5
Tim Kalita, Erie 5
Greg Wooten, Tacoma 5
Sam Marsonek, Tampa 5
Taylor Buchholz, Lakewood 5

SAVES

Jackson Markert, Hagerstown 39
Ed Almonte, Birmingham 36
Scott Chiasson, West Tenn/Iowa 34
Scotty Layfield, Potomac 31
Greg Runser, Charlotte (FSL) 30
Luke Anderson, San Jose 30
Justin Huisman, Asheville 30

INNINGS

Tim Kalita, Erie 200
Jared Fernandez, Louisville 196
Mike Nannini, Lexington 190
John Stephens, Bowie/Rochester 190
Mike Smith, Charleston, W. Va./Tennessee .. 187
Brandon Claussen, Tampa/Norwich 187

WAGNER PHOTOGRAPHY

Jim Rushford: .354 average led minors

WALKS

Chad Hutchinson, Memphis 104
Scott Dunn, Mudville/Chattanooga 102
Carlos Chantres, Indianapolis 93
Steve Sparks, Altoona/Nashville 89
Dave Elder, Tulsa/Oklahoma 86
Anthony Pluta, Lexington 86

STRIKEOUTS

Brandon Claussen, Tampa/Norwich 220
Josh Beckett, Brevard County/Portland (EL) .. 203
Matt Thornton, San Bernardino 192
John Stephens, Bowie/Rochester 191
Jake Peavy, Lake Elsinore/Mobile 188

STRIKEOUTS/9 INNINGS*
(Starters)
Josh Beckett, Brevard County/Portland (EL) .. 13.05
Jake Peavy, Lake Elsinore/Mobile 12.69
Nick Neugebauer, Huntsville/Indianapolis .. 12.05
Boof Bonser, Hagerstown 11.96
Francisco Rodriguez, Rancho Cucamonga .. 11.64

STRIKEOUTS/9 INNINGS*
(Relievers)
Jose Valverde, El Paso 15.68
Alberto Garza, Columbus (SAL)/Kinston .. 14.24
Michael Neu, Mudville 14.20
Buddy Hernandez, Macon/Myrtle Beach .. 14.10
Chris Booker, West Tenn/Chattanooga .. 13.37

BATTING AVERAGE AGAINST*
(Starters)
Josh Beckett, Brevard County/Portland (EL) .. .170
Rafael Soriano, San Bernardino/San Antonio .. .174
Dennis Tankersley, LE/Mobile/Las Vegas .181
Tim Redding, Round Rock/New Orleans .. .187
Domingo Valdez, Savannah/Charlotte (FSL) .. .189

BATTING AVERAGE AGAINST*
(Relievers)
Alex Pacheco, Norwich .... .142
Joe Valentine, Kannapolis/Winston-Salem .... .152
Jeremy Hill, Burlington (MWL)/Wilmington (CL) .. .157
Arnaldo Munoz, Kannapolis .... .160
Buddy Hernandez, Macon/Myrtle Beach .. .165

MOST STRIKEOUTS IN ONE GAME

Randy Keisler, Columbus (IL) 18
Rick Ankiel, Johnson City 17
Aaron Krawiec, Lansing 17
Carlos Hernandez, Round Rock 16
Ben Howard, Lake Elsinore 16
Dave Martinez, Greensboro 16

MOST ERRORS

David Espinosa, ss, Dayton 48
Ramon Carvajal, ss, Potomac 48
Daryl Clark, 3b, Beloit 47
Corey Smith, 3b, Columbus (SAL) 45
Bill Hall, ss, High Desert/Huntsville 45
Kelly Johnson, ss, Macon 45

KEN BABBITT

MINOR LEAGUES

MINOR LEAGUE BEST TOOLS

	International League AAA	Pacific Coast League AAA	Eastern League AA	Southern League AA	Texas League AA	California League A	Carolina League A	Florida State League A	Midwest League A	South Atlantic League A
Best Batting Prospect	Toby Hall, Durham	Sean Burroughs, Portland	Juan Rivera, Norwich	Joe Borchard, Birmingham	Lyle Overbay, El Paso	Xavier Nady, Lake Elsinore	Covelli Crisp, Potomac	Hank Blalock, Charlotte	Adrian Gonzalez, Kane County	Kelly Johnson, Macon
Best Power Prospect	Adam Dunn, Louisville	Jack Cust, Tucson	Mike Rivera, Erie	Adam Dunn, Chattanooga	Jason Lane, Round Rock	Xavier Nady, Lake Elsinore	Ray Cabrera, Frederick	Mitch Jones, Tampa	Wily Mo Pena, Dayton	Kelly Johnson, Macon
Best Baserunner	Brian Roberts, Rochester	Tike Redman, Nashville	Esix Snead, New Haven	Chone Figgins, Carolina	Alfredo Amezaga, Arkansas	Carlos Rosario, Visalia	Chad Durham, Winston-Salem	Jesus Medrano, Brevard County	Chris Morris, Peoria	Manny Ravelo, Hickory
Fastest Baserunner	Henry Mateo, Ottawa	Corey Patterson, Iowa	Esix Snead, New Haven	Carl Crawford, Orlando	Esteban German, Midland	Carlos Rosario, Visalia	Alex Requena, Kinston	Wilken Ruan, Jupiter	Victor Hall, South Bend	Bernabel Castro, Greensboro
Best Pitching Prospect	Brandon Duckworth, Scranton/W-B	Denny Stark, Tacoma	Josh Beckett, Portland	Joe Kennedy, Orlando	Tim Redding, Round Rock	Rafael Soriano, San Bernardino	Brett Evert, Myrtle Beach	Josh Beckett, Brevard County	Chad Qualls, Michigan	Adam Wainwright, Macon
Best Fastball	Jesus Colome, Durham	Kris Foster, Las Vegas	Franklin Nunez, Reading	Nick Neugebauer, Huntsville	Tim Redding, Round Rock	Rafael Soriano, San Bernardino	Alex Herrera, Kinston	Josh Beckett, Brevard County	Jeremy Hill, Burlington	Seth McClung, Charleston, S.C.
Best Breaking Pitch	Brandon Duckworth, Scranton/W-B	Kurt Ainsworth, Fresno	Ron Chiavacci, Harrisburg	Matt Guerrier, Birmingham	Chris Capuano, El Paso	Dennis Tankersley, Lake Elsinore	Blake Williams, Potomac	Josh Beckett, Brevard County	Ben Hendrickson, Beloit	Bubba Nelson, Macon
Best Control	Brett Jodie, Columbus	Bud Smith, Memphis	Kevin Olsen, Portland	Mark DiFelice, Carolina	Travis Smith, Round Rock	Craig Anderson, San Bernardino	Brett Evert, Myrtle Beach	Nick Regilio, Charlotte	Beltran Perez, South Bend	Seung Song, Augusta
Best Reliever	Matt DeWitt, Syracuse	Luis Vizcaino, Sacramento	Mark Corey, Binghamton	Scott Chiasson, West Tenn	Jose Valverde, El Paso	Hans Smith, Bakersfield	Scotty Layfield, Potomac	Stephen Bess, Lakeland	Mike Steele, West Michigan	Jackson Markert, Hagerstown
Best Defensive Catcher	Toby Hall, Durham	Yorvit Torrealba, Fresno	Jason Phillips, Binghamton	Corky Miller, Chattanooga	Carlos Maldonado, Round Rock	Dane Sardinha, Mudville	Victor Martinez, Kinston	Ryan Jorgensen, Daytona	Rob Bowen, Quad City	Scott Heard, Savannah
Best Defensive First Baseman	Nick Johnson, Columbus	Larry Barnes, Salt Lake	Carlos Rivera, Altoona	Eric Battersby, Birmingham	Greg Connors, San Antonio	Xavier Nady, Lake Elsinore	Adam LaRoche, Myrtle Beach	Eric Sandberg, Fort Myers	Adrian Gonzalez, Kane County	Casey Rogowski, Kannapolis
Best Defensive Second Baseman	Cesar Izturis, Syracuse	Jose Ortiz, Sacramento	Ruben Salazar, New Britain	Orlando Hudson, Tennessee	David Matranga, Round Rock	Steve Scarborough, High Desert	Bo Hart, Potomac	Brian Shipp, St. Lucie	Andy Green, South Bend	Chris Amador, Kannapolis
Best Defensive Third Baseman	Joe Crede, Charlotte	Chris Truby, New Orleans	Brant Ust	Eric Riggs, Jacksonville	Josh Hochgesang, Midland	Lance Niekro, San Jose	Troy Cameron, Kinston	Hank Blalock, Charlotte	Josh Williamson, Kane County	Tony Blanco, Augusta
Best Defensive Shortstop	Felipe Lopez, Syracuse	Cody Ransom, Fresno	Omar Infante, Erie	Nate Frese, West Tenn	Alfredo Amezaga, Arkansas	Ranier Olmedo, Mudville	Wilson Betemit, Myrtle Beach	Anderson Machado, Clearwater	Todd West, Beloit	Jose Reyes, Capital City
Best Infield Arm	Jason Dellaero, Charlotte	Juan Uribe, Colorado Springs	Michael Cuddyer, New Britain	Jorge Nunez, Jacksonville	Alfredo Amezaga, Arkansas	Ranier Olmedo, Mudville	Wilson Betemit, Myrtle Beach	Brandon Phillips, Jupiter	Miguel Cabrera, Kane County	Juan Salas, Charleston, S.C.
Best Defensive Outfielder	Alex Escobar, Norfolk	Jason Conti, Tucson	Andres Torres, Erie	Jeremy Owens, Mobile	Ryan Ludwick, Midland	Chris Snelling, San Bernardino	Ryan Langerhans, Myrtle Beach	Wilken Ruan, Jupiter	Nook Logan, West Michigan	Rick Asadoorian, Augusta
Best Outfield Arm	Wady Almonte, Rochester	Mario Encarnacion, Colorado Springs	Abraham Nunez, Portland	Luke Allen, Jacksonville	Kyle Logan, Round Rock	Daylan Holt, Modesto	Jeremy Harts, Lynchburg	Wilken Ruan, Jupiter	Steve Smitherman, Dayton	Ryan Church, Columbus
Most Exciting Player	Adam Dunn, Louisville	Ramon Vazquez, Tacoma	Marlon Byrd, Reading	Adam Dunn, Chattanooga	Alfredo Amezaga, Arkansas	Bill Hall, High Desert	Wilson Betemit, Myrtle Beach	Nic Jackson, Daytona	Jamal Strong, Wisconsin	Kelly Johnson, Macon
Best Managerial Prospect	Eric Wedge, Buffalo	Dan Rohn, Tacoma	Gary Varsho, Reading	John Shoemaker, Jacksonville	Mike Brumley, Arkansas	Dave Oliver, Mudville	Brian Snitker, Myrtle Beach	Marty Pevey, Dunedin	Gary Thurman, Wisconsin	Randy Ingle, Macon

Selected at midseason 2001 by Baseball America correspondents in consultation with minor league managers

MINOR LEAGUES

FREITAS AWARDS

As the seasons wear on, it becomes more of a challenge for a minor league franchise to keep the turnstiles spinning. The Delmarva Shorebirds, the 2001 Bob Freitas Award recipients for Class A, have figured out how to do just that, combining cutting-edge business and marketing philosophies with the feel of a classic minor league town to produce a diehard fan base.

The Shorebirds set a South Atlantic League attendance record with 315,011 fans and advanced to the league championship series in their first season in 1996. They raised the bar higher the next season, drawing 9,000 more fans and winning the league title with a new affiliation, with the nearby Baltimore Orioles.

"Just like any organization, we have that Cinderella season or two, and then it's time to get to work," said Shorebirds general manager Jim Terrill. "What we've done is maintained our level of attendance on the way up. The secret is constantly listening to the fans."

The Freitas Awards annually recognize long-term success by minor league franchises at the Triple-A, Double-A, Class A and short-season levels. They are named for Bob Freitas, a longtime minor league operator, promoter and ambassador who died in 1989.

Franchises are eligible for the honor in their fifth year of operation. Once they've won the award, they aren't eligible again for another three years.

Other winners for 2001 were the Buffalo Bisons, the Mobile BayBears and the Salem-Keizer Volcanoes.

■ In 1991, the first time the Buffalo Bisons won the Freitas Award, they were coming off a season in which they drew nearly 1.2 million fans. Since then, the Bisons have remained on top of their league—whether the old American

Association or the current incarnation of the International League—every year save the 2000 season, when Louisville opened its new ballpark and outdrew Buffalo by 18,000 fans with six more home dates.

The franchise has benefited from its major league affiliations, first with the Pirates through their success in the early '90s, and now with the Indians through their run in the American League Central.

Both Pittsburgh and Cleveland are less than three hours from Dunn Tire Park, which was certainly considered the crown jewel of minor league ballparks when it opened as Pilot Field in 1988. It remains one of the best parks in the minors.

■ The Mobile BayBears have done nothing to hurt the reputation of Hank Aaron, for whom their stadium is named.

city children to the game. Five years ago, there were 200 children in the program; now, there are 500.

■ The minor leagues have just four privately financed stadiums, and the Volcanoes play in one of them. Volcanoes Stadium, in the bedroom community of Keizer just four miles from Salem, is a public-private partnership. The city of Keizer provided the land, and co-owners Jerry Walker and Bill Tucker paid for the construction of the ballpark, affectionately known as The Crater.

Walker presides over the operation in Oregon, while Tucker visits from his home in Long Island for four homestands every summer. The two bought the Bellingham Mariners in 1989 but were ready to move out of Washington after six years.

PREVIOUS WINNERS

Triple-A
1989—Columbus (International)
1990—Pawtucket (International)
1991—Buffalo (American Association)
1992—Iowa (American Association)
1993—Richmond (International)
1994—Norfolk (International)
1995—Albuquerque (Pacific Coast)
1996—Indianapolis (American Association)
1997—Rochester (International)
1998—Salt Lake (Pacific Coast)
1999—Louisville (International)
2000—Edmonton (Pacific Coast)

Double-A
1989—El Paso (Texas)
1990—Arkansas (Texas)
1991—Reading (Eastern)
1992—Tulsa (Texas)
1993—Harrisburg (Eastern)
1994—San Antonio (Texas)
1995—Midland (Texas)
1996—Carolina (Southern)
1997—Bowie (Eastern)
1998—Trenton (Eastern)
1999—Portland (Eastern)
2000—Reading (Eastern)

Class A
1989—Durham (Carolina)
1990—San Jose (California)
1991—Asheville (South Atlantic)
1992—Springfield (Midwest)
1993—South Bend (Midwest)
1994—Kinston (Carolina)
1995—Kane County (Midwest)
1996—Wisconsin (Midwest)
1997—Rancho Cucamonga (California)
1998—West Michigan (Midwest)
1999—Wilmington (Carolina)
2000—Charleston, S.C. (South Atlantic)

Short-Season
1989—Eugene (Northwest)
1990—Salt Lake City (Pioneer)
1991—Spokane (Northwest)
1992—Boise (Northwest)
1993—Billings (Pioneer)
1994—Everett (Northwest)
1995—Great Falls (Pioneer)
1996—Bluefield (Appalachian)
1997—Oneonta (New York-Penn)
1998—Hudson Valley (New York-Penn)
1999—Portland (Northwest)
2000—Lowell (New York-Penn)

In addition to success at the gate (more than 200,000 fans in each of its five seasons) and on the field (a Southern League championship in 1998), one of the team's most popular programs incorporates the Mobile Housing Authority and the Boys and Girls Clubs to bring inner-

After the team drew just over 48,000 and had 250 season-ticket holders in its final season in Bellingham in 1995, it sold double that number of season tickets in its first week in '97. Overall attendance has been consistently around 125,000 all five seasons.

—GEOFF WILSON

PROSPECT POSITION RANKINGS

After the 2001 season, we decided to take a quick glance at how the game's top prospects measure up position by position. We have included only those players who did not exhaust their major league rookie eligibility status—130 plate appearances for position players and 50 innings for pitchers.

Ages are as of Sept. 1, 2001. We have also indicated the highest level each player reached in 2001.

RIGHTHANDERS

Injuries always figure into the equation when evaluating pitchers. This deep class of righthanders is no different. Minor League Player of the Year Josh Beckett rebounded from an injury-filled 2000 season to dominate. Jon Rauch, Baseball America's 2000 Player of the Year, was derailed by shoulder surgery, and Nick Neugebauer had to have his shoulder cut on just two starts into his major league career. Chris Bootcheck (Angels) and Seung Song (Red Sox) lead a group on the verge of cracking the list.

Rank	Player, Team	Age	Highest Level
1.	Josh Beckett, Marlins	21	Majors
2.	Mark Prior, Cubs	21	Did Not Play
3.	Juan Cruz, Cubs	20	Majors
4.	Dennis Tankersley, Padres	22	Triple-A
5.	Nick Neugebauer, Brewers	21	Majors
6.	Jake Peavy, Padres	20	Double-A
7.	Boof Bonser, Giants	19	Class A
8.	Jon Rauch, White Sox	22	Triple-A
9.	Rafael Soriano, Mariners	21	Double-A
10.	Jerome Williams, Giants	19	Double-A
11.	Jimmy Journell, Cardinals	23	Double-A
12.	Adam Wainwright, Braves	20	Class A
13.	Brett Myers, Phillies	21	Double-A
14.	Ben Diggins, Dodgers	22	Class A
15.	Brett Evert, Braves	20	Class A

LEFTHANDERS

Ryan Anderson didn't throw a pitch in 2001, but his ceiling still

Ryan Anderson: Still No. 1 lefthander, despite mssing 2001 season

towers over the rest of an impressive field. Carlos Hernandez was outstanding in three big league starts before season-ending rotator cuff surgery. Ty Howington and Corwin Malone had breakthrough seasons as they blitzed up their organizational ladders, while Brandon Claussen emerged as the minor league strikeout leader. Brian Tallet (Indians), Sean Burnett (Pirates) and Jung Bong (Braves) are also among the most promising lefties.

Rank	Player, Team	Age	Highest Level
1.	Ryan Anderson, Mariners	22	Did Not Play
2.	Ty Howington, Reds	20	Double-A
3.	Corwin Malone, White Sox	21	Double-A
4.	Carlos Hernandez, Astros	21	Majors
5.	Brandon Claussen, Yankees	22	Double-A
6.	Jimmy Gobble, Royals	20	Class A
7.	Mark Phillips, Padres	19	Class A
8.	Mario Ramos, Athletics	23	Triple-A
9.	Billy Traber, Mets	22	Triple-A
10.	Chris Narveson, Cardinals	19	Class A

CATCHERS

High School Player of the Year Joe Mauer stepped into the Rookie-level Appalachian League and hit .400 after being selected with the No. 1 pick in June. J.R. House had a disappointing season, though he did put rumors to rest about his college football career. Josh Phelps made tremendous strides at the plate, bashing 31 home runs and drawing a career-best 80 walks. He still has to answer concerns over his defense, but the Blue Jays are loaded with catchers, including a rejuvenated Jayson Werth.

Rank	Player, Team	Age	Highest Level
1.	Joe Mauer, Twins	18	Rookie
2.	Josh Phelps, Blue Jays	23	Majors
3.	J.R. House, Pirates	21	Double-A
4.	Victor Martinez, Indians	22	Class A
5.	Ryan Christianson, Mariners	20	Class A

FIRST BASEMEN

As you might expect, this position is led by a number of premi-

Carlos Pena: Top first base prospect primed for Rangers

Rank	Player, Team	Age	Highest Level
1.	Sean Burroughs, Padres	20	Triple-A
2.	Hank Blalock, Rangers	20	Double-A
3.	Mark Teixeira, Rangers	21	Did Not Play
4.	Drew Henson, Yankees	21	Triple-A
5.	Michael Cuddyer, Twins	22	Double-A

SHORTSTOPS

The most athletic players are often found at shortstop, and you'll find plenty of young players with tools here, but not a lot of finished products. The Braves could rush Wilson Betemit into their lineup in 2002, as they've shown a willingness to do with exceptional young players. Jose Reyes was one of the 2001 season's most talked-about prospects, as his tools drew comparisons to Alfonso Soriano. Chris Burke (Astros), Kelly Johnson (Braves) and Ramon Vazquez (Mariners) are also strong candidates. Antonio Perez (Mariners) was the top player at the position going into the 2001 season, but an injury-plagued year raised doubts about his future.

Rank	Player, Team	Age	Highest Level
1.	Wilson Betemit, Braves	19	Majors
2.	Brandon Phillips, Expos	20	Double-A
3.	Angel Berroa, Royals	21	Majors
4.	Jose Reyes, Mets	18	Class A
5.	Miguel Cabrera, Marlins	18	Class A

OUTFIELDERS

Former Stanford quarterback Joe Borchard heads a relatively thin stable of outfielders with his plus-plus power potential. Josh Hamilton missed most of the year with injuries and was facing back surgery after a comeback attempt in the Arizona Fall League. Marlon Byrd has five tools and looks like a young Kirby Puckett. The only teenager on the list, Chris Snelling, won the Class A California League batting title.

Rank	Player, Team	Age	Highest Level
1.	Joe Borchard, White Sox	22	Double-A
2.	Marlon Byrd, Phillies	24	Double-A
3.	Austin Kearns, Reds	21	Double-A
4.	Josh Hamilton, Devil Rays	20	Double-A
5.	Juan Rivera, Yankees	23	Majors
6.	Chris Snelling, Mariners	19	Class A
7.	Jamal Strong, Mariners	23	Class A
8.	Jack Cust, Diamondbacks	22	Majors
9.	Jason Lane, Astros	24	Double-A
10.	Carl Crawford, Devil Rays	20	Double-A

Wilson Betemit: No. 1 shortstop prospect began '01 in Class A

um hitters—several of whom didn't make the cut. Carlos Pena could be one of the early favorites for 2002 Rookie of the Year, and Casey Kotchman, who played briefly in his professional debut, is primed for a breakthrough first full season next year. Lyle Overbay (Diamondbacks) finished just behind Rangers third-base prospect Hank Blalock for second in the minors with a .352 average, followed closely by Ken Harvey (Royals). The Tigers are still counting on Eric Munson as their first baseman of the future, while the Cubs wait for Hee Seop Choi to develop. Xavier Nady (Padres) also made huge strides in 2001. None of those last five cracked the list.

Rank	Player, Team	Age	Highest Level
1.	Carlos Pena, Rangers	23	Majors
2.	Nick Johnson, Yankees	22	Majors
3.	Adrian Gonzalez, Marlins	19	Class A
4.	Justin Morneau, Twins	20	Double-A
5.	Casey Kotchman, Angels	18	Rookie

SECOND BASEMEN

This isn't typically a position where you look for prospects, as many players move here when they break into the big leagues. Former shortstops Bobby Hill and Tim Hummel have already moved and hit well in their first full seasons, though Hill battled a groin injury for much of the summer. Orlando Hudson was a pleasant surprise, while Chase Utley's production was disappointing. Speedsters Juan Francia (Tigers), Domingo Cuello (Pirates) and Jason Bourgeois (Rangers) are worth watching in full-season leagues in 2002.

Rank	Player, Team	Age	Highest Level
1.	Bobby Hill, Cubs	23	Double-A
2.	Tim Hummel, White Sox	22	Double-A
3.	Orlando Hudson, Blue Jays	23	Triple-A
4.	Chase Utley, Phillies	22	Class A
5.	Michael Woods, Tigers	21	Class A

THIRD BASEMEN

This is the cream of the crop for position players. Two of baseball's brightest pure hitters top the list. Hank Blalock's future at the position is a hot topic with the presence of Mark Teixeira in the Rangers system. Michael Cuddyer and Cubs prospect Dave Kelton could find themselves on the move to the outfield. Tony Blanco (Red Sox) and Corey Smith (Indians) could make a charge toward the top of this list next season.

Joe Borchard: White Sox slugger hit .295 with 27 home runs

282 • BASEBALL AMERICA 2002 ALMANAC

As with most of the prospect lists that appear in Baseball America, the Minor League Top 20 Prospects lists are compiled with long-term major league potential in mind. That's why you won't find Phil Hiatt, who led the minor leagues with 44 home runs and was the Pacific Coast League MVP in 2001, on our lists. Hiatt was 32, and while we like to see players do well now, what we're really looking for are future major league stars.

These lists do bring a slightly different perspective than the organizational Top 10 Prospects that begin on page 279. Those lists have more of a scouting angle, while our league lists are based on conversations with league managers. Managers and scouts can often view players differently. Both look at a player's tools, but managers give more weight to what a player does on the field, while scouts look at what he might eventually do. We think both perspectives are useful, so we give you both even though they don't always agree.

For a player to qualify for a league prospect list, he must have spent at least one-third of the season in the league. Position players must have one plate appearance per league game. In other words, for a league that plays 140 games, a player is eligible if he has at least 140 plate appearances.

Pitchers must pitch ⅓ inning per league game. Relievers must make at least 20 appearances in a full-season league or 10 appearances in a short-season league.

TRIPLE-A

INTERNATIONAL LEAGUE
1. Adam Dunn, of, Louisville (Reds)
2. Toby Hall, c, Durham (Devil Rays)
3. Felipe Lopez, ss-3b, Syracuse (Blue Jays)
4. Nick Johnson, 1b, Columbus (Yankees)
5. Brandon Duckworth, rhp, Scranton/Wilkes-Barre (Phillies)
6. Tim Spooneybarger, rhp, Richmond (Braves)
7. Alex Escobar, of, Norfolk (Mets)
8. Erick Almonte, ss, Columbus (Yankees)
9. Juan Rivera, of, Columbus (Yankees)
10. Cesar Izturis, ss-2b, Syracuse (Blue Jays)
11. Joe Crede, 3b, Charlotte (White Sox)
12. Vernon Wells, of, Syracuse (Blue Jays)
13. Aaron Rowand, of, Charlotte (White Sox)
14. Drew Henson, 3b, Columbus (Yankees)
15. Marcus Giles, 2b, Richmond (Braves)
16. Eric Valent, of, Scranton/Wilkes-Barre (Phillies)
17. Dave Coggin, rhp, Scranton/Wilkes-Barre (Phillies)
18. Brian Roberts, ss, Rochester (Orioles)
19. Orlando Hudson, 2b, Syracuse (Blue Jays)
20. Brad Wilkerson, of, Ottawa (Expos)

PACIFIC COAST LEAGUE
1. Sean Burroughs, 3b, Portland (Padres)
2. Carlos Pena, 1b, Oklahoma (Rangers)
3. Corey Patterson, of, Iowa (Cubs)
4. Bud Smith, lhp, Memphis (Cardinals)
5. Juan Uribe, ss, Colorado Springs (Rockies)
6. Chris George, lhp, Omaha (Royals)
7. Ramon Vazquez, ss, Tacoma (Mariners)
8. Kurt Ainsworth, rhp, Fresno (Giants)
9. Tony McKnight, rhp, New Orleans (Astros)
10. Joel Pineiro, rhp, Tacoma (Mariners)
11. Carlos Zambrano, rhp, Iowa (Cubs)
12. Morgan Ensberg, 3b, New Orleans (Astros)
13. Denny Stark, rhp, Tacoma (Mariners)
14. Hee Seop Choi, 1b, Iowa (Cubs)
15. Joaquin Benoit, rhp, Oklahoma (Rangers)
16. Ryan Vogelsong, rhp, Fresno (Giants)/ Nashville (Pirates)
17. Mario Ramos, lhp, Sacramento (Athletics)
18. Jack Cust, of, Tucson (Diamondbacks)
19. Tony Torcato, of, Fresno (Giants)
20. Cesar Crespo, util, Portland (Padres)

DOUBLE-A

EASTERN LEAGUE
1. Josh Beckett, rhp, Portland (Marlins)
2. Marlon Byrd, of, Reading (Phillies)
3. Nate Cornejo, rhp, Erie (Tigers)
4. Michael Cuddyer, 3b-1b, New Britain (Twins)
5. Brad Thomas, lhp, New Britain (Twins)
6. Juan Rivera, of, Norwich (Yankees)

STEVE MOORE

Sean Burroughs: No. 1 in PCL

7. Brandon Claussen, lhp, Norwich (Yankees)
8. Marcus Thames, of, Norwich (Yankees)
9. Juan Rincon, rhp, New Britain (Twins)
10. Omar Infante, ss, Erie (Tigers)
11. Michael Restovich, of, New Britain (Twins)
12. Brandon Phillips, ss, Harrisburg (Expos)
13. Luis Pineda, rhp, Erie (Tigers)
14. Casey Fossum, lhp, Trenton (Red Sox)
15. Mike Rivera, c, Erie (Tigers)
16. Ryan Drese, rhp, Akron (Indians)
17. Carlos Silva, rhp, Reading (Phillies)
18. John Stephens, rhp, Bowie (Orioles)
19. Abraham Nunez, of, Portland (Marlins)
20. Robert Stratton, of, Binghamton (Mets)

SOUTHERN LEAGUE
1. Adam Dunn, of, Chattanooga (Reds)
2. Nick Neugebauer, rhp, Huntsville (Brewers)
3. Wilson Betemit, ss, Greenville (Braves)
4. Joe Kennedy, lhp, Orlando (Devil Rays)
5. Joe Borchard, of, Birmingham (White Sox)
6. Dennis Tankersley, rhp, Mobile (Padres)
7. Juan Cruz, rhp, West Tenn (Cubs)
8. Danny Wright, rhp, Birmingham (White Sox)
9. Josh Phelps, c, Tennessee (Blue Jays)
10. Carl Crawford, of, Orlando (Devil Rays)
11. Orlando Hudson, 2b, Tennessee (Blue Jays)

12. Dave Kelton, 3b, West Tenn (Cubs)
13. Matt Guerrier, rhp, Birmingham (White Sox)
14. Jorge Cantu, ss, Orlando (Devil Rays)
15. Ben Broussard, 1b, Chattanooga (Reds)
16. Chin-Feng Chen, of, Jacksonville (Dodgers)
17. Bobby Hill, 2b, West Tenn (Cubs)
18. Reed Johnson, of, Tennessee (Blue Jays)
19. Scott Chiasson, rhp, West Tenn (Cubs)
20. Austin Kearns, of, Chattanooga (Reds)

TEXAS LEAGUE
1. Hank Blalock, 3b, Tulsa (Rangers)
2. Tim Redding, rhp, Round Rock (Astros)
3. Carlos Hernandez, lhp, Round Rock (Astros)
4. Rafael Soriano, rhp, San Antonio (Mariners)
5. Jeff Heaverlo, rhp, San Antonio (Mariners)
6. Mario Ramos, lhp, Midland (Athletics)
7. Angel Berroa, ss, Wichita (Royals)
8. Lyle Overbay, 1b, El Paso (Diamondbacks)
9. Ken Harvey, 1b, Wichita (Royals)
10. Jason Lane, of, Round Rock (Astros)
11. Nathan Haynes, of, Arkansas (Angels)
12. Jerome Williams, rhp, Shreveport (Giants)
13. Ryan Ludwick, of, Midland (Athletics)
14. John Lackey, rhp, Arkansas (Angels)
15. Alfredo Amezaga, ss, Arkansas (Angels)
16. Jose Valverde, rhp, El Paso (Diamondbacks)
17. Kenny Kelly, of, San Antonio (Mariners)
18. Wilfredo Rodriguez, lhp, Round Rock (Astros)
19. Mike Tonis, c, Wichita (Royals)
20. Tom Shearn, rhp, Round Rock (Astros)

CLASS A ADVANCED

CALIFORNIA LEAGUE
1. Dennis Tankersley, rhp, Lake Elsinore (Padres)
2. Xavier Nady, 1b, Lake Elsinore (Padres)
3. Rafael Soriano, rhp, San Bernardino (Mariners)
4. Chris Snelling, of, San Bernardino (Mariners)
5. Jake Peavy, rhp, Lake Elsinore (Padres)
6. Jamal Strong, of, San Bernardino (Mariners)
7. Ryan Christianson, c, San Bernardino (Mariners)
8. Ben Howard, rhp, Lake Elsinore (Padres)
9. Bill Hall, ss, High Desert (Brewers)
10. Chris Bootcheck, rhp, Rancho Cucamonga (Angels)
11. Matt Thornton, lhp, San Bernardino (Mariners)
12. Tony Torcato, of, San Jose (Giants)
13. Ranier Olmedo, ss, Mudville (Reds)
14. Freddie Bynum, ss, Modesto (Athletics)
15. David Krynzel, of, High Desert (Brewers)
16. Ben Johnson, of, Lake Elsinore (Padres)
17. Dane Sardinha, c, Mudville (Reds)
18. Eric Cyr, lhp, Lake Elsinore (Padres)
19. Mike O'Keefe, of, Rancho Cucamonga (Angels)
20. Craig Anderson, lhp, San Bernardino (Mariners)

CAROLINA LEAGUE
1. Wilson Betemit, ss, Myrtle Beach (Braves)
2. Jimmy Journell, rhp, Potomac (Cardinals)
3. Angel Berroa, ss, Wilmington (Royals)
4. Ryan Kibler, rhp, Salem (Rockies)
5. Chris Narveson, lhp, Potomac (Cardinals)
6. Brett Evert, rhp, Myrtle Beach (Braves)
7. Bobby Bradley, rhp, Lynchburg (Pirates)
8. Jimmy Gobble, lhp, Wilmington (Royals)
9. Jason Young, rhp, Salem (Rockies)
10. Victor Martinez, c, Kinston (Indians)
11. Ken Harvey, 1b, Wilmington (Royals)
12. Ed Rogers, ss, Frederick (Orioles)
13. Blake Williams, rhp, Potomac (Cardinals)
14. Alex Herrera, lhp, Kinston (Indians)
15. Jung Bong, lhp, Myrtle Beach (Braves)
16. Erik Bedard, lhp, Frederick (Orioles)
17. Shane Wallace, lhp, Kinston (Indians)
18. Trey Hodges, rhp, Myrtle Beach (Braves)
19. Brian Tallet, lhp, Kinston (Indians)
20. Covelli Crisp, of, Potomac (Cardinals)

FLORIDA STATE LEAGUE
1. Josh Beckett, rhp, Brevard County (Marlins)
2. Hank Blalock, 3b, Charlotte (Rangers)
3. Brandon Phillips, ss, Jupiter (Expos)
4. Nic Jackson, of, Daytona (Cubs)
5. Ricardo Rodriguez, rhp, Vero Beach (Dodgers)
6. Justin Morneau, 1b, Fort Myers (Twins)
7. Brandon Claussen, lhp, Tampa (Yankees)
8. Billy Traber, lhp, St. Lucie (Mets)
9. Ryan Dittfurth, rhp, Charlotte (Rangers)
10. Miguel Ascencio, rhp, Clearwater (Phillies)
11. Anderson Machado, ss, Clearwater (Phillies)
12. Seung Song, rhp, Sarasota (Red Sox)
13. Gabe Gross, of, Dunedin (Blue Jays)
14. Wilken Ruan, of, Jupiter (Expos)
15. Chase Utley, 2b, Clearwater (Phillies)
16. Greg Montalbano, lhp, Sarasota (Red Sox)
17. Freddy Sanchez, ss, Sarasota (Red Sox)
18. Mitch Jones, of, Tampa (Yankees)
19. Luis Garcia, 1b, Sarasota (Red Sox)
20. Nick Regilio, rhp, Charlotte (Rangers)

CLASS A
MIDWEST LEAGUE
1. Adrian Gonzalez, 1b, Kane County (Marlins)
2. Justin Morneau, 1b, Quad City (Twins)
3. Wily Mo Pena, of, Dayton (Reds)
4. Clint Nageotte, rhp, Wisconsin (Mariners)
5. Chris Narveson, lhp, Peoria (Cardinals)
6. Garett Gentry, c, Michigan (Astros)
7. Jamal Strong, of, Wisconsin (Mariners)
8. Chris Burke, ss, Michigan (Astros)
9. Miguel Cabrera, ss, Kane County (Marlins)
10. Grady Sizemore, of, Clinton (Expos)
11. David Espinosa, ss, Dayton (Reds)
12. Will Smith, of, Kane County (Marlins)
13. Chad Qualls, rhp, Michigan (Astros)
14. Aaron Taylor, rhp, Wisconsin (Mariners)
15. Ben Hendrickson, rhp, Beloit (Brewers)
16. Beltran Perez, rhp, South Bend (Diamondbacks)
17. Jose Cueto, rhp, Lansing (Cubs)
18. Oliver Perez, lhp, Fort Wayne (Padres)
19. Josh Hall, rhp, Dayton (Reds)
20. Todd Wellemeyer, rhp, Lansing (Cubs)

SOUTH ATLANTIC LEAGUE
1. Boof Bonser, rhp, Hagerstown (Giants)
2. Jose Reyes, ss, Capital City (Mets)
3. Adam Wainwright, rhp, Macon (Braves)
4. Corwin Malone, lhp, Kannapolis (White Sox)
5. Kelly Johnson, ss, Macon (Braves)
6. Corey Smith, 3b, Columbus (Indians)
7. Seung Song, rhp, Augusta (Red Sox)
8. Anthony Pluta, rhp, Lexington (Astros)
9. Tony Blanco, 3b, Augusta (Red Sox)
10. Ben Kozlowski, lhp, Macon (Braves)
11. Dave Martinez, lhp, Greensboro (Yankees)
12. Guillermo Reyes, ss, Kannapolis (White Sox)
13. Sean Burnett, lhp, Hickory (Pirates)
14. Rich Rundles, lhp, Augusta (Red Sox)
15. Taylor Buchholz, rhp, Lakewood (Phillies)

Adrian Gonzalez: No. 1 in Midwest

16. Mike Nannini, rhp, Lexington (Astros)
17. Ben Diggins, rhp, Wilmington (Dodgers)
18. Seth McClung, rhp, Charleston, S.C. (Devil Rays)
19. Koyie Hill, c-dh, Wilmington (Dodgers)
20. Rocco Baldelli, of, Charleston, S.C. (Devil Rays)

SHORT-SEASON CLASS A
NEW YORK-PENN LEAGUE
1. John VanBenschoten, rhp-dh, Williamsport (Pirates)
2. Sean Henn, lhp, Staten Island (Yankees)
3. Jason Arnold, rhp, Staten Island (Yankees)
4. Juan Francia, 2b, Oneonta (Tigers)
5. Denny Bautista, rhp, Utica (Marlins)
6. John-Ford Griffin, of, Staten Island (Yankees)
7. Zach Miner, rhp, Jamestown (Braves)
8. Dustin McGowan, rhp, Auburn (Blue Jays)
9. Tyrell Godwin, of, Auburn (Blue Jays)
10. Domingo Cuello, 2b, Williamsport (Pirates)
11. Justin Pope, rhp, New Jersey (Cardinals)
12. Ryan Raburn, 3b, Oneonta (Tigers)
13. Chris Flinn, rhp, Hudson Valley (Devil Rays)
14. Angel Pagan, of, Brooklyn (Mets)
15. Jason Stokes, of, Utica (Marlins)
16. Luz Portobanco, rhp, Brooklyn (Mets)
17. Tony Pena Jr., ss, Jamestown (Braves)
18. Charlton Jimerson, of, Pittsfield (Astros)
19. Aaron Rifkin, 1b, Staten Island (Yankees)
20. Juan Camacho, 3b, Staten Island (Yankees)

NORTHWEST LEAGUE
1. J.J. Johnson, of, Boise (Cubs)
2. Jesse Foppert, rhp, Salem-Keizer (Giants)
3. Julian Benavidez, 3b, Salem-Keizer (Giants)
4. Angel Guzman, rhp, Boise (Cubs)
5. Jake Gautreau, 3b, Eugene (Padres)
6. Dontrelle Willis, lhp, Boise (Cubs)
7. Corey Slavik, 3b, Boise (Cubs)
8. Matt Allegra, of, Vancouver (Athletics)
9. Jason Bartlett, ss, Eugene (Padres)
10. Jose Lopez, ss, Everett (Mariners)
11. Condor Cash, of, Boise (Cubs)
12. Tim Merritt, 2b-ss, Everett (Mariners)
13. Justin Germano, rhp, Eugene (Padres)
14. Brad Hennessey, rhp, Salem-Keizer (Giants)
15. Gustavo Martinez, rhp, Everett (Mariners)
16. James Harden, rhp, Vancouver (Athletics)
17. Jorge Sosa, rhp, Everett (Mariners)
18. Travis Blackley, lhp, Everett (Mariners)
19. Keto Anderson, of, Boise (Cubs)
20. Kip Bouknight, rhp, Tri-City (Rockies)

ROOKIE ADVANCED
APPALACHIAN LEAGUE
1. Joe Mauer, c, Elizabethton (Twins)
2. Dan Denham, rhp, Burlington (Indians)
3. Jason Bourgeois, 2b, Pulaski (Rangers)
4. J.D. Martin, rhp, Burlington (Indians)
5. Bryan Digby, rhp, Danville (Braves)
6. Kris Honel, rhp, Bristol (White Sox)
7. Sandy Tejada, rhp, Elizabethton (Twins)
8. Rashad Eldridge, of, Burlington (Indians)
9. David Wright, 3b, Kingsport (Mets)
10. Jonny Gomes, of, Princeton (Devil Rays)
11. Toe Nash, of, Princeton (Devil Rays)
12. Justin Woodrow, of, Johnson City (Cardinals)
13. Justin Huber, c, Kingsport (Mets)
14. Scott Heard, c, Pulaski (Rangers)
15. Travis Foley, rhp, Burlington (Indians)
16. Yadier Molina, c, Johnson City (Cardinals)
17. Omar Rogers, 2b, Bluefield (Orioles)
18. C.J. Wilson, lhp, Pulaski (Rangers)
19. D.J. Houlton, rhp, Martinsville (Astros)
20. Brayan Pena, c, Danville (Braves)

PIONEER LEAGUE
1. Mike Jones, rhp, Ogden (Brewers)
2. Jesus Cota, 1b, Missoula (Diamondbacks)
3. Josh Barfield, 2b, Idaho Falls (Padres)
4. Brandon League, rhp, Medicine Hat (Blue Jays)
5. Dallas McPherson, 3b, Provo (Angels)
6. Jose Diaz, c, Great Falls (Dodgers)
7. Scott Hairston, 2b, Missoula (Diamondbacks)
8. Jose Garcia, of, Great Falls (Dodgers)
9. Jon Steitz, rhp, Ogden (Brewers)
10. J.J. Hardy, ss, Ogden (Brewers)
11. Corby Medlin, rhp, Missoula (Diamondbacks)
12. William Bergolla, 2b-ss, Billings (Reds)
13. Jeff Mathis, c, Provo (Angels)
14. Jayson Nix, ss, Casper (Rockies)
15. Michael Keirstead, rhp, Great Falls (Dodgers)
16. Gary Varner, of, Billings (Reds)
17. Edwin Encarnacion, 3b, Billings (Reds)
18. Clinton Hosford, rhp, Great Falls (Dodgers)
19. Jon Hart, 1b, Ogden (Brewers)
20. Mark O'Sullivan, rhp, Provo (Angels)

ROOKIE
ARIZONA LEAGUE
1. Chris Tritle, of, Athletics
2. Shin-Soo Choo, of, Mariners
3. Andy Gonzalez, ss, White Sox
4. Ryan Hannaman, lhp, Giants
5. Ronny Cedeno, ss, Cubs
6. Johan Santana, rhp, Angels
7. Anthony Webster, of, White Sox
8. Francisco Liriano, lhp, Giants
9. Leonel Cabrera, 2b, Giants
10. Pedro Esparragoza, c, Brewers
11. Bryan Simmering, rhp, Athletics
12. Alejandro Cadena, dh, Mariners
13. Aaron Kirkland, rhp, White Sox
14. Rene Rivera, c, Mariners
15. Andy Sisco, lhp, Cubs
16. Austin Nagle, of, Athletics
17. Emiliano Fruto, lhp, Mariners
18. Chris Collins, 3b, Mariners
19. Kory Wayment, ss, Athletics
20. Jimbo McAuliff, of, Giants

GULF COAST LEAGUE
1. Chad Petty, lhp, Tigers
2. Anderson Hernandez, ss, Tigers
3. Bronson Sardinha, ss, Yankees
4. Manny Delcarmen, rhp, Red Sox
5. Carlos Duran, of, Braves
6. Josh Thigpen, rhp, Red Sox
7. Victor Diaz, 2b, Dodgers
8. Ezequiel Astacio, rhp, Phillies
9. Gonzalo Lopez, rhp, Braves
10. Alan Moye, of, Reds
11. Carlos Rodriguez, ss, Phillies
12. Matt Cooper, 1b, Red Sox
13. Kole Strayhorn, rhp, Dodgers
14. Bryan Bass, ss, Orioles
15. Juan Gonzalez, 3b, Tigers
16. Jose Dominguez, rhp, Rangers
17. Allen Baxter, rhp, Marlins
18. Josh Burrus, ss, Braves
19. Alex Santa, of, Yankees
20. Elvin Andujar, of, Reds

MINOR LEAGUES

ROBERT GURGANUS

TOP 100 PROSPECTS

Through consultation with scouts and player-development people, Baseball America selected is annual list of the game's top 100 minor league prospects in March 2001. The list emphasizes long-range major league potential and considers only players in professional baseball who had not exhausted their major league rookie status entering the 2001 season. The highest level each prospect reached in 2001 is noted in parentheses.

1. Josh Hamilton, of, Devil Rays (AA)
2. Corey Patterson, of, Cubs (Majors)
3. Josh Beckett, rhp, Marlins (Majors)
4. Jon Rauch, rhp, White Sox (AAA)
5. Ben Sheets, rhp, Brewers (Majors)
6. Sean Burroughs, 3b, Padres (AAA)
7. C.C. Sabathia, lhp, Indians (Majors)
8. Ryan Anderson, lhp, Mariners (Injured)
9. Ichiro Suzuki, of, Mariners (Majors)
10. Nick Johnson, 1b, Yankees (Majors)
11. Carlos Pena, 1b, Rangers (Majors)
12. Vernon Wells, of, Blue Jays (Majors)
13. Roy Oswalt, rhp, Astros (Majors)
14. Drew Henson, 3b, Yankees (AAA)
15. Chin-Hui Tsao, rhp, Rockies (A)
16. Antonio Perez, ss, Mariners (AA)
17. Juan Cruz, rhp, Cubs (Majors)
18. Alex Escobar, of, Mets (Majors)
19. Jerome Williams, rhp, Giants (AA)
20. Bobby Bradley, rhp, Pirates (A)
21. J.R House, c, Pirates (AA)
22. Hee Seop Choi, 1b, Cubs (AAA)
23. Joe Borchard, of, White Sox (AA)
24. Austin Kearns, of, Reds (AA)
25. Chris George, lhp, Royals (Majors)
26. Donnie Bridges, rhp, Expos (AAA)
27. Alfonso Soriano, ss, Yankees (Majors)
28. Matt Belisle, rhp, Braves (Injured)
29. Wilson Betemit, ss, Braves (Majors)
30. Kurt Ainsworth, rhp, Giants (Majors)
31. Jimmy Rollins, ss, Phillies (Majors)
32. Felipe Lopez, ss, Blue Jays (Majors)
33. Adam Dunn, of, Reds (Majors)
34. Jose Ortiz, 2b, Rockies (Majors)
35. Brad Wilkerson, of, Expos (Majors)
36. Joe Crede, 3b, White Sox (Majors)
37. Ben Christensen, rhp, Cubs (AA)
38. Jack Cust, of-1b, Diamondbacks (Majors)
39. Bud Smith, lhp, Cardinals (Majors)
40. Jacob Peavy, rhp, Padres (AA)
41. Adam Johnson, rhp, Twins (Majors)
42. Albert Pujols, 3b, Cardinals (Majors)
43. Aubrey Huff, 3b, Devil Rays (Majors)
44. Matt Ginter, rhp, White Sox (Majors)
45. Wes Anderson, rhp, Marlins (A)
46. D'Angelo Jimenez, ss, Padres (Majors)
47. Brett Myers, rhp, Phillies (AA)

Corey Patterson: Cubs outfielder played 59 games in majors

48. Dee Brown, of, Royals (Majors)
49. Tim Redding, rhp, Astros (Majors)
50. Joe Torres, lhp, Angels (A)
51. Matt McClendon, rhp, Braves (AAA)
52. Jason Standridge, rhp, Devil Rays (Majors)
53. Wascar Serrano, rhp, Padres (Majors)
54. Marcus Giles, 2b, Braves (Majors)
55. Michael Cuddyer, 3b, Twins (Majors)
56. Kevin Mench, of, Rangers (AA)
57. Wilfredo Rodriguez, lhp, Astros (Majors)
58. Mike Bynum, lhp, Padres (AA)
59. Jason Hart, 1b, Athletics (AAA)
60. Tony Torcato, 3b, Giants (AAA)
61. Dan Wright, rhp, White Sox (Majors)
62. Alex Cintron, ss, Diamondbacks (Majors)
63. Pat Strange, rhp, Mets (AAA)
64. Brian Cole, of, Mets (deceased)
65. Jovanny Cedeno, rhp, Rangers (A)
66. Adrian Hernandez, rhp, Yankees (Majors)
67. Brandon Inge, c, Tigers (Majors)
68. Carlos Zambrano, rhp, Cubs (Majors)
69. Jesus Colome, rhp, Devil Rays (Majors)
70. Eric Munson, 1b, Tigers (Majors)
71. Francisco Rodriguez, rhp, Angels (A)
72. Carl Crawford, of, Devil Rays (AA)
73. Luis Montanez, ss, Cubs (A)
74. Dane Sardinha, c, Reds (A)
75. Abraham Nunez, of, Marlins (AA)
76. Brad Baker, rhp, Red Sox (A)
77. Dernell Stenson, 1b-of, Red Sox (AAA)
78. Brad Baisley, rhp, Phillies (AA)
79. Mike MacDougal, rhp, Royals (Majors)
80. Joel Pineiro, rhp, Mariners (Majors)
81. Ryan Ludwick, of, Athletics (AAA)
82. Xavier Nady, 3b, Padres (A)
83. Nick Neugebauer, rhp, Brewers (Majors)
84. Justin Miller, rhp, Athletics (AAA)
85. Lance Niekro, 3b, Giants (A)
86. Chin-Feng Chen, of, Dodgers (AA)
87. Tony Blanco, 3b, Red Sox (A)
88. Danys Baez, rhp, Indians (Majors)

89. Adrian Gonzalez, 1b, Marlins (A)
90. David Espinosa, ss-2b, Reds (A)
91. Miguel Cabrera, ss, Marlins (A)
92. Jason Marquis, rhp, Braves (Majors)
93. Luis Rivas, 2b, Twins (Majors)
94. Juan Uribe, ss, Rockies (Majors)
95. Ramon Santiago, ss, Tigers (A)

Josh Hamilton

96. Keith Reed, of, Orioles (AAA)
97. Adam Wainwright, rhp, Braves (A)
98. Chris Snelling, of, Mariners (AA)
99. Joe Lawrence, c, Blue Jays (AAA)
100. Matt White, rhp, Devil Rays (AAA)

Ben Sheets

ORGANIZATION TOP 10 PROSPECTS
ANAHEIM/ARIZONA

ANALYSIS BY JOSH BOYD
Player rankings from 2000-01 offseason; Ages as of Oct. 1, 2001

ANAHEIM ANGELS

A variety of injuries hindered the Angels' brightest pitching prospects in 2001, including Joe Torres, Francisco Rodriguez and Derrick Turnbow.

STEPPING FORWARD: Chris Bootcheck overcame an early bout with tendinitis to have a solid debut season, but another righthander, Johan Santana, emerged from the Angels' renewed interest in the Dominican Republic. Santana's 95-mph heat reminds the organization of Ramon Ortiz, and he could pass the disappointing Rodriguez before long.

STEPPING BACK: Rodriguez was expected to break through in 2001, but for the third consecutive season tendinitis held him back. The Angels have had high hopes for his lively mid-90s fastball, but were discouraged by his inconsistent command. He registered 301 strikeouts in 235 career innings before the age of 20, however.

TOP 10 PROSPECTS

Player, Pos.	Age	Club (Class)	AVG	AB	R	H	2B	3B	HR	RBI	SB
3. Brian Specht, ss	20	Arkansas (AA)	.265	155	14	41	9	2	2	15	2
		Rancho Cucamonga (A)	.242	264	45	64	13	6	7	31	17
8. Nathan Haynes, of	21	Arkansas (AA)	.310	316	49	98	11	5	5	23	33
9. Elpidio Guzman, of	22	Arkansas (AA)	.244	459	58	112	21	8	7	46	18
10. Jared Abruzzo, c	19	Rancho Cucamonga (A)	.2088	101	13	21	1	0	2	13	1
		Cedar Rapids (A)	.241	323	41	78	20	0	10	53	1

Player, Pos.	Age	Club (Class)	W	L	ERA	G	SV	IP	H	BB	SO
1. Joe Torres, lhp	18	Quad City (A)	0	3	5.82	4	0	17	16	14	14
		Provo (R)	2	2	4.02	9	8	0	15	39	
2. Francisco Rodriguez, rhp	19	Rancho Cucamonga (A)	5	7	5.38	20	0	114	127	55	147
4. John Lackey, rhp	22	Salt Lake (AAA)	3	4	6.71	10	0	58	75	16	42
		Arkansas (AA)	9	7	3.46	18	0	127	106	29	94
5. Chris Bootcheck, rhp	22	Arkansas (AA)	3	3	5.45	6	0	36	39	11	22
		Rancho Cucamonga (A)	8	4	3.93	15	0	87	84	23	86
6. Philip Wilson, rhp	20	Arkansas (AA)	1	1	11.37	2	0	6	10	7	5
		Rancho Cucamonga (A)	8	10	5.23	26	0	160	173	55	134
7. Derrick Turnbow, rhp	23	Arkansas (AA)	0	0	2.57	3	0	14	12	5	11

Joe Torres

MEL BAILEY

ARIZONA DIAMONDBACKS

The Diamondbacks, who had one of the oldest teams in the major leagues in 2001, are lacking in high-profile prospects, but they have established depth in the lower rungs of the farm system, namely in their young pitchers.

STEPPING FORWARD: Arizona boasts a slew of hard-throwing relievers, including Jose Valverde, P.J. Bevis, Jay Belflower and Brian Bruney, but sweet-swinging Lyle Overbay has done nothing but mash since signing as an 18th-rounder in 1999. Overbay hit .352 at El Paso in 2001 and raised his career mark to .346, while averaging nearly 100 RBIs per season.

STEPPING BACK: After a horrid start at low Class A South Bend, Luis Terrero was demoted to short-season Yakima and worked his way up to Double-A by the end of the season. However, the free-swinger fanned 96 times and drew seven walks in 348 at-bats.

Alex Cintron

STEVE MOORE

TOP 10 PROSPECTS

Player, Pos.	Age	Club (Class)	AVG	AB	R	H	2B	3B	HR	RBI	SB
1. Alex Cintron, ss	22	Arizona	.286	7	0	2	0	1	0	0	0
		Tucson (AAA)	.292	425	53	124	24	3	3	35	9
2. Jack Cust, of-1b	22	Arizona	.500	2	0	1	0	0	0	0	0
		Tucson (AAA)	.278	442	81	123	24	2	27	79	6
3. Luis Terrero, of	21	El Paso (AA)	.299	147	29	44	13	3	3	8	9
		Lancaster (A)	.451	71	16	32	9	1	4	11	5
		South Bend (A)	.157	89	4	14	2	0	1	8	3
		Yakima (A)	.317	41	7	13	2	1	0	0	6
5. Jerry Gil, ss	18	South Bend (A)	.215	363	40	78	14	5	2	31	19
6. Brad Cresse, c	23	El Paso (AA)	.289	429	55	124	39	1	14	81	0

Player, Pos.	Age	Club (Class)	W	L	ERA	G	SV	IP	H	BB	SO
4. John Patterson, rhp	23	Tucson (AAA)	2	7	5.85	13	0	68	82	31	40
		El Paso (AA)	1	2	4.26	5	0	25	30	9	19
		Lancaster (A)	0	0	5.79	2	0	9	9	3	9
7. Jeremy Ward, rhp	23	Tucson (AAA)	3	4	3.52	40	13	46	53	17	35
		El Paso (AA)	0	0	1.13	6	0	8	2	1	6
8. Chris Capuano, lhp	23	El Paso (AA)	10	11	5.31	28	0	159	184	75	167
9. Bret Prinz, rhp	24	Arizona	4	1	2.63	46	9	41	33	19	27
		Tucson (AAA)	0	0	0.00	5	3	6	1	0	6
10. Jose Valverde, rhp	22	El Paso (AA)	2	2	3.92	39	13	41	36	27	72

ATLANTA **BRAVES**

The Braves have been a pitching factory over the last decade, and 2001 was no different. Despite injuries to several of their up-and-coming arms, pitchers like Tim Spooneybarger, Gonzalo Lopez, Ben Kozlowski, Trey Hodges, Jose Capellan, Jung Bong, Brett Evert, Bubba Nelson and Zach Miner stepped up.

STEPPING FORWARD: Aside from all of the pitchers who asserted themselves, shortstop Kelly Johnson, 19, excelled in his full-season debut. A 2000 supplemental first-rounder, Johnson silenced critics by slugging .513 while playing a solid shortstop.

STEPPING BACK: Matt McClendon reversed course in 2001 thanks to bone spurs in his right elbow. After flashing overpowering stuff in 2000, the 6-foot-6, 220-pounder finished 2001 in the Class A Carolina League, where he began in 2000.

TOP 10 PROSPECTS

Player, Pos.	Age	Club (Class)	AVG	AB	R	H	2B	3B	HR	RBI	SB
1. Wilson Betemit, ss	19	Atlanta	.000	3	1	0	0	0	0	0	1
		Greenville (AA)	.355	183	22	65	14	0	5	19	6
		Myrtle Beach (A)	.277	318	38	88	20	1	7	43	8
3. Marcus Giles, 2b	23	Atlanta	.262	244	36	64	10	2	9	31	2
		Richmond (AAA)	.333	252	48	84	19	1	6	44	13
8. Wes Helms, 3b	25	Atlanta	.222	216	28	48	10	3	10	36	1

Player, Pos.	Age	Club (Class)	W	L	ERA	G	SV	IP	H	BB	SO
2. Matt McClendon, rhp	23	Richmond (AAA)	0	6	8.16	10	0	46	50	31	31
		Greenville (AA)	0	1	5.91	2	0	11	10	7	9
		Myrtle Beach (A)	1	2	8.68	8	0	9	7	9	10
		Kissimmee (R)	0	0	1.35	3	0	7	3	10	15
4. Matt Belisle, rhp	21				Injured—Did not pitch						
5. Jason Marquis, rhp	23	Atlanta	5	6	3.48	38	0	129	113	59	98
6. Billy Sylvester, rhp	24	Richmond (AAA)	0	4	5.11	36	11	37	28	27	41
		Greenville (AA)	1	0	2.37	26	12	30	18	24	41
7. Adam Wainwright, rhp	20	Macon (A)	10	10	3.77	28	0	165	144	48	184
9. Christian Parra, rhp	23	Greenville (AA)	3	8	5.44	18	0	89	87	56	82
10. Scott Sobkowiak, rhp	23	Greenville (AA)	2	5	5.54	12	0	65	71	40	48
		Kissimmee (R)	0	0	1.29	2	0	7	4	1	11

Wilson Betemit

RICK BATTLE

BALTIMORE **ORIOLES**

The progress of the Orioles farm system in 2001 was best illustrated by looking at the number of youngsters on the overachieving big league club. But as goes for the parent club, the farm is lacking bona fide stars.

STEPPING FORWARD: Lefthander Erik Bedard quietly put together a strong 2000 campaign at low Class A Delmarva, and was in the midst of an even better one in 2001 at high Class A Frederick when shoulder tendinitis interrupted his ascent. Bedard managed to hold opponents to a .198 average while punching out 130 in 98 innings.

STEPPING BACK: In 2000, Papy Ndungidi was earning comparisons to a young Darryl Strawberry. In 2001, he never seemed to recover from a troublesome Arizona Fall League stint, and his production suffered mightily.

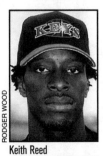

Keith Reed

RODGER WOOD

TOP 10 PROSPECTS

Player, Pos.	Age	Club (Class)	AVG	AB	R	H	2B	3B	HR	RBI	SB
1. Keith Reed, of	22	Rochester (AAA)	.311	74	11	23	7	1	2	11	1
		Bowie (AA)	.254	67	7	17	3	0	1	8	2
		Frederick (A)	.270	267	28	72	14	0	7	29	8
3. Ed Rogers, ss	20	Bowie (AA)	.199	191	11	38	10	1	0	13	10
		Frederick (A)	.260	292	39	76	20	3	8	41	18
4. Ntema Ndungidi, of	22	Bowie (AA)	.212	339	34	72	17	1	3	35	3
9. Octavio Martinez, c	22	Frederick (A)	.217	336	23	73	14	0	1	29	3
10. Brian Roberts, ss	23	Baltimore	.253	273	42	69	12	3	2	17	12
		Rochester (AAA)	.267	161	16	43	4	1	1	12	23
		Bowie (AA)	.296	81	12	24	7	0	1	7	10

Player, Pos.	Age	Club (Class)	W	L	ERA	G	SV	IP	H	BB	SO
2. Richard Stahl, lhp	20	Frederick (A)	1	1	1.95	6	0	32	26	15	24
		Delmarva (A)	2	3	2.67	6	0	34	24	15	31
		Sarasota (R)	0	0	0.00	1	0	2	1	1	1
5. Luis Rivera, rhp	23				Injured—Did not pitch						
6. Beau Hale, rhp	22	Bowie (AA)	1	5	5.11	12	0	62	74	15	40
		Frederick (A)	1	2	1.32	5	0	34	30	4	30
7. Matt Riley, lhp	22				Injured—Did not pitch						
8. Ryan Kohlmeier, rhp	24	Baltimore	1	2	7.30	34	6	41	48	19	29
		Rochester (AAA)	1	4	2.36	14	4	42	36	8	28

MINOR LEAGUES

BOSTON **RED SOX**

Dernell Stenson regained his No. 1 prospect status and went on to his worst effort in his third straight year in Triple-A. No. 2 prospect Brad Baker didn't fare much better, but teenage third baseman Tony Blanco showed tremendous offensive potential until shoulder surgery late in the season.

STEPPING FORWARD: Casey Fossum and Seung Song were two of the bright spots in the Top 10, while first baseman

Luis Garcia mashed his way to 62 extra-base hits and 89 RBIs between Class A Sarasota and Double-A Trenton.

STEPPING BACK: Sang-Hoon Lee signed a two-year major league contract worth more than $1 million following the 1999 season, and he appeared to be in line for a bullpen job. He was beaten out by Pete Schourek in spring training and spent an undistinguished season at Triple-A Pawtucket.

TOP 10 PROSPECTS

Player, Pos.	Age	Club (Class)	AVG	AB	R	H	2B	3B	HR	RBI	SB
1. Dernell Stenson, 1b-of	23	Pawtucket (AAA)	.237	464	53	110	18	1	16	69	0
3. Tony Blanco, 3b	19	Augusta (A)	.265	370	44	98	23	2	17	69	1
6. Steve Lomasney, c	24	Pawtucket (AAA)	.286	63	10	18	4	0	2	9	2
		Trenton (AA)	.249	209	24	52	14	2	10	29	0

Player, Pos.	Age	Club (Class)	W	L	ERA	G	SV	IP	H	BB	SO
2. Brad Baker, rhp	20	Sarasota (A)	7	9	4.73	24	0	120	132	64	103
4. Sun-Woo Kim, rhp	23	Boston	0	2	5.83	20	0	42	54	21	27
		Pawtucket (AAA)	6	7	5.36	19	0	89	93	27	79
5. Casey Fossum, lhp	23	Boston	3	2	4.87	13	0	44	44	20	26
		Trenton (AA)	3	7	2.83	20	0	118	102	28	130
7. Seung Song, rhp	21	Sarasota (A)	5	2	1.68	8	0	48	28	18	56
		Augusta (A)	3	2	2.04	14	0	75	56	18	79
8. Mauricio Lara, lhp	22	Sarasota (A)	1	3	10.50	27	1	30	40	28	29
		Augusta (A)	7	6	3.02	20	0	107	114	24	96
9. Paxton Crawford, rhp	24	Boston	3	0	4.75	8	0	36	40	13	25
		Pawtucket (AAA)	1	3	5.52	6	0	29	43	7	15
10. Sang-Hoon Lee, lhp	30	Pawtucket (AAA)	3	5	5.43	43	4	53	52	16	44

Dernell Stenson

CHICAGO **CUBS**

One of the deepest systems in baseball suffered some major setbacks to prospects in the upper levels in 2001, with injuries to Ben Christensen, Hee Seop Choi, David Kelton and Bobby Hill. However, the next wave of talent brewing in the lower levels looks promising, led by a prospect-laden club at short-season Boise.

STEPPING FORWARD: Ranked as the 30th-best prospect in

the organization prior to 2001, outfielder Nic Jackson showcased exciting five-tool potential to go with plus makeup at Class A Daytona.

STEPPING BACK: Top prospect Corey Patterson was uninspiring at Triple-A Iowa and then struggled to stay above .200 in an extended late-season callup.

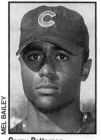

TOP 10 PROSPECTS

Player, Pos.	Age	Club (Class)	AVG	AB	R	H	2B	3B	HR	RBI	SB
1. Corey Patterson, of	22	Chicago	.221	131	26	29	3	0	4	14	4
		Iowa (AAA)	.253	367	63	93	22	3	7	32	19
3. Hee Seop Choi, 1b	22	Iowa (AAA)	.229	266	38	61	11	0	13	45	5
6. Luis Montanez, ss	19	Lansing (A)	.255	499	70	127	33	6	5	54	20
7. David Kelton, 3b	21	West Tenn (AA)	.313	224	33	70	9	4	12	45	1
8. Bobby Hill, 2b-ss	23	West Tenn (AA)	.301	209	30	63	8	1	3	21	20
10. Nate Frese, ss	24	West Tenn (AA)	.180	233	25	42	5	1	4	19	0

Player, Pos.	Age	Club (Class)	W	L	ERA	G	SV	IP	H	BB	SO
2. Juan Cruz, rhp	20	Chicago	3	1	3.22	8	0	45	40	17	39
		West Tenn (AA)	9	6	4.01	23	0	121	107	60	137
4. Ben Christensen, rhp	23	West Tenn (AA)	2	1	6.48	3	0	17	20	9	9
5. Carlos Zambrano, rhp	20	Chicago	1	2	15.26	6	0	8	11	8	4
		Iowa (AAA)	10	5	3.88	26	0	151	124	68	155
9. John Webb, rhp	22	Daytona (A)	1	1	5.40	5	0	20	23	7	20

MEL BAILEY

Corey Patterson

CHICAGO **WHITE SOX**

The White Sox continued to feed off their plentiful minor league chain in 2001. The system has produced pitchers Rocky Biddle, Mark Buehrle, Lorenzo Barcelo, Josh Fogg, Jon Garland, Matt Ginter and Danny Wright in the past two seasons. The well isn't dry, either. Corwin Malone, Matt Guerrier, Jason Stumm and Dennis Ulacia pace the next group.

STEPPING FORWARD: Malone and Guerrier had outstanding seasons in 2001. Malone went from a raw, hard thrower in low Class A to a dominating pitcher in Double-A by

season's end. Guerrier led the minors with 18 wins and looks like a polished product who is on the verge of joining the White Sox staff.

STEPPING BACK: Jon Rauch, Baseball America's 2000 Minor League Player of the Year, tried to pitch through pain, but that coupled with his ineffectiveness led to season-ending shoulder surgery in May. The White Sox expect the 6-foot-11 righthander to be back at full strength by spring training.

TOP 10 PROSPECTS

Player, Pos.	Age	Club (Class)	AVG	AB	R	H	2B	3B	HR	RBI	SB
2. Joe Borchard, of	22	Birmingham (AA)	.295	515	95	152	27	1	27	98	5
3. Joe Crede, 3b	23	Chicago	.220	50	1	11	1	1	0	7	1
		Charlotte (AAA)	.276	463	67	128	34	1	17	65	2
8. Aaron Rowand, of	24	Chicago	.293	123	21	36	5	0	4	20	5
		Charlotte (AAA)	.295	329	54	97	28	0	16	48	8

Player, Pos.	Age	Club (Class)	W	L	ERA	G	SV	IP	H	BB	SO
1. Jon Rauch, rhp	22	Charlotte (AAA)	1	3	5.79	6	0	28	28	7	27
4. Matt Ginter, rhp	23	Chicago	1	0	5.22	20	0	40	34	14	24
		Charlotte (AAA)	2	3	2.59	22	0	76	62	24	67
5. Dan Wright, rhp	23	Chicago	5	3	5.70	13	0	66	78	39	36
		Birmingham (AA)	7	7	2.82	20	0	134	112	41	128
6. Lorenzo Barcelo, rhp	24	Chicago	1	0	4.71	17	0	21	24	8	15
		Charlotte (AAA)	1	0	5.40	2	0	5	6	1	5
7. Brian West, rhp	21	Winston-Salem (A)	7	12	3.46	28	0	169	179	70	130
9. Josh Fogg, rhp	24	Chicago	0	0	2.03	11	0	13	10	3	17
		Charlotte (AAA)	4	7	4.79	40	4	115	129	30	89
10. Jason Stumm, rhp	20	AZL White Sox (R)	0	2	2.25	4	0	12	6	5	12

Jon Rauch

JOHN SPEAR

MINOR LEAGUES

CINCINNATI **REDS**

Outfielder Adam Dunn combined to hit 51 home runs at three levels in 2001, not including three he launched in all-star competition. No other Reds prospect in the Top 10 reached double digits.

STEPPING FORWARD: The Reds feel they landed a blossoming five-tool talent when they acquired Wily Mo Pena from the Yankees in spring training for Drew Henson.

STEPPING BACK: Austin Kearns was rated ahead of Dunn

prior to the 2001 season, but a hand injury sidelined him for most of the summer. Kearns was able to rebound late in the season, but Dane Sardinha and Gookie Dawkins never seemed to get going. In his pro debut, Sardinha's .259 on-base percentage left a lot to be desired, and Dawkins' third trip through the Double-A Southern League was more unimpressive than his second.

STEVE MOORE

Austin Kearns

TOP 10 PROSPECTS

Player, Pos.	Age	Club (Class)	AVG	AB	R	H	2B	3B	HR	RBI	SB
1. Austin Kearns, of	21	Chattanooga (AA)	.268	205	30	55	11	2	6	36	7
		GCL Reds (R)	.176	17	2	3	2	0	0	4	0
2. Adam Dunn, of	21	Cincinnati	.262	244	54	64	18	1	19	43	4
		Louisville (AAA)	.329	210	44	69	13	0	20	53	5
		Chattanooga (AA)	.343	140	30	48	9	0	12	31	6
3. *Drew Henson, 3b	21	Columbus (AAA)	.368	19	2	7	1	0	0	2	0
		Norwich (AA)	.222	270	29	60	6	0	11	38	2
		Tampa (A)	.143	14	2	2	0	0	1	3	1
4. Dane Sardinha, c	22	Mudville (A)	.235	422	45	99	24	2	9	55	0
5. David Espinosa, ss-2b	19	Dayton (A)	.262	493	88	129	29	8	7	37	15
8. Gookie Dawkins, 2b-ss	22	Chattanooga (AA)	.226	394	59	89	16	3	8	40	14

Player, Pos.	Age	Club (Class)	W	L	ERA	G	SV	IP	H	BB	SO
6. Ty Howington, lhp	20	Chattanooga (AA)	1	3	3.27	7	0	41	36	24	38
		Mudville (A)	3	2	2.43	7	0	37	33	20	44
		Dayton (A)	4	0	1.15	6	0	39	15	9	47
7. Dustin Moseley, rhp	19	Dayton (A)	10	8	4.20	25	0	148	158	42	108
9. John Riedling, rhp	26	Cincinnati	1	1	2.41	29	1	34	22	14	23
		Louisville (AAA)	0	0	0.00	1	0	1	0	1	1
10. Chris Reitsma, rhp	23	Cincinnati	7	15	5.29	36	0	182	209	49	96

*Traded to Yankees

CLEVELAND INDIANS

The Indians rejuvenated their system in 2001. A fruitful draft packed with live young arms provided a boost in the lower levels, while the parent club was able to rely on rookies C.C. Sabathia and Danys Baez down the stretch.

STEPPING FORWARD: Catcher Victor Martinez emerged as a double threat at Class A Kinston. Not only did he cut down basestealers with a strong, accurate arm, he broke out with 45 extra-base hits and a league-leading .329 average.

STEPPING BACK: Behind the Indians' top three starters, no pitchers made major progress in 2001. Jake Westbrook and Tim Drew struggled bouncing between Triple-A Buffalo and Cleveland, and the pen and the rotation. Zach Day was dealt for outfielder Milton Bradley and injuries cost Sean DePaula another season.

TOP 10 PROSPECTS

Player, Pos.	Age	Club (Class)	AVG	AB	R	H	2B	3B	HR	RBI	SB
3. Corey Smith, 3b	19	Columbus (A)	.260	500	59	130	26	5	18	85	10
4. Willy Taveras, of	19	Columbus (A)	.271	395	55	107	15	7	3	32	29
9. Maicer Izturis, ss	20	Kinston (A)	.240	433	47	104	16	6	1	39	32
10. Alex Requena, of	21	Kinston (A)	.212	259	30	55	7	4	2	13	32
		Columbus (A)	.255	137	22	35	6	0	2	13	15

Player, Pos.	Age	Club (Class)	W	L	ERA	G	SV	IP	H	BB	SO
1. C.C. Sabathia, lhp	21	Cleveland	17	5	4.39	33	0	180	149	95	171
2. Danys Baez, rhp	23	Cleveland	5	3	2.50	43	0	50	34	20	52
		Buffalo (AAA)	2	0	3.20	16	3	25	18	9	30
		Akron (AA)	0	0	0.00	1	0	2	1	0	2
5. Sean DePaula, rhp	27	Buffalo (AAA)	1	0	1.04	6	1	9	2	4	6
6. *Zach Day, rhp	23	Ottawa (AAA)	2	2	7.43	6	0	27	38	8	15
		Buffalo (AAA)	1	0	1.50	1	0	6	3	1	4
		Akron (AA)	9	10	3.10	22	0	137	123	45	94
7. Jake Westbrook, rhp	23	Cleveland	4	4	5.85	23	0	65	79	22	48
		Buffalo (AAA)	8	1	3.20	12	0	65	60	23	45
8. Tim Drew, rhp	23	Cleveland	0	2	7.97	8	0	35	51	16	15
		Buffalo (AAA)	8	6	3.92	18	0	108	115	27	75

*Traded to Expos

C.C. Sabathia

STEVE MOORE

COLORADO ROCKIES

Chin-Hui Tsao

STEVE MOORE

The ongoing turnover under general manager Dan O'Dowd's regime led the Rockies into a rebuilding phase in which they leaned heavily on the minor leagues in 2001. Righthanders Shawn Chacon and Jason Jennings, and shortstop Juan Uribe provided hope from the homegrown talent, while a three-way trade brought second baseman Jose Ortiz and outfielder Mario Encarnacion on board.

STEPPING FORWARD: Nobody enhanced his status more than Ryan Kibler, 20, who entered the year as the organization's No. 27 prospect. He rode his heavy sinker to 17 consecutive starts without a loss between three levels. Kibler's repertoire makes him an ideal candidate to handle the thin air at Coors Field.

STEPPING BACK: Choo Freeman was twice the organization's top prospect (1999-2000), but he has yet to translate tools into success above low Class A.

TOP 10 PROSPECTS

Player, Pos.	Age	Club (Class)	AVG	AB	R	H	2B	3B	HR	RBI	SB
2. Juan Uribe, ss	22	Colorado	.300	273	32	82	15	11	8	53	3
		Colorado Springs (AAA)	.310	281	40	87	27	7	7	48	11
		Carolina (AA)	.231	13	1	3	1	0	0	1	1
3. Choo Freeman, of	21	Salem (A)	.240	517	63	124	16	5	8	42	19
10. Matt Holliday, 3b-of	21	Salem (A)	.275	255	36	70	16	1	11	52	11

Player, Pos.	Age	Club (Class)	W	L	ERA	G	SV	IP	H	BB	SO
1. Chin-Hui Tsao, rhp	20	Salem (A)	0	4	4.67	4	0	17	23	5	18
4. Aaron Cook, rhp	22	Salem (A)	11	11	3.08	27	0	155	157	38	122
5. Jason Young, rhp	21	Salem (A)	6	7	3.44	17	0	105	104	28	91
6. Jason Jennings, rhp	23	Colorado	4	1	4.58	7	0	39	42	19	26
		Colorado Springs (AAA)	7	8	4.72	22	0	132	145	41	110
		Carolina (AA)	2	0	2.88	4	0	25	25	8	24
7. Craig House, rhp	24	Colorado Springs (AAA)	2	2	4.45	54	6	59	50	31	62
8. Shawn Chacon, rhp	23	Colorado	6	10	5.06	27	0	169	157	87	134
		Colorado Springs (AAA)	2	0	2.25	4	0	24	18	7	28
9. Josh Kalinowski, lhp	24	Carolina (AA)	7	8	4.06	25	0	137	151	65	116

MINOR LEAGUES

DETROIT **TIGERS**

Top prospect Brandon Inge was thrust into Detroit's starting lineup in 2001 when incumbent catcher Mitch Meluskey went down in spring training. Nate Cornejo joined the rotation and won a combined 20 games. And the Tigers are still waiting for Eric Munson to develop into their first baseman of the future.

STEPPING FORWARD: Catcher Mike Rivera, 24, emerged from obscurity by smacking 33 home runs and driving in 101 runs at Double-A Erie. His previous career high was 16 home runs.

STEPPING BACK: Injuries hampered two of the system's youngest and brightest prospects in 2001. Shortstop Ramon Santiago was limited to DH duty by offseason shoulder surgery, while righthander Matt Wheatland never could shake nagging arm problems in his first full season out of high school.

TOP 10 PROSPECTS

Player, Pos.	Age	Club (Class)	AVG	AB	R	H	2B	3B	HR	RBI	SB
1. Brandon Inge, c	24	Detroit	.180	189	13	34	11	0	0	15	1
		Toledo (AAA)	.289	90	11	26	11	1	2	15	1
		West Michigan (A)	.188	16	3	3	1	0	0	2	0
		GCL Tigers (R)	.100	10	1	1	0	0	1	2	0
2. Ramon Santiago, ss	20	Lakeland (A)	.268	429	64	115	16	3	2	46	34
3. Eric Munson, 1b	23	Detroit	.152	66	4	10	3	1	1	6	0
		Erie (AA)	.260	519	88	135	35	1	26	102	0
7. Andres Torres, of	23	Erie (AA)	.294	252	54	74	16	3	1	23	19
8. Omar Infante, ss	19	Erie (AA)	.302	540	86	163	21	4	2	62	27
10. Nook Logan, of	21	West Michigan (A)	.262	522	82	137	19	8	1	27	67

Player, Pos.	Age	Club (Class)	W	L	ERA	G	SV	IP	H	BB	SO
4. Matt Wheatland, rhp	19	West Michigan (A)	0	2	10.93	3	0	14	21	4	17
		GCL Tigers (R)	0	0	0.00	3	0	9	3	3	5
5. Nate Cornejo, rhp	21	Detroit	4	4	7.38	10	0	43	63	28	22
		Toledo (AAA)	4	0	2.12	4	0	30	24	7	22
		Erie (AA)	12	3	2.68	19	0	124	107	41	10
6. Shane Loux, rhp	22	Toledo (AAA)	10	11	5.78	28	0	151	203	73	72
9. Andy Van Hekken, lhp	22	Erie (AA)	5	0	4.69	8	0	48	63	8	29
		Lakeland (A)	10	4	3.17	19	0	111	105	33	82

Brandon Inge

MORRIS FOSTOFF

FLORIDA **MARLINS**

Injuries hit several of the Marlins top prospects, preventing Wes Anderson, Jason Stokes, Pablo Ozuna and Nate Rolison from progressing in 2001. Josh Beckett lived up to the hype, dominating at three levels a year after shoulder problems clouded his immediate future.

STEPPING FORWARD: Lefthander Nate Robertson rebounded from elbow surgery in 2000 to go 11-4, 2.88 in 19 starts at Class A Brevard County.

STEPPING BACK: The Marlins thought they stole a five-tool talent from the Diamondbacks when they acquired outfielder Abraham Nunez following the 1999 season. Nunez' tools are still evident, and he started to turn it around late in the year.

STEVE MOORE

Josh Beckett

TOP 10 PROSPECTS

Player, Pos.	Age	Club (Class)	AVG	AB	R	H	2B	3B	HR	RBI	SB
3. Miguel Cabrera, ss	18	Kane County (A)	.268	422	61	113	19	4	7	66	3
4. Adrian Gonzalez, 1b	19	Kane County (A)	.312	516	86	161	37	1	17	103	5
5. Abraham Nunez, of	21	Portland (AA)	.240	467	75	112	14	9	17	53	26
8. Jason Stokes, 1b	19	Utica (A)	.231	130	12	30	2	1	6	19	0
9. Pablo Ozuna, 2b	23		Injured—Did not play								
10. Nate Rolison, 1b	24	Calgary (AAA)	.167	12	1	2	0	0	0	1	0
		Portland (AA)	.211	19	1	4	1	0	0	2	0
		Brevard County (A)	.378	45	7	17	3	0	1	6	0
		GCL Marlins (R)	.500	4	1	2	0	0	0	1	0

Player, Pos.	Age	Club (Class)	W	L	ERA	G	SV	IP	H	BB	SO
1. Josh Beckett, rhp	21	Florida	2	2	1.50	4	0	24	14	11	24
		Portland (AA)	8	1	1.82	13	0	74	50	19	102
		Brevard County (A)	6	0	1.23	13	0	66	32	15	101
2. Wes Anderson, rhp	21	Brevard County (A)	1	6	5.63	8	0	32	48	21	17
		GCL Marlins (R)	0	1	27.00	1	0	3	1	0	
6. Claudio Vargas, rhp	22	Portland (AA)	8	9	4.19	27	0	159	122	67	151
7. Blaine Neal, rhp	23	Florida	0	0	6.75	4	0	5	7	5	3
		Portland (AA)	2	3	2.36	54	21	53	43	21	45

MINOR LEAGUES

HOUSTON **ASTROS**

Top-rated prospect Roy Oswalt established himself as one of the brightest young pitchers in baseball by posting a 14-3, 2.73 record after being recalled from Triple-A in May. Oswalt heads a deep stable of young guns.

STEPPING FORWARD: While pitching was the name of the game down on the Astros farm, nobody's performance was more surprising than that of outfielder Jason Lane, 24, at Double-A Round Rock. He ripped 78 extra-base hits and drove in 124 runs with a .318 batting average.

STEPPING BACK: Wilfredo Rodriguez began the 2001 season in the bullpen hoping to rediscover the command of his overpowering stuff. He still throws as hard as almost any lefthander around, and served up Barry Bonds' record-breaking home run on a 95-mph heater.

TOP 10 PROSPECTS

Player, Pos.	Age	Club (Class)	AVG	AB	R	H	2B	3B	HR	RBI	SB
6. Adam Everett, ss	24	Houston	.000	3	1	0	0	0	0	0	1
		New Orleans (AAA)	.249	441	69	110	20	8	5	40	24
8. John Buck, c	21	Lexington (A)	.275	443	72	122	24	1	22	73	4
10. Keith Ginter, 2b	25	New Orleans (AAA)	.269	457	76	123	31	5	16	70	8

Player, Pos.	Age	Club (Class)	W	L	ERA	G	SV	IP	H	BB	SO
1. Roy Oswalt, rhp	24	Houston	14	3	2.73	28	0	142	126	24	144
		New Orleans (AAA)	2	3	4.35	5	0	31	32	6	34
2. Wilfredo Rodriguez, lhp	22	Houston	0	0	15.00	2	0	3	6	1	3
		Round Rock (AA)	5	9	4.78	42	0	92	94	56	94
3. Tim Redding, rhp	23	Houston	3	1	5.50	13	0	56	62	24	55
		New Orleans (AAA)	4	1	4.54	6	0	38	22	19	42
		Round Rock (AA)	10	2	2.18	14	0	91	64	25	113
4. *Tony McKnight, rhp	24	Pittsburgh	2	6	5.19	12	0	69	88	21	36
		Houston	1	0	4.00	3	0	18	21	3	10
		New Orleans (AAA)	9	5	4.76	18	0	93	104	24	61
5. Robert Stiehl, rhp	20	Lexington (A)	2	3	1.98	14	0	50	28	34	59
7. Greg Miller, lhp	21	Round Rock (AA)	5	3	3.25	14	0	55	38	35	37
9. Mike Nannini, rhp	21	Lexington (A)	15	5	2.70	28	0	190	176	36	151
* Traded to Pirates											

Roy Oswalt

STEVE MOORE

KANSAS CITY **ROYALS**

After dealing young outfielders Johnny Damon and Jermaine Dye in 2001, it is apparent the Royals will need to draw from their minor league system frequently. It supplied lefthander Chris George and outfielder Dee Brown in 2001, with Angel Berroa (acquired in the Damon deal), Mike MacDougal, Jeff Austin and Ken Harvey on the cusp.

STEPPING FORWARD: Harvey was ranked among the organization's top prospects prior to the season, but by combining to hit .350 at two levels he solidified his status as a hitting machine.

STEPPING BACK: Kyle Snyder has pitched all of 26 innings since being drafted with the seventh overall pick in 1999. Arm injuries wiped out his 2001 season.

TOP 10 PROSPECTS

Player, Pos.	Age	Club (Class)	AVG	AB	R	H	2B	3B	HR	RBI	SB
2. Dee Brown, of	23	Kansas City	.245	380	39	93	19	0	7	40	5
		Omaha (AAA)	.297	37	5	11	0	0	2	6	0
6. Angel Berroa, ss	21	Kansas City	.302	53	8	16	2	0	0	4	2
		Wichita (AA)	.296	304	63	90	20	4	8	42	15
		Wilmington (A)	.317	199	43	63	18	4	6	25	10
7. Ken Harvey, 1b	23	Kansas City	.250	12	1	3	1	0	0	2	0
		Wichita (AA)	.338	314	54	106	20	3	9	63	3
		Wilmington (A)	.380	137	22	52	9	1	6	27	3
9. Alexis Gomez, of	21	Wichita (AA)	.281	342	55	96	15	6	4	34	16
		Wilmington (A)	.302	169	29	51	8	2	1	9	7

Chris George

JOHN SPEAR

Player, Pos.	Age	Club (Class)	W	L	ERA	G	SV	IP	H	BB	SO
1. Chris George, lhp	21	Kansas City	4	8	5.59	13	0	74	83	18	32
		Omaha (AAA)	11	3	3.53	20	0	117	103	51	84
3. Mike MacDougal, rhp	24	Kansas City	1	1	4.70	3	0	15	18	4	7
		Omaha (AAA)	8	8	4.68	28	0	144	144	76	110
4. Jimmy Gobble, lhp	20	Wilmington (A)	10	6	2.55	27	0	162	134	33	154
5. Jeff Austin, rhp	24	Kansas City	0	0	5.54	21	0	26	27	14	27
		Omaha (AAA)	3	7	6.88	28	2	71	89	27	55
8. Mike Stodolka, lhp	19	Burlington (A)	3	8	4.67	20	0	94	105	30	49
10. Kyle Snyder, rhp	23							Injured—Did not play			

MINOR LEAGUES

LOS ANGELES **DODGERS**

No team has staked claim to more rookie-of-the-year awards than the Dodgers, but the system's productivity has been in decline in recent years. However, an impressive crop of hard-throwing young arms is helping rebuild the tradition.

STEPPING FORWARD: Righthander Ricardo Rodriguez skipped two levels and led the Class A Florida State League in strikeouts during his first season above the Rookie level.

STEPPING BACK: Jason Repko has often been referred to as a five-tool prospect, but the 1999 first-rounder has made little progress in three years. If he has another year like 2001, it won't matter how many tools he has.

TOP 10 PROSPECTS

Player, Pos.	Age	Club (Class)	AVG	AB	R	H	2B	3B	HR	RBI	SB
2. Chin-Feng Chen, of	23	Jacksonville (AA)	.313	224	47	70	16	2	17	50	5
		Vero Beach (A)	.268	235	38	63	15	3	5	41	2
4. Jason Repko, ss	20	Wilmington (A)	.220	337	36	74	17	4	4	32	17
7. Willy Aybar, 3b	18	Vero Beach (A)	.286	7	0	2	0	0	0	0	0
		Wilmington (A)	.237	431	45	102	25	2	4	48	7
8. Hiram Bocachica, 2b-of	25	Los Angeles	.233	133	15	31	11	1	2	9	4
9. Joe Thurston, 2b	21	Jacksonville (AA)	.267	544	80	145	25	7	7	46	20

Player, Pos.	Age	Club (Class)	W	L	ERA	G	SV	IP	H	BB	SO
1. Ben Diggins, rhp	22	Wilmington (A)	7	6	3.58	21	0	106	88	48	79
3. Hong-Chih Kuo, lhp	20	GCL Dodgers (R)	0	0	2.33	7	0	19	13	4	21
5. Luke Prokopec, rhp	23	Los Angeles	8	7	4.88	29	0	138	146	40	91
		Las Vegas (AAA)	1	0	3.00	1	0	6	3	2	8
6. *Mike Judd, rhp	26	Texas	0	1	8.00	4	0	9	15	5	5
		Tampa Bay	1	0	4.05	8	0	20	19	10	11
		Oklahoma (AAA)	0	1	10.13	2	0	3	6	2	3
10. Chad Ricketts, rhp	26	Las Vegas (AAA)	1	3	2.91	48	3	59	49	25	70

*Traded to Devil Rays/Rangers

JOHN SPEAR

Ben Diggins

MILWAUKEE **BREWERS**

With the help of their top prospects, the Brewers assembled a promising young rotation in 2001, featuring Ben Sheets, Nick Neugebauer, Jamey Wright and Ruben Quevedo. But as has often been the case in Milwaukee, injuries were a factor.

STEPPING FORWARD: Righthander Ben Hendrickson, 20, went 8-9, 2.84 at low Class A Beloit. A 10th-round pick in 1999, he used a plus curveball and an above-average fastball to strike out 133 in 133 innings.

STEPPING BACK: Not everything went well for the Brewers' top-rated pitching prospects. Mike Penney had his best year in 2000 pitching out of the pen, but he shuffled between the rotation and the pen in 2001 and was demoted to Double-A Huntsville at midseason.

TOP 10 PROSPECTS

Player, Pos.	Age	Club (Class)	AVG	AB	R	H	2B	3B	HR	RBI	SB
3. David Krynzel, of	19	High Desert (A)	.277	383	65	106	19	5	5	33	34
		Beloit (A)	.305	141	22	43	1	1	1	19	11
4. Cristian Guerrero, of	20	High Desert (A)	.312	327	50	102	18	2	7	41	22
7. Kade Johnson, c	22	High Desert (A)	.254	370	57	94	21	1	21	67	9

Player, Pos.	Age	Club (Class)	W	L	ERA	G	SV	IP	H	BB	SO
1. Ben Sheets, rhp	23	Milwaukee	11	10	4.76	25	0	151	166	48	94
		Indianapolis (AAA)	1	1	3.38	2	0	11	14	3	6
2. Nick Neugebauer, rhp	21	Milwaukee	1	1	7.50	2	0	6	6	6	11
		Indianapolis (AAA)	2	1	1.50	4	0	24	10	9	26
		Huntsville (AA)	5	6	3.46	21	0	107	94	52	149
5. Allen Levrault, rhp	24	Milwaukee	6	10	6.06	32	0	131	146	59	80
		Indianapolis (AAA)	2	1	2.64	5	0	31	22	8	30
6. Jose Mieses, rhp	21	Indianapolis (AAA)	0	3	6.08	3	0	13	23	7	13
		Huntsville (AA)	0	0	2.22	5	0	24	21	3	35
		Ogden (R)	0	1	27.00	1	0	1	3	1	2
8. Mike Penney, rhp	24	Indianapolis (AAA)	4	3	5.37	22	1	57	70	23	35
		Huntsville (AA)	4	3	3.31	21	7	49	50	22	30
9. *Horacio Estrada, lhp	25	Colorado	1	1	14.54	4	0	4	8	1	4
		Colorado Springs (AAA)	8	4	4.73	16	0	91	102	20	77
10. Brandon Kolb, rhp	27	Milwaukee	0	0	13.03	10	0	10	16	8	8
		Indianapolis (AAA)	3	5	4.28	40	14	55	49	22	57

*Became free agent; signed by Rockies

MEL BAILEY

Ben Sheets

MINOR LEAGUES

MINNESOTA **TWINS**

The Cinderella story in the first half of the major league season, Minnesota did it with more homegrown flavor than any team in baseball.

STEPPING FORWARD: The Twins' bullpen was exploited during their second-half collapse, but help could be on the way as Australian righthander Grant Balfour, 23, led a dominant relief corps at Double-A New Britain. After going 2-1, 1.08 with 72 strikeouts and 13 saves in 50 innings, Balfour looks like a future closer with an above-average fastball/slider combination.

STEPPING BACK: Matt Kinney was in line for a shot at a spot in the Twins' rotation in spring training, but he was beset by shoulder soreness early in the season and dropped nine of his first 10 decisions at Triple-A Edmonton. He rallied to win four consecutive starts to end the season on a positive note.

TOP 10 PROSPECTS

Player, Pos.	Age	Club (Class)	AVG	AB	R	H	2B	3B	HR	RBI	SB
2. Michael Cuddyer, 3b	22	Minnesota	.222	18	1	4	2	0	0	1	1
		New Britain (AA)	.301	509	95	153	36	3	30	87	5
3. Michael Restovich, of	22	New Britain (AA)	.269	501	69	135	33	4	23	84	15
4. Luis Rivas, 2b	22	Minnesota	.266	563	70	150	21	6	7	47	31
5. Justin Morneau, 1b	20	New Britain (AA)	.158	38	3	6	1	0	0	4	0
		Fort Myers (A)	.294	197	25	58	10	3	4	40	0
		Quad City (A)	.356	236	50	84	17	2	12	53	0
7. Rob Bowen, c	20	Quad City (A)	.255	385	47	98	18	2	18	70	4
8. Bobby Kielty, of	25	Minnesota	.250	104	8	26	8	0	2	14	3
		Edmonton (AAA)	.287	341	58	98	25	2	12	50	5
10. B.J. Garbe, of	20	Fort Myers (A)	.242	463	55	112	14	4	6	61	13

Player, Pos.	Age	Club (Class)	W	L	ERA	G	SV	IP	H	BB	SO
1. Adam Johnson, rhp	22	Minnesota	1	2	8.28	7	0	25	32	13	17
		Edmonton (AAA)	1	1	5.70	4	0	24	19	10	25
		New Britain (AA)	5	6	3.82	18	0	113	105	39	110
6. Matt Kinney, rhp	24	Edmonton (AAA)	6	11	5.07	29	0	162	178	74	146
9. Brad Thomas, lhp	23	Minnesota	0	2	9.37	5	0	16	20	14	6
		New Britain (AA)	10	3	1.96	19	0	119	91	26	97

Adam Johnson

STEVE MOORE

MONTREAL **EXPOS**

As questions loom over the future of the Expos, their farm system is not as equipped as usual to fill the next void created by a fleeing free agent. They must continue to emphasize player development to stand a chance.

STEPPING FORWARD: Outfielder Ron Calloway wasn't a blip on the radar screen until he broke out with 19 home runs and 36 stolen bases between Double-A Harrisburg and Triple-A Ottawa in 2001. The Expos acquired Calloway, 24, from the Diamondbacks in a back-page trade in 1999 for catcher John Pachot.

STEPPING BACK: No. 1 prospect Donnie Bridges suffered through a disastrous season after winning 16 games in 2000. Bridges spent most of the year trying to rehab a tired arm, but never regained his dominant form.

TOP 10 PROSPECTS

Player, Pos.	Age	Club (Class)	AVG	AB	R	H	2B	3B	HR	RBI	SB
2. Brandon Phillips, ss	20	Harrisburg (AA)	.298	265	35	79	19	0	7	36	13
		Jupiter (A)	.284	194	36	55	12	2	4	23	17
3. Brad Wilkerson, of	24	Montreal	.205	117	11	24	7	2	1	5	2
		Ottawa (AAA)	.270	233	43	63	10	0	12	48	12
		Jupiter (A)	.231	26	3	6	3	0	0	1	0
6. Grady Sizemore, of	19	Clinton (A)	.268	451	64	121	16	4	2	61	32
7. Scott Hodges, 3b	22	Harrisburg (AA)	.275	305	30	84	11	2	5	32	3
9. Wilken Ruan, of	21	Harrisburg (AA)	.248	117	14	29	7	0	0	6	6
		Jupiter (A)	.283	293	41	83	8	2	2	26	25

Player, Pos.	Age	Club (Class)	W	L	ERA	G	SV	IP	H	BB	SO
1. Donnie Bridges, rhp	22	Ottawa (AAA)	3	5	7.48	13	0	55	60	43	49
		Harrisburg (AA)	1	2	3.24	3	0	17	14	13	14
		Jupiter (A)	0	1	6.75	1	0	4	7	3	2
4. Josh Girdley, lhp	21	Clinton (A)	0	2	3.68	6	0	29	28	18	21
5. Justin Wayne, rhp	22	Harrisburg (AA)	9	2	2.62	14	0	93	87	34	70
		Jupiter (A)	2	3	3.02	8	0	42	31	9	35
8. T.J. Tucker, rhp	23	Ottawa (AAA)	3	5	3.11	14	0	84	68	33	63
		Harrisburg (AA)	5	5	3.73	13	0	82	77	37	57
10. Luke Lockwood, lhp	20	Clinton (A)	5	10	2.70	26	0	163	152	49	114

JOHN SPEAR

Donnie Bridges

MINOR LEAGUES

NEW YORK **METS**

The Mets system hasn't been particularly productive in recent years, due in large part to injuries, and there isn't much knocking on the door. Only lefthander Billy Traber and outfielder Tsuyoshi Shinjo surpassed expectations among the organization's Top 10. Grant Roberts showed potential out of the Mets' bullpen down the stretch.

STEPPING FORWARD: Shortstop Jose Reyes emerged as a high-ceiling prospect oozing with tools at Class A Capital City. Reyes, 18, hit .307-5-48 with 30 steals in his first full-season league. Righthander Jae Seo was also a pleasant surprise, going 9-6, 2.77 at three levels, after arm injuries hampered him for three years.

STEPPING BACK: Coming off an impressive performance in the Arizona Fall League in 2000, Nick Maness failed to live up to raised expectations. Outfielder Brian Cole was killed in a car accident on his way home from spring training.

TOP 10 PROSPECTS

Player, Pos.	Age	Club (Class)	AVG	AB	R	H	2B	3B	HR	RBI	SB
1. Alex Escobar, of	22	New York	.200	50	3	10	1	0	3	8	1
		Norfolk (AAA)	.267	397	55	106	21	4	12	52	18
3. Brian Cole, of	—						Deceased				
4. Timo Perez, of	24	New York	.247	239	26	59	9	1	5	22	1
		Norfolk (AAA)	.359	192	37	69	10	2	6	19	15
6. Enrique Cruz, 3b	19	Capital City (A)	.251	438	60	110	20	2	9	59	33
9. Tsuyoshi Shinjo, of	29	New York	.268	400	46	107	23	1	10	56	4

Player, Pos.	Age	Club (Class)	W	L	ERA	G	SV	IP	H	BB	SO
2. Pat Strange, rhp	21	Norfolk (AAA)	1	0	0.00	6	0	6	4	1	6
		Binghamton (AA)	11	6	4.87	26	0	153	171	52	106
5. Grant Roberts, rhp	23	New York	1	0	3.81	16	0	26	24	8	29
		Norfolk (AAA)	3	5	4.52	30	2	68	80	19	54
7. Nick Maness, rhp	22	Binghamton (AA)	6	12	4.97	28	0	143	168	65	107
8. Billy Traber, lhp	21	Norfolk (AAA)	0	1	1.29	1	0	7	5	0	0
		Binghamton (AA)	4	3	4.43	8	0	43	50	13	45
		St. Lucie (A)	6	5	2.66	18	0	102	85	23	79
10. Dicky Gonzalez, rhp	22	New York	3	2	4.88	16	0	59	72	17	31
		Norfolk (AAA)	6	5	3.09	17	0	96	96	20	70

Alex Escobar

STEVE MOORE

NEW YORK **YANKEES**

The Yankees are still loaded with talent. They have flexibility in that they have prospects ready to step in—Nick Johnson, Juan Rivera, Erick Almonte, Brandon Claussen—and depth in the lower levels to be potentially used as trade bait to help restock.

STEPPING FORWARD: Claussen, 22, rode his way up the organizational ladder and led the minors with 220 strike-outs. Outfielder Rivera, 22, came on strong in his sixth season in the organization, hitting .322-28-98 between Double-A Norwich and Triple-A Columbus.

STEPPING BACK: Righthander Todd Noel was unable to return from shoulder surgery and has been limited to 10 innings since the beginning of 2000.

TOP 10 PROSPECTS

Player, Pos.	Age	Club (Class)	AVG	AB	R	H	2B	3B	HR	RBI	SB
1. Nick Johnson, 1b	22	New York	.194	67	6	13	2	0	2	8	0
		Columbus (AAA)	.256	359	68	92	20	0	18	49	9
2. Alfonso Soriano, ss	23	New York	.268	574	77	154	34	3	18	73	43
3. *D'Angelo Jimenez, ss	23	San Diego	.276	308	45	85	19	0	3	33	2
		Columbus (AAA)	.262	214	33	56	11	1	5	19	5
7. Erick Almonte, ss	23	New York	.500	4	0	2	1	0	0	0	2
		Columbus (AAA)	.287	345	55	99	19	3	12	55	4
		Norwich (AA)	.250	12	2	3	0	0	0	0	1
8. Deivi Mendez, ss	18	Greensboro (A)	.216	171	25	37	6	0	2	15	5
		Staten Island (A)	.231	186	23	43	10	2	1	21	2
9. +Wily Mo Pena, of	19	Dayton (A)	.264	511	87	135	25	5	26	113	26

Player, Pos.	Age	Club (Class)	W	L	ERA	G	SV	IP	H	BB	SO
4. Adrian Hernandez, rhp	27	New York	0	3	3.68	6	0	22	15	10	10
		Columbus (AAA)	8	7	5.51	21	0	118	116	60	97
5. Alex Graman, lhp	23	Norwich (AA)	12	9	3.52	28	0	166	174	60	138
6. Randy Keisler, lhp	25	New York	1	2	6.22	10	0	51	52	34	36
		Columbus (AAA)	5	7	5.18	18	0	97	111	39	88
10. Todd Noel, rhp	22					Injured—Did not play					

*Traded to Padres
+Traded to Reds

Nick Johnson

MINOR LEAGUES

OAKLAND **ATHLETICS**

The majority of the A's best young prospects have already made the transition to the majors. General Manager Billy Beane's small-market team shipped two of its top four prospects to the Rockies in a three-way trade for outfielder Jermaine Dye, after acquiring outfielder Johnny Damon for outfielder Ben Grieve and shortstop Angel Berroa in the spring.

STEPPING FORWARD: Lefthander Mario Ramos improved his career record to 30-9, 2.88 in 56 starts and finally

gained recognition as a top-notch pitching prospect. The A's are counting on him to join Tim Hudson, Barry Zito, Mark Mulder and Cory Lidle in the rotation in 2002.

STEPPING BACK: Jason Hart had his most disappointing season after crushing 31 bombs in Double-A in 2000. He was thought of as a potential backup plan for Jason Giambi, but Hart batted a career low and his power production dropped off.

TOP 10 PROSPECTS

Player, Pos.	Age	Club (Class)	AVG	AB	R	H	2B	3B	HR	RBI	SB
1. *Jose Ortiz, 2b	24	Colorado	.255	204	38	52	8	1	13	35	3
		Oakland	.167	42	4	7	0	0	0	3	1
		Sacramento (AAA)	.273	256	41	70	16	4	7	39	7
2. Jason Hart, 1b	23	Sacramento (AAA)	.247	494	71	122	26	1	19	75	3
3. Ryan Ludwick, of	23	Sacramento (AAA)	.228	57	10	13	3	0	1	7	2
		Midland (AA)	.269	443	82	119	23	3	25	96	9
4. *Mario Encarnacion, of	23	Colorado	.226	62	3	14	1	0	0	3	2
		Colorado Springs (AAA)	.303	231	37	70	13	2	14	43	4
		Sacramento (AAA)	.285	186	29	53	8	2	12	33	4
6. Freddie Bynum, ss	21	Modesto (A)	.261	440	59	115	19	7	2	46	28
9. Eric Byrnes, of	25	Oakland	.237	38	9	9	1	0	3	5	1
		Sacramento (AAA)	.289	415	81	120	23	2	20	51	25

Player, Pos.	Age	Club (Class)	W	L	ERA	G	SV	IP	H	BB	SO
5. Justin Miller, rhp	24	Sacramento (AAA)	7	10	4.75	29	0	165	174	64	134
7. Chad Harville, rhp	24	Oakland	0	0	0.00	3	0	3	2	0	2
		Sacramento (AAA)	5	2	3.98	33	8	41	35	12	55
		Visalia (A)	0	0	1.50	3	0	6	5	0	6
8. Mario Ramos, lhp	23	Sacramento (AAA)	8	3	3.14	13	0	80	74	27	82
		Midland (AA)	8	1	3.07	15	0	94	71	28	68
10. Bert Snow, rhp	24					Injured—Did not play					

* Traded to Rockies

COSIMO MELLACE

Jose Ortiz

PHILADELPHIA **PHILLIES**

Though the Phillies came up short in the National League East in 2001, it was a successful year in the organization. Shortstop Jimmy Rollins ignited their surprising pennant run while righthanders Brandon Duckworth and Dave Coggin stepped into the rotation down the stretch.

STEPPING FORWARD: On the heels of a nondescript season,

righthander Miguel Ascencio, 20, smoothed out his mechanics and posted a 12-5, 2.84 record at Class A Clearwater.

STEPPING BACK: Righthanders Brad Baisley and Ryan Madson were expected to ascend alongside Brett Myers, but both were stalled with nagging injuries.

TOP 10 PROSPECTS

Player, Pos.	Age	Club (Class)	AVG	AB	R	H	2B	3B	HR	RBI	SB
1. Jimmy Rollins, ss	22	Philadelphia	.274	656	97	180	29	12	14	54	46
5. Chase Utley, 2b	22	Clearwater (A)	.257	467	65	120	25	2	16	59	19
6. Anderson Machado, ss	20	Reading (AA)	.149	101	13	15	2	0	1	8	5
		Clearwater (A)	.261	272	49	71	5	8	5	36	23
7. Reggie Taylor, of	24	Philadelphia	.000	7	1	0	0	0	0	0	0
		Scranton/W-B (AAA)	.263	464	56	122	20	9	7	50	31
8. Eric Valent, of	24	Philadelphia	.098	41	3	4	2	0	0	1	0
		Scranton/W-B (AAA)	.272	448	65	122	30	2	21	78	0
10. Marlon Byrd, of	24	Reading (AA)	.316	510	108	161	22	8	28	89	32

Player, Pos.	Age	Club (Class)	W	L	ERA	G	SV	IP	H	BB	SO
2. Brett Myers, rhp	21	Reading (AA)	13	4	3.87	26	0	156	156	43	130
3. Brad Baisley, rhp	22	Reading (AA)	5	4	6.50	12	0	62	82	14	37
		Clearwater (A)	2	4	3.78	11	0	64	59	18	43
4. Ryan Madson, rhp	21	Clearwater (A)	9	9	3.90	22	0	118	137	49	101
9. Brandon Duckworth, rhp	25	Philadelphia	3	2	3.52	11	0	69	57	29	40
		Scranton/W-B (AAA)	13	2	2.63	22	0	147	122	36	150

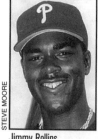

STEVE MOORE

Jimmy Rollins

MINOR LEAGUES

PITTSBURGH **PIRATES**

It was a miserable season in 2001 for the Pirates—both in the big leagues and down on the farm. The organization's Top 10 Prospects seemed to self-destruct. Righthander Bobby Bradley missed most of the season after elbow surgery, catcher J.R. House skipped a level and struggled and outfielder J.J. Davis remains an enigma.

STEPPING FORWARD: Lefthander Sean Burnett was one of the few bright spots, though the Pirates have to be excited about the development of several players in the lower levels, including Nate McLouth, Edwin Yan and Domingo Cuello. Six-foot-10 righthander Chris Young finally made his pro debut at midseason after graduating from Princeton.

STEPPING BACK: A season-long hamstring injury prevented Aron Weston from showcasing his five-tool potential.

TOP 10 PROSPECTS

Player, Pos.	Age	Club (Class)	AVG	AB	R	H	2B	3B	HR	RBI	SB
1. J.R. House, c	21	Altoona (AA)	.258	426	51	110	25	1	11	56	1
3. J.J. Davis, of	22	Altoona (AA)	.250	228	21	57	13	3	4	26	2
		GCL Pirates (R)	.471	17	3	8	1	0	2	6	0
4. Aron Weston, of	20	Hickory (A)	.122	74	8	9	2	1	0	2	5
5. Jose Castillo, ss	20	Lynchburg (A)	.245	485	57	119	20	7	7	49	23
6. Jack Wilson, ss	23	Pittsburgh	.223	390	44	87	17	1	3	25	1
		Nashville (AAA)	.369	103	20	38	6	1	1	6	2
10. Ryan Doumit, c	20	Altoona (AA)	.250	4	0	1	0	0	0	2	0
		Hickory (A)	.270	148	14	40	6	0	2	14	2
		GCL Pirates (R)	.235	17	2	4	2	0	0	3	0

Player, Pos.	Age	Club (Class)	W	L	ERA	G	SV	IP	H	BB	SO
2. Bobby Bradley, rhp	20	Lynchburg (A)	1	2	3.12	9	0	49	44	20	46
7. Chris Young, rhp	22	Hickory (A)	5	3	4.12	12	0	74	79	20	72
8. Sean Burnett, lhp	18	Hickory (A)	11	8	2.62	26	0	161	164	33	134
9. John Grabow, lhp	22	Altoona (AA)	2	5	3.38	10	0	51	30	39	42
		Lynchburg (A)	1	3	6.38	7	0	37	42	26	35
		GCL Pirates (R)	0	1	3.75	6	0	12	11	4	9

J.R. House

JOHN SPEAR

MINOR LEAGUES

ST. LOUIS **CARDINALS**

Despite lacking depth in their farm system, the Cardinals produced Rookie of the Year Albert Pujols and a Tom Glavine clone in Bud Smith.

STEPPING FORWARD: Righthander Jim Journell moved to the forefront of the system after proving he was completely recovered from Tommy John surgery. Armed with a plus fastball, Journell went 15-6, 2.39, including a seven-inning no-hitter in his only Double-A start.

STEPPING BACK: Control has never been a strong suit for righthander Chad Hutchinson, but after issuing 158 walks in 154 innings over the past two seasons, he is in jeopardy of losing his prospect status.

JOHN SPEAR

Bud Smith

TOP 10 PROSPECTS

Player, Pos.	Age	Club (Class)	AVG	AB	R	H	2B	3B	HR	RBI	SB
2. Albert Pujols, 3b	21	St. Louis	.329	590	112	194	47	4	37	130	1
7. Bill Ortega, of	26	St. Louis	.200	5	0	1	0	0	0	0	0
		Memphis (AAA)	.287	495	55	142	26	4	6	62	6
9. Luis Saturria, of	25	St. Louis	.200	5	0	1	1	0	0	1	1
		Memphis (AAA)	.225	413	63	93	16	5	13	49	6
		New Haven (AA)	.276	29	5	8	3	0	0	4	0

Player, Pos.	Age	Club (Class)	W	L	ERA	G	SV	IP	H	BB	SO
1. Bud Smith, lhp	21	St. Louis	6	3	3.83	16	0	85	79	24	59
		Memphis (AAA)	8	5	2.75	17	0	108	114	28	78
3. Chad Hutchinson, rhp	24	St. Louis	0	0	24.75	3	0	4	9	6	2
		Memphis (AAA)	4	9	7.92	27	0	98	99	104	111
4. Chance Caple, rhp	23				Injured—Did not pitch						
5. Nick Stocks, rhp	23	New Haven (AA)	2	12	5.16	16	0	82	89	33	63
6. Blake Williams, rhp	22	Potomac (A)	4	10	2.43	17	0	107	82	30	92
8. Gene Stechschulte, rhp	28	St. Louis	1	5	3.86	67	6	70	71	30	51
10. Josh Pearce, rhp	24	Memphis (AAA)	4	4	4.26	10	0	70	72	12	36
		New Haven (AA)	6	8	3.75	18	0	115	111	34	96

SAN DIEGO **PADRES**

Though Tony Gwynn played his last game in a Padres uniform in 2001, the future is bright in San Diego if the talent they have brewing in the minors is any indication. Sean Burroughs, Xavier Nady, Dennis Tankersley and Jake Peavy are among the best prospects in baseball.

STEPPING FORWARD: Righthander Ben Howard, 22, harnessed his lively 96-mph fastball and consistently located the strike zone for the first time in his career. He fanned 136 over 132 innings, while walking 47 between Class A Lake Elsinore and Double-A Mobile.

STEPPING BACK: Nobody in the Top 10 took a significant step in the wrong direction, but the organization suffered a devastating loss when righthander Gerik Baxter died in a car accident.

TOP 10 PROSPECTS

Player, Pos.	Age	Club (Class)	AVG	AB	R	H	2B	3B	HR	RBI	SB
1. Sean Burroughs, 3b	20	Portland (AAA)	.322	394	60	127	28	1	9	55	9
7. Xavier Nady, 1b	22	Lake Elsinore (A)	.302	524	96	158	38	1	26	100	6
8. Ben Johnson, of	20	Lake Elsinore (A)	.276	503	79	139	35	6	12	63	22

Player, Pos.	Age	Club (Class)	W	L	ERA	G	SV	IP	H	BB	SO
2. Jacob Peavy, rhp	20	Mobile (AA)	2	1	2.57	5	0	28	19	12	44
		Lake Elsinore (A)	7	5	3.08	19	0	105	76	33	144
3. Wascar Serrano, rhp	23	San Diego	3	3	6.56	20	0	47	60	21	39
		Portland (AAA)	6	5	4.53	27	0	93	98	35	73
4. Mike Bynum, lhp	23	Mobile (AA)	2	7	5.02	16	0	84	90	35	69
5. Gerik Baxter, rhp	—						Deceased				
6. Mark Phillips, lhp	19	Lake Elsinore (A)	2	1	2.57	5	0	28	19	14	34
		Fort Wayne (A)	4	1	2.64	5	0	31	19	14	27
		Eugene (A)	3	1	3.74	4	0	22	16	9	19
9. Dennis Tankersley, rhp	22	Portland (AAA)	1	2	6.91	3	0	14	16	8	16
		Mobile (AA)	4	1	2.07	13	0	70	44	24	89
		Lake Elsinore (A)	5	1	0.52	9	0	52	29	12	68
10. Junior Herndon, rhp	22	San Diego	2	6	6.33	12	0	43	55	25	14
		Portland (AAA)	9	5	4.58	21	0	116	132	39	47

Sean Burroughs

MEL BAILEY

SAN FRANCISCO **GIANTS**

The Giants are well-armed, starting at the top of the organization and trickling down. The 2001 season started inauspiciously for top pitchers Kurt Ainsworth and Jerome Williams, but they rebounded in the second half.

STEPPING FORWARD: The Giants surprised the industry by selecting righthander Boof Bonser with the 21st overall pick in 2000, and Bonser's impressive 16-win season was a pleasant surprise to everyone, including the Giants.

STEPPING BACK: Bill Mueller was dealt to the Cubs due in part to the presence of slugging rookie Pedro Feliz. Feliz shared a platoon with Russ Davis to open the season, and lost his job by the end of the year to Ramon Martinez.

TOP 10 PROSPECTS

Player, Pos.	Age	Club (Class)	AVG	AB	R	H	2B	3B	HR	RBI	SB
3. Tony Torcato, 3b	21	Fresno (AAA)	.320	150	20	48	8	1	2	8	0
		Shreveport (AA)	.293	147	13	43	9	1	1	23	0
		San Jose (A)	.341	258	38	88	21	2	2	47	9
4. Lance Niekro, 3b	22	San Jose (A)	.288	163	18	47	11	0	3	34	4
6. Sean McGowan, 1b	24	Fresno (AAA)	.286	391	59	112	30	2	14	65	1
		Shreveport (AA)	.304	125	11	38	6	0	3	17	0
7. Damon Minor, 1b	27	San Francisco	.156	45	3	7	1	0	0	3	0
		Fresno (AAA)	.308	406	74	125	22	3	24	71	1
8. Pedro Feliz, 3b	24	San Francisco	.227	220	23	50	9	1	7	22	2
9. Carlos Valderrama, of	23	Shreveport (AA)	.308	159	29	49	12	2	1	8	11

Player, Pos.	Age	Club (Class)	W	L	ERA	G	SV	IP	H	BB	SO
1. Jerome Williams, rhp	19	Shreveport (AA)	9	7	3.95	23	0	130	116	34	84
2. Kurt Ainsworth, rhp	22	San Francisco	0	0	13.50	2	0	2	3	2	3
		Fresno (AAA)	10	9	5.07	27	0	149	139	54	157
5. *Ryan Vogelsong, rhp	24	Pittsburgh	0	2	12.00	2	0	6	10	6	7
		San Francisco	0	3	5.65	13	0	29	29	14	17
		Nashville (AAA)	5	6	3.21	16	0	90	61	33	86
		Fresno (AAA)	3	3	2.79	10	0	58	38	18	53
10. Jeff Urban, lhp	24	Shreveport (AA)	7	11	3.91	27	0	157	178	32	117

*Traded to Pirates

MEL BAILEY

Jerome Williams

MINOR LEAGUES

SEATTLE **MARINERS**

Seattle has watched future Hall of Famers Randy Johnson, Ken Griffey and Alex Rodriguez depart, but they are far from devoid of talent at the big league level or throughout the minors.

STEPPING FORWARD: Where to begin? Rafael Soriano, Jamal Strong and Clint Nageotte made impressive strides, while 1998 first-rounder Matt Thornton, 25,

broke out in his fourth season. The lefthander went 14-7, 2.52 with 192 strikeouts in 157 innings at Class A San Bernardino.

STEPPING BACK: Shortstop Antonio Perez was one of the keys to the Griffey trade, and he showed why in his first Mariners season. In 2001, however, he was out of shape and a broken wrist kept him on the shelf almost all year.

TOP 10 PROSPECTS

Player, Pos.	Age	Club (Class)	AVG	AB	R	H	2B	3B	HR	RBI	SB
2. Ichiro Suzuki, of	27	Seattle	.350	692	127	242	34	8	8	69	56
3. Antonio Perez, ss	20	San Antonio (AA)	.143	21	3	3	0	0	0	0	0
5. Chris Snelling, of	19	San Bernardino (A)	.336	450	90	151	29	10	7	73	12
7. Willie Bloomquist, 2b	23	San Antonio (AA)	.255	491	59	125	23	2	0	28	34
8. Ryan Christianson, c	20	San Antonio (AA)	.249	527	65	131	42	5	12	85	3
10. Juan Silvestre, of	23	San Antonio (AA)	.228	372	29	85	13	0	8	39	0

Player, Pos.	Age	Club (Class)	W	L	ERA	G	SV	IP	H	BB	SO
1. Ryan Anderson, lhp	22				Injured—Did not pitch						
4. Joel Pineiro, rhp	22	Seattle	6	2	2.03	17	0	75	50	21	56
		Tacoma (AAA)	6	3	3.62	18	0	77	68	33	64
6. Jeff Heaverlo, rhp	23	San Antonio (AA)	11	6	3.12	27	0	179	164	40	173
9. Rafael Soriano, rhp	21	San Antonio (AA)	2	2	3.35	8	0	48	34	14	53
		San Bernardino (A)	6	3	2.53	15	0	89	49	39	98

Ryan Anderson

JEFF GOLDEN

TAMPA BAY **DEVIL RAYS**

STEVE MOORE

Josh Hamilton

Six of the Devil Rays' Top 10 Prospects reached the major leagues in 2001, and six more from the organization's Top 30 debuted in Tampa Bay.

STEPPING FORWARD: Toby Hall emerged as the catcher of the future, and lefthander Joe Kennedy enjoyed a rapid ascent from Double-A Orlando to Tampa Bay. He went 6-0, 0.98 in 11 starts between Orlando and Triple-A Durham.

STEPPING BACK: Regarded as the best prospect in baseball prior to the season, Josh Hamilton agonized through his second full year. Tampa Bay flirted with the idea of Hamilton cracking the Opening Day roster, while he struggled against major league pitching in spring training. Back and quadriceps injuries forced him to spend most of the season rehabbing.

TOP 10 PROSPECTS

Player, Pos.	Age	Club (Class)	AVG	AB	R	H	2B	3B	HR	RBI	SB
1. Josh Hamilton, of	20	Orlando (AA)	.180	89	5	16	5	0	0	4	2
		Charleston (A)	.364	11	3	4	1	0	1	2	0
3. Carl Crawford, of	20	Orlando (AA)	.274	537	64	147	24	3	4	51	36
4. Aubrey Huff, 3b	24	Tampa Bay	.248	411	42	102	25	1	8	45	1
		Durham (AAA)	.288	66	14	19	6	0	3	10	0
6. Brent Abernathy, 2b	23	Tampa Bay	.270	304	43	82	17	1	5	33	8
		Durham (AAA)	.302	252	45	76	20	0	4	23	11
9. Rocco Baldelli, of	19	Charleston (A)	.249	406	58	101	23	6	8	55	25

Player, Pos.	Age	Club (Class)	W	L	ERA	G	SV	IP	H	BB	SO
2. Jason Standridge, rhp	22	Tampa Bay	0	0	4.66	9	0	19	19	14	9
		Durham (AAA)	5	10	5.28	20	0	102	130	50	48
		Orlando (AA)	0	2	5.59	2	0	10	12	4	7
5. Jesus Colome, rhp	21	Tampa Bay	2	3	3.33	30	0	49	37	25	31
		Durham (AAA)	0	3	6.23	13	0	17	22	6	18
7. Matt White, rhp	23	Durham (AAA)	0	5	7.80	7	0	30	33	25	16
8. Bobby Seay, lhp	23	Tampa Bay	1	1	6.23	12	0	13	13	5	12
		Orlando (AA)	2	5	5.98	15	0	65	81	26	49
10. Travis Harper, rhp	25	Tampa Bay	0	2	7.71	2	0	7	15	3	2
		Durham (AAA)	12	6	3.70	25	0	156	140	38	115

TEXAS **RANGERS**

Not everything went wrong for the Rangers in 2001. First baseman Carlos Pena and third baseman Hank Blalock solidified their status as the cornerstones of the farm system. They could soon step in on the corners and join Alex Rodriguez in the infield. After a dismal season, the Rangers are encouraged by the development of young pitchers like Ryan Dittfurth, Joaquin Benoit and Colby Lewis, along with the acquisition of Justin Duchscherer.

STEPPING FORWARD: The Rangers stole Duchscherer from the Red Sox for journeyman catcher Bill Haselman. Duchscherer went 13-6, 2.47 overall.

STEPPING BACK: Jovanny Cedeno was drawing comparisons to Pedro Martinez based on his slight stature and nasty arsenal, but in 2001 he shared another similarity when he went down with an injured shoulder. Cedeno required surgery that limited him to three starts.

TOP 10 PROSPECTS

Player, Pos.	Age	Club (Class)	AVG	AB	R	H	2B	3B	HR	RBI	SB
1. Carlos Pena, 1b	23	Texas	.258	62	6	16	4	1	3	12	0
		Oklahoma (AAA)	.288	431	71	124	38	3	23	74	11
3. Jason Romano, of	22	Oklahoma (AAA)	.315	149	32	47	6	1	4	13	3
		Tulsa (AA)	.242	186	19	45	9	1	1	19	8
		Charlotte (A)	.400	10	3	4	2	0	0	1	1
		GCL Rangers (R)	.143	21	2	3	0	0	0	0	1
4. Kevin Mench, of	23	Tulsa (AA)	.265	475	78	126	34	2	26	83	4
7. Michael Young, 2b	24	Texas	.249	386	57	96	18	4	11	49	3
		Oklahoma (AAA)	.291	189	28	55	8	0	8	28	3
10. Hank Blalock, 3b	20	Tulsa (AA)	.327	272	50	89	18	4	11	61	3
		Charlotte (A)	.380	237	46	90	19	1	7	47	7

Player, Pos.	Age	Club (Class)	W	L	ERA	G	SV	IP	H	BB	SO
2. Jovanny Cedeno, rhp	21	Charlotte (A)	0	0	1.86	3	0	10	3	5	12
5. Joaquin Benoit, rhp	22	Texas	0	0	10.80	1	0	5	8	3	4
		Oklahoma (AAA)	9	5	4.19	24	0	131	113	73	142
		Tulsa (AA)	1	0	3.32	4	0	22	23	6	23
6. Colby Lewis, rhp	22	Tulsa (AA)	10	10	4.50	25	0	156	150	62	162
		Charlotte (A)	1	0	0.00	1	0	4	0	0	8
8. Aaron Myette, rhp	23	Texas	4	5	7.14	19	0	81	94	37	67
		Oklahoma (AAA)	4	3	3.73	12	0	70	64	30	76
		Tulsa (AA)	1	0	0.00	1	0	6	3	1	2
9. Andy Pratt, lhp	22	Tulsa (AA)	8	10	4.61	27	0	168	175	57	132

Carlos Pena

JOHN SPEAR

TORONTO **BLUE JAYS**

Rookies Vernon Wells, Felipe Lopez, Cesar Izturis, Brandon Lyon and Bob File provided the Blue Jays with a glimpse of their future in the second half of the 2001 season. Catcher Josh Phelps completed a monster offensive season in Double-A with 12 hitless at-bats for Toronto.

STEPPING FORWARD: Second baseman Orlando Hudson, 23, moved across the infield from third base and responded with a .306-8-79 season overall. A hard-nosed player, Hudson was drafted in the 43rd round in 1997.

STEPPING BACK: Charles Kegley showcased his live potential in his debut 2000 campaign, but shaky control accompanied it. Kegley didn't show any signs of improving his command in 2001 and has walked more than he's struck out in his career.

Vernon Wells

RICH ABEL

TOP 10 PROSPECTS

Player, Pos.	Age	Club (Class)	AVG	AB	R	H	2B	3B	HR	RBI	SB
1. Vernon Wells, of	22	Toronto	.312	96	14	30	8	0	1	6	5
		Syracuse (AAA)	.281	413	57	116	27	4	12	52	15
2. Felipe Lopez, ss-3b	21	Toronto	.260	177	21	46	5	4	5	23	4
		Syracuse (AAA)	.279	358	65	100	19	7	16	44	13
		Tennessee (AA)	.222	72	12	16	2	1	2	4	4
3. Cesar Izturis, ss	21	Toronto	.269	134	19	36	6	2	2	9	8
		Syracuse (AAA)	.292	342	32	100	16	3	2	35	24
4. Joe Lawrence, c	24	Syracuse (AAA)	.220	318	27	70	11	4	1	26	6
10. Josh Phelps, c	23	Toronto	.000	12	3	0	0	0	0	1	1
		Tennessee (AA)	.292	486	95	142	36	1	31	97	3

Player, Pos.	Age	Club (Class)	W	L	ERA	G	SV	IP	H	BB	SO
5. Bob File, rhp	24	Toronto	5	3	3.27	60	0	74	57	29	38
		Syracuse (AAA)	0	0	0.00	2	0	4	1	0	3
		Tennessee (AA)	0	0	3.00	3	1	3	3	0	2
6. Charles Kegley, rhp	21	Dunedin (A)	6	9	6.03	26	0	112	120	76	76
7. Brian Cardwell, rhp	20	Charleston (A)	3	10	5.18	19	0	92	101	33	60
8. Pasqual Coco, rhp	23	Toronto	1	0	4.40	7	0	14	12	6	9
		Syracuse (AAA)	8	6	4.66	22	0	122	128	50	82
		Tennessee (AA)	0	1	3.94	3	0	16	13	5	13
9. Matt Ford, lhp	20	Dunedin (A)	2	7	5.85	13	0	60	67	37	48
		Charleston (A)	4	4	2.42	11	0	71	62	22	69

INTERNATIONAL LEAGUE

BY MATT MICHAEL

The Louisville RiverBats did not apologize for winning the Governors' Cup championship in an abbreviated one-game series against the Scranton/Wilkes-Barre Red Barons.

But they did not celebrate it, either.

International League president Randy Mobley canceled the remainder of the five-game series after the Sept. 11 terrorist attacks on New York and Washington. Mobley declared Louisville the champion because the RiverBats had defeated Scranton 2-1 in the first game of the series played at Louisville Sept. 10.

"That's not the way you want to win it, but needless to say, we'll take it," RiverBats pitcher Matt Skrmetta said. "When stuff happens like it did, things that seemed so big in your life suddenly become very small. Baseball seems like a very small thing right now."

As the Louisville players packed their bags and headed home Sept. 13, a box of unopened champagne bottles sat on a clubhouse table.

"This isn't exactly like winning Game Five and popping the champagne," team president Gary Ulmer said. "It's not the kind of day you have a big celebration."

According to published reports, the Scranton/Wilkes-Barre players voted unanimously Sept. 11 not to play the rest of the Governors' Cup series. Scranton catcher Creighton Gubanich has a sister who works as a buyer for a department store near the World Trade Center, and his brother is a computer programmer who works across the street from the Pentagon. Fortunately, his sister was on vacation and his brother escaped harm.

Minor League Baseball president Mike Moore left it up to the IL and the other minor leagues to either resume their postseason series later or cancel the remaining games. Despite the Scranton players' earlier protests, Mobley said the Red Barons had agreed to play if the series resumed Sept. 13. But since all baseball games were postponed on that day, Mobley said he stuck with his earlier decision about canceling the rest of the series and making Louisville the champion.

Toby Hall: IL's MVP

Mobley said he never considered making Scranton and Louisville co-champions.

"I just didn't feel I could simply wipe that game out or it didn't take place or it didn't matter, because both clubs went out there trying to win a game," Mobley said. "It's not the best of circumstances, but nothing we dealt with has been anywhere near the best of circumstances."

While Scranton officials were upset with the ruling (the Lackawanna County Stadium Authority said it planned to file a letter of protest with the league), the Red Barons' coaching staff and players did not argue with it.

It was the second time in the 69-year history of the

STANDINGS

Page	EAST	W	L	PCT	GB	Manager(s)	Attendance (Avg.)	Last Penn.
114	Buffalo Bisons (Indians)	91	51	.641	—	Eric Wedge	652,245 (9,592)	1998
205	Scranton/W-B Red Barons (Phillies)	78	65	.545	13½	Marc Bombard/Jerry Martin	452,004 (6,457)	None
260	Syracuse SkyChiefs (Blue Jays)	71	73	.493	21	Omar Malave	423,405 (6,136)	1976
176	Ottawa Lynx (Expos)	68	76	.472	24	Stan Hough	205,916 (2,942)	1995
86	Pawtucket Red Sox (Red Sox)	60	82	.423	31	Gary Jones	647,928 (9,256)	1984
79	Rochester Red Wings (Orioles)	60	84	.417	32	Andy Etchebarren	455,123 (6,410)	1997
Page	**WEST**	**W**	**L**	**PCT**	**GB**	**Manager**	**Attendance (Avg.)**	**Last Penn.**
107	Louisville RiverBats (Reds)	84	60	.583	—	Dave Miley	649,232 (9,275)	2001
183	Columbus Clippers (Yankees)	67	76	.469	16½	Trey Hillman	503,824 (7,409)	1996
163	Indianapolis Indians (Brewers)	66	78	.458	18	Wendell Kim	604,407 (8,513)	2000
129	Toledo Mud Hens (Tigers)	65	79	.451	19	Bruce Fields	300,079 (4,349)	1967
Page	**SOUTH**	**W**	**L**	**PCT**	**GB**	**Manager**	**Attendance (Avg.)**	**Last Penn.**
191	Norfolk Tides (Mets)	85	57	.599	—	John Gibbons	498,950 (7,232)	1985
247	Durham Bulls (Devil Rays)	74	70	.514	12	Bill Evers	505,314 (7,219)	None
72	Richmond Braves (Braves)	68	76	.472	18	Carlos Tosca	447,020 (6,574)	1994
93	Charlotte Knights (White Sox)	67	77	.465	19	Nick Leyva	370,406 (5,368)	1999

GOVERNORS' CUP PLAYOFFS—Semifinals: Louisville defeated Norfolk 3-2 and Scranton/Wilkes-Barre defeated Buffalo 3-2 in best-of-5 series. **Finals:** Series canceled; Louisville declared champion after taking 1-0 lead over Scranton/Wilkes-Barre in best-of-5 series.

NOTE: Teams' individual batting and pitching statistics can be found on page indicated in lefthand column.

Governors' Cup that a champion was declared before the series ended. In the 1981 series that was shortened by several rainouts, Columbus beat Richmond 2-1 in what was supposed to be a best-of-five set.

The title was Louisville's first in the IL and the team's first since 1995, when it was in the American Association. The RiverBats, formerly known as the Redbirds, played in the IL from 1968-72 and rejoined the league in 1998 when the AA disbanded.

Runaway Winners

In a season in which just five of 14 IL clubs finished with records above .500, division winners Louisville (West), Buffalo (North) and Norfolk (South) each won by at least 12 games—a first for the league since it adopted three divisions in 1998.

Buffalo set a modern franchise record with 91 wins, the most in the IL since Columbus won 95 in 1992. Louisville also set a franchise record with 84 victories, while the Tides—with 85 wins—gave the IL three teams with at least 84 wins for the first time since 1961.

The IL's only interesting race was for the lone wild-card playoff berth, which Scranton clinched Aug. 31, three days before the season ended. The Red Barons reached the playoffs despite a managerial merry-go-round that included seven different skippers (Marc Bombard, 79 games; Jerry Martin, 38 games; Don Long, 20 games; Bill Dancy, three games; and Mick Billmyer, Milt Thompson and Ruben Amaro Sr., one game each).

Brandon Duckworth

"This has been a remarkable year for these guys," said Bombard, who spent half of the season in Philadelphia as a replacement for ill Phillies coach John Vukovich. "I don't think anyone in the world besides our players and coaches thought we had a chance when we were 20-30 in May."

The Red Barons advanced to the Governors' Cup finals by scoring four runs in the top of the 19th inning to defeat Buffalo 6-2 in the fifth and deciding game of their first-round series. No. 9 hitter Jason Knupfer, who was 0-for-16 in the series to that point, snapped a 2-2 tie with a two-run triple in the 19th.

In the other first-round series, starter Larry Luebbers and relievers Chris Nichting and Johnny Ruffin combined on a seven-hitter as the RiverBats blanked Norfolk 2-0 in the fifth game. After playing 19 innings Sept. 9, Scranton traveled to Louisville for the first game of the championship series Sept. 10 and lost 2-1 on Chris Sexton's bases-loaded walk in the seventh inning.

Award Winning

Durham Bulls catcher Toby Hall was named the IL's MVP even though he was promoted to the majors July 26. When Hall went up to the Devil Rays, he ranked among the top three batters in average (.335), home runs (19) and RBIs (72). He still led the IL in batting.

When most valuable pitcher and rookie of the year Brandon Duckworth of Scranton was promoted to Philadelphia Aug. 4, he was on track to become the IL's first pitching triple-crown winner since Rochester's Dennis Martinez in 1976. Duckworth tied for the IL lead in wins (13) and ranked first in ERA (2.63), but finished

third in strikeouts (150). Pitching dominated the league as there were just five .300 hitters.

While Hall and Duckworth earned the IL's top awards, managers named Louisville outfielder Adam Dunn the league's No. 1 prospect. Dunn, a 6-foot-6 former University of Texas quarterback, clouted 20 home runs with 53 RBIs in just 55 games for the RiverBats. He was named the IL's player of the week three times in a four-week stretch.

Veteran Norfolk pitcher Steve Trachsel, sent to the Tides after a horrendous start with the New York Mets, tossed the IL's only no-hitter of the season against the Ottawa Lynx May 29. The seven-inning gem was also the first no-hitter in the nine-year history of Norfolk's Harbor Park.

Four Buffalo pitchers (starter Jason Phillips and relievers Dario Veras, Scott Radinsky and Martin Vargas) nearly made IL history Aug. 3, when they came within two outs of a no-hitter against the Syracuse SkyChiefs. Had they completed the no-hitter, it would have been the first time in the IL's 118-year history that more than two pitchers combined on a no-hitter.

Pawtucket Red Sox outfielder Izzy Alcantara, who led the IL with 36 home runs, was suspended for six games and kicked off the IL all-star team for his part in a July 3 bench-clearing brawl with Scranton. But Alcantara got off easy compared to Durham outfielder Jose Guillen, who was suspended for 10 games in June for using a corked bat.

On Aug. 21 in Ottawa, Tim Raines Sr. and Tim Raines Jr. became the first father and son to play against each other in a regular season professional game at any level. Raines Sr., who was with the Lynx on an injury rehabilitation assignment, went 1-for-7 and Raines Jr. went 2-for-7 for Rochester as the teams split a doubleheader.

The Toledo Mud Hens, who haven't won an IL championship since 1967, had another losing season. But at least Toledo can look forward to the April opening of majestic Fifth Third Field, the IL's only new ballpark in 2002.

2001 INTERNATIONAL LEAGUE STATISTICS

CLUB BATTING

	AVG	G	AB	R	H	2B	3B	HR	BB	SO	SB
Louisville	.277	144	4978	728	1380	296	29	127	432	957	75
Durham	.273	144	4861	677	1329	256	28	133	406	896	110
Toledo	.268	144	4967	686	1332	277	39	152	449	996	95
Syracuse	.267	144	4905	690	1311	270	51	128	458	938	148
Richmond	.267	144	4861	559	1296	261	31	68	311	866	87
Indianapolis	.262	144	4941	666	1294	264	31	124	462	1065	72
Norfolk	.261	142	4727	602	1232	244	20	103	439	913	110
Buffalo	.259	142	4730	697	1225	238	30	149	471	979	92
Scranton/W-B	.259	143	4947	642	1281	276	32	100	495	989	131
Columbus	.258	143	4775	663	1234	239	35	148	478	982	101
Pawtucket	.257	142	4814	612	1235	237	15	171	412	1098	59
Charlotte	.256	144	4882	611	1251	253	19	155	388	922	72
Rochester	.251	144	4903	576	1230	243	27	95	398	1018	139
Ottawa	.248	144	4919	573	1222	242	37	106	451	1081	171

CLUB PITCHING

	ERA	G	CG	SHO	SV	IP	H	R	ER	BB	SO
Scranton/W-B	3.19	143	8	7	33	1300	1164	507	461	395	1095
Norfolk	3.55	142	4	10	52	1256	1246	565	495	411	919
Buffalo	3.59	142	8	11	53	1254	1212	569	500	395	988
Durham	3.76	144	4	10	37	1260	1228	611	527	418	925
Ottawa	3.88	144	5	11	40	1290	1241	639	557	432	996
Louisville	3.89	144	8	10	46	1287	1326	632	556	382	912
Charlotte	3.95	144	8	7	35	1268	1221	663	557	464	1029
Syracuse	4.08	144	5	9	37	1282	1293	655	581	433	935
Rochester	4.12	144	7	10	32	1288	1304	709	589	474	1100
Richmond	4.14	144	3	7	36	1275	1212	634	587	506	1046
Columbus	4.23	143	8	5	34	1240	1298	690	583	456	1039
Indianapolis	4.33	144	3	7	27	1279	1353	716	616	465	898
Toledo	4.36	144	5	3	32	1280	1402	722	620	462	910
Pawtucket	4.48	142	8	6	35	1237	1352	710	616	357	908

CLUB FIELDING

	PCT	PO	A	E	DP		PCT	PO	A	E	DP
Scranton/W-B	.982	3901	1546	100	127	Louisville	.975	3861	1632	138	140
Richmond	.980	3825	1442	105	115	Ottawa	.975	3871	1592	139	142
Buffalo	.978	3761	1437	117	147	Indianapolis	.973	3838	1506	149	133
Norfolk	.977	3768	1559	123	151	Pawtucket	.972	3711	1412	149	129
Charlotte	.977	3804	1493	123	121	Columbus	.971	3727	1335	151	127
Durham	.977	3780	1457	124	136	Toledo	.970	3839	1630	172	152
Syracuse	.977	3846	1545	129	147	Rochester	.963	3863	1325	197	109

INDIVIDUAL BATTING LEADERS
(Minimum 389 Plate Appearances)

	AVG	G	AB	R	H	2B	3B	HR	RBI	BB	SO	SB
Hall, Toby, Durham	.335	94	373	59	125	28	1	19	72	29	22	1
Rios, Brian, Toledo	.325	104	372	47	121	29	5	14	62	22	66	2
Forbes, P.J., Scranton/W-B	.305	133	514	79	157	29	2	5	61	48	72	5
Malloy, Marty, Louisville	.303	126	468	69	142	36	4	6	49	27	51	8
Smith, Bobby, Durham	.301	107	396	67	119	25	2	22	70	45	91	10
Gonzalez, Raul, Louisville	.299	142	539	90	161	39	1	11	66	64	70	6
Alcantara, Israel, Pawtucket	.297	119	451	80	134	26	1	36	90	57	107	9
Bridges, Kary, Columbus	.297	109	408	59	121	17	1	5	39	36	29	5
Scutaro, Marcos, Indianapolis	.295	132	495	87	146	29	3	11	50	62	83	11
Carter, Mike, Richmond	.294	104	388	55	114	16	3	2	20	10	45	10

INDIVIDUAL PITCHING LEADERS
(Minimum 115 Innings)

	W	L	ERA	G	GS	CG	SV	IP	H	R	ER	BB	SO
Duckworth, Brandon, Scranton/W-B	13	2	2.63	22	20	2	0	147	122	46	43	36	150
Beltran, Rigo, Scranton/W-B	2	2	2.96	37	11	0	2	116	87	40	38	41	113
Walker, Pete, Norfolk	13	4	2.99	26	26	0	0	168	145	64	56	46	106
Jodie, Brett, Columbus	10	4	3.01	19	19	2	0	120	123	46	40	25	59
Callaway, Mickey, Durham	11	7	3.07	29	21	2	0	129	131	50	44	24	81
Banks, Willie, Syracuse/Pawtucket	10	5	3.11	26	25	0	0	159	159	66	55	56	133
Bacsik, Mike, Buffalo	12	5	3.26	21	20	2	0	121	115	47	44	25	81
Moore, Trey, Richmond	9	8	3.31	26	25	2	0	163	140	64	60	41	122
Castillo, Carlos, Pawtucket	9	11	3.41	28	21	5	0	164	179	78	62	24	114
Douglass, Sean, Rochester	8	9	3.49	27	27	0	0	162	160	79	63	61	156

ALL-STAR TEAM

C—Toby Hall, Durham. **1B**—Calvin Pickering, Rochester. **2B**—P.J. Forbes, Scranton/Wilkes-Barre. **3B**—Kevin Orie, Scranton/Wilkes-Barre. **SS**—Cesar Izturis, Syracuse. **OF**—Karim Garcia, Buffalo; Eric Valent, Scranton/Wilkes-Barre; Chris Wakeland, Toledo. **DH**—Israel Alcantara, Pawtucket. **Util**—Brian Rios, Toledo. **SP**—Brandon Duckworth, Scranton/Wilkes-Barre. **RP**—Matt DeWitt, Syracuse.

Most Valuable Player: Toby Hall, Durham. **Most Valuable Pitcher**: Brandon Duckworth, Scranton/Wilkes-Barre. **Rookie of the Year**: Brandon Duckworth, Scranton/Wilkes-Barre. **Manager of the Year**: Eric Wedge, Buffalo.

DEPARTMENT LEADERS

BATTING

G	Raul Gonzalez, Louisville	142
AB	Chris Wakeland, Toledo	547
R	Raul Gonzalez, Louisville	90
H	Raul Gonzalez, Louisville	161
TB	Israel Alcantara, Pawtucket	270
XBH	Israel Alcantara, Pawtucket	63
2B	Raul Gonzalez, Louisville	39
3B	Henry Mateo, Ottawa	12
HR	Israel Alcantara, Pawtucket	36
RBI	Calvin Pickering, Roch./Lou.	99
SH	Jermaine Allensworth, Toledo	21
	Jesse Garcia, Richmond	21
SF	Pedro Swann, Richmond	10
BB	Nick Johnson, Columbus	81
IBB	Two tied at	8
HBP	Nick Johnson, Columbus	14
SO	Calvin Pickering, Roch./Lou.	151
SB	Henry Mateo, Ottawa	47
CS	Reggie Taylor, Scranton	15
GIDP	Wilton Veras, Pawtucket	24
OB%	Nick Johnson, Columbus	.407
SL%	Israel Alcantara, Pawtucket	.599

PITCHING

G	Brian Bowles, Syracuse	66
GS	Carlos Chantres, Indianapolis	28
	Jared Fernandez, Louisville	28
CG	Carlos Castillo, Pawtucket	5
ShO	Dicky Gonzalez, Norfolk	2
GF	Matt DeWitt, Syracuse	47
SV	Matt DeWitt, Syracuse	27
W	Brandon Duckworth, Scranton	13
	Pete Walker, Norfolk	13
L	Evan Thomas, Scranton	13
IP	Jared Fernandez, Louisville	196
H	Jared Fernandez, Louisville	218
R	John Snyder, Indianapolis	115
ER	Shane Loux, Toledo	97
HR	Travis Harper, Durham	25
HB	John Dillinger, Syracuse	15
	Shane Loux, Toledo	15
BB	Carlos Chantres, Indianapolis	93
SO	Brandon Knight, Columbus	173
WP	Jared Fernandez, Louisville	20
BK	Adam Bernero, Toledo	5
	Adrian Hernandez, Columbus	5

FIELDING

C	AVG	Matt Walbeck, Lou./Scr.	1.000
	PO	Brian Schneider, Ottawa	629
	A	Brian Schneider, Ottawa	79
	E	Frank Charles, Rochester	16
	DP	Matt Walbeck, Louis./Scranton	8
	PB	Joe Lawrence, Syracuse	15
1B	AVG	Ron Wright, Durham	.992
	PO	Ron Wright, Durham	980
	A	Ron Wright, Durham	66
	E	Three tied at	10
	DP	Ron Wright, Durham	102
2B	AVG	Marcos Scutaro, Indianapolis	.973
	PO	Henry Mateo, Ottawa	251
	A	Henry Mateo, Ottawa	328
		Pedro Santana, Toledo	328
	E	Pedro Santana, Toledo	31
	DP	Pedro Santana, Toledo	87
3B	AVG	Howard Battle, Richmond	.972
	PO	Wilton Veras, Pawtucket	128
	A	Brandon Larson, Louisville	279
	E	Wilton Veras, Pawtucket	26
	DP	Wilton Veras, Pawtucket	31
SS	AVG	Jason Dellaero, Charlotte	.968
	PO	Tomas de la Rosa, Ottawa	190
	A	Nick Punto, Scranton	398
	E	Erick Almonte, Columbus	27
	DP	John McDonald, Buffalo	81
OF	AVG	Mark Budzinski, Buffalo	1.000
	PO	Jermaine Allensworth, Toledo	318
	A	Tony Tarasco, Norfolk	13
		Chris Wakeland, Toledo	13
	E	Darnell McDonald, Rochester	12
	DP	Vernon Wells, Syracuse	5

BY JIM VAN VLIET

The 2001 season turned out to be something of an anticlimax for the Tacoma Rainiers.

Keeping up with the Seattle Mariners, their major league affiliate located 30 miles to the north, the Rainiers posted a wire-to-wire victory in the Pacific Coast League's Northern Division. Despite season-long rumors the team would be sold and moved to either Honolulu or Reno, the Rainiers won a league-high 85 games and finished 12½ games ahead of Calgary in the North.

Alas, there would be no celebration. The tragedy and terror that struck New York and Washington Sept. 11 wiped out the PCL championship series, and league president Branch Rickey III ruled Tacoma and the New Orleans Zephyrs would be considered co-champions for 2001.

"It sucks," Tacoma infielder Jason Grabowski said. "You want the ring yourself. You don't want to share it since both teams have come so far. But I understand."

It marked the second time the Tacoma franchise was forced to share a title. In 1978, the Tacoma Yankees were named co-champs when their series with Albuquerque was shut down because of inclement weather.

Arms Race

The 2001 season began and ended with solid pitching. Tacoma and New Orleans were first and second in the PCL in ERA—Tacoma at 3.74 and New Orleans at 3.75.

The Rainiers flourished despite losing Ryan "Space Needle" Anderson, the 6-foot-11 lefthander, to season-ending shoulder surgery in the spring. But righthander

Roosevelt Brown

Denny Stark: PCL leader in wins, ERA

COSIMO MELLACE

Denny Stark picked up the pieces for the Rainiers, leading the league with 14 wins and a 2.37 ERA.

Tacoma starters Brett Tomko and John Halama, both of whom spent considerable time in Seattle, also fired no-hitters within four days of each other. Tomko shut down Oklahoma 7-0 on July 3, allowing just a first-inning walk before retiring the final 25 batters. Halama not only no-

MINOR LEAGUES

JOHN SPEAR

STANDINGS

AMERICAN CONFERENCE

Page	EAST	W	L	PCT	GB	Manager	Attendance (Avg.)	Last Penn.
143	New Orleans Zephyrs (Astros)	82	57	.590	—	Tony Pena	385,447 (5,930)	2001
253	Oklahoma RedHawks (Rangers)	74	69	.517	10	DeMarlo Hale	447,077 (6,297)	None
212	Nashville Sounds (Pirates)	64	77	.454	19	Marty Brown	305,385 (4,426)	None
219	Memphis Redbirds (Cardinals)	62	81	.434	22	Gaylen Pitts	887,976 (12,507)	2000
Page	**CENTRAL**	**W**	**L**	**PCT**	**GB**	**Manager**	**Attendance (Avg.)**	**Last Penn.**
100	Iowa Cubs (Cubs)	83	60	.580	—	Bruce Kimm	475,342 (6,791)	None
58	Salt Lake Stingers (Angels)	79	64	.552	4	Garry Templeton	470,649 (6,629)	1979
149	Omaha Golden Spikes (Royals)	70	74	.486	13 ½	John Mizerock	359,038 (5,280)	None
122	Colorado Springs Sky Sox (Rockies)	62	79	.440	20	Chris Cron	269,904 (4,028)	1995

PACIFIC CONFERENCE

Page	NORTH	W	L	PCT	GB	Manager	Attendance (Avg.)	Last Penn.
240	Tacoma Rainiers (Mariners)	85	59	.590	—	Dan Rohn	320,329 (4,853)	2001
136	Calgary Cannons (Marlins)	72	71	.503	12 ½	Chris Chambliss	246,991 (3,920)	None
226	Portland Beavers (Padres)	71	73	.493	14	Rick Sweet	439,686 (6,193)	1994
170	Edmonton Trappers (Twins)	60	83	.420	24 ½	John Russell	372,244 (5,556)	1997
Page	**SOUTH**	**W**	**L**	**PCT**	**GB**	**Manager**	**Attendance (Avg.)**	**Last Penn.**
199	Sacramento RiverCats (Athletics)	75	69	.521	—	Bob Geren	901,214 (12,517)	None
233	Fresno Grizzlies (Giants)	68	71	.489	4 ½	Shane Turner	292,886 (4,184)	None
156	Las Vegas 51s (Dodgers)	68	76	.472	7	Rick Sofield	332,742 (4,621)	1988
65	Tucson Sidewinders (Diamondbacks)	65	77	.458	9	Tom Spencer	244,761 (3,653)	1993

PLAYOFFS—Semifinals: Tacoma defeated Sacramento 3-2 and New Orleans defeated Iowa 3-0 in best-of-5 series. **Finals:** Series cancelled; New Orleans and Tacoma declared co-champions.

NOTE: Teams' individual batting and pitching statistics can be found on page indicated in lefthand column.

hit Calgary 6-0 on July 7, but pitched the league's first-ever nine-inning perfect game and the first of any kind in 26 years.

In the Central Division, the Iowa Cubs staged a heated pennant race with the Salt Lake Stingers. After trailing Salt Lake for the majority of the season, the I-Cubs made a furious August rally to tie the Stingers with four games left, and the two teams met for those final four games. Iowa swept the series.

The I-Cubs, who planted "Field of Dreams" cornrows outside of Sec Taylor Stadium in Des Moines, used a combination of stout pitching and clutch hitting to win down the stretch. Behind Ruben Quevedo (9-5, 2.99) and Mike Meyers (7-4, 3.23), the I-Cubs finished third in the league in ERA at 3.85.

Iowa outfielder Roosevelt Brown led the league in batting at .346, then went up to Chicago and hit a game-winning home run in his first September game with the Cubs. Salt Lake lost despite a stellar season from veteran third baseman Jose Fernandez, who batted .338, hit 30 home runs and knocked in a league-leading 114 runs.

For most of the season, it wasn't much of a race in the South Division. On Aug. 3, all four teams were floundering under .500. But a trade by the parent Oakland Athletics inadvertently jump-started the defending champion Sacramento RiverCats. In late July, the A's made a three-team swap to land Jermaine Dye from the Kansas City Royals. The trade sent prospects Jose Ortiz, the PCL MVP in 2000, and Mario Encarnacion to the Colorado Rockies.

The RiverCats received second baseman Esteban German from Double-A Midland. German kick-started the Sacramento offense as the RiverCats immediately won eight in a row and 14 out of 15. German, who was named to the Texas League all-star team, batted .373 in 38 games for the RiverCats, scoring 40 runs and stealing 17 bases.

"I wasn't too sure about the trade," said veteran Sacramento righthander Steve Ontiveros. "But when I saw Esteban, then I understood."

Tacoma won its first-round playoff match, coming from a 2-1 deficit to win twice in Sacramento. New Orleans swept Iowa in three to advance to the championship series that never was.

Around The Bushes

Despite a slow start, the RiverCats broke the league's all-time attendance record for the second straight season, luring 901,214 into Raley Field. Sacramento became the first minor league team to eclipse 900,000 since the International League's Buffalo Bisons in 1995. Memphis also broke the old record by drawing 887,876 to Auto-Zone Park, but was passed on the final day of the season by Sacramento.

Phil Hiatt

The Redbirds might well have outlasted Sacramento in the season-long battle for the record but they lost one home game to weather, giving the RiverCats the slight edge. The success in both cities helped drive league-wide attendance up to a record 6,751,671.

The league welcomed back the Portland Beavers. Despite finishing 14 games out in the North, the Beavers averaged 6,193 fans a game at refurbished PGE Park.

Future Hall of Famer Rickey Henderson made a brief appearance in the PCL, 22 years after playing for Ogden. Henderson hit .275 in nine games for Portland while working himself into shape after being signed as a free agent by the parent San Diego Padres.

Lefthander Rick Ankiel also made a brief but unsuccessful appearance in the league after the parent St. Louis Cardinals sent him to Memphis to try and find a cure for his wildness. In three starts with the Redbirds, Ankiel went 0-2, 20.77 while walking 17 and throwing 12 wild pitches in four innings.

Multimillion-dollar stadium renovations approved in Albuquerque will signal the return of the PCL to that city in 2003. Calgary owner Russ Parker sold his team to Albuquerque interests during the 2001 season, and attendance predictably declined in Calgary. Only Tucson averaged fewer fans than the Cannons, who attracted an average of 3,920 a game.

The Cannons matched history on the final day of the season as B.J. Waszgis and Ryan McGuire both hit grand slams in the fourth inning as Calgary pummeled Tacoma 22-10. It was only the third time in league history, and first since 1991, that two grand slams were hit in the same inning.

The Las Vegas 51s' Phil Hiatt was the league's most proficient home run hitter. He was the league MVP with his 44 home runs—14 more than anybody else in the league. Las Vegas had success of its own, changing its nickname from Stars and working off a somewhat gimmicky relation to the famed Area 51 outside the city, where the U.S. military is rumored to harbor captured alien spacecraft. The otherworldly-themed merchandise surged to the top of minor league sales.

MINOR LEAGUES

LEAGUE CHAMPIONS

Last 30 Years

Year	Regular Season*	Pct.	Playoff
1971	Tacoma (Cubs)	.545	Salt Lake City (Angels)
1972	Albuquerque (Dodgers)	.622	Albuquerque (Dodgers)
1973	Tucson (Athletics)	.583	Spokane (Rangers)
1974	Spokane (Rangers)	.549	Spokane (Rangers)
1975	Hawaii (Padres)	.611	Hawaii (Padres)
1976	Salt Lake City (Angels)	.625	Hawaii (Padres)
1977	Phoenix (Giants)	.579	Phoenix (Giants)
1978	Tacoma (Yankees)	.584	#Tacoma (Yankees)
			#Albuquerque (Dodgers)
1979	Albuquerque (Dodgers)	.581	Salt Lake City (Angels)
1980	Tucson (Astros)	.595	Albuquerque (Dodgers)
1981	Albuquerque (Dodgers)	.712	Albuquerque (Dodgers)
1982	Albuquerque (Dodgers)	.594	Albuquerque (Dodgers)
1983	Albuquerque (Dodgers)	.594	Portland (Phillies)
1984	Hawaii (Pirates)	.621	Edmonton (Angels)
1985	Hawaii (Pirates)	.587	Vancouver (Brewers)
1986	Vancouver (Brewers)	.616	Las Vegas (Padres)
1987	Calgary (Mariners)	.596	Albuquerque (Dodgers)
1988	Albuquerque (Dodgers)	.605	Las Vegas (Padres)
1989	Albuquerque (Dodgers)	.563	Vancouver (White Sox)
1990	Albuquerque (Dodgers)	.641	Albuquerque (Dodgers)
1991	Albuquerque (Dodgers)	.580	Tucson (Astros)
1992	Colo. Springs (Indians)	.596	Colo. Springs (Indians)
1993	Portland (Twins)	.608	Tucson (Astros)
1994	Albuquerque (Dodgers)	.597	Albuquerque (Dodgers)
1995	Tucson (Astros)	.608	Colo. Springs (Rockies)
1996	Edmonton (Athletics)	.592	Edmonton (Athletics)
1997	Phoenix (Giants)	.615	Edmonton (Athletics)
1998	Iowa (Cubs)	.590	New Orleans (Astros)
1999	Vancouver (Athletics)	.592	Vancouver (Athletics)
2000	Salt Lake (Twins)	.629	Memphis (Cardinals)
2001	New Orleans (Astros)	.590	#New Orleans (Astros)
	Tacoma (Mariners)	.590	#Tacoma (Mariners)

*Best overall record #Co-champions

2001 PACIFIC COAST LEAGUE STATISTICS

MINOR LEAGUES

CLUB BATTING

	AVG	G	AB	R	H	2B	3B	HR	BB	SO	SB
Calgary	.292	143	4887	810	1425	315	21	187	408	1048	65
Colorado Springs	.290	141	4908	774	1424	293	35	146	424	1017	81
Salt Lake	.288	143	5017	820	1444	311	57	160	397	1016	114
Edmonton	.285	143	4887	719	1395	291	38	142	484	987	52
Tacoma	.285	144	4910	749	1399	316	39	118	445	968	83
Tucson	.277	142	4910	682	1361	269	37	118	428	968	74
Fresno	.277	139	4687	698	1297	250	33	170	358	1041	86
Las Vegas	.276	144	4932	740	1362	291	36	184	458	1047	101
Nashville	.276	141	4811	669	1326	244	32	130	372	987	85
Iowa	.276	143	4830	698	1331	302	36	139	395	1000	114
Oklahoma	.267	143	4843	690	1291	255	36	143	511	973	69
New Orleans	.266	139	4573	683	1217	256	32	130	461	1018	95
Sacramento	.266	144	4892	750	1300	269	20	173	561	1048	129
Omaha	.265	144	4795	684	1272	243	22	152	440	975	95
Memphis	.262	143	4868	643	1277	254	29	114	384	1017	55
Portland	.256	144	4840	623	1241	255	31	154	397	1138	96

CLUB PITCHING

	ERA	G	CG	SHO	SV	IP	H	R	ER	BB	SO
Tacoma	3.73	144	11	11	38	1250	1210	610	519	414	1079
New Orleans	3.75	139	8	8	41	1204	1211	591	501	331	959
Iowa	3.85	143	4	12	46	1263	1204	599	540	475	1228
Portland	4.18	144	0	11	36	1266	1300	653	588	390	998
Oklahoma	4.28	143	10	7	33	1266	1259	677	602	495	1107
Nashville	4.51	141	7	7	30	1222	1276	702	613	426	840
Salt Lake	4.55	143	9	4	34	1261	1320	716	638	392	1036
Tucson	4.57	142	4	6	33	1243	1405	757	632	402	937
Sacramento	4.70	144	7	4	27	1264	1359	741	660	465	1075
Omaha	4.80	144	2	2	34	1249	1359	731	666	442	967
Memphis	4.80	143	2	8	28	1252	1358	751	668	505	962
Edmonton	4.86	143	7	7	29	1229	1441	755	664	439	968
Las Vegas	4.98	144	5	10	33	1264	1412	780	700	474	1090
Fresno	5.02	139	1	4	40	1198	1297	745	669	497	983
Colorado Springs	5.25	141	5	6	21	1231	1459	826	718	400	1042
Calgary	5.34	143	3	5	34	1222	1492	801	725	376	977

CLUB FIELDING

	PCT	PO	A	E	DP		PCT	PO	A	E	DP
Portland	.980	3799	1466	110	114	Calgary	.976	3667	1444	124	121
Fresno	.978	3594	1380	110	129	Las Vegas	.976	3792	1425	127	150
Iowa	.978	3790	1325	114	117	Sacramento	.976	3799	1409	127	143
Tacoma	.978	3750	1403	116	112	Memphis	.976	3757	1411	129	115
Edmonton	.978	3687	1449	117	150	Salt Lake	.975	3784	1456	136	141
Omaha	.978	3748	1472	119	159	Colo. Spr.	.972	3693	1468	146	142
Oklahoma	.977	3799	1428	125	145	Tucson	.971	3729	1464	154	106
New Orleans	.977	3611	1459	122	133	Nashville	.969	3666	1533	165	145

INDIVIDUAL BATTING LEADERS
(Minimum 389 Plate Appearances)

	AVG	G	AB	R	H	2B	3B	HR	RBI	BB	SO	SB
Fernandez, Jose, Salt Lake	.338	122	452	99	153	37	1	30	114	105	91	9
McCracken, Quinton, Edmonton	.338	81	361	53	122	27	4	4	45	21	54	8
Castro, Ramon, Calgary	.336	108	390	81	131	33	0	27	90	38	74	1
Conti, Jason, Tucson	.331	92	362	68	120	23	6	9	52	33	54	2
Hiatt, Phil, Las Vegas	.330	113	436	107	144	29	5	44	99	52	109	6
LeCroy, Matthew, Edmonton	.328	101	396	53	130	17	0	20	80	36	95	0
Gulan, Mike, Calgary	.324	124	485	78	157	44	2	22	92	35	145	2
Huskey, Butch, Colo. Springs	.323	122	458	76	148	29	1	19	87	42	95	2
Burroughs, Sean, Portland	.322	104	394	60	127	28	1	9	55	37	54	9
Brumbaugh, Cliff, Okla./Colo. Spr.	.320	107	410	69	131	29	4	11	81	67	93	8

INDIVIDUAL PITCHING LEADERS
(Minimum 115 Innings)

	W	L	ERA	G	GS	CG	SV	IP	H	R	ER	BB	SO
Stark, Dennis, Tacoma	14	2	2.37	24	24	0	0	152	124	52	40	41	130
Quevedo, Ruben, Iowa	9	5	2.99	22	22	1	0	142	124	54	47	48	150
Arteaga, J.D., New Orleans	8	6	3.07	32	21	1	1	138	143	60	47	27	90
Powell, Brian, New Orleans	9	8	3.17	24	23	3	0	145	142	65	51	39	96
Meyers, Mike, Iowa	7	4	3.23	25	25	0	0	148	129	58	53	64	124
George, Chris, Omaha	11	3	3.53	20	20	0	0	117	103	54	46	51	84
D'Amico, Jeff, Omaha	5	7	3.54	32	20	0	0	140	151	65	55	40	92
Benes, Alan, Memphis	7	6	3.55	25	25	1	0	142	164	71	56	51	96
Dickey, R.A., Oklahoma	11	7	3.75	24	24	3	0	163	164	77	68	45	120
Driskill, Travis, New Orleans	11	5	3.78	26	24	1	0	179	175	83	75	33	145

ALL-STAR TEAM

C—Ramon Castro, Calgary. 1B—Todd Betts, Tacoma. 2B—Chad Meyers, Iowa. 3B—Jose Fernandez, Salt Lake. SS—Ramon Vazquez, Tacoma. OF—Roosevelt Brown, Iowa; Jason Conti, Tucson; Jack Cust, Tucson. DH—Phil Hiatt, Las Vegas. RHP—Denny Stark, Tacoma. LHP—Bud Smith, Memphis. RP—Jim Mann, New Orleans.

Most Valuable Player: Phil Hiatt, Las Vegas. **Pitcher of the Year**: Denny Stark, Tacoma. **Rookie of the Year**: Sean Burroughs, Portland. **Manager of the Year**: Dan Rohn, Tacoma.

DEPARTMENT LEADERS

BATTING

G	Kelly Dransfeldt, Oklahoma	143
AB	Kelly Dransfeldt, Oklahoma	551
R	Phil Hiatt, Las Vegas	107
H	Mike Gulan, Calgary	157
TB	Phil Hiatt, Las Vegas	315
XBH	Phil Hiatt, Las Vegas	78
2B	Chad Alexander, Tacoma	45
3B	Ross Gload, Iowa	10
	Tike Redman, Nashville	10
HR	Phil Hiatt, Las Vegas	44
RBI	Jose Fernandez, Salt Lake	114
SH	Alex Cintron, Tucson	20
SF	Butch Huskey, Colo. Springs	12
BB	Jack Cust, Tucson	102
IBB	Rob Ryan, Tucson/Sacramento	9
HBP	Chad Meyers, Iowa	26
SO	Jack Cust, Tucson	160
SB	Chad Meyers, Iowa	27
CS	Quinton McCracken, Edmonton	10
	Trenidad Hubbard, Omaha/Iowa	10
GIDP	Craig Wilson, Omaha	21
OB%	Jose Fernandez, Salt Lake	.421
SL%	Phil Hiatt, Las Vegas	.722

PITCHING

G	Robbie Crabtree, Fresno	63
GS	Two tied at	29
CG	Greg Wooten, Tacoma	5
ShO	Three tied at	2
GF	Bart Miadich, Salt Lake	54
SV	Jim Mann, New Orleans	27
	Bart Miadich, Salt Lake	27
W	Denny Stark, Tacoma	14
L	Robert Averette, Colo. Springs	14
	Dave Zancanaro, Memphis	14
IP	Travis Driskill, New Orleans	179
H	Eric Ireland, Sacramento	215
R	Robert Averette, Colo. Springs	131
ER	Robert Averette, Colo. Springs	113
HR	Robert Averette, Colo. Springs	29
HB	Justin Miller, Sacramento	16
BB	Chad Hutchinson, Memphis	104
SO	Mark Kiefer, Las Vegas	174
WP	Chad Hutchinson, Memphis	17
BK	Victor Alvarez, Las Vegas	5

FIELDING

C	AVG	Keith McDonald, Memphis	.998
	PO	Yorvit Torrealba, Fresno	.779
	A	Raul Chavez, New Orleans	62
		Yorvit Torrealba, Fresno	62
	E	Mel Rosario, Omaha/Tucson	12
	DP	Two tied at	10
	PB	Mel Rosario, Omaha/Tucson	8
1B	AVG	Todd Sears, Edmonton	.993
	PO	Jason Hart, Sacramento	1130
	A	Carlos Pena, Oklahoma	89
	E	Jason Hart, Sacramento	15
		Butch Huskey, Colo. Springs	15
	DP	Kit Pellow, Omaha	130
2B	AVG	Chad Meyers, Iowa	.965
	PO	Juan Melo, Fresno	200
	A	Stubby Clapp, Memphis	236
		Keith Ginter, New Orleans	236
	E	Chad Meyers, Iowa	15
	DP	Juan Melo, Fresno	71
3B	AVG	Sean Burroughs, Portland	.964
	PO	Sean Burroughs, Portland	79
		Tony Zuniga, Fresno	79
	A	Jose Fernandez, Salt Lake	234
	E	Mike Gulan, Calgary	18
	DP	Tony Zuniga, Fresno	24
SS	AVG	Cody Ransom, Fresno	.980
	PO	Kelly Dransfeldt, Oklahoma	268
	A	Kelly Dransfeldt, Oklahoma	400
	E	Alex Cintron, Tucson	30
	DP	Kelly Dransfeldt, Oklahoma	105
OF	AVG	Ryan Radmanovich, Port./Nash.	.995
	PO	Luis Saturria, Memphis	344
	A	Chris Prieto, Las Vegas	14
	E	Jack Cust, Tucson	11
	DP	Eric Byrnes, Sacramento	5

EASTERN LEAGUE

BY ANDREW LINKER

The matchup for the Eastern League championship series in 2001 surely was an intriguing one, with the prospect-packed New Britain Rock Cats against the prospect-lite, but gritty, Reading Phillies.

No one, though, ever saw it.

In the end, the champagne stayed packed. No one was celebrating as the EL, like nine other leagues in the minors, called off its playoffs after the terrorist attacks on New York and Washington. The finals, which were to begin the same day as the attacks of Sept. 11, never started. After three days of postponements, the league called off the series and declared New Britain and Reading co-champions.

RODGER WOOD

Mike Rivera

"You always want to be a champion in your own right," Phillies second baseman Brian Harris said, "but given the circumstances, I don't think you'll see anyone in here who has a problem with the decision."

The split title was the first in the EL since 1960, when rained canceled the finals between Williamsport and Springfield.

The 2001 season also started in the worst possible way for the Binghamton Mets, whose prized outfielder Brian Cole was killed in a single-vehicle accident at the end of spring training.

The 79th year in the history of the EL included a handful of records, feats and firsts, as well as its share of ignominious moments.

Reading center fielder Marlon Byrd, the league's MVP, came within two home runs of joining Jeromy Burnitz (Williamsport, 1991) as the only other player in league history to hit 30 homers and steal 30 bases in a season.

Erie's Mike Rivera (33, 101) and Eric Munson (26, 102) became the first teammates to hit at least 25 homers and drive in more than 95 runs in the same season since Cliff Floyd and Glenn Murray did so with the 1993 Harrisburg Senators.

New Haven center fielder Esix Snead stole 64 bases, the most in the EL since Ced Landrum stole 69 for Pittsfield in 1988. New Britain outfielder Lew Ford became the first player in EL history to hit four homers in a game, doing so in a 13-5 victory Aug. 19 in Binghamton.

Binghamton right fielder Rob Stratton, who became the first player since Greg Luzinski in 1970 to clear Reading's brick wall beyond left field, finished with 201 strikeouts to break the EL record of 184 set by former B-Mets first baseman Bryon Gainey in 1999.

The EL had six no-hitters, its most in one season since 1971. Only the no-hitter by Reading's Adam Walker, the first of the six, was a complete game that lasted nine innings. The nine-inning, complete-game no-hitter also was the league's first since Binghamton's Bill Pulsipher no-hit Harrisburg in Game Two of the 1994 finals.

Walker would finish the season in Binghamton after he was traded in midseason from Philadelphia to the New York Mets.

Three others—Bowie's John Stephens, and New Haven's duo of Les Walrond and Jimmy Journell—threw their no-hitters during seven-inning games of doubleheaders. Journell's came on the final day of the season in his only Double-A start.

The other two no-hitters were combined efforts, started by Donne Wall—on a major league injury rehab assignment with Binghamton—and top prospect Josh Beckett with the Portland Sea Dogs.

The 2001 season also featured the downfall of two champions. The New Haven Ravens, winners of the 2000 playoffs, went from champs to chumps as they changed affiliates from the Mariners to the Cardinals and led the minors with 95 losses.

In doing so, the Ravens became only the fourth team in EL history to go from first to worst and the first since the 1980 West Haven White Caps; New Haven's 95 losses also were the most in the league since Jersey City lost 97 games in 1977.

The other fallen champion was Harrisburg, winner of six titles since rejoining the EL in 1987. The Senators, considered among the preseason favorites, languished to a fourth-place finish in the Southern Division and missed the playoffs for just the second time in their 11 seasons as the Expos' Double-A affiliate.

STANDINGS

Page	NORTH	W	L	PCT	GB	Manager	Attendance (Avg.)	Last Penn.
170	New Britain Rock Cats (Twins)	87	55	.613	—	Stan Cliburn	261,331 (3,843)	2001
184	Norwich Navigators (Yankees)	83	59	.585	4	Stump Merrill	231,481 (3,455)	None
137	Portland Sea Dogs (Marlins)	77	65	.542	10	Rick Renteria	383,022 (5,803)	None
192	Binghamton Mets (Mets)	73	68	.518	13½	Howie Freiling	197,113 (2,899)	1994
87	Trenton Thunder (Red Sox)	67	75	.472	20	Billy Gardner	411,322 (5,876)	None
220	New Haven Ravens (Cardinals)	47	95	.331	40	Danny Sheaffer	186,301 (2,866)	2000
Page	SOUTH	W	L	PCT	GB	Manager	Attendance (Avg.)	Last Penn.
130	Erie SeaWolves (Tigers)	84	58	.592	—	Luis Pujols	246,404 (3,571)	None
206	Reading Phillies (Phillies)	77	65	.542	7	Gary Varsho	458,585 (6,948)	2001
115	Akron Aeros (Indians)	68	74	.479	16	Chris Bando	485,582 (7,037)	None
177	Harrisburg Senators (Expos)	66	76	.465	18	Luis Dorante	279,691 (4,113)	1999
213	Altoona Curve (Pirates)	63	79	.444	21	Dale Sveum	348,316 (5,122)	None
80	Bowie Baysox (Orioles)	59	82	.418	24½	Dave Machemer	350,127 (5,226)	None

PLAYOFFS—Semifinals: New Britain defeated Norwich 3-1 and Reading defeated Erie 3-1 in best-of-5 series. **Finals:** Series cancelled; New Britain and Reading declared co-champions.

NOTE: Teams' individual batting and pitching statistics can be found on page indicated in lefthand column.

2001 EASTERN LEAGUE STATISTICS

CLUB BATTING

	AVG	G	AB	R	H	2B	3B	HR	BB	SO	SB
Erie	.276	142	4789	741	1320	259	24	143	453	1014	120
Norwich	.269	142	4862	703	1309	287	22	141	413	1029	64
Trenton	.261	142	4784	625	1250	292	26	128	398	1029	87
New Britain	.261	142	4823	620	1259	250	34	126	379	892	60
Bowie	.261	141	4678	597	1219	238	24	91	426	1021	148
Reading	.260	142	4782	691	1243	237	34	134	421	872	123
Altoona	.258	142	4760	557	1226	267	38	91	376	1027	120
Binghamton	.255	141	4688	618	1196	252	20	143	427	1193	106
Akron	.255	142	4749	606	1210	260	30	135	351	996	108
Harrisburg	.252	142	4635	587	1169	203	39	98	398	950	161
Portland	.244	142	4688	590	1142	213	37	96	530	1097	131
New Haven	.233	142	4639	491	1079	211	24	81	335	1028	151

CLUB PITCHING

	ERA	G	CG	SHO	SV	IP	H	R	ER	BB	SO
New Britain	3.02	142	5	11	44	1268	1136	499	426	389	1148
Portland	3.23	142	4	12	38	1257	1067	517	452	356	1141
Norwich	3.27	142	7	13	40	1253	1129	578	455	463	1207
Altoona	3.73	142	4	8	30	1246	1257	613	516	430	872
Erie	3.85	142	16	11	42	1236	1216	612	529	395	1003
Akron	3.93	142	8	12	31	1236	1203	607	539	423	931
Reading	4.02	142	8	12	35	1248	1233	622	557	351	958
Harrisburg	4.14	142	10	6	30	1224	1244	666	563	440	958
Bowie	4.16	141	13	11	28	1228	1263	672	568	351	906
Trenton	4.21	142	1	9	34	1233	1298	683	577	380	1121
Binghamton	4.23	141	4	9	40	1232	1328	667	579	451	959
New Haven	4.25	142	4	9	24	1230	1248	690	580	478	944

CLUB FIELDING

	PCT	PO	A	E	DP		PCT	PO	A	E	DP
Portland	.980	3771	1317	105	108	Erie	.971	3707	1452	155	114
Akron	.978	3707	1518	120	131	Binghamton	.971	3695	1557	159	150
Reading	.974	3743	1504	139	114	New Haven	.970	3689	1434	157	128
Harrisburg	.972	3672	1349	144	120	Trenton	.970	3698	1426	158	121
New Britain	.972	3805	1523	153	115	Bowie	.968	3684	1422	167	109
Altoona	.972	3737	1513	153	126	Norwich	.962	3760	1337	204	107

INDIVIDUAL BATTING LEADERS
(Minimum 383 Plate Appearances)

	AVG	G	AB	R	H	2B	3B	HR	RBI	BB	SO	SB
Mohr, Dustan, New Britain	.336	135	518	90	174	41	3	24	91	49	111	9
Thames, Marcus, Norwich	.321	139	520	114	167	43	4	31	97	73	101	10
Burnham, Gary, Reading	.318	109	371	59	118	25	2	15	77	35	43	1
Byrd, Marlon, Reading	.316	137	510	108	161	22	8	28	89	52	93	32
Hooper, Kevin, Portland	.308	117	468	70	144	19	6	2	39	59	78	24
Harris, Willie, Bowie	.305	133	525	83	160	27	4	9	49	46	71	54
Infante, Omar, Erie	.302	132	540	86	163	21	4	2	62	46	87	27
Cuddyer, Michael, New Britain	.301	141	509	95	153	36	3	30	87	75	106	5
Figueroa, Frank, Bowie	.300	137	534	61	160	32	0	14	72	21	138	0
Salazar, Ruben, New Britain	.298	137	530	70	158	29	2	10	66	37	77	6

INDIVIDUAL PITCHING LEADERS
(Minimum 114 Innings)

	W	L	ERA	G	GS	CG	SV	IP	H	R	ER	BB	SO
Stephens, John, Bowie	11	4	1.84	18	17	3	0	132	95	32	27	21	130
Thomas, Brad, New Britain	10	3	1.96	19	19	1	0	119	91	37	26	26	97
Claussen, Brandon, Norwich	9	2	2.13	21	21	1	0	131	101	42	31	55	151
Olsen, Kevin, Portland	10	3	2.68	26	26	2	0	155	123	56	46	21	144
Cornejo, Nate, Erie	12	3	2.68	19	19	3	0	124	107	47	37	41	105
Flores, Randy, Norwich	14	6	2.78	25	25	3	0	159	156	64	49	63	115
Fossum, Casey, Trenton	3	7	2.83	20	20	0	0	118	102	47	37	28	130
Rincon, Juan, New Britain	14	6	2.88	29	23	2	0	153	130	60	49	57	133
Day, Zach, Akron	9	10	3.10	22	22	2	0	137	123	57	47	45	94
Spurling, Chris, Altoona	5	7	3.11	34	15	0	1	122	133	48	42	28	63

ALL-STAR TEAM

C—Mike Rivera, Erie. **1B**—Eric Munson, Erie. **2B**—Willie Harris, Bowie. **3B**—Michael Cuddyer, New Britain. **SS**—Omar Infante, Erie. **OF**—Marlon Byrd, Reading; Dustan Mohr, New Britain; Marcus Thames, Norwich. **DH**—Alejandro Freire, Erie. **Util**—J.P. Roberge, Reading. **RHP**—John Stephens, Bowie. **LHP**—Brad Thomas, New Britain. **RP**—Alex Pacheco, Norwich.

MINOR LEAGUES

BY DAVID JENKINS

The Los Angeles Dodgers were the new boys on the block at the beginning of the 2001 Southern League season. By September, they'd become the neighborhood bully.

Skippered skillfully by manager of the year John Shoemaker, the Dodgers' new Double-A affiliate at Jacksonville ran roughshod over the Southern League Eastern Division race, winning a league-high 83 games and both halves of the split-season race.

The Huntsville Stars needed five games to defeat the Birmingham Barons in the Western Division playoffs. They were named co-champions with Jacksonville when the final round of the SL playoffs was called off before a single contest was played following the suspension of play after September's terrorist attacks.

It marked the first time the Southern League named co-champions since opening for business in 1964. For Jacksonville, it was the city's first title since 1996; for the Stars, the shared title was their first pennant since 1994.

Don Mincher, named fulltime league president before the season, called giving up the playoffs "certainly the most difficult decision I have had to make as Southern League president."

Jacksonville dominated throughout, despite undergoing a near-total overhaul of its pitching staff between halves. Lefthander Victor Alvarez threw 29 consecutive scoreless innings beginning with the third inning of the Suns' Opening Day game, but his stinginess was overshadowed by Orlando Rays lefthander Joe Kennedy, who went five starts without giving up an earned run. Kennedy allowed only one earned run over 47 innings before being promoted to Triple-A and eventually the big leagues.

The league's top second-half player was Jacksonville outfielder Chin-Feng Chen. Joining the Suns at the split, Chen hit .313-17-50. Suns shortstop Jose Nunez stole a league-leading 44 bases, while Shoemaker's aggressive offense easily led the league with 165 steals.

Chattanooga, the only team in the East besides Jacksonville to post a winning record for the season, had the big story over the first five weeks of the season in outfielder Adam Dunn. Playing 39 games with the Lookouts, Dunn had at least one home run in every series and

BOB LIBBY
Chin-Feng Chen

STANDINGS: SPLIT SEASON

FIRST HALF					SECOND HALF			
EAST	W	L	PCT	GB	EAST	W	L	PCT	GB
Jacksonville	41	30	.577	—	Jacksonville	42	26	.618	—
Chattanooga	39	32	.549	2	Greenville	35	34	.507	7½
Carolina	31	39	.443	9½	Chattanooga	33	35	.485	9
Orlando	31	40	.437	10	Carolina	31	37	.456	11
Greenville	25	45	.357	15½	Orlando	28	41	.406	14½
WEST	W	L	PCT	GB	WEST	W	L	PCT	GB
Huntsville	42	29	.592	—	Birmingham	43	26	.623	—
Tennessee	41	30	.577	1	Tennessee	39	30	.565	4
Birmingham	37	34	.521	5	Huntsville	33	34	.493	9
West Tenn	34	37	.479	8	Mobile	32	35	.478	10
Mobile	33	38	.465	9	West Tenn	25	43	.368	17½

PLAYOFFS—Semifinals: Huntsville defeated Birmingham 3-2 and Jacksonville defeated Chattanooga 3-2 in best-of-5 series. **Finals:** Series canceled; Huntsville and Jacksonville declared co-champions.

moved up the ladder after hitting .343-12-31.

Tennessee Smokies catcher-DH Josh Phelps, who spent the entire season in the league, was a relatively easy choice as MVP. Phelps was a legitimate threat to win the league's triple crown, winning the home run title with 31, finishing one behind Birmingham Barons outfielder Joe Borchard with 97 RBIs and finishing sixth in average at .292, 28 points behind Chattanooga's Ben Broussard.

Broussard, at .320, became the 11th Lookouts hitter to claim a batting title since the city rejoined the SL in 1976. But the lefthanded-hitting first baseman was the first to win a title in the new Chattanooga ballpark, BellSouth Park.

A midseason callup for Huntsville, outfielder Jim Rushford, hit .342 in 187 at-bats for the Stars—too few to qualify for the league title. Including his Class A stats, .363 in the California League, Rushford finished the season with a .354 average, the highest in all of minor league baseball in 2001.

The league drew headlines from Opening Day, as a trio of Birmingham Barons pitchers—lefthanders Mike Porzio and Matt Beaumont and righthander Brian Tokarse—combined for a no-hitter against the Tennessee Smokies, 5-0, on April 5. Another Barons pitcher, Matt Guerrier, was the dominant SL starter for the first half with 11 wins. He later added seven Triple-A victories to lead all minor league pitchers with 18 wins.

Defending champion West Tenn struggled. The Diamond Jaxx pulled off the ignominious dual feat of being last in the SL in both batting average (.244) and ERA (4.26). The latter is all the more remarkable because lefthander Steve Smyth (2.54) won the league ERA title.

STANDINGS: OVERALL

Page		W	L	PCT	GB	Manager	Attendance (Avg.)	Last Penn.
157	Jacksonville Suns (Dodgers)	83	56	.597	—	John Shoemaker	225,362 (3,467)	2001
261	Tennessee Smokies (Blue Jays)	80	60	.571	3½	Rocket Wheeler	266,037 (3,856)	1978
94	Birmingham Barons (White Sox)	80	60	.571	3½	Nick Capra	311,362 (4,579)	1993
164	Huntsville Stars (Brewers)	75	63	.543	7½	Ed Romero	237,950 (3,838)	2001
108	Chattanooga Lookouts (Reds)	72	67	.518	11	Phillip Wellman	288,047 (4,236)	1988
227	Mobile BayBears (Padres)	65	73	.471	17½	Tracy Woodson	240,045 (3,583)	1998
123	Carolina Mudcats (Rockies)	62	76	.449	20½	Ron Gideon	257,558 (3,902)	1995
73	Greenville Braves (Braves)	60	79	.432	23	Paul Runge	243,900 (3,695)	1997
101	West Tenn Diamond Jaxx (Cubs)	59	80	.424	24	Dave Bialas	244,252 (3,758)	2000
247	Orlando Rays (Devil Rays)	59	81	.421	24½	Mike Ramsey	89,435 (1,376)	1999

NOTE: Teams' individual batting and pitching statistics can be found on page indicated in lefthand column.

CLUB BATTING

	AVG	G	AB	R	H	2B	3B	HR	BB	SO	SB
Tennessee	.271	140	4732	717	1282	257	37	135	504	1031	133
Birmingham	.268	140	4701	717	1262	261	27	129	547	978	82
Jacksonville	.260	139	4638	623	1206	248	37	103	479	993	165
Chattanooga	.258	139	4598	708	1187	265	17	155	513	1013	122
Orlando	.256	140	4657	514	1194	223	29	58	336	886	98
Huntsville	.255	138	4604	596	1174	227	16	121	420	946	90
Carolina	.252	138	4569	555	1152	239	29	76	472	957	131
Mobile	.249	138	4651	528	1159	234	30	87	459	1039	96
Greenville	.247	139	4596	541	1136	224	18	120	427	1095	75
West Tenn	.244	139	4620	590	1128	200	30	106	501	1104	100

CLUB PITCHING

	ERA	G	CG	SHO	SV	IP	H	R	ER	BB	SO
Jacksonville	3.29	139	2	8	42	1232	1109	530	451	417	1031
Huntsville	3.46	138	2	12	39	1216	1149	540	467	429	1085
Tennessee	3.75	140	14	14	38	1229	1155	576	512	386	874
Mobile	3.94	138	1	8	39	1226	1171	613	536	473	975
Greenville	3.96	139	4	7	33	1213	1181	614	534	484	1012
Birmingham	4.01	140	3	12	43	1230	1215	642	548	488	935
Chattanooga	4.04	139	6	14	30	1217	1206	625	546	497	1084
Orlando	4.04	140	3	13	30	1220	1242	640	548	457	956
Carolina	4.18	138	6	11	28	1210	1256	655	562	508	976
West Tenn	4.26	139	5	9	28	1216	1196	654	576	519	1114

CLUB FIELDING

	PCT	PO	A	E	DP		PCT	PO	A	E	DP
Mobile	.977	3677	1416	122	114	Birmingham	.972	3691	1550	151	137
Jacksonville	.976	3697	1381	126	109	Tennessee	.972	3687	1522	151	138
West Tenn	.975	3649	1246	127	103	Carolina	.972	3630	1471	149	115
Greenville	.972	3638	1483	146	112	Huntsville	.971	3647	1381	151	86
Orlando	.972	3661	1475	147	131	Chattanooga	.971	3650	1372	152	105

INDIVIDUAL BATTING LEADERS
(Minimum 378 Plate Appearances)

	AVG	G	AB	R	H	2B	3B	HR	RBI	BB	SO	SB
Broussard, Ben, Chattanooga	.320	100	353	81	113	27	0	23	69	61	69	10
Johnson, Reed, Tennessee	.314	136	554	104	174	29	4	13	74	45	79	42
Crosby, Bubba, Jacksonville	.302	107	384	68	116	22	5	6	47	37	60	22
Borchard, Joe, Birmingham	.295	133	515	95	152	27	1	27	98	67	158	5
Saunders, Chris, Birmingham	.294	118	442	74	130	33	0	10	68	60	85	4
Phelps, Josh, Tennessee	.292	136	486	95	142	36	1	31	97	80	127	3
Allen, Luke, Jacksonville	.290	125	486	74	141	32	6	16	73	42	111	13
Hummel, Tim, Chattanooga	.290	134	524	83	152	33	6	7	63	62	69	14
Burford, Kevin, Carolina	.289	101	363	51	105	21	4	6	35	45	79	4
Metcalfe, Mike, Chattanooga	.289	123	474	68	137	25	4	3	47	38	59	32

INDIVIDUAL PITCHING LEADERS
(Minimum 112 Innings)

	W	L	ERA	G	GS	CG	SV	IP	H	R	ER	BB	SO
Smyth, Steve, West Tenn	9	3	2.54	18	18	3	0	120	110	38	34	40	93
Gulin, Lindsay, Jacksonville	7	5	2.64	26	21	1	0	126	128	46	37	46	111
Wright, Danny, Birmingham	7	7	2.82	20	20	0	0	134	112	54	42	41	128
Magrane, Jim, Orlando	8	12	2.97	29	28	1	0	182	166	87	60	56	126
Dawley, Joey, Greenville	7	5	3.04	22	21	1	0	127	95	50	43	46	130
DiFelice, Mark, Carolina	6	4	3.15	19	18	2	0	123	108	47	43	23	99
Baker, Chris, Tennessee	15	6	3.37	28	26	4	1	179	162	73	67	42	121
Lee, Derek, Huntsville	7	11	3.38	28	28	0	0	162	173	76	61	39	109
Cumberland, Chris, Greenville	3	7	3.46	20	20	2	0	125	126	51	48	40	85
Junge, Eric, Jacksonville	10	11	3.46	27	27	1	0	164	143	72	63	56	116

ALL-STAR TEAM

C—Josh Phelps, Tennessee. **1B**—Ben Broussard, Chattanooga. **2B**—Orlando Hudson, Tennessee. **3B**—Josh Klimek, Huntsville. **SS**—Jorge Nunez, Jacksonville. **OF**—Luke Allen, Jacksonville; Joe Borchard, Birmingham; Bubba Crosby, Jacksonville; Reed Johnson, Tennessee. **Util**—Brooks Badeaux, Orlando. **RHP**—Chris Baker, Tennessee; Nick Neugebauer, Huntsville. **LHP**—Steve Smyth, West Tenn. **RP**—Ed Almonte, Birmingham.

Most Valuable Player: Josh Phelps, Knoxville. **Most Outstanding Pitcher:** Chris Baker, Tennessee. **Manager of the Year**: John Shoemaker, Jacksonville.

DEPARTMENT LEADERS

BATTING

G	Three tied at	136
AB	Reed Johnson, Tennessee	554
R	Reed Johnson, Tennessee	104
H	Reed Johnson, Tennessee	174
TB	Josh Phelps, Tennessee	273
XBH	Josh Phelps, Tennessee	68
2B	Josh Phelps, Tennessee	36
3B	Glenn Davis, Jacksonville	8
	Orlando Hudson, Tennessee	8
HR	Josh Phelps, Tennessee	31
RBI	Joe Borchard, Birmingham	98
SH	Five tied at	11
SF	Tim Hummel, Birmingham	10
BB	Graham Koonce, Mobile	89
IBB	Josh Klimek, Huntsville	8
HBP	Corky Miller, Chattanooga	19
SO	Darron Ingram, Birmingham	188
SB	Jorge Nunez, Jacksonville	44
CS	Carl Crawford, Orlando	20
GIDP	Tom Nevers, Chattanooga	17
OB%	Graham Koonce, Mobile	.429
SL%	Ben Broussard, Chattanooga	.592

PITCHING

G	Chris Booker, West Tenn/Chatt.	61
GS	Four tied at	28
CG	Chris Baker, Tennessee	4
	Scott Cassidy, Tennessee	4
ShO	Scott Cassidy, Tennessee	3
GF	Ed Almonte, Birmingham	48
SV	Ed Almonte, Birmingham	36
W	Chris Baker, Tennessee	15
	Mitch Wylie, Birmingham	15
L	Rick Guttormson, Mobile	16
IP	Jim Magrane, Orlando	182
H	Nathan Kent, Greenville	186
R	Rob Purvis, Birmingham	96
ER	Rob Purvis, Birmingham	82
HR	Chris Baker, Tennessee	22
HB	Juan Cruz, West Tenn	16
BB	Scott Dunn, Chattanooga	71
SO	Nick Neugebauer, Huntsville	149
WP	Luke Hudson, Carolina	18
BK	Stevenson Agosto, Orlando	4

FIELDING

C	AVG	Wilbert Nieves, Mobile	.996
	PO	Wilbert Nieves, Mobile	696
	A	Miguel Olivo, Birmingham	78
	E	Steve Torrealba, Greenville	14
	DP	Brian Moon, Huntsville	9
		Wilbert Nieves, Mobile	9
	PB	Miguel Olivo, Birmingham	19
1B	AVG	Eric Battersby, Birmingham	.995
	PO	Eric Battersby, Birmingham	1183
	A	Glenn Davis, Jacksonville	96
	E	Kevin Burford, Carolina	21
	DP	Eric Battersby, Birmingham	119
2B	AVG	Keoni DeRenne, Greenville	.986
	PO	Joe Thurston, Jacksonville	287
	A	Jeff Pickler, Huntsville	326
	E	Eddy de los Santos, Orlando	21
	DP	Tim Hummel, Birmingham	70
3B	AVG	Andrew Beinbrink, Orlando	.948
	PO	Michael Hessman, Greenville	74
	A	Glenn Williams, Tennessee	223
	E	Gabe Alvarez, Chattanooga	27
	DP	Glenn Williams, Tennessee	27
SS	AVG	Travis Dawkins, Chattanooga	.964
	PO	Cleatus Davidson, Mobile	178
	A	Cleatus Davidson, Mobile	343
	E	Jersen Perez, Tennessee	30
	DP	Jorge Cantu, Orlando	59
OF	AVG	Darrell Dent, Jacksonville	1.000
	PO	Joe Borchard, Birmingham	316
	A	Three tied at	15
	E	Joe Borchard, Birmingham	12
	DP	Jeremy Owens, Mobile	5
		Dewayne Wise, Tennessee	5

TEXAS LEAGUE

BY MICHAEL POINT

A season after Roy Oswalt, Bud Smith and Luke Prokopec overwhelmed Texas League batters on their way to big league success, the TL had several noteworthy hitting achievements in 2001—even as the circuit had only six hitters with .300 averages who had sufficient plate appearances to qualify for the batting title.

The most consistent and well-rounded offensive performance came from Round Rock outfielder Jason Lane, the TL player of the year. Lane led the minors with 124 RBIs while hitting .316 with 38 home runs. He also led the league with 103 runs, 320 total bases and 76 extra-base hits.

El Paso first baseman Lyle Overbay ran away with the batting title, hitting .352 while also leading the league in hits and doubles. Midland slugger

RODGER WOOD

Hank Blalock

Jacques Landry missed a rare 40-40 season, settling for 36 home runs and 37 stolen bases. Landry also led the league in strikeouts, fanning 148 times, the most since Rob Deer whiffed 185 times in 1983. After Lane and Landry staged an exciting first-half home run derby, with both entering July with 28 big flies, Wichita's Brandon Berger emerged as the leading second-half power hitter.

Berger ultimately passed Lane and Landry to take the home run title, becoming the first to hit 40 since 1964.

Perhaps the most amazing individual offensive feat of the season came from Tulsa's Hank Blalock. In just his sixth game after being called up from Class A Charlotte, where he was hitting .380, the Drillers third baseman hit for the cycle against Midland. Two nights later against the RockHounds, he did it again, becoming the first minor leaguer ever to hit for the cycle twice in one season.

"A lot of people were looking at me funny when I put him third in the lineup when he came up from A-ball," said Tulsa manager Paul Carey. "But like I told them, he goes out there and gets the job done."

The biggest story of the 2001 Texas League season, however, was the surprise postseason success of one of the league's weaker regular season teams and the controversy that ensued when president Tom Kayser abruptly ended the playoffs in the wake of the Sept. 11 terrorist tragedy.

The underdog Arkansas Travelers celebrated their first-year affiliation with the Anaheim Angels with an unexpected pennant run. Arkansas, which won the Eastern Division first-half title by a half game, had just a 66-70

STANDINGS: SPLIT SEASON

FIRST HALF					SECOND HALF			
EAST	**W**	**L**	**PCT**	**GB**	**EAST**	**W**	**L**	**PCT**	**GB**
Arkansas	38	32	.543	—	Wichita	43	27	.614	—
Wichita	36	31	.537	½	Tulsa	41	29	.586	2
Tulsa	28	41	.406	9½	Arkansas	28	38	.424	13
Shreveport	27	42	.391	10½	Shreveport	27	39	.409	14
WEST	**W**	**L**	**PCT**	**GB**	**WEST**	**W**	**L**	**PCT**	**GB**
Round Rock	50	20	.714	—	San Antonio	41	29	.586	—
Midland	43	27	.614	7	Round Rock	36	34	.514	5
San Antonio	29	38	.433	19½	El Paso	32	38	.457	9
El Paso	25	45	.357	25	Midland	28	42	.400	13

PLAYOFFS—Semifinals: Round Rock defeated San Antonio 3-2 and Arkansas defeated Wichita 3-1 in best-of-5 series. **Finals:** Series cancelled; Arkansas declared champion after leading Round Rock 2-0 in best-of-5 series.

regular season record, the league's sixth-best mark. But it eliminated Wichita in the divisional finals in four games, and had a 2-0 advantage over defending league champion Round Rock in the title series when play was stopped.

Despite a vehement protest from Round Rock, which had an 86-54 record in the regular season, Kayser declared Arkansas the league champion. While its playoff setback muddied an otherwise outstanding season on the field, Round Rock repeated its inaugural-year success at the turnstiles, extending its all-time Double-A attendance record to 668,792.

Behind the power pitching of Tim Redding, Carlos Hernandez, Brad Lidge and Greg Miller, Round Rock recorded a record-breaking 50-20 first-half mark. But with Redding, who was the league's pitcher of the year, and Hernandez promoted to the Astros—as well as Lidge and Miller on the disabled list—the team slipped in the final weeks. It lost the second-half title in the West to rival San Antonio. The Express ultimately won the West, though, in an extra-innings thriller in the playoffs.

Round Rock's pitching staff broke the league record for strikeouts, fanning 1,138. A Round Rock pitcher, either Redding or Hernandez, led the league in strikeouts until the final week of the season, when San Antonio's Jeff Heaverlo, who also led in complete games and shutouts, took the title in a game at Round Rock's Dell Diamond. Round Rock's Travis Smith, however, did lead the league in wins (15) and ERA (3.09).

The league infrastructure upgrade continued with new stadium construction in Midland and facility improvements in El Paso. But the spectacular failure of the Shreveport franchise, which barely averaged 900 fans a game, severely undercut that momentum, while also leading to a rash of rumors regarding relocation.

MINOR LEAGUES

STANDINGS: OVERALL

Page		W	L	PCT	GB	Manager	Attendance (Avg.)	Last Penn.
144	Round Rock Express (Astros)	86	54	.614	—	Jackie Moore	668,792 (9,554)	2000
150	Wichita Wranglers (Royals)	79	58	.577	5½	Keith Bodie	130,438 (2,070)	1999
241	San Antonio Missions (Mariners)	70	67	.511	14½	Dave Brundage	309,113 (4,480)	1997
200	Midland RockHounds (Athletics)	71	69	.507	15	Tony DeFrancesco	148,292 (2,149)	1975
254	Tulsa Drillers (Rangers)	69	70	.496	16½	Paul Carey	314,973 (4,500)	1998
59	Arkansas Travelers (Angels)	66	70	.485	18	Mike Brumley	185,905 (2,951)	2001
66	El Paso Diablos (Diamondbacks)	57	83	.407	29	Al Pedrique	253,994 (3,681)	1994
234	Shreveport Swamp Dragons (Giants)	54	81	.400	29½	Bill Russell	59,316 (913)	1995

NOTE: Teams' individual batting and pitching statistics can be found on page indicated in lefthand column.

CLUB BATTING

	AVG	G	AB	R	H	2B	3B	HR	BB	SO	SB
El Paso	.281	140	4862	650	1368	311	33	78	429	1054	95
Wichita	.280	137	4678	776	1308	252	39	146	420	842	116
Round Rock	.274	140	4812	713	1317	273	33	139	442	962	117
Arkansas	.266	136	4578	654	1217	255	43	110	418	948	146
Midland	.260	140	4764	742	1241	280	36	139	548	1031	123
Shreveport	.260	135	4589	564	1192	224	28	62	397	982	141
Tulsa	.257	139	4747	650	1218	260	35	116	473	965	87
San Antonio	.255	137	4729	615	1205	227	28	81	459	925	109

CLUB PITCHING

	ERA	G	CG	SHO	SV	IP	H	R	ER	BB	SO
Round Rock	3.62	140	3	17	39	1241	1136	569	499	461	1138
San Antonio	3.85	137	7	16	36	1236	1277	622	529	387	1062
Wichita	4.06	137	3	13	39	1200	1181	619	541	472	965
Shreveport	4.07	135	5	7	33	1193	1232	647	540	378	774
Tulsa	4.28	139	8	8	28	1237	1222	666	588	474	1063
Midland	4.40	140	1	8	33	1238	1379	709	605	433	926
Arkansas	4.77	136	9	3	27	1170	1246	722	621	434	757
El Paso	4.90	140	3	5	35	1220	1393	810	664	547	1024

CLUB FIELDING

	PCT	PO	A	E	DP		PCT	PO	A	E	DP
Round Rock	.976	3724	1390	127	115	Shreveport	.971	3580	1444	132	99
Wichita	.975	3600	1356	125	89	Arkansas	.970	3510	1442	151	114
Tulsa	.974	3712	1410	135	103	Midland	.968	3713	1574	176	116
San Antonio	.972	3708	1429	148	108	El Paso	.966	3660	1492	183	124

INDIVIDUAL BATTING LEADERS
(Minimum 378 Plate Appearances)

	AVG	G	AB	R	H	2B	3B	HR	RBI	BB	SO	SB
Overbay, Lyle, El Paso	.352	138	532	82	187	49	3	13	100	67	92	5
Dallimore, Brian, El Paso	.327	127	517	74	169	38	6	8	67	50	56	11
Lane, Jason, Round Rock	.316	137	526	103	166	36	2	38	124	61	98	14
Huffman, Royce, Round Rock	.309	137	511	75	158	35	1	4	49	51	90	13
Berger, Brandon, Wichita	.308	120	454	98	140	28	3	40	118	43	91	14
Matranga, Dave, Round Rock	.302	103	387	78	117	34	2	10	60	45	91	17
Castro, Nelson, Shreveport	.296	122	479	76	142	27	6	11	60	42	122	38
Quinlan, Robb, Arkansas	.295	129	492	82	145	33	7	14	79	53	84	0
Devore, Doug, El Paso	.294	128	476	67	140	32	11	15	74	46	118	11
Robinson, Bo, San Antonio	.293	133	474	75	139	23	1	13	74	81	56	3
Weber, Jake, San Antonio	.293	126	451	66	132	28	4	4	58	40	53	11

INDIVIDUAL PITCHING LEADERS
(Minimum 112 Innings)

	W	L	ERA	G	GS	CG	SV	IP	H	R	ER	BB	SO
Smith, Travis, Round Rock	15	8	3.09	29	22	1	1	160	154	66	55	26	85
Heaverlo, Jeff, San Antonio	11	6	3.12	27	27	4	0	179	164	75	62	40	173
Calero, Kiko, Wichita	14	5	3.33	27	19	0	0	124	110	57	46	51	94
Thurman, Corey, Wichita	13	5	3.37	25	25	0	0	155	117	66	58	61	148
Lackey, John, Arkansas	9	7	3.46	18	18	3	0	127	106	55	49	29	94
Cox, Ryan, Shreveport	8	8	3.69	24	24	1	0	137	145	70	56	24	61
Hernandez, Carlos, Round Rock	12	3	3.69	24	23	0	0	139	115	60	57	69	167
Putz, J.J., San Antonio	7	9	3.83	27	26	0	0	148	145	80	63	59	135
Affeldt, Jeremy, Wichita	10	6	3.90	25	25	0	0	145	153	74	63	46	128
Urban, Jeff, Shreveport	7	11	3.91	27	27	0	0	157	178	85	68	32	117

ALL-STAR TEAM

C—Brad Cresse, El Paso. **1B**—Lyle Overbay, El Paso. **2B**—Dave Matranga, Round Rock. **3B**—Hank Blalock, Tulsa. **SS**—Alfredo Amezaga, Arkansas. **OF**—Brandon Berger, Wichita; Jason Lane, Round Rock; Ryan Ludwick, Midland. **DH**—Jacques Landry, Midland. **Util**—Brian Dallimore, El Paso; Oscar Salazar, Midland. **P**—Jeremy Affeldt, Wichita; Jeff Heaverlo, San Antonio; Carlos Hernandez, Round Rock; Tim Redding, Round Rock; Travis Smith, Round Rock; Corey Thurman, Wichita.

Player of the Year: Jason Lane, Round Rock. **Pitcher of the Year**: Tim Redding, Round Rock. **Manager of the Year**: Jackie Moore, Round Rock.

DEPARTMENT LEADERS

BATTING

G	Lyle Overbay, El Paso	138
AB	Lyle Overbay, El Paso	532
R	Jason Lane, Round Rock	103
H	Lyle Overbay, El Paso	187
TB	Jason Lane, Round Rock	320
XBH	Jason Lane, Round Rock	76
2B	Lyle Overbay, El Paso	49
3B	Doug Devore, El Paso	11
HR	Brandon Berger, Wichita	40
RBI	Jason Lane, Round Rock	124
SH	Danny Solano, Tulsa	18
SF	Ken Harvey, Wichita	8
	Lyle Overbay, El Paso	8
BB	Bo Robinson, San Antonio	81
IBB	Jason Lane, Round Rock	11
	Lyle Overbay, El Paso	11
HBP	Jay Pecci, Midland	26
SO	Jacques Landry, Midland	184
SB	Nelson Castro, Shreveport	38
CS	Three tied at	15
GIDP	Greg Connors, San Antonio	19
OB%	Lyle Overbay, El Paso	.423
SL%	Brandon Berger, Wichita	.648

PITCHING

G	Travis Wade, Round Rock	60
GS	Ryan Baerlocher, Wichita	28
	Chris Capuano, El Paso	28
CG	Jeff Heaverlo, San Antonio	4
ShO	Jeff Heaverlo, San Antonio	4
GF	Travis Wade, Round Rock	54
SV	Travis Wade, Round Rock	23
W	Travis Smith, Round Rock	15
L	Dusty Bergman, Arkansas	13
IP	Ryan Baerlocher, Wichita	181
H	Justin Lehr, Midland	206
R	Chris Capuano, El Paso	109
ER	Chris Capuano, El Paso	94
	Justin Lehr, Midland	94
HR	Ryan Baerlocher, Wichita	26
HB	Colby Lewis, Tulsa	16
BB	Chris Capuano, El Paso	75
SO	Jeff Heaverlo, San Antonio	173
WP	Colby Lewis, Tulsa	16
BK	Oscar Villarreal, El Paso	11

FIELDING

C	AVG	Scott Maynard, San Antonio	.993
	PO	Brad Cresse, El Paso	665
	A	Brad Cresse, El Paso	83
	E	Brian Luderer, Midland	12
	DP	Scott Maynard, San Antonio	8
	PB	Brad Cresse, El Paso	17
1B	AVG	Charley Carter, Round Rock	.993
	PO	Todd Mensik, Midland	1178
	A	Robb Quinlan, Arkansas	97
	E	Todd Mensik, Midland	19
	DP	Todd Mensik, Midland	100
2B	AVG	Dave Matranga, Round Rock	.987
	PO	Rod Metzler, Wichita	197
	A	Dave Matranga, Round Rock	268
	E	Ryan Luther, Shreveport	20
	DP	Chris Lemonis, El Paso	59
3B	AVG	Henry Calderon, Wichita	.949
	PO	Julio Cordido, Shreveport	86
	A	Julio Cordido, Shreveport	245
	E	Royce Huffman, Round Rock	27
	DP	Brian Dallimore, El Paso	17
SS	AVG	Danny Solano, Tulsa	.971
	PO	Nelson Castro, Shreveport	207
	A	Nelson Castro, Shreveport	373
	E	Nelson Castro, Shreveport	32
	DP	Eric Bruntlett, Round Rock	67
OF	AVG	Mike Lockwood, Midland	.992
	PO	Barry Wesson, Round Rock	288
	A	Doug Devore, El Paso	11
	E	Doug Devore, El Paso	12
	DP	Three tied at	3

CALIFORNIA LEAGUE

BY PATRICK LAVERTY

As in most minor leagues, the California League playoffs came to an abrupt halt after the events of Sept. 11, causing San Jose and Lake Elsinore to be declared co-champions for the 2001 season. Despite the official wording, there was little debate over the best team in the league.

Loaded with top prospects like Dennis Tankersley, Jake Peavy and Xavier Nady, Lake Elsinore cruised to a minor league-best 91 victories in the regular season, 50 of those coming in the first half prior to the promotion of many of the Storm's top guns.

San Jose, winner of both halves in the Northern Division, did the majority of its damage with age and

LARRY GOREN

Jake Peavy

experience. Jeff Allen ranked among the league leaders in average (.305) and Tim Flaherty tied for the lead in homers (26), but both turned 25 during the season and had played more than 90 games at Double-A. Scoop McDowell led the league in triples with 11, but had played 361 games in three seasons in the California League. On the hill, Vance Cozier led the league with 15 wins, but he was in his second full season in the league after making 28 starts in 2000.

It was a far different story with Lake Elsinore, which relied on Nady, in his first professional season, and 19-year-old outfielder Ben Johnson to complement the best pitching staff in the league.

After losing three of their first four games to Rancho Cucamonga, the Storm didn't lose three in a row until the last three days in June. Over that span, Lake Elsinore put together four winning streaks of more than five games and lost back-to-back games twice.

San Bernardino entered the season as a back-to-back California League champion. After a slow start, the Stampede chased a third consecutive championship behind the league's second-best pitching staff and the aggressive nature of top prospects Chris Snelling and Jamal Strong.

But with Snelling, the league's batting champion, sidelined with a broken foot for the final two weeks of the season and the opening round of the playoffs, the Stampede fell to wild-card entrant High Desert.

Lake Elsinore had no such struggles with High Desert, sweeping the Mavericks in three games. Peavy pitched

the opener, allowing one run in six innings and striking out 10. Outfielder Vince Faison, ranked as the Padres' 13th-best prospect entering the season, was 4-for-5 with a game-ending homer in Game Two, as lefthander Eric Cyr struck out seven. Righthander Chris Rojas closed out High Desert with nine strikeouts in 6⅔ innings, as Nady provided the offensive punch with three hits, two runs and two RBIs.

While Lake Elsinore established itself as the best team on the field, it experienced tragedy off the field on July 29. Righthander Gerik Baxter, a former first-round pick who hadn't pitched during the season and was on a rehab assignment with the Storm after Tommy John surgery, died when his truck blew a tire and overturned on Interstate 10 outside Indo, Calif. Mark Hilde, a 32nd-round pick of the Athletics and former high school teammate of Baxter's, was also killed in the accident.

Also off the field, the Cal League attempted to stave off contraction of its own as Minor League Baseball offered Bakersfield and Mudville $3.9 million each for their franchises. The teams would then be moved to the Carolina League, but the plan never materialized.

Instead, the league purchased the Bakersfield club and will install a management team headed by Rancho Cucamonga owner Hank Stickney's Mandalay Sports Entertainment group. Stickney hoped to become involved more officially after discussions at baseball's Winter Meetings; current rules don't allow multiple-team ownership in the same league.

STANDINGS: SPLIT SEASON

FIRST HALF					SECOND HALF				
NORTH	**W**	**L**	**PCT**	**GB**	**NORTH**	**W**	**L**	**PCT**	**GB**
*San Jose	37	33	.529	—	San Jose	40	30	.517	—
Bakersfield	37	33	.529	—	Mudville	38	32	.543	2
Mudville	36	34	.514	1	Bakersfield	34	36	.486	6
Visalia	33	37	.471	4	Modesto	32	38	.457	8
Modesto	23	47	.329	14	Visalia	28	42	.400	12
SOUTH	**W**	**L**	**PCT**	**GB**	**SOUTH**	**W**	**L**	**PCT**	**GB**
Lake Elsinore	50	20	.714	—	San Bernardino	43	27	.614	—
High Desert	37	33	.529	13	Lake Elsinore	41	29	.586	2
Rancho Cuca.	35	35	.500	15	High Desert	34	36	.486	9
San Bernardino	33	37	.471	17	Lancaster	32	38	.457	11
Lancaster	29	41	.414	21	Rancho Cuca.	28	42	.400	15

*Won first meeting of second half, breaking first-half tie

PLAYOFFS—First Round: High Desert defeated San Bernardino 2-1 and Bakersfield defeated Mudville 2-1 in best-of-3 series. **Semifinals:** Lake Elsinore defeated High Desert 3-0 and San Jose led Bakersfield 2-1 in best-of-5 series. **Finals:** Series cancelled; Lake Elsinore and San Jose declared co-champions.

STANDINGS: OVERALL

Page		W	L	PCT	GB	Manager	Attendance (Avg.)	Last Penn.
228	Lake Elsinore Storm (Padres)	91	49	.650	—	Craig Colbert	223,712 (3,196)	2001
235	San Jose Giants (Giants)	77	63	.550	14	Lenn Sakata	145,225 (2,105)	2001
242	San Bernardino Stampede (Mariners)	76	64	.543	15	Daren Brown	151,832 (2,169)	2000
109	Mudville Nine (Reds)	74	66	.529	17	Dave Oliver	71,869 (1,073)	1992
165	High Desert Mavericks (Brewers)	71	69	.507	20	Frank Kremblas	143,361 (2,078)	1997
248	Bakersfield Blaze (Devil Rays)	71	69	.507	20	Charlie Montoyo	88,878 (1,288)	1989
60	Rancho Cucamonga Quakes (Angels)	63	77	.450	28	Tim Wallach	292,107 (4,173)	1994
201	Visalia Oaks (Athletics)	61	79	.436	30	Juan Navarrete	55,232 (812)	1978
67	Lancaster JetHawks (Diamondbacks)	61	79	.436	30	Scott Coolbaugh	173,621 (2,480)	None
200	Modesto A's (Athletics)	55	85	.393	36	Greg Sparks	141,337 (2,110)	1984

NOTE: Teams' individual batting and pitching statistics can be found on page indicated in lefthand column.

MINOR LEAGUES

2001 CALIFORNIA LEAGUE STATISTICS

CLUB BATTING

	AVG	G	AB	R	H	2B	3B	HR	BB	SO	SB
Lancaster	.281	140	4927	801	1385	269	51	145	511	1127	132
High Desert	.279	140	4887	837	1364	291	43	158	506	1267	211
Bakersfield	.273	140	4932	677	1344	292	31	96	348	1048	82
Lake Elsinore	.264	140	4806	683	1268	270	35	109	496	1167	124
San Jose	.262	140	4744	667	1245	258	38	89	462	1165	147
Visalia	.258	140	4813	763	1242	262	32	130	576	1215	160
Rancho Cucamonga	.257	140	4767	629	1226	256	47	88	379	1157	167
San Bernardino	.257	140	4895	689	1257	235	45	76	467	1112	137
Modesto	.254	140	4818	665	1225	233	38	90	554	1200	177
Mudville	.251	140	4755	623	1195	238	25	100	456	1066	102

CLUB PITCHING

	ERA	G	CG	SHO	SV	IP	H	R	ER	BB	SO
Lake Elsinore	3.03	140	1	13	44	1256	1069	534	423	427	1343
San Bernardino	3.45	140	2	12	36	1283	1133	598	492	487	1262
Mudville	3.60	140	3	9	38	1249	1204	618	500	548	1209
Bakersfield	4.04	140	1	9	41	1244	1268	668	559	471	1206
Modesto	4.24	140	1	5	23	1239	1313	721	584	447	1006
San Jose	4.32	140	1	7	40	1226	1233	686	588	460	954
Rancho Cucamonga	4.61	140	5	7	36	1239	1318	742	635	484	1110
Visalia	4.80	140	1	2	31	1233	1398	796	657	451	1133
Lancaster	4.95	140	3	6	26	1233	1423	827	678	463	1118
High Desert	5.26	140	1	4	30	1249	1392	844	731	517	1183

CLUB FIELDING

	PCT	PO	A	E	DP		PCT	PO	A	E	DP
San Jose	.971	3677	1459	153	117	Rancho Cuca.	.965	3716	1504	188	113
San Bernardino	.970	3849	1416	165	116	Visalia	.964	3698	1414	189	115
Bakersfield	.968	3733	1406	168	116	High Desert	.964	3748	1471	195	114
Lake Elsinore	.967	3767	1297	171	88	Lancaster	.960	3699	1429	213	130
Mudville	.966	3746	1353	178	106	Modesto	.960	3718	1488	218	97

INDIVIDUAL BATTING LEADERS
(Minimum 378 Plate Appearances)

	AVG	G	AB	R	H	2B	3B	HR	RBI	BB	SO	SB
Snelling, Chris, San Bernardino	.336	114	450	90	151	29	10	7	73	45	63	12
O'Keefe, Mike, Rancho Cuca.	.330	115	409	75	135	25	5	15	91	42	81	20
Diaz, Matt, Bakersfield	.328	131	524	79	172	40	2	17	81	24	73	11
Kaup, Nate, Bakersfield	.323	113	427	65	138	34	3	13	68	35	81	3
Strong, Jamal, San Bernardino	.311	81	331	74	103	11	2	0	32	51	60	47
Moore, Frank, Bakersfield	.307	129	505	75	155	29	6	7	60	25	106	9
Allen, Jeff, San Jose	.305	99	371	60	113	19	4	14	61	43	103	12
Gordon, Brian, Lancaster	.304	103	392	74	119	21	10	16	70	26	100	13
Hall, Bill, High Desert	.303	89	346	61	105	21	6	15	51	22	78	18
Nady, Xavier, Lake Elsinore	.302	137	524	96	158	38	1	26	100	62	109	6

INDIVIDUAL PITCHING LEADERS
(Minimum 112 Innings)

	W	L	ERA	G	GS	CG	SV	IP	H	R	ER	BB	SO
Anderson, Craig, San Bernardino	11	4	2.26	28	28	0	0	179	142	65	45	39	178
Gray, Brett, Mudville	10	4	2.42	29	18	0	0	141	133	48	38	37	110
Thornton, Matt, San Bernardino	14	7	2.52	27	27	0	0	157	126	56	44	60	192
Bazzell, Shane, Modesto	10	4	2.73	28	20	0	0	135	116	51	41	38	129
Rojas, Chris, Lake Elsinore	10	5	3.43	28	28	0	0	160	135	72	61	71	149
Walk, Mitch, San Jose	9	6	3.54	27	19	0	0	117	115	57	46	39	59
Cozier, Vance, San Jose	15	7	3.61	30	29	1	0	170	158	71	68	45	98
Cordova, Jorge, Mudville	9	8	3.72	30	25	0	0	155	157	81	64	67	132
Stokes, Brian, Bakersfield	8	6	3.92	32	20	1	1	129	118	65	56	64	92
Webb, Brandon, Lancaster	6	10	3.99	29	28	0	0	162	174	90	72	44	158
Wagner, Denny, Modesto	7	9	3.99	30	30	1	0	169	181	101	75	59	127

ALL-STAR TEAM

C—Lance Burkhart, High Desert. **1B**—Xavier Nady, Lake Elsinore. **2B**—Matt Kata, Lancaster. **3B**—Billy Martin, Lancaster. **SS**—Bill Hall, High Desert. **OF**—Matt Diaz, Bakersfield; Chris Snelling, San Bernardino; Jamal Strong, San Bernardino. **DH**—Nate Kaup, Bakersfield. **P**—Craig Anderson, San Bernardino; Luke Anderson, San Jose; Rafael Soriano, San Bernardino; Dennis Tankersley, Lake Elsinore; Matt Thornton, San Bernardino.

Most Valuable Player: Xavier Nady, Lake Elsinore. **Pitcher of the Year**: Matt Thornton, San Bernardino. **Rookie of the Year**: Xavier Nady, Lake Elsinore. **Manager of the Year**: Craig Colbert, Lake Elsinore.

BATTING

G	Steve Scarborough, High Desert	...	138
AB	Steve Scarborough, High Desert	...	546
R	Steve Scarborough, High Desert	...	101
H	Matt Diaz, Bakersfield	...	172
TB	Xavier Nady, Lake Elsinore	...	276
XBH	Xavier Nady, Lake Elsinore	...	65
2B	Marshall McDougall, Visalia	...	43
3B	Arturo McDowell, San Jose	...	11
HR	Three tied at	...	26
RBI	Billy Martin, Lancaster	...	106
SH	Carlos Gastelum, Rancho Cuca.	...	23
SF	Bill Scott, High Desert	...	9
BB	Billy Martin, Lancaster	...	95
IBB	Eric Welsh, Mudville	...	8
HBP	Jesus Basabe, Modesto	...	27
SO	Tim Flaherty, San Jose	...	162
SB	Carlos Rosario, Visalia	...	54
CS	Carlos Rosario, Visalia	...	24
GIDP	Ryan Christianson, San Bern.	...	17
OB%	Billy Martin, Lancaster	...	.420
SL%	Billy Martin, Lancaster	...	.551

PITCHING

G	Andy Shibilo, Lake Elsinore	...	60
GS	Denny Wagner, Modesto	...	30
CG	Rafael Soriano, San Bernardino	...	2
ShO	Six tied at	...	1
GF	Luke Anderson, San Jose	...	56
SV	Luke Anderson, San Jose	...	30
W	Vance Cozier, San Jose	...	15
L	Mark Gwyn, Modesto	...	13
IP	Craig Anderson, San Bernardino	...	179
H	Doug Slaten, Lancaster	...	207
R	Paul Stewart, High Desert	...	106
ER	Phil Wilson, Rancho Cuca.	...	93
HR	Paul Stewart, High Desert	...	23
HB	Brandon Webb, Lancaster	...	27
BB	Chris Rojas, Lake Elsinore	...	71
SO	Matt Thornton, San Bernardino	...	192
WP	Phil Wilson, Rancho Cuca.	...	19
BK	Doug Slaten, Lancaster	...	5

FIELDING

C	AVG	Ryan Christianson, San Bern.		.993
	PO	Ryan Christianson, San Bern.		993
	A	Dane Sardinha, Mudville	...	89
	E	Kade Johnson, High Desert	...	17
	DP	Danny Massiatte, Bakersfield	...	10
	PB	J.D. Closser, Lancaster	...	18
1B	AVG	Xavier Nady, Lake Elsinore	...	.989
	PO	Shawn McCorkle, San Bern.		1168
	A	Jeff Wanger, Rancho Cuca.	...	70
	E	Shawn McCorkle, San Bern.	...	17
	DP	Shawn McCorkle, San Bern.	...	105
2B	AVG	Carlos Gastelum, R. Cuca.	...	.982
	PO	Matt Kata, Lancaster	...	245
	A	Carlos Gastelum, R. Cuca.	...	330
	E	Matt Kata, Lancaster	...	25
	DP	Matt Kata, Lancaster	...	75
3B	AVG	Justin Leone, San Bern.	...	.928
	PO	Justin Leone, San Bern.	...	97
	A	Justin Leone, San Bern.	...	240
	E	Matt Howe, Modesto	...	28
	DP	Justin Leone, San Bern.	...	25
SS	AVG	Nestor Perez, Bakersfield	...	.967
	PO	Ranier Olmedo, Mudville	...	186
	A	Jhonny Carvajal, San Jose	...	350
	E	Ranier Olmedo, Mudville	...	40
	DP	Ranier Olmedo, Mudville	...	65
		Nestor Perez, Bakersfield	...	65
OF	AVG	Scott Daeley, San Jose	...	.984
	PO	Fernando Rios, Mudville	...	239
	A	Matt Diaz, Bakersfield	...	17
	E	Vince Faison, Lake Elsinore	...	12
		Ben Johnson, Lake Elsinore	...	12
	DP	Matt Diaz, Bakersfield	...	5

CAROLINA LEAGUE

BY DAVE UTNIK

Carolina League owners and general managers approved the addition of wild-card teams to the 2001 playoff format, believing it would add some drama to end-of-the-season pennant races. The wild card resulted in much more than drama—it also created history.

The Salem Avalanche, a distant runner-up in the Southern Division race during the regular season, became the first wild-card team to capture the Mills Cup championship when it defeated Northern Division champion Wilmington 6-4 in the deciding game of the best-of-five series. Salem had been soundly beaten in both halves of the CL's split-season schedule by Kinston. Wilmington also won both halves in the North.

Victor Martinez

Despite its expanded playoff, the Carolina League was the only full-season league in Minor League Baseball to complete its playoffs before the terrorist tragedy of Sept. 11 forced cancellation of all remaining playoff games throughout the minors.

Though the decision to expand the playoffs proved unpopular with some of the baseball purists within the league, the wild card accomplished its purpose even as it altered history.

"Even without the wild card the North would have been exciting, but in the South it meant more teams were in contention," Carolina League president John Hopkins said. "Salem wouldn't have gotten in without it."

The wild card added a new wrinkle to the Carolina League's split-season, two-division alignment for the first time in 21 years. It took some time to convince a majority of league owners to eliminate the bye format that had applied since two-division play began in 1980. But with the new system, both playoff races went to the wire.

"As a league, when we make decisions we are usually unified, but we weren't that way with this issue," Hopkins said. "It was among the most divided questions we've had come before us. We wrestled with it. The deciding factor was we wanted two rounds of playoffs every year."

Kinston, which had the league's best overall record at 89-51, was the first pennant winner affected by the change. The K-Tribe, led by league batting champion and MVP Victor Martinez and the league's best pitching staff, won both halves of the Southern Division pennant.

Under the old playoff system, the Indians would have

earned an automatic berth into the championship series. In 2001, however, the K-Tribe played second-half runner-up Salem in a best-of-three series.

The Avalanche edged the defending league champion Myrtle Beach Pelicans in a wild-card race that went down to the final week, and then upset Kinston two games to one. The Northern Division went to the wire as well. The Frederick Keys held off a challenge by the Potomac Cannons to clinch a wild-card berth in the North, but Wilmington—the pennant winner in each half—swept the Keys in the best-of-three division series.

Wilmington, one of the league's most successful franchises since its inception in 1993, nearly won its fifth championship. Wilmington forced a fifth and deciding game in the finals, but the Avalanche—behind a pair of homers from series MVP John Lindsey and solo homers from Seth Taylor and Dan Phillips—defeated Blue Rocks ace Jimmy Gobble in Game Five.

Avalanche righthander Ryan Price, who set a league record with 45 wild pitches, earned the team's two most important victories of the summer—the deciding game of the Southern Division series at Kinston and the championship clincher against Wilmington.

Price's postseason heroics exemplified a summer filled with outstanding individual performances. Kinston's Martinez hit for the cycle July 7 against Salem; Potomac's all-star left fielder, Covelli Crisp, had a league-high 162 hits; and Frederick's Doug Gredvig hit a league-best 20 homers. Lynchburg Hillcats outfielder Justin Martin got six hits in a May 19 game against Winston-Salem. Potomac's Jimmy Journell and Trey Hodges of Myrtle Beach shared pitcher-of-the-year honors. Journell went 14-6, 2.50, led the league in ERA and went 42⅓ innings without allowing an earned run—the longest streak in the minors in 2001. Hodges had the CL's most wins, going 15-8, 2.76, and was third in ERA.

STANDINGS: SPLIT SEASON

FIRST HALF					SECOND HALF				
NORTH	**W**	**L**	**PCT**	**GB**	**NORTH**	**W**	**L**	**PCT**	**GB**
Wilmington	39	31	.557	—	Wilmington	39	31	.557	—
Frederick	36	34	.514	3	Frederick	34	35	.493	4½
Potomac	35	35	.500	4	Potomac	31	39	.443	8
Lynchburg	27	40	.403	10½	Lynchburg	31	39	.443	8
SOUTH	**W**	**L**	**PCT**	**GB**	**SOUTH**	**W**	**L**	**PCT**	**GB**
Kinston	44	26	.629	—	Kinston	45	25	.643	—
Myrtle Beach	39	30	.565	4½	Salem	37	33	.529	8
Salem	33	35	.485	10	Myrtle Beach	32	37	.464	12½
Winston-Salem	24	46	.343	20	Winston-Salem	30	40	.429	15

PLAYOFFS—Semifinals: Wilmington defeated Frederick 2-0 and Salem defeated Kinston 2-1 in best-of-3 series. **Final:** Salem defeated Wilmington 3-2 in best-of-5 series.

STANDINGS: OVERALL

Page		W	L	PCT	GB	Manager	Attendance (Avg.)	Last Penn.
116	Kinston Indians (Indians)	89	51	.636	—	Brad Komminsk	133,169 (1,930)	1995
151	Wilmington Blue Rocks (Royals)	78	62	.557	11	Jeff Garber	336,074 (5,016)	1999
74	Myrtle Beach Pelicans (Braves)	71	67	.514	17	Brian Snitker	214,160 (3,196)	2000
124	Salem Avalanche (Rockies)	70	68	.507	18	Dave Collins	203,375 (3,035)	2001
81	Frederick Keys (Orioles)	70	69	.504	18½	Dave Cash	320,262 (4,710)	1990
221	Potomac Cannons (Cardinals)	66	74	.471	23	Joe Cunningham	181,758 (2,754)	1989
214	Lynchburg Hillcats (Pirates)	58	79	.423	29½	Curtis Wilkerson	112,310 (1,728)	1997
95	Winston-Salem Warthogs (White Sox)	54	86	.386	35	Wally Backman	141,164 (2,139)	1993

NOTE: Teams' individual batting and pitching statistics can be found on page indicated in lefthand column.

2001 CAROLINA LEAGUE STATISTICS

CLUB BATTING

	AVG	G	AB	R	H	2B	3B	HR	BB	SO	SB
Kinston	.252	140	4694	629	1182	233	34	92	460	1066	131
Potomac	.251	140	4619	532	1160	229	22	74	326	1003	127
Wilmington	.251	140	4583	610	1149	204	25	64	521	1091	110
Frederick	.249	139	4597	538	1146	209	16	84	348	964	134
Salem	.248	138	4540	558	1124	257	24	96	405	961	88
Lynchburg	.244	137	4542	538	1110	208	25	67	382	1144	123
Winston-Salem	.241	140	4658	507	1122	226	19	61	389	987	147
Myrtle Beach	.241	138	4499	553	1083	221	14	95	422	1147	97

CLUB PITCHING

	ERA	G	CG	SHO	SV	IP	H	R	ER	BB	SO
Kinston	2.73	140	6	17	46	1251	1073	461	380	390	1260
Frederick	3.21	139	8	10	40	1220	1127	526	435	372	1137
Potomac	3.26	140	8	12	38	1207	1128	566	437	348	909
Wilmington	3.27	140	2	13	35	1235	1115	537	449	379	1052
Myrtle Beach	3.36	138	4	16	39	1206	1086	526	450	347	1102
Winston-Salem	3.66	140	10	7	27	1244	1191	611	506	532	1022
Salem	3.77	138	3	12	44	1198	1165	607	502	458	985
Lynchburg	3.87	137	8	9	37	1192	1191	631	513	427	896

CLUB FIELDING

	PCT	PO	A	E	DP		PCT	PO	A	E	DP
Myrtle Beach	.972	3617	1381	144	102	Win.-Salem	.967	3731	1590	180	141
Wilmington	.971	3706	1408	154	109	Salem	.967	3594	1631	177	154
Frederick	.970	3660	1385	157	99	Lynchburg	.965	3576	1494	183	130
Kinston	.968	3754	1480	175	103	Potomac	.965	3621	1580	190	151

INDIVIDUAL BATTING LEADERS
(Minimum 378 Plate Appearances)

	AVG	G	AB	R	H	2B	3B	HR	RBI	BB	SO	SB
Martinez, Victor, Kinston	.329	114	420	59	138	33	2	10	57	39	60	3
Atkins, Garrett, Salem	.325	135	465	70	151	43	5	5	67	74	98	6
Crisp, Covelli, Potomac	.306	139	530	80	162	23	3	11	47	52	64	39
Haynes, Dee, Potomac	.290	114	417	45	121	24	3	13	72	14	82	5
Paulino, Ron, Lynchburg	.290	103	352	30	102	16	1	6	51	36	76	4
Langerhans, Ryan, Myrtle Beach	.287	125	450	66	129	30	3	7	48	55	104	22
Calzado, Napolean, Frederick	.287	121	464	50	133	20	2	5	41	16	52	34
Colina, Javier, Salem	.285	113	439	67	125	33	7	9	58	22	61	9
Cunningham, Marco, Wilmington	.284	138	497	82	141	22	4	4	61	95	119	17
Fiore, Curt, Myrtle Beach	.283	100	329	56	93	20	2	6	42	47	69	5

INDIVIDUAL PITCHING LEADERS
(Minimum 112 Innings)

	W	L	ERA	G	GS	CG	SV	IP	H	R	ER	BB	SO
Journell, Jim, Potomac	14	6	2.50	26	26	0	0	151	121	54	42	42	156
Gobble, Jimmy, Wilmington	10	6	2.55	27	27	0	0	162	134	58	46	33	154
Hodges, Trey, Myrtle Beach	15	8	2.76	26	26	1	0	173	156	64	53	41	146
Bong, Jung, Myrtle Beach	13	9	3.00	28	28	0	0	168	151	67	56	47	145
Tallet, Brian, Kinston	9	7	3.04	27	27	2	0	160	134	62	54	38	164
Lantigua, Eduardo, Win.-Salem	8	6	3.06	22	19	1	0	121	92	46	41	58	113
Cook, Aaron, Salem	11	11	3.08	27	27	0	0	155	157	73	53	38	122
Vance, Cory, Salem	10	8	3.10	26	26	1	0	154	129	65	53	65	142
Garcia, Sonny, Frederick	8	9	3.27	25	20	2	1	143	132	67	52	33	139
Natale, Mike, Wilmington	9	8	3.28	28	27	0	0	159	152	75	58	33	134

ALL-STAR TEAM

C—Victor Martinez, Kinston. **1B**—Garrett Atkins, Salem. **2B**—Javier Colina, Salem. **3B**—Troy Cameron, Myrtle Beach/Kinston. **SS**—Wilson Betemit, Myrtle Beach; Napolean Calzado, Frederick. **OF**—Covelli Crisp, Potomac; Ryan Langerhans, Myrtle Beach; Dan Phillips, Salem. **DH**—Ryan Hankins, Winston-Salem. **Util**—Dee Haynes, Potomac. **SP**—Jim Journell, Potomac. **RP**—Scotty Layfield, Potomac.

Most Valuable Player: Victor Martinez, Kinston. **Pitchers of the Year**: Trey Hodges, Myrtle Beach; Jim Journell, Potomac. **Manager of the Year**: Brad Komminsk, Kinston.

DEPARTMENT LEADERS

BATTING
G	Covelli Crisp, Potomac	139
AB	Covelli Crisp, Potomac	530
R	Marco Cunningham, Wilmington	82
H	Covelli Crisp, Potomac	162
TB	Covelli Crisp, Potomac	224
XBH	Doug Gredvig, Frederick	57
2B	Garrett Atkins, Salem	43
3B	Jose Castillo, Lynchburg	7
	Javier Colina, Salem	7
HR	Doug Gredvig, Frederick	20
RBI	Troy Cameron, M.B./Kinston	76
SH	Eric Nelson, Wilmington	16
SF	Javier Colina, Salem	12
BB	Marco Cunningham, Wilmington	95
IBB	Garrett Atkins, Salem	10
HBP	Marco Cunningham, Wilmington	19
	Curt Fiore, Myrtle Beach	19
SO	Donovan Ross, Wilmington	159
SB	Chad Durham, Winston-Salem	50
CS	Chad Durham, Winston-Salem	22
GIDP	Three tied at	15
OB%	Garrett Atkins, Salem	.421
SL%	Victor Martinez, Kinston	.488

PITCHING
G	Brian Jackson, Kinston	53
GS	Jung Bong, Myrtle Beach	28
	Brian West, Winston-Salem	28
CG	Dennis Ulacia, Winston-Salem	4
ShO	Twelve tied at	1
GF	Brian Jackson, Kinston	47
SV	Scotty Layfield, Potomac	31
W	Trey Hodges, Myrtle Beach	15
L	Franklin Tejeda, Potomac	14
IP	Trey Hodges, Myrtle Beach	173
H	Ryan Ledden, Lynchburg	184
R	Ryan Ledden, Lynchburg	112
ER	Ryan Ledden, Lynchburg	92
HR	Ryan Ledden, Lynchburg	18
HB	Matt Burch, Wilmington	21
BB	Ryan Price, Salem	85
SO	Brian Tallet, Kinston	164
WP	Ryan Price, Salem	45
BK	Andy Bent, Myrtle Beach	4
	Cory Vance, Salem	4

FIELDING
C	AVG	Ron Paulino, Lynchburg	.994
	PO	Victor Martinez, Kinston	967
	A	Octavio Martinez, Frederick	106
	E	Victor Martinez, Kinston	16
	DP	Jeff Winchester, Salem	11
	PB	Ron Paulino, Lynchburg	20
1B	AVG	Garrett Atkins, Salem	.995
	PO	Garrett Atkins, Salem	1200
	A	Donovan Ross, Wilmington	79
	E	Donovan Ross, Wilmington	13
	DP	Garrett Atkins, Salem	125
2B	AVG	Tommy Nicholson, Win.-Salem	.978
	PO	Tommy Nicholson, Win.-Salem	275
	A	Javier Colina, Salem	366
	E	Javier Colina, Salem	23
	DP	Javier Colina, Salem	94
3B	AVG	Troy Cameron, M.B./Kinston	.938
	PO	Napolean Calzado, Frederick	97
	A	Troy Cameron, M.B./Kinston	258
	E	Three tied at	25
	DP	Troy Cameron, M.B./Kinston	21
SS	AVG	Johnny Peralta, Kinston	.952
	PO	Jose Castillo, Lynchburg	220
	A	Ramon Carvajal, Potomac	428
	E	Ramon Carvajal, Potomac	48
	DP	Jose Castillo, Lynchburg	85
OF	AVG	B.J. Barns, Lynchburg	.990
	PO	Jeremy Harts, Lynchburg	260
	A	Chad Durham, Win.-Salem	16
		Jeremy Harts, Lynchburg	16
	E	Jeremy Harts, Lynchburg	14
	DP	Chad Durham, Win.-Salem	5

FLORIDA STATE LEAGUE

BY SEAN KERNAN

For the first time on record since the Florida State League was founded in 1919, the league had to name co-champions after the 2001 playoffs were halted for a variety of reasons, none bigger than the terrorist attacks that stunned the nation Sept. 11.

The Brevard County Manatees and Tampa Yankees were tied at one win each in the best-of-five championship series. The league postponed play that day and the next before canceling the series. FSL president Chuck Murphy cited additional factors, including an approaching tropical storm that would have prevented play from continuing for at least two days, and a requirement that playoffs conclude within 12 days of the regular season's end.

ROBERT GURGANUS

Nick Regilio

The Manatees won the FSL East in the second half and defeated the first-half champion Vero Beach Dodgers in the first round of the playoffs. The Yankees, second-half winners in the West, turned back the Charlotte Rangers in the best-of-3 playoff. Brevard County was credited with its first FSL title in its seven-year history, while the Yankees collected their sixth championship in 39 seasons.

Clearly the top prospect in the league was Manatees righthander Josh Beckett, who by the time the Manatees were in the playoffs had already pitched in the majors. The 21-year-old phenom headed the list of players on the FSL's postseason all-star team despite a midseason callup to Double-A Portland. Beckett, the Marlins' first draft pick in 1999 and the second player taken overall, has drawn comparisons to other hard-throwing pitchers from Texas. One of them is Kerry Wood, who pitched in the FSL in 1996 for the Daytona Cubs.

"Josh Beckett is probably the closest I've seen to the second coming of Kerry Wood coming through this league," said Daytona manager Dave Trembley, who has managed Wood on three different teams. "Beckett's very polished. He really has an idea of how to set up hitters. He knows he's in control. Those kinds of guys don't come along that often."

Beckett dominated FSL hitters. The only thing that held up his promotion to the Eastern League was the wait for warmer weather as a precautionary measure. He had missed most of 2000 with injuries.

"I've never taken anything for granted, and last year was tough," Beckett said. "To make two starts and then have to sit out—come back and have to sit out again—it was so hard. That's why I say I just thank God I'm healthy again."

Charlotte's Nick Regilio threw just the second perfect game in the last 26 years in the FSL when he stymied the Jupiter Hammerheads on June 10 in a 3-0 win at Roger Dean Stadium. The righthander struck out nine and coaxed 13 groundouts.

"It was one of those days when everything just clicked," Regilio said. "At the end I was just trying to pitch my game and stay calm. After the game I was shaking so hard I couldn't even sign autographs."

Two FSL managers joined the exclusive 1,000 career wins club during the season. Dave Huppert, skipper of the co-champion Manatees, and Trembley, who also has an FSL championship from 1995 on his resume, topped 1,000 within a month of each other.

Individually, St. Lucie's Marvin Seale hit for the cycle June 7 against Sarasota. Earlier in the year, Sarasota's Jesus Feliciano torched St. Lucie for six hits in a game.

STANDINGS: SPLIT SEASON

FIRST HALF

EAST
	W	L	PCT	GB
Vero Beach	40	28	.588	—
Brevard	39	29	.573	1
Lakeland	38	29	.567	1½
Daytona	37	30	.552	2½
St. Lucie	32	36	.471	8
Jupiter	29	38	.433	10½

WEST
	W	L	PCT	GB
Charlotte	35	33	.515	—
Dunedin	33	34	.493	1½
Clearwater	32	35	.478	2½
Fort Myers	32	36	.471	3
Tampa	29	38	.433	5½
Sarasota	29	39	.426	6

SECOND HALF

EAST
	W	L	PCT	GB
Brevard	41	26	.612	—
Jupiter	41	31	.569	2½
Daytona	31	38	.449	11
St. Lucie	31	40	.437	12
Lakeland	29	40	.420	13
Vero Beach	27	38	.415	13

WEST
	W	L	PCT	GB
Tampa	48	24	.667	—
Dunedin	38	30	.557	8
Fort Myers	36	33	.522	10½
Clearwater	36	34	.514	11
Charlotte	32	37	.464	14½
Sarasota	25	44	.362	21½

PLAYOFFS—Semifinals: Brevard County defeated Vero Beach 2-1 and Tampa defeated Charlotte 2-0 in best-of-3 series. **Finals:** Series cancelled; Brevard County and Tampa declared co-champions. Brevard County and Tampa were tied 1-1 in best-of-5 series.

STANDINGS: OVERALL

Page		W	L	PCT	GB	Manager	Attendance (Avg.)	Last Penn.
138	Brevard County Manatees (Marlins)	80	55	.593	—	Dave Huppert	118,307 (2,151)	2001
185	Tampa Yankees (Yankees)	77	62	.554	5	Brian Butterfield	102,998 (1,635)	2001
262	Dunedin Blue Jays (Blue Jays)	71	64	.526	9	Marty Peavy	47,514 (713)	None
158	Vero Beach Dodgers (Dodgers)	67	66	.504	12	Bob Mariano	49,177 (757)	1990
178	Jupiter Hammerheads (Expos)	70	69	.504	12	Tim Leiper	114,301 (1,657)	1991
102	Daytona Cubs (Cubs)	68	68	.500	12½	Dave Trembley	105,606 (1,790)	2000
171	Fort Myers Miracle (Twins)	68	69	.496	13	Jose Marzan	98,514 (1,470)	1985
207	Clearwater Phillies (Phillies)	68	69	.496	13	Ramon Aviles	76,406 (1,213)	1993
131	Lakeland Tigers (Tigers)	67	69	.493	13½	Kevin Bradshaw	21,280 (355)	1992
255	Charlotte Rangers (Rangers)	67	70	.489	14	Darryl Kennedy	31,312 (467)	1989
193	St. Lucie Mets (Mets)	63	76	.453	19	Tony Tijerina	67,141 (1,033)	1998
88	Sarasota Red Sox (Red Sox)	54	83	.394	27	Ron Johnson	51,125 (799)	1963

NOTE: Teams' individual batting and pitching statistics can be found on page indicated in lefthand column.

MINOR LEAGUES

2001 FLORIDA STATE LEAGUE STATISTICS

CLUB BATTING

	AVG	G	AB	R	H	2B	3B	HR	BB	SO	SB
Brevard County	.265	135	4469	677	1186	213	25	86	520	899	158
Dunedin	.265	135	4613	701	1224	232	33	71	494	1030	136
Clearwater	.256	137	4506	618	1152	230	33	81	447	923	189
Lakeland	.255	136	4506	625	1150	233	36	70	499	935	154
Daytona	.255	136	4455	604	1134	211	21	97	471	915	112
Vero Beach	.254	133	4336	517	1101	192	21	63	450	804	94
Fort Myers	.250	137	4602	614	1151	193	24	57	529	890	111
St. Lucie	.249	139	4473	590	1116	222	28	83	443	1016	191
Jupiter	.249	139	4535	578	1129	201	40	43	472	952	162
Charlotte	.247	137	4544	529	1123	219	38	62	401	910	97
Sarasota	.245	137	4576	550	1121	222	26	91	463	1039	101
Tampa	.244	139	4439	634	1083	233	40	112	555	1038	95

CLUB PITCHING

	ERA	G	CG	SHO	SV	IP	H	R	ER	BB	SO
Tampa	3.17	139	7	11	44	1194	1097	539	421	431	1132
Jupiter	3.21	139	4	13	37	1207	1131	551	431	406	875
Charlotte	3.37	137	5	9	41	1203	1050	566	451	491	986
Brevard County	3.43	135	4	14	38	1163	1119	579	443	438	828
Fort Myers	3.60	137	1	6	31	1212	1151	605	484	529	951
Vero Beach	3.69	133	5	9	42	1160	1070	557	476	504	1060
St. Lucie	3.75	139	5	5	27	1183	1132	594	493	468	895
Clearwater	3.81	137	9	6	38	1185	1160	601	502	513	931
Daytona	3.82	136	4	10	33	1167	1120	601	495	471	1020
Lakeland	3.92	136	6	9	41	1178	1158	607	514	521	847
Sarasota	4.13	137	2	5	26	1201	1242	701	551	443	990
Dunedin	4.66	135	5	4	35	1177	1240	736	610	529	836

CLUB FIELDING

	PCT	PO	A	E	DP		PCT	PO	A	E	DP
Clearwater	.973	3554	1451	139	133	Brevard	.967	3489	1423	167	134
Vero Beach	.972	3481	1516	136	86	Daytona	.967	3501	1306	165	86
Fort Myers	.972	3635	1596	151	150	Jupiter	.966	3620	1272	172	99
Lakeland	.971	3535	1473	150	119	Tampa	.965	3581	1440	180	105
Charlotte	.970	3610	1452	157	130	Dunedin	.965	3532	1466	180	133
St. Lucie	.970	3548	1548	159	125	Sarasota	.958	3603	1350	216	105

INDIVIDUAL BATTING LEADERS
(Minimum 378 Plate Appearances)

	AVG	G	AB	R	H	2B	3B	HR	RBI	BB	SO	SB
Watson, Matt, Jupiter	.330	124	446	70	147	33	4	5	74	63	45	17
Thompson, Rich, Dunedin	.311	112	454	90	141	14	6	1	60	44	72	39
Chapman, Travis, Clearwater	.307	96	329	39	101	22	0	4	50	44	39	3
Matthews, Lamont, Vero Beach	.307	107	349	61	107	26	3	10	57	95	106	1
Fagan, Shawn, Dunedin	.301	132	475	68	143	18	5	10	71	86	114	7
Vento, Mike, Tampa	.300	130	457	71	137	20	10	20	87	45	88	13
Roneberg, Brett, Brevard County	.299	88	331	49	99	20	4	11	63	50	54	5
Jackson, Nic, Daytona	.296	131	503	87	149	30	6	19	85	39	96	24
Padgett, Matt, Brevard County	.293	125	440	68	129	37	2	8	81	64	101	10
Deschaine, Jim, Daytona	.289	134	485	68	140	26	2	21	82	62	103	6

INDIVIDUAL PITCHING LEADERS
(Minimum 112 Innings)

	W	L	ERA	G	GS	CG	SV	IP	H	R	ER	BB	SO
Asencio, Miguel, Clearwater	12	5	2.84	28	21	2	0	155	124	62	49	70	123
Freed, Mark, Daytona	6	8	3.12	23	22	1	0	130	120	54	45	51	90
Rodriguez, Ricardo, Vero Beach	14	6	3.21	26	26	2	0	154	133	67	55	60	154
Sneed, John, Fort Myers	8	3	3.24	25	19	0	0	114	95	51	41	49	88
Sergent, Joe, Brevard County	12	6	3.33	27	25	0	0	143	154	70	53	32	89
Hannah, Shawn, Lakeland	7	5	3.35	34	17	0	0	129	128	63	48	54	55
Martinez, Anastacio, Sarasota	9	12	3.35	25	24	1	0	145	130	69	54	39	123
Dittfurth, Ryan, Charlotte	9	6	3.48	27	24	2	0	147	123	66	57	66	134
Klepacki, Ed, Jupiter	9	9	3.50	26	26	1	0	136	135	69	53	49	74
Marsonek, Sam, Tampa	8	8	3.51	24	23	5	0	138	128	67	54	39	120

ALL-STAR TEAM

C—Kevin Cash, Dunedin; Max St. Pierre, Lakeland. **1B**—Jason Jones, Charlotte. **2B**—Chase Utley, Clearwater. **3B**—Travis Chapman, Clearwater. **SS**—Jim Deschaine, Daytona. **OF**—Nic Jackson, Daytona; Mike Vento, Tampa; Matt Watson, Jupiter. **DH**—Mitch Jones, Tampa. **Util**—Nick Alvarez, Vero Beach; Rich Thompson, Dunedin. **RHP**—Miguel Ascencio, Clearwater; Josh Beckett, Brevard County; Ricardo Rodriguez, Vero Beach. **LHP**—Andy Van Hekken, Lakeland. **RHR**—Greg Runser, Charlotte. **LHR**—Anthony Ferrari, Jupiter.

Most Valuable Player: Mike Vento, Tampa. **Most Valuable Pitcher**: Ricardo Rodriguez, Vero Beach. **Manager of the Year**: Dave Huppert, Brevard County.

DEPARTMENT LEADERS

BATTING

G	Mitch Jones, Tampa	137
AB	Ramon Martinez, Charlotte	515
R	Jesus Medrano, Brevard County	93
H	Nic Jackson, Daytona	149
TB	Nic Jackson, Daytona	248
XBH	Mitch Jones, Tampa	60
2B	Matt Padgett, Brevard County	37
3B	Mike Vento, Tampa	10
HR	Three tied at	21
RBI	Mike Vento, Tampa	87
SH	Three tied at	14
SF	Andy Phillips, Tampa	10
BB	Lamont Matthews, Vero Beach	95
IBB	Hank Blalock, Charlotte	7
HBP	Nick Alvarez, Vero Beach	17
SO	Carlos Rodriguez, Sarasota	144
SB	Jesus Medrano, Brevard County	61
CS	Ramon Martinez, Charlotte	18
	Marvin Seale, St. Lucie	18
GIDP	Carlos Rodriguez, Sarasota	21
OB%	Lamont Matthews, Vero Beach	.458
SL%	Mike Vento, Tampa	.519

PITCHING

G	Greg Watson, Lakeland	57
GS	Edwin Moreno, Charlotte	28
CG	Sam Marsonek, Tampa	5
ShO	Three tied at	2
GF	Juan Padilla, Fort Myers	49
SV	Greg Runser, Charlotte	30
W	Ricardo Rodriguez, Vero Beach	14
L	Four tied at	12
IP	Martire Franco, Clearwater	161
H	Martire Franco, Clearwater	178
R	Aaron Dean, Dunedin	113
ER	Aaron Dean, Dunedin	97
HR	Frank Brooks, Clearwater	18
HB	Sam Marsonek, Tampa	21
BB	Calvin Chipperfield, Lakeland	81
SO	Ricardo Rodriguez, Vero Beach	154
WP	Ricardo Rodriguez, Vero Beach	18
BK	Byeong An, Sarasota	5

FIELDING

C	AVG	David Parrish, Tampa	.992
	PO	David Parrish, Tampa	812
	A	David Parrish, Tampa	89
	E	Kevin Cash, Dunedin	12
	DP	Three tied at	7
	PB	David Parrish, Tampa	34
1B	AVG	Mike Dzurilla, Daytona	.996
	PO	Pat Burns, St. Lucie	1148
	A	Nate Espy, Clearwater	90
	E	Pat Burns, St. Lucie	19
	DP	Nate Espy, Clearwater	101
2B	AVG	Josh McKinley, Jupiter	.975
	PO	Josh McKinley, Jupiter	255
	A	Brian Shipp, St. Lucie	327
	E	Pat Santoro, Sarasota	18
	DP	Brian Shipp, St. Lucie	79
3B	AVG	Matt Scanlon, Fort Myers	.925
	PO	Jose Santos, Brevard County	78
	A	Jose Santos, Brevard County	258
	E	Shawn Fagan, Dunedin	35
	DP	Shawn Fagan, Dunedin	25
SS	AVG	Rayner Bautista, Lakeland	.959
	PO	Chris Basak, St. Lucie	177
	A	Chris Basak, St. Lucie	392
	E	Jimmy Alvarez, Dunedin	36
	DP	Chris Basak, St. Lucie	76
OF	AVG	Jesus Feliciano, Vero Beach	1.000
	PO	Corey Richardson, Lakeland	321
	A	Cody Ross, Lakeland	23
	E	Carlos Rodriguez, Sarasota	12
		Mike Vento, Tampa	12
	DP	Douglas Garcia, Charlotte	4

MIDWEST LEAGUE

BY JOE BUSH

The Midwest League had its share of storylines in 2001. It dealt with one of the obstacles of its location, had its best regular season team finish on top in the play-offs, said goodbye to two of its stadiums, welcomed pro baseball's only female umpire, had another umpire resign amid evidence of biased calls, had its one-day attendance mark broken and its championship series shortened by the terrorist attacks of Sept. 11.

The first half of the season was dominated by two stories: the Kane County Cougars' explosive offense and the flooding and shutdown of Quad City's home, John O'Donnell Stadium.

ROBERT GURGANUS

Adrian Gonzalez

Kane County, led by three premium 2000 draftees—top overall pick Adrian Gonzalez, sixth-rounder Will Smith and fifth-rounder Jim Kavourias—and 1998 first-rounder Chip Ambres, won a first-half Western Division crown with a runaway offense that fueled a .691 winning percentage. It was the first postseason berth earned in the first half by the 11th-year franchise.

In mid-April, the Mississippi River exceeded its banks enough that even a sandbag wall couldn't keep its waters out of JOD. Not only did Quad City have to play its home games at a nearby junior college or, after Minor League Baseball mandated it, other MWL venues, most of its staff was fired as ownership looked into moving the team.

Through it all, the River Bandits—led by 1999 third-rounder Justin Morneau and corner infielder Terry Tiffee—challenged Kane County for the Western Division title. They got their home field back in early July after earning a first-half wild-card berth, while the franchise was sold to an entity in Eastlake, Ohio, where it will begin play in 2003. "If it has (been a distraction), they haven't shown it," Quad City manager Jeff Carter said of his players.

Umpire Ria Cortesio, a native of the Quad City area, earned a promotion from the Pioneer League and a post-season assignment. Another MWL ump, Erik Stahlbusch, resigned on Aug. 24, following an encounter with Cedar Rapids manager Tyrone Boykin.

Cedar Rapids played its last game in Memorial Stadium, while Peoria did likewise at Vonachen Stadium. The Kernels will play in a new stadium in 2002, while Peoria bid adieu to Vonachen Stadium after winning a legal battle to build a downtown ballpark.

Kane County's Kavourias began the on-field highlights May 9 against Peoria when he hit for the cycle. Dayton outfielder Wily Mo Pena slugged three homers in a game against Cedar Rapids Aug. 9, but three days later there wasn't much offense for the Dragons, as Quad City's Brian Wolfe no-hit Dayton 2-0.

Led by a pitching staff which had a postseason ERA of around 1.00, 1999 third-round pick Josh Wilson and Dominican center fielder Francisco Ferrand, Kane County swept its quarterfinal and semifinal matchups. Eastern Division wild-card South Bend also swept its first two rounds, beating top seeds Michigan and Dayton.

Kane County won the first game of the best-of-five title series 6-1 behind seven shutout innings from Dominican righty Ramon Castillo, who allowed one run in 14 playoff innings. After the terrorist attacks the next morning, the MWL eventually decided to cancel the series and declare Kane County the champion.

STANDINGS: SPLIT SEASON

FIRST HALF					SECOND HALF				
EAST	W	L	PCT	GB	**EAST**	W	L	PCT	GB
Dayton	41	29	.586	—	Michigan	44	25	.638	—
Michigan	38	30	.559	2	Dayton	41	28	.594	3
West Michigan	33	34	.493	6½	South Bend	38	31	.551	6
South Bend	32	35	.478	7½	Lansing	38	32	.543	6½
Fort Wayne	29	40	.420	11½	West Michigan	32	38	.457	12½
Lansing	27	43	.386	14	Fort Wayne	25	43	.368	18½
WEST	W	L	PCT	GB	**WEST**	W	L	PCT	GB
Kane County	47	21	.691	—	Wisconsin	42	26	.618	—
Wisconsin	42	26	.618	5	Kane County	41	29	.586	2
Quad City	42	26	.618	5	Quad City	38	31	.551	4½
Burlington	30	36	.455	16	Beloit	37	32	.536	5½
Cedar Rapids	30	37	.448	16½	Cedar Rapids	30	40	.429	13
Beloit	30	39	.435	17½	Peoria	29	39	.426	13
Clinton	28	41	.406	19½	Burlington	25	43	.368	17
Peoria	28	42	.400	20	Clinton	23	44	.343	18½

PLAYOFFS—Quarterfinals: South Bend defeated Michigan 2-0, Dayton defeated Lansing 2-0, Kane County defeated Beloit 2-0 and Wisconsin defeated Quad City 2-0 in best-of-3 series. **Semifinals:** Kane County defeated Wisconsin 2-0 and South Bend defeated Dayton 2-0 in best-of-3 series. **Finals:** Series canceled; Kane County declared champion after taking 1-0 lead over South Bend in best-of-5 series.

STANDINGS: OVERALL

Page		W	L	PCT	GB	Manager	Attendance (Avg.)	Last Penn.
139	Kane County Cougars (Marlins)	88	50	.638	—	Russ Morman	523,222 (7,694)	2001
242	Wisconsin Timber Rattlers (Mariners)	84	52	.618	3	Gary Thurman	207,823 (3,197)	1984
144	Michigan Battle Cats (Astros)	82	55	.599	5½	John Massarelli	66,088 (1,180)	2000
110	Dayton Dragons (Reds)	82	57	.590	6½	Donnie Scott	578,578 (8,385)	None
172	Quad City River Bandits (Twins)	80	57	.584	7½	Jeff Carter	129,961 (2,096)	1990
68	South Bend Silver Hawks (D'backs)	70	66	.515	17	Steve Scarsone	188,404 (3,039)	1993
165	Beloit Snappers (Brewers)	67	71	.486	21	Don Money	69,682 (1,089)	1995
131	West Michigan Whitecaps (Tigers)	65	72	.474	22½	Brent Gates	422,892 (6,219)	1998
103	Lansing Lugnuts (Cubs)	65	75	.464	24	Julio Garcia	404,429 (6,128)	1997
60	Cedar Rapids Kernels (Angels)	60	77	.438	27½	Tyrone Boykin	132,722 (1,952)	1994
222	Peoria Chiefs (Cardinals)	57	81	.413	31	Joe Hall	144,772 (2,161)	None
151	Burlington Bees (Royals)	55	79	.410	31	Joe Szekely	54,564 (853)	1999
228	Fort Wayne Wizards (Padres)	54	83	.394	33½	Tom Lawless	239,112 (3,569)	None
179	Clinton LumberKings (Expos)	51	85	.375	36	Steve Phillips	70,106 (1,062)	1991

NOTE: Team's individual batting and pitching statistics can be found on page indicated in lefthand column.

MINOR LEAGUES

CLUB BATTING

	AVG	G	AB	R	H	2B	3B	HR	BB	SO	SB
Michigan	.273	137	4628	764	1264	259	54	125	498	1033	222
Wisconsin	.271	136	4622	688	1254	248	40	74	431	946	245
Kane County	.271	138	4779	767	1295	268	37	108	515	899	120
South Bend	.270	136	4563	679	1232	221	49	74	399	946	211
Lansing	.270	140	4692	690	1266	270	42	121	453	990	91
Quad City	.262	137	4641	666	1218	239	32	85	413	880	114
Clinton	.258	137	4688	591	1208	192	33	59	415	955	175
Beloit	.254	138	4680	647	1191	234	12	100	389	1012	93
Cedar Rapids	.251	137	4608	639	1157	227	20	87	422	1057	167
West Michigan	.250	138	4610	616	1152	204	37	60	506	1009	205
Burlington	.248	134	4478	620	1109	225	34	81	435	965	101
Dayton	.247	139	4640	709	1145	259	31	144	434	1241	119
Peoria	.247	138	4566	599	1126	253	32	83	427	1092	249
Fort Wayne	.244	137	4556	560	1111	224	19	70	454	1000	156

CLUB PITCHING

	ERA	G	CG	SHO	SV	IP	H	R	ER	BB	SO
Wisconsin	2.96	136	4	16	34	1202	1049	513	395	398	1225
Quad City	3.60	137	7	14	42	1204	1112	594	482	454	1010
Dayton	3.67	139	6	13	40	1219	1226	613	498	396	1049
West Michigan	3.72	138	3	15	34	1215	1121	609	502	545	1054
South Bend	3.73	136	5	9	31	1177	1158	609	488	420	960
Kane County	3.86	138	1	4	39	1233	1223	619	528	373	865
Michigan	4.22	137	8	7	36	1189	1222	661	558	380	948
Beloit	4.23	138	2	5	35	1213	1156	696	570	586	1153
Fort Wayne	4.24	137	2	9	32	1185	1218	695	558	433	1035
Clinton	4.26	137	6	6	20	1197	1210	704	567	487	853
Lansing	4.32	140	8	8	35	1205	1293	731	579	483	1132
Cedar Rapids	4.37	137	7	3	33	1207	1218	738	587	456	1054
Peoria	4.38	138	3	4	30	1207	1286	761	588	395	878
Burlington	4.52	134	2	5	29	1151	1236	692	579	385	809

CLUB FIELDING

	PCT	PO	A	E	DP		PCT	PO	A	E	DP
Quad City	.968	3613	1467	167	103	Dayton	.962	3657	1487	201	100
Kane County	.968	3698	1536	174	124	South Bend	.961	3530	1458	200	112
Michigan	.967	3567	1380	170	108	Fort Wayne	.961	3554	1362	199	96
West Michigan	.966	3644	1404	178	121	Lansing	.960	3615	1427	209	111
Beloit	.965	3640	1410	183	113	Clinton	.960	3592	1560	216	119
Burlington	.964	3453	1437	183	94	Cedar Rapids	.956	3621	1369	228	90
Wisconsin	.963	3606	1398	194	113	Peoria	.953	3622	1598	258	125

INDIVIDUAL BATTING LEADERS
(Minimum 378 Plate Appearances)

	AVG	G	AB	R	H	2B	3B	HR	RBI	BB	SO	SB
Bay, Jason, Clinton	.363	87	318	67	115	20	4	13	61	48	62	15
Maule, Jason, Michigan	.347	124	412	101	143	23	5	1	63	74	62	56
Sadler, Ray, Lansing	.341	94	378	74	129	27	3	10	50	22	58	18
Castellano, John, Wisconsin	.334	99	377	59	126	34	0	14	81	19	35	13
Ansman, Craig, South Bend	.330	97	345	73	114	30	4	21	82	29	85	4
Reese, Kevin, Fort Wayne	.329	125	459	84	151	30	6	13	73	54	62	30
Watson, Brandon, Clinton	.327	117	489	74	160	16	9	2	38	29	65	33
Liriano, Pedro, Wisconsin	.326	113	442	76	144	28	3	4	47	30	50	65
Barbier, Blair, Lansing	.314	131	488	77	153	38	1	16	77	52	63	3
Campo, Mike, Cedar Rapids	.313	100	358	69	112	20	3	7	46	43	65	21

INDIVIDUAL PITCHING LEADERS
(Minimum 112 Innings)

	W	L	ERA	G	GS	CG	SV	IP	H	R	ER	BB	SO
Hall, Josh, Dayton	11	5	2.65	22	22	2	0	132	117	52	39	39	122
Lockwood, Luke, Clinton	5	10	2.70	26	26	3	0	163	152	78	49	49	114
Wolfe, Brian, Quad City	13	8	2.81	28	23	2	0	160	128	64	50	32	128
Perez, Beltran, South Bend	12	4	2.81	27	27	2	0	160	142	59	50	35	157
Hendrickson, Ben, Beloit	8	9	2.84	25	25	1	0	133	122	58	42	72	133
Snare, Ryan, Dayton	9	5	3.05	21	20	0	0	115	101	45	39	37	118
Nageotte, Clint, Wisconsin	11	8	3.13	28	26	0	0	152	141	65	53	50	187
Holubec, Ken, Quad City	4	8	3.22	27	22	1	1	134	107	57	48	63	129
Olore, Kevin, Wisconsin	13	4	3.32	27	27	0	0	155	134	70	57	40	158
Grunwald, Erik, Wisconsin	8	6	3.38	29	21	1	0	157	138	66	59	48	128

ALL-STAR TEAM

C—Garett Gentry, Michigan. **1B**—Adrian Gonzalez, Kane County. **2B**—Pedro Liriano, Wisconsin. **3B**—Blair Barbier, Lansing. **SS**—Miguel Cabrera, Kane County. **OF**—Wily Mo Pena, Dayton; Will Smith, Kane County; Jamal Strong, Wisconsin. **DH**—Jim Kavourias, Kane County; Samone Peters, Dayton. **LHP**—Luke Lockwood, Clinton. **RHP**—Chad Qualls, Michigan. **LHR**—Ferenc Jongejan, Lansing. **RHR**—Henry Bonilla, Quad City.

Most Valuable Player: Adrian Gonzalez, Kane County. **Prospect of the Year**: Adrian Gonzalez, Kane County. **Manager of the Year**: Russ Morman, Kane County.

DEPARTMENT LEADERS

BATTING

G	Wily Mo Pena, Dayton	135
AB	Will Smith, Kane County	535
R	Jason Maule, Michigan	101
H	Adrian Gonzalez, Kane County	161
TB	Adrian Gonzalez, Kane County	251
XBH	Steve Smitherman, Dayton	67
2B	Steve Smitherman, Dayton	45
3B	Four tied at	12
HR	Samone Peters, Dayton	28
RBI	Wily Mo Pena, Dayton	113
SH	Todd West, Beloit	26
SF	Forrest Johnson, West Michigan	10
BB	Chris Morris, Peoria	83
IBB	Garett Gentry, Michigan	8
HBP	Kevin West, Quad City	28
SO	Wily Mo Pena, Dayton	177
SB	Chris Morris, Peoria	111
CS	Chris Morris, Peoria	24
GIDP	Zach Roper, Cedar Rapids	18
OB%	Jason Maule, Michigan	.448
SL%	Craig Ansman, South Bend	.623

PITCHING

G	Steve Sawyer, Kane County	55
GS	Three tied at	28
CG	Luke Lockwood, Clinton	3
	Chad Qualls, Michigan	3
ShO	Four tied at	2
GF	Henry Bonilla, Quad City	47
SV	Henry Bonilla, Quad City	25
W	Ryan Mottl, Dayton	15
	Chad Qualls, Michigan	15
L	Duncan McAdoo, Fort Wayne	16
IP	Casey Daigle, South Bend	164
H	Aaron Krawiec, Lansing	183
R	Jon Leicester, Lansing	117
ER	Jon Leicester, Lansing	90
HR	Three tied at	19
HB	Jimmy Barrett, Michigan	24
BB	Justin Gordon, Beloit	84
SO	Clint Nageotte, Wisconsin	187
WP	Eddy Diaz, Lansing	20
BK	Jack Cassel, Fort Wayne	5

FIELDING

C	AVG	Rob Bowen, Quad City	.993
	PO	Rob Bowen, Quad City	751
	A	Ryan Hamill, Peoria	80
	E	Andres Pagan, Fort Wayne	20
	DP	Eliezer Alfonzo, Beloit	8
	PB	Andres Pagan, Fort Wayne	20
1B	AVG	Joe Dusan, Wisconsin	.994
	PO	Adrian Gonzalez, Kane County	1091
	A	Adrian Gonzalez, Kane County	85
	E	Samone Peters, Dayton	25
	DP	Adrian Gonzalez, Kane County	92
2B	AVG	Andy Green, South Bend	.973
	PO	Andy Green, South Bend	234
	A	Andy Green, South Bend	336
	E	Lee McCool, Fort Wayne	28
	DP	Andy Green, South Bend	63
3B	AVG	Mike Calitri, Dayton	.932
	PO	Vince Rooi, Clinton	83
	A	Vince Rooi, Clinton	265
	E	Daryl Clark, Beloit	47
	DP	Terry Tiffee, Quad City	18
SS	AVG	Todd West, Beloit	.983
	PO	Todd West, Beloit	214
	A	Todd West, Beloit	374
	E	David Espinosa, Dayton	48
	DP	Todd West, Beloit	72
OF	AVG	Will Smith, Kane County	.990
	PO	Chris Morris, Peoria	318
	A	Tim Lemon, Peoria	19
	E	Chris Morris, Peoria	17
	DP	Chip Ambres, Kane County	3
		Wily Mo Pena, Dayton	3

SOUTH ATLANTIC LEAGUE

BY GENE SAPAKOFF

The Lexington Legends and the Lakewood BlueClaws staged perhaps the most impressive race in South Atlantic League history, more turnstile spinning than SAL "Commissioner For Life" John H. Moss could have imagined when the cities received franchises for the 2001 season.

Lakewood (home attendance 482,206) edged Lexington (451,076) at the gate, but both clubs shattered the previous SAL single-season record set by the Delmarva Shorebirds in 1997 (324,412). The Legends also prevailed on the field. Lexington's Houston Astros farmhands were declared winners of the expanded 16-team league after

Corwin Malone

they led the Asheville Tourists 2-0 in what was going to be a best-of-five series before the terrorist attacks. Lexington had joined Wilmington as expansion franchises, and the team that had played in Fayetteville, N.C., as Cape Fear in 2000 moved to Lakewood, N.J.

Overall, the 16-team league attracted a record 2,950,630 fans. "We just have to tip our hats to an excellent Lexington team and see to it that our players get home safely," said Tourists general manager Ron McKee, who broke the news to the Legends as they prepared to practice for Game Three of the playoffs at Asheville's McCormick Field.

Lexington was consistent all season. The Legends hit .275 as a team, 22 points higher than runner-up Greensboro. Outfielder Jon Topolski and third baseman Ramon German finished 1-2 in the SAL in RBIs. The Lexington pitching staff was just as loaded as the batting order, led by righthanders Nick Roberts (10-1, 2.95), Rodrigo Rosario (13-4, 2.14), Mike Nannini (15-5, 2.70) and Anthony Pluta (12-4, 3.20).

Pitchers dominated the SAL's top prospect list as rarely before. Hagerstown Suns righthander Boof Bonser led the league in wins (16-4, 2.49) after making his nickname legally official during the offseason. Corwin Malone (11-4, 2.00)

of Kannapolis stood out among a bumper crop of lefties.

Macon's Adam Wainwright, a 6-foot-7 righthander, led the league in strikeouts and was named the SAL's best pitching prospect in BA's annual midseason survey of managers. Macon shortstop Kelly Johnson went from suspect first-round pick (the 38th overall in 2000) to shrewd investment, showing pop (.289-23-66) and speed (25 stolen bases). Johnson was named top big league prospect, best batting prospect, best power prospect and most exciting player in the BA survey.

And what would an SAL season be without a few wacky Mike Veeck promotions? This time, the Charleston RiverDogs' co-owner postponed Voodoo Night when he discovered it fell on Good Friday. Veeck allowed male fans into Riley Park on "Ladies Only Night"—if they were dressed as women (the gag lasted into the first inning).

On the field, Hickory third baseman Yurendell DeCaster (against Charleston, W.Va., on July 15) and Greensboro outfielder Jason Grove (against Delmarva on Aug. 7) hit for the cycle. And on the opening weekend of Lakewood's new GPU Energy Park, BlueClaws righthander Keith Bucktrot threw a seven-inning no-hitter against Hagerstown.

STANDINGS: SPLIT SEASON

FIRST HALF

NORTH	W	L	PCT	GB
Lexington	50	20	.714	—
Kannapolis	47	22	.681	2½
Hagerstown	38	32	.543	12
Greensboro	37	33	.529	13
Delmarva	30	40	.429	20
Hickory	29	41	.414	21
Lakewood	28	42	.400	28
Charleston, W.Va.	21	47	.309	28
SOUTH	**W**	**L**	**PCT**	**GB**
Augusta	42	28	.600	—
Columbus	39	30	.565	2½
Macon	37	30	.552	3½
Wilmington	38	32	.543	4
Capital City	30	36	.455	10
Charleston, S.C.	31	39	.443	11
Savannah	29	38	.433	11½
Asheville	27	43	.386	15

SECOND HALF

NORTH	W	L	PCT	GB
Hagerstown	45	25	.643	—
Lexington	42	28	.600	3
Hickory	38	32	.543	7
Greensboro	33	37	.471	12
Lakewood	32	37	.464	12½
Delmarva	31	39	.443	14
Charleston, W.Va.	30	40	.429	15
Kannapolis	29	41	.414	16
SOUTH	**W**	**L**	**PCT**	**GB**
Asheville	41	28	.594	—
Columbus	38	29	.567	2
Wilmington	37	31	.544	3½
Macon	35	31	.530	4½
Charleston, S.C.	33	37	.471	8½
Capital City	32	37	.464	9½
Augusta	32	37	.464	9½
Savannah	25	44	.362	16½

PLAYOFFS—Semifinals: Lexington defeated Hagerstown 2-0 and Asheville defeated Augusta 2-1 in best-of-3 series. **Finals:** Lexington led Asheville 2-0 in best-of-5 series; Lexington declared champion.

STANDINGS: OVERALL

Page		W	L	PCT	GB	Manager(s)	Attendance (Avg.)	Last Penn.
145	Lexington Legends (Astros)	92	48	.657	—	J.J. Cannon	451,076 (6,444)	2001
236	Hagerstown Suns (Giants)	83	57	.593	9	Bill Hayes	100,690 (1,503)	None
117	Columbus RedStixx (Indians)	77	59	.566	13	Ted Kubiak	115,569 (1,751)	None
96	Kannapolis Intimidators (White Sox)	76	63	.547	15½	Razor Shines	129,023 (2,150)	None
74	Macon Braves (Braves)	72	61	.541	16½	Randy Ingle	114,001 (1,754)	None
158	Wilmington Waves (Dodgers)	73	63	.537	17	Dino Ebel	135,548 (2,152)	None
89	Augusta GreenJackets (Red Sox)	74	65	.532	17½	Mike Boulanger	140,361 (2,127)	1999
186	Greensboro Bats (Yankees)	70	70	.500	22	Mitch Seoane	144,637 (2,260)	1982
125	Asheville Tourists (Rockies)	68	71	.489	23½	Joe Mikulik	159,886 (2,351)	1984
215	Hickory Crawdads (Pirates)	67	73	.479	25	Pete Mackanin	182,558 (2,685)	None
194	Capital City Bombers (Mets)	62	73	.459	27½	Ken Oberkfell	106,418 (1,716)	1998
249	Charleston, S.C., RiverDogs (Devil Rays)	64	76	.457	28	Buddy Biancalana	236,145 (3,633)	None
81	Delmarva Shorebirds (Orioles)	61	79	.436	31	Joe Ferguson	268,143 (3,886)	2000
207	Lakewood BlueClaws (Phillies)	60	79	.432	31½	Greg Legg	482,206 (6,889)	None
256	Savannah Sand Gnats (Rangers)	54	80	.403	35	Bill Slack/Pedro Lopez	101,295 (1,583)	1996
263	Charleston, W.Va., Alley Cats (Blue Jays)	51	87	.370	40	Rolando Pino	83,074 (1,298)	1990

NOTE: Teams' individual batting and pitching statistics can be found on page indicated in lefthand column.

2001 SOUTH ATLANTIC LEAGUE STATISTICS

CLUB BATTING

	AVG	G	AB	R	H	2B	3B	HR	BB	SO	SB
Lexington	.275	140	4799	781	1321	297	43	153	447	1089	221
Greensboro	.253	140	4625	637	1168	216	38	117	435	1087	123
Asheville	.252	139	4590	628	1157	206	26	116	444	1152	183
Columbia	.251	135	4473	615	1122	211	47	72	424	1000	193
Columbus	.250	136	4571	618	1143	204	45	89	430	1127	149
Wilmington	.250	138	4523	561	1130	205	39	56	366	994	278
Hagerstown	.249	140	4586	630	1143	239	21	83	504	1091	137
Hickory	.247	140	4585	570	1133	183	36	92	363	1032	211
Macon	.246	133	4479	614	1102	198	23	108	466	1008	176
Kannapolis	.245	139	4352	556	1067	159	37	69	375	1003	181
Delmarva	.241	140	4539	565	1096	175	39	57	454	982	92
Augusta	.238	139	4530	556	1080	196	21	71	428	1084	147
Lakewood	.236	139	4669	508	1101	240	26	61	371	1099	123
Savannah	.236	136	4470	524	1053	190	42	76	399	1146	149
Charleston, W.Va.	.232	138	4423	519	1028	199	28	60	405	1052	131
Charleston, S.C.	.225	140	4584	530	1031	198	36	79	364	1276	144

CLUB PITCHING

	ERA	G	CG	SHO	SV	IP	H	R	ER	BB	SO
Augusta	2.93	139	1	10	39	1214	1101	539	395	314	1087
Wilmington	3.03	138	2	12	44	1208	994	496	407	449	1058
Kannapolis	3.10	139	12	15	35	1180	1025	499	406	441	1128
Lexington	3.10	140	8	15	28	1245	1049	505	429	424	1235
Columbus	3.27	136	2	9	46	1207	1132	568	439	381	979
Charleston, S.C.	3.33	140	6	13	31	1234	1188	599	457	369	1107
Lakewood	3.37	139	12	11	31	1241	1130	602	465	412	1001
Macon	3.39	133	7	8	35	1181	1051	568	445	387	1104
Greensboro	3.49	140	7	11	37	1216	1116	581	471	485	1106
Hagerstown	3.69	140	1	12	52	1234	1154	606	506	472	1120
Hickory	3.73	140	8	4	34	1219	1215	628	505	423	1063
Columbia	3.73	135	2	6	33	1174	1120	592	486	416	1115
Charleston, W.Va.	3.84	138	10	6	23	1178	1137	645	503	391	963
Asheville	4.02	139	7	13	35	1200	1200	674	536	385	1001
Delmarva	4.02	140	5	8	34	1199	1175	660	536	405	991
Savannah	4.19	136	9	8	26	1181	1088	650	550	521	1164

CLUB FIELDING

	PCT	PO	A	E	DP
Lexington	.974	3736	1457	138	105
Hagerstown	.972	3703	1487	152	120
Kannapolis	.971	3539	1496	151	80
Wilmington	.970	3624	1448	155	102
Columbia	.965	3521	1469	180	90
Greensboro	.965	3647	1480	188	90
Macon	.964	3542	1374	182	87
Savannah	.964	3543	1291	182	102
Augusta	.963	3641	1456	194	76
Lakewood	.963	3723	1411	196	118
Asheville	.963	3599	1448	194	122
Hickory	.962	3657	1550	206	112
Delmarva	.961	3598	1399	203	89
Charl., S.C.	.960	3701	1510	216	92
Columbus	.959	3621	1425	214	115
Charl., W.Va.	.958	3534	1471	219	117

INDIVIDUAL BATTING LEADERS
(Minimum 378 Plate Appearances)

	AVG	G	AB	R	H	2B	3B	HR	RBI	BB	SO	SB
Reyes, Rene, Asheville	.322	128	484	71	156	27	2	11	61	28	80	53
Whiteman, Tommy, Lexington	.319	114	389	58	124	26	8	18	57	34	106	17
Kinchen, Jason, Greensboro	.309	134	489	81	151	24	1	30	82	50	102	2
Botts, Jason, Savannah	.309	114	392	63	121	24	2	9	50	53	88	13
Reyes, Jose, Capital City	.307	108	407	71	125	22	15	5	48	18	71	30
Hill, Mike, Lexington	.305	119	465	82	142	31	6	12	65	48	102	27
Hill, Koyie, Wilmington	.301	134	498	65	150	20	2	8	79	49	82	21
Coleman, Alph, Macon	.300	120	476	84	143	18	7	7	57	24	73	38
Ravelo, Manny, Hickory	.299	93	365	57	109	12	7	1	20	28	64	54
Grove, Jason, Greensboro	.296	115	446	68	132	21	8	15	68	36	108	0

INDIVIDUAL PITCHING LEADERS
(Minimum 112 Innings)

	W	L	ERA	G	GS	CG	SV	IP	H	R	ER	BB	SO
Malone, Corwin, Kannapolis	11	4	2.00	18		2	0	112	83	30	25	44	119
Rojas, Jose, Wilmington	10	3	2.12	24	23	1	0	136	107	42	32	42	116
Rosario, Rodrigo, Lexington	13	4	2.14	30	21	1	2	147	105	46	35	36	131
Rundles, Rich, Augusta	7	6	2.43	19	19	0	0	115	109	46	31	10	94
Kozlowski, Ben, Macon	10	7	2.48	26	23	1	0	145	134	60	40	27	147
Bonser, Boof, Hagerstown	16	4	2.49	27	27	0	0	134	91	40	37	61	178
Burnett, Sean, Hickory	11	8	2.62	26	26	1	0	161	164	63	47	33	134
Nannini, Mike, Lexington	15	5	2.70	28	27	4	0	190	176	70	57	36	151
Davis, Jason, Columbus	14	6	2.70	27	27	1	0	160	147	72	48	51	115
Miniel, Rene, Augusta	8	4	2.73	27	23	0	0	122	93	49	37	38	114

ALL-STAR TEAM

C—Koyie Hill, Wilmington. **1B**—Rene Reyes, Asheville. **2B**—Felix Escalona, Lexington. **3B**—Corey Smith, Columbus. **SS**—Kelly Johnson, Macon. **UTIL INF**—Tommy Whiteman, Lexington. **OF**—Ryan Church, Columbus; Manny Ravelo, Hickory; Jon Topolski, Lexington. **Util OF**—Yhency Brazoban, Greensboro. **DH**—Jason Kinchen, Greensboro. **RHP**—Boof Bonser, Hagerstown. **LHP**—Corwin Malone, Kannapolis.

Most Valuable Player—Rene Reyes, Asheville. **Most Valuable Pitcher**—Boof Bonser, Hagerstown. **Best Major League Prospect**—Kelly Johnson, Macon.

DEPARTMENT LEADERS

BATTING

G	Juan Richardson, Lakewood	137
AB	Jon Topolski, Lexington	550
R	Jon Topolski, Lexington	98
H	Jon Topolski, Lexington	158
TB	Jon Topolski, Lexington	271
XBH	Felix Escalona, Lexington	60
2B	Felix Escalona, Lexington	42
3B	B.J. Littleton, Delmarva	18
HR	Jason Kinchen, Greensboro	30
RBI	Jon Topolski, Lexington	96
SH	Bryan Gann, Hagerstown	20
SF	Alex Rios, Charleston, WV	14
BB	Jon Topolski, Lexington	75
IBB	Koyie Hill, Wilmington	14
HBP	J.J. Sherrill, Columbus	27
SO	Justin Schuda, Charleston, SC	166
SB	Bernabel Castro, Greensboro	67
CS	Edwin Yan, Hickory	21
GIDP	Alfredo Leon, Delmarva	18
OB%	Jason Botts, Savannah	.416
SL%	Tommy Whiteman, Lexington	.566

PITCHING

G	Jason Faigin, Greensboro	60
	Arnaldo Munoz, Kannapolis	60
GS	Three tied at	28
CG	Taylor Buchholz, Lakewood	5
ShO	Taylor Buchholz, Lakewood	3
GF	Jackson Markert, Hagerstown	55
SV	Jackson Markert, Hagerstown	39
W	Boof Bonser, Hagerstown	16
L	Taylor Buchholz, Lakewood	14
IP	Mike Nannini, Lexington	190
H	Doug Waechter, Charleston, S.C.	179
R	Doug Waechter, Charleston, S.C.	97
ER	Scott Dohmann, Asheville	83
HR	Scott Dohmann, Asheville	27
HB	David Mead, Savannah	19
BB	Anthony Pluta, Lexington	86
SO	Adam Wainwright, Macon	184
WP	Justin Echols, Savannah	21
BK	Roman Colon, Macon	4
	Arnaldo Munoz, Kannapolis	4

FIELDING

C	AVG	John Buck, Lexington	.994
	PO	John Buck, Lexington	1006
	A	John Buck, Lexington	118
	E	Koyie Hill, Wilmington	18
	DP	Koyie Hill, Wilmington	8
	PB	John Buck, Lexington	20
		Omar Fuentes, Greensboro	20
1B	AVG	Casey Rogowski, Kannapolis	.995
	PO	Casey Rogowski, Kannapolis	1051
	A	Mike Snyder, Charleston, WV	85
	E	Sean Swedlow, Columbus	23
	DP	Deivis Santos, Hagerstown	97
2B	AVG	Felix Escalona, Lexington	.979
	PO	Bryan Gann, Hagerstown	227
	A	Miguel Vilorio, Asheville	341
	E	Miguel Vilorio, Asheville	21
	DP	Bryan Gann, Hagerstown	71
3B	AVG	John Lackaff, Kannapolis	.970
	PO	Willy Aybar, Wilmington	106
	A	Rob Cosby, Charleston, WV	252
	E	Corey Smith, Columbus	45
	DP	Corey Smith, Columbus	23
SS	AVG	Jose Reyes, Capital City	.964
	PO	Nick Garcia, Delmarva	178
		Kenny Perez, Augusta	178
	A	Scott Youngbauer, Lakewood	335
	E	Kelly Johnson, Macon	45
	DP	Scott Youngbauer, Lakewood	72
OF	AVG	Jason Barnette, Lakewood	.996
	PO	B.J. Littleton, Delmarva	283
	A	Yhency Brazoban, Greensboro	19
	E	Reggie Abercrombie, Wilmington	15
	DP	Three tied at	4

NEW YORK-PENN LEAGUE

BY ADAM RUBIN

Jeff Dumas gets a sick feeling every time he arrives at the Staten Island Yankees' state-of-the-art ballpark.

Fans of his New York-Penn League club were treated to a breathtaking view of New York Harbor, the Statue of Liberty and the Manhattan skyline during 2001, the club's first season in the stadium.

But since the Sept. 11 terrorist attacks, the twin towers of the World Trade Center are notably absent beyond the outfield wall.

"I find myself looking directly at it," said Dumas, the Staten Island general manager. "It's actually difficult pulling in here every day."

New York mayor Rudolph Giuliani, now lauded as a symbol of strength as the Big Apple recovers, earlier had provided a pair of gems for the New York-Penn League and its fans. Giuliani, a vocal Yankees supporter, spearheaded construction of new ballparks in Staten Island and Coney Island, both of which debuted in 2001.

RICH ABEL

Jason Arnold

The $118 million initiative translated into a boon for the league. The Brooklyn Cyclones, in their first year as an affiliate of the New York Mets, drew a league-record 289,381 fans during their inaugural regular season, an average of 7,821 per game.

The Yanks, who had previously played at the College of Staten Island, lured an average of 4,951 per contest, third-best in the NY-P.

As a result, the NY-P shattered its attendance record. The league drew 1,638,335 fans during the regular season, an increase of nearly 300,000 from the previous best, in 1999.

Brooklyn beat host Williamsport 7-4 in Game One of the title series on Sept. 10, as the Cyclones ripped rehabbing major league righthander Jose Silva for four runs in

1⅔ innings. Brooklyn held another rehabbing Pirate, outfielder Adrian Brown, 0-for-4 with three strikeouts. After the tragedy the next day, the Crosscutters—making their first playoff appearance since 1968—and the Cyclones were declared co-champions.

The Crosscutters had dominated the Pinckney Division, posting a 48-26 record, 9½ games better than second-place Jamestown, which was swept in the opening round. Brooklyn owned the league's best record (52-24) as well as the top ERA (2.37).

The Cyclones topped Staten Island in a decisive third game, 4-1, for the McNamara Division postseason championship.

Brooklyn's Ross Peeples had the league's best ERA (1.34) and tied with teammate Harold Eckert for most wins (nine).

Other league leaders: Oneonta's Juan Francia (.340 batting average), Brooklyn's Frank Corr and Williamsport's Walter Young (13 homers), Staten Island's Juan Camacho (51 RBIs), Williamsport's Chris Duffy and Brooklyn's Angel Pagan (30 steals), Williamsport's Jeff Miller (15 saves) and Staten Island's Charlie Manning (87 strikeouts).

Staten Island's all-star righthander Jason Arnold tossed a no-hitter July 27 at Vermont. Two cycles were recorded within three weeks: Hudson Valley's Luis DePaula did it July 21 against Mahoning Valley, and Hector Pimentel of Jamestown returned the favor against Hudson Valley on Aug. 3.

The Pittsfield Astros, who will move to Troy, N.Y., for the 2002 season, had grand slams on three consecutive days in a series against Utica July 21-23. As for the Blue Sox, their future looked uncertain heading to the offseason, as rumors swirled about the imminent relocation of the franchise.

The Blue Sox were first thought to be heading for Washington, Pa., then for Pittsfield, but both of those deals fell through by October. Also a possibility for a new home: Aberdeen, Md., and the new ballpark being built by Cal Ripken's baseball foundation.

MINOR LEAGUES

STANDINGS

Page	PINCKNEY-STEDLER	W	L	PCT	GB	Manager	Attendance (Avg.)	Last Penn.
215	Williamsport Crosscutters (Pirates)	48	26	.649	—	Tony Beasley	72,258 (2,007)	2001
75	Jamestown Jammers (Braves)	39	36	.520	9½	Jim Saul	63,069 (1,752)	1991
132	Oneonta Tigers (Tigers)	37	37	.500	11	Gary Green	52.825 (1,554)	1998
208	Batavia Muckdogs (Phillies)	37	39	.487	12	Frank Klebe	43,257 (1,169)	1963
263	Auburn Doubledays (Blue Jays)	32	42	.432	16	Paul Elliott	54,994 (1,447)	1998
139	Utica Blue Sox (Marlins)	27	47	.365	21	Kevin Boles	47,135 (1,386)	1983
118	Mahoning Valley Scrappers (Indians)	26	49	.347	22½	Dave Turgeon	181,617 (5,045)	None
Page	McNAMARA	W	L	PCT	GB	Manager	Attendance (Avg.)	Last Penn.
195	Brooklyn Cyclones (Mets)	52	24	.684	—	Edgar Alfonso	289,381 (7,821)	2001
187	Staten Island Yankees (Yankees)	48	28	.632	4	David Jorn	188,127 (4,951)	2000
145	Pittsfield Astros (Astros)	45	30	.600	6½	Ivan DeJesus	56,747 (1,576)	1997
250	Hudson Valley Renegades (Devil Rays)	39	37	.513	13	Dave Howard	160,858 (4,348)	1999
222	New Jersey Cardinals (Cardinals)	35	41	.461	17	Brian Rupp	131,197 (3,644)	1994
89	Lowell Spinners (Red Sox)	33	43	.434	19	Arnie Beyeler	185,000 (5,000)	None
179	Vermont Expos (Expos)	28	47	.373	23½	Steve Balboni	115,560 (3,210)	1996

PLAYOFFS—Semifinals: Williamsport defeated Jamestown 2-0 and Brooklyn defeated Staten Island 2-1 in best-of-3 series. **Final:** Series canceled; Brooklyn led Williamsport 1-0 in best-of-3 series; Brooklyn and Williamsport declared co-champions.

NOTE: Teams' individual batting and pitching statistics can be found on page indicated in lefthand column.

2001 NEW YORK-PENN LEAGUE STATISTICS

CLUB BATTING

	AVG	G	AB	R	H	2B	3B	HR	BB	SO	SB
Brooklyn	.279	76	2548	368	711	143	14	58	199	524	97
Staten Island	.265	76	2561	383	678	138	25	46	265	498	71
Williamsport	.262	74	2432	374	637	125	25	36	243	489	132
Oneonta	.258	74	2450	327	631	98	35	25	244	597	73
Hudson Valley	.257	76	2700	352	694	143	24	41	210	579	41
New Jersey	.257	76	2545	330	653	142	24	29	325	580	89
Lowell	.252	76	2594	354	653	138	15	28	315	578	86
Pittsfield	.251	75	2492	398	625	139	25	35	290	600	133
Jamestown	.247	75	2452	292	606	115	20	26	217	511	68
Batavia	.241	76	2565	323	617	129	23	28	229	581	58
Auburn	.239	74	2547	306	610	107	19	33	206	507	94
Utica	.237	74	2479	297	588	103	19	38	244	649	41
Mahoning Valley	.226	75	2487	292	561	111	19	48	257	554	38
Vermont	.208	75	2432	264	506	85	13	21	232	638	66

CLUB PITCHING

	ERA	G	CG	SHO	SV	IP	H	R	ER	BB	SO
Brooklyn	2.37	76	1	6	31	671	505	223	177	261	644
Williamsport	2.91	74	2	5	23	640	550	275	207	229	567
Staten Island	3.22	76	4	5	22	664	556	284	238	240	633
New Jersey	3.27	76	0	5	24	676	630	317	246	234	621
Batavia	3.44	76	4	3	17	679	686	341	260	209	471
Pittsfield	3.46	75	1	4	18	670	644	349	258	260	564
Jamestown	3.48	75	1	3	20	651	603	297	252	242	556
Oneonta	3.53	74	3	6	18	634	630	357	249	223	529
Utica	3.82	74	0	3	14	649	598	356	275	231	458
Lowell	3.90	76	1	2	16	673	666	356	292	259	518
Hudson Valley	3.91	76	2	1	20	684	669	371	297	295	544
Auburn	3.96	74	0	5	14	675	631	349	297	306	685
Mahoning Valley	4.25	75	0	4	18	661	722	391	312	250	568
Vermont	4.45	75	1	1	12	651	680	394	322	237	527

CLUB FIELDING

	PCT	PO	A	E	DP		PCT	PO	A	E	DP
Jamestown	.972	1953	753	79	65	Hudson Valley	.961	2001	887	120	76
Staten Island	.971	1993	781	84	64	Utica	.960	1946	893	119	68
Williamsport	.967	1921	791	93	67	Mahoning	.959	1982	842	121	62
New Jersey	.967	2029	861	100	71	Batavia	.958	2038	782	124	64
Lowell	.966	2020	849	102	56	Pittsfield	.958	2010	910	129	69
Auburn	.966	2025	774	100	47	Oneonta	.956	1903	778	123	68
Brooklyn	.962	2013	869	113	61	Vermont	.955	1952	786	129	70

INDIVIDUAL BATTING LEADERS
(Minimum 205 Plate Appearances)

	AVG	G	AB	R	H	2B	3B	HR	RBI	BB	SO	SB
Francia, Juan, Oneonta	.340	47	191	30	65	5	2	0	8	11	32	17
Gonzalez, Edgar, Hudson Valley	.332	73	277	49	92	19	4	9	34	37	56	6
Caligiuri, Jay, Brooklyn	.328	66	238	38	78	14	3	5	34	26	31	4
Rabelo, Mike, Oneonta	.325	53	194	27	63	4	2	0	32	23	45	1
Rifkin, Aaron, Staten Island	.318	69	245	41	78	19	5	10	49	31	47	3
Youkilis, Kevin, Lowell	.317	59	183	52	58	14	2	3	28	70	28	4
Duffy, Chris, Williamsport	.317	64	221	50	70	12	4	1	24	33	33	30
Pagan, Angel, Brooklyn	.315	62	238	46	75	10	2	0	15	22	30	30
Griffin, John-Ford, Staten Island	.311	66	238	46	74	17	1	5	43	40	41	10
Kent, Mailon, Jamestown	.310	50	187	26	58	9	3	2	27	21	20	5

INDIVIDUAL PITCHING LEADERS
(Minimum 61 Innings)

	W	L	ERA	G	GS	CG	SV	IP	H	R	ER	BB	SO
Peeples, Ross, Brooklyn	9	3	1.34	16	15	1	0	80	63	19	12	29	67
Oquendo, Ian, Williamsport	7	0	1.39	10	9	1	0	65	55	16	10	10	56
Arnold, Jason, Staten Island	7	2	1.50	10	10	2	0	66	35	13	11	15	74
Ungs, Nick, Utica	3	1	1.62	12	11	0	0	61	57	14	11	0	40
Miner, Zach, Jamestown	3	4	1.89	15	15	0	0	91	76	26	19	16	68
Rodriguez, Juan, Williamsport	8	2	1.89	13	13	0	0	81	61	23	17	15	68
Portobanco, Luz, Brooklyn	5	2	2.04	13	12	0	0	71	51	20	16	29	52
Rodaway, Brian, Pittsfield	7	3	2.34	17	13	1	1	88	76	28	23	11	56
Flinn, Chris, Hudson Valley	3	4	2.36	15	10	0	2	69	54	33	18	21	72
Wilson, Mike, Batavia	4	4	2.58	14	14	1	0	80	89	37	23	23	51
Asahina, Jon, Utica	4	6	2.58	15	13	0	0	70	56	27	20	19	55

ALL-STAR TEAM

C—Mike Rabelo, Oneonta; Chris Shelton, Williamsport. **1B**—Aaron Rifkin, Staten Island. **2B**—Juan Francia, Oneonta. **3B**—Juan Camacho, Staten Island. **SS**—Tony Pena, Jamestown. **INF**—Edgar Gonzalez, Hudson Valley. **OF**—Frank Corr, Brooklyn; Chris Duffy, Williamsport; Angel Pagan, Brooklyn; Todd Self, Pittsfield. **DH**—Walter Young, Williamsport. **RHP**—Jason Arnold, Staten Island; Ian Oquendo, Williamsport. **LHP**—Ross Peeples, Brooklyn; Brian Rodaway, Pittsfield.
Most Valuable Player: Aaron Rifkin, Staten Island.

DEPARTMENT LEADERS

BATTING

G	Bill McCarthy, Jamestown	74
AB	Luis DePaula, Hudson Valley	303
R	Todd Self, Pittsfield	52
	Kevin Youkilis, Lowell	52
H	Edgar Gonzalez, Hudson Valley	92
TB	Edgar Gonzalez, Hudson Valley	146
XBH	Frank Corr, Brooklyn	35
2B	Ernie Durazo, Auburn	22
3B	Ryan Raburn, Oneonta	8
HR	Frank Corr, Brooklyn	13
	Walter Young, Williamsport	13
RBI	Juan Camacho, Staten Island	51
SH	Domingo Cuello, Williamsport	9
SF	Three tied at	6
BB	Kevin Youkilis, Lowell	70
IBB	Edgar Gonzalez, Hudson Valley	6
HBP	Chris Duffy, Williamsport	17
SO	Morrin Davis, Auburn	88
	Nom Siriveaw, Auburn	88
SB	Chris Duffy, Williamsport	30
	Angel Pagan, Brooklyn	30
CS	Angel Pagan, Brooklyn	18
GIDP	Andy Cannizaro, Staten Island	15
OBP	Kevin Youkilis, Lowell	.512
SLG	Frank Corr, Brooklyn	.594

PITCHING

G	Five tied at	29
GS	Ten tied at	15
CG	Three tied at	2
ShO	Il Kim, Batavia	2
GF	Oscar Bustillos, Hudson Valley	24
SV	Jeff Miller, Williamsport	15
W	Harold Eckert, Brooklyn	9
	Ross Peeples, Brooklyn	9
L	Four tied at	8
IP	Zach Miner, Jamestown	91
H	Nathan Cromer, Hudson Valley	94
R	John Dischiavo, Hudson Valley	58
ER	John Dischiavo, Hudson Valley	53
HR	Kyle Colton, Jamestown	9
HB	Luz Portobanco, Brooklyn	13
BB	Dustin McGowan, Auburn	49
SO	Charlie Manning, Staten Island	87
WP	Dustin McGowan, Auburn	16
BK	Toby David, Utica	3

FIELDING

C	AVG	Tim Whittaker, Auburn	.995
	PO	Dan Moylan, New Jersey	380
	A	Dan Moylan, New Jersey	67
	E	Edgar Martinez, Lowell	9
	DP	Brett Kay, Brooklyn	4
	PB	Josh Emmerick, Vermont	15
		Chris Shelton, Williamsport	15
1B	AVG	Jay Caligiuri, Brooklyn	.996
	PO	Aaron Rifkin, Staten Island	606
	A	Rickie Morton, Mahoning Valley	44
	E	Aaron Rifkin, Staten Island	8
	DP	Aaron Rifkin, Staten Island	47
2B	AVG	Richard Lewis, Jamestown	.975
	PO	Vince Harrison, Hudson Valley	127
	A	Brooks Conrad, Pittsfield	182
	E	Brooks Conrad, Pittsfield	14
	DP	Domingo Cuello, Williamsport	40
3B	AVG	Juan Camacho, Staten Island	.974
	PO	Nom Siriveaw, Auburn	48
	A	Juan Camacho, Staten Island	142
	E	Ryan Raburn, Oneonta	23
		Nom Siriveaw, Auburn	23
	DP	Fernando Cortez, Hudson Valley	16
SS	AVG	Deivi Mendez, Staten Island	.966
	PO	Daniel Gonzalez, Batavia	129
	A	Luis DePaula, Hudson Valley	210
	E	Tony Caracciolo, Vermont	26
	DP	Ryan Stegall, Pittsfield	47
OF	AVG	Jason Knoedler, Oneonta	1.000
	PO	Rod Perry, Batavia	155
	A	Mailon Kent, Jamestown	10
		Chris Kolodzey, Oneonta	10
	E	Jose Soto, Utica	10
	DP	Mario Campos, Lowell	5

NORTHWEST LEAGUE

BY SUSAN WADE

That's Professor Fred Stanley to you.

The Salem-Keizer Volcanoes skipper was the first in the Northwest League's 47-year history to be named manager of the year in consecutive seasons—and he has been in the league just two campaigns.

His skill in blending the proper team chemistry is what produced record-setting statistics and a second championship in four years for the San Francisco Giants affiliate in 2001.

Professor Stanley had his theories. "Play better at your position than your opponent" was one of them. Another was, "Play hard for us as long as it takes." Maybe the most effective one focused on positive reinforcement.

"We didn't have any true rah-rah, jump-up-and-get-it-done guys," he said, looking back at his 51-25 team that swept the Boise Hawks in the best-of-five championship series. "But everybody pulled for each other.

"Even if a guy got a sacrifice bunt or slid hard into second and broke up a double play—if a guy did anything unselfish—

Angel Guzman

MARC McCLINTOCK

everybody on that bench was up, ready to shake his hand when he got back to the dugout . . . just like he had hit a home run."

It took Stanley about 20 games to find the correct formula, as the Volcanoes began 9-11. The Giants added third baseman Julian Benavidez, their third-round draft pick in 2001 who signed July 12.

After Benavidez' July 16 arrival, Salem-Keizer was 40-13. The Volcanoes ended the season with six straight victories and 15 in their last 18 games to win their division by 14 games. Benavidez, who homered in his first start, hit .319-9-39 in 50 games.

The Volcanoes committed just 91 errors, an NWL record low (five fewer than the 2000 Yakima Bears). They had a strong infield, with Benavidez at third base, Mikey Miranda at shortstop, Derin McMains at second and Tyler Von Schell at first.

But Jesse Foppert stole the show as the NWL's most dominating righthander. The 6-foot-6, 210-pound University of San Francisco product finished with an 8-1 record and league-best 1.93 ERA. During the regular season, he struck out 88 in 70 innings, while walking just 23.

If Boise thought he was simply lucky, it learned different in the postseason. Foppert struck out 12 in six innings to lead Salem-Keizer to the first of two 5-0 triumphs at Boise. The Hawks had not been shut out at home all season and only once had been limited to one run there. On the road, they had been shutout victims just twice. But Foppert dismantled the team that led the NWL in hitting at .291.

Wes Hutchison (6-2, 1.64), the league leader in saves (10) in the regular season, came through to shut down the Hawks in Game Three. Rob Meyer, a .292 hitter who had been 1-for-10 in the championship series, hit a three-run homer for the 7-5 pennant-clinching victory.

The sweep was even more remarkable, considering Boise had routed the Volcanoes in Salem-Keizer in the season-opening series in June. "They kicked the hell out of us," Stanley remembered. "They scored 42 runs in four games against us."

Boise was a powerful opponent, indeed. The Eastern Division champions (52-23) led the NWL in team hitting (.291) and pitching (3.19 ERA). Outfielder Keto Anderson was the batting champion at .376. He also was first in hits (109), runs (70) and triples (six). Anderson served notice that he was ready for the season on Opening Night, June 19, when he went 6-for-6 in a win against Salem-Keizer.

The Hawks had the league's top three hitters, including Brad Bouras (.349) and Condor Cash (.347), and four of the top six. J.J. Johnson, the No. 6 hitter, led the league in RBIs (61).

Angel Guzman (9-1), No. 2 in ERA at 2.23 with 63 strikeouts and just 19 walks, had the most victories. He led a staff that landed five pitchers among the top 10 in ERA. Hawks pitchers allowed the fewest walks (216) and fewest home runs (34).

Eugene's Jon Benick pulled off a rare feat at the plate toward the end of the season, connecting for a grand slam against Vancouver on Aug. 27 and pulling it off again the next day against Everett.

The Tri-City Dust Devils, the offspring of the 2000 Portland Rockies who moved from Oregon when Triple-A baseball returned to Portland, recorded their first-ever no-hitter on Aug. 8, when righthanders Kip Bouknight and Pat Lynch combined to shut down the high-powered Hawks.

STANDINGS

Page	NORTH	W	L	PCT	GB	Manager	Attendance (Avg.)	Last Penn.
103	Boise Hawks (Cubs)	52	23	.693	—	Steve McFarland	99,840 (2,698)	1995
125	Tri-City Dust Devils (Rockies)	39	36	.520	13	Stu Cole	55,613 (1,464)	None
68	Yakima Bears (Diamondbacks)	33	42	.440	19	Greg Lonigro	59,000 (1,639)	2000
152	Spokane Indians (Royals)	22	54	.289	30½	Tom Poquette	181,214 (4,769)	1999

Page	SOUTH	W	L	PCT	GB	Manager	Attendance (Avg.)	Last Penn.
236	Salem-Keizer Volcanoes (Giants)	51	25	.671	—	Fred Stanley	115,340 (3,117)	2001
202	Vancouver Canadians (Athletics)	37	39	.487	14	Webster Garrison	118,357 (3,199)	None
243	Everett AquaSox (Mariners)	36	39	.480	14½	Terry Pollreisz	114.727 (3,187)	1985
229	Eugene Emeralds (Padres)	32	44	.421	19	Jeff Gardner	126,592 (3,516)	1980

PLAYOFFS—Salem-Keizer defeated Boise 3-0 in best-of-5 championship series.

NOTE: Teams' individual batting and pitching statistics can be found on page indicated in lefthand column.

MINOR LEAGUES

CLUB BATTING

	AVG	G	AB	R	H	2B	3B	HR	BB	SO	SB
Boise	.291	75	2637	441	768	157	26	62	238	517	82
Everett	.265	75	2636	376	698	141	18	55	230	628	91
Salem-Keizer	.261	76	2636	416	689	141	17	54	279	483	59
Eugene	.252	76	2540	361	641	116	16	57	270	681	80
Yakima	.248	75	2556	323	633	138	10	36	210	631	45
Spokane	.244	76	2608	327	637	94	22	25	253	615	82
Vancouver	.238	76	2508	320	597	129	17	44	280	713	72
Tri-City	.224	75	2513	322	563	126	30	28	236	669	84

CLUB PITCHING

	ERA	G	CG	SHO	SV	IP	H	R	ER	BB	SO
Boise	3.19	75	1	8	24	668	626	309	237	216	590
Vancouver	3.54	76	0	4	17	670	602	328	264	278	629
Tri-City	3.60	75	2	8	20	676	638	345	271	234	595
Salem-Keizer	3.79	76	0	7	20	686	676	338	289	223	660
Yakima	4.10	75	0	4	22	663	706	363	302	255	580
Everett	4.21	75	0	2	20	668	625	376	313	291	692
Eugene	4.22	76	3	3	14	649	638	373	304	240	593
Spokane	5.11	76	1	1	10	670	715	454	381	259	598

CLUB FIELDING

	PCT	PO	A	E	DP		PCT	PO	A	E	DP
Salem-Keizer	.970	2059	826	90	59	Everett	.960	2004	718	114	60
Yakima	.962	1990	797	110	60	Vancouver	.959	2011	745	118	42
Tri-City	.962	2023	762	110	55	Spokane	.959	2011	782	120	61
Eugene	.961	1946	755	109	44	Boise	.957	2003	843	128	52

INDIVIDUAL BATTING LEADERS
(Minimum 205 Plate Appearances)

	AVG	G	AB	R	H	2B	3B	HR	RBI	BB	SO	SB
Anderson, Syketo, Boise	.376	70	290	70	109	13	6	6	41	12	34	24
Bouras, Brad, Boise	.349	62	238	44	83	25	0	6	60	27	39	1
Cash, Condor, Boise	.347	66	245	33	85	18	4	10	49	26	37	6
Dobbs, Greg, Everett	.321	65	249	37	80	17	2	6	41	30	39	5
Benavidez, Julian, Salem-Keizer	.319	50	188	36	60	12	1	9	39	24	54	2
Johnson, J.J., Boise	.317	70	287	55	91	15	5	7	61	20	50	18
Figueroa, Eduardo, Everett	.310	49	187	35	58	10	2	3	24	17	45	7
Gautreau, Jake, Eugene	.309	48	178	28	55	19	0	6	36	22	47	1
Merritt, Tim, Everett	.306	51	196	33	60	13	3	5	30	9	35	11
Nettles, Marcus, Eugene	.300	55	213	37	64	3	0	0	10	27	54	35
Bartlett, Jason, Eugene	.300	68	267	49	80	12	4	3	37	28	47	12

INDIVIDUAL PITCHING LEADERS
(Minimum 61 Innings)

	W	L	ERA	G	GS	CG	SV	IP	H	R	ER	BB	SO
Foppert, Jesse, Salem-Keizer	8	1	1.93	14	14	0	0	70	35	18	15	23	88
Guzman, Angel, Boise	9	1	2.23	14	14	0	0	77	68	27	19	19	63
Martinez, Gustavo, Everett	5	3	2.67	15	15	0	0	84	62	30	25	34	100
Gonzalez, Christian, Vancouver	2	7	2.67	16	16	0	0	88	90	36	26	15	59
Bouknight, Kip, Tri-City	3	5	2.78	15	15	0	0	81	69	29	25	19	86
Wynegar, Adam, Boise	4	2	2.92	14	12	0	0	71	77	34	23	19	63
Nicholson, Scott, Tri-City	4	3	2.93	14	14	1	0	77	69	29	25	12	50
Willis, Dontrelle, Boise	8	2	2.98	15	15	0	0	94	76	36	31	19	77
Pignatiello, Carmen, Boise	7	3	3.00	16	12	0	1	78	70	37	26	22	83
Mitre, Sergio, Boise	8	4	3.07	15	15	1	0	91	85	37	31	18	71

ALL-STAR TEAM

C—Casey Myers, Vancouver. **1B**—Brad Bouras, Boise; Greg Dobbs, Everett. **2B**—Tim Merritt, Everett; Dan Uggla, Yakima. **3B**—Corey Slavik, Boise. **SS**—Jason Bartlett, Eugene. **OF**—Matt Allegra, Vancouver; Syketo Anderson, Boise; J.J. Johnson, Boise. **DH**—Greg Sain, Eugene. **RHP**—Angel Guzman, Boise. **LHP**—Dontrelle Willis, Boise. **RHR**—Wes Hutchison, Salem-Keizer; Jorge Sosa, Everett. **LHR**—Brett Price, Vancouver.

Most Valuable Player: J.J. Johnson, Boise. **Manager of the Year**: Fred Stanley, Salem-Keizer.

DEPARTMENT LEADERS

BATTING

G	Kyle Nichols, Yakima	75
	Tyler Von Schell, Salem-Keizer	75
AB	Tyler Von Schell, Salem-Keizer	293
R	Syketo Anderson, Boise	70
H	Syketo Anderson, Boise	109
TB	Syketo Anderson, Boise	152
XBH	Kyle Nichols, Yakima	36
	Greg Sain, Eugene	36
2B	Brad Bouras, Boise	25
3B	Syketo Anderson, Boise	6
HR	Greg Sain, Eugene	16
RBI	J.J. Johnson, Boise	61
SH	James Shanks, Spokane	10
SF	J.J. Johnson, Boise	7
BB	Corey Slavik, Boise	39
IBB	Chris Fallon, Spokane	5
HBP	Ashley Freeman, Tri-City	13
SO	Matt Allegra, Vancouver	104
SB	Marcus Nettles, Eugene	35
CS	Marcus Nettles, Eugene	17
GIDP	Derin McMains, Salem-Keizer	11
	Robbie Meyer, Salem-Keizer	11
OB%	Brad Bouras, Boise	.419
SL%	Condor Cash, Boise	.576

PITCHING

G	Darwin Soto, Eugene	30
GS	Christian Gonzalez, Vancouver	16
CG	Justin Germano, Eugene	2
ShO	Sergio Mitre, Boise	1
	Scott Nicholson, Tri-City	1
GF	Wes Hutchison, Salem-Keizer	25
SV	Wes Hutchison, Salem-Keizer	10
W	Angel Guzman, Boise	9
L	Four tied at	7
IP	Dontrelle Willis, Boise	94
H	Jon Castellanos, Yakima	100
R	Barry Armitage, Spokane	57
	Geoffrey Jones, Eugene	57
ER	Barry Armitage, Spokane	49
HR	Charles Merricks, Tri-City	9
	Anthony Pannone, Salem-Keizer	9
HB	Gustavo Martinez, Everett	18
BB	Phil Cullen, Everett	49
SO	James Harden, Vancouver	100
	Gustavo Martinez, Everett	100
WP	Kyle Middleton, Spokane	10
	Greg Valera, Yakima	10
BK	Jorge Vasquez, Spokane	10

FIELDING

C	AVG	Michael DiRosa, Yakima	.993
	PO	Keith Anderson, Salem	416
	A	Keith Anderson, Salem	48
	E	Warren Hanna, Boise	8
	DP	Keith Anderson, Salem	3
	PB	J.D. Alleva, Spokane	12
1B	AVG	Tyler Von Schell, Salem	.992
	PO	Tyler Von Schell, Salem	608
	A	Tyler Von Schell, Salem	47
	E	Greg Dobbs, Everett	12
		Dan Johnson, Vancouver	12
	DP	Tyler Von Schell, Salem	52
2B	AVG	Derin McMains, Salem	.966
	PO	Derin McMains, Salem	134
	A	Derin McMains, Salem	176
	E	Three tied at	13
	DP	Dan Uggla, Yakima	41
3B	AVG	Christian Reyes, Vancouver	.930
	PO	Corey Slavik, Boise	44
	A	Corey Slavik, Boise	129
	E	Miguel Villilo, Everett	18
	DP	Corey Slavik, Boise	10
SS	AVG	Jose Lopez, Everett	.954
	PO	Jose Lopez, Everett	115
	A	Jason Bartlett, Eugene	199
	E	Luis Cotto, Spokane	30
	DP	Jose Lopez, Everett	39
OF	AVG	Matt Huntingford, Salem	1.000
	PO	Matt Allegra, Vancouver	145
		James Shanks, Spokane	145
	A	Richie Barrett, Yakima	14
	E	Condor Cash, Boise	8
	DP	Three tied at	3

BY BLAIR LOVERN

The last time this much attention was paid to the Appalachian League was way back in . . . er, well, maybe never.

Three headliners brought out fans in 2001: Joe Mauer, the No. 1 overall draft pick; Rick Ankiel, working his way toward the majors again; and Toe Nash, with a litter trail of half-true media stories and hype.

"I would think this year beat anything in all of minor league baseball except when (Michael Jordan) played in the Southern League," said Appy League president Lee Landers, who has worked in professional baseball since 1959.

Mauer came from the same St. Paul, Minn., high school as Paul Molitor, and the 18-year-old catcher said he shared Molitor's approach to hitting by using all fields. Mauer didn't qualify for the Appy League batting title because he joined Elizabethton about halfway through the season after prolonged contract negotiations with the Twins. In 32 games, he hit

BILL SETLIFF

Rick Ankiel

.400-0-14.

"The first day I saw him, I looked at him and thought: He's young. But he plays like he's 25," said Elizabethton manager Rudy Hernandez. "He's real patient. He doesn't swing at too many bad pitches, and he's got an unbelievable arm and quickness behind the plate. I think he's going to be in the majors in probably three or four years."

Joe and his 22-year-old brother Jake—also drafted in June by the Twins—played on the same team for the first time since playing summer ball together in Minnesota. The Mauers helped Elizabethton win the Western Division title for the second straight year.

But Eastern Division winner Bluefield, with a .500 record in regular season play, beat the Twins in the championship series two games to one. Orioles first-round pick Bryan Bass scored the winning run in the deciding game when he led off the sixth inning with a triple and came home on a balk by Twins reliever Matt Vorwald.

Johnson City had the worst team in the West, but the Cardinals drew more fans than any other team in the league because they had Ankiel. The Cardinals' attendance was 42,816—almost double the figure of 2000.

When Ankiel wasn't pitching, he was usually the DH. Not only did he lead the league in strikeouts (158), he even made a run at the home run title (10). He finished the year 5-3, 1.33, while allowing 42 hits and 18 walks in 88 innings. He showed little of the wildness that plagued his once-promising major league career.

Ankiel stayed with Johnson City the entire season, following a demotion from Triple-A Memphis. St. Louis brought him to the majors again after Johnson City's season ended, but only to watch.

"We feel he's accomplished what he needs to do this year," St. Louis general manager Walt Jocketty said in August. "He's going to spend some time here in the major league environment, then go to the instructional league."

Nash was the big draw for Princeton, but even he admitted he wasn't sure why there was so much hype before his arrival. The left fielder hit .240-8-29 in 171 at-bats.

"It will take a while, but if he works hard I can see him being a star," said Devil Rays scout Benny Latino, who discovered Nash in the backwoods of Louisiana in 2000.

Nash's teammate, outfielder Jonny Gomes, was named the league's player of the year. A 19th-round pick in the 2001 draft, Gomes hit .291-16-44.

Three of the Indians' four first-round picks were assigned to Burlington: righthanders Dan Denham and J.D. Martin and outfielder Mike Conroy. Martin had the most success of the three, going 5-1, 1.38 with 72 strikeouts and 11 walks in 45 innings.

Other first-rounders in the league in 2001: third baseman David Wright of Kingsport (.302-4-16) and righthander Kris Honel of Bristol (2-3, 3.13).

STANDINGS

Page	EAST	W	L	PCT	GB	Manager	Attendance (Avg.)	Last Penn.
82	Bluefield Orioles (Orioles)	33	33	.500	—	Joe Almaraz	26,160 (1,006)	2001
146	Martinsville Astros (Astros)	31	37	.456	3	Jorge Orta	35,392 (1,106)	1999
119	Burlington Indians (Indians)	31	37	.456	3	Rouglas Odor	36,371 (1,137)	1993
75	Danville Braves (Braves)	30	38	.441	4	Ralph Henriquez	26,618 (832)	None
250	Princeton Devil Rays (Devil Rays)	28	39	.418	5½	Edwin Rodriguez	35,404 (1,264)	1994
Page	WEST	W	L	PCT	GB	Manager	Attendance (Avg.)	Last Penn.
172	Elizabethton Twins (Twins)	41	22	.651	—	Rudy Hernandez	20,878 (803)	2000
96	Bristol Sox (White Sox)	38	26	.594	3½	John Orton	19,300 (689)	1998
256	Pulaski Rangers (Rangers)	38	30	.559	5½	Bruce Crabbe	21,509 (672)	None
196	Kingsport Mets (Mets)	31	35	.470	11½	Joey Cora	20,384 (703)	1995
223	Johnson City Cardinals (Cardinals)	31	35	.470	11½	Chris Maloney	42,816 (1,381)	1976

PLAYOFFS—Bluefield defeated Elizabethton 2-1 in best-of-3 championship series.

NOTE: Teams' individual batting and pitching statistics can be found on page indicated in lefthand column.

CLUB BATTING

	AVG	G	AB	R	H	2B	3B	HR	BB	SO	SB
Bluefield	.264	66	2162	357	570	109	19	47	261	557	109
Elizabethton	.260	63	1972	271	512	109	14	28	184	456	58
Pulaski	.259	68	2247	382	583	124	19	59	231	637	97
Bristol	.257	65	2035	301	524	95	12	32	192	538	80
Kingsport	.257	67	2123	315	545	111	21	34	227	602	120
Princeton	.256	67	2175	338	557	99	17	66	201	596	54
Danville	.245	68	2250	265	551	111	14	27	184	617	48
Johnson City	.241	66	2105	286	508	95	13	48	232	558	38
Martinsville	.231	68	2153	230	498	96	15	26	126	515	75
Burlington	.223	68	2177	308	485	81	18	42	268	660	61

CLUB PITCHING

	ERA	G	CG	SHO	SV	IP	H	R	ER	BB	SO
Martinsville	3.04	68	3	6	14	573	494	243	194	212	575
Elizabethton	3.12	63	1	6	22	518	442	229	180	192	588
Johnson City	3.26	66	1	6	13	555	514	285	201	189	629
Bristol	3.58	65	5	4	15	531	514	267	211	149	486
Pulaski	3.71	68	2	4	19	575	546	307	237	191	555
Danville	3.79	68	2	4	17	583	529	327	246	238	623
Kingsport	4.11	67	1	1	11	565	588	320	258	215	552
Burlington	4.15	68	0	1	15	581	546	341	268	256	606
Bluefield	4.71	66	2	1	17	552	579	360	289	222	562
Princeton	5.13	67	2	3	11	552	581	374	315	242	560

CLUB FIELDING

	PCT	PO	A	E	DP		PCT	PO	A	E	DP
Martinsville	.969	1719	651	76	50	Kingsport	.955	1694	682	113	54
Elizabethton	.963	1554	564	82	30	Pulaski	.955	1725	755	118	51
Bristol	.961	1592	695	92	60	Bluefield	.953	1657	642	114	43
Burlington	.958	1744	663	106	40	Princeton	.952	1657	622	114	38
Danville	.956	1749	614	109	43	Johnson City	.951	1665	678	122	53

INDIVIDUAL BATTING LEADERS
(Minimum 184 Plate Appearances)

	AVG	G	AB	R	H	2B	3B	HR	RBI	BB	SO	SB
Pena, Brayan, Danville	.370	64	235	39	87	16	2	1	33	31	30	3
Francisco, Ruben, Bluefield	.327	57	199	35	65	16	0	3	21	17	32	18
Rogers, Omar, Bluefield	.323	63	226	41	73	12	1	2	32	29	41	22
Pittman, Sean, Kingsport	.320	47	181	24	58	11	3	1	26	21	36	17
Cavin, Jonathan, Bristol	.317	54	183	24	58	7	1	3	21	17	45	3
Huber, Justin, Kingsport	.314	47	159	24	50	11	1	7	31	17	42	4
Woodrow, Justin, Johnson City	.313	60	211	32	66	11	3	2	21	38	27	4
Bourgeois, Jason, Pulaski	.311	62	251	60	78	12	2	7	34	26	47	21
Perea, Jean, Pulaski	.305	68	256	40	78	15	0	3	39	24	53	13
Kochen, Ryan, Martinsville	.300	56	180	29	54	12	3	5	23	10	37	5
Tomlin, James, Elizabethton	.300	63	237	38	71	14	4	1	23	21	33	15

INDIVIDUAL PITCHING LEADERS
(Minimum 54 Innings)

	W	L	ERA	G	GS	CG	SV	IP	H	R	ER	BB	SO
Ankiel, Rick, Johnson City	5	3	1.33	14	14	1	0	88	42	20	13	18	158
Cabreja, Eny, Bluefield	4	3	1.58	12	12	1	0	74	54	19	13	20	67
Albertus, Roberto, Danville	3	2	2.39	16	5	0	2	60	46	20	16	13	41
Mattox, David, Kingsport	5	1	2.40	14	8	1	0	56	48	22	15	19	58
Gardner, Hayden, Bristol	4	4	2.48	13	13	2	0	83	71	32	23	15	70
Houlton, D.J., Martinsville	5	4	2.50	13	13	1	0	72	67	24	20	7	71
Merricks, Matt, Danville	4	5	2.79	12	11	0	0	58	42	19	18	18	78
Lubisich, Nik, Bristol	5	2	2.83	11	11	2	0	70	65	26	22	12	49
Szado, Craig, Bristol	2	3	3.05	15	8	0	1	56	52	23	19	12	56
Mabry, Barry, Danville	3	3	3.20	20	2	0	0	56	60	26	20	18	55
Tejada, Sandy, Elizabethton	5	3	3.20	11	10	0	0	56	43	26	20	20	87

ALL-STAR TEAM

C—Brayan Pena, Danville. **1B**—Andy Baxter, Burlington. **2B**—Omar Rogers, Bluefield. **3B**—Randall Shelley, Pulaski. **SS**—Sean Pittman, Kingsport. **OF**—Jonny Gomes, Princeton; James Tomlin, Elizabethton; Justin Woodrow, Johnson City. **DH**—Rick Ankiel, Johnson City. **Util**—Jason Bourgeois, Pulaski; Ruben Francisco, Bluefield; Brad Stockton, Pulaski. **RHP**—D.J. Houlton, Martinsville. **LHP**—Rick Ankiel, Johnson City. **RP**—Ryan Keefer, Bluefield.

Player of the Year: Jonny Gomes, Princeton. **Pitcher of the Year**: Rick Ankiel, Johnson City. **Manager of the Year**: Rudy Hernandez, Elizabethton.

DEPARTMENT LEADERS

BATTING

G	Jean Perea, Pulaski	68
AB	Jean Perea, Pulaski	256
R	Jason Bourgeois, Pulaski	60
H	Brayan Pena, Danville	87
TB	Jonny Gomes, Princeton	123
XBH	Andy Baxter, Burlington	31
2B	Randall Shelley, Pulaski	18
	Brad Stockton, Pulaski	18
3B	Rashad Eldridge, Burlington	6
HR	Jonny Gomes, Princeton	16
RBI	Andy Baxter, Burlington	46
SH	Randy Rojas, Martinsville	7
SF	Matt Knox, Burlington	5
	Randy Rojas, Martinsville	5
BB	Brad Stockton, Pulaski	40
IBB	John Fagan, Martinsville	3
HBP	Jonny Gomes, Princeton	26
SO	Jutt Hileman, Johnson City	81
	Randall Shelley, Pulaski	81
SB	Omar Rogers, Bluefield	22
CS	Omar Rogers, Bluefield	10
GIDP	Ruben Francisco, Bluefield	10
OB%	Jonny Gomes, Princeton	.442
SL%	Jonny Gomes, Princeton	.597

PITCHING

G	Ryan Keefer, Bluefield	29
GS	Rick Ankiel, Johnson City	14
	Matt Wright, Danville	14
CG	Three tied at	2
ShO	Hector Febles, Princeton	2
GF	Ryan Keefer, Bluefield	27
SV	Ryan Keefer, Bluefield	15
W	Five tied at	6
L	Mariano Gomez, Burlington	8
	Miguel Pinango, Kingsport	8
IP	Rick Ankiel, Johnson City	88
H	Matt Tate, Bluefield	80
R	Mariano Gomez, Burlington	47
ER	Mariano Gomez, Burlington	40
HR	Scott Patten, Bristol	12
HB	Omar Anez, Bluefield	10
BB	Brandon Kentner, Kingsport	36
SO	Rick Ankiel, Johnson City	158
WP	Bryan Digby, Danville	13
	Matt Wright, Danville	13
BK	Three tied at	5

FIELDING

C	AVG	Reinaldo Ruiz, Martinsville	.988
	PO	Yadier Molina, Johnson City	409
	A	Yadier Molina, Johnson City	81
	E	Hector Santana, Burlington	13
	DP	Gustavo Molina, Bristol	3
	PB	Cody Gunn, Johnson City	15
1B	AVG	John Fagan, Martinsville	.994
	PO	Jean Perea, Pulaski	628
	A	Jean Perea, Pulaski	46
	E	Garrett Jones, Danville	8
		Jean Perea, Pulaski	8
	DP	Jean Perea, Pulaski	45
2B	AVG	Randy Rojas, Martinsville	.965
	PO	Andrew Salvo, Bristol	106
	A	Jason Bourgeois, Pulaski	197
	E	Omar Rogers, Bluefield	19
	DP	Andrew Salvo, Bristol	39
3B	AVG	Randall Shelley, Pulaski	.924
	PO	Randall Shelley, Pulaski	48
	A	Randall Shelley, Pulaski	134
	E	Matt Abram, Elizabethton	18
	DP	Mike O'Kelly, Danville	11
SS	AVG	Ramon Mercedes, Princeton	.941
	PO	Pete Shier, Bluefield	90
	A	Pete Shier, Bluefield	148
	E	Jutt Hileman, Johnson City	27
	DP	Michael Morse, Bristol	29
OF	AVG	Woody Cliffords, Bluefield	1.000
	PO	Ardley Jansen, Danville	140
	A	Antwon Rollins, Pulaski	10
	E	Antwon Rollins, Pulaski	10
	DP	Antwon Rollins, Pulaski	4

PIONEER LEAGUE

BY JOHN ROYSTER

The Pioneer League draws its share of high draft picks each year. First-rounders in 2001 included first baseman Casey Kotchman of the Provo Angels and shortstop Jayson Nix of the Casper Rockies. There were a couple of first-rounders from past years, and a greater number of second-round picks.

But the overwhelming majority of the players are guys even Baseball America readers have never heard of. Players who get only a small bonus, a ticket to Big Sky Country and a wish of good luck. But a funny thing happens once they arrive. They seem to have acquired a tendency to win triple crowns.

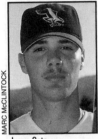

MARC McCLINTOCK

Jesus Cota

In 2001, Missoula Osprey first baseman Jesus Cota became the third such non-bonus baby to win one since 1997. Signed for $60,000 in the spring of 2001 as a 14th-round draft-and-follow, Cota tied for the home run lead (16) and led outright in batting (.368) and RBIs (71).

Greg Morrison and Jay Gibbons, both playing for Medicine Hat, won triple crowns in 1997 and '98. Before that, it had been done just once, by John Scoras for Lethbridge in 1976.

"There was a question mark regarding Jesus coming into minicamp in June," said Tommy Jones, farm director for the parent Diamondbacks. "He'd been injured a large portion of the year in junior college, and he kind of came into minicamp trying to get established."

Cota, a lefthanded hitter who attended Pima Community College in Tucson, truly dominated the league. He wasn't just in the top 10 in a lot of offensive categories.

He was first or second in doubles, extra-base hits, on-base percentage, slugging percentage and runs. And, of course, the triple-crown categories.

His "weakness" was in his number of hits. He was just third in that category, with two hits fewer than leader Gary Varner of the Billings Mustangs.

Varner and his teammates also walked away with the championship rings, eliminating Cota's team in the semifinals and Provo in the finals.

Billings lost its first playoff game, but then won four straight to take both of its best-of-three series. It also fell behind 4-0 early in the final game of the final series against Provo, but scored five runs in the sixth inning to win 5-4. The biggest hero was lefthander Cleris Severino, who pitched seven innings of four-hit, scoreless relief.

"When it was 4-0 I was thinking, 'OK, how are we going to get the pitching lined up for tomorrow?'" Billings manager Rick Burleson said. "But he kept getting them out, kept getting them out."

Provo had routed Casper in the other semifinal, outscoring the Rockies 30-9 in two games between the league's two newest cities.

The Provo franchise moved from Helena, Mont., where it had been the league's second Brewers affiliate, after the 2000 season. Casper, the first professional team in Wyoming since Cheyenne had a Western League club in 1941, moved from Butte, Mont., where it had been the Angels affiliate.

The two new teams played in the two smallest ballparks in the league, and they finished among the bottom three in attendance.

Both, though, had plans to improve their situations. Provo was working toward a new ballpark after playing the season at Brigham Young University's 2,000-seat Larry H. Miller Field.

"I have a lot of confidence in the city of Provo," Angels co-owner Linda Gach Ray said shortly before the season. "I'll admit it's taking slightly longer than I had hoped, but my optimism remains."

Casper at first thought it would move into new Mike Lansing Field sometime during the season, but construction delays forced it to play the whole year at 2,000-seat George Tani Memorial Field.

STANDINGS: SPLIT SEASON

FIRST HALF

NORTH	W	L	PCT	GB
Billings	25	12	.676	—
Missoula	25	13	.658	½
Great Falls	18	20	.474	7
Medicine Hat	9	29	.237	16½
SOUTH	**W**	**L**	**PCT**	**GB**
Provo	29	9	.763	—
Casper	16	22	.421	13
Ogden	14	22	.389	14
Idaho Falls	14	23	.378	14½

SECOND HALF

NORTH	W	L	PCT	GB
Missoula	27	11	.711	—
Billings	21	17	.553	6
Great Falls	19	19	.500	8
Medicine Hat	11	27	.289	16
SOUTH	**W**	**L**	**PCT**	**GB**
Provo	24	14	.632	—
Ogden	22	16	.579	2
Casper	21	17	.553	3
Idaho Falls	7	31	.184	17

PLAYOFFS—Semifinals: Billings defeated Missoula 2-1 and Provo defeated Casper 2-0 in best-of-3 series. **Final:** Billings defeated Provo 2-0 in best-of-3 series.

STANDINGS: OVERALL

Page		W	L	PCT	GB	Manager	Attendance (Avg.)	Last Penn.
61	Provo Angels (Angels)	53	23	.697	—	Tom Kotchman	51,919 (1,527)	1981
69	Missoula Osprey (Diamondbacks)	52	24	.684	1	Chip Hale	54,868 (1,483)	1999
110	Billings Mustangs (Reds)	46	29	.613	6½	Rick Burleson	104,524 (2,903)	2001
159	Great Falls Dodgers (Dodgers)	37	39	.487	16	Dave Silvestri	88,198 (2,321)	1990
126	Casper Rockies (Rockies)	37	39	.487	16	P.J. Carey	41,849 (1,131)	1984
166	Ogden Raptors (Brewers)	36	38	.486	16	Ed Sedar	109,360 (3,038)	None
230	Idaho Falls Padres (Padres)	21	54	.280	31½	Jake Molina	63,410 (1,669)	2000
264	Medicine Hat Blue Jays (Blue Jays)	20	56	.263	33	Tom Bradley	25,930 (682)	1982

NOTE: Teams' individual batting and pitching statistics can be found on the page indicated in lefthand column.

MINOR LEAGUES

2001 PIONEER LEAGUE STATISTICS

CLUB BATTING

	AVG	G	AB	R	H	2B	3B	HR	BB	SO	SB
Provo	.304	76	2631	557	801	145	23	69	315	607	82
Missoula	.284	76	2701	535	768	146	31	69	290	596	47
Ogden	.284	74	2575	460	731	143	18	48	246	499	107
Billings	.278	75	2637	452	734	131	25	54	266	533	84
Casper	.277	76	2614	448	724	127	25	74	277	686	108
Idaho Falls	.260	75	2619	405	680	130	20	43	247	722	60
Medicine Hat	.256	76	2640	361	675	111	14	55	223	594	63
Great Falls	.254	76	2590	400	657	109	22	42	273	496	137

CLUB PITCHING

	ERA	G	CG	SHO	SV	IP	H	R	ER	BB	SO
Missoula	3.63	76	1	4	21	670	689	375	270	222	532
Billings	3.77	75	2	4	18	661	654	350	277	196	608
Provo	3.97	76	2	6	20	656	670	365	290	226	688
Great Falls	4.64	76	0	5	18	676	725	454	349	247	668
Ogden	5.15	74	0	1	18	643	702	443	368	232	605
Casper	5.32	76	2	1	21	658	777	492	389	280	526
Medicine Hat	5.66	76	0	3	12	662	740	537	417	305	504
Idaho Falls	6.65	75	0	2	10	653	813	602	483	429	602

CLUB FIELDING

	PCT	PO	A	E	DP		PCT	PO	A	E	DP
Ogden	.964	1930	837	103	66	Idaho Falls	.952	1959	736	137	52
Casper	.959	1973	789	117	68	Great Falls	.947	2028	841	160	59
Billings	.959	1983	818	121	53	Missoula	.946	2009	835	161	65
Provo	.955	1969	788	131	54	Medicine Hat	.945	1987	860	167	70

INDIVIDUAL BATTING LEADERS
(Minimum 205 Plate Appearances)

	AVG	G	AB	R	H	2B	3B	HR	RBI	BB	SO	SB
Cota, Jesus, Missoula	.368	75	272	74	100	22	0	16	71	56	52	2
Corbeil, Al, Provo	.359	60	217	48	78	18	0	4	41	24	41	0
Swenson, Sam, Provo	.351	63	225	61	79	16	4	13	55	24	64	7
Varner, Gary, Billings	.351	72	291	55	102	20	5	8	55	29	64	7
Hairston, Scott, Missoula	.347	74	291	81	101	16	6	14	65	38	50	2
Chavez, Ender, Casper	.342	64	228	49	78	9	1	0	22	38	31	24
Hart, Jon, Ogden	.340	69	262	53	89	18	1	11	62	26	47	14
Santana, Ralph, Ogden	.337	68	261	57	88	6	1	1	26	37	37	30
McEachran, Aaron, Medicine Hat	.336	69	256	34	86	12	1	5	41	32	55	3
Tempesta, Nick, Medicine Hat	.335	72	263	49	88	16	1	8	46	24	51	3

INDIVIDUAL PITCHING LEADERS
(Minimum 61 Innings)

	W	L	ERA	G	GS	CG	SV	IP	H	R	ER	BB	SO
Dennis, Jason, Provo	5	0	2.05	14	13	0	0	75	53	20	17	21	79
Hosford, Clint, Great Falls	6	3	2.50	15	12	0	0	79	72	28	22	16	69
Holsten, Ryan, Missoula	9	3	2.53	17	12	0	0	89	84	33	25	12	60
Liriano, Pedro, Provo	11	2	2.78	14	14	0	0	78	80	39	24	31	76
Tisdale, Marlyn, Billings	7	4	3.05	14	14	1	0	83	88	31	28	13	76
Medina, Franklin, Missoula	8	2	3.39	15	14	1	0	88	89	42	33	28	55
Childress, Daylan, Billings	6	1	3.55	14	8	0	1	63	59	32	25	17	54
Mercedes, Gabriel, Missoula	8	3	3.71	15	14	0	0	80	81	47	33	30	66
McCracken, Vance, Great Falls	4	5	3.84	14	9	0	1	63	63	31	27	11	46
Severino, Cleris, Billings	3	3	4.30	15	13	1	0	67	66	37	32	30	54

ALL-STAR TEAM

C—Al Corbeil, Provo. **1B**—Jesus Cota, Missoula. **2B**—Scott Hairston, Missoula. **3B**—Florian Villanueva, Ogden. **SS**—Casey Smith, Provo. **OF**—Jose Garcia, Great Falls; Tony Miller, Casper; Sam Swenson, Provo. **DH**—Jesse Gutierrez, Billings. **RHP**—Pedro Liriano, Provo. **LHP**—Jason Dennis, Provo. **RP**—Nathan Cotton, Billings.

Most Valuable Player: Jesus Cota, Missoula. **Pitcher of the Year**: Pedro Liriano, Provo. **Manager of the Year**: Chip Hale, Missoula.

DEPARTMENT LEADERS

BATTING
G	Jesus Cota, Missoula	75
AB	Jose Garcia, Great Falls	306
R	Scott Hairston, Missoula	81
H	Gary Varner, Billings	102
TB	Scott Hairston, Missoula	171
XBH	Jesus Cota, Missoula	38
2B	Jose Garcia, Great Falls	23
3B	Jeramy Janz, Missoula	8
HR	Jesus Cota, Missoula	16
	Jesse Gutierrez, Billings	16
RBI	Jesus Cota, Missoula	71
SH	Casey Smith, Provo	9
SF	Jesse Gutierrez, Billings	7
BB	Jesus Cota, Missoula	56
IBB	Jesus Cota, Missoula	6
HBP	Mike Lopez, Missoula	16
SO	Jose Vasquez, Casper	96
SB	Manuel Nunez, Great Falls	32
CS	Ralph Santana, Ogden	12
GIDP	Jose Garcia, Great Falls	9
OB%	Jesus Cota, Missoula	.476
SL%	Sam Swenson, Provo	.631

PITCHING
G	Rusty Tucker, Idaho Falls	30
	Wilmer Villatoro, Idaho Falls	30
GS	Seven tied at	15
CG	Seven tied at	1
ShO	Four tied at	1
GF	Nathan Cotton, Billings	28
SV	Jesus Silva, Missoula	14
W	Pedro Liriano, Provo	11
L	Jon Huber, Idaho Falls	9
	David Pauley, Idaho Falls	9
IP	Ryan Holsten, Missoula	89
H	Jorge Buret, Casper	110
R	Charles Lawton, Idaho Falls	69
ER	Charles Lawton, Idaho Falls	58
HR	Charles Lawton, Idaho Falls	12
	Ismael Ramirez, Medicine Hat	12
HB	Brendan Fuller, Medicine Hat	10
BB	Rusty Tucker, Idaho Falls	50
SO	Jake Woods, Provo	84
WP	Jay Mitchell, Casper	15
BK	Francisco Rosario, Medicine Hat	6
	Jon Steitz, Ogden	6

FIELDING
C	AVG	Bryan Prince, Billings	.995
	PO	Jose Diaz, Great Falls	359
	A	Jose Diaz, Great Falls	52
		Bryan Prince, Billings	52
	E	Jose Diaz, Great Falls	9
	DP	Four tied at	3
	PB	John Blackburn, Medicine Hat	13
		Omar Falcon, Idaho Falls	13
1B	AVG	Jesse Gutierrez, Billings	.992
	PO	Dave Mulqueen, Casper	612
	A	Jesus Cota, Missoula	52
	E	Aaron McEachran, Medicine Hat	11
	DP	Dave Mulqueen, Casper	57
2B	AVG	Ralph Santana, Ogden	.961
	PO	Ralph Santana, Ogden	132
	A	Scott Hairston, Missoula	178
	E	Scott Hairston, Missoula	21
	DP	Eduardo Diaz, Casper	42
3B	AVG	Oscar Materano, Casper	.942
	PO	Cesar Martin, Medicine Hat	62
	A	Cesar Martin, Medicine Hat	160
	E	Cesar Martin, Medicine Hat	26
	DP	Mike Lopez, Missoula	14
SS	AVG	Jeff Bannon, Billings	.943
	PO	Juan Peralta, Medicine Hat	121
	A	Manuel Nunez, Great Falls	232
	E	Juan Peralta, Medicine Hat	35
	DP	Juan Peralta, Medicine Hat	44
OF	AVG	Jeramy Janz, Missoula	.989
	PO	Tony Miller, Casper	151
	A	Ender Chavez, Casper	11
	E	Jose Garcia, Great Falls	11
	DP	Ender Chavez, Casper	5

ARIZONA LEAGUE

BY ALLAN SIMPSON

As Chris Tritle and Shin-Soo Choo went, so went the Athletics and Mariners in the Rookie-level Arizona League in 2001.

Choo sizzled early for the Mariners, leading that team to the first-half title. As his performance slipped, Tritle picked up the pace and led the A's to the second-half crown. The Athletics then beat the Mariners in a one-game playoff for the league title.

"Tritle just took off at the halfway point of the season," Mariners manager Omer Munoz said. "He showed everything: power, speed, defense and an ability to take charge."

Just as the performance of those players had a profound effect on the Arizona League pennant race, Tritle's and Choo's tools also were at the forefront as managers identified the league's best major league prospects. Tritle, the league MVP, earned the nod as top prospect from six of the seven managers, while Choo gained the other first-place vote.

JOHN SPEAR
Chris Tritle

A 19th-round pick of the A's in 2000, Tritle made little impression on managers in his debut. But he was a different story in 2001, leading the league in homers, slugging percentage and stolen bases.

"He was from a small school in Iowa and the pro regimen was new to him last year," said A's scout John Kuehl, who managed Tritle in 2000. "He took it a lot more seriously this year, and he was a different player."

Ricky Nelson, who managed the A's in 2001, saw the same transformation. "He's really matured and now believes in his ability," Nelson said. "He's got the potential to be a consistent 30-30 player."

Choo sizzled in the first half for the Mariners, hitting .358. But he wound up batting only .302 overall, causing at least one manager to question his approach.

"Early on, he showed a lot of discipline at the plate," Nelson said. "But pitchers began to get him out by pounding him inside. He made a lot of adjustments in his stance as he began to press."

Managers were impressed with the all-around ability of the 19-year-old Korean, who starred as a pitcher at the 2000 world junior championship and later signed a $1.335 million bonus with Seattle as an outfielder. He generally adapted well to his new role.

"He's a very exciting player to watch," Munoz said. "He hits for average and power, runs well and has an excellent arm. He also works very hard and adapted nicely to the change in culture."

The key figure in the league's championship game was neither Tritle nor Choo, but A's righthander Bryan Simmering, an unassuming 20-year-old Towson University product who had a 57-5 strikeout-walk ratio during the regular season. Simmering was an easy choice to pitch the playoff game and combined with Jeff Muessig and Dave Beck to blank the Mariners 6-0 on three hits. The trio didn't walk a batter and combined for 13 strikeouts, 10 by Simmering. Choo struck out three times in the game.

While Simmering shone in postseason play, the best pitchers in the regular season were Giants lefthander Ryan Hannaman and White Sox righthander Aaron Kirkland. Hannaman was rated the league's best pitching prospect by managers, while Kirkland led the league in ERA.

Hannaman was second in ERA and strikeouts, a sharp contrast from his 2000 professional debut when he went 0-1, 21.60 and walked 11 in three innings.

"His command was all over the place last year and in extended spring training," Giants manager Keith Comstock said. "He made tremendous strides this summer. He's got a very easy arm action and found a niche that worked. He also learned to throw a slider with excellent bite."

Undrafted out of Troy State in June, the 22-year-old Kirkland led the league with a 0.40 ERA, 12 saves and a .158 opponents' batting average. His most eye-popping stat, however, was no unintentional walks in 45 innings.

"He's a strike-throwing machine," White Sox manager Jerry Hairston said.

The Arizona League abandoned its two-division format in 2001 as the Diamondbacks and Padres moved their clubs to the Northwest League, the Rockies to the Pioneer League and the Mexican Academy pulled up stakes altogether. Those teams were replaced in part by the Angels and Brewers, with all teams based in the Phoenix area.

STANDINGS: SPLIT SEASON

FIRST HALF	W	L	PCT	GB	SECOND HALF	W	L	PCT	GB
Mariners	18	10	.643	—	Athletics	20	8	.714	—
Brewers	16	12	.571	2	Mariners	16	12	.571	4
Athletics	15	13	.536	3	Giants	14	14	.500	6
Giants	15	13	.536	3	White Sox	13	15	.464	7
Cubs	14	14	.500	4	Cubs	12	16	.429	8
White Sox	10	18	.357	8	Angels	12	16	.429	8
Angels	10	18	.357	8	Brewers	11	17	.393	9

PLAYOFFS—Athletics defeated Mariners in one-game playoff.

STANDINGS: OVERALL

Page	Complex Site	W	L	PCT	GB	Manager	Last Penn.
202	Athletics	Phoenix	35	21	.625	—	Ricky Nelson	2001
244	Mariners	Peoria	34	22	.607	1	Omer Munoz	2000
237	Giants	Scottsdale	29	27	.518	6	Keith Comstock	None
167	Brewers	Phoenix	27	29	.482	8	Carlos Lezcano	1990
104	Cubs	Mesa	26	30	.464	9	Carmelo Martinez	1997
97	White Sox	Phoenix	23	33	.411	12	Jerry Hairston	None
62	Angels	Mesa	22	34	.393	13	Brian Harper	None

NOTE: Teams' individual batting and pitching statistics can be found on page indicated in lefthand column.

MINOR LEAGUES

2001 ARIZONA LEAGUE STATISTICS

CLUB BATTING

	AVG	G	AB	R	H	2B	3B	HR	BB	SO	SB
Mariners	.300	56	1974	360	592	110	26	26	188	391	34
Giants	.276	56	1987	301	549	87	29	10	145	371	56
Cubs	.268	56	1901	262	510	102	26	20	150	456	70
White Sox	.261	56	1941	259	507	95	20	9	158	405	76
Brewers	.258	56	1894	284	489	93	25	17	180	496	39
Athletics	.257	56	1926	311	495	80	38	22	235	479	104
Angels	.250	56	1869	258	467	63	25	11	168	435	81

CLUB PITCHING

	ERA	G	CG	SHO	SV	IP	H	R	ER	BB	SO
Athletics	3.31	56	0	1	17	502	480	244	185	127	469
White Sox	3.35	56	1	4	16	491	473	282	183	162	429
Giants	3.79	56	0	6	9	497	463	249	209	232	478
Angels	4.33	56	2	5	8	488	566	334	235	171	412
Brewers	4.36	56	0	0	9	493	546	293	239	171	373
Cubs	4.50	56	0	2	17	497	532	319	249	185	445
Mariners	4.59	56	1	1	17	486	549	314	248	176	427

CLUB FIELDING

	PCT	PO	A	E	DP		PCT	PO	A	E	DP
Athletics	.965	1507	618	78	31	Mariners	.946	1458	571	116	40
Giants	.963	1490	569	79	34	Angels	.937	1464	550	136	38
Brewers	.954	1479	612	101	46	White Sox	.937	1473	508	134	31
Cubs	.946	1492	558	117	44						

INDIVIDUAL BATTING LEADERS
(Minimum 151 Plate Appearances)

	AVG	G	AB	R	H	2B	3B	HR	RBI	BB	SO	SB
Cedeno, Ronny, Cubs	.350	52	206	36	72	13	4	1	17	13	32	17
Cordova, Roman, Mariners	.343	42	140	25	48	6	3	0	14	9	23	4
Collins, Chris, Mariners	.342	42	161	25	55	14	0	2	29	20	26	0
McAuliff, Jimbo, Giants	.337	43	172	41	58	14	3	1	18	23	35	6
Tritle, Chris, Athletics	.336	52	214	47	72	6	8	9	42	22	55	26
Cadena, Alejandro, Mariners	.333	56	222	41	74	23	1	8	60	14	23	0
Paulino, Robert, Cubs	.327	47	153	20	50	10	4	2	28	9	26	4
Williams, Jon, Giants	.324	39	136	24	44	7	3	3	26	16	14	1
Gonzalez, Andy, White Sox	.323	48	189	33	61	18	1	5	30	15	36	13
Cabrera, Leonel, Giants	.322	46	205	45	66	14	2	1	31	6	22	12

INDIVIDUAL PITCHING LEADERS
(Minimum 45 Innings)

	W	L	ERA	G	GS	CG	SV	IP	H	R	ER	BB	SO
Kirkland, Aaron, White Sox	0	2	0.40	29	0	0	13	45	25	5	2	4	62
Hannaman, Ryan, Giants	4	1	2.00	11	11	0	0	54	34	14	12	31	67
Steward, Jaime, Angels	5	3	2.02	19	4	1	1	49	47	19	11	11	40
Matos, Raymond, Giants	4	3	2.34	14	12	0	0	62	64	35	16	29	66
Simmering, Bryan, Athletics	2	2	2.40	13	6	0	0	49	41	16	13	5	57
Asencio, Domingo, White Sox	2	1	2.44	7	7	0	0	48	45	23	13	8	29
Oakes, Gerard, Brewers	2	4	2.85	12	7	0	0	54	50	24	17	25	44
Garcia, Jairo, Athletics	4	2	2.85	12	7	0	0	47	37	19	15	6	50
Perez, Armando, White Sox	3	3	2.98	15	5	1	0	63	56	27	21	23	44
Arias, Daniel, Angels	1	2	3.02	16	3	0	1	48	64	25	16	9	42

ALL-STAR TEAM

C—Pedro Esparragoza, Brewers. **1B**—Tripp Kelly, Athletics. **2B**—Leonel Cabrera, Giants. **3B**—Chris Collins, Mariners. **SS**—Andy Gonzalez, White Sox. **OF**—Shin-Soo Choo, Mariners; Chris Tritle, Athletics; Anthony Webster, White Sox. **DH**—Alejandro Cadena, Mariners. **RHP**—Johan Santana, Angels. **LHP**—Ryan Hannaman, Giants. **RHR**—Aaron Kirkland, White Sox. **LHR**—David Beck, Athletics.

Most Valuable Player: Chris Tritle, Athletics. **Manager of the Year**: Jerry Hairston, White Sox.

BATTING

G	Alejandro Cadena, Mariners	56
	Troy Gustafson, Giants	56
AB	Anthony Webster, White Sox	225
R	Shin-Soo Choo, Mariners	51
H	Alejandro Cadena, Mariners	74
TB	Alejandro Cadena, Mariners	123
XBH	Alejandro Cadena, Mariners	32
2B	Alejandro Cadena, Mariners	23
3B	Shin-Soo Choo, Mariners	10
HR	Chris Tritle, Athletics	9
RBI	Alejandro Cadena, Mariners	60
SH	Robinson Chirinos, Cubs	6
SF	Three tied at	4
BB	Shin-Soo Choo, Mariners	34
IBB	Francisco Aybar, White Sox	2
	Shin-Soo Choo, Mariners	2
HBP	Gary Banks, Cubs	11
SO	Gary Banks, Cubs	80
SB	Chris Tritle, Athletics	26
CS	Ronny Cedeno, Cubs	10
	Edgar Trinidad, Athletics	10
GIDP	Ozzie Chavez, Brewers	8
	Roman Cordova, Mariners	8
OB%	Tripp Kelly, Athletics	.433
SL%	Chris Tritle, Athletics	.565

PITCHING

G	Aaron Kirkland, White Sox	29
GS	Rylan Reed, White Sox	13
CG	Four tied at	1
ShO	Three tied at	1
GF	Aaron Kirkland, White Sox	29
SV	Aaron Kirkland, White Sox	13
W	Tanner Watson, Mariners	8
L	Ryan Burnau, Cubs	6
	Leonardo D'Amico, Angels	6
IP	Armando Perez, White Sox	63
H	Emiliano Fruto, Mariners	73
R	Rylan Reed, White Sox	46
ER	Deron Featherstone, Giants	31
HR	Domingo Asencio, White Sox	5
HB	Yimmy Nacar, Giants	11
BB	Johan Santana, Angels	35
SO	Johan Santana, Angels	69
WP	Alvin Jones, White Sox	13
BK	Cristian Batista, Brewers	5

FIELDING

C	AVG	Francisco D'Jesus, Giants	1.000
	PO	Richard Suomi, Athletics	295
	A	Pedro Esparragoza, Brewers	44
	E	Pedro Esparragoza, Brewers	10
	DP	Three tied at	3
	PB	Richard Suomi, Athletics	22
1B	AVG	Tripp Kelly, Athletics	.996
	PO	Tripp Kelly, Athletics	436
	A	Tripp Kelly, Athletics	30
	E	Sean Peless, Mariners	10
	DP	Sean Peless, Mariners	33
2B	AVG	Edgar Trinidad, Athletics	.971
	PO	Leonel Cabrera, Giants	75
	A	Edgar Trinidad, Athletics	116
	E	Roberto Paulino, Cubs	12
	DP	Leonel Cabrera, Giants	17
3B	AVG	Chris Ciesluk, Giants	.915
	PO	Christian Batista, Angels	38
	A	Chris Ciesluk, Giants	86
	E	Taylor McCormack, Brewers	17
	DP	Robinson Chirinos, Cubs	10
SS	AVG	Ozzie Chavez, Brewers	.933
	PO	Ronny Cedeno, Cubs	83
		Ozzie Chavez, Brewers	83
	A	Ozzie Chavez, Brewers	152
	E	Ronny Cedeno, Cubs	22
		Andy Gonzalez, White Sox	22
	DP	Ozzie Chavez, Brewers	24
OF	AVG	Chris Tritle, Athletics	1.000
	PO	Francisco Plasencia, Brewers	92
	A	Javerro January, Brewers	10
	E	Carlos Cleto, Giants	8
		Quan Cosby, Angels	8
	DP	Hector Miliano, Cubs	2

GULF COAST LEAGUE

BY ALLAN SIMPSON

The Dodgers made a grand return to the Gulf Coast League in 2001, posting the league's best overall record. They also boasted the best pitching staff and the batting champion. The only thing that stopped the season from being an unqualified success for the Dodgers was a setback in the league playoffs.

They were upended 2-1 in a best-of-three final by the Yankees, who won the third and deciding game 5-2. The Dodgers had earned a bye into the final by virtue of a 41-19 regular season record, best in the Eastern Division by an 11-game margin over the Braves.

The Yankees struggled to even reach the final round, winning the Northern Division by a single game over the Tigers. They then beat the Western Division champion Red Sox in a one-game semifinal.

Playing in the championship round for the second straight year, the Yankees then turned back the Dodgers. Righthander Josh Smith, the team's top winner, went the distance in the deciding game, walking none while allowing six hits and two unearned runs. Shortstop Bronson Sardinha, a supplemental first-round pick in June and the Yankees' leading hitter, provided all the offense Smith would need with a double, home run and three RBIs.

Chad Petty

The Dodgers rejoined the GCL after an eight-year absence. They pulled out of the league after the 1992 season, but returned when the organization made a renewed commitment to Vero Beach, Fla., as a year-round training base.

Besides leading the league with a 2.44 ERA, the Dodgers got a strong season from second baseman Victor Diaz, a 37th-round draft pick in 2000. The stocky Diaz signed as a draft-and-follow in May out of Grayson County (Texas) Community College and went on to lead the league with a .354 average, 69 hits, 104 total bases, 22 doubles and a .533 slugging percentage.

Unlike 2000, when records were set in all three triple-crown categories, the 2001 season had no significant offensive accomplishments. No one came close to the records that fell a year earlier. Red Sox first baseman Matt Cooper, a second-year player, led the league in homers with seven—well off the 13 hit a year earlier by former Red Sox teammates Tony Blanco and Bryan Barnowski.

Eight first-round draft picks played in the league in 2000, including No. 1 overall pick Adrian Gonzalez, but the GCL had just two first-rounders in 2001, both for the Braves. Neither distinguished himself as one of the league's best prospects. Lefthander Macay McBride, the 25th overall pick, went 4-4, 3.76 and was third in the league with 67 strikeouts in 55 innings. Shortstop Josh Burrus hit just .193-3-19 and committed 21 errors in 48 games.

If anything, pitching dominated the league. And no one was more dominant than Tigers lefthander Chad Petty, a 2000 draft pick who went 6-0. He was named the league's top prospect in Baseball America's annual poll of managers.

Petty made a cameo appearance in the league a year earlier after being Detroit's second-round pick in 2000. He led the league with a 1.11 ERA in his return engagement.

"He really learned how to pitch this year," Yankees manager Derek Shelton said. "He worked both sides of the plate and knew exactly what pitch to throw in each situation. He was very polished for the Gulf Coast League."

Petty showed the makings of three solid pitches. His fastball normally ranged from 87-89 mph, touched 90-91 and had excellent sinking action. His changeup also moved extremely well, while his curve acted more like a hard slider.

"He was head and shoulders the best pitcher in this division," Tigers manager Howard Bushong said.

STANDINGS

Page	EAST	Complex Site	W	L	PCT	GB	Manager	Last Penn.
160	Dodgers	Vero Beach	41	19	.683	—	Juan Bustabad	1990
76	Braves	Kissimmee	30	30	.500	11	Rick Albert	1964
140	Marlins	Melbourne	29	31	.483	12	Jon Deeble	None
180	Expos	Jupiter	20	40	.333	21	Dave Dangler	1991
Page	NORTH	Complex Site	W	L	PCT	GB	Manager	Last Penn.
188	Yankees	Tampa	35	25	.583	—	Derek Shelton	2001
133	Tigers	Lakeland	34	26	.567	1	Howard Bushong	None
209	Phillies	Clearwater	31	29	.517	4	Roly de Armas	None
152	Royals	Baseball City	20	40	.333	12	Lino Diaz	1992
Page	WEST	Complex Site	W	L	PCT	GB	Manager	Last Penn.
90	Red Sox	Fort Myers	37	22	.627	—	John Sanders	None
111	Reds	Sarasota	36	22	.621	½	Edgar Caceres	None
173	Twins	Fort Myers	32	26	.552	4 ½	Al Newman	None
257	Rangers	Port Charlotte	24	35	.407	13	Carlos Subero	2000
216	Pirates	Bradenton	22	34	.393	13 ½	Woody Huyke	None
83	Orioles	Sarasota	22	34	.393	13 ½	Jesus Alfaro	None

PLAYOFFS—Semifinals: Yankees defeated Red Sox in one-game playoff. **Final:** Yankees defeated Dodgers 2-1 in best-of-3 series.

NOTE: Teams' individual batting and pitching statistics can be found on page indicated in lefthand column.

MINOR LEAGUES

2001 GULF COAST LEAGUE STATISTICS

CLUB BATTING

	AVG	G	AB	R	H	2B	3B	HR	BB	SO	SB
Twins	.262	58	1819	237	477	100	24	14	182	376	77
Red Sox	.262	59	1892	278	496	97	14	43	207	400	66
Dodgers	.260	60	1983	315	516	84	13	20	188	461	70
Orioles	.257	56	1739	214	447	92	19	21	161	445	55
Yankees	.256	60	1905	298	487	87	18	27	209	434	69
Phillies	.251	60	1911	261	480	98	13	24	189	449	39
Reds	.248	58	1743	226	433	75	19	15	169	431	108
Tigers	.243	60	1872	253	454	54	21	20	185	405	110
Rangers	.240	59	1845	239	443	99	29	12	172	434	124
Royals	.236	60	1884	210	444	86	7	11	178	446	63
Braves	.227	60	1939	227	441	76	9	24	147	446	64
Marlins	.221	60	1923	209	425	80	7	10	166	490	100
Pirates	.221	56	1686	185	372	65	11	14	190	398	81
Expos	.216	60	1913	184	413	57	11	10	159	522	48

CLUB PITCHING

	ERA	G	CG	SHO	SV	IP	H	R	ER	BB	SO
Dodgers	2.43	60	0	7	15	517	400	171	140	149	442
Phillies	2.77	60	0	6	9	494	449	220	152	154	436
Marlins	2.77	60	1	5	14	519	427	226	160	148	460
Reds	2.79	58	3	6	18	475	397	185	147	176	477
Braves	2.80	60	1	9	19	518	433	221	161	163	562
Twins	3.49	58	2	7	21	477	457	224	185	176	434
Red Sox	3.50	59	0	3	21	492	440	217	191	176	440
Yankees	3.65	60	3	7	16	497	473	245	202	203	459
Orioles	3.72	56	1	0	8	454	440	251	188	196	354
Rangers	3.76	59	3	6	9	487	490	255	204	178	411
Tigers	3.84	60	4	5	15	492	453	257	210	218	468
Pirates	3.88	56	3	5	12	450	444	247	194	179	368
Royals	3.98	60	1	1	10	490	490	300	217	186	371
Expos	4.12	60	0	2	9	515	535	317	236	200	455

CLUB FIELDING

	PCT	PO	A	E	DP		PCT	PO	A	E	DP
Red Sox	.972	1475	595	60	47	Pirates	.961	1349	551	78	45
Dodgers	.970	1551	628	67	44	Marlins	.960	1558	635	92	45
Yankees	.966	1491	608	73	45	Braves	.957	1553	549	95	34
Rangers	.966	1462	598	73	64	Phillies	.951	1482	573	105	41
Reds	.964	1424	484	71	34	Royals	.951	1470	495	101	46
Tigers	.964	1475	570	77	41	Orioles	.951	1362	573	100	38
Twins	.963	1432	583	78	63	Expos	.945	1546	627	126	43

INDIVIDUAL BATTING LEADERS
(Minimum 162 Plate Appearances)

	AVG	G	AB	R	H	2B	3B	HR	RBI	BB	SO	SB
Diaz, Victor, Dodgers	.354	53	195	36	69	22	2	3	31	16	23	6
Gonzalez, Juan, Tigers	.333	54	192	30	64	6	0	3	33	19	30	19
Brackley, Carlos, Red Sox	.329	49	152	24	50	8	1	6	21	9	27	3
Legendre, Curtis, Royals	.321	48	168	23	54	15	2	0	29	16	25	7
Herrera, Christian, Dodgers	.320	46	153	24	49	3	0	0	20	12	23	9
Gotay, Ruben, Royals	.315	52	184	29	58	15	1	3	19	26	22	5
Duran, Carlos, Braves	.304	54	204	35	62	10	3	2	17	12	30	16
Sardinha, Bronson, Yankees	.303	55	188	42	57	14	3	4	27	28	51	11
Heath, Demetrius, Tigers	.303	50	175	34	53	5	6	0	19	18	16	21
Mendoza, Adrian, Dodgers	.302	52	172	34	52	7	1	4	37	29	55	9

INDIVIDUAL PITCHING LEADERS
(Minimum 48 Innings)

	W	L	ERA	G	GS	CG	SV	IP	H	R	ER	BB	SO
Petty, Chad, Tigers	6	0	1.11	12	10	2	0	57	35	11	7	13	52
Ferreira, Emilo, Twins	8	1	1.20	12	10	0	0	60	52	10	8	10	47
Cuen, David, Dodgers	4	0	1.42	13	6	0	0	51	32	14	8	17	49
Rosado, Hector, Royals	3	5	1.73	14	6	1	2	52	44	19	10	15	48
Sanchez, Rafael, Red Sox	5	1	1.78	10	8	0	0	51	36	12	10	7	45
Murray, A.J., Rangers	3	3	1.86	12	8	0	0	53	48	15	11	10	45
Smith, Jason, Yankees	5	2	1.93	11	11	2	0	61	52	25	13	11	41
Acuna, Jose, Expos	2	4	1.93	14	6	0	0	51	41	13	11	11	45
Lopez, Javier, Dodgers	5	1	2.04	14	7	0	1	62	46	20	14	12	45
Mata, Gustavo, Expos	3	4	2.05	10	9	0	0	48	44	27	11	13	38

ALL-STAR TEAM

C—Dioner Navarro, Yankees. **1B**—Adrian Mendoza, Dodgers. **2B**—Victor Diaz, Dodgers. **3B**—Juan Gonzalez, Tigers. **SS**—Bronson Sardinha, Yankees. **OF**—Elvin Andujar, Reds; Carlos Brackley, Red Sox; Carlos Duran, Braves. **SP**—Chad Petty, Tigers. **RP**—Jannio Gutierrez, Twins. **Manager of the Year:** Derek Shelton, Yankees.

MINOR LEAGUES

DEPARTMENT LEADERS

BATTING

G	Three tied at	58
AB	Travis Ezi, Dodgers	238
R	Bronson Sardinha, Yankees	42
H	Victor Diaz, Dodgers	69
TB	Victor Diaz, Dodgers	104
XBH	Victor Diaz, Dodgers	27
2B	Victor Diaz, Dodgers	22
3B	Anderson Hernandez, Tigers	11
HR	Matt Cooper, Red Sox	7
RBI	Adrian Mendoza, Dodgers	37
	Juan Tejeda, Tigers	37
SH	Travis Ezi, Dodgers	6
	Christian Herrera, Dodgers	6
SF	Brian Nickerson, Dodgers	7
BB	Paul Ciofrone, Phillies	33
	Alvaro Ruiz, Red Sox	33
IBB	Four tied at	3
HBP	Hector Perozo, Dodgers	17
SO	Travis Ezi, Dodgers	90
SB	Anderson Hernandez, Tigers	34
CS	Anthony Brewer, Marlins	10
GIDP	Luis Cruz, Red Sox	8
OB%	Ulises Cabrera, Rangers	.438
SL%	Victor Diaz, Dodgers	.533

PITCHING

G	Dimas Reina, Dodgers	25
GS	Nick Masset, Rangers	14
CG	Three tied at	2
ShO	Jason Smith, Yankees	2
GF	Jannio Gutierrez, Twins	21
SV	Jannio Gutierrez, Twins	16
W	Emilo Ferreira, Twins	8
L	Eddie Diaz, Expos	7
IP	Ronald Belizario, Marlins	73
H	Ronald Belizario, Marlins	62
	Leo Nunez, Pirates	62
R	Eddie Diaz, Expos	42
ER	Eddie Diaz, Expos	36
HR	Luis Diaz, Tigers	6
HB	Eddie Diaz, Expos	15
BB	Daniel Cabrera, Orioles	39
SO	Luis Diaz, Tigers	71
WP	Juan Figueroa, Tigers	12
BK	Juan Figueroa, Tigers	5

FIELDING

C	AVG	Dustin Smith, Rangers	.996
	PO	Alonzo Ruelas, Braves	300
	A	Dioner Navarro, Yankees	35
	E	Salomon Manriquez, Expos	9
	DP	Orlando Sulbaran, Rangers	4
	PB	Danilo Sanchez, Tigers	11
1B	AVG	Roberto Santana, Braves	.994
	PO	Matt Cooper, Red Sox	478
	A	Jared Pitney, Yankees	32
	E	Matt Cooper, Red Sox	7
		Luis Blanco, Expos	7
	DP	Anibal Figueroa, Royals	34
2B	AVG	Jose Gonzalez, Rangers	.985
	PO	Victor Diaz, Dodgers	88
	A	Victor Diaz, Dodgers	132
	E	Victor Diaz, Dodgers	12
		Ruben Gotay, Royals	12
	DP	Jose Gonzalez, Rangers	29
3B	AVG	Carlos Rijo, Orioles	.916
	PO	Carlos Rijo, Orioles	51
	A	Carlos Rijo, Orioles	102
	E	Carlos Rijo, Orioles	14
	DP	Three tied at	9
SS	AVG	Christian Herrera, Dodgers	.955
	PO	Anderson Hernandez, Tigers	90
	A	Christian Herrera, Dodgers	130
	E	Deni Mancebo, Expos	24
	DP	Anderson Hernandez, Tigers	28
OF	AVG	Sean Smith, Pirates	1.000
	PO	Anthony Brewer, Marlins	120
	A	Frank Diaz, Expos	9
	E	Mervin Williams, Royals	6
	DP	Masjid Khairy, Rangers	3
		Scott Whitrock, Twins	3

Success has been hard to come by of late for the Milwaukee Brewers, who have not had a winning season at the major league level since 1992 or a winning overall record in the minors since 1996. But the Brewers' Dominican Summer League entry has been a source of pride the last two years.

The DSL Brewers captured the league title in 2001, a year after finishing a close second in the 33-team league, the largest under the Minor League Baseball umbrella.

The Brewers went 51-21 during the regular season to beat the defending champion Dodgers by a healthy seven-game margin in the Santo Domingo East Division. They then turned back the Mets 2-1 in the first round of the playoffs and edged the Phillies 3-2 in a best-of-five final.

Milwaukee's recent success in the Dominican can be attributed to the hiring of Epy Guerrero as the club's director of international scouting in 1995, when the Brewers had almost no presence in the Dominican Republic. Guerrero, who once successfully mined Dominican talent for the Blue Jays, has been responsible for signing many of the top players in the Dominican, while his son Mike has managed the Brewers' DSL club.

The Brewers won the title despite playing without the league's RBI leader, third baseman Aldrin Gomez (.297-1-

59), in both rounds of the playoffs; and the team's top winner, lefthander Gabriel Mendoza (9-1, 1.91), in the final round. But outfielder Mario Mendez, who finished second in the league to Gomez in RBIs and was named the league MVP, stepped up in the final round by hitting two homers and driving in seven runs.

Mets lefthander Maikel DeLeon was the league's dominant pitcher. He went 8-0 and led the league with a 0.48 ERA while striking out 88 and walking nine in 94 innings to earn co-pitcher of the year honors. DeLeon also handed the Brewers their only loss in the semifinal round of the playoffs.

The Astros had the league's best regular-season record—.714, a mere six percentage points better than the Brewers—but went out in two straight games in the first round of the playoffs, losing to the Phillies.

The Dominican Summer League had 33 teams for the third straight year, with every major league club fielding a full roster for the first time. The Braves and Athletics fielded two teams, while the Indians and Red Sox shared a club.

The league played its first all-star game in 2001, with the American League defeating the National League 9-3. Tigers DH Edwin Williams went 3-for-4 with an RBI to earn game MVP honors.

ALL-STAR TEAM: C—Pedro Andujar, Dodgers. **1B**—Ruben Holguin, Mariners. **2B**—Valentin Mendez, Astros. **3B**—Aldrin Gomez, Brewers. **SS**—Albert Callaspo, Angels. **OF**—Carlos Arroyo, Mariners; Kelvin Guzman, White Sox; Mario Mendez, Brewers. **LHP**—Maikel DeLeon, Mets. **RHP**—Ambiorix Delgadillo, Angels. **RP**—Emilio Sanchez, Phillies.

Player of the Year: Mario Mendez, Brewers. **Co-Pitchers of the Year:** Maikel DeLeon, Mets; Emilio Sanchez, Phillies. **Manager of the Year:** Mike Guerrero, Brewers.

STANDINGS

SANTO DOMINGO EAST

	W	L	PCT	GB
Brewers	51	21	.708	—
Dodgers	44	28	.611	7
Mariners	42	29	.592	8½
Diamondbacks	37	34	.521	13½
Cardinals	35	36	.493	15½
Athletics East	33	39	.458	18
Tigers	33	39	.458	18
Giants	31	41	.431	20
Rockies	28	43	.394	22½
Marlins	24	48	.333	27

SANTO DOMINGO WEST

	W	L	PCT	GB
Mets	45	24	.652	—
Padres	39	29	.574	5½
Reds	35	33	.515	9½
Devil Rays	34	36	.486	11½
Cubs	32	35	.478	12
Athletics West	32	37	.464	13
Yankees	31	36	.463	13
Indians/Red Sox	25	43	.368	19½

SAN PEDRO de MACORIS

	W	L	PCT	GB
Astros	50	20	.714	—
Angels	45	25	.643	5
Blue Jays	43	27	.614	7
Expos	38	32	.543	12
Orioles	31	39	.443	19
Red Sox	28	42	.400	22
Pirates	27	43	.386	23
Rangers	18	52	.257	32

CIBAO

	W	L	PCT	GB
Phillies	43	29	.597	—
Indians	39	31	.557	3
White Sox	37	35	.514	6
Braves II	36	36	.500	7
Braves I	34	36	.486	8
Royals	33	39	.458	10
Twins	27	43	.386	15

PLAYOFFS: Semifinals—Phillies defeated Astros 2-0 and Brewers defeated Mets 2-1 in best-of-3 series. **Finals**—Brewers defeated Phillies 3-2 in best-of-5 series.

INDIVIDUAL BATTING LEADERS
(Minimum 150 Plate Appearances)

	AVG	AB	R	H	2B	3B	HR	RBI	SB
Montero, Danilo, Diamondbacks	.363	212	45	77	9	5	3	38	25
Tejeda, Ferdin, Yankees	.330	188	41	62	7	7	1	19	13
Callaspo, Albert, Angels	.356	275	55	98	11	4	2	39	14
Santiago, Ricardo, Diamondbacks	.355	276	60	98	19	13	3	36	22
Perez, Luis, Athletics East/West	.351	194	48	68	17	6	4	33	31
Williams, Edwin, Tigers	.352	159	36	56	6	3	1	25	17
Mendez, Valentin, Astros	.349	269	69	94	20	5	1	28	15
Arroyo, Carlos, Mariners	.348	253	52	88	22	2	1	43	19
Ramirez, Hanley, Red Sox	.345	197	32	68	18	2	5	34	13
Wispi, Jackson, Astros	.342	234	41	80	21	1	4	33	8
Guzman, Kelvin, White Sox	.337	270	64	91	14	8	0	39	13
Lopez, Angel, Mariners	.331	160	26	53	16	0	3	27	3
Mendez, Mario, Brewers	.330	279	58	92	18	1	3	57	25
Blanco, Gregor, Braves II	.330	215	45	71	6	10	0	18	21
Holguin, Ruben, Mariners	.315	267	43	84	9	5	10	53	5
Jose, Eugenio, Rockies	.315	235	40	74	16	4	6	41	29
Diaz, Robinson, Blue Jays	.312	253	49	79	17	2	2	45	4
Mendez, Victor, Tigers	.310	239	53	74	12	7	5	45	49
Cedano, Angelo, Red Sox	.307	241	44	74	10	1	0	19	18
Mallen, Yanel, Orioles	.306	209	34	64	10	3	5	32	7
Sarabia, Hamilton, Astros	.306	196	42	60	19	1	4	28	12
De Aza, Alejandro, Dodgers	.303	244	47	74	16	7	3	37	7
Ocumares, Omar, Indians	.303	264	33	80	23	3	5	47	6
Andujar, Pedro, Dodgers	.303	221	50	67	23	0	9	55	7
Suarez, Joel, Marlins	.302	225	49	68	13	6	3	25	10
DeJesus, Henry, Royals	.302	225	24	68	12	3	3	44	8
Paredes, Jeyson, Diamondbacks	.301	193	36	58	17	2	3	27	34
Garcia, Eustaquio, A's East	.300	260	44	78	9	5	1	40	20
Perez, Elvin, Devil Rays	.315	257	40	81	14	0	7	39	10
Prado, Martin, Braves II	.299	187	25	56	4	2	0	21	19
Garcia, Miguel, Mets	.298	168	24	50	13	1	2	25	5
Blanco, Andres, Royals	.298	188	39	56	0	3	0	16	9
Rosario, Robinson, Braves I	.298	238	48	71	12	10	0	39	26

	AVG	AB	R	H	2B	3B	HR	RBI	SB
Gomez, Aldrin, Brewers	.297	283	60	84	13	2	1	**59**	28
Cordova, Luis, Braves I	.297	209	22	62	18	1	1	38	3
Corzo, Erickson, Astros	.296	162	24	48	11	2	3	29	3
Tovar, Daniel, Athletics East/West	.295	156	30	46	3	1	0	23	6
Cespedes, Robinson, Astros	.294	313	59	92	13	7	1	37	26
Almonte, Sandy, Rockies	.294	218	47	64	14	5	2	18	24
Rivera, Johnny, White Sox	.294	248	44	73	6	4	4	30	18
Guzman, Edison, Twins	.294	180	15	53	5	2	0	23	7
Camarero, Rafael, Dodgers	.293	181	20	53	10	1	3	39	2
Arias, Yanuell, Indians	.293	242	44	71	6	3	1	22	37
Soto, Victor, Phillies	.293	167	23	49	2	4	0	18	10
Gomez, Galindo, Royals	.293	232	50	68	15	5	7	34	7
Rodriguez, Reynaldo, Expos	.292	185	33	54	6	1	1	30	19
Cruz, Waskar, White Sox	.292	264	44	77	**23**	0	4	51	9
Encarnacion, Victor, Blue Jays	.290	238	38	69	11	4	2	46	1
Bautista, Victor, Braves I	.290	231	46	67	12	6	1	27	16
Soto, Wilber, Angels	.289	228	39	66	7	3	0	41	18
Severino, Amaurys, Pirates	.289	197	22	57	7	2	0	22	10
Reyes, Jose, Cubs	.288	250	38	72	12	4	4	36	12
Rodriguez, Winston, Mariners	.287	237	54	68	10	3	0	35	36
Cerda, Antonio, Mets	.286	192	28	55	17	0	0	29	11
Nunez, Florentino, Rockies	.286	259	46	74	17	2	0	29	8
Melo, Manuel, Brewers	.285	260	64	74	12	0	0	26	**60**
Ferrer, Santos, Cardinals	.284	208	28	59	1	6	1	37	4
Robles, Manuel, Red Sox	.284	201	29	57	5	2	7	29	6
De la Cruz, Chris, Indians	.284	243	30	69	8	4	0	21	9
Rojas, Ricardo, Indians	.284	257	47	73	19	3	2	38	12
Dominguez, Raul, Yankees	.283	247	28	70	9	0	0	26	4
Perez, Angel, Cardinals	.283	219	44	62	8	6	0	31	16
Reid, Ivan, Devil Rays	.283	226	36	64	12	0	6	31	24
Lopez, Nelson, Cubs	.283	145	23	41	5	0	2	16	14
Castillo, Rogelio, Diamondbacks	.282	149	23	42	5	2	0	24	9
Batista, Jose, Marlins	.282	149	31	42	6	2	0	17	6
Sanchez, Washington, Mets	.282	131	19	37	7	5	0	10	8
Sanchez, Carlos, Cubs	.282	248	54	70	14	4	9	46	25
Gonzalez, Jose, Tigers	.281	192	31	54	10	3	0	22	10
Guillen, Rodolfo, Yankees	.281	231	38	65	13	2	**11**	41	11
Severino, Rolando, Padres	.280	164	31	46	3	3	2	17	9
#Campos, Tiago, Reds	.238	244	49	58	10	6	**11**	35	11

INDIVIDUAL PITCHING LEADERS
(Minimum 50 Innings)

	W	L	ERA	G	SV	IP	H	BB	SO
DeLeon, Maikel, Mets	8	0	**0.48**	15	0	94	51	9	88
Encarnacion, Alexis, Royals	5	2	0.88	27	8	72	45	15	55
Rodriguez, Rodney, Indians	6	2	0.99	19	4	54	31	13	57
Santiago, Victor, Dodgers	5	2	1.05	12	0	69	57	11	45
Nin, Antonio, Blue Jays	**11**	1	1.12	14	0	97	70	19	105
Ramirez, Elizardo, Phillies	10	1	1.26	14	0	93	71	9	81
Castillo, Jose, Angels	5	3	1.43	14	0	88	50	36	113
Delgadillo, Ambiorix, Angels	6	0	1.49	14	0	73	27	31	110
Garcia, Edwin, Twins	6	3	1.50	24	7	60	32	24	65
Cruz, Ramon, Mets	3	2	1.53	12	0	59	47	21	44
Garcia, Kelvin, Diamondbacks	7	4	1.55	15	0	81	55	13	80
Casimiro, Adolfo, Brewers	3	3	1.55	16	2	64	36	40	92
Valera, Jose, Brewers	8	1	1.57	12	0	74	48	26	70
De los Santos, Richard, Indians	6	2	1.58	13	0	80	67	13	41
Taveras, Rolando, Cardinals	6	2	1.78	13	1	61	53	23	63
Diaz, Carlos, Expos	6	4	1.83	19	1	69	66	12	59
Paulino, Gabriel, Tigers	1	3	1.84	29	14	54	30	12	74
Morales, Pablo, Astros	6	2	1.85	14	0	78	61	17	74
De la Cruz, Jesus, Devil Rays	8	3	1.88	13	0	91	58	49	**129**
Rivas, Juan, Pirates	6	5	1.90	16	1	76	63	9	77
Mendoza, Gabriel, Brewers	9	1	1.91	12	0	71	50	23	77
Lazuze, Enrique, Brewers	8	1	1.92	11	0	75	53	25	74
Valdez, Jose, Yankees	3	4	1.94	15	1	70	60	11	50
#Sanchez, Emilio, Phillies	2	2	1.97	32	**25**	32	18	11	30
Baez, Jose, White Sox	8	4	1.98	15	0	123	111	19	100
DePaula, Julio, Twins	5	3	1.98	19	2	68	51	23	49
Juarez, William, D'backs	6	1	1.98	10	0	59	50	13	64
Espinal, Jhovanny, Padres	4	3	2.00	13	0	54	42	15	46
Garcia, Abraham, Orioles	4	2	2.03	9	0	58	50	22	66
Silva, Erick, Diamondbacks	4	4	2.05	16	1	70	51	34	83
Ramirez, Jose, Orioles	3	2	2.06	12	0	70	66	9	58
Saint Hilaire, Algeni, White Sox	6	2	2.09	14	0	82	59	26	75
Abreu, Hector, Expos	2	4	2.13	14	0	55	52	20	37
Telemaco, Aneuri, Pirates	4	0	2.14	17	2	67	68	17	43
Lara, Juan, Indians	3	5	1.80	13	0	65	57	10	49
Alcantara, Kuintin, Cubs	5	2	2.20	12	0	57	62	15	51
Galvez, Willy, Red Sox	7	4	2.21	13	0	73	58	23	66
Corpas, Manuel, Rockies	2	1	2.24	15	2	56	56	17	41
Aguilar, Jhonneli, Astros	7	1	2.33	14	0	73	66	23	47
Berroa, Yeison, Blue Jays	7	5	2.33	14	0	85	83	23	74
Vega, Pablo, Royals	6	3	2.34	12	0	62	51	24	42
Avendano, Elvis, A's West	2	2	2.34	10	0	50	43	8	52
Tavarez, Carlos, Cubs	7	1	2.35	13	0	80	79	5	80
Sanchez, Adiel, A's West	7	5	2.44	14	0	92	100	22	70
Pascual, Jose, Devil Rays	4	2	2.44	16	1	55	44	19	35
Gonzalez, Hairo, Indians	2	4	2.45	12	0	62	57	7	58
Romero, David, Blue Jays	4	3	2.47	10	0	51	35	12	85
Ruelas, Heriberto, Dodgers	5	2	2.53	14	0	64	43	35	66
Hiraldo, Nelson, Indians	6	3	2.54	15	0	74	72	21	61
Brito, David, A's West	4	3	2.55	14	0	67	51	36	56
Rodriguez, Wascar, Marlins	5	4	2.56	25	6	63	49	28	70
Monges, Alvaro, Braves II	6	5	2.60	27	1	66	58	18	68
Moreno, Abel, Angels	8	3	2.61	13	0	90	87	17	53
Peguero, Tony, Devil Rays	5	3	2.62	15	1	89	68	24	50
Veras, Julio, Phillies	7	5	2.74	13	0	69	59	24	55
Hernandez, Santos, Rockies	3	6	2.64	15	0	78	60	26	76
Mercedes, Mirciades, Indians	3	6	2.66	12	0	61	44	27	69
Taveras, Nelson, A's East	10	3	2.68	15	0	91	77	21	80
Stewart, Scott, A's East	7	5	2.68	14	0	84	78	19	89
Vasquez, Esmerlyn, Reds	4	2	2.70	13	0	73	56	24	77
Gross, Pascual, Reds	5	3	2.72	15	0	79	66	37	53
Mejia, Andres, Mariners	7	3	2.76	32	10	59	47	27	66
Camilo, Elvis, Mets	7	1	2.77	13	0	62	54	15	46
Serrano, Ruben, Indians	3	7	2.77	14	0	65	49	33	62
Morales, Ruddy, White Sox	5	1	2.79	9	0	58	56	23	63
Gonzalez, Rodolfo, Dodgers	1	1	2.80	18	4	61	59	28	53
Rivera, Florentino, Brewers	5	2	2.81	13	1	77	65	12	63
German, Rafael, Reds	3	3	2.84	11	0	63	56	20	55
Gonzalez, Mailon, A's East/West	6	6	2.89	15	0	84	78	21	62
Malalla, Alexis, Braves I	6	6	2.90	15	0	81	78	21	69
Martinez, Ronnie, Astros	4	2	2.91	14	0	68	51	28	61
Mateo, Manuel, Braves II	6	7	2.93	15	0	92	93	18	48
Guzman, Braulio, Mets	4	0	2.95	13	0	55	48	34	44
Martinez, Kremlin, Twins	2	4	2.98	19	2	57	52	35	64
Concepcion, Felix, Phillies	3	4	2.99	14	0	66	49	41	66
Vilorio, Edikson, A's East	1	4	3.02	16	2	51	53	21	35
Pascual, Juan, Orioles	2	4	3.03	16	0	68	55	32	75
Made, Julin, Royals	2	8	3.06	14	0	71	81	21	48
Alvarez, Jesus, Braves II	1	2	3.07	10	0	56	54	23	37
Acosta, Richard, Orioles	2	4	3.09	12	0	64	54	11	41
Guzman, Ricardo, Braves I	4	2	3.11	13	0	84	77	20	46
Carmona, Fausto, Indians	4	2	3.11	14	0	75	69	12	47
Minaya, Francisco, Red Sox	4	6	3.12	13	0	69	87	15	47
Heredia, Jhonny, Cubs	4	6	3.14	14	0	80	72	27	54
Garcia, Anderson, Yankees	2	3	3.15	14	1	66	52	25	49
Lami, Onassis, Twins	5	3	3.15	11	0	54	63	20	26
Osoria, Frankelis, Dodgers	4	4	3.16	15	0	77	69	16	67

Statistics in boldface indicate league leader
#League leader but non-qualifier

VENEZUELAN SUMMER
LEAGUE

San Felipe dominated the Venezuelan Summer League in 2000, winning the regular season title with a 41-16, .716 record and scoring a clean sweep in the playoffs. It outdid itself in 2001—until the playoffs.

The Cleveland Indians farm club went 47-11, a league-record .810 clip, and won the Barquisimeto Division by 19½ games. But it stumbled in the playoffs, losing to Valencia Division champion Venoco 2-1 in a best-of-three series. It spoiled an otherwise dream season for San Felipe, which dominated the five-year-old league, compiling a team batting average (.306) that was 40 points lower than the next most prolific team, and a team ERA a full 0.49 runs greater than its closest pursuer.

San Felipe also had the league's dominant offensive performer, 5-foot-8, 140-pound switch-hitting center fielder Eider Torres, 18. He led the league in batting (.398), slugging percentage (.542), on-base percentage (.488), runs (67), hits (86), doubles (17) and stolen bases (41). Torres hit .310-0-19 a year earlier when San Felipe operated under a co-op arrangement with the Indians and Seattle Mariners.

Daniel Chirinos also topped pitchers with eight wins and a 1.23 ERA, but neither Torres nor Chirinos was much of a factor as San Felipe fell in the playoffs. Venoco, a Houston Astros farm club, knocked off San Felipe 6-2 in the deciding game as San Felipe committed five errors.

The VSL continued to expand in 2001, increasing from 10 to 12 clubs—doubling in size from its inaugural season in 1997. Twenty-two major league clubs provided players to the league, which is open to all Spanish-speaking players except those from the Dominican Republic and Puerto Rico. Most major league clubs shared teams in the league, the exceptions being Cleveland (San Felipe), Houston (Venoco) and the New York Mets (Universidad).

STANDINGS

BARQUISIMETO	W	L	PCT	GB
San Felipe	47	11	.810	—
Chivacoa	28	31	.474	19 ½
Cabudare	25	33	.441	22
Carora	17	42	.292	30 ½

VALENCIA	W	L	PCT	GB
Venoco	38	20	.653	—
San Joaquin	32	25	.559	5 ½
Mariara	32	25	.559	5 ½
Aguirre	28	29	.492	9 ½
La Pradera	28	29	.491	9 ½
Ciudad Alianza	25	30	.457	11 ½
Universidad	23	32	.424	13 ½
Cagua	20	36	.364	17

PLAYOFFS: Venoco defeated San Felipe 2-1 in best-of-3 series.
AFFILIATIONS: Aguirre (Mariners, Rockies), Cabudare (Orioles, Rangers), Cagua (Expos, Reds), Carora (Blue Jays, Cardinals), Chivacoa (Padres, Pirates), Ciudad Alianza (Cubs, Marlins), La Pradera (Dodgers, Yankees), Mariara (Devil Rays, Phillies), San Felipe (Indians), San Joaquin (Brewers, Red Sox, Twins), Universidad (Mets), Venoco (Astros).

INDIVIDUAL BATTING LEADERS
(Minimum 115 At-Bats)

	AVG	AB	R	H	2B	3B	HR	RBI	SB
Torres, Eider, San Felipe	.398	216	67	86	17	4	2	37	41
Gomez, Hose, San Felipe	.390	118	30	46	12	1	1	27	11
Canizalez, Jose, San Felipe	.367	109	29	40	7	4	0	16	8
Marin, Sergio, San Felipe	.362	116	24	42	7	1	1	21	8
Romero, Alexander, San Joaquin	.347	167	22	58	9	0	2	30	10
Huerta, Luis, San Felipe	.343	181	36	62	13	2	0	30	6
Cohen, Eleasaib, Universidad	.336	131	19	44	7	0	2	16	7
Gutierrez, Tonys, Cagua	.332	199	29	66	9	1	4	33	2
Perez, Miguel, Cagua	.331	163	20	54	3	1	0	19	6
Duran, Alexander, Mariara	.331	142	29	47	5	1	3	21	12
Colina, Yinner, Cagua	.324	170	30	55	9	0	2	30	1
Bencomo, Johan, San Felipe	.322	143	30	46	7	2	0	34	10
Torres, Saul, Venoco	.320	203	43	65	7	5	4	41	15
Aguilar, Trino, Mariara	.316	231	35	73	12	1	4	48	8
Araque, Marco, Cagua	.316	209	31	66	12	6	6	38	3
Martinez, Jose, Aguirre	.313	166	25	52	7	1	0	17	12
Golindano, Jesus, La Pradera	.310	197	30	61	12	2	4	31	5
Burgos, Omar, San Joaquin	.309	175	32	54	10	1	2	18	23
Gamero, Jesus, Universidad	.308	146	17	45	6	0	0	9	4
Martinez, Alirio, Cabudare	.308	133	23	41	5	1	0	13	15
Andrus, Erold, La Pradera	.305	223	44	68	14	0	1	23	10
Rodriguez, Marcos, Carora	.303	165	31	50	9	1	3	21	8
Antequera, Javier, Chivacoa	.302	126	20	38	6	4	0	16	12
Brito, Henry, Mariara	.301	183	32	55	8	3	2	23	7
Castro, Ismael, Aguirre	.300	200	34	60	7	4	2	21	23
Yepez, Marcos, Ciudad Alianza	.299	197	46	59	13	3	4	24	19
Soto, Illish, Universidad	.299	187	25	56	15	2	3	23	7

Roman, Jose, San Joaquin	.297	118	24	35	3	1	0	13	12
Marquez, Uriak, Ciudad Alianza	.295	149	18	44	10	3	4	29	7
Rivas, Kevin, San Felipe	.293	99	21	29	6	1	0	15	7
Perez, Jorge, San Joaquin	.292	202	43	59	7	1	2	26	14
Aponte, Jose, Ciudad Alianza	.288	205	38	59	13	1	5	37	15
Orozco, Dernier, San Joaquin	.287	108	18	31	7	0	0	12	5
Mora, Effison, San Felipe	.286	147	31	42	13	0	0	22	4
Orozco, Miguel, Aguirre	.286	119	17	34	7	0	0	22	3
Lambis, Alberto, Ciudad Alianza	.284	109	12	31	3	0	2	14	1
Vasquez, Domingo, San Felipe	.283	205	25	58	9	2	1	35	1
Chavez, Dirimo, San Joaquin	.278	180	26	50	12	2	0	16	9
Pulido, Gabriel, Carora	.278	158	18	44	12	0	0	19	4
Gimenez, Hector, Venoco	.278	144	27	40	12	3	5	34	4
Guerra, Alex, Cabudare	.277	191	29	53	7	0	1	24	16
Zerpa, Kleiver, Chivacoa	.277	130	19	36	11	1	2	17	3
Guerrero, Henry, Cabudare	.276	181	25	50	8	0	4	24	3
Caraballo, Francisco, Venoco	.275	142	16	39	5	2	0	22	2
Barboza, Nergio, La Pradera	.274	164	23	45	11	0	6	26	2
Colmenarez, Juan, Cabudare	.274	157	19	43	7	0	0	13	3
Dominguez, Freidy, Cabudare	.273	194	27	53	13	0	5	25	2
Marin, Limberth, Aguirre	.273	139	20	38	7	2	1	14	16
Guevara, Orlando, Mariara	.273	139	25	38	8	1	0	13	3
Hudson, Maximiliano, Venoco	.269	160	32	43	8	4	2	25	5
Leon, Adixon, Aguirre	.267	105	13	28	5	1	0	16	0
Rodriguez, Christian, Venoco	.264	208	34	55	11	1	6	35	8
Romero, Luis, La Pradera	.264	178	21	47	4	0	2	26	0
Herrera, Harold, Universidad	.264	159	25	42	12	0	0	15	7
Garcia, Antonio, Venoco	.263	194	25	51	13	1	4	31	3
Lopez, Geomar, Chivacoa	.263	160	15	42	9	1	1	20	4
Mago, Milwin, Chivacoa	.261	188	21	49	6	1	0	25	16
Meza, Jose, Universidad	.261	115	18	30	2	0	2	10	4
Galan, Jorman, Cagua	.260	131	24	34	6	0	2	8	3
Blanco, Franklin, Ciudad Alianza	.260	123	18	32	1	0	1	11	5
Maldonado, Jose, Aguirre	.259	166	25	43	10	1	4	19	10
Uribe, Melvin, Ciudad Alianza	.257	101	35	26	5	3	1	6	11
Martina, Sigmar, Mariara	.255	188	25	48	9	0	3	22	1
Perez, Randy, Carora	.255	165	22	42	6	3	1	21	5
Levi, Carlos, La Pradera	.254	193	26	49	12	0	10	34	11

INDIVIDUAL PITCHING LEADERS
(Minimum 46 Innings)

	W	L	ERA	G	SV	IP	H	BB	SO
Chirinos, Daniel, San Felipe	8	1	1.23	12	0	66	45	11	41
Guzman, Daniel, San Felipe	5	2	1.28	13	1	56	35	18	53
Veliz, Jesus, Cabudare	0	1	1.37	12	2	53	46	13	24
Delgado, Oscar, Aguirre	4	3	1.44	11	0	56	43	27	62
Escobar, Rodrigo, Venoco	3	2	1.68	12	0	70	53	9	69
Revilla, Cesar, Cabudare	4	2	1.81	15	1	50	39	24	44
Andres, Rafael, Aguirre	2	2	1.83	12	0	54	40	16	45
Morfee, Edgar, San Felipe	4	3	1.84	12	0	49	31	20	35
Chang, Kenly, Aguirre	3	4	1.91	14	0	61	41	12	31
Acosta, Nivaldo, Aguirre	4	3	1.96	16	0	55	47	7	30
Torrealba, Yoaan, Chivacoa	4	5	1.97	14	0	73	50	19	46
Zambrano, Oscar, Chivacoa	4	2	2.01	15	1	63	49	16	46
Almenar, Aristides, Universidad	3	4	2.08	12	0	61	52	14	57
Gonzalez, Jesus, Aguirre	1	2	2.10	14	0	56	40	24	27
Martinez, Javier, San Joaquin	4	1	2.18	14	0	62	48	28	42
Alvarado, Carlos, San Felipe	6	2	2.24	14	2	56	49	10	36
Mendoza, Luis, San Joaquin	6	0	2.27	13	1	67	46	10	61
De la Sierra, Antonio, Chivacoa	4	3	2.33	11	0	58	48	8	36
Heredia, Luis, Cagua	3	3	2.40	14	1	64	48	16	62
Bazardo, Yorman, Ciudad Alianza	7	2	2.43	12	0	70	59	18	62
Garcia, Rurik, Aguirre	1	5	2.56	15	0	46	35	25	28
Granado, Jan, Cagua	7	4	2.57	14	0	77	72	24	77
Blanco, Julio, San Joaquin	3	3	2.63	13	1	68	65	13	32
Dominguez, Carlos, Ciudad Alianza	7	3	2.70	15	1	77	53	19	80
Romero, Cesar, Mariara	1	3	2.73	10	0	56	41	33	31
Freites, Julio, Universidad	3	1	2.83	12	0	54	40	20	50
Machi, Jean, Mariara	8	3	2.86	14	2	57	40	30	56
Bravo, Mahler, Mariara	3	4	2.91	13	0	46	44	23	46
Contreras, Omar, Chivacoa	3	3	2.94	12	0	52	59	26	48
Oberto, Orlando, Mariara	1	4	2.94	12	0	52	35	17	41
Altuve, Juan, Cagua	3	3	3.00	13	0	54	52	31	46
Garcia, Javier, La Pradera	1	7	3.08	13	0	53	63	8	36
Rincon, Daniel, Carora	2	3	3.11	14	3	46	40	24	33
Salazar, Julio, Venoco	4	3	3.12	12	0	61	59	18	58
Sanchez, Anibal, San Joaquin	4	3	3.19	24	3	54	40	23	64
Strauss, Jonathan, Universidad	2	4	3.22	12	0	73	73	15	39
Vergara, Antonio, Venoco	4	0	3.26	14	3	50	45	13	32
Ochoa, Nehomar, Cagua	3	4	3.38	13	0	64	63	19	39
Gutierrez, Gilfran, San Joaquin	3	2	3.47	14	0	47	45	16	48
Escorcha, Orlando, Cagua	3	4	3.78	13	0	67	67	25	51
#Medina, Dennis, San Joaquin	2	4	4.24	26	12	34	33	15	33

INDEPENDENT

Northern League still sets standard; Eastern clubs continue to dominate

BY MARK DEREWICZ

After nine years, it's safe to say independent league baseball isn't going away. Hundreds of players have progressed into the affiliated minor leagues, several making it all the way to the big leagues. New ballparks have popped up in every independent league and fans continue to respond.

The gold standard remained the Northern League, even though a new team began play in one division and two teams ceased operations in the other in 2001.

In the Central Division, the Lincoln Saltdogs replaced the Madison Black Wolf, which was a huge upgrade. Commissioner Miles Wolff had been interested in Lincoln as an original franchise in 1993 but was unable to work out financing for a new stadium. That happened in 2001 and Cornhusker fans came out in droves to watch baseball.

Impressive debut: With Haymarket Park as its centerpiece, Lincoln drew 5,300 fans a game

The Saltdogs made it to the playoffs in their inaugural season and drew more than 5,300 fans a night at brand new Haymarket Park. With Madison out of the picture, only Duluth-Superior averaged less than 2,500 fans a night in the Central.

The Catskill Cougars and Waterbury Spirit dropped out of the NL's Eastern Division after the 2000 season, reducing the number of teams from eight to six. A handful of teams still needed to be addressed in the East but none were in dire straits. And the league planned to expand to eight teams again for 2002.

While teams in the East traditionally have not done as well attendance-wise as their counterparts in the Central, they have had no problem putting quality products on the field.

New Jersey beat Winnipeg in the NL championship series three games to one, marking the third consecutive time an East team had defeated a Central team since the Northern League merged with the Northeast League after the 1998 season. The East had also won the last two all-star games.

"I think it's a testament to our roster rules," league president Dan Moushon said of the East's success. "Each team must have four veterans and five rookies. There's no question the Central has better facilities, but not necessarily better players."

Allentown middle infielder Francisco Matos, the East's best player, hit .416 to set a Northern League record. Only Tim Howard, who hit .447 for Amarillo (Texas-Louisiana) in 1998, has put up a better mark in independent league history.

Matos struck out four times in 243 at-bats and at one point went 125 at-bats without a strikeout. He also hit safely in 31 consecutive games, but batted .456 at Allentown's Bicentennial Park, a quirky stadium with very little foul territory. The stadium features a tall left field fence considered too shallow for pro ball.

A New Look

Better ballparks have been the focal point in the Texas-Louisiana League's recent upgrade.

Edinburg, a small Texas town located 20 miles from the Mexican border, drew close to 3,000 fans a night in 2001. Three years earlier, no teams were drawing terribly well in that league and too many franchise changes had hurt the league's reputation.

Things began to change for the better with the addition of Springfield/Ozark in 1999. Horn Chen, who purchased the centrally operated league that year, made it a priority to leave poor markets once and for all.

The Greenville Bluesmen, who drew less than 400 fans a game in 2001, won't play in 2002. The league will most likely field six teams in 2002, while developing two new markets for 2003.

The Western League also had a facelift in 2001 while going from eight to six teams. The Feather River Mudcats, Tri-City Posse and Valley Vipers were dropped, while Long Beach, an original franchise, returned to the fold.

A new independent league was introduced in 2001. The All American Association debuted with six teams, stretching from Tyler, Texas, in the west to Albany, Ga., in the east.

While the Northern, Texas-Louisiana and Western

INDEPENDENT LEAGUES

PLAYER OF THE YEAR

Like most Atlantic League players, Somerset outfielder Mike Warner didn't want to spend the entire 2001 season in independent baseball. He wanted another shot with a major league organization.

With a few weeks left in the minor league season, a few teams finally called on Warner to fill a roster spot at Triple-A. Warner, though, decided to stick with Somerset, where he continued to post impressive numbers for arguably the strongest team in independent baseball.

"I'd rather stay here with this team and help in the postseason," Warner said. "I've had a good season. I'll take my chances on hooking up with a major league team in the offseason."

For his offensive onslaught and defense—not to mention his loyalty—Warner was named Baseball America's 2001 Independent Player of the Year.

Warner had a strong first half, batting .369-12-64 while leading the league in each triple-crown category. He lost pace in the home run race but finished the season .351-17-103.

The 5-foot-10, 170-pound New Jersey native led the league in average, RBIs and on-base percentage (.469). He finished second with 99 runs, 144 hits and a .571 slugging percentage.

His five second-half home runs were more indicative of coming down to earth than any late-summer swoon.

"I usually hit one home run every 10 games or so," he said. "In the first half, I hit five in one week. Once the second half started, teams did start to pitch around me a little bit. It was a combination of both. I started to hit more singles and doubles in the second half."

Warner, the Braves' 22nd-round pick in 1992, stayed in the Atlanta farm system for seven years but never produced enough at the higher levels to warrant a big league callup. He was granted free agency in 1998 and

Mike Warner

signed with the Dodgers. He batted .330-3-12 in 191 at-bats for Double-A San Antonio in 1999, but missed the final two months with a dislocated ankle.

The ankle healed very slowly, and he was barely able to walk by the time spring training started in 2000. He seriously considered quitting the game, but decided instead to give independent ball a shot. The Atlantic City Surf signed him in April 2000, but the team wasn't convinced he could play center field every day. He hadn't swung a bat or picked up a ball since the previous July, and his ankle was still a hindrance.

He made three plate appearances in 10 games before asking to be released. The Surf granted his request and Somerset signed him that same day. He wound up batting .303-9-53 with 47 stolen bases in 397 at-bats in 2000.

Healthy and hungry, Warner returned to Somerset in 2001 after spending the winter in the Venezuelan League.

With fast second baseman Billy Hall in the leadoff spot, Warner hit in the middle of the lineup all season, usually in the three-hole or cleanup.

"I know I can do the job the fourth outfielders are doing in the big leagues," he said. "But I won't get mad if I don't get another chance. I took a lot for granted when I was younger, but I've grown up as a person the past two years. When I came back after the injury, I was just playing because I love baseball."

Baseball America's 2001 independent all-star team:

C—Victor Sanchez, Solano (Western). **1B**—Ray Brown, Chico (Western). **2B**—Felix Pagan, Sioux Falls (Northern). **3B**—Josh Patton, Sioux City (Northern). **SS**—Francisco Matos, Allentown (Northern). **OF**—Michael Warner, Somerset (Atlantic); Carmine Cappuccio, Winnipeg (Northern); Charles Peterson, Sioux Falls (Northern). **DH**—Joe Hamilton, Alexandria (Texas-Louisiana).

SP—Clay Eason, Lincoln (Northern); Len Picota, Nashua (Atlantic); Ryan Harris, Edinburg (Texas-Louisiana); Rafael Gross, Winnipeg (Northern). **RP**—George Preston, Alexandria (Texas-Louisiana).

---

leagues build teams with similar roster requirements, the Frontier and Atlantic leagues continued to march to their own drummers with varying degrees of success.

The Frontier League has an age limit of 26, which precludes big-name veterans from playing. The league, though, has a solid history of providing places to play for nondrafted rookies and other young players.

Two more sanctuaries came into the fold in 2001. The Kalamazoo Kings had a great year at the gate, drawing close to 2,500 fans a night. The Gateway Grizzlies, on the other hand, drew less than 800 fans at a high school field. The team was supposed to play at a new stadium on the outskirts of St. Louis but funding got tied up prior to the season, halting construction.

The Atlantic League, which had a number of former big leaguers sprinkled throughout the league, has no rookie requirements and continued to successfully push itself as a Triple-A alternative to fans and players in the Northeast.

The Nashua Pride won the second-half North Division title after a disastrous first half. So many players landed on

the disabled list that the Pride tempted fate by holding a promotion called "Injury Night." Any fan with a brace or cast was admitted at half-price and escorted to the area of the grandstands where the most foul ball activity occurs.

The league still had to deal with its only black eye—the Lehigh Valley Black Diamonds. The Black Diamonds have never played in the Lehigh Valley because plans for a new stadium never got off the drawing board. Once scheduled to play in a new park near Easton, Pa., they spent 1998 in Newburgh, N.Y., 1999 on the road, 2000 in Quakertown, Pa., and 2001 back on the road.

The league absorbed the cost of keeping the team active but vowed it won't do the same in 2002.

The Atlantic League had another banner year at the gate, drawing well over 1.6 million in a 72-game home schedule. Somerset went 83-43 overall to break the league record for most wins in a season, and the Long Island Ducks broke their own attendance record from 2000.

The Ducks' average of 6,155 fell short of two Northern League teams. Winnipeg averaged 6,491 and St. Paul averaged 6,423 to lead independent baseball.

ALL-AMERICAN ASSOCIATION

The All-American Association kicked off its first season of independent league play in 2001 with a loosely-knit alignment of six teams spread over five states, from Texas in the west to Georgia in the east.

Just two of the six teams had decent fan support—the Fort Worth Cats averaged 1,483 and the Montgomery Wings drew 2,296 a game.

The Baton Rouge Blue Marlins won the inaugural championship series by taking three of five games from the Albany Alligators. DH Chris Cassels went 2-for-4 with a solo home run in the fifth inning of the final game to give the Blue Marlins a 3-2 lead.

The Blue Marlins also had the best team during the regular season, finishing with a 44-28 record. Baton Rouge dispatched Fort Worth in two straight in the semifinals.

Albany ace Rick Powalski defeated Tyler twice in the other series, including an inspired performance during a 12-inning 4-3 win in the final game. He entered the game in the fifth, after pitching a complete game two days earlier, and threw seven scoreless innings before his teammates finally pulled it out in the 12th inning.

Powalski, the league's pitcher of the year, had to pick up an extra share of the load when former major leaguer Jeff Sparks missed the playoffs when he hurt his elbow at the end of the season. Sparks went 8-2, 2.00 and struck out a league-leading 136 batters.

STANDINGS

	W	L	PCT	GB
Baton Rouge Blue Marlins	44	28	.611	—
Albany Alligators	41	31	.569	3
Tyler Roughnecks	39	32	.549	4½
Fort Worth Cats	37	35	.514	7
Montgomery Wings	34	38	.472	10
Tennessee T's	20	51	.282	23½

PLAYOFFS: Semifinals—Baton Rouge defeated Fort Worth 2-0 and Albany defeated Tyler 2-1 in best-of-3 series. **Finals**—Baton Rouge defeated Albany 3-2 in best-of-5 series.

MANAGERS: Albany—Tom Waelchli, Eddie Dixon. **Baton Rouge**—Scott Bethea. **Fort Worth**—Jim Gentile. **Montgomery**—Lou Thornton Jr. **Tennessee**—Jay Hemond. **Tyler**—Steve Maddock.

ATTENDANCE: Montgomery 78,069; Fort Worth 50,426; Albany 26,543; Tyler 18,973; Baton Rouge 16,616; Tennessee 10,343.

ALL-STAR TEAM: C—Gerard McCall, Montgomery. **1B**—Pedro Quero, Fort Worth. **2B**—Jason Williams, Baton Rouge. **3B**—Brennan Dees, Montgomery. **SS**—Erick Mejias, Tennessee. **OF**—Pat Hannon, Fort Worth; Brian Baker, Tennessee; Michael Kirkpatrick, Tyler. **DH**—Ben Brack, Montgomery. **SP**—Rich Powalski, Albany. **RP**—Rick Greene, Baton Rouge.

Most Valuable Player: Jason Williams, Baton Rouge. **Pitcher of the Year:** Rich Powalski, Albany. **Rookie of the Year:** Pat Hannon, Fort Worth. **Manager of the Year:** Scott Bethea, Baton Rouge.

INDIVIDUAL BATTING LEADERS
(Minimum 194 Plate Appearances)

	AVG	AB	R	H	2B	3B	HR	RBI	SB
Williams, Jason, Baton Rouge	.376	250	51	94	18	1	10	58	11
Matos, Malvin, Tyler	.375	112	24	42	10	1	6	30	1
Hannon, Pat, Fort Worth	.340	268	49	91	15	4	7	52	1
Brack, Ben, Montgomery	.330	221	39	73	11	1	9	43	1
Dees, Brennan, Mont.	.329	255	46	84	17	1	6	34	10
Perrett, Kevin, Baton Rouge	.328	235	52	77	17	0	4	44	7
Quero, Pedro, Fort Worth	.322	283	50	91	22	2	13	59	2
Bowden, Merrit, Mont.	.312	173	18	54	9	0	3	27	5
Brown, Eric, Baton Rouge	.309	181	33	56	9	1	4	20	5
Jackson, Gavin, Albany	.307	231	51	71	16	3	0	40	12

INDIVIDUAL PITCHING LEADERS
(Minimum 58 Innings)

	W	L	ERA	G	SV	IP	H	BB	SO
Guzman, Jose, Fort Worth	5	2	1.65	9	0	60	51	12	59
Powalski, Rich, Albany	8	4	1.81	34	10	89	59	16	132
Sparks, Jeff, Albany	8	2	2.00	14	0	86	62	27	136

Herbert, Russ, Tyler	6	1	3.18	9	0	62	52	26	67
Batson, Byron, Albany	6	2	3.20	11	0	76	77	9	54
Lewis, Roderick, Albany	8	2	3.29	18	0	93	86	40	67
Warren, David, Mont.	5	7	3.40	15	0	93	83	36	77
Wallace, Flint, Fort Worth	6	4	3.46	14	0	96	96	16	87
Melancon, Kory, Mont.	3	2	3.51	9	0	59	56	19	49
Shiery, Shawn, Mont.	6	4	3.55	15	0	96	92	29	98

ALBANY

BATTING	AVG	AB	R	H	2B	3B	HR	RBI	SB
Cormell, Eric, of	.228	149	26	34	6	0	0	11	9
Craddox, Kenny, of	.238	185	24	44	8	2	2	15	9
Datillo, Franco, ss	.203	69	10	14	5	0	0	7	1
Davila, Leonard, 3b-2b	.206	141	18	29	5	0	1	11	3
Denhan, T.J., 1b	.321	162	16	52	9	1	3	29	2
Fansler, Lindsay, of	.238	21	5	5	0	0	0	0	2
Feliciano, Edwin, 1b-c	.255	149	23	38	5	0	1	17	2
Griffin, Marcus, 2b-of	.182	22	4	4	2	0	0	3	5
Jackson, Gavin, ss	.307	231	51	71	16	3	0	40	12
Morabito, Mike, of	.200	15	3	3	0	0	0	3	1
Murphy, Darian, 1b	.059	17	1	1	0	0	0	0	1
Pope, Dwight, c	.189	143	12	27	5	1	1	10	0
Ransom, Grant, ss	.211	71	10	15	2	0	1	7	3
Scott, Donald, of	.221	86	7	19	2	1	0	9	3
Shemwell, Foy, 3b-2b	.289	204	38	59	11	0	2	36	7
Taylor, Lee, 2b	.269	175	35	47	7	1	0	9	9
Vizcaino, Romulo, of	.305	233	36	71	22	2	1	44	14
Walker, Steve, of	.300	280	61	84	20	4	6	51	29
PITCHING	**W**	**L**	**ERA**	**G**	**SV**	**IP**	**H**	**BB**	**SO**
Baez, Pedro	2	2	5.04	19	1	30	34	14	31
Baker, Jason	1	2	7.32	5	0	20	22	15	18
Batson, Byron	6	2	3.20	11	0	76	77	9	54
Brown, Ryan	1	4	4.67	21	0	54	58	20	50
Dixon, Eddie	0	1	5.52	4	0	15	17	1	12
Draper, Kris	0	0	6.00	4	1	6	13	3	5
Hendershot, Bob	0	0	2.19	5	1	12	11	2	6
Kuiper, David	1	2	2.70	4	0	17	16	5	17
Learson, John	1	2	5.59	5	0	19	26	13	16
Morgan, Shawn	2	2	6.11	7	0	35	54	18	30
Powalski, Rick	8	4	1.81	34	10	89	59	16	132
Roderick, Lewis	8	2	3.29	18	0	93	86	40	67
Sanders, John	2	2	6.88	9	0	34	23	41	24
Simmons, Tim	1	4	8.01	18	2	30	45	14	30
Sparks, Jeff	8	2	2.00	14	0	86	62	27	136

BATON ROUGE

BATTING	AVG	AB	R	H	2B	3B	HR	RBI	SB
Albaral, Randy, of	.133	15	3	2	0	0	0	0	0
Bethea, Scott, 3b-2b	.346	127	18	44	7	0	0	19	2
Bramble, Todd, of	.091	11	0	1	0	0	0	1	0
Brown, Eric, of	.309	181	33	56	9	1	4	20	5
Cassels, Chris, dh	.300	140	16	42	9	1	5	32	0
Healy, Liam, c	.207	145	17	30	10	0	3	22	1
Jarreau, James, of	.284	194	43	55	10	2	1	22	10
Keiser, Jason, 2b-ss	.257	171	35	44	9	2	0	14	22
Keith, Jason, ss	.276	163	21	45	11	1	2	25	3
Mendez, Rick, 1b-3b	.187	91	8	17	4	2	0	15	2
Perini, Mike, of	.301	143	26	43	8	2	2	22	5
Perret, Kevin, of-3b	.328	235	52	77	17	0	4	44	7
Salow, Josh, c	.196	92	8	18	2	0	1	12	0
Taylor, William, of	.255	102	16	26	2	2	0	7	14
Waguespack, Macky, 1b	.270	222	30	60	12	0	10	41	0
Williams, Jason, 2b-3b	.376	250	51	94	18	1	10	58	11
Wright, Ray, of-2b	.227	44	6	10	0	0	0	1	2
PITCHING	**W**	**L**	**ERA**	**G**	**SV**	**IP**	**H**	**BB**	**SO**
Babineaux, Darrin	5	2	2.52	16	2	39	27	11	43
Cuffia, Robby	3	2	4.57	15	0	41	45	19	20
Dicharry, Ben	4	4	5.33	15	0	79	87	50	55
Eby, Brian	0	2	3.19	19	1	31	26	9	22
Gray, Dave	1	0	1.46	16	1	12	9	4	12
Greene, Rick	1	1	1.33	27	21	27	14	7	27
Hebert, Cedric	3	4	4.99	15	0	67	70	35	48
Kaplan, Josh	3	0	3.79	17	0	36	34	17	38
Moran, Eric	6	0	2.70	8	0	43	41	10	54
Paugh, Rick	5	3	3.43	28	1	42	31	30	21
Robinson, Jeremy	11	3	3.73	16	0	103	114	22	81
Simpson, Cory	2	7	6.44	15	0	73	84	46	49

FORT WORTH

BATTING	AVG	AB	R	H	2B	3B	HR	RBI	SB
Austry, Mark, 1b	.263	259	39	68	10	0	1	45	2

BATTING	AVG	AB	R	H	2B	3B	HR	RBI	SB
Campaniello, Ed, dh	.286	206	47	59	9	0	3	31	11
Cubillian, Jose, of	.215	121	19	26	2	3	6	28	2
Fjelland, Ben, 2b-3b	.281	57	6	16	1	0	1	5	0
Guillen, Jose, ss	.279	129	25	36	6	0	0	8	14
Hannon, Pat, of	.340	268	49	91	15	4	7	52	1
Holland, Tapley, of	.185	27	3	5	2	0	0	4	0
Houser, Chris, 3b-2b	.226	221	28	50	11	0	1	28	2
Infante, Juan, 2b	.239	92	18	22	2	0	0	4	3
LeFlore, Alex, of	.167	48	6	8	2	0	0	2	1
Lopez, Anibal, 2b-ss	.258	124	13	32	2	0	0	8	3
O'Quine, Desmond, ss	.191	68	11	13	4	1	1	7	0
3-team (22 Tenn./6 Mont.)	.203	172	23	35	5	1	1	16	7
Ortmayer, Andy, c-3b	.289	97	17	28	9	0	1	11	1
Quero, Pedro, c-3b	.322	283	50	91	22	2	13	59	2
Walker, Keronn, c	.208	24	5	5	1	0	0	1	0
Whieldon, Andy, of	.269	108	14	29	5	2	0	14	0
Wood, Darren, of	.230	213	38	49	11	1	3	32	4

PITCHING	W	L	ERA	G	SV	IP	H	BB	SO
Canchola, Efren	1	0	3.71	6	0	17	25	5	10
2-team (9 Tyler)	5	2	4.32	15	0	58	73	17	35
Davidson, Jackie	6	3	4.99	17	0	49	60	6	36
Davis, Clint	1	2	3.00	27	2	33	39	6	46
Estivinson, Lina	3	5	3.97	9	0	48	39	23	53
Guzman, Jose	5	2	1.65	9	0	60	51	12	59
Houser, Kyle	0	2	5.79	22	6	23	30	10	33
Lewis, Ryan	0	1	10.03	9	0	13	20	3	11
McIntire, Bobby	0	0	3.86	4	0	7	8	7	7
Pape, Stace	1	2	6.14	5	0	22	32	14	22
Perio, Ian	0	1	1.63	14	2	28	23	9	42
Richards, Dave	3	6	3.86	15	0	84	75	27	94
Rojas, Francis	2	1	6.35	10	0	28	32	12	9
Rosales, Carlos	0	1	3.86	3	0	16	12	9	17
Wallace, Flint	6	4	3.46	14	0	96	96	16	87
Wright, Shane	6	6	3.71	16	0	85	90	16	50

MONTGOMERY

BATTING	AVG	AB	R	H	2B	3B	HR	RBI	SB
Bowden, Merrit, of	.312	173	18	54	9	0	3	27	5
Brack, Ben, dh-c	.330	221	39	73	11	1	9	43	1
Collins, Nick, c	.162	37	2	6	4	0	0	3	0
Dees, Brennan, of-2b	.329	255	46	84	17	1	6	34	10
Dees, Charlie, of-3b	.251	223	33	56	19	2	9	34	4
Devey, David, of	.200	100	9	20	2	0	0	8	0
Jernigan, Shannon, c	.091	11	2	1	1	0	0	0	0
McCall, Gerard, c	.297	229	33	68	9	1	2	27	1
Millhouse, D.J., 2b	.143	42	4	6	0	0	0	3	1
Mockabee, Nick, of	.213	47	6	10	0	1	0	3	3
Nash, Scott, 3b	.250	12	2	3	1	1	0	0	0
O'Quine, Desmond, ss.	.240	25	3	6	0	0	0	3	0
Pierson, Eddie, 1b	.308	13	1	4	1	0	0	1	0
Riley, Rusty, 1b	.245	229	33	56	13	0	7	36	2
Rivell, Warren, 2b-ss	.166	175	23	29	2	0	1	13	1
Scott, Reggie, 3b	.265	49	11	13	3	0	0	4	1
Still, Tim, of	.302	43	8	13	2	0	0	5	0
Thornton, Luis, 3b	.175	57	8	10	2	0	0	4	0
Tillis, Rashad, of	.272	103	14	28	4	1	0	16	2
Webster, Stephens, ss-3b	.245	241	35	59	13	0	4	26	2
Wooten, Corey, of	.193	57	6	11	2	0	0	3	2
Wright, Willie, 3b	.299	67	10	20	1	0	1	5	0

PITCHING	W	L	ERA	G	SV	IP	H	BB	SO
Blanchard, Jack	1	1	4.91	9	4	11	11	7	12
Brantley, Jim	2	3	3.74	23	6	34	35	14	23
Castillo, Brian	1	3	8.05	9	0	19	29	12	18
Drake, Heath	2	1	5.36	17	0	40	43	17	34
Long, Keith	0	5	3.72	13	0	46	51	20	33
McGill, Trea	4	3	4.08	8	0	57	51	16	57
Melancon, Kory	3	2	3.51	9	0	59	56	19	49
Palm, Jeremy	2	5	4.63	11	0	58	63	26	39
Schomas, Kevin	3	2	6.82	19	1	34	45	30	22
Shiery, Shawn	6	4	3.55	15	0	96	92	29	98
Smith, Bobby	2	0	5.93	19	2	30	34	14	30
Warren, David	5	7	3.40	15	0	93	83	36	77

TENNESSEE

BATTING	AVG	AB	R	H	2B	3B	HR	RBI	SB
Anderson, Marvin, 3b	.205	127	16	26	9	0	0	6	1
Baker, Brian, of	.295	261	52	77	17	3	13	45	25
Bowling, Reid, ss	.200	10	0	2	0	0	0	0	1
Evans, Jason, c	.217	23	0	5	0	0	0	1	0
Jernigan, Patrick, c	.097	31	3	3	0	0	0	2	0
Mejias, Erick, 2b-ss	.278	273	48	76	11	5	4	39	45
Nash, Scott, 3b	.167	12	0	2	0	0	0	1	0

BATTING	AVG	AB	R	H	2B	3B	HR	RBI	SB
2-team (3 Montgomery)	.208	24	2	5	1	1	0	1	0
O'Quine, Desmond, ss-2b	.203	79	9	16	1	0	0	6	7
Pierce, Brett, dh	.213	94	7	20	1	0	0	10	3
Preston, Doyle, 1b-3b	.298	255	30	76	16	0	3	32	1
Robinson, Coby, of	.000	11	0	0	0	0	0	0	1
Rottman, Paul, 1b	.194	31	2	6	0	0	0	2	0
Scala, Mickey, 3b-of	.216	139	28	30	5	0	2	14	6
Stanley, Derek, of	.227	203	24	46	10	1	4	22	20
Still, Tim, of	.500	4	0	2	0	0	0	0	0
2-team (12 Montgomery)	.319	47	8	15	2	0	0	5	0
Thomas, Kyle, of-c	.292	233	25	68	13	0	3	32	4
Tiller, Tim, of	.244	131	14	32	1	0	0	6	9
Van Winkle, Dave, c	.262	191	20	50	8	1	0	18	0
Worrell, Dustin, ss-2b	.268	183	23	49	10	0	0	24	11

PITCHING	W	L	ERA	G	SV	IP	H	BB	SO
Bloom, Tom	1	0	4.00	5	0	9	10	3	4
Bouie, Aaron	2	4	4.37	9	0	47	47	31	43
Coleman, Billy	1	0	1.56	9	2	17	10	6	21
Conino, Zack	0	0	9.00	2	0	6	11	2	5
Conrad, Jack	2	5	4.99	8	0	52	64	16	39
Jenkins, Aaron	0	2	5.59	7	0	10	10	4	9
Keener, Kevin	4	4	4.14	22	5	54	49	27	51
Langston, Mike	0	8	4.92	10	0	53	73	27	31
Lewis, Ryan	1	4	4.30	4	0	20	21	7	12
Meyer, John	1	3	7.71	7	0	33	34	27	24
Mullen, Trey	1	4	6.42	14	0	55	60	38	33
O'Donnell, Tony	0	2	5.31	19	0	42	52	11	39
Overstreet, Bobby	0	0	6.52	8	0	10	13	4	4
Patrylo, Ryan	2	3	3.79	6	0	36	35	18	23
Turrell, John	5	9	5.33	23	1	76	80	43	57
Tyus, Wayne	0	2	3.68	23	0	51	59	18	24

TYLER

BATTING	AVG	AB	R	H	2B	3B	HR	RBI	SB
Baird, Matt, of-1b	.281	167	27	47	9	2	4	19	2
Bethea, Larry, 1b	.133	75	9	10	1	0	2	10	9
Caraway, Doug, c	.167	12	1	2	0	0	0	1	0
Colon, Jose, of	.246	252	40	62	13	3	6	23	17
Deck, Ronnie, c	.145	76	7	11	1	0	0	5	2
Garcia, Vicente, ss	.242	215	34	52	10	0	0	21	5
Jaramillo, Tony, 2b-3b	.275	233	44	64	13	2	0	25	7
Johnson, Ryan, 2b-3b	.237	118	14	28	2	0	0	14	5
Kirkpatrick, Michael, of-1b	.293	242	47	71	20	5	9	37	11
Lane, Nolan, dh	.273	150	25	41	9	0	6	30	0
Matos, Malvin, dh	.375	112	24	42	10	1	6	30	1
Ramirez, Dan, of	.278	230	35	64	14	1	2	30	7
Ruiz, Ramon, 3b-ss	.242	240	42	58	8	2	11	36	6
Stevens, Brad, 1b	.100	20	3	2	0	0	0	2	0
Taylor, William, of	.286	98	18	28	2	0	0	7	21
2-team (29 Baton Rouge)	.270	200	34	54	4	2	0	14	35
Walker, Keronn, c	.252	139	12	35	9	0	0	23	9
2-team (9 Fort Worth)	.245	163	17	40	10	0	0	24	9

PITCHING	W	L	ERA	G	SV	IP	H	BB	SO
Ahearne, Paul	0	0	4.80	10	0	15	19	7	9
Boker, John	5	6	3.60	16	0	105	91	39	101
Brown, Stephen	3	3	2.27	17	0	36	37	10	26
Canchola, Efren	4	2	4.57	9	0	41	48	12	25
Flanagan, Chris	1	1	4.95	15	0	22	25	12	10
Herbert, Russ	6	1	3.18	9	0	62	52	26	67
Hitzeman, Travis	0	0	4.76	1	0	6	11	1	4
John, Tommy	7	5	3.83	15	0	92	84	27	72
Linares, Ramon	4	1	3.33	16	0	46	38	21	38
Maddock, Steve	0	0	2.00	1	0	9	4	0	3
Moore, Eric	1	4	7.12	23	1	30	42	7	30
Silverthorn, Will	2	2	5.98	12	0	47	61	16	35
Sokol, Trad	1	1	3.38	8	0	8	13	3	8
Turrentine, Rich	0	1	1.19	26	18	30	22	16	50
Ware, Jeff	4	4	4.26	10	0	57	57	29	41

ATLANTIC LEAGUE

Newark owner and former major league catcher Rick Cerone signed Jose Canseco, his brother Ozzie and a slew of former big leaguers including Jim Leyritz, Lance Johnson, Jaime Navarro and Pete Incaviglia to attract fans and build a winner in 2001.

It worked to a degree, as the Bears put together their best season in the Atlantic League's four-year history. But they were beaten by the Somerset Patriots in the league's championship series, attendance improved only marginally and the Canseco twins didn't last even half the season.

Jose Canseco had been released by the Anaheim Angels during spring training and signed with the Bears when no other major league club came calling. He batted .284-

Jose Canseco

7-27 with 40 walks and 39 strikeouts in 143 at-bats before signing with the Chicago White Sox. Once back in a big league clubhouse, he quickly slammed the Atlantic League in the press for inadequate facilities and a general feel of disorganization throughout the league. He spoke his mind, even after each Atlantic League franchise had pitched in money to pay his salary.

After his departure, the Bears released Ozzie, who batted .207-6-18 in 135 at-bats after hitting .299 with a league record 48 homers in 2000.

Newark was on the verge of winning the league playoffs as it took a 2-0 lead over Somerset in the best-of-5 final, but the Patriots came back to win the last three games. The Patriots had lost in the finals the previous three years.

Three Patriots pitchers shut down Newark 4-0 in Game Five and second baseman Emiliano Escandon went 2-for-4 with two RBIs to complete the comeback.

STANDINGS

FIRST HALF

NORTH
	W	L	PCT	GB
Newark Bears	38	25	.603	—
Nashua Pride	35	28	.556	3
Long Island Ducks	30	33	.476	8
Bridgeport Bluefish	30	33	.476	8

SOUTH
	W	L	PCT	GB
Somerset Patriots	39	24	.619	—
Atlantic City Surf	38	25	.603	1
Camden Riversharks	24	39	.381	15
Lehigh Valley Black Diamonds	18	45	.286	21

SECOND HALF

NORTH
	W	L	PCT	GB
Nashua Pride	38	25	.603	—
Newark Bears	37	26	.587	1
Bridgeport Bluefish	36	27	.571	2
Long Island Ducks	27	36	.429	11

SOUTH
	W	L	PCT	GB
Somerset Patriots	44	19	.698	—
Atlantic City Surf	26	37	.413	18
Camden Riversharks	25	38	.397	19
Lehigh Valley Black Diamonds	19	44	.302	25

PLAYOFFS: Semifinals—Newark defeated Nashua 2-1 in best-of-3 series. **Finals**—Somerset defeated Newark 3-2 in best-of-5 series.

MANAGERS: Atlantic City—Tommy Helms. **Bridgeport**—Duffy Dyer. **Camden**—Wayne Krenchicki, **Lehigh Valley**—Bob Flori. **Long Island**—Don McCormack. **Nashua**—Butch Hobson. **Newark**—Tom O'Malley. **Somerset**—Sparky Lyle.

ATTENDANCE: Long Island 443,142; Somerset 357,112; Camden 280,329; Bridgeport 245,073; Newark 243,255; Atlantic City 154,089; Nashua 132,450.

ALL-STAR TEAM: C—Francisco Morales, Long Island; Damian Sapp, Nashua. **1B**—Jose Velazquez, Atlantic City. **2B**—Steve Hine, Newark. **3B**—Billy Hall, Somerset. **SS**—Victor Gutierrez, Lehigh Valley. **OF**—Michael Warner, Somerset; Ric Johnson, Newark; Jose Malave, Nashua; Oreste Marrero, Bridgeport. **DH**—Doug Jennings, Long Island. **Util**—Brad Strauss, Camden. **RHP**—Len Picota, Nashua. **LHP**—Ricardo Jordan, Somerset. **RP**—John Briscoe, Somerset.

Player of the Year: Michael Warner, Somerset. **Pitcher of the Year:** Len Picota, Nashua. **Manager of the Year:** Butch Hobson, Nashua.

INDIVIDUAL BATTING LEADERS
(Minimum 340 Plate Appearances)

	AVG	AB	R	H	2B	3B	HR	RBI	SB
Warner, Michael, Somerset	.351	410	99	144	31	4	17	103	30
Gordon, Keith, Atlantic City	.339	354	69	120	23	3	18	58	11
Johnson, Ric, Newark	.317	398	53	126	12	3	4	53	30
Strauss, Brad, Camden	.314	437	82	137	31	4	13	51	8
Soto, Emison, Atlantic City	.312	391	56	122	26	0	21	68	7
Jennings, Doug, Long Island	.306	385	79	118	34	1	16	76	2
Polanco, Enohel, Atl. City	.303	419	75	127	15	2	6	41	23
Poe, Charles, Somerset	.302	364	60	110	15	1	12	75	12
Gutierrez, Vic, Lehigh	.299	468	57	140	12	12	4	50	36
Hall, Billy, Somerset	.296	500	113	148	20	10	6	38	72

INDIVIDUAL BATTING LEADERS
(Minimum 101 Innings)

	W	L	ERA	G	SV	IP	H	BB	SO
Henderson, Rod, LI	8	4	2.53	15	0	103	88	24	96
Pierson, Jason, Newark	6	3	2.85	34	0	110	108	25	100
Shepard, David, Newark	11	4	2.95	33	0	155	147	30	137
Picota, Len, Nashua	15	2	3.04	31	0	160	141	50	161
Jordan, Ricardo, Somerset	10	5	3.18	18	0	119	93	40	87
Heredia, Julian, Nashua	4	9	3.24	30	0	122	121	24	125
Schurman, Ryan, Camden	10	10	3.42	36	0	140	128	59	85
Armstrong, Jack, Newark	13	6	3.47	23	0	161	154	32	110
Dodd, Robert, Somerset	10	5	3.55	26	0	150	157	54	135
Walls, Doug, Somerset	9	6	3.55	24	0	129	125	46	93

ATLANTIC CITY

BATTING	AVG	AB	R	H	2B	3B	HR	RBI	SB
DeLeon, Sandy, c	.250	4	0	1	0	0	0	0	0
Dockery, Tim, c	.252	238	29	60	9	0	12	46	0
2-team (5 LV)	.249	245	30	61	9	0	12	46	0
Fowler, Maleke, of	.279	458	93	128	18	7	13	42	36
Gordon, Keith, of	.339	354	69	120	23	3	18	58	11
Henry, Santiago, 2b	.168	107	15	18	5	1	3	11	5
Hill, Willy, of	.331	118	19	39	3	2	0	9	3
Hunter, Brian, 1b	.327	153	38	50	14	0	12	38	0
Joffrion, Jack, ss-2b	.214	280	29	60	14	3	6	29	7
Llanos, Alex, 2b-ss	.273	256	28	70	23	0	3	31	1
Monell, Johnny, dh	.160	25	3	4	1	0	0	2	0
Morales, Jorge, c	.300	60	11	18	2	0	5	11	0
Olmeda, Jose, ss	.286	168	22	48	9	0	5	30	2
Pennyfeather, Will, of	.251	387	58	97	24	4	16	56	8
Perez, Danny, of	.279	369	60	103	23	1	12	54	5
Polanco, Enohel, 3b-ss	.303	419	75	127	15	2	6	41	23
Soto, Emison, c-1b	.312	391	56	122	26	0	21	68	7
Velazquez, Jose, 1b	.279	384	56	107	19	1	13	85	4
West, George, 3b	.256	180	19	46	6	1	2	20	1

PITCHING	W	L	ERA	G	SV	IP	H	BB	SO
Alberro, Jose	0	0	1.93	12	4	14	12	4	10
2-team (13 Newark)	3	2	5.72	25	4	28	31	12	18
Ali, Sam	12	5	4.88	30	1	138	143	60	94
Avrard, Corey	1	2	4.02	18	0	31	27	27	26
Barnett, Marty	1	4	8.20	7	0	26	33	16	32
Brown, Tighe	1	2	5.25	3	0	12	13	8	11
Dunham, Pat	0	4	5.53	34	3	68	67	58	60
Garcia, Ariel	9	8	4.53	25	0	161	164	44	96
High, Andy	9	2	3.20	14	0	90	89	20	75
Hoy, Wayne	0	1	20.25	1	0	3	0	0	0
2-team (3 Somerset)	0	4	14.73	4	0	11	25	8	4
Lane, Aaron	3	3	2.63	18	0	96	96	29	64
Mallard, Randi	6	5	3.46	43	11	52	52	24	47
Mangieri, John	4	2	5.76	41	5	50	55	38	30
Mastrolonardo, Dave	2	3	4.47	35	0	46	44	30	50
2-team (7 LV)	3	3	4.47	42	0	56	56	35	59
Mattson, Craig	0	1	2.00	5	0	9	7	4	4
2-team (21 LI)	2	3	4.54	26	0	38	40	22	21
Moody, Jason	0	1	3.50	37	4	36.0	40	17	20
Roque, Darryl	1	4	11.57	5	0	23	34	11	9
2-team (35 LV)	4	9	7.91	40	0	93	110	50	51
Shelby, Anthony	0	0	0.93	6	0	10	4	3	8
3-team (6 LI/4 Nashua)	1	0	2.96	16	0	24	21	10	18
Spivey, Chris	0	0	7.84	9	0	10	13	6	6
Stark, Zac	3	3	3.56	8	0	43	51	18	29
2-team (17 LV)	7	13	3.86	25	0	135	139	55	103
Taniguchi, Koichi	5	4	5.23	22	0	83	91	35	63
Taylor, Tommy	3	3	5.71	9	0	41	44	19	40
Williams, Mitch	4	3	3.86	11	0	44	46	11	35

BRIDGEPORT

BATTING	AVG	AB	R	H	2B	3B	HR	RBI	SB
Avila, Rolo, of	.269	435	72	117	21	1	4	45	41

	AVG	AB	R	H	2B	3B	HR	RBI	SB
Cole, Alex, of	.267	105	16	28	8	1	2	11	1
DeLeon, Sandy, c	.333	18	3	6	2	0	0	0	0
Delgado, Jose, ss-2b	.208	265	29	55	11	1	0	26	5
Devarez, Cesar, c	.179	56	6	10	1	0	2	6	1
Espada, Angel, ss-2b	.296	274	41	81	11	2	1	18	11
Jenkins, Dee, 2b-3b	.255	384	53	98	21	3	10	51	16
Kingman, Brendan, 3b-1b	.278	464	74	129	19	3	13	57	3
Lind, Jose, 2b	.244	45	3	11	3	0	0	7	1
Madonna, Chris, c-3b	.344	61	9	21	5	1	1	15	1
Marrero, Oreste, of-1b	.276	463	74	128	34	2	23	89	9
McGriff, Terry, c	.259	220	22	57	13	1	4	32	0
McQuiniff, Jason, c-3b	.267	135	14	36	4	1	0	7	2
2-team (20 LV)	.243	169	15	41	5	1	0	11	2
Ortiz, Asbel, 3b-1b	.111	9	3	1	1	0	0	2	0
2-team (69 LV)	.231	251	30	58	11	0	5	29	4
Pledger, Kinnis, 1b	.221	280	40	62	16	1	11	42	4
Rich, Billy, of	.264	265	42	70	16	2	6	31	14
Singleton, Duane, of	.250	304	35	76	13	1	5	40	16
Wearing, Mel, dh	.249	350	69	87	13	0	19	70	3
Williams, Reggie, of	.224	49	7	11	4	0	3	9	0
2-team (40 Newark)	.213	178	22	38	9	0	5	23	5

PITCHING	W	L	ERA	G	SV	IP	H	BB	SO
Cornett, Brad	0	1	2.25	2	0	12	10	1	9
Crawford, Joe	2	2	5.83	8	0	42	52	15	28
Davis, Keith	9	7	5.71	44	0	63	67	33	65
Della Ratta, Pete	1	1	3.02	32	4	48	43	12	43
Fesh, Sean	5	2	3.51	51	0	67	77	37	54
Frazier, Ron	9	8	4.02	28	1	116	135	31	52
Garcia, Apolinar	5	4	3.55	21	0	76	73	26	39
Guilfoyle, Mike	3	2	3.33	44	23	46	48	15	48
Imazeki, Masaru	1	6	4.95	24	0	80	92	41	72
Osteen, Gavin	4	8	4.62	25	0	115	130	37	76
Rosenkranz, Terry	2	1	5.66	36	1	56	48	56	45
Smetana, Steve	5	2	1.60	48	9	73	53	14	54
Sontag, Alan	11	8	4.33	24	0	148	175	37	87
Swanson, Dave	8	8	4.18	26	0	146	147	61	87
Wallace, Kent	1	0	0.00	6	1	9	3	2	7

CAMDEN

BATTING	AVG	AB	R	H	2B	3B	HR	RBI	SB
Abreu, Nelson, of	.235	200	12	47	4	2	1	17	10
Azuaje, Jesus, ss	.286	217	39	62	8	2	7	36	14
Batiste, Kim, 3b	.246	236	19	58	12	1	1	26	2
Brumfield, Jacob, of	.237	262	31	62	10	0	5	34	5
Dorman, John, ss-2b	.211	232	32	49	5	2	1	13	12
Duncan, Andres, 2b	.265	132	26	35	8	0	0	11	4
Garcia, Guillermo, c	.315	273	47	86	16	0	17	68	0
Goodwin, Joe, c	.238	172	19	41	8	1	0	21	1
Griffin, Justin, 2b	.120	25	2	3	0	0	0	1	1
Held, Dan, 1b	.270	440	64	119	20	4	10	52	1
Howard, Thomas, of	.307	150	20	46	12	0	4	23	1
Maness, Dwight, of	.246	350	58	86	14	4	16	52	22
Martinez, Gil, of	.294	231	27	68	22	2	3	40	1
Morales, Jorge, dh	.222	45	3	10	1	0	0	3	0
3-team (17 AC/27 LI)	.311	206	28	64	8	0	6	31	0
Mulligan, Sean, c	.178	73	7	13	2	0	2	6	0
Nicholas, Darrell, of	.272	298	43	81	16	3	6	34	19
Nunez, Isaias, 1b	.310	29	3	9	1	1	0	3	0
Raleigh, Matt, dh	.172	87	8	15	3	0	4	9	1
Rodarte, Raul, 2b-3b	.244	119	14	29	8	1	4	21	4
Sanchez, Yuri, ss-2b	.233	133	11	31	3	3	3	10	1
Sherlock, Brian, 2b	.192	151	18	29	6	0	1	9	4
Strauss, Brad, 3b-of	.314	437	82	137	31	4	13	51	8

PITCHING	W	L	ERA	G	SV	IP	H	BB	SO
Bauldree, Joe	0	0	6.06	10	0	16	20	9	6
Bolton, Rod	8	8	6.92	35	0	94	117	40	62
Briggs, Anthony	0	5	5.74	15	0	64	75	26	32
Busby, Mike	1	3	6.95	6	0	34	41	23	37
2-team (19 Nashua)	7	12	6.28	25	1	138	148	72	137
Censale, Silvio	1	4	8.38	12	0	19	27	14	12
Love, Jeff	5	6	4.90	41	3	90	111	35	55
Lowe, Benny	1	0	0.00	14	0	21	7	11	19
Mathews, Del	4	4	3.82	12	0	73	74	25	43
Mikkelson, Linc	4	5	3.75	15	0	101	95	33	81
Paredes, Carlos	0	1	3.82	26	0	35	35	22	22
Reed, Steve	0	2	4.24	10	1	17	17	6	11
2-team (12 Newark)	2	5	4.53	22	1	52	53	15	33
Roberts, Chris	1	3	5.61	7	0	43	58	14	21
Root, Derek	8	7	4.91	24	0	154	178	50	110
Sanders, Frankie	1	0	6.75	4	0	27	24	16	14
Schurman, Ryan	10	10	3.42	36	0	140	128	59	85
Seaver, Mark	2	5	6.32	12	0	47	56	30	26
Silva, Ted	3	5	5.77	28	0	78	93	21	57
Williams, Jimmy	1	8	3.09	47	23	58	62	26	51

LEHIGH VALLEY

BATTING	AVG	AB	R	H	2B	3B	HR	RBI	SB
Adams, John, of	.259	463	58	120	26	2	12	42	7
Bethea, Larry, 1b	.187	91	8	17	2	0	3	10	0
Cruz, Cirilo, of	.170	94	9	16	3	0	0	0	2
Darr, Ryan, 3b	.170	94	7	16	7	1	2	13	2
DeLeon, Sandy, c	.255	51	3	13	3	0	0	4	1
4-team (1 AC/12Bri./6 Som.)	.258	97	8	25	5	0	1	5	1
Fuentes, Joel, 2b	.250	260	32	65	4	5	1	14	5
Gambill, Chad, of	.268	426	45	114	26	1	12	63	0
Gutierrez, Vic, ss	.299	468	57	140	12	12	4	50	36
Hargrove, Harvey, of-2b	.242	434	53	105	19	1	9	46	7
Kuilan, Hector, c	.283	265	32	75	11	0	8	37	0
Lebron, Francisco, 1b	.303	264	36	80	18	1	11	41	1
McQuiniff, Jason, 1b	.147	34	1	5	1	0	0	4	0
Ortiz, Asbel, 1b-3b	.236	242	27	57	10	0	5	27	4
Piercy, Mike, of	.244	82	13	20	1	0	0	3	3
Rivera, Luis, c-1b	.150	40	2	6	1	0	0	2	0
Rodriguez, Juan, of	.140	107	10	15	2	1	2	4	1
Torres, Jason, c	.270	141	15	38	7	1	1	14	0
Tovar, Edgar, 3b-2b	.242	434	38	105	16	0	3	41	1
Van Rossum, Chris, of	.261	92	13	24	3	0	2	11	2
Williams, Mark, 3b-c	.196	112	4	22	3	0	0	6	2
Williams, P.J., of	.340	97	22	33	3	0	0	8	20

PITCHING	W	L	ERA	G	SV	IP	H	BB	SO
Carroll, Dave	1	4	3.98	57	2	75	76	39	42
Diaz, Antonio	0	5	7.03	23	0	40	63	17	21
Halpin, Jeremy	1	8	6.24	12	0	49	60	24	21
Hayden, Terry	0	6	10.33	7	0	27	50	22	32
Johnson, Craig	5	8	5.88	21	0	90	110	30	63
Lombardi, Justin	0	2	8.56	15	0	14	14	13	8
Martini, Mike	0	1	5.03	30	0	34	38	19	22
Mattson, Rob	0	4	5.13	4	0	26	28	7	11
Miranda, Angel	2	1	1.83	26	11	39	29	21	24
Numate, Hiroshi	4	7	5.27	17	1	84	102	25	70
Pizarro, Melvin	0	10	5.66	22	0	84	85	59	57
Ramirez, Jose	0	5	5.19	19	0	43	48	26	29
2-team (7 LI)	0	5	5.90	26	0	58	67	32	39
Roque, Darryl	3	5	6.69	35	0	70	76	39	42
Seaver, Mark	6	3	2.54	12	0	78	64	25	52
2-team (12 Camden)	8	8	3.96	24	0	125	120	55	78
Sheldon, Kyle	5	3	3.92	53	1	62	71	14	29
Stark, Zac	4	10	4.00	17	0	92	88	37	74
Walls, Doug	5	3	3.45	13	0	70	66	25	54
Weimer, Matt	1	3	4.37	49	7	47	55	12	27
Zallie, Chris	0	1	7.27	13	0	17	27	12	8

LONG ISLAND

BATTING	AVG	AB	R	H	2B	3B	HR	RBI	SB
Baerga, Carlos, 3b	.315	203	38	64	9	3	9	44	3
Bautista, Juan, ss	.240	417	49	100	13	9	2	37	21
Caputo, Tom, 3b	.243	70	7	17	5	0	0	7	2
Davies, Justin, of	.272	379	76	103	6	3	0	21	28
Durkac, Bo, 3b	.197	66	9	13	1	0	0	5	0
French, Anton, of	.253	245	34	62	6	4	1	22	22
Gibralter, Steve, of-3b	.367	30	6	11	1	1	1	6	5
Gonzalez, Jose, of-3b	.280	107	14	30	3	4	2	20	7
Gorecki, Ryan, 2b-3b	.238	130	13	31	4	0	0	19	1
Hage, Tom, of-1b	.288	413	54	119	21	2	7	55	0
Harrison, Adonis, 2b-ss	.269	391	63	105	13	6	4	48	17
Hernandez, Victor, of	.056	18	1	1	0	0	0	0	0
Jennings, Doug, of-1b	.306	385	79	118	34	1	16	76	2
Johnson, Michael, of	.111	9	1	1	0	0	0	1	0
2-team (3 LV)	.059	17	3	1	0	0	0	1	0
Moore, Michael, of	.213	141	18	30	9	1	4	14	2
Morales, Francisco, c-1b	.291	443	71	129	23	0	23	85	0
Morales, Jorge, dh	.356	101	14	36	5	0	1	17	0
Raven, Luis, dh	.313	147	21	46	6	0	7	27	2
Robles, Kevin, c	.298	114	11	34	7	1	1	19	0
Versailles, Greg, 3b	.111	18	1	2	0	0	0	0	0
Viera, Jose, dh	.237	211	29	50	16	0	9	47	0
Williams, P.J., of	.233	193	32	45	5	0	1	15	22
2-team (24 LV)	.269	290	54	78	8	0	1	23	42

PITCHING	W	L	ERA	G	SV	IP	H	BB	SO
Bullinger, Jim	6	1	2.28	9	0	47	42	14	25
Falteisek, Steve	4	5	3.92	11	0	64	69	10	39
Haring, Brett	3	4	2.86	12	0	44	39	13	31
Henderson, Rod	8	4	2.53	15	0	103	88	24	96
Lanfranco, Otoniel	1	3	3.57	14	0	71	62	22	56
Longo, Neil	1	3	9.00	14	0	18	24	15	13
Marrero, Kenny	0	1	11.05	2	0	7	10	7	6
Martin, Scott	0	0	3.38	4	0	5	5	3	2

	W	L	ERA	G	SV	IP	H	BB	SO
Mastrolonardo, Dave	1	0	4.50	7	0	10	12	5	9
Mattson, Craig	2	2	5.34	21	0	29	33	18	17
Mattson, Rob	1	1	10.80	2	0	10	20	4	3
2-team (4 LV)	1	5	6.69	6	0	36	48	11	14
Mays, Jarrod	0	0	3.86	15	0	19	23	5	11
McCoy, Chris	6	8	5.74	33	0	107	143	32	65
Mix, Greg	0	2	2.43	27	10	30	17	11	31
Paredes, Carlos	0	0	1.80	8	1	10	8	5	3
2-team (26 Camden)	0	1	3.38	34	1	45	43	27	25
Perez, Gil	9	3	3.63	16	0	89	81	21	61
Pontes, Dan	2	1	8.20	19	0	26	44	13	13
Ramirez, Jose	0	0	7.98	7	0	15	19	6	10
Ricken, Ray	8	7	4.27	19	0	110	105	38	73
Rutherford, Mark	1	2	1.82	23	7	30	24	10	21
2-team (10 Nashua)	1	6	5.59	33	7	58	64	19	34
Schaffer, Trevor	0	6	6.35	45	3	62	70	32	59
Shelby, Anthony	1	0	1.69	6	0	11	7	3	6
Smith, Byron	1	3	2.97	30	2	58	45	16	40
Smith, Matt	0	2	4.96	5	0	16	10	16	14
Theodile, Robert	4	3	4.18	9	1	52	49	20	31
Theodile, Simieon	0	1	14.73	3	0	7	15	5	7
Woodall, Brad	3	1	2.11	34	3	55	46	20	42

NASHUA

BATTING	AVG	AB	R	H	2B	3B	HR	RBI	SB
Batiste, Kim, 3b	.312	125	17	39	3	1	2	16	1
2-team (65 Camden)	.269	361	36	97	15	2	3	42	3
Bonds, Bobby, of	.264	72	8	19	4	1	2	9	1
Boston, D.J., 1b	.343	169	37	58	8	2	9	26	9
Brumfield, Jacob, of	.111	18	2	2	0	0	0	1	2
2-team (71 Camden)	.229	280	33	64	10	0	5	35	7
DiPace, Dan, of	.231	39	3	9	0	0	0	4	0
Fonville, Chad, 2b	.340	200	36	68	6	0	0	16	13
Horn, Sam, dh	.295	224	34	66	10	0	13	47	1
Howell, Pat, of-2b	.189	275	38	52	4	4	4	24	20
Hurst, Jimmy, of	.292	373	54	109	19	1	15	57	22
Larkin, Stephen, 1b-of	.259	370	55	96	21	3	5	47	9
Malave, Jose, of	.260	454	61	118	19	2	28	94	6
Mitchell, Mike, 1b-3b	.264	106	9	28	9	0	0	10	2
Mummau, Rob, 3b-2b	.232	388	47	90	14	5	6	35	4
Murray, Glenn, of	.307	137	27	42	7	1	8	28	5
Parra, Franklin, ss-2b	.308	227	40	70	14	3	4	23	18
Reyes, Jose, c-of	.206	252	36	52	5	3	4	27	6
Rodriguez, Juan, of-1b	.241	141	25	34	5	2	1	7	5
2-team (28 LV)	.198	248	35	49	7	3	3	11	6
Rodriguez, Tony, ss	.285	316	47	90	13	3	7	29	7
Sapp, Damian, c-3b	.259	352	54	91	18	0	26	70	3
Walton, Jerome, of	.158	38	6	6	1	0	2	4	6

PITCHING	W	L	ERA	G	SV	IP	H	BB	SO
Benz, Jake	2	2	3.84	55	0	63	63	27	55
Busby, Mike	6	9	6.06	19	1	104	107	49	100
Calandriello, Donato	4	2	3.19	46	0	59	50	29	41
Darley, Ned	3	1	2.93	51	18	55	38	26	44
Drumheller, Al	7	4	2.46	18	0	99	87	27	80
Heredia, Julian	4	9	3.24	30	0	122	121	24	125
Janzen, Marty	5	5	2.87	15	0	75	69	27	59
Lacy, Kerry	1	3	3.53	34	1	43	51	20	48
Miranda, Angel	1	0	3.38	4	0	3	2	3	3
Picota, Len	15	2	3.04	31	0	160	141	50	161
Roper, John	4	6	3.65	20	0	101	109	29	57
Rutherford, Mark	0	4	9.53	10	0	28	40	9	13
Shelby, Anthony	0	0	11.25	4	0	4	10	4	4
Thompson, Chris	10	4	4.09	51	1	101	91	46	79
Valera, Julio	0	3	7.64	7	0	33	47	8	18
Welch, Mike	5	4	3.25	45	4	53	44	23	50

NEWARK

BATTING	AVG	AB	R	H	2B	3B	HR	RBI	SB
Adriana, Sharnol, 1b	.254	63	14	16	3	0	4	10	1
Alguacil, Jose, ss	.265	343	49	91	10	2	2	26	19
Ashley, Billy, of-1b	.259	166	16	43	3	1	8	27	1
Ball, Jeff, 3b	.249	349	56	87	14	1	11	50	1
Canseco, Jose, of	.284	134	30	38	9	0	7	27	10
Canseco, Ozzie, 1b	.207	135	23	28	5	0	6	18	5
Felix, Lauro, ss-3b	.224	161	20	36	7	0	2	19	3
Fink, Marc, 1b	.190	84	8	16	6	0	2	9	0
Hine, Steve, 2b	.292	459	72	134	27	5	6	48	17
Incaviglia, Pete, dh	.353	187	30	66	11	0	9	43	2
Johnson, Lance, of	.306	85	17	26	5	4	0	12	8
Johnson, Ric, of	.317	398	53	126	12	3	4	53	30
Kanell, Danny, 1b	.237	76	11	18	2	2	1	6	2
Koeyers, Ramsey, c	.267	187	23	50	9	0	7	27	0

	AVG	AB	R	H	2B	3B	HR	RBI	SB
Leyritz, Jim, 3b	.296	71	15	21	3	0	4	15	1
Mathis, Joe, of	.295	224	49	66	9	8	3	28	31
Meulens, Hensley, of-1b	.245	139	26	34	10	1	10	30	3
Powell, Alonzo, of	.294	293	45	86	20	1	16	59	1
Ramirez, Peto, c-1b	.267	322	46	86	16	0	10	51	4
Reyes, Eduardo, of-3b	.184	147	17	27	2	0	1	15	4
Vasquez, Sandy, of	.163	43	6	7	4	0	0	4	0
Williams, Reggie, of	.209	129	15	27	5	0	2	14	5

PITCHING	W	L	ERA	G	SV	IP	H	BB	SO
Alberro, Jose	3	2	9.42	13	0	14	19	8	8
Armstrong, Jack	13	6	3.47	23	0	161	154	32	110
Butler, Adam	0	0	6.75	4	0	7	4	3	7
Cain, Tim	11	10	4.80	25	0	150	166	35	82
Censale, Silvio	0	0	6.00	6	0	9	14	4	6
2-team (12 Camden)	1	4	7.62	18	0	28	41	18	18
Diorio, Mike	1	1	2.70	25	1	30	20	10	26
Harris, Reggie	1	1	3.48	10	6	10	6	8	12
Henry, Dwayne	2	2	7.30	25	1	25	29	19	23
Jones, Calvin	3	2	2.36	37	10	42	23	13	54
Kubinski, Tim	3	0	3.00	5	0	21	17	3	21
Macey, Fausto	2	0	9.31	4	0	10	19	0	3
Moody, Jason	0	0	6.00	4	0	6	5	4	4
2-team (37 AC)	0	1	3.86	41	4	42	45	21	24
Navarro, Jaime	11	9	4.09	25	0	176	194	39	133
Pierson, Jason	6	3	2.85	34	0	110	108	25	100
Reed, Steve	2	3	4.67	12	0	35	36	9	22
Richards, Dave	0	0	7.04	6	0	8	14	6	6
Schmidt, George	4	2	1.41	20	2	45	29	7	37
Shepard, David	11	4	2.95	33	0	155	147	30	137
Thompson, Frank	2	3	3.40	45	12	48	47	17	36
Wagner, Hector	0	3	5.35	13	0	35	43	15	20
Yates, Chad	0	0	6.97	8	0	10	15	5	9

SOMERSET

BATTING	AVG	AB	R	H	2B	3B	HR	RBI	SB
Anderson, Jeff, 1b-2b	.238	126	15	30	4	0	1	11	0
Blosser, Greg, of	.270	311	52	84	15	0	21	78	4
Curl, John, 1b	.256	78	7	20	4	0	1	13	4
Dattola, Kevin, of-1b	.274	431	59	118	23	1	13	66	28
DeLeon, Sandy, c	.208	24	2	5	0	0	1	1	0
Escandon, Emiliano, 3b-2b	.286	399	80	114	28	2	2	38	3
Esposito, Paul, 3b-2b	.284	116	19	33	6	0	0	11	1
Glavine, Mike, 1b	.249	257	26	64	15	0	12	45	2
Hall, Billy, 2b-3b	.296	500	113	148	20	10	6	38	72
Martinez, Pablo, ss	.229	446	57	102	9	3	3	31	28
Pagan, Carlos, c	.204	250	32	51	15	1	10	35	0
Poe, Charles, of	.302	364	60	110	15	1	12	75	12
Sellers, Rick, c-1b	.246	199	23	49	4	0	5	26	1
Stovall, DaRond, of	.243	412	59	100	20	3	22	80	19
Warner, Michael, of	.351	410	99	144	31	4	17	103	30

PITCHING	W	L	ERA	G	SV	IP	H	BB	SO
Arroyo, Luis	8	0	2.52	40	5	61	53	22	52
Briscoe, John	5	1	2.70	53	22	60	53	24	50
Calmus, Lance	4	1	3.73	45	3	80	82	24	58
Dace, Derek	7	3	2.85	34	4	54	44	12	29
Davis, Ray	8	4	3.70	15	0	88	80	33	89
Dodd, Robert	10	5	3.55	26	0	150	157	54	135
Griffin, Kirk	3	2	3.59	50	2	85	80	28	53
Hoy, Wayne	0	3	13.97	3	0	10	22	8	4
Jordan, Ricardo	10	5	3.18	18	0	119	93	40	87
McMullen, Jerry	0	0	6.55	8	0	11	15	4	8
Mitchell, Dean	1	0	2.25	3	0	8	4	5	2
Renko, Steve	4	2	4.07	14	0	66	68	27	32
Rigby, Brad	2	1	3.94	5	0	16	21	2	13
Steed, Rick	7	7	4.80	25	0	114	122	57	68
Vasquez, Julian	4	1	3.33	30	1	49	37	15	51
Veniard, Jay	1	3	5.62	12	0	42	51	23	25
Walls, Doug	4	3	3.66	11	0	59	59	21	39
2-team (13 LV)	9	6	3.55	24	0	129	125	46	93
Winston, Darrin	5	2	2.12	31	5	59	59	8	51

FRONTIER LEAGUE

The Richmond Roosters finished second to the Chillicothe Paints in the Frontier League's Eastern Division in 2001, but turned the tables on the Paints in the playoffs. The Roosters won their first title since joining the league in 1995.

The Roosters pummeled the Paints 14-0 in Game Two to sweep the best-of-3 series. They scored 10 runs in the first inning and starter Mike Kraemer went seven strong innings en route to the easy win.

Richmond catcher Jeremiah Klosterman went 11-for-22 with eight RBIs in five playoff games, while third baseman Dave Leverett went 10-for-25 with seven RBIs. Klosterman was named MVP of the championship series.

The Frontier League, which began operating in 1993 just like the Northern League, expanded by two teams in 2001 for the second time in three years, adding Kalamazoo and Gateway.

STANDINGS

EASTERN DIVISION	W	L	PCT	GB
Chillicothe Paints	51	33	.607	—
Richmond Roosters	49	35	.583	2
Canton Crocodiles	47	37	.560	4
Johnstown Johnnies	44	40	.524	7
London Werewolves	37	47	.440	14
Kalamazoo Kings	25	59	.298	26

WESTERN DIVISION	W	L	PCT	GB
Dubois County Dragons	48	36	.571	—
River City Rascals	46	38	.548	2
Springfield Capitals	45	39	.536	3
Evansville Otters	44	40	.524	4
Gateway Grizzlies	37	44	.457	9½
Cook County Cheetahs	28	53	.346	18½

PLAYOFFS: Semifinals—Richmond defeated DuBois County 2-1 and Chillicothe defeated Canton 2-1 in best-of-3 series. **Finals**—Richmond defeated Chillicothe 2-0 in best-of-3 series.

MANAGERS: Canton—Jeff Isom. **Chillicothe**—Jamie Keefe. **Cook County**—Chad Epperson. **Dubois County**—Greg Tagert. **Evansville**—Dan Shwam. **Gateway**—Champ Summers. **Johnstown**—Mike Moore. **Kalamazoo**—Andy McCauley. **London**—Bruce Gray. **Richmond**—Fran Riordan. **River City**—Neil Fiala. **Springfield**—Dick Schofield.

ATTENDANCE: River City 153,905; Kalamazoo 103,031; Evansville 90,948; Cook County 65,627; Chillicothe 60,163; Johnstown 43,184; Richmond 42,976; London 42,061; Springfield 35,424; Canton 29,703; Gateway 28,898; Dubois County 23,302.

ALL-STAR TEAM: C—Adam Patterson, Chillicothe; Chuck Van Robays, Johnstown. **1B**—Fran Riordan, Richmond. **2B**—Kevin Connacher, Chillicothe. **3B**—Brian Fuess, River City; Johnny Poss, Johnstown. **SS**—Clay Snellgrove, Canton. **OF**—Kirk Taylor, Johnstown; Jon Weber, Canton; Jeremy Coronado, Evansville. **DH**—Steve Mitrovich, Richmond. **SP**—Rick Blanc, Chillicothe. **RP**—Brian Partenheimer, Dubois County.

Most Valuable Player: Kirk Taylor, Johnstown. **Most Valuable Pitcher:** Rick Blanc, Chillicothe. **Manager of the Year:** Greg Tagert, Dubois County.

INDIVIDUAL BATTING LEADERS
(Minimum 227 Plate Appearances)

	AVG	AB	R	H	2B	3B	HR	RBI	SB
Snellgrove, Clay, Canton	.364	343	49	125	21	1	3	45	8
Coronado, Jeremy, Evansville	.354	297	53	105	14	3	1	40	31
Taylor, Kirk, Johnstown	.350	331	65	116	22	6	17	72	19
McCay, Matt, Chillicothe	.345	325	62	112	14	0	1	48	8
Vanelderstine, Ben, London	.338	269	42	91	11	2	5	38	9
Robertson, Mike, River City	.335	218	46	73	11	3	14	46	6
Sellier, Brian, Gateway	.332	295	56	98	13	6	11	49	26
Delucchi, Dustin, DC	.331	236	44	78	16	0	6	41	22
Patterson, Adam, Chillicothe	.328	238	44	78	8	0	5	33	1
Graham, Dan, Springfield	.328	232	43	76	18	2	14	57	10

INDIVIDUAL PITCHING LEADERS
(Minimum 67 Innings)

	W	L	ERA	G	SV	IP	H	BB	SO
Thomas, Joe, Canton	9	0	1.36	11	0	86	82	22	55
Baber, Matt, Canton	8	3	2.33	17	0	120	98	32	96
Schweitzer, Matt, Richmond	5	3	2.64	39	3	72	58	20	79
Brand, Cliff, Evansville	4	4	2.73	17	0	96	97	25	80
Welch, Chris, Johnstown	8	3	3.08	14	0	85	98	29	61
LaMarsh, Rob, River City	8	7	3.19	17	0	118	120	28	74
Berry, Matt, Richmond	7	4	3.22	14	0	81	73	29	79
Blanc, Rick, Chillicothe	13	1	3.24	18	0	119	117	26	95
Yee, Damon, DC	6	6	3.28	17	0	93	85	33	70
Fisher, Cody, DC	6	3	3.30	19	1	87	89	21	71

CANTON

BATTING	AVG	AB	R	H	2B	3B	HR	RBI	SB
Alfieri, Frank, 3b	.252	147	21	37	9	0	5	22	5
Argento, Shaun, c	.220	277	34	61	13	1	3	35	5
Baderdeen, Kevin, 3b	.059	17	2	1	0	0	0	0	0
Butt, Gerald, of-c	.167	24	1	4	1	0	0	3	2
Callen, Tommy, 2b	.255	153	25	39	13	1	1	22	3
Copley, Travis, 1b-3b	.284	303	44	86	15	2	7	45	4
Coy, J.D., 2b	.220	141	16	31	2	1	0	18	4
Fischer, Aaron, dh-c	.262	183	31	48	3	0	4	26	13
Greenwell, William, 1b	.250	128	16	32	6	0	2	15	1
Langdon, Ryan, dh	.200	10	1	2	0	0	0	1	0
Livingston, Scott, of	.244	164	26	40	7	0	1	15	5
May, Freddy, of	.263	57	6	15	1	0	0	2	0
Morrison, Lee, of	.268	123	15	33	12	1	0	13	1
Snellgrove, Clay, ss	.364	343	49	125	21	1	3	45	8
Vollstedt, John, of	.289	201	34	58	6	0	1	9	27
Weber, Jon, of	.307	329	60	101	15	7	18	69	16
Wilke, Josh, of	.200	60	9	12	1	0	0	3	1
Wren, Cliff, 3b	.250	104	11	26	8	0	0	15	1

PITCHING	W	L	ERA	G	SV	IP	H	BB	SO
Baber, Matt	8	3	2.33	17	0	120	98	32	96
Bair, Dennis	8	5	3.51	13	0	92	92	31	82
Carlson, Ira	0	0	6.75	7	0	5	6	5	1
Durkee, Jeremy	0	0	3.98	16	0	20	21	16	25
Gallaty, Joe	4	3	3.36	12	1	59	63	18	35
Garvin, Robert	0	4	4.29	21	2	21	30	11	23
Goure, Sam	1	1	8.46	6	0	22	31	7	19
Kozol, Anthony	4	2	1.17	21	6	23	25	7	17
Litsinberger, Kevin	0	2	6.30	6	1	10	8	4	9
2-team (18 Richmond)	1	2	3.90	24	1	30	29	13	27
McEvoy, Casey	2	3	3.89	8	0	42	37	23	37
Mendoza, Juan	2	7	4.54	16	0	79	107	27	33
Meyer, Daniel	4	6	3.88	15	0	72	72	27	77
Montoya, Eric	1	0	2.31	11	0	23	10	19	27
Stephens, Riley	0	0	7.36	10	0	7	9	7	2
Stevens, Josh	2	0	0.77	11	6	12	6	2	24
Tallman, Scott	0	0	5.06	8	0	5	5	7	4
Thomas, Joe	9	0	1.36	11	0	86	82	22	55
Weltmer, Eric	2	1	5.23	13	1	21	23	8	15

CHILLICOTHE

BATTING	AVG	AB	R	H	2B	3B	HR	RBI	SB
Annicelli, Rob, ss-3b	.167	36	6	6	2	0	0	2	0
Cerni, Vincent, 3b-ss	.264	239	27	63	16	1	1	40	6
Colameco, Joe, of	.325	289	64	94	17	2	10	60	7
Connacher, Kevin, 2b	.282	330	72	93	19	2	16	46	29
Dalton, David, ss	.286	252	49	72	10	2	9	45	14
Estep, Joe, of	.276	170	20	47	8	1	1	14	9
Graham, Justin, of	.217	175	34	38	9	3	1	16	4
Guiseppe, John, c	.054	37	2	2	0	0	0	0	0
Kinsolving, Darin, 1b	.327	306	55	100	20	2	10	62	0
McCay, Matt, of	.345	325	62	112	14	0	1	48	8
Patterson, Adam, c	.328	238	44	78	8	0	5	33	1
Poulsen, Chris, c-3b	.269	156	17	42	8	0	2	18	3
See, Andrew, dh	.242	91	16	22	2	1	3	13	0
Swackhamer, Rustin, of	.245	94	13	23	4	0	6	15	0
Torres, Radames, 3b	.193	57	4	11	3	1	2	9	0
Warren, Phil, dh	.224	67	6	15	2	0	1	9	1

PITCHING	W	L	ERA	G	SV	IP	H	BB	SO
Blanc, Ric	13	1	3.24	18	0	119	117	26	95
Boesch, Sean	9	4	4.28	18	0	116	123	46	67
Bogs, Brian	2	0	4.13	30	1	52	57	16	56
Buirley, Kris	7	2	2.49	32	3	65	48	36	57
Fullenkamp, Woody	2	1	3.76	24	7	26	27	13	26
Goemann, Reed	2	2	3.80	21	0	21	22	22	17
Hampton, Matt	4	3	1.70	25	8	37	24	9	56
Harrison, Jason	5	5	4.70	19	0	100	103	51	112
Kisch, Greg	3	8	4.29	18	0	94	116	39	50
McGee, Denny	4	6	5.26	15	0	65	69	36	51
Quick, Dave	0	0	9.45	4	0	7	14	3	6
Robertson, Justin	0	1	19.44	2	0	8	23	6	4
See, Andrew	0	0	5.68	9	1	13	14	10	15
Tomco, Brad	0	0	8.53	4	0	6	4	1	5

COOK COUNTY

BATTING	AVG	AB	R	H	2B	3B	HR	RBI	SB
Bourhill, Scott, ss	.143	28	2	4	1	0	0	1	0
Butt, Gerald, 3b-of	.277	65	7	18	2	0	0	8	5
3-team (28 Spr./10 Can.)	.255	153	20	39	7	1	0	18	12
Conway, Rob, 3b	.296	152	18	45	6	1	0	13	5
Cook, Josh, dh	.220	59	6	13	1	0	2	5	1
DeFabbia, Rob, c-3b	.286	252	30	72	10	0	5	26	1
Feenker, Trent, of	.184	76	11	14	4	0	0	3	4
Flack, John, dh-1b	.125	48	3	6	1	0	0	3	0

	AVG	AB	R	H	2B	3B	HR	RBI	SB
2-team (42 Johnstown)	.307	153	18	47	11	1	1	18	0
Forsberg, Dana, 1b	.235	204	29	48	5	0	8	24	6
Friedman, Tim, 2b	.100	10	1	1	0	0	0	2	0
Goirigolzarro, Ray, of-2b	.259	228	28	59	12	3	4	23	15
Gourdin, Khalil, of	.048	21	3	1	1	0	0	2	0
Halstead, Jeff, of	.233	116	9	27	0	1	0	9	8
Johnson, Eunique, 3b	.212	33	7	7	2	0	1	4	1
Larreal, Roberto, 2b	.250	108	13	27	3	0	1	4	4
Longo, Troy, dh	.182	33	2	6	0	0	0	2	0
Marshall, Allen, 3b-ss	.227	110	24	25	5	0	4	16	7
Olmeda, Jose, ss	.233	73	6	17	2	0	2	6	0
Pierro, Justin, dh	.196	92	5	18	3	0	1	12	0
Rinne, James, of	.304	286	43	87	21	0	4	37	9
Schneider, Matt, of-1b	.225	213	30	48	12	2	9	36	3
Shanks, Eric, 2b	.259	112	16	29	4	1	3	15	5
Van Horn, Ryan, c	.204	142	15	29	6	0	2	19	1
Whitmer, Joe, of	.083	24	2	2	0	0	1	2	0
Williams, Justin, ss-2b	.239	117	12	28	5	0	0	5	1
Wright, Richard, of	.207	58	6	12	2	0	2	6	0

PITCHING	W	L	ERA	G	SV	IP	H	BB	SO
Bircher, Chad	0	3	3.03	30	11	30	33	5	25
Chinea, Julio	1	7	4.04	35	0	62	73	15	69
Classen, Ender	4	6	5.46	17	0	86	90	48	69
Fitzgerald, Ryan	0	0	7.71	7	0	9	13	5	7
Gonzalez, Giovanni	0	2	5.59	2	0	10	8	4	5
Hanrahan, Mark	1	1	3.89	20	0	35	32	15	30
Hardman, Steve	0	2	3.07	9	1	29	30	8	21
Houdek, Brian	6	2	4.50	16	1	36	36	26	38
Joseph, Glen	3	2	4.86	31	0	37	31	36	32
Kelley, Chris	2	2	4.05	5	0	27	24	20	30
McGill, Trae	1	1	3.95	4	0	27	28	4	39
Moore, Christopher	3	4	3.19	9	0	62	61	14	45
Odom, Lance	2	2	4.81	12	0	24	30	6	17
Roy, Angus	1	2	5.31	4	0	20	29	8	14
Shelley, Jason	2	8	4.79	17	0	92	86	42	88
White, Eric	2	4	4.40	21	0	76	83	49	56

DUBOIS COUNTY

BATTING	AVG	AB	R	H	2B	3B	HR	RBI	SB
Anderson, John, ss	.288	229	28	66	7	0	1	29	21
Bakich, Erik, of	.150	20	3	3	0	0	0	1	0
Balet, Pichi, 3b-ss	.329	149	23	49	6	0	2	26	2
Ballon, John, 3b-of	.274	266	43	73	18	0	7	43	2
Bronowicz, Scott, c	.245	151	13	37	4	1	2	17	1
Delucchi, Dustin, of	.331	236	44	78	16	0	6	41	22
Faulken, Matt, dh-1b	.257	109	16	28	3	0	2	14	3
Fillmore, Kurt, of	.269	268	49	72	7	2	4	26	10
Kalczynski, Joe, c	.310	168	26	52	12	0	4	34	0
Kobayashi, Mitsuru, ss-2b	.200	10	1	2	0	1	0	2	0
Krance, Max, of	.255	47	7	12	1	0	1	3	0
Matricardi, Fred, of	.214	42	7	9	1	0	0	8	6
Morey, Randy, 2b-of	.197	234	28	46	7	1	4	22	30
Olow, Adam, of	.275	200	39	55	6	1	4	19	8
Peerman, Mike, 1b	.271	229	33	62	11	2	1	26	4
Pelfrey, Dennis, 2b-3b	.289	152	37	44	4	1	6	24	16
Pierro, Justin, dh	.138	29	5	4	0	0	0	3	0
2-team (29 Cook County)	.182	121	10	22	3	0	1	15	0
Sapp, Curtis, 1b-3b	.235	187	18	44	3	0	2	22	0
Thompson, Todd, 2b	.143	21	3	3	0	1	0	1	0
Walsh, Patrick, 2b-of	.400	15	0	6	0	0	0	2	2

PITCHING	W	L	ERA	G	SV	IP	H	BB	SO
Bracho, Alejandro	2	2	5.11	17	0	37	30	19	28
Fisher, Cody	6	3	3.30	19	1	87	89	21	71
Fuqua, David	0	0	4.76	20	0	28	30	8	19
Gaines, Jamal	7	5	3.91	17	0	104	120	24	77
Kelley, Brent	5	4	2.79	30	4	48	39	14	43
Kuklis, Kevin	4	6	6.18	19	0	71	94	26	49
Lopez, Derek	7	3	4.50	16	0	84	102	19	72
Marshall, Gavin	3	0	5.44	28	2	45	56	17	42
Partenheimer, Brian	4	2	1.45	34	17	43	31	8	46
Perio, Ian	1	1	4.50	3	0	14	13	7	19
Turner, Jess	3	2	4.96	25	1	45	45	19	53
Viel, Chris	0	2	5.84	21	2	25	25	18	19
Yee, Damon	6	6	3.28	17	0	93	85	33	70

EVANSVILLE

BATTING	AVG	AB	R	H	2B	3B	HR	RBI	SB
Adams, Chris, 3b-of	.271	218	27	59	7	0	2	18	2
Brown, Todd, 3b	.265	117	11	31	2	0	1	19	3
Butler, Mike, ss-2b	.113	62	8	7	1	1	0	4	2
Carmona, Louis, of	.125	24	1	3	0	0	1	3	0
Coronado, Jeremy, of	.354	297	53	105	14	3	1	40	31

	AVG	AB	R	H	2B	3B	HR	RBI	SB
Cosbey, Chris, of	.295	251	48	74	8	4	2	24	38
Delgado, Gabriel, 2b	.338	148	30	50	6	2	1	22	7
2-team (31 London)	.313	256	49	80	10	2	2	39	12
Figueroa, Eduardo, 1b	.366	164	36	60	15	1	1	27	3
Godwin, Cliff, c	.129	31	1	4	0	0	0	0	0
Hardin, Travis, 2b	.200	35	0	7	1	0	0	6	2
Harrison, Brian, dh-1b	.273	139	20	38	6	0	3	24	0
Hudson, Josh, c	.215	65	10	14	2	0	0	7	0
Law, Keith, ss	.245	229	39	56	9	1	3	29	6
Martin, Craig, 2b-ss	.274	62	16	17	1	0	4	16	1
Mattingly, Brandon, c	.264	140	14	37	8	1	3	22	1
Nerei, Yuji, 3b	.327	153	33	50	10	0	10	40	0
Nouguier, Joe, 2b	.214	28	2	6	0	0	0	3	0
Raffo, John, 1b	.250	96	14	24	4	0	4	23	0
Ready, Alan, c	.207	58	8	12	3	0	1	6	0
2-team (26 London)	.197	142	27	28	6	0	3	16	1
Skinner, Rick, 2b	.105	19	3	2	0	0	0	1	0
Suraci, Scott, of	.183	71	14	13	1	1	2	13	3
Thomas, Mark, of-1b	.266	293	45	78	18	4	1	34	18
Williams, Jewell, of	.211	114	15	24	4	0	3	15	2

PITCHING	W	L	ERA	G	SV	IP	H	BB	SO
Blaylock, Don	1	0	5.85	17	0	20	23	11	19
Book, Jeremy	1	0	3.57	5	0	23	24	3	15
Boughey, William	1	0	6.75	5	0	9	15	9	5
Bowers, Rob	0	1	4.70	8	0	8	9	2	1
Brand, Cliff	4	4	2.73	17	0	96	97	25	80
Chavez, Jacob	0	0	3.09	8	0	12	11	7	11
Cooper, Eric	1	1	3.18	4	0	23	19	9	13
Fry, Nolan	8	3	3.74	16	0	99	92	44	59
Honda, Tomohiro	4	3	2.93	15	1	61	57	15	50
Howay, Chris	0	0	5.79	3	0	5	4	0	7
Love, Brad	1	7	6.72	19	1	68	85	43	53
Miller, Tom	9	5	3.70	18	0	112	120	27	87
Richter, William	3	3	1.09	29	11	33	21	13	25
Roe, Terrence	1	0	3.68	6	0	7	9	6	5
Smith, J.J.	0	2	7.36	9	0	15	15	7	8
Smuin, Shane	9	3	3.81	22	1	80	60	47	100
Steele, Bradley	0	4	7.56	10	0	17	24	5	4
Stelzner, Nick	1	2	4.13	26	4	28	27	18	26

GATEWAY

BATTING	AVG	AB	R	H	2B	3B	HR	RBI	SB
Bergheger, Jeremiah, ss	.219	215	31	47	7	1	3	18	4
Bugger, Mark, 2b	.275	244	48	67	12	1	3	30	2
Chinapen, Wayne, 1b	.200	30	2	6	1	0	1	4	0
Court, Rick, c	.268	97	14	26	2	0	1	5	0
DeGraffenreid, Todd, 3b-1b	.274	259	37	71	14	1	7	54	6
Dutter, Tony, 1b-of	.210	100	14	21	2	2	0	11	0
Essian, Jim, dh	.130	23	3	3	1	0	0	2	0
Filson, Gregory, 2b-3b	.294	102	17	30	2	0	1	15	4
Godwin, Cliff, dh	.270	63	10	17	5	0	2	11	0
2-team (9 Evansville)	.223	94	11	21	5	0	2	11	0
Haake, Brett, 3b	.253	91	12	23	3	3	2	12	0
Langlois, Jean, dh	.262	206	28	54	9	2	5	23	9
Lara, David, of	.253	292	37	74	15	2	11	58	3
Longo, Troy, 1b	.154	52	5	8	1	0	2	8	0
2-team (12 Cook County)	.165	85	7	14	1	0	2	10	0
Luebbert, Garet, ss	.282	39	6	11	1	0	0	7	1
Mateo, Jose, ss-2b	.167	36	6	6	1	0	0	5	0
Molinari, James, of	.274	314	65	86	10	1	7	34	27
Norrell, Troy, c	.159	69	9	11	5	0	3	5	1
Raybourn, Brendan, 1b	.091	11	1	1	0	0	0	1	0
Sandoval, Jhensy, dh	.118	17	0	2	1	0	0	2	0
Santiago, D.J., c	.182	137	16	25	3	0	1	9	1
2-team (25 River City)	.196	199	20	39	6	0	1	19	1
Sellier, Brian, of-1b	.332	295	56	98	13	6	11	49	26
Versailles, Greg, 2b-ss	.211	19	4	4	0	0	0	0	0

PITCHING	W	L	ERA	G	SV	IP	H	BB	SO
Anderegg, Jason	1	1	1.20	2	0	15	13	6	9
Beck, David	2	2	5.73	8	0	11	9	8	16
Buck, Pete	9	5	4.29	19	0	120	130	32	91
Cowan, Dustin	0	1	3.52	11	0	15	18	6	12
2-team (5 River City)	0	2	4.84	16	0	22	27	7	19
Ellison, Darrin	3	2	4.25	23	2	36	36	8	25
Giaudrone, Bret	3	4	3.76	9	0	55	55	22	47
Harris, James	0	1	5.06	3	0	5	8	1	3
Lee, Tymber	5	7	5.36	16	0	102	128	33	61
Lindsey, Bart	0	0	7.20	6	0	10	16	8	8
Mallonee, Mike	0	2	9.31	3	0	10	12	8	3
Meyer, Layne	1	2	1.63	27	16	28	13	15	45
Nelson, Nic	2	3	4.20	13	0	79	93	28	46
Schlenker, Jason	4	3	3.15	33	0	46	41	25	50
Shoemaker, Matt	1	1	4.01	19	0	34	39	21	30

INDEPENDENT LEAGUES

	W	L	ERA	G	SV	IP	H	BB	SO
Solano, Travis	1	1	4.63	3	0	12	13	8	6
Tippett, Royce	0	4	5.14	13	2	35	36	18	25
Warnecke, Ryan	3	2	5.05	7	0	41	51	12	17
2-team (6 River City)	3	3	7.50	13	0	48	73	12	20
Yost, Kyle	2	3	6.37	6	0	35	40	14	18

JOHNSTOWN

BATTING	AVG	AB	R	H	2B	3B	HR	RBI	SB
Constantino, Greg, dh	.260	73	5	19	4	0	0	9	0
Crowley, Ben, dh-of	.275	222	35	61	11	1	7	36	0
Deike, Mike, of	.307	313	39	96	15	2	4	44	1
Ferres, David, 2b	.297	343	64	102	21	4	3	50	7
Flack, John, 3b-1b	.390	105	15	41	10	1	1	15	0
Lewter, John, dh	.308	26	8	8	1	0	0	2	0
Memmert, Gabe, 1b	.228	263	32	60	17	0	4	35	0
Morse, Dan, of	.300	313	54	94	20	0	4	42	17
Paciorek, Mack, ss	.292	267	33	78	24	1	0	36	2
Passerelle, Matt, c	.219	32	0	7	1	0	0	4	0
Poss, John, 3b-ss	.307	352	57	108	22	2	4	37	1
Taylor, Kirk, of	.350	331	65	116	22	6	17	72	19
Van Robays, Charles, c	.323	260	41	84	10	1	1	31	3
Zachry, Drew, of-1b	.300	90	19	27	3	0	0	9	0

PITCHING	W	L	ERA	G	SV	IP	H	BB	SO
Barone, John	4	1	3.10	28	1	61	51	38	54
Bloom, Tom	1	1	9.12	5	0	26	44	4	22
Brown, B.J.	1	3	5.23	8	0	41	45	25	30
Brown, Kevin	0	4	9.82	4	0	15	24	4	6
Byrd, Stephen	2	3	3.43	6	0	42	41	11	35
2-team (11 Kalamazoo)	2	10	5.81	17	0	101	129	32	77
Chandler, Bobby	2	1	2.31	27	19	35	29	9	40
Creswell, Brandon	4	4	3.96	11	0	61	67	27	60
Crist, Ryan	3	4	5.77	10	0	58	59	36	69
Devine, Nathan	0	2	13.50	2	0	8	17	3	6
Ford, Sean	1	2	7.31	8	0	16	21	6	15
Fulmer, Bundy	5	1	5.88	8	0	49	66	14	23
Kawecki, Kevin	2	1	4.94	11	1	27	28	3	29
Lewter, John	0	0	6.65	8	2	23	26	14	18
Nemeth, Peter	7	4	4.72	23	1	55	64	15	58
Pilato, Chris	1	0	7.36	4	0	18	13	17	22
Sheets, Matt	3	5	5.26	10	0	63	77	29	34
Stoner, Simon	0	1	4.35	16	1	31	26	26	40
Vickroy, Steve	0	0	3.38	8	0	19	19	8	19
Welch, Chris	8	3	3.08	14	0	85	98	29	61

KALAMAZOO

BATTING	AVG	AB	R	H	2B	3B	HR	RBI	SB
Burgos, Tino, ss	.209	43	2	9	3	0	0	1	0
Cook, Josh, 1b	.280	50	6	14	4	0	1	9	0
2-team (19 Cook County)	.248	109	12	27	5	0	3	14	1
Doakes, Schuyler, of-2b	.311	328	45	102	11	2	3	35	48
Edwards, Dytarious, 2b	.287	150	14	43	3	1	0	18	9
Edwards, Willie, of-1b	.269	197	25	53	7	0	6	20	9
2-team (7 London)	.271	221	26	60	9	0	6	23	9
Gunderson, Jeff, ss-2b	.240	96	17	23	3	0	2	7	0
Harry, Russell, 1b	.227	66	7	15	2	0	0	5	0
Hills, Chris, of	.067	15	1	1	0	0	0	0	2
Hyott, Daniel, of	.063	16	1	1	0	0	0	0	0
Kent, Matt, c-1b	.227	154	12	35	5	0	2	16	0
Kruk, Delton, ss-2b	.175	57	4	10	2	0	1	3	0
Payne, Joe, 3b	.235	149	20	35	5	0	7	26	2
Peavey, Ryan, of	.239	197	22	47	5	1	3	14	9
2-team (16 Richmond)	.257	249	33	64	7	3	3	26	11
Peters, Ryan, dh	.222	45	4	10	4	0	1	2	0
Pohle, Ike, c	.262	267	25	70	19	0	3	37	1
Pujols, Raul, of-1b	.150	40	2	6	0	0	0	1	0
Raiburn, Josh, ss	.368	106	17	39	3	1	0	15	5
Seestadt, Joseph, dh	.145	62	8	9	2	0	1	3	0
Sowers, Will, 1b-2b	.291	230	25	67	14	0	4	30	2
Tharp, Zach, of-3b	.185	135	14	25	7	0	4	12	0
Williams, Marcus, of	.216	231	35	50	5	4	3	24	11
Wright, Richard, of	.214	14	3	3	1	1	0	3	2
Zardis, Alex, 2b	.184	87	11	16	0	0	1	5	1

PITCHING	W	L	ERA	G	SV	IP	H	BB	SO
Beckman, Jacob	1	2	7.32	8	0	20	28	14	5
Blaesing, Jamie	3	1	4.76	16	0	21	29	19	25
2-team (5 London)	3	2	5.64	21	0	30	40	24	30
Byrd, Stephen	0	7	7.52	11	0	59	88	21	42
Carr, Cory	0	0	4.37	8	0	23	26	8	18
2-team (8 London)	1	4	7.34	16	0	61	81	26	48
Clark, Mark	1	4	6.31	9	0	46	60	29	32
Goldwater, Kyle	0	0	5.14	18	2	21	22	7	15
Gunderson, Matt	3	10	4.06	16	0	93	85	39	81
Janecek, Eric	0	0	1.13	4	0	8	4	7	6

LONDON

	W	L	ERA	G	SV	IP	H	BB	SO
Lynn, Kevin	1	1	5.00	11	2	18	22	2	23
McWatters, David	2	7	3.95	18	0	82	89	20	85
Moriarity, Michael	1	8	5.96	17	1	77	104	42	48
Sheets, Matt	2	2	3.19	6	1	37	35	10	39
2-team (10 Johnstown)	5	7	4.50	16	1	100	112	39	73
Skinner, Corey	0	1	6.14	6	0	7	10	2	4
Takach, Ryan	6	8	3.43	17	0	113	113	29	91
Turnrose, Eric	0	0	2.35	5	0	8	1	3	7
Walters, Reggie	2	0	3.47	6	0	36	36	13	23
Wools, Jeff	2	5	4.66	30	1	37	40	23	39

LONDON

BATTING	AVG	AB	R	H	2B	3B	HR	RBI	SB
Babcock, Pete, 1b	.236	55	5	13	3	0	0	8	0
Bechard, Jess, 3b-1b	.288	285	45	82	20	1	6	37	6
Brock, Les, of	.163	202	22	33	6	0	3	18	12
Brown, Seth, 3b-ss	.277	191	37	53	9	0	3	15	4
Choron, Joey, dh	.200	50	4	10	3	0	1	6	0
Delgado, Gabriel, 2b	.278	108	19	30	4	0	1	17	5
Edwards, Willie, dh	.292	24	1	7	2	0	0	3	0
Forman, Wayne, c	.196	163	19	32	4	0	0	9	2
French, Ned, of	.283	254	33	72	12	0	4	35	20
Hendrickson, Justin, 1b	.297	256	35	76	17	0	10	42	1
Kitsch, Trent, dh	.248	113	11	28	5	0	1	17	2
Legacy, Toby, ss	.167	12	0	2	0	0	0	1	0
Lindberg, Ryan, c-of	.250	220	26	55	6	0	1	17	5
Lown, Ryan, ss	.263	57	6	15	1	1	0	6	4
Murphy, Sean, 2b-ss	.318	274	43	87	18	3	3	34	19
Ready, Alan, c	.190	84	19	16	3	0	2	10	1
Rittenhouse, Adam, 2b-ss	.289	180	23	52	12	0	3	21	4
Vanelderstine, Ben, of	.338	269	42	91	11	2	5	38	9
Wright, Richard, of	.185	92	11	17	4	2	1	13	2
3-team (6 Kal./19 CC)	.195	164	20	32	7	3	2	22	4

PITCHING	W	L	ERA	G	SV	IP	H	BB	SO
Allen, Mike	2	7	3.44	25	1	65	70	33	61
Bishop, Trevor	3	1	1.49	7	0	36	23	15	40
Blaesing, Jamie	0	1	8.22	5	0	8	11	5	5
Brazeal, Spencer	1	1	9.24	14	0	25	36	17	24
Buckle, Matt	7	7	3.97	17	0	104	108	27	56
Carr, Cory	1	4	9.08	8	0	39	55	18	30
Hartman, Kory	2	3	8.06	16	0	41	59	27	27
Harvey, Ian	2	2	2.40	31	11	41	36	16	47
Howay, Chris	0	2	3.92	6	0	21	20	13	19
2-team (3 Evansville)	0	2	4.26	9	0	25	24	13	26
Janecek, Eric	1	2	6.95	6	0	22	34	10	15
2-team (4 Kalamazoo)	1	2	5.40	10	0	30	38	17	21
Johnson, Jeff	1	0	6.07	14	0	27	36	13	32
Kojack, Phil	8	3	3.71	20	0	119	109	53	101
Levy, Tye	3	5	7.23	10	0	42	60	6	32
Lindberg, Ryan	3	1	2.53	9	1	32	29	9	31
Mosher, Craig	2	3	3.53	25	0	74	54	36	71
Reyes, Tom	0	0	15.43	4	0	5	13	3	2
Wigington, Jeff	0	5	7.04	7	0	31	39	21	21

RICHMOND

BATTING	AVG	AB	R	H	2B	3B	HR	RBI	SB
Burkhart, Damon, 2b	.285	214	48	61	9	2	1	29	13
Cruz, Raul, 2b-of	.260	154	29	40	8	2	12	32	3
Deakins, Jeremiah, of	.270	111	21	30	8	0	3	23	0
Halstead, Jeff, of	.253	170	17	43	0	1	0	11	11
2-team (32 Cook County)	.296	54	8	16	0	0	0	2	3
Klosterman, Jeremiah, c	.270	148	21	40	5	0	1	13	0
Leverett, Dave, 3b	.275	287	48	79	10	0	4	36	9
Marple, Scott, of	.308	159	31	49	8	3	5	19	4
Mitrovich, Steve, c	.304	283	42	86	20	1	12	65	1
Muro, Roy, dh-of	.224	98	18	22	7	0	3	15	0
Needle, Bryan, of	.224	98	19	22	3	0	1	10	3
Peavey, Ryan, of	.327	52	11	17	2	2	0	12	2
Riordan, Fran, 1b	.299	335	55	100	17	3	14	74	8
Schmitz, John, of	.326	233	51	76	19	0	4	36	11
Sledd, Aaron, of	.302	252	54	76	13	2	13	61	3
Tavares, John, ss	.280	336	75	94	13	2	6	52	5
Voshell, Key, 2b	.323	65	11	21	7	1	1	13	3
Wright, Paul, of	.188	16	3	3	1	0	1	0	0

PITCHING	W	L	ERA	G	SV	IP	H	BB	SO
Berry, Matt	7	4	3.22	14	0	81	73	29	79
Carver, Steve	10	3	3.91	16	0	104	108	33	90
Edmundson, Marcus	0	1	4.94	12	0	27	27	8	31
Ellison, Derrick	2	0	3.06	5	0	18	14	7	17
Engstrom, Jay	1	8	7.49	14	0	46	74	19	34
Fairbanks, Justin	6	1	2.56	9	0	53	48	18	45
Foster, Cory	2	2	4.18	16	0	28	33	12	40

	W	L	ERA	G	SV	IP	H	BB	SO
Fuller, Ryan	0	0	7.88	2	0	8	11	5	4
Immekus, Jason	1	2	9.58	4	0	10	21	4	4
Jelovcic, Rich	4	1	7.06	11	0	59	83	23	40
Kraemer, Mike	2	0	3.24	13	0	25	16	13	19
Litsinberger, Kevin	1	0	2.70	18	0	20	21	9	18
McGurk, Mike	3	5	5.37	16	0	67	86	19	33
Mierzwa, Aaron	3	0	3.38	9	0	13	6	10	12
Schweitzer, Matt	5	3	2.64	39	3	72	58	20	79
Sosebee, Chad	1	4	4.91	38	1	44	44	16	38
Ziroli, Mike	1	1	2.58	33	16	38	29	14	50

	W	L	ERA	G	SV	IP	H	BB	SO
Day, Kelvin	0	0	0.00	5	1	5	1	4	4
Harden, Tony	6	4	4.24	21	1	87	89	39	83
Harmon, Gary	2	5	5.06	19	0	78	89	45	43
Havens, Chris	1	2	3.94	27	6	30	34	12	22
Hernandez, Robert	1	0	5.56	12	0	23	26	21	18
Lockridge, Sherwin	1	0	7.82	15	1	13	19	10	9
Lucht, Scott	4	1	2.72	44	3	53	51	18	31
Miller, Kevin	4	5	3.95	43	5	41	32	25	43
Oksen, Andrew	6	7	4.51	18	0	108	104	50	78
St. Amant, John	3	0	4.66	24	0	39	39	17	42

RIVER CITY

BATTING	AVG	AB	R	H	2B	3B	HR	RBI	SB
Absher, Eric, of	.172	87	17	15	5	0	2	8	7
Annin, Justin, c	.254	134	13	34	7	1	4	18	0
Bates, Tyler, of	.258	155	31	40	4	2	1	17	20
Beckmann, Bryan, 3b-2b	.285	158	29	45	9	1	4	21	9
Boyd, Scott, of	.274	263	37	72	17	1	5	41	5
Cunningham, Ben, 1b	.207	29	5	6	0	0	0	0	0
Dawson, Travis, of	.280	214	41	60	7	1	0	11	24
Fuess, Brian, 3b-1b	.302	324	46	98	23	1	7	64	6
Jager, Corey, c	.272	81	11	22	4	0	0	9	0
Lucas, Kevin, ss	.233	240	36	56	10	2	4	30	11
Moore, Ryan, 2b	.275	265	40	73	15	0	6	31	12
Piatt, Ben, of	.188	32	3	6	2	0	1	4	1
Robertson, Mike, of	.335	218	46	73	11	3	14	46	6
Runnells, T.J., 2b-ss	.304	247	46	75	14	1	2	38	16
Santiago, D.J., c	.226	62	4	14	3	0	0	10	0
Strickland, Greg, of	.240	50	7	12	0	0	0	3	2
Urban, Joe, 1b	.278	252	38	70	10	2	4	38	6

PITCHING	W	L	ERA	G	SV	IP	H	BB	SO
Bauer, Ryan	5	6	4.28	13	0	82	79	28	70
Bracho, Alejandro	2	0	0.67	4	0	13	4	3	13
2-team (17 DuBois)	4	2	3.93	21	0	50	34	22	41
Castor, Henry	3	4	4.11	25	4	61	63	37	50
Coleman, Billy	1	2	6.28	6	0	29	36	13	22
Cowan, Dustin	0	1	7.71	5	0	7	9	1	7
Kinney, Josh	1	0	1.71	3	0	21	18	7	18
LaMarsh, Rob	8	7	3.19	17	0	118	120	28	74
Lindsey, Bart	1	1	6.41	10	0	20	22	18	14
2-team (6 Gateway)	1	1	6.67	16	0	30	38	26	22
Neubauer, Marc	1	1	2.57	20	9	28	21	14	30
Powell, Greg	4	2	3.09	9	0	55	43	16	32
Prather, Kendall	3	2	5.71	9	0	35	38	23	32
Rowland, Carl	11	4	3.44	18	0	105	103	34	77
Sansone, Pete	0	0	5.63	7	0	8	9	13	10
Shafer, Adam	0	2	1.83	26	13	34	23	14	28
Thomas, Tommy	6	4	4.85	18	1	65	52	36	59
Tippett, Roy	0	0	1.93	6	0	9	8	2	6
2-team (13 Gateway)	0	4	4.47	19	2	44	44	20	31
Tyler, Ryan	0	0	8.57	12	0	21	27	15	9
Warnecke, Ryan	0	1	21.86	6	0	7	22	0	3
Wood, Jared	0	1	7.71	5	0	5	6	3	8

SPRINGFIELD

BATTING	AVG	AB	R	H	2B	3B	HR	RBI	SB
Aragon, Rocky, 2b-ss	.125	24	5	3	0	0	1	4	2
Austin, Richard, of	.260	265	49	69	15	3	8	43	14
Ayres, Troy, c	.256	168	24	43	11	0	2	18	1
Bone, Billy, 2b	.179	117	19	21	5	0	3	14	8
Buchmeier, Brian, of	.100	50	10	5	2	0	2	5	3
Butt, Gerald, 3b-of	.266	64	12	17	4	1	0	7	5
Drobiak, Jayson, 3b	.295	271	48	80	17	3	12	36	12
Graham, Dan, of	.328	232	43	76	18	2	14	57	10
Jones, David, c	.233	30	2	7	1	0	1	4	2
Lindekugel, Tyson, dh	.225	276	34	62	19	2	8	40	5
Lockridge, Sherwin, ss	.246	134	17	33	4	1	2	18	6
Luebbert, Garet, 2b-ss	.286	213	39	61	12	2	6	29	7
2-team (11 Gateway)	.286	252	45	72	13	2	6	36	8
Luttbeg, Steve, 2b	.151	53	4	8	0	0	0	3	4
McDonald, Bobby, of	.244	266	29	65	12	1	4	30	1
Molina, Alfredo, ss-3b	.267	120	18	32	6	0	0	14	1
2-team (7 Canton)	.272	125	18	34	7	0	0	14	1
Oetting, Chad, c	.327	113	20	37	7	0	6	24	0
Pieczynski, Eddie, c	.440	25	7	11	0	0	0	3	2
Salyers, Cody, of	.238	164	24	39	11	1	4	20	7
Schelhaas, Greg, 1b	.295	305	50	90	16	1	15	51	4
Zambrano, Alvaro, 2b	.154	13	1	2	0	0	0	0	0

PITCHING	W	L	ERA	G	SV	IP	H	BB	SO
Balcer, David	4	7	6.20	17	0	97	123	29	51
Batthaver, Bryan	9	2	4.21	17	0	109	103	45	76
Cox, Jeremy	4	6	7.57	20	0	61	72	35	53

NORTHERN LEAGUE

When the Northern and Northeast leagues merged after the 1998 season, it was commonly held that Eastern Division teams (the former Northeast League) simply didn't have enough talent to complete with the Central Division teams.

Three years later, a team from the East had won every championship and two of three all-star games. Overall the East might be a little short on talent, but it certainly has enough to win when games really matter.

In 2001, the New Jersey Jackals handily defeated the Winnipeg Goldeyes three games to one. It was New Jersey's first Northern League title. The Jackals won the Northeast League title in 1998, the team's first year in Little Falls, N.J.

Trey Beamon

Jackals outfielder Trey Beamon went 9-for-14 with five RBIs, four stolen bases and three runs during the championship series to earn MVP honors.

New Jersey swept through three rounds of playoffs despite finishing last in its division in the first half and second in the second half. The Jackals defeated Albany-Colonie and Elmira, winners of both halves in their respective divisions, in the Eastern Division playoffs.

Winnipeg and Sioux Falls also won both halves of the split-season schedule in the Central Division.

It was a banner year, in particular, for Sioux Falls despite its premature exit from the playoffs. The Canaries finished with a 55-35 overall record and won both halves in the South Division to earn their first postseason berth in nine years. Lincoln also made a successful debut, drawing a number of capacity crowds to brand-new Haymarket Park. The Saltdogs went 52-38 overall, finishing second to Sioux Falls in both halves.

Doc Edwards, former manager of the Cleveland Indians, earned Northern League manager-of-the-year honors and three of his Sioux Falls players were named to the league's postseason all-star team.

Meanwhile, the once daunting St. Paul Saints sank to a new low, finishing well below .500 in the weak North Division. The Saints still led the league in wacky promotions and trailed only Winnipeg in attendance.

Francisco Matos

Allentown middle infielder Francisco Matos hit .416 to set a Northern League record and earn East Division player-of-the-year honors. He struck out four times in 243 at-bats. At one point, Matos went 125 at-bats without a strikeout. He also hit safely in 31 consecutive games.

INDEPENDENT LEAGUES

CENTRAL DIVISION

STANDINGS

FIRST HALF

NORTH

	W	L	PCT	GB
Winnipeg Goldeyes	29	16	.644	—
Duluth-Superior Dukes	21	24	.467	8
Schaumburg Flyers	18	27	.400	11
St. Paul Saints	17	28	.378	12

SOUTH

	W	L	PCT	GB
Sioux Falls Canaries	26	19	.578	—
Fargo-Moorhead RedHawks	25	20	.556	1
Lincoln Saltdogs	24	21	.533	2
Sioux City Explorers	20	25	.444	6

SECOND HALF

NORTH

	W	L	PCT	GB
Winnipeg Goldeyes	23	22	.511	—
St. Paul Saints	20	25	.444	3
Schaumburg Flyers	19	26	.422	4
Duluth-Superior Dukes	13	32	.289	10

SOUTH

	W	L	PCT	GB
Sioux Falls Canaries	29	16	.644	—
Lincoln Saltdogs	28	17	.622	1
Fargo-Moorhead RedHawks	26	19	.578	3
Sioux City Explorers	22	23	.489	7

PLAYOFFS: Semifinals—Winnipeg defeated Fargo-Moorhead 3-2 and Lincoln defeated Sioux Falls 3-1 in best-of-5 series. **Finals**—Winnipeg defeated Lincoln 3-1 in best-of-5 series.

MANAGERS: Duluth-Superior—Ed Nottle. **Fargo-Moorhead**—Doug Simunic. **Lincoln**—Kash Beauchamp, Les Lancaster. **St. Paul**—Doug Sisson. **Schaumburg**—Ron Kittle. **Sioux City**—Benny Castillo. **Sioux Falls**—Doc Edwards. **Winnipeg**—Hal Lanier.

ATTENDANCE: Winnipeg 292,095; St. Paul 282,613; Lincoln 240,022; Schaumburg 215,735; Fargo-Moorhead 185,288; Sioux City 123,821; Sioux City 112,115; Duluth-Superior 51,126.

ALL-STAR TEAM: C—Ryan Robertson, Winnipeg. **1B**—Jermaine Swinton, Sioux Falls. **2B**—Felix Pagan, Sioux Falls. **3B**—Josh Patton, Sioux City. **SS**—Brent Sachs, Winnipeg. **OF**—Charles Peterson, Sioux Falls; Carmine Cappuccio, Winnipeg; Ricky Freeman, Fargo-Moorhead. **DH**—Matt Nokes, Schaumburg. **LHP**—Jake Whitney, St. Paul. **RHP**—Clay Eason, Lincoln. **RP**—Chris Weidert, Lincoln.

Player of the Year: Clay Eason, Lincoln. **Rookie of the Year**: Kevin Sullivan, Lincoln. **Rookie Pitcher of the Year**: Billy Coleman, Schaumburg. **Manager of the Year**: Doc Edwards, Sioux Falls.

INDIVIDUAL BATTING LEADERS
(Minimum 243 Plate Appearances)

	AVG	AB	R	H	2B	3B	HR	RBI	SB
Peterson, Charles, SF	.364	374	69	136	20	2	16	76	16
Cappuccio, Carmine, Win	.359	379	70	136	39	1	9	80	10
Nokes, Matt, Schaumburg	.354	333	44	118	24	2	16	69	1
Lara, Eddie, Schaumburg	.336	295	53	99	20	2	10	56	15
Sullivan, Kevin, Lincoln	.333	315	41	105	15	3	6	39	5
Pagan, Felix, Sioux Falls	.331	384	76	127	33	3	19	66	13
Patton, Josh, Sioux City	.330	355	66	117	19	4	6	47	12
Prodanov, Peter, Win	.320	272	47	87	11	2	5	33	9
Colon, Cris, F-M	.318	343	45	109	14	2	4	51	0
Williams, Keith, St. Paul	.313	300	47	94	14	1	9	45	8

INDIVIDUAL PITCHING LEADERS
(Minimum 72 Innings)

	W	L	ERA	G	SV	IP	H	BB	SO
Eason, Clay, Lincoln	10	3	1.70	19	0	122	86	28	131
Gross, Rafael, Winnipeg	14	2	2.30	18	0	121	102	12	88
Whitney, Jacob, St. Paul	7	6	2.75	31	1	108	108	20	81
Jerue, Tristan, Sioux Falls	5	2	2.94	16	1	83	85	23	48
Albin, Scott, St. Paul	4	3	3.05	37	3	74	61	26	82
Onley, Shawn, Winnipeg	11	4	3.16	19	0	128	122	28	109
Johnston, Doug, F-M	9	6	3.36	19	0	112	129	21	80
Hyde, Rich, Sioux Falls	8	4	3.40	18	0	119	124	22	81
Martin, Scott, Sioux Falls	12	4	3.45	19	0	128	145	22	60
Coleman, Billy, Schaum.	9	8	3.50	20	0	139	117	44	100

DULUTH-SUPERIOR

BATTING

	AVG	AB	R	H	2B	3B	HR	RBI	SB
Bowers, Brent, of	.209	110	8	23	4	1	3	9	7
3-team (13 Fargo/34 SC)	.219	292	29	64	12	3	5	29	20
Briceno, David, c	.196	97	5	19	4	0	0	9	0
Cardona, Ruben, 2b	.245	372	33	91	14	1	3	27	12
Fauske, J.P., dh	.154	26	1	4	0	0	0	2	0

	AVG	AB	R	H	2B	3B	HR	RBI	SB
Gerald, Eddie, of	.295	173	38	51	12	3	8	28	12
Hunt, Tim, of-3b	.250	152	20	38	5	0	0	18	5
Kirkpatrick, Jay, dh-1b	.349	152	22	53	8	0	8	31	0
2-team (44 Sioux City)	.296	311	47	92	16	0	16	55	0
Lahti, Jeff, 2b-of	.283	60	9	17	2	0	0	4	2
Lantigua, Eddie, 3b	.248	322	37	80	22	1	7	35	5
Lepine, Chris, of	.157	51	7	8	1	0	0	2	1
Morrison, Greg, 1b	.294	354	59	104	29	3	6	43	8
Pernell, Brandon, of	.313	339	55	106	21	6	8	45	22
Radwan, Jason, c	.191	162	15	31	6	0	5	19	2
Reese, Nate, c	.125	16	0	2	0	0	0	0	0
Runk, Aaron, of	.294	255	41	75	13	4	3	26	16
Schwab, Chris, dh	.219	105	10	23	8	0	3	18	2
Serafin, Steve, ss	.161	93	16	15	6	0	0	5	1
Theoharis, Mike, ss	.222	212	23	47	5	1	0	17	10

PITCHING

	W	L	ERA	G	SV	IP	H	BB	SO
Book, Jeremy	3	2	4.20	20	2	45	48	11	33
Calvert, Klae	7	10	4.88	20	0	133	168	27	70
Correa, Amilcar	0	0	9.39	2	0	8	12	2	2
Doyle, Tom	5	7	4.77	18	0	115	133	48	85
Gooden, Derek	4	7	4.13	33	7	33	38	13	42
Guehne, Dan	2	1	2.31	37	5	35	36	13	23
Hill, Chris	6	9	4.41	20	0	129	128	46	85
Kemp, Corey	0	0	5.79	1	0	5	8	4	2
Koziara, Matt	4	4	3.60	29	0	55	55	18	35
Kozlowski, Kris	5	9	4.09	18	0	117	129	48	77
Maskivish, Joe	0	0	19.64	4	0	4	10	6	2
2-team (1 Sioux City)	0	0	15.43	5	0	5	10	7	3
Rochford, Duane	2	5	4.75	17	0	72	98	23	45
Turner, Eric	0	2	6.52	8	0	19	30	10	10
Vendela, Chris	0	0	3.63	13	0	17	21	7	9

FARGO-MOORHEAD

BATTING

	AVG	AB	R	H	2B	3B	HR	RBI	SB
Alvarez, Rafael, of	.310	142	24	44	8	1	3	19	10
Arnott, George, c-of	.240	100	15	24	5	0	1	9	1
Bowers, Brent, of	.208	48	5	10	5	0	0	4	4
Burke, Mark, dh	.247	77	9	19	2	0	2	7	0
Colon, Cris, 3b-ss	.318	343	45	109	14	2	4	51	0
Fauske, J.P., dh	.192	26	3	5	1	0	0	0	0
Freeman, Ricky, of-1b	.301	352	62	106	25	1	15	77	4
Hill, Jason, dh-3b	.267	45	6	12	1	0	1	9	0
2-team (69 St. Paul)	.311	299	41	93	13	1	9	50	9
Kay, Kevin, of-c	.307	254	37	78	14	2	3	43	5
Livingston, Doug, 2b	.229	301	35	69	7	0	2	32	15
Marcinczyk, T.R., 1b-3b	.258	361	64	93	17	1	20	71	13
McCallum, Geoff, ss	.250	96	15	24	2	0	0	11	3
Merriman, Terrell, of	.205	73	10	15	1	0	1	6	2
Pierce, Kirk, c	.278	216	28	60	10	0	8	33	0
Rivero, Eddie, of	.181	127	13	23	9	1	4	7	1
Spangler, Bob, ss	.275	51	6	14	1	0	0	3	1
Villacres, Gary, of	.247	146	30	36	2	2	0	9	12
Wilson, Andy, of-ss	.251	346	52	87	15	1	2	28	26
Wright, Dana, dh	.000	4	0	0	0	0	0	0	0

PITCHING

	W	L	ERA	G	SV	IP	H	BB	SO
Anderson, Brad	0	1	5.81	17	0	48	60	19	15
Bittiger, Jeff	2	1	4.58	8	0	35	42	13	25
Cana, Nelson	5	1	5.11	31	0	49	59	18	40
Fletschock, Justin	10	8	4.18	18	0	114	117	27	67
Gillow, Brian	2	4	3.89	7	0	44	41	12	39
Hooper, Jimmy	4	2	2.40	34	0	60	62	15	60
Johnston, Doug	9	6	3.36	19	0	112	129	21	80
Montgomery, Steve	3	2	3.86	32	17	40	37	16	44
Paull, Kalam	6	4	4.91	23	1	84	87	32	63
Salvevold, Greg	8	7	4.91	19	0	117	118	36	78
Stanton, Jeff	0	0	2.45	17	2	33	30	9	24
Stoner, Nat	2	3	3.98	32	1	61	60	17	44

LINCOLN

BATTING

	AVG	AB	R	H	2B	3B	HR	RBI	SB
Brinkley, Josh, 3b-c	.303	304	43	92	22	2	9	42	7
Britt, Bryan, of-1b	.252	330	51	83	11	2	18	52	5
Burton, Essex, of-2b	.303	357	59	108	14	1	3	34	31
Cano, Matt, 3b	.253	95	13	24	3	0	0	5	2
2-team (10 Winnipeg)	.227	128	18	29	4	0	0	6	2
De la Cruz, Lorenzo, of	.367	49	11	18	6	0	4	12	1
Delucchi, Dustin, of	.000	1	0	0	0	0	0	0	0
2-team (5 Winnipeg)	.188	16	4	3	1	0	0	2	0
Doskocil, Darren, ss-2b	.259	317	56	82	14	1	16	46	9
Fields, Jay, of	.045	22	2	1	0	0	0	1	0
Hernandez, Alexis, c	.423	26	4	11	3	0	2	8	0
James, Drue, c	.136	81	7	11	0	0	1	6	0

BATTING	AVG	AB	R	H	2B	3B	HR	RBI	SB
Jefferson, Dave, of	.262	225	28	59	11	3	3	24	12
Kobayashi, Mitsuru, ss	.194	98	13	19	3	2	0	11	6
Larreal, Roberto, 2b	.295	78	9	23	0	0	0	8	3
Maher, Jonathon, of	.000	11	0	0	0	0	0	0	0
Schell, Barry, of	.176	17	0	3	0	1	0	2	0
Schlosser, Mark, ss	.238	63	9	15	4	0	0	8	3
Sullivan, Kevin, c-of	.333	315	41	105	15	3	6	39	5
Vasquez, Chris, 1b	.292	342	41	100	14	2	9	48	7
Warner, Bryan, of	.324	216	33	70	13	0	6	37	11
Williams, Patrick, dh	.132	38	4	5	1	0	1	2	0
Zywica, Mike, of	.179	123	14	22	3	1	5	12	3

PITCHING	W	L	ERA	G	SV	IP	H	BB	SO
Bailey, Dave	0	0	4.66	5	0	10	12	3	5
Black, Brett	3	1	3.45	10	0	29	21	2	33
Eason, Clay	10	3	1.70	19	0	122	86	28	131
Embry, Byron	0	0	8.59	11	0	15	27	8	12
Ferretti, Ryan	1	0	5.00	13	0	18	17	8	11
Fitts, Brian	6	2	3.79	14	0	74	88	17	38
Green, Otis	0	2	10.61	2	0	9	11	5	6
James, Drue	2	1	4.91	21	0	33	39	15	21
Jones, Fontella	3	4	6.63	22	3	37	42	20	35
Lancaster, Les	5	1	2.89	9	0	56	58	11	43
Lee, Andy	1	1	3.57	35	2	23	27	9	27
Lewis, Peyton	2	2	4.75	15	0	61	59	27	65
Lewis, Rickey	7	5	4.32	16	0	94	99	42	58
Miller, Shawn	0	3	6.65	6	0	23	28	19	9
Piatkowski, Troy	0	0	16.88	5	0	5	7	8	3
Sherrill, Garrett	3	3	4.80	14	0	45	48	17	31
Silva, Troy	3	3	1.74	32	1	57	38	27	63
Vincent, Matt	2	1	5.22	20	0	29	36	9	21
Weidert, Chris	4	6	2.72	41	22	60	48	13	57

ST. PAUL

BATTING	AVG	AB	R	H	2B	3B	HR	RBI	SB
Arnott, George, c-of	.211	19	0	4	1	0	0	2	0
2-team (42 Fargo)	.235	119	15	28	6	0	1	11	1
Buckley, Reagan, c	.286	192	24	55	10	4	5	32	1
Burgess, Graham, c	.108	65	5	7	3	0	1	6	1
Camilli, Jason, 2b-ss	.247	85	7	21	2	0	2	9	0
Chance, Tony, 1b-of	.260	335	52	87	17	1	14	63	6
Dour, Craig, 1b	.103	39	3	4	1	0	0	1	0
Driskill, John, 2b-3b	.308	159	16	49	3	0	0	12	1
Dunaway, Jason, 3b-ss	.253	87	15	22	2	0	1	1	4
Fingleson, Gavin, 3b-2b	.298	168	19	50	9	0	1	23	4
Gomez, Ricardo, ss	.233	172	18	40	5	2	0	15	3
Hall, Noah, of-2b	.313	352	61	110	19	4	8	47	37
Hill, Jason, 3b-1b	.319	254	35	81	12	1	8	41	9
Ibarra, Jesse, 3b-c	.245	102	8	25	6	0	1	13	1
Metzger, Erik, c	.231	65	5	15	5	0	0	5	0
Nerei, Yuji, 1b-of	.275	109	8	30	5	0	1	13	3
Ruiz, Ryan, of	.310	297	52	92	8	2	1	16	16
Saucke, Casey, ss-2b	.200	50	3	10	4	0	0	3	0
Schlosser, Mark, 2b-ss	.139	36	3	5	1	0	0	1	2
2-team (20 Lincoln)	.202	99	12	20	5	0	0	9	5
Schwab, Chris, dh	.231	156	18	36	5	0	4	19	0
2-team (30 Duluth)	.226	261	28	59	13	0	7	37	2
Spangler, Bob, ss	.289	38	7	11	2	0	2	7	1
2-team (13 Fargo)	.281	89	13	25	3	0	2	10	2
White, Derrick, of	.327	52	10	17	3	1	2	10	1
Williams, Keith, of	.313	300	47	94	14	1	9	45	8

PITCHING	W	L	ERA	G	SV	IP	H	BB	SO
Akin, Aaron	0	0	12.86	4	0	7	18	3	7
Albin, Scott	4	3	3.05	37	3	74	61	26	82
Berroa, Oliver	0	1	17.36	2	0	5	8	4	4
Casteel, Ricky	0	2	8.10	4	0	7	7	4	1
Chambless, Chet	0	0	5.15	29	0	44	48	22	50
Cornejo, Jesse	0	1	5.59	9	0	10	16	10	10
Duff, Matt	0	3	4.83	22	3	32	38	11	41
Fleetham, Ben	3	2	4.43	17	4	22	29	9	26
2-team (16 Sioux Falls)	4	3	3.40	33	8	40	41	14	49
Friedman, Jason	1	0	3.55	21	0	25	31	11	21
Harrington, Matt	0	2	9.47	6	0	19	18	18	17
Honda, Tomohiro	0	4	7.01	9	0	26	35	10	20
Marini, Anthony	0	2	6.75	5	0	25	35	11	18
2-team (14 Sioux Falls)	3	5	5.06	19	0	107	143	28	69
Meyers, Kevin	0	0	3.46	12	0	13	17	3	6
Nunez, Maximo	1	1	4.61	5	0	14	15	3	10
Olean, Chris	0	1	15.43	2	0	5	11	1	4
Salyers, Jeremy	0	1	17.36	3	0	5	9	2	1
Smith, Dan	2	5	5.01	10	0	47	58	5	50
Swiatkiewicz, Chris	10	8	4.41	22	0	122	139	33	95
Veniard, Jay	1	5	3.52	11	0	61	60	26	45
Whitney, Jacob	7	6	2.75	31	1	108	108	20	81

PITCHING	W	L	ERA	G	SV	IP	H	BB	SO
Woodward, Finley	8	6	4.58	21	0	120	128	43	100

SCHAUMBURG

BATTING	AVG	AB	R	H	2B	3B	HR	RBI	SB
Chamberlain, Wes, 1b	.268	190	22	51	6	1	3	16	2
De la Garza, Gabe, 2b-ss	.241	133	23	32	4	1	1	11	5
Donohue, Matt, 3b	.211	19	1	4	1	0	0	2	0
Foley, Steve, of	.292	120	17	35	8	0	5	18	5
Franco, Christian, of-3b	.277	282	36	78	9	4	6	37	5
Galvan, Ron, c	.177	96	10	17	4	0	1	7	0
Gonzalez, Ender, 3b	.301	156	27	47	4	0	0	21	7
Klee, Chuck, ss	.200	20	1	4	1	0	0	0	0
Lane, Nolan, of	.230	126	14	29	6	0	3	12	0
Lara, Eddie, 2b	.336	295	53	99	20	2	10	56	15
Lichay, Donald, 3b	.067	15	1	1	0	0	0	0	0
Mackiewitz, Richard, 1b	.250	148	16	37	6	0	4	22	0
Matos, Malvin, of	.250	72	9	18	3	0	0	8	0
Nokes, Matt, dh	.354	333	44	118	24	2	16	69	1
Pomierski, Joe, of	.220	59	6	13	7	1	2	13	0
Ralph, Brian, of	.261	176	31	46	6	0	1	13	14
Shultz, Brian, of	.271	317	41	86	15	1	1	29	1
Sienko, Ryan, c-of	.244	246	36	60	12	0	8	31	1
Smith, Jeremy, ss	.270	248	33	67	4	0	1	27	4
Suraci, Scott, of	.130	23	0	3	0	0	0	0	0
Trahan, Mike, ss-3b	.226	53	5	12	3	0	0	3	1

PITCHING	W	L	ERA	G	SV	IP	H	BB	SO
Bair, Denny	0	1	6.59	5	0	14	20	9	4
Bedinger, Doug	1	4	4.74	34	10	44	50	22	31
Coleman, Billy	9	8	3.50	20	0	139	117	44	100
Craker, Justin	2	2	4.63	20	0	45	41	32	37
Donovan, T.J.	4	8	4.95	16	0	91	113	26	48
Fahrner, Evan	3	4	1.96	29	5	37	34	10	39
Genke, Todd	5	7	3.80	19	0	116	131	17	60
Kees, Justin	0	0	6.75	5	0	8	11	1	5
Mencas, Val	1	1	6.03	24	0	34	42	12	20
Newman, Damon	2	0	4.37	7	0	23	28	4	13
Poeck, Chad	4	4	4.58	10	0	57	66	10	49
Rohlfing, Jon	1	3	5.93	19	0	27	25	13	32
Rosengren, Phil	1	3	4.40	24	1	43	44	21	41
Stewart, John	0	2	18.41	2	0	7	17	5	5
Vardijan, Dan	0	0	4.50	4	0	6	5	6	1
Woodman, Hank	4	6	4.63	18	0	101	120	29	72

SIOUX CITY

BATTING	AVG	AB	R	H	2B	3B	HR	RBI	SB
Aldridge, Jon, of-2b	.214	84	14	18	4	0	0	3	7
Bowers, Brent, of	.231	134	16	31	3	2	2	16	9
Burke, Mark, 1b	.304	253	26	77	19	0	4	41	1
2-team (22 Fargo)	.291	330	35	96	21	0	6	48	1
Callen, Tommy, 2b-of	.156	32	3	5	1	0	1	6	0
Correa, Dalphie, ss	.230	244	30	56	10	1	0	8	12
Fauske, J.P., c	.230	165	18	38	11	0	5	23	0
3-team (8 Dul./7 Fargo)	.217	217	22	47	12	0	5	25	0
Garland, Tim, of	.274	84	10	23	2	1	1	10	9
2-team (15 Winnipeg)	.257	148	22	38	4	1	1	15	9
Johnson, E.D., of	.175	57	4	10	1	0	0	1	0
Keene, Andre, dh	.067	15	0	1	0	0	0	1	0
Kirkpatrick, Jay, 1b-c	.245	159	25	39	8	0	8	24	0
Kopacz, Derek, 3b-of	.314	172	31	54	12	0	8	37	8
Lee, Curt, 2b-ss	.259	320	46	83	13	0	0	34	5
Meggers, Mike, dh	.302	169	30	51	7	0	12	39	2
2-team (43 Winnipeg)	.260	350	52	91	14	0	24	78	3
Patton, Josh, 3b	.330	355	66	117	19	4	6	47	12
Rodrigues, Rich, c	.328	137	14	45	11	0	2	20	1
Sawyer, Chris, of	.143	42	6	6	0	0	0	4	0
Serafin, Steve, of-ss	.254	71	9	18	5	0	0	7	0
2-team (30 Duluth)	.201	164	25	33	11	0	0	12	1
Smith, Ira, of	.284	352	71	100	23	1	9	42	11
Thompson, Phil, of	.255	153	12	39	10	0	2	21	7
Vandernat, Jonathan, c	.150	20	2	3	0	0	1	1	0
Woodward, Steve, of	.277	47	2	13	2	0	1	4	1

PITCHING	W	L	ERA	G	SV	IP	H	BB	SO
Aragon, Angel	1	0	3.04	9	0	24	31	2	22
Duffy, John	4	2	3.68	40	3	64	57	30	36
Glick, David	7	9	3.95	20	0	130	139	37	80
Grote, Jason	2	3	3.38	20	2	32	37	7	25
Juden, Jeff	0	2	11.70	4	0	10	13	10	10
Kelley, Chris	0	0	4.34	12	0	19	10	11	13
LeRoy, John	0	0	7.50	2	0	6	7	3	8
Mazur, Graham	5	5	4.93	17	0	88	106	27	55
2-team (1 Sioux Falls)	6	5	4.61	18	0	94	108	27	71
Montgomery, Joe	0	3	7.29	7	0	21	26	9	12

	W	L	ERA	G	SV	IP	H	BB	SO
Pamus, Javier	5	5	3.88	30	7	56	57	16	50
Patino, Leonardo	1	2	3.91	9	0	25	27	9	15
Romero, Jordan	6	9	3.71	21	0	141	131	38	100
Runion, Tony	3	2	2.45	24	3	40	30	12	52
Springston, Adam	8	6	4.47	24	1	117	110	41	79
Wheeler, Josh	0	0	7.11	16	0	19	27	11	13

SIOUX FALLS

BATTING	AVG	AB	R	H	2B	3B	HR	RBI	SB
Bartolucci, Paul, ss	.244	312	43	76	7	1	0	25	4
Bozied, Taggert, 3b-of	.307	228	35	70	17	0	6	31	3
Busch, Mike, 3b-1b	.293	184	33	54	7	0	5	33	1
Campbell, Wylie, 2b	.189	53	8	10	3	1	0	2	0
Caston, Bernard, of	.281	292	45	82	11	1	6	37	18
Herrick, Jason, of	.284	81	12	23	10	1	3	13	1
Hunt, Brian, of	.211	19	2	4	1	0	0	1	0
Maluchnik, Gregg, c	.238	315	37	75	18	1	3	36	1
Murphy, Sean, dh	.241	319	49	77	16	3	10	50	7
Pagan, Felix, of-2b	.331	384	76	127	33	3	19	66	13
Pena, Bert, 2b-3b	.167	42	1	7	1	0	0	2	0
Peterson, Charles, of	.364	374	69	136	20	2	16	76	16
Rivero, Eddie, of	.283	120	26	34	5	1	13	32	1
2-team (36 Fargo)	.231	247	39	57	14	2	17	39	2
Swinton, Jermaine, 1b	.259	340	66	88	21	1	27	72	1
Troncoso, Dan, 2b-ss	.192	99	16	19	4	0	1	11	2

PITCHING	W	L	ERA	G	SV	IP	H	BB	SO
Anderson, Antwoine	4	3	3.79	29	0	55	60	20	38
Correa, Elvis	1	3	7.04	6	0	31	43	6	22
Delgado, Reymundo	0	2	3.38	7	0	11	22	2	7
Diaz, Antonio	1	1	2.74	18	0	23	23	2	14
Duff, Matt	4	0	1.74	17	7	21	16	6	29
2-team (22 St. Paul)	4	3	3.61	39	10	52	54	17	70
Fleetham, Ben	1	1	2.08	16	4	17	12	5	23
Hyde, Rich	8	4	3.40	18	0	119	124	22	81
Jerue, Tristan	5	2	2.94	16	1	83	85	23	48
Marini, Anthony	3	3	4.54	14	0	81	108	17	51
Martin, Scott	12	4	3.45	19	0	128	145	22	60
Mazur, Graham	1	0	0.00	1	0	6	2	0	6
Montgomery, Joe	1	0	4.50	6	0	8	13	3	4
2-team (7 Soiux City)	1	3	6.52	13	0	29	39	12	16
Pageler, Mick	1	1	2.73	27	4	30	30	3	29
Perez, Michelandy	1	0	3.92	14	0	21	21	9	17
Robell, Kevin	1	2	8.64	4	0	17	18	9	14
Sherrill, George	4	4	2.45	48	0	59	53	14	45
Smith, Matt	0	2	6.58	15	0	26	28	18	17
Ybarra, Jamie	7	3	3.79	11	0	74	78	20	59

WINNIPEG

BATTING	AVG	AB	R	H	2B	3B	HR	RBI	SB
Brown, Bobby, of	.267	330	36	88	18	2	1	40	3
Bunkley, Antuan, dh	.284	74	9	21	3	0	1	9	0
Cano, Matt, 3b	.152	33	5	5	1	0	0	1	0
Cappuccio, Carmine, of	.359	379	70	136	39	1	9	80	10
Clark, Jason, of	.270	63	14	17	0	2	1	6	2
Delucchi, Dustin, of	.200	15	4	3	1	0	0	2	0
Doan, Kory, of-c	.271	96	14	26	2	0	1	8	3
Garland, Tim, of	.234	64	12	15	2	0	0	5	0
Gieler, William, of	.167	12	0	2	0	0	0	1	0
Goodell, Steve, 1b-3b	.228	57	7	13	4	1	0	1	1
Kopacz, Derek, of-3b	.229	70	13	16	1	0	4	9	1
2-team (45 Sioux City)	.289	242	44	70	13	0	12	46	9
Leday, A.J., of-1b	.427	185	36	79	12	3	9	46	3
Meggers, Mike, dh	.221	181	22	40	7	0	12	39	1
Myrow, Brian, 2b	.386	88	27	34	9	0	10	36	2
Ortiz, Luis, 1b	.349	189	38	66	10	2	9	42	0
Osilka, Garret, 2b	.262	202	37	53	9	1	1	15	8
Pearson, Eddie, 1b	.313	80	11	25	5	0	3	11	0
Poulin, Max, 3b-ss	.265	181	24	48	5	4	1	13	5
Prodanov, Peter, 3b-of	.320	272	47	87	11	2	5	33	9
Robertson, Ryan, c	.310	303	37	94	18	0	7	44	1
Sachs, Brent, ss	.305	361	76	110	23	3	11	54	17

PITCHER	W	L	ERA	G	SV	IP	H	BB	SO
Bishop, Trevor	0	1	17.47	2	0	6	12	3	9
Conner, Scott	0	2	7.50	5	0	24	34	6	17
DeJesus, Tony	0	1	3.09	34	1	35	36	23	40
Franklin, Brent	5	1	4.00	13	0	54	56	19	41
Gross, Rafael	14	2	2.30	18	0	121	102	12	88
Hirose, Yasushi	1	1	5.92	11	0	24	27	11	23
Keppen, Jeff	2	3	4.83	7	0	41	39	13	36
Ochsner, Alan	4	2	4.91	39	1	48	52	18	50
Onley, Shawn	11	4	3.16	19	0	128	122	28	109
Orga, Kevin	2	6	5.76	10	0	55	70	23	28

	W	L	ERA	G	SV	IP	H	BB	SO
Smith, Donnie	2	3	4.37	35	0	56	61	12	56
Taylor, Donnie	5	4	4.94	19	0	89	105	29	50
Thomas, Steve	1	4	2.63	39	20	38	32	10	25
Vendela, Chris	1	2	3.93	11	0	18	17	9	12
2-team (13 Duluth)	1	2	3.79	24	0	36	38	16	21
Webb, Chris	4	1	6.24	15	0	62	92	16	34

EASTERN DIVISION

STANDINGS

FIRST HALF

NORTH	W	L	PCT	GB
Albany-Colonie Diamond Dogs	27	19	.587	—
Quebec Les Capitales	26	20	.565	1
Adirondack Lumberjacks	17	28	.378	9

SOUTH	W	L	PCT	GB
Elmira Pioneers	25	20	.556	—
Allentown Ambassadors	21	24	.467	4
New Jersey Jackals	20	25	.444	5

SECOND HALF

NORTH	W	L	PCT	GB
Albany-Colonie Diamond Dogs	23	22	.511	—
Adirondack Lumberjacks	20	24	.455	2 ½
Quebec Capitales	18	27	.400	5

SOUTH	W	L	PCT	GB
Elmira Pioneers	26	18	.591	—
New Jersey Jackals	25	20	.556	1 ½
Allentown Ambassadors	22	23	.489	4 ½

PLAYOFFS: Semifinals—New Jersey defeated Albany-Colonie 3-0 and Elmira defeated Allentown 3-0 in best-of-5 series. **Finals**—New Jersey defeated Elmira 3-2 in best-of-5 series.

MANAGERS: Adirondack—Darryl Motley. **Albany-Colonie**—Mike Marshall. **Allentown**—Joe Calfapietra. **Elmira**—Jon Debus. **New Jersey**—George Tsamis. **Quebec**—Jay Ward.

ATTENDANCE: Quebec 148,419; Allentown 110,059; New Jersey 109,126; Albany-Colonie 100,523; Elmira 64,110; Adirondack 59,223.

ALL-STAR TEAM: C—Scott McKee, Albany-Colonie. **1B**—Ryan Soules, Allentown. **2B**—Julio Zorrilla, Albany-Colonie. **3B**—Ryan Kane, New Jersey. **SS**—Francisco Matos, Allentown. **OF**—Brandon Curtis, Albany-Colonie; Tarrik Brock, Elmira; Rodney Clifton, Adirondack. **DH**—Marlon Roche, Albany-Colonie. **LHP**—Justin Stine, Elmira. **RHP**—Joel Bennett, New Jersey. **RP**—Ryan Halla, Elmira.

Player of the Year: Francisco Matos, Allentown. **Rookie of the Year**: B.J. Garrison, Quebec. **Rookie Pitcher of the Year**: Chris Brown, Elmira. **Manager of the Year**: Jon Debus, Elmira.

INDIVIDUAL BATTING LEADERS
(Minimum 243 Plate Appearances)

	AVG	AB	R	H	2B	3B	HR	RBI	SB
Matos, Francisco, Allentown	.416	243	39	101	26	2	3	45	11
Fera, Aaron, New Jersey	.355	231	46	82	19	2	18	54	7
Roche, Marlon, A-C	.336	283	46	95	14	1	10	48	5
Soules, Ryan, Allentown	.331	311	75	103	30	1	10	61	1
McKee, Scott, A-C	.328	360	56	118	32	1	7	49	0
Sergio, Tom, Allentown	.326	258	67	84	16	3	7	34	5
Bunkley, Antuan, Quebec	.318	258	36	82	14	0	5	43	2
Cornelius, Brian, Quebec	.315	327	57	103	22	0	13	59	3
Kane, Ryan, New Jersey	.314	331	49	104	33	2	11	58	3
Maxwell, Keith, Allentown	.312	349	57	109	22	2	11	62	5

INDIVIDUAL PITCHING LEADERS
(Minimum 72 Innings)

	W	L	ERA	G	SV	IP	H	BB	SO
Brassington, Phil, A-C	8	0	2.40	11	0	75	69	16	53
Bennett, Joel, New Jersey	10	5	2.57	22	3	129	104	42	118
Sano, Shigeki, Elmira	6	6	2.66	18	0	125	121	20	49
Shinada, Ayahito, Elmira	10	7	3.29	18	0	123	116	17	84
Keagle, Greg, Elmira	5	5	3.29	18	0	109	100	25	94
LeBlanc, Eric, D-C	10	6	3.44	18	0	118	132	34	104
Koutrouba, Tom, NJ	7	6	3.73	23	0	113	114	31	118
Von Haefen, Jason, A-C	9	4	3.90	18	0	99	91	32	98
Bond, Aaron, Allentown	9	4	3.90	19	1	111	126	25	102
Ward, Chad, Adirondack	6	10	3.96	21	1	114	134	22	101

ADIRONDACK

BATTING	AVG	AB	R	H	2B	3B	HR	RBI	SB
Aoki, Masayoshi, 2b-ss	.182	11	2	2	0	0	0	1	1
2-team (4 Albany)	.217	23	2	5	0	0	0	3	1
Briceno, David, c	.265	34	4	9	0	0	0	4	1
Clifton, Rodney, of	.290	334	50	97	21	7	20	68	7

BATTING	AVG	AB	R	H	2B	3B	HR	RBI	SB
Dour, Craig, 1b	.218	87	9	19	1	1	2	6	2
Finnegan, Chris, c-1b	.268	142	16	38	7	0	3	18	2
Flores, Ray, ss-3b	.209	177	18	37	9	1	1	18	2
Gonzalez, Ender, 3b-2b	.283	145	17	41	7	1	0	15	4
Goodwin, Keith, of	.242	157	21	38	6	1	4	23	11
Guerrero, Epy, 3b	.472	53	9	25	5	0	0	9	2
Hargreaves, Brad, c	.221	145	15	32	3	1	0	5	4
Ibarra, Jesse, 1b-3b	.229	214	32	49	8	1	10	32	1
James, Tony, 2b	.266	320	42	85	13	1	4	30	23
Kobayashi, Mitsuru, ss	.079	38	1	3	1	0	0	2	2
Mackiewitz, Richard, 1b	.324	68	13	22	4	0	2	10	0
Metzger, Erik, c	.148	27	0	4	0	1	0	4	0
Moeller, James, dh	.213	47	6	10	3	0	0	0	0
Motley, Darryl, dh	.258	252	39	65	11	1	11	39	6
Spangler, Bob, ss	.209	148	13	31	6	1	3	20	5
Spearman, Vernon, of	.291	358	58	104	17	3	1	20	40
Valera, Ramon, of-ss	.238	21	1	5	0	0	0	1	3
Vandernat, Jonathan, c	.152	33	1	5	0	0	0	2	1
White, Eric, 3b-of	.193	57	4	11	4	0	0	6	3
Zywica, Mike, of	.286	133	25	38	8	1	7	22	6

PITCHING	W	L	ERA	G	SV	IP	H	BB	SO
Anderson, Eric	1	4	5.40	7	0	35	44	12	14
Black, Brett	2	5	2.87	29	9	31	30	2	27
Campbell, Chad	2	3	5.14	25	0	56	61	31	34
Cary, Trae	0	3	3.23	25	0	53	56	16	26
Ferretti, Ryan	0	0	9.53	7	0	6	11	5	6
Gregg, James	0	0	4.54	24	0	34	46	13	17
Jones, Fontella	2	0	1.37	13	5	20	11	0	21
LaRoche, Jeff	1	0	2.08	4	0	4	6	3	1
2-team (3 Allentown)	1	0	4.50	7	0	10	13	3	3
Lima, Cory	2	7	5.65	19	0	80	104	36	53
Minton, Foye	1	1	6.53	13	0	21	27	12	17
Santiago, Derek	9	7	4.19	21	0	131	141	53	108
Scott, Cory	3	4	3.90	40	0	55	61	18	39
Ward, Chad	6	10	3.96	21	1	114	134	22	101
Zipser, Mike	8	8	4.29	20	0	128	146	19	95

ALBANY-COLONIE

BATTING	AVG	AB	R	H	2B	3B	HR	RBI	SB
Aoki, Masayoshi, ss	.250	12	0	3	0	0	0	2	0
Curtis, Brandon, 1b-of	.309	340	48	105	18	0	12	63	10
Darjean, John, of	.276	315	37	87	15	2	0	30	15
Davila, Vic, of-1b	.283	311	53	88	21	1	13	52	2
Dunaway, Jason, ss	.167	30	3	5	0	0	0	1	0
2-team (2 Adirondack)	.184	38	5	7	0	0	1	2	0
Espinal, Juan, 3b	.298	295	37	88	17	0	11	45	3
Gonzalez, Jose, of	.296	27	5	8	2	0	0	3	1
Goodwin, Keith, of	.224	58	8	13	4	2	1	5	1
2-team (44 Adirondack)	.237	215	29	51	10	3	5	28	12
Grice, Dan, ss	.243	111	16	27	8	0	1	13	3
Herz, Nick, c-1b	.160	131	11	21	9	0	0	11	0
McKee, Scott, c-1b	.328	360	56	118	32	1	7	49	0
Miyake, Chris, ss-2b	.238	126	16	30	4	0	1	10	5
2-team (43 New Jersey)	.206	281	32	58	10	2	3	30	9
Neubart, Adam, of	.322	180	31	58	9	3	2	20	17
Peel, Ricky, of	.202	203	24	41	6	0	1	21	4
Reinking, Kevin, c-of	.238	21	1	5	0	0	0	2	0
Roche, Marlon, dh-of	.336	283	46	95	14	1	10	48	5
Zorrilla, Julio, 2b	.285	319	46	91	13	5	4	28	13

PITCHING	W	L	ERA	G	SV	IP	H	BB	SO
Brassington, Phil	8	0	2.40	11	0	75	69	16	53
Chavez, Chris	4	1	1.91	39	14	57	41	25	79
Cosgrove, Mike	1	4	1.14	34	12	55	35	11	59
Deremer, Scott	2	2	5.56	6	0	23	24	7	8
Guess, Scott	3	6	6.35	27	1	89	119	20	65
Hasler, Jerry	1	1	2.87	3	0	16	13	8	7
Knollin, Christopher	1	3	7.23	7	0	24	34	12	29
Koutrouba, Tom	4	2	2.82	14	0	61	47	13	62
Lawton, Bill	4	6	5.64	30	1	81	107	30	59
LeBlanc, Eric	10	6	3.44	18	0	118	132	34	104
Marcotte, Trevor	2	1	4.97	8	0	29	27	15	20
Nieves, Ernie	0	1	2.79	5	0	10	10	2	6
Peel, Ricky	0	0	9.00	7	0	6	9	1	0
Scott, Cory	0	1	4.50	7	2	10	11	4	6
2-team (40 Adirondack)	3	5	3.99	4	2	65	72	22	45
Trufant, Jason	0	0	7.20	2	0	5	9	4	1
Valdez, Carlos	1	2	3.30	5	0	30	33	6	22
Von Haefen, Jason	9	4	3.90	18	0	99	91	32	98

ALLENTOWN

BATTING	AVG	AB	R	H	2B	3B	HR	RBI	SB
Alvarez, Rafael, of	.262	61	10	16	2	1	1	8	2
Azuaje, Jesus, ss	.228	184	26	42	4	0	1	13	7

BATTING	AVG	AB	R	H	2B	3B	HR	RBI	SB
Blen-Ferray, Damian, 2b	.247	154	22	38	5	2	4	22	1
Bordenick, Ryan, c	.274	215	33	59	16	0	6	30	0
Bunkley, Antuan, dh	.350	183	28	64	14	0	3	34	2
Caston, Bernard, of	.260	96	17	25	3	0	1	8	8
Gainer, Jay, dh	.331	172	32	57	12	1	7	38	1
Hall, Doug, of	.285	137	19	39	6	1	1	15	12
Herrick, Jason, of	.281	267	53	75	11	1	16	62	8
Leed, Adam, of	.245	229	34	56	10	1	8	33	2
Matos, Francisco, ss-2b	.416	243	39	101	26	2	3	45	11
Maxwell, Keith, 3b	.312	349	57	109	22	2	11	62	5
Piercy, Mike, of	.250	20	4	5	0	0	0	1	0
Samuels, Scott, of	.267	116	23	31	11	1	4	25	10
Sergio, Tom, of-2b	.326	258	67	84	16	3	7	34	5
Soules, Ryan, 1b-of	.331	311	75	103	30	1	10	61	1
Wittmeyer, Kevin, c	.216	162	22	35	8	2	4	20	4

PITCHING	W	L	ERA	G	SV	IP	H	BB	SO
Andujar, Luis	0	0	9.00	4	0	5	10	1	6
Bauldree, Joe	2	2	5.82	8	0	39	52	16	30
Bond, Aaron	9	4	3.90	19	1	111	126	25	102
Bradford, Josh	1	0	0.00	1	0	6	4	0	9
Clackum, Scott	1	2	1.80	8	1	15	12	0	10
Correa, Ed	1	2	6.39	5	0	13	17	2	7
Curtiss, Tom	1	2	3.93	27	0	37	32	23	31
Drahman, Brian	2	2	8.58	5	0	28	47	8	10
Ferretti, Ryan	0	0	5.63	4	0	8	11	1	3
2-team (7 Adirondack)	0	0	7.24	11	0	14	22	6	9
Fleck, Will	0	3	5.79	14	1	14	18	12	15
Fleming, Emar	0	0	17.36	3	0	5	14	1	2
Goebeler, Dan	5	7	5.11	20	0	88	115	30	52
LaRoche, Jeff	0	0	6.35	3	0	6	7	0	2
Leonards, Bake	4	1	3.60	17	0	25	33	7	27
Manwiller, Tim	1	1	6.88	3	0	17	26	3	5
Martinez, Romulo	0	0	8.59	7	0	7	15	2	3
McNally, Andrew	0	0	9.64	6	1	14	21	4	8
Mendoza, Marco	3	1	4.58	13	1	20	28	11	9
Moore, Peter	0	0	5.12	12	0	19	19	10	13
Pennington, Brad	4	2	5.86	8	0	54	64	23	17
Ramirez, Luis	3	2	3.55	38	3	46	52	10	39
Sanchez, Martin	0	4	7.76	6	0	27	49	4	18
Sexton, Patrick	2	3	7.14	10	0	47	68	21	22
Sigley, Jayson	0	1	10.95	5	0	12	19	11	11
Wagner, Matt	1	3	0.89	20	10	20	18	5	18
2-team (19 New Jersey)	1	3	1.82	39	20	40	37	9	36
Webb, Alan	1	2	11.57	9	0	35	51	30	30
2-team (9 New Jersey)	4	7	6.83	18	0	88	97	54	67
Williams, Larry	1	1	2.89	3	0	19	19	5	17
Zallie, Chris	1	2	6.17	13	1	42	42	21	21

ELMIRA

BATTING	AVG	AB	R	H	2B	3B	HR	RBI	SB
Ametller, Jesus, 2b	.143	14	1	2	1	0	0	2	0
Brock, Tarrik, of	.286	259	60	74	16	4	4	37	26
Bush, Ron, ss	.274	252	33	69	18	3	2	16	7
Fauske, J.P., 1b	.100	10	0	1	0	0	0	0	0
Greene, Allen, 1b-of	.196	51	6	10	3	0	0	7	1
Ingram, Garey, 2b-3b	.294	299	54	88	25	1	13	52	7
Kaeding, Clint, 3b-ss	.172	128	7	22	6	2	0	9	0
Lepine, Olivier, c	.323	93	8	30	8	1	2	13	0
2-team (22 Quebec)	.269	160	18	43	13	1	2	19	1
McDonald, Ashanti, dh-3b	.268	332	50	89	17	3	12	68	4
Moore, Kevin, of-3b	.272	202	30	55	13	1	4	28	2
Needle, Ben, c-3b	.233	30	1	7	2	0	0	3	1
Nelson, Chris, of	.250	20	5	5	2	0	0	1	3
Potter, Mike, of	.329	158	20	52	2	0	1	24	15
Reinoso, Nataniel, 1b	.268	220	25	59	9	1	4	37	4
Richardson, Brian, 3b-1b	.259	27	3	7	1	0	1	7	0
Simmons, Jerry, of	.295	156	29	46	7	2	5	25	14
Singletary, Dan, of	.272	261	42	71	12	7	5	28	18
Smith, Rod, 3b	.252	226	44	57	13	4	5	26	33
Vasquez, Sandy, 1b-of	.313	64	10	20	6	1	3	13	4
Wrenn, Michael, c	.237	232	29	55	10	0	2	22	3

PITCHING	W	L	ERA	G	SV	IP	H	BB	SO
Brack, A.J.	1	1	6.09	18	0	34	42	14	26
Brown, Chris	4	2	2.23	37	1	61	45	16	52
Estes, Eric	6	3	2.51	30	0	57	59	10	65
Halla, Ryan	2	3	1.70	36	18	37	28	16	46
Hasler, Jerry	4	2	4.79	8	1	41	50	11	27
Keagle, Greg	5	5	3.29	18	0	109	100	25	94
Sano, Shigeki	6	6	2.66	18	0	125	121	20	49
Shinada, Ayahito	10	7	3.29	18	0	123	116	17	84
Stine, Justin	9	2	4.23	21	1	106	110	32	73
Taczy, Craig	0	1	15.00	2	0	6	9	7	2
Thomas, Don	1	1	3.26	34	1	39	31	19	30
Totten, Kris	3	5	5.66	12	0	49	67	22	26

BATTING	AVG	AB	R	H	2B	3B	HR	RBI	SB
Abate, Mike, of	.178	45	3	8	2	0	1	1	0
Beamon, Trey, of	.348	138	33	48	7	1	2	23	9
Cano, Matt, 3b	.271	96	13	26	4	0	0	7	0
Capodieci, Adam, c	.203	74	14	15	0	1	0	7	0
Church, Mike, c	.266	241	21	64	10	0	3	27	0
Clark, Jason, of	.200	10	1	2	1	0	0	0	0
Conway, Craig, 2b-3b	.252	123	16	31	7	0	0	13	1
DeYoung, Peter, 1b-3b	.301	286	30	86	23	1	2	31	7
Fera, Aaron, of	.355	231	46	82	19	2	18	54	7
Hall, Doug, of	.253	194	31	49	8	2	3	22	5
2-team (32 Allentown)	.266	331	50	88	14	3	4	37	17
Kane, Ryan, 3b	.366	164	29	60	20	1	7	36	1
2-team (43 Quebec)	.314	331	49	104	33	2	11	58	3
Keene, Andre, dh	.312	77	8	24	2	0	2	11	2
Kennedy, David, 1b	.297	333	46	99	14	1	12	60	0
Mendoza, Angel, of	.260	123	12	32	2	1	0	7	4
Miyake, Chris, ss-2b	.181	155	16	28	6	2	2	20	4
Moreno, Juan, of	.298	352	61	105	20	4	4	29	17
Rossy, Eric, 2b-ss	.246	138	19	34	4	2	1	14	6
Samboy, Nelson, 2b	.274	117	23	32	6	0	0	7	11
Terni, Chaz, ss	.239	180	20	43	7	0	2	21	1
Walker, Ron, dh	.000	4	0	0	0	0	0	0	0

PITCHING	W	L	ERA	G	SV	IP	H	BB	SO
Allan, Scott	1	0	6.19	17	1	16	14	13	15
Bennett, Joel	10	5	2.57	22	3	129	104	42	118
Bertotti, Mike	6	2	3.80	12	0	71	48	37	99
Campbell, Chad	0	1	11.12	3	0	6	6	6	5
2-team (25 Adirondack)	2	4	5.69	28	0	62	67	37	39
Casteel, Ricky	1	4	4.78	5	0	26	34	8	7
Ennico, Chris	5	1	3.00	15	0	60	43	33	42
Fermin, Ramon	1	1	2.55	4	0	25	20	10	15
Fish, Steve	3	1	3.05	5	0	38	28	7	28
2-team (14 Quebec)	8	5	4.50	19	1	108	114	17	73
Grimmett, Darin	1	2	5.13	20	1	33	35	13	28
Hand, Jon	4	2	4.42	35	2	55	60	16	45
Herbert, Russ	2	4	5.27	7	0	41	46	20	39
Koutrouba, Tom	3	4	4.78	9	0	53	67	18	56
2-team (14 Albany)	7	6	3.73	23	0	113	114	31	118
Meady, Todd	3	3	2.61	33	4	41	40	17	24
Pincavitch, Kevin	1	2	9.85	5	0	25	36	11	17
Reichow, Bob	0	4	8.40	7	0	30	39	14	20
Sweeney, Mike	1	3	6.00	23	0	45	75	12	35
Wagner, Matt	0	0	2.79	19	10	19	19	4	18
Wambach, Trevor	0	1	4.50	1	0	6	6	1	3
2-team (9 Quebec)	5	2	3.93	10	0	53	58	14	22
Webb, Alan	3	5	3.71	9	0	53	46	24	37

BATTING	AVG	AB	R	H	2B	3B	HR	RBI	SB
Benes, Richie, 3b-ss	.261	69	10	18	2	0	0	8	2
2-team (2 Albany)	.250	76	10	19	2	0	0	8	2
Bunkley, Antuan, dh	.240	75	8	18	0	0	2	9	0
2-team (45 Allentown)	.318	258	36	82	14	0	5	43	2
Chimelis, Joel, 1b	.286	84	12	24	3	0	4	17	0
Cornelius, Brian, 1b-of	.315	327	57	103	22	0	13	59	3
DiPrima, Giancarlo, 2b	.260	334	43	87	12	1	0	33	15
Emond, Ben, of	.283	315	40	89	14	0	3	37	30
Garcia, Cipriano, c	.264	91	9	24	2	0	2	9	1
Garrison, B.J., of	.310	232	37	72	20	2	6	33	12
Henry, Santiago, of	.400	10	3	4	1	0	0	0	0
Kane, Ryan, 3b	.263	167	20	44	13	1	4	22	2
Kofler, Eric, of	.289	325	53	94	17	3	16	49	3
Lepine, Olivier, c	.194	67	10	13	5	0	0	6	1
Lewis, Marc, of	.228	57	10	13	2	0	3	9	4
Marval, Raul, ss	.263	331	42	87	14	1	5	41	3
Melendez, Luis, c	.228	136	13	31	3	0	0	8	1
Sawyer, Chris, of	.270	215	47	58	15	0	6	27	11
Scalabrini, Pat, 3b-1b	.241	241	39	58	7	0	5	24	12
Villacres, Gary, of	.270	111	15	30	5	0	0	13	7

PITCHING	W	L	ERA	G	SV	IP	H	BB	SO
Anderson, Eric	1	2	6.00	8	0	45	42	18	37
2-team (7 Adirondack)	2	6	5.74	15	0	80	86	30	51
Bacci, Tony	7	5	4.66	18	0	102	117	36	56
Blais, Joce	4	2	5.05	18	0	52	69	11	26
Chenard, Christian	2	2	4.26	39	1	57	55	29	37
Daniels, John	2	2	2.49	40	15	47	42	14	58
Fish, Steve	5	4	5.30	14	1	70	86	10	45
Goodmann, Joe	0	2	5.63	7	0	8	8	10	6
Hahn, Steve	4	8	5.77	41	0	48	61	19	31
Hasler, Jerry	6	3	4.44	13	1	71	77	25	40

	W	L	ERA	G	SV	IP	H	BB	SO
3-team (3 Alb./8 Elmira)	1	0	5.14	2	0	14	14	6	6
Lavenia, Mark	2	7	4.91	18	0	110	116	24	74
Lavigne, Martin	1	1	3.79	7	0	36	39	14	25
Nunez, Jose	2	1	2.30	5	0	31	29	3	26
Prata, Danny	3	4	5.77	11	0	58	66	28	36
Reichow, Bob	2	2	4.60	21	0	29	33	15	19
2-team (7 New Jersey)	2	6	6.52	28	0	59	72	29	39
Runion, Tony	0	0	5.40	5	1	7	11	2	7
Sherrill, Garrett	3	2	4.18	18	0	24	24	9	26
Smith, J.J.	0	1	8.44	9	0	16	25	7	10
Wambach, Trevor	5	1	3.86	9	0	47	52	13	19

TEXAS-LOUISIANA LEAGUE

The Edinburg Roadrunners put the finishing touches on a near-perfect inaugural season by winning three straight games to claim the 2001 Texas-Louisiana League championship.

The Roadrunners lost Game One of their best-of-five series with the San Angelo Colts 9-6 before winning the next three 10-0, 9-2 and 7-4.

Mario Rodriguez was perfect through five innings of relief in the deciding game to gain the victory, his only win of the playoffs. Roadrunners outfielder Evan Cherry batted .429-2-9 with nine runs in 21 postseason at-bats.

The Roadrunners went 62-34 overall to help their manager Chad Tredaway earn Baseball America's Independent League Manager of the Year award. The Edinburg native had never managed before the 2001 season, but he was familiar with the level of competition. He batted .382-17-69 in 2000 under San Angelo manager Dan Madsen, who helped Tredaway make a name for himself.

Tredaway heard the league wanted a franchise in Edinburg, so he immediately decided to put himself in a position to manage the team, which shares a new stadium with Texas-Pan American University, coached by Tredaway's father Reggie. Tredaway called Madsen, wound up having an all-star season in 2000 and then landed the job in Edinburg. A year later, he beat Madsen's club in the title series and was named the league's manager of the year.

STANDINGS

FIRST HALF

	W	L	PCT	GB
Edinburg Roadrunners	32	16	.667	—
Alexandria Aces	27	20	.574	4 ½
Amarillo Dillas	26	20	.565	5
San Angelo Colts	25	21	.543	6
Rio Grande Valley WhiteWings	22	26	.458	10
Springfield/Ozark Mountain Ducks	18	30	.375	14
Greenville Bluesmen	15	32	.319	16 ½

SECOND HALF

	W	L	PCT	GB
Alexandria Aces	34	14	.708	—
Edinburg Roadrunners	32	16	.667	2
Amarillo Dillas	23	25	.479	11
San Angelo Colts	22	26	.458	12
Springfield/Ozark Mountain Ducks	20	28	.417	14
Greenville Bluesmen	19	29	.396	15
Rio Grande Valley WhiteWings	18	30	.375	16

PLAYOFFS: Semifinals—Edinburg defeated Amarillo 2-0 and San Angelo defeated Alexandria 2-0 in best-of-3 series. **Finals**—Edinburg defeated San Angelo 3-1 in best-of-5 series.

MANAGERS: Alexandria—John O'Brien. **Amarillo**—Lonnie Maclin. **Edinburg**—Chad Tredaway. **Greenville**—Robin Harriss. **Springfield/Ozark**—Barry Jones. **Rio Grande Valley**—Eddie Dennis. **San Angelo**—Dan Madsen.

ATTENDANCE: Edinburg 135,360; Springfield/Ozark 134,485; San Angelo 114,957; Amarillo 102,155; Rio Grande Valley 84,448; Alexandria 57,305; Greenville 14,841.

ALL-STAR TEAM: C—Trey Salinas, Alexandria. **1B**—Lonnie Maclin,

Amarillo. **2B**—Sergio Guerrero, Edinburg. **3B**—Derek Henderson, Amarillo. **SS**—Will Roland, San Angelo. **OF**—Manny Lopez, San Angelo; Tyrone Pendergrass, Rio Grande Valley; Carlos Duncan, Rio Grande Valley; Andre Johnson, Springfield/Ozark. **Util**—Franklin Taveras, San Angelo. **DH**—Joe Hamilton, Alexandria. **P**—Rob Vael, Alexandria; Keith Dunn, Greenville; Ryan Harris, Edinburg; Pedro Flores, Edinburg; Mike Smith, Springfield/Ozark.

Player of the Year: Joe Hamilton, Alexandria. **Pitcher of the Year**: Ryan Harris, Edinburg. **Rookie of the Year**: Scott Fowler, Edinburg. **Manager of the Year**: Chad Tredaway, Edinburg.

INDIVIDUAL BATTING LEADERS
(Minimum 259 Plate Appearances)

	AVG	AB	R	H	2B	3B	HR	RBI	SB
Maclin, Lonnie, Amarillo	.390	308	56	120	26	3	7	72	4
Salinas, Trey, Alexandria	.351	262	53	92	23	0	12	61	4
Johnson, Andre, S/O	.347	375	67	130	25	0	19	80	15
Lopez, Manny, SA	.345	377	71	130	30	1	10	68	17
Alvarez, Jorge, Amarillo	.342	339	68	116	30	2	13	76	1
Pendergrass, Tyrone, RGV	.332	304	75	101	20	5	11	48	52
Henderson, Derek, Amarillo	.331	354	68	117	32	2	10	71	4
O'Sullivan, Patrick, Green.	.323	390	54	126	35	1	18	74	16
Duncan, Carlos, RGV	.320	353	71	113	19	7	14	70	50
Hamilton, Joe, Alexandria	.315	343	82	108	27	3	19	86	2

INDIVIDUAL PITCHING LEADERS
(Minimum 77 Innings)

	W	L	ERA	G	SV	IP	H	BB	SO
Harris, Ryan, Edinburg	11	5	2.00	19	0	144	110	34	136
McClain, Jeremy, SA	8	1	2.65	12	0	92	78	26	73
Dunn, Keith, Greenville	11	8	2.66	23	0	166	145	35	109
Madritsch, Bobby, SA	3	6	2.72	13	0	86	69	40	85
Flores, Pedro, Edinburg	11	7	2.87	21	0	141	103	59	170
Green, Scott, Edinburg	4	3	3.04	15	0	77	62	21	71
Smith, Mike, S/O	10	10	3.08	23	0	184	185	35	150
Smith, Clint, Edinburg	8	4	3.11	15	0	90	87	32	76
Wollscheid, James, S/O	8	5	3.16	18	0	120	121	48	83
Rodriguez, Mario, Edin.	6	3	3.18	13	0	82	81	26	63

ALEXANDRIA

BATTING	AVG	AB	R	H	2B	3B	HR	RBI	SB
Anderson, Danier, 2b	.077	13	2	1	1	0	0	1	0
Bethea, Larry, dh	.179	28	5	5	1	0	1	6	2
Cadwallader, Scott, of	.282	156	27	44	2	2	1	21	12
Coy, J.D., ss-2b	.286	147	28	42	8	0	1	12	2
Doughty, Griff, 3b-1b	.217	152	22	33	6	1	1	16	0
Ganter, Jason, of	.261	306	49	80	11	0	17	57	3
Hamilton, Joe, dh	.315	343	82	108	27	3	19	86	2
Hewes, Robert, 3b	.373	185	61	69	14	1	13	41	3
Hyers, Matt, ss-2b	.258	182	35	47	4	1	3	23	6
Matthews, Eric, 1b	.264	341	37	90	17	2	6	46	0
O'Brien, John, dh	.244	168	22	41	6	1	12	35	0
Pepper, Danny, c	.243	74	11	18	2	0	0	4	0
Roberts, Nick, ss	.260	73	13	19	4	1	1	7	1
Rothe, Ryan, of	.243	341	53	83	19	4	5	47	20
Salinas, Trey, c	.351	262	53	92	23	0	12	61	4
Trammell, Gary, 2b-of	.295	332	62	98	25	4	1	26	6
West, George, 3b	.261	142	19	37	10	1	3	38	1
PITCHING	W	L	ERA	G	SV	IP	H	BB	SO
Camp, Rusty	4	9	4.74	20	0	87	103	29	58
Craine, Shevin	10	9	4.90	25	1	125	151	39	65
DeJesus, Javier	14	6	4.12	23	0	166	167	38	109
Frisbie, James	0	0	11.32	7	0	10	19	5	3
Mathys, Jason	6	2	2.77	47	1	62	66	15	46
Olivera, Manny	7	1	4.30	16	0	67	71	23	48
Preston, George	1	0	2.47	45	32	47	38	26	61
Robell, Kevin	3	1	5.51	9	1	33	38	11	16
Snyder, Ryan	2	3	3.58	36	3	60	75	11	35
Vael, Rob	15	3	3.95	24	0	173	200	48	108

AMARILLO

BATTING	AVG	AB	R	H	2B	3B	HR	RBI	SB
Alvarez, Jorge, 2b	.342	339	68	116	30	2	13	76	1
Cepeda, Malcolm, 1b	.235	115	17	27	6	0	0	12	9
Cotto, Enrique, c	.233	73	16	17	2	0	0	5	2
Culwell, Nate, c-1b	.261	211	28	55	14	2	4	39	0
Deck, Ronnie, c	.214	42	9	9	2	1	0	4	0
Delgado, Daniel, ss	.274	314	46	86	12	5	0	53	9
Espinoza, Andres, of	.272	268	51	73	13	3	4	39	11
Garland, Tim, of	.295	88	17	26	5	2	0	3	10
Graser, Kenny, 2b-3b	.214	42	8	9	1	0	0	3	0
Hardge, Mike, 2b-of	.299	388	84	116	25	10	10	75	20
Henderson, Derek, 3b	.331	354	68	117	32	2	10	71	4

	AVG	AB	R	H	2B	3B	HR	RBI	SB
Horne, Tyrone, of	.295	332	67	98	25	1	5	51	6
Keith, Jason, ss-of	.083	12	1	1	0	0	0	0	0
Maclin, Lonnie, 1b	.390	308	56	120	26	3	7	72	4
Ricard, Toby, of	.282	394	65	111	21	1	7	48	10
Roun, Corey, c	.203	64	10	13	1	0	0	6	0
PITCHING	W	L	ERA	G	SV	IP	H	BB	SO
Brown, Stephen	1	1	5.40	4	0	10	10	1	4
Buchanan, Todd	3	2	4.86	32	1	50	56	22	23
Carpenter, Justin	2	1	7.56	3	0	17	23	11	13
Frazier, Harold	1	2	4.82	24	0	28	35	12	17
Harris, Pep	11	9	3.33	23	0	165	179	45	130
Hayes, Tim	0	0	8.54	18	0	26	38	12	11
Hill, Kendall	1	2	4.93	8	0	42	52	19	23
2-team (13 Greenville)	2	6	6.44	21	1	81	101	42	51
Leach, Mike	11	8	3.62	23	0	159	149	49	122
Patrick, Jason	2	4	6.09	6	0	34	50	7	21
Price, Tobias	0	2	8.04	8	0	16	24	7	3
Seely, Jason	4	5	4.17	42	12	45	50	22	23
Seivert, Kevin	6	5	5.38	26	0	95	111	47	70
Stewart, Cory	6	6	5.39	22	0	120	132	67	107

EDINBURG

BATTING	AVG	AB	R	H	2B	3B	HR	RBI	SB
Bartosh, T.J., dh	.214	42	7	9	1	1	2	5	0
Cherry, Evan, of	.272	372	57	101	16	4	2	31	17
Garcia, Ismael, 3b-1b	.266	271	29	72	15	1	7	39	1
Garza, O.J., of	.188	69	4	13	3	0	0	1	0
Gonzalez, Eric, 3b-of	.265	68	5	18	6	1	0	5	1
Guerrero, Sergio, 2b	.312	359	52	112	27	2	7	47	7
Hamilton, Mike, 3b-ss	.281	295	39	83	12	2	5	33	12
LaFlair, Jay, c	.243	309	36	75	10	1	5	28	10
Magdaleno, Ricky, ss	.262	325	47	85	10	0	8	41	9
Melo, Ramon, 2b	.182	22	3	4	0	0	0	2	0
Moore, Vince, of	.249	281	54	70	21	3	4	31	12
Querecuto, Juan, 1b-c	.276	355	28	98	12	0	5	42	3
Strickland, Greg, of	.314	140	21	44	9	2	4	24	4
Wilson, Michael, of	.309	320	44	99	24	4	9	53	15
PITCHING	W	L	ERA	G	SV	IP	H	BB	SO
Brown, Chris	6	6	4.55	20	0	117	141	52	84
Cervantes, Peter	8	2	2.67	32	2	57	50	24	61
Chapman, Billy	1	0	3.71	32	17	34	37	17	32
Flores, Pedro	11	7	2.87	21	0	141	103	59	170
Fowler, Scott	1	1	1.55	36	4	52	39	16	61
Green, Scott	4	3	3.04	15	0	77	62	21	71
Harris, Ryan	11	5	2.00	19	0	144	110	34	136
Rodriguez, Mario	6	3	3.18	13	0	82	81	26	63
Seale, Dustin	2	1	2.30	29	1	47	45	12	40
Smith, Clint	8	4	3.11	15	0	90	87	32	76

GREENVILLE

BATTING	AVG	AB	R	H	2B	3B	HR	RBI	SB
Bakich, Erik, 3b	.133	30	5	4	2	0	0	5	1
Brock, Todd, ss-2b	.277	346	61	96	16	6	13	44	16
Bustos, Saul, ss-2b	.220	173	21	38	9	1	4	22	3
Cepeda, Ali, of	.237	38	3	9	0	0	1	2	5
Cepeda, Malcolm, 1b	.298	161	22	48	9	3	2	17	11
Clark, Jamie, of	.241	79	10	19	4	0	4	10	1
Danzy, Ray, of	.213	155	24	33	4	1	7	17	5
Depew, Jeff, of	.168	107	9	18	4	0	3	16	3
Hymes, Mike, of	.211	161	29	34	7	0	0	9	17
Lebron, Jesus, of	.123	106	16	13	4	2	1	9	10
Moeller, Mike, of-1b	.254	173	28	44	10	2	4	16	2
Ness, Andrew, c-3b	.199	136	19	27	11	0	4	20	0
O'Sullivan, Patrick, dh-1b	.323	390	54	126	35	1	18	74	16
Patterson, Derek, 2b-3b	.311	148	22	46	11	0	7	29	12
Phipps, Tim, of	.270	270	45	73	12	7	4	28	19
Shanks, Sim, 2b	.241	199	26	48	6	4	0	11	8
Twombley, Dennis, c	.212	283	23	60	12	0	2	32	0
Valdez, Trovin, of	.241	54	9	13	1	1	0	2	9
White, Eric, 3b	.312	202	28	63	13	1	4	33	6
PITCHING	W	L	ERA	G	SV	IP	H	BB	SO
Cowling, Ross	5	6	6.02	19	1	61	77	30	41
Dunn, Keith	11	8	2.66	23	0	166	145	35	109
Hill, Kendall	1	4	8.08	13	1	39	49	23	28
Lowe, Matt	4	8	7.54	30	2	103	142	40	65
Morgan, Shawn	0	1	11.25	10	0	16	33	9	13
Pozza, Chris	6	7	6.22	16	0	97	127	51	66
Sanchez, Mike	3	11	5.15	23	0	124	134	67	86
Sasaki, Takahiro	0	2	4.45	22	0	32	39	13	19
Sexton, Jeff	2	3	2.68	23	6	44	32	10	54
Stout, Dan	5	9	4.88	36	0	83	93	35	62
Vaughn, Barton	0	4	8.86	28	3	42	61	25	36

SPRINGFIELD/OZARK

BATTING	AVG	AB	R	H	2B	3B	HR	RBI	SB
Benes, Richie, ss	.100	20	3	2	1	0	0	0	2
Cairo, Sergio, of	.303	366	46	111	19	4	7	51	13
Cole, Marvin, 2b	.285	386	65	110	21	4	1	44	26
Dettman, Matt, 3b-c	.282	333	49	94	18	1	6	35	13
Essian, James, c	.243	140	22	34	5	0	3	17	4
Fox, Brandon, of-1b	.257	113	18	29	6	0	2	11	2
Green, Terene, ss-of	.212	273	32	58	7	3	4	21	6
Heerman, Brian, ss-3b	.172	58	8	10	2	0	0	6	2
Holmberg, Brett, c	.235	68	11	16	2	0	0	7	1
Jasco, Elinton, ss-of	.284	155	26	44	2	0	0	17	3
Johnson, Andre, of	.347	375	67	130	25	0	19	80	15
Mora, Juan, of	.145	55	4	8	0	0	1	6	1
Thompson, Jason, of	.288	368	62	106	24	6	14	63	10
Underwood, Curtis, of	.262	317	28	83	14	0	5	42	2
Van Asselberg, Ricky, 3b-c	.191	220	24	42	4	0	3	13	3

PITCHING	W	L	ERA	G	SV	IP	H	BB	SO
Bowen, Patrick	0	3	14.00	3	0	9	18	9	8
Buitron, Andy	0	0	6.28	10	0	14	19	5	15
Collazo, Rafael	0	2	15.95	8	0	7	12	5	5
Dettman, Andy	2	3	6.55	25	1	69	86	41	43
Dill, Matt	2	3	5.68	12	0	32	37	15	20
Duperron, Mike	1	1	9.92	13	0	16	21	20	6
Ferguson, Tony	1	4	2.86	32	13	35	31	13	35
Hardcastle, John	4	12	5.63	19	0	113	152	48	64
2-team (1 Greenville)	4	12	5.59	20	0	114	154	49	64
Hays, Cody	2	2	4.38	4	0	25	25	7	21
Mozley, Brandon	8	9	3.77	25	0	138	150	55	73
O'Dell, Jason	0	1	8.31	9	0	13	16	11	9
Smith, Mike	10	10	3.08	23	0	184	185	35	150
Tremont, Harold	0	0	7.71	4	0	5	4	3	6
Turnrose, Erik	0	1	4.32	8	0	8	10	5	3
Vincent, Ryan	0	2	6.03	16	0	31	37	21	22
Wollscheid, James	8	5	3.16	18	0	120	121	48	83

RIO GRANDE VALLEY

BATTING	AVG	AB	R	H	2B	3B	HR	RBI	SB
Belk, J.J., of	.250	32	4	8	2	1	0	1	1
Branch, Jim, c	.157	51	5	8	2	0	0	0	3
Cepeda, Malcolm, 1b	.277	47	7	13	3	0	0	4	3
3-team (18 Amar/43 Green.)	.272	323	46	88	18	3	2	33	23
Clark, Jamie, of	.197	66	9	13	1	1	1	5	0
2-team (21 Greenville)	.221	145	19	32	5	1	5	15	1
Duncan, Carlos, of-2b	.320	353	71	113	19	7	14	70	50
Gainey, Bryon, 1b	.288	163	21	47	11	1	9	40	2
Greene, Shawn, dh-1b	.209	110	13	23	5	0	3	17	0
Keene, Andre, dh	.250	112	16	28	6	0	5	24	5
Kennedy, Nathan, 1b	.199	136	8	27	3	0	1	6	1
Medina, Luis, 3b	.268	302	25	81	14	1	1	19	1
Melo, Ramon, 2b-ss	.251	247	33	62	3	1	5	28	28
2-team (6 Edinburg)	.245	269	36	66	3	1	5	30	28
Oropeza, Willie, c	.280	296	35	83	12	0	8	41	2
Pendergrass, Tyrone, of	.332	304	75	101	20	5	11	48	52
Reyes, Armando, 2b	.294	17	2	5	0	0	0	0	1
Roland, William, ss-2b	.300	60	11	18	4	0	1	7	1
Shumpert, Derek, of	.208	77	8	16	2	1	2	8	0
Solis, John, of	.212	137	26	29	3	0	0	13	11
Thorpe, A.D., ss	.275	327	52	90	11	0	2	36	22
Ulises, Pedro, dh	.188	32	1	6	0	0	0	2	0
Van Allen, Larry, of	.203	69	9	14	4	0	0	3	0
Vasquez, Alejandro, of	.296	189	21	56	8	0	4	38	12
Vela, Manuel, 2b-ss	.120	25	2	3	0	0	0	1	1
Viegas, Clark, 3b	.167	12	0	2	1	0	0	0	0

PITCHING	W	L	ERA	G	SV	IP	H	BB	SO
Barreto, Joel	3	8	4.96	27	2	91	74	71	117
DeLeon, Jose	0	0	10.97	9	0	11	18	11	7
Engle, Jimmy	0	1	4.97	12	0	25	33	16	14
Feliciano, Ruben	0	3	7.64	5	0	18	19	15	15
Fretwell, Joseph	4	4	4.14	46	9	59	63	18	52
Kalchuk, Mike	0	0	7.36	3	0	7	12	8	4
Linares, Yfrain	4	7	3.60	19	0	80	70	51	83
Love, Farley	2	3	6.21	18	8	29	23	31	34
Madritsch, Bobby	3	4	3.15	10	0	60	55	34	58
Malloy, Bill	0	1	5.49	4	0	20	25	11	13
Martinez, Johnny	2	2	5.21	7	0	38	37	16	30
McDermott, Toby	2	2	2.87	7	0	47	39	22	28
2-team (6 San Angelo)	2	5	4.00	13	1	70	75	28	48
Montoya, Eric	2	0	4.32	4	0	8	3	8	12
Ortiz, Steve	4	3	3.83	8	0	54	51	24	45
2-team (9 San Angelo)	7	7	4.60	17	0	108	115	46	96
Perez, Pablo	8	6	4.33	21	1	123	133	47	101
Reyes, Pablo	0	1	13.50	3	0	7	12	3	4
Roundtree, Monte	0	0	1.50	5	1	6	4	8	6
Ryburn, Ty	0	0	9.82	11	0	15	18	14	10
Silva, Luis	0	1	15.88	4	0	11	23	4	13
Sokol, Trad	1	5	6.31	9	0	36	46	16	22
Trevino, Fabian	2	3	5.91	33	1	56	67	37	41
Willetts, Pete	2	2	6.08	6	0	24	28	12	9

SAN ANGELO

BATTING	AVG	AB	R	H	2B	3B	HR	RBI	SB
Bigham, Shawn, of	.208	48	5	10	0	1	1	4	0
Cotto, Enrique, c	.240	104	13	25	3	0	1	14	1
2-team (22 Amarillo)	.237	177	29	42	5	0	1	19	3
DeMarco, Tony, dh-of	.355	141	19	50	8	0	4	27	0
Donaldson, Rhodney, of	.282	124	25	35	7	1	3	26	4
Duross, Gabe, 1b	.301	409	59	123	23	1	7	53	0
Evans, Austin, of	.239	71	12	17	0	2	0	4	3
Giuffre, Guy, c	.192	255	46	49	15	0	13	35	1
Greene, Shawn, of-1b	.320	222	53	71	13	1	12	46	1
2-team (31 RGV)	.283	332	66	94	18	1	15	63	1
Kirkpatrick, Michael, of	.320	50	12	16	4	0	2	5	2
Lopez, Manny, of	.345	377	71	130	30	1	10	68	17
Martinez, David, 2b-3b	.239	197	31	47	8	1	3	28	1
Radcliff, Vic, dh	.333	27	5	9	4	0	0	1	2
Roland, William, ss	.314	296	68	93	21	1	6	39	0
2-team (16 RGV)	.312	356	79	111	25	1	7	46	1
Taveras, Frank, 3b-2b	.295	383	65	113	27	4	18	79	2
Taylor, T.D., c-3b	.234	47	8	11	2	0	2	10	1
Templeton, Garry, 2b	.167	30	1	5	2	0	0	1	0
Vaughn, Derek, of	.290	397	53	115	29	2	4	50	18
Vinh, Bao, 2b	.229	35	3	8	0	0	0	0	2
Waller, Chris, c	.194	31	7	6	1	0	0	0	0
White, Eric, 3b	.295	78	12	23	8	0	3	18	1
2-team (52 Greenville)	.307	280	40	86	21	1	7	51	7

PITCHING	W	L	ERA	G	SV	IP	H	BB	SO
Boker, John	0	2	4.71	3	0	21	16	12	20
Box, Shawn	4	4	4.12	36	10	39	33	15	51
Duwe, Josh	4	6	5.55	12	0	73	88	22	57
Gutierrez, Ricky	3	2	4.82	29	0	56	56	36	54
Hayden, Terry	2	0	0.75	2	0	12	13	3	7
Hessler, Landon	5	5	2.73	40	1	63	53	22	59
Linares, Ramon	1	0	7.24	3	0	14	19	8	14
Madritsch, Bobby	0	2	1.73	3	0	26	14	6	27
2-team (10 RGV)	3	6	2.72	13	0	86	69	40	85
Mahan, Dallas	10	6	5.05	20	0	128	149	51	104
Malloy, Bill	0	2	4.70	3	0	15	19	16	10
2-team (4 RGV)	0	3	5.14	7	0	35	44	27	21
Martin, Jeff	5	4	4.76	15	0	96	102	33	100
Martinez, Johnny	3	4	5.91	13	0	70	96	28	57
2-team (7 RGV)	5	6	5.67	20	0	108	133	44	87
McClain, Jeremy	8	1	2.65	12	0	93	78	26	73
McDermott, Toby	0	3	6.35	6	1	23	36	6	20
McGuire, Brandon	0	0	6.43	2	0	7	8	3	2
Ortiz, Steve	3	4	5.37	9	0	54	64	22	51
Sandler, Jared	1	2	4.71	22	0	36	47	10	23
Turrentine, Rich	0	0	3.00	5	1	6	4	4	11

WESTERN LEAGUE

Despite finishing the regular season 18 games below .500, the Long Beach Breakers defeated heavily favored Chico 3-2 in the Western League's best-of-five championship series.

The Breakers squeaked into the playoffs with a 21-24 second-half record, best in the Southern Division, while Chico finished 56-34, best overall.

Righthander Reggie Leslie outdueled league pitcher-of-the-year Greg Bicknell twice to lead Long Beach to the title. Leslie went seven strong innings in Game One of the title series in a 4-2 win, and defeated Bicknell again in Game Five, a 6-5 Breakers win.

Chico outfielder Buck McNabb homered twice in Game Five, including a solo shot in the ninth, but Long Beach reliever Rich Linares closed out the game for his only save of the playoffs. He pitched the final 3⅓ innings.

Losing in the championship series has become all too familiar to the faithful at Chico's Nettleton Stadium. The loss to Long Beach marked the third consecutive year

Chico had lost in the final. It lost in the semifinals in 1998 and won it all in 1997.

STANDINGS

FIRST HALF

NORTH

	W	L	PCT	GB
Chico Heat	31	14	.689	—
Solano Steelheads	25	20	.556	6
Sonoma County Crushers	23	22	.511	8

SOUTH

	W	L	PCT	GB
St. George Pioneerzz	21	24	.467	—
Yuma Bullfrogs	20	25	.444	1
Long Beach Breakers	15	30	.333	6

SECOND HALF

NORTH

	W	L	PCT	GB
Solano Steelheads	27	18	.600	—
Sonoma County Crushers	25	20	.556	2
Chico Heat	25	20	.556	2

SOUTH

	W	L	PCT	GB
Long Beach Breakers	21	24	.467	—
Yuma Bullfrogs	19	26	.422	2
St. George Pioneerzz	18	27	.400	3

PLAYOFFS: Semifinals—Long Beach defeated St. George 3-0 and Chico defeated Solano 3-1 in best-of-5 series. **Finals**—Long Beach defeated Chico 3-2 in best-of-5 series.

MANAGERS: Chico—Charley Kerfeld. **Long Beach**—Steve Yeager. **St. George**—Mike Littlewood. **Solano**—Bo Dodson. **Sonoma County**—Tim Ireland. **Yuma**—Bill Plummer.

ATTENDANCE: Chico 109,057; Solano 83,926; Yuma 83,046; Sonoma County 77,200; St. George 76,883; Long Beach 51,883.

ALL-STAR TEAM: C—Victor Sanchez, Solano. **1B**—Ray Brown, Chico. **2B**—Eric Martins, Long Beach. **3B**—Bo Durkac, Sonoma County. **SS**—Marc Gutfeld, Long Beach. **OF**—Brad Gennaro, Chico; Tim Howard, Yuma; Chris Powell, Sonoma County. **Util**—Jason Landreth, Solano. **DH**—Anthony Lewis, St. George. **P**—Greg Bicknell, Chico; Jason Olsen, Solano; Scott Navarro, Sonoma County; Gabe Sollecito, Chico; Mike Saipe, Long Beach.

Player of the Year: Victor Sanchez, Solano. **Pitcher of the Year:** Greg Bicknell, Chico. **Manager of the Year:** Charley Kerfeld, Chico.

INDIVIDUAL BATTING LEADERS
(Minimum 243 Plate Appearances)

	AVG	AB	R	H	2B	3B	HR	RBI	SB
Brown, Ray, Chico	.385	358	75	138	39	1	10	88	7
Gennaro, Brad, Chico	.366	361	64	132	27	1	14	89	4
Powell, Chris, SC	.363	306	77	111	18	3	5	40	25
Howard, Tim, Yuma	.350	340	65	119	25	4	7	63	6
Sanchez, Victor, Solano	.345	316	74	109	15	2	31	81	4
Sutherland, Alex, Yuma	.341	276	41	94	24	1	5	44	0
Durkac, Bo, SC	.336	324	58	109	13	0	3	67	1
Villalobos, Carlos, Yuma	.330	297	46	98	21	1	9	63	1
McNabb, Buck, Chico	.328	268	60	88	12	2	3	36	9
Torres, Paul, Solano	.315	232	47	73	17	2	10	46	2

INDIVIDUAL PITCHING LEADERS
(Minimum 72 Innings)

	W	L	ERA	G	SV	IP	H	BB	SO
Grant, Brian, SC	5	2	2.11	36	4	77	69	32	66
Bicknell, Greg, Chico	11	3	2.38	21	2	140	122	27	121
Navarro, Scott, Chico	10	2	2.55	15	0	92	88	32	67
Wood, Stanton, Solano	5	0	2.92	17	2	77	86	20	64
Saipe, Mike, LB	8	4	3.13	14	0	92	87	23	69
Olsen, Jason, Solano	8	2	3.44	18	0	110	100	29	110
Neboyia, Gabe, SC	4	6	3.52	16	0	79	91	16	68
McCall, Travis, LB	1	5	3.59	30	2	93	102	19	61
Harris, Jeff, Chico	11	7	3.94	21	0	130	144	46	99
Brosnan, Jason, Solano	8	5	4.11	17	0	105	109	25	86

CHICO

BATTING

	AVG	AB	R	H	2B	3B	HR	RBI	SB
Briones, Chris, c-of	.316	98	19	31	9	0	4	20	0
2-team (17 St. George)	.331	157	32	52	11	0	4	27	2
Brown, Ray, 1b	.385	358	75	138	39	1	10	88	7
Clark, Howie, 2b	.533	15	3	8	0	1	0	0	0
Cooper, Tim, ss-2b	.267	150	23	40	8	0	6	28	3
Daedelow, Craig, ss-3b	.272	309	42	84	20	1	2	33	5
Downing, Lance, 2b-3b	.265	347	44	92	9	2	9	57	6
Fitzpatrick, Eddie, c	.243	214	39	52	6	0	1	24	1
Gennaro, Brad, of	.366	361	64	132	27	1	14	89	4
Hyde, Brandon, c-1b	.204	49	5	10	4	0	1	3	0

	AVG	AB	R	H	2B	3B	HR	RBI	SB
Lewis, Danny, dh	.234	47	3	11	5	0	0	9	0
Macalutas, Jon, of-3b	.313	352	56	110	20	1	7	59	19
McNabb, Buck, of	.328	268	60	88	12	2	3	36	9
Rewers, Nate, dh-2b	.269	119	14	32	3	0	0	5	2
Scott, Shawn, of	.289	336	72	97	16	3	2	32	9
Vinh, Bao, 2b-of	.367	196	47	72	9	3	3	28	7

PITCHING

	W	L	ERA	G	SV	IP	H	BB	SO
Belovsky, Josh	4	2	2.09	40	20	43	33	23	39
Bennett, Erik	1	1	6.55	15	0	22	30	15	21
Bicknell, Greg	11	3	2.38	21	2	140	122	27	121
Borges, Reece	7	7	4.68	19	0	100	108	31	75
Brewer, Jim	2	2	8.54	20	0	45	71	34	39
Cuccias, Jon	0	0	4.32	4	0	8	4	6	8
2-team (2 Long Beach)	0	0	3.38	6	0	11	4	6	10
Doughty, Brian	4	2	4.71	8	0	42	60	8	35
Gallaty, Joe	2	1	3.66	6	0	32	32	10	9
Harris, Jeff	11	7	3.94	21	0	130	144	46	99
Madritsch, Bobby	0	1	11.74	5	0	8	14	6	12
Navarro, Scott	10	2	2.55	15	0	92	88	32	67
Ortiz, John	1	1	2.15	42	0	38	32	14	28
Parker, Daniel	0	0	10.57	6	0	8	18	2	8
Sanders, Frankie	0	1	3.18	5	0	6	3	5	4
Smith, Mike	1	2	4.44	4	0	26	29	7	31
2-team (15 St. George)	8	6	5.49	19	0	126	158	37	105
Sollecito, Gabe	3	2	1.06	35	5	51	36	8	55

LONG BEACH

BATTING

	AVG	AB	R	H	2B	3B	HR	RBI	SB
Anspach, Marc, 1b	.214	140	18	30	5	0	1	7	0
Betancourt, Tony, dh-c	.246	252	36	62	10	0	4	36	1
Cly, Jason, p	.264	72	6	19	2	0	1	16	1
Doherty, Steven, ss-3b	.188	32	5	6	1	1	1	8	0
Downs, Brian, c-1b	.276	341	41	94	12	1	6	44	4
Grebeck, Brian, 3b-2b	.256	78	12	20	3	0	2	12	1
2-team (47 St. George)	.277	256	43	71	14	0	7	40	1
Gutfeld, Marc, ss-3b	.281	270	34	76	15	0	1	33	4
Jones, Rafell, of	.234	308	38	72	16	3	5	38	8
Luke, Matt, 1b	.263	137	22	36	11	0	4	22	2
Martins, Eric, 2b-ss	.304	326	55	99	16	2	6	49	18
Miranda, Tony, of	.266	308	51	82	18	1	9	43	20
Norris, Sam, dh	.156	32	2	5	2	0	0	2	0
Sanchez, Toby, 3b	.286	234	36	67	13	0	7	41	5
Solano, Ben, 2b	.250	164	30	41	4	1	0	15	10
Vaughn, Lateef, of	.301	299	57	90	8	2	2	31	30
Yeager, Steve, of-c	.211	95	8	20	8	1	0	6	0

PITCHING

	W	L	ERA	G	SV	IP	H	BB	SO
Cly, Jason	6	5	5.04	17	0	84	104	19	44
Cuccias, Jon	0	0	0.00	2	0	2	0	0	2
Gonzalez, Gabe	1	4	1.47	29	5	43	38	9	30
Isaacson, Joe	1	4	4.05	28	0	47	51	19	30
Leslie, Reggie	8	6	5.33	21	1	106	121	42	86
Linares, Rich	2	1	4.03	6	0	38	40	12	21
3-team (12 SG/5 Sol.)	6	5	5.02	23	3	99	122	20	61
McCall, Travis	1	5	3.59	30	2	93	102	19	61
Pascarella, Josh	0	6	7.78	12	0	39	59	19	24
Russell, Eddie	2	2	6.65	6	1	22	25	13	14
Saipe, Mike	8	4	3.13	14	0	92	87	23	69
Samadani, A.J.	1	6	2.81	27	7	32	30	18	39
Sena, Jason	1	4	5.79	7	0	28	38	16	9
2-team (6 St. George)	1	5	6.64	13	0	41	55	28	20
Stephens, Shannon	0	1	3.24	2	0	8	10	2	6
Tomita, Wataru	0	0	4.05	12	0	20	20	12	15
Toriz, Steve	4	4	4.63	17	0	103	103	49	73
Turner, Eric	2	1	3.57	9	1	23	17	7	12
Verstratten, Robert	1	0	7.04	6	0	8	10	13	2
Wise, Andy	0	1	9.26	9	0	12	26	5	7

ST. GEORGE

BATTING

	AVG	AB	R	H	2B	3B	HR	RBI	SB
Ashley, Billy, dh	.278	79	19	22	5	1	7	21	2
Berry, Mike, 2b-3b	.310	142	24	44	9	1	5	30	1
Briones, Chris, c	.356	59	13	21	2	0	0	7	2
Bystrowski, Rob, of	.385	26	7	10	2	0	0	3	1
Craig, Benny, of	.283	276	53	78	18	1	16	54	2
Diaz, Alex, of	.313	16	3	5	2	0	0	3	0
Frank, Nick, ss-3b	.310	274	49	85	20	0	6	43	5
Fujimoto, Hiroshi, c-of	.274	62	14	17	4	1	0	8	1
Ging, Aaron, 2b-ss	.250	48	7	12	0	2	0	5	1
Grebeck, Brian, 2b-3b	.287	178	31	51	11	0	5	28	0
Huff, Jake, c-3b	.313	319	60	100	16	1	14	40	1
Jacobsen, Curtis, 3b-of	.500	28	6	14	2	0	0	6	0
Kolbach, Mike, of	.329	219	34	72	14	0	0	16	0

	AVG	AB	R	H	2B	3B	HR	RBI	SB
Lewis, Anthony, 1b	.248	379	49	94	24	5	22	90	3
Martinez, Greg, of	.455	101	27	46	11	4	0	22	15
McCall, Rob, dh	.254	189	30	48	5	0	12	32	0
Nelson, D.G., 3b-of	.233	43	9	10	3	1	0	2	2
Osuna, Ricky, of-ss	.307	218	44	67	10	6	1	38	7
Perry, Tyler, 2b-3b	.227	110	18	25	7	0	1	10	0
Romo, Pierre, c	.167	18	0	3	0	0	0	1	0
Sanchez, Toby, 3b	.242	62	15	15	1	0	4	9	0
2-team (64 Long Beach)	.277	296	51	82	14	0	11	50	5
Scott, Ed, of-2b	.146	48	9	7	0	0	0	7	5
Storke, Jon, ss-2b	.227	22	2	5	3	0	0	1	1
2-team (13 Sonoma)	.118	51	5	6	3	0	0	1	1
Trippy, Joe, of	.308	299	64	92	15	4	7	52	36

PITCHING	W	L	ERA	G	SV	IP	H	BB	SO
Buckles, Bucky	2	10	6.66	14	0	77	103	35	52
Butler, Adam	3	3	1.69	18	1	27	21	8	31
Caruso, Gene	2	4	8.49	7	0	35	57	19	20
Cepeda, Victor	0	2	6.00	5	0	21	31	3	11
Davison, Scott	3	0	3.25	28	8	36	38	7	30
Fahs, Derek	1	1	4.15	14	1	22	23	8	27
2-team (10 Sonoma)	2	1	6.97	24	2	31	38	15	38
Foster, Gabe	2	10	6.33	23	0	97	139	49	47
Gilich, Denny	0	0	4.50	2	0	2	2	2	2
Linares, Rich	3	3	6.82	12	3	33	47	6	21
Lubner, Ryan	5	7	7.62	14	0	65	92	35	38
Mercedes, Carlos	0	0	11.00	4	0	9	15	6	8
Meza, Nathan	2	1	6.88	25	0	34	44	27	23
Noe, Matthew	0	2	6.59	13	0	41	55	23	24
Pasqualicchio, Mike	4	1	6.00	40	1	57	64	32	43
Sena, Jason	0	1	8.53	6	0	13	17	12	11
Smith, Mike	7	4	5.76	15	0	100	129	30	74
Stockstill, Jason	3	1	6.00	22	0	48	59	29	36
Yeskie, Nate	2	1	9.18	9	0	49	90	15	25

SOLANO

BATTING	AVG	AB	R	H	2B	3B	HR	RBI	SB
Asencio, Alex, of	.285	263	41	75	14	3	0	28	9
Buckley, Mat, 2b-1b	.305	164	24	50	10	0	2	19	4
Cheatle, David, of-2b	.209	139	18	29	6	0	0	14	2
Clements, Jason, 2b-ss	.414	29	10	12	2	0	2	8	3
Escamilla, Roman, c	.326	89	8	29	2	0	0	12	5
Faggett, Ethan, of	.263	19	2	5	0	0	1	2	0
Goodwin, Curtis, of	.333	93	19	31	6	1	0	5	9
Gorman, Paul, 3b	.288	309	46	89	16	2	6	35	3
Hollins, Darontaye, of	.111	18	2	2	0	0	0	3	0
Kirby, Wayne, of	.267	131	21	35	8	0	4	18	5
Landreth, Jason, of	.299	341	59	102	22	12	13	61	20
Monahan, Shane, of-1b	.339	180	45	61	16	0	10	43	8
Ozuna, Rafael, ss	.286	343	50	98	22	4	5	46	8
Roth, Brett, c	.170	53	6	9	0	0	1	4	2
Sanchez, Victor, c-1b	.345	316	74	109	15	2	31	81	4
Torres, Paul, 1b-of	.315	232	47	73	17	2	10	46	2
Vopata, Nate, 2b	.236	216	31	51	10	4	5	30	2
Williams, Eddie, dh	.309	188	32	58	13	1	7	32	0

PITCHING	W	L	ERA	G	SV	IP	H	BB	SO
Brosnan, Jason	8	5	4.11	17	0	105	109	25	86
Brown, Darold	0	0	3.38	12	0	13	14	7	9
Caruso, Gene	2	4	8.91	13	1	34	53	22	29
2-team (7 St. George)	4	8	8.70	20	1	69	110	41	49
Davis, Jason	0	3	10.64	13	0	22	40	9	18
Kass, Mike	3	2	4.19	17	0	19	16	14	25
Lawrence, Mike	1	0	6.75	9	0	8	8	3	4
Linares, Rich	1	1	4.23	5	0	28	35	2	19
Lomon, Kevin	1	1	7.04	2	0	8	12	2	6
Luce, Rob	1	5	5.63	18	0	48	67	16	20
McDermott, Toby	4	1	3.69	9	0	63	62	25	37
McMullen, Mike	1	0	5.59	8	1	10	14	9	6
Menhart, Paul	1	2	7.03	5	0	24	33	9	22
Olsen, Jason	8	2	3.44	18	0	110	100	29	110
Rodriguez, Frankie	2	0	8.22	6	1	8	15	8	10
Sadler, Al	0	3	2.21	35	20	41	33	9	45
Shaw, Elliott	0	0	1.59	7	0	11	11	9	4
Stover, C.D.	8	2	2.77	41	1	65	66	13	55
Thompson, Jesse	6	5	5.51	26	0	78	89	40	64
Ugas, Juan	1	1	11.08	12	1	13	18	14	12
Wood, Stanton	5	0	2.92	17	2	77	86	20	64

SONOMA COUNTY

BATTING	AVG	AB	R	H	2B	3B	HR	RBI	SB
Adames, Winter, ss	.259	166	31	43	5	2	0	11	8
Bastida, Evel, 2b	.247	150	17	37	7	1	1	14	0
Capellan, Rene, 2b	.200	50	3	10	2	0	0	4	2
Durkac, Bo, 3b	.336	324	58	109	13	0	3	67	1

	AVG	AB	R	H	2B	3B	HR	RBI	SB
Lofton, James, ss	.212	52	10	11	2	0	0	2	1
Longmire, Marcel, of-1b	.323	65	10	21	4	1	1	6	2
McAffee, Josh, c	.191	230	38	44	11	0	8	32	1
Mitchell, Keith, of	.285	179	29	51	12	1	9	41	4
Montenegro, Jose, c-1b	.281	139	17	39	6	1	1	15	1
2-team (26 Yuma)	.275	233	32	64	10	1	1	23	1
Morales, Andy, 1b-3b	.286	35	4	10	2	0	1	8	0
Oglesby, Travis, 1b-of	.283	325	55	92	20	0	21	82	5
Patterson, Derek, 2b-ss	.264	140	21	37	11	1	4	23	4
Powell, Chris, of	.363	306	77	111	18	3	5	40	25
Pritchard, Jeff, of-c	.264	140	11	37	6	0	1	13	2
Rhein, Jeff, of	.143	21	1	3	1	0	0	4	1
2-team (59 Yuma)	.241	232	30	56	8	4	3	35	9
Rico, Diego, of	.255	216	42	55	16	0	2	25	4
2-team (26 Yuma)	.244	315	55	77	18	3	3	38	6
Rocha, Juan, of	.263	95	11	25	2	0	4	13	3
Sasaki, Makoto, dh	.290	314	52	91	12	3	6	42	10
Storke, Jon, ss-2b	.034	29	3	1	0	0	0	0	0
Templeton, Garry, ss-2b	.222	18	3	4	1	0	0	3	0
Valera, Ramon, dh	.188	16	2	3	0	0	0	5	0
Villalobos, Carlos, dh	.317	41	6	13	5	0	1	9	1

PITCHING	W	L	ERA	G	SV	IP	H	BB	SO
Davidson, Tim	4	6	6.37	18	0	82	105	43	56
Fahs, Derek	1	0	13.50	10	1	9	15	7	11
Garcia, Gabe	3	5	6.38	16	0	66	84	31	45
Gilich, Denny	0	0	10.80	3	0	5	8	5	3
2-team (2 St. George)	0	0	9.00	5	0	7	10	7	5
Grant, Brian	5	2	2.11	36	4	77	69	32	66
Hansen, N	3	2	4.58	18	0	55	62	17	40
Hooten, David	1	0	1.42	4	0	13	12	3	9
Kishita, Kirt	0	0	10.24	4	0	10	15	4	8
McCarter, Jason	0	2	9.00	4	0	11	21	9	3
Neboyia, Gabe	4	6	3.52	16	0	79	91	16	68
Pickford, Kevin	3	5	8.29	9	0	38	51	23	19
Pina, Rafael	2	2	4.26	5	0	25	31	4	12
Quintero, Mayque	2	3	4.33	11	0	44	46	23	46
Reeves, Scott	1	1	6.41	14	0	20	26	15	13
Roman, Rocky	7	4	4.79	18	0	92	95	37	66
Rose, Brian	3	2	1.55	25	8	41	28	10	39
2-team (15 Yuma)	4	5	2.64	40	9	61	67	17	46
Scott, Tim	3	0	0.91	27	15	30	20	3	44
Thompson, John	6	0	2.54	35	0	60	47	33	47

YUMA

BATTING	AVG	AB	R	H	2B	3B	HR	RBI	SB
Beauchamp, Kash, dh	.273	99	13	27	7	0	0	12	0
Capellan, Rene, of-2b	.187	107	11	20	2	0	0	9	1
2-team (18 Sonoma)	.191	157	14	30	4	0	0	13	3
Chapman, Scott, of	.157	51	1	8	2	1	0	8	0
Dighera, Nathan, c-1b	.167	24	0	4	0	0	0	1	0
Estrada, Marco, 3b-ss	.270	111	18	30	4	1	1	14	2
Funderburk, Levi, 1b	.265	234	27	62	8	1	4	25	0
Howard, Tim, of	.350	340	65	119	25	4	7	63	6
Kilburg, Joe, 2b-of	.287	356	65	102	15	5	3	31	5
Leon, Richy, ss-2b	.247	296	46	73	11	3	2	34	4
Longmire, Marcel, of-c	.288	212	32	61	7	4	4	30	4
2-team (20 Sonoma)	.296	277	42	82	11	5	5	36	6
Martinez, Jody, of	.056	18	0	1	0	0	0	0	0
Montenegro, Jose, 1b-c	.266	94	15	25	4	0	0	8	0
Rhein, Jeff, of	.251	211	29	53	7	3	3	31	8
Rico, Diego, of	.222	99	13	22	2	3	1	13	2
Roa, Hector, 3b	.304	316	50	96	19	4	5	47	10
Romo, Pierre, c	.000	7	1	0	0	0	0	0	0
2-team (7 St. George)	.120	25	1	3	0	0	0	1	0
Sutherland, Alex, c	.341	276	41	94	24	1	5	44	0
Villalobos, Carlos, 1b-of	.332	256	40	85	16	1	8	54	0
2-team (15 Sonoma)	.330	297	46	98	21	1	9	63	1

PITCHING	W	L	ERA	G	SV	IP	H	BB	SO
Bergan, Tom	5	5	6.03	17	0	78	112	31	47
Bond, Jason	5	5	6.15	23	0	101	99	60	91
Cowan, Bobby	4	2	3.18	48	3	65	61	27	46
Donnelly, Alex	2	4	5.47	24	0	26	36	7	17
Grzanich, Mike	0	1	10.43	7	0	15	23	17	11
Henderson, Ryan	3	4	4.15	30	9	61	56	38	52
Johnson, David	3	4	4.97	45	5	71	66	38	51
Lovett, George	0	0	5.40	3	0	10	16	3	6
Moore, Brad	6	8	4.80	24	0	96	88	49	84
Reyes, Pablo	1	4	4.12	8	0	44	54	12	27
Rose, Brian	1	3	4.79	15	1	21	39	7	16
Salcedo, Jose	3	3	2.93	10	0	55	44	19	52
Schourek, Pete	0	0	9.00	6	0	7	8	6	10
Sobkoviak, Jeff	4	3	5.51	21	0	83	108	21	51
Wilkerson, Steve	0	2	5.82	23	1	39	42	16	35
Zink, Charlie	0	0	5.40	4	0	4	4	6	9

FOREIGN

Tigers beat Reds in Mexico City final

BY JOHN ROYSTER

Any team that can lose a league batting champion and still average 8.3 runs per game has to be living the good life. That's what happened with the Mexico City Tigers, who were good enough to beat the Mexico City Red

MEXICO Devils four games to two in the 2001 Mexican League championship series.

The Tigers, who had the league's best regular-season record, actually had an easier time without Julio Franco, who left to join the Atlanta Braves at the Sept. 1 major league roster expansion. Franco, 40, who batted .437 in the Mexican League regular season, became the Braves' regular first baseman during their drive for the National League West title.

He left the Tigers on the eve of the Mexican League finals, just after they'd made up a 3-1 deficit to defeat the Monterrey Sultans in seven games in the semifinals.

There was much gnashing of teeth, but the Tigers went on to score in double figures four times in six games against the Red Devils. After spotting the Reds a 14-2 win in the first game, the Tigers won 11-6 and 11-8, lost 5-4 in 10 innings, then won 12-3 and 10-4. They made up a 4-0 deficit in Game Six.

Infielder Sergio Gastelum, who had just seven home runs during the regular season, had three in the pivotal Game Five. He drove in five runs.

The two Mexico City teams have played each other in four of the last five championship series, with the Tigers winning the last two. But the future of the rivalry was placed in jeopardy. Near the end of the regular season, Tigers owner Carlos Peralta threatened to move his team to Puebla for 2002.

Attendance for both of the Mexico City teams has lagged far behind their performance in recent years. Despite moving into the new Foro Sol Stadium in the middle of the 2000 season, the clubs have finished in the bottom half of the league in attendance in both 2000 and

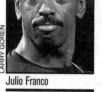

Julio Franco

LARRY GOREN

2001. In 2001, they finished in the bottom two spots in the 16-team league, averaging barely 1,000 fans per game.

Despite winning all four of the half-season championships in the Central Zone in that time, the league's two flagship franchises now draw much better on the road than they do at home.

"We draw fans everywhere else," Tigers president Chito Rodriguez said. "In Mexico City, we buy 1,500 giveaways and we'll have 500 left."

Barrera Eclipses Espino

The league had more than its share of notable on-field events in 2001, with easily the most notable being Nelson Barrera's establishment of a new career home runs record.

Barrera, who at the time was the Oaxaca Warriors'

manager and DH, hit No. 454 of his 25-year career on May 31, in the final game of the first half. It came on an 0-2 pitch in the second inning off Tabasco Cowboys righthander Gaudencio Aguirre.

The old record was established by Hector Espino over 24 seasons from 1962-84. Barrera, 43, opened the season needing eight homers to break it, and the chase became a distraction. He went without a home run from April 18 until he tied the record May 7, then went 24 days before breaking it.

"I hope things change for good on the team," Barrera said after hitting the record-breaker. "We are going to be calmer from here on out."

When Barrera got within two homers of the record, Espino's widow Carmen began traveling from park to park to be in atten-

Nelson Barrera

dance when the record fell. But after Barrera went into his homer drought, Mrs. Espino went home to Monterrey.

Barrera got even less respect from the Mexican media, which seemed underwhelmed by his achievement. He tied Espino's record in 9,650 at-bats, whereas Espino did it in 8,205 at-bats. Barrera was accused of using corked bats for part of his career, and he was trying to pass a player who remains a revered figure in the country four years after his death.

Barrera himself gave a nod to Espino after tying the record. "I'm not the best," he said. "Even in passing him, I would be equal to the best or a little below the best."

The final insult came about a month later, when the Warriors fired Barrera as manager and replaced him with coach Enrique Aguilar. Barrera remained as a player, but went on the disabled list shortly thereafter. He hit only one more home run after breaking the record.

Another Espino record fell when Red Devils center fielder and leadoff hitter Daniel Fernandez scored his 1,506th career run. Fernandez, 36 and in his 19th season with the Reds, broke the record with a solo homer in a 9-3 loss to the Union Laguna Cottoneers. It was just his 54th career home run.

Fernandez tried and failed to break another league record. After hitting .300 or more for a record-tying 14 straight seasons, he batted .290. Tigers first baseman Matias Carrillo will get a shot at the same record in 2002. He batted .309 to run his streak to 14 years, sandwiched around two stints in U.S. leagues. Carrillo has never failed to hit .300 in the Mexican League.

Saltillo Sarape Makers righthander Mike Romano pitched two of the season's four no-hitters, including the league's first ever in the playoffs. Romano, who pitched in three major league games for the Blue Jays in 1999, blanked Monterrey 9-0 in Game Six of a quarterfinal series.

Yucatan Lions lefthander Ravelo Manzanillo, who went 16-3 and won the ERA title at 1.52, no-hit the Campeche Pirates 1-0 in a seven-inning game.

STANDINGS

NORTH ZONE	W	L	T	PCT	GB
*Saltillo Sarape Makers	68	52	0	.567	—
Reynosa Broncos	69	53	0	.566	—
#Monclova Steelers	67	52	1	.563	½
Monterrey Sultans	68	53	0	.562	½
Union Laguna Cottoneers	61	59	0	.508	7
Two Laredos Owls	48	72	1	.400	20

CENTRAL ZONE	W	L	T	PCT	GB
*Mexico City Tigers	74	43	1	.632	—
#Mexico City Red Devils	69	51	0	.575	6½
Puebla Parrots	54	62	1	.466	19½
Oaxaca Warriors	50	69	1	.420	25
Cordoba Coffee Growers	38	78	0	.328	35½

SOUTH ZONE	W	L	T	PCT	GB
*Yucatan Lions	68	53	0	.562	—
#Campeche Pirates	62	56	0	.525	4½
Tabasco Cowboys	56	66	0	.459	12½
Veracruz Reds	55	66	0	.455	13
Cancun Lobstermen	49	71	1	.408	18½

*First-half champion #Second-half champion

PLAYOFFS—Quarterfinals: Monterrey defeated Saltillo 4-3; Mexico City Tigers defeated Campeche 4-2; Mexico City Red Devils defeated Yucatan 4-1; and Monclova defeated Reynosa 4-2 in best-of-7 series. **Semifinals:** Mexico City Tigers defeated Monterrey 4-3 and Mexico City Red Devils defeated Monclova 4-0 in best-of-7 series. **Finals:** Mexico City Tigers defeated Mexico City Red Devils 4-2 in best-of-7 series.

MANAGERS: Campeche—Eddie Diaz. **Cancun**—Javier Martinez, Marco Antonio Guzman. **Cordoba**—Noe Maduro, Gilberto Reyes. **Mexico City Red Devils**—Tim Johnson. **Mexico City Tigers**—Dan Firova. **Monclova**—Bernie Tatis. **Monterrey**—Derek Bryant. **Oaxaca**—Nelson Barrera, Enrique Aguilar. **Puebla**—Jose Juan Bellazetin. **Reynosa**—Raul Cano. **Tabasco**—Ramon Montoya. **Two Laredos**—Gerardo Sanchez, Andres Mora, Enrique Reyes. **Saltillo**—Houston Jimenez. **Union Laguna**—Francisco Chavez. **Veracruz**—Gilberto Reyes, Carlos Paz. **Yucatan**—Paquin Estrada.

REGULAR SEASON ATTENDANCE: Saltillo 613,551; Monterrey 536,351; Yucatan 501,370; Monclova 375,197; Oaxaca 193,868; Reynosa 169,994; Union Laguna 152,585; Two Laredos 125,299; Veracruz 122,632; Tabasco 122,084; Cordoba 111,237; Puebla 107,361; Campeche 103,961; Cancun 102,139; Mexico City Tigers 81,232; Mexico City Red Devils 74,198.

INDIVIDUAL BATTING LEADERS
(Minimum 329 Plate Appearances)

	AVG	AB	R	H	2B	3B	HR	RBI	SB
Franco, Julio, MC Tigers	.437	407	90	178	34	5	18	90	15
Orantes, Ramon, Monterrey	.363	355	46	129	15	0	10	50	0
Sherman, Darrell, Monclova	.355	403	83	143	15	1	6	43	30
Castellano, Pedro, MC Reds	.352	471	99	166	34	2	23	96	6
Bullett, Scott, Reynosa	.341	305	63	104	23	3	18	72	4
Chimelis, Joel, Laredo	.337	442	68	149	23	1	19	77	9
Iturbe, Pedro, Puebla	.337	356	51	120	24	3	9	46	8
Clark, Howie, Yucatan	.333	493	68	164	42	7	5	64	5
Garcia, Luis, MC Tigers	.332	368	73	122	25	5	19	82	16
Tellez, Alonso, Reynosa	.330	470	56	155	34	0	11	72	1
Zambrano, Roberto, Mont.	.329	340	43	112	19	1	8	49	1
Flores, Miguel, Monterrey	.328	390	75	128	26	1	11	56	28
Cruz, Fausto, UL	.325	421	75	137	20	3	14	70	5
Espinoza, Ramon, Reynosa	.321	523	83	168	30	1	9	44	15
Gastelum, Sergio, MC Tigers	.317	300	53	95	18	2	7	40	6
Mendez, Roberto, Oax/MC Reds	.314	366	67	115	27	1	15	70	12
Adriana, Sharnol, Campeche	.313	425	89	133	28	1	28	84	21
Contreras, Albino, Puebla	.313	294	45	92	16	6	6	52	7
Smith, Demond, Tab./Mont.	.313	326	68	102	21	9	10	39	36
Arredondo, Luis, Yucatan	.312	461	70	144	16	3	3	38	14
Ramirez, Jesus, Oaxaca	.312	295	38	92	16	0	0	31	2
Ojeda, Miguel, MC Reds	.310	422	78	131	17	3	16	65	4
Suarez, Luis, MC Tigers	.310	319	49	99	16	4	8	58	3
Vizcarra, Roberto, MC Tigers	.310	458	79	142	26	2	14	58	4
Mejia, Roberto, Tabasco	.310	329	46	102	18	3	12	49	8
Carrillo, Matias, MC Tigers	.309	369	64	114	20	0	14	66	3
Romero, Wilfredo, Saltillo	.308	325	75	100	22	2	12	53	23
Garcia, Cornelio, MC Reds	.307	280	35	86	9	1	1	33	2
Diaz, Remigio, Monterrey	.306	392	45	120	7	0	3	45	23
Seitzer, Brad, Can/Ver.	.306	327	33	100	19	1	5	51	0
Canizalez, Juan, Monterrey	.306	386	53	118	17	1	9	60	7
Pemberton, Rudy, Monclova	.306	396	63	121	34	1	14	84	9
Saenz, Ricardo, Monclova	.304	424	80	129	30	1	19	92	8
Barron, Tony, Can/Cam.	.304	392	65	119	23	0	22	66	4
Rodriguez, Boi, Monclova	.303	402	103	122	24	2	33	100	11
Newson, Warren, UL	.302	404	90	122	19	3	23	71	7

	AVG	AB	R	H	2B	3B	HR	RBI	SB
Sandoval, Jose, MC Reds	.301	395	52	119	22	1	11	64	1
Valdez, Francisco, Tabasco	.301	332	29	100	17	0	5	45	1
Gomez, Heber, Tabasco	.301	425	62	128	26	1	8	44	12
Otero, Ricky, Cancun	.301	402	60	121	22	7	8	35	8
Robles, Javier, MC Tigers	.300	383	53	115	22	3	20	68	5
Fornes, Daniel, Reynosa	.299	445	67	133	26	1	13	74	8
Munoz, Noe, Saltillo	.297	411	59	122	18	2	14	65	2
Robles, Oscar, Oaxaca	.296	466	71	138	26	2	5	51	4
White, Derrick, Mont/Lar.	.295	430	59	127	17	0	13	67	6
Diaz, Alex, UL	.295	315	53	93	18	1	13	60	9
Colina, Roberto, Puebla	.295	417	60	123	22	1	6	53	1
Sanchez, Roque, Campeche	.293	351	33	103	13	0	6	35	0
Rodarte, Raul, Rey/Cor.	.293	389	62	114	27	2	12	65	20
Brinkley, Darryl, Cam/Yuc.	.293	403	58	118	16	2	8	40	16

(Other Select Players)

	AVG	AB	R	H	2B	3B	HR	RBI	SB
Polonia, Luis, MC Tigers	.365	263	56	96	16	7	9	49	20
Benitez, Yamil, Reynosa	.347	121	21	42	6	1	5	28	6
Mendoza, Carlos, Saltillo	.319	72	9	23	3	0	0	6	4
Devarez, Cesar, Cordoba	.317	287	30	91	19	1	4	38	3
Magallanes, Bobby, Tigers/Pue	.310	187	27	58	22	0	3	34	2
Felix, Junior, Yucatan	.305	256	44	78	17	1	7	42	5
Malave, Jose, Ver/Salt.	.304	69	9	21	4	0	2	10	0
Ortiz, Luis, Mont/Tab.	.301	103	11	31	5	0	2	13	1
Magallanes, Ever, Monterrey	.300	150	23	45	3	0	3	16	1
Cedeno, Domingo, Cordoba	.296	247	38	73	4	5	4	18	12
Williams, Eddie, MC Reds	.295	241	51	71	11	0	12	54	0
Nunez, Raymond, Cor/Tab.	.294	337	47	99	17	2	11	41	0
De la Cruz, Lorenzo, Puebla	.291	344	48	100	16	3	13	67	9
Trapaga, Julio, MC Tigers	.288	52	13	15	2	0	0	8	2
Cappuccio, Carmine, Yucatan	.288	59	7	17	3	0	1	8	0
Garcia, Guillermo, Oaxaca	.288	132	22	38	7	0	8	24	0
Grijak, Kevin, MC Reds	.287	164	21	47	14	0	8	34	0
Tyler, Brad, Oaxaca	.286	255	44	73	12	3	11	54	9
Ball, Jeff, Cancun	.286	119	18	34	5	1	2	15	1
Amador, Jerry, UL	.286	7	1	2	0	0	0	1	1
Zazueta, Mauricio, Monclova	.285	369	60	105	15	0	11	55	23
Leday, A.J., Reynosa	.284	102	17	29	4	1	4	17	0
Velazquez, Guillermo, Salt.	.284	296	49	84	18	0	17	70	0
Pearson, Eddie, Tabasco	.284	194	26	55	6	0	9	38	0
Garcia, Omar, Ver/Yuc.	.282	354	48	100	19	0	13	75	1
Nava, Lipso, Ver/UL	.282	301	39	85	18	0	9	35	2
Brewer, Rod, Oax/Ver.	.282	404	83	114	21	0	26	86	3
Rodriguez, Carlos, Reynosa	.282	422	74	119	17	2	2	25	12
Gonzalez, Manny, Laredo	.281	167	22	47	6	1	3	21	6
Berroa, Geronimo, Camp.	.280	175	29	49	8	0	9	35	0
Presichi, Christian, Saltillo	.278	205	43	57	9	3	5	22	12
Smith, Bubba, Monterrey	.277	267	47	74	15	0	17	62	2
Garland, Tim, Tabasco	.277	130	14	36	5	1	0	9	5
Whiten, Mark, Veracruz	.277	376	80	104	13	0	33	78	5
Howard, Thomas, Monterrey	.274	84	11	23	6	0	3	16	0
Gibson, Derrick, Puebla	.270	259	44	70	11	1	13	45	1
Barrera, Nelson, Oaxaca	.268	265	30	71	12	0	9	43	0
Villanueva, Hector, Cor/Pue.	.266	289	35	77	16	0	9	46	0
Gordon, Keith, Saltillo	.266	94	11	25	4	2	5	23	1
Gorr, Rob, Tabasco	.265	98	15	26	4	0	3	11	1
Amettler, Jesus, Tabasco	.264	53	8	14	2	0	0	3	1
Murray, Glenn, Campeche	.261	222	39	58	13	1	18	50	1
Gainer, Jay, Tab/Cor.	.254	295	29	75	11	0	5	38	3
Jimenez, Houston, Saltillo	.250	8	1	2	0	0	0	0	0
Peters, Anthony, Yucatan	.250	44	4	11	1	0	0	3	3
Connell, Lino, Veracruz	.249	457	74	114	20	2	5	41	24
Boston, D.J., Cam/Can.	.244	311	44	76	7	0	9	37	8
Meulens, Hensley, Saltillo	.241	299	48	72	12	2	13	50	2
Lennon, Pat, Yucatan	.240	25	5	6	0	0	0	2	0
Amezcua, Adan, Monterrey	.238	147	9	35	8	0	1	12	3
Pacho, Juan, Yucatan	.238	265	21	63	5	1	0	23	0
Roberson, Kevin, Cor/UL	.235	153	16	36	12	0	2	19	0
Poe, Charles, Laredo	.233	30	3	7	1	0	0	3	0
Azocar, Oscar, Yucatan	.232	95	10	22	2	0	0	5	2
Matos, Malvin, Tabasco	.222	18	2	4	0	0	0	0	0
Powell, Corey, Reynosa	.220	91	7	20	2	0	3	10	0
Dattola, Kevin, Cam/Yuc.	.212	52	8	11	1	0	1	8	1
Sanchez, Gerardo, Lar./Tigers	.210	214	23	45	9	0	4	21	0
Samuels, Scott, Monterrey	.210	81	12	17	5	0	0	8	4
Pulliam, Harvey, Tabasco	.184	38	6	7	2	0	0	2	1
Ingram, Garey, Reynosa	.179	39	7	7	0	0	1	3	0
Myers, Rod, Monterrey	.167	30	1	5	0	0	0	1	1
Delgado, Alex, Tabasco	.150	40	3	6	1	0	0	4	0
Lewis, Anthony, Laredo	.147	34	1	5	2	0	0	3	0
Otanez, Willis, Monterrey	.143	56	5	8	1	0	1	5	0
Freeman, Ricky, Tabasco	.125	32	2	4	0	0	0	1	0
Anthony, Eric, Monterrey	.105	19	3	2	1	0	0	1	1
Peterson, Charles, UL	.000	10	0	0	0	0	0	1	1

INDIVIDUAL PITCHING LEADERS
(Minimum 98 Innings)

	W	L	ERA	G	SV	IP	H	BB	SO
Manzanillo, Ravelo, Yucatan	16	3	1.52	24	0	184	100	56	202
Lopez, Jose, Reynosa	5	4	1.79	70	41	101	76	33	94
Ruiz, Cecilio, Tabasco	14	2	1.94	19	0	121	114	20	67
Nunez, Jose, Laredo	6	5	2.80	14	0	106	87	16	82
Keppen, Jeff, Laredo	11	7	2.82	22	0	156	128	59	108
Romero, Alejandro, Monclova	9	3	2.83	23	0	156	129	42	102
Meza, Leobardo, Veracruz	7	4	2.84	21	0	124	125	34	67
Leyva, Edgar, Monterrey	10	5	2.91	22	0	127	109	34	125
Rios, Dan, UL	18	5	2.98	26	0	209	207	70	126
Kelley, Rich, Puebla	8	13	3.08	25	0	166	161	57	124
Campos, Francisco, Cam.	10	7	3.19	23	0	155	122	37	133
Quinonez, Enrique, Reynosa	9	8	3.24	25	0	147	148	38	76
Armenta, Alejandro, MC Tigers	15	4	3.26	23	0	149	127	59	110
Patrick, Bronswell, MC Reds	11	7	3.27	23	0	157	149	23	92
Manrique, Alberto, Reynosa	12	5	3.28	24	0	143	141	42	101
Rivera, Oscar, Veracruz	5	5	3.28	16	0	99	89	40	72
Munoz, Miguel, Cancun	11	6	3.30	22	0	136	138	26	56
Rivera, Lino, Monclova	14	6	3.34	22	0	151	138	37	65
Esquer, Mercedes, Reynosa	10	5	3.35	23	0	113	120	29	61
Delahoya, Javier, Saltillo	7	4	3.39	18	0	98	101	23	74
Pineda, Israup, Monterrey	5	2	3.40	39	1	103	98	45	89
Reyes, Nathanael, Saltillo	9	6	3.41	29	0	106	107	30	63
Theodile, Robert, Saltillo	6	6	3.42	18	0	108	106	45	64
Kammar, Emil, Monclova	9	5	3.44	18	0	102	97	36	34
Vega, Obed, Cancun	7	5	3.44	21	1	99	96	36	84
Olague, Jesus, Puebla	9	7	3.49	22	0	137	137	52	105
Mora, Eleazar, Veracruz	9	7	3.51	24	0	154	163	32	90
Palafox, Manuel, Monclova	13	7	3.52	23	0	156	155	43	62
Acosta, Aaron, Cor/Cam.	6	4	3.66	20	0	108	100	55	73
Ramirez, Roberto, MC Reds	9	3	3.66	16	0	98	111	19	67
Gonzalez, Arturo, Monterrey	10	7	3.68	22	0	120	117	35	49
Atondo, Sergio, Yucatan	4	6	3.69	24	0	107	104	48	109
Vargas, Joel, Tabasco	6	8	3.70	24	0	139	150	53	57
Drahman, Brian, Laredo	7	9	3.72	29	0	148	136	56	103
Henthorne, Kevin, MC Tigers	8	2	3.82	21	0	108	124	31	49
Cuervo, Bernardo, Yucatan	7	7	3.82	23	0	118	142	37	51
Perez, Leo, Cordoba	7	7	3.83	24	0	153	155	50	76
Moreno, Angel, UL	9	11	3.86	26	0	177	207	45	110
Morales, Luis, Veracruz	7	9	3.88	21	0	109	106	20	88

(Other Select Players)

	W	L	ERA	G	SV	IP	H	BB	SO
Lomon, Kevin, UL	1	0	0.00	4	1	5	3	2	5

	W	L	ERA	G	SV	IP	H	BB	SO
Palacios, Vicente, Saltillo	0	0	0.00	3	1	3	1	2	5
Chavez, Carlos, Yucatan	3	0	1.45	58	27	75	55	17	86
Mattson, Rob, Tabasco	4	6	1.91	26	3	33	29	7	12
Marquez, Isidro, Campeche	9	2	2.15	48	5	63	53	18	42
Hernandez, Santos, MC Tigers	3	2	2.30	53	38	63	55	28	66
Hartmann, Pete, Oaxaca	2	0	2.33	3	0	19	16	6	17
Magee, Danny, Monc/Cam.	7	6	2.61	15	0	90	76	47	88
Harris, Reggie, Veracruz	0	0	2.65	19	13	17	10	6	17
Parra, Jose, MC Reds/Oax.	5	5	2.70	57	33	63	50	30	63
Warren, Brian, Monterrey	0	2	2.87	16	13	16	14	4	10
Weaver, Eric, Puebla	0	0	2.93	13	0	15	15	10	15
Manzano, Adrian, MC Tigers	5	0	3.11	28	0	38	36	16	22
Rossiter, Mike, Tabsco	0	1	3.18	16	10	17	16	12	14
Huisman, Rick, Monterrey	0	0	3.27	11	0	11	11	6	8
Galvez, Randy, MC Reds	4	2	3.31	8	0	54	54	14	22
Burrows, Terry, Saltillo	4	3	3.36	10	0	59	57	31	35
Perez, Yorkis, MC Reds	2	4	3.51	57	0	51	52	15	56
Daniels, John, UL	0	2	3.52	6	2	8	8	5	8
Alberto, Jose, Saltillo	2	1	3.54	12	1	41	29	14	38
Wallace, Kent, Veracruz	1	2	3.68	19	13	22	20	4	22
Diaz, Rafael, Monterrey	1	6	3.76	13	0	53	55	27	48
Cecena, Jose, Monclova	3	3	3.78	36	2	50	57	17	32
Martinez, Pedro, Campeche	5	5	3.81	14	0	76	71	37	44
Ramos, Edgar, Oaxaca	4	8	3.88	17	0	107	116	28	91
Osuna, Ricardo, Tabasco	8	6	3.89	21	0	125	111	49	75
Dishman, Glenn, Reynosa	3	3	3.92	9	0	41	38	28	29
Romano, Mike, Saltillo	10	7	3.97	21	0	134	140	55	103
Perez, Dario, Oaxaca	5	8	4.06	16	1	89	100	12	32
Miranda, Angel, MC Reds/Oax.	4	4	4.22	22	0	64	61	31	48
Garcia, Ramon, Mont./Puebla	1	2	4.26	29	0	44	51	28	26
Andujar, Luis, Monterrey	3	2	4.67	13	3	17	20	10	12
Alvarez, Tavo, MC Reds	4	7	4.91	16	0	92	114	19	54
Newman, Jeff, Monclova	0	2	5.06	13	6	11	12	8	8
Flynt, Will, Saltillo	2	2	5.40	5	0	30	45	7	17
Mattson, Craig, Reynosa	2	2	5.79	22	0	33	34	29	17
Pujals, Denis, MC Tigers	1	1	6.27	16	1	19	21	12	10
Pina, Rafael, Oaxaca	1	2	6.65	4	0	22	27	10	10
Babineaux, Darrin, Laredo	1	5	7.90	6	0	27	36	14	14
Henry, Dwayne, Reynosa	1	0	8.80	13	0	15	18	10	15
Wagner, Matt, MC Tigs/Pue.	1	1	9.00	14	1	16	25	12	16
Ward, Chad, Campeche	0	2	10.38	4	0	13	18	7	6
Sak, James, Campeche	0	0	10.80	2	0	2	1	8	2
Davis, Ray, Veracruz	0	0	10.89	9	2	19	33	12	19
Garcia, Mike, MC Reds	0	2	11.45	12	3	11	21	4	11
Mathews, Del, Monterrey	0	1	17.18	2	0	4	7	4	5
Huntsman, Scott, Puebla	0	0	40.50	2	0	1	2	4	1

Santiago wins third straight title

BY MILTON JAMAIL

For the third straight season in 2001, Santiago de Cuba won the Serie Nacional championship. Santiago went 55-35 during the regular season, defeated Granma and Camaguey in the quarterfinals and semifinals, then took four of five games from Pinar del Rio to win the title.

CUBA

The 2000-2001 season, the 40th since Cuban baseball returned to an exclusively amateur status, was one of the most exciting ever. A new livelier ball, the Mizuno 150, resulted in a record number of home runs. The ball is the same one now used in international tournaments.

Outfielder Osmani Urrutia of Las Tunas won the batting title with a .431 average, and Villa Clara shortstop Eduardo Paret set a league record with 99 runs in a 90-game season. The home run lead was shared by Havana infielder Oscar Macias and Guantanamo outfielder Roberquis Videaux with 23.

Most of the pitching categories were dominated by righthander Maels Rodriguez of Sancti Spiritus. The 21-year-old sensation went 15-6, tying for the most wins in the league. He led the league in strikeouts (263), ERA (1.77), innings (178), starts (23) and walks (76).

His 263 strikeouts were the most ever by a pitcher in a Cuban League season—by far. The old record of 207 had stood since 1969. During the 1999-2000 season, Rodriguez—whose fastball touches 100 mph—pitched the first

STANDINGS

GROUP A	W	L	PCT	GB
Pinar del Rio	59	31	.656	—
Isla de la Juventud	53	37	.589	6
Metropolitanos	40	50	.444	19
Matanzas	36	54	.400	23

GROUP B	W	L	PCT	GB
Industriales	50	40	.556	—
Havana	50	40	.556	—
Sancti Spiritus	38	52	.422	12
Cienfuegos	28	62	.311	22

GROUP C	W	L	PCT	GB
Villa Clara	59	31	.656	—
Camaguey	53	37	.589	6
Ciego de Avila	35	55	.389	24
Las Tunas	25	65	.278	34

GROUP D	W	L	PCT	GB
Granma	55	35	.611	—
Santiago de Cuba	55	35	.611	—
Guantanamo	43	47	.478	12
Holguin	41	49	.456	14

PLAYOFFS—Quarterfinals: Santiago de Cuba defeated Granma, 3-1; Camaguey defeated Villa Clara 3-1; Havana defeated Isla de la Juventud 3-1; and Pinar del Rio defeated Industriales 3-2 in best-of-5 series. **Semifinals:** Santiago de Cuba defeated Camaguey 4-2 and Pinar del Rio defeated Havana 4-0 in best-of-7 series. **Finals:** Santiago de Cuba defeated Pinar del Rio 4-1 in best-of-7 series.

perfect game in the 40 years of the current Cuban league.

After the season, 50 players were selected to play on two teams in international tournaments in Holland, Italy and Venezuela, and in a series against Nicaragua in Cuba. That was followed by three weeks of training in Venezuela and three more in Japan, where the Cuban team faced the national teams of Korea, Taiwan, China and Italy in preparation for the World Cup in November in Taiwan.

The national included the infield quartet of Omar Linares, German Mesa, Antonio Pacheco and Orestes Kindelan—all in their mid-30s—that has been the cornerstone of Cuban baseball for more than a decade, as well as outfielder Yasser Gomez, 21, and infielder Michel Enriquez, 22. The strength of team lies in its pitching, which includes Rodriguez, Norge Vera, Jose Contreras, Pedro Lazo, Ciro Licea and Jose Ibar, and two young pitchers, Vicyohandry Odelin and lefthander Lemay de la Rosa.

Righthander Mayque Quintero and middle infielder Evel Bastida, both of whom played for Industriales, defected early in 2001 and signed with Sonoma of the independent Western League. Quintero, who was on the Cuban junior national team in 1995, was Industriales' best starting pitcher during the 1999-2000 season at 10-5, 1.90.

Another Industriales starter, lefthander Rolando Viera, also left Cuba during the year and signed with the Boston Red Sox. None of the players who left were in the mix for the Cuban national team.

INDIVIDUAL BATTING LEADERS
(Minimum 243 At-Bats)

	AVG	AB	R	H	2B	3B	HR	RBI
Urrutia, Osmani, Las Tunas	.431	290	62	125	14	0	16	65
Ramos, Alexander, IJ	.404	364	76	147	15	1	8	57
Perdomo, Michel, Villa Clara	.393	267	50	105	16	5	9	5
Rosell, Reemberto, Cienfuegos	.377	377	56	142	14	3	0	26
Scull, Antonio, Industriales	.375	285	73	107	25	0	16	74
Vega, Mario, Ciego de Avila	.373	338	66	126	22	0	4	41
Borrero, Ariel, Villa Clara	.371	337	63	125	21	10	17	83
Gonzalez, Ignacio, Havana	.364	308	69	112	24	1	16	67
Martinez, Issac, Ciego de Avila	.360	322	62	116	25	2	13	57
Gourriel, Luis, Sancti Spiritus ..	.354	316	47	112	15	6	6	46

INDIVIDUAL PITCHING LEADERS
(Minimum 90 Innings)

	W	L	ERA	G	IP	BB	SO
De la Rosa, Lemay, Havana	14	1	2.90	21	133	56	124
Montes de Oca, Eliecer, VC	15	3	2.98	24	166	45	121
Fernandez, Neury, Camaguey	12	4	3.89	22	137	41	72
Lazo, Pedro, Pinar del Rio	11	4	4.33	23	156	20	75
Garcia, Aleydis, IJ	8	3	3.42	29	100	22	49
Rodriguez, Maels, SS	15	6	1.77	24	178	76	263
Machado, Jorge Luis, Industriales	10	4	3.43	19	118	19	81
Odelin, Vicyohondri, Camaguey	12	5	2.54	22	149	38	130
Contreras, Jose. Pinar del Rio	14	6	3.50	24	159	45	188
Gonzalez, Orestes, Pinar del Rio	7	3	3.59	36	93	11	61

ASIA

Rhodes stars, but Yakult wins title

BY WAYNE GRACZYK

Japanese baseball actually survived its first season in eight years without Ichiro Suzuki, and the Yakult Swallows defeated the Osaka Kintetsu Buffaloes in a 2001 Japan Series between unlikely opponents.

JAPAN Central League champion Yakult won its first Japan Series crown since 1997, beating the Pacific League's Buffaloes four games to one. Kintetsu is the only one of Japan's 12 franchises never to have won a Japan Series.

The Swallows rose to the top after consecutive fourth-place finishes in 1998, 1999 and 2000, and the Buffaloes were last in the PL those latter two years. Preseason predictions by sportswriters and fans forecast the two teams would again finish in the second division.

But Yakult got 21 wins from three pitchers who walked into the club's fall camp for tryouts in October 2000, after being released by other teams. The Swallows also went virtually injury-free until mid-September, when star catcher Atsuya Furuta sprained a knee and missed three weeks.

Tuffy Rhodes
WAYNE GRACZYK

By that time the Swallows had built a sizable lead over the defending champion Tokyo Yomiuri Giants, the preseason favorite to win the CL again. Leading the Yakult charge was Venezuelan first baseman Roberto Petagine, whose 39 home runs and 127 RBIs led the league. Petagine also hit .322 and was named the CL's MVP.

Most of the excitement in the Pacific League, with Ichiro having left the Orix BlueWave for Seattle, was caused by American Tuffy Rhodes of the Buffaloes. He tied the single-season Japanese record for home runs with 55, matching Sadaharu Oh's total from 1964. Rhodes drove in 131 runs, scored 137 and batted .327 to earn PL MVP recognition.

Giants slugger Hideki Matsui, the 2000 CL homer and RBI leader thought to be a triple-crown candidate, won the batting title with a .333 average. Chiba Lotte Marines first baseman Kazuya Fukuura hit .346 to take the PL batting title, won by Ichiro the previous seven seasons.

Foreign pitchers winning individual titles in the PL were Marines righthander Nate Minchey, who led with a 3.26 ERA despite a 12-14 record, and Fukuoka Daiei Hawks closer Rod Pedraza, who had 34 saves.

The season was extended to 140 games, up from 135 in 2000, and the year saw the opening of the country's sixth all-weather stadium. The 43,000-capacity Sapporo Dome on the island of Hokkaido was unveiled June 26 when the Giants and Dragons played. The third and final game of the all-star series also was played at Sapporo Dome in July. The Pacific League won to take the series two games to one.

Four high-profile managers resigned at the end of the year, led by Shigeo Nagashima of the Giants. Also hanging up their thinking caps were Senichi Hoshino of Chunichi, Akira Ogi of Orix and Osamu Higashio of Seibu.

CENTRAL LEAGUE STANDINGS

	W	L	T	PCT	GB
Yakult Swallows	76	58	6	.567	—
Yomiuri Giants	75	63	2	.543	3
Yokohama BayStars	69	67	4	.507	8
Hiroshima Carp	68	65	7	.511	7½
Chunichi Dragons	62	74	4	.456	15
Hanshin Tigers	57	80	3	.416	20½

NOTE: Hiroshima had a higher winning percentage than Yokohama, but the BayStars were awarded third place on the basis of having more wins than the Carp.

FOREIGN LEAGUES

INDIVIDUAL BATTING LEADERS
(Minimum 434 Plate Appearances)

	AVG	AB	R	H	2B	3B	HR	RBI	SB
Matsui, Hideki, Giants	.333	481	107	160	23	3	36	104	3
Furuta, Atsuya, Swallows	.324	441	59	143	23	0	15	66	1
Petagine, Roberto, Swallows	.322	463	93	149	27	0	39	127	4
Suzuki, Takanori, BayStars	.315	454	56	143	22	1	6	57	15
Kanemoto, Tomoaki, Carp	.314	472	101	148	28	1	25	93	19
Manaka, Mitsuru, Swallows	.312	449	61	140	26	1	7	36	7
Inaba, Atsunori, Swallows	.311	527	94	164	32	5	25	90	5
Lopez, Luis, Carp	.308	493	53	152	21	0	32	100	0
Diaz, Eddy, Carp	.304	470	76	143	18	1	32	85	5
Saeki, Takahiro, BayStars	.302	490	58	148	18	2	14	73	11
Takahashi, Yoshinobu, Giants	.302	543	88	164	26	0	27	85	3
Hiyama, Shinjiro, Tigers	.300	406	52	122	24	0	12	57	7
Kiyohara, Kazuhiro, Giants	.298	467	67	139	29	0	29	121	0
Ishii, Takuro, BayStars	.295	580	81	171	34	4	8	36	26
Akahoshi, Norihiro, Tigers	.292	438	70	128	9	4	1	23	39
Tatsunami, Kazuyoshi, Dragons	.292	507	52	148	30	2	9	65	6
Motoki, Daisuke, Giants	.292	391	51	114	16	3	9	39	3
Iwamura, Akinori, Swallows	.287	520	79	149	24	4	18	81	15
Eto, Akira, Giants	.285	485	86	138	21	1	30	87	9
Ramirez, Alex, Swallows	.280	510	60	143	23	0	29	88	1
Nishi, Toshihisa, Giants	.273	597	83	163	29	1	20	59	20
Nomura, Kenjiro, Carp	.273	403	35	110	18	1	9	53	7
Kinjo, Tatsuhiko, BayStars	.271	480	68	130	19	2	3	49	10
Miyamoto, Shinya, Swallows	.270	477	74	129	15	0	1	17	11
Imaoka, Makoto, Tigers	.268	400	36	107	15	0	4	40	3
Nakamura, Takeshi, Dragons	.265	412	29	109	16	0	2	27	1
Ogawa, Hirofumi, BayStars	.264	420	48	111	16	0	15	65	3
Kimura, Takuya, Carp	.263	551	78	145	23	5	7	45	18
Hamanaka, Osamu, Tigers	.263	411	52	108	18	2	13	53	3
Higashide, Akihiro, Carp	.262	545	82	143	22	5	5	35	26
Ibata, Hirokazu, Dragons	.262	531	53	139	25	3	1	32	14
Tanishige, Motonobu, BayStars	.262	447	54	117	19	2	20	70	4
Fukudome, Kosuke, Dragons	.251	375	51	94	22	2	15	56	8
Dobashi, Katsuyuki, Swallows	.249	442	21	110	16	0	2	31	1

(Remaining U.S. and Latin America Players)

	AVG	AB	R	H	2B	3B	HR	RBI	SB
Zuber, Jon, BayStars	.310	232	19	72	14	2	2	27	1
Gomez, Leo, Dragons	.306	291	30	89	13	0	19	61	0
Doster Dave, BayStars	.272	309	35	84	14	0	9	27	3
Evans, Tom, Tigers	.242	124	7	30	4	0	2	14	1
Martinez, Domingo, Giants	.237	135	13	32	6	0	10	27	1
Cruz, Ivan, Tigers	.234	239	19	56	5	0	14	34	0
Timmons, Ozzie, Dragons	.228	272	30	62	9	1	12	45	1
Perez, Eduardo, Tigers	.222	167	20	37	11	0	3	19	3
Unroe, Tim, Dragons	.143	7	1	1	1	0	0	0	0
Sanders, Anthony, BayStars	.114	44	3	5	0	0	1	1	0

INDIVIDUAL PITCHING LEADERS
(Minimum 140 Innings)

	W	L	ERA	G	SV	IP	H	BB	SO
Noguchi, Shigeki, Dragons	12	9	2.46	26	0	194	167	28	187
Iguchi, Kei, Tigers	9	13	2.67	29	0	192	174	89	171
Miura, Daisuke, BayStars	11	6	2.88	26	0	169	137	53	135
Komiyama, Satoru, BayStars	12	9	3.03	24	0	149	150	30	74
Kuroda, Hiroki, Carp	12	8	3.03	27	0	190	175	45	146
Fujii, Shugo, Swallows	14	8	3.17	27	0	173	145	64	124
Bunch, Mel, Dragons	10	8	3.38	25	0	160	158	63	151
Ishii, Kazuhisa, Swallows	12	6	3.39	27	0	175	135	82	173
Hansell, Greg, Tigers	5	13	3.49	27	0	162	145	75	123
Sasaoka, Shinji, Carp	7	10	3.59	32	7	140	154	31	92
Yamamoto, Masahiro, Dragons	10	13	3.63	28	0	164	160	44	98
Iriki, Yusaku, Giants	13	4	3.71	27	1	162	143	58	137
Kawakami, Kenshin, Dragons	6	10	3.72	26	0	145	153	36	127
Carlyle, Buddy, Tigers	7	10	3.87	28	0	153	151	64	111
Maeda, Hirotsugu, Swallows	7	10	3.93	28	0	147	162	44	85
May, Darrell, Giants	10	8	4.13	26	0	159	160	45	168
Takahashi, Ken, Carp	10	8	4.27	30	0	173	165	60	132

(Remaining U.S. and Latin America Players)

	W	L	ERA	G	SV	IP	H	BB	SO
Gaillard, Eddie, Dragons	0	1	2.12	47	29	47	34	11	24
Young, Tim, Carp	0	0	3.00	5	0	3	4	2	0
Schullstrom, Erik, Carp	0	1	3.27	22	11	22	21	8	14
Hodges, Kevin, Swallows	5	3	3.80	12	0	66	73	34	30
Newman, Alan, Swallows	3	4	4.18	17	0	60	61	12	38
Bowers, Shane, BayStars	3	13	4.34	25	0	127	129	48	95
Ludwick, Eric, Carp	2	6	5.18	17	0	82	92	37	69
Hurst, Jonathan, Swallows	1	1	5.97	22	0	35	43	11	13
Almonte, Hector, Giants	0	1	7.36	4	0	4	5	3	5
Holzemer, Mark, BayStars	0	2	9.00	6	0	19	31	12	10

	W	L	T	PCT	GB
Osaka Kintetsu Buffaloes	78	60	2	.565	—
Fukuoka Daiei Hawks	76	63	1	.547	2 ½
Seibu Lions	73	67	0	.521	6
Orix BlueWave	70	66	4	.515	7
Chiba Lotte Marines	64	74	2	.464	14
Nippon Ham Fighters	53	84	3	.387	24 ½

INDIVIDUAL BATTING LEADERS
(Minimum 434 Plate Appearances)

	AVG	AB	R	H	2B	3B	HR	RBI	SB
Fukuura, Kazuya, Marines	.346	451	82	156	30	4	18	67	0
Ogasawara, Michihiro, Fighters	.339	576	108	195	40	2	32	86	1
Matsunaka, Nobuhiko, Hawks	.334	479	81	160	29	0	36	122	2
Rhodes, Tuffy, Buffaloes	.327	550	137	180	19	0	55	131	5
Tani, Yoshitomo, BlueWave	.325	547	99	178	52	3	13	79	27
Isobe, Koichi, Buffaloes	.320	537	82	172	42	4	17	95	7
Nakamura, Norihiro, Buffaloes	.320	525	109	168	25	0	46	132	3
Valdes, Pedro, Hawks	.310	526	95	163	31	0	21	81	1
Matsui, Kazuo, Lions	.308	552	94	170	28	2	24	76	26
Shibahara, Hiroshi, Hawks	.302	587	95	177	35	2	7	49	8
Mizuguchi, Eiji, Buffaloes	.290	403	48	117	10	0	3	30	1
Kokubo, Hiroki, Hawks	.290	535	108	155	32	1	44	123	6
Ide, Tatsuya, Fighters	.288	427	66	123	20	2	11	35	14
Cabrera, Alex, Lions	.282	514	96	145	23	0	49	124	3
May, Derrick, Marines	.282	490	59	138	31	0	31	91	0
Taguchi, So, BlueWave	.280	453	70	127	21	6	8	42	6
Ozeki, Tatsuya, Lions	.280	407	41	114	17	4	3	38	17
Bolick, Frank, Marines	.279	452	84	126	34	0	31	101	1
Vitiello, Joe, BlueWave	.275	407	52	112	21	0	22	83	0
Omura, Naoyuki, Buffaloes	.271	590	82	160	34	2	16	53	5
Katsuragi, Ikuro, BlueWave	.268	418	67	112	24	2	14	53	1
Yoshioka, Yuji, Buffaloes	.265	456	76	121	22	1	26	85	2
Oshima, Koichi, BlueWave	.263	414	67	109	19	0	1	31	4
Shiozaki, Makoto, BlueWave	.262	439	58	115	17	3	4	45	10
Kosaka, Makoto, Marines	.262	550	79	144	16	8	1	35	32
Arias, George, BlueWave	.262	543	70	142	19	1	38	97	3
Iguchi, Tadahiro, Hawks	.261	552	104	144	26	1	30	97	44
Jojima, Kenji, Hawks	.258	534	63	138	18	0	31	95	9
Tanaka, Yukio, Fighters	.255	491	46	125	22	0	20	77	2
Kataoka, Atsushi, Fighters	.254	401	57	102	18	1	16	62	1

(Remaining U.S. and Latin America Players)

	AVG	AB	R	H	2B	3B	HR	RBI	SB
Gilbert, Shawn, Buffaloes	.267	255	32	68	18	1	6	24	3
Obando, Sherman, Fighters	.259	201	29	52	7	0	15	51	0
McClain, Scott, Lions	.247	481	77	119	28	0	39	87	3
Wilson, Nigel, Fighters	.225	120	13	27	2	1	6	14	0
Mitchell, Tony. Hawks	.193	181	17	35	1	0	10	20	0
Garcia, Freddy, Buffaloes	.153	85	8	13	3	0	1	5	0

INDIVIDUAL PITCHING LEADERS
(Minimum 140 Innings)

	W	L	ERA	G	SV	IP	H	BB	SO
Minchey, Nate, Marines	12	14	3.26	30	0	204	196	63	102
Hsu, Ming-chieh, Lions	11	6	3.47	27	0	140	140	64	67
Matsuzaka, Daisuke, Lions	15	15	3.60	33	0	240	184	117	214
Ogura, Hisashi, BlueWave	11	7	3.62	26	0	164	156	26	128
Kato, Shinichi, BlueWave	11	7	3.69	27	0	168	175	45	92
Ono, Shingo, Marines	13	9	3.74	27	0	164	164	64	124
Tanoue, Keizaburo, Hawks	11	7	3.77	29	0	172	172	42	99
Kato, Kosuke, Marines	9	10	4.11	34	0	140	134	68	109
Hoshino, Junji, Hawks	13	9	4.35	30	0	176	197	50	82
Nishiguchi, Fumiya, Lions	13	9	4.35	28	0	165	156	85	143
Kanemura, Satoru, Fighters	7	13	4.89	25	0	142	164	66	94
Iwamoto, Tsutomu, Fighters	7	12	4.91	22	0	143	150	60	94
Maekawa, Katsuhiko, Buffaloes	12	9	5.89	28	0	141	140	85	84

(Remaining U.S. and Latin America Players)

	W	L	ERA	G	SV	IP	H	BB	SO
Mirabal, Carlos, Fighters	8	6	3.44	51	18	55	62	16	43
Pedraza, Rod, Hawks	4	4	3.65	54	34	57	63	10	32
Yarnall, Ed, BlueWave	4	3	3.93	15	0	73	52	47	82
Bergman, Sean, Buffaloes	10	4	4.18	18	0	108	117	28	59
Raggio, Brady, Hawks	9	6	4.31	22	0	125	145	58	66
Sanders, Scott, Fighters	3	5	4.36	24	0	87	87	45	70
Powell, Jeremy, Buffaloes	4	5	4.95	14	0	80	84	40	52
Elvira, Narciso, BlueWave	1	1	5.47	6	0	25	27	11	16
Del Toro, Miguel, Lions	1	1	5.59	14	0	19	28	5	19
Haney, Chris, Hawks	2	4	5.74	7	0	31	34	12	16
Sikorski, Brian, Marines	1	4	6.43	12	0	42	48	18	31
Pulido, Carlos, BlueWave	1	3	8.35	11	0	18	25	12	16
Ohme, Kevin, Fighters	0	2	14.85	3	0	7	10	3	4
Kubenka, Jeff, Marines	0	1	18.00	3	0	2	4	4	1
Flynt, Will, Buffaloes	0	0	27.00	1	0	0	2	1	0

FOREIGN LEAGUES

MVP Woods caps off huge season

BY THOMAS ST. JOHN

Doosan Bears first baseman Tyrone Woods came up huge as the Bears beat the Samsung Lions four games to two in the 2001 Korean Series..

Woods batted .391-4-10 and was the backbone of a team that showed it was hungrier than Samsung despite finishing 13½ games behind the first-place Lions in the regular season. Woods, in his fourth year in Korea, set a new career postseason record with 13 homers.

KOREA

He also became the first player to win the MVP awards for the regular season, the all-star game and the Korean Series. His final playoff homer was measured at more than 450 feet, easily sailing out of the Olympic Baseball Stadium in Seoul.

"We have worked so hard for this all season," Woods said. "We deserved this and it feels so good to be on top."

A partial power outage delayed the final out of the final game. With Doosan leading 6-5 with two outs, the Lions had two runners on base in the bottom of the ninth inning, with star slugger Lee Seung-yeop

Tyrone Woods

THOMAS ST. JOHN

advancing to the plate. A hit would likely tie the game, and an out would give the Bears their third Korean championship.

Doosan closer Jin Pil-jung had been a rock throughout the series, and Lee had been his usual clutch-hitting self. The next few pitches promised considerable drama. But as Lee stepped to the plate, the outfield lights went out and the game was delayed about 15 minutes until they were brought back on. Lee singled without a run scoring, and the next batter ended the game with a ground ball.

The series was odd in that both teams' pitching was slaughtered, especially in games 3-5 with a record 67 combined runs scored. Doosan broke the record for runs in an inning with 12 in Game Four. All pitchers were hit hard except lefthander Lee Hye-chun, 21, who picked up Doosan's first two wins.

The playoffs had been placed in jeopardy when the players' union threatened a boycott. The Korean Pro Baseball Players' Association campaigned during the latter half of the season for a reduction in the import-player limit from three to two per team. When the league didn't make a decision before the eve of the playoffs, the union decided to force the issue.

An 11th-hour agreement was reached to play the first round, and a second accord came later. The 2002 season will be the last with three foreign players per team. From 2003, just two will be allowed. Also, teams will be allowed to replace a released foreign player just once per season. Previously, teams could make unlimited changes.

"We are not against foreign players in the KBO," former KPBPA chairman Song Jin-woo said. "The league is not big enough to support three per team. Since foreigners usually occupy first and third base, fewer and fewer Korean amateurs are playing those positions."

Foreign players were prominent among the regular season statistical leaders. Woods won the RBI championship

and finished in the top three for home runs and runs. He batted .291-34-127.

Lotte Giants DH Felix Jose finished first in both slugging percentage (.695) and on-base percentage (.503). Hanwha Eagles outfielder Jay Davis finished with 166 hits, one behind the LG Twins' Lee Byung-kyu.

STANDINGS

	W	L	T	PCT	GB
Samsung Lions	81	52	0	.609	—
Hyundai Unicorns	72	57	4	.558	7
Doosan Bears	65	63	5	.508	13 ½
Hanwha Eagles	61	68	4	.473	18
Kia Tigers	60	68	5	.469	18 ½
LG Twins	58	67	8	.464	19
SK Wyverns	60	71	2	.458	20
Lotte Giants	59	70	4	.457	20

PLAYOFFS: Quarterfinals—Doosan defeated Hanwha 2-0 in best-of-3 series. **Semifinals**—Doosan defeated Hyundai 3-1 in best-of-5 series. **Finals**—Doosan defeated Samsung 4-2 in best-of-7 series.

INDIVIDUAL BATTING LEADERS

	AVG	AB	R	H	HR	RBI	BB	SO
Yang Joon-hyuk, LG	.355	439	79	156	14	92	80	55
Shim Jae-hak, Hyundai	.344	369	83	127	24	88	86	50
Herrera, Jose, SK	.344	418	61	142	15	63	24	53
Jose, Felix, Lotte	.335	367	90	123	36	102	127	72
Davis, Jay, Hanwha	.335	496	95	166	30	96	60	74
Ma Hae-yong , Samsung	.328	470	86	154	30	95	68	82
Chun Jun-ho, Hyundai	.325	400	85	130	4	35	65	51
Kim Jae-hyun, LG	.325	428	81	139	8	61	88	83
Kim Dong-joo, Doosan	.324	364	49	118	18	62	47	57
Brito, Tilson, SK	.320	422	59	135	22	80	57	53

(Remaining North Americans)

	AVG	AB	R	H	HR	RBI	BB	SO
De los Santos, Luis, Hai/Kia	.310	484	74	150	26	107	46	66
Woods, Tyrone, Doosan	.291	436	101	127	34	113	83	114
Martinez, Manny, Samsung	.278	482	93	134	25	96	57	79
Baerga, Carlos, Samsung	.275	120	18	33	4	17	10	12
Yan, Julian, Lotte	.270	330	52	89	17	62	54	88
Rohrmeier, Dan, LG	.268	60	28	55	11	47	25	50
Phillips, J.R. Hyundai	.261	66	37	60	15	46	25	62
Quinlan, Tom, Hyundai	.242	414	66	100	28	66	59	160
Tavarez, Jesus, Haitai	.237	46	24	42	1	14	16	26
Neel, Troy, Doosan	.193	57	7	11	1	3	10	15

INDIVIDUAL PITCHING LEADERS

	W	L	ERA	SV	IP	BB	SO
Park Seok-jin, Lotte	4	10	2.97	14	133	34	81
Shin Yoon-ho, LG	15	6	3.11	18	144	79	99
Lee Seung-ho, SK	14	14	3.54	2	221	115	165
Han Yong-duk, Hanwha	8	10	3.56	0	144	33	112
Oh Sang-min, SK	7	6	3.56	10	134	43	121
Lee Hye-chun, Doosan	9	6	3.62	3	142	72	107
Bae Yong-soo, Samsung	13	8	3.76	0	170	89	96
Song Jin-woo, Hanwha	10	8	3.83	2	185	86	139
Hernandez, Fernando, SK	14	13	3.89	0	234	134	215
Im Chang-yong, Samsung	14	6	3.89	1	185	62	136

(Remaining North Americans)

	W	L	ERA	G	SV	IP	BB	SO
Galvez, Balvino, Samsung	10	4	2.47	15	0	117	42	85
Rivera, Ben, Samsung	6	3	2.62	36	21	58	33	63
Leese, Brandon, Hanwha	7	7	3.16	18	0	100	50	62
Linton, Doug, LG	4	4	3.17	12	0	77	25	53
Chavez, Carlos, Hanwha	0	0	3.38	7	0	8	7	6
Warren, Brian, Hanwha	2	1	4.30	11	3	15	9	6
Harriger, Denny, LG	8	11	4.62	28	0	162	87	104
Valdez, Efrain, LG	10	9	4.65	30	0	165	85	80
Taylor, Kerry, Hyundai	8	10	4.75	29	0	155	115	94
Cole, Victor, Doosan	6	9	5.04	21	0	120	60	95
Giron, Emiliano, Lotte	4	2	5.48	10	0	48	30	42
Nunez, Jose, Hanwha	2	1	5.52	14	4	29	7	19
Farmer, Mike, Doosan	1	2	9.00	3	0	11	6	9
Winston, Darrin, Hanwha	1	0	9.39	9	0	8	3	5
Evans, David, Hanwha	0	1	13.50	2	0	6	4	7
Torres, Salomon, Samsung	0	2	20.25	2	0	5	10	5

FOREIGN LEAGUES

Taiwan to rally around Elephants

BY JEFFREY WILSON

A late-season Elephant charge might be the push Taiwanese baseball needs.

Traditionally Taiwan's most popular team, the Brother Elephants brought their legions of intensely loyal fans back

to the ballpark in 2001 by winning the second-half title in the Chinese Professional Baseball League. Brother then defeated the first-half champion President Lions four games to three in the league championship series, becoming the first CPBL team to rally from a 3-1 deficit.

The title was the first for Brother since 1994, a drought that included the aftereffects of a 1997 game-fixing scandal that almost destroyed the Taiwanese professional game. Brother's title put to rest longterm speculation that the pillar franchise would fold and take the league down with it.

The Elephants won with a maturing group of native players and Japanese import pitcher Tetsu Yofu, who figured in each win in the championship series with two victories and two saves. The team was the first in 12 years of pro ball in Taiwan to complete a season without using any North American, Latin American or Australian players.

The declining reliance on import players was further evidenced when just three foreigners won individual titles in Taiwan's two leagues. Yofu led the CPBL with 166 strikeouts. President's John Burgos led the CPBL in wins with an 18-4 record.

Richard Bell won the relief pitching title in the Taiwan Major League with 56 save points. Bell and his Taichung Agan team weren't challenged the entire season. They won the regular season by 11½ games, then defeated the Taipei Gida four games to two in the championship series.

Lack of balance in the TML was reflected by the hapless Chiayi Luka, who had the worst record ever in Taiwan pro baseball. After opening the season with six straight wins, the Luka finished 13-47 and won only once in their last 26 games.

TAIWAN MAJOR LEAGUE STANDINGS

STANDINGS	W	L	T	PCT	GB
Taichung Agan	43	16	1	.729	—
Taipei Gida	31	27	2	.534	11½
Kaohsiung Fala	31	28	1	.525	12
Chiayi Luka	13	47	0	.217	30½

PLAYOFFS: Taichung defeated Taipei 4-2 in best-of-7 series.

INDIVIDUAL BATTING LEADERS
(Minimum 185 Plate Appearances)

	AVG	AB	R	H	2B	3B	HR	RBI	SB
Lin Kun-han, Taipei	.368	163	28	60	11	1	3	36	0
Pan Chung-wei, Kaohsiung	.343	172	30	59	9	1	3	29	6
Tung Tsung-hui, Taichung	.331	251	44	83	16	2	6	45	5
Chen Feng-min, Chiayi	.324	189	29	59	7	1	1	19	2
Diaz, Freddie, Kaohsiung	.313	192	29	60	10	1	9	31	3

(Other Import Players)

	AVG	AB	R	H	2B	3B	HR	RBI	SB
Mejia, Roberto, Taichung	.415	41	13	17	4	1	4	15	2
Fingleson, Gavin, Chiayi	.369	103	19	38	7	3	1	15	4
Miller, Ryan, Taipei	.344	32	6	11	3	0	0	4	1
Vopata, Nate, Taipei	.318	66	15	21	5	2	3	10	0
Buckley, Matt, Chiayi	.310	100	15	31	7	2	1	13	7
Sanchez, Yuri, Chiayi	.309	110	13	34	6	1	1	18	4
Valenti, Jon, Taipei	.277	65	8	18	3	1	2	12	2
Martinez, Gil, Taichung	.269	78	11	21	5	2	2	13	1
Mitchell, Keith, Taichung	.269	26	5	7	1	0	2	4	0
Lewis, Anthony, Chiayi	.171	35	2	6	0	0	2	4	0

Hernandez, Victor, Taipei	.164	73	14	12	4	0	1	6	1
Durkac, Bo, Taichung	.000	8	0	0	0	0	0	0	0

INDIVIDUAL PITCHING LEADERS
(Minimum 60 Innings)

	W	L	ERA	G	SV	IP	H	BB	SO
Huang Chin-chih, Taichung	7	3	1.62	23	0	94	71	42	65
Li Yi-sung, Kaohsiung	3	4	2.43	16	1	63	58	6	36
Silva, Ted, Kaohsiung	3	4	2.45	10	0	62	53	22	39
Liang Ju-hao, Taipei	8	7	2.61	21	1	113	115	38	94
Hsu Chu-chien, Taichung	7	2	2.64	19	1	71	62	40	59

(Other Import Pitchers)

	W	L	ERA	G	SV	IP	H	BB	SO
Bennett, Shayne, Taipei	0	0	0.82	7	2	22	15	8	25
Bell, Richard, Taichung	2	2	1.62	33	22	55	34	31	69
Pageler, Mick, Kaohsiung	0	0	1.96	8	2	18	20	4	13
Bennett, Erik, Kaohsiung	0	1	1.98	10	4	13	6	7	16
Rodriguez, Frank, Kaohsiung	1	2	2.96	14	4	27	26	14	26
Davis, Jason, Kaohsiung	3	3	3.77	10	0	43	34	30	28
Quintanilla, Juan, Taichung	4	2	4.01	8	1	42	34	10	35
Juarbe, Ken, Taichung	4	1	4.81	10	0	48	53	34	37
Poeck, Chad, Kaohsiung	2	3	5.63	11	2	24	28	11	17
Rivera, Roberto, Chiayi	0	3	7.82	3	0	12	25	6	5
Rossiter, Mike, Chiayi	0	2	8.64	7	1	8	14	13	8
Ojeda, Jorge, Chiayi	0	6	8.76	9	0	37	59	21	12
Gonzalez, Lariel, Chiayi	0	1	10.80	1	0	1	3	3	2
Romo, Greg, Taipei	0	2	14.54	4	0	8	19	12	6

CPBL STANDINGS

FIRST HALF	W	L	T	PCT	GB
President Lions	27	14	4	.659	—
China Trust Whales	23	22	0	.511	6
Brother Elephants	17	23	5	.425	9½
Sinon Bulls	17	25	3	.405	10½

SECOND HALF	W	L	T	PCT	GB
Brother Elephants	27	16	2	.628	—
China Trust Whales	22	23	0	.489	6
Sinon Bulls	22	23	2	.489	6
President Lions	17	26	0	.395	10

PLAYOFFS: Brother defeated President 4-3 in best-of-7 series.

INDIVIDUAL BATTING LEADERS
(Minimum 284 Plate Appearances)

	AVG	AB	R	H	2B	3B	HR	RBI	SB
Luo Min-ching, President	.357	272	30	97	18	0	7	50	1
Yang Sung-hsien, CT	.312	337	50	105	23	1	4	29	30
Lin Ming-hsien, Brother	.305	285	45	87	13	9	3	32	13
Huang Chuan-chia, Pres.	.301	286	40	86	19	0	3	30	8
Chen Jui-chen, Brother	.298	319	46	95	13	3	1	40	14

(Other Import Players)

	AVG	AB	R	H	2B	3B	HR	RBI	SB
Miller, Orlando, China Trust	.308	169	23	52	6	0	5	32	1
Bell, Juan, China Trust	.261	115	21	30	7	0	4	15	4

INDIVIDUAL PITCHING LEADERS
(Minimum 90 Innings)

	W	L	ERA	G	SV	IP	H	BB	SO
Morales, Luis, Vera.	10	7	2.04	34	1	119	100	26	82
Flynt, Will, Saltillo	13	4	2.68	26	0	174	175	67	157
Hsiao Jen-wen, Brother	5	3	1.40	52	16	90	67	26	61
Burgos, John, President	18	4	2.03	28	0	199	178	40	143
Tetsu, Yofu, Brother	11	10	2.21	31	1	212	163	62	166
Hsieh Cheng-shun, CT	15	11	2.70	30	0	196	196	63	86
Martinez, Osvaldo, Sinon	11	10	2.84	37	4	209	192	77	139

(Other Import Pitchers)

	W	L	ERA	G	SV	IP	H	BB	SO
Parra, Jose, President	0	2	1.29	10	0	14	9	4	10
Lemon, Don, President	2	2	1.64	8	1	11	11	1	9
Dishman, Glenn, Sinon	2	4	2.72	13	0	56	48	44	40
Guzman, Domingo, CT	5	8	2.97	25	1	93	87	38	58
Heredia, Wilson, Sinon	5	8	3.67	32	4	77	87	39	57
Jordan, Ricardo, CT	3	7	4.02	14	0	53	55	33	44
De la Cruz, Fernando, President	2	2	4.23	7	0	27	26	21	8

Nettuno defeats Rimini for 16th title

Nettuno finally beat old nemesis Rimini to win the best-of-seven Italy Series in six games.

After defeating Bologna four games to one in the play-off semifinals, Nettuno lost the first two games of the finals. The defeats extended Nettuno's Italy Series losing streak to eight games, all against Rimini, dating to 1999. But Nettuno then beat the defending champion four straight times to claim its 16th national title. It was also Nettuno's ninth straight Italy Series appearance.

ITALY

Pitching dominated the 2001 series. Rimini and Nettuno ranked first and third in Serie A/1 with team batting averages of .315 and .294 in the regular season. They were held to .185 and .179 in the Series.

Yoshimune Wakita, the first Japanese import in Serie A/1 history, led Bologna to its highest finish since 1994. The 29-year-old righthander, a former United States independent leaguer, went 10-2, 1.59 to win the ERA title.

Former big league outfielder Jim Vatcher hit .353-8-65 and won his second straight RBI crown. Vatcher was one of four Rimini players among the top 10 batters.

The Italian national team, managed by former San Francisco Giants coach Jim Davenport, was upset by Russia in the semifinals of the European Championships. It was the first time since 1957 that Italy competed in the biennial competition and failed to finish in the top two.

—HARVEY SAHKER

STANDINGS

	W	L	PCT	GB
Rimini	43	11	.796	—
Bologna	39	15	.722	4
Nettuno	33	21	.647	10
Grosseto	33	21	.611	10
Caserta	29	25	.537	14
Parma	23	31	.426	20
Anzio	19	35	.352	24
Paterno	19	35	.352	24
Modena	19	35	.352	24
San Marino	13	41	.241	30

Vatcher, Jim, Rimini	.353	215	76	8	65
Patrone, Carlos Antonio, Nettuno	.342	193	66	2	28
Gaiardo, Alessandro, Rimini	.341	179	61	3	31
Ramos, Jairo, Grosseto	.337	208	70	15	54
DeFranceschi, Roberto, Nettuno	.336	211	71	4	40
Casolari, Franco, Nettuno	.335	185	62	8	56
Rovinelli, Dean, Rimini	.333	171	57	4	37
Dallospedale, Davide, Bologna	.333	213	71	1	23
Matteucci, Riccardo, Bologna	.325	163	53	1	21
Schiavetti, Igor, Nettuno	.321	184	59	2	23
Sforza, Marco, Paterno	.321	190	61	0	22

INDIVIDUAL PITCHING LEADERS

	W	L	ERA	SV	IP	SO
Wakita, Yoshimune, Bologna	10	2	1.59	0	96	115
Palazzetti, Angelo, Nettuno	8	3	1.82	0	94	112
Leslie, Reggie, San Marino	2	2	1.89	0	57	72
Kester, Tim, Rimini	5	2	1.99	0	54	46
Cossutta, Walter, Caserta	11	4	2.11	0	124	105
Kelly, John, Modena	9	5	2.20	0	131	184
Cabalisti, Roberto, Rimini	8	1	2.15	4	67	53
Mura, Christian, Bologna	10	6	2.23	0	101	80
Larreal, Guillermo, Paterno	10	7	2.36	0	145	135
Heredia, Maximo, Grosseto	6	3	2.35	0	61	50
Marchesano, Mike, Rimini	10	3	2.46	0	110	128
Newman, Dan, Bologna	11	4	2.51	0	129	108
Vigna, Juan Carlo, Nettuno	6	7	2.49	5	69	80
Ventura, Cipriano, Nettuno	7	4	2.69	0	131	129
Ginanneschi, Emiliano, Grosseto	7	4	2.86	2	104	65

INDIVIDUAL BATTING LEADERS

	AVG	AB	H	HR	RBI
Francois, Manny, Nettuno	.431	123	53	4	30
Tavarez, Ramon, Anzio	.388	178	69	9	44
Munoz, Orlando, Modena	.383	201	77	7	29
Marchiano, Mike, Rimini	.366	172	63	10	46
Santana, Ruben, Bologna	.362	221	80	11	52
Crociati, Filippo, Rimini	.358	212	76	3	41
Martinez, Sandy, Caserta	.358	232	83	2	31

Neptunas captures third crown

The 10-team Dutch Major League made news in 2001 by changing its structure in the middle of the season. The league adopted a split-season format for the first time, with the top six clubs qualifying for a "playoff pool," with games in the first half counting in the final standings.

HOLLAND

The remaining four clubs started from scratch in a promotion/relegation pool, along with the top two qualifiers from the First Division, the next level down from the DML. Those six clubs played for four places in the 2002 DML.

Neptunus defeated HCAW 3-1 in the best-of-five Holland Series. It was the third straight national crown for the Rotterdam club, making it the first to threepeat since Haarlem Nicols won four in a row from 1982-85. Neptunus also won the European Cup, the continental club championship.

There were several personnel changes at Neptunus before the season. Three key players retired, including ex-major league infielder Robert Eenhoorn. The club's player/manager in 2000, Eenhoorn was skipper of both

Neptunus and the Dutch national team in 2001. He resigned as manager of Neptunus at the end of the Holland Series.

Eenhoorn, 33, guided the Netherlands to first place at the European Championships, which took place in Germany. It was Holland's 17th continental title.

—HARVEY SAHKER

STANDINGS

PLAYOFF POOL	W	L	PCT	GB
Neptunus	34	12	.734	—
HCAW	34	13	.723	½
Kinheim	31	16	.660	3½
ADO	30	16	.649	4
Amsterdam Expos	30	17	.638	4½
PSV Eindhoven	11	36	.234	23½

PROMOTION/RELEGATION POOL	W	L	PCT	GB
Hoofddorp Pioniers	16	4	.800	—
Almere	13	7	.650	3
Sparta/Feyenoord	11	9	.550	5
RCH	10	10	.500	6
Oosterhout Twins	9	11	.450	7
Purmerend Flying Petrels	1	19	.050	15

FOREIGN LEAGUES

WINTER

Dominicans beat upstart Mexicans to capture Caribbean Series again

BY JOHN ROYSTER

Spirit may not be enough to conquer superior talent in baseball. But in the 2001 Caribbean Series, Mexican Pacific League entrant Hermosillo showed it can come pretty close.

The Hermosillo team was buoyed by phenomenal fan support at the Series site in Culiacan, Mexico, and showed a knack for comebacks, both within games and overall after losing two of its first three games.

The Orange Growers (3-3) reached the final game of the four-nation competition with a chance to win, but fell 5-3 to Aguilas (4-2) of the Dominican Republic. Aguilas won its last four games to capture the title, the sixth in 11 years by a team from the Dominican Republic.

The last time the four-nation series was played in Mexico, 1997, the Mexican Pacific League entrant also finished second to the Dominican Republic. In 30 events since the Caribbean Series was reborn in 1970, Mexico had finished last 14 times.

There was more hope than usual for Mexico in 2001, though, as big leaguers Vinny Castilla (Devil Rays) and Erubiel Durazo (Diamondbacks), the Series MVP, graced the Mexican League lineup. The perennial also-rans also had former big leaguers Trenidad Hubbard and Warren Newson to with a veteran pitching staff that included 41-year-old lefthander Fernando Valenzuela.

But they were still no match for the Dominicans, who were missing two-time Caribbean Series MVP Neifi Perez (Rockies), closer Antonio Alfonseca (Marlins) and outfielder Jose Guillen (Devil Rays), all last minute defections.

"Had it simply been a battle of wills, no one would have beaten us," Hermosillo manager Derek Bryant said. "For a while I thought that might be enough, but the Dominicans were just too good."

MEL BAILEY

Erubiel Durazo

Good enough, indeed, to lose their first two games in the six-game round-robin event in lackluster fashion, then roar back to take the title. Good enough, indeed, to do just that twice in five years. An Aguilas "dream team" lost its first two and won its last four in 1996.

This time that Aguilas comeback began in its first meeting with Hermosillo, a 4-2 victory on the third day. The loss dropped the Orange Growers to 1-2, but the Mexican fans gave them quite a show of support afterward, staying around to greet them tumultuously when they emerged from their clubhouse.

"It was a little disconcerting," Aguilas third baseman Tony Batista said. "We won, they were almost out of it and there was a party going on in the stadium when we came out. We were trying to figure out why."

Perhaps the fans knew inspiration would work. Just a day later, after beating Lara of Venezuela, Hermosillo had as good a chance to win as anybody. All four teams (including Puerto Rican representative Caguas) had 2-2 records.

2001 CARIBBEAN SERIES

Culiacan, Mexico
Feb. 2-7, 2001

ROUND-ROBIN STANDINGS

	W	L	PCT	GB
Dominican Republic (Aguilas)	4	2	.667	—
Venezuela (Lara)	3	3	.500	1
Mexico (Hermosillo)	3	3	.500	1
Puerto Rico (Caguas)	2	4	.333	2

INDIVIDUAL BATTING LEADERS
(Minimum 17 Plate Appearances)

	AVG	AB	R	H	2B	3B	HR	RBI	SB
Durazo, Erubiel, Mex	.455	22	3	10	1	0	3	6	0
Beltran, Carlos, PR	.409	22	6	9	2	0	2	7	0
Sojo, Luis, Venezuela	.391	23	3	9	0	0	1	2	0
Ortiz, David, DR	.381	21	3	8	1	0	1	2	0
Hernandez, Ramon, Ven.	.364	22	5	8	0	1	3	6	0
Matthews, Gary, PR	.360	25	4	9	2	0	2	6	0
Batista, Tony, DR	.333	24	2	8	2	0	1	6	0
Castilla, Vinny, Mex.	.333	24	6	8	0	0	2	6	0
Munoz, Jose, PR	.333	21	2	7	3	0	0	4	0
Polonia, Luis, DR	.333	21	4	7	2	0	0	3	1
Cabrera, Jolbert, Ven.	.333	21	5	7	4	0	0	3	0
Nelson, Bryant, Mex.	.320	25	4	8	1	0	0	3	1
Nieves, Jose, Venez.	.318	22	6	7	0	0	2	4	1
Raven, Luis, Venez.	.318	22	5	7	4	0	2	8	0
Cairo, Miguel, Venez.	.308	26	4	8	0	0	1	3	0
Nunez, Abraham, DR	.294	17	0	5	1	0	0	3	0
Freel, Ryan, Venezuela	.286	21	2	6	2	0	0	4	0
Hubbard, Trenidad, Mex.	.286	21	5	6	0	0	2	4	2

INDIVIDUAL PITCHING LEADERS
(Minimum 5 Innings)

	W	L	ERA	G	SV	IP	H	BB	SO
Glover, Gary, Venez.	1	0	0.00	2	0	5	3	1	5
Garcia, Jose, Mexico	1	0	0.96	2	0	9	5	6	8
Pena, Jesus, DR	0	0	1.17	3	1	8	7	2	8
Moreno, Angel, Mex.	0	0	1.50	1	0	6	3	1	5
Chacin, Gustavo, Ven.	0	0	1.80	2	0	5	5	4	5
Valenzuela, Fernando, Mex.	0	0	1.80	1	0	5	3	2	2
Bowie, Micah, DR	0	0	2.45	2	0	7	5	0	7
Ellis, Robert, DR	1	0	2.57	1	0	7	6	1	4
Calero, Kiko, PR	0	0	2.70	2	0	7	5	3	7
Miranda, Angel, PR	0	0	2.84	2	0	6	8	3	7
Arteaga, J.D., PR	1	0	3.00	1	0	6	3	6	3
Rodriguez, Frank, PR	1	1	3.18	2	0	11	8	2	8

Most Valuable Player—Erubiel Durazo, 1b, Mexico.

That set the stage for a thriller between Hermosillo and Caguas, which the Orange Growers won 6-4 in 10 innings. Hubbard hit two dramatic home runs. The first, which came after he fouled off three straight full-count pitches, gave the team a short-lived 3-2 lead in the seventh inning. The second, a two-run shot in the 10th after two failed sacrifice attempts, won the game.

Aguilas kept pace, scoring six runs in the second inning against Lara, then holding on for an 8-6 win.

The two results made the Aguilas-Hermosillo game on the final day a one-game showdown for the title, a scenario that had seemed highly unlikely just 72 hours before. Hermosillo was considered so far out of it that starting pitcher Elmer Dessens (Reds) had gone home, and had to be flown back to start the deciding game.

It was a wasted trip. Dessens gave up four runs in the first 2⅓ innings, as Aguilas built an early 5-1 lead. Hermosillo second baseman Miguel Flores accounted for all of the Mexicans' scoring, hitting a solo homer and a

PLAYER OF THE YEAR

Caguas closer Courtney Duncan saved a league-high 17 games during the Puerto Rican League regular season to lead his team to the regular season title, the Creoles' first in 14 years.

Courtney Duncan

Duncan, a righthander, then saved all four Caguas wins in its semifinal triumph over Santurce and four of its five wins in a 5-1 thrashing of Mayaguez, which propelled Caguas into the Caribbean Series in Mexico.

For his efforts, Duncan was selected Baseball America's 2000-2001 Winter League Player of the Year. Duncan spent the 2001 major league season with the Chicago Cubs.

PREVIOUS WINNERS

1999-2000—Morgan Burkhart, 1b, Navojoa (Mexican Pacific)
1998-1999—Bob Abreu, of, Caracas (Venezuela)
1997-1998—Jose Hernandez, ss, Mayaguez (Puerto Rico)
1996-1997—Bartolo Colon, rhp, Aguilas (Dominican Republic)
1995-1996—Darryl Brinkley, of, Mexicali (Mexican Pacific)
1994-1995—Carlos Delgado, c, San Juan (Puerto Rico)
1993-1994—John Hudek, rhp, Magallanes (Venezuela)
1992-1993—Matias Carrillo, of, Mexicali (Mexican Pacific)
1991-1992—Wilson Alvarez, lhp, Zulia (Venezuela)
1990-1991—Henry Rodriguez, of, Licey (Dominican Republic)
1989-1990—Edgar Martinez, 3b, San Juan (Puerto Rico)
1988-1989—Phil Stephenson, 1b, Zulia (Venezuela)
1987-1988—Jose Nunez, rhp, Escogido (Dominican Republic)
1986-1987—Vicente Palacios, rhp, Mexicali (Mexican Pacific)
1985-1986—Wally Joyner, 1b, Mayaguez (Puerto Rico)

two-run homer.

Aguilas righthander Miguel Batista gave up all three runs, but pitched seven strong innings before relievers Jose Garcia and Jesus Pena finished up.

Different Look

Winter baseball was pretty much status quo in the Arizona Fall League and the four traditional winter leagues in 2000-2001, but it had a different look elsewhere.

Major League Baseball abandoned its idea of a secondary development league on U.S. soil, after the California Fall League disbanded after a one-year run. Previous attempts had also failed in Hawaii and Maryland.

A new four-team league in Panama also failed to get off the ground as planned, but did start in 2001-02 with four teams and a 42-game schedule.

Winter ball in Australia was nearly extinct before a revamped format temporarily saved professional baseball in that country. In 1999-2000, the International Baseball League Australia played with no import players but its second attempt included players from several nations. The league, though, announced in the fall of 2001 that it would not play a 2001-02 season.

Two Players Killed

Recent winters have been marred by off-field tragedies, and in 2000-01 two players were killed in separate automobile accidents.

Former Astros and Padres shortstop Andujar Cedeno died after his car collided with a truck between Santo

Domingo and La Romana, Dominican Republic, on Oct. 28, 2000. Cedeno was 31.

Miguel Caldes, 30, a longtime utilityman on the Cuban national team, was killed Dec. 4, 2000, when his car was hit by a train near Camaguey, Cuba. He had batted .333-0-4 in 30 at-bats at the Sydney Olympics just weeks earlier.

Ex-Blue Jays lefthander Huck Flener was seriously injured on the field in a Venezuelan League playoff game in January. Flener was pitching for Lara when a line drive off the bat of Donaldo Mendez of the Magallanes Navigators struck him in the face. He sustained a detached retina in his right eye, a fractured cheekbone and a broken nose.

DOMINICAN LEAGUE

Aguilas' comeback victory in the Caribbean Series should have come as no surprise, considering the team had been practicing just such a thing for a week beforehand.

After falling behind Escogido two games to one in the Dominican League championship series, Aguilas won three straight games and its fifth league title in six years.

Felix Jose

Aguilas also won the regular season championship with a 32-18 record, but Escogido dominated the four-team, round-robin portion of the playoffs, going 14-4 while Aguilas finished second at just 9-9.

Estrellas outfielder Felix Jose, a star in Korea during the summer of 2001, won two-thirds of a Dominican League triple crown. Jose, who played briefly in the majors as recently as 2000, batted .377-8-33 and led the league in batting and RBIs.

He lost the home run title to Aguilas first baseman Andy Barkett, who hit 11 and later played well in the Caribbean Series before making his major league debut in 2001 with the Pirates.

Aguilas righthander Fernando Hernandez narrowly missed his third straight league strikeout title. He led with 60 after his last outing, but Azucareros righthander Miguel Batista pitched later and reached 61. Hernandez did lead the league in wins, going 7-2, 2.42 and reaching the six-victory plateau for the third straight season.

The season marked the return of Azucareros, the last team to resume play after Hurricane Georges heavily damaged Dominican ballparks in the late summer of 1998. Azucareros and Estrellas both sat out the '98-99 season before Estrellas returned in '99-00.

STANDINGS

REGULAR SEASON	W	L	PCT	GB
Aguilas	32	18	.640	—
Estrellas	29	21	.580	3
Escogido Lions	27	22	.551	4½
Azucareros	25	25	.500	7
Pollos	19	30	.388	12½
Licey Tigers	17	33	.340	15
PLAYOFFS	W	L	PCT	GB
Escogido Lions	14	4	.777	—
Aguilas	9	9	.500	5
Azucareros	7	11	.389	7
Estrellas	6	12	.333	8

Championship Series: Aguilas defeated Escogido, 4-2, in best-of-7 series.

Statistics in **boldface** indicate league leader.
#Indicates league leader but non-qualifier.

INDIVIDUAL BATTING LEADERS
(Minimum 137 Plate Appearances)

	AVG	AB	R	H	2B	3B	HR	RBI	SB
Jose, Felix, Estrellas	**.376**	125	20	47	12	2	8	**34**	1
Wilson, Desi, Estrellas	.341	164	22	**56**	14	3	0	17	5
Barkett, Andy, Aguilas	.339	121	26	41	**13**	1	**11**	25	0
Melo, Juan, Escogido	.315	143	26	45	6	1	3	19	5
Feliz, Pedro, Pollos	.304	168	19	51	10	0	4	18	1
Ortiz, David, Escogido	.283	145	14	41	9	3	5	27	0
Cesar, Dionys, Aguilas	.282	156	18	44	9	0	1	20	6
Encarnacion, Angelo, Pollos	.279	147	17	41	**13**	0	0	18	0
Bell, Juan, Azucareros	.279	140	19	39	9	5	1	15	0
Moreta, Ramon, Azu	.278	158	17	44	5	1	2	11	10
Nunez, Abraham, Esc	.261	138	14	36	5	3	1	10	4
German, Esteban, Azu	.253	150	**32**	38	4	1	1	16	**30**
Perez, Santiago, Pollos	.250	136	17	34	7	5	4	14	4
Wakeland, Chris, Esc	.246	126	18	31	7	0	3	9	0
Encarnacion, Mario, Agu	.244	160	23	39	8	1	3	19	2
Kingsale, Eugene, Est	.237	131	21	31	2	**6**	2	10	6
Martinez, Felix, Agu	.226	146	27	33	6	3	1	16	10
Castillo, Alberto, Agu	.205	117	11	24	1	0	3	11	1

INDIVIDUAL PITCHING LEADERS
(Minimum 40 Innings)

	W	L	ERA	G	SV	IP	H	BB	SO
#Vizcaino, Luis, Agu	0	1	0.81	23	**14**	22	13	6	30
Ellis, Robert, Azu	6	2	**1.55**	11	0	70	52	8	38
Telemaco, Amaury, Esc	3	1	1.88	10	0	48	44	13	34
Saipe, Mike, Estrellas	6	2	2.02	10	0	58	37	10	34
Valdez, Efrain, Pollos	6	5	2.36	12	0	69	56	25	27
Hernandez, Fernando, Agu	7	2	2.42	12	0	67	47	26	60
Roberts, Willis, Est	6	2	2.44	11	0	52	40	18	32
Aybar, Manny, Licey	4	2	2.94	9	0	49	43	14	35
Giron, Isabel, Pollos	1	5	3.04	11	0	53	54	16	35
Ozuna, Gab, Azucareros	3	4	3.05	13	0	41	32	14	22
Perez, Dario, Licey	0	3	3.24	9	0	42	40	11	27
Batista, Miguel, Azu	6	2	3.34	13	0	70	58	23	**61**
Estrella, Leo, Agu	2	4	3.57	10	0	40	46	12	12
Nunez, Vladimir, Licey	3	3	3.66	9	0	47	43	20	30
Padua, Geraldo, Azu	2	3	3.72	11	0	46	50	14	23
Murray, Dan, Pollos	0	5	3.79	10	0	40	34	32	34
Martinez, Jose, Pollos	2	4	4.08	10	0	46	55	12	22
Pena, Jesus, Aguilas	3	2	4.91	11	0	44	44	16	37

MEXICAN PACIFIC LEAGUE

JOHN SPEAR

Chris Hatcher

Lefthanders have a long shelf life these days, but this is ridiculous: Hermosillo's Angel Moreno, 45, threw a shutout in the deciding game of the Mexican Pacific League playoffs, beating Mazatlan 5-0.

Moreno is a former major leaguer, but forgive yourself if you don't remember it; he last pitched for the California Angels in 1982, at the end of a two-year career. Since then he's been playing in Mexico both summer and winter.

He and Fernando Valenzuela gave Hermosillo a formidable one-two punch of over-40 lefthanders. At one point in the playoffs, they combined for 14⅔ consecutive innings without giving up an earned run. The pair also played a key role as Hermosillo finished second in the Caribbean Series.

Moreno allowed just four hits against Mazatlan as the Orange Growers won the championship series three games to one. The playoffs reflected the regular season, in which Hermosillo and Mazatlan tied for the best record at 40-28, far ahead of their closest pursuers.

The top six hitters during the regular season were all import players, led by Bry Nelson (Hermosillo) with a .330 average. He was followed by Chris Hatcher (Culiacan) at .324, Jayson Bass (Los Mochis) at .317, Scott

Samuels (Mexicali) at .315, Virgil Chevalier (Navojoa) at .303 and Eddie Williams (Guasave) at .299.

Hatcher won the RBI title with 61, and three players shared the home run lead at 15: Hensley Meulens of Mexicali, Kevin Grijak of Mazatlan and Ricardo Saenz of Mexicali.

The league played its first season under new president Renato Vega, who came in a baseball-for-politics trade. A former governor of the Mexican state of Sinaloa, Vega replaced Arturo Leon, who left after 15 years and ran successfully for a seat in the Mexican congress.

STANDINGS

REGULAR SEASON	W	L	PCT	GB
*Mazatlan Deer	40	28	.588	—
*Hermosillo Orangemen	40	28	.588	—
Obregon Yaquis	33	34	.493	6½
Guasave Cottoneers	33	35	.485	7
Los Mochis Sugarcane Growers	32	34	.485	7
Navojoa Mayos	31	36	.463	8½
Mexicali Eagles	31	37	.456	9
Culiacan Tomato Growers	30	38	.441	10

*Split-season champion

PLAYOFFS—Quarterfinals: Obregon defeated Los Mochis 4-1; Hermosillo defeated Navojoa 4-2; and Mazatlan defeated Guasave 4-2, in best-of-7 series. **Semifinals**: Hermosillo defeated Guasave 4-0; and Mazatlan defeated Obregon, 4-2, in best-of-7 series. **Finals**: Hermosillo defeated Mazatlan, 4-1, in best-of-7 series.

INDIVIDUAL BATTING LEADERS
(Minimum 210 Plate Appearances)

	AVG	AB	R	H	2B	3B	HR	RBI	SB
Nelson, Bry, Her	**.330**	194	35	64	10	4	7	55	6
Hatcher, Chris, Cul	.324	222	35	**72**	17	2	12	**61**	2
Bass, Jayson, LM	.317	224	**51**	71	5	0	13	40	14
Samuels, Scott, Mex	.315	200	43	63	10	0	13	35	13
Williams, Eddie, Guas	.299	204	34	61	6	0	12	41	1
Chevalier, Virgil, Nav	.299	194	31	58	9	0	6	22	2
Garcia, Cornelio, Her	.296	223	42	66	6	0	1	20	1
Meulens, Hensley, Mex	.292	192	45	56	9	0	15	46	1
Arredondo, Luis, Obr	.289	204	23	59	8	3	4	23	11
Colina, Roberto, Mex	.286	248	36	71	7	0	9	44	0
Kirby, Wayne, Maz	.280	207	27	58	14	2	3	21	6
Maddox, Garry, Nav	.277	224	28	62	13	2	4	26	3
Flores, Miguel, Her	.276	210	44	58	10	0	6	23	6
Newson, Warren, Her	.273	220	34	60	7	0	11	45	1
Gastelum, Sergio, Mex	.271	262	35	71	13	1	9	40	5
Gil, Geronimo, Obr	.269	216	33	58	12	1	11	27	2
Grijak, Kevin, Maz	.267	240	26	64	3	0	**15**	36	1
Zuleta, Julio, Maz	.266	199	19	53	4	0	6	27	1
Carrillo, Matias, Maz	.262	195	21	51	8	0	6	23	2
Canizalez, Juan, Her	.261	199	29	52	13	0	6	34	0
Ingram, Garey, Nav	.261	199	26	52	8	1	7	29	2
Robles, Javier, Obr	.261	222	42	58	9	3	7	30	1
Sherman, Darrell, Cul	.261	245	46	64	7	1	6	18	17
Orantes, Ramon, LM	.260	219	27	57	11	0	6	31	1
Sandoval, Jose, Her	.256	207	30	53	10	0	9	35	3
Saenz, Ricardo, Mex	.252	226	33	57	16	3	**15**	40	1
Barron, Tony, Guas	.251	175	35	44	6	0	9	26	3
Jimenez, Eduardo, Mex	.249	225	39	56	8	0	13	39	0
Velazquez, Guillermo, Cul	.249	221	27	55	7	0	12	36	0
Garcia, Luis, Obr	.248	250	33	62	7	1	7	40	8
Magallanes, Ever, Cul	.247	243	34	60	10	2	3	21	0
Esquer, Ramon, Guas	.243	222	31	54	10	1	0	14	4
Guizar, Hector, Guas	.242	194	13	47	11	0	4	18	1
Stenson, Dernell, Nav	.241	249	36	60	9	0	11	36	0
Rojas, Homar, Obr	.241	191	23	46	1	0	10	29	0
Amezaga, Alfredo, Obr	.236	225	33	53	6	1	3	17	**24**
Pellow, Kit, Cul	.234	248	32	58	10	2	12	30	1
Brewer, Rod, Her	.225	204	24	46	6	1	10	37	1

INDIVIDUAL PITCHING LEADERS
(Minimum 68 Innings)

	W	L	ERA	G	SV	IP	H	BB	SO
Mora, Eleazar, Maz	7	3	**1.45**	12	0	74	60	17	58
Campos, Francisco, Maz	5	4	1.79	13	0	86	58	20	74
Alvarez, Victor, LM	6	4	1.95	13	0	78	56	28	61
Rivera, Oscar, Maz	6	5	1.98	13	0	77	54	34	58
Quinones, Enrique, Cul	7	2	2.34	16	0	73	59	27	40

WINTER LEAGUES

#Sinohui, David, Nav	0	2	2.51	30	**19**	29	21	9 32
Magee, Danny, Obr	3	6	2.68	13	0	77	53	49 **78**
Galvez, Randy, Guas	**8**	4	3.02	15	0	92	69	39 46
Villarreal, Oscar, Mex	6	5	3.14	15	0	80	62	39 66
Alvarez, Tavo, LM	4	7	3.65	13	0	81	69	18 64
Valenzuela, Fernando, Her	7	4	3.69	13	0	68	66	27 27
Garcia, Alfredo, Obr	5	4	3.82	15	0	75	77	42 54
Osuna, Ricardo, Nav	3	6	4.08	14	0	71	77	31 47
Montemayor, Humberto, Obr	1	4	4.15	15	0	80	92	20 66
Leyva, Edgar, Guas	7	5	4.18	15	0	75	76	25 52
Moreno, Angel, Her	5	3	4.43	14	0	69	72	37 51
Palafox, Juan, Nav	6	5	4.91	13	0	77	83	20 59

PUERTO RICAN LEAGUE

The Caguas Creoles, the dominant franchise for most of the Puerto Rican League's first four decades, won their first title in 14 years against a Mayaguez team that had dominated the last decade.

The biggest difference was Caguas closer Courtney Duncan, who saved a league-high 17 games during the regular season, all four Caguas wins in its semifinal triumph over Santurce and four of its five wins in their 5-1 thrashing of Mayaguez.

Another measure of Duncan's value came after he returned home instead of playing in the Caribbean Series in Culiacan,

Carlos Beltran

Mexico. The Creoles struggled in the bullpen without him, lost three straight games in the final inning and went 2-4 in the round-robin event.

Outfielder Carlos Beltran did all he could to offset Duncan's absence, and likely would have been the Caribbean Series MVP had the team fared better. Beltran, who played for the Bayamon Cowboys during the regular season, hit .409 with seven RBIs and six runs in Culiacan.

His first home run of the competition gave the Creoles a 4-3 lead over eventual champion Aguilas (Dominican Republic) in the eighth inning of a game they went on to lose 5-4. His second pulled Caguas even with runner-up Hermosillo (Mexico) at 2-2 in the seventh inning of a game the Creoles lost 6-4 in 10 innings.

The league MVP voting was a controversial choice between two players, and neither of them was Duncan or Beltran. Carolina Giants outfielder Yamil Benitez, who hit .327 and led the league with 35 RBIs, edged out Caguas second baseman Alex Cora, who led in home runs (10) and runs (37) while driving in 24 runs from the leadoff spot.

"Yamil's hitting had a big impact on the rest of that team. They might not have made the playoffs without him," Santurce manager Mako Oliveras said. "But Alex did so much for Caguas. He's valuable enough when you just consider what he does defensively. Throw in those offensive numbers and you understand why his teammates are upset."

STANDINGS

REGULAR SEASON	W	L	PCT	GB
Caguas Creoles	30	19	.612	—
Mayaguez Indians	28	21	.571	2
Santurce Crabbers	27	23	.540	3½
Carolina Giants	27	23	.540	3½
Bayamon Cowboys	21	29	.420	9½
Ponce Lions	16	34	.320	14½

PLAYOFFS—Semifinals: Caguas defeated Santurce, 4-1; and Mayaguez defeated Carolina, 4-2, in best-of-7 series. **Finals**: Caguas defeated Mayaguez, 5-1, in best-of-9 series.

INDIVIDUAL BATTING LEADERS
(Minimum 135 Plate Appearances)

	AVG	AB	R	H	2B	3B	HR	RBI	SB
Rodriguez, Victor, Car	**.364**	143	27	**52**	10	1	0	12	3
Bergeron, Peter, May	.331	136	22	45	9	**3**	1	15	10
Benitez, Yamil, Car	.327	159	23	**52**	**15**	1	7	**35**	0
Diaz, Alex, May	.327	153	24	50	12	1	4	20	2
Magee, Wendell, Ponce	.326	129	19	42	8	1	4	16	8
Valdes, Pedro, Car	.314	137	20	43	9	0	1	17	0
Lucca, Lou, Bay	.313	134	18	42	13	0	3	19	1
Lopez, Felipe, Sant	.310	155	32	48	10	1	6	23	7
Garcia, Omar, Bay	.306	134	22	41	8	1	7	23	1
Munoz, Jose, May	.305	167	28	51	13	2	2	27	1
Lopez, Luis, Sant	.304	158	19	48	9	0	6	24	0
Diaz, Edwin, Sant	.303	132	25	40	8	2	7	18	4
Crespo, Cesar, Car	.300	120	17	36	9	**3**	3	21	6
Gonzalez, Raul, Bay	.298	168	34	50	14	**3**	5	24	5
Rowand, Aaron, Bay	.297	148	14	44	12	0	3	14	2
Cintron, Alex, Cag	.294	163	20	48	7	2	2	21	3
Torres, Paul, May	.291	117	26	34	6	0	8	34	0
Figueroa, Luis, May	.288	160	20	46	11	2	0	19	3
Cora, Alex, Cag	.282	177	**37**	50	8	**3**	**10**	24	9
Cox, Darron, Bay	.282	124	18	35	6	1	3	23	2
Villanueva, Hector, Cag	.273	139	17	38	6	0	5	21	1
Leon, Donny, Ponce	.272	158	16	43	9	1	1	22	0
Echevarria, Angel, Ponce	.261	157	23	41	11	0	4	25	2
#Matos, Luis, Cag	.261	115	15	30	8	**3**	1	14	9
Tyler, Brad, Bay	.254	122	22	31	5	0	2	10	2
#Martinez, Gabby, Ponce	.246	65	11	16	1	**3**	1	5	2
Guzman, Edwards, May	.243	152	15	37	4	0	1	19	2
Rodriguez, Boi, May	.240	129	33	31	9	0	6	18	2
Ortiz, Nick, Bay	.236	123	20	29	9	1	6	20	1
Clemente, Edgard, Ponce	.223	112	10	25	4	1	2	14	1
Bocachica, Hiram, Sant	.211	133	23	28	6	0	2	10	**13**
Truby, Chris, May	.201	149	18	30	7	0	4	22	1

INDIVIDUAL PITCHING LEADERS
(Minimum 40 Innings)

	W	L	ERA	G	SV	IP	H	BB	SO
#Duncan, Courtney, Cag	1	0	1.03	25	**17**	26	17	11	25
Bones, Ricky, Ponce	3	0	**1.13**	7	0	40	27	14	15
Miranda, Angel, Cag	3	1	1.73	13	0	42	30	15	25
Powell, Jeremy, May	**7**	2	1.92	10	0	52	39	14	31
Hardwick, Bubba, Sant	4	1	2.26	12	0	56	40	28	**50**
Linton, Doug, May	6	1	2.38	10	0	64	56	20	41
Villegas, Ismael, Cag	4	1	2.52	11	0	54	40	16	37
Johnson, Mike, Ponce	1	3	3.05	8	0	41	39	14	26
Arteaga, J.D., May	**7**	2	3.50	10	0	54	54	8	35
Jordan, Ricardo, Bay	2	2	4.02	13	0	40	40	25	35
Sedlacek, Shawn, Car	4	2	4.03	11	0	51	59	23	26
McBride, Chris, May	1	0	4.20	9	0	41	41	13	14
DeSilva, John, Ponce	2	5	4.30	16	2	46	49	6	31
Reyes, Carlos, Car	1	3	4.60	9	0	45	52	6	25
Rojas, Chris, May	1	1	4.60	11	0	43	32	37	34
Calero, Kiko, May	3	4	4.67	9	0	44	42	25	34
Walker, Jamie, Car	2	2	6.20	14	1	41	46	7	26

VENEZUELAN LEAGUE

Lara defeated Magallanes four games to two in the league championship series, but the real playoff excitement came in the semifinal round-robin. The two finalists weren't determined until the final day, and one of the contenders was helped by that rarest of baseball rarities, a protest that was upheld.

Pastora apparently had defeated Magallanes 5-1 in an earlier game, but Magallanes manager Phil Regan filed a protest contending that Pastora closer Santos Hernandez, who led the league with 14 saves, hadn't been placed on the active list for the game.

Chris Jones

When Regan's protest was upheld, it created a doubleheader between the teams on the final day. A sweep by Pastora would have created a three-way tie for first in the round-robin, with Pastora, Magallanes and Lara all hav-

WINTER LEAGUES

ing 9-7 records. As it turned out, Magallanes swept, putting it in first place at 11-5 and Pastora all the way down to fourth at 7-9.

The playoffs featured another big story right from the start—the absence of Caracas in back-to-back years for the first time since the 1983-84 and '84-85 seasons. The Lions finished last in the Eastern Division in both 2000 and 2001, both times failing to overcome poor starts.

Caracas did get a good performance from outfielder Antonio Alvarez, who won the batting title with a .359 average. Alvarez, a Pirates farm hand, then joined Pastora for the round-robin playoff and led all hitters with a .373 average.

La Guaira outfielder Chris Jones led in RBIs with 47 and was named the league MVP.

STANDINGS

EASTERN DIVISION	W	L	PCT	GB
Magallanes Navigators	32	29	.525	—
La Guaira Sharks	30	31	.492	2
Oriente Caribbeans	26	35	.426	6½
Caracas Lions	26	36	.419	6½

WESTERN DIVISION	W	L	PCT	GB
Lara Cardinals	37	23	.617	—
Zulia Eagles	32	29	.525	5½
Pastora	31	29	.517	6
Aragua Tigers	29	31	.483	8

PLAYOFFS	W	L	PCT	GB
Magallanes Navigators	11	5	.688	—
Lara Cardinals	9	7	.563	2
Zulia Eagles	8	8	.500	3
Pastora	7	9	.438	4
La Guaira Sharks	5	11	.313	6

Championship Series: Lara defeated Magallanes, 4-2, in best-of-7 series.

INDIVIDUAL BATTING LEADERS
(Minimum 165 Plate Appearances)

	AVG	AB	R	H	2B	3B	HR	RBI	SB
Alvarez, Antonio, Car	.359	181	30	65	11	1	2	18	7
Salazar, Ruben, Ara	.342	231	33	79	14	0	4	38	2
Rodriguez, Liu, Car	.331	142	20	47	6	0	0	12	1
Mendoza, Carlos, LaG	.326	187	40	61	13	1	2	21	1
Rivera, Juan, Aragua	.324	188	25	61	11	1	7	29	4
#Machado, Robert, Mag	.315	130	16	41	14	0	4	22	0
Munoz, Orlando, Zulia	.315	143	17	45	5	0	0	17	2
Jones, Chris, LaG	.305	190	35	58	11	2	8	47	5
Taylor, Reggie, Zulia	.303	175	25	53	13	3	1	18	7
Jacobsen, Bucky, LaG	.303	142	27	43	8	1	8	28	0
Bolivar, Papo, Mag	.299	184	21	55	8	4	1	19	3
Zambrano, Roberto, Ara	.297	196	26	58	12	0	10	40	0
Colon, Cris, LaGuaira	.294	170	17	50	4	1	3	20	0
Hernandez, Ramon, Past	.293	157	18	46	9	0	5	25	1
Nieves, Jose, Ori	.290	155	28	45	6	3	8	25	2
Cabrera, Alex, Past	.289	194	28	56	13	1	13	45	1
Connell, Lino, Zulia	.288	170	25	49	10	2	3	22	1
Chavez, Endy, Mag	.284	204	36	58	10	5	0	15	9
Maldonado, Carlos, Zulia	.279	172	23	48	5	2	5	33	1
Wathan, Dusty, Ara	.276	170	21	47	7	0	2	17	0
Gonzalez, Wiki, Car	.276	181	14	50	5	0	3	27	1
Allen, Dusty, Car	.273	183	34	50	10	1	6	32	2
Izturis, Cesar, Lara	.272	206	30	56	6	2	0	19	12
Azocar, Oscar, LaG	.271	221	27	60	9	2	4	24	3
Sanchez, Alex, Past	.270	241	34	65	5	4	2	11	20
Mackowiak, Rob, Past	.269	212	32	57	10	2	7	29	6
Scutaro, Marcos, Past	.267	202	36	54	11	3	2	17	5
Carvajal, Johnny, Past	.264	178	24	47	5	2	2	17	4
Perez, Tomas, Ori	.263	198	28	52	13	2	2	19	1
Warner, Mike, Ori	.259	162	26	42	9	1	5	22	4
Raven, Luis, Lara	.257	210	37	54	9	1	9	39	3
Ensberg, Morgan, Car	.255	216	28	55	12	0	10	41	1
Smith, Nestor, Ara	.251	199	32	45	11	4	2	14	2
Freire, Alejandro, Ori	.250	172	29	43	10	1	8	21	1
Prieto, Alejandro, Zulia	.245	163	20	40	6	1	0	15	3
Perez, Robert, Lara	.242	198	25	48	9	3	6	24	5
#Alvarez, Rafael, Ara	.241	137	16	33	8	6	2	20	1

	AVG	AB	R	H	2B	3B	HR	RBI	SB
Rodriguez, Luis, Ori	.238	168	18	40	2	1	4	25	0
Helms, Wes, Mag	.236	157	24	37	10	1	9	26	2
Salazar, Oscar, Ara	.227	150	20	34	8	0	2	18	2
Gonzalez, Jesus, Zulia	.222	203	22	45	7	0	6	31	1

INDIVIDUAL PITCHING LEADERS
(Minimum 49 Innings)

	W	L	ERA	G	SV	IP	H	BB	SO
Silva, Douglas, Zulia	4	3	1.91	14	0	61	53	17	50
Rincon, Juan, Lara	0	3	1.95	11	0	51	38	19	33
#Hernandez, Santos, Past	1	1	2.25	26	14	32	25	8	35
Levrault, Allen, LaG	4	1	2.63	12	0	72	59	12	48
Laxton, Brett, Mag	3	4	2.69	11	0	64	59	23	53
Estrada, Horacio, Past	5	1	2.81	9	0	58	51	8	64
Polanco, Elvis, Zulia	1	3	2.82	13	0	51	47	19	19
Hazlett, Andy, LaG	3	2	2.96	29	0	52	41	13	50
Chacin, Gustavo, Lara	5	3	2.98	14	0	60	63	22	43
Simon, Ben, Past	3	3	3.13	13	0	63	75	14	51
Simontacchi, Jason, Ara	4	3	3.26	12	0	77	86	19	42
Evans, Keith, Past	3	5	3.27	13	0	77	74	17	57
Hurtado, Edwin, Lara	10	4	3.28	14	0	82	76	30	66
Luque, Roger, Car	4	4	3.46	13	0	65	61	10	46
Pacheco, Delvis, LaG	6	3	3.57	15	0	68	70	20	40
Romero, Josmir, Ara	6	3	3.63	12	0	62	53	18	32
Erdos, Todd, Mag	4	4	3.77	13	0	62	64	20	40
Flener, Huck, Ori	3	5	3.91	12	0	53	61	14	43
Quevedo, Ruben, Mag	2	4	4.09	12	1	51	55	15	57
Graterol, Beiker, Past	4	3	4.13	12	0	65	65	10	41
Robertson, Jeriome, Car	3	6	4.19	13	0	62	78	17	29
Conde, Argenis, Ori	6	4	4.29	14	0	80	88	26	38
#Solarte, Jose, Zulia	4	2	4.38	26	14	25	28	8	14

ARIZONA FALL LEAGUE

For a team that limped into the playoffs, it was only fitting that the Grand Canyon Rafters' postseason hero was a player who limped through both of the games.

Matthew LeCroy

Catcher Matthew LeCroy had the game-winning single in a 6-5 victory in Game One and had five RBIs in a 17-6 victory in Game Two as the Rafters swept the Phoenix Desert Dogs in the best-of-three championship series.

LeCroy, who spent much of the 2000 season with the Minnesota Twins, sprained an ankle on the last day of the regular season, but had to play in the one-tier playoff because the team's two other catchers already had gone home. He had four of the Rafters' 18 hits in Game Two, including two doubles and a home run.

"You have to suck it up," said LeCroy who was named the postseason MVP. "It was a pride issue to stay and play and finish it out. You made a commitment to play. You might as well play the whole time."

Grand Canyon went just 20-21 in the regular season, but won the Western Division by a game as four of the league's six teams had losing records. The two winning teams, Phoenix and the Scottsdale Scorpions, tied for the Eastern Division title at 25-16. Phoenix advanced to the playoffs based on its 5-3 head-to-head record against Scottsdale.

STANDINGS

EASTERN DIVISION	W	L	PCT	GB
Scottsdale Scorpions	25	16	.610	—
Phoenix Desert Dogs	25	16	.610	—
Mesa Solar Sox	15	26	.366	10

WESTERN DIVISION	W	L	PCT	GB
Grand Canyon Rafters	20	21	.488	—
Peoria Javelinas	19	22	.463	1
Maryvale Saguaros	19	22	.463	1

PLAYOFFS—Finals: Grand Canyon defeated Phoenix, 2-0, in best-of-3 series.

INDIVIDUAL BATTING LEADERS
(Minimum 100 Plate Appearances)

	AVG	AB	R	H	2B	3B	HR	RBI	SB
#Dina, Allen, Scott	.365	74	11	27	**10**	0	2	11	7
Giles, Marcus, Mesa	.359	92	19	33	9	1	2	14	3
Barnes, Larry, Phx	.355	121	18	43	9	4	1	24	2
McDonald, Donzell, Mary	.354	127	**29**	**45**	5	**5**	3	12	**18**
Mench, Kevin, GC	.354	99	20	35	6	3	4	12	3
Crosby, Bubba, Peoria	.346	104	12	36	6	1	3	13	3
Freel, Ryan, Scott	.341	91	18	31	8	3	0	9	10
Santana, Osmany, Phx	.327	107	13	35	1	1	0	7	6
Pujols, Albert, Scott	.323	93	15	30	5	1	4	21	3
Sorensen, Zach, Phx	.313	115	16	36	7	3	0	8	2
Brown, Richard, Mary	.311	106	16	33	2	2	2	20	5
LeCroy, Matthew, GC	.309	97	9	30	4	0	2	13	0
Redman, Tike, Peoria	.304	115	21	35	5	4	2	17	11
Clark, Brady, GC	.303	109	11	33	5	3	1	18	4
Randolph, Jaisen, Mesa	.302	96	13	29	3	1	0	7	2
Almonte, Erick, Mary	.301	103	19	31	2	4	4	21	4
Choi, Hee Seop, Mesa	.298	104	22	31	9	1	**6**	16	1
Hodges, Scott, Mary	.296	98	11	29	6	2	1	14	0
Ernster, Mark, Mary	.295	95	13	28	4	**5**	2	11	0
Crede, Joe, Phx	.293	116	19	34	6	1	1	11	0
Clapp, Stubby, Scott	.291	86	20	25	7	2	0	11	3
Bloomquist, Willie, Peoria	.289	90	14	26	7	1	0	8	3
Rollins, Jimmy, Mary	.286	98	13	28	4	4	0	12	11
Hall, Toby, Mesa	.286	98	14	28	6	0	1	13	0
Coffie, Ivanon, Mesa	.282	117	13	33	7	2	2	**26**	3
Kielty, Bobby, GC	.279	104	22	29	7	0	5	19	2
Brown, Dee, GC	.277	101	18	28	6	2	2	16	2
Hillenbrand, Shea, Phx	.275	102	13	28	7	1	4	22	0
Williams, Jason, GC	.274	95	10	26	6	0	0	9	7
Young, Mike, GC	.268	97	17	26	5	0	1	6	6
Kirby, Scott, Mary	.265	113	17	30	4	1	3	18	4
Curry, Mike, GC	.265	98	17	26	2	2	0	8	11
Byrnes, Eric, Phx	.265	117	16	31	5	0	5	14	5
Overbay, Lyle, Scott	.263	114	9	30	6	0	0	11	0
Wathan, Derek, Mesa	.263	95	14	25	1	1	0	7	2
Wilson, Craig, Peoria	.263	99	14	26	4	1	2	10	1
Allen, Luke, Peoria	.261	92	16	24	7	2	1	9	2
Hart, Jason, Phx	.259	116	19	30	6	0	**6**	23	0
Uribe, Juan, Peoria	.255	98	10	25	**10**	2	2	14	1
Rexrode, Jackie, Phx	.253	91	15	23	5	0	0	8	14
Wilson, Jack, Peoria	.253	99	9	25	2	1	0	5	3
Snead, Esix, Scott	.245	98	16	24	4	1	0	10	11
Hinske, Eric, Mesa	.227	97	11	22	4	1	1	10	5

INDIVIDUAL PITCHING LEADERS
(Minimum 20 Innings)

	W	L	ERA	G	SV	IP	H	BB	SO
Nina, Elvin, Phx	1	0	**0.41**	10	2	22	13	4	13
Miller, Matt, Scott	**5**	0	1.25	15	0	22	17	4	20
Reitsma, Chris, GC	2	0	1.44	13	2	25	18	4	21
Mattes, Troy, Mary	0	1	1.50	7	0	30	28	11	21
Kinney, Matt, GC	1	2	1.57	6	0	23	19	8	22
Lohse, Kyle, GC	3	0	1.80	10	0	35	32	7	35
Benoit, Joaquin, GC	2	2	1.91	8	0	33	22	6	28
Brummett, Sean, Phx	2	1	1.97	7	0	32	25	13	26
Kim, Sun-Woo, Phx	3	1	2.66	10	0	20	24	10	23
Hendrickson, Mark, Scott	2	3	2.67	7	0	30	31	12	19
Robbins, Jake, Mary	1	3	2.70	15	0	23	23	11	16
Taglienti, Jeff, Peoria	2	0	2.70	12	1	23	22	8	16
Herndon, Junior, Peoria	0	2	2.77	7	0	26	31	9	15
Andra, Jeff, Scott	2	2	2.86	8	0	35	28	6	20
Koplove, Mike, Scott	1	1	2.86	16	0	22	15	11	19
Teut, Nate, Mesa	1	0	3.00	7	0	27	24	5	25
Turman, Jason, Peoria	1	1	3.00	5	0	21	14	3	19
Pettyjohn, Adam, Scott	1	1	3.13	8	0	37	36	11	23
Knotts, Gary, Mesa	2	2	3.18	8	0	34	35	11	32
Parrish, John, Mesa	0	2	3.30	7	0	30	26	18	21
File, Bob, Scott	2	1	3.38	15	**5**	16	24	6	15
Persails, Mark, Mary	2	0	3.54	15	0	20	23	6	8
Miller, Justin, Phx	1	0	3.55	8	0	33	33	11	24
Lundberg, Spike, GC	2	3	3.67	15	1	27	24	4	9
Montgomery, Matt, Peoria	2	2	3.70	9	0	41	42	15	20
Garcia, Jose, Mary	0	1	3.75	10	0	24	24	12	23
Kessel, Kyle, Mary	0	2	3.86	8	0	28	28	8	15
Farnsworth, Jeff, Peoria	1	1	3.91	10	0	25	25	13	32
Maroth, Mike, Scott	2	2	3.97	8	0	34	32	13	21
Baez, Danys, Phx	1	2	4.01	6	0	25	21	8	22
Hodges, Kevin, Peoria	1	2	4.11	7	0	31	40	14	22
Spurling, Chris, Peoria	2	2	4.18	13	2	24	24	5	20
Harper, Travis, Mesa	2	2	4.22	7	0	32	35	9	25
Maness, Nick, Scott	2	0	4.36	8	0	33	32	17	23
Moss, Damian, Mesa	0	2	4.50	8	0	28	20	26	18

Condrey, Clay, Peoria	2	1	4.55	9	0	28	32	6	17
Cho, Jin-Ho, Phx	1	3	4.59	8	0	33	37	1	24
Hutchinson, Chad, Scott	2	1	4.64	8	0	33	26	23	**38**
Karnuth, Jason, Scott	3	1	4.70	15	0	23	24	8	9

IBL AUSTRALIA LEAGUE

The International Baseball League Australia made good on its name in 2000-01. After the league played its first season with just Australians, its four teams this time included players from several nations.

In fact, its most cosmopolitan team won the one-game playoff final, and in dramatic fashion. American first baseman A.J. Zapp singled home Troy Schader in the bottom of the ninth to give the Internationals, an amalgam of players from several countries, a 2-1 victory over Australia.

RICK BATTLE

A.J. Zapp

The league's other two teams were Taiwan and the MLB Stars, a collection of mostly American players from Major League Baseball organizations.

The final game marked the end of a sensational month for the Internationals, who had been in last place five weeks into the season. Their post-Christmas hot streak lifted them to both the regular season and playoff titles.

But there would be no 2001-02 season for the Internationals or any of the other clubs. The league went on hiatus in the fall of 2001.

STANDINGS

	W	L	T	PCT	GB
Internationals	25	15	3	.616	—
Taiwan	17	19	4	.475	6
Australia	17	19	2	.474	6
MLB Stars	17	25	1	.407	9

PLAYOFFS—Semifinals: Australia defeated Taiwan, 3-1; and Internationals defeated MLB Stars, 4-2, in one-game playoffs. **Finals:** Internationals defeated Australia, 2-1, in one-game playoff.

INDIVIDUAL BATTING LEADERS
(Minimum 100 Plate Appearances)

	AVG	AB	R	H	2B	3B	HR	RBI	SB
Hodges, Jarrod, Aus	.375	96	14	36	6	1	1	13	2
Zapp, A.J., Int	.373	153	**33**	**57**	**16**	**4**	4	32	5
Wilson, Travis, Int	.352	159	26	56	13	3	**7**	**38**	3
Huber, Justin, Aus	.323	96	9	31	3	1	3	18	1
Williams, Glenn, Aus	.315	130	18	41	3	1	5	22	4
Fingleson, Gavin, Aus	.314	156	26	49	6	1	2	19	5
Langerhans, Ryan, Int	.312	138	32	43	8	2	5	25	**12**
Schader, Troy, Int	.297	101	25	30	9	0	2	17	9
Roneberg, Brett, Aus	.294	143	24	42	9	3	1	20	6
Velazquez, Gilberto, MLB	.293	140	16	41	4	2	0	10	8
#Sohn Ji-Hwan, Int	.285	123	23	35	5	2	1	5	**12**
#Riggs, Eric, MLB	.272	136	29	37	7	**4**	4	16	8
#Stratton, Robert, MLB	.246	114	21	28	5	1	**7**	20	1

INDIVIDUAL PITCHING LEADERS
(Minimum 30 Innings)

	W	L	ERA	G	SV	IP	H	BB	SO
Dewey, Mark, Int	3	1	**0.63**	8	0	43	27	3	22
Tseng Chao-Hao, Tai	**5**	2	1.06	10	0	60	51	11	47
Lewis, Craig, Int	3	0	1.35	7	0	40	33	9	20
Bevis, P.J., Int	3	1	1.54	10	1	35	24	5	21
Chen Jung-Tsao, Tai	4	1	2.10	8	0	34	29	12	32
Guy, Brad, Int	2	4	2.48	11	0	58	57	14	**48**
Kim Kwang-Soo, Int	3	3	2.54	8	0	39	38	14	31
Joseph, Jake, MLB	**5**	3	2.68	12	0	47	49	7	39
Armitage, Barry, MLB	2	2	3.02	11	1	48	48	26	21
Yang Chien-Fu, Tai	2	0	3.16	11	1	31	34	15	26
#Voyles, Brad, Int	0	3	7.07	15	**5**	14	18	9	19

COLLEGE

Good times in Omaha
Miami celebrates its second College World Series triumph in three years

Hurricanes spoil West Coast party, deliver Morris second CWS crown

BY JOHN MANUEL

Skip Bertman already had one for his thumb. In 2001, he was looking for one for the road.

The legendary Louisiana State coach led the Tigers to their fifth College World Series championship in 10 years in 2000, then announced he would retire a year later. As a result, Bertman found a farewell celebration at every visiting ballpark he went to in 2001, honoring the coach's long, successful career.

The final farewell stop was supposed to take place in Omaha at the College World Series, everyone figured. No one would bet against Bertman leading his last LSU team to another national championship.

But while the 2001 CWS did acknowledge a coach at the pinnacle of the college game, it wasn't about Bertman. His Tigers were unceremoniously eliminated during a heated super-regional series with Tulane, their in-state rival which ended up making its first trip to Omaha.

It wasn't about Dave Van Horn, the 2001 Coach of the Year who turned Nebraska from an occasional regional contender to a CWS team. For the first time in the program's history, the Huskers played in Omaha in June, much to the delight of the local populace.

Instead, as Bertman ceded his place as college baseball's preeminent coach, Miami's Jim Morris slipped into his shoes. Morris already had earned a seat at the table of the game's top active coaches by taking the

Jim Morris

Hurricanes to their seventh CWS trip in his eight seasons at the helm.

But when his 2001 'Canes blistered Stanford 12-1 to claim the national championship, his second in three years, Morris replaced Bertman at the table's head.

The Right Ingredients

Prior to 1999, Morris was on his way to joining coaches such as Florida State's Mike Martin and Oklahoma State's Gary Ward who had made double-digit trips to Omaha without any hardware to show for it. Morris' Miami club beat Florida State for the national championship in 1999, though.

And now with the 2001 title and 897 career victories by age 49, Morris has a résumé few active coaches can rival.

The '99 title was won at the end of a long, difficult season for Miami, one tinged by the controversial departure of assistant coach and recruiting guru Turtle Thomas. In 2000, Miami failed to reach Omaha for the first time since 1993, but the No. 1-ranked Hurricanes left little doubt in 2001 that they were the best in the college game.

Technically, the Hurricanes were not the favorite in Omaha. Three West Coast powers—Cal State Fullerton, Southern California and Stanford—entered the Series as favorites thanks to their deep pitching staffs. Cal State Fullerton earned the No. 1 overall seed thanks mostly to a convincing three-game sweep of the Hurricanes in April at Mark Light

Stadium, the first time Miami ever had been swept at home.

But Miami did very little wrong after that, going 28-3 the rest of the year and winning its last 17 games. The formula was vintage Morris in that the multi-faceted 'Canes routinely demonstrated more than one way to win a game. That was obvious in Omaha, where Miami beat Tennessee in a pair of slugfests sandwiched around a tight 4-3 win against Southern California.

In the finale, the 'Canes left no doubt about overall superiority, dominating Stanford while tying the CWS record for the largest margin of victory in a championship game.

"Whether we win 2-1 or 21-13, our team has done what it's needed to do to win in the regionals, super-regionals and here," Morris said.

Developing an effective bullpen is a trait of Morris' Miami teams. After developing such closers as Jay Tessmer, Danny Graves, Robbie Morrison and Michael Neu over the years, Morris turned to junior Luke DeBold and freshman George Huguet in 2001. Both made a national-high 44 appearances.

Huguet finished with 14 saves, third in the nation, and a 2.03 ERA, while the sidearming DeBold was used mostly in a set-up role.

Senior righthander Tom Farmer started and won the national championship game, finishing the year at 15-2, 3.54. The Hurricanes had two other effective starters, but

DAVID GONZALEZ

Kevin Brown: five RBIs in title game

while sophomore righthander Kiki Bengochea (9-4, 4.10) had the staff's best stuff and left-hander Brian Walker (12-1, 4.22) won 24 of his last 27 decisions, Miami's pitching wasn't as dominant individually as it was taken as a whole.

Offensively, the Hurricanes' most obvious asset was speed. Miami stole 228 bases to lead Division I and featured four players with more than 30 swipes apiece: shortstop Javy Rodriguez (66), outfielder Mike Rodriguez (53), DH Marcus Nettles (44) and outfielder Charlton Jimerson (31).

Miami could also play the power game if it needed to, especially late in the season after senior first baseman Kevin Brown (.284-15-53) got hot. Brown had three homers and 10 RBIs in a regional win against Stetson and had five RBIs in the smashing of Stanford, giving him nine RBIs in a pair of title-game appearances.

"This was a total, total team effort," Morris said. "You can't ask any more of a team. We pitched great, we hit great and we played flawless defense."

Miami had 11 players selected in the 2001 draft, more than any other college team. And it was Jimerson, an Oakland native and fifth-round pick, who put all facets of Miami's game together.

Nicknamed "Chewdini" by teammate Greg Lovelady, Jimerson emerged as a legitimate talent late in his senior season after spending more than three years in a reserve role, honing his skills. His boundless enthusiasm and

COLLEGE WORLD SERIES

Omaha
June 8-16, 2001

STANDINGS

BRACKET ONE	W	L	RF	RA
Stanford	3	0	22	15
Cal State Fullerton	2	2	20	15
Tulane	1	2	19	29
Nebraska	0	2	9	11

Bracket One Final: Stanford 4, Cal State Fullerton 2

BRACKET TWO	W	L	RF	RA
Miami	3	0	37	22
Tennessee	2	2	48	47
Southern California	1	2	16	19
Georgia	0	2	17	30

Bracket Two Final: Miami 12, Tennessee 6
Championship Game: Miami 12, Stanford 1

INDIVIDUAL BATTING LEADERS
(Minimum 10 At-Bats)

PLAYER, TEAM	AVG	AB	R	H	2B	3B	HR	RBI	SB
Danny Matienzo, Miami	.588	17	7	10	1	0	3	9	0
Ryan Garko, Stanford	.583	12	5	7	1	0	2	4	0
David Coffey, Georgia	.545	11	4	6	1	0	1	6	0
Anthony Lunetta, USC	.545	11	1	6	3	0	0	1	0
Kevin Mannix, Miami	.538	13	3	7	1	0	0	3	0
Brandon Hopkins, Tenn	.533	15	7	8	0	1	1	7	0
Jeff Christensen, Tenn	.500	18	9	9	3	0	1	8	2
Andy Cannizaro, Tulane	.500	12	1	6	1	0	0	1	1
Anthony Giarratano, Tulane	.500	10	5	5	0	0	0	1	0
Kris Bennett, Tenn	.471	17	6	8	1	0	2	11	0

INDIVIDUAL PITCHING LEADERS
(Minimum 5 Innings)

PLAYER, TEAM	W	L	ERA	G	SV	IP	H	BB	SO
Darric Merrell, CS Fullerton	1	0	0.00	1	0	8	6	3	4
Kirk Saarloos, CS Fullerton	0	0	1.08	1	0	8	5	0	3
Luke DeBold, Miami	0	0	1.42	4	0	6	4	2	4
Brian Bannister, USC	0	0	1.80	2	0	5	3	1	2
R.D. Spiehs, Nebraska	0	0	3.60	1	0	5	5	0	1
Tom Farmer, Miami	2	0	4.22	2	0	11	10	4	8
Shane Komine, Nebraska	0	1	4.50	1	0	8	7	1	9

ALL-TOURNAMENT TEAM

C—Ryan Garko, Stanford. **1B**—Kevin Brown, Miami. **2B**—David Bacani, Cal State Fullerton. **3B**—Kris Bennett, Tennessee. **SS**—Chris Burke, Tennessee. **OF**—Jeff Christensen, Tennessee; Sam Fuld, Stanford; Charlton Jimerson, Miami. **DH**—Danny Matienzo, Miami. **P**—Jeff Bruksch, Stanford; Tom Farmer, Miami.
Most Outstanding Player—Charlton Jimerson, of, Miami.

CHAMPIONSHIP GAME
Miami 12, Stanford 1

STANFORD	ab	r	h	bi	MIAMI	ab	r	h	bi
O'Riordan 2b	4	0	0	0	Jimerson cf	5	0	1	0
Fuld cf	3	0	1	1	M Rodriguez lf	2	1	0	1
Garko c	3	0	2	0	J Rodriguez ss	4	3	2	0
Quentin rf	4	0	1	0	Matienzo dh	2	3	2	1
Ash dh	2	0	0	0	Nettles dh	1	0	0	0
Garza 3b	1	0	0	0	Howard 3b	4	3	2	1
Topham 3b-ss	3	0	0	0	Mannix rf	3	0	2	3
Swope ph	1	0	0	0	Burt rf	1	0	1	0
Hall lf-3b	3	0	0	0	Brown 1b	5	1	2	5
Naatjes ph	1	0	0	0	Clute 2b	4	1	1	0
Dragicevich ss	1	0	1	0	Lovelady c	4	0	0	0
Cooper ph-lf	2	0	0	0					
Van Zandt 1b	2	1	0	0					
Totals	30	1	5	1	Totals	35	12	13	11

Stanford	000 001 000—	1
Louisiana State	004 052 01x—	12

E—Quentin (8), Dragicevich (14). **DP**—Miami 2. **LOB**—Stanford 6, Miami 7. **2B**—Garko (16), J. Rodriguez (12), Matienzo (13), Mannix (10), Brown (17). **HR**—Brown (15). **SH**—Mannix (11). **SF**—M. Rodriguez (6). **SB**—M. Rodriguez (53).

STANFORD	ip	h	r	er	bb	so	MIAMI	ip	h	r	er	bb	so
Gosling L (7-3)	4	7	7	7	3	2	Farmer W (15-2)	5⅔	4	1	1	2	3
Bruksch	⅓	2	2	1	0	0	DeBold	2⅓	1	0	0	2	2
Wodnicki	⅔	1	2	2	2	0	Prendes	1	0	0	0	0	0
Hudgins	1	1	0	0	0	0							
McCally	1	0	0	0	0	1							
Willcox	1	2	1	0	0	1							

WP—Farmer (8). **HBP**—by Gosling (M. Rodriguez).
T—3:42. **A**—24,282.

charismatic leadership were on full display as the 'Canes surged down the stretch.

Jimerson led on and off the field, from calling a team meeting after the Cal State Fullerton sweep to help get Miami back on track, to hitting leadoff homers against Tennessee and Southern California in Omaha, to thwarting Southern California with a homer-stealing catch over the Rosenblatt Stadium wall. He hit .375-4-13 with 12 steals in nine postseason games and was named the CWS' most outstanding player.

The only performer to rival Jimerson at the CWS in 2001 was President George W. Bush, who became the first sitting president to attend the Series. The righthander threw out the first pitch prior to the opening Stanford-Tulane game, a fastball that fairly hummed across the plate.

Charlton Jimerson

"He did throw a great pitch," said Stanford catcher Ryan Garko, who had the honor of being on the receiving end of Bush's ceremonial toss. "It was a strike. He said we worked well together as a battery."

Season Of Stars

Beyond Miami's all-around contribution, college baseball had plenty of individual performers whose talent and accomplishments set them apart in 2001.

First and foremost was righthander Mark Prior, whose college career began when he turned down $1.5 million from the New York Yankees as a supplemental first-round draft pick in 1998. He attended Vanderbilt for a year before transferring to Southern California, where he joined the likes of Tom Seaver, Tom House, Randy Johnson, Seth Etherton and Barry Zito in

COLLEGE WORLD SERIES CHAMPIONS: 1947-2001

Year	Champion	Coach	Record	Runner-Up	MVP
1947	California*	Clint Evans	31-10	Yale	None selected
1948	Southern California	Sam Barry	40-12	Yale	None selected
1949	Texas*	Bibb Falk	23-7	Wake Forest	Charles Teague, 2b, Wake Forest
1950	Texas	Bibb Falk	27-6	Washington State	Ray VanCleef, of, Rutgers
1951	Oklahoma*	Jack Baer	19-9	Tennessee	Sid Hatfield, 1b-p, Tennessee
1952	Holy Cross	Jack Berry	21-3	Missouri	Jim O'Neill, p, Holy Cross
1953	Michigan	Ray Fisher	21-9	Texas	J.L. Smith, p, Texas
1954	Missouri	Hi Simmons	22-4	Rollins	Tom Yewcic, c, Michigan State
1955	Wake Forest	Taylor Sanford	29-7	Western Michigan	Tom Borland, p, Oklahoma State
1956	Minnesota	Dick Siebert	33-9	Arizona	Jerry Thomas, p, Minnesota
1957	California*	George Wolfman	35-10	Penn State	Cal Emery, 1b-p, Penn State
1958	Southern California	Rod Dedeaux	35-7	Missouri	Bill Thom, p, Southern California
1959	Oklahoma State	Toby Greene	27-5	Arizona	Jim Dobson, 3b, Oklahoma State
1960	Minnesota	Dick Siebert	34-7	Southern California	John Erickson, 2b, Minnesota
1961	Southern California*	Rod Dedeaux	43-9	Oklahoma State	Littleton Fowler, p, Oklahoma State
1962	Michigan	Don Lund	31-13	Santa Clara	Bob Garibaldi, p, Santa Clara
1963	Southern California	Rod Dedeaux	37-16	Arizona	Bud Hollowell, c, Southern California
1964	Minnesota	Dick Siebert	31-12	Missouri	Joe Ferris, p, Maine
1965	Arizona State	Bobby Winkles	54-8	Ohio State	Sal Bando, 3b, Arizona State
1966	Ohio State	Marty Karow	27-6	Oklahoma State	Steve Arlin, p, Ohio State
1967	Arizona State	Bobby Winkles	53-12	Houston	Ron Davini, c, Arizona State
1968	Southern California*	Rod Dedeaux	45-14	Southern Illinois	Bill Seinsoth, 1b, Southern California
1969	Arizona State	Bobby Winkles	56-11	Tulsa	John Dolinsek, of, Arizona State
1970	Southern California	Rod Dedeaux	51-13	Florida State	Gene Ammann, p, Florida State
1971	Southern California	Rod Dedeaux	53-13	Southern Illinois	Jerry Tabb, 1b, Tulsa
1972	Southern California	Rod Dedeaux	50-13	Arizona State	Russ McQueen, p, Southern California
1973	Southern California*	Rod Dedeaux	51-11	Arizona State	Dave Winfield, of-p, Minnesota
1974	Southern California	Rod Dedeaux	50-20	Miami (Fla.)	George Milke, p, Southern California
1975	Texas	Cliff Gustafson	56-6	South Carolina	Mickey Reichenbach, 1b, Texas
1976	Arizona	Jerry Kindall	56-17	Eastern Michigan	Steve Powers, dh-p, Arizona
1977	Arizona State	Jim Brock	57-12	South Carolina	Bob Horner, 3b, Arizona State
1978	Southern California*	Rod Dedeaux	54-9	Arizona State	Rod Boxberger, p, Southern California
1979	Cal State Fullerton	Augie Garrido	60-14	Arkansas	Tony Hudson, p, Cal State Fullerton
1980	Arizona	Jerry Kindall	45-21	Hawaii	Terry Francona, of, Arizona
1981	Arizona State	Jim Brock	55-13	Oklahoma State	Stan Holmes, of, Arizona State
1982	Miami (Fla.)*	Ron Fraser	57-18	Wichita State	Dan Smith, p, Miami (Fla.)
1983	Texas*	Cliff Gustafson	66-14	Alabama	Calvin Schiraldi, p, Texas
1984	Cal State Fullerton	Augie Garrido	66-20	Texas	John Fishel, of, Cal State Fullerton
1985	Miami (Fla.)*	Ron Fraser	64-16	Texas	Greg Ellena, dh, Miami (Fla.)
1986	Arizona	Jerry Kindall	49-19	Florida State	Mike Senne, of, Arizona
1987	Stanford	Mark Marquess	53-17	Oklahoma State	Paul Carey, of, Stanford
1988	Stanford	Mark Marquess	46-23	Arizona State	Lee Plemel, p, Stanford
1989	Wichita State	Gene Stephenson	68-16	Texas	Greg Brummett, p, Wichita State
1990	Georgia	Steve Webber	52-19	Oklahoma State	Mike Rebhan, p, Georgia
1991	Louisiana State*	Skip Bertman	55-18	Wichita State	Gary Hymel, c, Louisiana State
1992	Pepperdine*	Andy Lopez	48-11	Cal State Fullerton	Phil Nevin, 3b, Cal State Fullerton
1993	Louisiana State	Skip Bertman	53-17	Wichita State	Todd Walker, 2b, Louisiana State
1994	Oklahoma*	Larry Cochell	50-17	Georgia Tech	Chip Glass, of, Oklahoma
1995	Cal State Fullerton*	Augie Garrido	57-9	Southern California	Mark Kotsay, of-p, Cal State Fullerton
1996	Louisiana State*	Skip Bertman	52-15	Miami (Fla.)	Pat Burrell, 3b, Miami
1997	Louisiana State*	Skip Bertman	57-13	Alabama	Brandon Larson, ss, Louisiana State
1998	Southern California	Mike Gillespie	49-17	Arizona State	Wes Rachels, 2b, Southern California
1999	Miami*	Jim Morris	50-13	Florida State	Marshall McDougall, 2b, Florida State
2000	Louisiana State*	Skip Bertman	52-17	Stanford	Trey Hodges, rhp, Louisiana State
2001	Miami*	Jim Morris	53-12	Stanford	Charlton Jimerson, of, Miami

*Undefeated

PLAYER OF THE YEAR

BY JOHN MANUEL

Good pitching still beats good hitting in college baseball, no matter how many advantages hitters have. The evidence was all over the college baseball landscape in 2001, no matter where you looked. It was most obvious on Baseball America's All-America teams, which featured five pitchers with sub-2.00 ERAs.

This was a Year of the Pitcher.

The tone was set by Southern California's Mark Prior, who redefined dominant. Statistics tell part of the story as to why Prior was selected Baseball America's College Player of the Year, just the fourth pitcher to win the award. He joins Stanford's Jeff Austin (1998), Clemson's Kris Benson (1996) and Louisiana State's Ben McDonald (1989).

Benson and McDonald were selected first overall in the draft and Prior probably would have been as well had the Minnesota Twins not been scared off by his financial demands. Prior was selected second by the Chicago Cubs and signed a record five-year, $10.5 million major league contract after a 10-week holdout.

Mark Prior: 15-1, 1.69, 202 strikeouts

LARRY GOREN

Prior became just the 14th pitcher in Division I history to post 200 strikeouts in a season, and he did it in the most efficient manner possible. While going 15-1, 1.69 Prior struck out 202 while walking just 18 in 139 innings. He gave up 100 hits, just five of them home runs. In his lone College World Series start, Georgia patted itself on the back for scratching out four runs in seven innings during an 11-5 loss.

"I thought Mark Prior was everything he was advertised to be," Georgia coach Ron Polk said. "He's really good, and he's got a great future. We tried to get to him early in the count, and I thought we had some quality at-bats."

Apparently, other teams realized attacking Prior was their best way to answer his unique combination of power, command and poise. Early on, Prior thoroughly dominated his competition, leading long-time college baseball observers to proclaim him as the greatest pitcher in college history.

But in the month entering the CWS, Prior pitched in more mortal fashion.

He followed a 13-day layoff with his poorest start of the year, allowing six runs (four earned) in a seven-inning effort against Washington State. In his next start at Oregon State, he again was just mediocre—by his standards—striking out a season-low five in seven innings.

But he gave up three runs and got the win, which mattered most to the 6-foot-5, 220-pound junior righthander. He also wanted to make sure he was healthy, so he turned again to personal pitching guru Tom House for advice.

"I was a little tired and lost a little rhythm after the layoff," Prior said. "Tom told me the reason I wasn't pitching the way I did before the layoff was my body had gotten used to that time, to not working as hard. So I had to really step up my workouts and work hard to get my rhythm back.

"I was a little tired, but I felt I pitched well in the regional and super-regional."

By any standard—except maybe the Prior standard of 2001—he did. Against Pepperdine, Prior gave up 11 hits but just two runs while striking out 14 in eight innings. The Trojans rallied for a 4-3 win with three runs in the bottom of the ninth. In the super-regional, Prior was more efficient, giving up a first-inning run to Florida International before finishing with eight straight zeroes in a 5-1 victory.

Prior was primed to pitch a second game at the College World Series, but the Trojans were eliminated one game earlier. There was also considerable talk that he might help the Cubs in the September pennant race, but his late signing foiled that plan as well.

COLLEGE BASEBALL

PREVIOUS WINNERS

1981—Mike Sodders, 3b, Arizona State
1982—Jeff Ledbetter, of-lhp, Florida State
1983—Dave Magadan, 1b, Alabama
1984—Oddibe McDowell, of, Arizona State
1985—Pete Incaviglia, of, Oklahoma State
1986—Casey Close, of, Michigan
1987—Robin Ventura, 3b, Oklahoma State
1988—John Olerud, 1b-lhp, Washington State
1989—Ben McDonald, rhp, Louisiana State
1990—Mike Kelly, of, Arizona State
1991—David McCarty, 1b, Stanford
1992—Phil Nevin, 3b, Cal State Fullerton
1993—Brooks Kieschnick, dh-rhp, Texas
1994—Jason Varitek, c, Georgia Tech
1995—Todd Helton, 1b-lhp, Tennessee
1996—Kris Benson, rhp, Clemson
1997—J.D. Drew, of, Florida State
1998—Jeff Austin, rhp, Stanford
1999—Jason Jennings, rhp, Baylor
2000—Mark Teixeira, 3b, Georgia Tech

THE ROAD TO OMAHA

SUPER-REGIONALS

June 1-3; 16 teams, eight best-of-3 series (Winners advance to College World Series)

REGIONALS

May 25-27; 64 teams, 16 double-elimination tournaments (Winners advance to super-regionals)
*Automatic qualifier

CAL STATE FULLERTON

■ **Super-Regional Site:** Fullerton, Calif. (Cal State Fullerton).
Participants: Mississippi State (39-22) at Cal State Fullerton (44-16).
(Cal State Fullerton wins 2-0, advances to College World Series).

❑ **Regional Site:** Fullerton, Calif. (Cal State Fullerton).
Participants: *No. 1 Cal State Fullerton (41-15), No. 2 Arizona State (36-18), No. 3 Texas Tech (40-18), *No. 4 Temple (27-29).
Champion: Cal State Fullerton (3-1). **Runner-Up:** Texas Tech (3-2).
Outstanding Player: Shawn Norris, 3b, Cal State Fullerton.

❑ **Regional Site:** Columbus, Ohio (Ohio State).
Participants: *No. 1 Mississippi State (36-22), No. 2 Ohio State (43-16), *No. 3 Delaware (44-13), *No. 4 Kent State (30-28).
Champion: Mississippi State (3-0). **Runner-Up:** Kent State (2-2).
Outstanding Player: Matthew Brinson, 1b, Mississippi State.
(Miss. State advances to meet Cal State Fullerton in super-regional).

NEBRASKA

■ **Super Regional Site:** Lincoln, Neb. (Nebraska).
Participants: Rice (47-18) at Nebraska (48-14).
(Nebraska wins 2-0, advances to College World Series).

❑ **Regional Site:** Houston (Rice).
Participants: *No. 1 Rice (43-17), No. 2 Baylor (35-22), No. 3 Houston (29-28), *No. 4 Texas-Arlington (38-23).
Champion: Rice (4-1). **Runner-Up:** Baylor (2-2).
Outstanding Player: Jesse Roman, 1b, Rice.

❑ **Regional Site:** Lincoln, Neb. (Nebraska).
Participants: *No. 1 Nebraska (45-14), No. 2 Rutgers (40-15), *No. 3 Brigham Young (38-20), *No. 4 Northern Iowa (34-26).
Champion: Nebraska (3-0). **Runner-Up:** Rutgers (2-2).
Outstanding Player: Jeff Leise, of, Nebraska.
(Rice advances to meet Nebraska in super-regional).

TULANE

■ **Super Regional Site:** Metairie, La. (Tulane).
Participants: Louisiana State (43-20) at Tulane (53-10).
(Tulane wins 2-1, advances to College World Series).

❑ **Regional Site:** New Orleans (Tulane).
Participants: *No. 1 Tulane (50-10), No. 2 Mississippi (38-21), No. 3 Oklahoma State (40-20), *No. 4 Southern (43-10).
Champion: Tulane (3-0). **Runner-Up:** Oklahoma State (2-2).
Outstanding Player: Joey Charron, lhp, Tulane.

❑ **Regional Site:** Baton Rouge (Louisiana State).
Participants: No. 1 Louisiana State (40-19), No. 2 Virginia Commonwealth (38-17), No. 3 California (33-23), *No. 4 Minnesota (39-19).
Champion: Louisiana State (3-1). **Runner-Up:** Virginia Commonwealth (3-2).
Outstanding Player: Josh Arteaga, ss, Virginia Commonwealth.
(Louisiana State advances to meet Tulane in super-regional).

STANFORD

■ **Super Regional Site:** Stanford, Calif. (Stanford).
Participants: South Carolina (48-18) at Stanford (46-15).
(Stanford wins 2-1, advances to College World Series).

❑ **Regional Site:** Columbia, S.C. (South Carolina).
Participants: *No. 1 Central Florida (49-12), No. 2 South Carolina (44-17), *No. 3 The Citadel (38-22), *No. 4 Princeton (22-23).
Champion: South Carolina (4-1). **Runner-Up:** Central Florida (2-2).
Outstanding Player: Kip Bouknight, rhp, South Carolina.

❑ **Regional Site:** Stanford, Calif. (Stanford).
Participants: No. 1 Stanford (42-14), No. 2 Long Beach State (35-

21), No. 3 Texas (34-24), *No. 4 Marist (32-19).
Champion: Stanford (4-1). **Runner-Up:** Texas (2-2).
Outstanding Players: Ryan Garko, c, Stanford; Ben King, of-dh, Texas.
(South Carolina advances to meet Stanford in super-regional).

MIAMI

■ **Super Regional Site:** Coral Gables, Fla. (Miami).
Participants: Clemson (41-20) at Miami (47-12).
(Miami wins 2-0, advances to College World Series).

❑ **Regional Site:** Coral Gables, Fla. (Miami).
Participants: No. 1 Miami (44-12), No. 2 Florida (34-25), No. 3 Stetson (41-15), *No. 4 Bucknell (31-17).
Champion: Miami (3-0). **Runner-Up:** Stetson (2-2).
Outstanding Player: Kevin Brown, 1b, Miami.

❑ **Regional Site:** Clemson, S.C. (Clemson).
Participants: *No. 1 South Alabama (44-17), No. 2 Clemson (38-20), *No. 3 William & Mary (35-18), *No. 4 Seton Hall (32-21).
Champion: Clemson (3-0). **Runner-Up:** Seton Hall (2-2).
Outstanding Player: Michael Johnson, 1b, Clemson.
(Clemson advances to meet Miami in super-regional).

TENNESSEE

■ **Super Regional Site:** Kinston, N.C. (East Carolina).
Participants: Tennessee (44-18) at East Carolina (47-11).
(Tennessee wins 2-0, advances to College World Series).

❑ **Regional Site:** Knoxville, Tenn. (Tennessee).
Participants: *No. 1 Wake Forest (41-16), No. 2 Tennessee (41-17), No. 3 Middle Tennessee State (41-15), *No. 4 Tennessee Tech (32-28).
Champion: Tennessee (3-1). **Runner-Up:** Wake Forest (3-2).
Outstanding Player: Wyatt Allen, rhp, Tennessee.

❑ **Regional Site:** Wilson, N.C. (East Carolina).
Participants: No. 1 East Carolina (44-11), No. 2 Winthrop (46-14), No. 3 South Florida (32-29), *No. 4 Maryland-Baltimore County (31-18).
Champion: East Carolina (3-0). **Runner-Up:** Winthrop (2-2).
Outstanding Player: Chad Tracy, 3b, East Carolina.
(Tennessee advances to meet East Carolina in super-regional).

GEORGIA

■ **Super Regional Site:** Athens, Ga. (Georgia).
Participants: Florida State (46-17) at Georgia (45-19).
(Georgia wins 2-1, advances to College World Series).

❑ **Regional Site:** Athens, Ga. (Georgia).
Participants: No. 1 Georgia (41-18), No. 2 Georgia Tech (41-18), *No. 3 Coastal Carolina (40-18), No. 4 Georgia Southern (41-18).
Champion: Georgia (4-1). **Runner-Up:** Coastal Carolina (2-2).
Outstanding Player: Jeff Keppinger, ss, Georgia.

❑ **Regional Site:** Tallahassee, Fla. (Florida State).
Participants: No. 1 Florida State (43-17), No. 2 Auburn (35-19), No. 3 Jacksonville (38-23), *No. 4 Bethune-Cookman (26-32).
Champion: Florida State (3-0). **Runner-Up:** Auburn (2-2).
Outstanding Player: John-Ford Griffin, of, Florida State.
(Florida State advances to meet Georgia in super-regional).

SOUTHERN CALIFORNIA

■ **Super Regional Site:** Los Angeles (Southern California).
Participants: Florida International (43-19) at Southern California (42-17).
(Southern California wins 2-0, advances to College World Series).

❑ **Regional Site:** South Bend, Ind. (Notre Dame).
Participants: No. 1 Notre Dame (46-11), No. 2 UC Santa Barbara (39-15), No. 3 Florida International (40-18), *No. 4 Wisconsin-Milwaukee (39-16).
Champion: Florida International (3-1). **Runner-Up:** Notre Dame (3-2).
Outstanding Player: Willie Collazo, lhp, Florida International.

❑ **Regional Site:** Los Angeles (Southern California).
Participants: No. 1 Southern California (39-17), *No. 2 Pepperdine (41-16), No. 3 Fresno State (39-23), *No. 4 Oral Roberts (48-11).
Champion: USC (3-0). **Runner-Up:** Fresno State (2-2).
Outstanding Player: Michael Moon, 3b, Southern California.
(Florida International advances to meet USC in super-regional).

the program's pantheon of great pitchers.

Prior, the College Player of the Year, went 15-1, 1.69 with 202 strikeouts and 18 walks in 139 innings. He gave up just 100 hits while dominating college hitters week after week, game after game.

Prior entered the season ranked behind only Georgia Tech third baseman Mark Teixeira among the nation's top college prospects. Teixeira, the reigning POY, got off to a blazing start with 12 hits (four homers) and 11 RBIs in his first 24 at-bats. But he broke his right ankle going back on a ball in a game against Elon in early February and didn't return until May. In the meantime, preseason No. 1 Georgia Tech fell from the top spot in the rankings and eventually finished out of the Top 25 altogether.

Several pitchers challenged Prior for mound supremacy. Baseball America's entire staff on its All-America first team sported ERAs below 2.00. Middle Tennessee State's Dewon Brazelton gave up just 82 hits in 127 innings while striking out 154. Notre Dame's Aaron Heilman won all 15 of his starts with 12 complete games, while Central Florida's Justin Pope went 15-1 and broke Roger Clemens' Division I record by throwing 38 consecutive scoreless innings.

With Teixeira down, a shortstop and a two-way star bid for the title of best position player. Tennessee's Chris Burke, a second baseman his first two seasons, made two changes in his game to become one of the nation's top players. He moved to shortstop, handling the new defensive responsibilities with aplomb.

With a different stance providing him with more power, Burke made most of his noise at the plate, hitting .435-20-60. He led the nation with 105 runs (20 more than his nearest competitor) and 118 hits, adding 21 doubles, 11 triples and 49 stolen bases.

He tied for the national lead in total bases (221) with Kent State righthander/first baseman John VanBenschoten. VanBenschoten wasn't a known commodity coming into the season. He spent his summer at the IMG Academy in Bradenton, Fla., adding 17 pounds to his 6-foot-4 frame and improving his speed, cutting 0.3 seconds off his 60-yard time.

As a result, the 6-foot-4, 220-pounder blossomed into the country's top power hitter, leading the nation with 31 home runs and a .982 slugging percentage. VanBenschoten also had eight saves and led the Golden Flashes

President George W. Bush attended the opening of the CWS

to the Mid-America Conference tournament championship and resulting regional berth.

Both players became high first-round picks, with VanBenschoten going eighth overall to the Pirates while Burke went 10th to the Astros.

Not All Good News

Nebraska's appearance in the College World Series was the fourth by a team from the revamped Big 12 Conference; by going 0-2, the Huskers extended the league's losing streak in Omaha to eight games.

The league got more bad news in April when Iowa State announced it was discontinuing baseball effective at the end of the season. Iowa State, whose program dated back to 1892, became the latest Division I school to drop the sport. After losing eight of their first 10 games after the announcement, the Cyclones rallied to earn the eighth and final spot in the Big 12 tournament, where they eliminated Baylor before finishing their last season at 24-29.

"There are features about baseball that put it at a disadvantage at a school like Iowa State," Big 12 commissioner Kevin Weiberg said. "First is its inability to draw substantial revenue from baseball, and the second pretty much causes the first, and that's the weather."

Virginia almost met the same fate. An athletic department task force recommended gutting baseball and other men's non-revenue programs, a proposal that would

DAVID GONZALEZ

2001 COLLEGE ALL-AMERICA TEAM

Selected by Baseball America

John VanBenschoten

Dewon Brazelton

Chris Burke

Shelley Duncan

Aaron Heilman

FIRST TEAM

Pos.	Player, School	Hometown	YR	AVG	AB	R	H	2B	3B	HR	RBI	SB	Drafted/Round
C	Kelly Shoppach, Baylor	Fort Worth, Texas	Jr.	.397	234	51	93	20	2	12	69	4	Red Sox (2)
1B	John VanBenschoten, Kent State	Milford, Ohio	Jr.	.440	225	74	99	17	6	31	84	23	Pirates (1)
2B	Michael Woods, Southern	Baton Rouge	Jr.	.453	170	68	77	27	5	14	54	32	Tigers (1)
3B	Jeff Baker, Clemson	Woodbridge, Va.	So.	.369	233	66	86	13	2	23	75	5	Not eligible
SS	Chris Burke, Tennessee	Louisville	Jr.	.435	271	105	118	21	11	20	60	49	Astros (1)
OF	John Cole, Nebraska	Kanata, Ontario	Jr.	.418	239	71	100	15	4	11	61	28	Mariners (5)
OF	Shelley Duncan, Arizona	Tucson	Jr.	.338	228	64	77	9	1	24	78	3	Yankees (2)
OF	John-Ford Griffin, Florida State	Sarasota, Fla.	Jr.	.450	251	79	113	30	0	19	75	11	Yankees (1)
DH	Jake Gautreau, Tulane	McAllen, Texas	Jr.	.355	290	82	103	23	1	21	96	8	Padres (1)
UT	Cory Sullivan, Wake Forest	Pittsburgh	Sr.	.390	264	85	103	20	1	13	67	27	Rockies (7)

Pos.	Player, School	Hometown	YR	W	L	ERA	G	SV	IP	H	BB	SO	Drafted/Round
P	Dewon Brazelton, Middle Tennessee	Tullahoma, Tenn.	Jr.	13	2	1.42	15	0	127	82	24	154	Devil Rays (1)
P	Aaron Heilman, Notre Dame	Logansport, Ind.	Sr.	15	0	1.74	15	0	114	70	31	111	Mets (1)
P	Noah Lowry, Pepperdine	Ojai, Calif.	Jr.	14	2	1.71	18	1	121	88	41	142	Giants (1)
P	Justin Pope, Central Florida	Lake Worth, Fla.	Jr.	15	1	1.68	17	0	123	97	27	158	Cardinals (1)
P	Mark Prior, Southern California	Bonita, Calif.	Jr.	15	1	1.69	20	0	139	100	18	202	Cubs (1)
UT	Cory Sullivan, Wake Forest	Pittsburgh	Sr.	7	0	3.52	13	0	77	72	36	54	Rockies (7)

SECOND TEAM

Pos.	Player, School	Hometown	YR	AVG	AB	R	H	2B	3B	HR	RBI	SB	Drafted
C	Casey Myers, Arizona State	Casa Grande, Ariz.	Sr.	.395	223	53	88	17	0	7	69	2	Athletics (9)
1B	Dan Johnson, Nebraska	Coon Rapids, Minn.	Sr.	.361	230	77	83	13	1	25	86	7	Athletics (7)
2B	Chris O'Riordan, Stanford	San Diego	Jr.	.359	281	62	101	17	2	12	68	16	Not drafted
3B	Kevin Youkilis, Cincinnati	Cincinnati	Sr.	.405	210	81	85	7	2	18	61	22	Red Sox (8)
SS	Jeff Keppinger, Georgia	Auburn, Ga.	Jr.	.389	262	69	102	15	5	18	73	10	Pirates (4)
OF	Matt Davis, Virginia Commonwealth	Colonial Heights, Va.	Jr.	.396	227	84	90	7	2	3	26	49	Not drafted
OF	Greg Dobbs, Oklahoma	Moreno Valley, Calif.	Sr.	.428	243	53	104	25	2	10	62	12	Mariners (FA)
OF	Jason Knoedler, Miami (Ohio)	Springfield, Ill.	Jr.	.402	239	79	96	15	3	17	50	24	Tigers (6)
DH	Ryan Brunner, Northern Iowa	Charles City, Iowa	Sr.	.377	239	72	90	18	2	25	82	6	Red Sox (12)
UT	Dan Haren, Pepperdine	West Covina, Calif.	Jr.	.308	224	33	69	8	0	5	47	1	Cardinals (2)

Pos.	Player, School	Hometown	YR	W	L	ERA	G	SV	IP	H	BB	SO	Drafted
P	Jason Arnold, Central Florida	Palm Bay, Fla.	Sr.	14	3	1.97	19	0	119	82	32	150	Yankees (2)
P	Kenny Baugh, Rice	Houston	Sr.	13	2	2.17	22	0	141	106	54	163	Tigers (1)
P	Nate Fernley, Brigham Young	Long Beach	Sr.	16	3	3.12	21	0	153	136	32	133	Indians (FA)
P	Shane Komine, Nebraska	Honolulu	Jr.	14	2	3.35	18	0	132	129	36	157	Cardinals (19)
P	Kirk Saarloos, Cal State Fullerton	Long Beach	Sr.	15	2	2.18	25	4	153	99	23	153	Astros (3)
UT	Dan Haren, Pepperdine	West Covina, Calif.	Jr.	11	3	2.22	17	1	130	106	31	97	Cardinals (2)

THIRD TEAM

Pos.	Player, School	Hometown	YR	AVG	AB	R	H	2B	3B	HR	RBI	SB	Drafted
C	Tim Whittaker, South Carolina	Conway, S.C.	Sr.	.294	238	54	70	14	0	21	74	1	Blue Jays (38)
1B	Aaron Clark, Alabama	Ennis, Texas	Sr.	.335	212	66	71	15	2	20	71	5	Devil Rays (8)
2B	Dan Uggla, Memphis	Columbia, Tenn.	Jr.	.379	214	72	81	28	3	18	67	5	D'backs (11)
3B	Jack Hannahan, Minnesota	St. Paul, Minn.	Jr.	.372	226	65	84	20	4	15	63	16	Tigers (3)
SS	Brendan Harris, William & Mary	Queensbury, N.Y.	Jr.	.390	218	73	85	20	3	18	69	7	Cubs (5)
OF	Todd Linden, Louisiana State	Bremerton, Wash.	Jr.	.312	256	65	80	14	1	20	76	9	Giants (1)
OF	Steve Stanley, Notre Dame	Upper Arlington, Ohio	Jr.	.400	255	76	102	14	5	1	32	31	Marlins (50)
OF	Rickie Weeks, Southern	Altamonte Springs, Fla.	Fr.	.422	185	78	78	13	12	14	70	28	Not eligible
DH	Brian Baron, UCLA	Newhall, Calif.	Sr.	.443	237	39	105	17	0	2	47	1	Twins (DFE '00)
UT	Barry Matthews, Gonzaga	Northridge, Calif.	Sr.	.348	224	52	78	16	1	10	33	0	Tigers (FA)

Pos.	Player, School	Hometown	YR	W	L	ERA	G	SV	IP	H	BB	SO	Drafted
P	Willie Collazo, Fla. International	Carolina, Puerto Rico	Sr.	13	1	2.93	20	0	141	137	39	148	Braves (10)
P	Rik Currier, Southern California	Dana Point, Calif.	Jr.	12	3	2.59	17	0	118	112	40	120	Yankees (6)
P	Lee Gronkiewicz, South Carolina	Lancaster, S.C.	Sr.	2	1	1.31	36	19	62	31	23	77	Indians (FA)
P	Jeremy Guthrie, Stanford	Ashford, Ore.	So.	13	4	2.82	20	0	134	123	41	128	Pirates (3)
P	Ben Thurmond, Winthrop	Hopkins, S.C.	So.	14	3	2.88	20	1	150	132	42	148	Not eligible
UT	Barry Matthews, Gonzaga	Northridge, Calif.	Sr.	9	2	3.23	14	0	106	104	16	83	Tigers (FA)

COLLEGE BASEBALL

have made them "fourth-tier" sports without scholarship players and with very limited coaching and travel budgets.

But the Cavaliers program fought back, with students and boosters raising a chorus of protest. The tier proposal found little traction, and the recommendations were rejected. Moreover, an anonymous donor kick-started a $4 million ballpark initiative with a $2 million donation.

"I think the (tier proposal) was a wakeup call for athletic departments everywhere," Virginia coach Dennis Womack said. "A lot of ballparks are built with private funds, and the task force's report was a catalyst for folks to look at the situation and decide to help."

Virginia's vision came too late to help Indiana-Purdue at Indianapolis. In its third year as a Division I program, IUPUI had improved from seven wins to 10 to 17, finally escaping the cellar of the Mid-Continent Conference. But the school decided in May to kill the program. University officials cited the lack of an on-campus facility, weather and travel concerns as reasons for making IUPUI the 43rd Division I school without baseball.

Comings And Goings

California lost one coaching icon and will lose two more after the 2002 season. Long Beach State's Dave Snow, one of three two-time winners of Baseball America's Coach of the Year award, stepped down after the season at age 50. Snow resigned with a 510-291 career mark after the 49ers went 34-24 in 2001.

Fresno State's Bob Bennett and San Diego State's Jim Dietz both announced the 2002 season would be their last. Bennett has spent 45 years in coaching, 33 of them at Fresno State, and carries a 1,270-732 record into his final season. Dietz has had similar success—a career 1,188-727 mark—but his Aztecs clubs haven't reached regional play since 1991. Former Aztec Tony Gwynn, the namesake of the program's five-year-old stadium, was named to replace his former coach less than two weeks before he ended an illustrious career with the San Diego Padres.

Several significant posts changed hands after the 2001 season, with most movement in the Southeastern Conference. Florida started the carousel by firing Andy Lopez, who eventually landed at Arizona, where he replaced Jerry Stitt.

The Gators coaxed Florida native Pat McMahon to leave Mississippi State for Gainesville. McMahon was Ron Polk's hand-picked successor in Starkville, but Polk had since returned to coaching in 2000 at Georgia and led the Bulldogs to the College World Series in 2001.

Polk couldn't resist the opportunity to return home and replaced McMahon at Mississippi State. Georgia courted several prominent coaches, but every coach athletic director Vince Dooley contacted received a lucrative contract extension to stay put. Georgia ended up hiring assistant David Perno.

The coaching community lost one of its up-and-coming young stars when Texas-Arlington coach Clay Gould

Ron Polk

COACHING **CAROUSEL**

The biggest coaching change for the 2002 season at the Division I level was no surprise, as Louisiana State's Skip Bertman retired and handed the reins to Smoke Laval, his former assistant and the former coach at Louisiana-Monroe. The Southeastern Conference had more upheaval when Florida fired Andy Lopez and replaced him with ex-Mississippi State coach Pat McMahon, starting a chain reaction that had three schools with new coaches.

School	Old Coach	New Coach	Previous Position
Arizona	Jerry Stitt	Andy Lopez	Florida
Florida	Andy Lopez	Pat McMahon	Mississippi State
Georgia	Ron Polk	Dave Perno	Assistant
Hawaii	Les Murakami	Mike Trapasso	Assistant (Georgia Tech)
High Point	Jim Speight	Sal Bando Jr.	Wisconsin-Parkside
Hofstra	Reggie Jackson	Chris Dotolo	Assistant (St. John's)
Jacksonville State	Rudy Abbott	Jim Case	Assistant (Mississippi State)
Long Beach State	Dave Snow	Mike Weathers	Assistant
Louisiana State	Skip Bertman	Smoke Laval	Administrative Assistant
Mississippi State	Pat McMahon	Ron Polk	Georgia
Nevada-Las Vegas	Rod Soesbe	Jim Schlossnagle	Assistant (Tulane)
Northwestern State	John Cohen	Mitch Gaspard	Assistant (Alabama)
Quinnipiac	Joe Mattei	Dan Gooley	Administrator
Santa Clara	Mike Cummins	Mark O'Brien	Assistant (Stanford)
Texas-Arlington	Clay Gould	Jeff Curtis	Assistant
Villanova	George Bennett	Joe Godri	Assistant
Western Illinois	Kim Johnson	Stan Hyman	Rutgers-Newark

succumbed to colon cancer on June 23. Gould had missed part of the 2000 season battling the disease but returned to lead the Mavericks to early-season wins at Arizona State and Texas, and the team won the Southland Conference tournament while Gould was hospitalized.

Seton Hall coach Mike Sheppard missed the season after having triple-bypass surgery in early March. His son Rob, the program's associate head coach, led the Pirates to the Big East tournament crown. The elder Sheppard announced his return for 2002.

East Carolina's Keith LeClair disclosed in August that he was battling an unspecified neurological disorder. LeClair had not received an official diagnosis, but Lou Gehrig's disease (amyotrophic lateral sclerosis, or ALS) runs in his family.

In other news:

■ The NCAA's trends report showed offense continuing to slide gradually from the record numbers posted in Division I in 1998. Teams combined to hit .296, down from .306 in '98, with runs per game down from 7.12 to 6.44 over the same span of time.

■ The 64-team regional field did not include Wichita State for the first time since 1986. The Missouri Valley Conference received one bid—tournament champion Northern Iowa—much to the chagrin of the Shockers and regular season champion Southwest Missouri State.

■ Houston, 29-28 in the regular season, received a bid thanks to a nonconference schedule that included Baylor, Cal State Fullerton, Louisiana State, Rice and Southern California. The Cougars went 0-2 in regional play and finished the season with a losing record.

■ Florida State assistant coach Chip Baker became a hero when he jumped into the driver's seat and steered the Seminoles to safety when their bus driver had a fatal heart attack while at the wheel. The Seminoles were traveling on U.S. 101 from the San Francisco airport toward downtown after the team's arrival for its series against Stanford.

■ Washington State outfielder Adrian Thomas, 21, died in an Aug. 3 train-automobile collision near Price, Utah. He hit .339-4-19 as a junior for the Cougars.

COACH OF THE YEAR

Nebraska's Dave Van Horn became the first coach from a Big 12 Conference school to win Baseball America's Coach of the Year award.

Van Horn, 40, led the Huskers to their first-ever trip to the College World Series. In just four seasons, Van Horn has turned Nebraska from a Midwest also-ran into a national power. The Huskers have won three straight Big 12 tournament championships, won their first regular season crown since 1950 and finished the season ranked sixth nationally at 50-16. They also achieved their first-ever No. 1 ranking, occupying the top spot for two weeks during the season.

Van Horn arrived at Nebraska in January 1998, a month after the departure of John Sanders. Van Horn immediately instilled a new attitude in Lincoln, and an ambitious plan to emulate the program at Wichita State and become a Midwest power.

"When I came here, they just didn't think they could win, and I didn't think there was enough discipline for them to win," Van Horn said. "We had to change that, and we had to get better players."

Van Horn did that quickly, as the core of his first recruiting class led the Huskers to Omaha. He found speedy outfielders John Cole and Adam Stern in Canada, and Cole blossomed into a first-team All-American. DH/first baseman

Nebraska's Dave Van Horn

Matt Hopper led the nation's freshmen in homers in 2000 and was a key run-producer in 2001, while middle infielder Will Bolt provided solid defense at two positions.

Righthander Shane Komine, lured to the prairie from Hawaii, provided an ace for the rotation for three straight years. Komine, like Bolt and Hopper, returns for 2002.

Previously, Van Horn coached at Northwestern State, where he won two Southland Conference regular season titles. Van Horn also won a Division II national championship in one season at Central Missouri State after stints as an assistant at his alma mater, Arkansas, and a five-season stay as head coach at Texarkana (Texas) Community College.

"To me, the Midwest style was always to have big kids who swing hard and try to hit the ball out of the park," he said. "My style is good pitching and good defense off the bat. From there, I look at the offensive side. I like to have athletic players in the field, not three left fielders out there. We're not going to

make mistakes, and we're going to take advantage of the other team's mistakes."

Van Horn's turnaround enabled the Cornhuskers to join with the city of Lincoln and a new professional team, the Lincoln Saltdogs of the independent Northern League, to build a new ballpark. The $32 million Haymarket Park opened in June 2001 with a seating capacity of 4,500.

The last coach of a Midwestern school to win the Coach of the Year award was Wichita State's Gene Stephenson in 1993. Van Horn is the second coach from the state of Nebraska to win the award, joining Creighton's Jim Hendry (now the Chicago Cubs' assistant general manager), who won it in 1991.

—JOHN MANUEL

O'Connor top assistant

Paul Mainieri hired Brian O'Connor as an assistant baseball coach soon after he took over the Notre Dame program in 1994.

O'Connor was just 23 at the time, and remains one of the youngest top assistants in the nation. He's also become one of the best recruiters and pitching coaches in the country, which helped him earn the Baseball America/American Baseball Coaches Association Assistant Coach of

Brian O'Connor

the Year award. Stanford's Dean Stotz and Clemson's Tim Corbin were the first two honorees.

"It's very, very rare that someone comes in at age 23 and becomes a top assistant at a place like Notre Dame," said O'Connor, now 30. "I was at the right place at the right time."

Mainieri and Notre Dame feel the same way. The tandem has taken the Fighting Irish program to new heights, with seven consecutive 40-win seasons (extending the school's streak to 13), playing host to regionals in 1999 and 2001, a No. 1 national ranking in 2001 and bringing in one of the nation's top recruiting classes.

PREVIOUS WINNERS

1981—Ron Fraser, Miami
1982—Gene Stephenson, Wichita State
1983—Barry Shollenberger, Alabama
1984—Augie Garrido, Cal State Fullerton
1985—Ron Polk, Mississippi State
1986—Skip Bertman, Louisiana State
Dave Snow, Loyola Marymount
1987—Mark Marquess, Stanford
1988—Jim Brock, Arizona State
1989—Dave Snow, Long Beach State
1990—Steve Webber, Georgia
1991—Jim Hendry, Creighton
1992—Andy Lopez, Pepperdine
1993—Gene Stephenson, Wichita State
1994—Jim Morris, Miami
1995—Rod Delmonico, Tennessee
1996—Skip Bertman, Louisiana State
1997—Jim Wells, Alabama
1998—Pat Murphy, Arizona State
1999—Wayne Graham, Rice
2000—Ray Tanner, South Carolina

FRESHMAN OF THE YEAR

For the second time in three years, Tulane was home to Baseball America's Freshman of the Year.

In 1999, it was second baseman James Jurries. In 2001, it was left-hander/outfielder Michael Aubrey, one of the nation's top two-way players and a key cog in the Green Wave's first appearance in the College World Series.

Aubrey became just the second two-way player to be honored as the nation's top freshman, joining Texas' righthander/DH Brooks Kieschnick (1991). Kieschnick went on to be the national Player of the Year and a first-round draft pick of the Cubs as a junior in 1993.

Aubrey, a Shreveport, La., native, was expected to make more of an impact as a pitcher for Tulane. He pitched in all three games for Tulane in the CWS, earning a save and taking a loss, his first of the season. But Aubrey had a much better year with the bat—in part thanks to Jurries, who had moved to first base as a junior.

Jurries missed six weeks early in the season with a broken wrist, opening the door for Aubrey to get more time in the lineup. He never left.

Initially Aubrey played first base, but when Jurries returned Aubrey moved to the outfield. He eventually finished second on the Green Wave in average (.361) and home runs (13) while ranking third in RBIs (69).

Aubrey, who was not drafted out of high school, also was used primarily as a hitter during his summer stint with Team USA, and showed enough arm strength to profile as a corner outfielder down the line as a professional. But Tulane is happy to have him in his dual capacity for two more seasons.

"He's tremendous both ways," Tulane coach Rick Jones said. "At first base, he's the best defensively I've had in a long time."

Former Tulane assistant Jim Schlossnagle, who left after the season to become Nevada-Las Vegas' head coach, helped lure Aubrey into the Green Wave fold. During the CWS, he also praised Aubrey's versatility and wouldn't predict which part of the game would be in his pro future.

"Out of high school I would have said pitcher," Schlossnagle said. "Now he could go either way. I'd have to lean toward pitcher, because he's a lefthander who can throw in the high 80s and low 90s. But it's a hard call."

"We recruit freshmen who can make an immediate impact at

Michael Aubrey: .361-13-69

Tulane," Jones said, "and we have a couple who did that this year in Michael Aubrey and Anthony Giarratano."

Giarratano, a second baseman who is scheduled to play shortstop in 2002, joined Aubrey on Baseball America's All-Freshman first team. Cal State Fullerton also placed a pair of pitchers on the first team in Chad Cordero and Darric Merrell.

—JOHN MANUEL

FRESHMAN ALL-AMERICA TEAM

FIRST TEAM

Pos. Player, School	AVG	AB	R	H	2B	3B	HR	RBI	SB
C Mitch Maier, Toledo	.444	160	33	71	10	2	3	43	4
1B Jamie D'Antona, Wake Forest	.364	253	65	92	14	1	17	77	1
2B Anthony Giarratano, Tulane	.352	264	72	93	12	2	3	47	11
3B Myron Leslie, South Florida	.366	257	55	94	15	3	3	40	17
SS Omar Quintanilla, Texas	.367	196	36	72	22	2	2	37	8
OF Austin Davis, Rice	.346	257	73	89	18	2	6	29	5
OF Carlos Quentin, Stanford	.345	249	55	86	11	1	11	52	5
OF Rickie Weeks, Southern	.422	185	78	78	13	12	14	70	28
DH Rod Allen, Arizona State	.389	180	41	70	14	1	6	53	6
UT Michael Aubrey, Tulane	.361	277	74	100	17	4	13	69	9

	W	L	ERA	G	SV	IP	H	BB	SO
P Chad Cordero, Cal State Fullerton	3	4	1.83	38	14	64	43	12	63
P Clark Girardeau, South Alabama	10	4	3.87	22	2	98	83	36	70
P Paul Maholm, Mississippi State	8	4	4.06	16	0	95	106	30	87
P Darric Merrell, Cal State Fullerton	8	4	2.95	20	0	113	107	45	76
P Lane Mestepey, Louisiana State	11	3	3.75	22	1	139	158	37	79
UT Michael Aubrey, Tulane	3	1	5.15	17	1	72	75	33	46

SECOND TEAM

C–Javi Herrera, Tennessee (.296-7-45). **1B**–Bryan Zenchyk, Stetson (.383-4-39). **2B**–Steve Sollman, Notre Dame (.362-5-36, 23 SB). **3B**–Brian Snyder, Stetson (.341-7-49). **SS**–Brandon Green, Wichita State (.286-2-37). **OF**–Doug Deeds, Ohio State (.343-14-53); Sam Fuld, Stanford (.357-0-37); Sam Steidl, Minnesota (.401-0-32). **DH**–Matt Murton, Georgia Tech (.385-7-35).

P–George Huguet, Miami (1-0, 2.03, 14 SV); Sean Marshall, Virginia Commonwealth (9-4, 3.34); Brad Sullivan, Houston (6-7, 3.41); Chris Tracz, Marist (10-1, 3.13); Bob Zimmerman, Southwest Missouri State (7-3, 2.28, 6 SV). **UT**–Marc Kaiser, Arizona (.436-0-5; 8-6, 5.35).

N C A A
DIVISION I LEADERS

TEAM BATTING

BATTING AVERAGE	G	AVG
Bowling Green	54	.360
Wisconsin-Milwaukee	57	.352
Georgia Tech	61	.347
Southern	55	.345
Delaware State	42	.345
Tulane	69	.338
UC Santa Barbara	57	.338
Central Florida	65	.335
Nebraska	66	.334
Northern Iowa	63	.333

RUNS	G	R
Tulane	69	639
Nebraska	66	607
Georgia Tech	61	578
Louisiana State	67	574
Miami	65	557
New Mexico State	55	554
Wake Forest	62	546
Oklahoma State	64	543
Central Florida	65	543
Wisconsin-Milwaukee	57	537

DOUBLES	G	2B
Rice	67	163
Florida State	66	161
Central Florida	65	160
Baylor	61	157
Winthrop	65	156

TRIPLES	G	3B
Southern	55	38
Southwest Missouri State	58	36
New Mexico	60	34
Texas Christian	60	33
Brigham Young	60	32

HOME RUNS	G	HR
Ohio	54	122
Kent State	62	112
South Carolina	69	110
New Mexico State	55	108
Bowling Green	54	104
Louisiana State	67	98
Utah	56	91
Marshall	53	91
Ball State	58	87
Cincinnati	58	86
Southern Utah	60	86

STOLEN BASES	G	SB	ATT
Miami	65	228	273
Tennessee	68	160	201
North Carolina A&T	55	150	199
Oral Roberts	61	149	199
Florida	62	148	174
Tulane	69	146	174
Bethune-Cookman	60	140	193
Virginia Commonwealth	60	139	178
Coastal Carolina	62	138	170
Georgia Southern	62	131	163

TEAM PITCHING

W-L PERCENTAGE	W	L	PCT
Miami	53	12	.815
Tulane	56	13	.812
Delaware State	37	10	.787
Oral Roberts	48	13	.787
Notre Dame	49	13	.786
Central Florida	51	14	.785
East Carolina	47	13	.783
Southern	43	12	.782
Nebraska	50	16	.758
Winthrop	48	16	.750
Stanford	51	17	.750
Delaware	45	15	.750

EARNED RUN AVERAGE	G	ERA
Delaware State	47	2.99

Rice	67	3.03
Texas	62	3.17
UNC Wilmington	55	3.20
Notre Dame	63	3.22
Winthrop	65	3.28
South Carolina	69	3.44
Southern California	64	3.46
Florida State	66	3.47
Stanford	68	3.50

TEAM FIELDING

	G	AVG
Stanford	68	.977
San Jose State	60	.975
Southern California	64	.973
Central Florida	65	.973
Niagara	45	.973
Louisville	61	.972
Cal Poly	56	.972
Arkansas State	58	.971
Texas Tech	64	.971
Cal State Fullerton	66	.971

INDIVIDUAL BATTING

BATTING AVERAGE
(Minimum 125 At-Bats)

	Yr.	AVG	G	AB	R	H	2B	3B	HR	RBI	BB	SO	SB
Chris Tuttle, Wright State	So.	.478	54	203	43	97	9	3	1	49	29	19	11
Chris May, Penn	Sr.	.455	39	143	38	65	11	3	10	55	6	25	6
Michael Woods, Southern	Jr.	.453	47	170	68	77	27	5	14	54	26	69	32
John-Ford Griffin, Florida State	Jr.	.450	65	251	79	113	30	0	19	75	50	23	11
Mitch Maier, Toledo	Fr.	.444	44	160	33	71	10	2	3	43	11	23	4
Brian Baron, UCLA	Sr.	.443	56	237	39	105	17	0	2	47	20	26	1
John VanBenschoten, Kent State	Jr.	.440	61	225	74	99	17	6	31	84	55	50	23
Jason Law, Monmouth	Jr.	.436	53	204	58	89	20	0	16	77	28	21	8
Chris Burke, Tennessee	Jr.	.435	67	271	105	118	21	11	20	60	51	28	49
Phil Pilewski, Toledo	So.	.433	47	171	43	74	15	2	9	53	24	23	0
Scott Martin, Delaware State	So.	.432	44	162	60	70	19	2	16	77	18	17	6
Anthony Bocchino, Marist	Jr.	.430	49	200	51	86	20	6	7	64	13	13	4
Jon Hambelton, Maine	Sr.	.429	48	161	41	69	20	1	13	50	28	15	4
Greg Dobbs, Oklahoma	Sr.	.428	59	243	53	104	25	2	10	62	20	21	12
Michael Oliva, Albany	Sr.	.428	47	173	41	74	14	2	6	40	20	9	9
Bob Malek, Michigan State	So.	.427	56	206	53	88	15	3	4	42	24	10	11
Scott Gillitzer, Wis.-Milwaukee	Sr.	.424	57	229	68	97	18	2	10	66	28	14	8
Darin Haugom, Wis.-Milwaukee	Sr.	.423	49	194	61	82	15	4	6	48	22	38	20
Rickie Weeks, Southern	Fr.	.422	55	185	78	77	13	12	14	69	30	30	28
Billy McCarthy, Rutgers	Jr.	.421	59	216	51	91	21	2	7	65	26	22	11
Josh Renick, Middle Tennessee	Sr.	.420	56	224	74	94	20	2	8	38	31	22	24
John Cole, Nebraska	Jr.	.418	63	239	71	100	15	4	11	61	20	26	28
Chris Carter, Coastal Carolina	Sr.	.417	55	180	50	75	22	1	8	45	17	30	11
Dan Kantrovitz, Brown	Sr.	.417	46	163	42	68	12	3	5	41	27	9	11
Kevin Mitchell, McNeese State	Sr.	.415	51	193	48	80	20	0	19	64	21	28	3
Trevor Leu, Oral Roberts	Sr.	.415	45	135	27	56	17	1	6	38	19	18	4
Mike Scott, Connecticut	Jr.	.413	49	206	48	85	16	4	3	34	13	19	8
Josh Wilson, Texas A&M-CC	Sr.	.411	50	185	41	76	16	1	7	45	21	22	1
Robert Smith, CS Northridge	Sr.	.409	51	193	43	79	12	1	11	49	17	22	8
J.T. Stotts, CS Northridge	Jr.	.409	56	235	66	95	12	1	12	40	32	18	19
Chris Nelson, Southern Utah	Jr.	.408	53	179	65	73	11	2	8	43	32	23	6
Willie Core, La.-Monroe	Sr.	.408	58	211	52	86	15	0	12	56	39	38	7
Greg Graham, Western Michigan	Jr.	.406	51	187	35	76	14	0	14	43	11	25	0
Kendall Schlabach, Youngstown St.	Fr.	.406	55	197	50	80	9	1	1	25	24	20	19
Kevin Youkilis, Cincinnati	Sr.	.405	58	210	81	85	7	2	18	61	59	25	1
Mike LaBarbera, Rhode Island	Sr.	.404	50	198	41	80	8	6	2	44	7	5	35
Robert Deeb, Brown	Fr.	.404	45	156	42	63	9	3	0	20	12	32	15
Jason Knoedler, Miami (Ohio)	Jr.	.402	58	239	79	96	15	3	17	50	29	51	24
Mike Gillies, Nevada	Jr.	.402	50	189	43	76	14	1	4	35	19	17	2
Jeremy Kurella, Central Florida	Sr.	.401	63	247	63	99	16	1	7	49	22	24	17
Sam Stiedl, Minnesota	Fr.	.401	53	182	50	73	14	1	0	32	22	18	14
David Quattrociocchi, NW State	Jr.	.401	47	162	50	65	10	2	3	27	23	23	7
Steve Stanley, Notre Dame	Jr.	.400	63	255	76	102	14	5	1	32	29	17	31
Skip Schumaker, UCSB	So.	.400	57	250	65	100	19	3	1	41	32	31	22
Paul Henry, Ball State	So.	.400	58	230	53	92	20	1	12	62	22	19	3
Jeff Crandell, Xavier	Sr.	.400	54	200	51	80	18	1	5	41	26	15	3
Gregg Davies, Towson	Sr.	.399	60	218	57	87	21	2	15	74	24	20	8
Scott Henley, Ga. Southern	Sr.	.398	62	249	48	99	16	0	16	84	21	37	4
Kelly Williams, Delaware State	So.	.398	47	196	69	78	17	2	0	49	30	26	14
Kelly Shoppach, Baylor	Jr.	.397	61	234	51	93	20	2	12	69	24	52	4
Jared Pitney, Pepperdine	Sr.	.397	60	239	46	95	22	0	14	67	33	34	4
Len Elias, Bowling Green	Jr.	.397	53	204	62	81	15	2	13	58	26	24	8
Eddie Kim, James Madison	So.	.397	57	184	43	73	15	3	7	50	29	19	0
Tim Bittner, Marist	Jr.	.397	48	194	33	77	14	0	0	36	21	34	4
Matt Davis, VCU	Jr.	.396	60	227	84	90	7	2	3	26	45	17	49
Adam Brown, Delaware State	So.	.396	40	134	45	53	12	0	4	39	21	11	5
John Curry, Florida A&M	Fr.	.396	43	144	33	57	6	8	1	36	18	13	22
Andy Cannizaro, Tulane	Sr.	.395	69	299	80	118	34	3	3	70	26	21	52
Ernie Durazo, Arizona	Sr.	.395	56	238	66	94	23	4	7	57	30	37	6
Casey Myers, Arizona State	Sr.	.395	58	223	53	88	17	0	7	69	37	19	2
Chris Biles, Oregon State	So.	.395	49	177	36	70	8	1	9	48	8	28	4
Chad Peshke, UCSB	Sr.	.394	57	218	50	86	18	4	4	57	34	15	7
Andy Baxter, ETSU	Sr.	.394	55	221	65	87	25	1	12	49	26	34	8
Jared Dufault, Illinois State	Sr.	.394	53	203	58	80	10	7	8	47	27	20	4

RUNS

	Yr.	G	R
Chris Burke, Tennessee	Jr.	67	105
Cory Sullivan, Wake Forest	Sr.	62	85
Matt Davis, VCU	Jr.	60	84
Jake Gautreau, Tulane	Jr.	69	82
Kevin Youkilis, Cincinnati	Sr.	58	81
Andy Cannizaro, Tulane	Sr.	69	80
John-Ford Griffin, Florida State	Jr.	65	79
Jason Knoedler, Miami (Ohio)	Jr.	58	79
Jon Kaplan, Tulane	So.	68	79
Rickie Weeks, Southern	Fr.	55	78
Dan Johnson, Nebraska	Sr.	62	77
Richard Lewis, Georgia Tech	Jr.	61	77
A.J. Porfirio, Rice	Jr.	67	77
Steve Stanley, Notre Dame	Jr.	63	76
Chris Kolodzey, Delaware	Sr.	60	76

HITS

	Yr.	G	H
Chris Burke, Tennessee	Jr.	67	118
Andy Cannizaro, Tulane	Sr.	69	118
John-Ford Griffin, Florida State	Jr.	65	113
Brian Baron, UCLA	Sr.	56	105
Greg Dobbs, Oklahoma	Sr.	59	104
Cory Sullivan, Wake Forest	Sr.	62	103
Casey Stone, Clemson	Sr.	62	103
Jake Gautreau, Tulane	Jr.	69	103
Victor Menocal, Georgia Tech	Jr.	60	102
Steve Stanley, Notre Dame	Jr.	63	102
Jeff Keppinger, Georgia	Jr.	69	102
Chris O'Riordan, Stanford	Jr.	68	101
Richard Lewis, Georgia Tech	Jr.	61	100
John Cole, Nebraska	Jr.	63	100
Skip Schumaker, UCSB	So.	57	100
Greg Miller, James Madison	Sr.	60	100
Michael Aubrey, Tulane	Fr.	69	100

SLUGGING PERCENTAGE
(Minimum 125 At-Bats)

	Yr.	G	PCT
John VanBenschoten, Kent	Jr.	61	.982
Michael Woods, Southern	Jr.	47	.918
Scott Martin, Delaware State	So.	44	.870
Rickie Weeks, Southern	Fr.	55	.849
Jason Brooks, Marshall	Sr.	49	.829
Chris Burke, Tennessee	Jr.	67	.815
Kevin Mitchell, McNeese State	Sr.	51	.813
Jon Hambelton, Maine	Sr.	48	.807
John-Ford Griffin, Fla. State	Jr.	65	.797
Alex Trezza, Stony Brook	Jr.	51	.790
Dan Uggla, Memphis	Jr.	58	.790

TOTAL BASES

	Yr.	G	TB
John VanBenschoten, Kent	Jr.	61	221
Chris Burke, Tennessee	Jr.	67	221
John-Ford Griffin, Fla. State	Jr.	65	200
Jake Gautreau, Tulane	Jr.	69	191
Ryan Brunner, Northern Iowa	Sr.	63	187
Jeff Keppinger, Georgia	Jr.	69	181
Dan Johnson, Nebraska	Sr.	62	173
Jeff Baker, Clemson	So.	60	172
Ryan Barthelemy, Fla. State	Jr.	66	170
Dan Uggla, Memphis	Jr.	58	169
Josh Labandeira, Fresno State	Sr.	65	169
Jason Knoedler, Miami (Ohio)	Jr.	58	168
Andy Cannizaro, Tulane	Sr.	69	167

DOUBLES

	Yr.	G	2B
Andy Cannizaro, Tulane	Sr.	69	34
Ryan Kyes, Ohio	Sr.	54	32
John-Ford Griffin, Fla. State	Jr.	65	30
Todd Leathers, Winthrop	Sr.	65	28
Dan Uggla, Memphis	Jr.	58	28
Alec Porzel, Notre Dame	Jr.	63	28
Michael Woods, Southern	Jr.	47	27
Troy Cairns, New Mexico	So.	60	26
Adam Swann, Georgia	Jr.	69	26
Mike Fox, Central Florida	Jr.	65	26
Andy Baxter, East Tenn. St.	Sr.	55	25
Gregg Omori, Hawaii	Jr.	55	25
Greg Dobbs, Oklahoma	Sr.	59	25
Stevie Daniel, Tennessee	Jr.	67	25
Bryan Moore, Louisiana State	Jr.	65	25
Hunter Brown, Rice	Jr.	67	25
Chris Durbin, Baylor	So.	61	25
Ben Cunningham, Tenn. Tech	Sr.	62	25

TRIPLES

	Yr.	G	3B
Rickie Weeks, Southern	Fr.	55	12
Dante Brinkley, SW Mo. State	So.	56	12

BOB LIBBY

John-Ford Griffin: .450-19-75

	Yr.	G	
Chris Burke, Tennessee	Jr.	67	11
Eric Rico, Cornell	Jr.	38	8
John Curry, Florida A&M	Fr.	43	8
Marcus Chandler, Southern	Sr.	44	8
Doug Jackson, BYU	So.	55	8
Rudy Rivera, Texas Christian	Sr.	55	8

HOME RUNS

	Yr.	G	HR
John VanBenschoten, Kent	Jr.	61	31
Dan Johnson, Nebraska	Sr.	62	25
Ryan Brunner, Northern Iowa	Sr.	63	25
Shelley Duncan, Arizona	Jr.	56	24
Jason Brooks, Marshall	Sr.	49	23
Alex Trezza, Stony Brook	Jr.	51	23
Jeff Baker, Clemson	So.	60	23
Jake Gautreau, Tulane	Jr.	69	21
Tim Whittaker, So. Carolina	Sr.	68	21
Aaron Clark, Alabama	Sr.	55	20
Chris Burke, Tennessee	Jr.	67	20
Todd Linden, LSU	Jr.	66	20
Luke Scott, Oklahoma St.	Sr.	63	20
Kevin Mitchell, McNeese St.	Sr.	51	19
Jason Ricceri, Marshall	Sr.	53	19
Chris Shelton, Utah	Sr.	54	19
Jake Adams, La. Tech	Sr.	58	19
John-Ford Griffin, Fla. State	Jr.	65	19
Chad Oliva, Jacksonville	Jr.	65	19
Eric O'Brien, Kent State	So.	62	19
Ryan Clyde, Texas A&M-CC	Sr.	52	19
Cary Page, Morehead State	So.	53	18
Frank Corr, Stetson	Sr.	53	18
Lee Morrison, Bowling Green	Sr.	54	18
Stefan Bailie, Wash. State	So.	54	18
Jon Benick, Virginia	Sr.	55	18
Brendan Harris, Wm. & Mary	Jr.	55	18
Matt Carson, BYU	So.	56	18
Jeff Keppinger, Georgia	Jr.	69	18
Michael Johnson, Clemson	So.	62	18
Tyler Von Schell, UCSB	Jr.	57	18
Kevin Youkilis, Cincinnati	Sr.	58	18
Dan Uggla, Memphis	Jr.	58	18
Curtis Jacobsen, So. Utah	Sr.	59	18
Brian Wolotka, Valparaiso	Jr.	57	18
Todd Mitchell, Southern Utah	Sr.	60	18
Matt Carson, BYU	So.	56	18

RUNS BATTED IN

	Yr.	G	RBI
Jake Gautreau, Tulane	Jr.	69	96
Dan Johnson, Nebraska	Sr.	62	86
Matt Hopper, Nebraska	So.	64	85
John VanBenschoten, Kent	Jr.	61	84
Scott Henley, Ga. Southern	Sr.	62	84
Ryan Brunner, No. Iowa	Sr.	63	82
Shelley Duncan, Arizona	Jr.	56	78
Scott Martin, Del. State	So.	54	77
Jamie D'Antona, Wake Forest	Fr.	62	77
Todd Linden, LSU	Jr.	66	76
John-Ford Griffin, Fla. State	Jr.	65	75
Jeff Baker, Clemson	So.	60	75
Donovan Minero, West. Carolina	Jr.	56	74
Curtis Jacobsen, So. Utah	Sr.	59	74
Gregg Davies, Towson	Jr.	60	74
Tim Whittaker, So. Carolina	Sr.	68	74

	Yr.	G	
Jason Brooks, Marshall	Sr.	49	73
Jeff Keppinger, Georgia	Jr.	69	73
Jeff Christensen, Tennessee	Sr.	68	73
Ryan Barthelemy, Fla. State	Jr.	66	72
Chad Ehrnsberger, Central Fla.	Sr.	63	72
Aaron Clark, Alabama	Sr.	55	71
Andrew See, Ohio	Sr.	51	70
Rickie Weeks, Southern	Fr.	55	70
Matt Carson, BYU	So.	56	70
Josh Arteaga, VCU	Jr.	60	70
Andy Cannizaro, Tulane	Sr.	69	70

WALKS

	Yr.	G	BB
Dan Johnson, Nebraska	Sr.	62	63
Jason Burkley, Miss. State	Jr.	59	63
Clemente Bonilla, SE Mo. State	Jr.	52	61
Nick Swisher, Ohio State	So.	57	60
Kevin Youkilis, Cincinnati	Sr.	58	59

STRIKEOUTS

	Yr.	G	SO
Colt Morton, N.C. State	Fr.	60	76
Ryan Howard, SW Mo. State	Jr.	58	74
Kevin Brown, Miami	Sr.	62	72
Chad Hayes, UNC Greensboro	Jr.	59	70
Todd Mitchell, Southern Utah	Sr.	60	68
Doc Brooks, Georgia	Jr.	62	68

TOUGHEST TO STRIKE OUT
(Minimum 125 At-Bats)

	Yr.	AB	SO	Ratio
Mike LaBarbera, RI	Sr.	198	5	39.6
Casey Stone, Clemson	Sr.	274	10	27.4
Josh Harris, San Diego	Sr.	242	9	26.9
Jason Walker, Pacific	Jr.	215	10	21.5
Jeff Hoefler, Arkansas	Sr.	171	8	21.4

STOLEN BASES

	Yr.	G	SB	ATT
Javy Rodriguez, Miami	Jr.	63	66	82
Mike Rodriguez, Miami	Jr.	64	53	55
Andy Cannizaro, Tulane	Sr.	69	52	58
Chris Burke, Tennessee	Jr.	67	49	55
Matt Davis, VCU	Jr.	60	49	59
Stevie Daniel, Tennessee	Jr.	67	46	56
Marcus Nettles, Miami	Jr.	54	44	54
Aurelio Jackson, CS Sac.	Sr.	59	44	60
Chris Walker, Ga. Southern	Jr.	57	41	45
Matt Lemancyk, Sacred Heart	Jr.	45	40	44
Micah Simmons, Beth.-Cook.	Jr.	58	40	51
Kerry Hodges, Texas Tech	Jr.	64	38	43
Jason Tuttle, Elon	Sr.	57	38	48
Chris Graziano, Villanova	So.	42	37	41
Greg Landis, Monmouth	Sr.	53	37	41
Bartowski Cowasn, Ala. State	Jr.	47	37	41
Jason Battle, NC A&T	Jr.	55	37	48
Sean Hill, Miss. Valley St.	So.	46	36	42
Bobby Kingsbury, Fordham	So.	51	36	44
K.J. Hendricks, Tx.-Arl.	So.	64	36	45
Kevin Elrod, VCU	Sr.	55	36	46

HIT BY PITCH

	Yr.	G	HBP
Gabe Somarriba, Florida Atlantic	Jr.	59	27
Chris Nelson, Southern Utah	Jr.	53	26
Josh Persell, Southern California	Sr.	64	24
Karl Jernigan, Florida State	Sr.	57	23
Brian Houle, St. Mary's	Jr.	51	23

DAVID SCHOFIELD

Rickie Weeks: .422, 12 triples

INDIVIDUAL PITCHING

EARNED RUN AVERAGE
(Minimum 60 Innings)

	Yr.	W	L	ERA	G	GS	CG	SV	IP	H	R	ER	BB	SO
Lee Gronkiewicz, So. Carolina	Sr.	2	1	1.31	36	0	0	19	62	31	13	9	23	77
Todd Pennington, SE Missouri St.	Jr.	12	2	1.33	18	15	5	0	95	51	20	14	36	121
Dewon Brazelton, Middle Tenn.	Jr.	13	2	1.42	15	15	11	0	127	82	34	20	24	154
Justin Pope, Central Florida	Jr.	15	1	1.68	17	17	6	0	123	97	33	23	27	158
Mark Prior, Southern California	Jr.	15	1	1.69	20	18	6	0	139	100	32	26	18	202
Noah Lowry, Pepperdine	Jr.	14	2	1.71	18	17	3	1	121	88	32	23	41	142
Aaron Heilman, Notre Dame	Sr.	15	0	1.74	15	15	12	0	114	70	28	22	31	111
Chad Cordero, CS Fullerton	Fr.	3	4	1.83	38	0	0	14	64	43	16	13	12	63
Kyle Johnson, St. Bonaventure	So.	7	2	1.88	13	10	6	1	72	60	21	15	18	57
Casey Shumaker, Jacksonville	So.	7	6	1.91	33	3	1	12	75	48	20	16	40	117
Joe Engel, Pittsburgh	Jr.	5	5	1.92	10	10	6	0	70	55	26	15	27	69
Jonathan Stern, Brown	Jr.	5	4	1.92	9	8	4	0	61	57	29	13	24	53
Jason Mandryk, East Carolina	Jr.	7	1	1.95	13	12	0	0	74	66	20	16	23	52
Jason Arnold, Central Florida	Sr.	14	3	1.97	19	17	5	0	119	82	35	26	32	150
Eric Talbert, The Citadel	So.	8	3	2.06	17	16	3	0	113	93	41	26	28	96
John Sterling, Delaware State	So.	7	3	2.08	12	11	8	0	69	42	32	16	39	83
Kenny Baugh, Rice	Sr.	13	2	2.17	22	21	3	0	141	106	48	34	54	163
Kirk Saarloos, CS Fullerton	Sr.	15	2	2.18	25	18	7	4	153	99	41	37	23	153
Brian Whitaker, UNC Wilmington	Jr.	10	3	2.20	20	9	2	1	102	88	30	25	19	80
Dan Haren, Pepperdine	Jr.	11	3	2.22	17	16	6	1	130	106	48	32	31	97
John Rheinecker, SW Mo. St.	Sr.	5	4	2.27	12	12	6	0	91	79	37	23	22	106
Tim Vaillancourt, Delaware State	So.	8	3	2.27	16	11	6	4	79	64	29	20	24	63
Lance Cormier, Alabama	Jr.	9	5	2.30	17	14	6	2	110	109	41	28	29	73
Bobby Brownlie, Rutgers	So.	6	3	2.36	14	11	7	0	84	65	30	22	17	86
Steven Herce, Rice	So.	6	1	2.37	17	7	1	2	68	61	24	18	21	63
Michael Rogers, Oral Roberts	Jr.	14	1	2.37	18	17	3	1	121	99	36	32	46	137
Petersen Benjamin, Fla. Atlantic	Sr.	7	5	2.41	17	17	6	0	123	132	52	33	18	91
Tom Caple, San Diego	So.	5	3	2.43	25	6	3	9	85	72	27	23	23	77
Ryan Holsten, Fairfield	Sr.	6	4	2.45	11	11	1	0	73	69	37	20	16	53
Nic Ungs, Northern Iowa	Jr.	11	2	2.48	16	15	7	0	109	106	44	30	14	110
Taft Cable, UNC Greensboro	Jr.	5	2	2.50	34	3	0	9	68	55	29	19	13	60
Joe Brzeczek, Delaware State	Fr.	7	2	2.51	13	9	3	0	72	70	39	20	22	52
Steve Obenchain, Evansville	So.	8	3	2.53	27	4	1	2	68	53	24	19	11	61
Brian Lane, Richmond	Jr.	6	2	2.55	21	7	3	2	78	82	41	22	17	57
Roy Foster, Grambling State	Jr.	5	4	2.56	14	13	6	0	71	74	38	26	23	56
Shawn Kohn, Washington	Jr.	6	2	2.57	18	8	3	0	81	60	29	23	15	65
Troy Parton, Butler	Jr.	5	3	2.57	14	9	5	0	63	69	26	18	17	36
Steve Reba, Clemson	Jr.	12	3	2.58	18	17	2	0	108	84	39	31	31	103
Rik Currier, Southern California	Sr.	12	3	2.59	20	17	2	0	118	112	50	34	40	120
Jim Johnson, Brown	Sr.	5	4	2.59	11	9	5	1	66	62	27	19	16	73

Nate Fernley: 16 wins

WINS

	Yr.	W	L
Nate Fernley, Brigham Young	Sr.	16	3
Aaron Heilman, Notre Dame	Sr.	15	0
Mark Prior, Southern California	Jr.	15	1
Justin Pope, Central Florida	Jr.	15	1
Kirk Saarloos, Cal State Fullerton	Sr.	15	2
Tom Farmer, Miami	Jr.	15	2
Michael Rogers, Oral Roberts	Jr.	14	1
Shane Komine, Nebraska	Jr.	14	2
Noah Lowry, Pepperdine	Jr.	14	2
Jason Arnold, Central Florida	Sr.	14	3
Ben Thurmond, Winthrop	Jr.	14	3
Willie Collazo, Fla. International	Jr.	13	1
Kenny Baugh, Rice	Sr.	13	2
Dewon Brazelton, Middle Tenn	Jr.	13	2
Brandon Roberson, Texas Tech	Jr.	13	3
Jeremy Guthrie, Stanford	So.	13	4
Andy Torres, Arizona State	Jr.	13	4
Scott Sturkie, Char. Southern	Jr.	13	6
Sam Narron, East Carolina	So.	12	1
Brian Walker, Miami	Jr.	12	1
Jeremy Herauf, Winthrop	Sr.	12	2
Erik Weltmer, UMBC	Sr.	12	2
Todd Pennington, SE Mo. State	Jr.	12	2
Rik Currier, Southern California	Jr.	12	3
Steve Reba, Clemson	Jr.	12	3
John Maine, Charlotte	So.	12	6
Steve Carlson, Illinois-Chicago	Sr.	12	6

LOSSES

	Yr.	W	L
Mike Hughes, Howard	Sr.	3	13
Anthony Bernal, Hawaii-Hilo	Jr.	0	11
Robert Shimabuku, Hawaii-Hilo	So.	1	11
Erik Fisher, Air Force	Jr.	2	11
Jeremy Fuller, Texas A&M-CC	Sr.	4	11

APPEARANCES

	Yr.	G
Luke DeBold, Miami	Jr.	44
George Huguet, Miami	Fr.	44
Dave Bush, Wake Forest	Jr.	41
Ted Toler, UNC Greensboro	Sr.	40
Chad Cordero, CS Fullerton	Fr.	38

Kirk Saarloos: 15 wins, 153 innings

JEFF GOLDEN

COMPLETE GAMES

	Yr.	GS	CG
Aaron Heilman, Notre Dame	Sr.	15	12
Ben Thurmond, Winthrop	So.	18	12
Dewon Brazelton, Middle Tenn	Jr.	15	11
Scott Nicholson, Oregon State	Sr.	16	10
Jeff Barger, Xavier	Sr.	17	10
Eric Weltmer, UMBC	Sr.	22	10
Jason Bernard, Troy State	Sr.	17	10

SAVES

	Yr.	G	SV
Lee Gronkiewicz, So. Carolina	Sr.	36	19
Dave Bush, Wake Forest	Jr.	41	16
Chad Cordero, CS Fullerton	Fr.	38	14
George Huguet, Miami	Fr.	44	14
Casey Shumaker, Jacksonville	So.	33	12
Randy Corn, The Citadel	Jr.	34	12
Andy Hutchings, Charleston	So.	27	12
Justin Craker, Valparaiso	Sr.	30	12
Dallas Martin, Oral Roberts	So.	34	11
Justin Lord, Florida State	Jr.	30	11
Thom Ott, Nebraska	Jr.	29	11
Steve Haines, Wichita State	Jr.	27	11

INNINGS

	Yr.	G	IP
Kirk Saarloos, CS Fullerton	Sr.	25	153
Nate Fernley, Brigham Young	Sr.	21	153
Ben Thurmond, Winthrop	So.	20	150
Kenny Baugh, Rice	Sr.	22	141
Willie Collazo, Fla. International	Jr.	20	141

WALKS

	Yr.	IP	BB
Mike Hughes, Howard	Sr.	79	81
Brad Edwards, Indiana	Jr.	73	72
Mike Hale, New Mexico State	Jr.	97	71
Jason Anderegg, Belmont	Jr.	85	67
Brian Haskell, Cal Poly	Jr.	83	64

STRIKEOUTS

	Yr.	IP	SO
Mark Prior, So. California	Jr.	139	202
Kenny Baugh, Rice	Sr.	141	163
Justin Pope, Central Fla.	Jr.	123	158
Shane Komine, Nebraska	Jr.	132	157
Dewon Brazelton, Middle Tenn	Jr.	127	154
Kirk Saarloos, CS Fullerton	Sr.	153	153
Jason Arnold, Central Florida	Sr.	119	150
Willie Collazo, Fla. International	Jr.	141	148
Ben Thurmond, Winthrop	So.	150	148
John Maine, Charlotte	So.	134	144
Noah Lowry, Pepperdine	Jr.	121	142
Michael Rogers, Oral Roberts	Jr.	121	137
Scott Sturkie, Coastal Carolina	Sr.	133	133
Nate Fernley, Brigham Young	Sr.	153	133
Lenny DiNardo, Stetson	Jr.	112	131
Jon Switzer, Arizona State	Jr.	100	128
Jeremy Guthrie, Stanford	So.	134	128
Gerrit Simpson, Texas	Jr.	120	126
Brad Hennessey, Youngstown	Jr.	89	126

STRIKEOUTS/9 INNINGS
(Minimum 50 Innings)

	Yr.	IP	SO	AVG
Randy Corn, The Citadel	Jr.	56	88	14.1
Casey Shumaker, Jacksonville	So.	75	117	14.0
Mark Prior, So. California	Jr.	139	202	13.1
Brad Hennessey, Youngstown	Jr.	89	126	12.8
Pat Neshek, Butler	So.	85	118	12.5
Chris Flinn, Stony Brook	Jr.	89	121	12.3
Brandon Woodward, Mt. St. Mary's	So.	61	82	12.1
Neal Cotts, Illinois State	Jr.	87	113	11.6
Marcos Mendoza, San Diego State	Jr.	91	118	11.6
Justin Pope, Central Florida	Jr.	123	158	11.5
Brian Houdek, Western Ky.	Sr.	79	101	11.5
Craig Beslow, Yale	Jr.	52	66	11.5
Jon Switzer, Arizona State	Jr.	100	128	11.5
Todd Pennington, SE Mo. State	Jr.	95	121	11.5

COLLEGE
TOP 25

BATTERS: 10 or more at-bats. **PITCHERS:** 5 or more innings. **Boldface** indicates selected in 2001 draft.

1. MIAMI

Coach: Jim Morris   **Record:** 53-12

BATTING	YR	AVG	AB	R	H	2B	3B	HR	RBI	SB
Rodriguez, Javy, ss	Jr.	.382	241	63	92	12	4	5	60	66
Howard, Kevin, 3b	So.	.336	250	55	84	20	1	4	46	9
Rodriguez, Mike, of	Jr.	.329	231	68	76	15	2	5	43	53
Mannix, Kevin, of	So.	.328	189	42	62	10	2	4	38	8
Matienzo, Danny, dh-c	So.	.324	219	46	71	13	2	13	64	3
Nettles, Marcus, of	Sr.	.310	145	49	45	5	0	0	12	44
Jimerson, Charlton, of	Sr.	.302	162	47	49	7	2	10	41	31
Safchik, Brad, of	Jr.	.296	27	8	8	0	1	0	2	1
Brown, Kevin, 1b	Sr.	.284	176	50	50	17	1	15	53	2
Lovelady, Greg, c	Sr.	.269	78	12	21	3	0	3	16	0
Burt, Jim, of	Fr.	.260	73	13	19	4	0	2	13	0
Pratt, Haas, 1b-dh	Fr.	.258	97	14	25	6	0	2	17	0
Clute, Kris, 2b	So.	.254	193	45	49	13	0	3	39	9
DiRosa, Mike, c	Jr.	.235	98	39	23	3	0	9	30	2
Dryer, Matt, 2b	So.	.233	43	6	10	3	1	1	10	0

PITCHING		W	L	ERA	G	SV	IP	H	BB	SO
Prunty, T.J., lhp	Fr.	2	1	1.29	11	0	14	9	2	16
DeBold, Luke, rhp	Jr.	2	1	1.74	44	4	57	47	7	67
Huguet, George, rhp	Fr.	1	0	2.03	44	14	44	35	13	34
Smith, Dan, rhp	Jr.	6	0	2.42	13	0	26	18	12	22
Sheffield, Chris, rhp	Jr.	2	0	3.30	15	0	46	35	29	69
Farmer, Tom, rhp	Sr.	15	2	3.54	20	0	114	122	33	80
Bengochea, Kiki, rhp	So.	9	4	4.10	18	0	108	106	38	89
Walker, Brian, lhp	Jr.	12	1	4.22	19	0	100	109	38	68
Reboin, Jeff, rhp	Jr.	0	2	6.11	11	0	18	25	10	11
Vazquez, Vince, rhp	So.	2	1	6.43	15	0	14	15	9	20
Touchet, Danny, rhp	Fr.	1	0	6.48	13	1	17	17	9	22
Cohn, Andrew, lhp	Fr.	1	0	6.92	24	1	13	15	8	17
Prendes, Alex, lhp	Sr.	0	0	7.98	35	0	15	24	10	20

2. STANFORD

Coach: Mark Marquess   **Record:** 51-17

BATTING	YR	AVG	AB	R	H	2B	3B	HR	RBI	SB
Garko, Ryan, c	So.	.368	201	42	74	16	1	7	43	0
O'Riordan, Chris, 2b	Jr.	.359	281	62	101	17	2	12	68	16
Fuld, Sam, of	Fr.	.357	227	56	81	15	2	0	37	11
Quentin, Carlos, of	Fr.	.345	249	55	86	11	1	11	52	5
Ash, Jonny, dh	Fr.	.327	110	15	36	10	0	0	24	0
VanMeetren, Jason, of	Jr.	.320	178	33	57	14	3	7	33	7
Dragicevich, Scott, ss	Jr.	.320	253	47	81	14	0	5	34	6
Hall, Brian, of-3b	Fr.	.287	115	25	33	2	2	2	21	6
Topham, Andy, 3b	Jr.	.272	246	44	67	15	1	7	45	11
Cooper, Jason, of-dh	So.	.272	169	26	46	10	0	9	37	2
VanZandt, Arik, 1b	Jr.	.262	248	53	65	13	1	6	34	9
Tirpack, Ken, c	So.	.234	47	5	11	1	0	0	5	2
Garza, Mario, c	So.	.174	23	2	4	1	0	1	2	0
Naatjes, Darin, of	So.	.077	26	1	2	0	0	0	1	2

PITCHING		W	L	ERA	G	SV	IP	H	BB	SO
Willcox, J.D., rhp	Jr.	5	0	2.06	22	6	35	29	10	29
Ehrlich, Drew, lhp	Fr.	0	0	2.57	5	0	7	2	3	
McCally, Ryan, rhp	So.	2	1	2.62	26	3	34	27	9	22
Guthrie, Jeremy, rhp	So.	13	4	2.82	20	0	134	123	41	128
Bruksch, Jeff, rhp	Jr.	3	3	3.18	23	3	124	107	28	107
Cunningham, Tim, lhp	So.	6	0	3.62	18	0	75	59	40	54
Gosling, Mike, lhp	Jr.	7	3	3.94	17	0	82	65	28	77
Hudgins, John, rhp	Fr.	1	5	4.27	22	4	46	37	27	50
Wodnicki, Mike, rhp	Jr.	7	1	5.13	28	6	54	58	18	53
Luker, Jason, rhp	Jr.	1	0	8.03	6	1	12	18	5	7

3. CAL STATE FULLERTON

Coach: George Horton   **Record:** 48-18

BATTING	YR	AVG	AB	R	H	2B	3B	HR	RBI	SB
Costa, Shane, of	Fr.	.380	129	25	49	12	2	0	11	4
Rouse, Mike, ss	So.	.377	236	58	89	18	2	12	62	8
Stringfellow, Chris, of	Jr.	.345	206	40	71	13	2	4	36	10
Bacani, David, 2b	Sr.	.333	267	73	89	18	3	7	34	18
Corapci, Jason, of-dh	So.	.333	225	46	75	14	2	1	49	7
Kay, Brett, c	Jr.	.323	195	39	63	13	2	7	43	11
Guzman, Robert, of	Jr.	.317	230	44	73	18	1	3	37	12
Lamoure, Louie, of	Sr.	.316	76	14	24	4	0	4	15	6
Belfanti, Matt, dh	So.	.308	91	20	28	8	1	3	20	5
Rifkin, Aaron, 1b	Sr.	.300	240	62	72	18	0	16	60	2
Norris, Shawn, 3b	Jr.	.288	198	31	57	14	3	5	45	4
Boyer, Kyle, dh	Fr.	.220	50	9	11	1	1	1	4	1
Comfort, Geoff, dh	Jr.	.190	21	4	4	1	0	0	5	0
Pilittere, P.J., c	Fr.	.154	65	9	10	0	0	0	11	1
Martinez, Mike, 3b	So.	.119	42	5	5	1	1	0	4	0
Hilt, Cole, dh	Fr.	.062	16	1	1	0	0	0	1	0

PITCHING		W	L	ERA	G	SV	IP	H	BB	SO
Cordero, Chad, rhp	Fr.	3	4	1.83	38	14	64	43	12	63
Saarloos, Kirk, rhp	Sr.	15	2	2.18	25	4	153	99	23	153
Nunez, Mike, rhp	Sr.	2	0	2.66	14	0	20	14	11	26
Merrell, Darric, rhp	Fr.	8	4	2.95	20	0	113	107	45	76
Smith, Jon, lhp	Sr.	11	3	3.78	19	0	112	110	36	75
Zahari, Charlie, rhp	Jr.	2	1	4.15	14	0	39	39	20	27
Martin, Sean, rhp	So.	1	0	5.21	14	0	19	23	4	13
Waroff, Shane, rhp	Jr.	1	0	6.23	14	0	17	26	6	15
Littleton, Wes, rhp	Fr.	2	0	7.68	16	0	36	46	15	35
Lovato, Nick, lhp	So.	2	4	8.31	11	0	26	34	24	16

4. SOUTHERN CALIFORNIA

Coach: Mike Gillespie   **Record:** 45-19

BATTING	YR	AVG	AB	R	H	2B	3B	HR	RBI	SB
Morales, Michael, of	Sr.	.414	29	7	12	1	0	0	5	1
Barre, Brian, of	Jr.	.345	232	53	80	9	1	13	48	20
Davidson, Seth, ss	Sr.	.323	254	48	82	10	5	2	26	14
Concepcion, Alberto, c	So.	.321	224	37	72	17	3	7	41	4
Moon, Michael, 3b	Fr.	.313	227	40	71	8	3	6	35	11
Peavey, Bill, 1b	Sr.	.307	218	44	67	9	1	7	48	0
Lunetta, Anthony, 2b-dh	So.	.305	239	48	73	18	2	5	38	12
Persell, Josh, dh-1b	Sr.	.294	231	42	68	15	0	7	39	0
Garibaldi, Rob, of	Jr.	.281	135	22	38	5	1	1	25	2
Self, Josh, of	Sr.	.245	94	10	23	0	0	3	10	3
Brewster, Jon, of-2b	Fr.	.241	133	26	32	4	0	1	17	9
Montanez, Abel, of	Sr.	.238	84	16	20	4	0	3	15	2
Helland, Ricky, c	Jr.	.100	10	0	1	0	0	0	1	0

PITCHING		W	L	ERA	G	SV	IP	H	BB	SO
Prior, Mark, rhp	Jr.	15	1	1.69	20	0	139	100	18	202
Currier, Rik, rhp	Sr.	12	3	2.59	20	0	118	112	40	120
Bannister, Brian, rhp	So.	4	4	2.80	34	5	55	40	21	56
Reyes, Anthony, rhp	So.	5	4	3.72	19	0	109	111	25	97
Olson, Jordan, rhp	So.	2	1	5.06	21	0	27	30	20	24
Dizard, Fraser, lhp	Fr.	3	3	5.44	29	7	51	52	30	47
Rummonds, Josh, lhp	Fr.	0	0	6.00	6	0	6	7	2	2
Clark, Chad, rhp	So.	4	2	6.39	20	1	49	62	34	43
Todd, Mark, lhp	So.	0	0	6.75	4	0	5	5	6	4
Williams, Jon, rhp	Fr.	0	1	8.10	10	0	13	17	8	6

5. TULANE

Coach: Rick Jones   **Record:** 56-13

BATTING	YR	AVG	AB	R	H	2B	3B	HR	RBI	SB
Cannizaro, Andy, ss	Sr.	.395	299	80	118	34	3	3	70	52
Aubrey, Michael, of-1b	Fr.	.361	277	74	100	17	4	13	69	9
Kaplan, Jon, of	Sr.	.358	260	79	93	14	1	5	54	21
Gautreau, Jake, 3b	Jr.	.355	290	82	103	23	1	21	96	8
Groff, Matt, of	Sr.	.353	238	56	84	10	4	5	51	15
Giarratano, Anthony, 2b	Fr.	.352	264	72	93	12	2	3	47	11
Heintz, Jay, of	Sr.	.328	116	29	38	6	1	0	20	5
Jurries, James, 1b-dh	Jr.	.324	210	48	68	8	1	10	53	15
Shirley, Steve, 1b-dh	Jr.	.320	172	52	55	12	0	12	56	0
Madden, Scott, c	Fr.	.312	64	11	20	3	0	0	13	1
Feldman, Aaron, of	So.	.292	65	14	19	3	1	4	20	5
Mann, Matt, c	Fr.	.250	72	15	18	2	0	0	7	0
Bourgeois, Nick, dh	So.	.250	24	3	6	1	0	1	5	0
Burgess, James, of	So.	.236	72	9	17	3	0	1	19	1
Spencer, Wyn, c	Fr.	.136	44	7	6	0	0	0	3	1
VanDaele, Mike, of	So.	.091	11	2	1	0	0	0	2	0

COLLEGE BASEBALL

PITCHING		W	L	ERA	G	SV	IP	H	BB	SO
Searle, Chris, rhp	So.	1	0	2.70	6	0	7	7	5	9
Foster, Matt, rhp	So.	9	4	3.51	21	0	90	94	36	74
Charron, Joey, lhp	Fr.	9	2	3.52	29	2	64	75	20	63
Corona, Andrew, rhp	Jr.	8	1	3.65	15	1	62	60	34	41
Richardson, Beau, lhp	Jr.	8	1	4.24	21	1	85	88	32	66
Blades, Steven, rhp	So.	1	1	4.54	20	1	34	26	29	33
Kline, Kris, lhp	Fr.	1	0	4.91	8	0	18	21	10	18
Bourgeois, Nick, lhp	So.	3	1	5.01	14	0	50	48	38	50
Aubrey, Michael, lhp	Fr.	3	1	5.15	17	1	72	75	33	46
Walter, Will, rhp	Fr.	2	0	5.92	20	3	24	21	24	21
Melius, Barth, rhp	Sr.	10	2	6.02	24	4	102	115	35	66
Hoagland, Dirck, rhp	Fr.	1	0	7.00	9	1	9	12	1	3

6. NEBRASKA

Coach: Dave Van Horn   **Record:** 50-16

BATTING	YR	AVG	AB	R	H	2B	3B	HR	RBI	SB
Cole, John, of-2b	Jr.	.418	239	71	100	15	4	11	61	28
Leise, Jeff, of	So.	.380	245	67	93	14	5	7	48	17
Johnson, Dan, 1b-dh	Sr.	.361	230	77	83	13	1	25	86	7
Hopper, Matt, dh-1b	So.	.358	254	65	91	19	1	12	85	3
Seely, Justin, of	Jr.	.357	143	32	51	14	1	4	28	5
Morris, Jed, c	So.	.341	164	40	56	16	0	7	42	5
Blevins, Jeff, 3b	Jr.	.313	195	36	61	10	2	2	44	9
Eymann, Brandon, ss	Jr.	.307	101	31	31	5	0	3	31	2
Hesse, Josh, ss	Sr.	.297	138	26	41	6	1	1	20	1
Anderson, Drew, of	Fr.	.293	41	13	12	0	0	1	10	9
Stern, Adam, of	Jr.	.292	267	68	78	8	4	5	47	27
Rivera, Tito, c	Jr.	.275	80	14	22	3	0	1	7	0
Bolt, Will, 2b-ss	Jr.	.265	211	46	56	10	3	2	30	7
Jones, Willie, 2b	Jr.	.250	48	21	12	1	0	0	8	4

PITCHING		W	L	ERA	G	SV	IP	H	BB	SO
Penas, Brandon, lhp	Sr.	0	1	0.73	12	0	12	10	8	11
Blaesing, Jeff, rhp	So.	0	0	0.87	9	0	10	5	6	8
Conte, Derrick, rhp	Fr.	2	1	3.05	12	0	21	14	16	16
Byers, Waylon, rhp	So.	3	0	3.43	14	0	21	24	8	17
Pekarek, Justin, lhp	Fr.	0	1	3.86	3	1	7	3	2	6
Komine, Shane, rhp	Jr.	14	2	3.35	18	0	132	129	36	157
Ott, Thom, rhp	Jr.	5	2	4.03	29	11	58	52	23	42
Hale, Steve, rhp	So.	5	0	4.24	20	2	47	59	18	32
Spiehs, R.D., rhp	Jr.	8	3	4.78	21	1	79	89	19	76
Sillman, Mike, rhp	Fr.	2	1	4.84	9	0	22	23	11	15
Rodaway, Brian, lhp	Sr.	4	2	5.71	17	0	58	75	10	31
Rodrigue, Jamie, lhp	So.	6	3	6.03	17	0	78	106	20	66
Burch, Jason, rhp	Fr.	1	0	7.65	7	0	20	33	5	19

7. GEORGIA

Coach: Ron Polk   **Record:** 47-22

BATTING	YR	AVG	AB	R	H	2B	3B	HR	RBI	SB
Keppinger, Jeff, ss	Jr.	.389	262	69	102	15	5	18	73	10
Coffey, David, of-dh	Fr.	.358	173	44	62	9	0	5	33	7
Neufeld, Andy, 3b	Sr.	.334	287	71	96	20	1	10	38	5
Thornhill, Mark, 1b	Sr.	.332	262	37	87	21	0	2	49	0
Swann, Adam, of	Jr.	.326	270	58	88	26	1	6	62	5
Cavender, Matt, dh	Jr.	.310	71	14	22	3	0	5	10	1
Edge, Kris, of	Jr.	.304	168	37	51	7	1	0	21	9
Brooks, Doc, of-c	Jr.	.266	229	54	61	13	2	17	55	0
Bodenmiller, Blake, of	Fr.	.252	151	17	38	7	0	2	32	0
Blaze, Darryl, of	Jr.	.246	61	15	15	1	0	0	5	3
Pollock, Jody, 2b	Sr.	.234	273	42	64	16	3	2	31	4
Burchett, Tony, c	Sr.	.223	148	21	33	6	1	9	39	0
Mitchell, Lee, of	Fr.	.215	65	11	14	2	0	2	8	0
Armitage, Jon, ss	Fr.	.156	32	4	5	0	0	1	3	0

PITCHING		W	L	ERA	G	SV	IP	H	BB	SO
Lawson, Scott, lhp	Jr.	0	0	0.00	4	0	5	2	3	3
Magee, Kyle, rhp	Sr.	1	0	1.29	3	0	7	6	3	3
Friedman, Jody, rhp	Sr.	4	2	2.76	19	2	42	45	13	41
Carswell, Jeffery, rhp	Jr.	10	2	3.32	24	1	60	55	16	62
Sharpton, Bill, rhp	Jr.	5	1	3.81	24	0	50	48	22	37
Brown, Jeremy, rhp	Jr.	7	4	4.50	20	2	92	101	28	80
Hussion, Andy, rhp	Sr.	3	2	4.71	11	0	42	43	12	40
Moorhead, Brandon, rhp	So.	4	2	4.96	14	0	65	75	23	38
Helmey, Shaun, rhp	Sr.	3	1	5.16	13	0	45	62	4	40
Murphy, Scott, rhp	Jr.	4	2	5.53	16	0	86	100	35	76
Anglin, Brandon, lhp	Jr.	0	0	5.68	6	0	6	5	3	4
Moravek, Rob, rhp	Jr.	3	5	6.15	16	0	91	111	28	60
Havel, Max, rhp	Jr.	2	1	6.33	18	0	27	38	6	19

8. TENNESSEE

Coach: Rod Delmonico   **Record:** 48-20

BATTING	YR	AVG	AB	R	H	2B	3B	HR	RBI	SB
Burke, Chris, ss	Jr.	.435	271	105	118	21	11	20	60	49

BATTING										
Hopkins, Brandon, dh-of	Jr.	.367	128	30	47	6	1	4	24	4
Christensen, Jeff, of	Sr.	.341	258	59	88	22	3	12	73	24
Daniel, Stevie, 2b-3b	Jr.	.330	276	67	91	25	3	4	61	46
Bennett, Kris, 3b-2b	Sr.	.316	231	47	73	10	0	4	41	13
Case, Ryan, 1b	Jr.	.316	98	12	31	5	0	3	17	2
Herrera, Javi, c	Fr.	.296	213	32	63	14	1	7	45	2
Wilson, Dan, of	Jr.	.294	187	28	55	16	0	5	37	5
Parker, Justin, of-p	Sr.	.280	157	34	44	7	1	3	28	5
Gomez, Dennis, 1b	Jr.	.252	163	25	41	5	1	3	21	1
Bibee, Hal, c	Jr.	.250	80	15	20	3	0	3	22	1
Smith, Adam, of	Jr.	.250	48	9	12	2	0	0	6	1
Sternberg, Matt, 3b-of	Jr.	.236	144	22	34	7	1	3	17	0
Moffett, Ryan, of	Jr.	.207	116	23	24	6	2	2	9	3
Rigsby, Hunter, 2b	Fr.	.132	38	10	5	2	0	0	3	4

PITCHING	YR	W	L	ERA	G	SV	IP	H	BB	SO
Crowe, Brandon, rhp	So.	6	0	3.68	16	3	51	56	15	46
Curtiss, Will, lhp	Sr.	7	1	4.64	29	5	43	36	22	36
Johnson, Dusty, lhp	Fr.	4	1	4.72	14	0	48	55	8	18
Massey, Beau, rhp	Fr.	1	0	4.85	9	0	13	10	7	11
Gates, Brian, rhp	Jr.	6	5	5.03	19	3	77	89	28	76
Hicklen, Patrick, rhp	Fr.	5	4	5.27	16	3	80	92	23	61
Filsinger, Erik, rhp	Fr.	0	0	5.30	19	0	19	19	15	21
Nicholson, Devon, rhp	Sr.	3	2	5.93	18	0	44	50	33	45
Allen, Wyatt, rhp	Jr.	10	3	6.30	18	0	104	109	59	110
Parker, Justin, lhp	Sr.	4	3	6.40	15	0	52	55	36	58
Bertolino, Joe, lhp	Sr.	1	0	6.45	14	1	22	32	10	17
Samuels, Matt, rhp	Fr.	1	0	6.46	22	0	39	35	26	30
Gomez, Dennis, lhp	Fr.	0	1	6.75	5	0	9	15	3	6

9. LOUISIANA STATE

Coach: Skip Bertman   **Record:** 44-22

BATTING	YR	AVG	AB	R	H	2B	3B	HR	RBI	SB
Garidel, Jamin, c	Sr.	.400	10	2	4	0	0	0	1	0
Moore, Bryan, 1b	Jr.	.373	241	59	90	25	0	7	50	1
Theriot, Ryan, ss	Jr.	.353	266	67	94	18	3	1	48	17
Pontiff, Wally, 3b	So.	.347	268	47	93	9	1	7	58	3
Fontenot, Mike, 2b	Jr.	.339	221	64	75	13	0	14	50	7
Barker, Sean, dh	Jr.	.338	80	24	27	7	1	3	16	4
Raymer, David, of	Jr.	.324	148	42	48	13	1	4	30	11
Linden, Todd, of	Jr.	.312	256	65	80	14	1	20	76	9
Zinsman, Zeph, dh-1b	Jr.	.302	162	33	49	9	0	16	45	0
Hill, Aaron, of-2b	Fr.	.299	134	27	40	5	1	5	36	6
Heath, Matt, c	Jr.	.293	205	51	60	10	2	10	47	12
Wright, Ray, of	Sr.	.260	154	32	40	4	0	5	20	8
Thibodeau, Johnnie, of	Sr.	.256	121	29	31	4	0	5	21	3
Duncan, Trae, 3b	Jr.	.238	21	5	5	3	0	0	2	0
Brumfield, Victor, 3b	Jr.	.222	18	6	4	1	0	1	5	0
McBride, Billy, of	So.	.214	14	15	3	0	0	0	1	9
Phillips, Chris, of	Jr.	.190	42	3	8	2	0	0	4	0

PITCHING		W	L	ERA	G	SV	IP	H	BB	SO
Pettit, Bo, rhp	So.	4	0	2.42	7	0	26	21	7	25
Mestepey, Lane, lhp	Fr.	11	3	3.75	22	1	139	158	37	79
Nugent, Tim, lhp	Sr.	7	3	4.38	21	0	76	69	48	55
David, Brad, rhp	So.	2	1	4.40	24	3	31	25	23	32
Scobie, Jason, rhp	Sr.	4	3	4.69	21	0	96	109	31	59
Youman, Shane, lhp	Jr.	3	2	5.17	18	1	54	67	33	33
Corcoran, Roy, rhp	Jr.	8	4	5.48	28	0	69	67	31	62
Guidry, Weylin, rhp	Jr.	1	3	5.65	27	2	29	38	17	34
Wilson, Brian, rhp	Fr.	3	2	5.67	20	3	40	40	20	22
Hill, Justin, rhp	Jr.	1	1	6.16	18	2	19	14	17	27
Brian, Billy, rhp	Jr.	0	0	9.00	13	0	15	28	12	17

10. FLORIDA STATE

Coach: Mike Martin   **Record:** 47-19

BATTING	YR	AVG	AB	R	H	2B	3B	HR	RBI	SB
Griffin, John-Ford, of	Jr.	.450	251	79	113	30	0	19	75	11
Rogers, Nick, of	Jr.	.351	185	45	65	17	1	6	38	20
Futrell, Mike, of-dh	Jr.	.345	223	45	77	13	2	8	56	6
Barthelemy, Ryan, 1b-3b	Jr.	.343	280	55	96	22	5	14	72	3
Jernigan, Karl, of	Jr.	.305	200	52	61	16	2	5	44	28
Richie, Tony, c	Fr.	.291	206	27	60	15	1	3	32	1
Zech, Bryan, 2b	Fr.	.282	213	50	60	10	0	2	25	4
Groves, Brett, ss	Jr.	.272	81	16	22	6	0	0	14	14
Probst, Jeff, ss	Fr.	.267	161	31	43	11	1	2	27	2
McQuade, Tony, of	Fr.	.259	27	7	7	5	0	0	4	1
Hart, Chris, 3b-c	So.	.257	74	9	19	3	1	1	11	3
Toole, Scott, 3b-2b	Jr.	.223	184	34	41	7	3	2	17	5
Cole, Chris, 1b-of	Fr.	.211	71	15	15	2	0	3	11	0
Smith, Richie, of	Jr.	.207	58	20	12	2	1	1	2	10
McCaleb, Blair, c	Jr.	.185	54	10	10	2	0	0	5	1
Boyd, Scott, 1b-of	Sr.	.118	17	5	2	1	0	0	2	0

PITCHING		W	L	ERA	G	SV	IP	H	BB	SO
Roman, Eric, rhp	So.	4	2	0.89	27	1	40	24	14	30
Bentley, John, rhp	Sr.	0	0	1.93	4	0	5	6	0	7
Ginn, Chris, lhp	Sr.	0	0	2.92	20	0	12	12	6	9
Hodges, Daniel, hp	So.	4	3	3.05	27	4	59	65	15	55
Peterson, Trent, lhp	Fr.	5	1	3.16	16	0	57	50	20	45
Lord, Justin, rhp	Jr.	2	3	3.26	30	11	30	39	9	34
Whidden, Nick, rhp	So.	1	0	3.54	16	1	20	23	4	16
Lynch, Matt, lhp	So.	9	2	3.61	18	0	97	111	37	85
Varnes, Blair, rhp	Jr.	9	1	3.61	18	0	115	113	27	93
Read, Robby, rhp	So.	7	5	4.08	20	0	86	86	38	87
LaMacchia, Marc, rhp	Fr.	5	2	4.72	16	0	53	58	25	47
Pearson, Brent, lhp	Jr.	1	0	5.25	11	0	12	11	9	10

11. EAST CAROLINA

Coach: Keith LeClair — **Record:** 47-13

BATTING		YR	AVG	AB	R	H	2B	3B	HR	RBI	SB
Sugden, Jason, 2b	Fr.	.417	12	3	5	1	0	0	1	1
Ward, Bryant, 2b-3b	Jr.	.366	227	53	83	22	0	8	37	7
Delfino, Lee, ss	Jr.	.362	221	47	80	12	2	11	54	5
Tracy, Chad, 3b-1b	Jr.	.355	248	62	88	15	1	13	61	15
Williamson, John, of	Sr.	.349	218	58	76	22	0	11	56	7
Sorenson, Jedd, 2b	Jr.	.340	50	10	17	4	0	0	3	6
Hastings, Joseph, 1b	So.	.339	245	61	83	14	0	13	62	15
Godwin, Cliff, dh	Sr.	.322	183	40	59	14	3	15	45	1
Gaspar, Warren, of	Jr.	.309	243	49	75	9	3	2	30	16
McCullough, Clayton, c	Jr.	.301	163	28	49	6	2	4	28	3
Sanderson, Ben, of	So.	.288	73	14	21	4	0	0	6	3
Jones, Ryan, of	Fr.	.279	104	22	29	6	0	1	17	4
Paige, Jamie, of	Jr.	.261	23	2	6	0	0	0	3	0
Poppert, John, c	Fr.	.226	53	9	12	2	0	4	14	1
O'Sullivan, Kevin, 2b	So.	.188	16	5	3	0	0	1	3	1
Simons, Brad, of	Sr.	.186	43	5	8	3	0	1	6	3
Grieve, Kevin, 1b	Sr.	.156	32	4	5	0	0	1	3	6

PITCHING		YR	W	L	ERA	G	SV	IP	H	BB	SO
Mandryk, Jason, rhp	Jr.	7	1	1.95	13	0	74	66	23	52
Narron, Sam, lhp	So.	12	1	2.67	15	0	101	96	17	67
Sears, Neal, rhp	So.	6	1	2.94	24	3	52	52	7	35
Brinson, Will, rhp	So.	3	1	3.12	23	8	35	28	16	38
Speas, Todd, rhp	Fr.	0	0	3.60	5	0	5	7	2	4
Capps, Ashley, rhp	Fr.	3	2	3.89	16	0	42	39	21	26
Penny, Davey, rhp	So.	3	3	4.32	13	0	58	49	21	62
Tourangeau, Jason, rhp	So.	3	1	4.37	15	0	45	37	14	44
Tucker, Glenn, rhp	So.	2	2	4.60	27	2	45	52	15	35
Minton, Foye, lhp	Jr.	7	1	5.06	11	0	64	83	19	34
Greene, Scott, lhp	So.	0	0	5.40	2	1	5	4	1	6
Mattison, Kieran, rhp	Jr.	1	0	6.94	11	0	12	14	11	13

12. SOUTH CAROLINA

Coach: Ray Tanner — **Record:** 49-20

BATTING		YR	AVG	AB	R	H	2B	3B	HR	RBI	SB
Floyd, Michael, of	Jr.	.350	200	33	70	11	1	3	28	10
Gonce, Garris, of	Jr.	.338	204	51	69	18	2	9	35	6
Jeffcoat, Bryon, 2b	Sr.	.329	243	50	80	16	1	16	54	8
Meyer, Drew, ss	So.	.303	274	54	83	12	2	7	37	20
Whittaker, Tim, c-dh	Sr.	.294	238	54	70	14	0	21	74	1
Riddle, Matt, dh	So.	.292	24	4	7	0	0	0	2	0
Brown, Sheldon, of	Jr.	.288	52	16	15	4	0	1	7	6
Dees, Brennan, of-dh	Sr.	.286	203	45	58	6	0	13	40	7
McBeth, Marcus, of	Jr.	.280	279	58	78	21	1	17	58	12
Kelly, Tripp, 1b	Sr.	.259	166	40	43	9	1	9	30	4
Plummer, Chris, 3b	Sr.	.259	170	27	44	6	0	6	31	6
Adler, Tony, 3b-p	So.	.243	37	6	9	0	0	1	7	0
Thomas, Steve, inf	Jr.	.217	23	10	5	1	0	0	3	0
Bono, Chris, dh	Jr.	.200	25	3	5	2	0	1	4	0
Dyson, Trey, 1b-dh	Jr.	.186	97	10	18	5	0	1	15	1
Powell, Landon, c	Fr.	.169	77	15	13	4	0	3	13	0
Peters, Yaron, 1b	Jr.	.148	27	4	4	1	0	2	6	0

PITCHING		YR	W	L	ERA	G	SV	IP	H	BB	SO
Gronkiewicz, Lee, rhp	Sr.	2	1	1.31	36	19	62	31	23	77
MacLane, Tommy, lhp	Jr.	1	0	2.13	9	0	13	6	10	9
Carter, Chris, rhp	Fr.	0	0	2.84	7	0	6	5	3	6
Price, Brett, lhp	Jr.	6	1	2.95	26	0	37	31	30	44
Adler, Tony, rhp	So.	1	0	3.24	19	0	25	23	13	30
Taylor, Blake, rhp	Jr.	5	4	3.30	27	1	63	59	19	56
Bell, Gary, lhp	Jr.	10	5	3.46	20	0	101	99	42	74
Marchbanks, David, lhp	Fr.	7	1	3.63	15	0	57	55	15	46
Bouknight, Kip, rhp	Sr.	10	4	3.99	23	2	124	127	53	104
Spigner, Chris, rhp	Jr.	7	4	4.08	17	0	90	77	57	70
Bondurant, Steven, lhp	So.	0	0	4.76	9	0	11	11	7	8
Wilson, Matt, rhp	Jr.	0	0	5.30	11	0	19	28	7	13

13. RICE

Coach: Wayne Graham — **Record:** 47-20

BATTING		YR	AVG	AB	R	H	2B	3B	HR	RBI	SB
Davis, Austin, of	Fr.	.346	257	73	89	18	2	6	29	5
Porfirio, A.J., of	Jr.	.345	281	77	97	21	3	11	55	8
Brown, Hunter, 3b-of	Jr.	.335	260	46	87	25	2	7	44	5
Arnold, Eric, ss-3b	Jr.	.325	252	50	82	17	2	15	65	6
Jacobson, Billy, of-dh	Sr.	.320	100	19	32	5	1	0	7	3
Cunningham, Matt, dh-c	Jr.	.294	119	11	35	7	0	1	24	0
Roman, Jesse, 1b	Sr.	.291	258	43	75	21	4	6	67	1
Lorsbach, Mike, of	Jr.	.282	181	28	51	15	2	4	29	2
Cruz, Jose Enrique, 2b	Jr.	.270	122	31	33	7	1	6	19	8
Ghutzman, Phillip, c	Sr.	.267	221	37	59	11	0	4	34	0
Fox, Matt, 2b-ss	Sr.	.256	164	35	42	9	1	2	22	4
Bormaster, Brian, 2b	Fr.	.243	74	5	18	2	0	0	8	1
Blackinton, Jeff, c	Fr.	.194	36	1	7	1	0	0	6	0
Bryan, Bobby, 3b	Jr.	.167	36	4	6	3	0	1	6	0

PITCHING		W	L	ERA	G	SV	IP	H	BB	SO
Baugh, Kenny, rhp	Sr.	13	2	2.17	22	0	141	106	54	163
Herce, Steven, rhp	So.	6	1	2.37	17	2	68	61	21	63
Skaggs, Jon, rhp	Sr.	9	4	2.65	17	0	119	89	62	110
Gonzalez, Jonathan, lhp	So.	5	1	3.17	13	1	54	54	22	45
Barzilla, Philip, lhp	Sr.	3	4	3.17	30	10	54	57	16	46
Tribe, Philip, rhp	Jr.	4	2	3.19	26	1	73	70	41	79
Jacobson, Billy, rhp	Sr.	1	0	3.38	9	0	16	11	10	14
Wernecke, Dustin, rhp	Fr.	0	1	4.15	5	0	9	11	1	4
Martin, Nick, lhp	Jr.	2	1	5.03	11	0	20	24	15	19
Nichols, Jeff, rhp	Jr.	4	4	6.53	14	1	41	67	10	45

14. CENTRAL FLORIDA

Coach: Jay Bergman — **Record:** 51-14

BATTING		YR	AVG	AB	R	H	2B	3B	HR	RBI	SB
Kurella, Jeremy, ss	Sr.	.401	247	63	99	16	1	7	49	17
Johnson, Andy, dh	Jr.	.389	203	45	79	13	1	1	44	2
Cox, George, c	Jr.	.382	55	16	21	2	1	2	12	1
Fox, Mike, 2b-3b	Jr.	.354	229	47	81	26	1	9	61	3
Hanson, Ty, of-dh	Jr.	.349	63	13	22	4	1	0	15	0
Good, Greg, 1b	So.	.339	112	25	38	8	0	2	21	3
Ehrnsberger, Chad, 3b-2b	Jr.	.326	224	61	73	16	2	16	72	4
Frost, Jeremy, c-of	Jr.	.325	231	52	75	15	3	13	56	14
Summers, Wayne, of	Jr.	.320	197	47	63	15	1	2	34	15
Myers, Mike, of-ss	Jr.	.317	230	70	73	18	2	6	44	29
Oakley, Bill, 1b	Jr.	.310	116	29	36	11	0	0	18	8
Meath, Matt, of	Jr.	.307	101	27	31	4	1	2	15	3
Graham, Jason, of	Jr.	.279	122	29	34	7	2	1	25	16
Wallace, Rich, of	So.	.244	78	11	19	5	0	0	15	0
Schulte, Blaine, of	Fr.	.200	20	4	4	0	1	0	3	0

PITCHING			W	L	ERA	G	SV	IP	H	BB	SO
Pope, Justin, rhp	Jr.	15	1	1.68	17	0	123	97	27	158
Arnold, Jason, rhp	Sr.	14	3	1.97	19	0	119	82	32	150
Lubrano, Paul, lhp	Fr.	3	3	3.56	16	2	48	54	18	34
Sutton, Zach, rhp	Jr.	4	2	4.00	23	5	36	44	9	31
Clark, Burt, lhp	Fr.	5	1	4.12	10	0	39	31	30	38
Stertzbach, Von, rhp	So.	0	1	4.28	21	2	40	46	18	48
Cerrato, Justin, rhp	Fr.	1	0	4.50	13	0	36	41	21	37
Smietana, Mark, rhp	So.	2	0	5.02	9	0	14	24	4	17
Busbin, Brad, rhp	Jr.	6	2	6.99	20	0	76	106	18	64
Gonzalez, Abe, rhp	So.	1	1	8.31	10	0	13	22	6	16

15. NOTRE DAME

Coach: Paul Mainieri — **Record:** 49-13

BATTING		YR	AVG	AB	R	H	2B	3B	HR	RBI	SB
Stanley, Steve, of	Jr.	.400	255	76	102	14	5	1	32	31
Stavisky, Brian, of	So.	.386	210	46	81	19	4	10	66	9
Sollmann, Steve, 2b	Fr.	.362	221	52	80	9	2	5	36	23
Cooke, Ben, if	Sr.	.344	61	12	21	4	0	0	8	2
O'Toole, Paul, c-3b	Jr.	.323	201	40	65	12	2	4	35	15
Porzel, Alec, ss	Jr.	.295	251	53	74	28	2	8	59	6
Bok, Matt, dh	Jr.	.286	98	14	28	6	4	1	17	0
Thaman, Joe, 1b	So.	.284	208	29	59	15	1	2	25	1
Meyer, Ken, dh	Jr.	.271	107	16	29	5	0	3	20	1
Billmaier, Kris, of	So.	.257	183	34	47	9	0	3	37	4
Strickroth, Matt, of	So.	.245	49	7	12	2	1	4	9	0
Holba, Mike, 1b	So.	.211	19	2	4	1	0	0	2	0
Leahy, Soran, c	Fr.	.200	15	2	3	0	0	0	0	0
Sanchez, Javier, 3b	Fr.	.000	13	0	0	0	0	0	0	0

PITCHING			W	L	ERA	G	SV	IP	H	BB	SO
Heilman, Aaron, rhp	Sr.	15	0	1.74	15	0	114	70	31	111
Ogilvie, Peter, rhp	So.	5	1	1.90	8	0	52	44	11	30

	YR	W	L	ERA	G	SV	IP	H	BB	SO
Kalita, Ryan, rhp	So.	2	0	2.45	4	0	11	10	8	9
Tamayo, Danny, rhp	Sr.	8	3	2.72	15	0	113	96	17	106
Naumann, Mike, lhp	Sr.	3	1	3.02	16	0	42	52	7	12
Laird, Matt, rhp	So.	5	1	3.09	22	4	32	23	15	28
Viloria, Brandon, rhp	So.	3	1	3.32	12	2	22	21	5	8
Edwards, Aaron, rhp	Fr.	0	0	3.68	5	0	7	7	8	4
Buchmeier, Matt, rhp	Jr.	1	1	3.91	13	2	46	54	12	28
Duff, Drew, rhp	Jr.	2	0	4.99	13	0	31	34	9	28
Gagne, J.P., rhp	So.	5	5	5.35	17	0	71	79	21	47
Kaplan, Brian, rhp	Fr.	0	0	10.80	3	0	5	10	4	6

16. PEPPERDINE

Coach: Frank Sanchez **Record:** 42-18

BATTING	YR	AVG	AB	R	H	2B	3B	HR	RBI	SB
Pitney, Jared, 1b	Sr.	.397	239	46	95	22	0	14	67	4
Garcia, Danny, 2b	Jr.	.374	238	58	89	19	3	8	53	27
Garcia, Tony, ss	Jr.	.354	226	56	80	13	1	6	38	8
Cliffords, Woody, of	Jr.	.336	250	63	84	23	0	2	31	25
Ball, Dane, of	Sr.	.320	203	32	65	11	2	2	30	4
Haren, Daniel, dh-p	Jr.	.308	224	33	69	8	0	5	47	1
Payne, Jason, of	So.	.308	13	5	4	0	0	0	0	0
Mills, Rock, c	Jr.	.307	192	46	59	14	0	9	39	2
Kelly, Chris, of	Fr.	.269	182	30	49	8	0	6	24	2
Montague, Ed, 3b-of	So.	.262	126	22	33	5	1	0	13	6
Ferrer, Simon, ss-2b	So.	.227	44	7	10	0	1	0	9	0
Sardinha, Duke, 3b	So.	.225	120	12	27	6	1	3	18	0
Lopez, Andy, dh	Jr.	.174	23	1	4	0	0	0	1	0
Brightwell, Cory, dh	Fr.	.167	12	1	2	0	0	0	1	0
Harvick, Matt, c	Jr.	.087	23	2	2	0	0	0	1	0

PITCHING	YR	W	L	ERA	G	SV	IP	H	BB	SO
Lowry, Noah, lhp	Jr.	14	2	1.71	18	1	121	88	41	142
Haren, Daniel, rhp	Jr.	11	3	2.22	17	1	130	106	31	97
Decker, Dustin, rhp	So.	0	0	2.25	6	0	8	3	7	5
Beavers, Kevin, lhp	Jr.	2	2	3.45	15	3	29	22	10	18
Adams, Jay, rhp	Sr.	5	3	4.17	17	2	91	95	27	54
Ramirez, Greg, rhp	So.	5	4	4.95	24	3	73	80	27	55
Boesch, Brandon, rhp	Fr.	0	1	4.97	9	0	13	17	7	4
Barrack, Jacob, rhp	Fr.	4	1	6.75	18	2	24	31	20	18
Valenzuela, Eric, rhp	Sr.	1	2	7.20	13	1	40	52	32	23
Dolle, Nicholas, rhp	Fr.	0	0	7.94	4	0	6	8	4	4

17. CLEMSON

Coach: Jack Leggett **Record:** 41-22

BATTING	YR	AVG	AB	R	H	2B	3B	HR	RBI	SB
Stone, Casey, of	Sr.	.376	274	63	103	17	2	2	49	25
Baker, Jeff, 3b	Jr.	.369	233	66	86	13	2	23	75	5
Smith, Jon, c	Jr.	.364	22	6	8	3	0	1	6	0
Boyd, Patrick, of	Jr.	.333	3	2	1	1	0	0	0	0
Johnson, Michael, 1b	So.	.321	218	58	70	13	1	18	54	11
Miller, Seth, c	Jr.	.321	78	14	25	6	0	0	7	1
Greene, Khalil, ss	Jr.	.303	241	55	73	18	2	12	52	17
Schmidt, Jarrod, dh-1b	Jr.	.298	215	43	64	12	0	16	51	4
Riley, Ryan, 2b	Sr.	.291	220	52	64	10	2	6	29	11
Triplett, Russell, 2b-ss	Fr.	.291	79	15	23	6	0	0	7	0
Pyzik, Steve, c	So.	.275	142	14	39	6	0	0	26	1
Coder, Chad, of	So.	.270	222	43	60	12	2	5	30	18
Frank, Kyle, of	So.	.250	204	30	51	15	0	1	31	1
Green, Zane, of	Fr.	.234	107	22	25	5	0	0	19	3
Klosterman, Ryan, 3b	Fr.	.071	14	2	1	1	0	0	2	0

PITCHING	YR	W	L	ERA	G	SV	IP	H	BB	SO
Reba, Steve, rhp	Jr.	12	3	2.58	18	0	108	84	31	103
Henrie, Matt, rhp	So.	6	3	3.06	18	2	68	59	24	54
Glaser, Nick, rhp	Sr.	4	3	3.92	18	1	41	45	10	44
Cram, Josh, rhp	Jr.	4	2	4.20	28	6	41	48	11	38
Boozer, Thomas, lhp	Jr.	2	0	4.30	23	0	29	33	12	16
Schmidt, Jarrod, rhp	So.	7	3	4.34	16	0	75	73	35	59
Harrelson, Paul, lhp	Jr.	1	2	4.38	15	0	25	30	10	18
Lynn, Kevin, rhp	Sr.	2	2	4.75	22	0	55	64	17	47
Hogan, Patrick, rhp	Fr.	0	1	4.78	16	1	32	34	10	31
Jackson, Steven, rhp	Fr.	2	1	5.35	16	0	35	47	14	23
Childs, Ryan, rhp	So.	1	2	6.66	14	0	24	34	12	17
LaMura, B.J., rhp	So.	0	0	7.25	16	0	22	24	16	26

18. WAKE FOREST

Coach: George Greer **Record:** 44-18

BATTING	YR	AVG	AB	R	H	2B	3B	HR	RBI	SB
Sullivan, Cory, of-p	Sr.	.390	264	85	103	20	1	13	67	27
D'Antona, Jamie, 1b	Fr.	.364	253	65	92	14	1	17	77	1
Johnson, Ryan, of	So.	.363	157	33	57	9	3	3	31	2
Athas, Jamie, ss	Jr.	.332	226	58	75	14	2	2	31	22

	YR	AVG	AB	R	H	2B	3B	HR	RBI	SB
Aquilante, Jason, c-2b	Sr.	.332	196	41	65	10	2	2	42	7
Slavik, Corey, 3b	Sr.	.331	251	61	83	16	3	10	50	2
LeFaivre, Steve, dh	Fr.	.321	84	18	27	8	1	5	23	0
Brackley, Carlos, of	Sr.	.315	168	37	53	12	2	14	52	3
Hansen, Josh, of-c	Fr.	.311	122	29	38	8	1	4	30	0
Ghutzman, Stephen, c	So.	.308	117	23	36	7	0	4	30	1
Blue, Nick, 2b	So.	.291	196	47	57	6	0	1	31	18
Price, Matt, of	Sr.	.286	189	45	54	4	4	2	30	13

PITCHING	YR	W	L	ERA	G	SV	IP	H	BB	SO
Elbe, Ben, lhp	So.	0	0	2.63	8	0	14	15	2	8
Bush, Dave, rhp	Jr.	4	3	2.65	41	16	75	57	16	86
Maycroft, Eric, rhp	So.	0	0	3.38	6	0	5	4	5	2
Sullivan, Cory, lhp	Sr.	7	0	3.52	13	0	77	72	36	54
Braun, Ryan, rhp	So.	4	2	4.53	13	0	56	57	23	57
Siemon, Scott, rhp	Sr.	2	1	4.97	8	1	25	23	10	16
Sleeth, Kyle, lhp	Fr.	10	3	5.03	21	0	79	102	31	56
Clayton, Ben, lhp	So.	4	1	5.09	10	0	53	64	24	33
Hanson, Adam, rhp	Fr.	5	3	5.30	26	0	53	69	20	38
Bartlett, Josh, lhp	Sr.	3	2	5.64	23	0	59	67	33	45
Russell, Greg, rhp	Fr.	0	0	6.48	5	0	8	7	4	4
Lewis, Ryan, lhp	Jr.	4	2	6.92	17	0	26	31	13	9
Comer, Brad, rhp	Jr.	1	1	10.90	11	0	17	22	20	12

19. MISSISSIPPI STATE

Coach: Pat McMahon **Record:** 39-23

BATTING	YR	AVG	AB	R	H	2B	3B	HR	RBI	SB
Knott, Jon, of	Sr.	.359	195	36	70	9	3	8	41	4
Parks, Lee, c	Jr.	.333	12	1	4	1	0	0	1	0
Brinson, Matthew, 1b	Fr.	.328	198	37	65	6	1	7	46	1
Jones, Enrico, of	Jr.	.296	54	16	16	3	0	1	7	3
Burkley, Jason, c	Jr.	.286	192	43	55	10	1	3	44	3
Gendron, Steve, 3b	Fr.	.286	224	25	64	3	1	0	28	10
Brown, Michael, 2b	Jr.	.285	207	46	59	7	1	5	28	6
West, Josh, of	Sr.	.282	227	34	64	10	4	5	49	1
Lewis, Brent, dh	Fr.	.279	204	35	57	6	2	2	21	0
Long, Casey, of	Jr.	.246	57	11	14	4	0	3	11	2
Maniscalco, Matt, ss	So.	.232	241	42	56	13	1	0	24	10
Willingham, Phil, of-2b	Jr.	.213	216	32	46	4	1	4	31	11
Hutto, Brad, of	Fr.	.161	31	6	5	0	0	0	1	1
Henry, Chad, 2b-ss	Jr.	.147	34	7	5	1	0	0	3	0
Goodson, Robby, dh	Fr.	.097	31	5	3	1	0	0	1	0

PITCHING	YR	W	L	ERA	G	SV	IP	H	BB	SO
Lacher, Jeff, rhp	Fr.	2	0	1.12	3	0	8	4	2	9
Wooten, Josh, rhp	Sr.	3	5	1.87	23	5	43	32	9	39
Medders, Brandon, rhp	Jr.	6	3	2.13	17	6	51	34	14	56
Hunter, Jeff, rhp	Jr.	3	0	2.43	7	0	30	25	5	27
Young, Chris, rhp	So.	5	1	2.81	26	0	48	42	15	48
Dowe, Steven, lhp	So.	0	0	2.87	12	0	16	11	5	14
Collums, Joey, lhp	So.	3	3	3.71	16	0	53	50	20	47
Maholm, Paul, lhp	Fr.	8	4	4.06	16	0	95	106	30	87
Papelbon, Jonathan, rhp	Fr.	0	0	4.07	14	1	24	24	14	35
Hughes, Collins, rhp	Fr.	0	0	4.32	4	1	8	11	1	6
Brock, Tanner, rhp	Jr.	7	2	4.44	16	0	93	82	46	72
Carroll, Ryan, rhp	Jr.	0	0	4.60	16	0	29	32	14	32
Larson, Adam, rhp	Jr.	2	5	4.83	17	0	50	62	22	49
Nicholas, Todd, lhp	Fr.	0	0	8.31	7	0	9	8	9	9

20. FLORIDA INTERNATIONAL

Coach: Danny Price **Record:** 43-21

BATTING	YR	AVG	AB	R	H	2B	3B	HR	RBI	SB
Eldred, Brad, of-dh	So.	.411	73	22	30	5	0	9	28	1
Nunez, Hector, 1b	Fr.	.370	162	42	60	9	3	11	39	8
Pujols, Raul, 1b-3b	Jr.	.366	82	24	30	8	2	3	17	2
Bustamante, Daniel, dh-1b	Jr.	.340	141	28	48	14	0	4	28	6
Quintana, Mike, of	Jr.	.330	224	58	74	13	2	17	61	13
Huntingford, Matt, of	Jr.	.315	241	49	76	9	1	5	35	21
Paulk, Barry, of	Jr.	.310	255	56	79	12	1	1	28	30
Torello, Mickey, ss	Jr.	.301	216	46	65	22	2	5	43	13
Hines, Brendan, dh	Sr.	.300	90	19	27	6	0	5	17	1
New, Michael, c	Jr.	.293	99	23	29	7	0	3	16	1
Alfonso, Gus, 3b	Jr.	.288	198	41	57	11	1	4	42	10
Duenas, Tommy, c	Fr.	.264	121	23	32	8	0	6	24	2
Sherbinsky, Todd, 3b	So.	.250	64	11	16	3	0	1	6	3
Burgos, Tino, 2b	Jr.	.238	168	29	40	14	2	2	19	4
Gonzalez, Bernard, of	Jr.	.219	32	2	7	1	0	0	3	4

PITCHING	YR	W	L	ERA	G	SV	IP	H	BB	SO
Santos, Arthur, rhp	Fr.	3	1	2.65	23	2	37	32	9	29
Collazo, Willie, lhp	Jr.	13	1	2.93	20	0	141	137	39	148
Crandall, Matthew, rhp	Jr.	5	1	2.95	13	0	40	45	6	40
Banks, Joshua, rhp	Fr.	4	1	3.00	16	1	36	46	10	37
Jimenez, Steven, rhp	Sr.	0	0	3.24	5	0	8	6	5	8
Zervas, Paul, rhp	Jr.	7	4	3.84	20	0	101	93	30	78

	YR	W	L	ERA	G	SV	IP	H	BB	SO
Lugo, Ozzie, rhp	So.	0	1	4.11	15	6	15	11	14	29
Courtney, Jerry, rhp	Jr.	5	7	4.12	18	0	83	79	42	77
Baluja, Michael, rhp	Jr.	3	2	4.31	14	1	48	52	17	33
Mendez, Michael, rhp	Jr.	0	0	4.82	11	1	9	9	13	7
Gazitua, Luis, rhp	Fr.	3	3	5.27	16	1	27	21	23	22
Birch, Greg, lhp	So.	0	0	5.40	8	0	8	7	4	14

21. TEXAS TECH

Coach: Larry Hays
Record: 43-20

BATTING	YR	AVG	AB	R	H	2B	3B	HR	RBI	SB
Cranford, Austin, dh	Jr.	.387	181	46	70	15	2	7	36	1
Blankenship, Nick, 3b	Jr.	.353	272	53	96	20	2	10	61	2
Hodges, Kerry, of	Jr.	.339	251	61	85	11	6	8	46	38
Alvarez, Gera, ss	Jr.	.338	260	62	88	18	3	8	51	19
Arnerich, Tony, c	Jr.	.332	250	60	83	24	3	5	54	9
Rainey, Jason, of	Sr.	.312	208	51	65	13	7	10	55	13
Carson, Tyler, of	Jr.	.309	204	44	63	10	1	3	29	22
Burns, Brennan, 1b	Sr.	.294	17	5	5	0	0	0	3	0
Smith, Byron, 2b	Jr.	.293	225	50	66	8	4	9	52	3
Fossum, Brent, of	Fr.	.286	70	16	20	5	1	2	14	4
Leist, Stephen, of	Jr.	.266	79	16	21	6	1	0	19	5
Landry, Chad, 1b	Jr.	.246	191	37	47	7	1	10	43	0
Deichert, Matt, 2b	Jr.	.233	30	10	7	1	0	1	3	0
Williams, Shaud, 1b	So.	.200	15	2	3	0	0	0	2	1

PITCHING		W	L	ERA	G	SV	IP	H	BB	SO
Leist, Stephen, rhp	Jr.	0	0	1.04	10	0	9	7	3	10
Aragon, Phillip, rhp	Jr.	0	0	2.89	8	0	9	8	5	8
Fossum, Clancy, rhp	Sr.	1	0	3.00	9	0	12	10	3	3
Newman, J.J., rhp	Sr.	0	0	3.86	5	0	9	10	6	6
McGinley, Blake, lhp	Sr.	4	3	3.91	30	8	46	42	15	61
Harbin, Matt, lhp	Jr.	3	1	3.99	21	0	65	78	13	37
Phillips, Chris, rhp	Jr.	11	5	4.13	20	0	137	139	30	89
Roberson, Brandon, rhp	Sr.	13	3	4.18	19	0	116	113	26	105
Metzler, Cory, rhp	Jr.	6	3	4.28	19	1	80	87	12	54
Ertel, Chad, rhp	Jr.	3	4	5.17	18	0	56	63	25	34
Larsen, Mike, rhp	Jr.	0	1	7.27	10	0	9	10	4	1
Rowe, Steve, rhp	Jr.	1	0	8.31	14	1	9	13	3	7

22. ARIZONA STATE

Coach: Pat Murphy
Record: 37-20

BATTING	YR	AVG	AB	R	H	2B	3B	HR	RBI	SB
Myers, Casey, c	Sr.	.395	223	53	88	17	0	7	69	2
Allen, Rod, of	Fr.	.389	180	41	70	14	1	6	53	6
Duffy, Chris, of	Jr.	.373	201	46	75	6	2	4	37	20
Wyrick, Dennis, ss	So.	.360	172	31	62	8	0	0	27	4
Martin, Jonah, of	Sr.	.330	106	36	35	6	1	0	20	10
Lopez, Mike, 3b	Sr.	.310	184	49	57	19	0	3	49	6
Garrabrants, Steve, 2b-ss	Jr.	.307	140	31	43	5	5	0	23	16
West, Jeremy, 1b	Fr.	.307	140	34	43	8	4	6	34	2
Phelps, Jeff, 1b-dh	Sr.	.307	189	26	58	20	1	2	31	4
McKenna, Ryan, of	Fr.	.286	49	13	14	1	0	0	8	2
Conrad, Brooks, 2b	Jr.	.278	216	49	60	15	3	4	41	16
Walsh, Nick, dh	Fr.	.264	91	26	24	3	0	1	15	2
Sheaffer, Jon, of	Jr.	.261	23	8	6	0	0	0	3	3
Stocker, Mel, of	Jr.	.245	106	32	26	3	1	0	15	18
Keefner, Eric, inf	Fr.	.235	17	1	4	2	0	0	2	0

PITCHING		W	L	ERA	G	SV	IP	H	BB	SO
Friedberg, Drew, lhp	Sr.	4	2	2.03	24	1	53	40	13	55
Klusman, Aaron, rhp	Fr.	1	0	3.31	25	2	35	29	19	49
Switzer, Jon, lhp	Jr.	5	6	4.04	19	0	100	95	45	128
Esposito, Mike, rhp	Fr.	5	2	4.06	16	0	69	66	24	63
Torres, Andy, rhp	Jr.	13	4	4.30	27	1	92	104	29	74
Liebeck, Jared, lhp	So.	1	1	4.40	7	0	14	20	4	10
Doble, Eric, rhp	Sr.	3	2	5.59	17	1	37	47	14	40
Kartler, Bryce, lhp	So.	0	0	5.77	22	4	39	47	21	41
Ramirez, Angel, rhp	Jr.	0	0	6.00	5	0	6	6	4	5
Johnson, Ty, rhp	Sr.	0	0	6.00	9	0	12	13	9	12
Schroyer, Ryan, rhp	Fr.	2	2	7.31	13	0	28	28	22	29
Pezely, Franco, lhp	Jr.	3	1	8.27	18	0	21	30	9	22
Jackson, J.J., rhp	Fr.	0	0	8.68	9	0	9	10	9	13

23. SOUTH ALABAMA

Coach: Steve Kittrell
Record: 45-19

BATTING	YR	AVG	AB	R	H	2B	3B	HR	RBI	SB
Gretz, Nick, 1b-dh	Sr.	.375	208	40	78	13	0	10	53	2
Calahan, Scott, 2b	Sr.	.369	225	53	83	18	3	7	43	9
Davis, Brandon, c	Sr.	.360	25	3	9	2	2	0	7	1
Mulhern, Ryan, of	So.	.349	212	49	74	14	3	12	49	5
Hanna, Warren, c	So.	.333	180	32	60	9	0	3	29	4
Glasscock, Jason, 3b	So.	.333	12	2	4	2	0	0	3	0
Likely, Cameron, of	Sr.	.321	218	59	70	7	4	3	28	23
Stanky, Kyle, dh	Jr.	.310	100	14	31	8	0	2	25	0
Tsimpides, Boo, of	Sr.	.286	14	1	4	0	0	0	2	0
Merritt, Tim, ss	Sr.	.282	252	54	71	14	5	12	65	16
Touchstone, Josh, 3b	Fr.	.276	98	23	27	5	2	0	10	2
Smallwood, Erik, of	Jr.	.270	230	63	62	14	2	7	43	17
Piccotti, Tony, 1b	Sr.	.261	111	11	29	9	0	2	29	0
Remos, Craig, of	Sr.	.261	23	5	6	3	0	0	2	0
Nelson, Ben, 1b	So.	.229	35	4	8	2	0	1	9	0
Parker, Brett, 3b	So.	.228	123	31	28	9	0	1	9	3
Griffin, Brantley, of	Sr.	.188	48	21	9	2	0	0	3	5
Scoville, Shane, c	Jr.	.182	55	9	10	3	0	0	9	4

PITCHING	YR	W	L	ERA	G	SV	IP	H	BB	SO
Crosby, Caleb, rhp	Jr.	3	0	1.40	6	0	19	11	8	17
Glasscock, Jason, rhp	So.	1	0	1.80	13	2	25	25	7	30
Parnell, Adam, lhp	Jr.	0	1	2.13	9	0	13	9	11	15
Long, Joe, rhp	Sr.	3	2	2.45	24	5	55	49	27	46
Almond, Casey, rhp	Sr.	3	3	3.33	15	0	51	44	35	46
Spivey, Mel, rhp	Jr.	5	1	3.48	21	3	54	44	25	52
Smith, Sam, rhp	Jr.	5	1	3.56	17	0	48	58	18	31
Girardeau, Clark, rhp	Fr.	10	4	3.87	22	2	98	83	36	70
Neal, Tony, rhp	Jr.	9	3	3.89	19	0	106	99	39	86
Sulivant, Jason, rhp	So.	1	0	4.97	6	0	13	17	4	9
Heath, Bert, rhp	Fr.	2	3	5.06	12	0	27	29	15	31
Davis, Tim, lhp	Sr.	3	1	6.11	11	0	35	36	22	28

24. WINTHROP

Coach: Joe Hudak
Record: 48-16

BATTING	YR	AVG	AB	R	H	2B	3B	HR	RBI	SB
Leathers, Todd, of-3b	Jr.	.360	267	69	96	28	3	12	64	1
Swerdzewski, Stas, c	Jr.	.323	229	29	74	17	0	12	60	0
Colson, Jason, 3b-p	Sr.	.321	246	59	79	13	1	12	63	8
Friedman, Todd, of-dh	Jr.	.320	153	27	49	13	1	0	29	4
Ury, Josh, of	Sr.	.307	257	48	79	21	0	2	36	6
Gore, Jon, 2b	Fr.	.304	204	33	62	12	2	1	23	7
De la Rionda, Carlos, of	Sr.	.291	158	29	46	7	1	1	12	8
Webb, Jordan, ss	Sr.	.285	242	59	69	16	3	1	25	9
Stapf, Bennett, 1b	Fr.	.280	225	49	63	17	1	9	50	6
Thurmond, Ben, 2b-p	So.	.250	108	15	27	5	0	4	20	5
Funk, Conrad, of	So.	.211	90	12	19	3	0	3	13	0
Snyder, Brian, of	Fr.	.200	5	16	1	0	0	0	0	0
Neale, John, c	Jr.	.156	32	2	5	2	0	0	6	0
Matkovich, Matt, dh	Fr.	.111	36	2	4	2	1	0	4	0

PITCHING	YR	W	L	ERA	G	SV	IP	H	BB	SO
Terry, Jason, lhp	Fr.	1	0	2.00	7	0	9	11	1	4
Cheek, Geoff, lhp	Jr.	0	0	2.35	8	0	8	6	3	2
Reeves, Jeff, rhp	So.	1	2	2.41	17	2	41	31	22	48
Pawlish, Keith, rhp	Sr.	4	2	2.73	15	2	59	49	28	63
Thurmond, Ben, rhp	So.	14	3	2.88	20	1	150	132	42	148
Horner, Jason, lhp	Jr.	2	0	3.25	26	5	28	36	8	16
Herauf, Jeremy, rhp	Sr.	12	2	3.66	19	1	130	121	27	120
Tomsich, Christian, lhp	Sr.	3	2	3.80	19	2	45	47	9	35
Colson, Jason, rhp	Sr.	8	4	3.86	13	0	82	75	35	86
Chenard, Ryan, rhp	So.	3	1	4.15	24	3	26	35	14	29

25. RUTGERS

Coach: Fred Hill
Record: 42-17

BATTING	YR	AVG	AB	R	H	2B	3B	HR	RBI	SB
McCarthy, Billy, of	Jr.	.421	216	51	91	21	2	7	65	11
Majewski, Val, 1b-of	So.	.378	225	63	85	24	3	8	54	9
Wolski, Matt, 2b	Jr.	.346	214	53	74	12	1	3	36	4
Popowski, Mike, c	Jr.	.335	182	27	61	7	0	7	47	1
Marciniak, Jeff, ss-2b	Sr.	.313	67	8	21	5	0	0	17	0
Ciemniecki, Brian, of	Sr.	.300	230	50	69	8	3	1	23	9
Lillis, Ryan, 3b	Jr.	.282	202	20	57	9	1	0	24	1
Speedy, Todd, dh-of	Jr.	.265	151	12	40	6	0	2	16	1
Normane, Steve, 1b	Jr.	.262	65	11	17	3	0	3	10	0
Sweeney, Tim, ss	Jr.	.241	191	31	46	9	2	2	34	2
Badger, Graig, 2b	Fr.	.231	13	11	3	0	0	0	0	4
Shade, Leon, of	Jr.	.213	94	16	20	3	0	0	5	3
Vasquez, Alberto, c	So.	.173	75	10	13	3	0	0	4	2
Delehanty, Brian, dh	Jr.	.154	26	4	4	2	0	0	3	0
Rosario, Jamell, of	Fr.	.143	21	3	3	1	0	0	4	0

PITCHING		W	L	ERA	G	SV	IP	H	BB	SO
Atchison, Sean, lhp	So.	2	0	1.17	7	0	15	12	5	15
Brownlie, Bobby, rhp	So.	6	3	2.36	14	0	84	65	17	86
Brown, Eric, rhp	Sr.	2	1	2.83	23	8	29	22	6	31
Santiago, David, rhp	So.	5	0	3.15	13	0	40	42	19	38
Crohan, Tom, lhp	Jr.	6	2	3.38	17	0	75	69	27	43
Wheeler, Tom, rhp	Jr.	6	4	4.04	15	2	78	84	35	46
Molchan, Ryan, lhp	Jr.	3	2	4.06	24	0	38	37	13	22
Gallagher, Buddy, lhp	Jr.	6	4	4.20	15	0	79	84	17	69
Wilson, Jimmy, rhp	Sr.	4	2	5.40	14	0	37	28	28	24
Bergmann, Jason, rhp	So.	2	1	6.91	10	0	27	30	21	20
Winters, Brian, rhp	So.	0	0	15.00	6	0	6	12	4	4

CONFERENCE STANDINGS & LEADERS

AMERICA EAST CONFERENCE

	Conference		Overall	
	W	L	W	L
*Delaware	22	6	45	15
Maine	20	8	36	15
Towson	17	11	37	23
Northeastern	11	17	19	32
Drexel	11	17	15	38
Vermont	10	17	23	22
Hofstra	10	17	17	32
Hartford	10	18	14	35

ALL-CONFERENCE TEAM: C—Joe Drapeau, So., Maine. **1B**—Jon Hambelton, Sr., Maine. **2B**—Andrew Salvo, Sr., Delaware. **3B**—Peter Maestrales, Sr., Delaware. **SS**—Kris Dufner, So., Delaware. **OF**—Ben Beck, Jr., Northeastern; Gregg Davies, Jr., Towson; Chris Kolodzey, Sr., Delaware. **DH**—Jimmy Kittelberger, Sr., Towson. **P**—Bryan Simmering, Jr., Towson; Rusty Tucker, Jr., Maine.

Player of the Year: Gregg Davies, Towson. **Pitcher of the Year:** Rusty Tucker, Maine. **Rookie of the Year:** Mike Collar, Maine. **Coach of the Year:** Paul Kostacopoulos, Maine.

INDIVIDUAL BATTING LEADERS
(Minimum 125 At-Bats)

	AVG	AB	R	H	2B	3B	HR	RBI	SB
Hambelton, Jon, Maine	.429	161	41	69	20	1	13	50	4
Davies, Gregg, Towson	.399	218	57	87	21	2	15	74	8
Salvo, Andrew, Delaware	.372	242	55	90	15	1	7	45	14
Kittelberger, Jimmy, Towson	.364	198	63	72	22	2	8	40	5
Kolodzey, Chris, Delaware	.361	233	76	84	18	2	12	62	14
Vukovich, Vince, Delaware	.358	176	28	63	3	4	3	48	11
Cole, Mike, Vermont	.340	156	24	53	18	1	4	40	6
Gorecki, Reid, Delaware	.340	191	39	65	6	1	3	27	22
Barry, Jeff, Vermont	.336	146	39	49	12	3	0	19	22
Drapeau, Joe, Maine	.333	186	47	62	13	1	12	51	1
Costello, Mike, Towson	.333	135	30	45	7	1	8	41	0
Picard, Alain, Maine	.333	129	31	43	14	1	8	39	2
Marcozzi, Joey, Towson	.331	127	28	42	7	1	1	24	4
Bacon, Scott, Towson	.329	213	38	70	12	1	6	45	1
Dufner, Kris, Delaware	.328	189	36	62	14	4	3	34	1
Livulpi, Mike, Maine	.328	174	39	57	16	2	1	20	12
Sniecinski, Ben, Drexel	.328	180	25	59	9	4	0	33	5
Avila, Ryan, Towson	.317	218	62	69	20	1	5	42	5
Creaney, Eric, Hofstra	.317	145	32	46	6	1	0	10	16
Maestrales, Peter, Delaware	.315	213	75	67	19	5	10	52	15
Carlin, Luke, Northeastern	.315	165	42	52	7	1	6	38	13
Stidham, Casey, Towson	.315	178	37	56	14	2	10	38	0

INDIVIDUAL PITCHING LEADERS
(Minimum 45 Innings)

	W	L	ERA	G	SV	IP	H	BB	SO
#Walter, Jason, Towson	2	3	2.10	20	7	34	30	9	26
Robinson, Brian, Vermont	4	4	3.23	11	0	61	49	34	62
Tucker, Rusty, Maine	7	2	3.26	11	0	66	59	18	70
Simmering, Bryan, Towson	8	3	3.35	13	0	78	66	18	89
Sage, Vic, Delaware	11	3	3.49	19	0	101	87	30	64
Dixon, Jeff, Vermont	5	3	3.54	10	0	61	55	14	56
Collar, Mike, Maine	8	0	3.55	10	0	63	66	15	45
Brady, Matt, Towson	6	4	3.77	14	0	72	52	33	59
MacDonald, Mike, Maine	5	2	3.78	10	0	52	48	14	40
Nein, Matt, Towson	5	2	3.81	13	0	57	54	26	26
Horgan, Mark, Drexel	5	3	3.84	29	3	59	49	26	41
McGuire, Rich, Delaware	10	3	4.05	18	1	102	103	33	69
Marcotte, Trevor, Vermont	3	4	4.17	9	0	45	43	15	25
Summerlin, Jason, Towson	4	2	4.18	14	3	47	52	6	21
Mihalik, Mike, Delaware	5	3	4.76	17	1	70	79	42	46
Roy, Scott, Hartford	5	2	4.82	11	0	52	57	16	32
Mascaro, Brian, Hartford	3	6	4.99	14	2	49	60	19	36
Stoner, Simon, Maine	6	2	5.00	11	0	63	70	32	57

Jeff Baker: .369-23-75 for Clemson

BILL SETLIFF

ATLANTIC COAST CONFERENCE

	Conference		Overall	
	W	L	W	L
Florida State	20	4	47	19
Clemson	17	7	41	22
*Wake Forest	16	8	44	18
Georgia Tech	13	11	41	20
Duke	10	13	23	33
North Carolina	9	15	31	26
Virginia	9	15	25	31
North Carolina State	9	15	32	29
Maryland	4	19	17	37

ALL-CONFERENCE TEAM: C—Bryan Prince, Sr., Georgia Tech. **1B**—Ryan Barthelemy, Jr., Florida State. **2B**—Russ Adams, So., North Carolina. **3B**—Jeff Baker, So., Clemson. **SS**—Khalil Greene, Jr., Clemson. **OF**—John-Ford Griffin, Jr., Florida State; Cory Sullivan, Sr., Wake Forest; Brian Wright, Jr., North Carolina State. **Util**—Dan Street, So., Virginia. **DH**—Jarrod Schmidt, So., Clemson. **P**—Steve Reba, Jr., Clemson; Brandon Creswell, Sr., Virginia; Blair Varnes, Jr., Florida State. **RP**—Dave Bush, Jr., Wake Forest.

Player of the Year: John-Ford Griffin, Florida State. **Rookie of the Year:** Jamie D'Antona, Wake Forest. **Coach of the Year:** Mike Martin, Florida State.

INDIVIDUAL BATTING LEADERS
(Minimum 125 At-Bats)

	AVG	AB	R	H	2B	3B	HR	RBI	SB
Griffin, John-Ford, Fla. State	.450	251	79	113	30	0	19	75	11
Sullivan, Cory, Wake Forest	.390	264	85	103	20	1	13	67	27
Murton, Matt, Georgia Tech	.385	161	43	62	14	1	7	35	3
Menocal, Victor, Ga. Tech	.381	268	71	102	18	1	4	51	7
Lewis, Richard, Ga. Tech	.376	266	77	100	13	6	11	64	11
Stone, Casey, Clemson	.376	274	63	103	17	2	2	49	25
Mason, David, Duke	.370	208	36	77	9	2	2	39	6
Baker, Jeff, Clemson	.369	233	66	86	13	2	23	75	5
D'Antona, Jamie, Wake Forest	.364	253	65	92	14	1	17	77	1
Wyant, Hunter, Virginia	.363	237	48	86	16	7	8	50	8
Johnson, Ryan, Wake Forest	.363	157	33	57	9	2	3	31	2
Prosser, Chad, No. Carolina	.357	213	47	76	12	1	2	40	9
Rogers, Nick, Florida State	.351	185	45	65	17	1	6	38	20
Howell, Jason, No. Carolina	.350	160	29	56	13	2	1	29	4
Prince, Bryan, Georgia Tech	.349	238	54	83	16	0	6	63	1
Oursler, Steve, Maryland	.348	210	35	73	20	1	7	48	4
Wright, Brian, NC State	.347	248	58	86	21	2	10	62	10
Stockton, Brad, Ga. State	.346	162	42	56	10	5	7	44	1
Futrell, Mike, Florida State	.345	223	45	77	13	2	8	56	6
Boggs, Matthew, Ga. Tech	.345	206	56	71	10	1	0	35	7
Patenaude, Brian, Maryland	.345	194	42	67	16	0	2	29	6

COLLEGE BASEBALL

	AVG	AB	R	H	2B	3B	HR	RBI	SB
Barthelemy, Ryan, Fla. State	.343	280	55	96	22	5	14	72	3
Street, Dan, Virginia	.343	166	33	57	9	1	9	43	5
Stone, David, Virginia	.340	212	40	72	12	0	0	26	21
Perry, Jason, Georgia Tech	.337	187	59	63	9	1	14	57	7
Jerdan, Drew, Duke	.333	168	30	56	10	1	3	26	8
Basil, Jason, Georgia Tech	.333	234	64	78	12	0	14	64	8
Athas, Jamie, Wake Forest	.332	226	58	75	14	2	2	31	22
Alleva, J.D., Duke	.332	223	42	74	13	0	5	36	7
Aquilante, Jason, Wake Forest	.332	196	41	65	10	2	2	42	7
Slavik, Corey, Wake Forest	.331	251	61	83	16	3	10	50	2
Adams, Russ, No. Carolina	.331	239	52	79	13	2	1	41	28
Dutton, Jeremy, NC State	.328	247	52	81	20	6	3	36	12
Walsh, Sean, NC State	.328	229	40	75	14	2	5	39	19
Swope, Matt, Maryland	.328	204	44	67	10	0	7	34	10
Farrell, Sean, No. Carolina	.327	202	38	66	17	3	3	36	3
Caradonna, Troy, Duke	.322	202	30	65	8	0	1	30	0
Johnson, Michael, Clemson	.321	218	58	70	13	1	18	54	11
Brackley, Carlos, Wake Forest	.315	168	37	53	12	2	14	52	3
Shearin, Jamey, NC State	.315	219	33	69	18	1	6	41	0
Greenberg, Adam, No. Car.	.310	210	52	65	13	3	2	30	**29**

	AVG	AB	R	H	2B	3B	HR	RBI	SB
Myler, Jon, St. Bonaventure	.368	144	35	53	13	1	11	52	3
Brenning, Ty, Xavier	.368	204	49	75	20	0	3	37	2
Cisco, James, Fordham	.367	166	28	61	5	0	0	27	7
Kingsbury, Robert, Fordham	.363	190	44	69	15	**6**	8	47	**36**
Krimmel, Matt, Geo. Washington	.361	216	**58**	78	7	1	5	49	11
Bolinger, Shawn, Dayton	.359	231	53	**83**	18	4	8	45	2
Fuchs, Mike, LaSalle	.359	156	35	56	11	0	7	38	5
Vogel, Brooks, Dayton	.358	204	53	73	**23**	5	6	53	5
Sweppenhiser, Kyle, Temple	.358	187	42	67	13	0	7	47	9
Wald, Jake, Geo. Washington	.351	174	43	61	7	1	5	37	13
Reilly, Jim, St. Joseph's	.348	158	28	55	13	0	2	28	1
Kulak, Mike, Massachusetts	.347	147	32	51	8	4	4	36	12
Dokoupil, Tony, Geo. Wash.	.347	225	55	78	12	0	8	40	17
Lee, Gary, Duquesne	.344	125	15	43	8	1	0	30	3
Brown, Tony, Geo. Washington	.343	178	28	61	6	0	2	32	5
Altieri, Jeff, Massachusetts	.339	168	41	57	13	1	8	42	1
Andres, Mark, Xavier	.338	198	37	67	8	1	6	**55**	3
Bradshaw, Pace, St. Joseph's	.338	148	24	50	7	1	0	27	7
Rapacioli, Mike, St. Bonaventure	.336	137	36	46	13	0	**14**	42	4
Wilson, Eric, St. Bonaventure	.336	149	34	50	11	1	2	18	3
Jackson, Matt, Rhode Island	.336	134	19	45	7	1	4	29	15

INDIVIDUAL PITCHING LEADERS
(Minimum 50 Innings)

	W	L	ERA	G	SV	IP	H	BB	SO
Reba, Steve, Clemson	**12**	3	**2.58**	18	0	108	84	31	**103**
Bush, Dave, Wake Forest	4	3	1.66	41	**16**	75	57	16	86
Street, Dan, Virginia	4	4	2.76	10	0	75	62	24	36
Hodges, Daniel, Fla. State	4	3	3.05	27	4	59	65	15	55
Henrie, Matt, Clemson	6	3	3.06	18	2	68	59	24	54
Peterson, Trent, Fla. State	5	1	3.16	16	0	57	50	20	45
Creswell, Brandon, Virginia	7	4	3.42	14	0	100	113	33	75
Sullivan, Cory, Wake Forest	7	0	3.52	13	0	77	72	36	54
Lynch, Matt, Florida State	9	2	3.61	18	0	97	111	37	85
Varnes, Blair, Florida State	9	1	3.61	18	0	115	113	27	93
Roberts, Ralph, No. Carolina	3	1	4.03	12	0	51	47	22	31
Read, Robby, Florida State	7	5	4.08	20	0	86	86	38	87
Schmidt, Jarrod, Clemson	7	3	4.34	16	0	75	73	35	59
Blanton, Jason, NC State	5	1	4.40	19	0	76	89	31	61
Mattison, Corey, NC State	2	3	4.47	16	2	52	46	20	54
Braun, Ryan, Wake Forest	4	2	4.53	13	0	56	57	23	57
Kelly, Steve, Georgia Tech	7	5	4.56	16	0	113	117	37	93
Thompson, Kevin, Duke	7	3	4.56	14	0	81	91	19	48
LaMacchia, Marc, Fla. State	5	2	4.72	16	0	53	58	25	47
Lynn, Kevin, Clemson	2	2	4.75	22	0	55	64	17	47
Autrey, Scott, No. Carolina	3	3	4.76	14	0	68	76	25	42
Cameron, Kevin, Ga. Tech	6	2	4.84	16	2	67	76	31	55
Parrott, Rhett, Georgia Tech	9	5	4.89	16	0	105	106	43	84
McKee, Derek, NC State	3	4	4.92	16	0	71	80	22	56

INDIVIDUAL PITCHING LEADERS
(Minimum 50 Innings)

	W	L	ERA	G	SV	IP	H	BB	SO
Johnson, Kyle, St. Bonaventure	7	2	**1.88**	13	1	72	60	18	57
#Beggs, Bryan, Geo. Washington	2	2	2.86	28	**10**	35	37	17	30
Paolillo, Andrew, Fordham	6	4	3.41	24	2	58	62	17	37
Skutnik, Glen, Geo. Washington	4	4	3.66	14	0	64	66	26	47
Conden, Greg, Geo. Washington	8	6	3.72	15	0	77	92	31	36
Baker, Jason, Geo. Washington	7	5	3.81	14	0	90	78	18	70
Pearce, Dan, Rhode Island	6	4	3.82	12	0	73	66	31	55
Seales, Shaun, Fordham	0	2	3.88	16	0	56	56	20	17
Barger, Jeff, Xavier	7	6	3.93	19	0	110	117	24	71
Kerins, Mike, Dayton	7	5	3.98	14	0	93	106	13	57
Bruno, Brandon, Temple	5	3	4.20	21	1	60	72	22	41
Powell, Greg, Temple	7	8	4.37	22	2	105	113	32	**74**
O'Connor, Mike, Geo. Washington	1	1	4.45	26	1	57	53	33	53
Popp, Jim, Duquesne	3	4	4.55	12	0	61	62	25	37
Allen, Cory, Dayton	3	3	4.71	11	0	50	55	20	29
Christie, Ron, Geo. Washington	7	1	4.73	11	0	59	73	21	34
Rolih, Mike, Dayton	**9**	6	4.79	18	0	94	121	27	49
Santos, Jesse, Massachusetts	7	5	4.90	14	1	72	85	29	54
Niemczura, Kevin, St. Bona.	4	5	5.01	10	0	50	63	22	33

ATLANTIC-10 CONFERENCE

	Conference		Overall	
	W	L	W	L
Massachusetts	16	6	27	19
Dayton	15	7	32	26
*Temple	15	7	27	31
George Washington	13	9	38	23
St. Bonaventure	12	10	26	19
Rhode Island	10	12	27	23
St. Joseph's	10	12	23	27
Fordham	10	12	23	28
Xavier	8	14	21	34
La Salle	6	16	11	33
Duquesne	6	16	21	30

ALL-CONFERENCE TEAM: C—Jon Myler, Sr., St. Bonaventure. **1B**—Mark Andres, So., Xavier. **2B**—Kevin Kirkby, Sr., St. Joseph's. **3B**—Kyle Sweppenhiser, Sr., Temple. **SS**—Mike LaBarbera, Sr., Rhode Island. **OF**—Mike Bassett, Jr., George Washington; Gavin Clark, Sr., Massachusetts; Robert Kingsbury, So., Fordham. **DH**—Nick Gorneault, Sr., Massachusetts. **P**—Kyle Johnson, So., St. Bonaventure; Greg Powell, Sr., Temple. **RP**—Bryan Beggs, Sr., George Washington.

Player of the Year: Robert Kingsbury, Fordham. **Pitcher of the Year:** Kyle Johnson, St. Bonaventure. **Rookie of the Year:** Dan Batz, Rhode Island. **Coach of the Year:** Skip Wilson, Temple.

INDIVIDUAL BATTING LEADERS
(Minimum 125 At-Bats)

	AVG	AB	R	H	2B	3B	HR	RBI	SB
LaBarbera, Mike, Rh. Island	.404	198	41	80	8	**6**	2	44	35
Crandell, Jeff, Xavier	.400	200	51	80	18	1	5	41	3
Kirkby, Kevin, St. Joseph's	.392	171	38	67	10	0	2	41	6
Batz, Dan, Rhode Island	.375	152	39	57	9	1	2	23	7
Crowder, Travis, Geo. Wash.	.372	156	44	58	5	0	0	18	16
Gorneault, Nick, Mass.	.369	168	45	62	11	2	12	41	9

BIG EAST CONFERENCE

	Conference		Overall	
	W	L	W	L
Notre Dame	22	4	49	13
Rutgers	18	8	42	17
*Seton Hall	14	11	34	23
Virginia Tech	14	11	29	28
St. John's	13	13	31	22
Connecticut	13	13	26	25
West Virginia	12	14	27	26
Boston College	11	13	29	22
Villanova	10	16	25	25
Georgetown	7	19	17	39
Pittsburgh	6	18	18	27

ALL-CONFERENCE TEAM: C—Jeff Mackor, Jr., Boston College. **1B**—Val Majewski, So., Rutgers. **2B**—Steve Sollmann, Fr., Notre Dame. **3B**—Andy Bushey, Jr., Notre Dame. **SS**—Alec Porzel, Sr., Notre Dame. **OF**—Mike Scott, Jr., Connecticut; Steve Stanley, Jr., Notre Dame; Billy McCarthy, Jr., Rutgers. **DH**—Nick Piantek, Sr., Villanova. **Util**—Shawn Tarkington, Sr., Seton Hall. **P**—Bobby Brownlie, So., Rutgers; Aaron Heilman, Sr., Notre Dame; Danny Tamayo, Sr., Notre Dame.

Players of the Year: Mike Scott, Connecticut; Steve Stanley, Notre Dame. **Pitcher of the Year:** Aaron Heilman, Notre Dame. **Rookie of the Year:** Steve Sollmann, Notre Dame. **Coach of the Year:** Paul Mainieri, Notre Dame.

INDIVIDUAL BATTING LEADERS
(Minimum 125 At-Bats)

	AVG	AB	R	H	2B	3B	HR	RBI	SB
McCarthy, Billy, Rutgers	**.421**	216	51	91	21	2	7	65	11
Scott, Mike, UConn	.413	206	48	85	16	4	3	34	8
Stanley, Steve, Notre Dame	.400	255	**76**	**102**	14	**5**	1	32	31
Gorrie, Jon, UConn	.390	154	32	60	15	1	2	31	16
Stavisky, Brian, Notre Dame	.386	210	46	81	19	4	10	**66**	9
Majewski, Val, Rutgers	.378	225	63	85	24	3	8	54	9
Macchi, Brian, Boston Coll.	.376	189	44	71	12	0	**17**	56	3
Durkin, Brian, Boston Coll.	.373	169	37	63	9	2	8	28	4
Cuervo, Joe, Seton Hall	.370	216	51	80	20	4	6	39	23
Pizzini, Dave, Villanova	.369	179	35	66	10	1	2	25	8

	AVG	AB	R	H	2B	3B	HR	RBI	SB
Soteropoulos, Peter, UConn	.364	165	40	60	12	3	3	39	11
Sollmann, Steve, Notre Dame	.362	221	52	80	9	2	5	36	23
Grimm, Casey, Seton Hall	.360	222	42	80	11	3	5	46	6
Grimm, Eric, West Virginia	.358	179	29	64	12	1	2	30	7
West, John, Virginia Tech	.357	210	38	75	12	4	7	42	9
Graziano, Chris, Villanova	.357	157	40	56	6	0	0	17	37
Bilezikjian, Charles, St. John's	.352	196	50	69	16	3	2	36	26
Lenhart, Darrin, Pittsburgh	.350	160	30	56	14	1	2	26	4
Wolski, Matt, Rutgers	.346	214	53	74	12	1	3	36	4
Piantek, Nick, Villanova	.342	187	35	64	16	2	7	47	3
Carlini, Marc, Georgetown	.342	149	30	51	8	1	0	21	8
Kane, Jason, St. John's	.339	183	26	62	11	1	4	46	6
McCabe, Tim, West Virginia	.337	181	33	61	11	0	10	38	1
Colamarino, Brant, Pittsburgh	.337	169	31	57	18	0	7	33	2
Bowman, Addison, Va. Tech	.336	220	41	74	16	0	7	48	4
Bushey, Andrew, Notre Dame	.335	212	34	71	17	3	0	36	1
Popowski, Mike, Rutgers	.335	182	27	61	7	0	7	47	1
Cisneros, Josh, West Virginia	.324	142	20	46	8	0	0	14	2
O'Toole, Paul, Notre Dame	.323	201	40	65	12	2	4	35	15
Hutchison, Chris, Va. Tech	.320	203	47	65	14	3	4	25	7
#Porzel, Alec, Notre Dame	.295	251	53	74	28	2	8	59	6

INDIVIDUAL PITCHING LEADERS
(Minimum 50 Innings)

	W	L	ERA	G	SV	IP	H	BB	SO
Heilman, Aaron, Notre Dame	15	0	1.74	15	0	114	70	31	111
Ogilvie, Peter, Notre Dame	5	1	1.90	8	0	52	44	11	30
Engel, Joe, Pittsburgh	5	5	1.92	10	0	70	55	27	69
Brownlie, Bobby, Rutgers	6	3	2.36	14	0	84	65	17	86
Tamayo, Danny, Notre Dame	8	3	2.72	15	0	113	96	17	106
#Brown, Eric, Rutgers	2	1	2.83	23	8	29	22	6	31
McCracken, Vance, West Va.	3	5	2.91	11	0	65	60	17	52
Rhodes, Shane, West Virginia	7	2	2.92	14	0	86	83	34	89
Goldberg, Marc, St. John's	5	6	3.11	13	0	81	79	40	70
Reilly, Chris, Seton Hall	7	1	3.21	12	1	62	58	22	49
Orsogna, Geno, St. John's	5	2	3.32	12	1	76	62	32	42
Crohan, Tom, Rutgers	6	2	3.38	17	0	75	69	27	43
Pavlik, Isaac, Seton Hall	3	2	3.40	31	8	56	55	23	62
Saunders, Joe, Virginia Tech	9	3	3.48	17	0	116	121	40	87
Sullivan, Mark, Boston College	6	4	3.51	25	5	51	57	18	41
Reid, Joe, St. John's	3	2	3.69	11	0	54	51	38	47
Runyon, Chip, Virginia Tech	3	5	3.73	20	4	72	96	20	55
DeBrisco, Chris, UConn	3	4	3.87	16	2	77	76	17	37
Wheeler, Tom, Rutgers	6	2	4.04	15	2	78	84	35	46
Benik, B.J., Seton Hall	5	7	4.09	15	0	81	95	20	58
Sperone, Pat, UConn	6	5	4.16	12	0	76	78	24	36
Ostlund, Ian, Virginia Tech	8	5	4.17	19	0	101	126	15	60
Farino, Dan, Villanova	2	4	4.17	15	0	50	52	23	31
Gallagher, Buddy, Rutgers	6	4	4.20	15	0	79	84	17	69

BIG SOUTH CONFERENCE

	Conference		Overall	
	W	L	W	L
Winthrop	18	3	48	16
*Coastal Carolina	16	4	42	20
Liberty	14	7	35	21
Elon	12	9	30	27
UNC Asheville	8	12	15	39
High Point	5	14	21	33
Radford	5	16	12	38
Charleston Southern	3	16	12	37

ALL-CONFERENCE TEAM: C—Stas Swerdzewski, Jr., Winthrop. **1B**—Justin Owens, Jr., Coastal Carolina. **2B**—Michael Lowman, Jr., High Point. **3B**—Jason Colson, Sr., Winthrop. **SS**—Brian Ingram, So., Elon. **OF**—Chad Felty, Jr., Coastal Carolina; Trey Miller, Sr., Liberty; Todd Leathers, Jr., Winthrop. **DH**—Chris Carter, Sr., Coastal Carolina. **P**—Scott Sturkie, Sr., Coastal Carolina; Ben Thurmond, So., Winthrop; Jeremy Herauf, Sr., Winthrop.

Most Valuable Player: Jason Colson, Winthrop. **Rookie of the Year:** Jon Gore, Winthrop. **Coach of the Year:** Joe Hudak, Winthrop.

INDIVIDUAL BATTING LEADERS
(Minimum 125 At-Bats)

	AVG	AB	R	H	2B	3B	HR	RBI	SB
Carter, Chris, Co. Carolina	.417	180	50	75	22	1	8	45	11
Felty, Chad, Co. Carolina	.376	202	62	76	19	3	13	62	14
Tuttle, Jason, Elon	.374	222	54	83	5	3	0	25	38
Miller, Trey, Liberty	.373	185	48	69	19	1	8	54	12
Owens, Justin, Co. Carolina	.365	200	49	73	19	3	4	30	28
Ingram, Brian, Elon	.365	222	44	81	15	5	4	37	16
Kopczynski, Shaun, Elon	.363	212	46	77	20	1	6	43	11
York, Larry Wayne, Liberty	.363	135	26	49	8	2	1	32	13
Leathers, Todd, Winthrop	.360	267	69	96	28	3	12	64	1
Moncus, Curtis, UNCA	.343	207	34	71	14	0	10	44	3
Humay, Jon, Co. Carolina	.337	184	44	62	9	2	2	35	12

	AVG	AB	R	H	2B	3B	HR	RBI	SB
Bryant, Whit, Elon	.336	211	38	71	11	1	8	54	4
McGarvey, Randy, Co. Carolina	.335	161	24	54	12	0	5	35	5
Butler, Keith, Liberty	.328	189	51	62	14	3	3	33	14
Keim, Adam, Coastal Carolina	.326	233	50	76	19	3	11	57	13
Knouse, Kelly, Liberty	.324	145	40	47	13	0	7	42	7
Swerdzewski, Stas, Winthrop	.323	229	29	74	17	0	12	60	0
Colson, Jason, Winthrop	.321	246	59	79	13	1	12	63	8
Swenson, Jim, Elon	.321	137	20	44	6	1	5	24	3
Friedman, Todd, Winthrop	.320	153	27	49	13	1	0	29	4
Brunst, Keith, Radford	.317	180	30	57	11	0	9	39	1

INDIVIDUAL PITCHING LEADERS
(Minimum 50 Innings)

	W	L	ERA	G	SV	IP	H	BB	SO
#Brey, Josh, Liberty	3	1	1.87	27	10	34	32	14	30
Pawlish, Keith, Winthrop	4	2	2.73	15	2	59	49	28	63
Thurmond, Ben, Winthrop	14	3	2.88	20	1	150	132	42	148
Fischer, Brian, Co. Carolina	11	3	3.02	16	0	86	78	19	72
Pennix, Anthony, Liberty	8	3	3.16	14	0	80	62	28	83
Sturkie, Scott, Co. Carolina	13	6	3.32	21	0	133	119	18	133
Cantrell, Eric, Elon	2	3	3.34	18	0	57	44	44	63
Herauf, Jeremy, Winthrop	12	2	3.66	19	1	130	121	27	120
Carter, Steven, Co. Carolina	8	2	3.75	18	1	96	86	48	76
Colson, Jason, Winthrop	8	4	3.86	13	0	82	75	35	86
Bryant, Whit, Elon	5	4	4.01	16	0	90	93	50	67
Holcomb, Nathan, Elon	5	1	4.09	20	1	55	55	22	49
Dooley, Alex, Liberty	8	6	4.10	21	2	68	73	18	43
Pinkerton, Brad, Elon	4	6	4.13	20	1	89	87	58	84
Schuurman, Mark, UNCA	4	4	4.28	16	0	76	83	34	33
Sturge, Justin, Co. Carolina	3	3	4.72	29	0	69	75	23	71
Light, Scott, Elon	8	4	4.82	17	0	84	67	51	87

BIG TEN CONFERENCE

	Conference		Overall	
	W	L	W	L
Ohio State	20	7	43	18
Purdue	19	7	32	24
*Minnesota	19	8	39	21
Penn State	15	11	29	29
Illinois	13	14	29	28
Michigan	10	14	28	28
Northwestern	11	17	24	32
Michigan State	9	17	29	27
Iowa	8	17	19	29
Indiana	7	19	24	31

ALL-CONFERENCE TEAM: C—Chris Netwall, Sr., Penn State. **1B**—Nick Swisher, So., Ohio State. **2B**—David Blomberg, Sr., Purdue. **3B**—Jack Hannahan, Sr., Minnesota. **SS**—Mike Duursma, Sr., Purdue. **OF**—Mike Check, Sr., Ohio State; Bob Malek, So., Michigan State; Nate Sickler, Sr., Purdue. **DH**—Doug Deeds, Fr., Ohio State. **P**—Andy Dickinson, Jr., Illinois; Dave Gassner, Sr., Purdue; Mike Kobow, Jr., Minnesota; E.J. Laratta, Jr., Ohio State. **RP**—Cory Cox, Sr., Ohio State.

Player of the Year: Jack Hannahan, Minnesota. **Pitcher of the Year:** Andy Dickinson, Illinois. **Freshman of the Year:** Doug Deeds, Ohio State. **Coach of the Year:** Bob Todd, Ohio State.

INDIVIDUAL BATTING LEADERS
(Minimum 125 At-Bats)

	AVG	AB	R	H	2B	3B	HR	RBI	SB
Malek, Bob, Michigan State	.427	206	53	88	15	3	4	42	11
Stiedl, Sam, Minnesota	.401	182	50	73	14	1	0	32	14
Schutzenhofer, Andy, Illinois	.392	217	55	85	14	0	1	42	2
DeRenzo, Mike, Penn State	.387	163	36	63	11	4	1	34	9
Koman, Brock, Michigan	.383	196	49	75	19	2	14	60	1
Hannahan, Jack, Minnesota	.372	226	65	84	20	4	15	63	16
Sickler, Nate, Purdue	.369	195	50	72	21	5	8	54	12
Harrell, David, Purdue	.369	195	34	72	15	1	6	41	2
Wright, Donnie, Penn State	.369	168	38	62	13	1	10	37	1
Check, Mike, Ohio State	.363	215	54	78	13	3	0	37	32
Evans, Nick, Indiana	.359	131	20	47	8	1	1	19	0
Simmons, Luke, Illinois	.356	205	46	73	16	0	11	54	3
Fischer, Rob, Illinois	.350	220	48	77	14	4	12	55	9
Blomberg, Dave, Purdue	.349	212	52	74	17	2	3	28	18
Harris, Mike, Ohio State	.347	222	64	77	10	2	3	29	35
Haring, Kurt, Minnesota	.344	157	37	54	9	1	11	40	1
Deeds, Doug, Ohio State	.343	201	51	69	15	1	14	53	2
Welch, Scott, Minnesota	.342	228	55	78	9	4	6	42	6
Underwood, Daniel, Purdue	.342	190	51	65	8	3	4	33	11
Holthaus, Josh, Minnesota	.341	223	43	76	13	2	8	57	3
McIntyre, Nick, Purdue	.341	229	43	78	16	0	2	48	6
St. Clair, Blake, Indiana	.338	195	43	66	12	4	7	51	11
Smithlin, Zack, Penn State	.337	184	40	62	8	0	0	28	16
Mayor, John, Ohio State	.335	185	35	62	6	0	3	34	10

Arlis, Patrick, Illinois	.333	201	25	67	16	0	4	43	12
Ballard, Brady, Illinois	.332	223	59	74	20	3	6	42	14
Burrill, Brady, Mich. State	.331	142	17	47	12	0	2	44	1
Gusich, John, Purdue	.329	170	30	56	7	0	3	29	4
Perry, Rod, Penn State	.328	192	38	63	12	1	3	39	24
Wright, Nate, Michigan	.327	162	25	53	5	0	5	31	1
Tousa, Scott, Michigan	.325	206	52	67	4	2	4	24	14
Swisher, Nick, Ohio State	.322	174	60	56	16	0	15	56	2
Vitense, Kurt, Iowa	.322	174	27	56	7	0	2	24	7
Haegele, Dan, Indiana	.321	196	45	63	10	0	2	27	16
Kennedy, Jason, Minnesota	.321	215	55	69	18	3	10	39	12
Appert, Luke, Minnesota	.319	229	51	73	13	4	1	43	2
Blakeley, Eric, Indiana	.316	206	35	65	7	1	2	29	13
Koutnik, Jared, Mich. State	.316	155	33	49	10	0	4	23	3
Cantalames, Jordan, Michigan	.314	169	28	53	15	2	2	29	5
Lollio, Gino, Michigan	.311	132	25	41	8	1	4	19	5
Luce, Kris, Purdue	.309	194	31	60	12	1	5	35	3
Snavely, Christian, Ohio State	.307	140	28	43	6	2	8	36	3

INDIVIDUAL PITCHING LEADERS
(Minimum 50 Innings)

	W	L	ERA	G	SV	IP	H	BB	SO
#Cox, Cory, Ohio State	2	1	2.78	28	10	23	31	5	19
Korecky, Bobby, Michigan	6	4	3.36	13	0	102	114	19	60
Newman, Josh, Ohio State	8	3	3.50	15	0	72	74	26	51
Dickinson, Andy, Illinois	11	3	3.51	20	2	115	122	38	99
Gale, Bryan, Mich. State	9	1	3.53	21	2	64	55	26	59
Prenger, Greg, Ohio State	5	2	3.59	13	0	73	79	10	50
Gagner, Jay, Minnesota	3	3	3.60	16	1	60	55	21	39
Hill, Rich, Michigan	3	5	3.84	15	0	61	43	53	72
Schara, Zach, Northwestern	7	6	3.84	15	0	96	98	36	81
Nall, Mike, Northwestern	7	7	3.99	15	0	90	81	42	80
Laratta, E.J., Ohio State	9	3	4.08	14	0	104	119	24	66
McCall, Dan, Penn State	6	2	4.08	17	2	86	82	48	74
Blasko, Chadd, Purdue	6	6	4.23	14	0	83	97	20	54
Aardsma, David, Penn State	3	5	4.39	20	0	55	63	26	45
Cary, Jacob, Indiana	1	4	4.40	15	0	57	58	20	46
Blackwell, Chad, Iowa	4	4	4.50	12	0	64	64	16	46
Otte, Nick, Indiana	8	5	4.57	16	0	85	85	31	73
Kobow, Mike, Minnesota	10	3	4.65	17	0	108	110	50	88
Mentkowski, Ryan, Iowa	3	5	4.67	9	0	52	63	9	29
Quick, Ben, Purdue	7	5	4.67	14	0	98	113	26	79
Olson, Justin, Illinois	4	4	4.74	15	0	74	85	30	40
Sharpe, Steve, Iowa	0	4	4.80	9	0	51	66	16	30
Woodrow, C.J., Minnesota	7	4	4.82	16	0	93	115	16	74
O'Neil, Sean, Purdue	6	3	4.92	15	1	60	68	25	29
Huizinga, Jon, Mich. State	5	2	4.99	14	0	70	93	17	35
Jensen, Nick, Iowa	4	6	4.99	11	0	52	60	28	19

BIG 12 CONFERENCE

	Conference		Overall	
	W	L	W	L
*Nebraska	20	8	50	16
Texas Tech	19	10	43	20
Texas	19	11	36	26
Baylor	17	10	37	24
Oklahoma State	16	14	42	22
Texas A&M	15	15	33	27
Oklahoma	13	16	25	33
Iowa State	11	15	24	29
Kansas State	10	17	25	28
Missouri	11	19	31	24
Kansas	7	23	26	30

ALL-CONFERENCE TEAM: C—Kelly Shoppach, Jr., Baylor. **1B**—Dan Johnson, Sr., Nebraska. **2B**—Nebasett Brown, Jr., Oklahoma State. **3B**—Nick Blankenship, Jr., Texas Tech. **SS**—Omar Quintanilla, Fr., Texas. **OF**—Chris Durbin, So., Baylor; Greg Dobbs, Sr., Oklahoma; Pat Maloney, So., Kansas State; John Cole, Sr., Nebraska. **DH**—Matt Hopper, So., Nebraska. **Util**—Austin Cranford, Jr., Texas Tech. **P**—Shane Komine, Jr., Nebraska; Steven White, So., Baylor; Brandon Roberson, Sr., Texas Tech; Gerrit Simpson, Jr., Texas. **RP**—Thom Ott, Jr., Nebraska; Joe Weaver, Fr., Oklahoma.

Player of the Year: Kelly Shoppach, Baylor. **Pitcher of the Year:** Shane Komine, Nebraska. **Newcomer Player of the Year:** Greg Dobbs, Oklahoma. **Newcomer Pitcher of the Year:** Gerrit Simpson, Texas. **Freshman Player of the Year:** Omar Quintanilla, Texas. **Freshman Pitcher of the Year:** Justin Simmons, Texas; Joe Weaver, Oklahoma State. **Coach of the Year:** Dave Van Horn, Nebraska.

INDIVIDUAL BATTING LEADERS
(Minimum 125 At-Bats)

	AVG	AB	R	H	2B	3B	HR	RBI	SB
Dobbs, Greg, Oklahoma	.428	243	53	104	25	2	10	62	12
Cole, John, Nebraska	.418	239	71	100	15	4	11	61	28
Shoppach, Kelly, Baylor	.397	234	51	93	20	2	12	69	4

Cranford, Austin, Texas Tech	.387	181	46	70	15	2	7	36	1
Brown, Nebasett, Okla. State	.381	218	60	83	15	5	6	57	12
Leise, Jeff, Nebraska	.380	245	67	93	14	5	7	48	17
Quintanilla, Omar, Texas	.367	196	36	72	22	2	2	37	8
Cavender, Josh, Kan. State	.366	202	43	74	13	2	8	50	17
Evans, David, Texas A&M	.364	129	23	47	10	0	4	17	12
Johnson, Dan, Nebraska	.361	230	77	83	13	1	25	86	7
McAuliff, Jimbo, Okla. State	.360	186	59	67	10	2	4	34	23
Hopper, Matt, Nebraska	.358	254	65	91	19	1	12	85	3
Durbin, Chris, Baylor	.358	260	63	93	25	1	14	57	11
Seely, Justin, Nebraska	.357	143	32	51	14	1	4	28	5
Maloney, Pat, Kansas State	.355	197	43	70	7	2	11	44	9
Urban, Joe, Iowa State	.354	161	24	57	15	2	4	29	1
Blankenship, Nick, Texas Tech	.353	272	53	96	20	2	10	61	2
Freeman, Jeff, Texas A&M	.349	149	21	52	8	0	3	32	0
Morris, Jed, Nebraska	.341	164	40	56	16	0	7	42	5
Hodges, Kerry, Texas Tech	.339	251	61	85	11	6	8	46	38
Godsey, Jerome, Oklahoma	.339	236	41	80	4	3	3	22	11
Alvarez, Gera, Texas Tech	.338	260	62	88	18	3	8	51	19
Hubele, Ryan, Texas	.333	231	52	77	21	3	7	37	11
Arnerich, Tony, Texas Tech	.332	250	60	83	24	3	5	54	9
Scott, Luke, Oklahoma State	.323	220	56	71	13	1	20	62	10
Hartshorn, Tim, Baylor	.322	202	44	65	11	2	4	32	6
Klocksien, Ryan, Kansas	.321	196	42	63	15	0	4	37	5
Stephenson, Neal, Texas A&M	.319	144	24	46	10	1	7	31	3
Powell, Paul, Oklahoma State	.315	213	47	67	13	3	10	44	7
Rosenberg, Matt, Texas	.315	197	37	62	16	3	0	34	11
Blevins, Jeff, Nebraska	.313	195	36	61	10	2	2	44	9
Mote, Trevor, Baylor	.313	243	68	76	19	0	5	34	6
Conway, Rob, Iowa State	.313	214	35	67	14	3	4	49	2
Garner, Ty, Texas A&M	.313	195	39	61	11	1	2	25	7
Rainey, Jason, Texas Tech	.312	208	51	65	13	7	10	55	13
Nelson, John, Kansas	.312	215	48	67	8	6	4	27	31
King, Ben, Texas	.312	231	45	72	14	5	5	49	16
Garcia, Sergio, Oklahoma	.311	225	33	70	11	2	4	33	8
Carson, Tyler, Texas Tech	.309	204	44	63	10	1	3	29	22
Huggins, Mike, Baylor	.307	212	35	65	21	1	1	36	1

INDIVIDUAL PITCHING LEADERS
(Minimum 50 Innings)

	W	L	ERA	G	SV	IP	H	BB	SO
Montes, Albert, Texas	7	6	2.67	22	2	105	112	9	85
Simpson, Gerrit, Texas	5	2	2.74	17	0	122	92	39	128
Taylor, Justin, Baylor	8	2	2.86	18	0	91	91	22	68
Dale, Logan, Missouri	4	3	3.00	19	2	66	59	16	56
Smart, Pete, Kansas	9	4	3.20	16	0	115	111	33	92
Komine, Shane, Nebraska	14	3	3.35	18	0	132	129	36	157
Simmons, Justin, Texas	7	3	3.39	18	0	72	79	19	40
Moore, Justin, Texas A&M	7	3	3.39	17	0	77	79	17	49
White, Steven, Baylor	10	3	3.49	15	0	98	82	61	80
Clark, Ray, Texas	3	4	3.50	18	0	75	82	18	62
McCurdy, Nick, Okla. State	5	7	3.61	21	0	97	88	32	72
Farnum, Matt, Texas A&M	4	5	3.63	14	0	74	86	17	70
Scott, Josh, Baylor	4	4	3.65	15	0	89	83	38	51
Russ, Chris, Texas A&M	6	2	3.81	30	9	50	42	11	30
Theodorakos, Jared, Baylor	6	3	3.86	15	0	65	68	29	42
France, Ryan, Texas	5	4	3.86	13	1	51	55	12	60
Harbin, Matt, Texas A&M	3	1	3.99	21	0	65	78	13	37
Ott, Thom, Nebraska	5	2	4.03	29	11	58	52	23	42
Roberts, Mark, Oklahoma	3	2	4.03	27	4	51	51	17	45
Baker, Scott, Okla. State	3	2	4.05	11	0	53	47	20	40
Bomer, Alan, Iowa State	6	4	4.06	17	0	89	88	36	65
Hobbs, Matt, Missouri	8	5	4.06	16	0	82	89	36	55
Phillips, Chris, Texas A&M	11	5	4.13	20	0	137	139	30	89
Parcus, Kyle, Texas A&M	4	4	4.14	15	0	50	54	13	34
Mincks, Lincoln, Iowa State	4	6	4.17	16	0	91	88	32	50
Roberson, Brandon, Texas Tech	13	4	4.18	19	0	116	113	26	105
Thorp, Paul, Baylor	3	1	4.19	28	4	54	33	23	42
Metzler, Cory, Texas Tech	6	3	4.28	19	1	80	87	12	54
Lantz, Doug, Kansas	4	6	4.38	21	5	88	88	24	82
Merrigan, Josh, Okla. State	8	4	4.76	20	0	93	96	41	80
Spiehs, R.D., Nebraska	8	3	4.78	21	1	79	89	19	76

BIG WEST CONFERENCE

	Conference		Overall	
	W	L	W	L
Cal State Fullerton	14	4	48	18
UC Santa Barbara	12	6	40	17
Long Beach State	11	7	35	23
Cal State Northridge	9	9	34	22
Cal Poly	8	10	30	26
Pacific	5	13	25	30
Sacramento State	4	14	24	35

ALL-CONFERENCE TEAM: C—Brett Kay, Jr., Cal State Fullerton. **1B**—Tim Arroyo, Jr., Cal State Northridge. **2B**—David Bacani, Sr., Cal State Fullerton; Chad Peshke, Sr., UC Santa Barbara; Kevin Tillman, Sr., Cal Poly. **3B**—Dave Molidor, Sr., UC Santa Barbara. **SS**—Bobby Crosby, Jr., Long Beach State. **OF**—Jeff Jones, Sr., Long Beach State; Jared Schumaker, So., UC Santa Barbara; Ryan Spilborghs, So., UC Santa Barbara. **Util**—Jason Walker, Jr., Pacific. **DH**—Robert Smith, Sr., Cal State Northridge. **P**—James Garcia, Jr., UC Santa Barbara; Darric Merrell, Fr., Cal State Fullerton; Kirk Saarloos, Sr., Cal State Fullerton. **RP**—Chad Cordero, Fr., Cal State Fullerton.

Player of the Year: Bobby Crosby, Long Beach State. **Pitcher of the Year:** Kirk Saarloos, Cal State Fullerton. **Coach of the Year:** Bob Brontsema, UC Santa Barbara.

ALL-CONFERENCE TEAM: C—Cory Bauswell, Sr., Virginia Commonwealth; Magnus Pilegard, Jr., UNC Wilmington. **1B**—Joseph Hastings, Sr., East Carolina. **2B**—Bryant Ward, Jr., East Carolina. **3B**—Chad Tracy, Jr., East Carolina. **SS**—Brendan Harris, Jr., William & Mary. **OF**—Matt Davis, Jr., Virginia Commonwealth; Greg Miller, Sr., James Madison; John Williamson, Sr., East Carolina. **DH**—Cliff Godwin, Sr., East Carolina. **P**—Charlie Weatherby, Sr., UNC Wilmington; Sam Narron, So., East Carolina. **RP**—Jared Doyle, So., James Madison.

Player of the Year: Matt Davis, Virginia Commonwealth. **Rookie of the Year:** Sean Marshall, Virginia Commonwealth. **Coach of the Year:** Keith LeClair, East Carolina.

INDIVIDUAL BATTING LEADERS
(Minimum 125 At-Bats)

	AVG	AB	R	H	2B	3B	HR	RBI	SB
Smith, Robert, CS North.	.409	193	43	79	12	1	11	49	2
Stotts, J.T., CS Northridge	.409	235	66	95	12	1	12	40	19
Schumaker, Jared, UCSB	.400	250	65	100	19	3	1	41	22
Peshke, Chad, UCSB	.394	218	61	86	18	4	4	57	7
Molidor, Dave, UCSB	.387	230	55	89	18	1	10	67	1
Costa, Shane, CS Fullerton	.380	129	25	49	12	2	0	11	4
Rouse, Mike, CS Fullerton	.377	236	58	89	18	2	12	62	8
Spilborghs, Ryan, UCSB	.375	208	54	78	10	2	1	40	19
Arroyo, Tim, CS Northridge	.365	208	47	75	15	0	12	64	2
Kolbach, Mike, UCSB	.361	169	34	61	8	1	2	26	5
Nikolic, Adam, CS North.	.357	185	40	66	13	3	5	37	11
Stringham, Jed, UCSB	.355	169	39	60	10	2	14	51	1
Crosby, Bobby, LBSU	.353	218	56	77	16	0	9	39	11
Jones, Jeff, LBSU	.352	216	51	76	17	2	10	61	5
Reed, Jeremy, LBSU	.348	230	56	80	16	2	1	40	23
Stringfellow, Chris, CS Full.	.345	206	40	71	13	2	4	36	10
Walker, Jason, Pacific	.344	215	53	74	17	0	3	26	12
Jackson, Aurelio, Sacra. St.	.338	222	51	75	12	4	0	18	44
Bacani, David, CS Fullerton	.333	267	73	89	18	3	7	34	18
Corapci, Jason, CS Fullerton	.333	225	46	75	14	2	1	49	7
Wilson, Kyle, Cal Poly	.331	145	19	48	11	1	4	38	0
Hackett, Richard, Pacific	.327	214	40	70	13	6	9	52	12
Tillman, Kevin, Cal Poly	.325	197	36	64	15	3	3	39	10
Morales, Carlos, Sacra. State	.325	197	25	64	16	0	5	41	1
Kay, Brett, CS Fullerton	.323	195	39	63	13	2	7	43	11
Von Schell, Tyler, UCSB	.319	229	48	73	14	2	18	65	5
Morton, Rick, Pacific	.318	198	33	63	9	2	13	53	0
Guzman, Robert, CS Fullerton	.317	230	44	73	18	1	3	37	12
Gant, Bryan, Cal Poly	.316	155	33	49	7	1	2	24	11

INDIVIDUAL PITCHING LEADERS
(Minimum 50 Innings)

	W	L	ERA	G	SV	IP	H	BB	SO
Cordero, Chad, CS Fullerton	3	4	1.83	38	14	64	43	12	63
Saarloos, Kirk, CS Fullerton	15	2	2.18	25	4	153	99	23	153
Merrell, Darric, CS Fullerton	8	4	2.95	20	0	113	107	45	76
Demaria, Chris, LBSU	6	1	2.98	33	1	54	33	22	43
Pena, Matthew, Pacific	3	6	3.06	29	5	71	75	25	55
Loe, Kameron, CS North.	5	1	3.08	16	1	61	70	9	52
Garcia, James, UCSB	10	4	3.10	18	1	122	104	41	112
Davidson, Andy, CS North.	8	4	3.30	18	0	90	93	29	83
Houlton, D.J., Pacific	9	5	3.74	17	0	111	94	34	92
Smith, Jon, CS Fullerton	11	3	3.78	19	0	112	110	36	75
Beucler, Nate, LBSU	3	1	3.87	18	0	84	80	27	67
Vasquez, Matt, LBSU	5	4	3.95	16	0	68	77	19	49
Frick, Mike, CS Northridge	3	2	4.05	35	0	53	52	22	63
Murphy, Bill, CS Northridge	10	4	4.12	17	0	92	88	60	85
Ogle, Rylie, UCSB	10	2	4.15	16	0	98	103	33	61
Walker, Jason, Pacific	7	7	4.26	16	0	106	111	47	88
Dunn, Merrill, CS Northridge	3	3	4.37	35	0	56	64	14	53
Groeger, Jeffrey, Sacra. State	6	8	4.41	18	0	122	133	35	107
Miranda, Mike, Sacra. State	8	6	4.46	16	0	103	117	35	79
Paz, Matt, LBSU	8	4	4.49	19	0	106	120	28	60
Plouffe, Marshall, Sacra. State	3	1	4.64	20	0	52	47	22	41
JurvaKainen, Ryan, Pacific	3	2	4.73	25	3	51	66	8	36
Haskell, Brian, Cal Poly	3	5	4.90	15	0	83	76	64	72

INDIVIDUAL BATTING LEADERS
(Minimum 125 At-Bats)

	AVG	AB	R	H	2B	3B	HR	RBI	SB
Kim, Eddie, James Madison	.397	184	43	73	15	3	7	50	0
Davis, Matt, Va. Comm.	.396	227	84	90	7	3	26	49	49
Arteaga, Joshua, VCU	.393	224	62	88	15	1	9	70	16
Harris, Brendan, Wm. & Mary	.390	218	73	85	20	3	18	69	7
Miller, Greg, James Madison	.389	257	56	100	18	2	5	46	18
Ward, Bryant, East Carolina	.366	227	53	83	22	0	8	37	7
Delfino, Lee, East Carolina	.362	221	47	80	12	2	11	54	5
Walk, Mitch, William & Mary	.357	126	31	45	9	1	1	16	1
Tracy, Chad, East Carolina	.355	248	62	88	15	1	13	61	15
Johnson, Stephen, Geo. Mason	.353	190	46	67	11	3	9	35	16
Wakefield, Trey, Wm. & Mary	.352	236	47	83	22	1	3	50	7
Williamson, John, East Carolina	.349	218	58	76	22	0	11	56	7
Pritz, Bryan, Richmond	.349	218	52	76	5	4	3	29	22
Lindsey, Alan, James Madison	.345	171	50	59	16	3	4	25	7
Hastings, Joseph, East Carolina	.339	245	61	83	14	0	13	62	15
Pilegard, Magnus, UNCW	.339	186	32	63	10	3	0	31	4
Metheny, Brent, James Madison	.339	251	58	85	12	2	11	51	22
Tidball, Adam, Richmond	.337	181	36	61	10	0	10	40	1
Ballowe, Steve, James Madison	.330	206	50	68	14	3	6	38	12
Pabon, Jose, Va. Comm.	.329	222	42	73	20	1	6	34	8
Chiaravalloti, Vito, Richmond	.328	192	59	63	13	1	17	60	2
Godwin, Cliff, East Carolina	.322	183	40	59	14	3	15	45	1
Jordan, Eddie, George Mason	.319	182	43	58	14	3	10	40	13
Wright, Matt, UNCW	.318	198	30	63	9	1	3	51	5
Howard, Evan, George Mason	.315	162	30	51	12	3	3	21	5
Bauswell, Cory, Va. Comm.	.313	214	37	67	20	0	10	58	0
Brown, Michael, William & Mary	.310	213	41	66	13	1	8	43	4
Gaspar, Warren, East Carolina	.309	243	49	75	9	3	2	30	16
Ange, David, UNCW	.308	198	31	61	5	0	0	26	7
#Doyle, Nathan, James Madison	.283	205	39	58	18	4	5	38	7

INDIVIDUAL PITCHING LEADERS
(Minimum 50 Innings)

	W	L	ERA	G	SV	IP	H	BB	SO
Mandryk, Jason, ECU	7	1	1.95	13	0	74	66	23	52
Whitaker, Brian, UNCW	10	3	2.20	20	1	102	88	19	80
Lane, Brian, Richmond	6	2	2.55	21	2	88	82	17	57
Narron, Sam, East Carolina	12	1	2.67	15	0	101	96	17	67
Doyle, Jared, James Madison	3	1	2.75	23	6	56	47	20	48
McDonnell, Matt, UNCW	6	2	2.76	18	2	59	46	21	57
Evans, Kevin, Old Dominion	1	4	2.88	26	4	50	48	25	46
Weatherby, Charlie, UNCW	8	7	2.90	18	0	118	108	36	103
Sears, Neal, East Carolina	6	1	2.94	24	3	52	52	7	35
Saylor, Clark, William & Mary	9	2	2.99	22	3	96	91	31	83
Mullis, Jake, UNCW	7	5	3.01	15	0	93	90	27	71
#Brinson, Will, East Carolina	3	1	3.12	23	8	35	28	16	38
Marshall, Sean, Va. Comm.	9	4	3.34	21	0	73	65	30	69
Stauffer, Tim, Richmond	7	5	3.44	16	1	86	75	24	76
Martin, Thomas, Richmond	7	5	3.65	16	0	79	66	24	55
Acors, Bo, Va. Comm.	9	2	3.70	20	1	90	95	28	72
Hardman, Travis, George Mason	5	6	3.72	14	0	94	90	39	56
Cochran, Chris, James Madison	9	3	3.80	18	2	109	98	23	90
Baumann, Chad, Va. Comm.	4	3	3.93	28	5	66	74	12	40
Meyer, Dan, James Madison	8	4	4.04	15	1	76	72	25	67
Fisher, Marc, Va. Comm.	7	5	4.08	16	0	106	116	25	99
Farr, Whitt, William & Mary	9	6	4.13	19	0	105	92	34	116

COLONIAL ATHLETIC ASSOCIATION

	Conference		Overall	
	W	L	W	L
East Carolina	19	2	47	13
Virginia Commonwealth	12	8	41	19
*William & Mary	12	9	35	20
UNC Wilmington	11	9	33	23
James Madison	10	11	36	23
Richmond	7	13	27	26
Old Dominion	6	15	19	37
George Mason	5	15	21	32

CONFERENCE USA

	Conference		Overall	
	W	L	W	L
*Tulane	21	6	56	13
Houston	20	7	29	30
South Florida	16	11	33	31
Cincinnati	16	11	34	24
Memphis	13	14	34	24
Louisville	13	14	32	29
Southern Mississippi	11	16	27	32
Charlotte	10	17	24	31
Saint Louis	9	18	21	32
Alabama-Birmingham	6	21	25	30

ALL-CONFERENCE TEAM: C—Chris Hamblen, So., Cincinnati. **IF**—Andy Cannizaro, Sr., Tulane; Jake Gautreau, Jr., Tulane; James Jurries, Jr., Tulane; Dan Uggla, Jr., Memphis; Kevin Youkilis, Sr., Cincinnati. **OF**—Michael Aubrey, Fr., Tulane; Daniel Boyd, Jr., South Florida; Matt Groff, Sr., Tulane; Matt Singer, Sr., Cincinnati. **DH**—Steve Shirley, Sr., Tulane. **P**—Matt Foster, So., Tulane; Ben Hutton, Jr., Saint Louis; John Maine, So., Charlotte; Brad Sullivan, Fr., Houston. **RP**—Josh Ring, Jr., Louisville.

Player of the Year: Jake Gautreau, Tulane. **Pitcher of the Year:** John Maine, Charlotte. **Freshman of the Year:** Michael Aubrey, Tulane. **Coach of the Year:** Rick Jones, Tulane.

INDIVIDUAL BATTING LEADERS
(Minimum 125 At-Bats)

	AVG	AB	R	H	2B	3B	HR	RBI	SB
Youkilis, Kevin, Cincinnati	.405	210	81	85	7	2	18	61	22
Cannizaro, Andy, Tulane	.395	299	80	118	34	3	3	70	52
Uggla, Dan, Memphis	.379	214	72	81	28	3	18	67	5
Smith, Barrett, Memphis	.372	188	44	70	14	1	14	61	1
Leslie, Myron, So. Florida	.366	257	55	94	15	3	3	40	17
Aubrey, Michael, Tulane	.361	277	74	100	17	4	13	69	9
Kaplan, Jon, Tulane	.358	260	79	93	14	1	5	54	21
Gautreau, Jake, Tulane	.355	290	82	103	23	1	21	96	8
Groff, Matt, Tulane	.353	238	56	84	10	4	5	51	15
Giarratano, Anthony, Tulane	.352	264	72	93	12	2	3	47	11
Drawdy, Ben, South Florida	.348	233	46	81	12	0	1	16	21
Haley, Adam, Louisville	.347	167	45	58	7	2	1	14	2
Cook, Jeff, Southern Miss	.339	245	40	83	18	3	6	38	1
Sandel, George, Charlotte	.336	223	41	75	15	4	1	38	5
Singer, Matt, Cincinnati	.336	238	69	80	18	2	12	62	18
Eylward, Mike, So. Florida	.335	248	46	83	20	0	7	55	8
Erwin, Brad, Charlotte	.335	191	40	64	15	1	11	42	2
Orrico, Mike, St. Louis	.332	202	43	67	12	1	9	53	6
Boyd, Daniel, So. Florida	.330	230	55	76	11	3	12	48	12
Clark, Brett, Cincinnati	.329	255	70	84	18	0	10	48	7
Hamblen, Chris, Cincinnati	.329	240	49	79	15	0	12	66	6
Stegbauer, Rick, So. Florida	.326	175	24	57	7	1	5	40	1
Jurries, James, Tulane	.324	210	48	68	8	1	10	53	15
Garner, Mark, UAB	.324	185	32	60	10	0	2	31	4
Hook, Mike, Louisville	.321	190	44	61	8	0	5	32	25
Steiner, Nick, St. Louis	.321	196	38	63	12	0	3	27	9
Shirley, Steve, Tulane	.320	172	52	55	12	0	12	56	0
Tewes, Craig, Cincinnati	.317	199	47	63	18	0	5	50	2
Lamm, Brad, Charlotte	.316	206	43	65	11	1	2	35	9
Snyder, Chris, Houston	.316	212	29	67	13	0	13	53	4
Isbell, Brandon, UAB	.315	178	27	56	10	1	3	28	4
Nahorodny, Bill, So. Florida	.313	166	27	52	10	3	8	37	10
Budak, Mike, Louisville	.312	224	36	70	21	1	7	58	6
Isa, Fernando, Louisville	.310	203	27	63	12	0	1	26	2
Artman, Michael, So. Miss	.306	216	39	66	9	3	4	29	8
Shanks, Eric, Charlotte	.304	168	21	51	13	4	1	38	7
Bourn, Michael, Houston	.303	218	55	66	6	0	0	13	35
Bowman, Brian, Charlotte	.303	165	32	50	6	0	2	16	8
#Gatti, Bill, Louisville	.247	170	26	42	10	6	4	31	2

INDIVIDUAL PITCHING LEADERS
(Minimum 50 Innings)

	W	L	ERA	G	SV	IP	H	BB	SO
Parks, Andre, UAB	5	1	2.83	12	0	54	40	36	38
Rogers, Chad, So. Miss	6	6	3.28	15	0	85	94	14	55
Sullivan, Brad, Houston	6	7	3.41	18	1	95	98	47	98
Foster, Matt, Tulane	9	4	3.51	21	0	90	94	36	74
Charron, Joey, Tulane	9	2	3.52	29	2	64	75	20	63
Maynard, Tony, Cincinnati	4	0	3.54	13	0	56	54	28	32
Johnson, Matt, Charlotte	1	3	3.55	15	1	58	63	12	35
Douglas, Shea, So. Miss	6	5	3.59	14	0	93	79	34	92
Yarbrough, Joe, UAB	4	5	3.59	18	4	80	75	32	60
Corona, Andrew, Tulane	8	1	3.65	15	1	62	60	34	41
Flores, Gene, Houston	5	4	3.74	18	0	96	100	34	64
Maine, John, Charlotte	12	6	3.82	20	0	134	118	53	144
Dawson, Layne, Memphis	4	1	3.86	29	5	63	51	18	67
O'Malley, Ryan, Memphis	5	3	3.99	14	0	68	71	19	43
Gorham, John, South Florida	7	6	4.03	24	2	118	127	22	75
Richardson, Beau, Tulane	8	1	4.24	21	1	85	88	32	66
DiEduardo, Kyle, Cincinnati	5	4	4.26	26	0	70	68	20	49
Hutton, Ben, St. Louis	5	7	4.32	16	0	106	118	31	87
Williams, Denny, Louisville	7	7	4.45	17	0	93	98	39	52
Dobbins, Ross, UAB	5	4	4.52	15	0	80	85	34	62
Royal, Shannon, So. Florida	4	5	4.55	23	0	63	53	47	36
Castleman, Stephen, So. Miss	2	6	4.56	21	5	53	64	24	49
Faught, Austin, Houston	5	6	4.57	20	0	81	79	26	83
Wiedmeyer, Jason, Memphis	7	6	4.57	16	0	91	101	25	75
Ring, Josh, Louisville	4	6	4.63	28	10	89	91	24	74
Stewart, Daniel, Southern Miss	5	4	4.65	16	0	79	87	26	58
Rogers, Charlie, Southern Miss	3	3	4.94	15	0	58	65	30	36
Bourgeois, Nick, Tulane	3	1	5.01	14	0	50	48	38	50
Uhl, Jon, South Florida	4	5	5.08	16	0	80	96	40	63

IVY LEAGUE

	Conference		Overall	
GEHRIG	W	L	W	L
*Princeton	14	6	23	25
Columbia	10	10	20	27
Pennsylvania	8	12	22	18
Cornell	7	13	12	26
ROLFE	W	L	W	L
Dartmouth	12	8	22	18
Brown	12	8	23	23
Harvard	11	9	18	26
Yale	6	14	12	22

ALL-CONFERENCE TEAM: C—Mike Levy, Sr., Dartmouth. **1B**—Shaun Gallagher, Jr., Brown. **2B**—Robert Deeb, Fr., Brown. **3B**—Brian Nickerson, Sr., Dartmouth. **SS**—Dan Kantrovitz, Sr., Brown. **OF**—Chris May, Sr., Pennsylvania; Eric Rico, Jr., Cornell; Scott Shirrell, Fr., Dartmouth. **DH**—Nick Solaro, So., Columbia. **Util**—Andrew McCreery, So., Pennsylvania. **P**—Ryan Quillian, So., Princeton; Jim Johnson, Sr., Brown. **RP**—John Birtwell, Sr., Harvard.

Player of the Year: Chris May, Pennsylvania. **Pitcher of the Year:** Ryan Quillian, Princeton. **Rookie of the Year:** Scott Shirrell, Dartmouth.

INDIVIDUAL BATTING LEADERS
(Minimum 100 At-Bats)

	AVG	AB	R	H	2B	3B	HR	RBI	SB
May, Chris, Penn	.455	143	38	65	11	3	10	55	6
Kantrovitz, Dan, Brown	.417	163	42	68	12	3	5	41	11
Deeb, Robert, Brown	.404	156	42	63	9	3	0	20	15
Nickerson, Brian, Dart.	.383	149	36	57	15	1	7	35	0
Rico, Eric, Cornell	.381	139	37	53	10	8	5	32	10
Carter, Nick, Harvard	.380	158	41	60	14	1	8	30	3
McCreery, Andrew, Penn	.379	145	36	55	8	6	2	36	5
Shirrell, Scott, Dartmouth	.379	161	52	61	16	4	6	36	11
Gallagher, Shaun, Brown	.378	180	31	68	12	2	5	40	6
Gomez, Raul, Cornell	.372	129	21	48	5	2	7	29	1
Levy, Mike, Dartmouth	.369	149	35	55	7	2	8	33	6
Italiano, Nick, Penn	.362	141	42	51	13	1	0	14	7
Mager, Mark, Harvard	.343	169	24	58	11	0	0	33	5
Martin, Mickey, Princeton	.338	154	28	52	7	4	3	31	0
DeSantis, R.D., Yale	.336	119	11	40	7	0	0	18	6
Boran, Pat, Princeton	.335	197	46	66	19	0	2	25	17
Krance, Max, Princeton	.330	176	28	58	10	1	2	33	1
Buckmiller, Matt, Columbia	.327	150	42	49	13	2	5	18	14
Berti, Justin, Columbia	.326	138	38	45	5	1	2	20	5
Kutler, Matt, Brown	.326	175	28	57	15	4	2	36	6
#Lynn, Rick, Brown	.283	152	32	43	6	0	3	22	32

INDIVIDUAL PITCHING LEADERS
(Minimum 40 Innings)

	W	L	ERA	G	SV	IP	H	BB	SO
Stern, Jonathan, Brown	5	4	1.92	9	0	61	57	24	53
Johnson, Jim, Brown	5	4	2.59	11	1	66	62	16	73
Breslow, Craig, Yale	3	2	2.61	11	0	52	46	22	66
Steitz, Jon, Yale	2	4	2.66	11	0	64	49	39	81
Nyweide, Justin, Harvard	2	4	2.70	9	0	47	40	15	33
Birtwell, John, Harvard	4	5	2.72	10	0	56	59	12	51
McQuaid, Brendan, Cornell	5	2	2.86	9	0	66	71	7	35
Fitzgerald, Dan, Penn	4	1	3.13	10	1	46	35	13	30
McCreery, Andrew, Penn	5	2	3.40	8	0	50	49	19	36
Doveala, Brian, Columbia	2	1	3.43	10	1	42	36	15	38
Fey, Lawrence, Dartmouth	5	2	3.52	9	0	54	54	12	21
#Barnhorst, Nick, Penn	1	0	3.65	12	5	12	8	7	15
Schwartz, Adam, Columbia	3	4	3.66	10	0	64	74	23	42
Ronz, Kenon, Harvard	3	3	3.66	10	0	47	52	9	32
Crockett, Ben, Harvard	4	4	4.04	8	0	56	53	8	59
Quillian, Ryan, Princeton	6	3	4.19	12	0	69	75	11	59

METRO ATLANTIC CONFERENCE

	Conference		Overall	
	W	L	W	L
Siena	19	8	29	29
Rider	18	9	27	27
*Marist	17	10	33	21
Le Moyne	13	8	29	20
Niagara	15	11	25	20
Fairfield	14	13	17	28
Manhattan	9	13	20	25
Iona	8	13	17	32
Canisius	10	17	14	28
St. Peter's	4	23	4	39

ALL-CONFERENCE TEAM: C—Brett Woodcock, Jr., Le Moyne. **1B**—Ryan Bittner, Jr., Fairfield. **2B**—Kevin Roberts, Fr., Siena. **3B**—Kevin Riley, Jr., Rider. **SS**—Tim Superka, Sr., Rider. **OF**—Ryan Finn, Jr., Siena; Anthony Bocchino, Jr., Marist; Pete Nastasi, Sr., Niagara. **Util**—Luke Lambo, So., Iona. **DH**—Tim Bittner, Jr., Marist. **P**—Kevin Barry, Sr., Rider; Chris Begg, Sr., Niagara.

Player of the Year: Ryan Finn, Siena. **Pitcher of the Year:** Chris Begg, Niagara. **Rookie of the Year:** Chris Tracz, Marist. **Coach of the Year:** Tony Rossi, Siena; Sonny Pittaro, Rider.

INDIVIDUAL BATTING LEADERS
(Minimum 125 At-Bats)

	AVG	AB	R	H	2B	3B	HR	RBI	SB
Bocchino, Anthony, Marist	.430	200	51	**86**	**20**	**6**	7	**64**	4
Bittner, Tim, Marist	.397	194	33	77	14	0	0	36	4
Nastasi, Pete, Niagara	.380	171	52	65	16	3	9	38	**26**
Novalis, Jon, Fairfield	.380	158	33	60	7	3	5	26	7
McCurdy, Josh, Niagara	.375	184	40	69	15	3	5	41	6
O'Sullivan, Steven, Marist	.373	166	**62**	62	7	5	4	22	8
Brady, Ryan, Marist	.371	205	56	76	8	2	1	33	5
Domogala, Kyle, Canisius	.366	142	28	52	8	1	4	29	24
Bittner, Ryan, Fairfield	.364	173	30	63	12	1	2	31	2
Easton, Sean, Fairfield	.353	139	26	49	7	1	3	23	1
Loadenthal, Carl, Rider	.343	137	45	47	7	4	6	28	16
Burke, Jerry, Canisius	.336	137	20	46	12	0	2	23	4
Woodcock, Brett, Le Moyne	.333	147	30	49	3	0	1	27	6
Justice, Jeff, Le Moyne	.333	135	20	45	11	1	2	23	2
Pizarro, Manny, Iona	.332	187	36	62	10	1	7	31	14
Pecchia, Mike, Le Moyne	.326	172	43	56	15	0	6	39	1
Finn, Ryan, Siena	.325	206	41	67	15	2	**13**	51	13
Coleman, Jeff, Niagara	.325	154	17	50	10	1	2	27	1
Lambo, Luke, Iona	.325	154	24	50	9	2	7	38	9
Edwardsen, Scott, Le Moyne	.323	167	48	54	6	0	12	45	4
Superka, Tim, Rider	.319	210	36	67	6	2	4	38	10
Anderson, Wendell, Manhattan	.319	138	29	44	**20**	1	8	33	5
Riley, Kevin, Rider	.318	192	38	61	17	4	4	41	5
Murray, Chris, Niagara	.318	173	27	55	6	1	5	46	5
Pesaresi, Erinn, Rider	.317	183	43	58	5	**6**	2	27	14

INDIVIDUAL PITCHING LEADERS
(Minimum 50 Innings)

	W	L	ERA	G	SV	IP	H	BB	SO
Holsten, Ryan, Fairfield	5	4	**2.45**	11	0	73	69	26	50
Begg, Chris, Niagara	8	3	2.63	16	0	92	96	20	86
Ool, Kevin, Marist	5	4	2.71	23	2	100	93	20	87
Steward, Jaime, Le Moyne	8	4	2.76	12	0	75	51	28	71
Anderson, Wendell, Manhattan	3	2	3.04	11	1	68	55	36	58
#Turner, Tom, Manhattan	0	2	3.10	21	**8**	41	42	18	29
Tracz, Chris, Marist	**10**	1	3.13	14	0	86	92	17	74
Barry, Kevin, Rider	5	3	3.46	13	0	81	72	30	**91**
Wengert, Brent, Siena	5	6	3.54	13	0	61	53	32	38
Bittner, Tim, Marist	8	3	3.63	14	0	87	82	31	88
Martin, Scott, Manhattan	5	3	3.66	11	0	76	81	18	64
McNally, Matt, Niagara	3	2	3.71	13	0	53	48	24	36
Hoey, James, Rider	3	3	3.86	19	4	56	57	19	37
Sallustio, Phil, Iona	1	1	3.86	15	0	54	60	16	39
Barlow, Chris, Le Moyne	6	4	4.07	12	0	66	77	10	67
Darcy, Ryan, Manhattan	4	9	4.14	15	1	74	77	17	57
Mattoon, Brian, Le Moyne	2	5	4.25	14	1	53	65	18	39
Hosick, Tyler, Canisius	2	3	4.45	15	1	55	45	35	44
Copskey, Josh, Siena	5	5	4.48	14	0	70	86	17	31
Baltz, Brian, Iona	4	7	4.56	13	0	53	57	44	44
Young, Bob, Rider	7	5	4.64	16	0	76	89	19	47
Kondratowicz, Ryan, Marist	4	2	4.70	12	1	59	75	11	59

MID-AMERICA CONFERENCE

	Conference		Overall	
EAST	W	L	W	L
Bowling Green	18	9	36	18
*Kent State	16	11	32	30
Ohio	16	11	29	25
Miami (Ohio)	16	12	35	25
Marshall	11	17	24	29
Akron	9	18	16	34
Buffalo	5	23	11	39
WEST	W	L	W	L
Ball State	21	5	35	23
Central Michigan	16	12	35	24
Eastern Michigan	14	12	19	33
Western Michigan	15	13	26	28
Northern Illinois	10	17	28	27
Toledo	10	17	26	29

ALL-CONFERENCE TEAM: C—Mitch Maier, Fr., Toledo. **1B**—John VanBenschoten, Jr., Kent State. **2B**—Ryan Kyes, Sr., Ohio. **3B**—Matt Wood, Sr., Ball State. **SS**—Paul Henry, So., Ball State. **OF**—Lee Morrison, Sr., Bowling Green; Jason Knoedler, Jr., Miami; Andrew See, Sr., Ohio. **DH**—Greg Graham, Jr., Western Michigan. **Util**—Jason Brooks, Sr., Marshall. **P**—Bryan Bullington, So., Ball State; Jason Paul, Jr., Ball State; Chris Leonard, So., Miami; Denny McGee, Sr., Ohio. **RP**—Gavin Gillette, Jr., Central Michigan.

Player of the Year: John VanBenschoten, Kent State. **Pitcher of the Year:** Bryan Bullington, Ball State. **Freshman of the Year:** Mitch Maier, Toledo. **Coach of the Year:** Rick Maloney, Ball State.

INDIVIDUAL BATTING LEADERS
(Minimum 125 At-Bats)

	AVG	AB	R	H	2B	3B	HR	RBI	SB
Maier, Mitch, Toledo	**.444**	160	33	71	10	2	3	43	4
VanBenschoten, John, Kent	.440	225	74	**99**	17	**6**	**31**	**84**	23
Pilewski, Phil, Toledo	.433	171	43	74	15	2	9	53	0
Graham, Greg, West. Michigan	.406	187	35	76	14	0	14	43	0
Knoedler, Jason, Miami	.402	239	**79**	96	15	3	17	50	24
Henry, Paul, Ball State	.400	230	53	92	20	1	12	62	3
Elias, Len, BGSU	.397	204	62	81	15	2	13	58	8
Colangelo, David, Marshall	.392	217	71	85	13	**6**	3	25	15
Yost, Tom, Miami	.392	158	30	62	11	0	4	35	4
Kyes, Ryan, Ohio	.386	223	73	86	**32**	1	14	57	7
Christman, Aric, BGSU	.384	224	73	86	14	4	9	47	26
Morrison, Lee, BGSU	.382	204	55	78	17	0	18	63	7
Crowley, Matt, Cen. Michigan	.382	207	51	79	13	2	9	51	5
Lombardy, Chuck, Ohio	.379	145	38	55	14	1	0	46	0
Flamont, Sam, West. Michigan	.375	200	47	75	8	3	12	45	13
Brooks, Jason, Marshall	.374	187	52	70	14	1	23	73	10
Danielson, Noel, No. Illinois	.374	203	64	76	16	1	5	39	22
Nori, Brady, Miami	.371	259	59	96	16	2	4	47	20
Fox, Adam, Ohio	.371	197	51	73	18	1	12	51	7
Loomis, Corey, BGSU	.369	187	45	69	11	3	10	46	3
Miller, Tony, Toledo	.368	193	63	71	9	4	9	50	29
Huber, Eric, Buffalo	.367	188	36	69	12	0	4	34	1
Elrod, Nick, BGSU	.365	181	48	66	14	0	6	37	8
Scheurer, Bryan, Cen. Michigan	.365	197	52	72	18	4	4	33	22
Moorhead, Ty, Akron	.363	201	56	73	9	2	6	26	14
Carlin, Michael, Miami	.362	149	38	54	9	4	6	29	4
LoCascio, Phil, Kent State	.361	169	36	61	11	1	1	28	4
White, Clarke, Akron	.361	155	29	56	11	1	4	35	0
See, Andrew, Ohio	.355	217	57	77	14	2	17	70	2
Hunt, Kelly, BGSU	.353	201	48	71	14	2	14	49	1
Bullinger, Tim, Cen. Michigan	.348	227	54	79	16	4	4	47	21
Galloway, Mike, Cen. Michigan	.346	234	48	81	13	2	7	62	9
O'Brien, Eric, Kent State	.342	257	69	88	14	2	19	46	**33**
Meinhart, Mike, Toledo	.342	193	38	66	10	1	5	34	0
Scott, Mike, West. Michigan	.341	208	41	71	12	2	5	34	5
Mace, Clark, Miami	.339	251	62	85	18	**6**	9	59	17

INDIVIDUAL PITCHING LEADERS
(Minimum 50 Innings)

	W	L	ERA	G	SV	IP	H	BB	SO
#VanBenschoten, John, Kent	2	2	2.77	21	**8**	49	34	26	63
Paul, Jason, Ball State	**11**	2	**2.89**	17	0	97	104	22	78
McGee, Denny, Ohio	10	3	3.24	13	0	103	91	41	118
Richardson, Judd, Miami	6	3	3.32	13	0	81	73	37	61
Leonard, Chris, Miami	**11**	3	3.36	17	0	113	98	33	86
Menke, Craig, BGSU	6	1	3.45	11	0	60	48	17	66
Bullington, Bryan, Ball State	9	4	3.50	18	0	108	106	19	**119**
Misch, Pat, West. Michigan	7	2	4.00	15	0	79	84	34	99
Fowler, Steve, Marshall	5	3	4.07	14	0	86	98	32	71
Rodman, Don, Northern Illinois	5	2	4.35	14	0	52	63	19	40
Naylor, Kody, West. Michigan	3	8	4.44	15	0	81	79	33	72
Perez, Keith, West. Michigan	4	3	4.68	15	2	60	66	33	68
Bayer, Russ, Miami	5	3	5.01	17	1	74	86	31	51
Kommer, Phil, East. Michigan	5	3	5.01	14	0	65	76	29	60
Horvath, Dan, Cen. Michigan	6	4	5.18	20	0	97	111	33	102
DeLong, Mike, Toledo	3	0	5.19	15	0	52	71	20	48
Wechsler, Justin, Ball State	7	4	5.26	18	0	92	107	37	93
#Henry, Paul, Ball State	0	2	5.40	16	**8**	20	15	15	20

MID-CONTINENT CONFERENCE

	Conference		Overall	
	W	L	W	L
*Oral Roberts	24	1	48	13
Southern Utah	19	9	23	37
Valparaiso	14	10	28	29
Youngstown State	12	15	24	30
Indiana-Purdue-Indianapolis	11	17	17	37
Western Illinois	10	16	12	38
Chicago State	8	18	15	36
Oakland	7	19	11	43

ALL-CONFERENCE TEAM: C—Chris Nelson, Jr., Southern Utah; Todd Santore, Sr., Youngstown State. **1B**—Sean Munger, Sr., Western Illinois. **2B**—Todd Mitchell, Sr., Southern Utah. **3B**—Curtis Jacobsen, Sr., Southern Utah. **SS**—Steve Holm, Sr., Oral Roberts. **OF**—Billy Fitzwilson, Sr., Indiana-Purdue-Indianapolis; Mark Pedersen, Jr., Valparaiso; Kendall Schlabach, Fr., Youngstown State; Brian Wolotka, Jr., Valparaiso. **Util**—Wilton Reynolds, Jr., Oral Roberts. **DH**—Dan Wright, Sr., Southern Utah. **P**—Brad Hennessey, Jr., Youngstown State; Mark Pedersen, Jr., Valparaiso; Michael Rogers, Jr., Oral Roberts. **RP**—Dallas Martin, So., Oral Roberts.

Player of the Year: Mark Pedersen, Valparaiso. **Pitcher of the Year:** Michael Rogers, Oral Roberts; Brad Hennessey, Youngstown State. **Newcomer of the Year:** Brian Wolotka, Valparaiso. **Coach of the Year:** Paul Twenge, Valparaiso.

INDIVIDUAL BATTING LEADERS
(Minimum 125 At-Bats)

	AVG	AB	R	H	2B	3B	HR	RBI	SB
Leu, Trevor, Oral Roberts	.415	135	27	56	17	1	6	38	4
Nelson, Chris, Southern Utah	.408	179	65	73	11	2	8	43	6
Schlabach, Kendall, Young. State	.406	197	50	80	9	1	1	25	19
Jacobsen, Curtis, So. Utah	.390	228	64	89	16	2	18	74	0
Gaitano, Nick, Chicago State	.375	184	50	69	15	1	11	42	6
Santore, Todd, Young. State	.368	190	44	70	21	2	1	50	3
Dixon, Kellen, Young. State	.365	219	52	80	16	3	3	42	19
Pedersen, Mark, Valparaiso	.364	225	55	82	21	3	13	50	4
Newgent, Dan, Chicago State	.364	173	35	63	16	1	8	50	1
Harris, Kip, Oakland	.363	182	35	66	8	0	9	37	4
Gusso, Dominic, West. Illinois	.361	191	41	69	6	2	0	29	8
Sadler, Brandon, Valparaiso	.358	134	12	48	7	0	3	22	0
Tronick, Pete, Western Illinois	.357	157	36	56	11	1	10	43	4
Colin, Matt, Oral Roberts	.356	194	50	69	14	3	4	43	13
Longenecker, Joe, IUPUI	.354	195	36	69	8	1	7	33	9
Moore, Chris, Valparaiso	.343	207	46	71	19	1	10	38	8
Boyle, Danny, Oral Roberts	.341	223	58	76	10	3	2	37	35
Troy, Nick, Chicago State	.341	164	29	56	9	0	7	36	6
Stewart, Chad, Oral Roberts	.339	192	46	65	13	6	3	42	24
#Wolotka, Brian, Valparaiso	.327	211	50	69	14	5	18	55	3
#Mitchell, Todd, Southern Utah	.289	235	40	68	13	0	18	64	11

INDIVIDUAL PITCHING LEADERS
(Minimum 50 Innings)

	W	L	ERA	G	SV	IP	H	BB	SO
Rogers, Michael, Oral Roberts	14	1	2.37	18	1	121	99	46	137
Recio, Rene, Oral Roberts	8	2	2.63	18	0	89	75	32	91
Pedersen, Mark, Valparaiso	8	1	3.48	10	0	62	78	8	57
#Craker, Justin, Valparaiso	2	1	4.02	30	12	31	30	28	39
Hennessey, Brad, Young. State	6	5	4.06	16	0	89	82	42	126
Davis, Stockton, Oral Roberts	6	4	4.57	18	0	69	72	23	61
Leu, Trevor, Oral Roberts	8	3	4.62	15	0	86	81	41	102
Huysman, Neal, IUPUI	3	8	5.18	20	0	80	96	47	75
Gaitano, Nick, Chicago State	5	9	5.42	19	3	93	117	41	94
Anderson, James, So. Utah	5	5	5.53	13	0	81	110	25	45
Ousley, Matt, IUPUI	5	5	6.07	17	0	80	102	29	43
Carmosimo, Dominic, Oakland	2	4	6.37	15	0	59	66	43	51

MID-EASTERN CONFERENCE

	Conference		Overall	
NORTH	**W**	**L**	**W**	**L**
Delaware State	17	1	37	10
Howard	10	8	15	35
Coppin State	7	11	8	33
Maryland Eastern Shore	2	16	3	42
SOUTH	**W**	**L**	**W**	**L**
*Bethune-Cookman	11	5	26	34
North Carolina A&T	9	7	21	34
Florida A&M	9	7	19	27
Norfolk State	4	14	17	31

ALL-CONFERENCE TEAM: C—Dave Stevens, So., Delaware State. **IF**—George Bailey, Sr., Bethune-Cookman; Scott Martin, So., Delaware State; Joshua Melvin, So., Norfolk State; Jose Ramos, Jr., Bethune-Cookman. **OF**—Terrence Bain, Sr., Norfolk State; Jason Battle, Jr., North Carolina A&T; John Curry, Jr., Florida A&M. **DH**—Sharbel Torres, Jr., Bethune-Cookman. **P**—Travis Scott, Jr., North Carolina A&T.

Player of the Year: Jason Battle, North Carolina A&T. **Rookie of the Year:** Joe Brzeczek, Delaware State. **Coach of the Year:** Mervyl Melendez, Bethune-Cookman.

INDIVIDUAL BATTING LEADERS
(Minimum 100 At-Bats)

	AVG	AB	R	H	2B	3B	HR	RBI	SB
Martin, Scott, Del. State	.432	162	60	70	19	2	16	77	6
Williams, Kelly, Del. State	.398	196	69	78	17	2	0	49	14
Brown, Adam, Del. State	.396	134	45	53	12	0	4	39	5
Curry, John, Florida A&M	.396	144	33	57	6	8	1	36	22

	AVG	AB	R	H	2B	3B	HR	RBI	SB
Underwood, Bret, Del. State	.366	175	44	64	10	0	13	52	0
Torres, Sharbel, B-CC	.361	205	45	74	15	1	3	42	5
Melvin, Joshua, Norfolk State	.356	146	28	52	11	0	5	33	0
Branning, Chris, Florida A&M	.356	118	23	42	13	0	2	28	0
Maclin, Charles, Howard	.347	124	36	43	7	5	6	32	7
Smith, Adonis, NC A&T	.343	198	48	68	20	3	3	35	29
Battle, Jason, NC A&T	.343	207	54	71	12	5	3	32	37
Ramos, Jose, B-CC	.340	194	31	66	12	2	7	56	7
Linares, Eddy, Del. State	.327	107	33	35	5	3	1	27	4
Wilson, Duane, Florida A&M	.323	127	25	41	8	1	1	22	0
Fortune, Dwight, Howard	.323	133	34	43	13	1	7	31	14
Bailey, George, B-CC	.321	218	42	70	15	2	7	56	19
Palmer, Vince, Florida A&M	.317	139	29	44	15	1	6	31	1
August, Mike, Del. State	.316	133	38	42	15	0	1	35	2
Bain, Terence, Norfolk State	.315	165	35	52	7	3	2	16	11

INDIVIDUAL PITCHING LEADERS
(Minimum 40 Innings)

	W	L	ERA	G	SV	IP	H	BB	SO
Sterling, John, Del. State	7	3	2.08	12	0	69	42	39	83
Vaillancourt, Tim, Del. State	8	3	2.27	16	4	79	64	24	63
Brzeczek, Joe, Del. State	7	2	2.51	13	0	72	70	22	52
Montes de Oca, Cesar, B-CC	7	4	3.04	18	0	92	80	51	72
Scott, Travis, NC A&T	8	7	3.61	17	1	92	88	31	92
Dobbins, Gene, NC A&T	4	3	3.94	21	2	64	71	29	52
Clark, Claudell, Norfolk State	4	5	4.46	17	2	71	69	39	79
Garland, Noah, B-CC	1	3	4.50	23	2	48	63	30	29
Castillo, Joaquin, Florida A&M	4	1	4.70	25	3	44	45	11	52
Johnson, Travis, B-CC	4	4	5.00	19	0	68	86	29	51
Graham, Jason, B-CC	3	4	5.05	17	0	46	55	33	23

MIDWESTERN COLLEGIATE CONFERENCE

	Conference		Overall	
	W	**L**	**W**	**L**
*Wisconsin-Milwaukee	16	4	39	18
Illinois-Chicago	13	7	32	28
Wright State	12	8	31	27
Butler	8	12	25	30
Cleveland State	6	14	23	34
Detroit	5	15	12	41

ALL-CONFERENCE TEAM: C—Ryan Rumberger, Sr., Detroit. **1B**—Lance Links, Jr., Wright State. **2B**—Scott Gillitzer, Sr., Wisconsin-Milwaukee. **3B**—Bob Rosinski, Sr., Illinois-Chicago. **SS**—Keith Lillash, Sr., Cleveland State. **OF**—Eric Goerdt, Sr., Wisconsin-Milwaukee; Darin Haugom, Sr., Wisconsin-Milwaukee; Chris Tuttle, So., Wright State. **Util**—Jeff Steele, Jr., Butler. **DH**—Chuck Peters, So., Illinois-Chicago. **P**—Steve Carlson, Sr., Illinois-Chicago; Quintin Oldenburg, Jr., Wisconsin-Milwaukee.

Player of the Year: Darin Haugom, Wisconsin-Milwaukee. **Pitcher of the Year:** Quintin Oldenburg, Wisconsin-Milwaukee. **Newcomer of the Year:** Mike Bruszer, Illinois-Chicago; John VandenBerg, Wisconsin-Milwaukee; Trent Matthews, Wright State. **Coach of the Year:** Jerry Augustine, Wisconsin-Milwaukee.

INDIVIDUAL BATTING LEADERS
(Minimum 125 At-Bats)

	AVG	AB	R	H	2B	3B	HR	RBI	SB
Tuttle, Chris, Wright State	.478	203	43	97	9	3	1	49	11
Gillitzer, Scott, Wis.-Mil.	.424	229	68	97	18	2	10	66	8
Haugom, Darin, Wis.-Mil.	.423	194	61	82	15	4	6	48	20
Rosinski, Bob, Ill.-Chicago	.383	206	39	79	13	1	6	47	1
Guden, Steve, Wis.-Mil.	.379	161	42	61	13	0	9	38	6
Goerdt, Eric, Wis.-Milwaukee	.378	209	59	79	12	0	11	67	6
Houk, Matt, Wis.-Milwaukee	.355	231	63	82	16	2	6	31	14
VandenBerg, John, Wis.-Mil.	.346	182	48	63	10	2	10	46	7
Sinsabaugh, Jeremy, Butler	.344	183	32	63	11	1	8	31	14
Beaumier, Brian, Cleve. State	.343	198	27	68	13	2	10	48	1
Karpan, Chris, Ill.-Chicago	.338	139	25	47	8	3	2	21	4
Lillash, Keith, Cleveland St.	.337	199	30	67	16	2	5	39	6
Moran, J.P., Ill.-Chicago	.337	178	31	60	18	2	3	33	2
Ranstead, Chris, Wright State	.336	232	46	78	18	0	3	37	7
Pudlosky, Dave, Wis.-Mil.	.336	137	38	46	9	3	6	38	3
Rosner, John, Ill.-Chicago	.335	215	41	72	14	3	6	38	11
Morris, Jim, Wright State	.333	171	41	57	8	3	0	36	10
Shields, Nick, Wright State	.330	203	42	67	6	1	16	51	2
#Bowen, Weber, Ill.-Chicago	.318	179	45	57	24	3	5	32	1
#Steele, Jeff, Butler	.307	189	32	58	4	5	1	23	12
#Granderson, Curtis, Ill.-Chi.	.304	207	51	63	8	5	8	42	8

INDIVIDUAL PITCHING LEADERS
(Minimum 50 Innings)

	W	L	ERA	G	SV	IP	H	BB	SO
Parton, Troy, Butler	5	3	2.57	14	0	63	69	17	36
#Oberding, Eric, Wright State	3	3	2.90	24	6	40	43	15	32
Boyza, David, Cleve. State	5	5	3.14	24	0	83	66	50	86

	W	L	ERA	G	SV	IP	H	BB	SO
Carlson, Steve, Ill.-Chicago	**12**	6	3.55	22	1	99	90	40	99
Worm, Nick, Ill.-Chicago	4	2	4.08	13	0	57	83	14	37
Goerdt, Eric, Wis.-Mil.	5	1	4.09	12	1	51	58	15	33
Gilliam, Wes, Ill.-Chicago	2	6	4.16	13	0	63	57	25	62
Oldenburg, Quintin, Wis.-Mil.	9	4	4.20	17	0	94	113	33	79
Neshek, Pat, Butler	4	8	4.34	13	0	85	83	34	**118**
Greggor, Ben, Cleve. State	6	1	4.43	21	2	69	79	19	47
Banks, Larry, Ill.-Chicago	5	3	4.45	18	2	85	118	25	49
Long, Jerry, Cleveland State	4	10	4.50	16	0	94	86	56	90
Corcoran, John, Butler	4	4	4.52	14	0	64	71	19	53
Bushong, Aaron, Wis.-Mil.	5	1	4.57	14	1	67	85	14	41
Horvat, Jason, Detroit	3	6	4.84	13	1	67	82	12	28
Stephens, Brian, Wright State	3	3	4.87	9	1	57	69	14	46

MISSOURI VALLEY CONFERENCE

	Conference W	Conference L	Overall W	Overall L
Southwest Missouri State	22	10	36	22
Wichita State	21	11	42	24
Evansville	17	11	36	21
Illinois State	17	11	31	22
***Northern Iowa**	17	15	35	28
Indiana State	15	16	32	28
Creighton	11	21	21	31
Southern Illinois	10	21	19	36
Bradley	8	22	17	37

ALL-CONFERENCE TEAM: C—Ben Margalski, Jr., Southwest Missouri State. **1B**—Matt Gecan, Jr., Bradley. **2B**—Matt Gardner, Jr., Southwest Missouri State. **3B**—Aaron McEachran, So., Northern Iowa. **SS**—Wes Carroll, Sr., Evansville. **OF**—Ryan Brunner, Sr., Northern Iowa; Jared Dufault, Sr., Illinois State; Jason Frome, Sr., Indiana State. **Util**—Vince Serafini, Jr., Evansville. **DH**—Mike Saunches, So., Illinois State. **P**—Nic Ungs, Jr., Northern Iowa; Neal Cotts, Sr., Illinois State. **RP**—Bob Zimmermann, Fr., Southwest Missouri State; Steve Haines, Jr., Wichita State.

Player of the Year: Ryan Brunner, Northern Iowa. **Pitcher of the Year:** Nick Ungs, Northern Iowa. **Newcomer of the Year:** Jeremy Isenhower, Southwest Missouri State. **Freshman of the Year:** Bob Zimmermann, Southwest Missouri State.

INDIVIDUAL BATTING LEADERS

(Minimum 125 At-Bats)

	AVG	AB	R	H	2B	3B	HR	RBI	SB
Dufault, Jared, Illinois State	**.394**	203	58	80	10	7	8	47	4
Cantrell, Ryan, Illinois State	.380	184	40	70	16	4	2	22	4
Carroll, Wes, Evansville	.379	224	52	85	22	0	8	51	5
Brunner, Ryan, Northern Iowa	.377	239	**72**	90	18	2	**25**	**82**	6
Brinkley, Dant'e, SMSU	.374	227	52	85	16	**12**	1	42	18
McEachran, Aaron, No. Iowa	.367	248	56	**91**	18	1	9	63	6
Durazo, Willie, Northern Iowa	.366	224	63	82	11	1	2	24	6
Saunches, Mike, Illinois State	.363	201	45	73	14	0	13	68	4
Patterson, Seth, No. Iowa	.363	168	42	61	16	5	3	40	1
Pierce, Brad, Indiana State	.359	153	32	55	10	0	2	23	5
Hensel, Ron, Bradley	.355	138	24	49	8	1	7	43	1
Welsch, Travis, Northern Iowa	.354	237	57	84	13	1	0	35	17
Margalski, Ben, SMSU	.353	218	44	77	13	3	6	34	2
Burgamy, Brian, Wichita State	.353	241	50	85	**23**	1	5	47	15
Zaucha, Chad, Indiana State	.352	193	55	68	21	4	7	41	8
Sutherland, Marty, No. Iowa	.349	241	45	84	18	0	0	35	10
Lawler, Dan, Creighton	.349	186	33	65	15	2	7	46	3
Gecan, Matt, Bradley	.347	176	33	61	16	1	16	43	0
Schooley, Roman, So. Illinois	.346	182	26	63	10	0	7	36	6
Jeffers, Tommy, Indiana State	.344	163	34	56	15	1	7	44	2
Egli, Kevin, Indiana State	.343	169	39	58	11	2	7	37	4
Sorensen, Logan, Wich. State	.341	205	44	70	16	2	6	36	6
Allen, Scott, Creighton	.341	211	41	72	13	2	5	31	12
Spicer, Todd, Bradley	.333	156	29	52	4	0	1	12	5
Mazzuca, Joe, Creigton	.328	177	44	58	15	3	12	36	4
Rheinecker, John, SMSU	.327	147	28	48	11	1	5	28	7
Serafini, Mike, Evansville	.327	202	56	66	19	0	6	38	5
Gardner, Matt, SMSU	.324	250	46	81	13	2	12	52	5
Welch, Tanner, Wichita State	.322	152	23	49	6	0	0	20	7
Isenhower, Jeremy, SMSU	.321	224	57	72	15	6	5	28	9
Wright, Brad, Wichita State	.318	157	35	50	14	1	9	43	7
Maurath, Justin, So. Illinois	.316	136	19	43	9	3	3	30	3
Tolzien, Ed, Illinois State	.315	203	45	64	13	3	5	34	12
Frome, Jason, Indiana State	.315	235	54	74	10	6	17	57	**27**
Sullivan, Ryan, Bradley	.315	178	39	56	8	1	7	28	0
Serafini, Vince, Evansville	.314	188	35	59	9	0	9	39	2
Whealy, Blake, Evansville	.312	170	50	53	13	3	13	37	18
Purdom, John, Indiana State	.308	211	26	65	14	1	4	39	1
Nelson, Luke, So. Illinois	.307	218	35	67	7	2	2	29	13
Becker, Kent, Wichita State	.305	128	30	39	10	1	2	26	1
Davis, Wes, Evansville	.305	174	23	53	8	2	1	18	10

INDIVIDUAL PITCHING LEADERS

(Minimum 50 Innings)

	W	L	ERA	G	SV	IP	H	BB	SO
Rheinecker, John, SMSU	5	4	**2.27**	12	0	91	79	22	106
Zimmermann, Bob, SMSU	7	3	2.28	23	6	51	43	15	52
Ungs, Nic, Northern Iowa	**11**	2	2.48	16	0	109	106	14	110
Obenchain, Steve, Evansville	6	3	2.53	27	2	68	53	11	61
Cotts, Neal, Illinois State	8	3	2.89	13	0	87	60	34	**113**
Lucht, Scott, Southern Illinois	6	5	3.14	29	4	52	57	12	30
Kerbs, Reuben, Wichita State	2	2	3.18	25	2	51	47	15	40
Ziegler, Brad, SMSU	9	2	3.18	13	0	91	83	24	82
Reger, Caleb, Indiana State	5	4	3.23	30	4	53	50	33	45
Keiter, Ben, Wichita State	7	4	3.29	16	0	93	84	31	84
Green, Micah, Northern Iowa	7	2	3.30	22	4	74	71	24	62
Palmer, Matt, SMSU	6	3	3.65	14	0	94	86	35	91
Gray, Jeff, SMSU	3	3	3.72	13	0	58	59	20	38
Bryan, Erich, Wichita State	6	2	3.94	14	0	64	75	22	47
Hines, Matt, Illinois State	5	2	4.07	12	0	55	64	30	29
Zaleski, Matt, Indiana State	4	2	4.12	21	0	59	56	27	45
Maureau, Justin, Wichita State	6	3	4.18	18	1	88	78	31	91
Thatcher, Joe, Indiana State	5	4	4.20	15	0	71	89	29	56
Grasley, Steve, Creighton	3	5	4.28	24	5	61	62	22	57
Davis, Wes, Evansville	5	4	4.31	15	1	77	99	21	43
#Haines, Steve, Wichita State	4	2	4.37	28	**11**	35	45	5	33
Serafini, Vince, Evansville	8	5	4.39	19	2	105	115	23	81
Stetter, Mitch, Indiana State	2	8	4.39	13	0	84	86	35	72
Sanders, David, Wichita State	5	6	4.43	15	1	69	81	14	68
Hecker, Steve, Illinois State	9	3	4.46	15	0	75	87	28	63

MOUNTAIN WEST CONFERENCE

	Conference W	Conference L	Overall W	Overall L
***Brigham Young**	21	8	38	22
San Diego State	19	11	34	26
Utah	14	16	27	29
New Mexico	14	16	26	34
Nevada-Las Vegas	13	17	23	33
Air Force	8	21	23	33

ALL-CONFERENCE TEAM: C—Chris Shelton, Jr., Utah. **1B**—Nate Weese, Jr., Utah. **2B**—Troy Cairns, So., New Mexico. **3B**—Kainoa Obrey, So., Brigham Young. **SS**—Taber Lee, So., San Diego State. **OF**—Doug Jackson, So., Brigham Young; Matt Carson, So., Brigham Young; Andy Litteral, Sr., San Diego State. **DH**—Trent Kitsch, Sr., UNLV. **P**—Nate Fernley, Sr., Brigham Young; Marcos Mendoza, Jr., San Diego State; Ryan Bailey, Jr., Utah. **RP**—Royce Ring, So., San Diego State.

Player of the Year: Chris Shelton, Utah. **Freshman of the Year:** Mike Westfall, Utah. **Coach of the Year:** Vance Law, Brigham Young.

INDIVIDUAL BATTING LEADERS

(Minimum 125 At-Bats)

	AVG	AB	R	H	2B	3B	HR	RBI	SB
Obrey, Kainoa, BYU	**.381**	226	48	86	20	0	13	56	3
Shelton, Chris, Utah	.374	219	**63**	82	22	2	**19**	66	1
Trujillo, David, UNLV	.374	187	32	70	15	1	7	41	0
Jackson, Doug, BYU	.370	200	55	74	8	**8**	2	35	13
Swenson, Sam, Utah	.351	222	61	78	13	5	14	51	10
Shitanishi, Garett, UNLV	.351	208	39	73	7	1	0	14	9
Pierce, Sean, SDSU	.350	143	42	50	4	3	6	23	10
Stanley, Aaron, New Mexico	.349	169	31	59	10	3	0	26	**27**
Cairns, Troy, New Mexico	.349	275	57	**96**	**26**	6	2	32	12
Cota, Carlo, SDSU	.346	237	37	82	13	2	1	46	8
Lee, Taber, SDSU	.344	221	41	76	9	1	0	30	24
Westfall, Mike, Utah	.341	226	42	77	17	1	9	50	1
Coughlan, Cameron, BYU	.341	132	30	45	6	6	3	27	9
Johnson, Brent, UNLV	.340	197	39	67	20	1	1	33	15
Thiessen, Mike, Air Force	.339	180	48	61	15	0	9	41	12
Carson, Matt, BYU	.335	227	56	76	6	5	18	**70**	8
Leuthard, Ben, SDSU	.331	139	19	46	12	1	3	26	2
King, Seth, BYU	.328	183	38	60	14	2	9	42	4
Lovato, Anthony, New Mexico	.327	171	40	56	15	2	6	43	3
Labasco, Brian, Air Force	.325	191	26	62	13	2	1	24	12
Maestas, Tommy, Utah	.324	204	41	66	15	0	3	30	1
Sevieri, Donny, New Mexico	.324	225	48	73	14	1	9	40	12
Perry, Tyler, BYU	.323	158	28	51	7	3	2	30	3
Pannier, Brit, Utah	.321	234	45	75	20	2	10	45	2
Gwynn, Anthony, SDSU	.318	179	48	57	8	4	0	23	19
Saba, Donnie, Utah	.317	218	58	69	7	6	9	33	11

INDIVIDUAL PITCHING LEADERS

(Minimum 50 Innings)

	W	L	ERA	G	SV	IP	H	BB	SO
#Ring, Royce, SDSU	6	2	1.19	32	**9**	38	27	8	45
Fernley, Nate, BYU	**16**	3	**3.12**	21	0	153	136	32	**133**

Name	W	L	ERA	G	SV	IP	H	BB	SO
Skinner, John, SDSU	4	4	3.58	30	1	75	79	20	68
Mendoza, Marcos, SDSU	7	6	3.84	20	0	91	94	34	118
Adams, Ryan, BYU	6	2	4.10	12	0	53	66	22	21
Deyapp, Jeremy, New Mexico	4	3	4.32	17	0	73	81	20	58
Julianel, Ben, SDSU	5	5	5.00	18	0	54	54	22	60
Olson, Ryan, UNLV	4	4	5.09	11	0	69	86	22	42
Cooper, Chris, New Mexico	6	7	5.48	17	0	112	137	37	82
Hall, Courtney, UNLV	7	7	5.67	17	1	94	114	50	60
Wylie, Jason, UNLV	5	3	5.74	15	1	58	68	33	46
Shortell, Rory, SDSU	6	2	5.83	15	0	76	87	38	67
Palmer, Travis, Utah	5	5	5.91	17	0	99	116	35	59
Fisher, Erik, Air Force	2	11	6.07	18	0	92	130	37	77

NEW YORK STATE CONFERENCE

	Conference		Overall	
	W	L	W	L
Stony Brook	10	0	35	16
Binghamton	5	5	19	26
New York Tech	5	5	19	30
C.W. Post	4	6	12	29
Albany	3	7	15	32
Pace	3	7	19	29

ALL-CONFERENCE TEAM: C—Alex Trezza, Jr., Stony Brook. **1B**—Mike Bohlander, Jr., Pace. **2B**—Jelani Arnold, Fr., New York Tech. **3B**—Ryan Nevins, Sr., New York Tech. **SS**—Tim Macko, Sr., Binghamton. **OF**—Steve Martino, Jr., Pace; Michael Oliva, Sr., Albany; Jake Toms, Jr., Albany. **DH**—Doug Hehner, Fr., Pace. **Util**—Steve Checksfield, Sr., Albany. **P**—Chris Flinn, Jr., Stony Brook; Hector Duprey, Sr., C.W. Post. **RP**—Phil Artonio, So., Binghamton.

Player of the Year: Alex Trezza, Stony Brook. **Coach of the Year:** Matt Senk, Stony Brook.

INDIVIDUAL BATTING LEADERS
(Minimum 100 At-Bats)

	AVG	AB	R	H	2B	3B	HR	RBI	SB
Oliva, Michael, Albany	.428	173	41	74	14	2	6	40	9
Macko, Tim, Binghamton	.389	149	39	58	11	1	10	44	3
Goelz, Bryan, NY Tech	.388	206	62	80	9	1	7	37	15
Renner, Garrett, Stony Brook	.385	148	44	57	10	2	1	30	3
Graham, Rich, Stony Brook	.371	167	45	62	18	1	2	23	6
Whitaker, Dwayne, SB	.358	134	27	48	5	3	4	30	2
Nevins, Ryan, NY Tech	.357	182	42	65	19	0	13	52	11
Bohlander, Mike, Pace	.349	186	36	65	13	0	17	48	0
Toms, Jake, Albany	.345	168	38	58	14	0	4	35	8
Arnold, Jelani, NY Tech	.342	184	28	63	9	0	1	17	9
Mitchell, Brian, C.W. Post	.338	145	32	49	7	0	3	26	6
Trezza, Alex, Stony Brook	.337	181	59	61	13	0	23	68	1
St. George, Anthony, NY Tech	.328	137	28	45	9	0	5	26	2
Checksfield, Steve, Albany	.327	165	42	54	13	2	10	36	8
Gaffney, Mike, NY Tech	.323	158	35	51	2	0	1	20	11
#Martino, Steve, Pace	.307	192	53	59	12	3	6	36	9
#Scott, Eddie, Albany	.280	164	41	46	8	1	3	22	22

INDIVIDUAL PITCHING LEADERS
(Minimum 40 Innings)

	W	L	ERA	G	SV	IP	H	BB	SO
Reynolds, Lee, Stony Brook	8	1	2.87	14	0	69	64	20	41
Mischo, Dave, Stony Brook	3	0	3.46	18	0	42	42	28	29
Montani, Jeff, Binghamton	6	5	4.05	15	1	80	75	32	73
#Langford, Shelby, Pace	2	1	4.05	16	8	20	28	3	8
Flinn, Chris, Stony Brook	6	3	4.06	15	1	89	82	44	121
Duprey, Hector, C.W. Post	5	7	4.38	14	0	76	83	39	64
Lupo, Lenny, C.W. Post	1	3	4.84	14	0	58	69	20	35
Keinath, Tim, C.W. Post	2	1	4.91	7	0	40	33	20	33
Carle, Jeremy, Stony Brook	6	2	5.25	13	1	60	62	43	75
Taormina, Rob, NY Tech	4	6	5.43	16	0	70	93	14	40

NORTHEAST CONFERENCE

	Conference		Overall	
NORTH	W	L	W	L
Central Connecticut State	14	8	30	22
St. Franics (N.Y.)	14	8	25	22
Long Island	13	9	18	24
Sacred Heart	12	10	22	23
Quinnipiac	3	19	5	37
SOUTH	W	L	W	L
*Maryland-Baltimore County	17	5	31	20
Monmouth	17	5	29	24
Fairleigh Dickinson	9	13	13	27
Wagner	8	14	16	30
Mount St. Mary's	3	19	12	37

ALL-CONFERENCE TEAM: C—Scott Kosmicky, So., Maryland-Baltimore County. **1B**—Jeff Toth, Sr., Monmouth. **2B**—Chad Gerben, Sr., Maryland-Baltimore County. **3B**—Lance Koenig, So., Monmouth. **SS**—Jared Boyd, Jr., Maryland-Baltimore County. **OF**—Greg Deboy, Jr., Maryland-Baltimore County; Jason Law, Jr., Monmouth; Matt Lemanczyk, Jr., Sacred Heart. **DH**—Joe LaRocca, Jr., Wagner. **P**—Jason Fardella, Jr., St. Francis; Eric Weltmer, Sr., Maryland-Baltimore County.

Player of the Year: Jason Law, Monmouth. **Pitcher of the Year:** Jason Fardella, St. Francis. **Rookie of the Year:** Tim D'Aquila, Central Connecticut State. **Coach of the Year:** Charlie Hickey, Central Connecticut State.

INDIVIDUAL BATTING LEADERS
(Minimum 100 At-Bats)

	AVG	AB	R	H	2B	3B	HR	RBI	SB
Law, Jason, Monmouth	.436	204	58	89	20	0	16	67	8
Lemanczyk, Matt, SH	.392	181	46	71	12	4	2	30	40
Kosmicky, Scott, UMBC	.390	195	42	76	16	0	17	62	0
Molinini, Michael, St. Francis	.388	152	31	59	13	3	4	39	15
Toth, Jeff, Monmouth	.382	204	41	78	19	1	13	65	2
Mayette, John, CCSU	.378	156	41	59	15	1	0	32	6
Sottile, Joe, Long Island	.376	109	23	41	11	2	3	28	4
Gerben, Chad, UMBC	.372	207	56	77	20	3	4	57	2
Boyd, Jared, UMBC	.371	194	53	72	11	0	4	39	8
Bruckhorst, Brian, SH	.368	163	32	60	22	2	3	44	1
Early, Matthew, Long Island	.367	150	39	55	12	3	8	33	8
Marshall, Jonathon, LI	.364	143	34	52	13	3	3	29	4
Koenig, Lance, Monmouth	.355	200	63	71	19	0	4	50	24
D'Aquila, Tim, CCSU	.354	178	33	63	9	1	3	45	1
Fraley, Jeff, UMBC	.348	161	31	56	10	1	5	40	0
Deboy, Greg, UMBC	.344	157	38	54	10	2	7	47	1
Guarno, Rick, UMBC	.342	155	33	53	4	0	0	19	4
Shuler, John, UMBC	.338	207	52	70	11	2	3	29	5
Macellaro, Nick, CCSU	.337	172	31	58	13	1	1	27	3
Hagan, John, Fair. Dickinson	.337	104	15	35	5	1	1	14	1
Cerminaro, Mike, Wagner	.337	172	28	58	19	0	5	27	14
DiMichele, A.J., Fair. Dickinson	.333	120	22	40	12	0	1	18	6
Distefano, Bryan, Wagner	.333	159	26	53	10	0	0	13	15
LaPointe, Travis, Quinnipiac	.331	154	18	51	7	4	1	18	4
Hosgood, Robert, CCSU	.331	175	46	58	9	1	4	37	20

INDIVIDUAL PITCHING LEADERS
(Minimum 40 Innings)

	W	L	ERA	G	SV	IP	H	BB	SO
#Kelly, Mike, Monmouth	2	2	2.63	14	8	14	10	2	14
Fardella, Jason, St. Francis	8	4	2.68	16	0	81	74	24	86
Bushor, Eric, Sacred Heart	5	2	2.77	12	1	55	59	9	26
Weltmer, Erik, UMBC	12	2	2.86	22	2	123	129	10	85
Taylor, Robert, Mt. St. Mary's	2	4	3.06	22	2	50	48	31	59
Clarke, Jim, CCSU	2	3	3.18	12	1	74	75	14	53
Benfield, Mike, Monmouth	8	0	3.26	16	0	86	101	21	48
Genao, Enrique, Monmouth	5	4	3.79	13	1	78	70	48	56
Rosso, David, Sacred Heart	4	3	3.82	10	0	61	63	25	45
DeNicola, Anthony, St. Francis	4	4	4.02	16	0	65	75	18	58
Mayette, John, CCSU	5	4	4.13	10	0	61	58	31	19
Clark, Kevin, Fair. Dickinson	3	2	4.24	8	0	40	35	26	31
Facey, Andrew, Long Island	5	3	4.35	10	0	60	68	21	42
Bailey, Matt, St. Francis	3	3	4.53	17	1	44	49	13	30
Keeton, Glen, Monmouth	5	5	4.53	14	0	56	69	25	49
Hopper, Greg, UMBC	7	4	4.76	16	0	93	106	27	63
Scott, Dan, Sacred Heart	5	5	4.79	15	1	73	84	26	64

OHIO VALLEY CONFERENCE

	Conference		Overall	
	W	L	W	L
Eastern Illinois	19	1	35	20
Southeast Missouri State	15	6	34	20
*Tennessee Tech	12	9	33	30
Murray State	10	11	28	26
Austin Peay	9	12	32	30
Eastern Kentucky	8	12	25	31
Morehead State	7	14	19	35
Tennessee-Martin	3	18	8	46

ALL-CONFERENCE TEAM: C—Jeff Bourbon, Sr., Southeast Missouri. **1B**—A.J. Ellis, So., Austin Peay. **2B**—Clemente Bonilla, Jr., Southeast Missouri. **3B**—Rusty Moore, So., Austin Peay. **SS**—Zach Borowiak, Sr., Southeast Missouri. **OF**—Billy Moore, Jr., Murray State; Matt Curtis, Sr., Tennessee Tech; Bob VanHoorebeck, Sr., Eastern Illinois. **Util**—Ben Cunningham, Sr., Tennessee Tech. **DH**—Bret Pignatiello, So., Eastern Illinois. **P**—Todd Pennington, Jr., Southeast Missouri; Eddy Bushelman, Jr., Morehead State. **RP**—Mike Ziroli, Sr., Eastern Illinois.

Player of the Year: Clemente Bonilla, Southeast Missouri. **Pitcher of the Year:** Todd Pennington, Southeast Missouri. **Rookie of the Year:** Ben Duke, Eastern Illinois. **Coach of the Year:** Jim Schmitz, Eastern Illinois.

INDIVIDUAL BATTING LEADERS
(Minimum 125 At-Bats)

	AVG	AB	R	H	2B	3B	HR	RBI	SB
Cunningham, Ben, Tenn. Tech	.388	237	53	92	25	2	5	50	3
Bonilla, Clemente, SE Mo. State	.382	152	49	58	20	1	6	34	8
Moore, Billy, Murray State	.382	204	61	78	9	0	0	15	12
Duke, Ben, Eastern Illinois	.355	172	38	61	19	1	10	41	1
Beatty, Brad, SE Missouri State	.353	167	32	59	10	0	4	32	3
Anderson, Josh, East. Kentucky	.353	207	37	73	8	4	3	29	32
Moore, Rusty, Austin Peay	.351	242	64	85	21	1	7	37	28
Renaker, Will, Morehead State	.351	168	38	59	8	0	12	40	0
Matuszek, Kevin, More. State	.351	191	47	67	15	0	15	53	1
Johnson, Michael, Austin Peay	.341	226	56	77	11	2	15	45	21
Poynter, Chris, Austin Peay	.340	153	24	52	2	1	3	19	1
Curtis, Matt, Tennessee Tech	.339	227	58	77	23	1	10	51	13
Buzachero, Bubbie, Tenn. Tech	.338	139	21	47	9	1	4	35	9
Pirman, Pete, Eastern Illinois	.335	179	41	60	11	1	2	29	7
Landon, Josh, Eastern Illinois	.335	215	55	72	23	2	7	39	7
Ellis, A.J., Austin Peay	.335	224	44	75	17	1	10	58	2
VanHoorebeck, Bob, EIU	.333	162	42	54	9	3	6	34	6
Byars, Garner, Murray State	.333	210	44	70	11	2	2	40	10
Seets, Ronnie, Murray State	.331	157	36	52	12	1	2	42	3
#Martin, Chris, Eastern Illinois	.323	201	38	65	9	4	7	53	5
#Ridgway, Josh, Murray State	.305	210	35	64	16	4	1	40	12
#Hatton, Vern, SE Mo. State	.298	188	37	56	9	4	1	37	7

INDIVIDUAL PITCHING LEADERS
(Minimum 50 Innings)

	W	L	ERA	G	SV	IP	H	BB	SO
Pennington, Todd, SE Mo. St.	12	2	1.33	18	0	95	51	36	121
Ziroli, Mike, Eastern Illinois	8	2	2.63	30	8	65	55	35	55
Hilz, Jeffrey, SE Mo. State	5	3	3.26	27	2	50	34	22	64
Buzachero, Bubbie, Tenn. Tech	6	5	3.30	22	2	85	78	40	81
Russelburg, Aaron, Murray State	6	5	3.51	16	0	90	73	46	83
Long, Donnie, Tennessee Tech	7	6	3.98	21	2	97	102	42	97
Bachman, Dan, East. Kentucky	2	3	4.18	18	0	67	67	37	50
Lunski, Greg, SE Mo. State	4	3	4.26	22	1	57	48	30	54
Weel, Mike, Austin Peay	6	6	4.40	18	0	92	99	21	73
Warden, Jim Ed, Tenn. Tech	6	7	4.42	20	0	77	81	61	79
Smith, Dustin, Austin Peay	2	5	4.59	16	0	69	70	39	50
Thomas, Tommy, SE Mo. State	4	8	4.60	15	0	61	71	31	57
Metz, Scott, Eastern Illinois	5	2	4.85	12	0	65	76	29	41
Pew, Stephen, Austin Peay	8	4	4.85	23	1	82	90	25	60
Bushelman, Eddy, More. State	8	3	4.94	18	2	82	94	40	85
Purcell, Brad, SE Missouri State	5	2	5.04	16	1	64	67	35	44
Rhoades, Jesse, Murray State	5	3	5.10	17	0	60	67	37	45
#McCarty, Rick, Murray State	4	1	5.28	24	8	31	30	8	22

PACIFIC-10 CONFERENCE

	Conference W	L	Overall W	L
Southern California	18	6	45	19
Stanford	17	7	51	17
Arizona State	14	10	37	20
California	14	10	34	25
Arizona	12	12	33	23
Oregon State	11	13	31	24
UCLA	9	15	30	27
Washington	7	17	29	23
Washington State	6	18	15	39

ALL-CONFERENCE TEAM: C—Casey Myers, Sr., Arizona State; Bryan Ingram, Jr., Oregon State. **1B**—Stefan Bailie, So., Washington State; Ernie Durazo, Sr., Arizona. **INF**—Josh Canales, Sr., UCLA; Brooks Conrad, Jr., Arizona State; Chris O'Riordan, Jr., Stanford; Carson White, Jr., California. **OF**—Rod Allen, Fr., Arizona State; Brian Barre, Jr., Southern California; Chris Biles, So., Oregon State; Shelley Duncan, Jr., Arizona; Chris Duffy, Jr., Arizona State; Ben Francisco, So., UCLA; Sam Fuld, Fr., Stanford; Carlos Quentin, Fr., Stanford. **DH**—Brian Baron, Jr., UCLA. **P**—Rik Currier, Sr., Southern California; Scott Nicholson, Sr., Oregon State; Mark Prior, Sr., Southern California.

Player of the Year: Casey Myers, Arizona State. **Pitcher of the Year:** Mark Prior, Southern California. **Newcomer of the Year:** Carlos Quentin, Stanford. **Coach of the Year:** David Esquer, California.

INDIVIDUAL BATTING LEADERS
(Minimum 125 At-Bats)

	AVG	AB	R	H	2B	3B	HR	RBI	SB
Baron, Brian, UCLA	.443	237	39	105	17	0	2	47	1
Durazo, Ernie, Arizona	.395	238	66	94	23	4	7	57	6
Myers, Casey, Arizona State	.395	223	53	88	17	0	7	69	2
Biles, Chris, Oregon State	.395	177	36	70	8	1	9	48	4
Davis, Curtis, Oregon State	.390	146	25	57	12	1	2	26	1
Allen, Rod, Arizona State	.389	180	41	70	14	1	6	53	6
Canales, Josh, UCLA	.376	213	38	80	9	1	0	22	15
Duffy, Chris, Arizona State	.373	201	46	75	6	2	4	37	20
Anderson, Brian, Arizona	.370	181	40	67	9	6	4	38	8
Garko, Ryan, Stanford	.368	201	42	74	16	1	7	43	0
Barden, Brian, Oregon State	.367	226	51	83	11	2	8	55	5
Wyrick, Dennis, Arizona State	.360	172	31	62	8	0	0	27	4
O'Riordan, Chris, Stanford	.359	281	62	101	17	2	12	68	16
Fuld, Sam, Stanford	.357	227	56	81	15	2	0	37	11
Meyer, Rob, California	.355	214	47	76	6	0	10	44	3
Carter, Josh, Oregon State	.355	220	44	78	18	2	6	54	7
Abram, Matt, Arizona	.352	227	47	80	18	2	10	55	1
Bailie, Stefan, Wash. State	.352	210	55	74	9	1	18	56	2
Torres, Erik, Arizona	.350	237	48	83	15	6	5	35	1
Knight, Mike, Wash. State	.346	182	40	63	13	1	4	28	8
Barre, Brian, USC	.345	232	53	80	9	1	13	48	20
Quentin, Carlos, Stanford	.345	249	55	86	11	1	11	52	5
Done, Michael, Washington	.342	190	37	65	15	0	7	36	6
Duncan, Shelley, Arizona	.338	228	64	77	9	1	24	78	3
White, Carson, California	.338	225	44	76	19	4	8	49	6
Davidson, Tyler, Washington	.337	190	35	64	10	2	6	42	4
Baker, John, California	.331	169	29	56	13	0	3	29	0
Gates, Bookie, Wash. State	.327	211	43	69	16	0	8	60	8
Conley, Ben, California	.324	170	36	55	6	0	2	21	4
Davidson, Seth, USC	.323	254	48	82	10	5	2	26	14
Concepcion, Alberto, USC	.321	224	37	72	17	3	7	41	4
Hecker, Evan, Wash. State	.321	196	39	63	8	1	2	28	7
VanMeetren, Jason, Stanford	.320	178	33	57	14	3	7	33	7
Dragicevich, Scott, Stanford	.320	253	47	81	14	0	5	34	6
Pearl, Matt, UCLA	.317	246	44	78	13	1	6	42	5
Moon, Michael, USC	.313	227	40	71	8	3	6	35	11
Lopez, Mike, Arizona State	.310	184	49	57	19	0	3	49	6
Horwitz, Brian, California	.310	239	39	74	17	1	1	30	11
Francisco, Ben, UCLA	.309	236	48	73	10	1	6	42	15
Peavey, Bill, USC	.307	218	44	67	9	1	7	48	0
Garrabrants, Steve, Ariz. State	.307	140	31	43	5	5	0	23	16
West, Jeremy, Arizona State	.307	140	34	43	8	4	6	34	2
Phelps, Jeff, Arizona State	.307	189	26	58	20	1	2	31	4
Lunetta, Anthony, USC	.305	239	48	73	18	2	5	38	12
Garthwaite, Jay, Washington	.303	201	35	61	17	0	5	46	8
Dragicevich, Jeff, California	.302	169	26	51	6	0	3	21	1
Ingram, Bryan, Oregon State	.301	193	37	58	6	2	2	28	7
Persell, Josh, USC	.294	231	42	68	15	0	7	39	0

INDIVIDUAL PITCHING LEADERS
(Minimum 50 Innings)

	W	L	ERA	G	SV	IP	H	BB	SO
Prior, Mark, USC	15	1	1.69	20	0	139	100	18	202
Friedberg, Drew, Ariz. State	4	2	2.03	24	1	53	40	13	55
Kohn, Shawn, Washington	6	2	2.57	18	0	81	60	15	65
Currier, Rik, USC	12	3	2.59	20	0	118	112	40	120
Bannister, Brian, USC	4	4	2.80	34	5	55	40	21	56
Guthrie, Jeremy, Stanford	13	4	2.82	20	0	134	123	41	128
Bruksch, Jeff, Stanford	9	3	3.18	23	3	124	107	28	107
Karp, Josh, UCLA	5	2	3.26	15	0	80	75	32	92
Nicholson, Scott, Ore. State	11	2	3.58	16	0	131	137	21	73
Cunningham, Tim, Stanford	6	0	3.60	20	0	75	59	40	54
Reyes, Anthony, USC	5	4	3.72	19	0	109	111	25	97
Cash, David, California	10	3	3.77	28	4	93	90	35	94
Hutchinson, Trevor, California	6	7	3.85	17	1	115	141	28	91
Gosling, Mike, Stanford	7	3	3.94	17	0	82	65	28	77
Switzer, Jon, Arizona State	5	6	4.04	19	0	100	95	45	128
Esposito, Mike, Arizona State	5	2	4.06	16	0	69	66	24	63
Torres, Andy, Arizona State	13	4	4.30	27	1	92	104	29	74
Montalbo, Brian, California	4	1	4.38	23	0	62	65	37	47
Johnson, Thad, Oregon State	6	9	4.62	19	0	123	131	39	87
Rierson, Sean, Arizona	7	4	4.66	18	0	100	126	21	66
#Robertson, Scott, Washington	3	0	4.71	20	7	21	24	8	21
Brandt, Jon, UCLA	4	4	4.93	14	0	69	69	33	56
Wodnicki, Mike, Stanford	7	1	5.13	28	6	54	58	18	53
Little, Joe, Arizona	4	0	5.19	21	2	50	57	12	36
Kaiser, Marc, Arizona	8	6	5.35	17	0	101	122	57	70
Alwert, Garrett, Wash. State	2	6	5.40	15	0	58	72	17	23
Dizard, Fraser, USC	3	3	5.44	29	7	51	52	30	47

PATRIOT LEAGUE

	Conference W	L	Overall W	L
*Bucknell	14	4	31	19
Navy	14	6	21	25
Holy Cross	11	9	19	23
Army	10	10	17	27
Lehigh	6	14	14	28
Lafayette	5	15	10	32

ALL-CONFERENCE TEAM: C—Dale Johnson, So., Holy Cross. **1B**—Russ Lindberg, Sr., Bucknell. **2B**—Peter Summa, Jr., Holy Cross. **3B**—Nick Sylvester, Sr., Navy. **SS**—Buddy Gengler, Sr., Army. **OF**—Kyle Kalkwarf, Jr., Army; Ian Joseph, Sr., Bucknell; Mike Ritz, Sr., Bucknell. **DH**—Willie Gury, Sr., Navy. **P**—Buck Adams, Sr., Army; Matt Foster, So., Navy. **RP**—Gregg Farmery, Jr., Bucknell.

Player of the Year: Peter Summa, Holy Cross. **Pitcher of the Year:** Buck Adams, Army. **Coach of the Year:** Paul Pearl, Holy Cross.

INDIVIDUAL BATTING LEADERS
(Minimum 100 At-Bats)

	AVG	AB	R	H	2B	3B	HR	RBI	SB
D'Angelis, Vince, Lafayette	.402	107	29	43	11	3	5	24	5
Johnson, Dale, Holy Cross	.396	101	16	40	2	2	3	31	4
Rosenberg, Adam, Lafayette	.383	133	24	51	11	3	2	33	8
Gastellum, Miguel, Army	.376	149	32	56	7	2	0	20	31
Summa, Peter, Holy Cross	.368	155	38	57	11	3	6	44	6
Lindberg, Russ, Bucknell	.367	166	38	61	12	0	9	59	5
Novalis, Jesse, Lehigh	.357	140	27	50	17	1	4	40	6
Boyd, Jason, Lafayette	.356	132	40	47	8	4	3	23	5
Tambellini, Matt, Lafayette	.351	114	20	40	4	3	3	23	0
Gengler, Buddy, Army	.350	143	35	50	14	0	5	32	3
Kalkwarf, Kyle, Army	.338	145	36	49	7	1	4	37	6
Holden, Josh, Army	.329	155	38	51	7	0	2	20	23
Sylvester, Nick, Navy	.324	139	23	45	12	0	2	25	10
Gury, Willie, Navy	.320	128	24	41	7	1	2	24	1
Minney, Josh, Army	.317	145	39	46	5	0	0	29	13
Boyce, Brandon, Army	.314	140	20	44	14	1	2	23	1
McEvoy, Matt, Holy Cross	.313	150	32	47	15	1	3	27	9
Andruskevich, Bill, Holy Cross	.312	138	19	43	11	2	2	26	4
Ritz, Mike, Bucknell	.310	168	32	52	10	1	7	32	8
Czajka, Corey, Holy Cross	.307	150	39	46	8	2	3	21	10

INDIVIDUAL PITCHING LEADERS
(Minimum 40 Innings)

	W	L	ERA	G	SV	IP	H	BB	SO
#Farmery, Gregg, Bucknell	3	2	1.61	22	7	28	30	5	16
Cooney, Matt, Navy	5	3	3.63	11	0	52	42	20	45
Cerminaro, Dave, Lehigh	4	4	3.80	13	1	64	63	13	43
Miller, Kevin, Bucknell	7	0	3.86	18	2	51	43	19	29
McDevitt, Rich, Navy	3	5	3.99	10	0	50	47	14	19
Bumgardner, Wes, Army	5	3	4.06	9	0	51	52	18	29
Allen, Zachery, Bucknell	5	4	4.40	13	0	59	71	13	30
Andalman, Brian, Lehigh	0	8	4.88	11	0	63	74	28	35
Montano, Mike, Holy Cross	5	3	4.93	10	1	49	50	14	33
Vane, Scott, Navy	1	6	5.02	11	0	66	83	17	32
Foster, Matt, Navy	5	2	5.07	11	0	55	66	17	37
Duer, James, Lafayette	2	1	5.09	9	0	41	49	13	27
Tambellini, Matt, Lafayette	2	5	5.14	10	0	42	51	15	29
Adams, Buck, Army	5	3	5.32	15	1	71	89	23	51
Grant, R.J., Bucknell	3	1	5.63	10	0	40	40	34	28

SOUTHEASTERN CONFERENCE

EAST	Conference		Overall	
	W	L	W	L
Georgia	20	10	47	22
Tennessee	18	12	48	20
South Carolina	17	13	49	20
Florida	16	14	35	27
Vanderbilt	9	21	24	31
Kentucky	7	23	22	34
WEST	**W**	**L**	**W**	**L**
*Louisiana State	18	12	44	22
Mississippi State	17	13	39	24
Mississippi	17	13	39	23
Auburn	15	15	37	21
Alabama	15	15	32	23
Arkansas	11	19	27	29

ALL-CONFERENCE TEAM: C—Jeremy Brown, Jr., Alabama. **1B**—Aaron Clark, Sr., Alabama. **2B**—Mike Fontenot, So., Louisiana State. **3B**—Wally Pontiff, So., Louisiana State. **SS**—Chris Burke, Jr., Tennessee. **OF**—Gabe Gross, Jr., Auburn; Garris Gonce, Jr., South Carolina; Burney Hutchinson, Jr., Mississippi. **DH**—Doc Brooks, Jr., Georgia. **P**—Lane Mestepey, Fr., Louisiana State; Tanner Brock, Jr., Mississippi State. **RP**—Lee Gronkiewicz, Sr., South Carolina.

Player of the Year: Chris Burke, Tennessee. **Freshman of the Year:** Lane Mestepey, Louisiana State. **Coach of the Year:** Ron Polk, Georgia.

INDIVIDUAL BATTING LEADERS
(Minimum 125 At-Bats)

	AVG	AB	R	H	2B	3B	HR	RBI	SB
Burke, Chris, Tennessee	.435	271	105	118	21	11	20	60	49
Keppinger, Jeff, Georgia	.389	262	69	102	15	5	18	73	10

Moore, Bryan, LSU	.373	241	59	90	25	0	7	50	1
Hopkins, Brandon, Tenn.	.367	128	30	47	6	1	4	24	4
Brown, Jeremy, Alabama	.363	190	47	69	8	1	10	48	3
Knott, Jon, Miss. State	.359	195	36	70	9	3	8	41	4
Coffey, David, Georgia	.358	173	44	62	9	0	5	33	7
Hoefler, Jeff, Arkansas	.357	171	37	61	11	1	1	22	4
Hutchinson, Burney, Miss.	.356	219	69	78	15	6	14	63	15
Goss, Matt, Florida	.356	208	52	74	11	2	11	54	15
Theriot, Ryan, LSU	.353	266	67	94	18	3	1	48	17
Nystrom, Peter, Florida	.353	190	34	67	12	0	5	48	5
Christian, Josh, Mississippi	.351	222	44	78	17	3	14	58	4
Estrada, Kevin, Florida	.351	251	61	88	11	1	3	41	35
Floyd, Michael, So. Carolina	.350	200	33	70	11	1	3	28	10
Kent, Mailon, Auburn	.350	240	50	84	16	2	3	51	15
Pontiff, Wally, LSU	.347	268	47	93	9	1	7	58	3
Tyler, Gordon, Kentucky	.343	166	26	57	12	1	4	29	3
Christensen, Jeff, Tennessee	.341	258	59	88	22	3	12	73	24
McClanahan, Scott, Alabama	.341	220	50	75	13	3	4	35	15
Fontenot, Mike, LSU	.339	221	64	75	13	0	14	50	7
Sterbens, Chad, Mississippi	.339	218	45	74	7	0	0	24	4
Gonce, Garris, South Carolina	.338	204	51	69	18	2	9	35	6
Fletcher, Jeff, Arkansas	.338	154	22	52	7	1	4	30	6
Boyd, Brent, Alabama	.336	226	49	76	13	0	9	49	2
Clark, Aaron, Alabama	.335	212	66	71	15	2	20	71	5
Neufeld, Andy, Georgia	.334	287	71	96	20	1	10	38	5
Thornhill, Mark, Georgia	.332	262	37	87	21	0	2	49	0
Daniel, Stevie, Tennessee	.330	276	67	91	25	3	4	61	46
Jeffcoat, Bryon, So. Carolina	.329	243	50	80	16	1	16	54	8
Luellwitz, Sean, Vanderbilt	.328	198	33	65	15	2	6	38	0
Brinson, Matthew, Miss. State	.328	198	37	65	6	1	7	46	1
Gross, Gabe, Auburn	.327	208	51	68	19	1	15	67	11
Swann, Adam, Georgia	.326	270	58	88	26	1	6	62	5
Pickrell, Brad, Kentucky	.326	132	20	43	12	0	2	18	4
Raymer, David, LSU	.324	148	42	48	13	1	4	30	11
Stonard, Peter, Alabama	.320	194	34	62	11	2	0	32	7
Davidson, Aaron, Florida	.319	238	52	76	16	2	6	39	30
Bennett, Kris, Tennessee	.316	231	47	73	10	0	4	41	13
Kiger, Mark, Florida	.314	194	44	61	9	3	2	31	19
Linden, Todd, LSU	.312	256	65	80	14	1	20	76	9
Preston, Spencer, Kentucky	.312	202	36	63	12	0	8	36	1
Lafferty, Carl, Mississippi	.311	209	29	65	6	2	3	36	1
Pratt, Trent, Auburn	.308	201	46	62	19	2	7	41	2
Moran, Javon, Auburn	.306	255	54	78	14	3	1	36	24
Freeman, Ashley, Vanderbilt	.306	206	40	63	11	1	6	40	5
Edge, Kris, Georgia	.304	168	37	51	7	0	0	21	9
Harrison, Vince, Kentucky	.304	217	45	66	15	1	10	39	10
Meyer, Drew, South Carolina	.303	274	54	83	12	2	7	37	20
Zinsman, Zeph, LSU	.302	162	33	49	9	0	16	45	0
Crossett, Scott, Arkansas	.300	130	30	39	6	1	1	15	8

INDIVIDUAL PITCHING LEADERS
(Minimum 50 Innings)

	W	L	ERA	G	SV	IP	H	BB	SO
Gronkiewicz, Lee, So. Carolina	2	1	1.31	36	19	62	31	23	77
Medders, Brandon, Miss. State	6	3	2.13	17	6	51	34	14	56
Ramsey, Keith, Florida	4	3	2.24	31	9	52	48	14	56
Cormier, Lance, Alabama	9	5	2.30	17	2	110	109	29	73
Gliemmo, Hayden, Auburn	7	1	2.77	13	0	68	69	20	51
Taylor, Blake, So. Carolina	5	4	3.30	27	1	63	59	19	56
Carswell, Jeffery, Georgia	10	2	3.32	24	1	60	55	16	62
Montrenes, Pete, Mississippi	10	4	3.45	16	0	117	94	39	107
Bell, Gary, South Carolina	10	5	3.46	20	0	101	99	42	74
Brandon, Eric, Auburn	6	3	3.47	25	5	86	79	20	61
Speigner, Levale, Auburn	8	3	3.49	18	0	113	116	23	56
Roehl, Scott, Arkansas	4	4	3.54	15	0	53	56	16	31
Carter, Mark, Alabama	7	3	3.57	18	0	98	94	36	65
Marchbanks, David, So. Carolina	7	1	3.63	15	0	57	55	15	46
Crowe, Brandon, Tennessee	6	0	3.68	16	3	51	56	15	46
Collums, Joey, Miss. State	3	3	3.71	16	0	53	50	20	47
Hogan, Gary, Arkansas	3	4	3.73	11	0	51	47	22	24
Mestepey, Lane, LSU	11	3	3.75	22	1	139	158	37	79
Shapton, Bill, Georgia	5	1	3.81	24	0	50	48	22	37
Wade, Scott, Kentucky	4	9	3.84	16	0	103	117	25	52
Bradshaw, Nick, Mississippi	4	2	3.90	24	1	65	78	14	43
Bouknight, Kip, So. Carolina	10	4	3.99	23	2	124	127	53	104
Maholm, Paul, Miss. State	8	4	4.06	16	0	95	106	30	87
Paxton, Colby, Auburn	5	4	4.06	21	0	58	53	34	22
Spigner, Chris, So. Carolina	7	4	4.08	17	0	90	77	57	70
Green, B.J., Alabama	5	1	4.13	12	0	57	57	14	36
Nugent, Tim, LSU	7	3	4.38	21	0	76	69	48	55
Brock, Tanner, Miss. State	7	2	4.44	16	0	93	82	46	72
Brown, Jeremy, Georgia	7	4	4.50	20	2	92	101	28	80
Scobie, Jason, LSU	4	3	4.69	21	0	96	109	31	59
Yates, Adam, Mississippi	7	3	4.73	25	4	72	64	44	61
Larson, Adam, Miss. State	2	5	4.83	17	0	50	62	22	49

	W	L	ERA	G	SV	IP	H	BB	SO
Dueitt, Cory, Auburn	3	4	4.89	25	2	70	81	18	32
Ransom, Robert, Vanderbilt	4	2	4.92	24	2	71	81	30	48
Moorhead, Brandon, Georgia	4	2	4.96	14	0	65	75	23	58
Gates, Brian, Tennessee	6	5	5.03	19	3	77	89	28	76
Youman, Shane, LSU	3	2	5.17	18	1	54	67	33	33
Woodward, Jared, Alabama	3	3	5.17	25	2	56	65	12	39
Hicklen, Patrick, Tennessee	5	4	5.27	16	3	80	92	23	61
Corcoran, Roy, LSU	8	4	5.48	28	0	69	67	31	62
#Allen, Wyatt, Tennessee	10	3	6.30	18	0	104	109	59	**110**

SOUTHERN CONFERENCE

	Conference W	L	Overall W	L
Georgia Southern	21	9	42	20
The Citadel	20	10	38	24
Furman	18	11	30	25
Western Carolina	18	11	30	26
UNC Greensboro	17	12	31	28
Appalachian State	12	14	21	32
East Tennessee State	13	17	23	32
Charleston	10	16	24	28
Wofford	9	17	17	31
Davidson	10	20	19	32
Virginia Military Institute	8	19	15	32

ALL-CONFERENCE TEAM: C—Matt Lauderdale, So., Charleston; James Marino, Jr., Davidson. **1B**—Philip Hartig, Sr., The Citadel. **2B**—Shane Schumaker, Jr., UNC Greensboro. **3B**—Dallas McPherson, Jr., The Citadel. **SS**—Wes Timmons, Jr., Appalachian State. **OF**—Nathan Copeland, Sr., East Tennessee State; Donovan Minero, Jr., Western Carolina; Alan Beck, So., Western Carolina. **DH**—Scott Henley, Sr., Georgia Southern. **P**—Eric Talbert, Jr., The Citadel; Brett Lewis, Jr., Georgia Southern. **RP**—Randy Corn, Jr., The Citadel.

Player of the Year: Philip Hartig, The Citadel. **Pitcher of the Year:** Eric Talbert, The Citadel. **Rookie of the Year:** Derek Norman, Furman. **Coach of the Year:** Rodney Hennon, Georgia Southern.

INDIVIDUAL BATTING LEADERS
(Minimum 125 At-Bats)

	AVG	AB	R	H	2B	3B	HR	RBI	SB
Henley, Scott, Ga. Southern	.398	249	48	99	16	0	16	84	4
Baxter, Andy, East Tenn.	.394	221	65	87	25	1	12	49	8
Beck, Alan, West. Carolina	.385	179	56	69	20	0	13	62	7
Minero, Donovan, West. Car.	.379	219	49	83	12	0	17	74	8
Copeland, Nathan, East Tenn.	.379	214	53	81	23	2	17	67	3
Timmons, Wes, App. State	.374	190	55	71	21	1	5	36	12
Spearman, Jemel, Ga. Southern	.372	207	51	77	17	2	0	44	11
Etherington, Adam, Furman	.363	190	39	69	19	**6**	5	49	12
Norman, Derek, Furman	.362	210	49	76	17	5	5	42	7
Hartig, Philip, Citadel	.361	252	56	91	23	2	16	69	13
Herring, Matt, Ga. Southern	.353	218	50	77	12	0	12	54	4
Cross, Brandon, East Tenn.	.351	228	43	80	16	0	4	45	6
Cotugno, Chris, Wofford	.348	135	28	47	6	0	6	26	0
McPherson, Dallas, Citadel	.347	242	54	84	22	0	11	58	8
Buchanan, Todd, West. Car.	.344	215	47	74	16	0	5	45	6
Griffin, David, Citadel	.344	247	32	85	9	0	0	25	3
Ryan, Billy, Davidson	.342	152	22	52	9	1	4	36	0
Schumaker, Shane, UNCG	.341	223	58	76	16	4	8	52	28
Dantzler, Brook, Citadel	.341	126	20	43	13	0	0	16	2
Schade, Ryan, West. Carolina	.340	209	43	71	16	1	6	40	7
Hyder, Ryan, East Tennessee	.336	146	20	49	10	1	2	21	2
Catanzaro, Chris, VMI	.335	179	38	60	17	1	8	39	1
Lauderdale, Matt, Charleston	.333	159	32	53	18	1	3	40	3
Riley, Rob, VMI	.333	171	30	57	11	0	3	35	0
Little, Marko, App. State	.332	205	31	68	10	1	3	29	8
Hayes, Chad, UNCG	.330	209	41	69	17	0	2	33	12
Orlandos, Nick, Charleston	.328	201	31	66	6	0	0	25	3
Livingston, Chad, Wofford	.326	190	36	62	21	1	3	23	0
Purcell, Jack, Davidson	.326	193	44	63	7	2	3	27	10
Baker, Rocky, Ga. Southern	.323	217	47	70	13	5	4	42	16
Frend, Tim, Davidson	.323	198	46	64	12	1	9	39	6
Ramsey, Matt, VMI	.323	167	34	54	5	1	3	26	0
Balcom, Jasha, Charleston	.322	202	38	65	10	4	4	31	13
#Walker, Chris, Ga. Southern	.303	218	47	66	8	4	0	25	**41**

INDIVIDUAL PITCHING LEADERS
(Minimum 50 Innings)

	W	L	ERA	G	SV	IP	H	BB	SO
Talbert, Eric, Citadel	8	3	**2.06**	17	0	113	93	28	96
Corn, Randy, Citadel	8	3	2.50	35	**12**	58	45	24	88
Cable, Taft, UNCG	5	2	2.50	34	9	68	55	13	60
Mau, Ryan, Charleston	6	5	2.82	14	0	96	92	39	83
Toler, Ted, UNCG	6	5	2.89	40	3	72	74	32	67
Hancock, Everett, UNCG	6	4	3.13	23	1	95	98	47	54

	W	L	ERA	G	SV	IP	H	BB	SO
Hamer, Matt, Citadel	1	1	3.20	33	2	65	62	21	60
Lewis, Brett, Ga. Southern	**9**	2	3.25	16	0	114	121	38	95
#Hutchings, Andy, Charleston	3	2	3.25	27	**12**	28	25	16	28
David, Toby, Furman	8	4	3.32	15	0	103	94	20	58
Etheridge, Corey, Furman	4	4	3.62	15	0	80	73	31	57
Hendrix, Phil, VMI	3	2	3.72	29	6	75	80	20	58
Dove, Dennis, Ga. Southern	8	3	3.76	17	0	91	83	46	87
Williams, Paul, Citadel	2	3	3.97	25	0	66	63	25	61
Mincey, T.W., Citadel	6	4	4.03	20	2	60	63	26	40
Milner, Robby, Charleston	4	6	4.23	14	0	87	83	27	78
Fulmer, T.A., Citadel	6	4	4.29	17	0	84	98	26	65
Mastny, Tom, Furman	8	5	4.35	17	0	89	99	36	55
Osterman, Tate, Wofford	6	6	4.35	18	0	101	120	33	63
Michael, Scooter, UNCG	5	3	4.36	23	1	87	91	32	58
Foster, Seth, Western Carolina	5	4	4.54	17	0	69	75	20	43
Metzger, Jay, UNCG	1	2	4.85	24	1	69	74	19	54
Foley, Dan, Western Carolina	7	3	4.91	25	1	81	96	16	56
Burton, Jared, Western Carolina	5	2	5.01	19	0	93	119	23	67
Rogers, Brian, Ga. Southern	5	1	5.13	29	2	56	65	24	61
Lehr, George, Wofford	6	7	5.12	21	1	102	117	40	53
Casey, Reid, East Tennessee	3	8	5.22	20	1	117	139	49	**107**

SOUTHLAND CONFERENCE

	Conference W	L	Overall W	L
Northwestern State	19	8	38	17
Louisiana-Monroe	17	10	36	24
*Texas-Arlington	15	11	39	25
Southwest Texas State	15	11	36	22
Texas-San Antonio	15	12	30	29
Lamar	13	14	37	24
McNeese State	12	15	29	25
Nicholls State	12	15	26	30
Southeastern Louisiana	8	19	22	33
Sam Houston State	8	19	19	31

ALL-CONFERENCE TEAM: C—Matt McIntyre, Sr., Texas-San Antonio. **1B**—Kevin Mitchell, Sr., McNeese State. **2B**—David Quattrociocchi, Jr., Northwestern State. **3B**—Willie Core, Sr., Lousiana-Monroe. **SS**—Louie Carmona, Sr., Southwest Texas State. **OF**—Daniel Ortmeier, So., Texas-Arlington; Jordan Robison, Sr., Northwestern State; Lance Williams, Sr., Southwest Texas State. **DH**—Brad Hanson, Jr., Northwestern State. **P**—Jared Howton, Sr., Texas-San Antonio; Aaron Dobbins, Jr., Louisiana-Monroe; Pierce Loveless, So., Texas-Arlington.

Player of the Year: Willie Core, Louisiana-Monroe. **Hitter of the Year:** Willie Core, Louisiana-Monroe. **Pitcher of the Year:** Jared Howton, Texas-San Antonio. **Newcomer of the Year:** O.J. King, Northwestern State. **Freshman of the Year:** Josh Gray, Lamar. **Coach of the Year:** John Cohen, Northwestern State.

INDIVIDUAL BATTING LEADERS
(Minimum 125 At-Bats)

	AVG	AB	R	H	2B	3B	HR	RBI	SB
Mitchell, Kevin, McNeese State	.415	193	48	80	20	0	**19**	64	3
Core, Willie, La.-Monroe	.408	211	52	86	15	0	12	56	7
Quatrociocchi, David, NW State	.401	162	50	65	10	2	3	27	7
Hoffpauir, Micah, Lamar	.391	225	51	**88**	**24**	2	8	**65**	9
Hanson, Brad, NW State	.381	197	42	75	16	2	8	52	10
Williams, Lance, SW Texas State	.377	223	55	84	15	3	6	54	15
Pierce, Jeremy, Lamar	.377	175	41	66	14	1	7	48	4
Robison, Jordan, NW State	.372	207	**58**	77	14	**6**	**13**	56	20
Hale, Jeramie, NW State	.369	195	43	72	6	3	0	25	14
Hoorelbeke, Jesse, La.-Monroe	.366	232	38	85	13	2	10	46	4
Wright, C.J., Sam Houston	.365	159	19	58	11	1	4	27	4
Carmona, Louie, SW Texas	.360	186	39	67	11	0	2	28	5
Muller, Luke, Nicholls State	.349	215	43	75	13	3	7	43	1
Wenzel, Hunter, UTSA	.346	159	28	55	8	1	2	26	6
Ferrell, Lou, Sam Houston	.345	148	33	51	17	2	7	27	4
Hernandez, Mickey, Lamar	.342	234	47	80	18	1	4	44	6
Childers, Toby, La.-Monroe	.333	231	38	77	14	1	5	46	4
Topham, Drew, Lamar	.333	189	49	66	17	1	5	46	1
Cooksey, Wes, Lamar	.333	165	27	55	18	0	6	42	2
Anderson, Rondon, Nicholls St.	.330	212	46	70	15	2	15	51	6
Hendricks, K.J., UT-Arlington	.328	250	57	82	10	2	0	34	**36**
James, Jeremy, UTSA	.323	198	33	64	13	2	3	37	11
Ortmeier, Daniel, UT-Arlington	.322	236	40	76	17	4	4	37	15
Estrada, Jaime, La.-Monroe	.321	243	52	78	15	3	3	41	19
Cadwallader, Scott, La.-Monroe	.320	206	50	66	14	5	0	21	28
Schramek, Mark, UTSA	.319	191	40	61	13	3	10	39	3
McIntyre, Matt, UTSA	.317	164	36	52	13	2	3	32	2
Younk, Mark, SW Texas State	.316	190	52	60	12	0	12	51	3
Dieudonne, Aaron, Sam Houston	.313	134	18	42	9	1	3	20	2
Prince, Ran, McNeese State	.312	176	37	55	10	4	8	34	8
Durham, Tyler, NW State	.311	177	39	55	13	**6**	5	46	8

INDIVIDUAL PITCHING LEADERS
(Minimum 50 Innings)

	W	L	ERA	G	SV	IP	H	BB	SO
Walters, Cory, Sam Houston	4	4	2.33	17	0	58	52	14	45
Cooksey, Wes, Lamar	5	4	2.55	29	8	53	45	14	39
Gray, Josh, Lamar	5	2	2.69	14	0	70	75	21	53
Garza, Jarrett, UT-Arlington	7	3	3.02	28	5	54	47	12	48
Snapp, Michael, UT-Arlington	7	4	3.19	27	0	79	68	19	44
Loveless, Pierce, UT-Arlington	6	4	3.30	24	0	104	116	19	71
Howton, Jared, UTSA	9	3	3.35	17	0	99	87	29	86
Makowsky, Carl, NW State	5	0	3.35	18	0	94	87	31	78
Dobbins, Aaron, La.-Monroe	8	2	3.43	17	0	87	95	22	77
Darcey, Aaron, NW State	5	3	3.62	15	1	55	43	28	53
Sawicki, Bobby, SW Texas State	5	5	3.65	16	0	89	91	21	42
Sanches, Zach, NW State	7	3	3.72	22	1	65	67	12	44
Lind, Jason, La.-Monroe	6	5	3.95	18	0	87	88	27	75
King, J.J., NW State	8	2	4.03	15	0	80	68	28	62
Atlee, Thomas, Lamar	3	6	4.09	17	2	70	80	24	53
Olivera, Manuel, SW Texas State	6	2	4.17	14	1	73	82	25	54
Coffey, Charlie, UT-Arlington	4	4	4.20	16	0	56	65	14	29
Fletcher, Jeremy, La.-Monroe	3	5	4.28	12	0	55	62	14	38
Gothreaux, Jared, McNeese State	6	4	4.33	20	2	89	118	22	72
#Carro, Robert, La.-Monroe	4	2	4.58	27	9	37	36	14	36
Srp, Mike, Texas-San Antonio	5	5	4.61	17	0	92	110	18	48
McKeller, Laine, McNeese State	6	5	4.70	16	0	67	88	19	40
#Trosclair, Steve, SE Louisiana	5	6	5.62	13	0	75	75	54	93

SOUTHWESTERN ATHLETIC CONFERENCE

EAST	Conference		Overall	
	W	L	W	L
Alcorn State	21	8	26	19
Jackson State	18	9	29	23
Alabama A&M	15	17	20	29
Mississippi Valley State	10	16	12	36
Alabama State	9	23	14	33

WEST	W	L	W	L
*Southern	28	4	43	12
Texas Southern	22	10	24	28
Grambling State	16	14	27	25
Arkansas-Pine Bluff	7	25	12	37
Prairie View A&M	5	25	6	45

ALL-CONFERENCE TEAM: C—David Bell, Jr., Texas Southern. **1B**—Jason Roy, Sr., Texas Southern. **2B**—Michael Woods, Jr., Southern. **3B**—Byron Tillman, Jr., Alcorn State. **SS**—Ricardo Lee, Jr., Jackson State. **OF**—Stephen Cotton, Jr., Texas Southern; Brandon Tellis, Sr., Jackson State; Rickie Weeks, Fr., Southern. **DH**—Franco Blackburn, Sr., Southern. **P**—Candtobal Encarnacion, Sr., Alcorn State; Torik Harrison, Sr., Southern; Eric Thomas, Jr., Southern; Rashad Washington, Sr., Grambling State.
Player of the Year: Michael Woods, Southern. **Most Outstanding Hitter:** Michael Woods, Southern. **Most Outstanding Pitcher:** Torik Harrison, Southern. **Freshman of the Year:** Rickie Weeks, Southern.

INDIVIDUAL BATTING LEADERS
(Minimum 100 At-Bats)

	AVG	AB	R	H	2B	3B	HR	RBI	SB
Woods, Michael, Southern	.453	170	68	77	27	5	14	54	32
Weeks, Rickie, Southern	.425	181	78	77	13	12	14	70	28
Bell, David, Texas Southern	.382	152	50	58	16	2	9	42	11
Day, Dewan, Jackson State	.370	135	34	50	10	2	3	31	6
Puebla, Fernando, Southern	.367	177	42	65	7	2	1	49	3
Vital, Kevin, Southern	.366	123	38	45	14	0	3	47	0
DeLeon, Mario, Texas Southern	.363	135	31	49	7	1	4	26	4
Peters, Kris, Alcorn State	.359	103	32	37	4	1	0	17	7
Williams, Frank, Ark.-PB	.358	148	30	53	8	0	5	28	3
Chandler, Marcus, Southern	.349	146	51	51	10	8	4	45	13
Goss, Michael, Jackson State	.349	166	46	58	10	3	3	29	13
Turner, Charles, Ark.-PB	.349	126	35	44	8	1	2	29	6
Clayton, Marcus, Alcorn State	.346	136	45	47	10	3	6	43	10
Roy, Jason, Texas Southern	.346	136	40	47	12	0	14	44	4
Johnson, Jerel, Southern	.344	192	48	66	15	1	13	56	9
Ross, Cleitus, Ark.-Pine Bluff	.338	142	27	48	9	5	2	36	2
Willis, Mario, Alcorn State	.336	122	39	41	4	2	0	22	23
Tellis, Brandon, Jackson State	.331	181	44	60	16	1	11	49	15
Hill, Sean, Miss. Valley	.331	133	31	44	3	3	1	10	36
Kidd, Elston, Ark.-Pine Bluff	.331	133	28	44	9	4	2	26	3
Cowan, Bartowski, Ala. State	.327	165	46	54	8	3	2	34	37

INDIVIDUAL PITCHING LEADERS
(Minimum 40 Innings)

	W	L	ERA	G	SV	IP	H	BB	SO
#Primus, Carl, Southern	2	0	2.35	18	9	23	20	5	28
Foster, Roy, Grambling	5	4	2.56	14	0	71	74	23	56
Villanueva, Enrique, Grambling	5	2	3.19	12	0	59	73	21	48

Winder, Marcus, Texas Southern	5	6	3.28	11	0	64	58	37	56
Day, Dewan, Jackson State	3	4	3.29	10	0	55	46	20	39
Harrison, Torik, Southern	8	0	3.31	12	0	68	58	38	57
Encarnacion, Candtobal, Alc. St.	9	2	3.75	13	1	70	63	20	63
Thomas, Eric, Southern	8	1	4.04	13	0	65	60	29	69
Lane, Lavon, Jackson State	5	6	4.10	17	1	59	64	33	54
Johnson, Corey, Alcorn State	4	3	4.15	20	3	65	71	33	52
Washington, Rashad, Grambling	5	5	4.22	13	0	56	66	20	29
Liberto, Joseph, Miss. Valley	3	7	4.48	12	0	61	68	33	62
Anderson-Putman, Jason, South.	6	2	4.50	9	0	48	52	23	35
Pearson, Anthony, Jackson State	9	1	4.66	14	0	77	61	46	91
Jobe, John, Jackson State	6	2	5.05	14	0	52	59	31	62
Yelverton, Brandon, Miss. Valley	3	4	5.15	15	1	54	53	34	52

SUN BELT CONFERENCE

	Conference		Overall	
	W	L	W	L
Middle Tennessee State	17	10	41	17
*South Alabama	17	10	45	19
Florida International	16	11	43	21
Western Kentucky	14	13	32	27
New Orleans	13	14	25	32
Louisiana Tech	12	14	32	26
Arkansas-Little Rock	12	15	26	24
Arkansas State	12	15	22	36
Louisiana-Lafayette	12	15	28	28
New Mexico State	9	17	32	23

ALL-CONFERENCE TEAM: C—Ryan Cattell, Jr., Western Kentucky. **1B**—Nick Gretz, Sr., South Alabama. **2B**—Josh Renick, Sr., Middle Tennessee. **3B**—Brandon Johnson, Sr., Middle Tennessee. **SS**—Miguel Miranda, Sr., Arkansas-Little Rock. **OF**—Mike Quintana, Sr., Florida International; Jake Adams, Sr., Louisiana Tech; Justin Sims, So., Middle Tennessee. **Util**—Brian Houdek, Sr., Western Kentucky. **DH**—Brad Eldred, Jr., Florida International. **P**—Dewon Brazelton, Jr., Middle Tennessee; Willie Collazo, Sr., Florida International. **RP**—Joe Long, Sr., South Alabama.
Player of the Year: Josh Renick, Middle Tennessee. **Pitcher of the Year:** Dewon Brazelton, Middle Tennessee. **Newcomer of the Year:** Casey Blalock, Louisiana Tech. **Freshman of the Year:** Clark Girardeau, South Alabama. **Coach of the Year:** Steve Kittrell, South Alabama.

INDIVIDUAL BATTING LEADERS
(Minimum 125 At-Bats)

	AVG	AB	R	H	2B	3B	HR	RBI	SB
Renick, Josh, Mid Tenn	.420	224	74	94	20	2	8	38	24
Miranda, Miguel, Ark.-LR	.380	184	56	70	9	1	3	36	16
McMains, Derin, Ark.-LR	.379	182	54	69	15	0	11	58	13
Sims, Justin, Mid Tenn	.377	231	61	87	18	6	10	66	12
Wilkinson, Kurt, NMSU	.371	197	62	73	19	2	7	54	22
Gretz, Nick, South Alabama	.375	208	40	78	13	0	10	53	2
Nunez, Hector, Fla. Int.	.370	162	42	60	9	3	11	39	8
Calahan, Scott, South Alabama	.369	225	53	83	18	3	7	43	9
Fox, Matt, Western Ky.	.369	249	59	92	23	0	8	34	18
Dias, Chad, NMSU	.365	137	46	50	11	1	13	46	2
Veloz, Gabe, NMSU	.362	163	41	59	9	1	13	52	2
Montgomery, Craig, La. Tech	.358	226	55	81	18	0	8	37	7
Saloom, Brad, La.-Lafayette	.356	135	25	48	5	0	0	17	3
Moya, Jay, NMSU	.354	144	46	51	8	2	7	38	7
Gragg, John, Ark.-LR	.350	206	59	72	16	1	1	23	19
Mulhern, Ryan, South Alabama	.349	212	49	74	14	3	12	49	5
Nisbett, Marshall, Mid Tenn	.346	243	52	84	21	5	6	46	11
Kenning, Ryan, NMSU	.344	163	43	56	18	1	13	49	4
Bustamante, Daniel, Fla. Int.	.340	141	28	48	14	0	4	28	6
Hall, Chris, Ark.-Little Rock	.340	188	38	64	11	0	5	48	8
Miller, Jeff, New Orleans	.338	207	39	70	20	1	4	37	2
Hanna, Warren, South Alabama	.333	180	32	60	9	0	3	29	4
Quintana, Mike, Fla. Int.	.330	224	58	74	13	2	17	61	13
Turner, Nick, Western Ky.	.327	156	33	51	15	1	8	35	3
Houdek, Brian, Western Ky.	.325	237	49	77	20	3	3	30	7
Robinson, Wade, La. Tech	.323	229	46	74	19	2	0	25	4
Townsend, Tanner, Western Ky.	.322	149	30	48	10	0	4	18	6
Likely, Cameron, South Alabama	.321	218	59	70	7	4	3	28	23
Shelton, Robert, La.-Lafayette	.318	151	36	48	10	2	4	31	4
Simmons, Cullen, La. Tech	.318	198	49	63	11	0	8	45	12
Cattell, Ryan, Western Ky.	.317	161	32	51	11	0	11	41	1
Huntington, Matt, Fla. Int.	.315	241	49	76	9	1	5	35	21
#Bollich, Donnie, New Orleans	.278	223	36	62	4	1	0	12	31

INDIVIDUAL PITCHING LEADERS
(Minimum 50 Innings)

	W	L	ERA	G	SV	IP	H	BB	SO
Brazelton, Dewon, Mid Tenn	13	2	1.42	15	0	127	82	24	154
Long, Joe, South Alabama	3	2	2.45	24	5	55	49	27	46

Hutchison, Ryan, Western Ky.	9	7	2.87	17	0	122	109	35	100
Collazo, Willie, Fla. International	13	1	2.93	20	0	141	137	39	148
Moates, Jason, Mid Tenn	6	2	3.19	13	0	59	43	43	57
Almond, Casey, South Alabama	3	2	3.33	15	0	51	44	35	46
Ramon, Tim, La.-Lafayette	6	4	3.39	16	0	90	87	24	81
Spivey, Mel, South Alabama	5	1	3.48	21	3	54	44	25	52
Williams, John, Mid Tenn	7	1	3.59	14	0	83	68	43	60
Lipari, Tom, New Orleans	8	7	3.79	19	1	114	98	41	88
Zervas, Paul, Fla. Int.	7	4	3.84	20	0	101	93	30	78
Girardeau, Clark, South Alabama	10	4	3.87	22	2	98	83	36	70
Neal, Tony, South Alabama	9	3	3.89	19	0	106	99	39	86
Cuffia, Robby, Arkansas State	6	7	3.95	16	0	109	102	32	75
Templet, Eric, La.-Lafayette	7	5	4.10	16	0	90	79	33	109
#Lugo, Ozzie, Fla. Int.	0	1	4.11	15	6	15	11	14	29
Courtney, Jerry, Fla. Int.	5	7	4.12	18	0	83	79	42	77
Houdek, Brian, Western Ky.	7	4	4.22	18	2	79	75	28	101
Arthur, Tony, Arkansas State	8	8	4.35	20	0	122	133	33	87
Clapp, Marcus, La. Tech	4	2	4.41	28	2	51	56	22	41
Bartsch, John, Western Ky.	6	3	4.55	17	1	59	58	24	39
Blalock, Casey, La. Tech	5	4	4.62	18	1	103	104	28	106
Kirkendall, Adam, La. Tech	6	6	4.63	17	0	80	71	52	62
Gros, Andy, La.-Lafayette	2	6	4.72	30	2	74	85	20	70
Stander, Mark, New Orleans	6	5	4.78	13	0	75	79	20	75
Goforth, Tommy, Arkansas State	3	8	4.80	23	1	75	74	35	52

TRANSAMERICA CONFERENCE

	Conference		Overall	
	W	L	W	L
Central Florida	22	5	51	14
Stetson	19	8	43	17
Jacksonville	18	9	39	25
Campbell	17	10	33	21
Florida Atlantic	14	13	36	24
Troy State	12	15	27	28
Samford	12	15	20	34
Mercer	10	17	24	28
Georgia State	8	19	20	35
Jacksonville State	3	24	11	39

ALL-CONFERENCE TEAM: C—Chad Oliva, Jr., Jacksonville. **1B**—Bryan Zenchyk, Fr., Stetson. **2B**—Tony Della Costa, Sr., Campbell. **3B**—Chad Ehrnsberger, Sr., Central Florida. **SS**—Jeremy Kurella, Sr., Central Florida. **OF**—Frank Corr, Sr., Stetson; Jeff Christy, Jr., Stetson; L.J. Biernbaum, Jr., Florida Atlantic. **DH**—Scott Biernacki, Sr., Jacksonville. **P**—Jason Arnold, Sr., Central Florida; Lenny DiNardo, Jr., Stetson; Justin Pope, Jr., Central Florida. **RP**—Casey Shumaker, So., Central Florida.

Player of the Year: Justin Pope, Central Florida. **Freshman of the Year:** Bryan Zenchyk, Stetson. **Coach of the Year:** Jay Bergman, Central Florida.

INDIVIDUAL BATTING LEADERS
(Minimum 125 At-Bats)

	AVG	AB	R	H	2B	3B	HR	RBI	SB
Kurella, Jeremy, Cent. Fla.	.401	247	63	99	16	1	7	49	17
Johnson, Andy, Cent. Fla.	.389	203	45	79	13	1	1	44	2
Della Costa, Tony, Campbell	.388	201	52	78	17	5	7	60	11
Zenchyk, Bryan, Stetson	.383	206	40	79	16	0	4	39	1
Christy, Jeff, Stetson	.378	225	60	85	17	1	16	55	15
Evans, Robert, Samford	.376	178	43	67	16	1	6	30	9
Corr, Frank, Stetson	.374	203	55	76	13	3	18	60	3
Reier, Chris, Jacksonville	.372	164	48	61	11	1	0	20	11
Valdes, Mike, Fla. Atlantic	.371	202	44	75	16	0	6	38	6
Weed, B.J., Jacksonville	.371	229	52	85	17	2	2	29	18
Coates, Brad, Campbell	.368	182	35	67	15	4	0	21	10
Fields, Jay, Georgia State	.361	202	44	73	11	5	4	23	19
Levengood, Kyle, Mercer	.355	200	40	71	15	1	11	49	5
Fox, Mike, Cent. Fla.	.354	229	47	81	26	1	9	61	3
Harwell, David, Mercer	.349	195	49	68	14	0	4	35	11
Nover, Phil, Jacksonville	.343	207	54	71	11	2	8	49	9
Snyder, Brian, Stetson	.341	211	54	72	17	6	7	49	3
Wilson, Andy, Stetson	.341	220	50	75	17	0	11	47	2
Kendrick, Josh, Troy State	.340	200	33	68	12	1	8	33	9
Newton, Ryan, Mercer	.338	130	30	44	6	0	3	9	2
Newman, Lance, Troy State	.337	205	40	69	9	0	3	28	25
McDonough, James, Mercer	.335	167	48	56	13	0	10	30	20
Oliva, Chad, Jacksonville	.333	207	57	69	16	0	19	68	6
Blair, Brandon, Mercer	.330	179	30	59	12	1	13	54	0
Miller, Drew, Troy State	.328	183	38	60	20	0	8	33	2
Ehrnsberger, Chad, UCF	.326	224	61	73	16	2	16	72	4
Biernbaum, L.J., Fla. Atlantic	.326	221	53	72	13	1	13	54	19
Frost, Jeremy, Cent. Fla.	.325	231	52	75	15	3	13	56	14
Johnson, Dale, Jacksonville	.323	226	41	73	8	0	6	42	5
Summers, Wayne, UCF	.320	197	47	63	15	1	2	34	15
Beale, Rusty, Stetson	.319	188	34	60	3	2	4	38	12

Evans, Sae, Samford	.318	173	32	55	9	1	6	25	6
Myers, Mike, Cent. Fla.	.317	230	70	73	18	2	6	44	29
Keelan, Johnny, Campbell	.317	161	38	51	10	1	2	20	6
Smith, Casey, Troy State	.311	206	33	64	10	3	4	37	3
Carter, Nic, Campbell	.310	210	44	65	7	7	7	30	31
Sumner, Cory, Samford	.310	203	27	63	9	0	1	20	4

INDIVIDUAL PITCHING LEADERS
(Minimum 50 Innings)

	W	L	ERA	G	SV	IP	H	BB	SO
Pope, Justin, Central Florida	15	1	1.68	17	0	123	97	27	158
Shumaker, Casey, Jacksonville	7	6	1.91	33	12	75	48	40	117
Arnold, Jason, Cent. Florida	14	3	1.97	19	0	119	82	32	150
Lincoln, Bryan, Stetson	6	0	2.06	16	1	52	53	22	47
Petersen, Benjamin, Fla. Atlantic	7	5	2.41	17	0	123	132	18	97
Hepler, Wes, Campbell	11	4	2.61	20	0	131	107	22	97
Bernard, Jason, Troy State	11	4	2.78	17	0	130	116	35	93
Shippey, Steve, JSU	4	8	3.29	14	0	90	98	18	83
Oglesby, Jason, Stetson	9	4	3.46	18	0	83	95	25	51
Jones, Brian, Mercer	4	6	3.56	19	1	99	102	25	90
Sullivan, Brian, Stetson	6	3	3.69	19	0	83	87	21	65
DiNardo, Lenny, Stetson	10	3	3.78	20	0	112	111	31	131
Collins, Jack, Stetson	10	3	3.90	28	3	85	92	20	47
Truty, Darren, Jacksonville	9	5	4.00	20	0	81	78	40	73
Nix, Josh, Jacksonville State	2	5	4.03	22	1	58	60	22	59
Dedmon, Ty, Samford	4	6	4.09	19	1	95	80	47	72
Core, Danny, Fla. Atlantic	7	8	4.42	19	0	108	97	52	103
Corn, Jesse, JSU	2	7	4.50	13	1	60	71	12	50
Finch, Rob, Campbell	4	4	4.57	13	0	69	88	12	50
Poole, Shaun, Campbell	5	4	4.62	19	0	62	57	30	61
Hawkins, David, Georgia State	3	7	4.77	15	1	94	114	30	67
Jarrett, Brett, Mercer	7	4	4.78	25	2	85	88	33	65
Page, Jason, Mercer	9	7	4.84	23	0	110	100	44	86
Daws, Josh, Jacksonville	3	4	4.93	16	0	95	93	37	79

WEST COAST CONFERENCE

WEST	Conference		Overall	
	W	L	W	L
***Pepperdine**	25	5	42	18
San Diego	20	10	35	21
St. Mary's	10	20	18	36
Portland	9	21	20	34
COAST	W	L	W	L
Gonzaga	17	13	28	27
Santa Clara	17	13	23	33
San Francisco	14	16	28	26
Loyola Marymount	8	22	21	37

ALL-CONFERENCE TEAM: C—Kris Zacuto, Jr., Loyola Marymount. **1B**—Jared Pitney, Sr., Pepperdine. **2B**—Dan Garcia, Jr., Pepperdine. **3B**—Taggert Bozied, Sr., San Francisco. **SS**—Tony Garcia, Jr., Pepperdine. **OF**—Dane Ball, Sr., Pepperdine; Jack Headley, So., Santa Clara; Woody Cliffords, Jr., Pepperdine; Jared Hertz, Sr., Gonzaga. **DH**—Barry Matthews, Sr., Gonzaga. **Util**—Tom Caple, So., San Diego. **P**—Noah Lowry, Jr., Pepperdine; Dan Haren, Jr., Pepperdine; Ricky Barrett, So., San Diego.

Player of the Year: Dan Haren, Pepperdine. **Pitcher of the Year:** Noah Lowry, Pepperdine. **Freshman of the Year:** Joey Prast, San Diego. **Coach of the Year:** Steve Hertz, Gonzaga.

INDIVIDUAL BATTING LEADERS
(Minimum 125 At-Bats)

	AVG	AB	R	H	2B	3B	HR	RBI	SB
Pitney, Jared, Pepperdine	.397	239	46	95	22	0	14	67	4
Garcia, Danny, Pepperdine	.374	238	58	89	19	3	8	53	27
Teahen, Mark, St. Mary's	.369	203	40	75	17	6	1	36	4
Prast, Joey, San Diego	.365	170	34	62	16	1	4	38	4
Harris, Josh, San Diego	.360	242	50	87	14	1	3	30	13
Queen, Matt, Santa Clara	.356	222	42	79	21	1	7	57	1
Garcia, Tony, Pepperdine	.354	226	56	80	13	1	6	38	8
Spooner, Tim, St. Mary's	.354	209	29	74	10	2	3	38	2
Matthews, Barry, Gonzaga	.348	224	52	78	16	1	10	33	0
Janz, Jeramy, San Francisco	.342	193	40	66	17	0	7	42	4
Headley, Jack, Santa Clara	.341	217	53	74	15	2	1	25	16
Wayne, Brett, St. Mary's	.340	191	31	65	16	3	0	21	9
Cliffords, Woody, Pepperdine	.336	250	63	84	23	0	2	31	25
Bozied, Taggert, San Francisco	.335	212	51	71	13	2	12	38	20
Zacuto, Kris, LMU	.333	219	44	73	17	1	8	43	2
Sain, Greg, San Diego	.332	214	46	71	14	1	16	52	9
Booth, Steve, San Francisco	.327	171	24	56	7	0	2	24	3
Hertz, Jared, Gonzaga	.326	218	33	71	10	0	7	44	0
Hirsh, Robert, LMU	.324	176	27	57	8	1	0	29	5
Perez, Tommy, LMU	.321	168	38	54	7	2	10	41	1
Ball, Dane, Pepperdine	.320	203	32	65	11	2	2	30	4

Rodland, Eric, Gonzaga	.320	231	40	74	15	1	1	25	8
McCoy, Mike, San Diego	.320	241	49	77	13	3	4	42	20
Hanson, Travis, Portland	.316	212	31	67	14	2	4	35	4
Richardson, Kevin, Gonzaga	.315	197	32	62	8	0	11	34	0
Whitesell, Joshua, LMU	.314	172	21	54	10	0	4	30	0
Marian, Jason, San Diego	.313	201	35	63	15	0	7	45	8
Caple, Tom, San Diego	.313	195	53	61	14	2	3	33	11
Haren, Dan, Pepperdine	.308	224	33	69	8	0	5	47	1
Hull, Eric, Portland	.308	201	38	62	7	2	1	23	2
Lockin, Billy, LMU	.308	133	21	41	4	0	0	9	6

INDIVIDUAL PITCHING LEADERS
(Minimum 50 Innings)

	W	L	ERA	G	SV	IP	H	BB	SO
Lowry, Noah, Pepperdine	14	2	1.71	18	1	121	88	41	142
Haren, Dan, Pepperdine	11	3	2.22	17	1	130	106	31	97
Caple, Tom, San Diego	5	3	2.43	25	9	85	72	23	77
Yarbrough, Zach, Portland	4	2	2.91	17	0	59	62	17	43
Barrett, Ricky, San Diego	9	3	3.19	17	0	96	79	35	86
Matthews, Barry, Gonzaga	9	2	3.23	14	0	106	104	16	83
Gray, Chris, LMU	1	2	3.48	33	0	52	63	20	35
Wilson, Aaron, San Diego	5	1	3.54	13	1	61	52	21	37
Foppert, Jesse, San Francisco	8	4	3.75	16	1	98	104	38	112
Rose, Kevin, San Francisco	4	4	3.82	17	1	71	73	30	53
Hixson, David, Gonzaga	5	8	4.04	20	1	65	79	15	44
Kinney, Jeremy, San Francisco	2	4	4.04	22	0	65	76	19	47
Adams, Jay, Pepperdine	5	3	4.17	17	2	91	95	27	54
Dunkle, Peter, San Francisco	4	4	4.17	18	1	58	67	31	43
Redmond, John, Santa Clara	5	4	4.39	14	0	80	95	16	37
McConnell, Kellan, Santa Clara	4	2	4.43	16	0	63	64	14	43
Byer, Mike, St. Mary's	5	6	4.49	17	0	106	127	39	61
Corra, Kyle, Portland	3	4	4.55	16	1	63	73	18	26
Hollod, Matt, Portland	2	7	4.56	15	0	77	91	24	47
Hull, Eric, Portland	5	6	4.59	17	0	100	123	17	67
Diefenderfer, Joe, Santa Clara	5	6	4.92	16	0	90	111	23	62
Ramirez, Greg, Pepperdine	5	4	4.95	24	3	73	80	27	55
Cordova, Vincent, LMU	3	4	5.23	18	0	76	108	28	42
Thogersen, Chris, San Francisco	1	3	5.53	22	2	54	57	22	32

WESTERN ATHLETIC CONFERENCE

	Conference		Overall	
	W	L	W	L
Rice	26	10	47	20
Fresno State	22	14	41	25
Texas Christian	21	15	32	28
San Jose State	21	15	37	22
Nevada	17	19	30	26
Hawaii	16	20	29	27
Hawaii-Hilo	3	33	5	45

ALL-CONFERENCE TEAM: C—Brad Harper, Jr., Fresno State. **1B**—JaRell McIntyre, Jr., Nevada. **2B**—Gabe Lopez, Jr., San Jose State. **3B**—Hunter Brown, Jr., Rice. **SS**—Josh Labandeira, Sr., Fresno State. **OF**—Tom Bates, Sr., Texas Christian; Austin Davis, Fr., Rice; A.J. Porfirio, Jr., Rice; Chris Dickerson, Fr., Nevada. **DH**—Bo Bryant, Jr., Nevada. **Util**—Matthew Purtell, Sr., Hawaii. **P**—Kenny Baugh, Sr., Rice; Chris Bradshaw, Sr., Texas Christian; Jon Skaggs, Sr., Rice. **RP**—Stan Newton, Sr., Texas Christian.

Player of the Year: Josh Labandeira, Fresno State. **Pitcher of the Year:** Kenny Baugh, Rice. **Freshman of the Year:** Austin Davis, Rice. **Coach of the Year:** Bob Bennett, Fresno State.

INDIVIDUAL BATTING LEADERS
(Minimum 125 At-Bats)

	AVG	AB	R	H	2B	3B	HR	RBI	SB
Gillies, Mike, Nevada	.402	189	43	76	14	1	4	35	2
McIntyre, JaRell, Nevada	.388	214	46	83	15	2	11	47	2
Ruiz, Junior, San Jose State	.374	206	60	77	15	3	4	43	23
Labandeira, Josh, Fresno State	.367	267	62	98	18	4	15	68	8
Omori, Gregg, Hawaii	.367	229	40	84	25	0	11	62	2
Lopez, Gabe, San Jose State	.353	258	62	91	18	5	5	40	14
Macha, Erick, Texas Christian	.350	243	51	85	9	4	5	33	18
Davis, Austin, Rice	.346	257	73	89	18	2	6	29	5
Maguire, Matt, Nevada	.346	205	41	71	6	0	4	30	5
Porfirio, A.J., Rice	.345	281	77	97	21	3	11	55	8
Bryant, Bo, Nevada	.339	180	48	61	4	2	13	37	0
Lopez, Oscar, Fresno State	.337	249	45	84	17	2	5	43	3
Brown, Hunter, Rice	.335	260	46	87	25	2	7	44	5
Arnold, Eric, Rice	.325	252	50	82	17	2	15	65	6
McGehee, Casey, Fresno State	.324	247	45	80	14	4	5	50	4
Hass, Michael, Nevada	.320	181	40	58	11	2	8	32	2
Frandsen, Kevin, SJSU	.319	185	31	59	4	0	2	28	2
Scalabrini, Patrick, Hawaii	.319	213	46	68	14	1	7	38	19
Dickerson, Chris, Nevada	.317	189	40	60	13	2	11	46	3
Trofholz, Terry, Texas Christian	.316	196	40	62	9	3	2	16	12
Olmstead, Walter, TCU	.308	227	43	70	18	3	10	53	4

Gemoll, Brandon, Fresno State	.306	255	47	78	22	1	13	58	3
Bates, Tom, Texas Christian	.306	222	37	68	14	2	9	55	3
Purtell, Matthew, Hawaii	.304	217	44	66	10	0	0	25	25
Settle, Mike, Texas Christian	.300	217	33	65	19	1	6	44	3
Harper, Brad, Fresno State	.297	222	42	66	16	0	8	42	0
Price, Jason, TCU	.295	200	38	59	15	3	5	22	4
Kimura, Danny, Hawaii	.294	201	22	59	12	0	2	36	3
Roman, Jesse, Rice	.291	258	43	75	21	4	6	67	1
Garcia, Nick, Fresno State	.289	190	30	55	13	2	0	26	6
Herrera, Joey, Nevada	.289	152	22	44	6	0	2	20	5
Rivera, Rudy, Texas Christian	.287	188	31	54	8	8	3	31	6

INDIVIDUAL PITCHING LEADERS
(Minimum 50 Innings)

	W	L	ERA	G	SV	IP	H	BB	SO
Baugh, Kenny, Rice	13	2	2.17	22	0	141	106	54	163
Herce, Steven, Rice	6	1	2.37	17	2	68	61	21	63
Skaggs, Jon, Rice	9	4	2.65	17	0	119	89	62	110
Moran, Nick, Fresno State	6	6	3.09	19	2	90	83	23	78
Sherman, Chris, San Jose State	9	6	3.10	18	0	107	125	30	69
Gonzalez, Jonathan, Rice	5	1	3.17	13	1	54	54	22	45
Barzilla, Philip, Rice	3	4	3.17	30	10	54	57	16	46
Tribe, Philip, Rice	4	2	3.19	26	1	73	70	41	79
Runyon, Bob, Fresno State	10	1	3.54	20	0	127	134	22	93
Cook, Andy, San Jose State	4	1	3.66	23	0	59	63	18	47
Coleman, Jeff, Hawaii	8	6	3.75	19	0	122	113	45	97
Minor, Zach, Fresno State	8	5	4.02	19	0	107	119	24	78
Bradshaw, Chris, TCU	8	5	4.10	17	0	101	103	31	93
Rogelstad, Jeremy, SJSU	5	5	4.18	20	1	95	111	16	76
Rasner, Darrell, Nevada	5	8	4.20	17	0	114	111	41	96
George, Jahseam, SJSU	5	1	4.47	18	0	54	58	16	43
Adinolfi, Tim, San Jose State	8	5	4.60	18	0	94	112	32	95
Fritz, Ben, Fresno State	3	5	4.65	27	7	72	71	28	58
Nieves, Francisco, Fresno State	7	4	4.67	26	0	104	111	36	51
Crowder, Justin, Texas Christian	7	6	4.81	17	0	95	119	28	71
Tombrella, David, TCU	5	5	4.88	14	0	63	73	10	30
Miramontes, Mateo, Nevada	10	3	5.13	17	0	102	115	50	76

INDEPENDENTS

	Overall	
	W	L
Miami	53	12
Belmont	30	23
Centenary	23	36
Texas A&M-Corpus Christi	18	36
Texas-Pan American	12	40

INDIVIDUAL BATTING LEADERS
(Minimum 100 At-Bats)

	AVG	AB	R	H	2B	3B	HR	RBI	SB
Wilson, Josh, TAMU-CC	.411	185	41	76	16	1	7	45	1
Rodriguez, Javy, Miami	.382	241	63	92	12	4	5	60	66
Grenda, B.J., Centenary	.374	227	43	85	23	1	9	58	0
Soukup, Dan, Belmont	.372	156	32	58	14	0	4	22	1
Duranski, Mark, Centenary	.353	221	52	78	12	2	1	39	9
Clyde, Ryan, TAMU-CC	.350	177	47	62	16	0	19	61	1
Howard, Kevin, Miami	.336	250	55	84	20	1	4	46	9
Shandler, Michael, TAMU-CC	.335	176	37	59	13	3	4	28	4
Winterer, Seth, Centenary	.330	188	36	62	12	1	2	36	6
Rodriguez, Mike, Miami	.329	231	68	76	15	2	5	43	53
Mannix, Kevin, Miami	.328	189	42	62	10	2	4	38	8
Sledge, Chris, Belmont	.328	131	28	43	6	1	5	24	6
Matienzo, Danny, Miami	.324	219	46	71	13	2	13	64	3
Braithwaite, Sean, TAMU-CC	.312	186	48	58	4	3	8	36	11
Nettles, Marcus, Miami	.310	149	49	45	5	0	0	12	44
Heinrichs, Darren, Texas-PA	.310	145	33	45	10	1	10	33	5
Schick, Jason, Centenary	.307	153	36	47	12	5	7	44	6
Warpool, Jason, Belmont	.305	151	23	46	11	2	5	28	2
Jimerson, Charlton, Miami	.302	162	47	49	7	2	10	41	31

INDIVIDUAL PITCHING LEADERS
(Minimum 40 Innings)

	W	L	ERA	G	SV	IP	H	BB	SO
DeBold, Luke, Miami	5	2	1.74	44	4	57	47	7	67
Huguet, George, Miami	1	0	2.03	44	14	44	35	13	34
Sheffield, Chris, Miami	2	0	3.30	15	0	46	35	29	69
Renes, Alex, Belmont	4	3	3.48	19	4	62	53	24	42
Farmer, Tom, Miami	15	2	3.54	20	0	114	122	33	80
Bengochea, Kiki, Miami	9	4	4.10	18	0	108	106	38	89
Walker, Brian, Miami	12	1	4.22	19	0	100	109	38	68
Jaggers, Brandon, Belmont	6	4	4.73	17	1	84	85	39	39
Fisher, Cody, Belmont	6	6	4.75	18	0	85	111	28	63
Garcia, Jason, Texas-PA	1	4	5.12	13	0	46	51	24	34
Bogy, Justin, Texas-PA	2	3	5.63	14	0	46	60	15	24

Bridesmaids no longer
After consecutive runner-up finishes, St. Thomas (Minn.) celebrates winning the Division III College World Series

Gutierrez' homers take St. Mary's to first Division II championship

Jesse Gutierrez capped an MVP tournament effort by going 4-for-4 with two home runs and four RBIs to lead St. Mary's (Texas) past Central Missouri State 11-3 in the championship game of the 2001 Division II College World Series. The win, in front of 2,738 at Paterson Field in Montgomery, Ala., earned the first national title for the Rattlers program.

Gutierrez, a transfer from Division I independent

NCAA DIVISION II

Texas-Pan American, capped his MVP effort with home runs No. 27 and 28 of the season, third-most in Division II history. Freshman righthander Clay Wentworth (9-0, 1.47) also shined for St. Mary's, pitching a complete-game six hitter. He struck out 11 and walked seven.

St. Mary's (50-13), which lost to Central Missouri (53-10) earlier in the tournament, overcame an early 2-0 deficit, scoring three runs in the first. It broke a 3-3 tie in the third on Gutierrez' first home run. From there Wentworth blanked the Mules, while the Rattlers' offense roughed up Central Missouri starter P.J. McGinnis, sending him to his first loss in 15 decisions.

Tampa, which entered the CWS as the top-ranked team in Division II, went out in two straight games.

NCAA DIVISION III

After runner-up finishes in 1999 and 2000, St. Thomas (Minn.) went 4-1 to claim the 2001 NCAA Division III College World Series in Appleton, Wis. St. Thomas beat Marietta (Ohio) 8-4 in the final. Nine seniors led the way for the Tommies, including outfielder Brad Bonine, the tournament MVP, and second baseman Jake Mauer, the older brother of No. 1 overall draft pick Joe Mauer.

The Tommies led Division III in batting at .372, with 11 players hitting .345 or better, and scored 458 runs, a per-game average of 9.3. The Tommies hit .391 in the CWS, and placed five players on the all-tournament team.

Bonine was named MVP after going 3-for-5 with four RBIs and three runs in the title game. Overall, he went 12-for-21 with seven runs, nine RBIs, three doubles and two homers. Bonine also played on the Toms' 1999-2000 ice hockey team that lost to Norwich (Ver.) in the national finals.

Mauer broke the Toms' school records for career runs and hits. He finished with a .391 career average and led

FINAL **POLL**	
NCAA Division II	
1. St. Mary's (Texas)	50-13
2. Central Missouri State	53-10
3. North Florida	47-17
4. Delta State (Miss.)	50-11
5. Tampa	49-10
6. Kennesaw State (Ga.)	45-15
7. Sonoma State (Calif.)	49-17
8. Alabama-Huntsville	41-17
9. Abilene Christian (Texas)	43-17
10. Georgia College	41-18

FINAL **POLL**	
NCAA Division III	
1. St. Thomas (Minn.)	39-10
2. Marietta (Ohio)	48-9
3. Montclair State (N.J.)	38-11
4. Salisbury State (Md.)	33-13
5. Cortland State (N.Y.)	34-11
6. Southern Maine	37-14
7. Chapman (Calif.)	37-11
8. Illinois Wesleyan	37-15
9. Emory (Ga.)	36-9
10. Allegheny (Pa.)	31-11

the 2001 team in batting (.449), hits (83) and RBIs (58). Like his younger brother, Mauer was drafted by the hometown Minnesota Twins.

The loss by Marietta spoiled an otherwise spectacular season by junior righthander Matt DeSalvo, who went 17-1, 1.50 and set a Division III record with 205 strikeouts in 120 innings.

NAIA

In its last season in NAIA competition before a move to NCAA Division I, Birmingham-Southern exceeded its wildest dreams.

The Panthers (55-11) defeated two-time defending champion Lewis-Clark State (Idaho) on its home field 11-3 in the title game, their second straight win against the Warriors in the tournament. The last team to beat LCSC

Mike Nickoli

two in a row on its home field was Washington State in 1993. Lewis-Clark State had won 11 NAIA titles and lost in the title game for the fifth time. It finished the year at 54-14.

Birmingham-Southern did its damage against Wes Hutchison, MVP of the 2000 CWS for the Warriors. A four-run fifth inning gave the Panthers the lead, and a three-run homer by Matt Lambert in the eighth put an exclamation mark on the game.

Righthander Mike Nickoli, a fourth-round pick of the Angels, moved to 9-2 on the season with six innings of work in the title game, striking out five while giving up seven hits and two runs in his second start of the CWS. Freshman third baseman Connor Robertson won the MVP award after going 13-for-27 (.481) with eight RBIs, eight runs and three homers. He went 1-for-4 in the deciding game.

Cumberland (Tenn.) lefthander/outfielder Chris Smith was selected Baseball America's Small College Player of the Year. Smith went 9-2, 2.13 with 115 strikeouts in 84 innings while also hitting .414-14-67. He was the seventh player selected in the June draft.

JUNIOR COLLEGES

After losing its opener, North Central Texas rallied to win its next six games and claim the 2001 National Junior College World Series Division I championship. It was the third straight year a team from Texas won the title.

The final game, a seesaw affair the Lions won 7-6 over Utah's Dixie State, didn't end until North Central closer Kevin Smiley struck out the final two batters he faced for his 15th save, stranding the potential tying run at second base.

"I wanted this more than anything," Smiley said. "And it worked out. This is incredible. We're the best team in the nation."

Freshman Michael Mora had the game-winning hit, which came after tournament MVP Blake Justice loaded the bases by getting hit in the face with a pitch. Justice stayed in the game and watched Mora line a two-run single to center for his second and third RBIs of the game.

Delaware Tech captured the NJCAA Division II national title by defeating Phoenix College 3-1 in the championship game. Sophomore righthander Mark Comolli, who shut out

PLAYERS OF THE YEAR

Chris Smith   Scott Hairston

MARC McCLINTOCK

Small College: Chris Smith, lhp-of, Cumberland (Tenn.)
After earning second-team All-America honors as a sophomore outfielder with Florida State, Smith transferred to Cumberland so he could get a chance to pitch more often. The 6-foot-1, 190-pounder went 9-2, 2.13 with 115 strikeouts in 84 innings, and was an All-American again as an outfielder. The Orioles drafted him seventh overall.

Junior College: Scott Hairston, 2b, Central Arizona JC
The latest progeny of the Hairston baseball family, Scott Hairston entered the season with momentum as the MVP of the 2000 National Baseball Congress World Series. He led the nation in batting and RBIs on his way to being the Diamondbacks' third-round pick.

PREVIOUS WINNERS
SMALL COLLEGE

1989—Steve DiBartolomeo, rhp, New Haven (Conn.)
1990—Sam Militello, rhp, Tampa
1991—Sid Roberson, lhp, North Florida
1992—Michael Tucker, ss, Longwood (Va.)
1993—Billy Wagner, lhp, Ferrum (Va.)
1994—Rick Ladjevich, 3b, Central Missouri State
1995—Tim Jorgensen, ss, Wisconin-Oshkosh
1996—Dave Townsend, rhp, Delta State (Miss.)
1997—Donnie Thomas, 1b-lhp, Marietta (Ohio)
1998—Keith Hart, 1b, Lubbock Christian (Texas)
1999—Andy Heimbach, rhp, Mount Vernon Nazarene (Ohio)
2000—Jim Kavouras, of, Tampa

JUNIOR COLLEGE

1989—David Evans, rhp, San Jacinto (Texas)
1990—Kelly Stinnett, c, Seminole (Okla.)
1991—Frank Rodriguez, ss-rhp, Howard (Texas)
1992—Benji Simonton, of, Diablo Valley (Calif.)
1993—Don Denbow, of, Blinn (Texas)
1994—Justin Bowles, of, Galveston (Texas)
1995—Brian Conley, ss, Volunteer State (Tenn.)
1996—Derek Baker, 3b, Rancho Santiago (Calif.)
1997—Aaron Akin, rhp, Cowley County (Kan.)
1998—Brian Cole, of, Navarro (Texas)
1999—Kade Johnson, c, Seminole (Okla.)
2000—Brandon Lyon, rhp, Dixie (Utah)

Phoenix in a first-round game, had a shutout going into the final inning of the championship game before he was replaced with one out. Overall, Comolli went 2-0 with 20 strikeouts in the tournament to earn MVP honors.

Eastfield (Texas) College won the NJCAA Division III crown, beating Columbus State (Ohio) Community College 5-1 in the final.

Riverside City College, which had more players drafted in 2001 than any junior college in the nation, won its second straight California Community College championship as it overwhelmed Fresno City College 13-6 in the championship game. California teams are not affiliated with the NJCAA.

SMALL COLLEGES

NCAA DIVISION II

Site: Montgomery, Ala.
Participants: Central Missouri State (49-8); Delta State, Miss. (47-9); Kutztown, Pa. (38-17); Massachusetts-Lowell (38-17); North Florida (45-15); St. Mary's, Texas (46-12); Southern Illinois-Edwardsville (40-25); Tampa (49-8).
Champion: St. Mary's (4-1).
Runner-Up: Central Missouri State (4-2).
Outstanding Player: Jesse Gutierrez, c/1b, St. Mary's

ALL-AMERICA TEAM

Pos.	Player, School	Yr.	AVG	HR	RBI
C	Eli Whiteside, Delta State (Miss.)	Jr.	.401	8	75
1B	Chris Umphres, Central Missouri State	Jr.	.448	11	89
2B	Mark Bugger, SIU-Edwardsville	Sr.	.409	7	70
3B	Marcus Van Every, Delta State (Miss.)	Sr.	.399	9	81
SS	Jon Cahill, Massachusetts-Lowell	Sr.	.422	8	51
IF	Jesse Gutierrez, St. Mary's (Texas)	Sr.	.424	28	97
OF	Tom Carrow, Tampa	Sr.	.423	14	57
	Lenny Carter, Massachusetts-Lowell	Sr.	.401	13	60
	Ray Danzy, Central Oklahoma	Sr.	.385	23	62
	Fehlandt Lentini, Sonoma State (Calif.)	Sr.	.427	4	57
DH	Brad Bouras, Columbus State (Ga.)	Sr.	.374	15	67
		Yr.	**W**	**L**	**ERA**
SP	Ricky Belk, Central Oklahoma	Jr.	14	0	3.41
	Corey Clinefelter, Central Missouri	Sr.	13	1	3.01
	Tod Ewasko, North Florida	Jr.	14	3	2.78
	Matt Incinelli, North Florida	Jr.	12	1	3.23
RP	Kris Sutton, Tampa	Sr.	2	2	2.09

Player of the Year: Chris Umphres, Central Missouri State. **Pitcher of the Year:** Kris Sutton, Tampa.

NATIONAL LEADERS

BATTING AVERAGE
(Minimum 100 At-Bats)

Player, School	Yr.	AB	H	AVG
Mike Mann, North Dakota St.	So.	116	60	.517
Kevin Webster, Texas Lutheran	Sr.	112	55	.491
Mike Aviles, Concordia (N.Y.)	So.	195	92	.472
Ken Kessaris, St. Anselm (N.H.)	Jr.	159	75	.472
Pete Rodriguez, Bridgeport (Conn.)	Jr.	149	70	.470
Jon Doyle, Adelphi (N.Y.)	Sr.	132	62	.470
Mike Goodman, Regis (Colo.)	Sr.	142	65	.458
Matt Meyr, Missouri Southern	Sr.	186	85	.457
Pete Cavouto, Queens (N.Y.)	Sr.	130	59	.454
Sam Christensen, So. Colorado	Jr.	208	94	.452
Craig Prausackas, So. Connecticut	Sr.	209	94	.450

Department Leaders: Batting

Dept.	Player, School	Yr.	G	Total
R	Craig Ringe, Central Missouri	Jr.	63	89
	Fehlandt Lentini, Sonoma State (Calif.)	Sr.	65	89
H	Fehlandt Lentini, Sonoma State (Calif.)	Sr.	65	117
TB	Jesse Gutierrez, St. Mary's (Texas)	Sr.	63	204
2B	Sam Christensen, Southern Colorado	Jr.	59	32
3B	Mike Rodriguez, Incarnate Word (Texas)	Sr.	56	13
HR	Jesse Gutierrez, St. Mary's (Texas)	Sr.	63	28
RBI	Jesse Gutierrez, St. Mary's (Texas)	Sr.	63	97
SB	Mike Scarinci, Molloy (N.Y.)	Jr.	50	63

EARNED RUN AVERAGE
(Minimum 50 Innings)

Player, School	Yr.	IP	ER	ERA
Dan Sowash, Lock Haven (Pa.)	Jr.	70	9	1.16
Clay Wentworth, St. Mary's (Texas)	Sr.	79	13	1.47
Luke Steidlmayer, UC Davis	So.	99	19	1.73
Josh King, Northeastern Oklahoma	Sr.	102	20	1.76
Aaron Taylor, Wisconsin-Parkside	Sr.	87	17	1.77
Jason Taylor, West Liberty (W.Va.)	So.	76	15	1.77
Bret Giaudrone, SIU-Edwardsville	Sr.	96	20	1.88
Bryan Larson, North Dakota	Sr.	51	11	1.94
Derek Johnson, Winona State (Minn.)	Sr.	55	12	1.98
Judd Songster, Southern Colorado	Jr.	63	14	2.00

Department Leaders: Pitching

Dept.	Player, School	Yr.	G	Total
W	Ricky Belk, Central Oklahoma	Jr.	19	14
	Tod Ewasko, North Florida	Jr.	22	14
	P.J. McGinnis, Central Missouri	Jr.	15	14
	Brian Rauch, North Florida	So.	22	14
	Brad Reed, Kennesaw State (Ga.)	Sr.	29	14
SV	Kris Sutton, Tampa	Sr.	31	19
SO	Fernando Tadefa, St. Mary's (Texas)	Jr.	17	133

NCAA DIVISION III

Site: Appleton, Wis.
Participants: Chapman, Calif. (37-9); Cortland State, N.Y. (33-9); Illinois Wesleyan (37-13); Marietta, Ohio (44-7); Montclair State, N.J. (35-9); Salisbury State, Md. (31-11); St. Thomas, Minn. (35-9); Southern Maine (36-12).
Champion: St. Thomas (4-1).
Runner-Up: Marietta (4-2).
Outstanding Player: Brad Bonine, of, St. Thomas.

ALL-AMERICA TEAM

Pos.	Player, School	Yr.	AVG	HR	RBI
C	Jay Coakley, Marietta (Ohio)	Jr.	.446	19	78
	Jose Cortez, Pomona-Pitzer (Calif.)	So.	.439	17	66
1B	Drew Caravella, Ohio Wesleyan	Jr.	.447	16	82
2B	Brad O'Connell, Wisconsin-Stout	Sr.	.524	12	42
3B	Craig Conway, Montclair State (N.J.)	Sr.	.446	9	52
SS	Nick Tempesta, Eastern Connecticut	Sr.	.418	6	49
OF	Bob Capaldo, College of New Jersey	Jr.	.500	5	51
	Travis Gaidos, York (Pa.)	Jr.	.490	7	54
	Eric Swedberg, Worcester State (Mass.)	Jr.	.462	14	70
DH	Dan Penberthy, Wooster (Ohio)	Jr.	.497	10	56
UT	Derek Johnson, Denison (Ohio)	Sr.	.492	6	45
		Yr.	**W**	**L**	**ERA**
SP	Ryan Donegan, Emory (Ga.)	Sr.	11	1	1.11
	Matt DeSalvo, Marietta (Ohio)	Jr.	17	1	1.50
	Andrew Tisdale, Chapman (Calif.)	So.	11	1	1.83
	Mike Howell, Cortland State (N.Y.)	Jr.	11	1	2.38
UT	Derek Johnson, Denison (Ohio)	Sr.	7	6	3.78

Player of the Year: Jay Coakley, Marietta (Ohio). **Pitcher of the Year:** Matt DeSalvo, Marietta (Ohio).

NATIONAL LEADERS

BATTING AVERAGE
(Minimum 100 At-Bats)

Player, School	Yr.	AB	H	AVG
Brad O'Connell, Wisconsin-Stout	Sr.	124	65	.524
Armando Reyes, Averett (Va.)	Jr.	119	62	.521
Robert Capaldo, College of New Jersey	Jr.	136	68	.500
Dan Penberthy, Wooster (Ohio)	Jr.	151	75	.497
Derek Johnson, Denison (Ohio)	Sr.	124	61	.492
Travis Gaidos, York (Pa.)	Jr.	153	75	.490
Steve Osborne, St. Joseph's (Maine)	Sr.	160	77	.481
Eric Haynoski, Pittsburgh-Bradford	So.	101	48	.475
Chris Chaffinch, Wesley (Del.)	Sr.	114	54	.474
Justin Shaw, Muskingum (Ohio)	Jr.	163	77	.472
Tony DeLude, Delaware Valley (Pa.)	Jr.	122	57	.467
Jaime Ricigliano, Fredonia St. (N.Y.)	Jr.	101	47	.465
Colin Renick, College of New Jersey	Jr.	155	72	.465
Jabe Bergeron, Williams (Mass.)	Fr.	158	73	.462
Eric Swedberg, Worcester St. (Mass.)	Jr.	156	72	.462

Department Leaders: Batting

Dept.	Player, School	Yr.	G	Total
R	Shaun Richardson, Southern Maine	Sr.	51	69
H	Craig Conway, Montclair State (N.J.)	Sr.	49	91
TB	Steve Osborne, St. Joseph's (Maine)	Sr.	44	165
2B	Kyle DeSpain, Hanover (Ind.)	Jr.	45	25
3B	Trevor Purcell, Mount St. Mary (N.Y.)	Jr.	40	11
HR	Steve Osborne, St. Joseph's (Maine)	Sr.	44	22
RBI	Drew Caravella, Ohio Wesleyan	Jr.	52	82
SB	Jude Burger, Wartburg (Iowa)	Jr.	47	43

EARNED RUN AVERAGE
(Minimum 40 Innings)

Player, School	Yr.	IP	ER	ERA
Trey Lamb, Marietta (Ohio)	So.	73	9	1.11
Ryan Donegan, Emory (Ga.)	Sr.	97	12	1.11
Yani Rosenberg, Johns Hopkins (Md.)	Sr.	68	10	1.32
Kevin Cadres, Bridgewater St. (Mass.)	Sr.	68	10	1.33
Star Kriger, Salisbury State (Md.)	So.	52	8	1.38
Ryan Costello, Montclair State (N.J.)	Jr.	78	12	1.39
Russ Berger, Johns Hopkins (Md.)	Fr.	50	8	1.45
Jeff Wilson, Brockport (N.Y.)	So.	48	8	1.49
Matt DeSalvo, Marietta (Ohio)	Jr.	120	20	1.50
Michael Frost, Trinity (Texas)	Fr.	54	9	1.50

Department Leaders: Pitching

Dept.	Player, School	Yr.	G	Total
W	Matt DeSalvo, Marietta (Ohio)	Jr.	21	17
SV	Rob George, Allegheny (Pa.)	Sr.	19	11
	Mike Spavento, Wheaton (Mass.)	Jr.	25	11
SO	Matt DeSalvo, Marietta (Ohio)	Jr.	21	205

SMALL COLLEGES

NAIA

WORLD SERIES

Site: Lewiston, Idaho.
Participants: Bellevue, Neb. (46-16); Biola, Calif. (45-11); Birmingham-Southern (50-10); Dallas Baptist (39-16); Indiana Tech (49-22); Lewis-Clark State, Idaho (50-12); Mobile, Ala. (40-18); Ohio Dominican (36-17); Warner Southern, Fla. (51-14); Western Oregon (38-18).
Champion: Birmingham-Southern (5-1).
Runner-Up: Lewis-Clark State (4-2).
Outstanding Player: Connor Robertson, 3b, Birmingham-Southern.

ALL-AMERICA TEAM

Pos.	Player, School	Yr.	AVG	HR	RBI
C	Bill Julson, NW Oklahoma State	Sr.	.410	17	87
	Gene Stajduhar, Lewis-Clark (Idaho)	Jr.	.354	8	36
1B	Adam Manley, Missouri Valley (Mo.)	Jr.	.379	29	77
2B	Justin Knolhoff, McKendree (Ill.)	Sr.	.421	8	56
3B	Justin Turner, Warner Southern (Fla.)	Jr.	.407	16	68
SS	Scott Hilinski, Warner Southern (Fla.)	Jr.	.359	14	75
IF	Donald Kelly, Point Park (Pa.)	Jr.	.450	2	45
OF	David Burkholder, Grand View (Iowa)	Sr.	.521	27	88
	Mario Delgado, Oklahoma City	Sr.	.465	19	90
	Matt Hellman, Lewis-Clark (Idaho)	Sr.	.381	10	67
	Chris Smith, Cumberland (Tenn.)	Sr.	.414	17	67
DH	Edwin Rodriguez, Mount Mercy (Iowa)	Jr.	.445	24	87
		Yr.	W	L	ERA
SP	Dave Beck, Cumberland (Tenn.)	Sr.	10	1	2.11
	Jeff Francis, British Columbia	So.	12	3	0.92
	Kory Melancon, Mobile (Ala.)	Sr.	14	1	2.47
	Chris Schroeder, Oklahoma City	Sr.	13	1	1.64
RP	Josh Harris, Auburn-Montgomery (Ala.)	Jr.	5	3	1.60

Player of the Year: Mario Delgado, Oklahoma City.

NATIONAL LEADERS

BATTING AVERAGE
(Minimum 100 At-Bats)

Player, School	Yr.	AB	H	AVG
Dave Burkholder, Grand View (Iowa)	Sr.	178	92	.521
Drew Phillips, NW Oklahoma State	Fr.	214	106	.495
Brian Ayers, Friends (Kan.)	Fr.	110	53	.482
Mike Morabite, Thomas (Ga.)	Sr.	157	75	.478
Aaron Brown, Park (Mo.)	Sr.	120	57	.475
Chris Moreside, Mayville State (N.D.)	Sr.	136	64	.471
Ben Colling, Olivet Nazarene (Ill.)	So.	180	84	.467
Mario Delgado, Oklahoma City	Sr.	243	113	.465
Craig Nevels, Tri-State (Ind.)	Sr.	119	55	.462
Devin Jones, Park (Mo.)	Sr.	126	58	.460
Joe Bolstad, Sioux Falls (S.D.)	Jr.	111	51	.459
Mike Waddell, Mt. Vernon Nazarene (Ohio)	Sr.	165	72	.436
Bret Shaffer, Friends (Kan.)	Sr.	139	60	.432
Aaron Bay, Evangel (Mo.)	Jr.	163	70	.429
Mark Ferrer, Oklahoma City	Jr.	166	71	.428
Brian Heerman, Evangel (Mo.)	Sr.	162	69	.426

Department Leaders: Batting

Dept.	Player, School	Yr.	G	Total
R	Drew Phillips, NW Oklahoma State	Fr.	61	81
	Dave Burkholder, Grand View (Iowa)	Sr.	51	81
H	Mario Delgado, Oklahoma City	Sr.	69	113
2B	Brandon Florence, Albertson (Idaho)	Sr.	60	28
3B	Ben Colling, Olivet Nazarene (Ill.)	So.	47	13
HR	Adam Manley, Missouri Valley (Mo.)	Jr.	64	29
RBI	Mario Delgado, Oklahoma City	Sr.	69	90
SB	Bret Shaffer, Friends (Kan.)	Sr.	44	45

EARNED RUN AVERAGE
(Minimum 50 Innings)

Player, School	Yr.	IP	ER	ERA
David McWatters, Bellevue (Neb.)	Sr.	114	20	1.57
Chris Schroeder, Oklahoma City	Sr.	88	16	1.64
Adam Heiden, Sioux Falls (S.D.)	So.	62	13	1.89
Dave Beck, Cumberland (Tenn.)	Sr.	102	24	2.11
Chris Smith, Cumberland (Tenn.)	Jr.	84	20	2.13
Matt Zach, Bellevue (Neb.)	So.	89	23	2.34
Nate Zettler, Union (Ky.)	Jr.	80	21	2.37
Jason Stefani, Albertson (Idaho)	Jr.	86	23	2.42
Trevor Bishop, Mayville State (N.D.)	Sr.	63	17	2.45
Chris Fontes, Friends (Kan.)	Sr.	51	15	2.63

Department Leaders: Pitching

Dept.	Player, School	Yr.	G	Total
W	Chris Schroeder, Oklahoma City	Sr.	15	13
SO	Dave Beck, Cumberland (Tenn.)	Sr.	17	136

JUNIOR COLLEGE

NJCAA DIVISION I

WORLD SERIES

Site: Grand Junction, Colo.
Participants: Central Alabama (35-20); Cowley County, Kan. (46-14); Dixie State, Utah (48-12); Eastern Oklahoma State (26-26); Iowa Western (40-17); Miami-Dade (45-10); Middle Georgia (38-23); North Central Texas (47-14); Spartanburg Methodist, S.C. (49-10); Texarkana, Texas (39-19).
Champion: North Central Texas (6-1).
Runner-Up: Dixie State (4-2).
Outstanding Player: Blake Justice, inf, North Central Texas.

ALL-AMERICA TEAM

C—Omir Santos, East Central (Mo.). **INF**—Scott Hairston, Central Arizona; Brett Brown, Allegany (Md.); Chip Briggs, Jackson State (Tenn.); Victor Diaz, Grayson County (Texas). **OF**—Adam Riddle, New Mexico JC; Victor Rosario, Lake City (Fla.); Tory Haven, Highland (Kan.). **DH**—Fernando Diaz, Southwestern (Iowa). **P**—Wes Detwiler, Cowley County (Kan.); Grant Reynolds, Wallace State (Ala.); Kevin Poenitzsch, Galveston (Texas).

Player of the Year: Scott Hairston, ss, Central Arizona.

NATIONAL LEADERS
BATTING AVERAGE
(Minimum 100 At-Bats)

Player, School	AB	H	AVG
Scott Hairston, Central Arizona	187	94	.503
Joe Guillon, Johnson County (Kan.)	152	75	.493
Clint Turman, Mississippi Delta	119	58	.487
Brett Brown, Allegany (Md.)	162	76	.469
Jerry Fulton, Allegany (Md.)	157	73	.465
Edwin Maysonet, Mississippi Delta	124	55	.444
Eric Allen, Logan (Ill.)	188	83	.441
David Cheek, Darton (Ga.)	132	58	.439
Michael Collins, Central Arizona	165	72	.436
Justin Galvan, El Paso	140	61	.436

Department Leaders: Batting

Dept.	Player, School	G	Total
HR	Matt Armstrong, Santa Fe (Fla.)	45	20
	Joe Guillon, Johnson County (Kan.)	47	20
RBI	Scott Hairston, Central Arizona	60	86
SB	Matt Ryan, Louisburg (N.C.)	33	59

EARNED RUN AVERAGE
(Minimum 50 innings)

Player, School	IP	ER	ERA
Zachery Quinonez, Mississippi Delta	61	10	1.48
Justin Toone, San Jacinto (Texas)	71	13	1.65
David Acosta, Central Arizona	108	21	1.76
Jonathan Albaladejo, Miami-Dade	98	20	1.85
Frank Yeilding, Central Alabama	88	21	2.14
Rich Harden, Central Arizona	97	23	2.14
Zach Parker, San Jacinto (Texas)	87	22	2.28
Mark Ferguson, Spart. Methodist (S.C.)	63	16	2.30
Benjamin Williams, Faulkner State (Ala.)	68	18	2.40
Lance Johnston, Rend Lake (Ill.)	81	22	2.45

Department Leaders: Pitching

Dept.	Player, School	G	Total
W	David Acosta, Central Arizona	19	12
SO	Rich Harden, Central Arizona	18	127

NJCAA DIVISION II

WORLD SERIES

Site: Millington, Tenn.
Participants: Bevill State, Ala. (35-24); Delaware Tech (36-5); Frederick, Md. (33-9); Grand Rapids, Mich. (40-21); Iowa Central (42-21); Parkland, Ill. (50-12); Phoenix College (29-29); St. Louis-Forest Park (40-20).
Champion: Delaware Tech (4-0).
Runner-Up: Phoenix College (4-2).
Outstanding Player: Mark Comolli, rhp, Delaware Tech.

NJCAA DIVISION III

WORLD SERIES

Site: Batavia, N.Y.
Participants: Columbus State, Ohio (46-19); Dawson, Montana (33-14); Dutchess, N.Y. (29-16); Eastfield, Texas (37-12); Gloucester County, N.J. (42-7); Hudson Valley, N.Y. (32-8); Montgomery, Md. (28-28); Quinsigamond, Mass. (32-12).
Champion: Eastfield (4-0).
Runner-Up: Columbus State (4-2).
Outstanding Player: Chris Meeks, Eastfield.

HIGHSCHOOL

Breathing a collective sigh of relief
Seminole overcame pressure to win the national high school championship

Seminole High overcomes adversity to go wire-to-wire in national prep poll

BY JOHN ROYSTER

Even in the fall of 2000, Seminole (Fla.) High looked like an unusually clear choice as the top high school team in the nation for the spring of 2001. But no one could have foreseen how accurate that analysis truly was.

The Warhawks, located in the Tampa Bay area of Florida, had two of the top eight high school prospects for the 2001 draft in first baseman Casey Kotchman and righthander Ryan Dixon. The supporting cast included at least three other players who were being heavily scouted. It had all the makings of being the best high school team ever.

Then shortstop Bryan Bass transferred over the winter from Westminster Academy in Fort Lauderdale, and Seminole suddenly had three of the top eight prospects.

The short way of telling the rest of the story is that Seminole did win the national championship. It won all 31 of its games—at least on the field—and went wire to wire as the No. 1 team in the Baseball America/National High School Baseball Coaches Association poll.

Officially, though, its record was 21-10. It forfeited its first 10 wins when the Florida High School Activities Association ruled Bass ineligible, after initially approving his transfer. The association's reversal came because it discovered a break in Bass' residence chain—he had lived with a host family in Fort Lauderdale, and with his mother after his transfer, a violation of the rules. In addition to the forfeits, Bass was ruled ineligible for the balance of the season.

About the same time, Dixon went down with partially

torn cartilage in his shoulder. He felt discomfort from the first pitch of his first start, but an MRI showed no damage. He tried to pitch in another game, but had to come out and a second, more specialized MRI revealed the damage. Dixon, who had been clocked up to 95 mph, had surgery and was out for the year.

So Seminole played most of the season without two of those top-eight prospects, and still ran the table. That's how good the original roster had been.

"The season felt like four seasons thrown together with all of the adversity," said first-year Seminole coach Scott Miller. "It was an unfortunate administrative error (with Bass), then the injuries. But these kids wouldn't quit. When they came against the wall they responded every time."

Some of the adversity came from tough opponents. Seminole had two regular season wins over nearby Dunedin, the preseason No. 4 team and another club that overcame injuries. One of the games was won on outfielder Donyelle Williams' single in the bottom of the seventh inning, breaking a 6-6 tie.

The Warhawks also won their last three games with late-inning rallies, including the regional championship game against Countryside of Clearwater and the state semifinal against Tate of Gonzalez.

But the biggest miracle was saved for last, as the Warhawks rallied from a 4-0, sixth-inning deficit against St. Thomas Aquinas of Fort Lauderdale in the 5-A state championship game.

Seminole tied the game in the top of the sixth with

PREVIOUS **WINNERS**
Previous No. 1-ranked teams in the Baseball America/National High School Baseball Coaches Association poll:
1992—Westminster Christian HS, Miami
1993—Greenway HS, Phoenix
1994—Sarasota (Fla.) HS
1995—Germantown (Tenn.) HS
1996—Westminster Christian HS, Miami
1997—Jesuit HS, Tampa
1998—Vestavia Hills (Ala.) HS
1999—Lassiter HS, Marietta, Ga.
2000—Gloucester Catholic HS, Gloucester City, N.J.

four runs on a two-run double by Kotchman, an RBI single by Errol Blumer and a sacrifice fly by Phil Stillwell. The winning run came in the top of the seventh in bizarre fashion, as St. Thomas Aquinas righthander Mike Gulla balked home Jon Riggleman with the bases loaded.

Gulla was called for moving after coming set. St. Thomas Aquinas didn't argue, and mounted a threat of its own in the bottom of the seventh. It put runners at first and second with one out before Steven Encinosa grounded into a double play.

"It just doesn't seem realistic to win a game like that," Miller said. "It's a shame the game ended like that. They played so well, and we fought so hard to come back and tie it."

Dunedin lost early in the state playoffs, 7-3 to Jefferson of Tampa in a 4-A regional quarterfinal, and was 19th in the final national poll.

Three of the Falcons' pitchers, including the top prospect, Kyle Schmidt, were injured when a car driven by

HIGH SCHOOL TOP 50

Baseball America's final 2000 Top 50, selected in conjunction with the National High School Baseball Coaches Association.

Rank	Team, City	Record	Accomplishment	Top Player
1	#Seminole (Fla.) HS	21-10	Florida 5-A champion	Casey Kotchman, 1b
2	Bishop Amat HS, La Puente, Calif.	27-2	CIF sectional champion	Miguel Sanchez, lhp
3	Chatsworth (Calif.) HS	31-2	Los Angeles city champion	*Joe Guntz, lhp
4	Daphne (Ala.) HS	37-4	Alabama 6-A champion	*Jeff Butts, of
5	Desert Vista HS, Phoenix	32-3	Arizona 5-A champion	Jason St. Clair, ss-rhp
6	Bellaire HS, Houston	34-2	Lost in playoffs	Trey George, of-rhp
7	St. Thomas Aquinas HS, Fort Lauderdale	30-5	Florida 5-A runnerup	Chris Niesel, rhp
8	Barbe HS, Lake Charles, La.	34-5	Louisiana 5-A champion	Austin Nagle, of
9	Parkview HS, Lilburn, Ga.	32-4	Georgia 5-A champion	*Jeff Francoeur, of
10	Cretin-Derham Hall HS, St. Paul, Minn.	25-1	Minnesota 3-A champion	Joe Mauer, c
11	Archbishop Rummel HS, Metairie, La.	32-4	Lost in playoffs	Ray Liotta, lhp
12	Tottenville HS, Staten Island, N.Y.	29-0	New York public school champ	Ray Rodriguez, rhp
13	Hart HS, Newhall, Calif.	27-2	Lost in playoffs	Bill Susdorf, of
14	Southridge HS, Miami	30-3	Lost in playoffs	Derek DeCarlo, rhp
15	Warren Central HS, Vicksburg, Miss.	36-3	Mississippi 5-A champion	Taylor Tankersley, lhp
16	Lee County HS, Sanford, N.C.	26-3	North Carolina 4-A champion	Jason Brown, c
17	Midland (Texas) HS	34-7	Texas 5-A champion	Jayson Nix, ss
18	Rancho Bernardo HS, San Diego	28-5	CIF sectional champion	Danny Putnam, of
19	Dunedin (Fla.) HS	25-3	Lost in playoffs	Bryan Banks, rhp
20	Arundel HS, Gambrills, Md.	25-2	Maryland 4-A champion	Jason Lively, rhp
21	Penn HS, Mishawaka, Ind.	34-2	Indiana 4-A champion	Dave Zachary, rhp
22	Ballard HS, Louisville	35-4	Kentucky runnerup	Jeremy Sowers, lhp
23	Toms River (N.J.) East HS	29-2	New Jersey Group V champion	*Ryan Doherty, lhp
24	Elkins HS, Sugar Land, Texas	31-7	Lost in playoffs	*Wardell Starling, rhp-of
25	Lakeland (Fla.) HS	29-3	Lost in playoffs	*Tommy Baumgardner, lhp
26	Buchanan HS, Clovis, Calif.	32-5	CIF sectional runnerup	Tony Mansolino, ss
27	Owasso (Okla.) HS	38-6	Oklahoma 6-A champion	Chuck Shurtleff, rhp
28	Tampa Catholic HS	27-5	Florida 3-A champion	Roberto Valiente, of
29	Round Rock (Texas) HS	28-6	Lost in playoffs	Joey Guajardo, rhp-ss
30	Green Valley HS, Henderson, Nev.	28-7	Nevada 4-A champion	Garrett Guzman, of
31	Jesuit HS, Sacramento	30-4	CIF sectional champion	J.P. Howell, lhp
32	Hialeah (Fla.) HS	27-8	Florida 6-A champion	*Comela Martinez, rhp
33	Columbus (Ga.) HS	27-5	Georgia 4-A runnerup	Garrett Groce, of
34	The Bolles School, Jacksonville	29-3	Lost in playoffs	Taylor Cobb, rhp
35	Steinert HS, Hamilton Township, N.J.	24-4	Lost in playoffs	Chris Neylan, lhp
36	Mater Dei HS, Santa Ana, Calif.	25-5	Lost in playoffs	*Sergio Santos, ss
37	Danvers (Mass.) HS	25-0	Massachusetts Div. II champion	Chris Bowser, rhp
38	Southside HS, Gadsden, Ala.	37-2	Alabama 5-A champion	Eric West, ss
39	Capistrano Valley HS, Mission Viejo, Calif.	23-8	CIF sectional champion	Travis Becktel, of
40	Pleasure Ridge Park HS, Louisville	31-3	Lost in playoffs	Craig Snipp, lhp
41	Klein HS, Spring, Texas	30-8	Lost in playoffs	Josh Barfield, 2b
42	Russellville (Ark.) HS	29-3	Arkansas 5-A champion	Abel Newton, rhp
43	Logan (W.Va.) HS	32-3	West Virginia 3-A champion	Brandon Chambers, rhp
44	Federal Way (Wash.) HS	23-3	Washington 4-A champion	*Shea McFeely, p
45	Christian Brothers HS, Memphis	35-9	Tennessee Div. II champion	Chad Farr, lhp-of
46	Gainesville (Ga.) HS	34-1	Georgia 3-A champion	*Micah Owings, rhp-1b
47	Dublin (Ohio) Coffman HS	24-7	Ohio Division I champion	Bart Hunton, c
48	Lamar HS, Houston	27-6	Lost in playoffs	Vincent Blue, of
49	Dallas Christian HS	34-0	Texas independent champion	Brooks Shankle, 3b
50	Bradley-Bourbonnais HS, Bradley, Ill.	30-7	Illinois AA champion	Wade Greenlee, rhp

Forfeited 10 games for use of ineligible player
* Junior

California (CIF) does not have a state championship

Schmidt hit a utility pole. Bryan Banks and Matt Cheek returned shortly afterward and won games on consecutive days. Schmidt sustained a broken left arm (he's righthanded) and missed most of the season.

Bishop Amat Challenge

Seminole never gave up the No. 1 spot in the nation, but there were other contenders. Bishop Amat High of La Puente, Calif., finished second with a 27-2 record, shooting up the charts in the second half of the season. The Lancers entered the rankings at No. 12 after winning the prestigious National Classic tournament in April, and won their last 16 games.

They took the California Interscholastic Federation's Southern Section championship in Division IV (there is no statewide playoff), beating Burroughs High of Ridgecrest 8-0 in the final game. It was one of just three losses all year for Burroughs ace J.D. Martin: two in high

school and one in the Rookie-level Appalachian League after he signed a professional contract with the Indians.

Bellaire (Texas) High was in second place all season, and undefeated at 34-0, until being eliminated in the state 5-A quarterfinals in surreal fashion.

The Cardinals lost nearly half of their starting lineup to injury—including their leadoff hitter, No. 3 hitter, cleanup hitter and ace pitcher—in the first five innings of the best-of-three series. Elkins High of Fort Bend, which also ousted Bellaire in the 2000 playoffs, swept the series 8-5 and 11-0.

Elkins went on to lose to Austin in the state semifinals. The state champion was Midland High, which got an outstanding pitching performance from Jayson Nix in the final four at Dell Diamond in Round Rock. Nix, a sandwich draft pick of the Rockies as a shortstop, earned a save with two scoreless innings in the semifinals against Klein High of Spring, then pitched a complete game as the Bulldogs beat Austin 4-2 in the final.

Sidd Finch Lives

Catcher Joe Mauer of Cretin-Derham Hall in St. Paul, Minn., was Baseball America's High School Player of the Year and the No. 1 overall pick in the draft (see sidebar), but another prep player surpassed him in folk-hero status.

All of the clichés applied to Marshall (Texas) High righthander Colt Griffin. He was powerfully built at 6-foot-4 and 220 pounds, but was a basic, unassuming Midwestern kid. Before the season, few scouts had ever heard of him. He had pitched little before his senior year, largely because a growth spurt between his freshman and sophomore years left him unable to throw enough strikes. He wasn't exactly from the middle of nowhere—Marshall has a population of 25,000 and is known as a progressive place—but he knew a lot more about Shreveport than about Broadway.

In baseball's version of the actress being discovered in the drug store, he burst onto the scene in a game in which scouts were looking at somebody else.

And, oh yes, he threw 100 mph.

A handful of scouts were present to see Natchitoches (La.) Central righthander Calvin Carpenter. But Griffin reached 98 mph, and he and coach Jackie Lloyd received hundreds of phone messages from scouts and recruiters the next day. The legend was cemented days later when Griffin reached 100 in another game.

Griffin had been an all-district first baseman and center fielder previously. When Lloyd had him raise his arm angle as a pitcher from low three-quarters—almost sidearm—to high three-quarters, it instantly added 3-6 mph to his fastball. It also improved his control, though that remained a question mark even after he was drafted in the first round by the Royals.

"It felt better," Griffin said. "It was just more fluid, kind of. And now I can still drop down and give the hitter something different. Yeah, it seemed like I was throwing harder, but not that much. I could tell a little difference."

It wound up making quite a difference in his bank account.

Carpenter, incidentally, became the Brewers' sixth-round draft pick.

Can't Go On Forever

State playoffs brought their usual surfeit of excitement, surprises, extended streaks and broken streaks.

Vestavia Hills High, the 1998 national champion, saw its streak of seven Alabama 6-A titles broken. The Rebels lost a three-game quarterfinal series to Bob Jones High of Madison. In the deciding game, Bob Jones spotted Vestavia three runs in the first inning before coming back to win 5-4.

The eventual state champion was Daphne, which had been an up-and-comer for years and finished fourth nationally in 2001. The Trojans beat Bob Jones 7-5 in the rain-shortened third game of the best-of-three final series. Game One, a 9-1 Daphne victory, ended on a triple play. With the bases loaded, left fielder Nelson Bauer made a diving catch of a fly ball. As he stood to throw, the ball fell out of his glove. Two runners who thought Bauer had dropped the ball were then doubled off base.

Owasso High won its third Oklahoma 6-A championship in four years, beating Stillwater 6-4 in the final. Owasso pitcher Michael Brown started the title game for the third straight year, and got a decision for the first time. He gave up 11 hits and worked out of several jams, but didn't walk a

PLAYER OF THE YEAR

Joe Mauer seems to do things with precision. No odd, hard-to-remember numbers for him. He hit exactly .600 during the spring 2001 high school season. He was selected first overall in the June draft. And then he hit exactly .400 for Elizabethton in the Rookie-level Appalachian League.

He also struck out precisely once in his high school career at Cretin-Derham Hall in St. Paul, Minn., a career that included one state championship. And he is the 10th Baseball America High School Player of the Year.

Mauer, a catcher, certainly deserved the award. He had the requisite numbers at .600-15-53, opening the season on a tear that included eight home runs in seven games, and 10 in 11 games. But more important was the way he came through when his team needed him most.

LINDA CULLEN

Joe Mauer

Cretin-Derham Hall's state-title victory over Mayo High of Rochester was a 13-2 cakewalk in which Mauer went 3-for-3 with a triple. But he had gotten the Raiders to that game almost by himself with his heroics in the semifinals against Brainerd.

He hit a three-run homer in the fifth inning to create a 4-4 tie, and pitched the last five innings in relief, keeping Brainerd scoreless long enough for his teammates to push across the winning run in the ninth.

"His character is unparalleled as a high school player," said his coach, Jim O'Neill. "He plays within himself. He had 20 or 30 scouts out at batting practice every time, and he played right through it."

It was at least partly because he was used to the attention. By the time his senior season of baseball rolled around, Mauer already had been named the national player of the year—in football. He signed a letter of intent with Florida State to play quarterback, following in the footsteps of another Cretin-Derham Hall graduate, Chris Weinke.

PREVIOUS WINNERS

1992—Preston Wilson, of-rhp, Bamberg-Ehrhardt (S.C.) HS
1993—Trot Nixon, of-lhp, New Hanover HS, Wilmington, N.C.
1994—Doug Million, lhp, Sarasota (Fla.) HS
1995—Ben Davis, c, Malvern (Pa.) Prep
1996—Matt White, rhp, Waynesboro Area (Pa.) HS
1997—Darnell McDonald, of, Cherry Creek HS, Englewood, Colo.
1998—Drew Henson, 3b-rhp, Brighton (Mich.) HS
1999—Josh Hamilton, of-lhp, Athens Drive HS, Raleigh, N.C.
2000—Matt Harrington, rhp, Palmdale (Calif.) HS

But that was before the Twins drafted him and gave him 5,150,000 reasons to forget about football. He signed late and squeezed in just 110 at-bats at Elizabethton, but that was enough for managers to unanimously name him the league's top prospect.

—JOHN ROYSTER

State	Class, School/City		State	Class, School/City
Alabama	6A—*Daphne HS			1A—Newton HS
	5A—*Southside HS, Gadsden			Summer—St. Charles East HS, St. Charles
	4A—Bibb County HS, Centreville		**Indiana**	4A—*Penn HS, Mishawaka
	3A—Northside HS, Northport			3A—Cathedral HS, Indianapolis
	2A—Leroy HS			2A—Northfield HS, Wabash
	1A—G.W. Long HS, Skipperville			1A—Triton HS, Bourbon
Alaska	Service HS, Anchorage		**Iowa**	4A—Dowling HS, West Des Moines
Arizona	5A—*Desert Vista HS, Phoenix			3A—Heelan Catholic HS, Sioux City
	4A—Douglas HS			2A—Emmetsburg HS
	3A—Fountain Hills HS			1A—Spalding Catholic HS, Granville
	2A—Willcox HS		**Kansas**	6A—Derby HS
	1A—St. David HS			5A—Shawnee Heights HS, Tecumseh
Arkansas	5A—*Russellville HS			4A—Hayden HS, Topeka
	4A—Malvern HS			3A—Wichita Collegiate HS
	3A—Booneville HS			2A/1A—St. Mary's Colgan HS, Pittsburg
	2A—Lavaca HS		**Kentucky**	Boyd County HS, Ashland
	1A—Scranton HS		**Louisiana**	5A—*Barbe HS, Lake Charles
California	No state championship			4A—Sam Houston HS, Lake Charles
Colorado	5A—Smoky Hill HS, Aurora			3A—E.D. White HS, Thibodaux
	4A—Niwot HS, Longmont			2A—Catholic HS, New Iberia
	3A—Eaton HS			1A—Oak Grove HS
	2A—Custer County HS, Westcliffe			B—Pine Prairie HS
Connecticut	LL—Stamford HS			C—Elizabeth HS
	L—Staples HS, Westport		**Maine**	A—Deering HS, Portland
	M—Sheehan HS, Wallingford			B—John Bapst Memorial HS, Bangor
	S—Immaculate HS, Danbury			C—Hall-Dale HS, Farmingdale
Delaware	Salesianum HS, Wilmington			D—Mattanawcook Academy, Lincoln
Florida	6A—*Hialeah HS		**Maryland**	4A—*Arundel HS, Gambrills
	5A—*Seminole HS			3A—Northeast HS, Pasadena
	4A—Godby HS, Tallahassee			2A—Centennial HS, Ellicott City
	3A—*Tampa Catholic HS			1A—St. Michael's HS
	2A—Kings Academy, West Palm Beach			Private—*Riverdale Baptist HS, Upper Marlboro
	1A—Arlington Country Day HS, Jacksonville		**Massachusetts**	I—Boston College HS, Dorchester
Georgia	5A—*Parkview HS, Lilburn			II—*Danvers HS
	4A—Shaw HS, Columbus			III—Nipmuc Regional HS, Upton
	3A—*Gainesville HS		**Michigan**	I—South HS, Grosse Pointe
	2A—Cartersville HS			II—Swan Valley HS, Saginaw
	1A—The Walker School, Marietta			III—Flat Rock HS
Hawaii	Kailua HS			IV—Harper Woods HS
Idaho	A-1/Div. I—Coeur d'Alene HS		**Minnesota**	3A—*Cretin-Derham Hall, St. Paul
	A-1/Div. II—Vallivue HS, Caldwell			2A—Cathedral HS, St. Cloud
	A-2—Buhl HS			1A—St. Agnes HS, St. Paul
	A-3—Potlach HS		**Mississippi**	5A—*Warren Central HS, Vicksburg
	A-4—Kendrick HS			4A—Pearl HS
Illinois	2A—*Bradley-Bourbonnais HS, Bradley			3A—West Lauderdale HS, Collinsville
				2A—Mooreville HS

batter. The Rams (38-6) won their last 26 games.

Barbe High of Lake Charles, La., matched Owasso's feat, taking its third 5-A title in four years by winning both the semifinal and final in the seventh inning. A two-out, solo home run by outfielder Austin Nagle gave the Bucs a 5-4 win in the title game against St. Amant. The Gators had eliminated the nation's No. 3 team, Archbishop Rummel of Metairie, in the semifinals.

Gilmer County of Glenville, W.Va., whose coach Dave Jaffre died of a heart attack on the field before a playoff game in 2000, won the 2001 Class A state championship. The Titans overcame a 3-0, sixth-inning deficit to beat Fayetteville 4-3 on Justin Townsend's hit in the eighth. Coach Joe Frashure, a 21-year-old student at Glenville State, took over after Jaffre died.

Righthander Nick Long earned a save in the first game and a complete-game victory in the second as Shaw of Columbus swept crosstown rival Columbus High in the Georgia 4-A championship series. Long didn't allow a hit until the seventh inning of the second game. He later was drafted in the fourth round by the Expos.

The two games were played on the same day in intense heat. Shaw's Jose Hernandez caught all 14 innings, then collapsed with leg cramps between the dugout and the first-base line as his teammates celebrated near the mound.

Shaw had also won the state football title earlier in the school year. Charles Flowers coached both teams. The baseball champion in 5-A, Georgia's highest division, was Parkview High of Lilburn, which beat defending champion Lowndes of Valdosta 10-8 and 12-4.

Chatsworth (Calif.) High finished third in the nation after winning the Los Angeles City Section championship. Lefthander Joe Guntz started both the semifinal and final games, and gave up one run in 14 innings.

Righthander Josh Tupper of Joplin (Mo.) High pitched a no-hitter in the 4-A state championship game, beating Francis Howell North of St. Charles 2-0. Tupper struck out seven and walked three.

Green Valley High of Henderson, Nev., won its seventh state 4-A title since 1993, beating Galena High of Reno 6-2 in the final.

No Slouch

The year had its usual share of individual feats, includ-

	1A—Hamilton HS		3A—The Dalles HS	
Missouri	4A—Joplin HS		2A/1A—Regis HS, Stayton	
	3A—Helias HS, Jefferson City	**Pennsylvania**	3A—Moon HS, Coraopolis	
	2A—Iberia HS		2A—Phoenixville Area HS	
	1A—Jasper HS		1A—Central Catholic HS	
Montana	No high school baseball	**Rhode Island**	A—Toll Gate HS, Warwick	
Nebraska	Creighton Prep, Omaha		B—West Warwick HS	
Nevada	*Green Valley HS, Henderson	**South Carolina**	4A—Richland Northeast HS, Columbia	
New Hampshire	I—*Goffstown Area HS		3A—A.C. Flora HS, Columbia	
	L—Nashua HS		2A—Chapin HS	
	M—Newmarket HS		1A—Lake View HS	
	S—Pittsfield HS	**South Dakota**	No high school baseball	
New Jersey	IV—*Toms River East HS	**Tennessee**	3A—Germantown HS	
	III—Ramapo HS, Franklin Lakes		2A—David Lipscomb HS, Nashville	
	II—Audubon HS		1A—University HS, Jackson	
	I—Emerson HS		II—*Christian Brothers HS, Memphis	
	Parochial 'A'—Seton Hall Prep, West Orange	**Texas**	5A—*Midland HS	
	Parochial 'B'—Gloucester Catholic HS, Gloucester City		4A—Western Hills HS, Fort Worth	
New Mexico	5A—Eldorado HS, Albuquerque		3A—La Grange HS	
	4A—Farmington HS		2A—Weimar HS	
	3A—New Mexico Military Institute, Roswell		1A—Bremond HS	
	2A/1A—Sandia Prep, Albuquerque	**Utah**	5A—Alta HS	
New York	A—Union-Endicott HS, Endicott		4A—Lone Peak HS, American Fork	
	B—Massena Central HS		3A—Carbon HS, Price	
	C—Notre Dame HS, Utica		2A—San Juan HS, Blanding	
	D—Parishville-Hopkinton Central HS, Parishville	**Vermont**	I—Brattleboro Union HS	
North Carolina	4A—*Lee County HS, Sanford		II—Mount Abraham HS, Bristol	
	3A—Franklin HS		III—Northfield HS	
	2A—Shelby HS	**Virginia**	3A—Lee-Davis HS, Mechanicsville	
	1A—Cherryville HS		2A—Poquoson HS	
North Dakota	A—Dickinson HS		1A—John Battle HS, Bristol	
	B—Bishop Ryan HS, Minot	**Washington**	4A—*Federal Way HS	
Ohio	I—*Dublin Coffman HS, Dublin		3A—Newport HS	
	II—Notre Dame Cathedral Latin HS, Chardon		2A—Pullman HS	
	III—Pleasant HS		1A—Brewster HS	
	IV—Country Day HS, Cincinnati		B—De Sales HS, Walla Walla	
Oklahoma	6A—*Owasso HS	**Washington, D.C.**	Woodrow Wilson HS	
	5A—Ada HS	**West Virginia**	3A—*Logan HS	
	4A—Byng HS, Ada		2A—Winfield HS	
	3A—Metro Christian Academy, Tulsa		1A—Gilmer County HS, Glenville	
	2A—Dale HS	**Wisconsin**	I—Logan HS, La Crosse	
	A—Fletcher HS		II—Turner HS, Beloit	
	B—Dover HS		III—De Soto HS	
Oregon	4A—Lakeridge HS, Lake Oswego	**Wyoming**	No high school baseball	

*Ranked in Baseball America/National High School Baseball Coaches Association poll

HIGH SCHOOL BASEBALL

ing a notable one that has now occurred three times in 11 years, and can only be attributed to the era of the aluminum bat.

Stevan Louch of Clare (Mich.) High became the fourth high school player ever to hit home runs in six straight at-bats. He went deep three times in each game of a doubleheader against Alma, tying the record held by Bob Squires of Waterloo (Ind.) in 1982, Tim Morgan of Northwest Whitfield in Tunnel Hill, Ga., in 1990 and Alberto Concepcion of El Segundo (Calif.) in 1999.

It's doubtful that any of the other three record-holders was a bigger surprise than Louch, a senior. He entered the doubleheader batting .217 with no home runs, and he was just 5-foot-11 and 150 pounds.

Two other players hit four homers in one game, including senior catcher Madison Edwards of the aforementioned Texas champions from Midland. Edwards had three homers and eight RBIs in the first two innings of a 22-9 win over Odessa. He finished with 10 RBIs after walking in his fifth and final time up.

Senior outfielder Tanner Abel of La Grande (Ore.) High hit two grand slams and went 5-for-5 against Hermiston.

With 14 RBIs, he accounted for all but one of his team's runs in the 15-8 win.

Keith Ebner of La Vernia (Texas) High must have wondered what it took to get a win after he struck out 27 batters in 12 innings against Bandera, but didn't get a decision. Ebner, a highly regarded prospect for the 2003 draft, left the mound when his hamstring tightened up, with the score 5-5. His teammates went on to win 6-5 in 13 innings in a game that featured five errors by each team.

Another 13-inning game featured 47 strikeouts by four pitchers from Jacksonville schools University Christian and Wolfson. Ross Lewis had 11 K's and Mitchell Shepherd 12 for University Christian, which won 4-1 as Wolfson committed two errors in the top of the 13th.

Josh Deel fanned 13 and freshman Eric Hurley 11 for Wolfson, which loaded the bases in the bottom of the 13th before shortstop Rashad Anderson made a diving catch of Deel's drive to end the game.

A similar game developed in Louisville between senior prospects Jeremy Sowers of Ballard High and Travis Foley of Butler. Each pitcher threw nine scoreless innings, allowing one hit. Sowers, who became the Reds' first-

Selected by Baseball America
*Junior

Casey Kotchman

Jayson Nix

J.D. Martin

Austin Nagle

FIRST TEAM

Pos.	Player	School, Hometown	AVG	AB	R	H	2B	3B	HR	RBI	SB	Drafted (Round)
C	Joe Mauer	Cretin-Derham Hall, St. Paul Minn.	.605	90	49	54	9	7	15	53	2	Twins (1)
1B	Casey Kotchman	Seminole (Fla.) HS	.465	88	46	41	18	1	5	39	2	Angels (1)
INF	J.J. Hardy	Sabino HS, Tucson	.455	99	40	45	4	0	8	34	15	Brewers (2)
INF	Jayson Nix	Midland (Texas) HS	.451	122	61	55	18	2	13	46	14	Rockies (1)
INF	David Wright	Hickory HS, Chesapeake, Va.	.544	57	35	31	5	2	6	20	10	Mets (1)
OF	Roscoe Crosby	Union HS, Buffalo, S.C.	.516	61	36	31	12	2	16	42	17	Royals (2)
OF	Danny Putnam	Rancho Bernardo HS, San Diego	.500	112	64	56	9	4	19	48	19	Not drafted
OF	Michael Wilson	Washington HS, Tulsa	.506	83	46	42	12	0	4	26	51	Mariners (2)
DH	Jon Zeringue	E.D. White HS, Thibodeaux, La.	.487	78	39	38	5	2	13	54	12	White Sox (3)
UT	Matt Chico	Fallbrook (Calif.) HS	.318	85	31	27	2	1	6	21	6	Red Sox (2)

Pos.	Player	School, Hometown	W	L	ERA	G	SV	IP	H	BB	SO	Drafted (Round)
P	J.P. Howell	Jesuit HS, Sacramento	10	1	0.10	14	2	71	32	21	136	Braves (2)
P	*Scott Kazmir	Cypress Falls HS, Houston	6	0	0.69	8	1	61	19	22	127	Not eligible
P	J.D. Martin	Burroughs HS, Ridgecrest, Calif.	11	1	0.64	14	2	76	31	20	136	Indians (1)
P	Chris Niesel	St. Thomas Aquinas HS, Ft. Lauderdale	12	0	0.34	13	1	74	37	11	117	Cubs (46)
P	Jeremy Sowers	Ballard HS, Louisville	10	1	0.51	12	0	82	32	15	148	Reds (1)
UT	Matt Chico	Fallbrook (Calif.) HS	10	1	0.84	13	0	75	45	25	116	

SECOND TEAM

Pos.	Player	School, Hometown	AVG	AB	R	H	2B	3B	HR	RBI	SB	Drafted (Round)
C	Jon DeVries	Irvine (Calif.) HS	.449	78	26	35	8	0	6	26	9	Red Sox (3)
1B	Bill Paganetti	Galena HS, Reno, Nev.	.432	147	51	51	13	1	13	45	8	Cardinals (45)
INF	Joe Mather	Mountain Pointe HS, Phoenix	.455	88	34	40	5	1	17	43	7	Cardinals (3)
INF	Joey Metropoulos	Monte Vista HS, Jamul, Calif.	.389	167	30	65	15	0	12	46	2	Tigers (16)
INF	*B.J. Upton	Greenbrier Academy, Chesapeake, Va.	.633	90	51	57	16	7	13	44	43	Not eligible
OF	*Jeff Francoeur	Parkview HS, Lilburn, Ga.	.500	112	49	56	7	3	20	49	27	Not eligible
OF	Garrett Guzman	Green Valley HS, Henderson, Nev.	.533	122	56	65	15	5	12	55	9	Twins (10)
OF	Austin Nagle	Barbe HS, Lake Charles, La.	.464	112	61	52	8	4	4	47	62	Athletics (6)
DH	Mike Sweeney	Riverdale Baptist HS, Chesapeake, Md.	.500	138	57	69	12	1	17	63	5	Not drafted
UT	Kyle Davies	Stockbridge (Ga.) HS	.450	82	34	40	6	2	3	30	12	Braves (4)

Pos.	Player	School, Hometown	W	L	ERA	G	SV	IP	H	BB	SO	Drafted (Round)
P	Gavin Flord	Mount St. Joseph HS, Baltimore	8	2	1.11	11	0	63	23	29	103	Phillies (1)
P	Colt Griffin	Marshall (Texas) HS	8	2	1.40	13	1	65	22	39	113	Royals (1)
P	Alan Horne	Marianna (Fla.) HS	9	2	1.12	13	1	81	39	14	147	Indians (1)
P	Macay McBride	Screven County HS, Sylvania, Ga.	11	2	1.32	14	1	79	29	35	160	Braves (1)
P	Taylor Tankersley	Warren Central HS, Vicksburg, Miss.	13	0	0.44	17	1	95	41	32	165	Royals (39)
UT	Kyle Davies	Stockbridge (Ga.) HS	9	3	1.07	14	1	72	52	12	109	

PLAYER OF THE YEAR: Joe Mauer, c, Cretin-Derham Hall, St. Paul, Minn.

round pick but didn't sign, struck out 20. Foley, the Indians' fourth-round pick, fanned 16. Ballard won 3-0 in 11 innings.

Center fielder Chad Lane of Viam (Okla.) High finished three stolen bases short of the national record. Lane swiped 93, second all-time to the 96 by Vicente Rosario of George Washington High of New York in 1996. Lane's career total of 193 is third all-time.

Zac Bellinger of Niwot (Colo.) High reached base in 16 straight plate appearances, with 14 hits and two walks. The streak, which covered four games, ended when Bellinger grounded into a double play his first time up against Valley High of Gilcrest.

Rutherford (N.J.) High pitchers threw no-hitters in three straight home games over a span of eight days. Righthander Jack Egbert pitched the first one to beat Essex Catholic 2-0. Two days later, righthander Jim Wladyka pitched a perfect game, beating Tenafly 10-0. Five days after that Wladyka struck again, no-hitting Ridgefield Park 9-0.

Rich Hofman, the coach at Westminster Academy in Fort Lauderdale, recorded his 800th career victory when the Lions defeated Sarasota 4-1. Hofman, in his third season at Westminster after 30 years at Westminster Christian in Miami, has won 10 state championships and national titles in 1992 and 1996. He's the winningest coach all-time in Florida, 10th nationally.

Team USA faces different challenge, but responds behind Brownlie, staff

BY JOHN MANUEL AND ALLAN SIMPSON

The college national team fielded by USA Baseball in 2001 had almost an impossible act to follow.

There was nothing on the international calendar that came close to rivaling the 2000 Olympics, which the United States won with a team of minor leaguers. It also was a tall order to top the accomplishments of Team USA's powerful 2000 college squad, which lost just three games.

The 2001 team lacked the star quality of the 2000 college club, perhaps Team USA's best-ever assemblage of talent. There was no Mark Prior or Mark Teixeira on the 2001 roster, no Dewon Brazelton or Chris Burke or Jake Gautreau. Instead, Team USA's best hitter was Jeremy Reed, a singles-hitting first baseman from Long Beach State, and its most talented everyday player was an obscure outfielder from Southern, freshman sensation Rickie Weeks.

So the fact Team USA put together a finishing kick that led to a 21-7-1 record, including a near-sweep of its games against many of the nation's top summer college leagues, confirmed that the best college players still want to spend their summers wearing Team USA on their chest.

Team USA represented itself well on the field, winning 14 of its last 16 games. The stretch run included a 12-game winning streak that started after a 10-inning, 1-0 loss in Minnesota against the Northwoods League all-stars.

While not quite on a par with the 2000 model, Team USA did have a star-studded rotation that put together a

Pat McMahon

DAVID SCHOFIELD

Bobby Brownlie: Led the pitching staff with a 7-0, 0.84 record

string of low-scoring games and helped post a team ERA of 1.78. Three righthanders—Bobby Brownlie (Rutgers), Kiki Bengochea (Miami) and Mike Esposito (Arizona State)—set the pace.

Brownlie cemented his status as the top college prospect for the 2002 draft with a dominating summer, going 7-0, 0.84 with 60 strikeouts and 11 walks in 53 innings. He started on three days' rest on the final day of the Red, White and Blue Tour to pitch in front of the home folks in New Jersey and picked up his seventh victory.

Bengochea and Esposito, two other top prospects for the 2002 draft, were only slightly behind Brownlie. Bengochea went 3-1, 0.92 in six starts while Esposito went 3-1, 1.56 in five starts.

"The entire staff and our team defense were the strengths of the club," coach Pat McMahon said. "Brownlie is blessed with great ability, but what sets him apart is his competitiveness. When the game is tight, he pitches his best.

"Bengochea was really a leader on the staff and really competed well. Esposito's last start was a 1-0 win against Taiwan's No. 1 starter, and he really improved his straight changeup."

McMahon threw USA Baseball a changeup when he switched jobs just before the tour began, moving from

TEAM USA: COLLEGE 2001

Red, White and Blue Tour (21-7-1)

HEAD COACH: Pat McMahon (U. of Florida).

BATTING	AVG	AB	R	H	2B	3B	HR	RBI	SB	College	Class
Jeremy Reed, 1b	.366	101	22	37	4	2	2	14	9	Long Beach State	So.
Sam Fuld, of	.310	84	13	26	4	1	0	4	3	Stanford	Fr.
Kevin Howard, ss-3b	.299	97	12	29	7	2	1	18	2	Miami	So.
Rickie Weeks, of	.277	83	20	23	1	1	2	10	8	Southern	Fr.
Carlos Quentin, of	.267	75	8	20	5	0	1	9	1	Stanford	Fr.
Anthony Giarratano, ss	.250	20	2	5	0	0	0	1	0	Tulane	Fr.
Ryan Hubele, of	.246	69	9	17	1	2	2	11	1	Texas	So.
Jeff Baker, 3b-ss	.237	93	14	22	7	1	2	15	1	Clemson	So.
Michael Aubrey, of	.233	60	8	14	2	1	2	8	3	Tulane	Fr.
Omar Quintanilla, 2b	.193	83	13	16	2	0	3	8	2	Texas	Fr.
Chris Snyder, c	.175	63	7	11	1	1	1	9	2	Houston	So.
Javi Herrera, c	.128	39	2	5	1	0	0	3	0	Tennessee	Fr.
Nick Swisher, 1b	.000	6	0	0	0	0	0	0	0	Ohio State	So.

PITCHING	W	L	ERA	G	SV	IP	H	BB	SO	College	Class
Michael Aubrey	0	0	0.00	1	0	1	1	0	0	Tulane	Fr.
Bobby Brownlie	7	0	0.84	9	0	53	32	11	60	Rutgers	So.
Kiki Bengochea	3	1	0.92	6	0	39	21	18	32	Miami	So.
Royce Ring	0	0	0.93	10	1	10	6	4	10	San Diego State	So.
Bob Zimmerman	0	1	1.06	14	6	17	7	7	20	SW Missouri State	Fr.
Mike Esposito	3	1	1.56	5	0	35	22	9	35	Arizona State	Fr.
Anthony Reyes	1	0	2.08	4	1	22	20	3	21	Southern California	So.
Ben Thurmond	4	2	2.83	9	0	29	22	7	30	Winthrop	So.
Tim Cunningham	1	1	3.38	5	0	11	7	16	9	Stanford	So.
Bryan Bullington	2	1	4.05	8	1	27	28	6	29	Ball State	So.

head coach at Mississippi State to Florida. But his attention to Team USA never waned despite the stress of a job change and relocation of his family.

"It's the only situation I would have left Mississippi State for," McMahon said, "but my first commitment this summer was to Team USA. I'm fortunate that my (Florida) assistants (John Cohen and Ross Jones) were able to coordinate the process, and my wife Cheri was able to handle so much with the move.

"I'm just so honored to have been a part of Team USA, and I'm proud of the players. They represented themselves, their universities and the United States in a first-class manner."

The team's strong finish came despite a spate of injuries that sapped a roster that started with just 21 players. The injuries began when first baseman Nick Swisher (Ohio State) aggravated a wrist injury and was sent home after playing in two games. Infielder Anthony Giarratano (Tulane) was next, playing just seven games before injuring his shoulder in Alaska.

Baseball America Freshman of the Year Michael Aubrey (Tulane), a two-way player, missed the final 10 games after pulling a hamstring in Torrington, Conn., making a running catch. And shoulder tightness forced righthander Anthony Reyes (Southern California) to go home early after making just four appearances.

"The club really held together well, and we had a pretty close-knit group of young men," McMahon said. "We showed tremendous improvement as the year went on offensively, and we were battling through injuries to do it."

Team USA opened its season in Japan with a renewal of its annual collegiate series with that country and lost three of five games. Unlike previous years, though, the team did not finish its season playing in a tournament or against major international competition. But the schedule served as a training ground for the 2002 World 22-and-under Championships, which will be played in Italy.

How many of the Team USA players, who were freshmen and sophomores, will make the trip to Italy is unclear. McMahon said he recommended a similar mix to national team director Steve Cohen.

"I'll sit down and talk with Steve about each player's performance, and a lot will depend on what happens next spring," McMahon said. "You need a mix of some veterans and some freshmen, but this group represented itself very well."

Team USA was scheduled to conclude its 2001 season at the IBAF World Cup, scheduled for Nov. 7-18 in Kaohsiung, Taiwan. Sixteen nations took part in the event, last contested in Italy in 1998 when the U.S. finished a distant ninth.

With the competition open to professional players, Major League Baseball and the Players Association permitted Team USA and other nations the use of professional players not on 40-man rosters. That sent Team USA, Baseball Canada and other governing bodies scrambling for players less than a month before the event began.

Former Phillies manager Terry Francona managed the U.S. entry in the tournament.

Juniors Earn Berth

Team USA's junior national team (18-and-under) captured second place at the COPABE Pan American qualifying tournament in Cuba in July, to secure a spot for the United States at the 2002 International Baseball Federation World Junior

TEAM USA: JUNIOR 2001

COPABE Qualifying Tournament, Cuba (9-2)
HEAD COACH: Dave Grant (Glendale, Ariz., Community College).

BATTING	AVG	AB	R	H	2B	3B	HR	RBI	SB	High School
Jeff Francoeur, of	.538	39	15	21	4	2	2	17	4	Lilburn HS, Parkview, Ga.
Mike Nickeas, c-1b	.531	32	18	17	7	0	2	14	2	Westlake HS, Westlake Village, Calif.
Jeff Butts, dh	.472	36	13	17	3	0	1	9	5	Daphne (Ala.) HS
Nick Crowe, 3b	.471	34	13	16	6	1	1	10	0	Science Hill HS, Johnson City, Tenn.
B.J. Upton, ss	.462	26	8	12	1	1	1	6	3	Greenbrier Academy, Chesapeake, Va.
Denard Span, of	.450	40	9	18	3	1	1	12	3	Tampa Catholic HS
Matt Chico, of-p	.435	23	5	10	4	1	0	5	0	Fallbrook (Calif.) HS
Clint Sammons, c-1b	.355	31	10	11	3	0	2	9	2	Parkview HS, Stone Mountain, Ga.
James Guerrero, 2b	.300	30	12	9	2	0	1	7	0	Fontana (Calif.) HS
Sergio Santos, ss-3b	.286	35	11	10	2	0	1	7	2	Mater Dei HS, Santa Ana, Calif.
Huston Street, 3b	.278	18	3	5	1	0	0	2	1	Westlake HS, Austin
Matt Whitney, of-3b	.172	29	3	5	1	0	1	7	1	Palm Beach Gardens (Fla.) HS
PITCHING	**W**	**L**	**ERA**	**G**	**SV**	**IP**	**H**	**BB**	**SO**	**High School**
Jeremy Sowers	3	0	0.00	3	0	18	9	8	28	Ballard HS, Louisville
Zach Segovia	1	0	0.00	4	0	8	5	1	15	Forney (Texas) HS
Mark Worrell	0	0	0.00	3	1	6	0	3	13	John I. Leonard HS, Boynton Beach, Fla.
Mark Rosen	0	0	0.00	4	0	5	1	2	6	Salisbury (Conn.) HS
Grant Johnson	2	0	0.93	2	0	10	4	2	6	Lyons Township HS, Burr Ridge, Ill.
J.P. Howell	0	0	0.93	5	0	10	8	4	18	Jesuit HS, Sacramento
Mark McCormick	1	0	1.50	2	0	6	4	3	11	Clear Creek HS, Clear Lake Shores, Texas
Scott Kazmir	1	2	3.95	3	0	14	5	11	31	Cypress Falls HS, Houston
Matt Chico	1	0	6.75	2	0	8	9	6	15	Fallbrook (Calif.) HS

TEAM USA: YOUTH 2001

World Youth Championship, Mexico (7-0)
HEAD COACH: Chris Brown (San Diego City College).

BATTING	AVG	AB	R	H	2B	3B	HR	RBI	SB	High School
Jeff Flaig, ss	.536	28	11	15	2	0	3	12	1	El Dorado HS, Placentia, Calif.
Lastings Milledge, of	.522	23	11	12	1	1	3	10	2	Northside Christian HS, St. Petersburg, Fla.
Mike Rogers, of	.483	29	9	14	4	2	0	8	3	Del City (Okla.) HS
Chris Valaika, 3b	.444	18	3	8	0	1	0	2	1	Hart HS, Newhall, Calif.
Daniel Perales, of	.375	24	3	9	4	0	1	5	2	Mater Dei HS, Santa Ana, Calif.
Jarrod Saltalamacchia, c	.316	19	3	6	0	0	1	4	0	Royal Palm Beach HS, West Palm Beach, Fla.
Chris Lubanski, of	.286	7	2	2	0	1	0	3	1	Kennedy-Kenrick HS, Schwenksville, Pa.
Xavier Paul, of	.250	4	2	1	1	0	0	1	0	Archbishop Rummel HS, Metairie, La.
Sean Rodriguez, 2b	.240	25	8	6	1	0	0	2	4	Coral Park HS, Miami
Justin Brashear, 1b	.200	20	6	4	0	0	0	3	1	Barbe HS, Lake Charles, La.
David Winfree, c	.200	5	1	1	0	0	1	2	0	First Colonial HS, Virginia Beach, Va.
Zechry Zincola, 3b	.167	12	2	2	1	0	0	0	0	Arlington HS, Riverside, Calif.
PITCHING	**W**	**L**	**ERA**	**G**	**SV**	**IP**	**H**	**BB**	**SO**	**High School**
Mike Rogers	1	0	0.00	1	0	5	2	4	5	Del City (Okla.) HS
Jeff Manship	1	0	0.00	2	0	3	0	2	8	Reagan HS, San Antonio
Jeff Flaig	0	0	0.00	1	1	1	0	0	2	El Dorado HS, Placentia, Calif.
Jay Sborz	1	0	0.00	2	0	1	1	1	1	Langley HS, Great Falls, Va.
Eric Hurley	0	0	1.08	3	0	8	3	2	7	Wolfson HS, Jacksonville
Chuck Lofgren	1	0	1.29	3	1	7	2	4	12	Serra HS, San Mateo, Calif.
Sean Watson	2	0	1.72	3	0	16	9	2	19	Gulliver Prep, Miami
Andy Beal	1	0	1.84	3	1	15	8	5	24	Peninsula HS, Palos Verdes Estates, Calif.
Zechry Zincola	0	0	3.86	1	0	2	4	3	1	Arlington HS, Riverside, Calif.

JUNIOR PAN AM GAMES
(18-and-under)

Camaguey, Cuba
July 1-12, 2001

ROUND ROBIN STANDINGS

	W	L	RF	RA
Cuba	9	0	95	15
United States	8	1	106	14
Panama	6	3	58	60
Venezuela	6	3	56	44
Brazil	5	4	65	51
Dominican Republic	4	5	70	79
Colombia	3	6	44	79
Mexico	2	7	48	55
Netherlands Antilles	2	7	40	79
Ecuador	0	9	14	120

GOLD MEDAL: Cuba. **SILVER MEDAL:** United States. **BRONZE MEDAL:** Panama (Top three teams qualify for 2002 World Junior Championship, Sherbrooke, Quebec; Canada, as host team, was ineligible to compete in qualifying tournament).

ALL-TOURNAMENT TEAM: C—Mike Nickeas, United States. **1B**—Jose Camarena, Panama. **2B**—Yulieski Gourriel, Cuba. **3B**—Nick Crowe, United States. **SS**—Tiago da Silva, Brazil. **LF**—Roberto Alvarez, Cuba. **CF**—Denard Span, United States. **RF**—Jeff Francoeur, United States. **DH**—Luis Lopez, Panama. **P**—Jeremy Sowers, United States. **Most Valuable Player:** Kendry Morales, Cuba.

INDIVIDUAL BATTING LEADERS
(Minimum 18 Plate Appearances)

	AVG	AB	R	H	2B	3B	HR	RBI	SB
Mike Nickeas, USA	.577	26	16	15	6	0	2	13	1
Nick Crowe, USA	.519	27	10	14	6	1	1	9	0
Jeff Francoeur, USA	.500	32	12	16	3	2	2	13	4
Jeff Crawford, USA	.500	30	10	15	3	0	0	7	4
B.J. Upton, USA	.480	25	8	12	1	1	1	7	3
Franklin Bautista, DR	.469	32	9	15	2	0	0	8	1
Denard Span, USA	.455	33	9	15	2	1	1	10	2
Roberto Alvarez, Cuba	.452	31	15	14	1	1	4	13	2
Yulieski Gourriel, Cuba	.433	30	9	13	3	0	2	10	1
Javier Blanco, Colombia	.429	21	5	9	4	0	0	1	0
Renan Sato, Brazil	.419	31	7	13	4	1	2	6	2
Kendry Morales, Cuba	.414	29	12	12	1	1	2	5	0
Joel Cordero, DR	.414	29	8	12	1	3	0	9	0
Ricardo Iturralde, Ecuador	.414	29	3	12	3	1	0	1	3
Tiago da Silva, Brazil	.414	29	3	12	1	0	0	11	0
Jose Camarena, Panama	.412	34	8	14	3	1	0	8	0
Juan Linares, Cuba	.400	25	7	10	1	0	3	11	1
Williams Uzcategui, Ven.	.400	30	8	12	3	0	1	9	0
Luis Lopez, Panama	.394	33	3	13	1	0	1	6	0
Matt Chico, USA	.389	18	5	7	3	1	0	4	0
Leandro Hasegawa, Brazil	.385	39	11	13	3	0	1	11	5
Carlos Vazquez, Cuba	.382	34	11	13	2	0	1	7	1

INDIVIDUAL PITCHING LEADERS
(Minimum 9 Innings)

	W	L	ERA	G	SV	IP	H	BB	SO
Jeremy Sowers, USA	2	0	0.00	2	0	11	5	7	21
Otoniel Vargas, DR	2	0	0.61	3	0	15	7	4	22
Juan Linares, Cuba	1	0	0.82	2	0	11	6	5	13
Grant Johnson, USA	1	0	0.93	2	0	10	5	2	6
Jose Martiz, Panama	2	0	1.32	3	0	14	13	6	10
Rodrigo Hirota, Brazil	1	0	1.38	4	0	13	12	8	14
Anderson Kudo, Brazil	0	0	1.93	3	0	9	6	3	4
Ifreidi Coss, Cuba	2	0	2.40	2	0	15	8	2	24
Simeon Checo, DR	1	0	2.51	3	0	14	23	0	6
Jorge Macuare, Venez.	1	1	2.51	2	0	14	16	3	6
Jorge Meza, Mexico	1	0	2.79	2	0	10	4	4	17
Fernando Sanchez, NA	0	0	2.89	3	0	9	13	3	6
Kendry Morales, Cuba	2	0	3.00	2	0	15	12	3	15
Dennis Suarez, Cuba	1	0	3.00	3	0	9	6	3	10

WORLD YOUTH CHAMPIONSHIP
(16-and-under)

Monterrey, Mexico
August 3-12, 2001

ROUND ROBIN STANDINGS

POOL A	W	L	RF	RA
United States	4	0	48	5
Mexico	3	1	25	17
Taiwan	2	2	32	20
Korea	1	3	17	32
South Africa	0	4	6	54

POOL B	W	L	RF	RA
Cuba	5	0	54	15
Australia	4	1	60	24
Venezuela	3	2	51	31
Japan	2	3	29	32
Czech Republic	1	4	17	58
Russia	0	5	4	55

GOLD MEDAL: United States. **SILVER MEDAL:** Venezuela. **BRONZE MEDAL:** Australia.

ALL-TOURNAMENT TEAM: C—Jayron Larrinaga, Cuba. **1B**—Ryan Hastie, Australia. **2B**—Chris Valaika, USA. **3B**—Carlos Arrieche, Venezuela. **SS**—Jeff Flaig, USA. **OF**—Michael Rogers, USA; Lastings Milledge, USA; Dong Kuk Shim, Korea.

INDIVIDUAL BATTING LEADERS
(Minimum 12 Plate Appearances)

	AVG	AB	R	H	2B	3B	HR	RBI	SB
Mike Rogers, USA	.667	15	6	10	2	2	0	5	3
Jeff Flaig, USA	.563	16	7	9	2	0	2	7	2
Anthony Reinke, Australia	.563	16	6	9	3	0	0	6	1
Konras Weitz, SA	.545	11	4	6	1	1	1	1	1
Jayron Larrinaga, Cuba	.529	17	4	9	3	0	1	10	0
Adolfo Gonzalez, Venez.	.524	21	6	11	1	0	0	3	1
Ryan Hastie, Australia	.500	20	10	10	2	0	2	11	0
Ji Hoon Jang, Korea	.500	14	1	7	0	0	0	3	1
Lastings Milledge, USA	.500	10	6	5	1	1	0	4	0
Michael Sadler, Australia	.500	12	4	6	2	0	0	7	2
Lin I Hung, Taiwan	.500	12	6	6	0	0	1	1	3
Taichi Kunugi, Japan	.474	19	5	9	2	0	1	7	0
Yoslin Fernandez, Cuba	.462	13	4	6	0	0	0	1	0
Trent T'Antonio, Aus.	.455	22	8	10	1	0	0	7	1
Matsura Sugiyama, Japan	.455	11	1	5	0	0	1	3	0
Jonarthan Gil, Venez.	.444	18	10	8	2	0	1	7	0
Carlos Arrieche, Venez.	.429	21	8	9	2	0	1	4	0
Mitch Graham, Australia	.412	17	6	7	3	0	0	3	3
Daniel Perales, USA	.417	12	3	5	3	0	1	3	1
Chiang-chien Ming, Taiwan	.412	17	3	7	2	0	0	5	3
Edimir Piminiti, Venez.	.412	17	4	7	1	0	0	5	0
Chang-sik Song, Taiwan	.400	10	3	4	2	0	0	3	1
Javier Lizarraga, Mexico	.400	10	1	4	1	0	0	1	0
Yusuit Moran, USA	.400	15	6	6	2	0	0	1	0
Jaroslav Jiilk, Czech	.400	10	2	4	1	0	0	1	0

INDIVIDUAL PITCHING LEADERS
(Minimum 5 Innings)

	W	L	ERA	G	SV	IP	H	BB	SO
Chuck Lofgren, USA	1	0	0.00	2	0	6	1	3	8
Cesar Rojas, Venezuela	1	0	0.00	1	0	7	1	6	7
Julio Canales, Mexico	0	0	0.00	2	0	5	6	2	4
Yusef Badia, Cuba	1	0	0.00	1	0	6	3	3	3
Liam Flaherty, Australia	1	0	0.00	2	0	7	2	3	9
Mike Rogers, USA	1	0	0.00	1	0	5	2	4	5
Andy Beal, USA	0	0	0.00	2	1	6	3	2	10
Motoi Matsuki, Japan	1	0	0.57	3	0	16	13	6	15
Sean Watson, USA	1	0	1.13	2	1	8	2	1	11
Joe Truchio, Australia	1	0	1.35	3	0	7	6	1	8
Lucas Vega, Mexico	1	0	2.84	2	0	6	6	2	2
Kenny Rodriguez, Cuba	2	0	3.21	2	0	14	9	2	12
Luis Bermudez, Venez.	0	0	3.60	2	0	5	7	1	3

Championships.

No. 1 seeded Cuba beat the second-seeded U.S. 3-2 in the gold-medal game despite a spectacular performance by left-hander Scott Kazmir (Cypress Falls HS, Houston), who came on with two outs in the bottom of the second and allowed one hit while striking out 15 in the final 6⅓ innings. But Cuba saddled Kazmir with the loss when it broke a 2-2 tie in the seventh on two walks and a sacrifice fly.

The second-place finish was the highest ever for the U.S. in an Americas qualifying tournament. Previously, the U.S. had won bronze medals in 1997, 1999 and 2000. The 2002 World Junior Championship will be played in

Sherbrooke, Quebec.

Overall, the U.S. went 9-2 in the 10-nation competition and outscored its opponents 120-17. Kazmir, the No. 1-ranked player in the draft class of 2002, lost both games for the U.S. He also lost to Cuba 4-1 in the preliminary round to finish 1-2, 3.95 with 31 strikeouts in 14 innings.

The unqualified star for the U.S. was another left-hander, Jeremy Sowers (Ballard HS, Louisville). The Cincinnati Reds' first-round draft pick pitched three shutouts while striking out 28 in 18 innings. He beat Panama 12-0 on a four-hitter in the semifinals to help the U.S. reach the gold-medal game.

Outfielder Jeff Francoeur, a rising senior at Parkview High in Lilburn, Ga., was the top hitter for the U.S. He hit .538-2-17. As a team, the U.S. hit .405.

Sowers, Francoeur, catcher Mike Nickeas, third baseman Nick Crowe and outfielder Denard Span were named to the all-tournament team.

Players were selected from Team USA's junior tryout camp in Joplin, Mo.

U.S. Wins Youth Title

The United States reaffirmed its world dominance at the 16-and-under level by going undefeated and capturing the

Jeremy Sowers, left, and Lastings Milledge led Team USA's junior and youth teams in international play in 2001. Sowers led the junior squad to a second-place finish at an Americas qualifying tournament in Cuba, pitching three straight shutouts. Milledge hit .522-3-10 to lead the youth team to a gold medal at the World Youth Championship in Mexico.

2001 International Baseball Federation AA World Youth Championship in Veracruz, Mexico.

Righthander Andrew Beal (Palos Verdes Estates, Calif.) struck out 14, and outfielder Lastings Milledge (Palmetto, Fla.) slammed his third home run in two games to lead Team USA to a 6-2 victory over Venezuela to earn the gold medal in the weeklong, 11-team tournament.

With the victory, the U.S. not only successfully defended its world title, last contested in 1998, but it stretched its winning streak in international competition to 25 games. It won all seven games it played in Mexico.

"For sure, 25 victories in a row is awesome," Team USA coach Chris Brown said. "When people talk about baseball around the world, they tend to identify baseball with the United States."

Cuba was expected to provide a stiff challenge for the U.S. as both teams went undefeated in their respective pools. But Cuba never played the U.S. as it was upset by Korea 3-2 in a quarterfinal game and ended up in seventh place.

The U.S. edged Japan 2-1 in its first playoff game, and then beat Australia 14-6 in a semifinal game as Milledge, the top-rated player in the draft class of 2003, had a pair of homers. He hit .522-3-10 overall.

That set up the championship final against surprising Venezuela, in which Beal allowed five hits and walked three. In two starts, Beal went 1-0, 0.84 and had 24 strikeouts in 15 innings. Righthander Sean Watson (Miami) also made two starts for the U.S., going 2-0, 1.72.

The big star throughout the tournament for the U.S., however, was shortstop Jeff Flaig (Placentia, Calif.), who led Team USA with a

GOLDEN SPIKES AWARD

MARC McCLINTOCK

Mark Prior

USA Baseball presents its annual Golden Spikes Award to the nation's best amateur player. In general, the organization shows loyalty by recognizing a player who made contributions to the governing body by playing for Team USA during the summer season.

In 2000, USA Baseball made an exception by giving its award to South Carolina righthander Kip Bouknight, who led college baseball with 17 wins but never was a member of Team USA. But in 2001, the award went back to its roots.

Southern California righthander Mark Prior, Baseball America's College Player of the Year and the No. 2 overall pick in the 2001 draft, won the Golden Spikes—a reward for his dominant 2001 college season as well as the two summers with Team USA that helped shape him as the nation's best amateur pitcher.

"I've probably done 90 percent of my developing with Team USA," said Prior, who went 15-1, 1.69 with a nation-leading 202 strikeouts during the college season. "Dealing with the travel and pitching to hitters from Japan and everything—it was a great experience."

While transferring from Vanderbilt to USC following his freshman year, Prior went 4-2, 2.52 for Team USA, tying for the team lead in wins. In the summer of 2000, Prior absorbed two of the team's three losses during a 27-3 wonder ride. He took a mini-sabbatical with that team to attend his brother's wedding and was nearly unhittable upon his return, throwing 24 consecutive scoreless innings and finishing the summer with 44 strikeouts in 34 innings. He gave up just 16 hits and had a 1.60 ERA—just a sign of the dominance that was to come in 2001.

—JOHN MANUEL

PREVIOUS **WINNERS**

1981—Mike Sodders, 3b, Arizona State
1982—Jeff Ledbetter, of-lhp, Florida State
1983—Dave Magadan, 1b, Alabama
1984—Oddibe McDowell, of, Arizona State
1985—Pete Incaviglia, of, Oklahoma State
1986—Casey Close, of, Michigan
1987—Robin Ventura, 3b, Oklahoma State
1988—John Olerud, 1b-lhp, Washington State
1989—Ben McDonald, rhp, Louisiana State
1990—Mike Kelly, of, Arizona State
1991—David McCarty, 1b, Stanford
1992—Phil Nevin, 3b, Cal State Fullerton
1993—Brooks Kieschnick, dh-rhp, Texas
1994—Jason Varitek, c, Georgia Tech
1995—Todd Helton, 1b-lhp, Tennessee
1996—Kris Benson, rhp, Clemson
1997—J.D. Drew, of, Florida State
1998—Jeff Austin, rhp, Stanford
1999—Jason Jennings, rhp, Baylor
2000—Kip Bouknight, rhp, South Carolina

SUMMER PLAYER OF THE YEAR

BY JOHN MANUEL

Bruce Springsteen was already one of rock and roll's biggest stars, but the album "Born in the USA" and its subsequent summer tour made The Boss rock's biggest name in the mid-1980s. Flash forward to 2001, when another New Jersey native cemented his place in his chosen field with a tour of the USA.

Rutgers rising junior righthander Bobby Brownlie had been one of college baseball's top pitchers for two years. But a dominating summer for Team USA during its Red, White and Blue Tour left little doubt that Brownlie is college baseball's premium player entering the 2002 season. His performance was so impressive that it earned him the distinction of Baseball America's Summer College Player of the Year.

"I'm a huge Springsteen fan," Brownlie said. "We stick together in New Jersey, and we have a lot to be proud of. I chose to stay home, and it's all part of what we're trying to do at Rutgers.

"A lot of the country thinks of the Northeast and doesn't think of college baseball. We're trying to change that and open some eyes. I welcome the pressure that comes with that."

Brownlie relished the chance to just pitch in the summer of 2001. He missed four starts during the spring with a fractured thumb and won just six games. Trying to make up for lost work, he made a team-high six starts for Team USA and entered three more games in relief.

He logged a team-high 53 innings, making his final start in front of many home fans at Trenton's Waterfront Park. He beat Taiwan 3-1 on three days' rest, making him 3-0 when pitching every fourth day. He won a pair of games in the Big East Conference tournament in 2000 on three days' rest as well.

Brownlie will wear the bullseye in 2002 as the nation's top pitching prospect. He went 7-0, 0.84 for Team USA, just falling short of breaking the 0.65 ERA record set in 2000 by Dewon Brazelton (Middle Tennessee State). That team also featured righthanders Josh Karp (UCLA) and Mark Prior (Southern California) and was one of the best in USA Baseball history. All three of those pitchers were selected in the first six picks of the 2001 draft.

"He's right there with those guys," said USA Baseball's Steve Cohen, who oversees the selection of Team USA's roster as director of national team operations. "He's got the stuff, the makeup—he's off the charts. He's clearly in the same league as those three guys."

SUMMER LEAGUE ALL-AMERICA TEAM

Selected by Baseball America

FIRST TEAM

Player	College	Club/League	AVG	AB	R	H	HR	RBI	SB
C Ben Fritz	Fresno State	Anch. Pilots (Alaska)	.306	170	28	52	2	25	1
1B Larry Broadway	Duke	Orleans (Cape Cod)	.264	159	24	42	6	27	4
2B Russ Adams	North Carolina	Orleans (Cape Cod)	.281	171	27	48	2	12	23
3B Chris Wright	Penn State	Winchester (Valley)	.339	177	30	60	8	38	10
SS Wes Timmons	Appalachian	Winchester (Valley)	.384	190	47	73	4	35	7
OF Matt Murton	Georgia Tech	Wareham (Cape Cod)	.324	145	23	47	2	28	19
OF Eric Reed	Texas A&M	Wareham (Cape Cod)	.365	167	29	61	1	15	22
OF Steve Stanley	Notre Dame	Delaware (Great Lakes)	.442	138	35	61	0	15	23
DH Jeremy Brown	Alabama	No. Ohio (Great Lakes)	.389	113	26	44	8	30	3

Pitcher	College	Club/League	W	L	ERA	IP	H	BB	SO
SP Bobby Brownlie	Rutgers	Team USA	7	0	0.84	53	32	11	60
SP Jeff Francis	British Columbia	Anch. Bucs (Alaska)	7	1	1.29	77	36	21	81
SP Chris Leonard	Miami (Ohio)	Wareham (Cape Cod)	6	0	0.98	55	42	11	64
SP Casey Schumaker	Jacksonville	Bourne (Cape Cod)	6	2	1.19	60	35	11	62
RP Ryan Speier	Radford	Bourne (Cape Cod)	0	0	0.00	20	10	6	35

SECOND TEAM

C—Mitch Maier, Lake Erie/Great Lakes (Toledo). 1B—Jeremy Reed, Team USA (Long Beach State). 2B—Shaun Larkin, Keene/New England (Cal State Northridge). 3B—Todd Leathers, Fairbanks/Alaska (Winthrop). SS—Kevin Howard, Team USA (Miami, Fla.). OF—Rod Allen, Anchorage Glacier Pilots/Alaska (Arizona State); Anthony Bocchino, Petersburg/Coastal Plain (Marist); Matt Mann, St. Cloud/Northwoods (North Dakota State). DH—Jason Perry, Hyannis/Cape Cod (Georgia Tech). SP—Kiki Bengochea, Team USA (Miami, Fla.); Jared Doyle, Durham/Coastal Plain (James Madison); Mike Esposito, Team USA (Arizona State); Steve Schilsky, Twin City/Central Illinois (Illinois Wesleyan). RP—David Bush, Chatham/Cape Cod (Wake Forest).

.536 average and 12 RBIs, and shared the team lead with Milledge with three homers.

"This is the best I have played in a short-term tournament and one of the best tournaments I have ever had," Flaig said. "This is the greatest feeling ever. I'll never forget this."

Flaig made his mark in the quarterfinal win against Japan, when he hit a two-run homer in the seventh and came on in relief to pitch a scoreless ninth, striking out two of the three hitters he faced.

The U.S. players were selected from Team USA's Junior Olympics competition that was played in Tucson and Jupiter, Fla., in late June, and from team trials that followed in Houston.

AMATEUR BASEBALL

SUMMER LEAGUES

While the Cape Cod League generally garners the best college prospects who don't end up with Team USA each summer, the most intriguing story of the 2001 summer season involved a Canadian who didn't play on the Cape.

Jeff Francis, a 6-foot-5 lefthander out of NAIA member British Columbia, took center stage both in the Alaska League, where he was named the MVP and top prospect, and at the National Baseball Congress World Series.

A projected first-round pick in the 2002 draft, Francis ran away with the Alaska League's player of the year award, going 7-1, 1.20 with 83 strikeouts in 76 innings. He threw a club-record six shutouts for the Anchorage Bucs. When that team failed to qualify for the NBC World Series, he was added to the rival Anchorage Glacier Pilots' roster and was named MVP of the 48-team tournament.

Francis worked 14 scoreless innings in the tournament, including 1⅔ in relief in the championship game as the Pilots beat the Hays Larks of the Jayhawk League 3-2.

It was the fifth NBC title in Glacier Pilots history, matching the Alaska Goldpanners for the most championships in the 66-year history of the NBC World Series. Alaska teams have won 15 of the last 33 tournaments.

Familiar Champ On Cape

In the Cape Cod League, another familiar face was winning a championship. The Wareham Gatemen, making their 12th consecutive appearance in the playoffs, hadn't won a game in the last two postseasons but changed that in 2001. They defeated Chatham in a best-of-three championship series two games to one to claim their third Arnold Mycock trophy in the last decade.

Wareham had squandered a 3-1 lead but rallied to win the rubber game of the series with a run in the bottom of the ninth. Gatemen shortstop Paul Henry (Ball State) beat out an infield single off Chatham relief ace Zane Carlson (Baylor), bringing home Keith Butler (Liberty) from third with the game-winner.

Wareham infielder Aaron Hill (Louisiana State), who went 8-for-20 with five RBIs, was named the playoff MVP, part of the team's sweep of the postseason league awards. Outfielder Matt Murton (Georgia Tech), who led the league in RBIs while batting .324-2-28, was named the regular sea-

Matt Murton

son MVP. Murton, a rising sophomore, had a .399 on-base percentage and was successful on 19 of 20 stolen-base attempts.

Murton ranked third on the Cape's Top 10 Prospects list, which was dominated by Atlantic Coast Conference performers. Orleans second baseman Russ Adams (North Carolina) was a surprise No. 1 based on his athletic ability, speed, good pop and consistency. Chatham reliever David Bush (Wake Forest), who didn't sign as the Devil Rays' fourth-round pick, was the No. 2 prospect.

In other summer amateur news:

■ The Danville Dans held off a furious Bluff City rally to force extra innings, then scored two in the 10th to win

LARRY SMITH

Jeff Francis: MVP in Alaska League, NBC World Series

the Central Illinois Collegiate League tournament championship for the third straight year.

■ Arlington dominated the Clark Griffith League again, posting the best regular season record, then sweeping Fauquier to win its fourth consecutive league championship. Arlington then went on to beat host Johnstown, Pa., twice on the final day of the annual All-American Amateur Baseball Association (AAABA) World Series, by scores of 6-3 and 8-2. It was the third AAABA title in four years for the Senators.

■ Durham swept its best-of-three Petitt Cup series against Wilson to claim its first Coastal Plain League championship.

■ Delaware claimed its second Great Lakes League championship in the past four years. The Cows set a league record with an .816 winning percentage; their 31-7 record was the best among all summer league teams.

■ The Newport Gulls won the New England Collegiate League championship, beating Keene 2-1 behind lefthander Joel Kirsten (Los Angeles Pierce JC). A 28th-round pick of the Blue Jays in June, Kirsten earned the victory with a dominating performance, striking out 10 without issuing a walk in eight innings.

■ Wisconsin, just 12-19 in the league's first half, won the Northwoods League championship when it defeated St. Cloud 5-3 in the third and final game of the title series. It denied the River Bats, who had won league titles in 1998 and 2000, their third championship.

■ Led by the league's pitcher and player of the year, Winchester edged Covington three games to two to win its 11th Shenandoah Valley League championship—its first since 1997. Shortstop Wes Timmons (Appalachian State), who had a 31-game hitting streak snapped in the championship series, was named player of the year. Righthander Chris Kees (Shenandoah, Va.) won the pitchers' award after accumulating 10 complete games in 11 starts.

COLLEGE
SUMMER LEAGUES

NCAA-CERTIFIED

ATLANTIC COLLEGIATE LEAGUE

WOLFF	W	L	PCT	GB
New Jersey Colts	26	14	.650	—
Quakertown Blazers	23	17	.575	3
Delaware Valley Gulls	20	20	.500	6
Scranton Red Soxx	16	24	.400	10

KAISER	W	L	PCT	GB
Newburgh Generals	29	8	.784	—
Long Island Collegians	22	18	.550	8½
Jersey Pilots	12	28	.300	18½
Metro New York Cadets	9	28	.243	20

PLAYOFFS: New Jersey defeated Long Island and Newburgh defeated Quakertown in one-game semifinals; New Jersey defeated Newburgh in one-game final.

Most Valuable Player: Mike Aviles, Newburgh (Concordia, N.Y.).
Outstanding Pitchers: Damien Myers, Newburgh (Concordia, N.Y.); Bob Young, Quakertown (Rider).

INDIVIDUAL BATTING LEADERS
(Minimum 100 Plate Appearances)

	AVG	AB	R	H	2B	3B	HR	RBI	SB
Lemanczyk, Matt, LI	.343	102	23	35	3	2	0	6	23
Kohlhausen, Dash, Delaware	.342	117	11	40	5	0	0	14	5
Lipschutz, Lee, Long Island	.342	120	26	41	7	3	3	19	9
Schneider, Mike, Quakertown	.333	123	22	41	13	0	2	20	0
Colon, Sam, Newburgh	.327	101	26	33	3	2	0	7	18
Aviles, Mike, Newburgh	.323	127	21	41	8	4	0	29	6
Caruso, Brian, New Jersey	.321	109	17	35	5	1	5	20	5
Staszewski, Tim, Quakertown	.315	124	22	39	9	0	1	13	14
Cueto, Ben, Newburgh	.306	111	14	34	3	0	0	21	2
Merkle, Thomas, Metro NY	.306	108	15	33	6	4	0	13	2
Schuck, Josh, Jersey	.304	92	12	28	2	0	1	7	17
Garcia, Travis, Newburgh	.302	96	23	29	8	0	2	20	5
Gaidos, Travis, New Jersey	.301	123	24	37	8	2	0	19	11
Helcoski, Jason, Scranton	.300	120	18	36	5	5	2	16	0
Tagel, Bryan, Scranton	.300	100	9	30	2	1	0	13	1

INDIVIDUAL PITCHING LEADERS
(Minimum 40 Innings)

	W	L	ERA	G	SV	IP	H	BB	SO
Szustowicz, Matt, Quakertown	4	2	1.20	12	2	45	29	16	32
Young, Bob, Quakertown	6	0	1.30	12	0	55	41	18	40
Trout, Jared, Quakertown	6	3	1.38	11	0	52	36	29	44
Pahucki, Dave, Newburgh	4	1	1.50	7	1	42	30	8	35
Midkiff, Matt, Newburgh	5	1	1.54	6	0	41	21	8	25
Myers, Damien, Newburgh	8	0	1.55	9	0	64	55	14	58
McKitish, Brian, Quakertown	3	4	1.75	9	0	46	22	9	40
Martin, Greg, Scranton	2	5	2.03	11	0	53	40	33	58
Carle, Jeremy, Newburgh	3	2	2.03	6	0	40	28	11	40
Worth, Chris, Jersey	1	2	2.05	12	0	57	47	19	54

CAPE COD LEAGUE

EAST	W	L	T	PCT	PTS
Yarmouth-Dennis Red Sox	25	19	0	.568	50
Chatham A's	25	19	0	.568	50
Orleans Cardinals	20	24	0	.455	40
Harwich Mariners	19	25	0	.432	38
Brewster Whitecaps	17	25	2	.405	36

WEST	W	L	T	PCT	PTS
Wareham Gatemen	25	18	1	.581	51
Bourne Braves	23	18	3	.561	49
Falmouth Commodores	23	19	2	.548	48
Cotuit Kettleers	20	20	4	.500	44
Hyannis Mets	17	27	0	.386	34

PLAYOFFS: Chatham defeated Yarmouth-Dennis 2-0 and Wareham defeated Bourne 2-0 in best-of-3 semifinals; Wareham defeated Chatham 2-1 in best-of-3 championship series.

Russ Adams: Cape Cod's top prospect

ALL-STAR TEAM: C—Troy Caradonna, Orleans (Duke). **1B**—Larry Broadway, Orleans (Duke). **2B**—Russ Adams, Orleans (North Carolina). **3B**—Aaron Hill, Wareham (Louisiana State). **SS**—Hunter Brown, Falmouth (Rice). **OF**—Jon Kaplan, Falmouth (Tulane); Bob Malek, Chatham (Michigan State); Matt Murton, Wareham (Georgia Tech); Eric Reed, Wareham (Texas A&M). **DH**—Jason Perry, Hyannis (Georgia Tech). **Util**—Mike McCoy, Chatham (San Diego). **SP**—Chris Leonard, Wareham (Miami, Ohio); Casey Shumaker, Bourne (Jacksonville); Ryan Speier, Bourne (Radford). **RP**—David Bush, Chatham (Wake Forest).
Most Valuable Player: Matt Murton, Wareham. **Pitcher of the Year:** Chris Leonard, Wareham.

TOP 10 PROSPECTS (selected by league managers): **1.** Russ Adams, 2b, Orleans (North Carolina). **2.** David Bush, rhp, Chatham (Wake Forest). **3.** Matt Murton, of, Wareham (Georgia Tech). **4.** Chris Leonard, lhp, Wareham (Miami, Ohio). **5.** Larry Broadway, 1b, Orleans (Duke). **6.** Joe Blanton, rhp, Bourne (Kentucky). **7.** Joe Saunders, lhp, Harwich (Virginia Tech). **8.** Ben Crockett, rhp, Wareham (Harvard). **9.** Aaron Hill, 3b, Wareham (Louisiana State). **10.** Chadd Blasko, rhp, Cotuit (Purdue).

INDIVIDUAL BATTING LEADERS
(Minimum 100 Plate Appearances)

	AVG	AB	R	H	2B	3B	HR	RBI	SB
Reed, Eric, Wareham	.365	167	29	61	5	1	1	15	22
Murton, Matt, Wareham	.324	145	23	47	7	0	2	28	19
Butler, Keith, Wareham	.312	125	11	39	7	1	0	16	6
Barthelemy, Ryan, Hyannis	.310	126	17	39	11	1	5	23	2
Caradonna, Troy, Orleans	.301	136	11	41	2	0	0	8	0
Brown, Hunter, Falmouth	.295	139	14	41	5	0	1	19	7
Schmidt, Jarrod, Falmouth	.292	154	16	45	3	0	2	15	2
Peavey, Bill, Cotuit	.288	132	19	38	8	1	5	22	0
Perry, Jason, Hyannis	.287	143	22	41	6	3	8	25	3
McCoy, Michael, Chatham	.283	145	25	41	6	0	3	15	23
Bourassa, Adam, Y-D	.282	149	22	42	3	1	0	9	6
Adams, Russ, Orleans	.281	171	27	48	5	1	2	12	23
Kaplan, Jon, Falmouth	.280	143	21	40	4	2	3	12	11
Huggins, Mike, Wareham	.274	157	16	43	6	1	2	20	5
Klocksien, Ryan, Y-D	.270	148	16	40	10	0	0	16	1
Sollmann, Steve, Y-D	.270	141	18	38	5	2	0	17	3
Greenberg, Adam, Chatham	.269	119	23	32	4	1	2	13	7
Carson, Matt, Brewster	.269	119	11	32	7	0	2	10	3
Reynolds, Tila, Y-D	.269	119	13	32	5	1	1	12	2
Henry, Paul, Wareham	.267	176	20	47	1	0	1	14	6
Broadway, Larry, Orleans	.264	159	24	42	6	1	6	27	4
Malek, Bob, Chatham	.263	152	10	40	8	0	1	18	6
Stavisky, Brian, Hyannis	.263	156	21	41	10	2	4	19	7
Hill, Aaron, Wareham	.259	166	22	43	10	0	0	19	6

Name	AVG	AB	R	H	2B	3B	HR	RBI	SB
Metheny, Brent, Cotuit	.256	160	16	41	11	0	2	12	1
Cleveland, Jeremy, Chatham	.252	119	16	30	6	0	2	22	0
Baker, John, Y-D	.250	132	15	33	6	0	2	20	0
Porfirio, A.J., Cotuit	.250	128	15	32	5	0	3	15	9
Barden, Brian, Brewster	.248	137	17	34	3	0	1	6	5
Davis, Matt, Harwich	.247	162	15	40	6	2	0	13	20
Cho, Hyung, Y-D	.245	151	20	37	4	0	3	18	2
Burgamy, Brian, Bourne	.244	164	16	40	4	1	1	13	7
Schuerholz, Jon, Brewster	.243	136	18	33	0	1	0	9	12
Italiano, Nick, Bourne	.242	99	9	24	1	0	0	9	1
Pontiff, Wally, Brewster	.240	150	15	36	7	0	1	9	2
Boran, Pat, Harwich	.238	143	10	34	2	0	0	10	11
English, Jed, Falmouth	.237	114	8	27	1	0	0	9	0
O'Riordan, Chris, Cotuit	.236	123	13	29	4	0	1	8	7
Frank, Kyle, Hyannis	.236	157	20	37	4	1	2	16	12
Nonemaker, Karl, Chatham	.235	98	8	23	2	0	0	10	0
Garko, Ryan, Hyannis	.233	120	14	28	2	1	3	19	1
Biernbaum, L.J., Hyannis	.233	86	16	20	5	0	1	5	3
Hamblen, Chris, Brewster	.232	151	16	35	4	1	1	16	7
Matienzo, Danny, Brewster	.230	113	7	26	7	0	2	12	2
Hutchinson, Burney, Har.	.230	122	11	28	6	0	2	10	9
Concepcion, Alberto, Cot.	.229	131	13	30	4	2	2	18	1
Verbryke, Erik, Y-D	.228	136	18	31	4	2	1	11	3
Oliva, Chad, Bourne	.227	154	18	35	7	1	3	15	3
Davidson, Tyler, Orleans	.226	155	14	35	6	2	1	13	9
Jackson, Conor, Bourne	.225	129	13	29	6	0	3	12	4
Majewski, Val, Bourne	.222	153	17	34	7	2	3	20	9
Brown, Mike, Hyannis	.222	99	10	22	3	0	0	8	3
King, Ben, Falmouth	.221	113	16	25	5	1	1	14	10

INDIVIDUAL PITCHING LEADERS
(Minimum 40 Innings)

Name	W	L	ERA	G	SV	IP	H	BB	SO
Leonard, Chris, Wareham	6	0	0.98	7	0	55	42	11	64
Saunders, Joe, Harwich	4	3	1.02	8	0	53	32	11	61
Moore, Daniel, Chatham	5	2	1.02	7	0	44	36	20	46
Shumaker, Casey, Bourne	6	2	1.19	11	0	60	35	11	62
Clark, Ray, Falmouth	3	1	1.31	14	3	41	21	10	53
Robertson, Luke, Harwich	3	3	1.46	9	1	55	32	14	59
Hutchinson, Trevor, Orleans	3	3	1.47	7	0	43	26	7	44
Stetter, Mitch, Cotuit	4	2	1.49	7	0	48	30	17	36
Meyer, Daniel, Cotuit	3	1	1.55	14	3	41	23	16	49
Lynch, Matt, Harwich	3	2	1.59	8	0	51	32	8	63
Crockett, Ben, Wareham	1	6	1.67	9	0	59	41	9	74
Combs, Ryan, Cotuit	2	3	1.74	9	0	57	48	15	33
White, Steven, Falmouth	3	1	1.75	9	0	51	34	17	56
Herce, Steven, Falmouth	2	4	1.79	8	0	40	31	13	34
Bayer, Russ, Wareham	4	1	1.80	9	0	55	44	19	36
Brauer, Jim, Y-D	2	3	1.84	8	0	49	41	15	41
Read, Robby, Bourne	3	3	1.88	13	0	67	39	26	58
Gloger, Ryan, Brewster	3	3	2.03	10	0	58	46	8	47
Blanton, Joe, Bourne	5	2	2.25	11	0	68	45	22	77
Clayton, Ben, Chatham	1	1	2.25	8	0	40	31	15	40
Saylor, Clark, Y-D	4	0	2.34	13	0	42	32	20	26
Blasko, Chadd, Cotuit	3	3	2.34	9	0	42	24	16	36
Girardeau, Clark, Wareham	4	2	2.35	9	0	61	39	23	65
Hogan, Gary, Falmouth	4	2	2.66	9	0	47	40	13	35
Jackson, Steven, Falmouth	1	1	2.66	8	0	44	25	13	24
McGuire, Rich, Chatham	5	3	2.68	9	0	57	51	16	30
Ponder, Steve, Y-D	5	3	2.73	9	0	53	41	26	65
Korecky, Bobby, Y-D	3	3	2.72	7	0	46	40	9	29
Sleeth, Kyle, Cotuit	3	1	2.76	8	0	49	47	11	47
Dennison, Mike, Bourne	3	2	2.76	29	0	42	46	8	41
Copeland, Stephen, Brew.	3	3	2.83	10	0	48	42	9	33
Autrey, Scott, Orleans	2	2	2.83	9	0	54	49	14	59

CENTRAL ILLINOIS LEAGUE

EAST	W	L	PCT	GB
Danville Dans	31	15	.674	—
Twin City Stars	28	20	.583	4
Decatur Blues	16	30	.348	15

WEST	W	L	PCT	GB
Bluff City Bombers	26	22	.542	—
Quincy Gems	22	26	.458	4
Springfield Rifles	19	29	.396	7

PLAYOFF TOURNAMENT: Danville (3-1), Bluff City (2-1), Quincy (1-2), Twin City (0-2).

ALL-STAR TEAM: C—Wayne Austraskas, Bluff City (Kaskaskia, Ill., CC); David Harrell, Danville (Purdue); Tim Marks, Twin City (Butler). **1B**—Ron Hensel, Springfield (Bradley). **IF**—Seth Bynum, Quincy (Lincoln Trail, Ill., CC); Brian Fritzler, Springfield (Lewis, Ill.); Luke Humphrey, Bluff City (SIU-Edwardsville); Chad Opel, Bluff City (SIU-Edwardsville). **OF**—Mike Bowen,

Bluff City (Southwest Missouri State); John Brock, Twin City (Northern Illinois); David Coffey, Danville (Georgia); Tony Grana, Bluff City (Danville Area, Ill., CC); Ted Ledbetter, Springfield (Oklahoma State). **DH**—Eric Focht, Quincy (Indiana Tech); Justin Pouk, Decatur (Wabash Valley, Ill., CC); Mike Saunches, Twin City (Illinois State). **SP**—Brian Borgmann, Danville (Danville Area, Ill., CC); Bryan Gale, Bluff City (Michigan State); Luke Hagerty, Quincy (Ball State); Ryan Richard, Danville (San Diego); Dustin Scheffel, Danville (Sacramento CC), Steve Schilsky, Twin City (Illinois Wesleyan). **RP**—Eric Bowden, Danville (St. Mary's); Jordan Faircloth, Danville (Louisiana State); Greg Modica, Quincy (Culver-Stockton, Mo.); Eric Stults, Danville (Bethel, Ind.); Mark Sopko, Twin City (Arizona State).

Player of the Year: Chad Opel, Bluff City. **Pitcher of the Year:** Steve Schilsky, Twin City.

INDIVIDUAL BATTING LEADERS
(Minimum 100 Plate Appearances)

Name	AVG	AB	R	H	2B	3B	HR	RBI	SB
Opel, Chad, Bluff City	.370	162	34	60	6	8	2	34	11
Brock, John, Twin City	.337	166	25	56	3	1	1	19	23
Humphrey, Luke, BC	.333	114	22	38	3	2	2	15	13
Hensel, Ron, Springfield	.329	149	15	49	8	4	0	22	5
Fritzler, Brian, Springfield	.301	143	27	43	9	1	2	14	4
Marks, Tim, Twin City	.299	97	7	29	6	1	1	19	0
Ledbetter, Ted, Springfield	.298	104	19	31	7	1	4	17	2
Bynum, Seth, Quincy	.294	160	16	47	9	2	1	16	8
Bowen, Mike, Bluff City	.293	99	22	29	7	1	2	18	4
Astrauskas, Wayne, BC	.281	135	19	38	10	0	3	26	2
Coffey, David, Danville	.281	139	31	39	8	1	6	19	7
Grana, Tony, Bluff City	.277	177	39	49	6	3	0	23	15
Harrell, David, Danville	.276	152	20	42	9	4	1	24	3
Strickler, Steve, Twin City	.274	168	20	46	9	0	0	19	2
Varela, Edgar, Danville	.272	169	20	46	9	0	0	22	4

INDIVIDUAL PITCHING LEADERS
(Minimum 40 Innings)

Name	W	L	ERA	G	SV	IP	H	BB	SO
Schilsky, Steve, Twin City	8	0	0.54	9	0	67	38	20	72
Modica, Greg, Quincy	3	3	0.99	10	0	46	30	19	31
Gale, Bryan, Bluff City	7	1	1.30	10	0	62	46	20	54
Richard, Ryan, Danville	6	1	1.42	10	0	57	38	16	38
Borgmann, Brian, Danville	6	2	1.42	12	0	70	53	8	44
Hagerty, Luke, Quincy	6	0	1.51	10	0	60	36	16	85
Scheffel, Dustin, Danville	6	1	1.55	10	0	52	29	20	49
Stults, Eric, Danville	3	2	1.79	13	1	40	27	16	34
Evans, Rocky, Danville	2	1	2.06	8	0	44	41	10	32
Bough, Brett, Twin City	1	4	2.22	10	0	69	58	20	43

COASTAL PLAIN LEAGUE

NORTH	W	L	PCT	GB
*+Wilson Tobs	31	19	.620	—
Petersburg Generals	27	23	.540	4
Peninsula Pilots	24	27	.471	7 ½
Edenton Steamers	21	29	.420	10
Outer Banks Daredevils	17	31	.354	13

SOUTH	W	L	PCT	GB
*+Durham Braves	32	17	.653	—
+Fayetteville Swampdogs	31	18	.633	1
Asheboro Copperheads	24	25	.490	8
Thomasville Hi-Toms	23	27	.460	9 ½
Florence Redwolves	21	27	.438	10 ½
Wilmington Sharks	21	29	.420	11 ½

*First-half champion   +Second-half champion

PLAYOFFS: Durham defeated Fayetteville in one-game division playoff; Durham defeated Wilson 2-0 in best-of-3 series for league championship.

ALL-STAR TEAM: C—Greg Metzger, Wilson (Brown). **1B**—Michael Johnson, Florence (Clemson). **2B**—Chris Dunn, Durham (Southern Mississippi). **3B**—Trey Wakefield, Wilmington (William & Mary). **SS**—Brian Ingram, Fayetteville (Elon). **OF**—Anthony Bocchino, Petersburg (Marist); Jason Tuttle, Wilson (Elon); Chris Walker, Asheboro (Georgia Southern). **DH**—Bill Saul, Thomasville (Cal Poly San Luis Obispo). **Util**—Jason Battle, Thomasville (North Carolina A&T); Matt Lederhos, Outer Banks (Boston College). **RHP**—John Estes, Petersburg (Freed-Hardeman, Tenn.). **LHP**—Jared Doyle, Durham (James Madison). **RP**—Jason Walker, Asheboro (UNC-Asheville).

Most Valuable Player: Jared Doyle, Durham

TOP 10 PROSPECTS (selected by league managers): **1.** Tom Mastney, rhp, Wilson (Furman). **2.** Jared Doyle, lhp, Durham (James Madison). **3.** Michael Johnson, 1b, Florence (Clemson). **4.** Anthony Bocchino, of, Petersburg (Marist). **5.** Chris Walker, of, Asheboro (Georgia Southern). **6.** David Marchbanks, lhp, Wilmington (South Carolina). **7.** Blake Horsman, rhp, Edenton (Arkansas State). **8.** Jason Battle, of, Thomasville (North Carolina A&T). **9.** John Estes, rhp, Petersburg (Freed-Hardeman, Tenn.). **10.** Greg Metzger, c, Wilson (Brown).

INDIVIDUAL BATTING LEADERS
(Minimum 100 Plate Appearances)

	AVG	AB	R	H	2B	3B	HR	RBI	SB
Bocchino, Anthony, Pete.	.378	180	26	68	16	1	1	18	11
Tuttle, Jason, Wilson	.377	159	37	60	3	4	0	14	20
Beck, Ben, Peninsula	.347	98	14	34	2	3	2	17	2
Wakefield, Trey, Wilmington	.344	183	30	63	13	0	3	22	7
Saul, Bill, Thomasville	.344	160	31	55	8	1	0	11	5
Johnson, Michael, Florence	.338	157	30	53	10	0	3	22	4
Battle, Jason, Thomasville	.327	168	26	55	9	1	0	14	14
Dunn, Chris, Durham	.322	174	29	56	9	1	3	20	14
Lederhos, Matt, OB	.317	164	28	52	9	2	1	15	16
Ingram, Brian, Fayetteville	.316	190	34	60	10	1	2	22	15
Metzger, Greg, Wilson	.308	130	22	40	9	0	0	18	9
Correll, Brad, Asheboro	.307	189	24	58	11	1	4	22	6
Smithlin, Zack, Fayetteville	.301	176	30	53	4	1	0	12	21
Church, Brad, Fayetteville	.301	133	15	40	2	0	0	13	7
Maples, Chris, Durham	.301	103	18	31	3	0	3	21	7
Moyer, Wes, Outer Banks	.293	157	26	46	13	1	2	12	2
Nicolas, Cesar, Florence	.289	166	30	48	6	1	10	25	0
Triplett, Russ, Florence	.285	165	28	47	6	0	7	18	5
Vandiver, Josh, Wilmington	.282	188	20	53	10	1	3	29	1
Finn, Ryan, Petersburg	.279	154	24	43	7	0	3	23	3

INDIVIDUAL PITCHING LEADERS
(Minimum 40 Innings)

	W	L	ERA	G	SV	IP	H	BB	SO
Marchbanks, David, Wilmington	3	1	0.82	6	0	44	25	8	37
Woods, Matt, Wilmington	3	2	1.09	9	0	49	37	13	35
Doyle, Jared, Durham	7	1	1.29	13	2	70	45	31	80
Mastny, Tom, Wilson	3	5	1.43	10	0	69	43	17	72
Estes, John, Petersburg	7	1	1.63	14	0	99	80	6	63
Walker, Jason, Asheboro	5	2	1.65	28	10	49	41	7	44
Blocker, Tyson, Thomasville	5	1	1.79	11	0	45	36	4	46
Batton, Derek, Fayetteville	4	2	1.93	7	0	42	40	17	28
Watts, Marshall, Asheboro	4	3	1.97	9	0	64	56	17	37
McKee, Derek, Asheboro	4	3	2.07	9	0	61	47	23	48
Bondurant, Steve, Edenton	2	4	2.08	11	0	69	53	31	65
Hoffman, Brett, Outer Banks	4	4	2.11	11	0	68	50	23	60
Hager, Ben, Wilson	5	2	2.11	12	0	77	64	28	65
Olsen, Justin, Durham	5	3	2.18	9	0	66	46	31	55
Joaquin, Matt, Peninsula	4	3	2.19	9	0	62	50	28	56

GREAT LAKES LEAGUE

	W	L	PCT	GB
Delaware Cows	31	7	.816	—
Northern Ohio	29	11	.725	3
Columbus All-Americans	24	15	.615	7½
Grand Lake Mariners	22	17	.564	9½
Michigan Panthers	19	17	.527	11
Stark County Terriers	20	20	.500	12
Lima Locos	19	20	.487	12½
Lake Erie Monarchs	18	19	.486	12½
Motor City Marauders	10	28	.263	21
Youngstown Express	10	29	.256	21½
Pittsburgh Pandas	10	29	.256	21½

PLAYOFFS: Northern Ohio defeated Stark County in championship game of eight-team modified double-elimination tournament.

ALL-STAR TEAM: C—Rock Mills, Northern Ohio (Pepperdine); Mitch Maier, Lake Erie (Toledo). **1B**—Jeremy Brown, Northern Ohio (Alabama). **2B**—Trent Otis, Delaware (Grand Canyon). **3B**—Mike Martinez, Northern Ohio (Cal State Fullerton). **SS**—Victor Menocal, Northern Ohio (Georgia Tech). **OF**—Shane Costa, Northern Ohio (Cal State Fullerton); Ryan Goleski, Columbus (Eastern Michigan); Dan Lunsford, Delaware (Ohio); Steve Stanley, Delaware (Notre Dame). **DH**—Drew Caravella, Columbus (Ohio Wesleyan). **Util**—Shawn Bolinger, Delaware (Dayton). **SP**—Brian Burks, Northern Ohio (Georgia Tech); Dominic Carmosino, Delaware (Oakland); Jeff Garner, Michigan (Central Michigan); Dan Horvath, Lake Erie (Central Michigan). **RP**—Shawn Burchett, Lima (Ohio Wesleyan).

Most Valuable Players: Jeremy Brown, Northern Ohio; Steve Stanley, Delaware. **Pitcher of the Year:** Dominic Carmosino, Delaware.

TOP 10 PROSPECTS (selected by league managers): **1.** Dan Horvath, rhp, Lake Erie (Central Michigan). **2.** Jeremy Brown, 1b, Northern Ohio (Alabama). **3.** Matt DeSalvo, rhp, Delaware (Marietta, Ohio). **4.** Marcus Cornell, rhp, Delaware (Ohio). **5.** Rock Mills, c, Northern Ohio (Pepperdine). **6.** Jeff Garner, rhp, Michigan (Central Michigan). **7.** Drew Caravella, 1b, Columbus (Ohio Wesleyan). **8.** Steve Obenchain, rhp, Grand Lake (Evansville). **9.** Mitch Maie, c, Lake Erie (Toledo). **10.** Victor Menocal, ss, Northern Ohio (Georgia Tech).

INDIVIDUAL BATTING LEADERS
(Minimum 100 Plate Appearances)

	AVG	AB	R	H	2B	3B	HR	RBI	SB
Lunsford, Dan, Delaware	.506	89	25	45	10	1	4	20	2
Stanley, Steve, Delaware	.442	138	35	61	5	3	0	15	23
Caravella, Drew, Columbus	.414	99	18	41	6	1	1	21	0
Goleski, Ryan, Columbus	.406	96	22	39	9	0	1	15	3
Nisbett, Marshall, GL	.397	116	21	46	3	3	1	19	11
Brown, Jeremy, NO	.389	113	26	44	12	0	8	30	3
Costa, Shane, NO	.387	119	25	46	7	0	1	12	7
Smith, David, Grand Lake	.371	132	19	49	8	1	2	32	5
Gaffney, Mike, Lima	.367	117	18	36	3	1	0	9	4
Rea, Brad, Pittsburgh	.367	128	19	47	10	2	7	29	0
Foreman, Jason, Pittsburgh	.351	94	22	33	3	0	5	21	1
Arbinger, Mike, Grand Lake	.350	157	34	55	10	2	2	27	3
Links, Lance, Delaware	.348	92	13	32	7	1	4	17	0
Contreras, Frankie, Del.	.345	116	23	40	10	1	1	18	5
Mills, Rock, Northern Ohio	.341	129	31	44	16	2	5	38	2

INDIVIDUAL PITCHING LEADERS
(Minimum 30 Innings)

	W	L	ERA	G	SV	IP	H	BB	SO
DeSalvo, Matt, Delaware	3	0	1.06	6	0	34	13	15	41
Carmosino, Dominic, Del.	5	0	1.29	9	0	35	34	16	33
Barrack, Jacob, NO	4	0	1.64	7	0	33	23	7	39
Henschen, Nathan, Lima	4	1	1.85	8	0	39	33	14	23
Lynch, Brian, Grand Lake	4	1	1.99	8	0	45	28	12	41
Burks, Brian, Northern Ohio	5	1	2.04	9	0	49	39	16	55
Horvath, Dan, Lake Erie	5	5	2.25	11	0	64	48	16	59
LaRatta, E.J., Columbus	2	1	2.32	9	3	31	32	9	26
Lucy, Patrick, Northern Ohio	4	0	2.33	9	0	31	30	9	18
Pleiness, Chad, Lake Erie	4	5	2.47	10	0	69	55	38	77

NEW ENGLAND COLLEGIATE LEAGUE

NATIONAL	W	L	PCT	GB
Torrington Twisters	25	15	.625	—
Keene Swamp Bats	24	16	.600	1
Mill City All-Americans	23	17	.575	2
Danbury Westerners	17	23	.425	8
Concord Quarry Dogs	16	24	.400	9
AMERICAN	**W**	**L**	**PCT**	**GB**
Newport Gulls	25	15	.625	—
Eastern Tides	24	16	.600	1
Riverpoint Royals	17	23	.425	8
Middletown Giants	16	24	.400	9
Manchester Silkworms	13	27	.325	12

PLAYOFFS: Keene defeated Torrington 2-1 and Newport defeated Eastern 2-1 in best-of-3 semifinal series; Newport defeated Keene 2-1 in best-of-3 championship series.

ALL-STAR TEAM: C—Eric Winegarden, Newport (New Mexico State). **1B**—Nate Gold, Torrington (Gonzaga). **2B**—Shaun Larkin, Keene (Cal State Northridge). **3B**—Kevin Wissner, Middletown (Connecticut). **SS**—Taber Lee, Torrington (San Diego State). **OF**—Joe Apotheker, Danbury (Barry, Fla.); Reid Gorecki, Manchester (Delaware); Billy Grasier (St. John's). **DH**—Kainoa Obrey, Newport (Brigham Young). **P**—Joel Kirsten, Newport (Los Angeles Pierce JC); John Velosky, Concord (Dartmouth); Brian Waack, Riverpoint (Lander, S.C.).

Most Valuable Player: Shaun Larkin, Keene. **Outstanding Pitcher:** John Velosky, Concord.

TOP 10 PROSPECTS (selected by league managers): **1.** Taber Lee, ss, Torrington (San Diego State). **2.** Shaun Larkin, 2b, Keene (Cal State Northridge). **3.** Mike Bohlander, 1b, Newport (Pace). **4.** Chris Westervelt, c, Keene (Stetson). **5.** John Velosky, rhp, Concord (Dartmouth). **6.** Matt Effeldt, rhp, Concord (Boston College). **7.** Joel Kirsten, lhp, Newport (Los Angeles Pierce JC). **8.** Kainoa Obrey, 3b, Newport (Brigham Young). **9.** Matt Tupman, c, Concord (Massachusetts-Lowell). **10.** Billy Grasier, of, Newport (St. John's).

INDIVIDUAL BATTING LEADERS
(Minimum 100 Plate Appearances)

	AVG	AB	R	H	2B	3B	HR	RBI	SB
Westervelt, Chris, Keene	.359	131	26	47	8	0	3	22	6
Larkin, Shaun, Keene	.358	148	30	53	9	0	8	27	1
Graiser, Billy, Newport	.341	138	25	47	10	1	0	10	32
Jackson, Doug, Newport	.328	128	28	42	6	3	1	20	8
Bohlander, Mike, Newport	.325	151	28	49	5	0	10	29	0
Henry, Chad, Newport	.324	102	24	33	4	0	4	17	6
Wissner, Kevin, Middletown	.323	133	28	43	9	0	7	31	2
Lee, Taber, Torrington	.321	137	22	44	6	2	0	10	14
McCutchan, Brett, Danbury	.317	123	18	39	7	0	3	27	3
Winegarden, Erik, Newport	.315	89	20	28	6	1	4	21	2
Kane, Jason, Newport	.311	132	19	41	7	2	2	29	4
Gold, Nate, Torrington	.310	113	18	35	7	2	5	28	0

Justin DiLucchio, Front Royal (Duke); Blair Hayden, Covington (Lynchburg); Chris Kees, Winchester (Shenandoah, Va.). **RP**—Ryan Molchan, Winchester (Rutgers); Klint Rommel, Covington (Austin Peay).

Most Valuable Player: Wes Timmons, Winchester. **Outstanding Pitcher:** Chris Kees, Winchester.

INDIVIDUAL BATTING LEADERS
(Minimum 100 Plate Appearances)

	AVG	AB	R	H	2B	3B	HR	RBI	SB
Timmons, Wes, Winchester	.384	190	47	73	18	2	4	35	7
Gragg, John, Winchester	.383	193	43	74	17	2	2	41	13
Honce, Joe, Covington	.352	182	27	64	7	3	1	21	18
Stephenson, Rick, NM	.343	99	14	34	3	0	0	16	6
Spearman, Jemel, FR	.339	171	33	58	9	3	0	24	21
Wright, Chris, Winchester	.339	177	30	60	13	2	8	38	10
Harrison, Ben, Harrisonburg	.336	113	28	38	9	0	1	23	18
Apple, Ryan, Front Royal	.333	129	21	43	9	3	0	20	13
Bennett, Ross, Harrisonburg	.326	92	14	30	3	1	0	14	5
Erwin, Brad, New Market	.321	112	19	36	7	2	1	8	2
Stone, David, Staunton	.317	145	42	46	6	2	1	10	21
Miller, Wade, Luray	.314	140	25	44	9	0	7	25	1
Carter, Chris, Waynesboro	.311	106	10	33	5	2	1	11	4
Harris, Gary, Covington	.308	146	34	45	7	2	3	15	20
Bibbs, Kennard, Harrisonburg	.303	195	46	59	5	1	0	15	29
Hearn, Scott, Covington	.303	178	23	54	12	1	1	24	4
Geswein, Kyle, Staunton	.299	137	23	41	10	0	9	34	2
Ennis, Adam, Winchester	.287	167	17	48	13	1	2	23	6
Mannix, Kevin, Staunton	.287	87	13	25	8	0	2	17	3
Webb, Trey, Harrisonburg	.287	160	24	46	8	1	0	30	7

INDIVIDUAL PITCHING LEADERS
(Minimum 40 Innings)

	W	L	ERA	G	SV	IP	H	BB	SO
Kalita, Ryan, Waynesboro	0	3	1.47	8	0	43	40	27	41
Kees, Chris, Winchester	8	2	1.48	11	0	97	70	12	72
Borsa, B.J., Winchester	6	1	1.63	10	0	61	47	17	67
Buzachero, Bubby, Staunton	3	2	1.77	13	1	56	35	21	80
Campbell, Casey, Covington	4	1	2.24	13	0	52	51	17	29
Johnson, Matt, New Market	3	2	2.25	7	0	44	50	7	25
Hayden, Blair, Covington	3	2	2.47	9	0	51	43	16	32
Uhl, Jon, Front Royal	3	2	2.61	8	0	48	47	18	40
Burton, Jared, New Market	4	3	2.67	8	0	57	42	14	62
Cerrato, Justin, Staunton	4	0	2.72	12	0	40	28	8	27
Hahn, Jeff, Winchester	4	2	2.80	10	0	71	64	17	29
Casey, Reid, Covington	4	2	2.84	10	0	57	56	28	70
Dooley, Jason, Winchester	4	1	2.87	9	0	63	72	14	63
Burdette, Jason, New Market	3	2	2.91	8	0	53	43	18	50
Ernst, John, Front Royal	2	2	2.91	23	5	43	37	9	36
Rew, Daniel, Covington	4	0	2.91	11	0	53	32	30	58
Moore, Justin, Harrisonburg	2	2	3.09	6	0	44	46	7	33
Burke, Greg, Front Royal	3	2	3.27	7	1	41	32	13	55
Foster, Seth, Waynesboro	1	5	3.32	8	0	57	54	15	66
Jarrett, Brett, Staunton	3	3	3.40	9	1	45	49	6	27

NON-AFFILIATED LEAGUES

ALASKA LEAGUE

	W	L	PCT	GB	Overall W	L
*Anchorage Glacier Pilots	24	11	.685	—	31	19
*Mat-Su Miners	21	14	.600	3	28	19
Anchorage Bucs	20	15	.571	4	31	19
Fairbanks Goldpanners	16	19	.457	8	26	27
Kenai Peninsula Oilers	13	20	.394	10	21	28
Athletes in Action	9	24	.273	14	11	32

*Advanced to National Baseball Congress World Series

ALL-STAR TEAM: C—David Wallace, Anchorage Bucs (Vanderbilt). **1B**—Luke Simmons, Kenai (Illinois). **2B**—Marc Teahen, Kenai (St. Mary's). **3B**—Todd Leathers, Goldpanners (Winthrop). **SS**—Marc Tugwell, Goldpanners (Virginia Tech). **OF**—Rod Allen, Anchorage Glacier Pilots (Arizona State); Ben Francisco, Anchorage Glacier Pilots (UCLA); Nick McIntyre, Mat-Su (Purdue). **DH/Util**—Ben Fritz, Anchorage Glacier Pilots (Fresno State). **SP**—Jeff Francis, Anchorage Bucs (British Columbia); Carl Makowsky, Anchorage Glacier Pilots (Northwestern State); Ryan McCally, Anchorage Bucs (Stanford); Luke Steidlmayer, Mat-Su (California-Davis). **RP**—Abe Alvarez, Mat-Su (Long Beach State).

Most Valuable Player: Jeff Francis, Anchorage Bucs.

TOP 10 PROSPECTS (selected by managers); **1.** Jeff Francis, lhp, Anchorage Bucs (British Columbia). **2.** Ben Fritz, c-rhp, Anchorage Glacier Pilots (Fresno State). **3.** Brian Finch, rhp, Anchorage Bucs (Texas A&M). **4.** Jamie D'Antona, 3b, Kenai (Wake Forest). **5.** Juan Serrato, rhp, Kenai (Riverside, Calif., CC). **6.** Ryan Wing, lhp, Kenai (Riverside, Calif., CC). **7.**

Ryan Molchan: 4-0, 0.82, five saves for Winchester

Koman, Brock, Concord	.298	141	16	42	8	1	3	15	2
Hubbard, Marshall, Danbury	.298	114	20	34	9	1	3	16	2
McCusker, Adam, Lowell	.298	151	20	45	4	1	2	19	7

INDIVIDUAL PITCHING LEADERS
(Minimum 40 Innings)

	W	L	ERA	G	SV	IP	H	BB	SO
Velosky, John, Concord	6	1	0.76	8	0	59	39	28	65
Stauffer, Tim, Keene	7	0	1.35	7	0	60	44	3	40
Kirsten, Joel, Newport	6	0	1.73	9	0	57	32	7	58
Schumey, Matt, Eastern	6	1	1.79	21	3	45	29	11	27
Gale, Chris, Keene	1	2	1.84	9	0	44	26	12	27
Waack, Brian, Riverpoint	4	2	1.89	9	0	62	43	19	43
Ribas, Gabe, Keene	6	2	2.01	9	0	72	61	17	60
Barlow, Chris, Newport	3	1	2.06	8	0	52	43	13	56
Thatcher, Joe, Danbury	5	2	2.11	7	0	47	41	21	25
Auth, Gerry, Concord	3	3	2.12	9	0	64	57	20	41

SHENANDOAH VALLEY LEAGUE

NORTH	W	L	PCT	GB
Winchester Royals	28	12	.700	—
Front Royal Cardinals	21	19	.525	7
New Market Rebels	20	20	.500	8
Luray Wranglers	13	27	.325	15

SOUTH	W	L	PCT	GB
Covington Lumberjacks	23	17	.575	—
Harrisonburg Turks	22	18	.550	1
Staunton Braves	21	19	.525	2
Waynesboro Generals	12	28	.300	11

PLAYOFFS: Winchester defeated Front Royal 3-2 and Covington defeated Harrisonburg 3-0 in best-of-5 semifinal series; Winchester defeated Covington 3-2 in best-of-5 championship series.

ALL-STAR TEAM: C—Lance Newman, Covington (Troy State). **1B**—Drew Miller, Luray (Troy State). **2B**—Joe Honce, Covington (West Virginia Wesleyan). **3B**—Chris Wright, Winchester (Penn State). **SS**—Wes Timmons, Winchester (Appalachian State). **OF**—Kennard Bibbs, Harrisonburg (Oklahoma City); John Gragg, Winchester (Arkansas-Little Rock); Gary Harris, Covington (Georgia College); David Stone, Staunton (Virginia). **DH**—Kyle Geswein, Staunton (Michigan State); Wade Miller, Luray (Troy State). **Util**—Blake Gill, Front Royal (Louisiana State); Jemel Spearman, Front Royal (Georgia Southern). **SP**—Bubby Buzachero, Staunton (Tennessee Tech);

Ben Francisco, of, Anchorage Glacier Pilots (UCLA). **8.** Rod Allen, of, Anchorage Glacier Pilots (Arizona State). **9.** Luke Steidlmayer, rhp, Mat-Su (California-Davis). **10.** Dave Wallace, c, Anchorage Bucs (Vanderbilt).

INDIVIDUAL BATTING LEADERS
(Minimum 100 Plate Appearances)

	AVG	AB	R	H	2B	3B	HR	RBI	SB
Simmons, Luke, Peninsula	.331	163	35	54	12	1	1	32	7
Schutt, Doug, Bucs	.317	120	18	38	3	4	0	10	12
Seely, Justin, Peninsula	.316	98	12	31	6	1	0	16	4
Donaldson, Erick, AIA	.315	165	25	52	12	0	1	11	24
Allen, Rod, Glacier Pilots	.314	188	31	59	12	1	2	23	24
Purdom, John, Fairbanks	.309	159	20	47	5	1	0	14	9
Leathers, Todd, Fairbanks	.308	195	22	60	9	0	8	40	3
Fritz, Ben, Glacier Pilots	.306	170	28	52	15	1	2	25	1
Crowder, Justin, Bucs	.297	111	11	33	8	0	1	10	0
Huddleston, Bob, Pilots	.297	101	12	30	5	1	0	10	0
Tugwell, Marc, Fairbanks	.296	186	29	55	11	1	3	25	10
Causey, Josh, AIA	.295	166	35	49	12	1	1	31	5
Teahen, Mark, Peninsula	.292	192	38	56	7	4	0	22	6
Heether, Adam, Glacier Pilots	.290	155	23	45	3	0	1	15	19
Francisco, Ben, Glacier Pilots	.287	157	24	45	9	1	4	26	17
Reynolds, Wilton, Peninsula	.287	157	30	45	10	3	2	20	16
D'Antona, Jamie, Peninsula	.284	134	15	38	7	3	3	32	1
McIntyre, Nick, Mat-Su	.281	128	11	36	8	0	0	19	6
Wallace, Dave, Bucs	.277	141	31	39	6	0	7	26	4
Anderson, Ryan, AIA	.269	104	22	28	4	1	1	6	5
Ortega, Jose, Glacier Pilots	.266	188	33	50	7	1	1	28	9
Porter, Jeremiah, AIA	.266	143	32	38	5	1	0	24	3
Isbell, Brandon, AIA	.264	129	26	34	8	0	0	11	6
Horwitz, Brian, Peninsula	.258	159	25	41	7	0	2	23	5

INDIVIDUAL PITCHING LEADERS
(Minimum 40 Innings)

	W	L	ERA	G	SV	IP	H	BB	SO
Steidlmayer, Luke, Mat-Su	4	2	0.64	6	0	42	24	11	42
Minor, Zach, Glacier Pilots	3	1	1.16	8	0	47	32	17	45
Francis, Jeff, Bucs	7	1	1.29	12	1	77	36	21	81
Serrato, Juan, Peninsula	3	3	1.66	8	0	49	32	41	41
Little, Joe, Mat-Su	3	2	1.79	8	0	50	27	22	56
Davidson, Andy, Fairbanks	6	6	1.98	11	0	71	61	18	72
Makowsky, Carl, Glacier Pilots	6	2	2.24	9	0	52	39	23	56
Reilly, Chris, Peninsula	3	3	2.53	9	0	53	42	20	48
Felten, Brian, Fairbanks	3	1	2.41	7	0	52	51	12	40
McCally, Ryan, Bucs	5	1	2.65	8	0	58	48	19	44
Bostick, Ricky, Bucs	2	2	2.70	18	3	47	43	3	35
Blair, Buddy, Glacier Pilots	3	4	2.72	10	1	56	49	30	29
Lopez, Nelson, Peninsula	4	3	2.89	8	0	56	46	20	27
Olson, Jordan, Bucs	4	0	2.89	7	0	44	33	15	40
Pawelk, Reed, Glacier Pilots	4	0	2.94	11	0	52	46	21	25

CLARK GRIFFITH COLLEGIATE LEAGUE

	W	L	PCT	GB
*Arlington Senators	26	13	.667	—
+Fauquier Gators	24	15	.615	2
Vienna Mustangs	20	16	.556	4½
Bethesda Big Train	20	20	.500	6½
Germantown Black Rox	15	19	.441	8½
Silver Spring-Takoma Thunderbolts	15	21	.417	9½
Reston Hawks	10	29	.278	14½

*First-half champion   +Second-half champion

PLAYOFFS:. Arlington defeated Fauquier 3-0 in best-of-5 championship series.

INDIVIDUAL BATTING LEADERS
(Minimum 100 Plate Appearances)

	AVG	AB	R	H	2B	3B	HR	RBI	SB
Dixon, Kellen, Fauquier	.348	115	28	40	7	0	0	9	22
Clinton, Kurtis, Germantown	.336	125	18	42	9	0	2	28	1
Gilvin, Casey, Bethesda	.322	90	13	29	6	1	0	9	5
Beall, Kyle, Fauquier	.321	134	23	43	4	0	0	10	25
Hickman, Chuck, Arlington	.315	149	27	47	11	1	1	16	19
Edick, Denver, Vienna	.296	108	21	32	7	1	0	15	3
Consuegra, Cory, Germ.	.295	105	29	31	5	0	0	9	10
Ryan, Matthew, Fauquier	.294	126	24	37	0	1	0	10	22
Robertson, Connor, Fauquier	.287	136	22	39	8	0	5	26	7
Mattison, Justin, Arlington	.282	85	10	24	5	2	2	14	4
Deuchler, Matt, Arlington	.278	133	18	37	5	1	3	20	3
Reaver, David, Bethesda	.278	115	17	32	7	0	0	18	5
Street, Matt, Reston	.277	101	21	28	2	0	0	3	12
McKenna, Brian, Germ.	.273	121	16	33	8	0	0	16	4
Jones, Blake, Fauquier	.269	119	13	32	11	2	0	14	1

INDIVIDUAL PITCHING LEADERS
(Minimum 40 Innings)

	W	L	ERA	G	SV	IP	H	BB	SO
Binda, Byron, Fauquier	3	0	1.05	18	5	43	21	15	50
Kline, Steven, Bethesda	4	3	1.20	12	0	53	39	7	55
Johnson, Kyle, Arlington	5	1	1.44	10	1	63	45	16	44
Kondratowicz, Ryan, Vienna	5	3	1.52	9	0	59	50	10	54
Isenberg, Kurt, Arlington	5	3	1.68	11	1	59	40	16	61
Sterling, John, Arlington	5	1	1.68	9	0	59	38	22	46
Werts, Matt, SS-Takoma	2	2	1.79	12	1	60	54	7	41
Wunderlich, Jeremy, Germ.	5	4	2.19	10	0	70	48	17	60
Atchley, Chip, Fauquier	4	3	2.37	8	0	49	45	22	50
Hayhurst, Dirk, Bethesda	2	0	2.62	8	1	48	35	16	69

NORTHWOODS LEAGUE

NORTH	W	L	PCT	GB
+St. Cloud River Bats	39	25	.609	—
Mankato Mashers	36	28	.563	3
*Brainerd Mighty Gulls	25	37	.403	13
Alexandria Beetles	24	38	.387	14

SOUTH	W	L	PCT	GB
*Waterloo Bucks	37	27	.578	—
+Wisconsin Woodchucks	32	31	.508	4½
Rochester Honkers	31	33	.484	6
Madison Mallards	29	35	.453	8

*First-half champion   +Second-half champion

PLAYOFFS: St. Cloud defeated Brainerd 2-0 and Wisconsin defeated Waterloo 2-1 in best-of-3 divisional playoffs; Wisconsin defeated St. Cloud 2-1 in best-of-3 championship series.

ALL-STAR TEAM: C—Tony Arnerich, St. Cloud (Texas Tech); Chris Miller, Rochester (Cuesta, Calif., JC). **1B**—Andy Schutzenhofer, Waterloo (Illinois). **2B**—Matt Fisher, Mankato (Oklahoma). **3B**—Wes Long, St. Cloud (Alabama-Huntsville). **SS**—Josh Arteaga, Waterloo (Virginia Commonwealth). **OF**—T.J. Bohn, Brainerd (Iowa State); Gino Lollio, Alexandria (Michigan); Matt Mann, St. Cloud (North Dakota State); Ryan Spiborghs, Madison (UC Santa Barbara). **DH**—Travis McAndrews, Mankato (Los Angeles Harbor JC). **Util**—Ryan Ruiz, Madison (UNLV). **P**—Chris Demaria, St. Cloud (Long Beach State); Mike Egger, Waterloo (Northern Iowa); John Forrest, St. Cloud (El Camino, Calif., CC); Kevin Jenson, Mankato (Loyola Marymount); Mike Kunes, St. Cloud (UCLA); Tim McNab, Wisconsin (Florida Atlantic); Chad Mulholland, Waterloo (Logan, Ill., JC); Quintin Oldenburg, Wisconsin (Wisconsin-Milwaukee); Tom Oldham, Wisconsin (Creighton); Jaymie Russ, Rochester (Belmont Abbey, N.C.); Zach Schreiber, Waterloo (Duke); J.D. Seger, St. Cloud (Santa Rosa, Calif., CC); Vern Sterry, Mankato (Cypress, Calif., JC).

Most Valuable Player: Tony Arnerich, St. Cloud.

INDIVIDUAL BATTING LEADERS
(Minimum 150 Plate Appearances)

	AVG	AB	R	H	2B	3B	HR	RBI	SB
Arnerich, Tony, St. Cloud	.355	214	45	76	12	2	3	29	2
Mann, Matt, St. Cloud	.355	220	38	78	15	3	4	43	5
Spiborghs, Ryan, Madison	.331	175	28	58	13	1	0	20	14
Granderson, Curtis, Man.	.328	134	28	44	8	2	1	17	15
Lollio, Gino, Alexandria	.321	224	34	72	17	2	6	46	11
Bohn, T.J., Brainerd	.320	228	36	73	15	0	3	25	18
Deeds, Doug, Mankato	.301	133	17	40	6	3	1	21	6
Allen, Scott, Waterloo	.297	138	20	41	5	0	4	24	11
Fisher, Matt, Mankato	.295	176	21	52	11	0	1	25	11
Arteaga, Josh, Waterloo	.291	148	19	43	8	0	1	20	12
Schutzenhofer, Andy, Wat.	.288	226	38	65	12	0	0	31	3
Bowen, Weber, Wisconsin	.283	205	26	58	13	0	2	20	4
Stone, Wayne, Wisconsin	.278	162	30	45	6	1	1	13	7
Schuler, Tony, Wisconsin	.277	155	15	43	11	0	1	23	2
Steidl, Sam, Alexandria	.277	166	21	46	7	0	1	12	16
Cunningham, Mike, Roch.	.276	225	27	62	8	0	1	21	31

INDIVIDUAL PITCHING LEADERS
(Minimum 50 Innings)

	W	L	ERA	G	SV	IP	H	BB	SO
Oldham, Tom, Wisconsin	6	1	0.74	12	0	73	56	24	55
Mulholland, Chad, Waterloo	4	1	1.16	10	0	54	39	19	39
Castillo, Mike, Mankato	5	2	1.39	17	2	52	31	13	58
Egger, Mike, Waterloo	4	0	1.58	27	3	51	39	12	38
Demaria, Chris, St. Cloud	10	1	1.66	14	0	92	59	17	91
Kunes, Mike, St. Cloud	4	2	1.89	8	0	52	42	14	23
Sterry, Vern, Mankato	6	1	2.06	11	0	74	71	30	63
Kougl, Josh, St. Cloud	5	2	2.24	14	1	56	59	15	32
Oldenburg, Quintin, Wis.	8	5	2.49	15	0	90	82	25	72
Prenger, Greg, Mankato	3	2	2.53	10	1	53	57	15	35

Japan won its second Little League (11-12) World Series title in three years in 2001 by scoring two runs in the bottom of the sixth and final inning to defeat Apopka, Fla., 2-1. The game attracted a record crowd of 44,800 that included president George W. Bush, as well as a record prime time network TV audience.

Nobuhisa Baba drilled a one-out single off the outstretched glove of Apopka shortstop Stuart Tapley to drive in the tying and winning runs as Japan won its fifth World Series title.

Japan also won the international championship game, 2-1 over Curacao, in the bottom of the sixth a day earlier on a dramatic two-run homer by Atsushi Mochizuki, the winning pitcher in the deciding game. Tapley struck out 11 and yielded four hits as Apopka beat the Bronx, N.Y., 8-2 in the United States championship game.

The New York team had won its four previous games to that point, two on spectacular pitching performances by Danny Almonte. The 5-foot-10 lefthander threw a 5-0 perfect game against Apopka in the opening round of pool play, striking out 16 of 18 batters. He then pitched a 16-strikeout, one-hitter three games later against Oceanside, Calif., winning 1-0. With his team relegated to a third-place game because of its loss to Apopka, Almonte finished with a 9-1 win over Curacao, striking out 14 more hitters.

His performance later became shrouded in controversy, however, when charges were made that Almonte, a Dominican Republic product, was actually 14 years old. The Bronx was stripped of its third-place medals.

■ The most impressive performance by a 12-year-old team was turned in by the San Diego Stars, who went undefeated in 10 games to win the AAU 12-year-old national tournament in Burnsville, Minn., for the fourth year in a row. The Stars beat the St. Petersburg, Fla., Stingers 6-2 in the final.

■ In Babe Ruth Baseball's Cal Ripken League (11-12) World Series, South Lexington, Ky., won twice on the final day to capture the title. Down 4-3 entering the bottom of the fifth of the championship game against Korea, South Lexington erupted for three runs with the last two scoring as a result of a ball-four wild pitch.

Winning One For Coach

The 75th American Legion World Series was won by a manager who had been with the same team for 50 of those years. But for Joe Barth, the 10th anniversary of Brooklawn, N.J., Post 72's only previous national championship was the number that counted.

"The first time we won, I had been coaching 40 years," said Barth, 79. "And I told the guys if I'm going to win another one and it takes 40 years, I'll be 110. So I saved 30 years."

Barth's team won 5-2 over Lewiston, Idaho, Post 13, the first team from that state to play in the championship game since the very first one in 1926.

Lewiston took a 2-0 lead with four doubles in the space of five batters in the bottom of the third inning; third baseman Allen Balmer could advance only to third base on second baseman Dustin Zager's double, the last of the four. After that, Brooklawn righthander Andrew Noe struck out first baseman Josh Burton and pitcher Julius Smith to get out of the inning.

At that point Noe had given up six hits and two walks. He allowed two more hits the rest of the way, and one Lewiston player got as far as third base.

"As the game goes on he always gets stronger and hits his spots a lot better," catcher Mike Rucci said of Noe, who struck out 10. "Once we got a lead it took the pressure off him, and that's what we needed. Once he's on, no one can really hit him."

Rucci, the tournament MVP and the only player ever to participate in four American Legion World Series, provided the lead at 4-2 with a long two-run homer to left field in the top of the sixth.

Banner Year For East Cobb

Georgia's East Cobb Baseball, the nation's premier youth program, had another successful summer season in 2001 as it won nine national tournament titles. They included the prestigious AAU 16-year-old Junior Olympics and the Connie Mack World Series.

The East Cobb Astros finished second at the Junior Olympics in 2000, ending a run of four consecutive titles, but reasserted their dominance by winning the 44-team championship. The Astros went undefeated in nine games, threw three consecutive no-hitters at one point and beat the Washington Baseball System 7-1 in the final.

"This was a different kind of team than we normally have," Astros coach Guerry Baldwin said, "because it was built more on pitching and defense. We didn't have some of the hitters we've had in the past."

The East Cobb Yankees won the Connie Mack World Series (17-18) for the second time in three years by beating the Dallas Mustangs 7-5 and Fairfax, Va., Barnstormers 8-4 on the final day.

Six-foot-5, 205-pound Micah Owings, a rising senior at Gainesville (Ga.) High and one of the nation's top two-way players, was named tournament MVP. He hit a grand slam and earned a save in the Yankees' win over Dallas, then hit a crucial three-run homer in the championship game against Fairfax. Overall, he hit .388-4-14 in the series and went 1-0 with 14 strikeouts and no walks in nine innings.

Repeat Champions

Host Mobile, Ala., won the Babe Ruth League 16-18 World Series for the second straight year, beating Northern Fairfax, Va., 4-2 in the championship game. Mobile first baseman Jeff Terrell, the tournament's outstanding player, scored the tying run in the sixth inning after a leadoff single and knocked in the winning run on a base hit an inning later.

■ Despite fielding a team composed mostly of 2001 high school graduates, the Ohio Warhawks won the National Amateur Baseball Federation College World Series for the second year in a row. Lefthander Aaron Braden (Wright State) won the championship game 1-0.

■ PONY Baseball (13-14) played its 50th anniversary World Series in Washington, Pa., with Ponce, Puerto Rico, beating Richmond. Xavier Cedeno won the championship game and two others for Ponce while striking out 22 and walking none in 14 innings. He also went 10-for-20 with three homers.

TEAM USA

HEADQUARTERS: Tucson, Ariz.

JUNIOR TEAM (18-and-under)

Event	Site	Champion	Runner-up
COPABE Pan American	Camaguey, Cuba	Cuba	United States

YOUTH TEAM (16-and-under)

Event	Site	Champion	Runner-up
World Championship	Veracruz, Mexico	United States	Venezuela
USA Junior Olympics—East	Jupiter, Fla.	Team Florida	Norcross (Ga.) Blue Devils
USA Junior Olympics—West	Tucson	South Bay (Calif.) Sharks	Riverside (Calif.) Bulldogs

ALL-AMERICAN AMATEUR BASEBALL ASSOCIATION (AAABA)

HEADQUARTERS: Zanesville, Ohio

Event	Site	Champion	Runner-up
World Series (21 &under)	Johnstown, Pa.	Arlington, Va., Senators	Johnstown, Pa.

AMATEUR ATHLETIC UNION (AAU)

HEADQUARTERS: Lake Buena Vista, Fla.

Event	Site	Champion	Runner-up
9 & Under	Orlando	San Diego Stallions	Tampa Stix
10 & Under (60-foot)	Des Moines	Central Florida Mustangs	Carolina Lightning
11 & Under	Orlando	Orange County (Calif.) Stallions	East Cobb (Ga.) Blazers
12 & Under	Burnsville, Minn.	San Diego Stars	St. Petersburg (Fla.) Stingers
13 & Under (90-foot)	Winter Haven, Fla.	Kernersville (N.C.) Cardinals	Jacksonville Stars
13 & Under (80-foot)	Sherwood, Ark.	East Cobb (Ga.) Astros	West Coast Rebels
14 & Under (90-foot)	Sarasota, Fla.	South Florida Lightning	Norwalk (Calif.) Stingrays
14 & Under (80-foot)	Tulsa	Texas Reds	Waco (Texas) Lightning
15 & Under	Kingsport, Tenn.	Jamestown (N.C.) Jaguars	Three teams tied
Junior Olympics/16 & u	Hampton Roads, Va.	East Cobb (Ga.) Astros	Washington Baseball System
17 & Under	Phoenix	San Diego Gamers	San Antonio Hackers
18 & Under	Orlando	Kansas City Monarchs	Cordova (Tenn.) Dulin's Dodgers

AMERICAN AMATEUR BASEBALL CONGRESS (AABC)

HEADQUARTERS: Marshall, Mich.

Event	Site	Champion	Runner-up
Roberto Clemente (8 & u)	McDonough, Ga.	Glenview, P.R.	McDonough (Ga.) Reds
Willie Mays (10 & u)	Knoxville	Knoxville Stars	Jacksonville Sting
Pee Wee Reese (12 & u)	Toa Baja, P.R.	Riverdale (Ga.) Aztecs	Lower Bucks (Pa.) Bandits
Sandy Koufax (14 & u)	Jersey City, N.J.	Dallas Tigers	Puerto Rico
Mickey Mantle (16 & u)	McKinney, Texas	Bell Port, N.Y.	Las Lomas (P.R.) Patros
Connie Mack (18 & u)	Farmington, N.M.	East Cobb (Ga.) Yankees	Virginia Barnstormers
Stan Musial (open)	Battle Creek, Mich.	Flint (Mich.) Halo Burger	Atlanta Yankees

AMERICAN LEGION BASEBALL

HEADQUARTERS: Indianapolis

Event	Site	Champion	Runner-up
World Series (19 & u)	Yakima, Wash.	Brooklawn, N.J.	Lewiston, Idaho

BABE RUTH BASEBALL

HEADQUARTERS: Trenton, N.J.

Event	Site	Champion	Runner-up
10 & under	Vincennes, Ind.	Glen Allen, Va.	Meridian, Miss.
Cal Ripken (11-12)	Vincennes, Ind.	South Lexington, Ky.	Korea
13	Wilson County, N.C.	Vancouver, Wash.	Taylorsville, Utah
14	Longview, Wash.	Modesto, Calif.	Vancouver, Wash.
13-15	Hamilton, N.J.	Honolulu	Jefferson Parish, La.
16	Gulfport, Miss.	San Gabriel, Calif.	Loudoun County, Va.
16-18	Loudoun County, Va.	Mobile, Ala.	Northern Fairfax, Va.

CONTINENTAL AMATEUR BASEBALL ASSOCIATION (CABA)

HEADQUARTERS: Westerville, Ohio

Event	Site	Champion	Runner-up
9 & under	Charles City, Iowa	Caguas, P.R.	Cincinnati
10 & under	Aurelia, Iowa	Omaha	Tulsa Tigers
11 & under	Tarkio, Mo.	Miami Lakes, Fla.	Tulsa Stars
12 & under	Omaha	Woolsey, Ga.	Burleson, Texas
13 & under	Broken Arrow, Okla.	Placentia, Calif.	Indianapolis
14 & under	Dublin, Ohio	Tulsa Aces	Kansas City, Mo.
15 & under	Crystal Lake, Ill.	Bayamon, P.R.	Akron, Ohio
16 & under	Dallas	Manassas, Va.	Arlington, Texas
High school age	Euclid, Ohio	Panama City, Fla.	Miami
18 & under	Homestead, Fla.	Marietta, Ga.	Nashville

COOPERSTOWN DREAMS PARK

HEADQUARTERS: Salisbury, N.C.

Event	Site	Champion	Runner-up
Tournament of Champions (12 & u.)	Cooperstown	Woolsey (Ga.) Yankees	East Cobb (Ga.) Aztecs

DIXIE BASEBALL

HEADQUARTERS: Montgomery, Ala.

Event	Site	Champion	Runner-up
Dixie Youth (9-10)	Bedford, Va.	Hilton Head Island, S.C.	Montgomery (Ala.) Green

Dixie Youth (12 & u)	Madison Heights, Va.	Searcy, Ark.	Columbia County North (Ga.)
Dixie 13	Sulphur, La.	Columbus County, N.C.	St. Charles, La.
Dixie Boys (13-14)	Sulphur, La.	Phenix City, Ala.	Columbus County, N.C.
Dixie Pre-Majors (15-16)	Florence, S.C.	Lakeland, Fla.	Valdosta, Ga.
Dixie Majors (15-18)	North Charleston, S.C.	Meridian, Miss.	North Charleston, S.C.

HAP DUMONT BASEBALL/National Baseball Congress

HEADQUARTERS: Wichita

Event	Site	Champion	Runner-up
10 & under	Harrison, Ark.	Kentucky Kids	Kansas Outlaws
11 & under	Russell, Kan.	Wichita Cubs	Wichita Heaters
12 & under	Roswell, Ga.	Tri-State (Ga.) Cannons	Memphis Travelers
13 & under	Casper, Wyo.	Wichita Cougars	Colorado Rebels
14 & under	Manhattan, Kan.	Kansas City White Sox	Dallas Texans
15 & under	Nashville	Ohio Panthers	Wichita Jets
16 & under	Brainerd, Minn.	Edmonds, Wash.	Cincinnati Cardinals
18 & under	Harrison, Ark.	Springfield (Ohio) WBLY	Topeka (Kan.) Stars

LITTLE LEAGUE BASEBALL

HEADQUARTERS: Williamsport, Pa.

Event	Site	Champion	Runner-up
Little League (11-12)	Williamsport, Pa.	Japan	Apopka, Fla.
Junior League (13-14)	Taylor, Mich.	Aiea, Hawaii	Zulia, Venezuela
Senior League (15-16)	Kissimmee, Fla.	Palm Harbor (Fla.) American	Coquivacoa, Venezuela
Big League (17-18)	Easley, S.C.	Westminster, Calif.	Valencia, Venezuela

NATIONAL AMATEUR BASEBALL FEDERATION (NABF)

HEADQUARTERS: Bowie, Md.

Event	Site	Champion	Runner-up
Rookie (10 & u)	Spokane, Wash.	Spokane (Wash.) Heat	Connetquot (N.Y.) Chiefs
Freshman (12 & u)	Hopkinsville, Ky.	Cincinnati Flames	East Cobb (Ga.) Mudcats
Sophomore (14 & u)	Dayton, Ohio	Farmington, Mich.	Kennewick (Wash.) Dirtdogs
Junior (16 & u)	Northville, Mich.	Indiana Bulls	Dayton (Ohio) Classics
High School (17 & u)	Memphis	Rawlings Nationals (Ohio)	Midwest Prospects (Mo.)
Senior (18 & u)	Wilmington, Del.	Central Florida Renegades	Lexington (Ky.) Dixie
College (22 & u)	Dayton, Ohio	Ohio Warhawks	Keystone Diamonds
Major (open)	Derby City, Ky.	Chicago Clout	Virginia Federal Lock/Safe

POLICE ATHLETIC LEAGUE (PAL)

HEADQUARTERS: North Palm Beach, Fla.

Event	Site	Champion	Runner-up
14 & under	Kissimmee, Fla.	Palm Bay (Fla.) Pirates	Suffolk (N.Y.) Rangers
16 & under	Kissimmee, Fla.	Hollywood, Fla.	Suffolk (N.Y.) Blue Knights

PONY BASEBALL

HEADQUARTERS: Washington, Pa.

Event	Site	Champion	Runner-up
Mustang (9-10)	Irving, Texas	Bayamon, P.R.	Tampa
Bronco (11-12)	Monterey, Calif.	Maui, Hawaii	Seoul, Korea
Pony (13-14)	Washington, Pa.	Ponce, P.R.	Richmond
Colt (15-16)	Lafayette, Ind.	San Dimas, Calif.	Hoosier North (Ind.)
Palomino (17-18)	Santa Clara, Calif.	Houston	Santa Clara, Calif.

REVIVING BASEBALL IN INNER CITIES (RBI)

HEADQUARTERS: New York

Event	Site	Champion	Runner-up
Junior (13-15)	Orlando	Los Angeles	Atlanta Juniors
Senior (16-18)	Orlando	Tampa	Cincinnati

U.S. AMATEUR BASEBALL ASSOCIATION (USABA)

HEADQUARTERS: Edmonds, Wash.

Event	Site	Champion	Runner-up
11 & under	Sherwood, Ore.	Willamette Valley, Ore.	Kennewick, Wash.
12 & under	Sherwood, Ore.	Sherwood, Ore.	Sunset, Ore.
13 & under	Hoquiam, Wash.	South Sound (Wash.) Cobras	Puyallup (Wash.) Bandits
14 & under	Pasco, Wash.	Seattle Brewers	Kennewick (Wash.) Dirt Daugs
15 & under	Bellevue, Wash.	Kirkland (Wash.) Heat	Lebanon, Ore.
16 & under	South Jordan, Utah	Utah Highlanders	Orem (Utah) Tigers
18 & under	Carson City, Nev.	San Jose	Washington Bombers

U.S. SPECIALTY SPORTS ASSOCIATION (USSSA)

HEADQUARTERS: Petersburg, Va.

Event	Site	Champion	Runner-up
9 & under/Majors	Lafayette, La.	Puerto Rico	Baton Rouge Tigers
10 & under/Majors	Ballwin, Mo.	Las Vegas Vipers	San Diego Wildcats
11 & under/Majors	Omaha	El Monte (Calif.) No Fear	Puerto Rico
12 & under/Majors	Atlanta	Houston Raiders	Arizona Landsharks
13 & under/Majors	Tulsa	Houston Sox	Southern Cal Mama's Boyz
14 & under/Majors	Lynchburg, Tenn.	Chatsworth (Calif.) Valley Heat	East Cobb (Ga.) Seminoles
15 & under/Majors	Winter Haven, Fla.	Apopka, Fla.	East Cobb (Ga.) Red Sox
16 & under/Majors	Oklahoma City	Shreveport (La.) Mariners	East Cobb (Ga.) Jackets
18 & under/Majors	Lakeland, Fla.	Carolina Hurricanes	Cordova (Tenn.) Dulin's Dodgers

AMATEUR BASEBALL

BASEBALL FOR THE AGES

No matter how you slice it, it was a good year for baseball in Houston in 2001. From the big league Astros, to Minor League Player of the Year Josh Beckett, to numerous youth league national champions, Houston produced more than its share of baseball highlights.

That success was clear in Baseball America's fourth annual Baseball For The Ages program, which recognizes the best up-and-coming baseball players in America, from 12 to 25.

In each case, the universal youth baseball birthdate cutoff of Aug. 1 was used to establish a player's age.

12 **RYAN STILL, ss/rhp, Houston**
The 5-foot-5, 130-pounder led two teams to major national titles. He won MVP honors at the United States Specialty Sports Association (USSSA) World Series, winning three games and hammering three homers as the Houston Raiders, the nation's No. 2-ranked 12-year-old team, won the title. Still later joined the Woolsey (Ga.) Yankees and helped them win the Cooperstown Dreams Park National Tournament of Champions. He went 24-for-33, hammered 13 homers in 12 games and won three games against tough California teams. As a leadoff hitter, Still batted .580-32-82 overall in 58 games. He also went 16-0 as a pitcher and was clocked at 77 mph.

13 **RYAN MITCHELL, rhp, Houston**
At 6-foot-4 and 218 pounds, Mitchell is a man among boys. The Magnolia High freshman dominated his competition in 2001 with a fastball that topped out at 90 mph—unheard of for a player his age. As a member of the Houston Sox, the nation's No. 1 13-year-old team, he was MVP of the USSSA national tournament. He also earned MVP honors for the Houston Force at the Triple Crown national tournament. He made an impact on the international stage as well, leading the strongest collection of American 13-year-old all-stars ever assembled to the Santo

Ryan Mitchell

Domingo Classic championship in the Dominican Republic. Despite facing teams of players as old as 16, Mitchell went unbeaten.

14 **TREVOR BELL, 3b/rhp, Crescenta Valley, Calif.**
The 6-foot-1, 170-pound Bell wasn't a big factor as his summer team, the Valley Heat, won the USSSA 14-year-old national championship, but he was the unquestioned star. He has one of the most potent bats in the country and hit better than .600 on the season. He also has three effective pitches, with a fastball in the high 80s, and posted a sub-1.00 ERA. Bell is a freshman at Crescenta Valley High, where he is so advanced for his age that he already plays for the Padres scout

team, normally for 16- and 17-year-olds.

15 **ANDREW BEAL, rhp, Palos Verdes Estates, Calif.**
As a freshman at Peninsula High, he went 7-2, 0.63 with 73 strikeouts in 44 innings and was California's freshman of the year. He topped that performance as a member of Team USA at the world youth championships in Mexico, striking out 14 in the gold-medal game as the U.S. beat Venezuela 6-2. Overall he went 3-0 and struck out 53 in 34 innings for Team USA. He ranks as the nation's top high school player in the Class of 2004. Despite his 5-foot-11, 175-pound frame, Beal's fastball sits at 89-91 mph and touches 93.

Andrew Beal

16 **LASTINGS MILLEDGE, of, St. Petersburg, Fla.**
Milledge is an exceptional hitter. He has a quick bat, with above-average power potential and outstanding plate coverage. He runs the 60-yard dash in 6.5 seconds. At the world youth championship in Mexico in August, he homered twice in the championship game as Team USA defeated Venezuela 6-2. Overall, he hit .522-3-10 and was named the tournament's outstanding center fielder. He led all players with eight homers and 32 RBIs on Team USA's summer tour. At Northside Christian High in St. Petersburg, Milledge earned all-state honors as a sophomore by hitting .548-6-42 with 23 stolen bases.

17 **SCOTT KAZMIR, lhp, Houston**
Kazmir's stature and explosive velocity draw comparisons to another Houston lefty, Billy Wagner. As the only junior on BA's High School All-America team after going 6-0, 0.69, Kazmir was unhittable. The 6-foot, 175-pound lefthander, who throws a fastball ranging from 90-96 mph and a plus curveball, pitched four no-hitters, including three in a row. In one stretch, he gave up one single over 36 innings and fanned 55. He surrendered 19 hits and 22 walks, while striking out 127 in 61 innings on the season, but he was just getting started. He was named the No. 1 prospect at

Scott Kazmir

the Perfect Game USA Showcase at Tropicana Field, the Team USA Tournament of Stars in Joplin, Mo., and the Area Code Games.

18 **JOE MAUER, c, Twins**
The No. 1 pick in the 2001 draft and High School Player of the Year keeps adding to his trophy case. He spurned a scholarship to play quarterback at Florida State when he signed with the hometown Twins for a $5.15 million bonus. He hit a three-run homer and pitched five scoreless innings of relief—striking out nine—in a state semifinal game for Cretin-Derham Hall, then went 3-for-3 in the championship game. He kept it up in his pro debut, hitting .400-0-14 with 19 walks and 10 strikeouts in 110 at-bats for Rookie-level Elizabethton.

GREG WAGNER

FIRST-YEAR DRAFT

Twins play it safe in 2001 draft, take local boy with No. 1 selection

BY JIM CALLIS

The Twins owned the No. 1 overall pick in the 2001 first-year player draft, which could have been interpreted as either a blessing or a curse.

The last time Minnesota led off the draft, it chose Tim Belcher in 1983 but couldn't sign him. The Twins also couldn't get first-rounders Jason Varitek (1993) and Travis Lee (1996) under contract.

Just one year earlier, they let supplemental first-rounder Aaron Heilman and second-rounder Taggert Bozied get away. Minnesota wanted to draft high school righthander Matt Harrington with the No. 2 overall pick, but concerns about his bonus demands led the club to strike a predraft deal with Cal State Fullerton righty Adam Johnson. On pure talent, Johnson deserved to go about 10 choices later, though he reached the majors in his first full pro season.

Come draft day, the Twins made the best of their situation. Unable to get a firm grasp as to what it would take to sign Southern California righthander Mark Prior, the consensus top prospect, they played it safe and took Cretin-Derham Hall catcher Joe Mauer.

Mark Prior

Cretin-Derham is located in St. Paul, just eight miles from the Metrodome in Minneapolis. But Mauer wasn't picked because he's a hometown favorite. He was the top high school prospect in the nation, a rare catcher who's athletic and is a potential five-tool player. He also was the national high school football player of the year, a coveted quarterback recruit of Florida State.

"He's a legitimate No. 1 pick," Twins scouting director Mike Radcliff said. "I know a number of teams thought he may be the best guy in the draft. We had four guys we thought were legitimate No. 1 picks. We were fortunate in that regard.

"But let's be honest. We've had trouble signing players in our recent history. We are who we are. We have limit-

Joe Mauer: Drafted No. 1 by hometown team

ed resources and we have to deal with it. Joe was the best fit."

Besides Prior and Mauer, the Twins also considered Georgia Tech third baseman Mark Teixeira and Middle Tennessee State righthander Dewon Brazelton for the top choice. Minnesota contacted the families or representatives of all four players on the day of the draft, seeing if a predraft agreement might be reached, but ultimately had to make its decision without a deal in place.

Radcliff said the Twins went to great lengths to determine if they could sign Prior, whose camp never divulged a bonus request but reportedly was looking at Drew Henson money. They Yankees gave Henson, a Michigan quarterback projected as a possible No. 1 pick in the 2002 NFL draft, a $17 million contract when he left football behind in the spring of 2001.

"We did everything we could," Radcliff said. "We had hours of conversation with them and we watched every game he pitched all spring. I don't know what else we could have done. No one had really any idea where that one would end up."

Ability Trumps Signability

The selection of Mauer kicked off a development that had to rank as stunning by baseball's standards. The top five prospects in the draft actually went in the first five picks.

That scenario hadn't unfolded since Darin Erstad, Ben Davis, Jose Cruz Jr., Kerry Wood and Ariel Prieto led off the 1995 draft. Since then, there were charades such as 1997, when just two of the top prospects went in the top five and the other three all went 19th or lower; and 2000,

HISTORICAL SIGNIFICANCE

The week of Aug. 20-26, 2001, was one of the most eventful in draft history, as righthander Mark Prior signed the richest guaranteed contract ever for a draft pick and teams handed out four of the six largest signing bonuses in draft history. Below are the 10 largest bonuses for players who signed with the teams that drafted them:

Player, Pos.	Club, Year (Round)	Bonus
1. Joe Borchard, of	White Sox '00 (1)	$5,300,000
2. Joe Mauer, c	Twins '01 (1)	5,150,000
3. *Mark Teixeira, 3b	Rangers '01 (1)	4,500,000
4. *Dewon Brazelton, rhp	Devil Rays '01 (1)	4,200,000
Gavin Floyd, rhp	Phillies '01 (1)	4,200,000
6. *Mark Prior, rhp	Cubs '01 (1)	4,000,000
7. Josh Hamilton, of	Devil Rays '99 (1)	3,960,000
8. Corey Patterson, of	Cubs '98 (1)	3,700,000
9. *Josh Beckett, rhp	Marlins '99 (1)	3,625,000
10. *Eric Munson, 1b	Tigers '99 (1)	3,500,000

*Signed major league contract

when 10 of the first 11 picks were determined by the player's willingness to sign a predraft deal.

That year, club officials went out of their way to proclaim that none of the players were comparable to Josh Hamilton, Josh Beckett and Eric Munson, the top three picks from 1999—all of whom either set a bonus record or signed a major league contract. But in 2001, no one disparaged or avoided the available talent.

Some scouts considered Prior the best college pitcher of all time. Teixeira had more to offer than any recent slugger. Maryland high school righthander Gavin Floyd, who came from the same high school that produced Teixeira, headlined an exceptional group of prep righthanders. Brazelton had two dominant pitches and wasn't expected to require much of an apprenticeship in the minors.

"The better guys, the upper echelon, are more high profile," said an official from a team with an early selection who requested anonymity. "The top three or four guys have high ceilings. When you have a Mark Prior and a Mark Teixeira coming out of college in the same year, there was no one like that last year. Maybe Joe Borchard, but he's not up there with Teixeira."

Mark Teixeira

Like the Twins, the Cubs also were uncertain as to what Prior would cost, but they decided they couldn't pass him up with the No. 2 pick. Chicago's John Stockstill, running his first draft as scouting director, said his club determined in March to take Prior if he was available. They learned on the morning of the draft that Prior would be.

Baseball America's 2001 College Player of the Year, Prior overmatched hitters all spring with his 94-97 mph fastball and sharp curveball. He also has size (6-foot-5, 220 pounds), control, mound presence and work ethic. Stockstill stopped just short of calling him the top college pitching prospect ever.

RICHEST CONTRACTS

With major league contracts and other innovative deals that have been signed in the last several years, it no longer is fair to judge the highest compensation paid to draft picks strictly on the basis of cash signing bonuses. Here are the top 15 guaranteed incentive packages of the draft era:

Player, Pos.	Club, Year (Round)	Bonus	Guarantee
1. +Mark Prior, rhp	Cubs '01 (1)	$4,000,000	$10,500,000
2. *Matt White, rhp	Devil Rays '96 (FA)	10,200,000	10,200,000
3. *Travis Lee, 1b	Diamondbacks '96 (FA)	10,000,000	10,000,000
4. +Mark Teixeira, 3b	Rangers '01 (1)	4,500,000	9,500,000
5. +Pat Burrell, 1b	Phillies '98 (1)	3,150,000	8,000,000
6. +Josh Beckett, rhp	Marlins '99 (1)	3,625,000	7,000,000
7. +J.D. Drew, of	Cardinals '98 (1)	3,000,000	7,000,000
8. +Eric Munson, c	Tigers '99 (1)	3,500,000	6,750,000
9. *John Patterson, rhp	Diamondbacks '96 (FA)	6,075,000	6,075,000
10. ^Joe Borchard, of	White Sox '00 (1)	5,300,000	5,300,000
11. Joe Mauer, c	Twins '01 (1)	5,150,000	5,150,000
12. +Dewon Brazelton, rhp	Devil Rays '01 (1)	4,200,000	4,800,000
13. Gavin Floyd, rhp	Phillies '01 (1)	4,200,000	4,200,000
14. Josh Hamilton, of	Devil Rays '99 (1)	3,960,000	3,960,000
15. #Drew Henson, 3b	Yankees '98 (3)	2,000,000	3,900,000

* First-round draft pick; declared free agent because of incorrect contract tendering.

+ Signed multiyear, major league contract with guaranteed incentives.

Signed contract with a sliding incentive scale; minimum incentive of $1.9 million was paid if Henson became a full-time baseball player after fourth year of college.

^ Signed contract with payments spread over five years; bonus reflects value of contract at time of signing.

"There are pitchers who had better stuff, maybe a better curveball or threw 99 rather than 96-97," Stockstill said. "But Mark's a very good pitcher. He has the best college command I've seen in the last 10 years."

The Devil Rays, who had trouble meeting payroll in May, took Brazelton with the No. 3 selection. He outpitched Prior on Team USA in the summer of 2000, and has a similar fastball to go with what was the best changeup in college baseball in 2001.

Choosing fourth, the Phillies opted for Floyd. Scott Boras, Teixeira's adviser, reportedly warned both Tampa Bay and Philadelphia that his client wouldn't sign with either club. The Rangers, whose major league-high 6.10 ERA on draft day underscored their crying need for pitching, couldn't resist taking Teixeira.

"We thought there was a chance he might get to us," Rangers first-year scouting director Tim Hallgren said. "Everyone said, 'You've got to take a pitcher,' but when it got to us the pitchers remaining didn't match up to him. We were always looking for the best available talent with the fifth pick."

Radcliff, whose Twins set the tone, said it was nice to see the best players go to the teams picking at the top of the draft.

"All of us agree that the way the draft is set up, it behooves everyone if the selections go the way they went this time," Radcliff said. "There was a pretty good consensus that the five or six top guys went first."

Signings Take All Summer

Of course, selecting the players was easier than signing them. Though Mauer had the leverage of football—he might have emerged as the Seminoles' successor to fellow Cretin-Derham alum and 2000 Heisman Trophy winner Chris Weinke—he was by far the quickest to agree to terms.

MARK THIS DOWN

The acknowledged two top talents in the 2001 draft received the two top contracts. Mark Prior's contract is for five years, Mark Teixeira's for four. Player option years are noted with an asterisk:

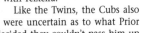

	Mark Prior	Mark Teixeira
Signing Bonus	$4,000,000	$4,500,000
Base Salaries		
2002	$250,000	$250,000
2003	$650,000	$750,000
2004	$1,600,000	$1,500,000
2005	*$2,000,000	$2,500,000
2006	*$2,000,000	n/a
Total Guaranteed	$10,500,000	$9,500,000
Bonuses		
•Cy Young Award, MVP, Rookie of Year, all-star	#$500,000 for 1st place; $250,000 for 2nd-5th place	n/a
•Roster	n/a	$135,000 each for 60, 90, 120, 140 days on major league roster

#Amount added to subsequent year

DRAFT '01 TOP 100 PICKS

Signing bonuses do not include scholarships, incentive bonus plans or salaries from a major league contract.
*Highest level of professional baseball attained   #Signed major league contract

Rank. Team, Player, Pos.	School	Hometown	Bonus	B'date	B-T	Ht.	Wt.	AVG	AB	H	HR	RBI	SB	2001 Assignment*
1. Twins, Joe Mauer, c	Cretin-Derham Hall	St. Paul, Minn.	$5,150,000	4-19-83	L-R	6-4	215	.605	90	54	15	53	2	Elizabethton (R)
5. #Rangers, Mark Teixeira, 3b	Georgia Tech	Severna Park, Md.	4,500,000	4-11-80	B-R	6-2	215	.419	62	26	5	20	2	Did not play
8. Pirates, John VanBenschoten, 1b	Kent State U.	Milford, Ohio	2,400,000	4-14-80	R-R	6-4	215	.440	225	99	31	84	23	Williamsport (A)
10. Astros, Chris Burke, ss	U. of Tennessee	Louisville	2,125,000	3-11-80	R-R	5-11	190	.435	271	118	20	60	49	Michigan (A)
13. Angels, Casey Kotchman, 1b	Seminole HS	Seminole, Fla.	2,075,000	2-22-83	L-L	6-3	190	.465	88	41	5	39	2	Provo (R)
14. Padres, Jake Gautreau, 3b	Tulane U.	McAllen, Texas	1,875,000	11-14-79	L-R	5-11	185	.355	290	103	21	96	8	Portland (AAA)
15. Blue Jays, Gabe Gross, of	Auburn U.	Dothan, Ala.	1,865,000	10-21-79	L-R	6-3	205	.327	208	68	15	67	11	Tennessee (AA)
19. Orioles, Mike Fontenot, 2b	Louisiana State U.	Slidell, Ala.	1,300,000	6-09-80	L-R	5-8	180	.339	221	75	14	50	7	Did not play
23. Yankees, John-Ford Griffin, of	Florida State U.	Sarasota, Fla.	1,200,000	11-19-79	L-L	6-2	195	.450	251	113	19	75	11	Staten Island (A)
25. Athletics, Bobby Crosby, ss	Long Beach State U.	Cypress, Calif.	1,350,000	1-12-80	R-R	6-3	195	.353	218	77	9	39	11	Modesto (A)
29. Braves, Josh Burrus, ss	Wheeler HS	Marietta, Ga.	1,250,000	8-20-83	R-R	6-1	180	.397	68	27	7	23	12	GCL Braves (R)
31. Orioles, Bryan Bass, ss	Seminole HS	Seminole, Fla.	1,150,000	4-12-82	B-R	6-1	180	.414	29	12	1	7	5	Bluefield (R)
32. Tigers, Michael Woods, 2b	Southern U.	Baton Rouge	1,100,000	9-11-80	R-R	6-0	200	.453	170	77	14	54	32	Provo (R)
33. Angels, Jeff Mathis, c	Marianna HS	Marianna, Fla.	850,000	3-31-83	R-R	6-0	180	.506	87	44	10	31	6	Provo (R)
34. Yankees, Bronson Sardinha, ss	Kamehameha, HS	Kahuku, Hawaii	1,100,000	4-06-83	L-R	6-0	190	.391	46	18	2	13	6	Did not play
36. Mariners, Michael Garciaparra, ss	Don Bosco HS	La Habra, Calif.	2,000,000	4-02-83	R-R	6-1	160	.417	12	5	0	2	0	Did not play
38. Mets, David Wright, 3b	Hickory HS	Chesapeake, Va.	960,000	12-20-82	R-R	6-0	198	.544	57	31	6	20	10	Kingsport (R)
40. Angels, Richard Lewis, 2b	Georgia Tech	Marietta, Ga.	850,000	6-29-80	R-R	6-1	185	.376	266	100	11	64	11	Jamestown (A)
41. Giants, Todd Linden, of	Louisiana State U.	Bremerton, Wash.	750,000	6-30-80	B-R	6-3	225	.312	256	80	20	76	9	Did not play
43. Indians, Michael Conroy, of	Boston College HS	Dorchester, Mass.	870,000	10-03-82	L-L	6-3	195	.431	51	22	3	12	6	Burlington (R)
44. Rockies, Jayson Nix, ss	Midland HS	Midland, Texas	925,000	8-26-82	R-R	5-11	175	.451	122	55	13	46	14	Casper (R)
48. Red Sox, Kelly Shoppach, c	Baylor U.	Fort Worth	737,500	4-29-80	R-R	5-11	185	.397	234	93	12	69	4	Did not play
49. Mariners, Rene Rivera, c	Papa Juan XXIII HS	Bayamon, P.R.	688,000	7-31-83	R-R	5-10	190	No spring team						Everett (A)
53. Royals, Roscoe Crosby, of	Union HS	Buffalo, S.C.	1,750,000	2-06-83	R-R	6-2	205	.516	61	31	16	42	16	Did not play
54. Astros, Mike Rodriguez, of	U. of Miami	Cooper City, Fla.	675,000	10-15-80	L-L	5-10	175	.329	231	76	5	43	53	Pittsfield (A)
56. Brewers, J.J. Hardy, ss	Sabino HS	Tucson	735,000	8-19-82	R-R	6-1	175	.455	99	45	8	34	15	Ogden (R)
57. Angels, Dallas McPherson, 3b	The Citadel	Randleman, N.C.	660,000	7-23-80	L-R	6-3	215	.346	231	80	11	56	8	Provo (R)
62. Yankees, Shelley Duncan, of	U. of Arizona	Tucson	655,000	9-29-79	R-R	6-5	210	.338	228	77	24	78	3	Staten Island (A)
67. Mariners, Michael Wilson, of	Booker T. Washington HS	Tulsa	900,000	6-29-83	R-R	6-2	215	.506	83	42	4	26	51	Did not play
70. Mets, Alhaji Turay, of	Auburn HS	Auburn, Wash.	515,000	9-22-82	R-R	6-0	200	.441	73	30	11	35	10	Kingsport (R)
73. Braves, Cole Barthel, 3b	Decatur HS	Decatur, Ala.	475,000	8-11-82	R-R	6-2	205	.400	75	30	1	18	17	GCL Braves (R)
76. Mets, Corey Ragsdale, ss	Nettleton HS	Jonesboro, Ark.	550,000	11-10-82	R-R	6-4	180	.402	102	41	3	29	38	Kingsport (R)
77. Twins, Jose Morales, ss	Academia La Providencia HS	Rio Piedras, P.R.	490,000	2-20-83	B-R	6-0	175	No spring team						GCL Twins (R)
78. Cubs, Ryan Theriot, ss	Louisiana State U.	Baton Rouge	480,000	12-07-79	R-R	5-11	175	.353	266	94	5	48	17	Daytona (A)
80. Mariners, Lazaro Abreu, c	Westminster Academy	Fort Lauderdale	450,000	9-27-82	R-R	6-1	190	.412	196	65	15	50	25	AZL Mariners (R)
85. Reds, Alan Moye, of	Southridge HS	Miami	450,000	12-02-81	L-R	6-2	180	.444	90	40	7	26	20	
87. Tigers, Jack Hannahan, 3b	U. of Minnesota	St. Paul, Minn.	435,000	3-04-80	R-R	6-2	200	.372	226	84	15	63	16	West Michigan (A)
90. Padres, Taggert Bozied, 3b	U. of San Francisco	Denver	Did not sign	7-24-79	R-R	6-3	215							Northern League
91. Blue Jays, Tyrell Godwin, of	U. of North Carolina	Council, N.C.	480,000	7-10-79	L-R	6-1	190	.335	212	71	12	38	20	Auburn (A)
93. Red Sox, Jon DeVries, c	Irvine HS	Irvine, Calif.	450,000	8-22-82	R-R	6-3	210	.449	78	35	6	26	9	GCL Red Sox (R)
94. Rockies, Jason Frome, of	Indiana State U.	Appleton, Wis.	420,000	7-03-79	L-R	6-0	192	.332	196	65	15	50	25	Tri-City (A)
96. Reds, Jason Roberts, of	Pine Tree HS	Longview, Texas	400,000	10-08-82	R-R	6-2	190	.444	90	40	7	26	20	GCL Reds (R)
98. D'backs, Scott Hairston, 2b	Central Arizona JC	Tucson	400,000	5-25-80	R-R	6-1	180	.503	165	83	18	77	24	Missoula (R)
99. Mariners, Tim Merritt, ss	U. of South Alabama	Cantonment, Fla.	400,000	2-07-80	R-R	6-4	185	.296	240	71	12	63	15	Wisconsin (A)

Rank. Team, Player, Pos.	School	Hometown	Bonus	B'date	B-T	Ht.	Wt.	W-L	ERA	IP	H	BB	SO	2001 Assignment*
2. #Cubs, Mark Prior, rhp	U. of Southern California	San Diego	$4,000,000	9-07-80	R-R	6-5	225	15-1	1.69	139	100	18	202	Did not play
3. #Devil Rays, Dewon Brazelton, rhp	Middle Tennessee State U.	Tullahoma, Tenn.	4,200,000	6-16-80	R-R	6-4	205	13-2	1.42	127	82	24	154	Did not play
4. Phillies, Gavin Floyd, rhp	Mount St. Joseph HS	Severna Park, Md.	4,200,000	1-27-83	R-R	6-6	210	8-2	1.11	63	23	29	103	Did not play
6. Expos, Josh Karp, rhp	UCLA	Bothell, Wash.	2,650,000	6-05-79	R-R	6-5	195	5-2	3.26	80	75	32	92	Did not play
7. Orioles, Chris Smith, lhp	Cumberland (Tenn.) U.	Wantagh, N.Y.	2,175,000	12-10-79	B-L	5-11	190	9-2	2.13	84	58	34	115	GCL Orioles (R)
9. Royals, Colt Griffin, rhp	Marshall HS	Marshall, Texas	2,400,000	9-29-82	R-R	6-4	198	8-2	1.40	65	22	39	113	Spokane (A)

Signing bonuses do not include scholarships, incentive bonus plans or salaries from a major league contract.
*Highest level of professional baseball attained   #Signed major league contract

Rank. Team, Player, Pos.	School	Hometown	Bonus	B'date	B-T	Ht.	Wt.	W-L	ERA	IP	H	BB	SO	2000 Assignment*
11. Tigers: Kenny Baugh, rhp	Rice U.	Houston	1,800,000	2-05-79	R-R	6-4	195	13-2	2.17	141	106	54	163	Erie (AA)
12. Brewers: Mike Jones, rhp	Thunderbird HS	Phoenix	2,075,000	4-23-83	R-R	6-5	210	5-1	1.16	48	27	13	89	Ogden (R)
16. White Sox: Kris Honel, rhp	Providence Catholic HS	New Lenox, Ill.	1,500,000	11-07-82	R-R	6-5	190	8-0	1.08	45	25	4	59	Bristol (R)
17. Indians: Dan Denham, rhp	Deer Valley HS	Antioch, Calif.	1,860,000	12-24-82	R-R	6-1	195	9-2	1.42	74	39	23	134	Burlington (R)
18. Mets: Aaron Heilman, rhp	U. of Notre Dame	Logansport, Ind.	1,508,705	11-12-78	R-R	6-5	225	15-0	1.74	114	70	31	111	St. Lucie (A)
20. Reds: Jeremy Sowers, lhp	Ballard HS	Louisville	Did not sign	5-17-83	L-L	6-1	165	10-1	0.51	82	32	15	148	Did not play
21. Giants: Brad Hennessey, rhp	Youngstown State U.	Toledo	1,382,500	2-07-80	R-R	6-2	180	6-5	4.06	89	40	42	126	Salem-Keizer (A)
22. Diamondbacks: Jason Bulger, rhp	Valdosta State U.	Snellville, Ga.	950,000	12-06-78	R-R	6-4	200	7-2	1.47	49	26	26	64	Did not play
24. Braves: Macay McBride, lhp	Screven County HS	Sylvania, Ga.	1,340,000	10-24-82	L-L	5-11	185	11-2	1.32	79	29	35	160	GCL Braves (R)
26. Athletics: Jeremy Bonderman, rhp	Pasco HS	Pasco, Wash.	1,350,000	10-28-82	R-R	6-1	210	3-1	3.60	35	25	12	54	Did not play
27. Indians: Alan Horne, rhp	Marianna HS	Marianna, Fla.	Did not sign	1-05-83	R-R	6-3	190	9-2	1.12	81	39	14	147	Did not sign
28. Cardinals: Justin Pope, rhp	U. of Central Florida	Lake Worth, Fla.	900,000	11-08-79	B-R	6-0	180	15-1	1.68	123	97	27	158	New Jersey (A)
30. Giants: Noah Lowry, lhp	Pepperdine U.	Ojai, Calif.	1,175,000	10-10-80	L-L	6-2	190	14-1	1.51	113	82	39	137	Salem-Keizer (A)
35. Indians: J.D. Martin, rhp	Burroughs HS	Ridgecrest, Calif.	975,000	1-02-83	B-R	6-4	165	11-1	0.64	76	31	20	136	Burlington (R)
37. Athletics: John Rheinecker, lhp	SW Missouri State U.	Waterloo, Ill.	600,000	5-29-79	L-L	6-2	215	5-4	2.27	91	79	22	106	Modesto (A)
39. White Sox: Wyatt Allen, rhp	U. of Tennessee	Brentwood, Tenn.	872,500	4-12-80	R-R	6-4	205	10-3	6.30	104	109	59	110	Kannapolis (A)
43. Indians: Jon Skaggs, rhp	Rice U.	Sugar Land, Texas	600,000	3-27-78	R-R	6-5	225	9-4	2.65	119	89	62	110	Staten Island (A)
45. Twins: Scott Tyler, rhp	Downingtown HS	Downingtown, Pa.	875,000	8-20-82	R-R	6-2	215	6-1	1.63	52	32	20	110	GCL Twins (R)
46. Cubs: Andy Sisco, lhp	Eastlake HS	Sammamish, Wash.	1,000,000	1-13-83	L-L	6-9	260	2-2	1.38	30	22	11	59	AZL Cubs (R)
47. Devil Rays: Jon Switzer, lhp	Arizona State U.	Houston	850,000	8-13-79	L-L	6-2	189	5-6	4.04	100	95	45	128	Hudson Valley (A)
50. Expos: Donald Levinski, rhp	Weimar HS	Weimar, Texas	825,000	10-20-82	R-R	6-4	200	8-1	0.39	54	14	19	103	GCL Expos (R)
51. Indians: Jake Dittler, rhp	Green Valley HS	Henderson, Nev.	750,000	11-24-82	R-R	6-3	200	4-2	1.51	37	23	7	46	Burlington (R)
52. Braves: J.P. Howell, lhp	Jesuit HS	Sacramento	Did not sign	4-25-83	L-L	6-0	170	10-0	0.10	71	32	21	136	Did not play
55. Tigers: Preston Larrison, rhp	U. of Evansville	Aurora, Ill.	685,000	11-19-80	R-R	6-4	215	8-4	5.25	94	102	36	77	Oneonta (A)
58. Padres: Matt Harrington, rhp	St. Paul (Northern)	Palmdale, Calif.	Did not sign	2-01-82	R-R	6-2	185	No school team						Did not play
59. Blue Jays: Brandon League, rhp	St. Louis School	Honolulu	660,000	3-16-83	R-R	6-2	180	5-2	3.30	60	47	10	75	Medicine Hat (R)
60. Marlins: Garrett Berger, rhp	Carmel HS	Carmel, Ind.	795,000	5-11-83	R-R	6-2	200	7-1	1.22	63	34	21	102	Did not play
61. Red Sox: Matt Chico, lhp	Fallbrook HS	Fallbrook, Calif.	Did not sign	6-10-83	L-L	5-11	175	10-1	0.84	75	45	25	116	Did not play
63. Yankees: Jason Arnold, rhp	U. of Central Florida	Palm Bay, Fla.	400,000	5-02-79	R-R	6-3	210	14-3	1.97	119	82	32	150	Staten Island (A)
64. Reds: Justin Gillman, rhp	Mosley HS	Panama City, Fla.	625,000	6-27-83	R-R	6-2	185	8-3	1.59	62	32	24	94	Billings (R)
65. Tigers: Matt Coenen, lhp	Charleston Southern U.	St. Michael's, Md.	620,000	3-13-80	L-L	6-6	230	5-7	5.38	97	118	52	102	Oneonta (A)
66. Diamondbacks: Mike Gosling, lhp	Stanford U.	Salt Lake City	2,000,000	9-23-80	L-L	6-2	215	7-3	3.94	82	65	28	77	Did not play
66. Dodgers: Brian Pilkington, rhp	Santiago HS	Garden Grove, Calif.	600,000	9-17-82	R-R	6-5	210	10-2	0.90	77	35	7	97	Great Falls (R)
69. Athletics: Neal Cotts, lhp	Illinois State U.	Lebanon, Ill.	525,000	3-25-80	L-L	6-2	198	8-3	2.89	87	60	34	113	Visalia (A)
71. White Sox: Ryan Wing, lhp	Riverside (Calif.) CC	Murrieta, Calif.	575,000	2-01-82	L-L	6-2	170	12-1	2.35	113	71	54	113	Bristol (R)
74. Cardinals: Dan Haren, rhp	Pepperdine U.	West Covina, Calif.	530,000	9-17-80	R-R	6-5	220	11-3	2.22	130	106	31	97	New Jersey (A)
74. Giants: Jesse Foppert, rhp	U. of San Francisco	San Rafael, Calif.	520,000	7-10-80	R-R	6-6	210	8-4	3.75	98	104	38	118	Salem-Keizer (A)
75. Rockies: Trey Taylor, lhp	Mansfield HS	Mansfield, Texas	Did not sign	11-12-82	R-L	6-2	185	9-2	2.58	65	45	33	107	Did not play
79. Devil Rays: Chris Flinn, rhp	U. of Stony Brook	Levittown, N.Y.	466,000	8-18-80	R-R	6-2	185	4-7	4.06	89	82	44	121	Hudson Valley (A)
81. Angels: Steven Shell, rhp	El Reno HS	El Reno, Okla.	460,000	3-10-83	R-R	6-5	195	4-7	2.56	71	51	17	117	Provo (R)
82. Expos: Mike Hinckley, lhp	Moore HS	Moore, Okla.	425,000	10-05-82	L-L	6-2	170	10-2	1.16	79	41	32	114	GCL Expos (R)
84. Orioles: Dave Crouthers, rhp	SIU-Edwardsville	Edwardsville, Ill.	425,000	12-18-79	R-R	6-3	210	9-6	3.03	104	84	48	110	Bluefield (R)
86. Pirates: Jeremy Guthrie, rhp	Stanford U.	Ashland, Ore.	Did not sign	4-08-79	R-R	6-1	195	13-4	2.82	134	123	41	128	Did not play
86. Astros: Kirk Saarloos, rhp	Cal State Fullerton	Long Beach, Calif.	300,000	5-23-79	R-R	6-0	180	15-2	2.18	153	99	23	153	Lexington (A)
88. Brewers: Jon Steitz, rhp	Yale U.	Branford, Conn.	440,000	9-05-80	R-R	6-3	205	2-4	2.66	64	49	39	81	Ogden (R)
89. Angels: Jacob Woods, lhp	Bakersfield (Calif.) JC	Kingsburg, Calif.	442,500	9-03-81	L-L	6-1	195	7-5	2.16	103	90	28	132	Provo (R)
91. Marlins: Allen Baxter, rhp	Varina HS	Sandston, Va.	450,000	7-06-83	R-R	6-4	215	6-3	1.40	55	37	10	84	Utica (A)
95. Yankees: Chase Wright, lhp	Iowa Park HS	Iowa Park, Texas	400,000	2-08-83	L-L	6-3	205							GCL Yankees (R)
97. Indians: Nick Moran, rhp	Fresno State U.	Elk Grove, Calif.	400,000	1-03-80	B-R	6-6	200	6-6	3.09	90	83	23	78	Mahoning Valley (A)
100. Dodgers: David Taylor, rhp	Southlake HS	Clermont, Fla.	385,000	12-04-82	B-R	6-5	190	4-4	2.35	57	39	34	79	GCL Dodgers (R)

FIRST-YEAR DRAFT

Mauer accepted a $5.15 million bonus on July 17. The only drafted player ever to receive more from the team that selected him is Borchard, a Stanford outfielder/quarterback who got $5.3 million from the White Sox as the No. 12 overall pick in 2000. Minnesota used Mauer's football ability to its advantage, spreading his bonus over five years as permitted by Major League Baseball rules applying to two-sport athletes.

One of the few stumbling blocks was exactly how the bonus would be stretched out. The Twins wanted to backload the contract to protect themselves in case Mauer eventually decided to resume his football career, but the two sides agreed to split the bonus between the front and back ends of the deal.

"What was in question was how you allocated the dollars," Radcliff said. "That was the key and we were both satisfied. They wanted some security up front, and we wanted some security in the back end. That was the crux of the negotiations."

Mauer's pro debut was a smashing success. He joined his brother Jake, Minnesota's 23rd-round pick in 2001, at Rookie-level Elizabethon, where Joe batted .400 in 32 games and was rated as the Applalachian League's top prospect.

None of the other top five picks signed in time to make their pro debut in 2001. The Cubs didn't begin negotiating in earnest with Prior until Aug. 5, and signed him 17 days later. He got a five-year major league contract worth $10.5 million, the largest guaranteed payout ever to a drafted player. It included a $4 million bonus, several incentives and player options on the final two years, giving Prior flexibility in the event he becomes eli-

MAJOR LEAGUE CONTRACTS

In what clearly has become a trend in the draft's evolution, three more players were signed to major league contracts in 2001. Such contracts require players to be placed immediately on the selecting team's 40-man roster. The 2001 signings increased the number of major league contracts to 17 since Bo Jackson agreed to a major league deal with the Royals in 1986 as a condition of his being pried away from a promising NFL career. Here's the full list, including the bonus the player received as well as the amount he was guaranteed in major league salaries and roster bonuses.

Year	Club (Round)	Player, Pos.	Bonus	Guar. Amount
1986	Royals (4)	Bo Jackson, of	$100,000	$1,066,000
1989	Orioles (1)	Ben McDonald, rhp	350,000	824,000
	Blue Jays (3)	John Olerud, 1b	575,000	800,000
1990	Athletics (1)	*Todd Van Poppel, rhp	500,000	1,200,000
1993	Mariners (1)	*Alex Rodriguez, ss	1,000,000	1,300,000
1998	Phillies (1)	Pat Burrell, 1b-of	3,150,000	8,000,000
	Cardinals (1)	J.D. Drew, of	3,000,000	7,000,000
		Chad Hutchinson, rhp	2,300,000	3,400,000
1999	Marlins (1)	*Josh Beckett, rhp	3,625,000	7,000,000
	Tigers (1)	Eric Munson, c	3,500,000	6,750,000
2000	Reds (1)	*David Espinosa, ss	None	2,950,000
	Reds (2)	Dane Sardinha, c	None	1,950,000
	Padres (2)	Xavier Nady, 3b	1,100,000	2,850,000
	Devil Rays (5)	Jace Brewer, ss	450,000	1,200,000
2001	Cubs (1)	Mark Prior, rhp	4,000,000	10,500,000
	Devil Rays (1)	Dewon Brazelton, rhp	4,200,000	4,800,000
	Rangers (1)	Mark Teixeira, 3b	4,500,000	9,500,000

* High school signee

NO. 1 PICKS, 1965-2001

Year	Club, Player, Pos.	School	Hometown	Highest Level (G#)	2001 Team	Bonus
1965	A's. Rick Monday, of	Arizona State U.	Santa Monica, Calif.	Majors (1,996)	Out of Baseball	$104,000
1966	Mets. Steve Chilcott, c	Antelope Valley HS	Lancaster, Calif.	Triple-A (2)	Out of Baseball	75,000
1967	Yankees. Ron Blomberg, 1b	Druid Hills HS	Atlanta	Majors (461)	Out of Baseball	75,000
1968	Mets. Tim Foli, ss	Notre Dame HS	Sherman Oaks, Calif.	Majors (1,696)	Out of Baseball	75,000
1969	Senators. Jeff Burroughs, of	Wilson HS	Long Beach	Majors (1,689)	Out of Baseball	88,000
1970	Padres. Mike Ivie, c	Walker HS	Decatur, Ga.	Majors (857)	Out of Baseball	80,000
1971	White Sox. Danny Goodwin, c	Central HS	Peoria, Ill.	Majors (252)	Out of Baseball	DNS
1972	Padres. Dave Roberts, 3b	U. of Oregon	Corvallis, Ore.	Majors (709)	Out of Baseball	60,000
1973	Rangers. David Clyde, lhp	Westchester, HS	Houston	Majors (84)	Out of Baseball	125,000
1974	Padres. Bill Almon, ss	Brown U.	Warwick, R.I.	Majors (1,236)	Out of Baseball	90,000
1975	Angels. Danny Goodwin, c	Southern U.	Peoria, Ill.	Majors (252)	Out of Baseball	125,000
1976	Astros. Floyd Bannister, lhp	Arizona State U.	Seattle	Majors (431)	Out of Baseball	100,000
1977	White Sox. Harold Baines, of	St. Michaels HS	St. Michaels, Md.	Majors (2,830)	White Sox	40,000
1978	Braves. Bob Horner, 3b	Arizona State U.	Glendale, Ariz.	Majors (1,020)	Out of Baseball	175,000
1979	Mariners. Al Chambers, of	Harris HS	Harrisburg, Pa.	Majors (57)	Out of Baseball	60,000
1980	Mets. Darryl Strawberry, of	Crenshaw HS	Los Angeles	Majors (1,583)	Out of Baseball	152,500
1981	Mariners. Mike Moore, rhp	Oral Roberts U.	Eakly, Okla.	Majors (450)	Out of Baseball	100,000
1982	Cubs. Shawon Dunston, ss	Jefferson HS	New York	Majors (1,678)	Cardinals	100,000
1983	Twins. Tim Belcher, rhp	Mt. Vernon Naz. Coll.	Sparta, Ohio	Majors (362)	Out of Baseball	DNS
1984	Mets. Shawn Abner, of	Mechanicsburg HS	Mechanicsburg, Pa.	Majors (392)	Out of Baseball	150,000
1985	Brewers. B.J. Surhoff, c	U. of North Carolina	Rye, N.Y.	Majors (2,004)	Braves	150,000
1986	Pirates. Jeff King, 3b	U. of Arkansas	Colorado Springs	Majors (1,201)	Out of Baseball	160,000
1987	Mariners. Ken Griffey Jr., of	Moeller HS	Cincinnati	Majors (1,791)	Reds	169,000
1988	Padres. Andy Benes, rhp	U. of Evansville	Evansville, Ind.	Majors (385)	Cardinals	235,000
1989	Orioles. Ben McDonald, rhp	Louisiana State U.	Denham Springs, La.	Majors (211)	Out of Baseball	*350,000
1990	Braves. Chipper Jones, ss	The Bolles School	Jacksonville	Majors (1,094)	Braves	275,000
1991	Yankees. Brien Taylor, lhp	East Carteret HS	Beaufort, N.C.	Double-A (27)	Out of Baseball	1,550,000
1992	Mets. Phil Nevin, 3b	Cal State Fullerton	Placentia, Calif.	Majors (672)	Padres	700,000
1993	Mariners. Alex Rodriguez, ss	West. Christian HS	Miami	Majors (952)	Rangers	*1,000,000
1994	Mets. Paul Wilson, rhp	Florida State U.	Orlando	Majors (74)	Devil Rays	1,550,000
1995	Angels. Darin Erstad, of	U. of Nebraska	Jamestown, N.D.	Majors (785)	Angels	1,575,000
1996	Pirates. Kris Benson, rhp	Clemson U.	Kennesaw, Ga.	Majors (63)	Pirates	2,000,000
1997	Tigers. Matt Anderson, rhp	Rice U.	Louisville	Majors (210)	Tigers	2,505,000
1998	Phillies. Pat Burrell, 3b	U. of Miami	Boulder Creek, Calif.	Majors (266)	Phillies	*3,150,000
1999	Devil Rays. Josh Hamilton, of	Athens Drive HS	Raleigh, N.C.	Double-A (23)	Devil Rays (AA)	3,960,000
2000	Marlins. Adrian Gonzalez, 1b	Eastside HS	Chula Vista, Calif.	Class A (135)	Marlins (A)	3,000,000
2001	Twins. Joe Mauer, c	Cretin-Derham Hall	St. Paul, Minn.	Rookie (32)	Twins (R)	5,150,000
	#No. of games at that level	DNS—Did not sign				

FIRST-YEAR DRAFT

gible for major league arbitration or of a big league work stoppage.

The Priors, who purposefully never floated a specific dollar figure before the draft and refused to negotiate in the press, were somewhat frustrated that it took so long to close a deal.

"We didn't want to hold out," said Jerry Prior, Mark's father. "We knew this would establish some new standards and that it could take time to negotiate, but the process leaves you twisting in the wind. The inaction was more frustrating than anything else. We wound up in the exact same position as the clients of some of the more volatile agents."

Boras has a reputation for being volatile, and he got a similar contract for Teixeira, who signed on the same day as Prior. The Rangers, who paid Boras client Alex Rodriguez a record $252 million as a free agent during the offseason, anted up a four-year major league deal worth a guaranteed $9.5 million for Teixeira. It included a $4.5 million signing bonus and easily attainable roster bonuses.

Dewon Brazelton

Aug. 22 also marked the second day of the fall semester at Middle Tennessee State, and the Devil Rays would have lost the rights to Brazelton as soon as he attended his first class. And late that afternoon, Phillies farm and scouting director Mike Arbuckle announced his team had concluded negotiations with Floyd, who was set to attend South Carolina.

The Floyds had turned down what Arbuckle characterized as the club's final offer of $4 million. The family initially had asked for a $7 million bonus, then a major league contract and then a bonus comparable to Mauer's.

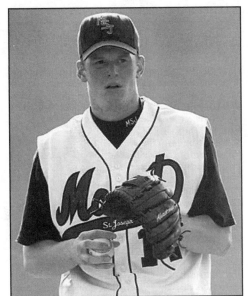
Gavin Floyd: Lengthy holdout netted $4.2 million bonus

That evening, Gavin and his older brother Mike, an outfielder whom Philadelphia drafted in the 22nd round, began the drive to Columbia.

On Aug. 23, Floyd's adviser Ron Shapiro called Arbuckle to see if a deal still could be worked out. The Phillies slightly increased their offer and signed Gavin shortly before midnight for a $4.2 million bonus. Mike also signed for $65,000, a generous bonus considering his draft status.

Meanwhile, cash-strapped Tampa Bay was trying to come up with a creative way to land Brazelton. Discussions went nowhere for most of the summer, as the Devil Rays offered just $250,000 up front as part of a five-year contract, a proposal Brazelton dismissed as "chump change."

Ultimately, the lure of an immediate big league callup got Brazelton into the Tampa Bay fold. On Aug. 26, he accepted a five-year, $4.8 million major league contract, which included a $4.2 million bonus spread over the length of the deal. He joined Tampa Bay in September but didn't appear in a game after a summer-long layoff.

"It's something I wanted more than anything," Brazelton said of becoming an instant big leaguer. "I realized they were not going to give me all the money, but that's something you can't put a price tag on. If I get to play some that would be fine, but you can't put a price tag on being able to live the life of a major league ballplayer. I feel like the next time won't be my first time, that I'll already have major league experience.

"I will probably seem like a little girl to them because I'm pretty sure the first time I step on that field I'll probably break down in tears or something."

First-Round Bonuses Rise 15 Percent

When UCLA righthander Josh Karp, the No. 6 overall pick, signed with the Expos for a $2.65 million bonus on Sept. 28, the entire first round was resolved. Twenty-eight of the first 30 picks turned pro for an average signing bonus of $2,162,723, a new record and a 15-percent increase over the 2000 average of $1,872,586. That com-

RELATIVELY SPEAKING

Players drafted in 2001 who are related to current or former big leaguers:

Player, Pos.	Club (Round)	Relative
Jon Ashford, of	Blue Jays (20)	Son of Tucker
Josh Barfield, 2b	Padres (4)	Son of Jesse
Robert Coomer, rhp	Pirates (25)	Brother of Ron
Joe Coppinger, rhp	Orioles (7)	Brother of Rocky
Josh Crede, 3b	White Sox (48)	Brother of Joe
Bobby Crosby, ss	Athletics (1)	Son of Ed
Tim Dillard, c	Brewers (15)	Son of Steve
Stephen Drew, ss	Pirates (11)	Brother of J.D., Tim
Shelley Duncan, of	Yankees (2)	Son of Dave
Ernie Durazo, 1b	Blue Jays (12)	Brother of Erubiel
Jared Eichelberger, rhp	Cubs (44)	Son of Juan
Daniel Foli, rhp	Cubs (31)	Son of Tim
Sean Gamble, of	Blue Jays (11)	Son of Oscar
Michael Garciaparra, ss	Mariners (1)	Brother of Nomar
Dustin Hahn, of	Orioles (21)	Son of Don
Scott Hairston, 2b	Diamondbacks (3)	Son of Jerry
Isaac Iorg, ss	Blue Jays (19)	Son of Garth
Bryan Kennedy, c	Twins (24)	Brother of Adam
Kaulana Kuhaulua, 2b	Twins (12)	Son of Fred
Taylor McCormack, 3b	Brewers (7)	Son of Don
Kevin McDowell, lhp	Tigers (15)	Son of Sam
Andy Myette, rhp	Rangers (44)	Brother of Aaron
Matt Pagnozzi, c	Cubs (40)	Son of Tom
John Palmer, rhp	Reds (21)	Son of David
Eric Patterson, ss	Rockies (23)	Brother of Corey
Josh Renick, ss	Twins (11)	Son of Rick
Daron Roberts, c	Devil Rays (25)	Son of Dave
Chad Scarbery, rhp	Expos (50)	Son of Randy
Vince Vukovich, of	Phillies (20)	Son of John
Dustin Yount, 1b	Orioles (9)	Son of Robin

pares to $1,809,767 in 1999 and $1,637,667 in 1998.

The averages represent only the present value of bonuses and don't consider additional payments that are part of major league contracts or scholarship plans. Fourteen players in 2001 received bonuses of $2 million or more— 12 of the first 13 choices, plus Mariners supplemental first-rounder Michael Garciaparra and Diamondbacks second-rounder Mike Gosling—compared to 15 a year earlier.

Two first-round picks went unsigned in the same draft for the first time since 1997, when J.D. Drew signed with the Northern League's St. Paul Saints rather than with the Phillies and Tyrell Godwin spurned the Yankees for the University of North Carolina. This time, lefthander Jeremy Sowers, the 20th overall selection, chose Vanderbilt over the Reds, while righty Alan Horne, chosen 27th, turned down the Indians for the University of Mississippi.

ERIC WILLIAMS

Jeremy Sowers

A Cincinnati club official acknowledged the Reds took Sowers because they knew they couldn't sign him. Sowers, who comes from a well-to-do family that wanted him to attend college, set an asking price in the neighborhood of $3 million. The Reds never offered him more than $1.4 million and were quite content to save first-round bonus money and get a supplemental first-rounder in the 2002 draft. The Reds will pick third in the '02 draft.

Cincinnati's bonus budget has been thin since it spent $2.1 million to purchase outfielder Alejandro Diaz from Japan's Hiroshima Toyo Carp in March 1999. The Reds signed 1999 first-rounder Ty Howington with $1.75 million they took from their 2000 budget. In 2000, they gave major league contracts with no bonuses to first-rounder David Espinosa and second-rounder Dane Sardinha, and signed supplemental first-rounder Dustin Moseley with $937,000 they took from their 2001 budget.

"We didn't take him with the idea that we knew we could sign him," a Reds official said of Sowers. We've found a way to get this kind of player done in the past. But we knew it was a

Matt Harrington

longshot."

Just one 2000 first-rounder didn't sign, and he still was without a team in November 2001. Matt Harrington was the consensus top prospect in the 2000 draft and went seventh overall to the Rockies, but negotiations turned ugly. Harrington's agent, Tommy Tanzer, claimed that Colorado promised his client a $4.95 million bonus, which the team denies.

Harrington ultimately turned down a $3.75 million bonus and signed with St. Paul to showcase himself for the 2001 draft. The Padres took him in the second round, but control and shoulder problems led to a 9.47 ERA in 18 innings with St. Paul. Harrington replaced Tanzer with Boras in September as talks continued with San Diego.

Requisite Draft Tidbits

■ The Pirates didn't surprise anyone when they took

NCAA Division I home run leader John VanBenschoten with the eighth overall pick. But they did turn a few heads when they opted to make VanBenschoten, a two-way star at Kent State whom most teams projected as a prototype right fielder, a pitcher. VanBenschoten, who signed for $2.4 million, was named the top prospect in the short-season New York-Penn League after going 0-2, 3.51 in nine starts. He also batted .227-0-8 in 32 games as a DH.

■ Seminole (Fla.) High, which was ranked No. 1 wire-to-wire in Baseball America's national poll, became the first high school to have six players selected in one draft.

The first choice was first baseman Casey Kotchman, who went 13th overall to the Angels—who employ his father Tom as a scout and minor league manager. Tom also served as the agent for Casey, who received a $2.075 million bonus.

■ For the first time, a high school junior was drafted. Pasco (Wash.) High righthander Jeremy Bonderman, Team USA's ace at the 2000 World Junior Championships, passed his GED test and asked to enter the draft. The Athletics selected him 26th overall and signed him for $1.35 million.

■ Mauer was just one of four first-round picks taken by his home state club. The White Sox chose New Lenox, Ill., high school righthander Kris Honel 16th overall, while the Braves had three of the top 40 picks and used them all on Georgia players: Sylvania high school lefty Macay McBride (24th overall), Marietta prep shortstop Josh Burrus (29th) and Georgia Tech second baseman Richard Lewis (40th). "It doesn't matter what area of the country they were from," Atlanta scouting director Roy Clark said of his picks. "These are guys we're proud to have. In the last 10 years, the talent and the players in Georgia have gotten so much better. I'm not sure if it's the amateur programs or a spinoff of the Braves' success, but it just keeps getting better and better."

■ McLennan (Texas) Community College lefthander Sean Henn received the largest bonus ever given to a draft-and-follow, accepting $1.7 million from the Yankees, who drafted him in the 26th round in 2000. Henn threw as hard as 98 mph in the spring but hurt his elbow after turning pro and had Tommy John surgery.

■ South Carolina high school outfielder Roscoe Crosby initially projected as one of the top 10 picks in the draft, but he also had NFL potential as a wide receiver and a football scholarship from Clemson. The Royals, who strongly considered him with the No. 9 overall pick, took him instead in the second round. He signed for a $1.75 million bonus spread over five years and will continue to play both sports. "The only player I can compare him to in the last 20 years is Junior Griffey," said Royals senior adviser Art Stewart, who began scouting in 1953. "He has those kinds of tools Junior had in high school. The same ability—arm strength, running speed, raw power—all the ingredients."

■ A rare three-brother combination from Georgia was drafted in 2001. Righthander Jason Bulger of Valdosta State was an unexpected first-round pick of the Diamondbacks, while his younger brothers were both picked by the Giants—Kevin, a shortstop from Brookwood High in the 43rd round and Brian, a righthander from South Georgia JC, in the 49th round. Three sets of twins were picked: Jason (Tigers, sixth round) and Justin Knoedler (Giants, fifth); Matt (Brewers, 43rd) and Vince Serafini (Twins, sixth); and Mark (Blue Jays, 29th) and P.J. McDonald (Blue Jays, 43rd).

■ Bronson Sardinha, the highest-drafted Hawaii high school player ever (34th overall), was a supplemental first-round pick of the Yankees. His older brother Duke was selected in the 41st round by the Rockies; his oldest brother Dane was a second-round pick of the Reds in 2000. Stephen Drew (Pirates, 11th) follows in the footsteps of older brothers J.D. and Tim, both former first-rounders. And Michael Cust (Cardinals, 35th) is the third brother in his family to have been drafted. Neither Drew nor Cust chose to sign.

DRAFT 2001

CLUB-BY-CLUB SELECTIONS

• Order of selection indicated in parentheses
• Boldface indicates player signed

ANAHEIM (13)

1. **Casey Kotchman, 1b, Seminole (Fla.) HS**
1. **Jeff Mathis, c, Marianna (Fla.) HS** (Supplemental pick—33rd—for loss of Type A free agent Mark Petkovsek).
2. **Dallas McPherson, 3b, The Citadel**
3. **Steven Shell, rhp, El Reno (Okla.) HS** (Choice from Rangers—81st—for loss of Type A free agent Mark Petkovsek).
3. **Jacob Woods, lhp, Bakersfield (Calif.) JC**
4. **Mike Nickoli, rhp, Birmingham-Southern College**
5. **Brad Pinkerton, lhp, Elon College**
6. **Quan Cosby, of, Mart (Texas) HS**
7. Rich Hill, lhp, U. of Michigan
8. **Justin Turner, 3b, Warner Southern (Fla.) College**
9. Devin Ivany, c, Cardinal Gibbons HS, Fort Lauderdale
10. **Matt Brown, 3b, Coeur d'Alene (Idaho) HS**
11. **Johnathon Shull, rhp, Eastside HS, Butler, Ind.**
12. **Ryan Budde, c, Oklahoma State U.**
13. **Tony Arthur, lhp, Arkansas State U.**
14. **Jason Dennis, lhp, U. of California**
15. Micah Posey, rhp, North Florida Christian HS, Tallahassee, Fla.
16. **Al Corbiel, c, Florida Southern College**
17. Mike Galloway, lhp, Allen (Texas) HS
18. **Ed Tolzien, 1b, Illinois State U.**
19. **Nick Gorneault, of, U. of Massachusetts**
20. Justin Nelson, of, Rancho Buena HS, Vista, Calif.
21. **David Gates, of, U. of Alabama-Huntsville**
22. Brock Keffer, rhp, LaSalle-Peru (Ill.) Township HS
23. Mitchell Arnold, rhp, New Mexico JC
24. William Robbins, rhp, Lockhart HS, Sharon, S.C.
25. **Mark O'Sullivan, rhp, Rollins (Fla.) College**
26. Jason Durbin, of, Atwater (Calif.) HS
27. Kelly Sisco, lhp, Connors State (Okla.) JC
28. **Ryan Nevins, ss, New York Tech**
29. Carlos Corporan, 1b, Francisco Oller HS, Catano, P.R.
30. **Kris Sutton, rhp, U. of Tampa**
31. **Ryan Bailey, rhp, U. of Utah**
32. **Steve Andrade, rhp, Cal State Stanislaus**
33. Scott Lewis, lhp, Washington HS, Washington Court House, Ohio
34. **Casey Smith, 2b, Troy State U.**
35. **Blake Allen, rhp, U. of Alabama-Birmingham**
36. Steven Trosclair, rhp, Southeastern Louisiana U.
37. James Morris, lhp, Eldorado (Ill.) HS
38. Thomas Sgueglia, 2b, Mt. Saint Michael HS, Bronx, N.Y.
39. **Jaime Steward, lhp, LeMoyne College**
40. Alan Crigger, rhp, Okaloosa Walton (Fla.) CC
41. **Brent Del Chiaro, c, U. of Kansas**
42. **Ryan Webb, 3b, Chico State (Calif.) U.**
43. David Bartelt, rhp, Jesuit HS, Odessa, Fla.
44. **Mike Eylward, 3b, U. of South Florida**
45. **Greg Porter, 3b, Texas A&M U.**
46. Alberto Marrero, c, Luis Pales Matos HS, Bayamon, P.R.
47. Jorge Marrero, of, Jose Collazo Colon HS, Juncos, P.R.
48. Collin Mahoney, c, Mount St. Michael HS, Bronx, N.Y.
49. Stephen Nielsen, rhp, Triton (Ill.) JC
50. Kevin Letz, rhp, Hanks HS, El Paso, Texas

ARIZONA (22)

1. **Jason Bulger, rhp, Valdosta State U.**
2. **Mike Gosling, lhp, Stanford U.**
3. **Scott Hairston, 2b, Central Arizona JC**
4. **Justin Wechsler, rhp, Ball State U.**
5. **Richie Barrett, of, Ursinas (Pa.) College**
6. Matt Fox, rhp, Stoneman Douglas HS, Parkland, Fla.
7. **Chad Tracy, 3b, East Carolina U.**
8. **Brandon Medders, rhp, Mississippi State U.**
9. **Jared Ball, of, Tomball (Texas) HS**
10. Matt Durkin, rhp, Willow Glen HS, San Jose, Calif.
11. **Dan Uggla, 2b, U. of Memphis**
12. **Erick Macha, 2b-ss, Texas Christian U.**
13. **Shane Waroff, rhp, Cal State Fullerton**
14. **Josh Clark, rhp, Southern Illinois U.-Edwardsville**
15. **Sam Taulli, lhp, Chipola (Fla.) JC**
16. **Michael DiRosa, c, U. of Miami**
17. **Jay Belflower, rhp, U. of Florida**
18. **Mike Garber, lhp, San Diego State U.**
19. **Dustin Vugteveen, of, Grand Valley State (Mich.) U.**

Casey Kotchman: Angels' first-round pick

RICK BATTLE

20. Eddie Bonine, rhp, Glendale (Ariz.) CC
21. Brett Smith, rhp, Sonora HS, La Habra, Calif.
22. Ryan Holsten, rhp, Fairfield U.
23. Scott Hilinski, ss, Warner Southern (Fla.) College
24. Phil Avlas, c, Kennedy HS, North Hills, Calif.
25. Chase Bassham, lhp, Western Hills HS, Benbrook, Texas
26. Ian Kinsler, ss-2b, Central Arizona JC
27. Cliff McMachen, lhp, CC of Southern Nevada
28. Clark Mace, of, Miami (Ohio) U.
29. Ryan Coffin, rhp, Chandler Gilbert (Ariz.) CC
30. Alex Frazier, of, Lurleen B. Wallace State (Ala.) JC
31. Jason Bingham, lhp, Pima (Ariz.) CC
32. Jeramy Janz, of, U. of San Francisco
33. Daniel Morris, lhp, Mosley HS, Southport, Fla.
34. Trent Pratt, c, Auburn U.
35. Chad Halbert, lhp, Cypress HS, Buena Park, Calif.
36. Marland Williams, of, North Florida CC
37. Brett Dowdy, 3b, Manatee (Fla.) JC
38. Quinn Stewart, of, Dallas Christian HS, Rowlett, Texas
39. Brian Cooper, ss, Bakersfield (Calif.) HS
40. Cary Nelson, of, Channelview (Texas) HS
41. Jesse Torborg, of, Connetquot HS, Ronkonkoma, N.Y.
42. Mike Thiessen, of, Air Force Academy
43. Matthew Raguse, rhp, St. Louis CC-Forest Park
44. Jonathan Felfoldi, lhp, La Jolla, Calif.
45. Matt Wilkinson, rhp, Southern Illinois U.-Edwardsville
46. Arlow Hanen, of, North HS, Phoenix
47. Matt Grooms, of, St. James HS, Montgomery, Ala.
48. Seth Smith, of, Hillcrest Christian HS, Jackson, Miss.
49. Troy Pickford, rhp, Fresno CC
50. Scott Foresman, rhp, American Heritage HS, Miramar, Fla.

ATLANTA (29)

1. Macay McBride, lhp, Screven County HS, Sylvania, Ga. (Choice from Dodgers—24th—as compensation for Type A free agent Andy Ashby).
1. Josh Burrus, ss, Wheeler HS, Marietta, Ga.
1. Richard Lewis, 2b, Georgia Tech (Supplemental pick—40th—for loss of Ashby).
2. J.P. Howell, lhp, Jesuit HS, Sacramento (Choice from Pirates—52nd—as compensation for Type B free agent Terry Mulholland).
2. Cole Barthel, 3b, Decatur (Ala.) HS
3. Adam Stern, of, U. of Nebraska
4. Kyle Davies, rhp, Stockbridge (Ga.) HS
5. Matt Esquivel, of, McArthur HS, San Antonio

6. Billy McCarthy, of, Rutgers U.
7. Roberto Nieves, rhp, Ileana de Gracia HS, Vega Alta, P.R.
8. Alonzo Ruelas, c, Grayson County (Texas) CC
9. Donnie Furnald, rhp-3b, Cal Poly Pomona
10. Willie Collazo, lhp, Florida International U.
11. Anthony Lerew, rhp, Northern Senior HS, Wellsville, Pa.
12. Mailon Kent, of, Auburn U.
13. Bryon Jeffcoat, 2b, U. of South Carolina
14. Kevin Barry, rhp, Rider (N.J.) College
15. Dexter Cooper, rhp, Etowah HS, Woodstock, Ga.
16. Roberto Santana, of, Colon HS, Las Piedras, P.R.
17. Anthony Mandel, rhp, Pensacola (Fla.) Catholic HS
18. Justin Parker, lhp, U. of Tennessee
19. Kevin Brown, 1b, U. of Miami
20. Greg Miller, of, James Madison U.
21. Adam Sokoll, rhp, Oakland (Mich.) U.
22. Dewayne Jones, c, Jackson State U.
23. Brian Strong, c, Ferrum (Va.) College
24. Fred Wray, rhp, UNC Wilmington
25. Travis Anderson, c, Burney, Calif.
26. Alex Trommelen, rhp, Pace (Fla.) HS
27. Cesar Montes de Oca, rhp, Bethune-Cookman College
28. Dominique Partridge, of, Northgate HS, Newnan, Ga.
29. Delwyn Young, 2b, Riverside (Calif.) CC
30. Tyler Jones, rhp, Martin HS, Arlington, Texas
31. Justin Willis, of, Parkland (Ill.) JC
32. Jeff Howell, c, Merritt Island (Fla.) HS
33. Ken Livesley, rhp, Stagg HS, Stockton, Calif.
34. Andrew Alvarado, rhp, James Logan HS, Union City, Calif.
35. John Grose, c, Chandler-Gilbert (Ariz.) JC
36. Jesse Craig, rhp, Basic HS, Henderson, Nev.
37. Robert Mason, lhp, Walnut (Calif.) HS
38. Matt Mercurio, ss, Avon Park (Fla.) HS
39. Matt Campbell, lhp, Hillcrest HS, Simpsonville, S.C.
40. Brandon Williams, c, Coeur d'Alene (Idaho) HS
41. Ryan Morgan, 3b, Boston College HS, Weymouth, Mass.
42. Paco Figueroa, ss, Gulliver Prep, Miami
43. Tim McClendon, rhp, Valencia (Fla.) CC
44. Adam Horner, 3b, University HS, Irvine, Calif.
45. Andrew Bowdish, rhp, St. Michaels Prep, San Jose, Calif.
46. Dallas Braden, lhp, Amos Alonzo Stagg HS, Stockton, Calif.
47. Curtis White, lhp, Seward County (Kan.) CC
48. Danny Figueroa, of, Gulliver Prep, Miami
49. Adam Hilzendeger, rhp, Moorpark (Calif.) JC
50. Vontrez Wilson, U. of Southern Colorado

BALTIMORE (7)

1. Chris Smith, lhp, Cumberland (Tenn.) U.
1. Mike Fontenot, 2b, Louisiana State U. (Choice from Yankees—19th—as compensation for Type A free agent Mike Mussina).
1. Bryan Bass, ss, Seminole (Fla.) HS (Supplemental pick—31st—for loss of Mussina).
2. (Choice to Indians as compensation for Type A free agent David Segui).
3. Dave Crouthers, rhp, Southern Illinois U.-Edwardsville
4. Rommie Lewis, lhp, Newport HS, Bellevue, Wash.
5. James Johnson, rhp, Endicott-Union HS, Endicott, N.Y.
6. Eli Whiteside, c, Delta State (Miss.) U.
7. Joe Coppinger, rhp, Seminole State (Okla.) JC
8. Chris Britton, rhp, Plantation (Fla.) HS
9. Dustin Yount, 1b, Chaparral HS, Phoenix
10. Woody Cliffords, of, Pepperdine U.
11. John Hardy, ss, Centennial HS, Boise, Idaho
12. T.W. Mincey, lhp, The Citadel
13. Richard Salazar, lhp, Miami-Dade CC
14. Cory Keylor, of, Ohio U.
15. Cory Morris, rhp, Dallas Baptist U.
16. Brad Edwards, lhp, Indiana U.
17. James Tiller, rhp, Elysian Field (Texas) HS
18. Trevor Caughey, lhp, San Luis Obispo (Calif.) HS
19. Adam Thomas, of, Abilene Christian U.
20. Andrew Perkins, lhp, Cal Poly Pomona
21. Dustin Hahn, of, Galena HS, Reno, Nev.
22. Adam Larson, rhp, Mississippi State U.
23. Josh Potter, rhp, Philipsburg Osceola HS, Philipsburg, Pa.
24. Adam Manley, 1b, Missouri Valley (Mo.) College
25. Richard Hackett, of, U. of the Pacific
26. Brent Burger, rhp, Paso Robles (Calif.) HS
27. Antoan Richardson, of, American Heritage School, Delray Beach, Fla.
28. Adam Dunavant, lhp, Prince George HS, Disputania, Va.
29. Kyle Schmidt, rhp, Dunedin (Fla.) HS
30. Coby Mavroulis, of, Cooper HS, Abilene, Texas
31. Evan Seibly, lhp, Moorpark (Calif.) HS
32. Lorenzo Mack, of, Larue County HS, Hodgenville, Ky.

33. Daniel Hanna, c, Eastern Arizona JC
34. Michael Coles, of, Hammond (Ind.) HS
35. Joshua Wilkening, rhp, Green River (Wash.) CC
36. Jeff Montani, rhp, SUNY Binghamton
37. Dwayne Carter, rhp, East Bakersfield (Calif.) HS
38. Sean Letsinger, rhp, Glen Oaks (Mich.) CC
39. Jesse Saunders, lhp, Eastside Catholic HS, Seattle
40. Michael Done, 3b, U. of Washington
41. Eric Blevins, rhp, Sullivan East HS, Bluff City, Tenn.
42. Josh Palm, rhp, Conneaut Lake (Pa.) HS
43. Justin Maxwell, of, Sherwood HS, Olney, Md.
44. Doug Brubaker, rhp, Hill (Texas) JC
45. Tabor Woolard, rhp, Antonian HS, San Antonio, Texas
46. Jonathon Fowler, lhp, Kirk Academy, Grenada, Miss.
47. Anthony Cupps, rhp, University Christian HS, Madison, Miss.
48. Bryan Johnson, lhp, Selah (Wash.) HS
49. Oscar Serrato, rhp, Riverside (Calif.) CC

BOSTON (17)

1. (Choice to Indians as compensation for Type A free agent Manny Ramirez).
2. Kelly Shoppach, c, Baylor U. (Choice from Phillies—48th—as compensation for Type B free agent Rheal Cormier).
2. Matt Chico, lhp, Fallbrook (Calif.) HS
3. Jonathan DeVries, c, Irvine (Calif.) HS
4. Stefan Bailie, 1b, Washington State U.
5. Eric West, ss, Southside HS, Gadsden, Ala.
6. Justin James, rhp, Yukon (Okla.) HS
7. Rolando Viera, lhp, Cuba
8. Kevin Youkilis, 3b, U. of Cincinnati
9. Billy Simon, rhp, Wellington (Fla.) Community HS
10. Ben Crockett, rhp, Harvard U.
11. Shane Rhodes, lhp, West Virginia U.
12. Ryan Brunner, of, U. of Northern Iowa
13. Alec Porzel, ss, U. of Notre Dame
14. Chris Farley, rhp, Mahar Regional HS, Orange, Mass.
15. Ryan Carroll, rhp, Mississippi State U.
16. Tony Gonzalez, of, Framingham (Mass.) HS
17. Michael Grant, rhp, Danville Area (Ill.) JC
18. Brian Lane, rhp, U. of Richmond
19. Jeremy Brown, c, U. of Alabama
20. Devoris Williams, ss, Greensboro (Ala.) HS
21. Charlie Weatherby, rhp, UNC Wilmington
22. Jed Rogers, rhp, Boston College
23. Pedro Suarez, rhp, Mount Miguel HS, Spring Valley, Calif.
24. Jason Ramos, ss, Braddock HS, Miami
25. Kris Coffey, of, Dallas Baptist U.
26. Ken Trapp, rhp, Dallas Baptist U.
27. Bryan Kent, 2b, Southwest Texas State U.
28. Steven Ponder, lhp, Texas A&M U.
29. Mario Campos, 3b, Trevecca Nazarene (Tenn.) U.
30. Rick Sander, rhp, Cal State San Bernardino
31. Brett Rudrude, rhp, Cal State San Bernardino
32. Kyle Jackson, rhp, Alvirne HS, Litchfield, N.H.
33. Chris Honsa, rhp, Corona del Sol HS, Chandler, Ariz.
34. Floyd Brown, 3b, Auburn (Ala.) HS
35. Koley Kolberg, rhp, Coppell (Texas) HS
36. Adam Sabari, 1b, Cardinal Mooney HS, Sarasota, Fla.
37. Emmanuel Lopez, 1b, Globe (Ariz.) HS
38. Jacob Almestica, rhp, Medardo Carazo HS, Trujillo Alta HS, P.R.
39. Richard Bauer, rhp, Mid Pacific (Hawaii) Institute
40. Josh Bolen, of, Illinois Central JC
41. Bart Braun, lhp, Napa Valley (Calif.) JC
42. Tom Major, rhp, Briarcliffe (N.Y.) JC
43. Tanner Wootan, ss, Mountain View HS, Mesa, Ariz.
44. Terrence Taylor, of, Marin (Calif.) CC
45. Brent Tarbett, of, CC of Southern Nevada
46. Chris Keeran, of, Eastlake HS, Chula Vista, Calif.
47. Donald Benson, 3b, Mt. San Jacinto (Calif.) JC

CHICAGO/AL (27)

1. Kris Honel, rhp, Providence Catholic HS, New Lenox, Ill. (Choice from Marlins—16th—as compensation for Type A free agent Charles Johnson).
1. (Choice to Indians as compensation for Type A free agent Sandy Alomar).
1. Wyatt Allen, rhp, U. of Tennessee (Supplemental pick—39th—for loss of Johnson).
2. Ryan Wing, lhp, Riverside (Calif.) CC
3. Jonathan Zeringue, c, E.D. White HS, Thibodeaux, La.
4. Jay Mattox, of, Conway (Ark.) HS
5. Andy Gonzalez, ss, Florida Air Academy, Melbourne, Fla.
6. Stevie Daniel, 2b-ss, U. of Tennessee
7. Brandon Camardese, lhp, Chaminade-Madonna HS, Cooper City, Fla.

8. Andrew Fryson, rhp, Wallace State (Ala.) JC
9. Jim Bullard, lhp, UC Santa Barbara
10. Tim Bittner, lhp, Marist U.
11. Tim Huson, 3b, Central Arizona JC
12. Chris Stewart, c, Riverside (Calif.) CC
13. Brian Sager, rhp, Georgia Tech
14. Matt Mitchell, rhp, JC of Lake County (Ill.)
15. Anthony Webster, of, Riverside HS, Parsons, Tenn.
16. Chris Young, of, Bellaire (Texas) HS
17. Jason McCurdy, lhp, South Dade HS, Miami
18. Justin Dowdy, lhp, Rancho Bernardo HS, San Diego
19. Wes Swackhamer, of, Delbarton HS, Morristown, N.J.
20. Brian Miller, rhp, Charlotte (Mich.) HS
21. Louis Palmisano, c, St. Thomas Aquinas HS, Fort Lauderdale, Fla.
22. Andrew Salvo, 2b, U. of Delaware
23. Josh Fields, rhp, Mesa (Ariz.) CC
24. Charlie Lisk, c, Fort Mill (S.C.) HS
25. Charles Haeger, rhp, Catholic Central HS, Plymouth, Mich.
26. Dustin Roddy, c, Searcy (Ark.) HS
27. Tom Collaro, of, Piper HS, Sunrise, Fla.
28. Jonathan Forest, rhp, Edouard Montpetit HS, St. Hubert, Quebec
29. Matthew Sibigtroth, ss, Hampshire (Ill.) HS
30. Heath Dobyns, rhp, U. of Northern Colorado
31. Nik Lubisich, lhp, Willamette (Ore.) U
32. Heath Castle, lhp, St. Catharine (Ky.) JC
33. Sean Kramer, rhp, Cornwall HS, New Windsor, N.Y.
34. Tim Tisch, lhp, Mesa (Ariz.) JC
35. Mike Moljewski, lhp, De la Salle Collegiate HS, Shelby, Mich.
36. Brent Speck, lhp, Broward (Fla.) JC
37. Juan Razzo, rhp, San Diego CC
38. Kenyatta Davis, of, Harlem Community Academy, Chicago
39. J.D. Johnson, rhp, Del Norte HS, Moriarty, N.M.
40. Chris Roque, 3b, Monsignor Pace HS, Opa Locka, Fla.
41. Chris Martinez, of, Florida Christian HS, Miami
42. Nick McMillan, rhp, El Dorado HS, Placentia, Calif.
43. Freddie LeBron, 2b, New Mexico JC
44. Ken Pridgeon, rhp, Cy Fair HS, Cypress, Texas
45. Gerron McGary, lhp-of, Texarkana (Texas) JC
46. Roy Irle, rhp, Anderson (Ind.) Madison Heights HS
47. Adrian Casanova, c, Coral Park HS, Miami
48. Josh Crede, 3b, Fatima HS, Westphalia, Mo.
49. Richard Morman, of, Fayetteville (Ark.) HS
50. Zach Jackson, lhp, Seneca Valley HS, Cranberry Township, Pa.

CHICAGO/NL (2)

1. Mark Prior, rhp, U. of Southern California
2. Andy Sisco, lhp, Eastlake HS, Sammamish, Wash.
3. Ryan Theriot, ss, Louisiana State U.
4. Ricky Nolasco, rhp, Rialto (Calif.) HS
5. Brendan Harris, ss, College of William & Mary
6. Adam Wynegar, lhp, James Madison U.
7. Sergio Mitre, rhp, San Diego CC
8. Warren Hanna, c, U. of South Alabama
9. Alan Bomer, rhp, Iowa State U.
10. Corey Slavik, 3b, Wake Forest U.
11. Geovany Soto, c, American Military Academy, Rio Piedras, P.R.
12. Jason Blanton, rhp, North Carolina State U.
13. Tony Garcia, ss, Pepperdine U.
14. Khalil Greene, ss, Clemson U.
15. Kevin Hairr, of, UNC Wilmington
16. Dwaine Bacon, of, Florida A&M U.
17. Nick Martin, lhp, Rice U.
18. Steve Ellis, rhp, Bradley U.
19. Mark Carter, lhp, U. of Alabama
20. Josh Arteaga, ss, Virginia Commonwealth U.
21. Brad Bouras, 1b, Columbus State (Ga.) U.
22. Jeff Carlsen, rhp, U. of Washington
23. B.J. Benik, rhp, Seton Hall U.
24. Luis Reyes, rhp, East Central (Mo.) JC
25. Eric Servais, 3b, U. of Wisconsin-Oshkosh
26. Jake Krause, rhp, Columbia City (Ind.) HS
27. Chad Farr, lhp, Christian Brothers HS, Memphis
28. Tony Sipp, lhp, Moss Point (Miss.) HS
29. Rick Devinney, c, Western HS, Fullerton, Calif.
30. Kyle DuBois, rhp, Cox HS, Virginia Beach, Va.
31. Daniel Foli, rhp, Walters State (Tenn.) CC
32. Jeff Larish, ss, McClintock HS, Tempe, Ariz.
33. Brian Stavisky, of, U. of Notre Dame
34. Charlie Isaacson, rhp, U. of Arkansas
35. Justin McCarty, of, Wichita State U.
36. Aaron O'Dell, rhp, Bend (Ore.) HS
37. Edwar Gonzalez, of, Seminole State (Okla.) JC
38. Jeff Teasley, rhp, Grossmont HS, La Mesa, Calif.
39. Jesse Chavez, rhp, A.B. Miller HS, Fontana, Calif.
40. Matt Pagnozzi, c, Highland HS, Gilbert, Ariz.

41. Wes Whisler, lhp, Noblesville (Ind.) HS
42. Mark Jecmen, rhp, Diamond Bar (Calif.) HS
43. Kevin Culpepper, lhp, Stephens County School, Toccoa, Ga.
44. Jared Eichelberger, rhp, Marian Catholic HS, San Diego
45. Jamil Knight, rhp, Shelton State (Ala.) CC
46. Chris Niesel, rhp, St. Thomas Aquinas HS, Fort Lauderdale
47. Taylor Gartz, lhp, Clear Lake HS, Seabrook, Texas
48. Kevin Randel, ss, Riverside (Calif.) CC
49. Mike Pete, lhp, Armwood HS, Brandon, Fla.
50. Patrick McIntyre, c, Vallivue HS, Caldwell, Idaho

CINCINNATI (20)

1. Jeremy Sowers, lhp, Ballard HS, Louisville
2. **Justin Gillman, rhp, Mosley HS, Panama City, Fla.**
3. **Alan Moye, of, Pine Tree HS, Longview, Texas**
4. **Steve Kelly, rhp, Georgia Tech**
5. **Daylan Childress, rhp, McLennan (Texas) CC**
6. **Scott Light, rhp, Elon College**
7. **Bobby Basham, rhp, U. of Richmond**
8. Jose Rodriguez, c, Warren HS, Downey, Calif.
9. **Junior Ruiz, of-2b, San Jose State U.**
10. **Bryan Prince, c, Georgia Tech**
11. Keith Ramsey, lhp, U. of Florida
12. Craig Bartosh, of, Duncanville (Texas) HS
13. Tanner Brock, rhp, Mississippi State U.
14. **David Molidor, 3b, UC Santa Barbara**
15. **Matt McWilliams, lhp, Cumberland (Tenn.) U.**
16. **Jason Vavao, 1b, Los Angeles Harbor CC**
17. **Richard Bartel, rhp, Grapevine (Texas) HS**
18. **Jeff Bannon, ss, UC Santa Barbara**
19. **Justin Davis, of, Cal Poly Pomona**
20. **Jesse Gutierrez, c, St. Mary's (Texas) U.**
21. John Palmer, rhp, Georgia Perimeter JC
22. **Ryan Fry, c, Young Harris (Ga.) JC**
23. **Joe Powers, rhp, Wright State U.**
24. **Jay Adams, rhp, Pepperdine U.**
25. **Curtus Moak, lhp, U. of Cincinnati**
26. Will Crouch, 1b, Westlake HS, Austin, Texas
27. **Weston Burnette, rhp, Young Harris (Ga.) JC**
28. Brian Martin, lhp, Texas City (Texas) HS
29. Seth Epstein, lhp, JC of the Canyons (Calif.)
30. Darin Blackburn, rhp, Fort Myers (Fla.) HS
31. Aaron Trolia, rhp, Edmonds (Wash.) CC
32. David Shafer, rhp, Central Arizona JC
33. David Asher, lhp, University HS, Orlando
34. **Domonique Lewis, 2b, Southwest Texas State U.**
35. Nick Markakis, lhp, Woodstock (Ga.) HS
36. Isaac Dillon, of, Nettleton HS, Jonesboro, Ark.
37. Erik Meyer, rhp, La Mirada (Calif.) HS
38. Justin Myers, rhp, Symmes Valley HS, Scottown, Ohio
39. Miles Carpenter, rhp, Pickens (Ga.) HS
40. Ben Rulon, lhp, Columbus (Ga.) HS
41. Douglas Curley, c, Granite Bay HS, Roseville, Calif.
42. Brandon Moorhead, rhp, U. of Georgia
43. Kyle Broussard, ss, Carencro (La.) HS
44. Francis Poni, c, Carson (Calif.) HS
45. Mark Schramek, rhp-3b, U. of Texas-San Antonio
46. Bart Hunton, c, Dublin (Ohio) Coffman HS
47. Raymond Gonzalez, of, Jose Campeche HS, San Lorenzo, P.R.
48. Jeffrey Crinklaw, c, Ohlone (Calif.) JC
49. Trey Hearne, of, Lufkin (Texas) HS
50. Clay Alarcon, ss, Sequoia HS, Redwood City, Calif.

CLEVELAND (21)

1. **Dan Denham, rhp, Deer Valley HS, Antioch, Calif.** (Choice from Red Sox—17th—as compensation for Type A free agent Manny Ramirez).
1. (Choice to Giants as compensation for Type A free agent Ellis Burks).
1. **Alan Horne, rhp, Marianna (Fla.) HS** (Choice from White Sox—27th— as compensation for Type A free agent Sandy Alomar).
1. **J.D. Martin, rhp, Burroughs HS, Ridgecrest, Calif.** (Supplemental pick—35th—for loss of Ramirez).
1. **Michael Conroy, of, Boston College HS, Dorchester, Mass.** (Supplemental pick—43rd—for loss of Type A free agent David Segui).
2. **Jake Dittler, rhp, Green Valley HS, Henderson, Nev.** (Choice from Orioles—51st—as compensation for Segui).
2. (Choice to Tigers as compensation for Type A free agent Juan Gonzalez).
3. **Nick Moran, rhp, Fresno State U.**
4. **Travis Foley, rhp, Butler HS, Louisville**
5. **Marcos Mendoza, rhp, San Diego State U.**
6. **Jim Ed Warden, rhp, Tennessee Tech**
7. **Josh Noviskey, of, Newton (N.J.) HS**
8. **Mike Quintana, of, Florida International U.**
9. **Luke Scott, of, Oklahoma State U.**
10. Brian Harrison, rhp, Dalton (Ga.) HS

11. **Brad Guglielmelli, c, Allan Hancock (Calif.) JC**
12. **Scott Sturkie, rhp, Coastal Carolina U.**
13. **Matt Knox, of, Millersville (Pa.) U.**
14. **Doug Lantz, rhp, U. of Kansas**
15. Martin Vergara, rhp, DePaul HS, Wayne, N.J.
16. Sean Smith, rhp, College Park HS, Pleasant Hill, Calif.
17. David Jensen, 1b, Brigham Young U.
18. T.J. Burton, rhp, Notre Dame HS, Ottawa, Ontario
19. **Luis Alvarado, lhp, U. of Puerto Rico**
20. Michael Rogers, rhp, Oral Roberts U.
21. **Richard Spaulding, lhp, Lexington (Ky.) CC**
22. **Jimmy Schultz, rhp, Klein Forest HS, Houston**
23. **Kent Myers, c, Mesa State (Colo.) College**
24. **Matt Blethen, lhp, West Virginia U.**
25. **Rickie Morton, of, U. of the Pacific**
26. **Bryce Uegawachi, ss, Hawaii Pacific U.**
27. Josh Lex, c, Sacramento CC
28. Brandon Harmsen, rhp, Grand Rapids (Mich.) CC
29. Chris Hunter, rhp, Lindon, Utah.
30. **Keith Lillash, 2b, Cleveland State U.**
31. **Brian Kirby, c, U. of Arkansas**
32. **Andy Baxter, 1b, East Tennessee State U.**
33. **Chad Peshke, 2b, UC Santa Barbara**
34. Aaron Mardsen, lhp, Hutchinson (Kan.) CC
35. **Chris Cooper, lhp, U. of New Mexico**
36. Jose Cruz, of, Metropolitan (P.R.) U.
37. **Todd Culp, rhp, U. of the Pacific**
38. Neto Quiroz, lhp, Saddleback (Calif.) CC
39. **Brian Farman, rhp, Pacific Lutheran (Wash.) U.**
40. Aaron Russell, rhp, Cerro Coso (Calif.) CC
41. Ross Lewis, rhp-of, University Christian HS, Jacksonville, Fla.
42. Kyle Allen, lhp, Trabuco Hills HS, Rancho Santa Margarita, Calif.
43. Vincent Davis, lhp, New Mexico JC
44. Garrett Mock, rhp, North Shore HS, Houston
45. Brett Ashmun, rhp, Modesto (Calif.) JC
46. **Todd Pennington, rhp, Southeast Missouri State U.**
47. Billy Brian, rhp, Louisiana State U.
48. Douglas Brooks, rhp, Henry Ford (Mich.) CC
49. Jason Columbus, 1b, New Mexico JC
50. James Burok, rhp, Valley View HS, Archbald, Pa.

COLORADO (18)

1. (Choice to Mets as compensation for Type A free agent Mike Hampton).
1. **Jayson Nix, ss, Midland (Texas) HS** (Supplemental pick—44th—for failure to sign 2000 first-round pick Matt Harrington).
2. (Choice to Yankees as compensation for Type A free agent Denny Neagle).
2. **Trey Taylor, lhp, Mansfield (Texas) HS** (Supplemental pick—75th— for Type C free agent Julian Tavarez).
3. **Jason Frome, of, Indiana State U.**
4. **Jay Mitchell, rhp, LaGrange (Ga.) HS**
5. **Gerrit Simpson, rhp, U. of Texas**
6. **Jamie Tricoglou, rhp, Kennesaw State U.**
7. **Cory Sullivan, of, Wake Forest U.**
8. **Scott Nicholson, lhp, Oregon State U.**
9. **James Sweeney, c, Bellaire (Texas) HS**
10. **Tony Miller, of, U. of Toledo**
11. **Jay Fardella, rhp, St. Francis (N.Y.) College**
12. **Bryan Ingram, c, Oregon State U.**
13. **Kip Bouknight, rhp, U. of South Carolina**
14. **Levi Frary, rhp, U. of Texas-Pan American**
15. **David Burkholder, 1b, Grand View (Iowa) College**
16. **Beau Dannemiller, rhp, Kent State U.**
17. **Josh Songster, rhp, U. of Southern Colorado**
18. **Buddy Gallagher, lhp, Rutgers U.**
19. **Ashley Freeman, 3b, Vanderbilt U.**
20. Matt Palmer, rhp, Southwest Missouri State U.
21. Roberto Martinez, rhp, Riverview HS, Brandon, Fla.
22. **Trey George, of, Bellaire HS, Houston**
23. Eric Patterson, ss, Harrison HS, Kennesaw, Ga.
24. **Casey Lambert, ss, U. of Alabama**
25. Mike Huggins, 1b, Baylor U.
26. Jake Glanzmann, lhp, West Springfield (Va.) HS
27. **Jeff Cruz, lhp, Long Beach State U.**
28. Adam Heether, 3b, Modesto (Calif.) JC
29. **Peter Greenbush, rhp, Massachusetts College**
30. Jonathan Varcarcel, lhp, Margarita Janer HS, Guaynabo, P.R.
31. Rejino Gonzalez, lhp, CC of Southern Nevada
32. Josh Merino, lhp, Kirkwood (Iowa) CC
33. Sean Hofferd, of, Bend (Ore.) HS
34. Chris Gimenez, c, Gilroy (Calif.) HS
35. Jeff MacDonald, rhp, Lethbridge (Alberta) CC
36. Brandon Freese, rhp, Skyview HS, Vancouver, Wash.
37. Chris Buechner, rhp, Little Cypress-Mauriceville HS, Orange, Texas

38. Vern Sterry, rhp, Cypress (Calif.) JC
39. Lucas Gaskamp, lhp, Northeast Texas CC
40. Pedro Diaz, rhp, Seminole State (Okla.) JC
41. Duke Sardinha, 3b, Pepperdine U.
42. Coby Hughes, of, Branson HS, Walnut Shade, Mo.
43. Kelly Castles, rhp, McLaughlin HS, Milton Freewater, Ore.
44. Josh Bryant, rhp, Wallace State (Ala.) CC
45. Brandon Young, of, Springfield (Ohio) North HS
46. Sergio Silva, rhp, JC of the Sequoias (Calif.)
47. John Toffey, rhp, St. Sebastian's HS, Barnstable, Mass.
48. Andrew York, c, JC of the Siskiyous, (Calif.)
49. J.R. Revere, of, Georgia Southern U.
50. Mike Marksbury, rhp, Miami (Ohio) U.

DETROIT (11)

1. **Kenny Baugh, rhp, Rice U.**
1. **Michael Woods, 2b, Southern U.** (Supplemental pick—32nd—for loss of Type A free agent Juan Gonzalez).
2. **Preston Larrison, rhp, U. of Evansville**
2. **Matt Coenen, lhp, Charleston Southern U.** (Choice from Indians—65th—as compensation for Gonzalez).
3. **Jack Hannahan, 3b, U. of Minnesota**
4. **Mike Rabelo, c, U. of Tampa**
5. **Ryan Raburn, 3b, South Florida CC**
6. **Jason Knoedler, of, Miami (Ohio) U.**
7. **Tom Farmer, rhp, U. of Miami**
8. **Don Kelly, ss, Point Park (Pa.) College**
9. **David Mattle, of, Kent State U.**
10. **Vincent Blue, of, Lamar HS, Houston**
11. Eric Thomas, rhp, Briarcliffe (N.Y.) JC
12. **Jamie Gonzales, rhp, UC Santa Barbara**
13. **Landon Stockman, rhp, Kennesaw State U.**
14. **Matt Williams, of, Fontana (Calif.) HS**
15. **Kevin McDowell, lhp, Bucknell U.**
16. Joey Metropoulos, 3b, Monte Vista HS, Jamul, Calif.
17. **Dan Smith, rhp, U. of Miami**
18. **Alex Trezza, c, U. at Stony Brook**
19. **Billy Ryan, 3b, Briarcliffe (N.Y.) JC**
20. **Jason Moates, rhp, Middle Tennessee State U.**
21. Tim Dorn, 1b, Monrovia (Calif.) HS
22. **Francisco Rosado, of, Antelope Valley (Calif.) JC**
23. **Mike Scott, of, U. of Connecticut**
24. John Schneider, c, U. of Delaware
25. **Chris Kolodzey, of, U. of Delaware**
26. **Herman Dean, c, Citrus (Calif.) JC**
27. **Mike Kobow, rhp, U. of Minnesota**
28. **Jon Connolly, lhp, Oneonta (N.Y.) HS**

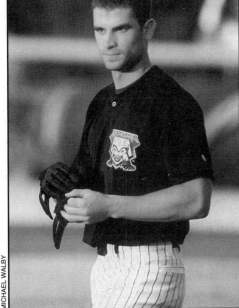

Chris Burke: Tennessee All-American picked in first round by Astros

29. Garth McKinney, of, Walters State (Tenn.) CC
30. **John Birtwell, rhp, Harvard U.**
31. Humberto Sanchez, rhp, Rockland (N.Y.) CC
32. **Trevor Leu, of, Oral Roberts U.**
33. **Michael Howell, rhp, SUNY Binghamton**
34. **Ian Ostlund, lhp, Virginia Tech**
35. **Chuck Lombardy, rhp, Ohio U.**
36. **Jed Stringam, of, UC Santa Barbara**
37. Kevin Miller, lhp, Cuesta (Calif.) JC
38. Adam Harben, rhp, Central Arkansas Christian HS, Little Rock
39. Robert White, lhp, Spartanburg Methodist (S.C.) JC
40. **Tom Lyons, rhp, Downers Grove (Ill.) North HS**
41. Trey Holloway, lhp, Booneville (Ark.) HS
42. Coby Judd, lhp, Simi Valley (Calif.) HS
43. Sean Richardson, c, Vista (Calif.) HS
44. Brent Hale, rhp, Peninsula HS, Rancho Palos Verde, Calif.
45. Lonnie Patterson, rhp, Harlan HS, Chicago

FLORIDA (16)

1. (Choice to White Sox as compensation for Type A free agent Charles Johnson).
2. **Garrett Berger, rhp, Carmel (Ind.) HS**
3. **Allen Baxter, rhp, Varina HS, Sandston, Va.**
4. **Chris Resop, rhp-of, Barron Collier HS, Naples, Fla.**
5. Tyler Lumsden, lhp, Cave Spring HS, Roanoke, Va.
6. **Adam Bostick, rhp, Greensburg-Salem HS, Greensburg, Pa.**
7. **Lincoln Holdzkom, rhp, Arizona Western CC**
8. **Jeff Fulchino, rhp, U. of Connecticut**
9. **Dustin Kupper, rhp, Pima (Ariz.) CC**
10. **Kody Naylor, rhp, Western Michigan U.**
11. **Rex Rundgren, ss, Sacramento CC**
12. **Nick Ungs, rhp, U. of Northern Iowa**
13. **Lance Davis, rhp, George County HS, Lucedale, Miss.**
14. **Michael Tucker, 3b, Florida Southern College**
15. Doug Boone, c, Ball State U.
16. **Hunter Wyant, ss, U. of Virginia**
17. **Kevin Cave, rhp, Xavier U.**
18. **Josh Coffey, c, Lee-Davis HS, Mechanicsville, Va.**
19. **Louis Evans, lhp, San Jose (Calif.) CC**
20. **Carl Lafferty, c, U. of Mississippi** (contract voided)
21. Dane Mason, rhp, Cherokee HS, Marlton, N.J.
22. **Jason Helps, ss, Central Michigan U.**
23. **Wes McCrotty, lhp, U. of Arkansas**
24. **John Skinner, rhp, San Diego State U.**
25. **Philip Hartig, 1b, The Citadel**
26. Adam Russell, rhp, North Olmsted (Ohio) HS
27. **Franco Blackburn, of, Southern U.**
28. Jonathan Hunton, rhp, North Plainfield (N.J.) HS
29. **Gooby Gerlits, c-of, Stoneman Douglas HS, Parkland, Fla.**
30. Nicholas Pesco, rhp, Tokay HS, Lodi, Calif.
31. Chris Johnston, rhp, Smoky Hills HS, Aurora, Colo.
32. Sergio Roman, c, Bishop Carroll HS, Wichita, Kan.
33. **Torik Harrison, rhp, Southern U.**
34. **Steve Thomas, rhp, Nova Southeastern U.**
35. **Marc Rittenhouse, 2b, U. of Washington**
36. **Kevin Halamicek, rhp, Cal State Dominguez Hills**
37. **Kris Clute, 2b, U. of Miami**
38. **Ronnie Goodwin, rhp, U. of Mississippi**
39. Justin Ottman, lhp, Rockland (N.Y.) CC
40. **Tyson Graham, of, North Gaston HS, Dallas, N.C.**
41. Eric Otero, 2b, Monignor Pace HS, Miami
42. Josh Perrault, rhp, South Mountain (Ariz.) CC
43. Isaac Garza, rhp, Odem (Texas) HS
44. Paris Dancy, of, Pine Forest HS, Pensacola, Fla.
45. Nick Blasi, of, Butler County (Kan.) CC
46. Andrew Vansickle, of, Senatobia (Miss.) HS
47. Chas Taylor, rhp, Westlake HS, Austin, Texas
48. Derek Hutton, ss, Palm Beach Gardens (Fla.) HS
49. Phillip Coke, lhp, Sonora HS, Twain Harte, Calif.
50. Steve Stanley, of, U. of Notre Dame

HOUSTON (10)

1. **Chris Burke, 2b-ss, U. of Tennessee**
2. **Mike Rodriguez, of, U. of Miami**
3. **Kirk Saarloos, rhp, Cal State Fullerton**
4. **Phillip Barzilla, lhp, Rice U.**
5. **Charlton Jimerson, of, U. of Miami**
6. **Russ Rohlicek, lhp, Long Beach State U.**
7. **Ryan Stegall, ss, U. of Missouri**
8. **Brooks Conrad, 2b, Arizona State U.**
9. **Kerry Hodges, of, Texas Tech**
10. Lance Cormier, rhp, U. of Alabama
11. **D.J. Houlton, rhp, U. of the Pacific**
12. **Chris Little, lhp, St. Louis CC-Forest Park**

13. Kendall Jones, c, Texarkana (Texas) CC
14. Clint Hoover, 1b, U. of California
15. Trevor Mote, 2b, Baylor U.
16. Brian Rodaway, lhp, U. of Nebraska
17. Thomas Bayrer, rhp, Campbell U.
18. Jose Deleon, rhp, Nixon-Smiley HS, Nixon, Texas
19. Ryan Kochen, ss, Western Michigan U.
20. Mark Obradovich, c, Gadsden State (Ala.) CC
21. Jeff Derrickson, c, Bryan Station HS, Lexington, Ky.
22. Justin Humphries, c, Episcopal HS, Richmond, Texas
23. Matt Albers, rhp, Clements HS, Sugar Land, Texas
24. Cameron Likely, of, U. of South Alabama
25. Chad Durham, rhp, Texas Christian U.
26. Steven Checksfield, of, U. of Albany
27. Henry Colbert, rhp, Columbia Basin (Wash.) CC
28. Seth Bobbit, rhp, Birmingham-Southern College
29. Raymar Diaz, of, Luis Hernaiz Verone HS, Canovanas, P.R.
30. Jjallil Sandoval, ss, Cal State Los Angeles
31. Brian Middleton, rhp, West Viginia State College
32. Billy Jacobson, of, Rice U.
33. John Fagan, 1b, San Jose State U.
34. Brandon Macchi, of, San Jose State U.
35. Travis Teeter, rhp, Rensselaer Polytechnic (N.Y.) Institute
36. Andrew Perry, rhp, Cal State Pomona
37. Jared Gothreaux, rhp, McNeese State U.
38. Ryan McKeller, rhp, Pflugerville (Texas) HS
39. Paul Hazeres, rhp, Carolina Forest HS, Conway, S.C.
40. Osvaldo Diaz, rhp, Cuba
41. Chris Saywers, rhp-ss, Edmonds (Wash.) CC
42. Pat Wells, lhp, West Jordan (Utah) HS
43. James McNair, rhp, Virginia Commonwealth U.
44. Lance Dawkins, ss, Meridian (Miss.) CC
45. Kyle Thompson, rhp, Valley Center HS, Escondido, Calif.
46. Justin Ard, of, Clear Lake HS, Houston
47. Eric Turnbow, lhp, Jordan HS, Sandy, Utah
48. Ben Leuthard, of, San Diego State U.
49. Kevin House, of, Alabama Southern JC

KANSAS CITY (9)

1. Colt Griffin, rhp, Marshall (Texas) HS
2. Roscoe Crosby, of, Union HS, Buffalo, S.C.
3. Matt Ferrara, 3b, Westminster Academy, Fort Lauderdale
4. John Draper, c, Cal State Los Angeles
5. Chamar McDonald, 1b, Madison (Miss.) Central HS
6. Clint Frost, rhp, Jordan HS, Columbus, Ga.
7. Chris Tierney, lhp, Lockport (Ill.) HS
8. Ira Brown, rhp, Willis (Texas) HS
9. Justin Nelson, lhp-of, Platte Valley HS, Kersey, Colo.
10. Danny Tamayo, rhp, U. of Notre Dame
11. Angel Sanchez, of, Florencia Garcia HS, Las Piedras, P.R.
12. Victor Rosario, of, Lake City (Fla.) CC
13. Cedric Watkins, of, Bassett (Va.) HS
14. Devon Lowery, rhp, South Point HS, Belmont, N.C.
15. Daniel Zell, lhp, Angelina (Texas) JC
16. Mel Stocker, of, Arizona State U.
17. Marcus Chandler, of, Southern U.
18. Alexis Alexander, of, Medical Lake (Wash.) HS
19. Mervin Williams, of, East St. John HS, Garyville, La.
20. Peter Gunny, of, Los Angeles Pierce JC
21. Brian Melnyk, lhp, Point Park (Pa.) College
22. Chris Fallon, 1b, St. John's U.
23. Jermaine Johnson, of, Glynn (Ga.) Academy
24. J.D. Alleva, c, Duke U.
25. Rick Zary, rhp, Limestone (S.C.) College
26. Derek DeCarlo, rhp, Southridge HS, Miami
27. Derrik Lytle, of, Mesa (Ariz.) CC
28. Lucas Palmer, rhp, Baker HS, Baker City, Ore.
29. Bryan McCaulley, rhp, Barbe HS, Lake Charles, La.
30. Ezekiel Parraz, ss, Green Valley HS, Henderson, Nev.
31. Jacob Guzman, c, Palomar (Calif.) JC
32. Julio Medina, rhp, Elk Grove (Ill.) HS
33. John Barnett, rhp, Arizona Western CC
34. Erik Dean, ss, West Valley (Calif.) JC
35. Barry Richardson, rhp, Lake City (Fla.) CC
36. Chris Washington, rhp, Port St. Lucie (Fla.) HS
37. Brad Knox, rhp, Blinn (Texas) JC
38. James Dayley, rhp, Utah Valley CC
39. Taylor Tankersley, lhp, Warren Central HS, Vicksburg, Miss.
40. Jason Snyder, rhp, Alta HS, Sandy, Utah
41. Rene Pablos, lhp, Cochise County (Ariz.) CC
42. Nick Cadena, c, Apollo HS, Glendale, Ariz.
43. Stephen Green, of, Moahalua HS, Honolulu
44. Brady Everett, c, Federal Way HS, Kent, Wash.
45. Curtis Legendre, 3b-c, Angelina (Texas) JC

46. Bret Berglund, 3b, Kent Denver HS, Englewood, Colo.
47. Caleb Irwin, rhp, Temple (Texas) JC
48. Ryan Coiner, rhp, Las Vegas HS
49. Ryan Patterson, of, Rowlett (Texas) HS
50. Bo Baker, rhp, Eastern Arizona JC

LOS ANGELES (24)

1. (Choice to Braves as compensation for Type A free agent Andy Ashby).
2. Brian Pilkington, rhp, Santiago HS, Garden Grove, Calif.
3. David Taylor, rhp, Southlake HS, Clermont, Fla.
4. Kole Strayhorn, rhp, Shawnee HS, Seminole, Okla.
5. Steve Nelson, rhp, Cole Harbour District HS, Dartmouth, Nova Scotia
6. Edwin Jackson, of, Shaw HS, Columbus, Ga.
7. David Cuen, lhp, Cibola HS, Somerton, Ariz.
8. David Cardona, of, San Jose de Calasanza HS, Trujillo Alta, P.R.
9. Sean Pierce, of, San Diego State U.
10. Thom Ott, rhp, U. of Nebraska
11. Luis Gonzalez, lhp, Florida Air Academy, Melbourne, Fla.
12. Cedric Benson, of, Lee HS, Midland, Texas
13. Matt Kauffman, lhp, San Jose State U.
14. Ryan Carter, of, Riverdale HS, Fort Myers, Fla.
15. Jimmy Stewart, rhp, Sabino HS, Tucson
16. Josh Canales, ss, UCLA
17. Jerry Johnson, of, U. of Arkansas-Little Rock
18. Vance McCracken, rhp, West Virginia U.
19. John Urick, 1b, Cowley County (Kan.) CC
20. William Malone, 2b, Robert Morris (Ill.) College
21. Jereme Milons, of, Starkville (Miss.) HS
22. Scott Gillitzer, 2b, U. of Wisconsin-Milwaukee
23. Les Dykes, lhp, Parklane Academy, McComb, Miss.
24. Ryan Lennerton, lhp, Brookswood SS, Langley, B.C.
25. Garrett Murdy, rhp, Mission Viejo HS, Laguna Hills, Calif.
26. Jay Sadlowe, rhp, Farragut HS, Knoxville, Tenn.
27. Eric Hutcheson, lhp, Florala HS, Lockhart, Ala.
28. Kyle Crist, rhp, Granite Bay HS, Grant, Calif.
29. Dennis Bigley, 1b, Dallas Christian HS, Lancaster, Texas
30. Tom Wilson, lhp, Central Cabarrus HS, Concord, N.C.
31. David Parker, rhp, Sisler HS, Winnipeg, Manitoba
32. Michael Hollimon, ss, Jesuit Prep, Dallas
33. Jason Stefani, lhp, Albertson (Idaho) College
34. Brian Devereaux, rhp, Hollywood (Fla.) Christian HS
35. Chris Casey, lhp, Hunstville (Texas) HS
36. Brian Cleveland, ss, San Jose CC
37. Dustin Schroer, rhp, Surrey, B.C.
38. Ryan Hamilton, ss, Klein HS, Spring, Texas
39. William Johnson, 1b, North Springs HS, College Park, Ga.
40. Cameron Feightner, rhp, Beaverton HS, Portland, Ore.
41. Jim Gregory, lhp, Crockett (Texas) HS
42. Jordan Kissock, of, Delphi Academy, Surrey, B.C.
43. Clint Sammons, c, Parkview HS, Stone Mountain, Ga.
44. Clay Wehner, c, Thomasville (Ga.) HS
45. Michael Rodriguez, rhp, Sierra (Calif.) JC
46. Michael Lynch, c, South Suburban (Ill.) JC
47. Devin Monds, rhp, Nepean HS, Ottawa, Ontario
48. Danny Desclouds, rhp, Connors State (Okla.) JC
49. Jason Schuler, c, Lake County (Ill.) JC
50. Brooks Bollinger, 3b, U. of Wisconsin

MILWAUKEE (12)

1. Mike Jones, rhp, Thunderbird HS, Phoenix
2. J.J. Hardy, ss, Sabino HS, Tucson
3. Jon Steitz, rhp, Yale U.
4. Brad Nelson, 1b, Bishop Garrigan HS, Algona, Iowa
5. Judd Richardson, rhp, Miami (Ohio) U.
6. Calvin Carpenter, rhp, Natchitoches (La.) Central HS
7. Taylor McCormack, 3b, Dunedin (Fla.) HS
8. Brandon Gemoll, 1b, Fresno State U.
9. Dennis Sarfate, rhp, Chandler-Gilbert (Ariz.) CC
10. Greg Moreira, rhp, Lake Brantley HS, Apopka, Fla.
11. David Slevin, 2b, Indian River (Fla.) JC
12. Ray Liotta, lhp, Archbishop Rummel HS, Metairie, La.
13. Travis Hinton, 1b, Chandler-Gilbert (Ariz.) CC
14. Aaron Sheffield, rhp, Young Harris (Ga.) JC
15. Tim Dillard, c, Saltillo (Miss.) HS
16. Gene DeSalme, lhp, Northwestern State (La.) U.
17. Justin Wilson, lhp, Chandler (Ariz.) HS
18. Jeff Eure, c, Old Dominion U.
19. Joel Alvarado, c, U. of Texas-Arlington
20. Josh Smith, rhp, Lake Havasu (Ariz.) City HS
21. Orlando Viera, of, Cuevas HS, Gurabo, P.R.
22. Damarius Bilbo, of, Moss Point (Miss.) HS
23. David Nolasco, rhp, Riverside (Calif.) CC

24. **Daniel Kolb, rhp, Manatee (Fla.) CC**
25. **Chris Barnwell, ss, Flagler (Fla.) College**
26. Manuel Parra, lhp, American River (Calif.) JC
27. **Daniel Boyd, of, U. of South Florida**
28. **Chris Saenz, rhp, Pima (Ariz.) CC**
29. Jamie McAlister, rhp, Clearwater HS, Piedmont, Mo.
30. **Chris Gittings, rhp, De Sales HS, Louisville**
31. Andrew Sigerich, rhp, Downers Grove (Ill.) North HS
32. John Calmes, rhp, Eastlake HS, Sammamish, Wash.
33. Greg Esteves, ss, River Ridge HS, New Port Richey, Fla.
34. Fuarieuir Miller, of, Laney (Calif.) JC
35. Stephen Hunt, of, Chandler-Gilbert (Ariz.) CC
36. **Rusty Huggins, lhp, Central Florida CC**
37. **Thomas Carrow, of, U. of Tampa**
38. Ross Hawley, rhp, Augustana (S.D.) College
39. Travis Johnson, of, Shannon (Miss.) HS
40. Jeremy Wilson, c, Catholic Central HS, Burlington, Wis.
41. Hubert Pruett, rhp, Kamehameha (Hawaii) HS
42. **Ralph Santana, ss, Lake Sumter (Fla.) CC**
43. **Matt Serafini, c, U. of Evansville**
44. **Corry Parrott, of, Long Beach State U.**
45. Jason Costello, lhp, Clearwater (Fla.) HS
46. Jordi Szabo, of, Carlsbad (Calif.) HS
47. Joseph Costentino, of, Bishop Gorman HS, Henderson, Nev.
48. Brian Harper, lhp, North Little Rock (Ark.) HS
49. Nicholas Stillwagon, c, Biloxi (Miss.) HS
50. **Chris Haggard, c, Oklahoma U.**

MINNESOTA (1)

1. **Joe Mauer, c, Cretin-Derham Hall, St. Paul, Minn.**
2. **Scott Tyler, rhp, Downingtown (Pa.) HS**
3. **Jose Morales, ss, Academie la Providencia HS, Rio Piedras, P.R.**
4. **Angel Garcia, rhp, Nicolas Sevilla HS, Dorado, P.R.**
5. **Jeremy Brown, rhp, U. of Georgia**
6. **Vince Serafini, lhp, U. of Evansville**
7. **Matt Vorwald, rhp, U. of Illinois**
8. **Jared Hemus, lhp, Grossmont (Calif.) JC**
9. **Dusty Gomon, 1b, Terry Parker HS, Jacksonville, Fla.**
10. **Garrett Guzman, of, Green Valley HS, Henderson, Nev.**
11. **Josh Renick, ss, Middle Tennessee State U.**
12. **Kaulana Kuhaulua, 2b, Long Beach State U.**
13. **Kevin Cameron, rhp, Georgia Tech**
14. Ryan Anderson, lhp, Gaither HS, Tampa
15. **Brett Lawson, rhp, Northwestern Oklahoma State U.**
16. Brian Stitt, rhp, Wellington Community (Fla.) HS
17. Matt Macri, ss, Dowling HS, Clive, Iowa
18. **Robert Guzman, of, Cal State Fullerton**
19. **Scott Whitrock, of, Madison (Wis.) Area Tech CC**
20. Anthony Albano, of, Brother Rice HS, Chicago
21. **Felix Molina, 2b, Eugenio Maria de Hostos HS, Trujillo Alto, P.R.**
22. **Ryan Smith, c, Citrus (Calif.) JC**
23. **Jake Mauer, 2b, U. of St. Thomas (Minn.)**
24. **Bryan Kennedy, c, Long Beach State U.**
25. **Josh Johnson, c, Ridgway (Pa.) HS**
26. John Herrera, rhp, Redlands (Calif.) HS
27. Justin Elliott, c, Lake Gibson HS, Lakeland, Fla.
28. **Brian Gates, rhp, U. of Tennessee**
29. Nick Blackburn, rhp, Seminole State (Okla.) JC
30. **Josh Daws, rhp, Jacksonville U.**
31. Ben Thomas, 3b, Central HS, Rapid City, S.D.
32. Jason Wilmes, lhp, Somerset (Wis.) HS
33. Ryan Gehring, lhp, Burlington (Wis.) Catholic Central HS
34. Marshall Hendon, lhp, Christian Brothers HS, Sacramento
35. Bookie Gates, 2b, Washington State U.
36. **Kenny Huff, of, U. of Arizona**
37. **Shawn Tarkington, lhp, Seton Hall U.**
38. **Matt Abram, 2b-of, U. of Arizona**
39. **Nick Niedbalski, lhp, East Central (Mo.) JC**
40. **Erik Lohse, rhp, Sacramento CC**
41. **Ryan Spataro, of, St. Peters SS, Barrie, Ontario**
42. **Pat Tingley, lhp, Indiana State U.**
43. Jason Vargas, lhp, Apple Valley (Calif.) HS
44. Jacob Hader, lhp, Belton (Mo.) HS
45. Josh Smith, of, Canyon Springs HS, Moreno Valley, Calif.
46. Mitchell Pruemer, rhp, Rend Lake (Ill.) JC
47. Daniel Smith, c, Eau Gallie HS, Melbourne, Fla.
48. William Guzman, ss, Northwest Christian Academy, Miami
49. Jason Paul, rhp, Ball State U.
50. Robert Strickland, 2b, Frostproof (Fla.) HS

MONTREAL (6)

1. **Josh Karp, rhp, UCLA**
2. **Donald Levinski, rhp, Weimar (Texas) HS**
3. **Mike Hinckley, lhp, Moore (Okla.) HS**

4. Nick Long, rhp, Shaw HS, Columbus, Ga.
5. **Reggie Fitzpatrick, of, McNair HS, Atlanta**
6. **Josh Labandiera, ss, Fresno State U.**
7. **Chad Bentz, lhp, Long Beach State U.**
8. **Greg Thissen, 3b, Triton (Ill.) JC**
9. **Shawn Norris, 3b, Cal State Fullerton**
10. **Eddie Diaz, rhp, Colonial HS, Orlando**
11. Kyle Pawelczyk, lhp, Chipola (Fla.) JC
12. **Danny Kahr, c, Durango HS, Las Vegas**
13. **Tyler Kirkman, rhp, Mt. Carmel (Ill.) HS**
14. **Jason Walker, lhp, U. of the Pacific**
15. **Tory Imotichy, lhp, Purcell (Okla.) HS**
16. **Warmar Gomez, rhp, Casiano Cepeda HS, Rio Grande, P.R.**
17. **David Maust, lhp, West Virginia U.**
18. **Rob Caputo, rhp, U. of Alabama-Birmingham**
19. **Chris Schroeder, rhp, Oklahoma City U.**
20. **Jason Greene, ss, Minford (Ohio) HS**
21. Tim Wood, rhp, Sabino HS, Tucson
22. Arlandus Brown, of, Copiah-Lincoln (Miss.) JC
23. Ja'mar Clanton, ss, Triton (Ill.) JC
24. Jimmy Treece, rhp, Riverside (Calif.) Poly HS
25. Zach Lerch, rhp, Prairie HS, Cedar Rapids, Iowa
26. Jerrell Jackson, rhp, Altoona (Pa.) Area HS
27. Daniel Smith, rhp, Sacramento CC
28. Michael Richardson, rhp, Richland (Wash.) HS
29. Mark Rodrigues, rhp, Kauai HS, Koloa, Hawaii
30. Jared Brown, lhp, Notre Dame Catholic HS, Milford, Conn.
31. Jamieson Boulanger, lhp, Concordia (Quebec) U.
32. Jean-Sabestien Varney, rhp, Edouard Montpetit HS, St. Hubert, Quebec
33. Jeremey White, lhp, Victor Valley (Calif.) CC
34. Henry Gutierrez-Portalatin, c, Florida Air Academy, Melbourne, Fla.
35. Michael Springsteen, rhp, Marshalltown (Iowa) CC
36. Cole Zumbro, rhp, Franklin (Miss.) HS
37. P.J. Connelly, lhp, Beloit (Wis.) Memorial HS
38. David LeClerc, lhp, Laval, Quebec
39. Jecorey Matthews, of, Northwest Classen HS, Oklahoma City
40. Fred Perkins, of, Brookhaven (Miss.) HS
41. Travis Becktel, of, Capistrano Valley HS, Mission Viejo, Calif.
42. John Taylor, lhp, Northside HS, Northport, Ala.
43. Joseph Gullion, ss, Johnson County (Kan.) CC
44. Brian Hipps, of, San Diego Mesa CC
45. Franklyn Jimenez, 2b, Muscatine (Iowa) CC
46. Josh Ranson, of, Chatfield HS, Littleton, Colo.
47. Ross Wolf, rhp, Newton HS, Wheeler, Ill.
48. Chris Jones, c, Edison HS, Fresno
49. Matthew Hayes, lhp, Effingham (Ill.) HS
50. Chad Scarbery, rhp, Fresno (Calif.) CC

NEW YORK/AL (19)

1. (Choice to Orioles as compensation for Type A free agent Mike Mussina).
1. **John-Ford Griffin, of, Florida State U.** (Choice from Mariners—23rd—as compensation for Type A free agent Jeff Nelson).
1. **Bronson Sardinha, ss, Kamehameha HS, Honolulu** (Supplemental pick—34th—for loss of Type A free agent Denny Neagle).
1. **Jon Skaggs, rhp, Rice U.** (Supplemental pick—42nd—for loss of Nelson).
2. **Shelley Duncan, of, U. of Arizona**
2. **Jason Arnold, rhp, U. of Central Florida** (Choice from Rockies—62nd—as compensation for Neagle).
3. **Chase Wright, lhp, Iowa Park (Texas) HS**
4. **Aaron Rifkin, 1b, Cal State Fullerton**
5. **Jeff Christensen, of, U. of Tennessee**
6. **Rik Currier, rhp, U. of Southern California**
7. **Andy Cannizaro, ss, Tulane U.**
8. Adam Peterson, rhp, Wichita State U.
9. **Charles Manning, lhp, U. of Tampa**
10. **Jared Pitney, 1b, Pepperdine U.**
11. **Brian Strelitz, rhp, Texas A&M U.**
12. **Chris Russ, rhp, Texas A&M U.**
13. **Adam Wheeler, rhp, Campbell HS, Smyrna, Ga.**
14. Trent Henderson, rhp, Pratt (Kan.) CC
15. **John Picco, lhp, Villanova HS, LaSalle, Ontario**
16. Nic Touchstone, lhp, Okaloosa-Walton (Fla.) JC
17. Quinton Robertson, rhp, Texarkana (Texas) JC
18. Josh Smith, rhp, Navarro (Texas) JC
19. Mike McGowan, rhp, Newman Smith HS, Carrollton, Texas
20. Jason McMillan, lhp, Dundee Crown HS, Carpentersville, Ill.
21. **Omir Santos, c, East Central (Mo.) JC**
22. **Todd Faulkner, 1b, Auburn U.**
23. **Kaazim Summerville, of, St. Mary's (Calif.) College**
24. **Bobby Wood, rhp, U. of Michigan**
25. Harold Edwards, c, Midland (Texas) HS

26. Andrew Marcus, rhp, Tyler (Texas) JC
27. Jeffrey Tuttle, of, Cypress (Calif.) JC
28. Brandon Jones, of, Liberty Eylau HS, Texarkana, Texas
29. Philip Humber, rhp, Carthage (Texas) HS
30. Danny Schwab, 1b, Arvada (Colo.) West HS
31. Ricky Stover, lhp, Navarro (Texas) JC
32. Aaron Edwards, c, John A. Logan (Ill.) JC
33. Chris Weakley, ss, Albany HS, El Cerrito, Calif.
34. Chris Kemlo, rhp, McLaughlin HS, Oshawa, Ontario
35. **Kevin Goodrum, lhp, Ohio State U.**
36. Fernando Fuentes, c, Weehawken (N.J.) HS
37. Josh Kerschen, rhp, CC of Southern Nevada
38. Brent Jackson, lhp, Henderson (Texas) HS
39. Tate Wallis, rhp, Ennis (Texas) HS
40. Hans Gleason, of, El Modena HS, Orange, Calif.
41. Jonathan Mercer, of, Jefferson (Mo.) JC
42. Greg Taylor, ss, St. Louis CC-Forest Park
43. Michael Bass, rhp, Santana HS, Santee, Calif.
44. Eric Hullinger, rhp, Oak Forest (Ill.) HS
45. Jose Robles, rhp, East Central (Mo.) JC
46. Domenic Ficco, lhp, Regis Jesuit HS, Aurora, Colo.
47. Chad Borek, rhp, Northmont HS, Dayton, Ohio
48. Brian Carpenter, of, Fairfield (Ohio) HS
49. Aneury Pichardo, ss, Miramar (Fla.) HS
50. Brandon Boggs, of, Pope HS, Marietta, Ga.

NEW YORK/NL (26)

1. **Aaron Heilman, rhp, U. of Notre Dame** (Choice from Rockies—18th—as compensation for Type A free agent Mike Hampton).
1. (Choice to Athletics as compensation for Type A free agent Kevin Appier).
1. **David Wright, 3b, Hickory HS, Chesapeake, Va.** (Supplemental pick—38th—for loss of Hampton).
2. **Alhaji Turay, of, Auburn (Wash.) HS**
2. **Corey Ragsdale, ss, Nettleton HS, Jonesboro, Ark.** (Supplemental pick—76th—for loss of Type C free agent Bobby Jones).
3. **Lenny DiNardo, lhp, Stetson U.**
4. **Brian Walker, lhp, U. of Miami**
5. **Danny Garcia, 2b, Pepperdine U.**
6. **Jason Weintraub, c, Jefferson HS, Tampa**
7. **Tyler Beuerlein, c, Grand Canyon (Ariz.) U.**
8. **Brett Kay, c, Cal State Fullerton**
9. **Jayson Weir, lhp, Boone HS, Orlando**
10. **Ryan Olson, lhp, U. of Nevada-Las Vegas**
11. **David Mattox, rhp, Anderson (S.C.) College**
12. **Darren Watts, of, U. of British Columbia**
13. **Jay Caligiuri, 3b, Cal State Los Angeles**
14. Kyle Larsen, 1b, Eastlake HS, Sammamish, Wash.
15. **Jason Scobie, rhp, Louisiana State U.**
16. **Joe Hietpas, c, Northwestern U.**
17. **Frank Corr, of, Stetson U.**
18. Justin Barnes, ss, Merritt Island (Fla.) HS
19. Josh Alliston, rhp, Long Beach State U.
20. Trevor Hutchinson, rhp, U. of California
21. **Blake McGinley, lhp, Texas Tech**
22. **David Bacani, 2b, Cal State Fullerton**
23. **John Toner, of, Western Michigan U.**
24. Josh Deel, rhp, Wolfson HS, Jacksonville
25. Nathaniel Craft, lhp, Palm Harbor (Fla.) University HS
26. **Justin Sassanella, of, De Kalb HS, Auburn, Ind.**
27. **Eric Templet, rhp, U. of Louisiana-Lafayette**
28. **Rylie Ogle, lhp, UC Santa Barbara**
29. **Domingo Acosta, rhp, Palm Beach (Fla.) JC**
30. **Chris Sherman, rhp, San Jose State U.**
31. Buddy Hausmann, lhp, Seton Hall U.
32. Cole Armstrong, c, Delphi Academy, Surrey, B.C.
33. Taylor George, rhp, Cypress (Calif.) JC
34. **Richard Pittman, ss-2b, North Georgia College**
35. Wayne Foltin, rhp, Centennial HS, Bakersfield, Calif.
36. Phillip Tyson, rhp, Katella HS, Anaheim
37. Jose Torres, c, Centennial HS, Corona, Calif.
38. Luis Roberts, lhp, Dartmouth (Nova Scotia) HS
39. Michael Almand, lhp, Stockbridge (Ga.) HS
40. John Sawatski, lhp, Westark (Ark.) CC
41. **Sean Farrell, lhp, Briarcliffe (N.Y.) JC**
42. Chris Davis, rhp, Fresno CC
43. Michael Schaeffer, rhp, Wilson HS, Sinking Springs, Pa.
44. Randy Wells, c, Southwestern Illinois JC
45. Edward Cannon, rhp, South Florida CC
46. Karnie Vertz, rhp, Porterville (Calif.) JC
47. Michael Hawkins, of, Eisenhower HS, Rialto, Calif.
48. Jamar Hill, 3b, Santa Ana (Calif.) JC
49. Paul Labiche, rhp, Reserve Christian HS, La Place, La.
50. DeWayne Carver, rhp, Santa Fe (Fla.) CC

OAKLAND (25)

1. **Bobby Crosby, ss, Long Beach State U.**
1. **Jeremy Bonderman, rhp, Pasco (Wash.) HS** (Choice from Mets—26th—as compensation for Type A free agent Kevin Appier).
1. **John Rheinecker, lhp, Southwest Missouri State U.** (Supplemental pick—37th—for loss of Appier).
2. **Neal Cotts, lhp, Illinois State U.**
3. **J.T. Stotts, ss, Cal State Northridge**
4. **Marcus McBeth, of, U. of South Carolina**
5. **Jeff Bruksch, rhp, Stanford U.**
6. **Austin Nagle, of, Barbe HS, Lake Charles, La.**
7. **Dan Johnson, 1b, U. of Nebraska**
8. **Mike Frick, rhp, Cal State Northridge**
9. **Casey Myers, c, Arizona State U.**
10. **Mike Wood, rhp, U. of North Florida**
11. **J.R. Crider, rhp, Lewis-Clark State (Idaho) College**
12. **Jeff Christy, of, Stetson U.**
13. **Chris Mabeus, rhp, Lewis-Clark State (Idaho) College**
14. **Brett Price, rhp, U. of South Carolina**
15. **Jason Basil, of, Georgia Tech**
16. Steve Reba, rhp, Clemson U.
17. Pete Montrenes, rhp, U. of Mississippi
18. Jacob Dixon, 1b, Rowva HS, Oneida, Ill.
19. **J.J. Pierce, of, Wayland Baptist (Texas) U.**
20. **Jeff Muessig, rhp, Briarcliffe (N.Y.) JC**
21. **Jeff Coleman, rhp, U. of Hawaii**
22. **Harold Holbert, 2b, Locke HS, Los Angeles**
23. **Kory Wayment, ss, Salt Lake CC**
24. Dylan Putnam, rhp, Michigan State U.
25. **Andy Neufeld, 3b, U. of Georgia**
26. **Chris Gill, rhp-3b, Phoenix JC**
27. **Bryan Simmering, rhp, Towson State U.**
28. **Matt Groff, of, Tulane U.**
29. **Leonard Landeros, lhp, JC of the Sequoias (Calif.)**
30. Thomas Braun, rhp, Kingwood (Texas) HS
31. **Brian Rooke, of, U. of Hawaii-Hilo**
32. Mark Hilde, 3b, Woodway HS, Edmonds, Wash.
33. Daniel Fyvie, rhp, Fenton (Mich.) HS
34. Adolfo Garza, rhp, Walla Walla (Wash.) CC
35. Trenton Froehlich, lhp, Lompoc (Calif.) HS
36. Cooper Fouts, c, Bishop Gorman HS, Las Vegas
37. Andre Ethier, of, Chandler-Gilbert (Ariz.) CC
38. Rob Lacheur, rhp, Prairie Baseball Academy, Lethbridge, Alberta
39. Nick Crosta, of, Highline HS, Seattle

PHILADELPHIA (4)

1. **Gavin Floyd, rhp, Mount St. Joseph HS, Severna Park, Md.**
2. (Choice to Red Sox as compensation for Type B free agent Rheal Cormier).
3. (Choice to Mariners as compensation for Type B free agent Jose Mesa).
4. **Terry Jones, ss, Upland (Calif.) HS**
5. **Ryan Howard, 1b, Southwest Missouri State U.**
6. **Bryan Hansen, of, Longwood HS, Coram, N.Y.**
7. **Vinny DeChristofaro, lhp, Richmond Hill (Ga.) HS**
8. **Taft Cable, rhp, UNC Greensboro**
9. Chris Roberson, of, Feather River (Calif.) JC
10. Rocky Cherry, rhp, U. of Oklahoma
11. **Matt Sweeney, rhp, Steinert HS, Yardville, N.J.**
12. Rod Perry, of, Penn State U.
13. **Andre Marshall, of, U. of Washington**
14. Mario Delgado, of, Oklahoma City U.
15. **Tim Davis, lhp, U. of South Alabama**
16. **Ben Margalski, c, Southwest Missouri State U.**
17. **Ryan Hutchison, rhp, Western Kentucky U.**
18. **Ben Ally, rhp, Warner Southern (Fla.) College**
19. **Matt Squires, lhp, Whitworth (Wash.) College**
20. **Vince Vukovich, of, U. of Delaware**
21. Julian Williams, of, Upland (Calif.)HS
22. **Michael Floyd, of, U. of South Carolina**
23. **Josh Cisneros, c, West Virginia U.**
24. **Kris Lammers, lhp, Middle Tennessee State U.**
25. **Josh Scott, lhp, Baylor U.**
26. Layne Dawson, rhp, U. of Memphis
27. Jason Bernard, rhp, Troy State U.
28. Mike Nall, rhp, Northwestern U.
29. Jeremy Kurella, ss, U. of Central Florida
30. **Kris Bennett, 3b, U. of Tennessee**
31. **Ryan Johnston, c, Sonoma State (Calif.) U.**
32. **Josh Miller, rhp, North Carolina State U.**
33. **Dan McCall, lhp, Penn State U.**
34. **Brian Schriner, rhp, U. of Louisiana-Monroe**
35. **Nick Glaser, rhp, Clemson U.**
36. **Jeff Phelps, 3b, Arizona State U.**

37. **Wes Carroll, ss, U. of Evansville**
38. Jaime Martinez, 1b, Hueneme HS, Oxnard, Calif.
39. Jason Jaramillo, c, Racine Case HS, Franksville, Wis.
40. Arnold Hughey, lhp, Venice (Fla.) HS
41. Dustin Miller, rhp, Diamond Bar (Calif.) HS
42. William Thompson, 1b, Loyola Sacred Heart HS, Missoula, Mont.
43. Andy Lytle, rhp, Highlands Ranch (Colo.) HS
44. Humberto Gonzales, ss-2b, Rainier Beach HS, Seattle
45. Jared Birrenkott, c, Granite Hills HS, El Cajon, Calif.
46. Allen Hicks, of, King HS, Tampa
47. **Sean Walsh, 3b-of, North Carolina State U.**
48. **Maximo Reyes, rhp, St. Petersburg (Fla.) JC**

PITTSBURGH (8)

1. **John VanBenschoten, rhp-1b, Kent State U.**
2. (Choice to Braves as compensation for Type B free agent Terry Mulholland).
3. Jeremy Guthrie, rhp, Stanford U.
4. **Jeff Keppinger, ss, U. of Georgia**
5. **Travis Chapman, 1b, Indian River (Fla.) CC**
6. **Drew Friedberg, lhp, Arizona State U.**
7. **Michael McCuistion, c, Yucaipa (Calif.) HS**
8. **Chris Duffy, of, Arizona State U.**
9. Jason Fellows, 1b, Berkmar HS, Lawrenceville, Ga.
10. Aaron Bulkley, ss, Port Byron (N.Y.) HS
11. Stephen Drew, ss, Lowndes HS, Valdosta, Ga.
12. **Tim Brown, 1b, Sheldon HS, Eugene, Ore.**
13. **Jeff Dutremble, lhp, Dartmouth U.**
14. **Jason Kiley, rhp, St. Charles (Ill.) East HS**
15. **Jeff Miller, rhp, U. of New Orleans**
16. Jon Smith, lhp, Cal State Fullerton
17. Tim Morley, lhp, Stevenson HS, Buffalo Grove, Ill.
18. **Lino Mariot, ss, Woodbridge (N.J.) HS**
19. **Jonathan Albaladejo, rhp, Miami-Dade CC**
20. **Zach Duke, lhp, Midway HS, Clifton, Texas**
21. Tim Pahuta, c-1b, Hunterdon Central HS, Whitehouse Station, N.J.
22. Jon Koch, rhp, Berrien Springs (Mich.) HS
23. **Casey Shumaker, rhp, Jacksonville U.**
24. Marcus Davila, rhp, Tallahassee (Fla.) CC
25. Robert Coomer, rhp, John Logan (Ill.) JC
26. **Jhosandy Morel, lhp, Emerson HS, Union City, N.J.**
27. **Dan D'Amato, lhp, North Carolina State U.**
28. **Claudell Clark, lhp, Norfolk State U.**
29. Scott Tower, lhp, Temple (Texas) JC
30. Kody Kirkland, 3b, Pocatello (Idaho) HS
31. **Brady Borner, lhp, Wayne State (Neb.) College**
32. Chris Torres, c, Vero Beach (Fla.) HS
33. **Chris Shelton, c, U. of Utah**
34. Brett Korth, rhp, Kishwaukee (Ill.) JC
35. Renardo Pitts, of, Jones County HS, Gray, Ga.
36. Adam Riddle, of, New Mexico JC
37. Eddie Elias, rhp, Brito Private HS, Miami
38. **Rajai Davis, 2b, U. of Connecticut-Avery Point JC**
39. Taylor Johnson, of, Skyview HS, Vancouver, Wash.
40. Jase Turner, 1b, Skyline HS, Oakland
41. Scott Wearne, 2b, Chipola (Fla.) JC
42. Preston Simms, rhp, Bethany HS, Oklahoma City
43. **Shane Youman, lhp, Louisiana State U.**
44. Joseph Martinez, rhp, Seton Hall Prep HS, West Orange, N.J.
45. Brent Sportsman, rhp, Elgin (Ill.) CC
46. Matthew Davis, lhp-of, Terry Parker HS, Jacksonville
47. Joshua MacDonald, rhp, Notre Dame HS, Milford, Conn.
48. Anthony Cekovsky, rhp, Southington (Conn.) HS
49. Jeb Gibbs, rhp, Pope HS, Villa Ricca, Ga.
50. **Justin Rethwisch, of, Antelope Valley (Calif.) JC**

ST. LOUIS (28)

1. **Justin Pope, rhp, U. of Central Florida**
2. **Dan Haren, rhp, Pepperdine U.**
3. **Joe Mather, ss, Mountain Pointe HS, Phoenix**
4. **Josh Brey, lhp, Liberty U.**
5. **Skip Schumaker, of, UC Santa Barbara**
6. **John Killalea, lhp, Seminole (Fla.) HS**
7. **Tyler Adamczyk, rhp, Westlake HS, Westlake Village, Calif.**
8. **John Nelson, ss, U. of Kansas**
9. **Rhett Parrott, rhp, Georgia Tech**
10. **Seth Davidson, ss, U. of Southern California**
11. **Jesse Roman, 1b, Rice U.**
12. **Ben Julianel, rhp, San Diego State U.**
13. **Chris Netwall, c, Penn State U.**
14. **Jordan Robison, of, Northwestern State (La.) U.**
15. **Matt Williams, 3b, Baylor U.**
16. **Mike Wodnicki, rhp, Stanford U.**
17. **Josh Merrigan, lhp, Oklahoma State U.**

Jake Gautreau: picked in first round by Padres

18. **Neal Simoneaux, ss, U. of Louisiana-Lafayette**
19. Shane Komine, rhp, U. of Nebraska
20. Bryce Kartler, lhp, Arizona State U.
21. **Cody Gunn, c, Brewster (Wash.) HS**
22. **Bryan Moore, 1b, Louisiana State U.**
23. Kevin Correia, rhp, Cal Poly San Luis Obispo
24. **Aaron Ledbetter, rhp, Westark (Ark.) CC**
25. **Dan Kantrovitz, 2b, Brown U.**
26. **Aaron Russelburg, rhp, Murray State U.**
27. Lee Gwaltney, rhp, Louisiana Tech
28. Blake Hawksworth, rhp, Eastlake HS, Sammamish, Wash.
29. **Pilar Amaya, ss, San Diego State U.**
30. **Jeff Jones, of, Long Beach State U.**
31. Marcus Markray, lhp, Springhill (La.) HS
32. **Andrew Davie, 1b, Central Arkansas Christian HS, Little Rock, Ark.**
33. Jacob Nowlen, rhp, U. of Arkansas-Monticello
34. **Matt Pearl, of, UCLA**
35. Michael Cust, of, Immaculata HS, Whitehouse Station, N.J.
36. Billy Biggs, rhp, West Virginia U.
37. Richard Quihuis-Bell, 1b, Central Arizona JC
38. **Jared Blasdell, rhp, Cal Poly San Luis Obispo**
39. **Dan Shouse, lhp, St. Louis U.**
40. **Steven Green, of, U. of Arkansas-Monticello**
41. **Travis Palmer, rhp, U. of Utah**
42. **Anthony Rawson, lhp, U. of Southern Mississippi**
43. Jesse Kozlowski, rhp, Los Angeles Pierce JC
44. Shane Reedy, rhp, Utah Valley State JC
45. Billy Paganetti, of, Galena HS, Reno, Nevada
46. Drew Davidson, of, Dowling HS, West Des Moines, Iowa
47. Michael Evans, 3b, Middle Georgia JC
48. **Michael Levy, c, Dartmouth College**
49. Sam Fisher, rhp, U. of Dayton
50. **Mike Fox, ss, U. of Central Florida**

SAN DIEGO (14)

1. **Jake Gautreau, 3b, Tulane U.**
2. Matt Harrington, rhp, St. Paul (Northern League)
3. Taggert Bozeid, 1b-3b, U. of San Francisco
4. **Josh Barfield, 2b, Klein HS, Spring, Texas**
5. **Greg Sain, c-3b, U. of San Diego**
6. **Jason Weidmeyer, lhp, U. of Memphis**
7. **Doc Brooks, of, U. of Georgia**
8. **David Pauley, rhp, Longmont (Colo.) HS**
9. **Jon Benick, 1b, U. of Virginia**
10. **Ben Fox, lhp, Dixie State (Utah) JC**
11. **Marcus Nettles, of, U. of Miami**
12. **Jordan Pickens, 1b, Cuesta (Calif.) JC**

13. Jason Bartlett, ss, U. of Oklahoma
14. Josh Carter, of, Oregon State U.
15. Carlos Fisher, rhp, Duarte (Calif.) HS
16. Jon Brandt, rhp, UCLA
17. Trevor Brown, c, Lewis-Clark State (Idaho) College
18. Scott Shapiro, rhp, St. Augustine HS, Oceanside, Calif.
19. Jason Anderegg, rhp, Belmont (Tenn.) U.
20. Jeremy Slayden, of, Oakland HS, Murfreesboro, Tenn.
21. Rusty Tucker, lhp, U. of Maine
22. Drew Macias, of, Alta Loma HS, Rancho Cucamonga, Calif.
23. Kyle Cullinan, 3b, Fullerton (Calif.) HS
24. Joseph Hastings, 1b, East Carolina U.
25. Scott Kelly, lhp, Missouri Valley College
26. Matt Hellman, of, Lewis-Clark State (Idaho) College
27. Elliot Singletary, 2b, North Fort Myers (Fla.) HS
28. Michael Watson, lhp, Midland (Texas) JC
29. Brendan Katin, c, Fort Myers (Fla.) HS
30. Matt Hobbs, lhp, U. of Missouri
31. Hunter Brown, 3b, Rice U.
32. Irving Falu, 2b, Angel P. Millan HS, Carolina, P.R.
33. Rashad Smith, of, Lambuth (Tenn.) U.
34. Zachary Wykoff, rhp, Oxford, Ga.
35. Chad Etheridge, of, Friendship Christian HS, Old Hickory, Tenn.
36. Shawn LeBlanc, rhp, Bourgeois HS, Gray, La.
37. John Coker, of, Muskogee (Okla.) HS
38. Anthony Lester, of, Hillsborough (Fla.) CC
39. Nick Walter, of, Hun School, Princeton, N.J.
40. Josh Archer, c, Henry County HS, Paris, Tenn.
41. Marcos Martinez, 1b, Chaffey (Calif.) JC

SAN FRANCISCO (30)

1. Brad Hennessey, rhp, Youngstown State U. (Choice from Indians—21st—as compensation for Type A free agent Ellis Burks).
1. Noah Lowry, lhp, Pepperdine U.
1. Todd Linden, of, Louisiana State U. (Supplemental pick—41st—for loss of Burks).
2. Jesse Foppert, rhp, U. of San Francisco
3. Julian Benavidez, 3b, Diablo Valley (Calif.) CC
4. Josh Cram, rhp, Clemson U.
5. Justin Knoedler, rhp, Miami (Ohio) U.
6. David Cash, rhp, U. of California
7. Jamie Athas, ss, Wake Forest U.
8. Jason Waddell, lhp, Riverside (Calif.) CC
9. T.J. Large, rhp, Seminole (Fla.) HS
10. Wesley Hutchinson, rhp, Lewis-Clark State (Idaho) College
11. Derin McMains, 2b, U. of Arkansas-Little Rock
12. Albert Montes, rhp, U. of Texas
13. Juan Serrato, rhp, Riverside (Calif.) CC
14. Jeff Timmons, c, Nova HS, Hollywood, Fla.
15. Tyler Von Schell, 1b, UC Santa Barbara
16. Craig James, rhp, Killian HS, Miami
17. Steve Holm, ss-c, Oral Roberts U.
18. Dayton Buller, c, Fresno (Calif.) CC
19. Robert Meyer, of, U. of California
20. Richard Giannotti, of, St. Thomas Aquinas HS, Fort Lauderdale, Fla.
21. Miguel Miranda, ss, U. of Arkansas-Little Rock
22. Karl Jernigan, of, Florida State U.
23. Petersen Benjamin, rhp, Florida Atlantic U.
24. T.J. Healey, rhp, Cardinal Gibbons HS, Fort Lauderdale, Fla.
25. Ryan Meaux, lhp, Lamar (Colo.) CC
26. Bobby Wilson, c, Seminole (Fla.) HS
27. Keith Anderson, c-3b, Cal Poly San Luis Obispo
28. David Hixson, rhp, Gonzaga U.
29. Matt Huntingford, of, Florida International U.
30. Joe Mercer, c, American River (Calif.) JC
31. Chris Ciesluk, ss, Taunton (Mass.) HS
32. Brian Stirm, rhp, West Valley (Calif.) JC
33. R.D. Spiehs, rhp, U. of Nebraska
34. Aaron Hornostaj, 2b, Saint Thomas of Villanova HS, Waterloo, Ontario
35. Chris Hamblen, c, U. of Cincinnati
36. Matt Hopper, rhp-1b, U. of Nebraska
37. Todd Mattaner, rhp, Dade Christian HS, Cooper City, Fla.
38. Lamont Jordan, 2b, Dinwiddie (Va.) HS
39. Matthew Somnis, rhp, Tumwater HS, Olympia, Wash.
40. Rudy Garcia, rhp, Lake Worth (Fla.) HS
41. Austin Allen, ss, Mount Hood (Ore.) CC
42. P.J. Hiser, rhp, Hagerstown (Md.) JC
43. Kevin Bulger, ss, Brookwood HS, Snellville, Ga.
44. Jon Williams, c, U. of Missouri
45. Karl Amonite, 1b, Connors State (Okla.) JC
46. Brent Adcock, rhp, Lebanon HS, Watertown, Tenn.
47. Scott Munter, rhp, Butler County (Kan.) CC
48. Paul O'Toole, c, U. of Notre Dame
49. Brian Bulger, rhp, South Georgia JC
50. P.J. McGinnis, rhp, Central Missouri State U.

SEATTLE (23)

1. (Choice to Yankees as compensation for Type A free agent Jeff Nelson).
1. Michael Garciaparra, ss, Don Bosco HS, La Habra Heights, Calif. (Supplemental pick—36th—for loss of Type A free agent Alex Rodriguez).
2. Rene Rivera, c, Papa Juan XXIII HS, Bayamon, P.R. (Choice from Rangers—49th—as compensation for Rodriguez).
2. Michael Wilson, of, Booker T. Washington HS, Tulsa, Okla.
3. Lazaro Abreu, c, Southridge HS, Miami (Choice from Phillies—80th—for loss of Type B free agent Jose Mesa).
3. Tim Merritt, ss, U. of South Alabama
4. Bobby Livingston, lhp, Trinity Christian HS, Lubbock, Texas
5. John Cole, 2b-of, U. of Nebraska
6. Justin Ockerman, rhp, Garden City (Mich.) HS
7. John Axford, rhp, Assumption College SS, Brantford, Ontario
8. Jeff Ellena, ss, Cal Poly Pomona
9. Justin Blood, lhp, Franklin Pierce (N.H.) College
10. Beau Hintz, lhp, Fresno State U.
11. Josh Ellison, of, Westminster Academy, Fort Lauderdale, Fla.
12. Mike Hrynio, 3b, Dover HS, Mine Hill, N.J.
13. Jason Van Meetren, of, Stanford U.
14. Blake Woods, ss, Grand Canyon (Ariz.) U.
15. Chris Colton, of, Newnan (Ga.) HS
16. Sean Peless, 1b, Edmonds (Wash.) CC
17. Ramon Royce, rhp, Lewis-Clark State (Idaho) College
18. John Williamson, of, East Carolina U.
19. Brian Sabourin, rhp, Dakota Collegiate HS, Winnipeg, Manitoba
20. David Purcey, lhp, Trinity Christian Academy, Dallas
21. Matthew Ware, of, Loyola HS, Malibu, Calif.
22. Ladd Hall, rhp, Buena HS, Hereford, Ariz.
23. Aaron Braithwaite, of, Killian HS, Miami
24. Garry Bakker, rhp, Suffern HS, Sloatsburg, N.Y.
25. Eddie Olszta, c, Butler U.
26. Jonathan Nelson, 3b, Dixie State (Utah) JC
27. Tim Bausher, rhp, Kutztown (Pa.) U.
28. David Morrow, rhp, Grayson County (Texas) CC
29. Kyle Aselton, lhp, West HS, Chehalis, Wash.
30. William Sadler, rhp, Pensacola (Fla.) JC
31. Jason Rainey, of, Texas Tech
32. Bryan Vickers, c, Perrysburg (Ohio) HS
33. Thomas Keefer, rhp, Byng HS, Sasakwa, Okla.
34. Trevor Heid, of, Dixie State (Utah) JC
35. Todd Holliday, lhp, South Charleston (W.Va.) HS
36. Ben Hudson, c, Truett-McConnell (Ga.) JC
37. Miguel Martinez, lhp, Miami-Dade JC
38. Bob Cramer, lhp, Long Beach State U.
39. Aaron Ruchti, c, Klein Forest HS, Houston
40. Marquis Pettis, of, Diablo Valley (Calif.) JC
41. Kevin Guyette, rhp, Chaparral HS, Paradise Valley, Ariz.
42. Ryan Brincat, of, Mira Costa HS, Manhattan Beach, Calif.
43. Bradley Pahs, c, Chesterton HS, Porter, Ind.
44. William Keyes, rhp, St. James (Md.) HS
45. Brandon Fusilier, of, Navarro (Texas) JC
46. Alan Gannaway, rhp, Bessemer Academy, McCalla, Ala.
47. Ethan Katz, rhp, University HS, Los Angeles
48. Luis DeJesus, ss, Teodoro Aguilar Mora HS, Yabucoa, P.R.
49. Nick Hamilton, of, West Lowndes HS, Starkville, Miss.
50. Brandon Espinosa, rhp, Santa Ana (Calif.) JC

TAMPA BAY (3)

1. Dewon Brazelton, rhp, Middle Tennessee State U.
2. Jon Switzer, lhp, Arizona State U.
3. Chris Flynn, rhp, U. at Stony Brook
4. David Bush, rhp, Wake Forest U.
5. Chris Seddon, lhp, Canyon HS, Santa Clarita, Calif.
6. Matt Rico, of, Fresno (Calif.) CC
7. Tim King, lhp, Deer Park (Texas) HS
8. Aaron Clark, of, U. of Alabama
9. Fernando Cortez, ss, Grossmont (Calif.) CC
10. Jason St. Clair, ss, Desert Vista HS, Phoenix
11. Mark Worrell, rhp, John I. Leonard HS, Boynton Beach, Fla.
12. Pierre Blount, of, Chaffey (Calif.) JC
13. Vince Harrison, 2b, U. of Kentucky
14. Tommy Nichols, 1b, Armijo HS, Fairfield, Calif.
15. Eric Miller, lhp, Gulf Coast HS, Naples, Fla.
16. Tim Layden, lhp, Deer Park (N.Y.) HS
17. Mike Navaroli, rhp, Indian River (Fla.) CC
18. Jonny Gomes, of, Santa Rosa (Calif.) CC
19. Jason Hammel, rhp, Treasure Valley (Ore.) CC
20. Jake Carney, rhp, U. of Dallas
21. Jarod Matthews, rhp, Yelm HS, Olympia, Wash.
22. John Paul Davis, 1b, Arkansas Tech
23. Brent Cordell, c, Cosumnes River (Calif.) JC
24. Brian Wolotka, of, Valparaiso U.

25. Daron Roberts, c, Westview HS, Portland, Ore.
26. John Asanovich, 2b, Highland HS, Gold Canyon, Ariz.
27. Gabriel Martinez, 1b, Blanca Malaret HS, Sabana Grande, P.R.
28. Mumba Rivera, rhp, Marshalltown (Iowa) CC
29. Joshua Parker, rhp, Wallace State (Ala.) CC
30. Matt Wilkerson, of, Santa Margarita HS, Trabuco Canyon, Calif.
31. Diego Lopez, rhp, Calexico (Calif.) HS
32. Joey Gathright, of, La Place, La.
33. Tyson Thompson, rhp, Washington State U.
34. Chad Gaudin, rhp, Crescent City Baptist HS, Harahan, La.
35. Bryan Banks, rhp, Dunedin (Fla.) HS
36. Michael White, lhp, Countryside (Fla.) HS
37. Michael Rider, rhp, Armijo HS, Fairfield, Calif.
38. Thomas Diamond, rhp, Archbishop Rummel HS, Metairie, La.
39. Greg Dini, c, Bishop Moore School, Longwood, Fla.
40. Brett Davis, 1b, Southern Union State (Ala.) JC
41. Derek Acosta, rhp, Capistrano Valley HS, Mission Viejo, Calif.
42. Kevin Bertrand, rhp, JC of the Sequoias (Calif.)
43. Griffin Zarbrough, lhp, Wallace State (Ala.) CC
44. Dan Van Ruiten, 3b, St. John Bosco HS, LaMirada, Calif.
45. Matt Lukevics, 2b, Jesuit HS, Tampa
46. Chris Eickhorst, c, Kean (N.J.) U.
47. Eric Beattie, rhp, Riverview HS, Valrico, Fla.
48. Brad Davis, c, Capistrano Valley HS, Mission Viejo, Calif.
49. Darwin Pittman, 1b, East St. John HS, Garyville, La.
50. Nicholas Aiello, lhp, Oklahoma Christian U.

TEXAS (5)

1. Mark Teixeira, 3b, Georgia Tech
2. (Choice to Mariners as compensation for Type A free agent Alex Rodriguez).
3. (Choice to Angels as compensation for Type A free agent Mark Petkovsek).
4. Josh Baker, rhp, Memorial HS, Houston
5. C.J. Wilson, lhp, Loyola Marymount U.
6. Ben Keiter, rhp, Wichita State U.
7. Patrick Boyd, of, Clemson U.
8. Masjid Khairy, of, Los Angeles CC
9. Gerald Smiley, rhp, Rainier Beach, Seattle
10. Rob Moravek, rhp, U. of Georgia
11. Greg Buscher, 3b, Terry Parker HS, Jacksonville, Fla.
12. Paul Abraham, rhp, Shippensburg (Pa.) U.
13. Michael Paustian, rhp, Fresno (Calif.) CC
14. Chris Bradshaw, rhp, Texas Christian U.
15. Ryan Dixon, rhp, Seminole (Fla.) HS
16. Royce Hampton, lhp, Lehi (Utah) HS
17. Randall Shelley, 3b, UCLA
18. Nathan Bright, rhp, U. of Northern Colorado

MICHAEL WALBY

Gabe Gross: Blue Jays picked Auburn outfielder in first round

19. Craig Frydendall, lhp, Cowley County (Kan.) CC
20. Jason Patty, ss, Fort Hays (Kan.) State
21. Chad Oliva, c, Jacksonville U.
22. Brad Stockton, of, Georgia Tech
23. Scott Beerer, rhp, Orange Coast (Calif).CC
24. Richie Gardner, rhp, Santa Rosa (Calif.) JC
25. Ryan Rote, rhp, Kettle Moraine HS, Delafield, Wis.
26. Dustin Scheffel, rhp, Sacramento CC
27. Tim Lloyd, of, Christian Brothers HS, Memphis
28. Troy Roberson, rhp, U. of Miami
29. Ryan Mask, rhp, Bakersfield (Calif.) JC
30. Andrew Campbell, lhp, Linn-Benton (Ore.) CC
31. Brandon Alford, lhp, Marshall (Texas) HS
32. Brandon Cornwell, rhp, James Madison U.
33. Jeff Moye, rhp, Cowley County (Kan.) CC
34. Dane De la Rosa, rhp, Elsinore HS, Wildomar, Calif.
35. Jarvis Hicks, rhp, Durant HS, Plant City, Fla.
36. Tony Irvin, rhp, Chamberlain HS, Tampa
37. Jason Ward, rhp, Spanish Fork (Utah) HS
38. Drake Wade, of, George Jenkins HS, Lakeland, Fla.
39. Jeremy Zick, rhp, Riverside (Calif.) CC
40. Jose Romo, lhp, Riverside HS, El Paso
41. Clay Timpner, lhp-of, LaBelle HS, Alva, Fla.
42. Reid Santos, lhp, Saddleback (Calif.) JC
43. Jason Windsor, rhp, West Valley (Calif.) JC
44. Andy Myette, rhp, JC of Southern Idaho
45. Luke Steidlmayer, rhp, U. of California-Davis
46. Jarle Brooks, rhp, Puyallup (Wash.) HS
47. Joldy Watts, rhp, Eastern Utah CC
48. Joseph Martinson, rhp, Payson (Utah) HS
49. Travis Kassebaum, of, Auburn (Wash.) HS
50. Clayne Garrett, 3b, Murray (Utah) HS

TORONTO (15)

1. Gabe Gross, of, Auburn U.
2. Brandon League, rhp, St. Louis HS, Honolulu
3. Tyrell Godwin, of, U. of North Carolina
4. Chris Sheffield, rhp, U. of Miami
5. Michael Rouse, ss, Cal State Fullerton
6. Lee Delfino, ss, East Carolina U.
7. Jason Colson, rhp, Winthrop U.
8. Sean Grimes, rhp, Saunders SS, London, Ontario
9. Luke Hetherington, of, Kentwood HS, Covington, Wash.
10. Ryan Costello, lhp, Montclair State (N.J.) U.
11. Sean Gamble, of, Jefferson Davis HS, Montgomery, Ala.
12. Ernie Durazo, 1b, U. of Arizona
13. Brendan Fuller, rhp, U. of South Florida
14. David Corrente, c, Chatham-Kent SS, Chatham, Ontario
15. Nick Thomas, rhp, Laguna Creek HS, Elk Grove, Calif.
16. Rock Mills, c, Pepperdine U.
17. Chris Neylan, lhp, Steinert HS, Trenton, N.J.
18. Aaron McEachran, 3b, U. of Northern Iowa
19. Isaac Iorg, ss, Knoxville, Tenn.
20. Jon Ashford, of, Covington (Tenn.) HS
21. Jeff Fiorentino, of, Nova HS, Hollywood, Fla.
22. Darren Heal, rhp, Oklahoma State U.
23. Garrick Evans, of, Lake Braddock HS, Burke, Va.
24. Dave Gassner, lhp, Purdue U.
25. Mark Comolli, rhp, Delaware Tech & CC
26. Nick Tempesta, ss, Eastern Connecticut State U.
27. Adam Daniels, lhp, North Vancouver, B.C.
28. Joel Kirsten, lhp, Los Angeles Pierce JC
29. Mark McDonald, rhp, Robinson HS, Burlington, Ontario
30. Javier Lopez, of, Northwest Christian Academy, Hollywood, Fla.
31. Robert Grana, c, Cimarron Memorial HS, Las Vegas
32. Adam Sanabria, lhp, Lake Mary HS, Longwood, Fla.
33. Kellen Ludwig, rhp, Lee County HS, Leesburg, Ga.
34. Brian Ennis, rhp, Harding University HS, Charlotte, N.C.
35. Nicholas Gor, rhp, Saddleback (Calif.) CC
36. Brian McFadden, of, Lake City (S.C.) HS
37. Felix Peguero, of, Bladensburg (Md.) HS
38. Tim Whittaker, c, U. of South Carolina
39. Adam Rodgers, c, Grapevine (Texas) HS
40. Alex Castellvi, c, Plant HS, Tampa
41. Ryan Olivo, 2b, Grapevine (Texas) HS
42. Jared Sanders, rhp, Mount Hood (Ore.) CC
43. P.J. McDonald, rhp, Robinson HS, Burlington, Ontario
44. Kevin Johnston, rhp, Matheson HS, Surrey, B.C.
45. Lawrence Best-Berfet, 2b, CC of Morris County (N.J.)
46. Sean Barker, inf, Louisiana State U.
47. Chris Jones, 1b, Heritage HS, Colleyville, Texas
48. Scott Shoemaker, rhp, Grossmont (Calf.) CC
49. Kenny Holmberg, 2b, Dunedin (Fla.) HS
50. Floyd Albert, lhp, Kernohan Park HS, St. Catharines, Ontario

OBITS/INDEX

OBITUARIES
NOVEMBER 2000-OCTOBER 2001

Tommie Agee, one of the heroes of the 1969 Miracle Mets, died of a heart attack Jan. 22 in New York. He was 58. Agee is best remembered for his exploits in Game Three of the '69 World Series against the Orioles, in which he homered to lead off the bottom of the first inning and made two spectacular catches in the outfield. A two-time all-star and the 1966 American League rookie of the year, Agee batted .255-130-433 in 12 major league seasons with the Indians (1962-64), White Sox (1965-67), Mets (1968-72), Astros (1973) and Cardinals (1973).

Hugh Alexander, a giant in the scouting profession, died Nov. 25, 2000, in Oklahoma City. He was 83. Alexander's scouting career began early (at the age of 20) because of a tragic accident and spanned eight decades, a career that saw him sign more than six dozen big league players. For nearly two decades he was the trusted right-hand man of Dallas Green, helping mold the 1980 Phillies into a World Series winner and the 1984 Cubs into a division champion. Alexander worked over the years for the Indians, Dodgers, White Sox, Phillies and Cubs.

Santos Amaro, a star in the Mexican and Cuban leagues during the 1930s, '40s and '50s, and the father and grandfather of Ruben Amaro Sr. and Jr., died May 31 in Veracruz, Mexico. He was 93. Amaro was a good-hitting outfielder with an outstanding arm. He played with Tampico and Veracruz in Mexico during the summer, and Santa Clara and Almendares in the Cuban winter league. He is a member of both countries' halls of fame. His only playing experience in the United States came in 1935 as a member of the barnstorming La Junta de Nuevo Laredo team—a club that included Mexicans, Mexican-Americans and Cubans.

George Archie, a former first baseman-third baseman for three major league teams, died Sept. 20 in Nashville. He was 87. Archie batted .273-3-53 in 121 big league games with the Tigers (1938), Washington Senators (1941) and St. Louis Browns (1941, 1946). He lost four prime years to military service in World War II.

Johnny Babich, a former Brooklyn Dodgers, Boston Braves and Philadelphia Athletics righthander, died Jan. 19 in Richmond, Calif. He was 87. Babich went 30-45 with the Dodgers (1934-35), Braves (1936) and A's (1940-41).

Red Barkley, a longtime scout and former big league infielder, died Dec. 12, 2000, in Waco, Texas. He was 87. In what must be some kind of record, Barkley played in three major league seasons, all for different teams, and all for teams that later moved to other cities: He was a St. Louis Brown in 1937, a Boston Brave in 1939 and a Brooklyn Dodger in 1943. He batted .264-0-21 in 63 big league games. Barkley is better known for his long scouting career (1948, 1964-88) with the Tigers, Cardinals, Yankees and the Major League Scouting Bureau.

Gerik Baxter, a righthander and a Padres 1999 first-round draft pick, was killed July 29 when he crashed his truck near Indio, Calif. He was 21. Baxter had been rated San Diego's fifth-best prospect by Baseball America entering the 2001 season. He was with high Class A Lake Elsinore for rehabilitation after Tommy John surgery but hadn't pitched in 2001. He went 10-6, 3.19 in two seasons in the San Diego organization.

Curt Blefary, the 1965 American League rookie of the year, died Jan. 28 in Pompano Beach, Fla. He was 57. Blefary, an outfielder, won the AL rookie-of-the-year award after hitting .260-22-70 for the Orioles. Overall, he batted .237-112-382 in eight major league seasons with the Orioles (1965-68), Astros (1969), Yankees (1970-71), Athletics (1971-72) and Padres (1972).

Lou Boudreau, the Indians' Hall of Fame shortstop and manager, and a longtime Cubs broadcaster, died of a heart attack Aug. 10 in Olympia Fields, Ill. He was 84. Boudreau, an eight-time all-star, was the player/manager of the last Indians team to win a World Series, in 1948. That also was his best year on the field; he batted .355-18-106. He won the American League batting title in 1944 with a .327 average, led the league in doubles three times and led AL shortstops in fielding percentage eight times. Overall, he batted .295-68-789 in 15 big league seasons with the Indians (1938-50) and Red Sox (1951-52). Boudreau managed the Indians from 1942-50, the Red Sox from 1952-54, the Kansas City Athletics from 1955-57 and the Cubs in 1960.

Lou Boudreau

George Bradley, a special assistant to White Sox general manager Ken Williams and one of the top scouts in baseball, died of a heart attack Sept. 14 in Tampa. He was 58. While Bradley briefly served as head of the Yankees' front office, scouting was the primary assignment of his 34-year career. He worked for the Phillies, Tigers, Angels and Yankees before being hired by the White Sox in 1991 and serving in various positions since.

Jimmy Bragan, whose varied career included a long stint as president of the Southern League, died of cancer June 2 in Sterrett, Ala. He was 72. Bragan was a schoolboy star at Phillips High in suburban Birmingham and went on to play collegiately at Mississippi State. He played in both the Dodgers and Reds organizations. After his playing career, he coached in the minors and finally made it to the majors as a coach with the Reds. He also coached with the Expos and Brewers, and at Mississippi State for two years before becoming SL president, a post he held from 1981-94.

Ike Brown, a Tigers utilityman in the late 1960s and early 1970s, died May 17 in Memphis. He was 60. Brown played in the majors from 1969-74, all with the Tigers, and batted .256-20-65 in 280 games.

Bob Buhl, a righthander who went 18-7, 2.74 for the '57 Braves, died Feb. 22 in Titusville, Fla. He was 72. In 1962, he set a ignominious record as a hitter by going 0-for-70 with the Braves and Cubs. As a pitcher, though, he went 166-132, 3.55 and was a key cog in the '50s Braves rotations that included Warren Spahn and Johnny Sain.

Nelson Burbrink, the former Mets scouting director who signed Tom Seaver, died April 12 in Largo, Fla. He was 79. Burbrink also had a 15-year playing career as a catcher, reaching the major leagues as a 33-year-old with the 1955 Cardinals. He batted .276-0-15 in 58 games with St. Louis, and actually made the majors as a player after first being a minor league manager. His scouting career included a stint with the Milwaukee Braves as well as the Mets.

Tom Chandler, longtime Texas A&M head coach and a former professional player, manager and scout, died Oct. 18 in Bryan, Texas, after battling progressive supranuclear palsy, a rare form of Parkinson's Disease. He was 75. Chandler coached 999 games from 1959-84, going 660-329-10 and piloted the Aggies to a College World Series trip in 1964. He worked as a scout for the Indians organization for 10 years after leaving Texas A&M, managing for three seasons in their farm system, and also scouted for the Dodgers and Tigers.

Bubba Church, one of the "Whiz Kids" of the 1950 Phillies, died Sept. 17 in Birmingham. He was 77. Church, a righthander, went 8-6, 2.73 as a 25-year-old rookie in 1950, on a young Phillies team that won the National League pennant. He didn't appear in the World Series as the Phils used five pitchers in getting swept by the Yankees. Overall, he went 36-37, 4.10 in six major league seasons with the Phillies (1950-52), Reds (1952-53) and Cubs (1953-55).

Brian Cole, an outfielder and the No. 3-ranked prospect in the Mets organization, was killed in an auto accident March 31 near Marianna, Fla. He was 22. Cole died from injuries suffered when he was thrown from his new-model SUV after the vehicle had, according to a highway patrol report, overturned 1 3/4 times on a Florida interstate near the Georgia border. He was Baseball America's Junior College Player of the Year in 1998 at Navarrro (Texas) JC. He stole 69 bases and hit 19 homers between Class A St. Lucie and Double-A Binghamton in 2000.

Eddie Collins Jr., the son of the Hall of Famer and himself a major league outfielder, died Nov. 2, 2000, in Kennett Square, Pa. He was 83. Collins Jr. played for the Philadelphia Athletics in 1939, 1941 and 1942, batting .241-0-16 in 132 big league games. His father also played for the A's for about half of his 25-year career.

Tony Criscola, a former major league outfielder, died July 10 in La Jolla, Calif. He was 86. Criscola played for the St. Louis Browns (1942-43) and the Reds (1944), batting .248-1-28 in 184 big league games.

John Dagenhard, a righthander who appeared in two games for the 1943 Boston Braves, died July 16 in Bolivar, Ohio. He was 84. Dagenhard worked in a defense-related industry and retired from baseball twice during the war, once for the 1942 season and again permanently in 1944. He pitched 11 innings for the Braves, winning one game and allowing just two unearned runs.

Crash Davis, the former Philadelphia Athletics infielder who inspired the fictional character of the same name in "Bull Durham," died Aug. 31 in Greensboro, N.C. He was 82. Davis played three seasons in the majors as a middle infielder after graduating from Duke in 1940, all with Connie Mack's Philadelphia Athletics. In 148 games, he hit .230. He enlisted in the Navy ROTC in 1942 and served during the war. He spent 1946-52 in the minors and never played again. Davis became a celebrity after "Bull Durham's" release and dropped by stadiums across America. He worked as a motivational speaker, talking about his days as a player and later a coach of championship high school and American Legion teams.

Crash Davis

Miguel Del Toro, a former Giants righthander who pitched in Japan in 2001, was killed in an automobile accident Oct. 6 near Obregon, Mexico. He was 29. Del Toro spent the summer with the Seibu Lions in the Japanese Pacific League, where he went 2-1, 2.33. He made 23 appearances with the Giants in 1999-2000, going 2-0, 4.61 in 41 innings.

Harry Dorish, a longtime major league pitcher, coach and scout, died Dec. 31, 2000, in Wilkes-Barre, Pa. He was 79. Dorish, a righthander, was one of the first relief specialists, starting just 40 times in 323 big league appearances. He went 45-43, 3.83 in 10 seasons with the Red Sox (1947-49, 1956), St. Louis Browns (1950), White Sox (1951-55) and Orioles

(1955-56). He led the American League with 11 saves in 1952, and finished second with 18 the next year. In later years he coached for the Red Sox and Braves, coached in the minors for the Reds and scouted for the Pirates and Indians.

Clem Dreisewerd, a distinguished minor league lefthander who also pitched in four major league seasons, died Sept. 11 of head injuries sustained in a fall while vacationing in Ocean Springs, Miss. He was 85. He made his major league debut in his 11th professional season, and went 6-8, 4.54 in 46 career games with the Red Sox (1944-46), St. Louis Browns (1948) and New York Giants (1948). He appeared briefly in the '46 World Series for the Red Sox.

Joe Duff, longtime coach at Navy, died of pulmonary fibrosis July 30 in Annapolis, Md. He was 78. Duff went 595-332-11 in 32 seasons, and also served as an assistant basketball coach and physical education professor. His baseball teams went to three NCAA tournaments.

Ferris Fain, the American league batting champion in 1951 and '52, died of leukemia Oct. 18 in Georgetown, Calif. He was 80. Known for his fiery disposition, Fain was a five-time all-star for the Athletics and White Sox. He also played with the Tigers and Indians during his major league career, hitting .290-48-570 in nine seasons.

Peggy Freitas, the widow of longtime minor league executive Bob Freitas, died of leukemia March 26 in Tualatin, Ore. She was 80. Baseball America's Freitas Awards are named for Bob Freitas, who was at different times a franchise broker, league president and field representative for the National Association. Peggy Freitas wasn't officially part of his business, but effectively was during the years when her husband worked out of their home in Eugene, Ore.

Len Gabrielson, a first baseman who appeared in five games for the 1939 Phillies, died Nov. 14, 2000, in Stanford, Calif. He was 85. Gabrielson went 4-for-18 with an RBI for the Phillies.

Jody Gajewski, who had just transferred from Saint Louis to Southeast Missouri State, died Sept. 30 in an automobile accident less than a quarter-mile from his home in Ashley, Ill. He was 19. Gajewski, a catcher/first baseman who took a redshirt in 2001, apparently fell asleep at the wheel and his car crashed into a tree.

Ford Garrison, a former Red Sox and Philadelphia Athletics outfielder, died June 6 in Largo, Fla. He was 85. Garrison batted .262-6-56 in four big league seasons, playing for the Red Sox from 1943-44 and the A's from 1944-46. He was a starter for Philadelphia in '44 before military service limited him to six games the next year.

Lloyd Gearhart, a heralded prospect who wound up playing just one season in the big leagues, died April 2 in Dayton. He was 77. Gearhart, an outfielder, batted .246-6-17 in 1945. He played for eight more seasons without returning to the majors.

Clay Gould, head coach at Texas-Arlington and a former outfielder in the independent Texas-Louisiana League, died of cancer June 23 in Dallas. He was 29. Gould was the only person to be a member of all three of the school's NCAA regional teams, participating on the 1990 and '92 teams as a player and coaching them to a berth in 2001. He led the Mavericks to a 63-55 overall record in his two years as the team's skipper.

Brendon Grant, a Senior Babe Ruth player, died in Cambridge, Mass., of injuries sustained in a collision with another fielder during a game in Belmont. He was 18. Grant, a student at American International (Mass.), was playing left field when he and the center fielder collided while pursuing a fly ball. He sustained chest and neck injuries. The center fielder was not injured.

Ralph Hamner, a former righthander for both of Chicago's major league teams, died May 22 in Little Rock, Ark. He was

84. Hamner went 8-20, 4.58 in a four-year big league career with the White Sox (1946) and Cubs (1947-49).

Arne Harris, the producer-director of Cubs television broadcasts on WGN, died Oct. 6 in Chicago. He was 67. Harris collapsed while having dinner at a downtown Chicago restaurant with his wife Arlene and broadcaster Chip Caray, hours after working the next-to-last game of the season. Though he never appeared on camera, the announcers' frequent references to Harris made him almost as famous as them.

Sam Harshaney, a former St. Louis Browns catcher, died Feb. 1 in San Antonio. He was 90. Harshaney batted .238-0-15 in four seasons (61 games) in the majors, all with the Browns from 1937-40. He played in the minors for 17 seasons, the last six as a player/manager for Texas teams in the lower minors.

Mark Hilde, a third baseman and the Athletics' unsigned 32nd-round draft pick in 2001, was killed July 29 with Padres prospect Gerik Baxter in a truck wreck near Indio, Calif. He was 18.

Mel Hoderlein, a former Red Sox and Washington Senators utility infielder, died May 21 in Mount Carmel, Ohio. He was 77. Hoderlein batted .252-0-24 in four big league seasons with Boston (1951) and Washington (1952-54).

Bert Hodge, a third baseman who appeared in eight games for the 1942 Phillies, died Jan. 8 in Knoxville. He was 83. Hodge went 2-for-11 for the Phillies, and played in the minors from 1937-42 and again in 1946.

Chief Hogsett, a longtime Tigers lefthander, died July 17 in Hays, Kan. At 97, he was among the oldest ex-major leaguers. Hogsett was old as a pitcher, too: In 1944, he made a three-game comeback with the Tigers (plus 31 more games in the American Association) at age 40, six years after last appearing in the big leagues. Overall he went 63-87, 5.02 in 11 major league seasons with the Tigers (1929-36, 1944), St. Louis Browns (1936-37) and Senators (1938).

Mary Holtz, an executive with several minor league clubs along with her late husband Ed, died of complications from a stroke July 12 in Appleton, Wis. She was 70. The Holtzes most recently ran the Macon team in the South Atlantic League in the middle 1990s, and previously had worked in Knoxville, Chattanooga, Tucson and Sumter, S.C.

Wally Hood, a righthander who appeared in two games for the 1949 Yankees, died June 16 in Glendale, Calif. He was 75. Hood worked 2 1/3 innings for New York, getting no decisions and allowing no runs or hits. He played pro ball from 1948-54, all in the majors and high minors.

Jack Horenberger, longtime baseball coach, basketball coach and athletic director at Illinois Wesleyan University, died Dec. 1, 2000, in Bloomington, Ill. He was 87. Horenberger, a 1936 Illinois Wesleyan graduate, was the school's basketball coach from 1945-65, and its baseball coach from 1942-81 except for 2 1/2 years during World War II. He was athletic director from 1947 until his retirement in 1981.

Jim Hughes, who pitched in the majors for seven seasons, died Aug. 13 in Chicago. He was 78. He went 15-13, 3.83 in his six-year major league career. In 1954, he led the National League in appearances with 60 and saves with 24.

Sam Jethroe, the oldest player to win rookie-of-the-year honors in the major leagues, died June 16 in Erie, Pa. He was 83. Jethroe, an outfielder, had been a star with the Cleveland Buckeyes in the Negro Leagues before he joined the Boston Braves in 1950. He became National League rookie of the year at age of 32 after batting .273-18-58 with a league-leading 35 stolen bases. He led the league in steals again the next year with 35 more, and overall batted .261-49-181 in the majors with the Braves (1950-52) and Pirates (two games in 1954).

Jake Jones, a major league first baseman before and after serving in World War II as a Navy ace pilot, died Dec. 13 in Delhi, La., at 80. Jones made his major league debut with the White Sox in 1941 and also played for Chicago in 1942, '46 and '47. He was with the Red Sox from 1947-48 to wrap up a big league career in which he hit .229-23-117 in 790 at-bats.

Bob Keegan, an all-star righthander for the White Sox, died June 20 in Rochester, N.Y. He was 80. Keegan was an American League all-star in 1954, when he went 16-9, 3.09 in his second major league season. Overall, he went 40-36, 3.66 in six big league seasons, all with the White Sox, from 1953-58.

Bob Keely, who had a brief career as a major league catcher and a longer one as a major league coach and scout, died May 20 in Sarasota, Fla. He was 91. Keely appeared with the Cardinals for a game each in 1944 and '45, going 0-for-1 as a hitter. He was a big league coach for the Boston and Milwaukee Braves for the next 10 years before becoming a scout for the club.

Newt Kimball, a righthanded reliever for four major league teams, died March 22 in Las Vegas. He was 85. Kimball went 11-9, 3.78 in 94 big league games (13 starts) for the Cubs (1937-38), Brooklyn Dodgers (1940, 1941-43), Cardinals (1940) and Phillies (1943).

Dick Kimble, a shortstop who appeared in 20 games for the 1945 Washington Senators, died May 7 in Toledo. He was 85. Kimble went 12-for-49 with one RBI for the Senators.

Leo Labossiere, a professional scout for the Astros and a veteran of 50 years in the business, died of a heart attack Sept. 17 in Providence. He was 75. Labossiere was a right-hand man for big league executive Roland Hemond for years. They hailed from the same hometown of Central Falls, R.I., started their baseball careers in the same year (1951) and worked together with the Boston and Milwaukee Braves, the Los Angeles and California Angels, the White Sox and the Orioles.

Al Lary, a former major league righthander and the brother of Tigers all-star Frank Lary, died July 9 in Northport, Ala. He was 71. Lary pitched in one game for the Cubs in 1954 and played in four games the next year as a pinch-runner. He didn't resurface in the majors until 1962, when he pitched in 15 more games for Chicago for career totals of 0-1, 6.52.

Nolan LeMar, an outfielder for College of the Canyons, a California junior college, was killed in an auto accident April 9 in Santa Clarita, Calif. He was 19. LeMar was co-captain of the junior college's team and its second-leading hitter at .368-2-19.

John LeRoy, a righthander for Sioux City of the independent Northern League who also made one big league appearance with the Braves, died of a brain aneurysm June 25 in Sioux City, Iowa. He was 26. LeRoy, the Braves' 15th-round draft pick in 1993, earned a win in his only major league appearance.

Lou Lombardo, a lefthander who appeared in two games for the '48 Giants, died June 11 in Rock Hill, S.C. He was 72. Lombardo pitched 5⅓ innings for New York, with no decisions and four earned runs allowed.

Joe Lovitto, a Rangers outfielder from 1972-75, died May 19 in Arlington, Texas. He was 50. Lovitto batted .216-4-53 for the Rangers, his only major league team. His career ended in 1975, when he was 24.

Jack Maguire, a utilityman for three major league clubs during two seasons, died Sept. 28 in Kerrville, Texas. He was 76. Maguire batted .240-2-21 in 94 major league games with the New York Giants (1950) and three teams in 1951: the Giants, Pirates and St. Louis Browns.

Mickey Mantle, son of the Hall of Famer of the same name, died Dec. 20, 2000, in Dallas. He was 47. His uncles

Ray and Roy also played professional baseball. Mantle hit .070-0-2 in 57 at-bats as an outfielder for Alexandria (Carolina) in 1978.

Willard Marshall, a three-time all-star outfielder for the New York Giants, died Nov. 5, 2000, in Norwood, N.J. He was 79. Marshall batted .274-130-604 in 11 big league seasons with the Giants (1942-49), Boston Braves (1950-52), Reds (1952-53) and White Sox (1954-55). He was an all-star in 1942, '47 and '49.

Eddie Mathews, a Hall of Fame third baseman who spent most of his career with the Braves, died Feb. 18 in La Jolla, Calif. He was 69. Mathews had more home runs by the age of 30 than teammate Henry Aaron did. He was part of a World Series champion with the Braves in 1957 and a pennant winner in 1958, then went 1-for-3 in two games in the '68 World Series. He hit 512 homers in a 17-year major league career.

Eddie Mathews

Pat McKernan, longtime general manager of the Pacific Coast League's Albuquerque Dukes, died of cancer July 10 in Albuquerque. He was 60. McKernan had a reputation for being gruff during his days with the Dukes, but he was a revered member of the Albuquerque community. His health had declined after the Dukes moved to Portland, Ore., after the 2000 season.

Jerry McQuaig, an outfielder who had a hit and an RBI in 16 at-bats for the Philadelphia Athletics in 1934, died Feb. 5 in Buford, Ga. He was 89.

Jo-Jo Moore, a six-time all-star outfielder for the Giants, died April 1 in Bryan, Texas. He was 92. Moore was a National League all-star every year from 1934-38, and again in 1940. He batted .298-79-513 in 12 major league seasons, all with the Giants, and appeared in the 1933, 1936 and 1937 World Series.

Bitsy Mott, a shortstop who played one season for the Phillies, died Feb. 25 in Brandon, Fla. He was 82. Mott batted .221-0-22 in 1945 in his only major league time. He played in the minors for 12 seasons from 1939-53, then made a three-game comeback with Tampa (Florida State) in '57.

Hugh Mulcahy, the first major leaguer to be drafted during World War II, died of complications from cancer and pneumonia Oct. 19 in Aliquippa, Pa. He was 88. Mulcahy spent most of his major league career with the Phillies, including an all-star season in 1940. He returned to Philadelphia after the war in 1945 and finished out his career with the Pirates in '47, ending with overall marks of 45-89, 4.49 in nine seasons.

Kevin Murphy, a professional scout for the Indians, died of cancer Feb. 16 in Santa Monica, Calif. He was 38.

Alex Nahigian, former head coach at Providence and Harvard, died July 30 in Cranston, R.I. Nahigian coached at Providence from 1960-78, going 221-173 with six NCAA tournament appearances. He was at Harvard from 1979-90, going 249-152 with three more NCAA appearances. He also served as a football assistant at Brown and Harvard, and as a high school teacher and coach.

Red Nonnenkamp, a former major league outfielder, died Dec. 3, 2000, in Little Rock, Ark. He was 89. Nonnenkamp batted .262-0-24 in 155 big league games with the Pirates (1933) and Red Sox (1938-40).

Chuck Olson, a member of the ownership group that moved the Braves from Milwaukee to Atlanta, died June 2 in Chicago. He was 73. Olson's group bought the Braves in 1962 and moved them to Atlanta in '66. The group, by then known as the Atlanta LaSalle Corporation, sold the

team to Ted Turner in the mid-1970s.

Roy Partee, a longtime scout for the Mets and a former major league catcher, died Dec. 26, 2000, in Eureka, Calif. He was 83. Partee caught in pro ball each season from 1938-57, except when he served during World War II in 1945. In the big leagues he batted .250-2-114 in five seasons with the Red Sox (1943-44, 1946-47) and St. Louis Browns (1948).

Tom Poholsky, a righthander who spent most of a six-season big league career with the Cardinals, died Jan. 6 in Kirkwood, Mo. He was 71. Poholsky went 31-52, 3.93 in the majors with the Cardinals (1950-51, 1954-56) and Cubs (1957).

Lou "Crip" Polli, one of the oldest former major leaguers, died Dec. 19, 2000, in Berlin, Vt. He was 99. Polli, a righthander, had two brief stints in the big leagues, 12 years apart. He appeared in five games for the 1932 St. Louis Browns and 19 games for the 1944 New York Giants, going a combined 0-2, 4.68.

John Powers, an outfielder for the Pirates, Reds, Orioles and Indians from 1955-60, died Sept. 25 in Birmingham. He was 72. Powers hit .195-6-14 in 215 at-bats over his six seasons.

Tot Pressnell, the starting pitcher for the Brooklyn Dodgers on the night Johnny Vander Meer pitched the second of his back-to-back no-hitters for the Reds, died Jan. 6 in Findlay, Ohio. He was 94. Pressnell debuted in the majors with a shutout, and went on to a 32-30, 3.80 career in five seasons with the Dodgers (1938-40) and Cubs (1941-42).

Hank Riebe, a former Tigers backup catcher, died April 16 in Cleveland. He was 79. Riebe batted .212-0-11 in 61 big league games, all with Detroit, in 1942 and 1947-49.

Bill Rigney, a special assistant for the Athletics who spent more than 60 years in the game, died Feb. 19. He was 83. Rigney was an infielder for the New York Giants from 1946-53 and manager of the San Francisco Giants from 1956-60 and in 1976. Rigney also managed the Los Angeles Angels (1061-69) and Minnesota Twins (1970-72). He later served as a scout, executive and broadcaster.

Alex Sabo, who appeared in five big league games as a catcher but was better known as a football player, died Jan. 3 in Tuckertown, N.J. He was 90. Sabo was one of the famed Seven Blocks of Granite, the linemen for Fordham in the middle 1930s. One of the others was Vince Lombardi. Sabo signed a baseball contract after graduating in 1936, and reached the majors with the Washington Senators briefly that year and the next. He went 3-for-8 in the big leagues.

Hank Sauer, a major league outfielder/first baseman for 15 years between 1941-59, died August 24 in Burlingame, Calif. He was 82. Sauer spent 36 games with the Reds in 1945 and the next two seasons with Syracuse before getting called up for good in 1948. He spent the next 12 major league seasons with the Reds, Cubs, Cardinals and Giants. He batted .266-288-876 in his 15 seasons and played in two All-Star Games with the Cubs in 1950 and '52. He led the National League with 37 home runs and 121 RBIs in 1952.

Dick Selma, the National League record holder for strikeouts in a single season by a relief pitcher, died of liver cancer Aug. 29 in Clovis, Calif. He was 57. Pitching for the Phillies in 1970, Selma fanned 153 batters in 134 relief innings to set the record. He also recorded the expansion Padres' first win in 1969. Overall, he went 42-54, 3.62 in 10 major league seasons with the Mets (1965-68), Padres (1969), Cubs (1969), Phillies (1970-73), Angels (1974) and Brewers (1974).

Jim Smith, Louisiana State's head coach from 1966-78, died Jan. 17 in Baton Rouge. He was 69. Smith was 238-251 with the Tigers, including a 40-16 team in 1975—LSU's best record in the pre-Skip Bertman era.

Bill Stafford, a mainstay on the Yankees' World Series teams of the early 1960s, died Sept. 19 in Canton, Mich. Stafford, a righthander, joined the Yankees late in the 1960 season and was an immediate hit, going 3-1, 2.25 in eight starts and three relief appearances. He went 14-9 in each of the next two years. Overall, he was 43-40, 3.52 in eight big league seasons with the Yankees (1960-65) and Kansas City Athletics (1966-67).

Willie Stargell, the Hall of Fame first baseman for the Pirates, died April 9 in Wilmington, N.C., of a stroke caused by complications from a longtime battle with diabetes and kidney disease. He was 61. Stargell spent his entire 21-year career with the Pirates from 1962-82 and leads the franchise in home runs (475), RBIs (1,540) and extra-base hits (953). He's best known for lifting the Pirates to their last World Series title in 1979, serving as their captain and acquiring the nickname "Pops" while hitting the decisive home run against the Orioles in Game Seven and garnering the MVP award. He also shared the National League MVP with the Cardinals' Keith Hernandez that season and was named MVP of the Pirates' NL Championship Series sweep of the Reds. Stargell died the day the Pirates opened brand-new PNC Park.

Willie Stargell

Joe Stephenson, a former major league catcher and legendary scout, died Sept. 20 in Fullerton, Calif. He was 80. Stephenson scouted for the Red Sox for nearly 50 years and signed more than 50 major leaguers, including Fred Lynn, Ken Brett, Glenn Hoffman, Bill Lee and Dwight Evans. As a player, Stephenson was a light hitter even in the minor leagues, but he made it to the majors for 29 games with the New York Giants (1943), the Cubs (1944) and the White Sox (1947). He batted .179-0-4.

Harry Taylor, the Brooklyn Dodgers' starting pitcher in the famous 1947 World Series game that ended with Cookie Lavagetto's pinch hit, died Nov. 5, 2000, in Terre Haute, Ind. He was 81. Lavagetto's two-run double in the ninth inning simultaneously broke up a no-hit bid by the Yankees' Bill Bevens and won Game Four for the Dodgers 3-2. Taylor went 19-21, 4.10 in six big league seasons with the Dodgers (1946-48) and Red Sox (1950-52).

Bud Thomas, a righthander for three American League teams in the 1930s and early '40s, died May 20 in Charlottesville, Va. He was 90. Thomas went 25-34, 4.96 in seven big league seasons with the Washington Senators (1932-33, 1939), Philadelphia Athletics (1937-39) and the Tigers (1939-41).

Adrian Thomas, a Washington State outfielder, was killed in an automobile-train crash Aug. 4 near Wellington, Utah. As a junior in 2001, Thomas hit .339-4-19 in 35 games after transferring from the College of Southern Idaho.

Leo Thomas, a former major league third baseman, died March 5 in Concord, Calif. He was 77. Thomas batted .212-1-27 in 95 big league games with the Browns (1950, 1952) and White Sox (1952). In a 13-year minor league career, he reached 100 RBIs twice and narrowly missed three more times, reaching 95, 97 and 99.

Lou Thuman, a righthander who appeared briefly with the Washington Senators in 1939 and '40, died Dec. 19 in Baltimore. He was 84. Thuman pitched five times for the Nats, going 0-1, 12.00 in nine innings.

Eric Tipton, a former major league outfielder and a member of the college football hall of fame, died of heart failure Aug. 29 in Newport News, Va. He was 86. As a running back and punter, Tipton starred on the powerful Duke football teams of the late 1930s, including the 1938 team which went through the regular season without giving up a point. He was in the Philadelphia Athletics outfield a year after that, and batted .270-22-151 in seven big league seasons with the A's (1939-41) and Reds (1942-45).

Sandy Ullrich, a Washington Senators righthander in 1944 and '45, died April 21 in Miami. He was 79. Ullrich went 3-3, 5.04 in 31 games for the Nats, all but three in 1945. A Cuban native, he played in the Mexican League and became a star for Havana's Florida International League entry for four years after his major league career.

Al Vincent, who had a long and varied career in pro ball, died Dec. 14, 2000, in Beaumont, Texas. He was 93. Vincent is best known as a major league coach with the Tigers, Orioles, Phillies and Kansas City Athletics, but he also was a longtime minor league manager and player. He managed in the minors from 1937-54, except for three years as a coach and scout for the Tigers, and occasionally appeared as a player as late as 1951.

Jim Whatley, longtime coach at the University of Georgia, died May 31 in Athens, Ga. He was 88. Whatley was a former American Baseball Coaches Association president and Georgia's coach from 1950-75. He was also an assistant football coach and head basketball coach but compiled a 336-327-3 record as Bulldogs coach. He entered the ABCA hall of fame in 1987.

Mike Weinberg, a New York firefighter and former outfielder in the Tigers system, was killed in the collapse of the World Trade Center on Sept. 11. He was 34. Weinberg was off-duty and about to tee off at a golf course in Queens when he heard about the first plane hitting one of the towers. Concerned for his sister's safety, Weinberg, a member of one of the oldest firefighting companies in New York City—Manhattan Company, Engine 1—went to help her and others. He rushed to the scene with chaplain Mychal Judge and Capt. Daniel Brethel. None of the three was in either of the towers when they collapsed; all three were killed in the street by falling debris.

Butch Wensloff, a righthander who had a brief but successful major league career, died Feb. 18 in San Rafael, Calif. He was 85. Wensloff went 16-13, 2.60 in three big league seasons with the Yankees (1943, 1947) and Indians (1948).

Hal White, a longtime Tigers righthander, died after a stroke April 21 in Venice, Fla. He was 82. White went 46-54, 3.78 in 12 major league seasons with the Tigers (1941-43, 1946-52), St. Louis Browns (1953) and Cardinals (1953-54).

Terry Wilshusen, a righthander who appeared in one game for the California Angels in 1973, died Dec. 1, 2000, in Lomita, Calif. He was 51. Wilshusen threw just a third of an inning for the Angels, walking two batters and allowing three earned runs.

Gene Woodling, a longtime major league outfielder for several clubs but most notably the Yankees, died June 2 in Barberton, Ohio. He was 78. Woodling appeared in five straight World Series with the Yankees from 1949-53, batting .318-3-6 in those games. He appeared in one All-Star Game (in 1959 when he was 36) and batted .284-147-830 in 17 big league seasons with the Indians (1943, 1946, 1955-57), Pirates (1947), Yankees (1949-54), Orioles (1955, 1958-60) and Washington Senators (1961-62), before finishing his career at 40 with the famously awful 1962 Mets.

Joe Zapustas, another Fordham football player who appeared briefly in the majors, died Jan. 14 in Randolph, Mass. He was 93. Zapustas, an outfielder, got into two games for the 1933 Philadelphia Athletics, going 1-for-5. He played just two other seasons in the minors and is better known for his post-baseball career as a longtime coach and athletic director at Massachusetts high schools, and as a top-level boxing referee.

INDEX MAJOR & MINOR LEAGUE CLUBS

NOTES